True to the work of
Yah Veh Elohim -
Adonay - Eternal I AM -
Creator - Judge.

True to the mission of
Yah Shua Messiah
- Adonay - Eternal I AM
- Creator - Saviour.

EDC
HEBREW ENGLISH BIBLE

a literal translation and transliteration of Scripture

SERIES 2

Everday Church, Inc.

True to the ministry
of the Holy Spirit -
Indwelling Paraclete -
Endower of Spirituals -
Birther of Eternal Life.

True to the enduements
of the Holy Spirit
- Ministries of Service
- Energies of Dynamis
- Attributes of Charismata.

Ruach ha-kodesh

First Edition,
The AUTHORIZED KING JAMES VERSION of 1611 in exeGeses,
© 1992 by Herb Jahn, Exegete.

The Second Edition,
exeGeses ready research BIBLE,
© 1993 by Herb Jahn, Exegete.

The Third Edition,
exeGeses companion BIBLE,
© 1994 by Herb Jahn, Exegete.

This Fourth Edition,
exeGeses BIBLE,
© 1994 by Herb Jahn, Exegete.

ISBN: 978-1-63950-139-7 (sc)
ISBN: 978-1-63950-140-3 (e)

Writers Apex

Gateway Towards Success
8063 MADISON AVE #1252
Indianapolis, IN 46227
+13176596889
www.writersapex.com

LEXICON:

You will particularly appreciate the LEXICON beginning on page 1866. All the *exeGeses* are verifiable by the expository critiques in the LEXICON, and by Strong's Exhaustive Concordance.

The LEXICON thoroughly explains the importance of the word word – and why it is used in both verbal and nounal forms. The SUMMARIES give you a thorough digest of certain subjects and roots of words.

Now you can easily satisfy your desire for deeper research – for every word in the LEXICON is number coded to Strong's Exhaustive Concordance. This is especially helpful because more and more of the old reliable research materials are being republished, also number coded to Strong's Exhaustive Concordance.

My petition is that Adonay Yah Shua Messiah be pleased to place His seal on the work of my life by spiritually enriching the work of your life.

In the name of Adonay Yah Shua Messiah,
Herb Jahn, Exegete

I invite all exegetes to critique this *EDC Hebrew / English Bible* in the hope that future editions may be less imperfect.

Everyday Church give all credits to Herb Jahn, as we go forward with this future edition. Others in the future may be less imperfect. Also, "However" Isaiah 55:11 "So shall my word be that goeth forth out of my mouth: it shall not return unto me void, but it shall accomplish that wich I please, and it shall prosper in the thing where to I ser it."

Acknowledgement

Thank you, Dawn,
for your
encouragement, endurance,
and
editorial excellence.

TABLE OF CONTENTS

VOLUME THREE: POETRY

VOLUME FOUR: PROPHETS

VOLUME THREE

POETRY

Ruth And Noomiy

1 *Now it came to pass* **And so be it,**
in the days when the judges *ruled* **judged,**
that there was a famine in the land.
And a *certain* man
of *Bethlehemjudah* **Beth Lechem Yah Hudah**
went to sojourn in the *country* **fields** of Moab,
he, and his *wife* **woman,** and his two sons.
2 And the name of the man
was *Elimelech* **Eli Melech,**
and the name of his *wife Naomi* **woman**
Noomiy, and the name of his two sons
Mahlon **Machlon** and *Chilion* **Kilyon,**
Ephrathites **Ephrathiym**
of *Bethlehemjudah* **Beth Lechem Yah Hudah.**
And they came into the *country* **fields** of Moab,
and continued there.
3 And *Elimelech* **Eli Melech**
Naomi's husband **Noomiy's man** died;
and she *was left* **survived,** and her two sons.
4 And they *took them wives*
of the **bore** women of Moab:
the name of the one was Orpah,
and the name of the *other* **second** Ruth:
and they *dwelled* **settled** there about ten years.
5 And *Mahlon* **Machlon** and *Chilion* **Kilyon**
died also both of them;
and the woman *was left* **survived**
of her two *sons* **children** and her *husband* **man.**
6 Then she arose with her daughters in law,
that she might return from the *country* **fields** of Moab:
for she had heard in the *country* **fields** of Moab
how that *the LORD* **Yah Veh** had visited his people
in giving them bread.
7 Wherefore she went forth
out of the place where she was,
and her two daughters in law with her;
and they went on the way
to return unto the land of *Judah* **Yah Hudah.**
8 And *Naomi* **Noomiy**
said unto her two daughters in law,
Go, return each **woman** to her mother's house:
the LORD deal kindly **Yah Veh work mercy** with you,
as ye have *dealt* **worked** with the dead, and with me.
9 *The LORD grant* **Yah Veh give** you
that ye may find rest,
each *of you* **woman** in the house of her *husband* **man.**
Then she kissed them;
and they lifted up their voice, and wept.
10 And they said unto her,
Surely we *will* **shall** return with thee unto thy people.
11 And *Naomi* **Noomiy** said,
Turn *again* **back,** my daughters:
why *will* **shall** ye go with me?
are there yet *any more* sons in my *womb* **inwards,**
that they may be your *husbands* **men?**
12 Turn *again* **back,** my daughters, go *your way;*
for I am too old to have *an husband* **a**
man. If I should say, I have hope,
if I should have *an husband* **a man** also to night,
and should also *bear* **birth** sons;
13 *Would* **Should** ye *tarry for* **await** them
till they were grown?
would **should** ye *stay for* **ban** them
from having *husbands* **men?**
nay, my daughters;
for it *grieveth* **embittereth** me *much* **mightily**
for your sakes
that the hand of *the LORD* **Yah Veh**
is gone *out* against me.
14 And they lifted up their voice, and wept again:
and Orpah kissed her mother in law;
but Ruth *clave* **adhered** unto her.
15 And she said, Behold,
thy sister in law is *gone back* **returned** unto her people,
and unto her *gods* **elohim:**
return thou after thy sister in law.
16 And Ruth said, *Intreat*
Intercede me not to leave thee,
or to return from following after thee:
for whither thou goest, I *will* **shall** go;

Ruth And Noomiy

1 And so be it,
in the days the judges judge,
a famine is in the land.
And a man of Beth Lechem Yah Hudah
goes to sojourn in the fields of Moab;
he and his woman and his two sons.
2 And the name of the man, Eli Melech
and the name of his woman, Noomiy
and the name of his two sons, Machlon and Kilyon
—Ephrathiym of Beth Lechem Yah Hudah.
And they come into the fields of Moab
and continue there.
3 And Eli Melech, the man of Noomiy dies;
and she and her two sons survive.
4 And they birth women of Moab;
the name of the one, Orpah

and the name of the second, Ruth;
and they settle there about ten years.
5 And both Machlon and Kilyon also die;
and the woman survives
her two children and her man.
6 And she rises with her daughters in law,
to return from the fields of Moab:
for she heard
that Yah Veh visits his people in the fields of Moab
in giving them bread.
7 So she goes with her two daughters in law
from the place she was;
and they go on the way
to return to the land of Yah Hudah.
8 And Noomiy says to her two daughters in law,
Go, each woman,
return to the house of your mother;
Yah Veh work mercy with you,
as you worked with the dead and with me.
9 Yah Veh give you to find rest,
each woman in the house of her man.
—and she kisses them.
And they lift their voice and weep
10 and say to her,
Surely we return with you to your people.
11 And Noomiy says,
Turn back, my daughters! Why go with me?
Are there yet sons in my inwards to be your men?
12 Turn back, my daughters! Go!
For I am too old to have a man.
If I say, I have hope,
and even have a man tonight and even birth sons
13 —await you them until they be grown?
—ban yourselves from having men?
No, my daughters;
for it embitters me mightily for your sakes
that the hand of Yah Veh goes against me.
14 And they lift their voice and weep again;
and Orpah kisses her mother in law;
and Ruth adheres to her;
15 and says, Behold,
your sister in law returns to her people
and to her elohim;
you return after your sister in law.
16 And Ruth says, Intercede not that I leave you,
or return from following after you;
for where you go, I go;
and where thou *lodgest* **stayest overnight**,
I *will lodge* **shall stay overnight**:
thy people shall be my people,
and thy *God* **Elohim** my *God* **Elohim**:
17 Where thou diest, *will* **shall** I die,
and there *will* **shall** I be *buried* **entombed**:
the LORD do so **Yah Veh work** to me, and *more* **add** also,
if ought but death *part* **separate** thee and me.
18 When she saw that she
was stedfastly minded **strengthened herself**
to go with her,
then she *left speaking* **ceased wording** unto her.
19 So they two went
until they came to *Bethlehem* **Beth Lechem**.
And **so be** it *came to pass*,
when they were come to *Bethlehem* **Beth Lechem**,
that all the city *was moved* **quaked** about them,
and they said, Is this *Naomi* **Noomiy**?
20 And she said unto them,
Call me not *Naomi* **Noomiy**,
call me *Mara* **Bitter**:
for *the Almighty* **Shadday**
hath *dealt very bitterly with* **mightily embittered** me.
21 I went out full
and *the LORD* **Yah Veh**
hath *brought me home again empty* **turned me back**:
why *then* call ye me *Naomi* **Noomiy**,
seeing *the LORD* **Yah Veh**
hath *testified* **answered** against me,
and *the Almighty* **Shadday** hath *afflicted* **vilified** me?
22 So *Naomi* **Noomiy** returned,
and Ruth the *Moabitess* **Moabiyth**, her daughter in law,
with her,
which returned out of the *country* **fields** of Moab:
and they came to *Bethlehem* **Beth Lechem**
in the beginning of barley harvest.

RUTH AND BOAZ

2 And *Naomi* **Noomiy** had a *kinsman* **kin**
of her *husband's* **man**,
a mighty man of *wealth* **valuables**,
of the family of *Elimelech* **Eli Melech**;
and his name was Boaz.
2 And Ruth the *Moabitess* **Moabiyth**
said unto *Naomi* **Noomiy**,
Let me now go to the field,
and glean ears *of corn* after him
in whose *sight* **eyes** I shall find *grace* **charism**.
And she said unto her, Go, my daughter.
3 And she went, and came,
and gleaned in the field after the *reapers* **harvesters**:
and her *hap was* **happening happened** to light
on *a part* **an allotment** of the field *belonging* unto Boaz,

who was of the *kindred* **family** of *Elimelech* **Eli Melech**.
4 And, behold, Boaz came from
Bethlehem **Beth Lechem**,
and said unto the *reapers* **harvesters**,
The LORD **Yah Veh** be with you.
And they *answered* **said to** him,
The LORD **Yah Veh** bless thee.
5 Then said Boaz unto his *servant* **lad**
that was *set* **stationed** over the *reapers* **harvesters**,
Whose *damsel* **lass** is this?
6 And the *servant* **lad**
that was *set* **stationed** over the *reapers* **harvesters**
answered and said,
It is the Moabitish *damsel* **lass**
that *came back* **returned** with *Naomi* **Noomiy**
out of the *country* **fields** of Moab:
7 And she said, I *pray* **beseech** you,
let me glean and gather after the *reapers* **harvesters**
among the *sheaves* **omers**:
so she came, and hath *continued* **stayed**
even from the morning until now,
that she *tarried* **settled** a little in the house.
8 Then said Boaz unto Ruth,
Hearest thou not, my daughter?
Go not to glean in another field,
neither *go* **pass** from hence,
but *abide* **adhere** here *fast* by my *maidens* **lasses**:
9 Let thine eyes be on the field
that they do *reap* **harvest**,
and where you stay overnight, I stay overnight;
your people *are* my people
and your Elohim, my Elohim;
17 where you die, I die and there I entomb;
Yah Veh work to me and add also,
if aught but death separate you and me.
18 And she sees
that she strengthens herself to go with her;
and she ceases wording to her.
19 And the two go until they
come to Beth Lechem.
And so be it,
they come to Beth Lechem,
and the whole city quakes about them
and they say, Is this Noomiy?
20 And she says to them,
Call me not Noomiy/Pleasant; call me Bitter;
for Shadday has mightily embittered me.
21 I go out full
and Yah Veh turns me back.
Why call me Noomiy,
seeing Yah Veh answers against me
and Shadday vilifies me?
22 And Noomiy returns
with her daughter in law, Ruth the Moabiyth
who return from the fields of Moab;
and they come to Beth Lechem
in the beginning of barley harvest.

RUTH AND BOAZ

2 And Noomiy has a kin of her man;
a mighty man of valuables
of the family of Eli Melech;
and his name, Boaz.
2 And Ruth the Moabiyth says to Noomiy,
Let me go, I beseech, to the field
and glean ears after him
in whose eyes I find charism.
And she says to her, Go, my daughter.
3 And she goes
and comes and gleans in the field
after the harvesters;
and her happening
happens to light on an allotment of the field to Boaz
of the family of Eli Melech.
4 And, behold, Boaz comes from Beth Lechem
and says to the harvesters,
Yah Veh be with you.
And they say to him, Yah Veh bless you.
5 Then Boaz says to his lad
who is stationed over the harvesters,
Whose lass is this?
6 And the lad stationed over the harvesters
answers and says,
The Moabitish lass who returned with Noomiy
from the fields of Moab;
7 and she says, I beseech you,
let me glean and gather after the harvesters
among the omers;
so she comes and stays
from the morning until now,
and settles a little in the house.
8 And Boaz says to Ruth,
Hear you not, my daughter?
Neither go to glean in another field,
nor pass from here;
but adhere here by my lasses;
9 may your eyes be on the field they harvest,
and go thou after them:
have I not *charged* **misvahed** the *young men* **lads**
that they shall not touch thee?

and when thou *art athirst* **thirstest**,
go unto the *vessels* **instruments**, and drink of that
which the *young men* **lads** have *drawn* **bailed**.
10 Then she fell on her face,
and *bowed* **prostrated** herself to the *ground* **earth**,
and said unto him,
Why have I found *grace* **charism** in thine eyes,
that thou shouldest *take knowledge of* **recognize** me,
seeing I am a stranger?
11 And Boaz answered and said unto her,
In being told, It hath *fully* been *shewed* **told** me,
all that thou hast *done* **worked** unto thy mother in law
since the death of *thine husband* **thy man**:
and how thou hast left thy father and thy mother,
and the land of thy nativity,
and art come unto a people which thou knewest not
heretofore **three yesters ago**.
12 *The LORD* **Yah Veh**
recompense **shalam** thy *work* **deed**,
and a *full reward* **complete hire** be given thee
of *the LORD God* **Yah Veh Elohim** of *Israel* **Yisra El**,
under whose wings thou art come to *trust* **seek refuge**.
13 Then she said,
Let me find *favour* **charism** in thy *sight* **eyes**,
my *lord* **adoni**;
for that thou hast *comforted* **sighed over** me,
and for that
thou hast *spoken friendly* **worded to the heart**
unto *thine handmaid* **thy maid**,
though I be not
like unto one of *thine handmaidens* **thy maids**.
14 And Boaz said unto her,
At *mealtime come thou hither* **foodtime approach**,
and eat of the bread,
and dip thy morsel in the *vinegar* **fermentation**.
And she *sat* **settled** beside the *reapers* **harvesters**:
and he *reached* **snatched** her parched *corn*,
and she did eat, and was *sufficed* **satisfied**,
and *left* **remained**.
15 And when she was risen up to glean,
Boaz *commanded* **misvahed** his *young men* **lads**, saying,
Let her glean even among the *sheaves* **omers**,
and *reproach* **shame** her not:
16 And *let fall also some of the handfuls of purpose*
of the spoilings, let fistfuls be spoiled for her,
and leave them, that she may glean them,
and rebuke her not.
17 So she gleaned in the field until even,
and *beat out* **threshed** that she had gleaned:
and it was about an ephah of barley.
18 And she *took* **lifted** it *up*, and went into the city:
and her mother in law saw what she had gleaned:
and she brought forth,
and gave to her that *she had reserved* **which remained**
after she was *sufficed* **satisfied**.
19 And her mother in law said unto her,
Where hast thou gleaned to day?
and where *wroughtest* **workedst** thou?
blessed be he that *did take knowledge of* **recognized** thee.
And she *shewed* **told** her mother in law
with whom she had *wrought* **worked**, and said,
The man's name with whom I *wrought* **worked** to day
is Boaz.
20 And *Naomi* **Noomiy** said
unto her daughter in law,
Blessed be he of *the LORD* **Yah Veh**,
who hath not *left off* **forsaken** his *kindness* **mercy**
to the living and to the dead.
And *Naomi* **Noomiy** said unto her,
The man is near *of kin* unto us,
one of our *next kinsmen* **redeemers**.
21 And Ruth the *Moabitess* **Moabiyth** said,
He said unto me also,
Thou shalt *keep fast* **stick** by my *young men* **lads**,
until they have *ended* **finished** all my harvest.
22 And *Naomi* **Noomiy** said
unto Ruth her daughter in law,
and you go after them.
Misvahed I not the lads to not touch you?
And when you thirst, go to the instruments
and drink from what the lads bail.
10 And she falls on her face
and prostrates herself to the earth and says to him,
Why find I charism in your eyes,
that you recognize me—and I, a stranger?
11 And Boaz answers and says to her,
In being told, I am told,
of all you worked to your mother in law
after the death of your man;
and how you left your father and your mother
and the land of your nativity
and come to a people you knew not
three yesters ago.
12 May Yah Veh shalam your deed
and a complete hire be given you
of Yah Veh Elohim of Yisra El,
under whose wings you come to seek refuge.
13 And she says,
May I find charism in your eyes, my adoni;
for sighing over me

and for wording to the heart of your maid
though I—I am not as one of your maids.
14 And Boaz says to her,
Approach at food time and eat of the bread
and dip your morsel in the fermentation.
And she settles beside the harvesters;
and he snatches her parched
and she eats and is satisfied and remains.
15 And she rises to glean,
and Boaz misvahs his lads, saying,
Let her glean even among the omers
and shame her not;
16 and of the spoilings, let
fistfuls be spoiled for her
and leave them so that she gleans them
—and rebuke her not.
17 And she gleans in the field until evening
and threshes what she gleaned
—about an ephah of barley.
18 And she lifts it and goes into the city;
and her mother in law sees what she gleaned;
and she brings and gives her what remained
after she was satisfied.
19 And her mother in law says to her,
Where have you gleaned today?
And where have you worked?
Blessed—he who recognizes you.
And she tells her mother in law
whom she worked with, and says,
The name of the man I worked with today, Boaz.
20 And Noomiy says to her daughter in law,
Blessed—he of Yah Veh
who forsakes not his mercy
to the living and to the dead.
And Noomiy says to her,
The man is near to us—of our redeemers.
21 And Ruth the Moabiyth says,
He says to me also,
Stick by my lads until they finish all my harvest.
22 And Noomiy says to Ruth her daughter in law,
It is good, my daughter,
that thou go *out* with his *maidens* **lasses**,
that they meet thee not in any other field.
23 So she *kept fast* **stuck** by
the *maidens* **lasses** of Boaz
to glean unto the *end* **finish**
of barley harvest and of wheat harvest; and
dwelt **settled** with her mother in law.

BOAZ REDEEMS RUTH

3 Then *Naomi* **Noomiy** her mother in law
said unto her,
My daughter, shall I not seek rest for thee,
that it may *be well with* **well—please** thee?
2 And now is not Boaz of our *kindred* **kin**,
with whose *maidens* **lasses** thou wast?
Behold,
he winnoweth barley to night in the threshingfloor.
3 *Wash* **Baptise** thyself therefore, and anoint thee,
and *put* **set** thy *raiment* **clothes** upon thee,
and *get* **descend** thee *down* to the *floor* **threshingfloor**:
but make not thyself known unto the man,
until he shall have *done* **finished** eating and drinking.
4 And **so be** it *shall be*, when he lieth down,
that thou shalt *mark* **know** the place where he shall lie,
and thou shalt go in, and *uncover* **expose** his feet,
and lay thee down;
and he *will* **shall** tell thee what thou shalt *do* **work**.
5 And she said unto her,
All that thou sayest unto me I *will do* **shall work**.
6 And she *went down* **descended**
unto the *floor* **threshingfloor**,
and *did* **worked** according to all
that her mother in law *bade* **misvahed** her.
7 And when Boaz had eaten and drunk,
and his heart was *merry* **well—pleased**,
he went to lie down at the end of the *heap of corn* **heaps**:
and she came *softly* **undercover**,
and *uncovered* **exposed** his feet, and laid her down.
8 And **so be** it *came to pass*, at midnight,
that the man *was afraid* **trembled**,
and *turned himself* **clasped**:
and, behold, a woman lay at his feet.
9 And he said, Who art thou?
And she *answered* **said**,
I am Ruth *thine handmaid* **thy maid**:
spread therefore thy *skirt* **wing**
over *thine handmaid* **thy maid**;
for thou art a *near kinsman* **redeemer**.
10 And he said,
Blessed be thou of *the LORD* **Yah Veh**, my daughter:
for thou hast *shewed* **well—pleased** more *kindness* **mercy**
in the latter end than at the beginning,
inasmuch as
thou *followedst* **goest** not *young men* **after youths**,
whether poor or rich.
11 And now, my daughter, *fear* **awe** not;
I *will do* **shall work** to thee all that thou *requirest* **sayest**:
for all the *city* **portal** of my people
doth know that thou art a virtuous woman.
12 And now *it is true that* **truly**

I am thy *near kinsman* **redeemer**:
howbeit there is a *kinsman* **redeemer** nearer than I.
13 *Tarry this night* **Stay overnight**,
and **so be** it *shall be* in the morning,
that if he
will perform unto thee the part of a kinsman, well
shall redeem thee, good;
let him *do the kinsman's part* **redeem thee**:
but if he *will* **shall** not **delight**
do the part of a kinsman to **redeem** thee,
then *will I do the part of a kinsman*
to **shall I redeem** thee,
as *the LORD* **Yah Veh** liveth:
lie down until the morning.
14 And she lay at his feet until the morning:
and she rose up
before one could know another **ere**
man recognized friend.
And he said, Let it not be known
that a woman came into the *floor* **threshingfloor**.
15 Also he said,
It is good, my daughter, to go with his lasses,
so that they not meet you in any other field.
23 —and she sticks by the lasses of Boaz
to glean the finish
of barley harvest and of wheat harvest;
and settles with her mother in law.

BOAZ REDEEMS RUTH

3 And Noomiy her mother in law says to her,
My daughter,
seek I not rest for you, to well—please you?
2 And now, is not Boaz of our kin,
with whose lasses you were?
Behold,
he winnows barley in the threshingfloor tonight.
3 And you, baptise and anoint yourself
and set your clothes upon you
and descend to the threshingfloor;
and that the man not know you
until he finishes eating and drinking:
4 and so be it, when he lies down,
that you know the place where he lies;
and you go in and expose his feet and lie down;
and he tells you what to work.
5 And she says to her,
I work all you say to me.
6 —and she descends to the threshingfloor
and works according to all
her mother in law misvahs her.
7 And Boaz eats and drinks
and well—pleases his heart,
and he goes and lies down at the end of the heaps;
and she comes undercover
and exposes his feet and lies down.
8 And so be it, at midnight,
the man trembles and clasps;
and behold, a woman lies at his feet:
9 and he says, Who are you?
And she says, I am Ruth your maid;
you have spread your wing over your maid;
for you *are* a redeemer.
10 And he says,
Blessed—you of Yah Veh, my daughter;
for you well—please more mercy
in the latter end than at the beginning
by not going after youths
whether poor or rich.
11 And now, my daughter, awe not;
I work to you all that you say;
for all the portal of my people
know you are a virtuous woman.
12 And now truly I *am* a redeemer;
however there is a redeemer nearer than I.
13 Stay overnight;
and so be it, in the morning,
if he redeems you, good;
he redeems you;
but if he delights not to redeem you,
then as Yah Veh lives, I redeem you;
lie down until the morning.
14 —and she lies at his feet until the morning;
and she rises ere man recognizes friend.
And he says, Let it not be known
that a woman came into the threshingfloor.
15 And he says,
Bring the vail that thou hast **Give the cloak** upon thee,
and hold it.
And when she held it,
he measured six *measures of* barley,
and *laid* **placed** it on her:
and she went into the city.
16 And when she came to her
mother in law, she said,
Who art thou, my daughter?
And she told her
all that the man had *done* **worked** to her.
17 And she said,
These six *measures of* barley gave he me;
for he said to me, Go not empty unto thy mother in law.

18 Then said she, *Sit still* **Settle**, my daughter,
until thou know how the *matter will* **word shall**
fall: for the man *will* **shall** not *be in* rest,
until he have finished the *thing* **word** this day.

Boaz Marries Ruth

4 Then *went* Boaz **ascended** *up* to the *gate* **portal**,
and *sat him down* **settled** there: and, behold,
the *kinsman* **redeemer** of whom Boaz *spake* **worded**
came **passed** by;
unto whom he said, Ho, such a one!
turn aside, *sit down* **settle** here.
And he turned aside, and *sat down* **settled**.
2 And he took ten men of the elders of the city,
and said, *Sit* **Settle** ye *down* here.
And they *sat down* **settled**.
3 And he said unto the *kinsman* **redeemer**,
Naomi **Noomiy**,
that *is come again* **returned**
out of the *country* **fields** of Moab,
selleth *a parcel* **an allotment** of *land* **field**,
which was our brother *Elimelech's* **Eli Melech's**:
4 And I *thought* **said** to *advertise*
thee **expose in thine ear**,
saying,
Buy it before **Chattel in front of** the *inhabitants* **settlers**,
and *before* **in front of** the elders of my people.
If thou *wilt* **shalt** redeem it, redeem it:
but if thou *wilt* **shalt** not redeem it,
then tell me, that I may know:
for there is none to redeem it *beside* **except** thee;
and I am after thee.
And he said, I *will* **shall** redeem it.
5 Then said Boaz,
What day thou *buyest* **chattelest** the field
of the hand of *Naomi* **Noomiy**,
thou *must buy it* **chattelest** also
of Ruth the *Moabitess* **Moabiyth**,
the *wife* **woman** of the dead,
to raise up the name of the dead upon his inheritance.
6 And the *kinsman* **redeemer** said,
I cannot redeem it for myself,
lest I *mar* **ruin** mine own inheritance:
redeem thou my *right* **redemption** to thyself;
for I cannot redeem it.
7 Now this was
the manner in former time in Israel
at the face of Yisra El
concerning redeeming
and concerning *changing* **exchanging**,
for to confirm all *things* **words**;
a man *plucked* **drew** off his shoe,
and gave it to his *neighbour* **friend**:
and this was a *testimony* **witness** in *Israel* **Yisra El**.
8 Therefore the *kinsman*
redeemer said unto Boaz,
Buy it **Chattel** for thee. So he drew off his shoe.
9 And Boaz said unto the
elders, and *unto* all the people,
ye are witnesses this day,
that I have *bought* **chatteled** all
that was *Elimelech's* **Eli Melech's**,
and all that was *Chilion's* **Kilyon's**
and *Mahlon's* **Machlon's**,
of the hand of *Naomi* **Noomiy**.
10 Moreover Ruth the *Moabitess* **Moabiyth**,
the *wife* **woman** of *Mahlon* **Machlon**,
have I *purchased* **chatteled** to be my *wife* **woman**,
Give the cloak upon you, and hold it.
—and she holds it,
and he measures six barley and places it on her;
and she goes to the city.
16 And she comes to her mother in law,
and she says, Who *are* you, my daughter?
—and she tells her all the man worked to her.
17 And she says,
He gave me these six barley;
for he says to me,
Go not empty to your mother in law.
18 Then she says, Settle, my daughter,
until you know how the word falls;
for the man rests not
until he finishes the word this day.

Boaz Marries Ruth

4 And Boaz ascends to the
portal and settles there;
and behold,
the redeemer of whom Boaz worded passes by;
to whom he says, Ho, such a one!
Turn aside! Settle here!
—and he turns aside and settles.
2 And he takes ten men of the elders of the city
and says, You settle here.
—and they settle.
3 And he says to the redeemer,
Noomiy,
who returned from the fields of Moab,
sold an allotment of field,
of our brother Eli Melech;

4 and I say to expose in your ear, saying,
Chattel in front of the settlers
and in front of the elders of my people
—if you redeem, redeem;
but if you redeem not,
then tell me, so that I know;
for there is no one to redeem except you;
and I after you.
And he says, I redeem.
5 And Boaz says,
The day you chattel the field
of the hand of Noomiy,
you also chattel of Ruth the Moabiyth,
the woman of the dead,
to raise up the name of the dead
upon his inheritance.
6 And the redeemer says,
I cannot redeem it for myself,
lest I ruin my own inheritance;
redeem my redemption to yourself;
for I cannot redeem it.
7 Now at the face of Yisra El
concerning redeeming and concerning exchanging
to confirm all words was this;
a man draws his shoe and gives it to his friend;
and this is the witness in Yisra El.
8 And the redeemer says to Boaz,
Chattel for yourself.
—and he draws off his shoe.
9 And Boaz says to the elders
and to all the people,
you *are* witnesses this day,
that I chatteled all that of Eli Melech
and all that of Kilyon and Machlon,
of the hand of Noomiy;
10 and I also chatteled
Ruth the Moabiyth the woman of Machlon,
to be my woman,
to raise up the name of the dead upon his inheritance,
that the name of the dead be not cut off
from among his brethren,
and from the *gate* **portal** of his place:
ye are witnesses this day.
11 And all the people that were in the *gate* **portal**,
and the elders, said, We are witnesses.
The LORD **Yah Veh**
make **give** the woman that is come into thine house
like Rachel and like Leah,
which two did build the house of *Israel* **Yisra El**:
and *do* **work** thou
worthily **to get valuables** in *Ephratah* **Ephrath**,
and *be famous* **call out thy name**
in *Bethlehem* **Beth Lechem**:
12 And let thy house be like
the house of *Pharez* **Peres**,
whom Tamar *bare* **birthed** unto *Judah* **Yah Hudah**,
of the seed which *the LORD* **Yah Veh** shall give thee
of this *young woman* **lass**.
13 So Boaz took Ruth, and she was his *wife* **woman**:
and when he went in unto her,
the LORD **Yah Veh** gave her conception,
and she *bare* **birthed** a son.
14 And the women said unto *Naomi* **Noomiy**,
Blessed be *the LORD* **Yah Veh**,
which hath not *left* **ceased** thee this day
without a *kinsman* **redeemer**,
that his name may be *famous* **called**
out in *Israel* **Yisra El**.
15 And he shall be unto thee
a restorer of thy *life* **soul**,
and a *nourisher* **sustainer** of *thine old age* **thy grayness**:
for thy daughter in law, which loveth thee,
which is better to thee than seven sons,
hath *born* **birthed** him.
16 And *Naomi* **Noomiy** took the child,
and *laid* **placed** it in her bosom,
and *became nurse unto* **nursed** it.
17 And the women her
neighbours **fellow tabernaclers**
gave it a name **called out**, saying,
There is a son *born* **birthed** to *Naomi* **Noomiy**;
and they called his name Obed:
he is the father of *Jesse* **Yishay**, the father of David.

THE GENERATIONS OF PERES

18 Now these are the generations of *Pharez* **Peres**:
Pharez begat Hezron **Peres birthed Hesron**,
19 And *Hezron begat* **Hesron birthed** Ram,
and Ram *begat Amminadab* **birthed Ammi Nadab**,
20 And *Amminadab begat* **Ammi**
Nadab birthed Nahshon,
and Nahshon *begat Salmon* **birthed Salmah**,
21 And *Salmon begat* **Salmah birthed** Boaz,
and Boaz *begat* **birthed** Obed,
22 And Obed *begat Jesse* **birthed Yishay**,
and *Jesse begat* **Yishay birthed** David.
to raise up the name of the dead
upon his inheritance,
that the name of the dead not be cut off
from among his brothers

and from the portal of his place;
you are witnesses this day.
11 And all the people in the portal, and the elders,
say, We are witnesses.
Yah Veh give the woman
who comes into your house
as Rachel and as Leah;
which two built the house of Yisra El;
and work you to get valuables in Ephrath
and call out your name in Beth Lechem;
12 and that your house be as the house of Peres,
whom Tamar *bare* **birthed** to Yah Hudah,
of the seed which Yah Veh gives you of this lass.
13 And Boaz takes Ruth
and she becomes his woman;
and he goes in to her
and Yah Veh gives her conception
and she births a son.
14 And the women say to Noomiy,
Blessed—Yah Veh,
who has not ceased you this day
without a redeemer,
to call out his name in Yisra El.
15 And he becomes a restorer of your soul
and a sustainer of your grayness;
for your daughter in law, who loves you,
who is better to you than seven sons,
births him.
16 And Noomiy takes the child
and places it in her bosom and nurses it.
17 And the women, her fellow tabernaclers,
call out, saying,
There a son *is* birthed to Noomiy;
and they call his name Obed
—he is the father of Yishay, the father of David.

The Generations Of Peres

18 And these are the generations of Peres;
Peres births Hesron
19 and Hesron births Ram
and Ram births Ammi Nadab
20 and Ammi Nadab births Nahshon
and Nahshon births Salmah
21 and Salmah births Boaz
and Boaz births Obed
22 and Obed births Yishay
and Yishay births David.

Vashti The Sovereigness

1 *Now it came to pass* **And so be it,**
in the days of *Ahasuerus* **Achash Rosh,**
(this is *Ahasuerus* **Achash Rosh** which reigned,
from *India* **Hodu** even unto *Ethiopia* **Kush,**
over an hundred and seven and twenty
provinces **jurisdictions:)**
2 That in those days,
when the *king Ahasuerus* **sovereign Achash Rosh**
sat **settled** on the throne of his *kingdom* **sovereigndom,**
which was in Shushan the palace,
3 In the third year of his reign,
he *made* **worked** a *feast* **banquet**
unto all his *princes* **governors** and his servants;
the *power* **virtuous** of Persia and *Media* **Maday,**
the nobles and *princes* **governors**
of the *provinces* **jurisdictions,**
being before him **at his face:**
4 When he *shewed* **had them see** the riches
of the honour of his *glorious kingdom* **sovereigndom**
and the *honour* **esteem**
of the adornment of his *excellent majesty* **greatness**
many days,
even an hundred and *fourscore* **eighty** days.
5 And when these days were *expired* **fulfilled,**
the *king made* **sovereign worked** a *feast* **banquet**
unto all the people
that were *present* **found** in Shushan the palace,
both unto great and small, seven days,
in the court of the garden
of the *king's* **sovereign's** palace;
6 Where were white, *green*
byssus, and blue, *hangings,*
fastened **held** with cords
of *fine linen* **bleached cotton** and purple
to silver rings and pillars of **white** marble:
the beds were of gold and silver,
upon a pavement of *red* **bright,**
and *blue* **white marble,** and *white* **pearl,**
and *black, marble* **black tile.**
7 And they gave them drink
in *vessels* **instruments** of gold,
(the *vessels* **instruments**
being diverse one **differing** from *another* **instruments,)**
and *royal* wine **of the sovereigndom** in abundance,
according to the *state* **hand** of the *king* **sovereign.**
8 And the drinking was
according to the *law* **edict;**
none *did compel* **insisted:**
for so the *king* **sovereign** had *appointed* **founded**
to all the *officers* **great** of his house,
that they should *do* **work** according to
every man's **the** pleasure **of man to man.**
9 Also Vashti the *queen* **sovereigness**
made **worked** a *feast* **banquet** for the women
in the *royal* house **of the sovereigndom**
which belonged to king Ahasuerus
of sovereign Achash Rosh.
10 On the seventh day,
when the heart of the *king* **sovereign**
was *merry* **good** with wine,
he *commanded* **said to** Mehuman,
Biztha, Harbona, Bigtha, and Abagtha,
Zethar, and *Carcas* **Karcas,**
the seven *chamberlains* **eunuchs** that *served* **ministered**
in the presence **at the face**
of *Ahasuerus* **Achash Rosh** the *king* **sovereign,**
11 To bring Vashti the *queen* **sovereigness**
before **at the face of** the *king* **sovereign**
with the *crown royal* **diadem of the sovereigndom,**
to *shew* **have** the people and the *princes* **governors**
see her beauty:
for she was *fair to look on* **good of visage.**
12 But the *queen* **sovereigness** Vashti refused
to come at the *king's commandment* **sovereign's word**
by **the hand of** his *chamberlains* **eunuchs:**
therefore
was the *king very wroth* **sovereign mighty enraged,**
and his *anger* **fury** burned in him.
13 Then the *king* **sovereign** said to the wise men,
which knew the times,

Vashti The Sovereigness

1 And so be it,
in the days of Achash Rosh
—Achash Rosh who reigns
from Hodu even to Kush
—a hundred and twenty—seven jurisdictions;
2 in those days,
the sovereign Achash Rosh
settles on the throne of his sovereigndom
in Shushan palace;
3 in the third year of his reign,
he works a banquet
to all his governors and his servants;
the virtuous of Persia and Maday,
the nobles and governors of the jurisdictions
at his face;
4 and he shows them the riches

of the honor of his sovereigndom
and the esteem of the adornment of his greatness
many days—even a hundred and eighty days.
5 And in the fulfilling of these days
the sovereign works a banquet
to all the people found in Shushan palace
both to great and small
seven days
in the court of the garden
of the palace of the sovereign;
6 —white, byssus and blue
held with cords of bleached cotton and purple
to silver rings and pillars of white marble;
the beds of gold and silver
on a pavement of bright and white marble
and pearl and black tile;
7 and they give them drink in instruments of gold
—instruments differing from instruments
and wine of the sovereigndom in abundance
according to the hand of the sovereign.
8 And the drinking is according to the edict;
no one insisting;
for thus the sovereign founded
to all the great of his house;
to work according to the pleasure of man to man.
9 Also Vashti the sovereigness
works a banquet for the women
in the house of the sovereigndom
of sovereign Achash Rosh.
10 On the seventh day,
when the heart of the sovereign is good with wine,
he says to Mehuman, Biztha, Harbona,
Bigtha and Abagtha, Zethar and Karcas,
the seven eunuchs who minister
at the face of Achash Rosh the sovereign,
11 to bring Vashti the sovereigness
at the face of the sovereign
with the diadem of the sovereigndom
—for the people and the governors
to see her beauty
—for she is of good visage.
12 And the sovereigness Vashti refuses
to come at the word of the sovereign
by the hand of his eunuchs;
and the sovereign enrages mightily,
and his fury burns within him.
13 And the sovereign says
to the wise men who know the times
(for so was the *king's manner* **sovereign's word**
toward **at the face of** all
that knew *law* **edict** and *judgment* **pleading**:
14 And *the next* **near** unto him
was *Carshena* **Karshena**,
Shethar, Admatha, Tarshish,
Meres, Marsena, and *Memucan* **Memuchan**,
the seven *princes* **governors** of Persia and *Media* **Maday**,
which saw the *king's* **sovereign's** face,
and *which sat* **settled** the first
in the *kingdom* **sovereigndom**;)
15 What shall we *do* **work**
unto the *queen* **sovereigness** Vashti
according to *law* **edict**,
because
she hath not *performed* **worked** the *commandment* **edict**
of the *king Ahasuerus* **sovereign Achash Rosh**
by **the hand of** the *chamberlains* **eunuchs**?
16 And *Memucan answered* **Memuchan said**
before **at the face**
of the *king* **sovereign** and the *princes* **governors**,
Vashti the *queen* **sovereigness**
hath not *done wrong* **bent** to the *king* **sovereign** only,
but also to all the princes,
and to all the people
that are in all the *provinces* **jurisdictions**
of the *king Ahasuerus* **sovereign Achash Rosh**.
17 For this *deed* **word** of the *queen* **sovereigness**
shall *come abroad* **go** unto all women,
so that they shall despise their *husbands* **masters**
in their eyes,
when it shall be reported **saying**,
The king Ahasuerus **Sovereign Achash Rosh**
commanded **said to** Vashti the *queen* **sovereigness**
to be brought in *before him* **at his face**,
but she came not.
18 Likewise shall the *ladies* **governesses** of Persia
and *Media* **Maday** say this day
unto all the *king's princes* **sovereign's governors**,
which have heard
of the *deed* **word** of the *queen* **sovereigness**.
Thus shall there arise
too much contempt **enough despite** and *wrath* **rage**.
19 If it *please* **be good with** the *king* **sovereign**,
let there go
a *royal commandment* **word of the sovereigndom**
from *him* **his face**,
and let it be *written* **inscribed** among the *laws* **edicts**
of the Persians and the *Medes* **Maday**,
that it *be not altered* **pass not away**,
That Vashti come no more
before **at the face of**

king Ahasuerus **sovereign Achash Rosh;**
and let the *king* **sovereign**
give her *royal estate* **sovereigndom**
unto *another* **her friend** that is better than she.
20 And when the *king's decree* **sovereign's sentence**
which he shall *make* **work**
shall be *published* **heard**
throughout all his *empire* **sovereigndom,**
(for it is great,)
all the *wives* **women**
shall give to their *husbands honour* **masters esteem,**
both to great and small.
21 And the *saying* **word**
well—pleased **the eyes of** the *king* **sovereign**
and the *princes* **governors;**
and the *king did* **sovereign worked**
according to the word of *Memucan* **Memuchan:**
22 For he sent *letters* **scrolls**
into all the *king's provinces* **sovereign's jurisdictions,**
into every province—**jurisdiction by jurisdiction**
according to the *writing* **inscribing** thereof,
and to *every people* **people by people**
after their *language* **tongue,**
that every man should bear rule in his own house,
and that it should be *published* **worded**
according to the *language* **tongue** of every people.
—for thus is the word of the sovereign
at the face of all who know edict and pleading;
14 and near to him, Karshena, Shethar, Admatha,
Tarshish, Meres, Marsena and Memuchan
—the seven governors of Persia and Maday,
who see the face of the sovereign
—who settle first in the sovereigndom;
15 What work we according to the edict
to the sovereigness Vashti
—because she works not the edict
of the sovereign Achash Rosh
by the hand of the eunuchs?
16 And Memuchan
at the face of the sovereign and the governors says,
Vashti the sovereigness
bends not to the sovereign only,
but also to all the princes and to all the people
in all the jurisdictions of the sovereign Achash Rosh.
17 For this word of the sovereigness
goes to all women,
so that they despise their masters in their eyes,
saying,
Sovereign Achash Rosh said
to bring Vashti the sovereigness at his face;
but she comes not.
18 Yes, this day
the governesses of Persia and Maday say to all the
governors of the sovereign who hear of the word of the
sovereigness. Thus there rises enough despite and rage.
19 If it be good with the sovereign,
let a word of the sovereigndom
go from his face
—inscribed among the edicts
of the Persians and the Maday
that it not pass away,
that Vashti come no more
at the face of sovereign Achash Rosh;
and that the sovereign
give her sovereigndom to her friend
who is better than she.
20 And when the sentence the sovereign works
is heard throughout all his sovereigndom,
—for it is great
all the women give their masters esteem;
both to great and small.
21 And the word well—pleases
the eyes of the sovereign and the governors:
and the sovereign works
according to the word of Memuchan:
22 and he sends scrolls
to all the jurisdictions of the sovereign
—jurisdiction by jurisdiction
according to the inscribing thereof
and to people by people after their tongue,
that every man bears rule in his own house;
and that it be worded
according to the tongue of every people.

A Sovereigness Is Sought

2 After these *things* **words,**
when the *wrath* **fury**
of *king Ahasuerus* **sovereign Achash Rosh**
was *appeased* **assuaged,**
he remembered Vashti, and what she had *done* **worked,**
and what was *decreed* **cut** against her.
2 Then said the *king's servants* **sovereign's lads**
that ministered unto him,
Let there be *fair young* **lasses of good visage**
—virgins sought for the *king* **sovereign:**
3 And let the *king* **sovereign**
appoint officers **oversee overseers**
in all the *provinces* **jurisdictions**
of his *kingdom* **sovereigndom,**
that they may gather together

all the *fair young* **lasses of good visage**
—virgins unto Shushan the palace,
to the house of the women,
unto the *custody* **hand** of Hege
the *king's chamberlain* **sovereign's eunuch,**
keeper **guard** of the women;
and let their *things for* purification be given them:
4 And let the *maiden* **lass**
which **well**—pleaseth **the eyes of** the *king* **sovereign**
be queen **reign** instead of Vashti.
And the *thing* **word**
well—pleased **the eyes of** the *king* **sovereign;**
and he *did* **worked** so.
5 Now in Shushan the palace
there was a *certain Jew* **man—a Yah Hudiy,**
whose name was *Mordecai* **Mordekay,**
the son of *Jair* **Yair,** the son of *Shimei* **Shimi,**
the son of *Kish* **Qish,** a *Benjamite* **man of Ben Yamin;**
6 Who had been *carried away* **exiled**
from *Jerusalem* **Yeru Shalem** with the *captivity* **exile**
which had been *carried away* **exiled**
with *Jeconiah* **Yekon Yah**
king **sovereign** of *Judah* **Yah Hudah,**
whom *Nebuchadnezzar* **Nebukadnets Tsar**
the *king* **sovereign** of *Babylon* **Babel**
had *carried away* **exiled.**
7 And he *brought up* **fostered** Hadassah,
that is, *Esther* **Ester,** his uncle's daughter:
for she had neither father nor mother,
and the *maid* **lass** was *fair* **beautiful of form**
and *beautiful* **good of visage;**
whom *Mordecai* **Mordekay,**
when her father and mother *were dead* **died,**
took for his own daughter.

Ester Well—Pleases The Eyes Of The Sovereign

8 *So it came to pass* **And so be it,**
when the *king's commandment* **sovereign's word**
and his *decree* **edict** was heard,
and when many *maidens* **lasses** were gathered *together*
unto Shushan the palace, to the *custody* **hand** of Hegai,
that *Esther* **Ester** was *brought* **taken** *also*
unto the *king's* **sovereign's** house,
to the *custody* **hand** of Hegai,
keeper **guard** of the women.
9 And the *maiden* **lass well**—pleased *him* **his eyes,**
and she *obtained kindness of him* **bore mercy at his face;**
and he *speedily gave her* **hastened**
her *things for purification* **purifications,**
with *such things as belonged to her* **her portions,**
and seven *maidens* **lasses,**
which were *meet* **seen** to be given her,
out of the *king's* **sovereign's** house:
and he *preferred* **changed** her and her *maids* **lasses**
unto the best *place* of the house of the women.
10 *Esther* **Ester** had not *shewed* **told** her people
nor her kindred:
for *Mordecai* **Mordekay** had *charged* **misvahed** her
that she should not *shew* **tell** it.
11 And *Mordecai* **Mordekay**
walked *every* day **by day**
before **at the face of** the court of the women's house,
to know *how Esther did* **the shalom of Ester,**
and what should *become* **be worked** of her.

A Sovereigness Is Sought

2 After these words,
the fury of sovereign Achash Rosh assuages,
and he remembers Vashti and what she worked
and what was cut against her.
2 And the lads of the sovereign
who minister to him say,
Seek out virgin lasses of good visage
for the sovereign;
3 and have the sovereign oversee overseers
in all the jurisdictions of his sovereigndom,
to gather all the virgin lasses of good visage
to Shushan palace to the house of the women,
to the hand of Hegai the eunuch of the sovereign,
guard of the women;
and give them their purification;
4 and have the lass
who well—pleases the eyes of the sovereign
reign instead of Vashti.
—and the word
well—pleases the eyes of the sovereign;
and thus he works.
5 And there is a man in Shushan palace
—a Yah Hudiy—his name,
Mordekay the son of Yair the son of Shimi
the son of Qish,
a man of Ben Yamin
6 who was exiled from Yeru Shalem
with the exile which was exiled
with Yekon Yah sovereign of Yah Hudah,
whom Nebukadnets Tsar the sovereign of Babel
exiled.
7 And he fosters Hadassah,
that is, Ester, the daughter of his uncle;

for she has neither father nor mother
and the lass *is* beautiful of form and good of visage;
whom, when her father and mother died,
Mordekay took for his own daughter.

Ester Well—Pleases The Eyes Of The Sovereign

8 And so be it,
the word and the edict of the sovereign is heard;
and many lasses gather to Shushan palace
to the hand of Hegai:
and Ester is taken to the house of the sovereign
to the hand of Hegai the guard of the women.
9 And the lass well—pleases his eyes
and he mercies her at his face;
and he hastens her purifications with her portions
and seven lasses from the house of the sovereign,
are seen to be given her;
and he changes her and her lasses
to the best of the house of the women.
10 Ester told neither her people nor her kindred;
for Mordekay misvahed her to not tell:
11 and Mordekay walks day by day
at the face of the court of the house of the women,
to know the shalom of Ester
and what is worked of her.
12 Now when every *maid's* **lasses'** turn
was *come* **reached**
to go in to *king Ahasuerus* **sovereign Achash Rosh,**
after that she had been **at the end of** twelve months,
according to the *manner* **edict** of the women,
(for so were the days of their purifications
accomplished **fulfilled,** *to wit,*
six months with oil of myrrh,
and six months with *sweet odours* **spices,**
and with other *things for the purifying* **purifications**
of the women;)
13 Then thus came *every maiden* **the lasses**
unto the *king* **sovereign;**
whatsoever she *desired* **said** was given her
to go with her out of the house of the women
unto the *king's* **sovereign's** house.
14 In the evening she went,
and on the *morrow* **morning** she returned
into the second house of the women, to
the *custody* **hand** of Shaashgaz,
the *king's chamberlain* **sovereign's eunuch,**
which *kept* **guarded** the concubines:
she came in unto the *king* **sovereign** no more,
except the *king* **sovereign** delighted in her,
and that she were called by name.
15 Now when the turn of *Esther* **Ester,**
the daughter of *Abihail* **Abi Hail**
the uncle of *Mordecai* **Mordekay,**
who had taken her for his daughter,
was *come* **reached** to go in unto the *king* **sovereign,**
she *required nothing* **sought no word**
but what Hegai
the *king's chamberlain* **sovereign's eunuch,**
the *keeper* **guard** of the women, *appointed* **said.**
And *Esther obtained favour* **Ester received charism**
in the *sight* **eyes** of all them that *looked upon* **saw** her.
16 So *Esther* **Ester** was taken
unto *king Ahasuerus* **sovereign Achash Rosh**
into *his house royal* **the house of his sovereigndom**
in the tenth month, which is the month Tebeth,
in the seventh year of his *reign* **sovereigndom.**

Sovereigness Ester

17 And the *king* **sovereign**
loved *Esther* **Ester** above all the women,
and she *obtained grace* **received**
charism and *favour* **mercy**
in his sight **at his face** more than all the virgins;
so that he set
the *royal crown* **diadem of the sovereigndom**
upon her head,
and made her *queen* **reign** instead of Vashti.
18 Then the *king* **sovereign**
made **worked** a great *feast* **banquet**
unto all his *princes* **governors** and his servants,
even *Esther's feast* **Ester's banquet;**
and he *made* **worked** a *release* **rest**
to the *provinces* **jurisdictions,**
and gave *gifts* **loads,**
according to the *state* **hand** of the *king* **sovereign.**

Mordekay Saves The Sovereign

19 And when the virgins
were gathered *together* the second time,
then *Mordecai* **Mordekay**
sat **settled** in the *king's gate* **sovereign's portal.**
20 *Esther* **Ester** had not *yet shewed* **told** her kindred
nor her people;
as *Mordecai* **Mordekay** had *charged* **misvahed** her:
for *Esther did* **Ester worked**
the *commandment* **edict** of *Mordecai* **Mordekay,**
like as when she was *brought up with* **tutored by** him.
21 In those days,
while *Mordecai* **Mordekay**

sat **settled** in the *king's gate* **sovereign's portal,**
two of the *king's chamberlains* **sovereign's eunuchs,**
Bigthan and Teresh,
of those which kept **guards of** the *door* **threshold,**
were *wroth* **enraged,**
and sought to *lay* **send their** hand
on *the king Ahasuerus* **sovereign Achash Rosh.**
22 And the *thing* **word** was
known to *Mordecai* **Mordekay,**
12 And at the end of twelve months
every lass reaches her turn
to go in to sovereign Achash Rosh
—according to the edict of the women,
—for thus are the days of their purifications fulfilled;
six months with oil of myrrh
and six months with spices
and with other purifications of the women
13 —and thus the lasses come to the sovereign;
and whatever she says is given her
to go with her from the house of the women
to the house of the sovereign.
14 In the evening she goes;
and in the morning she returns
into the second house of the women
to the hand of Shaashgaz
the eunuch of the sovereign
who guards the concubines;
she comes in to the sovereign no more,
unless the sovereign delights in her
and calls her name.
15 And the turn of Ester,
the daughter of Abi Hail the uncle of Mordekay
who took her for his daughter,
is reached to go in to the sovereign;
and she seeks no word
but what Hegai the eunuch of the sovereign
the guard of the women says.
And Ester receives charism
in the eyes of all who see her:
16 and they take Ester to sovereign Achash Rosh
to the house of his sovereigndom
in the tenth month, the month Tebeth,
in the seventh year of his sovereigndom.

SOVEREIGNESS ESTER

17 And the sovereign
loves Ester above all the women
and she receives charism and mercy
at his face more than all the virgins;
so that he sets the diadem of the sovereigndom
on her head
and has her reign instead of Vashti.
18 And the sovereign works a great banquet
to all his governors and his servants,
—the banquet of Ester;
and he works a rest to the jurisdictions
and gives loads
according to the hand of the sovereign.

MORDEKAY SAVES THE SOVEREIGN

19 And the virgins gather the second time,
and Mordekay settles in the portal of the sovereign.
20 Ester tells neither her kindred nor her people
as Mordekay misvahed her;
for Ester worked the edict of Mordekay,
as when he tutored her.
21 In those days,
Mordekay settles in the portal of the sovereign,
and two of the eunuchs of the sovereign,
Bigthan and Teresh, guards of the threshold,
enrage;
and seek to send their hand
on sovereign Achash Rosh.
22 And the word is known to Mordekay,
who told it unto *Esther* **Ester** the *queen* **sovereigness;**
and *Esther certified* **Ester said it to**
the *king thereof* **sovereign**
in *Mordecai's* **Mordekay's** name.
23 And when *inquisition* **the word**
was *made of the matter* **researched,**
it was found out;
therefore they were both hanged on a tree:
and it was *written* **inscribed** in the *book* **scroll**
of the *chronicles* **words of the days**
before **at the face of** the *king* **sovereign.**

HAMAN PLOTS AGAINST THE YAH HUDIY

3 After these *things* **words**
did king Ahasuerus **sovereign Achash Rosh**
promote **greatened** Haman
the son of *Hammedatha* **Medatha** the *Agagite* **Agagiy,**
and *advanced* **lifted** him,
and set his seat
above all the *princes* **governors** that were with him.
2 And all the *king's* **sovereign's** servants,
that were in the *king's gate* **sovereign's portal,**
bowed, and *reverenced* **prostrated to** Haman:
for the *king* **sovereign** had so *commanded* **misvahed**
concerning him.

But *Mordecai* **Mordekay** bowed not,
nor *did him reverence* **prostrated.**
3 Then the *king's* **sovereign's** servants,
which were in the *king's gate* **sovereign's**
portal, said unto *Mordecai* **Mordekay**,
Why *transgressest* **trespassest** thou
the *king's commandment* **sovereign's misvah**?
4 *Now it came to pass* **And so be it**,
when they *spake daily* **said day by day** unto him,
and he hearkened not unto them, that they told Haman,
to see whether *Mordecai's matters* **Mordekay's words**
would **should** stand:
for he had told them that he was *a Jew* **Yah Hudiy**.
5 And when Haman saw
that *Mordecai* **Mordekay** bowed not,
nor *did him reverence* **prostrated to him**,
then was Haman *full of wrath* **filled with fury**.
6 And *he thought scorn* **despicable in his eyes**
to *lay* **send forth** hands on *Mordecai* **Mordekay** alone;
for they had *shewed* **told** him **of** the people
of *Mordecai* **Mordekay**:
wherefore Haman
sought to *destroy* **desolate** all the *Jews* **Yah Hudiym**
that were throughout the whole *kingdom* **sovereigndom**
of *Ahasuerus* **Achash Rosh**,
even the people of *Mordecai* **Mordekay**.
7 In the first month, that is, the month Nisan,
in the twelfth year
of *king Ahasuerus* **sovereign Achash Rosh**,
they *cast* **felled** Pur, that is, the *lot* **pebble**,
before **at the face of** Haman from day to day,
and from month to month,
to the twelfth *month*, that is, the month Adar.
8 And Haman said
unto *king Ahasuerus* **sovereign Achash Rosh**,
There is *a certain* **one** people scattered *abroad*
and *dispersed* **spread** among the people
in all the *provinces* **jurisdictions**
of thy *kingdom* **sovereigndom**;
and their *laws* **edicts** are diverse from all people;
neither *keep* **work** they the *king's laws* **sovereign's edicts**:
therefore it is not **equated**
for the *king's profit* **sovereign** to *suffer* **allow** them.
9 If it *please* **be good with** the *king* **sovereign**,
let it be *written* **inscribed** that they may be destroyed:
and I *will pay* **shall weigh**
ten thousand *talents* **rounds** of silver
to the hands of *those that have the charge* **the workers**
of the *business* **work**,
to bring it into the *king's* **sovereign's** treasuries.
10 And the *king* **sovereign**
took **twisted off** his *ring* **signet** from his hand,
and gave it unto Haman
the son of *Hammedatha* **Medatha** the *Agagite* **Agagiy**,
the *Jews' enemy* **Yah Hudiym's tribulator**.
11 And the *king* **sovereign** said unto Haman,
who tells it to Ester the sovereigness;
and Ester says it to the sovereign
in the name of Mordekay.
23 And they research the word,
and find out;
and hang them both on a tree;
and inscribe it
in the scroll of the words of the days
at the face of the sovereign.

HAMAN PLOTS AGAINST THE YAH HUDIY

3 After these words
sovereign Achash Rosh greatens Haman
the son of Medatha the Agagiy
and lifts him
and sets his seat above all the governors with him.
2 And all the servants of the sovereign
in the portal of the sovereign
bow and prostrate to Haman;
for thus the sovereign misvahs concerning him.
—and Mordekay neither bows nor prostrates.
3 And the servants of the sovereign
in the portal of the sovereign
say to Mordekay,
Why trespass you the misvah of the sovereign?
4 And so be it,
day by day they say to him;
and he hearkens not to them,
and they tell Haman
to see whether the words of Mordekay stand;
for he had told them that he *is* a Yah Hudiy.
5 And Haman sees
that Mordekay neither bows nor prostrates to him;
and Haman fills with fury:
6 and it is despicable in his eyes
to send forth hands on Mordekay by himself;
for they tell him of the people of Mordekay;
and Haman seeks to desolate all the Yah Hudiym
throughout the whole sovereigndom
of Achash Rosh
—the people of Mordekay.
7 In the first month—the month Nisan
in the twelfth year of sovereign Achash Rosh,
they fell Pur, that *is*, the pebble,

at the face of Haman from day to day
and from month to month
to the twelfth—that *is*, the month Adar.
8 And Haman says to sovereign Achash Rosh,
There is one people scattered
and spread among the people
in all the jurisdictions of your sovereigndom;
and their edicts are diverse from all people;
they work not the edicts of the sovereign;
and it equates not that the sovereign allow them.
9 If it be good with the sovereign,
inscribe to destroy them;
and I weigh ten thousand rounds of silver
to the hands of the workers of the work
to bring it into the treasuries of the sovereign.
10 And the sovereign twists
his signet from his hand
and gives it to Haman
the son of Medatha the Agagiy
the tribulator of the Yah Hudiym.
11 And the sovereign says to Haman,
The silver is given to thee, the people also,
to *do* **work** with them
as it seemeth good *to thee* **in thine eyes**.
12 Then were the *king's* **sovereign's** scribes called
on the thirteenth *day* of the first month,
and there was *written* **inscribed**
according to all that Haman had *commanded* **misvahed**
unto the *king's lieutenants* **sovereign's satraps**,
and to the governors that were over
every province **jurisdiction by jurisdiction**,
and to the *rulers* **governors**
of *every people* **people by people**
of *every province* **jurisdiction by jurisdiction**
according to the *writing* **inscribings** thereof,
and to *every people* **people by people**
after their *language* **tongue**;
in the name of *king Ahasuerus* **sovereign Achash Rosh**
was it *written* **inscribed**,
and sealed with the *king's ring* **sovereign's signet**.
13 And the *letters* **scrolls** were sent
by *posts* **the hand of runners**
into all the *king's provinces* **sovereign's jurisdictions**,
to *destroy* **desolate**, to *kill* **slaughter**,
and to *cause to perish* **destroy**, all *Jews* **Yah Hudiym**,
both young and old **from lad to old man**,
little children **toddlers** and women, in one day,
even upon the thirteenth *day* of the twelfth month,
which is the month Adar,
and *to take the spoil of them for a*
prey **spoil their plunder**.
14 The *copy* **transcript** of the *writing* **inscribings**
for *a commandment* **an edict** to be given
in every province **jurisdiction by jurisdiction**
was *published* **exposed** unto all people,
that they should be ready against that day.
15 The *posts* **runners** went out,
being hastened
by the *king's commandment* **sovereign's word**,
and the *decree* **edict** was given in Shushan the palace.
And the *king* **sovereign** and Haman sat *down* to drink;
but the city Shushan was perplexed.

ESTER TOLD OF THE PLOT OF HAMAN

4 When *Mordecai* **Mordekay**
perceived all that was *done* **worked**,
Mordecai rent **Mordekay ripped** his clothes,
and *put on sackcloth* **enrobed saq** with ashes,
and went out into the midst of the city,
and cried with a *loud* **great** and a bitter cry;
2 And came even
before **at the face of** the *king's gate* **sovereign's portal**:
for none might enter
into the *king's gate* **sovereign's portal**
clothed **enrobed** with *sackcloth* **saq**.
3 And in *every province*
jurisdiction by jurisdiction,
whithersoever **whatever place**
the *king's commandment* **sovereign's word**
and his *decree came* **edict touched**,
there was great mourning among the *Jews* **Yah Hudiym**,
and fasting, and weeping, and *wailing* **chopping**;
and many *lay* **spread** in *sackcloth* **saq** and ashes.
4 So *Esther's maids* **Ester's lasses**
and her *chamberlains* **eunuchs** came and told *it* her.
Then was the *queen* **sovereigness**
exceedingly grieved **mightily writhed**;
and she sent *raiment* **clothes**
to *clothe Mordecai* **enrobe Mordekay**,
and to *take away* **turn aside** his *sackcloth* **saq** from him:
but he *received* **took** it not.
5 Then called *Esther* **Ester** for *Hatach* **Hathach**,
one of the *king's chamberlains* **sovereign's eunuchs**,
whom he had *appointed* **stood** to *attend upon* **face** her,
and *gave him a commandment* **misvahed**
to Mordecai **for Mordekay**,
to know what it was, and why it was.
6 So *Hatach* **Hathach** went
forth to *Mordecai* **Mordekay**
unto the *street* **broadway** of the city,
which was before **at the face**

of the *king's gate* **sovereign's portal.**
7 And *Mordecai* **Mordekay** told him
of all that had happened unto him,
The silver is given to you—the people also
to work with them as *is* good in your eyes.
12 Then they call the scribes of the sovereign
on the thirteenth of the first month;
and they inscribe
according to all that Haman misvahed
to the satraps of the sovereign
and to the governors
over jurisdiction by jurisdiction;
and to the governors of people by people
of jurisdiction by jurisdiction;
according to the inscribings thereof;
and to people by people after their tongue;
inscribed in the name of sovereign Achash Rosh
and sealed with the signet of the sovereign.
13 And they send scrolls by the hand of runners
into all the jurisdictions of the sovereign
—to desolate, to slaughter and to destroy
all Yah Hudiym—from lad to old man,
toddlers and women, in one day,
upon the thirteenth of the twelfth month
—the month Adar
and spoil their plunder;
14 the transcript of the inscribings for an edict
to be given jurisdiction by jurisdiction
is exposed to all people
to be ready against that day.
15 The runners go,
hastened by the word of the sovereign
and the edict is given in Shushan palace.
And the sovereign and Haman sit to drink;
and the city Shushan is perplexed.

Ester Told Of The Plot Of Haman

4 And Mordekay perceives all that was worked,
and Mordekay rips his clothes
and enrobes saq with ashes;
and goes midst the city
and cries a great and a bitter cry;
2 and he even comes
at the face of the portal of the sovereign
—for no one enters the portal of the sovereign
enrobed with saq.
3 And in jurisdiction by jurisdiction
whatever place
the word of the sovereign and his edict touches,
there is great mourning among the Yah Hudiym
and fasting and weeping and chopping;
and many spread in saq and ashes.
4 And the lasses of Ester
and her eunuchs come and tell her.
And the sovereigness writhes mightily;
and she sends clothes to enrobe Mordekay
and to turn aside his saq from him;
but he takes it not.
5 And Ester calls for Hathach,
one of the eunuchs of the sovereign
whom he stands at her face;
to misvah for Mordekay to know what and why.
6 And Hathach goes forth to Mordekay
to the broadway of the city
at the face of the portal of the sovereign.
7 And Mordekay tells him
all that happened to him
and of the sum of the *money* **silver**
that Haman had *promised* **said**
to *pay* **weigh** to the *king's* **sovereign's** treasuries
for the *Jews* **Yah Hudiym**, to destroy them.
8 Also he gave him
the *copy* **transcript** of the *writing* **inscribing**
of the *decree* **edict** that was given at Shushan
to *destroy* **desolate** them,
to *shew it unto Esther* **have Ester see,**
and to declare it unto her,
and to *charge* **misvah** her
that she should go in unto the *king* **sovereign,**
to *make supplication unto* **beseech charism of** him,
and to *make request before him* **beseech at his face**
for her people.
9 And *Hatach* **Hathach**
came and told *Esther* **Ester**
the words of *Mordecai* **Mordekay.**
10 *Again Esther spake* **And Ester**
said unto *Hatach* **Hathach,**
and *gave him commandment* **misvahed**
unto Mordecai **for Mordekay;**
11 All the *king's* **sovereign's**
servants, and the people
of the *king's provinces* **sovereign's jurisdictions,**
do know, that whosoever, whether man or woman,
shall come unto the *king* **sovereign** into the inner court,
who is not called,
there is one *law* **edict** of his to *put* **deathify** him *to death,*
except **apart from** such to whom the *king* **sovereign**
shall *hold out* **spread** the golden *sceptre* **scion,**
that he may live:
but I have not been called

to come in unto the *king* **sovereign** these thirty days.
12 And they told to *Mordecai*
Mordekay *Esther's* **Ester's** words.
13 Then *Mordecai* **Mordekay**
commanded to answer Esther **said to respond to Ester,**
Think **Consider** not with *thyself* **thy soul**
that thou shalt escape in the *king's* **sovereign's** house,
more than all the *Jews* **Yah Hudiym.**

The Mission Of Sovereigness Ester

14 For if **in hushing,**
thou *altogether holdest thy peace* **hushest** at this time,
then shall *there enlargement* **respite**
and *deliverance arise* **rescue stand**
to the *Jews* **Yah Hudiym** from another place;
but thou and thy father's house shall be destroyed:
and who knoweth whether
thou *art come to* **touchest** the *kingdom* **sovereigndom**
for *such* a time as this?
15 Then *Esther bade them* **Ester said to**
return *Mordecai* **Mordekay** this *answer,*
16 Go, gather *together* all the *Jews* **Yah Hudiym**
that are *present* **found** in Shushan, and fast ye for me,
and neither eat nor drink three days, night or day:
I also and my *maidens will* **lasses shall** fast likewise;
and *so will* **thus shall** I go in unto the *king* **sovereign,**
which is not according to the *law* **edict:**
and if I *perish* **destruct,** I *perish* **destruct.**
17 So *Mordecai went his way* **Mordekay passed,**
and *did* **worked** according to all
that *Esther* **Ester** had *commanded* **misvahed** him.

The Petition Of Sovereigness Ester

5 *Now it came to pass* **And**
so be it, on the third day,
that *Esther* **Ester**
put on **enrobed** her *royal* **sovereigndom** *apparel,*
and stood in the inner court
of the *king's* **sovereign's** house,
over against **opposite** the *king's* **sovereign's** house:
and the *king sat* **sovereign settled**
upon *his royal throne* **the throne of his sovereigndom**
in the *royal house* **house of the sovereigndom,**
over against **opposite** the *gate* **portal** of the house.
2 And it was so,
when the *king* **sovereign**
saw *Esther* **Ester** the *queen* **sovereigness**
standing in the court,
that she *obtained* **received charism** in his *sight* **eyes:**
and the *king held out* **sovereign extended** to *Esther* **Ester**
the golden *sceptre* **scion** that was in his hand.
So *Esther drew near* **Ester approached,**
and touched the top of the *sceptre* **scion.**

and of the sum of the silver that Haman said
to weigh to the treasuries of the sovereign
to destroy the Yah Hudiym:
8 and he gives him the transcript of the inscribing
of the edict given at Shushan to desolate them;
to have Ester see and to declare it to her;
and to misvah to her to go in to the sovereign,
to beseech charism of him
and to beseech at his face for her people.
9 And Hathach comes and tells Ester
the words of Mordekay:
10 and Ester says to Hathach
and misvahs for Mordekay;
11 All the servants and the people of the sovereign
of the jurisdictions of the sovereign know,
that whoever—whether man or woman,
come to the sovereign into the inner court,
who is not called,
there is one edict of his—to deathify him
—apart from such to whom the sovereign
spreads the golden scion—then they live;
but I am not called
to come in to the sovereign these thirty days.
12 —and they tell Mordekay the words of Ester.
13 And Mordekay says to respond to Ester,
Consider not in your soul
that being in the house of the sovereign
you escape any more than all the Yah Hudiym.

The Mission Of Sovereigness Ester

14 But if in hushing, you hush at this time,
then respite and rescue to the Yah Hudiym
stands from another place;
but you and the house of your father is destroyed;
and who knows
whether you reach the sovereigndom
for a time as this?
15 Then Ester says to return this to Mordekay,
16 Go, gather all the Yah
Hudiym found in Shushan
and fast you for me;
and neither eat nor drink three days, night or day;
I and also my lasses fast likewise;
and thus I go in to the sovereign,
which is not according to the edict;
and if I destruct, I destruct.

17 So Mordekay passes
and works according to all Ester misvahs him.

The Petition Of Sovereigness Ester

5 And so be it, on the third day,
Ester enrobes her sovereigndom;
and stands in the inner court
of the house of the sovereign,
opposite the house of the sovereign;
and the sovereign
settles on the throne of his sovereigndom
in the house of the sovereigndom,
opposite the portal of the house.
2 And so be it,
the sovereign sees Ester the sovereigness
stand in the court,
and she receives charism in his eyes;
and the sovereign extends
the golden scion in his hand to Ester:
and Ester approaches
and touches the top of the scion.
3 Then said the *king* **sovereign** unto her,
What *wilt thou* **to thee**, *queen Esther* **sovereigness Ester**?
and what is thy request?
so be it *shall be* even given thee
to the half of the *kingdom* **sovereigndom**.
4 And *Esther answered* **Ester said**,
If it *seem* **be** good unto the *king* **sovereign**,
let the *king* **sovereign** and Haman come this day
unto the banquet that I have *prepared* **worked** for him.
5 Then the *king* **sovereign** said,
Cause Haman to make haste,
that he may *do* **work** as *Esther* **Ester** hath *said* **worded**.
So the *king* **sovereign** and Haman came
to the banquet that *Esther* **Ester** had *prepared* **worked**.
6 And the *king* **sovereign** said unto *Esther* **Ester**
at the banquet of wine,
What is thy petition?
and **so be** it *shall be granted* **given** thee:
and what is thy request?
even to the half of the *kingdom* **sovereigndom**
so be it *shall be performed* **worked**.
7 Then answered *Esther* **Ester**, and said,
My petition and my request is;
8 If I have found *favour* **charism**
in the *sight* **eyes** of the *king* **sovereign**,
and if it *please* **be good with** the *king* **sovereign**
to *grant* **give** my petition,
and to *perform* **work** my request,
let the *king* **sovereign** and Haman come to the banquet
that I shall *prepare* **work** for them,
and I *will do* **shall work** to morrow
as the king hath said
according to the word of the sovereign.

Haman Filled With Fury

9 Then went Haman forth that day
joyful **cheerful** and with a *glad* **good** heart:
but when Haman saw *Mordecai* **Mordekay**
in the *king's gate* **sovereign's portal**,
that he *stood* **arose** not *up*, nor *moved* **agitated** for him,
he was *full of indignation* **filled with fury**
against *Mordecai* **Mordekay**.
10 Nevertheless Haman
refrained **restrained** himself:
and when he came *home* **to his house**,
he sent and called for his *friends* **loved ones**,
and Zeresh his *wife* **woman**.
11 And Haman *told* **scribed** them
of the *glory* **honour** of his riches,
and the *multitude* **abundance** of his *children* **sons**,
and all *the things* **those**
wherein the *king* **sovereign** had
promoted **greatened** him,
and how he had *advanced* **lifted** him
above the *princes* **governors** and servants
of the *king* **sovereign**.
12 Haman said moreover,
Yea, *Esther* **Ester** the *queen* **sovereigness**
did let no man come in with the *king* **sovereign**
unto the banquet that she had *prepared* **worked**
but myself;
and to morrow am I *invited* **called** unto her also
with the *king* **sovereign**.
13 Yet all this *availeth* **equateth**
me *nothing* **naught**,
so long as **all the time**
that I see *Mordecai* **Mordekay** the *Jew* **Yah Hudiy**
sitting **settled** at the *king's gate* **sovereign's portal**.
14 Then said Zeresh his *wife* **woman**
and all his *friends* **loved ones** unto him,
Let a *gallows* **tree** be *made* **worked** of fifty cubits high,
and *to morrow* **in the morning**
speak **say** thou unto the *king* **sovereign**
that *Mordecai* **Mordekay** may be hanged thereon:
then go thou in *merrily* **cheerfully**
with the *king* **sovereign**
unto the banquet.
And the *thing* **word well**—pleased **the face of** Haman;
and he caused the *gallows* **tree** to be *made* **worked**.

MORDEKAY HONOURED

6 On that night
could not the king sleep **the sovereign's sleep fled away,**
and he *commanded* **said** to bring the *book* **scroll**
of *records* **memorial** of the *chronicles* **words of the days;**
3 And the sovereign says to her,
What to you, sovereigness Ester?
And what *is* your request?
so be it even given you to the half of the sovereigndom.
4 And Ester says,
If it be good to the sovereign,
may the sovereign and Haman come this day
to the banquet I worked for him.
5 And the sovereign says,
Have Haman hasten to work as Ester words.
—and the sovereign and Haman come
to the banquet Ester worked.
6 And the sovereign says to Ester
at the banquet of wine,
What is your petition?
and so be it given you?
And what is your request?
—even to the half of the sovereigndom
so be it worked.
7 And Ester answers and says,
My petition and my request is;
8 If I find charism in the eyes of the sovereign
and if it is good with the sovereign
to give my petition and to work my request,
may the sovereign and Haman
come to the banquet I work for them;
and tomorrow
I work according to the word of the sovereign.

HAMAN FILLED WITH FURY

9 And that day Haman goes
—cheerful and with a good heart;
and Haman sees Mordekay
in the portal of the sovereign;
that he neither rises nor agitates for him,
he is filled with fury against Mordekay.
10 And Haman restrains himself;
and comes to his house:
and he sends and calls for his loved ones
and Zeresh his woman:
11 and Haman scribes them
of the honor of his riches
and the abundance of his sons
and all those wherein the sovereign greatens him;
and how he lifts him
above the governors and servants of the sovereign.
12 And Haman says,
Yes, Ester the sovereigness
has no man come in with the sovereign
to the banquet she works, except me;
and tomorrow also
I am called to her with the sovereign.
13 And all this equates me naught,
all the time I see Mordekay the Yah Hudiy
settling at the portal of the sovereign.
14 And Zeresh his woman
and all his loved ones say to him,
Work a tree fifty cubits high;
and in the morning
say to the sovereign to hang Mordekay thereon;
then go in cheerfully with the sovereign
to the banquet.
—and the word well—pleases the face of Haman;
and he works the tree.

MORDEKAY HONORED

6 On that night, the sleep of the sovereign flees;
and he says to bring
the scroll of memorial of the words of the days;
and they were *read* **called out**
before **at the face of** the *king* **sovereign.**
2 And it was found *written* **inscribed,**
that *Mordecai* **Mordekay**
had told of Bigthana and Teresh,
two of the *king's chamberlains* **sovereign's eunuchs,**
the *keepers* **guards** of the *door* **threshold,**
who sought to *lay* **send their** hand
on the *king Ahasuerus* **sovereign Achash Rosh.**
3 And the *king* **sovereign** said,
What *honour* **esteem** and *dignity* **greatness**
hath been *done* **worked** to *Mordecai* **Mordekay** for this?
Then said the *king's servants* **sovereign's lads**
that ministered unto him,
There is nothing done **No word hath been worked**
for him.
4 And the *king* **sovereign**
said, Who is in the court?
Now Haman was come
into the outward court of the *king's* **sovereign's** house,
to *speak* **say** unto the *king* **sovereign**
to hang *Mordecai* **Mordekay** on the *gallows* **tree**
that he had prepared for him.
5 And the *king's servants*
sovereign's lads said unto him,

Behold, Haman standeth in the court.
And the *king* **sovereign** said, Let him come in.
6 So Haman came in.
And the *king* **sovereign** said unto him,
What shall be *done* **worked** unto the man
whom the *king* **sovereign** delighteth to *honour* **esteem**?
Now Haman *thought* **said** in his heart,
To whom *would* **should** the *king* **sovereign** delight
to *do honour* **work esteem** more than to myself?
7 And Haman *answered*
said to the *king* **sovereign**,
For the man
whom the *king* **sovereign** delighteth to *honour* **esteem**,
8 Let the *royal apparel* **robe of the sovereigndom**
be brought
which the *king useth to wear* **sovereign enrobeth**,
and the horse that the *king* **sovereign** rideth upon,
and the *crown royal* **diadem of the sovereigndom**
which is *set* **given** upon his head:
9 And let this *apparel* **robe** and horse
be *delivered* **given** to the hand of *one* **the man**
of the *king's* **sovereign's** most noble *princes* **governors**,
that they may *array* **enrobe** the man *withal*
whom the *king* **sovereign** delighteth to *honour* **esteem**,
and *bring him* **have him ride** on horseback
through the *street* **broadway** of the city,
and *proclaim before him* **call out at his face**,
Thus shall it be *done* **worked** to the man
whom the *king* **sovereign** delighteth to *honour* **esteem**.
10 Then the *king* **sovereign** said to Haman,
Make haste, *and* take the *apparel* **robe** and the horse,
as thou hast *said* **worded**,
and *do* **work** even so
to *Mordecai* **Mordekay** the *Jew* **Yah Hudiy**,
that *sitteth* **settleth** at the *king's gate* **sovereign's portal**:
let *nothing fail* **no word fall**
of all that thou hast *spoken* **worded**.
11 Then took Haman the
apparel **robe** and the horse,
and *arrayed Mordecai* **enrobed Mordekay**,
and *brought him on horseback* **had him ride**
through the *street* **broadway** of the city,
and *proclaimed before him* **called out at his face**,
Thus shall it be *done* **worked** unto the man
whom the *king* **sovereign** delighteth to *honour* **esteem**.
12 And *Mordecai* **Mordekay**
came again **returned** to the *king's*
gate **sovereign's portal**.
But Haman hasted to his house mourning,
and having his head covered.
13 And Haman *told* **scribed**
to Zeresh his *wife* **woman**
and all his *friends* **loved ones**
every thing **all** that had befallen him.
Then said his wise men and Zeresh his *wife* **woman**
unto him,
If *Mordecai* **Mordekay** be of the seed
of the *Jews* **Yah Hudiym**,
and they call them out at the face of the sovereign.
2 And they find inscribed,
that Mordekay had told of Bigthana and Teresh,
two of the eunuchs of the sovereign
—guards of the threshold
who seek to send their hand
on the sovereign Achash Rosh.
3 And the sovereign says,
What esteem and greatness
was worked to Mordekay for this?
And the lads of the sovereign
who minister to him say,
No word was worked for him.
4 And the sovereign says, Who is in the court?
—and Haman comes into the outward court
of the house of the sovereign,
to say to the sovereign
to hang Mordekay on the tree
he prepared for him.
5 And the lads of the sovereign say to him,
Behold, Haman stands in the court.
And the sovereign says, Have him come in.
6 —and Haman comes in.
And the sovereign says to him,
What work we to the man
whom the sovereign delights to esteem?
And in his heart, Haman says,
Who delights the sovereign to work esteem
more than myself?
7 And Haman says to the sovereign,
For the man
whom the sovereign delights to esteem,
8 bring the robe of the sovereigndom
which the sovereign enrobes
and the horse the sovereign rides
and give the diadem of the sovereigndom
upon his head;
9 and give this robe and horse
to the hand of the man
of the most noble governors of the sovereign
—to enrobe the man
whom the sovereign delights to esteem;

and ride him horseback
through the broadway of the city
and call out at his face;
thus work to the man
whom the sovereign delights to esteem.
10 And the sovereign says to Haman,
Hasten, take the robe and the horse as you word,
and work even thus to Mordekay the Yah Hudiy
who settles at the portal of the sovereign;
fell no word of all you word.
11 And Haman takes the robe and the horse
and enrobes Mordekay
and rides him through the broadway of the city
and calls out at his face,
Thus be it worked to the man
whom the sovereign delights to esteem.
12 And Mordekay
returns to the portal of the sovereign;
and Haman hastens to his house mourning
and covers his head:
13 and Haman scribes to Zeresh his woman
and all his loved ones of all that befalls him.
And his wise men and Zeresh his woman
say to him,
If Mordekay is of the seed of the Yah Hudiym,
before **at the face of** whom thou hast begun to fall,
thou shalt not prevail against him,
but **in falling,** shalt *surely* fall *before him* **at his face.** 14
And while they were yet *talking* **wording** with him,
came the king's chamberlains
the sovereign's eunuchs touched,
and hasted to bring Haman unto the banquet
that *Esther* **Ester** had *prepared* **worked.**

HAMAN HANGED

7 *So* **And** the *king* **sovereign** and Haman
came to *banquet* **drink**
with *Esther* **Ester** the *queen* **sovereigness.**
2 And the *king* **sovereign** said
again unto *Esther* **Ester**
on the second day at the banquet of wine,
What is thy petition, *queen Esther* **sovereigness Ester**?
and **so be** it *shall be granted* **given** thee:
and what is thy request?
and **so be** it *shall be performed* **worked,**
even to the half of the *kingdom* **sovereigndom.**
3 Then *Esther* **Ester** the *queen* **sovereigness**
answered and said,
If I have found *favour* **charism** in thy *sight* **eyes,**
O *king* **sovereign,**
and if it *please* **be good with** the *king* **sovereign,**
let my *life* **soul** be given me at my petition,
and my people at my request:
4 For we are sold, I and my people,
to be *destroyed* **desolated,**
to be *slain* **slaughtered,** and to *perish* **destruct.**
But if **Even though** we had been sold
for *bondmen* **servants** and *bondwomen* **maids,**
I had *held my tongue* **hushed,**
although the *enemy* **tribulator**
could not countervail **equated not**
the *king's* **sovereign's** damage.
5 Then *the king Ahasuerus*
sovereign Achash Rosh
answered
and said unto *Esther* **Ester** the *queen* **sovereigness,**
Who is he, and where is he,
that durst presume in his heart **whose**
heart hath filled him
to do so **thus to work**?
6 And *Esther* **Ester** said,
The *adversary* **tribulator** and enemy
is this *wicked* **evil** Haman.
Then Haman was *afraid before* **frightened at the face**
of the *king* **sovereign** and the *queen* **sovereigness.**
7 And the *king* **sovereign** arising
from the banquet of wine
in his *wrath* **fury** went into the palace garden:
and Haman stood up
to *make request* **beseech** for his *life* **soul**
to *Esther* **Ester** the *queen* **sovereigness;**
for he saw that there was evil
determined **finished** against him by the *king* **sovereign.**
8 Then the *king* **sovereign**
returned out of the palace garden
into the *place* **house** of the banquet of wine;
and Haman was fallen upon the bed
whereon *Esther* **Ester** was.
Then said the *king* **sovereign,**
Will **Shall** he *force* **subdue** the *queen* **sovereigness**
also *before* **in front of** me in the house?
As the word went out of *king's* **sovereign's** mouth,
they covered Haman's face.
9 And Harbonah, one of the
chamberlains **eunuchs,**
said *before* **at the face of** the *king* **sovereign,**
Behold also, the *gallows* **tree** fifty cubits high,
which Haman had *made* **worked**
for *Mordecai* **Mordekay,**
who had *spoken* **worded** good for the *king* **sovereign,**

standeth in the house of Haman.
Then the *king* **sovereign** said, Hang him thereon.
10 So they hanged Haman on the *gallows* **tree**
that he had prepared for *Mordecai* **Mordekay**.
Then was the *king's wrath* **sovereign's fury**
pacified **assuaged**.

MORDEKAY PROMOTED

8 On that day
did the *king Ahasuerus* **sovereign Achash Rosh**
give the house of Haman
at the face of whom you begin to fall,
you prevail not against him:
but in falling, fall at his face.
14 And as they still word with him,
the eunuchs of the sovereign touch
and hasten to bring Haman to the banquet
Ester worked.

HAMAN HANGED

7 And the sovereign and Haman
come to drink with Ester the sovereigness.
2 And the sovereign also says to Ester
on the second day at the banquet of wine,
What is your petition, sovereigness Ester?
and so be it given you;
And what is your request?
and so be it worked to the half of the sovereigndom.
3 And Ester the sovereigness answers and says,
If I find charism in your eyes, O sovereign
and if it be good with the sovereign,
may my soul be given me at my petition
and my people at my request;
4 for we have been sold, I and my people,
to desolate, to slaughter and to destruct.
Even though we have been sold
for servants and maids,
I hushed;
although the tribulator
equated not the damage of the sovereign.
5 And sovereign Achash Rosh answers
and says to Ester the sovereigness,
Who is he and where is he,
whose heart has filled him thus to work?
6 And Ester says,
The tribulator and enemy is this evil Haman.
—and Haman is frightened at the face
of the sovereign and the sovereigness.
7 And the sovereign rises
from the banquet of wine,
and in his fury goes into the palace garden;
and Haman stands
to beseech for his soul to Ester the sovereigness;
for he sees that there is evil finished against him
by the sovereign.
8 And the sovereign returns
from the palace garden
to the house of the banquet of wine;
and Haman falls upon the bed whereon Ester *is*.
And the sovereign says,
Subdues he also the sovereigness
in front of me in the house?
As the word goes from the mouth of the sovereign,
they cover the face of Haman.
9 And Harbonah, one of the eunuchs,
says at the face of the sovereign,
Behold also, the tree fifty cubits high,
which Haman worked for Mordekay
who worded good for the sovereign,
stands in the house of Haman.
And the sovereign says, Hang him thereon.
10 —and they hang Haman on the tree
he prepared for Mordekay
—and the fury of the sovereign is assuaged.

MORDEKAY PROMOTED

8 On that day
sovereign Achash Rosh gives the house of Haman
the tribulator of the Yah Hudiym
the *Jews' enemy* **Yah Hudiym's tribulator**
unto *Esther* **Ester** the *queen* **sovereigness**.
And *Mordecai* **Mordekay**
came *before* **at the face of** the *king* **sovereign**;
for *Esther* **Ester** had told what he was unto her.
2 And the *king took* **sovereign**
twisted off his *ring* **signet**,
which he had *taken* **passed** from Haman,
and gave it unto *Mordecai* **Mordekay**.
And *Esther* **Ester** set *Mordecai* **Mordekay**
over the house of Haman.
3 And *Esther spake yet again* **Ester added to word**
before **at the face of** the *king* **sovereign**,
and fell down at **the face of** his feet,
and besought **charism of** him with *tears* **weeping**
to *put away* **pass over** the *mischief* **evil**
of Haman the *Agagite* **Agagiy**,
and his *device* **fabrication** that he had *devised* **fabricated**
against the *Jews* **Yah Hudiym**.

4 Then the *king* **sovereign**
held out **spread** the golden *sceptre* **scion**
toward *Esther* **Ester.**
So *Esther* **Ester** arose,
and stood *before* **at the face of** the *king* **sovereign,**
5 And said, If it *please* **be good**
with the *king* **sovereign,**
and if I have found *favour* **charism** in his *sight* **face,**
and the *thing seem right* **word prosper**
before **at the face of** the *king* **sovereign,**
and I be *pleasing* **goodly** in his eyes
let it be *written* **inscribed**
to *reverse* **return** the *letters* **scrolls**
devised by **the fabrication of** Haman
the son of *Hammedatha* **Medatha** the *Agagite* **Agagiy,**
which he *wrote* **inscribed**
to destroy the *Jews* **Yah Hudiym**
which are in all
the *king's provinces* **sovereign's jurisdictions:**
6 For how can I *endure to*
see the evil that shall *come unto* **find** my people?
or how can I *endure to*
see the destruction of my kindred?
7 Then *the king Ahasuerus*
sovereign Achash Rosh
said unto *Esther* **Ester** the *queen* **sovereigness**
and to *Mordecai* **Mordekay** the *Jew* **Yah Hudiy,** Behold,
I have given *Esther* **Ester** the house of Haman,
and him they have hanged upon the *gallows* **tree,**
because he *laid* **spread** his hand
upon the *Jews* **Yah Hudiym.**
8 *Write* **Inscribe** ye also for the *Jews* **Yah Hudiym,**
as it *liketh you* **be good in your eyes,**
in the *king's* **sovereign's** name,
and seal it with the *king's ring* **sovereign's signet:**
for the *writing* **inscribing**
which is *written* **inscribed** in the
king's **sovereign's** name,
and sealed with the *king's ring* **sovereign's signet,**
may **that** no man *reverse* **overturneth.**
9 Then were the *king's* **sovereign's** scribes
called at that time in the third month,
that is, the month Sivan,
on the three and twentieth *day* thereof;
and it was *written* **inscribed** according to all
that *Mordecai commanded* **Mordekay misvahed**
unto the *Jews* **Yah Hudiym,**
and to the *lieutenants* **satraps,** and
the *deputies* **governors**
and *rulers* **governors** of the *provinces* **jurisdictions**
which are from *India* **Hodu** unto *Ethiopia* **Kush,**
an hundred twenty and seven *provinces* **jurisdictions,**
unto *every province* **jurisdiction by jurisdiction**
according to the *writing* **inscribing** thereof,
and unto *every* people **by people**
after their language,
and to the *Jews* **Yah Hudiym**
according to their *writing* **inscribings,**
and according to their *language* **tongue.**
10 And he *wrote* **inscribed**
in *the king Ahasuerus'* **sovereign Achash Rosh's** name,
and sealed it with the *king's ring* **sovereign's signet,**
and sent *letters* **scrolls**
by *posts* **the hand of runners** on horseback,
and riders on *mules* **stallions,** *camels* **mules,**
and *young dromedaries* **sons of mares:**
to Ester the sovereigness:
and Mordekay comes at the face of the sovereign;
for Ester had told what he was to her.
2 And the sovereign twists the signet
he passed from Haman,
and gives it to Mordekay;
and Ester sets Mordekay over the house of Haman:
3 and Ester adds to word at
the face of the sovereign
and falls at the face of his feet;
and with weeping beseeches his charism
to pass over the evil of Haman the Agagiy
and the fabrication he fabricated
against the Yah Hudiym.
4 —and the sovereign
spreads the golden scion toward Ester.
And Ester rises
and stands at the face of the sovereign,
5 and says, If it be good with the sovereign
and if I find charism in his face
and the word prospers at the face of the sovereign
and I be goodly in his eyes,
inscribe to return the scrolls
—the fabrication of Haman
the son of Medatha the Agagiy,
wherein he inscribed to destroy the Yah Hudiym
in all the jurisdictions of the sovereign.
6 For how can I see the evil
which finds my people?
Or how can I see the destruction of my kindred?
7 And sovereign Achash Rosh
says to Ester the sovereigness
and to Mordekay the Yah Hudiy,
Behold, I give Ester the house of Haman;

and they hanged him upon the tree
because he spread his hand on the Yah Hudiym.
8 And you, you inscribe also for the Yah Hudiym
as *is* good in your eyes,
in the name of the sovereign;
and seal it with the signet of the sovereign;
for the inscribing
inscribed in the name of the sovereign
and sealed with the signet of the sovereign
so that no man overturns.
9 And at that time,
in the third month—the month Sivan,
on the twenty—third thereof,
they call the scribes of the sovereign
and inscribe according to all
Mordekay misvahed to the Yah Hudiym
—and to the satraps and the governors
and governors of the jurisdictions
from Hodu to Kush
—a hundred and twenty—seven jurisdictions
—jurisdiction by jurisdiction
according to the inscribing thereof;
and to people by people after their language;
and to the Yah Hudiym according to their inscribings
and according to their tongue.
10 And in the name of sovereign Achash Rosh
he inscribes and seals it
with the signet of the sovereign;
and sends scrolls
by the hand of runners on horseback
and riders on stallions, mules and sons of mares;
11 Wherein the *king* **sovereign**
granted **gave** the *Jews* **Yah Hudiym**
which were in *every* city **by city**
to *gather themselves together* **congregate**,
and to stand for their *life* **soul**,
to *destroy* **desolate**, to *slay* **slaughter**,
and to *cause to perish* **destroy**,
all the *power* **virtuous** of the people and province
that *would assault* **should besiege** them,
both little ones **toddlers** and women,
and *to take the spoil of them for a
prey* **spoil their plunder**,
12 Upon one day in all the *provinces* **jurisdictions**
of *king Ahasuerus* **sovereign Achash Rosh**, *namely*,
upon the thirteenth *day* of the twelfth month,
which is the month Adar.
13 The *copy* **transcript** of the *writing* **inscribing**
for *a commandment* **an edict** to be given
in every province **jurisdiction by jurisdiction**
was *published* **exposed** unto all people,
and that the *Jews* **Yah Hudiym**
should be ready against that day
to avenge themselves on their enemies.
14 So the *posts* **runners**
that rode upon *mules* **stallions** and camels went *out*,
being hastened and *pressed on* **hastened**
by the *king's commandment* **sovereign's word**.
And the *decree* **edict** was given at Shushan the palace.
15 And *Mordecai* **Mordekay** went out
from the *presence* **face** of the *king* **sovereign**
in *royal apparel* **a robe of the sovereigndom**
of blue and white,
and with a great crown of gold,
and with a *garment* **robe**
of *fine linen* **bleached cotton** and purple:
and the city of Shushan
rejoiced **resounded** and *was glad* **cheered**.
16 The *Jews* **Yah Hudiym** had light,
and *gladness* **cheerfulness**,
and *joy* **rejoicing**, and *honour* **esteem**.
17 And *in every province*
jurisdiction by jurisdiction,
and *in every* city **by city**,
whithersoever **whatever place**
the *king's commandment* **sovereign's word**
and his *decree came* **edict touched**,
the *Jews* **Yah Hudiym**
had *joy* **cheer** and *gladness* **rejoicing**,
a *feast* **banquet** and a good day.
And many of the people of the land
became Jews **Yah Hudahized**;
for the fear of the *Jews* **Yah Hudiym** fell upon them.

THE DOMINATION OF THE YAH HUDIYM

9 Now in the twelfth month,
that is, the month Adar,
on the thirteenth day of the same,
when the *king's commandment* **sovereign's word**
and his *decree drew near* **edict touched**
to be *put in execution* **worked**,
in the day that the enemies of the *Jews* **Yah Hudiym**
hoped **expected** to *have power* **dominate** over them,
(though it *was turned to the contrary* **turned out**
that the *Jews had rule* **Yah Hudiym
dominated** over them
that hated them;)
2 The *Jews* **Yah Hudiym**
gathered themselves together **congregated** in their cities
throughout all the *provinces* **jurisdictions**

of *the king Ahasuerus* **sovereign Achash Rosh,**
to *lay* **send his** hand on such as sought their *hurt* **evil**:
and no man could *withstand them* **stand at their face**;
for the fear of them fell upon all people.
3 And all the *rulers* **governors**
of the *provinces* **jurisdictions,**
and the *lieutenants* **satraps**, and the *deputies* **governors,**
and *officers* **those that did the work**
of the *king* **sovereign,**
helped **lifted** the *Jews* **Yah Hudiym**;
because the fear of *Mordecai* **Mordekay** fell upon them.
4 For *Mordecai* **Mordekay** was great
in the *king's* **sovereign's** house,
and his fame
went out throughout all the *provinces* **jurisdictions**:
11 wherein the sovereign gives the Yah Hudiym
in city by city
to congregate and to stand for their soul,
to desolate, to slaughter, and to destroy,
all the virtuous of the people and province
and of the toddlers and women who besiege them
and spoil their plunder.
12 On one day
in all the jurisdictions of sovereign Achash Rosh,
on the thirteenth of the twelfth month
—the month Adar
13 —a transcript of the inscribing for an edict
given jurisdiction by jurisdiction
is exposed to all the people;
and that the Yah Hudiym be ready against that day
to avenge themselves on their enemies.
14 So the runners
ride upon stallions and camels go hastening
—hastened by the word of the sovereign:
—and the edict is given at Shushan palace.
15 And Mordekay
goes from the face of the sovereign
in a robe of the sovereigndom of blue and white
and with a great crown of gold
and with a robe of bleached cotton and purple;
and the city of Shushan resounds and cheers.
16 The Yah Hudiym have light and cheerfulness
and rejoicing and esteem.
17 And jurisdiction by jurisdiction and city by city,
and whatever place
the word and edict of the sovereign touches,
the Yah Hudiym cheer and rejoice
—a banquet and a good day.
And many of the people of the land Yah Hudahize;
for the fear of the Yah Hudiym falls upon them.

THE DOMINATION OF THE YAH HUDIYM

9 And in the twelfth month—the month Adar,
on the thirteenth day of the same,
when they touch to work
the word and edict of the sovereign
—in the day the enemies of the Yah Hudiym
expect to dominate over them,
it turns out that the Yah Hudiym
dominate over them who hate them
2 —the Yah Hudiym congregate in their cities
throughout all the jurisdictions
of sovereign Achash Rosh,
to send his hand on such as seek their evil;
and no man stands at their face;
for the fear of them falls on all people:
3 and all the governors of the jurisdictions
and the satraps and the governors
and those working the work of the sovereign,
lift the Yah Hudiym:
because the fear of Mordekay falls upon them:
4 for Mordekay is great
in the house of the sovereign
and his fame goes throughout all the jurisdictions;
for this man *Mordecai* **Mordekay**
waxed greater **walked** and *greater* **greatened.**
5 Thus the *Jews* **Yah Hudiym**
smote all their enemies
with the stroke of the sword,
and slaughter, and destruction,
and *did* **worked** *what they would*
according to their pleasure
unto those that hated them.
6 And in Shushan the palace
the *Jews* **Yah Hudiym**
slew **slaughtered** and destroyed five hundred men.
7 And Parshandatha, and Dalphon, and Aspatha,
8 And Poratha, and *Adalia* **Adalya**, and Aridatha,
9 And Parmashta, and Arisai, and *Aridai* **Ariday**,
and *Vajezatha* **Vayezatha,**
10 The ten sons of Haman
the son of *Hammedatha* **Medatha,**
the *enemy* **tribulator** of the *Jews* **Yah Hudiym,**
slew **slaughtered** they;
but on the *spoil laid* **plunder** they **spread** not their hand.
11 On that day
the number of those that were *slain* **slaughtered**
in Shushan the palace
was brought *before* **at the face of** the *king* **sovereign.**
12 And the *king* **sovereign**

said unto *Esther* **Ester** the *queen* **sovereigness,**
The *Jews* **Yah Hudiym** have *slain* **slaughtered**
and destroyed five hundred men in Shushan the palace,
and the ten sons of Haman;
what have they *done* **worked** in the *rest* **survivors**
of the *king's provinces* **sovereign's jurisdictions**?
now what is thy petition?
and **so be** it *shall be granted* **given** thee:
or what is thy request *further* **again**?
and **so be** it *shall be done* **worked.**
13 Then said *Esther* **Ester,**
If it *please* **be good with** the *king* **sovereign,**
let it be *granted* **given**
to the *Jews* **Yah Hudiym** which are in Shushan
to *do* **work** to morrow also
according unto this day's *decree* **edict,**
and let Haman's ten sons
be hanged upon the *gallows* **tree.**
14 And the *king* **sovereign**
commanded **said** it so to be *done* **worked:**
and the *decree* **edict** was given at Shushan;
and they hanged Haman's ten sons.
15 For the *Jews* **Yah Hudiym** that were in Shushan
gathered themselves together **congregated**
on the fourteenth day also of the month Adar,
and *slew* **slaughtered** three hundred men at Shushan;
but on the *prey* **plunder**
they *laid* **spread** not their hand.
16 But the *other Jews* **Yah Hudiym survivors**
that were in the *king's provinces*
sovereign's jurisdictions
gathered themselves together **congregated,**
and stood for their *lives* **souls,**
and *had rest* **rested** from their enemies,
and *slew* **slaughtered** of their *foes* **haters**
seventy and five thousand,
but they *laid* **spread** not their hands
on the *prey* **plunder,**
17 On the thirteenth day of the month Adar;
and on the fourteenth day of the same rested they,
and *made* **worked** it
a day of *feasting* **banqueting** and *gladness* **cheerfulness.**
18 But the *Jews* **Yah Hudiym** that were at Shushan
assembled together **congregated**
on the thirteenth *day* thereof,
and on the fourteenth thereof;
and on the fifteenth *day* of the same they rested,
and *made* **worked** it
a day of *feasting* **banqueting** and *gladness* **cheerfulness.**
19 Therefore the *Jews* **Yah**
Hudiym of the *villages* **courts,**
that *dwelt* **settled**
in the *unwalled towns* **cities of the suburbs,**
made **worked** the fourteenth day of the month Adar
a day of gladness **cheerfulness** and *feasting* **banqueting,**
and a good day,
and of sending portions *one* **man** to *another* **friend.**
for this man Mordekay walks and greatens.
5 Thus the Yah Hudiym smite all their enemies
with the stroke of the sword
and slaughter and destruction;
and work according to their pleasure
to them who hate them:
6 and in Shushan palace the Yah Hudiym
slaughter and destroy five hundred men:
7 and Parshandatha and Dalphon and Aspatha,
8 and Poratha and Adalya and Aridatha,
9 and Parmashta and Arisai
and Ariday and Vayezatha
10 —the ten sons of Haman the son of Medatha,
the tribulator of the Yah Hudiym,
they slaughter;
but they spread not their hand on the plunder.
11 On that day,
they bring the number
of those slaughtered in Shushan palace
at the face of the sovereign:
12 and the sovereign says to Ester the sovereigness,
The Yah Hudiym slaughtered
and destroyed five hundred men in Shushan palace
and the ten sons of Haman;
What work they in the survivors
of the jurisdictions of the sovereign?
And what is your petition?
—and so be it given you;
And what is your request again?
—and so be it worked.
13 And Ester says,
If it is good with the sovereign,
give work to the Yah Hudiym in Shushan tomorrow
also according to the edict of this day;
and hang the ten sons of Haman upon the tree.
14 And the sovereign says to work thus;
and gives the edict at Shushan;
and they hang the ten sons of Haman.
15 And the Yah Hudiym in
Shushan also congregate
on the fourteenth day of the month Adar
and slaughter three hundred men at Shushan;

and they spread not their hand on the plunder.
16 And the survivors of the Yah Hudiym
in the jurisdictions of the sovereign
congregate and stand for their souls;
and rest from their enemies;
and slaughter seventy—five thousand of their haters;
and they spread not their hands on the plunder.
17 On the thirteenth day of the month Adar;
and on the fourteenth day of the same
they rest
and work a day of banqueting and cheerfulness.
18 And the Yah Hudiym at Shushan
congregate on the thirteenth thereof
and on the fourteenth thereof;
and on the fifteenth of the same they rest
and work a day of banqueting and cheerfulness.
19 So the Yah Hudiym of the courts,
settling in the cities of the suburbs,
work the fourteenth day of the month Adar
cheerfulness and banqueting
—a good day of sending portions man to friend.

THE DAYS OF PURIM

20 And *Mordecai* **Mordekay**
wrote **inscribed** these *things* **words,**
and sent *letters* **scrolls** unto all the *Jews* **Yah Hudiym**
that were in all the *provinces* **jurisdictions**
of the *king Ahasuerus* **sovereign Achash Rosh,**
both nigh and far,
21 To *stablish* **raise** *this* among them,
that they should *keep* **work**
the fourteenth day of the month Adar,
and the fifteenth day of the same, *yearly* **year by year,**
22 As the days
wherein the *Jews* **Yah Hudiym**
rested from their enemies,
and the month which was turned unto them
from *sorrow* **grief** to *joy* **cheer,**
and from mourning into a good day:
that they should *make* **work** them
days of *feasting* **banqueting** and *joy* **cheer,**
and of sending portions *one* **man** to *another* **friend,**
and gifts to the *poor* **needy.**
23 And the *Jews* **Yah Hudiym**
undertook to *do* **work** as they had begun,
and as *Mordecai* **Mordekay** had *written* **inscribed**
unto them;
24 Because Haman
the son of *Hammedatha* **Medatha,** the *Agagite* **Agagiy,**
the *enemy* **tribulator** of all the *Jews* **Yah Hudiym,**
had *devised* **fabricated** against the *Jews* **Yah Hudiym**
to destroy them,
and had *cast* **felled** Pur, that is, the *lot* **pebble,**
to *consume* **agitate** them, and to destroy them;
25 But when *Esther* **Ester** came
before **at the face of** the *king* **sovereign,**
he *commanded* **said** by *letters* **scrolls** that
his *wicked device* **evil fabrication,**
which he *devised* **fabricated**
against the *Jews* **Yah Hudiym,**
should return upon his own head,
and that he and his sons should be hanged
on the *gallows* **tree.**
26 Wherefore they called these days Purim
after the name of Pur.
Therefore for all the words of this *letter* **epistle,**
and of that which they had seen
concerning *this matter* **thus,**
and which *had come* **touched** unto them,
27 The *Jews ordained* **Yah Hudiym arose,**
and took upon them, and upon their seed,
and upon all such as joined themselves unto them,
so as it should not *fail* **pass away,**
that they *would keep* **should work** these two days
according to their *writing* **inscribing,**
and according to their *appointed time* **appointment**
every year **by year;**
28 And that these days
should be remembered and *kept* **worked**
throughout every generation **by generation,**
every family **by family,**
every province **jurisdiction by jurisdiction,**
and every city **by city;**
and that these days of Purim should not *fail* **pass away**
from among the *Jews* **Yah Hudiym,**
nor the memorial of them
perish **be consumed** from their seed.
29 Then *Esther* **Ester** the *queen* **sovereigness,**
the daughter of *Abihail* **Abi Hail,**
and *Mordecai* **Mordekay** the *Jew* **Yah Hudiy,**
wrote **inscribed** with all *authority* **power,**
to *confirm* **raise** this second *letter* **epistle** of Purim.
30 And he sent the *letters* **scrolls**
unto all the *Jews* **Yah Hudiym,**
to the hundred twenty and seven *provinces* **jurisdictions**
of the *kingdom* **sovereigndom** of
Ahasuerus **Achash Rosh,**
with words of *peace* **shalom** and truth,
31 To *confirm* **raise** these days of Purim
in their *times appointed* **appointment,**
according as *Mordecai* **Mordekay** the *Jew* **Yah Hudiy**

THE DAYS OF PURIM

20 And Mordekay inscribes these words
—and sends scrolls to all the Yah Hudiym
in all the jurisdictions of sovereign Achash Rosh
—near and far
21 to raise among them,
to work the fourteenth day of the month Adar,
and the fifteenth day of the same, year by year,
22 as the days
wherein the Yah Hudiym rested from their enemies;
and the month which turned them
from grief to cheer
and from mourning to a good day;
to work them days of banqueting and cheer
and of sending portions man to friend
and gifts to the needy.
23 And the Yah Hudiym
undertake to work as they began
and as Mordekay inscribed to them;
24 because Haman the son of Medatha the Agagiy,
the tribulator of all the Yah Hudiym,
had fabricated against the Yah Hudiym
to destroy them;
and felled Pur—the pebble,
to agitate them and to destroy them;
25 and when it comes at the face of the sovereign,
he says by scrolls,
Return the evil fabrication
he fabricated against the Yah Hudiym
upon his own head;
and hang him and his sons on the tree.
26 So they call these days Purim
after the name of Pur.
So for all the words of this epistle
and for what they saw concerning thus
—and which touched to them,
27 the Yah Hudiym rise
and take upon them and upon their seed
and upon all such as join themselves to them,
so that it not pass away
—that they work these two days
according to their inscribing
and according to their appointment year by year;
28 and that these days be remembered and worked
generation by generation
family by family
jurisdiction by jurisdiction
city by city;
and that neither these days of Purim pass away
from among the Yah Hudiym,
nor the memorial of them
consume from their seed.
29 And Ester the sovereigness
the daughter of Abi Hail
and Mordekay the Yah Hudiy
inscribe with all power
to raise this second epistle of Purim.
30 And he sends the scrolls to all the Yah Hudiym,
—to the hundred and twenty—seven jurisdictions
of the sovereigndom of Achash Rosh,
words of shalom and truth,
31 to raise these days of Purim
in their appointment,
according as Mordekay the Yah Hudiy
and *Esther* **Ester** the *queen* **sovereigness**
had *enjoined* **raised** them,
and as they had *decreed* **raised**
for *themselves* **their souls** and for their seed,
the *matters* **words** of the fastings and their cry.
32 And the *decree* **edict** of *Esther* **Ester**
confirmed **raised** these *matters* **words** of Purim;
and it was *written* **inscribed** in the *book* **scroll**.

THE GREATNESS OF MORDEKAY

10 And *the king Ahasuerus* **sovereign Achash Rosh**
laid a tribute **set a vassal** upon the land,
and upon the isles of the sea.
2 And all the *acts* **works** of
his power and of his might,
and the *declaration* **sum**
of the greatness of *Mordecai* **Mordekay**,
whereunto the *king advanced* **sovereign greatened** him,
are they not *written* **inscribed** in the *book* **scroll**
of the *chronicles* **words of the days**
of the *kings* **sovereigns** of *Media* **Maday** and Persia?
3 For *Mordecai* **Mordekay** the *Jew* **Yah Hudiy**
was *next* **second**
unto *king Ahasuerus* **sovereign Achash Rosh**,
and great among the *Jews* **Yah Hudiym**,
and *accepted* **pleased**
of the *multitude* **abundance** of his brethren,
seeking the *wealth of* **goodness for** his people,
and *speaking peace* **wording shalom** to all his seed.
and Ester the sovereigness raised them;
and as they raised for their souls and for their seed,
the words of the fastings and their cry.
32 And the edict of Ester raises
these words of Purim;
and it is inscribed in the scroll.

The Greatness Of Mordekay

10 And sovereign Achash Rosh
sets a vassal on the land and on the isles of the sea.
2 And all the works of his power and of his might
and the sum of the greatness of Mordekay,
whereunto the sovereign greatened him,
are they not inscribed in the scroll
of the words of the days
of the sovereigns of Maday and Persia?
3 For Mordekay the Yah Hudiy
is second to sovereign Achash Rosh
and great among the Yah Hudiym
and pleased by the abundance of his brothers,
seeking the goodness for his people
and wording shalom to all his seed.

1 There was a man in the land of *Uz* **Us**,
whose name was *Job* **Iyob**;
and that man was *perfect* **integrious**
and *upright* **straight**,
and one that *feared God* **awed Elohim**,
and *eschewed* **turned aside from** evil.
2 And there were *born* **birthed** unto him
seven sons and three daughters.
3 His *substance* **chattel** also
was seven thousand *sheep* **flocks**,
and three thousand camels,
and five hundred yoke of oxen,
and five hundred she *asses* **burros**,
and a *very* **mighty** great *household* **servantry**;
so that this man
was the greatest of all the men of the east.
4 And his sons went
and *feasted* **worked a banquet** in their houses,
every one **each man** his day;
and sent and called for their three sisters
to eat and to drink with them.
5 And **so be** it *was so*,
when the days of *their feasting* **banqueting**
were gone about **revolved**,
that *Job* **Iyob** sent and *sanctified* **hallowed** them,
and *rose up* **started** early in the morning,
and *offered burnt offerings* **holocausted holocausts**
according to the number of them all:
for *Job* **Iyob** said,
It may be that **Perhaps** my sons have sinned,
and cursed God **yet blessed Elohim** in their hearts.
Thus *did Job* **worked Iyob** continually.

The First Challenge Of Satan

6 *Now there was* **And so be it,**
a day when the sons of *God* **Elohim** came
to *present* **station** themselves
before the LORD **by Yah Veh**,
and Satan came also *among* **midst** them.
7 And *the LORD* **Yah Veh** said unto Satan,
Whence comest thou?
Then Satan answered *the LORD* **Yah Veh**, and said,
From *going* **flitting** to and fro in the earth,
and from walking *up* **forth** and *down* **back** in it.
8 And *the LORD* **Yah Veh** said unto Satan,
Hast thou *considered* **set thy heart**
on my servant *Job* **Iyob**,
that there is none like him in the earth,
a perfect **an integrious** and *an upright* **straight** man,

one that *feareth God* **aweth Elohim,**
and *escheweth* **turneth aside from** evil?
9 Then Satan answered *the*
LORD **Yah Veh**, and said,
Doth *Job* **Iyob** fear *God for naught* **Elohim gratuitously**?
10 Hast not thou made an hedge about him,
and *about* **throughout** his house,
and *about* **throughout** all that he hath
on every side **all around**?
thou hast blessed the work of his hands,
and his *substance* **chattel**
is increased **breaketh forth** in the land.
11 But *put forth* **spread** thine hand *now* **I beseech**,
and touch all that he hath,
and he will curse **whether he shall bless** thee to thy face.
12 And *the LORD* **Yah Veh**
said unto Satan, Behold,
all that he hath is in thy *power* **hand**;
only upon himself *put* **spread** not *forth* thine hand.
So **And** Satan went forth
from the *presence* **face** of *the LORD* **Yah Veh**.

The First Test Of Iyob

13 And **so be it,** *there was* a day
when his sons and his daughters
were eating and drinking wine
in their *eldest* **firstbirthed** brother's house:
14 And there came *a messenger*
an angel unto *Job* **Iyob**,
and said, The oxen were plowing,
and the *asses feeding* **she burros tending**
beside them **at their hands**:
15 And the Sabeans *fell upon* **felled** them,
and took them away;

1 There was a man in the land of Us,
his name, Iyob;
and that man being integrious and straight;
and one awing Elohim and turning aside from evil.
2 And seven sons and three daughters
are birthed to him;
3 and his chattel:
seven thousand flocks
and three thousand camels
and five hundred yoke of oxen
and five hundred she burros
and a mighty great servantry;
so that this man is the greatest
of all the men of the east.
4 And his sons go
and work a banquet in their houses
—each man *on* his day;
and they send and call for their three sisters
to eat and to drink with them.
5 And so be it, as the days of banqueting revolve,
Iyob sends and hallows them;
and starts early in the morning
and holocausts holocausts
according to their number;
for Iyob says,
Perhaps my sons have sinned,
yet blessed Elohim in their hearts.
—thus worked Iyob continually.

The First Challenge Of Satan

6 And so be it,
a day arrives when the sons of Elohim
come to station themselves by Yah Veh;
and Satan also comes in their midst.
7 And Yah Veh says to Satan,
Whence come you?
And Satan answers Yah Veh and says,
From flitting to and fro in the earth
and from walking forth and back in it.
8 And Yah Veh says to Satan,
Have you set your heart on my servant Iyob,
that there is none like him in the earth?
—an integrious and straight man,
one who awes Elohim
and turns aside from evil?
9 And Satan answers Yah Veh and says,
Iyob, fears he Elohim gratuitously?
10 Make you not a hedge about him
and throughout his house
and throughout all he has all around?
You bless the work of his hands
and his chattel break forth in the land.
11 And yet, spread your hand, I beseech,
and touch all that he has,
whether he blesses you to your face.
12 And Yah Veh says to Satan,
Behold, all he has is in your hand;
only spread not your hand on his self.
—and Satan goes from the face of Yah Veh.

The First Test Of Iyob

13 And so be it,
a day his sons and his daughters
are eating and drinking wine
in the house of their firstbirthed brother;
14 and an angel comes to Iyob and says,

The oxen were plowing
and the she burros tending at their hands;
15 and the Sabeans felled them
and took them away;
yea, they have *slain* **smitten** the *servants* **lads**
with the *edge* **mouth** of the sword;
and I only am escaped alone to tell thee.
16 While he was yet *speaking* **wording**,
there came also another, and said,
The fire of *God* **Elohim** is fallen
from *heaven* **the heavens**,
and hath burned up the *sheep* **flocks**,
and the *servants* **lads**, and consumed them;
and I only am escaped alone to tell thee.
17 While he was yet *speaking* **wording**,
there came also another, and said,
The *Chaldeans made* **Kesediym**
set out three *bands* **heads**,
and *fell upon* **stripped** the camels,
and have *carried* **taken** them away, yea,
and *slain* **smitten** the servants
with the *edge* **mouth** of the sword;
and I only am escaped alone to tell thee.
18 While he was yet *speaking* **wording**,
there came also another, and said,
Thy sons and thy daughters
were eating and drinking wine
in their *eldest* **firstbirthed** brother's house:
19 And, behold,
there came a great wind from **across** the wilderness,
and *smote* **touched** the four corners of the house,
and it fell upon the *young men* **lads**, and they are dead;
and I only am escaped alone to tell thee.
20 Then *Job* **Iyob** arose, and
rent **ripped** his mantle,
and *shaved* **sheared** his head,
and fell down upon the *ground* **earth**,
and *worshipped* **prostrated**.
21 And said,
Naked came I out of my mother's *womb* **belly**,
and naked shall I return thither:
the LORD **Yah Veh** gave,
and *the LORD* **Yah Veh** hath taken away;
blessed be the name of *the LORD* **Yah Veh**.
22 In all this *Job* **Iyob** sinned not,
nor *charged God* **attributed Elohim**
foolishly **with frivolity**.

The Second Challenge Of Satan

2 *Again there was* **And so be it,**
a day when the sons of *God* **Elohim**
came to *present* **station** themselves
before the LORD **by Yah Veh,**
and Satan came also among them
to *present* **station** himself *before the LORD* **by Yah Veh**.
2 And *the LORD* **Yah Veh** said unto Satan,
From whence comest thou?
And Satan answered *the LORD* **Yah Veh**, and said,
From *going* **flitting** to and fro in the earth,
and from walking *up* **forth** and *down* **back** in it.
3 And *the LORD* **Yah Veh** said unto Satan,
Hast thou *considered* **set thy heart**
on my servant *Job* **Iyob**,
that there is none like him in the earth,
a perfect **an integrious** and *an upright* **straight** man,
one that *feareth God* **aweth Elohim,**
and *escheweth* **turneth aside from** evil?
and still he *holdeth fast* **upholdeth** his integrity,
although thou *movedst* **goadest** me *against him*,
to *destroy* **swallow** him *without cause* **gratuitously**.
4 And Satan answered *the*
LORD **Yah Veh**, and said,
Skin for skin, yea,
all that a man hath *will* **shall** he give for his *life* **soul**.
5 But *put forth* **spread** thine hand *now* **I beseech**,
and touch his bone and his flesh,
and he will curse **whether he shall bless** thee to thy face.
6 And *the LORD* **Yah Veh**
said unto Satan, Behold,
he is in thine hand; but *save* **guard** his *life* **soul**.

The Second Test Of Iyob

7 So went Satan forth
from the *presence* **face** of *the LORD* **Yah Veh**,
and smote *Job* **Iyob** with *sore boils* **evil ulcers**
from the sole of his foot unto his *crown* **scalp**.
yes, they smote the lads
with the mouth of the sword;
and I—I only escaped alone to tell you.
16 While he is yet wording,
another also comes and says,
The fire of Elohim fell from the heavens
and burned up the flocks and the lads
and consumed them;
and I—I only escaped alone to tell you.
17 While he is yet wording,
another also comes and says,
The Kesediym set out three heads
and stripped the camels and took them away;
yes, and smote the servants
with the mouth of the sword;

and I—I only escaped alone to tell you.
18 While he is yet wording,
another also comes and says,
Your sons and your daughters
were eating and drinking wine
in the house of their firstbirthed brother;
19 and behold,
a great wind came from across the wilderness
and touched the four corners of the house
and it fell upon the lads and they are dead;
and I—I only escaped alone to tell you.
20 Then Iyob rises and rips his mantle
and shears his head
and falls down on the earth and prostrates
21 and says,
Naked came I from the belly of my mother
and naked I return;
Yah Veh gives and Yah Veh takes;
blessed—the name of Yah Veh.
22 In all this Iyob neither sinned
nor attributed Elohim with frivolity.

The Second Challenge Of Satan

2 And so be it,
the day the sons of Elohim
come to station themselves by Yah Veh;
and Satan also comes among them
to station himself by Yah Veh.
2 And Yah Veh says to Satan,
Whence come you?
And Satan answers Yah Veh and says,
From flitting to and fro in the earth
and from walking forth and back in it.
3 And Yah Veh says to Satan,
Have you set your heart on my servant Iyob
—that there is no one like him in the earth;
an integrious and straight man;
one who awes Elohim and turns aside from evil?
And still he upholds his integrity
although you goad me to swallow him gratuitously.
4 And Satan answers Yah Veh and says,
Skin for skin;
yes, all a man has he gives for his soul;
5 but spread your hand, I beseech and touch his bone
and his flesh, whether he blesses you to your face.
6 And Yah Veh says to Satan,
Behold, he is in your hand; but guard his soul.

The Second Test Of Iyob

7 And Satan goes from the face of Yah Veh
and smites Iyob with evil ulcers
from the sole of his foot to his scalp.
8 And he took him a potsherd
to scrape himself *withal*;
and he *sat down* **settled** among the ashes.
9 Then said his *wife* **woman** unto him,
Dost **Shalt** thou still *retain* **uphold** thine integrity?
curse God **bless Elohim**, and die.
10 But he said unto her, Thou *speakest* **wordest**
as one of the foolish *women speaketh* **wordeth.**
What? **Yea,**
shall we *receive* **take** good at the hand of *God* **Elohim,**
and shall we not *receive* **take** evil?
In all this *did not Job sin* **Iyob sinned not** with his lips.

The Three Friends Of Iyob

11 *Now* when *Job's* **Iyob's** three friends
heard of all this evil that was come upon him,
they came *every one* **each man** from his own place;
Eliphaz **Eli Phaz** the *Temanite* **Temaniy,**
and Bildad the *Shuhite* **Shuachiy,**
and *Zophar* **Sophar** the *Naamathite* **Naamahiy:**
for they had *made an appointment* **congregated** together
to come to *mourn* **wag** with him
and to *comfort* **sigh with** him.
12 And when they lifted up their eyes afar off,
and *knew* **recognized** him not,
they lifted up their voice, and wept;
and they *rent every one* **ripped each man** his mantle,
and sprinkled dust upon their heads
toward *heaven* **the heavens.**
13 So they *sat down* **settled**
with him upon the ground
seven days and seven nights,
and none *spake* **worded** a word unto him:
for they saw that *his grief* **the pain**
was *very* **mighty** great.

Iyob Speaks

3 After this opened *Job* **Iyob** his mouth,
and *cursed* **abased** his day.
2 And *Job spake* **Iyob answered**, and said,
3 Let the day *perish* **destruct**
wherein I was *born* **birthed,**
and the night in which it was said,
There is a *man* **mighty** child conceived.
4 Let that day be darkness;
let not *God regard* **Elohah require** it from above,
neither let the light shine upon it.
5 Let darkness and the shadow
of death *stain* **redeem** it;

let a *cloud dwell* **cloudiness tabernacle** upon it;
let the *blackness* **eclipses** of the day *terrify* **frighten** it.
6 As for that night, let darkness *seize upon* **take** it;
let it not *be joined* **rejoice** unto the days of the year,
let it not come into the number of the *months* **moons**.
7 *Lo* **Behold**, let that night be *solitary* **sterile**,
let no *joyful voice* **shout** come therein.
8 Let them curse it that curse the day,
who are ready to
raise up their mourning **waken a leviathan**.
9 Let the stars of the *twilight*
thereof **evening breeze**
be dark **darken**;
let it *look for* **await** light, but have none;
neither let it see the *dawning* **eyelids** of the *day* **dawn**:
10 Because it shut not *up*
the doors of my *mother's womb* **belly**, nor
hid *sorrow* **toil** from mine eyes.
11 Why died I not from the womb?
why did I not give up the ghost
—**expire** when I came out of the belly?
12 Why did the knees *prevent* **anticipate** me?
or why the breasts that I should suck?
13 For now should I have lain *still* **down**
and *been quiet* **rested,**
I should have slept: then had I been at rest,
14 With *kings* **sovereigns** and
counsellors of the earth,
which built *desolate places* **parched areas** for themselves;
15 Or with *princes* **governors** that had gold,
who filled their houses with silver:
16 Or as an hidden *untimely birth* **miscarriage**
I had not been;
as infants which never saw light.
17 There the wicked cease
from *troubling* **commotion**;
and there the *weary be at* **wearied of force** rest.
18 There the *prisoners rest* **bound relax** together;
they hear not the voice of the *oppressor* **exactor**.
8 And he takes a potsherd to scrape himself;
and he settles among the ashes.
9 And his woman says to him,
You still uphold your integrity!
Bless Elohim and die.
10 And he says to her,
You word as one of the foolish word.
yes, take we good at the hand of Elohim
—and not take evil?
—in all this Iyob sinned not with his lips.

THE THREE FRIENDS OF IYOB

11 And the three friends of Iyob
hear of all this evil coming upon him,
and each man comes from his own place;
Eli Phaz the Temaniy
and Bildad the Shuachiy
and Sophar the Naamahiy;
for they come to congregate together
to wag with him and to sigh with him.
12 And they lift their eyes afar off
and recognize him not,
and they lift their voice and weep;
and each man rips his mantle
and sprinkles dust on his head toward the heavens:
13 and they settle with him on the ground
seven days and seven nights
—and no one words a word to him;
for they see the pain is mighty great.

IYOB SPEAKS

3 After this Iyob opens his mouth
and abases his day;
2 and Iyob answers and says,
3 Destroy the day I was birthed;
and the night that says,
A mighty child is conceived;
4 O that that day be darkness:
that Elohah neither require it from above,
nor the light shine on it;
5 that darkness and the
shadow of death redeem it;
that a cloudiness tabernacle on it;
that the eclipses of the day frighten it;
6 as for that night, O that darkness take it;
that it not rejoice to the days of the year; that it
not come into the number of the moons.
7 Behold, O that that night be sterile,
that no shout come therein;
8 that they curse, who curse the day
who are ready to waken a leviathan;
9 O that the stars of the evening breeze darken;
that it await light, but have none;
that it not see the eyelids of the dawn;
10 because it neither shut the doors of my belly,
nor hide toil from my eyes.
11 Why died I not from the womb?
—expire when I came from the belly?
12 Why *did* the knees anticipate me?
Or why the breasts I suck?

13 For now I lie down and rest;
had I slept, then had I been at rest,
14 with sovereigns and counsellors of the earth,
who build parched areas for themselves;
15 or with governors who have gold
—who fill their houses with silver;
16 or I had not been as a hidden miscarriage
—as infants who never see light.
17 There the wicked cease from commotion;
and there the wearied of force rest;
18 there the bound relax together;
they hear not the voice of the exactor;
19 The small and great are there;
and the servant is *free* **liberated** from his *master* **adoni.**
20 Wherefore is light given to him that is in misery,
and life unto the bitter *in* soul;
21 Which *long for* **await** death,
but it *cometh* **be** not;
and dig for it more than for hid treasures;
22 Which *rejoice exceedingly* **cheer and twirl,**
and *are glad* **rejoice,**
when they can find the *grave* **tomb**?
23 *Why is light given to a man*
—To the mighty whose way is hid,
and whom *God* **Elohah** hath hedged in?
24 For my sighing cometh
before I eat **at the face of my bread,**
and my roarings are poured out like the waters.
25 For the *thing which I greatly*
feared **dread I dreaded**
is come upon me,
and that which I *was afraid of* **feared** is come unto me.
26 I was not *in safety* **serenified,** neither had I rest,
neither *was I quiet* **rested I**; yet
trouble **commotion** came.

Eli Phaz Answers

4 Then *Eliphaz* **Eli Phaz** the *Temanite* **Temaniy**
answered and said,
2 If we *assay to commune* **test a word** with thee,
wilt **shalt** thou *be grieved* **weary**?
but who can *withhold* **refrain** himself
from *speaking* **utterances**?
3 Behold, thou hast instructed many,
and thou hast strengthened the weak hands.
4 Thy *words* **utterances** have *upholden* **raised** him
that *was falling* **faltered,**
and thou hast strengthened the *feeble* **kneeling** knees.
5 But now it is come upon thee,
and thou *faintest* **weariest**;
it toucheth thee, and thou art *troubled* **terrified.**
6 Is not this thy *fear* **awe,**
thy confidence, thy hope,
and the *uprightness* **integrity** of thy ways?
7 Remember, I pray thee,
who ever *perished* **destructed,** being innocent?
or where were the *righteous* **straight** cut off?
8 Even as I have seen,
they that plow *iniquity* **mischief,**
and *sow wickedness* **seed toil,**
reap the same **thus harvest.**
9 By the *blast* **breath** of *God* **Elohah**
they *perish* **destruct,**
and by the *breath* **spirit/wind** of his nostrils
are they *consumed* **finished off.**
10 The roaring of the lion,
and the voice of the *fierce* **roaring** lion,
and the teeth of the *young lions* **whelps,**
are *broken* **pulled.**
11 The old lion *perisheth* **destructeth**
for lack of **without** prey,
and the *stout* **roaring** lion's whelps
are *scattered abroad* **separated.**
12 Now a *thing* **word** was *secretly* **by stealth**
brought to me,
and mine ear *received a little* **took an inkling** *thereof.*
13 In *thoughts* **sentiments** from
the visions of the night,
when deep sleep falleth on men,
14 *Fear came upon* **Dread**
confronted me, and trembling,
which *made all* my **abundant** bones *to shake* **dreaded.**
15 Then a spirit passed *before* **in front of** my face;
the hair of my flesh stood *up* **on end**:
16 It stood *still,*
but I could not *discern* **recognize**
the *form* **visage** *thereof*:
an image **a manifestation** was *before*
in front of mine eyes,
there was silence, **Stillness!** and I heard a voice, *saying,*
17 Shall mortal man be more
just than *God* **Elohah**?
shall *a man* **the mighty** be more pure
than his *maker* **Worker**?
18 Behold, he put no trust in his servants;
and his angels he *charged* **set** with *folly* **braggadocio**:
19 *How much less in them* **Yea, they**
that *dwell* **tabernacle** in houses of clay,
whose foundation is in the dust,
which are crushed *before* **at the face of** the moth?

20 They are *destroyed* **crushed**
from morning to evening:
19 the small and great are there;
and the servant *is* liberated from his adoni.
20 Why gives he light to him in misery
and life to the bitter soul;
21 who await death, and so be it not;
and dig for it more than for hid treasures;
22 who cheer and twirl and rejoice,
when they can find the tomb?
23 —to the mighty whose way is hid
whom Elohah hedges in?
24 For my sighing comes at the face of my bread
and my roarings pour as the waters.
25 For the dread I dreaded comes on me
and what I feared comes to me.
26 I neither serenified, nor had I rest,
nor rested I; yet commotion came.

Eli Phaz Answers

4 And Eli Phaz the Temaniy answers and says,
2 If one tests a word with you, you weary;
but who can refrain himself from utterances?
3 Behold, you instructed many
and you strengthened the weak hands;
4 your utterances raised him who falters
and you strengthened the kneeling knees.
5 But now it comes on you, and you weary;
it touches you, and you terrify.
6 Is not this your awe, your confidence,
your hope and the integrity of your ways?
7 Remember, I pray you,
whoever destructs, being innocent? or,
Where are the straight cut off?
8 Even as I see,
they who plow mischief and seed toil,
harvest thus.
9 By the breath of Elohah, they destruct
and by the spirit/wind of his nostrils, they finish off.
10 The roaring of the lion
and the voice of the roaring lion
and the teeth of the whelps
—all are pulled.
11 Without prey, the old lion destructs,
and the whelps of the roaring lion separate.
12 And by stealth, a word is brought to me
and my ear takes an inkling.
13 In sentiments from the visions of the night,
when deep sleep falls on men,
14 dread and trembling confront me
—which my abundant bones dread.
15 And a spirit passes in front of my face;
the hair of my flesh stands on end;
16 it stands:
but I recognize not the visage;
a manifestation in front of my eyes:
stillness—and I hear a voice,
17 Is mortal man more just than Elohah?
The mighty more pure than his Worker?
18 Behold, he puts no trust in his servants;
and he sets his angels with braggadocio;
19 yes, they who tabernacle in houses of clay,
whose foundation is in the dust
crush at the face of the moth
20 —crushed from morning to evening;
they *perish for ever* **destruct in perpetuity**
without *any regarding* **setting** it.
21 Doth not their *excellency*
remainder which is in them
go away **pull stakes**?
they die, even without wisdom.

5 Call *now* **I beseech**,
if there be any that *will* **shall** answer thee;
and to which of the *saints wilt* **holy shalt** thou *turn* **face**?
2 For *wrath killeth* **vexation**
slaughtereth the foolish *man*,
and envy *slayeth* **deathifieth** the *silly one* **enticed**.
3 I have seen the foolish taking root:
but suddenly I cursed his habitation **of rest**.
4 His children are far from *safety* **salvation**,
and they are crushed in the *gate* **portal**, neither
is there any to *deliver* **rescue** them.
5 Whose harvest the *hungry* **famished** eateth up,
and taketh it even *out of* **through** the thorns,
and the robber
swalloweth up **gulpeth** their *substance* **valuables**.
6 Although *affliction* **mischief**
cometh not forth of the dust,
neither *doth trouble* **toil**
spring **sprout** out of the *ground* **soil**;
7 Yet *man* **humanity** is *born*
birthed unto *trouble* **toil**,
as the *sparks* **sons of the burning
coal lift and** fly *upward*.
8 **But** I *would* **should** seek unto *God* **El**,
and unto *God* **Elohim**
would **should** I *commit* **set** my *cause* **word**:
9 Which *doeth* **worketh** great *things*
and unsearchable **not to be probed**;
marvellous things **marvels** without number:

10 Who giveth rain upon the **face of the** earth,
and sendeth waters upon the *fields* **face of the outways**:
11 To set *up on high* **in the heights**
those that be low **the lowly**;
that *those which mourn* **the darkened**
may be *exalted to safety* **lifted unto salvation**.
12 He *disappointeth* **breaketh down**
the *devices* **fabrications** of the *crafty* **subtle,**
so that their hands
cannot perform **work not** their *enterprise* **substance**.
13 He *taketh* **captureth** the
wise in their own craftiness:
and the counsel of the *froward* **twisters**
is *carried headlong* **hastened**.
14 They meet with darkness in the *daytime* **day**,
and grope in the noonday as in the night.
15 But he saveth the *poor* **needy** from the sword,
from their mouth,
and from the hand of the *mighty* **strong**.
16 So the poor *hath* **becometh** hope,
and *iniquity stoppeth* **wickedness shutteth** her mouth.
17 Behold, *happy* **blithe** is the man
whom *God correcteth* **Elohah reproveth**:
therefore *despise* **spurn** not thou
the *chastening* **discipline** of *the Almighty* **Shadday**:
18 For he *maketh sore* **paineth**, and bindeth *up*:
he *woundeth* **striketh**, and his hands *make whole* **heal**.
19 He shall *deliver* **rescue** thee
in six *troubles* **tribulations**:
yea, in seven there shall no evil touch thee.
20 In famine he shall redeem thee from death:
and in war from the *power* **hand** of the sword.
21 Thou shalt be hid from the
scourge **lash** of the tongue:
neither shalt thou *be afraid of*
destruction **awe devastation**
when it cometh.
22 At *destruction* **devastation** and *famine* **hunger**
thou shalt laugh:
neither shalt thou *be afraid of* **awe** the
beasts **live beings** of the earth.
23 For *thou shalt be in league* **thy covenant shall be**
with the stones of the field:
and the beasts of the field
shall be at *peace* **shalom** with thee.
24 And thou shalt know that thy *tabernacle* **tent**
shall be in *peace* **shalom**;
and thou shalt visit thy habitation **of rest**,
and shalt not sin.
25 Thou shalt know also that
thy seed shall be great,
and thine offspring as the *grass* **herbage** of the earth.
26 Thou shalt come to thy *grave*
tomb in *a full age* **maturity**,
they destruct in perpetuity without setting:
21 those remaining pull stakes
—they die, even without wisdom.

5 Call, I beseech,
if there be any who answer you;
and to which of the holy *do* you face?
2 For vexation slaughters the foolish
and envy deathifies the enticed.
3 I see the foolish taking root;
but suddenly I curse his habitation of rest.
4 His children are far from salvation
—crushed in the portal, none to rescue them;
5 whose harvest the famished eat
and even take it through the thorns
and the robber gulps their valuables.
6 For neither comes mischief from the dust,
nor sprouts toil from the soil;
7 yet humanity is birthed to toil,
as the sons of the burning coal lift and fly.
8 Yet I—I seek to El
and to Elohim I set my word;
9 who works great—not to be probed;
marvels without number;
10 who gives rain on the face of the earth
and sends waters on the face of the outways;
11 to set the lowly in the heights;
to lift the darkened to salvation.
12 He breaks down the fabrications of the subtle
so that their hands not work their substance:
13 he captures the wise in their own craftiness;
and hastens the counsel of the twisters.
14 They meet with darkness in the day
and grope in the noonday as in the night.
15 And he saves the needy from the sword,
from their mouth and from the hand of the strong.
16 And so be it, hope to the poor
and wickedness shuts her mouth.
17 Behold, blithe—the man
whom Elohah reproves;
so spurn not the discipline of Shadday;
18 for he pains and binds;
he strikes and his hands heal.
19 He rescues you in six tribulations;
yes, in seven no evil touches you.
20 In famine he redeems you from death;
and in war from the hand of the sword.
21 You are hid from the lash of the tongue;

awe not devastation when it comes.
22 You laugh at devastation and hunger;
and awe not the live beings of the earth.
23 For your covenant *is* with the stones of the field;
and the beasts of the field are at shalom with you.
24 And you know that your tent *is* in shalom;
and you visit your habitation of rest and sin not.
25 You know also that your seed *is* great
and your offspring as the herbage of the earth.
26 You come to your tomb in maturity,
like as a *shock of corn cometh* **heap ascendeth**
in his *season* **time**.
27 *Lo* **Behold** this,
we have *searched* **probed** it, so **be** it *is*;
hear it, and know thou it for thy good.
as a heap ascends in his time.
27 Behold this, we probe, and so be it;
hear and know for your own good.

Iyob Answers

6 But *Job* **Iyob** answered and said,
2 Oh that *my grief* **in weighing,**
my vexation were *throughly* weighed,
and my calamity *laid* **lifted** in the balances together!
3 For now it *would* **should** be heavier
than the sand of the sea:
therefore my words are *swallowed up* **gulped**.
4 For the arrows of *the Almighty*
Shadday are within me,
the poison whereof drinketh up my spirit:
the terrors of *God* **Elohah**
do set themselves in array **line up** against me.
5 *Doth* **Shall** the wild *ass* **runner** bray
when he hath *grass* **sprouts**?
or *loweth* **belloweth** the ox over his fodder?
6 *Can that which is unsavoury*
Shall slime be eaten
without salt?
or is there *any* taste in the *white* **slime** of an egg?
7 *The things* **Those** that my soul refused to touch
are as my *sorrowful meat* **bloody bread**.
8 *Oh* **Who giveth** that I might
have my *request* **petition**;
and that *God* **Elohah**
would grant me the thing that I long for
should give me hope!
9 *Even that it would please*
God **Though Elohah willeth**
to *destroy* **crush** me;
that he *would* **should** let loose his hand, and cut me off!
10 Then should *I yet have comfort*
yet my sighing be; yea,
I *would harden myself in sorrow*
should jump with pangs:
let him not spare;
for I have not concealed
the *words* **sayings** of the Holy One.
11 What is my *strength* **force**,
that I should *hope* **await**?
and what is mine end,
that I should prolong my *life* **soul**?
12 Is my *strength* **force** the *strength* **force** of stones?
or is my flesh of *brass* **copper**?
13 Is not my help in me?
and is *wisdom* **substance** driven quite from me?
14 To him that *is afflicted* **melteth,**
pity **mercy** should be *shewed* from his friend;
but he forsaketh the *fear* **awe** of *the Almighty* **Shadday**.
15 My brethren have *dealt deceitfully* **covered over**
as a *brook* **wadi,**
and as the *stream* **reservoir** of *brooks* **wadies**
they pass away;
16 Which are *blackish* **darkened**
by *reason of* the ice,
and wherein the snow is *hid* **concealed**:
17 What time they *wax warm* **dissipate**,
they *vanish* **are exterminated**:
when it is hot,
they are *consumed* **extinguished** out of their place.
18 The paths of their way are turned aside;
they *go* **ascend** to *nothing* **waste**, and *perish* **destruct**.
19 The *troops* **paths** of Tema looked,
the *companies* **caravans** of Sheba
waited for **awaited** them.
20 They were *confounded* **shamed**
because they had hoped;
they came thither, and *were ashamed* **blushed**.
21 For now ye are *nothing* **nought**;
ye see my casting down, and *are afraid* **awe**.
22 Did I say, Bring unto me?
or, *Give a reward for* **Bribe** me of your substance?
23 Or, *Deliver* **Rescue** me
from the *enemy's* hand **of the tribulator**?
or, Redeem me from the hand of the *mighty* **tyrant**?
24 Teach me, and I *will hold my tongue* **shall hush**:
and cause me to *understand* **discern**
wherein I have **inadvertently** erred.
25 How *forcible* **reinforcing**
are *right words* **sayings of straightness**!
but what doth your *arguing* **reproving** reprove?

26 Do ye *imagine* **fabricate** to
reprove *words* **utterances**,

IYOB ANSWERS

6 And Iyob answers and says,
2 Oh that in weighing, my vexation were weighed
and my calamity lifted in the balances together!
3 For now it is heavier than the sand of the sea;
so I gulp my words;
4 for the arrows of Shadday are within me,
whereof the poison drinks up my spirit;
the terrors of Elohah line up against me.
5 Brays the wild runner when he has sprouts?
Bellows the ox over his fodder?
6 Is slime eaten without salt?
Is there taste in the slime of an egg?
7 What my soul refuses to touch
is as my bloody bread.
8 O that I be given my petition;
and that Elohah give me hope!
9 O that Elohah wills to crush me
—to loose his hand and cut me off!
10 And yet it is my sighing;
I jump with pangs; he spares not:
for I conceal not the sayings of the Holy One.
11 What is my force, that I await?
What is my end, that I prolong my soul?
12 Is my force the force of stones?
Is my flesh of copper?
13 Is not my help within me?
Is substance quite driven from me?
14 He who melts, has mercy from his friend;
but he forsakes the awe of Shadday.
15 My brothers cover up as a wadi
and as the reservoir of wadies,
they pass away;
16 —darkened by the ice
wherein the snow conceals;
17 by the time they dissipate
they are exterminated;
when it is hot
they are extinguished from their place.
18 The paths of their way are turned aside;
they ascend to waste and destruct.
19 The paths of Tema look;
the caravans of Sheba await them;
20 they shame because they had hoped;
there they come and blush.
21 Surely now you are naught;
you see my casting down and awe.
22 Said I, Bring me?
or, Bribe me of your substance?
23 or, Rescue me from the hand of the tribulator?
or, Redeem me from the hand of the tyrant?
24 Teach me, and I hush;
and I discern wherein I have inadvertently erred.
25 How reinforcing the sayings of straightness!
And what *does* your reproving reprove?
26 Fabricate you to reprove utterances
and the *speeches* **sayings** of *one*
that is desperate **a quitter**,
which are—as wind?
27 Yea, ye *overwhelm* **fell** the *fatherless* **orphan**,
and ye dig *a pit* for your friend.
28 Now therefore *be content*,
look upon **will to face** me;
for it is evident unto *you* **your face** if I lie.
29 Return, I *pray* **beseech** you,
let it not be *iniquity* **wickedness**;
yea, return again, my *righteousness* **justness** is in it.
30 Is there *iniquity* **wickedness** in my tongue?
cannot my *taste* **palate**
discern *perverse things* **calamity**?

7 Is there not *an appointed time* **a hostility**
to man upon earth?
are *not* his days also like the days of an hireling?
2 As a servant *earnestly*
desireth **gulpeth** the shadow,
and as an hireling
looketh **awaiteth** for *the reward of* his *work* **deeds**:
3 *So am I made to possess* **Thus have I inherited**
months **moons** of vanity,
and *wearisome nights* **nights of toil**
are *appointed* **numbered** to me.
4 When I lie down, I say, When shall I arise
and the *night* **evening** be *gone* **flown**?
and I am *full* **satiated** of tossings to and fro
unto the *dawning of the day* **evening breeze**.
5 My flesh is *clothed* **enrobed**
with *worms* **maggots** and clods of dust;
my skin is *broken* **split**,
and *become loathsome* **dissipateth**.
6 My days are swifter than
a *weaver's shuttle* **weaver**,
and are *spent* **finished off** without hope.
7 O remember that my life is *wind* **wind/spirit**:
mine eye shall *no more* **not return to** see good.
8 The eye of him that hath seen me
shall *see me no more* **not lurk**:
thine eyes are upon me, and I am not.

9 *As* the cloud *is consumed* **finisheth off**
and *vanisheth away* **goeth**:
so he that *goeth down* **descendeth** to *the grave* **sheol**
shall *come up no more* **ascend not again**.
10 He shall return *no more* **not again** to his house,
neither shall his place
know **recognize** him *any more* **again**.
11 Therefore I *will* **shall** not
refrain **spare** my mouth;
I *will speak* **shall word**
in the *anguish* **tribulation** of my spirit;
I *will complain* **shall meditate**
in the bitterness of my soul.
12 Am I a sea, or a *whale* **monster**,
that thou settest a *watch* **guard** over me?
13 When I say,
My *bed* **bedstead** shall *comfort* **sigh for** me,
my *couch* **bed** shall *ease* **lift** my *complaint* **meditation**;
14 Then thou *scarest* **terrifiest** me with dreams,
and *terrifiest* **frightenest** me through visions:
15 So that my soul chooseth strangling,
and death rather than my *life* **bones**.
16 I *loathe* **spurn** it;
I *would* **shall** not live *alway* **eternally**:
let me *alone* **decease**; for my days are vanity.
17 What is man,
that thou shouldest *magnify* **greaten** him?
and that thou shouldest set thine heart upon him?
18 And that thou shouldest
visit him every morning,
and *try* **proof** him every *moment* **blink**?
19 How long
wilt **shalt** thou not *depart* **look away** from me,
nor let me *alone* **loose** till I swallow down my *spittle* **spit**?
20 I have sinned; what shall I do unto thee,
O thou *preserver* **guardian** of *men* **humanity**?
why hast thou set me as a *mark* **target** against thee,
so that I am a burden to myself?
21 And why dost thou not
pardon **lift** my *transgression* **rebellion**,
and *take* **pass** away my *iniquity* **perversity**?
for now shall I *sleep* **lie** in the dust;
and thou shalt seek me *in the morning* **early**,
but I shall not be.
and the sayings of a quitter as wind?
27 Yes, you fell the orphan
and you dig for your friend.
28 And now, will to face me;
for it is evident to your face if I lie.
29 Return, I beseech you,
that it not be wickedness;
yes, return, my justness is in it.
30 Is there wickedness in my tongue?
Cannot my palate discern calamity?

7 Is there not a hostility to man on earth?
Are his days also as the days of an hireling?
2 As a servant gulps the shadow
—as a hireling awaits his deeds;
3 thus I inherit moons of vanity
and nights of toil are numbered to me.
4 I lie down and I say, When *do* I arise?
and the evening flies *away*
and I am satiated by tossings to and fro
until the evening breeze.
5 My flesh enrobes with
maggots and clods of dust;
my skin splits and dissipates:
6 my days are swifter than a weaver
—finished off without hope.
7 O remember that my life is wind/spirit;
my eye returns not to see good.
8 The eye of him who sees me lurks not;
your eyes are on me, and I am not.
9 the cloud finishes off and goes;
thus he who descends to sheol ascends not again;
10 he neither returns to his house,
nor his place recognizes him again.
11 Also I—I spare not my mouth;
I word in the tribulation of my spirit;
I meditate in the bitterness of my soul.
12 Am I a sea or a monster
that you set a guard over me?
13 When I say, My bedstead sighs for me,
my bed lifts my meditation;
14 and you terrify me with dreams
and frighten me through visions;
15 so that my soul chooses strangling and death
rather than my bones.
16 I spurn; I live not eternally;
let me decease; for my days are vanity.
17 What is man, that you greaten him?
—that you set your heart on him?
18 —that you visit him every morning?
—and proof him every blink?
19 Until when look you not from me?
—nor loose me until I swallow my spit?
20 I sinned; what do I to you,
O you guardian of humanity?
Why set me as a target against you,
so that I am a burden to myself?
21 And why lift you not my rebellion

and pass away my perversity?
for now I lie in the dust;
and you seek me early—but I am not.

Bildad Answers

8 Then answered Bildad the *Shuhite* **Shuachiy**,
and said,
2 *How long* **Until when**
wilt **shalt** thou *speak* **utter** these *things*?
and how long shall the words—**the sayings of thy mouth**
be *like a strong* **much** wind?
3 Doth *God pervert* **El twist** judgment?
or doth *the Almighty* **Shadday** *pervert*
justice **twist justness**?
4 If thy children have sinned against him,
and he have *cast* **sent** them away
for **by the hand of** their *transgression* **rebellion**;
5 If thou *wouldest* **shouldest** seek unto *God* **El**
betimes **early**
and *make thy supplication* **seekest charism**
to the Almighty **of Shadday**;
6 If thou wert pure and *upright* **straight**;
surely now he *would* **should** awake for thee,
and *make* **shalam** the habitation **of rest** of
thy *righteousness prosperous* **justness**.
7 Though thy beginning was *small* **little**,
yet thy *latter end* **finality** should
greatly **mightily** increase.
8 For enquire, I *pray* **beseech**
thee, of the *former* **first** age,
and prepare thyself
to the *search* **probing** of their fathers:
9 (For we are *but* of yesterday,
and know *nothing* **naught**,
because our days upon earth are a shadow:)
10 Shall not they teach thee, and *tell* **say to** thee,
and utter *words* **utterances** out of their heart?
11 Can the rush *grow up* **rise** without mire?
can the *flag grow* **bulrush increase** without water?
12 Whilst it is yet in his *greenness* **unripeness**,
and not *cut down* **plucked**,
it withereth *before* **at the face of** any *other* herb.
13 So are the paths of all that forget *God* **El**;
and the *hypocrite's* **profaner's** hope shall *perish* **destruct**:
14 Whose hope shall be cut off,
and whose *trust* **confidence**
shall be a spider's *web* **house**.
15 He shall lean upon his house,
but it shall not stand:
he shall *hold* **strengthen** it *fast*,
but it shall not *endure* **arise**.
16 He is *green before* **moist at the face of** the sun,
and his *branch* **sprout** shooteth forth in his garden.
17 His roots are *wrapped* **entwined** about the heap,
and seeth the *place* **house** of stones.
18 If he *destroy him* **be swallowed** from his place,
then it shall deny him, *saying*, I have not seen thee.
19 Behold, this is the joy of his way,
and out of the *earth* **dust** shall others *grow* **sprout**.
20 Behold,
God will **El shall** not *cast away* **spurn**
a perfect man **the integrious**,
neither *will* **shall** he *help* **strengthen the hand**
of the *evil doers* **vilifiers**:
21 Till he fill thy mouth with laughing,
and thy lips with *rejoicing* **shouting**.
22 They that hate thee
shall be *clothed* **enrobed** with shame;
and the *dwelling place* **tent** of the wicked
shall come to nought.

Iyob Answers

9 Then *Job* **Iyob** answered and said,
2 **Truly** I know it is so *of a truth*:
but how should man be *just* **justified** with *God* **El**?
3 If he *will* **desireth to** contend with him,
he cannot answer him one of a thousand.
4 He is wise in heart, and *mighty*
strong in *strength* **force**:
who hath hardened *himself* against him,
and hath *prospered* **shalamed**?
5 Which removeth the
mountains, and they know not:
which overturneth them in his *anger* **wrath**.
6 Which shaketh the earth out of her place,
and the pillars thereof tremble.
7 Which *commandeth* **saith**
to the sun, and it riseth not;
and sealeth up the stars.
8 Which alone spreadeth out the heavens,

Bildad Answers

8 And Bildad the Shuachiy answers and says,
2 Until when utter you these?
—the sayings of your mouth so much wind?
3 El—twists he judgment?
Or Shadday—twists he justness?
4 If your children sin against him
and he sends them away

by the hand of their rebellion;
5 if you seek El early and
seek charism of Shadday;
6 if you are pure and straight;
surely now he wakes for you
and shalams the habitation of rest of your justness.
7 Though your beginning be little,
yet your finality mightily increases.
8 I beseech you, enquire of the first age;
prepare yourself to the probing of their fathers;
9 —for we are of yesterday and know naught,
because our days on earth are a shadow.
10 Teach they not and say to you?
—and utter utterances from their heart?
11 Rises the rush without mire?
Increases the bulrush without water?
12 While it is yet in unripeness and not plucked,
it withers at the face of any herb.
13 Thus are the paths of all who forget El;
and the hope of the profaner destructs
14 —whose hope is cut off
and whose confidence is the house of a spider.
15 He leans on his house, and it stands not;
he strengthens, and it rises not:
16 he is moist at the face of the sun
and his sprout shoots forth in his garden:
17 his roots entwine around the heap
and see the house of stones.
18 If he is swallowed from his place,
then they deny *saying*, I see you not.
19 Behold the joy of his way,
and others sprout from the dust.
20 Behold, El neither spurns the integrious,
nor strengthens the hand of the vilifiers;
21 until he fills your mouth with laughing
and your lips with shouting;
22 and they who hate you enrobe with shame;
and the tent of the wicked comes to nought.

IYOB ANSWERS

9 And Iyob answers and says,
2 Truly I know, and so be it;
and how is man justified with El?
3 If he desires to contend with him,
he cannot answer him one of a thousand.
4 He is wise in heart and strong in force.
Who hardens against him and shalams?
5 Who removes mountains and they know not?
Who overturns them in his wrath?
6 Who shakes the earth from her place
and the pillars thereof tremble?
7 Who says to the sun and it rises not?
And seals the stars?
8 Who alone spreads out the heavens
and treadeth upon the *waves* **bamahs** of the sea.
9 Which *maketh Arcturus*
worketh Ash, *Orion* **Kesil**,
and *Pleiades* **Kimah**, and the chambers of the south.
10 Which *doeth* **worketh** great *things*
past finding out—**unable to be probed**; yea,
and *wonders* **marvels** without number.
11 *Lo* **Behold**, he *goeth* **passeth**
by me, and I see him not:
he passeth on also, but I *perceive* **discern** him not.
12 Behold, he *taketh away* **seizeth**,
who *can hinder* **turneth** him **back**?
who *will* **shall** say unto him, What *doest* **workest** thou?
13 If *God* **Elohah**
will **shall** not *withdraw* **turn back** his *anger* **wrath**,
the proud helpers *do stoop* **prostrate** under him.
14 How much less shall I answer him,
and choose out my words *to reason* with him?
15 Whom, though I were *righteous* **justified**,
yet *would* **should** I not answer,
but I *would make supplication* **should seek charism**
to **from** my judge.
16 If I had called, and he had answered me;
yet *would* **should** I not *believe* **trust**
that he had hearkened unto my voice.
17 For he *breaketh* **crusheth**
me with a *tempest* **whirling**,
and *multiplieth* **aboundeth** my wounds
without cause **gratuitously**.
18 He *will* **shall** not *suffer* **give** me
to *take* **return** my *breath* **spirit**,
but *filleth* **satiateth** me with *bitterness* **bitternesses**.
19 If *I speak of strength* **of force**,
lo **behold**, he is strong:
and if of judgment,
who shall *set me a time to plead* **congregate to me**?
20 If I justify myself,
mine own mouth shall *condemn me* **judge me wicked**:
if *I say*, I am *perfect* **integrious**,
it shall also *prove me perverse* **pervert me**.
21 *Though I were perfect* **I am integrious**,
yet *would* **should** I not know my soul:
I *would despise* **should spurn** my life.
22 This is one *thing*, therefore I said it,
He *destroyeth* **finisheth off**
the *perfect* **integrious** and the wicked.

23 If the *scourge slay* **whip deathify** suddenly,
he *will laugh* **shall deride**
at the *trial* **testing** of the innocent.
24 The earth is given into the hand of the wicked:
he covereth the faces of the judges *thereof*;
if not, where, and who is he?
25 Now my days are swifter than a *post* **runner**:
they flee away, they see no good.
26 They are passed away as
the *swift* ships **of yearning**:
as the eagle that *hasteth to the prey* **pounceth for food.**
27 If I say, I *will* **shall** forget
my *complaint* **meditation**,
I *will leave off* **shall forsake** my *heaviness* **face**,
and *comfort* **relax** *myself*:
28 I *am afraid of* **fear** all my *sorrows* **contortions**,
I know that thou
wilt **shalt** not *hold* **exonerate** me *innocent*.
29 If I be wicked, why then labour I in vain?
30 If I *wash* **bathe** myself with snow water,
and *make my hands never so clean*
cleanse my palms in purity;
31 Yet shalt thou *plunge* **dip**
me in the *ditch* **pit of ruin**,
and mine own clothes shall abhor me.
32 For he is not a man, as I *am*,
that I should answer him,
and we should come together in judgment.
33 Neither is there any *daysman*
reprover betwixt us,
that might *lay* **place** his hand upon us both.
34 Let him *take his rod away*
turn aside his scion from me,
and let not his *fear terrify* **terror frighten** me:
35 Then *would* **should** I *speak* **word**,
and not *fear* **awe** him;
but it is not so with me.

10 My soul *is weary of my* **loatheth** life;
I *will leave* **shall forsake** my *complaint* **meditation**
upon myself;
I *will speak* **shall word** in the bitterness of my soul.
and treads on the bamahs of the sea?
9 Who works Ash, Kesil and Kimah
and the chambers of the south?
10 Who works great—unable to be probed?
Yes, and marvels without number?
11 Behold, he passes by me and I see him not;
and he passes on, and I discern him not.
12 Behold, he seizes! Who turns him back?
Who says to him, What work you?
13 Elohah turns not back his wrath;
the proud helpers prostrate under him.
14 How much less answer I him?
—choose out my words with him?
15 Whom, though I am justified, yet I answer not;
but seek charism from my judge.
16 Though I call and he answers me not
yet I trust that he hearkens to my voice;
17 *though* he crushes me with a whirling
and abounds my wounds gratuitously;
18 *though* he gives to not return my spirit
but satiates me with bitternesses—
19 If of force, behold, he is strong!
If of judgment, who congregates to me?
20 If I justify myself,
my own mouth judges me wicked;
I—integrious, it also perverts me;
21 I—integrious, yet I know not my soul;
I spurn my life.
22 This is one, so I say,
He finishes off the integrious and the wicked.
23 If the whip suddenly deathifies,
he derides at the testing of the innocent.
24 He gives the earth into the hand of the wicked;
he covers the faces of the judges;
If not, where and who is he?
25 My days are swifter than a runner;
they flee away; they see no good;
26 they pass away as the ships of yearning
—as the eagle pounces for food.
27 If I say,
I forget my meditation
I forsake my face and relax
28 I fear all my contortions
—I know you exonerate me not.
29 I—I am wicked! Why this?
Why labor I in vain?
30 If I bathe myself with snow water
and cleanse my palms in purity;
31 yet you dip me in the pit of ruin
and my own clothes abhor me.
32 For he is not a man as I,
that I answer him
and we come together in judgment.
33 There is no reprover between us
to place his hand on us both.
34 He turns aside his scion from me;
his terror frightens me not;
35 I word, and awe him not;
but not so with me.

10 My soul loathes life;
I forsake my self—meditation;
I word in the bitterness of my soul.
2 I *will* **shall** say unto *God* **Elohah,**
Do not condemn me **Judge me not wicked**;
shew me **let me know**
wherefore thou contendest with me.
3 Is it good unto thee that thou shouldest oppress,
that thou shouldest *despise* **spurn**
the *work* **labour** of *thine hands* **thy palms,**
and shine upon the counsel of the wicked?
4 Hast thou eyes of flesh? or
seest thou as man seeth?
5 Are thy days as the days of man?
are thy years as *man's* days **of the mighty**,
6 That thou *enquirest* **seekest**
after *mine iniquity* **my perversity**,
and searchest after my sin?
7 Thou knowest that I am not wicked;
and there is none
that can *deliver* **escape** out of thine hand.
8 Thine hands have *made* **formed** me
and *fashioned* **worked** me together round about;
yet thou *dost destroy* **swallowest** me.
9 Remember, I beseech thee,
that thou hast *made* **worked** me as the clay;
and *wilt* **shalt** thou *bring* **return** me into dust *again*?
10 Hast thou not poured me out as milk,
and curdled me like cheese?
11 Thou hast *clothed* **enrobed**
me with skin and flesh,
and hast *fenced* **hedged** me with bones and sinews.
12 Thou hast *granted* **worked**
me life and *favour* **mercy**,
and thy visitation hath *preserved* **guarded** my spirit.
13 And these *things* hast thou hid in thine heart:
I know that this is with thee.
14 If I sin, then thou *markest* **guardest** me,
and thou *wilt* **shalt** not *acquit* **exonerate** me
from mine iniquity.
15 If I be wicked, woe unto me;
and if I be *righteous* **justified**,
yet *will* **shall** I not lift *up* my head.
I am *full of confusion* **satiated with abasement**;
therefore see thou *mine affliction* **my humiliation**;
16 For it *increaseth* **riseth**.
Thou huntest me as a *fierce* **roaring** lion:
and *again* **turnest back;**
thou shewest thyself marvellous upon me.
17 Thou renewest thy witnesses against me,
and *increasest thine indignation* **aboundest thy vexation**
upon **with** me;
changes and *war* **hostility** are against me.
18 Wherefore then hast thou brought me forth
out of the womb?
Oh that I had *given up the ghost* **expired**,
and no eye had seen me!
19 *I should have been* **As not being**
as though I had not been **I have become**;
I should have been carried—**brought**
from the *womb* **belly**
to the *grave* **tomb**.
20 Are not my days few?
cease *then, and let me alone* **set away from me**,
that I may *take comfort* **relax** a little,
21 Before I go *whence I shall* **and** not return,
even to the land of darkness and the shadow of death;
22 A land of darkness, as darkness *itself*;
and of the shadow of death, without any order,
and where the *light* **shining** is as darkness.

11 Then answered
Zophar **Sophar** the *Naamathite* **Naamahiy**, and said,
2 Should not the *multitude* **abundance** of words
be answered?
and should a man full of *talk* **lips** be justified?
3 Should thy lies make men *hold their peace* **hush**?
and when thou *mockest* **deridest**,
shall no *man make thee ashamed* **one shame thee**?
4 For thou hast said, My doctrine is pure,
and I am *clean* **pure** in thine eyes.
5 But *oh that God would speak*
who giveth that Elohah should word,
and open his lips against thee;
2 I say to Elohah, Judge me not wicked;
let me know why you contend with me.
3 Is it good to you that you oppress?
That you spurn the labor of your palms? And
shine on the counsel of the wicked?
4 Have you eyes of flesh?
See you as man sees?
5 Are your days as the days of man?
—your years as days of the mighty
6 that you seek after my perversity
and search after my sin?
7 You know I am not wicked;
and there is no escape from your hand.
8 Your hands formed me
and worked me together all around;
yet you swallow me.
9 Remember, I beseech you,

that you worked me as the clay;
and return me to dust.
10 Pour you not me out as milk?
—curdle me as cheese?
11 You enrobe me with skin and flesh
and hedge me with bones and sinews:
12 you work me life and mercy
and your visitation guards my spirit;
13 and you hide these in your heart;
I know this is with you.
14 If I sin, you guard me
—you exonerate me not from my iniquity.
15 If I be wicked, woe to me;
and if I be justified, yet I lift not my head.
I satiate with abasement; you see my humiliation;
16 for it rises;
you hunt me as a roaring lion; you turn back;
you show yourself marvellous in me;
17 you renew your witnesses against
me and abound your vexation with me;
changes and hostility are against me.
18 Why then brought you
me forth from the womb?
Oh that I had expired and no eye had seen me!
19 As not being I became;
—brought from the belly to the tomb.
20 Are my days not few?
Cease, set away from me that I relax a little
21 —ere I go and not return
to the land of darkness and the shadow of death;
22 —a land of darkness as darkness;
of the shadow of death without any order
where the shining is as darkness.

Sophar Answers

11 And Sophar the Naamahiy answers and says,
2 Answer we not this abundance of words?
—justify a man full of lips?
3 —that your lies hush men?
—and when you deride, that no one shames you?
4 And you say, My doctrine is pure!
and, I am pure in your eyes!
5 But who gives that Elohah words
and opens his lips against you;
6 And that he *would shew* **should tell** thee
the *secrets* **concealments** of wisdom,
that they are *double to that which is* **a double substance**!
Know that *God* **Elohah** exacteth of thee
less than thine iniquity deserveth **thy perversity**.
7 Canst thou by *searching*
probing find out *God* **Elohah**?
canst thou find out
the *Almighty unto perfection* **conclusion of Shadday**?
8 It is as high as *heaven* **the heavens**;
what *canst* **doest** thou *do*?
deeper than *hell* **sheol**;
what *canst* **knowest** thou *know*?
9 The measure thereof is longer than the earth,
and broader than the sea.
10 If he *cut off* **pass by**, and shut up,
or *gather together* **congregate**,
then who *can hinder* **shall turn** him **back**?
11 For he knoweth vain men:
he seeth *wickedness* **mischief** *also*;
will he not then consider **shall no one discern** it?
12 For *vain* **empty** man *would
be wise* **disheartenneth**,
though *man* **humanity** be *born* **birthed**
like a wild *ass's* **runner's** colt.
13 If thou prepare thine heart,
and *stretch out thine hands* **spread
thy palms** toward him;
14 If *iniquity* **mischief** be in thine hand,
put **remove** it far away,
and let not wickedness
dwell **tabernacle** in thy *tabernacles* **tents**.
15 For then shalt thou lift *up* thy face
without spot **apart from blemish**;
yea, thou shalt be *stedfast* **firmed**, and shalt not *fear* **awe**:
16 Because thou shalt forget thy *misery* **toil**,
and remember it as waters that pass away:
17 And *thine age* **transcience**
shall *be clearer than* **arise above** the noonday:
thou shalt *shine forth* **fly**, thou shalt be as the morning.
18 And thou shalt *be secure* **confide**,
because there is hope;
yea, thou shalt dig *about thee*,
and thou shalt *take thy rest in safety*
lie down confidently.
19 Also thou shalt *lie down* **repose**,
and none shall *make* **tremble** thee *afraid*;
yea many shall *make suit unto thee* **stroke thy face**.
20 But the eyes of the wicked
shall *fail* **be finished off**,
and *they shall not escape* **flight destructeth
from them**, and their hope shall be
as the *giving up* **expiration** of the *ghost* **soul**.

Iyob Answers

12 And *Job* **Iyob** answered and said,
2 *No doubt* **Truly** but ye are the people,
and wisdom shall die with you.
3 *But* **Yea,**
I have *understanding as well* **such a heart** as you;
I am not *inferior to* **fallen lower than** you:
yea, who knoweth not such *things* as these?
4 I am as one *mocked* **ridiculed**
of his *neighbour* **friend,**
who calleth upon *God* **Elohah,** and he answereth him:
the just *upright man*, **the integrious**
is *laughed to scorn* **ridiculed.**
5 He that *is ready to slip*
prepareth to waver with his feet
is as a *lamp despised* **flambeau disrespected**
in the *thought* **thoughts** of him that *is at ease* **relaxeth.**
6 The *tabernacles* **tents** of *robbers* **ravagers**
prosper **serenify,**
and they that provoke *God* **El** are *secure* **confident;**
into whose hand *God* **Elohah** bringeth *abundantly.*
7 But ask *now* **I beseech** the *beasts* **animals,**
and they shall teach thee;
and the *fowls* **flyers** of the air,
and they shall tell thee:
8 Or *speak* **meditate** to the earth,
and it shall teach thee:
and the fishes of the sea
shall *declare* **scribe** unto thee.
9 Who knoweth not in all these
that the hand of *the LORD* **Yah Veh**
hath *wrought* **worked** this?
10 In whose hand is the soul
of *every* **all** living *thing,*
6 and tells you the concealments of wisdom,
that they are a double substance!
Know that Elohah exacts your perversity of you.
7 By probing, find you Elohah?
—find the conclusion of Shadday?
8 As high as the heavens; what do you?
Deeper than sheol; what know you?
9 The measure thereof
is longer than the earth and broader than the sea.
10 If he passes by, and shuts up or congregate,
who then turns him back?
11 For he knows vain men;
he sees mischief; no one discerns!
12 For empty man disheartens,
and humanity births *as* the colt of a wild runner.
13 If you prepare your heart
and spread your palms toward him;
14 if mischief be in your hand, remove it far away;
tabernacle no wickedness in your tents.
15 Then lift your face apart from blemish;
yes, be firmed and awe not;
16 because you forget your toil
and remember it as passing waters;
17 and transcience rises above the noonday;
you fly—you are as the morning;
18 and you confide because there is hope;
yes, you dig and lie down confidently;
19 and you repose and no one trembles you;
yes, many stroke your face.
20 And the eyes of the wicked finish off
and flight destructs from them
and their hope is as the expiration of the soul.

Iyob Answers

12 And Iyob answers and says,
2 Truly you *are* the people;
and with you, wisdom dies.
3 Yes, I have a heart as you;
I fall not lower than you;
yes, who knows not such as these?
4 I am as one ridiculed by his friend,
who calls on Elohah and he answers him;
he ridicules the just, the integrious.
5 He who prepares to waver with his feet
is as a flambeau disrespected
in the thoughts of him who relaxes.
6 The tents of ravagers serenify
and they who provoke El *are* confident;
into whose hand Elohah brings.
7 And yet, I beseech,
ask the animals to teach you;
and the flyers of the air to tell you;
8 or meditate to the earth to teach you;
and the fishes of the sea to scribe to you.
9 Who knows not that in all these
the hand of Yah Veh worked this?
10 In whose hand *is* the soul of all living
and the *breath* **spirit** of all *mankind* **flesh of man.**
11 Doth not the ear *try words* **proof utterances?**
and the *mouth* **palate** taste his *meat* **food?**
12 With the *ancient* **aged** is wisdom;
and in length of days understanding.
13 With him is wisdom and *strength* **might,**
he hath counsel and understanding.
14 Behold, he breaketh down,

and it cannot be built *again*:
he shutteth up a man,
and there *can* be no opening.
15 Behold, he *withholdeth* **restraineth** the waters,
and they dry *up*:
also he sendeth them out,
and they overturn the earth.
16 With him is strength and *wisdom* **substance**:
the deceived **they that err inadvertently**
and *the deceiver* **they that cause to err inadvertently**
are his.
17 He *leadeth* **walketh** counsellors
away *spoiled* **stripped**,
and maketh the judges *fools* **to halal**.
18 He looseth the bond of *kings* **sovereigns**,
and *girdeth* **bindeth** their loins with a girdle.
19 He *leadeth princes* **walketh priests**
away *spoiled* **stripped**,
and *overthroweth* **perverteth** the *mighty* **perennial**.
20 He *removeth away* **turneth aside**
the *speech* **lip** of the *trusty* **trustworthy**,
and taketh away the *understanding* **taste** of the aged.
21 He poureth *contempt* **disrespect**
upon *princes* **volunteers**,
and *weakeneth* **looseth** the *strength* **girdle**
of the *mighty* **gatherers**.
22 He *discovereth deep things* **exposeth depths**
out of darkness,
and bringeth out to light the shadow of death.
23 He increaseth the *nations* **goyim**,
and destroyeth them:
he *enlargeth* **spreadeth** the *nations* **goyim**,
and *straiteneth* **leadeth** them *again*.
24 He *taketh away* **turneth aside** the heart
of the *chief* **head** of the people of the earth,
and causeth them to *wander* **staggar** in a *wilderness* **void**
where there is no way.
25 They grope in the dark without light,
and he maketh them to stagger
like a drunken man **as intoxicated**.

13 *Lo* **Behold**, mine eye hath seen all this,
mine ear hath heard and *understood it* **discerned**.
2 *What ye know* **As to your knowledge**,
the same do I know also:
I am *not inferior to* **no more fallen than** you.
3 *Surely I would speak* **But I word**
to *the Almighty* **Shadday**,
and I desire to *reason with God* **reprove El**.
4 But ye are *forgers* **patchers** of *lies* **falsehoods**,
ye are all *physicians of no value* **worthless healers**.
5 *O that* **Who giveth, that in hushing,**
ye *would altogether hold your peace* **should hush**!
and it should be your wisdom.
6 Hear *now* **I beseech,** my *reasoning* **reproof**,
and hearken to the *pleadings* **defence** of my lips.
7 *Will* **Shall** ye *speak wickedly* **word wickedness**
for *God* **El**?
and *talk* **word** deceitfully for him?
8 *Will* **Shall** ye *accept his person* **lift his face**?
will **shall** ye contend for *God* **El**?
9 Is it good that he should *search* **probe** you *out*?
or as one *man* mocketh *another* **a man**,
do ye so mock **ye** him?
10 **In reproving,** He *will surely* **shall** reprove you,
if ye *do secretly accept persons* **covertly lift faces**.
11 Shall not his *excellency* **exalting**
make **frighten** you *afraid*?
and his dread fall upon you?
12 Your *remembrances*
memorials are like unto ashes,
your *bodies* **backs** to *bodies* **backs** of clay.
13 *Hold your peace* **Hush**, let me alone,
that I may *speak* **word**,
and the spirit of all flesh of man.
11 *Does* not the ear proof utterances?
—the palate taste food?
12 With the aged *is* wisdom;
and in length of days understanding;
13 with him, wisdom and might,
to him, counsel and understanding.
14 Behold, he breaks down and no one builds;
he shuts a man and no one opens.
15 Behold, he restrains the waters, and they dry;
he sends them out and they overturn the earth.
16 With him is strength and substance;
they who err inadvertently
and they who cause to err inadvertently
are his.
17 He walks counsellors away stripped
and has the judges halal;
18 he loosens the bond of sovereigns
and binds their loins with a girdle;
19 he walks priests away stripped
and perverts the perennial;
20 he turns aside the lip of the trustworthy
and takes away the taste of the aged;
21 he pours disrespect on volunteers
and loosens the girdle of the gatherers;
22 he exposes depths from darkness
and brings the shadow of death to light.
23 He increases the goyim and destroys them;

he spreads the goyim and leads them;
24 he turns aside the heart
of the head of the people of the earth;
and staggars them in a void
where there is no way;
25 they grope in the dark without light
and he staggers them as intoxicated.

13 Behold, my eye sees all,
my ear hears and discerns.
2 As to your knowledge, I also know;
I am no more fallen than you.
3 Yet I word to Shadday
and I desire to reprove El:
4 and yet, you are patchers of falsehoods,
you all—worthless healers.
5 Who gives, that in hushing, you hush;
that it be your wisdom.
6 I beseech, hear my reproof
and hearken to the defence of my lips.
7 Word you wickedness for El?
—word deceitfully for him?
8 —lift his face?—contend for El?
9 Is it good that he probe you?
As one mocks a man, mock you him?
10 In reproving, he reproves you,
if you covertly lift faces.
11 His exaltings, frighten they you not?
—his dread falling on you?
12 Your memorials *are* to ashes,
as your backs to backs of clay.
13 Hush, leave me alone to word;
and let *come on me what will* **whatever pass over me**.
14 Wherefore do I *take* **lift** my flesh in my teeth,
and *put* **set** my *life* **soul** in *mine hand* **my palm**?
15 *Though he slay* **Behold, he severeth** me,
yet *will I trust in him* **I shall not await**:
but I *will maintain* **shall reprove** mine own ways
before him **at his face**.
16 He also shall be my salvation:
for *an hypocrite* **a profaner**
shall not come *before him* **at this face**.
17 *Hear diligently my speech*
Hearken! Hear my utterances,
and my *declaration* **utterance** with your ears.
18 Behold *now* **I beseech**,
I have *ordered* **lined up** my *cause* **judgment**;
I know that I shall be justified.
19 Who is he that *will plead*
shall contend with me?
for now, if I *hold my tongue* **hush**,
I shall *give up the ghost* **expire**.
20 Only *do* **work** not **these** two *things* unto me:
then *will* **shall** I not hide myself from *thee* **thy face**.
21 *Withdraw thine hand* **Remove**
thy palm far from me:
and let not thy *dread make* **terror frighten** me *afraid*.
22 Then call thou, and I *will answer* **shall respond**:
or let me *speak* **word**, and answer thou me.
23 How many
are *mine iniquities* **my perversities** and sins?
make **have** me to know
my *transgression* **rebellion** and my sin.
24 Wherefore hidest thou thy face,
and *holdest* **fabricatest** me for thine enemy?
25 *Wilt* **Shalt** thou
break a leaf driven to and fro **terrify a dispersed leaf**?
and *wilt* **shalt** thou pursue the dry stubble?
26 For thou *writest bitter things*
inscribest bitternesses
against me,
and makest me
to possess the *iniquities* **perversities** of my youth.
27 Thou *puttest* **settest** my feet also in the stocks,
and *lookest narrowly* **guardest** unto all my
paths; thou *settest a print* **engravest**
upon the *heels* **roots** of my feet.
28 And he, as *a rotten thing* **rotteness,**
consumeth **weareth out**,
as *a garment* **clothing** that is moth eaten.

14 *Man that is born* **Humanity birthed** of a woman
is of few **be short of** days
and *full of trouble* **satiated with commotion**.
2 He cometh forth like a *flower* **blossom**,
and is *cut down* **clipped**:
he fleeth also as a shadow,
and *continueth* **standeth** not.
3 And dost thou open thine
eyes upon such an one,
and bringest me into judgment with thee?
4 Who *can bring a clean thing* **shall give purity**
out of *an unclean* **foul**?
not one.
5 Seeing his days are *determined* **appointed**,
the number of his months are with thee,
thou hast *appointed* **worked** his *bounds* **statutes**
that he cannot pass;
6 *Turn* **Look away** from him,
that he may *rest* **cease**,
till he shall *accomplish* **please**, as an hireling, his day.
7 For there is hope of a tree, if it be cut down,

that it *will sprout* **shall change** again,
and that the *tender branch* **sprout** *thereof*
will **shall** not cease.
8 Though the root *thereof*
wax old **age** in the earth,
and the *stock* **stump** *thereof* die in the *ground* **dust**;
9 *Yet* through the scent of water
it *will bud* **shall blossom**,
and *bring forth boughs* **work harvest** like a plant.
10 *But man* **The mighty** dieth,
and *wasteth away* **decayeth**:
yea, *man giveth up the ghost* **humanity expireth**,
and where is he?
11 *As* the waters *fail* **gad about** from the sea,
and the flood *decayeth* **parcheth** and drieth *up*:
12 So man lieth down, and riseth not:
till the heavens be no more, they shall not awake,
nor *be raised* **waken** out of their sleep.
and whatever passes over me.
14 Why lift I my flesh in my teeth?
—set my soul in my palm?
15 Behold, he severs me, yet I await not;
surely I reprove my own ways at his face.
16 Also he is my salvation;
for no profaner comes at this face.
17 Hearken! Hear my utterances!
—my utterance with your ears.
18 Behold, I beseech,
I line up my judgment;
I know I am justified.
19 Who contends with me?
for now, if I hush, I expire.
20 Only work not these two to me:
that I not hide from your face;
21 remove your palm far from me
and let not your terror frighten me.
22 And you call and I—I respond;
or, I word and you answer me.
23 How many are my perversities and sins?
—have me know my rebellion and my sin?
24 Why hide your face
and fabricate me for your enemy?
25 Terrify you a dispersed leaf?
—pursue the dry stubble?
26 For you inscribe bitternesses against me
that I possess the perversities of my youth.
27 You also set my feet in the stocks
and guard all my paths;
you engrave on the roots of my feet;
28 and as rotteness
he wears out as moth eaten clothing.

14 Humanity, birthed of a woman,
is short of days and satiated with commotion.
2 He comes forth as a blossom, and *is* clipped;
and he flees as a shadow, and stands not.
3 And open you your eyes on such a one
and bring me into judgment with you?
4 Who gives purity from foul? No one!
5 Seeing his days are appointed,
the number of his months *are* with you,
you work his statutes and he passes not;
6 look away from him, so that he ceases,
until as a hireling, he *is* pleased in his day.
7 For there is hope of a tree, if it is cut down,
that it change again, that its sprout not cease.
8 Though the root age in the earth
and the stump die in the dust;
9 and blossoms through the scent of water
and works harvest as a plant;
10 the mighty dies and decays;
yes, humanity expires—and where is he?
11 The waters gad about from the sea
and the flood parches and dries:
12 thus man lies down and rises not;
until the heavens be no more
they waken not
—waken not from their sleep.
13 *O* **Who giveth**
that thou *wouldest* **shouldest** hide me in *the grave* **sheol**,
that thou *wouldest* **shouldest** keep me secret,
until thy wrath be *past* **turned**,
that thou *wouldest* **shouldest**
appoint **set** me a *set time* **statute**,
and remember me!
14 If *a man* **the mighty** die,
shall he *live again* **enliven**?
all the days of my *appointed time* **hostility**
will **shall** I *wait* **await**,
till my change come.
15 Thou shalt call, and I *will* **shall** answer thee:
thou *wilt have a desire* **shalt yearn**
to **for** the work of thine hands.
16 For now thou *numberest*
scribest my *steps* **paces**:
dost thou not *watch* **guard** over my sin?
17 My *transgression* **rebellion**
is sealed up in a *bag* **bundle**,
and thou *sewest up mine iniquity* **patchest my perversity**.
18 *And surely* **But** the mountain falling
cometh to nought **withereth**,

and the rock is removed out of his place.
19 The waters *wear* **pulverize** the stones:
thou *washest away* **overflowest**
the *things which grow out* **spontaneous growth**
of the dust of the earth;
and thou destroyest the hope of man.
20 Thou prevailest *for ever* **in**
perpetuity against him,
and he passeth:
thou *changest* **alterest** his *countenance* **face,**
and sendest him away.
21 His sons *come to honour* **be honoured,**
and he knoweth it not;
and they are *brought low* **belittled,**
but he *perceiveth* **discerneth** it not of them.
22 But his flesh upon him shall *have* pain,
and his soul within him shall mourn.

15 Then answered
Eliphaz **Eli Phaz** the *Temanite* **Temaniy,**
2 and said, Should *a* **the** wise *man*
utter vain **answer spirit/wind** knowledge,
and fill his belly with the *east wind* **easterly**?
3 Should he *reason* **reprove**
with *unprofitable talk* **useless words**?
or with *speeches* **utterances**
wherewith he *can do no good* **benefiteth not**?
4 Yea, thou *castest off fear* **violatest awe,**
and *restrainest prayer* **diminishest**
meditation *before God* **at the face of El.**
5 For thy mouth
uttereth thine iniquity **teacheth thy perversity,**
and thou choosest the tongue of the *crafty* **subtle.**
6 Thine own mouth *condemneth*
judgeth thee **wicked,**
and not I:
yea, thine own lips *testify* **answer** against thee.
7 Art thou the first *man* **human**
that was *born* **birthed**?
or wast thou *made before* **whirled at the face of** the hills?
8 Hast thou heard
the *secret* **private counsel** of *God* **Elohah**?
and dost thou *restrain* **diminish** wisdom to thyself?
9 What knowest thou, that we know not?
what *understandest* **discernest** thou, which is not in us?
10 With us are both the *grayheaded* **grayed**
and *very* **the** aged *men,*
much elder **more advanced in days** than thy father.
11 Are the consolations of *God*
small **El petty** with thee?
is there any *secret thing* **gentle word** with thee?
12 Why doth thine heart *carry* **take** thee away?
and what do thy eyes *wink* **twinkle** at,
13 That thou turnest thy spirit against *God* **El,**
and lettest *such words* **utterances** go out of thy mouth?
14 What is man, that he should be *clean* **purified**?
and he which is born **birthed** of a woman,
that he should be *righteous* **justified**?
15 Behold,
he *putteth no trust* **trusteth not** in his *saints* **holy;**
yea, the heavens are not clean in his *sight* **eyes.**

13 Who gives, that you hide me in sheol?
—that you secret me, until your wrath turns?
—that you set me a statute and remember me?
14 If the mighty die, enlivens he?
All the days of my hostility, I wait
—until my change comes.
15 You call and I answer you;
you yearn for the work of your hands.
16 But now you scribe my paces;
You guard not over my sin:
17 you seal my rebellion in a bundle
and you patch my perversity.
18 And yet, the falling mountain withers
and the rock removes from its place;
19 the waters pulverize the stones;
you overflow the spontaneous growth
of the dust of the earth;
and you destroy the hope of man.
20 You prevail in perpetuity against him
and he passes;
you alter his face and send him away.
21 His sons are honored, and he knows it not;
and they are belittled, but he discerns it not of them.
22 Surely his flesh on him pains
and his soul within him mourns.

15 And Eli Phaz the Temaniy answers,
2 and says,
Answers the wise knowledge of spirit/wind?
—fills his belly with the easterly?
3 Reproves he with useless words?
—utterances of no benefit?
4 Yes, you violate awe and diminish meditation
at the face of El.
5 Your mouth teaches your perversity
and you choose the tongue of the subtle;
6 your own mouth judges you wicked—not I;
yes, your own lips answer against you.
7 Are you the first birthed human?
Were you whirled at the face of the hills?
8 Hear you the private counsel of Elohah?

Diminish you wisdom to yourself?
9 What know you, that we know not?
—what discern you, that is not in us?
10 With us are both the grayed and the aged,
more advanced in days than your father.
11 Are the consolations of El petty with you?
Is there any gentle word with you?
12 Why *does* your heart take you away?
At what *do* your eyes twinkle?
13 —that you turn your spirit against El
—that utterances go from your mouth?
14 What is man—birthed of a woman
that he be purified? that he be justified?
15 Behold, he trusts not in his holy;
yes, the heavens are not clean in his eyes.
16 How much more *abominable* **abhorrent**
and *filthy* **muddled** is man,
which drinketh *iniquity* **wickedness** like water?
17 I *will* **shall** shew thee, hear me;
and that which I have seen I *will declare* **shall scribe**;
18 Which **the** wise *men* have
told from their fathers,
and have not *hid* **concealed** it:
19 Unto whom alone the earth was given,
and no stranger passed among them.
20 The wicked *man*
travaileth with pain **writheth** all his days,
and the number of years
is hidden to the *oppressor* **tyrant**.
21 A *dreadful sound* **voice of dread** is in his ears:
in *prosperity* **shalom**
the *destroyer* **ravager** shall come upon him.
22 He *believeth* **trusteth** not
that he shall return out of darkness,
and he is *waited* **watched** for of the sword.
23 He wandereth abroad for
bread, *saying*, Where is it?
he knoweth that the day of darkness
is *ready* **prepared** at his hand.
24 *Trouble* **Tribulation** and *anguish* **distress**
shall *make* **frighten** him *afraid*;
they shall prevail against him,
as a *king* **sovereign** ready to the *battle* **tumult**.
25 For he *stretcheth out* **spreadeth**
his hand against *God* **El**,
and *strengtheneth himself* **prevaileth**
mightily against *the Almighty* **Shadday**.
26 He runneth upon him, *even on* **upon** his neck,
upon the thick bosses of his *bucklers* **shields**:
27 Because he covereth his face with his *fatness* **fat**,
and *maketh collops of fat on* **worketh plump** his flanks.
28 And he *dwelleth* **tabernacleth**
in *desolate* **cut off** cities,
and in houses which no man *inhabiteth* **settleth**,
which are ready to *become heaps* **heap**.
29 He shall not *be rich* **enrich**,
neither shall his *substance continue* **valuables arise**,
neither shall he
prolong **spread** the *perfection* **acquisitions** *thereof*
upon the earth.
30 He shall not *depart* **turn aside** out of darkness;
the flame shall *dry up* **wither** his *branches* **sprouts**,
and by the *breath* **wind/spirit** of his mouth
shall he *go away* **turn aside**.
31 Let not him that *is deceived*
strayeth trust in vanity:
for vanity shall be his *recompence* **exchange**.
32 **so be** it *shall be accomplished* **not be fulfilled**
before **in** his *time* **day**,
and his *branch* **palm leaf** shall not *be* green.
33 He shall *shake off* **violate** his *unripe* **sour** grape
as the vine,
and shall cast *off* his *flower* **blossom**
as the olive.
34 For the *congregation* **witness**
of *hypocrites* **profaners**
shall be *desolate* **sterile**,
and fire shall consume the *tabernacles* **tents** of bribery.
35 They conceive *mischief* **toil**,
and *bring forth vanity* **birth mischief**,
and their belly prepareth deceit.

Iyob Answers

16 Then *Job* **Iyob** answered and said,
2 I have heard many *such things* **of these**:
miserable comforters **sighers of toil** are ye all.
3 Shall *vain* words **of wind/spirit** have an end?
or what *emboldeneth* **reinforceth** thee
that thou answerest?
4 I also *could speak* **had worded** as ye *do*:
if **O that** your soul were in my soul's stead,
I could *heap up words* **charm utterances** against you,
and shake mine head at you.
5 But I *would* **should** strengthen
you with my mouth,
and the moving of my lips
should *asswage your grief* **spare you**.
6 Though I *speak* **word**,
my *grief* **pain** is not *asswaged* **spared**:
and though I *forbear* **cease**, what *am I eased* **goes**?
7 But now he hath *made* **wearied** me *weary*:

thou hast *made desolate* **desolated**
all my *company* **witnesses.**
16 How much more abhorrent
and muddled is man,
who drinks wickedness as water?
17 I show you, you hear me; what I see I scribe;
18 what, from their fathers,
the wise have told, and not concealed;
19 to whom alone the earth was given
and no stranger passed in their midst.
20 The wicked writhes all his days
and the number of years is hidden to the tyrant.
21 A voice of dread is in his ears;
in shalom, the ravager comes upon him.
22 He trusts not that he returns from darkness
and he is watched by the sword.
23 He wanders abroad for bread! Where is it?
He knows that the day of darkness
is prepared at his hand.
24 Tribulation and distress frighten him;
—prevail against him
as a sovereign ready to the tumult;
25 he spreads his hand against El
and prevails mightily against Shadday.
26 He runs on him—on his neck
—on the thick bosses of his shields;
27 because he covers his face with fat
and works his flanks plump;
28 and he tabernacles in cut off cities
and in houses which no man settles
—ready to be heaped.
29 He neither enriches,
neither his valuables arise,
nor his acquisitions spread on the earth;
30 nor turns aside from darkness.
The flame withers his sprouts
and by the wind/spirit of his mouth he turns aside.
31 He who strays, trusts not in vanity;
for vanity is his exchange;
32 —so be it neither fulfilled in his day
nor his palm leaf green;
33 he violates his sour grape as the vine
and casts his blossom as the olive.
34 For the witness of profaners sterilizes;
and fire consumes the tents of bribery:
35 they conceive toil and birth mischief
and their belly prepares deceit.

Iyob Answers

16 And Iyob answers and says,
2 I hear many such as these;
sighers of toil—all of you.
3 Is there an end to words of wind/spirit?
What reinforces you to answer?
4 I also word as you;
O that your soul were in the stead of my soul
to charm utterances against you
and shake my head at you.
5 I strengthen you by my mouth
that the moving of my lips spare you.
6 Though I word, my pain is not spared;
and though I cease, what goes?
7 But now I weary;
you desolate all my witnesses;
8 And thou hast *filled* **plucked** me *with wrinkles,*
which is **for** a witness *against me*:
and my *leanness* **emaciation** rising up in me
beareth witness **answereth** to my face.
9 He teareth me in his wrath,
who *hateth* **opposeth** me:
he gnasheth upon me with his teeth;
mine enemy **my tribulator** sharpeneth his eyes
upon me.
10 They have gaped upon me with their mouth;
they have smitten me upon the cheek reproachfully;
they have *gathered themselves together* **fulfilled**
against me.
11 *God* **El** hath *delivered* **shut**
me to the *ungodly* **pervert,**
and *turned* **hurled** me *over* into the hands of the wicked.
12 I was *at ease* **serene**, but he
hath broken me *asunder*:
he hath also taken me by my neck,
and *shaken* **shattered** me *to pieces,*
and *set me up* **raised me** for his *mark* **target.**
13 His archers *compass* **surround** me *round about,*
he cleaveth my reins *asunder,*
and *doth* **spareth** not *spare;*
he poureth out my *gall* **bitters** upon the *ground* **earth.**
14 He *breaketh* **breacheth** me
with **at the face of** breach upon breach,
he runneth upon me like *a giant* **the mighty.**
15 I have sewed *sackcloth* **saq** upon my skin,
and *defiled* **exploited** my horn in the dust.
16 My face *is foul* **foameth** with weeping,
and on my eyelids is the shadow of death;
17 Not for *any injustice* **violence**
in *mine hands* **my palms:**
also my prayer is pure.
18 O earth, cover not thou my blood,

and let my cry have no place.
19 Also now, behold,
my witness is in *heaven* **the heavens**,
and my *record is on high* **witness in the heights**.
20 My friends scorn me:
but mine eye *poureth out tears*
drippeth unto *God* **Elohah**.
21 O that one might *plead*
reprove for *a man* **the mighty**
with *God* **Elohah**
as a *man* **son of humanity** *pleadeth*
for his *neighbour* **friend**!
22 When *a few* years **of number** are come,
then I shall go the way whence I shall not return.

17 My *breath* **spirit** is *corrupt* **despoiled**,
my days are extinct,
the *graves* **tombs** are *ready* for me.
2 Are there not *mockers* **mockeries** with me?
and doth not mine eye
continue **stay** in their *provocation* **rebelling**?
3 *Lay down now* **Set, I beseech**,
put me in a surety **my pledge** with thee;
who is he that *will strike* **shall clap** hands with me?
4 For thou hast hid their heart
from *understanding* **comprehension**:
therefore shalt thou not exalt them.
5 He that *speaketh* **telleth**
flattery **smoothing it over** to his friends,
even the eyes of his children shall *fail* **finish off**.
6 He hath *made* **set** me also
a *byword* **proverb** of the people;
and aforetime **at the face of when** I was as *a tabret* **spit**.
7 Mine eye also is dim *by*
reason of sorrow **of vexation**,
and all my *members are* **forms** as a shadow.
8 *Upright men* **The straight**
shall be astonied at this,
and the innocent shall *stir up himself* **waken**
against the *hypocrite* **profaner**.
9 The *righteous* **just** also shall hold on his way,
and he that hath *clean* **pure** hands
in strengthening,
shall *be stronger and stronger* **strengthen**.
10 But as for you all,
do ye return **ye**, and come *now* **I beseech**:
for I *cannot find one* **find none** wise *man* among you.
11 My days are past,
my *purposes* **intrigues** are *broken off* **torn**,
even the *thoughts* **possessions** of my heart.
12 They *change* **set** the night into day:

8 you pluck me for a witness;
my emaciation rises within me
and answers to my face:
9 in his wrath, my opponent tears me;
he gnashes on me with his teeth;
my tribulator sharpens his eyes on me;
10 they gape on me with their mouth;
they smite me on the cheek reproachfully;
they fulfill against me.
11 El shuts me to the pervert
and hurls me to the hands of the wicked.
12 I am serene, and he breaks me;
and he takes me by my neck and shatters me;
he raises me for his target;
13 his archers surround me;
he cleaves my reins and spares not;
he pours out my bitters on the earth;
14 he breaches me at the face of breach on breach;
he runs on me as the mighty.
15 I sew saq on my skin
and exploit my horn in the dust;
16 my face foams with weeping
and on my eyelids is the shadow of death;
17 no violence *is* in my palms;
and my prayer is pure.
18 O earth, cover not my blood
that there be no place for my cry.
19 Also now, behold,
my witness in the heavens; my witness in the heights.
20 My friends scorn me;
but my eye drips to Elohah.
21 O that one reprove for the mighty with Elohah
as a son of humanity for his friend!
22 When years of number come,
I go the way of no return.

17 My spirit is despoiled;
my days extinct;
the tombs *are* for me.
2 If not, mockeries *are* with me
and my eye *is* stayed in their rebelling?
3 I beseech, Set my pledge with you.
Who is he who claps hands with me?
4 For you hide their heart from comprehension;
so you exalt them not.
5 He who tells his friends—smoothing it over,
even the eyes of his children are finished off.
6 and he sets me—a proverb of the people;
at whose face I am as spit;
7 and my eye is dim of vexation
and all my forms as a shadow;

8 the straight astonish at this
and the innocent waken against the profaner;
9 and the just holds his way;
and in strengthening,
he who has pure hands, strengthens.
10 But as for you all,
return and come, I beseech;
for I find none wise among you.
11 My days pass
my intrigues *are* torn
—the possessions of my heart.
12 They set the night into day;
the light is *short* **near**
because of **at the face of the** darkness.
13 If I *wait* **await**, *the grave* **sheol** is mine house:
I have *made* **spread** my bed in the darkness.
14 I have *said* **called** to *corruption* **the pit of ruin**,
Thou art my father:
to the *worm* **maggot**,
Thou art my mother, and my sister.
15 And where is now my hope?
as for my hope, who shall *see* **observe** it?
16 They shall *go down* **descend**
to the *bars* **veins** of *the pit* **sheol**,
when our rest together is in the dust.

BILDAD ANSWERS

18 Then answered Bildad the *Shuhite* **Shuachiy**,
and said,
2 *How long will it be* **Until when**
ere **set** ye *make* an end of *words* **utterances**?
mark **discern**, and afterwards we *will speak* **shall word**.
3 Wherefore are we
counted **machinated** as *beasts* **animals**,
and *reputed vile* **foul** in your *sight* **eyes**?
4 He teareth *himself* **his soul** in his *anger* **wrath**:
shall the earth be forsaken for thee?
and shall the rock be removed out of his place?
5 Yea, the light of the wicked
shall *be put out* **extinguish**,
and the *spark* **flame** of his fire
shall not *shine* **illuminate**.
6 The light shall *be dark*
darken in his *tabernacle* **tent**,
and his *candle* **lamp**
shall *be put out* **extinguish** with him.
7 The *steps* **paces** of his strength
shall *be straitened* **constrict**,
and his own counsel shall cast him down.
8 For he is *cast* **sent** into a net by his own feet,
and he walketh upon a *snare* **netting**.
9 The *gin* **snare** shall *take* **hold** him by the heel,
and the robber shall prevail against him.
10 The *snare* **cord** is *laid* **hid**
for him in the *ground* **earth**,
and a trap for him in the *way* **path**.
11 Terrors shall *make* **frighten** him *afraid*
on every side **round about**,
and shall *drive* **scatter** him to his feet.
12 His strength shall *be hungerbitten* **famish**,
and *destruction* **calamity** shall be *ready* **prepared**
at his side.
13 It shall devour the strength of his *skin* **veins**:
even the *firstborn* **firstbirthed** of death
shall devour his *strength* **veins**.
14 His confidence
shall be *rooted* **torn** out of his *tabernacle* **tent**,
and it shall *bring* **pace** him to the
king **sovereign** of terrors.
15 It shall *dwell* **tabernacle** in his *tabernacle* **tent**,
because it is none of his **without him**:
brimstone **sulphur** shall be *scattered* **winnowed**
upon his habitation **of rest**.
16 His roots shall *be dried up* **wither** beneath,
and above shall his *branch* **harvest** be *cut off* **clipped**.
17 His *remembrance* **memorial**
shall *perish* **destruct** from the earth,
and he shall have no name
in the street **at the face of the outways**.
18 He shall be *driven* **exiled**
from light into darkness,
and chased out of the world.
19 He shall neither have son nor *nephew* **posterity**
among his people,
nor *any remaining* **survivors** in his
dwellings **sojournings**.
20 They that come after him
shall be astonied at his day,
as *they that went before* **the ancients**
were *affrighted* **whirled away**.
21 Surely such
are the *dwellings* **tabernacles** of the wicked,
and this is the place of him that knoweth not *God* **El**.

IYOB ANSWERS

19 Then *Job* **Iyob** answered and said,
2 How long *will* **shall** ye *vex* **grieve** my soul,
and *break* **crush** me *in pieces* with *words* **utterances**?
3 These ten times have ye *reproached* **shamed** me:
the light is near the face of the darkness.

13 If I await, sheol is my house;
I spread my bed in the darkness.
14 I call out to the pit of ruin, My father;
to the maggot, My mother! My sister!
15 And where is my hope now?
As for my hope, who observes?
16 They descend to the veins of sheol,
we rest together in the dust.

Bildad Answers

18 And Bildad the Shuachiy answers and says,
2 Until when set you an end of utterances?
Discern—and afterwards we word.
3 Why are we machinated as animals?
—and foul in your eyes?
4 He tears his soul in his wrath.
Is the earth forsaken for your sake?
Is the rock removed from its place?
5 Yes, the light of the wicked extinguishes
and the flame of his fire illuminates not;
6 the light darkens in his tent
and his lamp extinguishes with him;
7 the paces of his strength constrict
and his own counsel casts him down.
8 For he is sent into a net by his own feet
and he walks on a netting;
9 the snare holds him by the heel
and the robber prevails against him;
10 his cord is hidden in the earth
—his trap in the path.
11 Terrors frighten him all around
and scatter him to his feet;
12 his strength famishes
and calamity prepares at his side.
13 It devours the strength of his veins
—the firstbirthed of death devours his veins.
14 His confidence is torn from his tent
and paces him to the sovereign of terrors.
15 It tabernacles in his tent without him;
sulphur is winnowed on his habitation of rest.
16 His roots wither below
and above his harvest is clipped:
17 his memorial destructs from the earth
and he has no name at the face of the outways:
18 he is exiled from light into darkness
and chased from the world.
19 He has neither son nor posterity
among his people,
nor survivors in his sojournings.
20 They who come after him astonish at his day
as the ancients whirl away.
21 Surely such are the tabernacles of the wicked
and this is the place of him who knows not El.

Iyob Answers

19 And Iyob answers and says,
2 Until when grieve you my soul
and crush me with utterances?
3 These ten times you shame me
exeGeses ready research BIBLE
ye are not ashamed **yet ye shame not**
that ye *make yourselves strange to* **injure** me.
4 And be it *indeed* **truly** that
I have erred **inadvertently**,
mine error *remaineth* **stayeth** with myself.
5 If *indeed* **truly**
ye *will magnify yourselves* **shall greaten** against me,
and *plead* **reprove** against me my reproach:
6 Know now
that *God* **Elohah** hath *overthrown* **twisted** me,
and hath *compassed* **surrounded** me with his *net* **lair**.
7 Behold, I cry out of *wrong* **violence**,
but I am not *heard* **answered**:
I cry *aloud*, but there is no judgment.
8 He hath *fenced up* **walled in**
my way that I cannot pass,
and he hath set darkness in my paths.
9 He hath stripped me of my *glory* **honour**,
and *taken* **turned aside** the crown from my head.
10 He hath *destroyed me* **pulled me down**
on every side **all around**,
and I am gone:
and mine hope hath he *removed* **plucked** like a tree.
11 He hath also kindled his wrath against me,
and he *counteth* **fabricated** me unto him
as one of his *enemies* **tribulators**.
12 His troops come together,
and raise *up* their way against me,
and encamp round about my *tabernacle* **tent**.
13 He hath *put* **removed** my brethren *far* from me,
and *mine acquaintance* **they whom I know** are verily estranged from me.
14 My *kinsfolk* **neighbours**
have *failed* **deceased**,
and *my familiar friends* **they whom I know**
have forgotten me.
15 They that *dwell* **sojourn** in
mine house, and my maids,
count **fabricate** me for a stranger:
I am an alien in their *sight* **eyes**.

16 I called my servant,
and he *gave me no answer* **answered me not**;
I *intreated him* **sought his charism** with my mouth.
17 My *breath* **spirit** is strange to my *wife* **woman**,
though I intreated **and my charism**
for the children's sake of mine own
body **to the sons of my belly**.
18 Yea, *young children despised*
sucklings spurned me;
I arose, and they *spake* **worded** against me.
19 All my *inward friends* **private**
councilmen abhorred me:
and they whom I loved are turned against me.
20 My bone
cleaveth **adhereth** to my skin and to my flesh,
and I am escaped with the skin of my teeth.
21 *Have pity upon me* **Grant me charism**,
have pity upon me **grant me charism**, O ye my friends;
for the hand of *God* **Elohah** hath touched me.
22 Why do ye *persecute* **pursue** me as *God* **El**,
and are not satisfied with my flesh?
23 *Oh* **Who giveth**
that my *words* **utterances** were now *written!* **inscribed?**
oh **Who giveth** that they were *printed* **inscribed**
in a *book!* **scroll?**
24 That they were *graven* **hewn**
with an iron *pen* **stylus**
and lead in the rock *for ever* **eternally**!
25 For I know that my redeemer liveth,
and that he shall *stand* **arise** at the latter *day*
upon the *earth* **dust**:
26 And *though*
after my skin *worms destroy this body* **be stricken**,
yet in my flesh shall I see *God* **Elohah**:
27 Whom I shall see for myself,
and mine eyes shall *behold* **see**,
and not *another* **a stranger**;
though my reins be *consumed* **finished off**
within *me* **my bosom**.
28 But ye should say, Why
persecute **pursue** we him,
seeing the root of the *matter* **word** is found in me?
29 *Be* **Dodge** ye *afraid* **at the face** of the sword:
for *wrath bringeth the punishments*
furious are the perversities of the sword,
that ye may know there is *a judgment* **the plea**.
yet you shame not that you injure me.
4 And also, I truly erred inadvertently;
my error stays with me.
5 If you truly greaten against me
and reprove against my reproach;
6 know now that Elohah twisted me
and surrounded me with his lair.
7 Behold, I cry from violence, but no answer;
I cry, but no judgment:
8 he walls in my way so I cannot pass;
and sets darkness in my paths:
9 he strips me of my honor
and turns aside the crown from my head:
10 he pulls me *down* all around, and I go;
and he plucks my hope as a tree:
11 He kindles his wrath against me
and fabricates me as one of his tribulators.
12 His troops come together
and raise their way against me
and encamp around my tent:
13 he removes my brothers from me;
and they whom I know
are verily estranged from me:
14 my neighbours decease
and they whom I know forget me:
15 they who sojourn in my house and my maids
fabricate me for a stranger
—an alien in their eyes.
16 I call my servant and he answers not;
I seek his charism with my mouth:
17 my spirit is strange to my woman
and my charism to the sons of my belly:
18 yes, sucklings spurn me;
I rise and they word against me:
19 all my private councilmen abhor me
and they whom I love turn against me:
20 my bone adheres to my skin and to my flesh
and I escape with the skin of my t`eeth.
21 Grant me charism
—grant me charism, O my friends; for
the hand of Elohah touches me.
22 Why pursue you me as El?
—and not satisfied with my flesh?
23 Who gives that my utterances be inscribed?
Who gives that they be inscribed in a scroll
24 —hewn eternally
with an iron stylus and lead in the rock!
25 I know that my redeemer lives
and rises at the latter on the dust;
26 and after my skin becomes stricken,
yet in my flesh I see Elohah
27 —see for myself
—my eyes see and not a stranger;
though my reins finish off within my bosom.

28 But you say, Why pursue we him
seeing the root of the word is found in me?
29 Dodge you at the face of the sword?
Furious are the perversities of the sword,
so that you know there is the plea.

SOPHAR ANSWERS

20 Then answered
Zophar **Sophar** the *Naamathite* **Naamahiy**, and said,
2 Therefore do my *thoughts* **sentiments**
cause me to *answer* **respond**, and
for this I *make haste* **hasten**.
3 I have heard the *check*
discipline of my reproach,
and the spirit of my *understanding* **discernment**
causeth me to answer.
4 Knowest thou *not* this *of old* **eternally**,
since *man* **humanity** was placed upon earth,
5 That the *triumphing* **shout**
of the wicked is short,
and the *joy* **cheer** of the *hypocrite* **profaner**
but for a *moment* **blink**?
6 Though his *excellency* **exaltation**
mount up **ascend** to the heavens,
and his head reach unto the **thick** clouds;
7 Yet he shall *perish for ever*
destruct in perpetuity
like his own dung:
they which have seen him shall say, Where is he?
8 He shall fly *away* as a dream,
and shall not be found:
yea, he shall be chased away as a vision of the night.
9 The eye also which *saw* **scanned** him
shall **not add to** see him *no more*;
neither shall his place any more *behold* **observe** him.
10 His *children* **sons** shall seek to please the poor,
and his hands shall restore their *goods* **strength**.
11 His bones are full of *the sin of* his youth,
which shall lie down with him in the dust.
12 Though *wickedness* **evil**
be sweet **sweeteneth** in his mouth,
though he *hid* **concealeth** it under his tongue;
13 Though he spare it, and forsake it not;
but *keep* **withhold** it still within his *mouth* **palate**:
14 Yet his *meat* **bread** in his
bowels **inwards** is turned,
it is the *gall* **venom** of asps within him.
15 He hath swallowed *down riches* **valuables**,
and he shall vomit them up *again*:
God **El** shall *cast* **dispossess** them out of his belly.
16 He shall suck the *poison* **rosh** of asps:
the *viper's* **hisser's** tongue shall *slay* **slaughter** him.
17 He shall not see the *rivers* **rivulets**, the floods,
the *brooks* **wadies** of honey and butter.
18 That which he laboured for shall he restore,
and shall not swallow *down*:
according to his *substance* **valuables**
thus shall the *restitution* **exchange** be,
and he shall not *rejoice therein* **leap for joy**.
19 Because he hath *oppressed* **crushed**
and hath forsaken the poor;
because he hath *violently taken away* **stripped** an house
which he builded not;
20 Surely he shall not *feel quietness* **know serenity**
in his belly,
he shall not *save* **rescue** of that which he desired.
21 There shall none of his
meat be left **food survive**;
therefore **none** shall *no man look for* **writhe** his goods.
22 In the fulness of his *sufficiency* **gluttony**
he shall be *in straits* **constricted**:
every hand of the wicked shall come upon him.
23 When he is about to fill his belly,
God **He** shall *cast* **send** the *fury* **fuming** of his wrath
upon him,
and shall rain it upon him while he is eating.
24 He shall flee from the iron *weapon* **armour**,
and the bow of *steel* **copper**
shall *strike* **pass** him through.
25 It is drawn, and cometh out of the body;
yea, the *glittering* **lightning** sword cometh out of his gall:
terrors are upon him.
26 All darkness shall be hid in
his *secret places* **hideouts**:
a fire not *blown* **puffed** shall consume him;
it shall go *ill* **evilly** with him
that *is left* **surviveth** in his *tabernacle* **tent**.
27 The *heaven* **heavens**
shall *reveal* **expose** his *iniquity* **perversity;**
and the earth shall rise *up* against him.
28 The *increase* **produce** of his house
shall *depart* **be exposed**,

SOPHAR ANSWERS

20 And Sophar the Naamahiy answers and says,
2 So my sentiments have me respond
and for this I hasten.
3 I hear the discipline of my reproach
and my spirit of discernment answers.
4 Know you this eternally

—since placing humanity on earth,
5 that the shouting of the wicked *is* near?
and the cheer of the profaner *is* for a blink?
6 Though his exaltation ascend to the heavens
and his head touch the thick clouds;
7 as his own dung, he destructs in perpetuity;
they who see him say, Where is he?
8 He flies as a dream and is not found;
yes,—chased away as a vision of the night.
9 Neither the eye scans to add to see him;
nor his place observes him any more.
10 His sons seek to please the poor
and his hands restore their strength.
11 His bones lie down with him in the dust;
—full of his youth.
12 Though evil sweetens in his mouth,
though he conceals it under his tongue;
13 though he spares it and forsakes it not;
and withholds it still within his palate;
14 yet his bread in his inwards turns
—the venom of asps within him.
15 He swallows valuables and vomits them;
El dispossess them from his belly;
16 he sucks the rosh of asps
the tongue of the hisser slaughters him;
17 he sees not the rivulets, the floods,
the wadies of honey and butter.
18 He restores that for which he labors
but swallows not;
as his valuables, thus the exchange
—and he leaps not for joy.
19 He crushes—he forsakes the poor;
he strips a house he built not;
20 surely he knows no serenity in his belly;
he rescues none of his desires:
21 none of his food survives;
so no one writhes his goods.
22 In the fulness of his gluttony, he constricts;
every hand of the wicked comes on him.
23 In the fulness of his belly,
he sends his fuming wrath on him
—rains on him while he eats.
24 He flees from the iron armour
and the bow of copper passes through him;
25 —drawn and comes from his body;
yes, the lightning sword comes from his gall;
with terrors on him.
26 All darkness hides in his hideouts;
a fire not puffed consumes him;
it goes evilly with him who survives in his tent.
27 The heavens expose his perversity;
and the earth rises against him:
28 the produce of his house exposes
and *his goods* shall flow away in the day of his wrath.
29 This is the *portion* **allotment**
of *a* wicked *man* **humanity** from *God* **Elohim**,
and the *heritage* **inheritance**
appointed unto him by God **of his sayings of El**.

IYOB ANSWERS

21 But *Job* **Iyob** answered and said,
2 *Hear diligently my speech*
In hearing, hear my utterances,
and let this be your consolations.
3 *Suffer* **Allow** me that I may *speak* **word**;
and after that I have *spoken* **worded**, *mock on* **deride**.
4 As for me,
is my *complaint* **meditation** to *man* **humanity**?
and if it were *so*,
why should not my spirit be *troubled* **curtailed**?
5 *Mark* **Face** me, and be astonished,
and *lay* **set** your hand upon your mouth.
6 Even when I remember I *am afraid* **terrify**,
and trembling taketh hold on my flesh.
7 Wherefore do the wicked
live, *become old* **antiquate**,
yea, *are mighty* **prevail mightily** in *power* **valour**?
8 Their seed is established
in their sight with them **at their face**,
and their offspring *before* **at** their eyes.
9 Their houses are *safe* **at**
shalom from *fear* **dread**,
neither is the *rod* **scion** of *God* **Elohah** upon them.
10 Their *bull gendereth* **ox passeth**,
and *faileth* **loatheth** not;
their *cow calveth* **heifer slippeth away**,
and *casteth* **aborteth** not her calf.
11 They send forth their *little*
ones **sucklings** like a flock,
and their children dance.
12 They *take* **lift** the *timbrel* **tambourine** and harp,
and *rejoice* **cheer**
at the *sound* **voice** of the *organ* **woodwind**.
13 They *spend* **wear away,**
finishing off their days in *wealth* **good**,
and in a *moment* **blink**,
go down **descend** to *the grave* **sheol**.
14 *Therefore* they say unto *God*
El, *Depart* **Turn** from us;
for we desire not the knowledge of thy ways.
15 What is *the Almighty* **Shadday**,

that we should serve him?
and what *profit* **benefit** should we have,
if we *pray* **intercede** unto him?
16 *Lo* **Behold**, their good is not in their hand:
the counsel of the wicked is far from me.
17 How oft is the *candle* **lamp** of the wicked
put out **extinguished**!
and *how oft* cometh their *destruction*
calamity upon them!
God distributeth sorrows **lie apportioneth pangs**
in his *anger* **wrath**.
18 They are as *stubble* **straw**
before **at the face of** the wind,
and as chaff
that the *storm carrieth away* **hurricane stealeth**.
19 *God* **Elohah**
layeth up his *iniquity* **punishment of mischief**
for his *children* **sons**:
he *rewardeth* **doth shalam** him, and he shall know it.
20 His eyes shall see his destruction,
and he shall drink
of the *wrath* **fury** of *the Almighty* **Shadday**.
21 For what *pleasure* **delight** hath he
in his house after him,
when the number of his months
is *cut off* **severed** in *the midst* **half**?
22 Shall any teach *God* **El** knowledge?
seeing he judgeth those that are *high* **lofted**.
23 One dieth in *his full strength*
the integrity of his bones,
being wholly *at ease* **serene** and *quiet* **secure**.
24 His *breasts* **pails** are full of milk,
and his bones are moistened with marrow.
25 And another dieth in the bitterness of his soul,
and never eateth *with pleasure* **good**.
26 They shall lie *down alike* **together** in the dust,
and the *worms* **maggots** shall cover them.
27 Behold,
and flows away in the day of his wrath.
29 This is the allotment of wicked humanity
by Elohim
and the inheritance of his sayings
by El.

Iyob Answers

21 And Iyob answers and says,
2 In hearing, hear my utterances
—this your consolation.
3 Allow me to word;
and after I word, deride.
4 As for me,
Is my meditation to humanity?
Why then is my spirit not curtailed?
5 Face me and astonish
and set your hand on your mouth.
6 Yes, when I remember I terrify
and trembling takes hold on my flesh.
7 Why *do* the wicked live? antiquate?
—yes, prevail mightily in valour?
8 Their seed establishes at their face
and their offspring at their eyes;
9 their houses are at shalom from dread,
the scion of Elohah is not on them.
10 Their ox passes and loathes not;
their heifer slips away and aborts not her calf.
11 They send forth their sucklings as a flock
and their children dance;
12 they lift the tambourine and harp
and cheer at the voice of the woodwind;
13 they wear away—finish off their days in good;
and in a blink, descend to sheol.
14 They say to El, Turn from us;
for we desire not the knowledge of your ways.
15 Who is Shadday, that we serve him?
and what benefit have we if we intercede to him?
16 Behold, their good is not in their hand;
the counsel of the wicked is far from me.
17 How often the lamp of the wicked extinguishes!
And their calamity comes on them!
He apportions pangs in his wrath;
18 —as straw at the face of the wind
and as chaff stolen by the hurricane.
19 Elohah lays up his punishment of mischief
for his sons;
—shalam him so that he knows.
20 His eyes see his destruction
and he drinks of the fury of Shadday.
21 For how delights he in his house after him,
when the number of his months is severed in half?
22 Whoever teaches El knowledge
—seeing he judges the lofty?
23 One dies in the integrity of his bones,
wholly serene and secure:
24 his pails are full of milk
and his bones moistened with marrow.
25 Another dies with bitter soul
and never eats good.
26 Together they lie in the dust;
the maggots cover them.
27 Behold,

I know your *thoughts* **fabrications**
and the *devices* **intrigues**
which ye *wrongfully imagine* **violate** against me.
28 For ye say,
Where is the house of the *prince* **volunteer**?
and where are the *dwelling places* **tents**
—the tabernacles of the wicked?
29 Have ye not asked them that *go* **pass** by the way?
and do ye not *know* **recognize** their *tokens* **signs**,
30 That the *wicked* **evil** is *reserved* **spared**
to the day of *destruction* **calamity**?
they shall be brought forth to the day of *wrath* **fury**.
31 Who shall *declare* **tell** his way to his face?
and who shall *repay* **shalam** him
for what he hath *done* **worked**?
32 Yet shall he be brought to the *grave* **tomb**,
and shall *remain* **watch** in the *tomb* **heap**.
33 The clods of the *valley* **wadi**
shall *be sweet* **sweeten** unto him,
and *every man* **all humanity** shall draw after him,
as there are innumerable *before him* **at his face**.
34 How then *comfort* **sigh** ye **over** me in vain,
seeing in your *answers* **responses**
there *remaineth falsehood* **surviveth treason**?

Eli Phaz Answers

22 Then *Eliphaz* **Eli Phaz** the *Temanite* **Temaniy**
answered and said,
2 *Can a man be profitable* **Be**
the mighty useful unto God,
as he that *is wise* **comprehendeth**
may be *profitable* **useful** unto himself?
3 Is it any *pleasure* **delight**
to *the Almighty* **Shadday**,
that thou art *righteous* **justified**?
or is it gain to him,
that thou makest thy ways *perfect* **integrious**?
4 *Will* **Shall** he reprove thee for *fear* **awe** of thee?
will **shall** he enter with thee into judgment?
5 Is not thy *wickedness* **evil** great?
and *thine iniquities infinite* **thy perversities endless**?
6 For thou hast taken a pledge from thy brother
for nought **gratuitously**,
and stripped the naked of their clothing.
7 Thou hast not given water
to the *weary* **languid** to drink,
and thou hast withholden bread
from the *hungry* **famished**.
8 But as for the *mighty* man **of arm**,
he had the earth;
and the *honourable man* **face of the exalted**
dwelt **settled** in it.
9 Thou hast sent widows away empty,
and the arms of the *fatherless* **orphan**
have been *broken* **crushed**.
10 Therefore snares are round about thee,
and sudden *fear troubleth* **dread terrifieth** thee;
11 Or darkness, that thou canst not see;
and abundance of waters cover thee.
12 Is not *God* **Elohah**
in the height of *heaven* **the heavens**?
and *behold* **see** the *height* **head** of the stars,
how high they are!
13 And thou sayest, How *doth God* **shall El** know?
can he judge through the *dark cloud* **dripping darkness**?
14 Thick clouds are a covering
to him, that he seeth not;
and he walketh
in the *circuit* **circle** of *heaven* **the heavens**.
15 Hast thou *marked* **regarded** the *old* **eternal** way
which *wicked* **mischievous** men have trodden?
16 Which were *cut down* **plucked** out of time,
whose foundation was *overflown* **poured** with a flood:
17 Which said unto *God* **El**,
Depart **Turn away** from us:
and what can *the Almighty* **Shadday** do for them?
18 Yet he filled their houses with good *things*:
but the counsel of the wicked is far from me.
19 The *righteous* **just** see it, and *are glad* **cheer**:
and the innocent *laugh* **deride** them *to scorn*.
20 Whereas our *substance*
opponent is not cut *down* **off**,
but the *remnant* **remainder** of them the fire consumeth.
21 *Acquaint now thyself* **Be accustomed, I beseech,**
with him,
I know the fabrications and intrigues
you violate against me:
28 for you say,
Where is the house of the volunteer?
and where are the tents
—the tabernacles of the wicked?
29 Ask you not of them who pass by the way?
Recognize you not their signs
30 —that the evil are spared to the day of calamity?
—to be brought forth to the day of fury?
31 Who tells his way to his face?
Who shalams him for what he works?
32 Yet he—he is brought to the tomb
and watches in the heap:
33 the clods of the wadi sweeten to him

and he draws all humanity after him
—innumerable at his face.
34 How then sigh you over me in vain,
seeing that treason survives in your responses?

Eli Phaz Answers

22 And Eli Phaz the Temaniy answers and says,
2 Is the mighty as useful to God
as he who comprehends is useful to himself?
3 Is it any delight to Shadday
that you are justified?
Or gain to him that your ways be integrious?
4 Reproves he because of your awe?
Enters he into judgment with you?
5 Is not your evil great?—your perversity endless?
6 Gratuitously you take a
pledge from your brother
and strip the naked of their clothing:
7 you give the languid no water to drink;
you withhold bread from the famished.
8 The man of arm has the earth
and the exalted face settles therein:
9 you send widows away empty
and crush the arms of the orphan.
10 So snares surround you
and sudden dread terrifies you:
11 or darkness, you see not;
and abundance of waters cover you.
12 Is not Elohah in the height of the heavens?
See the head of the stars—how high!
13 And you say, El knows what?
Judges he through the dripping darkness?
14 Thick clouds are his
covering that he not be seen;
and he walks in the circle of the heavens.
15 Regard you the eternal way
which mischievous men have trodden?
16 —who were plucked from time?
—whose foundation was poured with a flood?
17 Who says to El, Turn from us?
What does Shadday for them?
18 Yet he fills their houses with good;
but the counsel of the wicked is far from me:
19 the just see and cheer;
and the innocent deride.
20 Surely our opponent is not cut off,
and fire consumes them who remain.
21 I beseech, be accustomed with him
and *be at peace* **shalam**:
thereby good shall come unto thee.
22 Receive, I *pray* **beseech** thee,
the *law* **torah** from his mouth,
and *lay up* **set** his *words* **sayings** in thine heart.
23 If thou return to *the Almighty* **Shadday**,
thou shalt be built *up*,
thou shalt *put away iniquity* **remove wickedness**
far from thy *tabernacles* **tents**.
24 Then shalt thou *lay up gold* **set diggings** as dust,
and *the gold* of Ophir
as the *stones* **rocks** of the *brooks* **wadies**.
25 Yea, *the Almighty* **Shadday**
shall be thy *defence* **diggings**,
and thou shalt have *plenty* **strengths** of silver.
26 For then shalt thou have thy delight
in *the Almighty* **Shadday**,
and shalt lift *up* thy face unto *God* **Elohah**.
27 Thou shalt *make thy prayer* **intreat** unto him,
and he shall hear thee,
and thou shalt *pay* **shalam** thy vows.
28 Thou shalt also *decree a thing* **cut a saying**,
and it shall *be established* **arise** unto thee: and the
light shall *shine upon* **illuminate** thy ways.
29 When *men are cast down* **abased**,
then thou shalt say, There is *lifting up* **arrogance**;
and he shall save the *humble person* **downcast eye**.
30 He shall *deliver* **rescue** the
island of the innocent:
and it *is delivered* **escapeth**
by the *pureness* **purity** of *thine hands* **thy palms**.

Iyob Answers

23 Then *Job* **Iyob** answered and said,
2 Even to day
is my *complaint bitter* **meditation rebellious**:
my *stroke* **hand** is heavier than my *groaning* **sighing**.
3 *Oh* **Who giveth** that I knew
where I might find him!
that I might come *even* to his *seat* **place**!
4 *I would order my cause* **O**
that I line up my judgment
before him **at his face**,
and fill my mouth with *arguments* **reproofs**.
5 *I would* **O that I** know the *words* **utterances**
which he *would* **should** answer me,
and *understand* **discern**
what he *would* **should** say unto me.
6 *Will* **Shall** he *plead* **contend** against me
with his *great power* **abundant force**?
No; but he *would put strength* **should set it** in me.
7 There the *righteous* **straight**

might *dispute with* **reprove** him;
so should I be *delivered* **slipped away**
for ever **in perpetuity** from my judge.
8 Behold, I go *forward*
eastward, but he is not there;
and backward, but I cannot *perceive* **discern** him:
9 On the left *hand*, where he *doth work* **worketh**,
but I cannot *behold him* **see**:
he *hideth* **shroudeth** himself on the right *hand*,
that I cannot see *him*:
10 But he knoweth the way *that I take* **of mine**:
when he hath *tried* **proofed** me,
I shall come forth as gold.
11 My foot hath held his steps,
his way have I *kept* **guarded**, and not *declined* **perverted**.
12 Neither have I gone back
from the *commandment* **misvah** of his lips;
I have *esteemed* **treasured**
the *words* **sayings** of his mouth
more than my *necessary food* **statutes**.
13 But he is in one mind, and who can turn him?
and what his soul desireth, even that he *doeth* **worketh**.
14 For he *performeth* **shall shalam**
the thing that is appointed for me **my statute**:
and many such *things* are with him.
15 Therefore am I *troubled*
terrified at his *presence* **face**:
when I *consider* **discern**, I *am afraid of* **dread** him.
16 For *God maketh* **El tenderizeth** my heart *soft*,
and *the Almighty troubleth* **Shadday terrifieth** me:
17 Because I was not *cut off* **exterminated**
before **at the face of** the darkness,
neither hath he covered the darkness from my face.
and shalam;
thereby good comes to you.
22 I beseech you,
receive the torah from his mouth
and set his sayings in your heart.
23 If you return to Shadday, you are built up;
remove wickedness far from your tents:
24 so as to set your diggings as dust
—as the rocks of the wadies of Ophir.
25 Yes, Shadday becomes your diggings
and silver your strengths.
26 For then you have your delight in Shadday
—lift your face to Elohah.
27 Intreat to him
and he hears you shalam your vows:
28 and cut a saying and it rises to you;
and the light illuminates your ways.
29 When abased, say, This is arrogance!
—and he saves the downcast eye;
30 he rescues the island of the innocent;
it escapes by the purity of your palms.

Iyob Answers

23 And Iyob answers and says,
2 Even today my meditation *is* rebellious
—my hand heavier than my sighing.
3 Who gives that I know
—that I find him—that I come to his place!
4 O that I line up my judgment at his face
and fill my mouth with reproofs.
5 O that I know the utterances he answers me
and discern what he says to me.
6 Contends he against me
with his abundant force?
No; but he sets it in me.
7 There the straight reprove him;
and in perpetuity, I slip away from my judge.
8 Behold, I go eastward, and he is not;
and backward, and I discern him not;
9 on the left where he works,
and I see not;
he shrouds himself on the right,
and I see not.
10 For he knows my way;
he proofs me; I come forth as gold.
11 My foot holds to his steps; I guard his way;
and neither pervert
12 nor go back from the misvah of his lips:
I treasure the sayings of his mouth
more than my statutes.
13 And he is in one—and who can turn him?
and what his soul desires, he works.
14 For he shalams my statute;
and many such others with him.
15 So I terrify at his face;
I discern; I dread him.
16 for El tenderizes my heart
and Shadday terrifies me;
17 for I neither exterminate
at the face of the darkness;
nor covers he the darkness from my face.

24 Why,
seeing times are not hidden from *the Almighty* **Shadday**,
do they that know him not see his days?
2 *Some remove* **They overtake**
the *landmarks* **borders**;

they *violently take away flocks* **strip**
droves, and feed *thereof.*
3 They drive away the *ass* **she burro**
of the *fatherless* **orphan**,
they take the widow's ox for a pledge.
4 They *turn* **pervert** the needy out of the way:
the *poor* **humble** of the earth hide *themselves together.*
5 Behold, as wild *asses* **runners**
in the *desert* **wilderness**,
go they forth to their *work* **deeds**;
rising *betimes* **early** for a prey:
the *wilderness yieldeth food* **plains for bread**
for them and for their *children* **lads**.
6 They *reap every one his*
corn **harvest their fodder**
in the field:
and they *gather* **glean** the *vintage*
vineyard of the wicked.
7 They cause the naked
to *lodge* **stay overnight** without *clothing* **robe**,
that they have no covering in the cold.
8 They are *wet* **moist**
with the *showers* **floods** of the mountains,
and embrace the rock for want of a *shelter* **refuge**.
9 They *pluck* **strip** the *fatherless*
orphan from the breast,
and take a pledge of the *poor* **humble**.
10 They cause him to go naked
without *clothing* **robe**,
and they take away the *sheaf* **omer**
from the *hungry* **famished**;
11 Which *make* **press** oil
within **between** their walls,
and tread their *winepresses* **troughs**, and *suffer* thirst.
12 Men groan from out of the city,
and the soul of the *wounded* **pierced** crieth out:
yet *God layeth* **Elohah setteth** not *folly* **frivolity** to them.
13 They are of those that rebel against the light;
they *know* **recognize** not the ways *thereof,*
nor *abide* **settle** in the paths *thereof.*
14 The murderer rising with the light
killeth **severeth** the *poor* **humble** and
needy, and in the night is as a thief.
15 The eye also of the adulterer
waiteth **guardeth** for the *twilight* **evening breeze**,
saying, No eye shall *see* **observe** me:
and *disguiseth* **setteth** his face **covertly**.
16 In the dark they dig through houses,
which they had *marked* **sealed** for themselves
in the *daytime* **day**:
they know not the light.
17 For **together,** the morning is to them
even as the shadow of death:
if one *know* **recognize** them,
they are in the terrors of the shadow of death.
18 He is swift *as* **at the face of** the waters;
their *portion* **allotment** is *cursed* **abased** in the earth:
he *beholdeth* **faceth** not the way of the vineyards.
19 *Drought* **Parch** and heat
consume **strip** the snow waters:
so *doth the grave* **shall Sheol** those which have sinned.
20 The womb shall forget him;
the *worm* **maggot** shall *feed sweetly on* **suck** him;
he shall be no more remembered;
and wickedness shall be broken as a tree.
21 He *evil entreateth* **tendeth** the *barren* **sterile**
that *beareth* **birtheth** not:
and *doeth not good to* **well—pleaseth not** the widow.
22 He draweth also the mighty
with his *power* **force**:
he riseth up, and no *man is sure of* **one trusteth his** life.
23 *Though it be given him to be in safety*
lie giveth him confidence,
whereon he *resteth* **leaneth**;
yet his eyes are upon their ways.
24 They are exalted for a little *while,*
but are gone and *brought low* **subdued;**
they are *taken out of the way* **shut up** as all other,
and *cut off* **clipped** as the tops of the ears *of corn.*
25 And if *it be* not *so now,* who
will **shall** make me a liar,
and *make* **set** my *speech nothing*
worth **utterances as nought**?

24 Why are not times from Shadday treasured?
Why *do* they who know him not see his days?
2 They overtake the borders;
they strip droves and feed;
3 they drive away the she burro of the orphan;
they take the ox of the widow for a pledge;
4 they pervert the needy from the way;
the humble of the earth hide.
5 Behold, as wild runners in the wilderness,
they go to their deeds;
rising early for a prey;
to the plains for bread—for them and their lads;
6 they harvest their fodder in the field;
they glean the vineyard of the wicked;
7 they stay the naked overnight without robe
that they have no covering in the cold;
8 they are moist with the floods of the mountains
and embrace the rock for want of a refuge;

9 they strip the orphan from the breast
and take a pledge of the humble;
10 they have him go naked without robe;
they take away the omer from the famished;
11 they press oil between their walls
and tread their troughs—and thirst.
12 Men of the city groan
and the soul of the pierced cries out;
yet Elohah sets not frivolity to them.
13 They are of those who rebel against the light;
they neither recognize the ways
nor settle in the paths.
14 The murderer rising with the light
severs the humble and needy as a thief in the night:
15 the eye of the adulterer
guards for the evening breeze,
saying, No eye observes me!
—and covertly sets his face.
16 In the dark they dig through houses
which they sealed for themselves in the day;
they know not the light;
17 when they are together
morning is as the shadow of death;
if one recognizes them
they are in the terrors of the shadow of death.
18 He is swift at the face of the waters;
their allotment abases in the earth; he
faces not the way of the vineyards.
19 Parch and heat strip the snow waters
as Sheol to them who sin:
20 the womb forgets him;
the maggot sucks him;
—remembered no more:
and wickedness breaks as a tree.
21 He neither tends the sterile who birth
nor well—pleases the widow:
22 he draws the mighty with his force;
he rises, and no one trusts his life:
23 he gives him confidence whereon to lean
yet his eyes are on their ways.
24 They exalt for a little,
then go and subdue
—shut up as all the others
—clipped as the tops of the ears.
25 And if not, who proves me a liar?
Who sets my utterances as naught?

BILDAD ANSWERS

25 Then answered Bildad the *Shuhite* **Shuachiy**,
and said,
2 Dominion and *fear* **dread** are with him,
he *maketh peace* **worketh shalom**
in his *high places* **heights**.
3 Is there any number of his *armies* **troops**?
and upon whom doth not his light arise?
4 How then can man be justified with *God* **El**?
or how can he be *clean* **purified,**
that is *born* **birthed** of a woman?
5 Behold even to the moon, and it shineth not;
yea, the stars are not pure in his *sight* **eyes**.
6 How much less man,
that is a worm—**a maggot**?
and the son of *men* **humanity**,
which is a worm—**a maggot**?

IYOB ANSWERS

26 But *Job* **Iyob** answered and said,
2 How hast thou helped him
that *is without power* **hath no force**?
how savest thou the arm
that hath no strength?
3 How hast thou counselled
him that hath no wisdom?
and how hast thou
plentifully declared the thing as it is
abundantly made known his substance?
4 To whom hast thou *uttered*
words **told utterances**?
and whose *spirit* **breath** came from thee?
5 *Dead things are formed from* **Ghosts writhe**
under the waters,
and *the inhabitants thereof dwell*
they who tabernacle there.
6 *Hell* **Sheol** is naked *before* **in front of** him,
and *destruction* **Abaddon** hath no covering.
7 He *stretcheth out* **spreadeth** the north
over the *empty place* **void**,
and hangeth the earth upon *nothing* **naught whatever**.
8 He *bindeth up* **tribulateth**
the waters in his thick clouds;
and the cloud is not *rent* **split** under them.
9 He holdeth back the face of his throne,
and spreadeth his cloud upon it.
10 He hath *compassed* **circled**
the face of the waters
with *bounds* **statutes**,
until the *day* **light** and *night come*
to an end **dark conclude**.
11 The pillars of *heaven tremble* **the heavens quake**
and *are astonished* **marvel** at his *reproof* **rebuke**.

12 He *divideth* **splitteth** the
sea with his *power* **force**,
and by his *understanding* **discernment**
he *smiteth through* **striketh** the proud.
13 By his spirit he hath *garnished*
glorified the heavens;
his hand hath *formed* **writhed**
the *crooked* **fugitive** serpent.
14 *Lo* **Behold**, these are *parts* **the end** of his ways:
but how *little a portion* **an inkling of a word**
is heard of him?
but the thunder of his *power* **might**
who *can understand* **discerneth**?

27 *Moreover Job* **Iyob**
continued **added to lift** his *parable* **proverb**, and said,
2 *As God* **El** liveth,
who hath *taken away* **turned aside** my judgment;
and *the Almighty* **Shadday**,
who hath *vexed* **embittered** my soul;
3 All the while my breath is in me,
and the spirit of *God* **Elohah** is in my nostrils;
4 My lips shall not *speak* **word** wickedness,
nor my tongue *utter* **mutter** deceit.
5 *God forbid* **Far be it** that I should justify you:
till I *die* **expire**
I *will* **shall** not *remove* **turn aside**
from mine integrity *from me.*
6 My *righteousness* **justness** I *hold fast* **uphold**,
and *will* **shall** not *let it go* **slacken**:
my heart shall not reproach me
so long as I live **all my days**.
7 Let mine enemy be as the wicked,
and he that riseth up against me
as the *unrighteous* **wicked**.

BILDAD ANSWERS

25 And Bildad the Shuachiy answers and says,
2 Dominion and dread *are* with him;
he works shalom in his heights.
3 Is there any number of his troops?
On whom rises not his light?
4 How then is man justified with El?
How is he, birthed of a woman, purified?
5 Behold even to the moon and it shines not;
yes, in his eyes, the stars are not pure;
6 How much less man—a maggot?
and the son of humanity—a maggot?

IYOB ANSWERS

26 And Iyob answers and says,
2 How help you him who has no force?
—save the arm that has no strength?
3 —counsel him who has no wisdom?
—abundantly make known his substance?
4 To whom tell you utterances?
Whose breath came from you?
5 Ghosts writhe under the waters
with them who tabernacle there.
6 Sheol is naked in front of him
and Abaddon has no covering.
7 He spreads the north over the void
and hangs the earth on naught whatever;
8 he tribulates the waters in his thick clouds
and the cloud splits not under them;
9 he holds back the face of his throne
and spreads his cloud thereon;
10 he circles the face of the waters with statutes
until the light and dark conclude.
11 The pillars of the heavens quake
and marvel at his rebuke;
12 he splits the sea with his force;
by his discernment he strikes the proud:
13 by his spirit he glorifies the heavens;
his hand writhes the fugitive serpent.
14 Behold, these—the end of his ways;
And how an inkling of a word is heard of him?
And who discerns the thunder of his might?

27 And Iyob adds to lift his proverb, and says,
2 El lives—who turns aside my judgment;
and Shadday—who embitters my soul:
3 for all the while my breath *is* in me
and the spirit of Elohah in my nostrils:
4 neither my lips word wickedness
nor my tongue mutters deceit.
5 Far be it that I justify you;
until I expire I turn not aside from my integrity.
6 I uphold my justness and slacken not;
my heart reproaches me not all my days:
7 My enemy is as the wicked
and he who rises against me as the wicked.
8 For what is the hope of the *hypocrite* **profaner**,
though he hath gained,
when *God taketh away* **Elohah extracteth** his soul?
9 *Will God* **Shall El** hear his cry
when *trouble* **tribulation** cometh upon him?
10 *Will* **Shall** he delight himself
in *the Almighty* **Shadday**?
will **shall** he *always* **at all times** call upon *God* **Elohah**?
11 I *will* **shall** teach you by the hand of *God* **El**:
that which is with *the Almighty* **Shadday**

will **shall** I not conceal.
12 Behold, all ye yourselves have seen it;
why then are ye thus *altogether* **in being vain,** vain?
13 This is the *portion* **allotment**
of *a man* **wicked humanity**
with *God* **El,**
and the *heritage* **inheritance** of *oppressors* **tyrants,**
which they shall *receive* **take** of *the Almighty* **Shadday.**
14 If his *children be multiplied* **sons abound,**
it is for the sword:
and his offspring shall not be satisfied with bread.
15 *Those that remain of him* **His survivors**
shall be *buried* **entombed** in death:
and his widows shall not weep.
16 Though he heap *up* silver as the dust,
and prepare *raiment* **robes** as the clay;
17 He may prepare it, but the
just shall *put it on* **enrobe,**
and the innocent shall *divide* **allot** the silver.
18 He buildeth his house as a moth,
and as a *booth* **sukkoth/brush arbor**
that the *keeper maketh* **guardian worketh.**
19 The rich *man* shall lie down,
but *he* shall not be gathered:
he openeth his eyes, and he is not.
20 Terrors *take hold on* **overtake** him as waters,
a *tempest* **hurricane** stealeth him away in the night.
21 The *east wind carrieth*
easterly lifteth him *away,*
and he *departeth* **goeth**:
and *as a storm hurleth* **whirleth** him out of his place.
22 *For God* **And** shall cast
upon him, and not spare:
in fleeing, he *would fain flee* **fleeth** out of his hand.
23 *Men* **They** shall clap their *hands* **palms** at him,
and shall hiss him out of his place.

28 Surely there is a *vein* **source** for the silver,
and a place for gold where they *fine* **refine** it.
2 Iron is taken out of the *earth* **dust,**
and *brass* **copper** is *molten* **poured** out of the stone.
3 He setteth an end to darkness,
and *searcheth out* **probeth** all *perfection* **conclusion**:
the stones of darkness, and the shadow of death.
4 The *flood* **wadi** breaketh out
from the *inhabitant* **sojourner**;
even the waters—forgotten of the foot:
they *are dried up* **languish,**
they *are gone* **drift** away from men.
5 *As for* the earth, out of it cometh bread:
and under it is turned up as it were fire.
6 The stones of it are the place of sapphires:
and it hath dust of gold.
7 There is a path which no *fowl* **swooper** knoweth,
and which the *vulture's* **hawk's** eye
hath not *seen* **scanned**:
8 The *lion's whelps* **sons of**
pride have not trodden it,
nor the *fierce* **roaring** lion *passed by it* **attacked.**
9 He *putteth forth* **spreadeth**
his hand upon the *rock* **flint;**
he overturneth the mountains by the roots.
10 He *cutteth out* **splitteth** rivers among the rocks;
and his eye seeth *every precious thing* **all the esteemed.**
11 He bindeth the floods
from *overflowing* **weeping;**
and the *thing that is hid* **concealed**
bringeth he forth to light.
12 But where shall wisdom be found?
and where is the place of *understanding* **discernment**?
13 Man knoweth not the *price thereof* **appraisal;**
neither is it found in the land of the living.
14 The *depth* **abyss** saith, *It is* not in me:
and the sea saith, *It is* not with me.
15 *It cannot be gotten for gold*
Gold shall not be given for it,
neither shall silver be weighed for the price *thereof.*
8 For what *is* the hope of the profaner,
though he gains,
when Elohah extracts his soul?
9 Hears El his cry when
tribulation overcomes him?
10 Delights he in Shadday?
Calls he on Elohah at all times?
11 I teach you by the hand of El;
what *is* with Shadday I conceal not.
12 Behold, all you yourselves see;
why then, in being vain, are you so vain?
13 This is the allotment of
wicked humanity with El;
and the inheritance of tyrants
which they take of Shadday.
14 If his sons abound, it is for the sword;
and his offspring satisfy not with bread:
15 his survivors entomb in death
and his widows weep not:
16 though he heaps silver as the dust
and prepares robes as the clay:
17 he prepares, and the just enrobe;
and the innocent allot the silver:

18 he builds his house as a moth and as a sukkoth/
brush arbor which the guardian works.
19 The rich lies down, and he is not gathered;
he opens his eyes, and he is not:
20 terrors overtake him as waters;
a hurricane steals him away in the night:
21 the easterly lifts him and he goes
—whirls him from his place:
22 and casts on him and spares not;
in fleeing, he flees from his hand.
23 They clap their palms at him
and hiss him from his place.

28 Surely there is a source for the silver
and a place to refine gold;
2 iron is taken from the dust
and copper poured from the stone.
3 He sets an end to darkness
and probes all conclusion
—the stones of darkness
and the shadow of death.
4 The wadi breaks out from the sojourner;
—forgotten by the foot;
they languish;
they drift away from men.
5 The earth, from which comes bread;
and underneath, turns as fire.
6 The stones thereof are the place of sapphires;
and it has dust of gold.
7 There *is* a path
which neither the swooper knows
nor the eye of the hawk scans;
8 nor the sons of pride tread,
nor the roaring lion attacks.
9 He spreads his hand on the flint
he overturns the mountains by the roots:
10 he splits rivers among the rocks
and his eye sees all the esteemed:
11 he binds the floods from weeping
and brings the concealed to light.
12 And wisdom, where is it found?
Where is the place of discernment?
13 Man neither knows the appraisal;
nor finds it in the land of the living.
14 The abyss says, Not in me!
And the sea says, Not with me!
15 Neither *is* gold given for it
nor silver weighed for the price:
16 *It cannot be valued* **Nor balanced**
with the *gold* **ore** of Ophir,
with the *precious* **esteemed** onyx, or the sapphire.
17 The gold and the crystal
cannot equal **be not ranked with** it:
and the exchange of it **nor exchanged**
shall not be for *jewels* **instruments** of *fine* **pure** gold.
18 *No mention* **Nor remembered**
shall be *made of coral* **corals,** or *of* pearls:
for the *price* **sowing** of wisdom is above *rubies* **pearls.**
19 The topaz of *Ethiopia* **Kush**
shall not *equal* **be ranked with** it,
neither shall it be *valued* **balanced** with *pure gold* **ore.**
20 Whence then cometh wisdom?
and where is the place of *understanding* **discernment**?
21 Seeing it is *hid* **concealed**
from the eyes of all living,
and *kept close* **hidden**
from the *fowls* **flyers** of the *air* **heavens.**
22 *Destruction* **Abaddon** and death say,
We have heard the fame *thereof* with our ears.
23 *God understandeth* **Elohim**
discerneth the way *thereof,*
and he knoweth the place *thereof.*
24 For he looketh to the ends of the earth,
and seeth under the whole *heaven* **heavens;**
25 To *make* **work** the weight for the winds;
and he *weigheth* **gaugeth** the waters by measure.
26 When he *made* **worketh** a
decree **statute** for the rain,
and a way for the lightning of the *thunder* **voice:**
27 Then did he see it, and *declare* **scribe** it;
he prepared it, yea, and *searched* **probed** it *out.*
28 And unto *man* **humanity** he said, Behold,
the *fear* **awe** of *the Lord* **Adonay,**
that is wisdom;
and to *depart* **turn aside** from evil
is *understanding* **discernment.**

29 *Moreover Job* **Iyob**
continued **lifted to add** his *parable* **proverb**, and said,
2 *Oh* **Who giveth** that I were
as in *months past* **ancient moons,**
as in the days when *God preserved* **Elohah guarded** me;
3 When his *candle shined*
lamp halaled upon my head,
and when by his light I walked through darkness;
4 As I was in the days of *my youth* **winter,**
when the *secret* **private counsel** of *God*
Elohah was upon my *tabernacle* **tent;**
5 When *the Almighty* **Shadday** was yet with me,
when my *children* **lads** were **round** about me;
6 When I *washed* **bathed** my steps with butter,
and the rock poured me out *rivers* **rivulets** of oil;

7 When I went out to the *gate*
portal through the city,
when I prepared my *seat* **settlement**
in the *street* **broadway**!
8 The *young men* **lads** saw
me, and hid themselves:
and the aged arose, and stood up.
9 The *princes* **governors**
refrained *talking* **uttering**,
and *laid* **set** their *hand* **palm** on their mouth.
10 The *nobles held* **eminent hid** their *peace* **voice**,
and their tongue *cleaved* **adhered**
to *the roof of* their *mouth* **palate**.
11 When the ear heard *me*,
then it *blessed* **called** me **blithesome**;
and when the eye saw me,
it gave witness to me:
12 Because I *delivered* **rescued**
the *poor* **humble** that cried,
and the *fatherless* **orphan**,
and him that had *none to help him* **no helper**.
13 The blessing of him that
was ready to *perish* **destruct**
came upon me:
and I caused the widow's heart to *sing for joy* **shout**.
14 I *put on righteousness* **enrobed justness**,
and it *clothed* **enrobed** me:
my judgment was as a *robe* **mantle** and a *diadem* **turban**.
15 I was eyes to the blind,
and feet was I to the lame.
16 I was a father to the *poor* **needy**:
and the *cause* **contention** which I knew not
I *searched out* **probed**.
17 And I brake the *jaws* **molars** of the wicked,
and *plucked* **cast** the *spoil* **prey** out of his teeth.
18 Then I said, I shall *die* **expire** in my nest,
16 nor balanced with the ore of Ophir
—with the esteemed onyx, or the sapphire.
17 Neither are the gold and
the crystal ranked with it
nor exchanged for instruments of pure gold:
18 nor corals or pearls remembered;
for the sowing of wisdom is above pearls.
19 Neither is the topaz of Kush ranked with it;
nor balanced with ore.
20 Whence then comes wisdom?
Where is the place of discernment?
21 —seeing it is concealed from the eyes
of all living
—hidden from the flyers of the heavens.
22 Abaddon and death say,
We hear the fame with our ears:
23 Elohim discerns the way
and he knows the place:
24 for he looks to the ends of the earth
and sees under the whole heavens
25 —to work the weight for the winds
—to gauge the waters by measure.
26 He works a statute for the rain,
and a way for the lightning of the voice;
27 then he sees and scribes;
he prepares, yes, and probes.
28 And to humanity he says, Behold,
to Adonay is wisdom;
and to turn aside from evil, discernment.

29 And Iyob lifts to add his proverb and says,
2 O that I were as in ancient moons
—as in the days Elohah guarded me;
3 when his lamp halaled on my head;
when by his light I walked the darkness;
4 as I was in the days of winter
with the private counsel of Elohah on my tent:
5 when Shadday was yet with me;
when my lads surrounded me;
6 when I bathed my steps with butter
and the rock poured me rivulets of oil;
7 when I went out to the portal through the city;
when I prepared my settlement in the broadway!
8 The lads saw me and hid themselves
and the aged rose and stood;
9 governors refrained uttering
and set their palm on their mouth;
10 the eminent hid their voice
and their tongue adhered to their palate.
11 When the ear heard, it called me blithesome;
and when the eye saw, it gave me witness;
12 because I rescued them who cried
—the humble and the orphan
and whoever had no helper.
13 The blessing of him who was ready to destruct
came on me;
and I caused the heart of the widow to shout.
14 I enrobed justness and it enrobed me;
my judgment *was* as a mantle and a turban;
15 I was eyes to the blind and feet to the lame;
16 —a father to the needy.
I probed contentions that I knew not;
17 I broke the molars of the wicked
and cast the prey from his teeth.
18 And I said, I expire in my nest

and *I shall multiply* **my days shall abound** as the sand.
19 My root was spread out by the waters,
and the dew
lay all night **stayed overnight** upon my *branch* **clippings.**
20 My *glory* **honour** was *fresh in* **new within** me,
and my bow was *renewed* **changed** in my hand.
21 Unto me *men gave ear* **they**
hearkened, and waited,
and *kept silence* **hushed** at my counsel.
22 After my words they *spake* **reiterated** not *again*;
and my *speech* **utterances** dropped upon them.
23 And they waited for me as for the rain;
and they *opened* **gaped** their mouth *wide*
as for the *latter* **after** rain.
24 *If* I laughed on them, they
believed it **trusted** not;
and the light of my *countenance* **face**
they *cast* **felled** not *down.*
25 I chose out their way, and
sat chief **settled as head,**
and *dwelt* **tabernacled** as a *king* **sovereign**
in the *army* **troops,**
as one that *comforteth* **sigheth over** the mourners.

30 But now they that are
younger **of fewer days** than I
have me in derision **ridicule me,**
whose fathers I *would* **should** have *disdained* **spurned**
to have set with the dogs of my flock.
2 Yea, *whereto might the strength* **what is the force**
of their hands *profit* **to** me,
in whom *old age was perished* **maturity destructed**?
3 For *want* **lack** and *famine* **hunger**
they were *solitary* **sterile;**
fleeing **gnawing** into the *wilderness* **parch**
in former time **of yesternight**
desolate **of devastation** and *waste* **ruin.**
4 Who *cut up* **plucked** mallows
by the *bushes* **shrubs,**
and juniper roots for their *meat* **bread.**
5 They were *driven forth* **exiled**
from *among men* **the back,**
(they *cried* **shouted** after them as after a thief;)
6 To *dwell* **tabernacle**
in the *cliffs* **chasms** of the *valleys* **wadies,**
in caves **holes** of the *earth* **dust**, and *in* the rocks.
7 Among the *bushes* **shrubs** they brayed;
under the nettles they were *gathered together* **scraped.**
8 *They were children* **Sons** of fools,
yea, *children* **sons** of *base* **nameless** men:
they were viler than **ejected from** the earth.
9 And now am I their *song* **strummer,**
yea, I am their *byword* **utterance.**
10 They abhor me, they flee far from me,
and spare not to spit in my face.
11 Because he hath loosed my cord,
and *afflicted* **humbled** me,
they have also *let loose* **sent away**
the bridle *before me* **from my face.**
12 Upon my right *hand* rise the *youth* **offspring;**
they *push* **send** away my feet,
and they raise up against me
the ways of their destruction.
13 They *mar* **tear up** my path,
they *set forward* **benefit** my calamity,
they have no helper.
14 They came *upon me*
as a *wide breaking in of waters* **broad breach:**
in **under** the *desolation* **devastation**
they rolled themselves *upon me.*
15 Terrors are turned upon me:
they pursue my *soul* **reputation** as the wind:
and my *welfare* **salvation** passeth away as a **thick** cloud.
16 And now my soul is poured out upon me;
the days of *affliction* **humiliation**
have taken hold upon me.
17 My bones *are pierced* **penetrate** in me
in the night *season*:
and my *sinews take no rest* **gnawing lieth not down.**
18 By the great force *of my disease*
is my *garment changed* **robe disguised:**
it bindeth me about as the *collar* **mouth** of my coat.
19 He hath cast me into the *mire* **clay,**
and I am become like dust and ashes.
20 I cry unto thee,
and thou *dost not hear* **answerest** me **not**:
and my days abound as the sand.
19 My root spreads to the waters
and the dew stays overnight on my clippings.
20 My honor is new within me
and my bow changes in my hand.
21 To me they hearken and wait
and hush at my counsel.
22 After my words they reiterated not;
and my utterances dropped on them;
23 they awaited me as for the rain;
they gaped their mouth as for the after rain.
24 I laughed on them, they trusted not;
and the light of my face they felled not.
25 I chose their way, and settled as head;

and tabernacled as a sovereign in the troops,
as one who sighs over the mourners.

30 And now they of fewer days than I
ridicule me;
whose fathers I spurned
to set with the dogs of my flock.
2 Yes, what is the force of their hands to me,
in whom maturity destructs?
3 For lack and hunger, they *are* sterile;
gnawing into the parch of yesternight
of devastation and ruin:
4 who pluck mallows by the shrubs
and juniper roots for their bread.
5 They are exiled from the back,
they shout at them as after a thief;
6 to tabernacle in the chasms of the wadies,
holes of the dust and the rocks;
7 among the shrubs they bray;
under the nettles they scrape:
8 sons of fools;
yes, sons of nameless men ejected from the earth;
9 and now I am their strummer;
yes, I am their utterance.
10 They abhor me; they flee far from me;
they spare not to spit in my face.
11 Because he loosed my cord
and humbled me,
they also sent away the bridle from my face.
12 At my right rise the offspring;
they send away my feet;
they raise their ways of destruction against me;
13 they tear up my path;
they benefit my calamity;
they have no helper:
14 they come as a broad breach;
they roll themselves under the devastation.
15 Terrors turn on me;
they pursue my reputation as the wind;
and my salvation passes as a thick cloud.
16 And now my soul pours out on me;
the days of humiliation take hold on me;
17 my bones penetrate within me in the night;
and my gnawing lies not down.
18 By the great force is my robe disguised;
it binds around me as the mouth of my coat.
19 He casts me into the clay
and I become as dust and ashes.
20 I cry to you, and you answer me not;
I stand up, and thou *regardest* **discernest** me not.
21 Thou *art become* **turnest** cruel to me:
with thy *strong* **mighty** hand
thou opposest *thyself against* me.
22 Thou liftest me up to the wind;
thou *causest me to ride upon it* **drivest me**,
and *dissolvest* **razest** my substance.
23 For I know
that thou *wilt bring* **shalt return** me to death,
and to the house *appointed* **of the congregation**
for all **of all the** living.
24 Howbeit he *will* **shall** not
stretch out **spread** his hand to the *grave* **prey**,
though they cry in his *destruction* **calamity**.
25 Did not I weep for him
that *was in trouble* **had a hard day**?
was not my soul grieved for the *poor* **needy**?
26 When I *looked for* **awaited** good,
then evil came *unto me*:
and when I waited for light,
there came darkness.
27 My *bowels* **inwards** boiled,
and *rested* **hushed** not:
the days of *affliction* **humiliation**
prevented **anticipated** me.
28 I went *mourning* **darkened**
without the *sun* **heat**:
I *stood up* **arose**, and I cried in the congregation.
29 I am a brother to *dragons* **monsters**,
and a *companion* **friend** to *owls* **daughters of the owl**.
30 My skin is black upon me,
and my bones are *burned* **scorched** with *heat* **parch**.
31 My harp also
is turned to **be into** mourning,
and my *organ* **woodwind**
into the voice of them that weep.

31 I *made* **cut** a covenant with mine eyes;
why then should I *think* **discern** upon a *maid* **virgin**?
2 For what *portion* **allotment** of *God* **Elohah**
is *there* from above?
and what inheritance of *the Almighty* **Shadday**
from *on high* **the heights**?
3 Is not *destruction* **calamity** to the wicked?
and a *strange punishment* **strangeness**
to the *workers* **doers** of *iniquity* **mischief**?
4 Doth not he see my ways,
and *count* **scribe** all my *steps* **paces**?
5 If I have walked with vanity,
or if my foot hath hasted to deceit;
6 Let me be weighed
in *an even* **a** balance **of justness**
that *God* **Elohah** may know mine integrity.

7 If my step hath *turned* **spread** out of the way,
and mine heart walked after mine eyes,
and if any *blot* **blemish**
hath *cleaved* **adhered** to *mine hands* **my palms**;
8 Then let me *sow* **seed**, and let another eat;
yea, let my offspring be rooted out.
9 If mine heart have been
deceived **enticed** by a woman,
or *if* I have *laid wait* **lurked**
at my *neighbour's door* **friend's portal**;
10 Then let my *wife* **woman** grind unto another,
and let others *bow down upon* **kneel to** her.
11 For this is *an heinous crime* **intrigue**; yea,
it is an iniquity to be punished by the judges
a judicial perversity.
12 For it is a fire that consumeth
to *destruction* **Abaddon**,
and *would* **should** root out all *mine*
increase **my produce**.
13 If I *did despise* **spurned** the *cause* **judgment**
of my *manservant* **servant** or of my *maidservant* **maid**,
when they contended with me;
14 What then shall I *do* **work**
when *God* **El** riseth *up*?
and when he visiteth, what shall I *answer* **respond** him?
15 Did not he that *made* **worked**
me in the *womb* **belly**
make **work** him?
and did not one *fashion* **prepare** us in the womb?
16 If I have withheld the poor from their desire,
or have *caused* **finished off** the eyes of the widow *to fail*;
17 Or have eaten my morsel myself alone,
and the *fatherless* **orphan** hath not eaten *thereof*;
I stand, and you discern me not:
21 you turn cruel to me;
with your mighty hand you oppose me:
22 you lift me to the wind;
you drive me and raze my substance.
23 For I know that you return me to death
and to the house of the congregation
of all the living.
24 Surely he spreads not his hand to the prey,
though they cry in his calamity.
25 Wept I not for him who had a hard day?
Grieved not my soul for the needy?
26 When I awaited good, evil came;
when I waited for light, darkness came:
27 my inwards boiled and hushed not;
the days of humiliation anticipated me.
28 I go darkened without heat;
I rise and I cry in the congregation.
29 I am a brother to monsters
and a friend to daughters of the owl.
30 My skin blackens on me;
my bones scorch with parch.
31 My harp becomes mourning
and my woodwind the voice of weeping.

31 I cut a covenant with my eyes;
and what—discern I a virgin?
2 What is the allotment of Elohah from above?
What is the inheritance of Shadday from the heights?
3 Is not calamity to the wicked?
—a strangeness to the doers of mischief?
4 Sees he not my ways?
—scribes all my paces?
5 If I walk with vanity
or my foot hastens to deceit
6 weigh me in a balance of justness;
Elohah knows my integrity.
7 If my step spreads from the way and my heart walks
after my eyes; if any blemish adheres to my palms;
8 then have me seed and another eat:
yes, uproot my offspring.
9 If a woman enticed my heart
or I lurked at the portal of my friend;
10 then have my woman grind to another
and others kneel to her.
11 For this is intrigue;
yes, a judicial perversity:
12 a fire that consumes to Abaddon
and roots out all my produce.
13 If I spurn the judgment
of my servant or of my maid
when they contend with me
14 What then work I when El rises?
When he visits, what respond I?
15 He who worked me in the belly
worked he not also him?
—that one who prepared us in the womb?
16 If I withhold the poor from their desire,
or finish off the eyes of the widow;
17 or eat my morsel myself alone
and the orphan eats not;
18 (For from my youth he *was*
brought **grew** up with me,
as *with* a father,
and I have *guided* **led** her from my mother's *womb* **belly**;)
19 If I have seen any *perish* **destruct**
for want of *clothing* **robe**,
or *any poor* without covering **to the needy**;

20 If his loins have not blessed me,
and *if* he were not *warmed* **heated**
with the fleece of my *sheep* **lambs;**
21 If I have *lifted up* **shaken** my hand
against the *fatherless* **orphan,**
when I saw my help in the *gate* **portal:**
22 Then let *mine arm* **my shoulder**
fall from my shoulder blade,
and mine arm
be broken from the *bone* **stem.**
23 For *destruction* **calamity** from *God* **El**
was a *terror* **dread** to me,
and by reason of his *highness* **exalting**
I *could not endure* **am not able.**
24 If I have *made* **set** gold my hope,
or have said to the *fine gold* **ore,** *Thou art* my confidence;
25 If I *rejoiced* **cheered**
because my *wealth was* **valuables were** great,
and because mine hand had *gotten* **found** much;
26 If I *beheld* **saw** the *sun* **light**
when it *shined* **halaled,**
or the moon walking in *brightness* **esteem;**
27 And my heart
hath been *secretly enticed* **covertly duped,**
or my mouth hath kissed my hand:
28 This also were
an iniquity to be punished by the judge
a judicial perversity:
for I should have denied *the God that is* **El** above.
29 If I *rejoiced* **cheered**
at the *destruction* **calamity** of him that hated me,
or *lifted up myself* **wakened** when evil found him:
30 Neither have I *suffered* **given**
my *mouth* **palate** to sin
by *wishing a curse* **asking an oath** to his soul.
31 If the men of my *tabernacle* **tent** said not,
Oh **Who giveth** that we had of his flesh!
we cannot be satisfied.
32 The *stranger* **sojourner**
did not lodge **stayed not overnight**
in the *street* **outways:**
but I opened my doors to the *traveller* **wayward.**
33 If I covered my *transgressions* **rebellions**
as *Adam* **humanity,**
by hiding mine *iniquity* **perversity** in my bosom:
34 *Did I fear* **Then I dreaded** a great multitude,
or did the *contempt* **disrespect** of families terrify me,
that I *kept silence* **hushed,**
and went not out of the *door?* **portal.**
35 *Oh* **Who giveth** that one *would* **should** hear me!
behold, my *desire* **mark** is,
that *the Almighty would* **Shadday should** answer me,
and that *mine adversary* **my man of contention**
had *written* **scribed** a *book* **scroll.**
36 Surely I *would take* **should**
lift it upon my shoulder,
and *bind* **fasten** it as a crown to me.
37 I *would declare unto* **should tell** him
the number of my *steps* **paces;**
as *a prince would* **an eminent should** I go near unto him.
38 If my *land* **soil** cry against me,
or that the furrows *likewise thereof*
complain **weep together;**
39 If I have eaten the *fruits thereof* **produce**
without *money* **silver,**
or have caused the *owners thereof* **masters**
to *lose* **expire** their *life* **soul:**
40 Let *thistles* **thorns** grow instead of wheat,
and *cockle* **stinkweed** instead of barley.

The words of *Job* **Iyob**
are ended **be consummated.**

32 So these three men
ceased to answer Job **shabbathized**
from answering Iyob,
because he was *righteous* **just** in his own eyes.
18 —for as a father
he grew up with me from my youth
—led her from the belly of my mother.
19 If I have seen any destruct for want of robe
or the needy without covering;
20 if neither his loins blessed me
nor heated with the fleece of my lambs;
21 if I shook my hand against the orphan
when I saw my help in the portal;
22 then *may* my shoulder fall from the blade
and my arm break at the stem:
23 for calamity from El is a dread to me
and by reason of his exalting I am not able.
24 If I set gold my hope
or said to the ore, My confidence!
25 if I cheer because my valuables are great
and because my hand found much;
26 if I see the light when it halals
or the moon walking in esteem;
27 and my heart covertly duped
or my mouth kiss my hand;
28 this also is a judicial perversity:
for I denied El above.
29 If I cheer at the calamity of my hater,
or waken when evil finds him;

30 I give not my palate to sin
by asking him to oath his soul.
31 If not, men of my tent, say you,
Who gives that we have of his flesh
—we are not satisfied.
32 The sojourner
stayed not overnight in the outways;
I opened my doors to the wayward.
33 If I covered my rebellions as humanity
by hiding my perversity in my bosom;
34 then I dread a great multitude
—and the disrespect of families terrify me—
and I hush and go not from the portal.
35 Who gives that someone hear me!
Behold, my mark!
Shadday, answer me!
Man of contention, scribe a scroll!
36 If not, I lift it on my shoulder
and fasten it to me as a crown.
37 I tell him my paces;
as an eminent I go near him.
38 If my soil cries against me,
and the furrows weep together;
39 if I have eaten the produce without silver
or caused the masters to expire their soul;
40 may thorns grow instead of wheat
and stinkweed instead of barley. The
words of Iyob are consummated.
32 And these three men
shabbathized from answering Iyob,
because he was just in his own eyes.

Eli Hu Kindles His Wrath

2 Then was kindled the wrath of *Elihu* **Eli Hu**
the son of *Barachel* **Barach El** the *Buzite*
Buziy, of the *kindred* **family** of Ram:
against *Job* **Iyob** was his wrath kindled,
because he justified *himself* **his soul**
rather than *God* **Elohim**.
3 Also against his three friends
was his wrath kindled,
because they had found no answer,
and *yet* had *condemned Job* **judged Iyob wicked**.
4 Now *Elihu* **Eli Hu**
had waited till *Job* **Iyob** had *spoken* **worded**,
because they were elder than he **by days**.
5 When *Elihu* **Eli Hu** saw
that there was no answer
in the mouth of *these* three men,
then his wrath was kindled.
6 And *Elihu* **Eli Hu,**
the son of *Barachel* **Barach El** the *Buzite* **Buziy**
answered and said,
I am *young* **of few days**, and ye are *very old* **aged**;
wherefore I *was afraid* **feared**,
and *durst not* **awed**
to shew you *mine opinion* **my knowledge**.
7 I said, Days should *speak* **word**,
and *multitude* **abundance** of years
should *teach* **make known** wisdom.
8 *But* **Surely** there is a spirit in man:
and the *inspiration* **breath** of *the Almighty* **Shadday**
giveth them *understanding* **discernment**.
9 **The** Great *men* are not *always wise* **enwisened**:
neither do the aged *understand* **discern** judgment.
10 Therefore I said, Hearken to me;
I also *will* **shall** shew *mine opinion* **my knowledge**.
11 Behold, I *waited for* **awaited** your words;
I gave ear to your reasons,
whilst ye *searched out what to say* **probed utterances**.
12 Yea, I *attended* **discerned** unto you, and, behold,
there was none of you that *convinced Job* **reproved**
Iyob, or that answered his *words* **sayings**:
13 Lest ye should say, We have found out wisdom:
God thrusteth **El disperseth** him *down*, not man.
14 Now he hath not *directed* **arranged**
his *words* **utterances** against me:
neither *will ! answer him* **shall I respond**
with **to** your *speeches* **sayings**.
15 They were *amazed* **dismayed**,
they answered no more:
they *left off speaking* **removed from uttering**.
16 When I *had waited* **awaited**,
(for they *spake* **worded** not,
but stood still, and answered no more;)
17 *! said*, I *will* **shall** answer
also my *part* **allotment**,
I also *will* **shall** shew *mine opinion* **my knowledge**.
18 For I am full of *matter* **utterances**,
the spirit *within me* **of my belly**
constraineth **distresseth** me.
19 Behold,
my belly is as wine which hath no *vent* **opening**;
it is ready to burst **to split** like new *bottles* **skins**.
20 I *will speak* **shall word**, that
I may *be refreshed* **respire**:
I *will* **shall** open my lips and answer.
21 Let me not, I *pray* **beseech** you,
accept any man's person **lift the face of humanity**,
neither *let me* give *flattering titles* **honorary degrees**

unto *man* **humanity.**
22 For I know not
to give *flattering titles* **honorary degrees;**
in so doing my *maker* **Worker**
would soon take **should shortly lift** me *away.*
33 *Wherefore* **But,** *Job* **Iyob,** I *pray* **beseech** thee,
hear my *speeches* **utterances,**
and hearken to all my words.
2 Behold, *now* **I beseech,** I
have opened my mouth,
my tongue hath *spoken* **worded** in my *mouth* **palate.**
3 My *words* **sayings**
shall be of the *uprightness* **straightness** of my heart:
and my lips shall utter knowledge *clearly* **purely.**
4 The spirit of *God* **El** hath *made* **worked** me,

Eli Hu Kindles His Wrath

2 And Eli Hu the son of Barach El the Buziy
of the family of Ram kindles his wrath—
kindles his wrath against Iyob,
because he justifies his soul—rather than Elohim.
3 He also kindles his wrath
against his three friends
because they find no answer
and judge Iyob wicked.
4 And Eli Hu waits until Iyob words,
because they are elder than he by days.
5 And Eli Hu sees there is no answer
in the mouth of the three men,
and kindles his wrath.
6 And Eli Hu the son of Barach El the Buziy
answers and says,
I *am* of few days and you *are* aged;
so I fear
and awe to show you my knowledge.
7 I say, Days word;
and abundance of years make wisdom known.
8 Surely there is a spirit in man;
and the breath of Shadday gives discernment.
9 Neither the great enwisen
nor the aged discern judgment.
10 So I say, Hearken to me;
I also show my knowledge.
11 Behold, I awaited your words;
I gave ear to your reasons as you probed utterances:
12 yes, I discerned you;
and behold, none of you reproved Iyob
or answered his sayings:
13 lest you say, We have found out wisdom;
El disperses him—not man.
14 Neither arranged he his utterances against me;
nor respond I to your sayings.
15 They are dismayed;
they answer no more;
they remove from uttering:
16 I await, they word not;
but stand still and answer no more.
17 I also answer my allotment;
I also show my knowledge:
18 for I am full of utterances,
the spirit of my belly distresses me.
19 Behold, my belly
—as unopened wine—to split as new skins.
20 I word, and I respire;
I open my lips, and answer.
21 I beseech you,
that I neither lift the face of humanity, nor
give honorary degrees to humanity:
22 for I know not to give honorary degrees;
in so doing my Worker shortly lifts me away.
33 And yet, I beseech you, Iyob,
hear my utterances and hearken to all my words:
2 behold, I beseech, I open my mouth;
my tongue words in my palate;
3 my sayings are of the straightness of my heart;
and my lips utter knowledge purely.
4 The Spirit of El works me
and the breath of *the Almighty* **Shadday**
hath *given* **enlivened** me *life.*
5 If thou canst *answer me* **respond,**
set thy words in order before me **line up at my face,**
stand up **get set.**
6 Behold,
I am according to thy *wish* **mouth** in *God's* **El's** stead:
I also am formed out of the clay.
7 Behold, my terror shall not
make **frighten** thee *afraid,*
neither shall my *hand* **burden** be heavy upon thee.
8 Surely thou hast *spoken* **said**
in *mine hearing* **my ears,**
and I have heard the voice of thy *words* **utterances,**
saying,
9 I am *clean* **pure** without *transgression* **rebellion,**
I am *innocent* **covered;**
neither is there *iniquity* **perversity** in me.
10 Behold, he findeth *occasions*
alienations against me,
he *counteth* **fabricateth** me for his enemy,
11 He *putteth* **setteth** my feet in the stocks,
he *marketh* **guardeth** all my paths.

12 Behold, in this thou art not *just* **justified**:
I *will* **shall** answer thee,
that *God* **Elohah** is greater than man.
13 Why dost thou strive against him?
for he *giveth* **answereth** not *account of*
any of his *matters* **words**.
14 For *God speaketh* **El wordeth** once, yea twice,
yet man perceiveth **he observeth** it not.
15 In a dream, in a vision of the night,
when deep sleep falleth upon men,
in *slumberings* **drowsiness** upon the bed;
16 Then he *openeth* **exposeth** the ears of men,
and sealeth their *instruction* **discipline**,
17 That he may *withdraw*
man **turn humanity aside**
from his *purpose* **work**,
and *hide pride* **cover over arrogance**
from *man* **the mighty**.
18 He *keepeth back* **spareth** his
soul from the pit **of ruin**,
and his life from *perishing* **passing** by the *sword* **spear**.
19 He is *chastened* **reproved** also
with *pain* **sorrow** upon his bed,
and the *multitude* **strife** of his bones
with strong pain **is perennial**:
20 So that his life *abhorreth* **loatheth** bread,
and his soul *dainty meat* **food of desire**.
21 His flesh is *consumed away* **finished off**,
that it cannot be seen;
and his bones that were not seen
stick out **are exposed**.
22 Yea, his soul draweth near
unto the *grave* **pit of ruin**,
and his life to the *destroyers* **deathifiers**.
23 If there be *a messenger* **an angel** with him,
an interpreter, one among a thousand,
to *shew unto man* **tell humanity**
his *uprightness* **straightness**:
24 Then *he is gracious* **granteth**
he charism unto him,
and saith, *Deliver* **Rescue** him
from *going down* **descending** to the pit **of ruin**:
I have found *a ransom* **a koper/an atonement**.
25 His flesh shall be *fresher* **rejuvinated**
than a child's **as ladhood**:
he shall return to the days of his youth:
26 He shall *pray unto God* **intreat Elohah**,
and he *will be favourable unto* **shall please** him:
and he shall see his face with *joy* **shouting**:
for he *will render* **shall restore** unto man
his *righteousness* **justness**.
27 He *looketh upon* **observeth** men,
and if any say, I have sinned,
and perverted that which was *right* **straight**,
and it profited me not;
28 He *will deliver* **shall redeem** his soul
from *going* **passing** into the pit **of ruin**,
and his life shall see the light.
29 *Lo* **Behold**,
all these *things worketh God* **doeth El**
oftentimes **twice and thrice** with *man* **the mighty**,
30 To *bring back* **return** his
soul from the pit **of ruin**,
to be enlightened with the light of the living.

and the breath of Shadday enlivens me;
5 respond if you are able;
line up at my face; get set!
6 Behold, I—your mouth in the stead of El;
I also am formed from the clay.
7 Behold, *may* neither my terror frighten you
nor my burden be heavy on you;
8 surely you said to my ears;
and I heard the voice of your utterances;
9 I am pure without rebellion
—covered—no perversity within me.
10 Behold, he finds alienations against me;
he fabricates me for his enemy;
11 he sets my feet in the stocks;
he guards all my paths.
12 Behold, in this you are not justified;
I answer you, Elohah is greater than man.
13 Why strive against him?
Of all his words, he answers none.
14 For El words once; yes, twice;
he observes not.
15 In a dream—in a vision of the night
when deep sleep falls on men
in drowsiness on the bed;
16 then he exposes the ears of men
and seals their discipline;
17 he turns humanity aside from his work
and covers over the arrogance of the mighty:
18 he spares his soul from the pit of ruin
and his life from the passing of the spear;
19 he is also reproved with sorrow on his bed
and the strife of his bones is perennial;
20 his life loathes bread
and his soul food of desire;
21 his flesh finishes off that it not be seen;
and his bones that have not been seen

be exposed.
22 Yes, his soul draws near to the pit of ruin
and his life to the deathifiers.
23 If there is an angel with him
an interpreter—one among a thousand
to tell humanity his straightness,
24 then he grants him charism and says,
Rescue him from descending to the pit of
ruin; I have found a koper/an atonement.
25 His flesh rejuvinates as ladhood;
he returns to the days of his youth;
26 he intreats Elohah and pleases him;
he sees his face with shouting; for he
restores his justness to man.
27 He observes men, and if any say,
I sinned and perverted the straight
and it profits me not;
28 he redeems my soul
from passing into the pit of ruin
and my life sees the light.
29 Behold, El does all these
—twice and thrice with the mighty;
30 to return his soul from the pit of ruin;
to enlighten with the light of the living.
31 Mark well, O *Job* **Iyob**, hearken unto me:
hold thy peace **hush**, and I *will speak* **shall word**.
32 If thou hast *any thing to say* **utterances**,
answer me **respond**:
speak **word**, for I desire to justify thee.
33 If not, hearken unto me:
hold thy peace **hush**,
and I shall teach thee wisdom.

34 *Furthermore Elihu* **Eli Hu** answered and said,
2 Hear my *words* **utterances**, O ye wise *men*;
and *give ear* **hearken** unto me,
ye that *have knowledge* **know**.
3 For the ear *trieth words* **proofeth utterances**,
as the *mouth* **palate** tasteth *meat* **to eat**.
4 Let us choose to us judgment:
let us know among ourselves what is good.
5 For *Job* **Iyob** hath said, I am *righteous* **justified**:
and *God* **El** hath *taken away* **turned aside** my judgment.
6 should I lie against my *right* **judgment**?
my *wound* **arrow** is incurable
without *transgression* **rebellion**.
7 What *man* **mighty** is like *Job* **Iyob**,
who drinketh up *scorning* **derision** like water?
8 Which *goeth* **caravaneth** in
company **companionship**
with the *workers* **doers** of *iniquity* **mischief**,
and walketh with *wicked men* **men of wickedness**.
9 For he hath said,
It profiteth a man nothing **Useless for the mighty**
that he should *delight himself* **be pleased**
with *God* **Elohim**.
10 Therefore hearken unto me
ye men of *understanding* **heart**:
far be it from *God* **El**, that he should do wickedness;
and from *the Almighty* **Shadday**,
that he should *commit iniquity* **do wickedness**.
11 For the *work* **deeds** of *a man* **humanity**
shall he *render unto* **shalam** him,
and *cause every man to find* **present to every man**
according to his ways.
12 Yea, *surely* **truly,** *God will*
El shall not do wickedly,
neither *will the Almighty* **shall Shadday**
pervert **twist** judgment.
13 Who hath given him a charge over the earth?
or who hath *disposed* **set** the whole world?
14 If he set his heart upon man,
if he gather unto himself his spirit and his breath;
15 All flesh shall *perish* **expire** together,
and *man* **humanity** shall *turn again* **return** unto dust.
16 If *now* thou hast *understanding*
discernment, hear this:
hearken to the voice of my *words* **utterances**.
17 Shall even he that hateth
right govern **judgment bind**?
and *wilt* **shalt** thou *condemn* **judge** him **wicked**
that is most just?
18 *Is it fit to say* **Sayest thou** to a *king* **sovereign**,
Thou art wicked **Beli Yaal**?
and to *princes* **volunteers**, *Ye are ungodly* **Wicked**?
19 *How much less to him*—that accepteth not
the *persons* **faces** of *princes* **governors**,
nor *regardeth* **recognizeth** the *rich* **opulent**
more than **the face of** the poor?
for they all are the work of his hands.
20 In a *moment* **blink** shall they die,
and the people shall *be troubled* **shake** at midnight,
and pass away:
and the mighty shall *be taken away* **turn aside**
without hand.
21 For his eyes are upon the ways of man,
and he seeth all his *goings* **paces**.
22 There is no darkness, nor shadow of death,
where the *workers* **doers** of *iniquity* **mischief**
may hide *themselves*.
23 For he *will* **shall** not *lay* **set**
upon man more *than right*;

that he should *enter* **go** into judgment with *God* **El.**
24 He shall *break in pieces* **shatter the** mighty *men*
without number **unable to probe,**
and *set* **stand** others in their stead.
25 Therefore he *knoweth*
recognizeth their *works* **acts,**
and he overturneth them in the night,
so that they are *destroyed* **crushed.**
31 Mark well, O Iyob, hearken to me;
hush and I word.
32 If you have utterances, respond;
word, for I desire to justify you.
33 If not, hearken to me;
hush—and I teach you wisdom.

34 And Eli Hu answers and says,
2 Hear my utterances, O you wise;
and hearken to me, you who know:
3 for the ear proofs utterances,
as the palate tastes to eat.
4 We choose judgment;
we know among ourselves what is good.
5 For Iyob said, I am justified
and El turned aside my judgment!
6 Lie I against my judgment?
my arrow is incurable—without rebellion.
7 Who is mighty as Iyob?
Who drinks derision as water?
8 Who caravans in companionship
with the doers of mischief?
Who walks with men of wickedness?
9 For he said,
Useless for the mighty to be pleased with Elohim.
10 So you men of heart, hearken to me;
far be it from El to do wickedness;
and from Shadday to do wickedness.
11 He shalams humanity for his deeds,
and presents every man according to his ways.
12 Yes truly, neither El does wickedly,
nor Shadday twists judgment.
13 Who gave him charge over the earth?
Who set the whole world?
14 If he sets his heart on man,
he gathers his spirit and his breath to himself.
15 All flesh expires together
and humanity returns to dust.
16 If there *is* discernment, hear this
—hearken to the voice of my utterances.
17 Binds he, he who hates judgment?
Judge you wicked, he who is most just?
18 Say you to a sovereign, Beli Yaal?
—or to volunteers, Wicked?
19 —of him who neither accepts faces of governors
nor recognize the opulent
more than the face of the poor?
—they all are the work of his hands.
20 In a blink they die;
the people shake at midnight and pass away;
and the mighty turn aside without hand.
21 For his eyes are on the ways of man
and he sees all his paces.
22 There is neither darkness
nor shadow of death
where the doers of mischief hide.
23 For he sets no more on man
than to go into judgment with El:
24 he shatters the mighty, unable to probe;
and stands others in their stead.
25 So he recognizes their acts
and overturns them in the night
and they are crushed.
26 He *striketh* **slappeth** them as wicked *men*
in the *open sight* **place** of *others* **seeing;**
27 Because they turned back from **after** him,
and *would* **comprehended** not *consider*
any of his ways:
28 So that they cause the cry of the poor
to come unto him,
and he heareth the cry of the *afflicted* **humble.**
29 When he *giveth quietness* **resteth,**
who then *can make trouble* **judgeth wicked?**
and when he hideth his face,
who then *can behold* **observeth** him?
whether *it be done* against a *nation* **goyim,**
or against *a man only* **humanity altogether:**
30 *That the hypocrite reign not*
From the reign of the profaner of humanity,
lest the people be ensnared.
31 *Surely it is meet to be said*
Sayeth one unto *God* **El,**
I have *borne chastisement* **spared,**
I *will* **have** not *offend any more* **despoiled:**
32 **Except** That which I see not teach thou me:
if I have done *iniquity* **wickedness,**
I will do no more **never again.**
33 Should it be according to thy mind?
he *will recompense* **shall shalam** it,
whether thou refuse, or whether thou choose;
and not I:
therefore *speak* **word** what thou knowest.
34 Let men of understanding *tell me* **say,**

and let a wise *man* **mighty** hearken unto me.
35 *Job* **Iyob** hath *spoken* **worded**
without *knowledge* **comprehending**, and
his words were without wisdom.
36 My *desire* **yearning** is that *Job* **Iyob**
may be *tried unto the end* **proofed in perpetuity**
because of his *answers* **responses**
for *wicked men* **men of mischief.**
37 For he addeth rebellion unto his sin,
he clappeth *his hands* among us,
and *multiplieth* **aboundeth** his *words* **sayings**
against *God* **El**.

35 *Elihu spake moreover* **Eli**
Hu answered, and said,
2 *Thinkest* **Fabricatest** thou
this to be *right* **judgment**,
that thou saidst,
My *righteousness* **justness** is more than *God's* **El's**?
3 For thou saidst,
What *advantage will* **use shall** it be unto thee?
and, What *profit* **benefit** shall I have,
if I be cleansed from my sin?
4 I *will answer* **shall respond** thee **utterances**,
and thy *companions* **friends** with thee.
5 Look unto the heavens, and see;
and *behold* **observe** the *clouds* **vapours**
which are *higher than thou* **high above thee**.
6 If thou sinnest, what *doest*
workest thou against him?
or if thy *transgressions* **rebellions** be
multiplied, what doest thou unto him?
7 If thou be *righteous* **justified**,
what givest thou him?
or what *receiveth* **taketh** he of thine hand?
8 Thy wickedness may *hurt*
be for a man as thou *art*;
and thy *righteousness* **justness**
may profit **for** the son of *man* **humanity**.
9 By reason of the *multitude*
abundance of oppressions
they *make the oppressed* **cause** to cry:
they cry out by reason of the arm of the *mighty* **great**.
10 But none saith,
Where is *God* **Elohah** my *maker* **Worker**,
who giveth *songs* **psalms** in the night;
11 Who teacheth us
more than the *beasts* **animals** of the earth,
and *maketh us wiser* **enwiseneth us more**
than the *fowls* **flyers** of *heaven* **the heavens**?
12 There they cry, but none
giveth answer **answereth**,
because **at the face** of the *pride* **pomp** of evil *men*.
13 Surely *God will* **El shall** not hear vanity,
neither *will the Almighty regard*
shall Shadday observe it.
14 Although thou sayest thou
shalt not *see* **observe** him,
yet judgment is before him **the plea is at his**
face; *therefore trust* **writhe** thou in him.

26 He slaps them as wicked in the place of seeing;
27 because they turn back from after him
and comprehend none of his ways;
28 so that they cause the cry of the poor
to come to him;
and he hears the cry of the humble.
29 And when he rests,
who judges wicked?
and when he hides his face,
who observes him?
—whether against a goyim,
or against humanity altogether;
30 from the reign of the profaner of humanity,
lest the people be ensnared.
31 Says any one to El,
I have spared; I have not despoiled.
32 Except, what I see not, you teach me;
if I have done wickedness, never again.
33 According to your mind,
he shalams what you refuse—what you choose;
and not I;
so word *only* what you know.
34 *May* men of understanding say,
and the wise mighty hearken to me.
35 Iyob words without comprehending
—words without wisdom.
36 I yearn that Iyob be proofed in perpetuity
because of his responses for men of mischief:
37 for he adds rebellion to his sin,
he claps among us
and abounds his sayings against El.

35 And Eli Hu answers and says,
2 Fabricate you this to be judgment,
that you said, My justness is more than of El?
3 that you said, What use is it to you?
and, What benefit I from my sin?
4 —I respond utterances
to you and your friends with you.
5 Look to the heavens and see;
observe the vapours high above you.

6 If you sin, what work you against him?
Or if your rebellions be multiplied,
what do you to him?
7 If you be justified, what give you him?
Or what takes he from your hand?
8 Your wickedness is for a man as you;
and your justness for the son of humanity.
9 By reason of the abundance of oppressions
they cause to cry out
—to cry out by reason of the arm of the great.
10 And no one says, Where is Elohah my Worker
—who gives psalms in the night?
11 —who teaches us
more than the animals of the earth?
—who enwisens us
more than the flyers of the heavens?
12 There they cry,
and he answers not at the face of the pomp of evil.
13 Surely El neither hears vanity
nor Shadday observes.
14 Yes, although you say you observe him not,
the plea is at his face; writhe in him.
15 But now, because it is not *so,*
he hath visited in his *anger* **wrath**;
yet he knoweth it not in *great*
extremity **mighty stupidity**:
16 Therefore doth *Job open*
Iyob gasp his mouth in vain;
he *multiplieth words* **weaveth utterances**
without knowledge.

36 *Elihu* **Eli Hu** also *proceeded* **added**, and said,
2 *Suffer me a little* **Stay around**,
and I *will* **shall** shew thee
that I have yet *to speak* **utterances**
on *God's* **Elohah's** behalf.
3 I *will fetch* **shall lift** my knowledge from afar,
and *will ascribe righteousness* **shall give justness**
to my *Maker* **Worker**.
4 For truly my *words* **utterances** shall not be false:
he that is *perfect* **integrious** in knowledge is with thee.
5 Behold,
God **El** is mighty, and *despiseth* **spurneth** not *any*:
he is—mighty in *strength* **force** and *wisdom* **heart**.
6 He *preserveth* **enliveneth**
not *the life of* the wicked:
but giveth *right* **judgment** to the *poor* **humble**.
7 He *withdraweth* **diminisheth** not his eyes
from the *righteous* **just**:
but with *kings are they* **sovereigns** on the throne;
yea, he *doth establish* **settleth** them
for ever **in perpetuity**,
and they are *exalted* **lifted**.
8 And if they be bound in *fetters* **bonds**,
and be *holden* **captured** in cords
of *affliction* **humiliation**;
9 Then he *sheweth* **telleth** them their *work* **deeds**,
and their *transgressions* **rebellions**
that they have *exceeded* **prevailed mightily**.
10 He *openeth* **exposeth** also their ear to discipline,
and *commandeth* **sayeth**
that they return from *iniquity* **mischief**.
11 If they *obey* **hearken** and serve him,
they shall *spend* **conclude** their days in *prosperity* **good**,
and their years in pleasures.
12 But if they *obey* **hearken** not,
they shall *perish* **pass away expired** by the *sword* **spear**,
and they shall die without knowledge.
13 But the *hypocrites* **profaners**
in heart *heap up* **set** wrath:
they cry not when he bindeth them.
14 *They die* **Their soul dieth** in *youth* **ladhood**,
and their life
is among the *unclean* **hallowed whoremongers**.
15 He delivereth the poor in
his *affliction* **humiliation**,
and *openeth* **exposeth** their ears in oppression.
16 Even so *would* **should** he have removed thee
out of the *strait* **mouth of the narrow**
into a *broad place* **broadness**,
where there is no *straitness* **narrowness under**;
and that which should *be set* **rest** on thy table
should be full of fatness.
17 But thou hast fulfilled the
judgment **plea** of the wicked:
judgment **the plea** and *justice* **judgment**
take hold on thee **are upheld**.
18 Because there is *wrath* **fury**,
beware lest he *take* **goad** thee *away*
with *his stroke* **gluttony**:
then a great *ransom* **koper/atonement**
cannot deliver **shall not spread to** thee.
19 *Will* **Shall** he *esteem* **appraise**
thy *riches* **opulence**?
no, not *gold* **mines**, nor all the forces of *strength* **force**.
20 *Desire* **Gulp** not the night,
when people *are cut off* **ascend** in their *place* **stead**.
21 *Take heed,* **On guard!** *regard*
face not *iniquity* **mischief**:
for this hast thou chosen

rather than *affliction* **humiliation.**
22 Behold, *God exalteth* **El**
lofteth by his *power* **force**:
who teacheth like him?
23 Who hath enjoined him his way?
or who can say,
Thou hast *wrought iniquity* **done wickedness**?
24 Remember that thou *magnify*
increase his *work* **deeds**,
which men behold.
25 *Every man* **All humanity** may see it;
man may *behold it* a**scan** far off.
26 Behold, *God* **El** is *great* **exceedingly excellent**,
and we know him not,
15 And now, because there is none,
he visits his wrath;
yet in mighty stupidity, he knows not:
16 and Iyob gasps his mouth in vain;
he weaves utterances without knowledge.

36 And Eli Hu also adds and says, Stay around;
and I show you
that I have yet utterances on behalf of Elohah.
3 I lift my knowledge from afar
and give justness to my Worker.
4 For truly my utterances *are* not false;
the integrious in knowledge *is* with you.
5 Behold, El *is* mighty and spurns not
—mighty in force and heart.
6 He enlivens not the wicked
and gives judgment to the humble;
7 he diminishes not his eyes from the just
and with sovereigns on the throne:
yes, he settles them in perpetuity
and they are lifted:
8 and if bound in bonds
and captured in cords of humiliation;
9 then he tells them their
deeds and their rebellions
because they prevail mightily:
10 and he exposes their ear to discipline
and says to them to return from mischief.
11 If they hearken and serve him,
they conclude their days in good
and their years in pleasures:
12 and if they hearken not,
they pass away expired by the spear,
and die without knowledge.
13 And the profaners in heart set wrath;
they cry not when he binds them:
14 their soul dies in ladhood
and their life *is* among the hallowed whoremongers.
15 He delivers the poor in their humiliation
and exposes their ears in oppression:
16 And he also removes you
from the mouth of the narrow into a broadness,
where there is no narrowness under;
and what rests on your table is full of fatness.
17 And you fulfill the plea of the wicked;
the plea and judgment are upheld:
18 because of fury,
lest he goad you with gluttony;
then a great koper/atonement spreads not to you.
19 Appraises he your opulence?
—your mines, your forces of force?
20 Gulp not the night,
when people ascend in their stead.
21 On guard! Face not mischief;
for you choose this, rather than humiliation.
22 Behold, El lofts by his force;
Who teaches as he?
23 Who visits him on his way?
or who says, You have done wickedness?
24 Remember to increase his deeds
for men to behold;
25 for all humanity to see;
for man to scan far off.
26 Behold, El is exceedingly excellent
and we know neither him,
neither can the number of his years
be *searched out* **probed**.
27 For he *maketh small*
diminisheth the drops of water:
they *pour down* **refine** rain
according to **into** the *vapour thereof* **mist**:
28 Which the *clouds do drop*
vapours flow and *distil* **drip**
upon *man* **humanity** abundantly.
29 Also can any *understand* **discern**
the spreadings of the **thick** clouds,
or the *noise* **clamorings**
of his *tabernacle* **sukkoth/brush arbor**?
30 Behold, he spreadeth his light upon it,
and covereth the *bottom* **roots** of the sea.
31 For by them *judgeth* **pleadeth** he
the cause of the people;
he giveth *meat* **food** in abundance.
32 With *clouds* **his two palms** he covereth the light;
and *commandeth* **misvaheth** it
not to shine by the cloud that cometh betwixt
and intercedeth.

33 The *noise thereof* **shouting**
sheweth **telleth** concerning *it* **him**,
the *cattle* **chattel** also *concerning*
and the *vapour* **holocaust**.

37 At this also my heart trembleth,
and is *moved* **loosed** out of his place.
2 **In hearing,**
Hear *attentively* the *noise* **commotion** of his voice,
and the *sound* **meditation** that goeth out of his mouth.
3 He *directeth* **releaseth** under
the whole *heaven* **heavens**,
and his lightning unto the *ends* **wings** of the earth.
4 After it a voice roareth:
he thundereth with the voice of *his excellency* **pomp**;
and he *will* **shall** not *stay* **restrain** them
when his voice is heard.
5 *God* **El** thundereth marvellously with his voice;
great *things doeth* **worketh** he,
which we *cannot comprehend* **perceive not**.
6 For he saith to the snow, Be thou on the earth;
likewise to the *small* **downpour of** rain,
and to the *great* **downpour of** rain of his strength.
7 He sealeth up the hand of
every man **all humanity**;
that all men may know his work.
8 Then the *beasts go into dens* **live beings lurk**,
and *remain* **tabernacle** in their *places* **habitations**.
9 Out of the *south* **chamber**
cometh the *whirlwind* **hurricane**: and
cold out of the *north* **scattering**.
10 By the breath of *God* **El** frost is given:
and the breadth of the waters is *straitened* **narrowed**.
11 Also by *watering* **showering**
he *wearieth* **overloadeth** the thick cloud: he
scattereth his *bright* **lightning** cloud:
12 And it is turned round about by his counsels:
that they may do
whatsoever he *commandeth* **misvaheth** them
upon the face of the world in the earth.
13 He causeth it to come,
whether for *correction* **a scion**, or
for his land, or for mercy.
14 Hearken unto this, O *Job* **Iyob**: stand *still*,
and *consider* **discern**
the *wondrous works* **marvels** of *God* **El**.
15 Dost thou know when *God*
disposed **Elohah set** them,
and caused the light of his cloud to shine?
16 Dost thou know the
balancings of the **thick** clouds,
the *wondrous works* **marvels** of him
which is *perfect* **integrious** in knowledge?
17 How thy *garments* **clothes** are *warm* **hot**,
when he *quieteth* **resteth** the earth
by the *south wind* **southerly**?
18 Hast thou with him
spread out **expanded** the *sky* **vapours**,
which is strong,
and as a *molten looking glass* **poured reflector**?
19 *Teach us* **Let us know** what
we shall say unto him;
for we cannot *order our speech* **line up**
by reason of **at the face of the** darkness.
20 Shall it be *told* **scribed** him that I *speak* **word**?

nor probe the number of his years:
27 for he diminishes the drops of water;
they refine rain into the mist;
28 which the vapours flow and drip abundantly
on humanity.
29 And discern you
the spreadings of the thick clouds?
or the clamorings of his sukkoth/brush arbor?
30 Behold, he spreads his light thereon
and covers the roots of the sea.
31 For by them he pleads the cause of the people;
he gives food in abundance;
32 with his two palms he covers the light
and misvahs and intercedes.
33 The shouting tells concerning him;
also the chattel and the holocaust.

37 Also, my heart trembles at this
—loosed from its place.
2 In hearing, hear the commotion of his voice
and the meditation coming from his mouth;
3 he releases under the whole heavens
and his lightning to the wings of the earth.
4 After, a voice roars;
he thunders his voice of pomp;
and he restrains not when his voice is heard.
5 El thunders marvellously with his voice;
he works great—and we perceive not.
6 For to the snow he says, Be on the earth;
likewise to the downpour of rain
and to the downpour of rain of his strength:
7 he seals the hand of all humanity
that all men know his work.
8 And the live beings lurk
and tabernacle in their habitations.
9 From the chamber comes the hurricane;
and cold from the scattering:

10 by the breath of El frost is given;
and the breadth of the waters narrows:
11 by showering, he overloads the thick cloud;
he scatters his lightning cloud:
12 and by his counsels, it turns around to do whatever
he misvahs them on the face of the world in the earth:
13 he causes it to come
whether for a scion, or for his land, or for mercy.
14 Hearken to this, O Iyob;
Stand and discern the marvels of El.
15 Know you when Elohah set them?
—and shined the light of his cloud?
16 Know you the balancings of the thick clouds?
The marvels of him who is integrious in knowledge?
17 How your clothes heat
when he rests the earth by the southerly?
18 Expand you the vapours with him
—strong as a poured reflector?
19 Know we what to say to him?
for we line not up at the face of the darkness.
20 Is it scribed to him that I word?
if a man *speak* **say**, surely he shall be swallowed *up*.
21 And now *men* **they** see not the bright light
which is in the *clouds* **vapours**:
but the wind passeth, and *cleanseth* **purifieth** them.
22 *Fair weather* **Clear sky** cometh out of the north:
with *God* **Elohah** is *terrible* **awesome** majesty.
23 *Touching the Almighty* **Shadday**,
we cannot find him out:
he is **exceedingly** excellent
in *power* **force**, and in judgment,
and *in plenty of justice* **abundant in justness**:
he *will* **shall** not *afflict* **humble**.
24 Men do therefore fear him:
he *respecteth* **seeth** not any that are wise of heart.

YAH VEH ANSWERS IYOB

38 Then *the LORD* **Yah Veh**
answered *Job* **Iyob** out of the *whirlwind* **storm**, and said,
2 Who is this that darkeneth counsel
by *words* **utterances** without knowledge?
3 Gird up *now* **I beseech,** thy
loins like a *man* **mighty**;
for I *will demand* **shall ask** of thee,
and *answer thou me* **let me know**.
4 Where wast thou
when I *laid the foundations of* **founded** the earth?
declare **tell**,
if thou *hast understanding* **knowest discernment**.
5 Who *hath laid* **set** the *measures*
measurements *thereof*,
if thou knowest?
or who hath stretched the line upon it?
6 Whereupon are the foundations
thereof fastened **sunk**?
or who *laid* **poured** the corner stone *thereof*;
7 When the morning stars *sang* **shouted** together,
and all the sons of *God* **Elohim** shouted *for joy*?
8 Or who *shut up* **hedged in** the sea with doors,
when it *brake forth* **gushed**,
as if it had **when it** issued out of the womb?
9 When I *made* **set** the cloud
the garment thereof **for a robe**,
and *thick* **dripping** darkness
a swaddling band for it **for a swathe**,
10 And brake up for it my *decreed place* **statute**,
and set bars and doors,
11 And said, Hitherto shalt thou come,
but *no further* **add not**:
and here shall *thy proud* **the pomp of thy** waves
be stayed **set**?
12 Hast thou *commanded* **misvahed** the morning
since thy days;
and caused the *dayspring* **dawn** to know his place;
13 That it might take hold of
the *ends* **wings** of the earth,
that the wicked might be shaken out of it?
14 It is turned as **a seal of** clay *to the seal*;
and they *stand* **set** as a *garment* **robe**.
15 And from the wicked their light is withholden,
and the *high* **lofted** arm shall be broken.
16 Hast thou entered
into the *springs* **fountains** of the sea?
or hast thou walked
in the search of **probing** the *depth* **abyss**?
17 Have the *gates* **portals** of death
been *opened* **exposed** unto thee?
or hast thou seen
the *doors* **portals** of the shadow of death?
18 Hast thou *perceived* **discerned**
the *breadth* **broadness** of the earth?
declare **tell** if thou knowest it all.
19 Where is the way where
light *dwelleth* **tabernacleth**?
and *as for* darkness, where is the place *thereof*,
20 That thou shouldest take it
to the *bound thereof* **border**,
and that thou shouldest *know* **discern** the paths
to the house *thereof*?
21 Knowest thou it, because
thou wast then *born* **birthed**?

or *because* the number of thy days is great?
22 Hast thou entered into the
treasures of the snow?
or hast thou seen the treasures of the hail,
23 Which I have *reserved* **spared**
against the time of *trouble* **tribulation,**
against the day of battle and war?
If a man says, surely he is swallowed.
21 And now they see not the bright light
in the vapours;
but the wind passes and purifies them:
22 clear sky comes from the north;
with Elohah is awesome majesty.
23 Shadday—we find him not out;
exceedingly excellent in force and in judgment
and abundant in justness:
he abases not.
24 So men fear him;
he sees not any wise of heart.

YAH VEH ANSWERS IYOB

38 And Yah Veh answers Iyob from the storm
and says,
2 Who is this who darkens counsel
by utterances without knowledge?
3 Gird up I beseech, your loins as a mighty;
for I ask of you—and you have me know.
4 Where were you when I founded the earth?
Tell, if you know discernment,
5 who set the measurements, if you know?
Who stretched the line thereon?
6 Whereon are the foundations sunk?
Who poured the corner stone
7 when the morning stars shouted together
and all the sons of Elohim shouted?
8 Who hedged in the sea with doors
when it gushed?
When it issued from the womb?
9 When I set the cloud for a robe
and dripping darkness for a swathe;
10 and broke it up for my statute
and set bars and doors;
11 and said, Come to here, but add not:
And set there the pomp of your waves?
12 Misvahed you the morning since your days?
And had the dawn to know his place?
13 And took hold of the wings of the earth
to shake the wicked therefrom?
14 It turns as a seal of clay;
and they set themselves as a robe;
15 and their light is withheld from the wicked
and the lofted arm broken.
16 Enter you the fountains of the sea?
Walk you probing the abyss?
17 Expose you the portals of death?
See you the portals of the shadow of death?
18 Discern you the broadness of the earth?
Tell, if you know it all.
19 Where *is* this, the way that light tabernacles?
And darkness, where *is* its place?
20 —to take it to the border
—to discern the paths to the house?
21 Know you, because you were then birthed?
—or that the number of your days greaten?
22 Enter you into the treasures of the snow?
See you the treasures of the hail
23 that I spare against the time of tribulation?
—against the day of battle and war?
24 *By what way* **Whence** is
the light *parted* **allotted,**
which scattereth the *east wind* **easterly** upon the earth?
25 Who hath divided a *watercourse* **channel**
for the overflowing of waters,
or a way for the lightning of *thunder* **voices**;
26 To cause it to rain on the
earth, where no man is;
on the wilderness, wherein there is no *man* **human**;
27 To satisfy the *desolate* **devastation**
and *waste ground* **ruin**;
and to cause the *bud* **source** of the *tender herb* **sprout**
to *spring forth* **sprout**?
28 Hath the rain a father?
or who hath *begotten* **birthed** the drops of dew?
29 Out of whose *womb* **belly** came the ice?
and the *hoary frost* **hoarfrost** of *heaven* **the heavens**,
who hath *gendered* **birthed** it?
30 The waters are hid as *with* a stone,
and the face of the *deep* **abyss** is *frozen* **captured**.
31 Canst thou bind
the *sweet influences* **bonds** of *Pleiades* **Kimah**,
or loose the *bands* **cords** of *Orion* **Kesil**?
32 Canst thou bring forth
Mazzaroth **the constellations**
in *his season* **their time**?
or canst thou *guide Arcturus* **lead Ash** with his sons?
33 Knowest thou
the *ordinances* **statutes** of *heaven* **the heavens**?
canst thou set the dominion *thereof* in the earth?
34 Canst thou lift up thy voice to the **thick** clouds,
that abundance of waters may cover thee?

35 Canst thou send lightnings,
that they may go and say unto thee, Here we are?
36 Who hath put wisdom in
the *inward parts* **reins?**
or who hath given *understanding* **discernment**
to the *heart* **observant?**
37 Who can *number* **scribe** the
clouds **vapours** in wisdom?
or who can *stay* **lay down**
the bottles of *heaven* **the heavens,**
38 When the dust *groweth*
firmeth into *hardness* **mire,**
and the clods *cleave fast together* **adhere?**
39 *Wilt* **Shalt** thou hunt the
prey for the **roaring** lion?
or fill the *appetite* **life** of the *young lions* **whelps,**
40 When they *couch* **prostrate**
in their *dens* **habitations,**
and *abide* **settle** in the *covert* **sukkoth/brush arbor**
to *lie in wait* **lurk?**
41 Who *provideth* **prepareth**
for the raven his *food* **hunt?**
when his *young ones* **children** cry unto *God* **El,**
they *wander for lack of meat* **stray without food.**

39 Knowest thou the time
when the wild goats of the rock *bring forth* **birth?**
or canst thou *mark* **guard**
when the hinds *do calve* **writhe?**
2 Canst thou *number* **scribe** the *months* **moons**
that they fulfil?
or knowest thou the time when they *bring forth* **birth?**
3 They *bow themselves* **kneel,**
they *bring forth* **adhere to** their *young ones* **children,**
they *cast out* **send** their *sorrows* **pangs.**
4 Their *young ones* **sons** are *in good liking* **plump,**
they *grow up* **abound** with *corn* **grain;**
they go forth, and return not unto them.
5 Who hath *sent out* **released** the *wild ass* **runner**
free **liberated?**
or who hath loosed the bands of the *wild ass* **onager?**
6 Whose house I have *made*
set the *wilderness* **plains,**
and the *barren* **salt** land his *dwellings* **tabernacles.**
7 He *scorneth* **ridiculeth** the multitude of the city,
neither *regardeth* **heareth** he
the *crying* **clamorings** of the *driver* **exactor.**
8 The *range* **gleanings** of the
mountains is his pasture,
and he searcheth after *every* **all the** green *thing.*
9 *Will* **Willeth** the *unicorn be willing* **reem**
to serve thee,
or *abide* **stay overnight** by thy *crib* **manger?**
10 Canst thou bind the *unicorn* **reem**
with his band in the furrow?
or *will* **shall** he harrow the valleys after thee?
11 *Wilt* **Shalt** thou *trust* **confide in** him,
because his *strength* **force** is great?
or *wilt* **shalt** thou leave thy labour to him?

24 Where is this—where light *is* allotted?
—which scatters the easterly on the earth?
25 Who divided
a channel for the overflowing of waters?
—a way for the lightning of voices?
26 —to rain on the earth, where no man *is*?
—on the wilderness, wherein no humanity *is*?
27 —to satisfy the devastation and ruin?
—to cause the source of the sprout to sprout?
28 Has the rain a father?
Who births the drops of dew?
29 From whose belly comes ice?
Who births the hoarfrost of the heavens?
30 The waters are hid as a stone
and the face of the abyss is captured.
31 Bind you the bonds of Kimah?
Loose you the cords of Kesil?
32 Bring you forth the constellations in their time?
—lead Ash with his sons?
33 Know you the statutes of the heavens?
Set you the dominion in the earth?
34 —lift your voice to the thick clouds
so that abundance of waters cover you?
35 —send lightnings to go to you,
and say, Here we are?
36 Who put wisdom in the reins?
Who gives discernment to the observant?
37 Who scribes the vapours in wisdom?
Who causes the bottles of the heavens to lie down
38 when the dust firms to
mire and the clods adhere?
39 —hunts the prey for the roaring lion?
—fills the life of the whelps
40 when they prostrate in their habitations,
and settle in the sukkoth/brush arbor to lurk?
41 Who prepares the hunt for the raven
—when his children cry to El?
—when they stray without food?

39 Know you the time of birthing
of the wild goats of the rock?
—observe the writhing of the hinds?
2 —scribe the moons that they fulfill?

—know the time they birth?
3 They kneel;
they adhere to their children;
they send their pangs;
4 their sons are plump;
they abound with grain;
they go forth never to return.
5 Who releases the runner liberated?
Who looses the bands of the onager?
6 —whose house I have set the plains
and the saltland his tabernacles.
7 He ridicules the multitude of the city;
he hears not the clamorings of the exactor;
8 the gleanings of the mountains is his pasture
and he searches after all the green.
9 The reem—wills he to serve you?
—to stay overnight by your manger?
10 —to bind the reem with his band in the furrow?
—to harrow the valleys after you?
11 —to confide in him because his force is great?
—to leave your labor to him?
12 *Wilt* **Shalt** thou *believe* **trust** him,
that he *will bring home* **shall return** thy seed,
and gather it into thy *barn* **threshingfloor**?
13 *Gavest thou the goodly wings* **Or pinions**
unto the peacocks **to leap for joy**?
or *wings and feathers* **plumage** unto the *ostrich* **stork**?
14 Which leaveth her eggs in the earth,
and *warmeth* **heateth** them in dust,
15 And forgetteth that the foot
may *crush* **squeeze** them,
or that the *wild beast* **field life** may *break* **trample** them.
16 She is hardened against her *young ones* **sons**,
as though they were not her's:
her labour is in vain without *fear* **dread**;
17 Because *God* **Elohah**
hath *deprived her of wisdom* **exacted wisdom of her**,
neither hath he *imparted* **allotted** to her
understanding **discernment**.
18 What time she *lifteth up herself* **flappeth**
on high **in the heights**,
she *scorneth* **ridiculeth** the horse and his rider.
19 Hast thou given the horse *strength* might?
hast thou *clothed* **enrobed** his neck with thunder?
20 Canst thou *make* **cause** him *afraid* **to quiver**
as a *grasshopper* **locust**?
the *glory* **majesty** of his nostrils is *terrible* **terror**.
21 He *paweth* **diggeth** in the valley,
and rejoiceth in his *strength* **force**:
he goeth on to *meet* **confront** the *armed men* **armour**.
22 He *mocketh at fear* **ridiculeth dread**,
and is not *affrighted* **dismayed**;
neither turneth he back from **the face of** the sword.
23 The quiver *rattleth* **whizzeth** against him,
the *glittering* **flaming** spear and the *shield* **dart**.
24 He swalloweth the *ground* **earth**
with *fierceness* **quaking** and *rage* **commotion**:
neither *believeth* **trusteth** he
that it is the *sound* **voice** of the *trumpet* **shophar**.
25 He saith among the *trumpets*
shophars, *Ha, ha* **Aha**;
and he *smelleth* **scenteth** the *battle* **war** afar off,
the thunder of the *captains* **governors**, and the shouting.
26 *Doth* **Soareth** the hawk *fly*
by thy *wisdom* **discernment**,
and *stretch* **spread** her wings toward the south?
27 *Doth* **Goeth** the eagle
mount up at thy *command* **mouth**,
and make her nest on high?
28 She *dwelleth* **tabernacleth**
and *abideth* **stayeth overnight** on the rock,
upon the crag of the rock,
and the *strong place* **hunthold**.
29 From thence she *seeketh the*
prey **exploreth for food**,
and her eyes *behold* **scan** afar off.
30 Her *young ones also* **chicks** suck up blood:
and where the *slain* **pierced** are, there is she.

40 Moreover
the LORD **Yah Veh** answered *Job* **Iyob**, and said,
2 Shall he that contendeth
with *the Almighty* **Shadday**
instruct **reprove** him?
he that reproveth *God* **Elohah**, let him answer it.

IYOB ANSWERS YAH VEH

3 Then *Job* **Iyob** answered *the*
LORD **Yah Veh**, and said,
4 Behold, I am *vile* **abased**;
what shall I *answer* **respond to** thee?
I *will lay mine* **shall set my** hand *upon* **unto** my mouth.
5 Once have I *spoken* **worded**;
but I *will* **shall** not answer:
yea, twice; but *I will proceed no further* **not again**.

YAH VEH ANSWERS IYOB

6 Then answered *the LORD*
Yah Veh unto *Job* **Iyob**
out of the *whirlwind* **storm**, and said,
7 Gird up thy loins *now* **I**
beseech, like a *man* **mighty**:

I *will demand* **shall ask** of thee,
and *declare thou unto me* **let me know**.
8 *Wilt* **Shalt** thou *also disannul*
break my judgment?
wilt **shalt** thou *condemn* **judge** me **wicked**,
that thou mayest be *righteous* **justified**?
9 Hast thou an arm like *God* **El**?
or *canst* shalt thou thunder with a voice like him?
12 —to trust him to return your seed?
—to gather it into your threshingfloor?
13 Or pinions to leap for joy?
Or plumage to the stork?
14 —who leaves her eggs in the earth
and heats them in dust;
15 and forgets that the foot may squeeze them;
or that the field life may trample them.
16 She hardens her sons
as though they *are* not hers;
her labor is in vain without dread:
17 for Elohah exacts wisdom from her;
he allots her no discernment;
18 at the time she flaps in the heights
she ridicules the horse and his rider.
19 Give you the horse might?
—enrobe his neck with thunder?
20 —quiver him as a locust?
The majesty of his nostrils is terror.
21 He digs in the valley and rejoices in his force;
he goes on to confront the armour.
22 He ridicules dread and is not dismayed;
he turns not back from the face of the sword;
23 the quiver whizzes against him
—the flaming spear and the dart:
24 he swallows the earth
with quaking and commotion;
he trusts not the voice of the shophar.
25 He says among the shophars, Aha!
And he scents the war afar off
—the thunder of the governors and the shouting.
26 Soars the hawk by your discernment?
—spreads her wings toward the south?
27 Comes the eagle at your mouth
and makes her nest on high?
28 She tabernacles and stays overnight on the rock
—on the crag of the rock and the hunthold;
29 from thence she explores for food;
her eyes scan afar off;
30 her chicks suck blood;
and where the pierced *are*, there she *is*.

40 Yah Veh answers Iyob and says,
2 Contends the reprover with Shadday?
Whoever reproves Elohah, answer!

Iyob Answers Yah Veh

3 And Iyob answers Yah Veh and says,
4 Behold, I am abased;
What respond I to you?
I set my hand to my mouth.
5 I worded once; but I answer not:
yes, twice; but not again.

Yah Veh Answers Iyob

6 And Yah Veh answers Iyob from the storm
and says,
7 Gird your loins, I beseech, as a mighty;
I ask of you; and have me know.
8 Break you my judgment?
Judge you me wicked to justify yourself?
9 Have you an arm like El?
Thunder with a voice like him?
10 *Deck* **Adorn** thyself *now* **I beseech,**
with *majesty* **pomp** and *excellency* **loftiness**;
and *array* **enrobe** thyself
with *glory* **majesty** and *beauty* **honour**.
11 *Cast abroad* **Scatter** the *rage* **fury** of thy wrath:
and *behold* **see** every one that is *proud* **pompous**,
and abase him.
12 *Look on* **See** every one that is *proud* **pompous**,
and *bring him low* **subdue him**;
and *tread down* **trample** the wicked in their place.
13 Hide them in the dust together;
and bind their faces in *secret* **hiding**.
14 Then *will* **shall** I also confess unto thee
that thine own right *hand can* **shall** save thee.
15 Behold *now* **I beseech,**
behemoth, which I *made* **worked** with thee;
he eateth grass as an ox.
16 *Lo now* **Behold I beseech,**
his *strength* **force** is in his loins,
and his *force* **strength** is in the navel of his belly.
17 He *moveth* **bendeth** his tail like a cedar:
the sinews of his *stones* **testis**
are *wrapped together* **entwined**.
18 His bones
are as *strong pieces* **gatherings** of *brass* **copper**;
his bones
are like bars **as forgings** of iron.
19 He is the *chief* **beginning** of the ways of *God* **El**:
he that made him can make his
sword to approach unto him

his Worker approacheth with his sword.
20 Surely the mountains
bring **bear** him *forth food* **produce,**
where all the *beasts* **live beings** of the field *play* **laugh.**
21 He lieth under the *shady trees* **lotuses,**
in the covert of the *reed* **stalk,** and *fens* **mire.**
22 The *shady trees* **lotuses** cover
him with their shadow;
the willows of the *brook* **wadi**
compass **surround** him *about.*
23 Behold, he drinketh up a river, and hasteth not:
he *trusteth* **is confident**
that he can *draw up Jordan* **gush Yarden** into his mouth.
24 He taketh it with his eyes:
his *nose pierceth* **nostrils pierce** through snares.

41 Canst thou draw out leviathan with an hook?
or **drown** his tongue with a cord
which thou lettest down?
2 Canst thou *put an hook* **set**
a rush into his *nose* **nostrils**?
or bore his jaw through with a thorn?
3 *Will* **Shall** he *make many* **abound**
with supplications unto thee?
will **shall** he *speak soft words* **word tenderly** unto thee?
4 *Will* **Shall** he *make* **cut** a covenant with thee?
wilt **shalt** thou take him for a servant *for ever* **eternally**?
5 *Wilt* **Shalt** thou *play* **laugh**
with him as with a bird?
or *wilt* **shalt** thou bind him for thy *maidens* **lasses**?
6 Shall *the* **his** companions
make a banquet of **market** him?
shall they *part* **halve** him among the merchants?
7 *Canst thou fill* **Fillest thou** his skin
with *barbed irons* **barbs**?
or his head with fish *spears* **harpoons**?
8 *Lay thine hand* **Set thy palm** upon him,
remember the *battle* **war,** *do no more* **add not.**
9 Behold, the hope of him *is in vain* **lieth:**
shall not one be cast down
even at the *sight* **visage** of him?
10 None is so fierce that *dare*
stir **they waken** him *up*:
who then *is able to stand before me* **setteth at my face**?
11 Who *hath prevented* **anticipateth** me,
that I should *repay* **shalam** him?
whatsoever is under the whole *heaven* **heavens** is mine.
12 I *will* **shall** not *conceal*
hush as to his *parts* **veins,**
nor **the word of** his *power* might,
nor **the beauty of** his *comely* proportion.
13 Who *can discover* **exposeth**
the face of his *garment* **robe**?
or who *can come* **cometh** to him with his double bridle?
14 Who *can open* **openeth** the doors of his face?
his teeth are *terrible* **a terror** round about.
15 His *scales* **strong shields** are his *pride* **pomp,**
shut up *together as with a close* **as a constricted** seal.

10 I beseech,
adorn yourself with pomp and loftiness;
enrobe yourself with majesty and honor;
11 scatter the fury of your wrath;
see everyone who is pompous and abase him;
12 see everyone who is pompous and subdue him;
and trample the wicked in their place:
13 hide them in the dust together
and bind their faces in hiding.
14 And I—I also confess to you
that your own right saves thee.
15 Behold, I beseech,
behemoth, whom I worked with you
—who eats grass as an ox.
16 Behold, I beseech,
his force in his loins
and his strength in the navel of his belly.
17 He bends his tail as a cedar;
the sinews of his testis entwine:
18 his bones—as gatherings of copper;
his bones—as forgings of iron:
19 he is the beginning of the ways of El;
his Worker approaches with his sword:
20 surely the mountains bear him produce
where all the live beings of the field laugh.
21 He lies under the lotuses,
in the covert of the stalk and mire;
22 the lotuses cover him with their shadow;
the willows of the wadi surround him:
23 behold, he drinks a river; he hastens not;
—confident that he can gush Yarden in his mouth:
24 he takes it with his eyes;
his nostrils pierce through snares.

41 You—draw you leviathan with a hook?
Drown his tongue with a cord?
2 Set a rush into his nostrils?
Bore his jaw through with a thorn?
3 Abounds he with supplications to you?
Words he tenderly to you?
4 Cuts he a covenant with you?
You—take you him for a servant eternally?
5 Laugh with him as with a bird?
Bind him for your lasses?

6 *Do* his companions market him?
—halve him among the merchants?
7 —fill his skin with barbs?
or his head with fish harpoons?
8 Set your palm on him;
remember the war; add not.
9 Behold, his hope lies.
Is no one cast down at his visage?
10 None is so fierce that he wakens him.
Who then sets at my face?
11 Who anticipates me, that I shalam him?
whatever is under the whole heavens is mine.
12 I neither hush as to his veins,
nor to the word of his might,
nor to the beauty of his proportion.
13 Who exposes the face of his robe?
Who comes to him with his double bridle?
14 Who opens the doors of his face?
His teeth are a terror all around;
15 his strong shields are his pomp
—shut up as a constricted seal.
16 One *is so near to another* **approacheth one,**
that no *air can come* **wind/spirit cometh** between them.
17 They *are joined one* **adhere**
man to *another* **brother,**
they stick together,
that they *cannot be sundered* **be not separated.**
18 By his *neesings* **sneezings**
a light *doth shine* **halaleth,**
and his eyes are like the eyelids of the *morning* **dawn.**
19 Out of his mouth go *burning lamps* **flambeaus,**
and sparks of fire *leap out* **escape.**
20 Out of his nostrils goeth smoke,
as out of a *seething pot* **pressure cooker** or *caldron* **rush.**
21 His *breath kindleth* **soul inflameth** coals,
and a flame goeth out of his mouth.
22 In his neck *remaineth* **stayeth** strength,
and *sorrow is turned into joy before him*
languish leapeth at his face.
23 The flakes of his flesh *are*
joined together **adhere:**
they are firm **firmed** in themselves;
they *cannot be moved* **totter not.**
24 His heart is *as firm* **firmed** as a stone; yea,
as hard **firmed** as a *piece* **slice** of the nether *millstone.*
25 *When he raiseth up himself* **He swells,**
the mighty *are afraid* **dodge him:**
by reason of breakings they purify themselves.
26 The sword of him that *layeth at* **overtaketh** him
cannot hold **riseth not:**
the spear, the *dart* **arrow,** nor the habergeon.
27 He *esteemeth* **fabricateth** iron as straw,
and *brass* **copper** as rotten *wood* **timber.**
28 The *arrow* **son of the bow**
cannot make him flee:
slingstones are turned with him into stubble.
29 *Darts* **Clubs** are *counted* **fabricated** as stubble:
he laugheth at the *shaking* **quaking** of a *spear* **dart.**
30 *Sharp stones* **Pieces of potsherd** are under him:
he spreadeth *sharp pointed things* **ore** upon the mire.
31 He *maketh* **setteth** the deep
to boil like a *pot* **caldron:**
he maketh the sea like a *pot of ointment* **spicy broth.**
32 He maketh a path to *shine* **enlighten** after him;
one would think **he fabricateth** the *deep* **abyss**
to be *hoary* **greyed.**
33 Upon *earth* **dust** there is not his like,
who is *made* **worked** without *fear* **terror.**
34 He *beholdeth* **seeth** all *high things* **the heights:**
he is *a king* **sovereign**
over all the *children* **sons** of pride.

IYOB ANSWERS YAH VEH

42 Then *Job* **Iyob** answered *the LORD* **Yah Veh,**
and said,
2 I know that thou *canst do*
every thing **art able in all,**
and that no *thought* **intrigue**
can be withholden **shall be cut off** from thee.
3 Who is he that *hideth* **concealeth** counsel
without knowledge?
therefore have I *uttered* **told**
that I *understood* **discerned** not;
things too *wonderful* **marvellous** for me,
which I knew not.
4 Hear, I beseech thee, and
I *will speak* **shall word:**
I *will demand* **shall ask** of thee,
and *declare thou unto me* **let me know.**
5 I have heard of thee by the hearing of the ear:
but now mine eye *seeth* **hath seen** thee.
6 Wherefore I *abhor myself* **spurn,**
and *repent* **sigh** in dust and ashes.

YAH VEH ANSWERS ELI PHAZ

7 And **so be** it *was so,*
that after *the LORD* **Yah Veh**
had *spoken* **worded** these words unto *Job* **Iyob,**
the LORD **Yah Veh**

said to *Eliphaz* **Eli Phaz** the *Temanite* **Temaniy**,
My wrath is kindled against thee,
and against thy two friends:
for ye have not *spoken* **worded** of me
the thing that *is right* **which be established**,
as my servant *Job hath* **Iyob**.
8 Therefore take unto you now
seven bullocks and seven rams,
and go to my servant *Job* **Iyob**,
16 One approaches one
so that no wind/spirit comes between them;
17 they adhere man to brother;
they stick together—not to be separated.
18 By his sneezings a light halals
and his eyes are as the eyelids of the dawn;
19 from his mouth go flambeaus
and sparks of fire escape;
20 from his nostrils comes smoke
as from a pressure cooker or rush;
21 his soul inflames coals
and a flame comes from his mouth;
22 strength stays in his neck
and languish leaps at his face;
23 the flakes of his flesh adhere
—firmed in themselves not to totter;
24 his heart *is* firmed as a stone;
yes, firmed as a slice of the nether.
25 He swells; the mighty dodge him;
they purify themselves from breakings;
26 the sword of him who overtakes
raises neither the spear, the arrow,
nor the habergeon.
27 He fabricates iron as straw
and copper as rotten timber;
28 he flees not the son of the bow;
he turns slingstones into stubble;
29 he fabricates clubs as stubble;
he laughs at the quaking of a dart;
30 pieces of potsherd are under him;
he spreads ore on the mire;
31 he sets the deep to boil as a caldron;
he makes the sea as a spicy broth;
32 he makes a path to enlighten after him;
he fabricates the abyss to be greyed.
33 On the dust there is none like him
who is worked without terror;
34 he sees all the heights;
he is sovereign over all the sons of pride.

Iyob Answers Yah Veh

42 Iyob answers Yah Veh and says,
2 I know that you are able in all;
and that no intrigue is cut off from you.
3 Who is he
who conceals counsel without knowledge?
so I tell, and I discern not
—too marvellous for me, and I know not.
4 Hear, I beseech you, and I word;
I ask you; you have me know.
5 I hear you by the hearing of the ear;
and now my eye sees you:
6 so I spurn and sigh in dust and ashes.

Yah Veh Answers Eli Phaz

7 And so be it,
after Yah Veh words these words to Iyob,
Yah Veh says to Eli Phaz the Temaniy,
I kindle my wrath against you
and against your two friends;
for you word not of me what is established
—as my servant Iyob.
8 And now,
take seven bullocks and seven rams
and go to my servant Iyob
and *offer up* **holocaust** for yourselves
a *burnt offering* **holocaust**;
and my servant *Job* **Iyob** shall pray for you:
for him *will I accept* **shall I lift from his face**:
lest I deal **so as not to work** with you *after your* folly,
in that ye have not *spoken* **worded** of me
the thing **that** which is *right* **established**,
like my servant *Job* **Iyob**.
9 So *Eliphaz* **Eli Phaz** the *Temanite* **Temaniy**
and Bildad the *Shuhite* **Shuachiy**
and *Zophar* **Sophar** the *Naamathite* **Naamahiy** went,
and *did* **worked** according
as *the LORD commanded* **Yah Veh worded** them:
the LORD **Yah Veh**
also accepted Job **lifted the face of Iyob**.

Yah Veh Doubles The Substance Of Iyob

10 And *the LORD* **Yah Veh**
turned the captivity of *Job* **Iyob**,
when he prayed for his friends:
also *the LORD gave Job* **Yah Veh added to Iyob**
twice as much as he had *before* **faced**.
11 Then came there unto him all his brethren,
and all his sisters,

and all they
that had *been of his acquaintance* **known his face**,
and did eat bread with him in his house:
and they *bemoaned* **wagged with** him,
and *comforted* **sighed over** him
over all the evil
that *the LORD* **Yah Veh** had brought upon him:
every man also gave him *a piece of money* **one ingot**,
and every *one an earring* **man one nosering** of gold.
12 So *the LORD* **Yah Veh**
blessed the *latter end* **finality** of *Job* **Iyob**
more than his beginning:
for he had fourteen thousand *sheep* **flocks**,
and six thousand camels,
and a thousand yoke of oxen,
and a thousand she *asses* **burros**.
13 He had also seven sons and three daughters.
14 And he called the name of
the first, *Jemima* **Yemima**;
and the name of the second, Kezia;
and the name of the third, *Kerenhappuch*
Qeren Hap Puch.
15 And in all the land
were no women found so *fair* **beautiful**
as the daughters of *Job* **Iyob**:
and their father gave them inheritance
among their brethren.
16 After this lived *Job* **Iyob** an
hundred and forty years,
and saw his sons, and his sons' sons,
even four generations.
17 So *Job* **Iyob** died,
being *old* **aged** and *full* **satisfied** of days.
and holocaust yourselves a holocaust;
and my servant Iyob prays for you;
as for him, I lift from his face;
so as not to work folly with you
—in that you word not of me what is established,
as my servant Iyob.
9 And Eli Phaz the Temaniy
and Bildad the Shuachiy
and Sophar the Naamahiy
go and work according as Yah Veh words them;
and Yah Veh lifts the face of Iyob.

YAH VEH DOUBLES THE SUBSTANCE OF IYOB

10 And Yah Veh turns the captivity of Iyob,
in praying for his friends;
and Yah Veh adds to Iyob
twice as much as he had faced.

11 Then all his brothers and all his sisters
and all who knew his face
come to him
and eat bread with him in his house;
and they wag with him and sigh over him
—over all the evil Yah Veh brought on him;
and every man gives him one ingot
and every man one nosering of gold.
12 And Yah Veh blesses the finality of Iyob
more than his beginning;
for he has fourteen thousand flocks
and six thousand camels
and a thousand yoke of oxen
and a thousand she burros:
13 and he has seven sons and three daughters.
14 And he called the name of the first, Yemima;
and the name of the second, Kezia;
and the name of the third, Qeren Hap Puch.
15 And in all the land
they find no women
as beautiful as the daughters of Iyob;
and their father gives them inheritance
among their brothers.
16 After this Iyob lives a hundred and forty years
and sees his sons and the sons of his sons
—four generations.
17 And Iyob dies—aged and satisfied of days.

Book I

1 *Blessed* **Blithe** *is* the man
that walketh not in the counsel of the *ungodly* **wicked**,
nor standeth in the way of sinners,
nor *sitteth* **settleth** in the *seat* **settlement** of the scornful.
2 But his delight is in the *law*
torah of *the LORD* **Yah Veh**;
and in his *law* **torah** doth he meditate day and night.
3 And he shall be like a tree
planted **transplanted** by the *rivers* **rivulets** of water,
that *bringeth forth* **giveth** his fruit in his *season* **time**;
his leaf also shall not wither;
and whatsoever he *doeth* **worketh** shall prosper.
4 The *ungodly* **wicked** are not so:
but are like the chaff
which the wind *driveth away* **disperseth**.
5 Therefore the *ungodly* **wicked**
shall not *stand* **rise** in the judgment,
nor sinners
in the *congregation* **witness** of the *righteous* **just**.
6 For *the LORD* **Yah Veh**
knoweth the way of the *righteous* **just**:
but the way of the *ungodly* **wicked** shall *perish* **destruct**.

2 Why do the *heathen rage* **goyim conspire**,
and the *people* **nations**
imagine a vain thing **meditate vanity**?
2 The *kings* **sovereigns** of the earth
set **station** themselves,
and the *rulers take* **potentates set** counsel together,
against *the LORD* **Yah Veh**,
and against his anointed, *saying*,
3 Let us *break* **tear** their bands *asunder*,
and cast *away* their *cords* **ropes** from us.
4 He that *sitteth* **settleth** in
the heavens shall laugh:
the Lord **Adonay** shall *have* **deride** them *in derision*.
5 Then shall he *speak* **word**
unto them in his wrath,
and *vex* **terrify** them in his *sore displeasure* **fuming**.
6 Yet have I *set* **anointed** my *king* **sovereign**
upon my holy *hill of Zion* **mount Siyon**.
7 I *will declare* **shall scribe** the *decree* **statute**:
the LORD **Yah Veh** hath said unto me,
Thou art my *Son* **Ben***; this day have
I *begotten* **birthed** thee.

*Ben: cp 2:12

8 Ask of me,
and I shall give thee the *heathen* **goyim**
for thine inheritance,
and the *uttermost parts* **finalities** of the earth
for thy possession.
9 Thou shalt *break* **shatter**
them with a *rod* **scion** of iron;
thou shalt *dash* **splatter** them *in pieces*
like a potter's vessel **as a formed instrument**.
10 *Be wise* **Comprehend** now therefore,
O ye *kings* **sovereigns**:
be *instructed* **disciplined**, ye judges of the earth.
11 Serve *the LORD* **Yah Veh** with *fear* **awe**,
and *rejoice* **twirl** with trembling.
12 Kiss the *Son* **Bar***, lest he be angry,
and ye *perish* **destruct** from the way,
when his wrath *is kindled* **burneth** but a little.
Blessed **Blithe** *are* all they
that *put their trust* **seek refuge** in him.

*Bar: cp 2:7

3 A Psalm of David,
when he fled from *Absalom* **the face
of Abi Shalom** his son.
1 *LORD* **Yah Veh**,
how are they increased that trouble me
how my tribulators abound by the myriads!
many are they that rise *up* against me.
2 Many there be which say of my soul,
There is no *help* **salvation** for him in *God* **Elohim**.
Selah.
3 But thou, O *LORD* **Yah Veh**,
art a *shield* **buckler** for me;
my *glory* **honour**, and the lifter *up* of mine head.
4 I *cried* **called** unto *the LORD*
Yah Veh with my voice,
and he *heard* **answered** me out of his holy *hill* **mountain**.
Selah.
5 I laid me down and slept; I awaked;
for *the LORD* **Yah Veh** sustained me.

Book I

1 Blithe—the man
who neither walks in the counsel of the wicked,
nor stands in the way of sinners,
nor settles in the settlement of the scornful.
2 But his delight *is* in the torah of Yah Veh;
and in his torah he meditates day and night;
3 and being as a tree
transplanted by the rivulets of water,
giving his fruit in his time:
his leaf withers not;
and whatever he works, prospers.

4 Not so the wicked;
but *are* as chaff which the wind disperses.
5 So, neither the wicked rise in the judgment,
nor sinners in the witness of the just.
6 For Yah Veh knows the way of the just;
and the way of the wicked destructs.

2 Why *do* the goyim conspire
and the nations meditate vanity?
2 The sovereigns of the earth station themselves
and the potentates set counsel together
against Yah Veh and against his anointed.
3 Tear their bands
and cast their ropes from us.
4 He who settles in the heavens laughs;
Adonay derides them;
5 then he words to them in his wrath
and terrifies them in his fuming.
6 And I—I anointed my sovereign
on my holy mount Siyon;
7 I scribe the statute!
Yah Veh says to me,
You are my Son/Ben*; this day I birthed you.

*Ben; cp 2:12

8 Ask of me;
and I give you the goyim for your inheritance
and the finalities of the earth for your possession.
9 You, shatter them with a scion of iron;
splatter them as a formed instrument.
10 And now, O you sovereigns, comprehend;
be disciplined, you judges of the earth.
11 Serve Yah Veh with awe
and twirl with trembling;
12 kiss the Son/Bar*, lest he be angry
and you destruct from the way
—when his wrath burns but a little.
Blithe—all who seek refuge in him.

*Bar: cp 2:7

3 A Psalm by David;
as he flees from the face of Abi Shalom his son.
1 Yah Veh,
how my tribulators abound by the myriads!
Many rise against me;
2 many say of my soul,
There is no salvation for him in Elohim.
Selah.
3 And you, O Yah Veh, my buckler,
my honor and the lifter of my head.
4 I call to Yah Veh with my voice,
and he answers me from his holy mountain.
Selah.
5 I lie down and sleep; I waken;
for Yah Veh sustains me.
6 I *will* **shall** not *be afraid* **awe**
of ten thousands **myriads** of people,
that have set *themselves* against me round about.
7 Arise, O *LORD* **Yah Veh**;
save me, O my *God* **Elohim**:
for thou hast smitten all mine enemies
upon the cheek bone;
thou hast broken the teeth of the *ungodly* **wicked**.
8 Salvation *belongeth* unto *the LORD* **Yah Veh**:
thy blessing is upon thy people.
Selah.

4 To *the chief Musician* **His Eminence**,
on *Neginoth* **Strummer**,
A Psalm of David.
1 *Hear* **Answer** me when I call,
O *God* **Elohim** of my *righteousness* **justness**:
thou hast enlarged me
when I was in *distress* **tribulation**;
have mercy upon me **grant me charism**,
and hear my prayer.
2 O ye sons of men,
how long *will ye turn my glory* **shall my honour**
into **be for** shame?
how long will—**shall** ye love vanity,
and seek after *leasing* **lies**?
Selah.
3 But know that *the LORD* **Yah Veh** hath set apart
him that is *godly* **mercied** for himself:
the LORD will **Yah Veh shall** hear when I call unto him.
4 *Stand in awe* **Quiver** and sin not:
commune **say** with your own heart upon your bed,
and be still.
Selah.
5 *Offer* **Sacrifice** the sacrifices
of *righteousness* **justness**,
and *put your trust* **confide** in *the LORD* **Yah Veh**.
6 There be many that say,
Who *will shew us any* **shall let us see** good?
LORD **O Yah Veh**,
lift thou up the light of thy *countenance* **face** upon us.
7 Thou hast *put gladness* **given**
cheerfulness in my heart,
more than in the time
that their *corn* **crop** and their *wine* **juice**
increased **abounded by the myriads**.
8 I *will both* **shall altogether**
lay me down in *peace* **shalom**, and sleep:

for thou, *LORD* **O Yah Veh**, only
makest me dwell in safety **settlest me confidently**.

5 To *the chief Musician* **His Eminence,**
upon *Nehiloth* **Flute**,
A Psalm of David.
1 *Give ear* **Hearken** to my *words* **sayings**,
O *LORD* **Yah Veh**,
consider **discern** my meditation.
2 Hearken unto the voice of my cry,
my *King* **Sovereign**, and my *God* **Elohim**:
for unto thee *will* **shall** I pray.
3 My voice shalt thou hear in the morning,
O *LORD* **Yah Veh**;
in the morning
will I direct my prayer **shall I arrange** unto thee,
and *will look up* **shall watch**.
4 For thou art not *a God* **an El**
that *hath pleasure* **delighteth** in wickedness:
neither shall evil *dwell* **sojourn** with thee.
5 *The foolish* **They that halal**
shall not *stand* **settle** in *thy sight* **thine eyes**:
thou hatest all *workers of iniquity* **working mischief**.
6 Thou shalt destroy them
that *speak leasing* **word lies**:
the LORD will **Yah Veh shall** abhor
the *bloody* **man of bloods** and *deceitful man* **deceit**.
7 But as for me, I *will* **shall** come into thy house
in the *multitude* **abundance** of thy mercy:
and in thy *fear will* **awe shall** I *worship* **prostrate**
toward thy holy *temple* **manse**.
8 Lead me, O *LORD* **Yah Veh**,
in thy *righteousness* **justness**
because of mine *enemies* **opponents**;
make **straighten** thy way *straight before* **at** my face.

6 I awe not myriads of people,
who set against me all around.
7 Rise, O Yah Veh! Save me, O my Elohim!
For you have smitten all my enemies
on the cheek bone;
you broke the teeth of the wicked.
8 Salvation to Yah Veh;
your blessing *is* on your people.
Selah.

4 To His Eminence; On Strummer;
A Psalm by David.
1 Answer me when I call,
O Elohim of my justness;
in my tribulation you enlarged me;
grant me charism and hear my prayer.
2 O you sons of men,
until when *is* my honor for shame
—you who love vanity and seek after lies?
Selah.
3 And know that Yah Veh set apart
the mercied for himself;
Yah Veh hears when I call to him.
4 Quiver and sin not;
say with your own heart on your bed
and be still.
Selah.
5 Sacrifice the sacrifices of justness;
confide in Yah Veh.
6 Many say, Who has us see good?
O Yah Veh, lift the light of your face on us.
7 You gave cheerfulness in my heart,
from the time their crop and their juice
abounded by the myriads.
8 I altogether lie down in shalom and sleep;
for you only, O Yah Veh, settle me confidently.

5 To His Eminence; On Flute;
A Psalm by David.
1 Hear my sayings, O Yah Veh;
discern my meditation:
2 hearken to the voice of my cry,
my Sovereign and my Elohim;
for I pray to you.
3 Hear my voice in the morning, O Yah Veh;
in the morning I arrange to you and watch.
4 For you *are* an El
who neither delights in wickedness;
nor sojourns with evil.
5 They who halal settle not at your eyes;
you hate all who work mischief:
6 you destroy them who word lies;
Yah Veh abhors the man of bloods and deceit.
7 And as for me,
I come into your house
in the abundance of your mercy;
and in your awe
I prostrate toward your holy manse.
8 O Yah Veh, Lead me in your justness
because of my opponents;
straighten your way at my face:
9 For there is *no faithfulness* **naught established**
in their mouth;
their *inward part is very wickedness*
inwards are calamities;
their throat is an open *sepulchre* **tomb**;
they *flatter* **smooth over** with their tongue.

10 *Destroy thou them* **They**
have guilted, O *God* **Elohim**;
let them fall by their own counsels;
cast **drive** them out in the *multitude* **abundance**
of their *transgressions* **rebellions**;
for they have rebelled against thee.
11 But let all those that *put their*
trust **seek refuge** in thee
rejoice **cheer**:
let them *ever* **eternally** shout *for joy*,
because thou *defendest* **coverest** them **over**:
let them also that love thy name
be joyful **jump for joy** in thee.
12 For thou, *LORD* **O Yah Veh**,
wilt **shalt** bless the *righteous* **just**;
with *favour* **pleasure**
wilt **shalt** thou *compass* **surround** him as *with* a shield.

6 To *the chief Musician* **His Eminence**,
on *Neginoth* **Strummer** upon *Sheminith* **Octave**,
A Psalm of David.
1 O *LORD* **Yah Veh**,
rebuke **reprove** me not in *thine anger* **thy wrath**,
neither *chasten* **discipline** me in thy *hot displeasure* **fury**.
2 *Have mercy upon me* **Grant me charism**,
O *LORD* **Yah Veh**;
for I *am weak* **languish**:
O *LORD* **Yah Veh**, heal me;
for my bones are *vexed* **terrified**.
3 My soul is also *sore vexed* **mighty terrified**:
but thou, O *LORD* **Yah Veh**, how long?
4 Return, O *LORD* **Yah Veh**,
deliver **rescue** my soul:
oh save me for thy mercies' sake.
5 For in death
there is no *remembrance* **memorial** of thee:
in *the grave* **sheol**
who shall *give* **spread** thee *thanks* **hands**?
6 I am *weary* **belaboured**
with my *groaning* **sighing**;
all the night make I my bed to swim;
I *water* **flow** my *couch* **bedstead** with my tears.
7 Mine eye is *consumed* **motheaten**
because of grief **in vexation**;
it *waxeth old* **antiquateth**
because of all *mine enemies* **my tribulators**.
8 *Depart* **Turn** from me,
all ye *workers of iniquity* **working mischief**;
for *the LORD* **Yah Veh**
hath heard the voice of my weeping.
9 *The LORD* **Yah Veh** hath heard my supplication;
the LORD will receive **Yah Veh shall take** my prayer.
10 Let all mine enemies *be ashamed* **shame**
and *sore vexed* **terrify mightily**:
let them return
and *be ashamed suddenly* **shame in a blink**.

7 *Shiggaion* **Lyric Poem** of David,
which he sang unto *the LORD* **Yah Veh**,
concerning the words of *Cush* **Kush**
the *Benjamite* **Ben Yaminiy**.
1 O *LORD* **Yah Veh** my *God* **Elohim**,
in thee *do I put my trust* **seek I refuge**:
save me from all them that *persecute* **pursue** me,
and *deliver* **rescue** me:
2 Lest he tear my soul like a lion,
rending **craunching** it *in pieces*,
while there is none to *deliver* **rescue**.
3 O *LORD* **Yah Veh** my *God* **Elohim**,
If I have *done* **worked** this;
if there be *iniquity* **wickedness** in my *hands* **palms**;
4 If I have *rewarded* **dealt** evil unto him
that *was at peace* **shalamed** with me;
(*yea*, I have *delivered* **rescued** him
that *without cause* **vainly** is *mine enemy* **my tribulator**:)

9 for naught is established in their mouth;
their inwards are calamities;
their throat is an open tomb;
they smooth over with their tongue.
10 They guilt, O Elohim;
fell them by their own counsels:
in the abundance of their rebellions
drive them away:
for they rebel against you.
11 And all who seek refuge in you cheer;
they eternally shout
because you cover them over;
may they who love your name jump for joy in you:
12 for you bless the just, O Yah Veh;
with pleasure you surround him as a shield.

6 To His Eminence; On Strummer; On Octave;
A Psalm by David.
1 O Yah Veh,
neither reprove me in your wrath, nor
discipline me in your fury.
2 Grant me charism, O Yah Veh, for I languish;
Heal me, O Yah Veh,
for my bones are terrified;
3 my soul is mighty terrified.
And you, O Yah Veh, until when?
4 Return, O Yah Veh, rescue my soul;
save me for sake of your your mercies:

5 for your memorial is not in death;
who spreads hands to you in sheol?
6 I belabor with my sighing;
all night my bed swims:
I flow my bedstead with my tears;
7 my eye is motheaten in vexation
—antiquates because of all my tribulators.
8 Turn from me,
all you working mischief;
for Yah Veh hears the voice of my weeping:
9 Yah Veh hears my supplication;
Yah Veh takes my prayer.
10 All my enemies shame and terrify mightily;
they return and shame in a blink.

7 Lyric Poem, by David,
which he sang to Yah Veh,
concerning the words of Kush the Ben Yaminiy.
1 O Yah Veh my Elohim, in you seek I refuge;
save me from all my pursuers and rescue me:
2 lest he tear my soul like a lion—craunching,
while there is none to rescue.
3 O Yah Veh my Elohim,
If I worked this;
if there is wickedness in my palms;
4 if I dealt evil to him who shalamed with me;
or rescued my tribulator in vain:
5 Let the enemy *persecute* **pursue** my soul,
and *take it* **overtake**;
yea, let him *tread down* **trample** my life upon the earth,
and *lay* **tabernacle** mine honour in the dust.
Selah.
6 Arise, O *LORD* **Yah Veh**,
in *thine anger* **thy wrath**,
lift up thyself
because of the *rage* **fury** of *mine enemies* **my tribulators**:
and awake for me *to* the judgment
that thou hast *commanded* **misvahed**.
7 *So* **Thus**
shall the *congregation* **witnesses** of the *people* **nations**
compass **surround** thee *about*:
for their sakes therefore
return thou *on high* **in the heights**.
8 *The LORD* **Yah Veh**
shall *judge* **plead the cause of** the people:
judge me, O *LORD* **Yah Veh**,
according to my *righteousness* **justness**,
and according to mine integrity that is in me.
9 *Oh* **I beseech**,
let the *wickedness* **evil** of the wicked
come to an end **cease**;
but establish the just:
for the *righteous God* **just Elohim**
trieth **proofeth** the hearts and reins.
10 My *defence* **buckler** is *of God* **upon Elohim**,
which saveth the *upright* **straight** in heart.
11 *God judgeth the righteous*
Elohim is a just judge,
and *God is angry with the wicked*
El is enraged every day.
12 If he turn not, he *will whet*
shall sharpen his sword;
he hath bent his bow, and *made it ready* **prepared**.
13 He hath also prepared for him
the instruments of death;
he *ordaineth* **heats** his arrows
against *the persecutors* **them who pursue**.
14 Behold, he *travaileth* **despoileth**
with *iniquity* **mischief**,
and hath conceived *mischief* **toil**,
and *brought forth* **hath birthed** falsehood.
15 He *made* **digged** a *pit* **well**, and digged it,
and is fallen into the *ditch which* **pit of ruin** he made.
16 His *mischief* **toil** shall
return upon his own head,
and his *violent dealing* **violence**
shall *come down* **descend** upon his own *pate* **scalp**.
17 I *will praise the LORD* **shall**
spread hands to Yah Veh
according to his righteousness:
and *will sing praise* **shall psalm**
to the name of *the LORD most high* **Yah Veh Elyon**.

8 To *the chief Musician* **His**
Eminence, upon Gittith,
A Psalm of David.
1 O *LORD* **Yah Veh**, our *Lord* **Adonay**,
how *excellent* **mighty** is thy name in all the earth!
who hast *set* **given** thy *glory* **majesty** above the heavens.
2 Out of the mouth of *babes* **infants** and sucklings
hast thou *ordained* **founded** strength
because of *thine enemies* **thy tribulators**,
that thou mightest
still **shabbathize** the enemy and the avenger.
3 When I *consider* **see** thy heavens,
the work of thy fingers,
the moon and the stars,
which thou hast *ordained* **established**;
4 What is man,
that thou *art mindful of* **rememberest** him?
and the son of *man* **humanity**,
that thou visitest him?

5 For thou hast made him
a little *lower* **less** than *the angels* **Elohim**,
and hast crowned him
with *glory* **honour** and *honour* **majesty**.
6 Thou *madest* **hast** him to *have dominion* **reign**
over the works of thy hands;
thou hast put all *things* under his feet:
7 *All sheep* **Flocks** and oxen,
yea, and the *beasts* **animals** of the field;
8 The *fowl* **birds** of the *air* **heavens**,
and the fish of the sea,
and whatsoever passeth through the paths of the seas.
5 *may* the enemy pursue and overtake my soul;
yes, trample my life on the earth
and tabernacle my honor in the dust.
Selah.
6 Rise, O Yah Veh, in your wrath,
lift yourself;
because of the fury of my tribulators:
and waken for me the judgment you misvahed.
7 Thus the witnesses of the nations surround you;
so for their sakes, return in the heights.
8 Yah Veh pleads the cause of the people;
O Yah Veh, judge me according to my justness
and according to my integrity within me:
9 I beseech, cease the evil of the wicked;
and establish the just:
for the just Elohim proofs the hearts and reins.
10 My buckler is on Elohim,
who saves the straight in heart:
11 Elohim is a just judge
and El enrages every day.
12 If he turns not, he sharpens his sword;
he bends his bow and prepares
13 —prepares the instruments of death for him;
he heats his arrows for them who pursue.
14 Behold, he despoils with mischief
and conceives toil and births falsehood:
15 he digs a well
—digs and falls in the pit of ruin he made:
16 his toil returns on his own head
and his violence descends on his own scalp.
17 I spread hands to Yah Veh
according to his righteousness;
and psalm to the name of Yah Veh Elyon.

8 To His Eminence; On Gittith;
A Psalm by David.
1 O Yah Veh, our Adonay,
how mighty your name in all the earth;
who gives your majesty above the heavens.
2 From the mouth of infants and sucklings
you founded strength;
because of your tribulators
—to shabbathize the enemy and the avenger.
3 For I see your heavens,
the work of your fingers;
the moon and the stars,
you established!
4 What is man, that you remember him?
—and the son of humanity, that you visit him?
5 For you lessen him than Elohim
and crown him with honor and majesty;
6 to reign over the works of your hands
and put all under his feet:
7 flocks and oxen,
yes, and the animals of the field;
8 the birds of the heavens,
and the fish of the sea
and whatever passes through the paths of the seas.
9 O *LORD* **Yah Veh** our *Lord* **Adonay**,
how excellent is thy name in all the earth!

9 To *the chief Musician* **His Eminence**,
upon *Muthlabben* **Muth Labben/Death of the Son**,
A Psalm of David.
1 I *will praise thee* **shall spread**
hands, O *LORD* **Yah Veh**,
with my whole heart;
I *will shew forth* **shall scribe** all thy marvellous works.
2 I *will be glad* **shall cheer**
and *rejoice* **jump for joy** in thee:
I *will sing praise* **shall psalm** to thy name,
O thou *most High* **Elyon**.
3 When mine enemies are turned back,
they shall *fall* **falter**
and *perish* **destruct** at thy *presence* **face**.
4 For thou hast *maintained* **worked**
my *right* **judgment** and my *cause* **plea**;
thou *satest* **settlest** in the throne judging *right* **justness**.
5 Thou hast rebuked the *heathen* **goyim**,
thou hast destroyed the wicked,
thou hast *put out* **erased** their name
for ever **eternally** and *ever* **eternally**.
6 O thou enemy,
destructions **parched areas**
are *come to a perpetual end*
consummated in perpetuity:
and thou hast *destroyed* **uprooted** cities;
their memorial *is perished* **destructeth** with them.
7 But *the LORD* **Yah Veh**
shall *endure for ever* **settle eternally**:

he hath prepared his throne for judgment.
8 And he shall judge the world
in *righteousness* **justness**,
he shall *minister judgment* **plead the cause**
to **of** the *people* **nations** in *uprightness* **straightnesses**.
9 *The LORD* **Yah Veh**
also will **shall** be a *refuge* **secure loft** for the oppressed,
a *refuge* **secure loft** in times of *trouble* **tribulation**.
10 And they that know thy name
will put their trust **shall confide** in thee:
for thou, *LORD* **O Yah Veh**,
hast not forsaken them that seek thee.
11 *Sing praises* **Psalm** to *the LORD* **Yah Veh**,
which *dwelleth* **settleth** in *Zion* **Siyon**: *declare*
tell among the people his *doings* **exploits**.
12 When he *maketh inquisition*
searcheth for blood,
he remembereth them:
he forgetteth not the cry of the humble.
13 *Have mercy upon me* **Grant me charism**,
O *LORD* **Yah Veh**;
consider **see** my *trouble* **humiliation**
which I suffer of them that hate me,
thou that liftest me *up* from the *gates* **portals** of death:
14 That I may *shew forth* **scribe** all thy *praise* **halal**
in the *gates* **portals** of the daughter of *Zion* **Siyon**:
I *will rejoice* **shall twirl** in thy salvation.
15 The *heathen* **goyim** are sunk down
in the pit **of ruin** that they *made* **worked**:
in the net which they hid
is their own foot *taken* **captured**.
16 *The LORD* **Yah Veh** is known
by the judgment which he *executeth* **worketh**:
the wicked is snared
in the *work* **deeds** of his own *hands* **palms**.
Higgaion **Meditation**.
Selah.
17 The wicked shall be turned into *hell* **sheol**,
and all the *nations* **goyim** that forget *God* **Elohim**.
18 For the needy
shall not *alway* be forgotten **in perpetuity**:
the *expectation* **hope** of the *poor* **humble**
shall not *perish for ever* **destruct eternally**.
19 Arise, O *LORD* **Yah Veh**;
let not man *prevail* **strengthen**:
let the *heathen* **goyim** be judged *in thy sight* **at thy face**.
20 Put them in *fear* **awe**, O *LORD* **Yah Veh**:
that the *nations* **goyim**
may know themselves to be but men.
Selah.

9 O Yah Veh our Adonay,
how excellent your name in all the earth!

9 To His Eminence;
On Muth Labben/Death of the Son;
A Psalm by David.
1 I spread hands, O Yah Veh,
with my whole heart;
I scribe all your marvellous works;
2 I cheer and jump for joy in you;
I psalm to your name, O you Elyon.
3 When my enemies return
they falter and destruct at your face.
4 For you work my judgment and my plea;
you settle in the throne judging justness;
5 you rebuke the goyim;
you destroy the wicked;
you erase their name eternally and eternally.
6 O you enemy,
your parched areas consummate in perpetuity;
and the cities you uprooted
—their memorial destructs with them.
7 And Yah Veh settles eternal;
he prepares his throne for judgment:
8 he judges the world in justness;
he pleads the cause of the nations in straightnesses.
9 Yah Veh is a secure loft for the oppressed
—a secure loft in times of tribulation:
10 and they who know your name confide in you;
for you forsake not them who seek you,
O Yah Veh.
11 Psalm to Yah Veh who settles in Siyon;
tell his exploits among the people:
12 he remembers them who search for blood;
he forgets not the cry of the humble.
13 Grant me charism, O Yah Veh;
see my humiliation of them who hate me
—you who lift me from the portals of death;
14 so that I scribe all your halal
in the portals of the daughter of Siyon:
I twirl in your salvation.
15 The goyim sink in the pit of ruin they worked;
—capture their foot in the net they hid.
16 Yah Veh is known by the judgment he works;
the wicked is snared in the deeds of his palms.
Meditation.
Selah.
17 The wicked turn to sheol
with all the goyim who forget Elohim.
18 Neither are the needy forgotten in perpetuity;
nor the hope of the humble destructs eternally.

19 Rise, O Yah Veh; strengthen not man:
judge the goyim at your face.
20 Put them in awe, O Yah Veh,
that the goyim know they *are* but men.
Selah.

10 Why standest thou afar off, O *LORD* **Yah Veh**?
why *hidest* **concealest** thou thyself
in times of *trouble* **tribulation?**
2 The wicked in his *pride* **pomp**
doth persecute **hotly pursueth** the *poor* **humble**:
let them be *taken* **grabbed** in the *devices* **intrigue**
that they have *imagined* **machinated.**
3 For the wicked
boasteth **halaleth** of his *heart's* **soul's** desire,
and blesseth the *covetous* **greedy**,
whom *the LORD abhorreth* **Yah Veh scorneth.**
4 The wicked,
through *the pride of his countenance* **lifted nostrils**,
will **shall** not seek *after God*:
God **Elohim** is not in all his *thoughts* **intrigues.**
5 His ways *are always grievous* **writhe at all times**;
thy judgments are *far above* **in the heights**
out of his sight:
as for all his *enemies* **tribulators**, he puffeth at them.
6 He hath said in his heart, I
shall not *be moved* **totter**:
generation to generation
for I shall never be in *adversity* **evil.**
7 His mouth is full of *cursing* **oaths**
and *deceit* **deceits** and fraud:
under his tongue is *mischief* **toil** and *vanity* **mischief.**
8 He *sitteth* **settleth**
in the *lurking places* **lurks** of the *villages* **courts**:
in the *secret places* **coverts**
doth he *murder* **slaughtereth** the innocent:
his eyes *are privily set* **hath he hid**
against **from** the *poor* **unfortunate.**
9 He *lieth in wait secretly* **lurketh in the coverts**
as a lion in his *den* **sukkoth/brush arbor**:
he *lieth in wait* **lurketh** to catch the *poor* **humble**:
he *doth catch* **catcheth** the *poor* **humble**,
when he draweth him into his net.
10 He *croucheth* **crusheth,**
and *humbleth* **prostrateth** *himself*,
that the *poor* **army of the unfortunates**
may fall by his *strong ones* **mighty.**
11 He hath said in his heart, *God* **El** hath forgotten:
he hideth his face;
he *will never* **shall not** see it **in perpetuity.**
12 Arise, O *LORD* **Yah Veh**;
O *God* **El**, lift up thine hand: forget not the humble.
13 Wherefore doth the wicked
contemn God **scorn Elohim**?
he hath said in his heart,
Thou *wilt* **shalt** not require it.
14 Thou hast seen it;
for thou *beholdest* **scannest**
mischief **toil** and *spite* **vexation**,
to *requite it with* **give into** thy hand:
the *poor* **unfortunate**
committeth himself **is left** unto thee;
thou art the helper of the *fatherless* **orphan.**
15 Break thou the arm of the
wicked and the evil *man*:
seek out his wickedness till thou find none.
16 *The LORD* **Yah Veh** is *King* **Sovereign**
for ever **eternally** and *ever* **eternally**:
the *heathen are perished* **goyim destruct** out of his land.
17 *LORD* **O Yah Veh,**
thou hast heard the desire of the humble:
thou *wilt* **shalt** prepare their heart,
thou *wilt cause* **shalt hearken** thine ear *to hear*:
18 To judge the *fatherless*
orphan and the oppressed,
that the man of the earth
may *no more oppress* **not terrify again.**

11 To *the chief Musician* **His Eminence,**
A Psalm of David.
1 In *the LORD put I my trust*
Yah Veh I seek refuge:
how say ye to my soul,
Flee **Wander** as a bird to your mountain?
2 For, *lo* **behold**, the wicked bend their bow,
they *make ready* **prepare** their
arrow upon the *string* **cord,**
that they may *privily* **in darkness**
shoot at the *upright* **straight** in heart.

10 Why stand you afar off, O Yah Veh?
Why conceal yourself in times of tribulation?
2 The pompous wicked hotly pursue the humble;
—grab them in the intrigue they machinate:
3 because the wicked halal the desire of his soul
and bless the greedy whom Yah Veh scorns.
4 The wicked, through lifted nostrils, seek not:
Elohim is not! *are* all his intrigues:
5 his ways writhe at all times.
Your judgments in the heights *are* from his sight;
as for all his tribulators, he puffs at them.
6 He says in his heart,
I totter not from generation to generation

—never in evil.
7 His mouth is full of oaths and deceits and fraud;
under his tongue is toil and mischief;
8 he settles in the lurks of the courts;
he slaughters the innocent in the coverts; he
hides his eyes from the unfortunate:
9 he lurks in the coverts
as a lion in his sukkoth/brush arbor;
he lurks to catch the humble;
he catches the humble
drawing him into his net.
10 He crushes; he prostrates;
his mighty fells the army of the unfortunates.
11 He says in his heart, El forgets!
he hides his face; he sees it not in perpetuity.
12 Rise, O Yah Veh; O El, lift your hand:
forget not the humble.
13 The wicked—why scorn they Elohim?
He says in his heart, Not required!
14 You see; for you scan toil and vexation,
they give into your hand;
they leave the unfortunate to you you—
the helper of the orphan.
15 Break the arm of the wicked and the evil;
seek out his wickedness until you find none.
16 Yah Veh *is* Sovereign eternally and eternally;
the goyim destruct from his land.
17 O Yah Veh,
you hear the desire of the humble;
you prepare their heart;
you hearken your ear;
18 to judge the orphan and the oppressed
that the man of the earth not terrify again.

11 To His Eminence; By David.
1 In Yah Veh I seek refuge;
how say you to my soul,
Wander as a bird to your mountain?
2 For, behold, the wicked bend their bow;
they prepare their arrow on the cord;
and in the darkness
shoot at the straight in heart.
3 If the foundations *be destroyed* **demolish,**
what can the *righteous* **just** do?
4 *The LORD* **Yah Veh** is in his holy *temple* **manse,**
the LORD'S **Yah Veh's** throne is in *heaven* **the heavens**:
his eyes *behold* **see,** his eyelids *try* **proof,**
the *children* **sons** of *men* **humanity.**
5 *The LORD trieth* **Yah Veh**
proofeth the *righteous* **just**:
but the wicked and him that loveth violence
his soul hateth.
6 Upon the wicked he shall rain snares,
fire and *brimstone* **sulphur,**
and *an horrible tempest* **a raging wind/spirit**:
this shall be the portion—**the allotment** of their cup.
7 For *the righteous LORD* **just Yah Veh**
loveth *righteousness* **justness**;
his *countenance* **face**
doth behold **seeth** the *upright* **straight.**

12 To *the chief Musician* **His Eminence,**
upon *Sheminith* **the Octave,**
A Psalm of David.
1 *Help* **Save,** *LORD* **O Yah Veh;**
for the *godly man ceaseth* **mercied have deceased;**
for the *faithful fail* **trustworthy have disappeared**
from among the *children* **sons** of *men* **humanity.**
2 They *speak* **word** every *one* **man**
vanity with his *neighbour* **friend:**
with *flattering* lips **that smooth it over**
and *with a double heart* **heart to heart**
do they *speak* **word.**
3 *The LORD* **Yah Veh** shall cut off
all *flattering* lips **that smooth it over,**
and the tongue
that *speaketh proud things* **wordeth greatnesses:**
4 Who have said,
With our tongue *will* **shall** we prevail **mightily;**
our lips are our own: who is *lord* **adoni** over us?
5 For the *oppression* **devastation**
of the *poor* **humble,**
for the *sighing* **shrieking** of the needy,
now *will* **shall** I arise, saith *the LORD* **Yah Veh;**
I *will* **shall** set him in safety from
him that puffeth at him.
6 The *words* **sayings** of *the LORD* **Yah Veh**
are pure *words* **sayings:**
as silver *tried* **refined** in a furnace of earth,
purified seven times **refined sevenfold.**
7 Thou shalt *keep* **guard** them, O *LORD* **Yah Veh,**
thou shalt *preserve them* **guard us** from this generation
for ever **eternally.**
8 The wicked walk *on every side* **round about,**
when the *vilest men* **violent sons of humanity**
are exalted.

13 To *the chief Musician* **His Eminence,**
A Psalm of David.
1 How long *wilt* **shalt** thou
forget me, O *LORD* **Yah Veh?**
for ever **in perpetuity?**
how long *wilt* **shalt** thou hide thy face from me?

2 How long shall I *take* **set** counsel in my soul,
having *sorrow* **grief** in my heart daily?
how long shall mine enemy *be exalted* **loft** over me?
3 *Consider* **Look** and *hear* **answer** me,
O *LORD* **Yah Veh** my *God* **Elohim**:
lighten mine eyes, lest I sleep *the sleep of* **in** death;
4 Lest mine enemy say, I have
prevailed against him;
and *those that trouble me rejoice* **my tribulators**
twirl when I *am moved* **totter**.
5 But I have *trusted* **confided** in thy mercy;
my heart shall *rejoice* **twirl** in thy salvation.
6 I *will* **shall** sing unto *the LORD* **Yah Veh**,
because he hath dealt *bountifully* with me.

14 To *the chief Musician* **His Eminence**,
A Psalm of David.
1 The fool hath said in his heart,
There is no God **Elohim is not**.
They *are corrupt* **have ruined**,
they have done abominable works—**abhorrent exploits**,
there is none that *doeth* **worketh** good.
3 If the foundations demolish,
what *are* the just to do?
4 Yah Veh is in his holy manse,
the throne of Yah Veh is in the heavens;
his eyes see;
his eyelids proof the sons of humanity.
5 Yah Veh proofs the just;
and the wicked who love violence
his soul hates.
6 On the wicked he rains snares
—fire and sulphur and a raging wind/spirit;
—the allotment of their cup.
7 For just Yah Veh loves justness;
his face sees the straight.
12 To His Eminence; On the Octave;
A Psalm by David.
1 Save, O Yah Veh;
for the mercied decease;
for the trustworthy disappear
from among the sons of humanity.
2 Every man words vanity with his friend;
with lips that smooth it over
they word heart to heart.
3 Yah Veh cuts off all lips that smooth it over
and the tongue that words greatnesses:
4 who say,
With our tongue we prevail mightily;
our lips are our own; who is adoni over us?
5 For the devastation of the humble,
for the shrieking of the needy,
I now rise, says Yah Veh;
I set him in safety from him who puffs at him.
6 The sayings of Yah Veh are pure sayings;
as silver refined in a furnace of earth
—refined sevenfold.
7 Guard them, O Yah Veh,
guard us from this generation eternally.
8 The wicked walk all around,
when the violent sons of humanity are exalted.

13 To His Eminence; A Psalm by David.
1 Until when forget you me, O Yah Veh?
In perpetuity?
Until when hide you your face from me?
2 Until when set I counsel in my soul
—having grief in my heart daily? Until
when lofts my enemy over me?
3 Look and answer me, O Yah Veh my Elohim!
Light my eyes, lest I sleep in death;
4 lest my enemy say, I prevailed against him;
and my tribulators twirl when I totter.
5 And I—I confide in your mercy;
my heart twirls in your salvation.
6 I sing to Yah Veh,
because he deals with me.

14 To His Eminence; By David.
1 The fool, in his heart, says, No Elohim!.
They ruin;—abhorrent exploits;
none works good.
2 *The LORD* **Yah Veh** looked
down from *heaven* **the heavens**
upon the *children* **sons** of *men* **humanity**,
to see if there were any
that *did understand* **comprehend**,
and seek *God* **Elohim**.
3 They are all *gone* **turned** aside,
they are *all* together *become filthy* **muddled**:
there is none that *doeth* **worketh** good, no, not one.
4 Have all the *workers* **doers** of *iniquity* **mischief**
no knowledge **not known**?
who eat up my people as they eat bread,
and call not upon *the LORD* **Yah Veh**.
5 *There were they in great fear*
In dreading, they dreaded:
for *God* **Elohim** is in the generation of the *righteous* **just**.
6 Ye have shamed the counsel of the *poor* **humble**,
because *the LORD* **Yah Veh** is his refuge.
7 *Oh* **Who giveth** that the
salvation of *Israel* **Yisra El**
were *come* out of *Zion* **Siyon**!

when *the LORD* **Yah Veh**
bringeth back **returneth** the captivity of his people,
Jacob **Yaaqov** shall *rejoice* **twirl**,
and Israel **Yisra El** shall *be glad* **cheer**.

15 A Psalm of David.
1 *LORD* **Yah Veh,**
who shall *abide* **sojourn** in thy *tabernacle* **tent**?
who shall *dwell* **tabernacle** in thy holy *hill* **mountain**?
2 He that walketh *uprightly* **integriously**,
and *worketh righteousness* **doeth justness**, and
speaketh **wordeth** the truth in his heart.
3 He that *backbiteth* **steppeth** not with his tongue,
nor *doeth* **worketh** evil to his *neighbour* **friend**, nor
taketh up **lifteth** a reproach against his neighbour.
4 In whose eyes
a *vile person* **spurner** is *contemned* **despised**;
but he honoureth them that *fear the LORD* **awe Yah Veh**.
He that *sweareth* **oatheth** to *his own hurt* **vilify**,
and changeth not.
5 He that *putteth* **giveth** not
out his *money* **silver** to usury,
nor taketh *reward* **bribe** against the innocent.
He that *doeth* **worketh** these *things*
shall *never be moved* **not totter eternally**.

16 *Michtam* **Poem** of David.
1 *Preserve* **Guard** me, O *God* **El**:
for in thee *do I put my trust* **I seek refuge**.
2 *O my soul,* thou hast said
unto *the LORD* **Yah Veh,**
Thou art my *Lord* **Adonay**:
my goodness *extendeth* not to thee;
3 But to the *saints* **holy** that are in the earth,
and to the *excellent* **mighty**, in whom is all my delight.
4 Their *sorrows* **contortions**
shall *be multiplied* **abound**
that hasten after another *god*:
their *drink offerings* **libations** of blood
will **shall** I not *offer* **libate,**
nor *take up* **lift** their names into my lips.
5 *The LORD* **Yah Veh** is the portion
of mine *inheritance* **allotment** and of my cup:
thou *maintainest* **upholdest** my *lot* **pebble**.
6 The lines are fallen unto me
in *pleasant places* **pleasure**;
yea, I have a *goodly heritage* **glorious inheritance**.
7 I *will* **shall** bless *the LORD* **Yah Veh**
who hath *given* **counselled** me *counsel*:
my reins also *instruct* **discipline** me in the night *seasons*.
8 I have set *the LORD* **Yah Veh**
always before **continually in front of** me:
because he is at my right *hand*,
I shall not *be moved* **totter**.
9 Therefore my heart *is glad* **cheereth**,
and my *glory rejoiceth* **honour twirleth**:
my flesh also shall *rest in hope* **tabernacle confidently**.
10 For thou *wilt* **shalt** not *leave*
forsake my soul in *hell* **sheol**;
neither *wilt* **shalt** thou *suffer* **give**
thine Holy **thy Mercied** One to see
corruption **the pit of ruin**.
11 Thou *wilt shew me* **shalt have
me know** the path of life:
in **at** thy *presence* **face**
is *fulness of joy* **satisfying cheerfulness**;
at thy right *hand*
there are pleasures *for evermore* **in perpetuity**.

2 Yah Veh, from the heavens,
looks down on the sons of humanity,
to see if there is one who comprehends
and seeks Elohim.
3 They all turn aside,
together they muddle;
no one works good—no, not one.
4 Have all doing mischief not known?
—who eat my people as they eat bread
—who call not on Yah Veh.
5 In dreading, they dread;
for Elohim is in the generation of the just.
6 You shame the counsel of the humble,
because Yah Veh is his refuge.
7 Who gives the salvation of Yisra El from Siyon?
When Yah Veh returns the captivity of his
people. Twirl, O Yaaqov! Cheer, O Yisra El!

15 A Psalm by David.
1 Yah Veh, Who sojourns in your tent?
Who tabernacles in your holy mountain?
2 He who walks integriously and does justness
and words the truth in his heart.
3 He neither steps with his tongue
nor works evil to his friend
nor lifts a reproach against his neighbour.
4 His eyes despise a spurner
but honor them who awe Yah Veh.
He who oaths to villify, and changes not;
5 he neither gives his silver to usury
nor takes bribe against the innocent; he
who works these totters not eternally.

16 Poem by David.
1 Guard me, O El; for in you I seek refuge.
2 You say to Yah Veh—you, my Adonay

my goodness is not to you;
3 but to the holy in the earth;
and to the mighty in whom *is* all my delight.
4 Their contortions abound
who hasten after another;
I neither libate their libations of blood;
nor lift their names to my lips.
5 Yah Veh is the portion
of my allotment and of my cup;
you uphold my pebble:
6 the lines fall to me in pleasure;
yes, I have a glorious inheritance.
7 I bless Yah Veh who counsels me;
also in the night my reins discipline me:
8 I set Yah Veh continually in front of me;
because he is at my right, I totter not:
9 so my heart cheers and my honor twirls;
and my flesh tabernacles confidently.
10 For you neither forsake my soul in sheol;
nor give your Mercied One to see the pit of ruin:
11 you have me know the path of life;
at your face is satisfying cheerfulness; at
your right are pleasures in perpetuity.

17 A Prayer of David.
1 Hear *the right* **justness**, O *LORD* **Yah Veh**,
attend **hearken** unto my *cry* **shouting**,
give ear **hearken** unto my prayer,
that goeth not out of feigned lips **of lips without deceit**.
2 Let my *sentence* **judgment**
come forth from thy *presence* **face**;
let thine eyes *behold* **see**
the things **those** that are *equal* **in straightnesses**.
3 Thou hast *proved* **proofed** mine heart;
thou hast visited me in the night;
thou hast *tried* **refined** me,
and shalt find *nothing* **naught**;
I *am purposed* **have plotted**
that my mouth shall not transgress.
4 Concerning the *works* **deeds** of *men* **humanity**,
by the word of thy lips
I have *kept* **guarded** me from the paths of the destroyer.
5 *Hold up* **Uphold** my *goings* **steps** in thy paths,
that my *footsteps slip* **steps totter** not.
6 I have called upon thee,
for thou *wilt hear* **shalt answer** me, O *God* **El**:
incline **spread** thine ear unto me,
and *hear* my *speech* **sayings**.
7 *Shew* **Distinguish** thy
marvellous *lovingkindness* **mercy**,
O thou that savest by thy right *hand*
them which *put their trust in thee* **seek refuge**
from those that rise *up against them*.
8 *Keep* **Guard** me as the *apple* **pupil**
—**the daughter** of the eye,
hide me under the shadow of thy wings,
9 From **the face of** the wicked
that *oppress* **ravage** me,
from my *deadly* **soul** enemies,
who *compass* **surround** me *about*.
10 They are *inclosed* **shut** in their own fat:
with their mouth they *speak proudly* **word pompously**.
11 They have now *compassed* **surrounded** us
in our steps:
they have set their eyes
bowing down **spreading** to the earth;
12 Like as a lion that *is greedy*
of **yearneth for** his prey,
and as *it were a young lion* **a whelp**
lurking **settling** in *secret places* **coverts**.
13 Arise, O *LORD* **Yah Veh**,
disappoint him **anticipate his face**,
cast him down **knuckle him under**:
deliver **slip away** my soul from the wicked,
which is thy sword:
14 From men which are thy
hand, O *LORD* **Yah Veh**,
from **transcient** men *of the world*,
which have their *portion* **allotment** in this life,
and whose belly
thou fillest with thy *hid* **treasured** treasure:
they are full of children **their sons satiate**,
and leave the *rest of their substance* **remainder**
to their *babes* **infants**.
15 As for me,
I *will behold* **shall see** thy face in *righteousness* **justness**:
I shall be satisfied, when I awake,
with thy *likeness* **manifestation**.

18 To *the chief Musician* **His Eminence**,
A Psalm of David, the servant of *the LORD* **Yah Veh**,
who *spake* **worded** unto *the LORD* **Yah Veh**
the words of this song
in the day that *the LORD delivered* **Yah Veh rescued** him
from the *hand* **palm** of all his enemies,
and from the hand of *Saul* **Shaul**:
And he said,
1 I *will love* **shall mercy** thee,
O *LORD* **Yah Veh**, my strength.
2 *The LORD* **Yah Veh** is my rock,
and my *fortress* **stronghold**, and my *deliverer* **escape**;
my *God* **El**, my *strength* **rock**,

in whom I *will trust* **seek refuge**;
my buckler, and the horn of my salvation,
and my *high tower* **secure loft**.

17 A Prayer by David.
1 Hear justness, O Yah Veh;
hearken to my shouting:
hearken to my prayer from lips without deceit.
2 My judgment comes from your face;
your eyes see them who are in straightnesses;
3 you proof my heart;
you visit me in the night;
you refine me; you find naught;
I plot that my mouth not transgress.
4 Concerning the deeds of humanity,
by the word of your lips
I guard me from the paths of the destroyer.
5 Uphold my steps in your paths
that my steps totter not.
6 I—I call you, for you answer me, O El;
spread your ear to me and my sayings:
7 distinguish your marvellous mercy,
O you,
who by your right saves them who seek refuge
from those who rise.
8 Guard me as the pupil—the daughter of the eye,
hide me under the shadow of your wings
9 from the face of the wicked who ravage me
—from my soul enemies who surround me.
10 They shut their fat;
their mouth words pompously:
11 they surround our steps;
they set their eyes spreading to the earth:
12 as as a lion yearning for his prey
—as a whelp settling in the coverts.
13 Rise, O Yah Veh,
anticipate his face; knuckle him under:
slip my soul from the wicked by your sword
14 —from men by your hand, O Yah Veh
—from transient men whose allotment is this life
—in whose belly you treasured treasure:
their sons satiate
and leave the remainder to their infants.
15 As for me, I see your face in justness;
I satsify when I waken with your manifestation.

18 To His Eminence;
By David the servant of Yah Veh:
who worded to Yah Veh the words of this song
in the day Yah Weh rescued him
from the palm of his enemies,
and from the hand of Shaul:
and he says,
1 I mercy you, O Yah Veh, my strength!
2 Yah Veh is my rock
and my stronghold and my escape;
my El, my rock in whom I seek refuge;
my buckler and the horn of my salvation;
my secure loft.
3 I *will* **shall** call *upon the LORD* **Yah Veh**,
who is worthy to be praised—**The Halaled One**:
so shall I be saved from mine enemies.
4 The *sorrows* **cords** of death
compassed **surrounded** me,
and the *floods* **wadies** of *ungodly men* **Beli Yaal**
made me afraid **frightened me**.
5 The *sorrows* **cords** of *hell* **sheol**
compassed **surrounded** me *about*:
the snares of death *prevented* **anticipated** me.
6 In my *distress* **tribulation**
I called upon *the LORD* **Yah Veh**,
and cried unto my *God* **Elohim**:
he heard my voice out of his *temple* **manse**,
and my cry came *before him* **at his face**,
even into his ears.
7 Then the earth shook and *trembled* **quaked**;
the foundations also of the *hills* **mountains**
moved **quaked** and were shaken,
because he was *wroth* **inflamed**.
8 There *went up* **ascended** a
smoke out of his nostrils,
and fire out of his mouth *devoured* **consumed**:
coals were *kindled* **burnt** by it.
9 He *bowed* **spread** the heavens also,
and *came down* **descended**:
and **dripping** darkness was under his feet.
10 And he rode upon a cherub, and *did fly* **flew**:
yea, he *did fly* **flew** upon the wings of the wind.
11 He *made* **set** darkness his *secret place* **covert**;
his *pavilion* **sukkoth/brush arbor** round about him
were dark waters
and thick clouds of *the skies* **vapours**.
12 At the *brightness* **brilliance**
that was *before* **in front of** him
his thick clouds passed, hail *stones* and coals of fire.
13 *The LORD* **Yah Veh** also
thundered in the heavens,
and the Highest **Elyon** gave his voice;
hail *stones* and coals of fire.
14 Yea, he sent out his arrows, and scattered them;
and he shot out lightnings,
and *discomfited* **scattered** them.

15 Then the *channels* **reservoirs**
of waters were seen,
and the foundations of the world
were *discovered* **exposed** at thy rebuke,
O *LORD* **Yah Veh,**
at the *blast* **breath**
of the *breath* **wind/spirit** of thy nostrils.
16 He sent from *above* **the heights,**
he took me, he drew me out of many waters.
17 He *delivered* **rescued** me from my strong enemy,
and from them which hated me:
for they were *too strong for me* **stronger than I.**
18 They *prevented* **anticipated** me
in the day of my calamity:
but *the LORD* **Yah Veh** was my *stay* **support.**
19 He brought me forth also
into *a large place* **an expanse;**
he *delivered* **rescued** me, because he delighted in me.
20 *The LORD rewarded* **Yah Veh dealt** me
according to my *righteousness* **justness;**
according to the *cleanness* **purity** of my hands
hath he *recompensed* **returned to** me.
21 For I have *kept* **guarded**
the ways of *the LORD* **Yah Veh,**
and have not **done** wickedly
departed from **against** my *God* **Elohim.**
22 For all his judgments were *before* **in front of** me,
and I did not *put away* **turn aside** his statutes from me.
23 I was also *upright before*
integrious in front of him,
and I *kept* **guarded** myself
from *mine iniquity* **my perversity.**
24 Therefore
hath *the LORD recompensed* **Yah Veh returned to** me
according to my *righteousness* **justness,**
according to the *cleanness* **purity** of my hands
in his *eyesight* **eyes.**
25 With the *merciful* **mercied,**
thou wilt shew thyself merciful;
with an *upright man* **integrious mighty,**
thou wilt shew thyself upright **integrious;**
3 I call Yah Veh, The Halaled One:
—saved from my enemies.
4 The cords of death surround me;
the wadies of Beli Yaal frighten me;
5 the cords of sheol surround me;
the snares of death anticipate me.
6 In my tribulation
I call on Yah Veh and cry to my Elohim;
he hears my voice from his manse,
and my cry comes at his face—to his ears.
7 And the earth shakes and quakes;
the foundations of the mountains quake and shake
because he *is* inflamed.
8 A smoke ascends from his nostrils
and fire from his mouth consumes
—it burns coals.
9 And he spreads the heavens, and descends;
dripping darkness *is* under his feet:
10 he rides on a cherub and flies;
yes, he flies on the wings of the wind:
11 he sets darkness for his covert;
his sukkoth/brush arbor surrounds him
—dark waters and thick clouds of vapours:
12 at the brilliance in front of him
his thick clouds pass—hail and coals of fire.
13 Yah Veh thunders in the heavens;
Elyon gives his voice—hail and coals of fire:
14 yes, he sends his arrows and scatters them;
he shoots lightnings and agitates them.
15 And the reservoirs of waters were seen,
and exposed are the foundations of the world
at your rebuke, O Yah Veh
—at the breath of the wind/spirit of your nostrils.
16 He sends from the heights;
he takes me; he draws me from many waters:
17 he rescues me from my strong enemy
—from them who hate me;
for they are stronger than I.
18 They anticipate me in the day of my calamity;
and Yah Veh is my support.
19 He brings me to an expanse;
he rescues me, because he delights in me:
20 Yah Veh deals according to my justness;
—returns according to the purity of my hands:
21 for I guard the ways of Yah Veh
—not done wickedly against my Elohim.
22 For all his judgments *are* in front of me
and I turn not aside his statutes from me:
23 and I am integrious in front of him
and I guard myself from my perversity:
24 and Yah Veh returns to me
according to my justness
—according to the purity of my hands in his eyes.
25 With the mercied, merciful;
with the mighty integrious, integrious;
exeGeses ready research BIBLE
26 With the pure,
thou wilt shew thyself pure **purified;**
and with the *froward* **pervert,**

thou wilt shew thyself froward **a wrestler.**
27 For thou *wilt* **shalt** save the
afflicted **humble** people;
but *wilt bring down high looks* **shalt abase lofted eyes.**
28 For thou *wilt* **shalt** light my *candle* **lamp**:
the LORD **Yah Veh** my *God* **Elohim**
will enlighten **shall illuminate** my darkness.
29 For by thee I have run through a troop;
and by my *God* **Elohim** have I leaped over a wall.
30 *As for God* **EL**, his way is *perfect* **integrious**:
the *word* **saying** of *the LORD* **Yah Veh** is *tried* **refined**:
he is a buckler to all those that *trust* **seek refuge** in him.
31 For who is *God* **Elohah**
save the LORD **except Yah Veh**?
or who is a rock
save **except** our *God* **Elohim**?
32 *It is God that* **El** girdeth
me with *strength* **valour**,
and *maketh* **giveth** my way *perfect* **integrious**.
33 He *maketh* **placeth** my feet *like* **as** hinds' *feet*,
and *setteth* **standeth** me upon my *high places* **bamahs**.
34 He teacheth my hands to war,
so that a bow of steel is *broken* **bent** by mine arms.
35 Thou hast also given me
the *shield* **buckler** of thy salvation:
and thy right *hand* hath holden me *up*,
and thy *gentleness* **humbleness**
hath made me *great* **abound**.
36 Thou hast enlarged my *steps* **paces** under me,
that my *feet did not slip* **ankles wavered not**.
37 I have pursued mine enemies,
and overtaken them:
neither *did I turn again* **returned I**
till they were *consumed* **finished off**.
38 I have *wounded* **struck** them
that they were not able to rise:
they are fallen under my feet.
39 For thou hast girded me
with *strength* **valour** unto the *battle* **war**:
thou hast *subdued* **knuckled** under me
those that rose *up against me*.
40 Thou hast also given me
the necks of mine enemies;
that I might *destroy* **exterminate** them that hate me.
41 They cried, but there was
none to save them **no savior**:
even unto *the LORD* **Yah Veh**, but he answered them not.
42 Then *did I beat* **I pulverized**
them *small* as the dust
before **at the face of** the wind:
I *did cast* **poured** them out
as the *dirt* **mire** in the *streets* **outways**.
43 Thou hast *delivered* **slipped** me **away**
from the strivings of the people;
and thou hast *made* **set** me
the head of the *heathen* **goyim**:
a people *whom* I have not known shall serve me.
44 *As soon as they hear of me*
At the hearing of the ear,
they shall *obey* **hearken unto** me:
the **sons of** strangers
shall *submit themselves unto* **disavow** me.
45 The **sons of** strangers shall *fade away* **wither**,
and *be afraid* **tremble** out of their *close places* **borders**.
46 *The LORD* **Yah Veh** liveth;
and blessed be my rock;
and let *the God* **Elohim** of my salvation be *exalted* **lofted**.
47 *It is God that avengeth me*
El giveth me vengeance,
and subdueth the people under me.
48 He *delivereth me* **slippeth**
me away from mine enemies:
yea, thou liftest me up above those
that rise *up against me*:
thou hast *delivered* **rescued** me
from the *violent man* **man of violence**.
49 Therefore
will I give thanks **shall I spread hands** unto thee,
O *LORD* **Yah Veh**, among the *heathen* **goyim**,
and *sing praises* **psalm** unto thy name.
50 *Great deliverance giveth he*
lie greateneth salvation
to his *king* **sovereign**;
and *sheweth* **worketh** mercy to his anointed,
to David, and to his seed *for evermore* **eternally**.
26 with the pure, purified;
with the pervert, a wrestler.
27 For you save the humble people
and abase the lofted eye.
28 For you—you light my lamp;
Yah Veh my Elohim illuminates my darkeness.
29 For by you, I run a troop;
and by Elohim I leap a wall.
30 El, his way *is* integrious;
the saying of Yah Veh *is* refined:
he is a buckler to all who seek refuge in him.
31 For who *is* Elohah, except Yah Veh?
Who is a rock, except our Elohim?
32 El girts me with valour
and gives my way integrious;

33 He places my feet as the hinds
and stands me on my bamahs;
34 he teaches my hands to war
so my arms bend a bow of steel.
35 You give me the buckler of your salvation;
your right upholds me;
and your humbleness abounds me:
36 you enlarge my paces under me;
my ankles waver not.
37 I pursue my enemies, and overtake them;
I return not until they are finished off:
38 I strike them who are not able to rise;
they fall under my feet.
39 For you girt me with valour to the war;
you knuckle them under who rise:
40 you give me the necks of my enemies;
to exterminate them who hate me.
41 They cry, and there is no savior;
—to Yah Veh, but he answers them not.
42 And I purlverize them as the dust
at the face of the wind;
I pour them out as mire in the outways.
43 You slip me away
from the strivings of the people;
and you set me at the head of the goyim:
a people I know not serve me.
44 At the hearing of the ear, they hearken to me;
the sons of strangers disavow me:
45 the sons of strangers wither,
and tremble from their borders.
46 Yah Veh lives; blessed be my rock;
and lofted be the Elohim of my salvation.
47 El gives me vengeance
—subdues all the people under me.
48 He slips me away from my enemies;
yes, you lift me above them who rise; you
rescue me from the man of violence.
49 So I spread hands to you,
O Yah Veh, among the goyim,
and psalm to your name.
50 He greatens salvation to his sovereign;
and works mercy to his anointed
—to David, and to his seed eternally.

19 To *the chief Musician* **His Eminence**,
A Psalm of David.
1 The heavens
declare **scribe** the *glory* **honour** of *God* **El**;
and the *firmament* **expanse**
sheweth **telleth** his handywork.
2 Day unto day *uttereth speech* **gusheth sayings**,
and night unto night sheweth knowledge.
3 There is no *speech* **saying** nor *language* **word**,
where their voice is not heard.
4 Their line is gone out through all the earth,
and their *words* **utterances** to the end of the world.
In them hath he set a *tabernacle* **tent** for the sun,
5 Which is as a *bridegroom* **groom**
coming out of his *chamber* **canopy**,
and rejoiceth as *a strong man* **the mighty**
to run *a race* **the path**.
6 His *going forth* **source**
is from the end of the *heaven* **heavens**.
and his circuit
unto the ends of it:
and there is *nothing* **naught** hid from the heat *thereof.*
7 The *law* **torah** of *the LORD* **Yah Veh**
is perfect,
converting **restoring** the soul:
the *testimony* **witness** of *the LORD* **Yah Veh**
is *sure* **trustworthy**,
making wise **enwisening** the *simple* **gullible**.
8 The *statutes* **precepts** of *the LORD* **Yah Veh**
are *right* **straight**,
rejoicing **cheering** the heart:
the *commandment* **misvah** of *the LORD* **Yah Veh**
is pure,
enlightening the eyes.
9 The *fear* **awe** of *the LORD* **Yah Veh**
is *clean* **pure**,
enduring for ever **standing eternally**:
the judgments of *the LORD* **Yah Veh**
are *true* **truth**;
and righteous **justified** altogether.
10 More to be desired *are they* than gold,
yea, than much *fine* **pure** gold:
sweeter also than honey
and **the droppings of** the honeycomb.
11 Moreover by them is thy
servant *warned* **enlightened**:
and in *keeping of* **guarding** them
there is great *reward* **final result**.
12 Who *can understand* **discerneth**
is **inadvertent** errors?
cleanse **exonerate** thou me from *secret faults* **the hidden**.
13 *Keep back* **Spare** thy servant also
from *presumptuous sins* **arrogance**;
let them not *have dominion* **reign** over me:
then shall I be *upright* **integrious**,
and I shall be *innocent* **exonerated**
from the great *transgression* **rebellion**.

14 Let the *words* **sayings** of my mouth,
and the meditation of my heart,
be *acceptable in thy sight* **pleasing at thy face**,
O *LORD* **Yah Veh**, my *strength* **rock**, and my redeemer.

20 To *the chief Musician* **His Eminence**,
A Psalm of David.
1 *The LORD hear* **Yah Veh answereth** thee
in the day of *trouble* **tribulation**;
the name of *the God* **Elohim** of *Jacob* **Yaaqov**
defend **lofteth** thee;
2 *Send* **He sendeth** thee help
from the *sanctuary* **holies**,
and *strengthen* **supporteth** thee out of *Zion* **Siyon**;
3 *Remember* **He remembereth** all thy offerings,
and *accept* **fatteneth** thy *burnt sacrifice* **holocausts**;
Selah.
4 *Grant* **He giveth** thee
according to thine own heart,
and *fulfil* **fulfilleth** all thy counsel.
5 We *will rejoice* **shall shout** in thy salvation,
and in the name of our *God* **Elohim**
we *will set up* **shall raise** our banners:
the LORD **Yah Veh** *fulfil* **fulfilleth**
all thy *petitions* **requests**.

19 To His Eminence; A Psalm by David.
1 The heavens scribe the honor of El;
and the expanse tells his handiwork.
2 Day to day gushes sayings
and night to night shows knowledge.
3 There is neither saying nor word
where their voice is not heard.
4 Their line goes throughout all the earth
and their utterances to the end of the world.
In them he sets a tent for the sun:
5 and he, as a groom coming from his canopy;
rejoices as the mighty to run the path.
6 His source is from the end of the heavens
and his circuit to the ends thereof; and
naught is hid from the heat.
7 The torah of Yah Veh is perfect,
restoring the soul;
the witness of Yah Veh is trustworthy,
enwisening the gullible;
8 the precepts of Yah Veh are straight,
cheering the heart;
the misvah of Yah Veh is pure,
enlightening the eyes;
9 the awe of Yah Veh is pure,
standing eternally;
the judgments of Yah Veh are truth,
justified altogether.
10 More to be desired than gold,
yes, than much pure gold;
and sweeter than honey
and the droppings of the honeycomb.
11 Also by them your servant enlightens;
and in guarding them is a great final result.
12 Inadvertent errors—who discerns?
Exonerate me from the hidden;
13 also spare your servant from the arrogant
that they not reign over me:
and I *am* integrious
and exonerated from the great rebellion.
14 *May* the sayings of my mouth
and the meditation of my heart,
be pleasing at your face,
O Yah Veh, my rock and my redeemer.

20 To His Eminence; A Psalm by David.
1 Yah Veh answers you in the day of tribulation;
the name of Elohim of Yaaqov lofts you;
2 he sends you help from the holies
and supports you from Siyon;
3 he remembers all your offerings
and fattens your holocausts.
Selah.
4 He gives you according to your own heart
and fulfills all your counsel.
5 We shout in your salvation
and in the name of our Elohim we raise our banners;
Yah Veh fulfills all your requests.
6 Now know I
that *the LORD* **Yah Veh** saveth his anointed;
he *will hear* **shall answer** him
from his holy *heaven* **heavens**
with the *saving strength* might **of salvation**
of his right *hand*.
7 Some *trust* in chariots, and some in horses:
but we *will* **shall** remember
the name of *the LORD* **Yah Veh** our *God* **Elohim**.
8 They *are brought down* **have**
knuckled under and fallen:
but we are risen, and *stand upright* **restored**.
9 Save, *LORD* **O Yah Veh**:
let the *king hear* **sovereign answer** us
when **the day** we call.

21 To *the chief Musician* **His Eminence**,
A Psalm of David.
1 The *king* **sovereign** shall
joy **cheer** in thy strength,
O *LORD* **Yah Veh**;

and in thy salvation
how *greatly* **mightily** shall he *rejoice* **twirl**!
2 Thou hast given him his heart's desire,
and hast not withholden the *request* **yearning** of his lips.
Selah.
3 For thou *preventest* **anticipatest** him
with the blessings of goodness:
thou settest a crown of pure gold on his head.
4 He asked life of thee, and thou gavest it him,
even length of days *for ever* **eternally** and *ever* **eternally**.
5 His *glory* **honour** is great in thy salvation:
honour and majesty hast thou *laid* **placed** upon him.
6 For thou hast *made* **set** him
most blessed for ever **for blessings eternally**:
thou hast *made* **cheered** him
exceeding glad **with cheerfulness**
with thy *countenance* **face**.
7 For the *king* **sovereign**
trusteth **confideth** in *the LORD* **Yah Veh**,
and through the mercy of *the most High* **Elyon**
he shall not *be moved* **totter**.
8 Thine hand shall find out all thine enemies:
thy right *hand* shall find out those that hate thee.
9 Thou shalt *make* **set** them as a fiery oven
in the time *of thine anger* **at thy face**:
the LORD **Yah Veh** shall swallow them *up* in his wrath,
and the fire shall *devour* **consume** them.
10 Their fruit shalt thou destroy from the earth,
and their seed
from *among* the *children* **sons** of *men* **humanity**.
11 For they *intended* **spread** evil against thee:
they *imagined a mischievous device*
machinated intrigue,
which they are not able *to perform*.
12 *Therefore shalt thou make them turn their back*
Thou shalt set their shoulder,
when thou shalt make ready thine arrows upon thy strings
thou shalt prepare thy cords
against the face of them.
13 Be thou *exalted* **lofted**, *LORD* **O Yah Veh**,
in thine own strength:
so *will* **shall** we sing and *praise* **psalm** thy *power* **might**.

22 To *the chief Musician* **His Eminence**,
upon Aijeleth Shahar **on the Hind of the Dawn**,
A Psalm of David.
1 My *God* **El**, my *God* **El**, why
hast thou forsaken me?
why art thou—so far from *helping me* **my salvation**,
and from the words of my roaring?
2 O my *God* **Elohim**, I *cry* **call** in the *daytime* **day**,
but thou *hearest* **answerest** not;
and in the night *season*, and am not silent.
3 But thou art holy,
O thou that *inhabitest* **settlest**
in the *praises* **halals** of *Israel* **Yisra El**.
4 Our fathers *trusted* **confided** in thee:
they *trusted* **confided**,
and thou *didst deliver them* **slipped them away**.
5 They cried unto thee, and
were delivered **escaped**:
they *trusted* **confided** in thee,
and *were not confounded* **shamed not**.
6 Now I know that Yah Veh saves his anointed;
he answers him from his holy heavens
with the might of salvation of his right
7 —some in chariots—some in horses;
and we remember the name
of Yah Veh our Elohim.
8 They—they knuckle under and fall;
and we rise restored.
9 Save, O Yah Veh;
the sovereign answers us the day we call.

21 To His Eminence; A Psalm by David.
1 The sovereign cheers in your strength,
O Yah Veh;
how mightily he twirls in your salvation:
2 you give him the desire of his heart
and withhold not the yearning of his lips.
Selah.
3 For you anticipate him
with the blessings of goodness;
you set a crown of pure gold on his head;
4 he asks life of you
and you give him length of days
eternally and eternally:
5 great is his honor in your salvation;
you place honor and majesty on him:
6 for you set him for blessings eternally;
you cheer him with cheerfulness by your face.
7 For the sovereign confides in Yah Veh
and through the mercy of Elyon he totters not:
8 your hand finds all your enemies;
your right finds them who hate you:
9 you set them as a fiery oven
at the time of your face:
Yah Veh swallows them in his wrath
and the fire consumes them:
10 you destroy their fruit from the earth
and their seed from the sons of humanity.
11 For they spread evil against you;

they machinate intrigue;
they are not able:
12 for you set their shoulder;
you prepare your cords against their face.
13 Be lofted, O Yah Veh, in your own strength;
we sing and psalm your might.

22 To His Eminence; On the Hind of the Dawn:
A Psalm by David.
1 My El, my El, why forsake you me?
—so far from my salvation
and from the words of my roaring?
2 O my Elohim,
I call by day, and you answer not;
and by night, and am not silent.
3 And you *are* holy
—you who settles in the halals of Yisra El.
4 Our fathers confided in you
—they confided and you slipped them away:
5 they cried to you and escaped;
they confided in you and shamed not.
6 But I am a *worm* **maggot**, and no man;
a reproach of *men* **humanity**,
and despised of the people.
7 All they that see me *laugh* **deride** me *to scorn*:
they *shoot* **bust** out the lip, they shake the head, *saying*,
8 He *trusted* **rolled** on *the LORD* **Yah Veh**
that he *would deliver* **should rescue** him:
let him *deliver* **slip** him **away**, seeing he delighted in him.
9 But thou art he that *took* **gushed**
me out of the *womb* **belly**:
thou didst make me *hope* **confident**
when I was upon my mother's breasts.
10 I was cast upon thee from the womb:
thou art my *God* **El** from my mother's belly.
11 Be not far from me; for
trouble **tribulation** is near;
for there is *none to help* **no helper**.
12 Many *bulls* **bullocks** have
compassed **surrounded** me:
strong bulls **the mighty** of Bashan
have *beset* **surrounded** me *round*.
13 They gaped upon me with their mouths,
as a *ravening* **tearing** and a roaring lion.
14 I am poured out like water,
and all my bones are *out of joint* **separated**:
my heart is like wax;
it is melted in the midst of my *bowels* **inwards**.
15 My *strength* **force** is dried up like a potsherd;
and my tongue *cleaveth* **adhereth** to my *jaws* **prey**;
and thou hast *brought* **set** me into the dust of death.
16 For dogs have *compassed* **surrounded** me:
the *assembly* **witness** of *the wicked* **vilifiers**
have *inclosed* **surrounded** me:
they pierced **as a lion** my hands and my feet.
17 I may *tell* **scribe** all my bones:
they look and *stare* **see** upon me.
18 They *part* **allot** my *garments*
clothes among them,
and *cast lots upon* **toss pebbles for** my *vesture* **robe**.
19 But be not thou far from me, O *LORD* **Yah Veh**:
O my *strength* **might**, haste thee to help me.
20 *Deliver* **Rescue** my soul from the sword;
my *darling* **only** from the *power* **hand** of the dog.
21 Save me from the lion's mouth:
for thou hast *heard* **answered** me
from the horns of the *unicorns* **reems**.
22 I *will declare* **shall scribe**
thy name unto my brethren:
in the midst of the congregation
will I praise **shall I halal** thee.
23 Ye that *fear the LORD* **awe**
Yah Veh, *praise* **halal** him;
all ye the seed of *Jacob* **Yaaqov**, *glorify* **honour** him;
and *fear* **dodge** him, all ye the seed of *Israel* **Yisra El**.
24 For he hath not despised
nor *abhorred* **abominated**
the *affliction* **humbling** of the *afflicted* **humble**;
neither hath he hid his face from him;
but when he cried unto him, he heard.
25 My *praise* **halal** shall be of thee
in the great congregation:
I *will pay* **shall shalam** my vows
before **in front of** them that *fear* **awe** him.
26 The *meek* **humble** shall eat and be satisfied:
they shall *praise the LORD* **halal Yah Veh** that seek him:
your heart shall live *for ever* **eternally**.
27 All the *ends* **finalities** of
the world shall remember
and turn unto *the LORD* **Yah Veh**:
and all the *kindreds* **families** of the *nations* **goyim**
shall *worship before thee* **prostrate at thy face**.
28 For the *kingdom* **sovereigndom**
is *the LORD'S* **Yah Veh's**:
and he is the *governor* **sovereign**
among the *nations* **goyim**.
29 All *they that be* **the** fat upon earth
shall eat and *worship* **prostrate**:
all they that *go down* **descend** to the dust
shall *bow before him* **kneel at his face**:
and none *can keep alive* **shall enliven** his own soul.

30 A seed shall serve him;
it shall be *accounted* **ascribed** to *the Lord* **Adonay**
for a generation.
31 They shall come,
and shall *declare* **tell** his *righteousness* **justness**
unto a people that shall be *born* **birthed**,
that he hath *done* **worked** *this*.
6 I am but a maggot—not a man;
a reproach of humanity despised of the people.
7 All who see me deride me;
they bust out the lip, they shake the head,
8 *saying*,
Roll on Yah Veh! He rescues him!
He slips him away, seeing he delights in him!
9 For you are he who gushed me from the belly;
to confide in you at the breasts of my mother.
10 I was cast on you from the womb;
you are my El from the belly of my mother.
11 Be not far from me; for tribulation is near:
for there is no helper.
12 Many bullocks surround me;
the mighty of Bashan surround me:
13 they gape on me with their mouths
as a tearing and a roaring lion.
14 I am poured as water
and all my bones separate;
my heart is as wax melted midst my inwards;
15 my force is dried as a potsherd; my tongue adheres
to my prey; you set me into the dust of death.
16 For dogs surround me;
the witness of vilifiers surround me:
my hands and my feet as a lion.
17 I scribe all my bones;
they look and see me;
18 they allot my clothes among them
and toss pebbles for my robe.
19 And you, O Yah Veh, be not far from me;
O my might, hasten to help me:
20 rescue my soul from the sword;
my only from the hand of the dog:
21 save me from the mouth of the lion;
from the horns of the reems, answer me.
22 I scribe your name to my brothers;
midst the congregation I halal you.
23 You who awe Yah Veh, halal him;
all you seed of Yaaqov, honor him;
and dodge him, all you seed of Yisra El.
24 For he neither despises nor abominates
the humbling of the humble;
nor hides his face from him;
and in crying to him, he hears.
25 My halal *is* of you in the great congregation;
I shalam my vows in front of them who awe him.
26 The humble eat—satisfied;
they who seek Yah Veh halal him;
your heart lives eternally.
27 All the finalities of the world remember
and turn to Yah Veh;
and all the families of the goyim
prostrate at your face.
28 For the sovereigndom is to Yah Veh;
he is the sovereign among the goyim.
29 All the fat on earth eat and prostrate;
all they who descend to the dust kneel at his face;
and none enlivens his own soul.
30 A seed serves him;
—ascribed to Adonay for a generation.
31 They come and tell his justness to a people
yet to be birthed—whom he has worked.

23 A Psalm of David.
1 *The LORD is my shepherd* **Yah Veh Raah**;
I shall not *want* **lack**.
2 He *maketh me to lie down* **reposeth me**
in *green pastures* **sprouting folds**:
he *leadeth* **guideth** me
beside the *still waters* **waters of rest**.
3 He restoreth my soul:
he leadeth me in the paths of *righteousness* **justness**
for his name's sake.
4 Yea, though I walk through the valley
of the shadow of death,
I *will fear* **shall awe** no evil:
for thou art with me;
thy *rod* **scion** and thy *staff* **crutch**
they *comfort* **sigh over** me.
5 Thou *preparest* **arrangest** a
table *before me* **at my face**
in the presence of *mine enemies* **my tribulators**:
thou anointest my head with *oil* **ointment**;
my cup *runneth over* **satiateth**.
6 Surely goodness and mercy
shall *follow* **pursue** me
all the days of my life:
and I *will dwell* **shall settle**
in the house of *the LORD* **Yah Veh**
for *ever* **a length of days**.

24 A Psalm of David.
1 The earth is *the LORD'S* **Yah Veh's**,
and the fulness *thereof*;
the world, and they that *dwell* **settle** therein.
2 For he hath founded it upon the seas,

and established it upon the *floods* **rivers.**
3 Who shall ascend
into the *hill* **mountain** of *the LORD* **Yah Veh**?
or who shall *stand* **rise** in his holy place?
4 He that hath *clean hands* **innocent palms,**
and a pure heart;
who hath not lifted up his soul unto vanity,
nor *sworn* **oathed** deceitfully.
5 He shall *receive* **lift** the blessing
from *the LORD* **Yah Veh,**
and *righteousness* **justness**
from *the God* **Elohim** of his salvation.
6 This is the generation of them that seek him,
that seek thy face, O *Jacob* **Yaaqov.**
Selah.
7 Lift up your heads, O ye *gates* **portals;**
and be ye lift up, ye *everlasting doors* **eternal portals;**
and the *King* **Sovereign** of *glory*
honour shall *come in* **enter.**
8 Who is this *King* **Sovereign** of *glory* **honour**?
The LORD **Yah Veh** strong and mighty, *the*
LORD **Yah Veh** mighty in *battle* **war.**
9 Lift up your heads, O ye *gates* **portals;**
even lift them up, ye *everlasting doors* **eternal portals;**
and the *King* **Sovereign** of *glory*
honour shall *come in* **enter.**
10 Who is this *King* **Sovereign** of *glory* **honour**?
The LORD of hosts **Yah Veh Sabaoth,**
he is the *King* **Sovereign** of *glory* **honour.**
Selah.

25 *A Psalm* of David.
1 Unto thee, O *LORD* **Yah**
Veh, *do* I lift up my soul.
2 O my *God* **Elohim,** I *trust* **confide** in thee:
let me not *be ashamed* **shame,**
let not mine enemies *triumph* **jump for joy** over me.
3 Yea, let none that *wait on*
await thee *be ashamed* **shame:**
let them *be ashamed* **shame**
which *transgress without cause* **deal vanity covertly.**
4 *Shew* **Have** me **know** thy
ways, O *LORD* **Yah Veh;**
teach me thy paths.
5 *Lead* **Aim** me in thy truth, and teach me:
for thou art *the God* **Elohim** of my salvation;
on thee do I wait **I await thee** all the day.
6 Remember, O *LORD* **Yah Veh,**
thy tender mercies
and thy *loving kindnesses* **kind mercies;**
for they *have been ever of old* **be eternal.**

23 A Psalm by David.
1 Yah Veh Raah;
I lack not.
2 He reposes me in sprouting folds;
he guides me beside the waters of rest:
3 He restores my soul;
he leads me in the paths of justness
for sake of his name.
4 Yes, though I walk through the valley
of the shadow of death,
I awe no evil;
for you are with me;
your scion and your crutch sigh over me:
5 you arrange a table at my face
in the presence of my tribulators;
you anoint my head with ointment;
my cup satiates.
6 Surely goodness and mercy pursue me
all the days of my life;
and I settle in the house of Yah Veh
for a length of days.

24 A Psalm by David.
1 Unto Yah Veh *is* the earth and the fulness;
the world and they who settle therein:
2 for he founded it on the seas
and established it on the rivers.
3 Who ascends into the mountain of Yah Veh?
Who rises in his holy place?
4 He who has innocent palms and a pure heart;
—who neither lifts his soul to vanity
nor oaths deceitfully:
5 he lifts a blessing from Yah Veh
and justness from Elohim of his salvation.
6 This is the generation of seekers
who seek your face, O Yaaqov.
Selah.
7 Lift your heads, O you portals;
be lifted, you eternal portals;
and the Sovereign of honor enters.
8 Who is this Sovereign of honor?
Yah Veh strong and mighty!
Yah Veh mighty in war!
9 Lift your heads, O you portals;
be lifted, you eternal portals;
and the Sovereign of honor enters.
10 Who is this Sovereign of honor?
Yah Veh Sabaoth,
he *is* the Sovereign of honor.
Selah.

25 By David.
1 To you, O Yah Veh, I lift my soul;
2 O my Elohim, I confide in you;
may I neither shame
nor my enemies jump for joy over me:
3 yes, *may* none who await you shame;
shame them who deal vanity covertly.
4 Have me know your ways, O Yah Veh;
teach me your paths:
5 aim me in your truth and teach me;
for you are Elohim of my salvation:
I await you all the day.
6 Remember, O Yah Veh,
your tender mercies and your kind mercies;
for they *are* eternal:
7 Remember not the sins of my youth,
nor my *transgressions* **rebellions**:
according to thy mercy
remember thou me for thy goodness' sake,
O *LORD* **Yah Veh.**
8 Good and *upright* **straight**
is *the LORD* **Yah Veh**:
therefore *will* **shall** he teach sinners in the way.
9 The *meek will* **humble shall**
he *guide* **aim** in judgment:
and the *meek will* **humble shall** he teach his way.
10 All the paths of *the LORD* **Yah Veh**
are mercy and truth
unto such as *keep* **guard** his covenant
and his *testimonies* **witnesses.**
11 For thy name's sake, O *LORD* **Yah Veh,**
pardon mine iniquity **forgive my
perversity**; for it is great.
12 What man is he that *feareth
the LORD* **aweth Yah Veh**?
him shall he teach in the way that he shall choose.
13 His soul shall *dwell at ease* **stay in goodness**;
and his seed shall *inherit* **possess** the earth.
14 The *secret* **private counsel** of *the LORD* **Yah Veh**
is with them that *fear* **awe** him;
and he *will shew* **shall have** them **know** his covenant.
15 Mine eyes
are *ever* **continually** toward *the LORD* **Yah Veh**;
for he shall pluck my feet out of the net.
16 *Turn thee unto* **Face** me,
and *have mercy upon me* **grant me charism**;
for I am *desolate* **alone** and *afflicted* **humble.**
17 The *troubles* **tribulations**
of my heart are enlarged:
O bring thou me out of my distresses.
18 *Look upon mine affliction* **See my humiliation**
and my *pain* **toil**;
and *forgive* **lift** all my sins.
19 *Consider* **See** mine enemies;
for they *are many* **abound by the myriads**;
and they hate me with *cruel* hatred **of violence.**
20 O *keep* **guard** my soul, and *deliver* **rescue** me:
let me not *be ashamed* **shame**;
for I *put* **seek** my *trust* **refuge** in thee.
21 Let integrity and *uprightness* **straightness**
preserve **guard** me;
for I *wait on* **await** thee.
22 Redeem *Israel* **Yisra El**, O *God* **Elohim**,
out of all his *troubles* **tribulations.**
7 remember neither the sins of my youth
nor my rebellions:
according to your mercy
remember me for sake of your goodness,
O Yah Veh.
8 Good and straight *is* Yah Veh;
so he teaches sinners in the way:
9 he aims the humble in judgment;
and he teaches the humble his way.
10 All the paths of Yah Veh are mercy and truth
to such as guard his covenant and his witnesses.
11 For sake of your name, O Yah Veh,
forgive my perversity; for it *is* great.
12 What man is he who awes Yah Veh?
He teaches him in the way he chooses.
13 His soul stays in goodness;
and his seed possesses the earth:
14 the private counsel of Yah Veh
is with them who awe him;
and he has them know his covenant.
15 My eyes are continually toward Yah Veh;
for he plucks my feet from the net.
16 Face me and grant me charism;
for I *am* alone and humble:
17 the tribulations of my heart enlarge;
bring me from my distresses.
18 See my humiliation and my toil;
and lift all my sins:
19 see my enemies;
for they abound by the myriads:
and they hate me with hatred of violence.
20 O guard my soul and rescue me
that I shame not;
for I seek my refuge in you:
21 Integrity and straightness guard me;
for I await you:

22 redeem Yisra El, O Elohim,
from all his tribulations.

26 By David.
1 Judge me, O Yah Veh; for I walk in my integrity:
I confide in Yah Veh; I waver not.
2 Proof me, O Yah Veh,
proof me—refine my reins and my heart.
3 For your mercy is in front of my eyes
and I walk in your truth:
4 I neither settle with vain men
nor go with imposters:
5 I hate the congregation of vilifiers
and settle not with the wicked:
6 I wash my palms in innocency;
I surround your sacrifice altar, O Yah Veh:
7 that they hear the voice of spread hands
and scribe of all your wondrous works.
8 O Yah Veh,
I love the habitation of your house
and the place of the tabernacle of your honor.
9 Neither gather my soul with sinners
nor my life with men of blood
10 —in whose hands is intrigue
and their right full of bribes.
11 But as for me, I walk in my integrity;
redeem me and grant me charism:
12 my foot stands straight;
I bless Yah Veh in the congregations.

26 *A Psalm* of David.
1 Judge me, O *LORD* **Yah Veh;**
for I have walked in mine integrity:
I have *trusted also* **confided** in *the LORD* **Yah Veh**;
therefore I shall not *slide* **waver**.
2 *Examine* **Proof** me, O *LORD* **Yah Veh,**
and prove **proof** me; *try* **refine** my reins and my heart.
3 For thy *lovingkindness* **mercy**
is *before* **in front of** mine eyes:
and I have walked in thy truth.
4 I have not *sat* **settled** with vain *persons* **men,**
neither *will* **shall** I go in with *dissemblers* **imposters**.
5 I have hated the congregation
of *evildoers* **vilifiers**;
and *will* **shall** not *sit* **settle** with the wicked.
6 I *will* **shall** wash *mine hands*
my palms in innocency:
so will I compass **thus shall I surround**
thine **thy sacrifice** altar,
O *LORD* **Yah Veh**:
7 That I may *publish with* **have them hear**
the voice of *thanksgiving* **spread hands,**
and *tell* **scribe** of all thy wondrous works.
8 *LORD* **O Yah Veh,**
I have loved the habitation of thy house,
and the place
where thine honour dwelleth
of the tabernacle of thy honour.
9 Gather not my soul with sinners,
nor my life with *bloody* men **of blood**:
10 In whose hands is *mischief* **intrigue,**
and their right *hand* is full of bribes.
11 But as for me, I *will* **shall** walk in mine integrity:
redeem me, and *be merciful unto me* **grant me charism**.
12 My foot standeth *in an even place* **straight**:
in the congregations *will* **shall** I
bless *the LORD* **Yah Veh**.

27 *A Psalm* of David.
1 *The LORD* **Yah Veh** is my
light and my salvation;
whom shall I *fear* **dread**?
the LORD **Yah Veh** is the *strength* **stronghold** of my life;
of whom shall I *be afraid* **dread**?
2 When the *wicked* **vilifiers,**
even mine enemies **my tribulators**
and *my foes* **mine enemies,**
came upon me to eat up my flesh,
they stumbled and fell.
3 Though *an host* **a camp**
should encamp against me,
my heart shall not *fear* **awe**:
though war should rise against me,
in this *will* **shall** I *be confident* **confide**.
4 *One thing* **This one**
have I *desired* **asked** of *the LORD* **Yah Veh,**
that *will* **shall** I seek after;
that I may *dwell* **settle** in the house of *the LORD* **Yah Veh**
all the days of my life,
to *behold* **see** the *beauty* **pleasantness**
of *the LORD* **Yah Veh,**
and to *enquire* **search** in his *temple* **manse**.
5 For in the *time* **day** of *trouble* **evil**
he shall hide me in his *pavilion* **sukkoth/brush arbor**:
in the *secret* **covert** of his *tabernacle* **tent**
shall he hide me;
he shall *set* **lift** me *up* upon a rock.
6 And now shall mine head be lifted *up*
above mine enemies round about me:
therefore *will I offer* **shall I sacrifice**
in his *tabernacle* **tent**
sacrifices of *joy* **shouting;**
I *will* **shall** sing, yea,

I *will sing praises* **shall psalm** unto *the LORD* **Yah Veh**.
7 Hear, O *LORD* **Yah Veh**,
when I *cry* **call** with my voice:
have mercy also upon me **grant me charism**,
and answer me.
8 *When thou saidst*, Seek ye my face;
my heart said unto thee,
Thy face, *LORD* **O Yah Veh**, *will* **shall** I seek.
9 Hide not thy face *far* from me;
put **pervert** not thy servant away in *anger* **wrath**:
thou hast been my help;
leave me not, neither forsake me,
O *God* **Elohim** of my salvation.
10 When my father and my mother forsake me,
then *the LORD will take* **Yah Veh shall gather** me *up*.
11 Teach me thy way, O *LORD* **Yah Veh**,
and lead me in a *plain* **straight** path,
because of mine enemies.
12 *Deliver* **Give** me not *over*
unto the *will* **soul** of *mine enemies* **my tribulators**:
for false witnesses are risen up against me,
and such as *breathe out cruelty* **exhale violence**.
13 *I had fainted*, unless I had *believed* **trusted**
to see the goodness of *the LORD* **Yah Veh**
in the land of the living.
14 *Wait on the LORD* **Await Yah Veh**:
be of good courage **prevail**,
and he shall strengthen thine heart:
wait, I say, on the LORD **yea, await Yah Veh**.

28 *A Psalm* of David.
1 Unto thee *will I cry* **shall I call**,
O *LORD* **Yah Veh** my rock;
be not silent **hush not** to me:
lest, if thou *be silent* **hush** to me,
I become like them
that *go down* **descend** into the *pit* **well**.
2 Hear the voice of my supplications,
when I cry unto thee,
when I lift *up* my hands
toward *thy holy oracle* **the pulpit of thy holies**.
3 Draw me not away with the wicked,
and with the *workers* **doers** of *iniquity* **mischief**,
which *speak peace* **word shalom**
to their *neighbours* **friends**,
but *mischief* **evil** is in their hearts.

27 By David.
1 Yah Veh is my light and my salvation;
whom dread I?
Yah Veh is the stronghold of my life;
whom dread I?
2 When the vilifiers
—my tribulators and my enemies
come on me to eat my flesh,
they stumble and fall.
3 Though a camp encamp against me
my heart awes not;
though war rises against me
in this I confide.
4 This one I ask of Yah Veh—I seek after:
to settle in the house of Yah Veh
all the days of my life;
to see the pleasantness of Yah Veh
and to search in his manse.
5 For in the day of evil
he hides me in his sukkoth/brush arbor
—in the covert of his tent he hides me
—lifts me on a rock.
6 And now
my head lifts above my enemies all around;
and in his tent
I sacrifice sacrifices of shouting;
I sing, yes, I psalm to Yah Veh.
7 Hear, O Yah Veh, my voice—I call!
Grant me charism and answer me.
8 My heart says to you, Seek my face;
Your face, O Yah Veh, I seek.
9 Neither hide your face from me
nor pervert your servant away in wrath;
you are my help:
neither leave me nor forsake me,
O Elohim of my salvation.
10 When my father and my mother forsake me
then Yah Veh gathers me.
11 Teach me your way, O Yah Veh
and lead me in a straight path
because of my enemies.
12 Give me not to the soul of my tribulators;
for false witnesses rise against me
—such as exhale violence.
13 I trusted not to see the goodness of Yah Veh
in the land of the living.
14 Await Yah Veh!
Prevail; and he strengthens your heart;
yes, await Yah Veh.

28 By David.
1 To you I call, O Yah Veh my rock;
hush not to me:
if you hush to me
I become as they who descend into the well.
2 Hear the voice of my supplications

when I cry to you
—when I lift my hands
toward the pulpit of your holies.
3 Draw me not away with the wicked
—with the doers of mischief;
who word shalom to their friends
but evil *is* in their hearts.
4 Give them according to their deeds,
and according to the *wickedness* **evil**
of their *endeavours* **exploits**:
give them after the work of their hands;
render **return** to them *their desert* **as they dealt.**
5 Because they *regard* **discern** not
the *works* **deeds** of *the LORD* **Yah Veh,**
nor the *operation* **work** of his hands,
he shall *destroy* **demolish** them, and not build them *up.*
6 Blessed be *the LORD* **Yah Veh,**
because he hath heard the voice of my supplications.
7 *The LORD* **Yah Veh**
is my strength and my *shield* **buckler**;
my heart *trusted* **confided** in him, and I am helped:
therefore my heart *greatly rejoiceth* **jumpeth for joy**;
and with my song
will I praise **shall I spread hands unto** him.
8 *The LORD* **Yah Veh** is their strength,
and he is the *saving strength* **stronghold of salvations**
of his anointed.
9 Save thy people, and bless thine inheritance:
feed **befriend** them also,
and lift them up *for ever* **eternally.**

29 A Psalm of David.
1 Give unto *the LORD* **Yah Veh,**
O ye *mighty* **sons of El,**
give unto *the LORD* **Yah Veh**
glory **honour** and strength.
2 Give unto *the LORD* **Yah Veh**
the *glory due unto* **honour of** his name;
worship the LORD **prostrate to Yah Veh**
in the *beauty* **majesty** of *holiness* **his holies.**
3 The voice of *the LORD* **Yah**
Veh is upon the waters:
the *God* **El** of *glory* **honour** thundereth:
the LORD **Yah Veh** is upon many waters.
4 The voice of *the LORD is*
powerful **Yah Veh hath force;**
the voice of *the LORD is full of* **Yah Veh in** majesty.
5 The voice of *the LORD* **Yah**
Veh breaketh the cedars;
yea, *the LORD* **Yah Veh** breaketh the cedars of Lebanon.
6 He maketh them also to *skip* **dance** like a calf;
Lebanon and *Sirion* **Shirion**
like a *young unicorn* **son of reems.**
7 The voice of *the LORD* **Yah Veh**
divideth **heweth** the flames of fire.
8 The voice of *the LORD* **Yah Veh**
shaketh **twirleth** the wilderness;
the LORD **Yah Veh**
shaketh **twirleth** the wilderness of *Kadesh* **Qadesh.**
9 The voice of *the LORD* **Yah Veh**
maketh **causeth** the hinds *to calve* **writhe,**
and *discovereth* **strippeth** the forests:
and in his *temple* **manse**
doth every one speak **all say** of his *glory* **honour.**
10 *The LORD sitteth* **Yah Veh**
settleth upon the flood;
yea, *the LORD sitteth King* **Yah Veh settleth Sovereign**
for ever **eternally.**
11 *The LORD* **Yah Veh**
will **shall** give strength unto his people;
the LORD **Yah Veh**
will **shall** bless his people with *peace* **shalom.**

30 A Psalm and Song
at the *dedication* **hanukkah** of the house of David.
1 I *will extol* **shall exalt** thee, O *LORD* **Yah Veh;**
for thou hast *lifted* **bailed** me up,
and hast not made my *foes* **enemies**
to *rejoice* **cheer** over me.
2 O *LORD* **Yah Veh** my *God* **Elohim,**
I cried unto thee, and thou hast healed me.
3 O *LORD* **Yah Veh,**
thou hast *brought up* **ascended** my soul
from *the grave* **sheol**:
thou hast *kept me alive* **enlivened me,**
that I should not *go down* **descend** to the *pit* **well.**
4 *Sing* **Psalm** unto *the LORD* **Yah Veh,**
O ye *saints* **mercied** of his,
and *give thanks* **spread hands**
at the *remembrance* **memorial** of his holiness.
4 Give them according to their deeds
and according to the evil of their exploits;
give them according to the work of their hands;
return to them as they deal.
5 For they neither discern the deeds of Yah Veh
nor the work of his hands;
he demolishes them and builds them not.
6 Blessed be Yah Veh;
for he hears the voice of my supplications.
7 Yah Veh is my strength and my buckler;
my heart confides in him and I am
helped: and my heart jumps for joy;

and with my song I spread hands to him.
8 Yah Veh is their strength
and he is the stronghold of salvations
of his anointed.
9 Save your people and bless your inheritance;
befriend them also and lift them eternally.

29 A Psalm by David.
1 Give to Yah Veh, O you sons of El;
give to Yah Veh honor and strength;
2 give to Yah Veh the honor of his name:
prostrate to Yah Veh in the majesty of his holies.
3 The voice of Yah Veh *is* on the waters:
the El of honor thunders; Yah Veh *is* on many waters:
4 —the voice of Yah Veh in force
the voice of Yah Veh in majesty:
5 the voice of Yah Veh breaks the cedars;
yes, Yah Veh breaks the cedars of Lebanon.
6 He has them dance as a calf
—Lebanon and Shirion as a son of reems;
7 the voice of Yah Veh hews the flames of fire:
8 the voice of Yah Veh twirls the wilderness;
Yah Veh twirls the wilderness of Qadesh:
9 the voice of Yah Veh causes the hinds to writhe
and strips the forests:
and in his manse all say of his honor.
10 Yah Veh settles on the flood;
yes, Yah Veh settles, Sovereign eternal!
11 Yah Veh gives strength to his people;
Yah Veh blesses his people with shalom.

30 A Psalm; A Song:
at the hanukkah of the house of David.
1 I exalt you, O Yah Veh;
for you bail me up
so that my enemies not cheer over me.
2 O Yah Veh my Elohim
I cry to you and you heal me.
3 O Yah Veh,
you ascend my soul from sheol;
you enliven me that I not descend to the well.
4 Psalm to Yah Veh, all you his mercied;
spread hands at the memorial of his holiness:
5 For his *anger endureth* **wrath**
is but a *moment* **blink**;
in his *favour* **pleasure** is life:
weeping may *endure* **stay** for *a night* **an evening**,
but *joy cometh* **shouting** in the morning.
6 And in my *prosperity* **serenity** I said,
I shall *never be moved* **not totter eternally**.
7 *LORD* **O Yah Veh**, by thy *favour* **pleasure**
thou hast made my mountain
to stand *strong* **in strength**:
thou *didst hide* **hid** thy face, and I was *troubled* **terrified**.
8 I *cried* **called** to thee, O *LORD* **Yah Veh**;
and unto *the LORD* **Yah Veh**
I *made supplication* **sought charism**.
9 What *profit* **gain** is there in my blood,
when I *go down* **descend** to the pit **of ruin**?
Shall the dust *praise* **spread hands unto** thee?
shall it *declare* **tell** thy truth?
10 Hear, O *LORD* **Yah Veh**,
and *have mercy upon me* **grant me charism**:
LORD **O Yah Veh**, be thou my helper.
11 Thou hast turned for me
my *mourning* **chopping** into **round** dancing:
thou hast *put off* **loosed** my *sackcloth* **saq**, and
girded me with *gladness* **cheerfulness**;
12 *To the end*
that my *glory* **honour** may *sing praise* **psalm** to thee
and not *be silent* **hush**.
O *LORD* **Yah Veh** my *God* **Elohim**,
I *will give thanks* **shall spread hands** unto thee
for ever **eternally**.

31 To *the chief Musician* **His Eminence**,
A Psalm of David.
1 In thee, O *LORD* **Yah Veh**,
do I put my trust **I seek refuge**;
let me *never be ashamed* **not eternally shame**:
deliver **slip** me **away** in thy *righteousness* **justness**.
2 *Bow down* **Spread** thine ear to me;
deliver **rescue** me *speedily* **quickly**:
be thou my *strong* rock **of stronghold**,
for an house of *defence* **stronghold** to save me.
3 For thou art my rock and
my *fortress* **stronghold**;
therefore for thy name's sake lead me, and guide me.
4 Pull me out of the net
that they have *laid privily* **hid** for me:
for thou art my *strength* **stronghold**.
5 Into thine hand I *commit* **oversee** my spirit:
thou hast redeemed me,
O *LORD God* **Yah Veh El** of truth.
6 I have hated them that
regard *lying* **vain** vanities:
but I *trust* **confide** in *the LORD* **Yah Veh**.
7 I *will be glad* **shall cheer** and *rejoice* **twirl**
in thy mercy: for thou hast *considered* **seen**
my *trouble* **humiliation**; thou hast known
my soul in *adversities* **tribulations**;
8 And hast not shut me up
into the hand of the enemy:

thou hast *set* **stood** my feet in *a large room* **an expansion**.
9 *Have mercy upon me* **Grant me charism**,
O *LORD* **Yah Veh**,
for I am *in trouble* **tribulated**:
mine eye is *consumed* **motheaten** with *grief* **vexation**,
yea, my soul and my belly.
10 For my life is *spent* **finished off** with grief,
and my years with sighing:
my *strength faileth* **force faltereth**
because of *mine iniquity* **my perversity**,
and my bones are *consumed* **motheaten**.
11 I was a reproach
among all *mine enemies* **my tribulators**,
but *especially* **mightily**
among my *neighbours* **fellow tabernaclers**,
and a *fear* **dread** to *mine acquaintance* **those I know**:
they that did see me without fled from me.
12 I am forgotten
as *a dead man out of mind* **one dead of heart**:
I am like *a broken vessel* **an**
instrument that destructeth.
13 For I have heard the slander of many:
fear was on every side **terror surrounded**:
while they *took* **set** counsel *together* against me,
they *devised* **intrigued** to take *away* my *life* **soul**.
5 his wrath is for but a blink;
in his pleasure is life:
weeping stays at evening
but shouting at morning:
6 and in my serenity I say, I totter not eternally.
7 O Yah Veh, at your pleasure
my mountain stands in strength; you
hide your face and I terrify.
8 I call to you, O Yah Veh;
and to Yah Veh I seek charism.
9 What gain is there in my blood
when I descend to the pit of ruin?
Does dust spread hands to you?
—tell your truth?
10 Hear, O Yah Veh, and grant me charism;
O Yah Veh, be my helper.
11 Turn my chopping into round dancing;
loose my saq and girt me with cheerfulness:
12 so that my honor *may* psalm to you
and not hush.
O Yah Veh my Elohim,
I spread hands to you eternally.

31 To His Eminence; A Psalm by David.
1 In you, O Yah Veh, I seek refuge;
shame me not eternally;
slip me away in your justness:
2 spread your ear to me;
rescue me quickly;
be my rock of stronghold
—a house of stronghold to save me:
3 for you are my rock and my stronghold;
for sake of your name lead me and guide me.
4 Pull me from the net they hide for me;
for you are my stronghold:
5 into your hand I oversee my spirit;
you redeemed me, O Yah Veh El of truth.
6 I hate them who regard vain vanities
and I confide in Yah Veh;
7 I cheer and twirl in your mercy
for you see my humiliation;
you know my soul in tribulations.
8 And you shut me not in the hand of the enemy;
you stand my feet in an expanse:
9 grant me charism, O Yah Veh, for I tribulate;
my eye, my soul and my belly
are motheaten with vexation.
10 For my life is finished off with grief
and my years with sighing;
my force falters because of my perversity
and my bones are motheaten.
11 I am a reproach among all my tribulators
and mighty among my fellow tabernaclers
and a dread to those I know;
they who see me outside flee from me.
12 I am forgotten as one dead of heart
—as an instrument that destructs:
13 for I hear the slander of many;
terror surrounds as they set counsel against me:
they intrigue to take my soul.
14 But I *trusted* **confided** in
thee, O *LORD* **Yah Veh**:
I said, Thou art my *God* **Elohim**.
15 My times are in thy hand:
deliver **rescue** me from the hand of mine enemies,
and from them that *persecute* **pursue** me.
16 *Make* **Light** thy face *to shine* upon thy servant:
save me for thy mercies' sake.
17 Let me not *be ashamed*
shame, O *LORD* **Yah Veh**;
for I have called upon thee:
let the wicked *be ashamed* **shame**,
and let them *be silent* **hush** in *the grave* **sheol**.
18 Let the *lying* **false** lips be *put to silence* **muted**;
which *speak grievous things* **word impudence**
proudly **with pomp** and *contemptuously* **disrespect**

against the *righteous* **just.**
19 *Oh* how great is thy goodness,
which thou hast *laid up* **treasured**
for them that *fear* **awe** thee;
which thou hast *wrought* **done**
for them that *trust* **seek refuge** in thee
before **in front of** the sons of *men* **humanity**!
20 Thou shalt hide them
in the *secret* **covert** of thy *presence* **face**
from the pride of man:
thou shalt *keep* **hide** them *secretly*
in a *pavilion* **sukkoth/brush arbor**
from the strife of tongues.
21 Blessed be *the LORD* **Yah Veh**:
for he hath shewed me his marvellous *kindness* **mercy**
in a *strong* city **with rampart.**
22 For I said in my haste,
I am cut off *from before* **in front of** thine eyes:
nevertheless **surely** thou heardest
the voice of my supplications
when I cried unto thee.
23 O love *the LORD* **Yah Veh,**
all ye his *saints* **mercied**:
for the LORD **Yah Veh**
preserveth **guardeth** the *faithful* **trustworthy,**
and *plentifully rewardeth* **shalameth**
the *proud doer* **pompous worker.**
24 *Be of good courage* **Prevail,**
and he shall strengthen your heart,
all ye that *hope in the LORD* **await Yah Veh.**

32 *A Psalm* of David, *Maschil* **On Comprehension.**
1 *Blessed* **Blithe** *is* he
whose *transgression* **rebellion** is *forgiven* **lifted,**
whose sin is covered.
2 *Blessed* **Blithe** *is the man* **humanity**
unto whom *the LORD* **Yah Veh**
imputeth **fabricateth** not *iniquity* **perversity,**
and in whose spirit there is no *guile* **deceit.**
3 When I *kept silence* **hushed,**
my bones *waxed old* **wore out**
through my roaring all the day long.
4 For day and night thy hand was heavy upon me:
my moisture is turned into the
drought **parch** of summer.
Selah.
5 I *acknowledged* **made known**
my sin unto thee,
and *mine iniquity* **my perversity**
have I not *hid* **covered over.**
I said, I *will confess* **shall spread hands**
for my *transgressions* **rebellions**
unto *the LORD* **Yah Veh**;
and thou *forgavest* **liftest** the *iniquity*
perversity of my sin.
Selah.
6 For this shall every one that is *godly* **mercied**
pray unto thee in a time when thou mayest be found:
surely in the *floods* **overflowing** of great waters
they shall not *come nigh unto* **touch** him.
7 Thou art my *hiding place* **covert**;
thou shalt *preserve* **guard** me from *trouble* **tribulation;**
thou shalt *compass* **surround** me *about*
with *songs* **shouts** of *deliverance* **escape.**
Selah.
8 I *will instruct* **shall have** thee **discern**
and teach thee in the way which thou shalt go:
I *will guide* **shall counsel** thee with mine eye.
14 And I—I confide in you, O Yah Veh;
I say, You are my Elohim.
15 My times *are* in your hand;
rescue me from the hand of my enemies
—from them who pursue me:
16 light your face on your servant;
save me for sake of your mercies:
17 shame me not, O Yah Veh;
for I call on you:
shame the wicked to hush in sheol;
18 mute the false lips
who with pomp and disrespect word
impudence against the just.
19 How great is your goodness
which you treasure for them who awe you;
which you work
for them who seek refuge in you
in front of the sons of humanity.
20 Hide them in the covert of your face
from the pride of man;
hide them in a sukkoth/brush arbor
from the strife of tongues.
21 Blessed—Yah Veh;
for he shows me his marvellous mercy
in a city with rampart.
22 And I—I say in my haste,
I am cut off in front of your eyes!
—surely you hear the voice of my supplications
when I cry to you.
23 O love Yah Veh, all you his mercied;
Yah Veh guards the trustworthy
and shalams the pompous worker.
24 Prevail! and he strengthens your heart,
all you who await Yah Veh.

32 By David; On Comprehension.
1 Blithe
—he whose rebellion is lifted;
whose sin is covered:
2 Blithe
—humanity
to whom Yah Veh fabricates not perversity
and in whose spirit is no deceit.
3 When I hush, my bones become worn
through my roaring all day long:
4 when by day and night
your hand is heavy on me;
my moisture turns into the parch of summer.
Selah.
5 My sin, you know;
and my perversity, I covered not:
I say, I spread hands for my rebellions to Yah Veh;
and you lift the perversity of my sin.
Selah.
6 For this all the mercied pray to you
in a time of finding you;
surely in the overflowing of great waters
they touch him not.
7 You are my covert;
you guard me from tribulation:
you surround me with shouts of escape.
Selah.
8 I have you discern
and teach you the way to go;
I counsel you with my eye.
9 Be ye not as the horse, or as the mule,
which *have no understanding* **discern not**:
whose mouth must be *held in* **muzzled**
with bit and bridle,
lest they come near unto thee.
10 Many sorrows shall be to the wicked:
but he that *trusteth* **confideth** in *the LORD* **Yah Veh**,
mercy shall *compass* **surround** him *about*.
11 *Be glad* **Cheer** in *the LORD* **Yah Veh**,
and *rejoice* **twirl**, ye *righteous* **just**:
and shout *for joy*,
all ye that are *upright* **straight** in heart.

33 *Rejoice* **Shout** in *the LORD* **Yah Veh**,
O ye *righteous* **just**:
for *praise is comely for* **halal befitteth**
the *upright* **straight**.
2 *Praise the LORD* **Spread**
hands to Yah Veh with harp:
sing **psalm** unto him with the *psaltery* **bagpipe**
and *an instrument of ten strings* **decachord**.
3 Sing unto him a new song;
play skilfully **strum well—pleasingly**
with a *loud noise* **blast**.
4 For the word of *the LORD*
Yah Veh is *right* **straight**;
and all his works *are done in truth* **trustworthy**.
5 He loveth *righteousness* **justness** and judgment:
the earth is full
of the *goodness* **mercy** of *the LORD* **Yah Veh**.
6 By the word of *the LORD* **Yah Veh**
were the heavens *made* **worked**;
and all the host of them
by the *breath* **spirit/wind** of his mouth.
7 He gathereth the waters of the sea
together as an heap:
he *layeth up the deep in storehouses*
giveth treasuries in the abyss.
8 Let all the earth *fear the LORD* **awe Yah Veh**:
let all *the inhabitants of* **that settle in** the world
stand in awe of **dodge** him.
9 For he *spake* **said**, and **so be** it *was done*;
he *commanded* **misvahed**, and it stood *fast*.
10 *The LORD bringeth* **Yah Veh voideth**
the counsel of the *heathen* **goyim** *to nought*:
he *maketh* **anulleth**
the *devices* **fabrications** of the people *of none effect*.
11 The counsel of *the LORD* **Yah Veh**
standeth *for ever* **eternally**,
the *thoughts* **fabrications** of his heart
to all generations **generation to generation**.
12 *Blessed* **Blithe** *is* the *nation* **goyim**
whose *God* **Elohim** is *the LORD* **Yah Veh**;
and the people whom he hath chosen
for his own inheritance.
13 *The LORD looketh* **Yah Veh**
seeth from *heaven* **the heavens**;
he beholdeth all the sons of *men* **humanity**.
14 From the *place* **establishment**
of his *habitation* **settlement**
he *looketh* **peereth** upon all
the inhabitants of **that settled on** the earth.
15 He *fashioneth* **formeth**
their hearts *alike* **together**;
he *considereth* **discerneth** all their works.
16 There is no *king* **sovereign** saved
by the *multitude* **abundance** of *an host* **valour**:
a **the** mighty *man* is not *delivered* **rescued**
by *much strength* **abundant force**.
17 An horse is a *vain thing*
falsehood for *safety* **salvation**:

neither shall he *deliver* **rescue** *any*
by his great *strength* **valour**.
18 Behold, the eye of *the LORD* **Yah Veh**
is upon them that *fear* **awe** him,
upon them that *hope in* **await** his mercy;
19 To *deliver* **rescue** their soul from death,
and to *keep* **enliven** them *alive* in famine.
20 Our soul *waiteth for the*
LORD **awaiteth Yah Veh**:
he is our help and our *shield* **buckler**.
21 For our heart shall *rejoice* **cheer** in him,
because we have *trusted* **confided** in his holy name.
22 Let thy mercy, O *LORD* **Yah Veh**, be upon us,
according as we *hope in* **await** thee.
9 Be not as the horse or as the mule
who discern not;
whose mouth is muzzled with bit and bridle
lest they come near to you.
10 Many *are* the sorrows of the wicked;
as for him who confides in Yah Veh,
mercy surrounds him.
11 Cheer in Yah Veh and twirl, you just;
and shout, all you straight in heart.
33 Shout in Yah Veh, O you just;
for halal befits the straight:
2 spread hands to Yah Veh with harp;
psalm to him with bagpipe and decachord:
3 sing to him a new song;
strum well—pleasingly with a blast.
4 For the word of Yah Veh *is* straight;
and all his works trustworthy:
5 he loves justness and judgment;
the earth is full of the mercy of Yah Veh.
6 By the word of Yah Veh
were the heavens worked;
and all their host
by the spirit/wind of his mouth:
7 he gathers the waters of the sea as a heap;
he gives treasuries in the abyss.
8 All in the earth, awe Yah Veh;
all settled in the world, dodge him.
9 For he says, and so be it;
he misvahs, and it stands.
10 Yah Veh voids the counsel of the goyim;
he annuls the fabrications of the people:
11 the counsel of Yah Veh stands eternal;
the fabrications of his heart generation to generation.
12 Blithe—the goyim
whose Elohim is Yah Veh;
and the people
whom he chose for his own inheritance.
13 Yah Veh sees from the heavens;
he beholds all the sons of humanity:
14 from the establishment of his settlement
he peers on all who settle on the earth:
15 he forms their hearts together;
he discerns all their works.
16 Neither is the sovereign saved
by the abundance of valour;
nor the mighty rescued
by the abundance of force.
17 A horse is a falsehood for salvation;
he rescues not by his great valour.
18 Behold, the eye of Yah Veh
is on them who awe him
—on them who await his mercy;
19 to rescue their soul from death
and to enliven them in famine.
20 Our soul awaits Yah Veh;
he is our help and our buckler.
21 For our heart cheers in him
because we confide in his holy name.
22 *May* your mercy, O Yah Veh, be on us,
according as we await you.

34 *A Psalm* of David,
when he *changed* **altered** his *behaviour* **taste**
before Abimelech **at the face of Abi Melech**;
who *drove him away* **exiled him**, and he *departed* **went**.
1 I *will* **shall** bless *the LORD* **Yah Veh** at all times:
his *praise* **halal** shall continually be in my mouth.
2 My soul shall *make her boast* **halal**
in *the LORD* **Yah Veh**:
the humble shall hear *thereof*, and *be glad* **cheer**.
3 O *magnify the LORD* **greaten Yah Veh** with me,
and let us exalt his name together.
4 I sought *the LORD* **Yah Veh**, and he heard me,
and *delivered* **rescued** me from all my *fears* **terrors**.
5 They looked unto him, and
were lightened **sparkled**:
and their faces *were* **blushed** not *ashamed*.
6 This *poor man cried* **humble one called**,
and *the LORD* **Yah Veh** heard *him*,
and saved him out of all his *troubles* **tribulations**.
7 The angel of *the LORD* **Yah Veh**
encampeth round about them that *fear* **awe**
him, and *delivereth* **rescueth** them.
8 O taste and see that *the LORD* **Yah Veh** is good:
blessed **blithe** *is* the *man* **mighty**
that *trusteth* **seeketh refuge** in him.
9 O *fear the LORD* **awe Yah**
Veh, ye his *saints* **holy**:

for there is no *want* **lack** to them that *fear* **awe** him.
10 The *young lions do* **whelps** lack,
and *suffer hunger* **famish**:
but they that seek *the LORD* **Yah Veh**
shall not *want* **lack** any good *thing*.
11 Come, ye *children* **sons**, hearken unto me:
I *will* **shall** teach you the *fear* **awe** of *the LORD* **Yah Veh**.
12 What man is he that desireth life,
and loveth *many* days, that he may see good?
13 *Keep* **Guard** thy tongue from evil,
and thy lips from *speaking guile* **wording deceit**.
14 *Depart* **Turn away** from evil, and *do* **work** good;
seek *peace* **shalom**, and pursue it.
15 The eyes of *the LORD* **Yah Veh**
are upon the *righteous* **just**,
and his ears *are open* unto their cry.
16 The face of *the LORD* **Yah Veh**
is against them that *do* **work** evil,
to cut off *the remembrance of them* **their memorial**
from the earth.
17 *The righteous* **They** cry,
and *the LORD* **Yah Veh** heareth,
and *delivereth* **rescueth** them
out of all their *troubles* **tribulations**.
18 *The LORD* **Yah Veh** is nigh unto them
that are of a *broken* **crushed** heart; and
saveth such as be of a contrite spirit.
19 Many are the *afflictions*
evils of the *righteous* **just**:
but *the LORD delivereth* **Yah Veh rescueth** him
out of them all.
20 He *keepeth* **guardeth** all his bones:
not one of them is broken.
21 Evil shall *slay* **deathify** the wicked:
and they that hate the *righteous* **just**
shall *be desolate* **have guilted**.
22 *The LORD* **Yah Veh**
redeemeth the soul of his servants:
and none of them that *trust* **seek refuge** in him
shall be desolate **hath guilted**.

35 *A Psalm* of David.
1 *Plead my cause* **Defend**, O *LORD* **Yah Veh**,
with them that *strive* **contend** with me:
fight *against* them that fight *against* me.
2 Take hold of *shield* **buckler** and *buckler* **shield**,
and *stand up* **arise** for mine help.
3 Draw out also the spear,
and *stop the way against* **shut up and confront** them
that *persecute* **pursue** me:
say unto my soul, I am thy salvation.

34 By David;
when he alters his taste at the face of Abi Melech;
who exiles him and he goes.
1 I bless Yah Veh at all times;
his halal is continually in my mouth:
2 my soul halals in Yah Veh;
the humble hear and cheer:
3 O greaten Yah Veh with me
and exalt his name together.
4 I seek Yah Veh and he hears me
—rescues me from all my terrors.
5 They look to him and sparkle;
and their faces blushed not.
6 This humble one calls
and Yah Veh hears
and saves him from all his tribulations.
7 The angel of Yah Veh
encamps around all who awe him;
and rescues them.
8 O taste and see that Yah Veh is good;
Blithe—the mighty who seek refuge in him.
9 Awe Yah Veh, you his holy;
for there is no lack to them who awe him.
10 The whelps lack and famish;
but they who seek Yah Veh lack not any good.
11 Come, you sons, hearken to me;
I teach you the awe of Yah Veh.
12 What man desires life and loves days
to see good?
13 Guard your tongue from evil
and your lips from wording deceit:
14 turn from evil and work good;
seek shalom and pursue it.
15 The eyes of Yah Veh *are* on the just
and his ears to their cry.
16 The face of Yah Veh *is* against all who work evil,
to cut off their memorial from the earth.
17 They cry and Yah Veh hears
and rescues them from all their tribulations:
18 Yah Veh is near the crushed heart;
and the contrite spirit he saves:
19 many are the evils of the just;
Yah Veh rescues him from them all.
20 He guards all his bones;
not one of them is broken.
21 Evil deathifies the wicked;
and they who hate the just guilt.
22 Yah Veh redeems the soul of his servants
and none who seek refuge in him guilts.

35 By David.

1 Defend, O Yah Veh,
from them who contend with me;
fight them who fight me:
2 uphold with buckler and shield
and rise for my help:
3 and draw the spear;
shut up and confront them who pursue me;
say to my soul, I am your salvation.
4 Let them *be confounded* **shame**
and *put to* shame **them** that seek *after* my soul:
let them *be turned back* **apostatize**
and *brought to confusion* **blush**
that *devise my hurt* **fabricate me evil.**
5 Let them be as chaff *before*
at the face of the wind:
and **in overthrowing,**
let the angel of *the LORD chase*
Yah Veh overthrow them.
6 Let their way be dark and slippery:
and let the angel of *the LORD* **Yah Veh**
persecute **pursue** them.
7 For *without cause* **gratuitously**
have they hid for me
their net in a pit **of ruin,**
which *without cause* **gratuitously** they have digged
for my soul.
8 Let *destruction* **devastation** come upon him
at unawares **as he hath not known**;
and let his net that he hath hid
catch himself **capture him**:
into that very *destruction* **devastation** let him fall.
9 And my soul
shall *be joyful* **twirl** in *the LORD* **Yah Veh**:
it shall rejoice in his salvation.
10 All my bones shall say, *LORD* **O Yah Veh,**
who is like unto thee,
which *deliverest* **rescuest** the *poor* **humble**
from him that is *too strong for him* **stronger than he,**
yea, the *poor* **humble** and the needy
from him that *spoileth* **strippeth** him?
11 *False witnesses* **Witnesses**
of violence did rise up;
they *laid to my charge things* **asked me** that I knew not.
12 They *rewarded* **shalamed** me evil for good
to the *spoiling* **bereaving** of my soul.
13 But as for me,
when they were sick, my *clothing* **robe** was *sackcloth* **saq**:
I humbled my soul with fasting;
and my prayer returned into mine own bosom.
14 I *behaved myself* **walked**
as though he *had been* **be** my friend or brother:
I *bowed down heavily* **prostrated darkened,**
as one that mourneth for *his* **a** mother.
15 But in *mine adversity* **my limping**
they *rejoiced* **cheered,**
and gathered *themselves* together:
yea, the *abject* **smiters**
gathered *themselves together* against me,
and I knew it not;
they *did tear me* **ripped**, and *ceased* **hushed** not:
16 With *hypocritical* **profaners,**
mockers in feasts **jeerers at bakings**, they
gnashed upon me with their teeth.
17 *Lord* **Adonay,**
how long *wilt* **shalt** thou *look on* **see** me?
rescue **restore** my soul
from their *destructions* **devastations,**
my *darling* **only** from the *lions* **whelps.**
18 I *will give thee thanks* **shall**
spread hands to thee
in the great congregation:
I *will praise* **shall halal** thee among *much* **mighty** people.
19 Let not them that are mine enemies
wrongfully rejoice **falsely cheer** over me:
neither let them wink—**blink** with the eye
that hate me *without a cause* **gratuitously.**
20 For they *speak* **word** not *peace* **shalom**:
but they *devise deceitful matters*
fabricate words of deceit
against them that *are quiet* **rest** in the land.
21 Yea,
they *opened* **enlarged** their mouth *wide* against me,
and said, Aha, aha, our eye hath seen it.
22 *This* thou hast seen, O *LORD* **Yah Veh**:
keep **hush** not *silence*:
O *Lord* **Adonay,** be not far from me.
23 *Stir up thyself* **Waken,** and
awake to my judgment,
even unto my *cause* **defence,**
my *God* **Elohim** and my *Lord* **Adonay.**
24 Judge me, O *LORD* **Yah Veh** my *God* **Elohim,**
according to thy *righteousness* **justness**; and
let them not *rejoice* **cheer** over me.
4 Shame them—shame them who seek my soul;
they who fabricate me evil
apostatize and blush:
5 they are as chaff at the face of the wind;
and in overthrowing,
the angel of Yah Veh overthrows them;
6 their way is dark and slippery;

and the angel of Yah Veh pursues them.
7 For gratuitously they hide their net for me
in a pit of ruin,
which they gratuitously dig for my soul:
8 devastation comes on him
such as he never knew;
and the net he hid captures him;
into that very devastation he falls.
9 My soul twirls in Yah Veh
—rejoices in his salvation.
10 All my bones say, O Yah Veh,
who is likened to you,
who rescues the humble
from him who is stronger than he?
—yes, the humble and the needy
from him who strips him?
11 Witnesses of violence rise;
they ask me what I know not:
12 they shalam me evil for good
to the bereaving of my soul.
13 And I, in their sickness, enrobe with saq;
I humble my soul with fasting:
and my prayer returns into my own bosom.
14 I walk as a friend or brother;
I prostrate darkened, as one mourns for a mother.
15 And in my limping
they cheer and gather together;
the smiters gather against me
and I know it not;
they rip and hush not.
16 With profaners, jeerers at bakings,
they gnash on me with their teeth.
17 Adonay, until when see you me?
Restore my soul from their devastations
—my only from the whelps.
18 I spread hands to you in the great congregation;
I halal you among mighty people.
19 May not my enemies cheer over me falsely;
—blink with the eye, who hate me gratuitously.
20 For they word not shalom;
but fabricate words of deceit
against them who rest in the land.
21 yes, they enlarge their mouth against me
and say, Aha, aha, our eye sees!
22 You see, O Yah Veh; hush not.
O Adonay, be not far from me.
23 Waken—waken to my judgment
—to my defence, my Elohim and my Adonay.
24 Judge me, O Yah Veh my Elohim,
according to your justness; that they not cheer over me:
25 Let them not say in their hearts,
Ah, so would we have it: **Aha, aha, O soul!** let
them not say, We have swallowed him *up*.
26 Let them *be ashamed* **shame**
and *brought to confusion* **blush** together
that *rejoice* **cheer** at mine *hurt* **evil**:
let them be *clothed* **enrobed** with shame and dishonour
that *magnify themselves* **greaten** against me.
27 Let them shout *for joy*, and *be glad* **cheer**,
that *favour* **delight in** my *righteous cause* **justness**:
yea, let them say continually,
Let the LORD **Yah Veh** be *magnified* **greatened**,
which *hath pleasure* **delighteth**
in the *prosperity* **shalom** of his servant.
28 And my tongue shall *speak* **meditate**
of thy *righteousness* **justness**
and of thy *praise* **halal** all the day long.

36 To *the chief Musician* **His Eminence**,
A Psalm of David the servant of *the LORD* **Yah Veh**.
1 The *transgression* **rebellion** of the wicked
saith **doth oracle** within my heart,
that there is no *fear* **dread** of *God* **Elohim**
before **in front of** his eyes.
2 For he *flattereth* **smootheth over** himself
in his own eyes,
until his *iniquity* **perversity** be found to be *hateful* **hated**.
3 The words of his mouth
are *iniquity* **mischief** and deceit:
he hath *left off to be wise* **ceased comprehending**,
and to *do good* **well—please**.
4 He *deviseth* **fabricateth** mischief upon his bed;
he setteth himself in a way that is not good;
he *abhorreth* **spurneth** not evil.
5 Thy mercy, O *LORD* **Yah Veh**, is in the heavens;
and thy *faithfulness* **trustworthiness**
reacheth unto the *clouds* **vapours**.
6 Thy *righteousness* **justness**
is like the *great mountains* **mountains of El**;
thy judgments are a great *deep* **abyss**:
O *LORD* **Yah Veh**,
thou *preservest man* **savest human** and *beast* **animal**.
7 How *excellent* **esteemed** is
thy *lovingkindness* **mercy**,
O *God* **Elohim**!
therefore the *children* **sons** of *men* **humanity**
put their trust **seek refuge** under
the shadow of thy wings.
8 They shall *be abundantly satisfied* **satiate**
with the fatness of thy house;
and thou shalt *make them drink* **water them**

of the *river* **wadi** of thy pleasures.
9 For with thee is the fountain of life:
in thy light shall we see light.
10 O *continue* **draw out** thy *lovingkindness* **mercy**
unto them that know thee;
and thy *righteousness* **justness**
to the *upright* **straight** in heart.
11 Let not the foot of *pride* **pomp** come against me,
and let not the hand of the wicked *remove* **waver** me.
12 There are the *workers* **doers**
of *iniquity* **mischief** fallen:
they are *cast down* **overthrown**,
and shall not be able to rise.

37 *A Psalm* of David.
1 *Fret* **Inflame** not *thyself*
because of *evildoers* **vilifiers**,
neither be thou envious
against the workers of *iniquity* **wickedness**.
2 For they shall *soon* **quickly** be *cut down* **clipped**
like the grass,
and wither as the green *herb* **sprout**.
3 *Trust* **Confide** in *the LORD*
Yah Veh, and *do* **work** good;
so **thus** shalt thou *dwell* **tabernacle** in the land, and
verily thou shalt be fed **tend to trustworthiness**.
4 Delight thyself also in *the LORD* **Yah Veh**:
and he shall give thee the *desires* **requests** of thine heart.
5 *Commit* **Roll** thy way unto *the LORD* **Yah Veh**;
trust **confide** also in him;
and he shall *bring it to pass* **work it**.
25 that they not say in their hearts,
Aha, aha, O soul!
that they not say, We swallowed him!
26 Shame and blush them together
who cheer at my evil;
enrobe them with shame and dishonor
who greaten against me:
27 that they who delight in my justness
shout and cheer;
yes, that they say continually,
Yah Veh is greatened,
who delights in the shalom of his servant.
28 And my tongue meditates of your justness
and of your halal all the day long.

36 To His Eminence;
by David the servant of Yah Veh.
1 The rebellion of the wicked
oracles within my heart;
the dread of Elohim is not in front of his eyes:
2 for he smooths it over in his own eyes
only to find out his perversity is hated.
3 The words of his mouth are mischief and deceit;
he ceases comprehending, and to well—please:
4 he fabricates mischief on his bed;
he neither sets himself in a good way
nor spurns evil.
5 Your mercy, O Yah Veh, *is* in the heavens;
your trustworthiness to the vapours;
6 your justness is as the mountains of El;
your judgments as a great abyss.
O Yah Veh, you save human and animal.
7 How esteemed *is* your mercy, O Elohim!
and the sons of humanity
seek refuge under the shadow of your wings:
8 they satiate with the fatness of your house;
you water them from the wadi of your pleasures:
9 for the fountain of life is with you;
in your light we see light.
10 Draw out your mercy to them who know you;
and your justness to the straight in heart:
11 that neither the foot of pomp come against me
nor the hand of the wicked waver me.
12 There the doers of mischief fall;
—overthrown—not able to rise.

37 By David.
1 Neither inflame because of vilifiers
nor envious against workers of wickedness.
2 For they are quickly clipped as the grass
and wither as the green sprout.
3 Confide in Yah Veh and work good;
thus you tabernacle in the land
and tend to trustworthiness.
4 And delight yourself in Yah Veh
and he gives you the requests of your heart.
5 Roll your way to Yah Veh; confide in him;
and he works
6 And he shall bring forth
thy *righteousness* **justness** as the light,
and thy judgment as the noonday.
7 *Rest* **Be still** in *the LORD* **Yah Veh**,
and *wait patiently* **writhe** for him:
fret **inflame** not *thyself*
because of him who prospereth in his way,
because of the man
who *bringeth wicked devices to pass* **worketh intrigue**.
8 *Cease from anger* **Slacken wrath**,
and forsake *wrath* **fury**:
fret **inflame** not *thyself in any wise to do evil* **to vilify**.
9 For *evildoers* **vilifiers** shall be cut off:
but those that *wait upon the LORD* **await Yah Veh**,

they shall *inherit* **possess** the earth.
10 For yet a little *while*,
and the wicked shall not be:
yea, thou shalt *diligently consider* **discern** his place,
and it shall not be.
11 But the *meek* **humble** shall
inherit **possess** the earth;
and shall delight themselves
in the abundance of *peace* **shalom**.
12 The wicked *plotteth* **intrigueth** against the just,
and gnasheth upon him with his teeth.
13 *The Lord* **Adonay** shall laugh at him:
for he seeth that his day is coming.
14 The wicked have drawn out the sword,
and have bent their bow,
to *cast down* **fell** the *poor* **humble** and needy,
and to *slay* **slaughter**
such as be of upright conversation **the straight of way**.
15 Their sword shall enter into their own heart,
and their bows shall be broken.
16 A little that *a righteous man* **the just** hath
is better than the *riches* **abundance** of many wicked.
17 For the arms of the wicked shall be broken:
but *the LORD* **Yah Veh** upholdeth the *righteous* **just**.
18 *The LORD* **Yah Veh**
knoweth the days of the *upright* **integrious**:
and their inheritance shall be *for ever* **eternal**.
19 They shall not *be ashamed*
shame in the evil time:
and in the days of famine
they shall *be satisfied* **satiate**.
20 But the wicked shall *perish* **destruct**,
and the enemies of *the LORD* **Yah Veh**
shall be as the *fat* **esteem** of *lambs* **rams**:
they shall consume—**finished off**;
into smoke shall they *consume away* **be finished off**.
21 The wicked borroweth,
and *payeth* **doth** not **shalam** *again*:
but the *righteous* **just**
sheweth mercy **granteth charism**, and giveth.
22 For such as be blessed of him
shall *inherit* **possess** the earth;
and they that be *cursed* **abased** of him
shall be cut off.
23 The *steps* **paces** of *a good man* **the mighty**
are *ordered* **established** by *the LORD* **Yah Veh**:
and he delighteth in his way.
24 Though he fall, he shall
not be *utterly* cast down:
for *the LORD* **Yah Veh** upholdeth him with his hand.
25 I have been *young* **a lad**,
and *now am old* **have aged**;
yet have I not seen the *righteous* **just** forsaken,
nor his seed *begging* **seeking** bread.
26 He *is ever merciful* **ever**
granteth charism all days,
and lendeth;
and his seed *is blessed* **shall be for blessings**.
27 *Depart* **Turn away** from evil, and *do* **work** good;
and *dwell for evermore* **tabernacle eternally**.
28 For *the LORD* **Yah Veh** loveth judgment,
and forsaketh not his *saints* **mercied**;
they are *preserved for ever* **guarded eternally**:
but the seed of the wicked shall be cut off.
29 The *righteous* **just** shall *inherit* **possess** the land,
and *dwell* **tabernacle** therein *for ever* **eternally**.
30 The mouth of the *righteous* **just**
speaketh **meditateth** wisdom,
and his tongue *talketh* **wordeth** of judgment.
6 and brings forth your justness as the light
and your judgment as the noonday.
7 Be still in Yah Veh and writhe for him;
inflame not
because of him who prospers in his way
—because of the man who works intrigue.
8 Slacken wrath and forsake fury;
inflame not to vilify.
9 For vilifiers are cut off;
and they who await Yah Veh possess the earth.
10 For yet a little, and the wicked are not;
yes, discern his place and it is not:
11 and the humble possess the earth;
and delight themselves in the abundance of shalom.
12 The wicked intrigues against the just
and gnashes on him with his teeth.
13 Adonay laughs at him;
for he sees his day coming.
14 The wicked draw the sword and bend their bow
to fell the humble and needy
and to slaughter the straight of way.
15 Their sword enters their own heart
—their bows break.
16 Better is the little of the just
than the abundance of many wicked.
17 For the arms of the wicked break
and Yah Veh upholds the just.
18 Yah Veh knows the days of the integrious
—that their inheritance is eternal.
19 They shame not in the evil time;
they satiate in the days of famine.

20 But the wicked destruct
and the enemies of Yah Veh,
as the esteem of rams, are finished off
—into smoke are finished off.
21 The wicked borrows and shalams not
and the just grants charism and gives:
22 for his blessed possess the earth;
and his abased are cut off.
23 The paces of the mighty
are established by Yah Veh;
and he delights in his way:
24 though he falls, he is not cast down
for Yah Veh upholds him with his hand.
25 I was a lad and am aged;
yet I neither saw the just forsaken
nor his seed seeking bread:
26 all days he grants charism and lends;
and his seed is for a blessing.
27 Turn from evil and work good;
and tabernacle eternally.
28 For Yah Veh loves judgment
and forsakes not his mercied
—guarded eternally;
and the seed of the wicked is cut off.
29 The just possess the land
and tabernacle therein eternally.
30 The mouth of the just meditates wisdom
and his tongue words judgment.
31 The *law* **torah** of his *God* **Elohim** is in his heart;
none of his steps shall *slide* **waver.**
32 The wicked watcheth the *righteous* **just**,
and seeketh to *slay* **deathify** him.
33 *The LORD* **Yah Veh**
will **shall** not *leave* **forsake** him in his hand,
nor *condemn* **judge** him **wicked** when he is judged.
34 *Wait on the LORD* **Await Yah Veh,**
and *keep* **guard** his way,
and he shall exalt thee to *inherit* **possess** the land:
when the wicked are cut off, thou shalt see it.
35 I have seen the wicked *in great power* **tyrant**,
and spreading himself **stripped naked**
like a green *bay tree* **native.**
36 Yet he passed away, and, *lo* **behold**, he was not:
yea, I sought him, but he could not be found.
37 *Mark* **Regard** the *perfect man* **integrious**,
and *behold* **see** the *upright* **straight**:
for the *end* **finality** of that man is *peace* **shalom.**
38 But the *transgressors* **rebels**
shall be *destroyed* **desolated** together:
the *end* **finality** of the wicked shall be cut off.
39 But the salvation of the *righteous* **just**
is of *the LORD* **Yah Veh**:
he is their strength—**their stronghold**
in the time of *trouble* **tribulation.**
40 And *the LORD* **Yah Veh** shall help them,
and *deliver* **slip** them **away**:
he shall *deliver* **slip** them **away** from the wicked,
and save them, because they *trust* **seek refuge** in him.

38 *A Psalm* of David,
to *bring to remembrance* **remember.**
1 O *LORD* **Yah Veh,**
rebuke **reprove** me not in thy *wrath* **rage**:
neither *chasten* **discipline** me in thy *hot displeasure* **fury.**
2 For thine arrows *stick fast in* **penetrate** me,
and thy hand *presseth* **penetrateth** me *sore.*
3 There is no *soundness* **integrity** in my flesh
because **at the face** of *thine anger* **thy rage**;
neither is there any *rest* **shalom** in my bones
because **at the face** of my sin.
4 For *mine iniquities* **my perversities**
are *gone* **passed** over mine head:
as an heavy burden they are too heavy for me.
5 My wounds stink and *are corrupt* **dissolve**
because **at the face** of my *foolishness* **folly.**
6 I am *troubled* **bent**;
I am *bowed down greatly* **prostrated mightily**;
I go *mourning* **darkened** all the day long.
7 For my *loins* **flanks**
are filled with *loathsome disease* **scorching**:
and there is no soundness in my flesh.
8 I am *feeble* **exhausted** and
sore broken **mighty crushed**:
I have roared
by reason of the *disquietness* **growling** of my heart.
9 *Lord* **Adonay**, all my desire
is *before* **in front of** thee;
and my *groaning* **sighing** is not hid from thee.
10 My heart *panteth* **palpitateth,**
my *strength faileth* **force forsaketh** me:
as for the light of mine eyes,
it also is *gone from* **not in** me.
11 My lovers and my friends
stand *aloof from* **against** my *sore* **plague**;
and my *kinsmen* **neighbours** stand afar off.
12 They also that seek after my *life* **soul**
lay snares for **snare** me:
and they that seek my *hurt* **evil**
speak mischievous things **word calamities,**
and *imagine* **meditate** deceits all the day long.
13 But I, as *a* deaf *man*, heard not;

and I was as a *dumb man* **mute**
that openeth not his mouth.
14 Thus I was as a man that heareth not,
and in whose mouth are no reproofs.
15 For in thee, O *LORD* **Yah Veh**, *do I hope* **I await**:
thou *wilt hear* **shalt answer**,
O *Lord* **Adonay** my *God* **Elohim**.
31 The torah of his Elohim is in his heart;
none of his steps waver.
32 The wicked watches for the just
and seeks to deathify him.
33 Yah Veh neither forsakes him in his hand,
nor judges him wicked when he is judged.
34 Await Yah Veh and guard his way
and he exalts you to possess the land;
when the wicked are cut off, you see.
35 I saw the wicked tyrant
stripped naked as a green native;
36 yet he passes away; and behold, he is not;
yes, I seek him, but find him not.
37 Regard the integrious and see the straight;
for the finality of that man is shalom.
38 The rebels desolate together
—the finality of the wicked is cut off;
39 the salvation of the just *is* of Yah Veh
—their stronghold in the time of tribulation.
40 Yah Veh helps them and slips them away
—slips them away from the wicked
and saves them,
because they seek refuge in him.

38 By David; To remember.
1 O Yah Veh,
neither reprove me in your rage
nor discipline me in your fury:
2 for your arrows penetrate me
and your hand penetrates me.
3 There is neither integrity in my flesh
at the face of your rage;
nor any shalom in my bones
at the face of my sin.
4 For my perversities pass over my head;
as a heavy burden, too heavy for me:
5 my wounds stink and dissolve
at the face of my folly:
6 I bend; I prostrate mightily;
I go darkened all the day long:
7 for my flanks are filled with scorching
—no soundness in my flesh.
8 I am exhausted and mighty crushed;
I roar from the growling of my heart:
9 Adonay, all my desire *is* in front of you;
and my sighing is not hid from you.
10 My heart palpitates; my force forsakes me;
as for the light of my eyes, they are not with me:
11 my lovers and my friends
stand against my plague;
my neighbours stand afar off:
12 they who seek my soul, snare me;
and they who seek my evil, word calamities
and meditate deceits all the day long.
13 And I, as deaf, hear not
—as a mute who opens not his mouth
14 —as a man who hears not
whose mouth reproofs not.
15 For in you, O Yah Veh, I await;
answer, O Adonay my Elohim.
16 For I said, *Hear me*,
lest *otherwise* they should *rejoice* **cheer** over me:
when my foot *slippeth* **tottereth**,
they *magnify* **greaten** *themselves* against me.
17 For I am *ready* **prepared** to *halt* **limp**,
and my sorrow is continually *before* **in front of** me.
18 For I *will declare mine iniquity*
shall tell my perversity;
I will **shall** be *sorry* **concerned** for my sin.
19 But mine enemies *are lively* **enliven**,
and they are *strong* **mighty**:
and they that hate me *wrongfully* **falsely**
are multiplied **abound by the myriads**.
20 They also that *render* **shalam** evil for good
are *mine adversaries* **my satans**; because I
follow the thing that is **pursue** good.
21 Forsake me not, O *LORD* **Yah Veh**:
O my *God* **Elohim**, be not far from me.
22 *Make haste* **Hasten** to help me,
O *Lord* **Adonay** my salvation.

39 To *the chief Musician* **His Eminence**,
even to Juduthun **Yeduthun/A Laudatory**,
A Psalm of David.
1 I said, I *will take heed to* **shall guard** my ways,
that I sin not with my tongue:
I *will keep* **shall guard** my mouth with a *bridle* **muzzle**,
while the wicked is *before* **in front of** me.
2 I was *dumb* **mute** with silence,
I *held my peace, even* **hushed** from good; and
my *sorrow* **pain** was *stirred* **troubled**.
3 My heart *was hot* **heated** within me,
while I *was musing* **meditated** the fire burned:
then *spake* **worded** I with my tongue,
4 *LORD* **O Yah Veh**, *make me*
to **let me** know mine end,

and the measure of my days, what it is:
that I may know how *frail* **forsaken** I am.
5 Behold, thou hast *made* **given** my days
as *an handbreadth* **a palm span**; and
mine age **my transcience**
is as *nothing before* **naught in front of** thee:
verily *every man at his best state* **all humanity**
is *altogether* **stationed in** vanity.
Selah.
6 Surely every man walketh
in *a vain shew* **an image**:
surely they *are disquieted* **roar** in vain:
he heapeth *up riches*,
and knoweth not who shall gather *them*.
7 And now, *Lord* **O Adonay**,
what *wait I for* **await I**?
my hope is in thee.
8 *Deliver* **Rescue** me from all
my *transgressions* **rebellions**:
make **set** me not the reproach of the foolish.
9 I was *dumb* **mute**, I opened not my mouth;
because thou *didst* **worked** it.
10 *Remove* **Turn aside** thy
stroke away **plague** from me:
I am *consumed* **finished off**
by the *blow* **choking** of thine hand.
11 When thou with *rebukes* **reproofs**
dost correct **disciplinest** man for *iniquity* **perversity**,
thou *makest* **dissolvest** his *beauty*
to consume away **desire**
like a moth:
surely *every man* **all humanity** is vanity.
Selah.
12 Hear my prayer, O *LORD* **Yah Veh**,
and give ear **hearken** unto my cry;
hold not thy peace **hush not** at my tears:
for I am a *stranger* **sojourner** with thee,
and a *sojourner* **settler**, as all my fathers *were*.
13 O *spare* **look on** me, that I
may *recover strength* **relax**,
before I go hence, and be no more.

40 To *the chief Musician* **His Eminence**,
A Psalm of David.
1 *I waited patiently for the LORD*
In awaiting, I awaited Yah Veh;
and he *inclined* **spread** unto me, and heard my cry.
2 He *brought* **ascended** me *up* also
out of *an horrible pit* **a roaring well**,
out of the miry *clay* **mire**,
and *set* **raised** my feet upon a rock,
and established my *goings* **steps**.
16 For I say, lest they cheer over me;
when my foot totters they greaten against me.
17 For I am prepared to limp
and my sorrow is continually in front of me.
18 For I tell my perversity
—concerned for my sin:
19 and my enemies enliven
and they are mighty:
they who hate me falsely
abound by the myriads;
20 they who shalam evil for good
are my satans
—because I pursue good.
21 Forsake me not, O Yah Veh;
O my Elohim, be not far from me.
22 Hasten to help me,
O Adonay my salvation.

39 To His Eminence; Yeduthun/A Laudatory;
A Psalm by David.
1 I say,
I guard my ways from sinning with my tongue;
I guard my mouth with a muzzle
while the wicked is ere in front of me.
2 I am mute with silence;
I hush from good;
and my pain troubles me:
3 my heart heats within me;
as I meditate, the fire burns.
I word with my tongue,
4 O Yah Veh, have me know my end
and the measure of my days, what they are;
so that I know how forsaken I am.
5 Behold, you give my days as a palm span;
my transcience is as naught in front of you;
verily all humanity *is* stationed in vanity.
Selah.
6 Surely every man walks in an image;
surely they roar in vain:
he heaps and knows not who gathers.
7 And now, O Adonay, what await I?
My hope is in you.
8 Rescue me from all my rebellions;
set me not a reproach of fools.
9 I am mute, I open not my mouth;
because you—you worked it.
10 Turn aside your plague from me;
I am finished off by the choking of your hand.
11 With reproofs

you discipline man for his perversity;
you dissolve his desire as a moth;
surely all humanity is vanity.
Selah.
12 Hear my prayer, O Yah Veh;
hearken to my cry;
hush not at my tears;
for I *am* a sojourner with you
—a settler, as all my fathers.
13 O look on me, that I *may* relax,
ere I go hence and am no more.

40 To His Eminence; A Psalm by David.
1 In awaiting, I await Yah Veh;
he spreads to me and hears my cry:
2 and he ascends me from a roaring well
—from the miry mire;
and raises my feet on a rock
and establishes my steps.
3 And he hath *put* **given** a new song in my mouth,
even praise **Halal** unto our *God* **Elohim**:
many shall see it, and *fear* **awe**,
and shall *trust* **confide** in *the LORD* **Yah Veh**.
4 *Blessed* **Blithe** *is* that *man* **mighty**
that *maketh the LORD* **setteth Yah Veh**
his *trust* **confidant**,
and *respecteth* **faceth** not the proud,
nor *such as turn aside* **swerveth** to lies.
5 Many, O *LORD* **Yah Veh** my *God* **Elohim**,
are thy *wonderful works* **marvels**
which thou hast *done* **worked**,
and thy *thoughts* **fabrications**
which are to us—ward **toward us**:
they cannot be reckoned up in order
none can line them up unto thee:
if I *would declare* **should tell** and *speak* **word** *of them*,
they are *more* **mightier** than can be *numbered* **scribed**.
6 Sacrifice and offering thou didst not desire;
mine ears hast thou *opened* **pierced**:
burnt offering **holocaust** and *sin offering* **for sin**
hast thou not *required* **asked**.
7 Then said I, *Lo* **Behold**, I come:
in the *volume* **roll** of the *book* **scroll**
it is *written* **inscribed** of me,
8 I delight to *do* **work** thy *will* **pleasure**,
O my *God* **Elohim**:
yea, thy *law* **torah** is within my *heart* **inwards**.
9 I have *preached righteousness*
evangelized justness
in the great congregation:
lo **behold**, I have not *refrained* **restrained** my lips,
O *LORD* **Yah Veh**, thou knowest.
10 I have not *hid* **covered** thy
righteousness **justness**
within my heart;
I have *declared* **said**
thy *faithfulness* **trustworthiness** and thy salvation:
I have not concealed
thy *lovingkindness* **mercy** and thy truth
from the great congregation.
11 *Withhold* **Restrain** not thou
thy tender mercies from me,
O *LORD* **Yah Veh**:
let thy *lovingkindness* **mercy** and thy truth
continually *preserve* **guard** me.
12 For innumerable evils
have *compassed* **surrounded** me *about*:
mine iniquities **my perversities**
have *taken hold upon* **overtaken** me,
so that I am not able to *look up* **see**;
they are *more* **mightier** than the hairs of mine head:
therefore my heart *faileth* **forsaketh** me.
13 Be pleased, O *LORD* **Yah**
Veh, to *deliver* **rescue** me:
O *LORD* **Yah Veh**, *make haste* **hasten** to help me.
14 Let them *be ashamed* **shame**
and *confounded* **blush** together
that seek after my soul to *destroy* **scrape** it **away**;
let them *be driven backward* **apostatize**
and *put to* shame
that *wish* **desire** me evil.
15 *Let them be desolate* **Desolate them**
for a reward **in the finality** of their shame
that say unto me, Aha, aha.
16 Let all those that seek thee
rejoice and *be glad* **cheer** in thee:
let such as love thy salvation say continually,
The LORD **Yah Veh** be *magnified* **greatened**.
17 But I am *poor* **humble** and needy;
yet *the Lord thinketh* **Adonay fabricateth** upon me:
thou art my help *and my deliverer*
who slippeth me away;
make no tarrying **tarry not**, O my *God* **Elohim**.

41 To *the chief Musician* **His Eminence**,
A Psalm of David.
1 *Blessed* **Blithe** *is* he
that *considereth* **comprehendeth** the poor:
the LORD will deliver **Yah Veh shall rescue** him
in *time* **the day** of *trouble* **evil**.
3 He gives a new song in my mouth,
Halal to our Elohim!

Many see and awe and confide in Yah Veh.
4 Blithe—the mighty
who set Yah Veh as his confidant;
who neither face the proud
nor swerve to lies.
5 Many, O Yah Veh my Elohim,
are the marvels
and the fabrications you worked toward us;
no one lines them up to you;
if I tell and word
they are mightier than are scribed.
6 Sacrifice and offering you desire not;
you pierce my ears;
holocaust and for sin you ask not.
7 Then I say, Behold, I come;
in the roll of the scroll it is inscribed of me,
8 I delight to work your pleasure,
O my Elohim;
yes, your torah is within my inwards.
9 I evangelize justness in the great congregation;
behold, I restrain not my lips;
O Yah Veh, you know.
10 I neither cover your justness within my heart
—I say—your trustworthiness and your salvation;
nor conceal your mercy and your truth
from the great congregation.
11 Restrain not your tender mercies from me,
O Yah Veh;
may your mercy and your truth
guard me continually.
12 For innumerable evils surround me;
my perversities overtake me
so that I am not able to see;
—mightier than the hairs of my head;
and my heart forsakes me.
13 Be pleased, O Yah Veh, to rescue me;
O Yah Veh, hasten to help me:
14 they shame and blush together
who seek after my soul to scrape it away;
they apostatize and shame
who desire me evil.
15 Desolate them in the finality of their shame
who say to me, Aha! Aha!
16 All who seek you, rejoice and cheer in you;
such as love your salvation continually say,
Yah Veh greatens!
17 And I *am* humble and needy;
yet Adonay fabricates on me;
you are my help who slips me away;
tarry not, O my Elohim.

41 To His Eminence; A Psalm by David.
1 Blithe—he who comprehends the poor:
Yah Veh rescues him in the day of evil;
2 *The LORD will preserve*
Yah Veh shall guard him,
and *keep* **enliven** him *alive*;
and he shall be *blessed* **blithesome** upon the earth:
and thou *wilt* **shalt** not *deliver* **give** him
unto the *will* **soul** of his enemies.
3 *The LORD will strengthen*
Yah Veh shall support him
upon the *bed* **bedstead** of *languishing* **bleeding**:
thou *wilt make all* **shalt turn** his bed in his sickness.
4 I said, *LORD* **O Yah Veh**,
be merciful unto me **grant me charism**:
heal my soul; for I have sinned against thee.
5 Mine enemies *speak* **say** evil of me,
When shall he die, *and* his name *perish* **destruct**?
6 And if he come to see me,
he *speaketh* **wordeth** vanity:
his heart gathereth *iniquity* **mischief** to itself; *when*
he goeth *abroad* **without**, he *telleth* **wordeth** it.
7 All that hate me *whisper*
enchant *together* against me:
against me do they *devise* **fabricate** my *hurt* **evil**.
8 *An evil disease* **A word of Beli Yaal**, *say they*,
cleaveth fast **is poured** unto him:
and now that he lieth
he shall rise *up no more* **never again**.
9 Yea, *mine own familiar*
friend **my man of shalom**,
in whom I *trusted* **confided**,
which did eat of my bread,
hath *lifted up* **greatened** his heel against me.
10 But thou, O *LORD* **Yah Veh**,
be merciful unto me **grant me charism**, and raise me *up*,
that I may *requite* **shalam** them.
11 By this I know that thou
favourest **delightest in** me,
because mine enemy
doth **shall** not *triumph* **blast** over me.
12 And as for me, thou upholdest
me in mine integrity,
and *settest* **stationest** me *before* **in front of** thy face
for ever **eternally**.
13 Blessed
be *the LORD God* **Yah Veh Elohim** of *Israel* **Yisra El**
from *everlasting* **eternity**, and to *everlasting* **eternity**.
Amen, and Amen.

BOOK II

42 To *the chief Musician* **His Eminence**,
Maschil **On Comprehension**,
for the sons of *Korah* **Qorach**.
1 As the hart
panteth **yearneth** after the water *brooks* **reservoirs**,
so *panteth* **yearneth** my soul after thee, O *God* **Elohim**.
2 My soul thirsteth for *God*
Elohim, for the living *God* **El**:
when shall I come
and *appear before God* **be seen at the face of Elohim**?
3 My tears have been my
meat **bread** day and night,
while they *continually* **all day** say unto
me, Where is thy *God* **Elohim**?
4 When I remember these *things*,
I pour out my soul in me:
for I had *gone* **passed on** with the multitude,
I *went* **walked gently** with them to
the house of *God* **Elohim**,
with the voice of *joy* **shouting**
and *praise* **spread hands**,
with a multitude that *kept holyday* **celebrated**.
5 Why *art thou cast down*
prostratest thou, O my soul?
and *why art thou disquieted* **roarest thou** in
me? *hope thou in God* **await Elohim**:
for I shall yet *praise* **spread hands unto** him
for the *help* **salvation** of his *countenance* **face**.
6 O my *God* **Elohim**,
my soul *is cast down* **prostrateth** within me:
therefore *will* **shall** I remember thee
from the land of *Jordan* **Yarden**,
and of the *Hermonites* **Hermoniym**,
from the *hill Mizar* **little mountain**.
7 *Deep* **Abyss** calleth unto *deep* **abyss**
at the *noise waterspouts* **voice culverts**:
all thy *waves* **breakers** and thy *billows* **waves**
are gone **have passed** over me.
8 Yet *the LORD will command*
Yah Veh shall misvah
his *lovingkindness* **mercy** in the *daytime* **day**,
and in the night his song shall be with me,
and my prayer unto *the God* **El** of my life.
2 Yah Veh guards him and enlivens him;
—blithesome on the earth;
gives him not to the soul of his enemies.
3 Yah Veh supports him on
a bedstead of bleeding;
and in his sickness, turns his bed.
4 I—I say, O Yah Veh, grant me charism;
heal my soul; for I sinned against you.
5 My enemies say evil of me,
When he dies, his name destructs:
6 and when he comes to see, he words vanity;
his heart gathers mischief to itself;
he goes outside; he words.
7 All who hate me enchant against me
—against me they fabricate evil to me:
8 a word of Beli Yaal pours on him;
he lies down—never to rise again:
9 —yes, my man of shalom, in whom I confided,
who ate of my bread,
greatened his heel against me.
10 And you, O Yah Veh,
grant me charism and raise me,
and I shalam them.
11 By this I know that you delight in me,
because my enemy blasts not over me:
12 and as for me, uphold me in my integrity
and station me in front of your face eternally.
13 Blessed—Yah Veh Elohim of Yisra El
from eternity to eternity.
Amen and Amen.

BOOK II

42 To His Eminence; On Comprehension:
For the sons of Qorach.
1 As the hart yearns after the reservoirs of water,
thus yearns my soul after you, O Elohim.
2 My soul thirsts for Elohim, for the living El.
When come I to see the face of Elohim?
3 My tears are my bread day and night,
while all day they say to me, Where is your Elohim?
4 When I remember these,
I pour my soul within me;
I pass with the multitude
—walk gently with them to the house of Elohim
with the voice of shouting and spread hands
—with a multitude who celebrate.
5 Why prostrate, O my soul?
Why roar within me?
Await Elohim;
for I still spread hands to him for
the salvation of his face.
6 O my Elohim, my soul prostrates within me;
so I remember you
from the land of Yarden and of the Hermoniym,
from the little mountain.

7 Abyss calls to abyss at the voice culverts;
all your breakers and your waves pass over me.
8 Yet Yah Veh misvahs his mercy in the day;
and in the night his song *is* with me: and
my prayer to the El of my life.
9 I *will* **shall** say unto *God* **El** my rock,
Why hast thou forgotten me?
why go I *mourning* **darkened**
because of the oppression of the enemy?
10 *As* with *a sword* **murder** in my bones,
mine enemies **my tribulators** reproach me;
while **all day** they say *daily* unto me,
Where is thy *God* **Elohim**?
11 Why *art* **prostratest** thou *cast down*, O my soul?
and why *art* **roarest** thou *disquieted* within me?
hope thou in *God* **Elohim**:
for I shall *yet praise* **spread hands to** him,
who is the *health* **salvation** of my *countenance* **face**,
and my *God* **Elohim**.

43 Judge me, O *God* **Elohim**,
and *plead* **defend** my *cause* **defence**
against an *ungodly nation* **unmercied goyim**:
O *deliver me* **slip me away** from the
deceitful **man of deceits** and *unjust man* **wickedness**.
2 For thou art *the God* **Elohim**
of my *strength* **stronghold**:
why dost thou cast me off?
why go I *mourning* **darkened**
because of the oppression of the enemy?
3 O send out thy light and
thy truth: let them lead me;
let them bring me unto thy holy *hill* **mountain**,
and to thy tabernacles.
4 Then *will* **shall** I go
unto the **sacrifice** altar of *God* **Elohim**,
unto *God* **El**, *my exceeding joy* **the cheer of my twirling**:
yea, upon the harp
will I praise **shall I spread hands unto** thee,
O *God* **Elohim** my *God* **Elohim**.
5 Why *art* **prostratest** thou *cast down*, O my soul?
and why *art* **roarest** thou *disquieted* within me?
hope in God **await Elohim**:
for I shall yet *praise* **spread hands unto** him,
who is the *health* **salvation** of my *countenance* **face**,
and my *God* **Elohim**.

44 To *the chief Musician* **His Eminence**,
for the sons of *Korah* **Qorach**,
Maschil **On Comprehension**.
1 We have heard with our ears, O *God* **Elohim**,
our fathers have *told* **scribed** us,
what work **the deeds** thou didst in their days,
in the *times of old* **former days**.
2 How thou *drive out*
dispossessed the *heathen* **goyim**
with thy hand,
and plantedst them;
how thou *didst afflict* **vilified** the *people* **nations**,
and *cast* **sent** them out.
3 For they *got* **possessed** not the land *in possession*
by their own sword,
neither did their own arm save them:
but thy right *hand*, and thine arm,
and the light of thy *countenance* **face**,
because thou hadst *a favour* **pleasure** unto them.
4 Thou art my *King* **Sovereign**, O *God* **Elohim**:
command deliverances **misvah salvations**
for *Jacob* **Yaaqov**.
5 Through thee
will **shall** we push down our *enemies* **tribulators**:
through thy name
will **shall** we *tread* **trample** them *under*
that rise up against us.
6 For I *will* **shall** not *trust* **confide** in my bow,
neither shall my sword save me.
7 But thou hast saved us from
our *enemies* **tribulators**,
and hast *put* **shamed** them *to shame* that hated us.
8 In *God* **Elohim** we *boast* **halal** all the day long,
and *praise* **halal** thy name *for ever* **eternally**.
Selah.
9 *But* **Yea** thou hast cast off,
and *put* **shamed** us *to shame*;
and goest not forth with our *armies* **hosts**.
10 Thou makest us to turn back
from the *enemy* **tribulator**:
and they which hate us *spoil* **despoil** for themselves.
9 I say to El my rock,
Why forget you me?
Why go I darkened
because of the oppression of the enemy?
10 With murder in my bones,
my tribulators reproach me;
all day they say to me, Where is your Elohim?
11 Why prostrate, O my soul?
Why roar within me?
Hope in Elohim;
for I spread hands to him
—the salvation of my face and my Elohim.

43 Judge me, O Elohim;
defend my defence against an unmercied goyim:

O slip me away
from the man of deceits and wickedness.
2 For you are the Elohim of my stronghold;
why cast you me off?
Why go I darkened by the oppression of an enemy?
3 O send out your light and your truth to lead me;
to bring me to your holy mountain
and to your tabernacles.
4 And I enter to the sacrifice altar of Elohim
—to El, the cheer of my twirling:
on the harp, I spread hands to you,
O Elohim my Elohim.
5 Why prostrate, O my soul?
and why roar within me?
Await Elohim;
for I still spread hands to him,
—the salvation of my face, and my Elohim.

44 To His Eminence; For the sons of Qorach:
On Comprehension.
1 We heard with our ears, O Elohim,
our fathers scribed to us,
the deeds you did in their days
—in the former days:
2 how you dispossessed the goyim with your hand
and planted them;
how you vilified the nations
and sent them out.
3 For they neither possessed the land
by their own sword,
nor by their own arm *were* they saved;
but by your right and your arm
and the light of your face:
because you had pleasure in them.
4 You are my Sovereign, O Elohim.
Misvah salvations for Yaaqov.
5 Through you
we push down our tribulators;
through your name
we trample them who rise against us.
6 For I confide neither in my bow,
nor my sword to save me.
7 For you saved us from our tribulators
and shamed them who hate us.
8 In Elohim we halal all the day long
—halal your name eternally.
Selah.
9 Yes, you cast us off and shame us;
you come not forth with our hosts:
10 You turn us back from the tribulator;
and they who hate us despoil for themselves:
11 Thou hast given us
like sheep appointed **as a flock** for *meat* **food**;
and hast *scattered* **winnowed** us
among the *heathen* **goyim**.
12 Thou sellest thy people for nought,
and *dost not increase* **aboundest not**
thy wealth by their price.
13 Thou *makest* **settest** us a reproach
to our *neighbours* **fellow tabernaclers**,
a *scorn* **derision** and a *derision* **ridicule**
to them that are round about us.
14 Thou *makest* **settest** us a *byword* **proverb**
among the *heathen* **goyim**,
a shaking of the head among the *people* **nations**.
15 My *confusion* **shame** is *continually* **all day**
before **in front of** me,
and the shame of my face hath covered me,
16 For the voice of him
that reproacheth and blasphemeth;
by reason **at the face** of the enemy and avenger.
17 All this is come upon us;
yet have we not forgotten thee,
neither have we *dealt falsely* **falsified** in thy covenant.
18 Our heart is not *turned back* **apostatized**,
neither have our steps *declined* **stretched** from thy way;
19 Though thou hast *sore broken* **crushed** us
in the place of *dragons* **monsters**, and
covered us with the shadow of death.
20 If we have forgotten the
name of our *God* **Elohim**,
or *stretched out* **spread** our *hands* **palms**
to a strange *god* **el**;
21 Shall not *God search* **Elohim probe** this *out*?
for he knoweth the *secrets* **concealments** of the heart.
22 Yea, for thy sake
are we *killed* **slaughtered** all the day long;
we are *counted* **machinated**
as *sheep* **flock** for the slaughter.
23 Awake, why sleepest thou, O *Lord* **Adonay**?
arise **awake**, cast us not off *for ever* **in perpetuity**.
24 Wherefore hidest thou thy face,
and forgettest
our *affliction* **humiliation** and our oppression?
25 For our soul *is bowed down* **sinketh** to the dust:
our belly *cleaveth* **adhereth** unto the earth.
26 Arise for our help,
and redeem us for thy mercies' sake.

45 To *the chief Musician* **His Eminence,**
upon Shoshannim/**Trumpets**,
for the sons of *Korah* **Qorach**,

Maschil **On Comprehension,**
A Song of *loves* **the Beloved.**
1 My heart *is inditing* **bubbleth**
a good *matter* **word**:
I *speak of the things which I have made* **say of my works**
touching **to** the *king* **sovereign**:
my tongue
is the *pen* **stylus** of a *ready writer* **skillful scribe.**
2 Thou art *fairer* **beautified**
than **above** the *children* **sons** of *men* **humanity**:
grace **charism** is poured into thy lips:
therefore *God* **Elohim** hath blessed thee
for ever **eternally.**
3 Gird thy sword upon thy
thigh **flank**, O *most* mighty,
with thy glory and thy majesty.
4 And in thy majesty ride **thou;**
prosperously **prosper thou** because **of thy word** of truth
and *meekness* **humbleness** and *righteousness* **justness**;
and thy right *hand*
shall teach thee *terrible things* **awesomenesses.**
5 Thine arrows are *sharp* **pointened**
in the heart of the *king's* **sovereign's** enemies;
whereby the people fall under thee.
6 Thy throne, O *God* **Elohim,**
is *for ever* **eternally** and *ever* **eternally**:
the *sceptre* **scion** of thy *kingdom* **sovereigndom**
is a *right sceptre* **straight scion.**
11 as a flock, you give us for food;
and winnow us among the goyim:
12 you sell your people for naught
and abound not by their price:
13 you set us a reproach to our fellow tabernaclers;
a derision and a ridicule to them all around us:
14 you set us a proverb among the goyim
—a shaking of the head among the nations:
15 all day my shame is in front of me;
the shame of my face covers me:
16 because of his voice
who reproaches and blasphemes
at the face of the enemy and avenger.
17 All this comes to us:
yet we neither forgot you
nor falsified in your covenant
18 nor apostatized our heart
nor stretched our steps from your way:
19 though you crushed us in the place of monsters
and covered us with the shadow of death.
20 If we forget the name of our Elohim
or spread our palms to a strange el;
21 is this not probed by Elohim?
—for he knows the concealments of the heart.
22 Yes, for your sake we are slaughtered all day;
—machinated as flocks for the slaughter.
23 Waken! Why sleep, O Adonay?
Waken! Cast us not off in perpetuity.
24 Why hide your face
and forget our humiliation and our oppression?
25 For our soul sinks to the dust;
our belly adheres to the earth:
26 rise for our help
and redeem us for sake of your mercies.

45 To His Eminence; On Shoshannim/Trumpets;
For the sons of Qorach; On Comprehension:
Song of the Beloved.
1 My heart bubbles a good word;
I say of my works to the sovereign;
my tongue is the stylus of a skillful scribe.
2 You—beautified above the sons of humanity;
charism pours into your lips;
so Elohim blesses you eternally.
3 Gird your sword on your flank, O mighty,
with your glory and your majesty:
4 and in your majesty, ride;
prosper because of your word of truth
and humbleness and justness;
that your right teach you awesomenesses.
5 Your arrows pointen
in the heart of the enemies of the sovereign;
the people fall under you.
6 Your throne, O Elohim, *is* eternal and eternal;
the scion of your sovereigndom is a straight scion:
7 Thou lovest *righteousness* **justness,**
and hatest wickedness:
therefore *God* **Elohim,**
thy *God* **Elohim,** hath anointed thee
with the *oil* **ointment** of *gladness* **rejoicing**
above thy *fellows* **companions.**
8 All thy *garments* **clothes**
smell of myrrh, and aloes, and cassia,
out of the ivory *palaces* **manses,**
whereby they **whose strummings**
have *made* **cheered** thee *glad.*
9 *Kings'* **Sovereigns'** daughters
were among thy *honourable women* **esteemed**:
upon thy right *hand*
did stand the *queen* **mistress** in *gold* **ore** of Ophir.
10 Hearken, O daughter, and *consider* **see,**
and *incline* **spread** thine ear;
forget *also* thine own people, and thy father's house;

11 *So* shall the *king greatly* **sovereign** desire thy beauty:
for he is thy *Lord* **adoni**;
and *worship* **prostrate** thou **to** him.
12 And the daughter of *Tyre* **Sor**
shall be there with *a gift* **an offering**;
even the rich among the people
shall *intreat* **stroke** thy *favour* **face**.
13 The *king's* **sovereign's** daughter
is all *glorious* **honourable** within:
her *clothing* **robe** is of *wrought gold* **gold brocade**.
14 She shall be brought unto the *king* **sovereign**
in *raiment of needlework* **embroidery**:
the virgins her *companions that follow* **friends behind** her
shall be brought unto thee.
15 With *gladness* **cheerfulness** and rejoicing
shall *they* be brought:
they shall enter into the *king's palace* **sovereign's manse**.
16 Instead of thy fathers**,** shall be thy *children* **sons**,
whom thou mayest
make princes **set governors** in all the earth.
17 I *will* **shall** make thy name to be remembered
in all generations **generation to generation**:
therefore shall the people *praise* **spread hands unto** thee
for ever **eternally** and *ever* **eternally**.

46 To *the chief Musician* **His Eminence,**
for the sons of *Korah* **Qorach**,
A Song *upon Alamoth* **for Virgins**.
1 *God* **Elohim** is our refuge and strength,
a *very present* **mighty found** help in *trouble* **tribulation**.
2 Therefore *will* **shall** not we *fear* **awe**,
though the earth *be removed* **changeth**,
and *though* the mountains *be carried* **totter**
into the *midst* **heart** of the *sea* **seas**;
3 *Though* the waters *thereof*
roar and *be troubled* **foam**,
though the mountains *shake* **quake**
with the *swelling* **pomp** *thereof.*
Selah.
4 There is a river,
the streams whereof **whose rivulets**
shall *make glad* **cheer** the city of *God* **Elohim**,
the *holy place* **holies** of the tabernacles
of *the most High* **Elyon**.
5 *God* **Elohim** is in the midst of her;
she shall not *be moved* **totter**:
God **Elohim** shall help her,
and that right early **at the face of the morning**.
6 The *heathen raged* **goyim roared**,
the *kingdoms were moved* **sovereigndoms tottered**:
he *uttered* **gave** his voice, the earth melted.
7 *The LORD of hosts* **Yah Veh Sabaoth** is with us;
the *God* **Elohim** of *Jacob* **Yaaqov**
is our *refuge* **secure loft**.
Selah.
8 Come,
behold **see** the *works* **deeds** of *the LORD* **Yah Veh**,
what desolations he hath *made* **set** in the earth.
9 He *maketh* **shabbathizeth** wars *to cease*
unto the end of the earth;
he breaketh the bow,
and *cutteth* **choppeth** the spear *in sunder*;
he burneth the *chariot* **wagon** in the fire.

7 you love justness and hate wickedness;
so Elohim—your Elohim
anoints you with the ointment of rejoicing
above your companions:
8 all your clothes of myrrh and aloes and cassia
—from the manses of ivory
—whose strummings cheer you.
9 Daughters of Sovereigns
are among your esteemed;
on your right
stands a mistress in the ore of Ophir.
10 Hearken, O daughter,
and see and spread your ear;
forget your own people
and the house of your father;
11 the sovereign desires your beauty;
for he is your adoni;
prostrate to him.
12 The daughter of Sor with an offering,
even the rich among the people stroke your face.
13 Inwardly, the daughter of the sovereign
is all honorable;
her robe *is* of gold brocade
14 —brought to the sovereign in embroidery;
the virgins her friends behind her
—brought to you
15 —brought with cheerfulness and rejoicing;
they enter the manse of the sovereign.
16 Your sons, in the stead of your fathers,
whom you set as governors in all the earth.
17 I memorialize your name
generation to generation;
so the people spread hands to you
eternally and eternally.

46 To His Eminence; For the sons of Qorach;
A song for Virgins.

1 Elohim *is* our refuge and strength;
a mighty help to find in tribulation;
2 so we awe not:
the earth changes;
the mountains totter into the heart of the seas;
3 the waters roar and foam;
the pompous mountains quake.
Selah.
4 *There is* a river,
whose rivulets cheer the city of Elohim
—the holies of the tabernacles of Elyon.
5 Elohim *is* in her midst; she totters not:
Elohim helps her at the face of the morning.
6 The goyim roar;
the sovereigndoms totter:
he gives his voice: the earth melts.
7 Yah Veh Sabaoth is with us;
the Elohim of Yaaqov is our secure loft.
Selah.
8 Come see the deeds of Yah Veh,
who set desolations in the earth;
9 —shabbathizes wars to the end of the earth;
—breaks the bow and chops the spear;—
burns the wagon in the fire.
10 *Be still* **Let go**, and know
that I *am God*—**Elohim**:
I will **shall** be *exalted* **lofted** among the *heathen* **goyim**,
I will **shall** be *exalted* **lofted** in the earth.
11 *The LORD of hosts* **Yah Veh Sabaoth** is with us;
the God **Elohim** of *Jacob* **Yaaqov**
is our *refuge* **secure loft**.
Selah.

47 To *the chief Musician* **His Eminence**,
A Psalm for the sons of *Korah* **Qorach**.
1 O clap your *hands* **palms**, all ye people;
shout unto *God* **Elohim** with the
voice of *triumph* **shouting**.
2 For *the LORD most high* **Yah Veh Elyon**
is *terrible* **awesome**;
he is a great *King* **Sovereign** over all the earth.
3 He shall subdue the people under us,
and the nations under our feet.
4 He shall choose our inheritance for us,
the *excellency* **pomp** of *Jacob* **Yaaqov** whom he loved.
Selah.
5 *God is gone up* **Elohim hath**
ascended with a *shout* **blast**,
the LORD **Yah Veh** with the *sound*
voice of a *trumpet* **shophar**.
6 *Sing praises* **Psalm** to *God* **Elohim**,
sing praises **psalm**:
sing praises **psalm** unto our *King* **Sovereign**,
sing praises **psalm**.
7 For *God* **Elohim** is the *King*
Sovereign of all the earth:
sing ye praises **psalm**
with understanding **comprehendingly**.
8 *God* **Elohim** reigneth over the *heathen* **goyim**:
God sitteth **Elohim settleth**
upon the throne of his holiness.
9 The *princes* **volunteers** of the people
are gathered *together*,
even the people of the *God* **Elohim** of Abraham:
for the *shields* **bucklers** of the earth
belong **be** unto *God* **Elohim**:
he is *greatly exalted* **mightily ascended**.

48 A Song and Psalm for the
sons of *Korah* **Qorach**.
1 Great is *the LORD* **Yah Veh**,
and *greatly to be praised* **mightily halaled**
in the city of our *God* **Elohim**,
in the mountain of his holiness.
2 Beautiful for *situation* **elevation**,
the joy of the whole earth,
is mount *Zion* **Siyon**, on the *sides* **flanks** of the north,
the city of the great *King* **Sovereign**.
3 *God* **Elohim** is known in her *palaces* **citadels**
for a *refuge* **secure loft**.
4 For, *lo* **behold**,
the *kings were assembled* **sovereigns congregated**,
they passed by together.
5 They saw *it*, *and* so they marvelled;
they were *troubled* **terrified**, and hasted away.
6 *Fear* **Trembling** took hold upon them there,
and pain **pangs**, as of *a woman in travail* **birthing**.
7 Thou breakest the ships of
Tarshish with an east wind.
8 As we have heard, so have we seen
in the city of *the LORD of hosts* **Yah Veh Sabaoth**,
in the city of our *God* **Elohim**:
God will **Elohim shall** establish it *for ever* **eternally**.
Selah.
9 We have *thought of* **compared**
thy *lovingkindness* **mercy**,
O *God* **Elohim**, in the midst of thy *temple* **manse**.
10 According to thy name, O *God* **Elohim**,
so is thy *praise* **halal** unto the ends of the earth:
thy right *hand* is full of *righteousness* **justness**.
11 Let mount *Zion rejoice* **Siyon cheer**,
let the daughters of *Judah be glad* **Yah Hudah twirl**,

because of thy judgments.
12 *Walk about Zion* **Surround Siyon,**
and go round about **surround** her: *tell*
scribe to the towers *thereof.*
13 *Mark ye well* **Set your heart**
on her *bulwarks* **trenches,**
consider **contemplate** her *palaces* **citadels;**
that ye may *tell* **scribe** it to the generation *following* **after.**
14 For this *God* **Elohim** is our *God* **Elohim**
for ever **eternally** and *ever* **eternally:**
he *will be our guide even unto* **shall drive us over** death.
10 Slacken and know that I—Elohim
loft among the goyim—loft in the earth.
11 Yah Veh Sabaoth *is* with us;
Elohim of Yaaqov *is* our secure loft.
Selah.

47 To His Eminence;
A Psalm for the sons of Qorach.
1 O clap your palms, all you people;
shout to Elohim with the voice of shouting:
2 for Yah Veh Elyon *is* awesome
—a great Sovereign over all the earth:
3 he subdues the people under us
and the nations under our feet:
4 he chooses our inheritance for us
—the pomp of Yaaqov whom he loves.
Selah.
5 Elohim ascends with a blast
—Yah Veh with the voice of a shophar.
6 Psalm to Elohim! Psalm!
Psalm to our Sovereign! Psalm!
7 For Elohim *is* the Sovereign of all the earth;
Psalm comprehendingly!
8 Elohim reigns over the goyim;
Elohim settles on the throne of his holiness.
9 The volunteers of the people gather
—the people of the Elohim of Abraham;
for to Elohim be the bucklers of the earth;
—mightily ascended.

48 A Song, a Psalm, for the sons of Qorach.
1 Great *is* Yah Veh!
Mightily halaled in the city of our Elohim
the mountain of his holiness.
2 Beautiful for elevation
the joy of the whole earth
—mount Siyon on the flanks of the north;
the city of the great Sovereign.
3 Elohim is in her citadels—
known for a secure loft.
4 For behold,
the sovereigns congregate; they pass by together:
5 they see; thus they marvel:
they terrify; and haste away:
6 trembling holds them there
—pangs, as of birthing.
7 You break the ships of
Tarshish with an east wind.
8 As we hear, thus we see;
in the city of Yah Veh Sabaoth
—in the city of our Elohim;
Elohim establishes it eternally.
Selah.
9 We compare your mercy, O Elohim,
midst your manse:
10 as your name, O Elohim,
thus *is* your halal to the ends of the earth:
your right *is* full of justness.
11 Mount Siyon cheers;
the daughters of Yah Hudah twirl
because of your judgments.
12 Surround Siyon! Surround her!
Scribe to the towers!
13 Set your heart on her trenches;
contemplate her citadels:
scribe it to the generation after.
14 For this Elohim *is* our Elohim
eternally and eternally;
he—he drives us over death.

49 To *the chief Musician* **His Eminence,**
A Psalm for the sons of *Korah* **Qorach.**
1 Hear this, all ye people;
give ear **hearken,**
all ye *inhabitants of* **transcients settled in** the world:
2 Both *low* **sons of humanity**
and *high* **sons of man,**
rich and *poor* **needy,** together.
3 My mouth shall *speak* **word** of wisdom;
and the meditation of my heart
shall be of *understanding* **discernment.**
4 I *will* **shall** incline mine
ear to a *parable* **proverb:**
I *will* **shall** open my *dark saying* **riddle** upon the harp.
5 Wherefore should I *fear* **awe** in the days of evil,
when the *iniquity* **perversity** of my heels
shall *compass* **surround** me *about?*
6 They that *trust* **confide**
in their *wealth* **valuables,**
and *boast* **halal** themselves
in the *multitude* **abundance** of their riches;
7 *None of them can by any means*

In redeeming, no man shall redeem his brother,
nor give to *God* **Elohim**
a *ransom* **koper/an atonement** for him:
8 (For the redemption of their
soul is *precious* **esteemed,**
and it ceaseth *for ever* **eternally**:)
9 That he should still live *for ever* **in perpetuity,**
and not see *corruption* **the pit of ruin.**
10 For he seeth that wise men die,
likewise **together**
the fool and the *brutish person perish* **stupid destruct,**
and leave their *wealth* **valuables** to others.
11 Their inward thought is,
that their houses shall *continue for ever* **be eternal,**
and their *dwelling places* **tabernacles**
to all generations **generation to generation;**
they call their *lands* **soil** after their own names.
12 *Nevertheless man being in honour abideth not*
Humanity stayeth not in esteem:
he is like the *beasts* **animals** that *perish* **decease.**
13 This their way is their folly:
yet their posterity
approve **is pleased with** their *sayings* **mouth.**
Selah.
14 *Like sheep* **As a flock**
they are *laid* **set** in *the grave* **sheol;**
death shall *feed on* **tend** them;
and the *upright* **straight**
shall *have dominion over* **subjugate**
them in the morning;
and their *beauty* **form**
shall *consume* **wear out** in *the grave* **sheol**
from their *dwelling* **residence.**
15 But *God will* **Elohim shall** redeem my soul
from the *power* **hand** of *the grave* **sheol:**
for he shall *receive* **take** me.
Selah.
16 *Be not thou afraid* **Awe not**
when *one is made rich* **man enricheth,**
when the *glory* **honour** of his house
is increased **aboundeth;**
17 For when he dieth
he shall *carry nothing away* **take naught:**
his *glory* **honour** shall not descend after him.
18 Though while he lived he blessed his soul:
and *men will praise* **they shall spread hands unto** thee,
when thou *doest well to* **well—pleasest** thyself.
19 He shall go to the generation of his fathers;
they shall never see light **in perpetuity.**
20 *Man* **Humanity** that is in *honour* **esteem,**
and *understandeth* **discerneth** not,
is like the beasts that perish.

50 A Psalm of Asaph.
1 *The mighty God, even the LORD* **El—Elohim**
Yah Veh hath *spoken* **worded,**
and called the earth from the rising of the sun
unto the *going down* **entry** *thereof.*
2 Out of *Zion* **Siyon,** the perfection of beauty,
God **Elohim** hath shined.

49 To His Eminence;
A Psalm for the sons of Qorach.
1 Hear this, all you people!
Hearken, all you transcients settled in the world!
2 Both sons of humanity and sons of man!
Rich and needy, together!
3 My mouth words of wisdom;
and the meditation of my heart of discernment:
4 I incline my ear to a proverb;
I open my riddle on the harp.
5 Why awe I in the days of evil,
when the perversity of my heels surround me?
6 They who confide in their valuables
—in the abundance of their riches
halal themselves.
7 In redeeming,
man neither redeems his brother,
nor gives Elohim a koper/an atonement for him;
8 and esteemed *is* the redemption of their soul:
and ceases eternally;
9 and still he lives in perpetuity
and sees not the pit of ruin.
10 For he sees wise men die;
the fool and the stupid destruct together
and leave their valuables to others.
11 Inwardly they think their houses *are* eternal
and their tabernacles generation to generation;
they call their soil after their own names.
12 Humanity stays not in esteem;
he is as the animals who decease.
13 This their way *is* their folly;
yet their posterity *is* pleased with their mouth.
Selah.
14 As a flock they set themselves in sheol;
death tends them:
and the straight subjugate them in the morning;
and their form wears out:
sheol is their residence.
15 Surely Elohim redeems my soul
from the hand of sheol;
for he takes me.

Selah.
16 Awe not when man enriches
—when the honor of his house abounds:
17 for when he dies he takes naught;
his honor descends not after him.
18 For while he lives he blesses his soul;
and they spread hands to you when
you well—please yourself.
19 He goes to the generation of his fathers;
never to see light in perpetuity.
20 Humanity in esteem who discerns not,
is as the beasts that perish.

50 A Psalm; by Asaph.
1 El of Elohim—Yah Veh words;
and he calls to the earth:
from the rising of the sun to the entry;
2 from Siyon, the perfection of beauty,
Elohim shines.
3 Our *God* **Elohim** shall come,
and shall not *keep silence* **hush**:
a fire shall *devour before him* **consume at his face**,
and it shall *be very tempestuous* **whirl mightily**
round about him.
4 He shall call to the heavens from above,
and to the earth,
that he may *judge* **plead the cause of** his people.
5 Gather my *saints* **mercied** together unto me;
those that have *made* **cut** a covenant with me
by sacrifice.
6 And the heavens
shall *declare* **tell** his *righteousness* **justness**:
for *God* **Elohim** is judge himself.
Selah.
7 Hear, O my people, and I *will speak* **shall word**;
O *Israel* **Yisra El**,
and I *will testify* **shall witness** against thee:
I *am God*—**Elohim**, *even* thy *God* **Elohim**.
8 I *will* **shall** not reprove thee
for thy sacrifices or thy *burnt offerings* **holocausts**,
to have been continually *before* **in front of** me.
9 I *will* **shall** take no bullock out of thy house,
nor he goats out of thy folds.
10 For every beast of the forest is mine,
and the *cattle* **animals** upon a thousand *hills* **mountains**.
11 I know all the *fowls* **flyers** of the mountains:
and the *wild beasts* **creatures** of the field
are mine **with me**.
12 If I *were hungry* **famished**,
I *would* **should** not *tell* **say to** thee:
for the world is mine, and the fulness *thereof*.
13 *Will* **Shall** I eat the flesh of *bulls* **the mighty**,
or drink the blood of **he** goats?
14 *Offer* **Sacrifice** unto *God* **Elohim**
thanksgiving **spread hands**;
and *pay* **shalam** thy vows unto *the most High* **Elyon**:
15 And call upon me in the
day of *trouble* **tribulation**:
I *will deliver* **shall rescue** thee,
and thou shalt *glorify* **honour** me.
16 But unto the wicked *God* **Elohim** saith,
What hast thou to do to *declare* **scribe** my statutes,
or that thou shouldest *take* **lift** my covenant
in thy mouth?
17 Seeing thou hatest *instruction* **discipline**,
and castest my words behind thee.
18 When thou sawest a thief,
then thou *consentedst* **wast pleased** with him,
and hast *been partaker* **allotted** with adulterers.
19 Thou *givest* **spreadest** thy mouth to evil,
and thy tongue *frameth* **contriveth** deceit.
20 Thou *sittest* **settlest**
and *speakest* **wordest** against thy brother;
thou *slanderest* **givest to trip**
thine own mother's son.
21 These *things* hast thou *done* **worked**,
and I *kept silence* **hushed**;
thou *thoughtest* **equatest**
that I *was altogether such an one* **had become** as thyself:
but I *will* **shall** reprove thee,
and *set them in order before* **line them up at** thine eyes.
22 *Now* **I beseech,** *consider* **discern** this,
ye that forget *God* **Elohah**,
lest I tear *you* in pieces,
and there be none to *deliver* **rescue**.
23 Whoso *offereth praise* **sacrificeth spread hands**
glorifieth **honoureth** me:
and to him
that *ordereth his conversation aright* **setteth his way**
will I shew **shall I have see** the salvation of *God* **Elohim**.
3 Our Elohim comes and hushes not;
a consuming fire at his face
whirls mightily all around him.
4 He calls to the heavens above
and to the earth
to plead the cause of his people.
5 Gather my mercied to me
—to cut a covenant with me by sacrifice.
6 The heavens tell his justness;
for Elohim himself is judge.
Selah.

7 Hear, O my people, and I word;
O Yisra El, and I witness against you;
I—Elohim, your Elohim.
8 I reprove you not
yes, your sacrifices or your holocausts
are continually in front of me.
9 I take neither bullock from your house
nor he goats from your folds:
10 for every beast of the forest is mine
and the animals on a thousand mountains:
11 I know all the flyers of the mountains
and the creatures of the field with me.
12 If I famish, I say naught to you;
for the world is mine and the fulness.
13 Eat I the flesh of the mighty?
Drink I the blood of he goats?
14 Sacrifice spread hands to Elohim;
shalam your vows to Elyon;
15 call on me in the day of tribulation:
I rescue you and you honor me.
16 And to the wicked Elohim says,
What *is it* to you to scribe my statutes?
—to lift my covenant in your mouth?
17 Seeing you hate discipline
and cast my words behind you.
18 When you see a thief,
he pleases you;
and you allot with adulterers:
19 you spread your mouth to evil
and contrive your tongue to deceit:
20 you settle and word against your brother;
you give to trip the son of your own mother.
21 These you work, and I hush;
you equate that I become as your;
but I reprove you
and line them up at your eyes.
22 I beseech, discern this,
you who forget Elohah,
lest I tear in pieces and there be no one to rescue.
23 Whoever sacrifices spread hands honors me;
and he who sets his way
I have see the salvation of Elohim.

51 To *the chief Musician* **His Eminence**,
A Psalm of David,
when Nathan the prophet came unto him,
after he had gone in to *Bath—sheba* **Bath Sheba**.
1 *Have mercy upon me* **Grant me charism**,
O *God* **Elohim**,
according to thy *lovingkindness* **mercy**:
according unto the *multitude* **abundance**
of thy tender mercies
blot **wipe** out my *transgressions* **rebellions**.
2 *Wash* **Launder** me *throughly* **aboundingly**
from *mine iniquity* **my perversity**,
and *cleanse* **purify** me from my sin.
3 For I *acknowledge* **know** my
transgressions **rebellions**:
and my sin is *ever before* **continually in front of** me.
4 Against thee, thee only, have I sinned,
and *done* **worked** this evil in *thy sight* **thine eyes**:
that thou mightest be justified
when thou *speakest* **wordest**,
and be *clear* **pure** when thou judgest.
5 Behold, I was *shapen* **writhed**
in *iniquity* **perversity**;
and in sin did my mother conceive me.
6 Behold, thou desirest truth
in the *inward parts* **reins**:
and in the hidden *part*
thou shalt *make* **have** me to know wisdom.
7 *Purge* **Purify** me with hyssop,
and I shall be *clean* **purified**:
wash **launder** me, and I shall be whiter than snow.
8 Make me to hear
joy **rejoicing** and *gladness* **cheerfulness**;
that the bones which thou hast *broken* **crushed**
may *rejoice* **twirl**.
9 Hide thy face from my sins,
and *blot* **wipe** out all *mine iniquities* **my perversities**.
10 Create in me a *clean* **pure** heart, O *God* **Elohim**;
and renew a *right* **steadfast** spirit within me.
11 Cast me not away from thy *presence* **face**;
and take not thy *holy spirit* **Ruach ha-Kodesh** from me.
12 Restore unto me the *joy*
rejoicing of thy salvation;
and uphold me with thy free **voluntary** spirit.
13 Then *will* **shall** I teach
transgressors **rebels** thy ways;
and sinners shall *be converted* **return** unto thee.
14 *Deliver* **Rescue** me from *bloodguiltiness* **bloods**,
O *God* **Elohim**, *thou God* **Elohim** of my salvation:
and my tongue
shall *sing aloud* **shout** of thy *righteousness* **justness**.
15 O *Lord* **Adonay**, open thou my lips;
and my mouth shall *shew forth* **tell** thy *praise* **halal**.
16 For thou desirest not sacrifice;
else *would* **should** I give it:
thou delightest not in *burnt offering* **holocaust**.
17 The sacrifices of *God*
Elohim are a broken spirit:

a broken and a *contrite* **crushed** heart, O *God* **Elohim**,
thou *wilt* **shalt** not despise.
18 *Do good* **Well—please** in thy good pleasure
unto *Zion* **Siyon**:
build thou the walls of *Jerusalem* **Yeru Shalem**.
19 Then shalt thou *be pleased* **delight**
with **in** the sacrifices of *righteousness* **justness**,
with *burnt offering* **holocaust,**
and *whole burnt offering* **total holocaust**:
then shall they *offer* **holocaust** bullocks
upon *thine* **thy sacrifice** altar.

52 To *the chief Musician* **His Eminence**,
Maschil **On Comprehension**,
A Psalm of David,
when Doeg the *Edomite* **Edomiy**
came and told *Saul* **Shaul**,
and said unto him,
David is come to the house of *Ahimelech* **Achi Melech**.
1 Why *boastest* **halalest** thou
thyself in *mischief* **evil**,
O mighty *man*?
the *goodness* **mercy** of *God* **El**
endureth continually **is all day**.
2 The tongue *deviseth mischiefs*
fabricateth calamities;
like a *sharp* **sharpened** razor, working deceitfully.

51 To His Eminence; Psalm by David:
when Nathan the prophet comes to him,
after he went in to Bath Sheba.
1 Grant me charism, O Elohim,
according to your mercy;
according to the abundance of your tender mercies
wipe out my rebellions:
2 launder me aboundingly from my perversity
and purify me from my sin:
3 for I know my rebellions;
and my sin is continually in front of me.
4 Against you—you only, I sinned
and worked this evil in your eyes;
so that you are just when you word
and pure when you judge.
5 Behold, I writhed in perversity;
and in sin my mother conceived me.
6 Behold, you desire truth in the reins;
and in the hidden you have me know wisdom.
7 Purify me with hyssop, and I am purified;
launder me, and I am whiter than snow:
8 have me hear rejoicing and cheerfulness;
so that the bones you crush twirl.
9 Hide your face from my sins
and wipe out all my perversities;
10 create a pure heart within me, O Elohim;
and renew a steadfast spirit within me.
11 Neither cast me from your face;
nor take your *holy spirit* **Ruach ha-Kodesh** from me:
12 restore to me the rejoicing of your salvation;
and uphold me with your free voluntary spirit.
13 I teach rebels your ways;
and sinners return to you.
14 Rescue me from bloods, O Elohim
—Elohim of my salvation;
and my tongue shouts of your justness:
15 O Adonay, open my lips;
and my mouth tells your halal.
16 For you desire not sacrifice; else I give it:
you delight not in holocaust.
17 The sacrifices of Elohim *are* a broken spirit;
a broken and a crushed heart, O Elohim,
you despise not.
18 Well—please in your good pleasure to Siyon;
build the walls of Yeru Shalem:
19 then delight in the sacrifices of justness
with holocaust and total holocaust;
then they holocaust bullocks on your sacrifice altar.

52 To His Eminence; On Comprehension:
By David,
when Doeg the Edomiy comes and tells Shaul,
and says to him,
David came to the house of Achi Melech.
1 Why halal yourself in evil, O mighty?
The mercy of El is all day.
2 The tongue fabricates calamities
—as a sharpened razor, working deceitfully.
3 Thou lovest evil more than good;
and *lying* **falsehood**
rather than to *speak righteousness* **word justness**.
Selah.
4 Thou lovest all *devouring* **swallowing** words,
O thou deceitful tongue.
5 *God* **El** shall *likewise destroy* **pull** thee **down**
for ever **in perpetuity**,
he shall take thee away,
and *pluck* **uproot** thee out of thy *dwelling place* **tent**,
and *root* **uproot** thee out of the land of the living.
Selah.
6 The *righteous* **just** also shall see, and *fear* **awe**,
and shall laugh at him:
7 *Lo* **Behold**, *this is* the *man* **mighty**
that *made* **set** not *God* **Elohim** his *strength* **stronghold**;
but *trusted* **confided** in the abundance of his riches,

and strengthened himself in his *wickedness* **calamity**.
8 But I am like a green olive tree
in the house of *God* **Elohim**:
I *trust* **confide** in the mercy of *God* **Elohim**
for ever **eternally** and *ever* **eternally**.
9 I *will praise* **shall spread hands unto** thee
for ever **eternally**,
because thou hast *done* **worked** it:
and I *will wait on* **shall await** thy name;
for it is good *before* **in front of** thy *saints* **mercied**.

53 To *the chief Musician* **His Eminence**,
upon *Mahalath* **Stroking**,
Maschil **On Comprehension**, *A Psalm* of David.
1 The fool hath said in his heart,
There is no *God* **Elohim**.
Corrupt are they **They have ruined**,
and have done
abominable iniquity **abhorrent wickedness**:
there is none that *doeth* **worketh** good.
2 *God* **Elohim** looked down
from *heaven* **the heavens**
upon the *children* **sons** of *men* **humanity**,
to see if there were any that *did understand* **discerned**,
that *did* seek *God* **Elohim**.
3 Every one of them *is gone*
back **hath apostatized**:
they are altogether *become filthy* **muddled**;
there is none that *doeth* **worketh** good, no, not one.
4 Have the *workers* **doers** of *iniquity* **mischief**
no knowledge **not known**?
who eat up my people as they eat bread:
they have not called upon *God* **Elohim**.
5 *There were they in great fear*
In dreading, they dreaded,
where no *fear* **dread** was:
for *God* **Elohim** hath scattered the bones
of him that encampeth against thee:
thou hast *put* **shamed** them *to shame*,
because *God* **Elohim** hath *despised* **spurned** them.
6 *Oh* **Who giveth** that the
salvation of *Israel* **Yisra El**
were come out of *Zion* **Siyon**!
When *God bringeth* **Elohim turneth** back
the captivity of his people,
Jacob **Yaaqov** shall *rejoice* **twirl**,
and *Israel* **Yisra El** shall *be glad* **cheer**.

54 To *the chief Musician* **His Eminence**,
on *Neginoth* **Strummer**,
Maschil **On Comprehension**, *A Psalm* of David,
when the *Ziphims* **Ziphiym** came and said to *Saul* **Shaul**,
Doth not David hide himself with us?
1 Save me, O *God* **Elohim**, by thy name,
and *judge me* **plead my cause** by thy *strength* **might**.
2 Hear my prayer, O *God* **Elohim**;
give ear **hearken** to the *words* **sayings** of my mouth.
3 For strangers are risen *up* against me,
and *oppressors* **tyrants** seek after my soul:
they have not set *God before* **Elohim in front of** them.
Selah.
4 Behold, *God* **Elohim** is mine helper:
the Lord **Adonay** is with them that uphold my soul.
5 He shall *reward* **return** evil
unto mine *enemies* **opponents**:
cut **exterminate** them *off* in thy truth.
3 You love evil more than good;
and falsehood rather than to word justness.
Selah.
4 You love all swallowing words,
O you deceitful tongue.
5 Also, El pulls you down in perpetuity
—takes you and uproots you from your tent
—uproots you from the land of the living.
Selah.
6 And the just see and awe; and laugh at him:
7 behold the mighty
who sets not Elohim as his stronghold
—*who* confides in the abundance of his riches
—*who* strengthens himself in his calamity.
8 And I, as a green olive tree
in the house of Elohim,
confide in the mercy of Elohim
eternally and eternally:
9 I spread hands to you
eternally, because you work;
and I await your name;
for it is good in front of your mercied.

53 To His Eminence;
On Stroking; On Comprehension: By David.
1 The fool says in his heart, No Elohim!
They ruin and *do* abhorrent wickedness;
no one works good.
2 Elohim, from the heavens,
looks down on the sons of humanity
to see if there are any discerners who seek Elohim.
3 Everyone apostatizes;
they are altogether muddled;
no one works good—no, not one.
4 Know not the doers of mischief
—who eat my people as they eat bread?
—who call not on Elohim?

5 In dreading, they dread where no dread is;
for Elohim scatters the bones
of him who encamps against you;
you shame them; for Elohim spurns them.
6 Who gives the salvation of Yisra El from Siyon?
When Elohim turns back the captivity of his people,
Yaaqov twirls and Yisra El cheers.

54 To His Eminence; On Strummer;
On Comprehension: By David:
when the Ziphiym come and say to Shaul,
Hides not David himself with us?
1 Save me, O Elohim, by your name;
plead my cause by your might;
2 hear my prayer, O Elohim;
hearken to the sayings of my mouth:
3 for strangers rise against me
and tyrants seek after my soul:
they set not Elohim in front of them.
Selah.
4 Behold, Elohim my helper;
Adonay *is* with them who uphold my soul.
5 Return evil to my opponents;
exterminate them in your truth.
6 I *will freely* **shall voluntarily** sacrifice unto thee:
I *will praise* **shall spread hands unto** thy name,
O *LORD* **Yah Veh**;
for it is good.
7 For he hath *delivered* **rescued** me
out of all *trouble* **tribulation**:
and mine eye hath seen *his desire upon* mine enemies.

55 To *the chief Musician* **His Eminence,**
on *Neginoth* **Strummer,**
Maschil **A Discerning**, *A Psalm* of David.
1 Give ear to my prayer, O *God* **Elohim**;
and *hide* **conceal** not thyself from my supplication.
2 *Attend* **Hearken** unto me, and *hear me* **answer**:
I *mourn* **ramble on** in my *complaint* **meditation**,
and *make a noise* **quake**;
3 Because of the voice of the enemy,
because **at the face** of the oppression of the wicked:
for they *cast iniquity* **topple mischief** upon me,
and in wrath they *hate* **oppose** me.
4 My heart *is sore pained* **writheth** within me:
and the terrors of death are fallen upon me.
5 *Fearfulness* **Awe** and
trembling are come upon me,
and horror hath *overwhelmed* **covered over** me.
6 And I said, Oh **who giveth**
that I had *wings* **pinions** like a dove!
for then *would* **should** I fly *away*,
and *be at rest* **tabernacle**.
7 *Lo* **Behold**, then *would* **should** I wander far off,
and *remain* **stay overnight** in the wilderness.
Selah.
8 I *would* **should** hasten my escape
from the *windy storm* **rushing wind** and *tempest* **storm**.
9 *Destroy* **Swallow**, O *Lord* **Adonay**,
and divide their tongues:
for I have seen violence and strife in the city.
10 Day and night
they *go about it upon* **surround** the walls *thereof*:
mischief also and *sorrow* **toil** are in the midst of it.
11 *Wickedness* **Calamity** is in the midst *thereof*:
deceit **fraud** and *guile* **deceit**
depart not from her *streets* **broadways**.
12 For it was not an enemy that reproached me;
then I could have borne it:
neither was it he that hated me
that *did magnify himself* **greatened** against me;
then I *would* **should** have hid myself from him:
13 But *it was* thou, a man mine
equal, my *guide* **chiliarch**,
and mine acquaintance **whom I know**.
14 We *took sweet* **sweetened**
private counsel together,
and walked unto the house of *God* **Elohim**
in *company* **conspiracy**.
15 Let *death seize upon* **desolations deceive** them,
and let them *go down quick* **descend alive**
into *hell* **sheol**:
for wickedness **evil** is in their *dwellings* **sojournings**,
and among them.
16 As for me, I *will* **shall** call upon *God* **Elohim**;
and *the LORD* **Yah Veh** shall save me.
17 Evening, and morning, and at noon,
will **shall** I *pray* **meditate**, and *cry aloud* **roar**:
and he shall hear my voice.
18 He hath *delivered* **redeemed**
my soul in *peace* **shalom**
from the battle that was against me: for
there *were* **be** many with me.
19 *God* **El** shall hear, and *afflict* **answer** them,
even he that *abideth* **settleth** of *old* **antiquity**.
Selah.
Because they have no changes,
therefore they *fear* **awe** not *God* **Elohim**.
20 He hath *put forth* **spread** his hands
against such as be at *peace* **shalom** with him:
he hath *broken* **profaned** his covenant.
21 *The words of* his mouth

were smoother **was more tender** than butter,
but war was in his heart:
his words were softer than *oil* **ointment**,
yet were they *drawn swords* **openings**.
6 I voluntarily sacrifice to you;
I spread hands to your name, O Yah Veh;
for *it is* good.
7 For he rescues me from all tribulation;
and my eye sees my enemies.

55 To His Eminence; On Strummer;
A Discerning: By David.
1 Give ear to my prayer, O Elohim;
conceal not yourself from my supplication:
2 hearken to me and answer;
I ramble on in my meditation and quake
3 —because of the voice of the enemy
at the face of the oppression of the wicked:
for they topple mischief on me;
in wrath they oppose me.
4 My heart writhes within me
and the terrors of death fall on me:
5 awe and trembling come on me
and horror covers over me.
6 And I say,
Oh that they give me pinions as a dove!
for then I fly and tabernacle!
7 Behold, then I wander afar
and stay overnight in the wilderness!
Selah.
8 I hasten my escape
from the rushing wind and storm.
9 Swallow them, O Adonay;
divide their tongues:
for I see violence and strife in the city.
10 Day and night they surround the walls;
mischief also and toil *are* in their midst;
11 calamity *is* in the midst:
fraud and deceit depart not from her broadways.
12 For neither an enemy reproaches me
—or I had borne it;
nor he who hates me greatens against me;
—or I had hid myself from him:
13 but you—a man my equal,
my chiliarch whom I know.
14 We sweetened private counsel together
—walked to the house of Elohim in conspiracy.
15 Desolations deceive them;
they descend alive into sheol;
evil is in their sojournings among them.
16 As for me, I call on Elohim;
and Yah Veh saves me:
17 evening and morning and noon
I meditate and roar;
and he hears my voice.
18 He redeems my soul in shalom
from the battle against me;
for many are with me:
19 El hears and answers them
—he who settled from antiquity.
Selah.
He neither changes, nor awes Elohim;
20 he spreads his hands
against such as are at shalom with him;
he profanes his covenant;
21 his mouth is more tender than butter
but in his heart, war;
his words are softer than ointment,
yet, openings.
22 Cast *thy burden* **that which he giveth thee**
upon *the LORD* **Yah Veh**,
and he shall sustain thee:
he shall *never suffer* **not give** the *righteous* **just**
to *be moved* **totter eternally**.
23 But thou, O *God* **Elohim**,
shalt *bring* **descend** them *down*
into the *pit* **well** of *destruction* **the pit of ruin**:
bloody and deceitful men **men of bloods and deceit**
shall *not live out half* **halve** their days;
but I *will trust* **shall confide** in thee.

56 To *the chief Musician* **His Eminence,**
on *Jonath—elem—rechokim* **The Mute Distant Dove**,
Michtam **Poem** of David,
when the *Philistines* **Peleshethiym**
took hold of him in Gath.
1 *Be merciful unto me* **Grant**
me charism, O *God* **Elohim**:
for man *would swallow* **should gulp** me *up*;
he fighting daily oppresseth me.
2 Mine *enemies* **opponents**
would **should** daily *swallow* **gulp** me *up*:
for they be many that fight against me,
O thou *most High* **Elyon**.
3 *What time I am afraid* **The day I awe**,
I *will trust* **shall confide** in thee.
4 In *God* **Elohim** I *will praise* **shall halal** his word,
in *God* **Elohim** I *have put my trust* **shall confide**;
I *will* **shall** not *fear* **awe**
what flesh *can do* **shall work** unto me.
5 Every day they *wrest* **contort** my words:
all their *thoughts* **fabrications** are against me for evil.

6 They *gather themselves together* **dodge**,
they hide *themselves*,
they *mark* **guard** my *steps* **heelprints**,
when they *wait for* **await** my soul.
7 Shall they escape by *iniquity* **mischief**?
in *thine anger cast down* **thy wrath descend** the people,
O *God* **Elohim**.
8 Thou *tellest* **scribest** my wanderings:
put **set** thou my tears into thy *bottle* **skin**:
are they not in thy *book* **scroll**?
9 *When I cry unto thee* **The day I call**,
then shall mine enemies turn back: this
I know; for *God* **Elohim** is for me.
10 In *God* **Elohim**
will I praise his **shall I halal the** word:
in *the LORD* **Yah Veh**
will I praise his **shall I halal the** word.
11 In *God have I put my trust* **Elohim I confide**:
I *will* **shall** not *be afraid* **awe**
what *man can do* **humanity shall work** unto me.
12 Thy vows are upon me, O *God* **Elohim**:
I *will render* **shall shalam**
praises **spread hands** unto thee.
13 For thou hast *delivered*
rescued my soul from death:
wilt **shalt** not thou *deliver* my feet from falling,
that I may walk *before God* **at the face of Elohim**
in the light of the living?

57 To *the chief Musician* **His Eminence**,
Al—taschith **Al Tashcheth/Ruin Not**,
Michtam **Poem** of David,
when he fled from **the face of** *Saul* **Shaul** in the cave.
1 *Be merciful unto me* **Grant**
me charism, O *God* **Elohim**,
be merciful unto me **grant me charism**:
for my soul *trusteth* **seeketh refuge** in thee:
yea, in the shadow of thy wings
will I make my **shall I seek** refuge,
until these calamities be overpast.
2 I *will cry* **shall call** unto *God*
most high **Elohim Elyon**;
unto *God* **El**
that *performeth* **consummateth** all *things* for me.
3 He shall send from *heaven* **the heavens**,
and save me from the reproach of him
that *would* **should** swallow *me up* **after me**.
Selah.
22 Cast what he gives you on Yah Veh
and he sustains you;
he gives not the just to totter eternally.
23 And you, O Elohim,
descend them into the well of the pit of ruin;
men of bloods and deceit halve their days;
but I confide in you.

56 To His Eminence; On the Mute Distant Dove;
A Poem by David,
when the Peleshethiym hold him in Gath.
1 Grant me charism, O Elohim, for man gulps me;
fighting daily, he oppresses me:
2 my opponents gulp me daily;
for they are many who fight against me, O Elyon.
3 The day I awe, I confide in you:
4 In Elohim I halal his word; in Elohim I confide:
I awe not what flesh works to me.
5 Every day they contort my words;
all their fabrications are against me for evil.
6 They dodge; they hide;
they guard my heelprints; they await my soul;
7 they escape by mischief:
in wrath the people descend, O Elohim.
8 You scribe my wanderings
—set my tears into your skin;
are they not in your scroll?
9 The day I call, my enemies turn back:
this I know; for Elohim is for me.
10 In Elohim, I halal the word;
in Yah Veh, I halal the word;
11 in Elohim, I confide:
I awe not what humanity works to me.
12 Your vows are on me, O Elohim;
I shalam spread hands to you:
13 for you rescue my soul from death.
Do you not also my feet from falling
—so that I walk at the face of Elohim
in the light of the living?

57 To His Eminence; Al Tashcheth/Ruin Not:
A Poem by David,
as he flees the face of Shaul in the cave.
1 Grant me charism, O
Elohim; grant me charism;
for my soul seeks refuge in you:
yes, in the shadow of your wings I seek refuge
until these calamities overpass.
2 I call to Elohim Elyon
—to El who consummates all for me.
3 He sends from the heavens and saves me
from the reproach of him who swallows after me.
Selah.
God **Elohim** shall send *forth* his mercy and his truth.
4 My soul is among **roaring** lions:

and I lie even among them that are *set on fire* **inflamed,**
even the sons of *men* **humanity,**
whose teeth are spears and arrows,
and their tongue a sharp sword.
5 Be thou *exalted* **lofted,** O *God* **Elohim,**
above the heavens;
let thy glory be **thy honour**
above all the earth.
6 They have prepared a net for my steps;
my soul is bowed down:
they have digged a pit *before me* **at my face,**
into the midst whereof they are fallen *themselves.*
Selah.
7 My heart is *fixed* **prepared,** O *God* **Elohim,**
my heart is *fixed* **prepared:**
I *will* **shall** sing and *give praise* **psalm.**
8 Awake *up,* my *glory* **honour;**
awake, *psaltery* **bagpipe** and harp:
I *myself will* **shall** awake early.
9 I *will praise* **shall spread hands unto** thee,
O *Lord* **Adonay,** among the people:
I *will sing* **shall psalm** unto thee among the nations.
10 For thy mercy is great unto the heavens,
and thy truth unto the *clouds* **vapours.**
11 Be thou *exalted* **lofted,** O *God* **Elohim,**
above the heavens:
let thy glory be **thy honour**
above all the earth.

58 To *the chief Musician* **His Eminence,**
Al—taschith **Al Tashcheth/Ruin Not,**
Michtam **Poem** of David.
1 *Do* **Truly, word** ye *indeed*
speak righteousness **justness,**
O *congregation* **mute?**
do ye judge uprightly **judge ye in straightnesses,**
O ye sons of *men* **humanity?**
2 Yea, in heart ye *work* **do** wickedness;
ye weigh the violence of your hands in the earth.
3 The wicked are estranged from the womb:
they *go astray* **stray**
as soon as they be born **from the belly,**
speaking **wording** lies.
4 Their poison is like the poison of a serpent:
they are like the deaf *adder* **asp**
that *stoppeth* **shutteth** her ear;
5 Which *will* **shall** not hearken
to the voice of charmers,
charming *never* **charms** so wisely.
6 Break their teeth, O *God*
Elohim, in their mouth:
break **pull** out the *great* **grinder** teeth
of the *young lions* **whelps,** O *LORD* **Yah Veh.**
7 Let them *melt away* **dissipate** as waters
which *run* **pass** continually:
when he *bendeth his bow to shoot* **aimeth** his arrows,
let them be as cut *in pieces* **off.**
8 As a snail *which melteth* **dissolveth,**
let *every one of* them pass away:
like the *untimely birth* **miscarriage** of a woman,
that they may not see the sun.
9 Before your *pots can feel*
caldrons discern the thorns,
he shall *take* **whirl** them away *as with a whirlwind,*
both living **alive,** and *in his wrath* **fuming.**
10 The *righteous* **just** shall *rejoice* **cheer**
when he seeth the *vengeance* **avengement:**
he shall wash his *feet* **steps** in the blood of the wicked.
11 So that *a man* **humanity** shall say,
Verily there is a *reward* **fruit** for the *righteous* **just:**
verily he is *a God* **Elohim** that judgeth in the earth.

59 To *the chief Musician* **His Eminence,**
Al—taschith **Al Tashcheth/Ruin Not,**
Michtam **Poem** of David;
when *Saul* **Shaul** sent,
and they *watched* **guarded** the
house to *kill* **deathify** him.
1 *Deliver* **Rescue** me from mine enemies,
O my *God* **Elohim:**
defend **loft** me from them that rise *up against me.*
Elohim sends his mercy and his truth.
4 My soul is among roaring lions;
and I lie *among* the inflamed
—the sons of humanity
whose teeth *are* spears and arrows
and their tongue a sharp sword.
5 Be lofted, O Elohim, above the heavens;
your honor above all the earth.
6 They prepare a net for my steps;
I bow my soul:
they dug a pit at my face;
they fall into its midst.
Selah.
7 My heart is prepared, O Elohim;
my heart is prepared:
I sing and psalm.
8 Waken, my honor!
Waken, bagpipe and harp!
I waken early.
9 I spread hands to you, O Adonay,
among the people;

I psalm to you among the nations.
10 For your mercy is great to the heavens
and your truth to the vapours.
11 Be lofted, O Elohim, above the heavens;
your honor above all the earth.

58 To His Eminence; Al Tashcheth/Ruin Not:
A Poem by David.
1 Is it true that you word justness, O mute?
—judge in straightnesses, O you sons of humanity?
2 Yes, in heart you do wickedness;
you weigh the violence of your hands in the earth.
3 The wicked estrange from the womb;
they stray from the belly, wording lies:
4 their poison is as the poison of a serpent;
as the deaf asp who shuts her ear
5 —who hearkens not to the voice of charmers,
charming charms so wisely.
6 O Elohim, break their teeth in their mouth;
pull out the grinder teeth of the whelps, O Yah Veh;
7 dissipate them as waters which pass continually;
he aims his arrows as though they are cut off:
8 as a snail dissolving,
they pass away;
as the miscarriage of a woman,
they see not the sun.
9 Ere your caldrons discern the thorns,
he whirls them away, alive and fuming.
10 The just cheers when he sees the avengement;
he washes his steps in the blood of the wicked.
11 So that humanity says,
Surely there is a fruit for the just;
surely Elohim judges in the earth.

59 To His Eminence; Al Tashcheth/Ruin Not:
A Poem by David;
when Shaul sends
and they guard the house to deathify him.
1 Rescue me from my enemies, O my Elohim;
loft me from them who rise:
2 *Deliver* **Rescue** me
from the *workers* **doers** of *iniquity* **mischief**,
and save me from *bloody men* **men of blood**.
3 For, *lo* **behold**, they *lie in wait* **lurk** for my soul:
the *mighty are gathered* **strong dodge** against me;
not for my *transgression* **rebellion**,
nor for my sin, O *LORD* **Yah Veh**.
4 They run and prepare themselves
without *my fault* **perversity**:
awake to *help* **meet** me, and *behold* **see**.
5 Thou therefore,
O *LORD God of hosts* **Yah Veh Elohim Sabaoth**,
the God **Elohim** of *Israel* **Yisra El**,
awake to visit all the *heathen* **goyim**:
be **grant** not *merciful* **charism**
to any *wicked transgressors* **who deal covertly**.
Selah.
6 They return at evening:
they *make a noise* **roar** like a dog,
and go round about the city.
7 Behold, they *belch* **gush** *out* with their mouth:
swords are in their lips: for who, *say they*, doth hear?
8 But thou, O *LORD* **Yah
Veh**, shalt laugh at them;
thou shalt *have* **deride** all the *heathen in derision* **goyim**.
9 *Because of his strength* **O my Strength,**
will I wait upon **shall I regard** thee: for *God*
Elohim is my *defence* **secure loft**.
10 The *God* **Elohim** of my mercy
shall *prevent* **anticipate** me:
God **Elohim** shall *let* **have** me see *my desire upon*
mine *enemies* **opponents**.
11 *Slay* **Slaughter** them not, lest my people forget:
scatter **stagger** them by thy *power* **valour**;
and *bring* **topple** them *down*,
O *Lord* **Adonay** our *shield* **buckler**.
12 For the sin of their mouth
and the words of their lips
let them even be *taken* **captured** in their *pride* **pomp**:
and for *cursing* **oathing** and *lying* **deception**
which they *speak* **scribe**.
13 *Consume* **Finish** them **off** in *wrath* **fury**,
consume **finish** them **off**, that they may not be:
and let them know
that *God ruleth* **Elohim reigneth** in *Jacob* **Yaaqov**
unto the *ends* **finality** of the earth.
Selah.
14 And at evening *let them* **they** return;
and let them make a noise **they roar** like a dog,
and go round about the city.
15 *Let them* **They** wander *up
and down for meat* **to eat,**
and *grudge* **murmer** if they be not satisfied.
16 But I *will* **shall** sing of thy power;
yea, I *will sing aloud* **shall shout** of thy mercy
in the morning:
for thou hast been my *defence* **secure loft**
and *refuge* **retreat**
in the day of my *trouble* **tribulation**.
17 Unto thee, O my strength, *will* **shall** I sing:
for *God* **Elohim** is my *defence* **secure loft**,
and the God **Elohim** of my mercy.

60 To *the chief Musician* **His Eminence,**
upon *Shushan—eduth* **Trumpet of Witness,**
Michtam **Poem** of David,
when he strove with *Aram—naharaim* **Aram Naharaim**
and with *Aram—zobah* **Aram Sobah,**
when *Joab* **Yah Ab** returned,
and smote of Edom
in the *valley of salt* **Valley of Salt/Gay Melach**
twelve thousand.
1 O *God* **Elohim**, thou hast cast us off,
thou hast *scattered* **breached** us,
thou hast been *displeased* **angry**;
O *turn thyself* **return** to us *again*.
2 Thou hast *made* **quaked** the earth *to tremble*;
thou hast broken it:
heal the breaches *thereof*; for it *shaketh* **tottereth**.
2 rescue me from the doers of mischief
and save me from men of blood.
3 For, behold, they lurk for my soul;
the strong dodge against me:
neither for my rebellion,
nor for my sin, O Yah Veh.
4 Without perversity
they run and prepare themselves; they
waken to meet me and see.
5 And You, O Yah Veh Elohim Sabaoth,
Elohim of Yisra El,
Waken to visit all the goyim;
grant not charism to any who deal covertly.
Selah.
6 They return at evening;
they roar as a dog and go all around the city:
7 behold, they gush with their mouth;
swords are in their lips: Who hears?
8 And you, O Yah Veh, laugh at them;
you deride all the goyim.
9 O my Strength, I regard you;
for Elohim is my secure loft.
10 The Elohim of my mercy anticipates me;
Elohim shows my opponents.
11 Slaughter them not, lest my people forget;
stagger them by your valour:
and topple them, O Adonay our buckler.
12 The sin of their mouth is the words of their lips
—captured in their own pomp;
and for oathing and deception which they scribe.
13 Finish them off in fury,
finish them off, that they are not;
and so they know that Elohim reigns in Yaaqov
to the finality of the earth.
Selah.
14 And at evening they return;
they roar like a dog and go all around the city:
15 they wander to eat
and murmer if they are not satisfied.
16 And I—I sing of your power;
yes, I shout of your mercy in the morning:
for being my secure loft and retreat
in the day of my tribulation.
17 To you, O my strength, I sing; for Elohim
is my secure loft—Elohim of my mercy.

60 To His Eminence; On Trumpet of Witness:
A Poem by David,
when he strives
with Aram Naharaim and with Aram Sobah,
when Yah Ab returns
and smites twelve thousand of Edom
in the Valley of Salt/Gay Melach.
1 O Elohim, you cast us off;
you breached us; you angered:
O return to us!
2 You quaked the earth; you broke it:
heal the breaches; for it totters:
3 Thou hast *shewed* **had** thy people
hard things **see hardship**:
thou hast made us to drink
the wine of *astonishment* **staggering**.
4 Thou hast given *a banner* **an ensign**
to them that *fear* **awe** thee,
that it may *be displayed* **flutter**
because **at the face** of *the truth* **trueness**.
Selah.
5 That thy beloved may be *delivered* **rescued**;
save with thy right *hand*, and *hear me* **answer**.
6 *God* **Elohim** hath spoken in his holiness;
I *will rejoice* **shall jump for joy**,
I *will divide* **shall allot** Shechem,
and *mete* **measure** out
the valley of *Succoth* **Sukkoth/Brush Arbors**.
7 *Gilead* **Gilad** is mine,
and *Manasseh* **Menash Sheh** is mine;
Ephraim **Ephrayim** also
is the *strength* **stronghold** of mine head;
Judah **Yah Hudah** is my *lawgiver* **statute setter**;
8 Moab is my *wash pot* **bath caldron**;
over Edom *will* **shall** I cast out my shoe:
Philistia **Pelesheth**, *triumph* **shout** thou because of me.
9 Who *will* **shall** bring me
into the *strong* city **with rampart**?
who *will* **shall** lead me into Edom?

10 *Wilt* **Shalt** not thou, O *God* **Elohim**,
which hadst cast us off?
and thou, O *God* **Elohim**,
which didst not go out with our *armies* **hosts**?
11 Give us help from *trouble* **tribulation**:
for vain is the *help* **salvation** of *man* **humanity**.
12 Through *God* **Elohim** we
shall *do* **work** valiantly:
for he it is
that shall *tread down* **trample** our *enemies* **tribulators**.

61 To *the chief Musician* **His Eminence**,
upon *Neginah* **Strings**,
A Psalm of David.
1 Hear my *cry* **shouting**, O *God* **Elohim**;
attend **hearken** unto my prayer.
2 From the end of the earth
will I cry **shall I call** unto thee,
when my heart *is overwhelmed* **languisheth**:
lead me to the rock that is *higher* **loftier** than I.
3 For thou hast been a *shelter* **refuge** for me,
and a strong tower **a tower of strength**
from **the face of** the enemy.
4 I *will abide* **shall sojourn** in thy *tabernacle* **tent**
for ever **eternally**:
I *will trust* **shall seek refuge** in the covert of thy wings.
Selah.
5 For thou, O *God* **Elohim**, hast heard my vows:
thou hast given me the *heritage* **possession**
of those that *fear* **awe** thy name.
6 Thou *wilt prolong* **shalt add**
to the *king's life* **sovereign's days**:
and **to** his years
as many generations **generation to generation**.
7 He shall *abide before God*
settle at the face of Elohim
for ever **eternally**:
O *prepare* **number** mercy and truth,
which may *preserve* **guard** him.
8 So *will I sing praise* **shall I psalm** unto thy name
for ever **eternally**,
that I may *daily perform* **day by day shalam** my vows.

62 To *the chief Musician* **His Eminence**,
to Jeduthun **Yeduthun/A Laudatory**, A Psalm of David.
1 Truly my soul *waiteth upon*
God **is silent unto Elohim**:
from him *cometh* **be** my salvation.
2 He only is my rock and my salvation;
he is my defence **my secure loft**;
I shall not *be* **totter** greatly *moved*.
3 You had your people see hardship;
you had us drink the wine of staggering:
4 you gave an ensign to them who awe you,
to flutter at the face of trueness.
Selah.
5 So as to rescue your beloved
save *with* your right and answer:
6 Elohim speaks in his holiness;
I jump for joy; I allot Shechem
—measure out the valley of Sukkoth/Brush Arbors.
7 Gilad *is* mine and Menash Sheh *is* mine;
and Ephrayim *is* the stronghold of my
head: Yah Hudah *is* my statute setter;
8 Moab *is* my bath caldron;
over Edom I cast my shoe;
Pelesheth, shout because of me.
9 Who brings me to the city with rampart?
Who leads me into Edom?
10 Is it not you, O Elohim?
Cast you us, O Elohim?
Go you not with our hosts?
11 Give us help from tribulation;
for vain is the salvation of humanity:
12 through Elohim we work valiantly;
for he tramples our tribulators.

61 To His Eminence; On Strings: By David.
1 Hear my shouting, O Elohim;
hearken to my prayer.
2 From the end of the earth I call to you;
my heart languishes:
lead me to the rock that is loftier than I.
3 For you are a refuge for me
—a tower of strength from the face of the enemy:
4 I sojourn in your tent eternally;
I seek refuge in the covert of your wings.
Selah.
5 For you, O Elohim, hear my vows;
you give me the possession
of them who awe your name.
6 You add days to the sovereign;
and years generation to generation.
7 He settles eternally at the face of Elohim;
O number mercy and truth to guard him.
8 Thus I psalm to your name eternally;
day by day I shalam my vows.

62 To His Eminence; Yeduthun/A Laudatory:
A Psalm by David.
1 Truly my soul is silent to Elohim;
—from him *is* my salvation:
2 he only is my rock and my salvation;
my secure loft; I totter not greatly.

3 How long *will* **shall** ye
imagine mischief **assail** against a man?
ye shall be *slain* **murdered** all of you:
as a *bowing* **spread** wall *shall ye be,*
and as a tottering fence—**an overthrown wall.**
4 They only *consult* **counsel**
to *cast* **drive** him *down* from his *excellency* **exaltation**:
they *delight in lies* **lie to please**:
they bless with their mouth,
but they *curse* **abase** inwardly.
Selah.
5 My soul, *wait* **hush** thou only upon *God* **Elohim**;
for my *expectation* **hope** is from him.
6 He only is my rock and my salvation:
he is my defence **my secure loft**;
I shall not *be moved* **totter.**
7 In *God* **Elohim** is my salvation
and my *glory* **honour**:
the rock of my strength, *and* my refuge,
is in *God* **Elohim.**
8 *Trust* **Confide** in him at all times;
ye people, pour out your heart *before him* **at his face**:
God **Elohim** is a refuge for us.
Selah.
9 Surely *men of low degree*
sons of humanity are vanity,
and *men of high degree* **sons of men** are a lie:
to be *laid* **ascended** in the balance,
they are altogether *lighter than vanity* **vain.**
10 *Trust* **Confide** not in oppression,
and become not vain in robbery:
if *riches increase* **thy valuables flourish,**
set not your heart *upon them.*
11 *God* **Elohim** hath *spoken* **worded** once;
twice have I heard this;
that *power belongeth unto God* **strength be with Elohim.**
12 Also unto thee, O *Lord*
Adonay, *belongeth* mercy:
for thou *renderest* **shalt shalam**
to *every man* **each** according to his work.

63 A Psalm of David,
when he was in the wilderness of *Judah* **Yah Hudah.**
1 O *God* **Elohim**, thou art my *God* **El**;
early *will* **shall** I seek thee:
my soul thirsteth for thee,
my flesh *longeth* **yearneth** for thee
in a *dry* **parched** and *thirsty* **languid** land,
where no **without** water *is*;
2 To see thy *power* **strength** and thy *glory* **honour**,
so as **thus** I have seen thee in the *sanctuary* **holies.**
3 Because thy *lovingkindness*
mercy is better than life,
my lips shall *praise* **laud** thee.
4 Thus *will* **shall** I bless thee while I live:
I *will* **shall** lift *up* my *hands* **palms** in thy name.
5 My soul shall be satisfied
as *with* marrow and *fatness* **fat;**
and my mouth shall *praise* **halal** *thee*
with *joyful* **shouting** lips:
6 When I remember thee upon my bed,
and meditate on thee in the *night* watches.
7 Because thou hast been my help,
therefore in the shadow of thy wings
will I rejoice **shall I shout.**
8 My soul *followeth hard* **adhereth** after thee:
thy right *hand* upholdeth me.
9 But those that seek my soul,
to *destroy it* **devastation,**
shall go into the *lower parts of the* **nethermost** earth.
10 They shall *fall* **flow** by **the hands of** the sword:
they shall *be a portion* **become an allotment** for foxes.
11 But the *king* **sovereign**
shall *rejoice* **cheer** in *God* **Elohim;**
every one that *sweareth* **oatheth** by him shall *glory* **halal:**
but the mouth of them that *speak lies* **word falsehoods**
shall be *stopped* **shut.**

64 To *the chief Musician* **His Eminence,**
A Psalm of David.
1 Hear my voice, O *God* **Elohim,**
in my *prayer* **meditation**:
preserve **guard** my life
from *fear* **dread** of the enemy.
3 Until when assail you against a man?
you are murdered—all of you
—as a wall spread—a wall overthrown.
4 Surely
they counsel to drive him from his exaltation;
they lie to please:
with their mouth, they bless;
but inwardly, abase.
Selah.
5 My soul, hush only on Elohim;
for my hope is from him:
6 Surely he is my rock and my salvation;
my secure loft; I totter not:
7 in Elohim *is* my salvation and my honor;
the rock of my strength:
my refuge is in Elohim.
8 Confide in him at all times, you people;
pour out your heart at his face:

Elohim *is* our refuge.
Selah.
9 Surely sons of humanity are vanity
and sons of men a lie;
they ascend in the balance—altogether vain.
10 Neither confide in oppression nor rob in vain;
if your valuables flourish, set not your heart.
11 Elohim worded once;
twice I heard this;
that strength *is* with Elohim;
12 and with you, O Adonay, mercy:
for you shalam each according to his work.

63 A Psalm by David:
when he is in the wilderness of Yah Hudah.
1 O Elohim, you are my El;
I seek you early;
my soul thirsts for you—my flesh yearns for you
in a parched and languid land without water;
2 I see you in the holies
—see your strength and your honor.
3 Because your mercy is better than life,
my lips laud you.
4 Thus I bless you while I live;
I lift my palms in your name:
5 my soul is satisfied as marrow and fat
and my mouth halals with shouting lips:
6 when I remember you on my bed
I meditate on you in the watches:
7 for you are my help;
in the shadow of your wings, I shout:
8 my soul adheres after you;
your right upholds me.
9 And they who seek to devastate my soul
go into the nethermost earth:
10 they flow by the hands of the sword
—an allotment for foxes:
11 and the sovereign cheers in Elohim;
every one who oaths by him halals:
but the mouth of them who word falsehoods, shuts.

64 To His Eminence: A Psalm by David.
1 Hear my voice, O Elohim, in my meditation;
guard my life from dread of the enemy:
2 Hide me
from the *secret* **private** counsel of the *wicked* **vilifiers**;
from the *insurrection* **conspiracy**
of the *workers* **doers** of *iniquity* **mischief**:
3 Who *whet* **pointen** their tongue like a sword,
and *bend their bows to shoot* **aim** their arrows,
even bitter words:
4 That they may shoot *in secret* **from the coverts**
at the *perfect* **integrious**:
suddenly *do* they shoot *at* him, and *fear* **awe** not.
5 They *encourage* **strengthen** themselves
in an evil *matter* **word**:
they *commune* **scribe** of *laying* **hiding** snares *privily*;
they say, Who shall see *them*?
6 They search out *iniquities* **wickednesses**;
in searching,
they *accomplish* **consummate** a *diligent* search:
both the inward *thought of every one of them* **man**
and the heart, is deep.
7 But *God* **Elohim** shall shoot
at them with an arrow;
suddenly shall they be *wounded* **struck**.
8 So they shall *make* **trip upon** their own tongue
to fall upon themselve:
all that see them shall flee away.
9 And all *man* **humanity** shall *fear* **awe**,
and shall *declare* **tell** the *work* **deeds** of *God* **Elohim**;
for they shall
wisely consider of **comprehend** his *doing* **work**.
10 The *righteous* **just** shall *be glad* **cheer**
in *the LORD* **Yah Veh**,
and shall *trust* **seek refuge** in him;
and all the *upright* **straight** in heart shall *glory* **halal**.

65 To *the chief Musician* **His Eminence**,
A Psalm**,** *and* Song of David.
1 *Praise waiteth* **Halal is silent** for thee,
O *God* **Elohim**, in *Sion* **Siyon**:
and unto thee shall **they shalam** the vow *be performed*.
2 O thou that hearest prayer,
unto thee shall all flesh come.
3 *Iniquities* **Words of perversities**
prevail **mightily** against me:
as for our *transgressions* **rebellions**,
thou shalt *purge* **kapar/atone** them *away*.
4 *Blessed is the man* **Blithe—**
they whom thou choosest,
and *causest to approach* **drawest nigh** *unto thee*,
that he may *dwell* **tabernacle** in thy courts:
we shall be satisfied with the goodness of thy house,
even of thy holy *temple* **manse**.
5 *By terrible things in righteousness*
In awesome justness
wilt **shalt** thou answer us,
O *God* **Elohim** of our salvation;
who art the confidence of all the ends of the earth,
and of them that are afar off upon the sea:
6 Which by his *strength* **force**
setteth fast **establisheth** the mountains;

being girded with *power* **might**:
7 Which *stilleth* **laudeth** the
noise **roaring** of the seas,
the *noise* **roaring** of their waves,
and the *tumult* **roar** of the *people* **nations**.
8 They also
that *dwell* **settle** in the *uttermost parts* **extremities**
are afraid **awe** at thy *tokens* **signs**:
thou makest the *outgoings* **risings**
of the morning and evening to *rejoice* **shout**.
9 Thou visitest the earth, and
waterest **overflowest** it:
thou greatly enrichest it
with the *river* **rivulet** of *God* **Elohim**,
which is—full of water:
thou preparest them *corn* **crop**,
when thou hast so *provided* **prepared** for it.
10 Thou *waterest* **saturatest** the *ridges* **furrows**
thereof abundantly:
thou *settlest* **descendest in** the furrows *thereof*:
thou *makest* **dissolvest** it *soft* with showers:
thou blessest the *springing* **sprouting** *thereof*.
11 Thou crownest the year with thy goodness;
and thy *paths drop* **routes drip** fatness.
2 hide me from the private counsel of vilifiers
—from the conspiracy of doers of mischief
3 who pointen their tongue as a sword
and aim their arrows, bitter words:
4 to shoot the integrious from the coverts;
shoot suddenly, and not awe.
5 They strengthen themselves in an evil word;
they scribe of hiding snares:
they say, Who sees?
6 They search for wickednesses;
in searching, they consummate a search:
both the inward man and the heart is deep.
7 And Elohim shoots them an arrow;
suddenly they are struck:
8 they trip on their own tongue;
all who see them flee.
9 All humanity awes and
tells the deeds of Elohim;
for they comprehend his work:
10 the just cheer in Yah Veh
and seek refuge in him;
and all the straight in heart halal.

65 To His Eminence; A Psalm: A Song by David.
1 Silence to you! Halal O Elohim, in Siyon!
And to you, shalam the vow!
2 O you who hears prayer,
to whom all flesh comes.
3 Words of perversities
prevail mightily against me;
as for our rebellions, you kapar/atone them.
4 Blithe—they whom you choose and draw near
to tabernacle in your courts:
we satisfy with the goodness of your house
—your holy manse.
5 In awesome justness you answer us,
O Elohim of our salvation;
the confidence of all the ends of the earth
and of them afar off on the sea:
6 who by his force establishes the mountains;
girt with might:
7 who lauds the roaring of the seas
the roaring of their waves
and the roar of the nations.
8 And they who settle in the extremities
awe at your signs;
the risings of the morning and evening
you cause to shout.
9 You visit the earth and overflow it;
you greatly enrich it with the rivulet of Elohim
—full of water:
you prepare them crop
when you thus prepare for it:
10 you saturate the furrows;
you descend in the furrows;
you dissolve it with showers;
you bless the sprouting:
11 you crown the year with your goodness;
and your routes drip fatness.
12 They *drop* **drip**
upon the *pastures* **folds** of the wilderness:
and the *little hills* **mountains**
rejoice on every side **are girt with twirling round about**.
13 The *pastures* **rams**
are *clothed* **enrobed** with flocks;
the valleys also
are *covered over* **shrouded** with *corn* **grain**;
they shout *for joy*, they *also* sing.

66 To *the chief Musician* **His Eminence**,
A Song *or* Psalm.
1 *Make a joyful noise* **Shout ye** unto *God* **Elohim**,
all ye *lands* **earth**:
2 *Sing* **Psalm** forth the honour of his name:
make **set** his *praise glorious* **halal honoured**.
3 Say unto *God* **Elohim**,
How *terrible art thou in* **awesome** thy works!
through the greatness of thy *power* **strength**
shall thine enemies *submit themselves*
emaciate unto thee.

4 All the earth shall *worship* **prostrate unto** thee,
and shall *sing* **psalm** unto thee;
they shall *sing to* **psalm** thy name.
Selah.
5 Come and see the *works* **deeds** of *God* **Elohim**:
he is terrible in his doing **his awesome exploits**
toward the *children* **sons** of *men* **humanity**.
6 He turned the sea into dry *land*:
they *went* **passed** through the *flood* **river** on foot:
there did we *rejoice* **cheer** in him.
7 He *ruleth* **reigneth** by his *power* **might**
for ever **eternally**;
his eyes *behold* **watch** the *nations* **goyim**:
let not the *rebellious exalt* **revolters loft** themselves.
Selah.
8 O bless our *God* **Elohim**, ye people,
and *make* **have them hear**
the voice of his *praise* **halal** *to be heard*:
9 Which *holdeth* **setteth** our soul in life,
and *suffereth* **giveth** not our feet to *be moved* **topple**.
10 For thou, O *God* **Elohim**,
hast *proved* **proofed** us:
thou hast *tried* **refined** us, as silver is *tried* **refined**.
11 Thou broughtest us into the *net* **stronghold**;
thou *laidst affliction* **settest oppression** upon our loins.
12 Thou hast caused men to ride over our heads;
we went through fire and *through* water:
but thou broughtest us out *into a wealthy place* **satiated**.
13 I *will* **shall** go into thy house
with *burnt offerings* **holocausts**:
I *will pay* **shall shalam** thee my vows,
14 Which my lips have *uttered* **gasped**, and my mouth
hath *spoken* **worded**, when I was in *trouble* **tribulation**.
15 I *will offer* **shall holocaust** unto thee
burnt sacrifices **holocausts** of fatlings,
with the incense of rams;
I *will offer* **shall work** bullocks with **he** goats.
Selah.
16 Come and hear, all ye that *fear God* **awe Elohim**,
and I *will declare* **shall scribe**
what he hath *done* **worked** for my soul.
17 I *cried* **called** unto him with my mouth,
and he was *extolled with* **exalted under** my tongue.
18 If I *regard iniquity* **see mischief** in my heart,
the Lord will **Adonay shall** not hear me:
19 *But verily God* **Surely Elohim** hath heard *me*;
he hath *attended* **hearkened** to the voice of my prayer.
20 Blessed be *God* **Elohim**,
which hath not turned away my prayer,
nor his mercy from me.

67 To *the chief Musician* **His Eminence,**
on *Neginoth* **Strummer,**
A Psalm *or* Song.
1 *God be merciful* **Elohim grant charism** unto us,
and bless us;
and cause his face to *shine* **lighten** upon us;
Selah.
12 They drip on the folds of the wilderness;
and the mountains gird with twirling all around:
13 the rams enrobe with flocks;
and the valleys shroud with grain.
They shout! They sing!

66 To His Eminence: A Song: A Psalm.
1 Shout to Elohim, all you earth;
2 psalm forth the honor of his name;
set his halal honored.
3 Say to Elohim, How awesome your works!
Through the greatness of your strength
your enemies emaciate to you:
4 all the earth prostrates to
you and psalms to you;
they psalm your name.
Selah.
5 Come and see the deeds of Elohim;
his awesome exploits toward the sons of humanity.
6 He turned the sea into dry;
they passed through the river on foot:
there we cheered in him.
7 He reigns by his might eternally;
his eyes watch the goyim:
the revolters loft not themselves.
Selah.
8 O bless our Elohim, you people;
hear the voice of his halal
9 —who sets our soul in life
and gives that our feet topple not.
10 For you, O Elohim, proof us;
you refine us as refined silver;
11 you bring us to the stronghold;
you set oppression on our loins;
12 you ride men over our heads: we go through
fire and water; but you bring us out satiated.
13 I enter your house with holocausts;
I shalam you my vows:
14 my lips gasp
and my mouth words in my tribulation:
15 I holocaust to you
holocausts of fatlings with the incense of rams;
I work bullocks with he goats.
Selah.

16 Come and hear, all you who awe Elohim;
and I scribe what he works for my soul.
17 I call to him with my mouth
and exalt him under my tongue.
18 If I see mischief in my heart
Adonay hears me not:
19 surely Elohim hears;
he hearkens to the voice of my prayer.
20 Blessed—Elohim,
who neither turns away my prayer,
nor his mercy from me.

67 To His Eminence; On Strummer:
A Psalm; a Song.
1 Elohim grants us charism and blesses us;
and lightens his face on us;
Selah.
2 That thy way may be known upon earth,
thy *saving health* **salvation** among all *nations* **goyim**.
3 Let the people *praise* **spread hands unto** thee,
O *God* **Elohim**;
let all the people *praise* **spread hands unto** thee.
4 O let the nations *be glad*
cheer and *sing for joy* **shout**:
for thou shalt judge the people *righteously* **straightly**,
and *govern* **lead** the nations upon earth.
Selah.
5 Let the people *praise* **spread hands unto** thee,
O *God* **Elohim**;
let all the people *praise* **spread hands unto** thee.
6 Then shall the earth *yield*
give her *increase* **produce**;
and *God* **Elohim**,
even our own God **our Elohim**, shall bless us.
7 *God* **Elohim** shall bless us;
and all the *ends* **finality** of the earth shall *fear* **awe** him.

68 To *the chief Musician* **His Eminence,**
on *Neginoth* **Strummer,**
A Psalm *or* Song of David.
1 Let *God* **Elohim** arise, let
his enemies be scattered:
let them also that hate him flee *before him* **from his face.**
2 As smoke is *driven away*
dispersed, *so* drive them away:
as wax melteth *before* **at the face of** the fire,
so let the wicked *perish* **destruct**
at the *presence* **face** of *God* **Elohim.**
3 *But let the righteous be glad* **The just cheer**;
let them rejoice **they jump for joy** *before*
God **at the face of Elohim**:
yea, let them exceedingly **they cheerfully** rejoice.
4 Sing unto *God* **Elohim**, *sing*
praises **psalm** to his name:
extol him that rideth upon the *heavens* **plains**
by his name *JAH* **Yah**,
and *rejoice before him* **jump for joy at his face.**
5 A father of the *fatherless* **orphan**,
and a *judge of* **pleader for** the widows, is
God **Elohim** in his holy habitation.
6 *God* **Elohim** setteth the *solitary* **lonely**
in *families* **households**:
he bringeth out those which are bound
with chains **into prosperity**:
but the *rebellious* **revolting**
dwell in a *dry land* **parch**.
7 O *God* **Elohim,**
when thou wentest forth
before **at the face of** thy people,
when thou *didst march* **pacest**
through the *wilderness* **desolation**;
Selah:
8 The earth *shook* **quaked**,
the heavens also dropped
at the *presence* **face** of *God* **Elohim**:
even Sinai itself was moved **thus also Sinay**
at the *presence* **face** of *God* **Elohim,**
the God **Elohim** of *Israel* **Ysra El.**
9 Thou, O *God* **Elohim,**
didst send a plentiful rain
hast shaken an abundant downpour,
whereby thou *didst confirm*
establishest thine inheritance,
when it *was weary* **wearied.**
10 Thy *congregation hath dwelt*
therein **lives have settled**:
thou, O *God* **Elohim,**
hast prepared of thy goodness for the *poor* **humble.**
11 *The Lord* **Adonay** gave the *word* **saying**:
great was the *company of those* **host**
that *published* **evangelized** it.
12 *Kings of armies did flee apace*
In fleeing, sovereigns of hosts fled:
and she *that tarried* **whose habitation of rest is** at home
divided **allotted** the spoil.
13 Though ye have *lien* **lain** among the *pots* **stalls,**
yet shall ye be as the
as wings of a dove covered with silver,
and her feathers **as pinions** with *yellow gold* **green ore.**
14 When *the Almighty* **Shadday**
scattered kings **spread sovereigns** in it,
it was *white as snow* **snowwhite** in Salmon.

2 That your way be known on earth
and your salvation among all goyim.
3 The people spread hands to you, O Elohim;
all the people spread hands to you:
4 the nations cheer and shout;
for you judge the people straightly
and lead the nations on earth.
Selah.
5 The people spread hands to you, O Elohim;
all the people spread hands to you:
6 the earth gives her produce;
and Elohim—our Elohim, blesses us
7 —Elohim blesses us:
and all the finality of the earth awes him.

68 To His Eminence; On Strummer:
A Psalm; a Song by David.
1 Elohim rises; his enemies scatter:
they who hate him flee from his face.
2 As smoke disperses, driven away;
as wax melts at the face of the fire;
the wicked destruct at the face of Elohim:
3 the just cheer;
they jump for joy at the face of Elohim;
they cheerfully rejoice.
4 Sing to Elohim! Psalm to his name!
Extol him who rides on the plains,
by his name Yah;
and jump for joy at his face.
5 Father of the orphan; pleader for the widows:
Elohim in his holy habitation.
6 Elohim sets the lonely in households;
he brings the bound into prosperity:
but they who revolt dwell in a parch.
7 O Elohim;
as you come at the face of your people,
as you pace them through the desolation;
Selah.
8 The earth quakes;
yes, the heavens drop at the face of Elohim;
thus also Sinay at the face of Elohim,
O Elohim of Ysra El.
9 You, O Elohim,
shake an abundant downpour,
whereby you established your inheritance
when it wearies.
10 Your living settle therein;
you, O Elohim,in your goodness,
prepare for the humble.
11 Adonay gives the saying;
great is the host that evangelizes.
12 In fleeing, sovereigns of hosts flee;
and she whose habitation of rest is at home
allots the spoil
13 —though you lie among the stalls
—as wings of a dove covered with silver,
—as pinions with green ore.
14 When Shadday spreads sovereigns therein,
it is snowwhite in Salmon.
15 The *hill* **mountain** of *God* **Elohim**
is as the *hill* **mountain** of Bashan;
an high hill **peaks of the mountain**
as the *hill* **mountain** of Bashan.
16 Why *leap* **stand** ye **guard**,
ye *high hills?* **peaks of the mountains**
this is the hill—**the mountain**
which God **Elohim** desireth to *dwell in;* **settle?**
yea, *the LORD will dwell* **Yah Veh shall tabernacle** in it
for ever **in perpetuity**.
17 The chariots of *God* **Elohim**
are *twenty thousand* **two myriads**,
even thousands of *angels* **reinforcements**:
the Lord **Adonay** is among them,
as in *Sinai* **Sinay**, in the *holy place* **holies**.
18 Thou hast ascended *on high* **the heights**,
thou hast *led captivity captive* **captured the captives**:
thou hast *received* **taken** gifts for *men* **humanity**;
yea, *for* the *rebellious* **revolters** also,
that *the LORD God* **Yah Elohim**
might *dwell among them* **tabernacle**.
19 Blessed be *the Lord* **Adonay**,
who *daily* **day by day** loadeth us *with benefits*,
even the God—**El** of our salvation.
Selah.
20 *He that is our God is the God of salvation*
El—our El of salvations;
and unto *GOD the Lord* **Yah Veh Adonay**
belong **be** the issues from death.
21 But *God* **Elohim**
shall *wound* **strike** the head of his enemies,
and the hairy scalp of such an one
as goeth on still in his *trespasses* **guilt**.
22 *The Lord* **Adonay** said,
I *will bring again* **shall return**
from Bashan,
I *will bring my people again* **shall return**
from the depths of the sea:
23 That thy foot may be *dipped* **stricken**
in the blood of thine enemies,
and the tongue of thy dogs in the same.
24 They have seen thy *goings* **ways**, O *God* **Elohim**;

even the *goings* **ways** of my *God* **El**, my *King*
Sovereign, in the *sanctuary* **holies**.
25 The singers *went before* **preceded**,
the *players on instruments followed* **strummers** after;
among them were the *damsels* **virgins**
playing with timbrels **tambourining**.
26 Bless ye *God* **Elohim** in the congregations,
even the Lord **Adonay**,
from the fountain of *Israel* **Yisra El**.
27 There is *little Benjamin*
insignificant Ben Yamin
with their *ruler* **subjugator**,
the *princes* **governors** of *Judah* **Yah Hudah**
and their *council* **company**,
the *princes* **governors** of Zebulun,
and the *princes* **governors** of Naphtali.
28 Thy *God* **Elohim** hath *commanded*
misvahed thy strength:
strengthen, O *God* **Elohim**,
that which thou hast *wrought* **done** for us.
29 Because of thy *temple* **manse**
at *Jerusalem* **Yeru Shalem**
shall *kings* **sovereigns** bring presents unto thee.
30 Rebuke the *company of spearmen* **live stalkers**,
the *multitude* **witnesses** of the *bulls* **mighty**,
with the calves of the people,
till every one submit himself **each prostrating**
with *pieces* **fragments** of silver:
scatter thou the people that delight in war.
31 *Princes* **Wealth** shall come
out of *Egypt* **Misrayim**;
Ethiopia **Kush** shall *soon stretch out* **run** her hands
unto *God* **Elohim**.
32 Sing unto *God* **Elohim**,
ye *kingdoms* **sovereigndoms** of the earth;
O *sing praises* **psalm** unto *the Lord* **Adonay**;
Selah:
33 To him that rideth upon
the heavens of **the** heavens,
which were of *old* **antiquity**;
lo **behold**, he *doth send out* **giveth** his voice,
and that a mighty voice—**a voice of strength**.
15 The mountain of Elohim
is as the mountain of Bashan;
peaks of the mountain as the mountain of Bashan.
16 Why stand guard, you mountain peaks
—the mountain Elohim desires to settle?
—yes, Yah Veh tabernacles therein in perpetuity.
17 The chariots of Elohim are two myriads
—thousands of reinforcements;
Adonay is among them in the holies, as in Sinay.
18 You ascended the heights;
you captured the captives;
you took gifts for humanity;
yes, the revolters also,
that Yah Elohim *may* tabernacle.
19 Blessed
—Adonay, who day by day loads us
—El of our salvation.
Selah.
20 To El—our El of salvations
and to Yah Veh Adonay
are the issues of death.
21 Surely Elohim strikes the head of his enemies
and the hairy scalp of such who still go on in guilt.
22 Adonay says, I return from Bashan,
I return from the depths of the sea;
23 so that you strike your foot
in the blood of your enemies,
and the tongue of your dogs in the same.
24 They see your ways, O Elohim;
the ways of my El, my Sovereign, in the holies.
25 The singers precede; the strummers after:
the virgins tambourining among them.
26 Bless Elohim in the congregations
and Adonay from the fountain of Yisra El.
27 There *is* insignificant Ben
Yamin their subjugator,
the governors of Yah Hudah and their company,
the governors of Zebulun,
and the governors of Naphtali.
28 Your Elohim misvahs your strength.
Strengthen, O Elohim, what you do for us.
29 Because of your manse at Yeru Shalem
sovereigns bring presents to you.
30 Rebuke the live stalkers
the witnesses of the mighty
with the calves of the people
—each prostrating with fragments of silver:
scatter the people who delight in war.
31 Wealth comes from Misrayim;
Kush runs her hands to Elohim.
32 Sing to Elohim,
you sovereigndoms of the earth;
O psalm to Adonay;
Selah.
33 To him who rides
on the heavens of the heavens from antiquity;
behold, he gives his voice—a voice of strength.
34 *Ascribe* **Give** ye strength unto *God* **Elohim**:

his *excellency* **pomp** is over *Israel* **Yisra El**,
and his strength is in the clouds.
35 *O God, thou art terrible* **Awesome, O Elohim**
out of thy *holy places* **hallowed refuge**:
the God of Israel **El of Yisra El** is he
that giveth strength and *power* **mights**
unto *his* **the** people.
Blessed be *God* **Elohim**.

69 To *the chief Musician* **His Eminence**,
upon Shoshannim/**Trumpets**,
A Psalm of David.
1 Save me, O *God* **Elohim**;
for the waters are come in unto *my* **the** soul.
2 I sink in deep mire,
where there is no *standing* **foothold**:
I am come into *deep* **depths of** waters,
where the *floods* **streams** overflow me.
3 I am *weary* **belaboured** of my *crying* **calling**:
my throat is *dried* **scorched**:
mine eyes *fail* **are finished off**
while I *wait for* **await** my *God* **Elohim**.
4 They that hate me *without a cause* **gratuitously**
are more than the hairs of mine head
abound by the myriads:
they that *would destroy* **should exterminate** me,
being mine enemies *wrongfully* **of falseness**, are mighty:
then I restored that which I *took* **stripped** not *away*.
5 O *God* **Elohim**, thou
knowest my *foolishness* **folly**;
and my *sins* **guiltinesses** are not
hid **concealed** from thee.
6 Let not them that *wait on* **await** thee,
O *Lord GOD of hosts* **Adonay Yah Veh Sabaoth**,
be *ashamed* **shamed** for my sake:
let not those that seek thee
be confounded **shame** for my sake,
O *God* **Elohim** of *Israel* **Yisra El**.
7 Because for thy sake I have borne reproach;
shame hath covered my face.
8 I am become a stranger unto my brethren,
and *an alien* **a stranger** unto my mother's *children* **sons**.
9 For the zeal of thine house hath eaten me *up*;
and the reproaches of them that reproached thee
are fallen upon me.
10 When I wept,
and chastened my soul with fasting
in the fasting of my soul,
that was to my reproach.
11 I *made sackcloth* **gave saq** also my *garment* **robe**;
and I became a proverb to them.
12 They that *sit* **settle** in the *gate* **portal**
speak **meditate** against me;
and I was the song
of *the drunkards* **them drinking intoxicants**.
13 But as for me,
my prayer is unto thee, O *LORD* **Yah Veh**,
in *an acceptable* **a pleasant** time:
O *God* **Elohim**,
in the *multitude* **abundance** of thy
mercy *hear me* **answer**,
in the truth of thy salvation.
14 *Deliver* **Rescue** me out of the
mire, and let me not sink:
let me be *delivered* **rescued** from them that hate
me, and out of the *deep* **depths of** waters.
15 Let not the *waterflood*
water streams overflow me,
neither let the deep swallow me *up*,
and let not the *pit* **well** shut her mouth upon me.
16 *Hear me* **Answer**, O *LORD* **Yah Veh**;
for thy *lovingkindness* **mercy** is good:
turn unto **face** me
according to the *multitude* **abundance**
of thy tender mercies.
17 And hide not thy face from thy servant;
for I am *in trouble* **tribulated**:
hear **answer** me *speedily* **hastily**.
18 Draw nigh unto my soul, *and* redeem it:
deliver **redeem** me because of mine enemies.
19 Thou hast known my reproach,
and my shame, and my dishonour:
mine adversaries **my tribulators** are
all *before* **in front of** thee.

34 Give strength to Elohim;
his pomp is over Yisra El
and his strength in the clouds.
35 Awesome, O Elohim, from
your hallowed refuge;
El of Yisra El is he
who gives strength and might to the people.
Blessed—Elohim.

69 To His Eminence; On Shoshannim/Trumpets:
By David.
1 Save me, O Elohim;
for the waters come to the soul.
2 I sink in deep mire, where there is no foothold;
I come into depths of waters;
the streams overflow me:
3 I belabored of my calling;
my throat scorches;

my eyes finish off as I await my Elohim.
4 They who hate me gratuitously
—my exterminators abound by the myriads;
my enemies of falseness, are mighty;
I restored what I stripped not.
5 O Elohim, you know my folly;
and my guiltinesses are not concealed from you.
6 O Adonay Yah Veh Sabaoth,
may they who await you, not shame for my sake;
may they who seek you, not shame for my sake,
O Elohim of Yisra El.
7 Because of you, I bear reproach;
shame covers my face:
8 I become a stranger to my brothers
and a stranger to the sons of my mother:
9 for the zeal of your house eats me;
and the reproaches of them who reproach you
fall on me.
10 I weep in the fasting of my soul—my reproach;
11 I give saq for my robe;
and I become a proverb to them.
12 They who settle in the
portal meditate against me;
—I the song of them drinking intoxicants.
13 And as for me, my prayer *is* to you, O Yah Veh:
in a pleasant time, O Elohim,
in the abundance of your mercy
answer in the truth of your salvation.
14 Rescue me from the mire so that I not sink;
—rescue from them who hate me
and from the depths of waters:
15 *may* neither the water streams overflow me,
nor the deep swallow me
nor the well shut her mouth upon me.
16 Answer, O Yah Veh; for your mercy is good;
face me according to the abundance
of your tender mercies:
17 hide not your face from your servant;
for I tribulate:
answer me hastily.
18 Draw near my soul; redeem
—because of my enemies, redeem me.
19 You know my reproach
and my shame and my dishonor;
my tribulators are all in front of you.
20 Reproach hath broken my heart;
and I am full of heaviness:
and I *looked for some* **awaited one** to *take pity* **wag**,
but there was none;
and for *comforters* **sighers**, but I found none.
21 They gave me also *gall for*
my meat **rosh to chew**;
and in my thirst
they gave me *vinegar* **fermentation** to drink.
22 Let their table become a snare
before them **at their face**:
and *that which should have been*
for their *welfare* **shalom**,
let it become a *trap* **snare**.
23 Let their eyes be darkened, that they see not;
and make their loins continually to *shake* **waver**.
24 Pour out *thine indignation* **thy rage** upon them,
and let thy *wrathful anger* **fuming wrath**
take hold of **overtake** them.
25 Let their *habitation be* **walls** desolate;
and let none *dwell* **settle** in their tents.
26 For they *persecute him* **pursue**
whom thou hast smitten;
and they *talk* **scribe** to the *grief* **sorrow**
of *those whom thou hast wounded* **thy pierced**.
27 *Add iniquity* **Give perversity**
unto **for** their *iniquity* **perversity**:
and let them not come into thy *righteousness* **justness**.
28 Let them be *blotted* **wiped** out
of *the book* **scroll** of the living,
and not be *written* **scribed** with the *righteous* **just**.
29 But I am *poor* **humble** and *sorrowful* **pained**:
let thy salvation, O *God* **Elohim**,
set me up on high **loft me**.
30 I *will praise* **shall halal** the name of *God* **Elohim**
with a song,
and *will magnify* **shall greaten** him
with *thanksgiving* **spread hands**.
31 This also shall **well**—please *the LORD* **Yah Veh**
better than an ox or bullock
that hath horns **horned** and *hoofs* **hoofed**.
32 The humble shall see *this*, and *be glad* **cheer**:
and your heart shall live that seek *God* **Elohim**.
33 For *the LORD* **Yah Veh** heareth the *poor* **needy**,
and despiseth not his *prisoners* **bound**.
34 Let the *heaven* **heavens**
and earth *praise* **halal** him,
the seas, and *every thing* **all** that
moveth **creepeth** *therein*.
35 For *God will* **Elohim shall** save *Zion* **Siyon**,
and *will* **shall** build the cities of *Judah* **Yah Hudah**:
that they may *dwell* **settle** there,
and *have* **possess** it *in possession*.
36 The seed also of his servants shall inherit it:
and they that love his name

shall *dwell* **tabernacle** *therein.*

70 To *the chief Musician* **His Eminence,**
A Psalm of David,
to *bring to remembrance* **remember.**
1 *Make haste,* O *God* **Elohim,**
to *deliver* **rescue** me;
make haste **hasten** to help me, O *LORD* **Yah Veh.**
2 Let them *be ashamed* **shame**
and *confounded* **blush**
that seek after my soul:
let them *be turned backward* **apostatize,**
and *put to confusion* **shame,** that desire my *hurt* **evil.**
3 *Let them be turned back* **Return them**
for *a reward* **finality** of their shame that say, Aha, aha.
4 Let all those that seek thee
rejoice and *be glad* **cheer** in thee:
and let such as love thy salvation say continually,
Let God **Elohim** be *magnified* **greatened.**
5 But I am *poor* **humble** and needy:
make haste **hasten** unto me, O *God* **Elohim:**
thou art my help *and my deliverer*
who slippeth me away;
O *LORD* **Yah Veh,** *make no tarrying* **tarry not.**

71 In thee, O *LORD* **Yah Veh,**
do I put my trust **I seek refuge:**
let me never be *put to confusion* **eternally shamed.**
2 *Deliver* **Rescue** me in thy *righteousness* **justness,**
and *cause me to escape* **slip me away:**
incline **spread** thine ear unto me, and save me.

20 Reproach breaks my heart;
I am full of heaviness;
I await someone to wag, and there is no one;
and for sighers, and I find none.
21 They give me rosh to chew;
and in my thirst, fermentation to drink.
22 Their table becomes a snare at their face
—a snare for their shalom:
23 their eyes darken that they see not;
and they continually waver their loins.
24 Pour your rage on them
so that your fuming wrath overtakes them.
25 Desolate their walls
so that no one settles in their tents.
26 For they pursue whom you smite;
and they scribe to the sorrow of your pierced.
27 Give perversity for their perversity;
that they come not into your justness:
28 —wiped out of the scroll of the living
—not scribed with the just.
29 And I humble *myself* and pain;
your salvation, O Elohim, lofts me:
30 I halal the name of Elohim with a song
and greaten him with spread hands:
31 And this well—pleases Yah Veh
better than an ox or bullock—horned and hoofed.
32 The humble see, and cheer;
your heart lives—you who seek Elohim.
33 For Yah Veh hears the needy
and despises not his bound.
34 The heavens and earth halal him
—the seas and every creeper.
35 For Elohim saves Siyon
and builds the cities of Yah Hudah;
for them to settle there and possess.
36 The seed also of his servants inherit;
and they who love his name tabernacle therein.

70 To His Eminence, by David: A Reminder.
1 O Elohim, rescue me;
hasten to help me, O Yah Veh:
2 *may* they who seek my soul
shame and blush;
—apostatize and shame them who desire my evil.
3 Return final shame to them who say, Aha! Aha!
4 *May* all who seek you rejoice and cheer in you;
and such as love your salvation continually say,
Elohim be greatened.
5 And I *am* humble and needy;
hasten to me, O Elohim:
you are my help who slips me away;
O Yah Veh, tarry not.

71 In you, O Yah Veh, I seek refuge;
may I never shame eternally:
2 rescue me in your justness and slip me away;
spread your ear to me and save me:
3 Be thou my *strong* **rock—my** habitation,
whereunto I may continually resort:
thou hast *given commandment* **misvahed** to save me;
for thou art my rock and my *fortress* **stronghold.**
4 *Deliver me* **Slip me away,** O my *God* **Elohim,**
out of the *hand* **palm** of the wicked,
out of the hand
of the *unrighteous* **wicked** and *cruel* **embittered** *man.*
5 For thou art my hope, O
Lord GOD **Adonay Yah Veh:**
thou art my *trust* **confidant** from my youth.
6 By thee have I been holden
up from the *womb* **belly:**
thou art he
that *took* **cut** me out of my mother's *bowels* **inwards:**
my *praise* **halal** shall be continually of thee.

7 I am as *a wonder* **an omen** unto many;
but thou art my *strong* refuge **of strength.**
8 Let my mouth be filled with thy *praise* **halal**
and with thy *honour* **beauty** all the day.
9 Cast me not off in the time of old age;
forsake me not
when my *strength faileth* **force be finished off.**
10 For mine enemies *speak* **say** against me;
and they that *lay wait* **guard** for my soul
take counsel together,
11 Saying, *God* **Elohim** hath forsaken him:
persecute **pursue** and *take* **grab** him; for
there is none to *deliver him* **rescue.**
12 O *God* **Elohim,** be not far from me:
O my *God* **Elohim,** *make haste* **hasten** for my help.
13 Let them be *confounded* **shamed**
and *consumed* **finished off**
that are *adversaries* **satans** to my soul;
let them be covered with reproach and dishonour
that seek my *hurt* **evil.**
14 But I *will hope* **shall await** continually,
and *will yet praise* **shall halal** thee
more and more **increasingly.**
15 My mouth shall *shew forth* **scribe**
thy *righteousness* **justness** and thy salvation all the day;
for I know not the *numbers thereof* **scribing.**
16 I *will* **shall** go in the *strength* **might**
of *the Lord GOD* **Adonay Yah Veh:**
I *will make mention of* **shall remember**
thy *righteousness* **justness,** *even of* thine only.
17 O *God* **Elohim,** thou hast
taught me from my youth:
and hitherto
have I *declared* **told** thy *wondrous works* **marvels.**
18 Now also when I am *old*
aged and *greyheaded* **greyed,**
O *God* **Elohim,** forsake me not;
until I have *shewed thy strength* **told of thine arm**
unto *this* **a** generation,
and thy *power* **might** to every one that is to come.
19 Thy *righteousness* **justness** also, O *God* **Elohim,**
is *very high* **in the heights,**
who hast *done* **worked** great *things*:
O *God* **Elohim,** who is like unto thee!
20 Thou, which hast *shewed* me **see**
great and *sore troubles* **evil tribulations,**
shalt *quicken me again* **enliven me,**
and shalt *bring me up again* **ascend me**
from the *depths* **abysses** of the earth.
21 Thou shalt *increase* **abound** my greatness,
and *comfort* **surround** me *on every side* **and sigh.**
22 I *will* **shall** also *praise* **spread hands unto** thee
with the *psaltery* **instrument of bagpipe,**
even thy truth, O my *God* **Elohim:**
unto thee *will I sing* **shall I psalm** with the harp,
O thou Holy One of *Israel* **Yisra El.**
23 My lips shall *greatly rejoice* **shout**
when I *sing* **psalm** unto thee;
and my soul,
which thou hast redeemed.
24 My tongue also
shall *talk* **meditate** of thy *righteousness* **justness**
all the day long:
for they *are confounded* **shame,**
for they *are brought unto shame* **blush,**
that seek my *hurt* **evil.**
3 be my rock—my habitation;
to resort continually therein:
you misvahed to save me;
for you are my rock and my stronghold.
4 Slip me away, O my Elohim
from the palm of the wicked
—from the hand of the wicked and embittered:
5 for you *are* my hope, O Adonay Yah Veh
—my confidant from my youth
6 —from the belly
—who cut me from the inwards of my mother;
my halal *is* continually of you.
7 I am as an omen to many;
but you are my refuge of strength:
8 my mouth is filled *with* your halal
and *with* your beauty all the day.
9 Cast me not off in the time of old age;
forsake me not when my force finishes off.
10 For my enemies say against me;
and they who guard for my soul counsel together,
11 saying, Elohim forsook him;
pursue and grab him:
for there is no one to rescue.
12 O Elohim, be not far from me;
O my Elohim, hasten for my help:
13 shame them and finish them off
—these satans to my soul;
cover them with reproach and dishonor
who seek my evil.
14 I await you continually
and halal you increasingly.
15 My mouth scribes your justness and your
salvation all the day; for I know not the scribings.
16 I go in the might of Adonay Yah Veh;

I remember your justness—yours only:
17 O Elohim, you taught me from my youth;
and until now I tell your marvels:
18 and now that I age and grey;
O Elohim, forsake me not
until I tell of your arm to a generation
and of your might to every one to come.
19 Your justness, O Elohim, *is* in the heights,
who works great;
O Elohim, who liken we to you
20 —you,
who shows me great and evil tribulations;
enliven me and ascend me
from the abysses of the earth:
21 abound my greatness
and surround me and sigh.
22 I spread hands to you
with the instrument of bagpipe,
to your truth, O my Elohim;
to you I psalm with the harp
O Holy One of Yisra El:
23 my lips shout when I psalm to you;
and my soul which you redeemed:
24 my tongue meditates of your justness
all the day long;
for they shame;
for they blush who seek my evil.

72 *A Psalm for Solomon* **For Shelomoh.**
1 Give the *king* **sovereign** thy
judgments, O *God* **Elohim,**
and thy *righteousness* **justness**
unto the *king's* **sovereign's** son.
2 He shall *judge* **plead the cause of** thy people
with *righteousness* **justness,**
and thy *poor* **humble** with judgment.
3 The mountains shall *bring peace* **lift shalom**
to the people,
and the little hills, by *righteousness* **justness.**
4 He shall judge the *poor* **humble** of the people,
he shall save the *children* **sons** of the needy, and
shall *break in pieces* **crush** the oppressor.
5 They shall *fear* **awe** thee
as long as **at the face of** the sun and moon *endure,*
throughout all generations **generation to generation.**
6 He shall *come down* **descend** like rain
upon the mown *grass* **fleece:**
as showers that water the earth.
7 In his days shall the *righteous*
flourish **just blossom;**
and abundance of *peace* **shalom**
so long as the moon endureth **until there be no moon.**
8 He shall *have dominion also*
subjugate from sea to sea,
and from the river unto the *ends* **finalities** of the earth.
9 *They that dwell in the wilderness* **Desertdwellers**
shall *bow before him* **kneel at his face;**
and his enemies shall lick the dust.
10 The *kings* **sovereigns**
of Tarshish and of the *isles* **islands**
shall *bring presents* **return offerings:**
the *kings* **sovereigns** of Sheba and Seba
shall *offer gifts* **oblate their hire.**
11 Yea, all *kings* **sovereigns**
shall *fall down before* **prostrate in front of** him:
all *nations* **goyim** shall serve him.
12 For he shall *deliver* **rescue**
the needy when he crieth;
the *poor* **humble** also, and him that hath no helper.
13 He shall spare the poor and needy,
and shall save the souls of the needy.
14 He shall redeem their soul
from *deceit* **fraud** and violence:
and *precious* **esteemed** shall their blood be
in his *sight* **eyes.**
15 And he shall live,
and to him shall be given of the gold of Sheba:
prayer also shall be made for him **he shall be prayed for**
continually;
and daily **all day** shall he be *praised* **blessed.**
16 There shall be an *handful* **increase** of *corn* **grain**
in the earth upon the top of the mountains;
the fruit thereof shall *shake* **quake** like Lebanon:
and they of the city shall flourish
like *grass* **herbage** of the earth.
17 His name shall *endure for ever* **be eternal:**
his name shall be *continued as long as* **perpetuated**
at the face of the sun:
and *men* **they themselves** shall be blessed in him:
all *nations* **goyim** shall call him *blessed* **blithesome.**
18 Blessed be *the LORD God* **Yah Veh Elohim,**
the God **Elohim** of *Israel* **Yisra El,**
who *only doeth wondrous things* **alone worketh marvels.**
19 And blessed be his *glorious* **honoured** name
for ever **eternally:**
and let the whole earth be filled with his *glory* **honour;**
Amen, and Amen.
20 The prayers of David the son of *Jesse* **Yishay**
are *ended* **concluded.**

BOOK III

73 A Psalm of Asaph.
1 Truly *God* **Elohim** is good to *Israel* **Yisra El**,
even to such as are of a clean **to the pure of** heart.
2 But as for me, my feet were *almost gone* **spread**;
my steps had *well nigh slipped* **not poured**.
3 For I was envious at *the foolish* **them that halal**,
when I saw the *prosperity* **shalom** of the wicked.
4 For there are no bands in their death:
but their *strength* **might** is *firm* **fat**.

72 By Shelomoh.
1 Give the sovereign your judgments, O Elohim
and your justness to the son of the sovereign:
2 He pleads for your people with justness
and your humble with judgment.
3 The mountains lift shalom to the people
and the little hills, by justness.
4 He judges the humble of the people;
he saves the sons of the needy
and crushes the oppressor.
5 They awe you at the face of the sun and moon
—generation to generation.
6 He descends as rain on the mown fleece
—as showers that water the earth.
7 The just blossom in their day;
and abundance of shalom until there is no moon.
8 He subjugates from sea to sea
—from the river to the finalities of the earth:
9 desertdwellers kneel at his face
and his enemies lick the dust.
10 The sovereigns of Tarshish and of the islands
return offerings;
the sovereigns of Sheba and Seba
oblate their hire;
11 yes, all sovereigns prostrate ere in front of him;
all goyim serve him.
12 For he rescues the needy who cries
—the humble and he who has no helper;
13 he spares the poor and needy
and saves the souls of the needy:
14 he redeems their soul from fraud and violence;
and esteems their blood in his eyes:
15 and he lives
and gives him of the gold of Sheba;
and prays for him continually;
—blesses him all day.
16 There is an increase of grain in the earth;
the top of the mountains
quake their fruit as Lebanon;
and they of the city flourish
as herbage of the earth.
17 His name, Eternal;
his name perpetuates at the face of the sun;
and they bless themselves in him:
all goyim call him blithesome.
18 Blessed—Yah Veh Elohim,
Elohim of Yisra El, who alone works marvels.
19 And blessed—his honored name eternally;
and may the whole earth fills with his honor;
Amen and Amen.
20 The prayers by David the son of Yishay
are concluded.

BOOK III

73 A Psalm: By Asaph.
1 Surely Elohim is good to Yisra El
—to the pure of heart.
2 But as for me, my feet spread;
my steps unpour.
3 For I envy them who halal
when I see the shalom of the wicked:
4 for there are no bands in their death:
their might fattens;
5 They are not in *trouble as other* **toil of** men;
neither are they *plagued* **touched**
like *other men* **humans**.
6 Therefore *pride compasseth*
pomp choketh them
about as a chain;
violence *covereth* **shroudeth** them
as a **masculine** garment.
7 Their eyes stand out with *fatness* **fat**:
they *have more than the heart could wish*
surpass the imagination of the heart.
8 They *are corrupt* **blaspheme**,
and *speak wickedly* **word evil** concerning oppression:
they *speak* **word** loftily.
9 They set their mouth against the heavens,
and their tongue walketh through the earth.
10 Therefore his people return hither:
and waters of *a full cup* **fulness** are wrung out to them.
11 And they say, How doth *God* **El** know?
and is there knowledge in *the most High* **Elyon**?
12 Behold, these are the *ungodly* **wicked**,
who *prosper in the world* **be eternally serene**;
they increase in *riches* **valuables**.
13 Verily I have *cleansed* **purified** my heart in vain,
and washed my *hands* **palms** in innocency.

14 For all the day long have
I been *plagued* **touched,**
and *chastened every morning* **reproofed mornings.**
15 If I say, I *will speak* **shall scribe** thus;
behold, I should *offend* **deal covertly** *against*
with the generation of thy *children* **sons.**
16 When I *thought* **fabricated** to know this,
it was *too painful for me* **toilsome in mine eyes;**
17 Until I went
into the *sanctuary* **hallowed refuge** of *God* **El;**
then *understood* **discerned** I their *end* **finality.**
18 Surely thou didst set them
in *slippery* **smooth** places:
thou castedst them down into *destruction* **ruins.**
19 How are they *brought* into desolation,
as in a *moment* **blink!**
in consuming, they are *utterly* consumed with terrors.
20 As a dream *when one awaketh* **upon awakening;**
so, O *Lord* **Adonay,** when thou awakest,
thou shalt despise their image.
21 Thus my heart *was grieved* **embittered**
and I was pricked in my reins.
22 So *foolish* **stupid** was I, and *ignorant* **knew not:**
I was as *a beast before* **an animal in front of** thee.
23 Nevertheless I am continually with thee:
thou hast holden me by my right hand.
24 Thou shalt *guide* **lead** me with thy counsel,
and afterward *receive* **take** me to *glory* **honour.**
25 Whom have I in *heaven but thee* **the heavens?**
and there is none upon earth that I desire beside thee.
26 My flesh and my heart *faileth* **finisheth off:**
but *God* **Elohim** is the *strength* **rock** of my heart,
and my *portion for ever* **allotment eternally.**
27 For, *lo* **behold,**
they that are far from thee shall *perish* **destruct:**
thou hast *destroyed* **exterminated** all them
that *go a whoring* **whore** from thee.
28 But it is good for me to
draw near to *God* **Elohim:**
I have put my *trust* **refuge**
in *the Lord GOD* **Adonay Yah Veh,**
that I may *declare* **scribe** all thy works.

74 *Maschil* **On Comprehension** of Asaph.
1 O *God* **Elohim,**
why hast thou cast us off *for ever* **in perpetuity?**
why doth *thine anger* **thy wrath** smoke
against the *sheep* **flock** of thy pasture?
2 Remember thy *congregation* **witness,**
which thou hast *purchased* **chattelized** of *old* **antiquity;**
the *rod* **scion** of thine inheritance,
which thou hast redeemed;
this mount *Zion* **Siyon,**
wherein thou hast *dwelt* **tabernacled.**
3 Lift up thy *feet* **steps**
unto the perpetual *desolations* **ruins;**
even all that the enemy hath *done wickedly* **vilified**
in the *sanctuary* **holies.**

5 they are neither in toil of man
nor touched as humans.
6 So pomp chokes them;
violence shrouds them as a masculine garment:
7 their eyes stand out with fat;
they surpass the imagination of the heart:
8 they blaspheme
and word evil concerning oppression;
they word loftily:
9 they set their mouth against the heavens
and their tongue walks through the earth.
10 So his people return here;
and waters of fulness wring out to them.
11 And they say, How knows El?
Is there knowledge in Elyon?
12 Behold, these are the wicked,
—eternally serene who increase in valuables.
13 Surely I purify my heart in vain
and wash my palms in innocency.
14 For all the day long I am touched
and reproofed in the morning.
15 If I say, I scribe thus;
behold,
I deal covertly with the generation of your sons:
16 when I fabricated to know this,
it is toilsome in my eyes
17 —until I go into the hallowed refuge of El
—then I discern their finality.
18 Surely you set them in smooth places;
you cast them down into ruins:
19 how they become a desolation—as in a blink!
in consuming, they *are* consumed with terrors.
20 As a dream on wakening, O Adonay,
when you waken, you despise their image.
21 Thus my heart embitters
and I am pricked in my reins:
22 I am stupid and know not
—as an animal in front of you.
23 And I am continually with you;
you hold me by my right hand;
24 you lead me with your counsel
and afterward take me to honor.
25 Whom have I in the heavens?

I desire no one on earth beside you.
26 My flesh and my heart finish off;
but Elohim is the rock of my heart
and my allotment eternally.
27 For behold,
they who are far from you destruct;
you exterminate all who whore away from you.
28 and *it is* good for me to draw near to Elohim;
I put my refuge in Adonay Yah Veh,
so that I scribe all your works.

74 On Comprehension: By Asaph.
1 O Elohim,
why cast us off in perpetuity?
why smoke your wrath
against the flock of your pasture?
2 Remember the witness you
chattelized of antiquity
—the scion of your inheritance you redeemed
—this mount Siyon wherein you tabernacle.
3 Lift your steps to the perpetual ruins;
to all that the enemy vilified in the holies.
4 *Thine enemies* **Thy tribulators** roar
in the midst of thy congregations;
they set up their ensigns for signs.
5 *A man was famous* **He was known**
according as he had lifted up axes upon the thick trees.
6 But now they *break down* **hammer**
the *carved work* **engravings** *thereof*
at once **together** with axes and **sledge** hammers.
7 They have *cast* **sent** fire
into thy *sanctuary* **hallowed refuge**
they have *defiled by casting down* **profaned**
the *dwelling place* **tabernacle** of thy name
to the *ground* **earth**.
8 They said in their hearts,
Let us *destroy* **oppress** them together:
they have burned *up*
all the *synagogues* **congregations** of *God* **El** in the land.
9 We see not our signs: there
is no more any prophet:
neither is there among us
any that knoweth *how long* **until when**.
10 O *God* **Elohim**, *how long* **until when**
shall the *adversary* **tribulator** reproach?
shall the enemy *blaspheme* **scorn** thy name
for ever **in perpetuity**?
11 Why *withdrawest* **turnest** thou thy hand,
even thy right *hand*?
pluck **finish** it out of thy bosom.
12 For *God* **Elohim** is my *King*
Sovereign of *old* **antiquity**,
working **doing** salvation in the midst of the earth.
13 Thou *didst divide* **brakest** the sea
by thy strength:
thou brakest the heads of the *dragons* **monsters**
in the waters.
14 Thou *brakest* **crushest** the
heads of leviathan *in pieces*,
and gavest him *to be meat* **for food** to the people
inhabiting the wilderness—**the desertdwellers**.
15 Thou *didst cleave* **splittest**
the fountain and the *flood* **wadi**:
thou driedst up *mighty* **perennial** rivers.
16 The day is thine, the night also is thine:
thou hast prepared the light and the sun.
17 Thou hast *set* **stationed** all
the borders of the earth:
thou hast *made* **formed** summer and winter.
18 Remember this,
that the enemy hath reproached, O *LORD* **Yah Veh**,
and that the foolish people
have *blasphemed* **scorned** thy name.
19 O *deliver* **give** not the soul of thy turtledove
unto the *multitude of the wicked* **live beings**:
forget not the *congregation* **lives** of thy *poor* **humble**
for ever **in perpetuity**.
20 *Have respect* **Look** unto the covenant:
for the *dark places* **darknesses** of the earth
are full of the *habitations* **folds** of *cruelty* **violence**.
21 O let not the oppressed
return *ashamed* **shamed**:
let the *poor* **humble** and needy *praise* **halal** thy name.
22 Arise, O *God* **Elohim**,
plead **defend** thine own *cause* **defence**:
remember *how the foolish man reproacheth thee daily*
your reproach of the fool all the day.
23 Forget not the voice of *thine*
enemies **thy tribulators**:
the *tumult* **roaring** of those that rise *up against*
thee increaseth **ascendeth** continually.

75 To *the chief Musician* **His Eminence**,
Al—taschith **Al Taschcheth/Ruin Not**,
A Psalm *or* Song of Asaph.
1 Unto thee, O *God* **Elohim**,
do we give thanks **we spread hands**,
unto thee do we give thanks **we spread hands**:
for that thy name is near
thy *wondrous works declare* **marvels scribe**.
2 When I shall *receive* **take** the congregation

I *will* **shall** judge *uprightly* **in straightnesses.**
3 The earth
and all *the inhabitants thereof* **that settle therein**
are dissolved:
I *bear up* **gauge** the pillars of it.
Selah.
4 Your tribulators roar midst your congregations;
they set up their ensigns for signs;
5 he is known for lifting axes on the thick trees:
6 and now they hammer the engravings
with axes and sledge hammers;
7 they sent fire to your hallowed refuge;
they profaned the tabernacle of your name
to the earth.
8 They say in their hearts, Oppress them together!
They burn all the congregations of El in the land.
9 We neither see our signs;
nor is there any prophet;
nor is there among us any who knows until when.
10 O Elohim,
until when reproaches the tribulator?
—the enemy scorn your name in perpetuity?
11 Why turn your hand back—even your right?
Finish it from your bosom.
12 And Elohim *is* my Sovereign from antiquity
—working salvation midst the earth.
13 You broke the sea by your strength;
you broke the heads of the monsters in the waters:
14 you crushed the heads of leviathan
and gave him for food to the people
—the desertdwellers:
15 you split the fountain and the wadi;
you dried up perennial rivers.
16 The day *is* yours, the night *is* yours;
you prepared the light and the sun;
17 you stationed all the borders of the earth;
you formed summer and winter.
18 Remember this:
an enemy reproaches Yah Veh;
and the foolish people scorn your name.
19 O give not the soul of your turtledove
to the live beings;
forget not the lives of your humble
in perpetuity:
20 look to the covenant;
for the darknesses of the earth
are full of the folds of violence.
21 O that the oppressed not return shamed;
that the humble and needy halal your name.
22 Rise, O Elohim, defend your own defence;
remember your reproach of a fool all the day:
23 forget not the voice of your tribulators;
the roaring of those who rise ascends continually.

75 To His Eminence; Al Tashcheth/Ruin Not;
A Psalm by Asaph: A Song.
1 To you, O Elohim, we spread hands;
we spread hands, for your name, near:
they scribe your marvels.
2 When I take the congregation
I judge in straightnesses.
3 The earth and all who settle therein dissolve;
I gauge the pillars thereof.
Selah.
4 I said unto *the fools* **them that halal,**
Deal not foolishly **Halal not**:
and to the wicked, Lift not up the horn:
5 Lift not up your horn *on high* **to the heights**:
speak not with a stiff **or word with an impudent** neck.
6 For *promotion cometh* **the mount of exaltation**
is neither from the *east* **source**,
nor from *the west* **duskward**, nor
from the *south* **wilderness**.
7 But *God* **Elohim** is the judge: he *putteth down*
abaseth one, and *setteth up* **exalteth** another.
8 For in the hand of *the LORD*
Yah Veh there is a cup,
and the wine *is red* **foameth**; it is full of mixture;
and he poureth out *of the same* **thus**:
but the dregs *thereof*,
all the wicked of the earth
shall wring them out, and drink them.
9 But I *will declare for ever* **shall tell eternally**;
I will sing praises **I shall psalm**
to *the God* **Elohim** of *Jacob* **Yaaqov**.
10 All the horns of the wicked
also *will* **shall** I cut off;
but the horns of the *righteous* **just** shall be exalted.

76 To *the chief Musician* **His Eminence,**
on *Neginoth* **Strummer,**
A Psalm *or* Song of Asaph.
1 In *Judah* **Yah Hudah** is *God* **Elohim** known:
his name is great in *Israel* **Yisra El**.
2 In Salem also *is* **are** his
tabernacle **sukkoth/brush arbors,**
and his *dwelling place* **habitation** in *Zion* **Siyon**.
3 There brake he the *arrows*
burning flash of the bow,
the *shield* **buckler**, and the sword, and the *battle* **war**.
Selah.

4 Thou art more *glorious*
lightened and *excellent* **mighty**
than the mountains of prey.
5 The *stouthearted* **mighty of heart** are spoiled,
they have *slept* **slumbered** their sleep:
and none of the men of *might* **valour**
have found their hands.
6 At thy rebuke, O *God* **Elohim** of *Jacob* **Yaaqov**,
both the chariot and horse
are cast into a dead sleep **sleep soundly**.
7 Thou, *even* thou, art *to be feared* **awesome**:
and who may stand *in thy sight* **at the face of thine eyes**
when once thou art angry **since thy wrath**?
8 Thou didst cause *judgment* **their plea**
to be heard from *heaven* **the heavens**; the
earth *feared* **awed**, and *was still* **rested**,
9 When *God* **Elohim** arose to judgment,
to save all the *meek* **humble** of the earth.
Selah.
10 Surely the *wrath* **fury** of *man* **humanity**
shall *praise* **spread hands unto** thee:
the *remainder* **survivors** of *wrath* **fury**
shalt thou *restrain* **gird**.
11 Vow, and *pay* **shalam**
unto *the LORD* **Yah Veh** your *God* **Elohim**:
let all that be round about him bring presents
unto *him that ought to be feared* **the awesome one**.
12 He shall cut off the spirit
of *princes* **the eminent**:
he is *terrible* **awesome**
to the *kings* **sovereigns** of the earth.

77 To *the chief Musician* **His Eminence**,
to Jeduthun **Yeduthun/A Laudatory**, A Psalm of Asaph.
1 I cried unto *God* **Elohim** with my voice,
even unto *God* **Elohim** with my voice; and
he *gave ear* **hearkened** unto me.
2 In the day of my *trouble* **tribulation**
I sought *the Lord* **Adonay**:
my *sore* **hand** ran in the night, and *ceased* **exhaled** not:
my soul refused to *be comforted* **sigh**.
3 I remembered *God* **Elohim**,
and *was troubled* **roared**:
I *complained* **meditated**,
and my spirit *was overwhelmed* **languished**.
Selah.
4 Thou holdest mine *eyes waking* **eye guards**:
I am so *troubled* **agitated** that I cannot *speak* **word**.
4 I say to them who halal, Halal not!
And to the wicked, Lift not the horn!
5 Lift not your horn to the heights
or word with an impudent neck:
6 for the mount of exaltation
is neither from the source
nor from duskward
nor from the wilderness.
7 But Elohim *is* judge;
he abases one and exalts another.
8 For there is a cup in the hand of Yah Veh:
the wine foams; it is full of mixture:
and he pours thus;
surely, all the wicked of the earth
wring out and drink the dregs.
9 And I—I tell eternally;
I psalm to Elohim of Yaaqov:
10 All the horns of the wicked I cut off;
and exalt the horns of the just.

76 To His Eminence; On Strummer;
A Psalm by Asaph: A Song.
1 In Yah Hudah, Elohim *is* known;
in Yisra El, his name *is* great;
2 and in Salem, his sukkoth/brush arbors;
and his habitation in Siyon.
3 There he broke the burning flash of the bow
—the buckler and the sword and the war.
Selah.
4 You are more enlightened and mighty
than the mountains of prey.
5 The mighty of heart spoil;
they slumber away their sleep;
and none of the men of valour find their hands.
6 At your rebuke, O Elohim of Yaaqov,
both the chariot and horse sleep soundly.
7 You—you *are* awesome;
and who stands at the face of your eyes
since your wrath?
8 You hear their plea from the heavens;
the earth awes and rests;
9 as Elohim rises to judgment
—to save all the humble of the earth.
Selah.
10 Surely the fury of humanity
spreads hands to you;
you gird the survivors of fury;
11 vow and shalam to Yah Veh your Elohim
all you who surround him:
bring presents to the awesome one.
12 He cuts off the spirit of the eminent;
—awesome to the sovereigns of the earth.

77 To His Eminence; Yeduthun/A Laudatory:
A Psalm by Asaph.

1 My voice *is* to Elohim; I cry:
—my voice *is* to Elohim; and he hearkens to me:
2 in the day of my tribulation I seek Adonay;
my hand runs in the night, and exhale not;
my soul refuses to sigh.
3 I remember Elohim, and roar;
I meditate, and my spirit languishes.
Selah.
4 You hold my eye guards:
I am agitated; I cannot word:
5 I have *considered* **fabricated**
the days of *old* **antiquity**,
the years of *ancient times* **eternity**.
6 I *call to remembrance*
remember my *song* **strumming**
in the night:
I *commune* **meditate** with mine own heart:
and my spirit *made diligent search* **searched**.
7 *Will the Lord* **Shall Adonay**
cast off *for ever* **eternally**?
and *will he be favourable no more*
shall he never again be pleased?
8 Is his mercy *clean gone for*
ever **ceased in perpetuity**?
doth his *promise fail* **saying cease**
for evermore **generation to generation**?
9 Hath *God* **El** forgotten to
be gracious **grant charism**?
hath he in *anger* **wrath** shut up his tender mercies?
Selah.
10 And I said, This is my *infirmity* **stroke**:
but I will remember
—the years of the right *hand* of *the most High* **Elyon**.
11 I *will* **shall** remember
the *works* **exploits** of *the LORD* **Yah**:
surely I *will* **shall** remember thy *wonders* **marvels**
of *old* **antiquity**.
12 I *will* **shall** meditate also of all thy *work* **deeds**,
and *talk* **meditate** of thy *doings* **exploits**.
13 Thy way, O *God* **Elohim**,
is in the *sanctuary* **holies**:
who is so great *a God* **an El** as *our God* **Elohim**?
14 Thou art *the God* **El**
that *doest wonders* **workest marvels**:
thou hast *declared* **made known** thy strength
among the people.
15 Thou hast with thine arm redeemed thy people,
the sons of *Jacob* **Yaaqov** and *Joseph* **Yoseph**.
Selah.
16 The waters saw thee, O *God* **Elohim**,
the waters saw thee; they *were afraid* **writhed**:
the depths also *were troubled* **quaked**.
17 The **thick** clouds *poured out* **flooded** water:
the *skies sent out a sound* **vapours gave**
voice: thine arrows also went abroad.
18 The voice of thy thunder
was in the *heaven* **whirlwind**:
the lightnings lightened the world:
the earth *trembled* **quivered** and *shook* **quaked**.
19 Thy way is in the sea,
and thy path in the great waters,
and thy *footsteps* **heelprints** are not known.
20 Thou leddest thy people like a flock
by the hand of *Moses* **Mosheh** and *Aaron* **Aharon**.

78 *Maschil* **A Discerning** of Asaph.
1 *Give ear* **Hearken**, O my
people, to my *law* **torah**:
incline **spread** your ears
to the *words* **sayings** of my mouth.
2 I *will* **shall** open my mouth in a *parable* **proverb**:
I *will utter dark sayings* **shall gush**
riddles of *old* **antiquity**:
3 Which we have heard and known,
and our fathers have *told* **scribed unto** us.
4 We *will* **shall** not *hide* **conceal them**
from their *children* **sons**,
shewing **scribing** to the generation *to come* **after**
the *praises* **halals** of *the LORD* **Yah Veh**,
and his strength, and his *wonderful works* **marvels**
that he hath *done* **worked**.
5 For he *established* **raised** a *testimony* **witness**
in *Jacob* **Yaaqov**,
and *appointed* **set** a *law* **torah** in *Israel* **Yisra El**,
which he *commanded* **misvahed** our fathers,
that they should make them known
to their *children* **sons**:
6 That the generation *to come*
after might know them,
even the children which should—
the sons to be *born* **birthed**;
who should arise
and *declare* **scribe** them to their *children* **sons**:
7 That they might set their hope in *God* **Elohim**,
and not forget the works of *God* **El**,
but *keep* **guard** his *commandments* **misvoth**:
8 And might not be as their fathers,
a *stubborn* **revolting** and rebellious generation;
a generation that *set* **prepared** not their heart *aright*,
and whose spirit was not *stedfast*
trustworthy with *God* **El**.

5 I fabricate the days of antiquity
—the years of eternity:
6 I remember my strumming in the night;
I meditate with my heart;
my spirit searches.
7 Adonay—casts he off eternally?
—never again to please?
8 —cease his mercy in perpetuity?
—cease his sayings generation to generation?
9 —forgets El to grant charism?
—in wrath shuts his tender mercies?
Selah.
10 I say, This is my stroke;
—the years of the right of Elyon.
11 I remember the exploits of Yah;
surely I remember your marvels from antiquity.
12 I meditate on all your deeds
and meditate of your exploits;
13 your way, O Elohim, *is* in the holies.
Who is so great an El as Elohim?
14 You El, work marvels;
you have your strength known among the people;
15 and with your arm redeemed your people
the sons of Yaaqov and Yoseph.
Selah.
16 The waters see you, O Elohim;
the waters see you; they writhe:
the depths quake;
17 the thick clouds flood water;
the vapours give voice; your arrows go abroad.
18 The voice of your thunder *is* in the whirlwind;
the lightnings light the world;
the earth quivers and quakes:
19 your way is in the sea
and your path in the great waters and
your heelprints are not known:
20 you led your people as a flock
by the hand of Mosheh and Aharon.

78 A Discerning by Asaph.
1 Hearken, O my people, to my torah;
spread your ears to the sayings of my mouth.
2 I open my mouth in a proverb;
I gush riddles of antiquity
3 which we hear and know;
which our fathers scribed unto us;
4 we conceal them not from their sons
—scribing to the generation after
the halals of Yah Veh:
and his strength and his marvels he worked.
5 And he raises a witness in Yaaqov
and sets a torah in Yisra El
—which he misvahed our fathers
to make known to their sons;
6 that the generation after
—that the sons yet to be birthed know them;
—who then rise and scribe to their sons
7 to set their hope in Elohim
and not forget the works of El
—but guard his misvoth:
8 and not be as their fathers
—a revolting and rebellious generation
—a generation that prepared not their heart
—whose spirit *was* not trustworthy with El.
9 The *children* **sons** of *Ephraim* **Ephrayim**,
being armed, *and carrying* **hurling** bows,
turned back in the day of battle.
10 They *kept* **guarded** not the
covenant of *God* **Elohim**,
and refused to walk in his *law* **torah**;
11 And forgat his *works* **exploits**,
and his *wonders* **marvels** that he had *shewed* them **see**.
12 *Marvellous things did* **Marvels worked** he
in *the sight* **front** of their fathers,
in the land of *Egypt* **Misrayim**, in the field of *Zoan* **Soan**.
13 He *divided* **split** the sea,
and *caused* **passed** them *to pass* through;
and he *made* **stationed** the waters *to stand* as an heap.
14 In the *daytime* **day** also
he led them with a cloud,
and all the night with a light of fire.
15 He *clave* **split** the rocks in the wilderness,
and gave them drink as out of the great *depths* **abysses**.
16 He brought *streams* **flows** also out of the rock,
and caused waters to *run down* **descend** like rivers.
17 And they sinned yet *more* **again** against him
by *provoking the most High* **rebelling against Elyon**
in the *wilderness* **parch**.
18 And they *tempted God* **tested El** in their heart
by asking *meat* **food** for their *lust* **soul**.
19 Yea, they *spake* **worded** against *God* **Elohim**;
they said,
Can God furnish **Arrangeth El** a table in the wilderness?
20 Behold, he smote the rock,
that the waters *gushed out* **flowed**,
and the *streams* **wadies** overflowed;
can he give **giveth he** bread also?
can he provide **prepareth he** flesh for his people?
21 Therefore *the LORD* **Yah Veh** heard this,
and was wroth:
so a fire was kindled against *Jacob* **Yaaqov**,

and *anger* **wrath**
also *came up* **ascended** against *Israel* **Yisra El**;
22 Because they *believed*
trusted not in *God* **Elohim**,
and *trusted* **confided** not in his salvation:
23 Though he had
commanded **misvahed** the *clouds* **vapours** from above,
and opened the doors of *heaven* **the heavens**,
24 And had rained down manna upon them to eat,
and had given them
of the *corn* **crop** of *heaven* **the heavens**.
25 Man *did eat angels' food* **ate**
the bread of the mighty:
he sent them *meat* **hunt** to *the full* **satiate**.
26 He *caused an east wind to*
blow **plucked an easterly**
in the *heaven* **heavens**:
and by his *power* **strength**
he *brought in* **drove** the *south wind* **southerly**.
27 He rained flesh also upon them as dust,
and *feathered fowls* **winged flyers**
like as the sand of the sea:
28 And he *let it fall* **felled them**
in the midst of their camp,
round about their *habitations* **tabernacles**.
29 So they did eat, and were
well filled **mightily satiated**:
for he gave them their own desire;
30 They were not estranged from their *lust* **desire**.
But while their *meat* **food** was yet in their mouths,
31 The wrath of *God came*
Elohim ascended upon them,
and *slew* **slaughtered** the fattest of them,
and *smote the chosen men* **caused the youths**
of *Israel* **Yisra El to kneel**.
32 For all this they sinned still,
and *believed* **trusted** not for his
wondrous works **marvels**.
33 Therefore their days
did he consume **he finished off** in vanity,
and their years in *trouble* **terror**.
34 When he *slew* **slaughtered** them,
then they sought him:
and they returned
and *enquired* **sought** early after *God* **El**.
35 And they remembered
that *God* **Elohim** was their rock,
and *the high God* **El Elyon** their redeemer.
36 *Nevertheless* **But**
they *did flatter* **duped** him with their mouth,

and they lied unto him with their tongues.
9 The sons of Ephrayim, armed, hurling bows,
turn back in the day of battle;
10 they guard not the covenant of Elohim
and refuse to walk in his torah;
11 they forget his exploits and his marvels
he shows them;
12 —marvels he worked in front of their fathers,
in the land of Misrayim, in the field of Soan.
13 He splits the sea and passes them through;
he stations the waters as a heap:
14 in the day he leads them with a cloud
and all the night with a light of fire:
15 he splits the rocks in the wilderness
and gives them drink from great abysses:
16 he brings flows from the rock
so the waters descend as rivers:
17 and they add to sin against him
by rebelling against Elyon in the parch.
18 They test El in their heart
by asking food for their soul;
19 yes, they word against Elohim;
they say, El—arranges he a table in the wilderness?
20 Behold, he smites the rock, and waters flow;
yes, wadies overflow.
Gives he bread?
Prepares he flesh for his people?
21 Yah Veh hears this and wroths;
and he kindles a fire against Yaaqov and
ascends wrath against Yisra El:
22 because they neither trusted in Elohim
nor confided in his salvation.
23 He misvahs the vapours from above
and opens the doors of the heavens;
24 —he rains manna on them to eat
and gives them the crop of the heavens:
25 man eats the bread of the mighty
he sends them hunt to satiate.
26 He plucks an easterly in the heavens
and by his strength he drives the southerly;
27 he rains flesh on them as dust
and winged flyers as the sand of the sea;
28 he fells them midst their camp
all around their tabernacles:
29 and they eat and satiate mightily;
for he gives them their own desire;
30 they are not estranged from their desire.
and their food still being in their mouths,
31 the wrath of Elohim ascends on them
and slaughters their fattest

and has the youths of Yisra El to kneel.
32 For all this they still sin
and trust not his marvels:
33 and he finishes off their days in vanity
and their years in terror.
34 When he slaughters them,
then they seek him
—return and seek early after El;
35 and they remember
Elohim is their rock and El Elyon their redeemer.
36 And they dupe him with their mouth
and lie to him with their tongue:
37 For their heart was not
right **established** with him,
neither were they *stedfast* **trustworthy** in his covenant.
38 But he, *being full of compassion* **the merciful,**
forgave **did kapar/atone** their *iniquity*
perversity, and *destroyed* **ruined** them not:
yea, many a time **and he abounded**
turned he his anger away **to turn his wrath,**
and *did not stir up all* **wakened not** his *wrath* **fury.**
39 For he remembered that they were *but* flesh;
a wind that passeth *away,*
and *cometh not again* **returneth not.**
40 How oft did they *provoke* **rebel against** him
in the wilderness,
and *grieve* **contort** him in the *desert* **desolation**!
41 Yea, they turned back and
tempted God **tested El,**
and *limited* **branded** the Holy One of *Israel* **Yisra El.**
42 They remembered not his hand,
nor the day when he *delivered* **redeemed** them
from the *enemy* **tribulator.**
43 How he had *wrought* **set** his
signs in *Egypt* **Misrayim,**
and his *wonders* **omens** in the field of *Zoan* **Soan**:
44 And had turned their rivers into blood;
and their *floods* **flows**, that they could not drink.
45 He sent *divers sorts of flies* **swarms** among them,
which devoured them;
and frogs, which *destroyed* **ruined** them.
46 He gave also
their *increase* **produce** unto the caterpiller,
and their labour unto the locust.
47 He *destroyed* **slaughtered** their vines with hail,
and their sycomore trees with *frost* **aphis.**
48 He *gave* **shut** up their *cattle*
also **beasts** to the hail,
and their *flocks* **chattel**
to *hot thunderbolts* **burning flashes.**
49 He *cast* **sent** upon them
the fierceness of his *anger* **fuming wrath,**
wrath **fury**, and *indignation* **rage,**
and *trouble* **tribulation,**
by sending evil angels *among them.*
50 He *made a way* **weighed a**
path to his *anger* **wrath;**
he spared not their soul from death,
but *gave* **shut up** their life *over* to the pestilence;
51 And smote all the *firstborn*
firstbirthed in *Egypt* **Misrayim;**
the *chief* **firstfruits** of their strength
in the *tabernacles* **tents** of Ham:
52 But made his own *people*
to *go forth* **pull stakes** like *sheep* **a flock,**
and *guided* **drove** them in the wilderness
like a *flock* **drove.**
53 And he led them on *safely* **confidently,**
so that they *feared* **dreaded** not:
but the sea *overwhelmed* **covered over** their enemies.
54 And he brought them
to the border of his *sanctuary* **holies,**
even to—this mountain,
which his right *hand* had *purchased* **chattelized.**
55 He *cast out* **exiled** the *heathen also* **goyim**
before them **from their face,**
and *divided* **felled** them an inheritance by line,
and made the *tribes* **scions** of *Israel* **Yisra El**
to dwell **tabernacle** in their tents.
56 Yet they *tempted* **tested** and *provoked* **rebelled**
the most high God **against Elohim Elyon,**
and *kept* **guarded** not his *testimonies* **witnesses**:
57 But *turned back* **apostatized,**
and dealt *unfaithfully* **covertly** like their fathers:
they were turned aside like a deceitful bow.
58 For they *provoked* **vexed** him *to anger*
with their *high places* **bamahs,**
and moved him to jealousy
with their *graven images* **sculptiles.**
59 When *God* **Elohim** heard this, he was wroth,
and *greatly abhorred Israel* **mightily spurned Yisra El**:
60 So that he forsook the tabernacle of Shiloh,
the tent
which he *placed* **tabernacled** among *men* **humanity;**
61 And *delivered* **gave** his strength into captivity,
and his *glory* **beauty** into the *enemy's* **tribulator's** hand.
62 He *gave* **shut up** his people
over also unto the sword;
and *was wroth with* **passed over** his inheritance.
37 for neither is their heart established with him,

nor are they trustworthy in his covenant.
38 And he, the merciful,
kapars/atones their perversity and ruins them not;
he abounds to turn his wrath
and wakens not his fury:
39 and he remembers they are flesh
—a passing wind that never returns.
40 How often
they rebelled against him in the wilderness
and contorted him in the desolation!
41 Yes, they turned back and tested El
and branded the Holy One of Yisra El:
42 they remembered neither his hand,
nor the day he redeemed them from the tribulator
43 —how he set his signs in Misrayim
and his omens in the field of Soan;
44 and turned their rivers to blood
and they drank not their flows:
45 he sent swarms among them to devour them;
and frogs to ruin them:
46 he gave their produce to the caterpiller
and their labor to the locust:
47 he slaughtered their vines with hail
and their sycomore trees with aphis:
48 he shut their beasts to the hail
and their chattel to burning flashes:
49 he sent on them his fuming wrath
—fury and rage and tribulation
by sending evil angels.
50 He weighed a path to his wrath;
he spared not their soul from death:
yes, shut their life to the pestilence;
51 and smote all the firstbirthed in Misrayim
—the firstfruits of their strength in the tents of Ham:
52 and has his own pull stakes as a flock
and drove them as a drove in the wilderness:
53 and he led them on
confidently; they dreaded not;
and the sea covered their enemies:
54 he brought them to the border of his holies
—this mountain which his right chattelized:
55 he exiled the goyim from their face
and felled them an inheritance by line:
and had the scions of Yisra El
tabernacle in their tents.
56 Yet they tested and rebelled
against Elohim Elyon
and guarded not his witnesses;
57 and apostatized and dealt
covertly as their fathers
—turned aside as a deceitful bow:
58 and they vex him with their bamahs
and move him to jealousy with their sculptiles.
59 Elohim heard; he *was* wroth;
and spurned Yisra El mightily;
60 so that he forsook the tabernacle of Shiloh
—the tent he tabernacled among humanity;
61 and gave his strength to captivity
and his beauty into the hand of the tribulator;
62 he shut up his people to the sword
and passed over his inheritance.
63 The fire consumed their *young men* **youths**;
and their *maidens* **virgins**
were not *given to marriage* **halaled**.
64 Their priests fell by the sword;
and their widows *made no lamentation* **wept not**.
65 Then *the Lord* **Adonay**
awaked as *one* out of sleep,
and like *a* **the** mighty *man*
that shouteth *by reason* of wine.
66 And he smote his *enemies* **tribulators**
in the hinder parts **behind**:
he *put* **gave** them to *a perpetual* **an eternal** reproach.
67 Moreover
he *refused* **spurned** the *tabernacle* **tent** of *Joseph* **Yoseph**,
and chose not the *tribe* **scion** of *Ephraim* **Ephrayim**:
68 But chose the *tribe* **scion** of *Judah* **Yah Hudah**,
the mount *Zion* **Siyon** which he loved.
69 And he built his *sanctuary* **hallowed refuge**
like high palaces **lofty**,
like the earth
which he hath *established for ever* **founded eternally**.
70 He chose David also his servant,
and took him from the *sheepfolds* **flock folds**:
71 *From following the ewes* **After the sucklings**
great with young
he brought him to *feed Jacob* **tend Yaaqov** his people,
and *Israel* **Yisra El** his inheritance.
72 So he *fed* **tended** them
according to the integrity of his heart;
and *guided* **led** them
by the *skilfulness* **discernment** of his *hands* **palms**.

79 A Psalm of Asaph.
1 O *God* **Elohim**,
the *heathen* **goyim** are come into thine inheritance;
thy holy *temple* **manse** have they *defiled* **fouled**;
they have *laid Jerusalem* **set Yeru Shalem** on heaps.
2 The *dead bodies* **carcases** of thy servants
have they given *to be meat* **for food**
unto the *fowls* **flyers** of the *heaven* **heavens**,

the flesh of thy *saints* **mercied**
unto the *beasts* **live beings** of the earth.
3 Their blood have they *shed* **poured** like water
round about *Jerusalem* **Yeru Shalem**;
and there was none to *bury them* **entomb**.
4 We are become a reproach
to our *neighbours* **fellow tabernaclers**,
a *scorn* **derision** and *derision* **ridicule**
to them that are round about us.
5 How long, *LORD* **O Yah Veh**?
wilt **shalt** thou be angry *for ever* **in perpetuity**?
shall thy jealousy burn like fire?
6 Pour out thy *wrath* **fury**
upon the *heathen* **goyim**
that have not known thee,
and upon the *kingdoms* **sovereigndoms**
that have not called upon thy name.
7 For they have devoured *Jacob* **Yaaqov**,
and *laid waste* **desolated**
his *dwelling place* **habitation of rest**.
8 O remember not against us
former iniquities **first perversities**:
let thy tender mercies
speedily prevent **hastily anticipate** us:
for we are *brought very low* **mightily languished**.
9 Help us, O *God* **Elohim** of our salvation,
for the *glory* **word of the honour** of thy name:
and *deliver* **rescue** us,
and *purge away* **kapar/atone** our sins,
for thy name's sake.
10 Wherefore should the *heathen* **goyim** *say*,
Where is their *God* **Elohim**?
let him be known among the *heathen* **goyim** in our sight
by the *revenging* **vengeance** of the blood of thy servants
which is *shed* **poured**.
11 Let the *sighing* **shrieking** of the *prisoner* **bound**
come before thee **be at thy face**;
according to the greatness of *thy power* **thine arm**
preserve thou those that are appointed to die
let the sons of death remain;
63 Fire consumed their youths
and their virgins *were* not halaled;
64 their priests fell by the sword
and their widows wept not.
65 And Adonay wakened as from sleep
as the mighty shouting from wine:
66 and he smote his tribulators behind;
he gave on them an eternal reproach:
67 he spurned the tent of Yoseph
and chose not the scion of Ephrayim;
68 but chose the scion of Yah Hudah
—the mount Siyon he loved:
69 and he built his hallowed refuge lofty
—eternal as the earth he founded.
70 He chose David his servant
and took him from the flock folds;
71 after the sucklings, great with young,
he brought him to tend Yaaqov his people
and Yisra El his inheritance;
72 thus he tended them
according to the integrity of his heart;
and led them
by the discernment of his palms.

79 Psalm: By Asaph.
1 O Elohim,
the goyim come into your inheritance
—foul your holy manse
—set Yeru Shalem on heaps;
2 —give carcases of your servants
for food to the flyers of the heavens;
—the flesh of your mercied
to the live beings of the earth;
3 they pour their blood as water
all around Yeru Shalem;
and no one entombs.
4 We are a reproach to our fellow tabernaclers;
a derision and ridicule to all around us.
5 Until when, O Yah Veh?
Anger you in perpetuity? Burns your jealousy as fire?
6 Pour out your fury on the goyim
who know you not;
and on the sovereigndoms
who call not on your name:
7 for they devour Yaaqov
and desolate his habitation of rest.
8 O remember not our first
perversities against us;
may your tender mercies hastily anticipate us;
for we languish mightily:
9 help us, O Elohim of our salvation
for the word of the honor of your name;
and rescue us and kapar/atone our sins
for sake of your name.
10 Why say the goyim, Where is their Elohim?
may it be known among the goyim in our sight
by the vengeance of the blood of your servants
which is poured.
11 *May* the shrieking of the bound be at your face;
according to the greatness of your arm
may the sons of death remain;

12 And *render* **return**
unto our *neighbours* **fellow tabernaclers** sevenfold
into their bosom their reproach,
wherewith they have reproached thee, O *Lord* **Adonay.**
13 So we thy people and *sheep* **flock** of thy pasture
will give thee thanks **shall spread hands unto thee**
for ever **eternally**:
we *will shew forth* **shall scribe** thy *praise* **halal**
to all generations **generation to generation.**

80 To *the chief Musician* **His Eminence,**
upon Sho—shannim—Eduth/**Trumpets of Witness,**
A Psalm of Asaph.
1 *Give ear* **Hearken**, O *Shepherd*
Raah of *Israel* **Yisra El,**
thou that *leadest Joseph* **drivest Yoseph** like a flock;
thou that *dwellest* **settlest**
between **among** the *cherubims* **cherubim,**
shine forth.
2 *Before Ephraim* **At the face of Ephrayim**
and *Benjamin* **Ben Yamin** and *Manasseh* **Menash Sheh**
stir up **waken** thy *strength* **might,**
and come *and save us* **be our salvation.**
3 *Turn us again* **Return to us**, O *God* **Elohim,**
and cause thy face to *shine* **lighten**;
and we shall be saved.
4 O *LORD God of hosts* **Yah Veh Elohim Sabaoth,**
how long *wilt* **shalt** thou *be angry* **fume**
against the prayer of thy people?
5 Thou feedest them with the bread of tears;
and givest them **triple** tears to drink *in great measure.*
6 Thou *makest* **settest** us a
strife unto our neighbours:
and our enemies *laugh* **deride** among themselves.
7 *Turn us again* **Return us,**
O *LORD God of hosts* **Yah Veh Elohim Sabaoth,**
and *cause* **lighten** thy face *to shine*;
and we shall be saved.
8 Thou hast *brought* **plucked** a vine
out of *Egypt* **Misrayim**:
thou hast *cast out* **exiled** the *heathen* **goyim,**
and planted it.
9 *Thou preparedst room before it*
In facing, thou hast faced,
and **in rooting,** didst cause it to *take deep* root,
and it filled the land.
10 The *hills* **mountains** were covered
with the shadow of it,
and the *boughs thereof* **branches**
were like the *goodly* cedars **of El.**
11 She sent out her *boughs* **harvest** unto the sea,
and her branches unto the river.
12 Why hast thou then
broken down **breached** her *hedges* **walls,**
so that all they which pass by the way *do* pluck her?
13 The *boar* **hog** out of the *wood* **forest**
doth waste **wasteth** it,
and the *wild beast* **creature** of the field
doth devour **tendeth** it.
14 Return, we beseech thee,
O *God of hosts* **Elohim Sabaoth**:
look down from *heaven* **the heavens,**
and *behold* **see**, and visit this vine;
15 And the *vineyard* **plant**
which thy right *hand* hath planted,
and the *branch* **son**
that thou *madest strong* **strengthened** for thyself.
16 *It is*—burned with fire, *it is*—cut down:
they *perish* **destruct**
at the rebuke of thy *countenance* **face.**
17 Let thy hand be upon the man of thy right *hand*,
upon the son of *men* **humanity**
whom thou *madest strong* **strengthened** for thyself.
18 So *will* **shall** not we go
back **apostatize** from thee:
quicken **enliven** us, and we *will* **shall** call upon thy name.
19 *Turn us again* **Return us,**
O *LORD God of hosts* **Yah Veh Elohim Sabaoth,**
cause thy face to *shine* **lighten**; and we shall be saved.

12 and return sevenfold to the bosom
of our fellow tabernaclers
—for the reproach
wherewith they reproach you, O Adonay.
13 and we your people and flock of your pasture
—we spread hands to you eternally;
we scribe your halal generation to generation.

80 To His Eminence;
On Sho—shannim—Eduth/Trumpets of Witness:
A Psalm by Asaph.
1 Hearken, O Raah of Yisra El,
who drives Yoseph as a flock;
who settles among the cherubim;
shine forth
2 at the face of Ephrayim
and Ben Yamin and Menash Sheh;
waken your might and come for our salvation.
3 Return us, O Elohim;
light your face that we be saved.
4 O Yah Veh Elohim Sabaoth,
until when
fume you against the prayer of your people?

5 You feed them bread of tears
and give them triple tears to drink;
6 you set us a strife to our neighbours
and our enemies deride among themselves.
7 Return us, O Yah Veh Elohim Sabaoth;
light your face that we be saved.
8 You pluck a vine from Misrayim;
you exile the goyim and plant it.
9 In facing, you face it;
and in rooting, you root it;
and it fills the land:
10 the mountains cover with the shadow thereof;
and the branches as the cedars of El:
11 she sends her harvest to the sea
and her branches to the river.
12 Why breach you her walls,
so that all who pass by the way pluck her?
13 The hog from the forest wastes it
and the creature of the field tends it.
14 Return, we beseech you, O Elohim Sabaoth;
look down from the heavens and see and visit this vine
15 and the plant your right planted;
and the son you strengthened for yourself
16 —burnt with fire—cut down;
they destruct at the rebuke of your face.
17 *May* your hand be on the man by your right
—the son of humanity
whom you strengthen for yourself:
18 and we apostatize not from you;
enliven us and we call on your name.
19 Return us, O Yah Veh Elohim Sabaoth;
light your face that we be saved.

81 To *the chief Musician* **His Eminence,**
upon Gittith, *A Psalm* of Asaph.
1 *Sing aloud* **Shout** unto *God* **Elohim**
our strength:
make a joyful noise **shout** unto *the God* **Elohim**
of *Jacob* **Yaaqov.**
2 *Take* **Lift** a psalm,
and *bring hither* **give** the *timbrel* **tambourine,**
the pleasant harp with the *psaltery* **bagpipe.**
3 *Blow up* **Blast** the *trumpet*
shophar in the new moon,
in the *time appointed* **full moon,**
on our *solemn feast* **celebration** day.
4 For this was a statute for *Israel* **Yisra El,**
and a *law* **judgment** of *the God* **Elohim** of *Jacob* **Yaaqov.**
5 This he *ordained* **set** in *Joseph* **Yoseph**
for a *testimony* **witness,**
when he went out through the land of *Egypt* **Misrayim:**
where I heard a *language* **lip** that I *understood* **knew** not.
6 I *removed* **turned aside** his shoulder
from the burden:
his *hands were delivered* **palms passed away**
from the *pots* **boilers.**
7 Thou calledst in *trouble* **tribulation,**
and I *delivered* **rescued** thee;
I answered thee in the *secret place* **covert** of thunder:
I *proved* **proofed** thee at the waters of *Meribah* **Strife.**
Selah.
8 Hear, O my people,
and I *will testify* **shall witness** unto thee:
O *Israel* **Yisra El,** if thou *wilt* **shalt** hearken unto me;
9 There shall no strange *god* **el** be in thee;
neither shalt thou *worship* **prostrate**
to any strange *god* **el.**
10 I *am the LORD*—**Yah Veh** thy *God* **Elohim,**
which *brought* **ascended** thee
out of the land of *Egypt* **Misrayim:**
open **enlarge** thy mouth *wide*, and I *will* **shall** fill it.
11 But my people *would* **willed**
to not hearken to my voice;
and *Israel would* **Yisra El had** none of me.
12 So I *gave* **sent** them *up*
unto *their own hearts' lust* **the warp of their heart:**
and they walked in their own counsels.
13 Oh that my people had hearkened unto me,
and *Israel* **Yisra El** had walked in my ways!
14 I should *soon* **shortly** have
subdued their enemies,
and turned my hand against their
adversaries **tribulators.**
15 The haters of *the LORD* **Yah Veh**
should have submitted themselves unto
emaciated in front of him:
but their time
should have *endured for ever* **become eternal.**
16 He should have fed them also
with the *finest* **fat** of the wheat:
and with honey out of the rock
should I have satisfied thee.

82 A Psalm of Asaph.
1 *God standeth* **Elohim stationeth**
in the *congregation* **witness** of *the mighty* **El;**
he judgeth among the *gods* **elohim.**
2 How long *will* **shall** *ye* judge *unjustly* **wickedly,**
and *accept* **lift** the *persons* **faces** of the wicked?
Selah.
3 *Defend* **Judge** the poor and *fatherless* **orphan:**
do justice to **justify**

the *afflicted* **humble** and *needy* **impoverished.**
4 *Deliver* **Slip away** the poor and needy:
rid **rescue** them out of the hand of the wicked.
5 They know not, neither *will*
shall they *understand* **discern;**
they walk on in darkness:
all the foundations of the earth *are out of course* **totter.**
6 I have said, Ye are *gods* **elohim;**
and all of you are *children* **sons** of *the most High* **Elyon.**
7 *But* ye shall **surely** die like *men* **humanity,**
and fall like one of the *princes* **governors.**
8 Arise, O *God* **Elohim,** judge the earth:
for thou shalt inherit all *nations* **goyim.**

81 To His Eminence; On Gittith: By Asaph.
1 Shout to Elohim our strength;
shout to Elohim of Yaaqov:
2 lift a psalm and give the tambourine
—the pleasant harp with the bagpipe:
3 blast the shophar in the new moon
—in the full moon on our celebration day.
4 For this *is* a statute to Yisra El
—a judgment of Elohim of Yaaqov;
5 which he set in Yoseph for a witness
when he went through the land of Misrayim.
I hear a lip I know not;
6 I turn aside his shoulder from the burden;
pass his palms from the boilers.
7 You call in tribulation and I rescue you;
I answer you in the covert of thunder;
I proof you at the waters of Meribah/Strife.
Selah.
8 Hear, O my people, and I witness to you;
O Yisra El, if you hearken to me;
9 neither have a strange el in you;
nor prostrate to any strange el.
10 I—Yah Veh your Elohim,
who ascended you from the land of Misrayim;
enlarges your mouth; and I fill it.
11 But my people will to not hearken to my voice;
and Yisra El has none of me:
12 and I send them in the warp of their own heart;
and they walk in their own counsels.
13 Oh that my people hearken to me
and Yisra El walk in my ways:
14 then had I shortly subdued their enemies
and turned my hand against their tribulators.
15 The haters of Yah Veh emaciate in front of him;
but their time is eternal:
16 he feeds them with the fat of the wheat;
and satisfies you with honey from the rock.

82 A Psalm by Asaph.
1 Elohim stations in the witness of El;
he judges among the elohim:
2 until when judge you wickedly
and lift the faces of the wicked?
Selah.
3 Judge the poor and orphan;
justify the humble and impoverished;
4 slip away the poor and needy;
rescue them from the hand of the wicked.
5 They neither know nor discern;
they walk on in darkness;
all the foundations of the earth totter.
6 I—I have said, You *are* elohim;
—and sons of Elyon, all of you;
7 you die as humanity
and fall as one of the governors.
8 Rise, O Elohim, judge the earth;
inherit among all the goyim.

83 A Song *or* Psalm of Asaph.
1 *Keep not thou silence* **Quiet not,** O *God* **Elohim:**
hold not thy peace **hush not,**
and be not still **rest not,** O *God* **El.**
2 For, *lo* **behold,** thine enemies
make a tumult **roar:**
and they that hate thee have lifted up the head.
3 They have *taken crafty*
strategized private counsel
against thy people,
and *consulted* **counseled**
against thy *hidden* **treasured** ones.
4 They have said, Come,
and let us cut them off from *being a nation* **the goyim;**
that the name of *Israel* **Yisra El**
may be no more *in remembrance* **remembered.**
5 For they have *consulted* **counseled** together
with one *consent* **heart:**
they *are confederate* **have cut a covenant** against thee:
6 The *tabernacles* **tents** of Edom,
and the *Ishmaelites* **Yishma Eliym;**
of Moab, and the *Hagarenes* **Hagariym;**
7 Gebal, and Ammon, and *Amalek* **Amaleq;**
the *Philistines* **Peleshethiym**
with the *inhabitants* **settlers** of *Tyre* **Sor;**
8 *Assur* **Ashshur** also is joined with them:
they have *holpen* **been an arm to**
the *children* **sons** of Lot.
Selah.
9 *Do* **Work** unto them as unto
the Midianites **Midyan;**

as *to* Sisera, as *to Jabin* **Yabiyn**,
at the *brook* **wadi** of *Kison* **Qishon**:
10 *Which perished* **desolated** at *Endor* **En Dor**:
they became as dung for the *earth* **soil**.
11 *Make* **Place** their *nobles* **volunteers** like Oreb,
and like *Zeeb* **Zebach**:
yea, all their *princes* **libations** as *Zebah* **Zebach**,
and as *Zalmunna* **Sal Munna**:
12 Who said,
Let us *take to ourselves* **possess**
the *houses* **folds** of *God in possession* **Elohim**.
13 O my *God* **Elohim**, *make*
place them like a wheel;
as the stubble *before* **at the face of** the wind.
14 As the fire burneth a *wood* **forest**,
and as the flame *setteth* **inflameth**
the mountains *on fire*;
15 So *persecute* **pursue** them
with thy *tempest* **storm**,
and *make* **terrify** them *afraid* with thy *storm* **hurricane**.
16 Fill their faces with *shame* **abasement**;
that they may seek thy name, O *LORD* **Yah Veh**.
17 Let them *be confounded* **shame**
and *troubled for ever* **terrify eternally**;
yea, let them *be put to shame* **blush**, and *perish* **destruct**:
18 That *men* **they** may know that thou,
whose name alone is *JEHOVAH* **Yah Veh**, art
the most high **Elyon** over all the earth.

84 To *the chief Musician* **His Eminence,**
upon Gittith,
A Psalm for the sons of *Korah* **Qorach**.
1 How *amiable* **beloved** are thy tabernacles,
O *LORD of hosts* **Yah Veh Sabaoth**!
2 My soul *longeth* **yearneth**,
yea, even *fainteth* **finisheth off**
for the courts of *the LORD* **Yah Veh**:
my heart and my flesh
crieth out **shouteth** for the living *God* **El**.
3 Yea, the *sparrow* **bird** hath found an house,
and the swallow a nest for herself,
where she may *lay* **set** her *young* **chicks**,
even thine **thy sacrifice** altars,
O *LORD of hosts* **Yah Veh Sabaoth**,
my *King* **Sovereign**, *and* my *God* **Elohim**.
4 *Blessed* **Blithe** *are* they that
dwell **settle** in thy house:
they *will be* **shall** still *praising* **halal** thee.
Selah.
5 *Blessed* **Blithe** *is the man* **humanity**
whose strength is in thee;
in whose heart are the *ways* **highways** of them.
6 Who passing through the
valley of *Baca* **Weeping**
make **place** it a *well* **fountain**;
the **early** rain also *filleth the pools*
covereth with blessings.

83 A Song: A Psalm by Asaph.
1 Quiet not, O Elohim;
hush not, rest not, O El.
2 For, behold, your enemies roar;
they who hate you lift their head;
3 they strategize private counsel
against your people;
and counsel against your treasured ones.
4 They say, Come;
and we cut them off from the goyim;
that the name of Yisra El be no more remembered.
5 For they counseled together with one heart;
they cut a covenant against you
6 —the tents of Edom and the Yishma Eliym,
of Moab and the Hagariym,
7 Gebal and Ammon and Amaleq,
the Peleshethiym with the settlers of Sor
8 and Ashshur joins with them
—an arm to the sons of Lot.
Selah.
9 Work them as to Midyan;
as Sisera, as Yabiyn, at the wadi of Qishon;
10 desolated at En Dor,
to become as dung for the soil.
11 Place their volunteers as Oreb, as Zebach;
yes, all their libations as Zebach, as Sal Munna;
12 Who say, Possess the folds of Elohim!
13 O my Elohim, place them as a wheel;
as the stubble at the face of the wind;
14 as the fire burning a forest;
and as the flame enflaming the mountains:
15 thus pursue them with your storm
and terrify them with your hurricane:
16 fill their faces with abasement;
so that they seek your name, O Yah Veh.
17 Shame and terrify them eternally;
yes, that they blush and destruct;
18 so that they know that you,
whose name alone is Yah Veh, *are*
Elyon over all the earth.

84 To His Eminence; On Gittith:
A Psalm for the sons of Qorach.
1 How beloved your tabernacles,
O Yah Veh Sabaoth!

2 My soul yearns,
yes, finishes off for the courts of Yah Veh;
my heart and my flesh shout for the living El:
3 yes, the bird finds a house,
and the swallow a nest for herself
to set her chicks;
your sacrifice altars,
O Yah Veh Sabaoth, my Sovereign, my Elohim.
4 Blithe—they who settle in your house;
they still halal you.
Selah.
5 Blithe—humanity whose strength is in you;
whose highways are in their heart;
6 who, passing through the valley of weeping,
place it a fountain:
the early rain covers with blessings.
7 They go from *strength* **valour** to *strength* **valour**,
every one of them in Zion appeareth before God
to be seen of Elohim in Siyon.
8 O *LORD God of hosts* **Yah Veh Elohim Sabaoth**,
hear my prayer:
give ear **hearken**, O *God* **Elohim** of *Jacob* **Yaaqov**.
Selah.
9 *Behold* **See**, O *God* **Elohim** our *shield* **buckler**,
and look upon the face of thine anointed.
10 For a day in thy courts is
better than a thousand.
I *had rather* **choose to** be a *doorkeeper*
threshhold waiter
in the house of my *God* **Elohim**,
than to *dwell* **twirl** in the tents of wickedness.
11 For *the LORD God* **Yah Veh Elohim**
is a sun and shield:
the LORD **Yah Veh**
will give grace **shall grant charism** and *glory* **honour**:
no good *thing will* **shall** he withhold
from them that walk *uprightly* **integriously**.
12 O *LORD of hosts* **Yah Veh Sabaoth**,
blessed **blithe** *is* the *man* **human**
that *trusteth* **confideth** in thee.

85 To *the chief Musician* **His Eminence**,
A Psalm for the sons of *Korah* **Qorach**.
1 *LORD* **Yah Veh**,
thou *hast been favourable* **art pleased** unto thy land:
thou hast brought back the captivity of *Jacob* **Yaaqov**.
2 Thou hast *forgiven* **lifted** the *iniquity* **perversity**
of thy people,
thou hast covered all their sin.
Selah.
3 Thou hast taken away all thy *wrath* **fury**:
thou hast turned *thyself*
from the *fierceness* **fuming** of *thine anger* **thy wrath**.
4 *Turn* **Return to** us, O *God*
Elohim of our salvation,
and *cause thine anger to cease* **break thy vexation**
toward us.
5 *Wilt* **Shalt** thou be angry
with us *for ever* **eternally**?
wilt **shalt** thou draw out thine anger
to all generations **generation to generation**?
6 *Wilt* **Shalt** thou not *revive us*
again **return to enliven us**:
that thy people may *rejoice* **cheer** in thee?
7 *Shew us* **Let us see** thy mercy, O *LORD* **Yah Veh**,
and *grant* **give** us thy salvation.
8 I *will* **shall** hear
what *God the LORD will speak* **El Yah Veh shall word**:
for he *will speak peace* **shall word shalom**
unto his people, and to his *saints* **mercied**:
but let them not turn again to folly.
9 Surely his salvation is nigh
them that *fear* **awe** him;
that *glory* **honour** may *dwell* **tabernacle** in our land.
10 Mercy and truth are met together;
righteousness **justness** and *peace* **shalom**
have kissed *each other*.
11 Truth shall *spring* **sprout** out of the earth;
and *righteousness* **justness** shall look *down*
from *heaven* **the heavens**.
12 Yea, *the LORD* **Yah Veh**
shall give *that which is* good;
and our land shall yield her *increase* **produce**.
13 *Righteousness* **Justness** shall
go *before him* **at his face**;
and shall set us in the way of his steps.

86 A Prayer of David.
1 *Bow down* **Spread** thine ear, O *LORD* **Yah Veh**,
hear **answer** me: for I am *poor* **humble** and needy.
2 *Preserve* **Guard** my soul; for I am *holy* **mercied**:
O thou my *God* **Elohim**,
save thy servant that *trusteth* **confideth** in thee.
3 *Be merciful unto me* **Grant**
me charism, O *Lord* **Adonay**:
for I *cry* **call** unto thee *daily* **all day**.
4 *Rejoice* **Cheer** the soul of thy servant:
for unto thee, O *Lord* **Adonay**, do I lift *up* my soul.
5 For thou, *Lord* **O Adonay**,
art good, and *ready to forgive* **forgiving**;
and *plenteous* **abundant** in mercy
unto all them that call upon thee.

6 *Give ear* **Hearken,** O *LORD*
Yah Veh, unto my prayer;
and *attend* **hearken** to the voice of my supplications.
7 They go from valour to valour
—seen by Elohim in Siyon.
8 O Yah Veh Elohim Sabaoth, hear my prayer;
hearken, O Elohim of Yaaqov.
Selah.
9 See, O Elohim, our buckler;
and look on the face of your anointed.
10 For a day in your courts
is better than a thousand.
I choose to be a threshhold waiter
in the house of my Elohim,
rather than to twirl in the tents of wickedness.
11 For Yah Veh Elohim is a sun and shield;
Yah Veh grants charism and honor;
he withholds no good
from them who walk integriously.
12 O Yah Veh Sabaoth,
blithe—the human who confides in you.

85 To His Eminence:
A Psalm for the sons of Qorach.
1 You are pleased, O Yah Veh, of your land;
you brought back the captivity of Yaaqov;
2 you lifted the perversity of your people;
you covered all their sin.
Selah.
3 You took away all your fury;
you turned from the fuming of your wrath.
4 Return to us, O Elohim of our salvation,
and break your vexation toward us.
5 Anger you with us eternally?
—draw out your anger generation to generation?
6 —not to return to enliven us
so that your people cheer in you?
7 Have us see your mercy, O Yah Veh,
and give us your salvation.
8 I hear what El Yah Veh words;
for he words shalom
to his people and to his mercied;
and they return not to folly.
9 Surely his salvation is near them who awe him;
whose honor tabernacles in our land.
10 Mercy and truth meet together;
justness and shalom kiss;
11 truth sprouts from the earth;
and justness looks from the heavens:
12 yes, Yah Veh gives good
and our land yields her produce;
13 justness goes at his face
and sets us in the way of his steps.

86 A Prayer by David.
1 Spread your ear, O Yah Veh;
answer me; for I am humble and needy:
2 guard my soul; for I am mercied:
O you, my Elohim,
save your servant who confides in you;
3 grant me charism, O Adonay,
for I call to you all day:
4 cheer the soul of your servant
for to you, O Adonay, I lift my soul:
5 for you, O Adonay, are good and forgiving
—abundant in mercy to all who call on you.
6 Hearken, O Yah Veh, to my prayer;
hearken to the voice of my supplications:
7 In the day of my *trouble* **tribulation**
I *will* **shall** call upon thee:
for thou *wilt* **shalt** answer me.
8 Among the *gods* **elohim**
there is none like unto thee,
O *Lord* **Adonay**;
neither are there any works like unto thy works
no works like thine.
9 All *nations* **goyim** whom
thou hast *made* **worked**
shall come and *worship before thee* **prostrate at thy face**,
O *Lord* **Adonay**;
and shall *glorify* **honour** thy name.
10 For thou *art* great,
and *doest wondrous things* **workest marvels**:
thou art *God* **Elohim** alone.
11 Teach me thy way, O *LORD* **Yah Veh**;
I *will* **shall** walk in thy truth:
unite my heart to *fear* **awe** thy name.
12 I *will praise* **shall spread hands unto** thee,
O *Lord* **Adonay** my *God* **Elohim**, with all my heart:
and I *will glorify* **shall honour** thy name
for evermore **eternally**.
13 For great is thy mercy toward me:
and thou hast *delivered* **rescued** my soul
from the *lowest hell* **nethermost sheol**.
14 O *God* **Elohim**,
the *proud* **arrogant** are risen against me,
and the *assemblies* **witnesses** of *violent men* **tyrants**
have sought after my soul;
and have not set thee *before* **in front of** them.
15 But thou, O *Lord* **Adonay**,
art *a God* **an El** full of *compassion* **mercy**,
and *gracious* **charismatic**, *longsuffering* **slow to wrath**,

and *plenteous* **abundant** in mercy and truth.
16 O *turn unto* **face** me,
and *have mercy upon me* **grant me charism**;
give thy strength unto thy servant,
and save the son of *thine handmaid* **thy maid.**
17 *Shew* **Work** me a *token* **sign** for good;
that they which hate me may see it,
and *be ashamed* **shame**:
because thou, *LORD* **O Yah Veh**,
hast *holpen* **helped** me, and *comforted* **sighed over** me.

87 A Psalm *or* Song for the sons of *Korah* **Qorach.**
1 His foundation is in the holy mountains.
2 *The LORD* **Yah Veh**
loveth the *gates* **portals** of *Zion* **Siyon**
more than all the *dwellings* **tabernacles** of *Jacob* **Yaaqov.**
3 *Glorious things* **Honours**
are *spoken* **worded** of thee,
O city of *God* **Elohim.**
Selah.
4 I *will make mention of* **shall remember**
Rahab and *Babylon* **Babel**
to them that know me:
behold *Philistia* **Pelesheth**,
and *Tyre* **Sor**, with *Ethiopia* **Kush**;
this *man* was *born* **birthed** there.
5 And of *Zion* **Siyon** it shall be said,
This **man** and that man was *born* **birthed** in her:
and *the highest* **Elyon** himself shall establish her.
6 *The LORD* **Yah Veh** shall *count* **scribe**,
when he *writeth up* **charteth** the people,
that this *man* was *born* **birthed** there.
Selah.
7 As well the singers
as the *players on instruments* **pluckers** shall be there:
all my *springs* **fountains** are in thee.

88 A Song *or* Psalm for the sons of *Korah* **Qorach**,
to *the chief Musician* **His Eminence,**
upon Mahalath Leannoth **on Stroking the Humbled**,
Maschil **On Comprehension** of Heman
the *Ezrahite* **Zerachiy.**
1 O *LORD God* **Yah Veh Elohim** of my salvation,
I have cried day and night *before* **in front of** thee:
2 Let my prayer come *before thee* **at thy face**:
incline **spread** thine ear unto my *cry* **shouting**;
3 For my soul *is full of troubles* **satiateth with evil**:
and my life *draweth nigh* **toucheth** unto *the grave* **sheol.**
7 in the day of my tribulation I call on you
for you answer me:
8 Among the elohim,
no one is likened to you, O Adonay;
no works like yours.
9 All the goyim you worked
come and prostrate at your face, O Adonay,
and honor your name:
10 for you are great and work marvels;
you alone are Elohim.
11 Teach me your way, O Yah Veh;
I walk in your truth:
unify my heart to awe your name.
12 I spread hands to you, O Adonay my Elohim,
with all my heart;
and honor your name eternally.
13 For great *is* your mercy toward me;
you rescue my soul from the nethermost sheol.
14 O Elohim, the arrogant rise against me
and the witnesses of tyrants seek my soul;
they set you not in front of them.
15 But you, O Adonay, are El
—full of mercy and charismatic;
slow to wrath and abundant in mercy and truth.
16 O face me, and grant me charism;
give your servant strength
and save the son of your maid:
17 work me a sign for good;
that they who hate me see it and shame:
because you, O Yah Veh,
help me and sigh over me.

87 A Psalm: A Song for the sons of Qorach.
1 His foundation *is* in the holy mountains;
2 Yah Veh loves the portals of Siyon
more than all the tabernacles of Yaaqov:
3 honors are worded of you, O city of Elohim.
Selah.
4 I remember Rahab and Babel
to them who know me;
behold Pelesheth and Sor with Kush;
this *one* was birthed there.
5 And of Siyon it says,
This man and that man *were* birthed in her;
and Elyon himself establishes her.
6 When he charts the people,
Yah Veh scribes, this *one* was birthed there.
Selah.
7 The singers as well as the pluckers
—all my fountains *are* in you.

88 A Song, a Psalm for the sons of Qorach;
To His Eminence; On Stroking the Humbled;
On Comprehension: By Heman the Zerachiy.
1 O Yah Veh Elohim of my salvation,
in the day I cry; and at night in front of you;

2 my prayer comes at your face:
spread your ear to my shouting;
3 for my soul satiates with evil
and my life touches to sheol:
4 I am *counted* **fabricated** with them
that *go down* **descend** into the *pit* **well**:
I *am as a man*—**a mighty** that hath no *strength* **might**:
5 *Free* **Liberated** among the dead,
like the *slain* **pierced** that lie in the *grave* **tomb**,
whom thou rememberest no more:
and they are cut off from thy hand.
6 Thou hast *laid* **placed** me
in the *lowest pit* **nethermost well**,
in darkness, in the deeps.
7 Thy *wrath lieth hard* **fury proppeth** upon me,
and thou hast *afflicted* **humbled** me with all thy waves.
Selah.
8 Thou hast *put away* **far removed**
mine acquaintance far from me **them whom I know**;
thou hast *made* **placed** me
an *abomination* **abhorrence** unto them:
I am shut up—**restrained**, and I cannot come forth.
9 Mine eye *mourneth* **languisheth**
by reason of affliction **from humiliation**:
LORD **O Yah Veh**, I have called daily upon thee,
I have *stretched out* **spread** my *hands* **palms** unto thee.
10 *Wilt* **Shalt** thou *shew wonders* **work marvels**
to the dead?
shall the *dead* **ghosts** arise
and *praise* **spread hands unto** thee?
Selah.
11 Shall thy *lovingkindness* **mercy**
be *declared* **scribed** in the *grave* **tomb**?
or thy *faithfulness* **trustworthiness**
in *destruction* **Abaddon**?
12 Shall thy *wonders* **marvels**
be known in the dark?
and thy *righteousness* **justness**
in the land of *forgetfulness* **oblivion**?
13 But unto thee have I cried, O *LORD* **Yah Veh**;
and in the morning
shall my prayer *prevent* **anticipate** thee.
14 *LORD* **O Yah Veh**, why castest thou off my soul?
why hidest thou thy face from me?
15 I am *afflicted* **humbled**
and ready to die—**expiring**
from my youth up **since ladhood**:
while I *suffer* **bear** thy terrors I am *distracted* **perplexed**.
16 Thy *fierce wrath goeth* **fuming passeth** over me;
thy terrors *have cut me off* **exterminate me**.
17 They *came round about*
surround me *daily* **all day**
like water;
they *compassed me about* **surround me** together.
18 Lover and friend
hast thou *put far* **far removed** from me,
and *mine acquaintance* **they whom**
I know into darkness.

89 *Maschil* **On Comprehension**
of Ethan the *Ezrahite* **Zerachiy**.
1 I *will* **shall** sing of the mercies
of *the LORD* **Yah Veh**
for ever **eternally**:
with my mouth
will **shall** I make known thy
faithfulness **trustworthiness**
to all generations **generation to generation**.
2 For I have said,
Mercy shall be built up *for ever* **eternally**:
thy *faithfulness* **trustworthiness**
shalt thou establish in the very heavens.
3 I have *made* **cut** a covenant with my chosen,
I have *sworn* **oathed** unto David my servant,
4 Thy seed *will* **shall** I establish *for ever* **eternally**,
and build up thy throne
to all generations **generation to generation**.
Selah.
5 And the heavens
shall *praise* **spread hands unto** thy *wonders* **marvels**,
O *LORD* **Yah Veh**:
thy *faithfulness* **trustworthiness** also
in the congregation of the *saints* **holy**.
6 For who in the *heaven* **vapours**
can **shall** be *compared* **ranked**
unto the LORD **with Yah Veh**?
who among the sons of *the mighty* **El**
can **shall** be likened unto *the LORD* **Yah Veh**?
4 I am fabricated with them descending the well;
I—a mighty having no might;
5 liberated among the dead
as pierced lying in the tomb
whom you remember no more:
and they are cut off from your hand.
6 You place me in the nethermost well
—in darkness—in the deeps:
7 your fury props on me
and you humble me with all your waves.
Selah.
8 You far removed them whom I know;
you place me an abhorrence to them

—restrained—I come not forth:
9 my eye languishes from humiliation;
O Yah Veh, I call on you daily;
I spread my palms to you.
10 Work you marvels to the dead?
Rise the ghosts? Spread they hands to you?
Selah.
11 Is your mercy scribed in the tomb?
—your trustworthiness in Abaddon?
12 —your marvels known in the dark?
—your justness in the land of oblivion?
13 And I—to you I cried, O Yah Veh;
and in the morning my prayer anticipates you.
14 O Yah Veh, why cast you my soul?
Why hide your face from me?
15 I *am* humbled—expiring since ladhood;
I bear your terrors—perplexed;
16 your fuming passes over me;
your terrors exterminate me;
17 surrounding me all day as water:
they altogether surround me.
18 You far removed lover and friend from me
and they whom I know into darkness.

89 On Comprehension: By Ethan the Zerachiy.
1 I sing of the mercies of Yah Veh eternally;
with my mouth I make known your trustworthiness
generation to generation.
2 For I say, your mercy builds eternally;
your trustworthiness
establishes in the very heavens:
3 I cut a covenant with my chosen;
I oathed to David my servant:
4 your seed establishes eternally
and builds your throne generation to generation.
Selah.
5 And the heavens spread hands to your marvels,
O Yah Veh;
to your trustworthiness
in the congregation of the holy:
6 Who in the vapours ranks with Yah Veh?
Who among the sons of El likens to Yah Veh?
7 *God* **El** is greatly to be *feared* **awed**
in the *assembly* **private counsel** of the *saints* **holy**,
and *to be had in reverence* **awed**
of **over** all them that are about him.
8 O *LORD God of hosts* **Yah Elohim Sabaoth**,
who is a *strong LORD* **powerful Yah** like unto thee?
or to thy *faithfulness* **trustworthiness** round about thee?
9 Thou *rulest* **reignest** the *raging* **rising** of the sea:
when the waves *thereof* arise, thou *stillest* **laudest** them.
10 Thou hast *broken* **crushed** Rahab *in pieces*,
as one that is *slain* **pierced**;
thou hast scattered thine enemies
with thy *strong* arm **of strength**.
11 The heavens are thine, the earth also is thine:
as for the world and the fulness *thereof*,
thou hast founded them.
12 The north and the *south*
right thou hast created them:
Tabor and Hermon shall *rejoice* **shout** in thy name.
13 Thou hast *a mighty arm* **an arm of might**:
strong **strengthened** is thy hand, *and*
high **lofted** is thy right *hand*.
14 *Justice* **Justness** and judgment
are the *habitation* **establishment** of thy throne:
mercy and truth shall *go before* **anticipate** thy face.
15 *Blessed* **Blithe** *is* the people
that know the *joyful sound* **shout**:
they shall walk, O *LORD* **Yah Veh**,
in the light of thy *countenance* **face**.
16 In thy name shall they *rejoice* **twirl** all the day:
and in thy *righteousness* **justness**
shall they be *exalted* **lofted**.
17 For thou art the *glory* **beauty** of their strength:
and *in* **at** thy *favour* **pleasure**
our horn shall be *exalted* **lofted**.
18 For *the LORD* **Yah Veh** is our *defence* **buckler**;
and the Holy One of *Israel* **Yisra**
El is our *king* **sovereign**.
19 Then thou *spakest* **wordest** in vision
to thy *holy* **mercied** one, and saidst,
I have *laid* **placed** help upon one that is mighty;
I have exalted one chosen out of the people.
20 I have found David my servant;
with my holy *oil* **ointment** have I anointed him:
21 With whom my hand shall be established:
mine arm also shall strengthen him.
22 The enemy shall not exact upon him;
nor the son of wickedness *afflict* **abase** him.
23 And I *will beat down* **shall**
crush his *foes* **tribulators**
before **at** his face,
and *plague* **smite** them that hate him.
24 But my *faithfulness*
trustworthiness and my mercy
shall be with him:
and in my name shall his horn be *exalted* **lofted**.
25 I *will* **shall** set his hand *also* in the sea,
and his right *hand* in the rivers.
26 He shall *cry* **call** unto me, Thou *art*—my father,

my *God* **El**, and the rock of my salvation.
27 Also I *will make* **shall give** him
to be my *firstborn* **firstbirthed**,
higher than the kings **Elyon of the**
sovereigns of the earth.
28 My mercy *will I keep* **shall I guard** for him
for evermore **eternally**,
and my covenant shall *stand fast*
be trustworthy with him.
29 His seed also *will I make* **shall I set**
to endure for ever **eternal**,
and his throne as the days of *heaven* **the heavens**.
30 If his *children* **sons** forsake my *law* **torah**,
and walk not in my judgments;
31 If they *break* **profane** my statutes,
and *keep* **guard** not my *commandments* **misvoth**;
32 Then *will* **shall** I visit their
transgression **rebellion**
with the *rod* **scion**,
and their *iniquity* **perversity** with *stripes* **plagues**.
33 Nevertheless my *lovingkindness* **mercy**
will **shall** I not *utterly take from him* **void**,
nor *suffer* **falsify** my *faithfulness to fail* **trustworthiness**.
34 My covenant *will* **shall** I not *break* **profane**,
nor alter the *thing that is gone out*
proceedings of my lips.
35 Once have I *sworn* **oathed** by my holiness
that I *will* **shall** not lie unto David.
7 El is greatly to be awed
in the private counsel of the holy;
and awed over them who *are* all around him.
8 O Yah Elohim Sabaoth,
Who is a powerful Yah likened to you?
Or to your trustworthiness all around you?
9 You reign over the rising of the sea;
the waves rise, you laud them:
10 you crush Rahab as one pierced;
you scattered your enemies
with your arm of strength;
11 the heavens are yours—the earth is yours
—the world and the fulness you founded;
12 the north and the right you created.
Tabor and Hermon shout in your name.
13 You have an arm of might;
strengthened is your hand;
lofted is your right;
14 justness and judgment
are the establishment of your throne:
mercy and truth
anticipate your face.
15 Blithe—the people who know the shout;
they walk, O Yah Veh,
in the light of your face:
16 in your name they twirl all the day;
and in your justness they are lofted.
17 For you are the beauty of their strength;
and at your pleasure our horn is lofted.
18 For Yah Veh is our buckler
and the Holy One of Yisra El our sovereign.
19 Then you worded in vision
to your mercied one and said,
I placed help on one who is mighty;
I exalted one chosen from the people:
20 I found David my servant;
with my holy ointment I anoint him;
21 with whom I establish my hand;
my arm strengthens him:
22 neither the enemy exacts from him;
nor the son of wickedness abase him:
23 I crush his tribulators at his face
and smite them who hate him.
24 And my trustworthiness and my mercy
are with him;
and in my name his horn is lofted.
25 I set his hand on the sea
and his right on the rivers.
26 He calls to me, You—my father,
my El and the rock of my salvation.
27 I also give him to be my firstbirthed,
Elyon of the sovereigns of the earth.
28 I guard my mercy for him eternally
and my trustworthy covenant with him;
29 I set his seed eternal
and his throne as the days of the heavens.
30 If his sons forsake my torah
and walk not in my judgments;
31 if they profane my statutes
and guard not my misvoth;
32 then I visit their rebellion with the scion
and their perversity with plagues:
33 I neither void my mercy
nor falsify my trustworthiness;
34 neither profane my covenant
nor alter the proceedings of my lips.
35 Once I oath by my holiness; I lie not to David:
36 His seed shall *endure for ever* **be eternal**,
and his throne as the sun before me.
37 It shall be established *for*
ever **eternally** as the moon,
and as a *faithful* **trustworthy** witness

in *heaven* **the vapours.**
Selah.
38 But thou hast cast off and *abhorred* **spurned,**
thou hast *been wroth with* **passed over** thine anointed.
39 Thou hast *made void* **rejected**
the covenant of thy servant:
thou hast profaned his *crown* **separatism**
by casting it to the *ground* **earth.**
40 Thou hast *broken down*
breached all his *hedges* **walls;**
thou hast *brought* **set** his *strong holds* **fortresses** to ruin.
41 All that pass by the way spoil him:
he is a reproach to his *neighbours* **fellow tabernaclers.**
42 Thou hast *set up* **exalted**
the right *hand* of his *adversaries* **tribulators;**
thou hast made all his enemies to *rejoice* **cheer.**
43 Thou hast also turned the
edge **form** of his sword,
and hast not *made* **raised** him to *stand in the battle* **war.**
44 Thou hast *made* **shabbathized**
his *glory to cease* **purity,**
and *cast* **precipitated** his throne
down to the *ground* **earth.**
45 The days of his youth hast
thou *shortened* **curtailed:**
thou hast covered him with shame.
Selah.
46 How long, *LORD* **O Yah Veh?**
wilt **shalt** thou hide thyself *for ever* **in perpetuity?**
shall thy *wrath* **fury** burn like fire?
47 Remember how *short my time is* **transcient:**
wherefore hast thou
made **created** all *men* **sons of humanity** in vain?
48 What *man is he that* **mighty** liveth,
and shall not see death?
shall he *deliver* **rescue** his soul
from the hand of *the grave* **sheol?**
Selah.
49 *Lord* **Adonay,**
where are thy *former lovingkindnesses* **first mercies,**
which thou *swarest* **oathest** unto David
in thy *truth* **trustworthiness?**
50 Remember, *Lord* **Adonay,**
the reproach of thy servants;
how I *do* bear in my bosom *the reproach of*
all the *mighty* **great** people;
51 Wherewith thine enemies have reproached,
O *LORD* **Yah Veh;**
wherewith they have reproached
the *footsteps* **heelprints** of thine anointed.
52 Blessed be *the LORD for*
evermore **Yah Veh eternally.**
Amen, and Amen.

BOOK IV

90 A Prayer of *Moses* **Mosheh**
the man of *God* **Elohim.**
1 *Lord* **Adonay,**
thou hast been our *dwelling place* **habitation**
in all generations **generation to generation.**
2 Before the mountains were
brought forth **birthed,**
or ever thou *hadst formed* **writhed**
the earth and the world,
even from *everlasting* **eternity** to *everlasting* **eternity,**
thou *art God*—**El.**
3 Thou turnest man to *destruction* **be crushed;**
and sayest, Return, ye *children* **sons** of *men* **humanity.**
4 For a thousand years in thy *sight* **eyes**
are *but* as yesterday when it is past,
and as—a watch in the night.
5 Thou *carriest* **causest** them
away as with a flood **to be floodborne;**
they are as a sleep:
in the morning they are like grass
which *groweth up* **changeth.**
6 In the morning it flourisheth,
and *groweth up* **changeth;**
in the evening it is cut *down*, and withereth.
7 For we are *consumed* **finished off**
by *thine anger* **thy wrath,**
and by thy *wrath* **fury** are we *troubled* **terrified.**
36 his seed is eternal
and his throne as the sun in front of me;
37 —established eternally as the moon
and as a trustworthy witness in the vapours.
Selah.
38 And you—you cast off and spurn;
you pass over your anointed.
39 you reject the covenant of your servant;
you profane his separatism to the earth;
40 you breach all his walls;
you set his fortresses to ruin.
41 All who pass by the way spoil him;
—a reproach to his fellow tabernaclers.
42 You exalt the right of his tribulators;
you have all his enemies cheer;
43 you turn the form of his sword
and raise him to not war;
44 you shabbathized his purity

and precipitate his throne to the earth:
45 you curtailed the days of his youth;
you covered him with shame.
Selah.
46 Until when, O Yah Veh, hide you yourself?
In perpetuity?—Burn your fury as fire?
47 Remember how transcient!
Created you all sons of humanity in vain?
48 What mighty lives and sees not death?
—rescues his soul from the hand of sheol?
Selah.
49 Where are your first mercies, O Adonay,
which you oathed to David in your trustworthiness?
50 Remember, O Adonay,
the reproach of your servants;
how in my bosom I bear all the great people;
51 whom your enemies reproached, O Yah Veh
—reproached the heelprints of your anointed.
52 Blessed—Yah Veh eternally.
Amen and Amen.

Book IV

90 A Prayer of Mosheh, the man of Elohim.
1 Adonay, you have been our habitation
generation to generation.
2 ere the mountains were birthed;
or ever you writhed the earth and the world;
even from eternity to eternity—you *are* El.
3 You return man to crush;
and say, Return, you sons of humanity.
4 For a thousand years in your eyes
are as yesterday when it is past
—a watch in the night.
5 Floodborne, as asleep;
in the morning, as grass that changes.
6 In the morning, flourishes and changes;
in the evening, cut and withered:
7 for we are finished off by your wrath
and terrified by your fury.
8 Thou hast set our *iniquities* **perversities**
before **in front of** thee,
our *secret sins* **concealed**
in the light of thy *countenance* **face**.
9 For all our days *are passed*
away **have turned face**
in thy *wrath* **fury**:
we *spend* **finish off** our years as a
tale that is told **meditation**.
10 The days of our years
are *threescore years and ten* **seventy years**;
and if by *reason of strength* **might**
they be *fourscore* **eighty** years,
yet is their *strength* **pride,** *labour*
toil and *sorrow* **mischief**;
for it is *soon cut off* **quickly passed over**,
and we fly away.
11 Who knoweth the *power* **strength**
of *thine anger* **thy wrath**?
even according to thy fear **as thy**
awe, so *is* thy *wrath* **fury**.
12 So *teach us* **have us know** to number our days,
that we may apply our hearts unto wisdom.
13 Return, O *LORD* **Yah Veh**, how long?
and *let it repent thee* **sigh thou** concerning thy servants.
14 O satisfy us *early* **mornings** with thy mercy;
that we may *rejoice* **shout** and *be glad* **cheer** all our days.
15 *Make us glad* **Cheer us** according to the days
wherein thou hast *afflicted* **humbled** us, and
the years *wherein* we have seen evil.
16 Let thy *work appear* **deeds**
be seen unto thy servants,
and thy *glory* **majesty** unto their *children* **sons**.
17 And let the *beauty* **pleasantness**
of *the LORD* **Yah Veh** our *God* **Elohim** be upon us:
and establish thou the work of our hands upon us;
yea, the work of our hands establish thou it.

91 He that *dwelleth* **settleth**
in the *secret place of the most High* **covert of Elyon**
shall *abide* **stay**
under the shadow of *the Almighty* **Shadday**.
2 I *will* **shall** say of *the LORD* **Yah Veh**,
He is my refuge and my *fortress* **stronghold**:
my *God* **Elohim**; in him *will I trust* **shall I confide**.
3 *Surely* he shall *deliver* **rescue** thee
from the snare of the *fowler* **snarer**,
and from the *noisome* **calamitous** pestilence.
4 He shall cover thee with his *feathers* **pinions**,
and under his wings shalt thou *trust* **seek refuge**:
his truth shall be thy shield and buckler.
5 Thou shalt not *be afraid* **awe**
for the *terror* **dread** by night;
nor for the arrow that flieth by day;
6 Nor for the pestilence that walketh in darkness;
nor for the *destruction* **ruin**
that *wasteth* **devastateth** at noonday.
7 A thousand shall fall at thy side,
and *ten thousand* **myriads** at thy right *hand*;
but it shall not *come nigh* **approach** thee.
8 Only with thine eyes shalt thou *behold* **look**
and see the *reward* **retribution** of the wicked.

9 Because thou hast *made the LORD* **set Yah Veh,**
which is my refuge, *even the most High* **Elyon,**
thy habitation;
10 There shall no evil *befall* **happen** thee,
neither shall any plague come nigh thy *dwelling* **tent.**
11 For he shall *give* **misvah**
his angels *charge* over thee,
to *keep* **guard** thee in all thy ways.
12 They shall *bear* **lift** thee
up in their *hands* **palms,**
lest thou *dash* **stub** thy foot against a stone.
13 Thou shalt tread upon the
roaring lion and *adder* **asp:**
the *young lion* **whelp** and the *dragon*
monster shalt thou trample under feet.
14 Because he hath
set his love upon **attached himself to** me,
therefore *will I deliver* **shall I slip** him **away:**
I *will set* **shall loft** him *on high,*
because he hath known my name.
15 He shall call upon me, and
I *will* **shall** answer him:
I *will* **shall** be with him in *trouble* **tribulation;**
I *will deliver* **shall rescue** him, and honour him.
16 With *long life will* **length**
of days shall I satisfy him,
and *shew him* **let him see** my salvation.
8 You set our perversities in front of you,
our concealments in the light of your face.
9 For all our days turn face in your fury;
we finish off our years as a meditation:
10 the days of our years, seventy years;
and if by might, eighty years;
yet their pride is toil and mischief
—quickly passed over and we fly away.
11 Who knows the strength of your wrath?
As your awe, thus your fury.
12 So have us know to number our days,
so that we apply our hearts to wisdom.
13 Return, O Yah Veh! Until when?
Sigh concerning your servants!
14 O satisfy us mornings with your mercy;
so that we shout and cheer all our days:
15 cheer us according to the days you humbled us
and the years we saw evil;
16 show your deeds to your servants
and your majesty to their sons;
17 that the pleasantness of Yah Veh our Elohim
be on us:
establish the work of our hands on us; yes,
the work of our hands, establish it.

91 He who settles in the covert of Elyon
stays under the shadow of Shadday.
2 I say of Yah Veh, My refuge and my stronghold;
my Elohim; in him I confide:
3 he rescues you from the snare of the snarer
—from the calamitous pestilence:
4 he covers you with his pinions
and under his wings you seek refuge:
his truth *are* your shield and buckler.
5 Neither awe for the dread of night
nor the arrow that flies by day;
6 neither for the pestilence that walks in darkness
nor for the ruin that devastates at noonday.
7 A thousand fall at your side
and myriads at your right;
but they approach you not.
8 But look with your eyes
and see the retribution of the wicked.
9 Because you, O Yah Veh, my refuge
set Elyon your habitation.
10 Neither evil happens you,
nor any plague approach your tent;
11 for he misvahs his angels over you,
to guard you in all your ways:
12 hey lift you in their palms
lest you stub your foot against a stone:
13 you tread on the roaring lion and asp;
and trample the whelp and the monster under foot.
14 Because he attaches himself to me,
I slip him away;
loft him, because he knows my name.
15 He calls on me and I answer him;
I *am* with him in tribulation; I
rescue him and honor him:
16 with length of days I satisfy him
and have him see my salvation.

92 A Psalm *or* Song
for the *sabbath* **shabbath** day.
1 It is *a* good *thing*
to *give thanks* **spread hands** unto *the LORD* **Yah Veh,**
and to *sing praises* **psalm** unto thy name,
O *most High* **Elyon:**
2 To *shew forth* **tell** thy *lovingkindness* **mercy**
in the morning,
and thy *faithfulness* **trustworthiness**
every night **in the nights,**
3 Upon *an instrument of ten*
strings **the decachord,**
and upon the *psaltery* **bagpipe;**
upon the harp with a *solemn sound* **meditation.**

4 For thou, *LORD* **O Yah Veh,**
hast *made* **cheered** me *glad* through thy *work* **deeds:**
I *will triumph* **shall shout** in the works of thy hands.
5 O *LORD* **Yah Veh,** how *great*
greatened are thy works!
and thy *thoughts* **fabrications**
are very deep **mightily deepened.**
6 A *brutish* **stupid** man knoweth not;
neither *doth* a fool *understand this* **discern.**
7 When the wicked *spring*
blossom as the *grass* **herbage,**
and when all the *workers* **doers** of *iniquity* **mischief**
do flourish;
it is that they shall be *destroyed* **desolated**
for ever **eternally:**
8 But thou, *LORD* **O Yah Veh,**
art *most high for evermore* **in the heights eternally.**
9 For, *lo* **behold,** thine
enemies, O *LORD* **Yah Veh,**
for, *lo* **behold,** thine enemies shall *perish* **destruct;**
all the *workers* **doers** of *iniquity* **mischief**
shall be *scattered* **separated.**
10 But my horn shalt thou exalt
like *the horn of an unicorn* **a reem:**
I shall be anointed with *fresh oil* **green ointment.**
11 Mine eye also shall *see* **look**
my desire on mine enemies **on my observers,**
and mine ears shall hear
my desire of the wicked **the vilifiers**
that rise up against me.
12 The *righteous* **just** shall *flourish* **blossom**
like the palm tree:
he shall *grow* **increase** like a cedar in Lebanon.
13 Those that be *planted* **transplanted**
in the house of *the LORD* **Yah Veh**
shall *flourish* **blossom** in the courts of our *God* **Elohim.**
14 They shall still *bring forth fruit* **germinate**
in *old age* **greyness;**
they shall be fat and *flourishing* **green;**
15 To *shew* **tell** that *the LORD*
Yah Veh is *upright* **straight:**
he is—my rock,
and there is no *unrighteousness* **wickedness** in him.

93 *The LORD* **Yah Veh** reigneth,
he *is clothed* **hath enrobed** with *majesty* **pomp;**
the LORD is clothed **Yah Veh hath**
enrobed with strength,
wherewith he hath girded himself:
the world also is stablished,
that it *cannot be moved* **totter not.**
2 Thy throne is established *of old* **since then:**
thou art from *everlasting* **eternity.**
3 The *floods* **rivers** have lifted
up, O *LORD* **Yah Veh,**
the *floods* **rivers** have lifted *up* their voice;
the *floods* **rivers** lift *up* their waves.
4 *The LORD on high* **Yah Veh in the heights**
is mightier than the *noise* **voice** of many waters,
yea, than the mighty waves of the sea.
5 Thy *testimonies* **witnesses**
are *very sure* **mighty trustworthy:**
holiness *becometh* **befitteth** thine house,
O *LORD* **Yah Veh,** *for ever* **to length of days.**

92 A Psalm; A Song: For the shabbath day.
1 It is good to spread hands to Yah Veh
and to psalm to your name, O Elyon:
2 to tell your mercy in the morning
and your trustworthiness in the nights:
3 on the decachord and on the bagpipe;
on the harp with a meditation.
4 For you, O Yah Veh,
cheer me through your deeds;
I shout in the works of your hands.
5 O Yah Veh, how your works greaten!
How mightily your fabrications deepen!
6 Neither the stupid man knows;
nor the fool discerns this:
7 when the wicked blossom as the herbage
and when all the doers of mischief flourish
to be desolated eternally.
8 But you, O Yah Veh,
are in the heights eternally.
9 For behold, your enemies, O Yah Veh,
for behold, your enemies destruct; all
the doers of mischief separate.
10 But you exalt my horn as a reem
—anoint with green ointment.
11 My eye also sees my observers
and my ears hear the vilifiers who rise against me.
12 The just blossom as the palm tree;
he increases as a cedar in Lebanon:
13 they who are transplanted
in the house of Yah Veh
blossom in the courts of our Elohim:
14 they still germinate in greyness—fat and green;
15 to tell that Yah Veh is straight
—my rock
and there is no wickedness in him.

93 Yah Veh reigns—enrobed with pomp;
Yah Veh enrobes with strength; he girts himself:

the world is established that it totter not:
2 your throne is established since then;
yours—from eternity.
3 The rivers lift, O Yah Veh;
the rivers lift their voice; the rivers lift their waves:
4 Yah Veh in the heights
is mightier than the voice of many waters
—than the mighty waves of the sea.
5 Your witnesses are mighty trustworthy;
holiness befits your house, O Yah Veh,
to length of days.

94 *O LORD God, to whom vengeance belongeth*
O El of vengeance;
O God, to whom vengeance belongeth
O Yah Veh El of vengeance,
shew thyself **shine.**
2 Lift up thyself, thou judge of the earth:
render a reward **return a dealing** to the *proud* **pompous.**
3 *LORD* **O Yah Veh,** how long shall the wicked,
how long shall the wicked *triumph* **jump for joy?**
4 How long shall they *utter* **gush**
and *speak hard things* **word impudence?**
and all the *workers* **doers** of *iniquity* **mischief**
boast themselves **say?**
5 They *break in pieces* **crush** thy people,
O *LORD* **Yah Veh,**
and *afflict* **humble** thine *heritage* **inheritance.**
6 They *slay* **slaughter**
the widow and the *stranger* **sojourner,**
and murder the *fatherless* **orphan.**
7 Yet they say, *The LORD* **Yah Veh** shall not see,
neither shall *the God* **Elohim** of *Jacob* **Yaaqov**
regard **discern** *it.*
8 *Understand* **Discern,** ye *brutish*
stupid among the people:
and *ye* fools, when *will* **shall** ye *be wise* **discern?**
9 He that planted the ear, shall he not hear?
he that formed the eye, shall he not *see* **scan?**
10 He that *chastiseth* **disciplineth**
the *heathen* **goyim,**
shall not he *correct* **reprove?**
he that teacheth *man* **humanity** knowledge,
shall not he know?
11 *The LORD* **Yah Veh**
knoweth the *thoughts* **fabrications** of *man* **humanity,**
that they are vanity.
12 *Blessed* **Blithe** *is the man*—**the mighty**
whom thou *chastenest* **disciplinest,** O *LORD* **Yah,**
and teachest him out of thy *law* **torah;**
13 That thou mayest *give him* rest **him**
from the days of *adversity* **evil,**
until the pit **of ruin** be digged for the wicked.
14 For *the LORD* **Yah Veh**
will **shall** not *cast off* **abandon** his people,
neither *will* **shall** he forsake his inheritance.
15 But judgment shall return
unto *righteousness* **justness:**
and all the *upright* **straight** in heart
shall *follow* **be after** it.
16 Who *will* **shall** rise *up* for me
against the *evildoers* **vilifiers?**
or who *will stand up* **shall set** for me
against the *workers* **doers** of *iniquity* **mischief?**
17 Unless *the LORD* **Yah Veh** had been my help,
my soul had almost *dwelt* **tabernacled** in silence.
18 When I said, My foot *slippeth* **tottereth;**
thy mercy, O *LORD* **Yah Veh,** *held* **supported** me *up.*
19 In the *multitude* **abundance**
of my thoughts within me
thy *comforts* **consolations** delight my soul.
20 Shall the throne of *iniquity* **calamity**
have fellowship **join** with thee,
which *frameth mischief* **formeth toil** by a *law* **statute?**
21 They *gather themselves together* **troop**
against the soul of the *righteous* **just**
and *condemn* **judge wicked** the innocent blood.
22 But *the LORD* **Yah Veh** is
my *defence* **secure loft;**
and my *God* **Elohim** is the rock of my refuge.
23 And he shall *bring* **turn** upon them
their own *iniquity* **mischief,**
and shall *cut* **exterminate** them *off*
in their own *wickedness* **evil:**
yea, the LORD **Yah Veh** our *God* **Elohim**
shall *cut* **exterminate** them *off.*

95 O come, let us *sing* **shout**
unto *the LORD* **Yah Veh:**
let us *make a joyful noise* **shout**
to the rock of our salvation.
2 Let us *come before* **anticipate** his *presence* **face**
with *thanksgiving* **spread hands,**
and *make a joyful noise* **shout** unto him with psalms.

94 O El of vengeance;
O Yah Veh El of vengeance, shine!
2 Lift yourself, O judge of the earth;
return a dealing to the pompous.
3 O Yah Veh, until when the wicked
—until when jump the wicked for joy?
4 They gush; they word impudence
and all the doers of mischief say.

5 They crush your people, O Yah Veh,
and humble your inheritance;
6 they slaughter the widow and the sojourner
and murder the orphan:
7 and they say, neither Yah Veh sees,
nor Elohim of Yaaqov discerns.
8 Discern, you stupid among the people;
and fools, when discern you?
9 He who plants the ear, hears he not?
He who forms the eye, scans he not?
10 He who disciplines the goyim, reproves he not?
—he who teaches humanity knowledge?
11 Yah Veh knows
that the fabrications of humanity *are* vanity.
12 Blithe—the mighty whom
you discipline, O Yah;
—whom you teach from your torah;
13 so that you rest him from the days of evil,
until they dig the pit of ruin for the wicked.
14 For Yah Veh neither abandons his people
nor forsakes his inheritance;
15 for judgment returns to justness;
and all the straight in heart after it.
16 Who rises for me against the vilifiers?
Who sets for me against the workers of mischief?
17 Unless Yah Veh had been my help,
my soul had almost tabernacled in silence.
18 When I say, My foot totters;
your mercy, O Yah Veh, supports me.
19 In the abundance of my thoughts inside me
your consolations delight my soul.
20 Is the throne of calamity joined with you
—which forms toil by a statute?
21 They troop against the soul of the just
and innocent blood, thet judge wicked:
22 and Yah Veh is my secure loft;
and my Elohim is the rock of my refuge:
23 and he returns their own mischief on them
and exterminates them in their own evil: Yah
Veh our Elohim exterminates them.

95 O come; we shout to Yah Veh
—shout to the rock of our salvation;
2 —anticipate his face with spread hands
and shout to him with psalms.
3 For *the LORD* **Yah Veh** is a great *God* **El**,
and a great *King* **Sovereign** above all *gods* **elohim**.
4 In his hand
are the *deep places* **innermost depths** of the earth:
the *strength* **strengths** of the *hills* **mountains**
is **are** his also.
5 The sea is his, and he *made* **worked** it:
and his hands formed the dry *land*.
6 O come, let us *worship*
prostrate and *bow down* **kneel**:
let us kneel *before the LORD* **at the face of Yah Veh**
our *maker* **Worker**.
7 For he is our *God* **Elohim**;
and we are the people of his pasture,
and the *sheep* **flock** of his hand.
To day if ye *will* **shall** hear his voice,
8 Harden not your heart, as
in the *provocation* **strife**,
and as in the day of *temptation* **testing** in the wilderness:
9 When your fathers *tempted* **tested** me,
proved **proofed** me, and saw my *work* **deeds**.
10 Forty years long
was I grieved with **loathed I** this generation, and said,
It is a people that *do err* **stray** in their heart,
and they have not known my ways:
11 Unto whom I *sware* **oathed** in my wrath
that they should not enter into my rest.

96 O sing unto *the LORD* **Yah Veh** a new song:
sing unto *the LORD* **Yah Veh**, all the earth.
2 Sing unto *the LORD* **Yah Veh**, bless his name;
shew forth **evangelize** his salvation from day to day.
3 *Declare* **Scribe** his *glory* **honour**
among the *heathen* **goyim**,
his *wonders* **marvels** among all people.
4 For *the LORD* **Yah Veh** is great,
and *greatly* **mightily** to be praised:
he is *to be feared* **awesome** above all *gods* **elohim**.
5 For all the *gods* **elohim** of
the *nations* **people** are idols:
but *the LORD made* **Yah Veh worked** the heavens.
6 Honour and majesty are *before him* **at his face** :
strength and beauty are in his
sanctuary **hallowed refuge**.
7 Give unto *the LORD* **Yah Veh**,
O ye *kindreds* **families** of the people,
give unto *the LORD* **Yah Veh**
glory **honour** and strength.
8 Give unto *the LORD* **Yah Veh**
the *glory due unto* **honour of** his name:
bring **lift** an offering, and come into his courts.
9 O *worship the LORD* **prostrate to Yah Veh** in
the *beauty* **majesty** of *holiness* **his holies**: *fear
before him* **writhe at his face**, all the earth.
10 Say among the *heathen* **goyim,**
that the LORD **Yah Veh** reigneth:
the world also shall be established

that it shall not *be moved* **totter**:
he shall *judge* **plead the cause of** the people
righteously **in straightnesses**.
11 Let the heavens *rejoice* **cheer**,
and let the earth *be glad* **twirl**;
let the sea *roar* **thunder**, and the fulness *thereof*.
12 Let the field *be joyful* **jump for joy**,
and all that is therein:
then shall all the trees of the *wood rejoice* **forest shout**.
13 *Before the LORD* **At the face of Yah Veh**:
for he cometh, for he cometh to judge the earth:
he shall judge the world with *righteousness* **justness**,
and the people with his *truth* **trustworthiness**.

97 *The LORD* **Yah Veh** reigneth;
let the earth *rejoice* **twirl**;
let the *multitude of isles* **great islands**
be glad thereof **cheer**.
2 Clouds and **dripping** darkness
are round about him:
righteousness **justness** and judgment
are the *habitation* **establishment** of his throne.
3 A fire goeth *before* **at the face of** him,
and *burneth up* **inflameth** his *enemies* **tribulators**
round about.
4 His lightnings enlightened the world:
the earth saw, and *trembled* **writhed**.

3 For Yah Veh *is* a great El
and a great Sovereign above all elohim.
4 In his hand are the innermost
depths of the earth;
the strengths of the mountains *are* his;
5 the sea is his—he worked it;
and his hands formed the dry.
6 O come, we prostrate and kneel
—kneel at the face of Yah Veh our Worker;
7 for he *is* our Elohim
and we *are* the people of his pasture
—the flock of his hand.
Today if you hear his voice,
8 harden not your heart as in the strife
and as in the day of testing in the wilderness:
9 when your fathers tested me
—proofed me and saw my deeds.
10 Forty long years
I loathed this generation and said,
A people who stray in their heart;
who know not my ways:
11 whom I oathed in my wrath
that they not enter to my rest.

96 O sing to Yah Veh a new song;
sing to Yah Veh, all the earth;
2 sing to Yah Veh, bless his name;
evangelize his salvation from day today:
3 scribe his honor among the goyim
—his marvels among all people:
4 for Yah Veh is great and mightily praised
—awesome above all elohim.
5 For all the elohim of the people *are* idols;
and Yah Veh worked the heavens:
6 Honor and majesty *are* at his face;
strength and beauty *are* in his hallowed refuge.
7 Give to Yah Veh, O you families of the people;
give to Yah Veh honor and strength;
8 give to Yah Veh the honor of his name;
lift an offering and come into his courts.
9 O prostrate to Yah Veh in
the majesty of his holies;
writhe at his face, all the earth.
10 Say among the goyim, Yah Veh reigns!
The world *is* established; it totters not:
he pleads the cause of the people in straightnesses.
11 Cheer, O heavens;
twirl, O earth;
thunder, O sea and its fulness;
12 jump for joy, O field and all therein;
shout, all trees of the forest
13 at the face of Yah Veh:
for he comes—for he comes to judge the earth
—to judge the world in justness
and the people in his trustworthiness.

97 Yah Veh reigns;
twirl, O earth;
cheer, O great islands.
2 Clouds and dripping darkness surround him;
justness and judgment establish his throne.
3 A fire comes from his face
and inflames all around his tribulators:
4 his lightnings light the world;
the earth sees and writhes:
5 The *hills* **mountains** melted like wax
at the *presence* **face** of *the LORD* **Yah Veh**,
at the *presence* **face**
of *the Lord* **Adonay** of the whole earth.
6 The heavens *declare* **tell**
his *righteousness* **justness**,
and all the people see his *glory* **honour**.
7 *Confounded* **Shamed** be all they
that serve *graven images* **sculptiles**,
that *boast* **halal** themselves of idols:
worship **prostrate to** him, all ye *gods* **elohim**.
8 *Zion* **Siyon** heard, and *was glad* **cheered**;

and the daughters of *Judah rejoiced* **Yah Hudah twirled**
because of thy judgments, O *LORD* **Yah Veh.**
9 For thou, *LORD* **O Yah Veh,**
art *high* **Elyon** above all the earth:
thou art *exalted far* **ascended mightily**
above all *gods* **elohim.**
10 Ye that love *the LORD* **Yah Veh,** hate evil:
he *preserveth* **guardeth** the souls of his *saints* **mercied;**
he *delivereth* **rescueth** them
out of the hand of the wicked.
11 Light is *sown* **seeded** for the *righteous* **just,**
and *gladness* **cheerfulness** for the
upright **straight** in heart.
12 *Rejoice in the LORD* **Cheer in Yah Veh,**
ye *righteous* **just;**
and *give thanks* **spread hands**
at the remembrance of his holiness.

98 A Psalm.
1 O sing unto *the LORD* **Yah Veh** a new song;
for he hath *done marvellous things* **worked marvels:**
his right *hand*, and his holy arm,
hath gotten him the victory **saveth.**
2 *The LORD* **Yah Veh** hath
made known his salvation:
his *righteousness* **justness** hath he
openly shewed **exposed**
in the *sight* **eyes** of the *heathen* **goyim.**
3 He hath remembered his mercy
and his *truth* **trustworthiness**
toward the house of *Israel* **Yisra El:**
all the *ends* **finalities** of the earth
have seen the salvation of our *God* **Elohim.**
4 *Make a joyful noise* **Shout**
unto *the LORD* **Yah Veh,**
all the earth:
make a loud noise **break forth,**
and *rejoice* **shout,** and *sing praise* **psalm.**
5 *Sing* **Psalm** unto *the LORD*
Yah Veh with the harp;
with the harp, and the voice of a psalm.
6 With trumpets and *sound*
voice of *cornet* **shophar**
make a joyful noise **shout**
before the LORD **at the face of Yah Veh,**
the *King* **Sovereign.**
7 Let the sea *roar* **thunder,**
and the fulness *thereof*;
the world, and they that *dwell* **settle** *therein.*
8 Let the *floods* **rivers** clap their *hands* **palms:**
let the *hills be joyful* **mountains shout** together
9 *Before the LORD* **At the face of Yah Veh;**
for he cometh to judge the earth:
with *righteousness* **justness** shall he judge the world,
and the people *with equity* **in straightnesses.**

99 *The LORD* **Yah Veh** reigneth;
let the people *tremble* **quiver:**
he *sitteth* **settleth**
between the cherubims **on the cherubim;**
let the earth *be moved* **quake.**
2 *The LORD* **Yah Veh** is great in *Zion* **Siyon;**
and he is high above all the people.
3 Let them *praise* **spread hands**
unto thy great and *terrible* **awesome** name; *for* it is holy.
4 The *king's* **sovereign's**
strength also loveth judgment;
thou *dost establish equity* **establishest**
straightnesses, thou *executest* **workest** judgment
and *righteousness* **justness** in *Jacob* **Yaaqov.**
5 Exalt ye *the LORD* **Yah Veh** our *God* **Elohim,**
and *worship* **prostrate** at *his footstool*
the stool of his feet;
for he is holy.
5 the mountains melt as
wax at the face of Yah Veh
—at the face of Adonay of the whole earth:
6 the heavens tell his justness
and all the people see his honor.
7 Shamed are all they who serve sculptiles
—who halal themselves with idols:
prostrate to him, all you elohim.
8 Siyon hears and cheers
and the daughters of Yah Hudah twirl
because of your judgments, O Yah Veh.
9 For you, O Yah Veh,
are Elyon over all the earth:
you ascend mightily over all elohim.
10 You who love Yah Veh, hate evil;
he guards the souls of his mercied;
he rescues them from the hand of the wicked.
11 Light *is* seeded for the just
and cheerfulness for the straight in heart:
12 Cheer in Yah Veh, you just;
and spread hands
at the remembrance of his holiness.

98 A Psalm.
1 O sing to Yah Veh a new song;
for he works marvels:
his right and his holy arm saves.
2 Yah Veh makes known his salvation
—exposes his justness in the eyes of the goyim:

3 he remembers his mercy
and his trustworthiness toward the house of Yisra El;
all the finalities of the earth
see the salvation of our Elohim.
4 Shout to Yah Veh, all the earth;
break forth, and shout and psalm:
5 psalm to Yah Veh with the harp
—with the harp and the voice of a psalm:
6 with trumpets and voice of shophar
shout at the face of Yah Veh the Sovereign.
7 The sea thunders and its fulness;
the world and they who settle therein:
8 the rivers clap their palms;
the mountains shout together
9 at the face of Yah Veh:
for he comes to judge the earth;
with justness he judges the world
and the people in straightnesses.

99 Yah Veh reigns; the people quiver:
he settles on the cherubim; the earth quakes.
2 Yah Veh is great in Siyon
—high above all the people.
3 They spread hands
to your great and awesome name
—it is holy.
4 And the strength of the
sovereign loves judgment;
you establish straightnesses,
you work judgment and justness in Yaaqov.
5 Exalt Yah Veh our Elohim;
prostrate at the stool of his feet;
—he is holy.
6 *Moses* **Mosheh** and *Aaron* **Aharon**
among his priests,
and *Samuel* **Shemu El**
among them that call upon his name;
they called upon *the LORD* **Yah Veh**,
and he answered them.
7 He *spake* **worded** unto them
in the *cloudy* pillar **of cloud**:
they *kept* **guarded** his *testimonies* **witnesses**,
and the *ordinance* **statute** that he gave them.
8 Thou answeredst them,
O *LORD* **Yah Veh** our *God* **Elohim**:
thou wast *a God* **an El** that *forgavest* **bore** them,
though thou
tookest vengeance of **avenged** their *inventions* **exploits**.
9 Exalt *the LORD* **Yah Veh** our *God* **Elohim**,
and *worship* **prostrate** at his holy *hill* **mountain**;
for *the LORD* **Yah Veh** our *God* **Elohim** is holy.

100 A Psalm of *praise* **spread hands**.
1 *Make a joyful noise* **Shout**
unto *the LORD* **Yah Veh**,
all ye *lands* **earth**.
2 Serve *the LORD* **Yah Veh**
with *gladness* **cheerfulness**:
come *before* **at** his *presence* **face** with *singing* **shouting**.
3 Know ye that *the LORD*
Yah Veh he is *God* **Elohim**:
it is he that hath made **he hath worked** us,
and not we ourselves;
we are his people, and the *sheep* **flock** of his pasture.
4 Enter into his *gates* **portals**
with *thanksgiving* **spread hands**,
and into his courts with *praise* **halal**:
be thankful **spread hands** unto him, *and* bless his name.
5 For *the LORD* **Yah Veh** is good;
his mercy is *everlasting* **eternal**;
and his *truth* **trustworthiness**
endureth to all generations **generation to generation**.

101 A Psalm of David.
1 I *will* **shall** sing of mercy and judgment:
unto thee, O *LORD* **Yah Veh**, *will I sing* **shall I psalm**.
2 I *will behave myself wisely* **shall discern**
in *a perfect* **an integrious** way.
O when *wilt* **shalt** thou come unto me?
I *will* **shall** walk within my house *with*
a perfect **in integrity of** heart.
3 *I will* **shall** set no *wicked thing* **word of Beli Yaal**
before **in front of** mine eyes:
I hate the work of *them that turn aside* **swervers**;
it shall not *cleave* **adhere** to me.
4 A *froward* **perverted** heart
shall *depart* **turn aside** from me:
I *will* **shall** not know *a wicked person* **evil**.
5 Whoso *privily slandereth*
covertly tongue—lasheth
his *neighbour* **friend**,
him *will I cut off* **shall I exterminate**:
him that hath an high look **a lofty eye**
and *a proud* **an enlarged** heart,
will not I suffer **I am not able**.
6 Mine eyes
shall be upon the *faithful* **trustworthy** of the land,
that they may *dwell* **settle** with me:
he that walketh in *a perfect* **an integrious** way,
he shall *serve* **minister to** me.
7 He that worketh deceit
shall not *dwell* **settle** within my house:
he that *telleth lies* **wordeth falsehoods**

shall not *tarry in my sight* **be established in my eyes.**
8 *I will early destroy* **Mornings**
I shall exterminate
all the wicked of the land;
that I may cut off all *wicked doers* **the mischievous**
from the city of *the LORD* **Yah Veh.**
6 Mosheh and Aharon among his priests
and Shemu El among them who call on his name;
they called on Yah Veh and he answered them:
7 he worded to them in the pillar of cloud;
they guarded his witnesses and the statute he gave them.
8 You answered them, O Yah Veh our Elohim
—you are an El who spared them, though
you avenged their exploits.
9 Exalt Yah Veh our Elohim
and prostrate at his holy mountain;
for Yah Veh our Elohim *is* holy.

100 A Psalm of Spread Hands.
1 Shout to Yah Veh, all the earth;
2 serve Yah Veh with cheerfulness;
come at his face with shouting:
3 know that Yah Veh—he *is* Elohim;
he worked us, and not we ourselves;—his
people and the flock of his pasture.
4 Enter his portals with spread hands
and into his courts with halal:
spread hands to him; bless his name.
5 For Yah Veh is good; his mercy eternal:
and his trustworthiness generation to generation.

101 A Psalm by David.
1 I sing of mercy and judgment;
to you, O Yah Veh, I psalm:
2 I discern in an integrious way.
O when come you to me?
I walk within my house in integrity of heart;
3 I set no word of Beli Yaal in front of my eyes;
I hate the work of swervers;
it adheres not to me.
4 The perverted heart turns aside from me;
I know not evil:
5 whoever covertly tongue—lashes his friend,
I exterminate:
a lofty eye and an enlarged heart, I am not able.
6 My eyes are on the trustworthy of the land
to settle with me;
he who walks in an integrious way
ministers to me;
7 he who works deceit
settles not within my house;
he who words falsehoods
is not established in my eyes.
8 Mornings I exterminate
all the wicked of the land;
to cut off all mischievous from the city of Yah Veh.

102 A Prayer of the *afflicted* **humble,**
when he *is overwhelmed* **languisheth,**
and poureth out his *complaint* **meditation**
before the LORD **at the face of Yah Veh.**
1 Hear my prayer, O *LORD* **Yah Veh,**
and let my cry come unto thee.
2 Hide not thy face from me
in the day *when* I am in *trouble* **tribulation;**
incline **spread** thine ear unto me:
in the day *when* I call answer me *speedily* **hastily.**
3 For my days are *consumed*
finished off like smoke,
and my bones are *burned* **scorched**
as *an hearth* **a burning.**
4 My heart is smitten, and
withered like *grass* **herbage;**
so that I forget to eat my bread.
5 By reason of the voice of my *groaning* **sighing**
my bones *cleave* **adhere** to my *skin* **flesh.**
6 I am like a pelican of the wilderness:
I am *like* **likened to** an owl of the *desert* **parched areas.**
7 I watch,
and am as a *sparrow* **bird** alone upon the *house top* **roof.**
8 Mine enemies reproach me all the day;
and they that *are mad against* **halaled** me
are sworn **have oathed** against me.
9 For I have eaten ashes like bread,
and *mingled* **mixed** my drink with weeping.
10 *Because* **At the face** of thine indignation
and thy *wrath* **rage:**
for thou hast lifted me up, and cast me down.
11 My days are like a shadow
that *declineth* **spreadeth;**
and I am withered like *grass* **herbage.**
12 But thou, O *LORD* **Yah Veh,**
shall *endure for ever* **settle eternal;**
and thy *remembrance* **memorial**
unto all generations **generation to generation.**
13 Thou shalt arise,
and *have* **shall** mercy *upon Zion* **Siyon:**
for the time to *favour* **grant** her **charism,**
yea, the *set time* **season,** is come.
14 For thy servants
take pleasure **are pleased** in her stones,
and *favour* **grant charism unto** the dust *thereof.*
15 So the *heathen* **goyim**

shall *fear* **awe** the name of *the LORD* **Yah Veh**,
and all the *kings* **sovereigns** of the
earth thy *glory* **honour**.
16 When *the LORD* **Yah Veh**
shall build *up Zion* **Siyon**,
he shall *appear* **be seen** in his *glory* **honour**.
17 He *will regard* **shall face** the prayer
of the *destitute* **naked**,
and not despise their prayer.
18 This shall be *written* **inscribed**
for the generation *to come* **after**:
and the people which shall be created
shall *praise the LORD* **halal Yah**.
19 For he hath *looked down* **seen**
from the height of his *sanctuary* **holies**;
from *heaven* **the heavens**
did the LORD behold **Yah Veh scanned** the earth;
20 To hear the *groaning* **shrieking**
of the *prisoner* **bound**;
to loose *those that are appointed to* **the sons of** death;
21 To *declare* **scribe**
the name of *the LORD* **Yah Veh** in *Zion* **Siyon**,
and his *praise* **halal** in *Jerusalem* **Yeru Shalem**;
22 When the people are gathered *together*,
and the *kingdoms* **sovereigndoms**,
to serve *the LORD* **Yah Veh**.
23 He *weakened* **humbled** my
strength **force** in the way;
he *shortened* **curtailed** my days.
24 I said, O my *God* **El**,
take **ascend** me not *away* in the midst of my days:
thy years are
throughout all generations **generation to generation**.
25 *Of old* **At thy face**
hast thou *laid the foundation of* **founded** the earth:
and the heavens are the work of thy hands.

102 A Prayer of the humble when he languishes
and pours out his meditation at the face of Yah Veh.
1 Hear my prayer, O Yah Veh
so that my cry comes to you.
2 Hide not your face from me
in the day of my tribulation;
spread your ear to me;
in the day I call, hasten—answer me.
3 For my days finish off as smoke
and my bones scorch as a burning:
4 my heart is smitten and withers as herbage;
so that I forget to eat my bread:
5 by reason of the voice of my sighing
my bones adhere to my flesh:
6 I am likened to a pelican of the wilderness
—as an owl of the parched areas.
7 I watch; and I am as a bird alone on the roof:
8 my enemies reproach me all the day
and they who halal me oath against me.
9 For I eat ashes as bread
and mix my drink with weeping
10 at the face of your indignation and your rage:
for you lift me up and cast me down:
11 my days spread as a shadow;
and I wither as herbage.
12 And you, O Yah Veh, settle eternal;
and your memorial generation to generation:
13 You—you rise; you mercy Siyon;
for the time to grant her charism
—yes, the season has come.
14 For your servants are pleased in her stones
and grant charism to the dust.
15 And the goyim awe the name of Yah Veh
and all the sovereigns of the earth your honor.
16 Yah Veh built Siyon; he appears in his honor:
17 he faces the prayer of the naked
and despises not their prayer:
18 inscribe this for the generation after;
and the people to be created, to halal Yah.
19 For he sees from the height of his holies:
from the heavens Yah Veh scans the earth
20 —to hear the shrieking of the bound;
to loose the sons of death;
21 to scribe the name of Yah Veh in Siyon
and his halal in Yeru Shalem;
22 in the gathering of the people
and the sovereigndoms to serve Yah Veh.
23 He humbles my force in the way;
he curtails my days.
24 I say, O my El,
ascend me not midst my days;
your years are generation to generation.
25 At your face you founded the earth;
and the heavens are the work of your hands:
26 They shall *perish* **destruct**,
but thou shalt *endure* **stand**:
yea, all of them shall *wax old* **wear out**
like *a garment* **clothes**;
as a *vesture* **robe** shalt thou change them,
and they shall be changed:
27 But thou art the same,
and thy years shall *have no end* **not consummate**.
28 The *children* **sons** of thy servants
shall *continue* **tabernacle**,
and their seed shall be established
before thee **at thy face**.

103 *A Psalm* of David.
1 Bless *the LORD* **Yah Veh,** O my soul:
and all that is within me, *bless* his holy name.
2 Bless *the LORD* **Yah Veh,** O my soul,
and forget not all his *benefits* **dealings**:
3 Who forgiveth all *thine*
iniquities **thy perversities**;
who healeth all thy *diseases* **sicknesses**;
4 Who redeemeth thy life from
destruction **the pit of ruin**;
who crowneth thee with *lovingkindness* **mercy**
and tender mercies;
5 Who satisfieth thy mouth with good *things*;
so that thy youth is renewed like the eagle's.
6 *The LORD executeth* **Yah Veh worketh**
righteousness **justness** and judgment
for all that are oppressed.
7 He made known his ways unto *Moses* **Mosheh**,
his *acts* **exploits** unto the *children* **sons** of *Israel* **Yisra El.**
8 *The LORD* **Yah Veh** is merciful
and *gracious* **charismatic**,
slow to *anger* **wrath**, and *plenteous* **abundant** in mercy.
9 He *will* **shall** not *always*
chide **contend in perpetuity**:
neither *will* **shall** he *keep his anger* **guard**
for ever **eternally**.
10 He hath not *dealt* **worked** with us
after our sins;
nor *rewarded* **dealt with** us
according to our *iniquities* **perversities**.
11 For as the *heaven* **heavens**
is high **be lofted** above the earth,
so great is **thus prevaileth mightily** his mercy
toward them that *fear* **awe** him.
12 As far as the *east* **rising** is from the *west* **dusk**,
so far hath he removed
our *transgressions* **rebellions** from us.
13 Like as a father *pitieth*
mercieth his *children* **sons**,
so the LORD **thus Yah Veh**
pitieth **mercieth** them that *fear* **awe** him.
14 For he knoweth our *frame* **form**;
he remembereth that we are dust.
15 *As for*—man, his days are as grass: as a *flower*
blossom of the field, so he *flourisheth* **blossometh**.
16 For the wind passeth over it, and it is gone;
and the place *thereof* shall *know* **recognize** it no more.
17 But the mercy of *the LORD* **Yah Veh**
is from *everlasting* **eternity** to *everlasting* **eternity**
upon them that *fear* **awe** him,
and his *righteousness* **justness**
unto *children's children* **sons' sons**;
18 To such as *keep* **guard** his covenant,
and to those that remember his *commandments* **precepts**
to *do* **work** them.
19 *The LORD* **Yah Veh**
hath prepared his throne in the heavens;
and his *kingdom ruleth* **sovereigndom reigneth** over all.
20 Bless *the LORD* **Yah Veh**, ye his angels,
that excel **mighty** in *strength* **force**,
that *do* **work** his *commandments* **words**,
hearkening unto the voice of his word.
21 Bless ye *the LORD* **Yah Veh**, all *ye* his hosts;
ye ministers of his, that *do* **work** his pleasure.
22 Bless *the LORD* **Yah Veh,**
all his works in all places of his *dominion* **reign**:
bless *the LORD* **Yah Veh**, O my soul.
26 they—they destruct, and you stand;
yes, they all wear out as clothes;
as a robe you change them
and changed they are;
27 and you are the same
and your years consummate not.
28 The sons of your servants tabernacle
and their seed establishes at your face.

103 By David.
1 Bless Yah Veh, O my soul,
and all that is within me—his holy name:
2 bless Yah Veh, O my soul
and forget not all his dealings
3 —who forgives all your perversities;
who heals all your sicknesses;
4 who redeems your life from the pit of ruin;
who crowns you with mercy and tender mercies;
5 who satisfies your mouth with good;
—renews your youth as the eagle.
6 Yah Veh works justness and judgment
for all the oppressed;
7 he made his ways known to Mosheh;
his exploits to the sons of Yisra El:
8 Yah Veh is merciful and charismatic;
slow to wrath and abundant in mercy.
9 He neither contends in perpetuity
nor guards eternally:
10 he neither works with us after our sins
nor deals with us according to our perversities.
11 For as the heavens loft above the earth,
thus his mercy prevails mightily
toward them who awe him:
12 as far as the rising from the dusk,

thus far he removes our rebellions from us:
13 as a father mercies his sons
thus Yah Veh mercies them who awe him.
14 For he knows our form;
he remembers that we are dust.
15 Man—his days *are* as grass
—as a blossom of the field, thus he blossoms.
16 For the wind overpasses and is not;
and recognizes the place no more:
17 and the mercy of Yah Veh
from eternity to eternity on them who awe him:
and his justness to sons of sons
18 —to them who guard his covenant
and to them who remember his precepts
to work them.
19 Yah Veh prepared his throne in the heavens;
and his sovereigndom reigns over all.
20 Bless Yah Veh, you his angels,
mighty in force, who work his words,
to hearken to the voice of his word:
21 bless Yah Veh, all you his hosts;
you ministers of his, who work his pleasure:
22 bless Yah Veh,
all his works in all places of his reign;
bless Yah Veh, O my soul.

104 Bless *the LORD* **Yah Veh**, O my soul.
O *LORD* **Yah Veh** my *God* **Elohim**,
thou art *very great* **greatened mightily**;
thou art *clothed* **enrobed** with honour and majesty.
2 Who coverest *thyself* with
light as with a *garment* **cloth**:
who *stretchest out* **spreadest** the heavens like a curtain:
3 Who *layeth* **felleth** the beams
of his *chambers* **upper room** in the waters:
who *maketh the* **setteth thick** clouds his chariot:
who walketh upon the wings of the wind:
4 Who *maketh* **worketh** his angels spirits;
his ministers a flaming fire:
5 Who *laid* **founded**
the *foundations* **establishments** of the earth,
that *it* **they** should not *be removed* **totter**
for ever **eternally and eternally**.

*see Hebrews 1:7—14

6 Thou coveredst it with the *deep* **abyss**
as *with a garment* **a robe**:
the waters stood above the mountains.
7 *At* **From** thy rebuke they fled;
at **from** the voice of thy thunder they hasted away.
8 They *go up* **ascend** by the mountains;
they *go down* **descend** by the valleys
unto the place which thou hast founded for them.
9 Thou hast set a *bound* **border**
that they may not pass over;
that they turn not again to cover the earth.
10 He sendeth the springs into the *valleys* **wadies**,
which *run* **pass** among the *hills* **mountains**.
11 They give drink to every
beast **live being** of the field:
the wild *asses quench* **runners break** their thirst.
12 By them shall the *fowls*
flyers of the *heaven* **heavens**
have their habitation **tabernacle**,
which *sing among* **give voice between** the branches.
13 He *watereth* **moisteneth** the *hills* **mountains**
from his *chambers* **upper room**:
the earth is satisfied with the fruit of thy works.
14 He causeth the grass to *grow* **sprout**
for the *cattle* **animals**,
and herb for the service of *man* **humanity**:
that he may bring forth *food* **bread** out of the earth;
15 And wine that *maketh glad*
cheereth the heart of man,
and *oil* **ointment** to make his face to shine,
and bread which *strengtheneth* **supporteth** man's heart.
16 The trees of *the LORD* **Yah**
Veh are *full of sap* **satiated**;
the cedars of Lebanon, which he hath planted;
17 Where the birds *make their nests* **nest**:
as for the stork, the *fir trees* **firs** are her house.
18 The high *hills* **mountains**
are a refuge for the wild goats;
and the rocks for the conies.
19 He *appointed* **worked** the moon for seasons:
the sun knoweth his *going down* **entry**.
20 Thou *makest* **settest** darkness, and it is night:
wherein
all the *beasts* **live beings** of the forest *do* creep *forth*.
21 The *young lions* **whelps** roar after their prey,
and seek their *meat* **food** from *God* **El**.
22 The sun ariseth, they gather themselves *together*,
and *lay them down* **crouch** in their *dens* **habitations**.
23 *Man* **Humanity** goeth forth unto his *work* **deeds**
and to his *labour* **service** until the evening.
24 O *LORD* **Yah Veh**,
how *manifold are* thy works **abound by the myriads**!
in wisdom hast thou *made* **worked** them all:
the earth is full of thy *riches* **chattel**.
25 So is this great and *wide* **broad hand of the** sea,

wherein are *things creeping* **creepers** innumerable,
both small and great *beasts* **live beings**.
26 There go the ships:
there is that leviathan,
whom thou hast *made* **formed** to *play* **laugh** *therein*.
27 These *wait* **expect** all upon thee;
that thou mayest give them their *meat* **food**
in due season **on time**.
28 That thou givest them, they *gather* **gleen**:
thou openest thine hand, they are
filled **satiated** with good.

104 Bless Yah Veh, O my soul!
O Yah Veh, my Elohim,
you are mightily greatened;
—enrobed with honor and majesty:
2 who covers himself with light as a cloth;
who spreads the heavens as a curtain;
3 who fells the beams
of his upper room in the waters;
who sets thick clouds his chariot;
who walks on the wings of the wind;
4 who works his angels spirits
—his ministers a flaming fire*;
5 who founded the establishments of the earth
that they not totter eternally and eternally.

*see Hebrews 1:7—14

6 You covered the abyss as a robe;
the waters stand above the mountains;
7 from your rebuke they flee;
from the voice of your thunder they hasten away:
8 they ascend by the mountains;
they descend by the valleys
to the place you founded for them.
9 You set a border
that they neither pass over
nor turn again to cover the earth:
10 —who sends the springs into the wadies
passing among the mountains:
11 they moisten every live being of the field;
the wild runners break their thirst:
12 by them the flyers of the heavens tabernacle,
who give voice between the branches:
13 he moistens the mountains
from his upper room;
the earth satiates with the fruit of your works
14 so that the grass sprouts for the animals
and herbs for the service of humanity; to
bring forth bread from the earth:
15 and wine to cheer the heart of man
and ointment to shine his face and bread
to support the heart of man.
16 The trees of Yah Veh satiate
—the cedars of Lebanon he planted
17 —where the birds nest:
as for the stork, the firs *are* her house;
18 the high mountains, a refuge for the wild goats
and the rocks for the conies.
19 He worked the moon for seasons;
the sun knows his entry.
20 You set darkness and it is night;
wherein all the live beings of the forest creep:
21 the whelps roar after their prey
and seek their food from El:
22 the sun rises; they gather themselves;
they crouch in their habitations:
23 humanity goes on to his deeds and to his service
until the evening.
24 O Yah Veh,
how your works abound by the myriads!
In wisdom you worked them all;
the earth is full of your chattel:
25 thus this great and wide hand of the sea
wherein are creepers innumerable
—both small and great live beings:
26 there go the ships;
leviathan, whom you have formed to laugh.
27 These all expect you
to give them their food on time:
28 You give them, they gleen:
you open your hand, they satiate with good:
29 Thou hidest thy face, they are *troubled* **terrified**:
thou *takest away* **gatherest** their *breath* **spirit**,
they *die* **expire**, and return to their dust.
30 Thou sendest forth thy spirit, they are created:
and thou renewest the face of the *earth* **soil**.
31 The *glory* **honour** of *the LORD* **Yah Veh**
shall *endure for ever* **be eternal**:
the LORD **Yah Veh** shall *rejoice* **cheer** in his works.
32 He looketh on the earth, and it trembleth:
he toucheth the *hills* **mountains**, and they smoke.
33 I *will* **shall** sing unto *the LORD* **Yah Veh**
as long as I live **during my life**:
I *will sing praise* **shall psalm** to my *God* **Elohim**
while I *have my being* **still be**.
34 My meditation of him shall *be sweet* **please**:
I *will be glad* **shall cheer** in *the LORD* **Yah Veh**.
35 Let the sinners be consumed out of the earth,
and let the wicked be no more.
Bless thou *the LORD* **Yah Veh**, O my soul.
Praise ye the LORD **Halalu Yah**.

105 O *give thanks* **spread hands**
unto *the LORD* **Yah Veh**;
call upon his name:
make known his *deeds* **exploits** among the people.
2 Sing unto him, *sing psalms* **psalm** unto him:
talk **meditate** ye of all his *wondrous works* **marvels**.
3 *Glory* **Halal** ye in his holy name:
let the heart of them *rejoice* **cheer**
that seek *the LORD* **Yah Veh**.
4 Seek *the LORD* **Yah Veh**, and his strength:
seek his face *evermore* **continually**.
5 Remember his *marvellous works* **marvels**
that he hath *done* **worked**;
his *wonders* **omens**, and the judgments of his mouth;
6 O ye seed of Abraham his servant,
ye *children* **sons** of *Jacob* **Yaaqov** his chosen.
7 He is *the LORD* **Yah Veh** our *God* **Elohim**:
his judgments are in all the earth.
8 He hath remembered his
covenant *for ever* **eternally**,
the word which he *commanded* **misvahed**
to a thousand generations.
9 Which *covenant he made* **he cut** with Abraham,
and his oath unto *Isaac* **Yischaq**;
10 And *confirmed* **stood** the same
unto *Jacob* **Yaaqov** for a *law* **statute**,
and to *Israel* **Yisra El** for an *everlasting* **eternal** covenant:
11 Saying,
Unto thee *will* **shall** I give the land of *Canaan* **Kenaan**,
the *lot* **cord** of your inheritance:
12 When they were *but a* few *men* in number;
yea, very few, and *strangers* **sojourned** in it.
13 When they went from one
nation **goyim** to another,
from *one kingdom* **sovereigndom** to another people;
14 He *suffered* **allowed** no *man* **human**
to *do them* wrong **them**:
yea, he reproved *kings* **sovereigns** for their sakes;
15 *Saying*, Touch not mine anointed,
and *do* **vilify not** my prophets *no harm*.
16 *Moreover* he called for a famine upon the land:
he brake the whole *staff* **rod** of bread.
17 He sent a man *before them* **at their face**,
even Joseph **Yoseph**, who was sold for a servant:
18 Whose feet they *hurt* **humbled** with fetters:
he **his soul** was laid in iron:
19 Until the time that his word came:
the *word* **saying** of *the LORD tried* **Yah Veh refined** him.
20 The *king* **sovereign** sent and loosed him;
even the *ruler* **sovereign** of the people,
and *let him go free* **loosed him**.
21 He *made* **set** him *lord* **adoni** of his house,
and *ruler* **sovereign** of all his *substance* **chattel**:
22 To bind his *princes* **governors**
at his *pleasure* **soul**;
and *teach* **enwisen** his *senators wisdom* **elders**.
23 *Israel* **Yisra El** also came into *Egypt* **Misrayim**;
and *Jacob* **Yaaqov** sojourned in the land of Ham.
24 And *he increased* his people
greatly **became mighty fruitbearing**;
and *made them stronger* **mightier**
than their *enemies* **tribulators**.
29 you hide your face, they terrify:
you gather their spirit, they expire
—return to their dust:
30 you send your spirit, they are created:
and you renew the face of the soil.
31 The honor of Yah Veh is eternal.
Yah Veh cheers in his works.
32 He looks on the earth and it trembles;
he touches the mountains and they smoke.
33 I sing to Yah Veh during my life;
I psalm to my Elohim while I still am:
34 pleasing is my meditation of him;
I cheer in Yah Veh.
35 The sinners are consumed from the earth
and the wicked are no more.
Bless you Yah Veh, O my soul.
Halalu Yah.

105 O spread hands to Yah Veh;
call on his name;
make known his exploits among the people:
2 sing to him; psalm to him;
meditate of all his marvels:
3 halal in his holy name;
the heart of them who seek Yah Veh cheers.
4 Seek Yah Veh and his strength;
seek his face continually:
5 remember the marvels he worked
—his omens and the judgments of his mouth
6 O you seed of Abraham his servant,
you sons of Yaaqov his chosen.
7 He—Yah Veh our Elohim;
his judgments *are* in all the earth:
8 he remembers his covenant eternally
—the word he misvahed to a thousand generations
9 —which he cut with Abraham
and his oath to Yischaq:
10 and stood the same to Yaaqov for a statute

and to Yisra El for an eternal covenant:
11 saying,
I give you the land of Kenaan
the cord of your inheritance
12 —when they were few in number
—yes, very few and sojourned therein:
13 and they went from one goyim to another
from sovereigndom to another people:
14 he allowed no human to wrong them;
yes, he reproved sovereigns for their sakes;
15 *saying,*
Neither touch not my anointed
nor vilify my prophets!
16 He called for a famine on the land;
he broke the whole rod of bread;
17 he sent a man at their face
—Yoseph, who was sold for a servant
18 whose feet they humbled with fetters
—laid his soul in iron.
19 Until the time his word arrived
the saying of Yah Veh refined him;
20 the sovereign sent and loosed him
—the sovereign of the people, and loosed him;
21 he set him adoni of his house
and sovereign of all his chattel;
22 to bind his governors at his soul;
and enwisen his elders.
23 Yisra El also came to Misrayim;
and Yaaqov sojourned in the land of Ham;
24 and his people became mighty fruitbearing
—mightier than their tribulators:
25 He turned their heart to hate his people,
to *deal subtilly with* **deceive** his servants.
26 He sent *Moses* **Mosheh** his servant;
and *Aaron* **Aharon** whom he had chosen.
27 They *shewed* **set words of**
his signs among them,
and *wonders* **omens** in the land of Ham.
28 He sent darkness, and *made it dark* **it darkened**;
and they rebelled not against his word.
29 He turned their waters into blood,
and *slew* **deathified** their fish.
30 Their land
brought forth **teemed with** frogs *in abundance*,
in the chambers of their *kings* **sovereigns**.
31 He *spake* **said,**
and there came *divers sorts of flies* **swarms**,
and *lice* **stingers** in all their *coasts* **borders**.
32 He gave them hail for *rain* **downpour**,
and flaming fire in their land.
33 He smote their vines also and their fig trees;
and brake the trees of their *coasts* **borders**.
34 He *spake* **said,**
and the locusts came, and *caterpillers* **cankerworms**,
and that without number—**inummerable**,
35 And did eat up all the herbs in their land,
and devoured the fruit of their *ground* **soil**.
36 He smote also all the *firstborn*
firstbirthed in their land,
the *chief* **firstfruits** of all their strength.
37 He brought them forth also with silver and gold:
and *there was* not one *feeble person*
faltered among their *tribes* **scions**.
38 *Egypt was glad* **Misrayim**
cheered when they departed:
for the *fear* **dread** of them fell upon them.
39 He spread a cloud for a covering;
and fire to *give light* **lighten** in the night.
40 *The people* **They** asked, and he brought quails,
and satisfied them with the bread of *heaven* **the heavens**.
41 He opened the rock,
and the waters *gushed out* **flowed**;
they *ran* **walked** in the *dry places* **parch** like a river.
42 For he remembered his holy *promise* **word**,
and Abraham his servant.
43 And he brought forth his
people *with joy* **rejoicing**,
and his chosen *with gladness* **shouting**:
44 And gave them the lands of the *heathen* **goyim**:
and they *inherited* **possessed**
the *labour* **toil** of the *people* **nations**;
45 That they might *observe* **guard** his statutes,
and *keep* **guard** his *laws* **torah**.
Praise ye the LORD **l-lalalu Yah.**

106 *Praise ye the LORD* **l-lalalu Yah.**
O *give thanks* **spread hands** unto *the LORD* **Yah Veh**;
for he is good:
for his mercy *endureth for ever* **is eternal.**
2 Who can utter the *mighty acts* **might**
of *the LORD* **Yah Veh**?
who can *shew forth* **hear** all his *praise* **halal**?
3 *Blessed* **Blithe** *are* they
that *keep* **guard** judgment,
and he that *doeth righteousness* **worketh justness**
at all times.
4 Remember me, O *LORD* **Yah Veh**,
with the *favour that thou bearest* **pleasure**
unto **of** thy people:
O visit me with thy salvation;
5 That I may see the good of thy chosen,

that I may *rejoice* **cheer**
in the *gladness* **cheerfulness** of thy *nation* **goyim**,
that I may *glory* **halal** with thine inheritance.
6 We have sinned with our fathers,
we have *committed iniquity* **perverted**,
we have done wickedly.
7 Our fathers *understood* **comprehended** not
thy *wonders* **marvels** in *Egypt* **Misrayim**;
they remembered not
the *multitude* **abundance** of thy mercies;
but *provoked him* **rebelled** at the sea,
even at the *Red* **Reed** sea.
8 *Nevertheless* he saved them for his name's sake,
that he might make his *mighty*
power to be **might** known.
25 he turned their heart to hate his people
—to deceive his servants;
26 he sent Mosheh his servant
and Aharon whom he chose:
27 they set words of his signs among them
and omens in the land of Ham:
28 he sent darkness and it darkened;
they rebelled not against his word;
29 he turned their waters into blood
and deathified their fish;
30 their land teemed with frogs
in the chambers of their sovereigns.
31 He said,
and swarms and stingers
arrived in all their borders:
32 he gave them hail for downpour
and flaming fire in their land:
33 he smote their vines and their fig trees
and broke the trees of their borders.
34 He said,
and the locusts and cankerworms arrived
—inummerable;
35 and ate all the herbs in their land
and devoured the fruit of their soil:
36 he smote all the firstbirthed in their land
—the firstfruits of all their strength:
37 he brought them forth with silver and gold;
and not one among their scions faltered.
38 Misrayim cheered when they departed
for the dread of them fell upon them:
39 he spread a cloud for a covering
and fire to light in the night:
40 they asked, and he brought quails
and satiated them with the bread of the heavens:
41 he opened the rock and the waters flowed:
they walked in the parch as a river:
42 —for he remembered
his holy word and Abraham his servant;
43 and he brought forth his people rejoicing
and his chosen shouting;
44 and gave them the lands of the goyim;
and they possessed the toil of the nations
45 —to guard his statutes and guard his torah.
Halalu Yah.

106 Halalu Yah.
O spread hands to Yah Veh;
for good; for his mercy eternal.
2 Who utters the might of Yah Veh?
Who hears all his halal?
3 Blithe—they who guard judgment
who work justness at all times.
4 Remember me, O Yah Veh,
with the pleasure of your people;
O visit me with your salvation:
5 to see the good of your chosen,
to cheer in the cheerfulness of your goyim,
to halal with your inheritance.
6 We sinned with our fathers;
we perverted;
we did wickedly.
7 Our fathers
neither comprehended your marvels in Misrayim;
nor remembered the abundance of your mercies;
but rebelled at the sea—the Reed sea:
8 he saved them for sake of his name
to make his might known:
9 He rebuked the *Red* **Reed** sea also,
and it *was dried up* **parched**:
so he *led* **walked** them through the *depths* **abysses**,
as through the wilderness.
10 And he saved them
from the hand of him that hated them,
and redeemed them from the hand of the enemy.
11 And the waters covered
their *enemies* **tribulators**:
there was not one **none** of them *left* **remained**.
12 Then *believed* **trusted** they his words;
they sang his *praise* **halal**.
13 They *soon forgat* **hasted to forget** his works;
they waited not for his counsel:
14 But *lusted exceedingly* **in desiring,**
desired in the wilderness,
and *tempted God* **tested El** in the *desert* **desolation**.
15 And he gave them their *request* **petition**;
but sent *leanness* **emaciation** into their soul.

16 They envied *Moses* **Mosheh** also in the camp,
and *Aaron* **Aharon** the *saint* **holy** of *the LORD* **Yah Veh**.
17 The earth opened and swallowed *up* Dathan
and covered the *company* **witness** of *Abiram* **Abi Ram**.
18 And a fire *was kindled* **burnt**
in their *company* **witness**;
the flame burned *up* the wicked.
19 They *made* **worked** a calf in Horeb,
and *worshipped* **prostrated to** the molten *image*.
20 Thus they changed their *glory* **honour**
into the *similitude* **pattern** of an ox
that eateth *grass* **herbage**.
21 They forgat *God* **El** their saviour,
which had *done* **worked** great *things* in *Egypt* **Misrayim**;
22 *Wondrous works* **Marvels** in the land of Ham,
and terrible things **awesomenesses** by the *Red* **Reed** sea.
23 *Therefore* he said
that he *would destroy* **should desolate** them,
had not Moses **unless Mosheh** his chosen
stood *before him* **at his face** in the breach,
to turn away his *wrath* **fury**,
lest he should *destroy* **ruin** *them*.
24 Yea, they *despised* **spurned**
the *pleasant* land **of desire**,
they *believed* **trusted** not his word:
25 But *murmured* **rebelled** in their tents,
and hearkened not unto the voice of *the LORD* **Yah Veh**.
26 Therefore he lifted up his hand against them,
to *overthrow* **fell** them in the wilderness:
27 To *overthrow* **fell** their seed also
among the *nations* **goyim**,
and to *scatter* **winnow** them in the lands.
28 They joined *themselves also*
unto Baalpeor **Baal Peor**,
and ate the sacrifices of the dead.
29 Thus they *provoked* **vexed** him *to anger*
with their *inventions* **exploits**:
and the plague brake in upon them.
30 Then stood up *Phinehas* **Pinechas**,
and *executed judgment* **prayed**:
and *so* the plague was *stayed* **restrained**.
31 And that was *counted* **fabricated** unto him
for *righteousness* **justness**
unto all generations **generation to generation**
for evermore **eternally**.
32 They *angered* **enraged** him
also at the waters of strife,
so that it went *ill* **evilly** with *Moses* **Mosheh**
for their sakes:
33 Because they *provoked*
rebelled against his spirit,
so that he *spake unadvisedly* **babbled** with his lips.
34 They *did not destroy* **desolated**
not the *nations* **people**,
concerning whom
the LORD commanded **Yah Veh said to** them:
35 But were mingled among the *heathen* **goyim**,
and learned their works.
36 And they served their idols:
which were a snare unto them.
37 Yea, they sacrificed their
sons and their daughters
unto *devils* **demons**,
38 And *shed* **poured** innocent blood,
even the blood of their sons and of their daughters,
whom they sacrificed unto the idols of *Canaan* **Kenaan**:
and the land was *polluted* **profaned** with blood.
9 he rebuked the Reed sea and it parched;
thus he walked them through the abysses
as through the wilderness:
10 and he saved them
from the hand of him who hated them
and redeemed them from the hand of the enemy:
11 and the waters covered their tribulators;
not one of them remained.
12 Then they trusted his words; they sang his halal:
13 they hastened to forget his works;
they awaited not his counsel:
14 and in desiring, they desired in the wilderness
and tested El in the desolation:
15 He gave them their petition
and sent emaciation to their soul:
16 they envied Mosheh in the camp
and Aharon the holy of Yah Veh:
17 the earth opened and swallowed Dathan
and covered the witness of Abi Ram:
18 a fire burnt in their witness
—the flame burnt the wicked:
19 they worked a calf in Horeb
and prostrated to the molten:
20 they changed their honor
into the pattern of an ox that eats herbage:
21 they forgot El their saviour
who worked great in Misrayim
22 —marvels in the land of Ham;
awesomenesses by the Reed sea.
23 He said to desolate them,
except Mosheh his chosen
stood at his face in the breach,

to turn away his fury, lest he ruin.
24 Yes, they spurned the land of desire;
they trusted not his word;
25 they rebelled in their tents
and hearkened not to the voice of Yah Veh.
26 He lifted his hand against them
to fell them in the wilderness;
27 to also fell their seed among the goyim
and to winnow them in the lands.
28 They joined Baal Peor
and ate the sacrifices of the dead:
29 thus they vex him with their exploits;
and the plague breaks on them:
30 and Pinechas stands and prays;
and the plague restrains:
31 and it was fabricated to him for justness
generation to generation eternally.
32 They enraged him at the
waters of Meribah/strife,
so that it went evilly with Mosheh for their sakes:
33 for they rebelled against his spirit
so that he babbled with his lips:
34 they desolated not the people,
concerning whom Yah Veh had said to them;
35 but mingled among the goyim
and learned their works;
36 and served their idols—a snare to them:
37 yes, they sacrificed their
sons and their daughters
to demons,
38 and poured innocent blood
—the blood of their sons and of their daughters,
whom they sacrificed to the idols of Kenaan:
and profaned the land with blood.
39 Thus were they *defiled*
fouled with their own works,
and *went a whoring* **whored**
with **in** their *own inventions* **exploits.**
40 Therefore was the wrath of *the LORD* **Yah Veh**
kindled against his people,
insomuch that he abhorred his own inheritance.
41 And he gave them into the
hand of the *heathen* **goyim**;
and they that hated them *ruled* **reigned** over them.
42 Their enemies also oppressed them,
and they were *brought into subjection* **subdued**
under their hand.
43 Many times did he *deliver* **rescue** them;
but they *provoked him* **rebelled** with their counsel,
and were *brought low* **subdued** for
their *iniquity* **perversity**.
44 *Nevertheless*
he *regarded* **saw** their *affliction* **tribulation,**
when he heard their *cry* **shouting**:
45 And he remembered for them his covenant,
and *repented* **sighed**
according to the *multitude* **abundance** of his mercies.
46 He *made* **gave** them also to be *pitied* **mercied**
at the face of all those
that *carried* **captured** them *captives.*
47 Save us, O *LORD* **Yah Veh** our *God* **Elohim,**
and gather us from among the *heathen* **goyim,**
to *give thanks* **spread hands** unto thy holy name,
and to *triumph* **laud** in thy *praise* **halal.**
48 Blessed
be *the LORD God* **Yah Veh Elohim** of *Israel* **Yisra El**
from *everlasting* **eternity** to *everlasting* **eternity**:
and let all the people say, Amen.
Praise ye the LORD **Halalu Yah.**

Book V

107 O *give thanks* **spread hands**
unto *the LORD* **Yah Veh,**
for he is good:
for his mercy *endureth for ever* **is eternal.**
2 Let the redeemed of *the LORD* **Yah Veh** say *so,*
whom he hath redeemed
from the hand of the *enemy* **tribulator;**
3 And gathered them out of the lands,
from the *east* **rising,** and from *the west* **duskward,**
from the north, and from *the south* **seaward.**
4 They *wandered* **strayed** in the wilderness
in a *solitary* way **of desolation;**
they found no city *to dwell in* **of settlement.**
5 *Hungry* **Famished** and thirsty,
their soul *fainted* **languished** in them.
6 Then they cried unto *the LORD* **Yah Veh**
in their *trouble* **tribulation,**
and he *delivered* **rescued** them out of their distresses.
7 And he *led* **aimed** them *forth*
by the *right* **straight** way,
that they might go to a city of *habitation* **settlement.**
8 *Oh that men would praise the LORD*
Spread hands unto Yah Veh
for his *goodness* **mercy,**
and for his *wonderful works* **marvels** to
the *children* **sons** of *men* **humanity**!
9 For he satisfieth the *longing* **yearning** soul,
and filleth the *hungry* **famished** soul with goodness.

10 Such as *sit* **settle** in darkness
and in the shadow of death,
being bound in *affliction* **humiliation** and iron;
11 Because they rebelled
against the *words* **sayings** of *God* **El**,
and *contemned* **scorned** the counsel
of *the most High* **Elyon**:
12 *Therefore*
he *brought down* **subdued** their heart with *labour* **toil**;
they *fell down* **stumbled**,
and there was *none to help* **no helper.**
13 Then they cried unto *the LORD* **Yah Veh**
in their *trouble* **tribulation**,
and he saved them out of their distresses.
14 He brought them out of darkness
and the shadow of death,
and *brake* **tore** their bands *in sunder.*
39 Thus they fouled with their own works
and whored in their exploits.
40 Yah Veh kindled his wrath against his people
so that he abhored his own inheritance;
41 and he gave them into the hand of the goyim:
and they who hated them reigned over them:
42 their enemies oppressed them
and subdued them under their hand.
43 Many times he rescued them;
but they rebelled with their counsel
and they are subdued in their perversity.
44 He saw their tribulation
when he heard their shouting;
45 and he remembers his covenant and sighs
according to the abundance of his mercies:
46 he gave them to be mercied
at the face of all who captured them.
47 Save us, O Yah Veh our Elohim
and gather us from among the goyim,
to spread hands to your holy name
and to laud in your halal.
48 Blessed—Yah Veh Elohim of Yisra El
from eternity to eternity!
And all the people say, Amen.
Halalu Yah.

Book V

107 O spread hands to Yah Veh,
for good; for his mercy eternal.
2 Say it, you redeemed of Yah Veh
—whom he redeemed
from the hand of the tribulator;
3 and gathered from the lands
—from the rising and from duskward,
from the north and from seaward.
4 They strayed in the wilderness
in a way of desolation;
they found no city of settlement;
5 famished; yes, thirsty;
their soul languished therein.
6 They cried to Yah Veh in their tribulation
and he rescued them from their distresses;
7 he aimed them by the straight way
to go to a city of settlement.
8 Spread hands to Yah Veh for his mercy
and for his marvels to the sons of humanity!
9 For he satisfies the yearning soul
and the famished soul he fills with goodness
10 —such as settle in darkness
and in the shadow of death
—bound in humiliation and iron:
11 because they rebel against the sayings of El
and scorn the counsel of Elyon:
12 he subdues their heart with toil;
they stumble and there is no helper.
13 And they cry to Yah Veh in their tribulation
and he saves them from their distresses:
14 he brings them from darkness
and the shadow of death;
and tears their bands.
15 *Oh that men would praise the LORD*
Spread hands unto Yah Veh
for his *goodness* **mercy**,
and for his *wonderful works* **marvels** to
the *children* **sons** of *men* **humanity**!
16 For he hath broken the
gates **doors** of *brass* **copper**,
and cut the bars of iron *in sunder.*
17 Fools *because* **by way** of
their *transgression* **rebellion**,
and *because* **by way** of their *iniquities* **perversities**,
are *afflicted* **humbled**.
18 Their soul abhorreth all manner of *meat* **food**;
and they *draw near* **touch**
unto the *gates* **portals** of death.
19 Then they cry unto *the LORD* **Yah Veh**
in their *trouble* **tribulation**,
and he saveth them out of their distresses.
20 He sent his word, and healed them,
and *delivered* **rescued** them
from their *destructions* **pitfalls**.
21 *Oh that men would praise the LORD*
Spread hands unto Yah Veh

for his *goodness* **mercy,**
and for his *wonderful works* **marvels** to
the *children* **sons** of *men* **humanity**!
22 And let them sacrifice the sacrifices
of *thanksgiving* **spread hands,**
and *declare* **scribe** his works with *rejoicing* **shouting.**
23 They that *go down* **descend** to the sea in ships,
that *do business* **work** in great waters;
24 These see the works of *the LORD* **Yah Veh,**
and his *wonders* **marvels** in the deep.
25 For he *commandeth* **sayeth,**
and *raiseth* **stayeth** the stormy wind,
which lifteth up the waves *thereof.*
26 They *mount up* **ascend** to the *heaven* **heavens,**
they *go down again* **descend** to the *depths* **abysses:**
their soul is melted because of *trouble* **evil.**
27 They *reel to and fro* **celebrate,**
and stagger like *a drunken man* **one intoxicated,**
and *are at their wit's end* **all their wisdom is swallowed.**
28 Then they cry unto *the LORD* **Yah Veh**
in their *trouble* **tribulation,**
and he bringeth them out of their distresses.
29 He *maketh* **raiseth** the storm *a calm* **to hush,**
so that the waves *thereof are still* **hush.**
30 Then *are* they *glad* **cheer** because they *be*
quiet **hush**; so he *bringeth* **leadeth** them
unto *their desired* **the** haven **of their desire.**
31 *Oh that men would praise the LORD*
Spread hands unto Yah Veh
for his *goodness* **mercy,**
and for his *wonderful works* **marvels** to
the *children* **sons** of *men* **humanity**!
32 Let them exalt him *also*
in the congregation of the people,
and *praise* **halal** him
in the *assembly* **settlement** of the elders.
33 He *turneth* **setteth** rivers
into a wilderness,
and the *watersprings* **springs of waters**
into *dry ground* **thirst;**
34 A fruitful land into *barrenness* **salt,**
for the *wickedness* **evil** of them that *dwell* **settle** therein.
35 He *turneth* **setteth** the wilderness
into a *standing* **marsh of** water,
and *dry ground* **parched earth**
into *watersprings* **springs of waters.**
36 And there
he *maketh the hungry to dwell* **settleth the famished,**
that they may prepare a city for *habitation* **settlement;**
37 And *sow* **seed** the fields, and plant vineyards,
which may *yield* **work** fruits of *increase* **produce.**
38 He blesseth them also,
so that they *are multiplied greatly* **abound mightily;**
and *suffereth* **diminisheth** not
their *cattle* **animals** *to decrease.*

15 Spread hands to Yah Veh for his mercy
and for his marvels to the sons of humanity!
16 For he broke the doors of copper
and cut the bars of iron.
17 Fools by way of their rebellion
and by way of their perversities
are humbled:
18 their soul abhors all their food;
and they touch to the portals of death.
19 And they cry to Yah Veh in their tribulation;
he saves them from their distresses:
20 he sends his word and heals them
and rescues them from their pitfalls.
21 Spread hands to Yah Veh for his mercy
and for his marvels to the sons of humanity!
22 Sacrifice the sacrifices of spread hands
and scribe his works with shouting.
23 They who descend to the sea in ships
—who work in great waters;
24 these see the works of Yah Veh
and his marvels in the deep.
25 He says,
and the stormy wind which lifts the waves stay:
26 they ascend to the heavens; they descend to
the abysses; their soul melts because of evil.
27 They celebrate and stagger as intoxicated
—swallow all their wisdom:
28 and they cry to Yah Veh in their tribulation
and he brings them from their distresses:
29 he raises the storm to hush
and the waves hush:
30 and they cheer because they hush;
and he leads them to their haven of desire.
31 Spread hands to Yah Veh for his mercy
and for his marvels to the sons of humanity!
32 Exalt him in the congregation of the people
and halal him in the settlement of the elders.
33 He sets rivers to a wilderness
and the springs of waters to thirst;
34 a fruitful land to salt
for the evil of them who settle therein.
35 He sets the wilderness to a marsh of water
and parched earth to springs of waters:
36 and there he settles the famished
to prepare a city for settlement

37 —to seed the fields and plant vineyards;
to work fruits of produce:
38 he blesses them to abound mightily;
and diminishes not their animals.
39 *Again,* they *are minished* **diminish**
and *brought low* **prostrate**
through *oppression* **restraint,**
affliction **evil,** and *sorrow* **grief.**
40 He poureth *contempt* **disrespect**
upon *princes* **volunteers,**
and causeth them to *wander* **stray**
in the *wilderness* **waste,**
where there is no way.
41 Yet *setteth he the poor on*
high **he lofteth the needy**
from affliction **after humiliation,**
and *maketh him* **setteth** families like a flock.
42 The *righteous* **straight** shall
see it, and *rejoice* **cheer:**
and all *iniquity* **wickedness** shall *stop* **shut** her mouth.
43 Whoso is wise,
and *will observe* **shall guard** these *things,*
even they shall *understand* **discern**
the *lovingkindness* **mercy** of *the LORD* **Yah Veh.**

108 A Song *or* Psalm of David.
1 O *God* **Elohim,** my heart is *fixed* **prepared;**
I *will* **shall** sing and *give praise* **psalm,**
even with my *glory* **honour.**
2 Awake, *psaltery* **bagpipe** and harp:
I *myself will* **shall** awake early.
3 I *will praise* **shall spread hands unto** thee,
O *LORD* **Yah Veh,**
among the people:
and I *will sing praises* **shall psalm** unto thee
among the *nations* **people.**
4 For thy mercy is great above the heavens:
and thy truth *reacheth* unto the *clouds* **vapours.**
5 Be thou *exalted* **lofted,** O *God* **Elohim,**
above the heavens:
and thy *glory* **honour** above all the earth;
6 That thy beloved may be *delivered* **rescued:**
save with thy right *hand,* and answer me.
7 *God* **Elohim** hath *spoken*
worded in his holiness;
I *will rejoice* **shall jump for joy,**
I *will divide* **shall allot** Shechem,
and mete out the valley of *Succoth*
Sukkoth/Brush Arbors.
8 *Gilead* **Galad** is mine; *Manasseh*
Menash Sheh is mine;
Ephraim **Ephrayim** also
is the *strength* **stronghold** of mine head;
Judah **Yah Hudah** is my *lawgiver* **statute setter;**
9 Moab is my *wash pot* **bath caldron;** over
Edom *will* **shall** I cast out my shoe; over
Philistia will **Pelesheth shall** I triumph.
10 Who *will* **shall** bring me into
the *strong* **fortressed** city?
who *will* **shall** lead me into Edom?
11 *Wilt* **Shalt** not thou, *O God* **Elohim,**
who hast cast us off?
and *wilt* **shalt** not thou, O *God* **Elohim,**
go *forth* with our hosts?
12 Give us help from *trouble* **tribulation:**
for vain is the *help* **salvation** of *man* **humanity.**
13 Through *God* **Elohim** we
shall *do* **work** valiantly:
for he *it is that* shall tread down our *enemies* **tribulators.**

109 To *the chief Musician* **His Eminence,**
A Psalm of David.
1 *Hold not thy peace* **Hush not,**
O *God* **Elohim** of my *praise* **halal;**
2 For the mouth of *the wicked* **wickedness**
and the mouth of *the deceitful* **deceit**
are opened against me:
they have *spoken* **worded** against me
with a *lying* **false** tongue.
3 They *compassed about* **surrounded me**
also with words of hatred;
and fought against me *without a cause* **gratuitously.**
4 For my love they are my *adversaries* **satans:**
but I *give myself unto*—prayer.
5 And they have *rewarded*
set upon me evil for good,
and hatred for my love.
6 Set thou a wicked *man* over him:
and let Satan stand at his right *hand.*
7 When he shall be judged,
let him be *condemned* **judged wicked:**
and let his prayer become sin.
39 They diminish and prostrate
through restraint, evil, and grief:
40 he pours disrespect on volunteers
to stray in the way where there is no way:
41 and he lofts the needy from humiliation
and sets families as a flock.
42 The straight see and cheer;
and all wickedness shuts her mouth.
43 Who is wise and guards these,
discerns the mercy of Yah Veh.

108 A Song: A Psalm by David.
1 O Elohim, my heart is prepared;
I sing and psalm, even with my honor:
2 waken, bagpipe and harp; I waken early.
3 I spread hands to you, O Yah Veh,
among the people;
and I psalm to you among the people:
4 for your mercy—great above the heavens;
and your truth to the vapours.
5 Be lofted, O Elohim, above the heavens;
and your honor above all the earth:
6 that your beloved may be rescued;
save with your right and answer me.
7 Elohim words in his holiness;
I jump for joy:
I allot Shechem;
I mete out the valley of Sukkoth/Brush Arbors:
8 Galad *is* mine; Menash Sheh *is* mine;
Ephrayim *is* the stronghold of my head;
Yah Hudah *is* my statute setter;
9 Moab *is* my bath caldron;
over Edom I cast out my shoe;
over Pelesheth I triumph.
10 Who brings me to the fortressed city?
Who leads me into Edom?
11 Have you not, O Elohim cast us off?
Have you not, O Elohim, gone with our hosts?
12 Give us help from tribulation;
for vain is the salvation of humanity:
13 through Elohim we work valiantly
for he treads down our tribulators.

109 To His Eminence: A Psalm by David.
1 Hush not, O Elohim of my halal;
2 for the mouth of wickedness
and the mouth of deceit open against me: they
word against me with a false tongue;
3 they surround me with words of hatred;
and fight against me gratuitously:
4 instead of my love, they *are* my satans;
but I—prayer:
5 and against me, they set evil for good
and hatred for my love.
6 Set the wicked over him;
and stand Satan at his right:
7 in judging, judge him with the wicked;
and that his prayer become sin
8 Let his days be few;
and let another take his *office* **oversight**.
9 Let his *children* **sons** be *fatherless* **orphans**,
and his *wife* **woman** a widow.
10 *Let his children be continually vagabonds*
In wandering, let his sons wander,
and beg **ask**:
let them seek *their bread also*
out of their *desolate places* **parched areas.**
11 Let the *extortioner catch* **exactor snare** all that
he hath;
and let the strangers *spoil* **plunder** his labour.
12 Let there be none to *extend* **draw out** mercy
unto him:
neither let there be any to *favour* **grant charism**
to his *fatherless children* **orphans**.
13 Let his posterity be cut off;
and in *the* **another** generation *following*
let their name be *blotted* **wiped** out.
14 Let the *iniquity* **perversity** of his fathers
be remembered with *the LORD* **Yah Veh**;
and let not the sin of his mother be *blotted* **wiped** out.
15 Let them be
before the LORD **in front of Yah Veh** continually,
that he may cut off the *memory* **memorial** of them
from the earth.
16 Because
hat he remembered not to *shew* **work** mercy,
but *persecuted* **pursued** the *poor* **humble** and
needy man, that he might *even slay* **deathify**
the *broken* **dejected** in heart.
17 As he loved *cursing* **to abase**,
so let it come unto him:
as he delighted not in blessing, so let it be far from him.
18 As he *clothed* **enrobed** himself with *cursing*
abasing like as with his *garment* **tailoring**,
so let it come into his *bowels* **inwards** like water,
and like *oil* **ointment** into his bones.
19 Let it be unto him
as the *garment* **clothes** which covereth him,
and for a girdle wherewith he is girded continually.
20 Let this be *the reward* **for the deeds** of *mine*
adversaries **my satans**
from *the LORD* **Yah Veh**,
and of them that *speak* **word** evil against my soul.
21 But *do* **work** thou for me,
O *GOD the Lord* **Yah Veh Adonay**, for thy name's sake:
because thy mercy is good, *deliver* **rescue** thou me.
22 For I am *poor* **humble** and needy,
and my heart is *wounded* **pierced** within me.
23 I am gone like the shadow
when it *declineth* **spreadeth**:
I am *tossed up and down* **shaken** as the locust.
24 My knees *are weak* **falter** through fasting;

and my flesh *faileth* **emaciates** of *fatness* **ointment.**
25 I became also a reproach unto them:
when they looked upon **they see** me,
they *shaked* **shake** their heads.
26 Help me, O *LORD* **Yah Veh** my *God* **Elohim**:
O save me according to thy mercy:
27 That they may know that this is thy hand;
that thou, *LORD* **O Yah Veh**, hast *done* **worked** it.
28 Let them *curse* **abase**, but bless thou:
when they arise, let them *be ashamed* **shame**;
but let thy servant *rejoice* **cheer**.
29 Let *mine adversaries* **my satans**
be clothed **enrobe** with shame,
and let them cover themselves
with their own *confusion* **shame**, as with a mantle.
30 *I will greatly praise the LORD*
I shall mightily halal Yah Veh with my mouth;
yea, I *will praise* **shall spread hands unto** him
among the *multitude* **great**.
31 For he shall stand at the
right *hand* of the *poor* **needy**,
to save him from those that *condemn* **judge** his soul.
8 and his days become few
and another take his oversight:
9 and his sons become orphans
and his woman a widow:
10 in wandering, that his sons wander;
yes, ask; and seek from their parched areas.
11 The exactor snares all he has
and the strangers plunder his labor;
12 neither is there any to draw out mercy to him
nor any to grant charism to his orphans:
13 his posterity becomes cut off;
and in another generation
their name is wiped out:
14 the perversity of his fathers
is remembered to Yah Veh;
and the sin of his mother *is* not wiped out;
15 they become in front of Yah Veh continually
to cut off their memorial from the earth:
16 because he remembered not to work mercy
and pursued the humble and needy man
to deathify the dejected in heart.
17 As he loves to abase,
thus it approaches him;
as he delights not in blessing,
so be it far from him:
18 he enrobes abasing as tailoring,
thus it enters his inwards as water
—as ointment into his bones:
19 so be it as the clothes that cover him
and for a girdle to continually gird:
20 this *is* for the deeds of my satans from Yah Veh
and for them who word evil against my soul.
21 But work for me, O Yah Veh Adonay,
for sake of your name;
because your mercy is good, rescue me.
22 For I *am* humble and needy
and my heart pierces within me
23 —gone—spread as the shadow
—shaken as the locust:
24 my knees falter through fasting;
my flesh emaciates of ointment;
25 I—I am a reproach to them;
they see me; they shake their heads.
26 Help me, O Yah Veh my Elohim;
O save me according to your mercy;
27 so that they know this is your hand;
that you, O Yah Veh, worked it.
28 They abase and you bless;
they rise and shame:
and your servant cheers.
29 My satans enrobe with shame
—cover themselves with their own shame
as with a mantle.
30 I mightily halal Yah Veh with my mouth;
yes, I spread hands to him among the great:
31 for he stands at the right of the needy
to save him from those who judge his soul.

110 A Psalm of David.
1 *The LORD said* **An oracle of Yah Veh**
unto my *Lord* **Adonay**,
Sit **Settle** thou at my right *hand*,
until I *make* **set** thine enemies
thy footstool **the stool of thy feet**.
2 *The LORD* **Yah Veh** shall
send the rod of thy strength
out of *Zion* **Siyon**:
rule **subjugate** thou in the midst of thine enemies.
3 Thy people shall *be willing* **volunteer**
in the day of thy *power* **valour**,
in the *beauties* **majesties** of holiness
from the womb of the *morning* **dawn**:
thou hast the dew of thy *youth* **childhood**.
4 *The LORD hath sworn* **Yah Veh oathed**,
and *will* **shall** not *repent* **sigh**,
Thou art a priest *for ever* **eternally**
after the *order* **word** of *Melchizedek* **Malki Sedeq**.
5 *The Lord* **Adonay** at thy right *hand*
shall strike *through kings* **sovereigns**
in the day of his wrath.

6 He shall *judge among* **plead the cause**
of the *heathen* **goyim**,
he shall fill the places with the *dead* bodies;
he shall *wound* **strike** the heads
over *many countries* **the great land.**
7 He shall drink of the *brook* **wadi** in the way:
therefore shall he lift *up* the head.

111 *Praise ye the LORD* **l-lalalu Yah.**
I *will praise the LORD* **shall spread hands unto Yah Veh**
with my whole heart,
in the *assembly* **private counsel** of the *upright* **straight**,
and in the *congregation* **witness.**
2 The works of *the LORD* **Yah Veh** are great,
sought out of all them that *have pleasure* **delight** therein.
3 His *work* **deed** is honourable
and *glorious* **majestic**:
and his *righteousness* **justness**
endureth for ever **standeth eternal.**
4 He hath *made* **worked** his
wonderful works **marvels**
to be remembered—**a memorial**:
the LORD **Yah Veh** is *gracious* **charismatic**
and *full of compassion* **merciful.**
5 He hath given *meat* **prey** unto them that
fear **awe** him: he *will ever* **shall eternally**
be mindful of **remember** his covenant.
6 He hath *shewed* **told** his people
the *power* **force** of his works,
that he may give them
the *heritage* **inheritance** of the *heathen* **goyim.**
7 The works of his hands are
verity **truth** and judgment;
all his commandments are *sure* **trustworthy.**
8 They *stand fast* **sustain**
for ever **eternally** and *ever* **eternally**,
and are *done* **worked**
in truth and *uprightness* **straightness.**
9 He sent redemption unto his people:
he hath *commanded* **misvahed** his covenant
for ever **eternally**:
holy and *reverend* **awesome** is his name.
10 The *fear* **awe** of *the LORD* **Yah Veh**
is the beginning of wisdom:
a good *understanding* **comprehension**
have all they that *do his commandments* **work them**:
his *praise endureth for ever* **halal standeth eternal.**

112 *Praise ye the LORD* **l-lalalu Yah.**
Blessed **Blithe** *is* the man
that *feareth the LORD* **aweth Yah Veh,**
that delighteth *greatly* **mightily**
in his *commandments* **misvoth.**
2 His seed shall be mighty upon earth:
the generation of the *upright* **straight** shall be blessed.
3 Wealth and riches shall be in his house:
and his *righteousness* **justness**
endureth for ever **standeth eternal.**

110 A Psalm: By David.
1 An oracle of Yah Veh to my Adonay;
Settle at my right
until I set your enemies the stool of your feet.
2 Yah Veh sends the rod of your strength
from Siyon.
Subjugate midst your enemies.
3 Your people volunteer in the day of your valour
—in the majesties of holiness
from the womb of the dawn;
you have the dew of your childhood.
4 Yah Veh oaths and sighs not!
You are a priest eternally
after the word of Malki Sedeq.
5 Adonay at your right
struck sovereigns in the day of his wrath:
6 he pleads among the goyim;
he fills with bodies;
he strikes him—the head over the great land:
7 he drinks of the wadi in the way;
so he lifts the head.

111 Halalu Yah!
I spread hands to Yah Veh with my whole heart
in the private counsel of the straight
and in the witness.
2 The works of Yah Veh are great
—sought by all who delight therein:
3 his deed is honorable and majestic
and his justness stands eternal:
4 he worked his marvels—a memorial;
Yah Veh *is* charismatic and merciful.
5 he gives the prey to them who awe him;
he eternally remembers his covenant:
6 he told his people the force of his works
to give them the inheritance of the goyim.
7 The works of his hands are truth and judgment;
all his commandments are trustworthy:
8 they sustain eternally and eternally
—worked in truth and straightness:
9 he sends redemption to his people; he misvahs his
covenant eternally: holy and awesome *is* his name.
10 The awe of Yah Veh is the beginning of wisdom;
all who work them have good comprehension;
his halal stands eternal.

112 Halalu Yah!
Blithe—the man who awes Yah Veh
—who delights mightily in his misvoth.
2 His seed is mighty on earth;
the generation of the straight is blessed;
3 wealth and riches *are* in his house;
and his justness stands eternal.
4 Unto the *upright* **straight**
there ariseth light in the darkness:
he is *gracious* **charismatic**,
and *full of compassion* **merciful**, and *righteous* **just**.
5 A good man *sheweth favour* **granteth charism**,
and lendeth:
he *will guide* **shall sustain** his *affairs* **words**
with *discretion* **judgment**.
6 Surely he shall not *be moved*
for ever **totter eternally**:
the *righteous* **just**
shall be *in everlasting remembrance*
an eternal memorial.
7 He shall not *be afraid of* **awe** evil *tidings* **reports**:
his heart is *fixed* **established**,
trusting **confiding** in *the LORD* **Yah Veh**.
8 His heart is *established* **sustained**,
he shall not *be afraid* **awe**,
until he see his *desire upon his enemies* **tribulators**.
9 He hath *dispersed* **scattered**,
he hath given to the *poor* **needy**;
his *righteousness* **justness**
endureth for ever **standeth eternal**;
his horn shall be *exalted* **lofted** with honour.
10 The wicked shall see it, and be *grieved* **vexed**;
he shall gnash with his teeth, and melt away: the
desire of the wicked shall *perish* **destruct**.

113 *Praise ye the LORD* **l-lalalu Yah**.
Praise **l-lalal**, O ye servants of *the LORD* **Yah Veh**,
praise **halal** the name of *the LORD* **Yah Veh**.
2 Blessed be the name of *the LORD* **Yah Veh**
from this time forth and *for evermore* **eternally**.
3 From the rising of the sun
unto the *going down* **entry** *of the same*
the LORD'S **Yah Veh's** name is to be *praised* **halaled**.
4 *The LORD is high* **Yah Veh be lofted**
above all *nations* **goyim**,
and his *glory* **honour**
above the heavens.
5 Who is like unto *the LORD*
Yah Veh our *God* **Elohim**,
who *dwelleth on high* **lofteth in his settlement**,
6 Who *humbleth* **abaseth** *himself*
to *behold the things that are in heaven* **see in the heavens**,
and in the earth!
7 He raiseth *up* the poor out of the dust,
and lifteth the needy out of the dunghill;
8 That he may set him with *princes* **volunteers**,
even with the *princes* **volunteers** of his people.
9 He *maketh* **causeth** the *barren woman* **sterile**
to *keep* **settle** house,
and to be a *joyful* **cheerful** mother of *children* **sons**.
Praise ye the LORD **l-lalalu Yah**.

114 *When Israel* **Yisra El** went
out of *Egypt* **Misrayim**,
the house of *Jacob* **Yaaqov**
from a people *of strange language* **unintelligible**;
2 *Judah* **Yah l-ludah** was his *sanctuary* **holies**,
and Israel **Yisra El** his *dominion* **reign**.
3 The sea saw it, and fled:
Jordan was driven **Yarden turned** back.
4 The mountains *skipped* **danced** like rams,
and the *little* hills like *lambs* **sons of flocks**.
5 What *ailed thee*, O thou sea, that thou fleddest?
thou *Jordan* **Yarden**, that thou *wast driven* **turnest** back?
6 Ye mountains, that ye *skipped* **danced** like rams;
and ye *little* hills, like *lambs* **sons of flocks**?
7 *Tremble* **Writhe**, thou earth,
at the *presence* **face** of *the Lord* **Adonay**,
at the *presence* **face** of *the God* **Elohah** of *Jacob* **Yaaqov**;
8 Which turned the rock into
a *standing* **marsh** water,
the flint into a fountain of waters.

115 Not unto us, O *LORD* **Yah Veh**, not unto us,
but unto thy name give *glory* **honour**,
for thy mercy, and for thy truth's sake.
2 Wherefore should the *heathen* **goyim** say,
Where is *now* **I beseech**, their *God* **Elohim**?
3 But our *God* **Elohim** is in the heavens:
he hath *done* **worked** whatsoever
he hath *pleased* **desired**.
4 To the straight, light rises in the darkness;
he is charismatic and merciful and just:
5 a good man grants charism and lends;
he sustains his words with judgment:
6 surely he totters not eternally;
the just are an eternal memorial:
7 he awes not evil reports;
his heart is established, confiding in Yah Veh:
8 his heart sustains; he awes not
—until he sees his tribulators:
9 he scatters; he gives to the needy;
his justness stands eternal; his horn is lofted with honor.

10 The wicked sees and vexes
—gnashes his teeth and melts away; the
desire of the wicked destructs.

113 Halalu Yah!
Halal, O you servants of Yah Veh;
halal the name of Yah Veh:
2 blessed—the name of Yah Veh
from this time forth and eternally
3 —from the rising of the sun to the entry:
halal the name of Yah Veh;
4 loft Yah Veh above all goyim
and his honor above the heavens.
5 Who *is* as Yah Veh our Elohim?
Who lofts in his settlement?
6 Who abases to see
on the heavens and on the earth?
7 He raises the poor from the dust
and lifts the needy from the dunghill
8 to set them with volunteers
—the volunteers of his people.
9 He settles the sterile in the house
—a cheerful mother of sons.
Halalu Yah!

114 Yisra El came from Misrayim;
the house of Yaaqov from a people unintelligible;
2 Yah Hudah became his holies; Yisra El his reign.
3 The sea sees and flees; Yarden returns;
4 the mountains dance as rams;
the hills as sons of flocks.
5 What , O sea, that you flee?
O Yarden, that you return?
6 O mountains, that you dance as rams?
O hills, as sons of flocks?
7 Writhe, O earth, at the face of Adonay
—at the face of Elohah of Yaaqov;
8 who turned the rock into a marsh water;
the flint into a fountain of waters.

115 Not to us, O Yah Veh,
not to us, but unto your name give honor;
for your mercy; for your truth.
2 Why say the goyim,
Where I beseech, *is* their Elohim?
3 Our Elohim is in the heavens;
he works whatever he desires.
4 Their idols are silver and gold,
the work of *men's* **human** hands.
5 They have mouths, but they *speak* **word** not:
eyes have they, but they see not:
6 They have ears, but they hear not:
noses **nostrils** have they, but they *smell* **scent** not:
7 They have hands, but they *handle* **touch** not:
feet have they, but they walk not:
neither *speak* **mutter** they through their throat.
8 They that *make* **work** them are like unto them;
so is every one that *trusteth* **confideth** in them.
9 O *Israel* **Yisra El**,
trust **confide** thou in *the LORD* **Yah Veh**:
he is their help and their *shield* **buckler**.
10 O house of *Aaron* **Aharon**,
trust **confide** in *the LORD* **Yah Veh**:
he is their help and their *shield* **buckler**.
11 Ye that *fear the LORD* **awe Yah Veh**,
trust **confide** in *the LORD* **Yah Veh**:
he is their help and their *shield* **buckler**.
12 *The LORD* **Yah Veh** hath been mindful of us:
he *will* **shall** bless us;
he *will* **shall** bless the house of *Israel* **Yisra El**;
he *will* **shall** bless the house of *Aaron* **Aharon**.
13 He *will* **shall** bless them
that *fear the LORD* **awe Yah Veh**, *both* small and great.
14 *The LORD* **Yah Veh** shall
increase you *more and more*,
you and your *children* **sons**.
15 Ye are blessed of *the LORD* **Yah Veh**
which *made heaven* **worked the heavens** and earth.
16 The *heaven* **heavens**,
even the heavens, are *the LORD'S* **Yah Veh's**:
but the earth
hath he given to the *children* **sons** of *men* **humanity**.
17 The dead *praise* **halal** not *the LORD* **Yah**,
neither any that *go down* **descend** into silence.
18 But we *will* **shall** bless *the LORD* **Yah**
from this time *forth* and *for evermore* **eternally**.
Praise the LORD **Halalu Yah**.

116 I love *the LORD* **Yah Veh**,
because he hath heard my voice and my supplications.
2 Because he hath *inclined*
spread his ear unto me,
therefore
will **shall** I call *upon him as long as I live* **all my days**.
3 The *sorrows* **cords** of death
compassed **surrounded** me,
and the *pains of hell* **straits of sheol**
gat hold upon **found** me:
I found *trouble* **tribulation** and *sorrow* **grief**.
4 Then called I upon the
name of *the LORD* **Yah Veh**;
O *LORD* **Yah Veh**, I beseech thee,
deliver **rescue** my soul.

5 *Gracious* **Charismatic** is *the LORD* **Yah Veh**,
and *righteous* **just**;
yea, our *God is merciful* **Elohim mercieth**.
6 *The LORD* **Yah Veh**
preserveth **guardeth** the *simple* **gullible**:
I *was brought low* **languished**, and he *helped* **saved** me.
7 Return unto thy rest, O my soul;
for *the LORD* **Yah Veh** hath dealt *bountifully* with thee.
8 For thou hast *delivered*
rescued my soul from death,
mine eyes from tears,
and my feet from falling.
9 I *will* **shall** walk *before the*
LORD **at the face of Yah Veh**
in the land of the living.
10 I *believed* **trusted**, therefore
have I *spoken* **worded**:
I was *greatly afflicted* **mightily humbled**:
11 I said in my haste, All *men* **humans** are liars.
12 What shall I *render* **return**
unto *the LORD* **Yah Veh**
for all his benefits toward me?
13 I *will take* **shall lift** the cup of salvation,
and call upon the name of *the LORD* **Yah Veh**.
14 I *will pay* **shall shalam** my vows
unto *the LORD* **Yah Veh**
now in the presence of all his people.
15 *Precious* **Esteemed**
in the *sight* **eyes** of *the LORD* **Yah Veh**
is the death of his *saints* **mercied**.
4 Their idols are silver and gold
the work of human hands:
5 mouths have they, but they word not;
eyes have they, but they see not;
6 ears have they, but they hear not;
nostrils have they, but they scent not;
7 hands have they, but they touch not;
feet have they, but they walk not; they
mutter not through their throat.
8 They who work them are like them;
thus is every one who confides in them.
9 O Yisra El, confide in Yah Veh;
he is their help and their buckler:
10 O house of Aharon, confide in Yah Veh;
he is their help and their buckler:
11 you who awe Yah Veh, confide in Yah Veh;
he is their help and their buckler.
12 Yah Veh has been mindful of us; he blesses:
he blesses the house of Yisra El;
he blesses the house of Aharon;
13 he blesses them who awe Yah Veh
—small and great.
14 Yah Veh increases you—you and your sons
15 —you, blessed of Yah Veh
who worked the heavens and earth.
16 The heavens—the heavens, are to Yah Veh;
but he gives the earth to the sons of humanity.
17 Neither the dead halal Yah
nor any who descend into silence;
18 and we—we bless Yah
from this time and eternally.
Halalu Yah!

116 I love,
because Yah Veh hears
my voice, my supplications;
2 because he spreads his ear to me;
all my days I call:
3 the cords of death surround me
and the straits of sheol find me:
I find tribulation and grief:
4 I call on the name of Yah Veh;
O Yah Veh, I beseech you, rescue my soul.
5 Yah Veh is charismatic and just;
yes, our Elohim mercies:
6 Yah Veh guards the gullible;
I languish; he saves me:
7 return to your rest, O my soul;
for Yah Veh deals with you.
8 For you rescued my soul from death;
my eyes from tears;
my feet from falling:
9 I walk at the face of Yah Veh
in the land of the living:
10 I trust; I word:
I—I am mightily humbled.
11 I said in my haste, All humans are liars.
12 What return I to Yah Veh
for all his benefits toward me?
13 I lift the cup of salvation
and call on the name of Yah Veh;
14 I shalam my vows to Yah Veh
in the presence of all his people.
15 Esteemed in the eyes of Yah Veh
is the death of his mercied.
16 **I beseech,** *O LORD* **O Yah Veh**,
truly I *am* thy servant;
I *am* thy servant,
and the son of *thine handmaid* **thy maid**:
thou hast loosed my bonds.
17 I *will offer* **shall sacrifice** to thee

the sacrifice of *thanksgiving* **spread hands,**
and *will* **shall** call upon the name of *the LORD* **Yah Veh.**
18 I *will pay* **shall shalam** my vows
unto *the LORD* **Yah Veh**
now in the presence of all his people,
19 In the courts of *the LORD'S* **Yah Veh's** house,
in the midst of thee, O *Jerusalem* **Yeru Shalem.** *Praise ye the LORD* **l-lalalu Yah.**

117 O *praise the LORD* **halal Yah Veh,**
all ye *nations* **goyim:**
praise **laud** him,
all ye *people* **nations.**
2 For his *merciful kindness* **mercy**
is great **prevaileth mightily** toward us:
and the truth of *the LORD* **Yah Veh**
endureth for ever **is eternal.**
Praise ye the LORD **l-lalalu Yah.**

118 O *give thanks* **spread hands**
unto *the LORD* **Yah Veh;**
for he is good:
because his mercy *endureth for ever* **is eternal.**
2 Let *Israel now* **Yisra El, I beseech,** say,
that his mercy *endureth for ever* **is eternal.**
3 Let the house of *Aaron now*
Aharon I beseech, say,
that his mercy *endureth for ever* **is eternal.**
4 Let them, *now* **I beseech,**
that *fear the LORD* **awe Yah Veh** say,
that his mercy *endureth for ever* **is eternal.**
5 I called upon *the LORD*
Yah in *distress* **the straits:**
the LORD **Yah** answered me,
and set me in a large place **from an expanse.**
6 *The LORD* **Yah Veh** is on my side;
I *will* **shall** not *fear* **awe:**
what *can man do* **shall humanity work** unto me?
7 *The LORD* **Yah Veh** taketh my part
with *them that help me* **my helpers:**
therefore shall I see *my desire upon* them that hate me.
8 *It is* better to *trust* **seek**
refuge in *the LORD* **Yah Veh**
than to *put confidence* **confide** in *man* **humanity.**
9 *It is* better to *trust* **seek**
refuge in *the LORD* **Yah Veh**
than to *put confidence* **confide** in *princes* **volunteers.**
10 All *nations compassed* **goyim**
surrounded me *about*:
but in the name of *the LORD* **Yah Veh**
will I destroy **I shall cut** them **off.**
11 They *compassed* **surrounded** me *about*;
yea, they *compassed* **surrounded** me *about*:
but in the name of *the LORD* **Yah Veh**
I *will destroy* **shall cut** them **off.**
12 They *compassed* **surrounded**
me *about* like bees:
they are *quenched* **extinguished** as the fire of thorns:
for in the name of *the LORD* **Yah Veh**
I *will destroy* **shall cut** them **off.**
13 **In overthrowing,**
Thou hast *thrust sore at me* **overthrown me**
that I might fall:
but *the LORD* **Yah Veh** helped me.
14 *The LORD* **Yah** is my strength and *song* **psalm,**
and is become my salvation.
15 The voice of *rejoicing* **shouting** and salvation
is in the *tabernacles* **tents** of the *righteous* **just:**
the right *hand* of *the LORD* **Yah Veh**
doeth **worketh** valiantly.
16 The right *hand* of *the LORD* **Yah Veh** is exalted:
the right *hand of the LORD* **Yah Veh**
doeth **worketh** valiantly.
17 I shall not die, but live,
and *declare* **scribe** the works of *the LORD* **Yah.**
18 **In disciplining,**
The LORD **Yah** hath *chastened* **disciplined** me *sore*:
but he hath not given me over unto death.

16 I beseech, O Yah Veh, I your servant
—I your servant, the son of your maid;
you loosed my bonds.
17 I sacrifice to you
the sacrifice of spread hands
and call on the name of Yah Veh:
18 I shalam my vows to Yah Veh
in the presence of all his people
19 —in the courts of the house of Yah Veh;
in your midst, O Yeru Shalem.
Halalu Yah!

117 O halal Yah Veh, all you goyim;
laud him, all you nations:
2 for his mercy prevails mightily toward us;
and the truth of Yah Veh *is* eternal.
Halalu Yah!

118 O spread hands to Yah Veh;
for good; his mercy eternal.
2 I beseech, Yisra El say,
his mercy eternal.
3 I beseech, house of Aharon say,
his mercy eternal.
4 I beseech, you who awe Yah Veh say,
his mercy eternal.

5 I calle on Yah in the straits;
Yah answers me from an expanse:
6 Yah Veh is on my side;
I awe not what humanity works to me:
7 Yah Veh takes my part among my helpers;
I—I see them who hate me.
8 Better to seek refuge in Yah Veh
than to confide in humanity;
9 better to seek refuge in Yah Veh
than to confide in volunteers.
10 all goyim surround me;
in the name of Yah Veh, I cut them off:
11 they surround me; yes, they surround me;
in the name of Yah Veh, I cut them off:
12 they surround me as bees;
they are extinguished as a fire of thorns; for
in the name of Yah Veh I cut them off.
13 In overthrowing,
you overthrew me that I fell;
and Yah Veh helped me.
14 Yah *is* my strength and psalm
—become my salvation
15 The voice of shouting and salvation
is in the tents of the just;
the right of Yah Veh works valiantly:
16 the right of Yah Veh exalts;
the right of Yah Veh works valiantly.
17 I die not, but live;
and scribe the works of Yah.
18 In disciplining, Yah disciplines me;
but gives me not over to death.
19 Open to me the *gates* **portals**
of *righteousness* **justness**:
I *will* **shall** go into them,
and I *will praise the LORD* **shall spread hands unto Yah**:
20 This *gate* **portal** of *the LORD* **Yah Veh**,
into which the *righteous* **just** shall enter.
21 I *will praise* **shall spread hands unto** thee:
for thou hast *heard* **answered** me,
and art become my salvation.
22 The stone *which* the builders refused
is become the head *stone* of the corner.
23 This is *the LORD'S* **Yah Veh's** doing;
it is marvellous in our eyes.
24 This is the day
which the LORD **Yah Veh** hath *made* **worked**;
we *will rejoice* **shall twirl** and *be glad* **cheer** in it.
25 Save now* **I beseech**,
I beseech thee, O *LORD* **Yah Veh**:
O *LORD* **Yah Veh**, I beseech thee,
send now prosperity **prosper, I beseech.**

*Hoshia Nah

26 Blessed be he
that cometh in the name of *the LORD* **Yah Veh**:
we have blessed you
out of the house of *the LORD* **Yah Veh.**
27 *God* **El** is *the LORD* **Yah Veh,**
which hath *shewed us light* **enlightened us**:
bind the *sacrifice* **celebration** with *cords* **ropes,**
even unto the horns of the **sacrifice** altar.
28 Thou art my *God* **El,**
and I *will praise* **shall spread hands unto** thee:
thou art my *God* **Elohim,** I *will* **shall** exalt thee.
29 O *give thanks* **spread hands**
unto *the LORD* **Yah Veh**;
for he is good:
for his mercy *endureth for ever* **is eternal.**

119 ALEPH.
1 *Blessed* **Blithed** *are* the
undefiled **integrious** in the way,
who walk in the *law* **torah** of *the LORD* **Yah Veh.**
2 *Blessed* **Blithed** *are* they
that *keep* **guard** his *testimonies* **witnesses,**
and that seek him with the whole heart.
3 They also do no *iniquity* **wickedness**:
they walk in his ways.
4 Thou hast *commanded* **misvahed** *us*
to *keep* **guard** thy precepts *diligently* **mightily.**
5 O that my ways
were *directed* **prepared** to *keep* **guard** thy statutes!
6 Then shall I not *be ashamed* **shame,**
when I *have respect* **look**
unto all thy *commandments* **misvoth.**
7 I *will praise* **shall spread hands unto** thee
with *uprightness* **straightness** of heart,
when I shall have learned
thy *righteous judgments* **judgments of justness.**
8 I *will keep* **shall guard** thy statutes:
O forsake me not *utterly* **mightily.**

BETH.
9 Wherewithal shall a young
man *cleanse* **purify** his way?
by *taking heed thereto* **guarding** according to thy word.
10 With my whole heart have I sought thee:
O let me not *wander* **err inadvertantly**
from thy *commandments* **misvoth.**
11 Thy *word* **sayings** have I *hid*
treasured in mine heart,
that I might not sin against thee.

12 Blessed *art* thou, O *LORD* **Yah Veh**:
teach me thy statutes.
13 With my lips
have I *declared* **scribed** all the judgments of thy mouth.
14 I have rejoiced
in the way of thy *testimonies* **witnesses**,
as *much as in all riches* **over all wealth**.
15 I *will* **shall** meditate in thy precepts,
and *have respect* **scan** unto thy ways.
16 I *will* **shall** delight myself in thy statutes:
I *will* **shall** not forget thy word.
19 Open to me the portals of justness;
I go in and I spread hands to Yah;
20 this portal of Yah Veh, wherein the just enter:
21 I spread hands to you;
for you answered me and become my salvation.
22 The stone the builders refused
becomes the head of the corner.
23 This becomes from Yah Veh
—marvellous in our eyes.
24 This *is* the day Yah Veh worked;
we twirl and cheer therein.
25 Save now* I beseech,
I beseech you, O Yah Veh;
O Yah Veh, I beseech you,
prosper, I beseech.

*Hoshia Nah

26 Blessed
—he who comes in the name of Yah Veh; we
bless you from the house of Yah Veh.
27 El *is* Yah Veh; he enlightens us: bind the celebration
with ropes to the horns of the sacrifice altar.
28 You *are* my El, and I spread hands to you;
you are my Elohim, I exalt you.
29 O spread hands to Yah Veh;
for good; for his mercy eternal.

119 ALEPH.

1 Blithed—the integrious in the way,
who walk in the torah of Yah Veh:
2 blithed—they who guard his witnesses
—who seek him with the whole heart:
3 they do no wickedness;
they walk in his ways.
4 You misvahed us
to guard your precepts mightily.
5 O that I prepared my ways
to guard your statutes!
6 Then I shame not
when I look to all your misvoth:
7 I spread hands to you with straightness of heart
when I learn your judgments of justness:
8 I guard your statutes:
O forsake me not mightily.

BETH.

9 How purifies a young man his way?
By guarding according to your word.
10 With my whole heart I sought you;
that I not err inadvertantly from your misvoth:
11 I treasure your sayings in my heart
that I not sin against you.
12 Blessed you, O Yah Veh;
teach me your statutes.
13 With my lips
I scribe all the judgments of your mouth;
14 I rejoice in the way of your witnesses
as over all wealth;
15 I meditate in your precepts
and scan to your ways;
16 I delight myself in your statutes
—I forget not your word.

GIMEL.

17 Deal *bountifully* with thy servant,
that I may live, and *keep* **guard** thy word.
18 *Open* **Expose** thou mine eyes,
that I may behold *wondrous things* **marvels**
out of thy *law* **torah**.
19 I am a *stranger* **sojourner** in the earth:
hide not thy *commandments* **misvoth** from me.
20 My soul *breaketh* **crusheth**
for the *longing* **desire**
that it hath unto thy judgments at all times.
21 Thou hast rebuked the *proud* **arrogant**
that are cursed,
which *do* err **inadvertently**
from thy *commandments* **misvoth**.
22 *Remove* **Roll away** from me
reproach and *contempt* **disrespect**;
for I have *kept* **guarded** thy *testimonies* **witnesses**.
23 *Princes* **Governors** also
did sit **settled** and *speak* **worded** against me:
but thy servant *did meditate* **meditated** in thy statutes.
24 Thy *testimonies* **witnesses** also are my delight
and my *counsellors* **councilmen**.

DALETH.

25 My soul *cleaveth* **adhereth** unto the dust:
quicken **enliven** thou me according to thy word.
26 I have *declared* **scribed** my ways,
and thou *heardest* **answerest** me:
teach me thy statutes.

27 *Make* **Have** me to *understand* **discern**
the way of thy precepts:
so shall I *talk* **meditate** of thy *wondrous works* **marvels**.
28 My soul *melteth* **drippeth** for *heaviness* **grief**:
strengthen **raise** thou me according unto thy word.
29 *Remove* **Turn aside** from me
the way of *lying* **falsehoods**:
and *grant me thy law graciously*
with thy torah grant me charism.
30 I have chosen the way of *truth* **trustworthiness**:
thy judgments have I *laid* **placed** *before me*.
31 I have *stuck* **adhered** unto
thy *testimonies* **witnesses**:
O *LORD* **Yah Veh**, *put me not to* shame **me not**.
32 I *will* **shall** run the way of
thy *commandments* **misvoth**,
when thou shalt enlarge my heart.
HE.
33 Teach me, O *LORD* **Yah**
Veh, the way of thy statutes;
and I shall *keep* **guard** it unto the end.
34 *Give me understanding* **Have me discern**,
and I shall *keep* **guard** thy *law* **torah**;
yea, I shall *observe* **guard** it with my whole heart.
35 *Make* **Aim** me *to go*
in the path of thy *commandments* **misvoth**;
for therein do I delight.
36 *Incline* **Spread** my heart unto
thy *testimonies* **witnesses**,
and not to *covetousness* **greed**.
37 *Turn away* **Pass** mine eyes
from *beholding* **seeing** vanity;
and *quicken* **enliven** thou me in thy way.
38 *Stablish* **Raise up** thy *word*
sayings unto thy servant,
who *is devoted to thy fear* **aweth thee**.
39 *Turn away* **Pass** my reproach which I fear:
for thy judgments are good.
40 Behold, I have *longed* **desired** after thy precepts:
quicken **enliven** me in thy *righteousness* **justness**.
VAU.
41 Let thy mercies come also unto me,
O *LORD* **Yah Veh**,
even thy salvation, according to thy *word* **sayings**.
42 So shall I have *wherewith* **a word**
to answer him that reproacheth me:
for I *trust* **confide** in thy word.
43 And *take* **strip** not the word of truth
utterly **mightily** out of my mouth;
for I have *hoped in* **awaited** thy judgments.
44 So shall I *keep* **guard** thy *law* **torah** continually
for ever **eternally** and *ever* **eternally**.
GIMEL.
17 Deal with your servant
—I live and guard your word;
18 expose my eyes
to behold the marvels of your torah:
19 I *am* a sojourner in the earth;
hide not your misvoth from me:
20 my soul crushes for the desire
unto your judgments at all times.
21 You rebuke the cursed arrogant
who err inadvertently from your misvoth;
22 roll reproach and disrespect away from me
for I guard your witnesses:
23 governors settle and word against me
but your servant meditates in your statutes;
24 your witnesses
are my delight and my councilmen.
DALETH.
25 My soul adheres to the dust;
enliven me according to your word.
26 I scribe my ways and you answer me;
teach me your statutes:
27 have me discern the way of your precepts;
I meditate of your marvels:
28 my soul drips of grief;
raise me according to your word:
29 turn aside the way of falsehoods from me;
and with your torah grant me charism:
30 I choose the way of trustworthiness;
I placed your judgments:
31 I adhere to your witnesses;
O Yah Veh, shame me not:
32 I run the way of your misvoth;
you enlarge my heart.
HE.
33 Teach me, O Yah Veh, the way of your statutes;
and I guard it *to* the end:
34 have me discern, and I guard your torah;
yes, I guard it with my whole heart:
35 aim me in the path of your misvoth;
for therein I delight:
36 spread my heart to your witnesses
and not to greed:
37 pass my eyes from seeing vanity;
and enliven me in your way:
38 raise up your sayings to your servant
who awes you:
39 pass away my reproach which I fear;

for your judgments are good.
40 Behold, I desire after your precepts;
enliven me in your justness.
VAU.
41 Your mercies come to me, O Yah Veh,
your salvation, according to your sayings:
42 and I word to answer him who reproaches me;
for I confide in your word:
43 and strip not the word of truth
mightily from my mouth; for I await your judgments:
44 I guard your torah continually
—eternally and eternally:
45 And I *will* **shall** walk at *liberty* **large**:
for I seek thy precepts.
46 I *will speak* **shall word** of
thy *testimonies* **witnesses**
also *before kings* **in front of sovereigns**,
and *will* **shall** not *be ashamed* **shame**.
47 And I *will* **shall** delight myself
in thy *commandments* **misvoth**,
which I have loved.
48 My *hands* **palms** also
will **shall** I lift up unto thy *commandments* **misvoth**,
which I have loved;
and I *will* **shall** meditate in thy statutes.
ZAIN.
49 Remember the word unto thy servant,
upon which thou hast caused me to *hope* **await**.
50 This is my *comfort* **sighing**
in my *affliction* **humiliation**:
for thy *word hath quickened* **sayings have enlivened** me.
51 The *proud* **arrogant**
have *had me greatly in derision* **mightily scorned me**:
yet have I not *declined* **stretched** from thy *law* **torah**.
52 I remembered thy judgments of *old* **eternity**,
O *LORD* **Yah Veh**;
and have *comforted* **sighed over** myself.
53 *Horror* **Raging** hath taken hold upon me
because of the wicked that forsake thy *law* **torah**.
54 Thy statutes have been my *songs* **psalms**
in the house of my *pilgrimage* **sojournings**.
55 I have remembered thy
name, O *LORD* **Yah Veh**,
in the night,
and have *kept* **guarded** thy *law* **torah**.
56 This I had, because I *kept* **guarded** thy precepts.
CHETH.
57 *Thou art my portion*, O *LORD*
Yah Veh is my allotment:
I have said that I *would keep* **should guard** thy words.
58 I *intreated* **stroked** thy *favour*
face with my whole heart:
be merciful unto **grant** me **charism**
according to thy *word* **sayings**.
59 I *thought on* **fabricated** my ways,
and turned my feet unto thy *testimonies* **witnesses**.
60 I *made haste* **hastened**, and *delayed* **lingered** not
to *keep* **guard** thy *commandments* **misvoth**.
61 The *bands* **cords** of the wicked
have *robbed* **surrounded** me:
but I have not forgotten thy *law* **torah**.
62 At midnight I *will* **shall** rise
to *give thanks* **spread hands** unto thee
because of thy *righteous* judgments **of justness**.
63 I am a companion of all them that *fear* **awe** thee,
and of them that *keep* **guard** thy precepts.
64 The earth, O *LORD* **Yah**
Veh, is full of thy mercy:
teach me thy statutes.
TETH.
65 Thou hast *dealt well* **worked**
good with thy servant,
O *LORD* **Yah Veh**, according unto thy word.
66 Teach me good *judgment* **taste** and knowledge:
for I have *believed* **trusted** thy *commandments* **misvoth**.
67 Before I was *afflicted* **humbled**
I *went astray* **erred inadvertently**:
but now have I *kept* **guarded** thy *word* **sayings**.
68 Thou art good, and doest good;
teach me thy statutes.
69 The *proud* **arrogant**
have *forged a lie* **patched falsehood** against me:
but I *will keep* **shall guard** thy precepts
with my whole heart.
70 Their heart is *as fat as grease* **fattened**;
but I delight in thy *law* **torah**.
71 It is good for me that I have
been *afflicted* **humbled**;
that I might learn thy statutes.
72 The *law* **torah** of thy mouth
is better unto me than thousands of gold and silver.
45 And I walk at large
for I seek your precepts:
46 I word of your witnesses in front of sovereigns
and shame not:
47 I delight myself in your misvoth which I love;
48 I lift my palms to your misvoth which I love;
and I meditate in your statutes.
ZAIN.
49 Remember the word to your servant,

on which you have me await:
50 this is my sighing in my humiliation;
for your sayings enliven me.
51 The arrogant scorn me mightily;
yet I spread not from your torah:
52 I remember your judgments of eternity,
O Yah Veh;
and sigh over myself:
53 raging seizes me
because of the wicked who forsake your torah.
54 Your statutes became my psalms
in the house of my sojournings:
55 I remembered your name, O Yah Veh,
in the night;
and guarded your torah:
56 this became me
because I guarded your precepts.

CHETH.

57 Yah Veh *is* my allotment;
I say to guard your words:
58 I stroke your face with my whole heart;
grant me charism according to your sayings:
59 I fabricate my ways
and turned my feet to your witnesses:
60 I hasten, and linger not to guard your misvoth.
61 The cords of the wicked surround me;
I forget not your torah:
62 at midnight I rise to spread hands to you
because of your judgments of justness:
63 I *am* a companion to all who awe you
and to them who guard your precepts.
64 The earth, O Yah Veh, is full of your mercy;
teach me your statutes.

TETH.

65 You work good with your servant,
O Yah Veh, according to your word:
66 teach me good taste and knowledge;
for I trust your misvoth.
67 Ere I humbled, I erred inadvertently;
and now I guard your sayings:
68 you are good and do good;
teach me your statutes:
69 the arrogant patch falsehood against me;
I guard your precepts with my whole heart:
70 their heart fattens;
I—I delight in your torah:
71 *it is* good for me to be humbled
—to learn your statutes:
72 the torah of your mouth is better to me
than thousands of gold and silver.

JOD.

73 Thy hands
have *made* **worked** me and *fashioned* **established** me:
give me understanding **have me discern**,
that I may learn thy *commandments* **misvoth**.
74 They that *fear* **awe** thee
will be glad **shall cheer** when they see me;
because I have *hoped in* **awaited** thy word.
75 I know, O *LORD* **Yah Veh**,
that thy judgments are *right* **justness**,
and that thou in *faithfulness* **trustworthiness**
hast *afflicted* **humbled** me.
76 Let, I pray thee,
thy *merciful kindness* **mercy** be for my *comfort* **sighing**,
according to thy *word* **sayings** unto thy servant.
77 Let thy tender mercies come
unto me, that I may live:
for thy *law* **torah** is my delight.
78 Let the *proud be ashamed* **arrogant shame**;
for they
dealt perversely with me without a cause
twisted me falsely:
but I *will* **shall** meditate in thy precepts.
79 Let those that *fear* **awe** thee turn unto me,
and those that have known thy *testimonies* **witnesses**.
80 Let my heart be *sound*
integrious in thy statutes;
that I *be* **shame** not *ashamed.*

CAPH.

81 My soul *fainteth* **is finished**
off for thy salvation:
but I *hope in* **await** thy word.
82 Mine eyes *fail* **are finished**
off for thy *word* **sayings**,
saying, When *wilt* **shalt** thou *comfort* **sigh over** me?
83 For I am become like a *bottle* **skin** in the smoke;
yet do I not forget thy statutes.
84 How many are the days of thy servant?
when *wilt* **shalt** thou *execute* **work** judgment
on them that *persecute* **pursue** me?
85 The *proud* **arrogant** have digged pits for me,
which are not after thy *law* **torah**.
86 All thy *commandments* **misvoth**
are *faithful* **trustworthy**:
they *persecute* **pursue** me *wrongfully* **falsely**;
help thou me.
87 They had almost *consumed* **finished** me **off**
upon earth;
but I forsook not thy precepts.

88 *Quicken* **Enliven** me after
thy *lovingkindness* **mercy**;
so shall I *keep* **guard** the *testimony*
witness of thy mouth.
LAMED.
89 *For ever* **Eternally,** O *LORD* **Yah Veh,**
thy word is *settled* **stationed** in *heaven* **the heavens.**
90 Thy *faithfulness* **trustworthiness**
is unto all generations **generation to generation**:
thou hast established the earth, and it *abideth* **standeth.**
91 They *continue* **stand** this day
according to *thine ordinances* **thy judgments**:
for all are thy servants.
92 Unless thy *law* **torah** had been my delights,
I should then have *perished* **destructed**
in *mine affliction* **my humiliation.**
93 I *will never* **shall eternally**
not forget thy precepts:
for with them thou hast *quickened* **enlivened** me.
94 I am thine, save me: for I
have sought thy precepts.
95 The wicked have *waited for*
awaited me to destroy me:
but I *will consider* **shall discern**
thy *testimonies* **witnesses.**
96 I have seen an end of all *perfection* **conclusion**:
but thy *commandment* **misvah** is
exceeding **mighty** broad.
MEM.
97 O how love I thy *law* **torah**!
it is my meditation all the day.
98 *Thou through thy commandments* **Thy misvoth**
hast made me wiser **have enwisened me**
than **above** mine enemies:
for they are *ever* **eternally** with me.
99 I *have* **comprehend** more *understanding*
than all my teachers:
for thy *testimonies* **witnesses** are my meditation.
JOD.
73 Your hands worked me and established me:
have me to discern; to learn your misvoth.
74 They who awe you cheer when they see me;
because I await your word:
75 I know, O Yah Veh,
your judgments are justness
and in trustworthiness you humble me.
76 I pray you,
that your mercy be for my sighing,
according to your sayings to your servant.
77 Your tender mercies come to me; I live:
your torah is my delight.
78 Shame the arrogant
—for they twist me falselyShame
I meditate in your precepts.
79 May they who awe you turn to me;
with them who know your witnesses.
80 May my heart be integrious in your statutes;
that I not shame.
CAPH.
81 My soul finishes off for your salvation;
for I await your word:
82 my eyes finish off for your sayings,
saying, When sigh you over me?
83 For I become as a skin in smoke;
yet I forget not your statutes.
84 How many are the days of your servant?
When work you judgment on my pursuers?
85 The arrogant dig pits for me
which are not according your torah.
86 All your misvoth *are* trustworthy;
they pursue me falsely; help me!
87 They almost finish me off on earth;
and I—I forsake not your precepts.
88 Enliven me after your mercy;
and I guard the witness of your mouth.
LAMED.
89 Eternally, O Yah Veh,
your word is stationed in the heavens;
90 your trustworthiness generation to generation:
you established the earth and it stands.
91 They stand this day
according to your judgments;
for all *are* your servants.
92 Unless your torah *were* my delights
I had destructed in my humiliation:
93 I forget not your precepts eternally;
for with them you enliven me.
94 I am yours; save me:
for I seek your precepts:
95 the wicked await me to destroy me;
I discern your witnesses:
96 I see the end of all conclusion;
your misvah *is* mighty broad.
MEM.
97 O how I love your torah
—my meditation all the day:
98 your misvoth enwisen me above my enemies;
for they are eternally with me:
99 I comprehend more than all my teachers;
for your witnesses are my meditation:

exeGeses ready research BIBLE

100 I *understand* **discern** more
than the *ancients* **elders**,
because I *keep* **guard** thy precepts.
101 I have *refrained* **restrained** my feet
from every evil way,
that I might *keep* **guard** thy word.
102 I have not *departed* **turned aside**
from thy judgments:
for thou hast taught me.
103 How *sweet* **smooth** are thy *words* **sayings**
unto my *taste* **palate**!
yea, sweeter—than honey to my mouth!
104 Through thy precepts I *get*
understanding **discern**:
therefore I hate every false way.

NUN.

105 Thy word is a lamp unto my feet,
and a light unto my path.
106 I have *sworn* **oathed**,
and I *will perform* **shall raise** it,
that I *will keep* **shall guard**
thy *righteous* judgments **of justness**.
107 I am *afflicted very much* **humbled mightily**:
quicken **enliven** me, O *LORD* **Yah Veh**,
according unto thy word.
108 *Accept* **Be pleased**, I beseech thee,
the *freewill offerings* **voluntaries** of my mouth, O
LORD **Yah Veh**, and teach me thy judgments.
109 My soul is continually in my *hand* **palm**:
yet do I not forget thy *law* **torah**.
110 The wicked have *laid* **given** a snare for me:
yet I *erred* **strayed** not from thy precepts.
111 Thy *testimonies* **witnesses**
have I *taken as an heritage for ever* **inherited eternally**:
for they are the rejoicing of my heart.
112 I have *inclined* **spread** mine heart
to *perform* **work** thy statutes *alway* **eternally**,
even unto the end.

SAMECH.

113 I hate *vain thought* **skeptics**:
but thy *law do* **torah** I love.
114 Thou art my *hiding place* **covert**
and my *shield* **buckler**:
I *hope in* **await** thy word.
115 *Depart* **Turn away** from
me, ye *evildoers* **vilifiers**:
for I *will keep* **shall guard**
the *commandments* **misvoth** of my *God* **Elohim**.
116 Uphold me according unto thy *word* **sayings**,
that I may live:
and let me not *be ashamed* **shame**
of my *hope* **expectation**.
117 Hold thou me up, and I shall be *safe* **saved**:
and I *will have respect* **shall look**
unto thy statutes continually.
118 Thou hast *trodden down* **trampled** all them
that err **inadvertently** from thy statutes:
for their deceit is falsehood.
119 Thou *puttest away* **shabbathizest**
all the wicked of the earth like dross:
therefore I love thy *testimonies* **witnesses**.
120 My flesh *trembleth* **standeth on end**
for *fear* **dread** of thee;
and I *am afraid of* **awe** thy judgments.

AIN.

121 I have *done* **worked** judgment
and *justice* **justness**:
leave me not to mine oppressors.
122 *Be surety* **Pledge** for thy servant for good:
let not the *proud* **arrogant** oppress me.
123 Mine eyes *fail* **are finished off** for thy salvation,
and for the *word* **sayings** of thy *righteousness* **justness**.
124 *Deal* **Work** with thy servant
according unto thy mercy,
and teach me thy statutes.
125 I am thy servant;
give **have** me *understanding* **discern**,
that I may know thy *testimonies* **witnesses**.
126 It is time *for thee, LORD* **O Yah Veh**, to work:
for they have *made void* **broken** thy *law* **torah**.
100 I discern more than the elders;
because I guard your precepts:
101 I restrain my feet from every evil way
to guard your word:
102 I turn not aside from your judgments;
for you taught me.
103 How smooth your sayings to my palate!
—than honey to my mouth!
104 Through your precepts I discern;
so I hate every false way.

NUN.

105 Your word is a lamp to my feet
—a light to my path:
106 I oath and I raise
to guard your judgments of justness:
107 I am humbled mightily; enliven me,
O Yah Veh, according to your word.
108 Be pleased, I beseech you,

by the voluntaries of my mouth,
O Yah Veh, and teach me your judgments.
109 My soul *is* continually in my palm;
yet I forget not your torah:
110 the wicked give a snare for me;
yet I stray not from your precepts:
111 I inherited your witnesses eternally
—the rejoicing of my heart:
112 I spread my heart to work your statutes
—eternally—to the end.
SAMECH.
113 I hate skeptics; and your torah I love.
114 You are my covert and my buckler;
I await your word.
115 Turn away from me, you vilifiers;
for I guard the misvoth of my Elohim.
116 Uphold me according to your sayings,
that I live;
that I not shame because of my expectation:
117 uphold me and I am saved;
and I look to your statutes continually.
118 You trample them all
who err inadvertently from your statutes;
for their deceit is falsehood:
119 you shabbathize all the wicked of the earth
as dross:
so I love your witnesses.
120 My flesh stands on end for dread of you;
and I awe your judgments.
AIN.
121 I worked judgment and justness;
leave me not to my oppressors:
122 pledge for your servant for good;
that the arrogant not oppress me:
123 my eyes finish off for your salvation
and for the sayings of your justness.
124 Work with your servant according to
your mercy; and teach me your statutes.
125 I *am* your servant;
have me discern to know your witnesses.
126 It is time, O Yah Veh, to work;
for they break your torah.
127 Therefore
I love thy *commandments* **misvoth** above gold;
yea, above *fine* **pure** gold.
128 Therefore I *esteem* **straighten** all thy precepts
concerning all things to be **all** right;
and I hate every false way.
PE.
129 Thy *testimonies* **witnesses**
are *wonderful* **marvels**:
therefore *doth* my soul *keep* **guardeth** them.
130 The entrance of thy words giveth light;
it giveth understanding unto the simple
so that the gullible may discern.
131 I *opened* **gaped** my mouth, and *panted* **gulped**:
for I longed for thy *commandments* **misvoth.**
132 *Look thou upon* **Face** me,
and *be merciful unto me* **grant me charism,**
as thou usest to do **and judgment**
unto those that love thy name.
133 *Order* **Establish** my steps in thy *word* **sayings**:
and let not any *iniquity* **mischief**
have dominion over **dominate** me.
134 Deliver me from the
oppression of *man* **humanity**:
so *will I keep* **shall I guard** thy precepts.
135 *Make* **Lighten** thy face *to*
shine upon thy servant;
and teach me thy statutes.
136 *Rivers* **Rivulets** of waters
run down **descend** mine eyes,
because they *keep* **guard** not thy *law* **torah.**
TZADDI.
137 *Righteous* **Just** art thou, O *LORD* **Yah Veh,**
and *upright* **straight** are thy judgments.
138 Thy *testimonies* **witnesses**
that thou hast *commanded* **misvahed**
are *righteous* **justness**
and *very faithful* **mighty trustworthy.**
139 My zeal hath *consumed* **exterminated** me,
because
mine enemies **my tribulators** have forgotten thy words.
140 Thy *word* **saying** is *very pure* **mighty refined**:
therefore thy servant loveth it.
141 I am *small* **insignificant** and despised:
yet do not I forget thy precepts.
142 Thy *righteousness* **justness**
is an *everlasting righteousness* **eternal justness,**
and thy *law* **torah** is the truth.
143 *Trouble* **Tribulation** and *anguish* **distress**
have *taken hold on* **found** me:
yet thy *commandments* **misvoth** are my delights.
144 The *righteousness* **justness**
of thy *testimonies* **witnesses**
is *everlasting* **eternal**:
give me understanding **have me discern**, and I shall live.
KOPH.
145 I *cried* **called** with my whole heart;

hear me **answer**, O *LORD* **Yah Veh**:
I *will keep* **shall guard** thy statutes.
146 I *cried* **called** unto thee; save me,
and I shall *keep* **guard** thy *testimonies* **witnesses**.
147 I *prevented* **anticipated**
the *dawning of the morning* **evening breeze**, and cried:
I *hoped in* **awaited** thy word.
148 Mine eyes *prevent* **anticipate** the *night* watches,
that I might meditate in thy *word* **sayings**.
149 Hear my voice
according unto thy *lovingkindness* **mercy**:
O *LORD* **Yah Veh**,
quicken **enliven** me according to thy judgment.
150 They draw nigh
that *follow after mischief* **pursue intrigue**:
they are far from thy *law* **torah**.
151 Thou art near, O *LORD* **Yah Veh**;
and all thy *commandments* **misvoth** are truth.
152 *Concerning thy testimonies* **Thy witnesses**,
I have known of *old* **antiquity**
that thou hast founded them *for ever* **eternally**.
127 So I love your misvoth above gold
—yes, above pure gold:
128 so I straighten all your precepts
to be all right:
I hate every false way.
PE.
129 Your witnesses are marvels;
so my soul guards them:
130 the entrance of your words enlighten;
so that the gullible discern:
131 I gape my mouth and gulp;
for I yearn for your misvoth.
132 Face me;
and grant me charism and judgment
to them who love your name:
133 establish my steps in your sayings;
that no mischief dominate me:
134 deliver me from the oppression of humanity;
I guard your precepts.
135 Light your face on your servant;
and teach me your statutes.
136 Rivulets of waters descend my eyes,
because they guard not your torah.
TZADDI.
137 You *are* just, O Yah Veh,
and straight *are* your judgments:
138 your witnesses you misvahed *are* justness
—mighty trustworthy:
139 my zeal exterminates me
because my tribulators forget your words:
140 your saying is mighty refined;
your servant loves it.
141 I—insignificant and despised;
yet I forget not your precepts:
142 your justness—an eternal justness
and your torah—truth.
143 Tribulation and distress find me;
yet your misvoth *are* my delights.
144 The justness of your witnesses *is* eternal;
have me discern, and I live.
KOPH.
145 I call with my whole heart;
answer, O Yah Veh:
I guard your statutes.
146 I call to you;
save me,
and I guard your witnesses.
147 I anticipate the evening breeze and cry;
I await your word:
148 my eyes anticipate the watches
to meditate in your sayings:
149 hear my voice, according to your mercy,
O Yah Veh,
enliven me according to your judgment.
150 They who pursue intrigue draw nigh
—far from your torah:
151 you are near, O Yah Veh,
and all your misvoth are truth.
152 I have known your witnesses from antiquity
—that you founded them eternally.
RESH.
153 *Consider mine affliction* **See my humiliation**,
and *deliver* **rescue** me:
for I do not forget thy *law* **torah**.
154 *Plead* **Defend** my *cause* **defence**, and deliver me:
quicken **enliven** me according to thy *word* **sayings**.
155 Salvation is far from the wicked:
for they seek not thy statutes.
156 Great are thy tender mercies, O *LORD* **Yah Veh**:
quicken **enliven** me according to thy judgments.
157 Many are my *persecutors* **pursuers**
and *mine enemies* **my tribulators**;
yet *do I not decline* **I spread not** from
thy *testimonies* **witnesses**.
158 I *beheld* **saw them**
the transgressors **that deal covertly**,
and *was grieved* **loathed**;
because they *kept* **guarded** not thy *word* **sayings**.

159 *Consider* **See** how I love thy precepts:
quicken **enliven** me, O *LORD* **Yah Veh**,
according to thy *lovingkindness* **mercy**.
160 *Thy word is true from the beginning*
The sum of thy word is truth:
and every one of thy *righteous* judgments **of justness**
endureth for ever **is eternal**.
SCHIN.
161 *Princes* **Governors** have *persecuted* **pursued** me
without a cause **gratuitously**:
but my heart *standeth in awe of* **dreadeth** thy word.
162 I rejoice at thy *word* **sayings**,
as one that findeth great spoil.
163 I hate and abhor *lying* **falsehood**
but thy *law do* **torah** I love.
164 Seven times a day *do I praise* **I halal** thee
because of thy *righteous* judgments **of justness**.
165 Great *peace* **shalom**
have they which love thy *law* **torah**:
and *nothing shall offend them*
they have no stumblingblock.
166 *LORD* **O Yah Veh**,
I have *hoped for* **expected** thy salvation,
and *done* **worked** thy *commandments* **misvoth**.
167 My soul hath *kept* **guarded**
thy *testimonies* **witnesses**;
and I love them *exceedingly* **mightily**.
168 I have *kept* **guarded**
thy precepts and thy *testimonies* **witnesses**:
for all my ways are *before* **in front of** thee.
TAU.
169 Let my *cry* **shouting**
come near *before thee* **at thy face**,
O *LORD* **Yah Veh**:
give **have** me *understanding* **discern**
according to thy word.
170 Let my supplication come *before thee* **at thy face**:
deliver **rescue** me according to thy *word* **sayings**.
171 My lips shall *utter praise* **gush halal**,
when thou hast taught me thy statutes.
172 My tongue shall *speak*
answer of thy *word* **sayings**:
for all thy *commandments* **misvoth**
are *righteousness* **justness**.
173 Let thine hand help me;
for I have chosen thy precepts.
174 I have *longed* **desired** for thy salvation,
O *LORD* **Yah Veh**;
and thy *law* **torah** is my delight.
175 Let my soul live, and it shall *praise* **halal** thee;
and let thy judgments help me.
176 I have *gone astray* **strayed** like a lost *sheep* **lamb**;
seek thy servant;
for I *do not* forget **not** thy *commandments* **misvoth**.

120 A Song of degrees.
1 In my *distress* **tribulation**
I *cried* **called** unto *the LORD* **Yah Veh**,
and he *heard* **answered** *me*.
2 *Deliver* **Rescue** my soul, O *LORD* **Yah Veh**,
from *lying* **false** lips, *and* from a deceitful tongue.

RESH.
153 See my humiliation and rescue me;
for I forget not your torah:
154 defend my defence and deliver me;
enliven me according to your sayings
155 Salvation is far from the wicked
for they seek not your statutes:
156 Great are your tender mercies, O Yah Veh;
enliven me according to your judgments:
157 many are my pursuers and my tribulators;
yet I spread not from your witnesses:
158 I see them who deal covertly, and I loathe;
because they guard not your sayings.
159 See how I love your precepts;
enliven me, O Yah Veh, according to your mercy.
160 The sum of your word is truth;
and every one of your judgments of justness
is eternal.
SCHIN.
161 Governors pursue me gratuitously;
because of your words, my heart dreads.
162 I rejoice at your sayings,
as one who finds great spoil:
163 I hate and abhor falsehood
but love your torah:
164 seven times a day I halal you
because of your judgments of justness.
165 Great shalom have they who love your torah;
they have no stumblingblock.
166 O Yah Veh,
I await your salvation and work your misvoth:
167 my soul guards your witnesses;
and I love them mightily:
168 I guard your precepts and your witnesses;
all my ways are in front of you.
TAU.
169 My shouting comes near at your face,
O Yah Veh;
have me discern according to your word:

170 my supplication comes at your face;
rescue me according to your sayings:
171 my lips gush halal
for you teach me your statutes;
172 my tongue answers of your sayings;
for all your misvoth are justness:
173 your hand helps me;
for I chose your precepts.
174 I desire your salvation, O Yah Veh,
and your torah is my delight:
175 my soul lives and halals you;
your judgments help me:
176 I strayed as a lost lamb;
seek your servant; for I forget not your misvoth.

120 A Song of Degrees.
1 In my tribulation
I call to Yah Veh and he answers.
2 Rescue my soul, O Yah Veh,
from false lips—from a deceitful tongue.
3 What shall be given unto thee?
or what shall be *done* **added** unto thee,
thou *false* **deceitful** tongue?
4 *Sharp* **Pointened** arrows of the mighty,
with coals of juniper.
5 Woe is me, that I sojourn in *Mesech* **Meshech**,
that I dwell in the tents of *Kedar* **Qedar**!
6 My soul hath *long dwelt* **greatly tabernacled**
with him that hateth *peace* **shalom**.
7 I am for *peace* **shalom**:
but when I *speak* **word**, they are for war.

121 A Song of degrees.
1 I *will* **shall** lift up mine eyes
unto the *hills* **mountains**,
from whence cometh my help.
2 My help *cometh* from *the LORD* **Yah Veh**,
which *made heaven* **worked the heavens** and earth.
3 He *will* **shall** not *suffer* **give**
thy foot to *be moved* **topple**:
he that *keepeth* **guardeth** thee *will* **shall** not slumber.
4 Behold, he that *keepeth Israel* **guardeth Yisra El**
shall neither slumber nor sleep.
5 *The LORD* **Yah Veh** is thy *keeper* **guard**:
the LORD **Yah Veh** is thy shade upon thy right hand.
6 The sun shall not smite thee by day,
nor the moon by night.
7 *The LORD* **Yah Veh**
shall *preserve* **guard** thee from all evil:
he shall *preserve* **guard** thy soul.
8 *The LORD* **Yah Veh**
shall *preserve* **guard** thy going out and thy coming in
from this time *forth*, and even *for evermore* **eternally**.

122 A Song of degrees of David.
1 I *was glad* **cheered** when they said unto me,
Let us go into the house of *the LORD* **Yah Veh**.
2 Our feet shall stand within thy *gates* **portals**,
O *Jerusalem* **Yeru Shalem**.
3 *Jerusalem* **Yeru Shalem** is builded
as a city *that is compact* **joined** together:
4 *Whither* **And there** the
tribes go up **scions ascend**,
the *tribes* **scions** of *the LORD* **Yah**,
unto the *testimony* **witness** of *Israel* **Yisra El**,
to *give thanks* **spread hands**
unto the name of *the LORD* **Yah Veh**.
5 For there are *set* **settled** thrones of judgment,
the thrones of the house of David.
6 *Pray* **Ask** for the *peace* **shalom**
of *Jerusalem* **Yeru Shalem**:
they shall *prosper* **be content** that love thee.
7 *Peace* **Shalom** be within thy *walls* **trenches**,
and *prosperity* **serenity** within thy *palaces* **citadels**.
8 For my brethren and *companions'* **friend's** sakes,
I *will now say* **shall beseech a word**,
Peace **Shalom** be within thee.
9 Because of the house
of the *LORD* **Yah Veh** our *God* **Elohim**
I *will* **shall** seek thy good.

123 A Song of degrees.
1 Unto thee lift I up mine eyes,
O thou that *dwellest* **settlest** in the heavens.
2 Behold, as the eyes of servants *look*
unto the hand of their *masters* **adonim**,
and as the eyes of a *maiden* **maid**
unto the hand of her *mistress* **lady**;
so our eyes
wait upon the LORD **unto Yah Veh** our *God* **Elohim**,
until that he *have mercy upon* **grant** us **charism**.
3 *Have mercy upon* **Grant** us **charism**,
O *LORD* **Yah Veh**,
have mercy upon **grant** us **charism**:
for we are *exceedingly filled* **abundantly satiated**
with *contempt* **disrespect**.
4 Our soul is *exceedingly*
filled **abundantly satiated**
with the *scorning* **derision** of those that *are at ease* **relax**,
and with the *contempt* **disrespect** of the *proud* **pompous**.
3 What gives he to you?
What adds he to you,
you deceitful tongue?
4 Pointened arrows of the mighty

with coals of juniper.
5 Woe is me; I sojourn in Meshech;
I dwell in the tents of Qedar!
6 How greatly my soul tabernacles
with him who hates shalom.
7 I *am* for shalom;
and when I word, they are for war.

121 A Song of Degrees.
1 I lift my eyes to the mountains.
Whence comes my help?
My help *is* from Yah Veh
who worked the heavens and earth.
3 He gives not your foot to topple;
your guards slumbers not:
4 behold, he who guards Yisra El
neither slumbers nor sleeps:
5 Yah Veh—your guard;
Yah Veh—your shade at your right;
6 neither the sun smites you by day
nor the moon by night.
7 Yah Veh guards you from all evil
—guards your soul:
8 Yah Veh guards
your going and your coming
from this time and even eternally.

122 A Song of Degrees: By David.
1 I cheer when they say to me,
To the house of Yah Veh we go.
2 Our feet stand within your
portals, O Yeru Shalem.
3 Yeru Shalem *is* built; as a city joined together:
4 and there the scions ascend
—the scions of Yah to the witness of Yisra El;
to spread hands to the name of Yah Veh:
5 for there the thrones of judgment settle
—the thrones of the house of David.
6 Ask *for* the shalom of Yeru Shalem;
they who love you are content:
7 shalom be within your trenches
and serenity within your citadels:
8 for sake of my brothers and friends
I beseech a word,
Shalom—within you.
9 Because of the house of Yah Veh our Elohim
I seek your good.

123 A Song of Degrees.
1 To you I lift my eyes, O settler in the heavens!
2 Behold,
as the eyes of servants to the hand of their adonim;
as the eyes of a maid to the hand of her lady;
thus our eyes to Yah Veh our Elohim,
until he grants us charism.
3 Grant us charism, O Yah Veh, grant us charism;
for we abundantly satiate with disrespectsake
4 our soul abundantly satiates
with the derision of them who relax
—with the disrespect of the pompous.

124 A Song of degrees of David.
1 If it had not been *the LORD* **for Yah Veh**
who was on our side,
now **I beseech,** may *Israel* **Yisra El** say;
2 If it had not been *the LORD* **for Yah Veh**
who was on our side,
when *men* **humanity** rose *up* against us:
3 Then they had swallowed us *up quick* **alive,**
when their wrath was kindled against us:
4 Then the waters had
overwhelmed **overflowed** us,
the *stream* **wadi** had *gone* **passed** over our soul:
5 Then the *proud* **overflowing** waters
had *gone* **passed** over our soul.
6 Blessed be *the LORD* **Yah Veh,**
who hath not given us as a prey to their teeth.
7 Our soul *is* escaped
as a bird out of the snare of the *fowlers* **ensnarers**:
the snare is broken, and we *are* escaped.
8 Our help is in the name of *the LORD* **Yah Veh,**
who *made heaven* **worked the heavens** and earth.

125 A Song of degrees.
1 They that *trust* **confide** in *the LORD* **Yah Veh**
shall be as mount *Zion* **Siyon,**
which *cannot be removed* **shall not totter,**
but *abideth for ever* **settleth eternally**.
2 As the mountains
are round about Jerusalem **surround Yeru Shalem,**
so *the LORD* **Yah Veh**
is round about **surroundeth** his people
from *henceforth* **this time** even *for ever* **eternally**.
3 For the *rod* **scion** of *the wicked* **wickedness**
shall not rest upon the *lot* **pebble** of the *righteous* **just**;
lest the *righteous* **just**
put forth **spread** their hands unto *iniquity* **wickedness**.
4 Do good, O *LORD* **Yah Veh,**
unto *those that be* **the** good,
and to *them that are upright* **the straight** in their hearts.
5 As for such as *turn aside* **pervert**
unto their *crooked ways* **crookednesses,**
the LORD **Yah Veh** shall *lead* **walk** them *forth*
with the *workers* **doers** of *iniquity* **mischief**:
but *peace* **shalom** shall be upon *Israel* **Yisra El.**

126 A Song of degrees.
1 When *the LORD turned*
again **Yah Veh returned**
the *captivity* **returning** of *Zion* **Siyon,**
we were like them that dream.
2 Then was our mouth filled with laughter,
and our tongue with *singing* **shouting:**
then said they among the *heathen* **goyim,**
The LORD **Yah Veh**
hath *done great things* **worked greatly** for them.
3 *The LORD* **Yah Veh**
hath *done great things* **worked greatly** for us;
whereof we *are glad* **cheer.**
4 *Turn again* **Return** our
captivity, O *LORD* **Yah Veh,**
as the *streams* **reservoirs** in the south.
5 They that *sow* **seed** in tears
shall *reap* **harvest** in *joy* **shouting.**
6 **In going,** He that goeth *forth* and weepeth,
bearing *precious* **sowing** seed,
shall doubtless come again with *rejoicing* **shouting,**
bringing **bearing** his sheaves *with him.*

127 A Song of degrees for *Solomon* **Shelomoh.**
1 Except *the LORD* **Yah Veh** build the house,
they *labour* **toil** in vain that build it:
except *the LORD keep* **Yah Veh guard** the city,
the *watchman waketh but* **guard guardeth** in vain.
2 It is vain for you to *rise up* **start** early,
to *sit up* **settle down** late,
to eat the bread of *sorrows* **contorting:**
for so **thus** he giveth his beloved sleep.
3 *Lo* **Behold,** *children* **sons**
are an *heritage* **inheritance**
of *the LORD* **Yah Veh:**
and the fruit of the *womb* **belly** is his *reward* **hire.**

124 A Song of Degrees by David.
1 Unless Yah Veh had been for us
I beseech, O Yisra El, say,
2 Unless Yah Veh had been for us,
when humanity rose against us;
3 then they had swallowed us alive
when they kindled their wrath against us:
4 the waters had overflowed us;
the wadi had passed over our soul;
5 the overflowing waters
had passed over our soul.
6 Blessed—Yah Veh,
who gave us not as a prey to their teeth:
7 our soul escaped as a bird
from the snare of the ensnarers; the
snare broke and we escaped.
8 Our help is in the name of Yah Veh,
who worked the heavens and earth.

125 A Song of Degrees.
1 They who confide in Yah
Veh *are* as mount Siyon;
it totters not; it settles eternally.
2 As the mountains surround Yeru Shalem,
thus Yah Veh surrounds his people
—from this time—even eternally.
3 For the scion of wickedness
rests not on the pebble of the just;
lest the just spread their hands to wickedness.
4 Do good, O Yah Veh,
to the good and to the straight in heart:
5 as for such as pervert to their crookednesses,
Yah Veh walks them with the doers of mischief.
Shalom on Yisra El.

126 A Song of Degrees.
1 When Yah Veh returned the returning of Siyon,
we were as dreamers:
2 our mouth filled with laughter
and our tongue with shouting.
Then they among the goyim say,
Yah Veh worked greatly for them;
3 Yah Veh worked greatly for us
—whereof we cheer.
4 Return our captivity, O Yah Veh,
as the reservoirs in the south.
5 They who seed in tears
shout in harvesting:
6 in going, he who comes weeping,
bearing his seed, and seeding,
doubtless comes again with shouting,
bearing his sheaves.

127 A Song of Degrees: By Shelomoh.
1 Except Yah Veh build the house
the builders toil in vain;
except Yah Veh guard the city
the guards guard in vain:
2 how vain for you to start early,
to settle down late,
to eat the bread of contorting; thus
he gives his beloved sleep.
3 Behold, sons are an inheritance of Yah Veh;
the fruit of the belly is his hire:
4 As arrows *are* in the hand of a mighty man;
so are *children* **sons** of the youth.

5 *Happy* **Blithe** *is* the *man* **mighty**
that hath his quiver full of them:
they shall not *be ashamed* **shame**,
but they shall *speak* **word**
with the enemies in the *gate* **portal**.

128 A Song of degrees.
1 *Blessed* **Blithed** *is* every one
that *feareth the LORD* **aweth Yah Veh**;
that walketh in his ways.
2 For thou shalt eat the labour
of *thine hands* **thy palms**:
happy **blithe** shalt thou be,
and it shall be *well* **good** with thee.
3 Thy *wife* **woman** shall be as
a *fruitful* **fruitbearing** vine
by the *sides* **flanks** of thine house:
thy *children* **sons** like olive *plants* **transplants**
round about **surrounding** thy table.
4 Behold, that thus shall the
man **mighty** be blessed
that *feareth the LORD* **aweth Yah Veh**.
5 *The LORD* **Yah Veh** shall
bless thee out of *Zion* **Siyon**:
and thou shalt see the good of *Jerusalem* **Yeru Shalem**
all the days of thy life.
6 Yea, thou shalt see thy
children's children **sons' sons**,
and *peace* **shalom** upon *Israel* **Yisra El**.

129 A Song of degrees.
1 *Many a time* **Greatly** have
they *afflicted* **tribulated** me
from my youth,
may *Israel now* **Yisra El, I beseech,** say:
2 *Many a time* **Greatly** have
they *afflicted* **tribulated** me
from my youth:
yet they have not prevailed against me.
3 The plowers plowed upon my back:
they *made long* **lengthened** their furrows.
4 *The LORD* **Yah Veh** is *righteous* **just**:
he hath *cut asunder* **chopped** the
cords **ropes** of the wicked.
5 Let them *all be confounded* **shame**
and *turned back* **apostatize**
that hate *Zion* **Siyon**.
6 Let them be as the grass
upon the *house tops* **roofs**,
which withereth *afore it groweth up* **ere it is drawn**:
7 Wherewith the mower
filleth not his *hand* **palm**;
nor he that bindeth *sheaves* his bosom.
8 Neither do they which *go* **pass** by say,
The blessing of *the LORD* **Yah Veh** be upon you:
we bless you in the name of *the LORD* **Yah Veh**.

130 A Song of degrees.
1 Out of the depths
have I *cried* **called** unto thee, O *LORD* **Yah Veh**.
2 *Lord* **Adonay**, hear my voice:
let thine ears *be attentive* **hearken** to
the voice of my supplications.
3 If thou, *LORD* **O Yah**,
shouldest *mark iniquities* **regard perversities**,
O *Lord* **Adonay**, who shall stand?
4 But there is forgiveness with thee,
that thou mayest be *feared* **awed**.
5 I *wait for the LORD* **await Yah Veh**,
my soul *doth wait* **awaiteth**,
and in his word *do I hope* **I await**.
6 My soul *waiteth for the Lord* **be for Adonay**
more than they that *watch* **guard** for the morning:
I say, more than—they that *watch*
guard for the morning.
7 Let *Israel hope in the LORD*
Yisra El await Yah Veh:
for with *the LORD* **Yah Veh** there is mercy,
and with him *is plenteous* **aboundeth** redemption.
8 And he shall redeem *Israel* **Yisra El**
from all his *iniquities* **perversities.**
4 as arrows in the hand of a mighty man
thus are sons of the youth.
5 Blithe—the mighty
who fills his quiver with them;
they shame not,
for they word with the enemies in the portal.

128 A Song of Degrees.
1 Blithed—every one who awes Yah Veh;
who walks in his ways:
2 for you eat the labor of your palms;
blithed—and good with you
3 —your woman as a fruitbearing vine
by the flanks of your house:
your sons as olive transplants
surrounding your table.
4 Behold, thus are the mighty;
blessed—who awe Yah Veh.
5 Yah Veh blesses you from Siyon;
and you see the good of Yeru Shalem
all the days of your life.
6 Yes, you see the sons of your sons.
Shalom on Yisra El!

129 A Song of Degrees.
1 Greatly they tribulated me from my youth;
O Yisra El, I beseech, say;
2 Greatly they tribulated me from my youth;
yet they prevailed not against me:
3 the plowers plow on my back;
they lengthen their furrows.
4 Yah Veh is just:
he chops the ropes of the wicked.
5 Shame and apostatize, you who hate Siyon;
6 as the grass on the roofs,
withering ere they *are* drawn:
7 which fill neither the palm of the mower
nor the bosom of the binder:
8 neither say they who pass by,
The blessing of Yah Veh *is* upon you;
we bless you in the name of Yah Veh.

130 A Song of Degrees.
1 From the depths I call you, O Yah Veh:
2 Adonay, hear my voice;
hearken your ears to the voice of my supplications.
3 If, O Yah, you regard perversities,
O Adonay, who stands?
4 But with you *is* forgiveness,
that you be awed.
5 I await Yah Veh; my soul awaits:
in his word I await.
6 My soul *is* for Adonay
more than they who guard for morning
—who guard for morning.
7 Yisra El, await Yah Veh;
for with Yah Veh there is mercy
and with him redemption abounds;
8 and he redeems Yisra El
from all his perversities.

131 A Song of degreesof David.
1 *LORD* **O Yah Veh,**
my heart is not *haughty* **lifted**, nor
mine eyes *lofty* **lofted**:
neither *do I exercise myself* **walk I**
in *great matters* **greatness**,
or in *things too high for me* **marvels**.
2 Surely I have *behaved* **placed myself**
and *quieted myself* **hushed my soul**,
as a child that is weaned of his mother:
my soul is even as *a* weaned *child*.
3 Let *Israel hope in the LORD*
Yisra El await Yah Veh
from *henceforth* **this time** and *for ever* **eternally**.

132 A Song of degrees.
1 *LORD* **O Yah Veh**,
remember David, and all his *afflictions* **humblings**:
2 How he *sware* **oathed** unto *the LORD* **Yah Veh**,
and vowed unto the *mighty God*
Almighty of *Jacob* **Yaaqov**;
3 Surely I *will* **shall** not come
into the *tabernacle* **tent** of my house,
nor *go up* **ascend** into *my bed* **the bedstead of my beds**;
4 I *will* **shall** not give sleep to mine eyes,
or *slumber* **drowsiness** to mine eyelids,
5 Until I find out a place for *the LORD* **Yah Veh**,
an habitation **tabernacles**
for the *mighty God* **Almighty** of *Jacob* **Yaaqov**.
6 *Lo* **Behold**, we heard of it at *Ephratah* **Ephrath**:
we found it in the fields of the *wood* **forest**.
7 We *will* **shall** go into his tabernacles:
we *will worship* **shall prostrate**
at *his footstool* **the stool of his feet**.
8 Arise, O *LORD* **Yah Veh**, into thy rest;
thou, and the ark of thy strength.
9 Let thy priests
be clothed **enrobe** with *righteousness* **justness**;
and let thy *saints* **mercied** shout *for joy*.
10 For thy servant David's sake
turn not away the face of thine anointed.
11 *The LORD* **Yah Veh** hath *sworn* **oathed** in truth
unto David;
he *will* **shall** not turn from it;
Of the fruit of thy *body* **belly**
will **shall** I set upon thy throne.
12 If thy *children will keep* **sons**
shall guard my covenant
and my *testimony* **witness** that I shall teach them,
their *children* **sons** shall also *sit* **settle** upon thy throne
for evermore **eternally**.
13 For *the LORD* **Yah Veh** hath chosen *Zion* **Siyon**;
he hath desired it for his *habitation* **settlement**.
14 This is my rest *for ever* **eternally**:
here *will I dwell* **shall I settle**; for I have desired it.
15 **In blessing,**
I *will abundantly* **shall** bless her *provision* **hunt**:
I *will* **shall** satisfy her *poor* **needy** with bread.
16 I *will* **shall** also
clothe **enrobe** her priests with salvation:
and **in shouting**, her *saints* **mercied** shall shout
aloud for joy.
17 There *will I make* **shall I**
sprout the horn of David
to bud:

I have *ordained* **arranged** a lamp for mine anointed.
18 His enemies *will I clothe*
shall I enrobe with shame:
but upon himself shall his *crown* **separatism** flourish.

133 A Song of degrees of David.
1 Behold, how good and how pleasant *it is*
for brethren to *dwell* **settle** together in unity!
2 It is like the *precious* **good**
ointment upon the head,
that ran down **descending** upon the beard,
even Aaron's **Aharon's** beard:
that *went down* **descended**
to the skirts of his *garments* **tailoring**;
3 As the dew of Hermon,
and as the dew
that descended upon the mountains of *Zion* **Siyon**:
for there *the LORD* **Yah Veh**
commanded **misvahed** the blessing,
even life for evermore **life eternal**.

131 A Song of Degrees: By David.
1 O Yah Veh,
neither my heart lifts, nor my eyes loft;
nor walk I in greatness or in marvels:
2 surely I place myself and hush my soul,
as a child weaned from his mother;
—my soul as weaned.
3 Yisra El, await Yah Veh
from this time and eternally.

132 A Song of Degrees.
1 O Yah Veh,
remember David and all his humblings;
2 who oathed to Yah Veh
and vowed to the Almighty of Yaaqov.
3 I neither come into the tent of my house;
nor ascend into the bedstead of my beds;
4 nor give sleep to my eyes
or drowsiness to my eyelids
5 until I find a place for Yah Veh
—tabernacles for the Almighty of Yaaqov.
6 Behold, we heard thereof at Ephrath;
we found thereof in the fields of the forest:
7 we enter his tabernacles;
we prostrate at the stool of his feet.
8 Rise, O Yah Veh, into your rest
—you and the ark of your strength.
9 Your priests enrobe with justness;
and your mercied shout.
10 For sake of your servant David
turn not away the face of your anointed.
11 Yah Veh oathed truth to David;
he turns not from it:
I set the fruit of your belly on your throne.
12 If your sons guard my covenant
and the witness I teach them,
their sons also settle on your throne eternally.
13 For Yah Veh chose Siyon;
he desires it for his settlement:
14 this is my rest eternally;
here I settle; for I desire it.
15 In blessing, I bless her hunt;
I satisfy her needy with bread;
16 and I enrobe her priests with salvation;
and in shouting, her mercied shout:
17 there I sprout the horn of David;
I arrange a lamp for my anointed;
18 I enrobe his enemies with shame;
and on him, his separatism flourishes.

133 A Song of Degrees: By David.
1 Behold, how good and how pleasant
for brothers to settle together in unity
2 —as the good ointment on the head
descending on the beard—the beard of Aharon;
descending to the skirts of his tailoring;
3 as the dew of Hermon
descending on the mountains of SiyonAharon's
for there Yah Veh misvahed the blessing,
life eternal.

134 A Song of degrees.
1 Behold, bless ye *the LORD* **Yah Veh**,
all *ye* servants of *the LORD* **Yah Veh**,
which by night stand in the house of *the LORD* **Yah Veh**.
2 Lift up your hands in the *sanctuary* **holies**,
and bless *the LORD* **Yah Veh**.
3 *The LORD* **Yah Veh**
that *made heaven* **worked the heavens** and earth
bless thee out of *Zion* **Siyon**.

135 *Praise ye the LORD* **l-lalalu Yah**.
Praise **l-lalal** ye the name of *the LORD* **Yah Veh**;
praise him **halal**, O ye servants of *the LORD* **Yah Veh**.
2 Ye that stand in the house
of *the LORD* **Yah Veh**,
in the courts of the house of our *God* **Elohim**.
3 *Praise the LORD* **l-lalalu Yah**;
for *the LORD* **Yah Veh** is good:
sing praises **psalm** unto his name; for it is pleasant.
4 For *the LORD* **Yah**
hath chosen *Jacob* **Yaaqov** unto himself,
and Israel **Yisra El** for his peculiar treasure.

5 For I know that *the LORD* **Yah Veh** is great,
and that our *Lord* **Adonay** is above all *gods* **elohim**.
6 Whatsoever *the LORD pleased* **Yah Veh desired**,
that *did* **worked** he in *heaven* **the heavens**,
and in earth, in the seas, and all *deep places* **abysses**.
7 He causeth the vapours
to ascend from the ends of the earth;
he *maketh* **worketh** lightnings for the rain;
he bringeth the wind out of his treasuries.
8 Who smote the *firstborn*
firstbirthed of *Egypt* **Misrayim**,
both of *man and beast* **human unto animal**.
9 Who sent *tokens* **signs** and *wonders* **omens**
into the midst of thee, O *Egypt* **Misrayim**, upon
Pharaoh **Paroh**, and upon all his servants.
10 Who smote great *nations* **goyim**,
and *slew* **slaughtered** mighty *kings* **sovereigns**;
11 *Sihon king* **Sichon sovereign**
of the *Amorites* **Emoriy**,
and Og *king* **sovereign** of Bashan,
and all the *kingdoms* **sovereigndoms** of *Canaan* **Kenaan**:
12 And gave their land for an *heritage* **inheritance**,
an *heritage* **inheritance** unto *Israel* **Yisra El** his people.
13 Thy name, O *LORD* **Yah Veh**,
endureth for ever **is eternal**;
and thy memorial, O *LORD* **Yah Veh**,
throughout all generations **generation to generation**.
14 For *the LORD* **Yah Veh**
will judge **shall plead the cause of** his people,
and he *will repent himself* **shall sigh**
concerning his servants.
15 The idols of the *heathen*
goyim are silver and gold,
the work of *men's* **human** hands.
16 They have mouths, but they *speak* **word** not;
eyes have they, but they see not;
17 They have ears, but they *hear* **hearken** not;
neither is there *any breath* **spirit/wind** in their mouths.
18 They that *make* **work** them are like unto them:
so is every one that *trusteth* **confideth** in them.
19 Bless *the LORD* **Yah Veh**,
O house of *Israel* **Yisra El**:
bless *the LORD* **Yah Veh**, O house of *Aaron* **Aharon**:
20 Bless *the LORD* **Yah Veh**, O house of Levi:
ye that *fear the LORD* **awe Yah Veh**,
bless *the LORD* **Yah Veh**.
21 Blessed be *the LORD* **Yah Veh** out of *Zion* **Siyon**,
which *dwelleth* **tabernacleth** at *Jerusalem* **Yeru Shalem**.
Praise ye the LORD **Halalu Yah**.

136 O *give thanks* **spread hands**
unto *the LORD* **Yah Veh**;
for he is good:
for his mercy *endureth for ever* **is eternal**.
2 O *give thanks* **spread hands**
unto the *God* **Elohim** of *gods* **elohim**:
for his mercy *endureth for ever* **is eternal**.
3 O *give thanks* **spread hands**
to *the Lord* **Adonay** of *lords* **adonim**:
for his mercy *endureth for ever* **is eternal**.

134 A Song of Degrees.
1 Behold, bless Yah Veh
all you servants of Yah Veh
—who stand by night in the house of Yah Veh:
2 lift your hands in the holies and bless Yah Veh:
3 Yah Veh who worked the heavens and earth
blesses you from Siyon.

135 Halalu Yah!
Halal the name of Yah Veh;
halal, O you servants of Yah Veh;
2 you who stand in the house of Yah Veh
—in the courts of the house of our Elohim.
3 Halalu Yah!
Yah Veh is good.
Psalm to his name; for it is pleasant:
4 for Yah chose Yaaqov for himself;
Yisra El for his peculiar treasure.
5 For I know that Yah Veh is great
and that our Adonay is above all elohim.
6 Yah Veh works whatever he desires
in the heavens and in earth in the seas and all abysses:
7 he ascends the vapours
from the ends of the earth;
works lightnings for the rain;
brings the wind from his treasuries:
8 who smote the firstbirthed of Misrayim
—both of human to animal:
9 who sent signs and omens
into your midst, O Misrayim
—on Paroh and on all his servants:
10 who smote great goyim
and slaughtered mighty sovereigns
11 —Sichon sovereign of the Emoriy
and Og sovereign of Bashan
and all the sovereigndoms of Kenaan;
12 and gave their land for an inheritance
—an inheritance to Yisra El his people.
13 O Yah Veh,
your name, eternal;

O Yah Veh,
your memorial, generation to generation:
14 for Yah Veh pleads the cause of his people
and he sighs concerning his servants.
15 The idols of the goyim *are* silver and gold
—the work of human hands:
16 mouths, and they word not;
eyes, and they see not;
17 ears, and they hearken not;
nose, and their is no spirit/wind in their mouth.
18 They who work them are likened to them;
thus every one who confides in them.
19 O house of Yisra El, bless Yah Veh;
O house of Aharon, bless Yah Veh;
20 O house of Levi, bless Yah Veh;
you who awe Yah Veh, bless Yah Veh.
21 Blessed—Yah Veh from Siyon
who tabernacles at Yeru Shalem.
Halalu Yah!

136 O Spread hands to Yah Veh;
for good;
for his mercy eternal:
2 O spread hands to the Elohim of elohim;
for his mercy eternal:
3 O spread hands to Adonay of adonim;
for his mercy eternal:
4 To him who alone
doeth **worketh** great *wonders* **marvels**:
for his mercy *endureth for ever* **is eternal**.
5 To him that by *wisdom* **discernment**
made **worked** the heavens:
for his mercy *endureth for ever* **is eternal**.
6 To him
that *stretched out* **expandeth** the earth above the waters:
for his mercy *endureth for ever* **is eternal**.
7 To him that *made* **worked** great lights:
for his mercy *endureth for ever* **is eternal**:
8 The sun to *rule* **reign** by day:
for his mercy *endureth for ever* **is eternal**:
9 The moon and stars to *rule* **reign** by night:
for his mercy *endureth for ever* **is eternal**.
10 To him that smote *Egypt* **Misrayim**
in their *firstborn* **firstbirthed**:
for his mercy *endureth for ever* **is eternal**:
11 And brought out *Israel*
Yisra El from among them:
for his mercy *endureth for ever* **is eternal**:
12 With a strong hand, and with
a *stretched out* **spread** arm:
for his mercy *endureth for ever* **is eternal**.
13 To him
which *divided* **cut** the *Red* **Reed** sea into *parts* **pieces**:
for his mercy *endureth for ever* **is eternal**:
14 And made *Israel* **Yisra El**
to pass through the midst of it:
for his mercy *endureth for ever* **is eternal**:
15 But *overthrew Pharaoh* **shook off Paroh**
and his *host* **valiant** in the *Red* **Reed** sea: for
his mercy *endureth for ever* **is eternal**.
16 To him
which *led* **walked** his people through the wilderness:
for his mercy *endureth for ever* **is eternal**.
17 To him which smote great *kings* **sovereigns**:
for his mercy *endureth for ever* **is eternal**:
18 And *slew famous kings*
slaughtered mighty sovereigns:
for his mercy *endureth for ever* **is eternal**:
19 *Sihon king* **Sichon sovereign**
of the *Amorites* **Emoriy**:
for his mercy *endureth for ever* **is eternal**:
20 And Og the *king* **sovereign** of Bashan:
for his mercy *endureth for ever* **is eternal**:
21 And gave their land for an *heritage* **inheritance**:
for his mercy *endureth for ever* **is eternal**:
22 Even an *heritage* **inheritance**
unto *Israel* **Yisra El** his servant:
for his mercy *endureth for ever* **is eternal**.
23 Who remembered us in
our *low estate* **lowliness**:
for his mercy *endureth for ever* **is eternal**:
24 And hath *redeemed* **separated** us
from our *enemies* **tribulators**:
for his mercy *endureth for ever* **is eternal**.
25 Who giveth *food* **bread** to all flesh:
for his mercy *endureth for ever* **is eternal**.
26 O *give thanks* **spread hands**
unto *the God* **El** of *heaven* **the heavens**: for
his mercy *endureth for ever* **is eternal**.

137 By the rivers of *Babylon* **Babel**,
there we *sat down* **settled**,
yea, we wept, when we remembered *Zion* **Siyon**.
2 We hanged our harps upon the willows
in the midst *thereof*.
3 For there they that *carried*
captured us *away captive*
required **asked** of us **the words of** a song;
and they that *wasted* **caused us to howl,**
required of us mirth **cheerfulness**, *saying*,
Sing us *one* of the songs of *Zion* **Siyon**.
4 How shall we sing *the LORD'S* **Yah Veh's** song

in a strange *land* **soil?**
5 If I forget thee, O *Jerusalem* **Yeru Shalem,**
let my right *hand* forget *her cunning.*
6 If I do not remember thee,
let my tongue
cleave to the roof of my mouth **adhere to my palate;**
if I *prefer* **ascend** not *Jerusalem* **Yeru Shalem**
above my *chief joy* **head cheer.**
4 to him who alone works great marvels;
for his mercy eternal:
5 to him who by discernment worked the heavens;
for his mercy eternal:
6 to him who expanded the
earth above the waters;
for his mercy eternal:
7 to him who worked great lights;
for his mercy eternal:
8 the sun to reign by day;
for his mercy eternal:
9 the moon and stars to reign by night;
for his mercy eternal:
10 to him who smote Misrayim—their firstbirthed;
for his mercy eternal:
11 and brought Yisra El from among them;
for his mercy eternal:
12 with a strong hand and spread arm;
for his mercy eternal:
13 to him who cut the Reed sea into pieces;
for his mercy eternal:
14 and passed Yisra El through the midst;
for his mercy eternal:
15 and shook Paroh and his valiant in the Reed sea;
for his mercy eternal:
16 to him who walked his people in the wilderness;
for his mercy eternal:
17 to him who smote great sovereigns;
for his mercy eternal:
18 and slaughtered mighty sovereigns;
for his mercy eternal:
19 Sichon sovereign of the Emoriy;
for his mercy eternal:
20 and Og the sovereign of Bashan;
for his mercy eternal:
21 and gave their land for an inheritance;
for his mercy eternal:
22 even an inheritance to Yisra El his servant;
for his mercy eternal:
23 who remembered us in our lowliness;
for his mercy eternal:
24 and has separated us from our tribulators;
for his mercy eternal:
25 who gives bread to all flesh;
for his mercy eternal:
26 O spread hands to El of the heavens;
for his mercy eternal.

137 By the rivers of Babel, there we settled;
yes, we wept, when we remembered Siyon;
2 we hung our harps midst the willows:
3 for there our captors asked
us the words of a song
—our howlers, of cheer,
Sing us a song of Siyon!
4 How sing we a song of Yah Veh in a strange soil?
5 If I forget you, O Yeru Shalem,
my right forgets:
6 if I remember you not,
my tongue adheres to my palate
—if I ascend not Yeru Shalem,
above the head of my cheer.
7 Remember, O *LORD* **Yah Veh,**
the *children* **sons** of Edom
in the day of *Jerusalem* **Yeru Shalem;**
who said, *Rase it* **Strip naked,** *rase it* **strip naked,**
even to the foundation *thereof.*
8 O daughter of *Babylon* **Babel,**
who art to be *destroyed* **ravaged;**
happy **blithed** shall he be,
that *rewardeth* **shall shalam** thee
as **the deeds** thou hast *served* **dealt** us.
9 *Happy* **Blithed** shall he be,
that taketh and *dasheth* **splattereth**
thy *little ones* **infants**
against the *stones* **rocks.**

138 *A Psalm* of David.
1 I *will praise* **shall spread hands unto** thee
with my whole heart:
before the gods before **in front of Elohim/elohim,**
will I sing praise **shall I psalm** unto thee.
2 I *will worship* **shall prostrate**
toward thy holy *temple* **manse,**
and *praise* **spread hands unto** thy name
for thy *lovingkindness* **mercy** and for thy truth:
for thou hast *magnified* **greatened** thy *word* **saying**
above all thy name.
3 In the day when I *cried*
called thou answeredst me,
and *strengthenedst* **encouragedst** me
with strength in my soul.
4 All the *kings* **sovereigns** of the earth
shall *praise* **spread hands unto** thee, O *LORD* **Yah Veh,**

when they hear the *words* **sayings** of thy mouth.
5 Yea, they shall sing in the
ways of *the LORD* **Yah Veh**:
for great is the *glory* **honour** of *the LORD* **Yah Veh**.
6 Though *the LORD* **Yah Veh** be high,
yet *hath* he *respect* **seeth** unto the lowly: but
the *proud* **lofty** he knoweth afar off.
7 Though I walk in the midst
of *trouble* **tribulation**,
thou *wilt revive* **shalt enliven** me:
thou shalt *stretch forth* **spread** thine hand
against the wrath of mine enemies,
and thy right *hand* shall save me.
8 *The LORD* **Yah Veh**
will perfect **shall consummate** that
which concerneth me:
thy mercy, O *LORD* **Yah Veh**,
endureth for ever **is eternal**:
forsake **slacken** not the works of thine own hands.

139 To *the chief Musician* **His Eminence**,
A Psalm of David.
1 O *LORD* **Yah Veh**,
thou hast *searched* **probed** me, and known *me*.
2 Thou knowest my *downsitting* **settling**
and mine uprising,
thou *understandest* **discernest**
my *thought* **intention** afar off.
3 Thou *compassest* **winnowest** my path
and my *lying down* **reposing**,
and art *acquainted with* **accustomed to** all my ways.
4 For there is not *a word* **an**
utterance in my tongue,
but, lo **behold**, O *LORD* **Yah Veh**,
thou knowest it altogether.
5 Thou hast *beset* **besieged** me behind and before,
and *laid thine hand* **placed thy palm** upon me.
6 Such knowledge is too
wonderful **marvellous** for me;
it is high **lofty**, *! cannot attain unto* **I am not able for** it.
7 Whither shall I go from thy spirit?
or whither shall I flee from thy *presence* **face**?
8 If I ascend *up* into *heaven* **the heavens**,
thou art there:
if I *make my bed in hell* **bed down in sheol**,
behold, thou *art there*.
9 If I *take* **lift** the wings of the *morning* **dawn**,
and *dwell* **tabernacle**
in the *uttermost parts* **finality** of the sea;
10 Even there shall thy hand lead me,
and thy right *hand* shall hold me.

11 If I say, Surely the darkness
shall *cover* **crush** me;
even the night shall be light *about* **to** me.
7 Remember, O Yah Veh,
the sons of Edom in the day of Yeru Shalem
who say,
Strip naked—strip naked to the foundation!
8 O daughter of Babel, O ravaged;
blithed—he who shalams your deed to you
as you dealt us.
9 Blithed—he who takes and splatters your infants
against the rocks.

138 By David.
1 I spread hands to you with my whole heart;
in front of Elohim/the elohim, I psalm to you:
2 I prostrate toward your holy manse
and spread hands to your name
—for your mercy and for your truth:
for you greatened your saying
above all your name.
3 In the day I called
you answered me and encouraged me
with strength in my soul.
4 All the sovereigns of the earth
spread hands to you, O Yah Veh,
when they hear the sayings of your mouth.
5 Yes, they sing in the ways of Yah Veh;
for great is the honor of Yah Veh.
6 For Yah Veh is high,
and he sees the lowly;
and he knows the lofty afar off.
7 If I walk midst tribulation, you enliven me;
you spread your hand
against the wrath of my enemies
and your right saves me.
8 Yah Veh consummates what concerns me.
Your mercy, O Yah Veh, *is* eternal;
slacken not the works of your own hands.

139 To His Eminence: A Psalm by David.
1 O Yah Veh, you probed me and know;
2 you know my settling and my uprising;
you discern my intention afar off;
3 you winnow my path and my reposing
and are accustomed to all my ways;
4 for there is not an utterance in my tongue.
Behold, O Yah Veh, you know altogether;
5 you besiege me behind and in front
and placed your palm on me.
6 Such knowledge is too marvellous for me;
too lofty; I am not able for it.

7 Where go I from your spirit?
Where flee I from your face?
8 If I ascend into the heavens, you are there;
if I bed down in sheol, behold—you;
9 if I lift the wings of the dawn
and tabernacle in the finality of the sea;
10 even there your hand leads me
and your right holds me:
11 if I say, Surely the darkness crushes me;
even the night is light to me.
12 Yea, the darkness *hideth*
darkeneth not from thee;
but the night *shineth* **enlighteneth** as the day:
the darkness and the light are both alike to thee
as the darkness, so the light.
13 For thou hast *possessed* **chattelized** my reins:
thou hast covered me in my mother's *womb* **belly**.
14 I *will praise* **shall spread hands unto** thee;
for I am
fearfully and wonderfully made
awesomely distinguished:
marvellous are thy works;
and that my soul knoweth right well.
15 My *substance* **might** was not
hid **concealed** from thee,
when I was *made in secret* **covertly worked**,
and *curiously wrought* **embroidered**
in the *lowest parts* **nethermost** of the earth.
16 Thine eyes did see my *substance* **embryo**,
yet being unperfect;
and in thy *book* **scroll**
all my members were written **were they inscribed**,
which in continuance were fashioned
in the days they were formed,
when *as yet there* was none *of* **among** them.
17 How *precious* **esteemed** also
are thy *thoughts* **intentions** unto me,
O *God* **El**!
how *great* **mighty** is the *sum* **head** of them!
18 If I should *count* **scribe** them,
they *are* **abound** more *in number* than the sand:
when I awake, I am still with thee.
19 Surely thou *wilt slay* **shalt severe** the wicked,
O *God* **Elohah**:
depart **turn aside** from me therefore,
ye *bloody* men **of blood**.
20 For they *speak* **say** against
thee *wickedly* **intrigue**,
and thine enemies *take thy name* **be lifted** in *vain* **vanity**.
21 Do not I hate them, O *LORD*
Yah Veh, that hate thee?
and *am not I grieved with those* **do I not loathe**
them that *rise up against* **resist** thee?
22 I hate them with *perfect* **conclusive** hatred:
I count them mine enemies.
23 *Search* **Probe** me, O *God* **El**, and know my heart:
try **proof** me, and know my thoughts:
24 And see
if there be *any wicked* **a contorting** way in me,
and lead me in the way *everlasting* **eternal**.

140 To *the chief Musician* **His Eminence**,
A Psalm of David.
1 *Deliver* **Rescue** me, O *LORD* **Yah Veh**,
from the evil *man* **humanity**:
preserve **guard** me from the *violent* man **of violence**;
2 Which *imagine mischiefs*
machinate evils in their heart;
continually are **all day**
they *gathered* **sojourn** together *for* war.
3 They have *sharpened* **pointened** their tongues
like a serpent;
adders' **asp's** poison is under their lips.
Selah.
4 *Keep* **Guard** me, O *LORD* **Yah Veh**,
from the hands of the wicked;
preserve me from the *violent* man **of violence**;
who have *purposed* **machinated**
to overthrow my *goings* **steps**.
5 The *proud* **pompous**
have hid a *snare* **line** for me, and cords;
they have spread a net
by the *wayside* **hand of the route**;
they have set *gins* **snares** for me.
Selah.
6 I said unto *the LORD* **Yah**
Veh, Thou art my *God* **El**:
hear **hearken unto** the voice of my supplications,
O *LORD* **Yah Veh**.
7 O *GOD the Lord* **Yah Veh Adonay**,
the strength of my salvation,
thou hast covered my head
in the day of *battle* **armament**.
12 Yes, the darkness darkens not from you;
and night lights as the day;
as the darkness, thus the light.
13 For you—you chattelized my reins;
you covered me in the belly of my mother:
14 I spread hands to you;
for I am awesomely distinguished;

marvellous are your works
—and my soul knows that right well.
15 My might was not concealed from you,
when I was covertly worked and embroidered
in the nethermost of the earth:
16 your eyes saw my embryo;
and in your scroll they were inscribed
in the days they were formed
—and no one among them.
17 How esteemed—your intentions to me, O El!
How mighty their head!
18 If I scribe them, they
abound more than the sand;
when I waken, I am still with you.
19 Surely you sever the wicked, O Elohah;
so turn aside from me, you men of blood:
20 for they say intrigue against you;
lift your enemies in vanity.
21 Hate I not them, O Yah Veh, who hate you?
and loathe I not them who resist you?
22 I hate them with conclusive hatred;
I count them my enemies.
23 Probe me, O El, and know my heart;
proof me and know my thoughts:
24 and see if there be a contorting way in me
and lead me in the way eternal.

140 To His Eminence: A Psalm by David.
1 Rescue me, O Yah Veh, from evil humanity;
guard me from the man of violence
2 who machinates evils in the heart:
all day they sojourn for war;
3 they pointen their tongues as a serpent;
the poison of asps is under their lips.
Selah.
4 Guard me, O Yah Veh,
from the hands of the wicked;
preserve me from the man of violence;
who machinates to overthrow my steps.
5 The pompous hide a line for me—and cords;
they spread a net by the hand of the route;
they set snares for me.
Selah.
6 I say to Yah Veh, You are my El;
hearken, O Yah Veh,
to the voice of my supplications:
7 O Yah Veh Adonay,
the strength of my salvation,
you covered my head in the day of armament:
8 *Grant* **Give** not, O *LORD* **Yah Veh**,
the desires of the wicked:
further **promote** not his *wicked device* **intrigue**;
lest they *exalt themselves* **be lofted**.
Selah.
9 As for the head of those
that *compass* **surround** me *about*,
let the *mischief* **toil** of their own lips cover them.
10 Let *burning coals fall* **coals topple** upon them:
let them be cast—**fell them** into the fire; into
deep pits, that they rise not *up again*.
11 Let *not an evil speaker* **no man of tongue**
be established in the earth:
evil shall hunt the *violent* man **of violence**
to overthrow him.
12 I know that *the LORD* **Yah Veh**
will maintain **shall work**
the *cause* **plea** of the *afflicted* **humble**,
and the *right* **judgment** of the *poor* **needy**.
13 Surely the *righteous* **just**
shall *give thanks* **spread hands** unto thy name:
the *upright* **straight** shall *dwell* **settle**
in thy presence **at thy face**.

141 A Psalm of David.
1 *LORD* **O Yah Veh**, I *cry* **call** unto thee:
make haste **hasten** unto me;
give ear **hearken** unto my voice,
when I *cry* **call** unto thee.
2 Let my prayer
be *set forth before thee* **prepared at thy face** as incense;
and the *lifting up* **burden** of my *hands* **palms**
as the evening *sacrifice* **offering**.
3 Set a *watch* **guard**, O *LORD* **Yah Veh**,
before my mouth;
keep **guard** the door of my lips.
4 *Incline* **Spread** not my heart
to any evil *thing* **word**,
to *practise* **exploit** wicked *works* **exploits**
with men that *work iniquity* **do mischief**:
and let me not eat of their *dainties* **delicacies**.
5 *Let the righteous smite me; it shall be a kindness*
The just hammer me in mercy:
and *let him* reprove me;
it shall be an *excellent oil* **ointment**,
which *shall not break* my head **shall not disallow**:
for yet my prayer also
shall be *in* **against** their *calamities* **evil**.
6 When their judges are *overthrown* **released**
in stony places **by the hands of the rocks**,
they shall hear my *words* **sayings**;
for they are *sweet* **pleasing**.

7 Our bones are scattered at
the grave's **sheol's** mouth,
as when one *cutteth* **cleaveth** and *cleaveth wood* **splitteth**
upon the earth.
8 But mine eyes are unto thee,
O *GOD the Lord* **Yah Veh Adonay**:
in thee *is my trust* **I seek refuge**;
leave **strip** not my soul *destitute* **naked**.
9 *Keep* **Guard** me from the **hands of the** snares
which they have *laid* **ensnared** for me,
and the *gins* **snares**
of the *workers* **doers** of *iniquity* **mischief**.
10 Let the wicked fall into their own nets,
whilst that I *withal escape* **altogether pass on**.

142 *Maschil* **On Comprehension** of David:
A Prayer when he was in the cave.
1 I cried unto *the LORD* **Yah Veh** with my voice;
with my voice unto *the LORD* **Yah Veh** *did I*
make my supplication **sought I charism**.
2 I poured out my *complaint* **meditation**
before him **at his face**;
I shewed before him my trouble
I told my tribulation to his face.
3 When my spirit *was overwhelmed*
languished within me,
then thou knewest my path.
In the way wherein I walked
have they *privily laid* **hid** a snare for me.
8 give not, O Yah Veh, the wicked their desires;
promote not his intrigue; lest they be lofted.
Selah.
9 As for the heads of them who surround me,
cover them with the toil of their own lips;
10 topple coals on them;
fell them in the fire
—in deep pits that they rise not.
11 Establish no man of tongue in the earth;
evil hunts the man of violence—to overthrow him.
12 I know Yah Veh works the plea of the humble
—the judgment of the needy.
13 Surely the just spread hands to your name;
the straight settle at your face.

141 A Psalm by David.
1 O Yah Veh, I call to you; hasten to me;
hearken to my voice when I call to you:
2 I prepare my prayer at your face as incense;
and the burden of my palms as the evening offering.
3 Set a guard, O Yah Veh, in front of my mouth;
guard the door of my lips;
4 spread not my heart to any evil word
—to exploit wicked exploits
with men who work mischief
—that I not eat of their delicacies.
5 The just hammer me in mercy, and reprove me;
an ointment of the head
—which my head disallows not;
for my prayer *is* yet against their evil.
6 Their judges are released
by the hands of the rocks;
they hear my sayings; they are pleased.
7 Our bones are scattered at the mouth of sheol
as one cleaving and splitting the earth.
8 But to you, O Yah Veh Adonay, are my eyes;
in you I seek refuge; strip not my soul naked:
9 guard me from the hands of the snares
they ensnare for me
—and the snares of the doers of mischief.
10 Fell the wicked into their own nets,
until I pass over.

142 On Comprehension: By David:
A Prayer when he is in the cave.
1 My voice to Yah Veh, I cry;
my voice to Yah Veh, I seek charism:
2 I pour my meditation at his face;
I tell my tribulation to his face:
3 when my spirit languishes within me,
then you know my path:
in the way I walk, they hide a snare for me.
4 I looked *on my* **to the** right
hand, and *beheld* **saw**,
but there was no *man* **one**
that *would know* **should recognize** me:
refuge failed **retreat destructed from** me;
no *man cared for* **one sought** my soul.
5 I cried unto thee, O *LORD* **Yah Veh**: I said,
Thou art my refuge and my *portion* **allotment**
in the land of the living.
6 *Attend* **Hearken** unto my *cry* **shouting**;
for I am *brought very low* **mightily languished**:
deliver **rescue** me from my *persecutors* **pursuers**;
for they are *stronger* **more strengthened** than I.
7 Bring my soul out of *prison* **the lockup**,
that I may *praise* **spread hands to** thy name:
the *righteous* **just** shall *compass* **surround** me *about*;
for thou shalt deal *bountifully* with me.

143 A Psalm of David.
1 Hear my prayer, O *LORD* **Yah Veh**,
give ear **hearken** to my supplications:
in thy *faithfulness* **trustworthiness** answer me,
and in thy *righteousness* **justness**.

2 And enter not into judgment with thy servant:
for *in* **at** thy *sight* **face** shall no *man*
one living be justified.
3 For the enemy hath *persecuted* **pursued** my soul;
he hath *smitten* **crushed** my life
down to the *ground* **earth**;
he hath *made me to dwell* **settled me** in darkness,
as those that have been *long* **eternally** dead.
4 *Therefore is*
my spirit *overwhelmed* **languisheth** within me;
my heart within me *is desolate* **desolateth**.
5 I remember the days of *old* **antiquity**;
I meditate on all thy *work* **deeds**;
I *muse* **meditate** on the work of thy hands.
6 I *stretch forth* **spread** my hands unto thee:
my soul
thirsteth after thee, as a thirsty land
is as a languid land for thee.
Selah.
7 *Hear* **Answer** me *speedily*
hastily, O *LORD* **Yah Veh**:
my spirit *faileth* **finisheth off**:
hide not thy face from me,
lest I be like unto them
that *go down* **descend** into the *pit* **well**.
8 Cause me to hear thy *lovingkindness* **mercy**
in the morning;
for in thee do I *trust* **confide**:
cause me to know the way wherein I should walk;
for I lift up my soul unto thee.
9 *Deliver* **Rescue** me, O *LORD* **Yah Veh**,
from mine enemies:
I flee unto thee to hide me **Cover me with thyself**.
10 Teach me to *do* **work** thy *will* **pleasure**;
for thou art my *God* **Elohim**:
thy spirit is good;
lead me into the land of *uprightness* **straightness**.
11 *Quicken* **Enliven** me, O *LORD* **Yah Veh**,
for thy name's sake:
for thy *righteousness'* **justness'** sake
bring my soul out of *trouble* **tribulation**.
12 And of thy mercy cut off mine enemies,
and *destroy* **exterminate** all them
that *afflict* **tribulate** my soul:
for I am thy servant.

144 *A Psalm* of David.

1 Blessed be *the LORD* **Yah Veh** my *strength* **rock**
which teacheth my hands to war,
and my fingers to *fight* **war**:
2 My *goodness* **mercy**, and my *fortress* **stronghold**;
my *high tower* **secure loft**,
and my deliverer **who slippeth me away**;
my *shield* **buckler**, *and he* in whom I *trust* **seek refuge**;
who subdueth my people under me.
3 *LORD* **O Yah Veh**, what is *man* **humanity**,
that thou *takest knowledge of* **knowest** him!
or the son of man,
that thou *makest account of* **fabricatest** him!
4 I look to the right and see;
no one recognizes me:
retreat destructs from me;
no one seeks of my soul.
5 I cry to you, O Yah Veh; I say,
You are my refuge and my allotment
in the land of the living;
6 hearken to my shouting
for I am mightily languished:
rescue me from my pursuers
for they are stronger than I:
7 bring my soul from the lockup
to spread hands to your name;
the just surround me; when you deal with me.

143 A Psalm: By David.

1 Hear my prayer, O Yah Veh;
hearken to my supplications:
in your trustworthiness answer me
—in your justness.
2 And enter not into judgment with your servant;
for at your face no one living is justified;
3 for an enemy pursues my soul;
he crushes my life to the earth;
he settles me in darkness as the eternal dead:
4 my spirit within me languishes;
my heart within me desolates:
5 I remember the days of antiquity;
I meditate on all your deeds;
I meditate on the work of your hands:
6 I spread my hands to you;
my soul is as a languid land for you.
Selah.
7 Answer me hastily, O Yah Veh;
my spirit finishes off:
hide not your face from me;
lest I be as they who descend in the well:
8 that I hear your mercy in the morning;
for in you I confide:
that I know the way wherein I walk;
for I lift up my soul to you.
9 Rescue me, O Yah Veh, from my enemies
—cover me with yourself;

10 teach me to work your pleasure
for you *are* my Elohim;
your spirit *is* good;
lead me into the land of straightness.
11 Enliven me, O Yah Veh, for sake of your name;
for sake of your justness
bring my soul from tribulation:
12 and by your mercy cut off my enemies
and exterminate all who tribulate my soul;
for I am your servant.

144 By David.
1 Blessed—Yah Veh my rock
who teaches my hands to war
and my fingers to war:
2 my mercy and my stronghold;
my secure loft, who slips me away;
my buckler, in whom I seek refuge;
who subdues my people under me.
3 O Yah Veh,
what is humanity, that you know him?
—the son of man, that you fabricate him?
4 *Man* **Humanity** is *like* **likened** to vanity:
his days are as a shadow that passeth away.
5 *Bow* **Spread** thy heavens, O *LORD* **Yah Veh**,
and *come down* **descend**:
touch the mountains, and they shall smoke.
6 *Cast forth* **Lightning the**
lightning, and scatter them:
shoot out **send** thine arrows, and *destroy* **agitate** them.
7 Send thine hand from *above* **the heights**;
rid **tear** me **loose**,
and *deliver* **rescue** me out of great waters,
from the hand of strange *children* **sons**;
8 Whose mouth *speaketh* **wordeth** vanity,
and their right *hand* is a right *hand* of falsehood.
9 I *will* **shall** sing a new song
unto thee, O *God* **Elohim**:
upon a *psaltery* **bagpipe**
and *an instrument of ten strings* **a decachord**
will I sing praises **shall I psalm** unto thee.
10 *It is he that*
—**Who** giveth salvation unto *kings* **sovereigns**:
who *delivereth* **releaseth** David his servant
from the *hurtful* **evil** sword.
11 *Rid* **Tear** me **loose**, and *deliver* **rescue** me
from the hand of strange *children* **sons**,
whose mouth *speaketh* **wordeth** vanity,
and their right *hand* is a right *hand* of falsehood:
12 That our sons
may be as plants grown up in their youth;
that our daughters
may be as **prominent** corner *stones* **pillars**,
polished after **carved in** the *similitude* **pattern**
of a *palace* **manse**:
13 That our *garners* **granaries** may be full,
affording all manner of store
producing species by species:
that our *sheep* **flock**
may bring forth *thousands* **a thousandfold**
and *ten thousands* **abound by the myriads**
in our *streets* **outways**:
14 That our *oxen* **chiliarchs**
may *be strong to labour* **bear**;
that there be no *breaking in* **breaching**, nor going out;
that there be no *complaining* **outcry**
in our *streets* **broadways**.
15 *Happy* **Blithe** *is* that people,
that is *in such a case* **thus**:
yea, *happy* **blithe** *is* that people,
whose *God* **Elohim** is *the LORD* **Yah Veh**.

145 David's *Psalm of Praise* **Halal**.
1 I *will extol* **shall exalt** thee, my *God* **Elohim**,
O *king* **sovereign**;
and I *will* **shall** bless thy name
for ever **eternally** and *ever* **eternally**.
2 Every day *will* **shall** I bless thee;
and I *will praise* **shall halal** thy name *for*
ever **eternally** and *ever* **eternally**
3 Great is *the LORD* **Yah Veh**,
and *greatly* **mightily** to be *praised* **halaled**;
and his greatness is *unsearchable* **not to be probed**.
4 *One generation* **Generation to generation**
shall *praise* **laud** thy works *to another*, and
shall *declare* **tell** thy *mighty acts* **might**.
5 I *will speak* **shall meditate**
of the glorious honour of thy majesty,
and of thy *wondrous works* **marvellous words**.
6 And *men* shall *speak* **say**
of the *might* **strength** of thy *terrible* **awesome** acts:
and I *will declare* **shall scribe** thy greatness.
7 They shall *abundantly utter* **gush**
the *memory* **memorial** of thy great goodness,
and shall *sing* **shout** of thy *righteousness* **justness**.
8 *The LORD* **Yah Veh** is *gracious* **charismatic**,
and *full of compassion* **merciful**;
slow to *anger* **wrath**, and of great mercy.
9 *The LORD* **Yah Veh** is good to all:
and his tender mercies are over all his works.
10 All thy works shall *praise*
spread hands unto thee,

O *LORD* **Yah Veh**;
and thy *saints* **mercied** shall bless thee.
11 They shall *speak* **say**
of the *glory* **honour** of thy *kingdom* **sovereigndom**,
and *talk* **word** of thy *power* might;
4 Humanity is likened to vanity;
his days are as a passing shadow.
5 Spread your heavens, O Yah Veh, and descend;
touch the mountains, and they smoke;
6 lightning the lightning and scatter them;
send your arrows and agitate them;
7 send your hand from the heights;
tear me loose and rescue me from great waters
—from the hand of strange sons
8 whose mouth words vanity
whose right is a right of falsehood.
9 O Elohim, I sing you a new song;
on a bagpipe and a decachord, I psalm to you
10 —who gives salvation to sovereigns;
who release David his servant from the evil sword.
11 Tear me loose and rescue me
from the hand of strange sons
—whose mouth words vanity
whose right is a right of falsehood.
12 Because our sons as plants
become grown in their youth;
and our daughters as prominent corner pillars
carved in the pattern of a manse;
13 our granaries fill up
—producing species by species;
our flocks bring forth a thousandfold
and abound by the myriads in our outways;
14 our chiliarchs bear
—neither breaching nor going out;
nor cry out in our broadways.
15 Blithe—that people, who is thus;
yes, blithe—that people, whose Elohim *is* Yah Veh.

145 Halal: By David.
1 I exalt you, my Elohim, O sovereign;
and I bless your name eternally and eternally:
2 every day I bless you;
and I halal your name eternally and eternally:
3 great is Yah Veh and mightily to be halaled;
and his greatness is not to be probed:
4 generation to generation
lauds your works and tells your might:
5 I meditate on the glorious honor of your majesty
and on your marvellous words:
6 and say of the strength of your awesome acts;
I scribe your greatness:
7 they gush the memorial of your great goodness
and shout of your justness.
8 Yah Veh is charismatic and merciful;
slow to wrath and of great mercy:
9 Yah Veh *is* good to all;
and his tender mercies *are* over all his works.
10 All your works spread hands to you, O Yah Veh;
and your mercied bless you:
11 they say of the honor of your sovereigndom
and word of your might;
12 To make known to the sons of *men* **humanity**
his *mighty acts* **might**,
and the *glorious* **honour of** majesty of his kingdom.
13 Thy *kingdom* **sovereigndom**
is an *everlasting kingdom* **eternal sovereigndom**,
and thy *dominion* **reign**
endureth throughout all generations
generation to generation.
14 *The LORD* **Yah Veh** upholdeth all that fall,
and raiseth up all *those* that be bowed down.
15 The eyes of all *wait upon* **expect** thee;
and thou givest them
their *meat in due season* **food on time**.
16 Thou openest thine hand,
and satisfiest the *desire* **pleasure** of *every* **all** living *thing*.
17 *The LORD* **Yah Veh** is
righteous **just** in all his ways,
and *holy* **mercied** in all his works.
18 *The LORD* **Yah Veh** is nigh
unto all them that call upon him,
to all that call upon him in truth.
19 He *will fulfil* **shall work**
thc *desirc* **pleasure** of them
that *fear* **awe** him:
he also *will* **shall** hear their cry, and *will* **shall** save them.
20 *The LORD* **Yah Veh**
preserveth **guardeth** all them that love him:
but all the wicked *will* **shall** he *destroy* **desolate**.
21 My mouth shall *speak* **word**
the *praise* **halal** of *the LORD* **Yah Veh**:
and let all flesh bless his holy name
for ever **eternally** and *ever* **eternally**.

146 *Praise ye the LORD* **l-lalalu Yah**.
Praise the LORD **l-lalal Yah Veh**, O my soul.
2 *While I live* **In my life**
will I praise the LORD **I shall halal Yah Veh**:
I *will sing praises* **shall psalm** unto my *God* **Elohim**
while I *have any being* **be**.
3 *Put not your trust* **Confide**
not in *princes* **volunteers**,

nor in the son of *man* **humanity**,
in whom there is no *help* **salvation.**
4 His *breath* **spirit** goeth forth,
he returneth to his *earth* **soil**;
in that very day his thoughts *perish* **destruct.**
5 *Happy* **Blithed** *is* he
that hath *the God* **El** of *Jacob* **Yaaqov** for his help,
whose *hope* **expectation**
is in *the LORD* **Yah Veh** his *God* **Elohim**:
6 Which *made heaven* **worked**
the heavens, and earth,
the sea, and all that therein is:
which *keepeth* **guardeth** truth *for ever* **eternally**:
7 Which *executeth* **worketh**
judgment for the oppressed:
which giveth *food* **bread** to the *hungry* **famished.**
The LORD **Yah Veh** looseth the *prisoners* **bound**:
8 *The LORD* **Yah Veh** openeth
the eyes of the blind:
the LORD **Yah Veh** raiseth them that are bowed
down: *the LORD* **Yah Veh** loveth the *righteous* **just**:
9 *The LORD* **Yah Veh**
preserveth **guardeth** the *strangers* **sojourners**;
he *relieveth* **restoreth** the *fatherless* **orphan** and widow:
but the way of the wicked
he *turneth upside down* **twisteth.**
10 *The LORD* **Yah Veh** shall
reign *for ever* **eternally**,
even thy *God* **Elohim**, O *Zion* **Siyon**,
unto all generations **generation to generation.**
Praise ye the LORD **l-lalalu Yah.**

147 *Praise ye the LORD* **l-lalalu Yah**:
for it is good to *sing praises* **psalm** unto our *God* **Elohim**;
for it is pleasant;
and *praise is comely* **halal befitteth.**
2 *The LORD* **Yah Veh**
doth build up Jerusalem **buildeth Yeru Shalem**:
he gathereth *together*
the *outcasts* **overthrown** of *Israel* **Yisra El.**
3 He healeth the broken in heart,
and bindeth up their *wounds* **contortions.**
4 He *telleth* **numbereth** the number of the stars;
he calleth them all by their names.
12 to make his might known
to the sons of humanity
—and the honor of majesty of his kingdom.
13 Your sovereigndom is an eternal sovereigndom
and your reign generation to generation.
14 Yah Veh upholds all who fall
and raises all who *are* bowed down:
15 the eyes of all expect you;
and you give them their food on time:
16 you open your hand
and satisfy the pleasure of all living.
17 Yah Veh is just in all his ways
and mercied in all his works:
18 Yah Veh is near all who call on him
—to all who call on him in truth:
19 he works their pleasure, who awe him;
he hears their cry and saves them:
20 Yah Veh guards all who love him;
and desolates all the wicked.
21 My mouth words the halal of Yah Veh;
all flesh blesses his holy name
eternally and eternally.

146 Halalu Yah!
Halal Yah Veh, O my soul.
2 I halal Yah Veh in my life *time*;
I psalm to my Elohim while I *still* am.
3 Confide not in volunteers—
in a son of humanity
—in whom there is no salvation:
4 his spirit goes; he returns to his soil;
that very day his thoughts destruct.
5 Blithe—he who has El of Yaaqov for his help;
whose expectation is in Yah Veh his Elohim
6 —who worked the heavens and earth,
the sea and all therein:
who guards truth eternally;
7 who works judgment for the oppressed;
who gives bread to the famished.
Yah Veh looses the bound;
8 Yah Veh opens the blind; Yah Veh raises
the bowed; Yah Veh loves the just;
9 Yah Veh guards the sojourners;
he restores the orphan and widow; and
twists the way of the wicked.
10 Yah Veh reigns eternal;
your Elohim, O Siyon, generation to generation.
Halalu Yah!

147 Halalu Yah!
For *it is* good to psalm to our Elohim;
for *it is* pleasant; and befits halal:
2 Yah Veh builds Yeru Shalem;
he gathers the overthrown of Yisra El;
3 he heals the broken in heart
and binds their contortions;
4 he numbers the number of the stars;
he calls them all by names.

5 Great is our *Lord* **Adonay**,
and of great *power* **force**:
his *understanding is infinite* **discernments innumerable.**
6 *The LORD* **Yah Veh**
lifteth up **restoreth** the *meek* **humble**:
he *casteth* **abaseth** the wicked *down* to the *ground* **earth**.
7 *Sing unto the LORD* **Answer Yah Veh**
with *thanksgiving* **spread hands;**
sing praise **psalm** upon the harp unto our *God* **Elohim**:
8 Who covereth the *heaven*
heavens with **thick** clouds,
who prepareth rain for the earth,
who *maketh* **sprouteth** grass *to grow*
upon the mountains.
9 He giveth to the *beast* **animal** his *food* **bread**,
and to the *young* **sons of** ravens which *cry* **call**.
10 He delighteth not in the
strength **might** of the horse:
he taketh not pleasure in the legs of a man.
11 *The LORD* **Yah Veh** taketh pleasure
in them that *fear* **awe** him,
in those that *hope* **await** in his mercy.
12 *Praise the LORD* **Laud Yah Veh,**
O *Jerusalem* **Yeru Shalem;**
praise **halal** thy *God* **Elohim**, O *Zion* **Siyon.**
13 For he hath strengthened the bars
of thy *gates* **portals;**
he hath blessed thy *children* **sons** within thee.
14 He *maketh peace* **setteth shalom** in thy borders,
and *filleth* **satisfieth** thee with the *finest* **fat** of the wheat.
15 He sendeth forth his *commandment* **sayings**
upon earth:
his word runneth very *swiftly* **quickly**.
16 He giveth snow like wool:
he scattereth the hoarfrost like ashes.
17 He casteth forth his ice like morsels:
who can stand *before* **at the face of** his cold?
18 He sendeth out his word, and melteth them:
he causeth his wind to blow, and the waters flow.
19 He *sheweth* **telleth** his word unto *Jacob* **Yaaqov**,
his *statutes* **words** and his judgments
unto *Israel* **Yisra El**.
20 He hath not *dealt* **worked**
so with any *nation* **goyim**:
and as for his judgments, they have not known
them. *Praise ye the LORD* **l-lalalu Yah.**

148 *Praise ye the LORD* **l-lalalu Yah.**
Praise ye the LORD **l-lalal Yah Veh** from the heavens:
Praise **l-lalal** him in the heights.
2 *Praise* **l-lalal** ye him, all his angels:
praise **halal** ye him, all his hosts.
3 *Praise* **l-lalal** ye him, sun and moon:
praise **halal** him, all ye stars of light.
4 *Praise* **l-lalal** him, ye heavens of **the** heavens,
and ye waters that be above the heavens.
5 Let them *praise* **halal** the
name of *the LORD* **Yah Veh**:
for he *commanded* **misvahed**, and they were created.
6 He hath also *stablished* **stood** them
for ever **eternally** and *ever* **eternally**:
he hath *made* **given** a *decree* **statute**
which shall not pass.
7 *Praise the LORD* **l-lalal Yah Veh** from the earth,
ye *dragons* **monsters**, and all *deeps* **abysses**:
8 Fire, and hail; snow, and *vapours* **smoke**;
stormy wind *fulfilling* **working** his word:
9 Mountains, and all hills;
fruitful trees, and all cedars:
10 *Beasts* **Live beings**, and all *cattle* **animals**;
creeping things **creepers**, and *flying fowl* **birds of wing**:
11 *Kings* **Sovereigns** of the
earth, and all *people* **nations**;
princes **governors**, and all judges of the earth:
12 Both *young men* **youths**, and maidens;
old men **aged**, and *children* **lads**:
13 Let them *praise* **halal** the
name of *the LORD* **Yah Veh**:
for his name alone is *excellent* **lofted;**
his *glory* **majesty**
is above the earth and *heaven* **the heavens.**
14 He also exalteth the horn of his people,
the *praise* **halal** of all his *saints* **mercied;**
even of the *children* **sons** of *Israel* **Yisra El,**
a people near unto him.
Praise ye the LORD **l-lalalu Yah.**

5 Great *is* our Adonay and great of force;
his discernments innumerable:
6 Yah Veh restores the humble;
he abases the wicked to the earth.
7 Answer Yah Veh with spread hands;
psalm on the harp to our Elohim
8 —who covers the heavens with thick clouds;
who prepares rain for the earth;
who sprouts grass on the mountains;
9 who gives his bread to the animal
and to the sons of ravens who call.
10 He neither delights in the might of the horse;
nor takes pleasure in the legs of a man.
11 Yah Veh takes pleasure
in them who awe him; who await his mercy.
12 Laud Yah Veh, O Yeru Shalem;
halal your Elohim, O Siyon.

13 For he strengthens the bars of your portals;
he blesses your sons within you;
14 who sets shalom in your borders
and satisfies you with the fat of the wheat;
15 who sends his sayings on earth;
whose word runs very quickly;
16 who gives snow as wool:
he scatters the hoarfrost as ashes;
17 he casts his ice as morsels.
Who stands at the face of his cold?
18 He sends his word and they melt;
he blows his wind; the waters flow;
19 he tells his word to Yaaqov
—his words and his judgments to Yisra El.
20 He worked not thus with any goyim;
and as to judgments, they know them not.
Halalu Yah!

148 Halalu Yah!
Halal Yah Veh from the heavens;
halal him in the heights;
2 halal him, all his angels;
halal him, all his hosts;
3 halal him, sun and moon;
halal him, all you stars of light;
4 halal him, you heavens of the heavens
and you waters above the heavens:
5 Halal the name of Yah Veh;
for he misvahed and they were created.
6 He stands them eternally and eternally;
he gave a statute; they pass not over.
7 Halal Yah Veh from the earth
you monsters and all abysses;
8 fire and hail; snow and smoke;
stormy wind working his word;
9 mountains and all hills;
fruitful trees and all cedars;
10 live beings and all animals;
creepers and birds of wing;
11 sovereigns of the earth and all nations;
governors and all judges of the earth;
12 both youths and maidens;
aged and lads!
13 Halal the name of Yah Veh;
for his name alone is lofted;
his majesty *is* above the earth and the heavens:
14 he exalts the horn of his people
—the halal of all his mercied;
of the sons of Yisra El—a people near him.
Halalu Yah!

149 *Praise ye the LORD* **l-lalalu Yah.**
Sing unto *the LORD* **Yah Veh** a new song,
and his *praise* **halal** in the congregation
of *saints* **mercied.**
2 Let *Israel rejoice* **Yisra El cheer**
in him that *made* **worked** him:
let the *children* **sons** of *Zion* **Siyon**
be joyful **twirl** in their *King* **Sovereign.**
3 Let them *praise* **halal** his
name in the **round** dance:
let them *sing praises* **psalm** unto him
with the *timbrel* **tambourine** and harp.
4 For *the LORD* **Yah Veh**
taketh pleasure in his people:
he *will beautify* **shall adorn** the *meek* **humble**
with salvation.
5 Let the *saints* **mercied**
be joyful **jump for joy** in *glory* **honour**:
let them *sing aloud* **shout** upon their beds.
6 Let the *high praises of God* **exaltations of El**
be in their *mouth* **throat,**
and a *twoedged* sword **of teeth** in their hand;
7 To *execute* **work** vengeance
upon the *heathen* **goyim,**
and *punishments* **reproofs** upon the *people* **nations;**
8 To bind their *kings* **sovereigns**
with *chains* **bonds,**
and their *nobles* **honoured** with fetters of iron;
9 To *execute* **work** upon them
the judgment *written* **inscribed**:
this *honour* **majesty** have all his *saints* **mercied.**
Praise ye the LORD **l-lalalu Yah.**

150 *Praise ye the LORD* **l-lalalu Yah.**
Praise God **l-lalal El** in his *sanctuary* **holies**:
praise **halal** him
in the *firmament* **expanse** of his *power* **strength.**
2 *Praise* **l-lalal** him
for his *mighty acts* **might**:
praise **l-lalal** him
according to his *excellent* **abundant** greatness.
3 *Praise* **l-lalal** him
with the *sound* **blast** of the *trumpet* **shophars**:
praise **halal** him
with the *psaltery* **bagpipe** and harp.
4 *Praise* **l-lalal** him
with the *timbrel* **tambourine** and **round** dance:
praise **halal** him
with *stringed instruments* **strummers**
and *organs* **woodwinds.**
5 *Praise* **l-lalal** him
upon the *loud* **hearkening** cymbals:

praise **halal** him
upon the *high sounding* **clanging** cymbals.
6 Let *every thing that hath*
breath **all that breatheth**
praise the LORD **halal Yah.**
Praise ye the LORD **l-lalalu Yah.**

149 Halalu Yah!
Sing Yah Veh a new song
and his halal in the congregation of the mercied.
2 Yisra El cheers in his Worker;
the sons of Siyon twirl in their Sovereign:
3 they halal his name in the round dance;
they psalm to him with tambourine and harp;
4 for Yah Veh takes pleasure in his people;
he adorns the humble with salvation.
5 The mercied jump for joy in honor;
they shout on their beds;
6 the exaltation of El *is* in their throat
and a sword of teeth in their hand
7 —to work vengeance on the goyim
and reproofs on the nations:
8 to bind their sovereigns with bonds
and their honored with fetters of iron:
9 to work on them the inscribed judgment
—a majesty for all his mercied.
Halalu Yah!

150 Halalu Yah!
Halal El in his holies;
halal him in the expanse of his strength;
2 halal him for his might;
halal him according to his abundant greatness;
3 halal him with the blast of the shophar;
halal him with the bagpipe and harp;
4 halal him with the
tambourine and round dance;
halal him with strummers and woodwinds;
5 halal him on the hearkening cymbals;
halal him on the clanging cymbals.
6 All you who breathe, halal Yah.
Halalu Yah!

1 The proverbs of *Solomon* **Shelomoh**
the son of David,
king **sovereign** of *Israel* **Yisra El**;
2 To know wisdom and *instruction* **discipline**;
to *perceive the words* **discern sayings**
of *understanding* **discernment**;
3 To *receive the instruction* **take discipline**
of *wisdom* **comprehension**, *justice* **justness**,
and judgment, and *equity* **straightnesses**;
4 To give *subtilty* **strategy** to the *simple* **gullible**,
to the *young man* **lad** knowledge and *discretion* **intrigue**.
5 *A* **The** wise *man will* **shall** hear,
and *will* **shall** increase *learning* **doctrine**;
and *a man of understanding* **the discerning**
shall *attain* **chattelize** unto wise counsels:
6 To *understand* **discern** a proverb,
and the *interpretation* **satire**;
the words of the wise, and their *dark sayings* **riddles**.
7 The *fear* **awe** of *the LORD* **Yah Veh**
is the beginning of knowledge:
but fools
despise **disrespect** wisdom and *instruction* **discipline**.
8 My son, hear the *instruction*
discipline of thy father,
and *forsake* **abandon** not the *law* **torah** of thy mother:
9 For they shall be
an ornament **a wreath** of *grace* **charism** unto thy head,
and *chains about* **chokers around** thy *neck* **throat**.
10 My son, if sinners entice thee,
consent thou **shalt** not **will**.
11 If they say, Come with us,
let us *lay wait* **lurk** for blood,
let us *lurk privily* **hide out** for the innocent
without cause **gratuitously**:
12 Let us swallow them up alive as *the grave* **sheol**;
and *whole* **integrious**,
as those that *go down* **descend** into the *pit* **well**:
13 We shall find all *precious*
substance **esteemed wealth**,
we shall fill our houses with spoil:
14 *Cast in* **Fell** thy *lot* **pebble** among us;
let us all have one *purse* **pouch**:
15 My son, walk not thou in the way with them;
refrain **withhold** thy foot from their path:
16 For their feet run to evil,
and *make haste* **hasten** to *shed* **pour** blood.
17 Surely *in vain* **gratuitously**
the net is *spread* **winnowed**
in the *sight* **eye** of any *bird* **master of wing**.
18 And they *lay wait* **lurk** for their own blood;
they *lurk privily* **hide out** for their own *lives* **souls**.
19 So are the ways
of every one that is greedy of *gain* **greed**;
which taketh away
the *life* **soul** of *the owners thereof* **their masters**.
20 Wisdom *crieth without* **shouteth out**;
she *uttereth* **giveth** her voice in the *streets* **broadways**:
21 She *crieth* **calleth out**
in the *chief place* **top** of *concourse* **the roaring**,
in the *openings* **portals** of the *gates* **portals**:
in the city she *uttereth* **sayeth** her *words* **sayings**, *saying*,
22 How long, ye *simple ones* **gullible**,
will **shall** ye love *simplicity* **gullibility**?
and the scorners delight in their scorning,
and fools hate knowledge?
23 Turn you at my reproof:
behold, I *will pour out* **shall gush** my spirit unto you,
I *will* **shall** make known my words unto you.
24 Because I have called, and ye refused;
I have *stretched out* **spread** my hand,
and no *man regarded* **one hearkened**;
25 But ye have *set at nought* **loosed** all my counsel,
and *would* **willed** none of my reproof:
26 I also *will* **shall** laugh at your calamity;
I *will mock* **shall deride** when your *fear* **dread** cometh;
27 When your *fear* **dread**
cometh as *desolation* **devastation**,
and your *destruction* **calamity**
cometh as a *whirlwind* **hurricane**;
when *distress* **tribulation** and *anguish* **distress**
cometh upon you.

1 The proverbs of Shelomoh
the son of David sovereign of Yisra El:
2 to know wisdom and discipline;
to discern sayings of discernment;
3 to take discipline of comprehension, justness,
judgment and straightnesses;
4 to give strategy to the gullible;
to the lad knowledge and intrigue.
5 The wise hear and increase doctrine;
and the discerning chattelize to wise counsels:
6 to discern a proverb and the satire;
the words of the wise and their riddles.
7 to awe of Yah Veh is the
beginning of knowledge;
fools disrespect wisdom and discipline.
8 My son, hear the discipline of your father
and abandon not the torah of your mother:
9 —a wreath of charism to your head

and chokers around your throat.
10 My son, if sinners entice you, be not willing:
11 if they say, Come with us, we lurk for blood,
we hide out gratuitously for the innocent;
12 we swallow them alive as sheol;
the integrious,
as those who descend into the well;
13 we find all esteemed wealth;
we fill our houses with spoil;
14 fell your pebble among us;
we all have one pouch!
15 —my son, walk not in the way with them;
withhold your foot from their path:
16 for their feet run to evil
and hasten to pour blood.
17 Surely the net is winnowed gratuitously
in the eye of any master of wing:
18 they lurk for their own blood;
they hide out for their own souls:
19 thus are the ways of all the greedy of greed;
who take away the soul of their masters.
20 Wisdom shouts;
she gives her voice in the broadways;
21 she calls out in the top of the roaring
—in the portals of the portals;
in the city she says her sayings,
22 Until when, O gullible, love you gullibility?
and scorners delight in their scorning?
and fools hate knowledge?
23 Turn at my reproof;
behold, I gush my spirit to you; I make
known my words to you.
24 Because I called and you refuse;
I spread my hand and no one hearkens;
25 you loose all my counsel
and will none of my reproof.
26 I laugh at your calamity;
I deride when your dread comes
27 —when your dread comes as devastation
and your calamity comes as a hurricane; when
tribulation and distress come on you.
28 Then shall they call upon me,
but I *will* **shall** not answer;
they shall seek me early, but they shall not find me:
29 For that they hated knowledge,
and did not choose the *fear* **awe** of *the LORD* **Yah Veh**:
30 They *would* **willed** none of my counsel:
they *despised* **scorned** all my reproof.
31 Therefore shall they eat of
the fruit of their own way,
and be *filled* **satiated** with their own *devices* **counsels**.
32 For the *turning away* **apostasy**
of the *simple* **gullible**
shall *slay* **slaughter** them,
and the *prosperity* **serenity** of fools shall destroy them.
33 But whoso hearkeneth unto me
shall *dwell safely* **tabernacle confidently**,
and shall *be quiet* **relax** from *fear* **dread** of evil.

2 My son,
if thou *wilt receive* **shalt take** my *words* **sayings**,
and hide my *commandments* **misvoth** with thee;
2 So that thou *incline* **hearken**
thine ear unto wisdom,
and *apply* **spread** thine heart to
understanding **discernment**;
3 Yea, if thou *criest* **callest**
after *knowledge* **discernment**,
and *liftest up* **givest** thy voice for
understanding **discerning**;
4 If thou seekest her as silver,
and searchest for her as for hid treasures;
5 Then shalt thou *understand* **discern**
the *fear* **awe** of *the LORD* **Yah Veh**,
and find the knowledge of *God* **Elohim**.
6 For *the LORD* **Yah Veh** giveth wisdom:
out of his mouth
cometh knowledge and *understanding* **discernment**.
7 He *layeth up sound wisdom*
treasureth substance
for the *righteous* **straight**:
he is a buckler to them that walk *uprightly* **integriously**.
8 He *keepeth* **guardeth** the paths of judgment,
and *preserveth* **guardeth** the way of his *saints* **mercied**.
9 Then shalt thou
understand righteousness **discern justness**,
and judgment, and *equity* **straightnesses**;
yea, every good *path* **route**.
10 When wisdom entereth into thine heart,
and knowledge *is pleasant unto* **pleaseth** thy soul;
11 *Discretion* **Intrigue** shall *preserve* **guard** thee,
understanding **discernment** shall *keep* **guard** thee:
12 To *deliver* **rescue** thee
from the way of *the* evil *man*,
from the man
that *speaketh froward things* **wordeth perversions**;
13 Who *leave* **forsake**
the paths of *uprightness* **straightness**,
to walk in the ways of darkness;
14 Who *rejoice* **cheer** to *do* **work** evil,
and *delight* **twirl**

in the *frowardness* **perversions** of *the wicked* **evil**;
15 Whose ways *are crooked* **pervert**,
and they froward—**pervert** in their *paths* **routes**:
16 To *deliver* **rescue** thee from the strange woman,
even from the stranger
which *flattereth* **smootheth over** with her *words* **sayings**;
17 Which forsaketh the *guide*
chiliarch of her youth,
and forgetteth the covenant of her *God* **Elohim**.
18 For her house *inclineth* **sinketh** unto death,
and her *paths* **routes** unto *the dead* **ghosts**.
19 None that go unto her return *again*,
neither *take* **overtake** they *hold* of the paths of life.
20 That thou mayest walk in the way of good *men*,
and *keep* **guard** the paths of the *righteous* **just**.
21 For the *upright* **straight**
shall *dwell* **tabernacle** in the land,
and the *perfect* **integrious** shall remain in it.
22 But *the wicked* **they that deal covertly**
shall be cut off from the earth,
and the transgressors shall be *rooted out of it* **uprooted**.
28 Then they call me, and I answer not;
they seek me early, and they find me not;
29 because they hate knowledge
and choose not the awe of Yah Veh;
30 they will not my counsel;
they scorn all my reproof;
31 they eat of the fruit of their own way
and satiate with their own counsels:
32 for the apostasy of the gullible slaughters them
and the serenity of fools destroys them.
33 And whoever hearkens to me
tabernacles confidently;
and relaxes from dread of evil.

2 My son, if you take my sayings
and hide my misvoth with you
2 —to hearken your ear to wisdom
and spread your heart to discernment;
3 yes, if you call after discernment
and give your voice for discerning;
4 if you seek her as silver
and search for her as hid treasures
5 —then you discern the awe of Yah Veh
and find the knowledge of Elohim.
6 For Yah Veh gives wisdom
—from his mouth knowledge and discernment:
7 he treasures substance for the straight;
a buckler to them who walk integriously:
8 he guards the paths of judgment
and guards the way of his mercied.
9 Then you discern justness
and judgment and straightnesses
—every good route:
10 then wisdom enters your heart
and knowledge pleases your soul;
11 intrigue guards you;
discernment guards you;
12 to rescue you from the way of evil
—from the man who words perversions:
13 who forsakes the paths of straightness
to walk in the ways of darkness;
14 who cheers to work evil
and twirls in the perversions of evil;
15 whose ways pervert—pervert in their routes:
16 to rescue you from the strange woman
—from the stranger
who smoothes it over with her sayings;
17 who forsakes the chiliarch of her youth
and forgets the covenant of her Elohim.
18 For her house sinks to death
and her routes to ghosts.
19 Neither return they who go to her
nor overtake they of the paths of life.
20 So walk in the way of good
and guard the paths of the just:
21 for the straight tabernacle in the land
and the integrious remain therein:
22 and they who deal covertly
are cut off from the earth;
and the transgressors uprooted.

3 My son, forget not my *law* **torah**;
but let thine heart
keep **guard** my *commandments* **misvoth**:
2 For length of days, and *long* **years of** life,
and *peace* **shalom**, shall they add to thee.
3 Let not mercy and truth forsake thee:
bind them about thy *neck* **throat**;
write **inscribe** them upon the *table* **slab** of thine heart:
4 So shalt thou find *favour* **charism**
and good *understanding* **comprehension**
in the *sight* **eye** of *God* **Elohim** and *man* **humanity**.
5 *Trust* **Confide** in *the LORD*
Yah Veh with all thine heart;
and lean not unto thine own
understanding **discernment**.
6 In all thy ways *acknowledge* **know** him,
and he shall *direct* **straighten** thy paths.
7 Be not wise in thine own eyes: *fear the LORD*
awe Yah Veh, and *depart* **turn aside** from evil.
8 *It* **healing** shall be *health* to thy navel,

and *marrow* **moisture** to thy bones.
9 Honour *the LORD* **Yah Veh**
with thy *substance* **wealth**,
and with the firstfruits of all *thine increase* **thy produce**:
10 *So* **Thus** shall thy *barns* **ingatherings**
be filled with *plenty* **sufficiency**,
and thy *presses* **troughs** shall *burst out* **break forth**
with *new wine* **juice**.
11 My son, *despise* **spurn** not
the *chastening* **discipline** of *the LORD* **Yah Veh**;
neither *be weary of* **abhor** his *correction* **reproof**:
12 For whom *the LORD* **Yah Veh** loveth
he *correcteth* **reproveth**;
even as a father the son
in whom he *delighteth* **be pleased**.
13 *Happy is* **Blithe be** the *man* **human**
that findeth wisdom,
and the *man* **human**
that *getteth understanding* **produceth discernment**.
14 For the merchandise of it
is better than the merchandise of silver,
and the *gain* **produce** thereof than *fine gold* **ore**.
15 She is more *precious*
esteemed than *rubies* **pearls**:
and all *the things thou canst desire* **thy desires**
are not to be compared unto her.
16 Length of days is in her right *hand*;
and in her left *hand* riches and honour.
17 Her ways are ways of pleasantness,
and all her paths are *peace* **shalom**.
18 She is a tree of life
to them that *lay hold upon* **uphold** her:
and *happy is every one* **blithesome be they**
that *retaineth* **uphold** her.
19 *The LORD* **Yah Veh** by wisdom
hath founded the earth;
by *understanding* **discernment**
hath he established the heavens.
20 By his knowledge
the *depths* **abysses** are *broken up* **split**,
and the *clouds drop down* **vapours drip** the dew.
21 My son, let not them *depart*
pervert from thine eyes:
keep sound wisdom **guard substance**
and *discretion* **intrigue**:
22 So shall they be life unto thy soul,
and *grace* **charism** to thy *neck* **throat**.
23 Then shalt thou walk in
thy way *safely* **confidently**,
and thy foot shall not *stumble* **stub**.
24 When thou liest down,
thou shalt not *be afraid* **dread**:
yea, thou shalt lie down,
and thy sleep shall *be sweet* **please**.
25 *Be* **Awe** not *afraid of* sudden fear,
neither of the *desolation* **devastation** of the wicked,
when it cometh.
26 For *the LORD* **Yah Veh** shall
be thy *confidence* **hope**,
and shall *keep* **guard** thy foot from *being taken* **capture**.
27 Withhold not good
from *them to whom it is due* **thy masters**,
when it is in the *power* **El** of thine hand to *do* **work** it.
28 Say not unto thy *neighbour* **friend**,

3 My son, forget not my torah;
and your heart guard my misvoth;
2 for they add to you
length of days and years of life and shalom:
3 forsake not mercy and truth;
bind them about your throat;
inscribe them on the slab of your heart:
4 thus you find charism and good comprehension
in the eye of Elohim and humanity.
5 Confide in Yah Veh with all your heart
and lean not to your own discernment:
6 in all your ways know him
and he straightens your paths:
7 be not wise in your own eyes;
awe Yah Veh and turn aside from evil
8 —healing to your navel
and moisture to your bones.
9 Honor Yah Veh with your wealth
and with the firstfruits of all your produce:
10 thus are your ingatherings
filled with sufficiency
and your troughs break forth with juice.
11 My son,
neither spurn the discipline of Yah Veh
nor abhor his reproof:
12 for whom Yah Veh loves, he reproves
—even as a father the son who pleases him.
13 Blithe—the human who finds wisdom
and the human who produces discernment:
14 better, the merchandise thereof
than the merchandise of silver;
and the produce thereof than ore:
15 she is more esteemed than pearls
and all your desires are not comparable to her:
16 length of days is in her right;
and in her left, riches and honor:

17 her ways are ways of pleasantness
and all her paths are shalom:
18 she is a tree of life to them who uphold her;
and blithesome to them who uphold her.
19 Yah Veh, by wisdom, founded the earth;
by discernment, he established the heavens;
20 by knowledge, he split the abysses
and the vapours drip the dew.
21 My son, pervert them not from your eyes;
guard substance and intrigue
22 —life to your soul and charism to your throat.
23 Then you walk your way confidently
and stub not your foot:
24 you lie down; you dread not:
yes, you lie down and your sleep pleases.
25 Neither awe sudden fear;
nor the devastation of the wicked when it comes:
26 for Yah Veh is your hope
and he guards your foot from capture.
27 Withhold not good from your masters
when it is in the El of your hand to work it:
28 say not to your friend,
Go, and *come again* **return**,
and to morrow I *will* **shall** give;
when thou hast it by thee.
29 *Devise* **Inscribe** not evil
against thy *neighbour* **friend**,
seeing he *dwelleth securely* **settleth confidently** by thee.
30 Strive not with *a man* **humanity**
without cause **gratuitously**,
if he have *done* **dealt** thee no *harm* **evil**.
31 Envy thou not the *oppressor* **man of violence**,
and choose none of his ways.
32 For *the froward* **he that perverteth**
is *abomination* **abhorrence** to *the LORD* **Yah Veh**:
but his *secret* **private counsel**
is with the *righteous* **straight**.
33 The curse of *the LORD* **Yah Veh**
is in the house of the wicked:
but he blesseth the habitation **of rest** of the just.
34 Surely he scorneth the scorners:
but he giveth *grace* **charism** unto the *lowly* **humble**.
35 The wise shall inherit *glory* **honour**:
but *shame* **abasement**
shall be the *promotion* **exaltation** of fools.

4 Hear, ye *children* **sons**,
the *instruction* **discipline** of a father,
and *attend* **hearken** to know
understanding **discernment**.
2 For I give you good doctrine,
forsake ye not my *law* **torah**.
3 For I was my father's son,
tender and only *beloved*
in the sight **at the face** of my mother.
4 He taught me also, and said unto me,
Let thine heart *retain* **uphold** my words:
keep **guard** my *commandments* **misvoth**, and live.
5 *Get* **Chattelize** wisdom,
get understanding **chattelize discernment**:
forget it not;
neither *decline* **spread**
from the *words* **sayings** of my mouth.
6 Forsake her not, and she
shall *preserve* **guard** thee:
love her, and she shall *keep* **guard** thee.
7 Wisdom is the *principal thing* **firstfruits**;
therefore get **chattelize** wisdom:
and with all thy *getting* **chattelizing**
get understanding **chattelize discernment**.
8 Exalt her, and she shall *promote* **exalt** thee:
she shall bring thee to honour,
when thou dost embrace her.
9 She shall give to thine head
an ornament **a wreath** of *grace* **charism**:
with a crown of *glory* **beauty**
shall she *deliver to* **shield** thee.
10 Hear, O my son, and *receive* **take** my sayings;
and the years of thy life shall *be many* **abound**.
11 I have taught thee in the way of wisdom;
I have *led* **aimed** thee in *right paths*
routes of straightness.
12 When thou goest,
thy *steps* **paces** shall not be straitened;
and when thou runnest, thou shalt not stumble.
13 *Take fast hold of instruction* **Uphold discipline**;
let her not go:
keep **guard** her; for she is thy life.
14 Enter not into the path of the wicked,
and go not **nor be blithesome** in the way of evil *men*.
15 Avoid it, pass not by it,
turn **deviate** from it, and pass away.
16 For they sleep not,
except they have *done mischief* **vilified**;
and their sleep is *taken away* **stripped**,
unless they cause some to *fall* **trip**.
17 For they eat the bread of wickedness,
and drink the wine of violence.
18 But the path of the just is as
the *shining* **brilliant** light,
that *shineth* **goeth on and lighteneth** more and
more unto *the perfect* **establishing the** day.

19 The way of the wicked is as darkness:
they know not at what they stumble.
20 My son, *attend* **hearken** to my words;
incline **spread** thine ear unto my sayings.
Go and return, and tomorrow I give
—when you have it by you:
29 inscribe not evil against your friend
seeing he settles confidently by you:
30 strive not with humanity gratuitously
if he deals you no evil:
31 neither envy the man of violence
nor choose his ways:
32 for he who perverts is abhorrence to Yah Veh;
and his private counsel is with the straight.
33 The curse of Yah Veh
is in the house of the wicked;
and he blesses the habitation of rest of the just.
34 Surely he scorns the scorners;
yet he gives charism to the humble:
35 the wise inherit honor;
and abasement is the exaltation of fools.

4 Hear, you sons, the discipline of a father;
and hearken to know discernment;
2 for I give you good doctrine:
forsake not my torah.
3 For I was a son of my father—tender;
an only at the face of my mother:
4 and teaches me and says to me,
O that your heart uphold my words;
guard my misvoth and live.
5 Chattelize wisdom; chattelize discernment:
neither forget nor spread
from the sayings of my mouth.
6 Forsake her not, and she guards you;
love her, and she guards you:
7 the firstfruits, wisdom; chattelize wisdom:
and with all your chattelizing chattelize discernment.
8 Exalt her and she exalts you;
she honors you when you embrace her:
9 she gives your head a wreath of charism;
with a crown of beauty she shields you.
10 Hear, O my son, and take my sayings;
and abound the years of your life:
11 I teach you in the way of wisdom;
I aim you in routes of straightness:
12 so that as you walk, your paces constrain not;
and as you run, you stumble not.
13 Uphold discipline; let not go:
guard her; for she is your life:
14 neither enter the path of the wicked
nor blithe in the way of evil.
15 Avoid, pass not in;
deviate therefrom, and pass on:
16 for they sleep not unless they vilify;
and they strip their sleep until they trip some:
17 for they eat the bread of wickedness
and drink the wine of violence.
18 And the path of the just is as the brilliant light
that goes and lights more and more
to establish the day.
19 The way of the wicked is as darkness;
they know not at what they stumble.
20 My son, hearken to my words;
spread your ear to my sayings:
21 Let them not *depart* **pervert** from thine eyes;
keep **guard** them in the midst of thine heart.
22 For they are life unto those that find them,
and *health* **healing** to all their flesh.
23 *Keep* **Guard** thy heart *with*
all diligence **under guard**;
for out of it are the issues of life.
24 *Put away* **Turn aside** from thee
a *froward* **perverted** mouth,
and perverse lips *put* **remove** far from thee.
25 Let thine eyes look *right on* **straightforward**,
and let thine eyelids
look straight before **straighten in front of** thee.
26 *Ponder* **Weigh** the *path* **route** of thy feet,
and let all thy ways be established.
27 *Turn* **Spread** not to the
right *hand* nor to the left:
remove **turn** thy foot from evil.

5 My son, *attend* **hearken** unto my wisdom,
and bow **spread** thine ear to my
understanding **discernment**:
2 That thou mayest regard *discretion* **intrigue**,
and that thy lips may *keep* **guard** knowledge.
3 For the lips of a *strange woman* **stranger**
drop as an honeycomb,
and her *mouth* **palate** is smoother than *oil* **ointment**:
4 But her *end* **finality** is bitter as wormwood,
sharp as a *twoedged* sword **of mouths**.
5 Her feet *go down* **descend** to death;
her *steps* **paces** take hold on *hell* **sheol**.
6 Lest thou shouldest *ponder*
weigh the path of life,
her *ways are moveable* **routes drift**,
that thou *canst* not know them.
7 Hear me now therefore, O ye *children* **sons**,
and *depart* **turn** not **aside**

from the *words* **sayings** of my mouth.
8 Remove thy way far from her,
and come not nigh the *door* **portal** of her house:
9 Lest thou give thine honour unto others,
and thy years unto the cruel:
10 Lest strangers be *filled* **satiated**
with thy *wealth* **produce**;
and thy *labours* **contorting** be in the house of a stranger;
11 And thou *mourn* **growl** at the *last* **finality**,
when thy flesh and thy *body* **meat**
are *consumed* **finished off**,
12 And say, How have I hated
instruction **discipline**,
and my heart *despised* **scorned** reproof;
13 And have not obeyed the voice of my teachers,
nor *inclined* **spread** mine ear
to them that *instructed* **taught** me!
14 I was almost in all evil
in the midst of the congregation and *assembly* **witness**.
15 Drink waters out of thine own *cistern* **well**,
and *running waters* **flowings** out of thine own well.
16 Let thy fountains
be *dispersed abroad* **shattered in the outways**,
and *rivers* **rivulets** of waters
in the *streets* **broadways**.
17 Let them be only thine own,
and not strangers' with thee.
18 Let thy fountain be blessed:
and *rejoice* **cheer** with the *wife* **woman** of thy youth.
19 Let her be as the *loving* hind **of loves**
and *pleasant* roe **of charism**;
let her *breasts* **nipples** satisfy thee at all times;
and *be thou ravished* **err inadvertently**
always **continually** with her love.
20 And why *wilt* **shalt** thou, my son,
be ravished **err inadvertently**
with a *strange woman* **stranger**,
and embrace the bosom of a stranger?
21 For the ways of man
are *before* **in front of** the eyes of *the LORD* **Yah Veh**,
and he *pondereth* **weigheth** all his *goings* **routes**.
22 His own *iniquities* **perversities**
shall *take* **capture** the wicked himself,
and he shall be *holden* **upheld** with the cords of his sins.
23 He shall die without *instruction* **discipline**;
and in the greatness of his folly
he shall *go astray* **err inadvertently**.
21 pervert them not from your eyes;
guard them midst your heart:
22 for they are life to them who find them
and healing to all their flesh:
23 guard your heart under guard;
for from it are the issues of life:
24 turn aside from a perverted mouth
and perverse lips remove far from you
25 —your eyes looking straightforward
and straightening your eyelids in front of you:
26 weigh the route of your feet
and establish all your ways:
27 spread neither to the right nor to the left;
turn aside your foot from evil.
5 My son, hearken to my wisdom;
spread your ear to my discernment:
2 to regard intrigue
and your lips guard knowledge:
3 for the lips of a stranger drip as a honeycomb
and her palate is smoother than ointment:
4 but her finality is bitter as wormwood
sharp as a sword of mouths:
5 her feet descend to death;
her paces hold on to sheol:
6 lest you weigh the path of life
her routes drift so that you know them not.
7 Hear me now, O you sons,
and turn not aside from the sayings of my mouth:
8 remove your way far from her
and come not near the portal of her house;
9 lest you give your honor to others
and your years to the cruel:
10 lest strangers satiate with your produce;
and your contorting be in the house of a stranger:
11 and you growl at the finality
when your flesh and your meat finish off,
12 and say, How I hated discipline
and my heart scorned reproof:
13 and I neither obeyed the voice of my teachers
nor spread my ear to them who taught me:
14 I was almost in all evil
midst the congregation and witness.
15 Drink waters from your own well
and flowings from your own well:
16 why shatter the fountains in the outways
and rivulets of waters in the broadways?
17 They are only your own
and not strangers with you.
18 Blessed—your fountain.
Cheer with the woman of your youth;
19 she is as the hind of loves and the roe of
charism:
her nipples satisfy you at all times;

and continually err inadvertently with her love.
20 And why, my son,
err inadvertently with a stranger?
—embrace the bosom of a stranger?
21 For the ways of man
are in front of the eyes of Yah Veh
and he weighs all his routes.
22 His own perversities capture the wicked
—upheld by the cords of his own sins:
23 he dies without discipline;
and in the greatness of his folly
he errs inadvertently.

6 My son, if thou *be surety* **pledgest**
for thy friend,
if thou hast *stricken* **clapped** thy *hand* **palm**
with a stranger,
2 Thou art snared
with the *words* **sayings** of thy mouth,
thou art *taken* **captured**
with the *words* **sayings** of thy mouth.
3 *Do* **Work** this now, my son, and deliver thyself,
when thou art come into the *hand* **palm** of thy friend;
go, *humble thyself* **prostrate**,
and *make sure* **encourage** thy friend.
4 Give not sleep to thine eyes,
nor *slumber* **drowsiness** to thine eyelids.
5 Deliver thyself
as a *roe* **gazelle** from the hand *of the hunter*,
and as a bird from the hand of the *fowler* **snarer**.
6 Go to the ant, thou *sluggard* **sloth**;
consider **see** her ways, and *be wise* **enwisen**:
7 Which having no *guide* **commander**,
overseer **officer**, or *ruler* **sovereign**,
8 *Provideth* **Prepareth** her
meat **bread** in the summer,
and *gathereth* **harvesteth** her food in the harvest.
9 How long *wilt* **shalt** thou *sleep* **lie down**,
O *sluggard* **sloth**?
when *wilt* **shalt** thou arise out of thy sleep?
10 *Yet* a little sleep, a little *slumber* **drowsiness**,
a little *folding* **clasping** of the hands to *sleep* **lie down**:
11 So shall thy poverty come
as one that *travelleth* **walketh**,
and thy *want* **lack** as *an armed* **a** man **with buckler**.
12 A *naughty person* **human Beli Yaal**,
a *wicked man* **man of mischief**,
walketh with a *froward* **perverted** mouth.
13 He *winketh* **blinketh** with his eyes,
he *speaketh* **uttereth** with his feet, he
teacheth **pointeth** with his fingers;
14 *Frowardness* **Perversion** is in his heart,
he *deviseth mischief* **inscribeth evil**
continually **at all times**;
he *soweth discord* **sendeth contention**.
15 Therefore shall his calamity come suddenly;
suddenly **in a blink** shall he be broken
without *remedy* **healing**.
16 These six *things*
doth the LORD hate **Yah Veh hateth**:
yea, seven
are an *abomination* **abhorrence** unto *him* **his soul**:
17 A *proud look* **lofty eye**, a *lying* **false** tongue,
and hands that *shed* **pour** innocent blood,
18 An heart that *deviseth* **inscribeth**
wicked imaginations **mischievous fabrications**,
feet that *be swift* **hasten** in running to *mischief* **evil**,
19 A false witness that *speaketh* **breatheth** lies,
and he that *soweth discord* **spreadeth contention**
among brethren.
20 My son,
keep **guard** thy father's *commandment* **misvah**,
and *forsake* **abandon** not the *law* **torah** of thy mother:
21 Bind them continually upon thine heart,
and *tie* **fasten** them about thy *neck* **throat**.
22 When thou goest, it shall lead thee;
when thou *sleepest* **liest down**, it shall *keep* **guard** thee;
and when thou awakest, it shall *talk* **meditate** with thee.
23 For the *commandment* **misvah** is a lamp;
and the *law* **torah** is light;
and reproofs of *instruction* **discipline** are the way of life:
24 To *keep* **guard** thee from the evil woman,
from the *flattery of the* tongue
of a *strange woman* **stranger that smoothes it over**.
25 *Lust* **Desire** not after her beauty in thine heart;
neither let her take thee with her eyelids.
26 *For by means of a whorish woman*
a man is brought to a piece of bread:
For as a woman whoreth for a round of bread,
and the adulteress **so a man's woman**
will **shall** hunt for the *precious life* **esteemed soul.**
27 Can a man take fire in his bosom,

6 My son,
if you pledge for your friend,
clap your palm with a stranger,
2 snare yourself by the sayings of your mouth,
capture yourself by the sayings of your mouth;
3 work this now, my son, and deliver yourself:
when you come to the palm of your friend
go, prostrate and encourage your friend;
4 neither give sleep to your eyes

nor drowsiness to your eyelids;
5 deliver yourself as a gazelle from the hand
—as a bird from the hand of the snarer.
6 Go to the ant, you sloth;
see her ways and enwisen:
7 who, having no commander,
officer, or sovereign,
8 prepares her bread in the summer
and harvests her food in the harvest.
9 Until when lie you down, O sloth?
When rise you from your sleep?
10 A little sleep; a little drowsiness;
a little clasping of the hands to lie down:
11 thus comes your poverty—as one who walks
and your lack—as a man with buckler.
12 A human Beli Yaal—a man of mischief
walks with a perverted mouth;
13 he blinks with his eyes; he utters with
his feet; he points with his fingers:
14 perversion is in his heart;
he inscribes evil at all times;
he sends contention:
15 so his calamity comes suddenly;
in a blink—broken without healing.
16 These six Yah Veh hates;
yes, seven are an abhorrence to his soul;
17 a lofty eye; a false tongue;
and hands pouring innocent blood;
18 a heart inscribing mischievous fabrications;
feet hastening to run to evil;
19 a false witness breathing lies;
—spreading contention among brothers.
20 My son, guard the misvah of your father
and abandon not the torah of your mother:
21 bind them continually on your heart
and fasten them about your throat.
22 in going, it leads you;
in lying down, it guards you;
and in wakening, it meditates with you.
23 For the misvah is a lamp;
and the torah a light;
and reproofs of discipline, the way of life
24 to guard you from the evil woman:
from the tongue of a stranger
who smoothes it over.
25 Neither desire her beauty in your heart;
nor *be* overtaken by her eyelids:
26 for a woman whores for a round of bread;
and a woman of a man hunts for the esteemed soul.
27 Takes a man fire in his bosom
and his clothes not be burned?
28 Can *one* **a man** go upon *hot* coals,
and his feet not *be burned* **blister**?
29 *So* **Thus** he
that goeth in to his *neighbour's wife* **friend's woman**;
whosoever toucheth her
shall not be *innocent* **exonerated**.
30 *Men do not* despise **not** a thief, if he steal to
satisfy **fill** his soul when he *is hungry* **famisheth**;
31 But if he be found,
he shall *restore* **shalam** sevenfold;
he shall give all the *substance* **wealth** of his house.
32 But whoso *committeth adultery* **adulterizeth**
with a woman
lacketh *understanding* **heart**:
he that *doeth* **worketh** it *destroyeth* **ruineth** his own soul.
33 A *wound* **plague** and *dishonour* **abasement**
shall *he get* **find him**;
and his reproach shall not be wiped away.
34 For jealousy is the *rage*
fury of *a man* **the mighty**:
therefore he *will* **shall** not spare
in the day of *vengeance* **avengement**.
35 He *will* **shall** not *regard* **lift the face**
of any *ransom* **koper/atonement**;
neither *will he rest content* **shall he will**
though thou *givest many gifts* **aboundest bribes**.

7 My son, *keep* **guard** my *words* **sayings**,
and *lay up* **treasure** my *commandment*
misvoth with thee.
2 *Keep* **Guard** my *commandments*
misvoth, and live;
and my *law* **torah** as the *apple* **pupil** of thine eye.
3 Bind them upon thy fingers,
write **inscribe** them upon the table of thine heart.
4 Say unto wisdom, Thou art my sister;
and call *understanding* **discernment** thy *kinswoman* **kin**:
5 That they may *keep* **guard**
thee from the strange woman,
from the stranger
which *flattereth* **smootheth over** with her *words* **sayings**.
6 For at the window of my house
I looked through my *casement* **lattice**,
7 And *beheld* **saw** among the *simple ones* **gullible**,
I discerned among the *youths* **sons**,
a *young man void of understanding* **lad lacking heart**,
8 Passing through the street
near **beside** her corner;
and he *went* **paced** the way to her house,
9 In the *twilight* **evening breeze**,

in the evening **of the day,**
in the *black and dark night* **darkness of midnight**:
10 And, behold, there met him a woman
with the *attire* **masculine garment** of *an harlot* **a whore,**
and subtil of **with guarded** heart.
11 (She *is loud* **roareth** and *is stubborn* **revolteth;**
her feet *abide* **tabernacle** not in her house:
12 *Now is she without* **At this time in the outways,**
now in the streets **at that time in the broadways,**
and *lieth in wait at* **lurketh beside** every corner.)
13 So she *caught* **held** him, and kissed him,
and with *an impudent* **strengthened** face said unto him,
14 I have *peace offerings* **shelamim** with me;
this day have I *payed* **shalamed** my vows.
15 Therefore came I forth to meet thee,
diligently to seek **seeking early** thy face,
and I have found thee.
16 I have *decked* **spread** my *bed* **bedstead**
with *coverings of tapestry* **spreads,**
with *carved works* **carvings,**
with *fine linen* **tapestry** of *Egypt* **Misrayim.**
17 I have *perfumed* **rubbed** my bed with myrrh,
aloes, and cinnamon.
18 Come, let us *take our fill*
of love **satiate with loves**
until the morning:
let us *solace ourselves* **leap for joy** with loves.
19 For the *goodman* **man** is not at home,
he is gone a *long* **far** journey:
20 He hath taken a *bag* **bundle** of *money* **silver**
with him **in his hand,**
and *will* **shall** come home
at the day *appointed* **of thc full moon.**
and not burn his clothes?
28 —a man go on coals
and not blister his feet?
29 Thus he who goes in to the woman of his friend;
whoever touches her is not exonerated.
30 Despise not a thief
if he steals to fill his soul when he famishes;
31 and being found out, he shalams sevenfold;
he gives all the wealth of his house.
32 He who adulterizes with a woman, lacks heart;
he who thus works ruins his own soul:
33 he finds plague and abasement;
and his reproach wipes not away.
34 For jealousy is the fury of the mighty;
and he spares not in the day of avengement;
35 he neither lifts the face of any koper/atonement;
nor wills he though you abound bribes.

7 My son, guard my sayings
and treasure my misvoth with you:
2 guard my misvoth and live;
and my torah as the pupil of your eye:
3 bind them on your fingers;
inscribe them on the table of your heart:
4 say to wisdom, You are my sister;
and call discernment your kin
5 to guard you from the strange woman
—from the stranger
who smoothes it over with her sayings.
6 For at a window of my house
I look through my lattice;
7 and see among the gullible:
I discern among the sons
a lad lacking heart
8 passing through the street beside her corner:
and he paces the way to her house
9 in the evening breeze
—in the evening of the day in the darkness of midnight:
10 and behold, a woman meets him
with the masculine garment of a whore:
with guarded heart
11 she roars and revolts;
her feet tabernacle not in her house
12 —at this time in the outways at that time
in the broadways and lurks beside every corner.
13 She holds him and kisses him
and with strengthened face says to him,
14 I have shelamim with me;
this day I shalamed my vows:
15 so I come to meet you
early seeking your face, and I find you:
16 I spread my bedstead with spreads,
with carvings, with tapestry of Misrayim:
17 I rubbed my bed
with myrrh, aloes and cinnamon:
18 come, we satiate with loves until the morning
—leap for joy with loves:
19 for the man is not in his house;
—gone on a far journey:
20 he took a bundle of silver in his hand;
and comes home at the day of the full moon.
21 With her *much fair speech* **abundant doctrine**
she caused him to *yield* **spread,**
with the *flattering* **smoothing over** of her lips
she *forced* **drove** him.
22 He goeth after her *straightway* **suddenly,**
as an ox goeth to the slaughter,
or as a fool

to the *correction* **discipline** of *the stocks* **tinklers**;
23 Till *a dart* **an arrow** strike through his liver;
as a bird hasteth to the snare,
and knoweth not that it is for his *life* **soul**.
24 Hearken unto me now
therefore, O ye *children* **sons**,
and *attend* **hearken** to the *words* **sayings** of my mouth.
25 Let not thine heart *decline* **deviate** to her ways,
go **stray** not *astray* in her paths.
26 For she hath cast down many *wounded* **pierced**:
yea, many *strong men* **mighty**
have been *slain* **slaughtered** by her.
27 Her house is the way to *hell* **sheol**,
going down **descending** to the chambers of death.

8 Doth not wisdom *cry* **call**?
and *understanding put forth* **discernment give** her voice?
2 She standeth in the top of
high places **the heights**,
by the way *in* **between** the *places* **houses** of the paths.
3 She *crieth* **shouteth** at the
gates **handle of the portals**,
at the *entry* **mouth** of the city,
at the *coming in* **entry** at the *doors* **portals**.
4 Unto you, O men, I call;
and my voice is to the sons of *man* **humanity**.
5 O ye *simple* **gullible**,
understand wisdom **discern strategy**:
and, ye fools,
be ye of *an understanding* **a discerning** heart.
6 Hear;
for I *will* **shall** speak of *excellent things* **eminence**;
and the opening of my lips
shall be *right things* **straightnesses**.
7 For my *mouth* **palate** shall *speak* **meditate** truth;
and wickedness is an *abomination*
abhorrence to my lips.
8 All the *words* **sayings** of my mouth
are in *righteousness* **justness**;
there is *nothing froward* **naught twisted**
or *perverse* **perverted** in them.
9 They are all *plain* **straightforward**
to him that *understandeth* **discerneth**,
and *right* **straight** to them that find knowledge.
10 *Receive* **Take** my *instruction*
discipline, and not silver;
and knowledge rather than choice *gold* **ore**.
11 For wisdom is better than *rubies* **pearls**;
and all *the things that may be desired* **those desires**
are not to be compared to it.
12 I wisdom dwell with *prudence* **strategy**,
and find out knowledge of *witty inventions* **intrigue**.
13 The *fear* **awe** of *the LORD*
Yah Veh is to hate evil:
pride **pomp**, and *arrogancy* **pompousness**,
and the evil way,
and the *froward* mouth **of perversions**, do I hate.
14 Counsel is mine, and *sound wisdom* **substance**:
I am *understanding* **discernment**; I have *strength* **might**.
15 By me *kings* **sovereigns** reign,
and *princes* **potentates**
decree justice **set statutes of justness**.
16 By me *princes rule* **governors govern**,
and *nobles* **volunteers**, *even* all the judges of the earth.
17 I love them that love me;
and those that seek me early shall find me.
18 Riches and honour are with me;
yea, durable riches **expensive antiques**
and *righteousness* **justness**.
19 My fruit is better than *gold* **ore**,
yea, than *fine* **pure** gold;
and my *revenue* **produce** than choice silver.
20 I *lead* **walk** in the way of *righteousness* **justness**,
in the midst of the paths of judgment:
21 That I may cause *those that love me* **my lovers**
to inherit substance; and I *will* **shall** fill their treasures.
22 *The LORD possessed* **Yah Veh chattelized** me
in the beginning of his way,

21 With her abundant doctrine,
she spreads him out;
with the smoothing over of her lips she drives him:
22 suddenly he goes after her
—as an ox going to the slaughter
—as a fool to the discipline of tinklers:
23 until an arrow strikes through his liver;
as a bird hastens to the snare
and knows not it is for his soul.
24 Now, you sons, hearken to me;
hearken to the sayings of my mouth:
25 neither deviate your heart to her ways;
nor stray in her paths:
26 for she casts down many pierced;
slaughters many mighty:
27 her house is the way to sheol
descending to the chambers of death.

8 Wisdom, calls she not?
And discernment, give her voice?
2 She stands in the top of the heights by the way
between the houses of the paths;
3 she shouts at the handle of the portals
—at the mouth of the city at the entry at the portals.

4 To you, O men, I call;
and my voice to the sons of humanity:
5 to you, O gullible, discern strategy;
and you, O fools, discern heart:
6 hear; for I speak of eminence;
and the opening of my lips of straightnesses:
7 for my palate meditates truth;
and wickedness is an abhorrence to my lips:
8 all the sayings of my mouth are in justness;
naught of them *is* twisted or perverted:
9 they are all straightforward to him who discerns
and straight to them who find knowledge.
10 Take my discipline and not silver;
and knowledge rather than choice ore:
11 better, wisdom than pearls;
and all those desires not comparable.
12 I—wisdom dwell with strategy
and find out knowledge of intrigue.
13 The awe of Yah Veh is to hate evil;
pomp and pompousness and the evil way
and the mouth of perversions, I hate:
14 counsel and substance *are* mine;
I—discernment; I have might:
15 by me sovereigns reign
and potentates set statutes of justness:
16 by me governors govern;
and volunteers; all the judges of the earth.
17 I love them who love me;
and they who seek me early find me:
18 riches and honor are with me;
expensive antiques and justness:
19 better, my fruit than ore; yes, than pure gold;
and my produce than choice silver.
20 I walk in the way of justness
midst the paths of judgment;
21 that my lovers inherit substance;
and I fill their treasures.
22 Yah Veh chattelized me
in the beginning of his way
before **in** his *works of old* **ancient deeds.**
23 I was *set up* **libated** from *everlasting* **eternity,**
from the *beginning* **top,**
or ever the earth was **from the antiquity of the earth.**
24 When there were no *depths* **abysses,**
I was *brought forth* **writhed;**
when there were no fountains
abounding **heavy** with water.
25 Before the mountains were *settled* **sunk,**
before **at the face of** the hills was I *brought forth* **writhed:**
26 While as yet he had not *made* **worked** the earth,
nor the *fields* **outways,**
nor the *highest part* **top** of the dust of the world.
27 When he prepared the heavens, I was there:
when he *set a compass* **engraved a circle**
upon the face of the *depth* **abyss:**
28 When he *established* **strengthened**
the *clouds* **vapours** above:
when he strengthened
the *fountains* **eyes** of the *deep* **abyss:**
29 When he *gave* **set** to the sea his *decree* **statute,**
that the waters
should not pass his *commandment* **mouth:**
when he *appointed* **prescribed**
the foundations of the earth:
30 Then I was *by* **beside** him,
as one brought up *with him*:
and I was *daily* **day by day** his delight,
rejoicing always **laughing at all times**
before him **by his face;**
31 *Rejoicing* **Laughing**
in the *habitable part* **world** of his earth;
and my delights were with the sons of *men* **humanity.**
32 Now therefore hearken unto
me, O ye *children* **sons:**
for *blessed* **blithe** are they that *keep* **guard** my ways.
33 Hear *instruction* **discipline,**
and *be wise* **enwisen,**
and refuse it not.
34 *Blessed* **Blithe** is the *man*
human that heareth me,
watching daily **guarding day by day** at my gates,
waiting at the posts of my *doors* **portals.**
35 For whoso findeth me findeth life,
and shall *obtain favour* **promote pleasure**
of *the LORD* **Yah Veh.**
36 But he that sinneth against me
wrongeth **violateth** his own soul:
all they that hate me love death.

9 Wisdom hath builded her house,
she hath hewn out her seven pillars:
2 She hath *killed* **slaughtered** her *beasts* **slaughter;**
she hath *mingled* **mixed** her wine;
she hath also *furnished* **arranged** her table.
3 She hath sent forth her *maidens* **lasses:**
she *crieth* **calleth**
upon the *highest places* **high arches** of the city,
4 Whoso is *simple* **gullible,** let him turn in hither:
as for him that wanteth understanding
whoever lacketh heart, she saith to him,
5 Come, eat of my bread,

and drink of the wine which I have *mingled* **mixed.**
6 Forsake the *foolish* **gullible**, and live;
and go **blithesome**
in the way of *understanding* **discernment**.
7 He that *reproveth* **disciplineth** a scorner
getteth **taketh** to himself *shame* **abasement**:
and he that *rebuketh a* **reproveth the** wicked *man*
getteth himself a blot **shall be blemished.**
8 Reprove not a scorner, lest he hate thee:
rebuke **reprove** a wise *man*, and he *will* **shall** love thee.
9 Give *instruction to a wise man* **to the wise**,
and he *will be yet wiser* **shall enwisen**:
teach a just man **let the just know**,
and he *will* **shall** increase in *learning* **doctrine**.
10 The *fear* **awe** of *the LORD* **Yah Veh**
is the beginning of wisdom:
and the knowledge of the holy
is *understanding* **discernment**.
11 For by me thy days shall *be multiplied* **abound**,
and the years of thy life shall *be increased* **increase**.
—in his ancient deeds.
23 I was libated from eternity
—from the top—from the antiquity of the earth.
24 When there were no abysses, I was writhed;
when there were no fountains heavy with water:
25 ere the mountains were sunk
at the face of the hills, I was writhed:
26 while as yet he had neither worked the earth
nor the outways
nor the top of the dust of the world:
27 when he prepared the heavens, I was there;
when he engraved a circle on the face of the abyss;
28 when he strengthened the vapours above;
when he strengthened the eyes of the abyss;
29 when he set his statute to the sea,
that the waters not pass his mouth;
when he prescribed the foundations of the earth;
30 then I am beside him, as one brought up;
and day by day I am his delight,
at all times laughing by his face;
31 laughing in the world of his earth;
and my delights *are* with the sons of humanity.
32 Now, O sons, hearken to me,
for blithe—they who guard my ways;
33 hear discipline and enwisen and refuse it not:
34 Blithe—the human who hears me; guarding day by
day at my gates; waiting at the posts of my portals.
35 For whoever finds me finds life
and promotes the pleasure of Yah Veh:
36 and whoever sins against me
violates his own soul;
all who hate me love death.

9 Wisdom built her house;
she hewed her pillars—seven;
2 she slaughtered her slaughter;
she mixed her wine;
she arranged her table;
3 she sent forth her lasses;
she calls on the high arches of the city,
4 Whoever is gullible, turn in here!
Whoever lacks heart, she says to him,
5 Come, eat of my bread
and drink of the wine I mixed!
6 Forsake the gullible and live;
blithesome in the way of discernment.
7 He who disciplines a scorner
takes abasement to himself:
and he who reproves the wicked
blemishes.
8 Reprove not a scorner, lest he hate you;
reprove a wise, and he loves you:
9 give to the wise and he enwisens;
the just know, and increase in doctrine.
10 To awe Yah Veh is the beginning of wisdom;
and the knowledge of the holy is discernment:
11 for by me your days abound
and the years of your life increase:
12 *If thou be wise* **In enwisening**,
thou shalt be *wise for thyself* **enwisened**:
but if thou scornest, thou alone shalt bear it.
13 A foolish woman *is clamorous* **roareth**:
she is simple—**gullible**, and knoweth *nothing* **not what**.
14 For she *sitteth* **settleth** at
the *door* **portal** of her house,
on a *seat* **throne** in the *high places* **heights** of the city,
15 To call *passengers* **them who pass by the way**
who go right on **to straighten** their ways:
16 Whoso is *simple* **gullible**, let him turn in hither:
and *as for him that wanteth understanding*
whoever lacketh heart, she saith to him,
17 Stolen waters *are sweet* **sweeten**,
and *bread eaten in secret* **covert bread**
is pleasant **pleaseth**.
18 But he knoweth not that
the dead **ghosts** are there;
and that her *guests* **called ones**
are in the depths of *hell* **sheol**.

10 The proverbs of *Solomon* **Shelomoh**.
A wise son *maketh a glad* **cheereth a** father:
but a foolish son is the *heaviness* **grief** of his mother.

2 Treasures of wickedness
profit nothing **benefit naught**:
but *righteousness delivereth* **justness**
rescueth from death.
3 *The LORD will* **Yah Veh shall** not *suffer* **allow**
the soul of the *righteous* **just** to famish:
but he *casteth away* **expelleth**
the *substance* **calamity** of the wicked.
4 He *becometh poor* **impoverisheth**
that *dealeth with a slack hand* **worketh a deceitful palm**:
but the hand of the *diligent* **decisive**
maketh rich **enricheth**.
5 He that *gathereth* **harvesteth** in summer
is a *wise* **comprehending** son:
but he that sleepeth **soundly** in harvest
is a son that *causeth shame* **shameth**.
6 Blessings are upon the head of the just:
but violence covereth the mouth of the wicked.
7 The *memory* **memorial** of the just
is *blessed* **for blessings**:
but the name of the wicked shall rot.
8 The wise in heart
will receive commandments **shall take misvoth**:
but a *prating* fool **of lips** shall fall.
9 He that walketh *uprightly* **integriously**
walketh *surely* **confidently**:
but he that perverteth his ways shall be known.
10 He that *winketh* **blinketh** with the eye
causeth sorrow **giveth contortion**:
but a *prating* fool **of lips** shall fall.
11 The mouth of *a righteous man* **the just**
is a *well* **fountain** of life:
but violence covereth the mouth of the wicked.
12 Hatred *stirreth up strifes* **waketh contentions**:
but love covereth all *sins* **rebellions**.
13 In the lips of him that *hath*
understanding **discerneth**
wisdom is found:
but a *rod* **scion** is for the back of him
that *is void of understanding* **lacketh heart**.
14 **The** Wise *men lay up* **treasure** knowledge:
but the mouth of the *foolish* **fool** is near *destruction* **ruin**.
15 The *rich man's* wealth **of the rich**
is his *strong* city **of strength**:
the *destruction* **ruin** of the poor is their poverty.
16 The *labour* **deed** of the
righteous tendeth **just be** to life:
the *fruit* **produce** of the wicked to sin.
17 He is in the way of life
that *keepeth instruction* **guardeth discipline**:
but he that *refuseth* **forsaketh** reproof *erreth* **strayeth**.
18 He that hideth hatred with *lying* **false** lips,
and he that uttereth a slander, is a fool.
19 In the *multitude* **abundance** of words
there wanteth not sin **rebellion ceaseth not**:
but he that *refraineth* **spareth** his lips
is wise **comprehendeth**.
20 The tongue of the just is as choice silver:
the heart of the wicked is little worth.
21 The lips of the *righteous*
feed **just befriend** many:
but fools die for *want* **lack** of *wisdom* **heart**.
12 in enwisening, enwisen;
but if you scorn, you bear it alone.
13 A foolish woman roars;
—gullible and knows not what:
14 and she settles at the portal of her house,
on a throne in the heights of the city,
15 to call them who pass by the way
to straighten their ways,
16 Whoever is gullible, turn in here!
—and to whoever lacks heart, she says,
17 Stolen waters sweeten
and covert bread pleases!
18 —and he knows not that ghosts are there;
and that her called ones are in the depths of sheol.

10 The Proverbs of Shelomoh.
A wise son cheers a father;
and a foolish son is the grief of his mother.
2 Treasures of wickedness benefit naught;
and justness rescues from death.
3 Yah Veh allows not the
soul of the just to famish;
and he expels the calamity of the wicked.
4 He who works a deceitful palm impoverishes;
and the hand of the decisive enriches.
5 He who harvests in summer
is a comprehending son;
he who sleeps soundly in harvest
is a son who shames.
6 Blessings *are* on the head of the just;
and violence covers the mouth of the wicked.
7 The memorial of the just *is* for blessings;
and the name of the wicked rots.
8 The wise in heart take misvoth;
and a fool of lips falls.
9 He who walks integriously walks confidently;
and he who perverts his ways is known.
10 He who blinks with the eye gives contortion;
and a fool of lips falls.

11 The mouth of the just *is* a fountain of life;
and violence covers the mouth of the wicked.
12 Hatred wakens contentions;
and love covers all rebellions.
13 In the lips of him who discerns
wisdom *is* found;
and a scion is for the back of him
who lacks heart.
14 The wise treasure knowledge;
and the mouth of the fool *is* near ruin.
15 The wealth of the rich *is* his city of strength;
the ruin of the poor *is* their poverty.
16 The deed of the just *is* to life;
the produce of the wicked to sin.
17 He *is* in the way of life who guards discipline;
and he who forsakes reproof strays.
18 He who hides hatred with false lips
and he who utters a slander, *is* a fool.
19 In the abundance of words, rebellion ceases not;
and he who spares his lips, comprehends.
20 The tongue of the just *is* as choice silver;
the heart of the wicked *is* of little worth.
21 The lips of the just befriend many;
and fools die for lack of heart.
22 The blessing of *the LORD* **Yah Veh**,
it maketh rich **enricheth**,
and he addeth no *sorrow* **contorting** with it.
23 It is as *sport* **ridicule** to a fool
to *do mischief* **work intrigue**:
but a man of *understanding* **discernment** hath wisdom.
24 The *fear* **terror** of the wicked,
it shall come upon him:
but the desire of the *righteous* **just**
shall be *granted* **given**.
25 As the *whirlwind* **hurricane** passeth,
so *is* the wicked *no more* **be not**:
but the *righteous* **just** is an *everlasting*
eternal foundation.
26 As vinegar to the teeth,
and as smoke to the eyes,
so is the *sluggard* **sloth** to them that send him.
27 The *fear* **awe** of *the LORD* **Yah Veh**
prolongeth **addeth** days:
but the years of the wicked
shall be *shortened* **curtailed**.
28 The hope of the *righteous* **just**
shall be *gladness* **cheerfulness**:
but the *expectation* **hope** of the wicked
shall *perish* **destruct**.
29 The way of *the LORD* **Yah Veh**
is strength **be a stronghold** to the *upright* **integrious**:
but *destruction* **ruin**
shall be to the *workers* **doers** of *iniquity* **mischief**.
30 The *righteous* **just**
shall never *be removed* **totter eternally**:
but the wicked shall not *inhabit* **tabernacle on** the earth.
31 The mouth of the just
bringeth forth **germinateth** wisdom:
but the *froward* tongue **of perversions** shall be cut out.
32 The lips of the *righteous* **just**
know what *is acceptable* **pleaseth**:
but the mouth of the wicked
speaketh frowardness **perverteth**.

11 *A false balance* **Balances of deceit**
is abomination **are an abhorrence** to *the LORD* **Yah Veh**:
but a *just weight* **stone of shalom** is his *delight* **pleasure**.
2 *When pride* **Arrogance** cometh,
then cometh *shame* **abasement**: but with
the *lowly* **humble** is wisdom.
3 The integrity of the *upright* **straight**
shall *guide* **lead** them:
but the perverseness
of *transgressors* **them who deal covertly**
shall *destroy* **ravage** them.
4 *Riches profit* **Wealth benefiteth** not
in the day of *wrath* **fury**:
but *righteousness delivereth* **justness**
rescueth from death.
5 The *righteousness* **justness**
of the *perfect* **integrious**
shall *direct* **straighten** his way:
but the wicked shall fall by his own wickedness.
6 The *righteousness* **justness**
of the *upright* **straight**
shall *deliver* **rescue** them:
but *transgressors* **they who deal covertly**
shall be *taken* **captured**
in their own *naughtiness* **calamity**.
7 When a wicked *man* **human** dieth,
his *expectation* **hope** shall *perish* **destruct**:
and the hope of *unjust men* **the mischievous**
perisheth **shall destruct**.
8 The *righteous* **just**
is *delivered* **rescued** out of *trouble* **tribulation**,
and the wicked cometh in his stead.
9 *An hypocrite* **A profaner** with his mouth
destroyeth **ruineth** his *neighbour* **friend**:
but through knowledge
shall the just be *delivered* **rescued**.
10 When it *goeth well* **be good**
with the *righteous* **just**,

the city *rejoiceth* **jumpeth for joy**:
and when the wicked *perish* **destruct**, there is shouting.
11 By the blessing of the *upright* **straight**
the city is *exalted* **lofted**:
but it is *overthrown* **demolished**
by the mouth of the wicked.
22 The blessing of Yah Veh enriches
and he adds no contorting with it.
23 It is as ridicule to a fool to work intrigue;
and to a man of discernment, wisdom.
24 The terror of the wicked comes on him;
and the desire of the just is given.
25 As the passing of the hurricane,
the wicked are not;
and the just are an eternal foundation.
26 As vinegar to the teeth,
and as smoke to the eyes,
thus *is* the sloth to them who send him.
27 To awe Yah Veh adds days;
and the years of the wicked curtail.
28 The hope of the just *is* cheerfulness;
and the hope of the wicked destructs.
29 The way of Yah Veh
is a stronghold to the integrious; and
ruin to the doers of mischief.
30 The just totter not eternally;
and the wicked tabernacle not on the earth.
31 The mouth of the just germinates wisdom;
and the tongue of perversions is cut out.
32 The lips of the just know what pleases;
and the mouth of the wicked perverts.

11 Balances of deceit
are an abhorrence to Yah Veh;
and a stone of shalom is his pleasure.
2 Arrogance comes; abasement comes:
and with the humble is wisdom.
3 The integrity of the straight leads them;
and the perverseness of them who deal covertly
ravages them.
4 Wealth benefits not in the day of fury;
and justness rescues from death.
5 The justness of the integrious
straightens his way;
and the wicked falls by his own wickedness.
6 The justness of the straight rescues them;
and they who deal covertly
are captured in their own calamity.
7 In the death of a wicked human,
his hope destructs;
and the hope of the mischievous destructs.
8 The just are rescued from tribulation;
and the wicked come in his stead.
9 A profaner, with his mouth, ruins his friend;
and through knowledge the just are rescued.
10 In the good of the just,
the city jumps for joy;
and in destruction of the wicked,
they shout.
11 By the blessing of the straight the city is lofted;
and by the mouth of the wicked, demolished.
12 *He that is void of wisdom*
Whoever lacketh heart
despiseth **disrespecteth** his *neighbour* **friend**:
but a man of *understanding* **discernment**
holdeth his peace **husheth**.
13 A **walking** talebearer
revealeth secrets **exposeth private counsel**:
but he that is of a *faithful* **trustworthy** spirit
concealeth the *matter* **word**.
14 *Where no counsel is* **Without counsels**,
the people fall:
but in the *multitude* **abundance** of counsellors
there is *safety* **salvation**.
15 He that *is surety* **pledgeth** for a stranger
shall *smart for it* **shout evil**:
and he that hateth *suretiship* **to clap** is *sure* **confident**.
16 A *gracious* woman **of charism**
retaineth **upholdeth** honour:
and *strong men retain* **tyrants uphold** riches.
17 The merciful man *doeth*
good **dealeth** to his own soul:
but he that is cruel troubleth his own flesh.
18 The wicked worketh a *deceitful work* **false deed**:
but to him that *soweth righteousness* **seedeth**
justness shall be a *sure reward* **hire of truth**.
19 As *righteousness tendeth* **justness** to life:
so he that pursueth evil *pursueth it* to his own death.
20 They that are of a *froward* **perverted** heart
are *abomination* **an abhorrence** to *the LORD* **Yah Veh**:
but *such as are upright* **the integrious** in their way
are his *delight* **pleasure**.
21 *Though* hand *join* in hand,
the *wicked* **evil** shall not be *unpunished* **exonerated**:
but the seed of the *righteous* **just**
shall *be delivered* **escape**.
22 As a *jewel* **nosering** of gold
in a *swine's* **hog's** snout,
so is a *fair* **beautiful** woman
which *is without discretion* **turneth aside from taste**.
23 The desire of the *righteous* **just** is only good:

but the *expectation* **hope** of the wicked is *wrath* **fury.**
24 There is that scattereth, and yet increaseth;
and there is **one**
that *withholdeth more than is meet* **spareth straightness,**
but *it tendeth to poverty* **lacketh.**
25 The *liberal soul* **soul for blessings**
shall be *made fat* **fattened:**
and he that *watereth* **saturateth**
shall *be watered* **flow** also himself.
26 He that withholdeth *corn* **grain,**
the *people* **nations** shall *curse* **pierce** him: but
blessing shall be upon the head of him
that *selleth it* **marketeth kernels.**
27 He that *diligently* **early** seeketh good
procureth favour **seeketh pleasure:**
but he that seeketh *mischief* **evil,**
it shall *come unto* **approach** him.
28 He that *trusteth* **confideth**
in his riches shall fall;
but the *righteous* **just**
shall *flourish* **blossom** as a *branch* **leaf.**
29 He that troubleth his own house
shall inherit the wind:
and the fool shall be servant to the wise of heart.
30 The fruit of the *righteous* **just** is a tree of life;
and he that *winneth* **taketh** souls is wise.
31 Behold,
the *righteous* **just** shall be *recompensed* **shalamed**
in the earth:
much more the wicked and the sinner.

12 Whoso loveth *instruction* **discipline**
loveth knowledge:
but he that hateth reproof is *brutish* **stupid.**
2 *A* **The** good *man*
obtaineth favour **produceth pleasure**
of *the LORD* **Yah Veh:**
but a man of *wicked devices* **intrigue**
will **shall** he *condemn* **judge wicked.**
3 A *man* **human** shall not be
established by wickedness:
but the root of the *righteous* **just**
shall not *be moved* **totter.**
4 A virtuous woman is a crown
to her *husband* **master:**
12 Whoever lacks heart disrespects his friend;
and a man of discernment hushes.
13 A walking talebearer exposes private counsel;
and he of a trustworthy spirit conceals the word.
14 Without counsels,
the people fall;
and in the abundance of counsellors,
there *is* salvation.
15 He who pledges for a stranger, shouts evil;
and he who hates to clap is confident.
16 A woman of charism upholds honor;
and tyrants uphold riches.
17 The merciful man deals to his own soul;
and he who is cruel troubles his own flesh.
18 The wicked work false deeds;
and he who seeds justness, a hire of truth.
19 As justness to life;
thus he who pursues evil to his own death.
20 They of a perverted heart
are an abhorrence to Yah Veh; and
the integrious in their way
are his pleasure.
21 Hand in hand, the evil *are* not exonerated;
and the seed of the just escapes.
22 As a nosering of gold in the snout of a hog,
thus a beautiful woman who turns aside from taste.
23 The desire of the just is only good;
and the hope of the wicked *is* fury.
24 One scatters and yet increases;
one sparingly in straightness, but lacks.
25 The soul for blessings fattens;
and he who saturates, also flows.
26 He who withholds grain, the nations pierce;
and blessing *is* on the head of him
who markets kernels.
27 He who early seeks good, seeks pleasure;
and he who seeks evil, it approaches him.
28 He who confides in his riches, falls;
and the just blossom as a leaf.
29 He who troubles his own house,
inherits the wind;
and the fool *is* servant to the wise of heart.
30 The fruit of the just is a tree of life;
and he who takes souls is wise.
31 Behold, the just are shalamed in the earth;
much more the wicked and the sinner.

12 Whoever loves discipline loves knowledge;
and whoever hates reproof is stupid.
2 The good produce the pleasure of Yah Veh;
and the man of intrigue he judges wicked.
3 A human is not established by wickedness;
and the root of the just totters not.
4 A virtuous woman is a crown to her master;
but she that *maketh ashamed* **shameth**
is as rottenness in his bones.
5 The *thoughts* **fabrications** of the *righteous* **just**

are *right* **justness**:
but the counsels of the wicked are deceit.
6 The words of the wicked
are to *lie in wait* **lurk** for blood:
but the mouth of the *upright* **straight**
shall *deliver* **rescue** them.
7 The wicked are *overthrown*
overturned, and are not:
but the house of the *righteous* **just** shall stand.
8 A man shall be *commended* **halaled**
according to
his wisdom **the comprehension of his mouth**:
but he that is of a *perverse* **perverted** heart
shall be *despised* **disrespected**.
9 He that is *despised* **abased**, and hath a servant,
is better than he that honoureth himself,
and lacketh bread.
10 *A righteous man regardeth* **The just knoweth**
the *life* **soul** of his *beast* **animal**:
but the tender mercies of the wicked are cruel.
11 He that *tilleth* **serveth** his *land* **soil**
shall be satisfied with bread:
but he that *followeth vain persons* **pursueth vanities**
is void of understanding **lacketh heart**.
12 The wicked desireth the *net* **lair** of evil *men*:
but the root of the *righteous yieldeth fruit* **just giveth**.
13 The *wicked is snared* **snare of evil**
is by the *transgression* **rebellion** of *his* lips:
but the just shall come out of *trouble* **tribulation**.
14 A man shall be satisfied with good
by the fruit of his mouth:
and the *recompence* **dealing** of *a man's* **human** hands
shall *be rendered* **return** unto him.
15 The way of a fool is *right*
straight in his own eyes:
but he that hearkeneth unto counsel is wise.
16 A fool's *wrath* **vexation** is
presently known **in a day**:
but *a prudent man* **the subtle**
covereth *shame* **abasement**.
17 He that *speaketh truth* **breatheth trustworthily**
sheweth forth righteousness **telleth**
justness: but a false witness deceit.
18 There is that *speaketh* **babbleth**
like the *piercings* **stabs** of a sword:
but the tongue of the wise is *health* **healing**.
19 The lip of truth shall be
established *for ever* **eternally**:
but a *lying* **false** tongue is but for a *moment* **blink**.
20 Deceit is in the heart of them
that *imagine* **inscribe** evil:
but to the counsellors of *peace* **shalom**
is *joy* **cheerfulness**.
21 There shall no *evil* **mischief** happen to the just:
but the wicked shall be filled with *mischief* **evil**.
22 *Lying* **False** lips
are *abomination* **abhorrence** to *the LORD* **Yah Veh**:
but they that *deal truly* **work trustworthily**
are his *delight* **pleasure**.
23 A *prudent man* **subtle human**
concealeth **covereth** knowledge:
but the heart of fools *proclaimeth*
foolishness **calleth folly**.
24 The hand of the *diligent*
decisive shall *bear rule* **reign**:
but the *slothful* **deceitful** shall be *under tribute* **a vassal**.
25 *Heaviness* **Concern** in the heart of man
maketh it stoop **prostrateth him**:
but a good word *maketh it glad* **cheereth**.
26 The *righteous* **just**
is more excellent than **exploreth** his *neighbour* **friend**:
but the way of the wicked seduceth them.
27 The *slothful man roasteth* **deceitful singeth** not
that which he took in hunting **his hunt**:
but the *substance* **wealth**
of a *diligent man* **decisive human**
is *precious* **esteemed**.
28 In the way of *righteousness* **justness** is life:
and in the pathway *thereof* there is no death.

13 A wise son
heareth his father's *instruction* **discipline**:
but a scorner heareth not rebuke.
2 A man shall eat good by the fruit of his mouth:
and she who shames as rottenness in his bones.
5 The fabrications of the just *are* justness;
the counsels of the wicked *are* deceit.
6 The words of the wicked are to lurk for blood;
and the mouth of the straight rescues them.
7 The wicked overturn, and are not;
and the house of the just stands.
8 A man is halaled
according to the comprehension of his mouth;
and he of a perverted heart *is* disrespected.
9 Better, the abased who has a servant,
than he who honors himself and lacks bread.
10 The just knows the soul of his animal;
and the tender mercies of the wicked *are* cruel.
11 He who serves his soil is satisfied with bread;
and he who pursues vanities lacks heart.

12 The wicked desire the lair of evil;
and the root of the just gives.
13 The snare of evil *is* by the rebellion of lips;
and the just come from tribulation.
14 A man *is* satisfied with good
by the fruit of his mouth;
and the dealing of human hands
returns to him.
15 The way of a fool *is* straight in his own eyes;
and he who hearkens to counsel is wise.
16 The vexation of a fool is known in a day;
and the subtle cover abasement.
17 He who breathes trustworthily, tells justness;
and a false witness, deceit.
18 The babbler is like the stabs of a sword;
and the tongue of the wise is healing.
19 The lip of truth establishes eternally;
and a false tongue *is* for a blink.
20 Deceit *is* in the heart of them who inscribe evil;
but to the counsellors of shalom *is* cheerfulness.
21 No mischief happens to the just;
and the wicked are filled with evil.
22 False lips are an abhorrence to Yah Veh;
and they who work trustworthily are his pleasure.
23 A subtle human covers knowledge;
and the heart of fools calls, Folly!
24 The hand of the decisive reigns;
and the deceitful are a vassal.
25 Concern prostrates the heart of man;
and a good word cheers.
26 The just explores his friend;
and the way of the wicked seduces them.
27 The deceitful singes not his hunt;
and the wealth of a decisive human esteems.
28 In the way of justness *is* life;
and in that pathway there *is* no death.

13 A wise son—the discipline of a father;
and a scorner hears not rebuke.
2 A man eats good by the fruit of his mouth;
but the soul of the *transgressors* **covert**
shall eat **hath** violence.
3 He that *keepeth* **guardeth** his mouth
keepeth **guardeth** his *life* **soul**:
but he that *openeth wide* **spreadeth** his lips
shall have *destruction* **ruin**.
4 The soul of the *sluggard* **sloth** desireth,
and hath *nothing* **naught**:
but the soul of the *diligent* **decisive**
shall *be made fat* **fatten**.
5 *A righteous man hateth lying*
The just hate false words:
but *a man is loathsome* **the wicked stink**,
and *cometh to shame* **blush**.
6 *Righteousness* **Justness**
keepeth him that is upright **guardeth the integrious**
in the way:
but wickedness *overthroweth* **perverteth** the sinner.
7 There is that *maketh* **enricheth** himself *rich*,
yet hath *nothing* **naught**:
there is that *maketh* **impoverisheth** himself *poor*,
yet hath great *riches* **wealth**.
8 The *ransom* **koper/**
atonement of a man's *life* **soul**
are his riches:
but the *poor* **impoverished** heareth not rebuke.
9 The light of the *righteous rejoiceth* **just cheereth**:
but the lamp of the wicked shall
be *put out* **extinguished**.
10 Only *by pride* **arrogance**
cometh contention **giveth strife**:
but with the *well advised* **counseled** is wisdom.
11 Wealth *gotten* by vanity shall
be diminished **diminish**:
but he that gathereth by *labour* **hand**
shall *increase* **abound**.
12 Hope *deferred* **drawn out**
maketh **wearieth** the heart *sick*:
but when the desire cometh, it is a tree of life.
13 Whoso *despiseth* **disrespecteth** the word
shall be *destroyed* **despoiled**:
but he that *feareth* **aweth** the *commandment* **misvah**
shall *be rewarded* **shalam**.
14 The *law* **torah** of the wise is a fountain of life,
to *depart* **turn aside** from the snares of death.
15 Good *understanding* **comprehension**
giveth *favour* **charism**:
but the way of *transgressors* **the covert**
is *hard* **perennial**.
16 *Every prudent man* **All the subtle**
dealeth **work** with knowledge:
but a fool *layeth open his* **spreadeth** folly.
17 A wicked *messenger* **angel**
falleth into *mischief* **evil**:
but a *faithful* **trustworthy** ambassador is *health* **healing**.
18 Poverty and *shame* **abasement**
shall be to him
that *refuseth instruction* **avoideth discipline**:
but he that regardeth reproof shall be honoured.
19 The desire *accomplished* **that becometh**
is *sweet* **pleasant** to the soul:
but it is *abomination* **abhorrence** to fools

to *depart* **turn aside** from evil.
20 He that walketh with **the** wise *men*
shall be *wise* **enwisened**:
but *a companion of* **he that befriendeth** fools
shall be destroyed **shouteth**.
21 Evil pursueth sinners:
but *to the righteous good shall be repayed*
good is the shalam of the just.
22 *A* **The** good *man*
leaveth an inheritance to his children's children
hath his sons' sons to inherit:
and the *wealth* **valuables** of the sinner
is *laid up* **treasured** for the just.
23 *Much* **Abundant** food
is in the tillage of the *poor* **impoverished**:
but there is that is *destroyed* **scraped away**
for want of judgment.
24 He that spareth his *rod* **scion** hateth his son:
but he that loveth him
chasteneth **rising early disciplineth** him *betimes*.
25 The *righteous* **just** eateth to
the satisfying of his soul:
but the belly of the wicked shall *want* **lack**.
and the soul of the covert has violence.
3 He who guards his mouth guards his soul;
he who spreads his lips has ruin.
4 The soul of the sloth desires and has naught;
and the soul of the decisive fattens.
5 The just hate false words;
and the wicked stink and blush.
6 Justness guards the integrious in the way;
and wickedness perverts the sinner.
7 One enriches himself, yet has naught;
one impoverishes himself, yet has great wealth.
8 The koper/atonement of the soul of a man
are his riches;
and the impoverished hear not rebuke.
9 The light of the just cheers;
and the lamp of the wicked extinguishes.
10 Arrogance gives strife;
and with the counseled *is* wisdom.
11 Wealth by vanity diminishes;
and he who gathers by hand abounds.
12 Hope drawn out wearies the heart;
and when desire comes, it is a tree of life.
13 Whoever disrespects the word is despoiled;
and he who awes the misvah, is shalamed.
14 The torah of the wise is a fountain of life
to turn aside from the snares of death.
15 Good comprehension gives charism;
and the way of the covert is perennial.
16 All the subtle work with knowledge;
and a fool spreads folly.
17 A wicked angel falls into evil;
and a trustworthy ambassador is healing.
18 Poverty and abasement
are to him who avoids discipline;
and he who regards reproof is honored.
19 The desire that becomes
is pleasant to the soul;
and abhorrence to fools
is to turn aside from evil.
20 He who walks with the wise, enwisens;
and he who befriends fools, shouts.
21 Evil pursues sinners;
and good is the shalam of the just.
22 The good have the sons of their sons to inherit;
and the valuables of the sinner
are treasured for the just.
23 Abundant food
is the tillage of the impoverished;
and *is* scraped away for want of judgment.
24 He who spares his scion hates his son;
and he who loves him
rises early and disciplines him.
25 The just eats to satisfy his soul;
and the belly of the wicked lacks.

14 Every wise woman buildeth her house:
but the foolish
plucketh it down **demolisheth** with her hands.
2 He that walketh in his *uprightness* **straightness**
feareth the LORD **aweth Yah Veh**:
but *he that is perverse* **the perverted** in his ways
despiseth him.
3 In the mouth of the *foolish*
fool is a rod of *pride* **pomp**:
but the lips of the wise shall *preserve* **guard** them.
4 Where no oxen are, the *crib*
manger is *clean* **empty**:
but *much increase* **abundant produce**
is by the *strength* **force** of the ox.
5 A *faithful* **trustworthy** witness *will* **shall** not lie:
but a false witness *will utter* **shall breathe** lies.
6 A scorner seeketh wisdom, and *findeth* it **is** not:
but knowledge is *easy* **swift**
unto him that *understandeth* **discerneth**.
7 Go from the *presence* **front** of a foolish man,
when thou perceivest not *in him* the lips of knowledge.
8 The wisdom of the *prudent* **subtle** is to *understand*
discern his way: but the folly of fools is deceit.

9 Fools *make a mock* **scorn** at *sin* **guilt**:
but among the *righteous* **straight**
there is *favour* **pleasure**.
10 The heart knoweth *his own* bitterness **of soul**;
and a stranger *doth* **mingleth** not *intermeddle*
with his *joy* **cheerfulness**.
11 The house of the wicked
shall be *overthrown* **desolated**:
but the *tabernacle* **tent** of the *upright* **straight**
shall *flourish* **blossom**.
12 There is a way which seemeth *right* **straight**
unto **at the face of** a man,
but the *end* **finality** *thereof* are the ways of death.
13 Even in laughter the heart *is sorrowful* **paineth**;
and the *end* **finality** of that *mirth* **cheerfulness**
is *heaviness* **grief**.
14 *The backslider* **Whoso apostatizeth** in heart
shall be *filled* **satiated** with his own ways:
and a good man *shall be satisfied from* **of** himself.
15 The *simple believeth* **gullible**
trusteth every word:
but the *prudent man* **subtle**
looketh well to **discerneth** his *going* **step**.
16 *A* **The** wise *man feareth* **aweth**,
and *departeth* **turneth aside** from evil:
but the fool *rageth* **passeth on**, and is confident.
17 He that *is soon angry* **hath quick wrath**
dealeth foolishly **worketh folly**:
and a man of *wicked devices* **intrigue** is hated.
18 The *simple* **gullible** inherit folly:
but the *prudent* **subtle**
are *crowned* **surrounded** with knowledge.
19 The evil *bow before* **prostrate**
at the face of the good;
and the wicked at the *gates* **portals** of the *righteous* **just**.
20 The *poor* **impoverished** is hated
even of his own *neighbour* **friend**:
but *the rich hath many friends*
many are they who love the rich.
21 He that *despiseth* **disrespecteth**
his *neighbour* **friend**
sinneth:
but he that
hath mercy **granteth charism** on the *poor* **humble**,
happy **blithe** is he.
22 Do they not *err* **stray** that *devise* **inscribe** evil?
but mercy and truth shall be to them
that *devise* **inscribe** good.
23 In all *labour* **contorting**
there is *profit* **advantage**:
but the *talk* **word** of the lips
tendeth **be** only to *penury* **lack**.
24 The crown of the wise is their riches:
but the *foolishness* **folly** of fools is folly.
25 A true witness *delivereth* **rescueth** souls:
but *a* **the** deceitful *witness speaketh* **breatheth** lies.
26 In the *fear* **awe** of *the LORD* **Yah Veh**
is strong confidence:
and his *children* **sons** shall have *a place of* refuge.
27 The *fear* **awe** of *the LORD*
Yah Veh is a fountain of life,
to *depart* **turn** from the snares of death.

14 Every wise woman builds her house;
and the foolish demolishes with her hands.
2 He who walks in his straightness awes Yah Veh;
and the perverted in his ways despises him.
3 In the mouth of the fool *is* a rod of pomp;
and the lips of the wise guard them.
4 Where no oxen are, the manger *is* empty;
and abundant *is* the produce by the force of the ox.
5 A trustworthy witness lies not;
and a false witness breathes lies.
6 A scorner seeks wisdom and it is not;
and knowledge is swift to him who discerns.
7 Go from the front of a foolish man,
when you perceive not the lips of knowledge.
8 The wisdom of the subtle *is* to discern his way;
and the folly of fools is deceit.
9 Fools scorn at guilt;
and among the straight there is pleasure.
10 The heart knows bitterness of soul;
and a stranger mingles not with his cheerfulness.
11 The house of the wicked desolates;
and the tent of the straight blossoms.
12 There is a way—straight at the face of a man,
and the finality, the ways of death.
13 Even in laughter the heart pains;
and the finality of that cheerfulness is grief.
14 Whoever apostatizes in heart
satiates of his own ways; but a good man of himself.
15 The gullible trusts every word;
but the subtle discerns his step.
16 The wise awes and turns aside from evil;
and the fool passes on, confident.
17 He of quick wrath works folly;
and a man of intrigue is hated.
18 The gullible inherit folly;
and the subtle are surrounded with knowledge.
19 The evil prostrate at the face of the good;
and the wicked at the portals of the just.

20 The impoverished is hated
even by his own friend;
and many *are* they who love the rich.
21 He who disrespects his friend, sins;
and he who grants charism on the humble, blithes.
22 Stray they not, who inscribe evil?
And mercy and truth to them who inscribe good?
23 In all contorting there is advantage;
and the word of the lips *is* only to lack.
24 The crown of the wise is their riches;
and the folly of fools *is* folly.
25 A true witness rescues souls;
and the deceitful breathe lies.
26 In the awe of Yah Veh *is* strong confidence;
and his sons have refuge.
27 The awe of Yah Veh is a fountain of life,
to turn from the snares of death.
28 In the *multitude* **abundance** of people
is the *king's honour* **sovereign's majesty**:
but in the *want* **finality** of *people* **nations**
is the *destruction* **ruin** of the *prince* **potentate**.
29 He that is slow to wrath
is of great *understanding* **discernment**:
but he that is *hasty* **quick** of spirit exalteth folly.
30 A *sound* heart **of healing** is the life of the flesh:
but envy the rottenness of the bones.
31 He that oppresseth the poor
reproacheth his *Maker* **Worker**:
but he that honoureth him
hath mercy **granteth charism** on the *poor* **needy**.
32 The wicked
is *driven away* **overthrown** in his *wickedness* **evil**:
but the *righteous hath hope* **just seeketh refuge**
in his death.
33 Wisdom resteth in the heart of him
that *hath understanding* **discerneth**:
but that which is in the midst of fools is made known.
34 *Righteousness* **Justness** exalteth a *nation* **goyim**:
but sin is a *reproach* **shame** to *any people* **all nations**.
35 The *king's favour* **sovereign's pleasure**
is toward a *wise* **comprehending** servant:
but his *wrath* **outburst of passion**
is *against him* **one** that *causeth shame* **shameth**.

15 A *soft* **tender** answer turneth away *wrath* **fury**:
but *grievous* **contorting** words *stir
up anger* **ascend wrath**.
2 The tongue of the wise
useth **well—pleaseth** knowledge *aright*:
but the mouth of fools
poureth out foolishness **gusheth folly**.
3 The eyes of *the LORD* **Yah
Veh** are in every place,
beholding **watching** the evil and the good.
4 A *wholesome* **healing** tongue is a tree of life:
but perverseness therein is a breach in the spirit.
5 A fool
despiseth **scorneth** his father's *instruction* **discipline**:
but he that regardeth reproof *is prudent* **strategizeth**.
6 In the house of the *righteous* **just**
is much *treasure* **wealth**:
but in the revenues of the wicked is trouble.
7 The lips of the wise *disperse* **winnow** knowledge:
but the heart of the foolish *doeth*—not so.
8 The sacrifice of the wicked
is an *abomination* **abhorrence** to *the LORD* **Yah Veh**:
but the prayer of the *upright* **straight**
is his *delight* **pleasure**.
9 The way of the wicked
is an *abomination* **abhorrence** unto *the LORD* **Yah Veh**:
but he loveth him
that *followeth after righteousness* **pursueth justness**.
10 *Correction* **Discipline** is *grievous* **evil**
unto him that forsaketh the way:
and he that hateth reproof shall die.
11 *Hell* **Sheol** and *destruction* **abaddon**
are *before the LORD* **in front of Yah Veh**:
how much more then
the hearts of the *children* **sons** of *men* **humanity**?
12 A scorner loveth not one that reproveth him:
neither *will* **shall** he go unto the wise.
13 A *merry* **cheerful** heart
maketh a cheerful countenance **well—pleaseth the face**:
but by *sorrow* **contortion** of the heart
the spirit is *broken* **stricken**.
14 The heart of him that *hath
understanding* **discerneth**
seeketh knowledge:
but the *mouth* **face** of fools
feedeth on foolishness **befriendeth folly**.
15 All the days of the afflicted are evil:
but he that is of a merry heart
hath a continual *feast* **banquet**.
16 Better is little with the *fear*
awe of *the LORD* **Yah Veh**
than great treasure *and trouble
therewith* **with confusion**.
17 Better is a *dinner* **ration** of
herbs **greens** where love is,
than a *stalled* **foddered** ox and hatred *therewith*.
18 A *wrathful* man **of fury**
stirreth up **throttleth** strife:

but he that is slow to *anger* **wrath**
appeaseth **resteth** strife.
28 In the abundance of people
is the majesty of the sovereign;
and in the finality of nations
is the ruin of the potentate.
29 He who is slow to wrath *is* of great discernment;
and he who is quick of spirit exalts folly.
30 A heart of healing is the life of the flesh;
and envy *is* the rottenness of the bones.
31 He who oppresses the poor
reproaches his Worker;
and he who honors him
grants charism on the needy.
32 The wicked is overthrown in his evil;
and the just seek refuge in his death.
33 Wisdom rests in the heart of him who discerns;
but that midst fools is made known.
34 Justness exalts a goyim;
and sin is a shame to all nations.
35 The pleasure of the sovereign
is toward a comprehending servant;
and his outburst of passion is on one who shames.

15 A tender answer turns away fury;
and contorting words ascend wrath.
2 The tongue of the wise well—pleases knowledge;
and the mouth of fools gushes folly.
3 The eyes of Yah Veh are in every place,
watching the evil and the good.
4 A healing tongue *is* a tree of life;
and perverseness therein *is* a breach in the spirit.
5 A fool scorns the discipline of his father;
and he who regards reproof strategizes.
6 In the house of the just *is* much wealth;
and in the revenues of the wicked *is* trouble.
7 The lips of the wise winnow knowledge;
and the heart of the foolish—not so.
8 The sacrifice of the wicked
is an abhorrence to Yah Veh;
and the prayer of the straight
is his pleasure.
9 The way of the wicked
is an abhorrence to Yah Veh;
and he loves him
who pursues justness.
10 Discipline is evil to him who forsakes the way;
and he who hates reproof dies.
11 Sheol and abaddon *are* in front of Yah Veh;
how much more then
the hearts of the sons of humanity?
12 A scorner neither loves his reprover;
nor goes to the wise.
13 A cheerful heart well—pleases the face;
but contortion of the heart strikes the spirit.
14 The heart of the discerner seeks knowledge;
and the face of fools befriends folly.
15 All the days of the afflicted are evil;
and he of a merry heart has a continual banquet.
16 Better, little with the awe of Yah Veh
than great treasure with confusion:
17 better, a ration of greens and love
than a foddered ox and hatred.
18 A man of fury throttles strife;
and he who is slow to wrath rests strife.
19 The way of the *slothful man* **sloth**
is as an hedge of thorns:
but the way of the *righteous* **straight**
is *made plain* **raised.**
20 A wise son *maketh a glad* **cheereth a** father:
but a foolish *man* **human** despiseth his mother.
21 Folly is *joy* **cheerfulness**
to him that *is destitute of wisdom* **lacketh heart**:
but a man of *understanding* **discernment**
walketh *uprightly* **straightly**.
22 Without **private** counsel
purposes **fabrications** are *disappointed* **broken**:
but in the *multitude* **abundance** of counsellors
they *are established* **rise.**
23 A man hath *joy* **cheerfulness**
by the answer of his mouth:
and a word *spoken in due season* **in time**, how good is it!
24 The way of life is above to
the *wise* **comprehending**,
that he may *depart* **turn aside**
from *hell beneath* **sheol below**.
25 *The LORD will destroy* **Yah Veh shall uproot**
the house of the *proud* **pompous**:
but he *will establish* **shall station**
the border of the widow.
26 The *thoughts* **fabrications** of *the wicked* **evil**
are an *abomination* **abhorrence** to *the LORD* **Yah Veh**:
but the *words* **sayings** of the pure are pleasant *words*.
27 He that is greedy of *gain* **greed**
troubleth his own house;
but he that hateth gifts shall live.
28 The heart of the *righteous* **just**
studieth **meditateth** to answer:
but the mouth of the wicked
poureth out **gusheth** evil *things*.
29 *The LORD* **Yah Veh** is far from the wicked:

but he heareth the prayer of the *righteous* **just**.
30 The light of the eyes
rejoiceth **cheereth** the heart:
and a good report *maketh* **fatteneth** the bones *fat*.
31 The ear that heareth the reproof of life
abideth **stayeth** among the wise.
32 He that *refuseth instruction* **avoideth discipline**
despiseth **spurneth** his own soul:
but he that heareth reproof getteth *understanding* **heart**.
33 The *fear* **awe** of *the LORD* **Yah Veh**
is the *instruction* **discipline** of wisdom;
and *before* **at the face of** honour is humility.

16 The *preparations* **arrangements** of the heart
in *man* **humanity**,
and the answer of the tongue,
is from *the LORD* **Yah Veh**.
2 All the ways of a man are
clean **pure** in his own eyes;
but *the LORD weigheth* **Yah Veh gaugeth** the spirits.
3 *Commit* **Roll** thy works
unto *the LORD* **Yah Veh**,
and thy *thoughts* **fabrications** shall be established.
4 *The LORD* **Yah Veh** hath made all *things*
for himself **to answer to him**:
yea, even the wicked for the day of evil.
5 Every one that is *proud* **lofty** in heart
is an *abomination* **abhorrence** to *the LORD* **Yah Veh**:
though hand join hand **hand by hand**,
he shall not be *unpunished* **exonerated**.
6 By mercy and truth
iniquity *is purged* **doth kapar/atone**:
and by the *fear* **awe** of *the LORD* **Yah Veh**
men depart **turn aside** from evil.
7 When a man's ways please *the LORD* **Yah Veh**,
he maketh even his enemies
to be at peace with **shalam** him.
8 Better is a little with *righteousness* **justness**
than great *revenues* **produce** without *right* **judgment**.
9 *A man's* **The human** heart
deviseth **fabricateth** his way:
but *the LORD* **Yah Veh**
directeth **establisheth** his *steps* **pace**.
10 *A divine sentence* **Divination**
is in the lips of the *king* **sovereign**:
his mouth *transgresseth* **treasoneth** not in judgment.
11 A just weight and balance
are *the LORD'S* **Yah Veh's**:
19 The way of the sloth *is* as a hedge of thorns;
and the way of the straight is raised.
20 A wise son cheers a father;
and a foolish human despises his mother.
21 Folly is cheerfulness to one lacking heart;
and a man of discernment walks straightly.
22 Without private counsel fabrications are broken;
and in the abundance of counsellors, they rise.
23 A man has cheerfulness
by the answer of his mouth;
and a word in time, how good!
24 The way of life to the comprehending is above,
to turn aside from sheol below.
25 Yah Veh uproots the house of the pompous;
and he stations the border of the widow.
26 The fabrications of evil
are an abhorrence to Yah Veh;
and the sayings of the pure *are* pleasant.
27 He who *is* greedy of greed
troubles his own house;
and he who hates gifts lives.
28 The heart of the just meditates to answer;
and the mouth of the wicked gushes evil.
29 Yah Veh *is* far from the wicked;
and he hears the prayer of the just.
30 The light of the eyes cheers the heart;
and a good report fattens the bones.
31 The ear that hears the reproof of life
stays among the wise:
32 he who avoids discipline
spurns his own soul:
and he who hears reproof gets heart.
33 The awe of Yah Veh is the discipline of wisdom;
and at the face of honor *is* humility.

16 The arrangements of the heart
are from humanity;
and the answer of the tongue
is from Yah Veh.
2 All the ways of a man are pure in his own eyes;
and Yah Veh gauges the spirits.
3 Roll your works unto Yah Veh
and your fabrications are established.
4 Yah Veh made all to answer to him;
yes, even the wicked for the day of evil.
5 The lofty heart *is* an abhorrence to Yah Veh;
hand by hand he is not exonerated.
6 By mercy and truth iniquity kapars/atones;
and by the awe of Yah Veh evil turns aside.
7 When the ways of man please Yah Veh,
even his enemies shalam him.
8 Better, a little with justness
than great produce without judgment.
9 The human heart fabricates his way;

and Yah Veh establishes his pace.
10 Divination *is* in the lips of the sovereign;
his mouth treasons not in judgment.
11 A just weight and balance *are* of Yah Veh;
all the *weights* **stones** of the *bag* **pouch** are his work.
12 It is an *abomination* **abhorrence**
to kings **for sovereigns** to *commit* **work** wickedness: for
the throne is established by *righteousness* **justness.**
13 *Righteous lips* **Lips of justness**
are the *delight* **pleasure** of *kings* **sovereigns;**
and they love him that *speaketh right* **wordeth straight.**
14 The *wrath* **fury** of a *king* **sovereign**
is as *messengers* **angels** of death:
but a wise man *will pacify it* **shall kapar/atone.**
15 In the light of the *king's*
countenance **sovereign's face**
is life;
and his *favour* **pleasure**
is as a **thick** cloud of the *latter* **after** rain.
16 How much better *is it to*
get **to chattelize** wisdom
than gold **above ore**!
and to *get understanding* **chattelize discernment**
rather to be chosen *than* **above** silver!
17 The highway of the *upright* **straight**
is to *depart* **turn aside** from evil:
he that *keepeth* **guardeth** his way
preserveth **guardeth** his soul.
18 *Pride* **Pomp**
goeth before destruction **faceth the breech,**
and *an haughty* **a lifted** spirit
before a fall **faceth the stumble.**
19 Better it is
to be *of an humble* **a lowly** spirit with the *lowly* **humble,**
than to *divide* **allot** the spoil with the *proud* **pompous.**
20 He that handleth
a *matter wisely* **word comprehendingly**
shall find good:
and whoso *trusteth* **confideth** in *the LORD* **Yah Veh,**
happy is he **O how blithe.**
21 The wise in heart shall be
called *prudent* **discerning:**
and the sweetness of the lips
increaseth *learning* **doctrine.**
22 *Understanding* **Comprehension**
is a *wellspring* **fountain** of life
unto *him that hath it* **its master:**
but the *instruction* **discipline** of fools is folly.
23 The heart of the wise
teacheth **comprehendeth** his mouth, and
addeth *learning* **doctrine** to his lips.
24 Pleasant *words* **sayings** are as an honeycomb,
sweet to the soul, and *health* **healing** to the bones.
25 There is a way that seemeth *right* **straight**
unto **at the face of** a man,
but the *end thereof* **finality** are the ways of death.
26 *He that laboureth* **The soul of the toiler**
laboureth **toileth** for himself;
for his mouth craveth it of him.
27 *An ungodly man* **A man of**
Beli Yaal diggeth *up* evil:
and in his lips there is as *a burning* **an inflamed** fire.
28 A *froward* man **of perversions**
soweth **sendeth** strife:
and a whisperer separateth *chief friends* **chiliarchs.**
29 A *violent* man **of violence**
enticeth his *neighbour* **friend,**
and *leadeth* **walketh** him into the way that is not good.
30 He shutteth his eyes
to *devise froward things* **fabricate perversions:**
moving **biting** his lips he *bringeth*
concludeth evil *to pass.*
31 *The hoary head* **Greyness**
is a crown of *glory* **beauty,**
if it be found in the way of *righteousness* **justness.**
32 He that is slow to *anger* **wrath**
is better than the mighty;
and he that *ruleth* **reigneth** his spirit
than he that *taketh* **captureth** a city.
33 The *lot* **pebble** is cast into the *lap* **bosom;**
but *the whole disposing* **all judgment** *thereof*
is of *the LORD* **Yah Veh.**

17 Better is a *dry* **parched** morsel,
and *quietness* **serenity** therewith,
than an house full of sacrifices with strife.
2 A *wise* **comprehending** servant
shall *have rule* **reign** over a son
that *causeth shame* **shameth,**
and shall *have part of* **be allotted** the inheritance
among the brethren.
all the stones of the pouch are his work.
12 It *is* an abhorrence
for sovereigns to work wickedness;
for the throne is established by justness.
13 Lips of justness *are* the pleasure of sovereigns;
and they love him who words straight.
14 The fury of a sovereign is as angels of death;
and a wise man kapars/atones.
15 In the light of the face of the sovereign *is* life;
and his pleasure *is* as a thick cloud of the after rain.
16 To chattelize wisdom;

how much better than ore!
and to chattelize discernment
to be chosen above silver!
17 The highway of the straight
is to turn aside from evil;
he who guards his way guards his soul.
18 Pomp *is* at the face of the breech
and a lifted spirit *is* at the face of the stumble.
19 Better, a lowly spirit with the humble,
than to allot the spoil with the pompous.
20 He who handles a word comprehendingly
finds good;
and whoever confides in Yah Veh,
O how blithe.
21 The wise in heart is called, Discerning;
and the sweetness of the lips increases doctrine.
22 Comprehension is a
fountain of life to its master;
and the discipline of fools is folly.
23 The heart of the wise comprehends his mouth
and adds doctrine to his lips.
24 Pleasant sayings are as a honeycomb
—sweet to the soul and healing to the bones.
25 There is a straight way, at the face of man;
and its finality, the ways of death.
26 The soul of the toiler toils for himself
for the craving of his mouth:
27 a man of Beli Yaal digs evil;
and in his lips, as an inflamed fire:
28 a man of perversions sends strife;
and a whisperer separates chiliarchs:
29 a man of violence entices his friend
and walks him into the way—not good:
30 He shuts his eyes to fabricate perversions;
bites his lips to conclude evil.
31 Greyness *is* a crown of beauty
found in the way of justness.
32 Better, slow to wrath, than mighty;
—to reign over the spirit, than to capture a city.
33 The pebble is cast into the bosom;
and all judgment *is* of Yah Veh.

17 Better, a parched morsel with serenity
than a house full of sacrifices with strife.
2 A comprehending servant
reigns over a son who shames;
and allots the inheritance among the brothers.
3 The *fining pot* **crucible** is for silver,
and the furnace for gold:
but *the LORD trieth* **Yah Veh proofeth** the hearts.
4 A *wicked doer* **vilifier**
giveth heed **hearkeneth** to *false* lips **of mischief**;
and a *liar* **falsifier**
giveth ear **hearkeneth** to a *naughty* tongue **of calamity**.
5 Whoso *mocketh* **derideth**
the *poor* **impoverished**
reproacheth his *Maker* **Worker**:
and he that *is glad* **cheereth** at calamities
shall not be *unpunished* **exonerated**.
6 *Children's children* **Sons' sons**
are the crown of *old men* **the aged**;
and the *glory* **beauty** of *children* **sons** are their fathers.
7 *Excellent speech* **A lip of rest**
becometh **befitteth** not a fool:
much less *do lying* **false** lips a *prince* **volunteer**.
8 A *gift* **bribe** is as a *precious* stone **of charism**
in the eyes of *him that hath it* **his master**:
whithersoever it *turneth* **faceth**,
it *prospereth* **comprehendeth**.
9 He that covereth a *transgression* **rebellion**
seeketh love;
but he that *repeateth* **reiterateth** a *matter* **word**
separateth *very* friends.
10 *A reproof entereth more* **Rebuke penetrateth**
into a *wise man* **discerner**
more than an hundred *stripes* **smitings**
into a fool.
11 *An evil man* **A rebel** seeketh *only rebellion* **evil**:
therefore a cruel *messenger* **angel**
shall be sent against him.
12 Let a bear *robbed* **bereaved**
of her whelps meet a man,
rather than **but not** a fool in his folly.
13 Whoso *rewardeth* **returneth** evil for good,
evil shall not depart from his house.
14 The beginning of strife
is as *when one letteth out* **a bursting of** water:
therefore leave off contention,
before it be meddled with **ere it faceth a quarrel**.
15 He that justifieth the wicked,
and he that *condemneth* **judgeth wicked** the just,
even they both are *abomination* **abhorrence**
to *the LORD* **Yah Veh**.
16 Wherefore is there a price in the hand of a fool
to *get* **chattelize** wisdom,
seeing he hath no heart to it?
17 A friend loveth at all times,
and a brother is *born* **birthed** for *adversity* **tribulation**.
18 A *man void of understanding*
human that lacketh heart
striketh hands **clappeth palms**,

and becometh *surety* **a pledge**
in the presence **at the face** of his friend.
19 He loveth *transgression*
rebellion that loveth strife:
and he that *exalteth* **lifteth** his *gate* **portal**
seeketh *destruction* **a breech**.
20 He that hath a *froward* **perverted** heart
findeth no good:
and he that hath a *perverse* **turned** tongue
falleth into *mischief* **evil**.
21 He that *begetteth* **birtheth** a fool
doeth it to his sorrow **hath grief**:
and the father of a fool hath no *joy* **cheer**.
22 A *merry* **cheerful** heart
doeth good **well—pleaseth** like a *medicine* **cure**:
but a *broken* **stricken** spirit drieth the bones.
23 *A* **The** wicked *man* taketh a
gift **bribe** out of the bosom
to pervert the ways of judgment.
24 Wisdom *is before* **faceth** him
that *hath understanding* **discerneth**;
but the eyes of a fool are in the ends of the earth.
25 A foolish son is a *grief* **vexation** to his father,
and bitterness to her that *bare* **birthed** him.
26 Also to *punish* **penalize** the just is not good,
nor to *strike princes* **smite volunteers**
for *equity* **straightness**.
27 He that *hath* **knoweth** knowledge
spareth his *words* **sayings**:
3 The crucible for silver; the furnace for gold;
and Yah Veh proofs the hearts.
4 A vilifier hearkens to lips of mischief;
and a falsifier hearkens to a tongue of calamity.
5 Whoever derides the impoverished
reproaches his Worker;
whoever cheers at calamities
is not exonerated.
6 Sons of sons *are* the crown of the aged;
and the beauty of sons *are* their fathers.
7 A lip of rest befits not a fool;
much less false lips a volunteer.
8 A bribe is as a stone of charism
in the eyes of his master;
wherever it faces, it comprehends.
9 He who covers a rebellion seeks love;
and he who reiterates a word separates friends.
10 Rebuke penetrates a discerner
more than a hundred smitings to a fool.
11 A rebel seeks evil;
a cruel angel is sent against him.
12 *May* a bereaved bear meet a man
but not a fool in his folly.
13 Whoever returns evil for good
evil departs not from his house.
14 The beginning of strife *is* as a bursting of water
leave off contention ere it faces a quarrel.
15 He who justifies the wicked
and he who judges wicked the just
—even they both *are* abhorrence to Yah Veh.
16 Why is there a price in the hand of a fool
to chattelize wisdom,
when he has no heart for it?
17 A friend loves at all times
and a brother is birthed for tribulation.
18 A human who lacks heart claps palms;
and becomes a pledge at the face of his friend.
19 He who loves rebellion, loves strife;
and he who lifts his portal, seeks a breech.
20 A perverted heart finds no good;
and a turned tongue falls into evil.
21 He who births a fool has grief;
and the father of a fool cheers not.
22 A cheerful heart well—pleases as a cure;
and a stricken spirit dries the bones.
23 The wicked take a bribe from the bosom
to pervert the ways of judgment.
24 Wisdom faces him who discerns;
and the eyes of a fool are in the ends of the earth.
25 A foolish son is a vexation to his father
and bitterness to her who birthed him.
26 Also, neither penalize the just for good,
nor smite volunteers for straightness.
27 He who knows knowledge spares his sayings;
and a man of *understanding* **discernment**
is of *an excellent* **cool** spirit.
28 Even a fool, when he *holdeth his peace* **husheth**,
is *counted* **fabricated** wise:
and he that shutteth his lips
is esteemed a man of understanding **a discerner**.

18 Through desire a man,
having separated himself,
seeketh and *intermeddleth* **quarreleth**
with all *wisdom* **evidence**.
2 A fool hath no delight in
understanding **discernment**,
but that his heart may *discover* **expose** itself.
3 When the wicked cometh,
then cometh also *contempt* **disrespect**, and
with *ignominy* **abasement** reproach.
4 The words of a man's mouth are as deep waters,

and the *wellspring* **fountain** of wisdom
as a *flowing brook* **gushing wadi.**
5 It is not good to *accept* **lift**
the *person* **face** of the wicked,
to *overthrow* **pervert** the *righteous* **just** in judgment.
6 A fool's lips enter into contention,
and his mouth calleth for *strokes* **poundings.**
7 A fool's mouth is his *destruction* **ruin,**
and his lips are the snare of his soul.
8 The words of a *talebearer* **whisperer**
are as wounds **inflame,**
and they *go down* **descend**
into the *innermost parts* **chambers** of the belly.
9 He also that *is slothful* **slacketh** in his work
is brother to him that is a *great waster* **master of ruin.**
10 The name of *the LORD* **Yah Veh**
is a *strong* tower **of strength:**
the *righteous* **just** runneth into it, and is *safe* **lofted.**
11 The *rich man's* wealth **of the rich**
is his *strong* city **of strength,**
and as *an high* **a lofted** wall
in his own *conceit* **imagination.**
12 *Before destruction* **At the face of the breech**
the heart of man is *haughty* **lifted,**
and before **at the face of** honour is humility.
13 He that *answereth* **respondeth** a *matter* **word**
before he heareth it,
it is folly and shame unto him.
14 The spirit of a man
will **shall** sustain his *infirmity* **disease;**
but a *wounded* **stricken** spirit who can bear?
15 The heart of the *prudent* **discerning**
getteth **chattelizeth** knowledge;
and the ear of the wise seeketh knowledge.
16 *A man's gift* **The gift of a human**
maketh room for **enlargeth** him,
and *bringeth* **leadeth** him
before great men **at the face of the great.**
17 He that is first in **presenting**
his own *cause* **defence**
seemeth **be** just;
but his *neighbour* **friend** cometh
and *searcheth* **probeth** him.
18 The *lot* **pebble**
causeth contentions to *cease* **shabbathize,** and
parteth **separateth** between the mighty.
19 A brother *offended* **rebelled against**
is harder to be won than a strong
city **is as a city of strength:**
and their contentions are like the bars of a *castle* **citadel.**
20 A man's belly shall be satisfied
with the fruit of his mouth;
and with the *increase* **produce** of his lips
shall he be *filled* **satisfied.**
21 Death and life are in the
power **hand** of the tongue:
and they that love it shall eat the fruit thereof.
22 Whoso findeth a *wife*
woman findeth *a* good *thing,*
and *obtaineth favour* **produceth pleasure**
of *the LORD* **Yah Veh.**
23 The *poor* **impoverished**
useth intreaties **wordeth supplications;** but
the rich answereth *roughly* **strongly.**
24 A man that hath friends
must shew himself friendly:
and there is a *friend* **lover**
that *sticketh* **adhereth** closer than a brother.
and a man of discernment *is* of cool spirit.
28 Even a fool, when he hushes, *is* fabricated wise;
he who shuts his lips is a discerner.

18 He who seeks his own desire
separates himself and quarrels with all evidence.
2 A fool has no delight in discernment;
but to expose his heart.
3 When the wicked come,
then also comes disrespect;
and with abasement, reproach.
4 The words of the mouth of a man
are as deep waters,
and the fountain of wisdom
as a gushing wadi.
5 It is not good
—to lift the face of the wicked
—to pervert the just in judgment.
6 The lips of a fool enter contention
and his mouth calls for poundings.
7 The mouth of a fool *is* his ruin
and his lips the snare of his soul.
8 The words of a whisperer inflame
—descending to the chambers of the belly.
9 He also who slacks his work
is brother to a master of ruin.
10 The name of Yah Veh *is* a tower of strength;
the just run to it and are lofted.
11 The wealth of the rich *is* his city of strength
—as a lofted wall in his own imagination.
12 At the face of the breech
the heart of man *is* lifted;
at the face of honor *is* humility.

13 He who responds to a word ere he hears
—folly and shame to him.
14 The spirit of a man sustains his disease;
and a stricken spirit who can bear?
15 The heart of the discerning
chattelizes knowledge;
and the ear of the wise seeks knowledge.
16 The gift of a human enlarges him
—leads him at the face of the great.
17 He who presents his own defence first, is just;
and his friend comes and probes him.
18 The pebble causes contentions to shabbathize
and separates between the mighty.
19 A brother rebelled against, *is* as a city of
strength;
and their contentions, as the bars of a citadel.
20 The belly of man
satiates with the fruit of his mouth
—satiates with the produce of his lips.
21 Death and life *are* in the hand of the tongue;
and they who love it eat the fruit thereof.
22 Whoever finds a woman finds good
and produces pleasure from Yah Veh.
23 The impoverished word supplications;
and the rich answer strongly.
24 A man with friends shows himself friendly;
and there is a lover
who adheres closer than a brother.

19 Better *is the poor* **the impoverished**
that walketh in his integrity,
than *he that is perverse* **the perverted**
in *his* lips, and is a fool.
2 Also,
that the soul be without knowledge, it is not good;
and he that hasteth with his feet sinneth.
3 The *foolishness* **folly** of *man* **humanity**
perverteth his way:
and his heart *fretteth* **rageth** against *the LORD* **Yah Veh.**
4 Wealth *maketh* **addeth** many friends;
but the poor is separated from his *neighbour* **friend.**
5 A false witness shall not be
unpunished **exonerated,**
and he that *speaketh* **breatheth** lies shall not escape.
6 Many *will intreat* **shall stroke** the *favour* **face**
of the *prince* **volunteer:**
and every man is a friend to *him*
that giveth **a man of** gifts.
7 All the brethren of the *poor*
impoverished do hate him:
how much more
do his *friends* **companions** go far from him?
he pursueth them with *words* **sayings,**
yet they are *wanting to him* **not.**
8 He that *getteth wisdom* **chattelizeth heart**
loveth his own soul:
he that *keepeth understanding* **guardeth discernment**
shall find good.
9 A false witness shall not be
unpunished **exonerated,**
and he that *speaketh* **breatheth** lies shall *perish* **destruct.**
10 Delight is not *seemly* **befitting** for a fool;
much less for a servant
to *have rule* **reign** over *princes* **governors.**
11 The *discretion* **comprehension** of a *man* **human**
deferreth **prolongeth** his *anger* **wrath;**
and it is his *glory* **beauty**
to pass over a *transgression* **rebellion.**
12 The *king's wrath* **sovereign's rage**
is as the *roaring* **growling** of a *lion* **whelp;**
but his *favour* **pleasure** is as dew upon the *grass* **herbage.**
13 A foolish son is the calamity of his father:
and the contentions of a *wife* **woman**
are a continual *dropping* **dripping.**
14 House and *riches* **wealth**
are the inheritance of fathers:
and a *prudent wife* **comprehending woman**
is from *the LORD* **Yah Veh.**
15 *Slothfulness casteth* **Sloth**
falleth into a deep sleep;
and *an idle* **a deceitful** soul shall *suffer hunger* **famish.**
16 He that *keepeth* **guardeth**
the *commandment* **misvah**
keepeth **guardeth** his own soul;
but he that despiseth his ways shall die.
17 He that *hath pity* **granteth**
charism upon the poor
lendeth unto *the LORD* **Yah Veh;**
and that which he hath *given* **dealt**
will he pay him again **shall he shalam.**
18 *Chasten* **Discipline** thy son while there is hope,
and *let* **lift** not thy soul *spare* for his *crying* **death.**
19 *A man* **One** of *great* **harsh** wrath
shall *suffer punishment* **bear the penalty:**
for if thou *deliver* **rescue** him, yet thou must do it again.
20 Hear counsel, and *receive*
instruction **take discipline,**
that thou mayest *be wise* **enwisen**
in thy *latter end* **finality.**
21 There are many *devices*
fabrications in a man's heart;

nevertheless the counsel of *the LORD* **Yah Veh**,
that shall *stand* **rise**.
22 The desire of a *man* **human**
is his *kindness* **mercy**:
and *a poor man* **the impoverished**
is better than a *liar* **man of lies**.
23 The *fear* **awe** of *the LORD*
tendeth **Yah Veh be** to life:
and he *that hath it* shall *abide* **stay** satisfied;
he shall not be visited with evil.
24 *A slothful man* **The sloth**
hideth his hand in his bosom,
and *will* **shall** not
so much as bring **return** it to his mouth *again*.
25 Smite a scorner,
and the *simple will beware* **gullible shall strategize**:
and reprove one that *hath understanding* **discerneth**,
and he *will understand* **shall discern** knowledge.

19 Better, the impoverished walking in integrity,
than the perverted in lips who *is* a fool.
2 Also, without knowledge, the soul *is* not good;
and he who hastens with his feet, sins.
3 The folly of humanity perverts his way;
whose heart rages against Yah Veh.
4 Wealth adds many friends;
and the poor is separated from his friend.
5 Neither is a false witness exonerated
nor escapes he who breathes lies.
6 Many stroke the face of the volunteer;
and all are a friend of a man of gifts.
7 All the brothers hate the impoverished;
how much more, his companions far from him.
he pursues them with sayings; yet they are not.
8 He who chattelizes heart loves his own soul;
he who guards discernment finds good.
9 A false witness is not exonerated
and he who breathes lies destructs.
10 Delight befits not a fool;
much less a servant to reign over governors.
11 The comprehension of a human
prolongs his wrath;
and his beauty *is* to pass over a rebellion.
12 The rage of the sovereign
is as the growling of a whelp;
and his pleasure
is as dew on the herbage.
13 A foolish son
is the calamity of his father;
and the contentions of a woman
are a continual dripping.
14 House and wealth are the inheritance of fathers;
and a comprehending woman *is* from Yah Veh.
15 Sloth falls into a deep sleep;
and a deceitful soul famishs.
16 Whoever guards the misvah,
guards his own soul;
and whoever despises his ways, dies.
17 Whoever grants charism to the poor
lends to Yah Veh;
and shalams what he deals.
18 Discipline your son while there is hope
and lift not your soul for his death.
19 One of harsh wrath must bear the penalty;
for if you rescue him, you must do it again.
20 Hear counsel and take discipline,
that you finally enwisen.
21 Many *are* the fabrications in the heart of man;
nevertheless the counsel of Yah Veh rises.
22 The desire of a human *is* his mercy;
better, impoverishment than a man of lies.
23 To awe Yah Veh is unto life;
he stays satisfied; he *is* not visited with evil.
24 The sloth hides his hand in his bosom
and returns it not to his mouth.
25 Smite a scorner, and the gullible strategize;
reprove the discerner, and he discerns knowledge.
26 He that *wasteth* **ravageth** his father,
and *chaseth* **fleeth** away his mother,
is a son that *causeth shame* **shameth**,
and *bringeth reproach* **blusheth**.
27 Cease, my son,
to hear the *instruction* **discipline**
that causeth to err **inadvertently**
from the *words* **sayings** of knowledge.
28 *An ungodly* **A** witness **of Beli
Yaal** scorneth judgment:
and the mouth of the wicked
devoureth iniquity **swalloweth mischief**.
29 Judgments are prepared for scorners,
and *stripes* **poundings** for the back of fools.

20 Wine *is a mocker* **scorneth**,
strong drink is raging **intoxicant roareth**:
and whosoever *is deceived* **erreth inadvertently** *thereby*
is not *wise* **enwisened**.
2 The *fear* **terror** of a *king* **sovereign**
is as the *roaring* **growling** of a *lion* **whelp**:
whoso *provoketh* **enrageth** him *to anger*
sinneth against his own soul.
3 It is an honour for a man
to *cease* **shabbathize** from strife:

but every fool *will be meddling* **shall quarrel.**
4 The *sluggard* **sloth**
will **shall** not plow *by reason of the cold* **in winter**;
therefore shall he *beg* **ask** in harvest,
and have *nothing* **naught.**
5 Counsel in the heart of man is like deep water;
but a man of *understanding* **discernment**
will draw it out **shall bail.**
6 *Most men* **An abundance of humanity**
will proclaim every one **shall each call out**
his own *goodness* **mercy**:
but a *faithful* **trustworthy** man who can find?
7 The just *man* walketh in his integrity:
his *children* **sons** are *blessed* **blithe** after him.
8 A *king* **sovereign**
that *sitteth* **settleth** in the throne of *judgment* **pleading**
scattereth **winnoweth** *away* all evil with his eyes.
9 Who can say, I have *made*
purified my heart *clean*,
I am *pure* **purified** from my sin?
10 *Divers weights* **A stone and a stone**,
and divers measures **an ephah and an ephah**,
yea, both of them
are *alike abomination* **abhorrence** to *the LORD* **Yah Veh.**
11 Even a *child* **lad**
is *known* **recognized** by his *doings* **exploits**,
whether his *work* **deeds** be pure,
and whether it be *right* **straight.**
12 The hearing ear, and the seeing eye,
the LORD **Yah Veh**
hath *made* **worked** even both of them.
13 Love not sleep,
lest thou *come to poverty* **be dispossessed**;
open thine eyes, and thou shalt be satisfied with bread.
14 *It is naught* **Evil,** *it is naught* **evil**!
saith the *buyer* **chattelizer**:
but when he *is gone his way* **hath gad about**,
then he *boasteth* **halaleth.**
15 There is gold,
and *a multitude* **an abundance** of *rubies* **pearls**:
but the lips of knowledge
are *a precious jewel* **an esteemed instrument.**
16 Take his *garment* **clothes**
that is *surety* **pledge** for a stranger:
and take a pledge of him
for a *strange woman* **stranger.**
17 Bread of *deceit* **falsehood**
is *sweet* **pleasant** to a man;
but afterwards his mouth shall be filled with gravel.
18 Every *purpose* **fabrication**
is established by counsel:
and with *good advice make* **counsels work** war.
19 He that goeth about as a talebearer
revealeth secrets **exposeth private counsel**:
therefore meddle not with him
that *flattereth* **enticeth** with his lips.
20 Whoso *curseth* **abaseth** his father or his mother,
26 Whoever ravages his father
and has his mother to flee,
is a son that shames and blushes.
27 Cease, my son, to hear the discipline
to err inadvertently from the sayings of knowledge.
28 A witness of Beli Yaal scorns judgment;
and the mouth of the wicked swallows mischief.
29 Judgments are prepared for scorners;
and poundings for the back of fools.

20 Wine scorns; intoxicants roar;
and whoever errs inadvertently enwisens not.
2 The terror of a sovereign *is* as a growling whelp;
whoever enrages him sins against his own soul.
3 Honor to the man who shabbathizes from strife;
and every fool quarrels.
4 The sloth plows not in winter;
he asks in harvest and has naught.
5 Counsel in the heart of man *is* as deep water;
and the man of discernment bails.
6 An abundance of humanity each calls out his
own mercy; and a man of trust, who finds?
7 The just walks in his integrity;
his sons are blithe after him.
8 A sovereign who settles
in the throne of pleading
winnows all evil with his eyes.
9 Who says,
I purified my heart; I am purified from my sin?
10 A stone and a stone; an ephah and an ephah:
yes, both are abhorrence to Yah Veh.
11 Even a lad is recognized by his exploits,
whether his deeds are pure; whether straight.
12 The hearing ear and the seeing eye,
Yah Veh worked even both.
13 Love not sleep, lest you become dispossessed;
open your eyes and become satisfied with bread.
14 Evil, evil! says the chattelizer;
and when he gads about, he halals.
15 There is gold and an abundance of pearls;
and the lips of knowledge
are an esteemed instrument.
16 Take his clothes, who pledges for a stranger;

and pledge him for a stranger.
17 Bread of falsehood is pleasant to a man;
and afterward his mouth is filled with gravel.
18 Every fabrication is established by counsel;
and with counsels, work war.
19 A talebearer exposes private counsel;
meddle not with him who entices with his lips.
20 Whoever abases his father or his mother,
his lamp shall be *put out* **extinguished**
in *obscure* **mid** darkness.
21 An inheritance
may be *gotten hastily* **obtained by avarice**
at the *beginning* **first**;
but the *end thereof* **finality** shall not be blessed.
22 Say not thou, I *will recompense*
shall shalam for evil;
but wait on the LORD **await Yah Veh**,
and he shall save thee.
23 *Divers weights* **A stone and a stone**
are an *abomination* **abhorrence**
unto *the LORD* **Yah Veh**;
and *a false balance is* **balances of deceit are** not good.
24 *Man's goings* **The paces of the mighty**
are of *the LORD* **Yah Veh**;
how can a *man then* **human**
understand **discern** his own way?
25 It is a snare to the *man* **human**
who *devoureth* **hastily cheweth** that which is holy,
and after vows to *make enquiry* **search**.
26 A wise *king* **sovereign**
scattereth **winnoweth** the wicked,
and *bringeth* **turneth** the wheel over them.
27 The *spirit* **breath** of *man* **humanity**
is the *candle* **lamp** of *the LORD* **Yah Veh**,
searching all the *inward parts* **chambers** of the belly.
28 Mercy and truth *preserve*
guard the *king* **sovereign**:
and his throne is upholden by mercy.
29 The *glory* **beauty** of *young men* **youths**
is their *strength* **force**:
and the *beauty* **majesty** of *old men* **elders**
is the *grey head* **greyness**.
30 The *blueness* **lashes** of a wound
cleanseth away **purify** evil:
so *do stripes* **strokes** the inward parts of the belly.

21 The *king's* **sovereign's** heart
is in the hand of *the LORD* **Yah Veh**,
as the *rivers* **rivulets** of water:
he *turneth* **spreadeth** it whithersoever he *will* **desire**.
2 Every way of a man is *right*
straight in his own eyes:
but *the LORD pondereth* **Yah Veh gaugeth** the hearts.
3 *To do* **Choose to work** justice and judgment
is more acceptable to the LORD **unto Yah Veh**
rather than sacrifice.
4 An high look, and a *proud* **broad** heart,
and the plowing of the wicked, is sin.
5 The *thoughts* **fabrications**
of the *diligent* **decisive**
tend **be** only to *plenteousness* **advantage**; but
of every one that is hasty only to want.
6 The *getting* **deeds** of treasures
by a *lying* **false** tongue
is a vanity
tossed to and fro **dispersed** of them that seek death.
7 The *robbery* **devastation** of the wicked
shall *destroy* **cut** them;
because they refuse to *do* **work** judgment.
8 The way of **a guilty** man is
froward and strange **perverse**:
but as for the pure, his *work* **deed** is *right* **straight**.
9 It is better to *dwell* **settle**
in a corner of the *housetop* **roof**,
than with a *brawling* **contentious** woman
in a *wide* **community** house.
10 The soul of the wicked desireth evil:
his *neighbour* **friend**
findeth **granteth** no *favour* **charism** in his eyes.
11 When the scorner is *punished* **penalized**,
the *simple is made wise* **gullible enwiseneth**:
and when the wise *is instructed* **comprehendeth**,
he *receiveth* **taketh** knowledge.
12 The *righteous man* **Just One**
wisely considereth **comprehendeth**
the house of the wicked:
but *God overthroweth* **perverteth** the wicked
for their *wickedness* **evil**.
13 Whoso *stoppeth* **shutteth** his ears
at the cry of the poor,
he also shall *cry* **call out** himself,
but shall not be *heard* **answered**.
14 A **covert** gift *in secret*
pacifieth anger **tameth wrath**:
and a *reward* **bribe** in the bosom strong *wrath* **fury**.
extinguishes his lamp in mid darkness.
21 An inheritance first obtained by avarice;
is not blessed at its finality.
22 Say not, I shalam for evil;
await Yah Veh and he saves you.

23 A stone and a stone
are an abhorrence to Yah Veh;
and balances of deceit are not good.
24 The paces of the mighty are of Yah Veh;
how discerns a human his own way?
25 It is a snare to the human
who hastily chews what is holy and
vows to search afterward.
26 A wise sovereign winnows the wicked
and turns the wheel over them.
27 The breath of humanity is the lamp of Yah Veh,
searching all the chambers of the belly.
28 Mercy and truth guard the sovereign;
and upholds his throne by mercy.
29 The beauty of youths is their force;
and the majesty of elders is the greyness.
30 The lashes of a wound purify evil;
thus strokes the inward parts of the belly.

21 The heart of the sovereign
is in the hand of Yah Veh;
as the rivulets of water
he spreads it wherever he desires.
2 Every way of a man is straight in his own eyes;
and Yah Veh gauges the heart.
3 To work justice and judgment
is chosen of Yah Veh, rather than sacrifice.
4 A high look and a broad heart
and the plowing of the wicked, *is* sin.
5 The fabrications of the decisive
are only to advantage;
and of all the hasty
only to want.
6 The deeds of treasures by a false tongue
is a vanity dispersed by them who seek death.
7 The devastation of the wicked cuts them;
because they refuse to work judgment.
8 Perverse *is* the way of a man of guilt;
and the deed of the pure *is* straight.
9 Better, to settle in a corner of the roof,
than with a contentious woman
in a community house.
10 The soul of the wicked desires evil;
his friend grants no charism in his eyes.
11 When the scorner is penalized,
the gullible enwisen;
and when the wise comprehend,
he takes knowledge.
12 The Just One comprehends
the house of the wicked;
perverting the wicked for their evil.
13 Whoever shuts his ears at the cry of the poor,
calls, but is not answered.
14 A covert gift tames wrath;
and a bribe in the bosom, strong fury.
15 It is *joy* **cheerfulness** to the
just to *do* **work** judgment:
but *destruction* **ruin** shall be
to the workers of *iniquity* **mischief**.
16 The *man* **human** that *wandereth* **strayeth**
out of the way of *understanding* **comprehension**
shall *remain* **rest** in the congregation of *the dead* **ghosts**.
17 He that loveth *pleasure* **cheerfulness**
shall be a *poor* man **of lack**:
he that loveth wine and *oil* **ointment**
shall not *be rich* **enrich**.
18 The wicked
shall be *a ransom* **a koper/an atonement**
for the *righteous* **just**,
and *the transgressor* **they who deal covertly**
for the *upright* **straight**.
19 It is better to *dwell* **settle** in
the **land of the** wilderness,
than with a *contentious* **woman of contentions**
and *an angry woman* **vexations**.
20 There is treasure to be desired and *oil* **ointment**
in the *dwelling* **habitation of rest** of the wise;
but a foolish *man spendeth* **human swalloweth** it up.
21 He that *followeth* **pursueth**
after righteousness **justness** and mercy
findeth life, *righteousness* **justness**, and honour.
22 *A* **The** wise *man scaleth* **ascendeth**
the city of the mighty,
and *casteth down* **toppleth**
the strength of the confidence *thereof*.
23 Whoso *keepeth* **guardeth**
his mouth and his tongue
keepeth **guardeth** his soul from *troubles* **tribulations**.
24 Proud, *and haughty* **arrogant:**
scorner is his name,
who *dealeth* **worketh**
in proud wrath **the fury of arrogance**.
25 The desire of the *slothful*
killeth **sloth deathifieth** him;
for his hands refuse to *labour* **work**.
26 *He coveteth greedily* **In desiring,**
he desireth all the day long:
but the *righteous* **just** giveth and spareth not.
27 The sacrifice of the wicked
is *abomination* **abhorrence**:
how much more,

when he bringeth it with *a wicked mind* **intrigue**?
28 A *false* witness **of lies** shall *perish* **destruct**:
but the man that heareth
speaketh constantly **wordeth in perpetuity**.
29 A wicked man *hardeneth*
strengtheneth his face:
but *as for the upright* **the straight**,
he *directeth* **establisheth** his way.
30 There is no wisdom nor
understanding **discernment**
nor counsel against *the LORD* **Yah Veh**.
31 The horse is prepared
against the day of *battle* **war**:
but *safety* **salvation** is of *the LORD* **Yah Veh**.

22 A *good* name
is rather to be chosen than great riches,
and *loving favour* **good charism**
rather than silver and gold.
2 The rich and *poor* **impoverished** meet together:
the LORD **Yah Veh** is the *maker* **Worker** of them all.
3 *A prudent man foreseeth*
The subtle seeth the evil,
and hideth himself:
but the *simple* **gullible** pass on,
and are *punished* **penalized**.
4 *By* **The finality of** humility
and the *fear* **awe** of *the LORD* **Yah Veh**
are riches, and honour, and life.
5 Thorns and snares
are in the way of the *froward* **pervert**:
he that *doth keep* **guardeth** his soul
shall be far from them.
6 *Train up a child* **Hanukkah a lad by mouth**
in the way he should go **about his way**:
and when he *is old* **ageth**,
he *will* **shall** not *depart* **turn aside** from it.
7 The rich *ruleth* **reigneth**
over the *poor* **impoverished**,
and the borrower is servant
to the *lender* **man that lendeth**.
8 He that *soweth iniquity* **seedeth wickedness**
shall *reap vanity* **harvest mischief**:
and the *rod* **scion** of his *anger* **fury**
shall *fail* **be finished off**.
15 For the just to work judgment is cheerfulness;
and ruin to the workers of mischief.
16 The human
who strays from the way of comprehension
rests in the congregation of ghosts.
17 Whoever loves cheerfulness is a man of lack;
whoever loves wine and ointment enriches not.
18 The wicked
are a koper/an atonement for the just;
and they who deal covertly
for the straight.
19 Better, to settle in the land of the wilderness,
than with a woman of contentions and vexations.
20 A treasure to be desired, and ointment
is in the habitation of rest of the wise;
and a foolish human swallows it.
21 He who pursues justness and mercy
finds life, justness and honor.
22 The wise ascend the city of the mighty
and topple the strength of the confidence.
23 Whoever guards his mouth and his tongue
guards his soul from tribulations.
24 Proud, arrogant: scorner is his name,
who works the fury of arrogance.
25 The desire of the sloth deathifies him;
for his hands refuse to work.
26 In desiring, he desires all the day long;
and the just gives and spares not.
27 The sacrifice of the wicked *is* abhorrence;
how much more, when he brings it with intrigue?
28 A witness of lies destructs;
and the man who hears, words in perpetuity.
29 A wicked man strengthens his face;
and the straight establishes his way.
30 There is neither wisdom nor discernment
nor counsel against Yah Veh.
31 The horse is prepared against the day of war;
and salvation is of Yah Veh.

22 Choose a name rather than great riches;
and good charism rather than silver and gold.
2 The rich and impoverished meet together;
Yah Veh is the Worker of them all.
3 The subtle sees the evil and hides himself;
and the gullible pass on and *are* penalized.
4 The finality of humility and to awe Yah Veh
are riches and honor and life.
5 Thorns and snares *are* in the way of the pervert;
he who guards his soul is far from them.
6 Hanukkah a lad by mouth about his way;
and when he ages, he turns not aside from it.
7 The rich reign over the impoverished
and the borrower is servant to the man who lends.
8 Whoever seeds wickedness, harvests mischief;
and the scion of his fury *is* finished off.
9 He that hath a *bountiful*
good eye shall be blessed;

for he giveth of his bread to the poor.
10 *Cast out* **Exile** the scorner,
and contention shall go out;
yea, *strife* **pleading** and *reproach*
abasement shall *cease* **shabbathize.**
11 He that loveth pureness of heart,
for the *grace* **charism** of his lips the *king*
sovereign shall be his friend.
12 The eyes of *the LORD* **Yah**
Veh preserve knowledge,
and he *overthroweth* **perverteth** the words
of *the transgressor* **them who deal covertly.**
13 The *slothful man* **sloth** saith,
There is a lion without, **A lion in the outways!**
I shall be *slain in* **murdered within**
the *streets* **broadways.**
14 The mouth of *strange women* **strangers**
is a *deep pit* **chasm:**
he that *is abhorred of the LORD* **enrageth Yah Veh**
shall fall therein.
15 *Foolishness* **Folly** is bound
in the heart of a *child* **lad;**
but the *rod* **scion** of *correction* **discipline**
shall *drive* **remove** it far from him.
16 He *that* oppresseth the poor to *increase his*
riches **abound,** and he *that* giveth to the rich,
shall surely come to want **only to lack.**
17 *Bow down* **Spread** thine ear,
and hear the words of the wise,
and *apply* **set** thine heart unto my knowledge.
18 For it is a *pleasant thing* **pleasure**
if thou *keep* **guard** them within *thee* **thy belly;**
they shall *withal be fitted* **be established** in thy lips.
19 That thy *trust* **confidence**
may be in *the LORD* **Yah Veh,**
I have made known to thee this day, even to thee.
20 Have not I *written* **scribed** to thee
excellent things **thrice** in counsels and knowledge,
21 That I might *make* **have** thee know
the *certainty* **truth** of the *words* **sayings** of truth;
that thou mightest *answer* **respond**
to the *words* **sayings** of truth
to them that send unto thee?
22 *Rob* **Strip** not the poor, because he is poor:
neither *oppress* **crush** the *afflicted* **humble**
in the *gate* **portal:**
23 For *the LORD* **Yah Veh**
will plead **shall defend** their *cause* **defence,**
and *spoil* **defraud** the soul
of those that *spoiled* **defrauded** them.
24 *Make no friendship* **Befriend not**
with an angry man **a master of fury;** and
with a furious man thou shalt not go:
25 Lest thou *learn* **be taught** his ways,
and *get* **take** a snare to thy soul.
26 Be not thou *one* of them that
strike hands **clap palms,**
or of them that *are sureties* **pledge** for *debts* **loans.**
27 If thou hast *nothing* **naught** to *pay* **shalam,**
why should he take away thy bed from under thee?
28 Remove not the *ancient*
landmark **eternal border,**
which thy fathers have *set* **worked.**
29 Seest thou a man *diligent*
skillful in his *business* **work?**
he shall *stand before kings* **set at the face of sovereigns;**
he shall not *stand* **set**
before mean men **at the face of darkness.**

23 When thou *sittest* **settlest**
to eat with a *ruler* **sovereign,**
consider diligently **in discerning,**
discern what is *before thee* **at thy face:**
2 And *put* **set** a knife to thy throat,
if *thou be a man given to appetite* **thy soul be thy master.**
3 *Be not desirous* **Desire not**
of his *dainties* **delicacies:**
for they are *deceitful meat* **a bread of lies.**
4 Labour not to *be rich* **enrich:**
cease from thine own *wisdom* **discernment.**
5 *Wilt* **Shalt** thou *set* **flit** thine eyes
upon that which is not?
for *riches certainly make themselves*
in working, they work wings;
they fly away as an eagle toward *heaven* **the heavens.**
9 He who has a good eye is blessed;
for he gives of his bread to the poor.
10 Exile the scorner and contention goes out;
yes, pleading and abasement shabbathize.
11 Whoever loves pureness of heart,
his lips *are* charism; the sovereign his friend.
12 The eyes of Yah Veh preserve knowledge
and he perverts the words
of them who deal covertly.
13 The sloth says, A lion in the outways!
I am murdered within the broadways.
14 The mouth of strangers is a chasm;
he who enrages Yah Veh falls therein.
15 Folly is bound in the heart of a lad;
and the scion of discipline removes it far from him.
16 He oppresses the poor to abound

and he gives to the rich only to lack.
17 Spread your ear and hear the words of the wise
and set your heart to my knowledge:
18 for they are a pleasure
if you guard them within your belly:
they are established for your lips:
19 that your confidence be in Yah Veh,
I make known to you this day—even to you.
20 Scribed I not thrice to you
in counsels and knowledge,
21 so that you know the truth
of the sayings of truth
—to respond to the sayings of truth
to them who send to you?
22 Neither strip the poor, because he *is* poor;
nor crush the humble in the portal;
23 for Yah Veh defends their defence
and defrauds the soul of their defrauders.
24 Neither befriend a master of fury;
nor go with a man of fury;
25 lest you *be* taught his ways
and take a snare to your soul.
26 Be not of them who clap palms,
or of them who pledge for loans.
27 If you have naught to shalam,
why take your bed from under you?
28 Remove not the eternal border,
your fathers worked.
29 See a man skillful in his work?
He sets at the face of sovereigns;
he sets not at the face of darkness.

23 When you settle to eat with a sovereign,
in discerning, discern what *is* at your face;
2 and set a knife to your throat,
if your soul *is* your master.
3 Neither desire his delicacies
for they are a bread of lies:
4 nor labor to enrich;
cease from your own discernment.
5 Flit your eyes thereon; and it is not:
for in working, they work wings;
they fly away as an eagle toward the heavens.
6 Eat thou not the bread of
him that hath an evil eye,
neither desire thou his *dainty meats* **delicacies**:
7 For as he *thinketh* **guardeth**
in his *heart* **soul**, so is he:
Eat and drink, saith he to thee;
but his heart is not with thee.
8 The morsel which thou hast eaten
shalt thou dost vomit *up*,
and *lose* **ruin** thy *sweet* **pleasant** words.
9 *Speak* **Word** not in the ears of a fool:
for he *will despise* **shall disrespect**
the *wisdom* **comprehension** of thy *words* **utterances**.
10 Remove not the *old landmark* **eternal border**;
and enter not into the fields of the *fatherless* **orphan**:
11 For their redeemer is *mighty* **strong**;
he shall *plead* **defend** their *cause* **defence** with thee.
12 Apply thine heart unto *instruction* **discipline**,
and thine ears to the words of knowledge.
13 Withhold not *correction*
discipline from the *child* **lad**:
for if thou beatest **when thou smittest**
him with the *rod* **scion**,
he shall not die.
14 Thou shalt *beat* **smite** him with the *rod* **scion**,
and shalt *deliver* **rescue** his soul from *hell* **sheol**.
15 My son, if thine heart *be wise* **enwisen**,
my heart shall *rejoice* **cheer**, even mine.
16 Yea, my reins shall rejoice,
when thy lips *speak right things* **word straightnesses**.
17 Let not thine heart envy sinners:
but *be thou in the fear of the LORD* **awe thou Yah Veh**
all the day long.
18 For surely there is *an end* **a finality**;
and thine *expectation* **hope** shall not be cut off.
19 Hear thou, my son, and *be wise* **enwisen**,
and *guide* **blithe** thine heart in the way.
20 Be not among *winebibbers* **wine carousers**;
among *riotous eaters* **gluttons** of flesh:
21 For the *drunkard* **carouser** and the glutton
shall *come to poverty* **be dispossessed**:
and drowsiness shall *clothe a man*
enrobe with *rags* **shreds**.
22 Hearken unto thy father that *begat* **birthed** thee,
and *despise* **disrespect** not thy mother
when she *is old* **ageth**.
23 *Buy* **Chattelize** the truth, and sell it not;
also wisdom, and *instruction* **discipline**,
and *understanding* **discernment**.
24 The father of the *righteous* **just**
in twirling, shall *greatly rejoice* **twirl**:
and he that *begetteth a* **birtheth the** wise *child*
shall *have joy of* **cheer in** him.
25 Thy father and thy mother shall *be glad* **cheer**,
and she that *bare* **birthed** thee shall *rejoice* **twirl**.
26 My son, give me thine heart,
and let thine eyes *observe* **guard** my ways.
27 For a whore is a deep *ditch* **chasm**;

and a *strange woman* **stranger** is a narrow *pit* **well.**
28 She also *lieth in wait* **lurketh**
as *for a prey* **a robber,**
and increaseth *the transgressors* **them who**
deal covertly among *men* **humanity.**
29 Who hath woe? who hath *sorrow* **the will**?
who hath contentions? who hath *babbling* **meditation**?
who hath wounds *without cause* **gratuitously**?
who hath *redness* **flushness** of eyes?
30 They that *tarry long* **linger** at the wine;
they that go to *seek mixed wine* **probe cocktails.**
31 *Look* **See** not thou upon the wine
when it *is red* **hath reddened,**
when it giveth his *colour* **eye** in the *cup* **pouch,**
when it *moveth itself aright* **passeth in straightnesses.**
32 *At the last* **Finally** it biteth like a serpent,
and *stingeth* **woundeth** like *an adder* **a hisser.**
33 Thine eyes shall *behold* **see** strange women,
and thine heart shall *utter perverse*
things **word perversions.**
34 Yea, thou shalt be
as he that lieth down in the *midst* **heart** of the sea,
or as he that lieth upon the top of a mast.
35 They have *stricken* **smitten** me, *shalt thou say,*
and I was not sick;
they have *beaten* **hammered** me, and I *felt* **knew** it not:
when shall I awake?
I *will* **shall** seek it *yet* again **and again.**
6 Neither eat the bread of an evil eye
nor desire his delicacies;
7 for as he guards in his soul, thus *is* he:
Eat and drink, he says to you;
but his heart *is* not with you.
8 Vomit the morsel you ate
and ruin your pleasant words.
9 Word not in the ears of a fool;
for he disrespects
the comprehension of your utterances.
10 Neither remove the eternal border;
nor enter the fields of the orphan;
11 for their redeemer is strong:
he defends their defence with you.
12 Apply your heart to discipline
and your ears to the words of knowledge.
13 Withhold not discipline from the lad;
when you smite him with the scion, he dies not:
14 smite him with the scion
and rescue his soul from sheol.
15 My son, if your heart enwisens,
my heart cheers—even mine.
16 yes, my reins rejoice
when your lips word straightnesses.
17 O that your heart not envy sinners;
and awe Yah Veh all the day long.
18 For surely there is a finality;
then your hope is not cut off.
19 Hear you, my son and enwisen
and blithe your heart in the way.
20 Be not among carousers of wine
—among gluttons of flesh;
21 for the carouser and the glutton
become dispossessed;
and drowsiness enrobes with shreds.
22 Hearken to your father who birthed you
and disrespect not your mother when she ages.
23 Chattelize the truth; sell it not
—wisdom and discipline and discernment.
24 In twirling, the father of the just twirls;
and he who births the wise cheers in him.
25 Your father and your mother cheer
and she who birthed you twirls.
26 My son, give me your heart
so that your eyes guard my ways.
27 For a whore *is* a deep chasm;
and a stranger *is* a narrow well.
28 She also lurks as a robber
and increases them
who deal covertly among humanity.
29 Who has woe?
Who has will?
Who has contentions?
Who has meditation?
Who has wounds gratuitously?
Who has flushness of eyes?
30 They who linger at the wine;
they who go to probe cocktails.
31 See not on the wine when it reddens—when it gives
its eye in the pouch—when it passes in straightnesses:
32 and finally bites as a serpent
and wounds as a hisser.
33 Your eyes see strange women
and your heart words perversions:
34 yes, you—as he who lies in the heart of the sea
—as he who lies on the top of a mast.
35 They smote me, and I was not sick;
they hammered me, and I knew it not.
When waken I?
I seek it again and again.

24 Be not thou envious against evil men,
neither desire to be with them.
2 For their heart

studieth destruction **meditateth devastation,**
and their lips *talk* **word** of *mischief* **toil.**
3 Through wisdom is an house builded;
and by *understanding* **discernment** it is established:
4 And by knowledge shall the chambers be filled
with all *precious* **esteemed** and pleasant *riches* **wealth.**
5 *A* **The** wise *man is strong* **is mighty in strength;**
yea, a man of knowledge
increaseth strength **strengtheneth force.**
6 For by *wise counsel* **counsels**
thou shalt *make* **work** thy war:
and in *multitude* **abundance** of counsellors
there is *safety* **salvation.**
7 Wisdom is too high for a fool:
he openeth not his mouth in the *gate* **portal.**
8 He that *deviseth* **fabricateth** to *do evil* **vilify**
shall be called a *mischievous person* **master of intrigue.**
9 The *thought* **intrigue** of *foolishness* **folly** is sin:
and the scorner
is an *abomination* **abhorrence** to *men* **humanity.**
10 If thou *faint* **slacken** in the
day of *adversity* **tribulation,**
thy *strength* **force** is *small* **tribulated.**
11 If thou *forbear* **spare** to *deliver* **rescue**
them that are *drawn* **taken** unto death,
and those that
are ready to be slain **totter from the slaughter;**
12 If thou sayest, Behold, we knew it not;
doth not he that *pondereth* **gaugeth** the heart
consider **discern** it?
and he that *keepeth* **guardeth** thy soul,
doth not he know it?
and shall not he *render* **return**
to *every man* **all humanity**
according to his *works* **deeds?**
13 My son, eat thou honey, because it is good;
and the honeycomb, which is sweet to thy *taste* **palate:**
14 So shall the knowledge of
wisdom be unto thy soul:
when thou hast found it,
then there shall be a *reward* **finality,**
and thy *expectation* **hope** shall not be cut off.
15 *Lay not wait* **Lurk not,** O wicked *man,*
against the *dwelling* **habitation of rest**
of the *righteous* **just;**
spoil **ravage** not his *resting place* **repose:**
16 For *a* **the** just *man* falleth seven *times,*
and riseth *up again:*
but the wicked shall fall into *mischief* **evil.**
17 *Rejoice* **Cheer** not when thine enemy falleth,
and let not thine heart *be glad* **twirl** when he stumbleth:
18 Lest *the LORD* **Yah Veh** see it,
and it *displease him* **vilify in his eye,**
and he turn away his wrath from him.
19 *Fret* **Inflame** not thyself
because of evil men **at vilifiers,**
neither be thou envious at the wicked:
20 For there shall be no *reward*
finality to the evil *man;*
the *candle* **lamp** of the wicked
shall be *put out* **extinguished.**
21 My son,
fear **awe** thou *the LORD* **Yah Veh** and the *king* **sovereign:**
and meddle not with them
that *are given to change* **reiterate:**
22 For their calamity shall rise suddenly;
and who knoweth the *ruin* **calamity** of them both?
23 These *things* also *belong* **be** to the wise.
It is not good
to *have respect of persons* **recognize faces** in judgment.
24 He that saith unto the wicked,
Thou art *righteous* **just;**
him shall the people *curse* **pierce,**
nations shall *abhor* **enrage at** him:
25 But *to* them that *rebuke* **reprove** him
shall be *delight* **pleased,**
and a good blessing shall come upon them.
26 *Every man* **lie** shall kiss *his* **the** lips that
giveth a right answer **respond straightforward words.**

24 Neither be envious against evil men
nor desire to be with them:
2 for their heart meditates devastation
and their lips word of toil.
3 By wisdom, the house is built;
and by discernment, established;
4 and by knowledge, the chambers filled
with all esteemed and pleasant wealth.
5 The wise *are* mighty in strength;
yes, a man of knowledge strengthens force.
6 For by counsels, you work war;
and in abundance of counsellors, there *is* salvation.
7 Wisdom is too high for a fool;
he opens not his mouth in the portal.
8 Whoever fabricates to vilify
they call a master of intrigue.
9 The intrigue of folly is sin;
and the scorner is an abhorrence to humanity.
10 If you slacken in the day of tribulation,
your force is tribulated.
11 If you spare to rescue them

who are taken to death
and them who totter from the slaughter;
12 if you say, Behold, we knew it not;
Discerns he not, who gauges the heart?
Knows he not, who guards your soul?
—who returns to humanity according to his deeds?
13 My son, eat honey, because it is good;
and the honeycomb—sweet to your palate;
14 thus *is* the knowledge of wisdom to your soul;
when you find, then there is a finality
and your hope is not cut off.
15 Lurk not, O wicked,
against the habitation of rest of the just;
ravage not his repose:
16 for the just fall and rise by sevens;
and the wicked fall into evil.
17 Neither cheer when your enemy falls
nor twirl your heart when he stumbles;
18 lest Yah Veh sees it and it vilifies in his eye
and he turns away his wrath from him.
19 Neither inflame at vilifiers,
nor be envious of the wicked;
20 for there is no finality to the evil;
the lamp of the wicked extinguishes.
21 My son, awe Yah Veh and the sovereign;
meddle not with them who reiterate;
22 for their calamity rises suddenly;
and who knows the calamity of them both?
23 These also to the wise:
It is not good
to recognize faces in judgment.
24 He who says to the wicked, You are just
—the people pierce, nations enrage at him;
25 and they who reprove him are pleased;
and a good blessing comes on them.
26 He kisses the lips
that respond straightforward words.
27 Prepare thy work *without* **in the outways**,
and *make it fit for thyself* **ready it** in the field;
and afterwards build thine house.
28 Be not a witness against thy *neighbour* **friend**
without cause **gratuitously**;
and *deceive* **entice** not with thy lips.
29 Say not, I *will do so* **shall work** to him
as he hath *done* **worked** to me:
I *will render* **shall return** to the man
according to his *work* **deeds**.
30 I *went* **passed** by the field
of the *slothful* **man of sloth**,
and by the vineyard of the *man* **human**
void of understanding **that lacketh heart**;
31 And, *lo* **behold**,
it was all *grown over* **ascended** with *thorns* **thistles**,
and nettles had covered the face *thereof*,
and the stone wall *thereof* was broken down.
32 Then I saw, and *considered it* **set my heart** well:
I *looked upon it* **saw**,
and *received instruction* **took discipline**.
33 *Yet* a little sleep, a little *slumber* **drowsiness**,
a little *folding* **clasping** of the hands to *sleep* **lie down**:
34 So shall thy poverty come as one that travelleth;
and thy *want* **lack** as *an armed man* **a man with buckler**.

25 These are also proverbs of *Solomon* **Shelomoh**,
which the men of *Hezekiah* **Yechizqi Yah,**
king **sovereign** of *Judah* **Yah Hudah**
copied out **transcribed**.
2 It is the *glory* **honour** of *God* **Elohim**
to *conceal* **hide** a *thing* **word**:
but the honour of *kings* **sovereigns** is to
search out **probe** a *matter* **word**.
3 The *heaven* **heavens** for height,
and the earth for depth,
and the heart of *kings* **sovereigns**
is unsearchable **are not to be probed**.
4 *Take away* **Remove** the dross from the silver,
and there shall come forth
a vessel **an instrument** for *the finer* **refining**.
5 *Take away* **Remove** the wicked
from *before* **the face of** the *king* **sovereign**,
and his throne
shall be established in *righteousness* **justness**.
6 *Put* **Esteem** not *forth* thyself
in the presence **at the face** of the *king* **sovereign**,
and stand not in the place of great *men*:
7 For better it is that it be said unto thee,
Come up **Ascend** hither;
than that thou shouldest be *put lower* **abased**
in the presence **at the face** of the *prince* **volunteer**
whom thine eyes have seen.
8 Go not forth hastily to strive,
lest *thou know not what to do* **what thou workest**
in the *end thereof* **finality**,
when thy *neighbour* **friend**
hath *put thee to shame* **shamed thee?**
9 *Debate* **Defend** thy *cause* **defence**
with thy *neighbour himself* **friend**;
and *discover* **expose** not a *secret* **private counsel**
to another:
10 Lest he that heareth *it put thee to* shame **thee**,
and thine *infamy* **slander** turn not away.

11 A word *fitly spoken* **roundly worded**
is *like* apples of gold in *pictures* **imageries** of silver.
12 As *an earring* **a nosering** of gold,
and an ornament of *fine gold* **ore**,
so is a wise reprover upon an *obedient* **hearkening** ear.
13 As the cold of snow in the *time* **day** of harvest,
so is a *faithful messenger* **trustworthy ambassador**
to them that send him:
for he *refresheth* **restoreth** the soul
of his *masters* **adonim**.
14 *Whoso boasteth* **The man who halaleth** himself
of a false gift
is *like clouds* **vapour** and wind without *rain* **downpour**.
15 By long *forbearing* **wrath**
is a *prince persuaded* **commander enticed**, and
a *soft* **tender** tongue breaketh the bone.
27 Prepare your work in the outways
and ready it in the field;
and afterward build your house.
28 Neither witness against your friend gratuitously;
nor entice with your lips.
29 Say not, I work to him as he worked to me;
—return to the man according to his deeds.
30 I passed by the field of the man of sloth
and by the vineyard of the human lacking heart;
31 and behold, it all ascends with thistles
and nettles cover the face
and the stone wall is broken down.
32 Then I see and set my heart well
—I see and take discipline.
33 A little sleep; a little drowsiness;
a little clasping of the hands to lie down:
34 and so be your poverty as one who travels;
and your lack as a man with buckler.

25 These are also proverbs of Shelomoh;
which the men of Yechizqi Yah,
sovereign of Yah Hudah, transcribed.
2 The honor of Elohim *is* to hide a word;
and the honor of sovereigns to probe a word.
3 The heavens for height, and the earth for depth,
and the heart of sovereigns, probe not.
4 Remove the dross from the silver
and an instrument for refining comes forth.
5 Remove the wicked from
the face of the sovereign
and his throne is established in justness.
6 Neither esteem yourself
at the face of the sovereign;
nor stand in the place of greatness.
7 Better to say to you, Ascend hither;
than abased at the face of the volunteer
whom your eyes have seen.
8 Go not forth hastily to strive,
What work you
when your friend finally shames you?
9 Defend your defence with your friend;
and expose not a private counsel to another;
10 lest he who hears shames you
and your slander turns not away.
11 A word roundly worded
is apples of gold in imageries of silver:
12 as a nosering of gold and an ornament of ore,
thus *is* a wise reprover to a hearkening ear.
13 As the cold of snow in the day of harvest,
thus is a trustworthy ambassador
to them who send him;
for he restores the soul of his adonim.
14 The man who halals himself of a false gift
is as vapour and wind without downpour.
15 By long wrath is a commander enticed
and a tender tongue breaks the bone.
16 Hast thou found honey?
eat so much as is sufficient for thee,
lest thou be *filled therewith* **satiated**, and vomit it.
17 *Withdraw* **Esteem** thy foot
from thy *neighbour's* **friend's** house;
lest he be *weary* **satiated** of thee, and *so* hate thee.
18 A man that *beareth* **answereth** false witness
against his *neighbour* **friend** is a *maul* **mallet**,
and a sword, and a *sharp* **pointened** arrow.
19 Confidence
in *an unfaithful man* **one who dealeth covertly**
in *time* **a day** of *trouble* **tribulation**
is *like* a broken tooth, and a **dislocated** foot *out of joint*.
20 As he that *taketh away a*
garment **removeth clothes**
in **on a** cold *weather* **day**,
and as vinegar upon nitre,
so is he that singeth songs to an *heavy* **evil** heart.
21 If *thine enemy be hungry* **he**
that hateth thee famish,
give him bread to eat;
and if he *be thirsty* **thirst**, give him water to drink:
22 For thou shalt *heap* **take**
coals *of fire* upon his head,
and *the LORD* **Yah Veh** shall *reward* **shalam** thee.
23 The north wind
driveth away rain **whirleth the downpour**:
so doth an *angry countenance* **enraged face**
a *backbiting* **covert** tongue.

24 It is better to *dwell* **settle**
in the corner of the *housetop* **roof**,
than with a *brawling* **contentious** woman
and in a *wide* **community** house.
25 As cold waters to a *thirsty* **languid** soul,
so is *good news* **a report** from a far *country* **land**.
26 *A righteous man falling down* **The just tottering**
before **at the face of** the wicked
is as *a troubled* **an agitated** fountain,
and a *corrupt spring* **ruined fountain**.
27 It is not good to eat *much* **abundant** honey:
so for men to search their own glory is not glory.
nor honour to probe their own honour.
28 *He that hath no rule* **The man without control**
over his own spirit
is *like* a city that is *broken down* **breached**,
and without walls.

26 As snow in summer, and as rain in harvest,
so honour is not *seemly* **befitting** for a fool.
2 As the bird by wandering,
as the swallow by flying,
so *the curse causeless* **abasing**
shall not come **gratuitously**.
3 A whip for the horse,
a *bridle* **bit** for the *ass* **he burro**,
and a *rod* **scion** for the fool's back.
4 Answer not a fool according to his folly,
lest thou also be *like* **likened** unto him.
5 Answer a fool according to his folly,
lest he be wise in his own *conceit* **eyes**.
6 He that sendeth *a message*
word by the hand of a fool
cutteth off the feet, and drinketh *damage* **violence**.
7 The legs of the lame *are not equal* **languish**:
so is a *parable* **proverb** in the mouth of fools.
8 As he that *bindeth* **bundleth** a stone
in a *sling* **stoneheap**,
so is he that giveth honour to a fool.
9 As a thorn *goeth up* **ascendeth**
into the hand of *a drunkard* **one intoxicated**, so
is a *parable* **proverb** in the mouths of fools.
10 *The great God that formed*
Great is the whirler of all *things*;
both rewardeth **he hireth** the fool,
and *rewardeth* **hireth** transgressors.
11 As a dog returneth to his vomit,
so a fool *returneth to* **repeateth** his folly.
12 Seest thou a man wise in his own *conceit* **eyes**?
there is more hope of a fool than of him.
13 The *slothful man* **sloth** saith,
There is a **A roaring** lion in the way; a
lion is in the *streets* **broadways**.
14 As the door turneth upon his hinges,
16 Find you honey?
eat as much as suffices you,
lest you satiate and vomit.
17 Esteem your foot from the house of your friend;
lest he be satiated of you and hate you.
18 A man
who answers false witness against his friend is a
mallet and a sword and a pointened arrow.
19 Confidence in one who deals covertly
in a day of tribulation
is as a broken tooth and a dislocated foot.
20 Whoever removes clothes on a cold day
is as vinegar on nitre
—as he who sings songs to an evil heart.
21 If he who hates you famishes,
give him bread to eat;
and if he thirsts,
give him water to drink:
22 for you take coals on his head,
and Yah Veh shalams you.
23 The north wind whirls the downpour;
and an enraged face, a covert tongue.
24 Better, to settle in the corner of the roof
than with a contentious woman
in a community house.
25 As cold waters to a languid soul,
thus *is* a report from a far land.
26 The just tottering at the face of the wicked
is as an agitated fountain and a ruined fountain.
27 It is neither good to eat abundant honey;
nor honor to probe their own honor.
28 The man without control over his own spirit
is as a city breached and without walls.

26 As snow in summer;
as rain in harvest;
thus honor befits not a fool:
2 As the bird by wandering;
as the swallow by flying;
thus abasing comes not gratuitously.
3 A whip for the horse; a bit for the he burro;
and a scion for the back of a fool.
4 Answer not a fool according to his folly
lest you also be likened to him—even you;
5 answer a fool according to his folly
lest he be wise in his own eyes.
6 He who sends word by the hand of a fool
cuts off the feet and drinks violence.

7 The legs of the lame languish;
as a proverb in the mouth of fools.
8 As he who bundles a stone in a stoneheap
thus he who gives honor to a fool.
9 As a thorn ascends into
the hand of the intoxicated
thus a proverb in the mouths of fools.
10 Great is the whirler of all;
he hires the fool and hires transgressors.
11 As a dog returns to his vomit,
thus a fool repeats his folly.
12 See a man wise in his own eyes?
More hope of a fool than of him.
13 The sloth says,
A roaring lion in the way
—a lion in the broadways.
14 As the door turns on its hinge,
so *doth* the *slothful* **sloth** upon his bed.
15 The *slothful* **sloth** hideth his hand in his bosom;
it *grieveth* **wearieth** him
to *bring* **return** it *again* to his mouth.
16 The *sluggard* **sloth** is wiser
in his own *conceit* **eyes**
than seven men that can *render a reason* **return taste**.
17 He that passeth by,
and meddleth with strife *belonging not to him* **not his**,
is *like* one that *taketh* **upholdeth** a dog by the ears.
18 As *a mad man* **the rabid**
who *casteth firebrands* **shooteth fiery darts**,
arrows, and death,
19 So is the man that deceiveth
his *neighbour* **friend**,
and saith, Am not I *in sport* **laughing**?
20 Where *no wood* **the final timber** is,
there the fire goeth out:
so where there is no *talebearer* **whisperer**,
the strife *ceaseth* **subsideth**.
21 As coals *are to burning* **to** coals,
and *wood* **timber** to fire;
so is a contentious man to *kindle* **scorch** strife.
22 The words of a *talebearer* **whisperer**
are as wounds **inflame**,
and they *go down* **descend**
into the *innermost parts* **chambers** of the belly.
23 *Burning* **Inflamed** lips
and *a wicked* **an evil** heart
are *like* a potsherd *covered* **overlaid** with silver dross.
24 He that hateth
dissembleth with **is recognized by** his lips,
and *layeth up* **placeth** deceit within him;
25 When *he speaketh fair* **his**
voice granteth charism,
believe **trust** him not:
for there are seven *abominations* **abhorrences**
in his heart.
26 Whose hatred is covered by deceit,
his *wickedness* **evil** shall be *shewed* **exposed**
before **in front of** the *whole* congregation.
27 Whoso diggeth a pit **of ruin** shall fall therein:
and he that rolleth a stone, it *will* **shall** return upon him.
28 A *lying* **false** tongue
hateth those that are *afflicted* **oppressed** by it;
and a *flattering* **smooth** mouth
worketh *ruin* **overthrow**.

27 *Boast* **Halal** not thyself
in the day of to morrow;
for thou knowest not what a day may *bring forth* **birth**.
2 Let another *man praise* **halal** thee,
and not thine own mouth;
a stranger, and not thine own lips.
3 A stone is heavy, and the sand weighty;
but a fool's *wrath* **vexation** is heavier than *them* both.
4 *Wrath* **Fury** is cruel,
and *anger is outrageous* **wrath overfloweth**;
but who is able to stand *before* **at the face of** envy?
5 *Open rebuke* **Exposed reproof**
is better than *secret* **hidden** love.
6 *Faithful* **Trustworthy** are
the wounds of a *friend* **lover**;
but the kisses of *an enemy are deceitful* **haters abound**.
7 The *full* **satiated** soul
loatheth **trampleth** an honeycomb;
but to the *hungry* **famished** soul
every **all** bitter *thing* is sweet.
8 As a bird that wandereth from her nest,
so is a man that wandereth from his place.
9 *Ointment* **Oil** and *perfume* **incense**
rejoice **cheer** the heart:
so *doth* the sweetness of a man's friend
by *hearty* **soul** counsel.
10 Thine own friend, and thy
father's friend, forsake not;
neither go into thy brother's house
in the day of thy calamity:
for better is a *neighbour* **fellow tabernacler** that is near
than a brother far off.
11 My son, *be wise* **enwisen**,
and *make* **cheer** my heart *glad*,
that I may *answer* **return a word**
to him that reproacheth me.

thus the sloth on his bed.
15 The sloth hides his hand in his bosom;
it wearies him to return it to his mouth.
16 The sloth is wiser in his own eyes
than seven men who return taste.
17 He who passes by
and meddles with strife not his,
is as one upholding a dog by the ears:
18 as the rabid
who shoot fiery darts, arrows and death,
19 thus the man who deceives his friend
and says, Am I not laughing?
20 Where the final timber *is*, the fire goes out;
thus where no whisperer *is*, the strife subsides.
21 As coals to coals, and timber to fire;
thus a contentious man to scorch strife.
22 The words of a whisperer inflame;
and they descend into the chambers of the belly.
23 Inflamed lips and an evil heart
are as a potsherd overlaid with silver dross.
24 He who hates *is* recognized by his lips
and places deceit within him;
25 when his voice grants charism, trust him not;
for there are seven abhorrences in his heart;
26 whose hatred is covered by deceit,
exposes his evil in front of the congregation.
27 Whoever digs a pit of ruin, falls therein;
and whoever rolls a stone, it returns on him.
28 A false tongue hates whom it oppresses;
and a smooth mouth works overthrow.

27 Halal not yourself in the day of tomorrow;
for you know not what a day births.
2 Have another halal you,
and not your own mouth;
a stranger, and not your own lips.
3 A stone is heavy and the sand weighty;
and the vexation of a fool is heavier than both.
4 Fury *is* cruel and wrath overflows;
and who is able to stand at the face of envy?
5 Exposed reproof is better than hidden love.
6 Trustworthy are the wounds of a lover;
and the kisses of haters abound.
7 The satiated soul tramples a honeycomb;
and to the famished soul all bitter is sweet.
8 As a bird wandering from her nest,
thus a man wandering from his place.
9 Oil and incense cheer the heart;
thus the sweetness of the friend of a man
by counsel of the soul.
10 Neither forsake your own friend
or the friend of your father;
nor go to the house of your brother
in the day of your calamity.
Better, a fellow tabernacler nearby
than a brother afar.
11 My son, enwisen and cheer my heart,
and I return word to him who reproaches me.
12 *A prudent man foreseeth*
The subtle seeth the evil,
and hideth *himself*;
but the *simple* **gullible** pass on,
and are *punished* **penalized**.
13 Take his *garment* **clothes**
that *is surety* **pledgeth** for a stranger,
and *take a pledge of him* **pledge it**
for a *strange woman* **stranger**.
14 He that blesseth his friend
with a *loud* **great** voice,
rising early in the morning,
it shall be *counted a curse* **fabricated**
an abasement to him.
15 A continual *dropping* **dripping**
in a *very rainy* **torrential** day
and a contentious woman are alike.
16 Whosoever *hideth* **treasureth** her
hideth **treasureth** the wind,
and the ointment of his right *hand,*
which bewrayeth itself **calleth out**.
17 Iron sharpeneth iron;
so a man sharpeneth the *countenance* **face** of his friend.
18 Whoso *keepeth* **guardeth** the fig tree
shall eat the fruit *thereof*:
so he that *waiteth on* **guardeth** his *master* **adoni**
shall be honoured.
19 As in water face *answereth* to face,
so the heart of *man* **humanity** to *man* **humanity**.
20 *Hell* **As sheol** and *destruction* **abaddon**
are never *full* **satisfied**;
so the eyes of *man* **humanity** are never satisfied.
21 As the *fining pot* **crucible** for silver,
and the furnace for gold;
so is a man *to his praise* **by the halal of his mouth**.
22 Though thou shouldest *bray* **pestle** a fool
in a *mortar* **pestle**
among *wheat* **grits** with a pestle,
yet *will* **shall** not his *foolishness* **folly**
depart **turn aside** from him.
23 *Be thou diligent to know the state*
In knowing, know the face of thy flocks,
and look well **set thy heart** to thy *herds* **droves**.

24 For *riches are* **wealth be** not *for ever* **eternal**:
and doth the crown endure **nor the separatism** *to every generation?* **generation to generation.**
25 The *hay appeareth* **grass exposeth**,
and the *tender grass sheweth itself* **sprout is seen**,
and herbs of the mountains are gathered.
26 The lambs are for thy *clothing* **robe**,
and the **he** goats are the price of the field.
27 And thou shalt have **doe** goats' milk enough
for thy *food* **bread**,
for the *food* **bread** of thy household,
and for the *maintenance for* **life of** thy *maidens* **lasses**.

28 The wicked flee when no *man* **one** pursueth:
but the *righteous* **just** are *bold* **confident** as a *lion* **whelp**.
2 For the *transgression* **rebellion** of a land
many are the *princes thereof* **governors**:
but by a *man of understanding* **human that discerneth**
and *knowledge* **knoweth such**
the state thereof shall be prolonged.
3 *A poor man* **An impoverished mighty**
that oppresseth the poor
is *like* a sweeping rain which leaveth no *food* **bread**.
4 They that forsake the *law* **torah**
praise **halal** the wicked:
but such as *keep* **guard** the *law* **torah**
contend with **throttle** them.
5 Evil men *understand* **discern** not judgment:
but they that seek *the LORD* **Yah Veh**
understand **discern** all *things*.
6 Better is the *poor* **impoverished**
that walketh in his *uprightness* **integrity**,
than he that *is perverse in* **perverteth** his ways,
though he be rich.
7 Whoso *keepeth* **guardeth** the *law* **torah**
is a *wise* **discerning** son:
but he that
is a companion of riotous men **befriendeth gluttons**
shameth his father.
12 The subtle see the evil and hide;
and the gullible pass on and are penalized.
13 Take his clothes, who pledges for a stranger,
and pledge it for a stranger.
14 He who blesses his friend with a great voice,
rising early in the morning,
is fabricated as an abasement to him.
15 A continual dripping in a torrential day
and a contentious woman are alike.
16 Whoever treasures her, treasures the wind;
and the ointment at his right calls out.
17 Iron sharpens iron;
thus a man sharpens the face of his friend.
18 Whoever guards the fig tree, eats the fruit;
thus he who guards his adoni, is honored.
19 As the water, face to face,
thus the heart, humanity to humanity.
20 As sheol and abaddon are never satisfied;
thus the eyes of humanity are never satisfied.
21 As the crucible for silver
and the furnace for gold;
thus a man by the halal of his mouth.
22 Though you pestle a fool in a pestle
among grits with a pestle,
yet his folly turns not aside from him.
23 In knowing, know the face of your flocks;
set your heart to your droves.
24 For neither is wealth eternal;
nor the separatism generation to generation.
25 The grass exposes and the sprout is seen;
and herbs of the mountains are gathered.
26 The lambs *are* for your robe
and the he goats *are* the price of the field.
27 And you have milk enough of the doe goats
for your bread
—for the bread of your household,
and for the life of your lasses.

28 The wicked flee when no one pursues;
and the just are confident as a whelp.
2 For the rebellion of a land
many *are* the governors;
and by a human who discerns and knows,
such is prolonged.
3 An impoverished mighty who oppress the poor
is a sweeping rain which leaves no bread.
4 They who forsake the torah, halal the wicked;
such as guard the torah, throttle them.
5 Evil men discern not judgment;
but they who seek Yah Veh discern all.
6 Better the impoverished, who walk in integrity,
than he who perverts his ways, though he be rich.
7 Whoever guards the torah is a discerning son;
and he who befriends gluttons shames his father.
8 He that by *usury* **interest**
and *unjust gain* **bounty**
increaseth **aboundeth** his *substance* **wealth**,
he shall gather it for him
that *will pity* **shall grant charism unto** the poor.
9 He that turneth away his ear
from hearing the *law* **torah**,
even his prayer shall be *abomination* **abhorrence**.
10 Whoso causeth the *righteous* **straight**

to *go astray* **err inadvertently** in an evil way,
he shall fall *himself* into his own pit:
but the *upright* **integrious**
shall *have* **inherit the** good *things in possession.*
11 The rich man is wise in his own *conceit* **eyes**;
but the poor that *hath understanding* **discerneth**
searcheth him out.
12 When *righteous men do*
rejoice **the just jump for joy,**
there is great *glory* **beauty**:
but when the wicked rise,
a man is hidden **humanity is searched**.
13 He that covereth his *sins* **rebellions**
shall not prosper:
but whoso *confesseth* **spreadeth hands**
and forsaketh *them*
shall *have mercy* **be mercied**.
14 *Happy* **Blithe** is the *man* **human**
that *feareth alway* **continually dreadeth**:
but he that hardeneth his heart
shall fall into *mischief* **evil**.
15 As a *roaring* **growling** lion, and a ranging bear;
so is a wicked *ruler* **sovereign** over the poor people.
16 The *prince* **eminent**
that *wanteth understanding* **lacketh discernment**
is also a great oppressor:
but he that hateth *covetousness* **greed**
shall prolong his days.
17 A *man* **human** that *doeth violence* **violateth**
to the blood of *any person* **a soul**
shall flee to the *pit* **well**;
let no man *stay* **uphold** him.
18 Whoso walketh *uprightly*
integriously shall be saved:
but he that *is perverse in* **perverteth** his ways
shall fall at once.
19 He that *tilleth* **serveth** his *land* **soil**
shall *have plenty of* **satiate with** bread:
but he that *followeth after vain persons* **pursueth vanity**
shall *have* **satiate with** poverty *enough.*
20 A *faithful* **trustworthy** man
shall abound with blessings:
but he that *maketh haste* **hasteth** to *be rich* **enrich**
shall not be *innocent* **exonerated**.
21 To *have respect of persons*
respect faces is not good:
for for a *piece* **morsel** of bread
that *man will transgress* **mighty shall rebel**.
22 *He* **The man** that hasteth to *be rich* **have wealth**
hath an evil eye,
and *considereth* **perceiveth** not
that *poverty* **lack** shall come upon him.
23 He that *rebuketh a man* **reproveth humanity**
afterwards shall find more favour
than he that *flattereth* **smootheth over** with the tongue.
24 Whoso *robbeth* **strippeth**
his father or his mother,
and saith, It is no *transgression* **rebellion**;
the same is the companion of a *destroyer* **man ruiner**.
25 He that is of *a proud* **an enlarged** heart
stirreth up **throttleth** strife:
but he that *putteth his trust* **confideth**
in *the LORD* **Yah Veh**
shall be *made fat* **fattened**.
26 He that *trusteth* **confideth**
in his own heart is a fool:
but whoso walketh *wisely* **in wisdom**,
he shall *be delivered* **escape**.
27 He that giveth unto the *poor* **impoverished**
shall not lack:
but he that *hideth* **concealeth** his eye
shall have many a curse.
28 When the wicked rise,
men **humans** hide *themselves*:
but when they *perish* **destruct**,
the *righteous increase* **just abound**.
8 He who by interest and bounty
abounds his wealth,
gathers for him who grants charism to the poor.
9 He who turns his ear from hearing the torah,
even his prayer *is* an abhorrence.
10 Whoever causes the straight
to err inadvertently in an evil way,
falls into his own pit;
and the integrious inherit the good.
11 The rich man is wise in his own eyes;
and the poor who discern, search him out.
12 When the just jump for
joy, there is great beauty;
and when the wicked rise, humanity is searched.
13 He who covers his rebellions
prospers not;
and whoever spreads hands and forsakes
is mercied.
14 Blithe—the human who continually dreads;
and he who hardens his heart, falls into evil.
15 As a growling lion and a ranging bear;
thus a wicked sovereign over the poor people.
16 The eminent who lacks discernment,
is also a great oppressor;

and he who hates greed,
prolongs his days.
17 A human who violates the blood of a soul
flees to the well;
no man upholds him.
18 Whoever walks integriously is saved;
and he who perverts his ways, falls at once.
19 He who serves his soil, satiates with bread;
and he who pursues vanity, satiates with poverty.
20 A trustworthy man abounds with blessings;
and he who hastens to enrich, is not exonerated.
21 To respect faces is not good;
for, for a morsel of bread, the mighty rebel.
22 The man who hastens to have wealth
has an evil eye
and perceives not that lack comes on him.
23 He who reproves humanity afterwards
finds more favour
than he who
smoothes it over with the tongue.
24 Whoever strips his father or his mother
and says, It is no rebellion!
—is the companion of a man ruiner.
25 He of an enlarged heart, throttles strife;
and he who confides in Yah Veh, fattens.
26 Whoever confides in his own heart is a fool;
and whoever walks in wisdom, escapes.
27 Whoever gives to the impoverished, lacks not;
and he who conceals his eye has many a curse.
28 When the wicked rise, humans hide;
and when they destruct, the just abound.

29 *He, that being often reproved* **A man of reproofs**
hardeneth his **with hardened** neck,
shall *suddenly be destroyed* **break in a blink,**
and that without *remedy* **healing.**
2 When the *righteous are*
in authority **just abound,**
the people *rejoice* **cheer:**
but when the wicked *beareth rule* **reign,**
the people *mourn* **sigh.**
3 *Whoso* **The man that** loveth wisdom
rejoiceth **cheereth** his father:
but he that
keepeth company with harlot **befriendeth whores**
spendeth **destroyeth** his *substance* **wealth.**
4 The *king* **sovereign** by judgment
establisheth **standeth** the land:
but *he* **the man** that receiveth *gifts* **exaltments**
overthroweth **demolisheth** it.
5 A *man* **mighty**
that *flattereth* **smootheth over** his *neighbour* **friend**
spreadeth a net for his *feet* **steps.**
6 In the *transgression* **rebellion** of an evil man
there is a snare:
but the *righteous* **just**
doth sing **shall shout** and *rejoice* **cheer.**
7 The *righteous* **just**
considereth **knoweth** the *cause* **plea** of the poor:
but the wicked *regardeth* **discerneth** not to know it.
8 Scornful men *bring* **puff on** a city *into a snare*:
but **the** wise *men* turn away wrath.
9 *If a* **A** wise man *contendeth*
judgeth with a foolish man,
whether he *rage* **quiver** or *laugh* **ridicule,**
there is no rest.
10 The *bloodthirsty* **men of blood**
hate the *upright* **integrious:**
but the *just* **straight** seek his soul.
11 A fool uttereth all his *mind* **spirit:**
but *a* **the** wise *man keepeth it in till* **laudeth** afterwards.
12 If a *ruler* **sovereign** hearken to *lies* **false words,**
all his *servants* **ministers** are wicked.
13 The *poor* **impoverished** and
the *deceitful* man **of frauds**
meet together:
the LORD **Yah Veh** lighteneth both their eyes.
14 The *king* **sovereign**
that *faithfully* judgeth the poor **in truth,**
his throne shall be established *for ever* **eternally.**
15 The *rod* **scion** and reproof give wisdom:
but a *child left to himself* **lad sent away**
bringeth **shameth** his mother *to shame.*
16 When the wicked *are multiplied* **abound,**
transgression increaseth **rebellion aboundeth:**
but the *righteous* **just** shall see their *fall* **ruin.**
17 *Correct* **Discipline** thy son,
and he shall give thee rest;
yea, he shall give *delight* **delicately** unto thy soul.
18 Where there is no vision,
the people *perish* **be exposed:**
but he that *keepeth* **guardeth** the *law* **torah,**
happy **blithe** is he.
19 A servant
will **shall** not be *corrected* **disciplined** by words:
for though he *understand* **discern**
he *will* **shall** not answer.
20 Seest thou a man that is hasty in his words?
there is more hope of a fool than of him.
21 He that *delicately bringeth*
up **pampereth** his servant

from a child **since ladhood**
shall have him become *his son* **successor**
at the *length* **finality.**
22 *An angry* **A** man **of wrath**
stirreth up **throttleth** strife,
and a *furious man* **master of fury**
aboundeth in *transgression* **rebellion.**
23 *A man's pride* **The pomp of humanity**
shall *bring* **abase** him *low*:
but honour shall uphold the *humble* **abased** in spirit.
24 Whoso *is partner* **allotteth** with a thief
hateth his own soul:
he heareth *cursing* **oaths**, and *bewrayeth* **telleth** it not.

29 A man of reproofs, with hardened neck,
breaks in a blink—and there is no healing.
2 When the just abound, the people cheer;
and when the wicked reign, the people sigh.
3 The man who loves wisdom cheers his father;
and he who befriends whores, destroys his wealth.
4 The sovereign by judgment stands the land;
and the man who receives exaltments demolishes it.
5 A mighty who smoothes over his friend
spreads a net for his steps.
6 In the rebellion of an evil man, there *is* a snare;
and the just shout and cheer.
7 The just know the plea of the poor;
and the wicked discern to not know it.
8 Scornful men puff on a city;
and the wise turn away wrath.
9 A wise man judges a foolish man;
he quivers; he ridicules; there is no rest.
10 The men of blood hate the integrious;
and the straight seek his soul.
11 A fool utters all his spirit;
and the wise lauds afterward.
12 A sovereign who hearkens to false words
—all his ministers are wicked.
13 The impoverished and the man of frauds
meet together;
Yah Veh lights both their eyes.
14 The sovereign who judges the poor in truth,
establishes his throne eternally.
15 The scion and reproof give wisdom;
and a lad sent away shames his mother.
16 When the wicked abound, rebellions abound;
and the just see their ruin.
17 Discipline your son and he gives you rest;
yes, he gives delicately to your soul.
18 Where there is no vision,
the people are exposed;
and he who guards the torah, blithe *is* he.
19 Discipline not a servant by words;
for though he discerns, he answers not.
20 See a man hasty in words?
There is more hope of a fool than of him.
21 Whoever pampers his servant since ladhood
has him become successor at the finality.
22 A man of wrath throttles strife
and a master of fury abounds in rebellion.
23 The pomp of humanity abases;
and honor upholds the abased in spirit.
24 Whoever allots with a thief, hates his own soul;
he hears oaths and tells it not.
25 The *fear* **trembling** of *man* **humanity**
bringeth **giveth** a snare:
but whoso *putteth his trust* **confideth**
in *the LORD* **Yah Veh**
shall be *safe* **lofted.**
26 Many seek the *ruler's favour* **sovereign's face**;
but *every* man's judgment
cometh **be** from *the LORD* **Yah Veh.**
27 *An unjust man* **A man of wickedness**
is an *abomination* **abhorrence** to the just:
and *he that is upright* **the straight** in the way
is *abomination* **abhorrence** to the wicked.

THE ORACLE OF AGUR

30 The words of Agur the son of *Jakeh* **Yaqeh,**
even the *prophecy* **burden**:
the *man spake* **oracle of a mighty** unto *Ithiel* **Ithi El,**
even unto *Ithiel* **Ithi El** and *Ucal* **Ukal,**
2 Surely I am more *brutish* **stupid** than *any* man,
and have not the *understanding* **discernment**
of *a man* **humanity.**
3 I neither learned wisdom,
nor *have* **know** the knowledge of the holy.

PROPHECY OF THE SON OF HUMANITY

4 Who hath ascended up into *heaven* **the heavens,**
or descended?
who hath gathered the wind in his fists?
who hath *bound* **narrowed** the
waters in a *garment* **cloth**?
who hath *established* **raised**
all the *ends* **finalities** of the earth?
what is his name, and what is his son's name,
if thou *canst tell* **knowest**?
5 Every *word* **saying** of *God*
Elohah is *pure* **refined**:
he is a *shield* **buckler**

unto them that *put their trust* **seek refuge** in him.
6 Add thou not unto his words,
lest he reprove thee, and thou be found a liar.
7 *Two things have I required*
These two ask I of thee;
deny me **withhold** them not before I die:
8 Remove far from me vanity and **words of** lies:
give me neither poverty nor riches;
feed me with food convenient **tear**
my statute bread for me:
9 Lest I *be full* **satiate**, and deny thee, and say,
Who is *the LORD* **Yah Veh**?
or lest I be *poor* **dispossessed**, and steal,
and take the name of my *God in vain* **Elohim**.
10 *Accuse* **Tongue—lash** not a servant
unto his *master* **adoni**,
lest he *curse* **abase** thee,
and thou *be found guilty* **hast guilted**.
11 There is a generation that
curseth **abaseth** their father,
and *doth not bless* **blesseth not** their mother.
12 There is a generation that
are pure in their own eyes,
and yet is **but** not washed from their *filthiness* **dung**.
13 There is a generation, O how lofty *are* their eyes!
and their eyelids *are* lifted *up*.
14 There is a generation, whose teeth are *as* swords,
and their *jaw teeth* **molars** *as* knives,
to devour the *poor* **humble** from off the earth,
and the needy from *among men* **humanity**.
15 The horseleach hath two
daughters, *crying*, Give, give.
There are **These** three *things that* are never
satisfied, yea, four *things* say not, *It is* enough:
16 *The grave* **sheol**; and the
barren **restrained** womb;
the earth that is not *filled* **satiated** with water;
and the fire that saith not, *It is* enough.
17 The eye that *mocketh at his* **derideth** father,
and *despiseth* **disrespecteth** to obey *his* mother,
the ravens of the *valley* **wadi** shall *pick* **bore** it *out*,
and the *young* **sons of** eagles shall eat it.
18 *There be* **These** three *things*
which are too *wonderful* **marvellous** for me,
yea, four which I know not:
19 The way of an eagle in the *air* **heavens**;
the way of a serpent upon a rock;
the way of a ship in the *midst* **heart** of the sea;
and the way of a *man* **mighty** with a *maid* **virgin**.
20 Such is the way of an adulterous woman;
she eateth, and wipeth her mouth,
and saith, I have done no *wickedness* **mischief**.
25 The trembling of humanity gives a snare;
and whoever confides in Yah Veh is lofted.
26 Many seek the face of the sovereign;
and the judgment of man *is* from Yah Veh.
27 A man of wickedness
is an abhorrence to the just;
and the straight in the way
is an abhorrence to the wicked.

THE ORACLE OF AGUR

30 The words of Agur the son of Yaqeh:
the burden:
the oracle of the mighty to Ithi El
—even to Ithi El and Ukal:
2 For I am more stupid than man
and have not the discernment of humanity:
3 neither learned I wisdom,
nor know the knowledge of the holy.

PROPHECY OF THE SON OF HUMANITY

4 Who ascended to the heavens? Or descended?
Who gathered the wind in his fists?
Who narrowed the waters in a cloth?
Who raised all the finalities of the earth?
What *is* his name?
What *is* the name of his son—if you know?
5 Every saying of Elohah is refined;
he is a buckler to them who seek refuge in him.
6 Add not to his words;
lest he reprove you and you be found a liar.
7 These two I ask of you;
withhold them not ere I die;
8 vanity and words of lies, remove far from me;
give me neither poverty nor riches;
tear my statute bread for me;
9 —lest I satiate and deny you and say,
Who is Yah Veh?
Or lest I become dispossessed and steal
and take the name of my Elohim.
10 Tongue—lash not a servant to his adoni,
lest he abase you and you have guilted.
11 There is a generation who abases their father
and blesses not their mother:
12 there is a generation—pure in their own eyes
but not washed from their own dung:
13 there is a generation—how lofty their eyes!
and their eyelids lifted:
14 there is a generation whose teeth are swords

and their molars knives,
to devour the humble from off the earth
and the needy from humanity.
15 The horseleach has two daughters, Give! Give!
These three are never satisfied;
yes, four say not, Enough!
16—sheol; the restrained womb; the earth not satiated
with water; and the fire that says not, Enough!
17 The eye that derides father
and disrespects to obey mother;
the ravens of the wadi bore through
and the sons of eagles eat.
18 These three are too marvellous for me;
yes, four which I know not:
19 the way of an eagle in the heavens;
the way of a serpent on a rock;
the way of a ship in the heart of the sea;
and the way of the mighty with a virgin.
20 Such *is* the way of an adulterous woman;
she eats and wipes her mouth
and says, I do no mischief.
21 *For* **These** three *things*
quake the earth *is disquieted*
and for four *which* it cannot bear:
22 For a servant when he reigneth;
and a fool when he is *filled* **satiated** with *meat* **bread**;
23 For *an odious woman* **she who hateth**
when she is married;
and *an handmaid* **a maid**
that *is heir to* **possesseth** her *mistress* **lady**.
24 *There be* **These** four *things*
which are little upon the earth,
but **in enwisening,**
they *are exceeding wise* **enwisen**:
25 The ants are a people not strong,
yet they prepare their *meat* **bread** in the summer;
26 The conies are *but a feeble*
folk **not a mighty people**,
yet *make* **set** they their houses in the rocks;
27 The locusts have no *king* **sovereign**,
yet go they forth all of them by *bands* **ranks**;
28 The *spider taketh hold* **lizard**
grabbeth with her hands,
and is in *kings' palaces* **sovereign's manses**.
29 *There be* **These** three *things*
which go well **pace good**,
yea, four *are comely* **well—please** in going:
30 A lion *which is strongest*
mighty among *beasts* **animals**,
and turneth not *away for any* **from the face**;
31 *A greyhound* **One girt in**
the loins; an he goat also;
and a *king* **sovereign**, against whom there is no rising *up*.
32 If thou hast *done foolishly*
follied in lifting *up* thyself,
or if thou hast *thought evil* **intrigued**,
lay thine hand upon thy mouth.
33 Surely the churning of milk
bringeth forth butter,
and the *wringing* **churning** of the *nose* **nostrils**
bringeth forth blood:
so the *forcing* **churning** of wrath
bringeth forth strife.

THE WORDS OF SOVEREIGN LEMU EL

31 The words of *king Lemuel* **sovereign Lemu El**,
the *prophecy* **burden**
that his mother *taught* **disciplined** him.
2 What, my *son* **bar**?
and what, the *son* **bar** of my *womb* **belly**?
and what, the *son* **bar** of my vows?
3 Give not thy *strength* **valour** unto women,
nor thy ways
to that which *destroyeth kings* **wipeth out sovereigns**.
4 It is not for *kings* **sovereigns**,
O *Lemuel* **Lemu El**,
it is not for *kings* **sovereigns** to drink wine;
nor for *princes strong drink* **potentates intoxicants**:
5 Lest they drink, and forget the *law* **statute**,
and *pervert* **alter** the *judgment* **plea**
of any of the *afflicted* **sons of humiliation**.
6 Give *strong drink* **intoxicants**
unto him that is *ready* to *perish* **destruct**,
and wine
unto those that be *of heavy hearts* **bitter of soul**.
7 Let him drink, and forget his poverty,
and remember his *misery* **toil** no more.
8 Open thy mouth for the *dumb* **mute**
in the *cause* **plea** of all
such as are appointed to destruction—**sons of survivors**.
9 Open thy mouth, judge *righteously* **justness**,
and plead the cause of the *poor* **humble** and needy.
10 Who can find a virtuous woman?
for her price is far above *rubies* **pearls**.
11 The heart of her *husband* **master**
doth safely trust **confideth** in her,
so that he shall have no *need* **lack** of spoil.
12 She *will do* **shall deal** him good and not evil
all the days of her life.
13 She seeketh wool, and flax,

and worketh *willingly* **with delight**
with her *hands* **palms.**
14 She is like the merchants' ships;
she bringeth her *food* **bread** from afar.
15 She riseth also while it is yet night,
and giveth *meat* **the prey** to her household,
and a *portion* **statute** to her *maidens* **lasses.**
16 She *considereth* **intrigueth**
a field, and *buyeth* **taketh** it:
with the fruit of her *hands* **palms**
she planteth a vineyard.
21 These three quake the earth;
and for four it cannot bear:
22 for a servant when he reigns;
and a fool when he satiates with bread;
23 for she who hates when she is married;
and a maid who possesses her lady.
24 These four are little on the earth;
and in enwisening, they enwisen:
25 the ants *are* a people, not strong,
yet they prepare their bread in the summer;
26 the conies *are* a people, not mighty,
yet set they their houses in the rocks;
27 the locusts have no sovereign,
yet they all go by ranks;
28 the lizard grabs with her hands
and is in the manses of sovereigns.
29 These three pace good;
yes, four well—please in going:
30 a lion mighty among animals
who turns not from the face;
31 one girt in the loins; also a he goat;
and a sovereign, against whom no one rises.
32 If you folly by lofting yourself,
or if you intrigue,
lay your hand on your mouth.
33 Surely the churning of milk brings forth butter
and the churning of the nostrils brings forth blood;
thus the churning of wrath brings forth strife.

THE WORDS OF SOVEREIGN LEMU EL

31 The words of sovereign Lemu El;
the burden his mother disciplined him:
2 What, my bar?
and what, the bar of my belly?
and what, the bar of my vows?
3 Neither give your valour to women
nor your ways to wiping out sovereigns.
4 Not for sovereigns, O Lemu El,
neither for sovereigns, to drink wine;
nor for potentates, intoxicants:
5 lest they drink and forget the statute
and alter the plea of any of the sons of humiliation.
6 Give intoxicants to those destructing
and wine to the bitter of soul
7 to drink and forget his poverty
to remember his toil no more.
8 Open your mouth for the mute
for the plea of all sons of survivors:
9 open your mouth, judge justness
and plead the cause of the humble and needy.
10 Who finds a virtuous woman?
yes, her price *is* far above pearls;
11 the heart of her master confides in her;
he lacks no spoil;
12 she deals him good and not evil
all the days of her life:
13 she seeks wool and flax
and works her palms with delight;
14 she is as the ships of merchants;
she brings her bread from afar;
15 she rises while it *is* yet night
and gives the prey to her household
and a statute to her lasses:
16 she *is* intrigued by a field and takes it;
with the fruit of her palms she plants a vineyard;
17 She girdeth her loins with strength,
and strengtheneth her arms.
18 She *perceiveth* **tasteth** that
her merchandise is good:
her *candle* **lamp** goeth not out by night.
19 She *layeth* **spreadeth** her hands to the spindle,
and her *hands hold* **palms uphold** the *distaff* **spindle.**
20 She *stretcheth out* **spreadeth** her *hand* **palm**
to the *poor* **humble;**
yea, she *reacheth forth* **spreadeth** her hands
to the needy.
21 She *is* **aweth** not *afraid of* the snow
for her household:
for all her household are *clothed* **enrobed** with scarlet.
22 She *maketh* **worketh** herself
coverings of tapestry **spreads;**
her *clothing* **robe** is *silk* **fine linen** and purple.
23 Her *husband* **master** is
known in the *gates* **portals,**
when he *sitteth* **settleth** among the elders of the land.
24 She *maketh fine linen*
worketh wraps, and selleth *it;*

and *delivereth* **giveth** girdles unto
the *merchant* **Kenaaniy**.
25 Strength and *honour* **majesty**
are her *clothing* **robe**;
and she shall *rejoice in time to come* **laugh the day after**.
26 She openeth her mouth with wisdom;
and in her tongue is the *law* **torah** of *kindness* **mercy**.
27 She *looketh well to* **watcheth**
the ways of her household,
and eateth not the bread of *idleness* **sloth**.
28 Her *children* **sons** arise *up*,
and call her *blessed* **blithesome**;
her *husband* **master** *also*, and he *praiseth* **halaleth** her.
29 Many daughters have *done* **worked** virtuously,
but thou *excellest* **ascendest** them all.
30 *Favour is deceitful* **Charism**
is false, and beauty is vain:
but a woman that *feareth the LORD* **aweth Yah Veh**,
she shall be *praised* **halaled**.
31 Give her of the fruit of her hands;
and let her own works
praise **halal** her in the *gates* **portals**.

17 she girds her loins with strength
and strengthens her arms;
18 she tastes that her merchandise is good:
her lamp goes not out by night;
19 she spreads her hands to the spindle
and her palms uphold the spindle;
20 she spreads her palm to the humble;
yes, she spreads her hands to the needy;
21 she awes not the snow for her household;
for all her household are enrobed *with* scarlet:
22 she works herself spreads;
her robe *is* fine linen and purple:
23 her master is known in the portals,
when he settles among the elders of the land:
24 she works wraps and sells;
and gives girdles to the Kenaaniy:
25 strength and majesty are her robe;
and she laughs the day after:
26 she opens her mouth with wisdom;
and in her tongue is the torah of mercy:
27 she watches the ways of her household
and eats not the bread of sloth:
28 her sons rise and call her blithesome;
her master halals her:
29 many daughters work virtuously,
you ascend them all.
30 Charism is false and beauty is vain;
Halal the woman who awes Yah Veh!
31 Give her of the fruit of her hands.
Her own works halal her in the portals!

THE WORDS OF THE CONGREGATIONER

1 The words of the *Preacher* **Congregationer**,
the son of David,
king **sovereign** in *Jerusalem* **Yeru Shalem**.
2 Vanity of vanities, saith the
Preacher **Congregationer**,
vanity of vanities; all is vanity.
3 What *profit* **advantage** hath *a man* **humanity**
of all his *labour* **toil**
which he *taketh* **toileth** under the sun?
4 *One* generation passeth *away*,
and *another* generation cometh:
but the earth *abideth for ever* **standeth eternal**.
5 The sun also ariseth, and the sun goeth *down*,
and *hasteth* **swalloweth** to his place where he arose.
6 The wind goeth toward the south,
and turneth about unto the north;
it *whirleth* **goeth** about continually,
and the wind returneth again according to his circuits.
7 All the *rivers run* **wadies go** into the sea;
yet the sea is not full;
unto the place from whence the *rivers* **wadies** come,
thither they return *again* **to go**.
8 All *things are full of labour* **words belabour**;
man cannot *utter* **word** it:
the eye is not satisfied with seeing,
nor the ear filled with hearing.
9 *The thing hath been* **What hath become**,
it is that which shall *be* **become**;
and that which is done **What was worked**
is that which shall be *done* **worked**:
and there is *no* **naught** new *thing* under the sun.
10 Is there any *thing* **word** whereof it may be said,
See, this is new?
it hath been already *of old time* **eternally**,
which was *before us* **at our face**.
11 There is no *remembrance* **memorial**
of *former things* **firsts**;
neither shall there be any *remembrance* **memorial**
of *things that are to come* **lasts**
with those that shall *come* **become** after.
12 I the *Preacher* **Congregationer**
was *king* **sovereign** over *Israel* **Yisra El**
in *Jerusalem* **Yeru Shalem**.
13 And I gave my heart to seek
and *search out* **explore** by wisdom
concerning all *things that are done* **those worked**
under *heaven* **the heavens**:
this *sore travail* **evil drudgery** hath *God* **Elohim** given
to the sons of *man* **humanity**
to be *exercised* **humbled** therewith.
14 I have seen all the works
that are *done* **worked** under the sun;
and, behold, all is vanity and *vexation* **gnawing** of spirit.
15 That which is *crooked* **twisted**
cannot be *made straight* **straightened**:
and that which is *wanting* **lacking**
cannot be numbered.
16 I *communed* **worded** with
mine own heart, saying,
Lo **Behold**, I *am come to great estate* **have greatened**,
and have *gotten* **increased** more wisdom
than all they *that have been before me* **at my face**
in *Jerusalem* **Yeru Shalem**:
yea, my heart *had* **hath seen**
great *experience of* wisdom and knowledge.
17 And I gave my heart to know wisdom,
and to know madness and folly:
I perceived that this also is *vexation* **gnawing** of spirit.
18 For in *much* **abundant** wisdom
is *much grief* **abundant vexation**:
and he that increaseth knowledge increaseth sorrow.

2 I said in mine heart, Go to, *now* **I beseech**,
I *will prove* **shall test** thee with *mirth* **cheerfulness**,
therefore enjoy pleasure **see good**:
and, behold, this also is vanity.
2 I said of laughter, *It is mad* **Halal**:
and of *mirth* **cheerfulness**, What *doeth* **worketh** it?
3 I *sought* **explored** in mine heart
to *give myself* **draw my flesh** unto wine,

THE WORDS OF THE CONGREGATIONER

1 Words of the Congregationer:
Son of David; Sovereign in Yeru Shalem.
2 Vanity of vanities, says the Congregationer:
Vanity of vanities; all is vanity.
3 What advantage has humanity
of all the toil he toils under the sun?
4 Generation passes and generation comes;
and the earth stands eternal:
5 also the sun rises and the sun goes
and swallows to the place it rose:
6 the wind goes toward the south
and turns around to the north
—turning around and turning around:
and the wind returns again according to its circuits:
7 all the wadies go into the sea;
yet the sea *is* not full:
from the place the wadies come,

they return to go.
8 All words belabor; man cannot word it:
neither the eye satisfies with seeing
nor the ear fills with hearing.
9 What became, becomes;
what was worked, is worked:
and naught is new under the sun.
10 Is there any word whereof is said,
See, this is new?
It already became—eternally at our face.
11 There is neither memorial of firsts;
nor memorial of lasts
with those to become afterward.
12 I the Congregationer
became sovereign over Yisra El in Yeru Shalem:
13 and I gave my heart
to seek and explore by wisdom
concerning all those worked under the heavens
—this evil drudgery
Elohim gave to the sons of humanity
to be humbled therewith.
14 I saw all the works worked under the sun;
and behold, all is vanity and gnawing of spirit.
15 The twisted cannot *be* straightened;
and the lacking cannot *be* numbered.
16 I worded with my own heart, saying,
I—behold,
I greatened and increased more in wisdom
than all at my face in Yeru Shalem;
yes, my heart saw great wisdom and knowledge:
17 I gave my heart to know wisdom
and to know madness and folly;
I perceived that this also is gnawing of spirit.
18 For in abundant wisdom
is abundant vexation;
and he who increases knowledge
increases sorrow.

2 I said in my heart, Go to, I beseech,
I test you with cheerfulness; see the good:
and behold, this also is vanity.
2 Of laughter, I say, Halal!
Of cheerfulness, What works?
3 I explored in my heart to draw my flesh to wine;
yet *acquainting* **driving** mine heart with wisdom;
and to lay hold on folly,
till I might see what was that good
for the sons of *men* **humanity**,
which they should *do* **work** under the *heaven* **heavens**
all **the number of** the days of their life.
4 I *made me great* **greatened my** works;
I builded me houses; I planted me vineyards:
5 I *made* **worked** me gardens and orchards,
and I planted trees in them of all *kind of* fruits:
6 I *made* **worked** me pools of water,
to *water* **wet** therewith the *wood* **forest**
that *bringeth forth* **sprouteth** trees:
7 I *got me* **chattelized** servants
and *maidens* **maids**,
and had *servants born in* **sons of** my house;
also I had *great possessions* **abundant chattel**
of *great and small cattle* **oxen and flocks**
above all that were in *Jerusalem* **Yeru Shalem**
before me **at my face**:
8 I gathered me also silver and gold,
and the peculiar treasure of *kings* **sovereigns**
and of the *provinces* **jurisdictions**:
I *gat* **worked** me
men singers **songsters** and *women singers* **songtresses**,
and the delights of the sons of *men* **humanity**,
as musical instruments, and that of all sorts
and mistresses of mistresses.
9 So I *was great* **greatened**,
and increased more than all
that were *before me* **at my face** in
Jerusalem **Yeru Shalem**:
also my wisdom *remained* **stayed** with me.
10 And whatsoever mine eyes *desired* **asked**
I *kept* **set** not **aside** from them,
I withheld not my heart from any *joy* **cheerfulness**;
for my heart *rejoiced* **cheered** in all my *labour* **toil**:
and this was my *portion* **allotment** of all my *labour* **toil**.
11 Then I *looked on* **faced** all the works
that my hands had *wrought* **worked**,
and on the *labour* **toil**
that I had *laboured* **toiled** to *do* **work**: and, behold,
all was vanity and *vexation* **gnawing** of spirit,
and there was no *profit* **advantage** under the sun.
12 And I turned *myself* **my**
face to *behold* **see** wisdom,
and madness, and folly:
for what *can the man do* **of the human**
that cometh after the *king* **sovereign**?
even that which hath been **is** already *done* **worked**.
13 Then I saw that wisdom
excelleth **advantageth over** folly,
as far as light *excelleth* **advantageth over** darkness.
14 The *wise man's* eyes **of the wise** are in his head;
but the fool walketh in darkness:
and I myself perceived also
that one *event* **happening** happeneth to them all.

15 Then said I in my heart,
As it happeneth to the fool, so it happeneth even to me;
and why was I then more *wise* **enwisened**?
Then I *said* **worded** in my heart, that this also is vanity.
16 For there is no *remembrance*
memorial of the wise
more than of the fool *for ever* **eternally**;
seeing that which now is in **that already**
the days to come shall all be forgotten. And
how dieth the wise *man*? as the fool.
17 Therefore I hated life;
because the work that is *wrought* **worked** under the sun
is *grievous* **evil** unto me:
for all is vanity and *vexation* **gnawing** of spirit.
18 Yea, I hated all my *labour* **toil**
which I had *taken* **toiled** under the sun:
because I should leave it unto *the man* **humanity**
that shall be after me.
19 And who knoweth
whether he shall be *a* wise *man* or *a* fool?
yet shall he *have rule* **dominate** over all my *labour* **toil**
wherein I have *laboured* **toiled**,
and wherein I have *shewed* **enwisened** myself *wise*
under the sun.
This is also vanity.
20 *Therefore I went about to cause*
I turned my heart **around**
yet driving my heart with wisdom:
and to lay hold on folly
until I see the good for the sons of humanity;
which they work under the heavens
the number of the days of their life.
4 I greatened my works;
I built houses; I planted vineyards;
5 I worked gardens and orchards;
and in them I planted trees of all fruits:
6 I worked pools of water
to wet the forest to sprout trees;
7 I chattelized servants and maids
and had sons of my house;
I also had abundant chattel of oxen and flocks
above all that were in Yeru Shalem at my face:
8 I also gathered silver and gold
and the peculiar treasure of sovereigns
and of the jurisdictions:
I worked songsters and songtresses
and the delights of the sons of humanity
and mistresses of mistresses.
9 Thus I greatened and increased more than all
ere my face in Yeru Shalem;
also my wisdom stayed with me:
10 and whatever my eyes asked
I set not aside from them,
nor withheld my heart from any cheerfulness;
for my heart cheered in all my toil:
and this was my allotment of all my toil.
11 Then I faced all the works my hands worked
and on the toil I toiled to work;
and behold, all *is* vanity and gnawing of spirit
and there is no advantage under the sun.
12 And I turned my face
to see wisdom and madness and folly:
but what of the human
who comes after the sovereign
—when that which is, was already worked?
13 And I saw that wisdom advantages over folly,
as far as light advantages over darkness.
14 The eyes of the wise *are* in his head;
and the fool walks in darkness;
and I also perceived
that what happens to one, happens to all.
15 And I said in my heart,
As happens to the fool, happens even to me.
Why then am I more enwisened?
And I worded in my heart, that this also is vanity.
16 For there is no memorial of the wise
more than of the fool eternally;
that in the days to come, all is forgotten.
And how die the wise? As the fool!
17 And I hated life;
because the work worked under the sun
is evil to me;
for all is vanity and gnawing of spirit.
18 Yes, I hated all the toil I toiled under the sun;
because I leave it to humanity after me.
19 And who knows
whether he be wise or fool?
—and yet dominates over all the toil I toiled
wherein I enwisened myself under the sun.
This is also vanity.
20 I turned my heart around
to *despair of* **quit** all the *labour* **toil**
which I *took* **toiled** under the sun.
21 For there is a *man* **human**
whose *labour* **toil** is in wisdom,
and in knowledge, and in *equity* **prosperity**;
yet to a *man* **human** that hath not
laboured **toiled** therein
shall he *leave* **give** it for his *portion* **allotment**.
This also is vanity and a great evil.

22 For what hath *man* **humanity**
of all his *labour* **toil**,
and of the *vexation* **gnawing** of his heart, wherein
he hath *laboured* **toiled** under the sun?
23 For all his days are sorrows,
and his *travail grief* **drudgery vexation**;
yea, his heart *taketh* **lieth** not *rest* **down** in the night.
This is also vanity.
24 There is *nothing* **naught**
better for a *man* **human**,
than that he should eat and drink,
and that he should *make* **delight** his soul
enjoy **to see** good in his *labour* **toil**.
This also I saw,
that it was from the hand of *God* **Elohim**.
25 For who can eat,
or who else can hasten *hereunto*, more than I?
26 *For God giveth to a man* **Giving humanity**
that is good *in his sight* **at his face**
wisdom, and knowledge, and *joy* **cheerfulness**:
but to the sinner he giveth *travail* **drudgery**,
to gather and to heap *up*,
that he may give to him
that is good *before God* **at the face of Elohim**.
This also is vanity and *vexation* **gnawing** of spirit.

3 To *every thing* **all** there is a season,
and a time to every *purpose* **desire**
under the *heaven* **heavens**:
2 A time to *be born* **birth**,
and a time to die;
a time to plant,
and a time to *pluck up that which is* **uproot the** planted;
3 A time to *kill* **slaughter**,
and a time to heal;
a time to *break down* **breach**,
and a time to build *up*;
4 A time to weep,
and a time to laugh;
a time to *mourn* **chop**,
and a time to dance;
5 A time to cast away stones,
and a time to gather stones *together*;
a time to embrace,
and a time to *refrain* **be far** from embracing;
6 A time to *get* **seek**,
and a time to *lose* **destroy**;
a time to *keep* **guard**,
and a time to cast *away*;
7 A time to *rend* **rip**,
and a time to sew;
a time to *keep silence* **hush**,
and a time to *speak* **word**;
8 A time to love,
and a time to hate;
a time of war,
and a time of *peace* **shalom**.
9 What *profit* **advantage** hath he that worketh
in that wherein he *laboureth* **toileth**?
10 I have seen the *travail* **drudgery**,
which *God* **Elohim**
hath given to the sons of *men* **humanity**
to be *exercised in it* **humbled therein**.
11 He hath *made every thing* **worked all**
beautiful in his time:
also he hath *set the world* **given eternally** in their heart,
so that no *man* **human** can find out the work
that *God maketh* **Elohim worketh**
from the *beginning* **top** to the end.
12 I know that there is no good *in* **for** them,
but *for a man to rejoice* **to cheer**,
and to *do* **work** good in his life.

to quit all the toil I toiled under the sun.
21 For there is a human whose toil *is* in wisdom
and in knowledge and in prosperity;
yet he gives his allotment
to a human who never toiled therein.
This also is vanity and a great evil.
22 For what has humanity of all his toil
and of the gnawing of his heart
wherein he toiled under the sun?
23 For all his days are sorrows
and his drudgery, vexation;
yes, his heart lies not down in the night.
This is also vanity.
24 Naught is better for a human,
than to eat and drink and to delight his soul
—to see good in his toil.
This also I saw,
that this is from the hand of Elohim.
25 For who eats, or who else hastens more than I?
26 —giving humanity what is good at his face
—wisdom and knowledge and cheerfulness;
and to the sinner he gives drudgery,
to gather and to heap,
to give him the good at the face of Elohim.
This also is vanity and gnawing of spirit.
3 To all there is a season
and a time to every desire under the heavens;
2 a time to birth
and a time to die;

a time to plant
and a time to uproot the planted;
3 a time to slaughter
and a time to heal;
a time to breach
and a time to build;
4 a time to weep
and a time to laugh;
a time to chop
and a time to dance;
5 a time to cast away stones
and a time to gather stones;
a time to embrace
and a time to be far from embracing;
6 a time to seek
and a time to destroy;
a time to guard
and a time to cast;
7 a time to rip
and a time to sew;
a time to hush
and a time to word;
8 a time to love
and a time to hate;
a time of war
and a time of shalom.
9 What advantage has he who works
in that wherein he toils?
10 I saw the drudgery
Elohim gave to the sons of humanity
to be humbled therein.
11 He worked all beautiful in his time;
also he gave eternally in their heart,
so that no human can find out
the work Elohim works
from the top to the end.
12 I know that there is no good for them,
but to cheer and to work good in their life.
13 And also
that *every man* **all humanity** should eat and drink,
and *enjoy* **see** the good of all his *labour* **toil,**
it is the gift of *God* **Elohim.**
14 I know that, whatsoever
God doeth **Elohim worketh,**
it shall be *for ever* **eternal:**
nothing **naught** can be *put to it* **augmented,**
nor *any thing taken from it* **aught diminished:**
and *God doeth it,* **Elohim worketh**
that *men* **one** should *fear before him* **awe at his face.**
15 That which *hath been* **became,**
is now **already is;**
and that which *is to be* **becomes,**
hath already been **already was;**
and *God requireth* **Elohim seeketh**
that which is *past* **pursued.**
16 And moreover
I saw under the sun the place of judgment,
that wickedness was there;
and the place of *righteousness* **justness,**
that *iniquity* **wickedness** was there.
17 I said in mine heart,
God **Elohim** shall judge the *righteous*
just and the wicked:
for there is a time there
for every *purpose* **desire** and for every work.
18 I said in mine heart
concerning the *estate* **word** of the sons of *men* **humanity,**
that *God* **Elohim** might *manifest* **purify** them,
and that they might see
that they themselves are *beasts* **animals.**
19 For that which
befalleth **happeneth to** the sons of *men* **humanity**
befalleth beasts **happeneth to animals;**
even *one thing befalleth* **this happeneth to** them:
as *the one* **this** dieth, so dieth *the other* **that;**
yea, they have all one *breath* **spirit;**
so that *a man* **humanity** hath no *preeminence* **advantage**
above *a beast* **an animal:**
for all is vanity.
20 All go unto one place;
all are of the dust, and all *turn* **return** to dust *again.*
21 Who knoweth the spirit of
man **the son of humanity**
that *goeth upward* **ascendeth,**
and the spirit of the *beast* **animal**
that *goeth downward* **descendeth** to the earth?
22 Wherefore I *perceive* **see** that
there is *nothing* **naught** better,
than that a *man* **human**
should *rejoice* **cheer** in his own works;
for that is his *portion* **allotment:**
for who shall bring him to see what shall be after him?

4 So I returned,
and *considered* **saw** all the oppressions
that are *done* **worked** under the sun:
and behold the tears of *such as were* **the** oppressed,
and they had no *comforter* **one to sigh;**
and *on the side* **in the hand** of their oppressors
there was *power* **force;**
but they had no *comforter* **one to sigh.**

2 *Wherefore I praised* **I lauded**
the dead which are already dead
more than the living which *are* yet *alive* **live.**
3 Yea, better is he than both they,
which hath not yet been,
who hath not seen the evil work
that is *done* **worked** under the sun.
4 Again, I *considered* **saw** all *travail* **the toil,**
and *every right* **all the prosperity of** work,
that for this a man is envied of his *neighbour* **friend.**
This is also vanity and *vexation* **gnawing** of spirit.
5 The fool *foldeth* **embraceth** his hands *together,*
and eateth his own flesh.
6 Better is *an handful* **a palm**
full with *quietness* **rest,**
than *both the hands* **fists** full with *travail* **toil**
and *vexation* **gnawing** of spirit.
7 Then I returned, and I
saw vanity under the sun.
8 There is one *alone*, and there is *not a* **no** second;
yea, he hath neither *child* **son** nor brother:
13 And also that all humanity eat and drink
and see the good of all his toil,
—the gift of Elohim.
14 I know that whatever Elohim works, is eternal;
neither augmented; nor diminished:
and Elohim works so that they awe at his face.
15 What became, already is;
and what becomes, already became:
and Elohim seeks what is pursued.
16 And again, I saw under the sun
the place of judgment
—that wickedness was there;
and the place of justness
—that wickedness was there.
17 I said in my heart,
Elohim judges the just and the wicked;
for there is a time
for every desire and for every work.
18 I said in my heart
concerning the word of the sons of humanity,
that Elohim purify them
—that they see that they themselves are animals.
19 For what happens to the sons of humanity
happens to animals
—even this happens to them;
as this dies, thus that dies;
yes, they all have one spirit;
so that humanity has no advantage over an animal;
for all *is* vanity.
20 All go to one place;
all became of dust; all return to dust.
21 Who knows the spirit of the son of humanity
that ascends;
and the spirit of the animal
that descends to the earth?
22 I see there is naught better,
than for a human to cheer in his own works;
for that is his allotment;
for who brings him to see what becomes after him?

4 And I return
and see all the oppressions worked under the sun;
and behold, the tears of the oppressed
who have no one to sigh;
and the force of the hand of their oppressors
who have no one to sigh.
2 I laud the dead who already died
more than the living who yet live.
3 Yes, better is he than they both
—who became not yet
—who saw not
the evil work worked under the sun.
4 And I see all the toil
and all the prosperity of work;
that for this man envies friend;
this is also vanity and gnawing of spirit.
5 The fool embraces his hands
and eats his own flesh;
6 better, a palm full with rest,
than fists full with toil and gnawing of spirit.
7 And I return; and I see vanity under the sun:
8 there is one; and there is no second:
yes, he has neither son nor brother;
yet is there no end of all his *labour* **toil;**
neither is his eye satisfied with riches;
neither saith he, For whom *do I labour* **toil I,**
and *bereave* **lack** my soul of good?
This is also vanity,
yea, it is *a sore travail* **an evil drudgery.**
9 Two are better than one;
because they have a good *reward*
hire for their *labour* **toil.**
10 For if they fall,
the one *will lift up* **shall raise** his *fellow* **companion:**
but woe to him that is *alone* **one** when he falleth;
for he hath *not another* **no second** to *help* **raise** him *up.*
11 *Again* **Yea,** if two lie together,
then they *have* heat:
but how can one be warm *alone*?
12 And if one prevail against him,

two shall withstand him;
and a *threefold cord* **triple thread**
is not quickly *broken* **torn.**
13 Better is a poor and a wise child
than an *old* **aged** and foolish *king* **sovereign,**
who *will* **shall perceive** no more
be admonished **to be enlightened.**
14 For out of *prison* **the house of binding**
he cometh to reign;
whereas also
he that is *born* **birthed** in his *kingdom* **sovereigndom**
becometh *poor* **impoverished.**
15 I *considered* **saw** all the living
which walk under the sun,
with the second child that shall stand *up* in his stead.
16 There is no end of all the people,
even of all that have been *before them* **at their face:**
they also *that come after* **the final**
shall not *rejoice* **cheer** in him.
Surely this also is vanity and *vexation* **gnawing** of spirit.

5 *Keep* **Guard** thy foot
when thou goest to the house of *God* **Elohim,**
and *be more ready* **approach** to hear,
than to give the sacrifice of fools:
for they *consider* **know** not that they *do* **work** evil.
2 *Be* **Terrify** not *rash* with thy mouth,
and let not thine heart *be hasty* **hasten**
to utter *any thing before God* **a word**
at the face of Elohim:
for *God* **Elohim** is in *heaven* **the heavens,**
and thou upon earth:
therefore let thy words be few.
3 For a dream cometh
through **by** the *multitude* **abundance**
of *business* **drudgery;**
and a fool's voice
is known by multitude **by the abundance** of words.
4 When thou vowest a vow unto *God* **Elohim,**
defer not to *pay* **shalam** it;
for he hath no *pleasure* **delight** in fools:
pay **shalam** that which thou hast vowed.
5 Better is it that thou shouldest not vow,
than that thou shouldest vow and not *pay* **shalam.**
6 *Suffer* **Give** not thy mouth
to cause thy flesh to sin;
neither say thou *before* **at the face of** the angel,
that it was an **inadvertent** error:
wherefore should God be angry
why enrage Elohim at thy voice,
and *destroy* **despoil** the work of thine hands?
7 For in the *multitude* **abundance** of dreams
and many words there are also divers
vanities **words and vanities abound:**
but *fear* **awe** thou *God* **Elohim.**
8 If thou seest the oppression
of the *poor* **impoverished,**
and *violent perverting* **stripping** of judgment
and *justice* **justness** in a *province* **jurisdiction,**
marvel not at the *matter* **desire:**
for he that is
higher than the highest **high above the high** regardeth;
and there be *higher than they* **the high above them.**
9 Moreover the *profit* **advantage**
of the earth is for all:
the *king* **sovereign** *himself* is served by the field.
10 He that loveth silver shall
not be satisfied with silver;
nor he that loveth abundance with *increase* **produce:**
this is also vanity.
11 When *goods increase* **good aboundeth,**
they *are increased* **abound by the myriads** that eat them:
yet he neither ends his toil
nor satisfies his eye with riches:
For whom toil I, that my soul lacks good?
This is also vanity; yes, an evil drudgery.
9 Two are better than one
because they have a good hire for their toil;
10 for if they fall, the one raises his companion:
but woe to the one when he falls,
who has no second to raise him.
11 Yes, if two lie together, they heat;
but how warms the one?
12 And if one prevails against him,
two withstand him:
a triple thread is not quickly torn.
13 Better a child, poor and a wise,
than a sovereign, aged and foolish
who no more perceives to be enlightened?
14 for from the house of binding
he comes to reign;
and he, in his sovereigndom
was birthed impoverished.
15 I see all the living walk under the sun,
with the second child who stands in his stead.
16 There is no end of all the people
—of all who became ere their face;
and the final cheer not in him:
surely this also is vanity and gnawing of spirit.

5 Guard your foot
when you go to the house of Elohim;

and approach to hear,
rather than to give the sacrifice of fools:
for they know not that they work evil.
2 Neither terrify with your mouth
nor hasten with your heart
to utter a word at the face of Elohim;
for Elohim is in the heavens
—and you on earth;
so be of few words.
3 The dream comes
by the abundance of drudgery;
and the voice of a fool
by the abundance of words.
4 When you vow a vow to Elohim,
defer not to shalam;
for he delights not in fools:
shalam your vow.
5 Better not to vow,
than to vow and not shalam.
6 Neither give your mouth that your flesh sin;
nor say at the face of the angel,
An inadvertent error!
Why enrage Elohim at your voice
and despoil the work of your hands?
7 For in the abundance of dreams
words and vanities abound;
but awe Elohim.
8 If you see the oppression of the impoverished
and stripping of judgment and justness
in a jurisdiction,
marvel not at the desire;
for he who is high above the high regards
—and then the high above them.
9 Moreover the advantage of the earth is for all;
the sovereign is served by the field.
10 Neither is he who loves silver,
satisfied with silver;
nor he who loves abundance, with produce:
this is also vanity.
11 When good abounds,
they who eat abound by the myriads;
and what *good* **prosperity** is there
to the *owners* **masters** *thereof,*
saving the beholding of them **except**
seeing with their eyes?
12 The sleep of a *labouring man* **server** is sweet,
whether he eat little or *much* **abound**:
but the *abundance* **sufficiency** of the rich
will **shall** not *suffer* **allow** him to sleep.
13 There is *a sore* **an** evil **stroke**
which I have seen under the sun,
namely,
riches *kept* **guarded** for the *owners* **masters** *thereof*
to **for** their *hurt* **evil**.
14 But those riches *perish* **destruct**
by evil *travail* **drudgery**:
and he *begetteth* **birtheth** a son,
and there is *nothing* **naught** in his hand.
15 As he came forth of his mother's *womb* **belly**,
naked shall he return to go as he came,
and shall *take nothing* **lift naught** of his *labour* **toil**,
which he may carry *away* in his hand.
16 And this also is *a sore* **an** evil **stroke**,
that *in all points* as he came, *so* **thus** shall he go:
and what *profit* **advantage** hath he
that hath *laboured* **toiled** for the *wind* **spirit/wind**?
17 All his days also he eateth in darkness,
and he *hath much sorrow* **aboundeth vexation**
and *wrath* **rage** with his sickness.
18 Behold that which I have seen:
it is good and *comely* **beautiful** *for*
one to eat and to drink,
and to *enjoy* **see** the good of all his *labour* **toil**
that he *taketh* **toileth** under the sun
all **the number of** the days of his life,
which *God* **Elohim** giveth him:
for it is his *portion* **allotment**.
19 *Every man* **All humanity** also
to whom *God* **Elohim**
hath given riches and *wealth* **holdings**,
and *hath given him power* **dominance** to eat *thereof,*
and to *take* **bear** his *portion* **allotment**,
and to *rejoice* **cheer** in his *labour* **toil**;
this is the gift of *God* **Elohim**.
20 For he shall not *much* **abound**
to remember the days of his life;
because *God answereth* **Elohim humbleth** him
in the *joy* **cheerfulness** of his heart.

6 There is an evil which I
have seen under the sun,
and it is *common* **abundant** among *men* **humanity**:
2 A man to whom *God* **Elohim** hath given riches,
wealth **holdings**, and honour,
so that he wanteth *nothing* **naught** for his soul
of all that he desireth,
yet *God* **Elohim** giveth him not
power **dominance** to eat *thereof,*
but a *stranger* **man** eateth it:
this is vanity, and it is an evil *disease* **sickness**.
3 If a man *beget* **birth** an hundred *children,*

and live many years,
so that the days of his years be many,
and his soul be not *filled* **satisfied** with good,
and also that he have no *burial* **tomb**;
I say,
that an untimely birth **a miscarriage** is better than he.
4 For he cometh in with vanity,
and *departeth* **goeth** in darkness,
and his name shall be covered with darkness.
5 Moreover he hath not seen the sun,
nor known *any thing* **aught**:
this hath more rest than the other.
6 *Yea,* **Even** though he live a thousand years
twice told **two times**,
yet hath he seen no good: do not all go to one place?
7 All the *labour* **toil** of *man*
humanity is for his mouth,
and yet the *appetite* **soul** is not filled.
8 For what hath the wise more than the fool?
what hath the *poor* **humble**,
that knoweth to walk *before* **in front of** the living?
9 Better is the *sight* **visage** of the eyes
than the *wandering* **walking** of the *desire* **soul**: this
is also vanity and *vexation* **gnawing** of spirit.
and what prosperity *is* there to the masters
—except seeing with their eyes?
12 How sweet the sleep of the server
whether he eats little or abounds;
and the sufficiency of the rich
allows him not to sleep.
13 There is an evil stroke I saw under the sun
—riches guarded for the master, for his evil:
14 and those riches destruct by evil drudgery;
and he births a son—and naught is in his hand.
15 As he came from the belly of his mother,
naked he returns to go as he came
—and lifts naught of his toil to carry in his hand.
16 And this also is an evil stroke:
as he came, thus he goes;
and what advantage has he
who toiled for the spirit/wind?
17 All his days he eats in darkness
and vexation and rage and sickness abound.
18 Behold, what I saw!
Good and beautiful to eat and to drink
and to see the good
of all the toil toiled under the sun
the number of the days of life Elohim gives;
for it is his allotment.
19 All humanity also
to whom Elohim gave riches and holdings
and dominance to eat
and to bear his allotment and to cheer in his toil
—this is the gift of Elohim.
20 For he abounds,
not to remember the days of his life;
for Elohim humbles him
in the cheerfulness of his heart.

6 There is an evil I saw under the sun
—abundant among humanity:
2 a man to whom Elohim gives riches,
holdings and honor,
so that, of all he desires, his soul wants naught;
and Elohim gives him not dominance to eat;
but a man—a stranger eats;
this is vanity—an evil sickness.
3 If a man births a hundred and lives many years
so that the days of his years be many
and his soul satisfies not with good
and also he has no tomb:
I say, a miscarriage is better than he:
4 for he comes in vanity and goes in darkness
—his name covered with darkness:
5 he neither sees the sun; nor knows aught:
this rests more than that;
6 even though he lives a
thousand years two times,
yet sees no good!
Go they not all to one place?
7 All the toil of humanity is for the mouth
and yet the soul fills not.
8 For what more has the wise than the fool?
what has the humble,
who knows to walk in front of thc living?
9 Better the visage of the eyes
than the walking of the soul;
this is also vanity and gnawing of spirit.
10 That which hath *been* **become**
is named **its name is** already **called**,
and it is known that it is *man* **humanity**:
neither may he *contend* **be able to plead his cause**
with him that is mightier than he.
11 *Seeing there be many things* **Abounding words**
that increase **abound** vanity,
what is *man* **humanity** the *better* **more**?
12 For who knoweth
what is good for *man* **humanity** in *this* life,
all **the number of** the days of his *vain* life **of vanity**
which he *spendeth* **worketh** as a shadow?
for who can tell *a man* **humanity**
what shall be after him under the sun?

7 A *good* name is better than *precious* ointment;
and the day of death than the day of *one's* birth.
2 It is better to go to the house of mourning,
than to go to the house of *feasting* **banqueting**:
for that is the end of all *men* **humanity**;
and the living *will lay* **shall give** it to his heart.
3 *Sorrow* **Vexation** is better than laughter:
for by the *sadness* **evil** of the *countenance* **face**
the heart is *made better* **well—pleased.**
4 The heart of the wise
is in the house of mourning;
but the heart of fools
is in the house of *mirth* **cheerfulness.**
5 It is better to hear the rebuke of the wise,
than for a man to hear the song of fools.
6 For as the *crackling* **voice** of
thorns under a *pot* **caldron,**
so is the laughter of the fool:
this also is vanity.
7 Surely oppression
maketh a wise man mad **causeth the wise to halal**;
and a gift destroyeth the heart.
8 Better is the *end of a thing* **final word**
than the beginning *thereof*:
and the *patient in* **long** spirit
is better than the *proud in* **lofty** spirit.
9 Be not hasty in thy spirit to be *angry* **vexed**:
for *anger* **vexation** resteth in the bosom of fools.
10 Say not thou, What *is the cause* **hath become**
that the *former* **first** days were better than these?
for thou dost not
enquire wisely **ask out of wisdom** concerning this.
11 Wisdom is good with an inheritance:
and *by it there is profit* **more** to them that see the sun.
12 For wisdom is a *defence* **shadow,**
and money **silver** is a *defence* **shadow**:
but the *excellency* **advantage** of knowledge is,
that wisdom
giveth life to them that have it **enliveneth its masters.**
13 *Consider* **See** the work of *God* **Elohim**:
for who can *make that straight* **straighten,**
which he hath *made crooked* **twisted?**
14 In the day of *prosperity* **good** be joyful,
but in the day of *adversity consider* **evil see**:
God **Elohim** also
hath *set* **worked** the one over against the other,
to the *end* **word**
that *man* **humanity** should find
nothing **naught** after him.
15 All *things* have I seen in the days of my vanity:
there is *a* **the** just *man*
that *perisheth* **destructeth** in his *righteousness* **justness,**
and there is *a* **the** wicked *man*
that prolongeth *his life* in his *wickedness* **evil.**
16 Be not *righteous over much* **aboundingly just**;
neither *make thyself over wise* **more enwisened**:
why shouldest thou *destroy* **desolate** thyself?
17 Be not *over much* **aboundingly** wicked,
neither be thou foolish:
why shouldest thou die before thy time?
18 It is good that thou shouldest take hold of this;
yea, also from this *withdraw* **leave** not thine hand:
for he that *feareth God* **aweth Elohim**
shall come forth of them all.
19 Wisdom strengtheneth the wise
more than ten *mighty men* **potentates**
which are in the city.
10 What became?
its name is already called;
and know that it *is* humanity:
he is not able to plead his cause
with him who is mightier than he.
11 Abounding words abound vanity!
What more *is* to humanity?
12 For who knows
what *is* good for humanity in life
—the number of the days of his life of vanity
which he works as a shadow?
Who tells humanity what is after him under the sun?
7 Better a name, than ointment;
and the day of death, than the day of birth:
2 better to go to the house of mourning
than to go to the house of banqueting;
for that is the end of all humanity;
and the living gives to his heart:
3 better vexation than laughter;
for by the evil of the face
the heart becomes well—pleased.
4 The heart of the wise *is* in
the house of mourning;
and the heart of fools in the house of cheerfulness.
5 Better to hear the rebuke of the wise,
than for a man to hear the song of fools.
6 For as the voice of thorns under a caldron,
thus the laughter of the fool;
this also is vanity.
7 Through oppression, the wise halal;
and a gift destroys the heart.
8 Better the final word than the beginning:
better the yearning spirit than the lofty spirit.

9 Be not hasty in your spirit to be vexed;
for vexation rests in the bosom of fools.
10 Say not, How be it so,
that the first days were better than these?
for you asked not by wisdom concerning this.
11 Wisdom is good with an inheritance;
and more to them who see the sun:
12 for wisdom *is* a shadow; silver *is* a shadow;
and the advantage of knowledge,
wisdom enlivens its masters!
13 See the work of Elohim;
for who can straighten what he twists?
14 In the day of good, be joyful;
and in the day of evil, see:
Elohim also worked this against that,
to the word,
so that humanity find naught after him.
15 I saw it all in the days of my vanity:
the just who destructs in his justness;
and the wicked who prolongs in his evil
16 —neither be aboundingly just;
nor more enwisened.
Why desolate yourself?
17 Neither be aboundingly wicked;
nor foolish:
Why die ere your time?
18 It *is* good to take hold of this;
yes, also leave not your hand from this;
for he who awes Elohim, goes out with them all.
19 Wisdom strengthens the wise
more than ten potentates in the city:
20 For there is not a just *man* **human** upon earth,
that *doeth* **worketh** good, and sinneth not.
21 Also *take no heed* **give not thine heart**
unto all words that are *spoken* **worded**; lest
thou hear thy servant *curse* **abase** thee:
22 For oftentimes also thine own heart knoweth
that thou thyself likewise hast *cursed* **abased** others.
23 All this have I *proved* **tested** by wisdom:
I said, I *will be wise* **shall enwisen**;
but it was far from me.
24 That which is far off, and *exceeding* **deep** deep,
who can find it out?
25 I *applied* **turned** mine heart **around** to know,
and to *search* **explore**, and to seek out wisdom,
and the *reason of things* **machinations**,
and to know the wickedness of folly,
even of *foolishness* **folly** and madness:
26 And I find more bitter than death the woman,
whose heart is *snares* **lairs** and *nets* **devoted**,
and her hands as bands:
whoso *pleaseth God* **be good at the face of Elohim**
shall escape from her;
but the sinner shall be *taken* **captured** by her.
27 *Behold* **See**, this have I found,
saith the *preacher* **Congregationer**, *counting* one by one,
to find out the *account* **machinations**:
28 Which yet my soul seeketh, but I find not:
one *man* **human** among a thousand have I found;
but a woman among all those have I not found.
29 *Lo* **See**, this only have I found,
that *God* **Elohim**
hath *made man upright* **worked humanity straight**;
but they have sought out many *inventions* **machinations**.

8 Who is as the wise *man*?
and who knoweth the interpretation of a *thing* **word**?
a man's **human** wisdom
maketh **lighteneth** his face *to shine*,
and the *boldness* **strength** of his face shall be changed.
2 *I counsel thee to keep the king's commandment*
Guard the sovereign's mouth,
and that *in regard* **word** of the oath of *God* **Elohim**.
3 Be not hasty to go *out of his sight* **from his face**:
stand not in an evil *thing* **word**;
for he *doeth* **worketh** whatsoever
pleaseth him **he desireth**.
4 Where the word of a *king* **sovereign** is,
there is *power* **dominion**:
and who may say unto him, What *doest* **workest** thou?
5 Whoso *keepeth* **guardeth**
the *commandment* **misvah**
shall *feel* **know** no evil *thing* **word**:
and *a wise man's heart* **the heart of the wise**
discerneth **knoweth** both time and judgment.
6 Because to every *purpose* **desire**
there is time and judgment,
therefore the *misery* **evil** of *man* **humanity**
is great upon him.
7 For he knoweth not that which shall be:
for who can tell him when it shall be?
8 There is no *man* **human**
that *hath power* **is potentate** over the spirit
to *retain* **restrain** the spirit;
neither hath he power in the day of death:
and there is no *discharge* **shooting** in that war;
neither shall wickedness
deliver those that are given to it **rescue its masters**.
9 All this have I seen,
and *applied* **gave** my heart unto every work
that is *done* **worked** under the sun:

there is a time wherein
one man ruleth over another **human dominateth human**
to his own *hurt* **evil.**
10 And *so* **thus** I saw the wicked *buried* **entombed,**
who had come and gone from the place of the holy,
and they were forgotten in the city
where they had so *done* **worked:**
this is also vanity.
11 Because sentence against an evil work
is not *executed speedily* **quickly worked,**
therefore the heart of the sons of *men* **humanity**
20 for there is not a just human on earth,
who works good and sins not.
21 Also, give not your heart
to all words that are worded;
lest you hear your servant abase you;
22 for often times also your own heart knows
that you yourself also abased others.
23 I tested all this by wisdom;
I said, I enwisen; and it *is* far from me.
24 That which is far off and deep deep,
who can find out?
25 I turned my heart around to know
and to explore and to seek out wisdom
and the machinations
and to know the wickedness of folly
—even of folly and madness;
26 and I find more bitter than death
the woman whose heart is lairs and devoted
and her hands as bands;
whoever is good at the face of Elohim
escapes from her;
and the sinner is captured by her.
27 See, I found this,
says the Congregationer, one by one,
to find out the machinations;
28 my soul still seeks, and I find not;
one human among a thousand I found;
but a woman among all those I found not.
29 See, this only I found,
that Elohim worked humanity straight;
and they—they sought out many machinations.

8 Who is as the wise?
Who knows the interpretation of a word?
Human wisdom lights his face
and the strength of his face changes.
2 Guard the mouth of the sovereign
and the word of the oath of Elohim.
3 Neither hasten to go from his face;
nor stand in an evil word:
for he works whatever he desires.
4 Where the word of a sovereign *is,*
there *is* dominion.
Who says to him, What work you?
5 Whoever guards the misvah
knows no evil word;
and the heart of the wise
knows both time and judgment.
6 Because to every desire
there is time and judgment,
so the evil of humanity upon him is great:
7 for he knows not what becomes;
for who can tell him when it became?
8 Neither is a human potentate over the spirit
to restrain the spirit;
nor has he power in the day of death:
neither shooting in that war;
nor wickedness to rescue its masters.
9 I saw all this;
and give my heart
to every work worked under the sun;
there is a time
wherein human dominates human to his own evil.
10 And thus I saw the wicked entombed
who came and went from the place of the holy
—forgotten in the city where they worked;
this is also vanity.
11 Because sentencing an evil work
works not quickly,
the heart of the sons of humanity
is fully set in them to *do* **work** evil.
12 Though a sinner *do* **work** evil an hundred times,
and *his days* be prolonged,
yet surely I know that it shall be *well* **good** with them
that *fear God* **awe Elohim,**
which *fear before him* **awe at his face:**
13 But it shall not be *well* **good** with the wicked,
neither shall he prolong his days,
which are as a shadow;
because he *feareth* **aweth** not
before God **at the face of Elohim.**
14 There is a vanity
which is *done* **worked** upon the earth;
that there be **the** just *men,*
unto whom it *happeneth* **toucheth**
according to the work of the wicked;
again, there be **the** wicked *men,*
to whom it *happeneth* **toucheth**
according to the work of the *righteous* **just:**
I said that this also is vanity.

15 Then I *commended mirth* **lauded cheerfulness**,
because *a man* **humanity**
hath no better *thing* under the sun,
than to eat, and to drink, and to *be merry* **cheer**:
for that shall *abide* **join** with him of his *labour* **toil**
the days of his life,
which *God* **Elohim** giveth him under the sun.
16 When I *applied* **gave** mine
heart to know wisdom,
and to see the *business* **drudgery**
that is *done* **worked** upon the earth:
(for also there is that neither day nor night
seeth sleep with his eyes:)
17 Then I *beheld* **saw** all the work of *God* **Elohim**,
that *a man* **humanity** cannot find out the work
that is *done* **worked** under the sun:
because though *a man labour*
humanity toil to seek it out,
yet he shall not find it; yea farther;
though *a* **the** wise *man think to*
know it **sayeth he knoweth**,
yet shall he not be able to find it.

9 For all this
I *considered* **gave** in my heart even to declare all this,
that the *righteous* **just**, and the wise,
and their *works* **service**,
are in the hand of *God* **Elohim**:
no *man* **human** knoweth either love or hatred
by all that *is before them* **at their face**.
2 All *things come alike to* **in** all:
there is one *event* **happening** to the *righteous* **just**,
and to the wicked;
to the good and to the *clean* **pure**,
and to the *unclean* **foul**;
to him that sacrificeth, and to him that sacrificeth not:
as *is* the good, so *is* the sinner;
and he that *sweareth* **oatheth**,
as he that *feareth* **aweth** an oath.
3 This is an evil among all *things*
that are *done* **worked** under the sun,
that there is one event **one happening** unto all:
yea, also
the heart of the sons of *men* **humanity** is full of evil,
and *madness* **folly** is in their heart while they live,
and after that *they go to*—**unto** the dead.
4 For to him that is joined to all the living
there is *hope* **confidence**:
for a living dog is better than a dead lion.
5 For the living know that they shall die:
but the dead know *not any thing* **naught**,
neither have they any more a *reward* **hire**;
for *the memory of them* **their memorial** is forgotten.
6 Also their love, and their hatred, and their envy,
is *now perished* **already destructed**;
neither have they any more
a portion for ever **an allotment eternally**
in *any thing* **aught** that is *done* **worked** under the sun.
7 Go thy way, eat thy bread with *joy* **cheerfulness**,
and drink thy wine with a *merry* **good** heart;
for *God* **Elohim**
now accepteth **is already pleased in** thy works.
fully sets to work evil.
12 Though a sinner works evil a hundred times
and prolongs,
yet surely I know that it is good with them
who awe Elohim
—who awe at his face:
13 but not good with the wicked:
he prolongs not his days as a shadow;
because he awes not at the face of Elohim.
14 A vanity works on the earth:
the just who are touched
according to the work of the wicked:
again, the wicked who are touched
according to the work of the just.
I say this also *is* vanity.
15 And I lauded cheerfulness,
because humanity has naught better under the sun
than to eat and to drink and to cheer;
to join with him of his toil
the days of his life Elohim gives him under the sun.
16 When I gave my heart to know wisdom
and to see the drudgery worked on the earth
—for there are also those who,
neither day nor night see sleep with their eyes.
17 Then I saw all the work of Elohim,
that humanity cannot find out
—the work worked under the sun;
because though humanity toils to seek it out,
yet he finds it not:
yes, farther,
though the wise says he knows,
yet he is not able to find it.

9 But all this
—I gave in my heart to declare all this:
that the just and the wise and their service
are in the hand of Elohim;
no human knows either love or hatred
by all that *is* at their face.
2 All in all; one happening:

to the just and to the wicked;
to the good and to the pure and to the foul;
to him who sacrifices and to him who sacrifices not;
as the good, thus the sinner;
he who oaths, as he who awes an oath.
3 This is an evil among all worked under the sun,
one happening to all;
and also,
the heart of the sons of humanity is full of evil;
and folly in their heart while they live:
and after that—unto the dead.
4 For to whomever joins all the living
there is confidence:
for a living dog is better than a dead lion.
5 For the living know that they die;
but the dead know naught:
they have no more a hire;
for their memorial is forgotten.
6 Also their love, also their hatred, also their envy
already destructed;
they have no more an allotment eternal
in aught worked under the sun.
7 Go your way; eat your bread with cheerfulness;
and drink your wine with a good heart:
for Elohim is already pleased in your works.
8 Let thy *garments* **clothes** be
always **at all times** white;
and let thy head lack no ointment.
9 *Live joyfully* **See life**
with the *wife* **woman** whom thou lovest
all the days of the life of thy vanity,
which he hath given thee under the sun,
all the days of thy vanity:
for that is thy *portion* **allotment** in *this* life,
and in thy *labour* **toil**
which thou *takest* **toilest** under the sun.
10 Whatsoever thy hand findeth to *do* **work**,
do **work** it with thy might **force**;
for there is no work, nor *device* **machination**,
nor knowledge, nor wisdom,
in *the grave* **sheol**, whither thou goest.
11 I returned, and saw under the sun,
that the race is not to the swift,
nor the *battle* **war** to the *strong* **mighty**,
neither yet bread to the wise,
nor yet riches to *men of understanding* **the discerning**,
nor yet *favour to men of skill* **charism to the knowing**;
but time and *chance* **coincidence** happeneth to them all.
12 For *man* **humanity** also knoweth not his time:
as the fishes that are *taken* **held** in an evil *net* **lure**,
and as the birds that are *caught* **held** in the snare;
so are the sons of *men* **humanity** snared in an evil time,
when it falleth suddenly upon them.
13 This wisdom have I seen also under the sun,
and it *seemed* **be** great unto me:
14 There was a little city, and few men within it;
and there came a great *king* **sovereign** against it,
and *besieged* **surrounded** it,
and built great *bulwarks* **lairs** against it:
15 Now there was found in it a poor wise man,
and he by his wisdom *delivered* **rescued** the city;
yet no *man* **human** remembered that same poor man.
16 Then said I, Wisdom is
better than *strength* **might**:
nevertheless the poor man's wisdom
the wisdom of the poor is despised,
and his words are not heard.
17 The words of **the** wise *men*
are heard in *quiet* **rest**
more than the cry of him
that *ruleth* **reigneth** among fools.
18 Wisdom is better than
weapons **instruments** of war:
but one sinner destroyeth *much* **abounding** good.

10 Dead flies
cause the ointment of the *apothecary* **perfumer**
to *send forth a stinking savour* **gush and stink**:
so *doth* a little folly
him that is in *reputation* **esteem** for wisdom and honour.
2 *A wise man's heart* **The heart of the wise**
is at his right *hand*;
but *a fool's heart* **the heart of a fool**
at his left.
3 Yea also, when he that is a
fool walketh by the way,
his *wisdom* **heart** faileth *him*,
and he saith to every one that he is a fool.
4 If the spirit of the *ruler* **sovereign**
rise up **ascend** against thee,
leave not thy place;
for *yielding pacifieth* **healing**
alloweth great *offences* **sins**.
5 There is an evil which I
have seen under the sun,
as an **inadvertent** error
which proceedeth from **the face of** the *ruler* **potentate**:
6 Folly is *set* **given** in great *dignity* **heights**,
and the rich *sit* **settle** in *low place* **lowliness**.
7 I have seen servants upon horses,
and *princes* **governors**

walking as servants upon the earth.
8 He that diggeth a pit shall fall *into it* **therein**;
and whoso *breaketh an hedge* **breacheth a wall**,
a serpent shall bite him.
9 Whoso *removeth* **plucketh** stones
shall be *hurt* **contorted** therewith;
and he that *cleaveth wood* **splitteth timber**
shall be *endangered* **cut** thereby.
10 If the iron be *blunt* **dull**,
and he do not *whet* **sharpen** the *edge* **face**,
8 Your clothes at all times become white;
and your head lacks no ointment.
9 See life with the woman you love
all the days of the life of your vanity
which he gives you under the sun
—all the days of your vanity;
for that *is* your allotment in life
and in the toil you toiled under the sun.
10 Whatever your hand finds to work,
work with your force;
for there is no work, or machination,
or knowledge, or wisdom in sheol,
where you go.
11 I returned and saw under the sun,
neither is the race to the swift
nor the war to the mighty
nor yet bread to the wise
nor yet riches to the discerning
nor yet charism to the knowing:
for time and coincidence happens to all.
12 For even humanity knows not his time
—as the fishes held in an evil lure
as the birds held in the snare
thus the sons of humanity,
snared in an evil time,
when it falls suddenly on them.
13 This wisdom I also saw under the sun
—great to me:
14 a little city and few men within;
and a great sovereign came against it
and surrounded it and built great lairs against it:
15 and within they found a poor wise man;
and by his wisdom he rescued the city;
yet no human remembered that same poor man.
16 Then I said, Better wisdom than might;
the wisdom of the poor is despised
and his words not heard.
17 The words of the wise are heard in rest
more than the cry of him who reigns among fools.
18 Better wisdom than instruments of war;
one sinner destroys abounding good.
10 Dead flies gush and stink
the ointment of the perfumer;
more esteemed than wisdom and honor
—a little folly.
2 The heart of the wise *is* at his right;
and the heart of a fool at his left:
3 yes also, when a fool walks by the way,
his heart fails,
and he says to every one that he is a fool.
4 If the spirit of the sovereign ascends against you,
leave not your place;
for healing allows great sins.
5 There is an evil I saw under the sun
—an inadvertent error
proceeding from the face of the potentate;
6 folly *is* given in great heights
and the rich settle in lowliness.
7 I saw servants on horses
and governors walking as servants on the earth.
8 Whoever digs a pit, falls therein;
and whoever breaches a wall, a serpent bites:
9 whoever plucks stones *is* contorted thereby;
and whoever splits timber *is* cut thereby.
10 If the iron be dull and he sharpens not the face,
then must he *put to more strength*
prevail mightily with valour:
but wisdom *is profitable* **advantageth** to *direct* **prosper**.
11 Surely the serpent *will* **shall**
bite without enchantment;
and a *babbler* **master of tongue**
is no better **advantageth not**.
12 The words of *a wise man's*
mouth **the mouth of the wise**
are gracious **have charism**;
but the lips of a fool *will* **shall** swallow *up himself*.
13 The beginning of the words of his mouth
is *foolishness* **folly**:
and the *end* **finality** of his talk is
mischievous **evil** madness.
14 A fool also *is full of* **aboundeth** words:
a man **humanity** cannot tell what shall be;
and what shall be after him, who can tell him?
15 The *labour* **toil** of the foolish
wearieth every one of **belaboureth** them, because
he knoweth not how to go to the city.
16 Woe to thee, O land,
when thy *king* **sovereign** is a *child* **lad**,
and thy *princes* **governors** eat in the morning!
17 *Blessed* **Blithe** art thou, O land,

when thy *king* **sovereign** is the son of nobles,
and thy *princes* **governors** eat *in due season* **on time**,
for *strength* **might**, and not for *drunkenness* **drinking**!
18 By much *slothfulness* **sloth**
the *building decayeth* **framing subdueth**;
and through idleness of the hands
the house droppeth through.
19 *A feast* **Bread** is *made* **worked** for laughter,
and wine *maketh merry* **cheereth the life**:
but *money* **silver** answereth all *things*.
20 *Curse* **Abase** not the *king* **sovereign**,
no not *in thy thought* **knowingly**;
and *curse* **abase** not the rich in thy bedchamber:
for a *bird* **flyer** of the *air* **heavens**
shall carry the voice,
and *that which hath* **the master of** wings
shall tell the *matter* **word**.

11 *Cast* **Send** thy bread
upon the **face of the** waters:
for thou shalt find it after *many* **abundant** days.
2 Give *a portion* **an allotment**
to seven, and also to eight;
for thou knowest not what evil shall be upon the earth.
3 If the **thick** clouds be full of *rain* **downpour**,
they *empty* **pour** *themselves* upon the earth:
and if the tree fall toward the south, or toward the north,
in the place where the tree falleth, *there* **so be** it *shall be*.
4 He that *observeth* **regardeth** the wind
shall not *sow* **seed**;
and he that *regardeth* **seeth** the **thick** clouds
shall not *reap* **harvest**.
5 As thou knowest not
what is the way of the *spirit* **wind/spirit**,
nor how the bones *do grow* in the *womb* **belly**
of her that is *with child* **full**:
even so thou knowest not the works of *God* **Elohim**
who *maketh* **worketh** all.
6 In the morning sow thy seed,
and in the evening *withhold* **leave** not thine hand:
for thou knowest not *whether* **which** shall prosper,
either this or that,
or whether they both shall be *alike* **one** good.
7 Truly the light is sweet,
and *a pleasant thing* **good** it is
for the eyes to *behold* **see** the sun:
8 But if *a man* **human** live
many **and abound in** years,
and *rejoice* **cheer** in them all;
yet let him remember the days of darkness;
for they shall *be many* **abound**.
All that cometh is vanity.
9 *Rejoice* **Cheer**, O *young*
man **youth**, in thy youth;
and let thy heart *cheer* **better** thee
in the days of thy youth,
and walk in the ways of thine heart,
and in the *sight* **visage** of thine eyes:
but know thou, that for all these *things*
God will **Elohim shall** bring thee into judgment.
then he must prevail mightily with valour;
and wisdom advantages to prosper.
11 If the serpent bites without enchantment;
a master of tongue advantages not.
12 The words of the mouth of the wise
have charism;
and the lips of a fool swallow.
13 The beginning of the words of his mouth, folly;
and the finality of his talk, evil madness.
14 A fool abounds words;
humanity knows not what;
and what *is* after him? Who can tell?
15 Toil belabors the foolish,
because they know not how to go to the city.
16 Woe to you, O land,
when your sovereign *is* a lad
and your governors eat in the morning!
17 Blithe—you, O land,
when your sovereign *is* the son of nobles
and your governors eat on time
—for might and not for drinking!
18 By much sloth
the framing subdues;
and through idleness of hands
the house drops through.
19 Work the bread for laughter and wine to
cheer the life; and silver answers for all.
20 Neither abase the sovereign;
nor abase the rich in your bedchamber;
for a flyer of the heavens carries the voice
and the master of wings tells the word.

11 Send your bread on the face of the waters;
for after abundant days, you find.
2 Give an allotment to seven and also to eight;
for you know not what evil is on the earth.
3 If the thick clouds are full of downpour,
they pour on the earth;
and if the tree falls
toward the south or toward the north,
in the place the tree falls, so be it.
4 He who regards the wind, seeds not;

and he who sees the thick clouds, harvests not.
5 As you know not the way of the wind/spirit,
as bones in the belly of her that is full,
even thus you know not the works of Elohim
who works all.
6 In the morning, sow your seed;
and in the evening, leave not your hand:
for you know not which prospers
—this or that;
or whether they both be one good.
7 Truly the light is sweet
and good for the eyes to see the sun;
8 but if a human lives and abounds in years
and cheers in them all;
yet he remembers the days of darkness
—and so be it.
All that comes *is* vanity.
9 Cheer, O youth, in your youth;
that your heart better you in the days of your youth;
walk in the ways of your heart
and in the visage of your eyes;
and know this:
that for all these Elohim brings you into judgment.
10 *Therefore remove sorrow* **Turn vexation aside**
from thy heart,
and *put away* **pass** evil from thy flesh:
for childhood and *youth* **dawn** are vanity.

12 Remember now thy Creator
in the days of thy youth,
while the evil days come not,
nor the years *draw nigh* **touch,**
when thou shalt say, I have no *pleasure* **delight** in them;
2 While the sun, or the light,
or the moon, or the stars,
be not darkened,
nor the **thick** clouds return after the *rain* **downpour**:
3 In the day when the *keepers* **guards** of the house
shall *tremble* **agitate,**
and the *strong* **valiant** men shall *bow themselves* **twist,**
and the grinders cease
because they are *few* **diminished,**
and those that look out of the windows be darkened,
4 And the doors shall be shut in the streets,
when the *sound* **voice** of the grinding is low,
and he shall rise *up* at the voice of the bird,
and all the daughters of *musick* **song**
shall *be brought low* **prostrate;**
5 Also when they shall *be afraid*
of **awe** that which is high,
and *fears* **terrors** shall be in the way,
and the almond tree shall flourish,
and the *grasshopper* **locust** shall be a burden,
and desire shall *fail* **break down:**
because *man* **humanity**
goeth to his *long home* **eternal house,**
and the *mourners* **choppers**
go about **turn around** the streets:
6 Or ever the silver cord be *loosed* **removed,**
or the golden bowl be broken,
or the pitcher be broken at the fountain,
or the wheel *broken* **cracked** at the *cistern* **well.**
7 Then shall the dust return to the earth as it was:
and the spirit shall return unto *God* **Elohim** who gave it.
8 Vanity of vanities,
saith the *preacher* **Congregationer;**
all is vanity.
9 And moreover,
because the *preacher* **Congregationer** was *wise* **wiser,**
he still taught the people knowledge;
yea, he *gave good heed* **hearkened,**
and *sought out* **probed,**
and set in order *many* **abounding** proverbs.
10 The *preacher* **Congregationer**
sought to find out *acceptable* words **of delight:**
and that which was *written* **inscribed**
was *upright* **straightness,** *even*—words of truth.
11 The words of the wise are as goads,
and as nails *fastened* **implanted**
by the masters of *assemblies* **gatherings,**
which are given from one *shepherd* **attendant.**
12 And *further* **moreover,** by these, my son,
be *admonished* **enlightened:**
of *making many books* **working abundant scrolls**
there is no end;
and *much* **abundant** study
is a weariness of **belaboureth** the flesh.
13 Let us hear the conclusion
of the whole *matter* **word:**
Fear God **Awe Elohim,**
and *keep* **guard** his *commandments* **misvoth:**
for this is the whole *duty of man* **of humanity.**
14 For *God* **Elohim** shall bring
every work into judgment,
with every *secret thing* **concealment,** whether
it be good, *or* whether *it be* evil.
10 Turn vexation from your heart
and pass evil from your flesh;
for childhood and dawn are vanity.

12 Remember your Creator
in the days of your youth,

where neither the evil days come
nor the years touch;
when you say, I delight not in them.
2 While neither the sun, or the light,
or the moon, or the stars, darken;
and the thick clouds return after the downpour;
3 in the day the guards of the house agitate
and the valiant men twist
and the grinders cease
because they diminished;
and they who look from the windows darken;
4 and the doors in the streets shut:
when the voice of the grinding is low
and he rises at the voice of the bird
and all the daughters of song prostrate;
5 and they awe the heights with terrors in the way;
and the almond tree flourishes;
and the locust becomes a burden;
and desire breaks down
because humanity goes to his eternal house
and the choppers turn around the streets:
6 ere the silver cord is not removed;
or the golden bowl broken;
or the pitcher broken at the fountain;
or the wheel cracked at the well:
7 and the dust returns to the earth as it was;
and the spirit returns to Elohim who gave.
8 Vanity of vanities!
says the Congregationer:
All is vanity.
9 And moreover,
because the Congregationer was wiser,
he still taught the people knowledge;
yes, he hearkened and probed
and set in order abounding proverbs.
10 The Congregationer
sought to find out words of delight;
inscribed by the straight
—words of truth.
11 The words of the wise *are* as goads
—as nails implanted by the masters of gatherings
—given by one attendant.
12 And moreover, by these, my son, be enlightened:
of working abundant scrolls there is no end;
and abundant study belabors the flesh.
13 Hear the conclusion of the whole word;
Awe Elohim! Guard his misvoth!
For this is the whole of humanity.
14 For Elohim brings every work into judgment,
with every concealment,
whether good; whether evil.

The Song Of Songs

1 The song of songs, which
is *Solomon's* **Shelomoh's**.

The Woman Speaks

2 Let him kiss me with the kisses of his mouth:
for thy *love is* **loves are** better than wine.
3 Because of the *savour* **scent**
of thy good ointments
thy name is as ointment poured forth,
therefore *do* the virgins love thee.
4 Draw me, we *will* **shall** run after thee:
the *king* **sovereign** hath brought me into his chambers:
we *will be glad* **shall cheer** and *rejoice* **twirl** in thee,
we *will* **shall** remember thy *love* **loves** more than wine:
the upright **they** love thee **in straightnesses**.
5 I am black, but comely,
O ye daughters of *Jerusalem* **Yeru Shalem**,
as the tents of *Kedar* **Qedar**,
as the curtains of *Solomon* **Shelomoh**.
6 *Look not upon* **See** me **not**, because I am black,
because the sun hath *looked upon* **tanned** me:
my mother's *children were angry with* **sons scorched** me;
they *made* **set** me the *keeper* **guard** of the vineyards;
but mine own vineyard have I not *kept* **guarded**.
7 Tell me, O thou whom my soul loveth,
where thou *feedest* **tendest**,
where thou *makest thy flock to rest* **resposest** at noon:
for why should I be as one that *turneth aside* **is veiled**
by the *flocks* **droves** of thy companions?

The Man Responds

8 If thou know not,
O thou *fairest* **beautiful** among women,
go thy way forth by the *footsteps* **heelprints** of the flock,
and *feed* **tend** thy kids
beside the *shepherds' tents* **tabernacles of the tenders**.
9 I have compared thee, O my *love* **friend**,
to a *company of horses* **mare** in
Pharaoh's **Paroh's** chariots.
10 Thy cheeks are comely with rows *of jewels*,
thy neck with *chains of gold* **beads**.
11 We *will make* **shall work**
thee *borders* **rows** of gold
with *studs* **sequins** of silver.

The Woman

12 While the *king sitteth at*
sovereign be in his *table* **circle**,
my *spikenard* **nard**
sendeth forth **giveth** the *smell* **scent** *thereof.*
13 A bundle of myrrh is my
well—beloved unto me;
he shall *lie all night* **stay overnight** betwixt my breasts.
14 My beloved is unto me as a cluster of camphire
in the vineyards of *Engedi* **En Gedi**.

The Man

15 Behold, thou art *fair* **beautiful**, my *love* **friend**;
behold, thou art *fair* **beautiful**; thou hast doves' eyes.

The Woman

16 Behold, thou art *fair* **beautiful**, my beloved,
yea, pleasant:
also our *bed* **bedstead** is green.
17 The beams of our house are cedar,
and our *rafters* **troughs** of *fir* **firs**.

2 I am the rose of Sharon,
and the lily of the valleys.
2 As the lily among thorns,
so is my *love* **friend** among the daughters.
and our troughs of firs.
3 As the apple tree among
the trees of the *wood* **forest**,
so is my beloved among the sons.
I sat down under his shadow
with great delight **and delighted**,
and his fruit was sweet to my *taste* **palate**.
4 He brought me to the *banqueting* house **of wine**,
and his banner over me was love.
5 *Stay* **Sustain** me with *flagons* **cakes**, *comfort*
spread me with apples: for I am *sick* **worn out** of love.

The Song Of Songs

1 The song of songs; by Shelomoh.

The Woman Speaks

2 He kisses me with the kisses of his mouth;
your loves are better than wine:
3 the scent of your ointments is good;
your name, as poured ointment;
so the virgins love you.
4 Draw me, we run after you;
the sovereign brings me into his chambers;
we cheer and twirl in you;
we remember your loves more than wine;
they love you in straightnesses.
5 I am black and comely

O you daughters of Yeru Shalem;
—as the tents of Qedar
—as the curtains of Shelomoh.
6 See me not, because I am black;
because the sun tanned me;
the sons of my mother scorched me;
they set me to guard the vineyards;
my vineyard—my own I guarded not.
7 Tell me, you whom my soul loves,
where you tend; where you respose at noon;
why am I as a veiled one
by the droves of your companions?

THE MAN RESPONDS

8 If you know not,
O you beautiful among women,
go the way of the heelprints of the flock;
and tend your kids
beside the tabernacles of the tenders.
9 I compare you, O my friend,
to a mare of the chariots of Paroh:
10 your cheeks are comely with rows;
your neck with beads;
11 we work you rows of gold with sequins of silver.

THE WOMAN

12 While the sovereign *is* in his circle,
my nard gives its scent;
13 a bundle of myrrh is my well—beloved to me;
between my breasts, he stays overnight;
14 my beloved to me
is a cluster of camphire in the vineyards of En Gedi.

THE MAN

15 Behold, you are beautiful, my friend;
behold, you are beautiful;
your eyes, of doves.

THE WOMAN

THE MAN

16 Behold, you are beautiful, my beloved,
yes, pleasant; yes, our bedstead is green:
17 the beams of our house are of cedar
2 I—a rose of Sharon.
A lily of the valleys
2 —as a lily among thorns
is my friend among the daughters.
3 As an apple tree among the trees of the forest,
thus *is* my beloved among the sons:
in his shadow I delight and sit;
his fruit is sweet to my palate;
4 he brings me to the house of wine;
his banner over me is love.
5 Sustain me with cakes; spread me with apples;
for I am worn from love.
6 His left *hand* is under my head,
and his right *hand doth embrace* **embraceth** me.
7 I *charge* **oath** you,
O ye daughters of *Jerusalem* **Yeru Shalem,**
by the *roes* **gazelles,** and by the hinds of the field,
that ye *stir not up* **not waken,**
nor awake *my* **the** love, till he *please* **desireth.**
8 The voice of my beloved!
behold, he cometh leaping upon the mountains,
skipping upon the hills.
9 My beloved is *like a roe* **likened to a gazelle**
or a *young* **fawn** hart:
behold, he standeth behind our wall,
he *looketh* **peereth** forth at the windows,
shewing himself **flourishing** through the lattice.
10 My beloved *spake* **answered,** and said unto me,
Rise up **Arise,** my *love* **friend,** my *fair one* **beautiful,**
and come away.
11 For, *lo* **behold,** the winter *is past* **hath passed,**
the *rain is over* **downpour hath passed** and gone;
12 The *flowers appear* **blossoms**
be seen on the earth;
the time of *the singing of birds* **psalming**
is come **hath touched,**
and the voice of the *turtle* **turtledove**
is heard in our land;
13 The fig tree *putteth forth*
ripeneth her *green* **unripe** figs,
and the vines with the *tender grape* **blossom**
give *a good smell* **their scent.**
Arise, my *love* **friend,** my *fair one* **beautiful,**
and come away.
14 O my dove, that art in the clefts of the rock,
in the *secret places* **coverts** of the *stairs* **steep steps,**
let me see thy *countenance* **visage,**
let me hear thy voice;
for *sweet* **pleasant** is thy voice,
and thy *countenance is* **visage** comely.
15 Take us the foxes,
the little foxes, that *spoil* **despoil** the *vines* **vineyards:**
for our *vines* **vineyards** have *tender grapes* **blossoms.**
16 My beloved is mine, and I am his:
he *feedeth* **tendeth** among the lilies.
17 Until the day *break* **breathe,**
and the shadows flee away,

turn *around*, my beloved,
and be thou *like* **likened to** a *roe* **gazelle**
or a *young* **fawn** hart
upon the mountains of Bether.

3 By night on my bed
I sought him whom my soul loveth:
I sought him, but I found him not.
2 I *will* **shall** rise *now* **I beseech**,
and go about the city in the streets,
and in the broadways
I *will* **shall** seek him whom my soul loveth:
I sought him, but I found him not.
3 The *watchmen* **guards** that
go about **surround** the city
found me: *to whom I said*,
Saw ye him whom my soul loveth?
4 It was but a little that I passed from them,
but I found him whom my soul loveth:
I held him, and *would* **did** not let him go,
until I had brought him into my mother's house,
and into the chamber of her that conceived me.
5 I *charge* **oath** you,
O ye daughters of *Jerusalem* **Yeru Shalem**,
by the *roes* **gazelles**, and by the hinds of the field,
that ye stir not up, nor awake *my* **the** love,
till he *please* **desireth**.
6 Who is this
that *cometh* **ascendeth** out of the wilderness
like *pillars* **columns** of smoke,
perfumed **incensed** with myrrh and frankincense,
with all powders of the merchant?
7 Behold his bed, which is *Solomon's* **Shelomoh's**;
threescore valiant men are about
sixty mighty surround it,
of the *valiant* **mighty** of *Israel* **Yisra El**.
8 They all hold swords, *being*
expert **taught** in war:
every man hath his sword upon his *thigh*
flank because of *fear* **dread** in the night.
6 His left is under my head
and his right embraces me.
7 I oath you, O you daughters of Yeru Shalem,
by the gazelles and by the hinds of the field,
that neither you waken,
nor waken the love, until he desires.
8 The voice of my beloved!
Behold, he comes
—leaping on the mountains—skipping on the hills.
9 My beloved *is* likened to a gazelle or a fawn hart;
behold, he stands behind our wall;
he peers at the windows
flourishing through the lattice.
10 My beloved answers and says to me,
Rise, my friend, my beautiful, and come away!
11 For, behold, the winter has passed;
the downpour has passed and gone;
12 the blossoms are seen on the earth;
the time of psalming touches
and the voice of the turtledove is heard in our land:
13 the fig tree ripens her unripe figs
and the vines with the blossom give their scent.
Rise, my friend, my beautiful, and come away.
14 O my dove, in the clefts of the rock
—in the coverts of the steep steps,
have me see your visage;
have me hear your voice;
for your voice is pleasant and your visage comely.
15 Take the foxes for us
—the little foxes that despoil the vineyards;
for our vineyards have blossoms.
16 My beloved *is* mine and I *am* his;
he tends among the lilies,
17 until the day breathes, and
the shadows flee away,
turn, my beloved, as a gazelle or a fawn hart
on the mountains of Bether.

3 By night on my bed
I seek him whom my soul loves;
I seek him, but I find him not.
2 I rise; I beseech:
I go about the city
—in the streets and in the broadways:
I seek him whom my soul loves;
I seek him, but I find him not.
3 The guards surrounding the city find me;
See you him whom my soul loves?
4 In a little I pass from them,
until I find him whom my soul loves;
I hold him and not let him go
until I bring him into the house of my mother
—into the chamber of her who conceived me.
5 I oath you, O you daughters of Yeru Shalem,
by the gazelles and by the hinds of the field,
that you neither stir nor waken the love
until he desires.
6 Who is this ascending from the wilderness
as columns of smoke?
—incensed with myrrh and frankincense
with all powders of the merchant?
7 Behold his bed, of Shelomoh;

sixty mighty surround it—of the mighty of Yisra El.
8 They all hold swords; taught in war;
every man with his sword on his flank
because of dread in the night.
9 *King Solomon* **Sovereign Shelomoh**
made **worked** himself a *chariot* **palanquin**
of the *wood* **timber** of Lebanon.
10 He *made* **worked** the pillars *thereof* of silver,
the *bottom* **railings** *thereof* of gold,
the *covering of it* **saddle** of purple,
the midst *thereof* being paved with love,
for the daughters of *Jerusalem* **Yeru Shalem**.
11 Go forth, O ye daughters of *Zion* **Siyon**,
and *behold king Solomon* **see sovereign Shelomoh**
with the crown wherewith his mother crowned him
in the day of his *espousals* **wedding**,
and in the day of the *gladness* **cheerfulness** of his heart.

THE MAN

4 Behold, thou art *fair* **beautiful**, my *love* **friend**;
behold, thou art *fair* **beautiful**;
thou hast doves' eyes *within* **through** thy *locks* **vail**:
thy hair is as a *flock* **drove** of **doe** goats,
that *appear* **eat** from mount *Gilead* **Gilad**.
2 Thy teeth are like a
flock of sheep that are even shorn **clipped drove**,
which *came up* **ascended** from the *washing* **bathing**;
whereof every one *bear twins* **twinned**,
and none is *barren* **bereft** among them.
3 Thy lips are like a thread of scarlet,
and thy speech is comely:
thy temples are like a *piece* **slice** of a pomegranate
within **through** thy *locks* **vail**.
4 Thy neck is like the tower of David
builded for *an armoury* **arsenals**,
whereon there hang a thousand bucklers,
all shields of mighty men.
5 Thy two breasts
are like two *young roes that are* **fawn gazelle** twins,
which *feed* **tend** among the lilies.
6 Until the day *break* **breathe**,
and the shadows flee away,
I *will get* **shall walk** me to the mountain of myrrh,
and to the hill of frankincense.
7 Thou art all *fair* **beautiful**, my *love* **friend**;
there is no *spot* **blemish** in thee.
8 Come with me from Lebanon, *my spouse* **bride**,
with me from Lebanon:
look **observe** from the top of *Amana* **Amanah**,
from the top of Shenir and Hermon,
from the *lions' dens* **habitations of lions**,
from the mountains of the leopards.
9 Thou hast *ravished my heart* **heartened me**,
my *sister, my spouse* **sister bride**;
thou hast *ravished my heart* **heartened me**
with one of thine eyes,
with one *chain* **choker** of thy neck.
10 How *fair is* **beautified** thy *love* **loves**,
my *sister, my spouse* **sister bride**!
how much better is thy love than wine!
and the *smell* **scent** of thine ointments than all spices!
11 Thy lips, O *my spouse* **bride**,
drop as the honeycomb:
honey and milk are under thy tongue;
and the *smell* **scent** of thy *garments* **clothes**
is like the *smell* **scent** of Lebanon.
12 A garden inclosed is my *sister,*
my spouse **sister bride**;
a *spring shut up* **wave inclosed**,
a fountain sealed.
13 Thy *plants* **branches**
are *an orchard* **a paradise** of pomegranates,
with *pleasant* **precious** fruits;
camphire, with *spikenard* **nard**,
14 *Spikenard* **Nard** and saffron;
calamus **stalk** and cinnamon,
with all trees of frankincense;
myrrh and aloes, with all the *chief* **head** spices:
15 A fountain of gardens, a well of living waters,
and *streams* **flowings** from Lebanon.
9 Sovereign Shelomoh works himself a palanquin
of the timber of Lebanon:
10 he works the pillars of silver
the railings of gold
the saddle of purple
the middle paved with love
for the daughters of Yeru Shalem.
11 Come, you daughters of Siyon
and see sovereign Shelomoh
with the crown his mother crowned him
in the day of his wedding
and in the day of the cheerfulness of his heart.

THE MAN

4 Behold, you are beautiful, my friend!
Behold, you are beautiful!
Your eyes,
as doves through your veil;
your hair,
as a drove of doe goats eating on mount Gilad:

2 your teeth,
as a clipped drove ascending from the bathing
—whereof every one twins
and none bereft among them.
3 Your lips, as a thread of scarlet;
and your speech comely;
your temples,
as a slice of a pomegranate through your veil;
4 your neck,
as the tower of David built for arsenals
whereon hang a thousand bucklers
—all shields of mighty men;
5 your two breasts,
as two fawn gazelle twins, tending among the lilies.
6 Until the day breathes and
the shadows flee away,
I walk me to the mountain of myrrh
and to the hill of frankincense.
7 You are all beautiful, my friend;
—no blemish in you.
8 Come with me from Lebanon, bride,
with me from Lebanon;
observe from the top of Amanah,
from the top of Shenir and Hermon,
from the habitations of lions,
from the mountains of the leopards.
9 You hearten me, my sister bride,
you hearten me with one of your eyes;
with one choker of your neck.
10 How beautified your loves, my, sister bride!
Better your love than wine
and the scent of your ointments than all spices.
11 Your lips, O bride, drip as the honeycomb;
honey and milk are under your tongue;
and the scent of your clothes
is as the scent of Lebanon.
12 A garden inclosed—my sister bride;
a wave inclosed; a fountain sealed:
13 your branches, a paradise of pomegranates,
with precious fruits; camphire, with nard;
14 nard and saffron;
stalk and cinnamon;
with all trees of frankincense;
myrrh and aloes;
with all the head spices;
15 a fountain of gardens;
a well of living waters and flowings from Lebanon.

THE WOMAN

16 Awake, O *north wind* **northerly**;
and come, thou *south* **southerly**;
blow **puff** upon my garden,
that the spices *thereof* may flow *out*.
Let my beloved come into his garden
and eat his *pleasant* **precious** fruits.

THE MAN

5 I am come into my garden,
my *sister, my spouse* **sister bride**:
I have *gathered* **plucked** my myrrh with my spice;
I have eaten my *honeycomb* **honey of the forest**
with my honey;
I have drunk my wine with my milk: eat, O friends;
drink, *yea, drink abundantly* **and intoxicate**, O beloved.

THE WOMAN QUOTES THE MAN

2 I sleep, but my heart waketh:
it is the voice of my beloved that knocketh,
saying, Open to me, my sister, my *love* **friend**,
my dove, my *undefiled* **integrious**:
for my head is filled with *dew* **dewdrops**,
and my locks with the *drops* **dewdrops** of the night.
3 I have *put off* **stripped** my coat;
how shall I *put it on* **enrobe**?
I have washed my feet; how shall I *defile* **foul** them?

THE WOMAN SPEAKS FOR HERSELF

4 My beloved *put in* **spread** his hand by the hole
of the door,
and my *bowels were moved* **inwards roared** for him.
5 I rose up to open to my beloved;
and my hands *dropped with* **dripped** myrrh,
and my fingers with *sweet smelling* myrrh,
that passeth upon the *handles* **palms** of the lock.
6 I opened to my beloved;
but my beloved had withdrawn himself,
and *was gone* **had passed**:
my soul failed when he *spake* **worded**:
I sought him, but I *could not find* **found** him **not**;
I called him, but he *gave me no answer* **answered not**.
7 The *watchmen* **guards**
that *went about* **surrounded** the city found me,
they smote me, they wounded me;
the *keepers* **guards** of the walls
took away **lifted** my veil from me.
8 I *charge* **oath** you,
O daughters of *Jerusalem* **Yeru Shalem**,
if ye find my beloved,
that ye tell him, that I am *sick* **worn out** of love.

THE DAUGHTERS

9 What is thy beloved more than *another* beloved,
O thou *fairest* **beautiful** among women?
what is thy beloved more than *another* beloved,
that thou *dost so charge* **thus oathest** us?

THE WOMAN

10 My beloved is *white* **clear** and *ruddy* **red**,
the *chiefest* **bannerbearer** among *ten thousand* **myriads**.
11 His head is as *the most fine* **ore of pure** gold,
his locks are *bushy* **pendulous**, and black as a raven.
12 His eyes are as *the eyes of* doves
by the *rivers* **reservoirs** of waters,
washed **bathed** with milk, and *fitly* **in fulness** set.
13 His cheeks are as a *bed* **furrow** of spices,
as *sweet flowers* **towers of spices**:
his lips like lilies,
dropping sweet smelling **dripping passing** myrrh.
14 His hands are as gold rings
set **filled** with the beryl:
his *belly is as bright* **inwards as fabricated**
ivory *overlaid* **covered** with sapphires.
15 His legs *are* as pillars of **white** marble,
set **founded** upon sockets of *fine* **pure** gold:
his *countenance is* **visage** as Lebanon,
excellent as the **as select** cedars.
16 His *mouth is most* **palate** sweet:
yea, he is altogether *lovely* **desirable**.
This is my beloved, and this is my friend,
O daughters of *Jerusalem* **Yeru Shalem**.

THE MAN

5 I come into my garden, my sister bride;
I pluck my myrrh with my spice;

THE WOMAN

16 Waken, O northerly! Come, you southerly!
Puff on my garden so the spices flow.
My beloved comes into his garden
and eats his precious fruits.

THE MAN

I eat my honey of the forest with my honey;
I drink my wine with my milk;
eat, O friends;
drink and intoxicate, O beloved.

THE WOMAN QUOTES THE MAN

2 I sleep, but my heart wakens;
the voice of my beloved knocks,
Open to me, my sister, my friend,
my dove, my integrious;
for my head fills with dewdrops
—my locks with the dewdrops of the night.
3 I strip my coat; how enrobe I?
I wash my feet; how foul I?

THE WOMAN SPEAKS FOR HERSELF

4 My beloved spreads his hand by the hole
and my inwards roar for him.
5 I rise to open to my beloved;
my hands drip myrrh—my fingers with myrrh;
it passes on the palms of the lock.
6 I open to my beloved;
but my beloved withdraws; he passes on;
my soul fails when he words:
I seek him, but I find him not;
I call him, but he answers not.
7 The guards surrounding the city find me,
they smite me; they wound me:
the guards of the walls lift my veil from me.
8 I oath you, O daughters of Yeru Shalem,
if you find my beloved,
that you tell him, I am worn from love.

THE DAUGHTERS

9 What *is* your beloved more than beloved,
O you beautiful among women?
What *is* your beloved more than beloved,
that you thus oath us?

THE WOMAN

10 My beloved is clear and red;
the bannerbearer among myriads:
11 his head, as ore of pure gold;
his locks,
as pendulous and black as a raven;
12 his eyes,
as doves by the reservoirs of waters
bathed with milk and set in fulness;
13 his cheeks,
as furrows of spices; as towers of spices;
his lips,
as lilies dripping, passing myrrh;
14 his hands,
as gold rings filled with beryl;
his inwards,
as fabricated ivory covered with sapphires;
15 his legs,

as pillars of white marble
founded on sockets of pure gold;
his visage,
as Lebanon; as select cedars;
16 his palate,
sweet:
yes, he is altogether desirable.
This *is* my beloved and this *is* my friend,
O daughters of Yeru Shalem.

The Daughters

6 Whither is thy beloved gone,
O thou *fairest* **beautiful** among women?
whither is thy beloved turned *aside* **his face**?
that we may seek him with thee.

The Woman

2 My beloved *is gone down*
descended into his garden,
to the *beds* **furrows** of spices,
to *feed in* **tend** the gardens, and to *gather* **gleen** lilies.
3 I am my beloved's, and my beloved is mine:
he *feedeth* **tendeth** among the lilies.

The Man

4 Thou art beautiful, O my *love* **friend**, as Tirzah,
comely as *Jerusalem* **Yeru Shalem**,
terrible **awesome** as *an army with*
banners **bannerbearers**.
5 Turn away thine eyes from me,
for they have *overcome* **encouraged** me:
thy hair is as a *flock* **drove** of **doe** goats
that *appear* **eat** from *Gilead* **Gilad**.
6 Thy teeth are as a *flock* **drove** of *sheep* **ewes**
which *go up* **ascend** from the *washing* **bathing**,
whereof every one *beareth twins* **twinneth**,
and there is not one *barren* **bereft** among them.
7 As a *piece* **slice** of a pomegranate are thy temples
within **throughout** thy *locks* **veil**.
8 *There are threescore queens*
Sixty sovereignesses,
and *fourscore* **eighty** concubines,
and virgins without number.
9 My dove, my *undefiled* **integrious** is *but* one;
she is the *only* one of her mother,
she is the *choice one* **pure** of her that *bare* **birthed** her.

Concerning Her Admirers

The daughters saw her,
and *blessed* **pronounced** her **blithesome**;
yea, the *queens* **sovereignesses** and the concubines,
and they *praised* **halaled** her.
10 Who is she that looketh
forth as the *morning* **dawn**,
fair **beautiful** as the moon,
clear as the sun **pure as heat**,
and *terrible* **awesome**
as *an army with banners* **bannerbearers**.

The Woman Speaks For Herself

11 I *went down* **descended** into the garden of nuts
to see the *fruits* **unripeness** of the *valley* **wadi**,
and to see whether the vine *flourished* **blossomed**
and the pomegranates budded.
12 Or ever I *was aware* **knew**,
my soul *made* **set** me
like the chariots of *Amminadib* **Ammi Nadib**.
13 Return, return, O *Shulamite* **Shulammith**;
return, return, that we may *look* **see** upon thee.
What *will* **shall** ye see in the Shulamite **Shulammith**?
As it were
the *company* **round dance** of *two armies* **Machanah.**

The Man

7 How *beautiful* **beautified**
are thy *feet* **steps** with shoes,
O *prince's* **volunteer's** daughter!
the *joints* **roundness** of thy *thighs* **flanks**
are like jewels **as ornaments**,
the work of the hands of *a cunning workman* **an expert**.
2 Thy navel *is like* **as** a round *goblet* **bowl**,
which *wanteth not liquor* **lacketh no cocktail**:
thy belly *is like* **as** an heap *of wheat*
set about **hedged** with lilies.
3 Thy two breasts *are like* **as**
two *young roes* **fawn gazelles**
that are—twins.
4 Thy neck *is* as a tower of ivory;
thine eyes *like* **as** the fishpools in Heshbon,
by the *gate* **portal** of *Bath—rabbim*
Daughter of Rabbim:
thy *nose* **nostrils** *is* as the tower of Lebanon
which *looketh* **watcheth**
toward Damascus **at the face of Dammeseq**.

The Daughters

6 Where has your beloved gone,
O you beautiful among women?
Where has your beloved turned his face?
—that we seek him with you.

The Woman

2 My beloved descends to his garden
to the furrows of spices;
to tend the gardens and to gleen lilies.
3 I, to my beloved; and my beloved, to me;
he tends among the lilies.

The Man

4 You are beautiful, O my friend, as Tirzah,
comely as Yeru Shalem,
awesome as bannerbearers.
5 Turn your eyes from me,
for they encourage me;
your hair,
as a drove of doe goats eating of Gilad;
6 your teeth,
as a drove of ewes ascending from the bathing
whereof every one twins
—not one bereft among them;
7 as a slice of a pomegranate,
your temples through your veil.
8 Sixty sovereignesses
and eighty concubines
and virgins without number.
9 One *is* my dove, my integrious;
she, the one of her mother;
she, the pure of her who birthed her.

Concerning Her Admirers

The daughters see her
and pronounce her blithesome;
the sovereignesses and the concubines halal her.
10 Who is this?
looks, as the dawn,
beautiful, as the moon,
pure, as heat,
awesome, as bannerbearers.

The Woman Speaks For Herself

11 I descend to the garden of nuts
to see the unripeness of the wadi;
to see whether the vine blossoms
and the pomegranates bud.
12 Or ere I know,
my soul sets me as the chariots of Ammi Nadib.
13 Return! Return, O Shulammith!
Return! Return, so that we see you.
What see you in the Shulammith?
As it were, the round dance of Machanah.

The Man

7 How beautified are your steps with shoes,
O daughter of a volunteer;
the roundness of your flanks,
as ornaments
—the work of the hands of an expert;
2 your navel,
as a round bowl which lacks no cocktail;
your belly,
as a heap hedged with lilies;
3 your two breasts,
as two fawn gazelles—twins;
4 your neck,
as a tower of ivory;
your eyes,
as the fishpools in Heshbon
by the portal of the Daughter of Rabbim;
your nostrils,
as the tower of Lebanon
watching at the face of Dammeseq;
5 Thine head upon thee *is*
like Carmel **as an orchard,**
and the *hair* **thrum** of thine head *like* **as** purple;
the *king* **sovereign** is *held* **bound** in the *galleries* **curls.**
6 How *fair* **beautified** and how
pleasant **pleasing** art thou,
O love, for delights!
7 This thy *stature* **height** is
like **likened** to a palm tree,
and thy breasts to clusters *of grapes.*
8 I said, I *will go up* **shall ascend** to the palm tree,
I *will* **shall** take hold of the *boughs* **twigs** *thereof*:
now also thy breasts shall be as clusters of the vine,
and the *smell* **scent** of thy *nose like* **nostrils as** apples;
9 And *the roof of thy mouth* **thy palate**
like the best **as good** wine for my beloved,
that goeth *down sweetly* **in straightnesses,**
causing the lips of those that are asleep
to *speak* **tranquilly flow.**

The Woman

10 I am my beloved's, and his desire is toward me.
11 Come, my beloved, let us go forth into the field;
let us *lodge* **stay overnight** in the villages.
12 Let us *get up* **start** early to the vineyards;
let us see if the vine *flourish* **blossom,**
whether the tender grape appear—**the blossom open,**
and the pomegranates bud forth:
there *will* **shall** I give thee my loves.

13 The mandrakes give a *smell* **scent**,
and at our *gates* **portals**
are all manner *of pleasant fruits* **preciousnesses**,
new and old, *which* I have *laid up* **treasured** for thee,
O my beloved.

8 O **who giveth** that thou wert as my brother,
that sucked the breasts of my mother!
when I should find thee *without* **in the outways**,
I *would* **should** kiss thee;
yea, I should not be *despised* **disrespected**.
2 I *would lead* **should drive** thee,
and bring thee into my mother's house,
who *would instruct* **should teach** me:
I *would cause* **should have** thee
to drink of *spiced* **perfumed** wine
of the **squeezed** juice of my pomegranate.
3 His left *hand* should be under my head,
and his right *hand* should embrace me.
4 I *charge* **oath** you,
O daughters of *Jerusalem* **Yeru Shalem**,
that ye *stir* not **waken** *up*,
nor awake *my* **the** love, until he *please* **desireth**.

The Daughters

5 Who is this
that *cometh up* **ascendeth** from the wilderness,
leaning upon her beloved?

The Woman

I *raised* **wakened** thee *up* under the apple tree:
there thy mother *brought* **pledged** thee *forth*:
there she *brought* **pledged** thee *forth*
that *bare* **birthed** thee.
6 Set me as a seal upon thine heart,
as a seal upon thine arm:
for love is strong as death;
jealousy is *cruel* **hard** as *the grave* **sheol**:
the *coals* **burning flashes** *thereof*
are *coals* **burning flashes** of fire,
which hath—a most vehement flame.
7 Many waters cannot quench love,
neither can the *floods drown* **rivers overflow** it:
if a man *would* **should** give
all the *substance* **wealth** of his house for love,
it would utterly be contemned
in disrespecting, he should be disrespected.

5 your head on you,
as an orchard;
and the thrum of your head,
as purple
—the sovereign bound in the curls.
6 How beautified and how pleasing are you,
O love, for delights!
7 This your height, likened to a palm tree
and your breasts to clusters.
8 I say, I ascend to the palm tree,
I hold the twigs;
yes, your breasts,
as clusters of the vine;
the scent of your nostrils,
as apples;
9 your palate,
as good wine for my beloved
—who goes in straightnesses
so that the lips of those who sleep tranquilly flow.

The Woman

10 I *am* to my beloved and his desire *is* to me.
11 Come, my beloved, we go to the field
—stay overnight in the villages
12 —start early to the vineyards
—see if the vine blossoms—the blossoms open
and the pomegranates bud forth;
there I give you my loves.
13 The mandrakes give scent
and at our portals *are* all manner preciousnesses,
new and old, which I treasure for you,
O my beloved.

8 O who gives that you be as my brother
sucking the breasts of my mother!
I find you in the outways:
I kiss you;
yes, they disrespect me not:
2 I drive you;
I bring you to the house of my mother:
she teaches me;
I have you drink of perfumed wine
—of the squeezed juice of my pomegranate.
3 His left is under my head
and his right embraces me.
4 I oath you, O daughters of Yeru Shalem,
that neither you waken,
nor waken the love until he desires.

The Daughters

5 Who *is* this ascending from the wilderness,
leaning on her beloved?

The Woman

I wakened you under the apple tree;

there your mother pledged you
—there she who birthed you pledged you.
6 Set me as a seal on your heart,
as a seal on your arm;
for love is as strong as death;
jealousy as hard as sheol;
its burning flashes as burning flashes of fire,
—a most vehement flame.
7 Neither are many waters able to quench love,
nor the rivers overflow it;
if a man give all the wealth of his house for love,
in disrespecting, they disrespect him.

The Daughters

8 We have a little sister, and she hath no breasts:
what shall we *do* **work** for our sister
in the day when she shall be *spoken* **worded** for?
9 If she be a wall,
we *will* **shall** build upon her a *palace* **wall** of silver:
and if she be a door,
we *will inclose* **shall besiege** her
with *boards* **a slab** of cedar.

The Woman

10 I am a wall, and my breasts like towers:
then was I in his eyes as one that found *favour* **shalom**.
11 *Solomon* **Shelomoh**
had a vineyard at *Baalhamon* **Baal Hamon**;
he *let out* **gave** the vineyard unto *keepers* **guards**;
every one **each man** for the fruit *thereof*
was to bring a thousand *pieces of* silver.
12 My vineyard, which is mine,
is *before me* **at my face**:
thou, O *Solomon* **Shelomoh**, *must have* **hast** a thousand,
and those that *keep* **guard** the fruit *thereof* two hundred.

The Man

13 Thou that *dwellest* **settlest** in the gardens,
the companions hearken to thy voice:
cause me to hear it.
14 *Make haste* **Flee**, my beloved,
and be thou *like* **likened** to a *roe* **gazelle**
or to a *young* **fawn** hart upon the mountains of spices.

The Daughters

8 We have a little sister; she has no breasts:
what work we for our sister
in the day they word for her?
9 If she is a wall,
we build on her a wall of silver;
and if she is a door,
we besiege her with a slab of cedar.

The Woman

10 I *am* a wall; and my breasts as towers;
then am I in his eyes as one finding shalom.
11 Shelomoh has a vineyard at Baal Hamon;
he gives the vineyard to guards;
and for the fruit, each man brings a thousand silver.
12 My vineyard—mine, is at my face;
you, O Shelomoh, have a thousand
and they who guard the fruit two hundred.

The Man

13 You who settle in the gardens,
the companions hearken to your voice;
hear me.
14 Flee, my beloved
—likened to a gazelle or to a fawn hart
on the mountains of spices.

The First Lamentation

1 How *doth the city sit* **hath she settled** solitary,
that was full of **the city abounding with** people!
how *is* **hath** she become as a widow!
she that was great among the *nations* **goyim**,
and *princess* **governess** among the
provinces **jurisdictions**,
how *is* **hath** she become *tributary* **a vassal**!
2 **In weeping,** She weepeth *sore* in the night,
and her tears are on her cheeks:
among all her lovers
she hath none to *comfort* **sigh over** her:
all her friends have dealt treacherously with her,
they are—become her enemies.
3 *Judah* **Yah Hudah** is *gone into captivity* **exiled**
because of *affliction* **humiliation**,
and because of *great* **abundant** servitude:
she *dwelleth* **settleth** among the *heathen* **goyim**,
she findeth no rest:
all her *persecutors* **pursuers** overtook her
between the straits.
4 The ways of *Zion do* **Siyon** mourn,
because none come
to the *solemn feasts* **congregation festivals**:
all her *gates* **portals** are desolate:
her priests sigh, her virgins *are afflicted* **grieve**,
and she is *in bitterness* **embittered**.
5 Her *adversaries* **tribulators**
are the chief **have become her heads**,
her enemies *prosper* **serenify**;
for *the LORD* **Yah Veh** hath *afflicted* **grieved** her
for the *multitude* **abundance**
of her *transgressions* **rebellions**:
her *children* **infants** are *gone into captivity* **captured**
before **at the face of** the *enemy* **tribulator**.
6 And from the daughter of *Zion* **Siyon**
all her *beauty* **majesty** is departed:
her *prince* **governors** are become like harts
that find no pasture,
and they are gone without *strength* **force**
before **at the face of** the pursuer.
7 *Jerusalem* **Yeru Shalem** remembered
in the days of her *affliction* **humiliation**
and of her *miseries* **persecutions**
all her *pleasant things* **desires**
that she had in the days of *old* **antiquity**,
when her people
fell into the hand of the *enemy* **tribulator**,
and *none did help her* **she had no helper**:
the *adversaries* **tribulators** saw her,
and *did mock at* **ridiculed** her *sabbaths* **shabbathisms**.
8 **In sinning,**
Jerusalem **Yeru Shalem** hath *grievously* sinned;
therefore she is removed:
all that honoured her *despise* **disesteem** her,
because they have seen her nakedness:
yea, she sigheth, and turneth backward.
9 Her *filthiness* **foulness** is in her *skirts* **hems**;
she remembereth not her *last end* **finality**;
therefore
she *came down wonderfully* **descended marvellously**:
she had *no comforter* **none to sigh**.
O *LORD* **Yah Veh**, *behold* **see** my *affliction* **humiliation**:
for the enemy hath *magnified* **greatened** *himself*.
10 The *adversary* **tribulator**
hath spread out his hand
upon all her *pleasant things* **desires**:
for she hath seen
that the *heathen* **goyim** entered
into her *sanctuary* **holies**,
whom thou didst command
that they should not enter into thy congregation.
11 All her people sigh, they seek bread;
they have given their *pleasant things*
desires for *meat* **food**
to relieve the soul:
see, O *LORD* **Yah Veh**, and *consider* **look**;
for I am become *vile* **a glutton**.
12 Is it *nothing* **naught** to you,
all ye that pass by **the way**?

The First Lamentation

1 How she settles solitary
—the city abounding with people
—become as a widow!
This great among the goyim
and governess among the jurisdictions
—becomes a vassal!
2 In weeping, she weeps in the night
—her tears on her cheeks;
of all her lovers, none sigh over her;
all her friends deal treacherously with her
—become her enemies.
3 Yah Hudah *is* exiled because of humiliation
and because of abundant servitude;
she settles among the goyim,
she finds no rest;
all her pursuers overtake her between the straits.
4 The ways of Siyon mourn;

no one comes to the congregation festivals;
all her portals are desolate;
her priests sigh; her virgins grieve;
she *is* embittered.
5 Her tribulators become her heads;
her enemies serenify;
for Yah Veh grieves her
for the abundance of her rebellions;
her infants are captured at the face of the tribulator:
6 all majesty departs from the daughter of Siyon;
her governors become as harts finding no pasture—
gone without force from the face of the pursuer.
7 Yeru Shalem remembers
the days of her humiliation and of her persecutions;
all her desires from the days of antiquity
—when her people
fell into the hand of the tribulator
and she had no helper:
the tribulators saw her
and ridiculed her shabbathisms.
8 In sinning, Yeru Shalem sinned;
so she is removed;
all who honored her, disesteem her;
because they see her nakedness:
yes, she sighs and turns backward.
9 Her foulness *is* in her hems;
she remembers not her finality:
she descends marvellously;
she has no one to sigh.
O Yah Veh, see my humiliation;
for the enemy greatens.
10 The tribulator spreads his
hand on all her desires;
for she sees the goyim enter her holies,
whom you commanded
to not enter your congregation.
11 All her people sigh; they seek bread;
they gave their desires for food to relieve the soul:
see, O Yah Veh, and look;
for I am a glutton.
12 Is it naught to you, all you who pass by the way?
Look and see if there be any sorrow
like to the sorrow exploited to me
—wherewith Yah Veh afflicted me
in the day of his fuming wrath.
13 From above the heights
he sends fire into my bones to subjugate;
he spreads a net for my feet;
he turns me back;
he gives me desolation and bleeding all the day:
14 the yoke of my rebellions is bound by his hand
—entwined and ascend on my neck;
he falters my force;
Adonay gives me into their hands;
I am not able to rise.
15 Adonay tramples all my mighty in my midst;
he calls a congregation against me
to break my young men;
as in a winepress
Adonay treads the virgin daughter of Yah Hudah.
16 I weep for these;
my eye—my eye cascades with water,
because the sigher to restore my soul
is far from me;
my sons desolate, for the enemy prevails mightily.
17 Siyon spreads her hands
and there is no one to sigh over her;
Yah Veh commands concerning Yaaqov,
that his tribulators surround him;
Yeru Shalem is excluded among them.
18 Yah Veh is just;
for I rebelled against his mouth;
hear, I pray you, all people and see my sorrow;
my virgins and my young men
—gone into captivity.
19 I call for my beloveds;
they—they deceive me;
my priests and my elders expire in the city
while they seek food to restore their souls.
20 See, O Yah Veh, for I tribulate;
my inwards foam; my heart turns within me;
in rebelling, I rebelled:
outwardly the sword bereaves;
as death in the house:
21 they hear that I sigh; no one sighs over me:
all my enemies hear of my evil;
they rejoice that you worked it;
you brought in the day that you called;
they are like me.
22 All their evil comes at your face;
exploit them as you exploit me for all my rebellions;
for my sighs are many and my heart bleeds.

The Second Lamentation

2 How Adonay
overclouds the daughter of Siyon in his wrath;
—casts the beauty of Yisra El
from the heavens to the earth;
and remembers not the stool of his feet
in the day of his wrath!

behold **look,**
and see if there be any sorrow like unto my sorrow,
which *is done* **be exploited** unto me,
wherewith *the LORD* **Yah Veh** hath afflicted me
in the day of his *fierce anger* **fuming wrath.**
13 From above **the heights**
hath he sent fire into my bones,
and it *prevaileth against* **subjugateth** them:
he hath spread a net for my feet,
he hath turned me back:
he hath *made* **given** me
desolate **desolation** and *faint* **bleeding** all the day.
14 The yoke of my *transgressions* **rebellions**
is bound by his hand:
they are *wreathed* **entwined,**
and *come up* **ascend** upon my neck:
he hath made my *strength* **force** to *fall* **falter,**
the Lord **Adonay**
hath *delivered* **given** me into their hands,
from whom—I am not able to rise *up.*
15 *The Lord* **Adonay**
hath *trodden under foot* **trampled** all my mighty *men*
in the midst of me:
he hath called *an assembly* **a congregation** against me
to *crush* **break** my young men:
the Lord **Adonay** hath trodden the virgin,
the daughter of *Judah* **Yah Hudah,**
as in a winepress **of virgins.**
16 For these *things* I weep;
mine eye, mine eye *runneth down* **cascadeth** with water,
because the *comforter* **sigher**
that should *relieve* **restore** my soul is far from me:
my *children* **sons** are desolate,
because the enemy prevailed **mightily.**
17 *Zion* **Siyon** spreadeth forth her hands,
and there is none to *comfort* **sigh over** her:
the LORD **Yah Veh** hath commanded
concerning *Jacob* **Yaaqov,**
that his *adversaries* **tribulators**
should be round about him:
Jerusalem **Yeru Shalem**
is *as a menstruous woman* **excluded among them.**
18 *The LORD* **Yah Veh** is *righteous* **just;**
for I have rebelled against his *commandment* **mouth:**
hear, I pray you, all people, and *behold* **see** my sorrow:
my virgins and my young men are gone into captivity.
19 I called for my *lovers* **beloveds,**
but they deceived me:
my priests and mine elders
gave up the ghost **expired** in the city,
while they sought *their meat* **food** to
relieve **restore** their souls.
20 *Behold* **See,** O *LORD* **Yah Veh;**
for I am *in distress* **tribulated:**
my *bowels are troubled* **inwards foam;**
mine heart is turned within me;
in rebelling, *for* I have *grievously* rebelled:
abroad **outwardly** the sword bereaveth,
at home there is as death.
21 They have heard that I sigh:
there is none to *comfort* **sigh over** me:
all mine enemies have heard of my *trouble* **evil;**
they *are glad* **rejoice** that thou hast *done* **worked** it:
thou *wilt* **shalt** bring the day that thou hast called,
and **so** they shall be like unto me.
22 Let all their *wickedness* **evil**
come *before thee* **at thy face;**
and *do* **exploit** unto them,
as thou hast *done* **exploited** unto me
for all my *transgressions* **rebellions:**
for my sighs are many, and my heart *is faint* **bleedeth.**

THE SECOND LAMENTATION

2 How hath *the Lord* **Adonay**
covered **overclouded** the daughter
of *Zion* **Siyon** *with a cloud*
in his *anger* **wrath,**
and cast down from *heaven* **the heavens** unto the earth
the beauty of *Israel* **Yisra El,**
and remembered not *his footstool* **the stool of his feet**
in the day of his *anger* **wrath!**
exeGeses ready research BIBLE
2 *The Lord* **Adonay** hath swallowed up
all the *habitations* **folds** of *Jacob* **Yaaqov,**
and hath not *pitied* **spared:**
he hath *thrown down* **demolished** in his *wrath* **fury**
the *strong holds* **fortresses**
of the daughter of *Judah* **Yah I-ludah;**
he hath *brought* **touched** them
down to the *ground* **earth:**
he hath *polluted* **profaned** the *kingdom* **sovereigndom**
and the *princes* **governors** *thereof.*
3 He hath cut off in his *fierce anger* **fuming wrath**
all the horn of *Israel* **Yisra El:**
he hath *drawn* **turned** back his right *hand*
from *before* **the face of** the enemy,
and he burned against *Jacob* **Yaaqov** like a flaming fire,
which *devoureth* **consumeth** round about.
4 He hath bent his bow like an enemy:
he *stood* **stationed** with his right *hand*

as *an adversary* **a tribulator**,
and *slew* **slaughtered** all
that were *pleasant* **a desire** to the eye
in the *tabernacle* **tent** of the daughter of *Zion* **Siyon**:
he poured out his fury like fire.
5 *The Lord* **Adonay** was as an enemy:
he hath swallowed *up Israel* **Yisra El**,
he hath swallowed *up* all her *palaces* **citadels**:
he hath *destroyed* **ruined** his *strong holds* **fortresses**,
and hath *increased* **abounded**
in the daughter of *Judah* **Yah I-ludah**
mourning and *lamentation* **sighing**.
6 And he hath *violently taken away* **violated**
his *tabernacle* **sukkoth/brush arbor**
as *if it were of* a garden:
he hath *destroyed* **ruined**
his *places of the assembly* **seasons**:
the LORD **Yah Veh** hath caused
the *solemn feasts* **seasons** and *sabbaths* **shabbaths**
to be forgotten in *Zion* **Siyon**,
and hath *despised* **scorned**
in the *indignation* **rage** of his *anger* **wrath**
the *king* **sovereign** and the priest.
7 *The Lord* **Adonay** hath
cast off his **sacrifice** altar,
he hath *abhorred* **rejected** his *sanctuary* **holies**,
he hath *given* **shut** up into the hand of the enemy
the walls of her *palaces* **citadels**;
they have *made a noise* **given voice**
in the house of *the LORD* **Yah Veh**,
as in the day of a *solemn feast* **season**.
8 *The LORD* **Yah Veh** hath *purposed* **machinated**
to *destroy* **ruin** the wall of the daughter of *Zion* **Siyon**:
he hath *stretched out* **spread** a line,
he hath not *withdrawn* **turned back** his hand
from *destroying* **swallowing**:
therefore he made the *rampart* **trench**
and the wall to lament;
they languished together.
9 Her *gates* **portals** are sunk
into the *ground* **earth**;
he hath destroyed and broken her bars:
her *king* **sovereign** and her *princes* **governors**
are among the *Gentiles* **goyim**:
the *law* **torah** is *no more* **not**;
her prophets also
find no vision from *the LORD* **Yah Veh**.
10 The elders of the daughter of *Zion* **Siyon**
sit **settle** upon the *ground* **earth**, and *keep silence* **hush**:
they have *cast up* **ascended** dust upon their heads;
they have girded themselves with *sackcloth* **saq**:
the virgins of *Jerusalem* **Yeru Shalem**
hang down **lower** their heads to the *ground* **earth**.
11 Mine eyes *do fail* **are finished off** with tears,
my *bowels are troubled* **inwards foam**,
my liver is poured upon the earth,
for the *destruction* **breech** of the daughter of my people;
because the *children* **infants** and the sucklings
swoon **languish** in the *streets* **broadways** of the city.
12 They say to their mothers,
Where is *corn* **crop** and wine?
when they *swooned* **languished** as the *wounded* **pierced**
in the *streets* **broadways** of the city,
when their soul was poured out
into their mothers' bosom.
2 Adonay swallows all the folds of Yaaqov
and spares not;
in his fury he demolishes the fortresses
of the daughter of Yah Hudah;
he touches them to the earth;
he profanes the sovereigndom and the governors;
3 in his fuming wrath
he cuts off all the horn of Yisra El;
he turns back his right from the face of the enemy;
and he burns against Yaaqov as a flaming fire
—consuming all around:
4 he bends his bow as an enemy;
he stations with his right as a tribulator
and slaughters all who *are* a desire to the eye
in the tent of the daughter of Siyon;
he pours out his fury as fire.
5 Adonay, as an enemy, swallows Yisra El,
he swallows all her citadels;
he ruins his fortresses;
and abounds mourning and sighing
in the daughter of Yah Hudah:
6 he violates his sukkoth/brush arbor as a garden;
he ruins his seasons;
Yah Veh has the seasons and shabbaths
to be forgotten in Siyon;
and in the rage of his wrath
scorns the sovereign and the priest:
7 Adonay casts off his sacrifice altar;
he rejects his holies;
he shuts the walls of her citadels
to the hand of the enemy;
they give voice in the house of Yah Veh
as in the day of seasons.
8 Yah Veh machinates
to ruin the wall of the daughter of Siyon:
he spreads a line;

he turns not back his hand from swallowing;
and he has the trench and the wall lament;
they languish together:
9 her portals sink into the earth;
he destroys and breaks her bars;
her sovereign and her governors
are among the goyim;
the torah is not;
her prophets also find no vision from Yah Veh:
10 the elders of the daughter of Siyon
settle on the earth and hush; they ascend dust
on their heads; they girt themselves with saq;
the virgins of Yeru Shalem
lower their heads to the earth.
11 My eyes finish off with tears; my inwards foam;
my liver pours on the earth
for the breech of the daughter of my people;
because the infants and the sucklings
languish in the broadways of the city.
12 They say to their mothers,
Where *are* crop and wine?
—as they languish as the pierced
in the broadways of the city;
as their soul pours into the bosom of their mothers.
13 What *thing* shall I take to witness for thee?
what *thing* shall I liken to thee,
O daughter of *Jerusalem* **Yeru Shalem**?
what shall I *equal* **equate** to thee,
that I may *comfort* **sigh over** thee,
O virgin daughter of *Zion* **Siyon**?
for thy breach is great like the sea:
who *can* **shall** heal thee?
14 Thy prophets have seen *vain* **thy vanity**
and *foolish things for thee* **thy slime**:
and they have not
discovered thine iniquity **exposed thy perversity**,
to turn away thy captivity;
but have seen for thee *false* **vain** burdens
and *causes of banishment* **seductions**.
15 All that pass by **the way**
clap their *hands* **palms** at thee;
they hiss and wag their head
at the daughter of *Jerusalem* **Yeru Shalem**,
saying, Is this the city that *men call* **is said**
The perfection of **Total** beauty,
The joy of the whole earth?
16 All thine enemies
have *opened* **gasped** their mouth against thee:
they hiss and gnash the teeth:
they say, We have swallowed her *up*:
certainly **surely** this is the day that
we *looked for* **awaited**;
we have found, we have seen *it*.
17 *The LORD* **Yah Veh**
hath *done* **worked** that which he had *devised* **intrigued**;
he hath *fulfilled* **cut** his *word* **saying**
that he had commanded in the days of *old* **antiquity**:
he hath *thrown down* **demolished**,
and hath not *pitied* **spared**:
and he hath caused thine enemy
to *rejoice* **cheer** over thee,
he hath *set* **lifted** *up* the horn
of *thine adversaries* **thy tribulators**.
18 Their heart cried unto *the Lord* **Adonay**,
O wall of the daughter of *Zion* **Siyon**,
let tears *run down* **cascade** like a
river **wadi** day and night:
give thyself no *rest* **breather**;
let not the *apple* **daughter** of thine eye *cease* **be stilled**.
19 Arise, cry out in the night:
in the *beginning* **head** of the watches
pour out thine heart like water
before the face of *the Lord* **Adonay**:
lift up thy *hands* **palms** toward him
for the *life* **soul** of thy *young children* **infants**,
that *faint* **languish** for *hunger* **famine**
in the top of *every street* **all the outways**.
20 *Behold* **See**, O *LORD* **Yah
Veh**, and *consider* **look**
to whom thou hast *done this* **exploited thus**.
Shall the women eat their fruit,
and children—**infants** of a **palm** span *long*?
shall the priest and the prophet be *slain* **slaughtered**
in the *sanctuary* **holies** of *the Lord* **Adonay**?
21 The *young* **lad** and the *old* **aged**
lie on the *ground* **earth** in the *streets* **outways**:
my virgins and my young men are fallen by the sword;
thou hast *slain* **slaughtered** them
in the day of *thine anger* **thy wrath**;
thou hast *killed* **slaughtered**, and not *pitied* **spared**.
22 Thou hast called as in a *solemn* day **of season**
my terrors round about,
so that in the day of *the LORD'S anger* **Yah Veh's wrath**
none escaped **there be no escapee**
nor *remained* **survivor**:
those that I have
swaddled **palm spanned** and *brought up* **abounded**
hath mine enemy consumed.

The Third Lamentation

3 I am the *man* **mighty**
that hath seen *affliction* **humiliation**
by the *rod* **scion** of his *wrath* **fury**.
2 He hath *led* **driven** me,
and *brought* **walked** me into darkness,
but not into **without** light.
13 What take I to witness for you?
What liken I to you, O daughter of Yeru Shalem?
What equate I to you, so that I sigh over you,
O virgin daughter of Siyon?
For your breach is great as the sea;
who heals you?
14 Your prophets see your vanity and your slime;
and they expose not your perversity
to turn your captivity;
but see for you vain burdens and seductions.
15 All who pass by the way
clap their palms at you;
they hiss and wag their head
at the daughter of Yeru Shalem,
Is this the city of whom is said, Total beauty?
—the joy of the whole earth?
16 All your enemies gasp their mouth against you;
they hiss and gnash the teeth;
they say, We swallowed her!
Surely this is the day we awaited!
We found! We saw!
17 Yah Veh works what he intrigued;
he cut the saying
he commanded in the days of antiquity;
he demolished and spared not;
and he has your enemy to cheer over you:
he lifts the horn of your tribulators.
18 Their heart cries to Adonay,
O wall of the daughter of Siyon,
they cascade tears as a wadi day and night;
give yourself no breather;
may the daughter of your eye not be stilled.
19 Rise! Cry out in the night,
in the head of the watches;
pour your heart as water at the face of Adonay;
lift your palms toward him
for the soul of your infants who languish for famine
in the top of all the outways.
20 See, O Yah Veh,
and look to whom you thus exploit.
Are the women to eat their fruit
—infants of a palm span?
—priest and the prophet slaughtered
in the holies of Adonay?
21 The lad and the aged
lie on the earth in the outways;
my virgins and my young men fall by the sword;
you slaughter them in the day of your wrath
—slaughter and spare not.
22 You call as in a day of season
my terrors all around,
so that in the day of the wrath of Yah Veh
there is neither escapee nor survivor;
they whom I palm spanned and abounded
my enemy consumed.

The Third Lamentation

3 I, the mighty,
saw humiliation by the scion of his fury:
2 he drove me and walked me
into darkness without light:
3 Surely against me is he turned;
he turneth his hand *against me* all the day.
4 My flesh and my skin hath
he *made old* **worn out**;
he hath broken my bones.
5 He hath builded against me,
and *compassed* **surrounded** me
with *gall* **rosh** and travail.
6 He hath set me in dark places,
as *they that be* **the** dead of old.
7 He hath *hedged* **walled** me *about* **in**,
that I cannot get out:
he hath *made* **weighted** my *chain heavy* **copper**.
8 Also when I cry and shout,
he shutteth out my prayer.
9 He hath *inclosed* **walled in**
my ways with hewn *stone*,
he hath *made* **bent** my paths *crooked*.
10 He was unto me *as* a bear *lying in wait* **lurking**,
and as a lion in *secret places* **coverts**.
11 He hath turned aside my ways, and *pulled*
me in pieces **torn me**: he hath *made* **set** me desolate.
12 He hath bent his bow,
and *set* **stationed** me as a *mark* **target** for the arrow.
13 He hath caused the *arrows* **sons** of his quiver
to enter into my reins.
14 I was a *derision* **ridicule** to all my people;
and their *song* **strumming** all the day.
15 He hath *filled* **satiated** me
with *bitterness* **bitternesses**,
he hath *made me drunken* **satiated me** with wormwood.

16 He hath also *broken* **crushed** my teeth
with gravel *stones*,
he hath covered me with ashes.
17 And thou hast removed my soul
far off from *peace* **shalom**:
I forgat *prosperity* **good**.
18 And I said,
My *strength* **perpetuity** and my hope is perished
from *the LORD* **Yah Veh**:
19 Remembering mine *affliction* **humiliation**
and my *misery* **persecution,**
the wormwood and the *gall* **rosh**.
20 **In remembering,**
My soul *hath them still in remembrance* **remembereth**,
and *is humbled* **sinketh** in me.
21 This I *recall* **return** to my *mind* **heart**,
therefore *have I hope* **I await**.
22 It is of *the LORD'S* **Yah Veh's** mercies
that we are not consumed,
because his *compassions* **tender mercies**
fail not **never finish**.
23 *They are new every morning* **New by mornings**:
great is thy *faithfulness* **trustworthiness.**
24 *The LORD* **Yah Veh** is my *portion* **allotment**,
saith my soul;
therefore *will I hope in* **shall I await** him.
25 *The LORD* **Yah Veh** is good
unto them that *wait for* **await** him,
to the soul that seeketh him.
26 It is good *that a man should both hope* **to await**
and quietly wait for—**to silently await** the salvation
of *the LORD* **Yah Veh**.
27 It is good for a *man* **mighty**
that he bear the yoke of his youth.
28 He *sitteth* **settleth** alone
and *keepeth silence* **husheth**,
because he hath borne it upon him.
29 He *putteth* **giveth** his mouth in the dust;
if so be there may be hope.
30 He giveth his cheek to him that smiteth him:
he is *filled full* **satiated** with reproach.
31 For *the Lord* **Adonay**
will **shall** not cast off *for ever* **eternally**:
32 But though he *cause grief* **grieve thee,**
yet *will* **shall** he *have compassion* **mercy**
according to the *multitude* **abundance** of his mercies.
33 For he *doth not afflict* **neither humbleth**
willingly **from his heart**
nor *grieve* **grieveth** the *children* **sons** of men.
34 To crush under his feet
all the *prisoners* **bound** of the earth.
35 To *turn aside* **pervert** the *right*
judgment of a *man* **mighty**
before **in front of** the face of *the most High* **Elyon**,
3 surely he turns against me
—turns his hand all the day:
4 he wears out my flesh and my skin;
he breaks my bones;
5 he builds against me
and surrounds me with rosh and travail;
6 he sets me in dark places as the dead of old;
7 he walls me in so I cannot get out;
he weights my copper:
8 also when I cry and shout,
he shuts out my prayer;
9 he walls in my ways with hewn;
he bends my paths:
10 he *is* to me as a bear lurking
—a lion in coverts:
11 he turns aside my ways and tears me;
he sets me desolate;
12 he bends his bow
and stations me as a target for the arrow;
13 he has the sons of his quiver enter my reins.
14 I am a ridicule to all my people;
and their strumming all the day:
15 he satiates me with bitternesses;
he satiates me with wormwood:
16 and he crushes my teeth with gravel;
he covers me with ashes.
17 And you remove my soul far from shalom;
I forget the good.
18 And I say,
My perpetuity and my hope from Yah Veh
destructs;
19 remember my humiliation and my persecution
—the wormwood and the rosh.
20 In remembering, my soul remembers
and sinks within me.
21 I turn this to my heart; so I await.
22 The mercies of Yah Veh!
We are not consumed,
because his tender mercies never finish:
23 new by mornings;
how great your trustworthiness.
24 Yah Veh *is* my allotment, says my soul;
so I await him.
25 Yah Veh *is* good to them who await him
—to the soul who seeks him:
26 —good to await

—to silently await the salvation of Yah Veh.
27 —good for the mighty
to bear the yoke of his youth.
28 He settles alone and hushes
because he bears it on himself:
29 he gives his mouth in the dust;
if so be there is hope:
30 he gives his cheek to his smiter;
he satiates with reproach.
31 For Adonay casts not off eternally;
32 for though he grieves you,
yet he mercies
according to the abundance of his mercies:
33 for he neither humbles from his heart
nor grieves the sons of men.
34 To crush all the bound of
the earth under his feet,
35 to pervert the judgment of the mighty
in front of the face of Elyon,
36 to twist a man in his defence,
Adonay sees not.
37 Who *is* this—who says, and it becomes
and Adonay commands not?
38 From the mouth of Elyon
proceeds not evil and good?
39 Why sighs any living human
—the mighty for his sins?
40 We search our ways and probe
and return to Yah Veh;
41 we lift our heart with palms
to El in the heavens;
42 we—we transgress and rebel:
you—you forgive not;
43 you cover with wrath and pursue us;
you slaughter; you spare not:
44 you cover with a cloud
so our prayer passes not through:
45 you set us the offscouring and refuse
midst the people:
46 all our enemies gasp their mouths against us;
47 dread and a pit comes on us
—desolation and breech.
48 My eye cascades with rivulets of water
for the breech of the daughter of my people:
49 my eye flows and ceases not
—without any relaxation.
50 Until Yah Veh looks down
and sees from the heavens,
51 my eye exploits my soul
because of all the daughters of my city.
52 In hunting, my enemies hunt me as a bird
—gratuitously;
53 they exterminate my life in the well
and hand toss a stone on me:
54 waters overflow my head;
I say, I am cut off.
55 I call on your name, O Yah Veh,
from the nether well.
56 You hear my voice;
conceal not your ear at my respiration; at my cry:
57 you drew near in the day I called on you;
you said, Awe not.
58 O Adonay,
you defended the defences of my soul;
you redeemed my life:
59 O Yah Veh, you saw my writhing;
judge my judgment.
60 You see all their vengeance
and all their machinations against me.
61 You hear their reproach, O Yah Veh,
and all their machinations against me;
62 the lips of those who rise against me
and their meditation against me all the day.
63 Look at their sitting and their rising;
I am their satire.
64 Return their dealings to them,
O Yah Veh, according to the work of their hands:
65 give them a covered heart
—your curse to them:
66 persecute and desolate them in wrath
from under the heavens of Yah Veh.

THE FOURTH LAMENTATION

4 How the gold fades
—the good ore changes;
—the stones of the holies
poured out in the top of all the outways!
2 The esteemed sons of Siyon,
balanced to pure gold,
36 To *subvert* **twist** a man in his *cause* **defence**,
the Lord approveth **Adonay seeth** not.
37 Who is he that saith, and it
cometh to pass **becometh**,
when *the Lord* **Adonay** commandeth it not?
38 Out of the mouth of *the most High* **Elyon**
proceedeth not evil and good?
39 Wherefore doth a living *man* **human** complain,
a *man* **mighty** for *the punishment of* his sins?
40 Let us search and *try* **probe** our ways,
and *turn again* **return** to *the LORD* **Yah Veh**.

41 Let us lift up our heart with *our hands* **palms**
unto *God* **El** in the heavens.
42 We have transgressed and have rebelled:
thou hast not *pardoned* **forgiven**.
43 Thou hast covered with *anger* **wrath**,
and *persecuted* **pursued** us:
thou hast slain, thou hast not *pitied* **spared**.
44 Thou hast covered thyself with a cloud,
that our prayer should not pass through.
45 Thou hast *made* **set** us *as*
the offscouring and refuse
in the midst of the people.
46 All our enemies
have *opened* **gasped** their mouths against us.
47 *Fear* **Dread** and a *snare* **pit** is come upon us,
desolation and *destruction* **breech**.
48 Mine eye *runneth down* **cascadeth**
with *rivers* **rivulets** of water
for the *destruction* **breech** of the daughter of my people.
49 Mine eye *trickleth down*
floweth, and ceaseth not,
without any *intermission* **relaxation**.
50 Till *the LORD* **Yah Veh** look down,
and *behold* **see** from *heaven* **the heavens**.
51 Mine eye *affecteth mine*
heart **exploiteth my soul**
because of all the daughters of my city
52 **In hunting,** Mine enemies
chased **hunted** me *sore*,
like a bird, *without cause* **gratuitously**.
53 They have *cut off* **exterminated** my life
in the *dungeon* **well**,
and *cast* **hand tossed** a stone upon me.
54 Waters *flowed over* **overflowed** mine head;
then I said, I am cut off.
55 I called upon thy name, O *LORD* **Yah Veh**,
out of the *low dungeon* **nether well**.
56 Thou hast heard my voice:
hide **conceal** not thine ear
at my *breathing* **respiration**, at my cry.
57 Thou drewest near in the
day that I called upon thee:
thou saidst, *Fear* **Awe** not.
58 O *Lord* **Adonay**,
thou hast *pleaded* **defended**
the *causes* **defences** of my soul;
thou hast redeemed my life.
59 O *LORD* **Yah Veh**,
thou hast seen my *wrong* **writhing**:
judge thou my *cause* **judgment**.
60 Thou hast seen all their vengeance
and all their *imaginations* **machinations** against me.
61 Thou hast heard their
reproach, O *LORD* **Yah Veh**,
and all their *imaginations* **machinations** against me;
62 The lips of those that rose *up* against me,
and their *device* **meditation** against me all the day.
63 *Behold* **Look at** their sitting
down, and their rising *up*;
I am their *musick* **satire**.
64 *Render* **Return** unto them
a recompence **their dealings**,
O *LORD* **Yah Veh**, according to the work of their hands.
65 Give them *sorrow* **covering** of heart,
thy curse unto them.
66 Persecute and *destroy*
desolate them in *anger* **wrath**
from under the heavens of *the LORD* **Yah Veh**.

THE FOURTH LAMENTATION

4 How is the gold *become dim* **faded**!
how is the most fine gold—**the good ore** changed!
the stones of the *sanctuary* **holies**
are poured out in the top of *every street* **all the outways**.
2 The *precious* **esteemed** sons of *Zion* **Siyon**,
comparable **balanced** to *fine* **pure** gold,
how are they *esteemed* **reckoned**
as *earthen pitchers* **pottery bottles**,
the work of the hands of the *potter* **former**!
3 Even the *sea* monsters *draw out* **strip** the breast,
they *give suck to* **suckle** their *young ones* **whelps**:
the daughter of my people is *become* cruel,
like the ostriches in the wilderness.
4 The tongue of the *sucking child* **suckling**
cleaveth to the roof of his mouth **adhereth to his palate**
for thirst:
the *young children* **infants** ask bread,
and no *man breaketh* **one spreadeth** it unto them.
5 They that did *feed* **eat** delicately
are *desolate* **desolated** in the *streets* **outways**:
they that were *brought up in* **entrusted with** scarlet
embrace dunghills.
6 For the *punishment of the iniquity* **perversity**
of the daughter of my people
is *greater than the punishment of* **greatened above**
the sin of Sodom,
that was *overthrown* **overturned** as in a *moment* **blink**,
and no hands *stayed on* **writhed over** her.
7 Her *Nazarites* **Separatists**
were *purer than* **purified as** snow,

they were **dazzling** whiter than milk,
they were more ruddy in body **their**
bones more reddened
than *rubies* **pearls,**
their *polishing* **separatism** was of sapphire:
8 Their *visage* **form** is *blacker*
darker than *a coal* **darkness**;
they are not *known* **recognized** in the *streets* **outways**:
their skin *cleaveth* **adhereth** to their bones;
it is withered, it is become like *a stick* **wood.**
9 They that be *slain* **pierced** with the sword
are better than they
that be *slain* **pierced** with *hunger* **famine**:
for these *pine* **flow** away,
stricken through **stabbed**
for *want of the fruits* **the produce** of the field.
10 The hands of the *pitiful* **mercied** women
have *sodden* **stewed** their own children:
they were their *meat* **chewing**
in the *destruction* **breech** of the daughter of my people.
11 *The LORD* **Yah Veh** hath accomplished his fury;
he hath poured out his fierce *anger* **wrath,**
and hath kindled a fire in *Zion* **Siyon,**
and it hath *devoured* **consumed** the foundations *thereof.*
12 The *kings* **sovereigns** of the earth,
and all *the inhabitants of* **that settled** the world,
would **should** not have *believed* **trusted**
that the *adversary* **tribulator** and the enemy
should have entered
into the *gates* **portals** of *Jerusalem* **Yeru Shalem.**
13 For the sins of her prophets,
and the *iniquities* **perversities** of her priests,
that have *shed* **poured** the blood of the just
in the midst of her,
14 They have wandered
as blind *men* in the *streets* **outways,**
they have polluted themselves with blood,
so that *men could not* **they are not able**
to touch their *garments* **robes.**
15 They *cried* **called** unto them,
Depart ye; **Turn aside!** *it is unclean;* **Foul!**
depart, depart **Turn aside! Turn aside!**
touch not: **Touch not!**
when they fled away and wandered,
they said among the *heathen* **goyim,**
They shall *no more* **not add to** sojourn there.
16 The anger of *the LORD* **Yah Veh**
hath *divided* **allotted** them;
he *will no more regard* **shall never again scan** them:
they *respected* **bore** not the persons of the priests,
they *favoured* **granted** not **charism to** the elders.
17 As for us,
our eyes as yet *failed* **are finished off** for our vain help:
in our watching we have watched for a *nation* **goyim**
that could not save *us.*
18 They hunt our *steps* **paces,**
that we cannot go in our *streets* **broadways:**
how they are reckoned as pottery bottles,
the work of the hands of the former!
3 Even the monsters strip the breast;
they suckle their whelps:
the daughter of my people is cruel,
as ostriches in the wilderness.
4 The tongue of the suckling
adheres to his palate for thirst;
the infants ask bread
and no one spreads to them;
5 they who ate delicately
desolate in the outways;
those entrusted with scarlet
embrace dunghills.
6 And the perversity of the daughter of my people
greatens above the sin of Sodom
—overturned as in a blink
and no hands writhed over her.
7 Her Separatists were purified as snow
—dazzling whiter than milk;
their bones more reddened than pearls;
their separatism of sapphire:
8 their form becomes darker than darkness
—not recognized in the outways;
their skin adheres to their bones
—withers; becomes as wood.
9 Those pierced with the sword
are better than those pierced with famine;
for they flow away stabbed
because of the produce of the field.
10 The hands of the mercied women
stew their own children;
they chew them
in the breech of the daughter of my people.
11 Yah Veh accomplishes his fury
—pours out his fierce wrath
and kindled a fire in Siyon;
and it consumes the foundations.
12 The sovereigns of the earth
and all who settle the world,
had never trusted
for the tribulator and the enemy
to enter into the portals of Yeru Shalem.

13 Because of the sins of her prophets
and the perversities of her priests,
who pour the blood of the just in her midst,
14 they wander as blind in the outways:
they pollute themselves with blood,—
not able to touch their robes.
15 They call to them, Turn aside! Foul!
Turn aside! Turn aside! Touch not!
As they flee and wander,
they say among the goyim, Add not to sojourn there.
16 The anger of Yah Veh allots them;
never again to scan them;
they neither lifted the face of the priests,
nor granted charism to the elders.
17 As for us,
our eyes as yet are finished off for our vain help:
in our watching,
we watched for a goyim that saves not:
18 they hunt our paces,
from going in our broadways;
our end is near, our days are fulfilled;
for our end is come.
19 Our *persecutors* **pursuers**
are swifter than the eagles of the *heaven* **heavens**:
they *hotly* pursued us upon the mountains,
they *laid wait* **lurked** for us in the wilderness.
20 The *breath* **spirit/wind** of our nostrils,
the anointed of *the LORD* **Yah Veh**,
was *taken* **captured** in their pits,
of whom we said,
Under his shadow
we shall live among the *heathen* **goyim**.
21 Rejoice and *be glad* **cheer**, O daughter of Edom,
that *dwellest* **settlest** in the land of *Uz* **Us**; the
cup also shall pass through unto thee:
thou shalt *be drunken* **intoxicate**,
and shalt *make* **strip** thyself naked.
22 *The punishment of thine iniquity* **Thy perversity**
is *accomplished* **consummated**, O
daughter of *Zion* **Siyon**;
he *will* **shall** no more *carry* **exile** thee *away into captivity*:
he *will* **shall** visit *thine iniquity* **thy perversity**,
O daughter of Edom;
he *will discover* **shall expose** thy sins.

THE FIFTH LAMENTATION

5 Remember, O *LORD* **Yah Veh**,
what is come upon us:
consider **look**, and *behold* **see** our reproach.
2 Our inheritance is turned to strangers,
our houses to *aliens* **strangers**.
3 We are orphans and fatherless,
our mothers are as widows.
4 We have drunken our water for money;
our *wood* **timber** is *sold* **priced** unto us.
5 *Our necks are under persecution*
They pursue our necks:
we labour, and *have no* rest **not**.
6 We have given the hand to
the *Egyptians* **Misrayim**,
and to the Assyrians **to Ashshuriym**,
to be satisfied with bread.
7 Our fathers have sinned, and are not;
and we have borne their *iniquities* **perversities**.
8 Servants have *ruled* **reigned** over us:
there is none that *doth deliver* **separateth** us
out of their hand.
9 We gat our bread *with the*
peril of our lives **by our souls**
because of the sword of the wilderness.
10 Our skin was *black* **shriveled** like an oven
because of the *terrible* **raging** famine.
11 They *ravished* **humbled** the women
in *Zion* **Siyon**,
and the *maids* **virgins**
in the cities of *Judah* **Yah Hudah**.
12 *Princes* **Governors** are hanged up by their hand:
the faces of elders were not *honoured* **esteemed**.
13 They *took* **lifted** the young men to grind,
and the *children* **lads**
fell **stumbled** under the *wood* **timber**.
14 The elders
have *ceased* **shabbathized** from the *gate* **portal**,
the young men from their *musick* **strumming**.
15 The joy of our heart *is ceased* **shabbathized**;
our **round** dance is turned into mourning.
16 The crown is fallen from our head:
woe unto us, that we have sinned!
17 For this our heart *is faint* **bleedeth**;
for these *things* our eyes *are dim* **darken**.
18 Because of the mountain of *Zion* **Siyon**,
which is desolate, the foxes walk upon it.
19 Thou, O *LORD* **Yah Veh**,
remainest for ever **settlest eternally**; thy
throne from generation to generation.
20 Wherefore dost thou forget
us *for ever* **in perpetuity**,
and forsake us *so long* **for length of days of** time?
21 *Turn thou* **Return** us unto
thee, O *LORD* **Yah Veh**,

and we shall *be turned* **return**;
renew our days as of *old* **antiquity**.
22 But **in spurning,**
thou hast *utterly rejected* **spurned** us;
thou art *very wroth* **mighty enraged** against us.
19 Our pursuers
are swifter than the eagles of the heavens:
they pursue us on the mountains;
they lurk for us in the wilderness:
20 the spirit/wind of our nostrils,
the anointed of Yah Veh, is captured in their pits
—of whom we say,
Under his shadow we live among the goyim.
21 Rejoice and cheer, O daughter of Edom,
who settles in the land of Us;
the cup also passes through to you;
intoxicate and strip yourself naked:
22 your perversity *is* consummated,
O daughter of Siyon;
he exiles you no more:
he visits your perversity, O daughter of Edom:
he exposes your sins.

THE FIFTH LAMENTATION

5 Remember, O Yah Veh, what becomes us;
look and see our reproach:
2 our inheritance is turned to strangers;
our houses to strangers:
3 we are orphans and fatherless;
our mothers as widows:
4 we drank our water for money;
our timber comes at a price;
5 they pursue our necks;
we labor and rest not:
6 we gave a hand to the
Misrayim—to Ashshuriym,
to satisfy with bread;
7 our fathers sinned and are not;
and we bear their perversities:
8 servants reign over us;
no one separates us from their hand:
9 we get our bread by our souls
because of the sword of the wilderness:
10 our skin shrivels as an oven
because of the raging famine.
11 They humble the women in Siyon
and the virgins in the cities of Yah Hudah;
12 governors are hanged by their hand;
the faces of elders are not esteemed:
13 they lift the young men to grind
and the lads stumble under the timber:
14 the elders shabbathize from the portal
—the young men from their strumming:
15 the joy of our heart shabbathizes;
our round dance turns into mourning;
16 the crown is fallen from our head;
woe to us, for we sinned!
17 For this our heart bleeds;
for these our eyes darken.
18 For the mountain of Siyon is desolate;
the foxes walk on it.
19 You, O Yah Veh, settle eternally;
your throne from generation to generation.
20 Why forget us in perpetuity?
—forsake us for length of days of time?
21 Return us to you, O Yah Veh
and we return;
renew our days as of antiquity.
22 For in spurning, you spurn us;
you enrage mightily against us.

VOLUME FOUR

PROPHETS

THE VISION OF YESHA YAH

1 The vision of *Isaiah* **Yesha**
Yah the son of *Amoz* **Amos**,
which he saw concerning
Judah **Yah Hudah** and *Jerusalem* **Yeru Shalem**
in the days of *Uzziah* **Uzzi Yah**, *Jotham* **Yah Tham**,
Ahaz **Ach Az**, and *Hezekiah* **Yechizq Yah**,
kings **sovereigns** of *Judah* **Yah Hudah**.
2 Hear, O heavens, and *give ear* **hearken**, O earth:
for *the LORD* **Yah Veh** hath *spoken* **worded**,
I have nourished and *brought up children* **raised sons**,
and they have rebelled against me.
3 The ox knoweth his *owner* **chatteler**,
and the *ass* **burro** his master's *crib* **manger**:
but *Israel* **Yisra El** doth not know,
my people doth not *consider* **discern**.
4 *Ah* **Ho** sinful *nation* **goyim**,
a people *laden* **heavy** with *iniquity* **perversity**,
a seed of *evildoers* **vilifiers**,
children **sons** that are *corrupters* **ruiners**:
they have forsaken *the LORD* **Yah Veh**,
they have *provoked* **scorned**
the Holy One of *Israel* **Yisra El** *unto anger*,
they are *gone away* **estranged** backward.
5 Why should ye be *stricken* **smitten** any more?
ye *will* **shall increase** revolt *more and more*:
the whole head is sick,
and the whole heart *faint* **bleedeth**.
6 From the sole of the foot even unto the head
there is no *soundness* **integrity** in it;
but wounds, and *bruises* **lashes**,
and *putrifying sores* **dripping wounds**:
they have not been *closed* **squeezed**, neither bound *up*,
neither *mollified* **tenderized** with ointment.
7 Your *country* **land** is desolate,
your cities are burned with fire:
your *land* **soil**, strangers devour it in your presence,
and it is desolate, as overthrown by strangers.
8 And the daughter of *Zion*
is left **Siyon remaineth**
as a *cottage* **sukkoth/brush arbor** in a vineyard,
as a *lodge* **hammock**
in a *garden of cucumbers* **cucumber field**,
as a *besieged* **guarded** city.
9 *Except the LORD of hosts*
Unless Yah Veh Sabaoth
had *left* **let remain** unto us
a very *small remnant* **few survivors**,
we should have been as *Sodom* **Sedom**,
and we should have been like unto *Gomorrah* **Amorah**.
10 Hear the word of *the LORD* **Yah Veh**,
ye *rulers* **commanders** of *Sodom* **Sedom**;
give ear **hearken** unto the *law* **torah** of our *God* **Elohim**,
ye people of *Gomorrah* **Amorah**.
11 *To what purpose* **Wherefore**
is the *multitude* **abundance** of your sacrifices unto me?
saith *the LORD* **Yah Veh**:
I am *full* **satiated**
of the *burnt—offerings* **holocausts** of rams,
and the fat of *fed beasts* **fatlings**;
and I delight not in the blood of bullocks,
or of lambs, or of he goats.
12 When ye come
to *appear before me* **be seen at my face**,
who hath *required* **besought** this at your hand,
to *tread* **trample** my courts?
13 *Bring* **Add** no more vain *oblations* **offerings**;
incense is an *abomination* **abhorrence** unto me;
the new moons and *sabbaths* **shabbaths**,
the calling of *assemblies* **convocations**,
I cannot *away with*;
it is *iniquity* **mischief**,
even the *solemn meeting* **private assembly**.
14 Your new moons and your
appointed feasts **seasons**
my soul hateth:
they are a *trouble* **burden** unto me;
I am weary to bear them.
15 And when ye spread *forth* your *hands* **palms**,
I *will hide* **shall conceal** mine eyes from you:
yea, when ye *make many* **abound** prayers,
I *will* **shall** not hear:
your hands are *full of* **filled with** blood.

THE VISION OF YESHA YAH

1 The vision Yesha Yah the son of Amos saw
concerning Yah Hudah and Yeru Shalem
in the days
of Uzzi Yah, Yah Tham, Ach Az, and Yechizq Yah
—sovereigns of Yah Hudah.
2 Hear, O heavens; and hearken, O earth:
for Yah Veh words,
I nourished and raised sons,
and they—they rebelled against me.
3 The ox knows his chatteler
and the burro the manger of his master:
Yisra El knows not;
my people discern not.
4 Ho sinful goyim;

a people heavy with perversity;
a seed of vilifiers; sons—ruiners:
they forsake Yah Veh;
they scorn the Holy One of Yisra El;
they estrange backward.
5 Why be smitten any more?
You increase revolt;
the whole head is sick;
and the whole heart bleeds:
6 from the sole of the foot to the head
there is no integrity therein:
—wounds and lashes and dripping wounds
—neither squeezed nor bound;
nor tenderized with ointment.
7 Your land, a desolation;
your cities, burned with fire:
your soil, strangers devour in your presence
—a desolation overthrown by strangers.
8 And the daughter of Siyon remains
as a sukkoth/brush arbor in a vineyard
—as a hammock in a cucumber field
—as a guarded city.
9 Unless Yah Veh Sabaoth
had a very few survivors remain,
we had become as Sedom; likened to Amorah.
10 Hear the word of Yah Veh
you commanders of Sedom;
hearken to the torah of our Elohim
you people of Amorah:
11 Why your abundant sacrifices to me?
says Yah Veh:
I am satiated by the holocausts of rams
and the fat of fatlings;
and I delight not in the blood of bullocks
or of lambs or of he goats.
12 When you come to be seen at my face,
who beseeches this at your hand
—to trample my courts?
13 Add no more vain offerings;
incense is an abhorrence to me;
the new moons and shabbaths,
the calling of convocations,
I cannot; it is mischief:
and the private assembly.
14 Your new moons and your
seasons my soul hates:
they are a burden to me;
I weary to bear them.
15 And in spreading your palms,
I conceal my eyes from you:
yes, your abounding prayers I hear not:
your hands are filled with blood.
16 *Wash you* **Baptize yourselves,**
make you clean **purify yourselves;**
put away **turn aside** the evil of your *doings* **exploitations**
from *before* **in front of** mine eyes;
cease to *do evil* **vilify;**
17 Learn to *do well* **well—please;**
seek judgment, *relieve* **blithe** the oppressed,
judge the *fatherless* **orphan,** plead for the widow.
18 Come *now* **I beseech,** and let us reason *together,*
saith *the LORD* **Yah Veh:**
though your sins be as scarlet,
they shall *be as white* **whiten** as snow;
though they be *red* **reddened** like crimson,
they shall be as wool.
19 If ye *be willing* **so** will and *obedient* **hearken,**
ye shall eat the good of the land:
20 But if ye refuse and rebel,
ye shall be devoured with the sword:
for the mouth of *the LORD* **Yah Veh**
hath *spoken it* **worded.**
21 How is the *faithful* **trustworthy** city
become an *harlot* **whore!**
it was full of judgment;
righteousness lodged **justness stayed overnight** in it;
but now murderers.
22 Thy silver is become dross,
thy *wine mixed* **potion diluted** with water:
23 Thy *princes are rebellious* **governors revolt,**
and—companions of thieves:
every one loveth *gifts* **bribes,**
and *followeth after rewards* **pursueth bribes:**
they judge not the *fatherless* **orphan,**
neither doth the *cause* **plea** of the widow
come unto them.
24 *Therefore saith the Lord, the LORD of hosts*
An oracle of Adonay Yah Veh Sabaoth,
the *mighty One* **Almighty** of *Israel* **Yisra El,**
Ah **Ho,** I *will ease me* **shall sigh**
of mine adversaries **over my tribulators,**
and avenge me of mine enemies:
25 And I *will* **shall** turn my hand upon thee,
and *purely purge* **in purity refine** away thy dross,
and *take away* **turn aside** all thy tin:
26 And I *will* **shall** restore thy judges as at the first,
and thy counsellors as at the beginning:
afterward thou shalt be called,
The city of *righteousness* **justness,**
the *faithful* **trustworthy** city.

27 *Zion* **Siyon** shall be redeemed with judgment,
and *her converts* **those of her that return**
with *righteousness* **justness.**
28 And the *destruction* **breaking**
of the *transgressors* **rebels**
and of the sinners shall be together,
and they that forsake *the LORD* **Yah Veh**
shall be *consumed* **finished off.**
29 For they shall *be ashamed* **shame**
of the **mighty** oaks which ye have desired,
and ye shall *be confounded* **blush**
for the gardens that ye have chosen.
30 For ye shall be as an oak
whose leaf *fadeth* **withereth,**
and as a garden that hath no water.
31 And the *strong* **powerful** shall be as *tow* **tuft,**
and *the maker of it* **his deeds** as a spark,
and they shall both burn together,
and none shall quench *them.*

THE LAST DAYS

2 The word that *Isaiah* **Yesha**
Yah the son of *Amoz* **Amos**
saw concerning
Judah **Yah Hudah** and *Jerusalem* **Yeru Shalem.**
2 And **so be** it *shall come to pass* in the last days,
that the mountain of the *LORD'S* house **of Yah Veh**
shall be established in the top of the mountains,
and shall be *exalted* **lifted** above the hills;
and all *nations* **goyim** shall flow unto it.
3 And many people shall go and say,
Come ye, and let us *go up* **ascend**
to the mountain of *the LORD* **Yah Veh,**
to the house of *the God* **Elohim** of *Jacob* **Yaaqov;**

16 Baptize yourself; purify yourself;
turn aside the evil of your exploitations
from in front of my eyes:
cease to vilify;
17 learn to well—please;
seek judgment; blithe the oppressed; judge
the orphan; plead for the widow.
18 Come, I beseech, and we reason,
says Yah Veh:
though your sins be as scarlet,
they whiten as snow;
though they be reddened like crimson,
they be as wool.
19 If you so will and hearken,
you eat the good of the land:
20 and if you refuse and rebel,
you *are* consumed with the sword: for
the mouth of Yah Veh words.
21 How the trustworthy city becomes a whore!
Filled with judgment!
Justness stayed overnight therein
—now murderers:
22 your silver becomes dross,
your potion dilutes with water:
23 your governors revolt—companions of thieves:
every one loves bribes and pursues bribes:
they neither judge the orphan,
nor comes the plea of the widow to them
24 —an oracle of Adonay Yah Veh Sabaoth
the Almighty of Yisra El.
Ho, I sigh over my tribulators
and avenge me of my enemies:
25 and I turn my hand upon you;
and in purity, refine away your dross,
and turn aside all your tin:
26 and I restore your judges as at the first
and your counsellors as at the beginning:
and afterward call you,
The City of Justness; The City Trustworthy.
27 Siyon is redeemed in judgment
and her returnees in justness:
28 and the breaking of the rebels
and of the sinners *is* together,
and they who forsake Yah Veh are finished off.
29 For they shame
because of the mighty oaks you desire,
and you blush
for the gardens you chose.
30 For you become as an oak whose leaf withers,
and as a garden without water:
31 and the powerful become as tuft
and his deeds as a spark;
and they both burn together,
and no one quenches.

THE LAST DAYS

2 The word Yesha Yah the son of Amos saw
concerning Yah Hudah and Yeru Shalem:
2 and so be it, in the last days,
the mountain of the house of Yah Veh
is established in the top of the mountains,
and lifted above the hills;
and all goyim flow to it.
3 And many people go and say,
Come, and we ascend to the mountain of Yah Veh
—to the house of Elohim of Yaaqov:

and he *will* **shall** teach us of his ways,
and we *will* **shall** walk in his paths:
for out of *Zion* **Siyon** shall go forth the *law* **torah**,
and the word of *the LORD* **Yah Veh**
from *Jerusalem* **Yeru Shalem.**
4 And he shall judge among the *nations* **goyim**,
and shall *rebuke* **reprove** many people:
and they shall *beat* **forge** their swords into plowshares,
and their spears into *pruninghooks* **psalmpicks**:
nation **goyim** shall not lift *up* sword
against *nation* **goyim**,
neither shall they learn war any more.
5 O house of *Jacob* **Yaaqov**, come ye,
and let us walk in the light of *the LORD* **Yah Veh**.
6 Therefore thou hast *forsaken*
abandoned thy people
the house of *Jacob* **Yaaqov**,
because they *be replenished* **fill full** from the east,
and are *soothsayers* **cloudgazers**
like the *Philistines* **Peleshethiym**,
and they *please themselves* **clap**
in **with** the children of strangers.
7 Their land also is *full* **filled** of silver and gold,
neither is there any end of their treasures;
their land is also *full* **filled** of horses,
neither is there any end of their chariots:
8 Their land also is *full* **filled** of idols;
they *worship* **prostrate to** the work of their own hands,
that which their own fingers have *made* **worked**:
9 And *the mean man boweth*
down **humanity prostrateth,**
and *the great man humbleth himself* **man**
abaseth: therefore *forgive* **lift** them not.
10 Enter into the rock, and hide thee in the dust,
for **at the face of** fear of *the LORD* **Yah Veh**,
and for the *glory* **majesty** of his *majesty* **pomp**.
11 The lofty *looks* **eyes** of *man* **humanity**
shall *be humbled* **abase**,
and the haughtiness of men shall
be bowed down **prostrate**,
and *the LORD* **Yah Veh** alone
shall be exalted in that day.
12 For the day of *the LORD*
of hosts **Yah Veh Sabaoth**
shall be upon
every one that is proud **all the pompous** and lofty,
and upon *every one* **all** that is lifted *up*;
and he shall be *brought low* **abased**:
13 And upon all the cedars of Lebanon,
that are high and lifted up,
and upon all the oaks of Bashan,
14 And upon all the high mountains,
and upon all the hills that are lifted *up*,
15 And upon every high tower,
and upon every *fenced* **fortified** wall,
16 And upon all the ships of Tarshish,
and upon all *pleasant pictures* **observations of desire**.
17 And the loftiness of *man* **humanity**
shall *be bowed down* **prostrate**,
and the haughtiness of men shall *be made low* **abase**:
and *the LORD* **Yah Veh** alone
shall be exalted in that day.
18 And the idols
he shall *utterly abolish* **totally pass away**.
19 And they shall go into the
holes **caves** of the rocks,
and into the caves of the *earth* **dust**,
for **at the face of** fear of *the LORD* **Yah Veh**,
and for the *glory* **majesty** of his *majesty* **pomp**,
when he ariseth to *shake terribly* **terrify** the earth.
20 In that day *a man* **humanity**
shall cast his idols of silver, and his idols of gold,
which they *made each one* **worked** for himself
to *worship* **prostrate to**,
to the *moles* **burrowers** and to the bats;
21 To go into the *clefts* **crevices** of the rocks,
and into the *tops* **clefts** of the *ragged* rocks,
for **at the face of** fear of *the LORD* **Yah Veh**,
and for the *glory* **majesty** of his *majesty* **pomp**,
when he ariseth to *shake terribly* **terrify** the earth.
22 Cease ye from *man* **humanity**,
whose breath is in his nostrils:
for wherein is he to be *accounted of* **fabricated**?
and he teaches us of his ways,
and we walk in his paths:
for from Siyon the torah goes forth,
and the word of Yah Veh from Yeru Shalem.
4 And he judges among the goyim
and reproves many people:
and they forge their swords into plowshares
and their spears into psalmpicks:
goyim neither lift sword against goyim,
nor learn war any more.
5 O house of Yaaqov, come,
and we walk in the light of Yah Veh.
6 For you forsake your people,
the house of Yaaqov,
because they fill full from the east
—cloudgazers like the Peleshethiym;
and they clap with the children of strangers:

7 and the land is filled with silver and gold
—no end of their treasures;
and the land is filled with horses,
—no end of their chariots:
8 and the land is filled with idols;
they prostrate to the work of their own hands
which their own fingers worked:
9 and humanity prostrates; and man abases:
and you, lift them not.
10 Enter the rock and hide in the dust
at the face of fear of Yah Veh,
and for the majesty of his pomp.
11 The lofty eyes of humanity abase,
and the haughtiness of men prostrates, and
Yah Veh alone is exalted in that day.
12 For the day of Yah Veh Sabaoth *is* upon all the
pompous and lofty; and upon all the lifted and abased;
13 and upon all the cedars of Lebanon
—high and lifted up;
and upon all the oaks of Bashan;
14 and upon all the high mountains;
and upon all the lifted hills;
15 and upon every high tower
and upon every fortified wall;
16 and upon all the ships of Tarshish
and upon all observations of desire:
17 and the loftiness of humanity prostrates
and the haughtiness of men abases: and
Yah Veh alone is exalted in that day.
18 And the idols, he totally passes away:
19 and they go into the caves of the rocks
and into the caves of the dust
—at the face of fear of Yah Veh
and for the majesty of his pomp
when he rises to terrify the earth.
20 In that day,
humanity casts his idols of silver and his idols of gold
that they work for him to prostrate to
—to the burrowers and to the bats;
21 to go into the crevices of the rocks
and into the clefts of the rocks
—at the face of fear of Yah Veh;
and for the majesty of his pomp
when he rises to terrify the earth.
22 Cease you from humanity,
whose breath is in his nostrils: for—
wherein is he fabricated?

Judgment On Yeru Shalem And Yah Hudah

3 For, behold,
the Lord, the LORD of hosts **Adonay Yah Veh Sabaoth**,
doth *take away* **turn aside**
from *Jerusalem* **Yeru Shalem** and
from *Judah* **Yah Hudah**
the *stay* **support** and the *staff* **support**,
the whole *stay* **support** of bread,
and the whole *stay* **support** of water,
2 The mighty *man*, and the man of war,
the judge, and the prophet,
and the *prudent* **diviner**, and the *ancient* **aged**,
3 The *captain* **governor** of fifty,
and the *honourable man* **lifted face**,
and the counsellor,
and the *cunning artificer* **wise engraver**,
and the *eloquent* **discerning** orator.
4 And I *will* **shall** give
children **lads** to be their *princes* **governors**,
and *babes* **freaks** shall *rule* **reign** over them.
5 And the people shall be *oppressed* **exacted**,
every one by another **man upon man**,
and every one by his neighbour
even man upon his friend:
the *child* **lad** shall *behave himself proudly* **abuse**
against the *ancient* **aged**,
and the base against the honourable.
6 When a man shall *take hold*
of **apprehend** his brother
of the house of his father, *saying*,
Thou hast clothing, be thou our *ruler* **commander**,
and let this *ruin* **stumblingblock** be under thy hand:
7 In that day shall he *swear* **lift his hand**,
saying, I *will* **shall** not be *an healer* **a binder**;
for in my house is neither bread nor clothing:
make **set** me not a *ruler* **commander** of the people.
8 For *Jerusalem is ruined*
Yeru Shalem hath faltered,
and *Judah is* **Yah Hudah hath** fallen:
because their tongue and their *doings* **exploitations**
are against *the LORD* **Yah Veh**,
to *provoke* **rebel against** the eyes of his *glory* **honour**.
9 The *shew* **partiality** of their *countenance* **face**
doth *witness* **answer** against them;
and they *declare* **tell** their sin as *Sodom* **Sedom**,
they *hide* **conceal** it not.
Woe unto their soul!
for they have *rewarded* **dealt** evil unto themselves.

10 Say ye to the *righteous* **just**,
that it shall be *well with him* **for good**:
for they shall eat the fruit of their *doings* **exploitations**.
11 Woe unto the wicked! *it*
shall be ill with him—**evil**:
for the *reward* **dealing** of his hands
shall be *given* **worked** him.
12 As for my people,
children **exploiters** are their *oppressors* **exactors**,
and women *rule* **reign** over them.
O my people, they which *lead* **blithe** thee
cause thee to *err* **stray**,
and *destroy* **swallow** the way of thy paths.
13 *The LORD standeth up* **Yah**
Veh stationeth to plead,
and standeth to *judge* **plead the cause of** the people.
14 *The LORD will* **Yah Veh**
shall enter into judgment
with the *ancients* **elders** of his people,
and the *princes* **governors** *thereof*:
for ye have *eaten up* **burnt** the vineyard;
the *spoil* **stripping** of the *poor* **humble** is in your houses.
15 What mean ye that ye *beat*
crush my people *to pieces*,
and grind the faces of the *poor* **humble**?
saith the Lord GOD of hosts
an oracle of Adonay Yah Veh Sabaoth.
16 *Moreover the LORD* **Yah Veh** saith,
Because the daughters of *Zion* **Siyon** are *haughty* **lifted**,
and walk with *stretched forth necks* **spread throats**
and *wanton eyes* **ogling**,
walking and *mincing* **waddling** *as* they go,
and *making a* tinkling with their feet:
17 Therefore *the Lord* **Adonay**
will smite with a scab **shall scrape**
the *crown of the head* **scalp**
of the daughters of *Zion* **Siyon**,
and *the LORD* **Yah Veh**
will discover **shall strip naked** their
secret parts **pudenda**.

JUDGMENT ON YERU SHALEM AND YAH HUDAH

3 For, behold,
Adonay Yah Veh Sabaoth
turns aside from Yeru Shalem and from Yah Hudah
the support and the support
—the whole support of bread
and the whole support of water:
2 the mighty and the man of war,
the judge and the prophet, and the diviner and the aged,
3 the governor of fifty,
and the lifted face and the counsellor,
and the wise engraver and the discerning orator:
4 and I give lads for governors
and freaks reign over them.
5 And the people exact, man upon man;
even man upon his friend:
the lads abuse against the aged
and the base against the honorable.
6 When man apprehends his brother
of the house of his father by the clothing,
and says, Be our commander;
and this stumblingblock *is* under your hand:
7 in that day he lifts his hand, saying,
I am not a binder;
and in my house is neither bread nor clothing:
set me not a commander of the people.
8 For Yeru Shalem falters and Yah Hudah falls:
because of their tongue and their exploitations
against Yah Veh
—to rebel against the eyes of his honor:
9 their partiality of face answers against them;
and they tell their sin as Sedom—they conceal not.
Woe to their soul!
for they deal themselves evil.
10 You, say to the just, It is for good:
for they eat the fruit of their exploitations.
11 Woe to the wicked—evil:
for the dealing of his hands works to himself.
12 As for my people,
exploiters exact from them
and women reign over them.
O my people, they who blithe you
cause you to stray,
and swallow the way of your paths.
13 Yah Veh stations himself to plead
and stands to plead the cause of the people.
14 Yah Veh enters into judgment
with the elders of his people and the governors:
for you burnt the vineyard;
the stripping of the humble is in your houses.
15 What mean you, to crush my people?
And grind the faces of the humble?
—an oracle of Adonay Yah Veh Sabaoth.
16 Yah Veh says,
Because the daughters of Siyon lift themselves
and walk with spread throats and ogling
—walking and waddling they go,
and tinkling with their feet:

17 Adonay also scrapes the scalp
of the daughters of Siyon;
and their pudenda, Yah Veh strips naked.
18 In that day
the Lord will take away **Adonay shall turn aside**
the bravery of their tinkling ornaments about their feet
their adornments of tinklers,
and their *cauls* **nets,**
and their *round tires like the moon* **ornaments,**
19 The *chains* **pendants,** and the bracelets,
and the *mufflers* **veils,**
20 The *bonnets* **tiaras,**
and the *ornaments of the legs* **anklets,**
and the *headbands* **bands,**
and the *tablets* **housings of the soul,**
and the *earrings* **amulets,**
21 The *rings* **signets,** and *nose jewels* **nostrilrings,**
22 The *changeable suits of apparel* **mantles,**
and the mantles,
and the *wimples* **cloaks,** and the *crisping pins* **pockets,**
23 The *glasses* **rolls,** and the *fine linen* **wraps,**
and the *hoods* **turbans,** and the vails.
24 And **so be** it *shall come to pass,*
that instead of sweet *smell* **spice**
there shall be *stink* **putridity;**
and instead of a girdle
a *rent* **noose;**
and instead of *well set hair* **the work of the curler**
baldness;
and instead of a *stomacher* **festive mantle**
a *girding* **girdle** of *sackcloth* **saq;**
and burning **scarring** instead of beauty.
25 Thy men shall fall by the sword,
and thy *mighty* **might** in the war.
26 And her *gates lament* **portals**
shall mourn and mourn;
and she being *desolate* **exonerated**
shall *sit* **settle** upon the *ground* **land.**

THE SPROUT OF YAH VEH

4 And in that day
seven women shall take hold of one man, saying,
We *will* **shall** eat our own bread,
and *wear* **enrobe** our own apparel: only
let us be called by thy name,
to *take away* **gather** our reproach.
2 In that day
shall the *branch* **sprout** of *the LORD* **Yah Veh**
be *beautiful* **splendid** and *glorious* **honourable,**
and the fruit of the earth
shall be *excellent* **for pomp** and *comely* **adornment**
for *them that are escaped* **the escapees** of *Israel* **Yisra El.**
3 And **so be** it *shall come to pass,*
that he that *is left* **surviveth** in *Zion* **Siyon,**
and he that remaineth in *Jerusalem* **Yeru Shalem,**
shall be *called* **said** holy,
even every one
that is *written among the living* **inscribed for life**
in *Jerusalem* **Yeru Shalem:**
4 When *the Lord* **Adonay**
shall have *washed away* **baptized** the *filth* **dung**
of the daughters of *Zion* **Siyon,**
and shall have *purged* **cleansed**
the blood of *Jerusalem* **Yeru Shalem**
from the midst *thereof*
by the spirit of judgment, and by the spirit of burning.
5 And *the LORD will* **Yah Veh shall** create
upon every dwelling place of mount *Zion* **Siyon,**
and upon her *assemblies* **convocations,**
a cloud and smoke by day,
and the *shining* **brilliance** of a flaming fire by night:
for upon all the *glory* **honour** shall be a *defence* **canopy.**
6 And there shall be *a tabernacle*
sukkoth/brush arbors
for a shadow in the *daytime* **day** from
the heat, and for a place of refuge,
and for a covert from *storm* **flood** and from rain.

SONG OF THE VINEYARD

5 *Now* **I beseech,**
will **shall** I sing to my *wellbeloved* **beloved**
a song of my beloved touching his vineyard.
My *wellbeloved* **beloved** hath a vineyard
in *a very fruitful hill* **the horn of the son of oil:**
2 And he *fenced* **walled** it,
and *gathered out* **stoned** the stones *thereof,*
18 In that day,
Adonay turns aside their adornments of tinklers,
and their nets and their ornaments;
19 the pendants and the bracelets and the veils;
20 the tiaras and the anklets and the bands
and the housings of the soul and the amulets;
21 the signets and nostrilrings;
22 the mantles and the mantles
and the cloaks and the pockets;
23 the rolls and the wraps
and the turbans and the veils:
24 and so be it,
that instead of sweet spice, putridity;
and instead of a girdle, a noose;

and instead of the work of the curler, baldness;
and instead of a festive mantle, a girdle of saq
—scarring instead of beauty.
25 Your men fall by the sword
and your might in the war.
26 And her portals mourn and mourn;
and being exonerated, she settles upon the land.

The Sprout Of Yah Veh

4 In that day,
seven women take hold of one man, saying,
We eat our own bread and enrobe our own apparel:
only call us by your name, to gather our reproach.
2 In that day,
the sprout of Yah Veh is splendid and honorable
and the fruit of the earth for pomp and adornment
for the escapees of Yisra El.
3 And so be it,
he who survives in Siyon,
and he who remains in Yeru Shalem
—holy is said of him
—of every one inscribed for life in Yeru Shalem:
4 when Adonay
baptizes the dung of the daughters of Siyon,
and cleanses the blood of Yeru Shalem
from their midst
by the spirit of judgment and by the spirit of burning:
5 and upon every dwelling place of mount Siyon
and upon her convocations,
Yah Veh creates a cloud and smoke by day
and the brilliance of a flaming fire by night
—a canopy upon all the honor:
6 and sukkoth/brush arbors
for a shadow in the day from the heat
and for a place of refuge;
and for a covert from flood and from rain.

Song Of The Vineyard

5 I beseech, that I sing to my beloved
—a song of my beloved touching his vineyard
—my beloved has a vineyard
in the horn of the son of oil:
2 and he walls it and stones the stones;
and planted it with the *choicest vine* **choice**,
and built a tower in the midst of it,
and also made a *winepress* **trough** therein:
and he *looked* **awaited**
that it should *bring forth* **work** grapes,
and it *brought forth wild grapes* **worked stinkweeds**.
3 And now,
O *inhabitants* **settlers** of *Jerusalem* **Yeru Shalem**,
and men of *Judah* **Yah Hudah**,
judge, I *pray* **beseech** you,
betwixt me and my vineyard.
4 What could have been
done **worked** more to my vineyard,
that I have not *done* **worked** in it?
wherefore **why**, when I *looked* **awaited**
that it should *bring forth* **work** grapes,
brought it forth wild grapes **it worked stinkweeds**?
5 And now go to;
I *will tell* **shall make** you **know**
what I *will do* **shall work** to my vineyard:
I *will take away* **shall turn aside** the hedge *thereof*,
and it shall be *eaten up* **burnt**;
and *break down* **breach** the wall *thereof*,
and it shall be *trodden down* **trampled**:
6 And I *will lay it waste* **shall place it desolate**:
it shall not be *pruned* **plucked**, nor *digged* **hoed**; but
there shall *come up* **ascend** briers and thorns:
I *will* **shall** also *command* **misvah** the **thick** clouds
that they rain no rain upon it.
7 For the vineyard of *the LORD*
of hosts **Yah Veh Sabaoth**
is the house of *Israel* **Yisra El**,
and the men of *Judah* **Yah Hudah**
his *pleasant* plant **of delights**:
and he *looked for* **awaited** judgment,
but behold oppression;
for *righteousness* **justness**,
but behold a cry.

Ho And Judgment

8 *Woe* **Ho** unto them that
join **touch** house to house,
that *lay* **approach** field to field,
till *there be no* **the final** place,
that they may be *placed* **settled** alone
in the midst of the earth!
9 In mine ears, *said the LORD*
of hosts **Yah Veh Sabaoth**,
Of a truth **If not** many houses shall *be* **become** desolate,
even great and *fair* **good**, without *inhabitant* **settler**.
10 *Yea* **Assuredly**, ten acres of vineyard
shall *yield* **work** one bath,
and the seed of an *homer* **chomer**
shall *yield* **work** an ephah.
11 *Woe* **Ho** unto them
that *rise up* **start** early in the morning,

that they may *follow strong drink* **pursue intoxicants**;
that *continue until night* **linger in the evening breeze**,
till wine inflame them!
12 And the harp, and the *viol* **bagpipe**,
the *tabret* **tambourine**, and pipe, and wine,
are in their *feasts* **banquets**:
but they *regard* **scan** not
the *work* **deeds** of *the LORD* **Yah Veh**,
neither *consider* **see** the *operation* **work** of his hands.
13 Therefore my people are
gone into captivity **exiled**,
because they have no knowledge:
and their honourable men are famished,
and their multitude *dried up* **parched** with thirst.
14 Therefore *hell* **sheol** hath
enlarged *herself* **her soul**,
and *opened* **gaped** her mouth without *measure* **statute**:
and their glory, and their multitude,
and their *pomp* **uproar**,
and he that *rejoiceth* **jumpeth for joy**,
shall descend into it.
15 And *the mean man* **humanity**
shall *be brought down* **prostrate**,
and *the mighty* man shall *be humbled* **abase**,
and the eyes of the lofty shall *be humbled* **abase**:
16 But *the LORD of hosts* **Yah Veh Sabaoth**
shall be *exalted* **lifted** in judgment,
and *God* **El** that is holy
shall be *sanctified* **hallowed** in *righteousness* **justness**.
and plants with the choice,
and builds a tower in the midst;
and also makes a trough therein:
and he awaits it to work grapes
and it works stinkweeds.
3 And now,
O settlers of Yeru Shalem and men of Yah Hudah,
judge, I beseech you, between me and my vineyard.
4 What more work I to my vineyard
that I worked not therein?
Why, when I awaited it to work grapes,
worked it stinkweeds?
5 And now go to;
I have you know what I work to my vineyard:
I turn aside the hedge and burn it;
and breach the wall to trample on:
6 and I place it desolate
—neither plucked nor hoed;
and briers and thorns ascend:
and I misvah the thick clouds to rain no rain thereon.
7 For the vineyard of Yah Veh Sabaoth
is the house of Yisra El,
and the men of Yah Hudah
his plant of delights:
and he awaits judgment; and behold, oppression:
for justness; and behold, a cry.

Ho And Judgment

8 Ho to them who touch house to house,
who approach field to field,
until the final place,
to settle alone midst the earth!
9 In my ears, Yah Veh Sabaoth,
surely many houses become desolate—
great and good, without settler.
10 For ten acres of vineyard work one bath,
and the seed of an chomer works an ephah.
11 Ho to them who start early in the morning
to pursue intoxicants;
who linger in the evening breeze
until wine inflames them:
12 and the harp and the bagpipe,
the tambourine and pipe
and wine are in their banquets:
yes, they neither scan the deeds of Yah Veh
nor see the work of his hands.
13 So my people *are* exiled,
because they have no knowledge:
and their honorable men are famished,
and their multitude parched with thirst.
14 So sheol enlarges her soul
and gapes her mouth without statute;
and their glory and their multitude and their uproar:
and he who jumps for joy, descends therein:
15 and humanity prostrates and man abases;
and the eyes of the lofty abase.
16 And Yah Veh Sabaoth is lifted in judgment
and holy El, hallowed in justness.
17 Then shall the lambs *feed* **graze**
after their *manner* **word**,
and the *waste places* **parched areas**
of the *fat ones* **fatlings**
shall *strangers* **sojourners** eat.
18 *Woe* **Ho** unto them that
draw *iniquity* **perversity**
with cords of vanity,
and sin as it were with a *cart* **wagon** rope:
19 That say, Let him *make speed* **hasten**,
and hasten his work, that we may see it:
and let the counsel of the Holy One of *Israel* **Yisra El**
draw nigh **approach** and come, that we may know it!

20 *Woe* **Ho** unto them that *call* **say**
concerning evil good, and good evil;
that *put* **set** darkness for light, and light for darkness;
that *put* **set** bitter for sweet, and sweet for bitter!
21 *Woe* **Ho** unto them that
are wise in their own eyes,
and *prudent* **discerning** in their *own sight* **face**!
22 *Woe* **Ho** unto them that
are mighty to drink wine,
and men of *strength* **valour**
to *mingle strong drink* **mix intoxicants**:
23 Which justify the wicked for *reward* **a bribe**,
and *take away* **turn aside**
the *righteousness* **justness** of the *righteous* **just** from him!
24 Therefore as the **tongue of**
fire devoureth the stubble,
and the flame *consumeth* **slacketh** the *chaff* **hay**,
so their root shall be as *rottenness* **putridity**,
and their blossom shall *go up* **ascend** as dust:
because they have *cast away* **spurned** the *law* **torah**
of *the LORD of hosts* **Yah Veh Sabaoth**,
and *despised* **scorned** the *word* **saying**
of the Holy One of *Israel* **Yisra El**.
25 Therefore is the *anger* **wrath**
of *the LORD* **Yah Veh**
kindled against his people,
and he hath *stretched forth* **spread**
his hand against them,
and hath smitten them:
and the hills *did tremble* **quaked**,
and their carcases were *torn* **sweepings**
in the midst of the *streets* **outways**.
For all this his *anger* **wrath** is not turned away,
but his hand is *stretched out* **spread** still.
26 And he *will* **shall** lift *up* an ensign
to the *nations* **goyim** from far,
and *will* **shall** hiss unto them from the end of the earth:
and, behold, they shall come *with speed* **quickly**, swiftly:
27 None shall *be weary* **languish** nor *stumble* **falter**
among them;
none shall slumber nor sleep;
neither shall the girdle of their loins be loosed,
nor the latchet of their shoes be *broken* **torn**:
28 Whose arrows are *sharp* **pointened**,
and all their bows bent,
their horses' hoofs shall be *counted* **fabricated** like flint,
and their *wheels* **whirlers** like a *whirlwind* **hurricane**:
29 Their roaring shall be like a **roaring** lion,
they shall roar like *young lions* **whelps**:
yea, they shall *roar* **growl**, and *lay* **take** hold of the prey,
and shall *carry* **slip** it away *safe*
and none shall *deliver it* **rescue**.
30 And in that day they shall
roar **growl** against them
like the *roaring* **growling** of the sea:
and if one look unto the land,
behold darkness and *sorrow* **tribulation**,
and the light is darkened in the *heavens* **setting** *thereof*.

THE VISION OF YESHA YAH

6 In the year that *king Uzziah*
sovereign Uzzi Yah died
I saw also *the Lord* **Adonay** sitting upon a throne,
high and lifted up,
and his *train* **drape** filled the *temple* **manse**.
2 Above it stood the *seraphims* **seraphim**:
each one had six wings—**six wings to one**;
with *twain* **two** he covered his face,
and with *twain* **two** he covered his feet,
and with *twain* **two** he *did fly* **flew**.
3 And one *cried* **called** unto another, and said,
Holy, holy, holy, *is the LORD of hosts* **Yah Veh**
Sabaoth: the whole earth is full of his glory.
4 And the *posts* **hinges** of the *door* **threshold**
moved **shook** at the voice of him that cried,
and the house was filled with smoke.
17 And the lambs graze after their word;
and sojourners eat the parched areas of the fatlings.
18 Ho to them who draw perversity
with cords of vanity,
and sin as a wagon rope:
19 who say, Hasten him:
hasten his work for us to see:
and that the counsel of the Holy One of Yisra El
approach and come, for us to know.
20 Ho to them who say to evil, good;
and to good, evil;
who set darkness for light; and light for darkness:
who set bitter for sweet; and sweet for bitter.
21 Ho to them, the wise in their own eyes,
and discerning in their own face!
22 Ho to them, the mighty to drink wine,
and men of valour to mix intoxicants:
23 who justify the wicked for a bribe,
and turn aside the justness of the just from him!
24 So as the tongue of fire devours the stubble
and the flame slacks the hay,
thus their root is as putridity
and their blossom ascends as dust:
because they spurn the torah of Yah Veh Sabaoth,

and scorn the saying of the Holy One of Yisra El.
25 So Yah Veh kindles his wrath against his people;
and spreads his hand against them and smites them:
and the hills quake;
and their carcase is as sweepings midst the outways.
For all this, his wrath turns not away,
and he still spreads his hand:
26 and he lifts an ensign to the goyim from afar,
and hisses to them from the end of the earth:
and, behold, they come quickly—swiftly:
27 no one languishes nor falters among them;
no one slumbers nor sleeps;
neither loosens the girdle of their loins,
nor tears the latchet of their shoes:
28 whose arrows are pointened
and all their bows bent;
the hoofs of their horses fabricate as flint
and their whirlers as a hurricane:
29 they roar like a roaring
lion; they roar like whelps:
yes, they growl,
and take hold of the prey and slip it away
and no one rescues.
30 And in that day,
they growl against them as the growling of the sea:
and if one looks to the land,
behold, darkness and tribulation;
and the light darkens in the setting.

The Vision Of Yesha Yah

6 In the year sovereign Uzzi Yah dies
I see Adonay sitting upon a throne
—high and lifted up,
and his drape fills the manse:
2 seraphim stand over it
—six wings—six wings to one;
with two he covers his face
and with two he covers his feet
and with two he flies.
3 And one calls to another, and says,
Holy, holy, holy, Yah Veh Sabaoth:
the fulness of the whole earth *is* his glory.
4 —and the hinges of the threshold
shake at the voice of him who cries;
and the house fills with smoke.
5 Then said I, Woe is me! for I am *undone* **mute**;
because I am a man of *unclean* **foul** lips,
and I *dwell* **settle** in the midst of a people
of *unclean* **fouled** lips:
for mine eyes have seen the *King* **Sovereign**,
the LORD of hosts **Yah Veh Sabaoth**.
6 Then flew one of the
seraphims **seraphim** unto me,
having a *live coal* **hot stone** in his hand,
which he had taken with the tongs
from off the **sacrifice** altar:
7 And he *laid* **touched** it upon my mouth,
and said, *Lo* **Behold**, this hath touched thy lips;
and thine *iniquity* **perversity** is *taken away* **turned aside**,
and thy sin *purged* **kapared/atoned**.

The Commission Of Yesha Yah

8 Also I heard the voice of
the Lord **Adonay**, saying,
Whom shall I send, and who *will* **shall** go for us?
Then said I, Here am I; send me.
9 And he said, Go, and *tell* **say to** this people,
In hearing, Hear ye *indeed*, but *understand* **discern** not;
and **in seeing,** see ye *indeed*, but *perceive* **know** not.
10 *Make* **Fatten** the heart of this people *fat*,
and *make* **burden** their ears *heavy*,
and *shut* **stroke** their eyes;
lest they see with their eyes, and hear with their ears,
and *understand* **discern** with their heart,
and convert, and be healed.
11 Then said I, *Lord* **Adonay**, how long?
And he *answered* **said**,
Until the cities be wasted without *inhabitant* **settler**,
and the houses without *man* **humanity**,
and the *land* **soil** be **wasted**
utterly desolate—**a desolation**,
12 And *the LORD* **Yah Veh**
have **far** removed *men far away* **humanity**,
and there be a great forsaking in the midst of the land.
13 But yet in it shall be a tenth, and it shall return,
and shall be *eaten* **burnt**:
as *a teil* **an oak** tree, and as an oak,
whose *substance* **stump** is in them,
when they cast *their leaves*:
so the holy seed shall be the *substance* **stumps** *thereof*.

War Against Yeru Shalem

7 And **so be** it *came to pass*
in the days of *Ahaz* **Ach Az**
the son of *Jotham* **Yah Tham**,
the son of *Uzziah* **Uzzi Yah**,
king **sovereign** of *Judah* **Yah Hudah**,
that *Rezin* **Resin** the *king* **sovereign** of *Syria* **Aram**,
and *Pekah* **Peqach** the son of *Remaliah* **Remal Yah**,
king **sovereign** of *Israel* **Yisra El**,

went up toward Jerusalem **ascended to Yeru Shalem**
to war against it, but could not *prevail* **fight** against it.
2 And it was told the house of David, saying,
Syria is confederate **Aram resteth**
with *Ephraim* **Ephrayim**.
And his heart *was moved* **shook**,
and the heart of his people,
as the trees of the *wood are moved* **forest shake**
with **at the face of** the wind.
3 Then said *the LORD* **Yah**
Veh unto *Isaiah* **Yesha Yah**,
Go forth *now* **I beseech**, to meet *Ahaz* **Ach Az**,
thou, and *Shearjashub* **Shear Yashub** thy son,
at the end of the *conduit* **channel**
of the *upper* **most high** pool
in the highway of the fuller's field;
4 And say unto him, *Take heed* **On guard**,
and *be quiet* **rest**; *fear* **awe** not,
neither *be fainthearted* **tenderize thy heart**
for the two tails of these smoking *firebrands* **brands**,
for the *fierce anger* **fuming wrath**
of *Rezin* **Resin** with *Syria* **Aram**,
and of the son of *Remaliah* **Remal Yah**.
5 Because *Syria* **Aram**, *Ephraim* **Ephrayim**,
and the son of *Remaliah* **Remal Yah**,
have *taken* **counselled** evil *counsel* against thee, saying,
6 Let us *go up* **ascend** against *Judah* **Yah Hudah**,
and *vex* **loathe** it,
and let us *make a breach therein* **split it** for us,
5 Then I say, Woe is me! for I am mute;
because I am a man of foul lips
and I settle midst a people of fouled lips:
for my eyes see the Sovereign, Yah Veh Sabaoth.
6 Then one of the seraphim flies to me
with a hot stone in his hand
—which he took with the tongs
from off the sacrifice altar:
7 and he touches it on my mouth, and says,
Behold, this touches your lips;
and your perversity is turned aside,
and your sin is kapared/atoned.

THE COMMISSION OF YESHA YAH

8 And I hear the voice of Adonay, saying,
Whom send I? and, Who goes for us?
And I say, Here—I! Send me!
9 And he says, Go, and say to this people,
In hearing, you hear, and discern not;
and in seeing, you see, and know not.
10 Fatten the heart of this people
and burden their ears and stroke their eyes;
lest they see with their eyes and hear with their ears
and discern with their heart
—and convert and heal.
11 Then I say, Adonay, until when?
And he says,
Until the cities waste away without settler,
and the houses without humanity,
and the soil wastes—a desolation;
12 and Yah Veh removes humanity far off,
with a great forsaking midst the land.
13 And yet there is a tenth therein that returns
to burn as an oak tree
and as an oak with its stump,
when they cast:
the holy seed is the stump.

WAR AGAINST YERU SHALEM

7 And so be it,
in the days of Ach Az the son of Yah Tham,
the son of Uzzi Yah sovereign of Yah Hudah,
that Resin the sovereign of Aram,
and Peqach the son of Remal Yah sovereign of Yisra El
ascend to Yeru Shalem to war against it
but cannot fight against it.
2 And they tell the house of David, saying,
Aram rests with Ephrayim.
And his heart shakes—and the heart of his people
as the trees of the forest shake at the face of the wind.
3 Then Yah Veh says to Yesha Yah,
Go, I beseech, to meet Ach Az
—you and Shear Yashub your son,
at the end of the channel of the most high pool
in the highway of the field of the fuller;
4 and say to him, On guard! and, Rest!
Neither awe nor tenderize your heart
for the two tails of these smoking brands
—for the fuming wrath of Resin and Aram
and the son of Remal Yah:
5 because Aram, Ephrayim,
and the son of Remal Yah
counsel evil against you, saying,
6 We ascend against Yah Hudah
and loathe it and split it for us,
and *set a king* **reign a sovereign** in the midst of it,
even the son of *Tabeal* **Tabe El**:
7 Thus saith *the Lord GOD* **Adonay Yah Veh**,
It shall not *stand* **rise**,
neither shall it *come to pass* **be**.
8 For the head of *Syria* **Aram**
is *Damascus* **Dammeseq**,

and the head of *Damascus* **Dammeseq** is *Rezin* **Resin**;
and within *threescore* **sixty** and five years
shall *Ephraim* **Ephrayim** be broken,
that it be not **from** a people.
9 And the head of *Ephraim* **Ephrayim**
is *Samaria* **Shomeron**,
and the head of *Samaria* **Shomeron**
is *Remaliah's* **Remal Yah's** son.
If ye *will* **shall** not *believe* **trust**,
surely ye shall not be *established* **trustworthy**.

THE SIGN OF IMMANU EL

10 Moreover *the LORD* **Yah Veh**
spake again **added to word** unto *Ahaz* **Ach Az**, saying,
11 Ask thee a sign of *the LORD*
Yah Veh thy *God* **Elohim**;
ask it either in *the depth* **deep**,
or in *the height* **high** above.
12 But *Ahaz* **Ach Az** said, I *will* **shall** not ask,
neither *will I tempt the LORD* **shall I test Yah Veh**.
13 And he said, Hear ye now, O house of David;
Is it *a small thing* **petty** for you to weary men,
but *will* **shall** ye weary my *God* **Elohim** also?
14 Therefore *the Lord* **Adonay** himself
shall give you a sign;
Behold, a virgin shall conceive, and *bear* **birth** a son,
and shall call his name *Immanuel* **Immanu El**.
15 Butter and honey shall he eat,
that he may know to refuse the evil,
and choose the good.
16 For *before* **ere** the *child* **lad**
shall know to refuse the evil,
and choose the good,
the *land* **soil** that thou abhorrest shall be forsaken
at the face of both her *kings* **sovereigns**.
17 *The LORD* **Yah Veh** shall bring upon thee,
and upon thy people, and upon thy father's house,
days that have not come,
from the day that *Ephraim* **Ephrayim**
departed **turned aside** from *Judah* **Yah Hudah**;
even the *king* **sovereign** of *Assyria* **Ashshur**.
18 And **so be** it *shall come to pass*, in that day,
that *the LORD* **Yah Veh** shall hiss for the fly
that is in the *uttermost part* **end**
of the rivers of *Egypt* **Misrayim**,
and for the bee that is in the land of *Assyria* **Ashshur**.
19 And they shall come, and shall rest all of them
in the *desolate valleys* **wadies of desolations**,
and in the holes of the rocks,
and upon all thorns, and upon all *bushes* **pastures**.
20 In the same day shall *the Lord* **Adonay**
shave with a razor *that is hired* **the hireling**,
namely, by them beyond the river,
by the *king* **sovereign** of *Assyria* **Ashshur**,
the head, and the hair of the feet:
and it shall also *consume* **scrape away** the beard.
21 And **so be** it *shall come to pass*, in that day,
that a man shall *nourish* **keep alive**
a young *cow* **heifer of the herd**, and two *sheep* **flock**;
22 And **so be** it *shall come to pass*,
for the abundance of milk that they shall *give* **work**
he shall eat butter:
for butter and honey shall every one eat
that *is left* **remaineth** in the land.
23 And **so be** it *shall come to pass* in that day,
so be it, that every place *shall be*,
where there were
a thousand vines at a thousand silverlings,
it shall *even* be for briers and thorns.
24 With arrows and with bows
shall *men* come thither;
because all the land shall become briers and thorns.
25 And on all hills
that shall be *digged* **hoed** with the *mattock* **hoe**,
there shall not come thither the fear of briers and thorns:
but it shall be for the sending forth of oxen,
and for the *treading* **trampling** of *lesser cattle* **lambs**.

and reign a sovereign in their midst
—the son of Tabe El.
7 Thus says Adonay Yah Veh,
It neither rises, nor becomes:
8 for the head of Aram is Dammeseq
and the head of Dammeseq is Resin:
and within sixty—five years
Ephrayim, as a people, breaks.
9 And the head of Ephrayim is Shomeron
and the head of Shomeron is the son of Remal Yah:
If you trust not,
surely you are not trustworthy.

THE SIGN OF IMMANU EL

10 And Yah Veh adds to word to Ach Az, saying,
11 You, ask a sign of Yah Veh your Elohim;
ask, either deep, or high above.
12 And Ach Az says, I neither ask nor test Yah Veh.
13 And he says, Hear now, O house of David;
Is it petty for you to weary men?
And also weary my Elohim?
14 So Adonay himself gives you a sign:
Behold, a virgin conceives and births a
son and calls his name Immanu El:

15 he eats butter and honey
to know to refuse the evil and choose the good:
16 for ere the lad knows to refuse the evil
and choose the good,
the soil you abhor is forsaken
at the face of both her sovereigns:
17 Yah Veh brings upon you
and upon your people
and upon the house of your father,
days *such as* came not
—even from the day Ephrayim
turned aside from Yah Hudah
by the sovereign of Ashshur.
18 And so be it, in that day,
Yah Veh hisses for the fly
in the end of the rivers of Misrayim
and for the bee in the land of Ashshur:
19 and they all come and rest
in the wadies of desolations
and in the holes of the rocks
and upon all thorns and upon all pastures.
20 In the same day,
Adonay, by the sovereign of Ashshur,
with a razor, shaves the hireling beyond the river
—the head, and the hair of the feet:
yes, also scrapes away the beard.
21 And so be it, in that day,
that a man keeps alive
a young heifer of the herd, and two flock;
22 and so be it,
for the abundance of milk that they work
he eats butter:
for every one who remains in the land
eats butter and honey.
23 And so be it, in that day,
so be it, that every place where there are
a thousand vines *worth* a thousand silverlings,
it becomes for briers and thorns:
24 he comes there with arrows and with bows;
because all the land becomes briers and thorns:
25 and on all hills hoed with the hoe,
there comes not the fear of briers and thorns:
but it becomes for the sending forth of oxen,
and for the trampling of lambs.

THE FALL OF DAMMESEQ AND SHOMERON

8 *Moreover the LORD* **Yah Veh** said unto me,
Take thee a great roll,
and *write* **inscribe** in it with a man's *pen* **stylus**
concerning *Mahershalalhashbaz*
Mahers Halal Hash Baz.
2 And I *took* **witnessed** unto me
faithful **trustworthy** witnesses to record,
Uriah **Uri Yah** the priest,
and *Zechariah* **Zechar Yah**
the son of *Jeberechiah* **Yeberech Yah**.
3 And I *went unto* **approached** the prophetess;
and she conceived, and *bare* **birthed** a son.
Then said *the LORD* **Yah Veh** to me,
Call his name
Mahershalalhashbaz **Mahers Halal Hash Baz**.
4 For before the *child* **lad** shall have knowledge
to *cry* **call out**, My father, and my mother,
the *riches* **valuables** of *Damascus* **Dammeseq**
and the spoil of *Samaria* **Shomeron**
shall be *taken away before* **lifted from the face
of** the *king* **sovereign** of *Assyria* **Ashshur**.
5 *The LORD* **Yah Veh**
spake also **added to word** unto me *again*, saying,
6 Forasmuch as this people
refuseth the waters of *Shiloah* **Shiloach**
that go *softly* **gently**, and *rejoice* **in joy**
in *Rezin* **Resin** and *Remaliah's* **Remal Yah's** son;
7 *Now* therefore, behold,
the Lord bringeth up **Adonay ascendeth** upon them
the waters of the river, *strong* **mighty** and many,
even the *king* **sovereign** of *Assyria* **Ashshur**,
and all his *glory* **honour**:
and he shall *come up* **ascend**
over all his *channels* **reservoirs**,
and go over all his banks:
8 And he shall pass through *Judah* **Yah Hudah**;
he shall overflow and *go* **pass** over,
he shall *reach even* **touch** to the neck;
and the *stretching out* **spreading** of his wings
shall fill the breadth of thy land,
O *Immanuel* **Immanu El**.
9 *Associate yourselves* **Be broken**, O ye people,
and ye shall be broken *in pieces*;
and *give ear* **hearken**, all ye of far *countries* **lands**:
gird *yourselves*, and ye shall be broken *in pieces*;
gird *yourselves*, and ye shall be broken *in pieces*.
10 **In counselling,** *Take* counsel *together*,
and it shall *come to nought* **break**;
speak **word** the word, and it shall not *stand* **rise**:
for *God* **El** is with us.
11 For *the LORD* **Yah Veh**
spake **said** thus to me with a strong hand,
and *instructed* **disciplined** me

that I should not walk in the way of this people, saying,
12 Say ye not, *A confederacy* **Conspiracy**,
to all them to whom this people shall say,
A confederacy **Conspiracy**;
neither *fear* **awe** ye their *fear* **awesomeness**,
nor be *afraid* **awed**.
13 *Sanctify* **Hallow**
the LORD of hosts **Yah Veh Sabaoth** himself;
and let him be your *fear* **awe**,
and let him be your dread.
14 And he shall be for a *sanctuary* **holies**;
but for a stone of *stumbling* **stubbing**
and for a rock of offence
to both the houses of *Israel* **Yisra El**,
for a *gin* **snare** and for a snare
to the *inhabitants* **settlers** of *Jerusalem* **Yeru Shalem**.
15 And many among them
shall *stumble* **falter**, and fall,
and be broken, and be snared, and *be taken* **captured**.
16 Bind up the *testimony* **witness**,
seal the *law* **torah** among my disciples.
17 And I *will wait upon the*
LORD **shall await Yah Veh**,
that hideth his face from the house of *Jacob*
Yaaqov, and I *will look for* **shall await** him.
18 Behold, I and the children
whom *the LORD* **Yah Veh** hath given me
are for signs and for *wonders* **omens** in *Israel* **Yisra El**
from *the LORD of hosts* **Yah Veh Sabaoth**,

THE FALL OF DAMMESEQ AND SHOMERON

8 Yah Veh says to me,
You, take a great roll;
and inscribe therein with the stylus of a man
concerning Mahers Halal Hash Baz.
2 And I witness trustworthy
witnesses to record for me
—Uri Yah the priest
and Zechar Yah the son of Yeberech Yah:
3 and I approach the prophetess;
and she conceives and births a son.
Then Yah Veh says to me,
Call his name Mahers Halal Hash Baz:
4 for ere the lad knows to call out,
My father! and, My mother!,
they lift the valuables of Dammeseq
and the spoil of Shomeron
from the face of the sovereign of Ashshur.
5 And Yah Veh adds to word to me, saying,
6 Because this people refuses
the waters of Shiloach
that come gently and in joy
with Resin and the son of Remal Yah;
7 so, behold,
Adonay ascends upon them
the waters of the river, mighty and many,
the sovereign of Ashshur and all his honor:
and he ascends over all his reservoirs
and goes over all his banks:
8 and he passes through Yah Hudah;
he overflows and passes over;
he touches to the neck:
and the spreading of his wings
fills the breadth of your land, O Immanu El.
9 Be broken, O you people—be broken;
and hearken, all you of lands afar:
gird, and be broken; gird, and be broken:
10 in counselling, counsel; and it breaks;
word the word, and it rises not:
for El is with us.
11 For thus Yah Veh says to me with a strong hand;
and disciplines me
to not walk in the way of this people, saying,
12 You, say not, Conspiracy,
to all them to whom this people say, Conspiracy;
neither awe their awesomeness,
nor be awed.
13 Hallow Yah Veh Sabaoth himself
to be your awe and to be your dread.
14 And he becomes for a holies;
and for a stone of stubbing and for a rock of offence
to both the houses of Yisra El for a snare;
and for a snare to the settlers of Yeru Shalem:
15 and among them, many falter and fall
—broken and snared and captured.
16 Bind up the witness,
seal the torah among my disciples.
17 And I await Yah Veh
who hides his face from the house of Yaaqov,
and I await him.
18 Behold, I and the children Yah Veh gives me
are for signs and for omens in Yisra El
—from Yah Veh Sabaoth
which *dwelleth* **tabernacleth** in mount *Zion* **Siyon**.
19 And when they shall say unto you,
Seek unto *them that have familiar spirits* **spiritists**,
and unto *wizards* **knowers**
that *peep* **chirp**, and that mutter:
should not a people seek unto their *God* **Elohim**?

for the living to the dead?
20 To the *law* **torah** and to the *testimony* **witness**:
if they *speak* **say** not according to this word,
it is because there is no *light* **dawn** in them.
21 And they shall pass through it,
hardly bestead **hardened** and *hungry* **famished**:
and **so be** it *shall come to pass*,
that when they shall *be hungry* **famish**,
they shall *fret themselves* **enrage** and *curse* **abase**
their *king* **sovereign** and their *God* **Elohim**,
and *look* **face** upward.
22 And they shall look unto the earth;
and behold *trouble* **tribulation** and darkness,
dimness **darkness** of *anguish* **distress**;
and they shall be *driven* **expelled** to darkness.

9 Nevertheless the *dimness*
obscurity shall not be such
as *was* in her *vexation* **narrowness**,
when at the first **time** he lightly afflicted
the land of Zebulun and the land of Naphtali,
and afterward *did more grievously afflict* **honoured** her
by the way of the sea, beyond *Jordan* **Yarden**,
in *Galilee* **Galiyl** of the *nations* **goyim**.

A PROMISE OF LIGHT

2 The people that walked in darkness
have seen a great light:
they that *dwell* **settle** in the land of the shadow of death,
upon them hath the light *shined* **illuminated**.
3 Thou hast *multiplied*
greatened the *nation* **goyim**,
and not *increased* **greatened** the *joy* **cheerfulness**:
they *joy before thee* **cheer at thy face**
according to the *joy* **cheerfulness** in harvest,
and *as men rejoice* **twirl** when they *divide* **allot** the spoil.
4 For thou hast broken the yoke of his burden,
and the *staff* **rod** of his shoulder,
the *rod* **scion** of his *oppressor* **exactor**,
as in the day of *Midian* **Midyan**.
5 For every *battle* **boot** of the *warrior* **booted**
is with confused noise **quaketh,**
and garments rolled in blood;
but this shall be with burning *and* fuel of fire.

A Child Is Born, A Son Is Given

6 For unto us a child is *born*
birthed, unto us a son is given:
and the *government* **dominion**
shall be upon his shoulder:
and his name* shall be called
Wonderful **Marvelous**, Counsellor,
The mighty God **Mighty El**,
The everlasting **Eternal** Father,
The Prince **Governor** of *Peace* **Shalom**.

*singular

7 Of the increase
of his *government* **dominion** and *peace* **shalom**
there shall be no end,
upon the throne of David,
and upon his *kingdom* **sovereigndom**,
to *order* **establish** it, and to *establish* **support** it
with judgment and with *justice* **justness**
from henceforth even *for ever* **eternally**.
The zeal of *the LORD of hosts* **Yah Veh Sabaoth**
will perform **shall work** this.

The Wrath Of Yah Veh

8 *The Lord* **Adonay** sent a
word into *Jacob* **Yaaqov**,
and it hath *lighted* **fallen** upon *Israel* **Yisra El**.
9 And all the people shall know,
even Ephraim **Ephrayim**
and the *inhabitant* **settler** of *Samaria* **Shomeron**,
that say **saying**
in the *pride* **pomp** and *stoutness* **greatness** of heart,
10 The bricks are fallen *down*,
but we *will* **shall** build with hewn stones:
the sycomores are cut down,
but we *will* **shall** change them into cedars.
11 Therefore *the LORD* **Yah Veh**
who tabernacles in mount Siyon.
19 And when they say to you,
Seek to spiritists and to knowers
who chirp and mutter:
Seek a people not to their Elohim?
—for the living to the dead?
20 To the torah and to the witness!
If they say not according to this word
it is because there is no dawn to them:
21 and they pass through, hardened and famished:
and so be it, they famish;
they enrage and abase
their sovereign and their Elohim,
and face upward:
22 and they look to the earth;
and behold tribulation and darkness
—darkness of distress;
—expelled to darkness.

9 Nevertheless the obscurity is not such
as in her narrowness,

as at the first time when he lightly afflicted
the land of Zebulun and the land of Naphtali;
and afterward honored her
by the way of the sea beyond Yarden
in Galiyl of the goyim.

A Promise Of Light

2 The people, walking in
darkness, see a great light:
settlers in the land of the shadow of death,
upon them the light illuminates.
3 You greaten the goyim;
you greaten their cheerfulness:
they cheer at your face
as the cheerfulness in harvest;
and twirl when they allot the spoil.
4 For you broke the yoke of his burden
and the rod of his shoulder
—the scion of his exactor as in the day of Midyan.
5 For every boot of the booted quakes,
and garments roll in blood;
but this becomes a burning—a fuel of fire.

A Child Is Born, A Son Is Given

6 For a child is birthed to us; a son is given to us
—and the dominion is on his shoulder:
and he calls his name*
Marvelous, Counsellor, Mighty El,
Eternal Father, Governor of Shalom.
*singular
7 Of the increase of his dominion and shalom
there is no end,
on the throne of David and on his sovereigndom;
to establish and to support
with judgment and with justness
from henceforth—even eternally.
The zeal of Yah Veh Sabaoth works this.

The Wrath Of Yah Veh

8 Adonay sent a word to Yaaqov
and it fell upon Yisra El:
9 and all the people knew
—Ephrayim and the settler of Shomeron,
saying, in the pomp and greatness of heart,
10 The bricks fall,
and we build with hewn stones:
the sycomores are cut down,
and we change them into cedars:
11 and Yah Veh
shall *set up* **loft** the *adversaries*
tribulators of *Rezin* **Resin**
against him,
and *join* **cover** his enemies *together*;
12 The *Syrians before* **Aramiym in front**,
and the *Philistines* **Peleshethiym** behind;
and they shall devour *Israel* **Yisra El** with open mouth.
For all this his *anger* **wrath** is not turned away,
but his hand is *stretched out* **spread** still.
13 For the people turneth not
unto him that smiteth them,
neither do they seek
the LORD of hosts **Yah Veh Sabaoth**.
14 Therefore *the LORD* **Yah Veh**
will **shall** cut off from *Israel* **Yisra El**
head and tail, *branch* **palm leaf** and rush, in one day.
15 The *ancient* **elder** and *honourable* **lifted face**,
he is the head;
and the prophet that teacheth *lies* **falsehood**,
he is the tail.
16 For *the leaders of* this people **that blithe them**
cause them to *err* **stray**;
and they that are *led* **blithed** *of them*
are *destroyed* **swallowed**.
17 Therefore *the Lord* **Adonay**
shall *have no joy* **not cheer** in their *young men* **youths**,
neither shall *have* **he** mercy *on*
their *fatherless* **orphans** and widows:
for every one
is *an hypocrite* **a profaner** and *an evildoer* **a vilifier**,
and every mouth *speaketh* **wordeth** folly.
For all this his *anger* **wrath** is not turned away,
but his hand is *stretched out* **spread** still.
18 For wickedness burneth as the fire:
it shall devour the briers and thorns,
and shall kindle in the thickets of the forest,
and they shall *mount up* **spiral upward,**
like the *lifting up* **rising** of smoke.
19 Through the wrath
of *the LORD of hosts* **Yah Veh Sabaoth**
is the land *darkened* **burnt**,
and the people shall be as the fuel of the fire:
no man shall spare his brother.
20 And he shall *snatch* **cut** on the right *hand*,
and *be hungry* **famish**;
and he shall eat on the left *hand*,
and *they* shall not *be satisfied* **satiate**:
they shall eat every man the flesh of his own arm:
21 *Manasseh* **Menash Sheh**, *Ephraim* **Ephrayim**;
and *Ephraim* **Ephrayim**, *Manasseh* **Menash Sheh**:
and they together shall be against *Judah* **Yah Hudah**.
For all this his *anger* **wrath** is not turned away,
but his hand is *stretched out* **spread** still.

Ho To The Scribes

10 *Woe* **Ho** unto them that
decree unrighteous decrees **engrave statutes of mischief,**
and that *write grievousness* **inscribe toil**
which they have *prescribed* **incribed;**
2 To *turn aside* **pervert** the *needy* **poor**
from *judgment* **pleading their cause,**
and *to take away* **strip** the *right* **judgment**
from the *poor* **humble** of my people,
that widows may be their *prey* **spoil,**
and that they may *rob* **plunder** the *fatherless* **orphan**!
3 And what *will* **shall** ye *do*
work in the day of visitation,
and in the *desolation* **devastation**
which shall come from far?
to whom *will* **shall** ye flee for help?
and where *will* **shall** ye leave your *glory* **honour**?
4 Without me
they shall *bow down* **kneel** under the *prisoners* **bound,**
and they shall fall under the *slain* **slaughtered.**
For all this his *anger* **wrath** is not turned away,
but his hand is *stretched out* **spread** still.
5 *O Assyrian* **Ho Ashshuri,**
the *rod* **scion** of *mine anger* **my wrath,**
and the *staff* **rod** in their hand
is *mine indignation* **my rage.**
6 I *will* **shall** send him
against *an hypocritical nation* **a goyim of profaners,**
and against the people of my wrath
lofts the tribulators of Resin against him
and covers his enemies
12 —the Aramiym in front
and the Peleshethiym behind;
and they devour Yisra El with open mouth.
For all this, he turns not his wrath
and still spreads his hand:
13 and the people
neither turn to him who smites them,
nor seek they Yah Veh Sabaoth:
14 and Yah Veh cuts off from Yisra El
head and tail, palm leaf and rush, in one day.
15 The elder and lifted face, he *is* the head;
and the prophet teaching falsehood, he *is* the tail.
16 For this people who blithe them
cause them to stray;
and the blithed are swallowed.
17 So Adonay
neither cheers in their youths,
nor mercies their orphans and widows:
for every one is a profaner and a vilifier
and every mouth words folly.
For all this he turns not away his wrath
and still spreads his hand.
18 For wickedness burns as the fire
consuming the briers and thorns;
kindling in the thickets of the forest;
spiraling upward as the rising of smoke.
19 Through the wrath of Yah Veh Sabaoth
the land burns,
and the people are as the fuel of the fire:
no man spares his brother.
20 And on the right, he cuts and famishes;
and on the left, he eats and satiates not:
every man eats the flesh of his own arm
21 —Menash Sheh, Ephrayim;
and Ephrayim, Menash Sheh:
and together they *are* against Yah Hudah.
For all this he turns not away his wrath,
and still spreads his hand.

Ho To The Scribes

10 Ho to them engraving statutes of mischief,
and inscribers incribing toil;
2 to pervert the poor
from pleading their cause;
and strip the judgment
from the humble of my people
—that widows be their spoil
and to plunder the orphan!
3 And what work you in the day of visitation
and in the devastation coming from afar?
To whom flee you for help?
And where leave you your honor?
4 Without me, they kneel under the bound,
and they fall under the slaughtered.
For all this he turns not away his wrath,
and still spreads his hand.
5 Ho, Ashshuri, the scion of my wrath;
and the rod in their hand, my rage:
6 I send him against a goyim of profaners
and against the people of my wrath;
will I give him a charge **shall I misvah him,**
to take the spoil, and to *take* **plunder** the *prey* **plunder,**
and to *tread them down* **set them for trampling**
like the *mire* **heap** of the *streets* **outways.**
7 Howbeit he *meaneth* **considereth** not so,
neither doth his heart *think* **fabricate** so;
but it is in his heart
to *destroy* **desolate** and cut off *nations* **goyim** not a few.
8 For he saith,
Are not my *princes* **governors**

altogether *kings* **sovereigns**?
9 Is not *Calno* **Kalneh** as
Carchemish **Karchemish**?
is not Hamath as Arpad?
is not *Samaria* **Shomeron** as *Damascus* **Dammeseq**?
10 As my hand
hath found the *kingdoms* **sovereigndoms** of the idol,
and *whose graven images did excel them* **sculptiles**
of *Jerusalem* **Yeru Shalem** and *of Samaria* **Shomeron**;
11 Shall I not **work**, as I have *done* **worked**
unto *Samaria* **Shomeron** and her idols,
so *do* **work** to *Jerusalem* **Yeru Shalem** and her idols?
12 Wherefore **so be** it *shall come to pass*,
that when *the Lord* **Adonay**
hath *performed* **clipped** his whole work
upon mount *Zion* **Siyon** and on *Jerusalem* **Yeru Shalem**,
I *will punish* **shall visit**
upon the fruit of the *stout* **greatness of** heart
of the *king* **sovereign** of *Assyria* **Ashshur**,
and the *glory* **adornment** of his *high looks* **haughty eyes**.
13 For he saith,
By the *strength* **force** of my hand I have *done* **worked** it,
and by my wisdom; for I *am prudent* **discern**:
and I have *removed* **turned aside**
the *bounds* **borders** of the people,
and have *robbed* **plundered** their treasures,
and I have *put* **brought** down the *inhabitants* **settlers**
like *a valiant man* **the mighty**:
14 And my hand hath found as a nest
the *riches* **valuables** of the people:
and as one gathereth eggs that are *left* **abandoned**,
have I gathered all the earth;
and there was none that *moved* **flapped** the wing,
or *opened* **gaped** the mouth, or *peeped* **chirped**.
15 Shall the ax boast itself
against him that heweth therewith?
or shall the *saw magnify* **rasp greaten** itself
against him that shaketh it?
as if the *rod* **scion** should shake itself
against them that lift it *up*,
or as if the *staff* **rod** should lift *up* itself,
as if it were no *wood* **timber**.
16 Therefore shall *the Lord* **Adonay**,
the Lord of hosts **Adonay Sabaoth**,
send among his *fat ones leanness* **fatness emaciation**;
and under his *glory* **honour**
he shall *kindle* **burn** a burning like the burning of a fire.
17 And the light of *Israel* **Yisra El** shall be for a fire,
and his Holy One for a flame:
and it shall burn and *devour* **consume** his
thorns and his briers in one day;
18 And shall *consume* **finish off**
the *glory* **honour** of his forest,
and of his *fruitful field* **orchard/Karmel**,
both soul and *body* **flesh**:
and they shall be as when
a standardbearer fainteth **an ensignbearer melteth**.
19 And the *rest* **survivors** of the trees of his forest
shall be *few* **numerable**,
that a *child* may *write* **lad inscribe** them.

THE SURVIVING ESCAPEES

20 And **so be** it *shall come to pass* in that day,
that the *remnant* **survivors** of *Israel* **Yisra El**,
and *such as are escaped* **the escapees**
of the house of *Jacob* **Yaaqov**,
shall *no more again* **not add**
stay **to lean** upon him that smote them;
but shall *stay* **lean** upon *the LORD* **Yah Veh**,
the Holy One of *Israel* **Yisra El**, in truth.
21 The *remnant* **survivors** shall return,
I misvah him to take the spoil and to
plunder the plunder; and to set them for
trampling as the heap of the outways:
7 and he—he neither considers thus,
nor fabricates his heart thus;
but in his heart
is to desolate and cut off goyim not a few.
8 —for he says,
Are not my governors altogether sovereigns?
9 Is not Kalneh as Karchemish?
Is not Hamath as Arpad?
Is not Shomeron as Dammeseq?
10 As my hand found the
sovereigndoms of the idol,
and their sculptiles of Yeru Shalem and Shomeron;
11 Work I not
as I worked to Shomeron and her idols? Work
thus to Yeru Shalem and her idols?
12 And so be it,
when Adonay clips his whole work
on mount Siyon and on Yeru Shalem,
I visit upon the fruit of the greatness of heart
of the sovereign of Ashshur
and the adornment of his haughty eyes.
13 For he said,
By the force of my hand, I worked;
and by my wisdom, I discerned:
and I turned aside the borders of the people
and plundered their treasures;
and I brought down the settlers as the mighty:

14 and my hand found, as a nest,
the valuables of the people:
and as one gathers abandoned eggs,
I gathered all the earth;
and no one flapped the wing
or gaped the mouth or chirped.
15 Boasts the ax over him who hews therewith?
Or greatens the rasp over him who shakes it?
—as a scion shakes them who lift it?
Or as a rod lifts itself with no timber?
16 So Adonay—Adonay Sabaoth
sends emaciation among his fatness;
and under his honor
he burns a burning as the burning of a fire:
17 and the light of Yisra El is for a fire,
and his Holy One for a flame:
and in one day
it burns and consumes his thorns and his briers;
18 and finishes off the honor of his forest
and of his orchard/Karmel
—both soul and flesh:
to become as when an ensignbearer melts:
19 and the survivors of the trees of his forest
become a number,
that even a lad *can* inscribe them.

The Surviving Escapees

20 And so be it, in that day,
the survivors of Yisra El
and the escapees of the house of Yaaqov
add not to lean upon him who smote them;
and lean upon Yah Veh,
the Holy One of Yisra El, in truth:
21 the survivors return
even the *remnant* **survivors** of *Jacob* **Yaaqov**,
unto the mighty *God* **El**.
22 For though thy people *Israel* **Yisra El**
be as the sand of the sea,
yet a remnant **the survivors** of them shall return:
the consumption *decreed* **appointed**
shall overflow with *righteousness* **justness**.
23 For *the Lord GOD of hosts*
Adonay Yah Veh Sabaoth
shall *make* **work** a *consumption* **final finish**,
even determined **appointed**, in the midst of all the land.
24 Therefore thus saith
the Lord GOD of hosts **Adonay Yah Veh Sabaoth**,
O my people that *dwellest* **settlest** in *Zion* **Siyon**,
be not afraid of **awe not** the *Assyrian* **Ashshuri**:
he shall smite thee with a *rod* **scion**,
and shall lift *up* his *staff* **rod** against thee,
after the *manner* **way** of *Egypt* **Misrayim**.
25 For yet a very little while,
and the *indignation* **rage** shall *cease* **conclude**,
and *mine anger* **my wrath**
in their *destruction* **consumption**.
26 And *the LORD of hosts* **Yah Veh Sabaoth**
shall *stir up* **waken** a *scourge* **whip** for him
according to the *slaughter* **striking** of *Midian* **Midyan**
at the rock of Oreb:
and as his rod was upon the sea,
so shall he lift it *up*
after the *manner* **way** of *Egypt* **Misrayim**.

The Ointment Despoils The Yoke

27 And **so be** it *shall come to pass*, in that day,
that his burden shall *be taken away* **turn aside**
from off thy shoulder,
and his yoke from off thy neck,
and the yoke shall *be destroyed* **despoil**
because **at the face** of the *anointing* **ointment**.
28 He is come to *Aiath* **Ayath**,
he is passed to Migron;
at Michmash
he *hath laid up* **mustereth** his *carriages* **instruments**:
29 They are *gone* **passed** over the passage:
they have taken up their lodging at Geba;
Ramah *is afraid* **trembleth**;
Gibeah **Gibah** of *Saul is fled* **Shaul fleeth**.
30 *Lift up* **Resound** thy voice,
O daughter of *Gallim* **heaps**:
cause it to be heard unto **hearken O** Laish,
O *poor* **humble** Anathoth.
31 Madmenah *is removed* **fleeth**;
the *inhabitants* **settlers** of *Gebim* **the way of the dugouts**
gather **withdraw** themselves *to flee*.
32 As yet shall he *remain* **stand** at Nob that day:
he shall shake his hand
against the mount of *the daughter of Zion* **Bath Siyon**,
the hill of *Jerusalem* **Yeru Shalem**.
33 Behold,
the Lord, the LORD of hosts **Adonay Yah Veh Sabaoth**,
shall lop the *bough* **foliage** with *terror* **violence**:
and the high ones of *stature* **height**
shall be *hewn* **cut** *down*,
and the *haughty* **lofty** shall be *humbled* **abased**.
34 And he shall *cut down* **strike**
the thickets of the forest
with iron,
and Lebanon shall **have a mighty** fall *by a mighty one*.

THE BRANCH

11 And there shall come forth a rod
out of the *stem* **stump** of *Jesse* **Yishay**,
and a Branch shall *grow* **bear fruit** out
of his roots: cp Yesha Yah 11:10
2 And the spirit of *the LORD*
Yah Veh shall rest upon him,
the spirit of wisdom and understanding,
the spirit of counsel and might,
the spirit of knowledge
and of the *fear* **awe** of *the LORD* **Yah Veh**;
3 And shall *make* **scent** him
of quick understanding
in the *fear* **awe** of *the LORD* **Yah Veh**:
and he shall not judge after the sight of his eyes,
neither reprove after the hearing of his ears:
4 But with *righteousness* **justness**
shall he judge the poor,
and reprove with *equity* **straightness**
for the *meek* **humble** of the earth:
—the survivors of Yaaqov to the mighty El.
22 For though your people Yisra El
become as the sand of the sea,
their survivors return:
the appointed consumption overflows with justness:
23 for Adonay Yah Veh Sabaoth
works a final finish,
appointed midst all the land.
24 So Adonay Yah Veh Sabaoth says thus:
O my people settling in Siyon, awe not the Ashshuri:
he smites you with a scion
and lifts his rod against you after the way of Misrayim:
25 for yet a very little *while*,
and I conclude the rage,
and my wrath in their consumption.
26 And Yah Veh Sabaoth wakens a whip for him
according to the striking of Midyan
at the rock of Oreb:
and as his rod *is* over the sea,
and he lifts it as in the way of Misrayim.

THE OINTMENT DESPOILS THE YOKE

27 And so be it, in that day,
he turns aside his burden from off your shoulder
and his yoke from off your neck;
and the yoke despoils at the face of the ointment.
28 He comes to Ayath; he passes to Migron;
he musters his instruments at Michmash:
29 they pass over the passage:
they take up their lodging at Geba;
Ramah trembles; Gibah of Shaul flees.
30 Resound your voice, O daughter of heaps!
Hearken, O Laish! Humble, O Anathoth!
31 Madmenah flees;
the settlers of the way of the dugouts withdraw.
32 As yet he stands that day at Nob:
the mount of Bath Siyon, the hill of Yeru Shalem
shakes his hand.
33 Behold,
Adonay Yah Veh Sabaoth
lops the foliage with violence:
and cuts the high ones of height
and abases the lofty:
34 and he strikes the thickets
of the forest with iron,
and Lebanon falls by the mighty.

THE BRANCH

11 And a Rod comes from the stump of Yishay
and a Branch from his roots bears
fruit: cp Yesha Yah 11:10
2 and the spirit of Yah Veh rests upon him
—the spirit of wisdom and understanding,
the spirit of counsel and might,
the spirit of knowledge,
and of the awe of Yah Veh;
3 and scents him in the awe of Yah Veh:
and he neither judges after the sight of his eyes,
nor reproves after the hearing of his ears:
4 and with justness he judges the poor,
and reproves with straightness
for the humble of the earth:
and he shall smite the earth
with the *rod* **scion** of his mouth,
and with the *breath* **spirit** of his lips
shall he *slay* **execute** the wicked.
5 And *righteousness* **justness**
shall be the girdle of his loins,
and *faithfulness* **trustworthiness**
the girdle of his *reins* **loins**.
6 The wolf also shall *dwell* **sojourn** with the lamb,
and the leopard shall *lie down* **crouch** with the kid;
and the calf and the *young lion* **whelp**
and the fatling together;
and a little *child* **lad** shall *lead* **drive** them.
7 And the *cow* **heifer** and
the bear shall *feed* **graze**;
their *young ones* **children** shall *lie down* **crouch**
together: and the lion shall eat straw like the ox.

8 And the *sucking child* **suckling**
shall *play* **stroke** on the hole of the asp,
and the weaned *child* shall *put* **spread** his hand
on the *cockatrice' den* **hisser's hole.**
9 They shall not *hurt* **vilify** nor *destroy* **ruin**
in all my holy mountain:
for the earth shall *be full* **fill**
of the knowledge of *the LORD* **Yah Veh,**
as the waters cover the sea.
10 And in that day there shall
be a root of *Jesse* **Yishay,**
which shall stand for an ensign of the people;
to it shall the *Gentiles* **goyim** seek:
and his rest shall be *glorious* **honourable.**

cp Yesha Yah 11:1

The Survivors Restored

11 And **so be** it *shall come to pass,* in that day,
that the Lord **Adonay**
shall set his hand again *the second time* **secondly**
to *recover* **chattel** the *remnant* **survivors** of his people,
which shall *be left* **survive,**
from *Assyria* **Ashshur,** and from *Egypt* **Misrayim,**
and from Pathros, and from *Cush* **Kush,** and from Elam,
and from Shinar, and from Hamath,
and from the islands of the sea.
12 And he shall *set up* **lift** an ensign
for the *nations* **goyim,**
and shall *assemble* **gather**
the *outcasts* **overthrown** of *Israel* **Yisra El,**
and gather *together*
the *dispersed* **scattered** of *Judah* **Yah Hudah**
from the four *corners* **wings** of the earth.
13 The envy also of *Ephraim* **Ephrayim**
shall *depart* **turn aside,**
and the *adversaries* **tribulators** of *Judah* **Yah Hudah**
shall be cut off:
Ephraim **Ephrayim**
shall not envy *Judah* **Yah Hudah,**
and *Judah* **Yah Hudah**
shall not *vex Ephraim* **tribulate Ephrayim.**
14 But they shall fly
upon the shoulders of the *Philistines* **Peleshethiym**
toward the west **seaward;**
they shall *spoil* **plunder**
them **the sons** of the east together:
they shall *lay* **spread** their hand upon Edom and Moab;
and the *children* **sons** of Ammon
shall *obey* **hearken unto** them.
15 And *the LORD* **Yah Veh**
shall *utterly destroy* **devote**
the tongue of the *Egyptian* **Misrayim** sea;
and with *his mighty wind* **the strength of his wind/spirit**
shall he shake his hand over the river,
and shall smite it in the seven *streams* **wadies,**
and *make* **hath** men *go over dryshod* **tread in shoes.**
16 And there shall be an highway
for the *remnant* **survivors** of his people,
which shall *be left* **survive,** from *Assyria* **Ashshur;**
like as it was to *Israel* **Yisra El**
in the day that he *came up* **ascended** out
of the land of *Egypt* **Misrayim.**

A Psalm Of Spread Hands

12 And in that day thou shalt
say, O *LORD* **Yah Veh,**
I *will praise* **shall spread hands unto** thee:
and he smites the earth with the scion of his mouth
and with the spirit of his lips he executes the wicked:
5 and justness is the girdle of his loins,
and trustworthiness the girdle of his loins.
6 And the wolf sojourns with the lamb
and the leopard crouches with the kid
—the calf and the whelp and the fatling together;
and a little lad drives them:
7 and the heifer and the bear graze—their children
crouch together: and the lion eats straw as the ox
8 and the suckling strokes on the hole of the asp,
and the weaned spreads his hand
on the hole of hisser.
9 They neither vilify nor ruin
in all my holy mountain:
for the earth fills with the knowledge of Yah Veh,
as waters cover the sea.
10 And in that day,
a Root of Yishay stands for an ensign of the people;
to him the goyim seek:
and his rest becomes honorable.

cp Yesha Yah 11:1

The Survivors Restored

11 And so be it, in that day,
Adonay adds to set his hand secondly
to chattel the survivors of his people who survive
—from Ashshur and from Misrayim
and from Pathros and from Kush and from Elam
and from Shinar and from Hamath
and from the islands of the sea:

12 and he lifts an ensign for the goyim
and gathers the overthrown of Yisra El
and gathers the scattered of Yah Hudah
from the four wings of the earth:
13 and turns aside the envy of Ephrayim,
and cuts off the tribulators of Yah Hudah:
neither Ephrayim envies Yah Hudah,
nor Yah Hudah tribulates Ephrayim:
14 and they fly seaward
on the shoulders of the Peleshethiym;
together they plunder the sons of the east:
Edom and Moab spread their hand
and the sons of Ammon hearken to them.
15 And Yah Veh
devotes the tongue of the Misrayim sea;
and with the strength of his wind/spirit
he shakes his hand over the river
and smites it in the seven wadies;
and has men tread it in shoes.
16 And so be it, a highway
for the survivors of his people of Ashshur who survive
—as it became to Yisra El
in the day he ascended from the land of Misrayim.

A PSALM OF SPREAD HANDS

12 And in that day you say, O Yah Veh,
I spread hands to you:
though thou wast angry with me,
thine anger **thy wrath** is turned away,
and thou *comfortedst* **sighedst over** me.
2 Behold, *God* **El** is my salvation;
I *will trust* **shall confide**, and not *be afraid* **fear**:
for *the LORD JEHOVAH* **Yah Yah Veh**
is my strength and *my song* **psalm**;
he also is become my salvation.
3 Therefore with *joy* **rejoicing**
shall ye *draw* **bail** water
out of the *wells* **fountains** of salvation.
4 And in that day shall ye say,
Praise the LORD **Spread hands unto Yah Veh**,
call upon his name,
declare his doings **make known his exploits**
among the people,
make mention **remember** that his name is exalted.
5 *Sing* **Psalm** unto *the LORD* **Yah Veh**;
for he hath *done excellent things* **worked pomp**:
this is known in all the earth.
6 *Cry out* **Resound** and shout,
thou *inhabitant* **settlers** of *Zion* **Siyon**:
for great is the Holy One of *Israel* **Yisra El**
in the midst of thee.

THE BURDEN OF BABEL

13 The burden of *Babylon* **Babel**,
which *Isaiah* **Yesha Yah** the son of *Amoz* **Amos** did see.
2 Lift ye up *a banner* **an ensign**
upon the *high* **barren** mountain,
exalt the voice unto them, shake the hand,
that they may go
into the *gates* **portals** of the *nobles* **volunteers**.
3 I have *commanded* **misvahed**
my *sanctified ones* **hallowed**,
I have also called my mighty *ones*
for *mine anger* **my wrath**,
even them
that *rejoice* **jump for joy** in my *highness* **pomp**.
4 The *noise* **voice** of a multitude in the mountains,
like as **in the likeness** of a great people;
a tumultuous **an uproar of** noise
of the *kingdoms* **sovereigndoms** of *nations* **goyim**
gathered *together*:
the LORD of hosts **Yah Veh Sabaoth**
mustereth the host of the *battle* **war**.
5 They come from a far *country* **land**,
from the end of *heaven* **the heavens**,
even the LORD **Yah Veh**,
and the *weapons* **instruments** of his *indignation* **rage**,
to *destroy* **despoil** the whole land.
6 Howl ye;
for the day of *the LORD is at hand*
Yah Veh approacheth;
it shall come as a *destruction* **ravage**
from *the Almighty* **Shadday**.
7 Therefore shall all hands *be faint* **slacken**,
and every man's heart shall melt:
8 And they shall *be afraid* **terrify**:
pangs **pains** and *sorrows* **pangs** shall take hold of them;
they shall *be in pain* **writhe**
as a woman *that travaileth* **birthing**:
they shall *be amazed* **marvel**
one at another **every man at friend**;
their faces shall be as flames.
9 Behold, the day of *the LORD* **Yah Veh** cometh,
cruel both with wrath and *fierce anger* **fuming wrath**,
to *lay* **set** the land desolate:
and he shall *destroy* **desolate** the sinners *thereof* out of it.
10 For the stars of *heaven* **the heavens**
and *the constellations thereof* **kesil**
shall not *give* **halal** their light:
the sun shall be darkened in his going forth,
and the moon

shall not *cause* **illuminate** her light *to shine.*
11 And I *will punish* **shall visit**
the world for their evil,
and the wicked for their *iniquity* **perversity**;
and I *will* **shall** cause
the *arrogancy* **pomp** of the *proud* **arrogant**
to *cease* **shabbathize**,
and *will lay low* **shall abase**
the *haughtiness* **pomp** of the *terrible* **tyrant**.
though you were angry with me,
you turn away your wrath and you sigh over me.
2 Behold, El *is* my salvation;
I confide, and fear not:
for Yah Yah Veh *is* my strength and psalm;
and he is my salvation.
3 and with rejoicing you bail water
from the fountains of salvation.
4 And in that day, you say,
Spread hands to Yah Veh! Call on his name!
Make known his exploits among the people!
Remember—his name is exalted!
5 Psalm to Yah Veh for he worked pomp!
—this is known in all the earth.
6 Resound and shout, you settlers of Siyon:
for great *is* the Holy One of Yisra El in your midst.

THE BURDEN OF BABEL

13 The burden of Babel
Yesha Yah the son of Amos saw:
2 You, lift an ensign upon the barren mountain;
exalt the voice to them;
shake the hand,
so that they go into the portals of the volunteers.
3 I misvah my hallowed;
I also call my mighty for my wrath
—those jumping for joy in my pomp.
4 The voice of a multitude in the mountains,
in the likeness of a great people;
an uproar of noise of the sovereigndoms of goyim
who gather:
Yah Veh Sabaoth musters the host of the war:
5 they come from a land afar
—from the end of the heavens
—Yah Veh and the instruments of his rage
to despoil the whole land.
6 You, howl!
for the day of Yah Veh approaches;
it comes as a ravage from Shadday.
7 So all hands slacken
and every heart of man melts;
8 and they terrify:
pains and pangs take hold of them;
they writhe as a woman birthing:
every man marvels at friend
—their faces as flames.
9 Behold, the day of Yah Veh comes—cruel
—with both wrath and fuming wrath
to set the land desolate:
and he desolates the sinners from it.
10 For the stars of the heavens and kesil
halal not their light:
the sun darkens in its going,
and the moon illuminates not its light.
11 And I visit the world for their evil
and the wicked for their perversity;
and I cause the pomp of the arrogant to shabbathize;
and abase the pomp of the tyrant.
12 I *will make* **shall esteem** a man
more precious than *fine* **pure** gold;
even a man—**humanity**
than the *golden wedge* **ore** of Ophir.
13 Therefore I *will shake* **shall quake** the heavens,
and the earth shall *remove* **quake** out of her place,
in the wrath of *the LORD of hosts* **Yah Veh Sabaoth**,
and in the day of his *fierce anger* **fuming wrath**.
14 And it shall be as the *chased roe* **driven gazelle**,
and as a *sheep* **flock**
that *no man taketh up* **none shall gather**:
they shall every man *turn to* **face** his own people,
and flee every *one* **man** into his own land.
15 Every one that is found shall be thrust through;
and every one that is *joined unto them* **scraped away**
shall fall by the sword.
16 Their *children* **sucklings** also
shall be *dashed to pieces* **splattered**
before **in front of** their eyes;
their houses shall be *spoiled* **plundered**,
and their *wives ravished* **women lain with and raped**.
17 Behold,
I *will stir up the Medes* **shall waken the Maday**
against them,
which shall not *regard* **fabricate** silver;
and as for gold, they shall not delight in it.
18 Their bows also
shall *dash* **splatter** the *young men* **lads** *to pieces*;
and they shall *have no pity on* **not mercy**
the fruit of the *womb* **belly**;
their eye shall not spare *children* **sons**.
19 And *Babylon* **Babel**,
the *glory* **splendour** of *kingdoms* **sovereigndoms**,

the *beauty* **adornment**
of the *Chaldees' excellency* **Kesediym's pomp**,
shall be as when *God* **Elohim**
overthrew *Sodom* **Sedom** and *Gomorrah* **Amorah**.
20 It shall never be *inhabited* **settled in perpetuity**,
neither shall it be *dwelt* **tabernacled** in
from generation to generation:
neither shall the *Arabian pitch* **Arabiy** tent there;
neither shall the *shepherds* **tenders**
make their fold **crouch** there.
21 But *wild beasts of the* desert **dwellers**
shall *lie* **crouch** there;
and their houses
shall be *full* **filled** of *doleful creatures* **howlers**;
and **daughters of the** owls shall *dwell* **tabernacle** there,
and *satyrs* **bucks** shall dance there.
22 And the *wild beasts of the islands* **island howlers**
shall *cry* **answer** in their *desolate houses*
abandonments, and *dragons* **monsters**
in their *pleasant palaces* **manses of luxury**:
and her time is near to come,
and her days shall not be *prolonged* **drawn out**.

YAH VEH MERCIES YAAQOV

14 For *the LORD* **Yah Veh**
will **shall** *have* mercy *on Jacob* **Yaaqov**,
and *will* **shall** yet choose *Israel* **Yisra El**,
and set them in their own *land* **soil**:
and the *strangers* **sojourners** shall be joined with them,
and they shall *cleave* **be scraped**
to the house of *Jacob* **Yaaqov**.
2 And the people shall take them,
and bring them to their place:
and the house of *Israel* **Yisra El**
shall *possess* **inherit** them
in the *land* **soil** of *the LORD* **Yah Veh**
for servants and *handmaids* **maids**:
and they shall *take them captives*, **be captured**
whose captives they were **by their captors**;
and they shall *rule over* **subjugate**
their *oppressors* **exactors**.
3 And **so be** it *shall come to pass*,
in the day that *the LORD* **Yah Veh**
shall *give thee* rest **thee** from thy *sorrow* **contortion**,
and from thy *fear* **quivering**,
and from the hard *bondage* **service**
wherein thou wast made to serve
which was served on thee,

12 I esteem a man more precious than pure gold;
and humanity *more* than the ore of Ophir.
13 So I quake the heavens
and quake the earth from her place in the wrath of
Yah Veh Sabaoth and in the day of his fuming wrath.
14 And so be it,
as the driven gazelle and as a flock,
no one gathers:
every man faces his own people
and every man flees to his own land:
15 every one found *is* thrust through;
and every one scraped away, falls by the sword:
16 and they splatter their sucklings
in front of their eyes:
plunder their houses
and lie down with their women and rape.
17 Behold,
I waken the Maday against them,
who fabricate not silver;
and as for gold, they delight not therein.
18 And their bows splatter the lads;
and they neither mercy the fruit of the belly
nor their eye spares sons.
19 And Babel, the splendour of sovereigndoms,
the adornment of the pomp of the Kesediym,
becomes as
when Elohim overthrew Sedom and Amorah
20 —neither to settle therein in perpetuity
nor to tabernacle therein from generation
to generation: neither the Arabiy tent
there; nor the tenders crouch there:
21 and desert dwellers crouch there;
and their houses are filled by howlers;
and daughters of the owls tabernacle there,
and bucks dance there:
22 and the island howlers
answer in their abandonments,
and monsters in their manses of luxury:
and her time comes near,
and her days are not drawn out.

YAH VEH MERCIES YAAQOV

14 Because Yah Veh mercies Yaaqov,
and yet chooses Yisra El,
and sets them in their own soil:
and the sojourners join with them
and scrape them to the house of Yaaqov:
2 and the people take them
and bring them to their place:
and the house of Yisra El
inherits them in the soil of Yah Veh
for servants and maids:

captives of their captors;
and they subjugate to their exactors.
3 And so be it,
in the day Yah Veh rests you from your contortion,
and from your quivering,
and from the hard service served on you
4 That thou shalt *take up* **lift** this proverb
against the *king* **sovereign** of *Babylon* **Babel**, and say,
How hath the *oppressor ceased* **exactor shabbathized**!
the *golden city* **extortioners of gold**
ceased **shabbathized**!
5 *The LORD* **Yah Veh**
hath broken the *staff* **rod** of the wicked,
and the *sceptre* **scion** of the *rulers* **sovereigns**.
6 He who smote the people in wrath
with a *continual stroke* **stroke without revolt,**
he that *ruled* **subjugated** the *nations* **goyim**
in *anger* **wrath**
is persecuted, *and* none *hindereth* **spareth**.
7 The whole earth is at rest, *and is quiet* **resteth**:
they break forth into *singing* **shouting**.
8 Yea, the fir trees *rejoice* **cheer** at thee,
and the cedars of Lebanon, *saying*,
Since thou art laid down,
no *feller is come up* **cutter ascendeth** against us.
9 *Hell* **Sheol** from beneath
is moved **quaketh** for thee
to meet thee at thy coming:
it *stirreth up* **wakeneth** the *dead* **ghost** for thee,
even all the *chief ones* **he goats** of the earth;
it hath raised up from their thrones
all the *kings* **sovereigns** of the *nations* **goyim**.
10 All they shall *speak* **answer** and say unto thee,
Art thou also *become weak* **worn** as we?
art thou become like unto us?
11 Thy pomp is brought down to *the grave* **sheol**,
and the *noise* **sound** of thy *viols* **bagpipes**:
the *worm* **maggot** is spread under thee,
and the *worms* **maggots** cover thee.

THE HALALED ONE

12 How art thou fallen from *heaven* **the heavens**,
O *Lucifer* **Halaled one**, son of the *morning* **dawn**!
how art thou cut down to the *ground* **earth**,
which didst *weaken* **vanquish** the *nations* **goyim**!
13 For thou hast said in thine heart,
I *will* **shall** ascend into *heaven* **the heavens**,
I *will* **shall** exalt my throne above the stars of *God* **El**:
I *will* **shall** sit also upon the mount of the congregation,
in the *sides* **flanks** of the north:
14 I *will* **shall** ascend
above the *heights* **bamahs** of the **thick** clouds;
I will be—like *the most High* **Elyon**.
15 Yet thou shalt be brought down to *hell* **sheol**,
to the *sides* **flanks** of the *pit* **well**.
16 They that see thee shall
narrowly look **peer** upon thee,
and consider **discern** thee, *saying*,
Is this the man that *made* **quaked** the earth *to tremble*,
that *did shake kingdoms* **quaked sovereigndoms**;
17 That *made* **set** the world as a wilderness,
and *destroyed* **demolished** the cities *thereof*;
that opened not the house of his *prisoners* **bound**?
18 All the *kings* **sovereigns** of the *nations* **goyim**,
even all of them, lie in *glory* **honour**,
every *one* **man** in his own house.

cp Yahn 12:31, Loukas 10:18, Apocalypse 12:7—12

19 But thou art cast out of thy *grave* **tomb**
like an *abominable* **abhorrent** branch,
and as the *raiment* **robe**
of *those that are slain* **the slaughtered**,
thrust through **stabbed** with a sword,
that *go down* **descend** to the stones of the *pit* **well**;
as a carcase *trodden under feet* **trampled**.
20 Thou shalt not be *joined* **united** with them
in *burial* **the tomb**,
because thou hast *destroyed* **ruined** thy land,
and *slain* **slaughtered** thy people:
the seed of *evildoers* **vilifiers**
shall never **eternally** be *renowned* **called out**.
21 Prepare slaughter for his *children* **sons**
for the *iniquity* **perversity** of their fathers;
that they do not rise, nor possess the land,
nor fill the face of the world with cities.
22 For I *will* **shall** rise *up* against them,
saith the LORD of hosts **an oracle of Yah Veh Sabaoth**,
and cut off from *Babylon* **Babel** the name,
4 —to lift this proverb against
the sovereign of Babel,
and say,
How the exactor shabbathizes!
The extortioners of gold shabbathize!
5 Yah Veh breaks the rod of the wicked
—the scion of the sovereigns:
6 he who smote the people in wrath
with a stroke without revolt,
who subjugates the goyim in wrath
persecutes; spares no one.
7 At rest—the whole earth rests;

they break forth into shouting:
8 Yes, the fir trees cheer at you
—the cedars of Lebanon.
Since you lay down,
no cutter ascends against us:
9 sheol from beneath quakes for you
to meet you at your coming:
it wakens the ghost for you
all the he goats of the earth;
it raises from their thrones
all the sovereigns of the goyim.
10 They all answer and say to you,
Become you also worn as we?
Become you like us?
11 Your pomp is brought down to sheol
with the sound of your bagpipes:
the maggot spreads under you
and the maggots cover you.

THE HALALED ONE

12 How you fell from the heavens,
O Halaled one, son of the dawn
—cut down to the earth:
who vanquished the goyim!
13 For you said in your heart,
I ascend into the heavens:
I exalt my throne above the stars of El:
and I sit upon the mount of the congregation
in the flanks of the north:
14 I ascend above the bamahs of the thick clouds
—like Elyon.
15 Surely you are brought down to sheol
—to the flanks of the well.
16 They who see you peer at you, discerning,
Is this the man who quakes the earth?
Who quakes sovereigndoms?
17 Who sets the world as a wilderness?
And demolishes the cities?
Who opens not the house of his bound?
18 All the sovereigns of the goyim
—all of them lie in honor,
every man in his own house.

cp Yahn 12:31, Loukas 10:18, Apocalypse 12:7—12

19 And you are cast from your tomb
as an abhorrent branch;
and as the robe of the slaughtered
stabbed with a sword;
descending to the stones of the well;
as a carcase trampled.
20 You unite not with them in the tomb
—because you ruined your land
and slaughtered your people:
the seed of vilifiers is never called out—eternally.
21 Prepare slaughter for his sons
for the perversity of their fathers;
that they neither rise nor possess the land
nor fill the face of the world with cities.
22 For I rise against them
—an oracle of Yah Veh Sabaoth and
from Babel I cut off the name
and *remnant* **survivors**, and *son* **offspring**,
and *nephew* **posterity**,
saith the LORD **an oracle of Yah Veh**.
23 I *will also make* **shall set** it
a possession for the bittern,
and *pools* **marshes** of water:
and I *will* **shall** sweep it
with the *besom* **broom** of *destruction* **desolation**,
saith the LORD of hosts **an oracle of Yah Veh Sabaoth**.

THE BURDEN OF ASHSHUR

24 *The LORD of hosts* **Yah Veh Sabaoth**
hath *sworn* **oathed**, saying,
Surely as I have *thought* **considered**,
so shall it *come to pass* **be**;
and as I have *purposed* **counselled**,
so shall it *stand* **rise**:
25 That I *will* **shall** break the *Assyrian* **Ashshuri**
in my land,
and upon my mountains *tread* **trample** him *under foot*:
then shall his yoke *depart* **turn aside** from off them,
and his burden *depart* **turn aside**
from off their shoulders.
26 This is the *purpose* **counsel**
that is *purposed* **counselled** upon the whole earth:
and this is the hand
that is *stretched out* **spread** upon all the *nations* **goyim**.
27 For *the LORD of hosts* **Yah Veh Sabaoth**
hath *purposed* **counselled**,
and who shall *disannul* **break it**?
and his hand is *stretched out* **spread**,
and who shall turn it back?

THE BURDEN OF PELESHETH

28 In the year that *king Ahaz*
sovereign Ach Az died
was this burden.
29 *Rejoice* **Cheer** not thou,
whole *Palestina* **Pelesheth**,

because the *rod* **scion** of him that smote thee is broken:
for out of the serpent's root
shall come forth a *cockatrice* **hisser**,
and his fruit shall be a *fiery* flying *serpent* **seraph**.
30 And the *firstborn* **firstbirthed**
of the poor shall *feed* **graze**,
and the needy shall *lie down in*
safety **crouch confidently**:
and I *will* **shall** kill thy root with famine,
and he shall *slay* **slaughter** thy *remnant* **survivors**.
31 Howl, O *gate* **portal**; cry, O city;
thou, whole *Palestina* **Pelesheth**, art dissolved:
for there shall come from the north a smoke,
and none shall be alone in his *appointed times* **seasons**.
32 What shall one then
answer the *messengers* **angels** of the *nation* **goyim**?
That *the LORD* **Yah Veh** hath founded *Zion* **Siyon**,
and the *poor* **humble** of his people
shall *trust* **seek refuge** in it.

THE BURDEN OF MOAB

15 The burden of Moab.
Because in the night
Ar of Moab is *laid waste* **ravaged**,
and *brought to silence* **rendered mute**;
because in the night
Kir **Qir** of Moab is *laid waste* **ravaged**,
and brought to silence **rendered mute**;
2 He *is gone up* **ascendeth** to
Bajith **Bayith**, and to Dibon,
the *high places* **bamahs**, *to weep* **weeping**:
Moab shall howl over Nebo, and over Medeba:
on all their heads shall be baldness,
and every beard cut off.
3 In their *streets* **outways**
they shall gird *themselves* with sackcloth:
on *the tops of* their *houses* **roofs**,
and in their *streets* **broadways**,
every one shall howl,
descending into weeping abundantly.
4 And Heshbon shall cry, and *Elealeh* **El Aleh**:
their voice shall be heard *even* unto *Jahaz* **Yahsah**:
therefore the *armed soldiers* **equipped** of Moab
shall *cry out* **shout**;
his *life* **soul** shall *be grievous* **tremble** unto him.
5 My heart shall cry out for Moab;
his fugitives *shall flee* unto *Zoar* **Soar**,
an heifer of three *years old*:
for by the *mounting up* **ascent** of *Luhith* **Luchith**
with weeping shall they *go it up* **ascend**;

and survivors and offspring and posterity
—an oracle of Yah Veh.
23 I set it a possession for the bittern,
and marshes of water:
and I sweep it with the broom of desolation
—an oracle of Yah Veh Sabaoth.

THE BURDEN OF ASHSHUR

24 Yah Veh Sabaoth oaths, saying,
Surely as I consider, so be it;
and as I counsel, so it rises:
25 that I break the Ashshuri in my land,
and trample him upon my mountains:
and turn aside his yoke from off them
and turn aside his burden from off their shoulders.
26 This is the counsel
counselled upon the whole earth:
and this is the hand
spread upon all the goyim.
27 For Yah Veh Sabaoth counsels,
and who breaks it?
and his hand spreads,
and who turns it back?

THE BURDEN OF PELESHETH

28 In the year sovereign Ach Az dies,
—this burden:
29 You, cheer not Pelesheth—all of you
because the scion of him who smote you is broken:
for from the root of the serpent comes forth a hisser;
and his fruit *is* a flying seraph.
30 And the firstbirthed of the poor graze
and the needy crouch confidently:
and I kill your root with famine
and he slaughters your survivors.
31 Howl, O portal! Cry, O city!
You are dissolved, Pelesheth, all of you:
for from the north comes smoke,
and no one is alone in his seasons.
32 What then, answers one,
of the angels of the goyim?
That Yah Veh founded Siyon,
and the humble of his people seek refuge therein.

THE BURDEN OF MOAB

15 The burden of Moab:
Because in a night
Ar of Moab is ravaged and rendered mute;
because in a night
Qir of Moab is ravaged and rendered mute:

2 he ascends to Bayith and to Dibon
—to the bamahs, weeping:
Moab howls over Nebo and over Medeba
—baldness on all their heads
—every beard cut off.
3 In their outways they gird with sackcloth:
on their roofs and in their broadways
every one howls
—descending into weeping abundantly.
4 And Heshbon cries, and El Aleh:
their voice is heard to Yahsah:
so the equipped of Moab shout;
his soul trembles.
5 My heart *is* toward Moab;
his fugitives cry out to Soar, an heifer of three:
for by the ascent of Luchith
they ascend with weeping;
for in the way of *Horonaim* **Horonayim**
they shall *raise up* **waken** a cry of *destruction* **breaking.**
6 For the waters of Nimrim
shall be *desolate* **desolations**:
for the hay is withered away,
the *grass faileth* **sprout finisheth,** there is no green *thing.*
7 Therefore the abundance
they have *gotten* **worked,**
and that which they have *laid up* **mustered,**
shall they *carry* **bear** away
to the *brook* **wadi** of the willows.
8 For the cry is gone round
about the borders of Moab;
the howling *thereof* unto *Eglaim* **Eglayim,**
and the howling *thereof* unto Beerelim.
9 For the waters of Dimon
shall be *full* **filled** of blood:
for I *will bring more* **shall place additions** upon Dimon,
lions upon *him that escapeth* **the escapees** of Moab,
and upon the *remnant* **survivors** of the *land* **soil.**

JUSTICE UPON MOAB

16 Send ye the *lamb* **ram**
to the *ruler* **sovereign** of the land
from *Sela* **the rock** to the wilderness,
unto the mount of the daughter of *Zion* **Siyon.**
2 For it shall be, *that,*
as a *wandering bird* **flapping flyer**
cast **sent** out of the nest,
so the daughters of Moab
shall be at the *fords* **passages** of Arnon.
3 Take counsel, *execute judgment* **work justice**;
make **place** thy shadow
as the night in the midst of the *noonday* **noon**;
hide the *outcasts* **expelled**;
bewray **expose** not him that *wandereth* **flappeth.**
4 Let mine *outcasts dwell*
expelled sojourn with thee,
Moab; be thou a covert to them
from the face of the *spoiler* **ravager**:
for the *extortioner is at an end* **oppressor ceaseth,**
the *spoiler ceaseth* **ravage finisheth,**
the *oppressors* **tramplers** are consumed out of the land.
5 And in mercy shall the throne be established:
and he shall sit upon it in truth
in the *tabernacle* **tent** of David, judging, and seeking
judgment, and hasting *righteousness* **justness.**
6 We have heard of the *pride* **pomp** of Moab;
he is *very proud* **mighty pompous**:
even of his *haughtiness* **pomp,**
and his *pride* **pomp,** and his wrath:
but his lies shall not be so.
7 Therefore shall Moab howl for Moab,
every one shall howl:
for the foundations of *Kirhareseth* **Qir Hareseth**
shall ye *mourn* **meditate**; surely they *are* **be** stricken.
8 For the fields of Heshbon languish,
and the vine of Sibmah:
the *lords* **masters** of the *heathen* **goyim**
have *broken down* **hammered**
the *principal plants* **grapevines** *thereof,*
they are *come* **touched** *even* unto *Jazer* **Yazer,**
they wandered through the wilderness:
her branches are *stretched out* **abandoned,**
they are *gone* **passed** over the sea.
9 Therefore I *will bewail* **shall weep**
with the weeping of *Jazer* **Yazer** the vine of Sibmah:
I *will water* **shall saturate** thee with my tears,
O Heshbon, and *Elealeh* **El Aleh**:
for the shouting for thy summer fruits
and for thy harvest is fallen.
10 And *gladness* **cheerfulness**
is *taken away* **gathered,**
and *joy* **twirling** out of the *plentiful*
field **orchard/Karmel**;
and in the vineyards there shall be no *singing* **shouting,**
neither shall there be shouting:
the treaders shall tread out no wine
in *their presses* **troughs**;
I have made their *vintage* shouting to *cease* **shabbathize.**
11 Wherefore my *bowels* **inwards** shall *sound* **roar**
like an harp for Moab,
and mine *inward parts* **inwards**

for *Kirharesh* **Qir Hareseth.**
12 And **so be** it *shall come to pass,*
when it is seen that Moab is weary
on the *high place* **bamah,**
for in the way of Horonayim
they waken a cry of breaking.
6 For the waters of Nimrim are desolations:
for the hay withers away,
the sprout finishes off; there is no green.
7 So the abundance they worked
and what they mustered
they bear away to the wadi of the willows.
8 For the cry goes around the borders of Moab
—the howling to Eglayim
and the howling to Beerelim:
9 for the waters of Dimon fill with blood:
for I place additions upon Dimon
—lions upon the escapees of Moab
and upon the survivors of the soil.

Justice On Moab

16 You, send the ram to the sovereign of the land
—from the rock to the wilderness
to the mount of the daughter of Siyon.
2 And so be it,
as a flapping flyer sent from the nest,
thus be the daughters of Moab
at the passages of Arnon.
3 Take counsel; work justice;
place your shadow as the night midst the noon;
hide the expelled;
expose not him who flaps.
4 My expelled sojourn with you, O Moab;
a covert from the face of the ravager:
for the oppressor ceases; the ravage finishes;
the tramplers are consumed from the land.
5 And established in mercy is the throne:
and he sits thereon in truth in the tent of David
—judging and seeking judgment
and hasting justness.
6 We hear of the pomp of Moab;
—mighty pompous:
even of his pomp—his pomp and his wrath:
not so his lies.
7 So Moab howls for Moab; every one howls:
for the foundations of Qir Hareseth you meditate;
surely they are stricken.
8 Because the fields of Heshbon languish
—the vine of Sibmah:
the masters of the goyim hammer the grapevines
—they touch to Yazer;
they wander through the wilderness:
abandon her branches;
they pass over the sea.
9 So I weep
with the weeping of Yazer the vine of Sibmah:
I saturate you with my tears,
O Heshbon and El Aleh:
for the shouting for your summer fruits
and for your harvest is fallen:
10 and cheerfulness is gathered
with twirling from the orchard/Karmel;
and in the vineyards they shout not,
they shout not:
the treaders tread no wine in troughs;
I shabbathize their shouting.
11 So my inwards, as a harp, roar for Moab;
and my inwards for Qir Hareseth.
12 And so be it,
we see Moab, weary on the bamah,
that he shall come to his *sanctuary* **holies** to pray;
but he shall not prevail.
13 This is the word
that *the LORD* **Yah Veh** hath *spoken* **worded**
concerning Moab **ever** since *that time.*
14 But now *the LORD* **Yah**
Veh hath *spoken* **worded,**
saying, Within three years, as the years of an
hireling, and the *glory* **honour** of Moab
shall be *contemned* **abased,**
with all that great multitude;
and the *remnant* **survivors**
shall be *very small and feeble* **little—few—not many.**

The Burden Of Dammeseq

17 The burden of *Damascus* **Dammeseq.**
Behold,
Damascus **Dammeseq** is *taken away* **turned aside**
from being a city,
and it shall be a ruinous *heap* **ruin.**
2 The cities of Aroer are forsaken:
they shall be for *flocks* **droves,**
which shall *lie down* **crouch,**
and none shall *make* **cause** them *afraid* **to tremble.**
3 The fortress also
shall *cease* **shabbathize** from *Ephraim* **Ephrayim,**
and the *kingdom* **sovereigndom**
from *Damascus* **Dammeseq,**
and the *remnant* **survivors** of *Syria* **Aram:**
they shall be as the *glory* **honour**

of the *children* **sons** of *Israel* **Yisra El**,
saith the LORD of hosts **an oracle of Yah Veh Sabaoth.**
4 And in that day **so be** it *shall come to pass*,
that the *glory* **honour** of *Jacob* **Yaaqov**
shall *be made thin* **languish**,
and the fatness of his flesh shall *wax lean* **emaciate.**
5 And it shall be
as when the *harvestman* **harvester**
gathereth the *corn* **stalks**,
and *reapeth* **harvesteth** the ears with his arm;
and it shall be
as he that gathereth ears in the valley of Rephaim.
6 Yet *gleaning grapes* **gleanings**
shall *be left* **survive** in it,
as the shaking of an olive *tree*,
two or three berries
in the top of the uppermost *bough* **branch**,
four or five
in the *outmost fruitful branches* **fruitbearing twigs**
thereof,
saith the LORD God of Israel
an oracle of Yah Veh Elohim of Yisra El.
7 At that day
shall *a man* **humanity** look to his *Maker* **Worker**,
and his eyes
shall *have respect* **see** to the Holy One of *Israel* **Yisra El.**
8 And he shall not look to the **sacrifice** altars,
the work of his hands,
neither shall *respect* **see**
that which his fingers have *made* **worked**,
either the *groves* **asherah**, or the *images* **sun icons.**
9 In that day shall his *strong* **stronghold** cities
be as a forsaken *bough* **forest**, and an uppermost branch,
which they *left* **forsook**
because **at the face** of the *children* **sons** of *Israel* **Yisra El**:
and there shall be desolation.
10 Because thou hast forgotten
the God **Elohim** of thy salvation,
and hast not *been mindful of* **remembered**
the rock of thy *strength* **stronghold**,
therefore shalt thou plant pleasant plants,
and shalt *set* **seed** it with strange *slips* **twigs**:
11 In the day shalt thou *make*
hedge thy plant *to grow*,
and in the morning shalt thou *make* **blossom** thy seed
to flourish:
but the harvest shall be a heap
in the day of grief and of desperate *sorrow* **pain.**
12 *Woe* **Ho** to the multitude of many people,
which *make a noise* **roar** like the *noise* **roar** of the seas;
and to the *rushing* **uproar** of nations,
that *make a rushing* **shall be wasted**
like the *rushing mighty* **wasting of many** waters!
come to his holies to pray;
and he prevails not.
13 This is the word
Yah Veh words ever since concerning Moab.
14 And now Yah Veh words, saying,
Within three years, as the years of an
hireling, the honor of Moab is abased,
with all that great multitude;
and the survivors little—few—not many.

The Burden Of Dammeseq

17 The burden of Dammeseq:
Behold, Dammeseq turns aside as a city
and becomes a ruinous ruin:
2 the cities of Aroer are abandoned:
they become for droves that crouch,
and no one trembles them:
3 and the fortress from Ephrayim shabbathizes
with the sovereigndom from Dammeseq;
and the survivors of Aram
become as the honor of the sons of Yisra El
—an oracle of Yah Veh Sabaoth.
4 And so be it, in that day,
the honor of Yaaqov languishes
and the fatness of his flesh emaciates:
5 and so be it,
as the harvester gathering the stalks
and harvests the ears with his arm;
and so be it,
as gathering ears in the valley of Rephaim:
6 yet gleanings survive therein,
as the shaking of an olive,
two or three berries
in the top of the uppermost branch,
and four or five in the fruitbearing twigs
—an oracle of Yah Veh Elohim of Yisra El.
7 In that day, humanity looks to his Worker,
and his eyes see to the Holy One of Yisra El:
8 and he neither looks to the sacrifice altars
—the work of his hands,
nor sees what his fingers worked, either
the asherah or the sun icons.
9 In that day his stronghold cities
become as a forsaken forest
and as an uppermost branch
they forsook at the face of the sons of Yisra El:
and becomes desolation.

10 Because you forgot Elohim of your salvation,
and remembered not the rock of your stronghold,
so you plant pleasant plants
and seed with strange twigs:
11 in the day, you hedge your plant;
and in the morning, you blossom your seed:
the harvest *is* as a heap
in the day of grief and of desperate pain.
12 Ho to the multitude of many people
who roar as the roar of the seas;
and to the uproar of nations who waste
as the wasting of many waters!
13 The nations shall *rush* **roar**
like the *rushing* **roaring** of many waters:
but God shall rebuke them **and shall be rebuked,**
and they shall flee far off,
and shall be *chased* **pursued**
as the chaff of the mountains
before **at the face of** the wind,
and like a *rolling thing* **whirler**
before **at the face of** the *whirlwind* **hurricane.**
14 And behold at *eveningtide* **evening time,**
trouble **terror;**
and *before* **ere** the morning he is not.
This is the *portion* **allotment** of them that spoil us,
and the *lot* **pebble** of them that *rob* **plunder** us.

THE BURDEN OF KUSH

18 *Woe* **Ho** to the land *shadowing*
whirring with wings,
which is beyond the rivers of *Ethiopia* **Kush:**
2 That sendeth ambassadors by the sea,
even in *vessels* **instruments** of bulrushes
upon the **face of the** waters, *saying,*
Go, ye swift *messengers* **angels,**
to a *nation scattered* **goyim drawn** and *peeled* **polished,**
to a people *terrible* **awesome**
from their beginning *hitherto* **and onward;**
a *nation meted out* **goyim lined up**
and *trodden down* **trampled,**
whose land the rivers have *spoiled* **split!**
3 All ye *inhabitants* **settlers** of the world,
and *dwellers* **tabernaclers** on the earth,
see ye, when he lifteth up an ensign on the mountains;
and when he *bloweth* **blasteth** a
trumpet **shophar,** hear ye.
4 For *so the LORD* **thus Yah Veh** said unto me,
I *will* **shall** *take my* rest,
and I *will consider* **shall scan** in my dwelling place
like a clear heat upon *herbs* **the light,**
and like a **thick** cloud of dew in the heat of harvest.
5 For, *afore* **ere the face of** the harvest,
when the *bud* **blossom** is *perfect* **consummated,**
and the sour grape is ripening in the *flower* **blossom,**
he shall both
cut off the sprigs with *pruning hooks* **psalmpicks,**
and *take away* **turn aside**
and *cut down* **lop off** the *branches* **tendrils.**
6 They shall be left together
unto the *fowls* **swoopers** of the mountains,
and to the *beasts* **animals** of the earth:
and the *fowls* **swoopers** shall summer upon them,
and all the *beasts* **animals** of the earth
shall winter upon them.
7 In that time shall the present be brought
unto *the LORD of hosts* **Yah Veh Sabaoth**
of a people *scattered* **drawn** and *peeled* **polished,**
and from a people *terrible* **awesome**
from their beginning *hitherto* **and onward;**
a *nation* **goyim**
meted out **lined up** and *trodden under foot* **trampled,**
whose land the rivers have *spoiled* **split,**
to the place of the name
of *the LORD of hosts* **Yah Veh Sabaoth,**
the mount *Zion* **Siyon.**

THE BURDEN OF MISRAYIM

19 The burden of *Egypt* **Misrayim.**
Behold,
the LORD **Yah Veh** rideth upon a swift **thick** cloud,
and shall come into *Egypt* **Misrayim:**
and the idols of *Egypt* **Misrayim**
shall *be moved* **totter** at his *presence* **face,**
and the heart of *Egypt* **Misrayim**
shall melt in the midst of it.
2 And I *will set* **shall hedge**
the *Egyptians* **Misrayim**
against the *Egyptians* **Misrayim:**
and they shall fight every *one* **man** against his brother,
and every one against his *neighbour* **friend;**
city against city,
and
kingdom **sovereigndom** against *kingdom* **sovereigndom.**
3 And the spirit of *Egypt* **Misrayim**
shall *fail* **evacuate** in the midst *thereof;*
and I *will destroy* **shall swallow up** the counsel *thereof:*
13 The nations roar as the roaring of many waters:
and he rebukes and they flee far off
—pursued as the chaff of the mountains
at the face of the wind

—as a whirler at the face of the hurricane.
14 And behold, at evening time, terror;
and ere the morning, is not.
This is the allotment of them who spoil us,
and the pebble of them who plunder us.

THE BURDEN OF KUSH

18 Ho to the land whirring with wings
beyond the rivers of Kush:
2 that sends ambassadors by the sea
even in instruments of bulrushes
on the face of the waters.
Go, you swift angels,
to a goyim drawn and polished;
to a people
awesome from their beginning and onward;
a goyim lined up and trampled
whose land the rivers split.
3 All you settlers of the world,
and tabernaclers on the earth,
as an ensign lifting on the mountains, you see;
and as a shophar blasting, you hear.
4 For thus Yah Veh says to me, I rest,
and in my dwelling place
I scan as a clear heat upon the light
—as a thick cloud of dew in the heat of harvest.
5 For, ere the face of the harvest,
when the blossom consummates,
and the sour grape ripens in the blossom,
he both cuts off the sprigs with psalmpicks,
and turns aside and lops off the tendrils
6 —to abandon together
to the swoopers of the mountains
and to the animals of the earth:
and the swoopers summer on them,
and all the animals of the earth winter on them.
7 In that time, they bring a
present to Yah Veh Sabaoth
from a people drawn and polished
—an awesome people
from their beginning and onward
—a goyim lined up and trampled
—whose land the rivers split
to the place of the name of Yah Veh Sabaoth,
the mount Siyon.

THE BURDEN OF MISRAYIM

19 The burden of Misrayim:
Behold, Yah Veh rides upon a swift thick cloud
and comes to Misrayim:
and the idols of Misrayim totter at his face,
and the heart of Misrayim melts in its midst:
2 and I hedge the Misrayim against the Misrayim:
and every man fights against his brother
and every one against his friend;
—city against city
and sovereigndom against sovereigndom:
3 and evacuate the spirit of Misrayim in its midst;
and I swallow up the counsel:
and they shall seek to the idols,
and to the *charmers* **spiritists,**
and to *them that have familiar spirits* **necromancers,**
and to the *wizards* **knowers.**
4 And the *Egyptians* **Misrayim**
will I give over **shall I shut**
into the hand of *a cruel lord* **hard adonim;**
and a *fierce king* **strong sovereign**
shall *rule* **reign** over them,
saith the Lord **an oracle of Adonay,**
the LORD of host **Yah Veh Sabaoth.**
5 And the waters shall *fail* **dry** from the sea,
and the river shall *be wasted* **parch**
and *dried up* **wither.**
6 And they shall turn the rivers far away;
and the *brooks* **rivers** of *defence* **rampart**
shall *be emptied* **languish** and *dried up* **parch:**
the *reeds* **stalks** and *flags* **reeds** shall wither.
7 The *paper reeds* **nakednesses**
by the *brooks* **rivers,**
by the mouth of the *brooks* **rivers,**
and every *thing sown* **plant** by the *brooks* **rivers,**
shall wither, *be driven away* **disperse,** and be no more.
8 The fishers also shall mourn,
and all they that cast *angle* **hooks** into the *brooks* **rivers**
shall *lament* **mourn,**
and they that spread nets upon the **face of the** waters
shall languish.
9 *Moreover* they that *work*
serve in *fine* **drawn** flax,
and they that weave *networks* **white linen,**
shall *be confounded* **shame.**
10 And they shall be *broken* **crushed**
in the purposes *thereof,*
all that *make sluices and ponds* **hire to work marshes**
for *fish* **souls.**
11 Surely the *princes* **governors**
of *Zoan* **Soan** are fools,
the counsel of the wise counsellors of *Pharaoh* **Paroh**
is become brutish:
how say ye unto *Pharaoh* **Paroh,**

I am the son of the wise,
the son of ancient *kings* **sovereigns**?
12 Where are they? where are thy wise *men*?
and let them tell thee, *now* **I beseech**,
and let them know what
the LORD of hosts **Yah Veh Sabaoth**
hath *purposed* **counselled** upon *Egypt* **Misrayim**.
13 The *princes* **governors** of *Zoan* **Soan**
are become *fools* **folly**,
the *princes* **governors** of Noph are deceived;
they have also *seduced Egypt* **strayed Misrayim**,
even they that are the stay **the chiefs**
of the *tribes thereof* **scions.**
14 *The LORD* **Yah Veh** hath *mingled* **mixed**
a *perverse spirit* **spirit of perversities**
in the midst *thereof*:
and they have caused *Egypt* **Misrayim** to *err* **stray**
in every work *thereof*,
as *a drunken man* **an intoxicated**
staggereth in his vomit.
15 Neither shall there be *any*
work for *Egypt* **Misrayim**,
which the head or tail, *branch* **palm leaf** or rush,
may *do* **work**.
16 In that day shall *Egypt*
Misrayim be like unto women:
and it shall *be afraid* **tremble** and *fear* **fear**
because **at the face** of the *shaking* **waving** of the hand
of *the LORD of hosts* **Yah Veh Sabaoth**,
which he shaketh over it.
17 And the *land* **soil** of *Judah* **Yah Hudah**
shall be a terror unto *Egypt thereof* **Misrayim**,
every one that *maketh mention* **remembereth**
shall *be afraid* **fear** in himself,
because **at the face** of the counsel
of *the LORD of hosts* **Yah Veh Sabaoth**,
which he hath *determined* **counselled** against it.
18 In that day
shall five cities in the land of *Egypt* **Misrayim**
speak the *language* **lip** of *Canaan* **Kenaan**,
and *swear* **oath** to *the LORD of hosts* **Yah Veh Sabaoth**;
of one shall be *called* **said**,
The city of *destruction* **demolition**.
19 In that day shall there be
an **a sacrifice** altar to *the LORD* **Yah Veh**
and they seek to the idols and to the spiritists
and to necromancers and to the knowers:
4 and I shut the Misrayim
into the hand of hard adonim;
and a strong sovereign reigns over them

—an oracle of Adonay Yah Veh Sabaoth.
5 And the waters from the sea dry
and the river parches and withers:
6 and they turn away the rivers afar
and the rivers of rampart languish and parch:
the stalks and reeds wither:
7 the nakednesses by the rivers—by the
mouth of the rivers, and every plant by the
rivers, withers, disperses, and is not:
8 and the fishers mourn,
and all who cast hooks into the rivers mourn,
and who spread nets upon the face of the waters
languish:
9 they who serve in drawn flax,
and they who weave white linen, shame:
10 and all who hire to work marshes for souls
become crushed in the purposes.
11 Surely the governors of Soan are fools,
the counsel of the wise counsellors of Paroh
become brutish:
how say you to Paroh,
I am the son of the wise
—the son of ancient sovereigns?
12 Where are they? Where are your wise?
Yes, have them tell you, I beseech,
and have them know
what Yah Veh Sabaoth counselled upon Misrayim.
13 The governors of Soan become folly;
the governors of Noph become deceived;
they also stray the Misrayim
—the chiefs of her scions.
14 Yah Veh mixes a spirit of
perversities in their midst:
and they stray Misrayim in every work
as an intoxicate staggering in his vomit;
15 there is no work for Misrayim,
for the head or tail, palm leaf or rush, to work.
16 In that day, Misrayim becomes as women:
and trembles and fears
at the face of the waving of the hand
which Yah Veh Sabaoth shakes over it.
17 And the soil of Yah Hudah
becomes a terror to Misrayim;
every one who remembers
fears for himself at the face of the counsel
Yah Veh Sabaoth counselled against it.
18 In that day,
five cities in the land of Misrayim
speak the lip of Kenaan,
and oath to Yah Veh Sabaoth;

of one is said, The city of demolition.
19 In that day, there is a sacrifice altar to Yah Veh
in the midst of the land of *Egypt* **Misrayim,**
and a *pillar at* **monolith beside** the border *thereof*
to *the LORD* **Yah Veh.**
20 And it shall be for a sign and for a witness
unto *the LORD of hosts* **Yah Veh Sabaoth**
in the land of *Egypt* **Misrayim:**
for they shall cry unto *the LORD* **Yah Veh**
because **at the face** of the oppressors,
and he shall send them a saviour, *and a* great *one*,
and he shall *deliver* **rescue** them.
21 And *the LORD* **Yah Veh**
shall be known to *Egypt* **Misrayim,**
and the *Egyptians* **Misrayim**
shall know *the LORD* **Yah Veh** in that day,
and shall *do* **serve** sacrifice and *oblation* **offerings;**
yea, they shall vow a vow unto *the LORD* **Yah Veh,**
and *perform it* **shalam.**
22 And *the LORD* **Yah Veh**
shall smite *Egypt* **Misrayim:**
he shall smite and heal it:
and they shall return *even* to *the LORD* **Yah Veh,**
and he shall be intreated of them, and shall heal them.
23 In that day shall there be a highway
out of *Egypt* **Misrayim** to *Assyria* **Ashshur,**
and the *Assyrian* **Ashshuri**
shall come into *Egypt* **Misrayim,**
and the *Egyptian* **Misrayim** into *Assyria* **Ashshur,**
and the *Egyptians* **Misrayim**
shall serve with the *Assyrians* **Ashshuri.**
24 In that day shall *Israel* **Yisra El** be the third
with *Egypt* **Misrayim** and with *Assyria* **Ashshur,**
even a blessing in the midst of the land:
25 Whom *the LORD of hosts* **Yah Veh Sabaoth**
shall bless, saying,
Blessed be *Egypt* **Misrayim** my people,
and *Assyria* **Ashshur** the work of my hands,
and *Israel* **Yisra El** mine inheritance.

THE BURDEN OF MISRAYIM AND KUSH

20 In the year that Tartan came unto Ashdod,
(when Sargon the *king* **sovereign** of *Assyria* **Ashshur**
sent him,)
and fought against Ashdod, and *took* **captured** it;
2 At the same time *spake the*
LORD **worded Yah Veh**
by *Isaiah* **the hand of Yesha Yah** the son of *Amoz* **Amos,**
saying, Go and loose the sackcloth from off thy loins,
and *put* **pull** off thy shoe from thy foot.
And he *did* **worked** so,
walking naked and *barefoot* **unshod.**
3 And *the LORD* **Yah Veh** said,
Like as my servant *Isaiah* **Yesha Yah**
hath walked naked and *barefoot* **unshod** three years
for a sign and *wonder* **omen**
upon *Egypt* **Misrayim** and upon *Ethiopia* **Kush;**
4 So shall the *king* **sovereign** of *Assyria* **Ashshur**
lead **drive** away the *Egyptians* **Misrayim** prisoners,
and the *Ethiopians captives* **Kushi exiles,**
young **lads** and *old* **aged,** naked and *barefoot* **unshod,**
even with their buttocks *uncovered* **stripped,**
to the *shame* **nakedness** of *Egypt* **Misrayim.**
5 And they shall *be afraid*
terrify and *ashamed* **shame**
of *Ethiopia* **Kush** their expectation,
and of *Egypt* **Misrayim** their *glory* **adornment.**
6 And the *inhabitant* **settler** of this *isle* **island**
shall say in that day,
Behold, *such* **thus** is our expectation,
whither we flee for help to be *delivered* **rescued**
from the king **at the face of the sovereign**
of *Assyria* **Ashshur:**
and how shall we escape?

THE BURDEN OF BABEL

21 The burden of the *desert* **wilderness** of the sea.
As *whirlwinds* **hurricanes** in the south pass through;
so it cometh from the *desert* **wilderness,**
from *a terrible* **an awesome** land.
2 A *grievous* **hard** vision is *declared* **told** unto me;
the *treacherous dealer* **coverter**
dealeth treacherously **coverteth,**
and the *spoiler spoileth* **ravager ravageth.**
Go up **Ascend,** O Elam: besiege, O *Media* **Maday;**
all the sighing *thereof* have I made to *cease* **shabbathize.**
midst the land of Misrayim;
and a monolith beside the border to Yah Veh:
20 and it is for a sign and for a witness
to Yah Veh Sabaoth in the land of Misrayim:
for they cry to Yah Veh
at the face of the oppressors
and he sends them a saviour—great;
and he rescues them.
21 And Yah Veh is known to Misrayim;
and the Misrayim know Yah Veh in that day,
and serve sacrifice and offerings;
yes, they vow a vow and shalam to Yah Veh:
22 and Yah Veh smites Misrayim
—he smites and heals it:

and they return to Yah Veh,
and they intreat him; and he heals them.
23 In that day,
there is a highway from Misrayim to Ashshur:
and the Ashshuri come to Misrayim
and the Misrayim to Ashshur,
and the Misrayim serve with the Ashshuri.
24 In that day, Yisra El becomes the third
with Misrayim and with Ashshur
—a blessing midst the land:
25 whom Yah Veh Sabaoth blesses, saying,
Blessed—Misrayim my people;
and Ashshur the work of my hands;
and Yisra El my inheritance.

THE BURDEN OF MISRAYIM AND KUSH

20 In the year Tartan comes to Ashdod,
when Sargon the sovereign of Ashshur sends him,
he fights Ashdod and captures it;
2 at the same time, Yah Veh words
by the hand of Yesha Yah the son of Amos, saying,
Go and loosen the sackcloth from your loins,
and pull your shoe from your foot.
—and thus he works, walking naked and unshod.
3 And Yah Veh says,
As my servant Yesha Yah
walks naked and unshod three years
for a sign and omen upon Misrayim and upon Kush;
4 thus the sovereign of Ashshur drives away
the Misrayim prisoners and the Kushi exiles
—lads and aged, naked and unshod,
even with their buttocks stripped
to the nakedness of Misrayim.
5 —and they terrify and shame
of Kush their expectation
and of Misrayim their adornment.
6 And the settler of this island
says in that day,
Behold, is our expectation thus?
Where flee we for help to be rescued
at the face of the sovereign of Ashshur?
And how escape we?

THE BURDEN OF BABEL

21 The burden of the wilderness of the sea:
As hurricanes in the south pass through;
thus it comes from the wilderness
—from an awesome land. 2
I am told a hard vision:
the coverter coverts and the ravager ravages.
Ascend, O Elam! Besiege, O Maday!
I shabbathize all its sighing.
3 Therefore are my loins filled with pain:
pangs have taken hold upon me,
as the pangs of a woman *that travaileth* **birthing**:
I *was bowed down* **twisted** at the hearing of it;
I *was dismayed* **terrified** at the seeing of it.
4 My heart *panted* **staggered**,
fearfulness **trembling** affrighted me:
the *night* **evening breeze** of my pleasure
hath he *turned* **set** into *fear* **trembling** unto me.
5 *Prepare* **Line up** the table,
watch in the watchtower,
eat, drink:
arise, ye *princes* **governors**,
and anoint the *shield* **buckler**.
6 For thus hath *the Lord* **Adonay** said unto me,
Go, *set* **stand** a *watchman* **watcher**,
let him *declare* **tell** what he seeth.
7 And he saw a chariot
with a *couple* **pair** of *horsemen* **cavalry**,
a chariot of *asses* **burros**, *and* a chariot of camels;
and **in hearkening,** he hearkened
diligently with much heed:
8 And he *cried* **called out**, A lion:
My Lord **Adonay**,
I stand continually upon the watchtower
in the *daytime* **day**,
and I am *set* **stationed** in my *ward* **guard** whole nights:
9 And, behold, here cometh a chariot of men,
with a *couple* **pair** of *horsemen* **cavalry**.
And he answered and said,
Babylon **Babel** is fallen, is fallen;
and all the *graven images* **sculptiles** of her *gods* **elohim**
he hath broken unto the *ground* **earth**.
10 O my threshing,
and the *corn* **sons** of my *floor* **threshingfloor**:
that which I have heard
of *the LORD of hosts* **Yah Veh Sabaoth**,
the God **Elohim** of *Israel* **Yisra El**,
have I *declared* **told** unto you.

THE BURDEN OF DUMAH

11 The burden of Dumah.
He calleth to me out of Seir,
Watchman **Guard**, what of the night?
Watchman **Guard**, what of the night?
12 The *watchman* **guard** said,
The morning cometh, and also the night:
if ye *will* **shall** enquire, enquire ye: return, come.

THE BURDEN OF ARABIA

13 The burden upon Arabia.
In the forest in Arabia shall ye *lodge* **stay overnight**,
O ye *travelling companies* **caravans** of Dedanim.
14 The *inhabitants* **settlers** of the land of Tema
brought water to **confront** him that was thirsty,
they *prevented* **anticipated** with
their bread him that fled.
15 For they fled from **the face of** the swords,
from **the face of** the drawn sword,
and from **the face of** the bent bow,
and from **the face of** the *grievousness* **heaviness** of war.
16 For thus hath *the Lord* **Adonay** said unto me,
Within a year, according to the years of an hireling, and
all the *glory* **honour** of *Kedar* **Qedar** shall *fail* **finish**:
17 And the *residue* **survivors**
of the number of *archers* **bows**,
the mighty *men* of the *children* **sons** of *Kedar* **Qedar**,
shall be diminished:
for *the LORD God* **Yah Veh Elohim** of *Israel* **Yisra El**
hath *spoken it* **worded**.

THE BURDEN OF GAY HIZZAYON

22 The burden of
the valley of vision **Gay Hizzayon/Valley of Vision**
What aileth thee now,
that thou art wholly *gone up* **ascended**
to the *housetops* **roofs**?
2 Thou that art full of *stirs* **clamors**,
a *tumultuous* **roaring** city,
a *joyous city* **city jumping for joy**:
thy *slain* **pierced** *men* are not slain with the sword,
nor dead in *battle* **war**.
3 All thy *rulers* **commanders** are fled together,
they are bound by the *archers* **bows**:
3 So my loins fill with pain:
pangs hold me
as pangs of a woman birthing:
I twist at hearing; I terrify at seeing:
4 my heart staggers; trembling frightens me:
he sets the evening breeze of my pleasure
to tremble me.
5 Arrange the table! Watch in the watchtower!
Eat! Drink!
Arise, you governors! Anoint the buckler!
6 For Adonay says thus to me,
Go, stand a watcher; to tell what he sees.
7 And he sees a chariot with a pair of cavalry,
a chariot of burros, a chariot of camels;
and in hearkening, he hearkens:
8 and he calls out, A lion!
Adonay,
I stand continually on the watchtower in the day
and I station in my guard whole nights:
9 and, behold, a chariot of men
comes with a pair of cavalry:
and he answers and says,
Fallen! Babel—fallen!
and he breaks all the sculptiles of her elohim
to the earth.
10 O my threshing,
and the sons of my threshingfloor:
whatever I heard
from Yah Veh Sabaoth, Elohim of Yisra El,
I tell you.

THE BURDEN OF DUMAH

11 The burden of Dumah:
A call to me from Seir,
Guard, what of the night? Guard, what of the night?
12 The guard says,
The morning comes and also the night:
if you enquire—enquire: return, come.

THE BURDEN OF ARABIA

13 The burden upon Arabia:
You, stay overnight in the forest in Arabia,
you caravans of Dedanim:
14 the settlers of the land of Tema
bring water to confront the thirsty,
with their bread they anticipate him who flees:
15 for they flee from the face of the swords
—from the face of the drawn sword
and from the face of the bent bow
and from the face of the heaviness of war.
16 For Adonay says thus to me,
Within a year, according to the years of a hireling,
all the honor of Qedar finishes off:
17 and the survivors of the number of bows
—the mighty of the sons of Qedar diminish:
for Yah Veh Elohim of Yisra El has worded.

THE BURDEN OF GAY HIZZAYON

22 The burden of Gay Hizzayon/Valley of Vision:
What ails you now—all of you
that you ascend to the roofs?
2 You, full of clamors,
a roaring city, a city jumping for joy:
your pierced are neither slain with the sword

nor dead in war:
3 all your commanders flee together
—bound by the bows:
all that are found in thee are bound together,
which have fled from far.
4 Therefore said I, Look away from me;
I *will weep bitterly* **am embittered in weeping,**
labour **hasten** not to *comfort* **sigh over** me,
because of the *spoiling* **ravage**
of the daughter of my people.
5 For it is a day of *trouble* **confusion,**
and of *treading down* **trampling,** and of perplexity
by *the Lord GOD of hosts* **Adonay Yah Veh Sabaoth**
in *the valley of vision* **Gay Hizzayon/Valley of Vision,**
breaking down **digging** the walls,
and of crying to the mountains.
6 And Elam bare the quiver
with chariots of *men* **humanity** and *horsemen* **cavalry,**
and *Kir uncovered* **Qir stripped**
naked the *shield* **buckler.**
7 And **so be** it *shall come to pass,*
that thy choicest valleys shall be *full* **filled** of chariots,
and *the horsemen shall set themselves in array*
in placing, the cavalry shall place themselves
at the *gate* **portal.**
8 And he *discovered* **exposed**
the covering of *Judah* **Yah Hudah,**
and thou didst look in that day
to the armour of the house of the forest.
9 Ye have seen also
the *breaches* **fissures** of the city of David,
that they *are many* **abound by the myriads:**
and ye gathered together
the waters of the *lower* **nether** pool.
10 And ye have *numbered* **scribed**
the houses of *Jerusalem* **Yeru Shalem,**
and the houses have ye *broken* **pulled** down
to fortify the wall.
11 Ye *made* **worked** also a *ditch* **reservoir**
between the two walls for the water of the old pool:
but ye have not looked unto the *maker* **worker** *thereof,*
neither *had respect* **saw** unto him
that *fashioned* **formed** it *long ago* **in the distant past.**
12 And in that day
did the Lord GOD of hosts **Adonay Yah Veh Sabaoth**
call **called** to weeping, and to *mourning* **chopping,**
and to baldness, and to girding with sackcloth:
13 And behold *joy* **rejoicing**
and *gladness* **cheerfulness,**
slaying **slaughtering** oxen,
and *killing sheep* **slaughtering flock,**
eating flesh, and drinking wine:
let us eat and drink; for to morrow we shall die.
14 And it was *revealed* **exposed** in mine ears
by *the LORD of hosts* **Yah Veh Sabaoth,**
Surely this *iniquity* **perversity**
shall not be *purged* **kapared/atoned** from you till ye die,
saith *the Lord GOD of hosts* **Adonay Yah Veh Sabaoth.**
15 Thus saith
the Lord GOD of hosts **Adonay Yah Veh Sabaoth,**
Go, get thee unto this *treasurer* **useful one,**
even unto Shebna, which is over the house, *and say,*
16 What hast thou here and whom hast thou here,
that thou hast hewed thee out a *sepulchre* **tomb** here,
as he that heweth him out a *sepulchre* **tomb** on high,
and *that graveth an habitation* **engraveth a tabernacle**
for himself in a rock?
17 Behold, *the LORD* **Yah Veh**
will carry thee away with a mighty captivity
in casting, shall cast thee, O mighty,
and *will surely* **in covering, shall** cover thee.
18 *He will surely violently turn*
and toss thee like a ball
In whirling, he whirleth
—he shall whirl thee as a whirler
into a *large country* **land large of hand:**
there shalt thou die,
and there the chariots of thy *glory* **honour**
shall be the *shame* **abasement**
of *thy lord's* **adoni's** house.
19 And I *will drive* **shall exile**
thee from thy station,
and from thy *state* **function**
shall he *pull* **break** thee *down.*
20 And **so be** it *shall come to pass* in that day,
all those found in you, who flee from far,
are bound together.
4 So I say, Look away from me:
I am embittered in weeping;
hasten not to sigh over me
because of the ravage of the daughter of my people.
5 For it is a day of confusion
and of trampling and of perplexity
by Adonay Yah Veh Sabaoth
in Gay Hizzayon/Valley of Vision
—digging the walls and crying to the mountains.
6 And Elam bears the quiver
with chariots of humanity and cavalry;
and Qir strips naked the buckler:
7 and so be it,
your choicest valleys fill with chariots;
and in placing,

the cavalry place themselves at the portal;
8 and he exposes the covering of Yah Hudah:
and in that day,
you look to the armour of the house of the forest:
9 you also see the fissures of the city of David
abounding by the myriads:
and you gather together the waters of the nether pool:
10 and you scribe the houses of Yeru Shalem
and you pull down the houses to fortify the wall:
11 and you work a reservoir
between the two walls for the water of the old pool:
and you neither look to the worker,
nor see to him who formed it in the distant past.
12 And in that day,
Adonay Yah Veh Sabaoth
calls to weeping and to chopping
and to baldness and to girding with sackcloth:
13 and behold, rejoicing and cheerfulness,
slaughtering oxen and slaughtering flock,
eating flesh and drinking wine.
Eat and drink—for tomorrow we die.
14 And Yah Veh Sabaoth exposes in my ears,
Surely this perversity
kapars/atones not to you until you die,
says Adonay Yah Veh Sabaoth.
15 Thus says Adonay Yah Veh Sabaoth,
Go, get you to this useful one—to Shebna
who is over the house,
16 What—to you here, and who—to you here,
that you hew a tomb here,
as one who hews a tomb on high
and engraves a tabernacle for himself in a rock?
17 Behold, in casting, Yah Veh casts you, O mighty,
and in covering, covers you:
18 in whirling, he whirls
—whirls you as a whirler into a land large of hand:
there you die,
and there the chariots of your honor
are the abasement of the house of adoni:
19 and I exile you from your station,
and he breaks you from your function.
20 And so be it, in that day,
that I *will* **shall** call my servant *Eliakim* **El Yaqim**
the son of *Hilkiah* **Hilqi Yah**:
21 And I *will clothe* **shall enrobe**
him with thy *robe* **coat**,
and strengthen him with thy girdle,
and I *will commit* **shall give** thy *government* **reign**
into his hand:
and he shall be a father
to the *inhabitants* **settlers** of *Jerusalem* **Yeru Shalem**,
and to the house of *Judah* **Yah Hudah**.
22 And the key of the house of David
will F lay **shall I give** upon his shoulder;
so he shall open, and none shall shut;
and he shall shut, and none shall open.
23 And I *will fasten* **shall stake** him
as a nail **stake** in a *sure* **trustworthy** place;
and he shall be for *a glorious* **an honourable** throne
to his father's house.
24 And they shall hang upon him
all the *glory* **honour** of his father's house,
the offspring and the *issue* **outcasts**,
all *vessels of small quantity* **lesser instruments**,
from the *vessels* **instruments** of *cups* **bowls**,
even to all the *vessels* **instruments** of *flagons* **bagpipes**.
25 In that day,
saith the LORD of hosts **an oracle of Yah Veh Sabaoth**,
shall the *nail* **stake**
that is *fastened* **staked** in the *sure* **trustworthy** place
be removed, and be cut down, and fall;
and the burden that was upon it shall be cut off:
for *the LORD* **Yah Veh** hath *spoken it* **worded**.

THE BURDEN OF SOR

23 The burden of *Tyre* **Sor**.
Howl, ye ships of Tarshish; for it is *laid waste* **ravaged**,
so that there is no house, no entering in:
from the land of *Chittim* **Kittim**
it is *revealed* **exposed** to them.
2 Be still, ye *inhabitants* **settlers** of the *isle* **island**;
thou whom the merchants of *Zidon* **Sidon**,
that pass over the sea, have *replenished* **fulfilled**.
3 And by great waters the seed of *Sihor* **Shichor**,
the harvest of the river, is her *revenue* **produce**;
and she is a *mart* **merchant** of *nations* **goyim**.
4 Be thou *ashamed* **shamed**, O *Zidon* **Sidon**:
for the sea hath *spoken* **said**,
even the *strength* **stronghold** of the sea, saying,
I *travail* **writhe** not, nor *bring forth children* **birth**,
neither do I nourish *up young men* **youths**,
nor *bring up* **raise** virgins.
5 As at the report concerning *Egypt* **Misrayim**,
so shall they *be sorely pained* **writhe**
at the report of *Tyre* **Sor**.
6 Pass ye over to Tarshish;
howl, ye *inhabitants* **settlers** of the *isle* **island**.
7 Is this your *joyous city* **city jumping for joy**,
whose antiquity is of ancient days?
her own feet shall *carry* **bear** her afar off to sojourn.
8 Who hath taken this counsel against *Tyre* **Sor**,

the *crowning city* **crown**,
whose merchants are *princes* **governors**,
whose *traffickers* **merchants**
are the honourable of the earth?
9 *The LORD of hosts* **Yah Veh Sabaoth**
hath *purposed* **counselled** it,
to *stain* **profane** the *pride* **pomp** of all *glory* **splendour**,
and to *bring into contempt* **abase**
all the honourable of the earth.
10 Pass through thy land as a river,
O daughter of Tarshish:
there is no more *strength* **girdle**.
11 He *stretched out* **spread** his hand over the sea,
he *shook* **quaked** the *kingdoms* **sovereigndoms**:
the LORD **Yah Veh** hath *given a commandment* **misvahed**
against *the merchant city* **Kenaan**,
to *destroy* **desolate** the strong holds *thereof*.
12 And he said,
Thou shalt *no more rejoice* **not add to jump for joy**,
O thou oppressed virgin, daughter of *Zidon* **Sidon**:
arise, pass over to *Chittim* **Kittim**;
there also shalt thou *have no* **not** rest.
I call my servant El Yaqim the son of Hilqi Yah:
21 and I enrobe him with your coat
and strengthen him with your girdle
and I give your reign into his hand:
and he becomes a father
to the settlers of Yeru Shalem
and to the house of Yah Hudah:
22 and I give the key of the house of David
on his shoulder;
thus he opens and no one shuts;
and he shuts and no one opens:
23 and I stake him a stake in a trustworthy place;
and he becomes for an honorable throne
to the house of his father:
24 and they hang on him
all the honor the house of his father
—the offspring and the outcasts,
all lesser instruments
—from the instruments of bowls
even to all the instruments of bagpipes.
25 In that day,
—an oracle of Yah Veh Sabaoth
the stake that is staked in the trustworthy place
is removed and cut down and felled;
and the burden thereon, cut off:
for Yah Veh has worded.

The Burden Of Sor

23 The burden of Sor:
Howl, you ships of Tarshish; for it is ravaged,
so that there is neither house nor entering in:
from the land of Kittim it was exposed to them.
2 Be still, you settlers of the island;
you whom the merchants of Sidon,
who, passing over the sea, fulfilled.
3 And by great waters *is* the seed of Shichor;
the harvest of the river *is* her produce;
and she is a merchant of goyim.
4 Shame, O Sidon:
for the sea says—even the stronghold of the sea says,
I neither writhe, nor birth;
neither nourish youths, nor raise virgins.
5 As *at* the report concerning Misrayim,
they writhe at the report of Sor.
6 You, pass over to Tarshish;
howl, you settlers of the island.
7 Is this your city jumping for joy
—whose antiquity is of ancient days?
—her own feet bear her afar off to sojourn.
8 Who takes this counsel against Sor, the crown
—whose merchants *are* governors?
—Whose merchants *are* the honorable of the earth?
9 Yah Veh Sabaoth counsels it
to profane the pomp of all splendour
and to abase all the honorable of the earth.
10 Pass through your land as a river,
O daughter of Tarshish:
there is no more girdle.
11 He spreads his hand over the sea,
he quakes the sovereigndoms:
Yah Veh misvahs against Kenaan
to desolate the strong holds.
12 And he says, You, add not to jump for joy,
O you oppressed virgin, daughter of Sidon:
rise, pass over to Kittim;
even there you rest not.
13 Behold the land of the *Chaldeans* **Kesediym**;
this people was not, *till* the *Assyrian* **Ashshuri** founded it
for *them that dwell in the wilderness* **the desert dwellers**:
they *set up* **raised** the towers *thereof*,
they *raised up* **stripped bare** the *palaces* **citadels** *thereof*;
and he *brought* **set** it to ruin.
14 Howl, ye ships of Tarshish:
for your *strength* **stronghold** is *laid waste* **ravaged**.
15 And **so be** it *shall come to pass* in that day,
that *Tyre* **Sor** shall be forgotten seventy years,

according to the days of one *king* **sovereign**:
after the end of seventy years
shall *Tyre* **it be to Sor**
sing as an harlot **as the song of a whore.**
16 Take an harp, go about the city,
thou *harlot* **whore** that hast been forgotten;
make sweet melody **strum well—pleasingly,**
sing many songs **abound the song,**
that thou mayest be remembered.
17 And **so be** it *shall come to pass*
after the end of seventy years,
that *the LORD will* **Yah Veh shall** visit *Tyre* **Sor,**
and she shall turn to her *hire* **payoff,**
and shall *commit fornication* **whore**
with all the *kingdoms* **sovereigndoms** of the *world* **earth**
upon the face of the *earth* **soil.**
18 And her merchandise and her *hire* **payoff**
shall be *holiness to the LORD* **holy to Yah Veh:**
it shall not be treasured nor *laid up* **hoarded;**
for her merchandise shall be for them
that *dwell before the LORD* **settle at the face of Yah Veh,**
to eat *sufficiently* **to satiation,**
and for *durable clothing* **antique covering.**

YAH VEH EVACUATES THE EARTH

24 Behold,
the LORD maketh **Yah Veh evacuateth** the earth *empty,*
and *maketh it waste* **wasteth it,**
and *turneth it upside* **twisteth it face** down,
and scattereth abroad the *inhabitants* **settlers** *thereof.*
2 And it shall be,
as with the people, so with the priest;
as with the servant, so with his *master* **adoni;**
as with the maid, so with her *mistress* **lady;**
as with the *buyer* **chatteler,** so with the seller;
as with the lender, so with the borrower;
as with the *taker of usury* **exactor,**
so with the *giver of usury to him* **exacted.**
3 **In evacuating,**
The land shall be *utterly emptied* **evacuated,**
and *utterly spoiled* **in plundering, shall be plundered:**
for *the LORD* **Yah Veh** hath *spoken* **worded** this word.
4 The earth mourneth and *fadeth away* **withereth,**
the world languisheth and *fadeth away* **withereth,**
the *haughty* **high** people of the earth *do* languish.
5 The earth also is *defiled* **profaned**
under the *inhabitants* **settlers** *thereof;*
because
they have *transgressed* **trespassed** the *laws* **torah,**
changed **passed over** the *ordinance* **statute,**
broken the *everlasting* **eternal** covenant.
6 Therefore hath the *curse*
oath devoured the earth,
and *they that dwell* **the settlers** therein
are desolate **have guilted:**
therefore the *inhabitants* **settlers** of the earth
are *burned* **scorched,** and few men *left* **survive.**
7 The *new wine* **juice** mourneth,
the vine languisheth,
all the *merryhearted do* **cheerful** sigh.
8 The *mirth* **joy** of *tabrets* **tambourines**
ceaseth **shabbathizeth,**
the *noise* **uproar** of them that *rejoice* **jump for joy**
endeth **ceaseth,**
the joy of the harp *ceaseth* **shabbathizeth.**
9 They shall not drink wine with a song;
strong drink shall *be bitter to*
embitter them that drink it.
10 The city of *confusion* **waste** is broken down:
every house is shut up, that no man may come in.
11 There is *a crying* **an outcry** for wine
in the *streets* **outways;**
all *joy* **cheerfulness** is *darkened* **obscured,**
13 Behold the land of the Kesediym:
this people was not;
the Ashshuri founded it for the desert dwellers:
they raise the towers;
they strip bare the citadels;
and he sets it to ruin.
14 Howl, you ships of Tarshish:
for your stronghold is ravaged.
15 And so be it, in that day,
that Sor is forgotten seventy years,
according to the days of one sovereign:
after the end of seventy years it becomes to Sor
as the song of the whore.
16 Take a harp;
go about the city, you forgotten whore:
strum well—pleasingly; abound the song;
so that they remember you.
17 And so be it, after the end of seventy years,
Yah Veh visits Sor;
and she turns to her payoff
and whores with all the sovereigndoms of the earth
upon the face of the soil:
18 and her merchandise and her payoff
are holy to Yah Veh
—neither treasured nor hoarded;
for her merchandise is for them
settling at the face of Yah Veh
—to eat to satiation; and for antique covering.

YAH VEH EVACUATES THE EARTH

24 Behold, Yah Veh evacuates the earth
and wastes it and twists it face down
and scatters the settlers abroad.
2 And so be it,
as with the people, thus with the priest;
as with the servant, thus with his adoni;
as with the maid, thus with her lady;
as with the chatteler, thus with the seller;
as with the lender, thus with the borrower; as
with the exactor, thus with the exacted.
3 In evacuating, the land is evacuated,
and in plundering, plundered;
for Yah Veh words this word:
4 The earth mourns and withers;
the world languishes and withers; the
high people of the earth languish:
5 and the earth *is* profaned under the settlers;
because they trespassed the torah,
passed over the statute,
broke the eternal covenant.
6 So the oath devours the earth,
and the settlers therein guilt:
so the settlers of the earth scorch
and few men survive:
7 the juice mourns; the vine languishes;
all the cheerful sigh:
8 the joy of tambourines shabbathizes;
the uproar of them who jump for joy ceases;
the joy of the harp shabbathizes:
9 they drink no wine with a song;
strong drink embitters them who drink:
10 the city of waste breaks down:
every house is shut so that no man comes in.
11 There is an outcry for wine in the outways:
all cheerfulness is obscured;
the *mirth* **joy** of the land is *gone* **exiled.**
12 In the city *is left* **surviveth** desolation,
and the *gate* **portal**
is *smitten* **crushed** with *destruction* **waste.**
13 When thus it shall be
in the midst of the land among the people,
there shall be as the shaking of an olive *tree,*
and as the *gleaning grapes* **gleanings**
when the *vintage* **crop** is *done* **finished.**
14 They shall lift up their voice,
they shall *sing* **shout**
for the *majesty* **pomp** of *the LORD* **Yah Veh,**
they shall *cry aloud* **resound** from the sea.
15 Wherefore *glorify* **honour** ye *the LORD* **Yah Veh**
in the *fires* **flames,**
even the name
of *the LORD God* **Yah Veh Elohim** of *Israel* **Yisra El**
in the *isles* **islands** of the sea.
16 From the uttermost *part* **wing** of the earth
have we heard songs,
even glory **splendour** to the *righteous* **just.**
But I said, My *leanness,* **emaciation!**
my *leanness,* **emaciation!** woe unto me!
the *treacherous dealers* **coverters**
have *dealt treacherously* **coverted;**
yea, the *treacherous dealers* **coverters**
have *dealt very treacherously* **coverted.**
17 Fear, and the pit, and the snare, are upon thee,
O *inhabitant* **settler** of the earth.
18 And **so be** it *shall come to pass,*
that he who fleeth from the *noise* **voice** of the fear
shall fall into the pit;
and he that *cometh up* **ascendeth**
out of the midst of the pit
shall be *taken* **captured** in the snare:
for the windows from on high are open,
and the foundations of the earth *do shake* **quake.**
19 **In shattering,**
The earth is *utterly broken down* **shattered,**
In breaking,
the earth is *clean dissolved* **broken,**
In toppling,
the earth is *moved exceedingly* **toppled.**
20 **In staggering,**
The earth shall *reel to and fro* **stagger**
like a drunkard **as intoxicated,**
and shall *be removed* **sway** like a *cottage* **hammock;**
and the *transgression* **rebellion** *thereof*
shall be heavy upon it;
and it shall fall, and not rise *again.*
21 And **so be** it *shall come to pass* in that day,
that *the LORD* **Yah Veh** shall *punish* **visit**
upon the host of the high ones *that are* on high,
and the *kings* **sovereigns** of the *earth* **soil**
upon the *earth* **soil.**
22 And they shall
be gathered together **gather a gathering,**
as *prisoners* **bound** are gathered in the *pit* **well,**
and shall be shut up in the *prison* **lockup,**
and after many days shall they be visited.
23 Then the moon shall *be confounded* **blush,**
and the sun *ashamed* **shame,**
when *the LORD of hosts* **Yah Veh Sabaoth**
shall reign in mount *Zion* **Siyon,**
and in *Jerusalem* **Yeru Shalem,**
and *before* **in front of** his *ancients*
gloriously **elders honourably.**

THE EXALTMENT OF SPREAD HANDS

25 O *LORD* **Yah Veh**, thou *art* my *God* **Elohim**;
I *will* **shall** exalt thee,
I *will praise* **shall spread hands unto** thy name;
for thou hast *done wonderful things* **worked marvels**;
thy counsels of *old* **the distant past**
are *faithfulness* **trustworthiness** and *truth* **amen**.
2 For thou hast *made* **set** of a city an heap;
of a *defenced* **fortified** city a ruin:
a *palace* **citadel** of strangers to be no city;
it shall *never* **eternally not** be built.
3 Therefore shall the strong
people *glorify* **honour** thee,
the city of the *terrible nations* **tyrant**
goyim shall fear thee.
the joy of the land is exiled:
12 desolation survives in the city;
and the portal is crushed *with* waste.
13 And so be it, midst the land among the people,
as the shaking of an olive
—as the gleanings when the crop finishes.
14 They lift their voice!
They shout for the pomp of Yah Veh!
They resound from the sea!
15 So honor Yah Veh in the flames,
the name of Yah Veh Elohim of Yisra El
in the islands of the sea.
16 From the uttermost wing
of the earth we hear songs
—the splendor of the just:
and I say, My emaciation! My emaciation!
Woe to me!
the coverters covert; yes, the coverters covert:
17 fear and the pit and the snare are upon you,
O settler of the earth.
18 And so be it,
he who flees from the voice of the fear
falls into the pit;
and he who ascends from midst the pit
is captured in the snare:
for the windows from on high open,
and the foundations of the earth quake:
19 in shattering, the earth shatters;
in breaking, the earth breaks;
in toppling, the earth topples;
20 in staggering, the earth staggers as intoxicated
and sways as a hammock;
and the rebellion thereon is heavy:
and it falls, and rises not.
21 And so be it, in that day,
Yah Veh visits upon the host of the high ones on high
and the sovereigns of the soil upon the soil:
22 and they gather a gathering
as they gather the bound in a well,
and shut them up in the lockup;
and after many days they are visited.
23 And the moon blushes and the sun shames
when Yah Veh Sabaoth
reigns in mount Siyon and in Yeru Shalem
—honorably in front of his elders.

THE EXALTMENT OF SPREAD HANDS

25 O Yah Veh, you my Elohim;
I exalt you: I spread hands to your name:
for you worked marvels;
your counsels of the distant past
are trustworthiness and amen.
2 For of a city, you set a heap;
of a fortified city, a ruin;
a citadel of strangers, no city
—not built eternally.
3 So a strong people honors you
the city of the tyrant goyim fears you:
4 For thou hast been a *strength*
stronghold to the poor,
a strength to the needy in his *distress* **tribulation**,
a refuge from the *storm* **flood**,
a shadow from the *heat* **parchedness**,
when the *blast* **wind** of the *terrible ones* **tyrants**
is as a *storm* **flood** against the wall.
5 Thou shalt *bring down* **subdue**
the *noise* **uproar** of strangers,
as the *heat* **parchedness** in a *dry place* **parch**;
even the heat with the shadow of a **thick** cloud:
the branch of the *terrible ones* **tyrants**
shall *be brought low* **answer**.
6 And in this mountain
shall *the LORD of hosts* **Yah Veh Sabaoth**
make **work** unto all people
a *feast* **banquet** of *fat things* **oil**,
a *feast* **banquet** of *wines on the lees* **dregs**,
of *fat things full of marrow* **marrowed oil**,
of *wines on the lees well refined* **filtered dregs**.
7 And he *will destroy* **shall**
swallow in this mountain
the face of the *covering* **veil**
cast **veiled** over all people,
and the vail that is spread over all *nations* **goyim**.
8 He *will* **shall** swallow *up*
death in *victory* **perpetuity**;

and *the Lord GOD* **Adonay Yah Veh**
will **shall** wipe away tears from off all faces;
and the rebuke of his people
shall he *take away* **turn aside** from off all the earth:
for *the LORD* **Yah Veh** hath *spoken it* **worded.**
9 And it shall be said in that day, *Lo* **Behold**, this is
our *God* **Elohim**; we have *waited for* **awaited** him,
and he *will* **shall** save us:
this is *the LORD* **Yah Veh**;
we have *waited for* **awaited** him,
we *will be glad* **shall twirl** and *rejoice* **cheer**
in his salvation.
10 For in this mountain
shall the hand of *the LORD* **Yah Veh** rest,
and Moab shall be *trodden down* **threshed** under him,
even as straw is *trodden down* **threshed**
for **in the water of** the dunghill.
11 And he shall spread *forth* his hands
in the midst of them,
as he that swimmeth spreadeth *forth his hands* to swim:
and he shall *bring down* **abase** their *pride* **pomp**
together with the *spoils* **lurkings** of their hands.
12 And the fortress of the *high*
fort **secure loft** of thy walls
shall he *bring down* **prostrate**, *lay low* **lower**,
and *bring* **touch** to the *ground* **earth**, *even* to the dust.

SONG OF THE LAND OF YAH HUDAH

26 In that day
shall this song be sung in the land of *Judah* **Yah Hudah**;
We have a strong city;
salvation *will God appoint* **shall he place**
for walls and *bulwarks* **trenches**.
2 Open ye the *gates* **portals**,
that the *righteous nation* **just goyim**
which *keepeth* **guardeth** the *truth* **trust** may enter in.
3 Thou *wilt keep* **shalt guard** him
in *perfect peace* **shalom shalom**,
whose *mind* **imagination** is *stayed* **propped** on thee:
because he *trusteth* **confideth** in thee.
4 *Trust* **Confide** ye
in *the LORD for ever* **Yah Veh eternally**:
for in *the LORD JEHOVAH* **Yah Yah Veh**
is *everlasting strength* **an eternal rock**:
5 For he *bringeth down* **prostrateth** them
that *dwell* **settle** on high;
the *lofty* **exalted** city, he *layeth it low* **lowereth**;
he *layeth it low* **lowereth**, *even* to the *ground* **earth**;
he *bringeth* **toucheth** it *even* to the dust.
6 The foot shall *tread* **trample** it *down*,
even the feet of the *poor* **humble**, *and*
the steps of the *needy* **poor**.
7 The way of the just is *uprightness* **straightness**:
thou, *most upright* **O straight**,
dost weigh the *path* **route** of the just.
8 Yea, in the way of thy
judgments, O *LORD* **Yah Veh**,

4 for you are a stronghold to the poor;
a strength to the needy in his tribulation;
a refuge from the flood;
a shadow from the parchedness
when the wind of the tyrants
is as a flood against the wall.
5 You subdue the uproar of strangers
as the parchedness in a parch;
the heat with the shadow of a thick cloud:
the branch of the tyrants answer.
6 And in this mountain
Yah Veh Sabaoth works to all people
a banquet of oil, a banquet of dregs,
of marrowed oil, of filtered dregs.
7 And in this mountain
he swallows the face of the veil
veiled over all people,
and the veil spread over all goyim.
8 He swallows death in perpetuity;
and Adonay Yah Veh
wipes away tears from off all faces;
and turns aside the rebuke of his people
from off all the earth
—for Yah Veh has worded.
9 And in that day, it is said,
Behold, this our Elohim;
we awaited him and he saves us:
this *is* Yah Veh;
we awaited him; we twirl and cheer in his salvation.
10 For in this mountain the hand of Yah Veh rests;
and Moab is threshed under him
even as straw is threshed in the water of the dunghill:
11 and he spreads his hands in their midst
as the swimmer spreading to swim:
and he abases their pomp
together with the lurkings of their hands.
12 And he prostrates
the fortress of the secure loft of your walls lower
—touches to the earth—to the dust.

SONG OF THE LAND OF YAH HUDAH

26 In that day,
this song is sung in the land of Yah Hudah:

A strong city, we;
he places salvation for walls and trenches.
2 You, open the portals
for the just goyim who guard the trust to enter in.
3 You, guard him; shalom shalom:
whose imagination is propped on you:
because he confides in you.
4 You, confide in Yah Veh eternally:
for in Yah Yah Veh *is* an eternal rock:
5 for he prostrates them who settle on high;
the exalted city, he lowers
—he lowers to the earth;
he touches to the dust:
6 the foot tramples
—the feet of the humble; the steps of the poor.
7 The way of the just *is* straightness:
you, O straight, weigh the route of the just.
8 Yes, in the way of your judgments, O Yah Veh,
have we *waited for* **awaited** thee;
the desire of our soul is to thy name,
and to the *remembrance* **memorial** of thee.
9 With my soul have I desired thee in the night;
yea, with my spirit within me *will* **shall** I seek thee early:
for when thy judgments are in the earth,
the *inhabitants* **settlers** of the world
will **shall** learn *righteousness* **justness**.
10 *Let favour be shewed* **Grant**
charism to the wicked,
yet *will* **shall** he not learn *righteousness* **justness**:
in the land of *uprightness* **straightforwardness**
will **shall** he deal *unjustly* **wickedly**,
and *will* **shall** not *behold* **see**
the *majesty* **pomp** of *the LORD* **Yah Veh**.
11 *LORD* **Yah Veh**, *when* thy hand is lifted up,
they *will* **shall** not see:
but they shall see, and *be ashamed* **shame**
for their envy at the people;
yea, the fire of *thine enemies* **thy tribulators**
shall *devour* **consume** them.
12 *LORD* **Yah Veh**,
thou *wilt ordain peace* **shalt set shalom** for us:
for thou also hast *wrought* **made** all our works in us.
13 O *LORD* **Yah Veh** our *God* **Elohim**,
other lords **adonim** beside thee
have *had dominion over* **mastered** us:
but by thee only
will **shall** we *make mention of* **memorialize** thy name.
14 *They are* dead, they shall not live;
they are deceased **ghosts**, they shall not rise:
therefore hast thou visited and
destroyed **desolated** them,
and *made* **destroyed**
all their *memory to perish* **memorial**.
15 Thou hast increased the *nation* **goyim**,
O *LORD* **Yah Veh**,
thou hast increased the *nation* **goyim**:
thou art *glorified* **honoured**:
thou hadst removed it far unto all the ends of the earth.
16 *LORD* **Yah Veh**,
in *trouble* **tribulation** have they visited thee,
they poured out *a prayer* **an enchantment**
when thy chastening *was* upon them.
17 *Like* **Such** as a woman *with*
child **having conceived**,
that *draweth near the time of* **approacheth**
her *delivery* **birthing**,
is in pain **writheth**, *and* crieth out in her pangs;
so have we been *in thy sight* **at thy face**,
O *LORD* **Yah Veh**.
18 We have *been with child* **conceived**,
we have *been in pain* **writhed**,
we have *as it were brought forth* **birthed** wind;
we have not *wrought* **worked** any *deliverance* **salvation**
in the earth;
neither have the *inhabitants* **settlers** of the world fallen.
19 Thy dead *men* shall live,
together with my *dead body* **carcase** shall they arise.
Awake and *sing* **shout**, ye that *dwell* **tabernacle** in dust:
for thy dew is as the dew of herbs,
and the
earth shall cast out the dead **land of ghosts shall fall**.
20 Come, my people,
enter thou into thy chambers,
and shut thy doors about thee:
hide thyself *as it were* for a little *moment* **blink**,
until the *indignation be overpast* **rage passeth over**.
21 For, behold,
the LORD **Yah Veh** cometh out of his place
to *punish* **visit upon** the *inhabitants* **settlers** of the earth
for their *iniquity* **perversity**:
the earth also shall *disclose* **expose** her blood,
and shall no more cover her *slain* **slaughtered**.

THE DELIVERANCE OF YISRA EL

27 In that day *the LORD* **Yah Veh**
with his *sore* **hard** and great and strong sword
shall *punish* **visit**
upon leviathan the *piercing* **fugitive** serpent,
even leviathan that crooked serpent;
and he shall slay the *dragon* **monster** that is in the sea.
2 In that day *sing* **answer** ye unto her,

we await you;
the desire of our soul
is to your name and to your memorial.
9 With my soul I desire you in the night;
yes, with my spirit within me I seek you early:
for when your judgments are in the earth,
the settlers of the world learn justness.
10 To the wicked, you grant charism;
yet he learns not justness:
in the land of straightforwardness
he deals wickedly,
and sees not the pomp of Yah Veh.
11 Yah Veh, your hand *is* lifted; they see not:
they see and shame for their envy at the people;
yes, the fire of your tribulators consumes them.
12 Yah Veh, you set shalom for us:
for you also made all our works in us.
13 O Yah Veh our Elohim,
adonim beside you mastered us:
but only by you, we memorialize your name.
14 Dead—they live not; ghosts—they rise not:
so you, visit and desolate them
and destroy all their memorial.
15 You increased the goyim, O Yah Veh,
you increased the goyim: you are honored: you
removed it afar to all the ends of the earth.
16 Yah Veh, in tribulation they visit you;
they pour an enchantment;
your chastening *is* on them.
17 Such as a woman having conceived,
who, approaching her birthing,
writhes, cries out in her pangs;
so are we at your face, O Yah Veh.
18 We conceive; we writhe;
we birth the wind;
we work no salvation in the earth;
and the settlers of the world fall not.
19 Your dead live; their carcase rises.
Waken and shout, you who tabernacle in the dust:
for your dew is as the dew of herbs,
and the land of ghosts falls.
20 Come, my people,
enter your chambers
and shut your doors around you:
hide yourself for a little blink
until the rage passes over.
21 For, behold,
Yah Veh comes from his place
to visit on the settlers of the earth for their perversity:
and the earth exposes her blood,
and no more covers her slaughtered.

THE DELIVERANCE OF YISRA EL

27 In that day,
Yah Veh, with his hard and great and strong sword,
visits upon leviathan the fugitive serpent
—even leviathan that crooked serpent
and slays the monster in the sea.
2 In that day, you answer her,
A vineyard of *red wine* **desire**.
3 I *the LORD do keep* **Yah Veh guard** it;
I *will water* **shall moisten** it every *moment* **blink**:
lest any *hurt* **visit upon** it,
I *will keep* **shall guard** it night and day.
4 Fury is not in me:
who would set the briers and thorns against me in battle
who shall give me briers—thorns in war?
I *would go* **should stride** through them,
I *would* **should** burn them together.
5 Or let him take hold of my *strength* **stronghold**,
that he may *make peace* **work shalom** with me;
and he shall *make peace* **work shalom** with me.
6 He shall cause them that come of *Jacob* **Yaaqov**
to *take* root:
Israel **Yisra El** shall blossom and bud,
and fill the face of the world with *fruit* **produce**.
7 Hath he smitten him, as he
smote those that smote him?
or is he *slain* **slaughtered**
according to the slaughter of them
that are *slain* **slaughtered** by him?
8 In *measure* **seah**, when it
shooteth forth **spreadeth**,
thou *wilt debate* **shalt strive** with it:
he *stayeth* **removeth** his *rough* **hard** wind
in the day of the *east wind* **easterly**.
9 By this therefore
shall the *iniquity* **perversity** of *Jacob* **Yaaqov**
be *purged* **kapared/atoned**;
and this is all the fruit to *take away* **turn aside** his sin;
when he *maketh* **setteth** all the stones
of the **sacrifice** altar
as *chalkstones* **lime** that are *beaten in sunder* **shattered**,
the *groves* **asherah** and *images* **sun icons**
shall not *stand up* **rise**.
10 Yet the *defenced* **fortified**
city shall be *desolate* **alone**,
and the habitation **of rest** *forsaken* **sent away**,
and left—**forsaken** like a wilderness:
there shall the calf *feed* **graze**,
and there shall he *lie down* **crouch**,
and *consume* **finish** the *branches* **twigs** *thereof*.

11 When the *boughs* **harvests** *thereof* are withered,
they shall be broken off:
the women come, and *set* **light** them *on fire* **up**:
for it is a people of no understanding:
therefore he that *made* **worked** them
will **shall** not *have* mercy *on* them,
and he that formed them
will shew them no favour **shall grant them no charism.**
12 And **so be** it *shall come to pass* in that day,
that *the LORD* **Yah Veh**
shall beat off from the *channel* **stream** of the river
unto the *stream* **wadi** of *Egypt* **Misrayim,**
and ye shall be gathered one by one,
O ye *children* **sons** of *Israel* **Yisra El.**
13 And **so be** it *shall come to pass* in that day,
that the great *trumpet* **shophar** shall *be blown* **blast,**
and they shall come
which were ready to perish **to those destructing**
in the land of *Assyria* **Ashshur,**
and the *outcasts* **expelled** in the land of *Egypt* **Misrayim,**
and shall *worship the LORD* **prostrate to Yah Veh**
in the holy mount at *Jerusalem* **Yeru Shalem.**

HO TO EPHRAYIM

28 *Woe* **Ho** to the crown of *pride* **pomp,**
to the *drunkards* **intoxicated** of *Ephraim* **Ephrayim,**
whose *glorious beauty* **adornment of splendour**
is a *fading flower* **withering blossom,**
which are on the head
of the *fat* valleys **of ointment**
of them that are *overcome* **hammered** with wine!
2 Behold, *the Lord* **Adonay**
hath a mighty and strong one,
which as a tempest of hail
and a *destroying storm* **ruinous whirling,**
as a flood of *mighty* **many** waters overflowing,
shall *cast down* **set** to the earth with the hand.
3 The crown of *pride* **pomp,**
the *drunkards* **intoxicated** of *Ephraim* **Ephrayim,**
shall be *trodden* **trampled** under feet:
4 And the *glorious beauty*
adornment of splendour,
A vineyard of desire.
3 I Yah Veh guard it; I moisten it every blink:
lest any visit thereon, I guard it night and day:
4 Fury is not in me.
Who gives me briers—thorns in war?
I stride through them; I burn them at once.
5 Or that he uphold my stronghold
to work shalom with me:
he works shalom with me.
6 He roots them who come of Yaaqov:
Yisra El blossoms and buds
and fills the face of the world with produce.
7 Smites he him as his smiters smote him?
Or slaughters he as his slaughters slaughtered?
8 In a seah, when it spreads,
you strive therewith:
he removes his hard wind in the day of the easterly.
9 So by this
is the perversity of Yaaqov kapared/atoned;
and this is all the fruit to turn aside his sin;
in setting all the stones of the sacrifice altar
as shattered lime;
the asherah and sun icons rise not.
10 For the fortified city is alone;
the habitation of rest is sent away
—forsaken as a wilderness:
there the calf grazes; and there he crouches;
and finishes the twigs:
11 when the harvests wither, they break them off:
the women come, and light them:
for it is a people of no understanding:
so he who worked them, mercies them not,
and he who formed them, grants them no charism.
12 And so be it, in that day,
Yah Veh beats off from the stream of the river
to the wadi of Misrayim;
and gathers you, one by one, O you sons of Yisra El.
13 And so be it, in that day,
the great shophar blasts;
and they come to them
who destruct in the land of Ashshur,
and the expelled in the land of Misrayim;
and they prostrate to Yah Veh
in the holy mount at Yeru Shalem.

HO TO EPHRAYIM

28 Ho, to the crown of pomp
—to the intoxicated of Ephrayim
whose adornment of splendor is a withering blossom
on the head of the valleys of ointment
of them who are hammered with wine!
2 Behold, might and strength to Adonay
—as a tempest of hail and a ruinous whirling;
as a flood of many waters overflowing
set to the earth with the hand.
3 The crown of pomp
—the intoxicated of Ephrayim
are trampled under foot:

4 and the adornment of splendor
which is on the head of the *fat* valley **of ointment**,
shall be a *fading flower* **withering blossom**,
and as the *hasty fruit before* **firstfruits ere** the summer;
which when he that *looketh* **seeth** upon it seeth,
while it is yet in his *hand* **palm**
he *eateth it up* **swalloweth**.
5 In that day shall *the LORD*
of hosts **Yah Veh Sabaoth**
be for a crown of *glory* **splendour**,
and for a *diadem* **corona** of *beauty* **adornment**,
unto the *residue* **survivors** of his people,
6 And for a spirit of judgment
to him that sitteth in judgment,
and for *strength* **might** to them
that turn the *battle* **war** to the *gate* **portal**.
7 But they also have erred
inadvertently through wine,
and through *strong drink* **intoxicants**
are out of the way **stagger**;
the priest and the prophet have erred **inadvertently**
through *strong drink* **intoxicants**,
they are swallowed *up* of wine,
they *are out of the way* **stagger** through *strong*
drink **intoxicants**; they err **inadvertently** in
vision **sight**, they *stumble* **waver** in judgment.
8 For all tables are *full* **filled**
of vomit and *filthiness* **dung**,
so that there is no place *clean*.
9 Whom shall he teach knowledge?
and whom shall he *make* **have**
to *understand doctrine* **discern the report**?
them that are weaned from the milk,
and *drawn* **weaned** from the breasts.
10 For *precept must be* **misvah**
upon *precept* **misvah**,
precept **misvah** upon *precept* **misvah**;
line upon line, line upon line;
here a little, *and* there a little:
11 For with *stammering* **jeering**
lips and another tongue
will **shall** he *speak* **word** to this people.
12 To whom he said, This is the rest *wherewith*
ye may *cause the weary to* rest **the languid**;
and this is the *refreshing* **rest**:
yet they *would* **willed to** not hear.
13 But the word of *the LORD*
Yah Veh was unto them
precept **misvah** upon *precept* **misvah**,
precept **misvah** upon *precept* **misvah**;
line upon line, line upon line;
here a little, *and* there a little;
that they might go, and *fall* **falter** backward,
and be broken, and snared, and *taken* **captured**.
14 Wherefore hear the word of *the LORD* **Yah Veh**,
ye scornful men, that *rule* **reign over** this
people which is in *Jerusalem* **Yeru Shalem**.
15 Because ye have said,
We have *made* **cut** a covenant with death,
and with *hell* **sheol**
are we at agreement **worked we seers**;
when the overflowing *scourge* **whip** shall pass through,
it shall not come unto us:
for we have *made* **set** lies our refuge,
and under falsehood have we hid ourselves:
16 Therefore thus saith *the*
Lord GOD **Adonay Yah Veh**,
Behold, I lay in *Zion* **Siyon** for a foundation a stone,
a *tried* **proofed** stone, a *precious* **esteemed** corner *stone*,
a *sure* **founded** foundation:
he that *believeth* **trusteth** shall not *make haste* **hasten**.
17 Judgment also *will I lay* **shall I set** to the line,
and *righteousness* **justness** to the *plummet* **plumb line**:
and the hail shall *sweep* **snatch** away the refuge of lies,
and the waters shall overflow the *hiding place* **covert**.
18 And your covenant with death
shall be *disannulled* **kapared/atoned**,
and your *agreement* **vision** with *hell* **sheol**
shall not *stand* **rise**;
when the overflowing *scourge* **whip** shall pass through,
then ye shall be *trodden down* **trampled** by it.
19 *From the time that it goeth forth*
As often as it passeth over
it shall take you:
for morning by morning shall it pass over,
by day and by night:
on the head of the valley of ointment
is a withering blossom,
—as the firstfruits ere the summer;
which when he who sees, sees;
and while it is yet in his palm, swallows.
5 In that day,
Yah Veh Sabaoth becomes for a crown of splendor;
and for a corona of adornment
to the survivors of his people;
6 and for a spirit of judgment
to him sitting in judgment;
and for might
to them turning the war to the portal.
7 And even they, through wine, err inadvertently;
and through intoxicants, stagger;
the priest and the prophet, through intoxicants,

err inadvertently—swallowed by wine:
they stagger through intoxicants;
they err inadvertently in sight;
they waver in judgment.
8 For all tables are filled with vomit and dung,
without *a clean* place.
9 By whom teaches he knowledge?
And by whom discerns he the report?
By those weaned from the milk
—weaned from the breasts.
10 For misvah upon misvah, misvah upon misvah;
line upon line, line upon line;
here a little, there a little:
11 for with jeering lips and another tongue
he words to this people
12 —to whom he says,
This is the rest! Rest the languid;
and, This is the rest!
—yet they will to not hear.
13 And the word of Yah Veh is to them
—misvah upon misvah, misvah upon misvah;
line upon line, line upon line;
here a little, there a little;
so that they go and falter backward,
—broken and snared and captured.
14 So hear the word of Yah Veh,
you scornful men
who reign over this people in Yeru Shalem:
15 because you say,
We cut a covenant with death
and with sheol we work seers:
when the overflowing whip passes through,
it comes not to us:
for we set lies our refuge,
and under falsehood we hide ourselves.
16 So Adonay Yah Veh says thus,
Behold, I lay a stone in Siyon for a foundation
—a proofed stone; an esteemed corner;
a founded foundation:
he who trusts, hastens not.
17 And I set judgment to the line
and justness to the plumb line:
and the hail snatches away the refuge of lies,
and the waters overflow the covert:
18 and your covenant with death is kapared/atoned
and your vision with sheol rises not;
when the overflowing whip passes through,
then you become trampled thereby.
19 As often as it passes over, it takes you:
for morning by morning it passes over
—by day and by night:
and it shall be *a vexation* **an agitation**
only to *understand* **discern** the report.
20 For the bed is shorter than
that a man can stretch himself on it **to spread thereon**:
and the covering narrower than
that he can wrap himself in it **to enfold therein**.
21 For *the LORD* **Yah Veh** shall rise *up*
as *in mount Perazim* **the mount of breaches**,
he shall *be wroth* **quiver**
as *in the valley of Gibeon* **Gay Gibon**,
that he may *do* **work** his work, his strange work;
and *bring to pass* **serve** his *act* **service**,
his strange *act* **service**.
22 Now therefore be ye not *mockers* **translators**,
lest your *bands* **bonds** be *made strong* **strengthened**:
for I have heard from
the Lord GOD of hosts **Adonay Yah Veh Sabaoth**
a *consumption* **final finish**,
even determined **appointed** upon the whole earth.
23 *Give ye ear* **Hearken ye**, and hear my voice;
hearken, and hear my *speech* **saying**.
24 Doth the *plowman* **plower** plow all day to sow?
doth he open
and *break the clods of his ground* **harrow his soil**?
25 When he hath *made plain*
equalized the face *thereof*,
doth he not *cast abroad* **scatter** the *fitches*
fennelflowers, and scatter the cummin,
and *cast in the principal* **set the** wheat **in rows**
and the *appointed* **designated** barley
and the *rie* **spelt** in their *place* **border**?
26 For his *God* **Elohim**
doth *instruct* **discipline** him to *discretion* **judgment**,
and doth teach him.
27 For the *fitches* **fennelflowers**
are not threshed with a *threshing instrument* **sickle**,
neither is a *cart* **wagon** wheel
turned about upon the cummin;
but the *fitches* **fennelflowers**
are *beaten out* **threshed** with a *staff* **rod**,
and the cummin with a *rod* **scion**.
28 Bread *corn* is *bruised* **pulverized**;
because **in threshing**,
he *will* **shall** not *ever be threshing it* **thresh in perpetuity**,
nor *break* **crusheth** it with the wheel of his *cart* **wagon**,
nor *bruise* **pulverize** it with his *horsemen* **cavalry**.
29 This also cometh forth
from *the LORD of hosts* **Yah Veh Sabaoth**,
which is wonderful—**marvellous** in counsel,
and *excellent in working* **greatened in support**.

HO TO ARI EL

29 *Woe* **Ho** to *Ariel* **Ari El**,
to Ariel **Ari El** the city *where* David *dwelt* **encamped**!
add ye **scrape ye up** year to year;
let them *kill sacrifices* **strike celebrations**.
2 Yet I *will* **shall** distress *Ariel* **Ari El**,
and there shall be
heaviness **mourning** and *sorrow* **sighing**:
and it shall be unto me as *Ariel* **Ari El**.
3 And I *will camp* **shall encamp** against thee
round about **as a whirler**,
and *will lay siege* **shall besiege** against thee
with a *mount* **station**,
and I *will* **shall** raise *forts* **ramparts** against thee.
4 And thou shalt be *brought down* **abased**,
and shalt *speak* **word** out of the *ground* **earth**,
and thy *speech* **saying**
shall *be low* **prostrate** out of the dust,
and thy voice shall be,
as of *one that hath a familiar spirit* **a spiritist**,
out of the *ground* **earth**,
and thy *speech* **saying** shall *whisper* **chirp** out of the dust.
5 Moreover the multitude of thy strangers
shall be *like small dust* **as pulverized**,
and the multitude of the *terrible ones* **tyrants**
shall be as chaff that passeth away:
yea, it shall be *at an instant* **in a blink** suddenly.
6 Thou shalt be visited
of *the LORD of hosts* **Yah Veh Sabaoth**
and it becomes an agitation
even to discern the report:
20 for the bed is shorter than to spread thereon:
and the covering narrower than to enfold therein.
21 For Yah Veh rises as the mount of breaches,
he quivers as Gay Gibon,
to work his work—his strange work;
and serve his service—his strange service.
22 So now be not translators,
lest your bonds be strengthened:
for from Adonay Yah Veh Sabaoth
I heard the final finish
appointed on the whole earth.
23 You, hearken, and hear my voice;
hearken, and hear my saying.
24 Plows the plower all day to seed?
Opens and harrows he his soil?
25 When he equalizes the face,
scatters he not the fennelflowers?
And scatters the cummin
and sets the wheat in rows?
And the designated barley
and the spelt in their border?
26 For his Elohim disciplines him to judgment,
and teaches him:
27 for neither are the fennelflowers
threshed with a sickle,
nor a wagon wheel
turned around on the cummin;
for the fennelflowers are threshed with a rod
and the cummin with a scion.
28 Bread is pulverized;
because in threshing,
he neither threshes in perpetuity
nor crushes with the wheel of his wagon
nor pulverizes with his cavalry.
29 This also comes from Yah Veh Sabaoth,
—marvellous in counsel and greatened in support.

HO TO ARI EL

29 Ho to Ari El! Ari El—the city David encamped!
You, scrape up year to year;
strike up the celebrations:
2 and I distress Ari El,
and there is mourning and sighing:
and it is to me as Ari El:
3 and I encamp against you as a whirler
and besiege against you with a station
and I raise ramparts against you
4 and abase you:
you word from the earth
and prostrate your saying from the dust;
and your voice is as of a spiritist from the earth
and your saying as a chirper from the dust.
5 And the multitude of your strangers pulverize,
and the multitude of the tyrants pass away as
chaff: yes, it becomes in a blink—suddenly:
6 Yah Veh Sabaoth visits you
with thunder, and with *earthquake* **quake**,
and great *noise* **voice**,
with *storm* **hurricane** and *tempest* **storm**,
and the flame of devouring fire.
7 And the multitude of all the *nations* **goyim**
that *fight* **host** against *Ariel* **Ari El**,
even all that *fight* **host** against her
and her *munition* **hunthold**,
and that distress her,
shall be as a dream of a night vision.
8 It shall even be
as when *an hungry man* **the famished** dreameth,

and, behold, he eateth;
but he awaketh, and his soul is empty:
or as when a thirsty man dreameth,
and, behold, he drinketh;
but he awaketh, and, behold, he is *faint* **languid**,
and his soul *hath appetite* **yearneth**:
so shall the multitude of all the *nations* **goyim** be,
that *fight* **host** against mount *Zion* **Siyon**.
9 *Stay yourselves* **Linger**, and *wonder* **marvel**;
cry ye out **stare**, *and cry* **yes, stare**:
they *are drunken* **intoxicate**, but not with wine;
they stagger, but not with *strong drink* **intoxicants**.
10 For *the LORD* **Yah Veh**
hath *poured out* **libated** upon you
the spirit of *deep* **sound** sleep,
and hath *closed* **bound** your eyes: the
prophets and your *rulers* **heads**,
the seers hath he covered.
11 And the vision of all is become unto you
as the words of a *book* **scroll** that is sealed,
which *men deliver* **be given**
to one that *is learned* **knoweth the scroll**, saying,
Read **Call out** this, I *pray* **beseech** thee:
and he saith, I cannot; for it is sealed:
12 And the *book* **scroll** is *delivered* **given** to him
that *is not learned* **knoweth not the scroll**, saying,
Read **Call out** this, *I pray thee*:
and he saith, I *am not learned* **know not the scroll**.
13 *Wherefore the Lord* **Adonay** said,
Forasmuch
as this people draw near *me* with their mouth,
and with their lips *do* honour me,
but have removed their heart far from me,
and their fear toward me
is taught by the *precept* **misvah** of men:
14 Therefore, behold,
I *will proceed* **shall add**
to do a *marvellous work* **marvel** among this people,
even a work and a wonder **a marvellous marvel**:
for the wisdom of their wise *men*
shall *perish* **destruct**,
and the understanding of their *prudent men* **discerning**
shall be hid.
15 *Woe* **Ho** unto them that *seek deep* **deepen**
to hide their counsel from *the LORD* **Yah Veh**,
and their works *are* **become** in the dark,
and they say, Who seeth us? and who knoweth us?
16 Surely your turning *of things* upside down
shall be *esteemed* **fabricated**
as the *potter's clay* **former's morter**:
for shall the work say of him that *made* **worked** it,
He *made* **worked** me not?
or shall the *thing framed* **former**
say of *him that framed it* **the former**,
He *had no understanding* **discerned not**?
17 Is it not yet a very little while,
and Lebanon shall be turned
into *a fruitful field* **an orchard/Karmel**,
and the *fruitful field* **orchard/Karmel**
shall be *esteemed* **fabricated** as a forest?
18 And in that day
shall the deaf hear the words of the *book* **scroll**,
and the eyes of the blind
shall see out of *obscurity* **thick darkness**,
and out of darkness.
19 The *meek* **humble** also
shall increase *their joy* **cheerfulness**
in *the LORD* **Yah Veh**,
with thunder and with quake and great voice;
with hurricane and storm
and the flame of devouring fire:
7 and the multitude of all the goyim
hosting against Ari El,
even all her host and her hunthold,
even those distressing her,
become as a dream of a night vision.
8 And so be it, as when the famished dream:
and behold, he eats;
and he wakens and his soul is empty:
or as when a thirsty man dreams,
and behold, he drinks;
and he wakens, and behold, he languishes,
and his soul yearns:
thus is the multitude of all the goyim
who host against mount Siyon.
9 Linger, and marvel; stare; yes, stare:
they intoxicate, and not with wine; they
stagger, and not with intoxicants.
10 For Yah Veh
libates the spirit of sound sleep upon you:
and binds your eyes—the prophets
and your heads—the seers, he covers.
11 And all the vision becomes to you
as the words of a sealed scroll
—which they give to one knowing the scroll,
saying, Call this out, I beseech you!
And he says, I cannot; for it *is* sealed!
12 And the scroll is given to him
who knows not the scroll, saying,
Call this out!

And he says, I know not the scroll!
13 Adonay says,
Because
as this people draws near with their mouth
and with their lips honor me
—and remove their heart far from me,
and their fear toward me
is taught by the misvah of men
14 —so behold,
I add to do a marvel among this people
—a marvellous marvel:
for the wisdom of their wise destructs
and the understanding of their discerning hides.
15 Ho to them
who deepen to hide their counsel from Yah Veh
and their works are in the dark;
and they say, Who sees us? and, Who knows us?
16 O your turning upside down!
Is the former fabricated as the morter?
Says the work of its worker,
He worked me not?
Or says the formed of the former,
He discerned me not?
17 Is it not yet a very little while,
and Lebanon turns into an orchard/Karmel
and the orchard/Karmel *is* fabricated as a forest?
18 And in that day,
the deaf hear the words of the scroll,
and the eyes of the blind
see from thick darkness—and from darkness:
19 and the humble
increase cheerfulness in Yah Veh
and *the poor among men* **needy humanity**
shall *rejoice* **twirl** in the Holy One of *Israel* **Yisra El.**
20 For the *terrible one* **tyrant**
is brought to nought **ceaseth,**
and the scorner is *consumed* **finished off,**
and all that watch for *iniquity* **mischief** are cut off:
21 That *make a man* **cause humanity**
an offender for a **to sin in** word,
and *lay a snare for* **ensnare** him
that reproveth in the *gate* **portal,**
and *turn aside* **pervert** the just
for a *thing of nought* **waste.**
22 Therefore thus saith *the LORD* **Yah Veh,**
who redeemed Abraham
concerning the house of *Jacob* **Yaaqov,**
Jacob **Yaaqov** shall not now *be ashamed* **shame,**
neither shall his face now *wax* pale.
23 But when he seeth his children,
the work of mine hands, in the midst of him,
they shall *sanctify* **hallow** my name,
and *sanctify* **hallow** the Holy One of *Jacob* **Yaaqov,**
and shall *fear the God* **awe Elohim** of *Israel* **Yisra El.**
24 They also that *erred* **strayed** in spirit
shall *come to* **know** understanding,
and they that *murmured* **rebelled** shall learn doctrine.

HO TO THE REVOLTING SONS

30 *Woe* **Ho** to the *rebellious*
children **revolting sons,**
saith the LORD **an oracle of Yah Veh,**
that *take* **work** counsel, but not of me;
and that *cover with a covering* **pour a pouring,**
but not of my spirit,
that they may *add* **scrape up** sin to sin:
2 That walk to *go down*
descend into *Egypt* **Misrayim,**
and have not asked at my mouth;
to strengthen themselves
in the *strength* **stronghold** of *Pharaoh* **Paroh,**
and to *trust* **seek refuge** in the
shadow of *Egypt* **Misrayim!**
3 Therefore
shall the *strength* **stronghold** of *Pharaoh* **Paroh**
be your shame,
and the trust in the shadow of *Egypt* **Misrayim**
your *confusion* **shame.**
4 For his *princes* **governors** were at *Zoan* **Soan,**
and his *ambassadors came to* **angels touched** Hanes.
5 They were all ashamed
of a people that *could not profit* **benefiteth** them **not,**
nor be an help nor *profit* **benefit,**
but a shame, and also a reproach.

THE BURDEN OF THE ANIMALS OF THE SOUTH

6 The burden of the *beasts* **animals** of the south:
into the land of *trouble* **tribulation** and *anguish* **distress,**
from whence *come* the *young* **roaring lion** and old lion,
the *viper* **hisser** and *fiery* flying *serpent* **seraph,**
they *will carry* **shall bear** their *riches* **valuables**
upon the shoulders of *young asses* **colts,**
and their treasures upon the *bunches* **humps** of camels,
to a people that shall not *profit* **benefit** them.
7 For the *Egyptians shall help*
in vain **Misrayim be vanity,**
and *to no purpose* **shall help in vain:**
therefore have I *cried* **called** concerning this,
Their *strength* **pride** is to *sit still* **shabbathize.**

8 Now go,
write **inscribe** it *before* **in front of** them in a *table* **slab**,
and *note* **engrave** it in a *book* **scroll**,
that it may be for the *time to come* **latter day**
for ever **eternally** and *ever* **eternally**:
9 That this is a rebellious people,
lying children **deceptive sons**,
children **sons** that will **to** not hear
the *law* **torah** of *the LORD* **Yah Veh**:
10 Which say to the seers, See not;
and to the *prophets* **seers**,
Prophesy **See** not unto us
right things **straightforwardnesses**,
speak **word** unto us smooth *things*,
prophesy deceits **see delusions**:
11 *Get you* **Turn ye aside** out of the way,
turn aside **pervert** out of the path,
and needy humanity
twirls in the Holy One of Yisra El.
20 For the tyrant ceases
and the scorner is finished off;
and all who watch for mischief are cut off
21 —who cause humanity to sin in word
and ensnare him who reproves in the portal
and pervert the just for a waste.
22 So Yah Veh who redeemed Abraham
says thus concerning the house of Yaaqov,
Yaaqov neither now shames
nor his face now pale.
23 For when he sees his children,
the work of my hands, in his midst,
they hallow my name
and hallow the Holy One of Yaaqov;
and awe Elohim of Yisra El.
24 And strayers in spirit know understanding,
and the rebellers learn doctrine.

Ho To The Revolting Sons

30 Ho to the revolting sons
—an oracle of Yah Veh
who work counsel, but not mine;
and who pour a pouring, but not of my spirit,
who scrape up sin to sin:
2 who walk to descend into Misrayim,
and ask not at my mouth;
to strengthen themselves in the stronghold of Paroh,
and to seek refuge in the shadow of Misrayim!
3 So the stronghold of Paroh
becomes your shame;
and the trust in the shadow of Misrayim your shame.
4 For his governors were at Soan
and his angels touched Hanes:
5 they all shame by a people who benefit them not
—neither a help nor benefit
—but for shame and also for reproach.

The Burden Of The Animals Of The South

6 The burden of the animals of the south:
Into the land of tribulation and distress
from whence the roaring lion and the old lion,
the hisser and flying seraph
—who bear their valuables on the shoulders of colts
and their treasures on the humps of camels
to a people who benefit them not.
7 Yes, the Misrayim are vanity and help in vain:
so concerning this, I call out,
Their pride is to shabbathize!
8 Now go, inscribe it in front of them in a slab
and engrave it in a scroll
so that it become for the latter day
eternally and eternally:
9 that this is a rebellious people—deceptive sons
—sons who will to not hear the torah of Yah Veh:
10 who say to the seers, See not;
and to the seers,
See not straightforwardnesses to us;
word smoothly to us; see delusions:
11 you, turn aside from the way;
pervert from the path;
cause the Holy One of *Israel* **Yisra El**
to *cease* **shabbathize** from *before us* **our face**.
12 Wherefore thus saith the
Holy One of *Israel* **Yisra El**,
Because ye *despise* **spurn** this word,
and *trust* **confide** in oppression and perverseness,
and *stay* **lean** thereon:
13 Therefore this *iniquity* **perversity** shall be to you
as a **falling** breach *ready to fall*,
swelling **bulging** out in a *high* **lofted** wall,
whose breaking cometh suddenly
at an instant **in a blink**.
14 And he shall break it
as the breaking of the *potters' vessel* **former's bag**
that is *broken in pieces* **crushed**;
he shall not spare:
so that there shall not be found
in the *bursting* **fracture** of it
a *sherd* **potsherd** to take fire from the *hearth* **burning**,
or to *take* **strip** water *withal* out of the *pit* **dugout**.

15 For thus saith *the Lord GOD* **Adonay Yah Veh**,
the Holy One of *Israel* **Yisra El**;
In returning and rest shall ye be saved;
in *quietness* **resting** and in confidence
shall be your *strength* **might**:
and ye *would* **willed** not.
16 But ye said, No; for we *will*
shall flee upon horses;
therefore shall ye flee:
and, We *will* **shall** ride upon the swift;
therefore shall they that pursue you be swift.
17 One thousand *shall flee*
at **the face of** the rebuke of one;
at **the face of** the rebuke of five shall ye flee:
till ye *be left* **remain** as a *beacon* **mast**
upon the top of a mountain,
and as an ensign on an hill.
18 And therefore *will the*
LORD **shall Yah Veh** wait,
that he may *be gracious* **grant charism** unto you,
and therefore *will* **shall** he be exalted,
that he may *have* mercy *upon* you:
for *the LORD* **Yah Veh** is *a God* **an Elohim** of judgment:
blessed **blithesome** are all they that wait for him.
19 For the people shall *dwell* **settle** in *Zion* **Siyon**
at *Jerusalem* **Yeru Shalem**:
in weeping, thou shalt **not** weep *no more*:
in granting charism,
he *will be very gracious* **shall grant charism**
unto thee at the voice of thy cry;
when he shall hear it, he *will* **shall** answer thee.
20 And *though the Lord* **Adonay**
give **giveth** you the bread of *adversity* **tribulation**,
and the water of *affliction* **oppression**,
yet shall not thy teachers
be removed into a corner **withdraw** any more,
but thine eyes shall see thy teachers:
21 And thine ears shall hear a word behind thee,
saying, This is the way, walk ye in it,
when ye turn to the right *hand*, and
when ye turn to the left.
22 Ye shall *defile* **foul** also the *covering* **overlay**
of thy *graven images* **sculptiles** of silver,
and the *ornament* **ephod**
of thy *molten images* **moltings** of gold:
thou shalt cast them away as a menstruous cloth;
thou shalt say unto it, Get thee hence.
23 Then shall he give the rain of thy seed,
that thou shalt *sow* **seed** the *ground* **soil** withal;
and bread of the *increase* **produce** of the *earth* **soil**,
and it shall be fat and *plenteous* **fattened**:
in that day shall thy *cattle feed* **chattel graze**
in *large pastures* **enlarged meadows**.
24 The oxen *likewise* and the *young asses* **colts**
that *ear* **serve** the *ground* **soil**
shall eat *clean provender* **seasoned fodder**,
which hath been winnowed
with the *shovel* **winnowing fork**
and with the *fan* **winnowing basket**.
25 And there shall be upon
every *high* **lifted** mountain,
and upon every high hill,
rivers **rivulets** and streams of waters
in the day of the great slaughter, when the towers fall.

shabbathize the Holy One of Yisra El from our face.
12 So the Holy One of Yisra El says thus,
Because you spurn this word
and confide in oppression and perverseness
and lean thereon:
13 so this perversity is to you
as a falling breach bulging out in a lofted wall
—whose breaking comes suddenly in a blink.
14 And he breaks it
as breaking the bag of the former
—crushed; he spares not:
so that no potsherd is found in the fracture thereof
to take fire from the burning,
or to strip water from the dugout.
15 For thus says Adonay Yah Veh
the Holy One of Yisra El,
In returning and rest you are saved;
in resting and in confidence is your might:
and you will not.
16 But you say, No; for we flee upon horses!
—so you, flee:
and, We ride upon the swift!—
so your pursuers are swift.
17 One thousand
at the face of the rebuke of one;
at the face of the rebuke of five you flee:
until you remain as a mast on the top of a mountain
and as an ensign on a hill.
18 and so Yah Veh waits to grant you charism
—he is exalted to mercy you:
for Yah Veh *is* an Elohim of judgment:
blithesome—all who await him.
19 For the people settle in Siyon at Yeru Shalem:
in weeping, weep not:
in granting charism,
he grants you charism at the voice of your cry;

when he hears, he answers you.
20 And Adonay gives you the bread of tribulation
and the water of oppression;
and your teachers withdraw no more
and your eyes see your teachers:
21 and your ears hear a word behind you,
saying, This is the way, walk therein,
when you turn to the right and the left.
22 And you foul the overlay
of your sculptiles of silver
and the ephod of your moltings of gold:
you cast them away as a menstruous cloth;
you say to it, Get you hence.
23 And he gives the rain of
your seed to seed the soil;
and bread of the produce of the soil;
and it is fat and fattened:
in that day, your chattel graze in enlarged meadows:
24 the oxen and the colts who serve the soil
eat seasoned fodder
winnowed with the winnowing fork
and with the winnowing basket.
25 And so be it,
on every lifted mountain and on every high hill,
rivulets and streams of waters
in the day of the great slaughter
when the towers fall:
26 Moreover the light of the moon
shall be as the light of the sun,
and the light of the sun shall be sevenfold,
as the light of seven days,
in the day that *the LORD* **Yah Veh**
bindeth up the breach of his people,
and healeth the stroke of their wound.
27 Behold,
the name of *the LORD* **Yah Veh** cometh from far,
burning with his *anger* **wrath**,
and the burden *thereof* is heavy:
his lips are *full of indignation* **filled with rage**,
and his tongue as a *devouring* **consuming** fire:
28 And his *breath* **spirit**, as an
overflowing *stream* **wadi**,
shall *reach to the midst of* **halve** the neck,
to sift the *nations* **goyim** with the sieve of vanity:
and there shall be a bridle in the jaws of the people,
causing them to *err* **stray**.
29 Ye shall have a song, as in the night
when a holy *solemnity* **celebration** is *kept* **hallowed**;
and *gladness* **cheerfulness** of heart,
as when one goeth with a pipe
to come into the mountain of *the LORD* **Yah Veh**,
to the *mighty One* **Rock** of *Israel* **Yisra El**.
30 And *the LORD* **Yah Veh** shall cause
his *glorious voice* **voice of majesty** to be heard,
and *shall shew the lighting down of his arm*
the resting of his arm shall be seen,
with the *indignation* **rage** of his *anger* **wrath**,
and *with* the flame of a *devouring* **consuming** fire,
with scattering, and *tempest* **flood**, and hailstones.
31 For through the voice of *the LORD* **Yah Veh**
shall the *Assyrian* **Ashshuri** be beaten
down, which smote with a *rod* **scion**.
32 And in every *place* **passage**
where the *grounded staff* **founded rod** shall pass,
which *the LORD* **Yah Veh** shall *lay* **rest** upon him,
it shall be with *tabrets* **tambourines** and harps:
and in *battles* **wars** of *shaking* **waving**
will **shall** he fight with it.
33 For *Tophet* **Topheth**
is *ordained of old* **lined up from yesterday**;
yea, for the *king* **sovereign** it is prepared;
he hath *made it deep* **deepened** and *large* **enlarged**:
the *pile* **fuel pile** *thereof*
is fire and *much wood* **abounding timber**;
the breath of *the LORD* **Yah Veh**,
like a *stream* **wadi** of *brimstone* **sulphur**,
doth *kindle* **burn** it.

HO TO THEM THAT LOOK NOT UPON THE HOLY ONE

31 *Woe* **Ho** to them
that *go down to Egypt* **descend to Misrayim** for help;
and *stay* **lean** on horses, and *trust* **confide** in chariots,
because they are many;
and in *horsemen* **cavalry**,
because they are *very strong* **mightily mighty**;
but they look not unto the Holy One of *Israel* **Yisra El**,
neither seek *the LORD* **Yah Veh**!
2 Yet he also is wise, and *will* **shall** bring evil,
and *will* **shall** not *call back* **turn aside** his words:
but *will* **shall** arise
against the house of the *evildoers* **vilifiers**,
and against the help of them that work *iniquity* **mischief**.
3 Now the *Egyptians* **Misrayim**
are *men* **human** and not *God* **El**;
and their horses flesh, and not spirit.
When *the LORD* **Yah Veh** shall
stretched out **spread** his hand,
both he that helpeth shall *fall* **falter**,
and he that is *holpen* **helped** shall fall *down*,

and they all shall *fail* **finish** together.
4 For thus hath *the LORD*
spoken **Yah Veh said** unto me,
Like as the lion and the *young lion* **whelp**
roaring **meditating** on his prey,
when a *multitude* **fulness** of *shepherds* **tenders**
is called forth against him,
he *will* **shall** not *be afraid* **terrify** of their voice,
nor *abase* **humble** himself
for the *noise of them* **multitude**:
26 and the light of the moon
becomes as the light of the sun,
and the light of the sun becomes sevenfold,
as the light of seven days,
in the day Yah Veh binds the breach of his people,
and heals the stroke of their wound.
27 Behold, the name of Yah Veh comes from far
burning with his wrath;
and the burden is heavy:
his lips fill with rage:
and his tongue, as a consuming fire
28 and his spirit, as an overflowing wadi
halve the neck,
to sift the goyim with the sieve of vanity:
and a bridle in the jaws of the people
to stray them.
29 You are as a song in the night
when a holy celebration is hallowed;
and cheerfulness of heart
as when one goes with a pipe
to come into the mountain of Yah Veh,
to the Rock of Yisra El.
30 And Yah Veh has
his voice of majesty to be heard;
and the resting of his arm to be seen
with the rage of his wrath
and the flame of a consuming fire
—scattering and flood and hailstones.
31 For through the voice of Yah Veh
the Ashshuri are beaten down
—he smites with a scion.
32 And in every passage the founded rod passes,
which Yah Veh rests upon him
—with tambourines and harps:
and in wars of waving, he fights with it.
33 For Topheth lined up since yesterday;
yes, prepared for the sovereign;
he deepens and enlarges:
the fuel pile is fire and abounding timber;
the breath of Yah Veh, as a wadi of sulphur, burns it.

Ho To Them Who Look Not Upon The Holy One

31 Ho to them who descend to Misrayim for help;
and lean on horses and confide in chariots
because they are many;
and in cavalry because they are mighty mighty;
and neither look to the Holy One of Yisra El
nor seek Yah Veh.
2 Yet he also is wise and brings evil
and turns not aside his words:
but rises against the house of the vilifiers,
and against the help of them who work mischief.
3 And the Misrayim *are* human, and not El;
and their horses flesh, and not spirit.
When Yah Veh spreads his hand
the helper falters and the helped falls
and they all finish together.
4 For Yah Veh says thus to me,
As the lion and the whelp meditate on his prey
when a fulness of tenders call against him,
he neither terrifies by their voice
nor humbles himself for the multitude:
so shall *the LORD of hosts* **Yah Veh Sabaoth**
come down **descend** to fight for mount *Zion* **Siyon**,
and for the hill *thereof.*
5 As birds flying,
so *will the LORD of hosts* **shall Yah Veh Sabaoth**
defend Jerusalem **garrison Yeru Shalem**;
defending **garrisoning** also he *will* **shall** deliver it;
and passing over he *will preserve* **shall rescue** it.
6 Turn ye unto him
from whom the *children* **sons** of *Israel* **Yisra El**
have *deeply revolted* **deepened revolt**.
7 For in that day every man shall *cast away* **spurn**
his idols of silver, and his idols of gold,
which your own hands
have *made* **worked** unto you for a sin.
8 Then shall the *Assyrian*
Ashshuri fall with the sword,
not of *a mighty* man;
and the sword, not of *a mean man* **humanity**,
shall *devour* **consume** him:
but he shall flee from **the face of** the sword,
and his *young men* **youths** shall be *discomfited* **vassals**.
9 And he shall pass over to his *strong hold* **rock**
for *fear* **terror**,
and his *princes* **governors**
shall *be afraid* **dismay** of the ensign,
saith the LORD **an oracle of Yah Veh**,
whose *fire* **flame** is in *Zion* **Siyon**,
and his furnace in *Jerusalem* **Yeru Shalem**.

The Reign Of Justness

32 Behold, a king shall reign
in *righteousness* **justness,**
and *princes* **governors** shall *rule* **govern** in judgment.
2 And a man shall be
as *an hiding place* **a refuge** from the wind,
and a covert from the *tempest* **flood;**
as *rivers* **rivulets** of water in a *dry place* **parch,**
as the shadow of a *great* **heavy** rock
in a *weary* **languid** land.
3 And the eyes of them that see
shall not *be dim* **look away,**
and the ears of them that hear shall hearken.
4 The heart also of the *rash* **hasty**
shall *understand* **discern** knowledge,
and the tongue of the stammerers
shall *be ready* **hasten** to *speak plainly* **word clearly.**
5 The *vile person* **fool**
shall be no more called *liberal* **volunteer,**
nor the *churl* **crafty** said to be *bountiful* **opulent.**
6 For the *vile person* **fool**
will speak villany **shall word folly,**
and his heart *will* **shall** work *iniquity* **mischief,**
to *practise hypocrisy* **work profanity,**
and to *utter* **word** error against *the LORD* **Yah Veh,**
to *make empty* **pour** the soul of the *hungry* **famished,**
and he *will* **shall** cause the drink
of the thirsty to *fail* **lack.**
7 The instruments also of the *churl* **crafty** are evil:
he *deviseth wicked devices* **counselleth intrigue**
to *destroy* **despoil** the *poor* **humble**
with *lying words* **false sayings,**
even when the needy *speaketh right* **wordeth judgment.**
8 But the *liberal* **volunteer**
deviseth liberal things **counselleth voluntarily;**
and by *liberal things* **volunteering** shall he *stand* **rise.**

Relaxed Women And Confident Daughters

9 Rise up, ye women that are *at ease* **relaxed;**
hear my voice, ye *careless* **confident** daughters;
give ear **hearken** unto my *speech* **saying.**
10 Many days and years shall ye *be troubled* **quiver,**
ye *careless women* **confiding:**
for the *vintage* **crop** shall *fail* **finish off,**
the *gathering* **ingathering** shall not come.
11 Tremble, ye women that are *at ease* **relaxed;**
be troubled **quiver,** ye *careless ones* **confiding:**
strip you, and *make you* **strip** bare,
and gird sackcloth—**a girdle** upon *your* loins.
12 They shall *lament* **chop** for the *teats* **breasts,**
for the *pleasant fields* **fields of desire,**
for the *fruitful* **fruitbearing** vine.
13 Upon the *land* **soil** of my people
shall *come up* **ascend** thorns and briers;
thus Yah Veh Sabaoth descends to fight
for mount Siyon and for the hill.
5 As birds flying,
thus Yah Veh Sabaoth garrisons Yeru Shalem:
and in garrisoning, he delivers;
and passing over he rescues.
6 You, turn to him
from whom the sons of Yisra El deepen revolt:
7 for in that day,
every man spurns his idols of silver
and his idols of gold
—which your own hands worked to you, a sin:
8 and the Ashshuri fall with
the sword, not of man;
and the sword, not of humanity, consumes
him: and he flees the face of the sword
and his youths become vassals:
9 and he passes over to his rock from terror,
and his governors dismay of the ensign
—an oracle of Yah Veh
whose flame is in Siyon
and his furnace in Yeru Shalem.

The Reign Of Justness

32 Behold, a sovereign reigns in justness
and governors govern in judgment:
2 and man is as a refuge from the wind
and a covert from the flood;
as rivulets of water in a parch
as the shadow of a heavy rock in a languid land:
3 and the eyes of them who see, look not away;
and the ears of them who hear, hearken:
4 and the heart of the hasty
discerns knowledge,
and the tongue of the stammerers
hastens to word clearly:
5 neither is the fool called to volunteer any more
nor the crafty said to be opulent:
6 for the fool words folly
and his heart works mischief
—to work profanity
and to word error against Yah Veh
—to pour the soul of the famished;
and causes the drink of the thirsty to lack:

7 and the instruments of the crafty are evil:
he counsels intrigue
to despoil the humble with false sayings
—even when the needy word judgment.
8 and the volunteer counsels voluntarily;
and by volunteering he rises.

RELAXED WOMEN AND CONFIDENT DAUGHTERS

9 Rise up, you relaxed women;
hear my voice, you confident daughters;
hearken to my saying,
10 Many days and years you quiver—you confide:
for the crop is finished off;
the ingathering comes not.
11 Tremble, you relaxed women;
quiver, you who confide:
strip, and strip bare with a girdle on the loins.
12 They chop for the breasts
for the fields of desire
—for the fruitbearing vine:
13 on the soil of my people
thorns and briers ascend;
yea, upon all the houses of joy
in the *joyous* city **of jumping for joy**:
14 Because the *palaces* **citadels**
shall be *forsaken* **abandoned**;
the multitude of the city shall be *left* **forsaken**;
the *forts* **mounds** and **lookout** towers
shall be for *dens for ever* **caves eternally**,
a joy of wild *asses* **runners**, a pasture of *flocks* **droves**;
15 Until the spirit be poured
out upon us from on high,
and the wilderness be *a fruitful*
field **an orchard/Karmel**,
and the *fruitful field* **orchard/Karmel**
be *counted* **fabricated** for a forest.
16 Then judgment
shall *dwell* **tabernacle** in the wilderness,
and *righteousness* **justness**
remain **settle** in the *fruitful field* **orchard/Karmel**.
17 And the work of *righteousness* **justness**
shall be *peace* **shalom**;
and the *effect* **service** of *righteousness* **justness**
quietness **resting** and *assurance* **confidence**
for ever **eternally**.
18 And my people shall *dwell* **settle**
in a *peaceable habitation* **habitation of shalom of rest**,
and in *sure dwellings* **confident tabernacles**,
and in *quiet* resting places **of relaxation**;
19 When it shall hail,
coming down **descending** on the forest;
and the city shall be *low* **lowered**
in a *low place* **lowland**.
20 *Blessed* **Blithesome** are ye
that *sow* **seed** beside all waters,
that send forth *thither* the feet of
the ox and the *ass* **burro**.

HO TO THE RAVAGER

33 *Woe* **Ho** to thee that *spoilest* **ravagest**,
and thou wast not *spoiled* **ravaged**;
and dealest *treacherously* **covertly**,
and *they dealt not treacherously with*
thee **are not dealt covertly**!
when thou shalt *cease* **consummate** to *spoil* **ravage**,
thou shalt be *spoiled* **ravaged**;
and when thou shalt *make an* end
to deal *treacherously* **covertly**,
they shall deal *treacherously* **covertly** with thee.
2 O *LORD* **Yah Veh**, *be gracious*
grant charism unto us;
we have *waited for* **awaited** thee:
be thou their arm *every morning* **mornings**,
our salvation also in the time of *trouble* **tribulation**.
3 At the *noise* **voice** of the *tumult* **multitude**
the people fled;
at *the lifting up of thyself* **thy exaltation**
the *nations* **goyim** were scattered.
4 And your spoil shall be gathered
like the *gathering* **ingathering** of the caterpiller:
as the running *to and fro* **about** of locusts
shall he *run* **yearn** upon them.
5 *The LORD* **Yah Veh** is exalted;
for he *dwelleth* **tabernacleth** on high:
he hath filled *Zion* **Siyon**
with judgment and *righteousness* **justness**.
6 And wisdom and knowledge
shall be the *stability* **trustworthiness** of thy times,
and *strength* **wealth** of salvation:
the *fear* **awe** of *the LORD* **Yah Veh** is his treasure.
7 Behold,
their *valiant ones* **heros** shall cry *without* **outwardly**:
the *ambassadors* **angels** of *peace* **shalom**
shall weep bitterly.
8 The highways lie *waste* **desolated**,
the *wayfaring man* **passer of the way**
ceaseth **shabbathizeth**:
he hath broken the covenant,
he hath *despised* **spurned** the cities,

he *regardeth* **fabricateth** no man.
9 The earth mourneth and languisheth:
Lebanon *is ashamed* **blusheth**
and *hewn down* **withereth**:
Sharon is like a *wilderness* **plain**;
and Bashan and *Carmel* **Karmel/orchard**
shake *off their fruits.*
10 Now *will* **shall** I rise, saith *the LORD* **Yah Veh**;
yes, on all the houses of joy
in the city of jumping for joy:
14 surely the citadels are abandoned
and the multitude of the city forsaken;
the mounds and lookout towers
become caves eternally
—a joy of wild runners—a pasture of droves;
15 until the spirit pours out on us from on high,
and the wilderness becomes an orchard/Karmel,
and the orchard/Karmel is fabricated for a forest.
16 Then judgment tabernacles in the wilderness,
and justness settles in the orchard/Karmel:
17 And the work of justness becomes shalom;
and the service of justness rest and confidence
eternally:
18 and my people settle
in a habitation of shalom of rest
and in confident tabernacles
and in resting places of relaxation;
19 though it hails, descending on the forest
and the city lowers into a lowland.
20 Blithesome—you who seed beside all waters,
who send forth the feet of the ox and the burro.

HO TO THE RAVAGER

33 Ho to you who ravage, and are not ravaged;
who deal covertly, and are not dealt covertly:
when you consummate ravaging,
they ravage you;
and when you end dealing covertly,
they deal covertly with you.
2 O Yah Veh, grant us charism; we await you:
become their arm mornings,
and our salvation in the time of tribulation.
3 At the voice of the multitude the people flee;
at your exaltation the goyim scatter:
4 and gather your spoil
as the ingathering of the caterpiller:
as the running about of locusts
he yearns on them.
5 Yah Veh is exalted; for he tabernacles on high:
he fills Siyon with judgment and justness:
6 and wisdom and knowledge
become the trustworthiness of your times
and wealth of salvation:
the awe of Yah Veh *is* his treasure.
7 Behold, their heros cry outwardly;
the angels of shalom weep bitterly;
8 the highways lie desolate;
the passers of the way shabbathize:
he breaks the covenant;
he spurns the cities;
he fabricates no man.
9 The earth mourns and languishes;
Lebanon blushes and withers;
Sharon is as a plain;
and Bashan and Karmel/orchard shake.
10 Now I rise, says Yah Veh;
now *will* **shall** I be exalted; now *will* **shall** I lift *up* myself.
11 Ye shall conceive *chaff* **hay**,
ye shall *bring forth* **birth** stubble:
your *breath* **spirit**, as fire, shall *devour* **consume** you.
12 And the people
shall be as the *burnings* **calcinations** of lime:
as thorns cut up shall they be burned in the fire.
13 Hear, ye that are far off,
what I have *done* **worked**;
and, ye that are near, acknowledge my might.
14 The sinners in *Zion are afraid* **Siyon fear**;
fearfulness **trembling**
hath *surprised* **holden** the *hypocrites* **profaners**.
Who among us shall *dwell* **sojourn**
with the *devouring* **consuming** fire?
who among us shall *dwell* **sojourn**
with *everlasting* **eternal** burnings?
15 He that walketh *righteously* **in justness**,
and *speaketh uprightly* **wordeth straightly**;
he that *despiseth* **spurneth** the gain of oppressions,
that shaketh his *hands* **palms**
from *holding of* **upholding** bribes,
that *stoppeth* **shutteth** his ears from hearing of blood,
and *shutteth* **bindeth** his eyes from seeing evil;
16 He shall *dwell* **tabernacle** on high:
his *place of defence* **secure loft**
shall be the *munitions* **huntholds** of rocks:
bread shall be given him;
his waters shall be *sure* **trustworthy**.
17 Thine eyes shall see the *king*
sovereign in his beauty:
they shall *behold* **see** the land that is very far off.
18 Thine heart shall meditate terror.
Where is the scribe? where is the *receiver* **weigher**?

where is he that *counted* **scribed** the towers?
19 Thou shalt not see *a fierce* **an obstinate** people,
a people of a deeper *speech* **lip**
than thou *canst perceive* **hearest**;
of a *stammering* **deriding** tongue,
that thou *canst* not understand.
20 *Look* **See** upon *Zion* **Siyon**,
the city of our *solemnities* **seasons**:
thine eyes shall see *Jerusalem* **Yeru Shalem**
a *quiet habitation* **habitation of rest and relaxation**,
a *tabernacle* **tent** that shall not *be taken down* **migrate**;
not one of the stakes *thereof*
shall *ever* be *removed* **pulled in perpetuity**,
neither shall any of the cords *thereof* be *broken* **torn**.
21 But there *the glorious LORD* **mighty Yah Veh**
will **shall** be unto us a place of
broad rivers and streams **rivers—rivers broad of hand**;
wherein shall go no *galley* **ships** with oars,
neither shall *gallant* **mighty** ship pass thereby.
22 For *the LORD* **Yah Veh** is our judge,
the LORD **Yah Veh** is our *lawgiver* **statute setter**,
the LORD **Yah Veh** is our *king* **sovereign**;
he *will* **shall** save us.
23 Thy *tacklings* **cords** are *loosed* **abandoned**;
they *could not well strengthen*
held not the base of their mast,
they *could not* spread **not** the sail:
then is the prey of a great spoil *divided* **allotted**;
the lame *take* **plunder** the *prey* **plunder**.
24 And the *inhabitant* **fellow**
tabernacler shall not say,
I am sick:
the people that *dwell* **settle** therein
shall *be forgiven* **bear** their *iniquity* **perversity**.

Yah Veh Judges The Goyim

34 *Come near* **Approach**, ye
nations **goyim**, to hear;
and hearken, ye *people* **nations**:
let the earth hear, and all *that is therein* **its fulness**;
the world,
and all *things that come forth of it* **its offspring**.
2 For the *indignation* **rage** of *the LORD* **Yah Veh**
is upon all *nations* **goyim**,
and his fury upon all their *armies* **hosts**:
he hath *utterly destroyed* **devoted** them,
he hath *delivered* **given** them to the slaughter.
3 Their *slain* **pierced** also shall be cast out,
and their stink shall *come up* **ascend**
out of their carcases,
and the mountains shall be melted with their blood.
now I am exalted; now I am lifted.
11 You conceive hay, you birth stubble:
your spirit, as fire, consumes you:
12 and the people become as
the calcinations of lime
—as thorns cut up—burned in the fire.
13 Hear, you who are far off, what I worked;
and, you who are near, acknowledge my might.
14 The sinners in Siyon fear;
trembling holds the profaners.
Who among us sojourns with the consuming fire?
Who among us sojourns with eternal burnings?
15 He who walks in justness and words straightly;
he who spurns the gain of oppressions;
who shakes his palms from upholding bribes;
who shuts his ears from hearing of blood
and binds his eyes from seeing evil:
16 he tabernacles on high;
his secure loft, the huntholds of rocks:
he is given bread;
his waters are trustworthy.
17 Your eyes see the sovereign in his beauty;
they see a land afar off:
18 your heart meditates terror.
Where *is* the scribe? Where *is* the weigher?
Where is he who scribed the towers?
19 You see not an obstinate people
—a people of a lip too deep to hear;
of a deriding tongue that you understand not.
20 See on Siyon, the city of our seasons:
your eyes see Yeru Shalem
—a habitation of rest and relaxation
—a tent that neither migrates
nor one of the stakes pulled in perpetuity
nor any of the cords torn.
21 But there mighty Yah Veh
is to us a place of rivers—rivers broad of hand;
wherein neither ships with oars go
nor mighty ships pass thereby.
22 For Yah Veh our judge;
Yah Veh our statute setter;
Yah Veh our sovereign; he saves us.
23 Your cords are abandoned;
they neither hold the base of their mast
nor spread the sail:
then they allot the prey of a great spoil:
and the lame plunder the plunder:
24 and the fellow tabernacler says not, I am sick:
the people who settle therein bear their perversity.

YAH VEH JUDGES THE GOYIM

34 Approach, you goyim, to hear;
and hearken, you nations:
hear, O earth, and all its fulness;
the world, and all its offspring:
2 for the rage of Yah Veh *is* on all goyim,
and his fury on all their hosts:
he devotes them; he gives them to the slaughter:
3 and their pierced are cast out
and their stink ascends from their carcases
and the mountains melt with their blood:
4 And all the host of *heaven* **the heavens**
shall be dissolved,
and the heavens shall be rolled together as a scroll:
and all their host shall *fall down* **wither,**
as the leaf *falleth off* **withereth** from the vine,
and as a *fading fig* **withering** from the fig tree.
5 For my sword
shall be *bathed* **saturated** in *heaven* **the heavens**:
behold,
it shall *come down* **descend** upon *Idumea* **Edom,**
and upon the people of my *curse* **devotement,**
to judgment.
6 The sword of *the LORD* **Yah**
Veh is filled with blood,
it is *made fat* **fattened** with *fatness* **fat,**
and with the blood of *lambs* **rams** and **he** goats,
with the fat of the *kidneys* **reins** of rams:
for *the LORD* **Yah Veh** hath a sacrifice in *Bozrah* **Bosrah,**
and a great slaughter in the land of *Idumea* **Edom.**
7 And the *unicorns* **reems**
shall *come down* **descend** with them,
and the bullocks with the *bulls* **mighty;**
and their land shall be *soaked* **saturated** with blood,
and their dust *made fat with fatness* **fatteneth with fat.**
8 For it is the day
of *the LORD'S vengeance* **Yah Veh's avengement,**
and the year of *recompences* **satisfactions**
for the *controversy* **strife** of *Zion* **Siyon.**
9 And the *streams* **wadies** *thereof*
shall be turned into *pitch* **asphalt,**
and the dust *thereof* into *brimstone* **sulphur,**
and the land *thereof* shall become burning *pitch* **asphalt.**
10 It shall not be quenched night nor day;
the smoke *thereof* shall *go up for ever* **ascend eternally**:
from generation to generation it shall lie *waste* **parched**;
none shall pass through *it for ever*
and ever **in perpetuity.**
11 But the *cormorant* **pelican** and the bittern
shall possess it;
the owl also and the raven shall *dwell* **tabernacle** in it:
and he shall *stretch out* **spread** upon it
the line of *confusion* **waste,** and the stones of emptiness.
12 They shall call the nobles
thereof to the kingdom,
but none shall be there,
and all her *princes* **governors** shall *be nothing* **decease.**
13 And thorns
shall *come up* **ascend** in her *palaces* **citadels,**
nettles **thistles** and *brambles* **thorns**
in the fortresses *thereof*:
and it shall be an habitation **of rest** of *dragons* **monsters,**
and a court for **daughters of the** owls.
14 The *wild beasts of the desert* **desert dwellers**
shall also meet
with the *wild beasts of the island* **island howlers,**
and the *satyr* **buck** shall *cry* **call** to his *fellow* **friend;**
the *screech owl* **night spectre** also shall rest there,
and find for herself a place of rest.
15 There shall *the great owl*
make her **arrowsnake** nest,
and *lay* **escape,** and *hatch* **split,**
and *gather* **brood** under her shadow:
there shall the *vultures* **falcons** also be gathered,
every *one* **woman** with her *mate* **friend.**
16 Seek ye out of the *book*
scroll of *the LORD* **Yah Veh,**
and *read* **call out:**
no one of these shall *fail* **lack,**
none **no woman** shall *want* **oversee** her mate:
for my mouth it hath *commanded* **misvahed,**
and his spirit it hath gathered them.
17 And he hath *cast* **felled** the *lot* **pebble** for them,
and his hand hath *divided* **allotted** it unto them by line:
they shall possess it *for ever* **eternally,**
from generation to generation
shall they *dwell* **tabernacle** therein.

THE WAY OF HOLINESS

35 The wilderness and the *solitary place* **parch**
shall *be glad* **rejoice** for them;
and the *desert* **plain** shall *rejoice* **twirl,**
and blossom as the rose.
2 **In blossoming,** It shall blossom *abundantly,*
and *rejoice* **twirl**
even with *joy* **twirling** and *singing* **shouting**:
4 and all the host of the heavens dissolves
and the heavens roll together as a scroll:
and all their host withers

as the leaf withers from the vine
—as a withering from the fig tree.
5 For my sword saturates in the heavens:
behold, it descends on Edom
and on the people of my devotement
to judgment.
6 The sword of Yah Veh fills with blood,
—fattens with fat
with the blood of rams and he goats;
with the fat of the reins of rams:
for Yah Veh—a sacrifice in Bosrah
and a great slaughter in the land of Edom.
7 And the reems descend with them
and the bullocks with the mighty;
and their land saturates with blood
and their dust fattens with fat:
8 for it *is* the day of avengement of Yah Veh
and the year of satisfactions for the strife of Siyon.
9 And the wadies turn into asphalt
and the dust into sulphur
and the land becomes burning asphalt
10 —not quenched night or day;
the smoke ascends eternally:
from generation to generation it lies parched;
no one passes through in perpetuity.
11 And the pelican and the bittern possess it;
and the owl and the raven tabernacle therein:
and thereon, he spreads the line of waste,
and the stones of emptiness.
12 They call the nobles to the kingdom
but no one is there;
and all her governors decease:
13 and thorns ascend in her citadels
—thistles and thorns in the fortresses:
and it becomes a habitation of rest of monsters
—a court for daughters of the owls:
14 and the desert dwellers
meet with the island howlers;
and the buck calls to his friend;
and the night spectre rests there,
and finds a place of rest for herself:
15 there the arrowsnake nests
and escapes and splits and broods under her shadow:
and there the falcons gather
—every woman with her friend.
16 Seek the scroll of Yah Veh, and call out!
Not one of these lack!
No woman oversees her mate:
for my mouth misvahs,
and his spirit gathers them:
17 and he fells the pebble for them,
and his hand allots to them by line:
they possess it eternally,
from generation to generation they tabernacle therein.

THE WAY OF HOLINESS

35 The wilderness and the parch rejoice for them;
and the plain twirls and blossoms as the rose.
2 In blossoming, it blossoms;
in twirling, it twirls and shouts:
the *glory* **honour** of Lebanon shall be given unto it,
the *excellency* **majesty**
of *Carmel* **Karmel/orchard** and Sharon,
they shall see the *glory* **honour** of *the LORD* **Yah Veh**,
and the *excellency* **majesty** of our *God* **Elohim**.
3 Strengthen ye the weak hands,
and *confirm* **strengthen** the *feeble* **faltering** knees.
4 Say to them that are of a *fearful* **hasty** heart,
Be strong, *fear* **awe** not:
behold, your *God* **Elohim!**
will come with vengeance **avengement shall come**,
even God with a recompence—**the dealing of Elohim**;
he *will* **shall** come and save you.
5 Then the eyes of the blind shall be opened,
and the ears of the deaf shall be unstopped.
6 Then shall the lame *man* leap as an hart,
and the tongue of the *dumb sing* **mute shout**:
for in the wilderness shall waters *break out* **split**,
and *streams* **wadies** in the *desert* **plain**.
7 And the *parched ground* **mirage**
shall become a *pool* **marsh**,
and the thirsty *land springs* **fountains** of water:
in the habitation **of rest** of *dragons* **monsters**,
where each lay **in its repose**,
shall be grass with *reeds* **stalks** and *rushes* **bulrushes**.
8 And an highway shall be there, and a way,
and it shall be called The way of holiness;
the *unclean* **foul** shall not pass over it;
but it shall be for those:
the wayfaring men **waywalkers**, though fools,
shall not err *therein*.
9 No lion shall be there,
nor any ravenous *beast* **live being**
shall *go up* **ascend** thereon,
it shall not be found there;
but the redeemed shall walk there:
10 And the *ransomed* **redeemed**
of *the LORD* **Yah Veh**
shall return,
and come to *Zion* **Siyon** with *songs* **shouting**

and *everlasting joy* **eternal cheerfulness**
upon their heads:
they shall *obtain* **attain**
joy **rejoicing** and *gladness* **cheerfulness**,
and *sorrow* **grief** and sighing shall flee away.

SANCHERIB APPREHENDS YAH HUDAH

36 *Now* **And so be** it *came to pass*
in the fourteenth year
of *king Hesekiah* **sovereign Yechizqi Yah**,
that Sennacherib **Sancherib**,
king **sovereign** of *Assyria* **Ashshur**
came up **ascended** against all the *defenced* **fortified** cities
of *Judah* **Yah Hudah**, and *took* **apprehended** them.
2 And the *king* **sovereign** of *Assyria* **Ashshur**
sent *Rabshakeh* **Rab Shaqeh**
from Lachish to *Jerusalem* **Yeru Shalem**
unto king *Hesekiah* **Yechizqi Yah**
heavy with *a great army* **valiant**.
And he stood
by the *conduit* **channel** of the *upper* **most high** pool
in the highway of the fuller's field.
3 Then came forth unto him *Eliakim* **El Yaqim**,
Hilkiah's **Hilqi Yah's** son, which was over the house,
and Shebna the scribe,
and *Joah* **Yah Ach**, Asaph's son,
the *recorder* **memorializer**.
4 And *Rabshakeh* **Rab Shaqeh** said unto them,
Say ye *now* **I beseech,** to *Hesekiah* **Yechizqi Yah**,
Thus saith the great *king* **sovereign**,
the *king* **sovereign** of *Assyria* **Ashshur**,
What confidence is this wherein thou *trustest* **confidest**?
5 I say, *sayest thou*,
(but *they are but vain* **only lip** words)
I have counsel and *strength* **might** for war:
now on whom *dost thou trust* **confidest thou**,
that thou rebellest against me?
6 *Lo* **Behold**, thou *trustest* **confidest**
in the *staff* **crutch** of this *broken reed* **crushed stalk**,
on *Egypt* **Misrayim**;
whereon if a man *lean* **prop**,

the honor of Lebanon is given to it
—the majesty of Karmel/orchard and Sharon:
they see the honor of Yah Veh
and the majesty of our Elohim:
3 strengthen the weak hands
and strengthen the faltering knees.
4 Say to the hasty heart,
Be strong! Awe not! Behold, your Elohim!
Avengement comes—the dealing of Elohim;
he comes and saves you.
5 Then the eyes of the blind open
and the ears of the deaf unstop;
6 then the lame leap as a hart
and the tongue of the mute shouts:
for the waters split in the wilderness
and wadies in the plain:
7 and the mirage becomes a marsh;
and the thirsty, fountains of water:
in the habitation of rest wherein monsters repose,
grass with stalks and bulrushes.
8 And there becomes a highway, and a way;
and it is called The way of holiness;
the foul pass not over;
and it *is* for them—waywalkers;
even fools err not.
9 No lion is there;
a ravenous live being ascends not thereon;
it is not found therein;
and the redeemed walk therein:
10 and the redeemed of Yah Veh return
and come to Siyon with shouting
and eternal cheerfulness on their heads:
they attain rejoicing and cheerfulness,
and grief and sighing flee away.

SANCHERIB APPREHENDS YAH HUDAH

36 And so be it,
in the fourteenth year of sovereign Yechizqi Yah,
Sancherib sovereign of Ashshur
ascends against all the fortified cities of Yah Hudah
and apprehends them:
2 and the sovereign of Ashshur
sends Rab Shaqeh from Lachish to Yeru Shalem
to king Yechizqi Yah—heavy with valiant:
and he stands by the channel of the most high pool
in the highway of the field of the fuller.
3 Then El Yaqim the son of Hilqi Yah
who is over the house
comes to him, with Shebna the scribe,
and Yah Ach the son of Asaph the memorializer.
4 And Rab Shaqeh says to them,
You, say, I beseech, to Yechizqi Yah,
Thus says the great sovereign
—the sovereign of Ashshur,
What is this confidence wherein you confide?
5 I say, surely, words of lips!
Counsel and might *are* for war!
Now on whom confide you, to rebel against me?
6 Behold,

you confide in the crutch of this crushed stalk
—on Misrayim;
whereon, if a man props,
it *will* **shall** go into his *hand* **palm**, and pierce it:
so is *Pharaoh* **Paroh** *king* **sovereign** of *Egypt* **Misrayim**
to all that *trust* **confide** in him.
7 But if thou say to me,
We *trust* **confide** in *the LORD* **Yah Veh** our *Cod* **Elohim**:
is it not he,
whose *high places* **bamahs** and whose **sacrifice** altars
Hesekiah **Yechizqi Yah** hath *taken away* **turned aside**,
and said
to *Judah* **Yah Hudah** and to *Jerusalem* **Yeru Shalem**,
Ye shall *worship* **prostrate**
before **at the face of** this **sacrifice** altar?
8 Now therefore *give pledges*
pledge, I *pray* **beseech** thee,
to my *master* **adoni**
the *king* **sovereign** of *Assyria* **Ashshur**,
and I *will* **shall** give thee two thousand horses,
if thou be able on thy part to *set* **give** riders upon them.
9 How then *wilt* **shalt** thou turn away the face
of one *captain* **governor**
of the *least* **lesser** of my *master's* **adoni's** servants,
and *put thy trust* **confide** on *Egypt* **Misrayim**
for chariots and for *horsemen* **cavalry**?
10 And am I now *come up* **ascended**
without *the LORD* **Yah Veh**
against this land to *destroy* **ruin** it?
the LORD **Yah Veh** said unto me,
Co up **Ascend** against this land, and *destroy* **ruin** it.
11 Then said
Eliakim **El Yaqim** and Shebna and *Joah* **Yah Ach**
unto *Rabshakeh* **Rab Shaqeh**,
Speak **Word**, I *pray* **beseech** thee,
unto thy servants in *the Syrian language* **Aramaic**;
for we *understand it* **hear**:
and *speak* **word** not to us
in *the Jews' language* **Yah Hudaic**,
in the ears of the people that are on the wall.
12 But *Rabshakeh* **Rab Shaqeh** said,
Hath my *master* **adoni** sent me to thy *master* **adoni**
and to thee to *speak* **word** these words?
hath he not *sent me* to the men that sit upon the wall,
that they may eat their own *dung* **excrements**,
and drink *their own piss* **the urine at their feet** with you?
13 Then *Rabshakeh* **Rab Shaqeh** stood,
and *cried* **called out** with a *loud* **great** voice
in *the Jews' language* **Yah Hudaic**, and said,
Hear ye the words of the great *king* **sovereign**,
the *king* **sovereign** of *Assyria* **Ashshur**.
14 Thus saith the *king* **sovereign**,
Let not *Hesekiah* **Yechizqi Yah** deceive you: for
he shall not be able to *deliver* **rescue** you.
15 Neither let *Hesekiah* **Yechizqi Yah**
make **have** you *trust* **confide** in *the LORD* **Yah Veh**,
saying,
The LORD will surely deliver
In rescuing, Yah Veh shall rescue us:
this city shall not be *delivered* **given**
into the hand of the *king* **sovereign** of *Assyria* **Ashshur**.
16 Hearken not to *Hesekiah* **Yechizqi Yah**:
for thus saith the *king* **sovereign** of *Assyria* **Ashshur**,
Make an agreement **Work** with me
by a present **a blessing**,
and come out to me:
and eat ye every *one* **man** of his vine,
and every *one* **man** of his fig tree,
and drink ye every *one* **man**
the waters of his own *cistern* **well**;
17 Until I come
and take you away to a land like your own land,
a land of *corn* **crop** and *wine* **juice**,
a land of bread and vineyards.
18 *Beware*
lest *Hesekiah persuade* **Yechizqi Yah goad** you,
saying, *the LORD will deliver* **Yah Veh shall rescue** us.
Hath any **man** of the *gods* **elohim** of the *nations* **goyim**
delivered **rescued** his land
out of the hand of the *king* **sovereign**
of *Assyria* **Ashshur**?
19 Where are the *gods* **elohim**
of Hamath and Arphad?
where are the *gods* **elohim** of *Sepharvaim* **Sepharvayim**?
it goes into his palm, and pierces:
thus *is* Paroh sovereign of Misrayim
to all who confide in him.
7 And if you say to me,
We confide in Yah Veh our Elohim!
—is it not he,
whose bamahs and whose sacrifice altars
Yechizqi Yah turned aside,
and said to Yah Hudah and to Yeru Shalem,
Prostrate you at the face of this sacrifice altar?
8 And now pledge, I beseech you,
to my adoni the sovereign of Ashshur,
and I give you two thousand horses,
if you are able on your part to give riders on them.
9 And how turn you away
the face of one governor

of the lesser of the servants of my adoni,
and confide on Misrayim for chariots and for cavalry?
10 And now ascend I without Yah Veh
against this land to ruin it?
Yah Veh said to me,
Ascend against this land, and ruin it.
11 And El Yaqim and Shebna and Yah Ach
say to Rab Shaqeh,
Word, I beseech you, to your servants in Aramaic;
for we hear:
and word not to us in Yah Hudaic,
in the ears of the people on the wall.
12 And Rab Shaqeh says,
Has my adoni sent me to your adoni
to word these words to you?
Is it not to the men who sit on the wall
to eat their own excrements
and drink the urine at their feet with you?
13 And Rab Shaqeh stands
and calls out with a great voice in Yah Hudaic,
and says,
You, hear the words of the great sovereign
the sovereign of Ashshur!
14 Thus says the sovereign,
Neither let Yechizqi Yah deceive you:
for he is not able to rescue you:
15 nor let Yechizqi Yah have
you confide in Yah Veh,
saying, In rescuing, Yah Veh rescues us.
This city is not given
into the hand of the sovereign of Ashshur.
16 Hearken not to Yechizqi Yah:
for thus says the sovereign of Ashshur,
Work a blessing with me and come out to me
and every man eat of his vine
and every man of his fig tree;
and every man drink the waters of his own well;
17 —until I come and take you away
to a land like your own land
—a land of crop and juice,
a land of bread and vineyards;
18 lest Yechizqi Yah goads you, saying,
Yah Veh rescues us.
Has any man of the elohim of the goyim
rescued his land
from the hand of the sovereign of Ashshur?
19 Where are the elohim of Hamath and Arphad?
Where are the elohim of Sepharvayim?
and have they *delivered Samaria* **rescued Shomeron**
out of my hand?
20 Who are they
among all the *gods* **elohim** of these lands,
that have *delivered* **rescued** their land out of my hand,
that *the LORD* **Yah Veh**
should *deliver Jerusalem* **rescue Yeru Shalem**
out of my hand?
21 But they *held their peace* **hushed**,
and answered him not a word:
for the *king's commandment* **sovereign's misvah** was,
saying, Answer him not.
22 Then came *Eliakim* **El Yaqim**, the son of
Hilkiah **Hilqi Yah**, that was over the household,
and Shebna the scribe,
and *Joah* **Yah Ach**, the son of Asaph,
the *recorder* **memorializer**,
to *Hesekiah* **Yechizqi Yah** with their clothes *rent* **ripped**,
and told him the words of *Rabshakeh* **Rab Shaqeh**.
37 And **so be** it *came to pass*,
when *king Hesekiah* **sovereign Yechizqi Yah** heard it,
that he *rent* **ripped** his clothes,
and covered himself with *sackcloth* **saq**,
and went into the house of *the LORD* **Yah Veh**.
2 And he sent *Eliakim* **El Yaqim**,
who was over the household,
and Shebna the scribe,
and the elders of the priests covered with *sackcloth* **saq**,
unto *Isaiah* **Yesha Yah** the prophet
the son of *Amoz* **Amos**.
3 And they said unto him,
Thus saith *Hesekiah* **Yechizqi Yah**,
This day is a day of *trouble* **tribulation**,
and of rebuke, and of *blasphemy* **scorning**:
for the *children* **sons** are come to the *birth* **matrix**,
and there is not strength to *bring forth* **birth**.
4 It may be *the LORD* **Yah Veh** thy *God* **Elohim**
will **shall** hear the words of *Rabshakeh* **Rab Shaqeh**,
whom the *king* **sovereign** of *Assyria* **Ashshur**
his *master* **adoni**
hath sent to reproach the living *God* **Elohim**,
and *will* **shall** reprove the words
which *the LORD* **Yah Veh** thy *God* **Elohim** hath heard:
wherefore lift up thy prayer
for the *remnant* **survivors** that *is left* **survive**.
5 So the servants
of *king Hesekiah* **sovereign Yechizqi Yah**
came to *Isaiah* **Yesha Yah**.
6 And *Isaiah* **Yesha Yah** said unto them,
Thus shall ye say unto your *master* **adoni**,
Thus saith *the LORD* **Yah Veh**,
Be not afraid **Awe not at the face**

of the words that thou hast heard,
wherewith the *servants* **lads**
of the *king* **sovereign** of *Assyria* **Ashshur**
have blasphemed me.
7 Behold, I *will send a blast*
shall give a spirit upon him,
and he shall hear a *rumour* **report**,
and return to his own land;
and I *will cause him to fall* **shall fell him**
by the sword in his own land.
8 So *Rabshakeh* **Rab Shaqeh** returned,
and found the *king* **sovereign** of *Assyria* **Ashshur**
warring **fighting** against Libnah:
for he had heard that he was departed from Lachish.
9 And he heard say concerning
Tirhakah **Tirhaqah,**
king **sovereign** of *Ethiopia* **Kush**,
He is come forth to *make war* **fight** with thee.
And when he heard it,
he sent *messengers* **angels** to *Hesekiah* **Yechizqi Yah**,
saying,
10 Thus shall ye *speak* **say** to
Hesekiah **Yechizqi Yah,**
king **sovereign** of *Judah* **Yah Hudah**, saying,
Let not thy *God* **Elohim**, in whom
thou *trustest* **confidest**,
deceive thee, saying,
Jerusalem **Yeru Shalem** shall not be given
into the hand of the *king* **sovereign** of *Assyria* **Ashshur**.
Rescued they Shomeron from my hand?
20 Who are they, among all
the elohim of these lands,
who rescued their land from my hand,
that Yah Veh rescue Yeru Shalem from my hand?
21 And they hush and answer him not a word:
for the misvah of the sovereign is, saying,
Answer him not.
22 And El Yaqim the son of Hilqi Yah
who is over the household,
comes with Shebna the scribe,
and Yah Ach the son of Asaph, the memorializer,
to Yechizqi Yah with their clothes ripped,
and tell him the words of Rab Shaqeh.

37 And so be it,
when sovereign Yechizqi Yah hears,
he rips his clothes and covers himself with saq,
and goes into the house of Yah Veh.
2 And he sends El Yaqim
who is over the household,
and Shebna the scribe and the elders of the priests
covered with saq,
to Yesha Yah the prophet the son of Amos:
3 and they say to him,
Thus says Yechizqi Yah,
This day is a day of tribulation
and of rebuke and of scorning:
for the sons come to the matrix
and there is no strength to birth.
4 Perhaps Yah Veh your Elohim
hears the words of Rab Shaqeh,
whom the sovereign of Ashshur his adoni
sent to reproach the living Elohim,
and to reprove the words
Yah Veh your Elohim heard:
and to lift your prayer for the survivors who survive.
5 And the servants of sovereign Yechizqi Yah
come to Yesha Yah:
6 and Yesha Yah says to them,
You, say thus to your adoni,
Thus says Yah Veh,
Awe not at the face of the words you heard,
wherewith the lads of the sovereign of Ashshur
blasphemed me.
7 Behold, I give a spirit on him,
and he hears a report,
and returns to his own land;
and I fell him by the sword in his own land.
8 And Rab Shaqeh returns,
and finds the sovereign of Ashshur
fighting Libnah:
for he heard that he departed from Lachish:
9 and he heard say
concerning Tirhaqah sovereign of Kush,
He comes to fight you.
And he hears,
and sends angels to Yechizqi Yah, saying,
10 You, say thus to Yechizqi Yah
sovereign of Yah Hudah, saying,
Let not your Elohim, in whom you confide,
deceive you, saying,
Yeru Shalem is not given
into the hand of the sovereign of Ashshur.
11 Behold, thou hast heard
what the *kings* **sovereigns** of *Assyria* **Ashshur**
have *done* **worked** to all lands
by *destroying* **devoting** them *utterly*;
and shalt thou be *delivered* **rescued**?
12 Have the *gods* **elohim** of the *nations* **goyim**
delivered **rescued** them
which my fathers have *destroyed* **ruined**,

as Gozan, and Haran, and *Rezeph* **Reseph**,
and the *children* **sons** of Eden which were in Telassar?
13 Where is the *king* **sovereign** of Hamath,
and the *king* **sovereign** of Arphad,
and the *king* **sovereign**
of the city of *Sepharvaim* **Sepharvayim**,
Hena, and *Ivah* **Avvah**?
14 And *Hesekiah* **Yechizqi Yah**
received **took** the *letter* **scroll**
from the hand of the *messengers* **angels**,
and *read it* **called it out**:
and *Hesekiah went up* **Yechizqi Yah ascended**
unto the house of *the LORD* **Yah Veh**,
and spread it *before the LORD* **at the face of Yah Veh**.
15 And *Hesekiah* **Yechizqi Yah**
prayed unto *the LORD* **Yah Veh**, saying,
16 O *LORD of hosts* **Yah Veh Sabaoth**,
God **Elohim** of *Israel* **Yisra El**,
that *dwellest* **settlest**
between **upon** the *cherubims* **cherubim**,
thou *art the God* **Elohim**, *even* thou alone,
of all the *kingdoms* **sovereigndoms** of the earth:
thou hast *made heaven* **worked the heavens** and earth.
17 *Incline* **Spread** thine ear, O
LORD **Yah Veh**, and hear;
open thine eyes, O *LORD* **Yah Veh**, and see:
and hear all the words of *Sennacherib* **Sancherib**,
which hath sent to reproach the living *God* **Elohim**.
18 *Of a truth* **Truly**, *LORD* **O Yah Veh**,
the *kings* **sovereigns** of *Assyria* **Ashshur**
have *laid waste* **parched** all the *nations* **lands**,
and their *countries* **lands**,
19 And have *cast* **given** their
gods **elohim** into the fire:
for they were no *gods* **elohim**,
but the work of *men's* **human** hands,
wood **timber** and stone:
therefore they have destroyed them.
20 Now therefore, O *LORD*
Yah Veh our *God* **Elohim**,
save us from his hand,
that all the kingdoms of the earth may know that
thou art *the LORD* **Yah Veh**, *even* thou only.
21 Then *Isaiah* **Yesha Yah** the son of *Amoz* **Amos**
sent unto *Hesekiah* **Yechizqi Yah**, saying,
Thus saith
the LORD God **Yah Veh Elohim** of *Israel* **Yisra El**,
Whereas thou hast prayed to me against
Sennacherib **Sancherib**,
king **sovereign** of *Assyria* **Ashshur**:
22 This is the word which *the LORD* **Yah Veh**
hath *spoken* **worded** concerning him;
The virgin, the daughter of *Zion* **Siyon**,
hath despised thee, *and laughed* **ridiculed** thee *to scorn*;
the daughter of *Jerusalem* **Yeru Shalem**
hath shaken her head *at* **behind** thee.
23 Whom hast thou reproached and blasphemed?
and against whom hast thou exalted thy voice,
and lifted up thine eyes on high?
even against the Holy One of *Israel* **Yisra El**.
24 By **the hand of** thy servants
hast thou reproached *the Lord* **Adonay**,
and hast said, By the *multitude*
abundance of my chariots
am I *come up* **ascended** to the height of the mountains,
to the *sides* **flanks** of Lebanon;
and I *will* **shall** cut down
the *tall* **height of the** cedars *thereof*,
and the choice fir trees *thereof*:
and I *will* **shall** enter into the height of his *border* **edge**,
and the forest of his *Carmel* **Karmel/orchard**.
25 I have digged, and drunk water;
and with the sole of my *feet* **steps**
have I *dried up* **parched**
all the rivers of the *besieged places* **rampart**.
11 Behold, you heard what
the sovereigns of Ashshur
worked to all lands by devoting them
—and rescue you?
12 The elohim of the goyim
whom my fathers ruined
—Gozan and Haran and Reseph
and the sons of Eden which were in Telassar
—rescued they them?
13 Where is the sovereign of Hamath?
And the sovereign of Arphad?
And the sovereign of the city of Sepharvayim,
Hena, and Avvah?
14 And Yechizqi Yah
takes the scroll from the hand of the angels,
and calls it out:
and Yechizqi Yah ascends to the house of Yah Veh
and spreads it at the face of Yah Veh:
15 and Yechizqi Yah prays to Yah Veh, saying,
16 O Yah Veh Sabaoth, Elohim of Yisra El,
who settles on the cherubim
—you Elohim—you only
of all the sovereigndoms of the earth;
who worked the heavens and earth:
17 spread your ear, O Yah Veh, and hear;

open your eyes, O Yah Veh, and see:
and hear all the words of Sancherib,
who sent to reproach the living Elohim.
18 Truly, O Yah Veh,
the sovereigns of Ashshur parched all the lands,
and their lands;
19 and gave their elohim into the fire:
for they *are* no elohim
—only the work of human hands, timber and stone:
they destroyed them.
20 And now, O Yah Veh our Elohim,
save us from his hand,
so that all the kingdoms of the earth know
that you are Yah Veh—you only.
21 And Yesha Yah the son of Amos
sends to Yechizqi Yah, saying,
Thus says Yah Veh Elohim of Yisra El,
That which you prayed to me
against Sancherib sovereign of Ashshur,
22 this is the word Yah Veh words concerning him:
The virgin, the daughter of Siyon,
despises you, ridicules you;
the daughter of Yeru Shalem
shakes her head behind you.
23 Whom reproach you? And blaspheme?
And against whom exalt you your voice?
And lift your eyes on high?
Against the Holy One of Yisra El!
24 By the hand of your servants
you reproach Adonay,
and say,
By the abundance of my chariots
I ascend to the height of the mountains
—to the flanks of Lebanon;
and I cut down the height of the cedars
and the choice fir trees:
and I enter the height of his edge
and the forest of his Karmel/orchard:
25 I dig and drink water;
and with the sole of my steps
I parch all the rivers of the rampart.
26 Hast thou not heard *long*
ago **in the distant past**,
how I have *done* **worked** it;
and of ancient *times* **days**, that I have formed it?
now have I brought it to *pass* **become**,
that thou shouldest
be to lay waste *defenced* **fortified** cities
into *ruinous* **desolated** heaps.
27 Therefore their *inhabitants* **settlers**
were *of small power* **short handed**,
they were dismayed and *confounded* **shamed**:
they were as the *grass* **herbage** of the field,
and as the green *herb* **sprouts**,
as the grass on the *housetops* **roofs**,
and as *corn blasted* **the field**
before it be grown up **at the face of the stalks**.
28 But I know thy *abode* **sitting**,
and thy going out, and thy coming in,
and thy *rage* **quaking** against me.
29 Because thy *rage* **quaking** against me,
and thy *tumult* **uproar**,
is come up **ascendeth** into mine ears,
therefore
will I put **I shall set** my hook in thy *nose* **nostrils**,
and my *bridle* **bit** in thy lips,
and I *will* **shall** turn thee back
by the way by which thou camest.
30 And this shall be a sign unto thee,
Ye shall eat this year
such as groweth of itself **the spontaneous growth**;
and the second year
that which springeth of the same
the spontaneous growth:
and in the third year sow ye, and *reap* **harvest**,
and plant vineyards, and eat the fruit *thereof*.
31 And the *remnant* **escapees**
that *is escaped* **survived**
of the house of *Judah* **Yah Hudah**
shall again take root downward,
and *bear* **work** fruit upward:
32 For out of *Jerusalem* **Yeru Shalem** shall go forth *a*
remnant **survivors**, and *they that escape* **the escapees**
out of mount *Zion* **Siyon**:
the zeal of *the LORD of hosts* **Yah Veh Sabaoth**
shall *do* **work** this.
33 Therefore thus saith *the LORD* **Yah Veh**
concerning the *king* **sovereign** of *Assyria* **Ashshur**,
He shall not come into this city,
nor shoot an arrow there,
nor *come before it* **anticipate** with *shields* **buckler**,
nor *cast* **pour** a bank against it.
34 By the way that he came,
by the same shall he return,
and shall not come into this city,
saith the LORD **an oracle of Yah Veh**.
35 For I *will defend* **shall**
garrison this city to save it
for mine own sake, and for my servant David's sake.
36 Then the angel of *the*
LORD **Yah Veh** went forth,
and smote in the camp of *the Assyrians* **Ashshur**

a hundred and *fourscore* **eighty** and five thousand:
and when they *arose* **started** early in the morning,
behold, they were all dead *corpses* **carcases**.
37 So *Sennacherib* **Sancherib,** *king* **sovereign**
of *Assyria* **Ashshur** *departed* **pulled stakes**,
and went and returned, and *dwelt* **settled** at Nineveh.
38 And **so be** it *came to pass*,
as he was *worshipping* **prostrating**
in the house of Nisroch his *god* **elohim**,
that *Adrammelech* **Adram Melech**
and *Sharezer* **Shareser**
his sons smote him with the sword;
and they escaped into the land of *Armenia* **Ararat**:
and *Esarhaddon* **Esar Chaddon** his son
reigned in his stead.

THE HEALING OF YECHIZQI YAH

38 In those days
was *Hesekiah* **Yechizqi Yah** sick unto death.
And *Isaiah* **Yesha Yah** the prophet
the son of *Amoz* **Amos**
came unto him, and said unto him,
Thus saith *the LORD* **Yah Veh**,
Set **Misvah concerning** thine house *in order*:
for thou shalt die, and not live.
26 Heard you not in the distant
past, that I worked it?
Of ancient days, that I formed it?
now I bring it to become,
for you to waste fortified cities into desolate heaps.
27 And their settlers are short handed
—dismayed and shamed
—as the herbage of the field
and as the green sprouts;
as the grass on the roofs
and as the field at the face of the stalks.
28 And I know your sitting
and your coming and your going;
and your quaking against me:
29 because of your quaking against me
your uproar ascends into my ears:
I set my hook in your nostrils and my bit in your lips;
and I turn you back by the way you came.
30 And this is a sign to you,
This year you eat the spontaneous growth;
and the second year the spontaneous growth:
and in the third year you seed and harvest
and plant vineyards and eat the fruit.
31 And the escapees of the house of Yah Hudah
who survive
again take root downward and work fruit upward:
32 for survivors come from Yeru Shalem
and the escapees from mount Siyon: the
zeal of Yah Veh Sabaoth works this.
33 So Yah Veh says thus
concerning the sovereign of Ashshur,
He neither comes into this city,
nor shoots an arrow there;
neither anticipates with buckler,
nor pours a bank against it.
34 By the way he came, by the same he returns,
and comes not into this city
—an oracle of Yah Veh.
35 For I garrison this city to
save it for my own sake
and for sake of my servant David.
36 And the angel of Yah Veh goes
and smites a hundred and eighty—five thousand
in the camp of Ashshur:
and they start early in the morning,
and behold, they are all dead carcases.
37 And Sancherib sovereign
of Ashshur pulls stakes,
and goes and returns and settles at Nineveh.
38 And so be it,
as he prostrates in the house of Nisroch his elohim,
that his sons Adram Melech and Shareser
smite him with the sword;
and they escape into the land of Ararat:
and Esar Chaddon his son reigns in his stead.

THE HEALING OF YECHIZQI YAH

38 In those days
Yechizqi Yah is sick unto death:
and Yesha Yah the prophet the son of Amos
comes to him and says to him,
Thus says Yah Veh,
You, misvah concerning your house:
for you die and live not.
2 Then *Hesekiah* **Yechizqi Yah**
turned his face toward the wall,
and prayed unto *the LORD* **Yah Veh**,
3 And said, Remember *now* **I beseech**,
O *LORD* **Yah Veh**, I beseech thee,
how I have walked *before thee* **at thy face** in truth
and with a *perfect* heart **of shalom**,
and have *done* **worked** that which is good
in thy *sight* **eyes**.
And *Hesekiah* **Yechizqi Yah**
wept *sore* **with great weeping**.

4 Then came the word of *the LORD* **Yah Veh**
to *Isaiah* **Yesha Yah**, saying,
5 Go, and say to *Hesekiah* **Yechizqi Yah**,
Thus saith *the LORD* **Yah Veh**,
the God **Elohim** of David thy father,
I have heard thy prayer, I have seen thy tears:
behold, I *will* **shall** add unto thy days fifteen years.
6 And I *will deliver* **shall rescue** thee and this city
out of the *hand* **palm**
of the *king* **sovereign** of *Assyria* **Ashshur**:
and I *will defend* **shall garrison** this city.
7 And this shall be a sign unto thee
from *the LORD* **Yah Veh**,
that *the LORD* **Yah Veh**
will do **shall work** this *thing* **word**
that he hath *spoken* **worded**;
8 Behold, I *will bring again* **shall turn back**
the shadow of the degrees,
which is *gone down* **descended**
in the sun dial of *Ahaz* **Ach Az**,
ten degrees backward.
So the sun *returned* **turned back** ten degrees,
by which degrees it was *gone down* **descended**.
9 The *writing* **inscribing** of
Hesekiah **Yechizqi Yah,**
king **sovereign** of *Judah* **Yah Hudah**,
when he had been sick,
and *was recovered* **livened** of his sickness:
10 I said in the *cutting off* **severing** of my days,
I shall go to the *gates* **portals** of *the grave* **sheol**:
I am *deprived* **overlooked**
of the *residue* **remnant** of my years.
11 I said, I shall not see *the LORD* **Yah**,
even the LORD—**Yah**, in the land of the living:
I shall *behold man* **scan humanity** no more
with the *inhabitants* **settlers** of the *world* **deceased**.
12 *Mine age is departed*
My generation hath pulled stakes,
and is *removed* **exiled** from me
as a *shepherd's* **tender's** tent:
I have *cut off* **severed** like a weaver my life:
he *will cut me off* **shall clip me**
with pining sickness **from the thrum**:
from day *even* to night
wilt **shalt** thou *make an end of* **shalam** me.
13 I *reckoned* **equated** till morning, *that,*
as a lion, so *will* **shall** he break all my bones:
from day *even* to night
wilt **shalt** thou *make an end of* **shalam** me.
14 Like a *crane* **horse** or a swallow,
so did I chatter **thus I chirped**:
I *did mourn* **cooed** as a dove:
mine eyes *fail with looking upward* **languish on high**:
O *LORD* **Yah Veh**, I am oppressed;
undertake for me **be my pledge**.
15 What shall I *say* **word**?
he hath *both spoken* **said** unto me, and
himself hath *done* **worked** *it*:
I shall *go softly* **walk gently** all my years
in the bitterness of my soul.
16 *O Lord* **Adonay**, by these *things men live* **is life**,
and in all these *things* is the life of my spirit:
so *wilt* **shalt** thou *recover* **fatten** me,
and *make me to live* **enliven me**.
17 Behold,
for *peace* **shalom**
I *had great bitterness* **was bitterly embittered**:
but thou hast in *love* **being attached** to my soul
delivered it from the pit of *corruption* **ruin**:
2 And Yechizqi Yah turns
his face toward the wall,
and prays to Yah Veh,
3 and says, Remember, I beseech;
O Yah Veh, I beseech you,
how I walked at your face in truth
and with a heart of shalom,
and worked what *is* good in your eyes.
—and Yechizqi Yah weeps with great weeping.
4 And the word of Yah Veh comes to Yesha Yah,
saying,
5 Go, and say to Yechizqi Yah,
Thus says Yah Veh, Elohim of David your father,
I hear your prayer; I see your tears:
behold, I add to your days fifteen years:
6 and I rescue you and this city
from the palm of the sovereign of Ashshur;
and I garrison this city:
7 and this *is* a sign to you from Yah Veh,
that Yah Veh works this word he worded:
8 Behold, I turn back the shadow of the degrees
which descends in the sun dial of Ach Az
ten degrees backward.
—thus the sun turns back ten degrees,
by which degrees it had descended.
9 The inscribing
of Yechizqi Yah sovereign of Yah Hudah,
concerning his sickness,
when he enlivened from his sickness:
10 I—I say, in the severing of my days,
I go to the portals of sheol:
I overlooked the remnant of my years.
11 I say, I see not Yah—Yah
in the land of the living:

I scan humanity no more
with the settlers of the deceased.
12 My generation pulls stakes
and exiles from me as the tent of a tender:
my life—severed as a weaver:
he clips me from the thrum:
from day to night you shalam me:
13 I equate until morning;
as a lion, thus he breaks all my bones:
from day to night you shalam me.
14 As a horse or a swallow, thus I chirp:
I coo as a dove: my eyes languish on high: O
Yah Veh, I am oppressed; be my pledge.
15 What word I?
He says to me and he works:
I walk gently all my years in the bitterness of my soul.
16 Adonay, by these is life,
and in all these is the life of my spirit:
thus you fatten me and enliven me.
17 Behold,
for shalom I was bitterly embittered:
and you attached to my soul from the pit of ruin:
for thou hast cast all my sins behind thy back.
18 For *the grave* **sheol**
cannot praise **spreadeth not hands unto** thee,
death *can not celebrate* **halaleth** thee **not**:
they that *go down* **descend** into the *pit* **well**
cannot hope for **shall not expect** thy truth.
19 The living, the living,
he shall *praise* **spread hands unto** thee,
as I *do* this day:
the father to the *children* **sons**
shall make known thy truth.
20 *The LORD* **Yah Veh** was ready to save me:
therefore we *will sing* **shall strum**
my *songs to the stringed instruments* **strummings**
all the days of our life
in the house of *the LORD* **Yah Veh**.
21 For *Isaiah* **Yesha Yah** had said,
Let them *take* **bear** a lump of figs,
and *lay it for a plaister* **massage it** upon the *boil* **ulcer**,
and he shall *recover* **live**.
22 *Hesekiah* **Yechizqi Yah** also had said,
What is the sign that I shall *go up* **ascend**
to the house of *the LORD* **Yah Veh**?

The Visitors From Babel

39 At that time *Merodachbaladan*
Merodach Bel Adoni,
the son of *Baladan* **Bel Adoni**,
king **sovereign** of *Babylon* **Babel**,
sent *letters* **scrolls** and *a present* **an offering**
to *Hesekiah* **Yechizqi Yah**:
for he had heard that he had been sick,
and *was recovered* **strengthened**.
2 And *Hesekiah* **Yechizqi Yah**
was glad of **cheered over** them,
and *shewed* **had** them **see**
the house of his *precious things* **spicery**,
the silver, and the gold, and the spices,
and the *precious* **good** ointment,
and all the house of his *armour* **instruments**,
and all that was found in his treasures:
there was *nothing* **no word** in his house,
nor in all his *dominion* **reign**,
that *Hesekiah shewed* **Yechizqi Yah had** them not **see**.
3 Then came *Isaiah* **Yesha Yah** the prophet
unto *king Hesekiah* **sovereign Yechizqi Yah**,
and said unto him, What said these men?
and from whence came they unto thee?
And *Hesekiah* **Yechizqi Yah** said,
They are come from a far *country* **land** unto me,
even from *Babylon* **Babel**.
4 Then said he, What have
they seen in thine house?
And *Hesekiah answered* **Yechizqi Yah said**,
All that is in mine house have they seen:
there is *nothing* **no word** among my treasures
that I *have not shewed them* **had them not see**.
5 Then said *Isaiah* **Yesha Yah**
to *Hesekiah* **Yechizqi Yah**,
Hear the word of *the LORD of hosts* **Yah Veh Sabaoth**:
6 Behold, the days come, that
all that is in thine house,
and that which thy fathers have
laid up in store **treasured**
until this day,
shall be *carried* **lifted** to *Babylon* **Babel**:
nothing **no word** shall *be left* **remain**,
saith *the LORD* **Yah Veh**.
7 And of thy sons that shall issue from thee,
which thou shalt *beget* **birth**, shall they take away;
and they shall be eunuchs in the *palace* **manse**
of the *king* **sovereign** of *Babylon* **Babel**.
8 Then said *Hesekiah* **Yechizqi**
Yah to *Isaiah* **Yesha Yah**,
Good is the word of *the LORD* **Yah Veh**
which thou hast spoken.
He said *moreover*,
For there shall be *peace* **shalom** and truth in my days.

THE SIGH OF ELOHIM

40 *Comfort* **Sigh** ye, *comfort*
ye **sigh ye over** my people,
saith your *God* **Elohim**.
2 *Speak ye comfortably to Jerusalem*
Word ye to the heart of Yeru Shalem,
and *cry* **call out** unto her,
that her *warfare* **hostility** is *accomplished* **fulfilled**,
that her *iniquity* **perversity** is *pardoned* **satisfied**:
for you cast all my sins behind your back.
18 For neither sheol spreads hands to you,
nor death halals you:
they who descend into the well expect not your truth.
19 The living—the living,
he spreads hands to you, as I this day:
the father makes known your truth to the sons.
20 Yah Veh—ready to save me:
so we strum my strummings
all the days of our life in the house of Yah Veh.
21 For Yesha Yah says,
Let them bear a lump of figs
and massage it on the ulcer, and live.
22 And Yechizqi Yah says,
What *is* the sign
that I ascend to the house of Yah Veh?

THE VISITORS FROM BABEL

39 At that time Merodach Bel Adoni
the son of Bel Adoni sovereign of Babel,
sends scrolls and an offering to Yechizqi Yah:
for he hears he *is* sick—and strengthens.
2 And Yechizqi Yah cheers over them,
and they see the house of his spicery
—the silver and the gold and the spices
and the good ointment
and all the house of his instruments
and all they find in his treasures:
there *is* no word in his house and in all his reign
that Yechizqi Yah has them not see.
3 Then Yesha Yah the prophet
comes to sovereign Yechizqi Yah,
and says to him,
What say these men?
and, Whence come they to you?
And Yechizqi Yah says,
They come to me from a land afar—from Babel.
4 And he says, What saw they in your house?
And Yechizqi Yah says,
All that *is* in my house they saw:
there is no word among my treasures
that I had them not see.
5 And Yesha Yah says to Yechizqi Yah,
Hear the word of Yah Veh Sabaoth:
6 Behold, days come, that all that *is* in your house,
and what your fathers treasured until this day,
is lifted to Babel:
no word remains, says Yah Veh.
7 And of your sons who issue from you,
whom you birthed, they take away
to become eunuchs
in the manse of the sovereign of Babel.
8 And Yechizqi Yah says to Yesha Yah,
Good *is* the word of Yah Veh which you speak.
and he says,
For shalom and truth become in my days.

THE SIGH OF ELOHIM

40 You, sigh—sigh over my people,
says your Elohim.
2 Word to the heart of Yeru Shalem
and call out to her
that her hostility is fulfilled
—that her perversity is satisfied:
for she hath *received* **taken**
of *the LORD'S* **Yah Veh's** hand double for all her sins.
3 The voice of him that crieth in the wilderness,
Prepare **Face** ye the way of *the LORD* **Yah Veh**,
make straight **straighten** in the *desert* **plain**
a highway for our *God* **Elohim**.
4 Every valley shall be *exalted* **lifted**,
and every mountain and hill shall be *made low* **lowered**:
and the crooked shall be *made straight* **straightened**,
and the *rough places plain* **ridges a plain valley**:
5 And the *glory* **honour** of *the LORD* **Yah Veh**
shall be *revealed* **exposed**,
and all flesh shall see it together:
for the mouth of *the LORD* **Yah Veh**
hath *spoken* **worded** it.
6 The voice said, *Cry* **Call**.
And he said, What shall I *cry* **call**?
All flesh is grass, and all the *goodliness* **mercy** *thereof*
is as the *flower* **blossom** of the field:
7 The grass withereth,
the *flower fadeth* **blossom withereth**:
because the spirit of *the LORD* **Yah Veh** bloweth upon it:
surely the people is grass.
8 The grass withereth,
the *flower fadeth* **blossom withereth**:
but the word of our *God* **Elohim**

shall *stand for ever* **rise eternally.**
9 O *Zion* **Siyon**, that *bringest*
good tidings **evangelizest,**
get **ascend** thee *up* into the high mountain;
O *Jerusalem* **Yeru Shalem,**
that *bringest good tidings* **evangelizest,**
lift up thy voice with *strength* **force;**
lift *it up, be* **awe** not *afraid;*
say unto the cities of *Judah* **Yah Hudah,**
Behold your *God* **Elohim!**
10 Behold, *the Lord GOD* **Adonay Yah Veh**
will **shall** come with *strong hand* **strength,**
and his arm shall *rule* **reign** for him:
behold, his *reward* **hire** is with him,
and his *work before him* **deeds at his face.**
11 He shall *feed* **tend** his *flock* **drove**
like a *shepherd* **tender:**
he shall gather the lambs with his arm,
and *carry* **bear** them in his bosom,
and shall gently *lead* **guide**
those that *are with young* **suckle.**
12 Who hath measured the waters
in *the hollow of his hand* **his palm,**
and *meted out heaven* **gauged the heavens**
with the span,
and *comprehended* **contained** the dust of the earth
in a *measure* **tierce,**
and weighed the mountains in *scales* **weights,**
and the hills in a balance?
13 Who hath *directed* **gauged**
the Spirit of *the LORD* **Yah Veh,**
or being his *counsellor* **councilman**
hath *taught* **made known to** him?
14 With whom *took he counsel* **counselled he,**
and *who instructed* **had** him **discern,**
and taught him in the path of judgment,
and taught him knowledge,
and *shewed* **made known** to him
the way of *understanding* **discernment?**
15 Behold,
the *nations* **goyim** are as a drop of a *bucket* **pail,**
and are *counted* **fabricated**
as the *small dust* **powder** of the balance:
behold, he *taketh up* **lifteth** the *isles* **islands**
as *a very little thing* **pulverized.**
16 And Lebanon is not sufficient to burn,
nor the *beasts* **live beings** *thereof* sufficient
for a *burnt offering* **holocaust.**
17 All *nations* **goyim**
before him are as nothing **are as naught in front of** him;
and they are *counted* **fabricated** to him
less than nothing **as deceased**, and *vanity* **waste.**
18 To whom then *will* **shall** ye liken *God* **El?**
or what likeness *will* **shall** ye *compare* **line up** unto him?

for she takes double
of the hand of Yah Veh for all her sins.
3 The voice of him crying out in the wilderness,
You, face the way of Yah Veh,
straighten in the plain a highway for our Elohim
4 —every valley becomes lifted
and every mountain and hill lowered:
and the crooked straightened
and the ridges become a plain valley:
5 and the honor of Yah Veh *is* exposed
and all flesh sees it together:
for the mouth of Yah Veh words it.
6 A voice says, Call.
And he says, What call I?
All flesh *is* grass
and all the mercy as the blossom of the field:
7 the grass withers; the blossom withers:
because the spirit of Yah Veh blows thereon:
surely the people *is* grass.
8 the grass withers; the blossom withers:
but the word of our Elohim rises eternally.
9 O Siyon, who evangelizes,
ascend into the high mountain;
O Yeru Shalem, who evangelizes,
lift your voice with force;
lift; awe not:
say to the cities of Yah Hudah,
Behold your Elohim!
10 Behold, Adonay Yah Veh comes with strength
and his arm reigns for him:
behold, his hire is with him,
and his deeds are at his face.
11 He tends his drove as a tender:
he gathers the lambs with his arm,
and bears them in his bosom,
and gently guides the suckling.
12 Who measures the waters in his palm?
And gauges the heavens with the span?
And contains the dust of the earth in a tierce?
And weighs the mountains in weights
and the hills in a balance?
13 Who gauges the Spirit of Yah Veh?
Or as his councilman makes known to him?
14 With whom counsels he and discerns him?
And teaches him in the path of judgment?
And teaches him knowledge?

And makes known to him the way of discernment?
15 Behold, the goyim—as a drop of a pail;
fabricated as the powder of the balance:
behold, he lifts the islands as pulverized.
16 And neither is Lebanon sufficient to burn,
nor the live beings sufficient for a holocaust.
17 All goyim are as naught in front of him;
—fabricated to him as deceased and waste.
18 To whom then liken you El?
Or what likeness line you up to him?
19 The *workman* **engraver**
melteth **poureth** a *graven image* **sculptile**,
and the *goldsmith* **refiner**
spreadeth it over **overlayeth** with gold,
and *casteth* **refineth** silver chains.
20 He that is so *impoverished* **cut off**
that he hath no *oblation* **exaltment**
chooseth a tree that *will* **shall** not rot;
he seeketh unto him a *cunning workman* **wise engraver**
to prepare a *graven image* **sculptile**,
that shall not *be moved* **topple**.
21 Have ye not known? have ye not heard?
hath it not been told you from the beginning?
have ye not *understood* **discerned**
from the foundations of the earth?
22 It is he that *sitteth* **settleth**
upon the circle of the earth,
and the *inhabitants* **settlers** *thereof*
are as *grasshoppers* **locusts**;
that *stretcheth out* **spreadeth** the
heavens as a *curtain* **veil**,
and spreadeth them out as a tent to *dwell* **settle** in:
23 That *bringeth* **giveth** the *princes* **potentates**
to *nothing* **naught**;
he *maketh* **worketh** the judges of the earth
as *vanity* **waste**.
24 Yea, they shall not be planted;
yea, they shall not be *sown* **seeded**:
yea, their *stock* **stump** shall not *take* root in the earth:
and he shall also *blow* **puff** upon them,
and they shall wither,
and the *whirlwind* **storm**
shall *take* **bear** them away as stubble.
25 To whom then *will* **shall** ye liken me,
or *shall I be equal* **equate**? saith the Holy One.
26 Lift up your eyes on high,
and *behold* **see** who hath created these *things*,
that bringeth out their host by number:
he calleth them all by names
by the greatness of his *might* **strength**,
for that he is strong in *power* **force**;
not one faileth **no man lacketh**.
27 Why sayest thou, O *Jacob* **Yaaqov**,
and *speakest* **wordest,** O *Israel* **Yisra El**,
My way is hid from *the LORD* **Yah Veh**,
and my judgment is passed over from my *God* **Elohim**?
28 Hast thou not known? hast thou not heard,
that the *everlasting God* **eternal Elohim**,
the LORD **Yah Veh**, the Creator of the ends of the earth,
fainteth **wearieth** not, neither *is weary* **belaboureth**?
there is no *searching* **probing**
of his *understanding* **discernment**.
29 He giveth *power* **strength** to the *faint* **weary**;
and to them that have no *might* **strength** he
increaseth strength **aboundeth might**.
30 Even the *youths* **lads**
shall *faint* **weary** and *be weary* **belabour**,
and **in faltering,**
the *young men* **youths** shall *utterly fall* **falter**:
31 But they that *wait upon*
the LORD **await Yah Veh**
shall *renew* **change** their *strength* **force**;
they shall *mount up* **ascend** with *wings* **pinions** as eagles;
they shall run, and not *be weary* **belabour**;
and they shall walk, and not *faint* **weary**.

THE FIRST AND THE FINAL

41 *Keep silence before* **Hush**
in front of me, O islands;
and let the *people* **nations**
renew **change** their *strength* **force**:
let them come near; then let them *speak* **word**:
let us *come near* **approach** together to judgment.
2 Who *raised up* **wakened** the *righteous man* **just**
from the *east* **rising**,
called him to his foot,
gave the *nations before him* **goyim at his face**,
and *made* **had** him *rule over kings* **subjugate sovereigns**?
he gave them as the dust to his sword,
and as *driven* **disbursed** stubble to his bow.
3 He pursued them, and passed *safely* **in shalom**;
even by the way that he had not gone with his feet.
4 Who hath *wrought* **made** and *done* **worked** it,
calling the generations from the beginning?
19 The engraver pours a sculptile;
and the refiner overlays with gold
and refines silver chains.
20 He who is so cut off that he has no exaltment
chooses a tree that rots not;
he seeks a wise engraver

to prepare a sculptile that topples not.
21 Know you not? Hear you not?
Were you not told from the beginning?
Discerned you not from the foundations of the earth?
22 It *is* he who settles on the circle of the earth,
and the settlers are as locusts
who spread the heavens as a veil,—
spreads them as a tent to settle in:
23 who gives the potentates to naught;
who works the judges of the earth as waste.
24 Yes, they are not planted;
yes, they are not seeded:
yes, their stump roots not in the earth:
and he also puffs on them, and they wither,
and the storm bears them away as stubble.
25 To whom then liken you me, or equate?
says the Holy One.
26 Lift your eyes on high, and
see who created these;
who brings out their host by number:
—calls them all by names
by the greatness of his strength
—for he is strong in force;
no man lacks.
27 Why, O Yaaqov, say you,
and, O Yisra El, word you,
My way is hid from Yah Veh;
and from my Elohim my judgment passes over?
28 Know you not? Hear you not?
that the eternal Elohim,
Yah Veh, the Creator of the ends of the earth
neither wearies nor belabors?
There is no probing of his discernment.
29 He gives strength to the weary;
and to them of no strength, he abounds might.
30 Even the lads weary and belabor,
and in faltering, the youths falter:
31 but they who await Yah Veh, change their force;
they ascend with pinions as eagles;
they run, and belabor not;
and they walk, and weary not.

THE FIRST AND THE FINAL

41 Hush in front of me, O islands.
The nations change their force:
they come near; then they word:
we approach judgment together.
2 Who wakens the just from the rising?
He calls him at his foot
gives the goyim at his face
and subjugates sovereigns:
he gives *them* as the dust to his sword
and as disbursed stubble to his bow:
3 he pursues them; he passes in shalom;
he goes not by the way with his feet.
4 Who made it and worked it
—calling the generations from the beginning?
I *the LORD* **Yah Veh**, the first, and *with* the *last* **final**;
I am he.
5 The *isles* **islands** saw it, and *feared* **awed**;
the ends of the earth *were afraid* **trembled**,
drew near **approached**, and came.
6 They helped every *one*
man his *neighbour* **friend**;
and *every one* said to his brother, *Be of good* courage.
7 So the *carpenter* **engraver**
encouraged **strengthened** the *goldsmith* **refiner**,
and he that smootheth with the hammer
him that *smote* **hammered** the anvil, saying,
It is *ready for the sodering* **good to be joined**:
and he *fastened* **strengthened** it with nails,
that it should not *be moved* **topple**.
8 But thou, *Israel* **Yisra El**, art my servant,
Jacob **Yaaqov** whom I have chosen, the
seed of Abraham my *friend* **beloved**.
9 Thou whom I have *taken* **strengthened**
from the ends of the earth,
and called thee from the *chief men* **nobles** *thereof*,
and said unto thee, Thou art my servant;
I have chosen thee, and not *cast* **spurned** thee *away*.
10 *Fear* **Awe** thou not; for I am with thee:
be not dismayed **look not around**;
for I am thy *God* **Elohim**:
I *will* **shall** strengthen thee; yea, I *will* **shall** help thee;
yea, I *will* **shall** uphold thee
with the right *hand* of my *righteousness* **justness**.
11 Behold,
all they that were *incensed* **inflamed** against thee
shall be *ashamed* **shamed** and confounded:
they shall be as *nothing* **naught**;
and *they that strive with thee* **the men of thy strife**
shall *perish* **destruct**.
12 Thou shalt seek them, and shalt not find them,
even them that contended **the men of contention**
with thee:
they **the men** that war against thee
shall be as *nothing* **deceased**, and as
a thing of *nought* **naught**.
13 For I *the LORD* **Yah Veh** thy *God* **Elohim**
will **shall** hold thy right *hand*, saying unto
thee, *Fear* **Awe** not; I *will* **shall** help thee.

14 *Fear* **Awe** not, thou *worm Jacob* **maggot Yaaqov**,
and ye men of *Israel* **Yisra El**; I *will* **shall** help thee,
saith the LORD **an oracle of Yah Veh**,
and thy redeemer, the Holy One of *Israel* **Yisra El**.
15 Behold, I *will make* **shall set** thee
a new *sharp* **sickle** threshing *instrument* **sledge**
having **a master of** teeth:
thou shalt thresh the mountains,
and *beat* **pulverize** them *small*,
and shalt *make* **set** the hills as chaff.
16 Thou shalt *fan* **winnow** them,
and the wind shall *carry* **bear** them away,
and the *whirlwind* **storm** shall scatter them:
and thou shalt *rejoice* **twirl** in *the LORD* **Yah Veh**,
and *shalt glory* **shall halal** in the
Holy One of *Israel* **Yisra El**.
17 When the *poor* **humble** and needy seek water,
and there is none,
and their tongue *faileth* **drieth** for thirst,
I *the LORD will hear* **Yah Veh shall answer** them,
I *the God* **Elohim** of *Israel* **Yisra El**
will **shall** not forsake them.
18 I *will* **shall** open rivers in
high places **the barrens**,
and fountains in the midst of the valleys:
I *will make* **shall set** the wilderness
a *pool* **marsh** of water,
and the *dry land* **land of parch** springs of water.
19 I *will plant* **shall give** in
the wilderness the cedar,
the shittah tree, and the myrtle, and the oil tree;
I *will* **shall** set in the *desert* **plain** the fir tree,
and the *pine* **oak**, and the *box tree* **cedar** together:
20 That they may see, and know,
and *consider* **set**, and *understand* **comprehend** together,
that the hand of *the LORD* **Yah Veh**
hath *done* **worked** this,
and the Holy One of *Israel* **Yisra El** hath created it.
21 *Produce* **Approach with** your *cause* **plea**,
saith *the LORD* **Yah Veh**;
bring forth your *strong reasons* **mights**,
saith the *King* **Sovereign** of *Jacob* **Yaaqov**.
I Yah Veh, the first, and the final;
I *am* he.
5 The islands see and awe;
the ends of the earth tremble,
they approach; yes, they come.
6 Every man helps his friend;
and says to his brother, Courage!
7 And the engraver strengthens the refiner,
and him who smoothes with the hammer
and him who hammers the anvil, saying,
Good to join/unite:
and he strengthens it with nails, that it topple not.
8 And you, Yisra El—my servant,
Yaaqov whom I chose,
the seed of Abraham my beloved,
9 whom I strengthened from the ends of the earth
and called you from the nobles,
and I said to you, You are my servant;
I chose you and spurned you not:
10 awe not; for I *am* with you:
look not around; for I *am* your Elohim:
I strengthen you; yes, I help you;
yes, I uphold you with the right of my justness.
11 Behold,
all who inflame against you shame and confound:
they become as naught;
and the men who strive with you destruct.
12 You seek them, and find them not
—these men who contend with you:
these men who war against you
are as deceased and as of naught.
13 For I, Yah Veh your Elohim, hold your right,
saying to you, Awe not; I help you.
14 Awe not, you maggot Yaaqov,
and you men of Yisra El; I help you
—an oracle of Yah Veh
your redeemer, the Holy One of Yisra El.
15 Behold, I set you for a new
sickle threshing sledge
having a master of teeth:
you thresh the mountains and pulverize them
and set the hills as chaff:
16 you winnow them
and the wind bears them away
and the storm scatters them:
and you twirl in Yah Veh,
and halal in the Holy One of Yisra El.
17 The humble and needy seek water
and there is none;
and their tongue dries for thirst
and I Yah Veh answer them;
I Elohim of Yisra El forsake them not.
18 I open rivers in the barrens
and fountains midst the valleys:
I set the wilderness a marsh of water
and the land of parch springs of water.
19 In the wilderness I give the cedar
—the shittah tree and the myrtle and the oil tree;
in the plain I set the fir tree
and the oak and the cedar together:

20 that they see and know and set
and comprehend together
that the hand of Yah Veh worked this
and the Holy One of Yisra El created it.
21 Approach with your plea, says Yah Veh;
bring forth your mights, says the Sovereign of Yaaqov.
22 Let them bring *them* forth,
and *shew* **tell** us what shall happen:
let them *shew* **tell** the former *things*, what they be,
that we may *consider* **set our heart on** them,
and know the latter end of them;
or
declare us things for to come **let us hear of the coming.**
23 *Shew the things* **Tell those**
that are to come *hereafter* **afterward**,
that we may know that ye are *gods* **elohim**:
yea, *do good* **well—please**, or *do evil* **vilify**,
that we may *be dismayed* **look around**,
and *behold* **see** it together.
24 Behold, ye are of *nothing* **naught**,
and your *work of nought* **deeds a hissing**:
an *abomination* **abhorrence** is he that chooseth you.
25 I have *raised up* **wakened** *one* from the north,
and he shall come:
from the rising of the sun shall he call upon my name:
and he shall come upon *princes* **prefects** as *upon* morter,
and as the *potter treadeth clay* **former trampleth mire.**
26 Who hath *declared* **told** from the beginning,
that we may know?
and *beforetime* **from the face**,
that we may say, *He is righteous* **Just?**
yea, there is none that *sheweth* **telleth**,
yea, there is none that *declareth* **hearkeneth**,
yea, there is none that heareth your *words* **sayings.**
27 *The first shall say to Zion* **First to Siyon**,
Behold, behold them:
and I *will* **shall** give to *Jerusalem* **Yeru Shalem**
one that *bringeth good tidings* **evangelizeth.**
28 For I *beheld* **saw**, and there was no man;
even among them, and there was no counsellor,
that, when I asked of them, could *answer a* **return** word.
29 Behold, they are all *vanity* **mischief**;
their works *are nothing* **ceased**:
their *molten images* **libations**
are wind and *confusion* **waste.**

THE SERVANT OF YAH VEH

42 Behold my servant, whom I uphold;
mine elect **my chosen**,
in whom my soul *delighteth* **is pleased**;
I have *put* **given** my spirit upon him:
he shall bring forth judgment to the *Gentiles* **goyim.**
2 He shall not cry, nor lift *up*,
nor cause his voice to be heard in the *street* **outway.**
3 A *bruised reed* **crushed stalk** shall he not break,
and the smoking flax shall he not quench: he
shall bring forth judgment unto truth.
4 He shall not *fail* **dim** nor *be discouraged* **crush**,
till he have set judgment in the earth:
and the *isles* **islands** shall *wait for* **await** his *law* **torah.**
5 Thus saith *God the LORD* **El Yah Veh**,
he that created the heavens, and
stretched **spread** them *out*;
he that *spread forth* **expanded** the earth,
and *that which cometh out of it* **its offspring**;
he that giveth breath unto the people upon it,
and spirit to them that walk therein:
6 I *the LORD* **Yah Veh**
have called thee in *righteousness* **justness**,
and *will* **shall** hold thine hand,
and *will keep* **shall guard** thee,
and give thee for a covenant of the people,
for a light of the *Gentiles* **goyim**;
7 To open the blind eyes,
to bring out the *prisoners* **bound**
from the *prison* **lock up**,
and them that sit in darkness out of the prison house.
8 I am *the LORD* **Yah Veh**: that is my name:
and my *glory will* **honour shall** I not give to another,
neither my *praise* **halal** to *graven images* **sculptiles.**
9 Behold,
the former *things are come to pass* **have become**,
and **the** new *things do I declare* **I tell**:
before **ere** they *spring forth* **sprout**
I *tell you* **let you hear** of them.

SING AND HALAL TO YAH VEH

10 Sing unto *the LORD* **Yah Veh** a new song,
and his *praise* **halal** from the end of the earth,
22 They bring forth, and tell us what happened:
—the former, what they *are*,
to set our heart on them,
and know the latter end of them;
or have us hear of the coming.
23 Tell us what comes afterward,
so that we know you are elohim:
yes, well—please, or vilify,
so that we look around and see it together.
24 Behold, you *are* of naught,
and your deeds a hissing:

an abhorrence to him who chooses you.
25 I waken from the north, and he comes;
from the rising of the sun, he calls on my name:
and he comes on prefects as morter,
and as the former tramples mire.
26 Who told from the beginning, so that we know?
and from the face, so that we say, Just?
Yes, there is no one who tells;
yes, there is no one who hearkens;
yes, there is no one who hears your sayings.
27 First to Siyon,
Behold! Behold them:
and I give to Yeru Shalem one who evangelizes.
28 For I see, and there is no man;
yes, there is no counsellor among them,
who, when I ask them, return word.
29 Behold, they are all mischief;
their works cease:
their libations *are* wind and waste.

The Servant Of Yah Veh

42 Behold my servant, whom I uphold;
my chosen, in whom my soul *is* pleased:
I give my spirit on him;
he brings judgment to the goyim:
2 he neither cries, nor lifts,
nor has his voice heard in the outway:
3 he neither breaks a crushed stalk nor quenches he
the smoking flax; he brings forth judgment to truth:
4 he neither dims nor crushes
until he sets judgment in the earth:
and the islands await his torah.
5 Thus says El Yah Veh,
who created the heavens and spread them;
who expanded the earth and its offspring;
who gave breath to the people thereon,
and spirit to them who walk therein:
6 I Yah Veh call you in justness
and hold your hand and guard you;
and give you for a covenant of the people
and a light of the goyim:
7 to open the eyes of the blind;
to bring the bound from the lock up;
those sitting in darkness from the prison house.
8 I—Yah Veh: that is my name:
and I neither give my honor to another,
nor my halal to sculptiles.
9 Behold, the former becomes, and the new I tell:
ere they sprout, I have you hear of them.

Sing And Halal To Yah Veh

10 Sing to Yah Veh a new song
and his halal from the end of the earth;
ye that *go down* **descend** to the sea,
and *all that is therein* **its fulness**;
the *isles* **islands**, and the *inhabitants* **settlers** *thereof.*
11 Let the wilderness and the cities *thereof*
lift *up their voice*,
the *villages* **courts** that *Kedar* **Qedar** doth *inhabit* **settle**:
let the *inhabitants* **settlers** of the rock *sing* **shout**,
let them shout from the top of the mountains.
12 Let them *give glory* **set honour**
unto *the LORD* **Yah Veh**,
and *declare* **tell** his *praise* **halal** in the islands.
13 *The LORD* **Yah Veh** shall
go forth as *a* mighty *man*,
he shall *stir up* **waken** jealousy like a man of war:
he shall *cry* **shout**, yea, *roar* **whoop**;
he shall prevail **mightily** against his enemies.
14 I have *long time holden my*
peace **eternally hushed**;
I have *been still* **hushed**, and refrained myself:
now will **shall** I *cry* **scream**
like a *travailing* **birthing** woman;
I *will destroy* **shall puff**
and *devour at once* **gulp altogether**.
15 I *will make waste* **shall parch**
the mountains and hills,
and *dry up* **wither** all their herbs;
and I *will make* **shall set** the rivers islands,
and I *will dry up* **shall wither** the *pools* **marshes**.
16 And I *will bring* **shall carry** the blind
by a way that they knew not;
I *will lead* **shall tread** them
in paths that they have not known:
I *will make* **shall set** darkness light
before them **at their face**,
and crooked *things* straight.
These *things will* **words shall** I *do* **work** unto them,
and not forsake them.
17 They shall *be turned back* **apostatize backward**,
they shall *be greatly ashamed* **shamingly shame**,
that *trust* **confide** in *graven images* **sculptiles**,
that say to the *molten images* **moltens**,
Ye *are* our *gods* **elohim**.
18 Hear, ye deaf; and look,
ye blind, that ye may see.
19 Who is blind, but my servant?
or deaf, as my *messenger* **angel** that I sent?
who is blind as he that *is perfect* **shalams**

and blind as *the LORD'S* **Yah Veh's** servant?
20 Seeing *many things* **much**,
but thou *observest* **guardest** not;
opening the ears, but he heareth not.
21 *The LORD is well pleased* **Yah Veh delighteth**
for his *righteousness'* **justness'** sake;
he *will magnify* **shall greaten** the *law* **torah**,
and make it honourable **mightily**.
22 But this is a people
robbed **plundered** and *spoiled* **plundered**;
they are all of them **all their youths are** snared *in holes*,
and they are hid in prison houses:
they are for a *prey* **plunder**,
and none *delivereth* **rescueth**;
for a *spoil* **plunder**, and none saith, Restore.
23 Who among you
will give ear to **shall hearken unto** this?
who *will* **shall** hearken
and hear *for the time to come* **afterward**?
24 Who gave *Jacob* **Yaaqov** for a *spoil* **plunder**,
and *Israel* **Yisra El** to the *robbers* **plunderers**?
did not *the LORD* **Yah Veh**,
he against whom we have sinned?
for they *would* **willed to** not walk in his ways,
neither *were* **hearkened** they
obedient unto his *law* **torah**.
25 Therefore he hath poured upon him
the fury of his *anger* **wrath**,
and the strength of *battle* **war**:
and it hath *set* **inflamed** him on fire round about,
yet he knew not;
and it burned him, yet he *laid* **set** it not to heart.

YAH VEH, THE REDEEMER

43 But now thus saith *the LORD* **Yah Veh**
that created thee, O *Jacob* **Yaaqov**,
and he that formed thee, O *Israel* **Yisra El**,
you who descend to the sea, and its fulness;
the islands, and the settlers.
11 The wilderness and the cities lift,
Qedar settles the courts:
the settlers of the rock shout;
they shout from the top of the mountains:
12 they set honor to Yah Veh
and tell his halal in the islands:
13 Yah Veh goes forth as mighty;
he wakens jealousy as a man of war:
he shouts! Yes, whoops!
He prevails mightily against his enemies.
14 I hush eternally;
I hush and refrain myself:
I scream as a birthing woman;
I puff and gulp together:
15 I parch the mountains and hills
and I wither all their herbs;
and I set the rivers islands
and I wither the marshes:
16 and I carry the blind by a way they know not;
I tread them in paths they know not:
I set darkness light at their face
and crooked straight:
I work these words to them and forsake them not.
17 They apostatize backward
shamingly they shame
—who confide in sculptiles,
—who say to the moltens,
You *are* our elohim.
18 Hear, you deaf!
And look, you blind, and see!
19 Who is blind, but my servant?
Or deaf, as my angel whom I send?
Who is blind as he who shalams
yes, blind as the servant of Yah Veh?
20 Seeing much, you guard not;
opening ears, but he hears not.
21 Yah Veh delights for sake of his justness;
he greatens the torah mightily.
22 And this is a people plundered and plundered;
all their youths are snared—hidden in prison houses;
they are for a plunder, and no one rescues;
for a plunder, and no one says, Restore.
23 Who among you hearkens to this?
Who hearkens and hears afterward?
24 Who gave Yaaqov for a plunder?
And Yisra El to the plunderers?
Is it not Yah Veh, against whom we sinned?
Yes, they will neither to walk in his ways,
nor hearken to his torah.
25 So he pours on him
the fury of his wrath and the strength of war:
and it inflames him on fire round about,
yet he knows it not;
and it burns him,
yet he sets it not to heart.

YAH VEH, THE REDEEMER

43 And now thus says Yah Veh
who created you, O Yaaqov,
and he who formed you, O Yisra El,
Fear **Awe** not: for I have redeemed thee,

I have called *thee by* thy name; thou art mine.
2 When thou passest through the waters,
I *will* **shall** be with thee;
and through the rivers, they shall not overflow thee:
when thou walkest through the fire,
thou shalt not *be burned* **blister**;
neither shall the flame *kindle* **burn** upon thee.
3 For I am *the LORD* **Yah Veh** thy *God* **Elohim**,
the Holy One of *Israel* **Yisra El**, thy Saviour:
I gave *Egypt* **Misrayim** for thy *ransom* **koper/atonement**,
Ethiopia **Kush** and Seba for thee.
4 Since thou wast precious in my *sight* **eyes**,
thou hast been honourable, and I have loved thee:
therefore *will* **shall** I give *men* **humanity** for thee,
and *people* **nations** for thy *life* **soul**.
5 *Fear* **Awe** not: for I am with thee:
I *will* **shall** bring thy seed from the *east* **rising**,
and gather thee from the *west* **dusk**;
6 I *will* **shall** say to the north, Give up;
and to the south, *Keep* **Refrain** not *back*:
bring my sons from far,
and my daughters from the ends of the earth;
7 *Even* every one that is called by my name:
for I have created him for my *glory* **honour**,
I have formed him;
yea, I have *made* **worked** him.
8 Bring forth the blind people that have eyes,
and the deaf that have ears.
9 Let all the *nations* **goyim** be gathered *together*,
and let the *people be assembled* **nations gather**:
who among them can *declare* **tell** this,
and *shew us* **let us hear the** former *things*?
let them *bring* **give** forth their witnesses,
that they may be justified:
or let them hear, and say, *It is* truth.
10 Ye are my witnesses,
saith the LORD **an oracle of Yah Veh**,
and my servant whom I have chosen:
that ye may know and *believe* **trust** me,
and *understand* **discern** that I am he:
before me **at my face** there was no *God* **El** formed,
neither shall there be after me.
11 I, *even* I, *am the LORD* **Yah Veh**;
and *beside* **except** me there is no saviour.
12 I have *declared* **told**, and have saved,
and I have *shewed* **had thee hear**,
when there was *no* **naught** strange *god* among you:
therefore ye are my witnesses,
saith the LORD **an oracle of Yah Veh**,
that *I am God* **I—El**.
13 Yea, before the day *was* I am he;
and *there is* none *that* can *deliver* **rescue** out of my hand:
I *will work* **shall do**, and who shall *let it* **turn it back**?
14 Thus saith *the LORD* **Yah Veh**, your redeemer,
the Holy One of *Israel* **Yisra El**;
For your sake I have sent to *Babylon* **Babel**,
and have brought down all their *nobles* **fugitives**,
and the *Chaldeans* **Kesediym**,
whose *cry* **shouting** is in the ships.
15 I am *the LORD* **Yah Veh**, your Holy One,
the creator of *Israel* **Yisra El**, your *King* **Sovereign**.
16 Thus saith *the LORD* **Yah Veh**,
which *maketh* **giveth** a way in the sea, and
a path in the *mighty* **strong** waters;
17 Which bringeth forth the chariot and horse,
the *army* **valiant** and the *power* **strong**;
they shall lie down together, they shall not rise:
they are *extinct* **extinguished**,
they are quenched as *tow* **flax**.
18 Remember ye not the former *things*,
neither *consider* **discern** the *things of old* **ancient**.
19 Behold, I *will do* **shall work** a new *thing*;
now it shall *spring forth* **sprout**; shall ye not know it?
I *will* **shall** even *make* **set** a way in the wilderness,
and rivers in the *desert* **desolation**.
Awe not, for I redeemed you;
I called your name; you are mine.
2 When you pass through the waters,
I *am* with you;
and through the rivers,
they overflow you not:
when you walk through the fire,
you neither blister, nor the flame burn on you.
3 For I—Yah Veh your Elohim,
the Holy One of Yisra El, your Saviour:
I gave Misrayim for your koper/atonement,
Kush and Seba for you.
4 Since you are precious in my eyes,
honorable, and I love you: so I give humanity
for you and nations for your soul.
5 Awe not: for I *am* with you:
I bring your seed from the rising, and
gather you from the dusk;
6 I say to the north, Give up!
and to the south, Refrain not!
Bring my sons from far
and my daughters from the ends of the earth
7—every one called by my name: for I created him
for my honor, I formed him; yes, I worked him.
8 Bring forth the blind people with eyes,
and the deaf with ears.
9 All the goyim gather; and the nations gather:

who among them tells this
and has us hear the former?
They give their witnesses,
to justify themselves:
and they hear, and say, Truth.
10 You are my witnesses
—an oracle of Yah Veh
and my servant whom I chose:
so that you know and trust me,
and discern I am he:
ere my face, no El was formed,
and none after me.
11 I—I—Yah Veh;
and except me, there is no saviour.
12 I—I told; and saved;
and I hearkened
when there is no stranger among you:
and you *are* my witnesses
—an oracle of Yah Veh
and I—El.
13 Yes, ere the day, I *am* he;
and no one rescues from my hand:
I work, and who turns it back?
14 Thus says Yah Veh, your redeemer,
the Holy One of Yisra El;
for your sake I sent to Babel,
and brought down all their fugitives,
and the Kesediym, whose shouting *is* in the ships.
15 I—Yah Veh, your Holy One,
the creator of Yisra El, your Sovereign.
16 Thus says Yah Veh,
who gives a way in the sea and a
path in the strong waters:
17 who brings forth the chariot and horse,
the valiant and the strong;
they lie down together, they rise not:
they are extinguished; they are quenched as flax.
18 Neither remember the former,
nor discern the ancient:
19 behold, I work a new *work*!
Now it sprouts; Know you not?
I even set a way in the wilderness
and rivers in the desolation:
20 The *beast* **live being** of
the field shall honour me,
the *dragons* **monsters** and the **daughters of the** owls:
because I give waters in the wilderness,
and rivers in the *desert* **desolation**,
to give drink to my people, my chosen.
21 This people have I formed for myself;
they shall *shew forth* **scribe** my *praise* **halal**.
22 But thou hast not called upon me,
O *Jacob* **Yaaqov**;
but thou hast been *weary* **belaboured** of me,
O *Israel* **Yisra El**.
23 Thou hast not brought me
the *small cattle* **lambs** of thy *burnt offering* **holocausts**;
neither hast thou honoured me with thy sacrifices.
I have not caused thee to serve with an offering,
nor *wearied* **belaboured** thee with incense.
24 Thou hast *bought* **chatteled** me
no sweet *cane* **stalk** with *money* **silver**,
neither hast thou *filled* **satiated** me
with the fat of thy sacrifices:
but thou hast *made* **caused** me
to serve with thy sins,
thou hast *wearied* **belaboured** me
with *thine iniquities* **thy perversities**.
25 I, *even* I, *am* he
that *blotteth* **wipeth** out thy *transgressions* **rebellions**
for mine own sake,
and *will* **shall** not remember thy sins.
26 *Put me in remembrance* **Remind me**:
let us plead together:
declare **scribe** thou, that thou mayest be justified.
27 Thy first father hath sinned,
and thy *teachers* **translators**
have *transgressed* **rebelled** against me.
28 Therefore I have profaned
the *princes* **governors** of the *sanctuary* **holies**,
and have given *Jacob* **Yaaqov** to the *curse* **devotement**,
and *Israel* **Yisra El** to *reproaches* **revilings**.

YISRA EL, THE CHOSEN OF YAH VEH

44 Yet now hear, O *Jacob* **Yaaqov** my servant;
and *Israel* **Yisra El**, whom I have chosen:
2 Thus saith *the LORD* **Yah**
Veh that *made* **worked** thee,
and formed thee from the *womb* **belly**,
which *will* **shall** help thee;
Fear **Awe** not, O *Jacob* **Yaaqov**, my servant;
and thou, *Jesurun* **Yeshurun**, whom I have chosen.
3 For I *will* **shall** pour water
upon him that is thirsty,
and *floods* **flows** upon the dry *ground*:
I *will* **shall** pour my spirit upon thy seed,
and my blessing upon thine offspring:
4 And they shall *spring up* **sprout**
as among **between** the grass,
as willows by the water *courses* **streams**.
5 One shall say, I am *the LORD'S* **Yah Veh's**;

and another shall call *himself*
by the name of *Jacob* **Yaaqov**;
and another shall *subscribe* **inscribe** with his hand
unto *the LORD* **Yah Veh**,
and *surname himself* **an honorary degree**
by the name of *Israel* **Yisra El**.
6 Thus saith *the LORD* **Yah Veh**
the *King* **Sovereign** of *Israel* **Yisra El**,
and his redeemer *the LORD of hosts* **Yah Veh Sabaoth**;
I am the first, and I am the *last* **final**;
and *beside* **except** me there is no *God* **Elohim**.
7 And who, as I, shall call, and shall *declare* **tell** it,
and *set it in order* **line it up** for me,
since I appointed **set** the *ancient* **original** people?
and *the things* **those** that are coming, and shall come,
let them *shew* **tell** unto them.
8 Fear ye not, neither *be afraid* **fear**:
have not I
told thee from that time **had thee hear ever since**,
and have *declared* **told** it? ye are even my witnesses.
Is there *a God beside* **an Elohah except** me?
yea, there is no *God* **rock**; I know not any.
9 They that *make* **form** a *graven image* **sculptile**
are all of them *vanity* **waste**;
and their *delectable things* **desires**
shall not *profit* **benefit**;
20 the live beings of the field honor me
—the monsters and the daughters of the owls:
because I give waters in the wilderness
and rivers in the desolation,
to give my people drink—my chosen.
21 I formed this people for myself;
they scribe my halal.
22 And you called not on me, O Yaaqov;
and you belabored of me, O Yisra El:
23 you neither brought me
the lambs of your holocausts;
nor honored me
with your sacrifices.
I neither had you serve with an offering;
nor belabored you with incense.
24 You neither chatteled me sweet stalk with silver,
nor satiated me with the fat of your sacrifices:
only you had me to serve with your sins;
you belabored me with your perversities.
25 I, I *am* he who wipes out your rebellions
for my own sake,
and remembers not your sins.
26 Remind me, so that we plead together:
scribe you, that you be justified.
27 Your first father sinned,
and your translators rebelled against me:
28 and I profaned the governors of the holies;
and gave Yaaqov to the devotement
and Yisra El to revilings.

YISRA EL, THE CHOSEN OF YAH VEH

44 And now hear, O Yaaqov my servant;
and Yisra El, whom I chose:
2 thus says Yah Veh who worked you
and formed you from the belly;
who helps you:
Awe not, O Yaaqov, my servant;
and you, Yeshurun, whom I chose.
3 For I pour water on him who is thirsty,
and flowings on the dry:
I pour my spirit on your seed
and my blessing on your offspring:
4 and they sprout between the grass
as willows by the water streams.
5 *One* says, I—Yah Veh:
and another calls by the name of Yaaqov:
and another inscribes with his hand to Yah Veh
and by an honorary degree, the name of Yisra El.
6 Thus says Yah Veh the Sovereign of Yisra El,
and his redeemer Yah Veh Sabaoth;
I—the first, and I—the final;
and except me, there is no Elohim.
7 And who as I, calls and tells it and lines it up
for me who set the original people?
And those coming, and those to come,
tell they them?
8 Neither fear, nor frighten:
Heard you not ever since, what I told you?
You *are* my witnesses.
Is there an Elohah except me?
Yes, there is no rock; I know none.
9 They who form a sculptile
all of them *are* a waste;
and their desires benefit not:
and they are their own witnesses;
they see not, nor know;
that they may *be ashamed* **shame**.
10 Who hath formed *a god* **an el**,
or *molten* **poured** a *graven image* **sculptile**
that is *profitable* **beneficial** for *nothing* **naught**?
11 Behold,
all his *fellows* **companions** shall *be ashamed* **shame**:
and the *workmen* **engravers**, they are of *men* **humanity**:
let them all be gathered together, let them stand up;

yet they shall fear,
and they shall *be ashamed* **shame** together.
12 The *smith* **engraver of iron** with the *tongs* **axe**
both worketh in the coals,
and *fashioneth* **formeth** it with hammers,
and *worketh* **maketh** it
with the *strength* **force** of his arms:
yea, he is *hungry* **famished**,
and his *strength faileth* **force is not**:
he drinketh no water, and *is faint* **wearieth**.
13 The *carpenter* **engraver of timber**
stretcheth out **spreadeth** his *rule* **line**;
he *marketh it out* **surveyeth** with a *line* **stylus**;
he *fitteth* **worketh** it with planes,
and he *marketh it out* **surveyeth** with the compass,
and *maketh* **worketh** it after the *figure* **pattern** of a man,
according to the *beauty* **adornment** of *a man* **humanity**;
that it may *remain* **settle** in the house.
14 He *heweth* **cuteth** him down cedars,
and taketh the cypress and the oak,
which he strengtheneth for himself
among the trees of the forest:
he planteth an ash,
and the *rain* **downpour** doth nourish it.
15 Then shall it be for *a man* **humanity** to burn:
for he *will* **shall** take *thereof*, and *warm* **heat** himself;
yea, he kindleth it, and baketh bread;
yea, he *maketh a god* **worketh an el**,
and *worshippeth it* **prostrateth**;
he maketh it a *graven image* **sculptile**,
and *falleth down* **prostrateth** thereto.
16 He burneth *part* **half** *thereof* in the fire;
with *part* **half** *thereof* he eateth flesh;
he roasteth roast, and *is satisfied* **satiates**:
yea, he *warmeth* **heateth** *himself*,
and saith, Aha, I am *warm* **heated**,
I have seen the *fire* **flame**:
17 And the *residue* **survivors** *thereof*
he *maketh a god* **worketh an el**,
even his *graven image* **sculptile**:
he *falleth down* **prostrateth** unto it,
and worshippeth it **prostrateth**, and prayeth unto it,
and saith, *Deliver* **Rescue** me; for thou art my *god* **el**.
18 They have not known nor
understood **discerned**:
for he hath *shut* **daubed** their eyes,
that they cannot see **from seeing**,
and their hearts,
that they cannot understand **from comprehending**.
19 And none *considereth in* **turneth to** his heart,
neither is there knowledge
nor *understanding* **discernment** to say,
I have burned *part of it* **half** in the fire;
yea, also I have baked bread upon the coals *thereof*;
I have roasted flesh, and eaten it:
and shall I *make* **work** the *residue* **remnant** *thereof*
an *abomination* **abhorrence**?
shall I *fall down* **prostrate** to the *stock* **product** of a tree?
20 He *feedeth* **grazeth** on ashes:
a *deceived* **mocked** heart hath *turned*
perverted him *aside*,
that he cannot *deliver* **rescue** his soul,
nor say, Is there not a *lie* **falsehood** in my right *hand*?
21 Remember these, O *Jacob*
Yaaqov and *Israel* **Yisra El**;
for thou art my servant:
I have formed thee; thou art my servant:
O *Israel* **Yisra El**, thou shalt not be forgotten of me.
22 I have blotted out, as a thick cloud,
thy *transgressions* **rebellions**,
and, as a **thick** cloud, thy sins:
return unto me; for I have redeemed thee.
and they *are* their own witnesses;
they neither see, nor know to shame.
10 Who ever formed an el or poured a sculptile
that is not beneficial?
11 Behold, all his companions shame:
and the engravers *are* of humanity:
they all gather; together they stand:
they fear; together they shame.
12 The engraver of iron
works with the ax in the coals
and forms with hammers
and makes with the force of his arms:
yes, he famishes and his force is not:
he drinks no water and wearies.
13 The engraver of timber spreads his line;
he surveys with a stylus; he works with planes:
and he surveys with the compass
and works after the pattern of a man
according to the adornment of humanity;
that it settle in the house:
14 he cuts down cedars;
and takes the cypress and the oak
which he strengthens for himself
among the trees of the forest:
he plants an ash, and the downpour nourishes:
15 and it becomes for humanity to burn:
for he takes and heats;
yes, he kindles and bakes bread:
yes, he works an el and prostrates;
he makes a sculptile, and prostrates thereto:

16 he burns half in the fire;
with half he eats flesh;
he roasts a roast, and satiates:
yes, he heats,
and says, Aha, I heat up; I see the flame:
17 and of what survives, he works an el
—his sculptile:
he prostrates thereto
—prostrates and prays thereto,
and says, Rescue me; for you are my el.
18 They neither know nor discern:
for he daubs their eyes from seeing,
and their hearts from comprehending:
19 and no one turns to his heart;
there is neither knowledge nor discernment to say,
I burn half in the fire;
yes, also I bake bread on the coals;
I roast flesh and eat:
and I work the remnant an abhorrence:
I prostrate to the product of a tree.
20 He grazes on ashes:
a mocked heart perverts him
that he neither rescues his soul,
nor says, Is there not a falsehood in my right?
21 Remember these, O Yaaqov and Yisra El;
for you are my servant:
I formed you; you are my servant:
O Yisra El, I forget you not.
22 As a thick cloud, I wipe out your rebellions;
and, as a thick cloud, your sins:
return to me; for I redeem you.
23 *Sing* **Shout**, O ye heavens;
for *the LORD* **Yah Veh** hath *done* **worked** it:
shout, ye *lower parts of the* **nethermost** earth:
break forth into *singing* **shouting**, ye mountains,
O forest, and every tree therein:
for *the LORD* **Yah Veh** hath redeemed *Jacob* **Yaaqov**,
and *glorified* **adorned** himself in *Israel* **Yisra El**.
24 Thus saith *the LORD* **Yah Veh**, thy redeemer,
and he that formed thee from the *womb* **belly**,
I am *the LORD* **Yah Veh** that *maketh* **worketh** all *things*;
that *stretcheth forth* **spreadeth** the heavens alone;
that *spreadeth abroad* **expandeth** the earth by myself;
25 That *frustrateth* **breaketh** the
tokens **signs** of *the liars* **lies**,
and *maketh* **exposeth** diviners mad;
that turneth wise *men* backward,
and *maketh* **follieth** their knowledge *foolish*;
26 That *confirmeth* **raiseth** the word of his servant,
and *performeth* **shalameth**
the counsel of his *messengers* **angels**;
that saith to *Jerusalem* **Yeru Shalem**,
Thou shalt be *inhabited* **settled**;
and to the cities of *Judah* **Yah Hudah**,
Ye shall be built,
and I *will* **shall** raise *up*
the *decayed places* **parched areas** *thereof*:
27 That saith to the *deep* **abyss**, *Be dry* **Parch**,
and I *will dry up* **shall wither** thy rivers:
28 That saith of *Cyrus* **Koresh**,
He is my *shepherd* **tender**,
and shall *perform* **shalam** all my *pleasure* **delight**:
even saying to *Jerusalem* **Yeru Shalem**,
Thou shalt be built;
and to the *temple* **manse**,
Thy foundation shall be laid **Thou shalt be founded**.

*found: as in founding a foundation.

KORESH, THE ANOINTED OF YAH VEH

45 Thus saith *the LORD* **Yah Veh** to his anointed,
to *Cyrus* **Koresh**,
whose right *hand* I have *holden* **strengthened**,
to subdue *nations before him* **goyim at his face**;
and I *will* **shall** loose the loins of *kings* **sovereigns**,
in opening, to open
before him **at his face** the *two leaved gates* **doors**;
and the *gates* **portals** shall not be shut;
2 I *will* **shall** go *before thee* **at thy face**,
and *make the crooked places straight*
straighten the esteemed:
I *will* **shall** break in pieces the gates of *brass* **copper**,
and cut *in asunder* **apart** the bars of iron:
3 And I *will* **shall** give thee
the treasures of darkness,
and hidden *riches* **treasures** of *secret places* **coverts**,
that thou mayest know that I, *the LORD* **Yah Veh**,
which call thee by thy name,
am *the God* **Elohim** of *Israel* **Yisra El**.
4 For *Jacob* **Yaaqov** my servant's sake,
and *Israel mine elect* **Yisra El my chosen**,
I have even called thee by thy name:
I have *surnamed thee* **given thee an honorary degree**,
though thou hast not known me.
5 *I am the LORD* **I—Yah
Veh**, and there is none else,
there is no *God* **Elohim** beside me:
I girded thee, though thou hast not known me:
6 That they may know from the rising of the sun,
and from the *west* **dusk**,
that there is none *beside* **final except** me.

I am the LORD **I—Yah Veh**, and there is none else.
7 I form the light, and create darkness:
I *make peace* **work shalom**, and create evil:
I *the LORD do* **Yah Veh work** all these *things*.
8 *Drop down* **Drip**, ye heavens, from above,
and let the *skies* **vapours**
pour down righteousness **flow justness**:
let the earth open,
and let them *bring forth* **bear fruit of** salvation,
and let *righteousness spring up* **justness sprout** together;
I *the LORD* **Yah Veh** have created it.
9 *Woe* **Ho** unto him that striveth
with his *Maker* **Former**!
Let the potsherd strive
with the potsherds of the *earth* **soil**.
Shall the *clay* **morter** say to him
that *fashioneth* **formeth** it,
23 Shout, O you heavens; for Yah Veh worked it:
shout, you nethermost earth:
break forth into shouting, you mountains;
O forest, and every tree therein:
for Yah Veh redeems Yaaqov,
and adorns himself in Yisra El.
24 Thus says Yah Veh your redeemer
—he who formed you from the belly,
I—Yah Veh who worked all;
who alone spread the heavens;
who expanded the earth by myself:
25 who breaks the signs of lies and exposes
diviners as mad; who turns the wise
backward and follies their knowledge;
26 who raises the word of his servant
and shalams the counsel of his angels;
who says to Yeru Shalem, You, settle!
and to the cities of Yah Hudah, You, build!
—and I raise the parched areas:
27 who says to the abyss, Parch!
—and I wither your rivers:
28 who says of Koresh my tender,
who shalams all my delight:
even saying to Yeru Shalem, You, Build!
and to the manse, You, Found!*.

*found: as in founding a foundation.

KORESH, THE ANOINTED OF YAH VEH

45 Thus says Yah Veh to his anointed,
to Koresh, whose right I strengthened,
to subdue goyim at his face;
yes, to loose the loins of sovereigns,
in opening, to open the doors at his face;
and not shut the portals:
2 I go at your face and straighten the esteemed:
I break in pieces the gates of copper
and cut apart the bars of iron:
3 and I give you the treasures of darkness
and hidden treasures of coverts
so that you know, I—Yah Veh,
who calls you by your name, Elohim of Yisra El.
4 For sake of my servant Yaaqov
and Yisra El my chosen,
I even call you by your name:
I give you an honorary degree,
though you know me not.
5 I—Yah Veh, and there is no one else,
there is no Elohim except me:
I girded you, though you know me not:
6 so that they know
from the rising of the sun and from the dusk
that there *is* no one final except me:
I—Yah Veh, and there is no one else:
7 I form the light and create darkness:
I work shalom and create evil:
I Yah Veh work all these.
8 Drip, you heavens, from above;
and the vapours, flow justness:
earth opens and bears fruit of salvation;
and justness sprouts together:
I Yah Veh created it.
9 Ho to him who strives with his Former!
—a potsherd among the potsherds of the soil.
Says the morter to the Former,
What *makest* **workest** thou?
or thy *work* **deeds**, He hath no hands?
10 *Woe* **Ho** unto him that saith unto his father,
What *begettest* **birthest** thou?
or to the woman,
What hast thou *brought forth* **whirled**?
11 Thus saith *the LORD* **Yah Veh**,
the Holy One of *Israel* **Yisra El**, and his *Maker* **Former**,
Ask me of *things* **those which are** to come
concerning my sons,
and concerning the *work* **deeds** of my hands
command **misvah** ye me.
12 I have *made* **worked** the earth,
and created *man* **humanity** upon it:
I, *even* my hands, have *stretched out* **spread** the heavens,
and all their host have I *commanded* **misvahed**.
13 I have *raised* **wakened** him *up*
in *righteousness* **justness**,

and I *will direct* **shall straighten** all his ways:
he shall build my city,
and he shall *let go* **send away** my *captives* **exiles**,
not for price nor *reward* **bribe**,
saith *the LORD of hosts* **Yah Veh Sabaoth**.
14 Thus saith *the LORD* **Yah Veh**,
The labour of *Egypt* **Misrayim**,
and merchandise
of *Ethiopia* **Kush** and of the *Sabeans* **Sebaiym**,
men of *stature* **measure**,
shall *come* **pass** over unto thee, and they shall be thine:
they shall come after thee;
in *chains* **bonds** they shall *come* **pass** over,
and they shall *fall down* **prostrate** unto thee,
they shall *make supplication* **pray** unto thee,
saying, Surely *God* **El** is in thee;
and there is none else, there is no God beside me
—final—Elohim.
15 *Verily* **Surely** thou art *a God*
an El that hidest thyself,
O *God* **Elohim** of *Israel* **Yisra El**, the Saviour.
16 They shall be *ashamed*
shamed, and also confounded,
all of them:
they shall go to *confusion* **shame** together
that are *makers* **engravers** of *idols* **molds**.
17 *But Israel* **Yisra El** shall be
saved in *the LORD* **Yah Veh**
with an *everlasting* **eternal** salvation:
ye shall not be *ashamed* **shamed** nor confounded
world without end **unto the eternal ages**.
18 For thus saith *the LORD* **Yah Veh**
that created the heavens;
God **Elohim** himself
that formed the earth and *made* **worked** it;
he hath established it,
he created it not *in vain* **a waste**,
he formed it to be *inhabited* **settled**:
I am the LORD **I—Yah Veh**; and there is none else.
19 I have not *spoken in secret* **worded covertly**,
in a dark place of the earth:
I said not unto the seed of *Jacob* **Yaaqov**,
Seek ye me in *vain* **waste**:
I *the LORD speak righteousness* **Yah Veh word justness**,
I *declare things that are right* **tell it straight**.
20 *Assemble yourselves* **Gather** and come;
draw near together,
ye *that are escaped* **escapees** of the *nations* **goyim**:
they have no knowledge
that *set up* **bear**
the *wood* **timber** of their *graven image* **sculptile**,
and pray unto *a god* **an el** that cannot save.
21 Tell ye, and bring them near;
yea, let them *take* counsel together:
who hath *declared* **caused** this **to be heard**
from *ancient time* **antiquity**?
who hath told it from that time?
have not I *the LORD* **Yah Veh**?
and *there is no God else beside* **no Elohim except** me;
a just *God* **El** and a Saviour;
there is none *beside* **final except** me.
22 *Look unto* **Face** me, and be ye saved,
all the *ends* **finalities** of the earth:
for *I am God* **I—El**, and there is none else.
What work you?
Or of your deeds, No hands?
10 Ho to him who says to his
father, What birth you?
Or to the woman, What whirl you?
11 Thus says Yah Veh,
the Holy One of Yisra El his Former,
Ask me of those to come concerning my sons
and concerning the deeds of my hands;
you, misvah me.
12 I worked the earth,
and created humanity thereon:
I, my hands, spread the heavens,
and all their host I misvahed.
13 I waken him in justness
and straighten all his ways:
he builds my city and he sends away my exiles
—neither for price nor bribe,
says Yah Veh Sabaoth.
14 Thus says Yah Veh,
The labor of Misrayim,
and merchandise of Kush and of the Sebaiym
—men of measure
pass over to you, and they are yours:
they become after you;
they pass over in bonds
and they prostrate to you;
they pray to you,
Surely El is in you, Elohim the final.
15 Surely you are an El who hides yourself,
O Elohim of Yisra El, the Saviour.
16 They shame; they even confound—all of them:
the engravers of molds go to shame together.
17 Yisra El is saved in Yah Veh
with an eternal salvation:
you neither shame nor confound to the eternal ages.

18 For thus says Yah Veh who created the heavens;
Elohim himself who formed the earth and worked it;
he established it; he created it not a waste;
he formed it to settle therein:
I—Yah Veh; and there is no one else.
19 I neither word covertly in
a dark place of the earth:
nor say I to the seed of Yaaqov,
You seek me in waste.
I Yah Veh word justness; I tell it straight.
20 Gather and come;
draw near together, you escapees of the goyim:
they who bear the timber of their sculptile, know not,
and pray to an el who saves not.
21 You, tell; bring near;
yes, they counsel together.
Who had this to be heard from antiquity?
Who told it from that time?
Was it not I—Yah Veh?
—and no Elohim except me; a just El and a Saviour;
there is no one final except me.
22 Face me, and be saved,
all you finalities of the earth:
for I—El; and there is no one else.
23 I have *sworn* **oathed** by myself,
the word is gone out of my mouth
in *righteousness* **justness**,
and shall not return,
That unto me every knee shall *bow* **kneel**,
every tongue shall *swear* **oath**.
Philippians 2:9—11
24 Surely, shall *one* **he** say,
in *the LORD* **Yah Veh**
have I *righteousness* **justness** and strength:
even to him shall *men* come;
and all that are *incensed* **inflamed** against him
shall *be ashamed* **shame**.
25 In *the LORD* **Yah Veh**
shall all the seed of *Israel* **Yisra El** be justified,
and shall *glory* **halal**.

THE IDOLS OF BABEL

46 Bel *boweth down* **kneeleth**, Nebo stoopeth,
their idols were upon the *beasts* **live beings**,
and upon the *cattle* **animals**:
your *carriages* **loads** were heavy loaden;
they are—a burden to the *weary beast* **languid**.
2 They stoop, they *bow down* **kneel** together;
they could not *deliver* **rescue** the burden,
but *themselves* **their souls** are gone into captivity.
3 Hearken unto me, O house of *Jacob* **Yaaqov**,
and all the *remnant* **survivors**
of the house of *Israel* **Yisra El**,
which are *borne by me* **laden** from the belly,
which are *carried* **borne** from the womb:
4 And even to your *old age* **agedness** I *am* he;
and *even* to *hoar hairs* **greyness**
will **shall** I *carry* **bear** *you*:
I have *made* **worked**, and I *will* **shall** bear;
even I *will carry* **shall bear**,
and *will deliver* **shall rescue** you.
5 To whom *will* **shall** ye liken me,
and *make me equal* **equate me**,
and *compare* **liken** me, that we may be like?
6 They *lavish* **scatter** gold out of the *bag* **pouch**,
and weigh silver in the *balance* **beam**,
and hire a *goldsmith* **refiner**;
and he *maketh* **worketh** it *a god* **an el**:
they *fall down* **prostrate**, yea, they *worship* **prostrate**.
7 They bear him upon the
shoulder, they *carry* **bear** him,
and set him in his place, and he standeth;
from his place shall he not *remove* **depart**:
yea, one shall cry unto him, yet can he not answer,
nor save him out of his *trouble* **tribulation**.
8 Remember this, *and shew*
yourselves men **be manly**:
bring it again to mind **restore heart**,
O ye *transgressors* **rebels**.
9 Remember the former
things of old **from eternity**:
for *I am God* **I—El**, and there is none else;
I am God **I—Elohim**, *and there is none like me*—**final**,
10 *Declaring* **Telling** the end from the beginning,
and from *ancient times* **antiquity**
the things **former** that are not *yet done* **worked**,
saying, My counsel shall *stand* **rise**,
and I *will do* **shall work** all my *pleasure* **delight**:
11 Calling a *ravenous bird*
swooper from the *east* **rising**,
the man that executeth my counsel
from a far *country* **land**:
yea, I have *spoken it* **worded**,
I *will* **shall** also bring it *to pass*;
I have *purposed* **formed** it, I *will* **shall** also *do* **work** it.
12 Hearken unto me, ye
stouthearted **mighty hearted**,
that are far from *righteousness* **justness**:
13 I bring near my *righteousness* **justness**;
it shall not be far *off* **removed**,

and my salvation shall not *tarry* **delay**:
and I *will* **shall** place salvation in *Zion* **Siyon**
for *Israel my glory* **Yisra El mine adornment**.

THE FALL OF BABEL

47 *Come down* **Descend**, and sit in the dust,
O virgin daughter of *Babylon* **Babel**,
sit on the *ground* **earth**:
there is no throne, O daughter of
the *Chaldeans* **Kesediym**:
for thou shalt *no more* **not add**
to be called tender and delicate.
23 I oath by myself;
the word goes from my mouth in justness,
and returns not,
That to me every knee kneels,
every tongue oaths.
Philippians 2:9—11
24 Surely in Yah Veh, he says,
I have justness and strength:
to him he comes;
and all who inflame against him, shame.
25 In Yah Veh all the seed of Yisra El is justified,
and halals.

THE IDOLS OF BABEL

46 Bel kneels; Nebo stoops;
their idols are for the live beings
and for the animals:
your loads are heavily loaded
—a burden to the languid.
2 They stoop; they kneel together; they cannot rescue
the burden; and their souls go into captivity.
3 Hearken to me, O house of Yaaqov,
and all survivors of the house of Yisra El
—who are loaded from the belly;
who are raised from the womb:
4 and even to your agedness, I *am* he;
and to greyness I bear:
I work and I bear; yes, I bear and rescue you.
5 To whom liken you me and equate me
—liken me, to be alike?
6 They scatter gold from the pouch
and weigh silver in the beam
and hire a refiner;
and he works an el thereof:
they prostrate; yes, they prostrate:
7 they bear him on the shoulder;
they bear him and set him in his place
and he stands;
he departs not from his place:
yes, one cries to him; yet he answers not
—saves him not from his tribulation.
8 Remember this, be manly:
restore heart, O you rebels.
9 Remember the former from eternity:
for I—El, and there is no one else;
I—Elohim the final:
10 telling the end from the beginning,
and what formerly *was* not worked from antiquity,
saying, My counsel rises and I work all my delight:
11 calling a swooper from the rising
and the man who executes my counsel
from a land afar:
yes, I word; yes, I bring it;
I formed; yes, I also work it.
12 Hearken to me, you mighty hearted
who are far from justness:
13 I bring my justness near; it *is* not far removed;
and delay not my salvation:
and I place salvation in Siyon
for Yisra El my adornment.

THE FALL OF BABEL

47 Descend, and sit in the dust;
O virgin daughter of Babel, sit on the earth;
there is no throne, O daughter of the Kesediym:
for you add not to be called tender and delicate.
2 Take the millstones, and grind *meal* **flour**:
uncover **expose** thy *locks* **vail**,
make bare the leg **strip the train**,
uncover **expose** the *thigh* **leg**, pass over the rivers.
3 Thy nakedness shall be *uncovered* **exposed**,
yea, thy *shame* **reproach** shall be seen:
I *will* **shall** take *vengeance* **avengement**,
and I *will* **shall** not meet thee as a *man* **human**.
4 *As for* our redeemer,
the LORD of hosts **Yah Veh Sabaoth** is his name,
the Holy One of *Israel* **Yisra El**.
5 Sit thou silent, and get thee into darkness,
O daughter of the *Chaldeans* **Kesediym**:
for thou shalt no more be called,
The lady of *kingdoms* **sovereigndoms**.
6 I was *wroth* **enraged** with my people,
I have *polluted* **profaned** mine inheritance,
and given them into thine hand:
thou didst *shew* **set** them no *mercy* **mercies**;
upon the *ancient* **aged**
hast thou *very heavily laid* **made mighty heavy** thy yoke.

7 And thou saidst,
I shall be a lady *for ever* **eternally**:
so that thou didst not *lay* **set** these *things* to thy heart,
neither didst remember the latter end of it.
8 Therefore hear now this,
thou *that art given to pleasures* **voluptuous**,
that *dwellest carelessly* **settlest confidently**,
that sayest in thine heart,
I am, and none else beside me **I—final**;
I shall not sit *as* a widow,
neither shall I know *the loss of children* **bereavement**:
9 But these two *things* shall come to thee
in a *moment* **blink** in one day,
the loss of children **bereavement**, and widowhood:
they shall come upon thee in their *perfection* **integrity**
for the *multitude* **abundance** of thy sorceries,
and for the *great abundance* **mighty might**
of *thine enchantments* **thy charms**.
10 For thou hast *trusted* **confided**
in thy *wickedness* **evil**:
thou hast said, None seeth me.
Thy wisdom and thy knowledge,
it hath *perverted* **turned** thee **away**;
and thou hast said in thine heart,
I am, and none else beside me **I—final**.
11 Therefore shall evil come upon thee;
thou shalt not know
from whence it riseth **the dawn thereof**:
and *mischief* **calamity** shall fall upon thee;
thou shalt not be able to *put it off* **kapar/atone it**:
and *desolation* **devastation**
shall come upon thee suddenly,
which thou shalt not know.
12 Stand *now* **I beseech,**
with *thine enchantments* **thy charms**,
and with the *multitude* **abundance** of thy sorceries,
wherein thou hast laboured from thy youth;
if so be thou shalt be able to *profit* **benefit**,
if so be thou mayest *prevail* **terrify**.
13 Thou art wearied
in the *multitude* **abundance** of thy counsels.
Let *now* **I beseech,**
the *astrologers* **horoscopists of the heavens**,
the *stargazers* **seers of stars**,
the *monthly prognosticators* **knowers of months**,
stand up, and save thee
from these *things* that shall come upon thee.
14 Behold, they shall be as stubble;
the fire shall burn them;
they shall not *deliver themselves* **rescue their souls**
from the *power* **hand** of the flame:
there shall not be a coal to *warm at* **heat**,
nor *fire* **flame** to sit before it.
15 Thus shall they be unto thee
with whom thou hast laboured,
even thy merchants, from thy youth:
they shall wander every *one to his quarter* **man beyond**;
none shall save thee **thou shalt have no saviour**.
2 Take the millstones and grind flour;
expose your veil; strip the train;
expose the leg; pass over the rivers.
3 Your nakedness *is* exposed,
yes, your reproach *is* seen:
I take avengement, and I meet you not as a human.
4 Our redeemer—Yah Veh Sabaoth *is* his name
—the Holy One of Yisra El.
5 Sit silent, and get into darkness,
O daughter of the Kesediym:
for they no more call you, The lady of sovereigndoms.
6 I enrage over my people;
I profane my inheritance;
and give them into your hand:
you set them no mercies;
you make your yoke on the aged mighty heavy.
7 And you say, I am a lady eternally:
so that you neither set these to your heart
nor rememer the latter end thereof.
8 And now hear this, you voluptuous *one*,
who settles confidently; who says in your heart,
I—final;
I neither sit a widow, nor know bereavement.
9 And these two come to you in a blink in one day
—bereavement and widowhood:
they come on you in their integrity
for the abundance of your sorceries,
and for the mighty might of your charms:
10 for you confide in your evil:
you say, No one sees me.
Your wisdom and your knowledge turn you away;
and you say in your heart, I—*the* final.
11 And evil comes on you;
you know not the dawn thereof:
and calamity falls on you;
you *are* not able to kapar/atone:
and devastation comes on you suddenly
which you know not.
12 Stand, I beseech, with your charms
and with the abundance of your sorceries
wherein you labored from your youth;
if perhaps you benefit; if perhaps you terrify.

13 You weary in the abundance of your counsels.
I beseech you,
have the horoscopists of the heavens,
the seers of stars, the knowers of months stand up
and save you from these that come on you.
14 Behold, they *are* as stubble;
the fire burns them;
they rescue not their souls from the hand of the flame:
there is neither coal to heat,
nor flame to sit in front of.
15 Thus *are* they with whom you labored to you
—your merchants, from your youth:
they wander every man beyond;
your saviour is not.

THE HARDNESS OF YISRA EL

48 Hear ye this, O house of *Jacob* **Yaaqov**,
which are called by the name of *Israel* **Yisra El**,
and are come forth
out of the waters of *Judah* **Yah Hudah**,
which *swear* **oath** by the name of *the LORD* **Yah Veh**,
and *make mention of* **memorialize**
the God **Elohim** of *Israel* **Yisra El**,
but not in truth, nor in *righteousness* **justness**.
2 For they call themselves of the holy city,
and *stay* **prop** themselves
upon *the God* **Elohim** of *Israel* **Yisra El**;
The LORD of hosts **Yah Veh Sabaoth** is his name.
3 I have *declared* **told** the former *things*
from the beginning **ever since**;
and they went forth out of my mouth,
and I *shewed* **had** them **hear**;
I *did* **worked** them suddenly,
and they *came to pass* **became**.
4 Because I knew that thou art *obstinate* **hard**,
and thy neck is an iron sinew,
and thy *brow brass* **forehead copper**;
5 I have even *from the beginning* **ever since**
declared **told** it to thee;
before **ere** it *came to pass* **became,**
I shewed it **I had** thee **hear**:
lest thou shouldest say,
Mine idol hath *done* **worked** them,
and my *graven image* **sculptile**,
and my *molten image* **libation**,
hath *commanded* **misvahed** them.
6 Thou hast heard, see all this;
and *will* **shall** not ye *declare* **tell** it?
I have *shewed* **had** thee **hear** new *things* from this time,
even hidden things—**the guarded**,
and thou didst not know them.
7 They are created now, and
not from the beginning;
even before **at the face of** the day
when thou heardest them not;
lest thou shouldest say, Behold, I knew them.
8 Yea, thou heardest not; yea, thou knewest not;
yea, from that time that thine ear was not opened:
for I knew that **in dealing covertly,**
thou *wouldest* **shouldest** deal
very treacherously **covertly**,
and wast called a *transgressor* **rebel**
from the *womb* **belly**.
9 For my name's sake
will **shall** I *defer mine anger* **prolong my wrath**,
and for my *praise* **halal**
will **shall** I *refrain* **restrain** for thee,
that I cut thee not off.
10 Behold, I have refined thee, but not with silver;
I have chosen thee
in the furnace of *affliction* **humiliation**.
11 For mine own sake,
even for mine own sake, *will* **shall** I *do* **work** it:
for how should *my name be polluted* **it be profaned**?
and I *will* **shall** not give my *glory* **honour** unto another.
12 Hearken unto me,
O *Jacob* **Yaaqov** and *Israel* **Yisra El**, my called;
I *am* he; *I am the* **I**—first, *I also am the last* **yes, I—final**.
13 Mine hand also hath
laid the foundation of **founded** the earth,
and my right *hand* **palm** hath spanned the heavens:
when I call unto them, they stand up together.
14 All ye, *assemble yourselves* **gather**, and hear;
which among them hath *declared* **told** these *things*?
The LORD **Yah Veh** hath loved him:
he *will do* **shall work** his *pleasure* **delight**
on *Babylon* **Babel**,
and his arm shall be on the *Chaldeans* **Kesediym**.
15 I, *even* I, have *spoken* **worded**;
yea, I have called him:
I have brought him,
and he shall *make* **prosper** his way *prosperous*.
16 *Come ye near* **Approach** unto me, hear ye this;
I have not *spoken in secret* **worded covertly**
from the beginning;
from the time that it was, there am I:

THE HARDNESS OF YISRA EL

48 Hear this, O house of Yaaqov
—called by the name of Yisra El coming from the
waters of Yah Hudah; who oaths by the name of
Yah Veh and memorializes Elohim of Yisra El

—neither in truth, nor in justness.
2 For they call themselves of the holy city,
and prop themselves on Elohim of Yisra
El; Yah Veh Sabaoth *is* his name.
3 I told of the former ever since;
and they come from my mouth,
and I hear them;
I work them suddenly; and they become.
4 Because I know you are hard, and your neck
an iron sinew and your forehead copper;
5 I even tell you ever since;
so that you hear ere it becomes:
lest you say, My idol worked them!
And my sculptile and my libation misvahed them!
6 Hear you? See you all this?
—and tell it not?
I have you hear the new from this time,
—the guarded, and you know them not.
7 They are now created—not from the beginning
from the face of the day when you heard
not; lest you say, Behold, I knew them.
8 Yes, you heard not; yes, you knew not;
yes, from the time your ear was not opened:
for I knew that in dealing covertly,
that you deal covertly—a rebel from the belly.
9 For sake of my name, I prolong my wrath;
and for my halal, I restrain for you,
that I not cut you off.
10 Behold, I refined you, but not with silver;
I chose you in the furnace of humiliation.
11 For my own sake—for my own sake, I work it.
For how *is* it profaned?
And I give not my honor to another.
12 Hearken to me,
O Yaaqov and Yisra El, my called;
I *am* he; I—first; yes, I—final.
13 Also, my hand founded the earth
and my right palm spanned the heavens:
I call to them; they stand together.
14 All of you, gather and hear;
who among them tells these?
Yah Veh loved him:
he works his delight on Babel,
and his arm on the Kesediym.
15 I—I worded; yes, I called him:
I brought him; and prospered his way.
16 Approach me; hear this;
I worded not covertly from the beginning;
from the time of its being, there I *am*:
and now *the Lord GOD* **Adonay Yah Veh**, and his Spirit,
hath sent me.
17 Thus saith *the LORD* **Yah Veh**, thy Redeemer,
the Holy One of *Israel* **Yisra El**;
I am the LORD **I—Yah Veh** thy *God* **Elohim**
which teacheth thee to *profit* **benefit**,
which *leadeth* **aimeth** thee
by the way that thou shouldest go.
18 O that thou hadst hearkened
to my *commandments* **misvoth**!
then had thy *peace* **shalom** been as a river,
and thy *righteousness* **justness** as the waves of the sea:
19 Thy seed also had been as the sand,
and the offspring of thy *bowels* **inwards**
like the *gravel* **belly** *thereof*;
his name should not have been cut off
nor destroyed from *before me* **my face**.
20 Go ye forth of *Babylon* **Babel**,
flee ye from the *Chaldeans* **Kesediym**,
with a voice of *singing declare* **shouting tell** ye,
tell **have us hear** this, utter it *even* to the end of the earth;
say ye, *The LORD* **Yah Veh**
hath redeemed his servant *Jacob* **Yaaqov**.
21 And they thirsted not
when he *led* **carried** them
through the *deserts* **parched areas**:
he caused the waters to flow out of the rock for them:
he *clave* **split** the rock *also*,
and the waters *gushed out* **flowed**.
22 There is no *peace* **shalom**,
saith *the LORD* **Yah Veh**,
unto the wicked.

THE SERVANT OF YAH VEH

49 *Listen* **Hearken**, O *isles* **islands**, unto me;
and hearken, ye *people* **nations**, from far;
The LORD **Yah Veh** hath called
me from the *womb* **belly**;
from the *bowels* **inwards** of my mother
hath he *made mention of* **mentioned** my name.
2 And he hath *made* **set** my
mouth like a sharp sword;
in the shadow of his hand hath he hid me,
and *made* **set** me a polished *shaft* **arrow**;
in his quiver hath he hid me;
3 And said unto me,
Thou art my servant, O *Israel* **Yisra El**,
in whom I *will* **shall** be *glorified* **adorned**.
4 Then I said, I have laboured in vain,
I have *spent* **finished off** my *strength* **force**
for *nought* **a waste**, and in vain:

yet surely my judgment is with *the LORD* **Yah Veh**,
and my *work* **deeds** with my *God* **Elohim**.
5 And now, saith *the LORD* **Yah Veh**
that formed me from the *womb* **belly** to be his servant,
to *bring Jacob again* **return Yaaqov** to him,
Though *Israel* **Yisra El** be not gathered,
yet shall I be *glorious* **honoured**
in the eyes of *the LORD* **Yah Veh**,
and my *God* **Elohim** shall be my strength.
6 And he said, It is *a light thing* **trifling**
that thou shouldest be my servant
to raise up the *tribes* **scions** of *Jacob* **Yaaqov**,
and to restore the *preserved* **guarded** of *Israel* **Yisra El**:
I *will* **shall** also give thee for a light
to the *Gentiles* **goyim**,
that thou mayest be my salvation
unto the end of the earth.
7 Thus saith *the LORD* **Yah Veh**,
the Redeemer of *Israel* **Yisra El**, *and* his Holy One,
to *him whom man despiseth*
the despised in soul,
to *him whom the nation abhorreth*
the abhorrent of the goyim,
to a servant of *rulers* **sovereigns**,
Kings **Sovereigns** shall see and arise,
princes **governors** also shall *worship* **prostrate**,
because of *the LORD* **Yah Veh**
that is *faithful* **trustworthy**,
and the Holy One of *Israel* **Yisra El**,
and he shall choose thee.

THE RESTORATION OF YISRA EL

8 Thus saith *the LORD* **Yah Veh**,
and now Adonay Yah Veh and his Spirit send me.
17 Thus says Yah Veh,
your Redeemer, the Holy One of Yisra El;
I—Yah Veh your Elohim
teaching you to benefit,
aiming you in the way to go.
18 O had you hearkened to my misvoth
then your shalom had become as a river,
and your justness as the waves of the sea:
19 and your seed as the sand;
and the offspring of your inwards as the belly;
and his name,
neither cut off nor destroyed from my face.
20 Come from Babel!
Flee from the Kesediym!
Tell with a voice of shouting what we hear!
Utter it to the end of the earth!
Say, Yah Veh redeems his servant Yaaqov.
21 And they thirst not;
he carried them through the parched areas:
he flowed the waters from the rock for them:
he split the rock and the waters flowed.
22 There is no shalom, says Yah Veh,
to the wicked.

THE SERVANT OF YAH VEH

49 Hearken, O islands, to me;
and hearken, you nations, from afar;
Yah Veh called me from the belly;
from the inwards of my mother
he mentioned my name:
2 and he set my mouth as a sharp sword;
in the shadow of his hand he hid me,
and set me *as* a polished arrow;
in his quiver he hid me.
3 And he says to me,
You are my servant, O Yisra El,
in whom I *am* adorned.
4 Then I say, I labored in vain;
I finished off my force for a waste, and in vain:
surely my judgment is with Yah Veh,
and my deeds with my Elohim.
5 And now, says Yah Veh
who formed me from the belly to be his servant,
to return Yaaqov to him,
Though Yisra El is not gathered,
yet I *am* honored in the eyes of Yah Veh,
and my Elohim is my strength.
6 And he says, It is trifling
that you become my servant
to raise up the scions of Yaaqov;
and to restore the guarded of Yisra El:
I also give you for a light to the goyim,
to become my salvation to the end of the earth.
7 Thus says Yah Veh,
the Redeemer of Yisra El, his Holy One,
to the despised in soul
to the abhorrent of the goyim
to a servant of sovereigns,
Sovereigns see and rise; and governors prostrate;
because of Yah Veh who is trustworthy
—the Holy One of Yisra El, and he chooses you.

THE RESTORATION OF YISRA EL

8 Thus says Yah Veh,
In *an acceptable* **a** time **of pleasure**
have I *heard* **answered** thee,

and in a day of salvation have I helped thee:
and I *will preserve* **shall guard** thee,
and give thee for a covenant of the people,
to *establish* **raise** the earth,
to cause to inherit
the *desolate heritages* **desolated inheritances**;
9 That thou mayest say to the
prisoners **bound**, Go forth;
to them that are in darkness, *Shew* **Expose** *yourselves.*
They shall *feed* **graze** in the ways,
and their pastures shall be in all *high places* **the barrens.**
10 They shall not *hunger* **famish** nor thirst;
neither shall *the heat* **glare** nor sun smite them:
for he that *hath mercy on* **mercieth** them
shall *lead* **drive** them,
even by the springs of water shall he guide them.
11 And I *will make* **shall set**
all my mountains a way,
and my highways shall be exalted.
12 Behold, these shall come from far:
and, *lo* **behold**, these from the north
and from the *west* **seaward**;
and these from the land of Sinim.
13 *Sing* **Shout**, O heavens; and
be joyful **twirl**, O earth;
and break forth into *singing* **shouting**, O mountains:
for *the LORD* **Yah Veh**
hath *comforted* **sighed over** his people,
and *will have* **shall** mercy
upon his afflicted **his humbled**.
14 But *Zion* **Siyon** said,
The LORD **Yah Veh** hath forsaken me,
and *my Lord* **Adonay** hath forgotten me.
15 Can a woman forget her *sucking child* **suckling**,
that she should not *have compassion on* **mercy**
the son of her *womb* **belly**?
yea, they may forget, yet *will* **shall** I not forget thee.
16 Behold,
I have *graven* **engraved** thee
upon the palms of my hands;
thy walls are continually *before* **in front of** me.
17 Thy *children* **sons** shall *make haste* **hasten**;
thy *destroyers* **demolishers**
and they that *made* **parched** thee *waste*
shall go forth of thee.
18 Lift up thine eyes round about, and *behold* **see**:
all these gather *themselves together*, and come to thee.
As I live, *saith the LORD* **an oracle of Yah Veh,**
thou shalt surely *clothe* **enrobe** thee with them all,
as with an ornament,
and bind them *on thee*, as a bride *doeth*.
19 For thy *waste* **parched areas**
and thy *desolate places* **desolated,**
and the land of thy destruction,
shall even now be too *narrow* **restricted**
by reason of the *inhabitants* **settlers,**
and they that swallowed thee *up*
shall be far *away* **removed.**
20 *The children which thou shalt have,*
after thou hast lost the other,
The sons of thy bereavements
shall say again in thine ears,
The place is too *strait* **tribulated** for me:
give place to **approach** me that I may *dwell* **settle.**
21 Then shalt thou say in thine heart,
Who hath *begotten* **birthed** me these,
seeing I have *lost my children* **aborted,**
and am *desolate* **sterile,**
a captive **an exile,** *and removing to and fro* **turned aside**?
and who hath *brought up* **nourished** these?
Behold, I *was left* alone **survived;**
these, where had they been?
22 Thus saith *the Lord GOD* **Adonay Yah Veh,**
Behold,
I *will* **shall** lift up mine hand to the *Gentiles* **goyim,**
and *set up* **lift** my *standard* **ensign** to the people:
and they shall bring thy sons in *their arms* **bosom,**
and thy daughters
shall be *carried* **borne** upon their shoulders.
In a time of pleasure I answered you;
and in a day of salvation I helped you:
and I guard you
and give you for a covenant of the people
to raise the earth;
to have them inherit the desolated inheritances;
9 to say to the bound, Come!
To them in darkness, Expose!
They graze in the ways
with their pastures in all the barrens:
10 they neither famish nor thirst;
neither glare nor sun smites them:
for he who mercies them, drives them;
and by the springs of water he guides them.
11 And I set all my mountains, a way,
and my highways, exalted.
12 Behold, these come from afar;
and behold, these from the north
and from the seaward;
and these from the land of Sinim.
13 Shout, O heavens! And twirl, O earth!
And break forth into shouting, O mountains!

For Yah Veh sighs over his people
and mercies his humbled.
14 And Siyon says, Yah Veh forsook me!
and, Adonay forgot me!
15 Forgets a woman her suckling?
Mercies she not the son of her belly?
Yes, they forget; but I—I forget you not.
16 Behold,
I engraved you on the palms of my hands;
your walls are continually in front of me.
17 Your sons hasten;
your demolishers and they who parched you
go from you.
18 Lift up your eyes all round, and see:
all these gather and come to you.
I live—an oracle of Yah Veh
surely you, as an ornament, enrobe them all,
and bind them as a bride.
19 For your parched areas and your desolated
and the land of your destruction
are even now too restricted by reason of the settlers;
and they who swallow you *are* far removed.
20 Again the sons of your bereavements
say in your ears,
The place is too tribulated for me:
approach me, and I settle *down*.
21 Then you say in your heart,
Who birthed me these,
seeing I aborted and *am* sterile
—an exile, turned aside?
And who nourished these?
Behold, I alone survive;
These—whence *are* they?
22 Thus says Adonay Yah Veh,
Behold, I lift my hand to the goyim
and lift my ensign to the people:
and they bring your sons in the bosom
and bear your daughters on their shoulders:
23 And *kings* **sovereigns**
shall be thy *nursing fathers* **nurturers**,
and their *queens* **governesses**
thy *nursing mothers* **sucklers**:
they shall *bow down* **prostrate** to thee
with their *face* **nostrils** toward the earth,
and lick up the dust of thy feet;
and thou shalt know that *I am the LORD* **I—Yah Veh**:
for they shall not *be ashamed* **shame**
that *wait for* **await** me.
24 Shall the prey be taken from the mighty,
or the *lawful* **just** captive *delivered* **rescued**?
25 But thus saith *the LORD* **Yah Veh**,
Even the captives of the mighty shall be taken away,
and the prey of the *terrible* **tyrant**
shall be *delivered* **rescued**:
for I *will* **shall** contend with him
that contendeth with thee,
and I *will* **shall** save thy *children* **sons**.
26 And I *will* **shall** feed them that oppress thee
with their own flesh;
and they shall *be drunken* **intoxicate**
with their own blood,
as with *sweet wine* **squeezed juice**:
and all flesh shall know that I *the LORD* **Yah Veh**
am thy Saviour and thy Redeemer,
the *mighty* **Almighty** One of *Jacob* **Yaaqov**.

The Sin Of Yisra El

50 Thus saith *the LORD* **Yah Veh**,
Where is the *bill* **scroll** of your mother's divorcement,
whom I have *put* **sent** away?
or **to** which of my *creditors* **exactors**
is it to whom I have sold you?
Behold,
for your *iniquities* **perversities** have ye sold yourselves,
and for your *transgressions* **rebellions**
is your mother *put* **sent** away.
2 Wherefore, when I came, was there no man?
when I called, was there none to answer?
In shortening, Is my hand shortened *at all*,
that it cannot redeem?
or have I no *power* **force** to *deliver* **rescue**?
behold, at my rebuke I *dry up* **parch** the sea,
I *make* **set** the rivers a wilderness:
their fish stinketh, because there is no water,
and dieth for thirst.
3 I *clothe* **enrobe** the heavens
with *blackness* **darkness**,
and I *make sackcloth* **set saq** their covering.

The Tongue Of The Discipled

4 *The Lord GOD* **Adonay Yah Veh**
hath given me the tongue of the *learned* **discipled**,
that I should know
how to *speak* **reinforce** a word *in season*
to *him that is* **the** weary:
he wakeneth morning by morning,
he wakeneth mine ear to hear as the *learned* **discipled**.
5 *The Lord GOD* **Adonay Yah**
Veh hath opened mine ear,
and I was not rebellious,
neither *turned away back* **apostatized backward**.

A Messianic Prophecy

6 I gave my back to the smiters,
and my cheeks to them that *plucked off the hair* **balden**:
I hid not my face from shame and spitting.
7 For *the Lord GOD will* **Adonay**
Yah Veh shall help me;
therefore shall I not be confounded:
therefore have I set my face like a flint,
and I know that I shall not *be ashamed* **shame**.
8 He is near that justifieth me;
who *will* **shall** contend with me?
let us stand together:
who is *mine adversary* **the master of my judgment**?
let him come near to me.
9 Behold,
the Lord GOD will **Adonay Yah Veh shall** help me;
who is he that shall *condemn* **declare** me **wicked**?
lo **behold**,
they all shall *wax old* **wear out** as *a garment* **clothes**;
the moth shall eat them *up*.
10 Who is among you that
feareth *the LORD* **Yah Veh**,
23 and sovereigns become your nurturers
and their governesses your sucklers:
they prostrate to you
with their nostrils toward the earth
and lick up the dust of your feet;
and you know I—Yah Veh:
for they who await me shame not.
24 Take they the prey from the mighty?
Or rescue the captive of the just?
25 For thus says Yah Veh,
Even the captives of the mighty *are* taken
and the prey of the tyrant *is* rescued:
for I contend with him who contends with you
and I save your sons:
26 and they who oppress you,
I feed with their own flesh;
and intoxicate with their own blood
as with squeezed juice:
that all flesh know I—Yah Veh
your Saviour and your Redeemer,
the Almighty One of Yaaqov.

The Sin Of Yisra El

50 Thus says Yah Veh,
Where is the scroll of divorcement of your mother
whom I sent away?
Or to which of my exactors have I sold you?
Behold, for your perversities you sold yourselves,
and for your rebellions *is* your mother sent away.
2 Why, when I came, was there no man?
I called, and no one answered?
In shortening, is my hand shortened,
that it cannot redeem?
Or have I no force to rescue?
Behold, at my rebuke I parch the sea;
I set the rivers a wilderness:
their fish stink because there is no water
and they die for thirst:
3 I enrobe the heavens with darkness
and I set saq their covering.

The Tongue Of The Discipled

4 Adonay Yah Veh
gives me the tongue of the discipled,
to know *how* to reinforce a word to the weary:
he wakens morning by morning;
he wakens my ear to hear as the discipled:
5 Adonay Yah Veh opens my ear,
and I neither rebel nor apostatize backward.

A Messianic Prophecy

6 I give my back to the smiters
and my cheeks to them who balden;
I hide not my face from shame and spitting;
7 and Adonay Yah Veh helps me:
so I confound not;
so I set my face as a flint;
and I know that I shame not.
8 He who justifies me is near;
Who contends with me?
We stand together:
Who is the master of my judgment?
Have him come near me.
9 Behold, Adonay Yah Veh helps me!
Who declares me wicked?
Behold, they all wear out as clothes;
the moth eats them.
10 Who among you fears Yah Veh?
that *obeyeth* **hearkeneth unto** the voice of his servant,
that walketh in darkness, and hath no *light* **brilliance**?
let him *trust* **confide** in the name of *the LORD* **Yah Veh**,
and *stay* **lean** upon his *God* **Elohim**.
11 Behold, all ye that kindle a fire,
that *compass yourselves about* **girt** with sparks:
walk in the *light* **flame** of your fire,
and in the sparks that ye have *kindled* **burnt**.
This shall ye have of mine hand;
ye shall lie down in *sorrow* **agony**.

THE ETERNAL SALVATION OF SIYON

51 Hearken to me,
ye that *follow after righteousness* **pursue justness**,
ye that seek *the LORD* **Yah Veh**:
look unto the rock whence ye are hewn,
and to the *hole* **quarry** of the *pit* **well**
whence ye are *digged* **bored**.
2 Look unto Abraham your father,
and unto Sarah that *bare* **writhed** you:
for **one,** I **have** called him *alone*,
and blessed him, and *increased* **abounded** him.
3 For *the LORD* **Yah Veh**
shall *comfort Zion* **sigh over Siyon**:
he *will comfort* **shall sigh over**
all her *waste places* **parched areas**;
and he *will make* **shall set** her wilderness like Eden,
and her *desert* **plain**
like the garden of *the LORD* **Yah Veh**;
joy **rejoicing** and *gladness* **cheerfulness**
shall be found therein,
thanksgiving **spread hands**,
and the voice of *melody* **psalm**.
4 Hearken unto me, my people;
and *give ear* **hearken** unto me, O my nation:
for a *law* **torah** shall proceed from me,
and I *will make* **shall rest** my judgment *to rest*
for a light of the people.
5 My *righteousness* **justness** is near;
my salvation is gone forth,
and mine arms shall judge the people;
the *isles* **islands** shall *wait upon* **await** me,
and on mine arm shall they *trust* **wait**.
6 Lift up your eyes to the heavens,
and look upon the earth beneath:
for the heavens shall vanish away like smoke,
and the earth shall *wax old* **wear out**
like *a garment* **clothes**,
and they that *dwell* **settle** therein
shall die *in like manner* **as stingers**:
but my salvation shall be *for ever* **eternal**,
and my *righteousness* **justness**
shall not be *abolished* **broken down**.
7 Hearken unto me, ye that
know *righteousness* **justness**,
the people in whose heart is my *law* **torah**;
fear **awe** ye not the reproach of men,
neither *be ye afraid* **terrify** of their revilings.
8 For the moth shall eat them
up like *a garment* **clothes**,
and the *worm* **moth** shall eat them like wool:
but my *righteousness* **justness** shall be *for ever* **eternal**,
and my salvation from generation to generation.
9 Awake, awake, *put on* **enrobe** strength,
O arm of *the LORD* **Yah Veh**;
awake, as in the ancient days,
in the generations *of old* **eternal**.
Art thou not it that hath *cut Rahab* **hewn Rahab/pride**,
and *wounded* **pierced** the *dragon* **monster**?
10 Art thou not it which hath
dried **parched** the sea,
the waters of the great *deep* **abyss**;
that hath *made* **set** the depths of the sea
a way for the *ransomed* **redeemed** to pass over?
11 Therefore
the redeemed of *the LORD* **Yah Veh** shall return,
and come with *singing* **shouting** unto *Zion* **Siyon**;
and *everlasting joy* **eternal cheerfulness**
shall be upon their head:
they shall *obtain* **attain**
gladness **rejoicing** and *joy* **cheerfulness**;
and sorrow **grief** and *mourning* **sighing** shall flee away.
12 I, *even* I, *am* he that
comforteth **sigheth over** you:
Who hearkens to the voice of his servant?
Who walks in darkness with no brilliance?
Have him confide in the name of Yah Veh
and lean on his Elohim.
11 Behold, all you who kindle a fire,
who girt with sparks:
walk in the flame of your fire
and in the sparks you burn.
This becomes you from my hand;
you lie down in agony.

THE ETERNAL SALVATION OF SIYON

51 Hearken to me, you who pursue justness,
you who seek Yah Veh:
look to the rock whence you were hewn
and to the quarry of the well whence you were bored:
2 look to Abraham your father,
and to Sarah who writhed you:
I, for one,
called him and blessed him and abounded him.
3 For Yah Veh sighs over Siyon:
he sighs over all her parched areas;
and he sets her wilderness as Eden
and her plain as the garden of Yah Veh;
rejoicing, yes, and cheerfulness are found therein
—spread hands and the voice of psalm.

4 Hearken to me, O my people;
and hearken to me, O my nation:
for a torah proceeds from me
and I rest my judgment for a light of the people.
5 My justness *is* near;
my salvation and my arms go forth;
they judge the people;
the islands await me and on my arm they await.
6 Lift your eyes to the heavens
and look to the earth beneath:
for the heavens vanish as smoke
and the earth wears out as clothes;
and they who settle therein die as stingers:
and my salvation *is* eternal,
and my justness breaks not down.
7 Hearken to me, you who know justness,
the people in whose heart my torah *is*;
neither awe the reproach of men
nor terrify of their revilings:
8 For the moth eats them as cloth
and the moth eats them as wool:
and my justness *is* eternal
and my salvation from generation to generation.
9 Waken! Waken!
Enrobe strength, O arm of Yah Veh!
Waken as in the ancient days
—in the generations eternal.
Is it not you who hews Rahab/pride?
—piercing the monster?
10 Is it not you who parches the sea
—the waters of the great abyss?
Who sets the depths of the sea
—a way for the redeemed to pass over?
11 And the redeemed of Yah Veh return
and come with shouting to Siyon;
with eternal cheerfulness on their head:
they attain rejoicing and cheerfulness;
grief and sighing flee away.
12 I—I—he who sighs over you.
who art thou,
that thou shouldest *be afraid of* **awe** a man that shall die,
and of the son of *man* **humanity**
which shall be *made* **given** as grass;
13 And forgettest *the LORD*
Yah Veh thy *maker* **worker,**
that hath *stretched forth* **spread** the heavens,
and laid the foundations of the earth;
and hast feared continually every day
because **at the face** of the fury of the oppressor,
as if he were *ready* **prepared** to *destroy* **ruin**?
and where is the fury of the oppressor?
14 The *captive exile* **stroller** hasteneth
that he may be loosed,
and that he should not die in the pit **of ruin**,
nor that his bread should *fail* **lack**.
15 But *I am the LORD* **I—Yah Veh** thy *God* **Elohim**,
that *divided* **split** the sea, whose waves roared: *The*
LORD of hosts **Yah Veh Sabaoth** is his name.
16 And I have *put* **set** my words in thy mouth,
and I have covered thee in the shadow of mine hand,
that I may plant the heavens,
and lay the foundations of the earth,
and say unto *Zion* **Siyon**, Thou *art* my people.

THE CUP OF THE FURY OF YAH VEH

17 Awake, awake,
stand up **arise**, O *Jerusalem* **Yeru Shalem**,
which hast drunk at the hand of *the LORD* **Yah Veh**
the cup of his fury;
thou hast drunken
the *dregs* **chalice** of the cup of *trembling* **staggering**,
and wrung *them* out.
18 There is none to guide her
among all the sons whom she hath
brought forth **birthed**;
neither is there any that *taketh* **holdeth** her by the hand
of all the sons that she hath *brought up* **nourished**.
19 These two *things are come unto* **confront** thee;
who shall *be sorry for* **wag over** thee?
desolation **ravage**, and *destruction* **breaking**,
and the famine, and the sword:
by whom shall I *comfort* **sigh over** thee?
20 Thy sons have *fainted* **languished**,
they lie at the head of all the *streets* **outways**,
as *a wild bull* **an antelope** in a net:
they are full of the fury of *the LORD* **Yah Veh**,
the rebuke of thy *God* **Elohim**.
21 Therefore hear *now* **I beseech** this,
thou *afflicted* **humbled**,
and *drunken* **intoxicated**, but not with wine:
22 Thus saith thy *Lord the LORD* **Adonay Yah Veh**,
and thy *God* **Elohim**
that pleadeth the cause of his people,
Behold, I have taken out of thine hand
the cup of *trembling* **staggering**,
even the *dregs* **chalice** of the cup of my fury;
thou shalt *no more* **not add to** drink it again:
23 But I *will put* **shall set** it
into the hand of them that *afflict* **grieve** thee;
which have said to thy soul,

Bow down **Prostrate**, that we may *go* **pass** over:
and thou hast *laid* **set** thy *body* **back** as the *ground* **earth**,
and as the *street* **outway**, to them that *went* **passed** over.

Siyon Redeemed

52 Awake, awake;
put on **enrobe** thy strength, O *Zion* **Siyon**;
put on **enrobe**
thy *beautiful garment* **clothes of adornment**,
O *Jerusalem* **Yeru Shalem**, the holy city:
for henceforth
there shall *no more* **not add to** come into thee
the uncircumcised and the *unclean* **foul**.
2 Shake thyself from the dust;
arise, *and* sit down, O *Jerusalem* **Yeru Shalem**:
loose thyself from the *bands* **bonds** of thy neck,
O captive daughter of *Zion* **Siyon**.
3 For thus saith *the LORD* **Yah Veh**,
Ye have sold yourselves *for nought* **gratuitously**;
and ye shall be redeemed without *money* **silver**.
4 For thus saith *the Lord GOD* **Adonay Yah Veh**,
Who are you to awe a man who dies?
and, of the son of humanity, given as grass?
13 And forgets Yah Veh your worker
who spread the heavens
and laid the foundations of the earth?
—who feared continually every day
at the face of the fury of the oppressor
as if he were prepared to ruin?
And where is the fury of the oppressor?
14 The stroller hastens to be loosed
that he neither dies in the pit of ruin
nor that he lacks bread.
15 And I—Yah Veh your Elohim,
who split the sea; who roared the waves:
Yah Veh Sabaoth *is* his name.
16 And I set my words in your mouth;
and I covered you in the shadow of my hand
to plant the heavens
and to lay the foundations of the earth,
and to say to Siyon, You *are* my people.

The Cup Of Te Fury Of Yah Veh

17 Waken! Waken! Rise, O Yeru Shalem
who, at the hand of Yah Veh,
drank the cup of his fury;
the chalice of the cup of staggering
you drank and wrung out.
18 There is neither one to guide her
among all the sons whom she birthed;
nor is there any, of all the sons she nourished,
who holds her by the hand.
19 These two confront you.
Who wags over you?
Ravage and breaking and the famine and the sword!
Who *except* me sighs over you?
20 Your sons languish;
they lie at the head of all the outways
as an antelope in a net:
they are full of the fury of Yah Veh
—the rebuke of your Elohim.
21 So I beseech, hear this,
O humbled and intoxicated—but not with wine.
22 Thus says your Adonay Yah Veh,
and your Elohim who pleads the cause of his people,
Behold, I take the cup of staggering from your hand
—the chalice of the cup of my fury;
add not to drink it again:
23 and I set it in the hand of them who grieve you;
who say to your soul,
Prostrate, and we pass over:
and you set your back as the earth,
and as the outway, to them who pass over.

Siyon Redeemed

52 Waken! Waken!
Enrobe your strength, O Siyon;
enrobe your clothes of adornment, O Yeru Shalem,
the holy city:
for henceforth the uncircumcised and the foul
add not to enter you.
2 Shake yourself from the dust;
Rise! Sit, O Yeru Shalem!
Loose yourself from the bonds of your neck,
O captive daughter of Siyon!
3 For thus says Yah Veh,
You, sold gratuitously;
and you, redeemed without silver.
4 For thus says Adonay Yah Veh,
My people *went down aforetime* **descended formerly**
into *Egypt* **Misrayim** to sojourn there;
and the *Assyrian* **Ashshuri** oppressed them
without cause **unceasingly**.
5 Now therefore, what have I here,
saith the LORD **an oracle of Yah Veh**,
that my people is taken away *for nought* **gratuitously**?
they that *rule* **reign** over them *make* **cause** them to howl,
saith the LORD **an oracle of Yah Veh**;
and my name
continually every day is *blasphemed* **scorned**.

6 Therefore my people shall know my name:
therefore *they shall know* in that day
that I *am*—he that doth speak: behold, *it is* I.

A Messianic Prophecy

7 How *beautiful* **befitting** upon the mountains
are the feet of him
that *bringeth good tidings* **evangelizeth**,
that *publisheth peace* **hearkeneth shalom**;
that *bringeth good tidings* **evangelizeth** of good,
that *publisheth* **hearkeneth** salvation;
that saith unto *Zion* **Siyon**, Thy *God* **Elohim** reigneth!
8 Thy *watchmen* **watchers** shall lift *up* the voice;
with the voice together shall they *sing*
shout: for they shall see eye to eye,
when *the LORD* **Yah Veh**
shall *bring again Zion* **return Siyon**.
9 Break forth into joy, *sing* **shout** together,
ye *waste places* **parched areas** of *Jerusalem* **Yeru Shalem**:
for *the LORD* **Yah Veh**
hath *comforted* **sighed over** his people,
he hath redeemed *Jerusalem* **Yeru Shalem**.
10 *The LORD* **Yah Veh**
hath *made bare* **stripped** his holy arm
in the eyes of all the *nations* **goyim**;
and all the *ends* **finalities** of the earth
shall see the salvation of our *God* **Elohim**.
11 *Depart* **Turn** ye **aside**, *depart* **turn** ye **aside**,
go ye out from thence,
touch *no unclean thing* **not the foul**;
go ye out of the midst of her;
be ye *clean* **purified**,
that bear the *vessels* **instruments** of *the LORD* **Yah Veh**.
12 For ye shall not go out with
haste, nor go by *flight* **retreat**:
for *the LORD* **Yah Veh**
will **shall** go *before you* **at thy face**;
and *the God* **Elohim** of *Israel* **Yisra El**
will be your rereward **shall gather you**.

A Messianic Prophecy

13 Behold, my servant shall
deal prudently **comprehend**,
he shall be exalted and *extolled* **lifted**,
and be *very high* **mightily lifted**.
14 As many were astonied at thee;
his visage was so *marred more than any* **ruined by** man,
and his form *more than* **by** the sons of *men* **humanity**:
15 So shall he sprinkle many *nations* **goyim**;
the *kings* **sovereigns** shall shut their mouths at him:
for that which had not been *told* **scribed** them
shall they see;
and that which they had not heard
shall they *consider* **discern**.

53 Who hath *believed* **trusted** our report?
and to whom
is the arm of *the LORD revealed* **Yah Veh exposed**?
2 For he shall *grow up before*
him **ascend at his face**
as a *tender plant* **sprout**,
and as a root out of *a dry ground* **parched earth**:
he hath no form nor *comeliness* **majesty**;
and when we shall see him,
there is no *beauty* **visage** that we should desire him.
3 He is despised and *rejected* **abandoned** of men;
a man of sorrows,
and *acquainted with grief* **knowing sickness**:
and we hid as it were our faces from him;
he was despised, and we *esteemed* **machinated** him not.
4 Surely he hath borne our *griefs* **sicknesses**,
and *carried* **borne** our sorrows:
yet we *did esteem* **machinated** him *stricken* **plagued**,
smitten of *God* **Elohim**, and *afflicted* **abased**.
Formerly my people descended into Misrayim
to sojourn there;
and the Ashshuri oppressed them unceasingly:
5 and now, what *is to* me here
—an oracle of Yah Veh
that my people *are* taken away gratuitously?
They who reign over them have them to howl
—an oracle of Yah Veh
and continually every day my name is scorned.
6 So my people know my name:
so in that day
surely I *am* he who speaks: Behold—I.

A Messianic Prophecy

7 How befitting on the mountains
are the feet of him who evangelizes:
who hearkens shalom;
who evangelizes of good;
who hearkens salvation;
who says to Siyon, Your Elohim reigns!
8 Your watchers lift the voice;
with the voice they shout together:
for they see eye to eye
when Yah Veh returns to Siyon.
9 Break forth in joy!
Shout together, you parched areas of Yeru Shalem!
For Yah Veh sighs over his people;

he redeems Yeru Shalem:
10 Yah Veh strips his holy arm
in the eyes of all the goyim;
and all the finalities of the earth
see the salvation of our Elohim.
11 You, turn aside! Turn aside!
Come out from thence! Touch not the foul!
You, come from her midst!
You, be purified,
who bear the instruments of Yah Veh.
12 For you neither go in haste
nor come in retreat:
for Yah Veh goes at your face;
and Elohim of Yisra El gathers you.

A Messianic Prophecy

13 Behold, my servant comprehends;
he is exalted and lifted—mightily lifted.
14 As many astonish at you;
his visage so ruined by man;
and his form by the sons of humanity:
15 thus he sprinkles many goyim;
the sovereigns shut their mouths at him:
for what *was* not scribed to them, they see;
and what they heard not, they discern.

53 Who trusts our report?
and to whom is the arm of Yah Veh exposed?
2 For he ascends at his face as a sprout
—as a root from parched earth:
he has neither form nor majesty when we see him;
nor visage when we desire him.
3 He is despised and abandoned of men;
a man of sorrows, and knowing sickness:
as one from whom we hide our face;
he was despised, and we machinated him not.
4 Surely he bore our sicknesses
and bore our sorrows:
yet we machinated him plagued
—smitten of Elohim and abased.
5 But he was *wounded* **pierced**
for our *transgressions* **rebellions**,
he was bruised **crushed** for our *iniquities* **perversities**:
the chastisement of our *peace* **shalom** was upon him;
and with his *stripes* **lashes** we are healed.
6 All we like *sheep* **a flock**
have *gone astray* **strayed**;
we have *turned* **faced** every *one* **man** to his own way;
and *the LORD* **Yah Veh** hath *laid* **met** on him
the *iniquity* **perversity** of us all.
7 *He was oppressed* **Of him they exacted,**
and he was *afflicted* **abased**,
yet he opened not his mouth:
he is brought as a lamb to the slaughter,
and as *a sheep* **an ewe**
before **at the face of** her shearers is *dumb* **muted**,
so he openeth not his mouth.
8 He was taken
from prison **by restraint** and *from* **by** judgment:
and who shall *declare* **meditate** his generation?
for he was cut off out of the land of the living:
for the *transgression* **rebellion** of my people
was *he stricken* **the plague upon him.**
9 And he *made* **gave** his *grave*
tomb with the wicked,
and with the rich in his death;
because he had *done* **worked** no violence,
neither was *any* deceit in his mouth.
10 Yet it *pleased the LORD* **delighted Yah Veh**
to *bruise* **crush** him;
he hath *put* **stroked** him *to grief*:
when thou shalt *make* **set** his soul
an offering for sin **for the guilt**,
he shall see his seed, he shall prolong his days,
and the *pleasure* **delight** of *the LORD* **Yah Veh**
shall prosper in his hand.
11 He shall see of the *travail* **toil** of his soul,
and shall be satisfied:
by his knowledge
shall my *righteous* **just** servant justify many;
for he shall bear their *iniquities* **perversities.**
12 Therefore *will* **shall** I *divide* **allot** him *a portion*
with the great,
and he shall *divide* **allot** the spoil
with the *strong* **mighty**;
because he hath poured out his soul unto death:
and he was numbered with the *transgressors* **rebels**;
and he bare the sin of many,
and *made intercession* **interceded**
for the *transgressors* **rebels**.

The Glory Of Siyon

54 *Sing* **Shout**, O *barren* **sterile**,
thou that *didst* **birthed** not *bear*;
break forth into *singing* **shouting**,
and *cry aloud* **resound**,
thou that *didst* **writhed** not *travail with child*:
for more are the *children* **sons** of the *desolate* **desolated**
than the *children* **sons** of the married *wife*,
saith *the LORD* **Yah Veh**.
2 Enlarge the place of thy tent,

and let them *stretch forth* **spread** the curtains
of *thine habitations* **thy tabernacles**:
spare not, lengthen thy cords, and strengthen thy stakes;
3 For thou shalt *break forth* **separate**
on the right *hand* and on the left;
and thy seed shall *inherit* **succeed** the *Gentiles* **goyim**,
and make **settle** the *desolate* **desolated** cities
to be inhabited.
4 *Fear* **Awe** not; for thou shalt
not *be ashamed* **shame**:
neither be thou *confounded* **ashamed**;
for thou shalt not *be put to shame* **blush**:
for thou shalt forget the shame of thy youth,
and shalt not remember
the reproach of thy widowhood any more.
5 For thy *Maker* **Worker** is
thine husband **thy master**;
the LORD of hosts **Yah Veh Sabaoth** is his name;
and thy Redeemer the Holy One of *Israel* **Yisra El**;
The *God* **Elohim** of the whole earth shall he be called.
6 For *the LORD* **Yah Veh** hath called thee
as a woman forsaken and *grieved* **contorted** in spirit,
and a *wife* **woman** of youth, when thou wast refused,
saith thy *God* **Elohim**.
7 For a small *moment* **blink** have I forsaken thee;
5 And he is pierced for our rebellions;
crushed for our perversities:
the chastisement of our shalom *is* on him;
and with his lashes we are healed.
6 We all strayed as a flock;
—every man faced to his own way;
and on him, Yah Veh met all our perversity.
7 Of him they exact, and him they abase;
yet he opens not his mouth:
brought as a lamb to the slaughter
and as an ewe at the face of her shearers:
he is mute, and opens not his mouth:
8 taken by restraint and by judgment:
and who meditates his generation?
For he is cut off from the land of the living:
—plagued for the rebellion of my people.
9 And he gives his tomb with the wicked
and with the rich in his death;
because he neither worked violence
nor is deceit in his mouth.
10 Yet Yah Veh delights to crush him;
he strokes him:
when you set his soul for the guilt,
he sees his seed; he prolongs his days:
and the delight of Yah Veh prospers in his hand.
11 He sees the toil of his soul, and satisfies:
by his knowledge my just servant justifies many;
for he bears their perversities.
12 So I allot him with the great,
and he allots the spoil with the mighty;
because he pours his soul to death:
numbered with the rebels;
and he bears the sin of many,
and intercedes for the rebels.

THE GLORY OF SIYON

54 Shout, O sterile;
you who birth not!
Break forth into shouting and resound,
you who writhe not!
for more are the sons of the desolated
than the sons of the married, says Yah Veh.
2 Enlarge the place of your tent,
and spread the curtains of your tabernacles:
Spare not! Lengthen your cords!
Strengthen your stakes!
3 For you separate on the right and on the left;
and your seed succeeds the goyim
and settle in the desolated cities.
4 Awe not;
neither shame nor be ashamed nor blush:
for you forget the shame of your youth
and remember no more
the reproach of your widowhood.
5 For your Worker is your master;
Yah Veh Sabaoth is his name;
and your Redeemer, the Holy One of Yisra El;
the Elohim of the whole earth he *is* called.
6 For Yah Veh called you
as a woman forsaken and contorted in spirit,
and a woman of youth when she is refused,
says your Elohim.
7 For a small blink I forsook you;
but with great mercies *will* **shall** I gather thee.
8 In *a little wrath* **an outburst of rage**
I hid my face from thee for a *moment* **blink**;
but with *everlasting kindness* **eternal mercy**
will I have mercy on **shall I mercy** thee,
saith *the LORD* **Yah Veh** thy Redeemer.
9 For this is as the waters of *Noah* **Noach** unto me:
for *as* I have *sworn* **oathed**
that the waters of *Noah* **Noach**
should no more *go* **pass** over the earth;
so have I *sworn* **oathed**
that I *would* **should** not be *wroth* **enraged** with thee,

nor rebuke thee.
10 For the mountains shall depart,
and the hills *be removed* **topple**;
but my *kindness* **mercy** shall not depart from thee,
neither shall the covenant of my *peace* **shalom**
be removed **topple**,
saith *the LORD* **Yah Veh**
that *hath mercy on* **mercieth** thee.
11 O thou *afflicted* **humbled**,
tossed with tempest **stormtossed**,
and not *comforted* **sighed over**,
behold, I *will lay* **shall crouch** thy stones
with *fair colours* **stribium**,
and lay thy foundations with sapphires.
12 And I *will make thy windows* **shall set thy sun**
of *agates* **rubies**,
and thy *gates* **portals** of *carbuncles* **carbuncle stones**,
and all thy borders of *pleasant* stones **of delight**.
13 And all thy *children* **sons**
shall be *taught* **discipled** of *the LORD* **Yah Veh**;
and great shall be the *peace* **shalom** of thy *children* **sons**.
14 In *righteousness* **justness**
shalt thou *be established* **establish thyself**:
thou shalt be far **removed** from oppression;
for thou shalt not *fear* **awe**:
and from *terror* **ruin**;
for it shall not *come near* **approach** thee.
15 Behold,
in sojourning, they shall *surely gather together* **sojourn**,
but not by me:
whosoever shall *gather together* **sojourn** against thee
shall fall for thy sake.
16 Behold, I have created the *smith* **engraver**
that *bloweth* **puffeth** the coals in the fire,
and that bringeth forth an instrument for his work;
and I have created the *waster* **ruiner** to *destroy* **ruin**.
17 No *weapon* **instrument**
that is formed against thee
shall prosper;
and every tongue that shall rise against thee in judgment
thou shalt *condemn* **declare wicked**.
This is the *heritage* **inheritance**
of the servants of *the LORD* **Yah Veh**,
and their *righteousness* **justness** is of me,
saith the LORD **an oracle of Yah Veh**.

THE OPEN INVITATION OF YAH VEH

55 Ho, every one that thirsteth,
come ye to the waters,
and he that hath no *money* **silver**;
come ye, *buy* **market for kernels**, and eat;
yea, come, *buy* **market for kernels** wine and milk
without *money* **silver** and without price.
2 Wherefore do ye *spend money* **weigh silver**
for that which is not bread?
and your labour for that which satisfieth not?
in hearkening, hearken *diligently* unto me,
and eat ye that which is good,
and let your soul delight itself in fatness.
3 *Incline* **Spread** your ear, and come unto me:
hear, and your soul shall live;
and I *will make* **shall cut**
an *everlasting* **eternal** covenant with you,
even the *sure* **trustworthy** mercies of David.
4 Behold, I have given him *for* a witness
to the *people* **nations**,
a leader **eminent** and *commander* **misvaher**
to the *people* **nations**.
but with great mercies I gather you:
8 in an outburst of rage
I hid my face from you for a blink; and in eternal
mercy I mercy you, says Yah Veh your Redeemer.
9 For this is as the waters of Noach to me:
in that I oathed
that the waters of Noach pass no more over the earth;
thus I oathed that I neither enrage over you
nor rebuke you.
10 For the mountains depart and the hills topple;
but neither my mercy departs from you,
nor the covenant of my shalom topple,
says Yah Veh who mercies you.
11 O you humbled; stormtossed; not sighed over:
behold, I crouch your stones with stribium,
and lay your foundations with sapphires:
12 and I set your sun of rubies,
and your portals of carbuncle stones,
and all your borders of stones of delight:
13 and disciple all your sons by Yah Veh;
and great is the shalom of your sons.
14 Establish yourself in justness
—far removed from oppression
for you awe not:
and from ruin;
for it approaches you not.
15 Behold, in sojourning, they sojourn,
but not by me:
whosoever sojourns against you
falls for your sake.
16 Behold, I created the engraver
who puffs the coals in the fire

and who brings forth an instrument for his work;
and I created the ruiner to ruin.
17 No instrument formed against you prospers;
and every tongue rising against you in judgment,
you declare wicked.
This is the inheritance of the servants of Yah Veh
and their justness is of me
—an oracle of Yah Veh.

The Open Invitation Of Yah Veh

55 Ho, every one who thirsts!
Come to the waters!
And he who has no silver,
come, market for kernels, and eat;
yes, come, market for kernels, wine and milk
—without silver and without price.
2 Why weigh silver for what is not bread?
And labor for what satisfies not?
In hearkening, hearken to me,
and eat what is good,
that your soul delight itself in fatness.
3 Spread your ear, and come to me;
hear, and your soul lives;
and I cut an eternal covenant with you
—the trustworthy mercies of David.
4 Behold, I give him—a witness to the nations
—eminent and misvaher to the nations.
5 Behold,
thou shalt call a *nation* **goyim** that thou knowest not,
and *nations* **goyim** that knew not
thee shall run unto thee
because of *the LORD* **Yah Veh** thy *God* **Elohim**,
and for the Holy One of *Israel* **Yisra El**;
for he hath *glorified* **adorned** thee.
6 Seek ye *the LORD* **Yah Veh**
while he may be found,
call ye upon him while he is near:
7 Let the wicked forsake his way,
and the *unrighteous* man **of mischief**
his *thoughts* **fabrications**:
and let him return unto *the LORD* **Yah Veh**,
and he *will* **shall** *have* mercy *upon* him;
and to our *God* **Elohim**,
for he *will abundantly pardon* **shall abound to forgive**.
8 For my *thoughts* **fabrications**
are not your *thoughts* **fabrications**,
neither are your ways my ways,
saith the LORD **an oracle of Yah Veh**.
9 For *as* the heavens are higher than the earth,
so are my ways higher than your ways,
and my *thoughts* **fabrications** than
your *thoughts* **fabrications**.
10 For as the *rain cometh down*
downpour descendeth,
and the snow from *heaven* **the heavens**,
and returneth not thither,
but *watereth* **saturateth** the earth,
and *maketh* it *bring forth* **birtheth** and *bud* **sprouteth**,
that it may give seed to the *sower* **seeder**,
and bread to the eater:
11 So shall my word be that
goeth forth out of my mouth:
it shall not return unto me void,
but it shall *accomplish* **work** that which I *please* **desire**,
and it shall prosper *in the thing* whereto I sent it.
12 For ye shall go out with *joy* **cheerfulness**,
and be led forth with *peace* **shalom**:
the mountains and the hills shall break forth
before you **at thy face** into *singing* **shouting**,
and all the trees of the field shall clap their *hands* **palms**.
13 Instead of the thorn
shall *come up* **ascend** the fir tree,
and instead of the brier
shall *come up* **ascend** the myrtle tree:
and it shall be to *the LORD* **Yah Veh** for a name,
for an *everlasting* **eternal** sign that shall not be cut off.

Salvation For All

56 Thus saith *the LORD* **Yah Veh**,
Keep **Guard** ye judgment, and *do justice* **work justness**:
for my salvation is near to come,
and my *righteousness* **justness** to be *revealed* **exposed**.
2 *Blessed* **Blithesome** is the
man that *doeth* **worketh** this,
and the son of *man* **humanity** that layeth hold on it;
that *keepeth* **guardeth** the *sabbath* **shabbath**
from *polluting* **profaning** it,
and *keepeth* **guardeth** his hand
from *doing* **working** any evil.
3 Neither let the son of the stranger,
that hath joined himself to *the LORD* **Yah Veh**,
speak **say**, saying,
In separating,
The LORD **Yah Veh** hath *utterly*
separated me from his people:
neither let the eunuch say, Behold, I am a dry tree.
4 For thus saith *the LORD*
Yah Veh unto the eunuchs
that *keep* **guard** my *sabbaths* **shabbaths**,
and choose *the things* **those** that *please* **delight** me,

and *take* hold *of* my covenant;
5 Even unto them
will **shall** I give in mine house and within my walls
a *place* **hand** and a name
better than of sons and of daughters:
I *will* **shall** give them an *everlasting* **eternal** name,
that shall not be cut off.
6 Also the sons of the stranger,
that join themselves to *the LORD* **Yah Veh,**
to *serve* **minister to** him,
and to love the name of *the LORD* **Yah Veh,**
to be his servants,
every one that *keepeth* **guardeth** the *sabbath* **shabbath**
from *polluting* **profaning** it,
and *taketh hold of* **holdeth** my covenant;
5 Behold, you call a goyim whom you know not,
and goyim whom know you not run to you
because of Yah Veh your Elohim,
and for the Holy One of Yisra El;
for he adorns you.
6 Seek Yah Veh while he is to be found;
call on him while he is near:
7 the wicked forsake his way;
and the man of mischief, his fabrications:
and he returns to Yah Veh, and he mercies him;
and to our Elohim, for he abounds to forgive.
8 For neither are my fabrications your fabrications
nor your ways my ways
—an oracle of Yah Veh.
9 For *as* the heavens are higher than the earth
thus are my ways higher than your ways
—and my fabrications than your fabrications.
10 For as the downpour and the snow
descend from the heavens, and returns not
—but saturates the earth and births and sprouts
—to give seed to the seeder and bread to the eater:
11 thus becomes my word that
comes from my mouth:
it returns not to me void
but works what I desire;
and it prospers whereto I send it.
12 For you go forth with cheerfulness
and lead forth with shalom:
the mountains and the hills
break forth into shouting at your face;
and all the trees of the field clap their palms.
13 Instead of the thorn, the fir tree ascends,
and instead of the brier, the myrtle tree ascends:
and it becomes to Yah Veh for a name,
for an eternal sign, not cut off.

SALVATION FOR ALL

56 Thus says Yah Veh,
You, guard judgment and work justness;
for my salvation comes near
and to expose my justness.
2 Blithesome—the man who works this
and the son of humanity who lays hold thereon;
who guards from profaning the shabbath
and guards his hand from working any evil.
3 Neither let the son of the stranger,
who joins himself to Yah Veh, say, saying,
In separating, Yah Veh separated me from his people:
nor let the eunuch say, Behold, I am a dry tree.
4 For thus says Yah Veh to the eunuchs
who guard my shabbaths
and choose what delights me and hold my covenant;
5 I give them in my house and within my walls
a hand and a name
better than of sons and of daughters:
I give them an eternal name that is not cut off.
6 And sons of the stranger
who join themselves to Yah Veh
to minister to him and to love the name of Yah Veh
—to be his servants,
every one who guards from profaning the shabbath
and holds my covenant;
7 Even them *will* **shall** I bring
to my holy mountain,
and *make* **cheer** them *joyful* in my house of prayer:
their *burnt offerings* **holocausts** and their sacrifices
shall be *accepted* **a pleasure**
upon *mine* **my sacrifice** altar;
for mine house shall be called
an house of **my** prayer for all people.
8 *The Lord GOD* **An oracle of Adonay Yah Veh,**
which gathereth
the *outcasts* **overthrown** of *Israel* **Yisra El** *saith,*
Yet *will* **shall** I gather *others* to him,
beside those that are gathered unto him.
9 All ye *beasts* **live beings** of
the field, come to devour,
yea, all ye *beasts* **live beings** in the forest.
10 His *watchmen* **watchers** are blind:
they *are all ignorant* **know not,**
they are all *dumb* **mute** dogs, they cannot bark;
sleeping **dreaming,** lying down, loving to slumber.
11 Yea, they are *greedy* dogs **strong of soul**
which *can never have enough* **know not
satisfaction,** and they are *shepherds* **tenders**

that *cannot understand* **know not to discern**:
they all *look to* **face** their own way,
every *one* **man** for his gain, from his *quarter* **end**.
12 Come ye, *say they*, I *will fetch* **shall take** wine,
and we *will fill ourselves* **shall carouse**
with *strong drink* **intoxicants**;
and to morrow shall be as this day,
and *much more abundant* **a mighty great remainder**.

THE JUST DESTRUCT

57 The *righteous perisheth* **just destructeth**,
and no man *layeth* **setteth** it to heart:
and merciful men are *taken away* **gathered**,
none *considering* **discerning**
that the *righteous* **just** is *taken away* **gathered**
from **the face of** the evil *to come*.
2 He shall enter into *peace* **shalom**:
they shall rest in their beds,
each one walking in his *uprightness*
straightforwardness.
3 But *draw near* **approach** hither,
ye sons of the *sorceress* **cloudgazer**,
the seed of the adulterer and the whore.
4 Against whom do ye *sport* **delight** yourselves?
against whom *make ye a wide* **enlarge ye the** mouth,
and *draw out* **lengthen** the tongue?
are ye not children of *transgression* **rebellion**,
a seed of falsehood,
5 *Enflaming yourselves* **Heating**
up with *idols* **elohim**
under every green tree,
slaying **slaughtering** the children in the *valleys* **wadies**
under the *clifts* **clefts** of the rocks?
6 Among the *smooth stones*
smooth stones/allotment
of the *stream* **wadi** is thy *portion* **allotment**;
they, they are thy *lot* **pebble**:
even to them hast thou poured a *drink offering* **libation**,
thou hast *offered a meat* **holocausted an** offering.
should I *receive comfort* **sigh** in these?
7 Upon a lofty and *high* **lifted** mountain
hast thou set thy bed:
even thither *wentest* **ascendest** thou *up*
to *offer* **sacrifice** sacrifice.
8 Behind the doors also and the posts
hast thou set up thy remembrance:
for thou hast *discovered* **exposed** thyself
to another than **from** me,
and art *gone up* **ascended**;
thou hast enlarged thy bed,
and *made* **cut** thee *a covenant* with them;
thou lovedst their bed where thou sawest it.
9 And thou *wentest* **strollest** to the *king* **sovereign**
with ointment,
and *didst increase* **abounded** thy perfumes,
and *didst send* **sent** thy *messengers* **ambassadors** far off,
and *didst debase* **debased** thyself *even* unto *hell* **sheol**.
10 Thou art *wearied* **belaboured**
in the greatness of thy way;
yet saidst thou not, *There is no hope* **I quit!**:
thou hast found the life of thine hand;
therefore thou wast not *grieved* **worn**.
7 I bring them to my holy mountain,
and cheer them in my house of prayer:
their holocausts and their sacrifices
are a pleasure on my sacrifice altar;
for my house is called
a house of my prayer for all people
8 —an oracle of Adonay Yah Veh
who gather the overthrown of Yisra El:
again I gather to him—to his gathered ones.
9 All you live beings of the field, come to devour
—all you live beings in the forest.
10 His watchers are blind; they know not:
they are all mute dogs; they cannot bark:
dreaming, lying down, loving to slumber.
11 Yes, they are dogs, strong of soul,
who know not satisfaction;
and they are tenders who know not to discern:
they all face their own way,
every man for his gain, from his end.
12 You, come; I take wine,
and we carouse with intoxicants;
and tomorrow is as this day
—a mighty great remainder.

THE JUSTDESTRUCT

57 The just destruct and no man sets it to heart:
and merciful men gather and no one discerns
that the just are gathered from the face of the evil.
2 He enters into shalom; they rest in their beds
—each walking in straightforwardness.
3 And approach here, you sons of the cloudgazer
—the seed of the adulterer and the whore.
4 Against whom delight you yourselves?
Against whom enlarge you the mouth
and lengthen the tongue?
Are you not children of rebellion?
A seed of falsehood
5 heating up with elohim under every green tree?

Slaughtering the children in the wadies
under the clefts of the rocks?
6 Among the smooth stones/allotments
of the wadi is your allotment;
they—they are your pebble:
also to them you pour a libation,
you holocaust an offering.
Sigh I in these?
7 On a lofty and lifted mountain
you set your bed:
also there you ascend to sacrifice sacrifice:
8 and behind the doors and the posts
you set up your remembrance:
for you expose yourself from me, and ascend;
you enlarge your bed and you cut with them;
you love their bed where you see it:
9 and you stroll to the sovereign with ointment
and abound your perfumes;
and send your ambassadors afar off
and debase yourself to sheol:
10 you belabor in the greatness of your way;
yet you say not, I quit!
You find the life of your hand;
so you are not worn.
11 And of whom
hast thou been *afraid* **concerned** or *feared* **awed**,
that thou hast lied, and hast not remembered me,
nor *laid* **set** it to thy heart?
have not I *held my peace even of old* **hushed eternally**,
and thou *fearest* **awest** me not?
12 I *will declare* **shall tell** thy
righteousness **justness**,
and thy works;
for they shall not *profit* **benefit** thee.
13 When thou criest,
let thy *companies deliver* **throngs rescue** thee;
but the wind shall *carry* **bear** them all away;
vanity shall take them:
but he that *putteth his trust* **seeketh refuge** in me
shall *possess* **inherit** the land,
and shall inherit my holy mountain;
14 And shall say, *Cast ye* **Raise** up, *cast ye* **raise** up,
prepare **face** the way,
take up **lift** the stumblingblock
out of the way of my people.
15 For thus saith the high and *lofty* **lifted** One
that *inhabiteth* **tabernacleth** eternity,
whose name is Holy;
I *dwell* **tabernacle** in the high and holy *place*,
with him also
that is of a *contrite* **crushed** and *humble* **lowly** spirit,
to *revive* **enliven** the spirit of the *humble* **lowly**,
and to *revive* **enliven** the heart
of the *contrite* **crushed** *ones*.
16 For I *will* **shall** not contend *for ever* **eternally**,
neither *will* **shall** I be *always wroth* **perpetually enraged**:
for the spirit should *fail before me* **languish at my face**,
and the *souls* **breaths** which I have *made* **worked**.
17 For the *iniquity* **perversity**
of his *covetousness* **greedy gain**
was I *wroth* **enraged**, and smote him:
I hid me, and was *wroth* **enraged**,
and he went on *frowardly* **apostate**
in the way of his heart.
18 I have seen his ways, and *will* **shall** heal him:
I *will lead* **shall guide** him also,
and *restore comforts* **shalam solaces** unto him
and to his mourners.
19 I create the fruit of the lips;
Peace **Shalom**, *peace* **shalom** to him that is far off,
and to him that is near, saith *the LORD* **Yah Veh**;
and I *will* **shall** heal him.
20 But the wicked are like the *troubled* **driven** sea,
when it cannot rest,
whose waters *cast up mire* **expel filth** and *dirt* **mire**.
21 There is no *peace* **shalom**,
saith my *God* **Elohim**,
to the wicked.

FASTING

58 *Cry aloud* **Call out with the throat**, spare not,
lift up thy voice like a *trumpet* **shophar**,
and *shew* **tell** my people their *transgression* **rebellion**,
and the house of *Jacob* **Yaaqov** their sins.
2 Yet they seek me *daily* **day by day**,
and delight to know my ways,
as a *nation* **goyim** that *did righteousness*
worked justness,
and forsook not the *ordinance*
judgment of their *God* **Elohim**:
they ask of me the *ordinances*
judgments of *justice* **justness**;
they take delight in approaching to *God* **Elohim**.
3 Wherefore have we fasted,
say they, and thou seest not?
wherefore have we *afflicted* **humbled** our soul,
and thou takest no knowledge?
Behold, in the day of your fast ye find *pleasure* **delight**,
and exact all your *labours* **contortions**.
4 Behold, ye fast for strife and *debate* **strive**,
and to smite with the fist of wickedness:
ye shall not fast as ye do this day,

to *make* **have** your voice to be heard on high.
5 Is it such a fast that I have chosen?
a day for *a man* **humanity** to *afflict* **humble** his soul?
is it to bow down his head as a bulrush,
and to spread *sackcloth* **saq** and ashes *under him*?
Wilt **Shalt** thou call this a fast,
and an acceptable **a** day **of pleasure**
to *the LORD* **Yah Veh**?
11 And of whom are you concerned or awed,
that you lie
and neither remember me nor set it to your heart?
Hushed I not eternally, and you awed me not?
12 I tell your justness and your works;
and they benefit you not.
13 You cry; your throngs rescue you;
and the wind bears them all away;
vanity takes them:
and he who seeks refuge in me inherits the land,
and inherits my holy mountain:
14 and says, Raise! Raise! Face the way!
Lift the stumblingblock from the way of my people.
15 For thus says the high and lifted One
who tabernacles eternally—whose name is Holy;
I tabernacle in the high and holy
and with the crushed and lowly spirit
—to enliven the spirit of the lowly,
and to enliven the heart of the crushed.
16 For I neither contend eternally
nor perpetually rage:
for the spirit languishes at my face,
and the breaths I work.
17 For the perversity of his greedy gain
I rage and smite him:
I hide myself and rage,
and he goes on apostate in the way of his heart.
18 I see his ways and heal him; yes, I guide him;
and shalam solaces to him and to his mourners.
19 I create the fruit of the lips;
shalom, shalom to him who is far off
and to him who is near, says Yah Veh; and I heal him.
20 And the wicked *are* as the driven sea,
when it cannot rest,
whose waters expel filth and mire.
21 There is no shalom, says
my Elohim, to the wicked.

FASTING

58 Call out with the throat! Spare not!
Lift your voice as a shophar
and tell my people their rebellion;
and the house of Yaaqov their sins.
2 Yet they seek me day by day
and delight to know my ways
—as a goyim who works justness
and forsakes not the judgment of their Elohim:
they ask me of the judgments of justness;
they take delight in approaching Elohim.
3 Why fast we
and you see not?
Why humble we our soul
and you take no knowledge?
Behold, in the day of your fast you find delight,
and exact all your contortions.
4 Behold, you fast for strife and strive
and to smite with the fist of wickedness:
you fast not as *this* day,
so that your voice is heard on high.
5 Is this such a fast as I chose?
A day for humanity to humble his soul?
To bow the head as a bulrush
and to spread saq and ashes?
Call you this a fast—a day of pleasure to Yah Veh?
6 Is not this the fast that I have chosen?
to loose the bands of wickedness,
to undo the *heavy burdens* **bundles of the yoke pole**,
and to *let* **send away** the *oppressed* **crushed**
go free **liberated**,
and that ye *break* **tear** every yoke **pole**?
7 Is it not to *deal* **separate** thy bread
to the *hungry* **famished**,
and that thou bring
the *poor that are cast out* **humble outcasts** to thy house?
when thou seest the naked, that thou cover him;
and that thou *hide* **conceal** not thyself
from thine own flesh?
8 Then shall thy light
break forth **split** as the *morning* **dawn**,
and thine health
shall *spring forth speedily* **sprout quickly**:
and thy *righteousness* **justness**
shall go *before thee* **at thy face**;
the *glory* **honour** of *the LORD* **Yah Veh**
shall *be thy rereward* **gather thee up**.
9 Then shalt thou call,
and *the LORD* **Yah Veh** shall answer;
thou shalt cry, and he shall say, *Here I am* **Behold, I**.
If thou *take away* **turn aside** from the midst of thee
the yoke **pole**,
the *putting forth* **spreading** of the finger,
and *speaking vanity* **wording mischief**;
10 And if thou *draw out* **produce** thy soul

to the *hungry* **famished,**
and satisfy the *afflicted* **humbled** soul;
then shall thy light rise in obscurity,
and thy darkness be as the noon *day:*
11 And *the LORD* **Yah Veh**
shall guide thee continually,
and satisfy thy soul in *drought* **parch,**
and *make fat* **fatten** thy bones:
and thou shalt be like a *watered* **saturated** garden,
and like a spring of water, whose waters fail not.
12 And they that shall be of thee
shall build the *old waste places* **original parched areas:**
thou shalt raise *up* the foundations
of *many generations* **generation and generation;**
and thou shalt be called,
The *repairer* **waller** of the breach,
The restorer of paths to *dwell* **settle** *in.*
13 If thou turn away thy foot
from the *sabbath* **shabbath,**
from *doing* **working** thy *pleasure*
delight on my holy day;
and call the *sabbath* **shabbath** a *delight* **luxury,**
the holy of *the LORD* **Yah Veh,** honourable;
and shalt honour him,
not *doing* **working** thine own ways,
nor finding thine own *pleasure* **delight,**
nor *speaking* **wording** thine own words:
14 Then shalt thou delight
thyself in *the LORD* **Yah Veh;**
and I *will* **shall** cause thee to ride
upon the *high places* **bamahs** of the earth,
and feed thee
with the *heritage* **inheritance** of *Jacob* **Yaaqov** thy father:
for the mouth of *the LORD* **Yah Veh**
hath *spoken it* **worded.**

SEPARATION FROM YAH VEH

59 Behold,
the LORD'S **Yah Veh's** hand is not shortened,
that it cannot save **from saving;**
neither his ear heavy, *that it cannot hear* **from hearing:**
2 But your *iniquities* **perversities** have separated
between you and **between** your *God* **Elohim,**
and your sins have hid his face from you,
that he *will* **shall** not hear.
3 For your *hands* **palms** are
defiled **profaned** with blood,
and your fingers with *iniquity* **perversity;**
your lips have *spoken lies* **worded falsehoods,**
your tongue hath muttered *perverseness* **wickedness.**
4 None calleth for *justice* **justness,**
nor any pleadeth for *truth* **trustworthiness:**
they *trust* **confide** in *vanity* **waste,**
and *speak lies* **word vanity;**
they conceive *mischief* **toil,**
and *bring forth iniquity* **birth mischief.**

6 Is not the fast I chose thus:
To loose the bands of wickedness?
To undo the bundles of the yoke pole?
And to send the crushed away liberated?
And to tear every yoke pole?
7 Is it not to separate your bread to the famished?
To bring the humble outcasts to your house?
To cover the naked when you see him?
To not conceal yourself from your own flesh?
8 Then your light splits as the dawn
and your health sprouts quickly
and your justness comes at your face:
the honor of Yah Veh gathers you.
9 Then you call and Yah Veh answers;
you cry and he says, Behold—I.
If you turn aside the yoke pole from your midst
—the spreading of the finger and wording mischief;
10 and if you produce your soul to the famished
and satisfy the humbled soul;
then your light rises in obscurity
and your darkness as the noon;
11 and Yah Veh guides you continually
and satisfies your soul in parch
and fattens your bones:
and you become as a saturated garden
and as a spring of water whose waters fail not.
12 And from you
they build the original parched areas:
and you raise the foundations
of generation and generation;
and they call you,
The waller of the breach!
The restorer of paths to settle!
13 If you turn away your foot from the shabbath
from working your delight on my holy day;
and call the shabbath, a luxury
and the holy of Yah Veh, honorable
and honor him;
neither working your own ways
nor finding your own delight
nor wording your own words,
14 then you delight yourself in Yah Veh;
and I ride you on the bamahs of the earth
and feed you the inheritance of Yaaqov your father:
for the mouth of Yah Veh has worded.

Separation From Yah Veh

59 Behold,
neither is the hand of Yah Veh shortened from saving
nor his ear heavy from hearing:
2 but your perversities separate
between you and between your Elohim; and
your sins hide his face from hearing you.
3 For you profane your palms with blood
and your fingers with perversity;
your lips word falsehoods
your tongue mutters wickedness:
4 no one calls for justness
and no one pleads for trustworthiness:
they confide in waste and word vanity;
they conceive toil and birth mischief:
5 They *hatch cockatrice'* **split hisser's** eggs,
and weave the spider's web:
he that eateth of their eggs dieth,
and that which is crushed
breaketh out **splitteth** into a *viper* **hisser.**
6 Their webs shall not become *garments* **clothes,**
neither shall they cover themselves with their works:
their works are works of *iniquity* **mischief,**
and the *act* **deed** of violence is in their *hands* **palms.**
7 Their feet run to evil,
and they *make haste* **hasten** to *shed*
pour innocent blood:
their *thoughts* **fabrications**
are *thoughts* **fabrications** of *iniquity* **mischief;**
wasting **ravage** and *destruction* **breaking**
are in their *paths* **highways.**
8 The way of *peace* **shalom** they know not;
and there is no judgment in their *goings* **route:**
they have made them *crooked* **perverted** paths:
whosoever *goeth* **treadeth** therein
shall not know *peace* **shalom.**
9 Therefore is judgment far **removed** from us,
neither doth *justice* **justness** overtake us:
we *wait for* **await** light, but behold obscurity;
for *brightness* **brilliancies,** but we walk in darkness.
10 We grope for the wall like the blind,
and we grope as if we had no eyes:
we *stumble* **falter** at noon *day*
as in the *night* **evening breeze;**
we are in *desolate places* **fertile fields** as dead *men.*
11 We roar all like bears,
and *mourn sore* **in cooing, coo** like doves:
we *look for* **await** judgment, but there is none;
for salvation, but it is far *off* **removed** from us.
12 For our *transgressions* **rebellions**
are multiplied before **abound by the**
myriads in front of thee,
and our sins *testify* **answer** against us:
for our *transgressions* **rebellions** are with us;
and as for our *iniquities* **perversities,** we know them;
13 In *transgressing* **rebelling** and lying
against *the LORD* **Yah Veh,**
and departing away from our *God* **Elohim,**
speaking **wording** oppression and revolt,
conceiving and *uttering* **muttering** from the heart
words of falsehood.
14 And judgment is *turned*
away **removed** backward,
and *justice* **justness** standeth afar off:
for truth *is fallen* **faltereth** in the *street* **broadway,**
and *equity* **straightforwardness** cannot enter.
15 Yea, truth *faileth* **lacketh;**
and he that *departeth* **turneth aside** from evil
maketh himself a prey **is spoiled:**
and *the LORD saw it* **Yah Veh seeth,**
and it *displeased him* **be evil in his eyes**
that there *was* **be** no judgment.

The Redeemer

16 And he saw that there was no man,
and *wondered* **astonisheth** that there was no intercessor:
therefore his arm *brought salvation unto* **saved** him;
and his *righteousness* **justness,** it sustained him.
17 For he *put on righteousness* **enrobed justness**
as a *breastplate* **habergeon,**
and an helmet of salvation upon his head;
and he *put on* **enrobed**
the *garment* **clothes** of *vengeance* **avengement**
for *clothing* **robes,**
and was *clad* **covered** with zeal as a *cloke* **mantle.**
18 According to their *deeds* **dealings,**
accordingly he *will repay* **shall shalam,**
fury to his *adversaries* **tribulators,**
recompence **dealing** to his enemies;
to the islands
he *will repay recompence* **shall shalam.**
19 So shall they *fear* **awe** the
name of *the LORD* **Yah Veh**
from the *west* **dusk,**
and his *glory* **honour** from the rising of the sun.
When the *enemy* **tribulator**
shall come in like a *flood* **river,**
the Spirit of *the LORD* **Yah Veh**
shall *lift up a standard against him* **cause him to flee.**

5 they split the eggs of the hisser,
and weave the web of the spider:
he who eats their eggs dies,
and the crushed *egg* splits into a hisser.
6 Neither their webs become clothes,
nor cover they themselves with their works:
their works are works of mischief
and the deed of violence *is* in their palms.
7 Their feet run to evil
and they hasten to pour innocent blood:
their fabrications are fabrications of mischief;
ravage and breaking *are* in their highways:
8 the way of shalom they know not
and there is no judgment in their route:
they make them perverted paths;
whoever treads therein knows not shalom.
9 So judgment removes far from us
and justness overtakes us not:
we await light; and behold, obscurity:
for brilliancies; and we walk in darkness:
10 we grope for the wall as the blind;
and we grope as if we have no eyes:
we falter at noon as in the evening breeze;
in fertile fields as the dead:
11 we roar as bears—we all;
and in cooing, coo as doves:
we await judgment, and there is none;
for salvation, and it removes far from us.
12 For our rebellions
abound by the myriads in front of you;
and our sins answer against us:
for our rebellions are with us;
and as for our perversities, we know them.
13 In rebelling and lying against Yah Veh;
and departing from our Elohim:
wording oppression and revolt;
conceiving and muttering from the heart
words of falsehood:
14 and judgment removes backward
and justness stands afar off:
for truth falters in the broadway
and straightforwardness cannot enter.
15 Yes, truth lacks;
and he who turns aside from evil, spoils:
and Yah Veh sees,
and it is evil in his eyes that there is no judgment.

THE REDEEMER

16 And he sees that there is no man
and astonishes that there is no intercessor:
and his own arm saves him;
and his justness sustains him:
17 and he enrobes justness as a habergeon
and an helmet of salvation on his head;
and for robes, he enrobes the clothes of avengement
and covers with zeal as a mantle.
18 According to their dealings,
thus he shalams fury to his tribulators,
dealing to his enemies;
he shalams to the islands.
19 Thus they awe the name
of Yah Veh from the dusk
and his honor from the rising of the sun.
When the tribulator comes in as a river
the Spirit of Yah Veh has him to flee.
20 And the Redeemer shall come to *Zion* **Siyon**,
and unto them that turn
from *transgression* **rebellion** in *Jacob* **Yaaqov**,
saith the LORD **an oracle of Yah Veh**.
21 As for me,
this is my covenant with them, saith *the LORD* **Yah Veh**;
My spirit that is upon thee,
and my words which I have *put* **set** in thy mouth,
shall not depart out of thy mouth,
nor out of the mouth of thy seed,
nor out of the mouth of thy seed's seed,
saith *the LORD* **Yah Veh**,
from henceforth and *for ever* **eternally**.

THE HONOUR OF SIYON

60 Arise, *shine* **enlighten**; for thy light is come,
and the *glory* **honour** of *the LORD* **Yah Veh**
is risen upon thee.
2 For, behold, the darkness shall cover the earth,
and *gross* **dripping** darkness the *people* **nation**:
but *the LORD* **Yah Veh** shall arise upon thee,
and his *glory* **honour** shall be seen upon thee.
3 And the *Gentiles* **goyim** shall come to thy light,
and *kings* **sovereigns**
to the *brightness* **brilliance** of thy rising.
4 Lift up thine eyes round about, and see:
all they gather *themselves together*, they come to thee:
thy sons shall come from far,
and thy daughters shall *be nursed* **nurture** at thy side.
5 Then thou shalt *see* **awe**, and flow together,
and thine heart shall fear, and *be enlarged* **enlarge**;
because the abundance of the sea
shall *be converted* **turn** unto thee,
the *forces* **valued** of the *Gentiles* **goyim**
shall come unto thee.

6 The *multitude* **throngs** of
camels shall cover thee,
the dromedaries of *Midian* **Midyan** and Ephah;
all they from Sheba shall come:
they shall *bring* **bear** gold and incense;
and they shall *shew forth* **evangelize**
the *praises* **halals** of *the LORD* **Yah Veh**.
7 All the flocks of *Kedar* **Qedar**
shall *be gathered* **gather** together unto thee,
the rams of *Nebaioth* **Nebayoth** shall minister unto thee:
they shall *come up* **ascend** with *acceptance* **pleasure**
on *mine* **my sacrifice** altar,
and I *will glorify* **shall adorn** the house
of my *glory* **adornment**.
8 Who are these that fly as a cloud,
and as the doves to their windows?
9 Surely the *isles* **islands** shall *wait for* **await** me,
and the ships of Tarshish first, to bring thy sons from far,
their silver and their gold with them,
unto the name of *the LORD* **Yah Veh** thy *God* **Elohim**,
and to the Holy One of *Israel* **Yisra El**,
because he hath *glorified* **adorned** thee.
10 And the sons of strangers
shall build up thy walls,
and their *kings* **sovereigns** shall minister unto thee:
for in my *wrath* **rage** I smote thee,
but in my *favour* **pleasure** *have I had
mercy on* **I mercied** thee.
11 Therefore thy *gates* **portals**
shall be open continually;
they shall not be shut day nor night;
that men may bring unto thee
the forces of the *Gentiles* **goyim**,
and that their *kings* **sovereigns** may be *brought* **driven**.
12 For the *nation* **goyim** and
kingdom **sovereigndom**
that *will* **shall** not serve thee shall *perish* **destruct**; yea,
those *nations* **goyim** shall be utterly *wasted* **parched**.
13 The *glory* **honour** of Lebanon
shall come unto thee,
the fir tree, the *pine* **oak** tree, and the *box* **cedar** together,
to *beautify* **adorn** the place of my *sanctuary* **holies**;
and I *will make* **shall honour**
the place of my feet *glorious*.
14 The sons also of them that
afflicted **humbled** thee
shall come *bending* **prostrating** unto thee;
and all they that *despised* **scorned** thee
shall *bow themselves down* **prostrate**
at the soles of thy feet;
and they shall call thee, The city of *the LORD* **Yah Veh**,
The *Zion* **Siyon** of the Holy One of *Israel* **Yisra El**.
20 And the Redeemer comes to Siyon,
and to them who turn from rebellion in Yaaqov
—an oracle of Yah Veh.
21 As for me,
this is my covenant with them, says Yah Veh;
My spirit which *is* on you,
and my words which I set in your mouth,
depart, neither from your mouth
nor from the mouth of your seed,
nor from the mouth of the seed of your seed,
says Yah Veh,
from henceforth and eternally.

THE HONOR OF SIYON

60 Rise! Enlighten! For your light comes
and the honor of Yah Veh rises on you:
2 for behold, the darkness covers the earth
and dripping darkness the nation:
and Yah Veh rises on you
and his honor is seen on you.
3 And the goyim come to your light
and sovereigns to the brilliance of your rising.
4 Lift your eyes all round, and see:
they all gather; they come to you:
your sons come from afar
and your daughters nurture at your side.
5 Then you awe and flow together;
and your heart fears and enlarges:
because the abundance of the sea turns to you;
the valued of the goyim come to you:
6 the throngs of camels cover you
—the dromedaries of Midyan and Ephah;
all they of Sheba come:
they bear gold and incense
and they evangelize the halals of Yah Veh:
7 all the flocks of Qedar gather to you;
the rams of Nebayoth minister to you:
they ascend with pleasure on my sacrifice altar
and I adorn the house of my adornment.
8 Who are these, flying as a cloud
and as the doves to their windows?
9 Surely the islands await me;
and the ships of Tarshish first
to bring your sons from afar
—their silver and their gold with them
to the name of Yah Veh your Elohim,
and to the Holy One of Yisra El,
because he adorns you.

10 And the sons of strangers build your walls
and their sovereigns minister to you:
for in my rage I smote you
and in my pleasure I mercied you:
11 and your portals open continually
—shut neither day nor night;
to bring you the forces of the goyim,
even their sovereigns are driven.
12 For the goyim and sovereigndom
who serve you not, destruct;
yes, those goyim are utterly parched.
13 The honor of Lebanon comes to you
—the fir tree, the oak tree, and the cedar together
to adorn the place of my holies;
and I honor the place of my feet.
14 And the sons of them who humbled you
come prostrating to you;
and all they who scorn you
prostrate at the soles of your feet;
and they call you, The city of Yah Veh
—The Siyon of the Holy One of Yisra El.
15 *Whereas* **Instead** thou hast
been forsaken and hated,
so that no man *went* **passed** through *thee*,
I *will make* **shall set** thee an eternal *excellency* **pomp**, a
joy of *many generations* **generation and generation**.
16 Thou shalt also suck the
milk of the *Gentiles* **goyim**,
and shalt suck the breast of *kings* **sovereigns**: and
thou shalt know that I *the LORD* **Yah Veh**
am thy Saviour and thy Redeemer,
the *mighty* **Almighty** One of *Jacob* **Yaaqov**.
17 For *brass* **copper** I *will* **shall** bring gold,
and for iron I *will* **shall** bring silver,
and for *wood brass* **timber copper**, and for stones iron:
I *will* **shall** also *make* **set** thy *officers* **overseers**
peace **shalom**,
and thine exactors
righteousness **justness**.
18 Violence shall no more be heard
in thy land,
wasting **ravage** nor *destruction* **breaking**
within thy borders;
but thou shalt call thy walls Salvation,
and thy *gates Praise* **portals Halal**.
19 The sun shall be no more thy light by day;
neither for *brightness* **brilliance**
shall the moon *give light unto* **lighten** thee:
but *the LORD* **Yah Veh** shall be unto thee
an *everlasting* **eternal** light,
and thy *God* **Elohim** thy *glory* **adornment**.
20 Thy sun shall no more go down;
neither shall thy moon *withdraw itself* **be gathered**:
for *the LORD* **Yah Veh**
shall be thine *everlasting* **eternal** light,
and the days of thy mourning
shall *be ended* **shalam**.
21 Thy people also shall be all *righteous* **just**:
they shall *inherit* **be successor of** the land
for ever **eternally**,
the branch of my planting, the work of my hands,
that I may be *glorified* **adorned**.
22 A little *one* shall become a thousand,
and a *small one a strong nation* **little a mighty goyim**:
I *the LORD will* **Yah Veh shall** hasten it in his time.

A Messianic Prophecy

61 The Spirit of *the Lord GOD* **Adonay Yah Veh**
is upon me;
because *the LORD* **Yah Veh** hath anointed me
to *preach good tidings* **evangelize** unto the *meek* **humble**;
he hath sent me to bind up the brokenhearted,
to *proclaim* **call out** liberty to the captives,
and *the opening of the prison to them that are bound*
in opening, an opening to the bound;
2 To *proclaim* **call out**
the *acceptable* year **of pleasure** of *the LORD* **Yah Veh**,
and the day of *vengeance* **avengement**
of our *God* **Elohim**;
to *comfort* **sigh over** all that mourn;
3 To *appoint* **set** unto them
that mourn in *Zion* **Siyon**,
to give unto them *beauty* **adornment** for ashes,
the oil of *joy* **rejoicing** for mourning,
the *garment* **mantle** of *praise* **halal**
for the spirit of heaviness;
that they might be called
trees **mighty oaks** of *righteousness* **justness**,
the planting of *the LORD* **Yah Veh**,
that he might be glorified **to be adorned**.
4 And they shall build
the *old wastes* **original parched areas**,
they shall raise *up*
the former *desolations* **desolated areas**,
and they shall *repair* **renovate** the *waste* **parched** cities,
the *desolations* **desolated areas**
of *many generations* **generation and generation**.
5 And strangers shall stand
and *feed* **tend** your flocks,
and the sons of the *alien* **stranger**
shall be your *plowmen* **cultivators**
and your vinedressers.

6 But ye shall be *named* **called**
the Priests of *the LORD* **Yah Veh**:
men shall call **it shall be said of** you,
the Ministers of our *God* **Elohim**:
15 Instead of being forsaken and hated
so that no man passes through,
I set you an eternal pomp
—a joy of generation and generation:
16 and you suck the milk of the goyim
and suck the breast of sovereigns:
and you know I—Yah Veh
—your Saviour and your Redeemer
—the Almighty One of Yaaqov.
17 For copper, I bring gold;
and for iron, I bring silver;
and for timber, copper; and for stones, iron:
and I set your overseers, shalom;
and your exactors, justness.
18 Violence is heard no more in your land
or ravage or breaking within your borders;
and you call your walls, Salvation,
and your portals, Halal.
19 Neither becomes the sun any more
your light by day;
nor for brilliance, the moon lighten you:
and Yah Veh becomes your eternal light
and your Elohim your adornment.
20 Neither your sun goes down any more;
nor *is* your moon gathered:
for Yah Veh becomes your eternal light;
and the days of your mourning shalam;
21 and all your people just
—successors of the land eternally
—the branch of my planting; the work of my hands;
to be adorned.
22 A little becomes a thousand
and a little a mighty goyim:
I Yah Veh hasten it in his time.

A Messianic Prophecy

61 The Spirit of Adonay Yah Veh is on me;
because Yah Veh anointed me
to evangelize to the humble:
he sent me to bind the brokenhearted;
to call out liberty to the captives;
and in opening, an opening to the bound:
2 to call out the year of pleasure of Yah Veh
and the day of avengement of our Elohim:
to sigh over all who mourn;
3 to set to them who mourn in Siyon;
to give to them adornment for ashes;
the oil of rejoicing for mourning;
the mantle of halal for the spirit of heaviness;
and he calls them, Mighty Oaks of Justness
—the planting of Yah Veh to adorn.
4 And they build the original parched areas;
they raise the former desolated areas;
and they renovate the parched cities
—the desolated areas of generation and generation.
5 And strangers stand and tend your flocks,
and the sons of the stranger
are your cultivators and your vinedressers:
6 and you are called, Priests of Yah Veh:
of you is said, The Ministers of Our Elohim:
ye shall *eat* **consume**
the *riches* **valuables** of the *Gentiles* **goyim**,
and *in* **exchange** their *glory shall ye*
boast yourselves **honour**.
7 For your shame *ye* shall *have* double;
and *for confusion* **shame**
they shall *rejoice* **shout** in their *portion* **allotment**:
therefore in their land they shall possess the double:
everlasting joy **eternal cheerfulness** shall be unto them.
8 For I *the LORD* **Yah Veh** love judgment,
I hate *robbery* **stripping** for *burnt offering* **holocaust**;
and I *will direct* **shall give** their *work* **deeds** in truth,
and I *will make* **shall cut** an *everlasting* **eternal** covenant
with them.
9 And their seed
shall be known among the *Gentiles* **goyim**,
and their offspring among the people:
all that see them shall acknowledge them,
that they *are* the seed which *the*
LORD **Yah Veh** hath blessed.
10 **In rejoicing,**
I *will* **shall** *greatly* rejoice in *the LORD* **Yah Veh**,
my soul shall *be joyful* **twirl** in my *God* **Elohim**;
for he hath *clothed* **enrobed** me
with the *garment* **clothes** of salvation,
he hath *covered* **clothed** me
with the *robe* **mantle** of *righteousness* **justness**,
as a bridegroom decketh *himself*
as a priest with ornaments,
and as a bride adorneth *herself* with
her jewels **instruments**.
11 For as the earth bringeth forth her *bud* **sprout**,
and as the garden
causeth the things that are sown in it to spring forth
sprouteth the seedling;
so *the Lord GOD* **Adonay Yah Veh**

will cause righteousness and praise to spring forth
shall sprout justness and halal
before **in front of** all the *nations* **goyim.**

THE NEW HOME OF SIYON

62 For *Zion's* **Siyon's** sake
will **shall** I not *hold my peace* **hush,**
and for *Jerusalem's* **Yeru Shalem's** sake
I *will* **shall** not rest,
until the *righteousness* **justness** *thereof*
go forth as *brightness* **brilliance,**
and the salvation thereof
as a *lamp* **flambeau** that burneth.
2 And the *Gentiles* **goyim**
shall see thy *righteousness* **justness,**
and all *kings* **sovereigns** thy *glory* **honour:**
and thou shalt be called by a new name,
which the mouth of *the LORD* **Yah Veh**
shall *name* **appoint.**
3 Thou shalt also be a crown of *glory* **adornment**
in the *hand* **palm** of *the LORD* **Yah Veh,**
and a royal *diadem* **turban**
in the hand of thy *God* **Elohim.**
4 *Thou shalt no more be termed*
Neither shall it be said of you,
Forsaken;
neither shall **it be said of** thy land *any more be termed,*
Desolate:
but thou shalt be called *Hephzibah* **Hephsi Bah,**
and thy land *Beulah* **Beulah/Married:**
for *the LORD* **Yah Veh** delighteth in thee,
and thy land shall be *married* **Beulah/Married.**
5 For *as* a *young man* **youth** marrieth a virgin,
so shall thy sons marry thee:
and as the bridegroom *rejoiceth* **joyeth** over the bride,
so shall thy *God* **Elohim** rejoice over thee.
6 I have *set watchmen* **guards**
to oversee upon thy walls,
O *Jerusalem* **Yeru Shalem,**
which shall *never hold their peace* **not hush continually**
day nor night:
ye that *make mention of the LORD* **remember Yah Veh,**
keep not *silence* **quiet,**
7 And give him no *rest* **quiet,** till he establish,
and till he *make Jerusalem* **set Yeru Shalem**
a *praise* **halal** in the earth.
you consume the valuables of the goyim
and exchange their honor:
7 Instead of your shame, double;
and shame they shout in their allotment:
so in their land they possess the double
—eternal cheerfulness *is* theirs.
8 For I Yah Veh love judgment;
I hate stripping for holocaust:
and I give their deeds in truth
and I cut an eternal covenant with them:
9 and their seed is known among the goyim
and their offspring among the people: all
who see them acknowledge them, that
they *are* the seed Yah Veh blesses.
10 In rejoicing, I rejoice in Yah Veh;
my soul twirls in my Elohim:
for he enrobes me with the clothes of salvation,
he clothes me with the mantle of justness
—as a bridegroom decks
—as a priest with ornaments
—as a bride adorns with instruments.
11 For as the earth brings forth her sprout
and as the garden sprouts the seedling
thus Adonay Yah Veh sprouts justness
and halals in front of all the goyim.

THE NEW HOME OF SIYON

62 For sake of Siyon, I hush not;
and for sake of Yeru Shalem, I rest not;
until the justness goes forth as brilliance
and the salvation thereof as a flambeau that burns:
2 and the goyim see your justness and all sovereigns
your honor; and call you by a new name
which the mouth of Yah Veh appoints:
3 and you become a crown of adornment
in the palm of Yah Veh,
and a royal turban
in the hand of your Elohim.
4 Neither is it said of you, Forsaken;
nor is it said of your land, Desolate:
but you are called Hephsi Bah/My Delight,
and your land Beulah/Married:
for Yah Veh delights in you,
and your land is married.
5 For *as* a youth marries a virgin,
thus your sons marry you:
and as the bridegroom joys over the bride,
thus your Elohim rejoices over you.
6 I guard to oversee on your
walls, O Yeru Shalem,
which hush not continually day and night:
you who remember Yah Veh, quiet not;
7 and give him no quiet until he establishes
and until he sets Yeru Shalem a halal in the earth.

8 *The LORD* **Yah Veh** hath *sworn* **oathed**
by his right *hand*, and by the arm of his strength,
Surely I *will* **shall** no more give thy *corn* **crop**
to be *meat* **food** for thine enemies;
and the sons of the stranger
shall not drink thy *wine* **juice**,
for the which thou hast laboured:
9 But they that have gathered it shall eat it,
and *praise the LORD* **halal Yah Veh**;
and they that have *brought it together* **gathered**
shall drink it in the courts of my *holiness* **holies**.
10 *Go* **Pass** through, *go* **pass**
through the *gates* **portals**;
prepare **face** ye the way of the people;
cast **raise** up, *cast* **raise** up the highway;
gather out **stone** the stones;
lift up *a standard* **an ensign** for the people.
11 Behold, *the LORD* **Yah Veh**
hath *proclaimed* **thee hear**
unto the end of the world,
Say ye to the daughter of *Zion* **Siyon**,
Behold, thy salvation cometh;
behold, his *reward* **hire** is with him,
and his *work before him* **deeds at his face**.
12 And they shall call them,
The holy people, The redeemed of *the LORD* **Yah Veh**:
and thou shalt be called,
Sought out, A city not forsaken.

THE DAY OF YAH VEH

63 Who is this that cometh from Edom,
with *dyed garment* **dazzling clothes** from Bozrah?
this that is *glorious* **esteemed** in his *apparel* **robe**,
travelling **strolling** in the greatness of his *strength* **force**?
I that speak in *righteousness* **justness**,
mighty **great** to save.
2 Wherefore art thou red in
thine apparel **thy robe**,
and thy *garment* **clothes**
like him that treadeth in the winefat?
3 I have trodden the *winepress* **press** alone;
and of the people there was *none* **no man** with me:
for I *will* **shall** tread them in *mine anger* **my wrath**,
and trample them in my fury;
and their *blood* **squeezings**
shall be sprinkled upon my *garment* **clothes**,
and I *will stain* **shall profane** all my *raiment* **robe**.
4 For the day of *vengeance*
avengement is in mine heart,
and the year of my redeemed is come.
5 And I looked, and there was none to help;
and I *wondered* **astonished** that
there was none to uphold:
therefore mine own arm
brought salvation unto **hath saved** me;
and my fury, it upheld me.
6 And I *will tread down* **shall trample** the people
in mine anger,
and *make* **intoxicate** them *drunk*
in my fury,
and I *will* **shall** bring down their *strength* **squeezings**
to the earth.
7 I *will mention* **shall remember**
the *lovingkindnesses* **mercies** of *the LORD* **Yah Veh**,
and the *praises* **halals** of *the LORD* **Yah Veh**,
according to all
that *the LORD* **Yah Veh** hath *bestowed on* **dealt** us,
and the great goodness
toward the house of *Israel* **Yisra El**,
which he hath *bestowed* **dealt** on them
according to his mercies,
and according to the *multitude* **abundance**
of his *lovingkindnesses* **mercies**.
8 For he said, Surely they are my people,
children **sons** that *will* **shall** not *lie* **falsify**:
so he was their Saviour.
9 In all their *affliction* **tribulation**
he was *afflicted* **tribulated**,
and the angel of his *presence* **face** saved them:
in his love and in his *pity* **compassion**
he redeemed them; and he bare them,
and *carried* **bore** them all the days of *old* **antiquity**.
10 But they rebelled, and *vexed* **contorted**
his *holy Spirit* **Ruach ha-Kodesh**:
therefore he was turned to be their enemy,
and he fought against them.
8 Yah Veh oaths by his right
and by the arm of his strength,
I neither give your crop any more
to be food for your enemies;
nor the sons of the stranger
to drink your juice for which you labored:
9 for they who gather, eat and halal Yah Veh;
and they who gather, drink in the courts of my holies.
10 Pass through! Pass through the portals!
Face the way of the people!
Raise! Raise the highway! Stone the stones!
Lift an ensign for the people!
11 Behold, Yah Veh hearkens
to the end of the world,

You, say to the daughter of Siyon,
Behold, your salvation comes!
Behold, his hire is with him
and his deeds at his face!
12 And they call them,
Holy People, Redeemed of Yah Veh:
and call you,
Sought Out, A City Not Forsaken.

THE DAY OF YAH VEH

63 Who is this coming from Edom
—with dazzling clothes from Bozrah?
This who is esteemed in his robe
strolling in the greatness of his force? I
speaking in justness, great to save.
2 Why are you red in your robe
and your clothes as treading in the winefat?
3 I tread the press by myself;
and of the people, no man is with me:
and I tread them in my wrath
and trample them in my fury:
and I sprinkle their squeezings on my clothes
and profane all my robe.
4 For the day of avengement *is* in my heart,
and the year of my redeemed is come.
5 And I look, and there is no one to help;
and I astonish that there is no one to uphold:
and my own arm saves me;
and my fury upholds me:
6 and I trample the people in my anger
and intoxicate them in my fury
and I bring down their squeezings to the earth.
7 I remember the mercies of Yah Veh,
the halals of Yah Veh,
according to all Yah Veh dealt us,
and the great goodness toward the house of Yisra El
which he dealt on them according to his mercies
and according to the abundance of his mercies.
8 And he says,
Surely they *are* my people; sons who falsify not:
he is their Saviour.
9 In all their tribulation, *he* tribulates not;
and the angel of his face saves them: in his love
and in his compassion he redeemed them and he
bore them—bore them all the days of antiquity.
10 And they rebelled and contorted
his *holy Spirit* **Ruach ha-Kodesh**:
and he turned to be their enemy
—he fought against them:
11 Then he remembered the days of *old* **antiquity**,
Moses **Mosheh**, and his people, *saying*,
Where is he that *brought* **ascended**
them *up* out of the sea
with the *shepherd* **tender** of his flock?
where is he that *put* **set** his *holy Spirit*
Ruach ha-Kodesh within him?
12 That *led* **carried** them
by the right *hand* of *Moses* **Mosheh** with
his *glorious* arm **of adornment**,
dividing **splitting** the water *before them* **at their face**,
to *make* **work** himself an *everlasting* **eternal** name?
13 That *led* **carried** them through the *deep* **abyss**,
as an horse in the wilderness,
that they should not *stumble* **falter**?
14 As *a beast* **an animal**
goeth down **descendeth** into the valley,
the Spirit of *the LORD* **Yah Veh**
caused him to rest **rested him**:
so didst thou *lead* **drive** thy people,
to *make* **work** thyself
a *glorious name* **name of adornment**.
15 Look down from *heaven* **the heavens**,
and *behold* **see**
from the *habitation* **residence** of thy holiness
and of thy *glory* **adornment**:
where is thy zeal and thy *strength* **might**,
the *sounding* **roar**
of thy *bowels* **inwards** and of thy mercies toward me?
are they restrained?
16 *Doubtless* **Assuredly** thou art our father,
though Abraham *be ignorant of* **knew** us **not**,
and *Israel acknowledge* **Yisra El acknowledged** us not:
thou, O *LORD* **Yah Veh**, art our father, our redeemer;
thy name is from *everlasting* **eternity**.
17 O *LORD* **Yah Veh**,
why hast thou made us to *err* **stray** from thy ways,
and hardened our heart from thy *fear* **awe**?
Return for thy servants' sake,
the *tribes* **scions** of thine inheritance.
18 The people of thy holiness
have possessed it but a little while:
our *adversaries* **tribulators**
have *trodden down* **trampled** thy *sanctuary* **holies**.
19 We are thine:
thou *never barest rule* **hast not**
eternally reigned over them;
they were not called by thy name.

A PRAYER FOR MERCY

64 Oh that thou

wouldest rend **shouldest rip** the heavens,
that thou *wouldest come down* **shouldest descend**,
that the mountains might *flow down* **quake**
at thy *presence* **face**,
2 As *when* the *melting* **brush**
fire *burneth* **kindleth**,
the fire causeth the waters to boil,
to make thy name known to thine
adversaries **tribulators**,
that the *nations* **goyim** may *tremble* **quiver**
at thy *presence* **face**!
3 When thou *didst terrible*
things **worked awesomenesses**
which we *looked* **awaited** not *for*,
thou *camest down* **descendest**,
the mountains *flowed down* **quaked** at thy *presence* **face**.
4 For since *the beginning of the world* **eternity**
men have not **neither was it** heard,
nor perceived by the ear,
neither hath the eye seen, O *God* **Elohim**, beside thee,
what he hath *prepared* **worked** for him
that waiteth for him.

1 Corinthians 2:9, 10

5 Thou meetest him
that rejoiceth and worketh *righteousness* **justness**,
those that remember thee in thy ways:
behold, thou art *wroth* **enraged**; for we have sinned:
in those is *continuance* **eternity**, and we shall be saved.
6 But we are all as *an unclean thing* **foul**, and all our
righteousnesses **justnesses** are as *filthy rags* **menstrual**
clothes; and we all *do fade* **wither** as a leaf;
and our *iniquities* **perversities**, like the wind,
have *taken* **borne** us away.
7 And there is none that calleth upon thy name,
11 and he remembered the days of antiquity
—Mosheh—his people.
Where *is* he who ascended them from the sea
with the tender of his flock?
Where is he who set his *holy Spirit*
Ruach ha-Kodesh within him?
12 Who carried them by the right of Mosheh
with his arm of adornment
—splitting the water at their face
to work himself an eternal name?
13 Who carried them through the abyss
as a horse in the wilderness
that they not falter?
14 As an animal descends into the valley,
the Spirit of Yah Veh rests him:
thus you drive your people,
to work yourself a name of adornment.
15 Look down from the heavens,
and see from the residence of your holiness
and of your adornment.
Where is your zeal and your might?
—the roar of your inwards
and of your mercies toward me?
Are they restrained?
16 Assuredly you are our father;
though Abraham knew us not
and Yisra El acknowledged us not:
you, O Yah Veh, are our father, our redeemer;
your name *is* from eternity.
17 O Yah Veh,
why stray us from your ways?
Harden our heart from your awe?
For sake of your servant,
return the scions of your inheritance.
18 The people of your holiness
possessed but a little while:
our tribulators trampled your holies.
19 We are yours:
you neither reigned over them eternally;
nor were they called by your name.

A Prayer For Mercy

64 Oh that you rip the heavens;
that you descend;
that the mountains quake at your face
2 —as the brush fire kindles
—as the fire boils the waters;
to make your name known to your tribulators
to quiver the goyim at your face!
3 When you worked awesomenesses
which we awaited not,
you descended:
the mountains quaked at your face.
4 Even since eternity
it was neither heard, nor perceived by the ear,
nor seen by the eye, O Elohim, beside you,
what he worked for him who awaits
him. 1 Corinthians 2:9,10
5 You meet him who rejoices and works justness
—who remembers you in your ways:
behold, you enrage when we sin:
in them is eternity and we are saved.
6 And we are all as foul—all of us
and all our justnesses as menstrual clothes:
and we wither as a leaf—all of us

and our perversities, as the wind, bear us away:
7 and no one calls on your name
that *stirreth up* **waketh** himself to take hold of thee:
for thou hast hid thy face from us,
and hast *consumed* **melted** us,
because **by the hand** of our *iniquities* **perversities.**
8 But now, O *LORD* **Yah Veh**, thou art our father;
we are the *clay* **morter**, and thou our *potter*
Former; and we all are the work of thy hand.
9 Be not *wroth very sore* **mightily enraged,**
O *LORD* **Yah Veh,**
neither remember *iniquity for ever* **perversity eternally**:
behold, *see* **look**, we beseech thee, we are all thy people.
10 Thy holy cities are a wilderness,
Zion **Siyon** is a wilderness,
Jerusalem **Yeru Shalem** a desolation.
11 Our *holy and our beautiful house*
holies of adornment,
where our fathers *praised* **halaled** thee,
is burned up with fire:
and all our *pleasant things* **desirables**
are *laid waste* **parched.**
12 *Wilt* **Shalt** thou refrain thyself for these *things*,
O *LORD* **Yah Veh?**
wilt **shalt** thou *hold thy peace* **hush,**
and *afflict* **humble** us *very sore* **mightily**?

JUDGMENT

65 I am sought of them that asked not *for me*;
I am found of them that sought me not:
I said, Behold me, behold me,
unto a *nation* **goyim** that was not called by my name.
2 I have spread out my hands all the day
unto a *rebellious* **revolting** people,
which walketh in a way that was not good,
after their own *thoughts* **fabrications;**
3 A people that *provoke* **vex** me *to anger*
continually to my face;
that sacrificeth in gardens,
and *burneth* incense upon altars of brick;
4 Which *remain* **settle** among the *graves* **tombs,**
and *lodge* **stay overnight** in the *monuments* **guards,**
which eat swine's flesh,
and *broth* **soup** of *abominable things* **stench**
is in their *vessels* **instruments;**
5 Which say, *Stand by thyself* **Approach,**
come not near to me;
for I am holier than thou **lest I hallow thee.**
These are a smoke in my *nose* **nostrils,**
a fire that burneth all the day.
6 Behold, it is *written before*
me **inscribed at my face**:
I *will* **shall** not *keep silence* **hush,**
but *will recompense* **shall shalam,**
even *recompense* **shalam** into their bosom,
7 Your *iniquities* **perversities,**
and the *iniquities* **perversities** of your fathers together,
saith *the LORD* **Yah Veh,**
which have *burned incense* **incensed**
upon the mountains,
and *blasphemed* **reproached** me upon the hills:
therefore *will* **shall** I measure their former *work* **deeds**
into their bosom.

PRESERVATION

8 Thus saith *the LORD* **Yah Veh,**
As the *new wine* **juice** is found in the cluster,
and one saith, *Destroy* **Ruin** it not; for a blessing is in it:
so *will* **shall** I *do* **work** for my servants' sakes,
that I may not *destroy* **ruin** them all.
9 And I *will* **shall** bring forth
a seed out of *Jacob* **Yaaqov,**
and out of *Judah* **Yah Hudah**
an inheritor **a possessor** of my mountains:
and *mine elect* **my chosen** shall *inherit it* **be successor,**
and my servants shall *dwell* **tabernacle** there.
10 And Sharon shall be a *fold*
habitation of rest of flocks,
and *the valley of Achor* **Gaymek Achor**
a place for the herds to *lie down in* **repose,**
for my people that have sought me.
11 But ye are they that forsake *the LORD* **Yah Veh,**
that forget my holy mountain,
that *prepare* **line up** a table for *that troop* **Gad,**
and that *furnish the drink offering* **fulfill the cocktails**
unto *that number* **Fate.**
—wakens himself to take hold of you:
for you hide your face from us,
and melt us by the hand of our perversities.
8 And now, O Yah Veh, you *are* our father;
we are the morter, and you our Former;
and we all are the work of your hand.
9 Neither enrage not mightily, O Yah Veh,
nor remember our perversity eternally:
behold, look, we beseech you,
—your people—all of us.
10 Your holy cities are a wilderness:
Siyon is a wilderness; Yeru Shalem a desolation:
11 our holies of adornment
where our fathers halaled you,
are burned with fire:

and all our desirables are parched.
12 Refrain you yourself for these, O Yah Veh?
You hush, and humble us mightily.

JUDGMENT

65 I am sought by them who ask not;
I am found of them who seek me not:
I say, Behold me! Behold me!
to a goyim not called by my name.
2 I spread my hands all the day
to a revolting people
who walk in a way not good
—after their own fabrications;
3 a people who vex me continually to my face;
who sacrifice in gardens
and incense on altars of brick;
4 who settle among the tombs
and stay overnight in the guards
—who eat flesh of swine;
and soup of stench is in their instruments;
5 who say, Approach!
—but come not near me; lest I hallow you.
These are a smoke in my nostrils,
a fire that burns all the day.
6 Behold, it is inscribed at my face:
I hush not, but shalam;
and into their bosom,
7 I shalam your perversities,
and the perversities of your fathers together,
says Yah Veh,
who incensed on the mountains
and reproached me on the hills:
and I measure their former deeds
into their bosom.

PRESERVATION

8 Thus says Yah Veh,
As the juice is found in the cluster,
and one says, Ruin not; for a blessing *is* therein:
thus I work for sake of my servants,
that I not ruin them all:
9 and I bring forth a seed from Yaaqov
and from Yah Hudah a possessor of my mountains:
and my chosen are the successors
and my servants tabernacle there:
10 and Sharon becomes a
habitation of rest of flocks,
and Gaymek Achor, a place for the herds to
repose, for my people who seek me.
11 And you are they who forsake Yah Veh
who forget my holy mountain;
who line up a table for Gad;
and who fulfill the cocktails to Fate:
12 Therefore *will* **shall** I number you to the sword,
and ye shall all *bow down* **kneel** to the slaughter:
because when I called, ye *did not answer* **answered not**;
when I *spake* **worded**, ye *did not hear* **heard not**;
but *did* **worked** evil *before* **in front of** mine eyes,
and *did choose* **chose** that wherein I delighted not.
13 Therefore thus saith *the*
Lord GOD **Adonay Yah Veh**,
Behold, my servants shall eat,
but ye shall *be hungry* **famish**:
behold, my servants shall drink,
but ye shall *be thirsty* **thirst**:
behold, my servants shall *rejoice* **cheer**,
but ye shall *be ashamed* **shame**:
14 Behold,
my servants shall *sing* **shout** for *joy* **goodness** of heart,
but ye shall cry for *sorrow* **pain** of heart,
and shall howl for *vexation* **breaking** of spirit.
15 And ye shall leave your name
for *a curse* **an oath** unto my chosen:
for *the Lord GOD* **Adonay Yah Veh**
shall *slay* **deathify** thee,
and call his servants by another name:
16 That he who blesseth himself in the earth
shall bless himself in the *God* **Elohim** of *truth* **amen**;
and he that *sweareth* **oatheth** in the earth
shall *swear* **oath** by the *God* **Elohim** of *truth* **amen**;
because the former *troubles* **tribulations** are forgotten,
and because they are hid from mine eyes.

NEW HEAVENS, NEW EARTH

17 For, behold, I create new
heavens and a new earth:
and the former shall not be remembered,
nor *come* **ascend** into *mind* **heart**.
18 But *be ye glad* **rejoice** and *rejoice* **twirl**
for ever **eternally**
in that which I create:
for, behold,
I create *Jerusalem* **Yeru Shalem** a *rejoicing* **twirling**,
and her people a joy.
19 And I *will rejoice* **shall twirl**
in *Jerusalem* **Yeru Shalem**,
and *joy* **rejoice** in my people:
and the voice of weeping shall be no more heard in her,
nor the voice of crying.
20 There shall be no more thence

an infant **a suckling** of days,
nor an *old man* **elder** that hath not filled his days:
for the *child* **lad** shall die **a son of** an hundred years *old*;
but the sinner *being* **a son of** an hundred years *old*
shall be *accursed* **abased**.
21 And they shall build houses,
and *inhabit* **settle** them;
and they shall plant vineyards, and eat the fruit of them.
22 They shall not build, and another *inhabit* **settle**;
they shall not plant, and another eat:
for as the days of a tree are the days of my people,
and *mine elect* **my chosen**
shall *long enjoy* **waste away** the work of their hands.
23 They shall not labour in vain,
nor *bring forth* **birth** for *trouble* **terror**;
for they are the seed
of the blessed of *the LORD* **Yah Veh**,
and their offspring with them.
24 And **so be** it *shall come to pass*,
that before they call, I *will* **shall** answer;
and while they are yet speaking, I *will* **shall** hear.
25 The wolf and the lamb
shall *feed together* **graze as one**,
and the lion shall eat straw like the bullock:
and dust shall be the serpent's *meat* **bread**.
They shall not *hurt* **vilify** nor *destroy* **ruin**
in all my holy mountain, saith *the LORD* **Yah Veh**.

THE THRONE OF YAH VEH

66 Thus saith *the LORD* **Yah Veh**,
The *heaven is* **heavens are** my throne,
and the earth is *my footstool* **the stool of my feet**:
where is the house that ye build unto me?
and where is the place of my rest?
2 For all those *things* hath
mine hand *made* **worked**,
and all those *things* have been,
saith the LORD **an oracle of Yah Veh**:
but to this man *will* **shall** I look,

12 and I number you to the sword
and you all kneel to the slaughter:
because when I called, you answered not;
when I worded, you heard not;
but worked evil in front of my eyes
and chose that wherein I delighted not.
13 So thus says Adonay Yah Veh,
Behold, my servants eat, and you famish:
behold, my servants drink, and you thirst:
behold, my servants cheer, and you shame:
14 behold, my servants shout for goodness of heart,
and you cry for pain of heart
and howl for breaking of spirit:
15 and you leave your name
for an oath to my chosen:
for Adonay Yah Veh deathifies you
and calls his servants by another name:
16 that he who blesses himself in the earth
blesses himself in the Elohim of amen;
and he who oaths in the earth
oaths by the Elohim of amen;
because the former tribulations are forgotten
and because they are hid from my eyes.

NEW HEAVENS, NEW EARTH

17 For, behold, I create new
heavens and a new earth:
and the former are neither remembered
nor ascend into the heart.
18 But rejoice and twirl eternally in what I create:
for behold, I create Yeru Shalem a twirling,
and her people a joy:
19 and I twirl in Yeru Shalem
and rejoice in my people:
and neither is the voice of weeping
heard in her any more,
nor the voice of crying:
20 nor any more a suckling of days,
nor an elder who fulfilled not his days:
for the lad dies a son of a hundred years;
but the sinner a son of a hundred years abases.
21 And they build houses, and settle them;
and they plant vineyards, and eat the fruit of them:
22 they build not *for* another to settle;
they plant not *for* another to eat:
for as the days of a tree are the days of my people,
and my chosen waste away the work of their hands.
23 They neither labor in vain nor birth for terror;
for they are the seed of the blessed of Yah
Veh, and their offspring with them.
24 And so be it,
ere they call, I answer;
and while they yet speak, I hear:
25 the wolf and the lamb graze as one
and the lion eats straw as the bullock:
and dust is the bread of serpents.
They neither vilify nor ruin
in all my holy mountain, says Yah Veh.

THE THRONE OF YAH VEH

66 Thus says Yah Veh,

The heavens *are* my throne
and the earth, the stool of my feet:
where *is* the house you build to me?
and where the place of my rest?
2 For all those my hand worked,
and they all became
—an oracle of Yah Veh:
and to this man I look
even to him that is poor—**the humbled**
and *of a contrite* **smitten of** spirit,
and trembleth at my word.
3 *He that killeth* **Whoever slaughtereth** an ox
is as if he slew **smiteth** a man;
he that **whoever** sacrificeth a lamb,
as if he *cut off* **breaketh** a dog's neck;
he that offereth **whoever holocausteth**
an *oblation* **offering**,
as if he offered—swine's blood;
he that burneth **whoever memorializeth with** incense,
as if he blessed an idol **blesseth mischief**.
Yea, they have chosen their own ways,
and their soul delighteth in their abominations.
4 I also *will* **shall** choose their *delusions* **exploits**,
and *will* **shall** bring their *fears* **terrors** upon them;
because when I called, none *did answer* **answered**;
when I *spake* **worded**, they *did not hear* **heard not**:
but they *did* **worked** evil *before* **in front of** mine eyes,
and chose that in which I delighted not.
5 Hear the word of *the LORD* **Yah Veh**,
ye that tremble at his word;
Your brethren that hated you,
that cast you out for my name's sake, said,
Let *the LORD* **Yah Veh** be *glorified* **honoured**:
but he shall *appear* **be seen** to your *joy* **cheerfulness**,
and they shall *be ashamed* **shame**.
6 A voice of *noise* **uproar** from the city,
a voice from the *temple* **manse**,
a voice of *the LORD* **Yah Veh**
that *rendereth recompence* **shalameth**
to his enemies.
7 Before she *travailed* **writhed**,
she *brought forth* **birthed**;
before her *pain* **pangs** came,
she was *delivered* **rescued** of a *man* **male** child.
8 Who hath heard such *a thing*?
who hath seen such *things*?
shall the earth *be made to bring forth* **writhe** in one day?
or shall a *nation be born* **goyim birth** at *once* **one time**?
for *as soon* **even** as *Zion travailed* **Siyon writhed**,
she *brought forth* **birthed** her *children* **sons**.
9 Shall I *bring* **break** to the birth,
and not *cause to bring forth* **birth**?
saith *the LORD* **Yah Veh**:
Shall I cause to *bring forth* **birth**,
and *shut the womb* **restrain**?
saith thy *God* **Elohim**.
10 Rejoice ye with *Jerusalem* **Yeru Shalem**,
and *be glad* **twirl** with her, all ye that love her:
rejoice for joy with her, all ye that mourn for her:
11 That ye may suck,
and be satisfied with the breasts of her consolations;
that ye may *milk* **suck** out,
and *be delighted* **delight**
with the *abundance* **full breast** of her *glory* **honour**.
12 For thus saith *the LORD* **Yah Veh**, Behold,
I *will extend peace* **shall spread shalom** to her
like a river,
and the *glory* **honour** of the *Gentiles* **goyim**
like a flowing *stream* **wadi**:
then shall ye suck, ye shall be borne upon her sides,
and be *dandled* **stroked** upon her knees.
13 As *one* **man**
whom his mother *comforteth* **sigheth over**,
so *will* **shall** I *comfort* **sigh over** you;
and ye shall be *comforted* **sighed over**
in *Jerusalem* **Yeru Shalem**.
14 And when ye see *this*, your heart shall rejoice,
and your bones shall *flourish* **blossom**
like *an herb* **a sprout**:
and the hand of *the LORD* **Yah Veh**
shall be known toward his servants,
and *his indignation* **rage** toward his enemies.
15 For, behold,
the LORD will **Yah Veh shall** come with fire,
and with his chariots like a *whirlwind* **hurricane**,
to *render* **turn** his *anger* **wrath** with fury,
and his rebuke with flames of fire.
16 For by fire and by his sword
—the humbled and smitten of spirit
who tremble at my word.
3 Whoever slaughters an ox, smites a man;
whoever sacrifices a lamb, breaks the neck of a dog;
whoever holocausts an offering, the blood of swine;
whoever memorializes with incense, blesses mischief:
yes, they choose their own ways
and their soul delights in their abominations.
4 I also—I choose their exploits,
and bring their terrors on them;
because when I call, no one answers;
when I word, they hear not:

but they work evil in front of my eyes
and choose that in which I delight not.
5 Hear the word of Yah Veh,
you who tremble at his word;
your brothers who hate you,
who cast you out for sake of my name,
say, Yah Veh is honored:
and we see your cheerfulness, and they shame:
6 a voice of uproar from the city;
a voice from the manse;
a voice of Yah Veh shalaming his enemies.
7 Ere she writhes, she births;
ere her pangs come, she *is* rescued of a male child.
8 Who *ever* heard such? Who *ever* saw such?
Writhed the earth in one day?
Or birthed a goyim at one time?
For even as Siyon writhes, she births her sons.
9 Break I to the birth, and not birth?
says Yah Veh:
I also restrain, says your Elohim.
10 You, rejoice with Yeru Shalem,
and twirl with her, all you who love her:
rejoice for joy with her, all you who mourn for her:
11 that you suck
and be satisfied with the breasts of her consolations;
that you suck out,
and delight with the full breast of her honor.
12 For thus says Yah Veh, Behold,
I spread her shalom as a river,
and the honor of the goyim as a flowing wadi:
and you suck,
borne on her sides, and stroked on her knees.
13 As man over whom his mother sighs,
thus sigh I over you;
yes, sigh over you in Yeru Shalem.
14 And when you see, your heart rejoices,
and your bones blossom as a sprout:
and the hand of Yah Veh
is known toward his servants
and his rage toward his enemies.
15 For, behold, Yah Veh comes with fire
and with his chariots as a hurricane
—to turn his wrath with fury
and his rebuke with flames of fire.
16 For by fire and by his sword
will the LORD plead with **shall Yah Veh judge** all flesh:
and the *slain* **pierced** of *the LORD* **Yah Veh**
shall *be many* **abound by the myriads**.
17 They that *sanctify* **hallow** *themselves*,
and purify *themselves*
in the gardens behind *one tree* in the midst,
eating swine's flesh,
and the abomination, and the mouse,
shall be consumed together,
saith the LORD **an oracle of Yah Veh**.
18 For *I know* their works and
their *thoughts* **fabrications**:
it shall come,
that I *will* **shall** gather all *nations* **goyim** and tongues;
and they shall come, and see my *glory* **honour**.
19 And I *will* **shall** set a sign among them,
and I *will* **shall** send
those that escape of them **the escapees**
unto the *nations* **goyim**,
to Tarshish, Pul, and Lud, that draw the bow,
to Tubal, and *Javan* **Yavan**, to the *isles* **islands** afar off,
that have not heard my fame,
neither have seen my *glory* **honour**;
and they shall *declare* **tell** my *glory* **honour**
among the *Gentiles* **goyim**.
20 And they shall bring all your brethren
for an offering unto *the LORD* **Yah Veh**
out of all *nations* **goyim**
upon horses, and in chariots, and in *litters* **palanquins**,
and upon mules, and upon *swift beasts* **prancers**,
to my holy mountain *Jerusalem* **Yeru Shalem**,
saith *the LORD* **Yah Veh**,
as the *children* **sons** of *Israel* **Yisra El**
bring an offering in a *clean vessel* **pure instrument**
into the house of *the LORD* **Yah Veh**.
21 And I *will* **shall** also take of them
for priests *and* for *Levites* **Leviym**,
saith *the LORD* **Yah Veh**.
22 For as the new heavens and the new earth,
which I *will make* **shall work**,
shall *remain before me* **stand at my face**,
saith the LORD **an oracle of Yah Veh**,
so shall your seed and your name *remain* **stand**.
23 And **so be** it *shall come to pass*,
that from *one* new moon to *another* **new moon**,
and **enough**
from *one sabbath* **shabbath** to *another* **shabbath**,
shall all flesh come to *worship before*
prostrate in front of me,
saith *the LORD* **Yah Veh**.
24 And they shall go *forth*,
and *look upon* **see** the carcases of the men
that have *transgressed* **rebelled** against me:
for their *worm* **maggot** shall not die,
neither shall their fire be quenched;

and they shall be an abhorring unto all flesh.
Yah Veh judges all flesh:
and the pierced of Yah Veh
abound by the myriads.
17 They who hallow and purify *themselves*
behind, midst the gardens,
eating flesh of swine;
and the abomination and the mouse
are consumed together
—an oracle of Yah Veh.
18 And I—their works and their fabrications
I come to gather all goyim and tongues;
and they come, and see my honor:
19 and I set a sign among them;
and I send the escapees to the goyim
—to Tarshish, Pul, and Lud—who draw the bow,
—to Tubal, and Yavan—to the islands afar,
who neither heard my fame nor saw my honor;
and they tell my honor among the goyim:
20 and they bring all your brothers
for an offering to Yah Veh
—from all goyim
on horses and in chariots and in palanquins
and on mules and on prancers
to my holy mountain Yeru Shalem, says Yah Veh;
as the sons of Yisra El
bring an offering in a pure instrument
into the house of Yah Veh.
21 And I also take of them for priests for Leviym,
says Yah Veh.
22 For as the new heavens and the new earth,
which I work, stand at my face
—an oracle of Yah Veh;
thus your seed and your name stand.
23 And so be it,
that from new moon to new moon
and enough from shabbath to shabbath
all flesh comes to prostrate in front of me,
says Yah Veh;
24 and they come and see the carcases
of the men who rebel against me:
for neither their maggot dies,
nor their fire quenches;
and they become an abhorrance to all flesh.

THE GENEALOGY OF YIRME YAH

1 The words of *Jeremiah* **Yirme Yah**
the son of *Hilkiah* **Hilqi Yah,**
of the priests that were in Anathoth
in the land of *Benjamin* **Ben Yamin**:
2 To whom the word of *the LORD* **Yah Veh** came
in the days of *Josiah* **Yoshi Yah**
the son of Amon *king* **sovereign** of *Judah* **Yah Hudah,**
in the thirteenth year of his reign.
3 It came also in the days of *Jehoiakim* **Yah Yaqim**
the son of *Josiah* **Yoshi Yah,**
king **sovereign** of *Judah* **Yah Hudah,**
unto the *end* **consummation**
of the eleventh year of *Zedekiah* **Sidqi Yah**
the son of *Josiah* **Yoshi Yah,**
king **sovereign** of *Judah* **Yah Hudah,**
unto the *carrying away* **exile**
of *Jerusalem captive* **Yeru Shalem** in the fifth month.

THE CALLING OF YIRME YAH

4 Then the word of *the LORD*
Yah Veh came unto me,
saying,
5 Before I formed thee in the belly
I knew thee;
and before thou camest forth out of the womb
I *sanctified* **hallowed** thee,
and I *ordained* **gave** thee
a prophet unto the *nations* **goyim.**
6 Then said I, *Ah* **Aha,** *Lord*
GOD **Adonay Yah Veh!**
behold, I *cannot speak* **know not how to word**:
for I am a *child* **lad.**
7 But *the LORD* **Yah Veh** said unto me,
Say not, I am a *child* **lad**:
for thou shalt go to all that I shall send thee,
and whatsoever I *command* **misvah** thee
thou shalt *speak* **word.**
8 *Be not afraid of* **Awe not** their faces:
for I am with thee to *deliver* **rescue** thee,
saith the LORD **an oracle of Yah Veh.**
9 Then *the LORD put forth*
Yah Veh spread his hand,
and touched my mouth.
And *the LORD* **Yah Veh** said unto me,
Behold, I have *put* **given** my words in thy mouth.
10 See, I have this day set thee **overseer**
over the *nations* **goyim**
and over the *kingdoms* **sovereigndoms,**
to *root out* **uproot,** and to pull down, and to destroy,
and to *throw down* **demolish,** to build, and to plant.

THE ALMOND SPROUT

11 Moreover the word of *the*
LORD **Yah Veh** came unto me,
saying, *Jeremiah* **Yirme Yah,** what seest thou?
And I said, I see a *rod* **sprout** of an almond tree.
12 Then said *the LORD* **Yah Veh** unto me,
Thou hast *well seen* **well—pleased in seeing**:
for I *will hasten* **shall watch** my word to *perform* **work** it.

THE PRESSURE CALDRON

13 And the word of *the LORD* **Yah Veh**
came unto me *the second time* **secondly,** saying,
What seest thou?
And I said, I see a *seething pot* **pressure caldron;**
and the face thereof is *toward* **at the face of** the north.
14 *Then the LORD* **Yah Veh** said unto me,
Out of the north an evil shall *break forth* **loosen**
upon all the *inhabitants* **settlers** of the land.
15 For, *lo* **behold,** I *will* **shall** call all the families
of the *kingdoms* **sovereigndoms** of the north,
saith the LORD **an oracle of Yah Veh;**
and they shall come,
and they shall *set* **give** every *one* **man** his throne
at the *entering* **opening** of the *gates* **portals**
of *Jerusalem* **Yeru Shalem,**
and against all the walls *thereof* round about,
and against all the cities of *Judah* **Yah Hudah.**
16 And I *will utter* **shall word**
my judgments against them
touching all their *wickedness* **evil,**
who have forsaken me,
and have *burned incense* **incensed**
unto other *gods* **elohim,**
and *worshipped* **prostrated**
unto the works of their own hands.

THE GENEALOGY OF YIRME YAH

1 The words of Yirme Yah the son of Hilqi Yah,
of the priests in Anathoth in the land of Ben Yamin:
2 and so be the word of Yah Veh to him
in the days of Yoshi Yah
the son of Amon sovereign of Yah Hudah
in the thirteenth year of his reign:
3 and so be it in the days of Yah Yaqim
the son of Yoshi Yah sovereign of Yah Hudah
to the consummation
of the eleventh year of Sidqi Yah

the son of Yoshi Yah sovereign of Yah Hudah:
to the exile of Yeru Shalem in the fifth month.

The Calling Of Yirme Yah

4 And so be the word of Yah Veh to me, saying,
5 Before I formed you in the belly, I knew you;
and ere you came from the womb, I hallowed you,
I gave you, a prophet to the goyim.
6 Then I say, Aha, Adonay Yah Veh!
Behold, I know not how to word: for I *am* a lad.
7 And Yah Veh says to me,
Say not, I *am* a lad:
go to all to whom I send you,
and word whatever I misvah you:
8 awe not their faces:
for I *am* with you to rescue you
—an oracle of Yah Veh.
9 And Yah Veh spreads his hand,
and touches my mouth:
and Yah Veh says to me,
Behold, I give my words in your mouth.
10 See, this day I set you overseer over the goyim
and over the sovereigndoms;
to uproot and to pull down
and to destroy and to demolish;
to build and to plant.

The Almond Sprout

11 And so be the word of Yah Veh to me, saying,
Yirme Yah, what see you?
And I say, I see a sprout from an almond tree.
12 And Yah Veh says to me,
You well—please in seeing:
for I watch my word to work it.

The Pressure Caldron

13 And so be the word of Yah Veh to me secondly,
saying, What see you?
And I say, I see a pressure caldron;
and the face thereof is at the face of the north.
14 Yah Veh says to me,
From the north an evil loosens
on all the settlers of the land:
15 for behold, I call all the families
of the sovereigndoms of the north
—an oracle of Yah Veh
and they come and they give every man his throne
at the opening of the portals of Yeru Shalem
and against all the walls all round
and against all the cities of Yah Hudah:
16 and I word my judgments against them
touching all their evil
—in that they forsake me
and incense to other elohim,
and prostrate to the works of their own hands.
17 Thou therefore gird up thy loins, and arise,
and speak **word** unto them
all that I *command* **misvah** thee:
be not dismayed at their faces,
lest I *confound* **break** thee *before them* **at their face**.
18 For, behold,
I have *made* **given** thee this day a *defenced* **fortified** city,
and an iron pillar, and *brasen* **copper** walls
against the whole land,
against the *kings* **sovereigns** of *Judah* **Yah Hudah**,
against the *princes* **governors** *thereof*,
against the priests *thereof*,
and against the people of the land.
19 And they shall fight against thee;
but they shall not prevail against thee;
for I *am* with thee,
saith the LORD **an oracle of Yah Veh**,
to *deliver* **rescue** thee.

Yisra El Abandons Yah Veh

2 Moreover
the word of *the LORD* **Yah Veh** came to me, saying,
2 Go and *cry* **call** in the ears
of *Jerusalem* **Yeru Shalem**,
saying, Thus saith *the LORD* **Yah Veh**;
I remember thee, the *kindness* **mercy** of thy youth,
the love of *thine espousals* **thy bethrothals**,
when thou wentest after me in the wilderness,
in a land that was not *sown* **seeded**.
3 *Israel* **Yisra El** was holiness
unto *the LORD* **Yah Veh**,
and the *firstfruits* **firstlings** of his *increase* **produce**:
all that devour him shall *offend* **guilt**;
evil shall come upon them, saith *the LORD* **Yah Veh**.
4 Hear ye the word of *the LORD* **Yah Veh**,
O house of *Jacob* **Yaaqov**,
and all the families of the house of *Israel* **Yisra El**:
5 Thus saith *the LORD* **Yah Veh**,
What *iniquity* **wickedness** have
your fathers found in me,
that they are *gone* far **removed** from me,
and have walked after vanity, and are become vain?
6 Neither said they, Where is *the LORD* **Yah Veh**
that *brought* **ascended** us
up out of the land of *Egypt* **Misrayim**,

that *led* **carried** us through the wilderness,
through a land of *deserts* **plains** and of *pits* **chasms**,
through a land of *drought* **parch**,
and of the shadow of death,
through a land that no man passed through,
and where no *man dwelt* **human settled**?
7 And I brought you
into a *plentiful country* **land of orchards/Karmel**,
to eat the fruit *thereof* and the goodness *thereof*;
but when ye entered, ye *defiled* **fouled** my land,
and *made* **set** mine *heritage* **inheritance**
an *abomination* **abhorrence**.
8 The priests said not, Where
is *the LORD* **Yah Veh**?
and they that *handle* **manipulate** the *law* **torah**
knew me not:
the *pastors* **tenders** also *transgressed* **rebelled** against me,
and the prophets prophesied by Baal,
and walked after *things* **those** that do not *profit* **benefit**.
9 Wherefore I *will* **shall** yet plead with you,
saith *the LORD* **Yah Veh**,
and with your *children's children* **sons' sons**
will **shall** I plead.
10 For pass over the *isles* **islands**
of *Chittim* **Kittim**, and see;
and send unto *Kedar* **Qedar**,
and *consider diligently* **discern mightily**,
and see if there be such *a thing*.
11 Hath a *nation* **goyim**
changed their *gods* **elohim**,
which are yet no *gods* **elohim**?
but my people have changed their *glory* **honour**
for that which doth not *profit* **benefit**.
12 Be astonished, O ye heavens, at this,
and *be horribly afraid* **shutter**,
be ye *very desolate* **mightily parched**,
saith *the LORD* **Yah Veh**.
13 For my people have
committed **worked** two evils;
they have forsaken me the fountain of living waters,
and hewed them out *cisterns* **wells**,
broken *cisterns* **wells**, that can hold no water.
17 So you, gird your loins and rise;
word to them all that I misvah you:
dismay not at their faces,
lest I break you at their face.
18 For, behold, I give you this day,
a fortified city and an iron pillar and copper walls
against the whole land
—against the sovereigns of Yah Hudah,
against the governors, against the priests,
and against the people of the land:
19 and they fight against you;
but they prevail not against you; for I *am* with you
—an oracle of Yah Veh
to rescue you.

YISRA EL ABANDONS YAH VEH

2 And so be the word of Yah Veh to me, saying,
2 Go and call out in the ears of Yeru Shalem,
saying, Thus says Yah Veh,
I remember you;
the mercy of your youth,
the love of your betrothals
—your going after me in the wilderness
in a land not seeded.
3 Yisra El is holiness to Yah Veh
and the firstlings of his produce:
all who devour him guilt;
evil comes on them, says Yah Veh.
4 You, hear the word of Yah Veh,
O house of Yaaqov,
and all the families of the house of Yisra El:
5 thus says Yah Veh,
What wickedness found your fathers in me,
that they removed afar from me
and walked after vanity and became vain?
6 And said not, Where is Yah Veh
who ascended us from the land of Misrayim?
Who carried us through the wilderness
—a land of plains and of chasms
—a land of parch and of the shadow of death
—a land where no man passed through
and where no human settled?
7 And I bring you into a land of orchards/Karmel
to eat the fruit and the goodness;
and you enter and foul my land
and set my inheritance an abhorrence.
8 The priests say not, Where is Yah Veh?
and they who manipulate the torah know me not
and the tenders rebel against me;
and the prophets prophesy by Baal
and walk after those who benefit not.
9 So I still plead with you, says Yah Veh
—an oracle of Yah Veh
and with the sons of your sons, I plead.
10 For pass over the islands of Kittim, and see;
and send to Qedar, and discern mightily;
and see if there be such.
11 Changes a goyim their elohim

to a non—elohim?
and my people change their honor
for that which benefits not.
12 Astonish, O you heavens, at this, and shutter;
parch mightily, says Yah Veh.
13 For my people work two evils:
they forsake me, the fountain of living waters;
and hew wells—broken wells that hold no water.
14 Is *Israel* **Yisra El** a servant?
is he *a homeborn slave* **housebirthed**?
why is he *spoiled* **a plunder**?
15 The *young lions* **whelps** roared upon him,
and yelled **gave their voice**,
and they *made* **placed** his land *waste* **desolate**:
his cities are burned without *inhabitant* **settler**.
16 Also the *children* **sons**
of Noph and *Tahapanes* **Tachpanches**
have *broken the crown of* **grazed** thy *head* **scalp**.
17 Hast thou not *procured*
worked this unto thyself,
in that thou hast forsaken
the LORD **Yah Veh** thy *God* **Elohim**,
when he led **the time he carried** thee by the way?
18 And now what hast thou to do
in the way of *Egypt* **Misrayim**,
to drink the waters of *Sihor* **Shichor**?
or what hast thou to do in the way of *Assyria* **Ashshur**,
to drink the waters of the river?
19 Thine own *wickedness* **evil**
shall *correct* **discipline** thee,
and thy *backslidings* **apostasies** shall reprove thee:
know therefore and see that it is *an* evil *thing* and bitter,
that thou hast forsaken
the LORD **Yah Veh** thy *God* **Elohim**,
and that my fear is not in thee,
saith the Lord GOD of hosts
an oracle of Adonay Yah Veh Sabaoth.
20 For of *old* **eternal** time I have broken thy yoke,
and *burst* **torn** thy *bands* **bonds**;
and thou saidst, I *will* **shall** not *transgress* **serve**;
when upon every high hill and under every green tree
thou *wanderest* **strollest**, *playing the harlot* **whoring**.
21 Yet I had planted thee *a noble vine*—**choice**,
wholly a *right seed* **seed of truth**:
how then
art thou turned into the *degenerate* **twisted** plant
of a strange vine unto me?
22 For though thou *wash* **launder** thee with nitre,
and *take thee much* **abound thy** soap,
yet *thine iniquity* **thy perversity** is *marked* **inscribed**
before me **at my face**,
saith the Lord GOD **an oracle of Adonay Yah Veh**.
23 How canst thou say, I am not *polluted* **fouled**,
I have not gone after Baalim?
see thy way in the valley,
know what thou hast *done* **worked**:
thou art a swift dromedary
traversing **entangling** her ways;
24 A wild *ass used* **runner**
discipled to the wilderness,
that *snuffeth up* **gulpeth** the wind
at *her pleasure* **the yearning of her soul**;
in her occasion who can turn her *away* **back**?
all they that seek her *will* **shall** not weary themselves;
in her month they shall find her.
25 Withhold thy foot from being unshod,
and thy throat from thirst:
but thou saidst, *There is no hope* **I quit!**: no;
for I have loved strangers, and after them *will* **shall** I go.
26 As the thief is *ashamed*
shamed when he is found,
so is the house of *Israel ashamed* **Yisra El shamed**
they, their *kings* **sovereigns**, their *princes* **governors**,
and their priests, and their prophets.
27 Saying to a *stock* **tree**, Thou art my father;
and to a stone, Thou hast *brought me forth* **birthed me**:
for they have
turned **faced the nape of** their *back* **neck** unto me,
and not their face:
but in the time of their *trouble* **evil** they *will* **shall** say,
Arise, and save us.
28 But where are thy *gods* **elohim**
that thou hast *made* **worked** thee?
let them arise,
if they can save thee in the time of thy *trouble* **evil**:
for *according to* the number of thy cities
are thy *gods* **elohim**, O *Judah* **Yah Hudah**.
29 Wherefore *will* **shall** ye plead with me?
ye all have *transgressed* **rebelled** against me,
saith the LORD **an oracle of Yah Veh**.
14 Is Yisra El a servant? Is he house birthed?
Why is he for a plunder?
15 The whelps roar on him; they give their voice;
and they place his land desolate:
his cities burn without settler.
16 Also the sons of Noph and Tachpanches
graze your scalp.
17 Worked you not this to yourself
—in that you forsook Yah Veh your Elohim
the time he carried you by the way?

18 And now what *is it* to you
in the way of Misrayim
to drink the waters of Shichor?
Or what *is it* to you in the way of Ashshur
to drink the waters of the river?
19 Your own evil disciplines you
and your own apostasies reprove you:
so know and see that it is evil and bitter
to forsake Yah Veh your Elohim,
and that my fear is not in you
—an oracle of Adonay Yah Veh Sabaoth.
20 For from eternal time I broke your yoke
and tore your bonds;
and you say, I serve not!
when on every high hill and under every green tree
you stroll, whoring.
21 Yet I planted you, choice, wholly a seed of truth:
how then turn you on me
—into the twisted plant of a strange vine?
22 But though you launder yourself with nitre,
and abound with soap,
yet your perversity is inscribed at my face
—an oracle of Adonay Yah Veh.
23 How say you,
I am not fouled: I go not after Baalim?
See your way in the valley;
know what you worked
—a swift dromedary entangling her ways;
24 a wild runner discipled to the wilderness
who gulps the wind at the yearning of her soul;
who, in her occasion, turns her back?
No one seeking her wearies themselves;
in her month they find her.
25 Withhold your foot from being unshod
and your throat from thirst.
And you say, I quit!
No; I love strangers and after them I go.
26 As the thief shames when he is found out,
thus the house of Yisra El shames
—they, their sovereigns, their governors,
and their priests, and their prophets:
27 saying to a tree, You are my father;
and to a stone, You birthed me:
for they face the nape of their neck to me
and not their face:
and in the time of their evil they say,
Rise! and, Save us!
28 And where *are* the elohim
you worked for yourself?
Have them rise,
if they can save you in the time of your evil:
for the number of your cities are your elohim,
O Yah Hudah.
29 Why plead you with me?
You all rebel against me
—an oracle of Yah Veh.
30 In vain have I smitten your *children* **sons**;
they *received* **took** no *correction* **discipline**:
your own sword hath devoured your prophets,
like a *destroying* **ruining** lion.
31 O generation, see ye the
word of *the LORD* **Yah Veh**.
Have I been a wilderness unto *Israel* **Yisra El**?
a land of darkness?
wherefore say my people, We *are lords* **ramble on**;
we *will* **shall** come no more unto thee?
32 Can a *maid* **virgin** forget her ornaments,
or a bride her *attire* **bands**?
yet my people have forgotten me days without number.
33 Why *trimmest* **well—pleasest** thou thy way
to seek love?
therefore hast thou also
taught the *wicked* **evil** ones thy ways.
34 Also in thy *skirts* **wings**
is found the blood of the souls
of the *poor* **needy** innocents:
I have not found it by *secret search* **digging**,
but upon all these.
35 Yet thou sayest, Because I
am *innocent* **exonerated**,
surely his *anger* **wrath** shall turn from me.
Behold, I *will plead with* **shall judge** thee,
because thou sayest, I have not sinned.
36 Why gaddest thou about so *much* **mightily**
to change thy way?
thou also shalt be *ashamed* **shamed** of *Egypt* **Misrayim**,
as thou wast *ashamed* **shamed** of *Assyria* **Ashshur**.
37 Yea, thou shalt go forth from him,
and thine hands upon thine head:
for *the LORD* **Yah Veh**
hath *rejected* **spurned** thy confidences,
and thou shalt not prosper in them.

The Whoredom Of Yisra El

3 *They say* **Saying**,
If a man *put* **send** away his *wife* **woman**,
and she go from him, and become another man's,
shall he return unto her again?
in profaning,
shall not that land be *greatly polluted* **profaned**?
but thou hast *played the harlot* **whored**

with many *lovers* **friends**;
yet return *again* to me,
saith the LORD **an oracle of Yah Veh.**
2 Lift up thine eyes unto the *high places* **barrens**,
and see where thou hast not been *lien with* **raped**.
In the ways hast thou sat for them,
as the *Arabian* **Arabiy** in the wilderness;
and thou hast *polluted* **profaned** the land
with thy whoredoms
and with thy *wickedness* **evil**.
3 Therefore the showers have been withholden,
and there hath been no *latter* **after** rain;
and thou hadst a **woman's—a** whore's forehead,
thou refusedst to *be ashamed* **shame**.
4 *Wilt* **Shalt** thou not from
this time *cry* **call** unto me,
My father,
thou art the *guide* **chiliarch** of my youth?
5 *Will* **Shall** he *reserve his anger*
for ever **guard eternally**?
will **shall** he *keep it to the end* **guard in perpetuity**?
Behold, thou hast *spoken* **worded**
and *done* **worked** evil *things* as thou couldest.

THE UNTRUSTWORTHINESS OF YISRA EL

6 *The LORD* **Yah Veh** said also unto me
in the days of *Josiah* **Yoshi Yah**, the *king* **sovereign**,
Hast thou seen that which
backsliding Israel **apostate Yisra El** hath *done* **worked**?
she is gone up upon every high mountain
and under every green tree,
and there *hath played the harlot* **whored**.
7 And I said after she had
done **worked** all these *things*,
Turn thou unto me. But she returned not.
And her *treacherous* **covert** sister
Judah **Yah Hudah** saw it.
8 And I saw, when for all the causes
whereby *backsliding Israel* **apostate Yisra**
El *committed adultery* **adulterized**
30 In vain I smote your sons;
they took no discipline:
your own sword devoured your prophets
as a ruining lion.
31 O generation, see the word of Yah Veh.
Am I a wilderness to Yisra El?
A land of darkness?
Why say my people,
We ramble on—we come no more to you?
32 Forgets a virgin her ornaments?
Or a bride her bands?
Yet my people forget me days without number.
33 Why well—please you your way to seek love?
So you also teach the evil ones your ways.
34 Also found in your wings
is the blood of the souls of the needy innocents:
I found it not by digging, but on all these.
35 Yet you say, Because I am exonerated,
surely his wrath turns from me.
Behold, I judge you, because you say, I sin not.
36 Why gad you about so mightily
to change your way?
Even of Misrayim, you shame
as you shamed of Ashshur.
37 Yes, you go forth from him,
with your hands on your head:
for Yah Veh spurns your confidences,
and you prosper not therein.

THE WHOREDOM OF YISRA EL

3 Saying,
If a man sends away his woman,
and she goes from him, and becomes to another man,
returns he to her again?
In profaning, is not that land profaned?
And you whore with many friends and return to me
—an oracle of Yah Veh.
2 Lift your eyes to the barrens and see!
Where have you not raped?
You sit for them in the ways
as the Arabiy in the wilderness;
and you profane the land
with your whoredoms and with your evil.
3 And the showers are withheld
and no after rain becomes;
you have the forehead of a woman—a whore;
you refuse to shame.
4 Call you not to me at this time,
My father, you are the chiliarch of my youth?
5 Guards he eternally?
Guards he in perpetuity?
Behold, you word and work *all* the evil you can.

THE UNTRUSTWORTHINESS OF YISRA EL

6 And Yah Veh says to me
in the days of Yoshi Yah the sovereign,
See you what apostate Yisra El works?
She goes on every high mountain
and under every green tree,
and whores there.

7 And I say, after she works all these,
You, return to me.
—and she returns not.
And her covert sister Yah Hudah sees:
8 and I see, when for all the causes
whereby apostate Yisra El adulterized
I had *put* **sent** her away,
and given her a *bill* **scroll** of divorce;
yet her *treacherous* sister *Judah* **Yah Hudah**
who dealeth covertly *feared* **awed** not,
but went and *played the harlot* **whored** also.
9 And it *came to pass* **became**
through the *lightness* **voice** of her whoredom,
that she *defiled* **profaned** the land,
and *committed adultery* **adulterized** with stones
and with *stocks* **timber**.
10 And yet for all this
her *treacherous* sister *Judah* **Yah Hudah**
who dealeth covertly
hath not turned unto me with her whole heart,
but *feignedly* **in falsehood**,
saith the LORD **an oracle of Yah Veh**.
11 And *the LORD* **Yah Veh** said unto me,
The *backsliding Israel* **apostate Yisra El**
hath justified *herself* **her soul**
more than *treacherous Judah*
Yah Hudah that dealeth covertly.
12 Go and *proclaim* **call out** these words
toward the north **northward**, and say,
Return, thou *backsliding Israel* **apostate Yisra El**,
saith the LORD **an oracle of Yah Veh**;
and I *will* **shall** not cause *mine anger* **my face**
to fall upon you: for I *am* merciful,
saith the LORD **an oracle of Yah Veh**,
and I *will* **shall** not *keep anger for ever* **guard eternally**.
13 Only acknowledge *thine iniquity* **thy perversity**,
that thou hast *transgressed* **rebelled**
against *the LORD* **Yah Veh** thy *God* **Elohim**,
and hast scattered thy ways to the strangers
under every green tree,
and ye have not *obeyed* **hearkened unto** my voice,
saith the LORD **an oracle of Yah Veh**.
14 Turn, O *backsliding children* **apostate sons**,
saith the LORD **an oracle of Yah Veh**;
for I am married unto you:
and I *will* **shall** take you one of a city,
and two of a family,
and I *will* **shall** bring you to *Zion* **Siyon**:
15 And I *will* **shall** give you *pastors* **tenders**
according to mine heart,
which shall *feed* **tend** you
with knowledge and *understanding* **comprehending**.
16 And **so be** it *shall come to pass*,
when ye *be multiplied* **abound** and *increased* **bear fruit**
in the land, in those days,
saith the LORD **an oracle of Yah Veh**,
they shall say no more,
The ark of the covenant of *the LORD* **Yah Veh**:
neither shall it *come* **ascend** to *mind* **heart**:
neither shall they remember it;
neither shall they visit it;
neither shall that be *done* **worked** any more.
17 At that time they shall call
Jerusalem **Yeru Shalem**
the throne of *the LORD* **Yah Veh**;
and all the *nations* **goyim**
shall *be gathered* **congregate** unto it,
to the name of *the LORD* **Yah Veh**,
to *Jerusalem* **Yeru Shalem**:
neither shall they walk any more
after the *imagination* **warp** of their evil heart.
18 In those days the house of *Judah* **Yah Hudah**
shall walk with the house of *Israel* **Yisra El**,
and they shall come together out of the land of the north
to the land that
I have given for an inheritance unto your fathers
your fathers shall inherit.
19 But I said,
How shall I *put* **place** thee among the *children* **sons**,
and give thee a *pleasant land* **land of desire**,
a *goodly heritage* **splendid inheritance**
of the hosts of *nations* **goyim**?
and I said, Thou shalt call me, My father;
and shalt not turn away from **after** me.
I sent her away and gave her a scroll of divorce;
yet her sister Yah Hudah who deals covertly
awes not,
and goes and whores also.
9 And so be it,
through the voice of her whoredom
she profanes the land,
and adulterizes with stones and with timber.
10 And yet for all this
her sister Yah Hudah who deals covertly
returns not to me with her whole heart,
but in falsehood
—an oracle of Yah Veh.
11 And Yah Veh says to me,
The apostate Yisra El justifies her soul
more than Yah Hudah who deals covertly.
12 Go and call out these words northward, and say,

Return, you apostate Yisra El
—an oracle of Yah Veh.
I fell not my face on you: for I *am* merciful
—an oracle of Yah Veh.
I guard not eternally:
13 only, acknowledge your perversity,
that you rebel against Yah Veh your Elohim
and scatter your ways to the strangers
under every green tree,
and hearken not to my voice
—an oracle of Yah Veh.
14 Turn, O apostate sons
—an oracle of Yah Veh
for I *am* married to you:
and I take you,
one of a city and two of a family
and I bring you to Siyon:
15 and according to my heart,
I give you tenders to tend you
with knowledge and comprehension:
16 and so be it,
when you abound and bear fruit in the land,
in those days
—an oracle of Yah Veh
they neither say any more,
The ark of the covenant of Yah Veh:
nor ascend it to heart
nor remember they it
nor visit they it;
nor work they it any more.
17 At that time
they call Yeru Shalem the throne of Yah Veh;
and all the goyim congregate to it,
to the name of Yah Veh to Yeru Shalem:
and they walk no more
after the warp of their evil heart.
18 In those days
the house of Yah Hudah
walks with the house of Yisra El;
and they come together from the land of the north
to the land your fathers inherited.
19 And I say,
How place I you among the sons
and give you a land of desire
—a splendid inheritance of the hosts of goyim?
And I say, Call me, My father;
and turn not away from after me.
20 Surely as a *wife* **woman**
treacherously departeth **dealeth covertly**
from her *husband* **friend**,
so have ye dealt *treacherously* **covertly** with me,
O house of *Israel* **Yisra El**,
saith the LORD **an oracle of Yah Veh**.
21 A voice was heard upon the *high places* **barrens**,
weeping *and* supplications
of the *children* **sons** of *Israel* **Yisra El**:
for they have perverted their way,
and they have forgotten
the LORD **Yah Veh** their *God* **Elohim**.
22 Return, ye *backsliding children* **apostate sons**,
and I *will* **shall** heal your *backslidings* **apostasies**.
Behold, we come unto thee;
for thou art *the LORD* **Yah Veh** our *God* **Elohim**.
23 *Truly* **Surely** in *vain* **falsehood**
is salvation hoped for from the hills,
and from the multitude of mountains:
truly **surely** in *the LORD* **Yah Veh** our *God* **Elohim**
is the salvation of *Israel* **Yisra El**.
24 For shame hath devoured
the labour of our fathers from our youth;
their flocks and their herds,
their sons and their daughters.
25 We lie down in our shame,
and our confusion covereth us:
for we have sinned
against *the LORD* **Yah Veh** our *God* **Elohim**,
we and our fathers, from our youth even unto this day,
and have not *obeyed* **hearkened unto** the voice
of *the LORD* **Yah Veh** our *God* **Elohim**.

YAH VEH PLEADS WITH YISRA EL

4 If thou *wilt* **shalt** return, O *Israel* **Yisra El**,
saith the LORD **an oracle of Yah Veh**,
return unto me:
and if thou *wilt put away* **shalt turn aside**
thine abominations *out of my sight* **from my face**,
then shalt thou not *remove* **wander**.
2 And thou shalt *swear* **oath**,
The LORD **Yah Veh** liveth,
in truth, in judgment, and in *righteousness* **justness**;
and the *nations* **goyim** shall bless themselves in him,
and in him shall they *glory* **halal**.
3 For thus saith *the LORD* **Yah Veh**
to the men
of *Judah* **Yah Hudah** and *Jerusalem* **Yeru Shalem**,
Break up **Till** your *fallow ground* **tillage**,
and *sow* **seed** not among thorns.
4 Circumcise yourselves to *the LORD* **Yah Veh**,
and *take away* **turn aside** the foreskins of your heart,
ye men of *Judah* **Yah Hudah**

and *inhabitants* **settlers** of *Jerusalem* **Yeru Shalem**:
lest my fury come forth like fire,
and burn that none can quench it,
because **at the face** of the evil
of your *doings* **exploitations.**

YAH VEH WARNS YISRA EL

5 *Declare* **Tell** ye in *Judah* **Yah Hudah,**
and *publish* **let it be heard** in *Jerusalem* **Yeru Shalem;**
and say, *Blow* **Blast** ye the *trumpet* **shophar** in the land:
cry **call out**, *gather together* **fulfill**, and say,
Assemble yourselves **Gather,**
and let us go into the *defenced* **fortified** cities.
6 *Set up* **Lift** the *standard*
ensign toward *Zion* **Siyon:**
retire **withdraw**, stay not:
for I *will* **shall** bring evil from the north,
and a great *destruction* **breaking.**
7 The lion is *come up* **ascended** from his thicket,
and the *destroyer* **ruiner** of the *Gentiles* **goyim**
is on his way;
he is gone forth from his place
to *make* **set** thy land desolate;
and thy cities shall *be laid waste* **set desolate,**
without *an inhabitant* **a settler.**
8 For this gird you with *sackcloth* **saq,**
lament **chop** and howl:
for the *fierce anger* **fuming wrath** of *the LORD* **Yah Veh**
is not turned back from us.
9 And **so be** it *shall come to pass* at that day,
20 Surely as a woman deals
covertly with her friend,
thus you deal covertly with me, O house of Yisra El
—an oracle of Yah Veh.
21 A voice on the barrens—hear!
Weeping supplications of the sons of Yisra El:
for they pervert their way
and they forget Yah Veh their Elohim.
22 Return, you apostate sons,
and I heal your apostasies.
Behold, we come to you;
for you are Yah Veh our Elohim.
23 Surely in falsehood from the hills
and from the multitude of mountains:
surely in Yah Veh our Elohim
is the salvation of Yisra El.
24 For shame devours the labor of our fathers
from our youth
—their flocks and their herds their
sons and their daughters:
25 we lie down in our shame,
and our confusion covers us:
for we sin against Yah Veh our Elohim
—we and our fathers
from our youth even to this day,
and hearken not to the voice of Yah Veh our Elohim.

YAH VEH PLEADS WITH YISRA EL

4 If you return, O Yisra El,
—an oracle of Yah Veh
return to me;
and if you turn aside your abominations
from my face,
then you wander not:
2 and you oath, Yah Veh lives!
—in truth, in judgment and in justness:
and the goyim bless themselves in him
and in him they halal.
3 For thus says Yah Veh
to the men of Yah Hudah and Yeru Shalem,
Till your tillage; seed not among thorns:
4 circumcise yourselves to Yah Veh
and turn aside the foreskins of your heart,
you men of Yah Hudah and settlers of Yeru Shalem:
lest my fury comes forth as fire
and burns so that no one can quench it
at the face of the evil of your exploitations.

YAH VEH WARNS YISRA EL

5 Tell it in Yah Hudah
and have it heard in Yeru Shalem;
and say, Blast the shophar in the land!
Call out, fulfill, and say,
Gather, and we go into the fortified cities.
6 Lift the ensign toward Siyon:
withdraw, stay not:
for I bring evil from the north and a great breaking.
7 The lion ascends from his thicket
and the ruiner of the goyim *is* on his way;
he comes from his place to set your land desolate;
and set your cities desolate; without a settler.
8 For this gird with saq; chop and howl:
for the fuming wrath of Yah Veh
turns not back from us.
9 And so be it, at that day,
exeGeses ready research BIBLE
saith the LORD **an oracle of Yah Veh,**
that the heart of the *king* **sovereign** shall *perish* **destruct,**
and the heart of the *princes* **governors;**
and the priests shall *be astonished* **astonish,**

and the prophets shall *wonder* **marvel.**
10 Then said I, *Ah* **Aha,** *Lord*
GOD **Adonay Yah Veh**!
in deceiving, *surely* thou hast *greatly* deceived
this people and *Jerusalem* **Yeru Shalem,** saying,
Ye shall have *peace* **shalom;**
whereas the sword *reacheth* **toucheth** unto the soul.
11 At that time shall it be said to this people
and to *Jerusalem* **Yeru Shalem,**
A *dry* **clear** wind of the *high places* **barrens**
in the wilderness
toward the daughter of my people,
not to *fan* **winnow,** nor to *cleanse* **purify,**
12 *Even* a full wind *from those places*
shall come unto me:
now also
will **shall** I *give sentence* **word judgment** against them.
13 Behold, he shall *come up* **ascend** as clouds,
and his chariots shall be as a *whirlwind* **hurricane**:
his horses are swifter than eagles.
Woe unto us! for we are *spoiled* **ravaged.**
14 O *Jerusalem* **Yeru Shalem,**
wash **launder** thine heart from *wickedness* **evil,**
that thou mayest be saved.
How long **Until when**
shall thy *vain thoughts* **fabrications of mischief**
lodge **stay overnight** within thee?
15 For a voice *declareth* **telleth** from Dan,
and *publisheth affliction* **hearkeneth mischief**
from mount *Ephraim* **Ephrayim.**
16 *Make ye mention to* **Remind** the *nations* **goyim;**
behold,
publish **let it be heard** against *Jerusalem* **Yeru Shalem,**
that *watchers* **guards** come from a far *country* **land,**
and give out their voice
against the cities of *Judah* **Yah Hudah.**
17 As *keepers* **guards** of a field,
are they against her round about;
because she hath been rebellious against me,
saith the LORD **an oracle of Yah Veh.**
18 Thy way and thy *doings* **exploitations**
have *procured* **worked** these *things* unto
thee; this is thy *wickedness* **evil,**
because it is bitter, because it reacheth unto thine heart.
19 My *bowels* **inwards,** my *bowels* **inwards**!
I *am pained at my very* **writhe at the walls of my** heart;
my heart *maketh a noise* **roareth** in me;
I cannot *hold my peace* **hush,**
because thou hast heard, O my soul,
the *sound* **voice** of the *trumpet* **shophar,**
the *alarm* **blast** of war.
20 *Destruction* **Breech** upon *destruction* **breech**
is *cried* **called out;**
for the whole land is *spoiled* **ravaged:**
suddenly are my tents *spoiled* **ravaged,**
and my curtains in a *moment* **blink.**
21 How long shall I see the *standard* **ensign,**
and hear the *sound* **voice** of the *trumpet* **shophar**?
22 For my people is foolish,
they have not known me;
they are *sottish children* **foolish sons,**
and they *have none understanding* **discern not**:
they are wise to *do evil* **vilify,**
but to *do good* **well—please** they have no knowledge.
23 I *beheld* **saw** the earth, and, *lo* **behold,**
it was *without form* **a waste,** and *void* **empty;**
and the heavens, and they had no light.
24 I *beheld* **saw** the mountains,
and, *lo* **behold,** they *trembled* **quaked,**
and all the hills *moved lightly* **abate.**
25 I *beheld* **saw,** and, *lo* **behold,**
there was no *man* **human,**
and all the *birds* **flyers** of the heavens were fled.
26 I *beheld* **saw,** and, *lo* **behold,**
the *fruitful place* **orchard/Karmel** was a wilderness,
and all the cities *thereof* were *broken* **pulled** down
at the *presence* **face** of *the LORD* **Yah Veh,**
and by his *fierce anger* **fuming wrath.**
—an oracle of Yah Veh
the heart of the sovereign destructs,
and the heart of the governors;
and the priests astonish and the prophets marvel.
10 And I say, Aha, Adonay Yah Veh!
In deceiving,
you deceive this people and Yeru Shalem, saying,
Shalom is yours!
—whereas the sword touches to the soul.
11 At that time
it is said to this people and to Yeru Shalem,
A clear wind of the barrens in the wilderness
toward the daughter of my people
—neither to winnow nor to purify:
12 a full wind comes to me:
now also, I word judgment against them.
13 Behold, he ascends as clouds,
and his chariots as a hurricane:
swifter than eagles are his horses.
Woe to us! For we are ravaged!
14 O Yeru Shalem, launder your heart from evil,
to be saved.
Until when stay your fabrications of mischief
overnight within you?

15 For a voice tells from Dan,
and hearkens mischief from mount Ephrayim.
16 Remind the goyim;
behold, that it be heard against Yeru Shalem;
that guards are coming from a land afar,
and give their voice against the cities of Yah Hudah.
17 As guards of a field,
they are against her all around;
because she rebels against me
—an oracle of Yah Veh.
18 Your way and your exploitations
work these to you;
this is your evil; because it is bitter;
because it reaches to your heart.
19 My inwards! My inwards!
I writhe at the walls of my heart;
my heart roars within me;
I cannot hush, because you hear, O my soul,
the voice of the shophar—the blast of war.
20 Breech upon breech is called out;
for the whole land is ravaged:
suddenly my tents are ravaged
—and my curtains in a blink.
21 Until when see I the ensign
and hear the voice of the shophar?
22 For my people *are* foolish, they know me not;
foolish sons and they discern not:
wise to vilify
and to well—please they know not.
23 I see the earth; and behold, waste and empty;
and the heavens, and no light:
24 I see the mountains, and behold, they quake;
and all the hills abate:
25 I see, and behold, no human;
and all the flyers of the heavens flee:
26 I see, and behold,
the orchard/Karmel is a wilderness;
and all the cities are pulled down
at the face of Yah Veh by his fuming wrath.
27 For thus hath *the LORD* **Yah Veh** said,
The whole land shall be desolate;
yet *will* **shall** I not *make* **work** a *full end* **final finish**.
28 For this shall the earth mourn,
and the heavens above *be black* **darken**;
because I have *spoken* **worded** it,
I have *purposed* **intrigued** *it*,
and *will* **shall** not *repent* **sigh**,
neither *will* **shall** I turn back from it.
29 The whole city shall flee
for the *noise* **voice** of the *horsemen* **cavalry**
and *bowmen* **they that hurl the bow**;
they shall go into *thickets* **thick clouds**,
and *climb up* **ascend** upon the rocks:
every city shall be forsaken,
and not a man *dwell* **settle** therein.
30 And *when thou art spoiled* **thou, O ravaged**,
what *wilt* **shalt** thou *do* **work**?
Though thou *clothest* **enrobest** thyself
with *crimson* **scarlet**,
though thou *deckest* **adornest** thee
with ornaments of gold,
though thou *rentest* **rippest** thy *face* **eyes**
with *painting* **stibium**,
in vain shalt thou *make* **beautify** thyself *fair*;
thy lovers will despise
they who pant after thee shall spurn thee,
they *will* **shall** seek thy *life* **soul**.
31 For I have heard a voice
as of *a woman in travail* **stroking**,
and the *anguish* **tribulation** as of her
that *bringeth forth her first child* **bursteth the matrix**,
the voice of the daughter of *Zion* **Siyon**,
that *bewaileth herself* **sigheth**,
that spreadeth her *hands* **palms**, *saying*,
Woe is me *now* **I beseech**!
for my soul *is wearied* **languisheth**
because of murderers.

THE SEARCH FOR THE MAN WHO WORKS JUDGMENT

5 *Run ye to and fro* **Flit**
through the *streets* **outways** of *Jerusalem* **Yeru Shalem**,
and see *now* **I beseech**, and know,
and seek in the *broad places* **broadways** *thereof*,
if ye can find a man,
if there be any that *executeth* **worketh** judgment,
that seeketh *the truth* **trustworthiness**;
and I *will pardon it* **shall forgive**.
2 And though they say, *The LORD* **Yah Veh** liveth;
surely they *swear* **oath** falsely.
3 O *LORD* **Yah Veh**,
are not thine eyes upon *the truth* **trustworthiness**?
thou hast *stricken* **smitten** them,
but they have not *grieved* **writhed**;
thou hast *consumed* **finished** them **off**,
but they have refused to *receive* **take** correction:
they have *made* **toughened** their faces
harder than **as** a rock;
they have refused to return.
4 Therefore I said,

Surely these are poor; they are *foolish* **follied**:
for they know not the way of *the LORD* **Yah Veh**,
nor the judgment of their *God* **Elohim**.
5 I *will* **shall** get me unto the great *men*,
and *will speak* **shall word** unto them;
for they have known the way of *the LORD* **Yah Veh**,
and the judgment of their *God* **Elohim**:
but these have altogether broken the yoke,
and burst **torn** the bonds.
6 Wherefore a lion out of the
forest shall *slay* **smite** them,
and a wolf of the *evenings* **plains** shall *spoil* **ravage** them,
a leopard shall watch over their cities:
every one that goeth out thence shall be torn *in pieces*:
because their *transgressions* **rebellions**
are many **abound by the myriads**,
and their *backslidings* **apostasies** are *increased* **mighty**.
7 How shall I *pardon* **forgive** thee for this?
thy *children* **sons** have forsaken me,
and *sworn* **oathed** by them that are no *gods* **elohim**:
27 For thus says Yah Veh,
The whole land becomes desolate;
yet I work not a final finish:
28 for this the earth mourns
and the heavens above darken
—because I worded it; I intrigued:
and I neither sigh nor turn back therefrom.
29 The whole city flees at the voice of the cavalry
and them who hurl the bow;
they go into thick clouds and ascend on the rocks:
every city is forsaken and not a man settles therein.
30 And you, O ravaged, what work you?
Though you enrobe yourself with scarlet,
though you adorn with ornaments of gold,
though you rip your eyes with stibium,
you beautify yourself in vain:
they who pant after you, spurn you;
they seek your soul.
31 For I hear a voice as of stroking
and the tribulation as of bursting the matrix
—the voice of the daughter of Siyon sighing
—who spreads her palms,
Woe is me I beseech!
for my soul languishes because of murderers.

THE SEARCH FOR THE MAN WHO WORKS JUDGMENT

5 Flit through the outways of Yeru Shalem;
and see, I beseech, and know;
and seek in the broadways
—if you find a man
—if there be any who work judgment
—who seek trustworthiness;
and I forgive.
2 And if they say, Yah Veh lives!
—surely they oath falsely.
3 O Yah Veh,
are not your eyes on trustworthiness?
you smite them, and they writhe not;
you finish them off, and they refuse to take correction:
they toughen their faces as a rock;
they refuse to return.
4 And I—I say,
Surely these are poor; they folly:
for they know neither the way of Yah Veh
nor the judgment of their Elohim.
5 I go to the great and word to them
—for they know the way of Yah Veh
and the judgment of their Elohim:
surely these altogether broke the yoke;
they tore the bonds.
6 So a lion from the forest smites them;
a wolf from the plains ravages them;
a leopard watches over their cities;
every one who comes out thence is torn
—because their rebellions abound by the myriads
and their apostasies are mighty.
7 How forgive I you for this?
Your sons forsake me,
and oath by them who are non—elohim:
when I had *fed* **oathed** them *to the full*,
they then *committed adultery* **adulterized**,
and *assembled themselves by troops* **trooped**
in the *harlots'* **whore** houses.
8 They *were* **wandered** as *fed* **nourished** horses
in the morning:
every *one neighed* **man sounded**
after his *neighbour's wife* **friend's woman**.
9 Shall I not visit for these *things*?
saith the LORD **an oracle of Yah Veh**:
and shall not my soul be avenged
on such a *nation* **goyim** as this?
10 *Go ye up* **Ascend ye** upon
her *walls* **fortifications**
and *destroy* **ruin**;
but *make* **work** not a *full end* **final finish**:
take away **turn aside** her *battlements* **tendrils**;
for they are not *the LORD'S* **Yah Veh's**.
11 For the house of *Israel* **Yisra El**
and the house of *Judah* **Yah Hudah**

in dealing covertly,
have dealt *very treacherously* **covertly** against me,
saith the LORD **an oracle of Yah Veh.**
12 They have *belied the LORD* **disowned Yah Veh,**
and said, *It is* not he;
neither shall evil come upon us;
neither shall we see sword nor famine:
13 And the prophets shall become wind/**spirit,**
and the word is not in them:
thus shall it be *done* **worked** unto them.
14 Wherefore thus saith
the LORD God of hosts **Yah Veh Elohim Sabaoth,**
Because ye *speak* **word** this word, behold,
I *will make* **shall give** my words in thy mouth fire,
and this people *wood* **timber,**
and it shall *devour* **consume** them.
15 *Lo* **Behold,**
I *will* **shall** bring a *nation* **goyim** upon you from far,
O house of *Israel* **Yisra El,**
saith the LORD **an oracle of Yah Veh:**
it is a *mighty nation* **perennial goyim,**
it is an *ancient nation* **eternal goyim,**
a *nation* **goyim** whose language thou knowest not,
neither *understandest* **hearest** what they *say* **word.**
16 Their quiver is as an open *sepulchre* **tomb,**
they are all mighty *men.*
17 And they shall eat *up* thine
harvest, and thy bread,
which thy sons and thy daughters should eat:
they shall eat *up* thy flocks and thine herds:
they shall eat *up* thy vines and thy fig trees:
they shall impoverish thy *fenced* **fortified** cities,
wherein thou *trustedst* **confidedst,** with the sword.
18 Nevertheless in those days,
saith the LORD **an oracle of Yah Veh,**
I *will* **shall** not *make* **work** a *full*
end **final finish** with you.
19 And **so be** it *shall come to*
pass, when ye shall say,
Wherefore *doeth* **worketh** *the LORD* **Yah Veh**
our *God* **Elohim** all these *things* unto us?
then shalt thou *answer* **say to** them,
Like as ye have forsaken me,
and served strange *gods* **elohim** in your land,
so shall ye serve strangers in a land that is not yours.
20 *Declare* **Tell** this in the house of *Jacob* **Yaaqov,**
and *publish* **let** it **be heard** in *Judah* **Yah Hudah,** saying,
21 Hear *now* **I beseech,** this, O foolish people,
and without *understanding* **heart;**
which have eyes, and see not;
which have ears, and hear not:
22 *Fear* **Awe** ye not me?
saith the LORD **an oracle of Yah Veh:**
will **shall** ye not *tremble* **writhe** at my *presence* **face,**
which have *placed* **set** the sand
for the *bound* **border** of the sea
by *a perpetual decree* **an eternal statute,**
that it cannot pass it:
and though the waves *thereof toss themselves* **agitate,**
yet can they not prevail;
though they roar,
yet can they not pass over it?
23 But this people hath a revolting
and a rebellious heart;
when I oath them,
they adulterize and troop in the whore houses:
8 they wander as nourished horses;
every man sounds after the woman of his friend.
9 Visit I not for these?
—an oracle of Yah Veh
and avenge I not my soul on such a goyim as this?
10 You, ascend on her fortifications, and ruin;
and work not a final finish:
turn aside her tendrils;
for they are not of Yah Veh.
11 For the house of Yisra El
and the house of Yah Hudah
in dealing covertly, deal covertly against me
—an oracle of Yah Veh.
12 They disown Yah Veh, and say, Not him!
Neither comes evil on us
nor see we sword or famine:
13 and the prophets become wind/spirit,
and the word is not in them: thus is it worked to them.
14 So thus says Yah Veh Elohim Sabaoth,
Because you word this word, behold,
I give my words in your mouth, fire,
and this people, timber,
and it consumes them.
15 Behold, I bring a goyim on you from afar,
O house of Yisra El,
—an oracle of Yah Veh
—a perennial goyim—an eternal goyim—a goyim
—you neither know their tongue
nor hear their word:
16 their quiver *is as* an open tomb;
they all *are* mighty:
17 and they eat your harvest and your bread
which your sons and your daughters eat: they eat
your flocks and your herds; they eat your vines

and your fig trees; they impoverish your fortified
cities, wherein you confide, with the sword.
18 And even in those days,
—an oracle of Yah Veh
I work not a final finish with you.
19 And so be it, when you say,
Why works Yah Veh our Elohim all these to us?
then you say to them,
As you forsook me
and served strange elohim in your land,
thus you serve strangers in a land that *is* not yours.
20 Tell this in the house of Yaaqov,
and have it heard in Yah Hudah, saying,
21 Hear this, I beseech,
O foolish people, and without heart;
having eyes, and seeing not;
having ears, and hearing not:
22 Awe you not me?
—an oracle of Yah Veh:
Writhe you not at my face
—who set the sand for the border of the sea
by an eternal statute, that it not pass?
And though the waves agitate, yet they prevail not?
And though they roar, yet they pass not over it?
23 And this people
has a revolting and a rebellious heart;
they are *revolted* **turned aside** and gone.
24 Neither say they in their heart,
Let us *now* **I beseech,**
fear the LORD **awe Yah Veh** our *God* **Elohim**,
that giveth *rain* **downpour**,
both the *former* **early** and the *latter* **after**,
in his *season* **time**:
he *reserveth* **guardeth** unto us
the *appointed* **statute** weeks of the harvest.
25 Your *iniquities* **perversities**
have *turned away these things* **perverted**,
and your sins have withholden good *things* from you.
26 For among my people are found wicked *men*:
they *lay wait* **observe**, as he that *setteth* **weaveth** snares;
they *set* **station** a *trap* **ruin**, they *catch* **captivate** men.
27 As a cage is full of *birds* **flyers**,
so are their houses full of deceit:
therefore they are *become great* **greatened**,
and *waxen rich* **enriched**.
28 They are *waxen fat* **fattened**, they shine:
yea, they overpass the *deeds* **words** of the *wicked* **evil**:
they *judge* **plead** not the cause,
the cause of the *fatherless* **orphan**, yet they prosper;
and the *right* **judgment** of the needy do they not judge.
29 Shall I not visit for these *things*?
saith the LORD **an oracle of Yah Veh**:
shall **I** not **avenge** my soul *be avenged*
on such a *nation* **goyim** as this?
30 A *wonderful* **desolation** and horrible *thing*
is *committed* **become** in the land;
31 The prophets prophesy falsely,
and the priests *bear rule* **subjugate**
by their *means* **hands**;
and my people love *to have* it so:
and what *will* **shall** ye *do* **work** in the end *thereof*?

Yeru Shalem Is Visited

6 O ye *children* **sons** of *Benjamin* **Ben Yamin**,
gather **withdraw** yourselves
to flee out of the midst of *Jerusalem* **Yeru Shalem**,
and *blow* **blast** the *trumpet* **shophar** in *Tekoa* **Teqoa**,
and *set up* **lift** a *sign of fire* **burden**
in *Bethhaccerem* **Beth Hak Kerem**:
for evil *appeareth* **looketh** out of the north,
and great *destruction* **breaking**.
2 I have *likened* **severed** the
daughter of *Zion* **Siyon**
to a *comely and delicate woman*
delicate habitation of rest.
3 The *shepherds* **tenders** with their *flocks* **droves**
shall come unto her;
they shall *pitch* **stake** their tents against her round about;
they shall *feed* **tend** every *one in* **man at** his *place* **hand**.
4 *Prepare* **Hallow** ye war against her;
arise, and let us *go up* **ascend** at noon.
Woe unto us! for the day *goeth* **faceth** away,
for the shadows of the evening are *stretched out* **spread**.
5 Arise, and let us *go* **ascend** by night,
and let us *destroy* **ruin** her *palaces* **citadels**.
6 For thus hath *the LORD of*
hosts **Yah Veh Sabaoth** said,
Hew **Cut** ye down trees,
and *cast* **pour** a mount against *Jerusalem* **Yeru Shalem**:
this is the city to be visited;
she is wholly oppression in the midst of her.
7 As *a fountain casteth out her*
digging a well for waters,
so she *casteth out* **diggeth** her *wickedness* **evil**:
violence and *spoil* **ravage** is heard in her;
before me **at my face** continually
is *grief* **sickness** and wounds.
8 Be thou instructed, O *Jerusalem* **Yeru Shalem**,
lest my soul depart from thee;
lest I *make* **set** thee desolate, a land not *inhabited* **settled**.

9 Thus saith *the LORD of hosts* **Yah Veh Sabaoth,**
They shall throughly glean
the *remnant* **survivors** of *Israel* **Yisra El** as a vine:
turn back thine hand
as a *grapegatherer* **clipper** into the baskets.
10 To whom shall I *speak* **word,**
and *give warning* **witness,** that they may hear?
behold,
their ear is uncircumcised, and they cannot hearken:
they turn aside and go on;
24 they say not in their heart,
We now awe Yah Veh our Elohim
—who gives downpour
—both the early and the after in his time:
he guards to us the statute weeks of the harvest.
25 Your perversities pervert
and your sins withhold good from you:
26 for wicked are found among my people:
they observe, as he who weaves snares; they
station a ruin, they captivate men:
27 as a cage full of flyers,
thus are their houses full of deceit:
so they greaten and enrich;
28 they fatten; they shine:
yes, they overpass the words of the evil:
they plead not the cause
—the cause of the orphan, yet they prosper;
and the judgment of the needy they judge not.
29 Visit I not for these?
—an oracle of Yah Veh:
Avenge I not my soul on such a goyim as this?
30 Desolation and horror is in the land:
31 the prophets prophesy falsely
and the priests subjugate by their hands;
and thus my people love it.
And what work you in the end?

YERU SHALEM IS VISITED

6 O you sons of Ben Yamin,
withdraw yourselves to flee from midst Yeru Shalem:
and blast the shophar in Teqoa
and lift a burden in Beth Hak Kerem:
for evil looks from the north,
and great breaking.
2 I severed the delicate daughter of Siyon
to a habitation of rest:
3 the tenders with their droves come to her;
they stake their tents against her all
round; every man tends at his hand.
4 You, hallow war against her!
Rise! We ascend at noon! Woe to us!
For the day faces away;
for the shadows of the evening spread.
5 Rise! We ascend by night and ruin her citadels.
6 For thus says Yah Veh Sabaoth,
Cut down trees;
and pour a mound against Yeru Shalem
—the city to visit;
total oppression is in her midst.
7 As digging a well for waters,
thus she digs her evil:
violence and ravage is heard in her;
at my face continually *is* sickness and wounds.
8 Be instructed, O Yeru Shalem,
lest my soul depart from you;
lest I set you desolate—a land not settled.
9 Thus says Yah Veh Sabaoth,
They throughly glean, as a vine,
the survivors of Yisra El:
turn back your hand, as a clipper, into the baskets.
10 To whom word I, and witness to them to hear?
Behold, their ear is uncircumcised
and they cannot hearken:
behold,
the word of *the LORD* **Yah Veh** is unto them a reproach;
they have no delight in it.
11 Therefore
I am *full* **filled** of the fury of *the LORD* **Yah Veh;**
I am weary *with holding in* **of containing:**
I *will* **shall** pour it out
upon the *children abroad* **suckling in the outways,**
and upon the *assembly* **private counsel**
of *young men* **youths** together:
for even the *husband* **man** with the *wife* **woman**
shall be *taken* **captured,**
the *aged* **elder** with him that is full of days.
12 And their houses shall be turned unto others,
with their fields and *wives* **women** together:
for I *will stretch out* **shall spread** my hand
upon the *inhabitants* **settlers** of the land,
saith the LORD **an oracle of Yah Veh.**
13 For from the least of them
even unto the greatest of them
every one
is given to covetousness **greedily gaineth to greedy gain;**
and from the prophet even unto the priest
every one *dealeth* **worketh** falsely.
14 They have healed also
the *hurt of the daughter* **breaking** of my people slightly,
saying, *Peace* **Shalom,** *peace* **shalom;**

when there is no *peace* **shalom.**
15 Were they *ashamed* **shamed** when they had
committed abomination **worked abhorrence**? nay,
they were not at all ashamed
in shaming, they shamed not,
neither *could they blush* **knew they to shame**:
therefore they shall fall among them that fall:
at the time that I visit them they
shall *be cast down* **falter**,
saith *the LORD* **Yah Veh**.
16 Thus saith *the LORD* **Yah Veh**,
Stand ye in the ways, and see,
and ask for the *old* **eternal** paths, where is the good way,
and walk therein,
and ye shall find *rest* **a resting place** for your souls.
But they said, We *will* **shall** not walk *therein.*
17 Also I *set watchmen* **raise watchers** over you,
saying, Hearken to the *sound* **voice** of the *trumpet*
shophar. But they said, We *will* **shall** not hearken.
18 Therefore hear, ye *nations* **goyim**,
and know, O *congregation* **witness**, what is among them.
19 Hear, O earth: behold,
I *will* **shall** bring evil upon this people,
even the fruit of their *thoughts* **fabrications**,
because they have not hearkened unto my words,
nor to my *law* **torah**, but *rejected* **spurned** it.
20 To what purpose cometh there to me
incense from Sheba,
and the *sweet cane* **good stalk** from a far *country* **land**?
your *burnt offerings* **holocausts**
are not *acceptable* **pleasing**,
nor your sacrifices *sweet* **pleasing** unto me.
21 Therefore thus saith *the*
LORD **Yah Veh**, Behold,
I *will lay* **shall give** stumblingblocks
before **in front of** this people,
and the fathers and the sons together
shall *fall* **falter** upon them;
the *neighbour* **fellow tabernacler** and his friend
shall *perish* **destruct**.
22 Thus saith *the LORD* **Yah Veh**,
Behold, a people cometh from the north *country* **land**,
and a great *nation* **goyim** shall be *raised* **wakened**
from the *sides* **flanks** of the earth.
23 They shall lay hold on bow and *spear* **dart**;
they are cruel, and *have no mercy* **mercy not**;
their voice roareth like the sea;
and they ride upon horses,
set in array **lined up** as men for war against thee,
O daughter of *Zion* **Siyon**.
24 We have heard the fame *thereof*:
our hands *wax feeble* **slacken**:
anguish **tribulation** hath taken hold of us,
and pain **pang**, as *of a woman in travail* **in birthing**.
25 Go not forth into the field, nor walk by the way;
behold, the word of Yah Veh is their reproach;
they delight not therein:
11 and I am filled with the fury of Yah Veh;
I am weary of containing:
I pour it out on the suckling in the outways
and on the private counsel of youths together:
for they even capture the man with the woman
—the elder with him who is full of days:
12 and turn their houses to others
together with their fields and women:
for I spread my hand on the settlers of the land
—an oracle of Yah Veh.
13 For from their least, even to their greatest,
every one greedily gains to greedy gain;
and from the prophet, even to the priest,
every one works falsely:
14 and they heal the breeching
of my people slightly,
saying, Shalom! Shalom! when there is no shalom.
15 Shame they when they work abhorrence?
No! In shaming, they neither shame
nor know *how* to shame:
so they fall among the fallen:
at the time I visit them, they falter, says Yah Veh.
16 Thus says Yah Veh,
You, stand in the ways, and see;
and ask for the eternal paths where the good way *is*
and walk therein;
and find a resting place for your souls.
And they say, We walk not.
17 And I raise watchers over you,
Hearken to the voice of the shophar.
And they say, We hearken not.
18 So hear, you goyim,
and know, O witness, what *is* among them.
19 Hear, O earth!
Behold, I bring evil on this people
—the fruit of their fabrications
because they hearken not to my words,
and my torah, they spurn.
20 Why to me, this incense from Sheba?
And the good stalk from a far land? neither *are* your
holocausts pleasing nor your sacrifices pleasing to me.
21 So thus says Yah Veh, Behold,
I give stumblingblocks in front of this people;

and the fathers and the sons together falter on them;
the fellow tabernacler and his friend destruct.
22 Thus says Yah Veh, Behold,
a people comes from the north land
and a great goyim
wakens from the flanks of the earth:
23 they lay hold on bow and dart;
they *are* cruel, and mercy not;
their voice roars as the sea;
and they ride on horses
—lined up as men for war against you,
O daughter of Siyon.
24 We hear the fame: our hands slacken:
tribulation takes hold of us
—pang, as in birthing.
25 Neither go forth into the
field nor walk by the way;
for the sword of the enemy and *fear* **terror**
is *on every side* **round about.**
26 O daughter of my people,
gird thee with *sackcloth* **saq**, and wallow thyself in ashes:
make **work** thee mourning, as for an only son,
a chopping most bitter *lamentation*:
for the *spoiler* **ravager** shall suddenly come upon us.
27 I have *set* **given** thee for a tower
and a fortress among my people,
that thou mayest know and *try* **proof** their way.
28 They are all
grievous revolters **turned aside by revolters,**
walking with *slanders* **talebearers**:
they are *brass* **copper** and iron;
they are all *corrupters* **ruiners.**
29 The bellows are *burned* **scorched,**
the lead is consumed of the fire;
the *founder melteth* **refiner refineth** in vain:
for the *wicked* **evil** are not *plucked* **torn** away.
30 *Reprobate* **Refuse** silver
shall *men call them* **they be called,**
because *the LORD* **Yah Veh** hath *rejected* **refused** them.

Message At The House Of Yah Veh

7 The word that came to *Jeremiah* **Yirme Yah**
from *the LORD* **Yah Veh**, saying,
2 Stand in the *gate* **portal**
of the *LORD'S* house **of Yah Veh,**
and *proclaim* **call out** there this word, and say,
Hear the word of *the LORD* **Yah Veh,**
all *ye* of *Judah* **Yah Hudah,**
that enter in at these *gates* **portals**
to *worship the LORD* **prostrate in front of Yah Veh.**
3 Thus saith *the LORD of hosts* **Yah Veh Sabaoth,**
the *God* **Elohim** of *Israel* **Yisra El,**
Amend **Well—prepare** your ways
and your *doings* **exploits,**
and I *will* **shall** cause you
to *dwell* **tabernacle** in this place.
4 *Trust* **Confide** ye not in
lying **false** words, saying,
The *temple* **manse** of *the LORD* **Yah Veh,**
The *temple* **manse** of *the LORD* **Yah Veh,** The
temple **manse** of *the LORD* **Yah Veh,**
are these.
5 For if **in well—preparing,**
ye *throughly amend* **well—prepare**
your ways and your *doings* **exploitations;**
if **in working,** ye *throughly execute* **work** judgment
between a man and his *neighbour* **friend;**
6 If ye oppress not the *stranger* **sojourner,**
the *fatherless* **orphan,** and the widow,
and *shed* **pour** not innocent blood in this place,
neither walk after other *gods* **elohim** to your *hurt* **evil:**
7 Then *will* **shall** I cause you
to *dwell* **tabernacle** in this place,
in the land that I gave to your fathers,
for ever **eternally** and *ever* **eternally.**
8 Behold, ye *trust* **confide** in *lying* **false** words,
that cannot *profit* **benefit.**
9 *Will* **Shall** ye steal, murder,
and *commit adultery* **adulterize,** and *swear* **oath** falsely,
and *burn* incense unto Baal,
and walk after other *gods* **elohim** whom ye know not;
10 And come and stand *before me* **at my face**
in this house, which is called by my name,
and say, We are *delivered* **rescued!**
to do **in order to work**
all these *abominations* **abhorrences?**
11 Is this house, which is called by my name,
become a *den* **cave** of *robbers* **tyrants** in
your eyes? Behold, even I have seen it,
saith the LORD **an oracle of Yah Veh.**
12 But go ye *now* **I beseech,**
unto my place which was in Shiloh,
where I *set* **tabernacle** my name at the first,
and see what I *did* **worked** to it
for the wickedness **at the face of the evil**
of my people *Israel* **Yisra El.**
13 And *now* **I beseech,**
because ye have *done* **worked** all these works,
for the sword of the enemy and terror is all around.
26 O daughter of my people,

gird with saq, and wallow yourself in ashes:
work your mourning, as for an only son
—a chopping most bitter:
for the ravager comes on us suddenly.
27 I give you for a tower and a fortress
among my people,
so that you know and proof their way.
28 They all are turned aside by revolters;
walking with talebearers:
they are copper and iron;
they all are ruiners:
29 the bellows are scorched,
the lead is consumed by the fire;
the refiner refines in vain;
for the evil are not torn away:
30 Refuse silver, they are called,
because Yah Veh refused them.

MESSAGE AT THE HOUSE OF YAH VEH

7 And so be the word to Yirme Yah from Yah Veh,
saying,
2 Stand in the portal of the house of Yah Veh
and call out this word, and say,
Hear the word of Yah Veh, all Yah Hudah,
who enter in at these portals
to prostrate in front of Yah Veh:
3 thus says Yah Veh Sabaoth
the Elohim of Yisra El,
Well—prepare your ways and your exploits,
and I tabernacle you in this place.
4 Confide not in false words, saying,
The manse of Yah Veh!
The manse of Yah Veh!
The manse of Yah Veh *are* they!
5 For if, in well—preparing,
you well—prepare your ways and your exploitations;
if in working, you work judgment
between a man and his friend;
6 if you oppress not the sojourner,
the orphan, and the widow,
and pour not innocent blood in this place,
and walk not after other elohim to your evil:
7 then I tabernacle you in this place
in the land I gave to your fathers
eternally and eternally.
8 Behold,
you confide in false words that benefit not;
9 you steal, murder, and adulterize,
and oath falsely and incense to Baal;
and walk after other elohim whom you know not:
10 and then you come and stand at my face
in this house on which my name is called,
and say, We are rescued!
in order to work all these abhorrences.
11 Becomes this house, on
which my name is called,
a cave of tyrants in your eyes?
Behold, even I see
—an oracle of Yah Veh.
12 But come, I beseech, to my place in Shiloh,
where I tabernacled my name at the first;
and see what I worked to it
at the face of the evil of my people Yisra El:
13 and I beseech, because you work all these works
saith the LORD **an oracle of Yah Veh,**
and I *spake* **worded** unto you,
rising up **starting** early and *speaking* **wording,**
but ye heard not;
and I called you, but ye answered not;
14 Therefore *will* **shall** I *do* **work** unto this house,
which is called by my name, wherein ye *trust* **confide,**
and unto the place
which I gave to you and to your fathers,
as I have *done* **worked** to Shiloh.
15 And I *will* **shall** cast you
out of **from** my *sight* **face,**
as I have cast out all your brethren,
even the whole seed of *Ephraim* **Ephrayim.**
16 Therefore pray not thou for this people,
neither lift *up cry* **shout** nor prayer for them,
neither *make intercession* **intercede** to me:
for I *will* **shall** not hear thee.
17 Seest thou not what they *do* **work**
in the cities of *Judah* **Yah Hudah**
and in the *streets* **outways** of *Jerusalem* **Yeru Shalem?**
18 The *children* **sons** gather *wood* **timber,**
and the fathers *kindle* **burn** the fire,
and the women knead their dough,
to *make cakes* **work wafers**
to the *queen* **sovereigness** of *heaven* **the heavens,**
and to *pour out drink offerings* **libate libations**
unto other *gods* **elohim,**
that they may *provoke* **vex** me *to anger.*
19 Do they *provoke* **vex** me *to anger?*
saith the LORD **an oracle of Yah Veh:**
do they not provoke **and not** themselves
to the *confusion* **shame** of their own faces?
20 Therefore thus saith *the*
Lord GOD **Adonay Yah Veh;**

Behold, *mine anger* **my wrath** and my fury
shall be poured out upon this place,
upon *man* **humanity**, and upon *beast* **animal**,
and upon the trees of the field,
and upon the fruit of the *ground* **soil**;
and it shall burn, and shall not be quenched.
21 Thus saith *the LORD of hosts* **Yah Veh Sabaoth**,
the God **Elohim** of *Israel* **Yisra El**;
Put **Scrape up** your *burnt offerings* **holocausts**
unto your sacrifices, and eat flesh.
22 For I *spake* **worded** not unto your fathers,
nor *commanded* **misvahed** them in the day
that I brought them out of the land of *Egypt* **Misrayim**,
concerning *burnt offerings* **holocausts** or sacrifices:
23 But this *thing commanded* **misvahed** I them,
saying, *Obey* **Hearken to** my voice,
and I *will* **shall** be your *God* **Elohim**,
and ye shall be my people:
and walk ye
in all the ways that I have *commanded* **misvahed** you,
that it may *be well unto* **well—please** you.
24 But they hearkened not, nor
inclined **spread** their ear,
but walked in the counsels
and in the *imagination* **warp** of their evil heart,
and went backward, and not *forward* **toward the face**.
25 Since the day that your fathers came forth
out of the land of *Egypt* **Misrayim** unto this day
I have even sent unto you all my servants the prophets,
daily *rising up* **starting** early and sending them:
26 Yet they hearkened not unto me,
nor *inclined* **spread** their ear, but hardened their neck:
they *did worse than* **vilified above** their fathers.
27 Therefore
thou shalt *speak* **word** all these words unto them;
but they *will* **shall** not hearken to thee:
thou shalt also call unto them;
but they *will* **shall** not answer thee.
28 But thou shalt say unto them,
This is a *nation* **goyim** that *obeyeth* **hearkeneth** not
unto the voice of *the LORD* **Yah Veh** their *God* **Elohim**,
nor *receiveth correction* **taketh discipline**:
truth is perished **trustworthiness destructeth**,
and is cut off from their mouth.
29 *Cut off thine hair* **Shear thy**
separatism, *O Jerusalem*,
and cast it away,
and *take up* **lift** a lamentation on
high places **the barrens**;
—an oracle of Yah Veh;

and I word to you, starting early and wording,
and you hear not;
and I call you, and you answer not.
14 I also work to this house,
on which my name is called, wherein you confide,
and to the place I gave to you and to your fathers,
as I worked to Shiloh:
15 and I cast you from my face
as I cast out all your brothers
—the whole seed of Ephrayim:
16 and neither pray for this people
nor lift shouts nor prayers for them;
nor intercede to me:
for I hear you not.
17 See you not what they work
in the cities of Yah Hudah
and in the outways of Yeru Shalem?
18 The sons gather timber
and the fathers burn the fire;
and the women knead their dough
to work wafers to the sovereigness of the heavens
and to libate libations to other elohim to vex me.
19 Vex they me?
—an oracle of Yah Veh:
And not themselves to the shame of their own faces?
20 So thus says Adonay Yah Veh;
Behold, my wrath and my fury
poured on this place
—on humanity and on animal
and on the trees of the field
and on the fruit of the soil:
and it burns and quenches not.
21 Thus says Yah Veh Sabaoth, Elohim of Yisra El;
Scrape up your holocausts to your sacrifices
and eat flesh:
22 for I neither worded to your fathers,
nor misvahed them
in the day I brought them from the land of Misrayim
concerning holocausts or sacrifices:
23 But this I misvahed them, saying,
Hearken to my voice, and I am your
Elohim and you are my people:
and walk in all the ways I misvah you,
that it well—please you.
24 And they neither hearken nor spread their ear;
but walk in the counsels
and in the warp of their evil heart;
and go backward; and not toward the face.
25 Since the day your fathers came forth
from the land of Misrayim,

to this day,
I even sent to you all my servants the prophets,
daily starting early and sending them:
26 yet they neither hearkened to me,
nor spread their ear;
and hardened their neck:
they vilified above their fathers.
27 And you, word all these words to them;
and they hearken not to you:
and also call to them;
and they answer you not:
28 and say to them,
This goyim neither hearkens
to the voice of Yah Veh their Elohim,
nor takes discipline:
trustworthiness destructs;
yes, it *is* cut off from their mouth.
29 Shear your separatism and cast it away;
and lift a lamentation on the barrens;
for *the LORD* **Yah Veh**
hath *rejected* **spurned** and *forsaken* **abandoned**
the generation of his wrath.
30 For the *children* **sons** of *Judah* **Yah Hudah**
have *done* **worked** evil in my *sight* **eyes,**
saith the LORD **an oracle of Yah Veh**:
they have set their abominations
in the house which is called by my name,
to *pollute* **foul** it.

THE BAMAHS OF TOPHETH

31 And they have built
the *high places* **bamahs** of *Tophet* **Topheth,**
which is in
the valley of the son of Hinnom
Gay Ben Hinnom/Valley of the Son of Burning,
to burn their sons and their daughters in the fire;
which I *commanded* **misvahed** *them* not,
neither *came* **ascended** it into my heart.
32 Therefore, behold, the days come,
saith the LORD **an oracle of Yah Veh,**
that it shall no more be *called* **said,** *Tophet* **Topheth**
nor *the valley of the son of Hinnom*
Gay Ben Hinnom/Valley of the Son of Burning,
but
the valley of slaughter **Gay Haregah/Valley of Slaughter**:
for they shall *bury* **entomb** in *Tophet* **Topheth,**
till there be no place.
33 And the carcases of this people shall be meat
for the *fowls* **flyers** of the *heaven* **heavens,**
and for the *beasts* **animals** of the earth;
and none shall *fray* **tremble** them away.
34 Then *will* **shall** I cause to *cease* **shabbathize**
from the cities of *Judah* **Yah Hudah,**
and from the *streets* **outways** of *Jerusalem* **Yeru Shalem,**
the voice of *mirth* **rejoicing,**
and the voice of *gladness* **cheerfulness,**
the voice of the bridegroom, and the voice of the bride:
for the land shall be *desolate* **parched.**

THE SIN OF YAH HUDAH

8 At that time,
saith the LORD **an oracle of Yah Veh,**
they shall bring out
the bones of the *kings* **sovereigns** of *Judah* **Yah Hudah,**
and the bones of his *princes* **governors,**
and the bones of the priests,
and the bones of the prophets,
and the bones
of the *inhabitants* **settlers** of *Jerusalem* **Yeru Shalem,**
out of their *graves* **tombs**:
2 And they shall spread them *before* **to** the sun,
and the moon, and all the host of *heaven* **the heavens,**
whom they have loved, and whom they have served,
and after whom they have walked,
and whom they have sought,
and **to** whom they have *worshipped* **prostrated**:
they shall not be gathered, nor be *buried* **entombed**;
they shall be for dung upon the face of the *earth* **soil.**
3 And death shall be chosen rather than life
by all the *residue of them* **survivors**
that *remain* **survive** of this evil family,
which *remain* **survive**
in all the places whither I have driven them,
saith the LORD of hosts **an oracle of Yah Veh Sabaoth.**
4 Moreover thou shalt say unto them,
Thus saith *the LORD* **Yah Veh**;
shall they fall, and not arise?
shall he turn away, and not return?
5 Why then is this people of
Jerusalem **Yeru Shalem**
slidden **turned** back by a perpetual *backsliding* **apostasy**?
they *hold fast* **uphold** deceit, they refuse to return.
6 I hearkened and heard,
but they *spake* **worded** not aright:
no man *repented* **sighed for** him of his *wickedness* **evil,**
saying, What have I *done* **worked**?
every one turned to his *course* **race,**
as the horse *rusheth* **overfloweth** into the *battle* **war.**
7 Yea, the stork in the *heaven* **heavens**
knoweth her *appointed times* **seasons**;

for Yah Veh spurns and abandons
the generation of his wrath:
30 for the sons of Yah Hudah work evil in my eyes
—an oracle of Yah Veh:
they set their abominations
in the house on which my name is called
to foul it.

The Bamahs Of Topheth

31 And they build the bamahs of Topheth
in Gay Ben Hinnom/Valley of the Son of Burning
to burn their sons and their daughters in the fire;
which I neither misvahed nor ascended into my heart.
32 So behold, days come,
—an oracle of Yah Veh
that they neither say any more, Topheth
nor Gay Ben Hinnom/Valley of the Son of Burning,
but Gay Haregah/Valley of Slaughter:
for they entomb in Topheth until there is no place:
33 and the carcases of this people
are meat for the flyers of the heavens
and for the animals of the earth;
and no one trembles them away.
34 Then I shabbathize from
the cities of Yah Hudah,
and from the outways of Yeru Shalem,
the voice of rejoicing and the voice of cheerfulness;
the voice of the bridegroom and the voice of the bride
—for the land becomes parched.

The Sin Of Yah Hudah

8 At that time,
—an oracle of Yah Veh
they bring the bones of the sovereigns of Yah Hudah
and the bones of his governors
and the bones of the priests
and the bones of the prophets
and the bones of the settlers of Yeru Shalem
from their tombs:
2 and they spread them to the sun and the moon
and all the host of the heavens
—whom they loved and whom they served
and after whom they walked and whom they sought
and to whom they prostrated:
they are neither gathered nor entombed;
they are for dung on the face of the soil:
3 and death is chosen rather than life
by all the survivors who survive of this evil family
who survive in all the places I drive them
—an oracle of Yah Veh Sabaoth.
4 And you say to them, Thus says Yah Veh;
Fall they, and rise not?
Turns he away, and returns not?
5 Why then turns this people
of Yeru Shalem away
by a perpetual apostasy?
They uphold deceit; they refuse to return.
6 I hearken and hear; they word not right:
no man sighs of his evil,
saying, What worked I?
Every one turns to his race
as a horse overflowing into the war.
7 Yes, the stork in the heavens knows her seasons;
and the *turtle* **turtledove**
and the *crane* **swallow** and the *swallow* **thrush**
observe **regard** the time of their coming;
but my people
know not the judgment of *the LORD* **Yah Veh**.
8 How do ye say, We are wise,
and the *law* **torah** of *the LORD* **Yah Veh** is with us?
Lo **Behold**,
certainly **surely** in *vain made* **falsehood worked** he it;
the *pen* **false stylus** of the scribes
is in vain **worketh falsehood**.
9 The wise *men* are ashamed,
they are dismayed and *taken* **captured**:
lo **behold**, they have *rejected* **spurned**
the word of *the LORD* **Yah Veh**;
and what wisdom is in them?
10 Therefore *will* **shall** I give their *wives* **women**
unto others,
and their fields
to them that shall *inherit them* **be their successors**:
for every one from the least even unto the greatest
is given to covetousness **greedily gaineth to greedy gain**,
from the prophet even unto the priest
every one *dealeth* **worketh** falsely.
11 For they have healed
the *hurt* **breech** of the daughter of my people slightly,
saying, *Peace* **Shalom**, *peace* **shalom**;
when there is no *peace* **shalom**.
12 Were they ashamed when they had
committed abomination **worked abhorrence**?
nay **in shaming**,
they *were not at all ashamed* **shamed not**,
neither *could* **knew** they **to** blush:
therefore shall they fall among them that fall:
in the time of their visitation
they shall *be cast down* **falter**,
saith *the LORD* **Yah Veh**.

13 **In consuming,** I *will* **shall** *surely* consume them,
saith the LORD **an oracle of Yah Veh**:
there shall be no grapes on the vine,
nor figs on the fig tree,
and the leaf shall *fade* **wither**;
and *the things* **those** that I have given them
shall pass away from them.
14 Why do we sit *still? assemble yourselves* **gather**,
and let us enter into the *defenced* **fortified** cities,
and let us *be silent* **hush** there:
for *the LORD* **Yah Veh** our *God* **Elohim**
hath *put* **hushed** us *to silence,*
and given us water of *gall* **rosh** to drink,
because we have sinned against *the LORD* **Yah Veh**.
15 We *looked for peace* **awaited shalom**,
but no good *came*;
and for a time of *health* **healing**,
and behold *trouble* **fright**!
16 The snorting of his horses was heard from Dan:
the whole land *trembled* **quaked** at the *sound* **voice**
of the neighing of his *strong ones* **mighty**;
for they are come, and have devoured the land,
and *all that is in it* **the fulness thereof**;
the city, and those that *dwell* **settle** therein.
17 For, behold,
I *will* **shall** send serpents, *cockatrices*
hissers, among you,
which *will not be charmed* **shall have no charmer**,
and they shall bite you,
saith the LORD **an oracle of Yah Veh**.
18 *When I would comfort* **I should cheer** myself
against *sorrow* **grief**,
my heart *is faint* **bleedeth** in me.
19 Behold!
the voice of the *cry* **shout** of the daughter of my people
because of them
that dwell in a far country **in a land afar off**:
Is not *the LORD* **Yah Veh** in *Zion* **Siyon**?
is not her *king* **sovereign** in her?
Why have they *provoked* **vexed** me *to anger*
with their *graven images* **sculptiles**,
and with strange vanities?
20 The harvest is past, the
summer is *ended* **concluded**,
and the turtledove and the swallow and the thrush
regard the time of their coming;
and my people know not the judgment of Yah Veh.
How say you,
We *are* wise and the torah of Yah Veh *is* with us?
Behold, surely it works falsehood;
the false stylus of the scribes works falsehood.
9 The wise shame:
they are dismayed and captured:
behold, they spurn the word of Yah Veh;
and what wisdom *is* in them?
10 So I give their women to others
and their fields to their successors:
for every one from the least even to the greatest
greedily gains to greedy gain
—from the prophet even to the priest
—every one works falsely.
11 And they heal
the breech of the daughter of my people slightly,
saying, Shalom! Shalom!
when there is no shalom.
12 Shame they when they work abhorrence?
No, in shaming, they neither shame,
nor know they to blush:
so they fall among the fallen:
—falter in the time of their visitation,
says Yah Veh.
13 In consuming, I consume them,
—an oracle of Yah Veh:
—neither grapes on the vine nor figs on the fig tree;
and the leaf withers;
and I give these to pass away from them.
14 Why sit we?
Gather together; and enter the fortified cities:
and hush there:
for Yah Veh our Elohim hushes us and gives us water
of rosh to drink—because we sin against Yah Veh.
15 We await shalom, and there is no good;
for a time of healing, and behold, fright!
16 The snorting of his horses is heard from Dan:
the whole land quakes at the voice
of the neighing of his mighty;
and they come and devour the land
and the fulness thereof
—the city, and they who settle therein.
17 For, behold, I send serpents—
hissers among you,
who have no charmer; and they bite you
—an oracle of Yah Veh.
18 I cheer myself against grief,
my heart bleeds within me.
19 Behold!
the voice of the shout from the daughter of my people
in a land afar:
Is not Yah Veh in Siyon?
Is not her sovereign in her?

Why vex they me with their sculptiles?
And with strange vanities?
20 The harvest passes; the summer concludes;
and we are not saved.
21 For the *hurt* **breech** of the
daughter of my people
am I *hurt* **breeched**; I am *black* **darkened**;
astonishment hath taken hold on **desolation holdeth** me.
22 Is there no balm in *Gilead* **Gilad**;
is there no *physician* **healer** there?
why *then is* **ascends** not the health
of the daughter of my people *recovered*?

A Lamentation Over Siyon

9 Oh **that it be** that my head were waters,
and mine eyes a fountain of tears,
that I might weep day and night
for the *slain* **pierced** of the daughter of my people!
2 Oh **that it be** that I had in the wilderness
a lodging place of *wayfaring men* **caravans**;
that I might *leave* **forsake** my people, and go from them!
for they be all adulterers,
an **a private** assembly
of treacherous men **who deal covertly**.
3 And they bend their tongues like their bow
for *lies* **falsehood**:
but they *are* **prevail** not *valiant* **mightily**
for *the truth* **trustworthiness** upon the earth;
for they proceed from evil to evil, and they know not me,
saith the LORD **an oracle of Yah Veh**.
4 *Take ye heed* **On guard** every *one* **man**
of his *neighbour* **friend**,
and *trust* **confide** ye not in any brother:
for **in tripping the heel,**
every brother *will utterly supplant* **shall trip the heel**,
and every *neighbour* **friend**
will **shall** walk with *slanders* **talebearers**.
5 And they *will deceive* **shall mock** every *one* **man**
his *neighbour* **friend**,
and *will* **shall** not *speak* **word** the truth:
they have taught their tongue
to *speak lies* **word falsehoods**,
and weary themselves to *commit iniquity* **pervert**.
6 *Thine habitation is* **Thou**
settlest in the midst of deceit;
through deceit they refuse to know me,
saith the LORD **an oracle of Yah Veh**.
7 Therefore thus saith
the LORD of hosts **Yah Veh Sabaoth**,
Behold, I *will melt* **shall refine**
them, and *try* **proof** them;
for how shall I *do* **work**
for **at the face of** the daughter of my people?
8 Their tongue is *as an* **a**
slaughtering arrow *shot out*;
it *speaketh* **wordeth** deceit:
one speaketh peaceably **wording shalom**
to his *neighbour* **friend** with his mouth,
but *in heart he layeth his wait* **setteth**
his inwards to lurk.
9 Shall I not visit them for these *things*?
saith the LORD **an oracle of Yah Veh**:
shall not my soul be avenged
on such a *nation* **goyim** as this?
10 For the mountains
will I take up **shall I lift**
a weeping and *wailing* **lamentation**,
and for the *habitations* **folds** of the wilderness
a lamentation,
because they are burned *up*,
so that *none* **no man** can pass through *them*;
neither can men **nor** hear the voice of the *cattle* **chattel**;
both the *fowl* **flyer** of the heavens and the *beast* **animal**
are fled; they are gone.
11 And I *will make Jerusalem*
shall give Yeru Shalem
to become heaps,
and a *den* **habitation** of *dragons* **monsters**;
and I *will make* **shall work** the
cities of *Judah* **Yah Hudah**
desolate, without *an inhabitant* **settler**.
12 Who is the wise man,
that may *understand this* **discern**?
and who is he to whom
the mouth of *the LORD hath spoken* **Yah Veh worded**,
that he may *declare* **tell** it,
for what the land *perisheth* **destructeth**
and is burned *up* like a wilderness,
that none passeth through?
13 And *the LORD* **Yah Veh** saith,
and we—we are not saved.
21 For the breech of the daughter of my people,
I breech;
I darken; Desolation holds me.
22 Is there no balm in Gilad?
Is there no healer there?
Why ascends not the health
of the daughter of my people?

A Lamentation Over Siyon

9 Oh that it be, that my head be as waters;
and my eyes as a fountain of tears;
and I weep day and night
for the pierced of the daughter of my people!
2 Oh that it be, that I be in the wilderness
as a lodging place of caravans;
and I forsake my people and go from them;
for they all adultererize
—a private assembly who deals covertly:
3 and they bend their tongues as their bow
for falsehood:
and as for trustworthiness,
they prevail not mightily on the earth;
for they proceed from evil to evil
and they know me not
—an oracle of Yah Veh.
4 On guard, every man, of his friend
and confide not in any brother:
for in tripping the heel
every brother trips the heel;
and every friend walks with talebearers:
5 and every man mocks his friend
and words not the truth:
they teach their tongue to word falsehoods
and weary themselves to pervert.
6 You settle midst deceit;
through deceit they refuse to know me
—an oracle of Yah Veh.
7 So thus says Yah Veh Sabaoth,
Behold, I refine them, and proof them;
for how work I
at the face of the daughter of my people?
8 Their tongue *is* a slaughtering arrow;
wording deceit:
wording shalom to his friend with his mouth,
but setting his inwards to lurk.
9 Visit I them not for these?
—an oracle of Yah Veh
Avenge I not my soul on such a goyim as this?
10 For the mountains
I lift a weeping and lamentation;
and for the folds of the wilderness
a lamentation:
because they burned
so that man neither passes through;
nor hears the voice of the chattel;
both the flyer of the heavens and the animal flee
—gone.
11 and I give Yeru Shalem to heaps
and a habitation of monsters;
and I work the cities of Yah Hudah desolate
without settler.
12 Who is the wise man, who discerns?
And he to whom the mouth of Yah Veh words?
And who tells?
Why destructs the land and burns as a wilderness
so that no one passes through?
13 And Yah Veh says,
Because they have forsaken my *law* **torah**
which I *set before them* **gave at their face**,
and have not *obeyed* **hearkened unto** my voice,
neither walked therein;
14 But have walked
after the *imagination* **warp** of their own heart,
and after Baalim,
which their fathers taught them:
15 Therefore
thus saith *the LORD of hosts* **Yah Veh Sabaoth**,
the God **Elohim** of *Israel* **Yisra El**;
Behold, I *will* **shall** feed them, *even* this people,
with wormwood,
and give them water of gall to drink.
16 I *will* **shall** scatter them also
among the *heathen* **goyim**,
whom neither they nor their fathers have known:
and I *will* **shall** send a sword after them,
till I have *consumed* **finished** them **off**.
17 Thus saith *the LORD of hosts* **Yah Veh Sabaoth**,
Consider **Discern** ye,
and call for the *mourning women* **lamenters**,
that they may come;
and send for *cunning women* **the wise**,
that they may come:
18 And let them *make haste* **hasten**,
and *take up* **lift** a *wailing* **lamentation** for us,
that our eyes may *run down* **drip** with tears,
and our eyelids *gush out* **flow** with waters.
19 For a voice of *wailing* **lamentation**
is heard out of *Zion* **Siyon**,
How are we *spoiled* **ravaged**!
we are *greatly confounded* **mightily shamed**,
because we have forsaken the land,
because our *dwellings* **tabernacles** have cast us out.
20 Yet hear the word of *the LORD* **Yah Veh**,
O ye women,
and let your ear *receive* **take** the word of his mouth,
and teach your daughters *wailing* **lamentation**,
and every *one* **woman** her *neighbour* **friend** lamentation.

21 For death is *come up*
ascended into our windows,
and is entered into our palaces,
to cut off the *children* **sucklings**
from *without* **the outways,**
and the *young men* **youths** from the *streets* **broadways.**
22 *Speak, Thus* **Word thus,**
saith the LORD **an oracle of Yah Veh,**
Even the carcases of *men* **humanity**
shall fall as dung upon the *open* **face of the** field,
and as the *handful* **omer** after the *harvestman* **harvester,**
and none shall gather *them.*
23 Thus saith *the LORD* **Yah Veh,**
Let not the wise *man glory* **halal** in his wisdom,
neither let the mighty *man glory* **halal** in his might,
let not the rich *man glory* **halal** in his riches:
24 But let him that *glorieth*
glory **halaleth halal** in this,
that he *understandeth* **comprehendeth** and
knoweth me, that *I am the LORD* **I—Yah Veh**
which *exercise lovingkindness* **work mercy,**
judgment, and *righteousness* **justness,** in the earth:
for in these *things* I delight,
saith the LORD **an oracle of Yah Veh.**
25 Behold, the days come,
saith the LORD **an oracle of Yah Veh,**
that I *will punish all* **shall visit upon** them
which are circumcised
with the uncircumcised **in the foreskin;**
26 *Egypt* **Misrayim,** and *Judah*
Yah Hudah, and Edom,
and the *children* **sons** of Ammon, and Moab,
and all that *are in the utmost corners* **chop the edges,**
that *dwell* **settle** in the wilderness:
for all these *nations* **goyim** are uncircumcised,
and all the house of *Israel* **Yisra El**
are uncircumcised in the heart.

THE HANDIWORK OF ENGRAVERS

10 Hear ye the word
which *the LORD speaketh* **Yah Veh wordeth** unto you,
O house of *Israel* **Yisra El:**
2 Thus saith *the LORD* **Yah Veh,**
Because they forsake my torah
which I gave at their face,
and neither hearken to my voice nor walk therein;
14 and walk after the warp of their own heart
and after Baalim which their fathers taught them.
15 So thus says Yah Veh Sabaoth,
Elohim of Yisra El;
Behold, I feed them, this people, with wormwood;
and give them water of gall to drink:
16 and I scatter them among the goyim
whom neither they nor their fathers knew:
and I send a sword after them until I finish them off.
17 Thus says Yah Veh Sabaoth,
You, discern; and call for the lamenters to come;
and send for the wise to come:
18 Hasten them to lift a lamentation for us
so that our eyes drip with tears
and our eyelids flow with waters.
19 For a voice of lamentation is heard from Siyon,
How ravaged!
We shame mightily because we forsook the land;
because they cast out our tabernacles.
20 Yet hear the word of Yah Veh, O you women,
and your ear take the word of his mouth;
and teach your daughters lamentation
and every woman her friend lamentation.
21 For death ascends into our windows;
it enters into our palaces
to cut off the sucklings from the outways,
and the youths from the broadways.
22 Word thus,
—an oracle of Yah Veh
The carcases of humanity
falls as dung on the face of the field;
and as the omer after the harvester:
and no one gathers.
23 Thus says Yah Veh,
O that the wise not halal in his wisdom
—the mighty not halal in his might;
the rich not halal in his riches:
24 But he who halals, halal in this,
that he comprehends and knows me;
that I—Yah Veh
work mercy, judgment, and justness in the earth
for in these I delight
—an oracle of Yah Veh.
25 Behold, days come,
—an oracle of Yah Veh
that I visit on them
who are circumcised in the foreskin
26 —Misrayim and Yah Hudah and Edom
and the sons of Ammon and Moab
and all who chop the edges
—who settle in the wilderness:
for all these goyim *are* uncircumcised,
and all the house of Yisra El
are uncircumcised in the heart.

The Handiwork Of Engravers

10 Hear the word, O house of Yisra El,
which Yah Veh words to you:
2 thus says Yah Veh,
Learn not the way of the *heathen* **goyim**,
and be not dismayed at the signs of *heaven* **the heavens**;
for the *heathen* **goyim** are dismayed at them.
3 For the *customs* **statutes** of the people are vain:
for one cutteth a tree out of the forest,
the work of the hands of the *workman* **engraver**,
with the ax.
4 They *deck* **beautify** it with silver and with gold;
they *fasten* **strengthen** it with nails and with hammers,
that it *move* **wiggle** not.
5 They are *upright* **round** as the palm tree,
but *speak* **word** not:
in bearing, they must *needs* be borne,
because they cannot *go* **pace**.
Be not *afraid* **awed** of them;
for they *cannot do evil* **vilify not**,
neither also is it in them to *do good* **well—please**.
6 Forasmuch as there is none like unto thee,
O *LORD* **Yah Veh**;
thou art great, and thy name is great in might.
7 Who *would* **should** not *fear* **awe** thee,
O *King* **Sovereign** of *nations* **goyim?**
for *to thee doth it appertain* **it becometh thee**:
forasmuch as among all the wise *men*
of the *nations* **goyim**,
and in all their *kingdoms* **sovereigndoms**,
there is none like unto thee.
8 But they are *altogether* brutish and foolish:
the *stock* **tree** is a *doctrine* **discipline** of vanities.
9 *Silver spread into plates* **Expanded silver**
is brought from Tarshish,
and gold from Uphaz,
the work of the *workman* **engraver**,
and of the hands of the *founder* **refiner**:
blue and purple is their *clothing* **robe**:
they are all the work of *cunning men* **wise**.
10 But *the LORD* **Yah Veh**
is the *true God* **Elohim of truth**,
he is the living *God* **Elohim**,
and *an everlasting king* **eternal sovereign**:
at his *wrath* **rage** the earth shall *tremble* **quake**,
and the *nations* **goyim**
shall not be able to *abide* **contain** his *indignation* **rage**.
11 Thus shall ye say unto them,
The *gods* **elah**
that have not made the heavens and the earth,
even they shall *perish* **destruct** from the earth,
and from under these heavens.
12 He hath *made* **worked** the
earth by his *power* **force**,
he hath established the world by his wisdom,
and hath *stretched out* **spread** the heavens
by his *discretion* **discernment**.
13 When he *uttereth* **giveth** his voice,
there is a multitude of waters in the
heavens, and he causeth the vapours
to ascend from the ends of the earth;
he *maketh* **worketh** lightnings with rain,
and bringeth forth the wind out of his treasures.
14 *Every man* **All humanity**
is brutish in *his* knowledge:
every *founder* **refiner**
is *confounded* **shamed** by the *graven image* **sculptile**:
for his *molten image* **libation** is falsehood,
and there is no *breath* **spirit** in them.
15 They are vanity, *and* the work of *errors* **frauds**:
in the time of their visitation they shall *perish* **destruct**.
16 The *portion* **allotment** of *Jacob* **Yaaqov**
is not like them:
for he is the former of all *things*;
and *Israel* **Yisra El** is the *rod* **scion** of his inheritance:
The LORD of hosts **Yah Veh Sabaoth** is his name.
17 Gather up thy *wares* **bundles** out of the land,
O *inhabitant* **settler** of the *fortress* **siege**.
18 For thus saith *the LORD* **Yah Veh**, Behold,
I *will* **shall** sling out the *inhabitants* **settlers** of the land
at *this once* **one time**,
and *will distress* **shall tribulate** them,
that they may *find it so* **be found out**.
19 Woe is me for my *hurt* **breech**!
my wound is *grievous* **stricken**;
Neither learn the way of the goyim
nor dismay at the signs of the heavens;
for the goyim dismay at them:
3 for the statutes of the people are vain:
for one cuts a tree from the forest
—the work of the hands of the engraver with the ax:
4 they beautify with silver and with gold;
they strengthen with nails and with hammers
so that it wiggles not:
5 round as the palm tree, but word not:
in bearing, they bear, because they pace not.
Awe them not, for they vilify not;
yes, it is not in them to well—please.
6 Because there is no one like you, O Yah Veh;

you are great, and your name *is* great in might.
7 Who awes you not, O Sovereign of goyim?
For it becomes you:
for among all the wise of the goyim,
and in all their sovereigndoms,
there is no one like you.
8 And as one, they are brutish and foolish:
the tree is a discipline of vanities.
9 They bring expanded silver from Tarshish
and gold from Uphaz
—the work of the engraver
and of the hands of the refiner:
blue and purple is their robe:
they are all the work of wise.
10 And Yah Veh *is* the Elohim of truth;
he is the living Elohim and eternal sovereign:
the earth quakes at his rage
and the goyim contain not his rage.
11 Thus you say to them,
The elah who made not the heavens and the earth
destructs from the earth
and from under these heavens.
12 He worked the earth by his force;
he established the world by his wisdom;
and spread the heavens by his discernment.
13 He gives his voice;
there is a multitude of waters in the heavens:
and he ascends the vapours
from the ends of the earth:
he works lightnings with rain
and brings forth the wind from his treasures.
14 All humanity is brutish in knowledge:
every refiner is shamed by the sculptile:
for his libation is falsehood
and there is no spirit in them:
15 they are vanity, the work of frauds:
in the time of their visitation they destruct.
16 The allotment of Yaaqov *is* not like them:
for he is the former of all;
and Yisra El *is* the scion of his inheritance:
Yah Veh Sabaoth *is* his name.
17 Gather up your bundles from the land,
O settler of the siege:
18 for thus says Yah Veh, Behold,
I sling out the settlers of the land at one time
and tribulate them that they are found out.
19 Woe to me for my breech;
my wound is stricken;
but I said,
Truly **Surely** this is a *grief* **stroke**, and I must bear it.
20 My *tabernacle* **tent** is *spoiled* **ravaged**,
and all my cords are *broken* **torn**:
my *children* **sons** are gone forth of me, and they are not:
there is none to *stretch forth* **spread** my tent any more,
and to *set up* **raise** my curtains.
21 For the *pastors* **tenders** are
become *brutish* **stupid**,
and have not sought *the LORD* **Yah Veh**:
therefore they shall not *prosper* **comprehend**,
and all their *flocks* **pastures** shall be scattered.
22 Behold, the *noise* **voice** of
the *bruit* **report** is come,
and a great *commotion* **quake**
out of the north *country* **land**,
to *make* **set** the cities of *Judah* **Yah Hudah** desolate,
and a *den* **habitation** of *dragons* **monsters**.
23 O *LORD* **Yah Veh**,
I know that the way of *man* **humanity**
is not in *himself* **humanity**:
it is not in man
that walketh to *direct* **establish** his *steps* **paces**.
24 O *LORD* **Yah Veh**, correct
me, but with judgment;
not in *thine anger* **thy wrath**,
lest thou *bring* **diminish** me *to nothing*.
25 Pour out thy fury
upon the *heathen* **goyim** that know thee not,
and upon the families that call not on thy name:
for they have *eaten up Jacob* **consumed Yaaqov**,
and *devoured* **consumed** him, and
consumed **finished** him **off**,
and have *made* **desolated** his habitation *desolate* **of rest**.

THE BROKEN COVENANT

11 The word that came to *Jeremiah* **Yirme Yah**
from *the LORD* **Yah Veh**, saying,
2 Hear ye the words of this covenant,
and *speak* **word** unto the men of *Judah* **Yah Hudah**,
and to the *inhabitants* **settlers** of
Jerusalem **Yeru Shalem**;
3 And say thou unto them,
Thus saith
the LORD God **Yah Veh Elohim** of *Israel* **Yisra El**;
Cursed be the man
that *obeyeth* **hearkeneth** not
unto the words of this covenant,
4 Which I *commanded* **misvahed** your fathers
in the day that I brought them forth
out of the land of *Egypt* **Misrayim**,
from the iron furnace, saying,

Obey **Hearken unto** my voice, and *do* **work** them,
according to all which I *command* **misvah** you:
so shall ye be my people,
and *I will be* **I am** your *God* **Elohim**:
5 That I may *perform* **raise** the oath
which I have *sworn* **oathed** unto your fathers,
to give them a land flowing with milk and honey,
as it is this day.
Then answered I, and said,
So be it **Amen**, O *LORD* **Yah Veh**.
6 Then *the LORD* **Yah Veh** said unto me,
Proclaim **Call out** all these words
in the cities of *Judah* **Yah Hudah**,
and in the *streets* **outways** of *Jerusalem* **Yeru Shalem**,
saying,
Hear ye the words of this covenant, and *do* **work** them.
7 For **in witnessing,**
I *earnestly protested* **witnessed** unto your fathers
in the day that I *brought* **ascended** them *up*
out of the land of *Egypt* **Misrayim**,
even unto this day,
rising **starting** early and *protesting* **witnessing**,
saying, *Obey* **Hearken unto** my voice.
8 Yet they *obeyed* **hearkened** not,
nor *inclined* **spread** their ear,
but walked every *one* **man**
in the *imagination* **warp** of their evil heart:
therefore I *will* **shall** bring upon them
all the words of this covenant,
which I *commanded* **misvahed** them to *do* **work**:
but they *did* **worked** them not.
9 And *the LORD* **Yah Veh** said unto me,
A conspiracy is found among the
men of *Judah* **Yah Hudah**,
and I say, Surely this is a stroke for me to bear.
20 My tent is ravaged
and all my cords are torn:
my sons *are* gone from me, and they are not:
there is no one to spread my tent any more
and to raise my curtains:
21 for the tenders are stupid and seek not Yah Veh:
so they comprehend not
and all their pastures are scattered.
22 The voice of the report! Behold, it comes!
Even a great quake from the north land
to set the cities of Yah Hudah desolate
—a habitation of monsters.
23 O Yah Veh,
I know that the way of humanity
is not within humanity:
it is not within man
who walks to establish his paces.
24 O Yah Veh, correct me; only with judgment;
not in your wrath; lest you diminish me.
25 Pour your fury on the goyim who know you not,
and on the families who call not on your
name: for they consume Yaaqov
—consume him and finish him off
and desolate his habitation of rest.

THE BROKEN COVENANT

11 So be the word to Yirme Yah from Yah Veh,
saying,
2 Hear the words of this covenant;
and word to the men of Yah Hudah
and to the settlers of Yeru Shalem;
3 and say to them,
Thus says Yah Veh Elohim of Yisra El:
Cursed *is* the man
who hearkens not to the words of this covenant,
4 which I misvahed your fathers
in the day I brought them from the land of Misrayim
—from the iron furnace,
saying, Hearken to my voice, and work them,
according to all I misvah you:
and you are my people,
and I am your Elohim:
5 to raise the oath I oathed to your fathers
—to give them a land flowing with milk and honey
as this day.
And I answer, and say, Amen, O Yah Veh.
6 And Yah Veh says to me,
Call all these words in the cities of Yah Hudah
and in the outways of Yeru Shalem, saying,
Hear the words of this covenant, and work them.
7 For in witnessing, I witnessed to your fathers
in the day I ascended them from the land of Misrayim
to this day
—starting early and witnessing,
saying, Hearken to my voice!
8 And they neither hearkened
nor spread their ear;
and every man walked in the warp of his evil heart:
and I brought on them all the words of this covenant
which I misvahed them to work:
and they worked them not.
9 And Yah Veh says to me,
A conspiracy is found among the men of Yah Hudah
and among the *inhabitants* **settlers**
of *Jerusalem* **Yeru Shalem**.

10 They are turned back
to the *iniquities* **perversities** of their forefathers,
which refused to hear my words;
and they went after other *gods* **elohim** to serve them:
the house of *Israel* **Yisra El**
and the house of *Judah* **Yah Hudah**
have broken my covenant
which I *made* **cut** with their fathers.
11 Therefore thus saith *the LORD* **Yah Veh**,
Behold, I *will* **shall** bring evil upon them,
which they shall not be able to escape;
and though they shall cry unto me,
I *will* **shall** not hearken unto them.
12 Then shall the cities of *Judah* **Yah Hudah**
and *inhabitants* **settlers** of *Jerusalem* **Yeru Shalem** go
and cry unto the *gods* **elohim**
unto whom they *offer* incense:
but **in saving,** they shall not save them *at all*
in the time of their *trouble* **evil**.
13 For *according to* the number of thy cities
were thy *gods* **elohim**, O *Judah* **Yah Hudah**;
and *according to* the number
of the *streets* **outways** of *Jerusalem* **Yeru Shalem**
have ye set up **sacrifice** altars to *that* **the** shameful *thing*,
even **sacrifice** altars to *burn* incense unto Baal.
14 Therefore pray not thou for this people,
neither lift up a *cry* **shout** or prayer for them:
for I *will* **shall** not *hear them* **hearken**
in the time that they *cry* **call out** unto me
for their *trouble* **evil**.
15 What hath my beloved to do in mine house,
seeing
she hath *wrought lewdness* **worked intrigue** with many,
and the holy flesh is passed from thee?
when thou doest evil, then thou *rejoicest* **jumpest for joy**.
16 *The LORD* **Yah Veh** called thy name,
A green olive *tree*, *fair* **beautiful**,
and of *goodly* **formed** fruit:
with the *noise* **voice** of a great *tumult* **rush**
he hath kindled fire upon it,
and the branches of it are *broken* **shattered**.
17 For *the LORD of hosts* **Yah Veh Sabaoth**,
that planted thee,
hath *pronounced* **worded** evil against thee,
for **because of** the evil of the house of *Israel* **Yisra El**
and of the house of *Judah* **Yah Hudah**,
which they have *done* **worked** against themselves
to *provoke* **vex** me *to anger*
in *offering incense* **incensing** unto Baal.
18 And *the LORD* **Yah Veh**
hath given me knowledge of it, and I know it:
then thou
shewedst me **hadst me see** their *doings* **exploitations**.
19 But I was like a lamb or *an ox* **a bullock**
that is brought to the slaughter;
and I knew not
that they had *devised devices* **fabricated fabrications**
against me, *saying*,
Let us *destroy* **ruin** the tree with the *fruit* **bread** *thereof*,
and let us cut him off from the land of the living,
that his name may be no more remembered.
20 But, O *LORD of hosts* **Yah Veh Sabaoth**,
that judgest *righteously* **justly**,
that *triest* **proofest** the reins and the heart,
let me see thy *vengeance* **avengement** on them:
for unto thee have I *revealed* **exposed** my *cause* **plea**.
21 Therefore thus saith *the LORD* **Yah Veh**
of the men of Anathoth, that seek thy *life* **soul**, saying,
Prophesy not in the name of *the LORD* **Yah Veh**,
that thou die not by our hand:
22 Therefore
thus saith *the LORD of hosts* **Yah Veh Sabaoth**,
Behold, I *will punish* **shall visit upon** them:
the *young men* **youths** shall die by the sword;
their sons and their daughters shall die by famine:
23 And there shall be no
remnant **survivors** of them:
for I *will* **shall** bring evil upon the men of
Anathoth, *even* the year of their visitation.
and among the settlers of Yeru Shalem:
10 they return to the perversities
of their forefathers
who refused to hear my words;
and go after other elohim to serve them:
the house of Yisra El and the house of Yah Hudah
break my covenant which I cut with their fathers.
11 So thus says Yah Veh,
Behold, I bring evil on them,
which they are not able to escape;
and though they cry to me
I hearken not to them:
12 and the cities of Yah Hudah
and settlers of Yeru Shalem
go and cry to the elohim to whom they incense:
and in saving,
they save them not in the time of their evil:
13 for *as* the number of your cities are your elohim,
O Yah Hudah;
and *as* the number of the outways of Yeru Shalem,
you set up sacrifice altars to the shameful

—sacrifice altars to incense to Baal.
14 And you—you neither pray for this people,
nor lift a shout or prayer for them:
for I hearken not
in the time they call to me for their evil.
15 What—to my beloved in my house,
her working intrigue with many
and pass the holy flesh from you?
when you work evil, you jump for joy.
16 Yah Veh calls your name,
Green Olive! Beautiful! Formed Fruit!
With the voice of a great rush
he kindles fire thereon,
and shatters the branches thereof.
17 And Yah Veh Sabaoth who plants you,
words evil against you,
because of the evil of the house of Yisra El
and of the house of Yah Hudah,
which they work against themselves
to vex me by incensing to Baal.
18 And Yah Veh gives me knowledge thereof
and I know it:
then you show me their exploitations:
19 and I *am* as a lamb or a bullock
brought to the slaughter;
and I know not
that they fabricate fabrications against me:
—we ruin the tree with the bread
and we cut him off from the land of the living
so that we remember his name no more.
20 And, O Yah Veh Sabaoth, who judges justly,
who proofs the reins and the heart,
I see your avengement on them:
for to you I expose my plea.
21 So thus says Yah Veh
of the men of Anathoth who seek your soul, saying,
Prophesy not in the name of Yah Veh,
that you die not by our hand.
22 So thus says Yah Veh Sabaoth,
Behold, I visit on them:
their youths die by the sword
their sons and their daughters die by famine:
23 and they have no survivors:
for I bring evil on the men of Anathoth,
the year of their visitation.

THE PRAYER OF YIRME YAH

12 *Righteous* **Just** art thou, O *LORD* **Yah Veh**,
when I plead with thee:
yet let me *talk* **word** with thee of thy judgments:
Wherefore doth the way of the wicked prosper?
wherefore are all they *happy* **serene**
that **in dealing covertly**, deal *very*
treacherously **covertly**?
2 Thou hast planted them, yea,
they have *taken root* **rooted**:
they grow, yea, they *bring forth* **work** fruit:
thou art near in their mouth, and far from their reins.
3 But thou, O *LORD* **Yah Veh**, knowest me:
thou hast seen me,
and *tried* **proofed** mine heart toward thee:
pull **tear** them out like *sheep* **flock** for the slaughter,
and *prepare* **hallow** them for the day of slaughter.
4 How long shall the land mourn,
and the herbs of every field wither,
for the *wickedness* **evil** of them that *dwell* **settle** therein?
the *beasts* **animals** are *consumed* **scraped away**,
and the *birds* **flyers**;
because they said, He shall not see our last end.
5 If thou hast run with *the footmen* **them on foot**,
and they have wearied thee,
then how canst thou *contend* **be inflamed** with horses?
and if in the land of *peace* **shalom**,
wherein thou *trustedst* **confidest**, *they wearied thee*,
then how *wilt* **shalt** thou *do* **work**
in the *swelling* **pomp** of *Jordan* **Yarden**?
6 For even thy brethren, and
the house of thy father,
even they have dealt *treacherously* **covertly** with thee;
yea, they have called a multitude after thee:
believe **trust** them not,
though they *speak fair* **word good** words unto thee.
7 I have forsaken mine house,
I have *left* **abandoned** mine *heritage* **inheritance**;
I have given the *dearly beloved* **love** of my soul
into the *hand* **palm** of her enemies.
8 Mine *heritage* **inheritance** is unto me
as a lion in the forest;
it crieth out **giveth her voice** against me:
therefore have I hated it.
9 Mine *heritage* **inheritance** is unto me
as a speckled *bird* **swooper**,
the *birds* **swoopers** round about are against her;
come ye,
assemble **gather** all the *beasts* **live beings** of the field,
come *to devour* **for food**.
10 Many *pastors* **tenders**
have *destroyed* **ruined** my vineyard,
they have *trodden* **trampled** my *portion* **allotment**
under foot,

they have *made* **given the allotment**
of my *pleasant portion* **desire**
a desolate wilderness.
11 They have *made* **set** it desolate,
and being desolate it mourneth unto me;
the whole land is *made desolate* **desolated,**
because no man *layeth* **setteth** it to heart.
12 The *spoilers* **ravagers** are come
upon all *high places* **the barrens** through the wilderness:
for the sword of *the LORD* **Yah Veh** shall devour
from the *one* end of the land
even to the *other* end of the land:
no flesh shall have *peace* **shalom.**
13 They have sown wheat, but
shall *reap* **harvest** thorns:
they have *put themselves to pain* **worn out,**
but shall not *profit* **benefit:**
and they shall *be ashamed* **shame**
of your *revenues* **produce**
because of the *fierce anger* **fuming**
wrath of *the LORD* **Yah Veh.**
14 Thus saith *the LORD* **Yah Veh**
against all mine evil *neighbours* **fellow tabernaclers,**
that touch the inheritance
which I have caused my people *Israel* **Yisra El** to inherit;
Behold,
I *will pluck* **shall uproot** them out of their *land* **soil,**
and *pluck out* **uproot** the house of *Judah* **Yah Hudah**
from among them.

12 You *are* just, O Yah Veh,
O that I plead with you
—word to you of judgments!
Why prospers the way of the wicked?
Why are all they serene
—who in dealing covertly, deal covertly?
2 You planted them; yes, they root:
they grow; yes, they work fruit:
you *are* near in their mouth and far from their reins.
3 And you, O Yah Veh, know me:
you see me and proof my heart toward you:
tear them as flock for the slaughter
and hallow them for the day of slaughter.
4 How long mourns the land?
And the herbs of every field wither
for their evil who settle therein?
The animals are scraped away, and the flyers;
because, they say, He sees not our final end.
5 If you run with them on
foot, and they weary you,
and how inflame you yourself with horses?
And if in the land of shalom, wherein you confide,
then how work you in the pomp of Yarden?
6 For even your brothers, and
the house of your father
—even they dealt covertly with you;
yes, they called a multitude after you:
trust them not,
though they word good words to you.
7 I forsook my house;
I abandoned my inheritance;
I gave the beloved of my soul
into the palm of her enemies:
8 To me, my inheritance is as a lion in the forest;
she gives her voice against me:
so I hate her.
9 To me, my inheritance is as a speckled swooper.
Are the swoopers all around against her?
Come, gather all the live beings of the field;
come for food.
10 Many tenders ruin my vineyard;
they trample my allotment;
they give the allotment of my desire
a desolate wilderness:
11 they set it desolate;
and desolate, it mourns to me;
the whole land is desolated
because no man sets it to heart.
12 The ravagers come
on all the barrens in the wilderness:
for the sword of Yah Veh devours
from the end of the land even to the end of the land
—no shalom to any flesh.
13 They seed wheat; and harvest thorns:
they wear out; they benefit not:
and they shame of your produce
because of the fuming wrath of Yah Veh.
14 Thus says Yah Veh
against all my evil fellow tabernaclers,
who touch the inheritance
that I have my people Yisra El to inherit:
behold, I uproot them from their soil;
and uproot the house of Yah Hudah
from among them.
15 And **so be** it *shall come to pass,*
after that I have *plucked* **uprooted** them *out*
I *will* **shall** return, and *have* compassion *on* them,
and *will bring* **shall return** them *again,*
every man to his *heritage* **inheritance,**
and every man to his land.
16 And **so be** it *shall come to pass,*
if they *will* **shall** diligently learn the ways of my people,

to *swear* **oath** by my name, *The LORD* **Yah Veh** liveth;
as they taught my people to *swear* **oath** by Baal;
then shall they be built in the midst of my people.
17 But if they *will* **shall** not *obey* **hearken**,
I will utterly pluck up **In uprooting, I shall uproot**
and destroy that *nation* **goyim**,
saith the LORD **an oracle of Yah Veh**.

THE FLAX GIRDLE

13 Thus saith *the LORD* **Yah Veh** unto me,
Go and *get* **chattel** thee a *linen* **flax** girdle,
and *put* **set** it upon thy loins, and put it not in water.
2 So I *got* **chatteled** a girdle
according to the word of *the LORD* **Yah Veh**,
and *put* **set** it on my loins.
3 And the word of *the LORD* **Yah Veh**
came unto me *the second time* **secondly**, saying,
4 Take the girdle that thou hast *got* **chatteled**,
which is upon thy loins,
and arise, go to Euphrates,
and hide it there in a hole of the rock.
5 So I went, and hid it by Euphrates,
as *the LORD commanded* **Yah Veh misvahed** me.
6 And **so be** it *came to pass*
after **at the end of** many days,
that *the LORD* **Yah Veh** said unto me,
Arise, go to Euphrates, and take the girdle from thence,
which I *commanded* **misvahed** thee to hide there.
7 Then I went to Euphrates, and digged,
and took the girdle from the place where I had hid it:
and, behold, the girdle was *marred* **ruined**,
it *was profitable* **prospered** for *nothing* **nought**.
8 Then the word of *the LORD*
Yah Veh came unto me,
saying,
9 Thus saith *the LORD* **Yah Veh**,
After this manner *will I mar* **shall I ruin**
the *pride* **pomp** of *Judah* **Yah Hudah**,
and the great *pride* **pomp** of *Jerusalem* **Yeru Shalem**.
10 This evil people, which refuse to hear my words,
which walk in the *imagination* **warp** of their heart,
and walk after other *gods* **elohim**,
to serve them, and to *worship* **prostrate to** them,
shall *even* be as this girdle,
which *is good* **prospereth** for *nothing* **nought**.
11 For as the girdle
cleaveth **adhereth** to the loins of a man, so
have I caused to *cleave* **adhere** unto me
the whole house of *Israel* **Yisra El**
and the whole house of *Judah* **Yah Hudah**,
saith the LORD **an oracle of Yah Veh**;
that they might be unto me for a people, and for a name,
and for a *praise* **halal**, and for *a glory* **an adornment**:
but they *would not hear* **hearkened not**.

WINEBAGS

12 *Therefore* thou shalt *speak*
say unto them this word;
Thus saith
the LORD God **Yah Veh Elohim** of *Israel* **Yisra El**,
Every *bottle* **bag** shall be filled with wine:
and they shall say unto thee,
In knowing, *Do we not certainly* know **we not**
that every *bottle* **bag** shall be filled with wine?
13 Then shalt thou say unto them,
Thus saith *the LORD* **Yah Veh**, Behold,
I *will* **shall** fill all the *inhabitants* **settlers** of this land,
even the *kings* **sovereigns** that sit upon David's throne,
and the priests, and the prophets,
and all the *inhabitants* **settlers** of
Jerusalem **Yeru Shalem**,
with *drunkenness* **intoxication**.
14 And I *will dash* **shall shatter** them
one **man** against *another* **brother**,
even the fathers and the sons together,
saith the LORD **an oracle of Yah Veh**:
15 And so be it,
after I uproot them, I return and compassion them,
return them—every man to his inheritance
and every man to his land.
16 And so be it,
if they diligently learn the ways of my people,
to oath by my name—Yah Veh lives!
As they taught my people to oath by Baal;
thus are they built midst my people.
17 And if they hearken not,
In uprooting, I uproot and destroy that goyim
—an oracle of Yah Veh.

THE FLAX GIRDLE

13 Thus says Yah Veh to me,
Go and chattel yourself a flax girdle;
and set it on your loins and put it not in water.
2 And I chatteled a girdle
according to the word of Yah Veh,
and set it on my loins.
3 And so be the word of Yah Veh to me secondly,
saying,
4 Take the girdle you chatteled, on your loins,
and rise, go to Euphrates,

and hide it there in a hole of the rock.
5 —and I go and hide it by Euphrates
as Yah Veh misvahed me.
6 And so be it, at the end of many days,
Yah Veh says to me,
Rise, go to Euphrates, and take the girdle from thence,
which I misvahed you to hide there.
7 And I go to Euphrates, and dig,
and take the girdle from the place I hid it:
and behold, the girdle is ruined
—prospering for naught.
8 And so be the word of Yah Veh to me, saying,
9 Thus says Yah Veh,
Thus I ruin the pomp of Yah Hudah and
the great pomp of Yeru Shalem.
10 This evil people, who refuses to hear my words,
who walk in the warp of their heart
and walk after other elohim
—to serve them and to prostrate to them,
becomes as this girdle, prospering for naught.
11 For as the girdle adheres to the loins of a man,
thus I have the whole house of Yisra El
and the whole house of Yah Hudah adhere to me
—an oracle of Yah Veh
to be to me for a people and for a name
and for a halal and for an adornment:
and they hearken not.

Winebags

12 Say this word to them;
Thus says Yah Veh Elohim of Yisra El,
Every bag is filled with wine.
And they say to you,
In knowing, know we not
that every bag is filled with wine?
13 Then you say to them,
Thus says Yah Veh, Behold,
I fill all the settlers of this land,
even the sovereigns who sit on the throne of David
and the priests and the prophets
and all the settlers of Yeru Shalem
with intoxication:
14 and I shatter them, man against brother
—even the fathers and the sons together
—an oracle of Yah Veh:
I *will* **shall** not *pity* **compassion**,
nor spare, nor *have* mercy,
but *destroy* **ruin** them.
15 Hear ye, and *give ear*
hearken; be not *proud* **lifted**:
for *the LORD* **Yah Veh** hath *spoken* **worded**

The Threat Of Exile

16 Give *glory* **honour**
to *the LORD* **Yah Veh** your *God* **Elohim**,
before he cause darkness,
and before your feet *stumble* **stub**
upon the *dark* **evening breeze of the** mountains,
and, while ye look for light,
he *turn* **set** it into the shadow of death,
and *make it gross* **place dripping** darkness.
17 But if ye *will* **shall** not hear it,
my soul shall weep in *secret places* **coverts**
for **at the face of** your *pride* **arrogance**;
and mine eye shall weep sore,
and *run down* **drip** with tears,
because the LORD'S flock **Yah Veh's drove**
is *carried away captive* **captured**.
18 Say unto the *king* **sovereign**
and to the *queen* **lady**,
Humble yourselves **Abase**, sit down:
for your *principalities* **headships**
shall *come down* **descend**,
even the crown of your *glory* **adornment**.
19 The cities of the south shall be shut up,
and none shall open *them*:
Judah **Yah Hudah** shall be *carried
away captive* **exiled** all of it,
it shall be *wholly carried away captive* **exiled in shalom**.
20 Lift up your eyes,
and *behold* **see** them that come from the north:
where is the *flock* **drove** that was given thee,
thy *beautiful* flock **of adornment**?
21 What *wilt* **shalt** thou say
when he shall *punish* **visit upon** thee?
for thou hast taught them to be *captains* **chiliarchs**,
and as chief over thee:
shall not *sorrows* **pangs** take thee,
as *a woman in travail* **in birthing**?
22 And if thou say in thine heart,
Wherefore *come* **confront** these *things* upon me?
For the greatness of *thine iniquity* **thy perversity**
are thy *skirts discovered* **drapings exposed**,
and thy heels *made bare* **violated**.
23 Can the *Ethiopian change*
Kushiy overturn his skin,
or the leopard his *spots* **streaks**?
then may ye also *do good* **be able to well—please**,
that are *accustomed* **discipled** to *do evil* **vilify**.
24 Therefore *will* **shall** I scatter them as the stubble
that passeth away by the wind of the wilderness.
25 This is thy *lot* **pebble**,

the portion of thy measures from me,
saith the LORD **an oracle of Yah Veh**;
because thou hast forgotten me,
and *trusted* **confided** in falsehood.
26 Therefore *will* **shall** I *discover*
strip thy *skirts* **drapings**
upon thy face,
that thy *shame* **abasement** may *appear* **be seen**.
27 I have seen thine adulteries, and thy neighings,
the *lewdness* **intrigue** of thy whoredom,
and thine abominations on the hills in the fields.
Woe unto thee, O *Jerusalem* **Yeru Shalem**!
wilt **shalt** thou not be *made clean* **purified**?
when shall it once be **until when**?

DROUGHT, FAMINE, SWORD, AND PESTILENCE

14 The word of *the LORD* **Yah Veh**
that came to *Jeremiah* **Yirme Yah** concerning the dearth.
2 *Judah* **Yah Hudah** mourneth,
and the *gates* **portals** *thereof* languish;
they are *black* **darkened** unto the *ground* **earth**;
and the *cry* **outcry** of *Jerusalem* **Yeru Shalem**
is gone up **ascendeth**.
3 And their *nobles* **mighty**
have sent their little *ones* to the waters:
they came to the *pits* **dugouts**, and found no water;
they returned with their *vessels* **instruments** empty;
they were *ashamed* **shamed** and *confounded* **ashamed**,
and covered their heads.
I neither compassion nor spare nor mercy
—for their ruin.
15 Hear! And hearken! Not lofted!
—for Yah Veh has worded.

THE THREAT OF EXILE

16 Give honor to Yah Veh your Elohim
ere he causes darkness;
and ere your feet stub
on the evening breeze of the mountains:
and while you look for light,
he sets it into the shadow of death
and places dripping darkness:
17 and if you hear it not,
my soul weeps in coverts
at the face of your arrogance;
and my eye weeps sore and drips with tears,
for the drove of Yah Veh is captured.
18 Say to the sovereign and to the lady,
Abase! Sit!
—for your headships descend
—even the crown of your adornment.
19 The cities of the south are shut
and no one opens:
Yah Hudah is exiled—all of her—exiled in shalom.
20 Lift your eyes,
and see them coming from the north!
Where is the drove that was given you
—your flock of adornment?
21 What say you when he visits on you?
—for you taught them to be chiliarchs,
and as chief over you:
pangs, overtake they you not, as in birthing?
22 And if you say in your heart,
Why confront these on me?
For the greatness of your perversity
your drapings are exposed and your heels violated.
23 Can the Kushiy turn his skin?
Or the leopard his streaks?
You also are able to well—please
—you who are discipled to vilify.
24 And I scatter them as the stubble
that passes away by the wind of the wilderness.
25 This is your pebble
—the portion of your measures from me
—an oracle of Yah Veh;
because you forget me and confide in falsehood.
26 I also strip your drapings in front of your face
so that your abasement is seen:
27 I see your adulteries and your neighings
—the intrigue of your whoredom
and your abominations on the hills in the fields!
Woe to you, O Yeru Shalem!
Purify you not yourselves? Until when?

DROUGHT, FAMINE, SWORD, AND PESTILENCE

14 And so be the word of Yah Veh to Yirme Yah
concerning the dearth:
2 Yah Hudah mourns and the portals languish
—darkened to the earth;
and the outcry of Yeru Shalem ascends:
3 and the mighty send their
little *ones* to the waters:
they come to the dugouts and find no water;
they return with their instruments empty:
they shame and are ashamed and cover their heads:
4 Because the *ground* **soil** is *chapt* **broken**,
for there was no *rain* **downpour** in the earth,
the *plowmen* **cultivators** were *ashamed* **shamed**,

they covered their heads.
5 Yea, the hind also *calved* **birthed** in the field,
and forsook it, because there was no *grass* **sprout**.
6 And the wild *asses* **runners**
did stand in the *high places* **barrens,**
they *snuffed up* **gulped** the wind like *dragons* **monsters**;
their eyes *did fail* **finished off**,
because there was no *grass* **herbage**.
7 O *LORD* **Yah Veh**,
though our *iniquities* **perversities**
testify **answer** against us,
do **workest** thou it for thy name's sake:
for our *backslidings* **apostasies**
are many **abound by the myriads**;
we have sinned against thee.
8 O the *hope* **expectation** of *Israel* **Yisra El**,
the saviour *thereof* in time of *trouble* **tribulation**,
why shouldest thou be
as a *stranger* **sojourner** in the land,
and as a *wayfaring man* **caravan**
that *turneth aside* **spreadeth**
to *tarry for a night* **stay overnight**?
9 Why shouldest thou be
as a man *astonied* **dumbfounded**,
as a mighty *man* that cannot save?
yet thou, O *LORD* **Yah Veh**, art in the midst of us,
and we are called by thy name; leave us not.
10 Thus saith *the LORD* **Yah Veh** unto this people,
Thus have they loved to wander,
they have not *refrained* **spared** their feet,
therefore *the LORD* **Yah Veh**
doth not accept **is not pleased in** them;
he *will now* **shall, I beseech,**
remember their *iniquity* **perversity**, and visit their sins.
11 Then said *the LORD* **Yah Veh** unto me,
Pray not for this people for their good.
12 When they fast, I *will* **shall**
not hear their *cry* **shout**;
and when they *offer burnt offering* **holocaust**
a holocaust and an *oblation* **offering**,
I will not accept them **they shall not please me**:
but I *will consume* **shall finish** them **off** by the sword,
and by the famine, and by the pestilence.
13 Then said I, *Ah* **Aha**, *Lord*
GOD **Adonay Yah Veh**!
behold, the prophets say unto them,
Ye shall not see the sword, neither shall ye have famine;
but I *will* **shall** give you
assured peace **shalom of truth** in this place.
14 Then *the LORD* **Yah Veh** said unto me,
The prophets prophesy *lies* **falsehoods** in my name:
I sent them not, neither have I
commanded **misvahed** them,
neither *spake* **worded** unto them:
they prophesy unto you a false vision and divination,
and *a thing of nought* **worthlessness**,
and the deceit of their heart.
15 Therefore thus saith *the LORD* **Yah Veh**
concerning the prophets that prophesy in my name,
and I sent them not,
yet they say, Sword and famine shall not be in this land;
By sword and famine shall those prophets be consumed.
16 And the people to whom they prophesy
shall be cast out
in the *streets* **outways** of *Jerusalem* **Yeru Shalem**
because **at the face** of the famine and the sword;
and they shall have none to *bury* **entomb** them,
them, their *wives* **women**,
nor their sons, nor their daughters:
for I *will* **shall** pour their *wickedness* **evil** upon them.
17 *Therefore* thou shalt say this word unto them;
Let mine eyes *run* **drip** with tears night and day,
and let them not cease:
for the virgin daughter of my people
is broken with a great *breach* **breaking**,
with a *very grievous blow* **mighty stroking stroke**.
18 If I go forth into the field,
then behold! the *slain* **pierced** with the sword!
and if I enter into the city,
then behold! *them that are sick with*
the sickness of famine!
4 because the soil is broken
for there is no downpour in the earth:
the cultivators shame; they cover their heads.
5 And even the hind births
in the field, and forsakes;
because there is no sprout:
6 and the wild runners stand in the barrens;
they gulp the wind as monsters;
their eyes finish off because there is no herbage.
7 O Yah Veh,
though our perversities answer against us,
work this for sake of your name:
for our apostasies abound by the myriads;
we sin against you.
8 O the expectation of Yisra El,
the saviour in time of tribulation!
Why are you as a sojourner in the land?
And as a caravan that spreads to stay overnight?
9 Why are you as a man dumbfounded

—as a mighty who cannot save?
Yet you, O Yah Veh, *are* among us;
and we are called by your name;
leave us not.
10 Thus says Yah Veh to this people,
Thus they love to wander; they spare not their feet:
so Yah Veh is not pleased in them;
now he remembers their perversity
and visits their sins.
11 And Yah Veh says to me,
Pray not for this people for their good.
12 When they fast,
I hear not their shout;
and when they holocaust a holocaust and an offering,
they please me not:
and I finish them off by the sword
and by the famine and by the pestilence.
13 And I say, Aha! Adonay Yah Veh!
Behold, the prophets say to them,
You neither see the sword, nor famine;
for I give you the shalom of truth in this place.
14 And Yah Veh says to me,
The prophets prophesy falsehoods in my name:
I neither sent them nor misvahed them
nor worded to them:
they prophesy to you a false vision and divination
and worthlessness and the deceit of their heart.
15 So thus says Yah Veh
concerning the prophets who prophesy in my name,
whom I sent not,
yet they say,
Sword and famine become not in this land;
the sword and famine consumes those prophets:
16 and the people to whom they prophesy
are cast out in the outways of Yeru Shalem
at the face of the famine and the sword:
and there is no one to entomb them
—them, their women, their sons and their daughters:
for I pour their evil on them.
17 You, say this word to them;
My eyes drip with tears night and day
and they cease not:
for the virgin daughter of my people
is broken with a great breaking
—with a mighty stroking stroke.
18 If I go forth into the field,
then behold, the pierced with the sword!
And if I enter the city,
then behold, the sickness of famine!
yea, both the prophet and the priest
go about **merchandise** into a land that they know not.
19 **In spurning,**
Hast thou *utterly rejected Judah* **spurned Yah Hudah**?
hath thy soul lothed *Zion* **Siyon**?
why hast thou smitten us, and there is no healing for us?
we *looked for peace* **awaited shalom,**
and there is no good;
and for the time of healing, and behold *trouble* **fright**!
20 We acknowledge, O *LORD*
Yah Veh, our wickedness,
and the *iniquity* **perversity** of our fathers:
for we have sinned against thee.
21 Do not *abhor* **scorn** us, for thy name's sake,
do not disgrace the throne of thy *glory* **honour**:
remember, break not thy covenant with us.
22 Are there any among the
vanities of the *Gentiles* **goyim**
that can cause *rain* **downpour**?
or can the heavens give showers?
art not thou he, O *LORD* **Yah Veh** our *God* **Elohim**?
therefore we *will wait upon* **shall await** thee:
for thou hast *made* **worked** all these *things*.

JUDGMENT

15 Then said *the LORD* **Yah Veh** unto me,
Though *Moses* **Mosheh** and *Samuel* **Shemu El**
stood *before me* **at my face**,
yet my *mind* **soul** could not be toward this people:
cast **send** them *out of my sight* **from my face**,
and let them go forth.
2 And **so be** it *shall come to pass*,
if they say unto thee, Whither shall we go forth?
then thou shalt *tell* **say to** them,
Thus saith *the LORD* **Yah Veh**;
Such as are for death, to death;
and such as are for the sword, to the sword;
and such as are for the famine, to the famine;
and such as are for the captivity, to the captivity.
3 And I *will appoint over* **shall visit upon** them
four *kinds* **families**,
saith the LORD **an oracle of Yah Veh**:
the sword to *slay* **slaughter**, and the dogs to *tear* **drag**,
and the *fowls* **flyers** of the *heaven* **heavens**,
and the *beasts* **animals** of the earth,
to devour and *destroy* **ruin**.
4 And I *will cause* **shall give** them
to be removed **for an agitation**
into all *kingdoms* **sovereigndoms** of the earth,
because of *Manasseh* **Menash Sheh**
the son of *Hesekiah* **Yechizqi Yah,**
king **sovereign** of *Judah* **Yah Hudah,**

for that which he *did* **worked** in *Jerusalem* **Yeru Shalem**.
5 For who shall *have pity upon* **compassion** thee,
O *Jerusalem* **Yeru Shalem**?
or who shall *bemoan* **wag over** thee?
or who shall *go* **turn** aside
to ask *how thou doest* **of thy shalom**?
6 Thou hast *forsaken* **abandoned** me,
saith the LORD **an oracle of Yah Veh**,
thou art gone backward:
therefore *will* **shall** I *stretch out*
spread my hand against thee,
and *destroy* **ruin** thee; I am weary
with *repenting* **sighing**.
7 And I *will* **shall** fan them
with a *fan* **winnowing basket**
in the *gates* **portals** of the land;
I *will* **shall** bereave them *of children*,
I *will* **shall** destroy my people
since they return not from their ways.
8 Their widows are *increased* **mighty** to me
above the sand of the seas: I have brought upon them
against the mother of the *young men* **youths**
a *spoiler* **ravager** at *noonday* **noon**:
I have caused *him* to fall upon it suddenly,
and terrors upon the city.
9 She that hath *borne* **birthed** seven languisheth:
she hath *given up* **expired** the *ghost* **soul**;
her sun is gone down while it was yet day:
she hath been *ashamed* **shamed**
and *confounded* **blushed**:
and the *residue* **survivors** of them
will I deliver **shall I give** to the sword
before **at the face of** their enemies,
Yes, both the prophet and the priest
merchandise into a land they know not.
19 In spurning, spurn you Yah Hudah?
Loathes your soul Siyon?
Why smite you us? And is there no healing for us?
We await shalom, and there is no good;
and for the time of healing, and behold, fright.
20 We acknowledge, O Yah Veh, our wickedness,
and the perversity of our fathers:
for we sinned against you.
21 Scorn us not, for sake of your name
—the throne of your honor:
remember, break not your covenant with us.
22 Are there any among the vanities of the goyim
who can cause downpour?
Or can the heavens give showers?
Are you not he, O Yah Veh our Elohim?
So we await you: for you worked all these.

JUDGMENT

15 And Yah Veh says to me,
Though Mosheh and Shemu El stand at my face,
yet my soul is not toward this people:
send them from my face, and go.
2 And so be it,
if they say to you, Where go we?
you say to them, Thus says Yah Veh:
Such as are for death, to death;
and such as are for the sword, to the sword;
and such as are for the famine, to the famine;
and such as are for the captivity, to the captivity:
3 and upon them I visit four families
—an oracle of Yah Veh
the sword to slaughter
and the dogs to drag
and the flyers of the heavens
and the animals of the earth
to devour and ruin:
4 and I give them for an agitation
into all sovereigndoms of the earth,
because of Menash Sheh
the son of Yechizqi Yah sovereign of Yah Hudah,
for what he worked in Yeru Shalem.
5 For who compassions you, O Yeru Shalem?
And who wags over you?
And who turns aside to ask of your shalom?
6 You abandoned me
—an oracle of Yah Veh;
you go backward:
and I spread my hand against you, and ruin you;
I weary with sighing:
7 and I fan them with a winnowing basket
in the portals of the land;
I bereave them;
I destroy my people
since they return not from their ways.
8 Their widows are mighty to me
above the sand of the seas:
I bring on them
—against the mother of the youths
a ravager at noon:
I fell her suddenly with terrors and anguish:
9 she who birthed seven, languishes;
her soul expires:
her sun goes down while it is yet day;
she shames and blushes:
and I give their survivors to the sword
at the face of their enemies

saith the LORD **an oracle of Yah Veh.**
10 Woe is me, my mother,
that thou hast *borne* **birthed** me a man of strife
and a man of contention to the whole earth!
I have neither lent on usury,
nor men have lent to me on usury;
yet every one of them doth *curse* **abase** me.
11 *The LORD* **Yah Veh** said,
Verily it shall be well with thy remnant
In releasing, I release you for good;
verily I will cause the enemy to entreat thee well
did I not intercede for thee with the enemy
in the time of evil
and in the time of *affliction.* **tribulation?**
12 *Shall iron break the northern iron*
Breaketh one iron—iron from the north
and the *steel* **copper?**
13 Thy *substance* **valuables** and thy treasures
will **shall** I give to the *spoil* **plunder** without price,
and that for all thy sins, even in all thy borders.
14 And I *will make* **shall cause** thee to pass
with thine enemies into a land which thou knowest not:
for a fire is kindled in *mine anger* **my wrath,**
which shall burn upon you.
15 O *LORD* **Yah Veh,** thou knowest:
remember me, and visit me,
and *revenge* **avenge** me of my *persecutors* **pursuers;**
take me not away
in *thy longsuffering* **the length of thy wrath:**
know that for thy sake
I have *suffered rebuke* **borne reproach.**
16 Thy words were found, and I did eat them;
and thy word was unto me
the *joy* **rejoicing** and *rejoicing*
cheerfulness of mine heart:
for I am called by thy name,
O *LORD God of hosts* **Yah Veh Elohim Sabaoth.**
17 I sat not in the *assembly* **private counsel**
of *the mockers* **them that ridicule,**
nor *rejoiced* **jumped for joy;**
I sat alone because of thy hand:
for thou hast filled me with *indignation* **rage.**
18 Why is my pain perpetual,
and my wound incurable,
which refuseth to be healed?
Wilt **Shalt** thou be altogether unto me as a liar,
and as waters that *fail* **are not trustworthy?**
19 Therefore thus saith *the LORD* **Yah Veh,**
If thou return, then *will* **shall** I bring thee again,
and thou shalt stand *before me* **at my face:**
and if thou take forth the *precious* **esteemed**
from the *vile* **glutton,**
thou shalt be as my mouth:
let them return unto thee; but
return not thou unto them.
20 And I *will make* **shall give** thee unto this people
a fenced *brasen* **copper** wall:
and they shall fight against thee,
but they shall not prevail against thee:
for I am with thee to save thee and to *deliver* **rescue** thee,
saith the LORD **an oracle of Yah Veh.**
21 And I *will deliver* **shall rescue** thee
out of the *hand* **palm** of the *wicked* **evil,**
and I *will* **shall** redeem thee
out of the hand of the *terrible* **tyrant.**

SWORD AND FAMINE

16 The word of *the LORD* **Yah**
Veh came also unto me,
saying,
2 Thou shalt not take thee a *wife* **woman,**
neither shalt thou have sons or daughters in this place.
3 For thus saith *the LORD* **Yah Veh**
concerning the sons and concerning the daughters
that are *born* **birthed** in this place,
and concerning their mothers that *bare* **birthed** them,
and concerning their fathers
that *begat* **birthed** them in this land;
4 They shall die *of grievous* deaths **of sicknesses;**
they shall not be *lamented* **chopped after;**
neither shall they be *buried* **entombed;**
but they shall be as dung upon the face of the *earth* **soil:**
and they shall be *consumed* **finished off**
by the sword, and by famine;
—an oracle of Yah Veh.
10 Woe is me, my mother,
that you birthed me—a man of strife
and a man of contention to the whole earth!
I neither lent on usury
nor men lent to me on usury;
every one of them abases me.
11 Yah Veh says,
In releasing, I release you for good;
Interceded I not for you with the enemy
in the time of evil and in the time of tribulation?
12 Breaks one iron—iron from the north?
And copper?
13 I give your valuables and your treasures
to the plunder without price;
and that for all your sins, even in all your borders:

14 and I pass you and your enemies
into a land you know not:
for a fire kindles in my wrath
which burns on you.
15 O Yah Veh, you know:
remember me and visit me
and avenge me of my pursuers;
take me not away in the length of your wrath:
know that for your sake, I bear reproach.
16 I found your words and I consume them;
and your word to me
is the rejoicing and cheerfulness of my heart:
for your name is called on me,
O Yah Veh Elohim Sabaoth.
17 I neither sat in the private counsel of ridiculers
nor jumped for joy:
I sat alone because of your hand:
for you filled me with rage.
18 Why becomes my pain perpetual
and my wound incurable
—refusing to be healed?
—altogether to me as a liar,
and as waters not trustworthy?
19 So thus says Yah Veh,
If you return,
then I return you and stand you at my face:
and if you take the esteemed from the glutton,
you become as my mouth:
have them return to you;
and you return not to them:
20 and I give this people to you
as a fenced copper wall: and they fight against you,
and they prevail not against you:
for I *am* with you to save you and to rescue you
—an oracle of Yah Veh
21 and I rescue you from the palm of the evil
and I redeem you from the hand of the tyrant.

SWORD AND FAMINE

16 And so be the word of Yah Veh to me, saying,
2 You, neither take a woman
nor have sons or daughters in this place:
3 for thus says Yah Veh
concerning the sons and concerning the daughters
birthed in this place,
and concerning their mothers who birth them,
and concerning their fathers who birth them
in this land:
4 they die deaths of sicknesses;
—neither chopped after nor entombed;
—as dung on the face of the soil:
—finished off by the sword and by famine;
exeGeses ready research BIBLE
and their carcases shall be meat
for the *fowls* **flyers** of *heaven* **the heavens**,
and for the *beasts* **animals** of the earth.
5 For thus saith *the LORD* **Yah Veh**,
Enter not into the house of **a feast of** mourning,
neither go to *lament* **chop** nor *bemoan* **wag over** them:
for I have *taken away* **gathered** my *peace* **shalom**
from this people,
saith the LORD **an oracle of Yah Veh**,
even *lovingkindness* **mercy** and mercies.
6 Both the great and the *small*
lesser shall die in this land:
they shall not be *buried* **entombed**,
neither *shall men lament for them* **chopped over**,
nor *cut* **incise** themselves,
nor *make* **balden** themselves *bald* for them:
7 Neither shall *men tear* **they separate** *themselves*
for them in mourning,
to *comfort* **sigh over** them for the dead;
neither shall *men give* **they cause** them
the cup of consolation to drink
for their father or for their mother.
8 Thou shalt not *also* go
into the house of *feasting* **banquets**, to
sit with them to eat and to drink.
9 For thus saith *the LORD*
of hosts **Yah Veh Sabaoth**,
the God **Elohim** of *Israel* **Yisra El**;
Behold,
I *will* **shall** cause to *cease* **shabbathize** out of this place
in your eyes, and in your days,
the voice of *mirth* **rejoicing**,
and the voice of *gladness* **cheerfulness**,
the voice of the bridegroom, and the voice of the bride.
10 And **so be** it *shall come to pass*,
when thou shalt *shew* **tell** this people all these words,
and they shall say unto thee,
Wherefore hath *the LORD* **Yah Veh**
pronounced **worded** all this great evil against us?
or what is our *iniquity* **perversity**?
or what is our sin that we have *committed* **sinned** against
the LORD **Yah Veh** our *God* **Elohim**?
11 Then shalt thou say unto them,
Because your fathers have forsaken me,
saith the LORD **an oracle of Yah Veh**,
and have walked after other *gods* **elohim**,
and have served them,

and have *worshipped* **prostrated to** them,
and have forsaken me,
and have not *kept* **guarded** my *law* **torah**;
12 And **in working,**
ye have *done worse* **worked vilifying**
than **above** your fathers;
for, behold, ye walk every *one* **man**
after the *imagination* **warp** of his evil heart,
that they may not hearken unto me:
13 Therefore *will* **shall** I cast you out of this land
into a land that ye know not, neither ye nor your fathers;
and there shall ye serve other *gods* **elohim** day and night;
where I *will* **shall** not *shew* **give** you *favour* **charism.**
14 Therefore, behold, the days come,
saith the LORD **an oracle of Yah Veh,**
that it shall no more be said, *The LORD* **Yah Veh** liveth,
that *brought up* **ascended**
the *children* **sons** of *Israel* **Yisra El** out
of the land of *Egypt* **Misrayim;**
15 But, *The LORD* **Yah Veh** liveth,
that *brought up* **ascended** the *children*
sons of *Israel* **Yisra El**
from the land of the north,
and from all the lands whither he had driven them:
and I *will bring* **shall return** them *again*
into their *land* **soil** that I gave unto their fathers.
16 Behold, I *will* **shall** send for many fishers,
saith the LORD **an oracle of Yah Veh,**
and they shall fish them;
and after *will* **shall** I send for many hunters,
and they shall hunt them from every mountain,
and from every hill, and out of the holes of the rocks.
17 For mine eyes are upon all their ways:
they are not hid from my face,
neither is their *iniquity* **perversity**
hid *from* **in front of** mine eyes.
and their carcases are meat
for the flyers of the heavens
and for the animals of the earth.
5 For thus says Yah Veh,
Neither enter the house of a feast of mourning,
nor go to chop nor wag over them:
for I gather my shalom from this people
—an oracle of Yah Veh
even mercy and mercies.
6 Both the great and the lesser die in this land:
neither entombed nor chopped over; neither
incise nor balden yourselves for them:
7 neither separate yourselves
for them in mourning
to sigh over them for the dead;
nor drink the cup of consolation
for their father or for their mother:
8 nor go into the house of banquets
to sit with them to eat and to drink.
9 For thus says Yah Veh
Sabaoth, Elohim of Yisra El;
Behold, from this place
—in your eyes and in your days
I shabbathize the voice of rejoicing
and the voice of cheerfulness:
the voice of the bridegroom
and the voice of the bride.
10 And so be it,
when you tell this people all these words,
and they say to you,
Why words Yah Veh all this great evil against us?
Yes, what *is* our perversity?
And what sin
sinned we against Yah Veh our Elohim?
11 Then you say to them,
Because your fathers forsook me
—an oracle of Yah Veh
and walked after other elohim
and served them and prostrated to them
—forsook me and not guarded my torah:
12 and in working,
you worked vilification above your fathers;
for behold, every man of you
walks after the warp of his evil heart
that they not hearken to me:
13 and I cast you from this land
into a land that you know not
—you or your fathers;
and there you serve other elohim day and night;
where I give you no charism.
14 So behold, days come,
—an oracle of Yah Veh
that it is no more said, Yah Veh lives!
—who ascended the sons of Yisra El
from the land of Misrayim:
15 but, Yah Veh lives!
—who ascended the sons of Yisra El
from the land of the north,
and from all the lands where he drove them:
and I return them to the soil I gave to their fathers.
16 Behold, I send for many fishers;
—an oracle of Yah Veh
and they fish them:
and afterward, I send for many hunters;

and they hunt them from every mountain
and from every hill and from the holes of the rocks.
17 For my eyes are on all their ways:
they neither hide from my face,
nor hide their perversity in front of my eyes.
18 And first I *will recompense* **shall shalam**
for their *iniquity* **perversity** and their sin double;
because they have *defiled* **profaned** my land,
they have filled mine inheritance
with the carcases of their *detestable* **abominations**
and *abominable things* **abhorrences**.
19 O *LORD* **Yah Veh**,
my strength, and my *fortress* **stronghold**,
and my *refuge* **retreat** in the day of *affliction* **tribulation**,
the *Gentiles* **goyim** shall come unto thee
from the *ends* **finalities** of the earth,
and shall say,
Surely our fathers have inherited *lies* **falsehoods**,
vanity, *and things* wherein there is no *profit* **benefit**.
20 Shall *a man make gods* **humanity work elohim**
unto himself,
and they *are no gods* **be no elohim**?
21 Therefore, behold,
I *will this once* **shall at this time** cause them to know,
I *will* **shall** cause them to know
mine hand and my might;
and they shall know
that my name is *The LORD* **Yah Veh**.

THE SIN OF YAH HUDAH

17 The sin of *Judah* **Yah Hudah**
is *written* **engraved** with a *pen* **stylus** of iron,
and with the *point* **nail** of a *diamond* **brier**:
it is *graven* **engraved** upon the table of their heart,
and upon the horns of your **sacrifice** altars;
2 Whilst their *children* **sons**
remember their **sacrifice** altars and their *groves* **asherah**
by the green trees upon the high hills.
3 O my mountain in the field,
I *will* **shall** give
thy *substance* **valuables** and all thy treasures
to the *spoil* **plunder**,
and thy *high places* **bamahs** for sin,
throughout all thy borders.
4 *And thou,* even thyself,
shalt *discontinue* **release** from thine *heritage* **inheritance**
that I gave thee;
and I *will* **shall** cause thee to serve thine enemies
in the land which thou knowest not:
for ye have kindled a fire in *mine anger* **my wrath**,
which shall burn *for ever* **eternally**.
5 Thus saith *the LORD* **Yah Veh**;
Cursed be the *man* **mighty**
that *trusteth* **confideth** in *man* **humanity**,
and *maketh* **setteth** flesh his arm,
and whose heart
departeth **turneth aside** from *the LORD* **Yah Veh**.
6 For he shall be like the *heath*
naked in the *desert* **plain**,
and shall not see when good cometh;
but shall *inhabit* **tabernacle**
in the *parched places* **scorches** in the wilderness,
in a salt land and not *inhabited* **settled**.
7 Blessed is the *man* **mighty**
that *trusteth* **confideth** in *the LORD* **Yah Veh**,
and whose *hope the LORD* **confidence Yah Veh** is.
8 For he shall be as a tree
planted **transplanted** by the waters,
and that spreadeth *out* her roots
by the *river* **stream**,
and shall not see when heat cometh,
but her leaf shall be green;
and shall not be *careful* **concerned**
in the year of drought,
neither shall *cease* **depart** from *yielding* **working** fruit.
9 The heart is *deceitful* **crooked** above all *things*,
and *desperately wicked* **incurable**:
who *can know* **knoweth** it?
10 I *the LORD search* **Yah Veh probe** the heart,
I try **proof** the reins,
even to give every man according to his ways,
and according to the fruit of his *doings* **exploitations**.
11 *As* the partridge *sitteth on eggs* **broodeth**,
and *hatcheth them* **birtheth** not;
so he that *getteth* **worketh** riches,
and not by *right* **judgment**,
shall *leave* **forsake** them in the *midst* **half** of his days,
and at his end shall be a fool.
18 And first I shalam double
for their perversity and their sin;
because they profaned my land
—they filled my inheritance
with the carcases of their abominations
and abhorrences.
19 O Yah Veh, my strength, and my stronghold;
and my retreat in the day of tribulation,
the goyim come to you
from the finalities of the earth, and say,
our fathers inherited falsehoods;
vanity, wherein no one benefits.

20 Works humanity elohim for himself?
They are non—elohim!
21 So behold,
at this time I have them know
—I have them know my hand and my might;
and they know my name *is* Yah Veh.

THE SIN OF YAH HUDAH

17 The sin of Yah Hudah
is engraved with a stylus of iron
and with the nail of a brier
—engraved on the table of their heart
and on the horns of your sacrifice altars;
2 as their sons remember
their sacrifice altars and their asherah by
the green trees; by the high hills.
3 O my mountain in the field,
I give your valuables and all your treasures
for plunder,
and your bamahs for sin throughout all your borders:
4 and you released yourself
from the inheritance I gave you;
and I had you to serve your enemies
in the land you knew not:
for you kindled a fire in my wrath
which burns eternally.
5 Thus says Yah Veh;
Cursed be the mighty who confide in humanity;
who set flesh as his arm;
who turns his heart from Yah Veh.
6 And he becomes as the naked in the plain,
and sees not when good comes;
and tabernacles in the scorches in the wilderness
—in a salt land, not settled.
7 Blessed—the mighty who confide in Yah Veh,
and whose confidence is in Yah Veh:
8 who is as a tree transplanted by the waters
who spreads her roots by the stream;
and sees not when heat comes,
her leaf is green
—neither concerned in the year of drought
nor departs from working fruit.
9 The heart is crooked above all and incurable:
who knows it?
10 I Yah Veh probe the heart; proof the reins;
even to give every man according to his ways
and according to the fruit of his exploitations.
11 The partridge broods, and births not:
thus is he who works riches, but not by justness
—who forsakes them in the half of his days
and at his end, is a fool.
12 A *glorious* **honourable** high
throne from the beginning
is the place of our *sanctuary* **holies**.
13 O *LORD* **Yah Veh**,
the *hope* **expectation** of *Israel* **Yisra El**,
all that forsake thee shall *be ashamed* **shame**,
and they that *depart* **turn aside** from me
shall be *written* **inscribed** in the earth,
because they have forsaken *the LORD* **Yah Veh**,
the fountain of living waters.
14 Heal me, O *LORD* **Yah
Veh**, and I shall be healed;
save me, and I shall be saved:
for thou art my *praise* **halal**.
15 Behold, they say unto me,
Where is the word of *the LORD* **Yah Veh**?
let it come *now* **I beseech**.
16 *As for me,* I have not hastened
from *being a pastor to follow* **tending after** thee:
neither have I desired the *woeful* **incurable** day;
thou knowest:
that which *came* **proceeded** out of my lips
was *right before thee* **straightforward at thy face**.
17 Be not a *terror* **ruin** unto me:
thou art my *hope* **refuge** in the day of evil.
18 Let them *be confounded* **shame**
that *persecute* **pursue** me,
but let not me *be confounded* **shame**:
let them *be dismayed* **dismay**,
but let not me *be dismayed* **dismay**:
bring upon them the day of evil,
and *destroy* **break** them
with double *destruction* **breaking**.

HALLOWING THE SHABBATH

19 Thus said *the LORD* **Yah Veh** unto me;
Go and stand in the *gate* **portal**
of the *children* **sons** of the people,
whereby the *kings* **sovereigns** of *Judah* **Yah Hudah**
come in, and by the which they go out,
and in all the *gates* **portals** of *Jerusalem* **Yeru Shalem**;
20 And say unto them,
Hear ye the word of *the LORD* **Yah Veh**,
ye *kings* **sovereigns** of *Judah* **Yah Hudah**,
and all *Judah* **Yah Hudah**,
and all the *inhabitants* **settlers** of
Jerusalem **Yeru Shalem**,
that enter in by these *gates* **portals**:
21 Thus saith *the LORD* **Yah Veh**;

Take heed to yourselves **Guard your souls**,
and bear no burden on the *sabbath* **shabbath** day,
nor bring it in
by the *gates* **portals** of *Jerusalem* **Yeru Shalem**;
22 Neither carry forth a burden out of your houses
on the *sabbath* **shabbath** day,
neither *do* **work** ye any work,
but hallow ye the *sabbath* **shabbath** day,
as I *commanded* **misvahed** your fathers.
23 But they *obeyed* **hearkened** not,
neither *inclined* **spread** their ear,
but *made* **hardened** their neck *stiff*,
that they might not hear,
nor *receive instruction* **take discipline**.
24 And **so be** it *shall come to pass*,
in hearkening, if ye *diligently hearken* **hearken** unto me,
saith the LORD **an oracle of Yah Veh,**
to bring in no burden
through the *gates* **portals** of this city
on the *sabbath* **shabbath** day,
but hallow the *sabbath* **shabbath** day,
to *do* **work** no work therein;
25 Then shall there enter into
the *gates* **portals** of this city
kings **sovereigns** and *princes* **governors**
sitting upon the throne of David,
riding in chariots and on horses, they,
and their *princes* **governors,**
the men of *Judah* **Yah Hudah,**
and the *inhabitants* **settlers** of *Jerusalem* **Yeru Shalem:**
and this city shall *remain for ever* **settle eternally.**
26 And they shall come
from the cities of *Judah* **Yah Hudah,**
and *from the places* **round** about *Jerusalem* **Yeru Shalem,**
and from the land of *Benjamin* **Ben Yamin,**
12 An honorable high throne from the beginning
is the place of our holies.
13 O Yah Veh, the expectation of Yisra El,
all who forsake you, shame;
and they who turn aside from me
are inscribed in the earth,
because they forsook Yah Veh
the fountain of living waters.
14 Heal me, O Yah Veh, and I am healed;
save me, and I am saved:
for you are my halal.
15 Behold, they say to me,
Where is the word of Yah Veh?
Come, I beseech!
16 I neither hasten from tending after you
nor desire I the incurable day:
you, you know that what proceeds from my lips
is straightforward at your face.
17 Be not my ruin:
you *are* my refuge in the day of evil.
18 Have them shame who pursue me;
and me, not shame:
have them dismay;
and me, not dismay:
bring on them the day of evil,
and break them with double breaking.

HALLOWING THE SHABBATH

19 Thus says Yah Veh to me;
Go and stand in the portal of the sons of the people
whereby the sovereigns of Yah Hudah come
and whereby they go;
and in all the portals of Yeru Shalem:
20 and say to them,
Hear the word of Yah Veh
—you sovereigns of Yah Hudah and all Yah Hudah
and all the settlers of Yeru Shalem
entering in by these portals.
21 Thus says Yah Veh, Guard your souls;
and neither bear a burden on the shabbath day
nor bring it in by the portals of Yeru Shalem:
22 neither carry forth a burden from your houses
on the shabbath day
nor work any work;
but hallow the shabbath day
as I misvahed your fathers:
23 and they neither hearken nor spread their ear;
and harden their neck
so that they neither hear nor take discipline.
24 And so be it,
in hearkening, if ye hearken to me
—an oracle of Yah Veh
to bring in no burden
through the portals of this city on the shabbath day
—and hallow the shabbath day
to work no work therein;
25 then there enter the portals of this city
sovereigns and governors on the throne of David
riding in chariots and on horses
—they and their governors
—the men of Yah Hudah
and the settlers of Yeru Shalem:
and they settle this city eternally:
26 and they come from the cities of Yah Hudah
and all around Yeru Shalem

and from the land of Ben Yamin
and from the *plain* **lowland**, and from the mountains,
and from the south,
bringing *burnt offerings* **holocausts**, and sacrifices,
and *meat* offerings, and incense,
and bringing *sacrifices of praise* **spread hands**,
unto the house of *the LORD* **Yah Veh**.
27 But if ye *will* **shall** not hearken unto me
to hallow the *sabbath* **shabbath** day,
and not to bear a burden,
even entering in
at the *gates* **portals** of *Jerusalem* **Yeru Shalem**
on the *sabbath* **shabbath** day;
then *will* **shall** I kindle a fire in the *gates* **portals** *thereof*,
and it shall devour
the *palaces* **citadels** of *Jerusalem* **Yeru Shalem**,
and it shall not be quenched.

The Former

18 The word which came to *Jeremiah* **Yirme Yah**
from *the LORD* **Yah Veh**, saying,
2 Arise,
and *go down* **descend** to the *potter's* **former's** house,
and there I *will* **shall** cause thee to hear my words.
3 Then I *went down* **descended**
to the *potter's* **former's** house, and, behold,
he *wrought* **worked** a work on the *wheels* **stones**.
4 And the *vessel* **instrument**
that he *made* **worked** of *clay* **morter**
was *marred* **ruined**
as morter in the hand of the *potter* **former**:
so he *made it again* **turned and worked**
another *vessel* **instrument**,
as seemed *good* **straight**
to the *potter* **former** to *make* **work** *it*.
5 Then the word of *the LORD*
Yah Veh came to me,
saying,
6 O house of *Israel* **Yisra El**,
cannot I *do* **work** with you as this *potter* **former**?
saith the LORD **an oracle of Yah Veh**.
Behold,
as the *clay is* **morter** in the *potter's* **former's** hand,
so are ye in mine hand, O house of *Israel* **Yisra El**.
7 At what *instant* **blink** I shall *speak* **word**
concerning a *nation* **goyim**,
and concerning a *kingdom* **sovereigndom**,
to *pluck up* **uproot**, and to pull down, and to destroy it;
8 If that *nation* **goyim**,
against whom I have *pronounced* **worded**,
turn from their evil,
I *will repent* **shall sigh** of the evil
that I *thought* **fabricated** to *do* **work** unto them.
9 And at what *instant* **blink** I shall *speak* **word**
concerning a *nation* **goyim**, and concerning
a kingdom, to build and to plant it;
10 If it *do* **work** evil in my *sight* **eyes**,
that it *obey* **hearken** not **unto** my voice,
then I *will repent* **shall sigh** of the good,
wherewith I said
I *would benefit them* **should well—please**.
11 Now therefore *go to* **I beseech**,
speak to the men of *Judah* **Yah Hudah**,
and to the *inhabitants* **settlers** of
Jerusalem **Yeru Shalem**,
saying, Thus saith *the LORD* **Yah Veh**;
Behold, I *frame* **form** evil against you,
and *devise* **fabricate** a *device* **fabrication** against you:
return ye *now* **I beseech,**
every *one* **man** from his evil way,
and *make* **well—please in** your ways
and your *doings good* **exploitations**.
12 And they said, *There is no hope* **I quit!**:
but we *will* **shall** walk after our
own *devices* **fabrications,**
and *we will every one* **shall each man**
do **work** the *imagination* **warp** of his evil heart.
13 Therefore thus saith *the LORD* **Yah Veh**;
Ask ye *now* **I beseech,** among the *heathen* **goyim**,
who hath heard such *things*:
the virgin of *Israel* **Yisra El**
hath *done a very horrible thing* **worked mighty horribly**.
14 *Will a man leave* **Shall** the
snow of Lebanon **cease**
which cometh from the rock of the field?
and from the lowland and from the mountains
and from the south
—bringing holocausts and sacrifices
and offerings and incense;
and bringing spread hands to the house of Yah Veh.
27 And if you hearken not to me
to hallow the shabbath day,
and to not bear a burden,
even entering at the portals of Yeru Shalem
on the shabbath day;
then I kindle a fire in the portals;
and it consumes the citadels of Yeru Shalem,
and quenches not.

THE FORMER

18 So be the word to Yirme Yah from Yah Veh,
saying,
2 Rise and descend to the house of the former;
and there you hear my words.
3 And I descend to the house of the former;
and, behold, he works a work on the stones:
4 and the instrument he works of morter ruins
—as morter in the hand of the former:
so he turns and works another instrument,
as seems straight in the eyes of the former to work.
5 And so be the word of Yah Veh to me, saying,
6 O house of Yisra El,
cannot I work with you as this former *works*?
—an oracle of Yah Veh.
Behold,
as the morter in the hand of the former,
so are you in my hand, O house of Yisra El.
7 At that blink, when I word concerning a goyim,
and concerning a sovereigndom,
to uproot—and to pull down—and to destroy
8 —if that goyim, against whom I word,
turns from their evil,
then I sigh of the evil I fabricate to work to them.
9 And at that blink, when I
word concerning a goyim
and concerning a kingdom—to build and to plant;
10 If it works evil in my eyes,
that it hearkens not to my voice,
then I sigh of the good wherewith I said
I *am* well—pleased.
11 And now I beseech,
speak to the men of Yah Hudah
and to the settlers of Yeru Shalem,
saying, Thus says Yah Veh;
Behold, I form evil against you,
and fabricate a fabrication against you:
you, return I beseech
—every man from his evil way,
and well—please in your ways
and your exploitations.
12 And they say, I quit!
For we walk after our own fabrications,
and each man works the warp of his evil heart.
13 So thus says Yah Veh;
Ask I beseech you, among the goyim,
Who *ever* heard such?
The virgin of Yisra El works mighty horribly.
14 Ceases the snow of Lebanon
from the rock of the field?
or shall the *cold* **strange cool** flowing waters
that come from another place be forsaken **be uprooted**?
15 Because my people hath forgotten me,
they have *burned incense* **incensed** to
vanity, and they have caused them
to *stumble* **falter** in their ways
from the *ancient* **eternal** paths,
to walk in paths, in a way not *cast* **raised** *up*;
16 To *make* **set** their land desolate,
and a perpetual **an eternal** hissing;
every one that passeth thereby
shall *be astonished* **astonish**, and wag his head.
17 I *will* **shall** scatter them as with an east wind
before **at the face of** the enemy;
I *will* **shall** *shew* **have** them **see** the *back* **neck**,
and not the face,
in the day of their calamity.
18 Then said they,
Come and let us *devise devices* **fabricate fabrications**
against *Jeremiah* **Yirme Yah**;
for the *law* **torah** shall not *perish*
destruct from the priest,
nor counsel from the wise,
nor the word from the prophet.
Come, and let us smite him with the tongue,
and let us not *give heed* **hearken**
to **unto** any of his words.
19 *Give heed* **Hearken** to me, O *LORD* **Yah Veh**,
and hearken to the voice of them that contend with me.
20 Shall evil *be recompensed* **shalam** for good?
for they have digged a *pit* **chasm** for my soul.
Remember that I stood *before thee* **at thy face**
to *speak* **word** good for them,
and to turn away thy *wrath* **fury** from them.
21 Therefore *deliver up* **give** their *children* **sons**
to the famine,
and pour **them** out *their blood*
by the *force* **hand** of the sword;
and let their *wives* **women** be bereaved *of their children*,
and be widows;
and let their men be *put to death* **slaughtered**;
let their *young men* **youths**
be *slain* **smitten** by the sword in *battle* **war**.
22 Let a cry be heard from their houses,
when thou shalt bring a troop suddenly upon them:
for they have digged a *pit* **chasm** to *take* **capture** me,
and hid snares for my feet.
23 Yet, *LORD* **Yah Veh**,
thou knowest all their counsel against me

to *slay* **execute** me:
forgive **kapar/atone** not their *iniquity* **perversity**,
neither *blot* **wipe** out their sin from thy *sight* **face**,
but *let* **fell** them *be overthrown before thee* **at thy face**;
deal **work** thus with them
in the time of *thine anger* **thy wrath**.

The Broken Instrument

19 Thus saith *the LORD* **Yah Veh**,
Go and *get* **chattel** a *potter's earthen*
former's potsherd bottle,
and take of the *ancients* **elders** of the people,
and of the *ancients* **elders** of the priests;
2 And go forth unto
the valley of the son of Hinnom
Gay Ben Hinnom/Valley of the Son of Burning,
which is by the *entry* **opening**
of the *east gate* **pottery portal**,
and *proclaim* **call out** there
the words that I shall *tell* **word** thee,
3 And say, Hear ye the word
of *the LORD* **Yah Veh**,
O *kings* **sovereigns** of *Judah* **Yah Hudah**,
and *inhabitants* **settlers** of *Jerusalem* **Yeru Shalem**;
Thus saith *the LORD of hosts* **Yah Veh Sabaoth**,
the God **Elohim** of *Israel* **Yisra El**;
Behold, I *will* **shall** bring evil upon this place,
the which whosoever heareth, his ears shall tingle.
4 Because they have forsaken me,
and have *estranged* **recognized** this place,
and have *burned incense* **incensed** in it
unto other *gods* **elohim**,
whom neither they nor their fathers have known,
nor the *kings* **sovereigns** of *Judah* **Yah Hudah**,

Or are the strange cool flowing waters uprooted?
15 But my people forget me,
they incense to vanity;
and they have them falter in their ways
from the eternal paths
—to walk in paths—in a way not raised;
16 to set their land desolate—an eternal hissing;
every one who passes by astonishes
and wags his head.
17 I scatter them as with an east wind
at the face of the enemy;
I have them see the neck and not the face
in the day of their calamity.
18 And they say, Come!
We fabricate fabrications against Yirme Yah;
for neither the torah destructs from the priest
nor counsel from the wise
nor the word from the prophet:
Come, and smite him with the tongue,
and hearken not to any of his words.
19 Hearken to me, O Yah Veh,
and hearken to the voice
of them that contend with me.
20 Shalam we evil for good?
For they dig a chasm for my soul.
Remember that I stood at your face
to word good for them
and to turn away your fury from them.
21 So give their sons to the famine
and pour them by the hand of the sword;
so that their women bereave and become widows;
and their men become slaughtered;
—their youths smitten by the sword in war.
22 Hear their cry from the houses
when you bring a troop suddenly on them:
for they dig a chasm to capture me
and hide snares for my feet.
23 Yet, O Yah Veh,
you know all their counsel against me
—to execute me:
neither kapar/atone their perversity
nor wipe out their sin from your face;
fell them at your face;
work thus with them in the time of your wrath.

The Broken Instrument

19 Thus says Yah Veh,
Go and chattel a potsherd bottle of the former,
of the elders of the people
and of the elders of the priests;
2 and go forth to
Gay Ben Hinnom/Valley of the Son of Burning
by the opening of the pottery portal;
and there call out the words I word you,
3 and say,
Hear the word of Yah Veh,
O sovereigns of Yah Hudah
and settlers of Yeru Shalem;
thus says Yah Veh Sabaoth, Elohim of Yisra El:
Behold, I bring evil on this place,
by which whoever hears, his ears tingle:
4 because they forsake me
and recognize this place;
and incense therein to other elohim
—whom neither they nor their fathers
nor the sovereigns of Yah Hudah knew;

and have filled this place with the blood of innocents;
5 They have built also the
high places **bamahs** of Baal,
to burn their sons with fire
for *burnt offerings* **holocausts** unto Baal,
which I *commanded* **misvahed** not, nor *spake* **worded** *it*,
neither *came* **ascended** it into my *mind* **heart**:
6 Therefore, behold, the days come,
saith the LORD **an oracle of Yah Veh,**
that this place shall no more be called *Tophet* **Topheth**,
nor *The valley of the son of Hinnom*
Gay Ben Hinnom/Valley of the Son of Burning,
but
the valley of slaughter **Gay Haregah/Valley of Slaughter**.
7 And I *will make void* **shall vacate**
the counsel of *Judah* **Yah Hudah**
and *Jerusalem* **Yeru Shalem** in this place;
and I *will* **shall** cause them to fall by the sword
before **at the face of** their enemies,
and by the hands of them that seek their *lives* **souls**:
and their carcases *will* **shall** I give to be *meat* **food**
for the *fowls* **flyers** of the *heaven* **heavens**,
and for the *beasts* **animals** of the earth.
8 And I *will make* **shall set** this city desolate,
and an hissing;
every one that passeth thereby
shall be astonished and hiss
because of all the *plagues* **wounds** *thereof*.
9 And I *will* **shall** cause them to *eat* **feed**
the flesh of their sons and the flesh of their daughters,
and they shall eat every *one* **man**
the flesh of his friend in the siege and *straitness* **distress**,
wherewith their enemies,
and they that seek their *lives* **souls**,
shall *straiten* **distress** them.
10 Then shalt thou break the bottle
in the *sight* **eyes** of the men that go with thee,
11 And shalt say unto them,
Thus saith *the LORD of hosts* **Yah Veh Sabaoth**;
Even so will **Thus shall** I break this people and this city,
as one breaketh a *potter's vessel* **former's instrument**,
that cannot be *made whole* **healed** again:
and they shall *bury* **entomb** them in *Tophet* **Topheth**,
till there be no place to *bury* **entomb**.
12 Thus *will I do* **shall I work** unto this place,
saith the LORD **an oracle of Yah Veh**,
and to the *inhabitants* **settlers** thereof,
and *even make* **give** this city as *Tophet* **Topheth**:
13 And the houses of *Jerusalem* **Yeru Shalem**,
and the houses
of the *kings* **sovereigns** of *Judah* **Yah Hudah**,
shall be *defiled* **fouled** as the place of *Tophet* **Topheth**,
because of all the houses upon whose roofs
they have *burned incense* **incensed**
unto all the host of *heaven* **the heavens**,
and have *poured out drink offerings* **libated libations**
unto other *gods* **elohim**.
14 Then came *Jeremiah* **Yirme**
Yah from *Tophet* **Topheth**,
whither *the LORD* **Yah Veh** had sent him to prophesy;
and he stood in the court
of the *LORD'S house* **house of Yah Veh**;
and said to all the people,
15 Thus saith *the LORD of hosts* **Yah Veh Sabaoth**,
the God **Elohim** of *Israel* **Yisra El**; Behold,
I *will* **shall** bring upon this city and upon all her towns
all the evil that I have *pronounced* **worded** against it,
because they have hardened their necks,
that they might not hear my words.

YIRME YAH IS PERSECUTED

20 *Now Pashur* **Pashchur** the
son of Immer the priest,
who was also *chief governor* **eminent overseer**
in the house of *the LORD* **Yah Veh**,
heard that *Jeremiah* **Yirme Yah**
prophesied these *things* **words**.
2 Then *Pashur* **Pashchur**
smote *Jeremiah* **Yirme Yah** the prophet,
and *put* **gave** him in the *stocks* **stockades** that were
in the **most** high *gate* **portal** of *Benjamin* **Ben Yamin**,
which was by the house of *the LORD* **Yah Veh**.
3 And **so be** it *came to pass* on the morrow,
and fill this place with the blood of innocents;
5 and build the bamahs of Baal
to burn their sons with fire for holocausts to Baal
—which I neither misvahed nor worded
—nor ascended into my heart.
6 So behold, days come,
—an oracle of Yah Veh
that this place is no more called Topheth,
or Gay Ben Hinnom/Valley of the Son of Burning,
but Gay Haregah/Valley of Slaughter:
7 and I vacate the counsel of Yah Hudah
and Yeru Shalem in this place; and
I fell them by the sword
at the face of their enemies,
and by the hands of them seeking their souls:
and I give their carcases for food
for the flyers of the heavens

and for the animals of the earth:
8 and I set this city desolate and a hissing:
every one who passes by astonishes and hisses
because of all the wounds.
9 And I feed them the flesh of their sons
and the flesh of their daughters;
and every man eats the flesh of his friend
in the siege and distress,
whereby their enemies and they seeking their souls,
distress them.
10 And you break the bottle
in the eyes of the men going with you,
11 and say to them,
Thus says Yah Veh Sabaoth:
Thus I break this people and this city,
as one breaks an instrument of the former
that it cannot be healed again:
and they entomb them in Topheth
until there is no place to entomb.
12 Thus I work to this place
—an oracle of Yah Veh
and to the settlers thereof;
and give this city as Topheth:
13 and so be the houses of Yeru Shalem
and the houses of the sovereigns of Yah Hudah
—fouled as the place of Topheth
because of all the houses on whose roofs
they incensed to all the host of the heavens
and libated libations to other elohim.
14 And Yirme Yah comes from Topheth
where Yah Veh sent him to prophesy;
and he stands in the court of the house of Yah Veh;
and says to all the people,
15 Thus says Yah Veh Sabaoth, Elohim of Yisra El:
Behold, I bring on this city and on all her towns
all the evil I worded against it;
because they harden their necks
to not hear my words.

Yirme Yah Is Persecuted

20 And Pashchur the son of Immer the priest
who is also eminent overseer in the house of Yah Veh
hears Yirme Yah prophesying these words:
2 and Pashchur smites Yirme Yah the prophet
and gives him in the stockades
in the most high portal of Ben Yamin
by the house of Yah Veh.
3 And so be it, on the morrow,
that *Pashur* **Pashchur** brought forth *Jeremiah* **Yirme Yah**
out of the *stocks* **stockades**.
Then said *Jeremiah* **Yirme Yah** unto him,
The LORD **Yah Veh**
hath not called thy name *Pashur* **Pashchur**,
but *Magormissabib*
Magor Mis Sabib/Terror Round About.
4 For thus saith *the LORD* **Yah Veh**,
Behold, I *will make* **shall give** thee a terror to thyself,
and to all thy *friends* **loved ones**:
and they shall fall by the sword of their enemies,
and thine eyes shall *behold* **see** it:
and I *will* **shall** give all *Judah* **Yah Hudah**
into the hand of the *king* **sovereign** of *Babylon* **Babel**,
and he shall *carry* **exile** them *captive* into *Babylon* **Babel**,
and shall *slay* **smite** them with the sword.
5 *Moreover ! will deliver* **I shall give**
all the *strength* **wealth** of this city,
and all the labours *thereof*,
and all the *precious* **esteemed** *things thereof*,
and all the treasures
of the *kings* **sovereigns** of *Judah* **Yah Hudah**
will **shall** I give into the hand of their enemies,
which shall *spoil* **plunder** them, and take them,
and carry them to *Babylon* **Babel**.
6 And thou, *Pashur* **Pashchur**,
and all that *dwell* **settle** in thine house
shall go into captivity:
and thou shalt come to *Babylon* **Babel**,
and there thou shalt die,
and shalt be *buried* **entombed** there,
thou, and all thy *friends* **loved ones**,
to whom thou hast prophesied *lies* **falsehoods**.

The Complaint Of Yirme Yah

7 O *LORD* **Yah Veh**,
thou hast *deceived* **deluded** me,
and I was *deceived* **deluded**;
thou art stronger than I, and hast prevailed:
I am *in derision* **ridiculed** daily, every
one *mocketh* **derideth** me.
8 For *since ! spake* **I have worded enough,**
I *cried* **called** out, I cried violence and *spoil* **ravage**;
because the word of *the LORD* **Yah Veh**
was made a reproach unto me,
and a *derision* **ridicule**, daily.
9 Then I said, I *will* **shall**
not *make* mention *of* him,
nor *speak* **word** any more in his name.
But *his word* **it** was in mine heart
as a burning fire *shut up* **restrained** in my bones,
and I was weary with *forbearing* **containing**,

and I *could not stay* **was not able.**
10 For I heard the *defaming* **slandering** of many,
fear on every side **terror round about.**
Report **Tell**, *say they*, and we *will report it* **shall tell.**
All my *familiars* **men of shalom**
watched for **guarded at** my *halting* **limping side**, *saying*,
Peradventure he *will* **shall** be *enticed* **deluded**,
and we shall prevail against him,
and we shall take our *revenge* **avengement** on him.
11 But *the LORD* **Yah Veh** is with me
as a mighty *terrible one* **tyrant**:
therefore my *persecutors* **pursuers** shall *stumble* **falter**,
and they shall not prevail:
they shall be *greatly ashamed* **mightily shamed**;
for they shall not *prosper* **comprehend**:
their *everlasting* **eternal** confusion
shall never be forgotten.
12 But, O *LORD of hosts* **Yah Veh Sabaoth**,
that *triest righteous* **proofest the just**,
and seest the reins and the heart,
let me see thy *vengeance* **avengement** on them:
for unto thee have I *opened* **exposed** my *cause* **plea.**
13 Sing unto *the LORD* **Yah Veh**,
praise **halal** ye *the LORD* **Yah Veh**:
for he hath *delivered* **rescued** the soul of the *poor* **needy**
from the hand of *evildoers* **vilifiers.**
14 Cursed be the day wherein I was *born* **birthed**:
let not the day wherein my mother *bare* **birthed** me
be blessed.
Pashchur brings Yirme Yah from the stockades;
and Yirme Yah says to him,
Yah Veh calls not your name Pashchur,
but Magor Mis Sabib/Terror All Around:
4 for thus says Yah Veh,
Behold, I give you a terror to yourself
and to all your loved ones:
and they fall by the sword of their enemies
and your eyes see it:
and I give all Yah Hudah
into the hand of the sovereign of Babel;
and he exiles them into Babel
and smites them with the sword:
5 and I give all the wealth of this city
—all the labors and all the esteemed
and all the treasures of the sovereigns of Yah Hudah
I give into the hand of their enemies
to plunder them and take them
and carry them to Babel:
6 and you, Pashchur,
and all who settle in your house go into captivity:
and you come to Babel,
and there you die and there you are entombed
—you, and all your loved ones
to whom you prophesied falsehoods.

The Complaint Of Yirme Yah

7 O Yah Veh,
you delude me and I am deluded:
you are stronger than I and you prevail:
I am ridiculed daily; every one derides me:
8 for I word enough;
I call out; I cry violence and ravage;
because of the word of Yah Veh
is a reproach to me; and a ridicule, daily.
9 Then I say, I neither mention him,
nor word any more in his name:
and it is in my heart as a burning fire
restrained in my bones:
and I am weary with containing
and I am not able:
10 for I hear the slandering of many:
terror is all around.
Tell, and we tell!
—all my men of shalom guard at my limping side,
Perhaps he is deluded; and we prevail against him;
and we take our avengement on him.
11 And Yah Veh is with me as a mighty tyrant:
so my pursuers falter and they prevail not:
they shame mightily; for they comprehend not:
their eternal confusion is not forgotten.
12 And O Yah Veh Sabaoth,
who proofs the just and sees the reins and the heart,
I see your avengement on them:
for to you I expose my plea.
13 Sing to Yah Veh; halal Yah Veh:
for he rescues the soul of the needy
from the hand of vilifiers.
14 Curse the day I was birthed;
bless not the day my mother birthed me.
15 Cursed be the man
who *brought tidings* **evangelized** to my father,
saying, A *man child* **male son** is *born* **birthed** unto thee;
making **in cheering, cheering** him *very glad.*
16 And let that man be as the cities
which *the LORD overthrew* **Yah Veh turned against**,
and *repented* **sighed** not:
and let him hear the cry in the morning,
and the shouting at *noontide* **noon time**;
17 Because he *slew* **executed** me not from the womb;
or that my mother might have been my *grave* **tomb**,
and her womb *to be always* **eternally** great *with me.*

18 Wherefore came I forth out of the womb
to see *labour* **toil** and *sorrow* **grief,**
that my days
should be *consumed* **finished off** with shame?

The Message Of Yirme Yah To Sidqi Yah

21 The word which came unto *Jeremiah* **Yirme Yah**
from *the LORD* **Yah Veh,**
when *king Zedekiah* **sovereign Sidqi Yah** sent unto him
Pashur **Pashchur** the son of *Melchiah* **Malki Yah,**
and *Zephaniah* **Sephan Yah**
the son of *Maaseiah* **Maase Yah** the priest, saying,
2 Enquire, I *pray* **beseech** thee,
of *the LORD* **Yah Veh** for us;
for *Nebuchadrezzar* **Nebukadnets Tsar**
king **sovereign** of *Babylon* **Babel**
maketh war **fighteth** against us;
if so be that
the LORD will deal **Yah Veh shall work** with us
according to all his *wondrous* **marvellous** works,
that he may *go up* **ascend** from us.
3 Then said *Jeremiah* **Yirme Yah** unto them,
Thus shall ye say to *Zedekiah* **Sidqi Yah:**
4 Thus saith
the LORD God **Yah Veh Elohim** of *Israel* **Yisra El;**
Behold, I *will* **shall** turn back the *weapons* **vessels** of war
that are in your hands,
wherewith ye fight
against the *king* **sovereign** of *Babylon* **Babel,**
and *against* the *Chaldeans* **Kesediym,**
which besiege you without the walls,
and I *will assemble* **shall gather** them
into the midst of this city.
5 And I myself *will* **shall** fight *against* you
with an *outstretched* **spread** hand and with a strong arm,
even in *anger* **wrath,** and in fury,
and in great *wrath* **rage.**
6 And I *will* **shall** smite the
inhabitants **settlers** of this city,
both *man* **human** and *beast* **animal:**
they shall die of a great pestilence.
7 And afterward,
saith the LORD **an oracle of Yah Veh,**
I *will deliver Zedekiah* **shall give Sidqi Yah,**
king **sovereign** of *Judah* **Yah Hudah,**
and his servants, and the people,
and such as *are left* **survive** in this city
from the pestilence,
from the sword, and from the famine,
into the hand of *Nebuchadrezzar* **Nebukadnets Tsar**
king **sovereign** of *Babylon* **Babel,**
and into the hand of their enemies,
and into the hand of those that seek their *life* **soul:**
and he shall smite them
with the *edge* **mouth** of the sword;
he shall not spare them,
neither *have pity* **spare,** nor *have* mercy.
8 And unto this people thou shalt say,
Thus saith *the LORD* **Yah Veh;**
Behold, I *set before you* **give at thy face**
the way of life, and the way of death.
9 He that *abideth* **settleth** in this city
shall die by the sword,
and by the famine, and by the pestilence:
but he that goeth out,
and falleth to the *Chaldeans* **Kesediym** that besiege you,
he shall live,
and his *life* **soul** shall be unto him for a *prey* **spoil.**
10 For I have set my face against this city for evil,
and not for good,
15 Curse the man who evangelized to my father,
saying, A male son is birthed to you;
in cheering, cheer him:
16 so be that man,
as the cities Yah Veh turned against and sighed not
—to hear the cry in the morning,
and the shout at noon time:
17 because he executed me not from the womb
that my mother become my tomb
and her womb eternally great.
18 Why came I forth from the womb
—to see toil and grief?
To finish off my days with shame?

The Message Of Yirme Yah To Sidqi Yah

21 So be the word to Yirme Yah from Yah Veh
when sovereign Sidqi Yah
sends Pashchur the son of Malki Yah
and Sephan Yah the son of Maase Yah the priest
to him, saying,
2 Enquire, I beseech you, of Yah Veh for us;
for Nebukadnets Tsar sovereign of Babel fights us:
perhaps Yah Veh works with us
according to all his marvellous works,
and ascends him from us.
3 Then says Yirme Yah to them,
Say thus to Sidqi Yah:
4 Thus says Yah Veh Elohim of Yisra El:
Behold, I turn back the vessels of war in your hands
with which you fight the sovereign of Babel

and the Kesediym
who besiege you outside the walls;
and I gather them midst this city:
5 and I—I fight you
with a spread hand and with a strong arm
—in wrath and in fury and in great rage:
6 and I smite the settlers of this city
—both human and animal
that they die of a great pestilence.
7 And afterward
—an oracle of Yah Veh
I give Sidqi Yah sovereign of Yah Hudah
and his servants and the people
and such as survive in this city from the pestilence
and from the sword and from the famine
into the hand of Nebukadnets Tsar sovereign of Babel
—and into the hand of their enemies
and into the hand of them who seek their soul:
and he smites them with the mouth of the sword;
he neither spares them
—neither spares nor mercies.
8 And to this people you say,
Thus says Yah Veh;
Behold, I give at your face
the way of life and the way of death.
9 He who settles in this city dies by the sword
and by the famine and by the pestilence:
and he who goes out
and falls to the Kesediym who besiege you,
he lives:
and his soul becomes to him for a spoil.
10 For I set my face against this city for evil
and not for good;
saith the LORD **an oracle of Yah Veh**:
it shall be given into the hand
of the *king* **sovereign** of *Babylon* **Babel**,
and he shall burn it with fire.
11 And *touching* **as to** the house
of the *king* **sovereign** of *Judah* **Yah Hudah**, *say*,
Hear ye the word of *the LORD* **Yah Veh**;
12 O house of David, thus saith *the LORD* **Yah Veh**;
Execute judgment **Plead the cause** in the morning,
and *deliver him that is spoiled* **rescue the stripped**
out of the hand of the oppressor,
lest my fury go out like fire,
and burn that none can quench *it*,
because **at the face** of the evil of your *doings* **exploits**.
13 Behold, I am against thee,
O *inhabitant* **settler** of the valley, and rock of the plain,
saith the LORD **an oracle of Yah Veh**;
which say, Who shall *come down* **descend** against us?
or who shall enter into our habitations?
14 But I *will punish* **shall visit upon** you
according to the fruit of your *doings* **exploits**,
saith the LORD **an oracle of Yah Veh**:
and I *will* **shall** kindle a fire in the forest *thereof*,
and it shall *devour* **consume** all *things* round about it.

THE JUDGMENT OF THE HOUSE OF YAH HUDAH

22 Thus saith *the LORD* **Yah Veh**;
Go down **Descend** to the house
of the *king* **sovereign** of *Judah* **Yah Hudah**,
and *speak* **word** there this word,
2 And say, Hear the word of *the LORD* **Yah Veh**,
O *king* **sovereign** of *Judah* **Yah Hudah**,
that sittest upon the throne of David,
thou, and thy servants,
and thy people that enter in by these *gates* **portals**:
3 Thus saith *the LORD* **Yah Veh**;
Execute **Work** ye judgment and *righteousness* **justness**,
and *deliver* **rescue** the *spoiled* **stripped**
out of the hand of the oppressor:
and do no wrong,
do no violence to **violate not** the *stranger* **sojourner**,
the *fatherless* **orphan**, nor the widow,
neither *shed* **pour** innocent blood in this place.
4 For if **in working,** ye *do*
work this *thing indeed* **word**,
then shall there enter in by the
gates **portals** of this house
kings **sovereigns** sitting upon the throne of David,
riding in chariots and on horses,
he, and his servants, and his people.
5 But if ye *will* **shall** not hear these words,
I *swear* **oath** by myself,
saith the LORD **an oracle of Yah Veh,**
that this house shall become a *desolation* **parched area.**
6 For thus saith *the LORD* **Yah Veh** unto
the *king's* house **of the sovereign** of *Judah* **Yah Hudah**;
Thou art *Gilead* **Gilad** unto me,
and the head of Lebanon:
yet surely I *will make* **shall place** thee a wilderness,
and cities which are not *inhabited* **settled.**
7 And I *will prepare destroyers*
shall hallow ruiners
against thee,
every *one* **man** with his *weapons* **instruments**:
and they shall cut down thy choice cedars,

and *cast* **fell** them into the fire.
8 And many *nations* **goyim** shall pass by this city,
and they shall say every man to his *neighbour* **friend**,
Wherefore hath *the LORD done* **Yah Veh worked** thus
unto this great city?
9 Then they shall *answer* **say**,
Because they have forsaken the covenant
of *the LORD* **Yah Veh** their *God* **Elohim**,
and *worshipped* **prostrated to** other *gods* **elohim**,
and served them.
10 Weep ye not for the dead,
neither *bemoan* **wag over** him:
but **in weeping,** weep *sore* for him that goeth away:
for he shall return no more,
nor see his native *country* **land**.
11 For thus saith *the LORD* **Yah Veh**
touching **as to** Shallum the son of *Josiah* **Yoshi Yah,**
king **sovereign** of *Judah* **Yah Hudah,**
—an oracle of Yah Veh:
—given into the hand of the sovereign of Babel
and he burns it with fire.
11 And as to the house of the
sovereign of Yah Hudah:
Hear the word of Yah Veh:
12 O house of David, thus says Yah Veh:
Plead the cause in the morning
and rescue the stripped
from the hand of the oppressor
lest my fury go out as fire
and burns so no one can quench
at the face of the evil of your exploits.
13 Behold, I *am* against you,
O settler of the valley and rock of the plain
—an oracle of Yah Veh
who say, Who descends against us?
or, Who enters into our habitations?
14 And I visit on you
according to the fruit of your exploits
—an oracle of Yah Veh
and I kindle a fire in the forest
and it consumes all around it.

The Judgment Of The House Of Yah Hudah

22 Thus says Yah Veh:
Descend to the house of the sovereign of Yah Hudah
and word there this word,
2 and say, Hear the word of Yah Veh,
O sovereign of Yah Hudah,
who sits on the throne of David
—you and your servants
and your people entering by these portals.
3 Thus says Yah Veh:
Work judgment and justness
and rescue the stripped
from the hand of the oppressor:
and neither wrong nor violate the sojourner,
the orphan and the widow;
nor pour innocent blood in this place.
4 For if in working, ye work this word,
then there enters in by the portals of this house
sovereigns sitting on the throne of David
riding in chariots and on horses
—he and his servants and his people:
5 and if you hear not these words,
I oath by myself
—an oracle of Yah Veh
that this house becomes a parched area.
6 For thus says Yah Veh
to the house of the sovereign of Yah Hudah:
You *are* my Gilad—the head of Lebanon:
surely I place you a wilderness, and cities not settled:
7 and I hallow ruiners against you,
—every man with his instruments:
and they cut down your choice cedars
and fell them in the fire.
8 And many goyim pass by this city
and they say every man to his friend,
Why works Yah Veh thus to this great city?
9 And they say,
Because they forsook the covenant
of Yah Veh their Elohim;
and prostrated to other elohim and served them.
10 Neither weep you for the dead
nor wag over him:
but in weeping, weep for him who goes away:
for he neither returns any more
nor sees his native land.
11 For thus says Yah Veh concerning Shallum
the son of Yoshi Yah sovereign of Yah Hudah
which reigned
instead **in the stead** of *Josiah* **Yoshi Yah** his father,
which went forth out of this place;
He shall not return thither any more:
12 But he shall die in the place
whither they have *led* **exiled** him *captive*,
and shall see this land no more.
13 *Woe* **Ho** unto him
that buildeth his house
by unrighteousness **without justness,**

and his *chambers* **upper rooms**
by wrong **without judgment;**
that useth his *neighbour's* **friend's** service
without wages **gratuitously,**
and giveth him not for his *work* **deeds;**
14 That saith,
I *will* **shall** build me a *wide* house **of measure**
and *large chambers* **breathtaking upper rooms,**
and *cutteth* **rippeth** him out windows;
and *it is* cieled with cedar,
and *painted* **anointed** with vermilion.
15 Shalt thou reign,
because thou *closest thyself* **art inflamed** in cedar?
did not thy father eat and drink,
and *do* **work** judgment and *justice* **justness,**
and then it was *well with him* **for his good?**
16 He *judged* **pleaded** the cause
of the *poor* **humble** and needy;
then it was *well with him* **for his good:**
was not this to know me?
saith the LORD **an oracle of Yah Veh.**
17 But thine eyes and thine heart
are not but for thy *covetousness* **greedy gain,**
and for to *shed* **pour** innocent blood, and for oppression,
and *for* **to work** violence, *to do it.*
18 Therefore thus saith *the*
LORD **Yah Veh** concerning
Jehoiakim **Yah Yaqim** the son of *Josiah* **Yoshi Yah,**
king **sovereign** of *Judah* **Yah Hudah;**
They shall not *lament* **chop** for him,
saying, *Ah* **Ho** my brother! or, *Ah* **Ho** sister!
they shall not *lament* **chop** for him, *saying,*
Ah lord **Ho adoni!** or, *Ah* **Ho** his *glory* **majesty!**
19 He shall be *buried* **entombed**
with the *burial* **tomb** of *an ass* **a burro,**
drawn **dragged** and cast forth
beyond the *gates* **portals** of *Jerusalem* **Yeru Shalem.**
20 *Go up* **Ascend** to Lebanon, and cry;
and *lift up* **give** thy voice in Bashan,
and cry from *the passages* **Abirim:**
for all thy lovers are *destroyed* **broken.**
21 I *spake* **worded** unto thee
in thy *prosperity* **serenity;**
but thou saidst, I *will* **shall** not hear.
This hath been thy *manner* **way** from thy youth,
that thou *obeyedst* **hearkenedst** not **unto** my voice.
22 The wind shall *eat up* **tend**
all thy *pastors* **tenders,**
and thy lovers shall go into captivity:
surely then shalt thou be *ashamed*
shamed and confounded
for all thy *wickedness* **evil.**
23 O *inhabitant* **settler** of Lebanon,
that *makest thy nest* **nestest** in the cedars,
how *gracious* **charismatic** shalt thou be
when pangs come upon thee,
the *pain* **pang** as *of a woman in travail* **in birthing!**
24 *As* I live, *saith the LORD* **an oracle of Yah Veh,**
though *Coniah* **Kon Yah** the son
of *Jehoiakim* **Yah Yaqim,**
king **sovereign** of *Judah* **Yah Hudah**
were the *signet* **seal** upon my right hand,
yet *would* **should** I *pluck* **tear** thee thence;
25 And I *will* **shall** give thee
into the hand of them that seek thy *life* **soul,**
and into the hand of them whose face thou fearest,
even into the hand of *Nebuchadrezzar*
Nebukadnets Tsar
king **sovereign** of *Babylon* **Babel,**
and into the hand of the *Chaldeans* **Kesediym.**
26 And I *will* **shall** cast thee out,
and thy mother that *bare* **birthed** thee,
into another *country* **land,** where
ye were not *born* **birthed;**
and there shall ye die.
27 But to the land
—who reigned in the stead of Yoshi Yah his father
—who went from this place,
He returns here no more;
12 he dies in the place they exiled him
and sees this land no more.
13 Ho to him who builds his
house without justness
and his upper rooms without judgment;
who uses the service of his friend gratuitously,
and gives him not for his deeds;
14 who says, I build me a house of measure
and breathtaking upper rooms;
and rip out windows and ciel with cedar
and anoint with vermilion.
15 Reign you, because you are inflamed in cedar?
Your father—ate and drank he not?
Yes, he worked judgment and justness
—and for his own good:
16 he pleaded the cause of the humble and needy;
—and for his good:
Was this not to know me?
—an oracle of Yah Veh.
17 But your eyes and your heart
are for naught but your greedy gain
and for pouring innocent blood

and for oppression and to work violence.
18 So thus says Yah Veh
concerning Yah Yaqim
the son of Yoshi Yah sovereign of Yah Hudah:
They chop not for him, saying,
Ho my brother! or, Ho sister!
they chop not for him,
Ho adoni! or, Ho his majesty!
19 He is entombed with the tomb of a burro
—dragged and cast forth
beyond the portals of Yeru Shalem.
20 Ascend to Lebanon and cry;
and give your voice in Bashan and cry from Abirim:
for all your lovers are broken.
21 I worded to you in your serenity;
you said, I hear not.
This is your way from your youth, that
you hearkened not to my voice.
22 The wind tends all your tenders
and your lovers go into captivity:
surely then you shame and confound for all your evil.
23 O settler of Lebanon, who nests in the cedars,
how charismatic are you
when pangs come on you
—the pang as in birthing!
24 I live,—an oracle of Yah Veh;
though Kon Yah
the son of Yah Yaqim sovereign of Yah Hudah
were seal on my right hand,
yet I tear you thence;
25 and I give you
into the hand of them who seek your soul
and into the hand of them whose face you fear
—even into the hand
of Nebukadnets Tsar sovereign of Babel
and into the hand of the Kesediym:
26 and I cast you and your mother who birthed you
into another land where you were not birthed;
and there you die.
27 And to the land
whereunto they *desire* **lift their soul** to return,
thither shall they not return.
28 Is this man *Coniah* **Kon Yah**
a despised *broken* **splattered** idol?
is he a vessel **an instrument**
wherein is no *pleasure* **delight**?
wherefore are they cast out, he and his seed,
and are cast into a land which they know not?
29 O earth, earth, earth,
hear the word of *the LORD* **Yah Veh**.
30 Thus saith *the LORD* **Yah Veh**,
Write **Inscribe** ye this man *childless* **barren**,
a *man* **mighty** that shall not prosper in his days:
for no man of his seed shall prosper,
sitting upon the throne of David,
and *ruling* **reigning** any more in *Judah* **Yah Hudah**.

THE JUST SPROUT

23 *Woe be* **Ho** unto the *pastors* **tenders**
that destroy and scatter the *sheep* **flock** of my pasture!
saith the LORD **an oracle of Yah Veh**.
2 Therefore thus
saith *the LORD God* **Yah Veh Elohim** of *Israel* **Yisra El**
against the *pastors* **tenders** that *feed* **tend** my people;
Ye have scattered my flock, and driven them away,
and have not visited them:
behold,
I *will* **shall** visit upon you the evil
of your *doings* **exploits**,
saith the LORD **an oracle of Yah Veh**.
3 And I *will* **shall** gather the
remnant **survivors** of my flock
out of all *countries* **lands** whither I have driven them,
and *will bring* **shall return** them *again*
to their *folds* **habitations of rest**;
and they shall be *fruitful* **fruitbearing**
and *increase* **abound**.
4 And I *will set up shepherds* **shall raise tenders**
over them which shall *feed* **tend** them:
and they shall *fear* **awe** no more, nor be dismayed,
neither shall they be *lacking* **oversighted**,
saith the LORD **an oracle of Yah Veh**.
5 Behold, the days come,
saith the LORD **an oracle of Yah Veh**,
that I *will* **shall** raise unto David
a *righteous Branch* **just Sprout**,
and a *King* **Sovereign**
shall reign and *prosper* **comprehend**,
and shall *execute* **work** judgment and *justice* **justness**
in the earth.
6 In his days *Judah* **Yah Hudah** shall be saved,
and *Israel* **Yisra El** shall dwell *safely* **confidently**:
and this is his name whereby he shall be called,
THE LORD OUR RIGHTEOUSNESS
7 Therefore, behold, the days come,
saith the LORD **an oracle of Yah Veh**,
that they shall no more say, *The LORD* **Yah Veh** liveth,
which *brought up* **ascended**
the *children* **sons** of *Israel* **Yisra El**
out of the land of *Egypt* **Misrayim**;

8 But, *The LORD* **Yah Veh** liveth,
which *brought up* **ascended** and which led
the seed of the house of *Israel* **Yisra El**
out of the north *country* **land,**
and from all *countries* **lands** whither I had driven them;
and they shall *dwell* **settle** in their own *land* **soil.**
9 Mine heart within me
is broken because of the prophets;
all my bones *shake* **flutter;**
I am like *a drunken* **an intoxicated** man,
and like a *man* **mighty**
whom wine hath *overcome* **overpassed,**
because **at the face** of *the LORD* **Yah Veh,**
and *because* **at the face** of the words of his holiness.
10 For the land is *full* **filled** of adulterers;
for *because* **at the face** of *swearing* **oathing**
the land mourneth;
the *pleasant places* **folds** of the wilderness
are *dried up* **withered,**
and their *course* **race** is evil,
and their *force* **might** is not right.
to which they lift their soul to return
they return not.
28 Is this man Kon Yah a despised splattered idol?
An instrument wherein is no delight?
Why are they cast out, he and his seed,
—cast into a land they know not?
29 O earth! Earth! Earth!
Hear the word of Yah Veh!
30 Thus says Yah Veh:
Inscribe this man barren,
a mighty who prospers not in his days:
for no man of his seed prospers
—sitting on the throne of David
and reigning any more in Yah Hudah.

THE JUST SPROUT

23 Ho to the tenders
who destroy and scatter the flock of my pasture
—an oracle of Yah Veh.
2 So thus says Yah Veh Elohim of Yisra El
against the tenders who tend my people:
You scatter my flock and drive them away
and visit them not:
behold, I visit the evil of your exploits on you
—an oracle of Yah Veh
3 and I gather the survivors of my flock
from all lands I drove them;
and return them to their habitations of rest;
and they bear fruit and abound:
4 and I raise tenders over them to tend them:
and they neither awe any more nor dismay
nor oversight
—an oracle of Yah Veh.
5 Behold, days come,
—an oracle of Yah Veh
that I raise to David a just Sprout,
and a Sovereign reigns and comprehends
and works judgment and justness in the earth.
6 In his days Yah Hudah is saved,
and Yisra El dwells confidently:
and this is his name whereby he is called,
Yah Veh Sidqenuw.
7 So behold, days come,
—an oracle of Yah Veh
that they no more say, Yah Veh lives,
who ascended the sons of Yisra El

YAH VEH SIDQENUW.

from the land of Misrayim;
8 but, Yah Veh lives,
who ascended and who led
the seed of the house of Yisra El
from the north land,
and from all lands I drove them:
and they settle in their own soil.
9 Concerning the prophets:
My heart within me is broken;
all my bones flutter;
I am as an intoxicated man
and as the mighty overpassed by wine
at the face of Yah Veh,
and at the face of the words of his holiness.
10 For the land is filled with adulterers;
for at the face of oathing, the land mourns;
the folds of the wilderness wither
and their race is evil;
and their might, not right.

exeGeses ready research BIBLE

11 For both prophet and priest are profane;
yea, in my house have I found their *wickedness* **evil,**
saith the LORD **an oracle of Yah Veh.**
12 Wherefore their way shall be unto them
as slippery *ways* in the darkness:
they shall be *driven on* **overthrown,** and fall therein:
for I *will* **shall** bring evil upon them,
even the year of their visitation,
saith the LORD **an oracle of Yah Veh.**
13 And I have seen *folly* **frivolity**
in the prophets of *Samaria* **Shomeron;**

they prophesied in Baal,
and caused my people *Israel* **Yisra El** to *err* **stray**.
14 I have seen also
in the prophets of *Jerusalem* **Yeru Shalem**
an horrible thing **a horror**:
they *commit adultery* **adulterize**,
and walk in *lies* **falsehoods**:
they strengthen also the hands of *evildoers* **vilifiers**,
that *none* **no man** doth return from his *wickedness* **evil**;
they are all of them unto me as *Sodom* **Sedom**,
and the *inhabitants* **settlers** *thereof*
as *Gomorrah* **Amorah**.
15 Therefore
thus saith *the LORD of hosts* **Yah Veh Sabaoth**
concerning the prophets;
Behold, I *will* **shall** feed them with wormwood,
and make them drink the water of gall:
for from the prophets of *Jerusalem* **Yeru Shalem**
is profaneness gone forth into all the land.
16 Thus saith *the LORD of hosts* **Yah Veh Sabaoth**,
Hearken not
unto the words of the prophets that prophesy unto you:
they make you vain:
they *speak* **word** a vision of their own heart,
and not out of the mouth of *the LORD* **Yah Veh**.
17 They say *still* **saying** unto
them that *despise* **scorn** me,
The LORD **Yah Veh** hath *said* **worded**,
Ye shall have *peace* **shalom**;
and they say unto every one
that walketh after the *imagination*
warp of his own heart,
No evil shall come upon you.
18 For who hath stood
in the **private** counsel of *the LORD* **Yah Veh**,
and hath *perceived* **seen** and heard his word?
who hath *marked* **hearkened unto**
his word, and heard it?
19 Behold,
a *whirlwind* **storm** of *the LORD* **Yah Veh**
is gone forth in fury,
even a *grievous whirlwind* **whirling storm**:
it shall *fall grievously* **whirl** upon the head of the wicked.
20 The *anger* **wrath** of *the LORD* **Yah Veh**
shall not return,
until he have *executed* **worked**,
and till he have *performed* **raised**
the *thoughts* **intrigue** of his heart:
in the latter days
ye shall *consider it perfectly* **discern with discernment**.

21 I have not sent these prophets, yet they ran:
I have not *spoken* **worded** to them, yet they prophesied.
22 But if they had stood in my **private** counsel,
and had caused my people to hear my words,
then they should have turned them from their evil way,
and from the evil of their *doings* **exploits**.
23 Am I *a God at hand* **an Elohim nearby**,
saith the LORD **an oracle of Yah Veh**,
and not *a God* **an Elohim** afar off?
24 Can *any* **man** hide himself
in *secret places* **coverts**
that I shall not see him?
saith the LORD **an oracle of Yah Veh**.
Do not I fill *heaven* **the heavens** and earth?
saith the LORD **an oracle of Yah Veh**.
25 I have heard what the prophets said,
that prophesy *lies* **falsehoods** in my name, saying,
I have dreamed, I have dreamed.
26 How long shall this be in
the heart of the prophets
that prophesy *lies* **falsehoods**?
yea, *they are* prophets of the deceit of their own heart;
11 For both prophet and priest profane;
yes, in my house I found their evil
—an oracle of Yah Veh.
12 So their way is to them
as slippery in the darkness:
they are overthrown and fall therein:
for I bring evil on them
—the year of their visitation
—an oracle of Yah Veh.
13 And I see frivolity in the prophets of Shomeron;
they prophesy in Baal,
and stray my people Yisra El:
14 and I see a horror
in the prophets of Yeru Shalem;
they adulterize and walk in falsehoods:
yes, they strengthen the hands of vilifiers
so that no man returns from his evil:
they all are to me as Sedom
and the settlers as Amorah.
15 So thus says Yah Veh Sabaoth
concerning the prophets:
Behold, I feed them with wormwood and have them
drink the water of gall: for from the prophets of
Yeru Shalem profaneness goes into all the land.
16 Thus says Yah Veh Sabaoth:
Hearken not to the words of the prophets
who prophesy to you:
they make you vain:

they word a vision of their own heart
—not from the mouth of Yah Veh.
17 In saying, they say to them who scorn me,
Yah Veh words, Shalom to you!
—and they say to every one
who walks after the warp of his own heart,
Evil comes not on you!
18 —for who stands in the
private counsel of Yah Veh
and sees and hears his word?
Who hearkens to his word, and hears?
19 Behold, a storm of Yah Veh comes in fury
—even a whirling storm:
whirling on the head of the wicked.
20 The wrath of Yah Veh turns
not back until he works
and until he raises the intrigue of his heart:
in the latter days you discern with discernment.
21 I sent not these prophets, yet they run:
I worded not to them, yet they prophesy.
22 But had they stood in my private counsel
and had my people heard my words,
then they had turned them from their evil way
and from the evil of their exploits.
23 I *am* an Elohim nearby
—an oracle of Yah Veh;
and not an Elohim afar off!
24 Hides man himself in coverts that I not see him?
—an oracle of Yah Veh.
Fill I not the heavens and earth?
—an oracle of Yah Veh.
25 I hear what the prophets say
—who prophesy falsehoods in my name, saying,
I dreamed! I dreamed!
26 Until when is this in the heart of the prophets
who prophesy falsehoods?
—yes, prophets of the deceit of their own heart;
27 Which *think* **fabricate**
to cause my people to forget my name
by their dreams which they *tell* **scribe**
every man to his *neighbour* **friend,**
as their fathers have forgotten my name for Baal.
28 The prophet that hath a dream,
let him *tell* **scribe** a dream; and he that hath my word,
let him *speak* **word** my word *faithfully* **in truth.**
What is the *chaff* **straw** to the *wheat* **grain**?
saith the LORD **an oracle of Yah Veh.**
29 Is not my word *like* **thus** as a fire?
saith the LORD **an oracle of Yah Veh**;
and like a hammer
that breaketh **shattereth** the rock *in pieces*?
30 Therefore, behold, I am against the prophets,
saith the LORD **an oracle of Yah Veh,**
that steal my words
every *one* **man** from his *neighbour* **friend.**
31 Behold, I am against the prophets,
saith the LORD **an oracle of Yah Veh,**
that *use* **take** their tongues, and say, *He saith.* **An oracle!**
32 Behold, I am against them
that prophesy false dreams,
saith the LORD **an oracle of Yah Veh,**
and *do tell* **scribe** them,
and cause my people to *err* **stray** by their *lies* **falsehoods,**
and by their *lightness* **frothiness;**
yet I sent them not, nor *commanded* **misvahed** them:
therefore **in benefitting,** they shall not *profit* **benefit**
this people *at all*,
saith the LORD **an oracle of Yah Veh.**
33 And when this people, or
the prophet, or a priest,
shall ask thee, saying,
What is the burden of *the LORD* **Yah Veh**?
thou shalt *then* say unto them, What burden?
I *will* **shall** even *forsake* **abandon** you,
saith the LORD **an oracle of Yah Veh.**
34 And as for the prophet, and
the priest, and the people,
that shall say, The burden of *the LORD* **Yah Veh,**
I *will* **shall** even *punish* **visit upon**
that man and his house.
35 Thus shall ye say
every *one* **man** to his *neighbour* **friend,**
and every *one* **man** to his brother,
What hath *the LORD* **Yah Veh** answered?
and, What hath *the LORD spoken* **Yah Veh worded**?
36 And the burden of *the LORD* **Yah Veh**
shall ye *mention* **remember** no more:
for every man's word shall be his burden;
for ye have perverted the words of
the living *God* **Elohim,**
of *the LORD of hosts* **Yah Veh Sabaoth** our *God* **Elohim.**
37 Thus shalt thou say to the prophet,
What hath *the LORD* **Yah Veh** answered thee?
and, What hath *the LORD spoken* **Yah Veh worded**?
38 But since ye say, The burden
of *the LORD* **Yah Veh;**
therefore thus saith *the LORD* **Yah**
Veh; Because ye say this word,
The burden of *the LORD* **Yah Veh,**
and I have sent unto you, saying,

Ye shall not say, The burden of *the LORD* **Yah Veh**;
39 Therefore, behold, I, *even I,*
will utterly **in forgetting, shall** forget you,
and I *will forsake* **shall abandon** you,
and the city that I gave you and your fathers,
and cast you out of my presence **from my face**:
40 And I *will bring* **shall give**
an *everlasting* **eternal** reproach upon you,
and *a perpetual* **an eternal** shame,
which shall not be forgotten.

THE FIG BASKETS

24 *The LORD shewed me* **Yah Veh had me see**,
and, behold, two baskets of figs
were set before **congregated at the face of**
the *temple* **manse** of *the LORD* **Yah Veh**,
after that *Nebuchadrezzar* **Nebukadnets Tsar**
king **sovereign** of *Babylon* **Babel**
had *carried away captive Jeconiah* **exiled Yechon Yah**
the son of *Jehoiakim* **Yah Yaqim,**
king **sovereign** of *Judah* **Yah Hudah**,
27 who fabricate to have my people forget my name
by the dreams they scribe every man to his friend
—as their fathers forgot my name for Baal.
28 The prophet, having a dream,
have him scribe a dream;
and he, having my word,
have him word my word in truth.
What is the straw to the grain?
—an oracle of Yah Veh.
29 Is not my word thus as a fire?
—an oracle of Yah Veh
and as a hammer shattering the rock?
30 So behold, I *am* against the prophets
—an oracle of Yah Veh
who steal my words, every man from his friend.
31 Behold, I *am* against the prophets
—an oracle of Yah Veh
who take their tongues and say,—an oracle!
32 Behold,
I *am* against them who prophesy false dreams
—an oracle of Yah Veh
and scribe them;
and stray my people by their falsehoods
and by their frothiness;
and I—I neither sent them nor misvahed them:
in benefitting, they benefit this people not
—an oracle of Yah Veh.
33 And when this people or the prophet or a priest
ask you, saying,
What is the burden of Yah Veh?
Say to them, What burden?
I abandoned you
—an oracle of Yah Veh.
34 And the prophet and the priest and the people
who say, The burden of Yah Veh!
I visit upon that man and upon his house.
35 You, say thus, every man to his friend,
and every man to his brother,
What answers Yah Veh?
And what words Yah Veh?
36 And you
—remember the burden of Yah Veh no more
for the word of every man is his burden;
for you perverted the words of the living Elohim
—of Yah Veh Sabaoth our Elohim.
37 Thus say to the prophet,
What answers Yah Veh?
And what words Yah Veh?
38 And since you say, The burden of Yah Veh!
—so thus says Yah Veh:
Because you say this word, The burden of Yah Veh!
—and I sent to you, saying,
Say not, The burden of Yah Veh!
39 —so, behold, in forgetting, I forget you;
and I abandon you
and the city I gave you and your fathers
from my face:
40 and I give on you
an eternal reproach and an eternal shame
which is not forgotten.

THE FIG BASKETS

24 Yah Veh has me see;
and behold, two baskets of figs
congregate at the face of the manse of Yah Veh,
after Nebukadnets Tsar sovereign of Babel
exiles Yechon Yah
the son of Yah Yaqim sovereign of Yah Hudah
and the *princes* **governors** of *Judah* **Yah Hudah**,
with the *carpenters* **engravers** and *smiths* **locksmiths**,
from *Jerusalem* **Yeru Shalem**,
and had brought them to *Babylon* **Babel**.
2 One basket had *very* **mighty** good figs,
even like the figs that are first ripe:
and the *other* **one** basket
had *very naughty* **mighty evil** figs,
which could not be eaten, they were so *bad* **evil**.
3 Then said *the LORD* **Yah Veh** unto me,
What seest thou, *Jeremiah* **Yirme Yah**?

And I said, Figs;
the good figs, *very* **mighty** good;
and the evil, *very* **mighty** evil,
that cannot be eaten, they are so evil.
4 Again the word of *the LORD*
Yah Veh came unto me,
saying,
5 Thus saith *the LORD* **Yah Veh**,
the God **Elohim** of *Israel* **Yisra El**;
Like these good figs,
so *will* **shall** I acknowledge
them that are carried away captive of Judah
the exiles of Yah Hudah,
whom I have sent out of this place
into the land of the *Chaldeans* **Kesediym** for *their* good.
6 For I *will* **shall** set mine
eyes upon them for good,
and I *will bring* **shall return** them *again* to this land:
and I *will* **shall** build them,
and not *pull them down* **break**;
and I *will* **shall** plant them,
and not *pluck them up* **uproot**.
7 And I *will* **shall** give them an heart to know me,
that *I am the LORD* **I—Yah Veh**:
and they shall be my people,
and I *will* shall be their *God* **Elohim**:
for they shall return unto me with their whole heart.
8 And as the evil figs, which cannot be eaten,
they are so evil;
surely thus saith *the LORD* **Yah Veh**,
So *will* **shall** I give *Zedekiah* **Sidqi Yah**
the *king* **sovereign** of *Judah* **Yah Hudah**,
and his *princes* **governors**,
and the *residue* **survivors** of *Jerusalem* **Yeru Shalem**,
that *remain* **survive** in this land,
and them that *dwell* **settle** in the
land of *Egypt* **Misrayim**:
9 And I *will deliver* **shall give** them
to be removed **for an agitation**
into all the *kingdoms* **sovereigndoms** of the earth
for *their hurt* **evil**,
to be—a reproach and a proverb,
a *taunt* **gibe** and *a curse* **an abasement**,
in all places whither I shall drive them.
10 And I *will* **shall** send the sword, the famine,
and the pestilence, among them,
till they be consumed from off the *land* **soil**
that I gave unto them and to their fathers.

THE SEVENTY YEAR CAPTIVITY

25 The word that came to *Jeremiah* **Yirme Yah**
concerning all the people of *Judah* **Yah Hudah**
in the fourth year of *Jehoiakim* **Yah Yaqim**
the son of *Josiah* **Yoshi Yah**
king **sovereign** of *Judah* **Yah Hudah**,
that was the first year of
Nebuchadrezzar **Nebukadnets Tsar**
king **sovereign** of *Babylon* **Babel**;
2 The which *Jeremiah* **Yirme Yah** the prophet
spake **worded** unto all the people of *Judah* **Yah Hudah**,
and to all the *inhabitants* **settlers**
of *Jerusalem* **Yeru Shalem**, saying,
3 From the thirteenth year of *Josiah* **Yoshi Yah**
the son of Amon *king* **sovereign** of *Judah* **Yah Hudah**,
even unto this day, that is the three and twentieth year,
the word of *the LORD* **Yah Veh** hath come unto me,
and I have *spoken* **worded** unto you,
rising **starting** early and *speaking* **wording**;
but ye have not hearkened.
4 And *the LORD* **Yah Veh** hath sent unto you
all his servants the prophets,
rising **starting** early and sending them;
and the governors of Yah Hudah
with the engravers and locksmiths from Yeru Shalem;
and brings them to Babel.
2 One basket of mighty good figs,
as the first ripe figs:
and the one basket of mighty evil figs,
which are not eaten, for evil.
3 Then says Yah Veh to me,
What see you, Yirme Yah?
And I say, Figs!
The good figs, mighty good;
and the evil, mighty evil,
not eaten, for evil.
4 And so be the word of Yah Veh to me, saying,
5 Thus says Yah Veh, Elohim of Yisra El;
As these good figs,
thus I acknowledge the exiles of Yah Hudah
—whom I sent from this place
into the land of the Kesediym for good:
6 and I set my eyes on them for good,
and I return them to this land:
and I build them, and not break;
and I plant them, and not uproot:
7 and I give them a heart to know me,
I—Yah Veh:
and they are my people,

and I am their Elohim:
for they return to me with their whole heart.
8 And as the evil figs, not eaten for their evil,
thus says Yah Veh:
Thus I give Sidqi Yah the sovereign of Yah Hudah
and his governors and the survivors of Yeru Shalem
who survive in this land
—who settle in the land of Misrayim:
9 and I give them for an agitation
into all the sovereigndoms of the earth for evil
—a reproach and a proverb
—a gibe and an abasement
in all places I drive them:
10 and I send the sword
the famine and the pestilence among them
—until they *are* consumed from off the soil
—I give to them and to their fathers.

The Seventy Year Captivity

25 And so be the word to Yirme Yah
concerning all the people of Yah Hudah
in the fourth year of Yah Yaqim
the son of Yoshi Yah sovereign of Yah Hudah,
—the first year of
Nebukadnets Tsar sovereign of Babel;
2 which Yirme Yah the prophet
words to all the people of Yah Hudah
and to all the settlers of Yeru Shalem, saying,
3 From the thirteenth year of Yoshi Yah the
son of Amon sovereign of Yah Hudah, even
to this day—the twenty—third year,
so be the word of Yah Veh to me,
and I worded to you, starting early and wording;
and you hearkened not:
4 and Yah Veh sent to you
all his servants the prophets
—starting early and sending them;
but ye have not hearkened,
nor *inclined* **spread** your ear to hear.
5 *They said* **Saying**, Turn ye again *now* **I beseech,**
every *one* **man** from his evil way,
and from the evil of your *doings* **exploits**,
and *dwell* **settle** in the *land* **soil**
that *the LORD* **Yah Veh**
hath given unto you and to your fathers
for ever **eternally** and *ever* **eternally**:
6 And go not after other *gods*
elohim to serve them,
and to *worship* **prostrate to** them,
and *provoke* **vex** me not *to anger*
with the works of your hands;
and I *will do you no hurt* **shall not vilify you.**
7 Yet ye have not hearkened unto me,
saith the LORD **an oracle of Yah Veh**;
that ye might *provoke* **vex** me *to anger*
with the works of your hands to your own *hurt* **evil**.
8 Therefore
thus saith *the LORD of hosts* **Yah Veh Sabaoth**;
Because ye have not heard my words,
9 Behold,
I *will* **shall** send and take all the families of the north,
saith the LORD **an oracle of Yah Veh**,
and *Nebuchadrezzar* **Nebukadnets Tsar**
king **sovereign** of *Babylon* **Babel**, my servant,
and *will* **shall** bring them against this land,
and against the *inhabitants* **settlers** *thereof*,
and against all these *nations* **goyim** round about,
and *will utterly destroy* **shall devote** them,
and *make* **set** them
an astonishment **a desolation**, and an hissing,
and *perpetual desolations* **eternal parched areas**.
10 *Moreover I will take* **I shall destroy** from them
the voice of *mirth* **rejoicing**,
and the voice of *gladness* **cheerfulness**,
the voice of the bridegroom, and the voice of the bride,
the *sound* **voice** of the millstones,
and the light of the *candle* **lamp**.
11 And this whole land
shall be a *desolation* **parched area**,
and *an astonishment* **a desolation**;
and these *nations* **goyim**
shall serve the *king* **sovereign** of *Babylon* **Babel**
seventy years.
12 And **so be** it *shall come to pass*,
when seventy years are *accomplished* **fulfilled**,
that I *will punish* **shall visit**
upon the *king* **sovereign** of *Babylon* **Babel**,
and that *nation* **goyim**,
saith the LORD **an oracle of Yah Veh**,
for their *iniquity* **perversity**,
and the land of the *Chaldeans* **Kesediym**,
and *will make* **shall set** it *perpetual* **eternal** desolations.
13 And I *will* **shall** bring upon that land
all my words
which I have *pronounced against it* **worded**,
even all that is *written* **inscribed** in this *book* **scroll**,
which *Jeremiah* **Yirme Yah** hath prophesied
against all the *nations* **goyim**.
14 For many *nations* **goyim**
and great *kings* **sovereigns**

shall serve themselves of them also:
and I *will recompense* **shall shalam** them
according to their deeds,
and according to the works of their own hands.
15 For thus saith
the LORD God **Yah Veh Elohim** of *Israel* **Yisra El**
unto me;
Take the wine cup of this fury at my hand,
and cause all the *nations* **goyim**, to whom I send thee,
to drink it.
16 And they shall drink,
and *be moved* **agitate**, and *be mad* **halal**,
because **at the face** of the sword
that I *will* **shall** send among them.
17 Then took I the cup at *the*
LORD'S **Yah Veh's** hand,
and made all the *nations* **goyim** to drink, unto
whom *the LORD* **Yah Veh** had sent me:
but you neither hearkened
nor spread your ear to hear:
5 saying, Turn back, I beseech,
every man from his evil way,
and from the evil of your exploits,
and settle in the soil Yah Veh
I gave to you and to your fathers
eternally and eternally:
6 and go not after other elohim
to serve them and to prostrate to them;
and vex me not with the works of your hands;
and I vilify you not.
7 And you hearkened not to me
—an oracle of Yah Veh
and vexed me with the works of your hands
to your own evil.
8 So thus says Yah Veh Sabaoth:
Because you heard not my words,
9 Behold,
I send and take all the families of the north
—an oracle of Yah Veh
and Nebukadnets Tsar sovereign of Babel my servant
—and bring them against this land
and against the settlers
and against all these goyim all around;
and devote them
and set them a desolation and a hissing;
and eternal parched areas:
10 I destroy from them the voice of rejoicing
and the voice of cheerfulness;
the voice of the bridegroom
and the voice of the bride;
the voice of the millstones
and the light of the lamp:
11 and this whole land
becomes a parched area and a desolation;
and these goyim
serve the sovereign of Babel seventy years:
12 and so be it,
when seventy years fulfill,
I visit on the sovereign of Babel and that goyim
—an oracle of Yah Veh
for their perversity
—and the land of the Kesediym
and set it eternal desolations:
13 and I bring on that land
all the words I worded
—all inscribed in this scroll
which Yirme Yah prophesied against all the goyim.
14 For many goyim and great sovereigns
are also served by them:
and I shalam them according to their deeds,
and according to the works of their own hands.
15 For thus says Yah Veh Elohim of Yisra El to me:
Take the wine cup of this fury at my hand,
and have all the goyim, to whom I send you, drink:
16 and they drink and agitate and halal
at the face of the sword I send among them.
17 And I take the cup from the hand of Yah Veh
and have all the goyim drink
—to whom Yah Veh sent me:
18 *To wit, Jerusalem* **Yeru Shalem**,
and the cities of *Judah* **Yah Hudah**,
and the *kings* **sovereigns** *thereof*,
and the *princes* **governors** *thereof*,
to *make* **give** them a *desolation* **parched area**,
an astonishment **a desolation**,
an hissing, and *a curse* **an abasement**; as it is this day;
19 *Pharaoh king* **Paroh**
sovereign of *Egypt* **Misrayim**,
and his servants, and his *princes* **governors**,
and all his people;
20 And all the *mingled people* **comingled**,
and all the *kings* **sovereigns** of the land of *Uz* **Us**,
and all the *kings* **sovereigns**
of the land of the *Philistines* **Peleshethiym**,
and *Ashkelon* **Ashqelon**, and Azzah, and *Ekron* **Eqron**,
and the *remnant* **survivors** of Ashdod,
21 Edom, and Moab, and the
children **sons** of Ammon,
22 And all the *kings* **sovereigns** of *Tyrus* **Sor**,
and all the *kings* **sovereigns** of *Zidon* **Sidon**,

and the *kings* **sovereigns** of the *isles* **islands**
which are beyond the sea,
23 Dedan, and Tema, and Buz,
and all that *are in the utmost corners* **chop the edges,**
24 And all the *kings* **sovereigns** of Arabia,
and all the *kings* **sovereigns**
of the *mingled people* **comingled**
that *dwell* **tabernacle** in the *desert* **wilderness,**
25 And all the *kings* **sovereigns** of Zimri,
and all the *kings* **sovereigns** of Elam,
and all the *kings* **sovereigns** of the *Medes* **Maday,**
26 And all the *kings* **sovereigns** of the north,
far and near, *one* **man** with *another* **brother,**
and all the *kingdoms* **sovereigndoms** of the *world* **earth,**
which are upon the face of the *earth* **soil:**
and the *kings* **sovereigns** of Sheshach
shall drink after them.
27 *Therefore* thou shalt say unto them,
Thus saith *the LORD of hosts* **Yah Veh Sabaoth,**
the God **Elohim** of *Israel* **Yisra El;**
Drink ye, and *be drunken* **intoxicate,**
and *spue* **vomit,** and fall, and rise no more,
because **at the face** of the sword
which I *will* **shall** send among you.
28 And *it shall be* **so be it,**
if they refuse to take the cup at thine hand to drink,
then shalt thou say unto them,
Thus saith *the LORD of hosts* **Yah Veh Sabaoth;**
In drinking, Ye shall *certainly* drink.
29 For, *lo* **behold,**
I begin to *bring evil on* **vilify** the city
which is called by my name,
and **in exonerating,**
should ye be *utterly unpunished* **exonerated?**
Ye shall not be unpunished:
for I *will* **shall** call for a sword
upon all the *inhabitants* **settlers** of the earth,
saith the LORD of hosts **an oracle of Yah Veh Sabaoth.**
30 Therefore prophesy thou
against them all these words,
and say unto them,
The LORD **Yah Veh** shall roar from on high,
and *utter* **give** his voice from his holy habitation **of rest;**
in roaring,
he shall *mightily* roar upon his habitation **of rest;**
he shall *give a shout* **answer,**
as they that tread *the grapes,*
against all the *inhabitants* **settlers** of the earth.
31 *A noise* **An uproar**
shall come *even* to the ends of the earth;
for *the LORD* **Yah Veh**
hath a controversy with the *nations* **goyim,**
he *will plead with* **shall judge** all flesh;
he *will* **shall** give them that are wicked to the sword,
saith the LORD **an oracle of Yah Veh.**
32 Thus saith *the LORD of hosts* **Yah Veh Sabaoth,**
Behold, evil shall go forth
from *nation* **goyim** to *nation* **goyim,**
and a great *whirlwind* **storm** shall be *raised up* **wakened**
from the *coasts* **flanks** of the earth.

18 Yeru Shalem and the cities of Yah Hudah;
and the sovereigns and the governors
—to give them a parched area, a desolation;
a hissing and an abasement; as this day:
19 Paroh sovereign of Misrayim
and his servants and his governors and all his people;
20 and all the comingled
and all the sovereigns of the land of Us;
and all the sovereigns of the land of the Peleshethiym;
and Ashqelon and Azzah and Eqron
and the survivors of Ashdod;
21 Edom and Moab and the sons of Ammon;
22 and all the sovereigns of Sor;
and all the sovereigns of Sidon;
and the sovereigns of the islands beyond the sea;
23 Dedan and Tema and Buz
and all who chop the edges;
24 and all the sovereigns of Arabia;
and all the sovereigns of the comingled
who tabernacle in the wilderness;
25 and all the sovereigns of Zimri;
and all the sovereigns of Elam;
and all the sovereigns of the Maday;
26 and all the sovereigns of the north,
far and near, man with brother;
and all the sovereigndoms of the earth
on the face of the soil:
and the sovereigns of Sheshach drink after them.
27 And say to them,
Thus says Yah Veh Sabaoth Elohim of Yisra El:
You, drink and intoxicate and vomit and fall
and rise no more
at the face of the sword I send among you.
28 And so be it,
if they refuse to take the cup at your hand to drink
then you say to them,
Thus says Yah Veh Sabaoth;
In drinking, drink!
29 For, behold,
I begin to vilify the city on which my name is called.

And in exonerating, are you exonerated?
You are not unpunished:
for I call for a sword on all the settlers of the earth
—an oracle of Yah Veh Sabaoth.
30 So prophesy all these words against them
and say to them,
Yah Veh roars from on high
and gives his voice from his holy habitation of rest;
in roaring, he roars on his habitation of rest;
he answers
as they who tread against all the settlers of the earth.
31 An uproar approaches the ends of the earth;
for Yah Veh has a controversy with the goyim:
he judges all flesh;
he gives the wicked to the sword
—an oracle of Yah Veh.
32 Thus says Yah Veh Sabaoth,
Behold, evil goes from goyim to goyim
and a great storm wakens from the flanks of the earth:
33 And the *slain* **pierced** of *the LORD* **Yah Veh**
shall be at that day from *one* end of the earth
even unto *the other* end of the earth:
they shall not be *lamented* **chopped over**,
neither gathered, nor *buried* **entombed**;
they shall be dung upon the *ground* **face of the soil**.
34 Howl, ye *shepherds* **tenders**, and cry;
and wallow yourselves *in the ashes*,
ye *principal* **mighty** of the flock:
for the days
of your slaughter and of your *dispersions* **scatterings**
are *accomplished* **fulfilled**;
and ye shall fall
like *a pleasant vessel* **an instrument of desire**.
35 And *the shepherds shall have no way to flee*
flight from the tenders shall destruct,
nor the principal of the flock to escape
and escape from the mighty of the flock.
36 A voice of the cry of the *shepherds* **tenders**,
and an howling of the *principal* **mighty** of the flock,
shall be heard:
for *the LORD* **Yah Veh**
hath *spoiled* **ravaged** their pasture.
37 And the *peaceable habitations* **folds of shalom**
are *cut down* **severed**
because **at the face** of the *fierce anger* **fuming wrath**
of *the LORD* **Yah Veh**.
38 He hath forsaken his *covert*
sukkoth/brush arbor,
as the *lion* **whelp**:
for their land is desolate
because **at the face** of the *fierceness* **fuming**
of the oppressor,
and *because* **at the face** of his *fierce anger* **fuming wrath**.

WARNING TO THE CITIES OF YAH HUDAH

26 In the beginning
of the *reign* **sovereigndom** of *Jehoiakim* **Yah Yaqim**
the son of *Josiah* **Yoshi Yah,**
king **sovereign** of *Judah* **Yah Hudah**
came this word from *the LORD* **Yah Veh**, saying,
2 Thus saith *the LORD* **Yah Veh**;
Stand in the court
of the *LORD'S* house **of Yah Veh**,
and *speak* **word** unto all the cities of *Judah* **Yah Hudah**,
which come to *worship* **prostrate**
in the *LORD'S* house **of Yah Veh**,
all the words
that I *command* **misvah** thee to *speak* **word** unto them;
diminish not a word:
3 If so be they *will* **shall** hearken,
and turn every man from his evil way,
that I may *repent* **sigh** me of the evil,
which I *purpose* **fabricate** to *do* **work** unto them
because **at the face** of the evil of their *doings* **exploits**.
4 And thou shalt say unto them,
Thus saith *the LORD* **Yah Veh**;
If ye *will* **shall** not hearken to me,
to walk in my *law* **torah**,
which I have set *before you* **at thy face**,
5 To hearken to the words of
my servants the prophets,
whom I sent unto you,
both rising up **starting** early, and sending *them*,
but ye have not hearkened;
6 Then *will I make* **shall I**
give this house like Shiloh,
and *will make* **shall give** this city *a curse* **an**
abasement to all the *nations* **goyim** of the earth.
7 So the priests and the
prophets and all the people
heard *Jeremiah* **Yirme Yah** speaking these
words in the house of *the LORD* **Yah Veh**.
8 *Now* **And so be** it *came to pass*,
when *Jeremiah* **Yirme Yah**
had *made an end of speaking* **finished wording** all that
the LORD **Yah Veh** had *commanded* **misvahed** him
to *speak* **word** unto all the people,
that the priests and the prophets and all the people
took **apprehended** him, saying,
In dying, Thou shalt *surely* die.

9 Why hast thou prophesied
in the name of *the LORD* **Yah Veh**, saying,
This house shall be like Shiloh,
33 And so be the pierced of Yah Veh at that day
from end of the earth even to end of the earth:
neither chopped over nor gathered nor entombed;
they become as dung on the face of the soil.
34 Howl, you tenders, and cry;
and wallow yourselves, you mighty of the flock:
for the days of your slaughter and of your scatterings
are fulfilled;
and you fall as an instrument of desire:
35 and flight destructs from the tenders
and escape from the mighty of the flock
36 —a voice of the cry of the tenders
and a howling of the mighty of the flock:
for Yah Veh ravages their pasture:
37 and severs the folds of shalom
at the face of the fuming wrath of Yah Veh.
38 He forsakes his sukkoth/
brush arbor as the whelp:
surely their land is desolate
at the face of the fuming of the oppressor
and at the face of his fuming wrath.

WARNING TO THE CITIES OF YAH HUDAH

26 In the beginning
of the sovereigndom of Yah Yaqim
the son of Yoshi Yah sovereign of Yah Hudah
so be this word from Yah Veh, saying,
2 Thus says Yah Veh:
Stand in the court of the house of Yah Veh;
and word to all the cities of Yah Hudah
who come to prostrate in the house of Yah Veh
all the words I misvah you to word to them;
diminish not a word:
3 perhaps they hearken
and every man turns from his evil way,
so that I sigh of the evil I fabricate to work to them
at the face of the evil of their exploits.
4 And you say to them, Thus says Yah Veh:
If you hearken not to me,
to walk in my torah which I set at your face,
5 to hearken to the words of
my servants the prophets
whom I send to you, starting early and sending,
and you hearken not:
6 then I give this house as Shiloh
and give this city
for an abasement to all the goyim of the earth.
7 And the priests and the
prophets and all the people
hear Yirme Yah
speaking these words in the house of Yah Veh.
8 And so be it,
Yirme Yah finishes wording
all Yah Veh misvahs him to word to all the people;
and the priests and the prophets and all the people
apprehend him, saying,
In dying, you die!
9 Why prophesy you in the
name of Yah Veh, saying,
This house becomes as Shiloh,
and this city shall be *desolate* **parched**
without *an inhabitant* **a settler?**
And all the people
were gathered **congregated** against *Jeremiah* **Yirme Yah**
in the house of *the LORD* **Yah Veh.**
10 When the *princes* **governors**
of *Judah* **Yah Hudah**
heard these *things* **words,**
then they *came up* **ascended**
from the *king's* **sovereign's** house
unto the house of *the LORD* **Yah Veh,**
and sat down in the *entry* **opening**
of the new *gate* **portal**
of the *LORD'S* house **of Yah Veh.**
11 Then *spake* **said** the priests and the prophets
unto the *princes* **governors** and to all the people, saying,
This man *is worthy to die* **hath judgment of death;**
for he hath prophesied against this city,
as ye have heard with your ears.
12 Then *spake Jeremiah* **said Yirme Yah**
unto all the *princes* **governors** and to all the people,
saying, *The LORD* **Yah Veh** sent me to prophesy
against this house and against this city
all the words that ye have heard.
13 Therefore now
amend **well—prepare** your ways
and your *doings* **exploits,**
and obey
the voice of *the LORD* **Yah Veh** your *God* **Elohim;**
and *the LORD will repent him* **Yah Veh shall sigh**
of the evil that he hath *pronounced* **worded** against you.
14 As for me, behold, I am in your hand:
do **work** with me as seemeth good
and *meet unto you* **straight in your eyes.**
15 But **in knowing,** know ye *for certain* **this,**
that if ye *put me to death* **deathify me,**
ye shall surely *bring* **give** innocent blood

upon yourselves, and upon this city,
and upon the *inhabitants* **settlers** *thereof*:
for of a truth *the LORD* **Yah Veh** hath sent me unto you
to *speak* **word** all these words in your ears.
16 Then said the *princes*
governors and all the people
unto the priests and to the prophets;
This man
is not worthy to die **hath not judgment of death**:
for he hath *spoken* **worded** to us
in the name of *the LORD* **Yah Veh** our *God* **Elohim**.
17 Then rose up *certain* **men**
of the elders of the land,
and *spake* **said**
to all the *assembly* **congregation** of the people, saying,
18 *Micah* **Michah Yah** the *Morasthite* **Moreshethiy**
prophesied in the days of *Hesekiah* **Yechizqi Yah,**
king **sovereign** of *Judah* **Yah Hudah,**
and *spake* **said** to all the people of *Judah* **Yah Hudah,**
saying, Thus saith *the LORD of hosts* **Yah Veh Sabaoth**;
Zion **Siyon** shall be plowed like a field,
and *Jerusalem* **Yeru Shalem** shall become heaps,
and the mountain of the house
as the *high places* **bamahs** of a forest.
19 Did *Hesekiah* **Yechizqi Yah**
king **sovereign** of *Judah* **Yah Hudah**
and all *Judah* **Yah Hudah**
put him at all to death **in deathifying, deathify him**?
did he not fear *the LORD* **Yah Veh,**
and *besought the LORD* **stroked the face of Yah Veh,**
and *the LORD repented him* **Yah Veh sighed** of the evil
which he had *pronounced* **worded** against them?
Thus might we *procure* **work** great evil against our souls.
20 And there was also a man
that prophesied in the name of *the LORD* **Yah Veh,**
Urijah **Uri Yah** the son of *Shemaiah* **Shema Yah**
of *Kirjathjearim* **Qiryath Arim,**
who prophesied against this city and against this land
according to all the words of *Jeremiah* **Yirme Yah**.
21 And when *Jehoiakim* **Yah**
Yaqim the *king* **sovereign,**
with all his mighty *men*, and all the *princes* **governors,**
heard his words,
the *king* **sovereign** sought to *put* **deathify** him *to death*:
but when *Urijah* **Uri Yah** heard it,
he *was afraid* **awed,**
and fled, and went into *Egypt* **Misrayim;**
22 And *Jehoiakim* **Yah Yaqim** the *king* **sovereign**
and this city parched without a settler?
—and all the people congregate against Yirme Yah
in the house of Yah Veh.
10 And the governors of Yah
Hudah hear these words,
and they ascend from the house of the sovereign
to the house of Yah Veh;
and sit in the opening of the new portal
of the house of Yah Veh.
11 And the priests and the prophets
say to the governors and to all the people, saying,
A judgment of death for this man;
for he prophesies against this city,
as you hear with your ears.
12 And Yirme Yah
says to all the governors and to all the people,
saying, Yah Veh sent me to prophesy
against this house and against this city
all the words you heard:
13 and now
well—prepare your ways and your exploits
and obey the voice of Yah Veh your Elohim;
so that Yah Veh sighs
concerning the evil he worded against you.
14 As for me, behold, I *am* in your hand:
work with me
as seems good and straight in your eyes.
15 Only in knowing, know this:
that if you deathify me
you surely give innocent blood on yourselves
and on this city and on the settlers:
for of a truth Yah Veh sent me to you
to word all these words in your ears.
16 Then the governors and all the people
say to the priests and to the prophets;
No judgment of death for this man:
for he words to us
in the name of Yah Veh our Elohim.
17 And men of the elders of the land rise
and say to all the congregation of the people, saying,
18 Michah Yah the Moreshethiy
was prophesying
in the days of Yechizqi Yah sovereign of Yah Hudah;
and said to all the people of Yah Hudah,
saying, Thus says Yah Veh Sabaoth;
Siyon becomes a plowed field;
and Yeru Shalem becomes heaps;
and the mountain of the house
as the bamahs of a forest.
19 Yechizqi Yah sovereign of Yah Hudah
—and all Yah Hudah
in deathifying, deathified he him?

Feared he not Yah Veh
and stroked the face of Yah Veh
—and Yah Veh sighed of the evil
he worded against them?
And we work great evil against our souls.
20 And also, so be a man
who prophesied in the name of Yah Veh
—Uri Yah the son of Shema Yah of Qiryath Arim
who prophesied against this city and against this land
according to all the words of Yirme Yah:
21 and when Yah Yaqim the sovereign
with all his mighty and all the governors,
heard his words,
the sovereign sought to deathify him:
but when Uri Yah heard
he awed and fled and went into Misrayim:
22 and Yah Yaqim the sovereign
sent men into *Egypt* **Misrayim,**
namely, Elnathan **El Nathan** the son of Achbor,
and *certain* men with him into *Egypt* **Misrayim.**
23 And they fetched forth *Urijah* **Uri Yah**
out of *Egypt* **Misrayim,**
and brought him
unto *Jehoiakim* **Yah Yaqim** the *king* **sovereign;**
who *slew* **smote** him with the sword,
and cast his *dead body* **carcase**
into the *graves* **tombs** of the *common* **sons of the** people.
24 Nevertheless the hand of
Ahikam the son of Shaphan
was with *Jeremiah* **Yirme Yah,**
that they should not give him into the hand of the people
to put **deathify** him *to death.*

YAH HUDAH UNDER NEBUKADNETS TSAR

27 In the beginning
of the *reign* **sovereigndom** of *Jehoiakim* **Yah Yaqim**
the son of *Josiah* **Yoshi Yah,**
king **sovereign** of *Judah* **Yah Hudah**
came this word unto *Jeremiah* **Yirme Yah**
from *the LORD* **Yah Veh,** saying,
2 Thus saith *the LORD* **Yah Veh** to me;
Make **Work** thee bonds and *yokes* **yoke poles,**
and *put* **give** them upon thy neck,
3 And send them to the *king* **sovereign** of Edom,
and to the *king* **sovereign** of Moab,
and to the *king* **sovereign** of the
Ammonites **sons of Ammon,**
and to the *king* **sovereign** of *Tyrus* **Sor,**
and to the *king* **sovereign** of *Zidon* **Sidon,**
by the hand of the *messengers* **angels**
which come to *Jerusalem* **Yeru Shalem**
unto *Zedekiah* **Sidqi Yah,**
king **sovereign** of *Judah* **Yah Hudah;**
4 And *command* **misvah** them
to say **saying** unto their *masters* **adonim,**
Thus saith *the LORD of hosts* **Yah Veh Sabaoth,**
the God **Elohim** of *Israel* **Yisra El;**
Thus shall ye say unto your *masters* **adonim;**
5 I have *made* **worked** the earth,
the man **with humanity** and the *beast* **animal**
that are upon the *ground* **face of the earth,**
by my great *power* **strength**
and by my *outstretched* **spread** arm,
and have given it unto whom
it *seemed meet unto me* **hath been straight in my eyes.**
6 And now have I given all these lands
into the hand of
Nebuchadnezzar **Nebukadnets Tsar**
king **sovereign** of *Babylon* **Babel,** my servant;
and the *beasts* **live beings** of the field
have I given him also to serve him.
7 And all *nations* **goyim** shall serve him,
and his son, and his son's son,
until the very time of his land come:
and then many *nations* **goyim** and great *kings* **sovereigns**
shall **cause him to** serve *themselves of him.*
8 And **so be** it *shall come to pass,*
that the *nation* **goyim** and *kingdom* **sovereigndom**
which *will* **shall** not serve the same
Nebuchadnezzar **Nebukadnets Tsar**
king **sovereign** of *Babylon* **Babel,**
and that *will* **shall** not *put* **give** their neck
under the yoke of the *king* **sovereign** of *Babylon* **Babel,**
that *nation will I punish* **goyim shall I visit upon,**
saith the LORD **an oracle of Yah Veh,**
with the sword,
and with the famine, and with the pestilence,
until I have consumed them by his hand.
9 Therefore hearken not ye to your prophets,
nor to your diviners, nor to your dreamers,
nor to your *enchanters* **cloudgazers,**
nor to your sorcerers,
which speak unto you, saying,
Ye shall not serve the *king* **sovereign** of *Babylon* **Babel:**
10 For they prophesy a *lie* **falsehood** unto you,
to remove you far from your *land* **soil;**
and that I should drive you out,
and ye should *perish* **destruct.**
11 But the *nations* **goyim** that bring their neck
sent men into Misrayim

—El Nathan the son of Achbor and
men with him into Misrayim:
23 and they fetched Uri Yah from Misrayim
and brought him to Yah Yaqim the sovereign;
who smote him with the sword
and cast his carcase
into the tombs of the sons of the people:
24 only the hand of Ahikam the son of Shaphan
was with Yirme Yah,
to not give him into the hand of the people
to deathify him.

Yah Hudah Under Nebukadnets Tsar

27 In the beginning
of the sovereigndom of Yah Yaqim
the son of Yoshi Yah sovereign of Yah Hudah,
so be the word to Yirme Yah from Yah Veh, saying,
2 Thus says Yah Veh to me;
Work yourself bonds and yoke poles
and give them on your neck;
3 and send them to the sovereign of Edom
and to the sovereign of Moab
and to the sovereign of the sons of Ammon
and to the sovereign of Sor
and to the sovereign of Sidon
by the hand of the angels who come to Yeru Shalem
—to Sidqi Yah sovereign of Yah Hudah:
4 and misvah them, saying to their adonim,
Thus says Yah Veh Sabaoth Elohim of Yisra El:
Thus say to your adonim:
5 I—I worked the earth with humanity
and the animal on the face of the earth
by my great strength and by my spread arm;
and gave it to whom *were* straight in my eyes.
6 And now I give all these lands into the hand of
Nebukadnets Tsar sovereign of Babel, my servant;
and I also give him the live beings of the field
to serve him:
7 and all goyim serve him
and his son and sons of his son
until the very time of his land comes:
and then many goyim and great sovereigns
have him to serve.
8 And so be it,
the goyim and sovereigndom
who serve not the same
Nebukadnets Tsar sovereign of Babel
—who give not their neck
under the yoke of the sovereign of Babel,
I visit on that goyim
—an oracle of Yah Veh,
with the sword
and with the famine and with the pestilence
until I consume them by his hand.
9 And you, hearken neither to your prophets
nor to your diviners nor to your dreamers
nor to your cloudgazers nor to your sorcerers
who speak to you, saying,
You, serve not the sovereign of Babel:
10 for they prophesy a falsehood to you
to remove you far from your soil:
and that I drive you out and you destruct.
11 And the goyim who bring their neck
under the yoke of the *king* **sovereign** of *Babylon* **Babel**,
and serve him,
those *will* **shall** I *let remain still* **leave**
in their own *land* **soil**,
saith the LORD **an oracle of Yah Veh**;
and they shall *till* **serve** it, and *dwell* **settle** therein.
12 I *spake* **worded** also
to *Zedekiah* **Sidqi Yah**
king **sovereign** of *Judah* **Yah Hudah**
according to all these words, saying,
Bring your necks
under the yoke of the *king* **sovereign** of *Babylon* **Babel**,
and serve him and his people, and live.
13 Why *will* **shall** ye die, thou and thy people,
by the sword, by the famine, and by the pestilence,
as *the LORD* **Yah Veh**
hath *spoken* **worded** against the *nation* **goyim**
that *will* **shall** not serve
the *king* **sovereign** of *Babylon* **Babel**?
14 Therefore hearken not unto
the words of the prophets
that *speak* **say** unto you, saying,
Ye shall not serve the *king* **sovereign** of *Babylon* **Babel**:
for they prophesy a *lie* **falsehood** unto you.
15 For I have not sent them,
saith the LORD **an oracle of Yah Veh**,
yet they prophesy a *lie* **falsehood** in my name;
that I might drive you out,
and that ye might *perish* **destruct**,
ye, and the prophets that prophesy unto you.
16 Also I *spake* **worded**
to the priests and to all this people, saying,
Thus saith *the LORD* **Yah Veh**;
Hearken not to the words of your prophets
that prophesy unto you, saying, Behold,
the *vessels* **instruments**
of the *LORD'S* house **of Yah Veh**

shall now *shortly be brought again* **be quickly returned**
from *Babylon* **Babel**:
for they prophesy a *lie* **falsehood** unto you.
17 Hearken not unto them;
serve the *king* **sovereign** of *Babylon* **Babel**, and live:
wherefore should this city be *laid waste* **parched**?
18 But if they be prophets,
and if the word of *the LORD* **Yah Veh** be with them,
let them *now* **I beseech,** *make intercession* **intercede**
to *the LORD of hosts* **Yah Veh Sabaoth**,
that the *vessels* **instruments** which *are left* **remain**
in the house of *the LORD* **Yah Veh**,
and in the house
of the *king* **sovereign** of *Judah* **Yah Hudah**,
and at *Jerusalem* **Yeru Shalem**,
go not to *Babylon* **Babel**.
19 For thus saith *the LORD*
of hosts **Yah Veh Sabaoth**
concerning the pillars,
and concerning the sea, and concerning the bases,
and concerning
the *residue* **rest** of the *vessels* **instruments**
that remain in this city,
20 Which *Nebuchadnezzar* **Nebukadnets Tsar**
king **sovereign** of *Babylon* **Babel** took not,
when he *carried away captive*
Jeconiah **exiled Yechon Yah**
the son of *Jehoiakim* **Yah Yaqim,**
king **sovereign** of *Judah* **Yah Hudah**
from *Jerusalem* **Yeru Shalem** to *Babylon* **Babel**,
and all the nobles
of *Judah* **Yah Hudah** and *Jerusalem* **Yeru Shalem**;
21 Yea, thus saith *the LORD*
of hosts **Yah Veh Sabaoth**,
the God **Elohim** of *Israel* **Yisra El**,
concerning the *vessels* **instruments**
that remain in the house of *the LORD* **Yah Veh**,
and in the house
of the *king* **sovereign** of *Judah* **Yah Hudah**
and of *Jerusalem* **Yeru Shalem**;
22 They shall be carried to *Babylon* **Babel**,
and there shall they be until the day that I visit them,
saith the LORD **an oracle of Yah Veh**;
then *will I bring them up* **shall I ascend them**,
and *restore* **return** them to this place.
under the yoke of the sovereign of Babel
and serve him,
I leave in their own soil
—an oracle of Yah Veh
to serve it and settle therein.

12 And I worded to Sidqi Yah
sovereign of Yah Hudah
according to all these words, saying,
Bring your necks
under the yoke of the sovereign of Babel;
and serve him and his people, and live.
13 Why die—you and your people,
by the sword, by the famine, and by the pestilence,
as Yah Veh worded against the goyim
who serve not the sovereign of Babel?
14 And hearken not to the words of the prophets
who say to you, saying,
You, serve not the sovereign of Babel:
for they prophesy a falsehood to you:
15 for I sent them not
—an oracle of Yah Veh:
yet they prophesy a falsehood in my name;
so that I drive you out and that you destruct
—you and the prophets who prophesy to you.
16 And I worded to the priests
and to all this people,
saying, Thus says Yah Veh:
Hearken not to the words of your prophets
who prophesy to you, saying,
Behold, the instruments of the house of Yah Veh
now return quickly from Babel!
—for they prophesy a falsehood to you.
17 Hearken not to them;
serve the sovereign of Babel, and live: why
have this city become parched?
18 And if they *are* prophets,
and if the word of Yah Veh *is* with them,
have them, I beseech, intercede to Yah Veh Sabaoth,
so that the instruments remaining
in the house of Yah Veh
and in the house of the sovereign of Yah Hudah
and at Yeru Shalem go not to Babel.
19 For thus says Yah Veh Sabaoth
concerning the pillars and concerning
the sea and concerning the bases,
and concerning the rest of the instruments
remaining in this city,
20 which Nebukadnets Tsar sovereign of Babel
took not,
when he exiled Yechon Yah
the son of Yah Yaqim sovereign of Yah Hudah
from Yeru Shalem to Babel,
and all the nobles of Yah Hudah and Yeru Shalem;
21 Yes, thus says Yah Veh Sabaoth,
Elohim of Yisra El,

concerning the instruments
that remain in the house of Yah Veh,
and in the house
of the sovereign of Yah Hudah
and of Yeru Shalem:
22 They are carried to Babel
—to be there until the day I visit them
—an oracle of Yah Veh:
then I ascend them and return them to this place.

HANAN YAH, THE PSEUDO PROPHET

28 And **so be** it *came to pass* the same year,
in the beginning of the *reign* **sovereigndom**
of *Zedekiah* **Sidqi Yah**
king **sovereign** of *Judah* **Yah Hudah,**
in the fourth year, *and* in the fifth month,
that Hananiah **Hanan Yah**
the son of *Azur* **Azzur** the prophet,
which was of *Gibeon* **Gibon,**
spake **said** unto me in the house of *the LORD* **Yah Veh,**
in the *presence* **eyes** of the priests and of all the people,
saying,
2 Thus *speaketh* **saith**
the LORD of hosts **Yah Veh Sabaoth,**
the God **Elohim** of *Israel* **Yisra El**, saying,
I have broken the yoke
of the *king* **sovereign** of *Babylon* **Babel.**
3 Within two *full* years **of days**
will I bring again **shall I restore** into this place
all the *vessels* **instruments**
of the *LORD'S* house **of Yah Veh,**
that *Nebuchadnezzar* **Nebukadnets Tsar**
king **sovereign** of *Babylon* **Babel**
took away from this place,
and carried them to *Babylon* **Babel**:
4 And I *will bring again* **shall restore** to this place
Jeconiah **Yechon Yah**
the son of *Jehoiakim* **Yah Yaqim**
king **sovereign** of *Judah* **Yah Hudah,**
with all the *captives* **exiles** of *Judah* **Yah Hudah,**
that went into *Babylon* **Babel,**
saith the LORD **an oracle of Yah Veh**:
for I *will* **shall** break the yoke
of the *king* **sovereign** of *Babylon* **Babel.**
5 Then the prophet *Jeremiah* **Yirme Yah**
said unto the prophet *Hananiah* **Hanan Yah**
in the *presence* **eyes** of the priests,
and in the *presence* **eyes** of all the people
that stood in the house of *the LORD* **Yah Veh,**
6 Even the prophet *Jeremiah*
Yirme Yah said, Amen:
the LORD do **Yah Veh work** so:
the LORD perform **Yah Veh raise** thy words
which thou hast prophesied,
to *bring again* **return** the *vessels* **instruments**
of the *LORD'S* house **of Yah Veh,**
and all *that is carried away captive* **the exiles,**
from *Babylon* **Babel** into this place.
7 Nevertheless hear thou *now* **I beseech,**
this word that I *speak* **word** in thine ears,
and in the ears of all the people;
8 The prophets that have
been *before me* **at my face**
and *before thee of old* **at thy face originally**
prophesied both against many *countries* **lands,**
and against great *kingdoms* **sovereigndoms,**
of war, and of evil, and of pestilence.
9 The prophet which
prophesieth of *peace* **shalom,**
when the word of the prophet
shall *come to pass* **become,**
then shall the prophet be known,
that *the LORD* **Yah Veh** hath *truly* **in truth** sent him.
10 Then *Hananiah* **Hanan Yah** the prophet
took the yoke **pole**
from off the prophet *Jeremiah's* **Yirme Yah's** neck,
and brake it.
11 And *Hananiah* **Hanan Yah**
spake **said** in the *presence* **eyes** of all the people,
saying, Thus saith *the LORD* **Yah Veh;**
Even so *will* **shall** I break the yoke
of *Nebuchadnezzar* **Nebukadnets Tsar**
king **sovereign** of *Babylon* **Babel**
from the neck of all *nations* **goyim**
within the space of two *full* years **of days.**
And the prophet *Jeremiah* **Yirme Yah** went his way.
12 Then the word of *the LORD* **Yah Veh**
came unto *Jeremiah* **Yirme Yah** *the prophet,*
after that *Hananiah* **Hanan Yah** the prophet
had broken the yoke **pole** from off the neck of
the prophet *Jeremiah* **Yirme Yah**, saying,
13 Go and *tell Hananiah* **say**
to Hanan Yah, saying,

HANAN YAH, THE PSEUDO PROPHET

28 And so be it, the same year,
in the beginning of the sovereigndom
of Sidqi Yah sovereign of Yah Hudah
—in the fourth year, in the fifth month,

Hanan Yah the son of Azzur the prophet, of Gibon,
says to me in the house of Yah Veh
in the eyes of the priests and of all the people
saying,
2 Thus says Yah Veh Sabaoth Elohim of Yisra El,
saying,
I broke the yoke of the sovereign of Babel.
3 Within two years of days
I return to this place
all the instruments of the house of Yah Veh,
that Nebukadnets Tsar sovereign of Babel
took from this place and carried to Babel:
4 and I restore to this place
Yechon Yah the son of Yah Yaqim
sovereign of Yah Hudah
with all the exiles of Yah Hudah who went into Babel
—an oracle of Yah Veh
for I break the yoke of the sovereign of Babel.
5 And the prophet Yirme Yah
says to the prophet Hanan Yah
in the eyes of the priests
and in the eyes of all the people
standing in the house of Yah Veh,
6 yes, the prophet Yirme Yah says,
Amen! Thus Yah Veh works!
Yah Veh raises the words you prophesied
—to return the instruments of the house of Yah Veh
and all the exiles from Babel to this place:
7 Only hear, I beseech you, this word I word in
your ears and in the ears of all the people;
8 the prophets who were at my face
and at your face originally
prophesied both against many lands
and against great sovereigndoms
—of war and of evil and of pestilence.
9 The prophet who prophesies of shalom,
when that word of the prophet becomes,
then it is known
that Yah Veh in truth sent that prophet.
10 And Hanan Yah the prophet takes the yoke pole
from off the neck of the prophet Yirme Yah
and breaks it:
11 and in the eyes of all the people,
Hanan Yah says, saying, Thus says Yah Veh:
Even thus I break the yoke
of Nebukadnets Tsar sovereign of Babel
from the neck of all goyim
within the space of two years of days.
—and the prophet Yirme Yah goes his way.
12 And so be the word of Yah Veh to Yirme Yah,
after Hanan Yah the prophet
breaks the yoke pole from off the neck
of the prophet Yirme Yah, saying,
13 Go and say to Hanan Yah, saying,
Thus saith *the LORD* **Yah Veh;**
Thou hast broken the *yokes* **yoke poles** of *wood* **timber;**
but thou shalt *make for them* **work in their stead,**
yokes **yoke poles** of iron.
14 For thus saith *the LORD*
of hosts **Yah Veh Sabaoth,**
the God **Elohim** of *Israel* **Yisra El;**
I have *put* **given** a yoke of iron
upon the neck of all these *nations* **goyim,**
that they may serve
Nebuchadnezzar **Nebukadnets Tsar**
king **sovereign** of *Babylon* **Babel;**
and they shall serve him:
and I have given him
the *beasts* **live beings** of the field also.
15 Then said the prophet *Jeremiah* **Yirme Yah**
unto *Hananiah* **Hanan Yah** the prophet,
Hear *now Hananiah* **I beseech Hanan Yah;**
The LORD **Yah Veh** hath not sent thee;
but thou *makest* **causest** this people
to *trust* **confide** in a *lie* **falsehood.**
16 Therefore thus saith *the LORD* **Yah Veh;**
Behold, I *will cast* **shall send** thee
from off the face of the *earth* **soil:**
this year thou shalt die,
because thou hast *taught rebellion* **worded revolt**
against *the LORD* **Yah Veh.**
17 So *Hananiah* **Hanan Yah** the prophet
died the same year in the seventh month.

THE SCROLL OF YIRME YAH TO THE EXILES

29 *Now* these are the words of the *letter* **scroll**
that *Jeremiah* **Yirme Yah** the prophet
sent from *Jerusalem* **Yeru Shalem**
unto the *residue* **remnant** of the elders
which were *carried away captives* **exiled,**
and to the priests, and to the prophets,
and to all the people whom
Nebuchadnezzar **Nebukadnets Tsar**
king **sovereign** of *Babylon* **Babel**
had *carried away captive* **exiled**
from *Jerusalem* **Yeru Shalem** to *Babylon* **Babel;**
2 (After that *Jeconiah* **Yechon**
Yah the *king* **sovereign,**
and the *queen* **lady,** and the eunuchs,
the *princes* **governors** of *Judah* **Yah Hudah**

and *Jerusalem* **Yeru Shalem**,
and the *carpenters* **engravers**, and
the *smiths* **locksmiths**,
were departed from *Jerusalem* **Yeru Shalem**;)
3 By the hand of *Elasah* **El**
Asah the son of Shaphan,
and *Gemariah* **Gemar Yah** the son of *Hilkiah* **Hilqi Yah**,
(whom *Zedekiah* **Sidqi Yah**
king **sovereign** of *Judah* **Yah Hudah**
sent unto *Babylon* **Babel**
to *Nebuchadnezzar* **Nebukadnets Tsar**
king **sovereign** of *Babylon* **Babel**) saying,
4 Thus saith *the LORD of hosts* **Yah Veh Sabaoth**,
the God **Elohim** of *Israel* **Yisra El**,
unto all that are *carried away captives* **exiled**,
whom I have caused to be *carried away* **exiled**
from *Jerusalem* **Yeru Shalem** unto *Babylon* **Babel**;
5 Build ye houses, and *dwell* **settle** *in them*;
and plant gardens, and eat the fruit of them;
6 Take ye *wives* **women**, and
beget **birth** sons and daughters;
and take *wives* **women** for your sons,
and give your daughters to *husbands* **men**,
that they may *bear* **birth** sons and daughters;
that ye may *be increased* **abound** there,
and not *diminished* **diminish**.
7 And seek the *peace* **shalom** of the city
whither I have caused you
to be *carried away captives* **exiled**,
and pray unto *the LORD* **Yah Veh** for it:
for in *the peace* **shalom** *thereof*
shall ye have *peace* **shalom**.
8 For thus saith *the LORD*
of hosts **Yah Veh Sabaoth**,
the God **Elohim** of *Israel* **Yisra El**;
Let not your prophets and your diviners,
that be in the midst of you, deceive you,
neither hearken to your dreams
which ye cause to be dreamed.
9 For they prophesy *falsely*
falsehood unto you in my name:
Thus says Yah Veh:
You broke yoke poles of timber;
and in their stead, I work yoke poles of iron.
14 For thus says Yah Veh
Sabaoth Elohim of Yisra El:
I give a yoke pole of iron
on the neck of all these goyim,
to serve Nebukadnets Tsar sovereign of Babel;
and they serve him:
and I also give him the live beings of the field.
15 And the prophet Yirme Yah
says to Hanan Yah the prophet,
Hear, I beseech, Hanan Yah;
Yah Veh sent you not;
and you have this people confide in a falsehood:
16 so thus says Yah Veh:
Behold, I send you from off the face of the soil:
this year you die,
because you word revolt against Yah Veh.
17 —and Hanan Yah the prophet
dies that same year in the seventh month.

THE SCROLL OF YIRME YAH TO THE EXILES

29 And these are the words of the scroll
Yirme Yah the prophet sent from Yeru Shalem
to the remnant of the elders of the exile
and to the priests and to the prophets
and to all the people
whom Nebukadnets Tsar sovereign of Babel
exiled from Yeru Shalem to Babel
2 —after Yechon Yah the sovereign
and the lady and the eunuchs
and the governors of Yah Hudah and Yeru Shalem
and the engravers and the locksmiths
departed from Yeru Shalem:
3 by the hand of El Asah the son of Shaphan
and Gemar Yah the son of Hilqi Yah,
—whom Sidqi Yah sovereign of Yah Hudah
sent to Babel
to Nebukadnets Tsar sovereign of Babel, saying,
4 Thus says Yah Veh Sabaoth Elohim of Yisra El
—to all the exiles
whom I exiled from Yeru Shalem to Babel,
5 Build houses and settle
and plant gardens and eat their fruit;
6 take women and birth sons and daughters;
and take women for your sons
and give your daughters to men
to birth sons and daughters;
so that you abound there and not diminish:
7 and seek the shalom of the city
where I exile you;
and pray to Yah Veh for it:
for in shalom, shalom becomes.
8 For thus says Yah Veh
Sabaoth Elohim of Yisra El:
See that your prophets and your diviners among you
deceive you not,
and hearken not to the dreams they have you dream:
9 for they prophesy falsehood to you in my name:

I have not sent them,
saith the LORD **an oracle of Yah Veh.**
10 For thus saith *the LORD* **Yah Veh,**
That *after* **according to my mouth,**
seventy years be *accomplished* **fulfilled**
at *Babylon* **Babel,**
I *will* **shall** visit you,
and *perform* **raise** my good word toward you,
in causing you to return to this place.
11 For I know the *thoughts* **fabrications**
that I *think* **fabricate** toward you,
saith the LORD **an oracle of Yah Veh,**
thoughts **fabrications** of *peace* **shalom,** and not of evil,
to give you an *expected end* **posterity and hope.**
12 Then shall ye call upon me,
and ye shall go and pray unto me, and
I *will* **shall** hearken unto you.
13 And *ye* shall seek me, and find me,
when ye shall search for me with all your heart.
14 And I *will* **shall** be found of you,
saith the LORD **an oracle of Yah Veh:**
and I *will turn away* **shall restore** your captivity,
and I *will* **shall** gather you from all the *nations* **goyim,**
and from all the places whither I have driven you,
saith the LORD **an oracle of Yah Veh;**
and I *will bring* **shall return** you *again* into the place
whence I caused you to be *carried away captive* **exiled.**
15 Because ye have said, *The LORD* **Yah Veh**
hath raised us up prophets in *Babylon* **Babel;**
16 *Know that*
thus saith *the LORD* **Yah Veh** of the *king* **sovereign**
that *sitteth* **settleth** upon the throne of David,
and of all the people that *dwelleth* **settleth** in this city,
and of your brethren that are not gone forth with you
into *captivity* **exile;**
17 Thus saith *the LORD of hosts* **Yah Veh Sabaoth;**
Behold, I *will* **shall** send upon them the sword,
the famine, and the pestilence,
and *will make* **shall give** them like *vile* **putrified** figs,
that cannot be eaten, they are so evil.
18 And I *will persecute* **shall pursue after** them
with the sword, with the famine, and with the pestilence,
and *will deliver* **shall give** them
to be removed **for an agitation**
to all the *kingdoms* **sovereigndoms** of the earth,
to be a curse **for an oath,**
and *an astonishment* **a desolation,**
and an hissing, and a reproach,
among all the *nations* **goyim**
whither I have driven them:
19 Because they have not hearkened to my words,
saith the LORD **an oracle of Yah Veh,**
which I sent unto them by my servants the prophets,
rising up **starting** early and sending them;
but ye *would not hear* **hearkened not,**
saith the LORD **an oracle of Yah Veh.**
20 Hear ye therefore the word
of *the LORD* **Yah Veh,**
all ye *of the captivity* **exiles,**
whom I have sent
from *Jerusalem* **Yeru Shalem** to *Babylon* **Babel:**
21 Thus saith *the LORD of hosts* **Yah Veh Sabaoth,**
the God **Elohim** of *Israel* **Yisra El,**
of *Ahab* **Ach Ab** the son of *Kolaiah* **Kola Yah,**
and of *Zedekiah* **Sidqi Yah**
the son of *Maaseiah* **Maase Yah,**
which prophesy a *lie* **falsehood** unto you in my name;
Behold, I *will deliver* **shall give** them
into the hand of *Nebuchadrezzar* **Nebukadnets Tsar**
king **sovereign** of *Babylon* **Babel,**
and he shall *slay* **smite** them *before* **in front of** your eyes;
22 And of them shall be taken
up *a curse* **an abasement**
by all the *captivity* **exiles** of *Judah* **Yah Hudah**
which are in *Babylon* **Babel,** saying,
The LORD make **Yah Veh set** thee
like *Zedekiah* **Sidqi Yah** and like *Ahab* **Ach Ab,**
whom the *king* **sovereign** of *Babylon* **Babel**
roasted **scorched** in the fire;
23 Because they have *committed*
villany **worked folly**
in *Israel* **Yisra El,**
I sent them not
—an oracle of Yah Veh.
10 For thus says Yah Veh:
According to my mouth,
when seventy years are fulfilled at Babel,
I visit you and raise my good word toward you
and return you to to this place.
11 For I know the fabrications
I fabricate toward you
—an oracle of Yah Veh:
fabrications of shalom and not of evil,
to give you a posterity and hope.
12 And you, call on me; and come and pray to me;
and I hearken to you:
13 and you, seek me and find me
when you search for me with all your heart:
14 and you find me
—an oracle of Yah Veh
and I return your captivity
and I gather you from all the goyim

and from all the places I drove you
—an oracle of Yah Veh
and I return you to the place
whence I exiled you;
15 because you said,
Yah Veh raised us prophets in Babel;
16 thus says Yah Veh of the sovereign
who settles on the throne of David,
and of all the people who settle in this city,
and of your brothers who were not exiled with you;
17 thus says Yah Veh Sabaoth:
Behold, I send on them the sword
the famine and the pestilence;
and give them as putrified figs,
not eaten for their evil:
18 and I pursue after them with the sword
with the famine and with the pestilence;
and give them for an agitation
to all the sovereigndoms of the earth
—for an oath and a desolation
and a hissing and a reproach
among all the goyim where I drove them:
19 because they hearken not to my words
—an oracle of Yah Veh
which I sent to them by my servants the prophets
—starting early and sending them;
but you hearken not
—an oracle of Yah Veh.
20 And you, hear the word
of Yah Veh, all you exiles,
whom I sent from Yeru Shalem to Babel:
21 Thus says Yah Veh Sabaoth Elohim of Yisra El,
of Ach Ab the son of Kola Yah
and of Sidqi Yah the son of Maase Yah
who prophesy a falsehood to you in my name;
Behold, I give them into the hand
of Nebukadnets Tsar sovereign of Babel
to smite them in front of your eyes;
22 and take an abasement from them
for all the exiles of Yah Hudah in Babel, saying,
Yah Veh sets you as Sidqi Yah and as Ach Ab,
whom the sovereign of Babel scorched in the fire;
23 because they worked folly in Yisra El
and have *committed adultery* **adulterized**
with their *neighbour's wives* **friend's women,**
and have *spoken lying* **worded false** words in my name,
which I have not *commanded* **misvahed** them;
even I know, and am a witness,
saith the LORD **an oracle of Yah Veh.**
24 Thus shalt thou also *speak* **say**
to *Shemaiah* **Shema Yah**, the *Nehelamite* **Nechlamiy**,
saying,
25 Thus *speaketh* **saith**
the LORD of hosts **Yah Veh Sabaoth,**
the God **Elohim** of *Israel* **Yisra El**, saying,
Because thou hast sent *letters* **scrolls** in thy name
unto all the people that are at *Jerusalem* **Yeru Shalem,**
and to *Zephaniah* **Sephan Yah**
the son of *Maaseiah* **Maase Yah** the priest,
and to all the priests, saying,
26 *The LORD* **Yah Veh** hath *made* **given** thee priest
in the stead of *Jehoiada* **Yah Yada** the priest,
that ye should be *officers* **overseers**
in the house of *the LORD* **Yah Veh,**
for every man that is *mad* **insane,**
and *maketh himself a prophet* **prophesieth,**
that thou shouldest *put* **give** him
in prison **to the stockade**, and in the stocks.
27 Now therefore why hast
thou not *reproved* **rebuked**
Jeremiah **Yirme Yah** of *Anathoth* **Anathothiy**, which
maketh himself a prophet **prophesieth** to you?
28 For therefore he sent unto us in *Babylon* **Babel,**
saying, This *captivity* is long:
build ye houses, and *dwell* **settle** *in them*;
and plant gardens, and eat the fruit of them.
29 And *Zephaniah* **Sephan Yah** the priest
read **called out** this *letter* **scroll**
in the ears of *Jeremiah* **Yirme Yah** the prophet.
30 Then came the word of *the LORD* **Yah Veh**
unto *Jeremiah* **Yirme Yah**, saying,
31 Send to all *them of the*
captivity **the exiles**, saying,
Thus saith *the LORD* **Yah Veh**
concerning *Shemaiah* **Shema Yah**
the *Nehelamite* **Nechlamiy;**
Because that *Shemaiah* **Shema Yah**
hath prophesied unto you, and I sent him not,
and he caused you to *trust* **confide** in a *lie* **falsehood:**
32 Therefore thus saith *the LORD* **Yah Veh;**
Behold, I *will punish* **shall visit upon**
Shemaiah **Shema Yah** the *Nehelamite* **Nechlamiy,**
and his seed:
he shall not have a man
to *dwell* **settle** among this people;
neither shall he *behold* **see** the good
that I *will do* **shall work** for my people,
saith the LORD **an oracle of Yah Veh;**
because he hath *taught rebellion* **worded revolt**
against *the LORD* **Yah Veh.**

YISRA EL RESTORED

30 The word that came to *Jeremiah* **Yirme Yah**
from *the LORD* **Yah Veh**, saying,
2 Thus *speaketh* **saith**
the LORD God **Yah Veh Elohim**
of *Israel* **Yisra El**, saying,
Write **Inscribe** thee all the words
that I have *spoken* **worded** unto thee in a *book* **scroll**.
3 For, *lo* **behold**, the days come,
saith the LORD **an oracle of Yah Veh**,
that I *will bring again* **shall restore**
the captivity of my people
Israel **Yisra El** and *Judah* **Yah Hudah**,
saith *the LORD* **Yah Veh**:
and I *will* **shall** cause them to return to the land
that I gave to their fathers, and they shall possess it.
4 And these are the words
that *the LORD spake* **Yah Veh worded**
concerning *Israel* **Yisra El**
and concerning *Judah* **Yah Hudah**.
5 For thus saith *the LORD* **Yah Veh**;
We have heard a voice of trembling, of
fear, and not of *peace* **shalom**.
6 Ask ye *now* **I beseech**, and see
whether a *man doth travail with child* **male shall birth**?
and adulterized with the women of their friends;
and worded false words in my name
which I misvahed them not;
—I know and witness
—an oracle of Yah Veh.
24 And say thus to Shema Yah the Nechlamiy,
saying,
25 Thus says Yah Veh Sabaoth Elohim of Yisra El,
saying,
Because you sent scrolls in your name
to all the people at Yeru Shalem
and to Sephan Yah the son of Maase Yah the priest
and to all the priests, saying,
26 Yah Veh gives you as priest
in the stead of Yah Yada the priest;
being overseers in the house of Yah Veh,
for every insane man who prophesies,
to give him to the stockade and in the stocks.
27 And now why rebuke you not
Yirme Yah of Anathothiy who prophesies to you?
28 For he sent to us in Babel, saying, This *is* long: build
houses and settle and plant gardens and eat their fruit.
29 —and Sephan Yah the priest calls out this scroll
in the ears of Yirme Yah the prophet.
30 And so be the word of Yah Veh to Yirme Yah,
saying,
31 Send to all the exiles, saying,
Thus says Yah Veh
concerning Shema Yah the Nechlamiy:
Because Shema Yah prophesied to you
and I sent him not;
and he had you confide in a falsehood:
32 so thus says Yah Veh:
Behold, I visit on Shema Yah the Nechlamiy
and his seed:
he neither has a man to settle among this people
nor sees the good I work for my people
—an oracle of Yah Veh
because he words revolt against Yah Veh.

YISRA EL RESTORED

30 So be the word to Yirme Yah from Yah Veh,
saying,
2 Thus says Yah Veh Elohim of Yisra El: saying,
Inscribe in a scroll all the words I word to you.
3 For, behold, days come,
—an oracle of Yah Veh
that I restore the captivity
of my people Yisra El and Yah Hudah,
says Yah Veh:
and I restore them to the land I gave to their fathers;
and they possess it.
4 And these are the words Yah Veh worded
concerning Yisra El and concerning Yah Hudah:
5 for thus says Yah Veh:
We hear a voice of trembling;
of fear, and not of shalom:
6 ask, I beseech, and see,
Is a male birthing?
wherefore do I see every *man* **mighty**
with his hands on his loins,
as *a woman in travail* **in birthing**,
and all faces are turned into *paleness* **pale green**?
7 *Alas* **Ho**! for that day is
great, so that none is like it:
it is even the time of *Jacob's trouble*
Yaaqov's tribulation,
but he shall be saved out of it.
8 *For* **And so be** it *shall come to pass*, in that day,
saith the LORD of hosts **an oracle of Yah Veh Sabaoth**,
that I *will* **shall** break his yoke from off thy neck,
and *will burst* **shall tear** thy bonds,
and strangers shall no more
cause him to serve *themselves of him*:

9 But they shall serve
the LORD **Yah Veh** their *God* **Elohim,**
and David their *king* **sovereign,**
whom I *will* **shall** raise *up* unto them.
10 Therefore *fear* **awe** thou not,
O my servant *Jacob* **Yaaqov,**
saith the LORD **an oracle of Yah Veh;**
neither be dismayed, O *Israel* **Yisra El:** for, *lo* **behold,**
I *will save thee* **am thy saviour** from afar,
and thy seed from the land of their captivity;
and *Jacob* **Yaaqov** shall return,
and shall *be in* rest, and *be quiet* **relax,**
and none shall make him *afraid* **tremble.**
11 For I am with thee,
saith the LORD **an oracle of Yah Veh,**
to save thee:
though I *make a full end* **work a final finish**
of all *nations* **goyim** whither I have scattered thee,
yet I *will* **shall** not *make a full end* **work a final finish**
of thee:
but I *will correct* **shall discipline** thee
in *measure* **judgment,**
and *will not leave thee altogether unpunished.*
in exonerating, shall not exonerate thee
12 For thus saith *the LORD* **Yah Veh,** Thy *bruise*
breech is incurable, and thy wound is *grievous* **worn.**
13 There is none to plead thy cause,
that thou mayest be *bound up* **bandaged:**
thou hast no *healing medicines* **bandage healers.**
14 All thy lovers have forgotten
thee; they seek thee not;
for I have *wounded* **smitten** thee
with the wound of an enemy,
with the chastisement of a cruel one,
for the *multitude* **abundance**
of *thine iniquity* **thy perversity;**
because thy sins were *increased* **mighty.**
15 Why criest thou for *thine affliction* **thy breech?**
thy sorrow is incurable
for the *multitude* **abundance**
of *thine iniquity* **thy perversity:**
because thy sins were *increased* **mighty,**
I have *done* **worked** these *things* unto thee.
16 Therefore all they that *devour* **consume** thee
shall be *devoured* **consumed;**
and all *thine adversaries* **thy tribulators,**
every one of them, shall go into captivity;
and they that *spoil* **plunder** thee
shall be *a spoil* **plundered,**
and all that *prey upon* **plunder** thee
will **shall** I give for a *prey* **plunder.**
17 For I *will restore* **shall ascend** health unto thee,
and I *will* **shall** heal thee of thy wounds,
saith the LORD **an oracle of Yah Veh;**
because they called thee *an Outcast* **Expelled,** *saying,*
This is *Zion* **Siyon,** whom no man seeketh after.
18 Thus saith *the LORD* **Yah Veh;** Behold,
I *will bring again* **shall restore**
the captivity of *Jacob's* **Yaaqov's** tents,
and *have* **shall** mercy *on* his *dwellingplaces* **tabernacles;**
and the city shall be builded upon her own heap,
and the *palace* **citadel** shall *remain* **be settled**
after the *manner* **judgment** *thereof.*
19 And out of them
shall proceed *thanksgiving* **spread hands**
and the voice of them that *make merry* **ridicule:**
Why see I all the mighty with his hands on his loins
as in birthing?
—and all faces turn into pale green?
7 Ho! for that day is great; none like it:
it is even the time of the tribulation of Yaaqov,
but he is saved from it.
8 For so be it, in that day,
—an oracle of Yah Veh Sabaoth
that I break his yoke from off your neck,
and tear your bonds,
and he no more serves strangers:
9 and they serve Yah Veh their Elohim;
and David their sovereign whom I raise to them.
10 And you, neither awe, O my servant Yaaqov
—an oracle of Yah Veh;
nor dismay, O Yisra El:
for behold, I am your saviour from afar
and your seed from the land of their captivity;
and Yaaqov returns and rests and relaxes
and no one trembles him.
11 For I *am* with you
—an oracle of Yah Veh
to save you:
though I work a final finish
of all goyim where I scattered you,
yet I not work a final finish of you:
and I discipline you in judgment,
and in exonerating, I exonerate you not.
For thus says Yah Veh:
Your breech is incurable and your wound *is* worn:
13 —no one pleads your cause
—bandages you, no bandage healers.
14 All your lovers forget you; they seek you not:
for I smite you with the wound of an enemy;

with the chastisement of a cruel one;
for the abundance of your perversity;
your sins are mighty.
15 Why cry for your breech?
your sorrow is incurable
for the abundance of your perversity:
your sins are mighty, I worked these to you.
16 So all who consume you are consumed;
and all your tribulators—every one of them
go into captivity;
and they who plunder you, are plundered;
and all who plunder you, I give for a plunder:
17 for I ascend health to you
and I heal you of your wounds
—an oracle of Yah Veh
because they called you, Expelled
—Siyon, whom no man seeks after.
18 Thus says Yah Veh:
Behold, I restore the captivity of the tents of Yaaqov
and mercy his tabernacles;
and build the city on her own heap,
and settle the citadel according to the judgment.
19 And spread hands proceed from them
and the voice of them who ridicule:
and I *will multiply* **shall abound** them,
and they shall not be *few* **diminished**;
I *will also glorify* **shall honour** them,
and they shall not be *small* **belittled**.
20 Their *children* **sons** also shall
be as *aforetime* **formerly**,
and their *congregation* **witness**
shall be established *before me* **at my face**,
and I *will punish* **shall visit upon** all that oppress them.
21 And their *nobles* **mighty** shall be of themselves,
and their *governor* **sovereign**
shall proceed from the midst of them;
and I *will* **shall** cause him to *draw near* **approach**,
and he shall approach unto me:
for who is this
that *engaged* **pleased** his heart to approach unto me?
saith the LORD **an oracle of Yah Veh**.
22 And ye shall be my people,
and I *will* **shall** be your *God* **Elohim**.
23 Behold, the *whirlwind*
storm of *the LORD* **Yah Veh**
goeth forth with fury,
a continuing *whirlwind* **storm**:
it shall *fall with pain* **whirl** upon the head of the wicked.
24 The *fierce anger* **fuming**
wrath of *the LORD* **Yah Veh**
shall not return,
until he hath *done* **worked** it,
and until he have *performed* **raised**
the *intents* **intrigue** of his heart:
in the latter days ye shall *consider* **discern** it.

THE ETERNAL LOVE OF YAH VEH

31 At the same time,
saith the LORD **an oracle of Yah Veh**,
will I **shall** be *the God* **Elohim**
of all the families of *Israel* **Yisra El**,
and they shall be my people.
2 Thus saith *the LORD* **Yah Veh**,
The people, *which were left* **the survivors** of the sword
found *grace* **charism** in the wilderness;
even Israel **Yisra El**, when I went to cause him to rest.
3 *The LORD* **Yah Veh**
hath *appeared* **been seen**
of old unto me **by me in the distance**, *saying*,
Yea, I have loved thee with an *everlasting* **eternal** love:
therefore with lovingkindness have I drawn thee.
4 Again I *will* **shall** build thee,
and thou shalt be built,
O virgin of *Israel* **Yisra El**:
thou shalt again be adorned
with thy *tabrets* **tambourines**,
and shalt go forth in the *dances* **round dancing**
of them that *make merry* **entertain**.
5 Thou shalt yet plant vines
upon the mountains of *Samaria* **Shomeron**:
the planters shall plant,
and shall *eat* **profane** them *as common things*.
6 For there shall be a day,
that the *watchmen* **guards**
upon the mount *Ephraim* **Ephrayim** shall *cry* **call**,
Arise ye, and let us *go up* **ascend** to *Zion* **Siyon**
unto *the LORD* **Yah Veh** our *God* **Elohim.**
7 For thus saith *the LORD* **Yah Veh**;
Sing **Shout** with *gladness* **cheerfulness** for *Jacob* **Yaaqov**,
and *shout* **resound** among the chief
of the *nations* **goyim**:
publish ye **hearken**, praise ye, and say,
O *LORD* **Yah Veh**, save thy people,
the *remnant* **survivors** of *Israel* **Yisra El**.
8 Behold,
I *will* **shall** bring them from the north *country* **land**,
and gather them from the *coasts*
flanks of the *earth* **land**,
and with them the blind and the lame,
the woman with child

and her that *travaileth with child* **birtheth** together:
a great *company* **congregation** shall return thither.
9 They shall come with weeping,
and with supplications *will* **shall** I lead them:
I *will* **shall** cause them
to walk by the *rivers* **wadies** of waters in a straight way,
wherein they shall not *stumble* **falter**:
for I am a father to *Israel* **Yisra El**,
and *Ephraim* **Ephrayim** is my *firstborn* **firstbirthed**.
10 Hear the word of *the LORD*
Yah Veh, O ye *nations* **goyim**,
and I abound them and they diminish not;
I honor them, and they *are* not belittled:
20 and his sons become as formerly
and their witness establish at my face:
and I visit on all who oppress them.
21 And their mighty become from themselves,
and their sovereign proceeds from their midst:
and I have him approach; and he approaches to me:
for who is this
who pleases his heart to approach to me?
—an oracle of Yah Veh.
22 And you are my people,
and I am your Elohim.
23 Behold, the storm of Yah
Veh goes forth with fury
—a continuing storm:
it whirls on the head of the wicked.
24 The fuming wrath of Yah Veh returns not
until he so works,
and until he raises the intrigue of his heart:
in the latter days we discern.

The Eternal Love Of Yah Veh

31 At the same time,
—an oracle of Yah Veh
I become Elohim of all the families of Yisra El,
and they become my people.
2 Thus says Yah Veh,
The people, the survivors of the sword
find charism in the wilderness;
Yisra El, when I go to rest him.
3 Yah Veh is seen by me in the distance, Yes, I love you
with an eternal love: so with lovingkindness I draw you:
4 in building, I build you again,
O virgin of Yisra El:
adorn you again with your tambourines
and you come forth
in the round dancing of entertainers:
5 again, you plant vines
on the mountains of Shomeron: the
planters plant and profane.
6 For there is a day,
that the guards call out on the mount Ephrayim,
Rise, and we ascend to Siyon
to Yah Veh our Elohim.
7 For thus says Yah Veh:
Shout with cheerfulness for Yaaqov
and resound among the chief of the goyim:
hearken, praise, and say,
O Yah Veh, save your people,
the survivors of Yisra El.
8 Behold, I bring them from the north land,
and gather them from the flanks of the land;
the blind and the lame
the woman with child and she who births
together among them:
a great congregation returns there:
9 they come with weeping;
and with supplications I lead them:
I walk them by the wadies of waters in a straight way
wherein they falter not:
for I *am* a father to Yisra El
and Ephrayim *is* my firstbirthed.
10 Hear the word of Yah Veh, O you goyim!
and *declare* **tell** it in the *isles* **islands** afar off, and say,
He that *scattered Israel* **winnowed Yisra El**
will **shall** gather him, and *keep* **guard** him,
as a *shepherd doth* **tender** his *flock* **drove**.
11 For *the LORD* **Yah Veh** hath
redeemed *Jacob* **Yaaqov**,
and *ransomed* **redeemed** him
from the hand *of him* that was stronger than he.
12 Therefore they shall come
and *sing* **shout** in the height of *Zion* **Siyon**,
and shall flow together
to the goodness of *the LORD* **Yah Veh**,
for *wheat* **crop**, and for *wine* **juice**, and for oil,
and for the *young* **sons** of the flock and of the herd:
and their soul shall be as a *watered* **saturated** garden;
and they shall not
sorrow any more at all **add to languish**.
13 Then shall the virgin
rejoice **cheer** in the *dance* **round dancing**,
both *young men* **youths** and *old* **elders** together:
for I *will* **shall** turn their mourning into *joy* **rejoicing**,
and *will comfort* **shall sigh over** them,
and *make* **cheer** them *rejoice* from their *sorrow* **grief**.
14 And I *will* **shall** satiate the
soul of the priests with fatness,

and my people shall be satisfied with my goodness,
saith the LORD **an oracle of Yah Veh.**
15 Thus saith *the LORD* **Yah Veh;**
A voice was heard in Ramah,
lamentation, *and bitter* weeping **of bitterness;**
Rahel **Rachel** weeping for her *children* **sons**
refused to *be comforted* **sigh** for her *children* **sons,**
because they were not.
16 Thus saith *the LORD* **Yah Veh;**
Refrain **Withhold** thy voice from weeping,
and thine eyes from tears:
for *thy work shall be rewarded*
thou shalt have a hire for thy deeds,
saith the LORD **an oracle of Yah Veh;**
and they shall *come again* **return**
from the land of the enemy.
17 And there is hope in thine end,
saith the LORD **an oracle of Yah Veh,**
that thy *children* **sons**
shall *come again* **return** to their own border.
18 **In hearing,** I have *surely*
heard *Ephraim* **Ephrayim**
bemoaning **wagging over** himself *thus;*
Thou hast *chastised* **disciplined** me,
and I was *chastised* **disciplined,**
as a *bullock unaccustomed to the yoke* **calf not trained:**
turn thou me, and I shall be turned;
for thou art *the LORD* **Yah Veh** my *God* **Elohim.**
19 *Surely* after that I *was turned*
returned, I *repented* **sighed;**
and after that I was instructed,
I *smote* **slapped** upon my *thigh* **flank:**
I was *ashamed* **shamed,** yea, even confounded,
because I did bear the reproach of my youth.
20 Is *Ephraim* **Ephrayim** my *dear* **esteemed** son?
is he a pleasant child—**a child of delights?** for
since I *spake* **worded sufficient** against him,
I do earnestly **In remembering, I** remember him still:
therefore my *bowels* **inwards** are troubled for him;
I will surely have mercy upon
In mercying, I shall mercy him,
saith the LORD **an oracle of Yah Veh.**
21 *Set thee up waymarks* **Station monuments,**
make **set** thee *high heaps* **pillars:**
set thine heart toward the highway,
even the way which thou wentest:
turn again, O virgin of *Israel* **Yisra El,**
turn again to these thy cities.
22 How long *wilt* **shalt** thou go about,
O thou *backsliding* **apostate** daughter?
for *the LORD* **Yah Veh**
hath created *a new thing* **newness** in the earth,
A *woman* **female** shall *compass* **surround** a *man* **mighty.**
23 Thus saith *the LORD of hosts* **Yah Veh Sabaoth,**
the God **Elohim** of *Israel* **Yisra El;**
As yet they shall *use* **say** this *speech* **word**
in the land of *Judah* **Yah Hudah** and in the cities *thereof,*
when I shall *bring again* **restore** their captivity;
And tell it in the islands afar off, and say,
He who winnows Yisra El
gathers him and guards him
as a tender to his drove.
11 For Yah Veh redeems Yaaqov
—redeems him
from the hand stronger than his:
12 and they come and shout in the height of Siyon;
and flow together to the goodness of Yah Veh
for crop and for juice and for oil
and for the sons of the flock and of the herd:
and their soul becomes as a saturated garden;
and they add not to languish.
13 Then the virgin cheers in the round dancing
—both youths and elders together
for I turn their mourning into rejoicing,
and sigh over them and cheer them from their grief:
14 and I satiate the soul of the priests with fatness
and satisfy my people with my goodness
—an oracle of Yah Veh.
15 Thus says Yah Veh:
A voice is heard in Ramah
—lamentation; weeping of bitterness:
Rachel weeping for her sons
refuses to sigh for her sons, because they are not.
16 Thus says Yah Veh:
Withhold your voice from weeping
and your eyes from tears:
there is a hire for your deeds
—an oracle of Yah Veh
and they return from the land of the enemy.
17 And there is hope in your end
—an oracle of Yah Veh
that your sons return to their own border.
18 In hearing, I hear Ephrayim
wagging over himself;
You disciplined me
—disciplined me as a calf not trained:
return me, and I return;
for you *are* Yah Veh my Elohim.
19 Surely after I returned, I sighed;
and after I *was* instructed, I slapped my flank:

I shamed, yes, even confounded,
because I bore the reproach of my youth.
20 Is Ephrayim my esteemed son?
A child of delights?
For since I worded sufficient against him,
in remembering, I remember him still:
so my inwards trouble for him;
In mercying, I mercy him
—an oracle of Yah Veh.
21 Station monuments! Set pillars!
Set your heart toward the highway in the way you go!
Return, O virgin of Yisra El!
Return to these your cities!
22 How long go you about,
O you apostate daughter?
for Yah Veh creates newness in the earth;
a female surrounds the mighty.
23 Thus says Yah Veh Sabaoth Elohim of Yisra El:
They still say this word
in the land of Yah Hudah and in the cities,
when I restore their captivity;
The LORD **Yah Veh** bless thee,
O habitation **of rest** of *justice* **justness**,
and mountain of holiness.
24 And there shall *dwell* **settle**
in *Judah* **Yah Hudah** itself,
and in all the cities *thereof* together,
husbandmen **cultivators**,
and they that go forth with *flocks* **droves**.
25 For I have satiated the *weary* **languid** soul,
and I have *replenished* **fulfilled** every
sorrowful **languishing** soul.
26 Upon this I awaked, and *beheld* **saw**;
and my sleep *was sweet unto* **pleased** me.
27 Behold, the days come,
saith the LORD **an oracle of Yah Veh**,
that I *will sow* **shall seed** the house of *Israel* **Yisra El**
and the house of *Judah* **Yah Hudah**
with the seed of *man* **humanity**,
and with the seed of *beast* **animal**.
28 And **so be** it *shall come to pass*,
that like as I have watched over them,
to *pluck up* **uproot**, and to break down,
and to *throw down* **demolish**, and to destroy,
and to *afflict* **vilify**;
so *will* **shall** I watch over them, to build, and to plant,
saith the LORD **an oracle of Yah Veh**.
29 In those days they shall say no more,
The fathers have eaten a sour grape,
and the *children's* **sons's** teeth are *set on edge* **dull**.
30 But every *one* **man** shall die
for his own *iniquity* **perversity**:
every man **all humanity** that eateth the sour grape,
his teeth shall be *set on edge* **dulled**.

Yah Veh Cuts A New Covenant

31 Behold, the days come,
saith the LORD **an oracle of Yah Veh**,
that I *will make* **shall cut** a new covenant
with the house of *Israel* **Yisra El**,
and with the house of *Judah* **Yah Hudah**:
32 Not according to the covenant
that I *made* **cut** with their fathers
in the day that I *took* **held** them by the hand
to bring them out of the land of *Egypt* **Misrayim**;
which my covenant they brake,
although I was *an husband* **a master** unto them,
saith the LORD **an oracle of Yah Veh**:
33 But this shall be the covenant
that I *will make* **shall cut** with the
house of *Israel* **Yisra El**;
After those days,
saith the LORD **an oracle of Yah Veh**,
I *will put* **shall give** my *law* **torah**
in their *inward parts* **inwards**,
and *write* **inscribe** it in their hearts;
and *will* **shall** be their *God* **Elohim**,
and they shall be my people.
34 And they shall teach no more
every man his *neighbour* **friend**,
and every man his brother, saying,
Know *the LORD* **Yah Veh**:
for they shall all know me,
from the least of them unto the greatest of them,
saith the LORD **an oracle of Yah Veh**:
for I *will* **shall** forgive their *iniquity* **perversity**,
and I *will* **shall** remember their sin no more.
35 Thus saith *the LORD* **Yah Veh**,
which giveth the sun for a light by day,
and the *ordinances* **statutes** of the moon and of the stars
for a light by night,
which *divideth* **spliteth** the sea
when the waves *thereof* roar;
The LORD of hosts **Yah Veh Sabaoth** is his name:
36 If those *ordinances* **statutes**
depart from *before me* **my face**,
saith the LORD **an oracle of Yah Veh**,
then the seed of *Israel* **Yisra El** also
shall *cease* **shabbathizeth**
from being a *nation before me* **goyim at my face**

for ever **all the days.**
37 Thus saith *the LORD* **Yah Veh;**
If *heaven* **the heavens** above can be measured,
Yah Veh bless you,
O habitation of rest of justness, mountain of holiness.
24 And settling in Yah Hudah
and in all the cities together
are cultivators and they who go forth with droves.
25 For I satiate the languid soul,
and I fill full every languishing soul.
26 On this I waken, and see;
and my sleep pleases me.
27 Behold, days come,
—an oracle of Yah Veh
that I seed the house of Yisra El
and the house of Yah Hudah
with the seed of humanity
and with the seed of animal.
28 And so be it, as I watched over them
to uproot and to break down
and to demolish and to destroy and to vilify,
thus I watch over them
to build and to plant
—an oracle of Yah Veh.
29 In those days, they say no more,
The fathers eat sour grapes,
and the teeth of the sons are dull.
30 But every man dies for his own perversity:
all humanity who eat the sour grape, dulls his teeth.

YAH VEH CUTS A NEW COVENANT

31 Behold, days come,
—an oracle of Yah Veh
that I cut a new covenant with the house of Yisra El
and with the house of Yah Hudah:
32 not according to the covenant
I cut with their fathers
in the day I held them by the hand
to bring them from the land of Misrayim
—my covenant which they broke,
although I was their master
—an oracle of Yah Veh:
33 For this *is* the covenant
I cut with the house of Yisra El:
After those days,
—an oracle of Yah Veh
I give my torah in their inwards and inscribe
it in their hearts; and I become their
Elohim and they become my people:
34 and no more teaches every man his friend,
and every man his brother, saying,
Know Yah Veh!
For they all know me
—from the least of them to the greatest of them
—an oracle of Yah Veh
for I forgive their perversity
and I remember their sin no more.
35 Thus says Yah Veh
who gives the sun for a light by day
and the statutes of the moon and of the stars
for a light by night:
who splits the sea when the waves roar;
Yah Veh Sabaoth *is* his name:
36 If those statutes depart from my face
—an oracle of Yah Veh
then the seed of Yisra El
also shabbathizes from being a goyim at my face
all days.
37 Thus says Yah Veh:
If you measure the heavens above,
and the foundations of the earth
searched out beneath **probed below,**
I *will* **shall** also
cast off **spurn** all the seed of *Israel* **Yisra El**
for all that they have *done* **worked,**
saith the LORD **an oracle of Yah Veh.**

THE NEW CITY

38 Behold, the days come,
saith the LORD **an oracle of Yah Veh,**
that the city shall be built to *the LORD* **Yah Veh**
from the tower of *Hananeel* **Hanan El**
unto the *gate* **portal** of the corner.
39 And the measuring line shall *yet* go forth
over against **in front of** it upon the hill Gareb, and
shall *compass about to Goath* **surround Goah.**
40 And the whole valley of
the *dead bodies* **carcases,**
and of the *ashes* **fat,**
and all the fields unto the *brook* **wadi** of *Kidron* **Qidron,**
unto the corner of the horse *gate* **portal**
toward the *east* **rising,**
shall be holy unto *the LORD* **Yah Veh;**
it shall not be *plucked up* **uprooted,**
nor thrown down any more *for ever* **eternally.**

YIRME YAH SHUT UP

32 The word that came to *Jeremiah* **Yirme Yah**
from *the LORD* **Yah Veh**
in the tenth year of *Zedekiah* **Sidqi Yah** *king* **sovereign**
of *Judah* **Yah Hudah,** which **year** was the eighteenth
year of *Nebuchadrezzar* **Nebukadnets Tsar.**

2 For then the *king* **sovereign**
of *Babylon's army* **Babel's valiant**
besieged *Jerusalem* **Yeru Shalem**:
and *Jeremiah* **Yirme Yah** the prophet
was shut up in the court of the *prison* **target area**,
which was in
the *king* **sovereign** of *Judah's* **Yah Hudah's** house.
3 For *Zedekiah* **Sidqi Yah**
king **sovereign** of *Judah* **Yah Hudah**
had shut him up, saying,
Wherefore dost thou prophesy, *and say* **saying**,
Thus saith *the LORD* **Yah Veh**,
Behold, I *will* **shall** give this city
into the hand of the *king* **sovereign** of *Babylon* **Babel**,
and he shall *take* **capture** it;
4 And *Zedekiah* **Sidqi Yah**
king **sovereign** of *Judah* **Yah Hudah**
shall not escape
out of the hand of the *Chaldeans* **Kesediym**,
but **in giving,** shall *surely* be *delivered* **given**
into the hand of the *king* **sovereign** of *Babylon* **Babel**,
and shall *speak* **word** with him mouth to mouth,
and his eyes shall *behold* **see** his eyes;
5 And he shall *lead Zedekiah* **carry Sidqi Yah**
to *Babylon* **Babel**,
and there shall he be until I visit him,
saith the LORD **an oracle of Yah Veh**:
though ye fight with the *Chaldeans* **Kesediym**,
ye shall not prosper.

YIRME YAH CHATTELS A FIELD

6 And *Jeremiah* **Yirme Yah** said,
The word of *the LORD* **Yah Veh** came unto me, saying,
7 Behold,
Hanameel **Hanam El** the son of Shallum thine uncle
shall come unto thee, saying,
Buy **Chattel** thee my field that is in Anathoth:
for the *right* **judgment** of redemption
is thine to *buy* **chattel** it.
8 So *Hanameel* **Hanam El** mine uncle's son
came to me in the court of the *prison* **target area**
according to the word of *the LORD* **Yah Veh**,
and said unto me,
Buy **Chattel** my field, I *pray* **beseech** thee,
that is in Anathoth,
which is in the *country* **land** of *Benjamin* **Ben Yamin**:
for the *right* **judgment** of *inheritance* **possession** is thine,
and the redemption is thine; *buy* **chattel** it for thyself.
Then I knew
that this was the word of *the LORD* **Yah Veh**.
and probe the foundations of the earth below,

I also spurn all the seed of Yisra El for all they worked
—an oracle of Yah Veh.

THE NEW CITY

38 Behold, days come,
—an oracle of Yah Veh
that the city to Yah Veh is built
from the tower of Hanan El
to the portal of the corner:
39 and the measuring line goes forth
in front of it to the hill Gareb;
and surrounds Goah.
40 And the whole valley of
the carcases and of the fat
and all the fields to the wadi of Qidron
to the corner of the horse portal toward the rising
are holy to Yah Veh
—neither uprooted
nor thrown down any more eternally.

YIRME YAH SHUT UP

32 So be the word to Yirme Yah from Yah Veh
in the tenth year of Sidqi Yah sovereign of Yah Hudah
—the year, the eighteenth year of Nebukadnets Tsar:
2 and then the valiant of the sovereign of Babel
besiege Yeru Shalem:
and shut Yirme Yah the prophet
in the court of the target area,
in the house of the sovereign of Yah Hudah:
3 where Sidqi Yah sovereign of Yah Hudah
shut him, saying,
Why prophesy you, saying,
Thus says Yah Veh: Behold,
I give this city into the hand of the sovereign of Babel,
to capture it?
4 And Sidqi Yah sovereign of Yah Hudah
escapes not from the hand of the Kesediym
but in giving,
is given into the hand of the sovereign of Babel;
and words with him mouth to mouth
and his eyes see his eyes;
5 and he carries Sidqi Yah to Babel
and is there until I visit him
—an oracle of Yah Veh
though you fight with the Kesediym,
you prosper not?

YIRME YAH CHATTELS A FIELD

6 And Yirme Yah says,
So be the word of Yah Veh to me, saying,

7 Behold, Hanam El the son
of Shallum your uncle
comes to you, saying,
Chattel my field in Anathoth:
for the judgment of redemption is yours to chattel.
8 And Hanam El the son of my uncle
comes to me in the court of the target area
according to the word of Yah Veh;
and says to me,
Chattel, I beseech you,
my field in Anathoth in the land of Ben Yamin:
for the judgment of possession is yours;
and the redemption is yours:
chattel it for yourself:
and I know this *is* the word of Yah Veh.
exeGeses ready research BIBLE
9 And I *bought* **chatteled** the
field of *Hanameel* **Hanam El**
my uncle's son, that was in Anathoth,
and weighed him the *money* **silver**,
even seventeen shekels of silver.
10 And I *subscribed* **inscribed** the *evidence* **scroll**,
and sealed *it*, and *took* witnesses **witnessed**,
and weighed him the *money* **silver** in the balances.
11 So I took the *evidence* **scroll**
of the *purchase* **chattel**,
both that which was sealed
according to the *law* **misvah** and *custom* **statute**,
and that which was *open* **exposed**:
12 And I gave the *evidence*
scroll of the *purchase* **chattel**
unto Baruch the son of *Neriah* **Neri Yah**,
the son of *Maaseiah* **Machse Yah**,
in the *sight* **eyes** of *Hanameel* **Hanam El**
mine uncle's *son*,
and in the *presence* **eyes** of the witnesses
that *subscribed* **inscribed** the *book* **scroll**
of the *purchase* **chattel**,
before **in the eyes of** all the *Jews* **Yah Hudiym**
that sat in the court of the *prison* **target area**.
13 And I *charged* **misvahed** Baruch
before them **in their eyes**, saying,
14 Thus saith *the LORD of hosts* **Yah Veh Sabaoth**,
the God **Elohim** of *Israel* **Yisra El**;
Take these *evidences* **scrolls**,
this *evidence* **scroll** of the *purchase* **chattel**,
both which is sealed,
and this *evidence* **scroll** which is *open* **exposed**;
and *put* **give** them
in *an earthen vessel* **a potsherd instrument**,
that they may *continue* **stand** many days.
15 For thus saith *the LORD*
of hosts **Yah Veh Sabaoth**,
the God **Elohim** of *Israel* **Yisra El**;
Houses and fields and vineyards
shall be *possessed* **chatteled** again in this land.
16 *Now when* **After** I had *delivered* **given**
the *evidence* **scroll** of the *purchase* **chattel**
unto Baruch the son of *Neriah* **Neri Yah**, I
prayed unto *the LORD* **Yah Veh**, saying,
17 *Ah Lord GOD* **Aha Adonay Yah Veh**! behold,
thou hast *made* **worked**
the *heaven* **heavens** and the earth
by thy great power and *stretched out* **spread** arm,
and there is *nothing* **no word**
too *hard* **marvellous** for thee:
18 Thou *shewest lovingkindness* **workest mercy**
unto thousands,
and *recompensest* **shalam**
iniquity **for the perversity** of the fathers
into the bosom of their *children* **sons** after them:
the Great, the Mighty *God* **El**,
the LORD of hosts **Yah Veh Sabaoth**, is his name,
19 Great in counsel, and *mighty*
great in *work* **exploits**:
for thine eyes are open
upon all the ways of the sons of *men* **humanity**:
to give every *one* **man** according to his ways,
and according to the fruit of his *doings* **exploits**:
20 Which hast set signs and *wonders* **omens**
in the land of *Egypt* **Misrayim**, *even* unto this day,
and in *Israel* **Yisra El**, and among *other men* **humanity**;
and hast *made* **worked** thee a name, as at this day;
21 And hast brought forth
thy people *Israel* **Yisra El**
out of the land of *Egypt* **Misrayim** with
signs, and with *wonders* **omens**,
and with a strong hand, and with a
stretched out **spread** arm,
and with great *terror* **awesomeness**;
22 And hast given them this land,
which thou didst *swear* **oath** to
their fathers to give them,
a land flowing with milk and honey;
23 And they came in, and possessed it;
but they *obeyed* **hearkened** not **unto** thy voice,
neither walked in thy *law* **torah**;
they have *done nothing* **not worked**
of all that thou *commandedst* **misvahedst** them
to *do* **work**:
therefore thou hast *caused* **confronted** all this evil

to come upon them:
24 Behold the *mounts* **mounds**,
9 And I chattel the field
of Hanam El the son of my uncle
in Anathoth;
and weigh him the silver
—seventeen shekels of silver:
10 and I inscribe the scroll and seal;
and witnesses witness
and weigh him the silver in the balances:
11 and I take the sealed scroll of the chattel
to the misvah and statute,
with the exposed *one*:
12 and I give the scroll of the chattel to Baruch
the son of Neri Yah the son of Machse Yah
in the eyes of Hanam El *the son* of my uncle,
and in the eyes of the witnesses
who inscribe the scroll of the chattel
in the eyes of all the Yah Hudiym
who sit in the court of the target area.
13 And I misvah Baruch in their eyes, saying,
14 Thus says Yah Veh Sabaoth Elohim of Yisra El:
Take these scrolls,
both this sealed scroll of the chattel,
and this exposed scroll;
and give them in a potsherd instrument
to stand many days.
15 For thus says Yah Veh
Sabaoth Elohim of Yisra El:
Again houses and fields and vineyards
are chatteled in this land.
16 After I give the scroll of the chattel
to Baruch the son of Neri Yah,
I pray to Yah Veh, saying,
17 Aha, Adonay Yah Veh! Behold,
you worked the heavens and the earth
by your great power and spread arm;
and there is no word too marvellous for you:
18 you work mercy to thousands
and shalam for the perversity of the fathers
into the bosom of their sons after them.
The Great! The Mighty El!
Yah Veh Sabaoth *is* his name:
19 great in counsel and great in exploits:
in that your eyes open on all the ways
of the sons of humanity:
to give every man according to his ways,
and according to the fruit of his exploits:
20 who set signs and omens
in the land of Misrayim
to this day;
and in Yisra El and among humanity;
and worked a name, as this day;
21 and brought forth your people Yisra El
from the land of Misrayim
with signs and with omens;
and with a strong hand and with a spread arm
and with great awesomeness;
22 and give them this land
which you oathed to their fathers to give them
—a land flowing with milk and honey;
23 and they came in and possessed;
and they neither hearkened to your voice,
nor walked in your torah;
nor worked all you misvahed them to work:
so you confronted all this evil on them.
24 Behold the mounds,
they are come unto the city to *take* **capture** it;
and the city
is given into the hand of the *Chaldeans* **Kesediym**,
that fight against it, *because* **at the face** of the sword,
and of the famine, and of the pestilence:
and what thou hast *spoken* **worded**
is *come to pass* **become**;
and, behold, thou seest it.
25 And thou hast said unto me,
O Lord GOD **Adonay Yah Veh**,
Buy **Chattel** thee the field for *money* **silver**,
and *take* **have** witnesses **witness**;
for the city
is given into the hand of the *Chaldeans* **Kesediym**.

The Response Of Yah Veh

26 Then came the word of *the LORD* **Yah Veh**
unto *Jeremiah* **Yirme Yah**, saying,
27 Behold,
I am the LORD **I—Yah Veh**, *the God* **Elohim** of all flesh:
is there any *thing* **word** too *hard* **marvellous** for me?
28 Therefore thus saith *the LORD* **Yah Veh**;
Behold,
I *will* **shall** give this city
into the hand of the *Chaldeans* **Kesediym**,
and into the hand of
Nebuchadrezzar **Nebukadnets Tsar**
king **sovereign** of *Babylon* **Babel**,
and he shall take it:
29 And the *Chaldeans* **Kesediym**,
that fight against this city,
shall come and *set* **kindle** fire on this city,
and burn it with the houses,
upon whose roofs

they have *offered incense* **incensed** unto Baal,
and *poured out drink offerings* **libated libations**
unto other *gods* **elohim**, to *provoke* **vex** me *to anger.*
30 For the *children* **sons** of *Israel* **Yisra El**
and the *children* **sons** of *Judah* **Yah Hudah**
have only *done* **worked** evil *before me* **in my eyes**
from their youth:
for the *children* **sons** of *Israel* **Yisra El**
have only *provoked* **vexed** me *to anger*
with the work of their hands,
saith the LORD **an oracle of Yah Veh.**
31 For this city hath been to me
as a provocation of *mine anger* **my wrath** and of my fury
from the day that they built it even unto this day;
that I should *remove it* **turn it aside**
from before **in front of** my face,
32 Because of all the evil
of the *children* **sons** of *Israel* **Yisra El**
and of the *children* **sons** of *Judah* **Yah Hudah,**
which they have *done* **worked** to
provoke **vex** me *to anger,*
they, their *kings* **sovereigns,**
their *princes* **governors,** their priests, and their prophets,
and the men of *Judah* **Yah Hudah,**
and the *inhabitants* **settlers** of *Jerusalem* **Yeru Shalem.**
33 And they have *turned* **faced**
unto me the *back* **neck,**
and not the face:
though I taught them,
rising up **starting** early and teaching them,
yet they have not hearkened
to *receive instruction* **take discipline.**
34 But they set their abominations in the house,
which is called by my name, to *defile* **foul** it.
35 And they built the *high places* **bamahs** of Baal,
which are in
the valley of the son of Hinnom
Gay Ben Hinnom/Valley of the Son of Burning,
to cause their sons and their daughters
to pass through *the fire* unto Molech;
which I *commanded* **misvahed** them not,
neither *came* **ascended** it into my *mind* **heart,**
that they should *do* **work** this *abomination* **abhorrence,**
to cause *Judah* **Yah Hudah** to sin.
36 And now therefore thus
saith *the LORD* **Yah Veh,**
the God **Elohim** of *Israel* **Yisra El,**
concerning this city, whereof ye say,
they come to the city to capture it
—to give the city into the hand of the Kesediym

who fight against it at the face of the sword
and of the famine and of the pestilence:
and what you worded, becomes;
and behold, you see.
25 And Adonay Yah Veh, you said to me,
Chattel you the field for silver,
and have witnesses witness;
for the city is given into the hand of the Kesediym.

THE RESPONSE OF YAH VEH

26 And so be the word of Yah Veh to Yirme Yah,
saying,
27 Behold, I—Yah Veh, Elohim of all flesh!
Is any word too marvellous for me?
28 So thus says Yah Veh:
Behold,
I give this city into the hand of the Kesediym,
and into the hand
of Nebukadnets Tsar sovereign of Babel;
and he takes it:
29 and the Kesediym who fight against this city
come and kindle fire on this city
—and burn it with the houses
on whose roofs they incensed to Baal
and libated libations to other elohim, to vex me:
30 for the sons of Yisra El and
the sons of Yah Hudah
surely work evil in my eyes from their youth:
for the sons of Yisra El
surely vex me with the work of their hands
—an oracle of Yah Veh.
31 And so be this city to me
—a provocation of my wrath and of my fury
from the day they built it even to this day;
that I turn it aside from in front of my face,
32 because of all the evil
the sons of Yisra El and the sons of Yah Hudah
work to vex me
—they, their sovereigns,
their governors, their priests, and their prophets,
and the men of Yah Hudah,
and the settlers of Yeru Shalem:
33 and they face their neck
to me and not their face:
though I taught them
—starting early and teaching them,
yet they hearken not to take discipline:
34 and they set their abominations in the house
on which my name is called
to foul it:

35 and they build the bamahs of Baal
in Gay Ben Hinnom/Valley of the Son of Burning,
to pass their sons and their daughters
through to Molech
—which I neither misvahed them
nor ascended it into my heart
that they work this abhorrence
to have Yah Hudah sin.
36 And so now,
thus says Yah Veh Elohim of Yisra El
concerning this city of which you say,
It shall be *delivered* **given** into the hand
of the *king* **sovereign** of *Babylon* **Babel**
by the sword, and by the famine, and by the pestilence;
37 Behold,
I *will* **shall** gather them out of all *countries* **lands,**
whither I have driven them in *mine anger* **my wrath,**
and in my fury, and in great *wrath* **rage;**
and I *will bring* **shall return** them *again* unto this place,
and I *will* **shall** cause them
to *dwell safely* **settle confidently:**
38 And they shall be my people,
and I *will* **shall** be their *God* **Elohim:**
39 And I *will* **shall** give them
one heart, and one way,
that they may *fear* **awe** me *for ever* **all days,**
for the good of them,
and of their *children* **sons** after them:
40 And I *will make* **shall cut**
an *everlasting* **eternal** covenant with them,
that I *will* **shall** not turn away from **after** them,
to *do* **well—please** them *good;*
but I *will put* **shall give** my fear in their hearts,
that they shall not *depart* **turn aside** from me.
41 Yea, I *will* **shall** rejoice over
them to do them good,
and I *will* **shall** plant them in this land
assuredly **in truth**
with my whole heart and with my whole soul.
42 For thus saith *the LORD* **Yah Veh;**
Like as I have brought all this great
evil upon this people,
so *will* **shall** I bring upon them all the good
that I have *promised* **worded** them.
43 And fields shall be *bought* **chatteled** in this land,
whereof ye say,
It is desolate without *man* **humanity** or *beast* **animal;**
it is given into the hand of the *Chaldeans* **Kesediym.**
44 Men shall *buy* **chattel** fields for *money* **silver,**
and *subscribe evidences* **inscribe scrolls,** and seal them,
and *take* **witness** witnesses
in the land of *Benjamin* **Ben Yamin,**
and *in the places* **round** about *Jerusalem* **Yeru Shalem,**
and in the cities of *Judah* **Yah Hudah,**
and in the cities of the mountains,
and in the cities of the *valley* **lowland,**
and in the cities of the south:
for I *will cause* **shall restore** their captivity *to return,*
saith the LORD **an oracle of Yah Veh.**

The Restoration By Yah Veh

33 Moreover the word of *the LORD* **Yah Veh**
came unto *Jeremiah* **Yirme Yah**
the second time **secondly,**
while he was yet *shut up* **restrained**
in the court of the *prison* **target area,** saying,
2 Thus saith *the LORD* **Yah Veh**
the *maker* **worker** *thereof,*
the LORD **Yah Veh** that formed it, to establish it;
the LORD **Yah Veh** is his name;
3 Call unto me, and I *will* **shall** answer thee,
and *shew* **tell** thee great and *mighty things* **fortified,**
which thou knowest not.
4 For thus saith *the LORD* **Yah Veh,**
the God **Elohim** of *Israel* **Yisra El,**
concerning the houses of this city,
and concerning the houses
of the *kings* **sovereigns** of *Judah* **Yah Hudah,**
which are *thrown* **pulled** down by the *mounts* **mounds,**
and by the sword;
5 They come to fight with
the *Chaldeans* **Kesediym,**
but it is to fill them
with the *dead bodies* **carcases** of *men* **humanity,**
whom I have *slain* **smitten**
in *mine anger* **my wrath** and in my fury,
and for all whose *wickedness* **evil**
I have hid my face from this city.
6 Behold,
I *will bring* **shall ascend** it health and *cure* **healing,**
and I *will cure* **shall heal** them,
and *will reveal* **shall expose** unto them
the abundance of *peace* **shalom** and truth.
7 And I *will cause* **shall restore**
the captivity of *Judah* **Yah Hudah**
to give into the hand of the sovereign of Babel
by the sword and by the famine
and by the pestilence,
37 Behold, I gather them from all lands,

where I drove them in my wrath and in my
fury and in great rage; and I return them to this
place: and have them settle confidently:
38 and they are my people,
and I am their Elohim:
39 and I give them one heart and one way,
so that they awe me all days,
for the good of them
and of their sons after them:
40 and I cut an eternal covenant with them
to not turn away from after them
to well—please them;
and I give my fear in their hearts
that they not turn aside from me.
41 Yes, I rejoice over them to do them good,
and I plant them in this land in truth with
my whole heart and with my whole soul.
42 For thus says Yah Veh:
As I brought all this great evil on this people,
thus I bring all the good I worded on them.
43 And chattel the fields in this land,
whereof you said,
Desolate! Without humanity or animal!
—it is given into the hand of the Kesediym.
44 Men chattel fields for silver
and inscribe scrolls and seal them;
and witnesses witness in the land of Ben Yamin
and all around Yeru Shalem
and in the cities of Yah Hudah
and in the cities of the mountains
and in the cities of the lowland
and in the cities of the south:
and I restore their captivity
—an oracle of Yah Veh.

The Restoration By Yah Veh

33 And so be the word of Yah Veh
to Yirme Yah secondly,
while he is still restrained
in the court of the target area, saying,
2 Thus says Yah Veh the worker
—Yah Veh former—who established;
Yah Veh is his name:
3 Call to me, and I answer you
and tell you great and fortified
which you know not.
4 For thus says Yah Veh Elohim of Yisra El
concerning the houses of this city
and concerning the houses
of the sovereigns of Yah Hudah
—which *are* pulled down by the mounds
and by the sword;
5 they come to fight the Kesediym,
and to to fill them with the carcases of humanity
whom I smote in my wrath and in my fury
—and for all whose evil I hid my face from this city.
6 Behold, I ascend health and healing
and I heal them;
and expose to them
the abundance of shalom and truth:
7 and I restore the captivity of Yah Hudah
and the captivity of *Israel* **Yisra El** *to return*,
and *will* **shall** build them, as at the first.
8 And I *will cleanse* **shall purify** them
from all their *iniquity* **perversity**,
whereby they have sinned against me;
and I *will pardon* **shall forgive**
all their *iniquities* **perversities**,
whereby they have sinned,
and whereby they have *transgressed* **rebelled** against me.
9 And it shall be to me a name of *joy* **rejoicing**,
a *praise* **halal** and an *honour* **adornment**
before **in front of** all the *nations* **goyim** of the earth,
which shall hear all the good that I *do* **work** unto them:
and they shall fear and *tremble* **quiver**
for all the goodness and for all the *prosperity* **shalom**
that I *procure* **work** unto it.
10 Thus saith *the LORD* **Yah Veh**;
Again there shall be heard in this place,
which ye say shall be *desolate* **parched dry**
without *man* **humanity** and without *beast* **animal**,
even in the cities of *Judah* **Yah Hudah**,
and in the *streets* **outways** of *Jerusalem* **Yeru Shalem**,
that are *desolate* **desolated**, without *man* **humanity**,
and without *inhabitant* **settler**, and
without *beast* **animal**,
11 The voice of *joy* **rejoicing**,
and the voice of *gladness* **cheerfulness**,
the voice of the bridegroom, and the voice of the bride,
the voice of them that shall say,
Praise **Spread hands**
the LORD of hosts **unto Yah Veh Sabaoth**:
for *the LORD* **Yah Veh** is good;
for his mercy *endureth for ever* **be eternal**:
and of them
that shall bring *the sacrifice of praise* **spread hands**
into the house of *the LORD* **Yah Veh**.
For I *will* **shall** cause to *return* **restore**
the captivity of the land, as at the first,
saith *the LORD* **Yah Veh**.

12 Thus saith *the LORD of hosts* **Yah Veh Sabaoth**;
Again in this place, which is *desolate* **parched dry**
without *man* **humanity** and without *beast* **animal**,
and in all the cities *thereof*,
shall be an habitation **of rest** of *shepherds* **tenders**
causing their flocks to *lie down* **crouch**.
13 In the cities of the mountains,
in the cities of the *vale* **lowland**,
and in the cities of the south,
and in the land of *Benjamin* **Ben Yamin**,
and in the places **round** about *Jerusalem* **Yeru Shalem**,
and in the cities of *Judah* **Yah Hudah**,
shall the flocks pass again
under the hands of him that telleth them,
saith *the LORD* **Yah Veh**.
14 Behold, the days come,
saith the LORD **an oracle of Yah Veh**,
that I *will perform* **shall raise** that good *thing* **word**
which I have *promised* **worded**
unto the house of *Israel* **Yisra El**
and to the house of *Judah* **Yah Hudah**.
15 In those days, and at that time,
will **shall** I cause
the *Branch* **Sprout** of *righteousness* **justness**
to *grow up* **sprout** unto David;
and he shall *execute* **work**
judgment and *righteousness* **justness** in the land.
16 In those days shall *Judah* **Yah Hudah** be saved,
and *Jerusalem* **Yeru Shalem**
shall *dwell safely* **tabernacle confidently**:
and this is the name wherewith she shall be called,
The LORD our righteousness **Yah Veh Sidqenuw**.
17 For thus saith *the LORD* **Yah Veh**;
David shall never *want* **cut** a man to sit upon the throne
of the house of *Israel* **Yisra El**;
18 Neither shall the priests the *Levites* **Leviym**
want **cut** a man *before me* **at my face**
to *offer burnt offerings* **holocaust holocausts**,
and to *kindle meat* **incense** offerings,
and to *do* **work** sacrifice continually.
and the captivity of Yisra El;
and build them as at the first:
8 and I purify them from all their perversity
whereby they sinned against me;
and I forgive all their perversities whereby they sinned
and whereby they rebelled against me.
9 And so be it to me, a name of rejoicing
—a halal and an adornment
in front of all the goyim of the earth
who hear of all the good I work to them:
and they fear and quiver
for all the goodness and for all the shalom
I work to it.
10 Thus says Yah Veh:
Again it *is* heard in this place,
which you say is parched dry
without humanity and without animal
—in the cities of Yah Hudah
and in the outways of Yeru Shalem that are desolated
—without humanity
and without settler and without animal,
11 The voice of rejoicing
and the voice of cheerfulness;
the voice of the bridegroom
and the voice of the bride;
the voice of them who say,
Spread hands to Yah Veh Sabaoth:
for Yah Veh *is* good; for his mercy *is* eternal:
—who bring spread hands to the house of Yah Veh.
For I restore the captivity of the land as at the first,
says Yah Veh.
12 Thus says Yah Veh Sabaoth;
Again in this place, which *is* parched dry
without humanity and without animal,
and in all the cities,
a habitation of rest of tenders
whose flocks crouch.
13 In the cities of the mountains
in the cities of the lowland
and in the cities of the south
and in the land of Ben Yamin
and in the places all around Yeru Shalem
and in the cities of Yah Hudah,
the flocks pass again
under the hands of him who tells them,
says Yah Veh.
14 Behold, days come,
—an oracle of Yah Veh,
that I raise that good word I worded
to the house of Yisra El
and to the house of Yah Hudah.
15 In those days, and at that time,
I sprout the Sprout of justness unto David; to
work judgment and justness in the land.
16 In those days Yah Hudah is saved,
and Yeru Shalem tabernacles confidently:
and this is what to call her:
Yah Veh Sidqenuw.
17 For thus says Yah Veh:
Neither David cut a man

to sit on the throne of the house of Yisra El;
18 nor the priests the Leviym cut a man at my face
to holocaust holocausts and to incense offerings
and to work sacrifice continually.
19 And **so be** the word of *the LORD* **Yah Veh**
came unto *Jeremiah* **Yirme Yah**, saying,
20 Thus saith *the LORD* **Yah Veh**;
If ye can break my covenant of the day,
and my covenant of the night,
and that there should not be day and night
in *their season* **time**;
21 Then may also my covenant be broken
with David my servant,
that he should not have a son to reign upon his throne;
and with the *Levites* **Leviym** the priests, my ministers.
22 As the host of *heaven* **the heavens**
cannot be *numbered* **scribed**,
neither the sand of the sea measured:
so *will* **shall** I *multiply* **abound**
the seed of David my servant,
and the *Levites* **Leviym** that minister unto me.
23 Moreover the word of *the LORD* **Yah Veh**
came to *Jeremiah* **Yirme Yah**, saying,
24 *Considerest* **Seest** thou not
what this people have *spoken* **worded**, saying,
The two families which *the LORD* **Yah Veh** hath chosen,
he hath *even cast them off* **spurned**?
thus they have *despised* **scorned** my people,
that they should be no more a *nation* **goyim**
before them **at their face**.
25 Thus saith *the LORD* **Yah Veh**;
If my covenant be not with day and night,
and if I have not *appointed* **set** the *ordinances* **statutes**
of *heaven* **the heavens** and earth;
26 Then *will* **shall** I *cast away* **spurn**
the seed of *Jacob* **Yaaqov** and David my servant,
so that I *will* **shall** not take *any* of his seed
to be *rulers* **sovereigns** over the seed of Abraham,
Isaac **Yischaq**, and *Jacob* **Yaaqov**:
for I *will cause* **shall restore** their captivity *to return*,
and *have* **shall** mercy *on* them.

THE WORD AGAINST SIDQI YAH

34 The word which came unto *Jeremiah* **Yirme Yah**
from *the LORD* **Yah Veh**,
when *Nebuchadnezzar* **Nebukadnets Tsar**
king **sovereign** of *Babylon* **Babel**,
and all his *army* **valiant**,
and all the kingdoms of the earth
of *his dominion* **the reign of his hand**,
and all the people,
fought against *Jerusalem* **Yeru Shalem**,
and against all the cities *thereof*, saying,
2 Thus saith
the LORD **Yah Veh**, *the God* **Elohim** of *Israel* **Yisra El**;
Go and *speak* **say** to *Zedekiah* **Sidqi Yah**
king **sovereign** of *Judah* **Yah Hudah**,
and *tell* **say to** him, Thus saith *the LORD* **Yah Veh**;
Behold, I *will* **shall** give this city
into the hand of the *king* **sovereign** of *Babylon* **Babel**,
and he shall burn it with fire:
3 And thou shalt not escape out of his hand,
but **in apprehending**,
shalt *surely be taken* **be apprehended**,
and *delivered* **given** into his hand;
and thine eyes shall *behold* **see**
the eyes of the *king* **sovereign** of *Babylon* **Babel**,
and he shall *speak* **word** with thee mouth to mouth,
and thou shalt go to *Babylon* **Babel**.
4 Yet hear the word of *the LORD* **Yah Veh**,
O *Zedekiah* **Sidqi Yah**
king **sovereign** of *Judah* **Yah Hudah**;
Thus saith *the LORD* **Yah Veh** of thee,
Thou shalt not die by the sword:
5 *But* thou shalt die in *peace* **shalom**:
and with the *burnings* **cremations** of thy fathers,
the former *kings* **sovereigns**
which were *before thee* **at thy face**,
so shall they burn *odours* for thee;
and they *will lament* **shall chop for** thee, *saying*,
Ah lord **Ho adoni**!
for I have *pronounced* **worded** the word,
saith the LORD **an oracle of Yah Veh**.
19 And so be the word of Yah Veh to Yirme Yah,
saying,
20 Thus says Yah Veh:
If you break my covenant of the day
and my covenant of the night
so that there is no day and night in time;
21 *then* I also break my covenant
with David my servant,
that he has no son reigning on his throne;
and with the Leviym the priests, my ministers.
22 As neither the host of the heavens *is* scribed,
nor the sand of the sea measured:
thus I abound the seed of David my servant,
and the Leviym who minister to me.
23 And so be the word of Yah Veh to Yirme Yah,
saying,
24 See you not what this people word, saying,

The two families Yah Veh chose, he spurns?
Thus they scorn my people,
that they are no more a goyim at their face.
25 Thus says Yah Veh:
If my covenant is not day and night;
if I set not the statutes of the heavens and earth;
26 then I also spurn
the seed of Yaaqov and David my servant,
that I not take of his seed to be sovereigns
over the seed of Abraham, Yischaq, and Yaaqov:
for I restore their captivity,
and mercy them.

THE WORD AGAINST SIDQI YAH

34 So be the word to Yirme Yah from Yah Veh
—when Nebukadnets Tsar sovereign of Babel
and all his valiant
and all the kingdoms of the earth
of the reign of his hand
and all the people fight against Yeru Shalem,
and against all the cities, saying,
2 Thus says Yah Veh Elohim of Yisra El:
Go and say to Sidqi Yah sovereign of Yah Hudah,
and say to him, Thus says Yah Veh:
Behold,
I give this city into the hand of the sovereign of Babel
to burn with fire;
3 and you escape not from his hand:
for in apprehending, you are apprehended
and given into his hand:
and your eyes see the eyes of the sovereign of Babel
and he words with you mouth to mouth;
and you go to Babel.
4 Yet hear the word of Yah Veh,
O Sidqi Yah sovereign of Yah Hudah;
Thus says Yah Veh of you:
You die not by the sword:
5 you die in shalom:
and with the cremations of your fathers
the former sovereigns at your face;
thus they burn for you: and they chop for you:
Ho adoni!
for the word I worded
—an oracle of Yah Veh.
6 Then *Jeremiah* **Yirme Yah** the prophet
spake **worded** all these words
unto *Zedekiah* **Sidqi Yah**
king **sovereign** of *Judah* **Yah Hudah**
in *Jerusalem* **Yeru Shalem**,
7 When the *king* **sovereign**
of *Babylon's army* **Babel's valiant**
fought against *Jerusalem* **Yeru Shalem**,
and against all the cities of *Judah* **Yah Hudah**
that *were left* **remained**,
against Lachish, and against *Azekah* **Azeqah**:
for these *defenced* **fortified** cities
remained of the cities of *Judah* **Yah Hudah**.
8 *This is* the word that came
unto *Jeremiah* **Yirme Yah**
from *the LORD* **Yah Veh**,
after that the *king Zedekiah* **sovereign Sidqi Yah**
had *made* **cut** a covenant with all the people
which were at *Jerusalem* **Yeru Shalem**,
to *proclaim* **call out** liberty unto them;
9 That every man should let
his *manservant* **servant**,
and every man his *maidservant* **maid**,
being an Hebrew or an Hebrewess,
go free **be sent away liberated**;
that none should serve himself of them,
to wit, of a *Jew* **Yah Hudahiy** his brother.
10 Now when all the *princes* **governors**,
and all the people,
which had entered into the covenant,
heard that every *one* **man**
should let his *manservant* **servant**,
and every *one* **man** his *maidservant* **maid**,
go *free* **liberated**,
that none should serve themselves of them any more,
then they *obeyed* **hearkened**, and *let* **sent** them *go* **away**.
11 But afterward they turned,
and caused the servants and the *handmaids* **maids**,
whom they had *let go free* **sent away liberated**, to return,
and brought them into subjection
for servants and for *handmaids* **maids**.
12 Therefore the word of *the LORD* **Yah Veh**
came to *Jeremiah* **Yirme Yah** from *the LORD* **Yah Veh**,
saying,
13 Thus saith *the LORD* **Yah Veh**,
the God **Elohim** of *Israel* **Yisra El**;
I *made* **cut** a covenant with your fathers
in the day that I brought them forth
out of the land of *Egypt* **Misrayim**,
out of the house of *bondmen* **servants**, saying,
14 At the end of seven years
let ye go **send ye away** every man his brother an Hebrew,
which hath been sold unto thee;
and when he hath served thee six years,
thou shalt *let him go free* **send him away liberated**
from thee:
but your fathers hearkened not unto me,

neither *inclined* **spread** their ear.
15 And ye were *now* **to day** turned,
and had *done right* **worked straight** in my *sight* **eyes**,
in *proclaiming* **calling out** liberty
every man to his *neighbour* **friend**;
and ye had *made* **cut** a covenant *before me* **at my face**
in the house which is called by my name:
16 But ye turned and *polluted* **profaned** my name,
and caused every man his servant,
and every man his *handmaid* **maid**,
whom he had *set at* **spread** liberty
at their *pleasure* **soul**,
to return, and brought them into subjection,
to be unto you for servants and for *handmaids* **maids**.
17 Therefore thus saith *the LORD* **Yah Veh**;
Ye have not hearkened unto me,
in *proclaiming* **calling out** liberty,
every *one* **man** to his brother,
and every man to his *neighbour* **friend**:
behold, I proclaim a liberty for you,
saith the LORD **an oracle of Yah Veh**,
to the sword, to the pestilence, and to the famine;
and I *will make* **shall give** you *to be*
removed **for an agitation**
into all the kingdoms of the earth.
6 And Yirme Yah the prophet
words all these words
to Sidqi Yah sovereign of Yah Hudah
in Yeru Shalem,
7 when the valiant of the sovereign of Babel
fight against Yeru Shalem
and against all the cities of Yah Hudah that remain
—against Lachish and against Azeqah:
for of the fortified cities
these cities of Yah Hudah remained.
8 So be the word to Yirme Yah from Yah Veh,
after the sovereign Sidqi Yah
cuts a covenant with all the people at Yeru Shalem
—to call out liberty to them;
9 that every man send away his servant
and every man his maid
—Hebrew or Hebrewess:
—liberated, that they serve no one
—a Yah Hudahiy by his brother.
10 And all the governors
and all the people who entered into the covenant
hear that every man liberated his servant
and every man his maid
so that no one be served by them any more;
and they hearken and send them away:
11 and afterward they turn,
and return the servants and the maids,
whom they sent away liberated;
and bring them into subjection
for servants and for maids.
12 And so be the word of Yah Veh to Yirme Yah
from Yah Veh, saying,
13 Thus says Yah Veh Elohim of Yisra El:
I cut a covenant with your fathers
in the day I brought them from the land of Misrayim
—from the house of servants, saying,
14 At the end of seven years
every man sends away his brother
—a Hebrew sold to you
—who serves you six years:
send him away liberated from you:
and your fathers neither hearkened to me,
nor spread their ear.
15 And today you turn and
work straight in my eyes
in calling out liberty—every man to his friend;
and you cut a covenant at my face
in the house on which my name is called:
16 and you turn and profane my name:
and every man has his servant
and every man his maid
to whom he spread liberty at their soul, to return,
and bring them into subjection
being for servants and for maids.
17 So thus says Yah Veh:
You hearken not to me, in calling out liberty
—every man to his brother
and every man to his friend:
behold, I proclaim a liberty for you
—an oracle of Yah Veh
to the sword, to the pestilence and to the famine;
and I give you for an agitation
into all the kingdoms of the earth:
18 And I *will* **shall** give the men
that have *transgressed* **tresspassed** my covenant,
which have not
performed **raised** the words of the covenant
which they had *made before me* **cut at my face**,
when they cut the calf in *twain* **two**,
and passed between the *parts* **sections** *thereof*,
19 The *princes* **governors** of *Judah* **Yah Hudah**,
and the *princes* **governors** of *Jerusalem* **Yeru Shalem**,
the eunuchs, and the priests,
and all the people of the land,
which passed between the *parts* **sections** of the calf;
20 I *will* **shall** even give them

into the hand of their enemies,
and into the hand of them that seek their *life* **soul**:
and their *dead bodies* **carcases** shall be for *meat* **food**
unto the *fowls* **flyers** of the *heaven* **heavens**,
and to the *beasts* **animals** of the earth.
21 And *Zedekiah* **Sidqi Yah**
king **sovereign** of *Judah* **Yah Hudah**
and his *princes* **governors**
will **shall** I give into the hand of their enemies,
and into the hand of them that seek their *life* **soul**,
and into the hand
of the *king* **sovereign** of *Babylon's army* **Babel's valiant**,
which are *gone up* **ascended** from you.
22 Behold, I *will command* **shall misvah**,
saith the LORD **an oracle of Yah Veh**, and
cause them to return to this city;
and they shall fight against it,
and *take* **capture** it, and burn it with fire:
and I *will make* **shall give** the cities of *Judah* **Yah Hudah**
a desolation without *an inhabitant* **a settler**.

THE OBEDIENCE OF THE HOUSE OF THE RECHABIYM

35 The word which came unto *Jeremiah* **Yirme Yah**
from *the LORD* **Yah Veh**
in the days of *Jehoiakim* **Yah Yaqim**
the son of *Josiah* **Yoshi Yah**
king **sovereign** of *Judah* **Yah Hudah**, saying,
2 Go unto the house of the
Rechabites **Rechabiym**,
and *speak* **word** unto them,
and bring them into the house of *the LORD* **Yah Veh**,
into one of the chambers, and give them wine to drink.
3 Then I took *Jaazaniah* **Yaazan Yah**
the son of *Jeremiah* **Yirme Yah**,
the son of *Habaziniah* **Chabatz Tzan Yah**,
and his brethren, and all his sons,
and the whole house of the *Rechabites* **Rechabiym**;
4 And I brought them
into the house of *the LORD* **Yah Veh**,
into the chamber of the sons of Hanan,
the son of *Igdaliah* **Yigdal Yah**, a man of *God* **Elohim**,
which was *by* **beside** the chamber
of the *princes* **governors**,
which was above the chamber of *Maaseiah* **Maase Yah**
the son of Shallum,
the *keeper* **guard** of the *door* **threshold**:
5 And I *set before* **gave at the face of** the sons
of the house of the *Rechabites* **Rechabiym**
pots **bowls** full of wine, and cups,
and I said unto them, Drink ye wine.
6 But they said, We *will* **shall** drink no wine:
for *Jonadab* **Yah Nadab**
the son of Rechab our father
commanded **misvahed** us, saying,
Ye shall drink no wine,
neither ye, nor your sons *for ever* **eternally**:
7 Neither shall ye build house,
nor *sow* **seed** seed, nor plant vineyard, nor have *any*:
but all your days ye shall *dwell* **settle** in tents;
that ye may live many days in the *land* **face of the soil**
where ye be *strangers* **sojourners**.
8 Thus have we *obeyed* **hearkened**
unto the voice of *Jonadab* **Yah Nadab**
the son of Rechab our father
in all that he hath *charged* **misvahed** us,
to drink no wine all our days,
we, our *wives* **women**, our sons, nor our daughters;
9 Nor to build houses for us to *dwell* **settle** in:
neither have we vineyard, nor field, nor seed:
18 and I give the men
who tresspass my covenant,
who raise not the words of the covenant
to cut at my face
—when they cut the calf in two
and passed between the sections
19 —the governors of Yah Hudah
and the governors of Yeru Shalem,
the eunuchs, and the priests
and all the people of the land
who passed between the sections of the calf;
20 yes, I give them into the hand of their enemies
and into the hand of them who seek their
soul: and their carcases become food
to the flyers of the heavens
and to the animals of the earth:
21 and I give Sidqi Yah sovereign of Yah Hudah
and his governors
into the hand of their enemies
and into the hand of them who seek their soul
and into the hand
of the valiant of the sovereign of Babel,
who ascend from you.
22 Behold, I misvah
—an oracle of Yah Veh
and return them to this city;
and they fight against it and capture it
and burn it with fire:
and I give the cities of Yah Hudah
a desolation without a settler.

THE OBEDIENCE OF THE HOUSE OF THE RECHABIYM

35 So be the word to Yirme Yah from Yah Veh
in the days of Yah Yaqim
the son of Yoshi Yah sovereign of Yah Hudah, saying,
2 Go to the house of the Rechabiym
and word to them,
and bring them into the house of Yah Veh
—into one of the chambers
and give them wine to drink.
3 And I take Yaazan Yah
the son of Yirme Yah the son of Chabatz Tzan Yah
and his brothers and all his sons
and the whole house of the Rechabiym;
4 and I bring them into the house of Yah Veh
—into the chamber of the sons of Hanan
the son of Yigdal Yah—a man of Elohim,
—beside the chamber of the governors
above the chamber of Maase Yah the son of Shallum
the guard of the threshold:
5 and at the face of the sons
of the house of the Rechabiym
I give bowls full of wine and cups,
and I say to them, Drink wine.
6 And they say, We drink no wine:
for Yah Nadab the son of Rechab our father
misvahed us, saying, Drink no wine
—neither you nor your sons eternally:
7 neither build house
nor seed seed nor plant vineyard: have none:
and settle all your days in tents;
so that you live many days in the face of the soil
where you sojourn.
8 Thus we hearkened to the voice of Yah Nadab
the son of Rechab our father
in all he misvahed us
—to drink no wine all our days
we, our women, our sons, and our daughters:
9 neither build houses for us to settle in:
nor vineyard, nor field, nor seed:
10 But we have *dwelt* **settled** in tents,
and have *obeyed* **hearkened**,
and *done* **worked** according to all
that *Jonadab* **Yah Nadab** our father
commanded **misvahed** us.
11 *But* **And so be** it *came to pass*,
when *Nebuchadrezzar* **Nebukadnets Tsar**
king **sovereign** of *Babylon* **Babel**
came up **ascended** into the land, that we said,
Come, and let us go to *Jerusalem* **Yeru Shalem**
for fear **from the face** of the *army* **valiant**
of the *Chaldeans* **Kesediym**,
and *for fear* **from the face** of the *army* **valiant**
of the *Syrians* **Aramiym**:
so we *dwell* **settle** at *Jerusalem* **Yeru Shalem**.
12 *Then came* **And so be** the
word of *the LORD* **Yah Veh**
unto *Jeremiah* **Yirme Yah**, saying,
13 Thus saith *the LORD of hosts* **Yah Veh Sabaoth**,
the God **Elohim** of *Israel* **Yisra El**;
Go and *tell* **say to** the men of *Judah* **Yah Hudah**
and the *inhabitants* **settlers** of *Jerusalem* **Yeru Shalem**,
will **shall** ye not *receive instruction* **take discipline**
to hearken to my words?
saith the LORD **an oracle of Yah Veh**.
14 The words of *Jonadab* **Yah Nadab**
the son of Rechab,
that he *commanded* **misvahed** his
sons not to drink wine,
are *performed* **raised**;
for unto this day they drink none,
but *obey* **hearken**
unto their father's *commandment* **misvah**:
notwithstanding I have *spoken* **worded** unto you
rising **starting** early and *speaking* **wording**;
but ye hearkened not unto me.
15 I have sent also unto you all
my servants the prophets,
rising up **starting** early and sending them, saying,
Return ye *now* **I beseech**, every man from his evil way,
and *amend* **well—prepare** your *doings* **exploits**,
and go not after other *gods* **elohim** to serve them,
and ye shall *dwell* **settle** in the *land* **soil**
which I have given to you and to your fathers:
but ye have not *inclined* **spread** your ear,
nor hearkened unto me.
16 Because the sons of *Jonadab* **Yah Nadab**
the son of Rechab
have *performed* **raised** the *commandment* **misvah**
of their father,
which he *commanded* **misvahed** them;
but this people hath not hearkened unto me:
17 Therefore thus saith
the LORD God of hosts **Yah Veh Elohim Sabaoth**,
the God **Elohim** of *Israel* **Yisra El**;
Behold, I *will* **shall** bring upon *Judah* **Yah Hudah**
and upon all
the *inhabitants* **settlers** of *Jerusalem* **Yeru Shalem**
all the evil that I have *pronounced* **worded** against them:

because I have *spoken* **worded** unto them,
but they have not heard;
and I have called unto them,
but they have not answered.
18 And *Jeremiah* **Yirme Yah** said
unto the house of the *Rechabites* **Rechabiym**,
Thus saith *the LORD of hosts* **Yah Veh Sabaoth**,
the God **Elohim** of *Israel* **Yisra El**;
Because ye have *obeyed* **hearkened**
unto the *commandment* **misvah**
of *Jonadab* **Yah Nadab** your father,
and *kept* **guarded** all his *precepts* **misvoth**,
and *done* **worked** according unto all
that he hath *commanded* **misvahed** you:
19 Therefore thus saith
the LORD of hosts **Yah Veh Sabaoth**,
the God **Elohim** of *Israel* **Yisra El**;
Jonadab **Yah Nadab** the son of Rechab
shall not *want* **cut** a man to stand *before me* **at my face**
for ever **all days**.

Yirme Yah Inscribes A Scroll

36 And **so be** it *came to pass*
in the fourth year of *Jehoiakim* **Yah Yaqim**
10 and we settle in tents,
and hearken and work according to all
Yah Nadab our father misvahed us.
11 And so be it,
Nebukadnets Tsar sovereign of Babel
ascends into the land, and we say,
Come, we go to Yeru Shalem
from the face of the valiant of the Kesediym,
and from the face of the valiant of the Aramiym:
thus we settle at Yeru Shalem.
12 And so be the word of Yah Veh to Yirme Yah,
saying,
13 Thus says Yah Veh Sabaoth Elohim of Yisra El:
Go and say to the men of Yah Hudah
and the settlers of Yeru Shalem,
Take you no discipline to hearken to my words?
—an oracle of Yah Veh.
14 The words that Yah Nadab the son of Rechab
misvahed his sons to not drink wine are raised:
for to this day they drink no one,
but hearken to the misvah of their father:
and I—I worded to you
starting early and wording;
and you hearkened not to me.
15 I also sent all my servants the prophets to you
—starting early, and sending them, saying,
Return, I beseech, every man from his evil way
and well—prepare your exploits;
and go not after other elohim to serve them;
and settle in the soil I gave to you and to your fathers:
and you neither spread your ear
nor hearkened to me.
16 Because the sons of Yah
Nadab the son of Rechab
raised the misvah their father misvahed them;
and this people hearken not to me:
17 so thus says Yah Veh Elohim Sabaoth,
Elohim of Yisra El,
Behold, I bring on Yah Hudah
and on all the settlers of Yeru Shalem
all the evil I worded against them:
because I worded to them, and they heard not;
and I called to them, and they answered not.
18 And Yirme Yah says
to the house of the Rechabiym,
Thus says Yah Veh Sabaoth Elohim of Yisra El:
Because you hearkened
to the misvah of Yah Nadab your father
and guarded all his misvoth;
and worked according to all he misvahed you:
19 so thus says
Yah Veh Sabaoth Elohim of Yisra El:
Yah Nadab the son of Rechab
cuts not off a man from standing at my face all days.

Yirme Yah Inscribes A Scroll

36 And so be it,
in the fourth year of Yah Yaqim
the son of *Josiah* **Yoshi Yah**
king **sovereign** of *Judah* **Yah Hudah**,
that this word came unto *Jeremiah* **Yirme Yah**
from *the LORD* **Yah Veh**, saying,
2 Take thee a roll of a *book* **scroll**,
and *write* **inscribe** therein
all the words that I have *spoken* **worded** unto thee
against *Israel* **Yisra El**, and against *Judah* **Yah Hudah**,
and against all the *nations* **goyim**,
from the day I *spake* **worded** unto thee,
from the days of *Josiah* **Yoshi Yah**, even unto this day.
3 *It may be that* **Perhaps** the
house of *Judah* **Yah Hudah**
will **shall** hear all the evil
which I *purpose* **fabricate** to *do* **work** unto them;
that they may return every man from his evil way;
that I may forgive their *iniquity* **perversity** and their sin.
4 Then *Jeremiah* **Yirme Yah**

called Baruch the son of *Neriah* **Neri Yah**:
and Baruch *wrote* **inscribed**
from the mouth of *Jeremiah* **Yirme Yah**
all the words of *the LORD* **Yah Veh,**
which he had *spoken* **worded** him,
upon a roll of a *book* **scroll.**
5 And *Jeremiah* **Yirme Yah**
commanded **misvahed** Baruch, saying,
I am *shut up* **restrained;**
I cannot go into the house of *the LORD* **Yah Veh**:
6 Therefore go thou, and *read* **call out** in the roll,
which thou hast *written* **inscribed** from my mouth,
the words of *the LORD* **Yah Veh** in the ears of the people
in the *LORD'S* house **of Yah Veh**
upon the fasting day:
and also thou shalt *read* **call** them **out**
in the ears of all *Judah* **Yah Hudah**
that come out of their cities.
7 *It may be* **Perhaps** they *will present* **shall fell**
before the LORD **at the face of Yah Veh**
their supplication
and *will* **shall** return every *one* **man** from his evil way:
for great is the *anger* **wrath** and the fury
that *the LORD* **Yah Veh** hath *pronounced* **worded**
against this people.
8 And Baruch the son of *Neriah* **Neri Yah**
did **worked** according to all
that *Jeremiah* **Yirme Yah** the prophet
commanded **misvahed** him,
reading **calling out** in the *book* **scroll**
the words of *the LORD* **Yah Veh**
in the *LORD'S* house **of Yah Veh.**
9 And **so be** it *came to pass*
in the fifth year of *Jehoiakim* **Yah Yaqim**
the son of *Josiah* **Yoshi Yah**
king **sovereign** of *Judah* **Yah Hudah,**
in the ninth month,
that they *proclaimed* **called** a fast
before the LORD **at the face of Yah Veh**
to all the people in *Jerusalem* **Yeru Shalem,**
and to all the people
that came from the cities of *Judah* **Yah Hudah**
unto *Jerusalem* **Yeru Shalem.**
10 Then *read* Baruch **called out** in the *book* **scroll**
the words of *Jeremiah* **Yirme Yah**
in the house of *the LORD* **Yah Veh,**
in the chamber of *Gemariah* **Gemar Yah**
the son of Shaphan the scribe,
in the *higher* **most high** court,
at the *entry* **opening** of the new *gate* **portal**
of the *LORD'S* house **of Yah Veh,**
in the ears of all the people.
11 When *Michaiah* **Michah Yah**
the son of *Gemariah* **Gemar Yah,** the son of Shaphan,
had heard out of the *book* **scroll**
all the words of *the LORD* **Yah Veh,**
12 Then he *went down* **descended**
into the *king's* **sovereign's** house,
into the scribe's chamber: and, *lo* **behold,**
all the *princes* **governors** sat there,
even Elishama **Eli Shama** the scribe,
and *Delaiah* **Dela Yah** the son of *Shemaiah* **Shema Yah,**
the son of Yoshi Yah sovereign of Yah Hudah,
so be the word to Yirme Yah from Yah Veh, saying,
2 Take a roll of a scroll,
and inscribe therein
all the words I worded to you
against Yisra El and against Yah Hudah
and against all the goyim
from the day I worded to you
—from the days of Yoshi Yah even to this day.
3 Perhaps the house of Yah Hudah
hears all the evil I fabricate to work to them;
so that every man returns from his evil way
and I forgive their perversity and their sin.
4 And Yirme Yah calls
Baruch the son of Neri Yah:
and from the mouth of Yirme Yah
Baruch inscribes all the words of Yah Veh,
that he words him on a roll of a scroll:
5 and Yirme Yah misvahs Baruch, saying,
I *am* restrained;
I cannot enter the house of Yah Veh:
6 but you enter, and call out in the roll,
what you inscribe from my mouth
—the words of Yah Veh in the ears of the people
in the house of Yah Veh on the day of fasting:
and also call them out in the ears of all Yah Hudah
who come from their cities:
7 perhaps they fell their supplications
at the face of Yah Veh
so that every man returns from his evil way:
for great is the wrath and the fury
Yah Veh words against this people.
8 And Baruch the son of Neri Yah works
according to all
Yirme Yah the prophet misvahs him
—calling out in the scroll the words of Yah Veh
in the house of Yah Veh.
9 And so be it

in the fifth year of Yah Yaqim
the son of Yoshi Yah sovereign of Yah Hudah,
in the ninth month,
they call a fast at the face of Yah Veh
to all the people in Yeru Shalem,
and to all the people
coming from the cities of Yah Hudah to Yeru Shalem.
10 And Baruch calls out in the scroll
the words of Yirme Yah in the house of Yah Veh
in the chamber of Gemar Yah
the son of Shaphan the scribe
—in the most high court
at the opening of the new portal
of the house of Yah Veh
—in the ears of all the people.
11 And Michah Yah
the son of Gemar Yah the son of Shaphan
hears all the words of Yah Veh from the scroll:
12 and he descends to the house of the sovereign
to the chamber of the scribe:
and behold, all the governors sit there
—Eli Shama the scribe
and Dela Yah the son of Shema Yah
and *Elnathan* **El Nathan** the son of Achbor,
and *Gemariah* **Gemar Yah** the son of Shaphan,
and *Zedekiah* **Sidqi Yah** the son of
Hananiah **Hanan Yah,**
and all the *princes* **governors.**
13 Then *Michaiah declared*
Michah Yah told unto them
all the words that he had heard,
when Baruch *read* **called out** the *book* **scroll**
in the ears of the people.
14 Therefore all the *princes* **governors** sent
Jehudi **Yah Hudiy** the son of *Nethaniah* **Nethan Yah,**
the son of *Shelemiah* **Shelem Yah,**
the son of *Cushi* **Kushiy,** unto Baruch, saying,
Take in thine hand the roll
wherein thou hast *read* **called out**
in the ears of the people,
and come.
So Baruch the son of *Neriah* **Neri Yah**
took the roll in his hand, and came unto them.
15 And they said unto him,
Sit down *now* **I beseech,**
and *read it* **call it out** in our ears.
So Baruch *read it* **called it out** in their ears.
16 *Now* **And so be** it *came to pass,*
when they had heard all the words,
they *were afraid both one* **feared man** and *other* **friend,**
and said unto Baruch,
In telling, We *will* **shall** *surely* tell the *king* **sovereign**
of all these words.
17 And they asked Baruch, saying,
Tell us *now* **I beseech,** ,
How didst thou *write* **inscribe** all these words
at his mouth?
18 Then Baruch *answered* **said to** them,
He *pronounced* **called out** all these words unto me
with his mouth,
and I *wrote them* **inscribed** with ink in the *book* **scroll.**
19 Then said the *princes* **governors** unto Baruch,
Go, hide thee, thou and *Jeremiah* **Yirme Yah;**
and let no man know where ye be.

Yah Yaqim Burns The Scroll Of Yirme Yah

20 And they went in to the *king*
sovereign into the court,
but they *laid up* **oversaw** the roll
in the chamber of *Elishama* **Eli Shama** the scribe,
and told all the words in the ears of the *king* **sovereign.**
21 So the *king* **sovereign** sent *Jehudi* **Yah Hudiy**
to *fetch* **take** the roll:
and he took it
out of *Elishama* **Eli Shama** the scribe's chamber.
And *Jehudi read it* **Yah Hudiy called it out**
in the ears of the *king* **sovereign,**
and in the ears of all the *princes* **governors**
which stood beside the *king* **sovereign.**
22 *Now* the *king* **sovereign** sat in the winterhouse
in the ninth month:
and *there was a fire* on the hearth
a burning *before him* **at his face.**
23 And **so be** it *came to pass,*
that when *Jehudi* **Yah Hudiy**
had *read* **called out** three or four leaves,
he *cut* **ripped** it with the *penknife* **scribe's knife,**
and cast it into the fire that was on the hearth,
until all the roll was consumed in the fire
that was on the hearth.
24 Yet they *were* **feared** not *afraid,*
nor *rent* **ripped** their *garments* **clothes,**
neither the *king* **sovereign,**
nor any of his servants that heard all these words.
25 Nevertheless *Elnathan* **El Nathan**
and *Delaiah* **Dela Yah** and *Gemariah* **Gemar Yah**
had *made intercession* **interceded** to the *king* **sovereign**
that he *would* **should** not burn the roll:
but he *would* **should** not hear them.
26 But the *king commanded* **sovereign misvahed**

Jerahmeel **Yerachme El** the son of *Hammelech* **Melech**,
and *Seraiah* **Sera Yah** the son of *Azriel* **Ezri El**,
and *Shelemiah* **Shelem Yah** the son of *Abdeel* **Abde El**,
to take Baruch the scribe
and *Jeremiah* **Yirme Yah** the prophet:
but *the LORD* **Yah Veh** hid them.
and El Nathan the son of Achbor
and Gemar Yah the son of Shaphan
and Sidqi Yah the son of Hanan Yah
with all the governors.
13 And Michah Yah tells them
all the words he heard
when Baruch called out the scroll
in the ears of the people.
14 And all the governors
send Yah Hudiy the son of Nethan Yah
the son of Shelem Yah the son of Kushiy
to Baruch, saying,
Take in your hand the roll
wherein you called out in the ears of the people
and come.
And Baruch the son of Neri Yah
takes the roll in his hand, and comes to them:
15 and they say to him,
Sit down, I beseech, and call it out in our ears.
—and Baruch calls it out in their ears.
16 And so be it, they hear all the words,
and man and friend fear;
and say to Baruch,
In telling, we tell all these words to the sovereign.
17 And they ask Baruch, saying,
Tell us, I beseech,
How inscribed you all these words at his mouth?
18 Then Baruch says to them,
He called out all these words to me with his mouth
and I inscribed with ink in the scroll.
19 Then the governors say to Baruch,
Go, hide—you and Yirme Yah;
so that no man knows where.

Yah Yaqim Burns The Scroll Of Yirme Yah

20 And they go in to the sovereign into the court,
and they oversee the roll
in the chamber of Eli Shama the scribe;
and tell all the words in the ears of the sovereign.
21 And the sovereign sends
Yah Hudiy to take the roll:
and he takes it
from the chamber of Eli Shama the scribe:
and Yah Hudiy calls it out
in the ears of the sovereign
and in the ears of all the governors
standing beside the sovereign:
22 and the sovereign is sitting in the winterhouse
in the ninth month:
and the hearth burns at his face.
23 And so be it,
when Yah Hudiy calls out three or four leaves,
he rips it with the knife of the scribe
and casts it into the fire on the hearth
—until all the roll consumes in the fire on the hearth:
24 and they neither fear nor rip their clothes
—neither the sovereign nor any of his servants
who hear all these words.
25 And El Nathan and Dela Yah and Gemar Yah
intercede to the sovereign to not burn the roll:
but he hears them not.
26 And the sovereign misvahs
Yerachme El the son of Melech
and Sera Yah the son of Ezri El
and Shelem Yah the son of Abde El
to take Baruch the scribe and Yirme Yah the prophet:
and Yah Veh hides them.

Yirme Yah Inscribes A Second Scroll

27 Then the word of *the LORD* **Yah Veh**
came to *Jeremiah* **Yirme Yah**,
after that the *king* **sovereign** had burned the roll,
and the words which Baruch *wrote* **inscribed**
at the mouth of *Jeremiah* **Yirme Yah**, saying,
28 **Return,** Take thee *again* another roll,
and *write* **inscribe** in it
all the former words that were in the first roll,
which *Jehoiakim* **Yah Yaqim**
the *king* **sovereign** of *Judah* **Yah Hudah** hath burned.
29 And thou shalt say to *Jehoiakim king* **Yah Yaqim**
sovereign of *Judah* **Yah Hudah**,
Thus saith *the LORD* **Yah Veh**;
Thou hast burned this roll, saying,
Why hast thou *written* **inscribed** therein, saying,
In coming, The *king* **sovereign** of *Babylon* **Babel**
shall *certainly* come and *destroy* **ruin** this land,
and shall cause to *cease* **shabbathize** from thence
man **humanity** and *beast* **animal**?
30 Therefore thus saith *the LORD* **Yah Veh**
of *Jehoiakim* **Yah Yaqim**
king **sovereign** of *Judah* **Yah Hudah**;
He shall have none to sit upon the throne of David:
and his *dead body* **carcase** shall be cast out
in the day to the *heat* **parchedness**,

and in the night to the frost.
31 And I *will punish* **shall visit upon** him
and his seed and his servants for
their *iniquity* **perversity**;
and I *will* **shall** bring upon them,
and upon
the *inhabitants* **settlers** of *Jerusalem* **Yeru Shalem**,
and upon the men of *Judah* **Yah Hudah**,
all the evil that I have *pronounced* **worded** against them;
but they hearkened not.
32 Then took *Jeremiah* **Yirme Yah** another roll,
and gave it to Baruch the scribe,
the son of *Neriah* **Neri Yah**;
who *wrote* **inscribed** therein
from the mouth of *Jeremiah* **Yirme Yah**
all the words of the *book* **scroll**
which *Jehoiakim* **Yah Yaqim**
king **sovereign** of *Judah* **Yah Hudah**
had burned in the fire:
and there were added besides unto them
many like words.

Yirme Yah Imprisoned

37 And *king Zedekiah* **sovereign Sidqi Yah**
the son of *Josiah* **Yoshi Yah** reigned
instead of *Coniah* **Kon Yah**
the son of *Jehoiakim* **Yah Yaqim**,
whom *Nebuchadrezzar* **Nebukadnets Tsar**
king **sovereign** of *Babylon* **Babel**
made *king* **sovereign** in the land of *Judah* **Yah Hudah**.
2 But neither he,
nor his servants, nor the people of the land,
did hearken unto the words of *the LORD* **Yah Veh**,
which he *spake* **worded**
by **the hand of** the prophet *Jeremiah* **Yirme Yah**.
3 And *Zedekiah* **Sidqi Yah** the *king* **sovereign**
sent *Jehucal* **Yehuchal** the son of *Shelemiah* **Shelem Yah**
and *Zephaniah* **Sephan Yah**
the son of *Maaseiah* **Maase Yah** the priest
to the prophet *Jeremiah* **Yirme Yah**, saying,
Pray *now* **I beseech,**
unto *the LORD* **Yah Veh** our *God* **Elohim** for us.
4 *Now Jeremiah* **Yirme Yah**
came in and went out among the people:
for they had not *put* **given** him
into **the** prison **house**.
5 Then *Pharaoh's army* **Paroh's valiant**
was come forth out of *Egypt* **Misrayim**:
and when the *Chaldeans* **Kesediym**
that besieged *Jerusalem* **Yeru Shalem**
heard *tidings* **the report** of them,
they *departed* **ascended** from *Jerusalem* **Yeru Shalem**.
6 Then came the word of *the LORD* **Yah Veh**
unto the prophet *Jeremiah* **Yirme Yah**, saying,

Yirme Yah Inscribes A Second Scroll

27 And so be the word of Yah Veh to Yirme Yah
after the sovereign burns the roll
with the words Baruch inscribed at the
mouth of Yirme Yah, saying,
28 Return, take another roll,
and inscribe therein
all the former words in the first roll
that Yah Yaqim the sovereign of Yah Hudah burned:
29 and say to Yah Yaqim sovereign of Yah Hudah,
Thus says Yah Veh:
You burned this roll, saying,
Why inscribed you therein, saying,
In coming,
the sovereign of Babel comes and ruins this land,
and shabbathizes humanity and animal from it?
30 So thus says Yah Veh
of Yah Yaqim sovereign of Yah Hudah;
No one of his is to sit on the throne of David
and his carcase is cast out
—to the parchness in the day
and to the frost in the night:
31 and I visit on him and his seed and his servants
for their perversity;
and I bring on them
and on the settlers of Yeru Shalem
and on the men of Yah Hudah
all the evil I worded against them:
and they hearken not.
32 And Yirme Yah takes another roll
and gives it to Baruch the scribe the son of Neri Yah;
who inscribes therein from the mouth of Yirme Yah
all the words of the scroll
Yah Yaqim sovereign of Yah Hudah
burned in the fire:
and added besides many like words to them.

Yirme Yah Imprisoned

37 And sovereign Sidqi Yah the son of Yoshi Yah
reigns in the stead of Kon Yah the son of Yah Yaqim
whom Nebukadnets Tsar sovereign of Babel
made sovereign in the land of Yah Hudah:
2 and neither he
nor his servants nor the people of the land
hearken to the words of Yah Veh

worded by the hand of the prophet Yirme Yah.
3 And Sidqi Yah the sovereign
sends Yehuchal the son of Shelem Yah
and Sephan Yah the son of Maase Yah the priest
to the prophet Yirme Yah, saying,
Pray, I beseech, to Yah Veh our Elohim for us.
4 —and Yirme Yah comes and goes
among the people
for they give him not into the prison house.
5 And the valiant of Paroh come from Misrayim:
and the Kesediym besieging Yeru Shalem
hear their report;
and they ascend from Yeru Shalem.
6 And so be the word of Yah Veh
to the prophet Yirme Yah, saying,
7 Thus saith *the LORD* **Yah Veh,**
the God **Elohim** of *Israel* **Yisra El;**
Thus shall ye say
to the *king* **sovereign** of *Judah* **Yah Hudah,**
that sent you unto me to enquire of me;
Behold, *Pharaoh's army* **Paroh's valiant,**
which is come forth to help you,
shall return to *Egypt* **Misrayim** into their own land.
8 And the *Chaldeans* **Kesediym**
shall *come again* **return,** and fight against this city,
and *take* **capture** it, and burn it with fire.
9 Thus saith *the LORD* **Yah Veh;**
Deceive not *yourselves* **your souls,** saying,
The *Chaldeans* **Kesediym**
shall *surely depart* **walk and go** from us:
for they shall not *depart* **go.**
10 For though ye had smitten
the whole *army* **valiant** of the *Chaldeans* **Kesediym**
that fight against you,
and there *remained* **survived**
but wounded men among them,
yet should they rise up every man in his tent,
and burn this city with fire.
11 And **so be** it *came to pass,*
that when the *army* **valiant** of the *Chaldeans* **Kesediym**
was broken up **ascended** from *Jerusalem* **Yeru Shalem**
for fear **from the face** of *Pharaoh's army* **Paroh's valiant,**
12 Then *Jeremiah* **Yirme Yah**
went forth out of *Jerusalem* **Yeru Shalem**
to go into the land of *Benjamin* **Ben Yamin,**
to *separate himself thence* **receive an allotment**
in the midst of the people.
13 And
when he was in the *gate* **portal** of *Benjamin* **Ben Yamin,**
a *captain* **master** of the *ward* **visitation** was there,
whose name was *Irijah* **Yiri Yah,**
the son of *Shelemiah* **Shelem Yah,**
the son of *Hananiah* **Hanan Yah;**
and he *took Jeremiah* **apprehended Yirme Yah**
the prophet, saying,
Thou fallest away to the *Chaldeans* **Kesediym.**
14 Then said *Jeremiah* **Yirme**
Yah, *It is false* **Falsehood;**
I fall not away to the *Chaldeans* **Kesediym.**
But he hearkened not to him:
so *Irijah took Jeremiah* **Yiri Yah**
apprehended Yirme Yah,
and brought him to the *princes* **governors.**
15 Wherefore the *princes* **governors**
were *wroth* **enraged** with *Jeremiah* **Yirme Yah,**
and smote him, and *put* **gave** him
in *prison* **the bond house**
in the house of *Jonathan* **Yah Nathan** the scribe:
for they had *made* **worked** that the prison **house.**
16 When *Jeremiah* **Yirme Yah** was entered
into the *dungeon* **well house,** and
into the *cabins* **prisons,**
and *Jeremiah* **Yirme Yah**
had *remained* **settled** there many days;
17 Then *Zedekiah* **Sidqi Yah,** the *king* **sovereign**
sent, and took him out:
and the *king* **sovereign** asked him *secretly* **covertly**
in his house, and said,
Is there *any* word from *the LORD* **Yah Veh?**
And *Jeremiah* **Yirme Yah** said, There is:
for, said he, thou shalt be *delivered* **given**
into the hand of the *king* **sovereign** of *Babylon* **Babel.**
18 Moreover *Jeremiah* **Yirme Yah**
said unto *king Zedekiah* **sovereign Sidqi Yah,**
What have I *offended* **sinned** against thee,
or against thy servants, or against this people,
that ye have *put* **given** me *in* **unto the** prison **house?**
19 Where are *now* your prophets
which prophesied unto you, saying,
The *king* **sovereign** of *Babylon* **Babel**
shall not come against you, nor against this land?
20 Therefore hear now, I *pray* **beseech** thee,
O my *lord* **adoni** the *king* **sovereign:**
let my supplication, I *pray* **beseech** thee,
be accepted before thee **fall at thy face;**
that thou cause me not to return
to the house of *Jonathan* **Yah Nathan** the scribe,
lest I die there.
7 Thus says Yah Veh Elohim of Yisra El:
Say thus to the sovereign of Yah Hudah,

who sent you to me to enquire of me:
Behold, the valiant of Paroh who come to help you
return to Misrayim into their own land:
8 and the Kesediym return
and fight against this city and capture it
and burn it with fire.
9 Thus says Yah Veh:
Deceive not your souls, saying,
The Kesediym walk and go from us!
—for they go not.
10 For though you smite
all the valiant of the Kesediym
who fight against you,
and there survives but wounded men among them,
every man rises from his tent
to burn this city with fire.
11 And so be it,
the valiant of the Kesediym
ascend from Yeru Shalem
from the face of the valiant of Paroh,
12 and Yirme Yah comes from Yeru Shalem
and goes to the land of Ben Yamin
—to receive an allotment among the people.
13 And so be it,
he is in the portal of Ben Yamin,
a master of the visitation is there
whose name *is* Yiri Yah
the son of Shelem Yah the son of Hanan Yah;
and he apprehends Yirme Yah the prophet, saying,
You fall to the Kesediym.
14 And Yirme Yah says, Falsehood!
I fall not to the Kesediym.
—and he hearkens not to him.
And Yiri Yah apprehends Yirme Yah,
and brings him to the governors:
15 and the governors enraged over Yirme Yah
and smite him and give him into the bond house
in the house of Yah Nathan the scribe:
which they worked for a prison house.
16 And Yirme Yah enters into the well house
and into the prisons;
and Yirme Yah settles there many days.
17 And Sidqi Yah the sovereign sends
and takes him out:
and in his house the sovereign asks him covertly,
and says, Is there a word from Yah Veh?
And Yirme Yah says, There is.
And he says,
You are given into the hand of the sovereign of Babel.
18 And Yirme Yah says to sovereign Sidqi Yah,
What sinned I against you
—or against your servants—or against this people
that you give me to the prison house?
19 Where are your prophets
who prophesied to you, saying,
The sovereign of Babel
comes not against you or against this land?
20 And now hearken, I beseech you,
O my adoni the sovereign:
that my supplication, I beseech you, fall at your face;
that you not return me
to the house of Yah Nathan the scribe,
lest I die there.
21 Then *Zedekiah* **Sidqi Yah**, the *king* **sovereign**
commanded **misvahed**
that they should *commit Jeremiah* **muster Yirme Yah**
into the court of the *prison* **target area**,
and that they should give him daily
a *piece* **round** of bread
out of the bakers' *street* **outway**,
until all the bread in the city were *spent* **consumed**.
Thus *Jeremiah remained* **Yirme Yah settled**
in the court of the *prison* **target area**.

YIRME YAH IN A PIT

38 Then *Shephatiah* **Shaphat**
Yah the son of Mattan,
and *Gedaliah* **Gedal Yah** the son of *Pashur* **Pashchur**,
and *Jucal* **Yuchal** the son of *Shelemiah* **Shelem Yah**,
and *Pashur* **Pashchur** the son of *Malchiah* **Malki Yah**,
heard the words that *Jeremiah* **Yirme Yah**
had spoken unto all the people, saying,
2 Thus saith *the LORD* **Yah Veh**,
He that *remaineth* **settleth** in this city
shall die by the sword,
by the famine, and by the pestilence:
but he that goeth forth to the *Chaldeans* **Kesediym**
shall live;
for he shall have his *life* **soul** for a *prey* **spoil**,
and shall live.
3 Thus saith *the LORD* **Yah Veh**,
In giving, This city shall *surely* be given into the hand
of the *king* **sovereign** of *Babylon's army* **Babel's valiant**,
which shall *take* **capture** it.
4 Therefore
the *princes* **governors** said unto the *king* **sovereign**,
We beseech thee, let this man be *put to death* **deathified**:
for thus he *weakeneth* **slackeneth** the hands
of the men of war that *remain* **survive** in this city,
and the hands of all the people,

in *speaking* **wording** such words unto them:
for this man seeketh not
the *welfare* **shalom** of this people,
but the *hurt* **evil.**
5 Then *Zedekiah* **Sidqi Yah,**
the *king* **sovereign** said,
Behold, he is in your hand:
for the *king* **sovereign** is not he
that can *do any thing* **word** against you.
6 Then took they *Jeremiah* **Yirme Yah,**
and cast him into the *dungeon* **well**
of *Malchiah* **Malki Yah** the son of *Hammelech* **Melech,**
that was in the court of the *prison* **target area:**
and they *let* **sent** down *Jeremiah* **Yirme Yah** with cords.
And in the *dungeon* **well** there was no water, but mire:
so *Jeremiah* **Yirme Yah** sunk in the mire.
7 *Now* when *Ebedmelech* **Ebed Melech**
the *Ethiopian* **Kushiy,** *one* **a man** of the eunuchs
which was in the *king's* **sovereign's** house,
heard that they had *put Jeremiah* **given Yirme Yah**
in the *dungeon* **well;**
the *king* **sovereign** then sitting
in the *gate* **portal** of *Benjamin* **Ben Yamin;**
8 *Ebedmelech* **Ebed Melech** went forth
out of the *king's* **sovereign's** house,
and *spake* **worded** to the *king* **sovereign,** saying,
9 **O** My *lord the king* **adoni sovereign,**
these men have *done evil* **vilified**
in all that they have *done* **worked**
to *Jeremiah* **Yirme Yah** the prophet,
whom they have cast into the *dungeon* **well;**
and he is like to die *for hunger* **at the face of famine**
in the place where he is:
for there is no more bread in the city.
10 Then the *king* **sovereign**
commanded Ebedmelech **misvahed Ebed Melech**
the *Ethiopian* **Kushiy,** saying,
Take from hence thirty men *with thee* **under thy hand,**
and *take up Jeremiah* **ascend Yirme Yah** the prophet
out of the *dungeon* **well,** *before* **ere** he die.
11 So *Ebedmelech* **Ebed Melech**
took the men *with him* **under his hand,**
and went into the house of the *king* **sovereign**
under the treasury,
21 And Sidqi Yah the sovereign
misvahs them to muster Yirme Yah
into the court of the target area,
and that they give him daily
a round of bread from the outway of the bakers,
until all the bread in the city is consumed.
Thus Yirme Yah settles in the court of the target area.

YIRME YAH IN A PIT

38 And Shaphat Yah the son of Mattan
and Gedal Yah the son of Pashchur
and Yuchal the son of Shelem Yah
and Pashchur the son of Malki Yah
hear the words Yirme Yah spoke to all the people,
saying,
2 Thus says Yah Veh:
He who settles in this city dies by the sword
by the famine and by the pestilence:
and he who goes to the Kesediym lives;
for his soul becomes for a spoil, and lives.
3 Thus says Yah Veh,
In giving, this city is given into the hand
of the valiant of the sovereign of Babel
who capture it.
4 And the governors say to the sovereign,
We beseech you, deathify this man:
for thus he slackens the hands
of the men of war who survive in this city
and the hands of all the people,
in wording such words to them:
for this man seeks not the shalom of this people,
but their evil.
5 Then Sidqi Yah the sovereign says,
Behold, he is in your hand:
for the sovereign cannot word against you.
6 And they take Yirme Yah and cast him
into the well of Malki Yah the son of Melech
in the court of the target area:
and they send Yirme Yah down with cords:
and there is no water in the well; only mire:
and Yirme Yah sinks in the mire.
7 And Ebed Melech the Kushiy
a man of the eunuchs in the house of the sovereign
hears that they give Yirme Yah in the well;
and the sovereign sits in the portal of Ben Yamin:
8 Ebed Melech comes from
the house of the sovereign
and words to the sovereign, saying,
9 O my adoni sovereign, these men vilify
in all that they work to Yirme Yah the prophet
—whom they cast into the well to die
at the face of famine in the place where he is:
for there is no more bread in the city.
10 And the sovereign
misvahs Ebed Melech the Kushiy, saying,
Take from here thirty men under your hand,
and ascend Yirme Yah the prophet from the well

ere he die.
11 So Ebed Melech takes the men under his hand
and goes into the house of the sovereign
under the treasury,
and took thence *old cast clouts* **decayed rags**
and *old* **decayed** rotten rags,
and *let* **sent** them down by cords
into the *dungeon* **well** to *Jeremiah* **Yirme Yah.**
12 And *Ebedmelech* **Ebed**
Melech, the *Ethiopian* **Kushiy**
said unto *Jeremiah* **Yirme Yah,**
Put now **Set I beseech,**
these *old cast clouts* **decayed rags** and rotten rags
under *thine armholes* **the elbow holes for thy hands**
under the cords.
And *Jeremiah did* **Yirme Yah worked** so.
13 So they drew up *Jeremiah*
Yirme Yah with cords,
and *took* **ascended** him *up* out of the *dungeon* **well**:
and *Jeremiah remained* **Yirme Yah settled**
in the court of the *prison* **target area.**
14 Then *Zedekiah* **Sidqi Yah**
the *king* **sovereign** sent,
and took *Jeremiah* **Yirme Yah** the prophet unto him
into the third entry
that is in the house of *the LORD* **Yah Veh**:
and the *king* **sovereign** said unto *Jeremiah* **Yirme Yah,**
I *will* **shall** ask thee a *thing* **word**;
hide nothing **conceal naught** from me.
15 Then *Jeremiah* **Yirme Yah**
said unto *Zedekiah* **Sidqi Yah,**
If I *declare it* **tell** unto thee,
in deathifying,
wilt **shalt** thou not *surely put me to death* **deathify me**?
and if I *give thee* counsel **thee,**
wilt **shalt** thou not hearken unto me?
16 So *Zedekiah* **Sidqi Yah** the *king* **sovereign**
sware secretly **oathed covertly** unto *Jeremiah* **Yirme Yah,**
saying, *As the LORD* **Yah Veh** liveth,
that *made* **worked** us this soul,
I *will* **shall** not *put* **deathify** thee *to death,*
neither *will* **shall** I give hee into the hand of these men
that seek thy *life* **soul.**
17 Then said *Jeremiah* **Yirme Yah**
unto *Zedekiah* **Sidqi Yah,**
Thus saith *the LORD* **Yah Veh,**
the God of hosts **Elohim Sabaoth,**
the God **Elohim** of *Israel* **Yisra El;**
If **in going,** thou *wilt assuredly* **shalt** go *forth*
unto the *king* **sovereign** of *Babylon's* **Babel's**
princes **governors,**
then thy soul shall live,
and this city shall not be burned with fire;
and thou shalt live, and thine house:
18 But if thou *wilt* **shalt** not go forth
to the *king* **sovereign** of *Babylon's* **Babel's**
princes **governors,**
then shall this city be given
into the hand of the *Chaldeans* **Kesediym,**
and they shall burn it with fire,
and thou shalt not escape out of their hand.
19 And *Zedekiah* **Sidqi Yah** the *king* **sovereign**
said unto *Jeremiah* **Yirme Yah,**
I am *afraid* **concerned** of the *Jews* **Yah Hudiym**
that are fallen to the *Chaldeans* **Kesediym,**
lest they *deliver* **give** me into their hand,
and they *mock* **exploit** me.
20 But *Jeremiah* **Yirme Yah** said,
They shall not *deliver* **give** thee.
Obey **Hear,** I beseech thee,
the voice of *the LORD* **Yah Veh,**
which I *speak* **word** unto thee:
so it shall *be well unto* **well—please** thee,
and thy soul shall live.
21 But if thou refuse to go forth,
this is the word
that *the LORD* **Yah Veh** hath *shewed* me **see:**
22 And, behold, all the women that *are left* **survive**
in the *king* **sovereign** of *Judah's* **Yah Hudah's** house
shall be brought forth
to the *king* **sovereign** of *Babylon's*
Babel's *princes* **governors,**
and those *women* shall say,
Thy *friends* **men of shalom** have *set* **goaded** thee *on,*
and have prevailed against thee:
thy feet are sunk in the mire,
and they are *turned away back* **apostatized backward.**
and takes decayed rags and decayed rotten rags
and sends them down by cords
into the well to Yirme Yah.
12 And Ebed Melech the Kushiy says to Yirme Yah,
Set, I beseech, these decayed rags and rotten rags
under the elbow holes for your hands
under the cords.
—and Yirme Yah works thus.
13 And they draw up Yirme Yah with cords
and ascend him from the well:
and Yirme Yah settles in the court of the target area.
14 And Sidqi Yah the sovereign sends,
and takes Yirme Yah the prophet to himself

into the third entry in the house of Yah Veh:
and the sovereign says to Yirme Yah,
I ask a word of you; conceal naught from me.
15 And Yirme Yah says to Sidqi Yah,
If I tell you,
in deathifying, deathify you me not?
And if I counsel you, you hearken not to me!
16 And Sidqi Yah the sovereign
oaths covertly to Yirme Yah,
saying, Yah Veh lives, who worked this soul of mine;
I neither deathify you
nor give you into the hand of these men
who seek your soul.
17 And Yirme Yah says to Sidqi Yah,
Thus says Yah Veh Elohim Sabaoth Elohim of Yisra El:
If in going,
you go to the governors of the sovereign of Babel,
your soul lives,
and this city is not burned with fire;
and you live—and your house:
18 and if you go not
to the governors of the sovereign of Babel,
then this city is given into the hand of the Kesediym
and they burn it with fire;
and you escape not from their hand.
19 And Sidqi Yah the sovereign says to Yirme Yah,
I am concerned for the Yah Hudiym
who fell to the Kesediym;
lest they give me into their hand and they exploit me.
20 And Yirme Yah says, They give you not.
Hear, I beseech you,
the voice of Yah Veh that I word to you:
so it well—pleases you, and your soul lives.
21 And if you refuse to go,
this is the word Yah Veh shows me:
22 and behold, they bring all
the women who survive
in the house of the sovereign of Yah Hudah
to the governors of the sovereign of Babel;
and they say,
Your men of shalom goaded you
and prevailed against you:
your feet have sunk in the mire,
and they apostatized backward.
23 So they shall bring out all thy *wives* **women**
and thy *children* **sons** to the *Chaldeans* **Kesediym**:
and thou shalt not escape out of their hand,
but shalt be *taken* **apprehended**
by the hand of the *king* **sovereign** of *Babylon* **Babel**:
and thou shalt cause this city to be burned with fire.
24 Then said *Zedekiah* **Sidqi Yah**
unto *Jeremiah* **Yirme Yah**,
Let no man know of these words, and thou shalt not die.
25 But if the *princes* **governors** hear
that I have *talked* **worded** with thee,
and they come unto thee, and say unto thee,
Declare **Tell** unto us *now* **I beseech,**
what thou hast *said* **worded** unto the *king* **sovereign**,
hide it **conceal** not from us,
and we *will* **shall** not *put* **deathify** thee *to death*;
also what the *king said* **sovereign worded** unto thee:
26 Then thou shalt say unto them,
I presented my supplication
before **at the face of** the *king* **sovereign**,
that he *would* **should** not cause me
to return to *Jonathan's house* **the house of Yah Nathan**,
to die there.
27 Then came all the *princes* **governors**
unto *Jeremiah* **Yirme Yah**,
and asked him:
and he told them according to all these words
that the *king* **sovereign** had *commanded* **misvahed**.
So they *left off speaking with him* **hushed**;
for the *matter* **word** was not *perceived* **heard**.
28 So *Jeremiah* **Yirme Yah**
abode **settled** in the court of the *prison* **target area**
until the day
that *Jerusalem* **Yeru Shalem** was *taken* **captured**:
and he was there
when *Jerusalem* **Yeru Shalem** was *taken* **captured**.

Yeru Shalem Captured

39 In the ninth year of *Zedekiah* **Sidqi Yah**
king **sovereign** of *Judah* **Yah Hudah**,
in the tenth month,
came *Nebuchadrezzar* **Nebukadnets Tsar**
king **sovereign** of *Babylon* **Babel**
and all his *army* **valiant** against *Jerusalem* **Yeru Shalem**,
and they besieged it.
2 And in the eleventh year of *Zedekiah* **Sidqi Yah**,
in the fourth month, the ninth *day* of the month,
the city was *broken up* **split**.
3 And all the *princes* **governors**
of the *king* **sovereign** of *Babylon* **Babel** came in,
and sat in the middle *gate* **portal**,
even *Nergalsharezer* **Nergal Shareser**,
Samgarnebo **Samgar Nebo**, Sarsechim,
Rabsaris **the rabbi eunuch**,
Nergalsharezer **Nergal Shareser**,
Rabmag **the rabbi magi**,

with all the *residue* **survivors** of the *princes* **governors**
of the *king* **sovereign** of *Babylon* **Babel.**
4 And **so be** it *came to pass,*
that when *Zedekiah* **Sidqi Yah**
the *king* **sovereign** of *Judah* **Yah Hudah** saw them,
and all the men of war,
then they fled, and went forth out of the city by night,
by the way of the *king's* **sovereign's** garden,
by the *gate* **portal** betwixt the two walls:
and he went out the way of the plain.
5 But the *Chaldean's army* **Kesediym's valiant**
pursued after them,
and overtook *Zedekiah* **Sidqi Yah**
in the plains of *Jericho* **Yericho**:
and when they had taken him,
they *brought him up* **ascended him**
to *Nebuchadnezzar* **Nebukadnets Tsar**
king **sovereign** of *Babylon* **Babel**
to Riblah in the land of Hamath,
where he *gave* **worded** judgment upon him.
6 Then the *king* **sovereign** of *Babylon* **Babel**
slew **slaughtered** the sons of *Zedekiah* **Sidqi Yah**
in Riblah *before* **in front of** his eyes:
also the *king* **sovereign** of *Babylon* **Babel**
23 And they bring all your women and your sons
to the Kesediym:
and you escape not from their hand,
for you are apprehended
by the hand of the sovereign of Babel:
and this city is burned with fire.
24 Then Sidqi Yah says to Yirme Yah,
No man is to know of these words; and you die not:
25 and if the governors hear
that I worded with you,
and they come to you, and say to you,
Tell us, I beseech,
what you worded to the sovereign;
conceal not from us; and we deathify you not;
and what the sovereign worded to you:
26 then you say to them,
I presented my supplication
at the face of the sovereign,
that he not return me to the house of Yah Nathan
to die there.
27 And all the governors come to Yirme Yah,
and ask him:
and he tells them according to all these words
the sovereign misvahed:
and they hush; for they hear not the word:
28 and Yirme Yah settles in
the court of the target area
until the day Yeru Shalem is captured:
and he is there when Yeru Shalem is captured.

YERU SHALEM CAPTURED

39 In the ninth year
of Sidqi Yah sovereign of Yah Hudah
in the tenth month,
Nebukadnets Tsar sovereign of Babel
and all his valiant
come against Yeru Shalem and besiege it:
2 and in the eleventh year of Sidqi Yah,
in the fourth month, the ninth of the month,
the city is split:
3 and all the governors of the sovereign of Babel
come in and sit in the middle portal
—Nergal Shareser, Samgar Nebo,
Sarsechim the rabbi eunuch,
Nergal Shareser the rabbi magi,
and all the survivors of the governors
of the sovereign of Babel.
4 And so be it,
Sidqi Yah the sovereign of Yah Hudah
and all the men of war see them,
and they flee, and go from the city by night
by the way of the garden of the sovereign
by the portal between the two walls:
and he goes the way of the plain.
5 And the valiant of the Kesediym pursue them
and overtake Sidqi Yah in the plains of Yericho:
and they take him and ascend him
to Nebukadnets Tsar sovereign of Babel
to Riblah in the land of Hamath
—where he words judgment on him.
6 And the sovereign of Babel
slaughters the sons of Sidqi Yah
in Riblah in front of his eyes:
yes, the sovereign of Babel
slew **slaughtered** all the nobles of *Judah* **Yah Hudah.**
7 Moreover
he *put out Zedekiah's* **blinded Sidqi Yah's** eyes,
and bound him with *chains* **coppers,**
to carry him to *Babylon* **Babel.**
8 And the *Chaldeans* **Kesediym**
burned the *king's* **sovereign's** house,
and the houses of the people, with fire,
and brake down the walls of *Jerusalem* **Yeru Shalem.**
9 Then *Nebuzaradan* **Nebu Zaradan**
the *captain of the guard* **rabbi slaughterer**

carried away captive **exiled** into *Babylon* **Babel**
the remnant of the people
that *remained* **survived** in the city,
and those that fell away, that fell to him,
with the *rest* **remnant** of the people
that *remained* **survived**.
10 But *Nebuzaradan* **Nebu Zaradan**
the *captain of the guard* **rabbi slaughterer**
left **let survive** of the poor of the people,
which had *nothing* **naught**,
in the land of *Judah* **Yah Hudah**,
and gave them vineyards and **plowed** fields
at the same time **that same day**.

Yirme Yah Spared

11 *Now Nebuchadrezzar* **Nebukadnets Tsar**
king **sovereign** of *Babylon* **Babel**
gave charge **misvahed** concerning *Jeremiah* **Yirme Yah**
to Nebuzaradan **by the hand of Nebu Zaradan**
the *captain of the guard* **rabbi slaughterer**, saying,
12 Take him, and *look well to*
set thine eyes unto him,
and *do* **work** him no *harm* **evil**;
but *do* **work** unto him
even as he shall *say* **word** unto thee.
13 So *Nebuzaradan* **Nebu Zaradan**
the *captain of the guard* **rabbi slaughterer** sent,
and *Nebushasban* **Nebu Shazban**,
Rabsaris **the rabbi eunuch**,
and *Nergalsharezer* **Nergal Shareser**,
Rabmag **the rabbi magi**,
and all the *king* **sovereign**
of *Babylon's princes* **Babel's rabbis**;
14 Even they sent, and took *Jeremiah* **Yirme Yah**
out of the court of the *prison* **target area**,
and *committed* **gave** him unto *Gedaliah* **Gedal Yah**
the son of Ahikam the son of Shaphan,
that he should carry him home:
so he *dwelt* **settled** among the people.
15 *Now* the word of *the LORD* **Yah Veh**
came unto *Jeremiah* **Yirme Yah**,
while he was *shut up* **restrained**
in the court of the *prison* **guard area**, saying,
16 Go and *speak* **say**
to *Ebedmelech* **Ebed Melech** the
Ethiopian **Kushiy**, saying,
Thus saith *the LORD of hosts* **Yah Veh Sabaoth**,
the God **Elohim** of *Israel* **Yisra El**; Behold,
I *will* **shall** bring my words upon this city for evil,
and not for good;
and they shall be *accomplished*
in that day *before thee* **at thy face**.
17 But I *will deliver* **shall rescue** thee in that day,
saith the LORD **an oracle of Yah Veh**:
and thou shalt not be given into the hand of the men
of whom thou *art afraid* **fearest to face**.
18 *For* **In rescuing,** I *will surely*
deliver **shall rescue** thee,
and thou shalt not fall by the sword,
but thy *life* **soul** shall be for a *prey* **spoil** unto thee:
because thou hast *put thy trust* **confided** in me,
saith the LORD **an oracle of Yah Veh**.

Yirme Yah Rescued

40 The word that came to *Jeremiah* **Yirme Yah**
from *the LORD* **Yah Veh**,
after that *Nebuzaradan* **Nebu Zaradan**
the *captain of the guard* **rabbi slaughterer**
had *let him go* **sent him away** from Ramah,
when he had taken him being bound in *chains* **manacles**
among all *that were carried away captive* **the exiles**
of *Jerusalem* **Yeru Shalem** and *Judah* **Yah Hudah**,
which were *carried away captive*
exiled unto *Babylon* **Babel**.
slaughters all the nobles of Yah Hudah:
7 and he blinds the eyes of Sidqi Yah
and binds him with coppers to carry him to Babel.
8 And the Kesediym
burn the house of the sovereign
and the houses of the people with fire,
and break down the walls of Yeru Shalem:
9 and Nebu Zaradan the rabbi slaughterer
exiles the remnant of the people
who survive in the city,
and those who fell—who fell to him,
with the remnant of the people who survive
to Babel:
10 and of the poor of the people who have naught
Nebu Zaradan the rabbi slaughterer
has them survive in the land of Yah Hudah;
and gives them vineyards and plowed fields
that same day.

Yirme Yah Spared

11 And Nebukadnets Tsar sovereign of Babel
misvahs concerning Yirme Yah
by the hand of Nebu Zaradan the rabbi slaughterer,
saying,
12 Take him, and set your eyes to him;
and work him no evil:

and work to him as he words to you.
13 And Nebu Zaradan the rabbi slaughterer sends;
and Nebu Shazban the rabbi eunuch,
and Nergal Shareser the rabbi magi,
and all the rabbis of the sovereign of Babel;
14 and they send,
and take Yirme Yah from the court of the target area
and give him to Gedal Yah
the son of Ahikam the son of Shaphan
to carry him home:
and he settles among the people.
15 And so be the word of Yah Veh to Yirme Yah,
who is restrained in the court of the guard area,
saying,
16 Go and say to Ebed Melech the Kushiy, saying,
Thus says Yah Veh Sabaoth Elohim of Yisra El:
Behold, I bring my words on this city for evil
and not for good;
to be at your face in that day:
17 and I rescue you in that day
—an oracle of Yah Veh
and give you not into the hand
of the men you fear to face.
18 In rescuing, I rescue you;
and you fall not by the sword,
and your soul becomes for a spoil to you:
because you confided in me
—an oracle of Yah Veh.

YIRME YAH RESCUED

40 And so be the word to Yirme Yah from Yah Veh
after Nebu Zaradan the rabbi slaughterer
sent him away from Ramah;
when he took him bound in manacles
among all the exiles of Yeru Shalem and Yah Hudah,
who were exiled to Babel.
2 And the *captain of the guard* **rabbi slaughterer**
took *Jeremiah* **Yirme Yah**, and said unto him,
The LORD **Yah Veh** thy *God* **Elohim**
hath *pronounced* **worded** this evil upon this place.
3 *Now the LORD* **Yah Veh** hath brought it,
and *done* **worked** according as he hath *said* **worded**:
because ye have sinned against *the LORD* **Yah Veh**,
and have not *obeyed* **hearkened unto** his voice,
therefore this *thing* is come upon you.
4 And now, behold, I loose thee this day
from the *chains* **manacles** which were upon thine hand.
If it seem good *unto thee* **in thine eyes**
to come with me into *Babylon* **Babel**, come;
and I *will look well* **shall set mine eyes** unto thee:
but if it seem *ill unto thee* **evil in thine eyes**
to come with me into *Babylon* **Babel**, *forbear* **cease**:
behold **see**, all the land is *before thee* **at thy face**:
whither it seemeth good
and *convenient for thee* **straight in thine eyes** to go,
thither go.
5 *Now* while he was not yet gone back, *he said*,
Go **Turn** back also to *Gedaliah* **Gedal Yah**
the son of Ahikam the son of Shaphan,
whom the *king* **sovereign** of *Babylon* **Babel**
hath made *governor* **overseer**
over the cities of *Judah* **Yah Hudah**,
and *dwell* **settle** with him among the people:
or go wheresoever it seemeth
convenient unto thee **straight in thine eyes** to go.
So the *captain of the guard* **rabbi slaughterer**
gave him *victuals* **rations** and a *reward* **load/burden**,
and *let* **sent** him *go* **away**.
6 Then went *Jeremiah* **Yirme Yah**
unto *Gedaliah* **Gedal Yah**
the son of Ahikam to *Mizpah* **Mispeh**;
and *dwelt* **settled** with him among the people
that *were left* **survived** in the land.
7 *Now* when all
the *captains* **governors** of the *forces* **valiant**
which were in the fields, *even* they and their men,
heard that the *king* **sovereign** of *Babylon* **Babel**
had made *Gedaliah* **Gedal Yah** the son of Ahikam
governor **overseer** in the land,
and had committed unto him men, and women,
and *children* **toddlers**, and of the poor of the land,
of them that were not
carried away captive **exiled** to *Babylon* **Babel**;
8 Then they came to *Gedaliah* **Gedal Yah**
to *Mizpah* **Mispeh**,
even *Ishmael* **Yishma El**
the son of *Nethaniah* **Nethan Yah**,
and *Johanan* **Yah Hanan** and *Jonathan* **Yah Nathan**
the sons of *Kareah* **Qareach**,
and *Seraiah* **Sera Yah** the son of *Tanhumeth* **Tachumeth**,
and the sons of *Ephai* **Ophay**
the *Netophathite* **Netophathiy**,
and *Jezaniah* **Yezan Yah**
the son of a *Maachathite* **Maachahiy**,
they and their men.
9 And *Gedaliah* **Gedal Yah**
the son of Ahikam the son of Shaphan
sware **oathed** unto them and to their men, saying,
Fear **Awe** not to serve the *Chaldeans* **Kesediym**:
dwell **settle** in the land,

and serve the *king* **sovereign** of *Babylon* **Babel**,
and it shall *be well with* **well—please** you.
10 As for me, behold,
I *will dwell* **shall settle** at *Mizpah* **Mispeh**,
to *serve the Chaldeans* **stand at the face of the Kesediym**,
which *will* **shall** come unto us:
but ye, gather ye wine, and summer fruits, and oil,
and *put* **set** them in your *vessels* **instruments**,
and *dwell* **settle** in your cities
that ye have *taken* **apprehended**.
11 Likewise
when all the *Jews* **Yah Hudiym** that were in Moab,
and among the *Ammonites* **sons of Ammon**,
and in Edom, and that were in all the *countries* **lands**,
heard that the *king* **sovereign** of *Babylon* **Babel**
2 And the rabbi slaughterer takes Yirme Yah,
and says to him,
Yah Veh your Elohim words this evil on this place:
3 Yah Veh brought and worked it as he worded:
because you sinned against Yah Veh,
and hearkened not to his voice,
even this is to you:
4 and now, behold, I loose you this day
from the manacles on your hand:
if it seems good in your eyes
to come with me to Babel,
come;
and I set my eyes to you:
and if it seem evil in your eyes
to come with me into Babel,
cease:
see, all the land is at your face:
where it seems good and straight in your eyes to go,
go:
5 —and he still replys not—
or turn back to Gedal Yah
the son of Ahikam the son of Shaphan,
whom the sovereign of Babel
made overseer over the cities of Yah Hudah;
and settle with him among the people:
or go wherever it seems straight in your eyes to go.
—and the rabbi slaughterer
gives him rations and a load/burden
and sends him away.
6 And Yirme Yah
goes to Gedal Yah the son of Ahikam to Mispeh;
and settles with him
among the people who survived in the land.
7 And all the governors of the valiant in the fields
—they and their men
hear that the sovereign of Babel
made Gedal Yah the son of Ahikam
overseer in the land,
and committed to him
men and women and toddlers
and of the poor of the land
—of them who were not exiled to Babel;
8 and they go to Gedal Yah to Mispeh
—even Yishma El the son of Nethan Yah,
and Yah Hanan and Yah Nathan the sons of Qareach
and Sera Yah the son of Tachumeth;
and the sons of Ophay the Netophathiy
and Yezan Yah the son of a Maachahiy
—they and their men.
9 And Gedal Yah
the son of Ahikam the son of Shaphan
oaths to them and to their men, saying,
Awe not to serve the Kesediym:
settle in the land and serve the sovereign of Babel,
and it well—pleases you.
10 As for me, behold, I settle at Mispeh,
to stand at the face of the Kesediym
who come to us:
and you, gather wine and summer fruits and oil;
and set them in your instruments:
and settle in the cities you apprehend.
11 And also, all the Yah Hudiym in Moab
and among the sons of Ammon and in Edom
and in all the lands,
hear that the sovereign of Babel
had *left a remnant* **given survivors** of *Judah* **Yah Hudah**,
and that he had *set over* **oversee** them
Gedaliah **Gedal Yah**
the son of Ahikam the son of Shaphan;
12 Even all the *Jews* **Yah Hudiym**
returned out of all places whither they were driven,
and came to the land of *Judah* **Yah Hudah**,
to *Gedaliah* **Gedal Yah**, unto *Mizpah* **Mispeh**,
and gathered wine and summer fruits
very much **mighty abounding**.
13 Moreover
Johanan **Yah Hanan** the son of *Kareah* **Qareach**,
and all the *captains* **governors** of the *forces* **valiant**
that were in the fields,
came to *Gedaliah* **Gedal Yah** to *Mizpah* **Mispeh**,
14 And said unto him,
In knowing, Dost thou *certainly* know that Baalis
the *king* **sovereign** of the *Ammonites* **sons of Ammon**
hath sent *Ishmael* **Yishma El**

the son of *Nethaniah* **Nethan Yah**
to *slay thee* **smite thy soul**?
But *Gedaliah* **Gedal Yah** the son of Ahikam
believed **trusted** them not.
15 Then *Johanan* **Yah Hanan**
the son of *Kareah* **Qareach**
spake **said** to *Gedaliah* **Gedal Yah** in *Mizpah* **Mispeh**
secretly **covertly** saying, Let me go, *I pray thee,*
and I *will slay Ishmael* **shall smite Yishma El**
the son of *Nethaniah* **Nethan Yah**,
and no man shall know it:
wherefore should he *slay thee* **smite thy soul**,
that all the *Jews* **Yah Hudiym**
which are gathered unto thee should be scattered,
and the *remnant* **survivors** in *Judah* **Yah Hudah**
perish **destruct**?
16 But *Gedaliah* **Gedal Yah** the son of Ahikam
said unto *Johanan* **Yah Hanan**
the son of *Kareah* **Qareach**,
Thou shalt not *do* **work** this *thing* **word**:
for thou *speakest* **wordest** falsely of *Ishmael* **Yishma El**.

GEDAL YAH EXECUTED

41 *Now* **And so be** it *came to*
pass in the seventh month,
that Ishmael **Yishma El** the son of
Nethaniah **Nethan Yah**
the son of *Elishama* **Eli Shama**,
of the seed *royal* **of the sovereigndom**,
and the *princes* **rabbis** of the *king* **sovereign**,
even ten men with him,
came unto *Gedaliah* **Gedal Yah** the son of Ahikam
to *Mizpah* **Mispeh**;
and there they did eat bread together in *Mizpah* **Mispeh**.
2 Then arose *Ishmael* **Yishma El**
the son of *Nethaniah* **Nethan Yah**,
and the ten men that were with him,
and smote *Gedaliah* **Gedal Yah**
the son of Ahikam the son of Shaphan with the sword,
and *slew* **executed** him,
whom the *king* **sovereign** of *Babylon* **Babel**
had made *governor* **overseer** over the land.
3 *Ishmael* **Yishma El** also *slew* **smote**
all the *Jews* **Yah Hudiym** that were with him,
even with *Gedaliah* **Gedal Yah**, at *Mizpah* **Mispeh**,
and the *Chaldeans* **Kesediym** that were found there,
and the men of war.
4 And **so be** it *came to pass* the second day
after he had *slain Gedaliah* **executed Gedal Yah**,
and no man knew it,
5 That there came *certain* **men** from Shechem,
from Shiloh, and from *Samaria* **Shomeron**,
even fourscore **eighty** men, having their beards shaven,
and their clothes *rent* **ripped**,
and having *cut themselves* **incised**,
with offerings and incense in their hand,
to bring them to the house of *the LORD* **Yah Veh**.
6 And *Ishmael* **Yishma El**
the son of *Nethaniah* **Nethan Yah**
went forth from *Mizpah* **Mispeh** to meet them,
weeping *all along* **and walking** as he went:
and **so be** it *came to pass*,
as he met them, he said unto them,
Come to *Gedaliah* **Gedal Yah** the son of Ahikam.
gives survivors of Yah Hudah,
and that he has
Gedal Yah the son of Ahikam the son of Shaphan
oversee them;
12 and all the Yah Hudiym
return from all the places they were driven
and come to the land of Yah Hudah
—to Gedal Yah, to Mispeh,
and gather wine and summer fruits
mighty abounding.
13 And Yah Hanan the son of Qareach
and all the governors of the valiant in the fields
go to Gedal Yah to Mispeh;
14 and say to him,
In knowing, know you that Baalis
the sovereign of the sons of Ammon
sends Yishma El the son of Nethan Yah
to smite your soul?
—and Gedal Yah the son of Ahikam trusts them not.
15 And Yah Hanan the son of Qareach
says covertly to Gedal Yah in Mispeh, saying,
Have me go, I beseech you,
and I smite Yishma El the son of Nethan Yah,
so that no man knows.
Why have him smite your soul,
that all the Yah Hudiym gathered to you scatter,
and the survivors in Yah Hudah destruct?
16 And Gedal Yah the son of Ahikam
says to Yah Hanan the son of Qareach,
Work not this word:
for you word falsely of Yishma El.

GEDAL YAH EXECUTED

41 And so be it, in the seventh month,
Yishma El the son of Nethan Yah the son of Eli Shama
of the seed of the sovereigndom,

and the rabbis of the sovereign
with ten men,
go to Gedal Yah the son of Ahikam to Mispeh;
and there they eat bread together in Mispeh.
2 And Yishma El the son of Nethan Yah
with the ten men
rise and smite Gedal Yah
the son of Ahikam the son of Shaphan
with the sword;
and execute him whom the sovereign of Babel
made overseer over the land.
3 And Yishma El smites all
the Yah Hudiym with him
—with Gedal Yah at Mispeh
—with the Kesediym they found there
and the men of war.
4 And so be it,
the second day after he executes Gedal Yah
—and no man knows,
5 men come from Shechem
from Shiloh and from Shomeron
—eighty men
with beards shaven and clothes ripped,
and having incised
—with offerings and incense in their hand
to bring to the house of Yah Veh.
6 And Yishma El the son of Nethan Yah
goes from Mispeh to meet them
—weeping and walking as he goes:
and so be it, as he meets them, he says to them,
Come to Gedal Yah the son of Ahikam.
7 And it was so,
when they came into the midst of the city,
that *Ishmael* **Yishma El** the son of
Nethaniah **Nethan Yah**
slew **slaughtered** them,
and cast them into the midst of the *pit* **well**,
he, and the men that were with him.
8 But ten men were found among them
that said unto *Ishmael* **Yishma El**, *Slay* **Execute** us not:
for we have **hidden** treasures in the field,
of wheat, and of barley, and of oil, and of honey.
So he *forbare* **ceased**,
and slew them not among their brethren.
9 Now the *pit* **well** wherein *Ishmael* **Yishma El**
had cast all the *dead bodies* **carcases** of the men,
whom he had *slain* **smitten**
because **under the hand** of *Gedaliah* **Gedal Yah**,
was it which Asa the *king* **sovereign** had *made* **worked**
for fear **at the face** of *Baasha* **Basha**
king **sovereign** of *Israel* **Yisra El**:
and Ishmael **Yishma El** the son of
Nethaniah **Nethan Yah**
filled it with them that were *slain* **pierced**.
10 Then *Ishmael carried away*
captive **Yishma El captured**
all the *residue* **survivors** of the people
that were in *Mizpah* **Mispeh**,
even the *king's* **sovereign's** daughters, and all the people
that *remained* **survived** in *Mizpah* **Mispeh**,
whom *Nebuzaradan* **Nebu Zaradan**
the *captain of the guard* **rabbi slaughterer**
had *committed* **mustered**
to *Gedaliah* **Gedal Yah** the son of Ahikam:
and *Ishmael* **Yishma El** the son of
Nethaniah **Nethan Yah**
carried **captured** them *away captive*,
and *departed to go* **went to pass** over
to the *Ammonites* **sons of Ammon**.

YAH HANAN RESCUES THE PEOPLE

11 But when
Johanan **Yah Hanan** the son of *Kareah* **Qareach**,
and all the *captains* **governors** of the *forces* **valiant**
that were with him,
heard of all the evil
that *Ishmael* **Yishma El** the son of
Nethaniah **Nethan Yah**
had *done* **worked**,
12 Then they took all the men,
and went to fight with *Ishmael* **Yishma El**
the son of *Nethaniah* **Nethan Yah**,
and found him
by the great waters that are in *Gibeon* **Gibon**.
13 *Now* **And so be** it *came to*
pass, that when all the people
which were with *Ishmael* **Yishma El**
saw *Johanan* **Yah Hanan** the son of *Kareah* **Qareach**,
and all the *captains* **governors** of the *forces* **valiant**
that were with him, *then* they *were glad* **cheered**.
14 So all the people that *Ishmael* **Yishma El**
had *carried away captive* **captured** from *Mizpah* **Mispeh**
cast about **turned around** and returned, and went
unto *Johanan* **Yah Hanan** the son of *Kareah* **Qareach**.
15 But *Ishmael* **Yishma El**
the son of *Nethaniah* **Nethan Yah**
escaped from *Johanan* **the face of Yah Hanan**
with eight men,
and went to the *Ammonites* **sons of Ammon**.
16 Then took *Johanan* **Yah Hanan**

the son of *Kareah* **Qareach**,
and all the *captains* **governors** of the *forces* **valiant**
that were with him,
all the *remnant* **survivors** of the people
whom he had *recovered* **returned**
from *Ishmael* **Yishma El**
the son of *Nethaniah* **Nethan Yah**,
from *Mizpah* **Mispeh**,
after *that* he had *slain* **smitten**
Gedaliah **Gedal Yah** the son of Ahikam,
even mighty men of war,
and the women, and the children, and the eunuchs,
whom he had
brought again **returned** from *Gibeon* **Gibon**:
17 And they departed, and *dwelt* **settled**
in the *habitation* **inn** of *Chimham* **Kimham**,
which is *by Bethlehem* **beside Beth Lechem**,
7 And so be it, they come midst the city,
and Yishma El the son of Nethan Yah
slaughters them midst the well
—he and the men with him.
8 And they find ten men among them
who say to Yishma El, Execute us not:
for we hid treasures in the field
—of wheat and of barley and of oil and of honey.
—and he ceases
and slaughters them not among their brothers.
9 And the well wherein Yishma El
cast all the carcases of the men,
whom he smote under the hand of Gedal Yah,
was the one Asa the sovereign worked
at the face of Basha sovereign of Yisra El:
Yishma El the son of Nethan Yah
fills it with the pierced:
10 and Yishma El captures
all the survivors of the people in Mispeh
—the daughters of the sovereign
and all the people who survived in Mispeh;
whom Nebu Zaradan the rabbi slaughterer mustered
to Gedal Yah the son of Ahikam:
and Yishma El the son of Nethan Yah captures them,
and goes to pass over to the sons of Ammon.

YAH HANAN RESCUES THE PEOPLE

11 And Yah Hanan the son of Qareach
and all the governors of the valiant with him
hear of all the evil
Yishma El the son of Nethan Yah works:
12 and they take all the men,
and go to fight with Yishma El the son of Nethan Yah:
and they find him by the great waters in Gibon.
13 And so be it,
all the people with Yishma El
see Yah Hanan the son of Qareach
and all the governors of the valiant with him,
and they cheer:
14 and all the people Yishma
El captured from Mispeh
turn around and return
and go to Yah Hanan the son of Qareach:
15 and Yishma El the son of Nethan Yah
escapes from the face of Yah Hanan with eight
men and goes to the sons of Ammon.
16 And Yah Hanan the son of Qareach
and all the governors of the valiant with him
take all the survivors of the people
whom he returned
from Yishma El the son of Nethan Yah
—from Mispeh,
after he smote Gedal Yah the son of Ahikam
—mighty men of war;
and the women and the children and the eunuchs
whom he returned from Gibon:
17 and they depart
and settle in the inn of Kimham beside Beth Lechem
to go to enter into *Egypt* **Misrayim**,
18 *Because* **At the face** of the *Chaldeans* **Kesediym**:
for they *were afraid of them* **awed at their face**,
because
Ishmael **Yishma El** the son of *Nethaniah* **Nethan Yah**
had *slain Gedaliah* **smitten Gedal Yah**
the son of Ahikam,
whom the *king* **sovereign** of *Babylon* **Babel**
made *governor* **overseer** in the land.

WARNING AGAINST APPROACHING MISRAYIM

42 Then all the *captains*
governors of the *forces* **valiant**,
and *Johanan* **Yah Hanan** the son of *Kareah* **Qareach**,
and *Jezaniah* **Yezan Yah** the son
of *Hoshaiah* **Hosha Yah**,
and all the people from the least even unto the greatest,
came near,
2 And said unto *Jeremiah* **Yirme Yah** the prophet,
Let, we beseech thee,
our supplication be accepted *before thee* **at thy face**,
and pray for us unto *the LORD*
Yah Veh thy *God* **Elohim**,
even for all *this remnant* **these survivors**;
(for we *are left* **survived**

but a few of *many* **an abundance,**
as thine eyes *do behold* **see** us:)
3 That *the LORD* **Yah Veh** thy *God* **Elohim**
may *shew* **tell** us the way wherein we may walk,
and the *thing* **word** that we may *do* **work.**
4 Then *Jeremiah* **Yirme Yah**
the prophet said unto them,
I have heard *you*; behold,
I *will* **shall** pray
unto *the LORD* **Yah Veh** your *God* **Elohim**
according to your words;
and **so be** it *shall come to pass,*
that whatsoever *thing* **word**
the LORD **Yah Veh** shall answer you,
I *will declare* **shall tell** it unto you;
I *will keep nothing back* **shall withhold no word**
from you.
5 Then they said to *Jeremiah* **Yirme Yah,**
The LORD **Yah Veh** be *a true* **in truth**
and **a** faithful witness between us,
if we *do* **work** not even according to all *things* **the word**
for the which *the LORD* **Yah Veh** thy *God* **Elohim**
shall send thee to us.
6 Whether *it be* good, or whether *it be* evil,
we *will obey* **shall hearken unto** the voice
of *the LORD* **Yah Veh** our *God* **Elohim,**
to whom we send thee;
that it may *be well with* **well—please** us,
when we *obey* **hearken unto** the voice
of *the LORD* **Yah Veh** our *God* **Elohim.**
7 And it *came to pass after*
became at the end of ten days,
that the word of *the LORD* **Yah Veh**
came unto *Jeremiah* **Yirme Yah.**
8 Then called he
Johanan **Yah Hanan** the son of *Kareah* **Qareach,**
and all the *captains* **governors** of the *forces* **valiant**
which were with him,
and all the people from the least even to the greatest,
9 And said unto them, Thus
saith *the LORD* **Yah Veh,**
the God **Elohim** of *Israel* **Yisra El,**
unto whom ye sent me
to *present* **fell** your supplication *before him* **at his face;**
10 If ye *will still abide* **shall**
return and settle in this land,
then *will* **shall** I build you, and not *pull* **break** you down,
and I *will* **shall** plant you, and not *pluck* **uproot** you *up*:
for I *repent me* **sigh** of the evil
that I have *done* **worked** unto you.
11 *Be* **Awe** not *afraid of*
the *king* **sovereign** of *Babylon* **Babel,**
of whom ye *are afraid* **fear at his face;**
be not *afraid* **awed** of him,
saith the LORD **an oracle of Yah Veh:**
for I am with you to save you,
and to *deliver* **rescue** you from his hand.
12 And I *will shew* **shall give** mercies unto you,
that he may *have* mercy *upon* you,
and *cause* **restore** you *to return* to your own *land* **soil.**
13 But if ye say,
We *will* **shall** not *dwell* **settle** in this land,
—to go to enter Misrayim
18 from the face of the Kesediym:
for they awed at their face,
because Yishma El the son of Nethan Yah
smote Gedal Yah the son of Ahikam
whom the sovereign of Babel
made overseer in the land.

Warning Against Approaching Misrayim

42 And all the governors of the valiant
and Yah Hanan the son of Qareach
and Yezan Yah the son of Hosha Yah
and all the people
from the least even to the greatest come near,
2 and say to Yirme Yah the prophet,
Accept, we beseech you,
our supplication at your face;
and pray for us to Yah Veh your Elohim
for all these survivors
—for only a few from an abundance survive
as your eyes see:
3 that Yah Veh your Elohim
tell us the way to walk
and the word to work.
4 And Yirme Yah the prophet says to them,
I hear!
Behold, I pray to Yah Veh your Elohim
according to your words:
and so be it,
whatever word Yah Veh answers you, I tell you;
I withhold no word from you.
5 And they say to Yirme Yah,
Yah Veh is, in truth,
a faithful witness between us,
if we work not according to all the word
for which Yah Veh your Elohim sends you to us:
6 whether good; whether evil;
we hearken to the voice of Yah Veh our Elohim,

to whom we send you
—that it well—please us
when we hearken
to the voice of Yah Veh our Elohim.
7 And so be it, at the end of ten days,
the word of Yah Veh comes to Yirme Yah:
8 and he calls Yah Hanan the son of Qareach
and all the governors of the valiant with him
and all the people from the least even to the greatest;
9 and says to them,
Thus says Yah Veh Elohim of Yisra El
to whom you sent me
to fell your supplication at his face:
10 If you return and settle in this land, then I build
you, and break you not; and I plant you, and uproot
you not: for I sigh of the evil I worked to you.
11 Awe not the sovereign of Babel
whose face you fear;
awe him not
—an oracle of Yah Veh
for I *am* with you to save you
and to rescue you from his hand:
12 and I give you mercies,
that he mercy you and restore you to your own soil.
13 And if you say,
We neither settle in this land
neither *obey* **hearken unto** the voice
of *the LORD* **Yah Veh** your *God* **Elohim,**
14 Saying, No;
but we *will* **shall** go into the land of *Egypt* **Misrayim,**
where we shall see no war,
nor hear the *sound* **voice** of the *trumpet* **shophar,**
nor have hunger of bread;
and there *will* **shall** we *dwell* **settle:**
15 And now therefore
hear the word of *the LORD* **Yah Veh,**
ye *remnant* **survivors** of *Judah* **Yah Hudah;**
Thus saith *the LORD of hosts* **Yah Veh Sabaoth,**
the God **Elohim** of *Israel* **Yisra El;**
If **in setting,** ye *wholly* set your faces
to enter into *Egypt* **Misrayim,** and go to sojourn there;
16 *Then* **And so be** it *shall come to pass,*
that the sword, which ye feared,
shall overtake you there in the land of *Egypt* **Misrayim,**
and the famine, whereof ye were *afraid* **concerned,**
shall *follow close after* **adhereth to** you
there in *Egypt* **Misrayim;** and there ye shall die.
17 *So* shall it be with all the men that set their faces
to go into *Egypt* **Misrayim** to sojourn
there; they shall die by the sword,
by the famine, and by the pestilence:
and *none of them* **there** shall *remain* **be no survivors**
escape **or escapees**
from **the face of** the evil that I *will*
shall bring upon them.
18 For thus saith *the LORD*
of hosts **Yah Veh Sabaoth,**
the God **Elohim** of *Israel* **Yisra El;**
As *mine anger* **my wrath** and my fury
hath been poured forth
upon the *inhabitants* **settlers** of *Jerusalem* **Yeru Shalem;**
so shall my fury be poured forth upon you,
when ye shall enter into *Egypt* **Misrayim:**
and ye shall be an *execration* **oath,**
and *an astonishment* **a desolation,**
and *a curse* **an abasement,** and a reproach;
and ye shall see this place no more.
19 *The LORD* **Yah Veh** hath
said **worded** concerning you,
O ye *remnant* **survivors** of *Judah* **Yah Hudah;**
Go ye **Enter** not *into Egypt* **Misrayim:**
in knowing, know *certainly*
that I have *admonished* **witnessed to** you this day.
20 For *ye dissembled in* your
hearts **souls have strayed,**
when ye sent me
unto *the LORD* **Yah Veh** your *God* **Elohim,** saying,
Pray for us unto *the LORD* **Yah Veh** our *God* **Elohim;**
and according unto all
that *the LORD* **Yah Veh** our *God* **Elohim** shall say,
so *declare* **tell** unto us, and we *will do* **shall work** it.
21 And *now* I have this day *declared* **told** it to you;
but ye have not *obeyed* **hearkened unto** the voice
of *the LORD* **Yah Veh** your *God* **Elohim,**
nor *any thing* **aught**
for the which he hath sent me unto you.
22 Now therefore **in knowing,**
know *certainly* that ye shall die by the sword,
by the famine, and by the pestilence,
in the place whither ye desire to go *and* to sojourn.

The Warning Of Yirme Yah

43 And **so be** it *came to pass,*
that when *Jeremiah* **Yirme Yah**
had *made an end of speaking* **concluded wording**
unto all the people
all the words of *the LORD* **Yah Veh** their *God* **Elohim,**
for which *the LORD* **Yah Veh** their *God* **Elohim**
had sent him to them, *even* all these words,
2 Then *spake* **said**

Azariah **Azar Yah** the son of *Hoshaiah* **Hosha Yah**,
and *Johanan* **Yah Hanan** the son of *Kareah* **Qareach**,
and all the *proud* **arrogant** men,
saying unto *Jeremiah* **Yirme Yah**, Thou speakest falsely:
the LORD **Yah Veh** our *God* **Elohim** hath not sent thee,
to say **saying**,
Go not into *Egypt* **Misrayim** to sojourn there:
3 But Baruch the son of *Neriah* **Neri Yah**
setteth **goadeth** thee *on* against us,
for to *deliver* **give** us into the hand
of the *Chaldeans* **Kesediym**,
nor hearken to the voice of Yah Veh your Elohim,
14 saying, No!
—but we enter the land of Misrayim
where we neither see war
nor hear the voice of the shophar
nor hunger for bread—and there we settle:
15 and now so, hear the word of Yah Veh
—you survivors of Yah Hudah;
Thus says Yah Veh Sabaoth Elohim of Yisra El:
If in setting, you set your faces to enter Misrayim
and go to sojourn there;
16 then so be it,
the sword you fear
overtakes you there in the land of Misrayim;
and the famine whereof you are concerned
adheres to you there in Misrayim
—and there you die:
17 and so be it with all the men who set their faces
to go into Misrayim to sojourn there:
they die by the sword
by the famine and by the pestilence:
and there are no survivors or escapees
from the face of the evil I bring on them.
18 For thus says Yah Veh
Sabaoth Elohim of Yisra El:
As my wrath and my fury
pours on the settlers of Yeru Shalem;
thus my fury pours on you
when you enter Misrayim:
and you become an oath and a desolation
and an abasement and a reproach;
and you see this place no more.
19 Yah Veh words concerning you,
O you survivors of Yah Hudah;
Enter not Misrayim:
in knowing, know that I witness to you this day:
20 for your souls strayed,
when you sent me to Yah Veh your Elohim, saying,
Pray for us to Yah Veh our Elohim;
and according to all Yah Veh our Elohim says,
tell us, and we work.
21 And this day I tell you;
but you neither hearken
to the voice of Yah Veh your Elohim
nor for aught for which he sent me to you.
22 And now,
in knowing, know that you die by the sword
by the famine and by the pestilence
in the place where you desire to go to sojourn.

THE WARNING OF YIRME YAH

43 And so be it,
Yirme Yah concludes wording all the words
of Yah Veh their Elohim to all the people,
for which Yah Veh their Elohim sent him to them
—all these words,
2 that Azar Yah the son of Hosha Yah
and Yah Hanan the son of Qareach
and all the arrogant men say to Yirme Yah,
saying, You speak falsely:
Yah Veh our Elohim sent you not,
saying, Go not into Misrayim to sojourn there.
3 —for Baruch the son of Neri Yah
goads you against us,
to give us into the hand of the Kesediym
that they might put us to death,
and *carry us away captives* **exile us** into *Babylon* **Babel**.
4 So *Johanan* **Yah Hanan** the
son of *Kareah* **Qareach**,
and all the *captains* **governors** of the *forces* **valiant**,
and all the people,
obeyed **hearkened** not **unto** the
voice of *the LORD* **Yah Veh**,
to *dwell* **settle** in the land of *Judah* **Yah Hudah**.
5 But *Johanan* **Yah Hanan** the son of *Kareah* **Qareach**,
and all the *captains* **governors** of the *forces* **valiant**,
took all the *remnant* **survivors** of *Judah* **Yah Hudah**,
that were returned from all *nations* **goyim**,
whither they had been driven,
to *dwell* **sojourn** in the land of *Judah* **Yah Hudah**;
6 *Even men* **Mighty**, and
women, and *children* **toddlers**,
and the *king's* **sovereign's** daughters,
and every *person* **soul** that *Nebuzaradan* **Nebu Zaradan**
the *captain of the guard* **rabbi slaughterer**
had left with *Gedaliah* **Gedal Yah**
the son of Ahikam the son of Shaphan,
and *Jeremiah* **Yirme Yah** the prophet,
and Baruch the son of *Neriah* **Neri Yah**.

7 So they came into the land of *Egypt* **Misrayim**:
for they *obeyed* **hearkened** not
unto the voice of *the LORD* **Yah Veh**:
thus came they *even* to *Tahpanhes* **Tachpanches**.
8 Then came the word of *the LORD* **Yah Veh**
unto *Jeremiah* **Yirme Yah** in *Tahpanhes* **Tachpanches**,
saying,
9 Take great stones in thine hand,
and hide them in the *clay* **cement** in the brickkiln,
which is at the *entry* **portal** of *Pharaoh's* **Paroh's** house
in *Tahpanhes* **Tachpanches**,
in the *sight* **eyes** of the men *of Judah* **Yah Hudah**;
10 And say unto them,
Thus saith *the LORD of hosts* **Yah Veh Sabaoth**,
the God **Elohim** of *Israel* **Yisra El**;
Behold, I *will* **shall** send and take
Nebuchadrezzar **Nebukadnets Tsar**
the *king* **sovereign** of *Babylon* **Babel**, my servant,
and *will* **shall** set his throne
upon these stones that I have hid;
and he shall spread his *royal* **glory** pavilion over them.
11 And when he cometh,
he shall smite the land of *Egypt* **Misrayim**,
and deliver such as are for death to death;
and such as are for captivity to captivity; and
such as are for the sword to the sword.
12 And I *will* **shall** kindle a fire
in the houses of the *gods* **elohim** of *Egypt* **Misrayim**;
and he shall burn them,
and *carry* **capture** them *away captives*:
and he shall *array* **cover** himself
with the land of *Egypt* **Misrayim**,
as a *shepherd* **tender**
putteth on **covereth with** his *garment* **clothes**;
and he shall go forth from thence in *peace* **shalom**.
13 He shall break also
the *images* **monoliths** of *Bethshemesh* **Beth Shemesh**,
that is in the land of *Egypt* **Misrayim**;
and the houses
of the *gods* **elohim** of the *Egyptians* **Misrayim**
shall he burn with fire.

WARNING CONCERNING IDOLATRY

44 The word that came to *Jeremiah* **Yirme Yah**
concerning all the *Jews* **Yah Hudiym**
which *dwell* **settle** in the land of *Egypt* **Misrayim**,
which *dwell* **settle** at Migdol,
and at *Tahpanhes* **Tachpanches**, and at Noph,
and in the *country* **land** of Pathros, saying,
2 Thus saith *the LORD of hosts* **Yah Veh Sabaoth**,
the God **Elohim** of *Israel* **Yisra El**;
Ye have seen all the evil that I have brought
upon *Jerusalem* **Yeru Shalem**,
and upon all the cities of *Judah* **Yah Hudah**;
and, behold, this day they are a *desolation* **parch**,
and no man *dwelleth* **settleth** therein,
3 *Because* **At the face** of their *wickedness* **evil**
which they have *committed* **worked**
to *provoke* **vex** me *to anger*,
so that they put us to death and exile us to Babel.
4 And Yah Hanan the son of Qareach
and all the governors of the valiant and all the people
hearken not to the voice of Yah Veh
to settle in the land of Yah Hudah:
5 and Yah Hanan the son of Qareach
and all the governors of the valiant
take all the survivors of Yah Hudah,
who returned from all goyim where they were driven,
to sojourn in the land of Yah Hudah;
6 —mighty and women and toddlers
and daughters of the sovereign
and every soul Nebu Zaradan the rabbi slaughterer
left with Gedal Yah
the son of Ahikam the son of Shaphan
and Yirme Yah the prophet
and Baruch the son of Neri Yah.
7 And they come to the land of Misrayim:
for they hearken not to the voice of Yah Veh:
thus they come to Tachpanches.
8 And so be the word of Yah Veh
to Yirme Yah in Tachpanches, saying,
9 Take great stones in your hand,
and hide them in the cement in the brickkiln
at the portal of the house of Paroh in Tachpanches
in the eyes of the men of Yah Hudah;
10 and say to them,
Thus says Yah Veh Sabaoth Elohim of Yisra El:
Behold, I send and take
Nebukadnets Tsar the sovereign of Babel, my servant,
and set his throne on these stones I hid:
and he spreads his glory pavilion over them:
11 and he comes and smites the land of Misrayim
—such as are for death, to death;
and such as are for captivity, to captivity;
and such as are for the sword, to the sword:
12 and I kindle a fire
in the houses of the elohim of Misrayim;
and he burns them and captures them:
and he covers himself with the land of Misrayim
as a tender covers with his clothes;

and he comes from there in shalom:
13 and he breaks the monoliths of Beth Shemesh
in the land of Misrayim;
and burns the houses of the elohim of the Misrayim
with fire.

WARNING CONCERNING IDOLATRY

44 And so be the word to Yirme Yah
concerning all the Yah Hudiym
who settle in the land of Misrayim
—who settle at Migdol
and at Tachpanches and at Noph and
in the land of Pathros, saying,
2 Thus says Yah Veh Sabaoth Elohim of Yisra El:
You see all the evil I bring on Yeru Shalem
and on all the cities of Yah Hudah;
and behold, this day they are a parch,
and no man settles therein
3 at the face of the evil they worked to vex me
in that they went to *burn* incense,
and to serve other *gods* **elohim**, whom they knew not,
neither they, ye, nor your fathers.
4 Howbeit I sent unto you all
my servants the prophets,
rising **starting** early and sending them, saying,
Oh **I beseech**, *do* **work** not
this *abominable thing* **word of abhorrence** that I hate.
5 But they hearkened not,
nor *inclined* **spread** their ear
to turn from their *wickedness* **evil**,
to *burn no* **not** incense unto other *gods* **elohim**.
6 Wherefore my fury and *mine anger* **my wrath**
was poured forth,
and was *kindled* **burnt** in the cities of *Judah* **Yah Hudah**
and in the *streets* **outways** of *Jerusalem* **Yeru Shalem**;
and they are *wasted* **parched** and desolate, as at this day.
7 Therefore now thus saith *the LORD* **Yah Veh**,
the God of hosts **Elohim Sabaoth**,
the God **Elohim** of *Israel* **Yisra El**;
Wherefore *commit* **work** ye this great evil
against your souls,
to cut off from you man and woman,
child **infant** and suckling,
out of *Judah* **the midst of Yah Hudah**,
to leave you **that in surviving,** none *to remain* **survive**;
8 In that ye *provoke* **vex** me *unto wrath*
with the works of your hands,
burning incense **incensing** unto other *gods* **elohim**
in the land of *Egypt* **Misrayim**,
whither ye be gone to *dwell* **sojourn**,
that ye might cut yourselves off,
and that ye might be
a curse **an abasement** and a reproach
among all the *nations* **goyim** of the earth?
9 Have ye forgotten the
wickedness **evil** of your fathers,
and the *wickedness* **evil**
of the *kings* **sovereigns** of *Judah* **Yah Hudah**,
and the *wickedness* **evil** of their *wives* **women**,
and your own *wickedness* **evil**,
and the *wickedness* **evil** of your *wives* **women**,
which they have *committed* **worked**
in the land of *Judah* **Yah Hudah**,
and in the *streets* **outways** of *Jerusalem* **Yeru Shalem**?
10 They are not *humbled*
crushed *even* unto this day,
neither have they *feared* **awed**,
nor walked in my *law* **torah**, nor in my statutes,
that I *set before you* **gave at your face**
and *before* **at the face of** your fathers.
11 Therefore
thus saith *the LORD of hosts* **Yah Veh Sabaoth**,
the God **Elohim** of *Israel* **Yisra El**;
Behold, I *will* **shall** set my face against you for evil,
and to cut off all *Judah* **Yah Hudah**.
12 And I *will* **shall** take
the *remnant* **survivors** of *Judah* **Yah Hudah**,
that have set their faces
to go into the land of *Egypt* **Misrayim** to sojourn there,
and they shall all be consumed,
and fall in the land of *Egypt* **Misrayim**;
they shall *even* be consumed
by the sword and by the famine:
they shall die, from the least even unto the greatest,
by the sword and by the famine:
and they shall be an *execration* **oath**,
and *an astonishment* **a desolation**,
and *a curse* **an abasement**, and a reproach.
13 For I *will punish* **shall visit upon** them
that *dwell* **settle** in the land of *Egypt* **Misrayim**,
as I have *punished Jerusalem* **visited upon Yeru Shalem**,
by the sword, by the famine, and by the pestilence:
14 So that none
of the *remnant* **survivors** of *Judah* **Yah Hudah**,
which are gone into the land of *Egypt* **Misrayim**
to sojourn there,
shall escape or remain—**escapees or survivors**
that they should return into the
land of *Judah* **Yah Hudah**,
to the which they *have a desire* **lift their soul**

to return to *dwell* **settle** there:
for none shall return but such as shall escape.
by going in to incense
and to serve other elohim whom they know not
—neither they, you, nor your fathers:
4 and I sent to you all my servants the prophets,
starting early and sending them,
saying, I beseech,
work not this word of abhorrence that I hate!
5 And they neither hearken
nor spread their ear to turn from their evil
to not incense to other elohim.
6 and I poured my fury and my wrath
and it burns in the cities of Yah Hudah
and in the outways of Yeru Shalem;
and they are parched and desolate, as this day.
7 And now thus says Yah Veh Elohim Sabaoth
Elohim of Yisra El;
Why work this great evil against your souls,
to cut off from you
man and woman, infant and suckling
from midst Yah Hudah,
that in surviving, none survive;
8 in that you vex me with
the works of your hands,
incensing to other elohim in the land of Misrayim
where you go to sojourn,
to cut yourselves off,
and that you become an abasement and a reproach
among all the goyim of the earth?
9 Forget you the evil of your fathers?
And the evil of the sovereigns of Yah Hudah?
And the evil of their women?
And your own evil?
And the evil your women worked
in the land of Yah Hudah
and in the outways of Yeru Shalem?
10 They are neither crushed to this day, nor awed;
nor walk in my torah
nor in my statutes I gave at your face
and at the face of your fathers.
11 So thus says Yah Veh
Sabaoth Elohim of Yisra El:
Behold, I set my face against you for evil,
and cut off all Yah Hudah:
12 and I take the survivors of Yah Hudah,
who set their faces
to enter the land of Misrayim to sojourn there:
and they all *are* consumed,
and fall in the land of Misrayim;
—consumed by the sword and by the famine:
they die, from the least even to the greatest,
by the sword and by the famine:
and they become an oath and a desolation
and an abasement and a reproach:
13 and I visit on them
who settle in the land of Misrayim,
as I visited on Yeru Shalem
—by the sword, by the famine, and by the pestilence:
14 so that not one of the survivors of Yah Hudah,
who go into the land of Misrayim to sojourn there
—escapees or survivors
return to the land of Yah Hudah,
to which they lifted their soul to return to settle there:
for no one returns except such as escape.
15 Then all the men which
knew that their *wives* **women**
had *burned incense* **incensed** unto other *gods* **elohim**,
and all the women that stood by,
a great *multitude* **congregation**,
even all the people that *dwelt* **settled**
in the land of *Egypt* **Misrayim**, in Pathros,
answered *Jeremiah* **Yirme Yah**, saying,
16 *As for* the word that thou hast *spoken* **worded**
unto us in the name of *the LORD* **Yah Veh**,
we *will* **shall** not hearken unto thee.
17 But **in working,** we *will certainly do* **shall work**
whatsoever *thing* goeth forth out of our own mouth,
to *burn* incense
unto the *queen* **sovereigness** of *heaven* **the heavens**,
and to *pour out drink offerings* **libate libations** unto her,
as we have *done* **worked**, we, and our fathers,
our *kings* **sovereigns**, and our *princes* **governors**,
in the cities of *Judah* **Yah Hudah**,
and in the *streets* **outways** of *Jerusalem* **Yeru Shalem**:
for then
had we plenty of victuals **were we satiated with bread**,
and were *well* **good**, and saw no evil.
18 But since we *left off to burn* **ceased to** incense
to the *queen* **sovereigness** of *heaven* **the heavens**,
and to *pour out drink offerings* **libate libations** unto her,
we have wanted all *things*,
and have been consumed
by the sword and by the famine.
19 And when we *burned incense* **incensed**
to the *queen* **sovereigness** of *heaven* **the heavens**,
and *poured out drink offerings* **libated libations** unto her,
did we *make* **work** her cakes to *worship* **idolize** her,
and *pour out drink offerings* **libate libations** unto her,
without our men?

20 Then *Jeremiah* **Yirme Yah**
said unto all the people,
to the *men* mighty, and to the women,
and to all the people
which had *given* **answered** him *that answer* **word**,
saying,
21 The incense that ye *burned* **incensed**
in the cities of *Judah* **Yah Hudah**,
and in the *streets* **outways** of *Jerusalem* **Yeru Shalem**,
ye, and your fathers, your *kings* **sovereigns**,
and your *princes* **governors**, and the people of the land,
did not *the LORD* **Yah Veh** remember them,
and *came* **ascended** it not into his *mind* **heart**?
22 So that *the LORD* **Yah Veh** could no longer bear,
because **at the face** of the evil of your *doings* **exploits**,
and *because* **at the face** of the *abominations* **abhorrences**
which ye have *committed* **worked**;
therefore is your land a *desolation* **parched area**,
and *an astonishment* **a desolation**,
and *a curse* **an abasement**,
without *an inhabitant* **a settler**, as at this day.
23 Because **at the face of that**
ye have *burned incense* **incensed**,
and because ye have sinned against *the LORD* **Yah Veh**,
and have not
obeyed **hearkened unto** the voice of *the LORD* **Yah Veh**,
nor walked in his *law* **torah**, nor in his statutes,
nor in his *testimonies* **witnesses**;
therefore this evil *is happened unto* **confronteth** you,
as at this day.
24 *Moreover*
Jeremiah **Yirme Yah** said unto all the people,
and to all the women,
Hear the word of *the LORD* **Yah Veh**,
all *Judah* **Yah Hudah**
that are in the land of *Egypt* **Misrayim**:
25 Thus saith *the LORD of hosts* **Yah Veh Sabaoth**,
the God **Elohim** of *Israel* **Yisra El**, saying;
Ye and your *wives* **women**
have both *spoken* **worded** with your mouths,
and fulfilled with your hand, saying,
In working, We *will surely perform* **shall work** our vows
that we have vowed,
to *burn* incense
to the *queen* **sovereigness** of *heaven* **the heavens**,
and to *pour out drink offerings* **libate libations** unto her:
15 Then all the men who know
that their women incense to other elohim,
and all the women who stand by
—a great congregation—even all the people
who settle in the land of Misrayim, in Pathros,
answer Yirme Yah, saying,
16 The word you worded to us
in the name of Yah Veh,
we hearkened not to you:
17 for in working,
we work whatever comes from our own mouth,
to incense to the sovereigness of the heavens
and to libate libations to her
as we worked—we and our fathers
our sovereigns and our governors
in the cities of Yah Hudah
and in the outways of Yeru Shalem:
for then we were satiated with bread
and were good and saw no evil:
18 and since we ceased to incense
to the sovereigness of the heavens
and to libate libations to her,
we *are* all in want,
—consumed by the sword and by the famine:
19 and when we incensed
to the sovereigness of the heavens,
and libated libations to her,
worked we cakes to idolize her,
and libated libations to her without our men?
20 Then Yirme Yah says to all the people,
—to the mighty and to the women
and to all the people who answer him words, saying,
21 The incense you incensed
in the cities of Yah Hudah
and in the outways of Yeru Shalem
—you and your fathers,
your sovereigns and your governors
and the people of the land
remembered not Yah Veh them?
and ascended it not into his heart?
22 And Yah Veh can no longer bear
at the face of the evil of your exploits
—and at the face of the abhorrences you worked;
so your land is a parched area
and a desolation and an abasement
without a settler, as this day.
23 Because at the face of your incensing
and because you sinned against Yah Veh,
and neither hearkened to the voice of Yah Veh
nor walked in his torah
nor in his statutes nor in his witnesses;
so this evil confronts you, as at this day.
24 Yirme Yah says to all the people,
and to all the women,

Hear the word of Yah Veh,
all Yah Hudah in the land of Misrayim:
25 Thus says Yah Veh Sabaoth Elohim of Yisra El,
saying;
You and your women
both worded with your mouths,
and fulfilled with your hand, saying,
In working, we work the vows we vowed,
to incense to the sovereigness of the heavens
and to libate libations to her:
in raising, ye *will surely accomplish*
shall raise your vows,
and **in working,** *surely perform* **ye shall work** your vows.
26 Therefore hear ye the word
of *the LORD* **Yah Veh,**
all *Judah* **Yah Hudah**
that *dwell* **settle** in the land of *Egypt* **Misrayim;**
Behold, I have *sworn* **oathed** by my great name,
saith *the LORD* **Yah Veh,**
that my name shall no more be *named* **called out**
in the mouth of any man of *Judah* **Yah Hudah**
in all the land of *Egypt* **Misrayim,** saying,
The Lord GOD **Adonay Yah Veh** liveth.
27 Behold,
I *will* **shall** watch over them for evil, and not for good:
and all the men of *Judah* **Yah Hudah**
that are in the land of *Egypt* **Misrayim**
shall be consumed by the sword and by the famine,
until *there be an end of them* **the consummation.**
28 Yet a *small number* **number of men,**
that escape—**escapees of** the sword
shall return out of the land of *Egypt* **Misrayim**
into the land of *Judah* **Yah Hudah,**
and all the *remnant* **survivors** of *Judah* **Yah Hudah,**
that are gone into the land of *Egypt* **Misrayim**
to sojourn there,
shall know whose words shall *stand* **rise,** mine, or theirs.
29 And this shall be a sign unto you,
saith the LORD **an oracle of Yah Veh,**
that I *will punish* **shall visit upon** you in this place,
that ye may know that my words
in rising, shall *surely stand* **rise** against you for evil:
30 Thus saith *the LORD* **Yah Veh;**
Behold, I *will* **shall** give
Pharaohhophra **Paroh Hophra**
king **sovereign** of *Egypt* **Misrayim**
into the hand of his enemies,
and into the hand of them that seek his *life* **soul;**
as I gave *Zedekiah* **Sidqi Yah**
king **sovereign** of *Judah* **Yah Hudah**
into the hand of
Nebuchadrezzar **Nebukadnets Tsar**
king **sovereign** of *Babylon* **Babel,**
his enemy, and that sought his *life* **soul.**

MESSAGE TO BARUCH

45 The word that *Jeremiah* **Yirme Yah** the prophet
spake **worded**
unto Baruch the son of *Neriah* **Neri Yah,**
when he had *written* **inscribed** these words
in a *book* **scroll**
at the mouth of *Jeremiah* **Yirme Yah,**
in the fourth year of *Jehoiakim* **Yah Yaqim**
the son of *Josiah* **Yoshi Yah**
king **sovereign** of *Judah* **Yah Hudah,** saying,
2 Thus saith *the LORD* **Yah Veh,**
the God **Elohim** of *Israel* **Yisra El,**
unto thee, O Baruch:
3 Thou *didst say* **saidst,**
Woe is me *now* **I beseech!**
for *the LORD* **Yah Veh** hath added grief to my sorrow;
I *fainted* **belaboured** in my sighing, and I find no rest.
4 Thus shalt thou say unto him,
The LORD **Yah Veh** saith thus; Behold,
that which I have built
will **shall** I break down,
and that which I have planted
I *will pluck up* **shall uproot,**
even this whole land.
5 And seekest thou great *things*
for thyself? seek *them* not:
for, behold, I *will* **shall** bring evil upon all flesh,
saith the LORD **an oracle of Yah Veh:**
but thy *life will* **soul shall** I give unto thee for a *prey* **spoil**
in all places whither thou goest.

MESSAGE AGAINST THE GOYIM

46 The word of *the LORD* **Yah Veh**
which came to *Jeremiah* **Yirme Yah** the prophet
against the *Gentiles* **goyim;**

MESSAGE AGAINST MISRAYIM

2 Against *Egypt* **Misrayim,**
against the *army* **valiant** of
Pharaohnecho **Paroh Nechoh**
king **sovereign** of *Egypt* **Misrayim,**
in raising, we raise our vows,
and in working, we work our vows.
26 So hear the word of Yah Veh,

all Yah Hudah who settles in the land of Misrayim;
Behold, I oath by my great name, says Yah Veh,
that my name no more becomes called out
in the mouth of any man of Yah Hudah
in all the land of Misrayim, saying,
Adonay Yah Veh lives.
27 Behold, I watch over them for evil,
and not for good:
and all the men of Yah Hudah in the land of Misrayim
are consumed by the sword and by the famine
until the consummation.
28 Yet a number of men—escapees from the sword
return from the land of Misrayim
to the land of Yah Hudah;
and all the survivors of Yah Hudah
who enter the land of Misrayim to sojourn there,
know whose words rise—mine or theirs.
29 And this is your sign
—an oracle of Yah Veh
that I visit on you in this place,
so that you know, that in rising,
my words rise against you for evil.
30 Thus says Yah Veh:
Behold, I give Paroh Hophra sovereign of Misrayim
into the hand of his enemies
and into the hand of them who seek his soul:
as I gave Sidqi Yah sovereign of Yah Hudah
into the hand of Nebukadnets Tsar sovereign of Babel
—his enemy who sought his soul.

MESSAGE TO BARUCH

45 The word Yirme Yah the prophet
worded to Baruch the son of Neri Yah
when he inscribed these words in a scroll
at the mouth of Yirme Yah,
in the fourth year of Yah Yaqim
the son of Yoshi Yah sovereign of Yah Hudah, saying,
2 Thus says Yah Veh Elohim of Yisra El
concerning you, O Baruch:
3 You had said,
Woe is me, I beseech!
for Yah Veh adds grief to my sorrow;
I belabor in my sighing and I find no rest.
4 Say thus to him:
Yah Veh says thus:
Behold, what I built, I break down;
and what I planted, I uproot
—even this whole land.
5 And seek you greatness for yourself?
Seek not!
For behold, I bring evil on all flesh
—an oracle of Yah Veh:
and I give your soul to you for a spoil
in all the places you go.

MESSAGE AGAINST THE GOYIM

46 So be the word of Yah Veh
to Yirme Yah the prophet
against the goyim:

MESSAGE AGAINST MISRAYIM

2 against Misrayim,
against the valiant of Paroh Nechoh
sovereign of Misrayim;
which was by the river Euphrates
in *Carchemish* **Karchemish,**
which *Nebuchadrezzar* **Nebukadnets Tsar**
king **sovereign** of *Babylon* **Babel**
smote in the fourth year of *Jehoiakim* **Yah Yaqim**
the son of *Josiah* **Yoshi Yah**
king **sovereign** of *Judah* **Yah Hudah.**
3 *Order* **Line up** ye the buckler and shield,
and draw near to *battle* **war.**
4 *Harness* **Hitch** the horses;
and *get up* **ascend,** ye *horsemen* **cavalry,**
and stand forth with *your* helmets;
furbish **polish** the *spears* **javelins,**
and put on **enrobe** the brigandines.
5 Wherefore have I seen
them *dismayed* **terrorized**
and *turned away back* **apostatized backward?**
and their mighty *ones are beaten down* **crushed,**
and are fled *apace* **to a retreat,** and *look* **face** not back:
for fear **terror** was round about,
saith the LORD **an oracle of Yah Veh.**
6 Let not the swift flee away,
nor the mighty *man* escape;
they shall stumble,
and *fall toward the north* **falter northward**
by **the hand of** the river Euphrates.
7 Who is this that *cometh up*
ascendeth as a *flood* **river,**
whose waters are *moved* **agitated** as the rivers?
8 *Egypt riseth up* **Misrayim**
ascendeth like a *flood* **river,**
and his waters are *moved* **agitated** like the rivers;
and he saith,
I *will go up* **shall ascend,** and *will* **shall** cover the earth;
I *will* **shall** destroy the city
and the *inhabitants* **settlers** *thereof.*

9 *Come up* **Ascend**, ye horses;
and rage **halal**, ye chariots;
and let the mighty *men* come forth;
the *Ethiopians* **Kushies** and the *Libyans* **Puties**,
that *handle* **manipulate** the *shield* **buckler**;
and the *Lydians* **Ludiym**,
that *handle* **manipulate** and bend the bow.
10 For this is the day
of *the Lord GOD of hosts* **Adonay Yah Veh Sabaoth**,
a day of *vengeance* **avengement**,
that he may avenge him of his *adversaries* **tribulators**:
and the sword shall devour,
and it shall be satiate
and *made drunk* **satiated** with their blood:
for *the Lord GOD of hosts* **Adonay Yah Veh Sabaoth**
hath a sacrifice in the north *country* **land**
by the river Euphrates.
11 *Go up* **Ascend** into *Gilead* **Gilad**, and take balm,
O virgin, the daughter of *Egypt* **Misrayim**:
in vain shalt thou *use many medicines* **abound healers**;
for thou shalt not be *cured* **bandaged**.
12 The *nations* **goyim**
have heard of thy *shame* **abasement**,
and thy *cry* **outcry** hath filled the land:
for the mighty *man*
hath *stumbled* **faltered** against the mighty,
and they are fallen both *together*.
13 The word that *the LORD* **Yah Veh**
spake **worded** to *Jeremiah* **Yirme Yah** the prophet,
how *Nebuchadrezzar* **Nebukadnets Tsar**
king **sovereign** of *Babylon* **Babel**
should come and smite the land of *Egypt* **Misrayim**.
14 *Declare* **Tell** ye in *Egypt* **Misrayim**, and
publish **be it heard** in Migdol, and *publish* **be it**
heard in Noph and in *Tahpanhes* **Tachpanches**:
say ye, Stand fast, and prepare thee;
for the sword shall *devour* **consume** round about thee.
15 Why are thy *valiant men* **mighty** swept away?
they stood not,
because *the LORD did drive* **Yah Veh exiled** them.
16 He *made many to fall* **hath**
abounded the falterer,
yea, *one* **man** fell upon *another* **friend**:
and they said,
Arise, and let us *go again* **return** to our own people,
and to the land of our *nativity* **kindred**,
from **the face of** the oppressing sword.
being by the river Euphrates in Karchemish,
whom Nebukadnets Tsar sovereign of Babel smote
in the fourth year of Yah Yaqim
the son of Yoshi Yah sovereign of Yah Hudah.
3 Line up your buckler and shield
and draw near to war:
4 hitch the horses and ascend, you cavalry
and stand with helmets:
polish the javelins; enrobe the brigandines.
5 Why see I them terrorized?
—apostatizing backward and their mighty crushed?
—fleeing to a retreat, and not facing back?
with terror all around?
—an oracle of Yah Veh.
6 Neither the swift flee nor the mighty escape;
they stumble and falter northward
by the hand of the river Euphrates.
7 Who is this—ascending as a river?
—whose waters agitate as the rivers?
8 Misrayim ascends as a river
and his waters agitate as the rivers:
and he says, I ascend and cover the earth;
I destroy the city and the settlers.
9 Ascend, you horses! Halal, you chariots!
Go forth, you mighty!
—Kushies and Puties, manipulating the buckler;
and Ludiym, manipulating and bending the bow:
10 for this is the day of Adonay Yah Veh Sabaoth
—a day of avengement,
to avenge him of his tribulators:
and the sword devours and satiates
—satiates with their blood
for a sacrifice to Adonay Yah Veh Sabaoth
in the north land by the river Euphrates.
11 Ascend into Gilad, and take balm,
O virgin, the daughter of Misrayim:
you abound your healers in vain
for they bandage you not.
12 The goyim hear of your abasement
and your outcry fills the land:
for the mighty falter against the mighty,
together they fall—both.
13 The word Yah Veh worded
to Yirme Yah the prophet
—concerning the coming
of Nebukadnets Tsar sovereign of Babel
and smiting the land of Misrayim:
14 Tell it in Misrayim
and have them hear in Migdol;
and have them hear in Noph and in Tachpanches!
Say, Stand fast and prepare!
For the sword consumes all around you!
15 Why are your mighty swept away?

They stand not because Yah Veh exiles them.
16 He abounds the falterer; yes, man fells friend:
and they say,
We rise and return to our own people
and to the land of our kindred
from the face of the oppressing sword.
17 They *did cry* **called out** there,
Pharaoh king **Paroh sovereign** of *Egypt* **Misrayim**
is but *a noise* **an uproar**;
he hath passed the *time appointed* **season**.
18 *As* I live, *saith* **an oracle of** the *King* **Sovereign**,
whose name is *the LORD of hosts* **Yah Veh Sabaoth**,
Surely as Tabor is among the mountains,
and as *Carmel* **Karmel/orchard** by the sea,
so shall he come.
19 O thou daughter *dwelling*
settling in *Egypt* **Misrayim**,
furnish **work vessels for** thyself to go into *captivity* **exile**:
for Noph shall be *waste* **desolate** and *desolate* **burned**
without *an inhabitant* **a settler**.
20 *Egypt* **Misrayim** is like a
very *fair* **beautiful** heifer,
but destruction **extermination** cometh;
it cometh out of the north.
21 Also her *hired men* **hirelings**
are in the midst of her like fatted *bullocks* **calves**;
for they also *are* turned **face** *back*,
and are fled away together:
they did not stand,
because the day of their calamity was come upon them,
and the time of their visitation.
22 The voice *thereof* shall go like a serpent;
for they shall march with *an army* **the valiant**,
and come against her with axes,
as *hewers* **choppers** of *wood* **timber**.
23 They shall cut down her forest,
saith the LORD **an oracle of Yah Veh**,
though it cannot be *searched* **probed**;
because they *are more* **abound by the myriads**
than **above** the grasshoppers, and are innumerable.
24 The daughter of *Egypt* **Misrayim**
shall *be confounded* **shame**;
she shall be *delivered* **given**
into the hand of the people of the north.
25 *The LORD of hosts* **Yah Veh Sabaoth**,
the God **Elohim** of *Israel* **Yisra El**, saith;
Behold, I *will punish* **shall visit**
upon the multitude of No,
and *Pharaoh* **Paroh**, and *Egypt* **Misrayim**,
with their *gods* **elohim**, and their *kings* **sovereigns**;
even *Pharaoh* **Paroh**,
and *all* them that *trust* **confide** in him:
26 And I *will deliver* **shall give** them
into the hand of those that seek their *lives* **souls**,
and into the hand of *Nebuchadrezzar* **Nebukadnets Tsar**
king **sovereign** of *Babylon* **Babel**,
and into the hand of his servants:
and afterward it shall be *inhabited* **tabernacled therein**,
as in the **ancient** days *of old*,
saith the LORD **an oracle of Yah Veh**.
27 But *fear* **awe** not thou, O
my servant *Jacob* **Yaaqov**,
and be not dismayed, O *Israel* **Yisra El**: for, behold,
I *will save thee* **shall be thy saviour** from afar off,
and thy seed from the land of their captivity;
and *Jacob* **Yaaqov** shall return,
and *be in* rest and *at ease* **relax**,
and none shall *make* **frighten** him *afraid*.
28 *Fear* **Awe** thou not, O *Jacob* **Yaaqov** my servant,
saith the LORD **an oracle of Yah Veh**:
for I *am* with thee;
for I *will make a full end* **shall work a final finish**
of all the *nations* **goyim** whither I have driven thee:
but I *will* **shall** not *make a full end*
work a final finish of thee,
but *correct* **discipline** thee in *measure* **judgment**;
yet *will I not leave thee wholly unpunished*
in exonerating, I shall not exonerate thee.

WORD AGAINST THE PELESHETHIYM

47 The word of *the LORD* **Yah Veh**
that came to *Jeremiah* **Yirme Yah** the prophet
against the *Philistines* **Peleshethiym**,
before that *Pharaoh* **Paroh** smote *Gaza* **Azzah**.
2 Thus saith *the LORD* **Yah Veh**; Behold,
waters *rise up* **ascend** out of the north,
and shall be an overflowing *flood* **wadi**,
and shall overflow the land, and *all*
that is therein **its fulness**;
the city, and them that *dwell* **settle** therein:
then *the men* **humanity** shall cry **out**,
and all the *inhabitants* **settlers** of the land shall howl.
17 And there they call out,
Paroh sovereign of Misrayim is but an uproar;
his season *has* passed.
18 I live—an oracle of the Sovereign
whose name is Yah Veh Sabaoth,
Surely as Tabor is among the mountains
and as Karmel/orchard by the sea,
thus he comes.

19 O you daughter settling in Misrayim,
work vessels for yourself to go into exile:
for Noph becomes desolate
and burns without a settler:
20 Misrayim is as a very beautiful heifer:
extermination comes—comes from the north:
21 even her hirelings are
among her as fatted calves;
for they also turn face:
they flee together; they stand not:
because the day of their calamity comes on them
—the time of their visitation.
22 Its voice comes as a serpent;
for they march with the valiant
and come against her with axes
—as choppers of timber:
23 they cut down her forest
—an oracle of Yah Veh
though it cannot be probed;
because they abound by the myriads
above the grasshoppers—innumerable.
24 The daughter of Misrayim shames;
she is given into the hand of the people of the north.
25 Yah Veh Sabaoth Elohim of Yisra El, says;
Behold, I visit on the multitude of No
and Paroh and Misrayim
with their elohim, and their sovereigns;
even Paroh, and they who confide in him:
26 and I give them into the hand
of them who seek their souls,
and into the hand
of Nebukadnets Tsar sovereign of Babel,
and into the hand of his servants:
and afterward they tabernacled therein
as in the ancient days
—an oracle of Yah Veh.
27 And you, awe not, O my servant Yaaqov;
and be not dismayed, O Yisra El:
for behold, I save you from afar
and your seed from the land of their captivity:
and Yaaqov returns; and rests and relaxes:
and no one frightens him.
28 Awe not, O Yaaqov my servant
—an oracle of Yah Veh
for I *am* with you;
for I work a final finish of all the goyim
wherever I drove you:
and I work not a final finish of you
and discipline you in judgment:
and in exonerating, I exonerate you not.

WORD AGAINST THE PELESHETHIYM

47 And so be the word of Yah Veh
to Yirme Yah the prophet
against the Peleshethiym ere Paroh smote Azzah.
2 Thus says Yah Veh:
Behold, waters ascending from the north
become an overflowing wadi;
and overflow the land and its fulness
—the city and they who settle therein:
and humanity cries out
and all the settlers of the land howl.

JEREMIAH 47, 48

exeGeses ready research BIBLE

3 At the *noise* **voice** of the stamping of the hoofs
of his *strong horses* **mighty**,
at the *rushing* **quake** of his chariots,
and at the *rumbling* **roar** of his wheels,
the fathers shall not *look* **face** back to *their children* **sons**
for *feebleness* **slackness** of hands;
4 Because of the day that cometh
to *spoil* **ravage** all the *Philistines* **Peleshethiym**,
and to cut off from *Tyrus* **Sor** and *Zidon* **Sidon**
every *helper* **survivor** that *remaineth* **helpeth**:
for *the LORD* **Yah Veh**
will spoil **shall ravage** the *Philistines* **Peleshethiym**,
the *remnant* **survivors**
of the *country* **island** of *Caphtor* **Kaphtor**.
5 Baldness is come upon *Gaza* **Azzah**;
Ashkelon is *cut off* **severed**
with the *remnant* **survivors** of their valley:
how long *wilt* **shalt** thou *cut* **incise** thyself?
6 *O* **Ho** thou sword of *the LORD* **Yah Veh**,
how long *will* **shall** it be ere thou *be quiet* **rest**?
put up thyself into **gather** thy *scabbard* **sheath**,
rest, and be still.
7 How can it *be quiet* **rest**,
seeing *the LORD* **Yah Veh**
hath *given it a charge* **misvahed** against Ashkelon,
and against the sea *shore* **haven**?
there hath he *appointed it* **congregated**.

MESSAGE AGAINST MOAB

48 Against Moab
thus saith *the LORD of hosts* **Yah Veh Sabaoth**,
the God **Elohim** of *Israel* **Yisra El**;
Woe **Ho** unto Nebo! for it is *spoiled* **ravaged**:
Kiriathaim **Qiryathaim**
is *confounded* **shamed** and *taken* **captured**:
Misgab **The secure loft**

is *confounded* **shamed** and dismayed.
2 There shall be no more *praise* **halal** of Moab:
in Heshbon they have *devised* **fabricated** evil against it;
come, and let us cut it off from *being* a *nation* **goyim**.
Also thou shalt be *cut down* **severed**, O Madmen;
the sword shall *pursue* **go after** thee.
3 A voice of crying shall be from Horonaim,
spoiling **ravage** and great *destruction* **breaking**.
4 Moab is *destroyed* **broken**;
her little *ones* have caused a cry to be heard.
5 For in the *going up* **ascent** of *Luhith* **Luchith**
in weeping, *continual* weeping shall *go up* **ascend**;
for in the *going down* **descent** of Horonaim
the *enemies* **tribulators**
have heard a cry of *destruction* **breaking**.
6 Flee, *save* **rescue** your *lives* **souls**,
and be like the *heath* **naked tree** in the wilderness.
7 For because thou hast *trusted* **confided**
in thy works and in thy treasures,
thou shalt also be *taken* **captured**:
and *Chemosh* **Kemosh** shall go forth into *captivity* **exile**
with his priests and his *princes* **governors** together.
8 And the *spoiler* **ravager**
shall come upon every city,
and no city shall escape:
the valley also shall *perish* **destruct**,
and the plain shall *be destroyed* **desolate**,
as *the LORD* **Yah Veh** hath *spoken* **said**.
9 Give wings unto Moab, that
it may flee and get away:
for the cities thereof shall be desolate,
without any to *dwell* **settle** therein.
10 Cursed be he
that *doeth* **worketh** the work of *the LORD* **Yah Veh**
deceitfully,
and cursed be he
that *keepeth back* **withholdeth** his sword from blood.
11 Moab hath *been at ease* **relaxed** from his youth,
and he hath *settled* **rested** on his *lees* **dregs**,
and hath not been *emptied* **poured out**
from *vessel* **instrument** to *vessel* **instrument**,
neither hath he gone into *captivity* **exile**:
therefore his taste *remained* **stood** in him,
and his scent is not changed.
12 Therefore, behold, the days come,
saith the LORD **an oracle of Yah Veh**,
3 At the voice of the stamping of the hoofs
of his mighty,
at the quake of his chariots,
and at the roar of his wheels,

the fathers face not the sons for slackness of hands;
4 because of the day that comes
to ravage all the Peleshethiym;
and to cut off from Sor and Sidon
every survivor who helps:
for Yah Veh ravages the Peleshethiym,
the survivors of the island of Kaphtor.
5 Baldness comes on Azzah;
Ashkelon is severed with the survivors of their valley:
How long incise you yourself?
6 Ho, you sword of Yah Veh,
how long ere you rest?
Gather your sheath; rest and hush.
7 How rests it,
seeing Yah Veh misvahs against Ashkelon?
—and against the sea haven?
There he congregates.

MESSAGE AGAINST MOAB

48 Against Moab:
Thus says Yah Veh Sabaoth Elohim of Yisra El;
Ho, Nebo! for it *is* ravaged:
Qiryathaim *is* shamed and captured:
the secure loft *is* shamed and dismayed.
2 The halal of Moab *is* no more:
in Heshbon they fabricated evil against it.
Come, and we cut it off from a goyim.
Also you, O Madmen, *are* severed;
the sword goes after you.
3 A voice of crying from Horonaim
—ravage and great breaking.
4 Moab is broken;
her little *ones cry* a cry to be heard.
5 For in the ascent of Luchith,
in weeping, weeping ascends;
for in the descent of Horonaim
the tribulators hear a cry of breaking.
6 Flee! Rescue your souls!
Become as the naked tree in the wilderness.
7 For, because you confide
in your works and in your treasures,
you also are captured:
and Kemosh goes into exile
together with his priests and his governors.
8 And the ravager comes on every city
and no city escapes:
and the valley destructs and the plain desolates,
as Yah Veh said.
9 Give wings to Moab
to flee and get away:

for the cities thereof desolate
without any to settle therein.
10 Cursed
—he who works the work of Yah Veh deceitfully:
and cursed
—he who withholds his sword from blood.
11 Moab relaxes from his
youth and rests on his dregs
—neither poured out from instrument to instrument
nor gone into exile:
so his taste stands within him
and his scent changes not.
12 So behold, days come,
—an oracle of Yah Veh
that I *will* **shall** send unto him *wanderers* **strollers**,
that shall cause him to *wander* **stroll**,
and shall *empty* **pour out** his *vessels* **instruments**,
and *break* **shatter** their *bottles* **bags**.
13 And Moab
shall be *ashamed* **shamed** of *Chemosh* **Kemosh**,
as the house of *Israel was ashamed* **Yisra El shamed**
of *Bethel* **Beth El** their confidence.
14 How say ye,
We are mighty and *strong* **valiant** men for the war?
15 Moab is *spoiled* **ravaged**,
and *gone up out of* **ascended** her cities,
and his chosen *young men* **youths**
are *gone down* **descended** to the slaughter,
saith the King **an oracle of the Sovereign**,
whose name is *the LORD of hosts* **Yah Veh Sabaoth**.
16 The calamity of Moab is near to come,
and his *affliction* **evil** hasteth *fast* **mightily**.
17 All ye that are **round** about him,
bemoan **wag over** him;
and all ye that know his name, say,
How is the *strong staff* **rod of strength** broken,
and the *beautiful rod* **staff of adornment**!
18 Thou daughter that *dost inhabit* **settlest** Dibon,
come down **descend** from thy *glory* **honour**,
and *sit* **settle** in thirst;
for the *spoiler* **ravager** of Moab
shall *come* **ascend** upon thee,
and he shall *destroy* **ruin** thy *strong holds* **fortresses**.
19 O *inhabitant* **settler** of Aroer,
stand by the way, and *espy* **watch**;
ask him that fleeth, and her that escapeth,
and say, What is done?
20 Moab is *confounded* **shamed**;
for it is broken down:
howl and cry;
tell ye it in Arnon, that Moab is *spoiled* **ravaged**,
21 And judgment is come upon
the plain *country* **land**;
upon Holon,
and upon *Jahazah* **Yahsah**, and upon Mephaath,
22 And upon Dibon, and upon Nebo,
and upon *Bethdiblathaim* **Beth Diblathayim**,
23 And upon *Kiriathaim* **Qiryathaim**,
and upon *Bethgamul* **Beth Gamul**,
and upon *Bethmeon* **Beth Meon**,
24 And upon *Kerioth* **Qerioth**, and upon Bozrah,
and upon all the cities of the land of Moab, far or near.
25 The horn of Moab is cut
off, and his arm is broken,
saith the LORD **an oracle of Yah Veh**.
26 *Make ye* **Intoxicate** him *drunken*:
for he *magnified* **greatened** *himself*
against *the LORD* **Yah Veh**:
Moab also shall *wallow* **slurp** in his vomit,
and he also shall be *in derision* **ridiculed**.
27 For was not *Israel* **Yisra El**
a *derision* **ridicule** unto thee?
was he found among thieves?
for since *thou spakest of him* **from thy sufficient words**,
thou *skippedst* **swayedst** for joy.
28 O ye that *dwell* **settle** in Moab,
leave the cities, and *dwell* **tabernacle** in the rock,
and be like the dove that *maketh her nest* **nesteth**
in the sides of the *hole's* **pit's** mouth.
29 We have heard the *pride* **pomp** of Moab,
(he is *exceeding proud* **mightily pompous**)
his *loftiness* **haughtiness**, and his *arrogancy* **pomp**,
and his *pride* **pomp**, and the haughtiness of his heart.
30 I know his wrath,
saith the LORD **an oracle of Yah Veh**;
but it shall not be so; his lies shall not so *effect* **work** it.
31 Therefore *will* **shall** I howl for Moab,
and I *will* **shall** cry out for all Moab;
mine heart shall mourn—**meditate**
for the men of *Kirheres* **Qir Hareseth**.
32 O vine of Sibmah, I *will* **shall** weep for thee
with the weeping of *Jazer* **Yazer**:
thy *plants* **tendrils** are *gone* **passed** over the sea,
they *reach even* **touch** to the sea of *Jazer* **Yazer**:
the *spoiler* **ravager** is fallen upon thy summer fruits
and upon thy *vintage* **crop**.
that I send him strollers who have him stroll,
and pour his instruments and shatter his bags.
13 And Moab shames because of Kemosh,
as the house of Yisra El shamed

of Beth El their confidence.
14 How say you,
We *are* mighty and valiant men for the war?
15 Moab *is* ravaged and ascends her cities;
and his chosen youths descend to the
slaughter—an oracle of the Sovereign
whose name is Yah Veh Sabaoth.
16 The calamity of Moab is near to come
and his evil hastens mightily.
17 All you who are all around him, wag over him;
and all you who know his name, say,
How the rod of strength is broken
—the staff of adornment!
18 You, daughter who settles in Dibon,
descend from your honor,
and settle in thirst;
for the ravager of Moab ascends on you;
he ruins your fortresses.
19 O settler of Aroer, stand by the way, and watch;
ask him who flees; and she who escapes;
and say, What becomes?
20 Moab shames; for it is broken down.
Howl and cry!
Tell it in Arnon, that Moab is ravaged:
21 and judgment comes on the plain land
—on Holon and on Yahsah
and on Mephaath,
22 and on Dibon and on Nebo
and on Beth Diblathayim
23 and on Qiryathaim and on Beth Gamul
and on Beth Meon
24 and on Qerioth and on Bozrah
and on all the cities of the land of Moab
far or near.
25 The horn of Moab is cut off and his arm broken
—an oracle of Yah Veh.
26 Intoxicate him:
for he greatens against Yah Veh:
Moab also slurps in his *own* vomit
and he also is ridiculed.
27 For was not Yisra El a ridicule to you?
Was he found among thieves?
For since your sufficient words, you sway for joy.
28 O you who settle in Moab,
leave the cities; and tabernacle in the rock:
and be as the dove
who nests in the sides of the mouth of the pit.
29 We hear the pomp of Moab
—mighty pompous
—his haughtiness and his pomp
—his pomp and the haughtiness of his heart.
30 I know his wrath
—an oracle of Yah Veh
but it is not thus; his lies work not thus.
31 So I howl for Moab,
and I cry for all Moab
—meditate for the men of Qir Hareseth.
32 O vine of Sibmah, I weep for you
with the weeping of Yazer:
your tendrils pass over the sea;
they touch to the sea of Yazer:
the ravager falls on your summer fruits
and on your crop:
33 And *joy* **cheerfulness** and *gladness* **twirling**
is *taken* **gathered** from the *plentiful*
field **orchard/Karmel**,
and from the land of Moab,
and I have caused wine to *fail* **shabbathize**
from the *winepresses* **troughs**:
none shall tread with shouting;
their shouting shall be no shouting.
34 From the cry of Heshbon
even unto *Elealeh* **El Aleh**,
and *even* unto *Jahaz* **Yahsah**,
have they *uttered* **given** their voice,
from *Zoar* **Soar** *even* unto Horonaim,
as an heifer of three *years old*:
for the waters also of Nimrim
shall be *desolate* **desolations**.
35 *Moreover*
I *will* **shall** cause to *cease* **shabbathize** in Moab,
saith the LORD **an oracle of Yah Veh**,
him that *offereth* **holocausteth** in
the *high places* **bamahs**,
and him that *burneth incense* **incenseth**
to his *gods* **elohim**.
36 Therefore
mine heart shall *sound* **roar** for Moab like pipes,
and mine heart shall *sound* **roar** like pipes
for the men of *Kirheres* **Qir Hareseth**:
because the riches that he hath *gotten* **worked**
are *perished* **destroyed**.
37 For every head shall *be bald* **balden**,
and every beard *clipped* **diminished**:
upon all the hands shall be *cuttings* **incisions**,
and upon the loins *sackcloth* **saq**.
38 There shall be *lamentation*
generally **chopping for all**
upon all the *housetops* **roofs** of Moab,
and in the *streets* **broadways** *thereof*:

for I have broken Moab like *a vessel* **an instrument**
wherein is no pleasure,
saith the LORD **an oracle of Yah Veh**.
39 They shall howl, *saying*, How is it broken down!
how hath Moab *turned* **faced** the *back* **neck**
with shame **shamed**!
so shall Moab be a *derision* **ridicule**
and a *dismaying* **ruin**
to all them **round** about him.
40 For thus saith *the LORD* **Yah Veh**;
Behold, he shall fly as an eagle, and shall
spread his wings over Moab.
41 *Kerioth* **Qerioth** is *taken* **captured**,
and the *strong holds* **huntholds**
are *surprised* **apprehended**,
and the mighty *men's* hearts in Moab at that day
shall be as the heart of a woman
in her *pangs* **tribulating**.
42 And Moab shall *be destroyed* **desolate**
from *being* a people,
because he hath *magnified* **greatened** *himself*
against *the LORD* **Yah Veh**.
43 Fear, and the pit, and the snare,
shall be upon thee, O *inhabitant* **settler** of Moab,
saith the LORD **an oracle of Yah Veh**.
44 He that fleeth from the **face of** fear
shall fall into the pit;
and he that *getteth up* **ascendeth** out of the pit
shall be *taken* **captured** in the snare:
for I *will* **shall** bring upon it, *even* upon Moab,
the year of their visitation,
saith the LORD **an oracle of Yah Veh**.
45 They that fled stood under
the shadow of Heshbon
because of the force:
but a fire shall come forth out of Heshbon,
and a flame from *the midst of Sihon* **within Sichon**,
and shall *devour* **consume** the *corner* **edge** of Moab,
and the *crown* **scalp**
of the *head* **sons** of *the tumultuous ones* **uproar**.
46 Woe be unto thee, O Moab!
the people of *Chemosh perisheth* **Kemosh destruct**:
for thy sons are taken **with the** captives,
and thy daughters *captives* **with the captivity**.
47 Yet *will* **shall** I *bring again*
return the captivity of Moab
in the latter days,
saith the LORD **an oracle of Yah Veh**.
Thus far **This** is the judgment of Moab.
33 and cheerfulness and twirling
are gathered from the orchard/Karmel
and from the land of Moab;
and I shabbathize the wine from the troughs:
no one treads with shouting;
in shouting, they shout not.
34 From the cry of Heshbon to El Aleh;
and to Yahsah they give their voice:
from Soar to Horonaim, a heifer of three:
for even the waters of Nimrim become desolations:
35 and I shabbathize in Moab
—an oracle of Yah Veh
he who holocausts in the bamahs,
and he who incenses to his elohim.
36 So my heart roars for Moab as pipes;
and my heart roars as pipes
for the men of Qir Hareseth:
because the riches he worked are destroyed.
37 For every head baldens,
and every beard diminishes:
on all the hands, incisions,
and on the loins, saq:
38 and chopping for all
on all the roofs of Moab and in the broadways:
for I break Moab
as an instrument wherein is no pleasure
—an oracle of Yah Veh.
39 They howl, How it is broken!
How Moab faces the neck shamed!
And Moab becomes a ridicule and a ruin to all
all around him.
40 For thus says Yah Veh;
Behold, he flies as an eagle
and spreads his wings over Moab.
41 Qerioth is captured,
and the huntholds apprehended;
and at that day,
the hearts of the mighty in Moab
become as the heart of a woman in her tribulating:
42 and Moab, as a people, desolates
because he greatens *himself* against Yah Veh.
43 Fear and the pit and the snare
snare on you, O settler of Moab
—an oracle of Yah Veh.
44 He who flees from the face of fear
falls into the pit;
and he who ascends from the pit
is captured in the snare:
for I bring thereon—on Moab,
the year of their visitation
—an oracle of Yah Veh.

45 They who flee stand under
the shadow of Heshbon
because of the force:
for a fire comes from Heshbon
and a flame from within Sichon
and consumes the edge of Moab,
and the scalp of the sons of uproar.
46 Woe to you, O Moab!
the people of Kemosh destruct:
for your sons are taken with the captives
and your daughters with the captivity.
47 And I restore the captivity of Moab
in the latter days
—an oracle of Yah Veh.
This is the judgment of Moab.

MESSAGE AGAINST THE SONS OF AMMON

49 Concerning the *Ammonites* **sons of Ammon**,
thus saith *the LORD* **Yah Veh;**
Hath *Israel* **Yisra El** no sons? hath he no *heir* **successor**?
why *then* doth their *king inherit* **sovereign succeed** Gad,
and his people *dwell* **settle** in his cities?
2 Therefore, behold, the days come,
saith the LORD **an oracle of Yah Veh,**
that I *will* **shall** cause *an alarm* **a blast** of war
to be heard in Rabbah of the
Ammonites **sons of Ammon;**
and it shall be a desolate heap,
and her daughters shall be burned with fire:
then shall *Israel* **Yisra El** be *heir* **successor** unto them
that were his *heirs* **successors,**
saith *the LORD* **Yah Veh.**
3 Howl, O Heshbon, for *Ai* **Ay** is *spoiled* **ravaged:**
cry, ye daughters of Rabbah, gird you with *sackcloth* **saq;**
lament **chop**, and *run to and fro* **flit** by the *hedges* **walls;**
for their *king* **sovereign** shall go into *captivity* **exile,**
and his priests and his *princes* **governors** together.
4 Wherefore *gloriest* **halalest** thou in the valleys,
thy flowing valley, O *backsliding* **apostate** daughter?
that *trusted* **confided** in her treasures, *saying,*
Who shall come unto me?
5 Behold, I *will* **shall** bring a fear upon thee,
saith the Lord GOD of hosts
an oracle of Adonay Yah Veh Sabaoth,
from all those that be **round** about thee;
and ye shall be driven out every man
right forth **from his face;**
and none shall gather *up* him that wandereth.
6 And afterward
I *will bring again* **shall return** the captivity
of the *children* **sons** of Ammon,
saith the LORD **an oracle of Yah Veh.**

MESSAGE AGAINST EDOM

7 Concerning Edom,
thus saith *the LORD of hosts* **Yah Veh Sabaoth;**
Is wisdom no more in Teman?
is counsel *perished* **destroyed**
from the *prudent* **discerning**?
is their wisdom *vanished* **spread thin**?
8 Flee ye, *turn* **face** back, *dwell* **settle** deep,
O *inhabitants* **settlers** of Dedan;
for I *will* **shall** bring the calamity
of *Esau* **Esav** upon him,
the time that I *will* **shall** visit him.
9 If *grapegatherers* **clippers** come to thee,
would **should** they not
leave some gleaning grapes **let gleanings remain**?
if thieves by night,
they *will destroy* **shall ruin** till they *have enough* **satiate.**
10 But I have *made Esau bare* **stripped Esav,**
I have *uncovered* **exposed** his *secret places* **coverts,**
and he shall not be able to hide himself:
his seed is *spoiled* **ravaged,**
and his brethren, and his *neighbours*
fellow tabernaclers,
and he is not.
11 Leave thy *fatherless children* **orphans,**
I *will preserve* **shall enliven** them *alive;*
and let thy widows *trust* **confide** in me.
12 For thus saith *the LORD* **Yah Veh;** Behold,
they whose judgment was not to drink of the cup
in drinking, have *assuredly* drunken;
and art thou he that **in exonerating,**
shall *altogether go unpunished* **be exonerated**?
thou shalt not *go unpunished* **be exonerated,**
but **in drinking,** thou shalt *surely* drink of it.
13 For I have *sworn* **oathed** by myself,
saith the LORD **an oracle of Yah Veh,**
that Bozrah shall become a desolation,
a reproach, a *waste* **parch**, and *a curse* **an abasement;**
and all the cities *thereof*
shall be *perpetual wastes* **eternal parched areas.**
14 I have heard a *rumour* **report**
from *the LORD* **Yah Veh,**
and an ambassador is sent unto the *heathen* **goyim,**
saying, Gather ye together, and come against her,
and rise up to the *battle* **war.**
15 For, *lo* **behold,**
I *will make* **shall give** thee small
among the *heathen* **goyim,**

Message Against The Sons Of Ammon

49 Concerning the sons of Ammon,
thus says Yah Veh:
Has Yisra El no sons?—No successor?
Why has their sovereign succeeded Gad?
—and his people settle in his cities?
2 So behold, days come,
—an oracle of Yah Veh
that I have a blast of war
to be heard in Rabbah of the sons of Ammon;
and it becomes a desolate heap:
and her daughters burn with fire:
and Yisra El posseses them who possessed him,
says Yah Veh.
3 Howl, O Heshbon, for Ay is ravaged!
Cry, you daughters of Rabbah; gird with saq;
chop, and flit by the walls;
for their sovereign goes into exile
together with his priests and his governors.
4 Why halal in the valleys
—your flowing valley, O apostate daughter?
Who confides in her treasures?
Who comes to me?
5 Behold, I bring a fear on you
—an oracle of Adonay Yah Veh Sabaoth
from all them all around you;
and they drive you out—every man from his face;
and no one gathers him who wanders:
6 And afterward
I restore the captivity of the sons of Ammon
—an oracle of Yah Veh.

Message Against Edom

7 Concerning Edom,
thus says Yah Veh Sabaoth:
Is wisdom no more in Teman?
Is counsel destroyed from the discerning?
Is their wisdom spread thin?
8 Flee you, face back, settle
deep, O settlers of Dedan;
for I bring the calamity of Esav on him
at the time I visit him.
9 If clippers come to you,
leave they not the gleanings?
If thieves by night,
they ruin until they satiate.
10 For I—I strip Esav; I expose his coverts;
and he cannot hide himself:
his seed is ravaged
—with his brothers and his fellow tabernaclers
—and he is not.
11 Leave your orphans, I enliven them;
—and your widows. Trust me!
12 For thus says Yah Veh:
Behold,
they whose judgment is to not drink of the cup
in drinking, they drink;
and are you he, who in exonerating, is exonerated?
You *are* not exonerated,
but in drinking, you drink thereof.
13 For I oath by myself
—an oracle of Yah Veh
that Bozrah becomes a desolation,
a reproach, a parch, and an abasement
—and all the cities eternal parched areas.
14 I hear a report from Yah Veh,
and an ambassador is sent to the goyim,
Gather yourselves
and come against her and rise to the war.
15 For, behold,
I give you, small among the goyim
and despised among *men* **humanity**.
16 Thy *terribleness* **trembling** hath deceived thee,
and the *pride* **arrogance** of thine heart,
O thou that *dwellest* **tabernaclest**
in the clefts of the rock,
that *holdest* **apprehendest** the height of the hill:
though thou shouldest *make* **heighten** thy nest
as high as the eagle,
I *will* **shall** bring thee down from thence,
saith the LORD **an oracle of Yah Veh.**
17 Also Edom shall be a desolation:
every one that *goeth* **passeth** by it shall be astonished,
and shall hiss at all the *plagues* **wounds** *thereof.*
18 As in the overthrow
of *Sodom* **Sedom** and *Gomorrah* **Amorah**
and the *neighbour cities* **nearby tabernacles** *thereof,*
saith *the LORD* **Yah Veh,**
no man shall *abide* **settle** there,
neither shall a son of *man dwell* **humanity sojourn** in it.
19 Behold, he shall *come up* **ascend** like a lion
from the *swelling* **pomp** of *Jordan* **Yarden**
against the habitation **of rest** of the *strong* **perennial**:
but I *will suddenly* **shall in a blink**
make him run away from her:
and who is a chosen *man,*
that I may *appoint over* **oversee** her?
for who is like me?
and who *will appoint me the time*
shall congregate with me?

and who is that *shepherd* **tender**
that *will* **shall** stand *before me* **at my face**?
20 Therefore hear the counsel
of *the LORD* **Yah Veh**,
that he hath *taken* **counselled** against Edom;
and his *purposes* **fabrications**,
that he hath *purposed* **fabricated**
against the *inhabitants* **settlers** of Teman:
Surely the *least* **lesser** of the flock
shall *draw* **drag** them out:
surely he shall *make* **desolate**
their habitations *desolate* **of rest** with them.
21 The earth *is moved* **quaketh**
at the *noise* **voice** of their fall,
at the cry the *noise* **voice** *thereof*
was heard in the *Red* **Reed** sea.
22 Behold, he shall *come up*
ascend and fly as the eagle,
and spread his wings over Bozrah:
and at that day shall the heart of
the mighty *men* of Edom
be as the heart of a woman in her *pangs* **tribulating**.

Message Against Dammeseq

23 Concerning *Damascus* **Dammeseq**.
Hamath is *confounded* **shamed**, and Arpad:
for they have heard evil *tidings* **reports**:
they are *fainthearted* **melted**;
there is *sorrow* **concern** on the sea;
it cannot *be quiet* **rest**.
24 *Damascus is waxed feeble* **Dammeseq slacketh**,
and *turneth* **faceth** *herself* to flee,
and *fear* **terror** hath *seized on* **holden** her:
anguish **tribulation** and *sorrows* **pangs** have taken her,
as *a woman in travail* **in birthing**.
25 How is the city of *praise* **halal** not *left* **forsaken**,
the city of my joy!
26 Therefore her *young men* **youths**
shall fall in her *streets* **broadways**,
and all the men of war
shall be *cut off* **severed** in that day,
saith the LORD of hosts **an oracle of Yah Veh Sabaoth**.
27 And I *will* **shall** kindle a fire
in the wall of *Damascus* **Dammeseq**,
and it shall consume
the *palaces* **citadels** of *Benhadad* **Ben Hadad**.

Message Against Qedar And Hazor

28 Concerning *Kedar* **Qedar**,
and concerning the *kingdoms* **sovereigndoms** of Hazor,
which *Nebuchadrezzar* **Nebukadnets Tsar**
king **sovereign** of *Babylon* **Babel** shall smite,
thus saith *the LORD* **Yah Veh**;
Arise ye, *go up* **ascend** to *Kedar* **Qedar**,
and *spoil* **ravage** the *men* **sons** of the east.
29 Their tents and their flocks shall they take away:
they shall *take* **bear** to themselves their curtains,
and despised among humanity:
16 your trembling deceives you
—and the arrogance of your heart,
O you who tabernacle in the clefts of the rock
—who apprehend the height of the hill:
though you heighten your nest as high as the eagle,
I bring you down from there
—an oracle of Yah Veh.
17 Also Edom becomes a desolation:
every one who passes by astonishes
and hisses at all the wounds.
18 As the overthrow of Sedom and Amorah
and the nearby tabernacles,
says Yah Veh,
neither man settles there
nor a son of humanity sojourns therein.
19 Behold,
he ascends as a lion from the pomp of Yarden
against the habitation of rest of the perennial:
and in a blink, I run him away from her:
and who is chosen, that I oversee her?
For who is like me?
And who congregates with me?
And who is that tender standing at my face?
20 So hear the counsel of Yah Veh,
that he counsels against Edom;
and the fabrications
he fabricates against the settlers of Teman:
surely the lesser of the flock drag them out:
surely he desolates their habitations of rest with them.
21 The earth quakes at the voice of their fall;
—the cry—the voice is heard in the Reed sea.
22 Behold, he ascends and flies as the eagle
and spreads his wings over Bozrah:
and at that day,
the heart of the mighty of Edom
become as the heart of a woman in her tribulating.

Message Against Dammeseq

23 Concerning Dammeseq:
Hamath and Arpad shame:
for they hear evil reports; they melt:
there is concern on the sea; it cannot rest.

24 Dammeseq slackens and faces to flee;
and terror holds her:
tribulation and pangs take her as in birthing.
25 How the city of halal is not forsaken
—the city of my joy!
26 So her youths fall in her broadways,
and all the men of war are severed in that day
—an oracle of Yah Veh Sabaoth
27 and I kindle a fire in the wall of Dammeseq
and it consumes the citadels of Ben Hadad.

Message Against Qedar And Hazor

28 Concerning Qedar
and concerning the sovereigndoms of Hazor,
which Nebukadnets Tsar sovereign of Babel smote:
Thus says Yah Veh:
Rise; ascend to Qedar:
and ravage the sons of the east.
29 They take their tents and their flocks:
they bear their curtains to themselves
and all their *vessels* **instruments**, and their camels;
and they shall *cry* **call out** unto them,
Fear **Terror** is *on every side* **round about**.
30 Flee, *get you far off* **bemoan mightily**,
dwell **settle** deep, O ye *inhabitants* **settlers** of Hazor,
saith the LORD **an oracle of Yah Veh**;
for *Nebuchadrezzar* **Nebukadnets Tsar**
king **sovereign** of *Babylon* **Babel**
hath *taken counsel* **counselled** against you,
and hath *conceived* **fabricated** a *purpose* **fabrication**
against you.
31 Arise,
get **ascend** you *up* unto the *wealthy nation* **serene goyim**,
that *dwelleth without care* **settleth confidently**,
saith the LORD **an oracle of Yah Veh**,
which have neither *gates* **doors** nor bars,
which *dwell* **tabernacle** alone.
32 And their camels shall be a *booty* **plunder**,
and the multitude of their *cattle* **chattel** a spoil:
and I *will scatter* **shall winnow** into all winds
them that *are in the utmost corners* **chop the edges**;
and I *will* **shall** bring their calamity
from all sides *thereof*,
saith the LORD **an oracle of Yah Veh**.
33 And Hazor shall be
a *dwelling for dragons* **habitation of monsters**,
and a desolation *for ever* **eternally**:
there shall no man *abide* **settle** there,
nor *any* **a** son of *man dwell* **humanity sojourn** in it.

Message Against Elam

34 The word of *the LORD* **Yah Veh**
that came to *Jeremiah* **Yirme Yah** the prophet
against Elam in the beginning of
the *reign* **sovereigndom**
of *Zedekiah* **Sidqi Yah**
king **sovereign** of *Judah* **Yah Hudah**, saying,
35 Thus saith *the LORD of hosts* **Yah Veh Sabaoth**;
Behold, I *will* **shall** break the bow of Elam,
the *chief* **beginning** of their might.
36 And upon Elam *will* **shall** I bring the four winds
from the four *quarters* **ends** of *heaven* **the heavens**,
and *will scatter* **shall winnow** them
toward all those winds;
and there shall be no *nation* **goyim**
whither the *outcasts* **expelled** of Elam shall not come.
37 For I *will* **shall** cause Elam to be dismayed
before **at the face of** their enemies,
and *before* **at the face of** them that seek their *life* **soul**:
and I *will* **shall** bring evil upon them,
even my *fierce anger* **fuming wrath**,
saith the LORD **an oracle of Yah Veh**;
and I *will* **shall** send the sword after them,
till I have *consumed* **finished** them **off**:
38 And I *will* **shall** set my throne in Elam,
and *will* **shall** destroy from thence
the *king* **sovereign** and the *princes* **governors**,
saith the LORD **an oracle of Yah Veh**.
39 *But* **And so be** it *shall come
to pass* in the latter days,
that I *will bring again* **shall return** the captivity of Elam,
saith the LORD **an oracle of Yah Veh**.

Message Against Babel

50 The word that *the LORD spake* **Yah Veh worded**
against *Babylon* **Babel**
and against the land of the *Chaldeans* **Kesediym**
by *Jeremiah* **the hand of Yirme Yah** the prophet.
2 *Declare* **Tell** ye among the *nations* **goyim**,
and *publish* **let it be heard**,
and *set up a standard* **lift an ensign**;
publish **let it be heard**, and conceal not:
say, *Babylon* **Babel** is *taken* **captured**,
Bel is *confounded* **shamed**,
Merodach is broken *in pieces*;
her idols are *confounded* **shamed**,
her *images* **idols** are broken *in pieces*.
3 For out of the north
there *cometh up* **ascendeth** a *nation* **goyim** against her,

which shall *make* **place** her land desolate,
and none shall *dwell* **settle** therein:
they shall *remove* **wander**, they shall depart,
both *man* **humanity** and *beast* **animal**.
4 In those days, and in that time,
with all their instruments and their camels:
and they call out to them,
Terror *is* all around!
30 Flee, bemoan mightily, settle deep,
O you settlers of Hazor
—an oracle of Yah Veh:
for Nebukadnets Tsar sovereign of Babel
counsels against you,
and fabricates a fabrication against you.
31 Rise;
ascend to the serene goyim who settle confidently
—an oracle of Yah Veh
with neither doors nor bars
who tabernacle alone.
32 And their camels become a plunder
and the multitude of their chattel a spoil:
and I winnow them who chop the edges
to all the winds;
and I bring their calamity from all sides
—an oracle of Yah Veh
33 and Hazor becomes a habitation of monsters
and a desolation eternally:
neither man settles there,
nor a son of humanity sojourns therein.

Message Against Elam

34 So be the word of Yah Veh
to Yirme Yah the prophet against Elam
in the beginning of the sovereigndom
of Sidqi Yah sovereign of Yah Hudah, saying,
35 Thus says Yah Veh Sabaoth:
Behold, I break the bow of Elam,
the beginning of their might:
36 and on Elam I bring the four winds
from the four ends of the heavens;
and winnow them toward all those winds;
so that no goyim becomes
where the expelled of Elam enter not.
37 For I dismay Elam at the face of their enemies
and at the face of them who seek their soul:
and I bring evil on them—my fuming wrath
—an oracle of Yah Veh
and I send the sword after them until I finish them off:
38 and I set my throne in Elam,
and destroy there the sovereign and the governors
—an oracle of Yah Veh.
39 And so be it, in the latter days,
I restore the captivity of Elam
—an oracle of Yah Veh.

Message Against Babel

50 The word Yah Veh words against Babel
and against the land of the Kesediym
by the hand of Yirme Yah the prophet.
2 Tell you among the goyim and have them hear;
and lift an ensign:
have them hear; and conceal not:
say, Babel *is* captured, Bel *is* shamed,
Merodach *is* broken:
her idols *are* shamed; her idols *are* broken.
3 For from the north
a goyim ascends against her
who places her land desolate;
and no one settles therein:
they wander; they depart;
—both humanity and animal.
4 In those days, and in that time,
saith the LORD **an oracle of Yah Veh**,
the *children* **sons** of *Israel* **Yisra El** shall come,
they and the *children* **sons** of *Judah* **Yah Hudah** together,
going and weeping: they shall go,
and seek *the LORD* **Yah Veh** their *God* **Elohim**.
5 They shall ask the way to *Zion* **Siyon**
with their faces thitherward, *saying*,
Come, and let us join ourselves to *the LORD* **Yah Veh**
in *a perpetual* **an eternal** covenant
that shall not be forgotten.
6 My people hath been lost *sheep* **flocks**
their *shepherds* **tenders**
have caused them to *go astray* **stray**,
they have *turned* **apostatized** them *away*
on the mountains:
they have gone from mountain to hill,
they have forgotten their *restingplace* **repose**.
7 All that found them have devoured them:
and their *adversaries* **tribulators** said,
We *offend* **have** not **guilted**,
because they have sinned against *the LORD* **Yah Veh**,
the habitation **of rest** of *justice* **justness**,
even *the LORD* **Yah Veh**,
the *hope* **expectation** of their fathers.
8 *Remove* **Wander** out of the
midst of *Babylon* **Babel**,
and go forth out of the land of the *Chaldeans* **Kesediym**,
and be as the he goats *before* **at the face of** the flocks.

9 For, *lo* **behold,** I *will raise* **shall waken**
and cause to *come up* **ascend** against *Babylon* **Babel**
an assembly **a congregation** of great *nations* **goyim**
from the north *country* **land:**
and they shall *set themselves in array* **line up** against her;
from thence she shall be *taken* **captured:**
their arrows shall be as of a mighty
expert man **discerner;**
none shall return in vain.
10 And *Chaldea* **Kesediym** shall be a spoil:
all that spoil her shall *be satisfied* **satiate,**
saith the LORD **an oracle of Yah Veh.**
11 Because ye *were glad* **cheered,**
because ye *rejoiced* **jumped for joy,**
O ye *destroyers* **plunderers** of mine *heritage* **inheritance,**
because ye are grown fat as the heifer at grass,
and *bellow* **resound** as *bulls* **mighty;**
12 Your mother shall *be sore*
confounded **mightily shame;**
she that *bare* **birthed** you shall *be ashamed* **blush:**
behold, the hindermost of the *nations* **goyim**
shall be a wilderness,
a *dry land* **parch,** and a *desert* **plain.**
13 Because of the *wrath* **rage** of *the LORD* **Yah Veh**
it shall not be *inhabited* **settled,**
but it shall be wholly desolate:
every one that *goeth* **passeth** by *Babylon* **Babel**
shall be astonished, and hiss at all her *plagues* **wounds.**
14 *Put yourselves in array* **Line**
up against *Babylon* **Babel**
round about:
all ye that bend the bow,
shoot **hand toss** at her, spare no arrows:
for she hath sinned against *the LORD* **Yah Veh.**
15 Shout against her round about:
she hath given her hand:
her foundations are fallen, her walls are thrown down:
for it is the *vengeance* **avengement**
of *the LORD* **Yah Veh:**
take vengeance **avenge** upon her;
as she hath *done* **worked,** *do* **work** unto her.
16 Cut off the *sower* **seeder** from *Babylon* **Babel,**
and him that *handleth* **manipulateth** the sickle
in the time of harvest:
for fear **at the face** of the oppressing sword
they shall *turn* **face** every *one* **man** to his people,
and they shall flee every *one* **man** to his own land.
17 *Israel* **Yisra El** is a scattered *sheep* **lamb;**
the lions have driven him away:
first
the *king* **sovereign** of *Assyria* **Ashshur**
hath devoured him;
and last
this *Nebuchadrezzar* **Nebukadnets Tsar**
king **sovereign** of *Babylon* **Babel**

—an oracle of Yah Veh
the sons of Yisra El come
—they and the sons of Yah Hudah together
coming and weeping:
they come and seek Yah Veh their Elohim:
5 they ask the way to Siyon
with their faces toward,
Come; we join ourselves to Yah Veh
in an eternal covenant, not forgotten.
6 My people became lost flocks
their tenders strayed them,
they apostatized them on the mountains:
going from mountain to hill
they forgot their repose.
7 All who find them devour them:
and their tribulators say,
We guilt not!
—because they sinned against Yah Veh
the habitation of rest of justness;
—Yah Veh, the expectation of their fathers.
8 Wander from the midst of Babel
and come from the land of the Kesediym;
and be as the he goats at the face of the flocks.
9 For, behold, I waken
and against Babel
I ascend a congregation of great goyim
from the north land:
and they line up against her;
from thence they capture her:
their arrows as of a mighty discerner;
no one returns in vain.
10 And Kesediym becomes a spoil:
all who spoil her satiate—an oracle of Yah Veh
11 because you cheer
—because you jump for joy
O you plunderers of my inheritance,
because you grow fat as the heifer at grass
and resound as the mighty;
12 your mother shames mightily;
she who birthed you blushes:
behold, the backword of the goyim
are a wilderness, a parch, and a plain:
13 because of the rage of Yah Veh
it is not settled
and becomes wholly desolate:
every one who passes by Babel
astonishes and hisses at all her wounds.

14 Line up against Babel, all around
—all you who bend the bow:
hand toss at her; spare no arrows:
for she sinned against Yah Veh.
15 Shout against her all around:
she gives her hand:
her foundations fallen; her walls overthrown:
for it *is* the avengement of Yah Veh:
avenge on her;
as she worked, work to her:
16 cut off the seeder from Babel;
and he who manipulates the sickle
in the time of harvest:
at the face of the oppressing sword;
every man faces to his people,
and every man flees to his own land.
17 Yisra El is a scattered lamb;
the lions drive him away:
first the sovereign of Ashshur devours him;
and last this Nebukadnets Tsar sovereign of Babel
hath *broken* **craunched** his bones.
18 Therefore thus saith
the LORD of hosts **Yah Veh Sabaoth**,
the God **Elohim** of *Israel* **Yisra El**;
Behold, I *will punish* **shall visit**
upon the *king* **sovereign** of *Babylon* **Babel** and his land,
as I have *punished* **visited**
upon the *king* **sovereign** of *Assyria* **Ashshur**.
19 And I *will bring Israel again*
shall turn Yisra El back
to his habitation **of rest**,
and he shall *feed* **tend**
on *Carmel* **Karmel/orchard** and Bashan,
and his soul shall *be satisfied* **satiate**
upon mount *Ephraim* **Ephrayim** and *Gilead* **Gilad**.
20 In those days, and in that time,
saith the LORD **an oracle of Yah Veh**,
the *iniquity* **perversity** of *Israel* **Yisra El**
shall be sought for,
and there shall be none;
and the sins of *Judah* **Yah Hudah**,
and they shall not be found:
for I *will pardon* **shall forgive** them
whom I *reserve* **let remain**.
21 *Go up* **Ascend**
against the land of *Merathaim* **Merathayim**,
even against it,
and against the *inhabitants* **settlers** of *Pekod* **Peqod**:
waste **parch** and *utterly destroy* **devote** after them,
saith the LORD **an oracle of Yah Veh**,
and *do* **work** according to all
that I have *commanded* **misvahed** thee.
22 A *sound* **voice** of *battle* **war** is in the land,
and of great *destruction* **breaking**.
23 How is the hammer of the whole earth
cut *asunder* **apart** and broken!
how is *Babylon* **Babel**
become a desolation among the *nations* **goyim**!
24 I have laid a snare for thee,
and thou art also *taken* **captured**, O *Babylon* **Babel**,
and thou *wast not aware* **knewest not**:
thou art found, and also *caught* **apprehended**,
because thou hast *striven* **throttled**
against *the LORD* **Yah Veh**.
25 *The LORD* **Yah Veh**
hath opened his *armoury* **treasury**,
and hath brought forth
the *weapons* **instruments** of his *indignation* **rage**:
for this is the work
of *the Lord GOD of hosts* **Adonay Yah Veh Sabaoth**
in the land of the *Chaldeans* **Kesediym**.
26 Come against her from the *utmost border* **end**,
open her *storehouses* **granaries**:
cast **raise** her *up* as heaps, and *destroy* **devote** her *utterly*:
let *nothing of her be left* **there be no survivors**.
27 *Slay* **Parch** all her bullocks;
let them *go down* **descend** to the slaughter:
woe **ho** unto them!
for their day is come, the time of their visitation.
28 The voice of them that flee and escape
out of the land of *Babylon* **Babel**,
to *declare* **tell** in *Zion* **Siyon** the *vengeance* **avengement**
of *the LORD* **Yah Veh** our *God* **Elohim**,
the *vengeance* **avengement** of his *temple* **manse**.
29 *Call together* **Hearken** the archers
against *Babylon* **Babel**:
all ye that bend the bow,
camp **encamp** against it round about;
let *none thereof escape* **there be no escapees**:
recompense **shalam to** her according to her *work* **deeds**;
according to all that she hath *done* **worked**,
do **work** unto her:
for she hath been proud against *the LORD* **Yah Veh**,
against the Holy One of *Israel* **Yisra El**.
30 Therefore shall her *young men* **youths**
fall in the *streets* **broadways**,
and all her men of war
shall be *cut off* **severed** in that day,
saith the LORD **an oracle of Yah Veh**.
31 Behold, I am against thee, O
thou most proud **arrogance**,
craunches his bones.

18 So thus says
Yah Veh Sabaoth Elohim of Yisra El;
Behold,
I visit on the sovereign of Babel and his land,
as I visited on the sovereign of Ashshur:
19 and I return Yisra El to his habitation of rest,
and he tends on Karmel/orchard and Bashan, and
his soul satiates on mount Ephrayim and Gilad.
20 In those days, and in that time,
—an oracle of Yah Veh
they seek the perversity of Yisra El,
and there is none;
and the sins of Yah Hudah,
and they find them not:
for I forgive them whom I leave remaining.
21 Ascend against the land of Merathayim,
—against it, and against the settlers of Peqod:
parch and devote after them
—an oracle of Yah Veh
and work according to all I misvahed you.
22 A voice of war *is* in the land,
and of great breaking.
23 How the hammer of the whole earth
is cut apart and broken!
How Babel becomes a desolation among the goyim!
24 I lay a snare for you,
and also capture you, O Babel,
and you know not:
you are found out and also apprehended
because you throttled against Yah Veh.
25 Yah Veh opens his treasury
and brings forth the instruments of his rage:
for this is the work of Adonay Yah Veh Sabaoth
in the land of the Kesediym.
26 Come against her from the end;
open her granaries:
raise her as heaps and devote her
that there be no survivors:
27 parch all her bullocks;
descend them to the slaughter.
Ho to them!
for their day *is* come—the time of their visitation.
28 The voice of them who flee and escape
from the land of Babel,
to tell in Siyon
the avengement of Yah Veh our Elohim
—the avengement of his manse.
29 Hearken the archers against Babel
all you who bend the bow:
encamp against it all around;
that there be no escapees:
shalam her according to her deeds;
work to her according to all she worked:
for she *is* proud against Yah Veh
—against the Holy One of Yisra El.
30 So fell her youths in the broadways
and sever all her men of war in that day
—an oracle of Yah Veh.
31 Behold, I *am* against you, O Arrogance!
saith the Lord GOD of hosts
an oracle of Adonay Yah Veh Sabaoth:
for thy day is come, the time that I *will* **shall** visit thee.
32 And the *most proud* **arrogant**
shall *stumble* **falter** and fall,
and none shall raise him up:
and I *will* **shall** kindle a fire in his cities,
and it shall *devour* **consume** all round about him.
33 Thus saith *the LORD of hosts* **Yah Veh Sabaoth**;
The *children* **sons** of *Israel* **Yisra El**
and the *children* **sons** of *Judah* **Yah Hudah**
were oppressed together:
and all that *took* **captured** them *captives*
held them *fast*;
they refused to *let* **send** them *go* **away**.
34 Their Redeemer is strong;
the LORD of hosts **Yah Veh Sabaoth** is his name:
in pleading, he shall *throughly* plead their *cause* **plea**,
that he may *give* rest *to* the land,
and *disquiet* **quake**
the *inhabitants* **settlers** of *Babylon* **Babel**.
35 A sword is upon the *Chaldeans* **Kesediym**,
saith the LORD **an oracle of Yah Veh**,
and upon the *inhabitants* **settlers** of *Babylon* **Babel**,
and upon her *princes* **governors**, and upon her wise *men*.
36 A sword is upon *the liars* **their lies**;
and they shall *dote* **folly**:
a sword is upon her mighty *men*;
and they shall be dismayed.
37 A sword is upon their horses,
and upon their chariots,
and upon all the *mingled people* **comingled**
that are in the midst of her;
and they shall become as women:
a sword is upon her treasures;
and they shall be *robbed* **plundered**.
38 A *drought* **parch** is upon her waters;
and they shall be dried up:
for it is the land of *graven images* **sculptiles**,
and they *are mad upon their idols* **halal bugaboos**.
39 Therefore the *wild beasts of*
the desert **desert dwellers**
with the *wild beasts of the islands* **island**
howlers shall *dwell* **settle** there,

and the **daughters of the** owls shall *dwell* **settle** therein:
and it shall be no more *inhabited* **settled**
for ever **in perpetuity**;
neither shall it be *dwelt* **tabernacled** in
from generation to generation.
40 As *God* **Elohim**
overthrew *Sodom* **Sedom** and *Gomorrah* **Amorah**
and the *neighbour cities* **nearby tabernacles** *thereof,*
saith the LORD **an oracle of Yah Veh**;
so shall no man *abide* **settle** there,
neither shall any son of *man* **humanity**
dwell **sojourn** therein.
41 Behold, a people shall come from the north,
and a great *nation* **goyim**,
and many *kings* **sovereigns** shall be *raised up* **wakened**
from the *coasts* **flanks** of the earth.
42 They shall hold the bow and the *lance* **dart**:
they are cruel, and *will* **shall** not *shew* mercy:
their voice shall roar like the sea,
and they shall ride upon horses,
every one put in array—**lined up**,
like a man to the *battle* **war**,
against thee, O daughter of *Babylon* **Babel**.
43 The *king* **sovereign** of *Babylon* **Babel**
hath heard the report of them,
and his hands *waxed feeble* **slackened**:
anguish **tribulation** took hold of him,
and pangs as *of a woman in travail* **in birthing**.
44 Behold, he shall *come up* **ascend** like a lion
from the *swelling* **pomp** of *Jordan* **Yarden**
unto the habitation **of rest** of the *strong* **perennial**:
but I *will make* **shall cause** them *suddenly* **in a blink**
run away from her:
and who is *a* chosen *man*, that I may appoint over her?
for who is like me?
and who *will appoint* **shall congregate with** me *the time*?
—an oracle of Adonay Yah Veh Sabaoth
for your day is come—to visit you:
32 and the arrogant to falter and fall
with no one to raise him:
and I kindle a fire in his cities,
and it consumes all all around him.
33 Thus says Yah Veh Sabaoth;
The sons of Yisra El and the sons of Yah Hudah
are oppressed:
and all who capture them hold them;
they refuse to send them away.
34 Their Redeemer is strong;
Yah Veh Sabaoth *is* his name:
in pleading, he pleads their plea
—to rest the land
and quake the settlers of Babel.
35 A sword *is* on the Kesediym
—an oracle of Yah Veh
and on the settlers of Babel
and on her governors and on her wise:
36 a sword *is* on their lies
and they folly;
a sword *is* on her mighty
and they dismay;
37 a sword *is* on their horses and on their chariots
and on all the comingled among her;
and they become as women:
a sword *is* on her treasures
and they are plundered;
38 a parch is on her waters
and they dry up;
for it is the land of sculptiles
and they halal bugaboos:
39 so the desert dwellers settle there
with the island howlers;
and the daughters of the owls settle therein:
and it *is* neither settled any more in perpetuity;
nor tabernacled in from generation to generation.
40 As Elohim overthrew Sedom and Amorah
and the nearby tabernacles
—an oracle of Yah Veh
thus neither man settles there,
nor any son of humanity sojourns therein.
41 Behold, a people come from the north
even a great goyim,
and many sovereigns waken
from the flanks of the earth:
42 they hold the bow and the dart;
they are cruel, and mercy not:
their voice roars as the sea
and they ride on horses
—lined up against you, O daughter of Babel,
as a man to the war.
43 The sovereign of Babel hears their report
and he slackens his hands:
tribulation takes hold of him
and pangs as in birthing.
44 Behold,
he ascends as a lion from the pomp of Yarden
to the habitation of rest of the perennial:
but I, in a blink, run them away from her.
And who is chosen? I appoint over her!
For who *is* like me?
And who congregates with me?
and who is that *shepherd* **tender**

that *will* **shall** stand *before me* **at my face?**
45 Therefore hear ye the counsel
of *the LORD* **Yah Veh,**
that he hath *taken* **counselled** against *Babylon* **Babel;**
and his *purposes* **fabrications,**
that he hath *purposed* **fabricated**
against the land of the *Chaldeans* **Kesediym:**
Surely the *least* **lesser** of the flock
shall *draw* **drag** them out:
surely he shall *make* **desolate**
their *habitation desolate* **habitation of rest** with them.
46 At the *noise* **voice**
of the *taking* **apprehending** of *Babylon* **Babel**
the earth is *moved* **quaked,**
and the cry is heard among the *nations* **goyim.**

THE JUDGMENT OF BABEL

51 Thus saith *the LORD* **Yah Veh;** Behold,
I *will raise up* **shall waken** against *Babylon* **Babel,**
and against them
that *dwell* **settle** in the *midst* **heart**
of them that *rise up against me* **rouse,**
a *destroying* **ruinous** wind/**spirit;**
2 And *will* **shall** send unto *Babylon* **Babel**
fanners **strangers,**
that shall *fan* **winnow** her,
and shall *empty* **evacuate** her land:
for in the day of *trouble* **evil**
they shall be against her round about.
3 Against him that bendeth
let the *archer* **bender** bend his bow,
and against him
that *lifteth himself up* **ascendeth** in his brigandine:
and spare ye not her *young men* **youths;**
destroy **devote** ye *utterly* all her host.
4 Thus the *slain* **pierced** shall fall
in the land of the *Chaldeans* **Kesediym,**
and they that are thrust through in her *streets* **outways.**
5 For *Israel* **Yisra El** hath not
been *forsaken* **abandoned,**
nor *Judah* **Yah Hudah** of his *God* **Elohim,**
of *the LORD of hosts* **Yah Veh Sabaoth;**
though their land was filled with *sin* **guilt**
against the Holy One of *Israel* **Yisra El.**
6 Flee out of the midst of *Babylon* **Babel,**
and *deliver* **rescue** every man his soul:
be not *cut off* **severed** in her *iniquity* **perversity;**
for this is the time
of *the LORD'S vengeance* **Yah Veh's avengement;**
he *will render* **in dealing shalom,**
he shall deal shalom unto her *a recompence.*
7 *Babylon* **Babel** hath been a golden cup
in *the LORD'S* **Yah Veh's** hand,
that *made* **intoxicated** all the earth *drunken:*
the *nations* **goyim** have drunken of her wine;
therefore the *nations are mad* **goyim halal.**
8 *Babylon* **Babel** is suddenly
fallen and *destroyed* **broken:**
howl for her;
take balm for her *pain* **sorrow,**
if so be she may be healed.
9 We *would* **should** have healed *Babylon* **Babel,**
but she is not healed:
forsake her,
and let us go every *one* **man** into his own *country* **land:**
for her judgment
reacheth **toucheth** unto *heaven* **the heavens,**
and is lifted up *even* to the *skies* **vapours.**
10 *The LORD* **Yah Veh**
hath brought forth our *righteousness* **justness:**
come, and let us *declare* **scribe** in *Zion* **Siyon**
the work of *the LORD* **Yah Veh** our *God* **Elohim.**
11 *Make bright* **Polish** the
arrows; *gather* **fill** the shields:
the LORD **Yah Veh** hath *raised up* **wakened**
the spirit of the *kings* **sovereigns** of the *Medes* **Maday:**
for his *device* **intrigue** is against *Babylon* **Babel,**
to *destroy* **ruin** it;
because it is the *vengeance* **avengement**
of *the LORD* **Yah Veh,**
the *vengeance* **avengement** of his *temple* **manse.**
12 *Set up* **Lift** the *standard* **ensign**
upon the walls of *Babylon* **Babel,** *make*
strengthen the *watch strong* **guard,**

And who *is* that tender who stands at my face?
45 So hear the counsel
Yah Veh counsels against Babel;
and the fabrications
he fabricates against the land of the Kesediym:
surely the lesser of the flock drag them out:
surely he desolates their habitation of rest with them.
46 At the voice of the apprehending of Babel
the earth quakes;
and the cry is heard among the goyim.

THE JUDGMENT OF BABEL

51 Thus says Yah Veh; Behold,
I waken a ruinous wind/spirit against Babel
and against them who settle in the heart of them
—who rouse:

2 and I send strangers to Babel
to winnow her and evacuate her land:
for in the day of evil
they are against her all around.
3 In bending,
the bender neither bends his bow,
nor ascends in his brigandine:
spare not her youths; devote all her host.
4 Thus the pierced fall in
the land of the Kesediym
and the thrust through in her outways.
5 For neither is Yisra El abandoned
nor Yah Hudah by his Elohim Yah Veh Sabaoth;
though their land is filled with guilt
against the Holy One of Yisra El.
6 Flee from midst Babel,
and rescue every man his soul:
be not severed in her perversity;
for this is the time
of the avengement of Yah Veh;
in dealing shalom, he deals shalom to her.
7 In the hand of Yah Veh, Babel *is* a golden cup
that intoxicates all the earth:
the goyim drink of her wine
and so the goyim halal.
8 Suddenly Babel falls and breaks:
howl for her; take balm for her sorrow,
if so be, she heals.
9 We heal Babel, and she heals not:
forsake her; and go every man into his own land:
for her judgment touches to the heavens,
—lifts to the vapours.
10 Yah Veh brings forth our justness:
come, and scribe in Siyon
the work of Yah Veh our Elohim:
11 polish the arrows; fill the shields:
Yah Veh wakens the spirit
of the sovereigns of the Maday:
for his intrigue *is* against Babel, to ruin therein;
because it *is* the avengement of Yah Veh
—the avengement of his manse.
12 Lift the ensign on the walls of Babel,
strengthen the guard;
set up **raise** the *watchmen* **guards**,
prepare the *ambushes* **lurks**:
for *the LORD* **Yah Veh** hath both *devised* **intrigued**
and *done* **worked** that which he spake
against the *inhabitants* **settlers** of *Babylon*
Babel. Apocalypse 18:1—17
13 O thou that *dwellest*
tabernaclest upon many waters,
abundant in treasures, thine end is come,
and the measure of thy *covetousness* **greedy gain**.
14 *The LORD of hosts* **Yah Veh Sabaoth**
hath *sworn* **oathed** by *himself* **his soul**, *saying*,
Surely I *will* **shall** fill thee with *men* **humanity**,
as with *caterpillers* **cankerworms**;
and they shall *lift up* **answer** a shout against thee.

THE FORCE OF YAH VEH

15 He hath *made* **worked** the
earth by his *power* **force**,
he hath established the world by his wisdom,
and hath *stretched out* **spread** the *heaven* **heavens**
by his *understanding* **discernment**.
16 When he *uttereth* **giveth** his voice,
there is a multitude of waters in the heavens;
and he causeth the vapours
to ascend from the ends of the earth:
he *maketh* **worketh** lightnings with rain,
and bringeth forth the wind out of his treasures.
17 *Every man* **All humanity** is
brutish by his knowledge;
every *founder* **refiner** is *confounded* **shamed**
by the *graven image* **sculptile**:
for his *molten image* **libation** is falsehood,
and there is no *breath* **spirit** in them.
18 They are vanity, the work of *errors* **frauds**:
in the time of their visitation they shall *perish* **destruct**.
19 The *portion* **allotment** of *Jacob* **Yaaqov**
is not like them;
for he is the former of all *things*:
and *Israel is* the rod of his inheritance:
the LORD of hosts **Yah Veh Sabaoth** is his name.
20 Thou art my *battle ax* **disintegrator**
and *weapons* **instruments** of war:
for with thee *will I break in pieces* **shall I shatter**
the *nations* **goyim**,
and with thee *will I destroy* **shall I ruin**
kingdoms **sovereigndoms**;
21 And with thee *will I break*
in pieces **shall I shatter**
the horse and his rider;
and with thee *will I break in pieces* **shall I shatter**
the chariot and his rider;
22 With thee also *will I break*
in pieces **shall I shatter**
man and woman;
and with thee *will I break in pieces* **shall I shatter**
old **aged** and *young* **lad**;
and with thee *will I break in pieces* **shall I shatter**
the *young man* **youth** and the *maid* **virgin**;

23 I *will* **shall** also *break in pieces with thee*
shatter the *shepherd* **tender** and his *flock* **tender drove**;
and with thee *will I break in pieces* **shall I shatter**
the *husbandman* **cultivator** and his yoke *of oxen*;
and with thee *will I break in pieces* **shall I shatter**
captains **governors** and *rulers* **prefects**.
24 And I *will render* **shall**
shalam unto *Babylon* **Babel**
and to all the *inhabitants* **settlers** of *Chaldea* **Kesediym**
all their evil that they have *done* **worked** in *Zion* **Siyon**
in your *sight* **eyes**,
saith the LORD **an oracle of Yah Veh**.
25 Behold, I am against thee,
O *destroying mountain* **mountain of ruin**,
saith the LORD **an oracle of Yah Veh**,
which *destroyest* **ruinest** all the earth:
and I *will stretch out* **shall spread** mine hand upon thee,
and roll thee down from the rocks,
and *will make* **shall give** thee a *burnt* **burning** mountain.
26 And they shall not take of
thee a stone for a corner,
nor a stone for foundations;
but thou shalt be desolate *for ever* **eternally**, *saith*
the LORD **an oracle of Yah Veh**. Apocalypse 8:8,9
27 *Set* **Lift** ye *up a standard* **an ensign** in the land,
blow **blast** the *trumpet* **shophar**
among the *nations* **goyim**,
prepare **hallow** the *nations* **goyim** against her,
raise the guards; prepare the lurks:
for Yah Veh both intrigues and works
what he speaks against the settlers of
Babel. Apocalypse 18:1—17
13 O you who tabernacles on many waters;
abundant in treasures; your end is come
—the measure of your greedy gain.
14 Yah Veh Sabaoth oaths by his soul,
Surely I fill you with humanity as with cankerworms;
and they answer a shout against you.

THE FORCE OF YAH VEH

15 He works the earth by his force;
he establishes the world by his wisdom
and spreads the heavens by his discernment:
16 he gives his voice,
and there is a multitude of waters in the heavens;
and he ascends the vapours
from the ends of the earth:
he works lightnings with rain
and brings forth the wind from his treasures.
17 All humanity is brutish by his knowledge;
every refiner shames by the sculptile:
for his libation is falsehood
and there is no spirit in them.
18 They are vanity—the work of frauds:
in the time of their visitation they destruct.
19 The allotment of Yaaqov *is* not like them;
for he is the former of all
and the rod of his inheritance:
Yah Veh Sabaoth *is* his name.
20 You are my disintegrator
and instruments of war:
and with you, I shatter the goyim;
and with you, I ruin sovereigndoms;
21 and with you, I shatter the horse and his rider;
and with you, I shatter the chariot and his rider;
22 and with you, I shatter man and woman;
and with you, I shatter aged and lad;
and with you, I shatter the youth and the virgin;
23 and I shatter the tender and his drove;
and with you, I shatter the cultivator and his yoke;
and with you, I shatter governors and prefects:
24 and I shalam to Babel
and to all the settlers of Kesediym
all the evil they worked in Siyon in your eyes
—an oracle of Yah Veh.
25 Behold, I *am* against you, O mountain of ruin
—an oracle of Yah Veh,
who ruins all the earth:
and I spread my hand on you
and roll you down from the rocks;
and give you as a burning mountain:
26 and they neither take of you a stone for a corner
nor a stone for foundations;
for you are desolated eternally
—an oracle of Yah Veh.
Apocalypse 8:8,9
27 Lift an ensign in the land!
Blast the shophar among the goyim!
Hallow the goyim against her,
call together **hearken** against her
the *kingdoms* **sovereigndoms** of Ararat,
Minni, and *Ashchenaz* **Ashkenaz**;
appoint a captain **muster an officer** against her;
cause the horses to *come up* **ascend**
as the *rough caterpillers* **shaggy cankerworms**.
28 *Prepare* **Hallow** against her the *nations* **goyim**
with the *kings* **sovereigns** of the *Medes*
Maday, the *captains* **governors** *thereof*,
and all the *rulers* **prefects** *thereof*,
and all the land of his *dominion* **reign**.
29 And the land shall tremble and *sorrow* **writhe**:
for every *purpose* **fabrication** of *the LORD* **Yah Veh**
shall *be performed* **rise** against *Babylon* **Babel**,

to *make* **set** the land of *Babylon* **Babel**
a desolation without *an inhabitant* **a settler**.
30 The mighty *men* of *Babylon* **Babel**
have *forborn* **ceased** to fight,
they have *remained* **settled** in their *holds* **huntholds**:
their might hath *failed* **withered**;
they became as women:
they have burned her *dwellingplaces* **tabernacles**;
her bars are broken.
31 *One post* **Runner** shall run
to meet *another* **runner**,
and *one messenger* **teller** to meet *another* **teller**,
to *shew* **tell** the *king* **sovereign** of *Babylon* **Babel**
that his city is *taken* **captured** at *one* **the** end,
32 And that the passages are *stopped* **apprehended**,
and the *reeds* **marshes** they have burned with fire,
and the men of war are *affrighted* **terrified**.
33 For thus saith *the LORD*
of hosts **Yah Veh Sabaoth**,
the God **Elohim** of *Israel* **Yisra El**;
The daughter of *Babylon* **Babel** is like a threshingfloor,
it is time to *thresh* **tread** her:
yet a little while, and the time of her harvest shall come.
34 *Nebuchadrezzar* **Nebukadnets Tsar**
the *king* **sovereign** of *Babylon* **Babel**
hath devoured me, he hath crushed me,
he hath *made* **set** me an empty *vessel* **instrument**,
he hath swallowed me up like a *dragon* **monster**,
he hath filled his belly with my *delicates* **pleasures**,
he hath *cast* **thrust** me *out* **away**.
35 *The violence done to me and to*
My violence, and that of my flesh
be upon *Babylon* **Babel**,
shall the *inhabitant* **settler** of *Zion* **Siyon** say;
and my blood
upon the *inhabitants* **settlers** of *Chaldea* **Kesediym**,
shall *Jerusalem* **Yeru Shalem** say.
36 Therefore thus saith *the LORD* **Yah Veh**;
Behold, I *will* **shall** plead thy *cause* **plea**,
and *take vengeance* **avenge avengement** for thee;
and I *will dry up* **shall parch** her sea,
and *make her springs* dry **her fountains**.
37 And *Babylon* shall **Babel** become heaps,
a *dwellingplace* **habitation** for *dragons* **monsters**,
an astonishment **a desolation**, and an hissing,
without *an inhabitant* **a settler**.
38 They shall roar together like *lions* **whelps**:
they shall *yell* **growl** as lions' whelps.
39 In their heat
I *will make* **shall place** their *feasts* **banquets**,
and I *will make* **shall intoxicate** them *drunken*,
that they may *rejoice* **jump for joy**,
and sleep *a perpetual* **an eternal** sleep, and not wake,
saith the LORD **an oracle of Yah Veh**.
40 I *will* **shall** bring them down
like *lambs* **rams** to the slaughter,
like rams with he goats.
41 How is Sheshach *taken* **captured**!
and how is the *praise* **halal** of the whole earth
surprised **apprehended**!
how is *Babylon* **Babel**
become *an astonishment* **a desolation**
among the *nations* **goyim**!
42 The sea is *come up* **ascended**
upon *Babylon* **Babel**:
she is covered with the multitude of the waves *thereof*.
43 Her cities are a desolation,
a *dry* **parched** land, and a *wilderness* **plain**,
a land wherein no man *dwelleth* **settleth**,
hearken against her
the sovereigndoms of Ararat, Minni, and Ashkenaz;
muster an officer against her;
ascend the horses as the shaggy cankerworms:
28 hallow the goyim against her
with the sovereigns of the Maday,
the governors and all the prefects
and all the land of his reign.
29 And the land trembles and writhes:
for every fabrication of Yah Veh rises against Babel
to set the land of Babel a desolation without a settler.
30 The mighty of Babel cease to fight;
they settle in their huntholds;
their might withers; they became as women:
they burn her tabernacles; they break her bars:
31 runner runs to meet runner
and teller to meet teller
to tell the sovereign of Babel
that his city is captured at the end:
32 and that the passages are apprehended
and the marshes burned with fire and
the men of war are terrified.
33 For thus says Yah Veh
Sabaoth Elohim of Yisra El:
The daughter of Babel *is* as a threshingfloor;
it is time to tread her:
yet a little while, and the time of her harvest comes.
34 Nebukadnets Tsar the sovereign of Babel
devours us; crushes us:
he sets me an empty instrument;
he swallows me up as a monster;
he fills his belly with my pleasures;
he thrusts me away.

35 My violence, and that of my flesh is on Babel,
say the settlers of Siyon;
and my blood on the settlers of Kesediym,
says Yeru Shalem.
36 So thus says Yah Veh:
Behold, I plead your plea,
and avenge your avengement:
and I parch her sea and dry her fountains:
37 and Babel becomes heaps
—a habitation for monsters
—a desolation and a hissing without a settler:
38 they roar together as whelps:
they growl as whelps of lions.
39 In their heat, I place their banquets;
and I intoxicate them so that they jump for joy
and sleep an eternal sleep and waken not
—an oracle of Yah Veh.
40 I bring them down as rams to the slaughter
—as rams with he goats.
41 How Sheshach is captured!
And how the halal of the whole earth is apprehended!
How Babel becomes a desolation among the goyim!
42 The sea ascends on Babel
—covered with the multitude of the waves:
43 her cities a desolation; a
parched land; and a plain:
a land wherein neither man settles
neither doth *any* **a** son of *man* **humanity**
pass *thereby* **therein**.
44 And I *will punish* **shall visit upon** Bel
in *Babylon* **Babel**,
and I *will* **shall** bring forth out of his mouth
that which he hath swallowed *up*:
and the *nations* **goyim**
shall not flow together *any* more unto him:
yea, the wall of *Babylon* **Babel** shall fall.
45 My people, go ye out of the midst of her,
and *deliver* **rescue** ye every man his soul
from the *fierce anger* **fuming wrath**
of *the LORD* **Yah Veh**.
46 And lest your heart *faint* **be tenderized**,
and ye *fear* **awe** for the *rumour* **report**
that shall be heard in the land;
a *rumour* **report** shall *both* come *one* **in a** year,
and after that in *another* **a** year
shall *come a rumour* **the report**,
and violence in the land,
ruler **sovereign** against *ruler* **sovereign**.
47 Therefore, behold, the days come,
that I *will do judgment* **shall visit**
upon the *graven images* **sculptiles** of *Babylon* **Babel**:
and her whole land shall *be confounded* **shame**,
and all her *slain* **pierced** shall fall in the midst of her.
48 Then the *heaven* **heavens** and the earth,
and all that is therein,
shall *sing* **shout** for *Babylon* **Babel**:
for the *spoilers* **ravagers** shall come unto her
from the north,
saith the LORD **an oracle of Yah Veh.**
49 As *Babylon* **Babel**
hath caused the *slain* **pierced** of *Israel* **Yisra El** to fall,
so at *Babylon* **Babel**
shall fall the *slain* **pierced** of all the earth.
50 Ye that have escaped the sword,
go away, stand not still:
remember *the LORD* **Yah Veh** afar off,
and let *Jerusalem* **Yeru Shalem**
come **ascend** into your *mind* **heart**.
51 We are *confounded* **shamed**,
because we have heard reproach:
shame hath covered our faces:
for strangers are come into the *sanctuaries* **holies**
of the *LORD'S* house **of Yah Veh**.
52 Wherefore, behold, the days come,
saith the LORD **an oracle of Yah Veh**,
that I *will do judgment* **shall visit**
upon her *graven images* **sculptiles**:
and through all her land
the *wounded* **pierced** shall *groan* **shriek**.
53 Though *Babylon* **Babel**
should *mount up to heaven* **ascend to the heavens**,
and though she should fortify the height of her strength,
yet from me shall *spoilers* **ravagers** come unto her,
saith the LORD **an oracle of Yah Veh**.
54 A *sound* **voice** of a cry
cometh from *Babylon* **Babel**,
and great *destruction* **breaking**
from the land of the *Chaldeans* **Kesediym**:
55 Because *the LORD* **Yah Veh**
hath *spoiled Babylon* **ravaged Babel**,
and destroyed out of her the great voice;
when her waves *do* roar like great waters,
a noise **an uproar** of their voice is *uttered* **given**:
56 Because the *spoiler* **ravager** is come upon her,
even upon *Babylon* **Babel**,
and her mighty *men* are *taken* **captured**,
every one of their bows is broken:
for *the LORD God* **Yah Veh El** of *recompences* **dealings in shalaming**, shall *surely requite* **shalam**.
57 And I *will make drunk* **shall intoxicate**
her *princes* **governors**,

and her wise *men*, her *captains* **governors**,
and her *rulers* **prefects**, and her mighty *men*:
and they shall sleep *a perpetual* **an eternal** sleep,
and not wake,
saith the King **an oracle of the Sovereign**,
whose name is *the LORD of hosts* **Yah Veh Sabaoth**.
nor a son of humanity passes therein.
44 And I visit on Bel in Babel,
and from his mouth
I bring forth what he swallowed:
and the goyim
flow together to him no more:
yes, the wall of Babel falls.
45 My people, come from among her
and rescue every man his soul
from the fuming wrath of Yah Veh.
46 And lest your heart be tenderized,
and you awe for the report heard in the land;
a report comes in a year:
and a year after the report, violence in the land
—sovereign against sovereign.
47 So behold, days come,
that I visit shame on the sculptiles of Babel
and her whole land;
and all her pierced fall in her midst.
48 And the heavens and the earth and all therein
shout against Babel:
for the ravagers come to her from the north
—an oracle of Yah Veh.
49 As Babel pierced Yisra El to fall,
thus at Babel
all the pierced of the earth fall.
50 You who escaped the sword, go away;
stand not still:
remember Yah Veh from afar
and ascend Yeru Shalem into your heart.
51 We shame, because we hear reproach:
shame covers our faces:
for strangers
come into the holies of the house of Yah Veh.
52 So behold, days come,
—an oracle of Yah Veh
that I visit on her sculptiles:
and through all her land the pierced shriek:
53 though Babel ascends to the heavens,
and though she fortify the height of her strength,
my ravagers come to her
—an oracle of Yah Veh.
54 A voice of a cry from Babel,
and great breaking from the land of the Kesediym:
55 because Yah Veh ravages Babel,
and destroys from her the great voice;
when her waves roar as great waters,
an uproar of their voice is given:
56 because the ravager comes on her—on Babel
and her mighty are captured;
every one of their bows break:
for Yah Veh El of dealings
in shalaming, shalams:
57 and I intoxicate her governors and her wise
—her governors and her prefects and her mighty:
and they sleep an eternal sleep and waken not
—an oracle of the Sovereign
whose name *is* Yah Veh Sabaoth.
58 Thus saith *the LORD of hosts* **Yah Veh Sabaoth**;
The broad walls of *Babylon* **Babel**
in stripping bare, shall be *utterly broken* **stripped bare**,
and her high *gates* **portals** shall be burned with fire;
and the people shall labour *in vain* **vainly enough**,
and the *folk* **nations** in the fire **enough**,
and they shall be weary.
59 The word which *Jeremiah*
Yirme Yah the prophet
commanded **misvahed**
Seraiah **Sera Yah** the son of *Neriah* **Neri Yah**,
the son of *Maaseiah* **Machse Yah**,
when he went with *Zedekiah* **Sidqi Yah**
the *king* **sovereign** of *Judah* **Yah Hudah**
into *Babylon* **Babel** in the fourth year of his reign.
And *this Seraiah* **Sera Yah**
was a *quiet prince* **restive governor**.
60 So *Jeremiah* **Yirme Yah**
wrote **inscribed** in *a book* **one scroll**
all the evil that should come upon *Babylon* **Babel**,
even all these words
that are *written* **inscribed** against *Babylon* **Babel**.
61 And *Jeremiah* **Yirme Yah**
said to *Seraiah* **Sera Yah**,
When thou comest to *Babylon* **Babel**, and shalt
see, and shalt *read* **call out** all these words;
62 Then shalt thou say, O *LORD* **Yah Veh**,
thou hast *spoken* **worded** against this place, to cut it off,
that none shall *remain* **settle** in it,
neither *man* **humanity** nor *beast* **animal**,
but that it shall be desolate *for ever* **eternally**.
63 And **so be** it *shall be*,
when thou hast *made an end of* **finished**
reading **calling out** this *book* **scroll**,
that thou shalt bind a stone to it,
and cast it into the midst of Euphrates:

64 And thou shalt say,
Thus shall *Babylon sink* **Babel drown,**
and shall not rise
from **the face of** the evil that I *will* **shall** bring upon her:
and they shall be weary.
Thus far are the words of *Jeremiah* **Yirme Yah.**

THE FALL OF YERU SHALEM

52 *Zedekiah* **Sidqi Yah**
was **a son of** one and twenty years *old*
when he began to reign,
and he reigned eleven years in *Jerusalem* **Yeru Shalem.**
And his mother's name was Hamutal
the daughter of *Jeremiah* **Yirme Yah** of Libnah.
2 And he *did* **worked** that which was evil
in the eyes of *the LORD* **Yah Veh,**
according to all that *Jehoiakim* **Yah**
Yaqim had *done* **worked.**
3 For through the *anger*
wrath of *the LORD* **Yah Veh**
so be it *came to pass*
in *Jerusalem* **Yeru Shalem** and *Judah* **Yah Hudah,**
till he had cast them out from his *presence* **face,**
that *Zedekiah* **Sidqi Yah** rebelled
against the *king* **sovereign** of *Babylon* **Babel.**
4 And **so be** it *came to pass*
in the ninth year of his reign,
in the tenth month, in the tenth *day* of the month,
that *Nebuchadrezzar* **Nebukadnets Tsar**
king **sovereign** of *Babylon* **Babel** came,
he and all his *army* **valiant,**
against *Jerusalem* **Yeru Shalem,**
and *pitched* **encamped** against it,
and built *forts* **battering towers** against it round about.
5 So the city was *besieged* **under siege**
unto the eleventh year
of *king Zedekiah* **sovereign Sidqi Yah.**
6 And in the fourth month, in
the ninth *day* of the month,
the famine *was sore* **prevailed** in the city,
so that there was no bread for the people of the land.
7 Then the city was *broken up* **split,**
and all the men of war fled,
and went forth out of the city by night
by the way of the *gate* **portal** between the two walls,
which was by the *king's* **sovereign's** garden;
(*now* the *Chaldeans* **Kesediym**
were by the city round about:)
and they went by the way of the plain.
58 Thus says Yah Veh Sabaoth:
In stripping bare,
the broad walls of Babel are stripped bare
and her high portals burned with fire:
and the people labor vainly enough
and the nations *are* in the fire enough;
and they weary.
59 The word Yirme Yah the prophet misvahs to
Sera Yah the son of Neri Yah the son of Machse Yah
when he goes
with Sidqi Yah the sovereign of Yah Hudah
into Babel in the fourth year of his reign.
—and Sera Yah is a restive governor.
60 Thus in one scroll
Yirme Yah inscribes all the evil coming on Babel
—all these words inscribed against Babel.
61 And Yirme Yah says to Sera Yah,
When you come to Babel,
and see, and call out all these words;
62 then you say, O Yah Veh,
you worded against this place, to cut it off,
so that no one becomes a settler therein
—neither humanity nor animal,
and that it becomes desolate eternally.
63 And so be it,
when you finish calling out this scroll,
bind a stone to it and cast it midst the Euphrates:
64 and say, Thus Babel drowns,
and rises not
from the face of the evil that I bring on her:
and they weary.
Thus far are the words of Yirme Yah.

THE FALL OF YERU SHALEM

52 Sidqi Yah *is* a son of twenty—one years
in beginning to reign;
and he reigns eleven years in Yeru Shalem:
and the name of his mother, Hamutal
the daughter of Yirme Yah of Libnah.
2 And he works evil in the eyes of Yah Veh
according to all Yah Yaqim worked.
3 For because of the wrath of Yah Veh
it is in Yeru Shalem and Yah Hudah,
until he casts them from his face;
and Sidqi Yah rebels against the sovereign of Babel.
4 And so be it, in the ninth year of his reign,
in the tenth month, in the tenth of the month,
Nebukadnets Tsar sovereign of Babel comes
—he and all his valiant against Yeru Shalem
and encamp against it;
and builds battering towers against it all around:

5 thus the city comes under siege
to the eleventh year of sovereign Sidqi Yah.
6 And in the fourth month,
in the ninth of the month,
the famine prevails in the city,
and there is no bread for the people of the land.
7 Then the city splits and all the men of war flee;
and go from the city by night
by the way of the portal between the two walls
by the garden of the sovereign
—the Kesediym are all around the city;
and they go by the way of the plain:
8 But the *army* **valiant** of
the *Chaldeans* **Kesediym**
pursued after the *king* **sovereign**,
and overtook *Zedekiah* **Sidqi Yah**
in the plains of *Jericho* **Yericho**;
and all his *army* **valiant** was scattered from him.
9 Then they *took* **apprehended**
the *king* **sovereign**,
and *carried* **ascended** him *up*
unto the *king* **sovereign** of *Babylon* **Babel**
to Riblah in the land of Hamath;
where he *gave* **worded** judgment upon him.
10 And the *king* **sovereign** of *Babylon* **Babel**
slew **slaughtered** the sons of *Zedekiah* **Sidqi Yah**
before **in front of** his eyes:
he *slew* **slaughtered** also
all the *princes* **governors** of *Judah* **Yah Hudah** in Riblah.
11 Then he *put out* **blinded** the eyes
of *Zedekiah* **Sidqi Yah**;
and the *king* **sovereign** of *Babylon* **Babel**
bound him in *chains* **coppers**,
and carried him to *Babylon* **Babel**,
and *put* **gave** him in *prison* **the house of visitation**
till the day of his death.
12 *Now* in the fifth month, in
the tenth *day* of the month,
which **year** was the nineteenth year
of *Nebuchadrezzar* **Nebukadnets Tsar**
king **sovereign** of *Babylon* **Babel**,
came *Nebuzaradan* **Nebu Zaradan**,
captain of the guard **rabbi slaughterer**,
which *served* **stood at the face**
of the *king* **sovereign** of *Babylon* **Babel**,
into *Jerusalem* **Yeru Shalem**,
13 And burned the house of *the LORD* **Yah Veh**,
and the *king's* **sovereign's** house;
and all the houses of *Jerusalem* **Yeru Shalem**,
and all the houses of the great *men*, burned he with fire:
14 And all the *army* **valiant** of
the *Chaldeans* **Kesediym**,
that were with the *captain of the*
guard **rabbi slaughterer**,
brake down all the walls of *Jerusalem* **Yeru Shalem**
round about.
15 Then *Nebuzaradan* **Nebu Zaradan**
the *captain of the guard* **rabbi slaughterer**
carried away captive **exiled**
certain of the poor of the people,
and the *residue* **remnant** of the people
that *remained* **survived** in the city,
and those that fell away,
that fell to the *king* **sovereign** of *Babylon* **Babel**,
and the *rest* **remnant** of the multitude.
16 But *Nebuzaradan* **Nebu Zaradan**
the *captain of the guard* **rabbi slaughterer**
left certain **let survive** of the poor of the land
for vinedressers and for *husbandmen* **plowers**.
17 Also the pillars of *brass* **copper**
that were in the house of *the LORD* **Yah Veh**,
and the bases, and the *brasen* **copper** sea that
was in the house of *the LORD* **Yah Veh**,
the *Chaldeans* **Kesediym** brake,
and *carried* **bore** all the *brass* **copper** of them
to *Babylon* **Babel**.
18 The caldrons also, and the shovels,
and the *snuffers* **tweezers**, and the *bowls* **sprinklers**,
and the *spoons* **hollow bowls**,
and all the *vessels* **instruments** of *brass* **copper**
wherewith they ministered, took they away.
19 And the basons, and the *firepans* **trays**,
and the *bowls* **sprinklers**, and the caldrons,
and the *candlesticks* **menorah**, and the spoons,
and the *cups* **exoneration basins**;
that which was of gold *in* gold,
and that which was of silver *in* silver,
took the *captain of the guard* **rabbi slaughterer** away.
20 The two pillars, one sea,
and twelve *brasen* **copper** bulls
that were under the bases,
which *king Solomon* **sovereign Shelomah**
had *made* **worked** in the house of *the LORD* **Yah Veh**:
the *brass* **copper** of all these *vessels* **instruments**
was without weight.
21 And *concerning* the pillars,
8 and the valiant of the Kesediym
pursue the sovereign
and overtake Sidqi Yah in the plains of Yericho;
and all his valiant scatter from him:

9 and they apprehend the sovereign,
and ascend him to the sovereign of Babel
—to Riblah in the land of Hamath;
where he words judgment on him.
10 And the sovereign of Babel
slaughters the sons of Sidqi Yah in front of his eyes:
he also slaughters
all the governors of Yah Hudah in Riblah:
11 and he blinds the eyes of Sidqi Yah;
and the sovereign of Babel binds him in coppers
and carries him to Babel;
and gives him in the house of visitation
until the day of his death.
12 And in the fifth month,
in the tenth of the month,
which year *is* the nineteenth year
of Nebukadnets Tsar sovereign of Babel,
Nebu Zaradan the rabbi slaughterer
who stands at the face of the sovereign of Babel,
comes to Yeru Shalem;
13 and burns the house of Yah Veh
and the house of the sovereign
and all the houses of Yeru Shalem:
and all the houses of the great he burns with fire:
14 and all the valiant of the Kesediym
with the rabbi slaughterer
break down all the walls of Yeru Shalem all around:
15 and Nebu Zaradan the rabbi slaughterer
exiles certain of the poor people
and the remnant of the people who survive in the city
and those who fell away
—who fell to the sovereign of Babel
with the remnant of the multitude:
16 and Nebu Zaradan the rabbi slaughterer
lets some of the poor of the land survive
for vinedressers and for plowers.
17 And the Kesediym break
the pillars of copper in the house of Yah Veh
and the bases
and the copper sea in the house of Yah Veh,
and bear all their copper to Babel
18 —with the caldrons and the shovels
and the tweezers and the sprinklers
and the hollow bowls:
and they take away all the instruments of copper
with which they ministered:
19 and the rabbi slaughterer takes away
the basons and the trays
and the sprinklers and the caldrons
and the menorah and the spoons
and the exoneration basins
of gold gold and of silver silver
20 —the two pillars, one sea,
and twelve copper bulls under the bases,
which sovereign Shelomah worked
in the house of Yah Veh:
the copper of all these instruments without weight:
21 and the pillars
the height of one pillar was eighteen cubits
and a *fillet* **thread** of twelve cubits
did *compass* **surround** it;
and the thickness *thereof* was four fingers: *it was* hollow.
22 And a *chapiter* **cap** of *brass* **copper** was upon it;
and the height of one *chapiter* **cap** was five cubits,
with *network* **netting** and pomegranates
upon the *chapiters* **caps** round about, all of *brass* **copper**.
The second pillar also and the pomegranates
were like unto these.
23 And there were ninety and six pomegranates
on a *side* **wind**;
and all the pomegranates upon the *network* **netting**
were an hundred round about.
24 And the *captain of the guard* **rabbi slaughterer**
took *Seraiah* **Sera Yah** the chief priest,
and *Zephaniah* **Sephan Yah** the second priest,
and the three *keepers* **guards** of the *door* **threshold**:
25 He took also out of the city *an* **one** eunuch,
which had the charge **an overseer** of the
men of war; and seven men of them
that *were near* **saw** the *king's person* **sovereign's face**,
which were found in the city;
and the *principal* scribe **of the governor** of the host,
who *mustered* **hosted** the people of the land;
and *threescore* **sixty** men of the people of the land,
that were found in the midst of the city.
26 So *Nebuzaradan* **Nebu Zaradan**
the *captain of the guard* **rabbi slaughterer** took them,
and *brought* **carried** them
to the *king* **sovereign** of *Babylon* **Babel** to Riblah.
27 And the *king* **sovereign** of
Babylon **Babel** smote them,
and *put* **deathified** them *to death* in Riblah
in the land of Hamath.
Thus *Judah* **Yah Hudah** was *carried away captive* **exiled**
out of his own *land* **soil**.
28 This is the people whom
Nebuchadrezzar **Nebukadnets Tsar**
carried away captive **exiled**:
in the seventh year
three thousand *Jews* and three and twenty **Yah Hudiym**:
29 In the eighteenth year

of *Nebuchadrezzar* **Nebukadnets Tsar**
he *carried away captive* **exiled**
from *Jerusalem* **Yeru Shalem**
eight hundred thirty and two *persons* **souls**:
30 In the three and twentieth year
of *Nebuchadrezzar* **Nebukadnets Tsar**
Nebuzaradan **Nebu Zaradan**
the *captain of the guard* **rabbi slaughterer**
carried away captive **exiled** of the *Jews* **Yah Hudiym**
seven hundred forty and five *persons* **souls**:
all the *persons* **souls** were four
thousand and six hundred.
31 And **so be** it *came to pass*
in the seven and thirtieth year
of the *captivity* **exile** of *Jehoiachin* **Yah Yachin**
king **sovereign** of *Judah* **Yah Hudah**,
in the twelfth month,
in the five and twentieth *day* of the month,
that *Evilmerodach* **Evil Merodach**
king **sovereign** of *Babylon* **Babel**
in the *first* year of his *reign* **sovereigndom**
lifted up the head of *Jehoiachin* **Yah Yachin**
king **sovereign** of *Judah* **Yah Hudah**,
and brought him forth out of **the** prison **house**.
32 And *spake kindly* **worded good** unto him,
and *set* **gave** his throne
above the throne of the *kings* **sovereigns**
that were with him in *Babylon* **Babel**,
33 And changed his prison *garment* **clothes**:
and he did continually eat bread *before him* **at his face**
all the days of his life.
34 And for his *diet* **ration**,
there was a continual *diet* **ration** given him
of the *king* **sovereign** of *Babylon* **Babel**,
every day a *portion* **word** until the day of his death,
all the days of his life.
—the height of one pillar eighteen cubits
and a thread of twelve cubits surrounds it;
and the thickness, four fingers—hollow:
22 with a cap of copper thereon;
and the height of one cap, five cubits;
with netting and pomegranates
on the caps all around—all of copper:
and the second pillar and the pomegranates
are like to these:
23 and there are ninety—six pomegranates
on a wind;
and all the pomegranates on the netting
are a hundred all around.
24 And the rabbi slaughterer
takes Sera Yah the chief priest
and Sephan Yah the second priest
and the three guards of the threshold:
25 and he also takes one eunuch of the city
—an overseer of the men of war;
and seven of their men
who see the face of the sovereign
whom they find in the city;
and the scribe of the governor of the host
who hosts the people of the land;
and sixty men of the people of the land
whom they find midst the city.
26 And Nebu Zaradan the rabbi slaughterer
takes them
and carries them to the sovereign of Babel to Riblah:
27 and the sovereign of Babel smites them
and deathifies them in Riblah in the land of Hamath.
Thus they exile Yah Hudah from his own soil.
28 This is the people Nebukadnets Tsar exiles:
in the seventh year
three thousand and twenty—three Yah Hudiym:
29 in the eighteenth year of Nebukadnets Tsar
he exiles eight hundred and thirty—two souls
from Yeru Shalem:
30 In the twenty—third year
of Nebukadnets Tsar,
Nebu Zaradan the rabbi slaughterer
exiles seven hundred and forty—five souls
of the Yah Hudiym:
all the souls *are* four thousand and six hundred.
31 And so be it,
in the thirty—seventh year
of the exile of Yah Yachin sovereign of Yah Hudah,
in the twelfth month,
in the twenty—fifth of the month,
Evil Merodach sovereign of Babel
in the year of his sovereigndom
lifts the head of Yah Yachin sovereign of Yah Hudah;
and brings him from the prison house;
32 and words good to him:
and gives his throne
above the throne of the sovereigns with him in Babel:
33 and changes his prison clothes:
and he continually eats bread at his face
all the days of his life.
34 And for his ration,
he is a given continual ration
of the sovereign of Babel
—a word day by day until the day of his death
all the days of his life.

THE VISIONS OF YECHEZQ EL

1 *Now* **And so be** it *came to*
pass in the thirtieth year,
in the fourth *month,* in the fifth *day* of the month,
as I was among the *captives* **exiles**
by the river of *Chebar* **Kebar,**
that the heavens were opened,
and I saw visions of *God* **Elohim.**
2 In the fifth *day* of the month,
which was the fifth year
of *king Jehoiachin's captivity* **sovereign**
Yah Yachin's exile,
3 The word of *the LORD* **Yah Veh** came expressly
unto *Ezekiel* **Yechezq El** the priest, the son of Buzi,
in the land of the *Chaldeans* **Kesediym**
by the river *Chebar* **Kebar;**
and the hand of *the LORD* **Yah Veh** was there upon him.

OMENS

4 And I *looked* **saw**, and, behold,
a *whirlwind* **windstorm** came out of the north,
a great cloud, and a fire *infolding* **overtaking** itself,
and a *brightness* **brilliance** was **round** about it,
and out of the midst *thereof*
as the *colour* **eyes** of *amber* **brilliant copper,**
out of the midst of the fire.

FOUR LIVE BEINGS

5 Also out of the midst *thereof*
came the likeness of four *living creatures* **live beings.**
And this was their *appearance* **visage;**
they **these** had the likeness of a *man* **human.**
6 And *every* one had four faces,
and *every* one had four wings.
7 And their feet were straight feet;
and the sole of their feet was like the sole of a calf's foot:
and they sparkled
like the *colour* **eye** of burnished *brass* **copper.**
8 And they had the hands of a *man* **human**
under their wings on their four *sides* **quarters;**
and they four had their faces and their wings.
9 Their wings were joined *one*
woman to *another* **sister;**
they turned not when they went;
they went every *one straight* **man face** forward.
10 As for the likeness of their faces,
they four had the face of a *man* **human,** and
the face of a lion, on the right *side*:
and they four had the face of an ox on the left *side*;
they four also had the face of an eagle.
11 Thus were their faces:
and their wings *were stretched* **spread** upward;
two *wings of every one* **of each man**
were joined *one* **man** to *another* **man,**
and two covered their bodies.
12 And they went *every one* **each man**
straight **face** forward:
whither the spirit was to go, they went;
and they turned not when they went.
13 As for the likeness of the
living creatures **live beings,**
their *appearance* **visage** was like burning coals of fire,
and like the *appearance* **visage** of *lamps* **flambeaus:**
it went up and down
among the *living creatures* **live beings;**
and the fire was *bright* **brilliant,**
and out of the fire went forth lightning.
14 And the *living creatures* **live**
beings ran and returned
as the *appearance* **visage** of a flash *of lightning.*

THE WHEEL MIDST A WHEEL

15 *Now* as I *beheld* **saw** the
living creatures **live beings,**
behold one wheel upon the earth
by the living creatures **beside the live beings,**
with his four faces.
16 The *appearance* **visage** of
the wheels and their work
was like unto the *colour* **eye** of a beryl:
and they four had one likeness:
and their *appearance* **visage** and their work
was as it were a wheel in the *middle* **midst** of a wheel.
17 When they went,
they went upon their four *sides* **quarters:**
and they turned not when they went.
18 As for their *rings* **rims,**
they were so high that they were *dreadful* **awesome;**

THE VISIONS OF YECHEZQ EL

1 And so be it, in the thirtieth year,
in the fourth, in the fifth of the month,
I *am* among the exiles by the river of Kebar;
the heavens open and I see visions of Elohim.
2 In the fifth of the month
of the fifth year of the exile of sovereign Yah Yachin:
3 and so be the word of Yah Veh expressly
to Yechezq El the priest the son of Buzi
in the land of the Kesediym by the river Kebar:
and the hand of Yah Veh *is* on him.

OMENS

4 And I see, and behold,
a windstorm coming from the north
—a great cloud and a fire overtaking itself
and a brilliance all around;
and from the midst
eyes as of brilliant copper from midst the fire.

FOUR LIVE BEINGS

5 And from the midst, the
likeness of four live beings:
and this *is* their visage; the likeness of a human:
6 and to *each* one four faces
and to *each* one four wings:
7 and their feet, straight feet;
and the sole of their feet,
as the sole of the foot of a calf:
and they sparkle as the eye of burnished copper:
8 and their hands as of a human
under their wings on their four quarters:
and they *have* four faces and wings.
9 Their wings join woman to sister;
they turn not as they go;
each man goes face forward:
10 as for the likeness of their faces, the four *have* the
face of a human and the face of a lion on the right;
and the four *have* the face of an ox on the left;
the four also *have* the face of an eagle;
11 thus *are* their faces:
and their wings spread upward
—two of each man join man to man
and two cover their bodies.
12 And each man goes face forward:
wherever the spirit goes, they go;
and they turn not as they go.
13 As for the likeness of the live beings:
their visage *is* as burning coals of fire
and as the visage of flambeaus:
going up and down among the live beings:
and the fire *is* brilliant;
and from the fire comes lightning:
14 and the live beings run and return
as the visage of a flash.

THE WHEEL MIDST A WHEEL

15 And I see the live beings, and behold,
one wheel on the earth
beside the live beings at their four faces.
16 The visage of the wheels and their work
is as the eye of a beryl:
and the four *have* one likeness:
and their visage and their work
is as a wheel midst a wheel.
17 In going, they go on their four quarters:
and they turn not as they go.
18 As for their rims,
they *are* so high that they *are* awesome;
and their *rings* **rims**
were full of eyes round about them four.
19 And when the *living creatures* **live beings** went,
the wheels went *by them* **along side**:
and when the *living creatures* **live beings**
were lifted *up* from the earth,
the wheels were lifted *up*.
20 Whithersoever the spirit was to go, they went,
thither was their spirit to go;
and the wheels were lifted *up*
over against **alongside** them:
for the spirit of the *living creature* **live being**
was in the wheels.
21 *When those went* **In their going**,
these went **they go**;
and when those stood **in their standing**,
these stood **they stand**;
and when those were **in their being** lifted *up*
from the earth,
the wheels *were* lifted *up over against* **alongside** them:
for the spirit of the *living creature* **live being**
was in the wheels.
22 And the likeness of the *firmament* **expanse**
upon the heads of the *living creature* **live being**
was as the *colour* **eye** of *the terrible* **awesome** crystal,
stretched forth **spread** over their heads above.
23 And under the *firmament* **expanse**
were their wings straight,
the one **woman** toward *the other* **sister**:
every one **each man** had two,
which covered *on this side* **here**,
and *every one* **each man** had two,
which covered *on that side* **there**,
their bodies.
24 And when they went,
I heard the *noise* **voice** of their wings,
like the *noise* **voice** of great waters,
as the voice of *the Almighty* **Shadday**,
the voice of *speech* **rushing**,
as the *noise* **voice** of *an host* **a camp**:
when they stood, they *let down* **lowered** their wings.

25 And there was a voice from
the *firmament* **expanse**
that was over their heads,
when they stood, and had *let down* **lowered** their wings.

THE THRONE OF HONOUR

26 And above the *firmament* **expanse**
that was over their heads
was the likeness of a throne,
as the *appearance* **visage** of a sapphire stone:
and upon the likeness of the throne
was the likeness
as the *appearance* **visage** of a *man* **human**
above upon it.
27 And I saw as the *colour* **eye**
of *amber* **brilliant copper**,
as the *appearance* **visage** of fire
round about *within it* **the housing**,
from the *appearance* **visage** of his loins
even upward,
and from the *appearance* **visage** of his loins
even downward,
I saw as it were the *appearance* **visage** of fire,
and it had *brightness* **brilliance** round about.
28 As the *appearance* **visage** of the bow
that is in the cloud in the day of *rain* **downpour**,
so was the *appearance* **visage** of the *brightness* **brilliance**
round about.
This was the *appearance* **visage** of the likeness
of the *glory* **honour** of *the LORD* **Yah Veh**.

THE CALL OF YECHEZQ EL

And when I saw *it*, I fell upon my face,
and I heard a voice of one that spake.

2 And he said unto me, Son of *man* **humanity**,
stand upon thy feet,
and I *will speak* **shall word** unto thee.
2 And the spirit entered into me
when he *spake* **worded** unto me,
and *set* **stood** me upon my feet,
that I heard him that spake unto me.
and their rims
are full of eyes all around all four.
19 And when the live beings go,
the wheels go beside:
and when the live beings lift off the earth,
the wheels lift:
20 wherever the spirit goes, they go:
there the spirit goes, and the wheels lift alongside them:
for a spirit of the live being *is* in the wheels.

21 In their going, they go;
in their standing, they stand;
in their lifting from the earth,
the wheels lift alongside them:
for the spirit of the live being *is* in the wheels.
22 And the likeness of the expanse
on the heads of the live being
is as the eye of awesome crystal,
spread over their heads above.
23 And under the expanse
their wings *are* straight, woman toward sister:
each man two, covering *their bodies* here;
and each man two, covering their bodies there.
24 And as they go,
I hear the voice of their wings
as the voice of great waters;
as the voice of Shadday:
the voice of rushing
as the voice of a camp:
when they stand, they lower their wings.
25 And there *is* a voice
from the expanse over their heads
when they stand and lower their wings.

THE THRONE OF HONOR

26 And above the expanse over their heads,
the likeness of a throne
as the visage of a sapphire stone:
and on the likeness of the throne,
the likeness as the visage of a human from above.
27 And I see as the eye of brilliant copper
as the visage of fire all around the housing
—from the visage of his loins upward
and from the visage of his loins downward;
I see as the visage of fire and it brilliance all around:
28 as the visage of the bow in the cloud
in the day of downpour,
thus *is* the visage of the brilliance all around.
This *is* the visage of the likeness
of the honor of Yah Veh.

THE CALL OF YECHEZQ EL

And I see; and I fall on my face;
and I hear a voice of one speaking:

2 and he says to me, Son of humanity,
stand on your feet, and I word to you.
2 And he words to me,
and the spirit enters into me
and stands me on my feet:
and I hear him who speaks to me:

3 And he said unto me, Son of *man* **humanity**,
I send thee to the *children* **sons** of *Israel* **Yisra El**,
to a *rebellious nation* **rebelling goyim**
that hath rebelled against me:
they and their fathers
have *transgressed* **rebelled** against me,
even unto this *very* **same** day.
4 For they are *impudent children* **hard faced sons**
and *stiffhearted* **strong hearted**.
I *do* send thee unto them;
and thou shalt say unto them,
Thus saith *the Lord GOD* **Adonay Yah Veh**.
5 And they, whether they *will* **shall** hear,
or whether they *will forbear* **shall desist**,
(for they are a rebellious house,)
yet shall know
that there hath been a prophet among them.
6 And thou, son of *man* **humanity**,
be not *afraid* **awed** of them,
neither be *afraid* **awed** of their words,
though *briers* **thistles** and *thorns* **prickles** be with thee,
and thou dost *dwell* **settle** among scorpions:
be not *afraid* **awed** of their words,
nor be dismayed at their *looks* **faces**,
though they be a rebellious house.
7 And thou shalt *speak* **word**
my words unto them,
whether they *will* **shall** hear,
or whether they *will forbear* **shall desist**:
for they are most rebellious.
8 But thou, son of *man* **humanity**,
hear what I say unto thee;
Be not thou rebellious like that rebellious house:
open **gape** thy mouth, and eat that I give thee.
9 And when I *looked* **saw**, behold,
an hand was sent unto me;
and, *lo* **behold**, a roll of a *book* **scroll** was therein;
10 And he spread it *before me* **at my face**;
and it was *written within* **inscribed on the face**
and *without* **on the back**:
and there was *written* **inscribed** therein lamentations,
and *mourning* **meditations**, and woe.

THE COMMISSION OF YECHEZQ EL

3 *Moreover* he said unto me,
Son of *man* **humanity**,
eat that thou findest; eat this roll,
and go *speak* **word** unto the house of
Israel **Yisra El**. *roll: a small scroll
2 So I opened my mouth,
and he *caused me to eat* **fed me** that roll.
3 And he said unto me, Son of *man* **humanity**,
cause **feed** thy belly *to eat*,
and fill thy *bowels* **inwards** with this roll that I give thee.
Then did I eat it;
and it was in my mouth as honey for sweetness.
4 And he said unto me, Son of *man* **humanity**,
go, get thee unto the house of *Israel* **Yisra El**,
and *speak* **word** with my words unto
them. Apocalypse 10:1—11
5 For thou art not sent to a people
of *a strange speech* **deep lip**
and of an *hard language* **heavy tongue**,
but to the house of *Israel* **Yisra El**;
6 Not to many people of a *strange speech* **deep lip**
and of an *hard language* **heavy tongue**,
whose words thou canst not *understand* **hear**.
Surely, had I sent thee to them,
they *would* **should** have hearkened unto thee.
7 But the house of *Israel* **Yisra El**
will **willeth to** not hearken unto thee;
for they *will* **willed to** not hearken unto me:
for all the house of *Israel* **Yisra El**
are *impudent* **strong foreheaded** and hardhearted.
8 Behold, I have *made* **given** thy face strong
against **alongside** their faces,
and thy forehead strong
against **alongside** their foreheads.
9 As *an adamant harder* **a
brier stronger** than flint
have I *made* **given** thy forehead:
fear **awe** them not, neither be
dismayed at their *looks* **faces**,
though they be a rebellious house.
3 and he says to me, Son of humanity,
I send you to the sons of Yisra El
—to a rebelling goyim who rebel against me:
they and their fathers rebel against me
to this same day:
4 for they, to whom I send you,
are hard faced sons, and strong hearted:
and say to them,
Thus says Adonay Yah Veh:
5 And they,
whether they hear, or whether they desist,
—for they are a rebellious house,
yet know a prophet becomes among them.
6 And you, son of humanity,
neither awe them nor awe their words
—though thistles and prickles *are* with you,

and you, settle among scorpions:
neither awe their words nor dismay at their faces
for they *are* a rebellious house:
7 and you, word my words to them,
whether they hear or whether they desist:
for they *are* most rebellious.
8 And you, son of humanity,
hear what I say to you;
Become not rebellious as that rebellious house:
gape your mouth and eat what I give you.
9 And I see, and behold, a hand sent to me;
and behold, a roll of a scroll therein;
10 and he spreads it at my face;
and it *is* inscribed on the face and on the back:
and inscribed therein
are lamentations and meditations and woe.

THE COMMISSION OF YECHEZQ EL

3 He says to me, Son of humanity,
eat what you find; eat this roll*;
and go word to the house of Yisra El.
*roll: a small scroll
2 So I open my mouth and he feeds me that roll;
3 and he says to me,
Son of humanity, feed your belly;
and fill your inwards with this roll I give you.
—and I eat it;
and in my mouth, it *is* as honey for sweetness.
4 And he says to me, Son of humanity,
Go, get to the house of Yisra El, and
word with my words to them.
Apocalypse 10:1—11
5 For you are not sent to a people
of deep lip and of a heavy tongue
—but to the house of Yisra El:
6 not to many people
of a deep lip and of a heavy tongue
whose words you hear not.
Had I sent you to them,
they had hearkened to you.
7 But the house of Yisra El
wills to not hearken to you;
for they will to not hearken to me:
for all the house of Yisra El
is strong foreheaded and hardhearted.
8 Behold, I give your face
strong alongside their faces
and your forehead strong alongside their foreheads:
9 as a brier stronger than
flint I give your forehead:
neither awe them nor dismay at their faces,
though they be a rebellious house.
10 *Moreover* he said unto me,
Son of *man* **humanity**,
all my words that I shall *speak* **word** unto thee
receive **take** in thine heart, and hear with thine ears.
11 And go, get thee to them of the *captivity* **exile**,
unto the *children* **sons** of thy people,
and *speak* **word** unto them, and *tell* **say to** them,
Thus saith *the Lord GOD* **Adonay Yah Veh**;
whether they *will* **shall** hear,
or whether they *will forbear* **shall desist**.
12 Then the spirit *took* **bore** me *up*,
and I heard behind me a voice of a great *rushing* **quake**,
saying,
Blessed be the *glory* **honour** of *the LORD* **Yah Veh**
from his place.
13 *I heard* also the *noise* **voice** of the wings
of the *living creatures* **live beings**
that *touched one another* **kissed woman to sister**,
and the *noise* **voice** of the wheels
over against **alongside** them,
and a *noise* **voice** of a great *rushing* **quake**.
14 So the spirit lifted me *up*, and took me away,
and I went in bitterness, in the *heat* **fury** of my
spirit; but the hand of *the LORD* **Yah Veh**
was strong upon **strengthened** me.
15 Then I came to them of the *captivity* **exile**
at *Telabib* **Tel Aviv**,
that *dwelt* **settled** by the river of *Chebar* **Kebar**,
and I *sat* **settled** where they *sat* **settled**,
and *remained* **settled** there
astonished among them seven days.

THE WARNING OF YAH VEH CONCERNING NOT WARNING

16 And **so be** it *came to pass*
at the end of seven days,
that the word of *the LORD* **Yah Veh** came unto me,
saying,
17 Son of *man* **humanity**,
I have *made* **given** thee a *watchman* **watcher**
unto the house of *Israel* **Yisra El**:
therefore hear the word at my mouth,
and *give* **enlighten** them *warning* from me.
18 *When I say* **In my saying** unto the wicked,
In dying, Thou shalt *surely* die;
and thou *givest* **enlightenest** him not *warning*,
nor *speakest* **wordest** to *warn* **enlighten** the wicked
from his wicked way,

to save his life **that he may live;**
the same wicked *man* shall die in his *iniquity* **perversity;**
but his blood *will* **shall** I *require* **seek** at thine hand.
19 Yet if thou *warn* **enlighten** the wicked,
and he turn not from his wickedness,
nor from his wicked way,
he shall die in his *iniquity* **perversity;**
but thou hast *delivered* **rescued** thy soul.
20 *Again,* When *a righteous man* **the just**
doth turn from his *righteousness* **justness,**
and *commit iniquity* **work wickedness,**
and I *lay* **give** a stumblingblock *before him* **at his face,**
he shall die:
because thou hast not *given* **enlightened** him *warning,*
he shall die in his sin,
and his *righteousness* **justness**
which he hath *done* **worked**
shall not be remembered;
but his blood *will* **shall** I *require* **seek** at thine hand.
21 Nevertheless
if thou *warn* **enlighten** the *righteous man* **just,**
that the *righteous* **just** sin not, and he doth not sin,
in living, he shall *surely* live,
because he is *warned* **enlightened;**
also thou hast *delivered* **rescued** thy soul.

YAH VEH REVEALS HIS HONOUR

22 And the hand of *the LORD* **Yah Veh**
was there upon me;
and he said unto me, Arise, go forth into the *plain* **valley,**
and *I will* **shall** there *talk* **word** with thee.
23 Then I arose, and went
forth into the *plain* **valley:**
and, behold,
the *glory* **honour** of *the LORD* **Yah Veh** stood there,
as the *glory* **honour** which I saw by
the river of *Chebar* **Kebar:**
and I fell on my face.
10 He says to me, Son of humanity,
all my words I word to you
take in your heart and hear with your ears:
11 and go, get to them of the exile
—to the sons of your people
and word to them, and say to them,
Thus says Adonay Yah Veh!
—whether they hear, or whether they desist.
12 And the spirit bears me,
and behind me, I hear a voice of a great quake,
Blessed—the honor of Yah Veh from his place!
13 And the voice of the wings of the live beings
kiss woman to sister;
and the voice of the wheels alongside them
and a voice of a great quake.
14 And the spirit lifts me, and takes me away;
and I go in bitterness, in the fury of my spirit;
and the hand of Yah Veh strengthens me.
15 And I come to them of the exile at Tel Aviv,
who settle by the river of Kebar,
and where they settle, I settle;
and settle there astonished among them seven days.

THE WARNING OF YAH VEH CONCERNING NOT WARNING

16 And so be it, at the end of seven days,
so be the word of Yah Veh to me, saying,
17 Son of humanity,
I give you, a watcher to the house of Yisra El:
so hear the word at my mouth,
and enlighten them from me.
18 In my saying to the wicked,
In dying, you die;
and you neither enlighten him,
nor word to enlighten the wicked
from the wicked way he lives;
the same wicked dies in his perversity;
and I seek his blood at your hand:
19 and *if* you enlighten the wicked
and he neither turns from his wickedness
nor from his wicked way,
he dies in his perversity;
and you rescue your soul.
20 And when the just turns from his justness
and works wickedness,
and I give a stumblingblock at his face, he dies:
because you enlighten him not, he dies in his sin;
and the justness he worked *is* not remembered;
and I seek his blood at your hand.
21 And if you enlighten the just,
that the just sin not, and he sins not,
in living, he lives—because he enlightened;
and you rescue your soul.

YAH VEH REVEALS HIS HONOR

22 And so be the hand of Yah Veh on me,
and he says to me, Rise, go into the valley,
and there I word with you.
23 And I rise, and go into the valley:
and behold, the honor of Yah Veh stands there,
as the honor I saw by the river of Kebar:
and I fall on my face:

24 Then the spirit entered into me,
and *set* **stood** me upon my feet,
and *spake* **worded** with me, and said unto me,
Go, shut thyself within thine house.
25 But thou, O son of *man* **humanity**, behold,
they shall *put bands* **give ropes** upon thee,
and shall bind thee with them,
and thou shalt not go out among them:
26 And I *will* **shall** make thy tongue
cleave **stick** to *the roof of* thy *mouth* **palate**,
that thou shalt be *dumb* **muted**,
and shalt not be to them a **man** reprover:
for they are a rebellious house.
27 But when I *speak* **word** with thee,
I *will* **shall** open thy mouth,
and thou shalt say unto them,
Thus saith *the Lord GOD* **Adonay Yah Veh**;
He that heareth, let him hear;
and he that *forbeareth* **desisteth**, let him *forbear* **desist**:
for they are a rebellious house.

THE SIEGE OF YERU SHALEM

4 Thou also, son of *man* **humanity**,
take thee a *tile* **brick**,
and *lay it before thee* **give it at thy face**,
and *pourtray* **engrave** upon it the city,
even Jerusalem **Yeru Shalem**:
2 And *lay* **give** siege against it,
and build a *fort* **battering tower** against it,
and *cast* **pour** a *mount* **mound** against it;
set **give** the camp also against it,
and set *battering* rams against it round about.
3 Moreover take thou unto
thee an iron *pan* **griddle**,
and *set* **give** it for a wall of iron
between thee and **between** the city:
and *set* **establish** thy face against it,
and it shall be *besieged* **under siege**,
and thou shalt *lay* siege against it.
This shall be a sign to the house of *Israel* **Yisra El**.
4 Lie thou also upon thy left side,
and *lay* **set** the *iniquity* **perversity**
of the house of *Israel* **Yisra El** upon it:
according to the number of the days
that thou shalt lie upon it
thou shalt bear their *iniquity* **perversity**.
5 For I have *laid* **given** upon thee
the years of their *iniquity* **perversity**,
according to the number of the days,
three hundred and ninety days:
so shalt thou bear the *iniquity* **perversity**
of the house of *Israel* **Yisra El**.
6 And when thou hast
accomplished **concluded** them,
lie *again* **secondly** on thy right side,
and thou shalt bear the *iniquity* **perversity**
of the house of *Judah* **Yah Hudah** forty days:
I have *appointed* **given** thee
each **a day for a year,** a day for a year.
7 Therefore thou shalt *set* **establish** thy face
toward the siege of *Jerusalem* **Yeru Shalem**,
and thine arm shall be *uncovered* **stripped**,
and thou shalt prophesy against it.
8 And, behold,
I *will lay bands* **shall give ropes** upon thee,
and thou shalt not turn thee
from *one* side to *another* **side**,
till thou hast *ended* **finished** the days of thy siege.
9 Take thou also unto thee wheat, and barley,
and beans, and lentiles, and millet, and *fitches* **spelt**,
and *put* **give** them in one *vessel* **instrument**,
and *make* **work** thee bread *thereof*,
according to the number of the days
that thou shalt lie upon thy side,
three hundred and ninety days shalt thou eat *thereof.*
10 And thy *meat* **food** which thou shalt eat
shall be by weight, twenty shekels a day:
from time to time shalt thou eat it.
11 Thou shalt drink water by measure,
the sixth *part* of an hin:
from time to time shalt thou drink.
12 And thou shalt eat it as barley *cakes* **ashcakes**,
24 and the spirit enters me
and stands me on my feet;
and words with me, and says to me,
Go, shut yourself within your house.
25 And you, O son of humanity,
behold, they give ropes on you
and bind you with them
that you go not among them:
26 and I stick your tongue to your palate
and mute you,
that you not become their man reprover:
for they are a rebellious house.
27 And I word with you, and I open your mouth,
and you say to them,
Thus says Adonay Yah Veh:
He who hears, hear;
and he who desists, desist
—for they are a rebellious house.

The Siege Of Yeru Shalem

4 And you, son of humanity,
take a brick and give it at your face;
and engrave thereon the city, Yeru Shalem:
2 and give siege against it
and build a battering tower against it
and pour a mound against it;
and give the camp against it,
and set rams against it all around:
3 and take an iron griddle to yourself;
and give it for a wall of iron
between you and between the city:
and establish your face against it;
and it becomes under siege
and you siege against it
—a sign to the house of Yisra El.
4 And lie on your left side
and set the perversity of the house of Yisra El thereon:
according to the number of the days you lie thereon
you bear their perversity:
5 and I—I give on you the years of their perversity
according to the number of the days
—three hundred and ninety days:
thus you bear the perversity of the house of Yisra El.
6 And when you conclude them,
lie secondly on your right side;
and bear the perversity of the house of Yah Hudah
forty days:
I give you a day for a year, a day for a year.
7 And establish your face
toward the siege of Yeru Shalem,
and strip your arm and prophesy against it.
8 And behold, I give ropes on you, that you not turn
from side to side, until you finish the days of your siege.
9 And take to yourself wheat
and barley and beans and lentiles and millet and spelt
and give them in one instrument;
and work bread
according to the number of the days
you lie on your side
—three hundred and ninety days you eat.
10 And the food you eat
—twenty shekels a day by weight:
from time to time you eat.
11 And drink water by
measure, the sixth of an hin:
from time to time you drink.
12 And eat it as barley ashcakes,
and thou shalt bake it with dung **balls**
that cometh out of man **of human excrement**,
in their *sight* **eyes**.
13 And *the LORD* **Yah Veh** said,
Even thus shall the *children* **sons** of *Israel* **Yisra El**
eat their *defiled* **fouled** bread among the *Gentiles* **goyim**,
whither I *will* **shall** drive them.
14 Then said I, *Ah Lord GOD*
Aha Adonay Yah Veh!
behold, my soul hath not been *polluted* **fouled**:
for from my youth up even till now
have I not eaten of *that which dieth of itself* **a carcase**,
or *is* torn *in pieces*;
neither came there
abominable **stench of** flesh into my mouth.
15 Then he said unto me, *Lo* **See**,
I have given thee *cow's* **cow** dung
for *man's dung* **human dung balls**,
and thou shalt *prepare* **work** thy bread therewith.
16 *Moreover* he said unto me,
Son of *man* **humanity**,
behold, I *will* **shall** break the *staff* **rod** of bread
in *Jerusalem* **Yeru Shalem**:
and they shall eat bread by weight,
and with *care* **concern**;
and they shall drink water by measure,
and with astonishment:
17 That they may want bread and water,
and be astonied *one* **man** with *another* **brother**,
and *consume away* **dissolve** for their *iniquity* **perversity**.

The Desolation Of Yeru Shalem

5 And thou, son of *man* **humanity**,
take thee a sharp *knife* **sword**, take thee a barber's razor,
and cause it to pass upon thine head and upon thy beard:
then take thee balances *to weigh* **for weights**,
and *divide the hair* **allot them**.
2 Thou shalt burn with *fire* **flame**
a third *part* in the midst of the city,
when the days of the siege are fulfilled:
and thou shalt take a third *part*,
and smite **round** about it with a *knife* **sword**:
and a third *part* thou shalt scatter in the wind;
and I *will* **shall** draw out a sword after them.
3 Thou shalt also take *thereof* a few in number,
and bind them in thy *skirts* **wings**.
4 Then take of them again,
and cast them into the midst of the fire,
and burn them in the fire;
for thereof shall a fire come forth
into all the house of *Israel* **Yisra El**.

5 Thus saith *the Lord GOD* **Adonay Yah Veh**;
This is *Jerusalem* **Yeru Shalem**:
I have set it
in the midst of the *nations* **goyim** and *countries* **lands**
that are round about her.
6 And she hath *changed* **rebelled**
against my judgments
into wickedness more than the *nations* **goyim**,
and my statutes more than the *countries* **lands**
that are round about her:
for they have refused my judgments and my statutes,
they have not walked in them.
7 Therefore thus saith *the*
Lord GOD **Adonay Yah Veh**;
Because ye multiplied more than the *nations* **goyim**
that are round about you,
and have not walked in my statutes,
neither have *kept* **worked** my judgments,
neither have *done* **worked** according to the judgments
of the *nations* **goyim** *that are* round about you;
8 Therefore thus saith *the*
Lord GOD **Adonay Yah Veh**;
Behold, I, even I, am against thee,
and *will execute* **shall work** judgments
in the midst of thee
in the *sight* **eyes** of the *nations* **goyim**.
9 And I *will do* **shall work** in thee
that which I have not *done* **worked**,
and whereunto
I *will* **shall** not *do* **work** any more the like,
because of all thine *abominations* **abhorrences**.
10 Therefore the fathers shall eat the sons
in the midst of thee,
and the sons shall eat their fathers;
and bake it with dung balls of human excrement
in their eyes.
13 And Yah Veh says,
Even thus the sons of Yisra El
eat their fouled bread among the goyim,
where I drive them.
14 And I say, Aha Adonay Yah Veh!
behold, my soul *is* not fouled:
for from my youth up even until now
I neither ate of a carcase or torn;
nor came stench of flesh into my mouth.
15 And he says to me, See,
I give you cow dung for human dung balls
and work your bread therewith.
16 And he says to me, Son of humanity,
behold, I break the rod of bread in Yeru Shalem:
and they eat bread by weight,
and with concern;
and they drink water by measure,
and with astonishment:
17 so that they lack bread and water
and astonish man with brother;
and dissolve for their perversity.

THE DESOLATION OF YERU SHALEM

5 And you, son of humanity,
take a sharp sword, take a razor of a barber,
and pass it over your head and over your beard:
and take balances of weights and allot them.
2 A third, burn with flame midst the city
when the days of the siege are fulfilled:
and take a third, and smite all around with a sword:
and a third, scatter in the wind;
and I draw a sword after them:
3 and take a few in number
and bind them in your wings:
4 and take of them again,
and cast them midst the fire and burn them in the fire;
and a fire comes forth into all the house of Yisra El.
5 Thus says Adonay Yah Veh:
This is Yeru Shalem:
I set it midst the goyim and lands all around her:
6 and she rebels against my judgments
in wickedness more than the goyim,
and my statutes more than the lands around her:
for they refuse my judgments and my statutes
and walk not in them.
7 So thus says Adonay Yah Veh:
Because you multiply
more than the goyim around you,
and neither walk in my statutes
nor work my judgments,
nor work according to the judgments
of the goyim around you;
8 so thus says Adonay Yah Veh:
Behold, I—even I *am* against you,
and work judgments midst you
in the eyes of the goyim:
9 and I work in you what I neither worked
nor work any more the like
because of all your abhorrences.
10 So the fathers eat the sons midst you;
and the sons eat their fathers:
and I *will execute* **shall work** judgments in thee,
and the whole *remnant* **survivors** of thee
will I scatter **shall I winnow** into all the winds.

11 Wherefore, *as* I live,
saith the Lord GOD **an oracle of Adonay Yah Veh**;
Surely,
because thou hast *defiled* **fouled** my *sanctuary* **holies**
with all thy *detestable things* **abominations**,
and with all thine *abominations* **abhorrences**,
therefore *will* **shall** I also diminish thee;
neither shall mine eye spare,
neither *will I have any pity* **shall I compassion**.
12 A third *part* of thee shall die with the pestilence,
and with famine shall they be *consumed* **finished off**
in the midst of thee:
and a third *part* shall fall by the sword round about thee;
and I *will scatter* **shall winnow** a third *part*
into all the winds,
and I *will* **shall** draw out a sword after them.
13 Thus shall *mine anger* **my wrath**
be *accomplished* **finished off**,
and I *will* **shall** cause my fury to rest upon them,
and I *will be comforted* **shall sigh**:
and they shall know that I *the LORD* **Yah Veh**
have *spoken it* **worded** in my zeal,
when I have *accomplished* **finished off** my fury in them.
14 *Moreover* I *will make* **shall give** thee
waste **for a parched area**,
and a reproach among the *nations* **goyim**
that are round about thee,
in the *sight* **eyes** of all that pass by.
15 So **be** it *shall be* a reproach
and a *taunt* **revilement**,
an instruction **a discipline**
and *an astonishment* **a desolation**
unto the *nations* **goyim** *that are* round about thee,
when I shall *execute* **work** judgments in thee
in *anger* **wrath** and in fury
and in *furious rebukes* **reproofs of fury**.
I *the LORD* **Yah Veh** have *spoken it* **worded**.
16 When I shall send upon them
the evil arrows of famine,
which shall be for their *destruction* **ruin**, *and*
which I *will* **shall** send to *destroy* **ruin** you: and
I *will* **shall** increase the famine upon you, and
will **shall** break your *staff* **rod** of bread:
17 So *will* **shall** I send upon you
famine and evil *beasts* **live beings**,
and they shall bereave thee:
and pestilence and blood shall pass through thee;
and I *will* **shall** bring the sword upon thee.
I *the LORD* **Yah Veh** have *spoken it* **worded**.

A PROPHECY AGAINST THE MOUNTAINS OF YISRA EL

6 And the word of *the LORD*
Yah Veh came unto me,
saying,
2 Son of *man* **humanity**,
set thy face toward the mountains of *Israel* **Yisra El**,
and prophesy against them,
3 And say, Ye mountains of *Israel* **Yisra El**,
hear the word of *the Lord GOD* **Adonay Yah Veh**;
Thus saith *the Lord GOD* **Adonay Yah Veh**
to the mountains, and to the hills,
to the *rivers* **reservoirs**, and to the valleys;
Behold, I, *even* I, *will* **shall** bring a sword upon you,
and I *will* **shall** destroy your *high places* **bamahs**.
4 And your **sacrifice** altars shall *be* desolate,
and your *images* **sun icons** shall be broken:
and I *will cast down* **shall fell** your *slain men* **pierced**
before **at the face of** your idols.
5 And I *will lay* **shall give** the *dead* carcases
of the *children* **sons** of *Israel* **Yisra El**
before **at the face of** their idols;
and I *will scatter* **shall winnow** your bones
round about your **sacrifice** altars.
6 In all your *dwellingplaces* **sites**
the cities shall be *laid waste* **parched**,
and the *high places* **bamahs** shall *be* desolate;
that your **sacrifice** altars may be *laid waste* **parched**
and *made desolate* **have guilted**,
and your idols may be broken and *cease* **shabbathize**,
and I work judgments in you,
and I winnow all your survivors into all the winds.
11 So—I live
—an oracle of Adonay Yah Veh
because you foul my holies
with all your abominations
and with all your abhorrences,
I also diminish you;
neither my eye spares nor I compassion.
12 A third of you die with the pestilence
—finished off with famine in your midst;
and a third fall by the sword all around you;
and a third I winnow into all the winds:
and I draw out a sword after them.
13 Thus I finish off my wrath
and I rest my fury on them, and sigh:
and they know that I Yah Veh word in my zeal
when I finish off my fury in them.
14 I give you for a parched area;

and for a reproach among the goyim around you
in the eyes of all who pass by:
15 and so be it, a reproach and a revilement,
a discipline and a desolation
to the goyim around you,
when I work judgments in you
in wrath and in fury and in reproofs of fury.
I Yah Veh have worded.
16 I send on them the evil arrows of famine
being for their ruin
—which I send to ruin you:
and I increase the famine on you
and break your rod of bread:
17 thus I send famine on you;
and evil live beings bereave you;
and pestilence and blood passes through you;
and I bring the sword on you.
I Yah Veh have worded.

A Prophecy Against The Mountains Of Yisra El

6 And so be the word of Yah Veh to me, saying,
2 Son of humanity,
set your face toward the mountains of Yisra El
and prophesy against them,
3 and say, Mountains of Yisra El,
hear the word of Adonay Yah Veh;
Thus says Adonay Yah Veh
to the mountains and to the hills
to the reservoirs and to the valleys:
Behold, I—I bring a sword on you
and I destroy your bamahs:
4 and desolate your sacrifice altars
and break your sun icons
and I fell your pierced at the face of your idols:
5 and I give the carcases of the sons of Yisra El
at the face of their idols;
and I winnow your bones
all around your sacrifice altars.
6 In all your sites the cities parch
and the bamahs desolate;
and your sacrifice altars parch and guilt
and your idols break and shabbathize
and your *images* **sun icons** may be cut down,
and your works may be *abolished* **erased**.
7 And the *slain* **pierced** shall
fall in the midst of you,
and ye shall know that *I am the LORD* **I—Yah Veh**.
8 Yet *will I leave a remnant*
shall I let some remain,
that ye may have
some that shall escape **escapees of** the sword
among the *nations* **goyim**,
when ye shall be *scattered* **winnowed**
through the *countries* **lands**.
9 And *they that escape of you* **the escapees**
shall remember me among the *nations* **goyim**
whither they shall be *carried captives* **captured**,
because I am broken with their whorish heart,
which hath *departed* **turned aside** from me,
and with their eyes,
which *go a whoring* **whore** after their idols:
and they shall lothe *themselves*
for **at the face of** the evils
which they have *committed* **worked**
in all their *abominations* **abhorrences**.
10 And they shall know that *I am the LORD* **I—Yah Veh**,
and that I have not *said in vain* **worded gratuitously**
that I *would do* **should work** this evil unto them.
11 Thus saith *the Lord GOD* **Adonay Yah Veh**;
Smite with thine *hand* **palm**, and stamp with thy foot,
and say, *Alas* **Ach!**
for all the evil *abominations* **abhorrences**
of the house of *Israel* **Yisra El**!
for they shall fall by the sword,
by the famine, and by the pestilence.
12 He that is far off shall die of the pestilence;
and he that is near shall fall by the sword;
and he that *remaineth* **surviveth**
and is *besieged* **under guard**
shall die by the famine:
thus *will I accomplish* **shall I finish**
off my fury upon them.
13 Then shall ye know that *I*
am the LORD **I—Yah Veh**,
when their *slain men* **pierced** shall be among
their idols round about their **sacrifice** altars,
upon every high hill, in all the tops of the mountains,
and under every green tree, and under every thick oak,
the place where they
did offer sweet savour **gave a scent of rest**
to all their idols.
14 So *will* **shall** I *stretch out*
spread my hand upon them,
and *make* **give** the land desolate,
yea, more *desolate* **desolation**
than the wilderness toward *Diblath* **Riblah**,
in all their *habitations* **sites**:
and they shall know that *I am the LORD* **I—Yah Veh**.

THE APPROACH OF THE END

7 Moreover
the word of *the LORD* **Yah Veh** came unto me, saying,
2 Also, thou son of *man* **humanity**,
thus saith *the Lord GOD* **Adonay Yah Veh**
unto the *land* **soil** of *Israel* **Yisra El**;
An end,
the end is come upon the four *corners* **wings** of the land.
3 Now is the end *come* upon thee,
and I *will* **shall** send *mine anger* **my wrath** upon thee,
and *will* **shall** judge thee according to thy ways,
and *will recompense* **shall give** upon thee
all thine *abominations* **abhorrences**.
4 And mine eye shall not spare thee,
neither *will I have pity* **shall I compassion**:
but I *will recompense* **shall give** thy ways upon thee,
and thine *abominations* **abhorrences**
shall be in the midst of thee:
and ye shall know that *I am the LORD* **I—Yah Veh**.
5 Thus saith *the Lord GOD* **Adonay Yah Veh**
An evil, *an only* **one** evil, behold, is come.
6 An end is come, the end is come:
it *watcheth* **waketh** for thee; behold, it is come.
7 The *morning* **corona** is come unto thee,
O thou that *dwellest* **settlest** in the land:
the time is come, the day of *trouble* **confusion** is near,
and not the *sounding again* **shouting** of the mountains.
8 Now *will* **shall** I *shortly* **soon**
pour out my fury upon thee,
and your sun icons cut down
and your works erase:
7 and the pierced fall in your midst
and you know I—Yah Veh.
8 Yet some remain
—escapees of the sword among the goyim as
you *are* winnowed through the lands:
9 and the escapees among the goyim
remember me where they are captured,
because I am broken with their whorish heart
who turn aside from me;
and with their eyes
which whore after their idols:
and they loathe at the face of the evils they worked
in all their abhorrences;
10 and they know I—Yah Veh:
and that I word not gratuitously
to work this evil to them.
11 Thus says Adonay Yah Veh:
Smite with your palm and stamp with your foot,
and say, Ach!
for all the evil abhorrences of the house of Yisra El!
for they fall by the sword
by the famine and by the pestilence:
12 he who is afar dies of the pestilence;
and he who is near falls by the sword;
and he who survives and is under guard
dies by the famine:
thus I finish off my fury on them:
13 and you know I—Yah Veh,
when their pierced become among their idols
all around their sacrifice altars
on every high hill
in all the tops of the mountains
and under every green tree and under every thick oak
—in all the places
they give a scent of rest to all their idols.
14 Thus I spread my hand on them
and give the land a desolatiom
—yes, more desolation
than the wilderness toward Riblah in all their sites:
and they know I—Yah Veh.

THE APPROACH OF THE END

7 And so be the word of Yah Veh to me, saying,
2 And you son of humanity,
thus says Adonay Yah Veh to the soil of Yisra El;
An end—
the end arrives on the four wings of the land:
3 now the end *is* on you;
and I send my wrath on you
and judge you according to your ways,
and give all your abhorrences on you.
4 And neither my eye spares
you nor I compassion:
and I give your ways on you,
for your abhorrences are midst you:
and you know I—Yah Veh.
5 Thus says Adonay Yah Veh:
An evil, one evil, behold, has arrived;
6 an end has arrived, the end arrives;
it wakens for you; behold, it arrives:
7 the corona arrives to you,
O you who settle in the land:
the time arrives; the day of confusion is near,
and not the shouting of the mountains.
8 Now, soon I pour my fury on you,
and *accomplish mine anger* **finish off my wrath**
upon thee:
and I *will* **shall** judge thee according to thy ways,

and *will recompense* **shall give** thee
for all thine *abominations* **abhorrences.**
9 And mine eye shall not spare,
neither *will I have pity* **shall I compassion**:
I *will recompense* **shall give** thee according to thy ways
and thine *abominations* **abhorrences**
that are in the midst of thee;
and ye shall know
that *I am the LORD* **I—Yah Veh** that smiteth.
10 Behold the day, behold, it is come:
the *morning* **corona** is gone forth;
the rod hath blossomed, *pride* **arrogance** hath budded.
11 Violence is risen up into a rod of wickedness:
none of them shall *remain*, nor of their
multitude, nor of any of *theirs* **abundance:**
neither shall there be *wailing* **lamentation** for them.
12 The time is come, the day
draweth near **toucheth**:
let not the *buyer rejoice* **chatteler cheer**,
nor the seller mourn:
for *wrath* **fuming** is upon all the multitude *thereof.*
13 For the seller shall not
return to that which is sold,
although
they were yet alive **their life was among the living**:
for the vision is touching the whole multitude *thereof,*
which shall not return;
neither shall *any* **man** strengthen himself
in the *iniquity* **perversity** of his life.
14 They have *blown* **blast** the *trumpet* **blast**,
even to *make all ready* **prepare**;
but none goeth to the *battle* **war**:
for my *wrath* **fuming** is upon all the multitude *thereof.*
15 The sword is without,
and the pestilence and the famine within **the house**:
he that is in the field shall die with the sword;
and he that is in the city,
famine and pestilence shall devour him.
16 But *they that escape of them* **the escapees**
shall escape,
and shall be on the mountains like doves of the valleys,
all of them *mourning* **roaring**,
every *one* **man** for his *iniquity* **perversity**.
17 All hands shall *be feeble* **slacken**,
and all knees shall *be weak as water* **go watery**.
18 They shall *also* gird
themselves with *sackcloth* **saq**,
and *horror* **trembling** shall cover them;
and shame shall be upon all faces,
and baldness upon all their heads.
19 They shall cast their silver
in the *streets* **outways**,
and their gold shall be *removed* **excluded**:
their silver and their gold
shall not be able to *deliver* **rescue** them
in the day of the wrath of *the LORD* **Yah Veh**:
they shall not satisfy their souls,
neither fill their *bowels* **inwards**:
because it is the stumblingblock
of their *iniquity* **perversity**.
20 As for the *beauty* **splendour** of his ornament,
he set it in *majesty* **pomp**:
but they *made* **worked** the images
of their *abominations* **abhorrences**
and of their *detestable things* **abominations** therein:
therefore have I *set it far* **given to exclude it** from them.
21 And I *will* **shall** give it
into the hands of the strangers for a *prey* **plunder**,
and to the wicked of the earth for a spoil;
and they shall *pollute* **profane** it.
22 My face *will* **shall** I turn also from them,
and they shall *pollute* **profane** my *secret place* **hideout**:
for the *robbers* **tyrants** shall enter into it,
and *defile* **profane** it.
23 *Make* **Work** a chain:
for the land is *full* **filled**
of *bloody crimes* **judgments of blood**,
and the city is *full* **filled** of violence.
24 Wherefore
I *will* **shall** bring the *worst* **evil** of the *heathen* **goyim**,
and finish off my wrath on you:
and I judge you according to your ways,
and give you for all your abhorrences.
9 And neither my eye spares, nor I compassion:
I give you according to your ways
and your abhorrences midst you;
and you know I—Yah Veh who smites.
10 Behold the day; behold, arrives:
the corona goes forth;
the rod blossoms; arrogance buds:
11 violence rises into a rod of wickedness:
neither one of them nor of their multitude
nor of any of abundance;
nor any lamentation for them.
12 The time arrives; the day touches;
neither the chatteler cheers
nor the seller mourn:
for fuming is on all the multitude.
13 For the seller returns not to what is sold
although their life is among the living:

for the vision touches the whole multitude;
not to return;
and man strengthens not himself
by the perversity of his life.
14 They blast the blast to prepare
and no one goes to the war;
for my fuming is on all the multitude:
15 the sword is outside
and the pestilence and the famine inside the house:
he who is in the field
dies with the sword;
and he who is in the city
famine and pestilence devour him:
16 and the escapees escape,
and are on the mountains as doves of the valleys
—all of them roaring
—every man for his perversity:
17 all hands slacken and all knees go watery:
18 they gird with saq and trembling covers them;
and shame *is* on all faces
and baldness on all their heads.
19 They cast their silver in the outways
and their gold becomes excluded:
their silver and their gold cannot rescue them
in the day of the wrath of Yah Veh:
they neither satisfy their souls
nor fill their inwards:
because it becomes
the stumblingblock of their perversity.
20 As for the splendor of his ornament,
he sets it in pomp:
and they work the images of their abhorrences
and of their abominations therein:
so I give to exclude it from them:
21 and I give it into the hands of the strangers
for a plunder;
and to the wicked of the earth
for a spoil;
and they profane it:
22 and I turn my face from them
and they profane my hideout;
for the tyrants enter it and profane it.
23 Work a chain:
for the land fills with judgments of blood,
and the city fills with violence.
24 And I bring the evil of the goyim
and they shall possess their houses:
I *will* **shall** also make the pomp of the strong
to *cease* **shabbathize**;
and their *holy places* **hallowed**
shall be *defiled* **profaned**.
25 *Destruction* **Severence** cometh;
and they shall seek *peace* **shalom**,
and there shall be none.
26 *Mischief* **Calamity** shall
come upon *mischief* **calamity**,
and *rumour* **report** shall *be* upon *rumour* **report**;
then shall they seek a vision of the prophet;
but the *law* **torah** shall *perish* **destruct** from the priest,
and counsel from the *ancients* **elders**.
27 The *king* **sovereign** shall mourn,
and the *prince* **hierarch**
shall be *clothed* **enrobed** with desolation,
and the hands of the people of the land
shall *be troubled* **terrify**:
I *will do* **shall work** unto them after their way,
and *according to* **after** their *deserts* **judgments**
will **shall** I judge them;
and they shall know that *I am the LORD* **I—Yah Veh**.

THE FIGURINE OF JEALOUSY

8 And **so be** it *came to pass* in the sixth year,
in the sixth *month*, in the fifth *day* of the month,
as I sat in mine house,
and the elders of *Judah* **Yah Hudah**
sat *before me* **at my face**,
that the hand of *the Lord GOD* **Adonay Yah Veh**
fell there upon me.
2 Then I *beheld* **saw**,
and *lo* **behold** a likeness as the *appearance* **visage** of fire:
from the *appearance* **visage** of his loins even downward,
fire;
and from his loins even upward,
as the *appearance* **visage** of *brightness*
brilliance, as the *colour* **eye** of *amber*
brilliant copper. Apocalypse 1:12—16
3 And he *put forth* **spread** the
form **pattern** of an hand,
and took me by a *lock* **tassel** of mine head;
and the spirit lifted me up
between the earth and **between** the *heaven* **heavens**,
and brought me in the visions of *God* **Elohim**
to *Jerusalem* **Yeru Shalem**,
to the *door* **opening** of the inner *gate* **portal**
that *looketh toward the north* **faceth northward**;
where was the seat of the *image* **figurine** of jealousy,
which provoketh to jealousy.
4 And, behold,
the *glory* **honour** of *the God* **Elohim** of *Israel* **Yisra El**
was there,

according to the *vision* **visage**
that I saw in the *plain* **valley**.
5 Then said he unto me, Son of *man* **humanity**,
lift up thine eyes *now* **I beseech,**
the way *toward the north* **northward**.
So I lifted up mine eyes
the way *toward the north* **northward**,
and behold northward
at the *gate* **portal** of the **sacrifice** altar
this *image* **figurine** of jealousy in the entry.
6 He said *furthermore* unto
me, Son of *man* **humanity**,
seest thou what they *do* **work**?
even the great *abominations* **abhorrences**
that the house of *Israel committeth*
Yisra El worketh here,
that I should *go* far *off* **remove**
from my *sanctuary* **holies**?
but turn thee yet again,
and thou shalt see greater abominations.
7 And he brought me to the
door **portal** of the court;
and when I *looked* **saw**, behold *a* **one** hole in the wall.
8 Then said he unto me, Son of *man* **humanity**,
dig *now* **I beseech,** in the wall:
and when I had digged in the wall,
behold *a door* **one opening**.
9 And he said unto me, *Go in* **Enter**,
and *behold* **see**
the *wicked abominations* **evil abhorrences**
that they *do* **work** here.
10 So I *went in* **entered** and saw; and behold
to possess their houses:
I also shabbathize the pomp of the strong;
to profane their hallowed.
25 Severence arrives; and they seek shalom,
and there *is* none.
26 Calamity on calamity arrives;
and report on report:
and they seek a vision of the prophet;
and the torah destructs from the priest
and counsel from the elders.
27 The sovereign mourns
and the hierarch enrobes with desolation
and the hands of the people of the land terrify:
I work to them after their way,
and judge them after their judgments;
and they know I—Yah Veh.

THE FIGURINE OF JEALOUSY

8 And so be it, in the sixth year,
in the sixth, in the fifth of the month,
I sit in my house
and the elders of Yah Hudah sit at my face
and the hand of Adonay Yah Veh falls on me there.
2 Then I see, and behold,
a likeness as the visage of fire:
from the visage of his loins even downward—fire;
and from his loins and upward
as the visage of brilliance
—as the eye of brilliant copper.
Apocalypse 1:12—16
3 And he spreads the pattern of a hand
and takes me by a tassel of my head;
and the spirit lifts me
between the earth and between the heavens,
and in visions of Elohim,
brings me to Yeru Shalem
to the opening of the inner portal facing northward;
to the seat of the figurine of jealousy
which provokes to jealousy.
4 And behold,
the honor of Elohim of Yisra El
is according to the visage I saw in the valley.
5 And he says to me, Son of humanity,
lift your eyes, I beseech, the way northward.
And I lift my eyes the way northward, and behold,
northward at the portal of the sacrifice altar
this figurine of jealousy in the entry.
6 He says to me,
Son of humanity, see you what they work?
the great abhorrences
the house of Yisra El works here
to remove afar from my holies?
And turn yet again,
and see greater abominations.
7 —and he brings me to the portal of the court;
and I see, behold one hole in the wall.
8 And he says to me, Son of humanity,
dig, I beseech, in the wall!
—and I dig in the wall, and behold, one opening.
9 And he says to me, Enter,
and see the evil abhorrences they work here.
10 —and I enter and see; and behold,
every *form* **pattern** of *creeping things* **creepers**,
and abominable *beasts* **animals**,
and all the idols of the house of *Israel* **Yisra El**,
pourtrayed **engraved** upon the wall

round about, **round about**.
11 And there stood *before* **at the face of** them
seventy men
of the *ancients* **elders** of the house of *Israel* **Yisra El**,
and in the midst of them
stood *Jaazaniah* **Yaazan Yah** the son of Shaphan,
with every man his censer in his hand;
and a *thick* **voluminous** cloud of incense
went up **ascended**.
12 Then said he unto me, Son of *man* **humanity**,
hast thou seen what the *ancients* **elders**
of the house of *Israel do* **Yisra El work** in the dark,
every man in the chambers of his imagery?
for they say, *The LORD* **Yah Veh** seeth us not;
the LORD **Yah Veh** hath forsaken the earth.
13 He said also unto me, Turn thee yet again,
and thou shalt see greater *abominations* **abhorrences**
that they *do* **work**.
14 Then he brought me
to the *door* **opening** of the *gate* **portal**
of the *LORD'S* house **of Yah Veh**
which was *toward the north* **northward**; and, behold,
there sat women weeping for Tammuz.
15 Then said he unto me,
Hast thou seen *this*, O son of *man* **humanity**?
turn thee yet again, and thou shalt see
greater *abominations* **abhorrences** than these.
16 And he brought me into the inner court
of the *LORD'S* house **of Yah Veh**, and, behold,
at the *door* **portal**
of the *temple* **manse** of *the LORD* **Yah Veh**,
between the porch and the **sacrifice** altar,
were about five and twenty men,
with their backs
toward the *temple* **manse** of *the LORD* **Yah Veh**,
and their faces *toward the east* **eastward**;
and they *worshipped* **prostrated to** the sun
toward the east **eastward**.
17 Then he said unto me,
Hast thou seen *this*, O son of *man* **humanity**?
Is it *a light thing* **trifling** to the
house of *Judah* **Yah Hudah**
that they *commit* **work** the *abominations* **abhorrences**
which they *commit* **work** here?
for they have filled the land with violence,
and have returned to *provoke* **vex** me *to anger*:
and, *lo* **behold**,
they *put* **spread** the *branch* **twig** to their *nose* **nostrils**.
18 Therefore *will* **shall** I also *deal* **work** in fury:
mine eye shall not spare,
neither *will I have pity* **shall I compassion**:
and though they *cry* **call out** in mine ears
with a *loud* **great** voice, yet *will* **shall** I not hear them.

SLAUGHTER OF IDOLATERS

9 He *cried* **called out** also in mine ears
with a *loud* **great** voice, saying,
Cause them that have charge over the city
to *draw near* **approach**,
even every man
with his *destroying weapon* **instrument of ruin**
in his hand.
2 And, behold, six men came
from the way of the *higher gate* **most high portal**,
which *lieth toward the north* **faceth northward**,
and every man
a *slaughter weapon* **disintegrator**
instrument in his hand;
and one man among them
was *clothed* **enrobed** with linen,
with a *writer's inkhorn* **scribe's inkwell**
by **upon** his *side* **loins**:
and they *went in* **entered**,
and stood beside the *brasen* **copper sacrifice** altar.
3 And the *glory* **honour**
of *the God* **Elohim** of *Israel* **Yisra El**
was gone up **ascended** from the cherub,
whereupon he was, to the threshold of the house.
every pattern of creepers and abominable animals
and all the idols of the house of Yisra El
engraved on the wall all around—all around.
11 And standing there at their face
seventy men of the elders of the house of Yisra El,
and Yaazan Yah the son of Shaphan
stands midst them;
every man with his censer in his hand;
and a voluminous cloud of incense ascends.
12 And says he to me, Son of humanity,
you see what the elders of the house of Yisra El
work in the dark
—every man in the chambers of his imagery?
for they say, Yah Veh sees us not;
Yah Veh forsook the earth.
13 And he says to me, Turn yet again,
and see greater abhorrences they work.
14 —and he brings me to the opening
of the portal of the house of Yah Veh northward;
and behold,
women sitting and weeping for Tammuz.
15 And he says to me,

See you, O son of humanity?
turn yet again
and see greater abhorrences than these.
16 And he brings me into the inner court
of the house of Yah Veh, and behold,
at the portal of the manse of Yah Veh
between the porch and the sacrifice altar
—about twenty—five men
with their backs toward the manse of Yah Veh
and their faces eastward;
and they prostrate eastward toward the sun.
17 And he says to me,
See you, O son of humanity?
Is it trifling to the house of Yah Hudah
to work the abhorrences they work here?
For they fill the land with violence
and return to vex me:
and behold, they spread the twig to their nostrils.
18 So I also work in fury:
neither my eye spares, nor I compassion:
and though they call out in my ears
with a great voice, yet I hear them not.

Slaughter Of Idolaters

9 And he calls out in my ears with a great voice,
saying,
Have them in charge over the city to approach,
even every man
with his instrument of ruin in his hand.
2 And behold,
six men come from the way of the most high portal
facing northward;
and every man
has a disintegrator instrument in his hand;
and one man among them is enrobed with linen
with an inkwell of a scribe on his loins:
and they enter
and stand beside the copper sacrifice altar:
3 and the honor of Elohim of Yisra El
ascends from the cherub on whom it
is to the threshold of the house.
And he called to the man *clothed* **enrobed** with linen,
which had the *writer's inkhorn* **scribe's inkwell**
by **upon** his *side* **loins**;
4 And *the LORD* **Yah Veh** said unto him,
Co **Pass** through the midst of the city,
through the midst of *Jerusalem* **Yeru Shalem**,
and *set* **tattoo** a *mark* **tattoo**
upon the foreheads of the men
that sigh and that *cry* **shriek**
for all the *abominations* **abhorrences**
that be *done* **worked** in the midst *thereof.*
5 And to the others he said in mine *hearing* **ears**,
Co **Pass** ye after him through the city, and smite:
let not your eye spare,
neither *have ye pity* **compassion**:
6 *Slay utterly* **Slaughter to ruin**
old **aged** and *young* **youth**,
both maids **and virgins**, and *little children* **toddlers**,
and women:
but come not near any man
upon whom is the *mark* **tattoo**;
and begin at my *sanctuary* **holies**.
Then they began at the *ancient* **aged** men
which were *before* **at the face of** the house.
7 And he said unto them, *Defile* **Foul** the house,
and fill the courts with the *slain* **pierced**: go *ye forth.*
And they went *forth*, and *slew* **smote** in the city.
8 And **so be** it *came to pass,*
while they were *slaying* **smiting** them,
and I *was left* **survived**,
that I fell upon my face, and cried, and said,
Ah Lord COD **Aha Adonay Yah Veh**!
wilt **shalt** thou *destroy* **ruin**
all the *residue* **survivors** of *Israel* **Yisra El**
in thy pouring out of thy fury
upon *Jerusalem* **Yeru Shalem**?
9 Then said he unto me,
The *iniquity* **perversity**
of the house of *Israel* **Yisra El** and *Judah* **Yah Hudah**
is *exceeding* **mighty** great,
and the land is *full* **filled** of blood,
and the city *full* **filled** of *perverseness* **distortion**:
for they say, *The LORD* **Yah Veh** hath forsaken the earth,
and *the LORD* **Yah Veh** seeth not.
10 And as for me also, mine eye shall not spare,
neither *will I have pity* **shall I compassion**,
but I will recompense **I shall give** their way
upon their head.
11 And, behold, the man
clothed **enrobed** with linen,
which had the *inkhorn by* **inkwell upon** his *side* **loins**,
reported the matter **returned word**, saying,
I have *done* **worked**
as thou hast *commanded* **misvahed** me.

The Honour Of Yah Veh Fills The House

10 Then I *looked* **saw**, and, behold,
in the *firmament* **expanse**
that was above the head of the *cherubims* **cherubim**

there appeared over them as it were a sapphire stone,
as the *appearance* **visage** of the likeness of a throne.
2 And he *spake* **said** unto the
man clothed with linen,
and said,
Co in **Enter** between the wheels, *even* under the cherub,
and fill thine *hand* **fist** with coals of fire
from between the *cherubims* **cherubim**,
and scatter them over the city.
And he *went in* **entered** in my *sight* **eyes**.
3 *Now* the *cherubims* **cherubim**
stood on the right side of the house,
when the man *went in* **entered**;
and the cloud filled the inner court.
4 Then the *glory* **honour** of *the LORD* **Yah Veh**
went up **lifted** from the cherub,
and stood over the threshold of the house;
and the house was filled with the cloud,
and the court was *full* **filled** of the *brightness* **brilliance**
of the *LORD'S glory* **honour of Yah Veh**.
5 And the *sound* **voice**
of the *cherubims'* **cherubim's** wings
was heard *even* to the outer court,
And he calls to the man enrobed with linen
with the inkwell of the scribe on his loins;
4 and Yah Veh says to him,
Pass through midst the city
—through midst Yeru Shalem;
and tattoo a tattoo on the foreheads
of the men who sigh and shriek
for all the abhorrences worked in our midst.
5 And to the others he says in my ears,
Pass after him through the city, and smite:
neither your eye spare nor compassion:
6 slaughter to ruin aged and youth
and virgin and toddler and women:
but come not near any man
on whom *is* the tattoo;
and begin at my holies.
—and they begin at the aged men
at the face of the house.
7 And he says to them, Foul the house,
and fill the courts with the pierced: Go!
—and they go and smite in the city.
8 And so be it, as they smite them,
and I—I survive,
I fall on my face, and cry, and say,
Aha! Adonay Yah Veh!
Ruin you all the survivors of Yisra El
in your pouring from your fury
on Yeru Shalem?
9 And he says to me,
The perversity of the house of Yisra El and Yah Hudah
is mighty mighty great,
and the land fills with blood
and the city fills with distortion:
for they say, Yah Veh forsakes the earth,
and Yah Veh sees not.
10 And I also,
neither my eye spares, nor I compassion:
I give their way on their head.
11 And behold, the man enrobed with linen
with the inkwell on his loins
returns word, saying,
I worked as you misvahed me.

THE HONOR OF YAH VEH FILLS THE HOUSE

10 And I see, and behold,
in the expanse above the head of the cherubim
there appears over them as a sapphire stone
—as the visage of the likeness of a throne:
2 and he says to the man clothed with linen,
saying, Enter between the wheels under the cherub
and fill your fist with coals of fire
from between the cherubim
and scatter them over the city.
—and he enters at my eyes.
3 And the cherubim stand
at the right side of the house
as the man enters;
and the cloud fills the inner court:
4 and the honor of Yah Veh lifts from the cherub
over the threshold of the house:
and the house fills with the cloud;
and the court fills
from the brilliance of the honor of Yah Veh:
5 and the voice of the wings of the cherubim
is heard to the outer court
as the voice of *the Almighty God* **El Shadday**
when he *speaketh* **wordeth**.
6 And **so be** it *came to pass*,
that when he had *commanded* **misvahed**
the man *clothed* **enrobed** with linen, saying,
Take fire from between the wheels,
from between the *cherubims* **cherubim**;
then he *went in* **entered**, and stood beside the wheels.
7 And *one* cherub *stretched forth* **spread** his hand
from between the *cherubims* **cherubim**
unto the fire that was between the *cherubims* **cherubim**,
and *took* **lifted** *thereof*,

and *put* **gave** it into the *hands* **fists**
of *him* **the one** that was *clothed* **enrobed** with linen:
who took it, and went out.
8 And there *appeared* **was seen**
in the *cherubims* **cherubim**
the *form* **pattern** of a *man's* **human** hand
under their wings.

THE WHEEL MIDST A WHEEL

9 And when I *looked* **saw**, behold
the four wheels *by* **beside** the *cherubims* **cherubim**,
one wheel *by* **beside** one cherub,
and *another* **one** wheel *by another* **beside one** cherub:
and the *appearance* **visage** of the wheels
was as the *colour* **eye** of a beryl stone.
10 And as for their *appearances* **visages**,
they four had one likeness,
as if a wheel had been in the midst of a wheel.
11 When they went,
they went upon their four *sides* **quarters**;
they turned not as they went,
but to the place whither the head *looked* **faced**
they *followed* **went after** it;
they turned not as they went.
12 And their whole *body* **flesh**, and their backs,
and their hands, and their wings, and the wheels,
were full of eyes round about,
even the wheels that they four had.
13 As for the wheels,
it was *cried* **called out** unto them in my *hearing* **ears**,
O wheel.
14 And *every* **each** one had four faces:
the first face was the face of a cherub,
and the second face was the face of a *man* **human**,
and the third the face of a lion,
and the fourth the face of an eagle.
15 And the *cherubims* **cherubim** were lifted *up*.
This is the *living creature* **live being** that
I saw by the river of *Chebar* **Kebar**.
16 And when the *cherubims* **cherubim** went,
the wheels went *by* **beside** them:
and when the *cherubims* **cherubim** lifted *up* their wings
to *mount up* **lift** from the earth,
the *same* wheels also turned not from beside them.
17 When they stood, these stood;
and when they *were* lifted *up*,
these lifted *up themselves also*:
for the spirit of the *living creature*
live being was in them.
18 Then the *glory* **honour** of *the LORD* **Yah
Veh** departed from off the threshold of the house,
and stood over the *cherubims* **cherubim**.
19 And the *cherubims* **cherubim**
lifted *up* their wings,
and *mounted* **lifted** *up* from the earth in my *sight* **eyes**:
when they went out, the wheels also were beside them,
and *every one* **each** stood
at the *door* **opening** of the east *gate* **portal**
of the *LORD'S* house **of Yah Veh**;
and the *glory* **honour** of *the God*
Elohim of *Israel* **Yisra El**
was over them above.
20 This is the *living creature* **live being** that I saw
under *the God* **Elohim** of *Israel* **Yisra El**
by the river of *Chebar* **Kebar**;
and I knew that they were the *cherubims* **cherubim**.
21 *Every* **Four,** *one* **each** had four faces *apiece*,
and *every one* **each** four wings;
and the likeness of the hands of a *man* **human**
was under their wings.
22 And the likeness of their faces
—as the voice of El Shadday when he words.
6 And so be it,
he misvahs the man enrobed with linen, saying,
Take fire from between the wheels
—from between the cherubim;
and he enters, and stands beside the wheels:
7 and a cherub spreads his hand
from between the cherubim
to the fire between the cherubim,
and lifts,
and gives it into the fists
of the one enrobed with linen:
who takes it and goes.
8 And there in the cherubim
the pattern of a human hand is seen under their wings.

THE WHEEL MIDST A WHEEL

9 And I see, and behold,
the four wheels beside the cherubim
—one wheel beside one cherub
and one wheel beside one cherub:
and the visage of the wheels
is as the eye of a beryl stone:
10 and as for their visages,
they four *each have* one likeness, as if
a wheel being midst a wheel:
11 in going, they go on their four quarters;
they turn not as they go,
but to the place where the head faces, they go after;
they turn not as they go.
12 And their whole flesh and their backs,

and their hands and their wings and the wheels
are full of eyes all around.
Their wheels *are* four:
13 and in my ears, one calls to the wheels,
O wheel!
14 And each one *has* four faces:
the first face, the face of a cherub;
and the second face, the face of a human;
and the third, the face of a lion;
and the fourth, the face of an eagle:
15 and the cherubim lift.
This is the live being I saw by the river of Kebar.
16 And when the cherubim go
the wheels go beside them:
and when the cherubim lift their wings
to lift from the earth,
the wheels, also turn not from beside them.
17 When they stand, these stand;
and when they lift, these lift:
because of the spirit of the live being within.
18 And the honor of Yah Veh
departs from off the threshold of the house,
and stands over the cherubim:
19 and the cherubim lift their wings,
and lift off from the earth in my eyes:
when they go, the wheels *are* also beside them;
and each stands at the opening of the east portal
of the house of Yah Veh:
and the honor of Elohim of Yisra El
is over above them.
20 This is the live being I saw
under Elohim of Yisra El
by the river of Kebar;
and I know they *are* the cherubim:
21 four—each four faces and each four wings;
and the likeness of the hands of a human
under their wings;
22 and the likeness of their faces
was the same faces
which I saw by the river of *Chebar* **Kebar**,
their *appearances* **visages** and themselves:
they went *every one straight* **each man face** forward.

JUDGMENT OF MEN WHO FABRICATE MISCHIEF

11 Moreover the spirit lifted me up,
and brought me unto the east *gate* **portal**
of the *LORD'S* house **of Yah Veh**,
which *looketh* **faceth** eastward:
and behold at the *door* **opening** of the *gate* **portal**
five and twenty men;
among whom I saw
Jaazaniah **Yaazan Yah** the son of *Azur* **Azzur**,
and *Pelatiah* **Pelat Yah** the son of *Benaiah* **Bena Yah**,
princes **governors** of the people.
2 Then said he unto me, Son of *man* **humanity**,
these are the men that *devise* **fabricate** mischief, *and*
give wicked **counsellors evil** counsel in this city:
3 Which say, It is not near; let us build houses:
this *city* is the caldron, and we be the flesh.
4 Therefore prophesy against them,
prophesy, O son of *man* **humanity**.
5 And the Spirit of *the LORD*
Yah Veh fell upon me,
and said unto me, Speak;
Thus saith *the LORD* **Yah Veh**;
Thus have ye said, O house of *Israel* **Yisra El**:
for I know the
things that come into your mind **degrees of your spirit**,
every one **each** of them.
6 Ye have *multiplied* **abounded** your *slain* **pierced**
in this city,
and ye have filled the *streets* **outways** *thereof*
with the *slain* **pierced**.
7 Therefore thus saith *the*
Lord GOD **Adonay Yah Veh**;
Your *slain* **pierced**
whom ye have *laid* **set** in the midst of it,
they are the flesh, and this *city* is the caldron:
but I *will* **shall** bring you forth out of the midst of it.
8 Ye have *feared* **awed** the sword;
and I *will* **shall** bring a sword upon you,
saith the Lord GOD **an oracle of Adonay Yah Veh**.
9 And I *will* **shall** bring you out of the midst *thereof*,
and *deliver* **give** you into the hands of strangers, and
will execute **shall work** judgments among you.
10 Ye shall fall by the sword;
I *will* **shall** judge you in the border of *Israel* **Yisra El**;
and ye shall know that *I am the LORD* **I—Yah Veh**.
11 This *city* shall not be your caldron,
neither shall ye be *the* **for** flesh in the midst *thereof*;
but I *will* **shall** judge you in the border of *Israel* **Yisra El**:
12 And ye shall know that *I*
am the LORD **I—Yah Veh**:
for ye have not walked in my statutes,
neither *executed* **worked** my judgments,
but have *done* **worked** after the *manners* **judgments**
of the *heathen* **goyim** that are round about you.
13 And **so be** it *came to pass*, when I prophesied,
that *Pelatiah* **Pelat Yah**

the son of *Benaiah* **Bena Yah** died.
Then fell I down upon my face,
and cried with a loud voice, and said,
Ah Lord GOD **Aha Adonay Yah Veh**!
wilt **shalt** thou *make a full end* **work a final finish**
of the *remnant* **survivors** of *Israel* **Yisra El**?
14 Again the word of *the LORD*
Yah Veh came unto me,
saying,
15 Son of *man* **humanity**, thy brethren,
even thy brethren, the men of thy *kindred* **redemption**,
and all the house of *Israel* **Yisra El** wholly,
are they unto whom
the *inhabitants* **settlers** of *Jerusalem* **Yeru Shalem**
have said,
Get you **Remove ye** far from *the LORD* **Yah Veh**:
unto us is this land given in possession.

Word Concerning The Restoration Of Yisra El

16 Therefore say,
Thus saith *the Lord GOD* **Adonay Yah Veh**;
Although I have *cast* **removed** them far off
among the *heathen* **goyim**,
is the same faces I saw by the river of Kebar
—their visages and themselves:
each man going face forward.

Judgment Of Men Who Fabricate Mischief

11 And the spirit lifts me
and brings me to the east portal
of the house of Yah Veh facing eastward:
and behold, at the opening of the portal,
twenty—five men;
among whom I see Yaazan Yah the son of Azzur
and Pelat Yah the son of Bena Yah
—governors of the people:
2 and he says to me, Son of humanity, these are the men
fabricating mischief counseling evil counsel in this city:
3 saying, It *is* not near; build houses:
this *is* the caldron, and we the flesh.
4 —so prophesy against them;
prophesy, O son of humanity.
5 And the Spirit of Yah Veh falls on me,
and says to me, Speak;
Thus says Yah Veh:
Thus you said, O house of Yisra El.
For I know the degrees of your spirit—each of you:
6 you abound your pierced in this city,
and you fill the outways with the pierced.
7 So thus says Adonay Yah Veh:
Your pierced whom you set in the midst,
they are the flesh and this is the caldron:
and I bring you forth from the midst thereof:
8 you awe the sword
and I bring a sword on you
—an oracle of Adonay Yah Veh
9 and I bring you from the midst
and give you into the hands of strangers,
and work judgments among you:
10 you fall by the sword;
I judge you in the border of Yisra El;
and you know I—Yah Veh.
11 This neither becomes your caldron
nor become you for flesh in the midst;
I judge you in the border of Yisra El:
12 and you know I—Yah Veh:
for you neither walk in my statutes
nor work my judgments;
but work after the judgments of the goyim
all around you.
13 And so be it, in prophesying,
Pelat Yah the son of Bena Yah dies
and I fall on my face and cry with a loud voice,
and say, Aha, Adonay Yah Veh;
work you a final finish of the survivors of Yisra El?
14 And so be the word of Yah Veh to me, saying,
15 Son of humanity, your brothers,
your brothers, the men of your redemption,
and all the house of Yisra El wholly
are those to whom the settlers of Yeru Shalem say,
Remove afar from Yah Veh:
this land is given to us in possession.

Word Concerning The Restoration Of Yisra El

16 So say, Thus says Adonay Yah Veh:
Although I remove them afar from among the goyim,
and although I have scattered them
among the *countries* **lands**,
yet *will* **shall** I be to them as a little *sanctuary* **holies**
in the *countries* **lands** where they shall come.
17 Therefore say,
Thus saith *the Lord GOD* **Adonay Yah Veh**;
I *will* **shall** even gather you from the people,
and assemble you out of the countries
where ye have been scattered,
and I *will* **shall** give you the *land* **soil** of *Israel* **Yisra El**.
18 And they shall come thither,

and they shall *take away* **turn aside**
all the *detestable things* **abominations** *thereof*
and all the *abominations* **abhorrences** *thereof*
from thence.
19 And I *will* **shall** give them one heart,
and I *will put* **shall give** a new spirit within you;
and I *will take* **shall turn aside** the *stony* heart **of stone**
out of their flesh,
and *will* **shall** give them an heart of flesh:
20 That they may walk in my statutes,
and *keep mine ordinances* **guard my judgments**,
and *do* **work** them:
and they shall be my people,
and I *will* **shall** be their *God* **Elohim**.
21 But as for them whose heart
walketh after the heart
of their *detestable things* **abominations**
and their *abominations* **abhorrences**,
I *will recompense* **shall give** their way
upon their own heads,
saith the Lord GOD **an oracle of Adonay Yah Veh**.
22 Then did the *cherubims*
cherubim lift *up* their wings,
and the wheels beside them;
and the *glory* **honour** of *the God*
Elohim of *Israel* **Yisra El**
was over them above.
23 And the *glory* **honour** of *the LORD* **Yah Veh**
went up **ascended** from the midst of the city,
and stood upon the mountain
which is *on the east side* **eastward** of the city.
24 Afterwards the spirit *took* **bore** me *up*,
and brought me in a vision by the Spirit of *God* **Elohim**
into *Chaldea* **Kesediym**, to them of the *captivity* **exile**.
So the vision that I had seen *went up* **ascended** from me.
25 Then I *spake* **worded** unto
them of the *captivity* **exile**
all the *things* **words**
that *the LORD* **Yah Veh** had *shewed* me **see**.

THE WORD OF YAH VEH CONCERNING THE EXILES

12 **So be** The word of *the LORD*
Yah Veh also *came* unto me,
saying,
2 Son of *man* **humanity**,
thou *dwellest* **settlest** in the midst of a rebellious house,
which have eyes to see, and see not;
they have ears to hear, and hear not:
for they are a rebellious house.
3 Therefore, thou son of *man* **humanity**,
prepare **work** thee *stuff* **instruments**
for *removing* **exiling**,
and *remove* **exile** by day in their *sight* **eyes**;
and thou shalt *remove* **exile** from thy place
to another place in their *sight* **eyes**:
it may be **perhaps** they *will consider* **shall see**,
though they be a rebellious house.
4 Then shalt thou bring forth
thy *stuff* **instruments**
by day in their *sight* **eyes**,
as *stuff* **instruments** for *removing* **exiling**:
and thou shalt go forth at even in their *sight* **eyes**,
as they that *go forth* **proceed** into *captivity* **exile**.
5 Dig thou through the wall in their *sight* **eyes**,
and carry out thereby.
6 In their *sight* **eyes** shalt thou
bear it upon thy shoulders,
and carry it forth in the *twilight* **dusk**:
thou shalt cover thy face,
that thou see not the *ground* **earth**:
for I have *set* **given** thee for *a sign* **an omen**
unto the house of *Israel* **Yisra El**.
7 And I *did* **worked** so as I
was *commanded* **misvahed**:
I brought forth my *stuff* **instruments** by day,
as *stuff* **instruments** for *captivity* **exile**,
and in the even
I digged through the wall with mine hand;
and although I scatter them among the lands,
yet I *am* to them as a little holies
in the lands where they go.
17 So say, Thus says Adonay Yah Veh:
And I gather you from the people,
and assemble you from the countries
where you scattered;
and I give you the soil of Yisra El
18 to go there,
and turn aside all the abominations
and all the abhorrences from there:
19 and I give them one heart
and I give a new spirit within you;
and I turn aside the heart of stone from their flesh
and give them an heart of flesh:
20 so that they walk in my statutes
and guard my judgments and work them:
and they are my people,
and I am their Elohim.
21 As for them
whose heart walks after the heart

of their abominations and their abhorrences,
I give their way on their own heads
—an oracle of Adonay Yah Veh.
22 And the cherubim lift their wings
and the wheels *are* beside them;
and the honor of Elohim of Yisra El over them above:
23 and the honor of Yah Veh
ascends from midst the city
and stands on the mountain eastward of the city.
24 Afterward the spirit bears me
and brings me in a vision by the Spirit of Elohim
into Kesediym to the exiles:
and the vision I see ascends from me:
25 and I word to the exiles
all the words Yah Veh has me see.

THE WORD OF YAH VEH CONCERNING THE EXILES

12 And so be the word of Yah Veh to me, saying,
2 Son of humanity,
you settle midst a rebellious house,
with eyes to see, and see not;
ears to hear, and hear not;
for they *are* a rebellious house:
3 and you, son of humanity,
work instruments of exile:
and exile by day in their eyes;
and exile from your place to another place
in their eyes:
perhaps they see, for they *are* a rebellious house:
4 and bring forth your
instruments by day in their eyes
as instruments of exile:
and go forth at evening in their eyes
as proceeding into exile.
5 Dig through the wall in their eyes
and carry out thereby:
6 in their eyes, bear it on your shoulders,
and carry it forth in the dusk:
and cover your face that you not see the earth:
for I give you for an omen to the house of Yisra El.
7 And thus I work as I *am* misvahed:
I bring my instruments by day, as instruments of exile,
and in the evening
I dig through the wall with my hand:
I brought it forth in the *twilight* **dusk**,
and I bare it upon my shoulder in their *sight* **eyes**.
8 And in the morning
came the word of *the LORD* **Yah Veh** unto me, saying,
9 Son of *man* **humanity**,
hath not the house of *Israel* **Yisra El**, the rebellious house,
said unto thee, What *doest* **workest** thou?
10 Say thou unto them,
Thus saith *the Lord GOD* **Adonay Yah Veh**;
This burden concerneth
the *prince* **hierarch** in *Jerusalem* **Yeru Shalem**,
and all the house of *Israel* **Yisra El**, that are among them.
11 Say, I am your *sign* **omen**:
like as I have *done* **worked**,
so shall it be *done* **worked** unto them:
in exiling, they shall *remove and go into captivity* **exile**.
12 And the *prince* **hierarch** that is among them
shall bear upon his shoulder in the *twilight* **dusk**,
and shall go forth:
they shall dig through the wall to carry out thereby:
he shall cover his face,
so that he see not the *ground* **earth** with his eyes.
13 My net also *will* **shall** I spread upon him,
and he shall be *taken* **apprehended** in my *snare* **lure**:
and I *will* **shall** bring him to *Babylon* **Babel**
to the land of the *Chaldeans* **Kesediym**;
yet shall he not see it, though he shall die there.
14 And I *will scatter* **shall winnow** toward every wind
all that are **round** about him to help him,
and all his bands;
and I *will* **shall** draw out the sword after them.
15 And they shall know that *I am the LORD* **I—Yah Veh**,
when I shall *scatter* **winnow** them
among the *nations* **goyim**,
and disperse them in the *countries* **lands**.
16 But I *will leave a few men* **shall let remain** of them
from the sword,
from the famine, and from the pestilence;
that they may *declare* **scribe**
all their *abominations* **abhorrences**
among the *heathen* **goyim** whither they come;
and they shall know that *I am the LORD* **I—Yah Veh**.
17 Moreover the word of *the LORD* **Yah Veh** came to me,
saying,
18 Son of *man* **humanity**, eat
thy bread with quaking,
and drink thy water with *trembling* **quivering**
and with *carefulness* **concern**;
19 And say unto the people of the land,
Thus saith *the Lord GOD* **Adonay Yah Veh**

of the *inhabitants* **settlers** of *Jerusalem* **Yeru Shalem**,
and of the *land* **soil** of *Israel* **Yisra El**;
They shall eat their bread with *carefulness* **concern**,
and drink their water with astonishment,
that her land may be desolate
from *all that is therein* **the fulness thereof**,
because of the violence
of all them that *dwell* **settle** therein.
20 And the cities that are *inhabited* **settled**
shall be *laid waste* **parched**,
and the land shall be desolate;
and ye shall know that *I am the LORD* **I—Yah Veh**.
21 And the word of *the LORD*
Yah Veh came unto me,
saying,
22 Son of *man* **humanity**,
what is that proverb that ye have
in the *land* **soil** of *Israel* **Yisra El**, saying,
The days are prolonged,
and every vision *faileth* **destructs**?
23 Tell them therefore,
Thus saith *the Lord GOD* **Adonay Yah Veh**;
I *will make* **shall cause** this proverb
to *cease* **shabbathize**,
and they shall no more *use* **proverbialize** it
as a proverb in *Israel* **Yisra El**;
but *say* **word** unto them,
The days *are at hand* **approach**,
and the *effect* **word** of every vision.
24 For there shall be no more any vain vision
nor *flattering* **smoothing** divination
within the house of *Israel* **Yisra El**.
I bring it forth in the dusk
and I bear it on my shoulder in their eyes.
8 And so be the word of Yah Veh to me
in the morning, saying,
9 Son of humanity, say they not to you,
the house of Yisra El—this rebellious house,
What work you?
10 You, say to them, Thus says Adonay Yah Veh:
This burden concerns the hierarch in Yeru Shalem
and all the house of Yisra El among them.
11 Say, I *am* your omen;
as I work, so be it worked to them:
in exiling, they exile:
12 and the hierarch among them
bears on his shoulder in the dusk,
and goes forth:
they dig through the wall to carry out thereby:
he covers his face
so that he sees not the earth with his eyes.
13 and I spread my net on him,
and apprehend him in my lure:
and I bring him to Babel
to the land of the Kesediym;
yet he sees it not, though he dies there:
14 and toward every wind
I winnow all who are all around him to help him
—and all his bands;
and I draw out the sword after them:
15 and they know I—Yah Veh
when I winnow them among the goyim
and disperse them in the lands.
16 And I leave of them remaining from the sword
from the famine and from the pestilence
so that they scribe all their abhorrences
among the goyim where they go;
and they know I—Yah Veh.
17 And so be the word of Yah Veh to me, saying,
18 Son of humanity, eat your bread with quaking
and drink your water with quivering
and with concern
19 and say to the people of the land,
Thus says Adonay Yah Veh
of the settlers of Yeru Shalem,
and of the soil of Yisra El:
They eat their bread with concern
and drink their water with astonishment
that her land be desolate from the fulness thereof,
because of the violence of all who settle therein.
20 And the settled cities parches
and the land desolates;
and you know I—Yah Veh.
21 And so be the word of Yah Veh to me, saying,
22 Son of humanity,
what is that proverb of you in the soil of Yisra El,
saying,
The days prolong; and every vision destructs?
23 So tell them,
Thus says Adonay Yah Veh:
I shabbathize this proverb
that they no more proverbialize it
as a proverb in Yisra El:
but word to them,
Days approach; and the word of every vision:
24 for there *is* neither any more a vain vision
nor smoothing divination within the house of Yisra El.
25 For *I am the LORD* **I—Yah Veh**:
I *will speak* **shall word**,
and the word that I shall *speak* **word**
shall *come to pass* **work**;
it shall be no more *prolonged* **drawn out**:

for in your days, O rebellious house,
will I say **shall I word** the word,
and *will perform* **shall work** it,
saith the Lord GOD **an oracle of Adonay Yah Veh**.
26 Again the word of *the LORD*
Yah Veh came to me,
saying,
27 Son of *man* **humanity**, behold,
they of the house of *Israel* **Yisra El** say,
The vision that he seeth is for many days *to come*,
and he prophesieth of the times that are far off.
28 Therefore say unto them,
Thus saith *the Lord GOD* **Adonay Yah Veh**;
There shall none of my words
be *prolonged* **drawn out** any more,
but the word which I have *spoken* **worded**
shall be *done* **worked**,
saith the Lord GOD **an oracle of Adonay Yah Veh**.

The Word Of Yah Veh Concerning Prophets

13 And the word of *the LORD*
Yah Veh came unto me,
saying,
2 Son of *man* **humanity**,
prophesy against the prophets of *Israel* **Yisra El**
that prophesy,
and say thou unto them
that prophesy out of their own hearts, Hear
ye the word of *the LORD* **Yah Veh**;
3 Thus saith *the Lord GOD* **Adonay Yah Veh**;
Woe **Ho** unto the foolish prophets,
that *follow* **walk after** their own spirit,
and have seen *nothing* **naught**!
4 O *Israel* **Yisra El**,
thy prophets
are like the foxes in the *deserts* **parched areas**.
5 Ye have not *gone up* **ascended**
into the *gaps* **breaches**,
neither *made up* **walled** the *hedge* **wall**
for the house of *Israel* **Yisra El** to stand in the *battle* **war**
in the day of *the LORD* **Yah Veh**.
6 They have seen vanity and
lying divination, saying,
The LORD saith **An oracle of Yah Veh**:
and *the LORD* **Yah Veh** hath not sent them:
and they have *made others to hope* **hoped**
that they *would* **should** confirm the word.
7 Have ye not seen a vain vision,
and have ye not *spoken* **said** a lying divination,
whereas ye say **saying**,
The LORD saith it **An oracle of Yah Veh**;
albeit I have not *spoken* **worded**?
8 Therefore thus saith *the*
Lord GOD **Adonay Yah Veh**;
Because ye have *spoken* **worded** vanity, and seen lies,
therefore, behold, I am against you,
saith the Lord GOD **an oracle of Adonay Yah Veh**.
9 And mine hand shall be upon the prophets
that see **seers of** vanity and *that divine* **diviners of** lies:
they shall not be
in the *assembly* **private counsel** of my people,
neither shall they be *written* **inscribed**
in the *writing* **inscribing** of the house of *Israel* **Yisra El**,
neither shall they enter into the
land **soil** of *Israel* **Yisra El**;
and ye shall know
that I *am the Lord GOD* **Adonay Yah Veh**.
10 Because, even because they
have seduced my people,
saying, *Peace* **Shalom**; and there was no *peace* **shalom**;
and one built up a wall, and, *lo* **behold**,
others daubed it with *untempered morter* **slime**:
11 Say unto them
which daub it with *untempered morter* **slime**,
that it shall fall:
there shall be an overflowing *shower* **downpour**;
and ye, O great hailstones, shall fall;
and a stormy wind shall *rend* **split** it.
12 *Lo* **Behold**, when the wall is fallen,
shall it not be said unto you,
Where is the daubing wherewith ye have daubed it?
13 Therefore thus saith *the*
Lord GOD **Adonay Yah Veh**;
25 For I—Yah Veh:
I word; and the word I word works;
it *is* no more drawn out:
for in your days, O rebellious house,
I word the word, and work it
—an oracle of Adonay Yah Veh.
26 And so be the word of Yah Veh to me, saying,
27 Son of humanity,
behold, the house of Yisra El says,
The vision he sees is for many days,
and he prophesies of the times afar off.
28 So say to them,
Thus says Adonay Yah Veh:
Not one of my words *is* drawn out any more:
and the word I word works
—an oracle of Adonay Yah Veh.

THE WORD OF YAH VEH CONCERNING PROPHETS

13 And so be the word of Yah Veh to me, saying,
2 Son of humanity,
prophesy against the prophets of Yisra El
who prophesy:
and to them who prophesy from their own hearts,
say, Hear the word of Yah Veh;
3 Thus says Adonay Yah Veh:
Ho to the foolish prophets
who walk after their own spirit, and see naught!
4 O Yisra El,
your prophets are as the foxes in the parched areas.
5 You neither ascend into the breaches
nor wall the wall
for the house of Yisra El to stand in the war
in the day of Yah Veh.
6 They see vanity and lying divination, saying,
—An oracle of Yah Veh!
and Yah Veh sent them not:
and they hope to confirm the word.
7 You saw neither a vain vision,
nor a lying divination say, saying,
—An oracle of Yah Veh!
Have I not worded?
8 So thus says Adonay Yah Veh:
Because you word vanity and see lies
—so behold, I *am* against you
—an oracle of Adonay Yah Veh
9 and my hand becomes on the prophets,
seers of vanity and diviners of lies:
they are neither in the private counsel of my people,
nor inscribed in the inscribing of the house of Yisra El,
nor enter they the soil of Yisra El;
and you know I—Adonay Yah Veh.
10 Because, even because they seduce my people,
saying, Shalom; and there *is* no shalom;
and one builds a wall;
and behold, others daub it with slime.
11 Say to them who daub it with slime, It falls!
There becomes an overflowing downpour;
and you, O great hailstones, fall:
and a stormy wind splits:
12 behold, when the wall falls,
say they not to you,
Where is the daubing with which you daubed?
13 So thus says Adonay Yah Veh:
I *will* **shall** even *rend* **split** it with a stormy wind
in my fury;
and there shall be an overflowing *shower* **downpour**
in *mine anger* **my wrath,**
and great hailstones in my fury to
consume **fully finish** it.
14 So *will I break down* **shall I demolish** the wall
that ye have daubed with *untempered morter* **slime,**
and bring it down **that it touch** to the *ground* **earth,**
so that the foundation *thereof*
shall be *discovered* **exposed,** and it shall fall,
and ye shall be *consumed* **finished off**
in the midst *thereof*:
and ye shall know that *I am the LORD* **I—Yah Veh.**
15 Thus *will I accomplish* **shall**
I finish off my *wrath* **fury**
upon the wall,
and upon them
that have daubed it with *untempered morter* **slime,**
and *will* **shall** say unto you,
The wall is *no more* **not,** neither they that daubed it;
16 *To wit,* the prophets of *Israel* **Yisra El**
which prophesy concerning *Jerusalem* **Yeru Shalem,**
and which see **seers of** visions of *peace* **shalom** for her,
and there is no *peace* **shalom,**
saith the Lord GOD **an oracle of Adonay Yah Veh.**
17 Likewise, thou son of *man* **humanity,**
set thy face against the daughters of thy people,
which prophesy out of their own heart;
and prophesy thou against them,
18 And say, Thus saith *the Lord*
GOD **Adonay Yah Veh;**
Woe to the women **Ho to them** that sew pillows
to all armholes **for all the elbow holes of my hands,**
and *make kerchiefs* **work vails**
upon the head of every *stature* **height** to hunt souls!
will **shall** ye hunt the souls of my people,
and *will* **shall** ye *save* **let** the souls *alive* **live**
that come unto you?
19 And *will* **shall** ye *pollute* **profane** me
among my people
for *handfuls* **palmfuls** of barley
and for *pieces* **bits** of bread,
to *slay* **execute** the souls that should not die,
and to *save the souls alive* **enliven**
that should not live,
by your lying to my people that hear *your* lies?
20 Wherefore thus saith *the*
Lord GOD **Adonay Yah Veh;**
Behold, I am against your pillows,
wherewith ye there hunt the souls
to *make them fly* **blossom,**

and I *will tear* **shall rip** them from your arms,
and *will let* **shall send away** the souls *go*,
even the souls that ye hunt to *make them fly* **blossom**.
21 Your *kerchiefs* **vails** also *will I tear* **shall I rip**,
and *deliver* **rescue** my people out of your hand,
and they shall be no more in your hand
to be *hunted* **lured**;
and ye shall know that *I am the LORD* **I—Yah Veh**.
22 Because with *lies* **falsehoods** ye have
made **pained** the heart of the *righteous sad*
just, whom I have not *made sad* **pained**;
and strengthened the hands of the *wicked* **evil**,
that he should not return from his wicked way,
by *promising* **enlivening** him *life*:
23 Therefore ye shall see no more vanity,
nor divine divinations:
for I *will deliver* **shall rescue** my people out of your hand:
and ye shall know that *I am the LORD* **I—Yah Veh**.

THE WORD OF YAH VEH CONCERNING IDOLATROUS ELDERS

14 Then came *certain* **men** of
the elders of *Israel* **Yisra El**
unto me,
and sat *before me* **at my face**.
2 And the word of *the LORD*
Yah Veh came unto me,
saying,
3 Son of *man* **humanity**,
these men have *set up* **ascended** their idols in their heart,
and *put* **gave** the stumblingblock of
their *iniquity* **perversity**
before **at** their face:
should I be enquired of at all by them?
4 Therefore *speak* **word** unto
them, and say unto them,

I split it with a stormy wind in my fury;
and so be it,
an overflowing downpour in my wrath
and great hailstones in my fury to fully finish it off:
14 thus I demolish the wall you daubed with slime
so that it touches to the earth,
so that the foundation exposes and falls
and finishes you off in the midst:
and you know I—Yah Veh.
15 Thus I finish off my fury on the wall
and on them who daubed it with slime
and say to you,
The wall *is* not: they who daubed it *are* not;
16 —the prophets of Yisra El
who prophesy concerning Yeru Shalem
—seers of visions of shalom for her
and there is no shalom
—an oracle of Adonay Yah Veh.
17 And you, son of humanity,
set your face against the daughters of your people
who prophesy from their own heart:
and prophesy against them,
18 and say, Thus says Adonay Yah Veh:
Ho to them
who sew pillows for all the elbow holes of my hands;
and work veils on the head of every height
to hunt souls;
Hunt you the souls of my people?
Leave you the souls to live with you?
19 Yes, you profane me among my people
for palmfuls of barley and for bits of bread
—to execute the souls that ought not die
and to enliven them that ought not live
—by your lying to my people—hearkening to lies.
20 So thus says Adonay Yah Veh;
Behold, I *am* against your pillows,
with which you hunt the souls to blossom;
and I rip them from your arms
and send away the souls
—the souls you hunt to blossom.
21 And I rip your veils
and rescue my people from your hand,
that they become no more in your hand to be lured;
and you know I—Yah Veh.
22 Because with falsehoods
you pain the heart of the just,
whom I pain not;
and strengthen the hands of the evil
that he not return from his wicked way,
by enlivening him:
23 so you neither see more vanity,
nor divine divinations:
for I rescue my people from your hand:
and you know I—Yah Veh.

THE WORD OF YAH VEH CONCERNING IDOLATROUS ELDERS

14 And men of the elders of Yisra El come to me
and sit at my face:
2 and so be the word of Yah Veh to me, saying,
3 Son of humanity,
these men ascend their idols
in their heart,
and give the stumblingblock of their perversity

at their face:
Inquire they at all of me?
4 So word to them, and say to them,
Thus saith *the Lord GOD* **Adonay Yah Veh**;
Every **Man by** man of the house of *Israel* **Yisra El**
that *setteth up* **ascendeth** his idols in his heart,
and *putteth* **setteth**
the stumblingblock of his *iniquity* **perversity**
before **at** his face,
and cometh to the prophet;
I *the LORD will* **Yah Veh shall** answer him that cometh
according to the *multitude* **abundance** of his idols;
5 That I may *take* **apprehend**
the house of *Israel* **Yisra El**
in their own heart,
because they are all estranged from
me through their idols.
6 Therefore say unto the house of *Israel* **Yisra El**,
Thus saith *the Lord GOD* **Adonay Yah Veh**;
Repent **Turn**, *and* turn *yourselves* from your idols;
and turn *away* **from** your faces
from all your *abominations* **abhorrences**.
7 For *every one* **each man** of
the house of *Israel* **Yisra El**,
or of the *stranger* **sojourner**
that sojourneth in *Israel* **Yisra El**,
which separateth himself from **after** me,
and *setteth up* **ascendeth** his idols in his heart,
and *putteth* **setteth**
the stumblingblock of his *iniquity* **perversity**
before **at** his face,
and cometh to a prophet
to enquire of him concerning me;
I *the LORD will* **Yah Veh shall** answer him by myself:
8 And I *will set* **shall give**
my face against that man,
and *will make* **shall desolate** him a sign and a proverb,
and I *will* **shall** cut him off from the midst of my people;
and ye shall know that *I am the LORD* **I—Yah Veh**.
9 And if the prophet be *deceived* **deluded**
when he hath *spoken* **worded** a *thing* **word**,
I *the LORD* **Yah Veh**
have *deceived* **deluded** that prophet,
and I *will stretch out* **shall spread** my hand upon him,
and *will destroy* **shall desolate** him
from the midst of my people *Israel* **Yisra El**.
10 And they shall bear
the punishment of their iniquity **their perversity**:
the *punishment* **perversity** of the prophet
shall be even as the *punishment* **perversity**
of him that *seeketh unto him* **enquires**;
11 That the house of *Israel* **Yisra El**
may *go* **stray** no more *astray* from me,
neither be *polluted* **fouled** any more
with all their *transgressions* **rebellions**;
but that they may be my people,
and I may be their *God* **Elohim**,
saith the Lord GOD **an oracle of Adonay Yah Veh**.
12 The word of *the LORD* **Yah Veh** came again to me,
saying,
13 Son of *man* **humanity**,
when the land sinneth against me
by *trespassing grievously* **treasoning a treason**,
then *will* **shall** I *stretch out* **spread** mine hand upon it,
and *will* **shall** break the *staff* **rod** of the bread *thereof*,
and *will* **shall** send famine upon it,
and *will* **shall** cut off
man **humanity** and *beast* **animal** from it:
14 Though these three men,
Noah **Noach**, *Daniel* **Dani El**, and *Job* **Iyob**,
were in *it* **the midst**,
they should *deliver but* **rescue** their own souls
by their *righteousness* **justness**,
saith the Lord GOD **an oracle of Adonay Yah Veh**.
15 If I cause *noisome beasts* **evil live beings**
to pass through the land,
and they *spoil* **bereave** *it*, so that it be desolate,
that no man may pass through
because **at the face** of the *beasts* **live beings**:
16 Though these three men were in **the midst of** it,
as I live,
saith the Lord GOD **an oracle of Adonay Yah Veh**,
they shall *deliver* **rescue** neither sons nor daughters;
they only shall be *delivered* **rescued**,
but the land shall be desolate.
17 Or *if* I bring a sword upon that land,
Thus says Adonay Yah Veh:
Man by man of the house of Yisra El
who ascends his idols in his heart,
and sets the stumblingblock of his perversity
at his face,
and goes to the prophet;
I Yah Veh give him who goes
an answer according to the abundance of his idols:
5 so that I apprehend the house of Yisra El
in their own heart;
because, through their idols,
they all estrange from me.
6 So say to the house of Yisra El,
Thus says Adonay Yah Veh:

Turn—turn from your idols;
and turn from your faces
—from all your abhorrences:
7 for each man of the house of Yisra El
or of the sojourner who sojourns in Yisra El,
who separates himself from after me,
and ascends his idols in his heart,
and sets the stumblingblock of his perversity
at his face,
and goes to a prophet
to inquire of him concerning me;
I Yah Veh answer him by myself:
8 and I give my face against that man
and desolate him—a sign and a proverb
and I cut him off from midst my people;
and you know I—Yah Veh.
9 And if the prophet, when he is deluded,
and words a word,
I Yah Veh delude that prophet,
and I spread my hand on him,
and desolate him from midst my people Yisra El.
10 And they bear their perversity:
the perversity of the prophet
even as the perversity of him who inquires;
11 that the house of Yisra El
neither stray from me any more
nor foul with all their rebellions any more;
and that they become my people
and I become their Elohim
—an oracle of Adonay Yah Veh.
12 And so be the word of Yah Veh to me, saying,
13 Son of humanity,
when the land sins against me
in treasoning a treason,
then I spread my hand thereon
and break the rod of the bread
and send famine thereon;
and cut off humanity and animal from it:
14 and there are three men in the midst,
—Noach, Dani El, and Iyob
who rescued their own souls by their justness
—an oracle of Adonay Yah Veh.
15 If I pass evil live beings through the land,
and they bereave, and it becomes desolate,
so that no man passes through
at the face of the live beings
16 —these three men in the midst thereof,
I live
—an oracle of Adonay Yah Veh
they rescue neither sons nor daughters;
they only *are* rescued,
and the land becomes desolate.
17 Or, I bring a sword on that land,
and say, Sword, *go* **pass** through the land;
so that I cut off *man* **humanity**
and *beast* **animal** from it:
18 Though these three men were in **the midst of** it,
as I live,
saith the Lord GOD **an oracle of Adonay Yah Veh,**
they shall *deliver* **rescue** neither sons nor daughters,
but they only shall be *delivered themselves* **rescued.**
19 Or *if* I send a pestilence into that land,
and pour out my fury upon it in blood,
to cut off from it *man* **humanity** and *beast* **animal**:
20 Though *Noah* **Noach**, *Daniel*
Dani El, and *Job* **Iyob**
were in **the midst of** it, *as* I live,
saith the Lord GOD **an oracle of Adonay Yah Veh,**
they shall *deliver* **rescue** neither son nor daughter;
they shall *but deliver* **rescue** their own souls
by their *righteousness* **justness.**
21 For thus saith *the Lord GOD* **Adonay Yah Veh;**
How much more
when I send my four *sore* **evil** judgments
upon *Jerusalem* **Yeru Shalem,**
the sword, and the famine,
and the *noisome beast* **evil live being**, and the pestilence,
to cut off from it *man* **humanity** and *beast* **animal**?
22 Yet, behold,
therein shall *be left a remnant* **remain escapees**
that shall be brought forth, *both* sons and daughters:
behold, they shall come forth unto you,
and ye shall see their way and their *doings* **exploits**:
and ye shall *be comforted* **sigh** concerning the evil
that I have brought upon *Jerusalem* **Yeru Shalem,**
even concerning all that I have brought upon it.
23 And they shall *comfort* **sigh over** you,
when ye see their ways and their *doings* **exploits**:
and ye shall know
that I have not *done without cause* **worked gratuitously**
all that I have *done* **worked** in it,
saith the Lord GOD **an oracle of Adonay Yah Veh.**

THE WORD OF YAH VEH
CONCERNING THE CONSUMED VINE

15 And the word of *the LORD*
Yah Veh came unto me,
saying,
2 Son of *man* **humanity,**
what is the vine tree more than any tree,

or than a branch which is
—**a twig** among the trees of the forest?
3 shall *wood* **timber** be taken *thereof*
to *do* **work** any work?
or *will men take a pin of it* **shall a stake be taken**
to hang any *vessel* **instrument** thereon?
4 Behold, it is *cast* **given** into the fire for fuel;
the fire *devoureth* **consumeth** both the ends of it,
and the midst of it is *burned* **scorched.**
Is it meet **Shall it prosper** for *any* work?
5 Behold, when it was *whole* **integrious,**
it *was meet for* **worked** no work:
how much less shall it *be meet* **work** yet *for any* work,
when the fire hath devoured it,
and *it is burned* **scorched?**
6 Therefore thus saith *the*
Lord GOD **Adonay Yah Veh;**
As the vine tree among the trees of the forest,
which I have given to the fire for fuel,
so *will* **shall** I give
the *inhabitants* **settlers** of *Jerusalem* **Yeru Shalem.**
7 And I *will set* **shall give** my face against them;
they shall go out from *one* fire,
and *another* fire shall *devour* **consume** them;
and ye shall know that *I am the LORD* **I—Yah Veh,**
when I set my face against them.
8 And I *will make* **shall give** the land desolate,
because they have
committed **treasoned** a *trespass* **treason,**
saith the Lord GOD **an oracle of Adonay Yah Veh.**

The Word Of Yah Veh Concerning Untrusting Yeru Shalem

16 Again the word of *the LORD*
Yah Veh came unto me,
saying,
2 Son of *man* **humanity,** cause
Jerusalem **Yeru Shalem**
to know her *abominations* **abhorrences,**
3 And say,
and say, Sword, pass through the land;
so that I cut off humanity and animal from it:
18 and these three men in the midst thereof
—I live
—an oracle of Adonay Yah Veh
they rescue neither sons nor daughters,
for they only *are* rescued.
19 Or, I send a pestilence into that land
and pour my fury thereon in blood
—to cut off humanity and animal therefrom:
20 and Noach, Dani El, and Iyob *are* in the midst
—I live
—an oracle of Adonay Yah Veh
they rescue neither son nor daughter;
they rescue their own souls by their justness.
21 For thus says Adonay Yah Veh;
How much more when I send
my four evil judgments on Yeru Shalem
—the sword and the famine
and the evil live being and the pestilence
—to cut it off from humanity and animal?
22 Yet behold,
escapees remain therein
to bring out sons and daughters:
behold, they come to you;
and you see their way and their exploits:
and you sigh concerning the evil
I bring on Yeru Shalem
concerning all I bring thereon:
23 and they sigh over you
when you see their ways and their exploits:
and you know, I work not gratuitously
all that I work therein
—an oracle of Adonay Yah Veh.

The Word Of Yah Veh Concerning The Consumed Vine

15 And so be the word of Yah Veh to me, saying,
2 Son of humanity,
what is the vine tree more than any tree,—a
twig among the trees of the forest?
3 *Is* timber taken to work any work?
Or a stake taken to hang any instrument thereon?
4 Behold, it *is* given into the fire for fuel;
the fire consumes both the ends thereof
and scorches the midst thereof.
Prospers it for work?
5 Behold, in being integrious, it works no work:
How much less work works it
when the fire consumes and scorches?
6 So thus says Adonay Yah Veh:
As I give the vine tree among the trees of the forest
as fire for fuel,
thus I give the settlers of Yeru Shalem:
7 and I give my face against them;
they come from the fire; and fire consumes them:
and you know I—Yah Veh
when I set my face against them:
8 and I give the land desolate, because they treason
a treason—an oracle of Adonay Yah Veh.

THE WORD OF YAH VEH CONCERNING UNTRUSTING YERU SHALEM

16 And so be the word of Yah Veh to me, saying,
2 Son of humanity,
have Yeru Shalem know her abhorrences;
3 and say,
Thus saith *the Lord GOD* **Adonay Yah Veh**
unto *Jerusalem* **Yeru Shalem;**
Thy *birth* **origin** and thy *nativity* **kindred**
is of the land of *Canaan* **Kenaan;**
thy father was an *Amorite* **Emoriy,**
and thy mother an *Hittite* **Hethiy.**
4 And as for thy *nativity* **kindred,**
in the day thou wast *born* **birthed** thy navel was not cut,
neither wast thou *washed* **baptized** in water
to supple thee **for inspection;**
in salting, thou wast not salted *at all,*
nor swaddled at all **in swathing, thou wast not swathed.**
5 None eye pitied thee,
to *do any* **work one** of these unto thee,
to *have* compassion *upon* thee;
but thou wast cast out in the *open* **face of the** field,
to the lothing of thy *person* **soul,**
in the day that thou wast *born* **birthed.**
6 And when I passed by thee,
and saw thee *polluted* **trampled** in thine own blood,
I said unto thee *when thou wast* in thy blood, Live;
yea, I said unto thee *when thou wast* in thy blood, Live.
7 I have *caused* **given** thee
to *multiply* **abound by the myriads**
as the *bud* **sprout** of the field,
and thou hast *increased* **abounded**
and *waxen great* **greatened,**
and thou art come
to *excellent* **an ornament of** ornaments:
thy breasts are fashioned,
and thine hair *is grown* **sprouted,**
whereas thou wast naked and *bare* **nude.**
8 *Now* when I passed by thee,
and *looked upon* **saw** thee,
behold, thy time was the time of love;
and I spread my *skirt* **wing** over thee,
and covered thy nakedness:
yea, I *sware* **oathed** unto thee,
and entered into a covenant with thee,
saith the Lord GOD **an oracle of Adonay Yah Veh,**
and thou becamest mine.
9 Then *washed* **baptized** I thee with water;
yea, I throughly washed away thy blood from thee,
and I anointed thee with oil.
10 I *clothed* **enrobed** thee also
with *broidered work* **embroidery,**
and shod thee with badgers' skin,
and I *girded* **bound** thee *about* with *fine* **white** linen,
and I covered thee with silk.
11 I *decked* **adorned** thee also with ornaments,
and I *put bracelets* **gave clasps** upon thy
hands, and a chain on thy *neck* **throat.**
12 And I *put* **gave** a *jewel* **nosering**
on thy *forehead* **nostrils,**
and earrings in thine ears,
and a *beautiful* crown **of adornment**
upon thine head.
13 Thus wast thou *decked*
adorned with gold and silver;
and thy *raiment* **robe** was of *fine* **white** linen,
and silk, and *broidered work* **embroidery;**
thou didst eat *fine* flour, and honey, and oil:
and thou wast *exceeding beautiful* **mightily beautified,**
and thou didst prosper into a *kingdom* **sovereigndom.**
14 And thy *renown* **name**
went forth among the *heathen* **goyim** for thy beauty:
for it was perfect through my *comeliness* **majesty,**
which I had *put* **set** upon thee,
saith the Lord GOD **an oracle of Adonay Yah Veh.**
15 But thou *didst trust* **confidedst**
in thine own beauty,
and *playedst the harlot* **whored**
because of thy *renown* **name,**
and pouredst out thy *fornications* **whoredoms**
on every one that passed by; his it was.
16 And of thy *garment* **clothes** thou didst take,
and *deckedst* **workedst** thy *high places* **bamahs**
with *divers colours* **patches,**
and *playedst the harlot* **whored** thereupon:
the like things **it** shall not come, neither shall it be so.
17 Thou hast also taken
thy *fair jewels* **instruments of adornment**
Thus says Adonay Yah Veh to Yeru Shalem;
Your origin and your kindred *is* of the land of Kenaan
—your father an Emoriy and your mother a Hethiy:
4 and as for your kindred,
in the day you *were* birthed,
neither *was* your navel cut
nor *were* you baptized in water for inspection;
in salting, you *were* not salted;
in swathing, you *were* not swathed:
5 no eye spared you, to work one of these to you
—to compassion you;

but you *were* cast out in the face of the field,
to the loathing of your soul,
in the day you *were* birthed.
6 And I pass you by
and see you trampled in your own blood;
and I say to you in your blood, Live!
Yes, I say to you in your blood, Live!
7 I give you to abound by the myriads
as the sprout of the field:
and you abound and greaten;
and you come with ornaments of ornaments:
your breasts fashion and your hair sprouts,
and you *are* naked and nude.
8 And I pass you by and see you;
behold, your time *is* a time of loves:
and I spread my wing over you
and cover your nakedness:
yes, I oath to you
and enter a covenant with you
—an oracle of Adonay Yah Veh
and you become mine:
9 and I baptize you with water;
yes, I throughly wash away your blood from you
and I anoint you with oil:
10 and I enrobe you with embroidery
and shod you with skin of badgers;
and I bind you with white linen
and I cover you with silk:
11 and I adorn you with ornaments
and I give clasps on your hands
and a chain on your throat:
12 and I give a nosering on your nostrils
and earrings in your ears
and a crown of adornment on your head:
13 and adorn you with gold and silver;
and your robe *is* of white linen
and silk and embroidery:
you eat flour and honey and oil:
and you *are* mightily beautified
and you prosper into a sovereigndom:
14 and because of your beauty
your name goes forth among the goyim:
for it *is* perfect through my majesty
which I set on you
—an oracle of Adonay Yah Veh.
15 And you confide in your own beauty
and whore because of your name;
and pour your whoredoms
on every one who passes by—to him.
16 And from your clothes, you take of the patches,
and work your bamahs and whore thereon:
such as neither has come, nor becomes.
17 And you take your instruments of adornment
of my gold and of my silver, which I had given thee,
and *madest* **workedst** to thyself images of *men* **males**,
and *didst commit whoredom* **whored** with them,
18 And tookest thy
broidered garment **clothes of embroidery**,
and coveredst them:
and thou hast *set* **given** mine oil and mine incense
before them **at their face**.
19 My meat also which I gave thee,
fine flour, and oil, and honey, *wherewith I fed thee* **to eat**,
thou hast even *set it before them* **given at their face**
for a *sweet savour* **scent of rest**:
and thus it *was* **became**,
saith the Lord GOD **an oracle of Adonay Yah Veh**.
20 Moreover thou hast taken
thy sons and thy daughters,
whom thou hast *borne* **birthed** unto me,
and these hast thou sacrificed
unto them to be *devoured* **eaten**.
Is this of thy whoredoms *a small matter* **trifling**,
21 That thou hast *slain*
slaughtered my *children* **sons**,
and *delivered* **gave** them
to cause them to pass through *the fire* for them?
22 And in all thine *abominations* **abhorrences**
and thy whoredoms
thou hast not remembered the days of thy youth,
when thou wast naked and *bare* **nude**,
and wast *polluted* **trampled** in thy blood.
23 And **so be** it *came to pass*
after all thy *wickedness* **evil**,
(woe, woe unto thee!
saith the Lord GOD **an oracle of Adonay Yah Veh**;)
24 That thou hast also built unto thee
an *eminent place* **arch**,
and hast *made* **worked** thee *an high place* **a ramah**
in every *street* **broadway**.
25 Thou hast built thy *high place* **ramah**
at every head of the way,
and hast made thy beauty to be abhorred,
and hast *opened* **spread** thy feet
to every one that passed by,
and *multiplied* **abounded** thy whoredoms.
26 Thou hast also *committed fornication* **whored**
with the *Egyptians* **sons of Misrayim**
thy *neighbours* **fellow tabernaclers**, great of flesh;
and hast *increased* **abounded** thy whoredoms,

to *provoke* **vex** me *to anger.*
27 Behold,
therefore I have *stretched out* **spread** my hand over thee,
and have diminished thine *ordinary food* **statute**,
and *delivered* **gave** thee
unto the *will* **soul** of them that hate thee,
the daughters of the *Philistines* **Peleshethiym**,
which are ashamed of thy *lewd* way **of intrigue**.
28 Thou hast *played the whore* **whored** also
with the *Assyrians* **sons of Ashshur**,
because thou wast *unsatiable* **not satisfied**;
yea, thou hast *played the harlot* **whored** with them,
and yet couldest not be satisfied.
29 Thou hast *moreover*
multiplied **abounded** thy *fornication* **whoredom**
in the land of *Canaan* **Kenaan** unto *Chaldea* **Kesediym**;
and yet thou wast not satisfied herewith.
30 How weak is thine heart,
saith the Lord GOD **an oracle of Adonay Yah Veh**,
seeing thou *doest* **workest** all these *things*,
the work of *an imperious* **a**
domineering whorish woman;
31 In that thou buildest thine *eminent place* **arch**
in the head of every way,
and *makest thine high place* **workest thy ramah**
in every *street* **broadway**;
and hast not been as *an harlot* **a whore**,
in that thou *scornest hire* **ridiculest payoff**;
32 But as a *one* **woman**
that *commiteth adultery* **adulterizeth**,
which taketh strangers instead of her *husband* **man**!
33 They give *gifts* **payoffs** to all whores:
but thou givest thy *gifts* **payoffs** to all thy lovers,
and hirest them,
that they may come unto thee *on every side* **round about**
for thy whoredom.
of my gold and of my silver, which I give you,
and work images of males to yourself
and whore with them;
18 and take your clothes of embroidery
and cover them:
and you give my oil and my incense at their face:
19 and the meat I give you
—flour and oil and honey to eat,
you even give at their face for a scent of rest:
and so be it,
—an oracle of Adonay Yah Veh.
20 And you take your sons and your daughters,
whom you birthed to me,
and you sacrifice them to be eaten.

Are these trifling—your whoredoms,
21 to slaughter my sons,
and give them to pass through?
22 And in all your abhorrences
and your whoredoms
you remember not the days of your youth,
when you *were* naked and nude,
and *were* trampled in your blood.
23 And so be it, after all your evil,
—woe, woe to you
—an oracle of Adonay Yah Veh
24 you also build an arch to yourself
and work a ramah in every broadway:
25 build your ramah at every head of the way
so that your beauty *is* abhorred;
and spread your feet to every one passing by
and abound your whoredoms.
26 And you whore with the sons of Misrayim
your fellow tabernaclers, great of flesh;
and abound your whoredoms to vex me.
27 Behold, I spread my hand over you
and diminish your statute;
and give you to the soul of them who hate you
—the daughters of the Peleshethiym
who shame over your way of intrigue.
28 And you whore with the sons of Ashshur,
because you *are* not satisfied;
yes, you whore with them,
and yet you *are* not satisfied.
29 You abound your whoredom
in the land of Kenaan to the Kesediym; and
yet you *are* not satisfied with this.
30 How weak your heart
—an oracle of Adonay Yah Veh
seeing you work all these
—the work of a domineering whorish woman;
31 building your arch in the head of every way;
and working your ramah in every broadway: and
not being as a whore who ridicules a payoff;
32 but as a woman who adulterizes,
who takes strangers instead of her man!
33 They give payoffs to all whores:
and you give payoffs to all your lovers,
and hire them to come to you from all around
for your whoredom.
34 And the contrary is in thee
from *other* women in thy whoredoms,
whereas none
followeth thee to commit whoredoms
whoreth after thee:

and in that thou givest a *reward* **payoff**,
and no *reward* **payoff** is given unto thee,
therefore thou art contrary.
35 Wherefore, O *harlot* **whore**,
hear the word of *the LORD* **Yah Veh**:
36 Thus saith *the Lord GOD* **Adonay Yah Veh**;
Because thy *filthiness* **copper** was poured out,
and thy nakedness *discovered* **exposed**
through thy whoredoms with thy lovers,
and with all the idols of thy *abominations* **abhorrences**,
and by the blood of thy *children* **sons**,
which thou didst give unto them;
37 Behold, therefore I *will*
shall gather all thy lovers,
with whom thou hast *taken pleasure* **been pleased**,
and all *them* that thou hast loved,
with all *them* that thou hast hated;
I *will* **shall** even gather them round about against thee,
and *will discover* **shall expose** thy nakedness unto them,
that they may see all thy nakedness.
38 And I *will* **shall** judge thee,
as *women* **adulteresses**
that *break wedlock and shed* **pour** blood
are judged **have judgments**;
and I *will* **shall** give thee blood in fury and jealousy.
39 And I *will* **shall** also give thee into their hand,
and they shall throw down thine *eminent place* **arch**,
and shall *break* **pull** down thy *high places* **ramahs**:
they shall strip thee also of thy clothes,
and shall take thy *fair jewels* **instruments of adornment**,
and leave thee naked and *bare* **nude**.
40 They shall also
bring up **ascend** a *company* **congregation** against thee,
and they shall stone thee with stones,
and *thrust* **section** thee *through* with their swords.
41 And they shall burn thine houses with fire,
and *execute* **work** judgments upon thee
in the *sight* **eyes** of many women:
and I *will* **shall** cause thee
to *cease* **shabbathize** from *playing the harlot* **whoring**,
and thou also shalt give no *hire* **payoff** any more.
42 So *will I make* **shall I rest**
my fury toward thee *to rest*,
and my jealousy shall *depart* **turn** from thee,
and I *will be quiet* **shall rest**,
and *will* **shall** be no more *angry* **vexed**.
43 Because
thou hast not remembered the days of thy youth,
but hast *fretted* me **quiver** in all these *things*;
behold,
therefore I also *will recompense* **shall give** thy way
upon thine head,
saith the Lord GOD **an oracle of Adonay Yah Veh**:
and thou shalt not *commit* **work** this *lewdness* **intrigue**
above all thine *abominations* **abhorrences**.
44 Behold, every one that *useth*
proverbializeth proverbs
shall *use* **proverbialize** this proverb against thee,
saying, As is the mother, so is her daughter.
45 Thou art thy mother's daughter,
that lotheth her *husband* **man** and her *children* **sons**;
and thou art the sister of thy sisters,
which lothed their *husbands* **men**
and their *children* **sons**:
your mother was an *Hittite* **Hethiy**,
and your father an *Amorite* **Emoriy**.
46 And thine *elder* **great** sister
is *Samaria* **Shomeron**,
she and her daughters that *dwell* **settle** at
thy left *hand*: and thy younger sister,
that *dwelleth* **settleth** at thy right *hand*,
is *Sodom* **Sedom** and her daughters.
47 Yet hast thou not walked after their ways,
nor *done* **worked** after their *abominations* **abhorrences**:
but, *as if that were a very little thing* **lothed as a trifling**,
thou wast *corrupted* **ruined** more than they
in all thy ways.
34 And the contrary is in you
of women in your whoredoms;
whereas no one whores after you:
and in that you give a payoff
and no payoff is given to you:
so you are contrary.
35 So, O whore,
hear the word of Yah Veh!
36 Thus says Adonay Yah Veh:
Because your copper *is* poured,
and your nakedness exposed
through your whoredoms with your lovers
and with all the idols of your abhorrences,
and by the blood of your sons,
which you give them;
37 behold,
so I gather all your lovers whom you pleased
and all whom you loved
with all whom you hated
—and I gather them all around against you
and expose your nakedness to them
so that they see all your nakedness.
38 And I judge you with judgments

as adulteresses who pour blood;
and I give you blood and fury and jealousy:
39 and I give you into their hand: and they
throw down your arch and pull down your
ramahs: and they strip you of your clothes
and take your instruments of adornment;
and leave you naked and nude:
40 and they ascend a congregation against you
and stone you with stones
and section you with their swords:
41 and they burn your houses with fire
and work judgments on you in the eyes of many women:
and I shabbathize you from whoring
and that you give a payoff no more.
42 Thus I rest my fury toward you; and turn my
jealousy from you: and I rest, and vex no more.
43 Because you remember not
the days of your youth,
and quiver me in all these:
behold, even I also give your way on your head
—an oracle of Adonay Yah Veh
that you not work this intrigue
above all your abhorrences.
44 Behold, every one who proverbializes proverbs
proverbializes this proverb against you, saying,
As the mother, thus her daughter.
45 You are the daughter of your mother who loathes
her man and her sons; and you are the sister of your
sisters, who loathe their men and their sons:
your mother *is* a Hethiy
and your father an Emoriy:
46 and your great sister is Shomeron
—she and her daughters who settle at your left:
and your younger sister who settles at your right
is Sedom and her daughters.
47 Yet you neither walk after their ways,
nor work after their abhorrences:
but loathe as a trifling:
in all your ways, you *are* ruined more than they.
48 I live
—an oracle of Adonay Yah Veh
Sodom **Sedom** thy sister hath not *done* **worked**,
she nor her daughters,
as thou hast *done* **worked**,
thou and thy daughters.
49 Behold, this was the *iniquity* **perversity**
of thy sister *Sodom* **Sedom**,
pride **pomp**, *fulness* **sufficiency** of bread,
and *abundance* **the serenity** of *idleness* **resting**
was in her and in her daughters,
neither did she strengthen the hand
of the *poor* **humble** and needy.
50 And they *were haughty* **lifted themselves**,
and *committed abomination* **worked abhorrence**
before me **at my face**:
therefore I took **turned** them *away* **aside** as I saw *good.*
51 Neither hath *Samaria* **Shomeron**
committed **sinned** half of thy sins; but
thou hast *multiplied* **abounded**
thine *abominations* **abhorrences** more than they,
and hast justified thy sisters
in all thine *abominations* **abhorrences**
which thou hast *done* **worked**.
52 Thou also, which hast judged thy sisters,
bear thine own shame for thy sins that thou hast
committed more *abominable* **abhorrent** than they:
they are more *righteous* **justified** than thou:
yea, be thou *confounded* **shamed** also,
and bear thy shame,
in that thou hast justified thy sisters.
53 When I shall *bring again* **return** their captivity,
the captivity of *Sodom* **Sedom**
and her daughters,
and the captivity of *Samaria* **Shomeron**
and her daughters,
then will I bring again **and** the captivity of thy captives
in the midst of them:
54 That thou mayest bear thine own shame,
and mayest be confounded
in all that thou hast *done* **worked**,
in that thou *art a comfort unto* **sighest over** them.
55 When thy sisters, *Sodom*
Sedom and her daughters,
shall return to their former estate,
and *Samaria* **Shomeron** and her daughters
shall return to their former estate,
then thou and thy daughters
shall return to your former estate.
56 For thy sister *Sodom* **Sedom**
was not *mentioned* **reported** by thy mouth
in the day of thy *pride* **pomp**,
57 Before thy *wickedness* **evil**
was *discovered* **exposed**,
as at the time of *thy* reproach
of the daughters of *Syria* **Aram**,
and all that are round about her,
the daughters of the *Philistines* **Peleshethiy**,
which despise thee round about.
58 Thou hast borne *thy lewdness* **thine intrigue**

and thine *abominations* **abhorrences**, *saith*
the LORD **an oracle of Yah Veh**.
59 For thus saith *the Lord GOD* **Adonay Yah Veh**;
I *will* **shall** even *deal* **work** with thee
as thou hast *done* **worked**,
which hast despised the oath in breaking the covenant.
60 *Nevertheless*
I *will* **shall** remember my covenant with thee
in the days of thy youth,
and I *will establish* **shall raise** unto thee
an *everlasting* **eternal** covenant.
61 Then thou shalt remember thy ways,
and *be ashamed* **shame**,
when thou shalt *receive* **take** thy sisters,
thine elder **thy greater** and thy younger:
and I *will* **shall** give them unto thee for daughters,
but not by thy covenant.
62 And I *will establish* **shall**
raise my covenant with thee;
and thou shalt know that *I am the LORD* **I—Yah Veh**:
63 That thou mayest remember,
and *be confounded* **shame**,
and never open thy mouth any more
because **at the face** of thy shame,
Sedom your sister
—neither she nor her daughters
work as you work
—you and your daughters.
49 Behold, this *is* the perversity
of your sister Sedom:
pomp, sufficiency of bread,
and the serenity of resting
are in her and in her daughters,
she strengthens not the hand
of the humble and needy:
50 and they lift themselves
and work abhorrence at my face: and
I turn them aside when I see.
51 As for Shomeron:
she sins not the half of your sins;
but you abound your abhorrences more than they
and justify your sisters
in all the abhorrences you work.
52 You also, who judge your sisters,
bear your own shame for your sins
—more abhorrent than theirs:
they are justified more than you:
yes you, shame also and bear your shame
in that you justify your sisters.
53 When I restore their captivity
—the captivity of Sedom and her daughters
and the captivity of Shomeron and her daughters
and the captivity of your captives in their midst:
54 that you bear your own shame and confound
in all you work in that you sigh over them.
55 When your sisters, Sedom and her daughters,
return to their former estate,
and Shomeron and her daughters return
to their former estate, then you and your
daughters return to your former estate.
56 For your mouth reports not your sister Sedom
in the day of your pomp
57 ere your evil *is* exposed
as at the time of reproach of the daughters of Aram
and all those around her,
the daughters of the Peleshethiy,
who despise you all around.
58 You bear your intrigue and your abhorrences
—an oracle of Yah Veh.
59 For thus says Adonay Yah Veh:
I work with you as you work
—who despise the oath to break the covenant.
60 I remember my covenant with you
in the days of your youth;
and I raise to you an eternal covenant.
61 Then you remember your ways and shame
—when you take your sisters
—your greater and your younger:
and I give them to you for daughters,
—and not by your covenant:
62 and I raise my covenant with you;
and you know, I—Yah Veh:
63 so that you remember, and shame;
that you not open your mouth any more
at the face of your shame,
when I am *pacified* **kapared/atoned** toward thee
for all that thou hast *done* **worked**,
saith the Lord GOD **an oracle of Adonay Yah Veh**.

TWO EAGLES AND A VINE

17 And the word of *the LORD* **Yah Veh**
came unto me, saying,
2 Son of *man* **humanity**, *put*
forth **propound** a riddle,
and *speak* **proverbialize** a *parable* **proverb**
unto the house of *Israel* **Yisra El**;
3 And say, Thus saith *the Lord*
GOD **Adonay Yah Veh**;
A great eagle with great wings,
longwinged **long pinioned**, full of *feathers* **plumage**,

which had divers colours **of embroidery**,
came unto Lebanon,
and took the *highest branch* **foliage** of the cedar:
4 He *cropped* **plucked** off
the top of his *young twigs* **sapplings**,
and carried it into a land of *traffick* **merchandise**;
he set it in *a city of merchants* **Kenaan**.
5 He took also of the seed of the land,
and *planted* **gave** it in a fruitful field;
he *placed* **took** it by great waters,
and set it as a willow tree.
6 And it *grew* **sprouted**,
and became a spreading vine of low *stature* **height**,
whose branches *turned toward* **faced** him,
and the roots *thereof* were under him:
so it became a vine, and *brought forth* **worked** branches,
and *shot forth sprigs* **spread foliage**.
7 There was also *another* **one** great eagle
with great wings and *many feathers* **much plumage**:
and, behold,
this vine *did bend* **bent** her roots toward him,
and *shot forth* **spread** her branches toward him,
that he might *water* **moisten** it
by the furrows of her plantation.
8 It was *planted* **transplanted**
in a good *soil* **field** by great waters,
that it might *bring forth* **work** branches,
and that it might bear fruit,
that it might be a *goodly* **mighty** vine.
9 Say thou, Thus saith *the*
Lord GOD **Adonay Yah Veh**;
shall it prosper?
shall he not *pull up* **tear** the roots *thereof*,
and *cut* **lop** off the fruit *thereof*, that it wither?
it shall wither in all the *leaves* **prey** of her *spring* **sprout**,
even without great power or many people
to *pluck* **bear** it up by the roots *thereof*.
10 Yea, behold, being *planted* **transplanted**,
shall it prosper?
in withering, shall it not *utterly* wither,
when the east wind toucheth it?
it shall wither in the furrows *where it grew* **of the sprout**.
11 Moreover
the word of *the LORD* **Yah Veh** came unto me, saying,
12 Say *now* **I beseech,** to the rebellious house,
Know ye not what these *things mean* **be**?
tell *them*, Behold, the *king* **sovereign** of *Babylon* **Babel**
is come to *Jerusalem* **Yeru Shalem**,
and hath taken the *king* **sovereign** *thereof*,
and the *princes* **governors** *thereof*,
and led them with him to *Babylon* **Babel**;
13 And hath taken of the
king's seed **of the kingdom**,
and *made* **cut** a covenant with him,
and hath taken an oath of him:
he hath also taken the mighty of the land:
14 That the *kingdom* might
sovereigndom be *base* **lowly**,
that it might not lift itself *up*,
but that by *keeping* **guarding** of his covenant
it might stand.
15 But he rebelled against him
in sending his *ambassadors* **angels** into *Egypt* **Misrayim**,
that they might give him horses and much people.
shall he prosper?
shall he escape that *doeth* **worketh** such *things*?
or shall he break the covenant,
and be *delivered* **rescued**?
when I kapar/atone for you for all you work
—an oracle of Adonay Yah Veh.

Two Eagles And A Vine

17 So be the word of Yah Veh to me, saying,
2 Son of humanity, propound a riddle,
and proverbialize a proverb
to the house of Yisra El;
3 and say, Thus says Adonay Yah Veh:
A great eagle, great winged,
long pinioned, full of plumage, of embroidery,
comes to Lebanon;
and takes the foliage of the cedar;
4 he plucks off the top of his sapplings
and carries it into a land of merchandise;
he sets it in Kenaan:
5 and he takes of the seed of the land
and gives it in a fruitful field;
he takes it by great waters
and sets it as a willow tree;
6 and it sprouts
and becomes a spreading vine of low height
whose branches face him;
with the roots under him:
and thus it becomes a vine
and works branches and spreads foliage.
7 And there is one great eagle
with great wings and much plumage:
and behold, this vine bends her roots toward him
and spreads her branches toward him
so that he moistens it
by the furrows of her plantation.

8 It *is* transplanted in a good field by great waters,
so as to work branches and to bear fruit
—to become a mighty vine.
9 Say, Thus says Adonay Yah Veh:
It prospers!
Tears he not the roots,
and lops off the fruit, so it withers?
It withers in all the prey of her sprout,
even without great power or many people
to bear it up by the roots.
10 Yes, behold, transplanting, it prospers!
In withering, withers it not
when the east wind touches it?
It withers in the furrows of the sprout.
11 And so be the word of Yah Veh to me, saying,
12 Say, I beseech, to the rebellious house,
Know you not what these *are*?
Tell, Behold,
the sovereign of Babel comes to Yeru Shalem,
and takes the sovereign and the governors
and leads them with him to Babel:
13 and takes of the seed of the kingdom
and cuts a covenant with him
and takes an oath of him:
he also takes the mighty of the land:
14 so that the sovereigndom becomes lowly
—that it not lift itself;
to guard his covenant, so that it stands.
15 And he rebels against him
by sending his angels into Misrayim,
so that they give him horses and much people.
Prospers he?
Escapes he who works such?
Or, breaks he the covenant and escapes?
16 I live
—an oracle of Adonay Yah Veh
surely in the place
where the king dwelleth **of the sovereign**
that *made* **caused** him *king* **to reign,**
whose oath he despised, and whose covenant he brake,
even with him in the midst of *Babylon* **Babel** he shall die.
17 Neither shall *Pharaoh* **Paroh**
with his *mighty army* **great valiant**
and great *company* **congregation**
make **work** for him in the war,
by *casting up* **pouring** mounts,
and building *forts* **battering towers,**
to cut off many *persons* **souls**:
18 Seeing he despised the oath
by breaking the covenant,
when, *lo* **behold,** he had given his hand,
and hath *done* **worked** all these *things*,
he shall not escape.
19 Therefore thus saith *the*
Lord GOD **Adonay Yah Veh**;
As I live, surely mine oath that he hath despised,
and my covenant that he hath broken,
even it *will I recompense* **shall I give** upon his own head.
20 And I *will* **shall** spread my net upon him,
and he shall be *taken* **apprehended** in my *snare* **lure,**
and I *will* **shall** bring him to *Babylon* **Babel,**
and *will* **shall** plead with him there
for his *trespass* **treason**
that he hath *trespassed* **treasoned** against me.
21 And all his fugitives with all his bands
shall fall by the sword,
and they that *remain* **survive**
shall be scattered toward all winds:
and ye shall know
that I *the LORD* **Yah Veh** have *spoken it* **worded.**
22 Thus saith *the Lord GOD* **Adonay Yah Veh**;
I *will* **shall** also take
of the *highest branch* **foliage** of the high cedar,
and *will set* **shall give** it;
I *will crop off* **shall pluck**
from the top of his *young twigs* **sprouts** a tender one,
and *will plant* **shall transplant** it
upon an high mountain and *eminent* **lofty**:
23 In the mountain of the height of *Israel* **Yisra El**
will I plant **shall I transplant** it:
and it shall *bring forth boughs* **bear branches,**
and *bear* **worketh** fruit, and be a *goodly* **mighty** cedar:
and under it
shall *dwell* **tabernacle** all *fowl* **bird** of every wing;
in the shadow of the branches *thereof*
shall they *dwell* **tabernacle.**
24 And all the trees of the field shall know
that I *the LORD* **Yah Veh**
have *brought down* **lowered** the high tree,
have *exalted* **heightened** the low tree,
have *dried up* **withered** the *green* **fresh** tree,
and have *made* **blossomed** the dry tree *to flourish*:
I *the LORD* **Yah Veh**
have *spoken* **worded** and have *done* **worked** it.

THE SINNING SOUL DIES

18 The word of *the LORD* **Yah**
Veh came unto me again,
saying,
2 What mean ye, that ye *use*
proverbialize this proverb

concerning the *land* **soil** of *Israel* **Yisra El**, saying,
The fathers have eaten sour grapes,
and the *children's* **sons'** teeth are *set on edge* **dull**?
3 *As* I live,
saith the Lord GOD **an oracle of Adonay Yah Veh**,
ye **it** shall not *have occasion* **become you** any more
to *use* **proverbialize** this proverb in *Israel* **Yisra El**.
4 Behold, all souls are mine;
as the soul of the father,
so also the soul of the son is mine:
the soul that sinneth, it shall die.

The Just Man Lives

5 But if a man be just,
and *do that which is lawful* **work judgment**
and *right* **justness**,
6 And hath not eaten upon the mountains,
neither hath lifted up his eyes
to the idols of the house of *Israel* **Yisra El**,
in the place of the sovereign who has him reign
—whose oath he despises
and whose covenant he breaks,
dies he not with him midst Babel?
17 Not even Paroh
with his great valiant and great congregation
works for him in the war
by pouring mounds,
and building battering towers to cut off many souls:
18 seeing he despises the oath
by breaking the covenant,
and behold, he gives his hand to work all these;
he escapes not.
19 So thus says Adonay Yah Veh: I live!
My oath that he despises,
and my covenant that he breaks,
give I not on his own head?
20 And I spread my net on him
and apprehend him in my lure;
and I bring him to Babel,
and there I plead with him
for the treason he treasons against me:
21 and all his fugitives with all his bands
fall by the sword;
and scatter them who survive toward all winds:
and you know that I Yah Veh have worded.
22 Thus says Adonay Yah Veh:
I also take of the foliage of the high cedar
and give it;
I pluck a tender one from the top of his sprouts
and transplant it on a high and lofty mountain
23 —transplant it
in the mountain of the height of Yisra El:
and it bears branches and works fruit
and becomes a mighty cedar:
and all birds of every wing tabernacle under it;
in the shadow of the branches they tabernacle:
24 and all the trees of the field
know that I Yah Veh
lower the high tree; heighten the low tree:
wither the fresh tree; and blossom the dry tree:
I Yah Veh word and work it.

The Sinning Soul Dies

18 And so be word of Yah Veh to me, saying,
2 What mean you, that you
proverbialize this proverb
concerning the soil of Yisra El, saying,
The fathers eat sour grapes,
and the teeth of the sons dull?
3 I live!
—an oracle of Adonay Yah Veh
it becomes you no more
to proverbialize this proverb in Yisra El.
4 Behold, all souls *are* mine;
as the soul of the father,
thus also the soul of the son *is* mine:
the soul who sins, dies.

The Just Man Lives

5 And a man, being just,
who works judgment and justness,
6 who:
neither eats on the mountains
nor lifts his eyes to the idols of the house of Yisra El;
neither hath *defiled* **fouled**
his *neighbour's wife* **friend's woman**,
neither hath *come near* **approached**
to a menstruous **an excluded** woman,
7 And hath not oppressed *any* **man**,
but hath restored to the debtor his pledge,
in stripping, hath *spoiled none by violence* **not stripped**,
hath given his bread to the *hungry* **famished**,
and hath covered the naked with *a garment* **clothes**;
8 He that hath not given forth upon usury,
neither hath taken any *increase* **bounty**,
that hath *withdrawn* **turned** his hand
from *iniquity* **wickedness**,
hath *executed true* **worked** judgment **in truth**
between man and man,
9 Hath walked in my statutes,

and hath *kept* **guarded** my judgments,
to *deal truly* **work in truth**;
he is just, **in living,** he shall *surely* live,
saith the Lord GOD **an oracle of Adonay Yah Veh**.

THE TYRANT SON OF A JUST MAN DIES

10 If he *beget* **birth** a son that is a *robber* **tyrant**,
a *shedder* **pourer** of blood,
and that *doeth the like to any one of these things*
worketh these to one of his brothers,
11 And that *doeth* **worketh** not any of those *duties*,
but even hath eaten upon the mountains,
and *defiled* **fouled** his *neighbour's wife* **friend's woman**,
12 Hath oppressed the *poor* **humble** and needy,
in stripping, hath *spoiled by violence* **stripped**,
hath not restored the pledge,
and hath lifted up his eyes to the idols,
hath *committed abomination* **worked abhorrence**,
13 Hath given forth upon usury,
and hath taken *increase* **bounty**:
shall he then live? he shall not live:
he hath *done* **worked**
all these *abominations* **abhorrences**;
in dying, he shall *surely* die;
his blood shall be upon him.

THE JUST SON OF THE UNJUST FATHER LIVES

14 *Now, lo* **behold**, if he *beget* **birth** a son,
that seeth all his father's sins which
he hath *done* **worked**,
and *considereth* **seeth**, and *doeth* **worketh** not such like,
15 That hath not eaten upon the mountains,
neither hath lifted up his eyes
to the idols of the house of *Israel* **Yisra El**,
hath not *defiled* **fouled**
his *neighbour's wife* **friend's woman**,
16 Neither hath oppressed *any* **man**, hath not
withholden the pledge, *neither hath spoiled by*
violence **in stripping, hath not stripped**,
but hath given his bread to the *hungry* **famished**,
and hath covered the naked with *a garment* **clothes**,
17 *That* hath *taken off* **turned** his hand
from the *poor* **humble**,
that hath not *received* **taken** usury nor *increase* **bounty**,
hath *executed* **worked** my judgments,
hath walked in my statutes;
he shall not die for the *iniquity* **perversity** of his father,
in living, he shall *surely* live.

THE UNJUST FATHER OF THE JUST SON DIES

18 *As* for his father,
because **in oppressing,** he *cruelly* oppressed,
spoiled **in stripping, stripped** his brother *by violence*,
and *did* **worked** that which is not good
among his people,
lo **behold**, even he shall die in his *iniquity* **perversity**.
19 Yet say ye, Why?
doth not the son bear the *iniquity*
perversity of the father?
When the son hath *done* **worked**
that which is lawful **judgment** and *right* **justness**,
and hath *kept* **guarded** all my statutes,
and hath *done* **worked** them,
in living, he shall *surely* live.
20 The soul that sinneth, it shall die.
The son shall not bear the *iniquity*
perversity of the father,
neither fouls the woman of his friend
nor approaches an excluded woman;
7 neither oppresses man;
restores the pledge to the debtor;
in stripping, strips not;
gives his bread to the famished;
and covers the naked with clothes;
8 neither gives on usury
nor takes any bounty;
turns his hand from wickedness;
works judgment in truth between man and man;
9 walks in my statutes and guards my judgments
to work in truth;
he is just: in living, he lives
—an oracle of Adonay Yah Veh.

THE TYRANT SON OF A JUST MAN DIES

10 And he births a son
—a tyrant—a pourer of blood
and has a brother work one of these
11 —*though the father* works none of those:
he eats on the mountains;
and fouls the woman of his friend;
12 oppresses the humble and needy;
in stripping, strips and restores not the pledge;
and lifts his eyes to the idols;
works abhorrences;
13 gives forth on usury and takes bounty:
Lives he? He lives not!
In working all these abhorrences,
in dying, he dies!
His blood becomes on him.

The Just Son Of The Unjust Father Lives

14 And behold, he births a son,
who sees all the sins his father worked
who sees, and works not likewise:
15 who neither eats on the mountains
nor lifts his eyes to the idols of the house of Yisra El;
nor fouls the woman of his friend;
16 neither oppresses man nor withholds
the pledge; in stripping, strips not;
gives his bread to the famished;
covers the naked with clothes;
17 turns his hand to the humble;
neither takes usury nor bounty,
works my judgments,
walks in my statutes:
he dies not for the perversity of his father:
in living, he lives.

The Unjust Father Of The Just Son Dies

18 His father,
because in oppressing, he oppresses,
in stripping, strips his brother,
and works what is not good among his people,
behold, even he dies in his perversity.
19 And say you, Why?
Bears not the son the perversity of the father?
The son who works judgment and justness;
guards all my statutes and works them;
in living, he lives.
20 The soul who sins, dies.
Neither the son bears the perversity of the father
neither shall the father bear the
iniquity **perversity** of the son:
the *righteousness* **justness** of the *righteous* **just**
shall be upon him,
and the wickedness of the wicked shall be upon him.

The Wicked Who Turns To Justness Lives

21 But if the wicked *will* **shall** turn from all his sins
that he hath *committed* **worked,**
and *keep* **guard** all my statutes,
and *do that which is lawful* **work judgment**
and *right* **justness,**
in living, he shall *surely* live, he shall not die.
22 All his *transgressions* **rebellions**
that he hath *committed* **worked,**
they shall not be *mentioned* **remembered** unto him:
in his *righteousness* **justness** that he hath *done* **worked**
he shall live.
23 Have I any *pleasure* **desire** at all
that the wicked should die?
saith the Lord GOD **an oracle of Adonay Yah Veh:**
and not that he should return from his ways, and live?
24 But when the *righteous* **just**
turneth away from his *righteousness* **justness,**
and *committeth iniquity* **worketh wickedness,**
and *doeth* **worketh**
according to all the *abominations* **abhorrences**
that the wicked *man doeth* **worketh,**
shall he live?
All his *righteousness* **justness** that he hath *done* **worked**
shall not be *mentioned* **remembered:**
in his *trespass* **treason** that he hath *trespassed* **treasoned,**
and in his sin that he hath sinned, in them shall he die.

The Gage Of Justness

25 Yet ye say,
The way of *the Lord is not equal* **Adonay gaugeth not.**
Hear *now* **I beseech,** O house of *Israel* **Yisra El;**
Is not my way *equal* **gauged?**
are not your ways *unequal* **ungauged?**
26 When *a righteous man* **the just**
turneth away from his *righteousness* **justness,**
and *committeth iniquity* **worketh wickedness,**
and dieth in them;
for his *iniquity* **wickedness** that he hath *done* **worked**
shall he die.
27 Again, when the wicked *man* turneth away
from his wickedness that he hath *committed* **worked,**
and *doeth that which is lawful* **worketh judgment**
and *right* **justness,**
he shall save his soul alive **his soul shall live.**
28 Because he *considereth* **seeth,**
and turneth away from all his *transgressions* **rebellions**
that he hath *committed* **worked,**
in living, he shall *surely* live, he shall not die.
29 Yet saith the house of *Israel* **Yisra El,**
The way of *the Lord* **Adonay** is not *equal* **gauged.**
O house of *Israel* **Yisra El,**
are not my ways *equal* **gauged?**
are not your ways *unequal* **not gauged?**
30 Therefore I *will* **shall** judge you,
O house of *Israel* **Yisra El,**
every *one* **man** according to his ways,
saith the Lord GOD **an oracle of Adonay Yah Veh.**
Repent, and turn *yourselves*
from all your *transgressions* **rebellions;**
so *iniquity* **perversity**
shall not be your *ruin* **stumblingblock.**

31 Cast *away* from you all your
transgressions **rebellions**,
whereby ye have *transgressed* **rebelled**;
and *make* **work** you a new heart and a new spirit:
for why *will* **shall** *ye* die, O house of *Israel* **Yisra El**?
32 For I have no *pleasure* **delight**
in the death of him that dieth,
saith the Lord GOD **an oracle of Adonay Yah Veh**:
wherefore turn *yourselves*, and live ye.

LAMENTATION

19 Moreover *take* **lift** thou *up* a lamentation
for the *princes* **hierarchs** of *Israel* **Yisra El**,
2 And say, What is thy mother? A **roaring** lioness:
she *lay down* **crouched** among lions,
nor the father bears the perversity of the son:
the justness of the just becomes on him,
and the wickedness of the wicked becomes on him.

THE WICKED WHO TURNS TO JUSTNESS LIVES

21 And if the wicked turns
from all his sins he works
and guards all my statutes
and works judgment and justness;
in living, he lives; he dies not:
22 all the rebellions he worked
are not remembered to him:
in the justness he works, he lives.
23 Desire I at all that the wicked die?
—an oracle of Adonay Yah Veh
and not that he return from his ways, and live?
24 But when the just turns from his justness,
and works wickedness,
and works according to all the abhorrences
the wicked work,
lives he?
All the justness he worked *are* not remembered:
in his treason, he treasoned,
and in the sin he sinned, he dies.

THE GAUGE OF JUSTNESS

25 And you say,
The way of Adonay gauges not.
Hear, I beseech, O house of Yisra El;
Is not my way gauged?
are not your ways ungauged?
26 When the just turns from his justness
and works wickedness
and dies in them,
for the wickedness he worked, he dies.
27 And when the wicked
turns from the wickedness he worked,
and works judgment and justness,
his soul lives:
28 because he sees
and turns from all the rebellions he worked;
in living, he lives: he dies not.
29 And the house of Yisra El says,
The way of Adonay is not gauged.
O house of Yisra El, are not my ways gauged?
Are not your ways not gauged?
30 So I judge you, O house of Yisra El,
every man according to his ways
—an oracle of Adonay Yah Veh.
Repent, and turn from all your rebellions;
so that perversity
becomes not your stumblingblock.
31 Cast from you all the rebellions you rebelled;
and work yourself a new heart and a new
spirit: and why die, O house of Yisra El?
32 For I delight not in the death of the dying
—an oracle of Adonay Yah Veh
and you, turn and live.

LAMENTATION

19 And you,
lift a lamentation for the hierarchs of Yisra El,
2 and say, What is your mother?
A roaring lioness!
She crouches among lions,
she *nourished* **greatened** her whelps
among *young lions* **whelps**.
3 And she *brought up* **ascended** one of her whelps:
it became a *young lion* **whelp**,
and it learned to *catch the* prey;
it devoured *men* **humanity**.
4 The *nations* **goyim** also heard of him;
he was *taken* **apprehended** in their pit **of ruin**,
and they brought him with *chains* **hooks**
unto the land of *Egypt* **Misrayim**.
5 *Now* when she saw that she had waited,
and her hope was lost/**destroyed**,
then she took *another* **one** of her whelps,
and *made* **set** him a *young lion* **whelp**.
6 And he went up and down among the lions,
he became a *young lion* **whelp**,
and learned to *catch the* prey,
and devoured *men* **humanity**.

7 And he knew their *desolate*
palaces **abandonments,**
and he *laid waste* **parched** their cities;
and the land was desolate, and the fulness thereof,
by the *noise* **voice** of his roaring.
8 Then the *nations set* **goyim gave** against him
on every side **round about**
from the *provinces* **jurisdictions,**
and spread their net over him:
he was *taken* **apprehended** in their pit **of ruin.**
9 And they *put* **gave** him in
ward **a cage** in *chains* **hooks,**
and brought him to the *king* **sovereign** of *Babylon* **Babel:**
they brought him into *holds* **huntholds,**
that his voice should no more be heard
upon the mountains of *Israel* **Yisra El.**
10 Thy mother is like a vine in thy blood,
planted **transplanted** by the waters:
she *was fruitful* **bore fruit** and *full of branches* **branched**
by reason of many waters.
11 And she had *strong* rods **of strength**
for the *sceptres* **scions** of them that *bare rule* **reigned,**
and her *stature* **height** was *exalted* **heightened**
among the *thick branches* **foliage,**
and she *appeared* **was seen** in her height
with the *multitude* **abundance** of her branches.
12 But she was *plucked up* **uprooted** in fury,
she was cast down to the *ground* **earth,**
and the east wind *dried up* **withered** her fruit:
her *strong* rods **of strength** were
broken **off** and withered;
the fire consumed them.
13 And now she is *planted*
transplanted in the wilderness,
in a *dry* **parched** and thirsty *ground* **earth.**
14 And fire is gone out of a rod of her branches,
which hath *devoured* **consumed** her fruit, so
that she hath no *strong* rod **of strength**
to be a *sceptre* **scion** to *rule* **reign.**
This is a lamentation, and shall be for a lamentation.

THE ABHORRENCES OF YISRA EL

20 And **so be** it *came to pass* in the seventh year,
in the fifth *month,* the tenth *day* of the month,
that *certain* **men** of the elders of *Israel* **Yisra El**
came to enquire of *the LORD* **Yah Veh,**
and sat *before me* **at my face.**
2 Then came the word of *the*
LORD **Yah Veh** unto me,
saying,
3 Son of *man* **humanity,**
speak **word** unto the elders of *Israel* **Yisra El,**
and say unto them,
Thus saith *the Lord GOD* **Adonay Yah Veh;**
Are ye come to enquire of me?
As I live,
saith the Lord GOD **an oracle of Adonay Yah Veh,**
I *will* **shall** not be enquired of by you.
4 *Wilt* **Shalt** thou judge them,
son of *man* **humanity,**
wilt **shalt** thou judge them?
cause them to know
the *abominations* **abhorrences** of their fathers:
5 And say unto them,
Thus saith *the Lord GOD* **Adonay Yah Veh;**
In the day when I chose *Israel* **Yisra El,**
and lifted up mine hand
unto the seed of the house of *Jacob* **Yaaqov,**
she greatens her whelps among whelps:
3 and she ascends one of her whelps:
it becomes a whelp that learns to prey;
it devours humanity:
4 and the goyim hear of him
and apprehend him in their pit of ruin:
and with hooks
they bring him to the land of Misrayim.
5 when she sees, that in
waiting, her hope destructs,
she takes one of her whelps,
and sets him a whelp:
6 and he goes up and down among the lions,
he becomes a whelp and learns to prey
and devours humanity.
7 And he knows their abandonments;
and he parches their cities;
and the land, and the fulness thereof desolates
by the voice of his roaring.
8 And the goyim give against him
from all around the jurisdictions;
and spread their net over him:
and apprehend him in their pit of ruin:
9 and with hooks they give him in a cage,
and bring him to the sovereign of Babel:
they bring him into the huntholds
so that his voice is heard no more
on the mountains of Yisra El.
10 Your mother is as a vine in your blood
transplanted by the waters:
she bears fruit and branches
by reason of many waters:

11 and she has rods of strength
for the scions of them who reign;
and her height heightens among the foliage,
and she is seen in her height
with the abundance of her branches:
12 and she *is* uprooted in fury
—cast down to the earth;
and the east wind withers her fruit:
her rods of strength break and wither;
the fire consumes them:
13 and now she is transplanted in the wilderness
—in a parched and thirsty earth:
14 and fire comes from a rod of her branches,
which consumes her fruit,
so that she has no rod of strength
to become a scion to reign.
This is a lamentation; and becomes for a lamentation.

THE ABHORRENCES OF YISRA EL

20 And so be it, in the seventh year,
in the fifth, in the tenth of the month,
men of the elders of Yisra El
come to enquire of Yah Veh, and sit at my face.
2 And so be the word of Yah Veh to me, saying,
3 Son of humanity,
word to the elders of Yisra El, and say to them,
Thus says Adonay Yah Veh:
Come you to enquire of me?
I live!
—an oracle of Adonay Yah Veh.
I *am* not enquired of by you.
4 Judge you them, son of humanity?
Judge you them?
Have them know the abhorrences of their fathers:
5 and say to them,
Thus says Adonay Yah Veh:
In the day I chose Yisra El,
and lifted my hand
to the seed of the house of Yaaqov,
and made myself known unto them
in the land of *Egypt* **Misrayim**,
when I lifted up mine hand unto them, saying,
I am the LORD **I—Yah Veh** your *God* **Elohim**;
6 In the day that I lifted up mine hand unto them,
to bring them forth of the land of *Egypt* **Misrayim**
into a land that I had *espied* **explored** for them,
flowing with milk and honey,
which is the *glory* **splendour** of all lands:
7 Then said I unto them,
Cast ye away every man the abominations of his eyes,
and *defile* **foul** not yourselves
with the idols of *Egypt* **Misrayim**:
I am the LORD **I—Yah Veh** your *God* **Elohim**.
8 But they rebelled against me,
and *would* **willed to** not hearken unto me:
they did not every man
cast away the abominations of their eyes,
neither did they forsake the idols of *Egypt* **Misrayim**:
then I said, I *will* **shall** pour out my fury upon them,
to *accomplish* **finish off** my *anger* **wrath** against them
in the midst of the land of *Egypt* **Misrayim**.
9 But I *wrought* **worked** for my name's sake,
that it should not be *polluted* **profaned**
before **in the eyes of** the *heathen* **goyim**,
among whom they were,
in whose *sight* **eyes** I made myself known unto them,
in bringing them forth out of the
land of *Egypt* **Misrayim**.
10 Wherefore I caused them to go forth
out of the land of *Egypt* **Misrayim**, and
brought them into the wilderness.
11 And I gave them my statutes,
and *shewed* **caused** them **to know** my judgments,
which if a *man do* **human work**,
he shall even live in them.
12 Moreover also I gave them
my *sabbaths* **shabbaths**,
to be a sign between me and **between** them,
that they might know that *I am the LORD* **I—Yah Veh**
that *sanctify* **hallow** them.
13 But the house of *Israel* **Yisra El**
rebelled against me in the wilderness:
they walked not in my statutes,
and they *despised* **spurned** my judgments,
which if a *man do* **human work**,
he shall even live in them;
and my *sabbaths* **shabbaths**
they *greatly polluted* **mightily profaned**:
then I said,
I *would* **should** pour out my fury upon them
in the wilderness, to consume them.
14 But I *wrought* **worked** for my name's sake, that it
should not be *polluted* **profaned** *before* **in the eyes of** the
heathen **goyim**, in whose *sight* **eyes** I brought them out.
15 Yet also
I lifted up my hand unto them in the wilderness,
that I *would* **should** not bring them into the land
which I had given them,
flowing with milk and honey,
which is the glory of all lands;

16 Because they *despised* **spurned** my judgments,
and walked not in my statutes,
but *polluted* **profaned** my *shabbaths* **shabbaths**:
for their heart went after their idols.
17 Nevertheless
mine eye spared them from *destroying* **ruining** them,
neither did I *make an end* **work a final finish**
of them in the wilderness.
18 But I said unto their *children*
sons in the wilderness,
Walk ye not in the statutes of your fathers,
neither *observe* **guard** their judgments,
nor *defile* **foul** yourselves with their idols:
19 *I am the LORD* **I—Yah Veh** your *God* **Elohim**;
walk in my statutes,
and *keep* **guard** my judgments, and *do* **work** them;
20 And hallow my *sabbaths* **shabbaths**;
and they shall be a sign between me and **between** you,
that ye may know
that *I am the LORD* **I—Yah Veh** your *God* **Elohim**.
and made myself known to them
in the land of Misrayim,
when I lifted my hand to them, saying,
I—Yah Veh your Elohim:
6 the day I lifted my hand to them,
to bring them from the land of Misrayim
to a land I explored for them
—flowing with milk and honey
—the splendor of all lands:
7 and I say to them,
You, every man
cast away the abominations of his eyes
and foul not yourselves with the idols of Misrayim:
I—Yah Veh your Elohim.
8 And they rebel against me
and will to not hearken to me:
they—every man
neither cast away the abominations of their eyes,
nor forsake the idols of Misrayim.
And I say, I pour my fury on them
to finish off my wrath against them
midst the land of Misrayim.
9 And for sake of my name,
I work to not profane it in the eyes of the goyim,
among whom they *are*
in whose eyes I make myself known to them
in bringing them from the land of Misrayim:
10 and I bring them from the land of Misrayim
and bring them into the wilderness:
11 and I give them my statutes
so that they know my judgments
—which, if a human works, he lives in them:
12 and also, I give them my shabbaths,
to become a sign between me and between them
so that they know that I Yah Veh hallow them.
13 And the house of Yisra El
rebels against me in the wilderness:
they walk not in my statutes
and they spurn my judgments
—which, if a human works, he lives in them;
and they mightily profane my shabbaths:
and I say,
I pour my fury on them in the wilderness
to consume them.
14 And for sake of my name,
I worked to not profane in the eyes of the goyim,
in whose eyes I brought them out.
15 And also,
I lifted my hand to them in the wilderness,
to not bring them into the land I gave them
—flowing with milk and honey
—the glory of all lands;
16 because they spurned my judgments
and walked not in my statutes;
and profaned my shabbaths:
for their heart went after their idols:
17 and my eye spared them from ruin:
and I worked not their final finish in the wilderness.
18 But I say to their sons in the wilderness,
Neither walk in the statutes of your fathers
nor guard their judgments
nor foul yourselves with their idols:
19 I—Yah Veh your Elohim!
Walk in my statutes
and guard my judgments and work them;
20 and hallow my shabbaths;
to become a sign between me and between you,
so that you know I—Yah Veh your Elohim.
21 Notwithstanding the *children*
sons rebelled against me:
they walked not in my statutes,
neither *kept* **guarded** my judgments to *do* **work** them,
which if a *man do* **human work**,
he shall even live in them;
they *polluted* **profaned** my *sabbaths* **shabbaths**:
then I said, I *would* **shall** pour out my fury upon them,
to accomplish my *anger* **wrath** against them
in the wilderness.
22 *Nevertheless I withdrew* **I turned** mine hand,

and *wrought* **worked** for my name's sake,
that it should not be *polluted* **profaned**
in the *sight* **eyes** of the *heathen* **goyim**,
in whose *sight* **eyes** I brought them forth.
23 I lifted up mine hand unto
them also in the wilderness,
that I *would* **should** scatter them
among the *heathen* **goyim**,
and *disperse* **winnow** them through the *countries* **lands**;
24 Because they had not *executed*
worked my judgments,
but had despised my statutes,
and had *polluted* **profaned** my *sabbaths* **shabbaths**,
and their eyes were after their fathers' idols.
25 Wherefore I gave them also
statutes that were not good,
and judgments whereby they should not live;
26 And I *polluted* **fouled** them
in their own *gifts* **offerings**,
in that they caused to pass through *the fire*
all that *openeth* **bursteth** the womb,
that I might *make them* desolate **them**,
to the end that
they might know that *I am the LORD* **I—Yah Veh**.
27 Therefore, son of *man* **humanity**,
speak **word** unto the house of *Israel* **Yisra El**,
and say unto them,
Thus saith *the Lord GOD* **Adonay Yah Veh**;
Yet in this your fathers have blasphemed me,
in that they have
committed **treasoned** a *trespass* **treason** against me.
28 For when I had brought them into the land,
for the which I lifted up mine hand to give it to them,
then they saw every high hill, and all the thick trees,
and they *offered* **sacrificed** there their sacrifices,
and there they *presented* **gave**
the *provocation* **vexation** of their *offering* **qorban**:
there also they *made* **set** their *sweet savour* **scent of rest**,
and *poured out* **libated** there
their *drink offerings* **libations**.
29 Then I said unto them,
What is the *high place* **bamah** whereunto ye go?
And the name *thereof* is called Bamah unto this day.

The Idolatry Of The House Of Yisra El

30 Wherefore say unto the house of *Israel* **Yisra El**,
Thus saith *the Lord GOD* **Adonay Yah Veh**;
Are ye *polluted* **fouled**
after the *manner* **way** of your fathers?
and *commit ye whoredom* **whore ye**
after their abominations?
31 For when ye *offer* **bear** your *gifts* **offerings**,
when ye *make* **cause** your sons to pass through the fire,
ye *pollute* **foul** yourselves with all your idols,
even unto this day:
and shall I be enquired of by you,
O house of *Israel* **Yisra El**?
As I live,
saith the Lord GOD **an oracle of Adonay Yah Veh**,
I *will* **shall** not be enquired of by you.
32 And that
which *cometh* **ascendeth** into your *mind* **spirit**
shall not be at all,
that ye say, We *will* **shall** be as the *heathen* **goyim**,
as the families of the *countries* **lands**,
to *serve wood* **minister timber** and stone.

The Judgment And Restoration Of Yisra El

33 *As* I live,
saith the Lord GOD **an oracle of Adonay Yah Veh**,
surely with a *mighty* **strong** hand,
and with a *stretched out* **spread** arm,
and with fury poured out,
will I rule **shall I reign** over you:
21 And the sons rebel against me:
and they neither walk in my statutes
nor guard my judgments to work them
—which, if a human works, he lives in them:
they profane my shabbaths.
And I say, I pour my fury on them
to accomplish my wrath against them
in the wilderness.
22 I turn my hand,
and work for sake of my name,
not to profane in the eyes of the goyim,
in whose eyes I brought them forth.
23 I also—I lift my hand to them in the wilderness
to scatter them among the goyim
and winnow them through the lands
24 because they work not my judgments;
and despise my statutes and profane my shabbaths:
and their eyes *are* after the idols of their fathers.
25 And I also—I give them statutes—not good
and judgments whereby they live not;
26 and I foul them in their own offerings
in that they pass through all who burst the womb
so that I desolate them
so that they know, I—Yah Veh.
27 So, son of humanity,

word to the house of Yisra El, and say to them,
Thus says Adonay Yah Veh:
Yet in this your fathers blasphemed me,
in treasoning a treason against me.
28 And I bring them into the land
for which I lifted my hand to give it to them,
and they see every high hill and all the thick trees;
and there they sacrifice their sacrifices,
and there they give the vexation of their qorban:
there they also set their scent of rest
and there they libate their libations.
29 And I say to them,
What is the bamah to which you go?
—and the name is called Bamah to this day.

THE IDOLATRY OF THE HOUSE OF YISRA EL

30 So say to the house of Yisra El,
Thus says Adonay Yah Veh:
Why foul you after the way of your fathers?
And whore after their abominations?
31 And when you bear your offerings
—when you pass your sons through the fire
you foul yourselves with all your idols to this day:
and *am* I inquired of by you, O house of Yisra El?
—I live
—an oracle of Adonay Yah Veh
I *am* not inquired of by you.
32 And that which ascends into your spirit,
saying, We become as the goyim
—as the families of the lands
to minister timber and stone
surely becomes not.

THE JUDGMENT AND RESTORATION OF YISRA EL

33 I live
—an oracle of Adonay Yah Veh
surely with a strong hand and with a spread arm
and with fury poured out
I reign over you:
34 And I *will* **shall** bring you out from the people,
and *will* **shall** gather you out of the *countries* **lands**
wherein ye are scattered,
with a *mighty* **strong** hand, and with
a *stretched out* **spread** arm,
and with fury poured out.
35 And I *will* **shall** bring you
into the wilderness of the people,
and there *will* **shall** I plead with you face to face.
36 Like as I pleaded with your fathers
in the wilderness of the land of *Egypt* **Misrayim**,
so *will* **shall** I plead with you,
saith the Lord GOD **an oracle of Adonay Yah Veh**.
37 And I *will* **shall** cause you
to pass under the *rod* **scion**,
and I *will* **shall** bring you into the bond of the covenant:
38 And I *will* **shall** purge out
from among you the rebels,
and them that *transgress* **rebel** against me:
I *will* **shall** bring them forth
out of the *country* **land** where they sojourn,
and they shall not enter into the
land **soil** of *Israel* **Yisra El**:
and ye shall know that *I am the LORD* **I—Yah Veh**.
39 As for you, O house of *Israel* **Yisra El**,
thus saith *the Lord GOD* **Adonay Yah Veh**;
Go ye, serve ye every *one* **man** his idols,
and *hereafter also* **afterward**,
if ye *will* **shall** not hearken unto me:
but *pollute* **profane** ye my holy name no more
with your *gifts* **offerings**, and with your idols.
40 For in mine holy mountain,
in the mountain of the height of *Israel* **Yisra El**,
saith the Lord GOD **an oracle of Adonay Yah Veh**,
there shall all the house of *Israel* **Yisra El**,
all of them in the land, serve me:
there *will I accept* **shall I be pleased with** them,
and there *will* **shall** I require your *offerings* **exaltments**,
and the *firstfruits* **firstlings**
of your *oblations* **loads/burdens**,
with all your *holy things* **holies**.
41 I *will accept you* **shall be pleased**
with your *sweet savour* **scent of rest**,
when I bring you out from the people,
and gather you out of the *countries* **lands**
wherein ye have been scattered;
and I *will* **shall** be *sanctified* **hallowed** in you
before **in the eyes of** the *heathen* **goyim**.
42 And ye shall know that *I*
am the LORD **I—Yah Veh**,
when I shall bring you into the *land*
soil of *Israel* **Yisra El**,
into the *country* **land** for the which I lifted up mine hand
to give it to your fathers.
43 And there shall ye remember your ways,
and all your *doings* **exploits**,
wherein ye have been *defiled* **fouled**;
and ye shall lothe yourselves in your own *sight* **face**
for all your evils that ye have *committed* **worked**.
44 And ye shall know that *I*
am the LORD **I—Yah Veh**,

when I have *wrought* **worked** with
you for my name's sake,
not according to your *wicked* **evil** ways,
nor according to your corrupt *doings* **exploits**,
O ye house of *Israel* **Yisra El**,
saith the Lord GOD **an oracle of Adonay Yah Veh**.

THE WORD OF YAH VEH CONCERNING THE SOUTH

45 Moreover
the word of *the LORD* **Yah Veh** came unto me, saying,
46 Son of *man* **humanity**,
set thy face *toward the south* **in the southerly way**,
and drop *thy word toward the south* **southward**,
and prophesy against the forest of the south field;
47 And say to the forest of the south,
Hear the word of *the LORD* **Yah Veh**;
Thus saith *the Lord GOD* **Adonay Yah Veh**;
Behold, I *will* **shall** kindle a fire in thee,
and it shall *devour* **consume** every
green **fresh** tree in thee,
and every dry tree:
the flaming flame shall not be quenched,
and all faces from the south to the north
shall be *burned* **inflamed** *therein*.
48 And all flesh shall see
that I *the LORD* **Yah Veh** have *kindled* **burnt** it:
it shall not be quenched.
34 and I bring you from the people
and gather you from the lands wherein you scatter
with a strong hand and with a spread arm
and pour with fury:
35 and I bring you into the
wilderness of the people,
and there I plead with you face to face:
36 as I pleaded with your fathers
in the wilderness of the land of Misrayim,
thus I plead with you
—an oracle of Adonay Yah Veh
37 and I pass you under the scion
and I bring you into the bond of the covenant:
38 and I purge the rebels from among you,
and they who rebel against me:
I bring them from the land where they sojourn
and they enter not into the soil of Yisra El:
and you know I—Yah Veh.
39 As for you, O house of Yisra El,
thus says Adonay Yah Veh:
You, go every man; serve his idols:
and afterward, if you neither hearken to me,
nor profane my holy name any more
with your offerings and with your idols—
40 for in my holy mountain
—in the mountain of the height of Yisra El
—an oracle of Adonay Yah Veh
there all the house of Yisra El
—all of them in the land, serve me:
there I *am* pleased with them,
and there I require your exaltments,
and the firstlings of your loads/burdens,
with all your holies.
41 I *am* pleased with your scent of rest
when I bring you out from the people;
and gather you from the lands wherein you scattered;
and I *am* hallowed in you in the eyes of the goyim:
42 and you know I—Yah Veh,
when I bring you into the soil of Yisra El,
into the land for which I lifted my hand
to give it to your fathers:
43 and there you remember your ways
and all your exploits wherein you fouled;
and you loathe yourselves in your own face
for all the evils you worked:
44 and you know I—Yah Veh,
when I work with you for sake of my name
—neither according to your evil ways
nor according to your corrupt exploits
O you house of Yisra El
—an oracle of Adonay Yah Veh.

THE WORD OF YAH VEH CONCERNING THE SOUTH

45 And so be the word of Yah Veh to me, saying,
46 Son of humanity,
set your face in the southerly way
and drop southward
and prophesy against the forest of the south field;
47 and say to the forest of the south,
Hear the word of Yah Veh;
Thus says Adonay Yah Veh:
Behold, I kindle a fire in you;
and it consumes every fresh tree in you
and every dry tree:
the flaming flame quenches not;
and all faces from the south to the north inflame:
48 and all flesh sees that I Yah Veh burn it:
it quenches not.
49 Then said I, *Ah Lord GOD*
Aha Adonay Yah Veh!
they say of me,
Doth he not *speak parables* **proverbialize proverbs**?

The Word Of Yah Veh Concerning Yisra El

21 And the word of *the LORD*
Yah Veh came unto me,
saying,
2 Son of *man* **humanity**,
set thy face toward *Jerusalem* **Yeru Shalem**,
and drop *thy word* toward the *holy places* **holies**,
and prophesy against the *land* **soil** of *Israel* **Yisra El**,
3 And say to the *land* **soil** of *Israel* **Yisra El**,
Thus saith *the LORD* **Yah Veh**;
Behold, I am against thee,
and *will* **shall** draw forth my sword out of his sheath,
and *will* **shall** cut off from thee
the *righteous* **just** and the wicked.
4 *Seeing then that I will* **Because I shall**
cut off from thee the *righteous* **just** and the wicked,
therefore shall my sword go forth out of his sheath
against all flesh from the south to the north:
5 That all flesh may know
that I *the LORD* **Yah Veh**
have drawn forth my sword out of his
sheath: it shall not return any more.
6 Sigh therefore, thou son of *man* **humanity**,
with the breaking of thy loins;
and with bitterness sigh *before* **in front of** their eyes.
7 And **so be** it *shall be*, when they say unto thee,
Wherefore sighest thou?
that thou shalt *answer* **say**, For the *tidings* **report**;
because it cometh:
and every heart shall melt,
and all hands shall *be feeble* **slacken**,
and every spirit shall *faint* **dim**,
and all knees shall be *weak* as water:
behold, it cometh, and shall be *brought to pass*,
saith the Lord GOD **an oracle of Adonay Yah Veh**.

The Word Of Yah Veh Concerning The Sword

8 Again the word of *the LORD*
Yah Veh came unto me,
saying,
9 Son of *man* **humanity**, prophesy, and say,
Thus saith *the LORD* **Yah Veh**;
Say, A sword,
a sword is sharpened, and *also furbished* **polished**:
10 It is sharpened to *make a*
sore **slaughter a** slaughter;
it is *furbished* **polished** *that it may glitter* **as lightning**:
should we then *make mirth* **rejoice**?
it *contemneth* **spurneth** the *rod* **scion**
of my son, as every tree.
11 And he hath given it to be *furbished* **polished**,
that it may be *handled* **manipulated by the palm**:
this sword is sharpened, and it is *furbished* **polished**,
to give it into the hand of the *slayer* **slaughterer**.
12 Cry and howl, son of *man* **humanity**:
for **so be** it *shall be* upon my people,
so be it *shall be* upon all the *princes*
hierarchs of *Israel* **Yisra El**:
terrors by reason of **precipitation as to** the sword
shall be upon my people:
smite **slap** therefore upon thy *thigh* **flank**.
13 Because it is *a trial* **to proof**,
and what if *the sword contemn* **it spurneth**
even the *rod* **scion**?
so be it *shall be* no more,
saith the Lord GOD **an oracle of Adonay Yah Veh**.
14 Thou therefore, son of
man **humanity**, prophesy,
and smite *thine hands* **thy palms** together.
and let the sword be doubled the third *time*,
the sword of the *slain* **pierced**:
it is the sword of the great *men* that are *slain* **pierced**,
which entereth into their privy **in their** chambers.
15 I have *set* **given** the *point* **brandish** of the sword
against all their *gates* **portals**,
that their heart may *faint* **melt**,
and their *ruins be multiplied* **stumblingblocks abound**:
ah **Ach**! it is made *bright* **lightning**,
it is wrapped up for the slaughter.
16 *Go thee one way or other,*
either **Unite** on the right *hand, or* **set** on the left,
whithersoever thy face *is set* **congregateth**.
17 I *will* **shall** also smite mine
hands **palms** together,
and I *will* **shall** cause my fury to rest:
I *the LORD* **Yah Veh** have *said it* **worded**.
49 Then I say, Aha, Adonay Yah Veh!
they say of me,
Proverbializes he not proverbs?

The Word Of Yah Veh Concerning Yisra El

21 And so be the word of Yah Veh to me, saying,
2 Son of humanity,
set your face toward Yeru Shalem
and drop toward the holies;
and prophesy against the soil of Yisra El:

3 and say to the soil of Yisra El,
Thus says Yah Veh: Behold, I *am* against you,
and draw my sword from its sheath;
and cut off from you the just and the wicked.
4 Because I cut off from you
the just and the wicked,
so my sword comes from its sheath
against all flesh from the south to the north:
5 so that all flesh knows that I Yah Veh
draw my sword from his sheath:
to return no more:
6 and you, son of humanity,
sigh with the breaking of your loins;
and sigh with bitterness in front of their eyes.
7 And so be it, when they
say to you, Why sigh you?
that you say, Because of the report; for it comes:
and every heart melts and all hands slacken
and every spirit dims and all knees as water:
behold, it comes, and so be it
—an oracle of Adonay Yah Veh.

The Word Of Yah Veh Concerning The Sword

8 And so be the word of Yah Veh to me, saying,
9 Son of humanity, prophesy;
and say, Thus says Yah Veh:
Say, A sword—a sword sharpened and polished
10 —sharpened to slaughter a slaughter
—polished as lightning:
Rejoice we?
It spurns the scion of my son, as every tree.
11 And he gives to polish
—to manipulate by the palm:
this sword, sharpened and polished,
to give into the hand of the slaughterer.
12 Cry and howl, son of humanity:
so be it on my people
—on all the hierarchs of Yisra El:
precipitation as to the sword:
so be it on my people:
so slap on your flank:
13 because it is to proof:
and what if it spurns even the scion?
So be it not
—an oracle of Adonay Yah Veh.
14 And you, son of humanity, prophesy;
and smite your palms together:
and double the sword thrice
—the sword of the pierced
—the sword of the great
who are pierced, in their chambers.
15 I give to brandish the sword
against all their portals;
to melt their heart
and abound their stumblingblocks:
Ach! it is made lightning,
—wrapped for the slaughter.
16 Unite on the right; set on the left:
—wherever your face congregates!
17 And I also—I smite my palms together,
and I rest my fury:
I Yah Veh have worded.
18 The word of *the LORD* **Yah
Veh** came unto me again,
saying,
19 Also, thou son of *man* **humanity**,
appoint **set** thee two ways,
that the sword of the *king* **sovereign** of *Babylon* **Babel**
may come:
both *twain* **two** shall come forth out of one land:
and choose thou a *place* **hand**,
choose **cut** it at the head of the way to the city.
20 *Appoint* **Set** a way,
that the sword may come
to *Rabbath* **Rabbah** of the *Ammonites* **sons of Ammon**,
and to *Judah* **Yah Hudah** in *Jerusalem* **Yeru Shalem**
the *defenced* **fortified**.
21 For the *king* **sovereign** of *Babylon* **Babel**
stood at the *parting* **mother** of the way,
at the head of the two ways, to *use* **divine** divination:
he *made* **sharpened** his arrows *bright*,
he *consulted with images* **asked of teraphim**,
he *looked* **saw** in the liver.
22 At his right *hand*
was the divination for *Jerusalem* **Yeru Shalem**,
to *appoint captains* **set rams**,
to open the mouth in the *slaughter* **murder**,
to lift up the voice with shouting,
to *appoint battering* **set** rams against the *gates* **portals**,
to *cast* **pour** a mount, and to build
a *fort* **battering tower**.
23 And **so be** it *shall be* unto them
as a *false* **vain** divination in their *sight* **eyes**,
to them that have *sworn* **oathed** oaths:
but he *will call to remembrance* **shall remember**
the *iniquity* **perversity**,
that they may be *taken* **apprehended**.
24 Therefore thus saith *the
Lord GOD* **Adonay Yah Veh**;

Because ye have
made **memorialized** your *iniquity* **perversity**
to be remembered,
in that your *transgressions* **rebellions**
are *discovered* **exposed,**
so that in all your *doings* **exploits**
your sins *do appear* **be seen;**
because, *I say,*
that ye *are come to remembrance* **have memorialized,**
ye shall be *taken* **apprehended** with the *hand* **palm.**
25 And thou,
profane wicked *prince* **hierarch** of *Israel* **Yisra El,**
whose day is come,
when *iniquity* **the time of perversity**
have an end **shall be ended,**
26 Thus saith *the Lord GOD* **Adonay Yah Veh;**
Remove **Turn aside** the *diadem* **tiara,**
and *take* **lift** off the crown: this shall not be the same:
exalt **lift** him that is low, and abase him that is high.
27 *I will overturn* **Perverted,** *overturn* **perverted,**
overturn, **perverted!**
I set it: and **so be** it *shall be* no more,
until he come whose *right* **judgment** it is;
and I *will* **shall** give it *him.*
28 And thou, son of *man*
humanity, prophesy and say,
Thus saith *the Lord GOD* **Adonay Yah Veh**
concerning the *Ammonites* **sons of Ammon,**
and concerning their reproach;
even say thou, The sword, the sword is *drawn* **loosed:**
for the slaughter it is *furbished* **polished,**
to consume because of the *glittering* **lightning:**
29 Whiles they see vanity unto thee,
whiles they divine a lie unto thee,
to *bring* **give** thee upon the necks
of them that are *slain* **pierced,**
of the wicked, whose day *is come* **has approached,**
when **the time of** their *iniquity* **perversity**
shall *have an* end.
30 Shall I cause it to return into his sheath?
I *will* **shall** judge thee
in the place where thou wast created,
in the land of thy *nativity* **origin.**
31 And I *will* **shall** pour out mine *indignation* **rage**
upon thee,
I *will blow* **shall puff** against thee
in the fire of my wrath,
18 And so be the word of Yah Veh to me, saying,
19 And you, son of humanity,
set you two ways,
for the sword of the sovereign of Babel to come:
the two both come forth from one land:
and choose a hand,
cut it at the head of the way to the city:
20 set a way for the sword to come
—to Rabbah of the sons of Ammon
and to Yah Hudah in Yeru Shalem, the fortified.
21 For the sovereign of Babel
stands at the mother of the way
—at the head of the two ways, to divine divination:
he sharpens his arrows; he asks of teraphim:
he sees in the liver:
22 at his right *is* the divination for Yeru Shalem:
to set rams,
to open the mouth in the murder,
to lift the voice with shouting,
to set rams against the portals,
to pour a mound
and to build a battering tower.
23 And so be it to them
as a vain divination in their eyes
—to them who oath oaths:
and he remembers the perversity,
to apprehend them.
24 So thus says Adonay Yah Veh:
Because you memorialize your perversity,
in that you expose your rebellions
so that your sins *are* seen in all your exploits:
because you memorialize,
you *are* apprehended by the palm.
25 And you, profane wicked hierarch of Yisra El,
whose day approaches
in the time of perversity of the end.
26 Thus says Adonay Yah Veh:
Turn aside the tiara, and lift off the crown:
this—not this
lift the low; and abase the high:
27 Perverted! Perverted! Perverted!
I set it: and so be it no more,
until he comes whose judgment it is;
and I give it.
28 And you, son of humanity, prophesy and say,
Thus says Adonay Yah Veh
concerning the sons of Ammon
and concerning their reproach:
and say, The sword! Loosen the sword!
—polished for the slaughter
to consume because of the lightning.
29 As they see vanity for you,

as they divine a lie for you,
to give you on the necks of the pierced—
of the wicked whose day approaches, the
time of the perversity of the end.
30 Return it to his sheath.
I judge you in the place you *were* created
—in the land of your origin:
31 and I pour my rage on you;
I puff against you in the fire of my wrath
and *deliver* **give** thee into the hand
of *brutish men* **men of burning,**
and *skilful* **engravers** to *destroy* **ruin.**
32 Thou shalt be for fuel to the fire;
thy blood shall be in the midst of the land;
thou shalt be no more remembered:
for I *the LORD* **Yah Veh** have *spoken it* **worded.**

THE WORD OF YAH VEH CONCERNING THE ABHORRENCES OF YISRA EL

22 Moreover
the word of *the LORD* **Yah Veh** came unto me, saying,
2 *Now,* thou son of *man* **humanity,**
wilt **shalt** thou judge,
wilt **shalt** thou judge the bloody city?
yea, thou shalt *shew* **make known to** her
all her *abominations* **abhorrences.**
3 *Then* say thou,
Thus saith *the Lord GOD* **Adonay Yah Veh,**
The city *sheddeth* **poureth** blood in the midst of it,
that her time may *come* **approach,**
and *maketh* **worketh** idols against herself
to *defile* **foul** herself.
4 Thou *art become guilty* **hast guilted**
in thy blood that thou hast *shed* **poured;**
and hast *defiled* **fouled** thyself
in thine idols which thou hast *made* **worked;**
and thou hast caused thy days to *draw near* **approach,**
and art come *even* unto thy years:
therefore have I *made* **given** thee
a reproach unto the *heathen* **goyim,**
and a *mocking* **ridicule** to all *countries* **lands.**
5 Those that be near, and
those that be far from thee,
shall *mock* **ridicule** thee,
which art infamous **O polluted of name**
and much *vexed* **confused.**
6 Behold, the *princes* **hierarchs** of *Israel* **Yisra El,**
every *one* **man** were in thee
to their power to *shed* **pour** blood.
7 In thee have they *set light by*
abased father and mother:
in the midst of thee
have they *dealt* **worked** by oppression
with the *stranger* **sojourner:**
in thee
have they vexed the *fatherless* **orphan** and the widow.
8 Thou hast despised mine *holy things* **holies,**
and hast profaned my *sabbaths* **shabbaths.**
9 In thee are men,
that carry tales **talebearers** to *shed* **pour** blood:
and in thee
they eat upon the mountains:
in the midst of thee
they *commit lewdness* **work intrigue.**
10 In thee
have they *discovered* **exposed** their fathers' nakedness:
in thee
have they *humbled* **debased** her
that was *set apart* **excluded** for *pollution* **foulness.**
11 And *one* **every man**
hath *committed abomination* **worked abhorrence**
with his *neighbour's wife* **friend's woman;**
and *another* **every man**
hath *lewdly defiled* **intriguingly fouled**
his daughter in law;
and *another* **every man** in thee
hath *humbled* **debased** his sister, his father's daughter.
12 In thee
have they taken *gifts* **bribes** to *shed* **pour** blood;
thou hast taken usury and *increase* **bounty,**
and thou hast greedily gained of thy *neighbours* **friends**
by extortion,
and hast forgotten me,
saith the Lord GOD **an oracle of Adonay Yah Veh.**
13 Behold, therefore I have
smitten *mine hand* **my palm**
at thy *dishonest* **greedy** gain
which thou hast *made* **worked,**
and at thy blood which hath been in the midst of thee.
14 Can thine heart *endure* **stand,**
or can thine hands be strong,
in the days that I shall *deal* **work** with thee?
and give you into the hand
of the men of burning and engravers to ruin:
32 you become fuel for the fire;
your blood midst the land
is remembered no more:
for I Yah Veh word.

THE WORD OF YAH VEH CONCERNING THE ABHORRENCES OF YISRA EL

22 And so be the word of Yah Veh to me, saying,
2 You, son of humanity,
Judge you? Judge you the city of blood? Yes,
have her know all her abhorrences,
3 saying,
Thus says Adonay Yah Veh:
The city pours blood in its midst,
so that her time approaches:
and she works idols against herself to foul herself.
4 You guilt in that you pour blood;
and foul yourself by the idols you work;
and you cause your days to approach,
and approach your years:
so I give you
—a reproach to the goyim
and a ridicule to all lands.
5 The near, and the far from you, *all* ridicule you,
O polluted of name and much confused.
6 Behold, the hierarchs of Yisra El,
every man of you,
according to his arm, pours blood:
7 in you they abase father and mother:
in your midst
they worked oppression with the sojourner:
in you they vex the orphan and the widow.
8 You despise my holies
and you profane my shabbaths:
9 in you are men
—talebearers to pour blood:
and in you
they eat on the mountains:
in your midst they work intrigue:
10 in you
they expose the nakedness of their fathers:
in you
they debase her who was excluded for foulness.
11 And every man works abhorrence
with the woman of his friend:
and every man intriguingly fouls his daughter in law:
and every man in you
debases his sister—the daughter of his father:
12 in you
they take bribes to pour blood:
you take usury and bounty
and you greedily gain of your friends by extortion:
and forget me
—an oracle of Adonay Yah Veh.
13 And behold, I smite my palm
at the greedy gain you work;
and at your blood in your midst.
14 Stands your heart?
Or *are* your hands strong
in the days I work with you?
I *the LORD* **Yah Veh** have *spoken it* **worded**,
and *will do it* **shall work**.
15 And I *will scatter* **shall winnow** thee
among the *heathen* **goyim**,
and disperse thee in the *countries* **lands**,
and *will* **shall** consume thy *filthiness*
foulness out of thee.
16 And thou shalt
take thine inheritance in **profane** thyself
in the *sight* **eyes** of the *heathen* **goyim**,
and thou shalt know that *I am the LORD* **I—Yah Veh**.
17 And the word of *the LORD*
Yah Veh came unto me,
saying,
18 Son of *man* **humanity**,
the house of *Israel* **Yisra El** is to me become dross:
all they are *brass* **copper**, and tin, and iron, and lead,
in the midst of the furnace;
they are *even the dross* **drosses** of silver.
19 Therefore thus saith *the*
Lord GOD **Adonay Yah Veh**;
Because ye are all become dross,
behold, therefore I *will* **shall** gather you
into the midst of *Jerusalem* **Yeru Shalem**.
20 *As* they gather silver, and *brass* **copper**,
and iron, and lead, and tin,
into the midst of the furnace,
to *blow* **puff** the fire upon it, to melt it;
so *will* **shall** I gather you
in *mine anger* **my wrath** and in my fury,
and I *will* **shall** leave you *there*, and melt you.
21 Yea, I *will* **shall** gather you,
and *blow* **puff** upon you in the fire of my wrath,
and ye shall be melted in the midst *thereof*.
22 As silver is melted in the midst of the furnace,
so shall ye be melted in the midst *thereof*;
and ye shall know that I *the LORD* **Yah Veh**
have poured out my fury upon you.
23 And the word of *the LORD*
Yah Veh came unto me,
saying,
24 Son of *man* **humanity**, say unto her,
Thou art the land that is not *cleansed* **purified**,
nor rained upon in the day of *indignation* **rage**.

25 There is a conspiracy of her prophets
in the midst *thereof*,
like a roaring lion *ravening* **tearing** the prey;
they have devoured souls;
they have taken
the *treasure* **wealth** and *precious things* **esteemed**;
they have *made* **abounded** her *many* widows
in the midst *thereof*.
26 Her priests have violated my *law* **torah**,
and have profaned mine *holy things* **holies**:
they have *put no difference* **not separated**
between the holy and profane,
neither have they *shewed difference* **made known**
between the *unclean* **foul** and the *clean* **pure**,
and have *hid* **concealed** their eyes
from my *sabbaths* **shabbaths**,
and I am profaned among them.
27 Her *princes* **governors** in the midst *thereof*
are like wolves *ravening* **tearing** the prey,
to *shed* **pour** blood, *and* to destroy souls,
to *get dishonest* **greedily gain greedy** gain.
28 And her prophets
have daubed them with *untempered morter* **slime**,
seeing **seers of** vanity, and divining lies unto them,
saying, Thus saith *the Lord GOD* **Adonay Yah Veh**,
when *the LORD* **Yah Veh** hath not *spoken* **worded**.
29 The people of the land
have used oppression **in oppressing, have oppressed**,
and *exercised robbery* **in stripping, have stripped**,
and have vexed the *poor* **humble** and needy:
yea, they have oppressed the *stranger* **sojourner**
wrongfully **without judgment**.
30 And I sought for a man among them,
that should *make* **wall** up the *hedge* **wall**,
and stand in the *gap* **breach**
before me **at my face** for the land,
that I should not *destroy* **ruin** it: but I found none.
31 Therefore
have I poured out mine *indignation* **rage** upon them;
I Yah Veh word and work:
15 and I winnow you among the goyim
and disperse you in the lands
and consume your foulness from you:
16 and you profane yourself
in the eyes of the goyim,
and you know I—Yah Veh.
17 And so be the word of Yah Veh to me, saying,
18 Son of humanity,
the house of Yisra El is to me become dross:
all they *are* copper and tin and iron and lead
midst the furnace
—drosses of silver.
19 So thus says Adonay Yah Veh:
Because you all become dross,
behold, so I gather you midst Yeru Shalem:
20 a gathering of silver
and copper and iron and lead and tin
midst the furnace,
to puff the fire thereon, to melt:
thus I gather you in my wrath and in my fury
and I leave you and melt you:
21 yes, I gather you,
and puff on you in the fire of my wrath,
and melt you in the midst:
22 as silver melts midst the furnace,
thus you melt in the midst:
and you know that I Yah Veh
pour my fury on you.
23 And so be the word of Yah Veh to me, saying,
24 Son of humanity, say to her,
You are the land
—neither purified nor rained on in the day of rage
25 —a conspiracy of prophets in her midst:
as a roaring lion tearing the prey, they devour souls:
they take the wealthy and esteemed;
they abound her widows in her midst:
26 her priests violate my torah
and profane my holies:
they neither separate between the holy and profane
nor make known between the foul and the pure;
and conceal their eyes from my shabbaths,
and I am profaned among them.
27 Her governors midst her
are as wolves tearing the prey,
to pour blood; to destroy souls;
to greedily gain greedy gain:
28 and her prophets daub them with slime
—seers of vanity, divining lies to them,
saying, Thus says Adonay Yah Veh:
when Yah Veh words not.
29 The people of the land
in oppressing, oppress;
and in stripping, strip;
and vex the humble and needy:
yes, they oppress the sojourner without judgment.
30 And I seek for a man among them,
to wall up the wall,
and stand in the breach at my face for the land
to not ruin it:
and I find no one:

31 and I pour my rage on them;
I have *consumed* **finished** them **off**
with the fire of my wrath:
their own way
have I *recompensed* **given** upon their heads,
saith the Lord GOD **an oracle of Adonay Yah Veh.**

WHORING IN MISRAYIM

23 The word of *the LORD* **Yah**
Veh came again unto me,
saying,
2 Son of *man* **humanity,**
there were two women, the daughters of one mother:
3 And they *committed whoredoms* **whored**
in *Egypt* **Misrayim;**
they *committed whoredoms* **whored** in their youth:
there were their breasts *pressed* **pierced,**
and there they *bruised* **worked** the *teats* **nipples**
of their virginity.
4 And the names of them were
Aholah **Oholah** the *elder* **greater,**
and *Aholibah* **Oholi Bah** her sister:
and they were mine,
and they *bare* **birthed** sons and daughters.
Thus were their names;
Samaria is Aholah **Shomeron is Oholah,**
and *Jerusalem Aholibah* **Yeru Shalem Oholi Bah.**
5 And *Aholah* **Oholah**
played the harlot when she was mine **whored under me;**
and she *doted on* **panted after** her lovers,
on the *Assyrians* **Ashshuri** her neighbours,
6 Which were *clothed* **enrobed** with blue,
captains **governors** and *rulers* **prefects,**
all of them *desirable young men* **youths of desire,**
horsemen **cavalry** riding upon horses.
7 Thus she *committed* **gave**
her whoredoms with them,
with all them
that were the chosen *men* **sons** of *Assyria* **Ashshur,**
and with all on whom she *doted* **panted after:**
with all their idols she *defiled* **fouled** herself.
8 Neither *left* **forsook** she her whoredoms
brought from *Egypt* **Misrayim:**
for in her youth they lay with her,
and they *bruised* **worked** the *breasts*
nipples of her virginity,
and poured their whoredom upon her.
9 Wherefore
I have *delivered* **given** her into the hand of her lovers,
into the hand of the *Assyrians* **sons of Ashshur,**
upon whom she *doted* **panted after.**
10 These *discovered* **exposed** her nakedness:
they took her sons and her daughters,
and *slew* **slaughtered** her with the sword:
and she became *famous* **a name** among women;
for they had *executed* **worked** judgment upon her.
11 And when her sister *Aholibah*
Oholi Bah saw this,
she was more *corrupt* **ruined**
in her *inordinate love* **panting** than she,
and in her whoredoms
more than her sister in her whoredoms.
12 She *doted upon* **panted after**
the *Assyrians* **sons of Ashshur**
her neighbours, *captains* **governors** and *rulers* **prefects**
clothed **enrobed** most *gorgeously* **splendidly,**
horsemen **cavalry** riding upon horses,
all of them *desirable young men* **youths of desire.**
13 Then I saw that she was *defiled* **fouled,**
that they *took* **be** both one way,
14 And that she increased her whoredoms:
for when she saw
men *pourtrayed* **engraved** upon the wall,
the images of the *Chaldeans* **Kesediym**
pourtrayed **engraved** with vermilion,
15 *Girded* **Girdled** with girdles upon their loins,
exceeding in dyed attire upon their heads,
all of them *princes to look to* **tertiaries in visage,**
after the *manner* **likeness**
of the *Babylonians* **sons of Babel** of *Chaldea* **Kesediym,**
the land of their *nativity* **kindred:**
16 And *as soon as she saw them* **at the sight**
with **of** her eyes,
she *doted upon* **panted after** them,
and sent *messengers* **angels** unto them
into *Chaldea* **Kesediym.**
I finished them off with the fire of my wrath:
I give their own way on their heads
—an oracle of Adonay Yah Veh.

WHORING IN MISRAYIM

23 And so be the word of Yah Veh to me, saying,
2 Son of humanity,
two women are the daughters of one mother,
3 and they whore in Misrayim;
they whore in their youth:
there they pierce their breasts
and there they work the nipples of their virginity:
4 and their names,
Oholah and Oholi Bah her sister:

and they *are* mine; and they birth sons and daughters.
As to their names:
Shomeron is Oholah and Yeru Shalem Oholi Bah.
5 And Oholah whores under me;
and she pants after her lovers
—on the neighboring Ashshuri
6 —governors and prefects enrobed with blue
—all youths of desire
—cavalry riding on horses.
7 Thus she gives her whoredoms with them
—with all the chosen sons of Ashshur
and with all whom she pants after: she
fouls herself with all their idols:
8 she forsakes not her whoredoms from Misrayim:
for in her youth they lie with her
and work the nipples of her virginity
and pour their whoredom on her.
9 So I give her into the hand of her lovers
—into the hand of the sons of Ashshur
whom she pants after.
10 They expose her nakedness:
they take her sons and her daughters
and slaughter her with the sword:
and she becomes a name among women;
and they work judgments on her.
11 And her sister Oholi Bah sees this,
and in her panting, she ruins more than her,
and in her whoredoms
more than her sister in her whoredoms.
12 She pants after the neighboring sons of Ashshur
—governors and prefects enrobed most splendidly,
—cavalry riding on horses
—all youths of desire.
13 Then I see her foul—one way to both;
14 and she increases her whoredoms:
for when she sees men engraved on the wall
—images of the Kesediym engraved with vermilion
15 girdled with girdles on their loins
exceeding in dyed attire on their heads
—all of them tertiaries in visage
after the likeness of the sons of Babel
of Kesediym, the land of their kindred.
16 And at the sight of her eyes,
she pants after them,
and sends angels to them to Kesediym:
exeGeses ready research BIBLE
17 And the *Babylonians* **sons of Babel** came to her
into the bed of love,
and they *defiled* **fouled** her with their whoredom,
and she was *polluted* **fouled** with them,
and her *mind* **soul** was alienated from them.
18 So she *discovered* **exposed** her whoredoms,
and *discovered* **exposed** her nakedness:
then my *mind* **soul** was alienated from her,
like as my *mind* **soul** was alienated from her sister.
19 Yet she *multiplied* **abounded** her whoredoms,
in *calling to remembrance* **remembering**
the days of her youth,
wherein she had *played the harlot* **whored**
in the land of *Egypt* **Misrayim**.
20 For she *doted upon* **panted after**
their *paramours* **concubines**,
whose flesh is as the flesh of *asses* **burros**,
and whose *issue* **flux** is like the *issue* **flux** of horses.
21 Thus thou *calledst to remembrance* **visitest**
the *lewdness* **intrigue** of thy youth,
in *bruising* **working** thy *teats* **nipples**
by the *Egyptians* **Misrayim**
for the *paps* **breasts** of thy youth.
22 Therefore, O *Aholibah* **Oholi Bah**,
thus saith *the Lord GOD* **Adonay Yah Veh**; Behold,
I *will raise up* **shall waken** thy lovers against thee,
from whom thy *mind* **soul** is alienated,
and I *will* **shall** bring them against thee
on every side **round about**;
23 The *Babylonians* **sons of Babel**,
and all the *Chaldeans* **Kesediym**,
Pekod, and Shoa, and Koa,
and all the *Assyrians* **sons of Ashshur** with them:
all of them *desirable young men* **youths of desire**,
captains **governors** and *rulers* **prefects**,
great *lords* **tertiaries** and *renowned* **called out**,
all of them riding upon horses.
24 And they shall come against thee
with *chariots* **weapons**, *wagons* **chariots**, and wheels,
and with *an assembly* **a congregation** of people,
which shall set against thee
buckler **shield** and *shield* **buckler** and helmet
round about:
and I *will set* **shall give** judgment
before them **at their face**,
and they shall judge thee according to their judgments.
25 And I *will set* **shall give**
my jealousy against thee,
and they shall *deal furiously* **work** with thee **in fury**:
they shall *take away* **turn aside**
thy *nose* **nostrils** and thine ears;
and thy *remnant* **posterity** shall fall by the sword:
they shall take thy sons and thy daughters;
and thy *residue* **posterity**

shall be *devoured* **consumed** by the fire.
26 They shall also strip thee out of thy clothes,
and take away thy *fair jewels*
instruments of adornment.
27 Thus *will* **shall** I make thy *lewdness* **intrigue**
to *cease* **shabbathize** from thee,
and thy whoredom *brought*
from the land of *Egypt* **Misrayim**:
so that thou shalt not lift up thine eyes unto them,
nor remember *Egypt* **Misrayim** any more.
28 For thus saith *the Lord GOD* **Adonay Yah Veh**;
Behold, I *will deliver* **shall give** thee
into the hand *of* them whom thou hatest,
into the hand of them
from whom thy *mind* **soul** is alienated:
29 And they shall *deal* **work**
with thee *hatefully* **in hatred**,
and shall take away all thy labour,
and shall *leave* **forsake** thee naked and *bare* **nude**:
and the nakedness of thy whoredoms
shall be *discovered* **exposed**,
both thy *lewdness* **intrigue** and thy whoredoms.
30 I *will do* **shall work** these *things* unto thee,
because thou hast *gone a whoring* **whored**
after the *heathen* **goyim**,
and because thou art *polluted* **fouled**
with their idols.
31 Thou hast walked in the way of thy sister;
therefore *will* **shall** I give her cup into thine hand.
17 and the sons of Babel come to her
into the bed of love,
and they foul her with their whoredom
and she is fouled by them;
and her soul alienates from them:
18 and she exposes her whoredoms
and exposes her nakedness:
and I alienate my soul from her
as I alienated my soul from her sister:
19 and she abounds her whoredoms
in remembering the days of her youth
wherein she whored in the land of Misrayim:
20 and she pants after their concubines—
whose flesh is as the flesh of burros and
whose flux is as the flux of horses.
21 You visit the intrigue of your youth,
in working your nipples by the Misrayim
for the breasts of your youth.
22 So, O Oholi Bah,
thus says Adonay Yah Veh:
Behold, I waken your lovers against you,
from whom you alienate your soul;
and I bring them against you all around
23 —the sons of Babel and all the Kesediym;
Pekod and Shoa and Koa
with all the sons of Ashshur
—all youths of desire, governors and prefects,
great tertiaries and called out
—all riding on horses:
24 and they come against you with weapons
chariots and wheels;
and with a congregation of people,
who set shield and buckler and helmet
against you all around:
and I give judgment at their face
to judge you according to their judgments:
25 and I give my jealousy against you
that they work with you in fury:
they turn aside your nostrils and your ears
and your posterity falls by the sword:
they take your sons and your daughters
and consume your posterity by the fire:
26 and they strip your clothes
and take your instruments of adornment:
27 thus I shabbathize your whoredom from you
and your intrigue from the land of Misrayim:
so that you neither lift your eyes to them
nor remember Misrayim any more.
28 For thus says Adonay Yah Veh:
Behold, I give you into the hand of whom you hate
—into the hand from whom your soul alienates:
29 and they work with you in hatred
and take away all your labor
and forsake you naked and nude:
and they expose the nakedness of your whoredoms
—both your intrigue and your whoredoms.
30 I work these to you
because you whore after the goyim;
because you foul with their idols:
31 you walk in the way of your sister;
and I give her cup into your hand.
32 Thus saith *the Lord GOD* **Adonay Yah Veh**;
Thou shalt drink of thy sister's cup deep and large:
thou shalt be *laughed to scorn* **ridiculed**
and *had in derision* **derided**;
it containeth *much* **an increase**.
33 Thou shalt be filled
with *drunkenness* **intoxication** and *sorrow* **grief**,
with the cup of *astonishment* **desolation** and desolation,
with the cup of thy sister *Samaria* **Shomeron**.

34 Thou shalt even drink it and suck it out,
and thou shalt *break* **craunch** the *sherds* **potsherds**
thereof,
and *pluck off* **tear** thine own breasts:
for I have *spoken it* **worded**,
saith the Lord GOD **an oracle of Adonay Yah Veh**.
35 Therefore thus saith *the*
Lord GOD **Adonay Yah Veh**;
Because thou hast forgotten me,
and cast me behind thy back,
therefore bear thou also
thy *lewdness* **intrigue** and thy whoredoms.
36 *The LORD* **Yah Veh** said *moreover* unto me;
Son of *man* **humanity**,
wilt **shalt** thou judge
Aholah **Oholah** and *Aholibah* **Oholi Bah**?
yea,
declare **tell** unto them their *abominations* **abhorrences**;
37 That they have *committed adultery* **adulterized**,
and blood is in their hands,
and with their idols
have they *committed adultery* **adulterized**,
and have also caused their sons,
whom they *bare* **birthed** unto me,
to pass for them through *the fire,*
to devour them **for fuel**.
38 Moreover this they have *done* **worked** unto me:
they have *defiled* **fouled** my *sanctuary* **holies**
in the same day,
and have profaned my *sabbaths* **shabbaths**.
39 For when they had
slain **slaughtered** their *children* **sons** to their idols,
then they came the same day
into my *sanctuary* **holies** to profane it;
and, *lo* **behold**,
thus have they *done* **worked** in the midst of mine house.
40 And *furthermore* **also**,
that ye have sent for men to come from far,
unto whom *a messenger* **an angel** was sent;
and, *lo* **behold**, they came:
for whom thou *didst wash* **baptizedst** thyself,
paintedst thy eyes,
and *deckedst* **adornedst** thyself with ornaments,
41 And satest upon a stately bed,
and a table *prepared before it* **arranged at its face**,
whereupon thou hast set mine incense and mine oil.
42 And a voice of a **serene** multitude *being at ease*
was with her:
and with the men
of the *common sort* **abundance of humanity**
were brought *Sabeans* **Sabaiym/carousers**
from the wilderness,
which *put bracelets* **gave clasps** upon their hands,
and *beautiful* crowns **of adornment** upon their heads.
43 Then said I unto *her* **the one**
that was *old* **worn out** in adulteries,
Will **Shall** they now *commit whoredoms* **whore** with her,
and she with them?
44 Yet they went in unto her,
as they go in unto a woman
that *playeth the harlot* **whoreth**:
so went they in
unto *Aholah* **Oholah** and unto *Aholibah* **Oholi Bah**,
the *lewd* **intriguing** women.
45 And the *righteous* **just** men,
they shall judge them
after the *manner* **judgment** of adulteresses,
and after the *manner* **judgment**
of women that *shed* **pour** blood;
because they are adulteresses,
and blood is in their hands.
46 For thus saith *the Lord GOD* **Adonay Yah Veh**;

32 Thus says Adonay Yah Veh:
Drink of the cup of your sister
—deep and large:
you are ridiculed and derided
—containing an increase
33 —filled with intoxication and grief
with the cup of desolation
and desolation with the cup of your sister Shomeron.
34 Drink and suck out;
craunch the potsherds and tear your own breasts:
for I have worded
—an oracle of Adonay Yah Veh.
35 So thus says Adonay Yah Veh:
Because you forget me
and cast me behind your back,
even thus
you also bear your intrigue and your whoredoms.
36 Yah Veh says to me;
Son of humanity,
Judge you Oholah and Oholi Bah?
Tell them their abhorrences:
37 that they adulterize and blood is in their hands;
and they adulterize with their idols;
and their sons whom they birthed to me
they also pass through for fuel.
38 Even yet, they work this to me:
they foul my holies
the same day they profane my shabbaths:

39 they slaughter their sons to their idols;
and the same day
they come into my holies to profane:
and behold, thus they work midst my house.
40 And also,
that you sent for men coming from afar,
to whom you sent an angel;
and behold, they come
—they, for whom you baptized yourself,
painted your eyes,
and adorned yourself with ornaments;
41 and you sit on a stately bed,
and arrange a table at its face,
whereon you set my incense and my oil.
42 And with her, a voice of a serene multitude:
and with the men of the abundance of humanity,
bring Sabaiym/carousers from the wilderness
who give clasps on their hands
and crowns of adornment on their heads.
43 And I say to the one worn out in adulteries,
Whore they now with her? And she with them?
44 And they go in to her,
as they go in to a woman who whores:
thus they go in to Oholah and to Oholi Bah
the intriguing women:
45 and the just men judge them
after the judgment of adulteresses
and after the judgment of women who pour blood
—because they are adulteresses
and blood is in their hands.
46 For thus says Adonay Yah Veh:
I *will bring up* **shall ascend** a *company* **congregation**
upon them,
and *will* **shall** give them to be removed
and *spoiled* **for plunder**.
47 And the *company* **congregation**
shall stone them with stones,
and *dispatch* **cut** them with their swords;
they shall *slay* **slaughter** their sons and their daughters,
and burn up their houses with fire.
48 Thus *will* **shall** I cause *lewdness* **intrigue**
to *cease* **shabbathize** out of the land,
that all women may be taught
not to *do* **work** after your *lewdness* **intrigue**.
49 And they shall
recompense **give** your *lewdness* **intrigue** upon you,
and ye shall bear the sins of your idols:
and ye shall know
that *I am the Lord GOD* **I—Adonay Yah Veh**.

THE CALDRON

24 Again in the ninth year,
in the tenth month, in the tenth *day* of the month,
the word of *the LORD* **Yah Veh** came unto me, saying,
2 Son of *man* **humanity**,
write **inscribe** thee the name of the day,
even of this same day:
the *king* **sovereign** of *Babylon* **Babel** *set* **propped** himself
against *Jerusalem* **Yeru Shalem** this same day.
3 And *utter* **proverbialize** a *parable* **proverb**
unto the rebellious house, and say unto them,
Thus saith *the Lord GOD* **Adonay Yah Veh**;
Set on a *pot* **caldron**, set it on,
and also pour water into it:
4 Gather the *pieces* **members** *thereof* into it,
even every good *piece* **member**,
the *thigh* **flank**, and the shoulder;
fill it with the choice bones.
5 Take the choice of the flock,
and *burn* **whirl** also the bones under it,
and *make it* **in boiling,** boil **it** well,
and let them seethe the bones *of it therein* **in its midst**.
6 Wherefore thus saith *the
Lord GOD* **Adonay Yah Veh**;
Woe to the bloody city,
to the *pot* **caldron** whose scum is therein,
and whose scum is not gone out of it!
bring it out *piece* **member** by *piece* **member**;
let no *lot* **pebble** fall upon it.
7 For her blood is in the midst of her;
she set it upon the *top* **clearing** of a rock;
she poured it not upon the *ground* **earth**,
to cover it with dust;
8 That it might cause fury to *come up* **ascend**
to *take vengeance* **avenge avengement**;
I have *set* **given** her blood
upon the *top* **clearing** of a rock,
that it should not be covered.
9 Therefore thus saith *the
Lord GOD* **Adonay Yah Veh**;
Woe to the bloody city!
I *will* **shall** even *make* **greaten** the pile for fire *great*.
10 *Heap on wood* **Abound the timber**,
kindle **inflame** the fire,
consume the flesh, and **in spicing,** spice it *well*,
and let the bones be *burned* **scorched**.
11 Then *set* **stand** it empty upon the coals *thereof*,
that the *brass* **copper** of it may be hot,
and may *burn* **scorch**,

and that the *filthiness* **foulness** of it
may be molten in *it* **its midst**,
that the scum of it may be consumed.
12 She hath wearied herself with *lies* **mischiefs**,
and her great scum went not forth out of
her: her scum shall be in the fire.
13 In thy *filthiness* **foulness** is *lewdness* **intrigue**:
because I have *purged* **purified** thee,
and thou wast not *purged* **purified**,
thou shalt not be *purged* **purified**
from thy *filthiness* **foulness** any more,
till I have caused my fury to rest upon thee.
14 I *the LORD* **Yah Veh** have *spoken it* **worded**:
so be it *shall come to pass*, and I *will do* **shall work** it;
I ascend a congregation on them,
and give them to be removed and for plunder.
47 And the congregation stones them with stones
and cuts them with their swords;
they slaughter their sons and their daughters,
and burn their houses with fire.
48 Thus I shabbathize intrigue from the land,
to teach all women to not work after your intrigue.
49 And they give your intrigue on you, and you bear the
sins of your idols: and you know I—Adonay Yah Veh.

THE CALDRON

24 And so be the word of Yah Veh to me,
in the ninth year, in the tenth month,
in the tenth of the month, saying,
2 Son of humanity,
inscribe the name of the day—this same day:
the sovereign of Babel props himself
against Yeru Shalem—this same day:
3 and proverbialize a proverb
to the rebellious house:
and say to them, Thus says Adonay Yah Veh:
Set a caldron;
set, and also pour water into it:
4 gather the members into
it—every good member
—the flank and the shoulder;
fill it with the choice bones:
5 take the choice of the flock
and also whirl the bones under it;
and in boiling, boil it well;
and seethe the bones midst it.
6 So, thus says Adonay Yah Veh:
Woe to the city of blood
—to the caldron whose scum is therein,
and whose scum comes not out of it:
bring it out member by member;
and that no pebble fall thereon.
7 For her blood is in her midst;
she sets it on the clearing of a rock;
she pours it not on the earth,
to cover it with dust;
8 —to ascend fury—to avenge avengement;
I give her blood on the clearing of a rock
—not covered.
9 So thus says Adonay Yah Veh:
Woe to the city of blood!
I—I greaten the pile for fire.
10 Abound the timber! Inflame the fire!
Consume the flesh! And in spicing, spice!
And scorch the bones:
11 and stand it empty on the coals,
that heat and scorch the copper thereof
so that the foulness thereof melts in the midst
—to consume the scum thereof.
12 She wearies herself with mischiefs
and her great scum goes not from her:
her scum *is* in the fire.
13 In your foulness *is* intrigue:
because I purify you; and you purify not:
you purify not from your foulness any more
until I rest my fury on you.
14 I Yah Veh have worded:
so be it; and I work it:
I *will* **shall** not *go back* **release**, neither *will* **shall** I spare,
neither *will* **shall** I *repent* **sigh**;
according to thy ways,
and according to thy *doings* **exploits**,
shall they judge thee,
saith the Lord GOD **an oracle of Adonay Yah Veh**.

THE DEATH OF THE WOMAN OF YECHEZQ EL

15 Also the word of *the LORD*
Yah Veh came unto me,
saying,
16 Son of *man* **humanity**, behold,
I take away from thee the desire of thine eyes
with a *stroke* **plague**:
yet neither shalt thou *mourn* **chop** nor weep,
neither shall thy tears run *down*.
17 *Forbear to cry* **Hush thy shrieking**,
make **work** no mourning for the dead,
bind *the tire of thine head* **thy tiara** upon thee,
and *put on* **set** thy shoes upon thy feet,
and cover not thy *lips* **upper lip**,
and eat not the bread of men.

18 So I *spake* **worded** unto
the people in the morning:
and at even my *wife* **woman** died;
and I *did* **worked** in the morning
as I was *commanded* **misvahed**.
19 And the people said unto me,
Wilt **Shalt** thou not tell us what these *things* are to us,
that thou *doest* **workest** *so*?
20 Then I *answered* **said to** them,
The word of *the LORD* **Yah Veh** came unto me, saying,
21 Speak unto the house of *Israel* **Yisra El**,
Thus saith *the Lord GOD* **Adonay Yah Veh**;
Behold, I *will* **shall** profane my *sanctuary* **holies**,
the *excellency* **pomp** of your strength,
the desire of your eyes,
and that which your soul *pitieth* **sympathizeth**;
and your sons and your daughters
whom ye have *left* **forsaken** shall fall by the sword.
22 And ye shall *do* **work** as I have *done* **worked**:
ye shall not cover your *lips* **upper lip**,
nor eat the bread of men.
23 And your *tires* **tiaras** shall be upon your heads,
and your shoes upon your feet:
ye shall not *mourn* **chop** nor weep;
but ye shall *pine away* **vanish**
for your *iniquities* **perversities**,
and *mourn one* **growl man** toward *another* **brother**.
24 Thus *Ezekiel* **Yechezq El** is
unto you *a sign* **an omen**:
according to all that he hath *done* **worked,**
shall ye *do* **work**:
and when this cometh,
ye shall know that *I am the Lord*
GOD **I—Adonay Yah Veh**.
25 Also, thou son of *man* **humanity**,
shall it not be in the day when I take from them
their *strength* **stronghold**,
the joy of their *glory* **adornment**, the desire of their eyes,
and *that whereupon they set*
the burden of their *minds* **souls**,
their sons and their daughters,
26 That *he that escapeth* **the escapees** in that day
shall come unto thee,
to cause thee to hear it with *thine* ears?
27 In that day shall thy mouth be opened
to *him which is escaped* **the escapees**,
and thou shalt *speak* **word**,
and be no more *dumb* **muted**:
and thou shalt be *a sign* **an omen** unto them;
and they shall know that *I am the LORD* **I—Yah Veh**.

THE WORD OF YAH VEH CONCERNING THE SONS OF AMMON

25 The word of *the LORD* **Yah Veh**
came again unto me, saying,
2 Son of *man* **humanity**,
set thy face against the *Ammonites* **sons of Ammon**,
and prophesy against them;
3 And say unto the *Ammonites* **sons of Ammon**,
Hear the word of *the Lord GOD* **Adonay Yah Veh**;
Thus saith *the Lord GOD* **Adonay Yah Veh**;
Because *thou saidst* **of thy saying**, Aha,
against my *sanctuary* **holies**, when it was profaned;
I neither release nor spare nor sigh:
according to your ways
and according to your exploits
they judge you
—an oracle of Adonay Yah Veh.

THE DEATH OF THE WOMAN OF YECHEZQ EL

15 And so be the word of Yah Veh to me, saying,
16 Son of humanity, behold,
I take the desire of your eyes away from you
with a plague:
yet you neither chop nor weep nor your tears run.
17 Hush your shrieking;
work no mourning for the dead;
bind your tiara on you
and set your shoes on your feet;
and neither cover your upper lip
nor eat the bread of men.
18 Thus I word to the people in the morning:
and at even my woman dies;
and in the morning I work as I *am* misvahed.
19 And the people say to me,
Tell you not us what these which you work
are to us?
20 And I say to them,
And so be the word of Yah Veh to me, saying,
21 Speak to the house of Yisra El, Thus says
Adonay Yah Veh: Behold, I profane my
holies—the pomp of your strength
the desire of your eyes
and the sympathy of your soul:
and your sons and your daughters whom you forsake
fall by the sword.
22 And you, work as I work:
neither cover your upper lip
nor eat the bread of men:
23 with your tiaras on your heads
and your shoes on your feet:

neither chop nor weep;
and you desolate for your perversities,
and growl—man toward brother.
24 Thus Yechezq El becomes an omen to you:
according to all he works, you work:
and when this comes,
you know I am Adonay Yah Veh.
25 And you, son of humanity,
is it not in the day I take their stronghold from them
—the joy of their adornment
—the desire of their eyes
and the burden of their souls
—their sons and their daughters?
26 In that day, the escapees come to you,
so that you hear with ears:
27 in that day you open your
mouth to the escapees,
and word—muted no more:
and you become an omen to them;
and they know I—Yah Veh.

THE WORD OF YAH VEH CONCERNING THE SONS OF AMMON

25 And so be the word of Yah Veh to me, saying,
2 Son of humanity,
set your face against the sons of Ammon
and prophesy against them:
3 and say to the sons of Ammon,
Hear the word of Adonay Yah Veh;
Thus says Adonay Yah Veh:
Because you say, Aha! against my holies,
when it profanes;
and against the *land* **soil** of *Israel* **Yisra El**,
when it was *desolate* **desolated**;
and against the house of *Judah* **Yah Hudah**,
when they went into *captivity* **exile**;
4 Behold, therefore I *will deliver* **shall give** thee
to the *men* **sons** of the east for a possession,
and they shall set their *palaces* **walls** in thee,
and *make* **give** their *dwellings* **tabernacles** in thee:
they shall eat thy fruit, and they shall drink thy milk.
5 And I *will make* **shall give** Rabbah
a *stable* **habitation of rest** for camels,
and the *Ammonites* **sons of Ammon**
a *couching* **resting** place for flocks:
and ye shall know that *I am the LORD* **I—Yah Veh**.
6 For thus saith *the Lord GOD* **Adonay Yah Veh**;
Because thou hast clapped *thine hands* **the hand**,
and stamped with the *feet* **foot**,
and *rejoiced* **cheered** in *heart* **soul**
with all thy despite against the *land*
soil of *Israel* **Yisra El**;
7 Behold,
therefore I *will stretch out* **shall**
spread mine hand upon thee,
and *will deliver* **shall give** thee for *a spoil* **plunder**
to the *heathen* **goyim**;
and I *will* **shall** cut thee off from the people,
and I *will* **shall** cause thee
to *perish* **destruct** out of the countries:
I *will destroy* **shall desolate** thee;
and thou shalt know that *I am the LORD* **I—Yah Veh**.

THE WORD OF YAH VEH CONCERNING MOAB AND SEIR

8 Thus saith *the Lord GOD* **Adonay Yah Veh**;
Because *that* **of the saying of** Moab and Seir *do say*,
Behold,
the house of Judah **Yah Hudah**
is like unto all the *heathen* **goyim**;
9 Therefore, behold,
I *will* **shall** open the *side* **shoulder** of Moab
from the cities,
from his cities which are on his *frontiers* **edges**,
the *glory* **splendour** of the country,
Bethjeshimoth **Beth Ha Yeshimoth**,
Baalmeon **Baal Meon**, and *Kiriathaim* **Qiryathaim**,
10 Unto the *men* **sons** of the east
with the *Ammonites* **sons of Ammon**,
and *will* **shall** give them in possession,
that the *Ammonites* **sons of Ammon**
may not be remembered among the *nations* **goyim**.
11 And I *will execute* **shall**
work judgments upon Moab;
and they shall know that *I am the LORD* **I—Yah Veh**.

THE WORD OF YAH VEH CONCERNING EDOM

12 Thus saith *the Lord GOD* **Adonay Yah Veh**;
Because that Edom hath *dealt* **worked**
against the house of *Judah* **Yah Hudah**
by *taking vengeance* **avenging avengement**,
and **in guilting,** hath *greatly offended* **guilted**,
and *revenged* **avenged** himself upon them;
13 Therefore thus saith *the*
Lord GOD **Adonay Yah Veh**;
I *will* **shall** also *stretch out* **spread**
mine hand upon Edom,
and *will* **shall** cut off
man **humanity** and *beast* **animal** from it;
and I *will make* **shall give** it *desolate* **parched**

from Teman;
and they of Dedan shall fall by the sword.
14 And I *will lay* **shall give**
my *vengeance* **avengement**
upon Edom
by the hand of my people *Israel* **Yisra El**:
and they shall *do* **work** in Edom
according to *mine anger* **my wrath**
and according to my fury;
and they shall know my *vengeance* **avengement**,
saith the Lord GOD **an oracle of Adonay Yah Veh**.

THE WORD OF YAH VEH CONCERNING THE PELESHETHIYM

15 Thus saith *the Lord GOD* **Adonay Yah Veh**;
Because the *Philistines* **Peleshethiym**
have *dealt* **worked** by *revenge* **avengement**,
and have *taken vengeance* **avenged**
with a despiteful *heart* **soul**,
to *destroy* **ruin** it for the *old hatred* **eternal enmity**;
16 Therefore thus saith *the*
Lord GOD **Adonay Yah Veh**;
and against the soil of Yisra El,
when it desolates;
and against the house of Yah Hudah,
when they go into exile;
4 behold, so I give you
to the sons of the east for a possession;
and they set their walls in you
and give their tabernacles in you:
they eat your fruit and they drink your milk:
5 and I give Rabbah as a
habitation of rest for camels
and the sons of Ammon as a place of rest for flocks:
and you know I—Yah Veh.
6 For thus says Adonay Yah Veh:
Because you clap the hand,
and stamp the foot,
and cheer in soul with all your despite
against the soil of Yisra El;
7 behold, so I spread my hand on you
and give you for plunder to the goyim;
and I cut you off from the people,
and I destroy you from the countries:
I desolate you; and you know I—Yah Veh.

THE WORD OF YAH VEH CONCERNING MOAB AND SEIR

8 Thus says Adonay Yah Veh:
Because of the saying of Moab and Seir,
Behold, Yah Hudah *is* as all the goyim;
9 so, behold,
I open the shoulder of Moab from the cities
—from his cities on his edges,
the splendor of the country
—Beth Ha Yeshimoth,
Baal Meon and Qiryathaim;
10 to the sons of the east with the sons of Ammon;
and give them in possession:
so that the sons of Ammon
are not remembered among the goyim:
11 and I work judgments on Moab;
and they know I—Yah Veh.

THE WORD OF YAH VEH CONCERNING EDOM

12 Thus says Adonay Yah Veh:
Because Edom works against the house of Yah Hudah
by avenging avengement,
and in guilting, guilts,
and avenges himself on them;
13 so thus says Adonay Yah Veh:
I also spread my hand on Edom
and cut off humanity and animal from it:
and I give it parched from Teman;
and they of Dedan fall by the sword:
14 and I give my avengement on Edom
by the hand of my people Yisra El:
and they work in Edom
according to my wrath and according to my fury;
and they know my avengement
—an oracle of Adonay Yah Veh.

THE WORD OF YAH VEH CONCERNING THE PELESHETHIYM

15 Thus says Adonay Yah Veh:
Because the Peleshethiym work avengement;
and avenge with a despiteful soul
to ruin the eternal enmity;
16 so thus says Adonay Yah Veh:
Behold, I *will stretch out* **shall spread** mine hand
upon the *Philistines* **Peleshethiym**,
and I *will* **shall** cut off the *Cherethims* **Kerethiym**,
and destroy the *remnant* **survivors**
of the sea *coast* **haven**.
17 And I *will execute* **shall work**
great vengeance **avengements**
upon them with *furious rebukes* **reproofs of fury**;
and they shall know that *I am the LORD* **I—Yah Veh**,
when I shall *lay my vengeance* **give my avengement**
upon them.

THE WORD OF YAH VEH CONCERNING SOR

26 And **so be** it *came to pass*
in the eleventh year, in the first *day* of the month,
that the word of *the LORD* **Yah Veh** came unto me,
saying,
2 Son of *man* **humanity**,
because that *Tyrus* **Sor**
hath said against *Jerusalem* **Yeru Shalem**, Aha,
she is broken
that was the gates—**the doors** of the people:
she is turned unto me:
I shall be *replenished* **fulfilled**,
now she is *laid waste* **parched**:
3 Therefore thus saith *the*
Lord GOD **Adonay Yah Veh**;
Behold, I *am* against thee, O *Tyrus* **Sor**,
and *will* **shall** cause many *nations* **goyim**
to *come up* **ascend** against thee,
as the sea causeth his waves to *come up* **ascend**.
4 And they shall *destroy* **ruin**
the walls of *Tyrus* **Sor**,
and break down her towers:
I *will* **shall** also scrape **off** her dust from her,
and *make* **give** her like the *top* **clearing** of a rock.
5 **So be** It *shall be a place* for the spreading of nets
in the midst of the sea:
for I have *spoken it* **worded**,
saith the Lord GOD **an oracle of Adonay Yah Veh**:
and *it shall become* **so be it** a *spoil* **plunder**
to the *nations* **goyim**.
6 And her daughters which are in the field
shall be *slain* **slaughtered** by the sword;
and they shall know that *I am the LORD* **I—Yah Veh**.
7 For thus saith *the Lord GOD* **Adonay Yah Veh**;
Behold, I *will* **shall** bring upon *Tyrus* **Sor**
Nebuchadrezzar **Nebukadnets Tsar**
king **sovereign** of *Babylon* **Babel**,
a *king* **sovereign** of *kings* **sovereigns**, from the north,
with horses, and with chariots,
and with *horsemen* **cavalry**,
and *companies* **congregations**, and much people.
8 He shall *slay* **slaughter** with the sword
thy daughters in the field:
and he shall *make* **give** a *fort*
battering tower against thee,
and *cast* **pour** a mount against thee,
and *lift up* **raise** the *buckler* **shield** against thee.
9 And he shall *set engines of*
war **give battering rams**
against thy walls,
and with his *axes* **sword**
he shall *break* **pull** down thy towers.
10 By *reason of the abundance*
the throngs of his horses
their dust shall cover thee:
thy walls shall *shake* **quake**
at the *noise* **voice** of the *horsemen* **cavalry**,
and of the wheels, and of the chariots,
when he shall enter into thy *gates* **portals**,
as *men enter* **entering** into a **split** city
wherein is made a breach.
11 With the hoofs of his horses
shall he *tread down* **trample** all thy *streets* **outways**:
he shall *slay* **slaughter** thy people by the sword,
and thy *strong garrisons* **monoliths of strength**
shall *go down* **lower** to the *ground* **earth**.
12 And they shall
make a spoil of **plunder** thy *riches* **valuables**,
and *make a prey of* **plunder** thy merchandise:
and they shall break down thy walls,
and *destroy* **pull down** thy pleasant houses:
and they shall *lay* **set** thy stones and thy timber
and thy dust in the midst of the water.
Behold, I spread my hand on the Peleshethiym
and I cut off the Kerethiym
and destroy the survivors of the sea
haven. 17 And I work on them
avengements with reproofs of fury;
and they know I—Yah Veh,
when I give my avengement on them.

THE WORD OF YAH VEH CONCERNING SOR

26 And so be it,
in the eleventh year, in the first of the month,
the word of Yah Veh is to me, saying,
2 Son of humanity,
because Sor says against Yeru Shalem, *saying*,
Aha, she is broken—the doors of the people:
she turns to me:
I am fulfilled; she is parched.
3 So thus says Adonay Yah Veh:
Behold, I *am* against you, O Sor,
and I ascend many goyim against you,
as the sea ascends his waves:
4 and they ruin the walls of Sor
and break down her towers:
and I scrape her dust from her
and give her as the clearing of a rock.
5 and so be it for the spreading
of nets midst the sea:

I—I have worded
—an oracle of Adonay Yah Veh
and so be it, a plunder to the goyim:
6 and her daughters in the field are slaughtered
by the sword; and they know I—Yah Veh.
7 For thus says Adonay Yah Veh:
Behold, I bring on Sor
Nebukadnets Tsar sovereign of Babel
—a sovereign of sovereigns, from the north,
with horses and with chariots and with cavalry
and congregations and much people.
8 He slaughters your daughters
with the sword in the field:
and he gives a battering tower against you
and pours a mound against you
and raises the shield against you:
9 and he give battering rams against your walls
and with his sword he pulls down your towers.
10 By the throngs of his horses
their dust covers you:
your walls quake at the voice of the cavalry
and of the wheels and of the chariots
—when he enters into your portals
is as entering into a split city.
11 With the hoofs of his horses
he tramples all your outways:
he slaughters your people by the sword
and lowers your monoliths of strength to the earth.
12 And they plunder your valuables
and plunder your merchandise:
and they break down your walls
and pull down your pleasant houses:
and they set your stones and your timber
and your dust midst the water.
13 And I *will* **shall** cause the *noise* **roar** of thy songs
to *cease* **shabbathize**;
and the *sound* **voice** of thy harps shall be no more heard.
14 And I *will make* **shall give** thee
like the *top* **clearing** of a rock:
thou shalt be a place to spread nets upon;
thou shalt be built no more:
for I *the LORD* **Yah Veh** have *spoken it* **worded**,
saith the Lord GOD **an oracle of Adonay Yah Veh**.
15 Thus saith *the Lord GOD* **Adonay Yah Veh**
to *Tyrus* **Sor**;
shall not the *isles shake* **islands quake**
at the *sound* **voice** of thy *fall* **ruin**,
when the *wounded cry* **pierced shriek**,
when the slaughter is *made* **slaughtered**
in the midst of thee?
16 Then all the *princes* **hierarchs** of the sea
shall *come down* **descend** from their thrones,
and *lay away* **turn aside** their *robes* **mantles**,
and *put off* **strip**
their *broidered garments* **clothes of embroidery**:
they shall *clothe* **enrobe** themselves with trembling;
they shall sit upon the *ground* **earth**,
and shall tremble *at every moment* **in a blink**,
and be astonished at thee.
17 And they shall *take up* **lift**
a lamentation for thee,
and say to thee, How art thou destroyed,
that wast *inhabited* **settled** of *seafaring men* **the seas**,
the renowned city, which wast strong in the sea,
she and her *inhabitants* **settlers**,
which *cause* **give** their terror
to be on all that *haunt* **settle** it!
18 Now shall the *isles* **islands** tremble
in the day of thy *fall* **ruin**;
yea, the *isles* **islands** that are in the sea shall
be troubled **terrify** at thy departure.
19 For thus saith *the Lord GOD* **Adonay Yah Veh**;
When I shall *make* **give** thee a *desolate* **parched** city,
like the cities that are not *inhabited* **settled**;
when I shall *bring up* **ascend** the *deep* **abyss** upon thee,
and great waters shall cover thee;
20 When I shall bring thee down
with them that descend into the *pit* **well**,
with the **original** people *of old time*,
and shall *set* **settle** thee
in the *low parts* **nethermost** of the earth,
in *places desolate of old* **the original parched areas**,
with them that *go down* **descend** to the *pit* **well**,
that thou be not *inhabited* **settled**;
and I shall *set glory* **give splendour**
in the land of the living;
21 I *will make* **shall give** thee *a terror* **terrors**,
and thou shalt be no more:
though thou be sought for,
yet shalt thou *never* **not eternally** be found again,
saith the Lord GOD **an oracle of Adonay Yah Veh**.

THE WORD OFYAH VEH CONCERNING THE LAMENTATION OF SOR

27 The word of *the LORD* **Yah Veh**
came again unto me, saying,
2 *Now*, thou son of *man* **humanity**,
take up **lift** a lamentation for *Tyrus* **Sor**;
3 And say unto *Tyrus* **Sor**,
O thou that *art situate* **settlest** at the entry of the sea,

which art a merchant of the people
for many *isles* **islands**,
Thus saith *the Lord GOD* **Adonay Yah Veh**;
O *Tyrus* **Sor**, thou hast said, I am of perfect beauty.
4 Thy borders are in the *midst* **heart** of the seas,
thy builders have perfected thy beauty.
5 They have made all thy *ship boards* **tables**
of fir trees of Senir:
they have taken cedars from Lebanon
to *make* **work** masts for thee.
6 Of the oaks of Bashan
have they *made* **worked** thine oars;
the *company* **daughters** of the *Ashurites* **Ashshuriym**
have *made* **worked** thy *benches* **boards** of ivory,
brought out of the *isles* **islands** of *Chittim* **Kittim**.
13 And I shabbathize the roar of your songs
and the voice of your harps are heard no more:
14 and I give you as the clearing of a rock
to spread nets on:
you are built no more:
for I Yah Veh have worded
—an oracle of Adonay Yah Veh.
15 Thus says Adonay Yah Veh to Sor:
Quake not the islands at the voice of your ruin
when the pierced shriek?
When the slaughter *is* slaughtered in your midst?
16 And all the hierarchs of the sea
descend from their thrones
and turn aside their mantles;
they strip their clothes of embroidery
and enrobe themselves with trembling;
they sit on the earth and tremble in a blink
and astonish at you:
17 and they lift a lamentation for you,
and say to you,
How you destruct, you settled of the seas;
the renowned city—strong in the sea;
she and her settlers,
who give their terror on all who settle it!
18 Now the islands tremble in the day of your ruin;
yes, the islands in the sea terrify at your departure.
19 For thus says Adonay Yah Veh:
When I give you as a parched city,
as the cities not settled;
when I ascend the abyss on you
and great waters cover you;
20 when I descend you
with them descending into the well
—to the original people,
and settle you in the nethermost of the earth
—in the original parched areas
with them descending to the well,
so that you not settle;
and I give splendor in the land of the living.
21 I give you as terrors, and you *are* no more:
though you are sought for,
yet you *are* not eternally found again
—an oracle of Adonay Yah Veh.

THE WORD OF YAH VEH CONCERNING THE LAMENTATION OF SOR

27 So be the word of Yah Veh to me, saying,
2 You, son of humanity, lift a lamentation for Sor;
3 and say to Sor,
O you who settles at the entry of the sea;
a merchant of the people for many islands;
Thus says Adonay Yah Veh:
O Sor, you—you who say, I *am* of perfect beauty:
4 your borders are in the heart of the seas,
your builders perfect your beauty:
5 they make all your tables of fir trees of Senir;
they take cedars from Lebanon to work your masts;
6 from the oaks of Bashan they work your oars;
the daughters of the Ashshuriym
work your boards of ivory
—brought from the islands of Kittim.
7 *Fine* **White** linen with
broidered work **embroidery**
from *Egypt* **Misrayim**
was *that which thou spreadest forth* **thy spreadings**
to be thy sail;
blue and purple from the *isles*
islands of *Elishah* **Eli Shah**
was that which covered thee.
8 The *inhabitants* **settlers** of
Zidon **Sidon** and Arvad
were thy *mariners* **paddlers**:
thy wise *men*, O *Tyrus* **Sor**, that were in thee,
were thy *pilots* **sailers**.
9 The *ancients* **elders** of Gebal
and the wise *men thereof*
were in thee thy *calkers* **breach holders**:
all the ships of the sea with their mariners were in thee
to *occupy* **pledge** thy merchandise.
10 They of Persia and of Lud and of *Phut* **Put**
were in thine *army* **valiant**, thy men of war:
they hanged the *shield* **buckler** and helmet in thee;
they *set* **gave** forth thy *comeliness* **majesty**.
11 The *men* **sons** of Arvad with thine *army* **valiant**
were upon thy walls round about,

and the *Gammadims* **warriors** were in thy towers:
they hanged their shields upon thy walls round about;
they have *made* **perfected** thy beauty *perfect.*
12 Tarshish was thy merchant
by reason **because** of the *multitude* **abundance**
of *all kind of riches* **wealth;**
with silver, iron, tin, and lead,
they *traded* **gave** in thy *fairs* **markets.**
13 *Javan* **Yavan,** Tubal, and Meshech,
they were thy merchants:
they *traded the persons* **gave the souls** of *men* **humanity**
and *vessels* **instruments** of *brass* **copper**
in **of** thy *market* **merchandise.**
Apocalypse 18:12, 13
14 They of the house of Togarmah
traded **gave** in thy *fairs* **markets**
with horses and *horsemen* **cavalry** and mules.
15 The *men* **sons** of Dedan were thy merchants;
many *isles* **islands** were the merchandise of thine hand:
they *brought thee for a present* **restored for their hire**
horns of ivory and *ebony* **ebonies.**
16 *Syria* **Aram** was thy merchant
by reason **because** of the *multitude* **abundance**
of *the wares of thy making* **thy works:**
they *occupied* **gave** in thy *fairs* **markets** with emeralds,
purple, and *broidered work* **embroidery,**
and *fine* **bleached** linen, and coral, and *agate* **rubies.**
17 *Judah* **Yah Hudah,** and
the land of *Israel* **Yisra El,**
they were thy merchants:
they *traded* **gave** in thy *market* **merchandise**
wheat of Minnith, and Pannag,
and honey, and oil, and balm.
18 *Damascus* **Dammeseq** was thy merchant
in the *multitude* **abundance** of the wares of thy making,
for the *multitude* **abundance** of all *riches* **wealth;**
in the wine of Helbon, and white wool.
19 *Dan also* **Vedan** and *Javan* **Yavan**
going to and fro **gadding about,**
occupied **gave** in thy *fairs* **markets:**
bright iron, cassia, and *calamus* **stalks,**
were in thy *market* **merchandise.**
20 Dedan was thy merchant
in *precious* clothes **of liberation** for chariots.
21 Arabia, and all the *princes*
hierarchs of *Kedar* **Qedar,**
they *occupied with thee* **merchandised**
in lambs, and rams, and **he** goats:
in these were *they thy* **the** merchants **of thy hand.**
22 The merchants of Sheba and Raamah,
they were thy merchants:
they *occupied* **gave** in thy *fairs* **markets**
with *chief of* all **head** spices,
and with all *precious* **esteemed** stones, and gold.
23 Haran, and *Canneh* **Kanneh,** and Eden,
the merchants of Sheba,
Asshur **Ashshur,** and *Chilmad* **Kilmad,**
were thy merchants.
24 These were thy merchants
in all sorts of things **of splendour,**
in blue *clothes* **robes,** and *broidered work* **embroidery,**
7 Of white linen with embroidery from Misrayim
become your spreadings to become your sail;
blue and purple from the islands of Eli Shah
becomes your cover;
8 the settlers of Sidon and Arvad
become your paddlers;
your wise, O Sor, become your sailers;
9 the elders of Gebal and her wise
become your breach holders;
all the ships of the sea with their mariners
become to pledge your merchandise:
10 they of Persia and of Lud and of Put
become your valiant, your men of war:
they hang the buckler and helmet in you;
they give forth your majesty.
11 The sons of Arvad with your valiant
are on your walls all around
and the warriors in your towers:
they hang their shields on your walls all around;
they perfect your beauty.
12 Tarshish *is* your merchant
because of the abundance of wealth
—with silver, iron, tin, and lead
they give in your markets.
13 Yavan, Tubal, and Meshech *are* your merchants:
they give the souls of humanity
and instruments of copper of your
merchandise. Apocalypse 18:12, 13
14 They of the house of Togarmah
give horses and cavalry and mules
in your markets.
15 The sons of Dedan *are* your merchants;
many islands *are* the merchandise of your hand:
for their hire
they restore horns of ivory and ebonies.
16 Aram *is* your merchant
because of the abundance of your works:
they give in your markets with emeralds
purple and embroidery

and bleached linen and coral and rubies.
17 Yah Hudah, and the land of Yisra El,
are your merchants:
in your merchandise
they give wheat of Minnith and Pannag;
and honey and oil and balm.
18 Dammeseq *is* your merchant
in the abundance of the wares of your making,
for the abundance of all wealth;
in the wine of Helbon and white wool.
19 Vedan and Yavan gad about,
and in your markets
they give bright iron, cassia,
and stalks in your merchandise.
20 Dedan *is* your merchant
in clothes of liberation for chariots.
21 Arabia and all the hierarchs of Qedar,
merchandise in lambs and rams and he goats:
these *are* the merchants of your hand.
22 The merchants of Sheba and Raamah
are your merchants:
and in your markets
they give all head spices,
and all esteemed stones, and gold.
23 Haran, and Kanneh, and Eden,
the merchants of Sheba,
Ashshur, and Kilmad,
are your merchants:
24 these *are* your merchants of splendor
in blue robes and embroidery
and in chests of rich *apparel* **damasks,**
bound with cords, and *made* of cedar,
among thy merchandise.
25 The ships of Tarshish
did sing of thee **strolled** in thy *market* **merchandise**:
and thou wast *replenished* **fulfilled,**
and *made very glorious* **mightily honoured**
in the *midst* **heart** of the seas.
26 Thy *rowers* **paddlers**
have brought thee into great waters:
the east wind
hath broken thee in the *midst* **heart** of the seas.
27 Thy *riches* **wealth**, and thy *fairs* **markets**,
thy merchandise,
thy mariners, and thy *pilots* **sailers**,
thy *calkers* **breach holders**,
and the *occupiers* **pledgers** of thy merchandise,
and all thy men of war, that are in thee,
and in all thy *company* **congregation**
which is in the *midst* **heart** of thee,
shall fall into the midst of the seas in the day of thy ruin.
28 The suburbs shall *shake* **quake**
at the *sound* **voice** of the cry of thy *pilots* **sailers.**
29 And all that *handle* **manipulate** the oar,
the mariners, and all the *pilots* **sailers** of the sea,
shall *come down* **descend** from their ships,
they shall stand upon the land;
30 And shall cause their voice
to be heard against thee,
and shall cry bitterly,
and shall *cast up* **ascend** dust upon their heads,
they shall wallow themselves in the ashes:
31 And **in balding,** they shall
make themselves utterly bald **balden themselves** for thee,
and gird them with *sackcloth* **saq,**
and they shall weep for thee with bitterness of *heart* **soul**
and bitter *wailing* **chopping.**
32 And in their *wailing* **lamentation**
they shall *take up* **lift** a lamentation for thee,
and lament over thee, *saying,*
What *city* is like *Tyrus* **Sor,**
like the *destroyed* **severed** in the midst of the sea?
33 When thy *wares* **markets**
went forth out of the seas,
thou *filledst* **satisfied** many people;
thou didst enrich the *kings* **sovereigns** of the earth
with the *multitude* **abundance** of thy *riches* **wealth**
and of thy merchandise.
34 In the time when thou
shalt be broken by the seas
in the depths of the waters
thy merchandise and all thy *company* **congregation**
in the midst of thee shall fall.
35 All the *inhabitants* **settlers** of the *isles* **islands**
shall be astonished at thee,
and their *kings* **sovereigns**
shall *be sore afraid* **shudder with horror,**
they shall be *troubled* **irritated** in their *countenance* **face.**
36 The merchants among the
people shall hiss at thee;
thou shalt be *a terror* **terrors,**
and *never shalt be any more* **shall not be eternally.**

THE WORD OF YAH VEH CONCERNING THE EMINENT OF SOR

28 The word of *the LORD* **Yah Veh**
came again unto me, saying,
2 Son of *man* **humanity,**
say unto the *prince* **eminent** of *Tyrus* **Sor,**
Thus saith *the Lord GOD* **Adonay Yah Veh**;
Because thine heart is *lifted up* **haughty,**

and thou hast said, I *am a God*—**El**,
I sit in the seat of *God* **Elohim**,
in the *midst* **heart** of the seas;
yet thou art *a man* **human**, and not *God* **El**,
though thou *set* **give** thine heart
as the heart of *God* **Elohim**:
3 Behold, thou art wiser than *Daniel* **Dani El**;
there is *no secret* **nought shut up**
that they can *hide* **shade** from thee:
4 With thy wisdom
and with *thine understanding* **thy discernment**
thou hast *gotten* **worked** thee *riches* **valuables**,
and hast *gotten* **worked** gold and
silver into thy treasures:
and in chests of rich damasks
—bound with cords and of cedar,
among your merchandise.
25 The ships of Tarshish stroll
in your merchandise:
and fulfill you
and mightily honor you in the heart of the seas.
26 Your paddlers bring you into great waters:
the east wind breaks you in the heart of the seas:
27 your wealth, and your markets,
your merchandise, your mariners, and your sailers,
your breach holders,
and the pledgers of your merchandise,
and all your men of war
—in you and in all your congregation among you
fall into the heart of the seas in the day of your ruin.
28 The suburbs quake
at the voice of the cry of your sailers:
29 and all who manipulate the oar
—the mariners and all the sailers of the sea
descend from their ships;
they stand on the land:
30 and hearken their voice
against you and cry bitterly
and ascend dust on their heads:
they wallow themselves in the ashes:
31 and in balding, they balden themselves for you,
and gird themselves with saq;
and they weep for you
with bitterness of soul and bitter chopping:
32 and in their lamentation
they lift a lamentation for you
and lament over you,
What is as Sor
—as the severed midst the sea?
33 In your markets going from the seas,
you satisfied many people;
you enriched the sovereigns of the earth
with the abundance of your wealth
and of your merchandise.
34 In the time you *are* broken by the seas
in the depths of the waters
your merchandise and all your congregation
fall in your midst.
35 All the settlers of the islands astonish at you
and their sovereigns shudder with horror
—irritated in their face:
36 the merchants among the people hiss at you;
you become terrors,
and *are* not eternal.

THE WORD OF YAH VEH CONCERNING THE EMINENT OF SOR

28 And so be the word of Yah Veh to me, saying,
2 Son of humanity, say to the eminent of Sor,
Thus says Adonay Yah Veh:
Because your heart is haughty, and you say, I—El;
I sit in the seat of Elohim, in the heart of the seas.
—yet you are human, and not El,
though you give your heart as the heart of Elohim:
3 behold, you are wiser than Dani El;
naught shut up *is* shaded from you:
4 with your wisdom and with your discernment
you work valuables for yourself;
and work gold and silver into your treasures:
exeGeses ready research BIBLE
5 By *thy great* **the greatness of thy** wisdom
and by thy *traffick* **merchandise**
hast thou *increased* **abounded** thy *riches* **valuables**,
and thine heart is lifted *up*
because of thy *riches* **valuables**:
6 Therefore thus saith *the*
Lord GOD **Adonay Yah Veh**;
Because thou hast *set* **given** thine heart
as the heart of *God* **Elohim**;
7 Behold, therefore I *will* **shall**
bring strangers upon thee,
the *terrible* **tyrant** of the *nations* **goyim**:
and they shall draw their swords
against the beauty of thy wisdom,
and they shall *defile* **profane** thy *brightness* **splendour**.
8 They shall bring thee down to the pit **of ruin**,
and thou shalt die the deaths of them
that are *slain* **pierced** in the *midst* **heart** of the seas.
9 **In saying,**

Wilt **Shalt** thou *yet* say *before him* **at his face**
that slayeth thee, *I am God* **I—Elohim?**
but thou shalt be *a man* **human**, and no *God* **El,**
in the hand of him that *slayeth* **slaughtereth** thee.
10 Thou shalt die the deaths of the uncircumcised
by the hand of strangers:
for I have *spoken it* **worded**,
saith the Lord GOD **an oracle of Adonay Yah Veh.**

The Word Of Yah Veh Concerning The Sovereign Of Sor

11 Moreover
the word of *the LORD* **Yah Veh** came unto me, saying,
12 Son of *man* **humanity**,
take up **lift** a lamentation
upon the *king* **sovereign** of *Tyrus* **Sor**, and say unto him,
Thus saith *the Lord GOD* **Adonay Yah Veh**;
Thou sealest up the *sum* **gauge**,
full of wisdom, and perfect in beauty.
13 Thou hast been in Eden
the garden of *God* **Elohim**;
every *precious* **esteemed** stone was thy covering,
the sardius, topaz, and the diamond,
the beryl, the onyx, and the jasper,
the sapphire, the emerald, and the carbuncle, and gold:
the workmanship of thy *tabrets* **tambourines** and of thy pipes
was prepared in thee in the day that thou wast created.
14 Thou art the *anointed* **overspreading** cherub
that covereth;
and I have *set* **given** thee *so*:
thou wast upon the holy mountain of *God* **Elohim**;
thou hast walked up and down
in the midst of the stones of fire.
15 Thou *wast perfect* **integrious** in thy ways
from the day that thou wast created,
till *iniquity* **wickedness** was found in thee.
16 By the *multitude* **abundance** of thy merchandise
they have filled the midst of thee with violence,
and thou hast sinned:
therefore I *will* **shall** cast thee as profane
out of the mountain of *God* **Elohim**:
and I *will* **shall** destroy thee, O covering cherub,
from the midst of the stones of fire.
17 Thine heart was *lifted up* **haughty**
because of thy beauty,
thou hast *corrupted* **ruined** thy wisdom
by reason of thy *brightness* **splendour**:
I *will* **shall** cast thee to the *ground* **earth**,
I *will lay* **shall give** thee
before kings **at the face of sovereigns**,
that they may *behold* **see** thee.
18 Thou hast *defiled* **profaned**
thy *sanctuaries* **holies**
by the *multitude* **abundance**
of *thine iniquities* **thy perversities**,
by the *iniquity* **wickedness** of thy *traffick* **merchandise**;
therefore *will* **shall** I bring forth a fire
from the midst of thee,
it shall devour thee,
and I *will bring* **shall give** thee to ashes upon the earth
in the *sight* **eyes** of all them that *behold* **see** thee.
19 All they that know thee among the people
shall be astonished at thee:
thou shalt be *a terror* **terrors**,
and *never shalt thou be any more* **thou art not eternal.**
5 by your great wisdom and by your merchandise
you abound your valuables;
and you lift your heart because of your valuables.
6 So thus says Adonay Yah Veh:
Because you give your heart as the heart of Elohim;
7 behold, so I bring strangers upon you
—the tyrants of the goyim: and they draw their swords
against the beauty of your wisdom
and they profane your splendor:
8 they bring you down to the pit of ruin
and you die the deaths of the pierced
in the heart of the seas.
9 In saying, say you, I *am* Elohim!
—at the face of him who slays you?
you *are* but human, and not El
in the hand of him who slaughters you:
10 you die the deaths of the uncircumcised
by the hand of strangers:
for I have worded
—an oracle of Adonay Yah Veh.

The Word Of Yah Veh Concerning The Sovereign Of Sor

11 And so be the word of Yah Veh to me, saying,
12 Son of humanity,
lift a lamentation on the sovereign of Sor,
and say to him, Thus says Adonay Yah Veh:
You seal the gauge
—full of wisdom and perfect in beauty.
13 You, were in Eden the garden of Elohim;
every esteemed stone, your covering
—the sardius, topaz, and the diamond;
the beryl, the onyx, and the jasper; the sapphire,
the emerald and the carbuncle and gold:

the workmanship of your tambourines
and of your pipes
was prepared in you in the day that you were created.
14 You, the overspreading cherub who covers;
and I gave you on the holy mountain of Elohim;
to walk up and down midst the stones of fire.
15 You, integrious in your ways
from the day of your creating,
until wickedness was found in you.
16 By the abundance of your merchandise
they filled your midst with violence,
and you sinned.
So I cast you as profane
from the mountain of Elohim:
and I destroy you, O covering cherub,
from midst the stones of fire:
17 your heart is haughty because of your beauty;
you ruin your wisdom because of your splendor:
I cast you to the earth;
I give you at the face of sovereigns
so that they see you:
18 you profaned your holies
by the abundance of your perversities
—by the wickedness of your merchandise;
and I bring a fire from your midst to consume you:
and I give you to ashes on the earth
in the eyes of all who see you.
19 All among the people who know you
astonish at you:
you become terrors,
and you are not eternal.

The Word Of Yah Veh Concerning Sidon

20 Again the word of *the LORD*
Yah Veh came unto me,
saying,
21 Son of *man* **humanity,**
set thy face against *Zidon* **Sidon**, and prophesy against it,
22 And say, Thus saith *the Lord*
GOD **Adonay Yah Veh;**
Behold, I am against thee, O *Zidon* **Sidon**;
and I *will* **shall** be *glorified* **honoured**
in the midst of thee:
and they shall know that *I am the LORD* **I—Yah Veh,**
when I shall have *executed* **worked** judgments in her,
and shall be *sanctified* **hallowed** in her.
23 For I *will* **shall** send into her pestilence,
and blood into her *streets* **outways;**
and the *wounded* **pierced**
shall be *judged* **felled** in the midst of her
by the sword upon her *on every side* **round about;**
and they shall know that *I am the LORD* **I—Yah Veh.**
24 And there shall be no more
a *pricking brier* **bitter prickle**
unto the house of *Israel* **Yisra El,**
nor *any grieving* **painful** thorn
of all that are round about them,
that despised them;
and they shall know
that I *am the Lord GOD*—**Adonay Yah Veh.**
25 Thus saith *the Lord GOD* **Adonay Yah Veh;**
When I shall have gathered the house of *Israel* **Yisra El**
from the people among whom they are scattered,
and shall be *sanctified* **hallowed** in them
in the *sight* **eyes** of the *heathen* **goyim,**
then shall they *dwell* **settle** in their *land* **soil**
that I have given to my servant *Jacob* **Yaaqov.**
26 And they shall *dwell safely*
settle confidently *therein,*
and shall build houses, and plant vineyards;
yea, they shall *dwell with confidence* **settle confidently,**
when I have *executed* **worked** judgments
upon all those that despise them round about them;
and they shall know
that *I am the LORD* **I—Yah Veh** their *God* **Elohim.**

The Word Of Yah Veh Concerning The Sovereign Of Misrayim

29 In the tenth year,
in the tenth *month*, in the twelfth *day* of the month,
the word of *the LORD* **Yah Veh** came unto me, saying,
2 Son of *man* **humanity,**
set thy face against *Pharaoh* **Paroh** *king*
sovereign of *Egypt* **Misrayim,**
and prophesy against him,
and against all *Egypt* **Misrayim:**
3 *Speak* **Word,** and say,
Thus saith *the Lord GOD* **Adonay Yah Veh;**
Behold, I am against thee,
Pharaoh king **Paroh sovereign** of *Egypt* **Misrayim,**
the great *dragon* **monster**
that *lieth* **croucheth** in the midst of his rivers,
which hath said,
My river is mine own,
and I have *made* **worked** it for myself.
4 But I *will put* **shall give** hooks in thy jaws,
and I *will* **shall** cause the fish of thy rivers
to stick unto thy scales,
and I *will bring* **shall ascend** thee *up*
out of the midst of thy rivers,

and all the fish of thy rivers shall stick unto thy scales.
5 And I *will leave* **shall abandon** thee
thrown into the wilderness,
thee and all the fish of thy rivers:
that thou shalt fall upon the *open* **face of the** fields;
that thou shalt not be *brought* **gathered** together,
nor gathered:
I have given thee for *meat* **food**
to the *beasts* **live beings** of the *field* **earth**
and to the *fowls* **flyers** of the *heaven* **heavens**.
6 And all the *inhabitants*
settlers of *Egypt* **Misrayim**
shall know that *I am the LORD* **I—Yah Veh**,
because they have been a *staff* **stalk** of *reed* **support**
to the house of *Israel* **Yisra El**.
7 When they *took hold of*
apprehended thee by thy *hand* **palm**,

The Word Of Yah Veh Concerning Sidon

20 And so be the word of Yah Veh to me, saying,
21 Son of humanity,
set your face against Sidon and prophesy against it,
22 and say, Thus says Adonay Yah Veh:
Behold, I *am* against you, O Sidon;
and I am honored in your midst:
and they know I—Yah Veh,
when I work judgments in her,
and am hallowed in her.
23 And I send her pestilence
and blood in her outways;
and fell the pierced in her midst
by the sword on her all around;
and they know I—Yah Veh.
24 And neither *is* there any more a bitter prickle
to the house of Yisra El,
nor painful thorn
of all who *are* all around them who despise them;
and they know I—Adonay Yah Veh.
25 Thus says Adonay Yah Veh:
When I gather the house of Yisra El
from the people among whom they scattered,
and *am* hallowed in them in the eyes of the goyim,
then they settle in their soil
that I gave to my servant Yaaqov:
26 and they settle confidently
and build houses and plant vineyards:
yes, they settle confidently,
when I work judgments
on all who despise them all around them;
and they know I—Yah Veh their Elohim.

The Word Of Yah Veh Concerning The Sovereign Of Misrayim

29 In the tenth year,
in the tenth, in the twelfth of the month,
so be the word of Yah Veh to me, saying,
2 Son of humanity,
set your face against Paroh sovereign of Misrayim
and prophesy against him
—and against all Misrayim.
3 Word and say, Thus says Adonay Yah Veh:
Behold, I *am* against you,
Paroh sovereign of Misrayim,
the great monster who crouches midst his rivers;
who says, My river is my own
and I work it for myself.
4 And I give hooks in your jaws
so that the fish of your rivers stick to your scales:
and I ascend you from midst your rivers,
and all the fish of your rivers stick to your scales:
5 and I abandon you in the wilderness
—you and all the fish of your rivers:
so that you fall on the face of the fields;
so that you *are* neither gathered together,
nor gathered:
I give you for food to the live beings of the earth
and to the flyers of the heavens:
6 and all the settlers of Misrayim know
I—Yah Veh,
because of their being a stalk of support
to the house of Yisra El.
7 They apprehend you by your palm;
thou didst *break* **crush**, and *rend* **split** all their shoulder:
and when they leaned upon thee, thou brakest,
and madest all their loins to *be at a stand* **shake**.
8 Therefore thus saith *the*
Lord GOD **Adonay Yah Veh**;
Behold, I *will* **shall** bring a sword upon thee,
and cut off *man* **humanity** and *beast* **animal** out of thee.
9 And the land of *Egypt* **Misrayim**
shall be desolate and *waste* **parched**;
and they shall know that *I am the LORD* **I—Yah Veh**:
because he hath said,
The river is mine, and I have *made* **worked** it.
10 Behold,
therefore I am against thee, and against thy rivers,
and I *will make* **shall give** the land of *Egypt* **Misrayim**
utterly waste **in parching, parched** and desolate,
from the tower of *Syene* **Seven**
even unto the border of *Ethiopia* **Kush**.

11 No foot of *man* **humanity** shall pass through
it, nor foot of *beast* **animal** shall pass through it,
neither shall it be *inhabited* **settled** forty years.
12 And I *will make* **shall give**
the land of *Egypt* **Misrayim**
desolate
in the midst of the *countries* **lands**
that are *desolate* **desolated**,
and her cities among the cities
that are *laid waste* **parched**
shall be desolate forty years:
and I *will* **shall** scatter the *Egyptians* **Misrayim**
among the *nations* **goyim**,
and *will disperse* **shall winnow** them
through the *countries* **lands**.
13 Yet thus saith *the Lord GOD* **Adonay Yah Veh**;
At the end of forty years
will **shall** I gather the *Egyptians* **Misrayim**
from the people whither they were scattered:
14 And I *will bring again* **shall return**
the captivity of *Egypt* **Misrayim**,
and *will* **shall** cause them to return
into the land of Pathros,
into the land of their *habitation* **origin**;
and they shall be there
a *base kingdom* **lowly sovereigndom**.
15 **So be** it *shall be*
the *basest* **lowliest** of the *kingdoms* **sovereigndoms**;
neither shall it exalt itself any more
above the *nations* **goyim**:
for I *will* **shall** diminish them,
that they shall no more
rule over **subjugate** the *nations* **goyim**.
16 And **so be** it *shall be*
no more the confidence of the house of *Israel* **Yisra El**,
which *bringeth* **remembereth**
their *iniquity to remembrance* **perversity**,
when they shall *look* **face** after them:
but they shall know
that *I am the Lord GOD* **I—Adonay Yah Veh**.
17 And **so be** it *came to pass*
in the seven and twentieth year,
in the first *month*, in the first *day* of the month,
the word of *the LORD* **Yah Veh** came unto me, saying,
18 Son of *man* **humanity**,
Nebuchadrezzar **Nebukadnets Tsar**
king **sovereign** of *Babylon* **Babel**
caused his *army* **valiant**
to serve a great service against *Tyrus* **Sor**:
every head was *made bald* **baldened**,
and every shoulder was peeled:
yet had he no *wages* **hire**, nor his *army* **valiant**,
for *Tyrus* **Sor**, for the service that
he had served against it:
19 Therefore thus saith *the*
Lord GOD **Adonay Yah Veh**;
Behold, I *will* **shall** give the land of *Egypt* **Misrayim**
unto *Nebuchadrezzar* **Nebukadnets Tsar**
king **sovereign** of *Babylon* **Babel**;
and he shall *take* **lift** her multitude,
and *take* **spoil** her spoil,
and *take her prey* **plundereth her plunder**;
and **so be** it *shall be* the *wages* **hire** for his *army* **valiant**.
20 I have given him the land of *Egypt* **Misrayim**
for his *labour* **deeds** wherewith he served against it,
you crush and split all their shoulder:
and when they lean on you,
you break and shake all their loins.
8 So thus says Adonay Yah Veh:
Behold, I bring a sword on you
and cut off humanity and animal from you;
9 and desolate and parch the land of Misrayim;
and they know I—Yah Veh:
because he says,
The river *is* mine and I work it.
10 So behold,
I *am* against you and against your rivers;
and in parching,
I give the land of Misrayim parched and desolate
—from the tower of Seven to the border of Kush:
11 neither foot of humanity passes through
nor foot of animal passes through;
nor *is* it settled forty years:
12 and I give the land of Misrayim desolate
midst the desolate lands;
and her cities among the parched cities
—desolate them forty years:
and I scatter the Misrayim among the goyim,
and winnow them through the lands.
13 Yet thus says Adonay Yah Veh:
At the end of forty years I gather the Misrayim
from the people where they are scattered:
14 and I restore the captivity of Misrayim
—restore them to the land of Pathros
to their land of origin;
and there they become a lowly sovereigndom;
15 so be it, of all the sovereigndoms, the lowliest;
no more to exalt itself above the goyim:
for I diminish them
so that they no more subjugate the goyim.

16 And so be it no more
the confidence of the house of Yisra El
—who remembers their perversity,
when they faced after them:
and they know I—Adonay Yah Veh.
17 And so be it, in the twenty—seventh year,
in the first, in the first of the month,
so be the word of Yah Veh to me, saying,
18 Son of humanity,
Nebukadnets Tsar sovereign of Babel
has his valiant to serve a great service against Sor:
every head baldens and every shoulder peels:
yet neither he nor his valiant have any hire from Sor
for the service he served against it.
19 So thus says Adonay Yah Veh:
Behold, I give the land of Misrayim
to Nebukadnets Tsar sovereign of Babel;
to lift her multitude and spoil her spoil
and plunder her plunder;
and so be it the hire for his valiant.
20 I give him the land of Misrayim
for the deeds he served against it
because they *wrought* **worked** for me,
saith the Lord GOD **an oracle of Adonay Yah Veh.**
21 In that day *will* **shall** I cause the horn
of the house of *Israel* **Yisra El** to *bud forth* **sprout,**
and I *will* **shall** give thee the opening of the mouth
in the midst of them;
and they shall know that *I am the LORD* **I—Yah Veh.**

THE WORD OF YAH VEH CONCERNING MISRAYIM

30 The word of *the LORD* **Yah Veh**
came again unto me, saying,
2 Son of *man* **humanity**, prophesy and say,
Thus saith *the Lord GOD* **Adonay Yah Veh**;
Howl ye, *Woe worth* **Hah** the day!
3 For the day is near,
even the day of *the LORD* **Yah Veh** is near, a cloudy day;
it shall be the time of the *heathen* **goyim.**
4 And **so be** the sword *shall*
come upon Egypt **Misrayim,**
and **so be** great pain *shall be* in *Ethiopia* **Kush,**
when the *slain* **pierced** shall fall in *Egypt* **Misrayim,**
and they shall take away her multitude,
and her foundations shall be broken *down.*
5 *Ethiopia* **Kush**, and *Libya* **Put**, and *Lydia* **Lud,**
and all the *mingled people* **comingled**, and *Chub* **Kub,**
and the *men* **sons** of the land that is in *league* **covenant,**
shall fall with them by the sword.
6 Thus saith *the LORD* **Yah Veh;**
They also that uphold *Egypt* **Misrayim** shall fall;
and the *pride* **pomp** of her *power* **strength**
shall *come down* **topple:**
from the tower of *Syene* **Seven**
shall they fall in it by the sword,
saith the Lord GOD **an oracle of Adonay Yah Veh.**
7 And they shall *be* desolate
in the midst of the *countries* **lands**
that *are desolate* **desolated,**
and her cities
shall be in the midst of the cities that are wasted.
8 And they shall know that *I*
am the LORD **I—Yah Veh,**
when I have *set* **given** a fire in *Egypt* **Misrayim**, and
when all her helpers shall be *destroyed* **broken.**
9 In that day shall *messengers* **angels**
go forth from *me* **my face** in ships
to make the *careless Ethiopians* **confident Kushies**
afraid **tremble,**
and great pain shall come upon them,
as in the day of *Egypt* **Misrayim:**
for, *lo* **behold**, it *cometh* **approacheth.**
10 Thus saith *the Lord GOD* **Adonay Yah Veh;**
I *will* **shall** also *make* **cause**
the multitude of *Egypt* **Misrayim** to *cease* **shabbathize**
by the hand of *Nebuchadrezzar* **Nebukadnets Tsar**
king **sovereign** of *Babylon* **Babel.**
11 He and his people with him,
the *terrible* **tyrant** of the *nations* **goyim,**
shall be brought to *destroy* **ruin** the land:
and they shall draw their swords
against *Egypt* **Misrayim,**
and fill the land with the *slain* **pierced.**
12 And I *will make* **shall work** the rivers dry,
and sell the land into the hand of the *wicked* **evil:**
and I *will make* **shall desolate** the land *waste,*
and *all that is therein* **the fulness thereof,**
by the hand of strangers:
I *the LORD* **Yah Veh** have *spoken it* **worded.**
13 Thus saith *the Lord GOD* **Adonay Yah Veh;**
I *will* **shall** also destroy the idols,
and I *will* **shall** cause their *images* **idols**
to *cease* **shabbathize** out of Noph;
and there shall be no more
a *prince* **hierarch** of the land of *Egypt* **Misrayim:**
and I *will put* **shall give** a fear
in the land of *Egypt* **Misrayim.**
14 And *I will make Pathros* **I**
shall desolate **Pathros,**

and *will set* **shall give** fire in *Zoan* **Soan,**
and *will execute* **shall work** judgments in No.
15 And I *will* **shall** pour my fury upon Sin,
the *strength* **stronghold** of *Egypt* **Misrayim;**
and I *will* **shall** cut off the multitude of No.
16 And I *will* **shall** set fire in *Egypt* **Misrayim**:
In writhing, Sin shall *have great pain* **writhe,**
because they worked for me
—an oracle of Adonay Yah Veh.
21 In that day,
I sprout the horn of the house of Yisra El,
and I give you
the opening of the mouth in their midst;
and they know I—Yah Veh.

THE WORD OF YAH VEH CONCERNING MISRAYIM

30 And so be the word of Yah Veh to me, saying,
2 Son of humanity, prophesy and say,
Thus says Adonay Yah Veh:
Howl! Hah! The day!
3 —for the day is near
—the day of Yah Veh is near;
a day of clouds; it is the time of the goyim:
4 and so be the sword on Misrayim
and so be great pain in Kush;
the pierced fall in Misrayim:
and they take away her multitude
and break her foundations:
5 Kush and Put and Lud
and all the comingled and Kub
and the sons of the land in covenant
fall with them by the sword.
6 Thus says Yah Veh;
And they who uphold Misrayim fall;
and the pomp of her strength topples:
from the tower of Seven they fall by the sword
—an oracle of Adonay Yah Veh
7 and they desolate midst the desolate lands;
and her cities midst the cities are wasted.
8 And they know I—Yah Veh,
when I give a fire in Misrayim
and when all her helpers *are* broken.
9 In that day, angels go from my face in ships
to make the confident Kushies tremble,
and great pain becomes them
as in the day of Misrayim:
for behold, it approaches.
10 Thus says Adonay Yah Veh:
I shabbathize the multitude of Misrayim
by the hand of Nebukadnets Tsar sovereign of Babel:
11 he and his people with him
—the tyrant of the goyim,
he brings the land to ruin:
and they draw their swords against Misrayim,
and fill the land with the pierced.
12 And I work the rivers dry
and sell the land into the hand of the evil:
and I desolate the land and the fulness thereof
by the hand of strangers:
I Yah Veh have worded.
13 Thus says Adonay Yah Veh:
And I destroy the idols
and I shabbathize their idols from Noph;
and there is no more
a hierarch of the land of Misrayim:
and I give a fear in the land of Misrayim:
14 and I desolate Pathros
and give fire in Soan and work judgments in No:
15 and I pour my fury on Sin
the stronghold of Misrayim;
and I cut off the multitude of No;
16 and I set fire in Misrayim:
in writhing, sin writhes,
and No shall be rent asunder,
and Noph shall have *distresses* **tribulations** daily.
17 The *young men* **youths** of *Aven* **mischief**
and of *Pibeseth* **Pi Beseth** shall fall by the sword:
and these cities shall go into captivity.
18 At *Tehaphnehes* **Tachpanches** also
the day shall be *darkened* **spared,**
when I shall break there
the *yokes* **yoke poles** of *Egypt* **Misrayim**:
and the pomp of her strength
shall *cease* **shabbathize** in her:
as for her, a cloud shall cover her,
and her daughters shall go into captivity.
19 Thus *will I execute* **shall I work** judgments
in *Egypt* **Misrayim**:
and they shall know that *I am the LORD* **I—Yah Veh.**
20 And **so be** it *came to pass* in the eleventh year,
in the first *month,* in the seventh *day* of the month,
that the word of *the LORD* **Yah Veh** came unto me,
saying,
21 Son of *man* **humanity,**
I have broken the arm of *Pharaoh* **Paroh**
king **sovereign** of *Egypt* **Misrayim;**
and, *lo* **behold,**

it shall *not be* **be not** bound *up*
to *be healed* **give to healers,**
to *put* **set** a *roller* **bandage** to bind it,
to *make* **strengthen** it *strong*
to *hold* **apprehend** the sword.
22 Therefore thus saith *the*
Lord GOD **Adonay Yah Veh;**
Behold, I am against *Pharaoh* **Paroh**
king **sovereign** of *Egypt* **Misrayim,**
and *will* **shall** break his arms,
the strong, and that which was broken;
and I *will* **shall** cause the sword to fall out of his hand.
23 And I *will* **shall** scatter the *Egyptians* **Misrayim**
among the *nations* **goyim,**
and *will* **shall** disperse them through the *countries* **lands.**
24 And I *will* **shall** strengthen the arms
of the *king* **sovereign** of *Babylon* **Babel,**
and *put* **give** my sword in his hand:
but I *will* **shall** break *Pharaoh's* **Paroh's** arms,
and he shall groan *before him* **at his face**
with the groanings of a *deadly wounded* **pierced** man.
25 But I *will* **shall** strengthen the arms
of the *king* **sovereign** of *Babylon* **Babel,**
and the arms of *Pharaoh* **Paroh** shall fall down;
and they shall know that *I am the LORD* **I—Yah Veh,**
when I shall *put* **give** my sword
into the hand of the *king* **sovereign** of *Babylon* **Babel,**
and he shall *stretch* **spread** it out
upon the land of *Egypt* **Misrayim.**
26 And I *will* **shall** scatter the *Egyptians* **Misrayim**
among the *nations* **goyim,**
and *disperse* **winnow** them among the *countries* **lands;**
and they shall know that *I am the LORD* **I—Yah Veh.**

THE WORD OF YAH VEH CONCERNING PAROH

31 And **so be** it *came to pass* in the eleventh year,
in the third *month*, in the first *day* of the month,
that the word of *the LORD* **Yah Veh** came unto me,
saying,
2 Son of *man* **humanity,**
speak unto *Pharaoh* **Paroh**
king **sovereign** of *Egypt* **Misrayim,**
and to his multitude;
Whom art thou like in thy greatness?
3 Behold, the *Assyrian* **Ashshuri**
was a cedar in Lebanon
with *fair* **beautiful** branches,
and with *a shadowing shroud* **an overshadowing forest,**
and of an high *stature* **height;**
and his *top* **foliage** was among the thick *boughs* **foliage.**
4 The waters *made* **greatened** him *great,*
the *deep set* **abyss lifted** him *up on high*
with her rivers *running* **passing** round about his plants,
and sent her *little rivers* **channels**
unto all the trees of the field.
5 Therefore his height was *exalted* **heightened**
above all the trees of the field,
and No rips *apart,*
and Noph tribulates daily.
17 The youths of mischief
and of Pi Beseth fall by the sword; and
these cities go into captivity:
18 and spare the day in Tachpanches,
when I break the yoke poles of Misrayim:
and the pomp of her strength shabbathizes in her:
as for her, a cloud covers her
and her daughters go into captivity.
19 Thus I work judgments in Misrayim:
and they know I—Yah Veh.
20 And so be it, in the eleventh year,
in the first, in the seventh of the month,
so be the word of Yah Veh to me, saying,
21 Son of humanity,
I broke the arm of Paroh sovereign of Misrayim;
and behold, it *is* not bound to give healing
to set a bandage to bind it,
to strengthen it to apprehend the sword.
22 So thus says Adonay Yah Veh:
Behold, I *am* against Paroh sovereign of Misrayim,
and I break his arms
—the strong and the broken:
and I fell the sword from his hand;
23 and I scatter the Misrayim among the goyim
and disperse them through the lands:
24 and I strengthen the arms
of the sovereign of Babel
and give my sword in his hand:
and I break the arms of Paroh, and he groans
the groanings of a pierced man at his face.
25 And I strengthen the arms
of the sovereign of Babel
and fell the arms of Paroh:
and they know I—Yah Veh,
when I give my sword
into the hand of the sovereign of Babel;
and he spreads it on the land of Misrayim:
26 and I scatter the Misrayim among the goyim
and winnow them among the lands:
and they know I—Yah Veh.

THE WORD OF YAH VEH CONCERNING PAROH

31 And so be it, in the eleventh year,
in the third, in the first of the month,
so be the word of Yah Veh to me, saying,
2 Son of humanity,
speak to Paroh sovereign of Misrayim
and to his multitude;
To whom are you likened in your greatness?
3 Behold, the Ashshuri,
a cedar in Lebanon with beautiful branches
with an overshadowing forest
and high in height;
with his foliage among the thick foliage:
4 the waters greaten him; the abyss lifts him;
and her rivers pass all around his plants
and send her channels to all the trees of the field.
5 So his height heightens
above all the trees of the field;
and his *boughs* **twigs** were *multiplied* **greatened**,
and his *branches became long* **foliage lengthened**
because of the *multitude* **abundance** of waters,
when he *shot* **spread** forth.
6 All the *fowls* **flyers** of *heaven* **the heavens**
made their nests **nested** in his *boughs* **twigs**,
and under his *branches* **foliage**
did all the *beasts* **live beings** of the field
bring forth **birth** their young,
and under his shadow
dwelt **settled** all great *nations* **goyim**.
7 Thus was he *fair* **beautified** in his greatness,
in the length of his branches:
for his root was by great waters.
8 The cedars in the garden of *God* **Elohim**
could not *hide* **shade** him:
the fir trees were not like his *boughs* **twigs**,
and the chesnut trees were not like his *branches* **foliage**;
nor any tree in the garden of *God* **Elohim**
was like unto him in his beauty.
9 I have *made* **worked** him *fair* **beautiful**
by the *multitude* **abundance** of his branches:
so that all the trees of Eden,
that were in the garden of *God* **Elohim**, envied him.
10 Therefore thus saith *the*
Lord GOD **Adonay Yah Veh**;
Because thou hast
lifted up thyself in **heightened thy** height,
and he hath *shot up* **given** his *top* **foliage**
among the thick *boughs* **foliage**,
and his heart is lifted *up* in his height;
11 I have therefore *delivered* **given** him
into the hand of the *mighty one* **el** of the *heathen* **goyim**;
in working, he shall *surely deal* **work** with him:
I have driven him out for his wickedness.
12 And strangers, the *terrible*
tyrants of the *nations* **goyim**,
have cut him off, and have *left* **abandoned** him:
upon the mountains and in all the valleys
his branches are fallen,
and his *boughs* **foliage** are broken
by all the *rivers* **reservoirs** of the *land* **earth**;
and all the people of the earth
are *gone down* **descended** from his shadow,
and have *left* **abandoned** him.
13 Upon his ruin shall **tabernacle**
all the *fowls* **flyers** of the *heaven remain* **heavens**,
and all the *beasts* **live beings** of the field
shall be upon his *branches* **foliage**:
14 To the end that none of
all the trees by the waters
exalt **heighten** themselves for their height,
neither *shoot up* **give** their *top* **foliage**
among the thick *boughs* **foliage**,
neither their *trees* **mighty oaks** stand up in their height,
all that drink water:
for they are all *delivered* **given** unto death,
to the *nether parts* **nethermost** of the earth,
in the midst of the *children* **sons** of *men* **humanity**,
with them that *go down* **descend** to the *pit* **well**.
15 Thus saith *the Lord GOD* **Adonay Yah Veh**;
In the day
when he *went down* **descended** to *the grave* **sheol**
I caused a mourning:
I covered the *deep* **abyss** for him,
and I *restrained* **withheld** the *floods* **rivers** *thereof*,
and the great waters were stayed:
and I caused Lebanon to *mourn* **darken** for him,
and all the trees of the field *fainted* **languished** for him.
16 I *made* **caused** the *nations* **goyim**
to *shake* **quake** at the *sound* **voice** of his *fall* **ruin**,
when I *cast* **brought** him down to *hell* **sheol**
with them that *descend* **descended** into the *pit* **well**:
and all the trees of Eden, the choice and best of Lebanon,
all that drink water, shall *be comforted* **sigh**
in the *nether parts* **nethermost** of the earth.
17 They also *went down* **descended** into *hell* **sheol**
with him
unto them that be *slain* **pierced** with the sword;
and they that *were* his arm,
that *dwelt* **settled** under his shadow

in the midst of the *heathen* **goyim**.
and his twigs greaten and his foliage lengthens
because of the abundance of waters
when he spreads forth:
6 all the flyers of the heavens nest in his twigs
and under his foliage
all the live beings of the field birth their young;
and all the great goyim settle under his shadow:
7 and he beautifies in his greatness
—in the length of his branches:
and so be his root by great waters:
8 the cedars in the garden
of Elohim shade him not:
neither are the fir trees like his twigs;
nor the chesnut trees like his foliage; nor
any tree in the garden of Elohim
like him in his beauty:
9 I worked him beautiful
in the abundance of his branches:
so that all the trees of Eden in the garden of Elohim
envy him.
10 So thus says Adonay Yah Veh:
Because you heighten in height,
and he gives his foliage among the thick foliage
and lifts his heart in height;
11 so I give him
into the hand of the el of the goyim;
in working, he works with him:
I drive him out for his wickedness:
12 and strangers, the tyrants of the goyim,
cut him off and abandon him:
his branches fall
on the mountains and in all the valleys;
and his foliage breaks
by all the reservoirs of the earth;
and all the people of the earth
descend from his shadow and abandon him:
13 all the flyers of the heavens,
tabernacle on his ruin;
and all the live beings of the field
are on his foliage:
14 so that none of all the trees by the waters
heighten themselves in height;
neither give their foliage among the thick foliage
nor their mighty oaks stand in their height
—all drinking waters:
for they are all given to death;
to the nethermost of the earth
midst the sons of humanity,
who descend with them to the well.
15 Thus says Adonay Yah Veh:
In the day he descends to sheol
I cause a mourning; I cover the abyss for him:
and I withhold the rivers and stay the great waters:
and I darken Lebanon for him
and all the trees of the field languish for him:
16 I quake the goyim at the voice of his ruin
when I bring him down to sheol
with them who descend into the well:
and all the trees of Eden
—the choice and best of Lebanon
—all who drink water
sigh in the nethermost of the earth:
17 they also descend into sheol with him
to the pierced with the sword;
and settles his arm under his shadow midst the goyim.
18 To whom art thou thus like in *glory* **honour**
and in greatness among the trees of Eden?
yet shalt thou be brought down with the trees of Eden
unto the *nether parts* **nethermost** of the earth:
thou shalt lie in the midst of the uncircumcised
with them that be *slain* **pierced** by the sword.
This is *Pharaoh* **Paroh** and all his multitude,
saith the Lord GOD **an oracle of Adonay Yah Veh**.

Lamentation Against Paroh

32 And **so be** it *came to pass* in the twelfth year,
in the twelfth month, in the first *day* of the month,
that the word of *the LORD* **Yah Veh** came unto me,
saying,
2 Son of *man* **humanity**, *take up* **lift** a lamentation
for *Pharaoh king* **Paroh sovereign** of *Egypt* **Misrayim**,
and say unto him,
Thou art like a *young lion* **whelp** of the *nations* **goyim**,
and thou art as *a whale* **monsters** in the seas:
and thou camest forth with thy rivers,
and troubledst the waters with thy feet,
and fouledst their rivers.
3 Thus saith *the Lord GOD* **Adonay Yah Veh**;
I *will* **shall** therefore spread out my net over thee
with a *company* **congregation** of many people;
and they shall *bring* **ascend** thee *up* in my net.
4 Then *will I leave* **shall I**
abandon thee upon the land,
I *will* **shall** cast thee forth upon
the *open* **face of the** field,
and *will* **shall** cause
all the *fowls* **flyers** of the *heaven* **heavens**
to *remain* **tabernacle** upon thee,
and I *will fill* **shall satiate** the *beasts* **live beings**

of the whole earth with thee.
5 And I *will lay* **shall give** thy
flesh upon the mountains,
and fill the valleys with thy *height* **carcase heaps**.
6 I *will* **shall** also *water* **wet** with thy blood
the land *wherein thou swimmest* **of thy swimming**,
even to the mountains;
and the *rivers* **reservoirs** shall be *full* **filled** of thee.
7 And when I shall put thee out,
I *will* **shall** cover the *heaven* **heavens**,
and *make* **darken** the stars *thereof dark*;
I *will* **shall** cover the sun with a cloud,
and the moon shall not *give her light* **lighten**.
8 All the *bright* lights
of the light of *heaven* **the heavens**
will I make dark **shall I darken** over thee,
and *set* **give** darkness upon thy land,
saith the Lord GOD **an oracle of Adonay Yah Veh**.
9 I *will* **shall** also vex the hearts of many people,
when I shall bring thy *destruction* **breech**
among the *nations* **goyim**,
into the *countries* **lands** which thou hast not known.
10 Yea, I *will make* **shall cause** many people
amazed **to astonish** at thee,
and their *kings* **sovereigns**
shall *be horribly afraid* **shudder with horror** *for thee*,
when I shall *brandish* **flutter** my sword
before them **at their face**;
and they shall tremble *at every moment* **in a blink**,
every man for his own *life* **soul**, in
the day of thy *fall* **ruin**.
11 For thus saith *the Lord GOD* **Adonay Yah Veh**;
The sword of the *king* **sovereign** of *Babylon* **Babel**
shall come upon thee.
12 By the swords of the mighty
will **shall** I cause thy multitude to fall,
the *terrible* **tyrants** of the *nations* **goyim**, all of them:
and they shall *spoil* **ravage** the pomp of *Egypt* **Misrayim**,
and all the multitude *thereof*
shall be *destroyed* **desolated**.
13 I *will* **shall** destroy also all
the *beasts* **animals** *thereof*
from beside the great waters;
neither shall the foot of *man* **humanity**
trouble them any more,
nor the hoofs of *beasts* **animals** trouble them.
14 Then *will* **shall** I make their waters *deep* **drown**,
and cause their rivers to *run* **go** like oil,
saith the Lord GOD **an oracle of Adonay Yah Veh**.
15 When I shall *make* **give** the
land of *Egypt* **Misrayim**

desolate,
18 To whom are you thus likened in honor
and in greatness among the trees of Eden?
Yet I bring you down with the trees of Eden
to the nethermost of the earth:
to lie among the uncircumcised
with the pierced by the sword
—thus *is* Paroh and all his multitude
—an oracle of Adonay Yah Veh.

Lamentation Against Paroh

32 And so be it, in the twelfth year,
in the twelfth month, in the first of the month,
so be the word of Yah Veh to me, saying,
2 Son of humanity,
lift a lamentation for Paroh sovereign of Misrayim,
and say to him,
You are like a whelp of the goyim
and as monsters in the seas:
and you come forth with your rivers
and trouble the waters with your feet
and foul their rivers.
3 Thus says Adonay Yah Veh:
And I spread my net over you
with a congregation of many people;
and they ascend you in my net:
4 and I abandon you on the land:
I cast you forth on the face of the field,
and all the flyers of the heavens tabernacle on you;
and with you,
I satiate the live beings of the whole earth:
5 and I give your flesh on the mountains
and fill the valleys with your carcase heaps:
6 and with your blood
I wet the land of your swimming
—even to the mountains;
and fill the reservoirs with you:
7 and when I put you out,
I cover the heavens and darken the stars:
I cover the sun with a cloud
and the moon lightens not:
8 all the lights of the light of the heavens
I darken over you
and give darkness on your land
—an oracle of Adonay Yah Veh.
9 And I vex the hearts of many people,
when I bring your breech among the goyim,
to the lands you know not.
10 Yes, many people astonish at you
and their sovereigns shudder with horror

when I flutter my sword at their face;
and in a blink, every man trembles for his own soul
in the day of your ruin.
11 For thus says Adonay Yah Veh:
The sword of the sovereign of Babel comes upon you.
12 By the swords of the mighty,
I fell your multitude
—the tyrants of the goyim—all of them:
and they ravage the pomp of Misrayim,
and all the multitude desolates:
13 and I destroy all the animals
from beside the great waters;
neither the foot of humanity troubles them any more
nor the hoofs of animals trouble them.
14 Then I drown their waters
that their rivers go as oil
—an oracle of Adonay Yah Veh.
15 I give the land of Misrayim desolate
and the *country* **land** hall be *destitute* **desolated** *of that*
whereof it was full **from the fulness thereof,** when
I shall smite all them that *dwell* **settle** therein, then
shall they know that *I am the LORD* **I—Yah Veh.**
16 This is the lamentation
wherewith they shall lament her:
the daughters of the *nations* **goyim** shall lament her:
they shall lament for her,
even for *Egypt* **Misrayim,** and for all her multitude,
saith the Lord GOD **an oracle of Adonay Yah Veh.**
17 **So be** it *came to pass*
also in the twelfth year, in the
fifteenth *day* of the month,
that the word of *the LORD* **Yah Veh** came unto me,
saying,
18 Son of *man* **humanity,**
wail **lament** for the multitude of *Egypt* **Misrayim,**
and *cast* **bring** them down, *even* her,
and the daughters of the *famous nations* **mighty goyim,**
unto the *nether parts* **nethermost** of the earth,
with them that *go down* **descend** into the *pit* **well.**
19 *Whom dost thou pass in beauty?*
With whom hast thou been most pleasant?
go down **descend,**
and be thou laid with the uncircumcised.
20 They shall fall in the midst of them
that are *slain* **pierced** by the sword:
she is *delivered* **given** to the sword:
draw her and all her multitudes.
21 The *strong among* **el of** the mighty
shall *speak* **word** to him
out of the midst of *hell* **sheol** with them that help him:
they *are gone down* **descend,**
they lie uncircumcised, *slain* **pierced** by the sword.
22 *Asshur* **Ashshur** is there
and all her *company* **congregation:**
his *graves* **tombs** are **round** about him:
all of them *slain* **pierced,** fallen by the sword:
23 Whose *graves* **tombs** are *set* **given**
in the *sides* **flanks** of the *pit* **well,**
and her *company* **congregation**
is round about her *grave* **tomb:**
all of them *slain* **pierced,** fallen by the sword,
which *caused* **gave** terror in the land of the living.
24 There is Elam and all her multitude
round about her *grave* **tomb,**
all of them *slain* **pierced,** fallen by the sword,
which are *gone* **brought** down uncircumcised
into the *nether parts* **nethermost** of the earth,
which *caused* **gave** their terror in the land of the living;
yet have they borne their shame
with them that *go down* **descend** to the *pit* **well.**
25 They have *set* **given** her a bed
in the midst of the *slain* **pierced** with all her multitude:
her *graves* **tombs** are round about him:
all of them uncircumcised, *slain* **pierced** by the sword:
though their terror
was *caused* **given** in the land of the living,
yet have they borne their shame with them
that *go down* **descend** to the *pit* **well:**
he is *put* **given** in the midst of them that be *slain* **pierced.**
26 There is Meshech, Tubal,
and all her multitude:
her *graves* **tombs** are round about him:
all of them uncircumcised, *slain* **pierced** by the sword,
though they *caused* **gave** their terror
in the land of the living.
27 And they shall not lie with the mighty
that are fallen of the uncircumcised,
which are *gone down* **descended** to *hell* **sheol**
with their *weapons* **instruments** of war:
and they have *laid* **given** their swords under their heads,
but their *iniquities* **perversities**
shall be upon their bones,
though they were the terror of the mighty
in the land of the living.
28 Yea,
thou shalt be broken in the midst of the uncircumcised,
and shalt lie with them
that are *slain* **pierced** with the sword.
29 There is Edom,
and desolate the land from the fulness thereof

and I smite all who settle therein:
and they know I—Yah Veh.
16 This is a lamentation; and they lament her:
the daughters of the goyim lament her:
they lament her,
for Misrayim and for all her multitude
they lament her
—an oracle of Adonay Yah Veh.
17 So be it,
in the twelfth year, in the fifteenth of the month,
so be the word of Yah Veh to me, saying,
18 Son of humanity,
lament for the multitude of Misrayim,
and descend them
—them and the daughters of the mighty goyim,
to the nethermost of the earth,
with them who descend into the well.
19 With whom have you been most pleasant?
Descend and lie with the uncircumcised.
20 They fall in their midst
—the pierced by the sword:
she is given to the sword:
they draw her and all her multitudes:
21 the el of the mighty words
to him from midst sheol
with them who help him:
they descend;
they lie uncircumcised; pierced by the sword.
22 There is Ashshur with all her congregation:
surrounded by his tombs:
all the pierced; the fallen by the sword:
23 whose tombs are given in the flanks of the well;
and her congregation surrounds her tomb:
all of the pierced; the fallen by the sword:
who give terror in the land of the living.
24 There is Elam with all her multitude:
surrounded her tomb,
all of the pierced; the fallen by the sword:
who descend the uncircumcised
into the nethermost of the earth;
who give their terror in the land of the living;
yet they bear their shame
with them who descend to the well.
25 They give her a bed midst the pierced
with all her multitude:
her tombs surround him:
all of the uncircumcised; the pierced by the sword:
for their terror *is* given in the land of the living,
yet they bear their shame
with them who descend to the well:
he *is* given midst the pierced.
26 There is Meshech, Tubal, and all her multitude:
surrounded by her tombs:
all of the uncircumcised; the pierced by the sword
for they give their terror in the land of the living:
27 and they not lie with the mighty
—the fallen of the uncircumcised,
who descend to sheol with their instruments of war:
and they give their swords under their heads,
and their perversities *are* on their bones,
for the terror of the mighty in the land of the living.
28 Yes,
you are broken among the uncircumcised,
and lie with them
who are pierced with the sword.
29 There is Edom,
her *kings* **sovereigns**, and all her *princes* **hierarchs**,
which with their might are *laid* **given**
by them that were *slain* **pierced** by the sword:
they shall lie with the uncircumcised,
and with them that *go down* **descend** to the *pit* **well**.
30 There be the princes of the north,
all of them, and all the *Zidonians* **Sidonians**,
which are *gone* **brought** down with the *slain* **pierced**;
with their terror they are ashamed of their might;
and they lie uncircumcised
with them that be *slain* **pierced** by the sword,
and bear their shame
with them that *go down* **descend** to the *pit* **well**.
31 *Pharaoh* **Paroh** shall see them,
and shall *be comforted* **sigh** over all his multitude,
even Pharaoh **Paroh** and all his *army* **valiant**
slain **pierced** by the sword,
saith the Lord GOD **an oracle of Adonay Yah Veh**.
32 For I have *caused* **given** my terror
in the land of the living:
and he shall be laid in the midst of the uncircumcised
with them that are *slain* **pierced** with the sword,
even Pharaoh **Paroh** and all his multitude,
saith the Lord GOD **an oracle of Adonay Yah Veh**.

YECHEZQ EL, THE WATCHER

33 Again the word of *the LORD* **Yah Veh**
came unto me, saying,
2 Son of *man* **humanity**,
speak **word** to the *children* **sons** of thy people,
and say unto them,
When I bring the sword upon a land,
if the people of the land
take *a* **one** man of their *coasts* **edges**,

and *set* **give** him for their *watchman* **watcher**:
3 If when he seeth the sword
come upon **approach** the land,
he *blow* **blast** the *trumpet* **shophar**,
and *warn* **enlighten** the people;
4 Then in **hearkening,**
whosoever *heareth* **hearkeneth**
the sound **unto the voice** of the *trumpet* **shophar**,
and taketh not warning;
if the sword come, and take him away,
his blood shall be upon his own head.
5 He heard the *sound* **voice** of the *trumpet* **shophar**,
and took not warning; his blood shall be upon him. But
he that taketh warning shall *deliver* **rescue** his soul.
6 But if the *watchman* **watcher**
see the sword come,
and *blow* **blast** not the *trumpet* **shophar**,
and the people be not warned; if the sword come,
and take *any person* **a soul** from among them,
he is taken away in his *iniquity* **perversity**;
but his blood *will* **shall** I require
at the *watchman's* **watcher's** hand.
7 So thou, O son of *man* **humanity**,
I have *set* **given** thee
a *watchman* **watcher** unto the house of *Israel* **Yisra El**;
therefore thou shalt hear the word at my mouth,
and *warn* **enlighten** them from me.
8 *When I say* **Saying** unto
the wicked, O wicked *man*,
in dying, thou shalt *surely* die;
if thou dost not *speak* **word**
to *warn* **enlighten** the wicked from his way,
that wicked *man* shall die in his *iniquity* **perversity**;
but his blood *will I require* **shall I seek** at thine hand.
9 Nevertheless,
if thou *warn* **enlighten** the wicked of his way
to turn from it;
if he do not turn from his way,
he shall die in his *iniquity* **perversity**;
but thou hast *delivered* **rescued** thy soul.
10 Therefore, O thou son of *man* **humanity**,
speak **say** unto the house of *Israel* **Yisra El**;
Thus ye *speak* **say**, saying,
If our *transgressions* **rebellions** and our sins be upon us,
and we *pine away* **vanish** in them,
how should we then live?
11 Say unto them, *As* I live,
saith the Lord GOD **an oracle of Adonay Yah Veh**,
I have no *pleasure* **delight** in the death of the wicked;
but that the wicked turn from his way and live:

her sovereigns, and all her hierarchs,
who in their might
are given with the pierced by the sword:
they lie with the uncircumcised,
and with them who descend to the well.
30 These *are* the princes of the north
—all of them and all the Sidonians
who descend with the pierced in their terror;
they shame of their might;
and they lie uncircumcised
with the pierced by the sword;
and bear their shame
with them who descend to the well.
31 Paroh sees them
and sighs over all his multitude
—Paroh and all his valiant pierced by the sword
—an oracle of Adonay Yah Veh.
32 For I give his terror in the land of the living:
and he lies among the uncircumcised
with the pierced of the sword
—Paroh and all his multitude
—an oracle of Adonay Yah Veh.

YECHEZQ EL, THE WATCHER

33 And so be the word of Yah Veh to me, saying,
2 Son of humanity,
word to the sons of your people, and say to them,
When I bring the sword on a land,
if the people of the land
take one man from their edges,
and give him for their watcher:
3 and he sees the sword approach the land,
he blasts the shophar and enlightens the people:
4 and in hearing, one hears
the voice of the shophar,
and takes not warning;
and the sword approaches and takes him away,
his blood is on his own head:
5 for he hears the voice of the shophar,
and takes not warning;
his blood is on himself:
and he who takes warning, rescues his soul.
6 And if the watcher sees the sword approach,
and neither blasts the shophar nor warns the people;
if the sword approaches
and takes a soul from among them,
he is taken away in his perversity;
and I require his blood
at the hand of the watcher.
7 Thus you, O son of humanity,

I give you as a watcher to the house of Yisra El:
so hear the word at my mouth
and enlighten them from me;
8 saying to the wicked, O wicked,
in dying, you die
if you word not to enlighten the wicked from his way:
that wicked dies in his perversity
and I seek his blood at your hand.
9 And you,
if you enlighten the wicked to turn from his way
and he turns not from his way,
he dies in his perversity and you rescue your soul.
10 And you, O son of humanity,
say to the house of Yisra El;
say thus, saying,
Surely our rebellions and our sins *are* on us,
and we vanish in them:
how then live we?
11 Say to them, I live
—an oracle of Adonay Yah Veh,
I delight not in the death of the wicked;
but that the wicked turn from his way and live:
turn ye, turn ye from your evil ways;
for why *will* **shall** ye die, O house of *Israel* **Yisra El**?
12 Therefore, thou son of *man* **humanity**,
say unto the *children* **sons** of thy people,
The *righteousness* **justness** of the *righteous* **just**
shall not *deliver* **rescue** him
in the day of his *transgression* **rebellion**:
as for the wickedness of the wicked,
he shall not *fall* **falter** thereby
in the day that he turneth from his wickedness;
neither shall the *righteous* **just** be able to live
for his righteousness **by it** in the day that he sinneth.
13 When I shall say to the *righteous* **just**,
that **in living,** he shall *surely* live;
if he *trust* **confide** to his own *righteousness* **justness**,
and *commit iniquity* **work wickedness**,
all his *righteousnesses* **justnesses**
shall not be remembered;
but for his *iniquity* **wickedness**
that he hath *committed* **worked**, he shall die for it.
14 *Again, when I say* **Saying** unto the wicked,
In dying, Thou shalt *surely* die;
if he turn from his sin,
and *do that which is lawful* **work judgment**
and *right* **justness**;
15 If the wicked restore the pledge,
give again **shalam** that **which** he had *robbed* **stripped**,
walk in the statutes of life,
without *committing iniquity* **working wickedness**;
in living, he shall *surely* live, he shall not die.
16 None of his sins that he hath *committed* **sinned**
shall be *mentioned* **remembered** unto him:
he hath *done* **worked**
that which is lawful **judgment** and *right* **justness**;
in living, he shall *surely* live.

THE WAY OF BALANCE

17 Yet the *children* **sons** of thy people say,
The way of *the Lord* **Adonay** is not *equal* **gauged**:
but as for them, their way is not *equal* **gauged**.
18 When the *righteous* **just**
turneth from his *righteousness* **justness**,
and *committeth iniquity* **worketh wickedness**,
he shall even die thereby.
19 But if the wicked turn from his wickedness,
and do that which is *lawful* **judgment** and *right* **justness**,
he shall live thereby.
20 Yet ye say,
The way of *the Lord* **Adonay** is not *equal* **gauged**.
O ye house of *Israel* **Yisra El**,
I *will* **shall** judge you every *one* **man** after his ways.

YERU SHALEM SMITTEN

21 And **so be** it *came to pass*
in the twelfth year of our *captivity* **exile**,
in the tenth *month*, in the fifth *day* of the month,
that one *that had escaped* **escapee**
out of *Jerusalem* **Yeru Shalem** came unto me, saying,
The city is smitten.
22 *Now* the hand of *the LORD* **Yah Veh**
was upon me in the evening,
afore he that was escaped came
at the face of the coming of the escapee;
and had opened my mouth,
until he came to me in the morning;
and my mouth was opened,
and I was no more *dumb* **mute**.
23 Then the word of *the LORD*
Yah Veh came unto me,
saying,
24 Son of *man* **humanity**,
they that *inhabit* **settle** those *wastes* **parched areas**
of the *land* **soil** of *Israel* **Yisra El** *speak* **say**, saying,
Abraham was one,
and he *inherited* **was successor of** the land:
but we are many;
the land is given us for *inheritance* **possession**.
25 Wherefore say unto them,

Thus saith *the Lord GOD* **Adonay Yah Veh**;
Ye eat with the blood,
and lift up your eyes toward your idols,
and *shed* **pour** blood:
turn—turn from your evil ways;
for why die, O house of Yisra El?
12 And you, son of humanity,
say to the sons of your people,
The justness of the just
rescues him not in the day of his rebellion:
as for the wickedness of the wicked,
he falters not in the day he turns from his wickedness;
and the just are not able to live by it
in the day he sins.
13 When I say to the just, In living, he lives!
—and he confides in his own justness
and works wickedness,
all his justnesses *are* not remembered:
and for the wickedness he works, he dies for it.
14 And saying to the wicked, In dying, you die;
if he turns from his sin,
and works judgment and justness;
15 if the wicked restores the pledge and shalams what
he stripped; and walks in the statutes of life without
working wickedness; in living, he lives; he dies not.
16 Not one of the sins he sinned
are remembered to him:
he works judgment and justness;
in living, he lives.

THE WAY OF BALANCE

17 And the sons of your people say,
The way of Adonay *is* not gauged:
and as for them, their way *is* not gauged.
18 When the just turns from his justness,
and works wickedness,
he dies thereby:
19 and if the wicked turns from his wickedness,
and does judgment and justness,
he lives thereby.
20 And you say, The way of Adonay is not gauged.
—O you house of Yisra El,
I judge every man of you after his ways.

YERU SHALEM SMITTEN

21 And so be it, in the twelfth year of our exile,
in the tenth, in the fifth of the month,
that one escapee from Yeru Shalem comes to me,
saying, The city is smitten.
22 the hand of Yah Veh is on me in the evening,
ere the face of the coming of the escapee;
and opens my mouth,
until he comes to me in the morning;
and my mouth opens
and I *am* no more mute.
23 And so be the word of Yah Veh to me, saying,
24 Son of humanity,
they who settle the parched areas
of the soil of Yisra El say, saying,
Abraham, being one, was successor of the land:
but we *are* many;
the land is given us for possession.
25 Why say to them, Thus says Adonay Yah Veh:
You eat with the blood
and lift your eyes toward your idols
and pour blood!
and shall ye possess the land?
26 Ye stand upon your sword,
ye work *abomination* **abhorrence**,
and ye *defiled* **fouled**
every *one* **man** his *neighbour's wife* **friend's woman**:
and shall ye possess the land?
27 Say thou thus unto them,
Thus saith *the Lord GOD* **Adonay Yah Veh**; *As* I live,
surely they that are in the *wastes* **parched areas**
shall fall by the sword,
and him that is in the *open* **face of the** field
will **shall** I give to the *beasts* **live beings** to be devoured,
and they that be in the *forts* **huntholds** and in the caves
shall die of the pestilence.
28 For I *will lay* **shall give** the land
most desolate **desolation and desolation**,
and the *pomp* **pomp** of her strength
shall *cease* **shabbathize**;
and the mountains of *Israel* **Yisra El** shall *be* desolate,
that none shall pass through.
29 Then shall they know that
I am the LORD **I—Yah Veh**,
when I have *laid* **given** the land
most desolate **desolation and desolation**
because of all their *abominations* **abhorrences**
which they have *committed* **worked**.
30 Also, thou son of *man* **humanity**,
the *children* **sons** of thy people
still *are talking* **wording** against thee *by* **beside** the walls
and in the *doors* **portals** of the houses,
and *speak* **word** one to *another* **one**,
every *one* **man** to his brother, saying,
Come, I *pray* **beseech** you, and hear what is the word
that cometh forth from *the LORD* **Yah Veh**.

31 And they come unto thee
as the people *cometh* **approach**,
and they sit *before thee* **at thy face** as my people,
and they hear thy words,
but they *will* **shall** not *do* **work** them:
for with their mouth they *shew*
much love **work pantings**,
but their heart goeth after their
covetousness **greedy gain**.
32 And, *lo* **behold**, thou art unto them
as a *very lovely* song **of pantings**
of one that hath a *pleasant* **beautiful** voice,
and can *play well* **strum goodly** on an instrument:
for they hear thy words, but they *do* **work** them not.
33 And when this *cometh to pass* **approacheth**,
(*lo* **behold**, it *will come* **shall approach**,)
then shall they know that a prophet
hath been among them.

THE WORD OF YAH VEH CONCERNING TENDERS

34 And **so be** the word of *the LORD came* **Yah Veh**
unto me, saying,
2 Son of *man* **humanity**,
prophesy against the *shepherds* **tenders** of *Israel* **Yisra El**,
prophesy, and say unto them,
Thus saith *the Lord GOD* **Adonay Yah Veh**
unto the *shepherds* **tenders**;
Woe be **Ho** to the *shepherds* **tenders** of *Israel* **Yisra El**
that *do feed* **tend** themselves!
should not the *shepherds feed* **tenders tend** the flocks?
3 Ye eat the fat, and ye *clothe*
enrobe you with the wool,
ye *kill them that are fed* **sacrifice the fattened**:
but ye *feed* **tend** not the flock.
4 The *diseased* **worn** have ye not strengthened,
neither have ye healed that which was sick,
neither have ye bound up that which was broken,
neither have ye *brought again* **restored**
that which was *driven away* **expelled**,
neither have ye sought that which was lost;
but with *force* **severity** and with *cruelty* **tyranny**
have ye *ruled* **subjugated** them.
5 And they were scattered,
because there is no *shepherd* **tender**:
and they became *meat* **food**
to all the *beasts* **live beings** of the field,
when they were scattered.
6 My *sheep wandered* **flock erred inadvertently**
through all the mountains, and upon every high hill:

yea, my flock was scattered upon all the face of the earth,
and none did search or seek *after them*.
Possess you the land?
26 You stand on your sword; you work abhorrence;
You foul the woman of the friend of every man:
Possess you the land?
27 You, say thus to them,
Thus says Adonay Yah Veh: I live!
Surely they in the parched areas fall by the sword,
and him in the face of the field
I give to the live beings to devour;
and they in the huntholds and in the caves
die of the pestilence.
28 And I give the land a desolation and desolate,
and the pomp of her strength shabbathizes;
and the mountains of Yisra El desolate
so that no one passes through:
29 and they know I—Yah Veh
when I give the land a desolation and desolate
because of all the abhorrences they work.
30 And you, son of humanity,
the sons of your people still word against you
beside the walls and in the portals of the houses;
and they word one to one, every man to his brother,
saying, Come, I beseech you,
and hear the word that comes from Yah Veh.
31 And they come to you as people approaching
and they sit at your face as my people;
and they hear your words, and work them not:
for they work pantings with their mouth
but their heart goes after their greedy gain:
32 and behold,
you are to them as a song of pantings
—of a beautiful voice
strumming goodly on an instrument:
for they hear your words, and they work them not.
33 And when this approaches
—behold, it approaches
then they know a prophet is among them.

THE WORD OF YAH VEH CONCERNING TENDERS

34 And so be the word of Yah Veh to me, saying,
2 Son of humanity,
prophesy against the tenders of Yisra El
—prophesy, and say to them,
Thus says Adonay Yah Veh to the tenders:
Ho to the tenders of Yisra El who tend themselves!
Tend the tenders not the flocks?
3 You eat the fat and you enrobe with the wool;

you sacrifice the fattened:
you tend not the flock.
4 you neither strengthen the
worn nor heal the sick;
nor bind the broken nor restore the expelled;
nor seek you the lost:
and with severity and with tyranny
you subjugate them.
5 And because there is no tender, they scatter:
and they become food
to all the live beings of the field;
yes, they scatter.
6 My flock errs inadvertently
through all the mountains and on every high hill:
yes, my flock scatters on all the face of the earth;
and no one searches or seeks.
7 Therefore, ye *shepherds* **tenders**,
hear the word of *the LORD* **Yah Veh**;
8 *As* I live,
saith the Lord GOD **an oracle of Adonay Yah Veh**,
surely because my flock became a *prey* **plunder**,
and my flock became *meat* **food**
to every *beast* **live being** of the field,
because there was no *shepherd* **tender**,
neither did my *shepherds* **tenders** search for my flock,
but the *shepherds fed* **tenders tended** themselves,
and *fed* **tended** not my flock;
9 Therefore, O ye *shepherds* **tenders**,
hear the word of *the LORD* **Yah Veh**;
10 Thus saith *the Lord GOD* **Adonay Yah Veh**;
Behold, I am against the *shepherds* **tenders**;
and I *will* **shall** require my flock at their hand,
and cause them to *cease* **shabbathize**
from *feeding* **tending** the flock;
neither shall the *shepherds feed* **tenders tend** themselves
any more;
for I *will deliver* **shall rescue** my flock from their mouth,
that they may not be *meat* **food** for them.

THE TENDER OF YISRA EL

11 For thus saith *the Lord GOD* **Adonay Yah Veh**;
Behold, I, *even* I,
will **shall** both search my *sheep* **flock**,
and *seek* **search** them out.
12 As a *shepherd* **tender**
seeketh **searcheth** out his *flock* **drove**
in the day
that he is among his *sheep* **flock** that are scattered;
so *will I seek* **shall I search** out my *sheep* **flock**,
and *will deliver* **shall rescue** them
out of all places where they have been scattered
in the cloudy and *dark* day **of dripping darkness**.
13 And I *will* **shall** bring them out from the people,
and gather them from the *countries* **lands**,
and *will* **shall** bring them to their own *land* **soil**,
and *feed* **tend** them upon the
mountains of *Israel* **Yisra El**
by the *rivers* **reservoirs**,
and in all the *inhabited places* **sites** of the *country* **land**.
14 I *will feed* **shall tend** them in a good pasture,
and upon the high mountains of *Israel* **Yisra El**
shall their *fold* **habitation of rest** be:
there shall they *lie* **crouch**
in a good *fold* **habitation of rest**,
and in a fat pasture shall they *feed* **graze**
upon the mountains of *Israel* **Yisra El**.
15 I *will feed* **shall tend** my flock,
and I *will* **shall** cause them to *lie down* **crouch**, *saith
the Lord GOD* **an oracle of Adonay Yah Veh**.
16 I *will* **shall** seek that which was lost,
and *bring again* **restore**
that which was *driven away* **expelled**,
and *will* **shall** bind up that which was broken,
and *will* **shall** strengthen that which was sick:
but I *will destroy* **shall desolate** the fat and the strong;
I *will feed* **shall tend** them with judgment.
17 And as for you, O my flock,
thus saith *the Lord GOD* **Adonay Yah Veh**;
Behold, I judge between *cattle* **lambs** and *cattle* **lambs**,
between the rams and the he goats.
18 *Seemeth it a small thing* **Be it belittling** unto you
to have *eaten up* **tended** the good pasture,
but ye must tread down **to have trampled** with your feet
the *residue* **remnant** of your pastures?
and to have drunk of the *deep* **pond** waters,
but ye must **to** foul *the residue* **that which remaineth**
with your feet?
19 And as for my flock,
they *eat* **tend** that
which ye have *trodden* **trampled** with your feet;
and they drink that
which ye have *fouled* **trampled** with your feet.
20 Therefore thus saith
the Lord GOD **Adonay Yah Veh** unto them;
Behold, I, *even* I,
will **shall** judge between the fat *cattle* **lambs**
and between the *lean cattle* **emaciated lambs**.
7 So, you tenders, hear the word of Yah Veh:
8 I live
—an oracle of Adonay Yah Veh

surely because my flock *are* a plunder
yes, my flock becomes food
to every live being of the field
because there *is* no tender;
my tenders search not for my flock:
and the tenders tend themselves
and tend not my flock.
9 So, O you tenders, hear the word of Yah Veh;
10 Thus says Adonay Yah Veh:
Behold, I *am* against the tenders;
and I require my flock at their hand,
and shabbathize them from tending the flock;
and the tenders tend themselves no more;
and I rescue my flock from their mouth,
so that they not become food for them.

The Tender Of Yisra El

11 For thus says Adonay Yah Veh;
Behold, I—I both search my flock
and search them out
12 as a tender searches his drove
in the day he is among his flock who scatter;
thus I search my flock and rescue them
from all places they scatter
in the day of cloud and dripping darkness:
13 and I bring them from the people
and gather them from the lands;
and bring them to their own soil
and tend them on the mountains of Yisra El
—by the reservoirs and in all the sites of the land:
14 I tend them in a good pasture,
and on the high mountains of Yisra El
is their habitation of rest:
there they crouch in a good habitation of rest
and in a fat pasture
they graze on the mountains of Yisra El.
15 I tend my flock and I crouch them
—an oracle of Adonay Yah Veh.
16 I seek the lost and restore the expelled
and bind up the broken and strengthen the sick:
and I desolate the fat and the strong;
I tend them with judgment.
17 And as for you, O my flock,
thus says Adonay Yah Veh:
Behold, I judge between lambs and lambs;
between the rams and the he goats.
18 Is it belittling to you to tend the good pasture?
To trample the remnant of your pastures
with your feet?
To drink of the pond waters?
To foul what remains with your feet?
19 And as for my flock,
they tend what you trample with your feet;
and they drink what you trample with your feet.
20 So thus says Adonay Yah Veh to them;
Behold, I—I judge between the fat lambs
and between the emaciated lambs:
21 Because ye have *thrust* **shoved**
with side and with shoulder,
and *pushed* **butted** all the *diseased* **worn**
with your horns,
till ye have scattered them *abroad* **to the outways**;
22 Therefore *will* **shall** I save my flock,
and they shall no more be a *prey* **plunder**;
and I *will* **shall** judge
between *cattle* **lambs** and *cattle* **lambs**.
23 And I *will set up* **shall raise**
one *shepherd* **tender** over them,
and he shall *feed* **tend** them, *even* my servant David;
he shall *feed* **tend** them,
and he shall be their *shepherd* **tender**.
24 And I *the LORD* **Yah Veh**
will **shall** be their *God* **Elohim**,
and my servant David a *prince* **hierarch** among them;
I *the LORD* **Yah Veh** have *spoken it* **worded**.

Yah Veh Cuts A Covenant Of Shalom

25 And I *will make* **shall cut** with them
a covenant of *peace* **shalom**,
and *will* **shall** cause the evil *beasts* **live beings**
to *cease* **shabbathize** out of the land:
and they shall *dwell safely* **settle confidently**
in the wilderness,
and sleep in the *woods* **forests**.
26 And I *will make* **shall give** them
and *the places* round about my hill a blessing;
and I *will* **shall** cause the *shower* **downpour**
to *come down* **descend** in his *season* **time**;
there shall be *showers* **downpours** of blessing.
27 And the tree of the field
shall *yield* **give** her fruit,
and the earth shall *yield* **give** her *increase* **produce**,
and they shall *be safe* **confide** in their *land* **soil**,
and shall know that *I am the LORD* **I—Yah Veh**,
when I have broken the *bands* **yoke poles** of their yoke,
and *delivered* **rescued** them
out of the hand of those that served themselves of them.
28 And they shall no more
be a *prey* **plunder** to the *heathen* **goyim**,

neither shall the *beast* **live being**
of the land devour them;
but they shall *dwell safely* **settle confidently**,
and none shall *make* **terrify** them *afraid.*
29 And I *will* **shall** raise up for them
a plant of *renown* **name**,
and they shall be no more *consumed* **gathered**
with *hunger* **famine** in the land,
neither bear the shame of the *heathen* **goyim** any more.
30 Thus shall they know
that I *the LORD* **Yah Veh** their *God*
Elohim am with them,
and *that* they, *even* the house of *Israel* **Yisra El**,
are my people,
saith the Lord GOD **an oracle of Adonay Yah Veh.**
31 And ye my flock, the flock of my pasture,
are *men* **human**,
and I *am*—your *God* **Elohim**,
saith the Lord GOD **an oracle of Adonay Yah Veh.**

THE WORD OF YAH VEH CONCERNING MOUNT SEIR

35 Moreover
the word of *the LORD* **Yah Veh** came unto me, saying,
2 Son of *man* **humanity**,
set thy face against mount Seir, and prophesy against it,
3 And say unto it,
Thus saith *the Lord GOD* **Adonay Yah Veh**;
Behold, O mount Seir, I am against thee,
and I *will stretch out* **shall spread**
mine hand against thee,
and I *will make* **shall give** thee
most desolate **desolation and desolation.**
4 I *will lay* **shall set** thy cities *waste* **parched**,
and thou shalt be desolate,
and thou shalt know that *I am the LORD* **I—Yah Veh.**
5 Because thou hast had
a perpetual hatred **an eternal enmity**,
and hast *shed the blood of* **poured out**
the *children* **sons** of *Israel* **Yisra El**
by the *force* **hands** of the sword
in the time of their calamity,
in the time that their *iniquity* **perversity** had an end:
6 Therefore, *as* I live,
21 because you shove with side and with shoulder
and butt all the worn with your horns
until you scatter them to the outways.
22 So I save my flock
and they are no more a plunder;
and I judge between lambs and lambs:
23 and I raise one tender over them
—my servant David; and he tends them; he
tends them and he becomes their tender.
24 And I Yah Veh become their Elohim,
and my servant David a hierarch among them;
I Yah Veh have worded.

YAH VEH CUTS A COVENANT OF SHALOM

25 And I cut a covenant of shalom with them
and shabbathize the evil live beings from the land:
and they settle confidently in the wilderness
and sleep in the forests:
26 and I give all them all around my hill a blessing;
and I descend the downpour in its time
—downpours of blessing:
27 and the tree of the field gives her fruit
and the earth gives her produce
and they confide in their soil;
and know I—Yah Veh
when I break the yoke poles of their yoke,
and rescue them
from the hand of them who serve themselves of them.
28 And they *are* a plunder to the goyim no more,
and the live being of the land devours them not;
and they settle confidently and no one terrifies them.
29 And I raise for them a plant of name,
and they gather no more with famine in the land
and bear the shame of the goyim no more.
30 Thus they know that I—Yah Veh their Elohim,
am with them,
and they, the house of Yisra El, *are* my people
—an oracle of Adonay Yah Veh.
31 And you, my flock—the flock of my pasture,
are human; and I *am* your Elohim
—an oracle of Adonay Yah Veh.

THE WORD OF YAH VEH CONCERNING MOUNT SEIR

35 And so be the word of Yah Veh to me, saying,
2 Son of humanity, set your
face against mount Seir,
and prophesy against it;
3 and say to it, Thus says Adonay Yah Veh:
Behold, O mount Seir, I *am* against you
and I spread my hand against you;
and I give you desolation and desolation.
4 I set your cities parched and desolate you;
and you know I—Yah Veh.
5 Because of your eternal enmity,

and you pour the sons of Yisra El
by the hands of the sword
in the time of their calamity
—in the time of the perversity of the end:
6 So, I live
saith the Lord GOD **an oracle of Adonay Yah Veh,**
I *will prepare* **shall work** thee unto blood,
and blood shall pursue thee:
since thou hast not hated blood,
even blood shall pursue thee.
7 Thus *will I make* **shall I give** mount Seir
most desolate **desolation and desolation,**
and cut off from it
him that passeth out and him that returneth.
8 And I *will* **shall** fill his mountains
with his *slain men* **pierced:**
in thy hills, and in thy valleys,
and in all thy *rivers* **reservoirs,**
shall they fall that are *slain* **pierced** with the sword.
9 I *will make* **shall give** thee
perpetual **eternal** desolations,
and thy cities shall not *return* **be settled:**
and ye shall know that *I am the LORD* **I—Yah Veh.**
10 Because *thou hast said* **saying,**
These two *nations* **goyim** and these two *countries* **lands**
shall be mine, and we *will* **shall** possess it;
whereas *the LORD* **Yah Veh** was there:
11 Therefore, *as* I live,
saith the Lord GOD **an oracle of Adonay Yah Veh,**
I *will* **shall** even *do* **work**
according to *thine anger* **thy wrath,**
and according to thine envy
which thou hast *used* **worked**
out of thy hatred against them;
and I *will* **shall** make myself known among them,
when I have judged thee.
12 And thou shalt know that *I*
am the LORD **I—Yah Veh,**
and that I have heard all thy *blasphemies* **scornings**
which thou hast *spoken* **said**
against the mountains of *Israel* **Yisra El,** saying,
They are *laid desolate* **desolated,**
they are given us *to consume* **for food.**
13 Thus with your mouth
ye have *boasted* **greatened** against me,
and have *multiplied* **abounded** your words against me:
I have heard them.
14 Thus saith *the Lord GOD* **Adonay Yah Veh;**
When the whole earth *rejoiceth* **cheereth,**
I *will make* **shall work** thee desolate.
15 As *thou didst rejoice* **thy cheerfulness**
at the inheritance of the house of *Israel* **Yisra El,**
because it was *desolate* **desolated,**
so *will I do* **shall I work** unto thee:
thou shalt be desolate,

O mount Seir, and all *Idumea* **Edom,** *even* all of it: and
they shall know that *I am the LORD* **I—Yah Veh.**

PROPHECY AGAINST THE MOUNTAINS OF YISRA EL

36 Also, thou son of *man* **humanity,**
prophesy unto the mountains of *Israel* **Yisra El,** and say,
Ye mountains of *Israel* **Yisra El,**
hear the word of *the LORD* **Yah Veh:**
2 Thus saith *the Lord GOD* **Adonay Yah Veh;**
Because the enemy hath said against you, Aha,
even the *ancient high places* **eternal bamahs**
are our's in possession:
3 Therefore prophesy and say,
Thus saith *the Lord GOD* **Adonay Yah Veh;**
Because they have *made* **desolated** you *desolate,*
and swallowed you *up on every side* **round about,**
that ye might be a possession
unto the *residue* **survivors** of the *heathen* **goyim,**
and ye are *taken up* **ascended**
in the lips of *talkers* **tongues,**
and are *an infamy* **a slander** of the people:
4 Therefore, ye mountains of *Israel* **Yisra El,**
hear the word of *the Lord GOD* **Adonay Yah Veh;**
Thus saith *the Lord GOD* **Adonay Yah Veh**
to the mountains, and to the hills,
to the *rivers* **reservoirs,** and to the valleys,
to the *desolate wastes* **desolated parches,**
and to the cities that are forsaken,
which became a *prey* **plunder** and derision
to the *residue* **survivors** of the *heathen* **goyim**
that are round about;
—an oracle of Adonay Yah Veh
I work you to blood; and blood pursues you:
since you hate not blood,
blood also pursues you.
7 And I give mount Seir
desolation and desolation;
and cut off from it
him who passes and him who returns:
8 and I fill his mountains with his pierced:
in your hills and in your valleys
and in all your reservoirs
the pierced fall with the sword.

9 I give you eternal desolations,
and settle not your cities: and you know I—Yah Veh.
10 Because saying,
These two goyim and these two lands are mine,
and we possess it;
whereas Yah Veh is *already* there:
11 So, I live
—an oracle of Adonay Yah Veh
and I work according to your wrath
and according to the envy you work
by your hatred against them;
and I make myself known among them
when I judge you:
12 and you know I—Yah Veh,
and that I hear all the scornings
you say against the mountains of Yisra El, saying,
They *are* desolated; they *are* given us for food.
13 And with your mouth you greaten against me;
and with your words abound against me:
I hear them.
14 Thus says Adonay Yah Veh:
When the whole earth cheers, I work you desolate
15 —as your cheerfulness
at the inheritance of the house of Yisra El,
because it *is* desolated,
thus I work to you:
you are desolate,
O mount Seir, and all Edom—all thereof:
and they know I—Yah Veh.

PROPHECY AGAINST THE MOUNTAINS OF YISRA EL

36 And you, son of humanity,
prophesy to the mountains of Yisra El, and say,
You mountains of Yisra El, hear the word of Yah Veh:
2 Thus says Adonay Yah Veh:
Because the enemy says against you, Aha,
even the eternal bamahs are for us in possession:
3 so prophesy and say,
Thus says Adonay Yah Veh:
Because—yes, because they desolate you
and swallow you all around
to be a possession to the survivors of the goyim,
and ascend you on the lips of tongues
—a slander of the people:
4 so, O mountains of Yisra El,
hear the word of Adonay Yah Veh;
Thus says Adonay Yah Veh
to the mountains and to the hills;
to the reservoirs and to the valleys;
to the desolated parches and to the forsaken cities
—to become a plunder and derision
to the survivors of the goyim all around;
5 Therefore thus saith *the*
Lord GOD **Adonay Yah Veh**;
Surely in the fire of my jealousy have I *spoken* **worded**
against the *residue* **survivors** of the *heathen* **goyim**,
and against all *Idumea* **Edom**,
which have *appointed* **given** my land
into their possession
with the *joy* **cheerfulness** of all their heart,
with despiteful *minds* **souls**,
to cast it out for a prey **a suburb to plunder**.
6 Prophesy therefore
concerning the *land* **soil** of *Israel* **Yisra El**,
and say unto the mountains, and to the hills,
to the *rivers* **reservoirs**, and to the valleys,
Thus saith *the Lord GOD* **Adonay Yah Veh**; Behold,
I have *spoken* **worded** in my jealousy and in my fury,
because ye have borne the shame of the *heathen* **goyim**:
7 Therefore thus saith *the*
Lord GOD **Adonay Yah Veh**;
I have lifted up mine hand,
Surely the *heathen* **goyim** that are **round** about you,
they shall bear their shame.
8 But ye, O mountains of *Israel* **Yisra El**,
ye shall *shoot forth* **give** your branches,
and *yield* **bear** your fruit to my people of *Israel* **Yisra El**;
for they *are at hand* **approach** to come.
9 For, behold, I am for you,
and I *will turn* **shall face** unto you,
and ye shall be *tilled* **served** and *sown* **seeded**:
10 And I *will multiply men* **shall abound humanity**
upon you,
all the house of *Israel* **Yisra El**, *even* all of it:
and the cities shall be *inhabited* **settled**,
and the *wastes* **parched areas** shall be builded:
11 And I *will multiply* **shall abound** upon you
man **humanity** and *beast* **animal**;
and they shall *increase* **abound** and *bring* **bear** fruit:
and I *will* **shall** settle you after your *old* **former** estates,
and *will* **shall** do better unto you
than at your beginnings:
and ye shall know that *I am the LORD* **I—Yah Veh**.
12 Yea, I *will* **shall** cause *men* **humanity**
to walk upon you,
even my people *Israel* **Yisra El**;
and they shall possess thee,
and thou shalt be their inheritance,
and thou shalt *no more henceforth* **not add**

to bereave them *of men*.
13 Thus saith *the Lord GOD* **Adonay Yah Veh**;
Because they say unto you,
Thou *land devourest up men* **eatest humans**,
and hast bereaved thy *nations* **goyim**:
14 Therefore thou shalt *devour*
men **eat humans** no more,
neither bereave thy *nations* **goyim** any more,
saith the Lord GOD **an oracle of Adonay Yah Veh**.
15 Neither *will* **shall** I cause *men* to hear in thee
the shame of the *heathen* **goyim** any more,
neither shalt thou
bear the reproach of the people any more,
neither shalt thou
cause thy *nations* **goyim** to *fall* **falter** any more,
saith the Lord GOD **an oracle of Adonay Yah Veh**.
16 Moreover
the word of *the LORD* **Yah Veh** came unto me, saying,
17 Son of *man* **humanity**,
when the house of *Israel* **Yisra El**
dwelt **settled** in their own *land* **soil**,
they *defiled* **fouled** it
by their own way and by their *doings* **exploits**:
their way was *before me* **at my face**
as the *uncleanness* **foulness**
of *a removed woman* **one excluded**.
18 Wherefore I poured my fury upon them
for the blood that they had *shed* **poured** upon the land,
and for their idols wherewith they had *polluted* **fouled** it:
19 And I scattered them among the *heathen* **goyim**,
and they were dispersed through the *countries* **lands**:
according to their way
and according to their *doings* **exploits** I judged them.
20 And when they entered unto the *heathen* **goyim**,
whither they went, they profaned my holy
name, *when they said* **saying** to them,

5 So thus says Adonay Yah Veh:
Surely in the fire of my jealousy I word
against the survivors of the goyim
and against all Edom,
who give my land as their own possession
with cheerfulness of all their heart,
with despite of soul
—a suburb to plunder.
6 So, prophesy concerning the soil of Yisra El;
and say to the mountains and to the hills;
to the reservoirs and to the valleys,
Thus says Adonay Yah Veh:
Behold, I word in my jealousy and in my fury
because you bear the shame of the goyim.
7 So thus says Adonay Yah Veh:
I lift my hand;
surely the goyim all around you bear their shame:
8 and you, O mountains of Yisra El,
give your branches
and bear your fruit to my people of Yisra El;
for they approach to come.
9 For, behold, I *am* for you and I face to you;
and serve and seed you:
10 and I abound humanity on you
—all the house of Yisra El—all thereof
to settle the cities and build the parched areas:
11 and I abound on you humanity and animal;
and they abound and bear fruit:
and I settle you after your former estates
and do better to you than at your beginnings:
and you know I—Yah Veh.
12 Yes, I walk humanity all over you
—my people Yisra El;
and they possess you
and you become their inheritance;
and you add not to bereave them.
13 Thus says Adonay Yah Veh:
Because they say to you,
You eat humans and bereave your goyim:
14 So you neither eat humans any more nor bereave
your goyim any more—an oracle of Adonay Yah Veh
15 —nor hear the shame of the goyim any more
nor bear the reproach of the people any more
nor that your goyim falter any more
—an oracle of Adonay Yah Veh.
16 And so be the word of Yah Veh to me, saying,
17 Son of humanity,
the house of Yisra El settles in their own soil;
they foul it by their own way and by their exploits:
their way *is* at my face
as the foulness of one excluded:
18 and I pour my fury on them
for the blood they pour on the land,
and for their idols with which they foul it:
19 and I scatter them among the goyim,
and disperse them through the lands:
according to their way and according to their exploits
I judge them:
20 and they approach the goyim
where they approach;
they profane my holy name, saying to them,

exeGeses ready research BIBLE
These are the people of *the LORD* **Yah Veh**,
and are gone forth out of his land.

21 But I *had pity for* **compassioned** mine holy name,
which the house of *Israel* **Yisra El** had profaned
among the *heathen* **goyim**, whither they went.
22 Therefore say unto the house of *Israel* **Yisra El**,
thus saith *the Lord GOD* **Adonay Yah Veh**;
I *do* **work** not this for your sakes,
O house of *Israel* **Yisra El**,
but for mine holy name's sake,
which ye have profaned among the *heathen* **goyim**,
whither ye went.
23 And I *will sanctify* **shall hallow** my great name,
which was profaned among the *heathen* **goyim**,
which ye have profaned in the midst of them;
and the *heathen* **goyim** shall know
that *I am the LORD* **I—Yah Veh**,
saith the Lord GOD **an oracle of Adonay Yah Veh**,
when I shall be *sanctified* **hallowed** in you
before **in front of** their eyes.
24 For I *will* **shall** take you
from among the *heathen* **goyim**,
and gather you out of all *countries* **lands**,
and *will* **shall** bring you into your own *land* **soil**.
25 Then *will* **shall** I sprinkle
clean **pure** water upon you,
and ye shall be *clean* **pure**:
from all your *filthiness* **foulness**, and from all your idols,
will I cleanse **shall I purify** you.
26 A new heart also *will* **shall** I give you,
and a new spirit *will I put* **shall I give** within you:
and I *will take away* **shall turn aside**
the stony heart out of your flesh,
and I *will* **shall** give you an heart of flesh.
27 And I *will put* **shall give** my spirit within you,
and *cause* **work** you to walk in my statutes,
and ye shall *keep* **guard** my judgments,
and *do* **work** them.
28 And ye shall *dwell* **settle**
in the land that I gave to your fathers;
and ye *shall* be my people,
and *I will be* **I AM** your *God* **Elohim**.
29 I *will* **shall** also save you
from all your *uncleannesses* **foulnesses**:
and I *will* **shall** call for the *corn* **crop**,
and *will increase* **shall abound** it,
and *lay* **give** no famine upon you.
30 And I *will multiply* **shall**
abound the fruit of the tree,
and the *increase* **produce** of the field,
that ye shall *receive* **take** no more reproach of famine
among the *heathen* **goyim**.
31 Then shall ye remember your own evil ways,
and your *doings* **exploits** that were not good,
and shall lothe *yourselves in your own sight* **at your face**
for your *iniquities* **perversities**
and for your *abominations* **abhorrences**.
32 Not for your sakes *do* **work** I this,
saith the Lord GOD **an oracle of Adonay Yah Veh**,
be it known unto you:
be *ashamed* **shamed** and confounded for your own ways,
O house of *Israel* **Yisra El**.
33 Thus saith *the Lord GOD* **Adonay Yah Veh**;
In the day that I shall *have cleansed* **purify** you
from all your *iniquities* **perversities**
I *will* **shall** also cause *you* to *dwell* **settle** in the cities,
and the *wastes* **parched areas** shall be builded.
34 And the *desolate* **desolated**
land shall be *tilled* **served**,
whereas it lay desolate
in the *sight* **eyes** of all that passed by.
35 And they shall say,
This land that was *desolate* **desolated**
is become like the garden of Eden;
and the *waste* **parched** and *desolate* **desolated**
and *ruined* **demolished** cities
are *become fenced* **fortified**, and are *inhabited* **settled**.
36 Then the *heathen* **goyim**
that *are left* **survive** round about you
shall know that I *the LORD* **Yah Veh**
build the *ruined places* **demolished**,
and plant that that was *desolate* **desolated**:
These *are* the people of Yah Veh,
who come from his land.
21 And I compassion my holy name
which the house of Yisra El
profanes among the goyim wherever they go.
22 So say to the house of Yisra El,
Thus says Adonay Yah Veh:
I work this, not for your sakes, O house of Yisra El,
but for sake of my holy name
—which you profane among the goyim,
wherever you go:
23 and I hallow my great name
profaned among the goyim
—which you profane among them;
and the goyim know I—Yah Veh
—an oracle of Adonay Yah Veh
when I *am* hallowed in you in front of their eyes.
24 For I take you from among the goyim
and gather you from all lands
and bring you into your own soil:

25 and I sprinkle pure water
on you and purify you:
from all your foulness and from all your idols
I purify you:
26 and I give you a new heart
and a new spirit I give within you:
and I turn aside the stony heart from your flesh
and I give you an heart of flesh:
27 and I give my spirit within you
so that you work to walk in my statutes and
guard my judgments and work them
28 and I settle you in the land I gave your fathers:
and you become my people
and I become your Elohim:
29 and I save you from all your foulnesses:
and I call for the crop and abound it;
and give no famine on you:
30 and I abound the fruit of the tree
and the produce of the field
that you take no more reproach of famine
among the goyim.
31 Then you remember your own evil ways
and your no good exploits;
and loathe at your face
for your perversities and for your abhorrences.
32 I work this not for your sakes
—an oracle of Adonay Yah Veh
thus be it known to you:
shame and confound for your own ways,
O house of Yisra El.
33 Thus says Adonay Yah Veh:
In the day I purify you from all your perversities
I also settle you in the cities,
and build the parched areas:
34 and the desolated land is served
instead of becoming desolate in the
eyes of all who pass by.
35 And they say,
This desolated land is as the garden of Eden;
and the parched and desolated and demolished cities
fortified and settled.
36 And the goyim who survive all around you
know that I—Yah Veh
build the demolished and plant the desolated:
I *the LORD* **Yah Veh** have *spoken it* **worded,**
and I *will do* **shall work** it.
37 Thus saith *the Lord GOD* **Adonay Yah Veh;**
I will **shall** yet for this be enquired of
by the house of *Israel* **Yisra El,** to *do* **work** it for them;
I *will increase* **shall abound** them with
men **humanity** like a flock.
38 As the holy flock,
as the flock of *Jerusalem* **Yeru Shalem**
in her *solemn feasts* **seasons;**
so shall the *waste* **parched** cities
be filled with flocks of *men* **humanity:**
and they shall know that *I am the LORD* **I—Yah Veh.**

The Vision Of The Valley Of Dry Bones

37 The hand of *the LORD* **Yah Veh** was upon me,
and carried me out in the spirit of *the LORD* **Yah Veh,**
and *set* **rested** me *down* in the midst of the valley
which was full of bones,
2 And caused me to pass by them
round about **and round about**: and, behold,
there were very many in the *open* **face of the** valley;
and, *lo* **behold,** they were *very* **mighty** dry.
3 And he said unto me,
Son of *man* **humanity,** can these bones live?
And I *answered* **said,**
O Lord GOD **Adonay Yah Veh,** thou knowest.
4 Again he said unto me,
Prophesy upon these bones, and say unto them,
O ye dry bones, hear the word of *the LORD* **Yah Veh.**
5 Thus saith *the Lord GOD* **Adonay**
Yah Veh unto these bones;
Behold, I *will* **shall** cause *breath* **the**
Spirit to enter into you,
and ye shall live:
6 And I *will lay* **shall give** sinews upon you,
and *will bring up* **shall ascend** flesh upon you,
and cover you with skin,
and *put breath* **give spirit** in you, and ye shall live;
and ye shall know that *I am the LORD* **I—Yah Veh.**
7 So I prophesied as I was *commanded* **misvahed:**
and as I prophesied, there was a *noise*
voice, and behold a *shaking* **quake,**
and the bones *came together* **approached,**
bone to his bone.
8 And when I *beheld* **saw,** *lo* **behold,**
the sinews and the flesh *came up* **ascended** upon them,
and the skin covered them above:
but there was no *breath* **spirit** in them.
9 Then said he unto me,
Prophesy unto the *wind* **Spirit,**
prophesy, son of *man* **humanity,**
and say to the *wind* **Spirit,**
Thus saith *the Lord GOD* **Adonay Yah Veh;**
Come from the four winds/**spirits,** O *breath* **Spirit,**

and *breathe* **puff** upon these *slain* **slaughtered**,
that they may live.
10 So I prophesied as he *commanded* **misvahed** me,
and the *breath* **Spirit** came into them,
and they lived, and stood up upon their feet,
an exceeding great army **a mighty great valiant**.

THE INTERPRETATION

11 Then he said unto me, Son of *man* **humanity**,
these bones are the whole house of *Israel* **Yisra El**:
behold, they say,
Our bones are *dried* **withered**, and our hope is lost:
we are cut off for our parts.
12 Therefore prophesy and say unto them,
Thus saith *the Lord GOD* **Adonay Yah Veh**;
Behold, O my people,
I *will* **shall** open your *graves* **tombs**,
and cause you to *come up* **ascend**
out of your *graves* **tombs**,
and bring you into the *land* **soil** of *Israel* **Yisra El**.
13 And ye shall know that *I am the LORD* **I—Yah Veh**,
when I have opened your *graves* **tombs**, O my people,
and *brought* **ascended** you *up* out of your *graves* **tombs**,
14 And shall *put* **give** my *spirit* **Spirit** in you,
and ye shall live,
and I shall *place* **set** you in your own *land* **soil**:
then shall ye know that I
the LORD **Yah Veh** have *spoken it* **worded**,
and *performed it* **worked**,
saith the LORD **an oracle of Yah Veh**.
I Yah Veh worded, and I work.
37 Thus says Adonay Yah Veh:
Yet for this I *am* enquired of by the house of Yisra El
to work it for them;
I abound them with humanity as a flock
38 —as the holy flock
—as the flock of Yeru Shalem in her seasons;
thus the parched cities
are filled with flocks of humanity:
and they know I—Yah Veh.

THE VISION OF THE VALLEY OF DRY BONES

37 And so be the hand of Yah Veh on me;
and he carries me in the spirit of Yah Veh
and rests me midst the valley full of bones:
2 and passes me by them
all around and all around:
and behold,
there *are* very many in the face of the valley;
and behold, they *are* mighty dry.
3 And he says to me,
Son of humanity, live these bones?
And I say, Adonay Yah Veh, you know.
4 And he says to me,
Prophesy on these bones, and say to them,
O you dry bones, hear the word of Yah Veh;
5 Thus says Adonay Yah Veh to these bones:
Behold, I enter a spirit into you, and you live:
6 and I give sinews on you
and ascend flesh on you
and cover you with skin
and give a spirit within you, and you live:
and you know I—Yah Veh.
7 And I prophesy as I was misvahed:
and as I prophesy, there *is* a voice;
and behold, a quake:
and the bones approach—bone to bone.
8 And I see, and behold,
the sinews and the flesh ascend on them,
and the skin covers them:
and there is no spirit in them.
9 And says he to me, Prophesy to the Spirit;
prophesy, son of humanity, and say to the Spirit,
Thus says Adonay Yah Veh:
From the four winds/spirits, come O Spirit,
and puff on these slaughtered so that they live.
10 And I prophesy as he misvahs me;
and the Spirit comes into them:
and they live and stand on their feet
—a mighty great valiant.

THE INTERPRETATION

11 And he says to me, Son of humanity,
these bones are the whole house of Yisra El:
behold, they say,
Our bones withers and our hope destructs:
we *are* cut off for our parts.
12 So prophesy and say to them,
Thus says Adonay Yah Veh; Behold, O my people,
I open your tombs
and ascend you from your tombs
and bring you to the soil of Yisra El:
13 and you know I—Yah Veh,
when I open your tombs, O my people,
and ascend you from your tombs;
14 and give my Spirit in you and you live;
and I set you in your own soil:
and you know I—Yah Veh have worded and worked
—an oracle of Yah Veh.

YAH HUDAH AND YISRA EL BECOME ONE

15 The word of *the LORD* **Yah**
Veh came again unto me,
saying,
16 Moreover, thou son of *man* **humanity**,
take thee one *stick* **tree**, and *write* **inscribe** upon it,
For *Judah* **Yah Hudah**,
and for the *children* **sons** of *Israel* **Yisra El**
his companions:
then take *another stick* **one tree**,
and *write* **inscribe** upon it,
For *Joseph* **Yoseph**, the *stick* **tree** of *Ephraim* **Ephrayim**
and for all the house of *Israel* **Yisra El** his companions:
17 And *join* **approach** them one to *another* **one**
into one *stick* **tree**;
and they shall become one in thine hand.
18 And when the *children* **sons** of thy people
shall *speak* **say** unto thee, saying,
wilt **shalt** thou not *shew* **tell** us
what *thou meanest by* these **be**?
19 *Speak* **Word** unto them,
Thus saith *the Lord GOD* **Adonay Yah Veh**;
Behold, I *will* **shall** take the *stick* **tree** of *Joseph* **Yoseph**,
which is in the hand of *Ephraim* **Ephrayim**,
and the *tribes* **scions** of *Israel* **Yisra El**
his *fellows* **companions**,
and *will put* **shall give** them with him,
even with the *stick* **tree** of *Judah* **Yah Hudah**,
and *make* **work** them one *stick* **tree**,
and they shall be one in mine hand.
20 And the *stick* **tree** whereon
thou *writest* **inscribest**
shall be in thine hand *before* **in front of** their eyes.
21 And *say* **word** unto them,
Thus saith *the Lord GOD* **Adonay Yah Veh**; Behold,
I *will* **shall** take the *children* **sons** of *Israel* **Yisra El**
from *among* **between** the *heathen* **goyim**,
whither they be gone,
and *will* **shall** gather them *on every side* **round about**,
and bring them into their own *land* **soil**:
22 And I *will make* **shall work**
them one *nation* **goyim**
in the land upon the mountains of *Israel* **Yisra El**;
and one *king* **sovereign**
shall be *king* **sovereign** to them all:
and they shall be no more two *nations* **goyim**,
neither shall they be *divided* **halved**
into two *kingdoms* **sovereigndoms** any more *at all* **still**.
23 Neither shall they *defile* **foul** themselves
any more with their idols,
nor with their *detestable things* **abominations**,
nor with any of their *transgressions* **rebellions**:
but I *will* **shall** save them out of all
their *dwellingplaces* **sites**,
wherein they have sinned,
and *will cleanse* **shall purify** them:
so shall they be my people,
and I *will* **shall** be their *God* **Elohim**.

THE SOVEREIGNDOM OF DAVID

24 And David my servant
shall be *king* **sovereign** over them;
and they all shall have one *shepherd* **tender**:
they shall also walk in my judgments,
and *observe* **guard** my statutes, and *do* **work** them.
25 And they shall dwell in the land
that I have given unto *Jacob* **Yaaqov** my servant,
wherein your fathers have *dwelt* **settled**
and they shall *dwell* **settle** therein,
even they, and their *children* **sons**,
and their *children's children for ever* **sons' sons eternally**:
and my servant David
shall be their *prince for ever* **hierarch eternally**.

THE ETERNAL COVENANT OF YAH VEH

26 Moreover
I *will make* **shall cut** a covenant of *peace* **shalom**
with them;
so be it *shall be* an *everlasting* **eternal**
covenant with them:
and I *will place* **shall give** them,
and *multiply* **abound** them,
and *will set* **shall give** my *sanctuary* **holies**
in the midst of them *for evermore* **eternally**.
27 My tabernacle also shall be with them:
yea, I *will* **shall** be their *God* **Elohim**,

YAH HUDAH AND YISRA EL BECOME ONE

15 And so be the word of Yah Veh to me, saying,
16 And you, son of humanity,
take one tree and inscribe thereon,
For Yah Hudah,
and for the sons of Yisra El his companions:
and take one tree and inscribe thereon,
For Yoseph, the tree of Ephrayim
and for all the house of Yisra El his companions:
17 and approach them one by one into one tree;
and they become one in your hand.
18 And when the sons of your people say to you,
saying, Tell you not us what these *are* to you?
19 Word to them, Thus says Adonay Yah Veh:

Behold, I take the tree of Yoseph,
in the hand of Ephrayim,
and the scions of Yisra El his companions,
and give them with him, with the tree of Yah Hudah,
and work them, one tree,
and they become one in my hand.
20 And the tree whereon you inscribe
becomes in your hand in front of their eyes.
21 And word to them, Thus says Adonay Yah Veh:
Behold,
I take the sons of Yisra El from between the goyim
where they went,
and gather them all around
and bring them into their own soil:
22 and I work them one goyim
in the land on the mountains of Yisra El;
and one sovereign becomes sovereign to them all:
and they neither becme two goyim any more, nor
halved into two sovereigndoms any more:
23 neither foul they themselves
with their idols any more
nor with their abominations
nor with any of their rebellions:
and I save them from all their sites
wherein they sinned
and purify them:
so they are my people, and I am their Elohim.

The Sovereigndom Of David

24 And David my servant *is* sovereign over them;
and their is one tender:
and they walk in my judgments
and guard my statutes and work them:
25 and they dwell in the land
I gave to Yaaqov my servant,
wherein your fathers settled:
and they settle therein—they and their sons,
and the sons of their sons eternally:
and my servant David *is* their hierarch eternally.

The Eternal Covenant Of Yah Veh

26 And I cut a covenant of shalom with them
—so be it, an eternal covenant with them:
and I give them and abound them;
and give my holies among them eternally.
27 My tabernacle also is with them:
yes, I am their Elohim
and they *shall* be my people.
28 And the *heathen* **goyim** shall know
that I *the LORD* **Yah Veh**
do sanctify Israel **hallow Yisra El**,
when my *sanctuary* **holies** shall be in the midst of them
for evermore **eternally**.

The Word Of Yah Veh Concerning Gog

38 And the word of *the LORD* **Yah Veh**
came unto me, saying,
2 Son of *man* **humanity**,
set thy face against Gog, the land of Magog,
the *chief prince* **Rosch hierarch**
of Meshech and Tubal,
and prophesy against him,
3 And say, Thus saith *the Lord*
GOD **Adonay Yah Veh**;
Behold, I am against thee, O Gog,
the *chief prince* **Rosch hierarch**
of Meshech and Tubal:
4 And I *will* **shall** turn thee back,
and *put* **give** hooks into thy jaws,
and I *will* **shall** bring thee forth,
and all thine *army* **valiant**, horses and *horsemen* **cavalry**,
all of them *clothed* **enrobed**
with *all sorts of armour* **splendour,**
even a great *company* **congregation**
with *bucklers* **shields** and *shields* **bucklers**,
all of them *handling* **manipulating** swords:
5 Persia, *Ethiopia* **Kush**, and *Libya* **Put** with them;
all of them with *shield* **buckler** and helmet:
6 Gomer, and all his bands;
the house of Togarmah of the north *quarters* **flanks**,
and all his bands: and many people with thee.
7 Be thou prepared, and prepare for thyself,
thou, and all thy *company* **congregation**
that are *assembled* **congregated** unto thee,
and be thou a guard unto them.
8 After many days thou shalt be visited:
in the latter years thou shalt come into the land
that is *brought back* **restored** from the sword,
and is gathered out of many people,
against the mountains of *Israel* **Yisra El,**
which have been *always waste* **continually parched**:
but it is brought forth out of the *nations* **goyim,**
and they shall *dwell safely* **settle confidently** all of them.
9 Thou shalt ascend and *come*
like a *storm* **devastation**,
thou shalt be like a cloud to cover the land, thou,
and all thy bands, and many people with thee.
10 Thus saith *the Lord GOD* **Adonay Yah Veh**;
It shall also *come to pass* **become**, that at the same time
shall *things come* **words ascend** into thy *mind* **heart**,

and thou shalt *think* **fabricate** an
evil *thought* **fabrication:**
11 And thou shalt say,
I *will go up* **shall ascend**
to the land of *unwalled villages* **suburbs;**
I *will* **shall** go to them that *are at* rest,
that *dwell safely* **settle confidently,**
all of them *dwelling* **settling** without walls,
and having neither bars nor *gates* **doors.**
12 To *take* **spoil** a spoil,
and to *take a prey* **plunder a plunder;**
to turn thine hand
upon the *desolate places* **parched areas**
that are now inhabited,
and upon the people
that are gathered out of the *nations* **goyim,**
which have *gotten* **worked**
cattle **chattel** and *goods* **chattel,**
that *dwell in* **settle on** the *midst* **summit** of the land.
13 Sheba, and Dedan, and the
merchants of Tarshish,
with all the *young lions* **whelps** *thereof,*
shall say unto thee, Art thou come to *take* **spoil** a spoil?
hast thou
gathered **congregated** thy *company* **congregation**
to *take* **plunder** a *prey* **plunder?**
to *carry* **bear** away silver and gold,
to take away *cattle* **chattel** and *goods* **chattel,**
to *take* **spoil** a great spoil?
14 Therefore, son of *man* **humanity,**
prophesy and say unto Gog,
and they become my people: 28 and the goyim know
that I Yah Veh hallow Yisra El,
when my holies is among them eternally.

THE WORD OF YAH VEH CONCERNING GOG

38 And so be the word of Yah Veh to me, saying,
2 Son of humanity,
set your face against Gog of the land of Magog
—the Rosch hierarch of Meshech and Tubal,
and prophesy against him,
3 and say, Thus says Adonay Yah Veh:
Behold, I *am* against you, O Gog,
the Rosch hierarch of Meshech and Tubal:
4 and I turn you back,
and give hooks in your jaws,
and I bring you forth,
and all your valiant, horses and cavalry
enrobed with splendor—all of them
—a great congregation with shields and bucklers,
all of them manipulating swords:
5 Persia, Kush, and Put with them;
all of them *with* buckler and helmet:
6 Gomer, and all his bands;
the house of Togarmah of the north flanks
with all his bands;
and many people with you.
7 Prepare—prepare for yourself
—you and all your congregation
who congregate to you,
and become their guard.
8 After many days you *are* visited:
in the latter years you enter the land
restored from the sword
—gathered from many people,
on the mountains of Yisra El,
being continually parched:
and it is brought forth from the goyim,
and they settle confidently—all of them.
9 You ascend as a devastation,
—as a cloud covers the land
—you and all your bands and many people with you.
10 Thus says Adonay Yah Veh;
and so be it, at the same time,
words ascend into your heart
and you fabricate an evil fabrication:
11 and you say, I ascend to the land of suburbs;
I go to them who rest—who settle confidently;
all of them settling without walls
and having neither bars nor doors;
12 to spoil a spoil and to plunder a plunder
—to turn your hand on the parched areas
now inhabited,
and on the people gathered from the goyim,
who work chattel and who chattel
—who settle on the summit of the land.
13 Sheba and Dedan and the merchants of Tarshish
with all their whelps,
say to you, Come you to spoil a spoil?
To congregate your congregation
to plunder a plunder?
To bear away silver and gold?
To take away chattel and to chattel?
To spoil a great spoil?
14 So, son of humanity,
prophesy and say to Gog,
Thus saith *the Lord GOD* **Adonay Yah Veh;**
In that day when my people of *Israel* **Yisra El**
dwelleth safely **settleth confidently,**
shalt thou not know it?

15 And thou shalt come
from thy place out of the north *parts* **flanks,**
thou, and many people with thee,
all of them riding upon horses,
a great *company* **congregation,**
and *a mighty army* **great valiant:**
16 And thou shalt *come up* **ascend**
against my people of *Israel* **Yisra El,**
as a cloud to cover the land;
so be it *shall be* in the latter days,
and I *will* **shall** bring thee against my land,
that the *heathen* **goyim** may know me
when I shall be *sanctified* **hallowed** in thee, O Gog,
before **in front of** their eyes.
17 Thus saith *the Lord GOD* **Adonay Yah Veh;**
Art thou he
of whom I have *spoken* **worded** in *old* **ancient** time
by **the hand of** my servants the
prophets of *Israel* **Yisra El,**
which prophesied in those days *many* years
that I *would* **should** bring thee against them?
18 And **so be** it *shall come to pass*
at the same time **in that day,**
when **the day** Gog shall come
against the *land* **soil** of *Israel* **Yisra El,**
saith the Lord GOD **an oracle of Adonay Yah Veh,**
that my fury shall *come up* **ascend** in my *face* **nostrils.**
19 For in my jealousy and in the fire of my wrath
have I *spoken* **worded,**
Surely in that day there shall be a great *shaking* **quake**
in the *land* **soil** of *Israel* **Yisra El;**
20 So that the fishes of the sea,
and the *fowls* **flyers** of the *heaven* **heavens,**
and the *beasts* **live beings** of the field,
and all *creeping things* **creepers**
that creep upon the *earth* **soil,**
and all the *men* **humans**
that are upon the face of the *earth* **soil,**
shall *shake* **quake** at my *presence* **face,**
and the mountains shall be *thrown down* **demolished,**
and the steep *places* **steps** shall fall,
and every wall shall fall to the *ground* **earth.**
21 And I *will* **shall** call for a sword against him
throughout all my mountains,
saith the Lord GOD **an oracle of Adonay Yah Veh:**
every man's sword shall be against his brother.
22 And I *will plead* **shall judge** against him
with pestilence and with blood;
and I *will* **shall** rain upon him, and upon his bands,
and upon the many people that are with him,
an overflowing *rain* **downpour,**
and great hailstones, fire, and *brimstone* **sulphur.**
23 Thus *will I magnify* **shall I greaten** myself,
and *sanctify* **hallow** myself;
and I *will* **shall** be known in the eyes
of many *nations* **goyim,**
and they shall know that *I am the LORD* **I—Yah Veh.**

39 Therefore, thou son of *man* **humanity,**
prophesy against Gog, and say,
Thus saith *the Lord GOD* **Adonay Yah Veh;**
Behold, I am against thee, O Gog,
the *chief prince* **Rosch hierarch**
of Meshech and Tubal:
2 And I *will* **shall** turn thee back,
and *leave but the sixth part of* **hexsect*** thee,
and *will* **shall** cause thee to *come up* **ascend**
from the north *parts* **flanks,**
and *will* **shall** bring thee
upon the mountains of *Israel* **Yisra El:**
3 And I *will* **shall** smite thy
bow out of thy left hand,
and *will* **shall** cause thine arrows
to fall out of thy right hand.
*hexsect: divide into sixths
4 Thou shalt fall upon the
mountains of *Israel* **Yisra El,**
thou, and all thy bands, and the people that is with thee:
I *will* **shall** give thee
unto the *ravenous* **swooper** birds of every *sort* **wing,**
Thus says Adonay Yah Veh:
In that day,
when my people of Yisra El settle confidently,
know you not thereof?
15 And you come from your place
—from the north flanks
—you and many people with you;
all of them riding on horses;
a great congregation and great valiant:
16 and you ascend against my people of Yisra El
as a cloud to cover the land;
and so be it in the latter days,
I bring you against my land,
so that the goyim know me
when I *am* hallowed in you, O Gog,
in front of their eyes.
17 Thus says Adonay Yah Veh;
Are you he of whom I worded in ancient time
by the hand of my servants the prophets of Yisra El,
who prophesied in those days—years
that I bring you against them?

18 And so be it, in that day,
the day Gog enters the soil of Yisra El—an oracle of
Adonay Yah Veh that my fury ascends in my nostrils.
19 For in my jealousy and in the fire of my wrath
—I have worded;
surely in that day
a great quake becomes in the soil of Yisra El;
20 so that the fishes of the sea
and the flyers of the heavens
and the live beings of the field
and all creepers creeping on the soil
and all the humans on the face of the soil
quake at my face:
and the mountains demolish
and the steep steps fall
and every wall falls to the earth:
21 and I call for a sword against him
throughout all my mountains
—an oracle of Adonay Yah Veh
—the sword of every man is against his brother:
22 and I judge against him
with pestilence and with blood;
and I rain on him and on his bands
and on the many people with him,
an overflowing downpour and great hailstones,
fire and sulphur.
23 Thus I greaten myself and hallow myself;
and I *am* known in the eyes of many goyim;
and they know I—Yah Veh.

39 And you, son of humanity,
prophesy against Gog,
and say, Thus says Adonay Yah Veh:
Behold, I *am* against you, O Gog,
the Rosch hierarch of Meshech and Tubal:
2 and I turn you back and hexsect* you
and ascend you from the north flanks and
bring you on the mountains of Yisra El:
3 and I smite your bow from your left hand
and fell your arrows from your right hand.
*hexsect: divide into sixths
4 You fall on the mountains of Yisra El
—you and all your bands
and the people with you:
I give you to the swooper birds of every wing
and to the *beasts* **live beings** of the field
to be devoured **for food.**
5 Thou shalt fall upon the *open* **face of the** field:
for I have *spoken it* **worded,**
saith the Lord GOD **an oracle of Adonay Yah Veh.**
6 And I *will* **shall** send a fire on Magog,
and among them that *dwell carelessly* **settle confidently**
in the *isles* **islands**:
and they shall know that *I am the LORD* **I—Yah Veh.**
7 So *will* **shall** I make my holy name known
in the midst of my people *Israel* **Yisra El;**
and I *will* **shall** not
let them pollute **profane** my holy name any more:
and the *heathen* **goyim** shall know
that *I am the LORD* **I—Yah Veh,**
the Holy One in *Israel* **Yisra El.**
8 Behold, it *is* **hath** come,
and it *is done* **hath become,**
saith the Lord GOD **an oracle of Adonay Yah Veh;**
this is the day whereof I have *spoken* **worded.**
9 And they that *dwell* **settle**
in the cities of *Israel* **Yisra El**
shall go forth,
and shall *set on fire* **burn**
and burn the *weapons* **armament,**
both the *shields* **bucklers** and the *bucklers* **shields,**
the bows and the arrows,
and the handstaves, and the *spears* **javelins,**
and they shall burn them with fire seven years:
10 So that they shall
take **lift** no *wood* **timber** out of the field,
neither *cut down* **chop** any out of the forests;
for they shall burn the *weapons* **armaments** with fire:
and they shall spoil those that spoiled them,
and *rob* **plunder** those that *robbed* **plundered** them,
saith the Lord GOD **an oracle of Adonay Yah Veh.**
11 And **so be** it *shall come to pass* in that day,
that I *will* **shall** give unto Gog
a place there of *graves* **tombs** in *Israel* **Yisra El,**
the valley of *the passengers* **passersby**
on the east of the sea:
and it shall stop the *noses of the passengers* **passersby**:
and there shall they *bury* **entomb** Gog
and all his multitude:
and they shall call it
The *valley of Hamongog*
Gay Hamon Gog/The Valley of the Multitude of Gog.
12 And seven months shall
the house of *Israel* **Yisra El**
be burying of **entomb** them,
that they may *cleanse* **purify** the land.
13 Yea, all the people of the land
shall *bury* **entomb** them;
and it shall be to them a *renown* **name**
the day that I shall be *glorified* **honoured,**
saith the Lord GOD **an oracle of Adonay Yah Veh.**

14 And they shall *sever out*
continually separate men
of continual employment, passing through the land
to *bury* **entomb** with the *passengers* **the passersby**
those that remain upon the face of the earth,
to *cleanse* **purify** it:
after the end of seven months shall they *search* **probe**.
15 And the *passengers* **passersby**
that pass through the land,
when any seeth *a man's* **human** bone,
then shall he set *up a sign by* **a monument beside** it,
till the *buriers* **entombers** have *buried* **entombed** it
in the *valley of Hamongog*
Valley of the Multitude of Gog/Gay Hamon Gog.
16 And also the name of the
city shall be Hamonah.
Thus shall they *cleanse* **purify** the land.
17 And, thou son of *man* **humanity**,
thus saith *the Lord GOD* **Adonay Yah Veh**;
Speak unto every *feathered fowl* **bird of wing**,
and to every *beast* **live being** of the field,
Assemble yourselves **Gather**, and come;
gather *yourselves on every side* **round about**
to my sacrifice that I *do* sacrifice for you,
even a great sacrifice
upon the mountains of *Israel* **Yisra El**, that
ye may eat flesh, and drink blood.
18 Ye shall eat the flesh of the mighty,
and drink the blood of the *princes* **hierarchs** of the earth,
and to the live beings of the field for food:
5 you fall on the face of the field:
for I have worded
—an oracle of Adonay Yah Veh
6 and I send a fire on Magog
and among them who settle confidently in the islands:
and they know I—Yah Veh.
7 Thus I make my holy name known
among my people Yisra El;
and I profane my holy name no more:
and the goyim know I—Yah Veh,
the Holy One in Yisra El.
8 Behold, it approaches, and so be it
—an oracle of Adonay Yah Veh this
is the day whereof I worded.
9 And they who settle in the cities of Yisra El
go forth and burn—burn the armament;
both the bucklers and the shields
the bows and the arrows
and the handstaves and the javelins
and they burn them with fire seven years:
10 so that they neither lift timber from the field
nor chop any from the forests;
for they burn the armaments with fire:
and they spoil them who spoil them
and plunder them who plunder them
—an oracle of Adonay Yah Veh.
11 And so be it, in that day,
I give Gog a place there—a tomb in Yisra El,
in the valley of passersby on the east of the sea:
and the passersby stop
and there they entomb Gog and all his multitude:
and they call it
Gay Hamon Gog/The Valley of the Multitude of Gog.
12 And for seven months
the house of Yisra El entombs them
to purify the land.
13 Yes, all the people of the land entomb them;
and it becomes to them for a name
the day they honor me
—an oracle of Adonay Yah Veh.
14 And they continually separate men
passing through the land
with the the passersby
to entomb them who remain on the face of the earth
—to purify it:
and after the end of seven months they probe:
15 and when the passersby pass through the land
and any sees a human bone,
he sets a monument beside it
until the entombers entombed it in
Gay Hamon Gog/The Valley of the Multitude of Gog:
16 and the name of the city *is* also Hamonah/
Multitude: thus they purify the land.
17 And you, son of humanity,
thus says Adonay Yah Veh:
Speak to every bird of wing,
and to every live being of the field,
Gather and come;
gather from all around
for the sacrifice I sacrifice for you
—a great sacrifice on the mountains of Yisra El
—to eat flesh and drink blood:
18 —to eat the flesh of the mighty
and drink the blood of the hierarchs of the earth,
of rams, of lambs, and of **he** goats, of bullocks,
all of them fatlings of Bashan.
19 And ye shall eat fat *till ye be full* **unto satiety**,
and drink blood till ye be *drunken* **intoxicated**,
of my sacrifice which I have sacrificed for you.
20 Thus ye shall be *filled* **satiated** at my table

with horses and chariots,
with mighty *men*, and with all men of war,
saith the Lord GOD **an oracle of Adonay Yah Veh**.
21 And I *will set* **shall give** my *glory* **honour**
among the *heathen* **goyim**,
and all the *heathen* **goyim** shall see my judgment
that I have *executed* **worked**,
and my hand that I have *laid* **set** upon them.
22 So the house of *Israel* **Yisra El** shall know
that *I am the LORD* **I—Yah Veh** their *God* **Elohim**
from that day and *forward* **beyond**.
23 And the *heathen* **goyim** shall know
that the house of *Israel* **Yisra El**
went into captivity **was exiled**
for their *iniquity* **perversity**:
because they *trespassed* **treasoned** against me,
therefore hid I my face from them,
and gave them
into the hand of their *enemies* **tribulators**:
so fell they all by the sword.
24 According to their *uncleanness* **foulness**
and according to their *transgressions* **rebellions**
have I *done* **worked** unto them,
and hid my face from them.

YAH VEH MERCIES YISRA EL

25 Therefore
thus saith *the Lord GOD* **Adonay Yah Veh**;
Now *will I bring again* **shall I return**
the captivity of *Jacob* **Yaaqov**,
and *have* mercy *upon* the whole house of *Israel* **Yisra El**,
and *will* **shall** be jealous for my holy name;
26 After that they have borne their shame,
and all their *trespasses* **treasons**
whereby they have *trespassed* **treasoned** against me,
when they *dwelt safely* **settled confidently**
in their *land* **soil**,
and none made them *afraid* **tremble**.
27 When I have *brought* **returned** them *again*
from the people,
and gathered them out of their enemies' lands,
and am *sanctified* **hallowed** in them
in the *sight* **eyes** of many *nations* **goyim**;
28 Then shall they know
that *I am the LORD* **I—Yah Veh** their *God* **Elohim**,
which caused them
to be *led into captivity* **exiled** among the *heathen* **goyim**:
but I have gathered them unto their own *land* **soil**,
and have *left* none of them **remain** any more there.
29 Neither *will* **shall** I hide my
face any more from them:
for I have poured out my spirit
upon the house of *Israel* **Yisra El**,
saith the Lord GOD **an oracle of Adonay Yah Veh**.

THE HOUSE IS MEASURED

cp Apocalypse 11:1,2

40 In the five and twentieth
year of our *captivity* **exile**,
in the beginning of the year,
in the tenth *day* of the month,
in the fourteenth year after that the city was smitten,
in the selfsame day
the hand of *the LORD* **Yah Veh** was upon me,
and brought me thither.
2 In the visions of *God* **Elohim**
brought he me into the land of *Israel* **Yisra El**,
and set **rested** me upon a *very* **mighty** high mountain,
by which was as the *frame* **building** of a city
on the south.
3 And he brought me thither, and, behold,
there was a man,
whose *appearance* **visage**
was like the *appearance* **visage** of *brass* **copper**,
with a line of flax in his hand,
and a measuring *reed* **stalk**;
and he stood in the *gate* **portal**.
of rams, of lambs, and of he goats, of bullocks,
of all the fatlings of Bashan:
19 and you,
eat fat to satiety and drink blood to intoxication
of the sacrifice I sacrifice for you.
20 Thus satiate at my table
with horses and chariots,
with mighty and with all men of war
—an oracle of Adonay Yah Veh.
21 And I give my honor among the goyim
and all the goyim see the judgment I worked,
and my hand that I set on them:
22 thus the house of Yisra El knows
I—Yah Veh their Elohim from that day and beyond:
23 and the goyim know that the house of Yisra El
is exiled for their perversity
because they treason against me:
so I hide my face from them,
and give them into the hand of their tribulators:
so they all fall by the sword
24 —according to their foulness
and according to their rebellions
that I work to them;

and I hide my face from them.

YAH VEH MERCIES YISRA EL

25 So, thus says Adonay Yah Veh;
Now I restore the captivity of Yaaqov
and mercy the whole house of Yisra El
and *am* jealous for my holy name;
26 after they bear their shame
for all the treasons they treason against me;
when they settle confidently in their soil
and no one trembles them.
27 When I restore them from the people
and gather them from the lands of their enemies
and *am* hallowed in them in the eyes of many goyim
28 —and they know I—Yah Veh their Elohim,
who exiled them among the goyim:
and I gather them to their own soil,
so that none of them remain there any more:
29 and I hide not my face from them any more:
for I pour my spirit on the house of Yisra
El—an oracle of Adonay Yah Veh.

THE HOUSE IS MEASURED

cp Apocalypse 11:1,2

40 In the twenty—fifth year of our exile,
in the beginning of the year,
in the tenth of the month,
in the fourteenth year after the city *is* smitten,
in this selfsame day,
and the hand of Yah Veh being on me,
brings me there
2 —in the visions of Elohim
he brings me into the land of Yisra El
and rests me on a mighty high mountain;
on which *is* as the building of a city on the south.
3 And he brings me there, and behold,
a man with a visage as the visage of copper
with a line of flax in his hand and a measuring stalk;
and he stands in the portal
4 And the man *said* **worded** unto me,
Son of *man* **humanity**,
behold **see** with thine eyes, and hear with thine ears,
and set thine heart
upon all that I shall *shew* **have** thee **see**;
for to the intent
that I might *shew* **have** them **see** unto thee
art thou brought hither:
declare **tell** all that thou seest to the
house of *Israel* **Yisra El**.
5 And behold a wall on the outside of the house
round about **and round about**,
and in the man's hand a measuring *reed* **stalk**
of six cubits *long* by the cubit
and *an hand breadth* **a palm span**:
so he measured the breadth of the building,
one *reed* **stalk**;
and the height, one *reed* **stalk**.
6 Then came he unto the *gate* **portal**
which *looketh toward the east* **faceth eastward**,
and *went up* **ascended** the *stairs* **steps** *thereof*, and
measured the threshold of the *gate* **portal**,
which was one *reed* **stalk** broad;
and the *other* **one** threshold *of the gate*,
which was one *reed* **stalk** broad.
7 And *every little* **each** chamber
was one *reed* **stalk** long,
and one *reed* **stalk** broad;
and between the *little* chambers were five cubits;
and the threshold of the *gate* **portal**
by **beside** the porch of the *gate* **portal**
within **from the house** was one *reed* **stalk**.
8 He measured also the porch of the *gate* **portal**
within **from the house**, one *reed* **stalk**.
9 Then measured he the porch of the *gate* **portal**,
eight cubits;
and the *posts* **pilasters** *thereof*, two cubits;
and the porch of the *gate* **portal**
was inward **from the house**.
10 And the *little* chambers
of the *gate eastward* **portal of the way of the east**
were three *on this side* **here**, and three *on that side* **there**;
they three were of one measure:
and the *posts* **pilasters** had one measure
on this side **from here** and *on that side* **from there**.
11 And he measured
the breadth of the *entry* **opening** of the *gate* **portal**,
ten cubits;
and the length of the *gate* **portal**, thirteen cubits.
12 The *space* **border** *also*
before **at the face of** the *little* chambers
was one cubit *on this side* **from here**,
and the *space* **border**
was one cubit *on that side* **from there**:
and the *little* chambers
were six cubits *on this side* **from here**, and
six cubits *on that side* **from there**:.
13 He measured then the *gate* **portal**
from the roof of *one little* chamber to the roof *of another*:
the breadth was five and twenty cubits,

door **portal** against *door* **portal**.
14 He *made* **worked** also *posts* **pilasters**
of *threescore* **sixty** cubits,
even unto the *post* **pilaster** of the court
round about **and round about** the *gate* **portal**.
15 And from the face of the
gate **portal** of the entrance
unto the face of the porch of the inner *gate* **portal**
were fifty cubits.
16 And there were *narrow* **shuttered** windows
to the *little* chambers,
and to their *posts* **pilasters** within the *gate* **portal**
round about **and round about**,
and likewise to the arches: and windows
were round about **and round about** *inward* **within**:
and upon each *post* **pilaster** were palm trees.

THE OUTWARD COURT

17 Then brought he me into the outward court,
and, *lo* **behold**, there were chambers,
and a pavement made for the court
round about **and round about**:
4 and the man words to me, Son of humanity,
see with your eyes and hear with your ears
and set your heart on all I show you;
for I bring you here to show you
—to tell all you see to the house of Yisra El.
5 And behold,
a wall outside the house all around and all around;
and in the hand of the man, a measuring stalk
six cubits by the cubit and a palm span:
so he measures the breadth of the building, one stalk;
and the height, one stalk:
6 and he comes to the portal facing eastward
and ascends the steps
and measures the threshold of the portal,
one stalk broad;
and the one threshold, one stalk broad:
7 and each chamber,
one stalk long, and one stalk broad;
and between the chambers, five cubits;
and the threshold of the portal
beside the porch of the portal
from the house, one stalk;
8 and he measures the porch of the portal
from the house, one stalk;
9 and he measures the porch of the portal,
eight cubits;
and the pilasters, two cubits;
and the porch of the portal from the house.
10 And the chambers of the portal
of the way of the east,
three here and three there;
they three of one measure:
and the pilasters,
one measure from here and from there.
11 And he measures
the breadth of the opening of the portal, ten cubits;
and the length of the portal, thirteen cubits:
12 the border at the face of the chambers,
one cubit from here;
and the border, one cubit from there:
and the chambers,
six cubits from here, and six cubits from there.
13 And he measures the portal of the chamber
from roof to roof:
the breadth, twenty—five cubits,
portal against portal.
14 He also works pilasters, sixty cubits,
even to the pilaster of the court
all around and all around the portal:
15 and from the face of the portal of the entrance
to the face of the porch of the inner portal,
fifty cubits;
16 with shuttered windows to the chambers,
and to their pilasters within the portal
all around and all around;
and likewise to the arches:
with windows all around and all around within:
and on each pilaster, palm trees.

THE OUTWARD COURT

17 And he brings me into the outward court,
and behold, chambers;
and a pavement made for the court
all around and all around;
thirty chambers were upon the pavement.
18 And the pavement
by the *side* **shoulder** of the *gates* **portals**
over against **alongside** the length of the *gates* **portals**
was the *lower* **nether** pavement.
19 Then he measured the breadth
from the *forefront* **face** of the *lower gate* **nether portal**
unto the *forefront of* **face of** the inner
court *without* **outward**,
an hundred cubits eastward and northward.

THE PORTAL AT THE FACE OF THE NORTHWARD WAY

20 And the *gate* **portal** of the outward court

that *looked toward* **faced** the *north* **northward way**
he measured the length *thereof*, and the breadth *thereof*.
21 And the *little* chambers *thereof*
were three *on this side* **from here**
and three *on that side* **from there**;
and the *posts* **pilasters** and the arches *thereof*
were after the measure of the first *gate* **portal**:
the length *thereof* was fifty cubits,
and the breadth five and twenty cubits.
22 And their windows, and their
arches, and their palm trees,
were after the measure of the *gate* **portal**
that *looketh toward* **faceth** the *east* **eastward way**;
and they *went up* **ascended** unto it by seven steps;
and the arches *thereof were before* **faced** them.
23 And the *gate* **portal** of the inner court
was over against the *gate* **portal**
toward the north **northward**,
and *toward the east* **eastward**;
and he measured from *gate* **portal** to *gate* **portal**
an hundred cubits.

The Portal Of The Southward Way

24 After that
he *brought* **carried** me *toward* the *south* **southward way**,
and behold a *gate* **portal**
toward the south **the southward way**:
and he measured the *posts* **pilasters** *thereof*
and the arches *thereof* according to these measures.
25 And there were windows in
it and in the arches *thereof*
round about **and round about**, like those windows:
the length was fifty cubits,
and the breadth five and twenty cubits.
26 And there were seven steps
to go up to it **of ascent**,
and the arches *thereof* were *before* **at the face of** them:
and it had palm trees,
one on this side **one from here**,
and *another on that side* **one from there**,
upon the *posts* **pilasters** *thereof*.
27 And there was a *gate* **portal** in the inner court
toward the south **the southward way**:
and he measured from *gate* **portal** to *gate* **portal**
toward the south **the southward way** an hundred cubits.

The Inner Court

28 And he brought me to the inner court
by the *south gate* **southward portal**
and he measured the *south gate* **southward portal**
according to these measures;
29 And the *little* chambers *thereof*,
and the *posts* **pilasters** *thereof*,
and the arches *thereof*, according to these measures:
and there were windows in it and in the arches *thereof*
round about **and round about**:
it was fifty cubits long, and five and twenty cubits broad.
30 And the arches round about **and round about**
were five and twenty cubits long, and five cubits broad.
31 And the arches *thereof*
were toward the *utter* **outer** court;
and palm trees were upon the *posts* **pilasters** *thereof*:
and the *going up to it* **ascent** had eight steps.
32 And he brought me into the inner court
toward **the way of** the east:
and he measured the *gate* **portal**
according to these measures.
33 And the *little* chambers *thereof*,
and the *posts* **pilasters** *thereof*, and the arches *thereof*,
were according to these measures:
and there were windows therein
and in the arches *thereof* round about **and round about**:
it was fifty cubits long, and five and twenty cubits broad.
with thirty chambers on the pavement:
18 and the pavement by the shoulder of the portals
alongside the length of the portals,
the nether pavement:
19 and he measures the breadth
from the face of the nether portal
to the face of the inner court outward,
a hundred cubits eastward and northward.

The Portal At The Face Of The Northward Way

20 And the portal of the outward court
facing the northward way,
he measures the length and the breadth:
21 and the chambers,
three from here and three from there;
and the pilasters and the arches
are after the measure of the first portal:
the length, fifty cubits,
and the breadth, twenty—five cubits.
22 And their windows, and their arches,
and their palm trees,
as the measure of the portal
facing the eastward way;
and they ascend to it by seven steps;
and the arches face them.
23 And the portal of the inner court

is over against the portal northward and eastward;
and he measures from portal to portal,
a hundred cubits.

The Portal Of The Southward Way

24 And after that, he carries
me the southward way,
and behold, a portal the southward way;
and he measures the pilasters
and the arches according to these measures:
25 with windows therein and in the arches
all around and all around
like those windows:
the length, fifty cubits;
and the breadth, twenty—five cubits:
26 with seven steps of ascent,
and arches at their face:
and palm trees
—one from here and one from there
on the pilasters:
27 with a portal in the inner
court the southward way:
and he measures from portal to portal
the southward way, a hundred cubits.

The Inner Court

28 And he brings me to the inner court
by the southward portal;
and he measures the southward portal
according to these measures:
29 and the chambers and the
pilasters and the arches
according to these measures:
with windows therein and in the arches
all around and all around,
fifty cubits long, and twenty—five cubits broad:
30 and the arches all around and all around,
twenty—five cubits long, and five cubits broad:
31 with the arches toward the outer court;
and palm trees on the pilasters,
and the ascent eight steps.
32 And he brings me into the inner court
the way of the east:
and he measures the portal
according to these measures:
33 and the chambers and the
pilasters and the arches
are according to these measures:
with windows therein
and in the arches all around and all around:
fifty cubits long, and twenty—five cubits broad:
34 And the arches *thereof* were
toward the outward court;
and palm trees were upon the *posts* **pilasters** *thereof*,
on this side **from here**, and *on that side* **from there**:
and the *going up to it* **ascent** had eight steps.
35 And he brought me to the north *gate* **portal**,
and measured it according to these measures;
36 The *little* chambers *thereof*,
the *posts* **pilasters** *thereof*, and the arches *thereof*,
and the windows to it round about **and round about**:
the length was fifty cubits,
and the breadth five and twenty cubits.
37 And the *posts* **pilasters** *thereof*
were toward the utter court;
and palm trees were upon the *posts* **pilasters** *thereof*,
on this side **from here**, and *on that side* **from there**:
and the *going up to it* **ascent** had eight steps.

The Chambers Of The Holocaust

38 And the chambers and
the *entries* **portals** *thereof*
were by the *posts* **pilasters** of the *gates*
portals, where they *washed* **cleansed**
the *burnt offering* **holocaust**.
39 And in the porch of the *gate* **portal**
were two tables *on this side* **from here**,
and two tables *on that side* **from there**,
to *slay* **slaughter** thereon the *burnt offering* **holocaust**
and *the sin offering* **that for the sin**
and *the trespass offering* **that for the guilt**.
40 And at the *side without* **shoulder outward**,
as one *goeth up* **ascendeth**
to the *entry* **opening** of thc north *gate* **portal**,
were two tables;
and on the other *side* **shoulder**,
which was at the porch of the *gate* **portal**,
were two tables.
41 Four tables were *on this side* **from here**,
and four tables *on that side* **from there**,
by the *side* **shoulder** of the *gate* **portal**;
eight tables,
whereupon they *slew their sacrifices* **slaughtered**.
42 And the four tables were of hewn stone
for the *burnt offering* **holocaust**,
of *a* **one** cubit and an half long,
and *a* **one** cubit and an half broad,
and one cubit high:
whereupon also they *laid* **set** the instruments
wherewith they *slew* **slaughtered**
the *burnt offering* **holocaust** and the sacrifice.

43 And *within* **in the house** were hooks,
an hand broad **one palm span,**
fastened **established** round about **and round about:**
and upon the tables was the flesh of the *offering* **qorban.**

THE CHAMBERS OF THE SINGERS

44 And *without* **outward** the inner *gate* **portal**
were the chambers of the singers in the inner court,
which was at the *side* **shoulder** of the north *gate* **portal;**
and their prospect **they faced**
was toward the south **the southward way:**
one at the *side* **shoulder** of the east *gate* **portal**
having the prospect **at the face**
toward the north **of the northward way.**

THE CHAMBERS OF THE PRIESTS

45 And he *said* **worded** unto me,
This chamber,
whose prospect is toward the south
at the face of the southerly way,
is for the priests,
the *keepers* **guards** of the *charge* **guard** of the house.
46 And the chamber
whose prospect is toward the north
at the face of the northward
is for the priests,
the *keepers* **guards**
of the *charge* **guard** of the **sacrifice** altar:
these are the sons of *Zadok* **Sadoq**
among the sons of Levi,
which *come near to the LORD* **approach Yah Veh**
to minister unto him.
47 So he measured the court,
an hundred cubits long, and an hundred cubits broad,
34 with the arches toward the outward court;
and palm trees on the pilasters
from here, and from there:
and the ascent eight steps.
35 And he brings me to the north portal
and measures it according to these measures:
36 the chambers and the pilasters and the arches
and the windows to it all around and all around:
the length, fifty cubits,
and the breadth, twenty—five cubits;
37 with the pilasters toward the utter court;
and palm trees on the pilasters
from here, and from there:
and the ascent eight steps.

THE CHAMBERS OF THE HOLOCAUST

38 And the chambers and the portals *are* by the pilasters
of the portals where they cleanse the holocaust:
39 and in the porch of the portal,
two tables from here, and two tables from there,
to slaughter thereon the holocaust
and that for the sin and that for the guilt.
40 And at the shoulder outward,
as one ascends to the opening of the north portal,
two tables;
and on the other shoulder at the porch of the portal,
two tables.
41 Four tables from here, and
four tables from there
by the shoulder of the portal;
eight tables, whereon they slaughter:
42 with four tables of hewn stone for the holocaust,
one and a half cubits long,
and one and a half cubits broad,
and one cubit high:
whereon they set the instruments
to slaughter the holocaust and the sacrifice:
43 and hooks in the house, one palm span,
established all around and all around: and
on the tables, the flesh of the qorban.

THE CHAMBERS OF THE SINGERS

44 And outward the inner portal,
the chambers of the singers in the inner court
at the shoulder of the north portal;
at the face of the southward way;
one at the shoulder of the east portal
at the face of the northward way.

THE CHAMBERS OF THE PRIESTS

45 And he words to me,
This chamber at the face of the southward way
is for the priests
—the guards who guard the house:
46 and the chamber at the face of the northward
is for the priests,
—the guards who guard the sacrifice altar:
these are the sons of Sadoq among the sons of Levi
who approach Yah Veh to minister to him:
47 and he measures the court,
a hundred cubits long, and a hundred cubits broad,
foursquare **square;**
and the **sacrifice** altar

that was before **at the face of** the house.

THE HOUSE

48 And he brought me to the porch of the house,
and measured each *post* **pilaster** of the porch,
five cubits *on this side* **from here,**
and five cubits *on that side* **from there:**
and the breadth of the *gate* **portal**
was three cubits *on this side* **from here,**
and three cubits *on that side* **from there.**
49 The length of the porch was twenty cubits,
and the breadth eleven cubits,
and *he brought me by* the steps
whereby they *went up* **ascended** to it:
and there were pillars by the *posts* **pilasters,**
one on this side **one from here,**
and *another on that side* **one from there.**

THE MANSE

41 Afterward he brought me to the *temple* **manse,**
and measured the *posts* **pilasters,**
six cubits broad *on the one side* **from here,**
and six cubits broad *on the other side* **from there,**
which was the breadth of the *tabernacle* **tent.**
2 And the breadth of the *door*
opening was ten cubits;
and the *sides* **shoulders** of the *door* **opening**
were five cubits *on the one side* **from here,**
and five cubits *on the other side* **from there:**
and he measured the length *thereof,* forty cubits:
and the breadth, twenty cubits.

THE HOLY OF HOLIES

3 Then went he *inward* **within,**
and measured the *post* **pilaster** of the *door* **opening,**
two cubits;
and the *door* **opening,** six cubits;
and the breadth of the *door* **opening,** seven cubits.
4 So he measured the length
thereof, twenty cubits;
and the breadth, twenty cubits
before **at the face of** the *temple* **manse:**
and he said unto me,
This is the *most holy place* **holy of holies.**
5 After he measured the wall
of the house, six cubits;
and the breadth of *every* side *chamber,* four cubits,
round about **and round about** the house
on every side **round about.**
6 And the *side chambers* **sides** were
three, one over another, and thirty in order
side by side thirty—three times;
and they entered into the wall which was of the house
for the *side chambers* **sides**
round about **and round about,**
that they might have hold,
but they had not **taken** hold in the wall of the house.
7 And there was an enlarging,
and a *winding* **spiraling** about
still upward **upward and upward**
to the *side chambers* **sides:**
for the *winding* **spiraling** about of the house
went *still upward* **upward and upward**
round about **and round about** the house:
therefore the breadth of the house
was *still upward* **upward and upward,**
and so *increased* **ascended**
from the *lowest* **nethermost** *chamber*
to the *highest* **most high** by the midst.
8 I saw also the height of the house
round about **and round about:**
the foundations of the *side chambers* **sides**
were a full *reed* **stalk** of six *great* **elbow** cubits.
9 The *thickness* **breadth** of the wall,
which was for the side *chamber without* **outward,**
was five cubits:
and that which was left was the *place* **house**
of the *side chambers that were within* **sides to the house.**
10 And between the chambers
was the *wideness* **breadth** of twenty cubits
round about **and round about** the house
on every side **round about.**
11 And the *doors* **openings**
of the *side chambers* **sides**
square;
and the sacrifice altar at the face of the house.

THE HOUSE

48 And he brings me to the porch of the house
and measures each pilaster of the porch;
five cubits from here, and five cubits from there:
and the breadth of the portal,
three cubits from here, and three cubits from there:
49 the length of the porch, twenty cubits,
and the breadth, eleven cubits,
and the steps whereby they ascend to it:
with pillars by the pilasters,
one from here, and one from there.

THE MANSE

41 And he brings me to the manse
and he measures the pilasters;
six cubits broad from here,
and six cubits broad from there
—the breadth of the tent:
2 and the breadth of the opening, ten cubits;
and the shoulders of the opening,
five cubits from here, and five cubits from there:
and he measures the length, forty cubits:
and the breadth, twenty cubits.

THE HOLY OF HOLIES

3 And he goes inward
and measures the pilaster of the opening, two cubits;
and the opening, six cubits;
and the breadth of the opening, seven cubits:
4 and he measures the length, twenty cubits;
and the breadth, twenty cubits
at the face of the manse.
And he says to me,
This is the holy of holies.
5 And he measures the wall
of the house, six cubits;
and the breadth of side, four cubits,
all around and all around the house all around:
6 and the sides, side by side, thirty—three times;
and they enter the wall of the house
for the sides all around and all around to hold,
but they are not to hold the wall of the house:
7 and there *is* an enlarging
and a spiraling around upward and upward
to the sides:
and the spiraling of the house
goes upward and upward
all around and all around the house:
thus the breadth of the house *is* upward and upward,
and thus ascends
from the nethermost to the most high by the midst.
8 And I see the height of the house
all around and all around:
the foundations of the sides,
a full stalk of six cubits by the elbow:
9 the breadth of the wall, for the side outward,
five cubits:
and what *is* left
are the side houses to the house.
10 And between the chambers,
the breadth of twenty cubits
all around and all around the house all around:
11 and the openings of the sides
exeGeses ready research BIBLE
were toward *the place* that **which** was left,
one *door* **opening**
toward **the way of** the north,
and *another door* **one opening**
toward the south **southerly**:
and the breadth of *the place* that **which** was left
was five cubits round about **and round about**.
12 *Now* the building
that was before **at the face**
of the *separate place* **separation**
at the *end toward the west* **edge of the way of the sea**
was seventy cubits broad;
and the wall of the building was five cubits *thick* **broad**
round about **and round about,**
and the length *thereof* ninety cubits.
13 So he measured the house,
an hundred cubits long;
and the *separate place* **separation**, and the building,
with the walls *thereof*, an hundred cubits long;
14 Also the breadth of the face of the house,
and of the *separate place* **separation**
toward the east **eastward,**
an hundred cubits.
15 And he measured the length of the building
over against **at the face of** the *separate place* **separation**
which was behind it,
and the galleries *thereof*
on the one side **from here**
and *on the other side* **from there,**
an hundred cubits,
with the inner *temple* **manse,**
and the porches of the court;
16 The *door posts* **thresholds,**
and the *narrow* **shuttered** windows, and the galleries
round about **and round about** on their three *stories*,
over against the *door* **threshold,**
cieled with wood **with shingles of timber**
round about **and round about,**
and from the *ground* **earth** up to the windows,
and the windows were covered;
17 To that above the *door* **opening,**
even unto the inner house,
and *without* **outward**, and by all the wall
round about **and round about**
within **inward** and *without* **outward**, by measure.
18 And it was made

with *cherubims* **cherubim** and palm trees,
so that a palm tree was between a cherub and a cherub;
and *every* cherub had two faces;
19 So that the face of a *man* **human**
was toward the palm tree *on the one side* **from here**,
and the face of a *young lion* **whelp**
toward the palm tree *on the other side* **from there**:
it was made through all the house
round about **and round about**.
20 From the *ground* **earth** unto
above the *door* **opening**
were *cherubims* **cherubim** and palm trees
made, and on the wall of the *temple* **manse**.
21 The posts of the *temple* **manse** were squared,
and the face of the *sanctuary* **holies**;
the *appearance of the one* **visage**
as the *appearance of the other* **visage**.
22 The **sacrifice** altar of *wood* **timber**
was three cubits high,
and the length *thereof* two cubits;
and the corners *thereof*, and the length *thereof*,
and the walls *thereof*, were of *wood* **timber**:
and he *said* **worded** unto me,
This is the table
that is *before the LORD* **at the face of Yah Veh**.
23 And the *temple* **manse** and the *sanctuary* **holies**
had two doors.
24 And the doors had two leaves *apiece*,
two *turning* **folding** leaves;
two *leaves* for the one door,
and two leaves for the other *door*.
25 And there were made on them,
on the doors of the *temple* **manse**, *cherubims* **cherubim**
and palm trees, like as were made upon the walls;
toward what *is* left;
one opening the northward way,
and one opening the southward;
and the breadth of what *is* left,
five cubits all around and all around.
12 The building at the face of the separation,
at the edge of the way of the sea,
seventy cubits broad:
and the wall of the building,
five cubits broad all around and all around;
and the length ninety cubits.
13 And he measures the house,
a hundred cubits long;
and the separation, and the building,
with the walls, a hundred cubits long;
14 and the breadth of the face of the house
and of the separation eastward,
a hundred cubits:
15 and he measures the length of the building
at the face of the separation behind it,
and the galleries,
from here, and from there, a hundred cubits,
with the inner manse, and the porches of the court:
16 the thresholds,
and the shuttered windows, and the galleries
all around and all around, three,
over against the threshold,
with shingles of timber all around and all around
and from the earth up to the windows;
and the covered windows;
17 to that above the opening
—even to the inner house and outward
and by all the wall all around and all around
inward and outward, by measure.
18 And it *is* made with cherubim and palm trees,
so that there *is* a palm tree
between cherub and cherub;
and *each* cherub *has* two faces;
19 with the face of a human
toward the palm tree from here,
and the face of a whelp
toward the palm tree from there
—made through all the house
all around and all around.
20 From the earth to above the opening
they make cherubim and palm trees,
and on the wall of the manse.
21 The posts of the manse *are* squared,
and the face of the holies;
the visage *is* as the visage.
22 The sacrifice altar *is* of timber,
three cubits high, and two cubits long;
and the corners and the length and the walls, timber.
And he words to me,
This is the table at the face of Yah Veh.
23 And the manse and the holies *have* two doors:
24 and the doors, two leaves—two folding leaves;
two for the one door, and two leaves for the other.
25 And make on them—on the doors of the manse,
cherubim and palm trees,
as those made on the walls
and there were thick *planks* **timbers** upon
the face of the porch *without* **outward**.

26 And there were
narrow **shuttered** windows and palm trees
on the one side **from here**
and *on the other side* **from there**,
on the *sides* **shoulders** of the porch,
and *upon* the *side chambers* **sides** of the house,
and thick planks.

THE CHAMBERS OF THE PRIESTS

42 Then he brought me forth
into the *utter* **outer** court,
the *way toward the north* **northward way**:
and he brought me into the chamber
that was over against the *separate place* **separation**,
and which was before the building
toward the north **northward**.
2 *Before* **At the face of** the
length of an hundred cubits
was the north *door* **opening**,
and the breadth was fifty cubits.
3 Over against the twenty *cubits*
which were for the inner court,
and over against the pavement
which was for the *utter* **outer** court,
was gallery *against* **at the face of** gallery
in *three stories* **tiers**.
4 And *before* **at the face of** the chambers
was a walk to ten cubits breadth inward,
a way of one cubit;
and their *doors toward the north* **openings northward**.
5 *Now* the *upper* **most high**
chambers were shorter:
for the galleries *were higher* **contained** more than these,
than the *lower* **nether**,
and than the middlemost of the building.
6 For they were in *three stories* **tiers**,
but had not pillars as the pillars of the courts:
therefore *the building was straitened* **it was set**
more than the *lowest* **nethermost** and the middlemost
from the *ground* **earth**.
7 And the wall that was *without* **outward**
over against **alongside** the chambers,
toward the utter **the way of the outer** court
on the forepart **at the face** of the chambers,
the length *thereof* was fifty cubits.
8 For the length of the chambers
that were in the *utter* **outer** court was fifty cubits:
and, *lo* **behold**, *before* **at the face of** the *temple* **manse**
were an hundred cubits.
9 And from under these chambers
was the entry on the east *side*,
as one goeth into them from the *utter* **outer** court.
10 The chambers were in the *thickness* **breadth**
of the wall of the court
toward the east **to the eastward way**,
over against **at the face of** the *separate place* **separation**,
and *over against* **at the face of** the building.
11 And the way *before them* **at their face**
was like the *appearance* **visage** of the chambers
which were *toward the north* **to the northward way**,
as long as they, **as their length,**
and as broad as they **thus their breadth**:
and all their *goings out* **proceedings** were both
according to their *fashions* **judgments**,
and according to their *doors* **openings**.
12 And according to the *doors*
openings of the chambers
that were *toward the south* **to the southward way**
was *a door* **an opening** in the head of the way,
even the way
directly before **turning at the face of** the wall
toward the east **to the eastward way**,
as one entereth into them.
13 Then said he unto me,
The *north* **northward** chambers
and the *south* **southward** chambers,
which are *before* **at the face of** the
separate place **separation**,
they be holy chambers,
where the priests that approach unto *the LORD* **Yah Veh**
shall eat the *most holy things* **holy of holies**:
there shall they *lay* **set**
the *most holy things* **holy of holies**,
and the *meat* offering,
with thick timbers on the face of the porch outward:
26 with shuttered windows and palm trees
from here and from there
on the shoulders of the porch
and the sides of the house
with thick planks.

THE CHAMBERS OF THE PRIESTS

42 And he brings me forth into the outer court,
the northward way:
and he brings me into the chamber
over against the separation,
in front of the building northward.

2 At the face,
the length of the north opening, a hundred cubits,
and the breadth, fifty cubits.
3 Over against the twenty for the inner court,
and over against the pavement for the outer court,
the gallery at the face of gallery, in tiers.
4 And at the face of the chambers,
a walk ten cubits broad to the inside,
a way of one cubit;
and their openings, northward.
5 And the most high chambers *are* shorter:
for the galleries contain more than these
—than the nether
and than the middlemost of the building.
6 For they *are* in tiers,
but not pillars as the pillars of the courts:
so it sets back from the earth
more than the nethermost and the middlemost.
7 And the outward wall alongside the chambers,
the way of the outer court at the face of the chambers,
the length, fifty cubits.
8 For the length of the chambers
in the outer court, fifty cubits:
and behold, at the face of the manse,
a hundred cubits.
9 And under these chambers,
the entry on the east,
as one enters them from the outer court:
10 with the chambers
in the breadth of the wall of the court
to the eastward way,
at the face of the separation,
and at the face of the building.
11 And the way at their face
is as the visage of the chambers
to the northward way;
as their length, thus their breadth:
and all their proceedings
according to their judgments,
and according to their openings.
12 And according to the openings of the chambers
to the southward way,
an opening in the head of the way;
the way,
turning at the face of the wall to the eastward way,
as one enters them.
13 Then says he to me,
The northward chambers
and the southward chambers
at the face of the separation,
are holy chambers,
where the priests who approach to Yah Veh
eat the holy of holies:
there they set the holy of holies and the offering
and *the sin offering* **that for the sin,**
and *the trespass offering* **that for the guilt**;
for the place is holy.
14 When the priests enter therein,
then shall they not go out of the *holy place* **holies**
into the *utter* **outer** court,
but there they shall *lay* **set** their *garments* **clothes**
wherein they minister;
for they are holy;
and shall *put on* **enrobe** other *garments* **clothes**,
and shall approach to those *things*
which are for the people.

THE MEASURING OF THE OUTWARD COURT

15 *Now* when he had *made an end of* **finished**
measuring the inner house,
he brought me forth *toward* **the way of** the *gate* **portal**
whose prospect is toward **at the face**
of the *east* **eastward way**,
and measured it round about **and round about.**
16 He measured the east *side* **wind/spirit**
with the measuring *reed* **stalk**,
five *hundred reeds* **cubits of stalks**,
with the measuring *reed* **stalk**
round about **and round about.**
17 He measured the north *side* **wind/spirit**,
five hundred *reeds* **stalks**,
with the measuring *reed* **stalk**
round about **and round about.**
18 He measured the *south side*
southerly wind/spirit,
five hundred *reeds* **stalks**, with the measuring *reed* **stalk.**
19 He turned about to the *west*
side **seaward wind/spirit**,
and measured five hundred *reeds* **stalks**
with the measuring *reed* **stalk.**
20 He measured it by the four *sides* **winds/spirits**:
it had a wall round about **and round about**,
five hundred *reeds* long, and five hundred broad,
to *make a separation* **separate**
between the *sanctuary* **holies** and the profane *place*.

THE HONOUR OF YAH VEH FILLS THE HOUSE

43 Afterward he *brought* **carried**
me to the *gate* **portal**,
even the *gate* **portal**

that *looketh toward* **faceth the way of** the east:
2 And, behold,
the *glory* **honour** of *the God* **Elohim** of *Israel* **Yisra El**
came from the way of the east:
and his voice was like a *noise* **voice** of many waters:
and the earth shined with his *glory* **honour**.
3 And it was according to the *appearance* **vision**
of the vision which I saw,
even according to the vision that I saw
when I came to *destroy* **ruin** the city:
and the visions were like the vision that I saw
by the river *Chebar* **Kebar**;
and I fell upon my face.
4 And the *glory* **honour** of *the LORD* **Yah Veh**
came into the house by the way of the *gate* **portal**
whose prospect is toward **at the face of the way**
of the east.
5 So the spirit *took* **bore** me *up*,
and brought me into the inner court; and, behold,
the *glory* **honour** of *the LORD* **Yah Veh** filled the house.
6 And I heard him speaking
unto me out of the house;
and the man stood *by* **beside** me.
7 And he said unto me, Son of *man* **humanity**,
the place of my throne,
and the place of the soles of my feet,
where I *will dwell* **shall tabernacle**
in the midst of the *children* **sons** of *Israel* **Yisra El**
for ever **eternally**,
and my holy name,
shall the house of *Israel* **Yisra El** no more *defile* **foul**,
neither they, nor their *kings* **sovereigns**,
by their whoredom,
nor by the carcases of their *kings* **sovereigns**
in their *high places* **bamahs**.
8 In their *setting* **giving** of their threshold
by my thresholds,
and their post *by* **beside** my posts,
and the wall between me and **between** them,
and that for the sin and that for the guilt;
for the place *is* holy.
14 When the priests enter therein,
they not go from the holies into the outer court;
but there they set their clothes wherein they minister;
for they are holy:
and enrobe other clothes,
and approach those which are for the people.

THE MEASURING OF THE OUTWARD COURT

15 And he finishes measuring the inner house;
and he brings me forth the way of the portal
at the face of the eastward way,
and measures it all around and all around.
16 He measures the east wind/spirit
with the measuring stalk, five cubits of stalks,
with the measuring stalk all around and all around.
17 He measures the north wind/spirit,
five hundred stalks,
with the measuring stalk all around and all around.
18 He measures the southerly wind/spirit,
five hundred stalks, with the measuring stalk.
19 He turns around to the seaward wind/spirit,
and measures five hundred stalks
with the measuring stalk:
20 he measures it by the four winds/spirits:
with a wall all around and all around,
five hundred long, and five hundred broad,
to separate between the holies and the profane.

THE HONOR OF YAH VEH FILLS THE HOUSE

43 And he carries me to the portal,
the portal facing the way of the east:
2 and behold,
the honor of Elohim of Yisra El
comes from the way of the east:
with his voice as a voice of many waters:
and the earth shines with his honor:
3 and it according to the vision
is the vision I saw,
—according to the vision I saw
when I came to ruin the city:
and the visions as the vision I saw by the river Kebar;
and I fall on my face:
4 and the honor of Yah Veh
comes into the house by the way of the portal
at the face of the way of the east:
5 and the spirit bears me
and brings me into the inner court;
and behold, the honor of Yah Veh fills the house.
6 And I hear him speak to me from the house;
with the man standing beside me,
7 and he says to me, Son of humanity,
the place of my throne,
and the place of the soles of my feet,
where I tabernacle
among the sons of Yisra El eternally,
and my holy name,
the house of Yisra El fouls no more
—neither they nor their sovereigns
by their whoredom,

nor by the carcases of their sovereigns
in their bamahs.
8 In their giving of their
threshold with my thresholds,
and their post beside my posts,
and the wall between me and between them,
they have even *defiled* **fouled** my holy name
by their *abominations* **abhorrences**
that they have *committed* **worked**:
wherefore I have *consumed* **finished** them **off**
in *mine anger* **my wrath**.
9 Now let them *put away* **far**
remove their whoredom,
and the carcases of their *kings* **sovereigns**,
remove far from me,
and I *will dwell* **shall tabernacle** in the midst of them
for ever **eternally**.
10 Thou son of *man* **humanity**,
shew **tell** the house**,** to the house of *Israel* **Yisra El**,
that they may be ashamed
of their *iniquities* **perversities**:
and let them measure the *pattern* **gauge**.
11 And if they be ashamed
of all that they have *done* **worked**,
shew **make** them **know** the form of the house,
and the *fashion* **structure** *thereof*,
and the *goings out* **exits** *thereof*,
and the *comings in* **entrances** *thereof*,
and all the forms *thereof*,
and all the *ordinances* **statutes** *thereof*,
and all the forms *thereof*,
and all the *laws* **torah** *thereof*:
and *write it* **inscribe** in their *sight* **eyes**,
that they may *keep* **guard** the whole form *thereof*,
and all the *ordinances* **statutes** *thereof*,
and *do* **work** them.
12 This is the *law* **torah** of the house;
Upon the top of the mountain
the whole *limit* **border** *thereof*
round about **and round about**
shall be *most holy* **the holy of holies**.
Behold, this is the *law* **torah** of the house.

The Altar Measured

13 And these are the measures of the **sacrifice** altar
after the cubits:
The cubit is a cubit and *an hand breadth* **palm span**;
even the *bottom* shall *be* **bosom** a cubit,
and the breadth a cubit,
and the border *thereof* by the *edge* **lip** *thereof*
round about shall be *a* **one** span:
and this shall be
the *higher place* **arch** of the **sacrifice** altar.
14 And from the *bottom upon*
bosom of the *ground* **earth**
even to the *lower settle* **nether ledge** shall be
two cubits, and the breadth one cubit;
and from the lesser *settle* **ledge**
even to the greater *settle* **ledge**
shall *be* four cubits,
and the breadth *one* cubit.
15 *So* **And** the altar shall be four cubits;
and from *the altar* **Ari El** and
upward shall be four horns.
16 And *the altar* **Ari El** shall be twelve *cubits* long,
twelve broad, square in the four *squares* **quarters** *thereof*.
17 And the *settle* **ledge** shall be fourteen *cubits* long
and fourteen broad in the four *squares* **quarters** *thereof*;
and the border **round** about it shall be half a cubit;
and the *bottom thereof* **bosom**
shall be a cubit **round** about;
and his *stairs* **steps** shall *look toward* **face** the east.

The Ordinances Of The Sacrifice Altar

18 And he said unto me, Son of *man* **humanity**,
thus saith *the Lord GOD* **Adonay Yah Veh**;
These are the ordinances of the **sacrifice** altar
in the day when they shall make it,
to *offer burnt offerings* **holocaust holocausts** thereon,
and to sprinkle blood thereon.
19 And thou shalt give to the priests
the *Levites* **Leviym** that be of the seed of *Zadok* **Sadoq**,
which approach unto me, to minister unto me,
saith the Lord GOD **an oracle of Adonay Yah Veh**,
a young **an ox son of a** bullock for *a sin offering* **the sin**.
20 And thou shalt take of the blood *thereof*,
and *put* **give** it on the four horns of it,
and on the four corners of the *settle* **ledge**,
and upon the border round about:
thus shalt thou cleanse and *purge* **kapar/atone** it.
and they foul my holy name
by the abhorrences they work:
and I finish them off in my wrath.
9 Now have them remove their whoredom
and remove the carcases of their sovereigns
far from me;
and I tabernacle midst them eternally.
10 You, son of humanity,
tell the house—the house of Yisra El,
to shame of their perversities;

and have them measure the gauge:
11 and if they shame of all they worked,
have them know the form of the house
and the structure and the exits and the entrances;
and all the forms of all the statutes
and all the forms of all the torah:
and inscribe in their eyes,
so that they guard the whole form and all the statutes
and work them.
12 This is the torah of the house:
on the top of the mountain
the whole border all around and all around
is the holy of holies.
Behold, this, the torah of the house.

THE ALTAR MEASURED

13 And these *are* the measures of the sacrifice altar
by cubits:
The cubit is a cubit and palm span;
and the bosom, a cubit;
and the breadth, a cubit;
and the border by the lip all around, one span:
and this *is* the arch of the sacrifice altar:
14 and from the bosom of the earth
to the nether ledge, two cubits; and the breadth,
one cubit; and from the lesser ledge
to the greater ledge, four cubits,
and the breadth, a cubit.
15 And the altar, four cubits;
and from Ari El and upward, four horns:
16 and Ari El *is* twelve long, twelve broad,
square in the four quarters:
17 and the ledge,
fourteen long and fourteen broad in the four quarters;
and the border all around, half a cubit:
and the bosom, a cubit all around:
and his steps face the east.

THE ORDINANCES OF THE SACRIFICE ALTAR

18 And he says to me, Son of humanity,
thus says Adonay Yah Veh:
These *are* the ordinances of the sacrifice altar
in the day they make it
to holocaust holocausts thereon
and to sprinkle blood thereon.
19 And you, give the priests
—the Leviym of the seed of Sadoq
who approach to me, to minister to me
—an oracle of Adonay Yah Veh
an ox son of a bullock for the sin:
20 and take of the blood and give it
on the four horns thereof
and on the four corners of the ledge
and on the border all around:
thus you cleanse and kapar/atone it.
21 Thou shalt take the bullock also
of *the sin offering* **that for the sin,**
and he shall burn it
in the *appointed* **specified** place of the house,
without the *sanctuary* **holies.**
22 And on the second day
thou shalt *offer a kid* **oblate a buck** of the **doe** goats
without blemish for a sin offering **integrious for the sin;**
and they shall cleanse the **sacrifice** altar,
as they *did cleanse it* **cleansed** with the bullock.
23 When thou hast *made an*
end of **finished** cleansing it,
thou shalt *offer a young* **oblate an ox son of**
a bullock, *without blemish* **integrious,**
and a ram out of the flock, *without blemish* **integrious.**
24 And thou shalt *offer* **holocaust** them
before the LORD **at the face of Yah Veh,**
and the priests shall cast salt upon them,
and they shall *offer* **oblate** them *up*
for a *burnt offering* **holocaust** unto *the LORD* **Yah Veh.**
25 Seven days shalt thou *prepare* **work** every day
a goat for a sin offering **a buck for the**
sin: they shall also *prepare* **work**
a young **an ox son of a** bullock,
and a ram out of the flock, *without blemish* **integrious.**
26 Seven days shall they
purge **kapar/atone** the **sacrifice** altar and purify it;
and they shall *consecrate themselves* **fill their hands.**
27 And when these days are *expired* **finished,**
so be it *shall be,*
that upon the eighth day, and *so forward* **beyond,**
the priests shall *make* **work**
your *burnt offerings* **holocausts** upon the **sacrifice** altar,
and your *peace offerings* **shelamim;**
and I *will accept* **shall be pleased with** you,
saith the Lord GOD **an oracle of Adonay Yah Veh.**

THE PORTAL OF YAH VEH SHUT

44 Then he *brought* **turned** me back
the way of the *gate* **portal** of the
outward *sanctuary* **holies**
which *looketh* **faceth** toward the east; and it was shut.
2 Then said *the LORD* **Yah Veh** unto me;
This *gate* **portal** shall be shut, it shall not be opened,
and no man shall enter in by it;

because
the LORD **Yah Veh**, *the God* **Elohim** of *Israel* **Yisra El**,
hath entered in by it, therefore it shall be shut.
3 It is for the *prince* **hierarch**;
the prince, he shall sit in it to eat bread
before the LORD **at the face of Yah Veh**;
he shall enter by the way of the porch of that *gate* **portal**,
and shall go out by the way of the same.
4 Then brought he me the
way of the north *gate* **portal**
before **at the face of** the house:
and I *looked* **saw**, and, behold,
the *glory* **honour** of *the LORD* **Yah Veh**
filled the house of *the LORD* **Yah Veh**:
and I fell upon my face.
5 And *the LORD* **Yah Veh** said unto me,
Son of *man* **humanity**, *mark well* **set thine heart**,
and *behold* **see** with thine eyes, and hear with thine ears
all that I say unto thee
concerning all the *ordinances* **statutes**
of the house of *the LORD* **Yah Veh**,
and all the *laws* **torah** *thereof*;
and *mark well* **set thy heart**
to the *entering in* **entrance** of the house,
with every *going forth* **exit** of the *sanctuary* **holies**.
6 And thou shalt say to the rebellious,
even to the house of *Israel* **Yisra El**,
Thus saith *the Lord GOD* **Adonay Yah Veh**;
O ye house of *Israel* **Yisra El**,
let it suffice you **Enough**
of all your *abominations* **abhorrences**,
7 In that ye have brought *into my*
sanctuary **in sons of** strangers,
uncircumcised in heart, and uncircumcised in flesh,
to be in my *sanctuary* **holies**, to *pollute* **profane** it,
even my house,
when ye *offer* **oblate** my bread, the fat and the blood,
and they have broken my covenant
because of **as to** all your *abominations* **abhorrences**.
21 And take the bullock of that for the sin
and burn it in the specified place of the house
outside the holies:
22 and on the second day
oblate an integrious buck of the doe goats
for the sin;
and cleanse the sacrifice altar
as they cleansed for the bullock:
23 when you finish cleansing,
oblate an integrious ox son of a bullock,
and an integrious ram from the flock
24 and holocaust them at the face of Yah Veh;
and the priests cast salt on them,
and they oblate them for a holocaust to Yah Veh.
25 Daily, for seven days
work a buck for the sin:
and also work an integrious ox son of a bullock
and a ram from the flock:
26 for seven days
kapar/atone the sacrifice altar and purify it;
and fill their hands.
27 And so be it, when these days are finished,
on the eighth day and beyond,
the priests work your holocausts
on the sacrifice altar
with your shelamim;
and I *am* pleased with you
—an oracle of Adonay Yah Veh.

THE PORTAL OF YAH VEH SHUT

44 And he turns me back to the way of the portal
of the outward holies facing eastward; and it is shut.
2 And Yah Veh says to me;
This portal is shut, not to be opened;
and no man enters in by it;
because Yah Veh Elohim of Yisra El,
enters in by it, thus it is shut.
3 It is for the hierarch;
the hierarch sits therein
to eat bread at the face of Yah Veh;
he enters by the way of the porch of that portal
and goes out by the same way.
4 Then he brings me the way of the north portal
at the face of the house:
and I see, and behold,
the honor of Yah Veh fills the house of Yah Veh:
and I fall on my face.
5 And Yah Veh says to me,
Son of humanity, set your heart,
and see with your eyes, and hear with your ears
all I say to you
concerning all the statutes of the house of Yah Veh,
and all the torah;
and set your heart to the entrance of the house
with every exit of the holies.
6 And you,
say to the rebellious—to the house of Yisra El,
Thus says Adonay Yah Veh:
O you house of Yisra El,
enough of all your abhorrences,

7 in that you bring in sons of strangers
uncircumcised in heart and uncircumcised in flesh
to be in my holies, to profane it—my house,
when you oblate my bread, the fat and the blood,
and they break my covenant
with all your abhorrences:
8 And ye have not *kept* **guarded** the *charge* **guard**
of mine *holy things* **holies**:
but ye have set *keepers* **guards** of my *charge* **guard**
in my *sanctuary* **holies** for yourselves.
9 Thus saith *the Lord GOD* **Adonay Yah Veh**;
No **son of a** stranger,
uncircumcised in heart, nor uncircumcised in flesh,
shall enter into my *sanctuary* **holies**,
of any **son of a** stranger
that is among the *children* **sons** of *Israel* **Yisra El**.

The Idolatrous Leviym

10 And the *Levites* **Leviym**
that *are gone away* far **removed** from me,
when *Israel went astray* **Yisra El strayed**,
which *went astray* **strayed** away
from me after their idols;
they shall even bear their *iniquity* **perversity**.
11 Yet they shall be ministers
in my *sanctuary* **holies**,
having charge at the *gates* **portals** of the
house, and ministering to the house:
they shall *slay* **slaughter** the *burnt offering* **holocaust**
and the sacrifice for the people,
and they shall stand *before* **at the face of** them
to minister unto them.
12 Because they ministered unto them
before **at the face of** their idols,
and *caused* **became to** the house of *Israel* **Yisra El**
to fall into iniquity **a stumblingblock of perversity**;
therefore have I lifted up mine hand against them,
saith the Lord GOD **an oracle of Adonay Yah Veh**,
and they shall bear their *iniquity* **perversity**.
13 And they shall not come near unto me,
to *do the office of a priest* **priest the priethood** unto me,
nor to come near to any of my *holy things* **holies**,
in the *most holy place* **holy of holies**:
but they shall bear their shame,
and their *abominations* **abhorrences**
which they have *committed* **worked**.
14 But I *will make* **shall give** them
keepers **guards** of the *charge* **guard** of the house,
for all the service *thereof*,
and for all that shall be *done* **worked** therein.

The Trustworthy Leviym

15 But the priests the *Levites* **Leviym**,
the sons of *Zadok* **Sadoq**,
that *kept* **guarded**
the *charge* **guard** of my *sanctuary* **holies**
when the *children* **sons** of *Israel* **Yisra El**
went astray **strayed** from me,
they shall *come near to* **approach** me
to minister unto me,
and they shall stand *before me* **at my face**
to *offer* **oblate** unto me the fat and the blood,
saith the Lord GOD **an oracle of Adonay Yah Veh**:
16 They shall enter into my *sanctuary* **holies**,
and they shall *come near to* **approach** my table,
to minister unto me,
and they shall *keep* **guard** my *charge* **guard**.
17 And **so be** it *shall come to pass*,
that when they enter in
at the *gates* **portals** of the inner court,
that they shall *be clothed* **enrobe**
with *linen garments* **flax clothes**;
and no wool shall *come* **ascend** upon them,
whiles they minister
in the *gates* **portals** of the inner court,
and *within* **the house**.
18 They shall have *linen bonnets* **flax tiaras**
upon their heads,
and shall have *linen* **flax** breeches upon their loins;
they shall not gird *themselves*
with any *thing that causeth sweat* **sweater**.
19 And when they go forth
into the *utter* **outer** court,
even into the *utter* **outer** court to the people,
they shall *put off* **strip** their *garments* **clothes**
wherein they ministered,
and *lay* **leave** them in the holy chambers,
and they shall put on other *garments* **clothes**;
and they shall not *sanctify* **hallow** the people
with their *garments* **clothes**.
8 and you guard not the guard of my holies:
and you set guards of my guard
in my holies for yourselves.
9 Thus says Adonay Yah Veh:
A son of a stranger,
neither uncircumcised in heart
nor uncircumcised in flesh,
enters into my holies
—of any son of a stranger among the sons of Yisra El.

The Idolatrous Leviym

10 And the Leviym who removed afar from me
when Yisra El strayed
—strayed from me after their idols;
they bear their perversity.
11 And they are ministers in my holies;
having charge at the portals of the house
and ministering to the house:
they slaughter the holocaust and the sacrifice
for the people,
and they stand at their face to minister to them.
12 Because they minister to them
at the face of their idols,
and become a stumblingblock of perversity
to the house of Yisra El;
so I lift my hand against them
—an oracle of Adonay Yah Veh
and they bear their perversity:
13 and they neither come near to me
to priest the priethood to me,
nor to come near to any of my holies
in the holy of holies:
and they bear the shame
and the abhorrences they worked:
14 and I give them
for guards of the guard of the house
—for all the service
and for all they work therein.

The Trustworthy Leviym

15 And the priests, the Leviym, the sons of Sadoq,
who guarded the guard of my holies
when the sons of Yisra El strayed from me,
they approach me to minister to me;
and they stand at my face
to oblate the fat and the blood to me
—an oracle of Adonay Yah Veh:
16 they enter my holies
and approach my table to minister to me,
and they guard my guard.
17 And so be it,
when they enter in at the portals of the inner court,
they enrobe with flax clothes;
and no wool ascends on them,
while they minister
in the portals of the inner court and the house
18 —flax tiaras on their heads
and flax breeches on their loins; they
gird not with any sweater.
19 And when they go forth into the outer court
into the outer court to the people,
they strip the clothes wherein they minister
and leave them in the holy chambers;
and they put on other clothes;
they neither hallow the people with their clothes.
20 Neither shall they shave their heads,
nor *suffer* **spread** their locks *to grow long*;
they shall only *poll* **shear** their heads.
21 Neither shall any priest drink wine,
when they enter into the inner court.
22 Neither shall they take for their *wives* **women**
a widow,
nor her that is *put away* **expelled**:
but they shall take *maidens* **virgins**
of the seed of the house of *Israel* **Yisra El**,
or a widow
that *had a priest before* **was the widow of a priest**.
23 And they shall teach my people
the difference between *the* holy and **between** profane,
and cause them to *discern* **know**
between *the unclean* **foul** and *the clean* **between pure**.
24 And *in* **concerning** controversy
they shall stand *in judgment* **and judge**;
and they shall judge *it* according to my judgments:
and they shall *keep* **guard** my *laws* **torah** and my statutes
in all *mine assemblies* **my congregations**;
and they shall hallow my *sabbaths* **shabbaths**.
25 And they shall come at no dead *person* **human**
to *defile* **foul** themselves:
but for father, or for mother, or for son, or for daughter,
for brother, or for sister that hath had no *husband* **man**,
they may *defile* **foul** *themselves*.
26 And after he is *cleansed* **purified**,
they shall *reckon* **scribe** unto him seven days.
27 And in the day that he goeth
into the *sanctuary* **holies**,
unto the inner court, to minister in the *sanctuary* **holies**,
he shall *offer his sin offering* **oblate for his sin**,
saith the Lord GOD **an oracle of Adonay Yah Veh**.
28 And it shall be unto them for an inheritance:
I am their inheritance:
and ye shall give them no possession in *Israel* **Yisra El**:
I am their possession.
29 They shall eat the *meat* offering,
and *the sin offering* **that for the sin**,
and *the trespass offering* **that for the guilt**:
and every *dedicated thing* **devotement** in *Israel* **Yisra El**
shall be theirs.

30 And the *first* **firstlings** of all
the firstfruits of all *things*,
and every *oblation* **exaltment** of all,
of *every sort* **all** of your *oblations* **exaltments**,
shall be the priest's:
ye shall also give unto the priest
the *first* **firstlings** of your dough,
that he may *cause* **rest** the blessing *to rest* in thine house.
31 The priests shall not eat
of any *thing that is dead of itself* **carcase**, or torn,
whether it be *fowl* **flyer** or *beast* **animal**.

FELLING THE LAND FOR INHERITANCE

45 *Moreover*, when ye shall
divide by lot **fell** the land for inheritance,
ye shall *offer* **lift** an *oblation* **exaltment**
unto *the LORD* **Yah Veh**,
an *holy portion* **holies** of the land:
the length
shall be the length of five and twenty thousand *reeds*,
and the breadth shall be ten thousand.
This shall be holy in all the borders *thereof* round about.
2 Of this there shall be for the *sanctuary* **holies**
five hundred *in length*, *with* **by** five hundred *in breadth*,
square round about;
and fifty cubits round about for the suburbs *thereof*.
3 And of this measure shalt thou measure
the length of five and twenty thousand,
and the breadth of ten thousand:
and in it shall be the *sanctuary* **holies**
and the *most holy place* **holy of holies**.
4 The *holy portion* **holies** of the land
shall be for the priests
the ministers of the *sanctuary* **holies**,
which shall *come near* **approach**
to minister unto *the LORD* **Yah Veh**:
and it shall be a place for their houses,
and an holy place for the sanctuary—**a holies**.
5 And the five and twenty thousand of length,
20 nor shave their heads nor spread their locks;
in shearing, they shear their heads.
21 No priest drinks wine
in entering the inner court.
22 Neither take they a widow for their women
nor her that is expelled:
but virgins of the seed of the house of Yisra El
or a widow being the widow of a priest:
23 and they teach my people
between holy and between profane,
and that they know between foul and between pure:
24 and concerning controversy,
they stand and judge;
and they judge according to my judgments:
and they guard my torah and my statutes
in all my congregations;
and they hallow my shabbaths:
25 and they approach no dead human
to foul themselves:
except for father or for mother
or for son or for daughter;
for brother or for sister:
so that they foul no man.
26 And after he purifies,
they scribe seven days to him:
27 and in the day he goes into the holies
—to the inner court to minister in the holies,
he oblates for his sin
—an oracle of Adonay Yah Veh
28 and so it becomes their inheritance;
I *am* their inheritance:
and you give them no possession in Yisra El;
I *am* their possession:
29 they eat the offering
and that for the sin and that for the guilt:
and every devotement in Yisra El
becomes theirs:
30 and the firstlings of all the firstfruits of all,
and every exaltment of all—of all of your exaltments
become for the priest:
and give the priest the firstlings of your dough
so that he rests the blessing in your house.
31 The priests eat not of any carcase or torn
—flyer or animal.

FELLING THE LAND FOR INHERITANCE

45 When you fell the land for inheritance,
lift an exaltment to Yah Veh
—a holies of the land:
the length, twenty—five thousand, the length;
and the breadth, ten thousand.
This *is* holy in all the borders all around:
2 and so be it, of this,
for the holies, five hundred by five hundred,
square all around;
and fifty cubits all around for the suburbs:
3 and of this measure,
measure the length, twenty—five thousand,
and the breadth, ten thousand:
and the holies and the holy of holies is therein.

4 The holies of the land, for the priests
—the ministers of the holies,
who approach to minister to Yah Veh:
and it is a place for their houses—a holies:
5 and the twenty—five thousand of length,
and the ten thousand of breadth,
shall *also* the *Levites* **Leviym**, the ministers of the house,
have for themselves,
for a possession for twenty chambers.
6 And ye shall *appoint* **give**
the possession of the city
five thousand broad, and five and twenty thousand long,
over against **alongside** the *oblation* **exaltment**
of the *holy portion* **holies**:
so be it *shall be* for the whole house of *Israel* **Yisra El**.
7 And *a portion shall be* **so**
be it for the *prince* **hierarch**
on the one side **from here**
and *on the other side* **from there**
of the *oblation* **exaltment** of the *holy portion* **holies**,
and of the possession of the city,
before the oblation **at the face of the exaltment**
of the *holy portion* **holies**,
and *before* **at the face of** the possession of the city,
from the *west side westward* **sea edge seaward**,
and from the east *side* **edge** eastward:
and the length shall be
over against **alongside** one of the *portions* **allotments**,
from the *west* **seaward** border unto the east border.
8 In the land shall be his
possession in *Israel* **Yisra El**:
and my *princes* **hierarchs**
shall no more oppress my people;
and *the rest of* the land
shall they give to the house of *Israel* **Yisra El**
according to their *tribes* **scions**.

THE BALANCE SYSTEM OF YAH VEH

9 *Thus saith the Lord GOD*
An oracle of Adonay Yah Veh;
Let it suffice **Enough of** you,
O *princes* **hierarchs** of *Israel* **Yisra El**:
remove **turn aside** violence and *spoil* **ravage**,
and *execute* **work** judgment and *justice* **justness**,
take away **lift** your *exactions*
expulsions from my people,
saith *the Lord GOD* **Adonay Yah Veh**.
10 *Ye shall have just balances* **Balances of justness**,
and a just ephah **an ephah of justness**,
and a just bath **a bath of justness**.
11 The ephah and the bath
shall be of one *measure* **gauge**, that
the bath may *contain* **bear**
the *tenth part* **tithe** of an *homer* **chomer**,
and the ephah the tenth *part* of an *homer* **chomer**:
the *measure* **quantity** *thereof* shall be
after the *homer* **chomer**.
12 And the shekel shall be twenty gerahs:
twenty shekels, five and twenty shekels, fifteen shekels,
shall be your maneh.

OFFERINGS

13 This is the *oblation* **exaltment**
that ye shall *offer* **lift**;
the sixth *part* of an ephah of an *homer* **chomer** of wheat,
and ye shall give the sixth part of—**hexsect**
an ephah of an *homer* **chomer** of barley:
14 Concerning the *ordinance* **statute** of oil,
the bath of oil,
ye shall *offer* the *tenth part* **tithe** of a bath out of the cor,
which is an *homer* **chomer** of ten baths;
for ten baths are an *homer* **chomer**:
15 And one lamb out of the
flock, out of two hundred,
out of the *fat pastures* **moist areas** of *Israel* **Yisra El**;
for *a meat* **an** offering,
and for a *burnt offering* **holocaust**,
and for *peace offerings* **shelamim**,
to *make reconciliation* **kapar/atone** for them,
saith the Lord GOD **an oracle of Adonay Yah Veh**.
16 All the people of the land
shall give this *oblation* **exaltment**
for the *prince* **hierarch** in *Israel* **Yisra El**.
17 And **so be** it *shall be* the *prince's part* **hierarch's**
to give burnt offerings **for holocausts**,
and *meat* offerings,
and *drink offerings* **libations**,
in the *feasts* **celebrations**,
and in the new moons, and in the *sabbaths* **shabbaths**,
in all *solemnities* **seasons** of the house of *Israel* **Yisra El**:
he shall *prepare the sin offering* **work that for the sin**,
and the ten thousand of breadth,
is for the Leviym, the ministers of the house
—for themselves,
for a possession for twenty chambers.
6 And you, give the possession of the city
five thousand broad,
and twenty—five thousand long,
alongside the exaltment of the holies:
so be it for the whole house of Yisra El.

7 And so be it for the hierarch
from here, and from there,
of the exaltment of the holies
and of the possession of the city;
at the face of the exaltment of the holies
and at the face of the possession of the city;
from the sea edge seaward
and from the east edge eastward:
and the length, alongside one of the allotments,
from the seaward border to the east border;
8 —and the land becomes
his possession in Yisra El:
and my hierarchs oppress my people no more;
and they give the land to the house of Yisra El
according to their scions.

THE BALANCE SYSTEM OF YAH VEH

9 An oracle of Adonay Yah Veh:
Enough of you, O hierarchs of Yisra El:
turn aside violence and ravage
and work judgment and justness;
lift your expulsions from my people,
says Adonay Yah Veh.
10 Balances of justness,
an ephah of justness, a bath of justness:
11 the ephah and the bath being one gauge,
so that the bath bears the tithe of a chomer,
and the ephah the tenth of a chomer:
the quantity being after the chomer.
12 And the shekel, twenty gerahs:
twenty shekels,
twenty—five shekels, fifteen shekels,
being your maneh.

OFFERINGS

13 This is the exaltment you lift:
the sixth of an ephah of a chomer of wheat,—
hexsect an ephah of a chomer of barley:
14 concerning the statute of oil,
the bath of oil, the tithe of a bath from the cor,
a chomer of ten baths;
for ten baths *are* a chomer:
15 and one lamb from the
flock, from two hundred,
from the moist areas of Yisra El;
for an offering and for a holocaust and for shelamim
to kapar/atone for them
—an oracle of Adonay Yah Veh.
16 All people of the land,
give this exaltment for the hierarch in Yisra El.
17 And so be it for the hierarch
for holocausts and offerings and libations
—in the celebrations
and in the new moons and in the shabbaths,
in all seasons of the house of Yisra El:
he works that for the sin
and the *meat* offering, and the *burnt offering* **holocaust**,
and the *peace offerings* **shelamim**,
to *make reconciliation* **kapar/atone**
for the house of *Israel* **Yisra El**.
18 Thus saith *the Lord GOD* **Adonay Yah Veh**;
In the first *month*, in the first *day* of the month,
thou shalt take *a young* **an ox son of a** bullock,
without blemish **integrious**,
and cleanse the *sanctuary* **holies**:
19 And the priest shall take of the blood
of *the sin offering* **that for the sin**,
and *put* **give** it upon the posts of the house,
and upon the four corners
of the *settle* **ledge** of the **sacrifice** altar,
and upon the posts of the *gate* **portal** of the inner court.
20 And so thou shalt *do* **work**
the seventh *day* of the month
for every *one* **man** that erreth **inadvertently**,
and for *him that is simple* **the gullible**:
so shall ye *reconcile* **kapar/atone** the house.
21 In the first *month*, in the
fourteenth day of the month,
ye shall have the *passover* **pasach**,
a *feast* **celebration** of *seven* **a week of** days;
unleavened bread **matsah** shall be eaten.
22 And upon that day shall the *prince* **hierarch**
prepare **work** for himself
and for all the people of the land
a bullock for *a sin offering* **the sin**.
23 And seven days of the *feast* **celebration**
he shall *prepare* **work** a *burnt offering* **holocaust**
to *the LORD* **Yah Veh**,
seven bullocks and seven rams
without blemish **integrious** daily the seven days;
and a *kid* **buck** of the **doe** goats daily
for *a sin offering* **the sin**.
24 And he shall *prepare a meat* **work an** offering
of an ephah for a bullock, and an ephah for a ram,
and an hin of oil for an ephah.
25 In the seventh *month*,
in the fifteenth day of the month,
shall he *do* **work** the like
in the *feast* **celebration** of the seven days,
according to the sin offering **as that for the sin**,

according to the burnt offering **so that for the holocaust,**
and according to the meat offering **as for the offering,**
and according to **so for** the oil.

The Offerings Of Rulers

46 Thus saith *the Lord GOD* **Adonay Yah Veh;**
The *gate* **portal** of the inner court
that *looketh* **faceth** toward the east
shall be shut the six *working days* **days of work;**
but on the *sabbath* **shabbath** it shall be opened,
and in the day of the new moon it shall be opened.
2 And the *prince* **hierarch** shall enter
by the way of the porch
of that *gate without* **portal outward,**
and shall stand by the post of the *gate* **portal,**
and the priests
shall *prepare* **work** his *burnt offering* **holocaust**
and his *peace offerings* **shelamim,**
and he shall *worship* **prostrate**
at the threshold of the *gate* **portal:**
then he shall go forth;
but the *gate* **portal** shall not be shut until the evening.
3 Likewise the people of the
land shall *worship* **prostrate**
at the *door* **opening** of this *gate* **portal**
before the LORD **at the face of Yah Veh**
in the *sabbaths* **shabbaths** and in the new moons.
4 And the *burnt offering* **holocaust**
that the *prince* **hierarch** shall *offer* **oblate**
unto *the LORD* **Yah Veh** in the *sabbath* **shabbath** day
shall be six lambs *without blemish* **integrious,**
and a ram *without blemish* **integrious.**
5 And the *meat* offering shall
be an ephah for a ram,
and the *meat* offering for the lambs
as he shall be *able to give* **the gift of his hand,**
and an hin of oil to an ephah.
6 And in the day of the new moon
and the offering and the holocaust and the shelamim,
to kapar/atone for the house of Yisra El.
18 Thus says Adonay Yah Veh:
In the first, in the first of the month,
take an integrious ox son of a bullock,
and cleanse the holies:
19 and the priest takes of the
blood of that for the sin
and gives it on the posts of the house
and on the four corners
of the ledge of the sacrifice altar
and on the posts of the portal of the inner court.
20 And thus you work the seventh of the month
for every man who errs inadvertently,
and for the gullible:
thus you kapar/atone the house.
21 In the first, in the fourteenth day of the month,
the pasach, a celebration of a week of days;
eat matsah:
22 and on the day the hierarch works for himself
and for all the people of the land,
a bullock for the sin.
23 And seven days of the celebration
he works a holocaust to Yah Veh
—seven integrious bullocks and seven rams
daily for seven days;
and a buck of the doe goats daily for the sin:
24 and he works an offering
of an ephah for a bullock and an ephah for a ram
—a hin of oil for an ephah:
25 and in the seventh,
in the fifteenth day of the month,
he works likewise
in the celebration of the seven days;
as that for the sin, thus for the holocaust,
as for the offering, thus for the oil.

The Offerings Of Rulers

46 Thus says Adonay Yah Veh:
The portal of the inner court facing eastward
is shut the six days of work;
and open on the shabbath;
and open in the day of the new moon:
2 and the hierarch enters
by the way of the porch of that portal outward
and stands by the post of the portal;
and the priests work his holocaust and his shelamim;
and he prostrates at the threshold of the portal:
and he goes forth;
and the portal *is* not shut until the evening.
3 And the people of the land
prostrate at the opening of this portal
at the face of Yah Veh,
in the shabbaths and in the new moons:
4 and the holocaust the
hierarch oblates to Yah Veh
in the shabbath day,
six integrious lambs and an integrious ram:
5 and the offering, an ephah for a ram,
and the offering for the lambs, the gift of his hand

and a hin of oil to an ephah:
6 and in the day of the new moon,
it shall be *a young* **an ox son of a** bullock
without blemish **integrious**,
and six lambs, and a ram:
they shall be *without blemish* **integrious**.
7 And he shall *prepare a meat* **work an** offering,
an ephah for a bullock, and an ephah for a ram,
and for the lambs
according as his hand shall *attain unto* **attain**,
and an hin of oil to an ephah.
8 And when the *prince* **hierarch** shall enter,
he shall *go in* **enter**
by the way of the porch of that *gate* **portal**,
and he shall *go forth* **exit** by the way *thereof.*
9 But when the people of the land
shall come *before the LORD* **at the face of Yah Veh**
in the *solemn feasts* **seasons**,
he that entereth in by the way of the north *gate* **portal**
to *worship* **prostrate**
shall *go out* **exit** by the way of the south *gate* **portal**;
and he that entereth by the way of the south *gate* **portal**
shall go forth by the way of the north *gate* **portal**:
he shall not *return* **exit** by the way of the *gate* **portal**
whereby he *came in* **entered**,
but shall *go forth over against* **exit opposite** it.
10 And the *prince* **hierarch** in the midst of them,
when they go in **in entering**, shall *go in* **enter**; and
when they go forth **in exiting**, shall *go forth* **exit**.
11 And in the *feasts* **celebrations**
and in the *solemnities* **seasons**
the *meat* offering shall be an ephah to a bullock,
and an ephah to a ram,
and to the lambs as *he is able to give* **the gift of his hand**,
and an hin of oil to an ephah.
12 Now when the *prince* **hierarch**
shall *prepare* **work** a voluntary *burnt offering* **holocaust**
or *peace offerings voluntarily* **voluntary shelamim**
unto *the LORD* **Yah Veh**,
one **he** shall then open him the *gate* **portal**
that *looketh* **faceth** toward the east,
and he shall *prepare* **work** his *burnt offering* **holocaust**
and his *peace offerings* **shelamim**,
as he *did* **worked** on the *sabbath* **shabbath** day:
then he shall *go forth* **exit**;
and after his *going forth* **exiting**
one **he** shall shut the *gate* **portal**.
13 Thou shalt daily *prepare* **work**
a *burnt offering* **holocaust** unto *the LORD* **Yah Veh**
of a lamb *of the first year* **a yearling son**
without blemish **integrious**:
thou shalt *prepare* **work** it
every morning **morning by morning**.
14 And thou shalt *prepare a*
meat **work an** offering for it
every morning **morning by morning**,
the sixth *part* of an ephah,
and the third part of an hin of oil,
to *temper* **sprinkle** with the *fine* flour;
a meat **an** offering continually
by *a perpetual ordinance* **an eternal statute**
unto *the LORD* **Yah Veh**.
15 Thus shall they *prepare* **work** the lamb,
and the *meat* offering, and the oil,
every morning **morning by morning**
for a continual *burnt offering* **holocaust**.

Rights Of Inheritance

16 Thus saith *the Lord GOD* **Adonay Yah Veh**;
If the *prince* **hierarch**
give a gift unto any **man** of his sons,
the inheritance *thereof* shall be his sons';
it shall be their possession by inheritance.
17 But if he give a gift of his inheritance
to one of his servants,
then it shall be his to the year of liberty;
after it shall return to the *prince* **hierarch**:
but his inheritance shall be his sons' for them.
18 Moreover the *prince* **hierarch**
shall not take of the people's inheritance by oppression,
to thrust them out of their possession;
but *he shall give* **that** his sons *inheritance* **shall inherit**
out of his own possession:
an integrious ox son of a bullock,
and six integrious lambs, and an *integrious* ram:
7 and he works an offering,
an ephah for a bullock and an ephah for a ram,
and for the lambs according as his hand attains,
and a hin of oil to an ephah.
8 And the hierarch enters,
and he enters by the way of the porch of that portal
and he exits by the *same* way.
9 And when the people of the land
enters at the face of Yah Veh in their
seasons, he who enters to prostrate
by the way of the north portal,
exits by the way of the south portal;
and he who enters in by the way of the south portal
exits by the way of the north portal:
he exits not by the way of the portal

whereby he enters,
but exits opposite.
10 And the hierarch among them,
in entering, enters;
and in exiting, exits:
11 and in the celebrations and in the seasons,
the offering, an ephah to a bullock
and an ephah to a ram;
and to the lambs as the gift of his hand,
and a hin of oil to an ephah.
12 And when the hierarch
works a voluntary holocaust
or voluntary shelamim to Yah Veh,
he opens for himself the portal facing eastward;
and he works his holocaust and his shelamim
as he worked on the shabbath day:
then he exits;
and shuts the portal after he exits.
13 And work a daily holocaust to Yah Veh
an integrious lamb—a yearling son:
work it morning by morning:
14 And morning by morning,
work an offering for it,
the sixth of an ephah and the third part of a hin of oil,
to sprinkle with the flour;
an offering by an eternal statute
continually to Yah Veh:
15 and work the lamb and the offering and the oil
morning by morning for a continual holocaust.

RIGHTS OF INHERITANCE

16 Thus says Adonay Yah Veh;
If the hierarch gives a gift to any man of his sons,
the inheritance *is* to his sons;
it becomes their possession by inheritance.
17 And if he gives a gift of his inheritance
to one of his servants,
it becomes his to the year of liberty;
afterward it returns to the hierarch:
and his inheritance becomes to his sons.
18 And the hierarch
takes no inheritance of the people by oppression
to thrust them from their possession;
but that his sons inherit from his own possession:
that my people be not scattered
every man from his possession.
19 After he brought me through the entry,
which was at the *side* **shoulder** of the *gate* **portal**,
into the holy chambers of the priests,
which *looketh toward the north* **faceth northward**:
and, behold, there was a place
on the two *sides westward* **flanks seaward**.

THE PLACE OF STEWING

20 Then said he unto me,
This is the place where the priests
shall *boil the trespass offering* **stew that for the guilt**
and *the sin offering* **that for the sin,**
where they shall bake the *meat* offering;
that they bear them not out into the *utter* **outer** court,
to *sanctify* **hallow** the people.
21 Then he brought me forth
into the *utter* **outer** court,
and caused me to pass by the four corners of the court;
and, behold,
in every corner of the court there was a court
a court in the corner of a court,
a court in the corner of a court.
22 In the four corners of the
court there were courts
joined **enclosed** of forty *cubits* long and thirty broad:
these four corners were of one measure.
23 And there was a row *of*
building round about in them,
round about them four,
and it was made with *boiling places* **hearths**
under the *rows* **walls** round about.
24 Then said he unto me,
These are the *places* **houses** of them that *boil* **stew**,
where the ministers of the house
shall *boil* **stew** the sacrifice of the people.

WATERS ISSUE FROM THE HOUSE

47 *Afterward he brought me*
again **And he returned me**
unto the *door* **opening** of the house;
and, behold, waters issued out
from under the threshold of the house eastward:
for the *forefront* **face** of the house
stood toward the east **is eastward,**
and the waters *came down* **descended**
from under from the right *side* **shoulder** of the house,
at the south *side* of the **sacrifice** altar.
2 Then brought he me
out of the way of the *gate* **portal** northward,
and *led* **turned** me about the way *without* **outward**
unto the *utter gate* **outward portal**
by the way that *looketh* **faceth** eastward;
and, behold,
there *ran out* **poured** waters on the right *side* **shoulder**.

THE WATERS MEASURED

3 And when the man that had the line in his hand
went forth eastward,
he measured a thousand cubits,
and he *brought* **passed** me through the waters;
the waters were to the ankles.
4 Again he measured a thousand,
and *brought* **passed** me through the waters;
the waters were to the knees.
Again he measured a thousand,
and *brought* **passed** me through;
the waters were to the loins.
5 Afterward he measured a thousand;
and it was a *river* **wadi** that I could not pass over:
for the waters were risen, waters to swim in,
a *river* **wadi** that could not be passed over.
6 And he said unto me,
Son of *man* **humanity**, hast thou seen *this*?
Then he *brought* **carried** me,
and caused me to return to the
brink **lip** of the *river* **wadi**.
7 *Now* when I had returned, behold,
at the *bank* **lip** of the *river* **wadi**
were *very* **mighty** many trees
on the one side **from here** and *on the other* **from there**.
8 Then said he unto me,
These waters issue out toward the east *country* **region**,
and *go down* **descend** into the *desert* **plain**,
and go into the sea:
which being brought forth into the sea,
so that every man of my people
not scatter of his possession.
19 And he brings me in through the entry
at the shoulder of the portal
into the holy chambers of the priests
facing northward:
and behold, a place on the two flanks seaward.

THE PLACE OF STEWING

20 And he says to me,
This is the place where the priests stew
that for the guilt and that for the sin
—where they bake the offering;
that they not bear them out into the outer court
to hallow the people.
21 And he brings me into the outer court,
and passes me by the four corners of the court;
and behold,
a court in the corner of a court
a court in the corner of a court
22—courts in the four corners of the court
enclosed, forty long and thirty broad:
these four corners of one measure:
23 and a row all around in them
—all around all four
—made with hearths under the walls all around.
24 And says he to me,
These are the houses of them who stew
—where the ministers of the house
stew the sacrifice of the people.

WATERS ISSUE FROM THE HOUSE

47 And he returns me to the opening of the house;
and behold, waters issue forth
from under the threshold of the house eastward;
for the face of the house is eastward:
and the waters descend
from under from the right shoulder of the house
at the south of the sacrifice altar:
2 and he brings me
from the way of the portal northward,
and turns me around to the way outward
to the outward portal
by the way that faces eastward;
and behold,
waters pour on the right shoulder.

THE WATERS MEASURED

3 And the man with the line
in his hand goes eastward
and he measures a thousand cubits;
and he passes me through water
—water to the ankles:
4 and he measures a thousand;
and passes me through water
—water to the knees:
and he measures a thousand;
and passes me through
—waters to the loins:
5 and he measures a thousand;
—a wadi I cannot pass over:
for the waters rise—waters to swim in,
a wadi not to pass over.
6 And he says to me, See you, son of humanity?
And he carries me,
and returns me to the lip of the wadi:
7 and I return, and behold, at the lip of the wadi,
mighty many trees from here, and from there.
8 And he says to me,

These waters issue forth toward the east region
and descend into the plain and enter the sea
—brought forth into the sea;
the waters shall be healed.
9 And **so be** it *shall come to pass,*
that every *thing* **soul** that liveth, which *moveth* **teemeth,**
whithersoever the *rivers* **wadies** shall come, shall live:
and there shall be a *very* **mighty** great multitude of fish,
because these waters shall come thither:
for they shall be healed;
and *every thing* **all** shall live
whither the *river* **wadi** cometh.
10 And **so be** it *shall come to pass,*
that the fishers shall stand upon it
from *Engedi* **En Gedi** even unto *Eneglaim* **En Eglayim;**
they shall *be a place* **become** to spread forth nets;
their fish shall be *according to their kinds* **in species,**
as the fish of the great sea, *exceeding* **mighty** many.
11 But the *miry places* **mires** *thereof*
and the *marishes* **dugouts** *thereof* shall not be healed;
they shall be given to salt.
12 And by the *river* **wadi** upon the *bank* **lip** *thereof,*
on this side **from here** and *on that side* **from there,**
shall *grow* **ascend** all trees for *meat* **food,**
whose leaf shall not *fade* **wither,**
neither shall the fruit *thereof* be consumed:
it shall bring forth new fruit according to his months,
because their waters
they issued out of the *sanctuary* **holies:**
and the fruit *thereof* shall be for *meat* **food,**
and the leaf *thereof* for *medicine* **healing.**

THE BORDERS OF THE LAND

13 Thus saith *the Lord GOD* **Adonay Yah Veh;**
This shall be the border,
whereby ye shall inherit the land
according to the twelve *tribes* **scions** of *Israel* **Yisra El:**
Joseph **Yoseph** shall have *two portions* **boundaries.**
14 And ye shall inherit it,
one as well **man** as *another* **brother:**
concerning the which I lifted up mine hand
to give it unto your fathers:
and this land shall fall unto you for inheritance.
15 And this shall be the border of the land
toward the north *side* **edge,**
from the great sea,
the way of Hethlon, as men go to *Zedad* **Sedad;**
16 Hamath, Berothah, *Sibraim* **Sibrayim,**
which is between the border of *Damascus* **Dammeseq**
and **between** the border of Hamath;
Hazar—hatticon **Hasar Hat Tichon,**
which is by the *coast* **border** of Hauran.
17 And the border from the sea
shall be *Hazarenan* **Hasar Enon,**
the border of *Damascus* **Dammeseq,**
and the north northward, and the border of Hamath.
And this is the north *side* **edge.**
18 And the east *side* **edge**
ye shall measure *from* **between** Hauran,
and *from Damascus* **between Dammeseq,**
and *from Gilead* **between Gilad,**
and *from* **between** the land of *Israel*
Yisra El by *Jordan* **Yarden,**
from the border unto the east sea.
And this is the east *side* **edge.**
19 And the south *side* **edge** southward,
from Tamar
even to *the waters of strife* **Mayim Meribah**
in *Kadesh* **Qadesh,**
the *river* **wadi** to the great sea.
And this is the south *side* **edge** southward.
20 The *west side* **seaward edge** also
shall be the great sea from the border,
till a man come over against Hamath.
This is the *west side* **seaward edge.**
21 So shall ye *divide* **allot** this land unto you
according to the *tribes* **scions** of *Israel* **Yisra El.**
22 And **so be** it *shall come to pass,*
that ye shall *divide it by lot* **fell it**
for an inheritance unto you,
and to the *strangers* **sojourners** that sojourn among you,
which shall *beget children* **birth sons** among you:
and they shall be unto you as *born in the country* **natives**
among the *children* **sons** of *Israel* **Yisra El;**
and the waters heal.
9 And so be it, every living soul that teems,
wherever the wadies enter, lives:
and there becomes a mighty great multitude of fish,
because these waters enter:
and they heal;
and wherever the wadi enters, they all live.
10 And so be it,
the fishers stand thereon
from En Gedi even to En Eglayim;
they become to spread nets;
their fish become in species,
as the fish of the great sea—mighty many.
11 And the mires and the dugouts heal not;
they *are* given to salt.
12 And by the wadi on the lip,

from here and from there,
all the trees ascend for food
—whose leaf neither withers,
nor *is* the fruit consumed:
it brings forth new fruit according to his months
because their waters issue from the holies:
and the fruit *is* for food and the leaf for healing.

THE BORDERS OF THE LAND

13 Thus says Adonay Yah Veh;
This *is* the border whereby you inherit the land
according to the twelve scions of Yisra El
—the boundaries of Yoseph:
14 and you inherit, man as brother:
I lifted my hand to give to your fathers:
and this land falls to you for inheritance.
15 And this, the border of the land the north edge:
from the great sea,
the way of Hethlon as men go to Sedad;
16 Hamath, Berothah, Sibrayim,
between the border of Dammeseq
and between the border of Hamath;
—Hasar Hat Tichon, by the border of Hauran:
17 and the border from the sea:
Hasar Enon, the border of Dammeseq,
and the north northward, and the border of Hamath:
and this is the north edge.
18 And the east edge:
measure between Hauran
and between Dammeseq and between Gilad
and between the land of Yisra El by Yarden
from the border to the east sea:
and this is the east edge.
19 And the south edge southward:
from Tamar even to Mayim Meribah in Qadesh,
the wadi to the great sea:
and this is the south edge southward.
20 And the seaward edge:
the great sea from the border
until a man comes over against Hamath:
and this is the seaward edge.
21 Allot this land to yourselves
according to the scions of Yisra El.
22 And so be it,
fell it for an inheritance to yourselves
and to the sojourners who sojourn among you
who birth sons among you:
and they are to you
as natives among the sons of Yisra El:
they shall *have* **fell an** inheritance with you
among the *tribes* **scions** of *Israel* **Yisra El.**
23 And **so be** it *shall come to pass,*
that in what *tribe* **scion** the *stranger*
sojourner sojourneth,
there shall ye give him his inheritance,
saith the Lord GOD **an oracle of Adonay Yah Veh.**

APPORTIONING THE LAND

48 *Now* these are the names of the *tribes* **scions.**
From the north end
to the *coast* **hand** of the way of Hethlon,
as one goeth to Hamath, *Hazarenan* **Hasar Enan,**
the border of *Damascus* **Dammeseq** northward,
to the *coast* **hand** of Hamath;
for these are his *sides* **edges** east and *west* **seaward;**
a portion for Dan**, one.**
2 And by the border of Dan,
from the east *side* **edge** unto the *west side* **seaward edge,**
a portion for Asher**, one.**
3 And by the border of Asher,
from the east side edge
even unto the *west side* **seaward edge,**
a portion for Naphtali**, one.**
4 And by the border of Naphtali,
from the east *side* **edge** unto the *west side* **seaward edge,**
a portion for *Menashsheh* **Menash Sheh, one.**
5 And by the border of *Manasseh* **Menash Sheh,**
from the east *side* **edge** unto the *side* **seaward**
edge, *a portion* for *Ephraim* **Ephrayim, one.**
6 And by the border of *Ephraim* **Ephrayim,**
from the east *side* **edge**
even unto the *west side* **seaward edge,**
a portion for Reu Ben**, one.**
7 And by the border of *Reuben* **Reu Ben,**
from the east *side* **edge** unto the *west side* **seaward edge,**
a portion for *Judah* **Yah Hudah, one.**

THE HALLOWED REFUGE

8 And by the border of *Judah* **Yah Hudah,**
from the east *side* **edge** unto the *west side* **seaward edge,**
shall be the *offering* **exaltment** which ye shall *offer* **lift**
of five and twenty thousand *reeds* in breadth,
and in length as one of the *other parts* **allotments,**
from the east *side* **edge** unto the *west side* **seaward edge:**
and the *sanctuary* **holies** shall be in the midst of it.
9 The *oblation* **exaltment**
that ye shall *offer* **lift** unto *the LORD* **Yah Veh**
shall be of five and twenty thousand in length,

and of ten thousand in breadth.
10 And for them, even for the priests,
shall be this holy *oblation* **exaltment**;
toward the north **northward**
five and twenty thousand *in length*,
and *toward the west* **seaward**
ten thousand in breadth,
and *toward the east* **eastward**
ten thousand in breadth,
and *toward the south* **southward**
five and twenty thousand in length:
and the *sanctuary* **holies** of *the LORD* **Yah Veh**
shall be in the midst *thereof*.
11 It shall be for the priests
that are *sanctified* **hallowed**
of the sons of *Zadok* **Sadoq**;
which have *kept* **guarded** my *charge* **guard**,
which *went* **strayed** not *astray*
when
the *children* **sons** of *Israel went astray* **Yisra El strayed**,
as the *Levites went astray* **Leviym strayed**.
12 And this *oblation* **exaltment** of the land
that is *offered* **out of the exaltment**
shall be unto them a *thing most holy* **holy of holies**
by the border of the *Levites* **Leviym**.
13 And *over against* **alongside**
the border of the priests
the *Levites* **Leviym** shall have
five and twenty thousand in length,
and ten thousand in breadth:
all the length shall be five and twenty thousand,
and the breadth ten thousand.
14 And they shall not sell of it, neither exchange,
nor *alienate* **pass away** the *firstfruits*
firstlings of the land:
for it is holy unto *the LORD* **Yah Veh**.
have them fell an inheritance with you
among the scions of Yisra El.
23 And so be it,
that in whatever scion the sojourner sojourns,
there you give him his inheritance
—an oracle of Adonay Yah Veh.

APPORTIONING THE LAND

48 These are the names of the scions.
From the north end
to the hand of the way of Hethlon,
as one goes to Hamath, Hasar Enan,
the border of Dammeseq northward,
to the hand of Hamath;
are his edges east and seaward;
for Dan, one.
2 And by the border of Dan:
from the east edge to the seaward edge;
for Asher, one.
3 And by the border of Asher:
from the east edge even to the seaward edge;
for Naphtali, one.
4 And by the border of Naphtali:
from the east edge to the seaward edge;
for Menash Sheh, one.
5 And by the border of Menash Sheh:
from the east edge to the seaward edge;
for Ephrayim, one.
6 And by the border of Ephrayim:
from the east edge even to the seaward edge;
for Reu Ben, one.
7 And by the border of Reu Ben:
from the east edge to the seaward edge;
for Yah Hudah, one.

THE HALLOWED REFUGE

8 And by the border of Yah Hudah:
from the east edge to the seaward edge,
is the exaltment you lift
—twenty—five thousand broad and long
—as one of the allotments,
from the east edge to the seaward edge;
and the holies are in the midst thereof:
9 the exaltment you lift to Yah Veh,
twenty—five thousand long,
and ten thousand broad.
10 And of these, the holy exaltment for the priests:
northward, twenty—five thousand;
and seaward, ten thousand broad,
and eastward, ten thousand broad,
and southward, twenty—five thousand long:
and the holies of Yah Veh is in the midst
11 —for the priests
—the hallowed of the sons of Sadoq;
who guarded my guard;
who strayed not when the sons of Yisra El strayed
as the Leviym strayed.
12 And this exaltment of the land
that is from the exaltment
is to them a holy of holies
by the border of the Leviym.
13 And alongside the border
of the priests, the Leviym:
twenty—five thousand long,

and ten thousand broad:
all the length, twenty—five thousand
and the breadth, ten thousand.
14 And they neither sell thereof nor exchange
nor pass away the firstlings of the land:
for *it is* holy to Yah Veh.

THE PROFANE

15 And the five thousand,
that *are left* **remain** in the breadth
over against **at the face of** the five and twenty thousand,
shall be *a* profane *place* for the city,
for *dwelling* **sites**, and for suburbs:
and the city shall be in the midst *thereof*.
16 And these shall be the measures *thereof*;
the north *side* **edge** four thousand and five hundred,
and the south *side* **edge** four thousand and five hundred,
and on the east *side* **edge**
four thousand and five hundred,
and the *west side* **seaward edge**
four thousand and five hundred.
17 And the suburbs of the city shall be
toward the north **northward** two hundred and fifty,
and *toward the south* **southward** two hundred and fifty,
and *toward the east* **eastward** two hundred and fifty,
and *toward the west* **seaward** two hundred and fifty.
18 And *the residue* **that which remaineth**
in length *over against* **alongside**
the *oblation* **exaltment** of the *holy portion* **holies**
shall be ten thousand eastward,
and ten thousand *westward* **seaward**:
and it shall be *over against* **alongside**
the *oblation* **exaltment** of the *holy portion* **holies**;
and the *increase* **produce** *thereof*
shall be for *food* **bread** unto them that serve the city.
19 And they that serve the city
shall serve it out of all the *tribes* **scions** of *Israel* **Yisra El**.
20 All the *oblation* **exaltment** shall be
five and twenty thousand by five and twenty thousand:
ye shall *offer* **lift** the holy *oblation* **exaltment,**
foursquare **a fourth**, with the possession of the city.

THE AREA OF THE HIERARCH

21 And *the residue* **that which remaineth**
shall be for the *prince* **hierarch**,
on the one side **from here** and *on the other* **from there**
of the holy *oblation* **exaltment**,
and of the possession of the city,
over against **at the face of** the five and twenty thousand
of the *oblation* **exaltment**
toward the east **to the eastward** border,
and *westward* **seaward**
over against **at the face of** the five and twenty thousand
toward the west **to the seaward** border,
over against **alongside** the *portions* **allotments**
for the *prince* **hierarch**:
and it shall be the holy *oblation* **exaltment**;
and the *sanctuary* **holies** of the house
shall be in the midst *thereof*.
22 Moreover from the possession
of the *Levites* **Leviym**,
and from the possession of the city,
being in the midst of that which is the *prince's* **hierarch's**,
between the border of *Judah* **Yah Hudah**
and the border of *Benjamin* **Ben Yamin**,
shall be for the *prince* **hierarch**.
23 As for the rest of the *tribes* **scions**,
from the east *side* **edge** unto the west *side* **edge**,
Benjamin shall have a portion **Ben Yamin, one**.
24 And by the border of *Benjamin* **Ben Yamin**,
from the east *side* **edge** unto the *west side* **seaward edge**,
Simeon shall have a portion **Shimon, one**.
25 And by the border of *Simeon* **Shimon**,
from the east *side* **edge** unto the *west side* **seaward edge**,
Issachar a portion **Yissachar, one**.
26 And by the border of *Issachar* **Yissachar**,
from the east *side* **edge** unto the *west side* **seaward edge**,
Zebulun *a portion*, **one**.
27 And by the border of Zebulun,
from the east *side* **edge** unto the *west side* **seaward edge**,
Gad, *a portion* **one**.
28 And by the border of Gad,
at the south side edge southward,
the border shall be even from Tamar
unto *the waters of strife* **Mayim Meribah**
in *Kadesh* **Qadesh**,
and to the *river* **wadi** toward the great sea.
29 This is the land which ye shall *divide by lot* **fell**

THE PROFANE

15 And the five thousand broad
remaining at the face of the twenty—five thousand
is profane;
it is for the city, for sites, and for suburbs:
and the city is in the midst.
16 And these *are* the measures:
the north edge, four thousand and five hundred;
and the south edge, four thousand and five hundred;
and on the east edge, four thousand and five hundred;
and the seaward edge,

four thousand and five hundred.
17 And the suburbs of the city:
northward, two hundred and fifty; and southward,
two hundred and fifty; and eastward, two hundred
and fifty; and seaward, two hundred and fifty.
18 And whatever remains in length
alongside the exaltment of the holies
—ten thousand eastward and ten thousand seaward
—being alongside the exaltment of the holies;
the produce is their bread who serve the city:
19 and they who serve the city
serve from all the scions of Yisra El.
20 All the exaltment,
twenty—five thousand by twenty—five thousand:
lift a fourth of the holy exaltment
with the possession of the city.

The Area Of The Hierarch

21 And whatever remains *is* for the hierarch
—from here and from there of the holy exaltment
and of the possession of the city
at the face of the twenty—five thousand
of the exaltment to the eastward border, and seaward,
at the face of the twenty—five thousand
to the seaward border,
alongside the allotments *is* for the hierarch:
being the holy exaltment;
and the holies of the house in the midst.
22 Moreover from the possession of the Leviym,
and from the possession of the city,
midst that which *is* of the the hierarch,
between the border of Yah Hudah
and the border of Ben Yamin,
is for the hierarch.
23 As for the rest of the scions:
from the east edge to the west edge;
Ben Yamin, one.
24 And by the border of Ben Yamin:
from the east edge to the seaward edge;
Shimon, one.
25 And by the border of Shimon:
from the east edge to the seaward edge;
Yissachar, one.
26 And by the border of Yissachar:
from the east edge to the seaward edge;
Zebulun, one.
27 And by the border of Zebulun:
from the east edge to the seaward edge;
Gad, one.
28 And by the border of Gad:
at the south side edge southward,
the border being from Tamar
to Mayim Meribah in Qadesh
and to the wadi toward the great sea.
29 This is the land you fell
unto the *tribes* **scions** of *Israel* **Yisra El** for inheritance,
and these are their *portions* **allotments**,
saith the Lord GOD **an oracle of Adonay Yah Veh**.

The Exits

30 And these are the *goings out* **exits** of the city
on the north *side* **edge**,
four thousand and five hundred measures.
31 And the *gates* **portals** of the city
shall be after the names
of the *tribes* **scions** of *Israel* **Yisra El**:
three *gates* **portals** northward;
one *gate* **portal** of *Reuben* **Reu Ben**,
one *gate* **portal** of *Judah* **Yah Hudah**,
one *gate* **portal** of Levi.
32 And at the east *side* **edge**
four thousand and five hundred:
and three *gates* **portals**;
and one *gate* **portal** of *Joseph* **Yoseph**,
one *gate* **portal** of *Benjamin* **Ben Yamin**,
one *gate* **portal** of Dan.
33 And at the south *side* **edge**
four thousand and five hundred measures:
and three *gates* **portals**;
one *gate* **portal** of *Simeon* **Shimon**,
one *gate* **portal** of *Issachar* **Yissachar**,
onc *gatc* **portal** of Zebulun.
34 At the *west side* **seaward edge**
four thousand and five hundred,
with their three *gates* **portals**;
one *gate* **portal** of Gad,
one *gate* **portal** of Asher,
one *gate* **portal** of Naphtali.
35 It was round about eighteen thousand *measures*:
and the name of the city from that day shall be,
The LORD is there **Yah Veh Sham**.
to the scions of Yisra El for inheritance,
and these are their allotments
—an oracle of Adonay Yah Veh.

The Exits

30 And these are the exits of the city:
on the north edge:

four thousand and five hundred measures:
31 and the portals of the city
as the names of the scions of Yisra El.
Three portals northward:
the portal of Reu Ben, one;
the portal of Yah Hudah, one;
the portal of Levi, one.
32 And at the east edge
four thousand and five hundred
with three portals:
the portal of Yoseph, one;
the portal of Ben Yamin, one;
the portal of Dan, one.
33 And at the south edge
four thousand and five hundred measures
with three portals;
the portal of Shimon, one;
the portal of Yissachar, one;
the portal of Zebulun, one.
34 At the seaward edge
four thousand and five hundred
with their three portals;
the portal of Gad, one;
the portal of Asher, one;
the portal of Naphtali, one
35 —eighteen thousand all around.
And the name of the city from that day on,
Yah Veh Sham.

NEBUKADNETS TSAR BESEIGES YERU SHALEM

1 In the third year
of the *reign* **sovereigndom** of *Jehoiakim* **Yah Yaqim,**
king **sovereign** of *Judah* **Yah Hudah**
came *Nebuchadnezzar* **Nebukadnets Tsar**
king **sovereign** of *Babylon* **Babel**
unto *Jerusalem* **Yeru Shalem,** and besieged it.
2 And *the Lord* **Adonay** gave
Jehoiakim **Yah Yaqim**
king **sovereign** of *Judah* **Yah Hudah** into his hand,
with part of the *vessels* **instruments**
of the house of *God* **Elohim:**
which he carried into the land of Shinar
to the house of his *god* **elohim;**
and he brought the *vessels* **instruments**
into the *treasure house* **treasury** of his *god* **elohim.**

NEBUKADNETS TSAR CHOOSES SONS OF YISRA EL FOR SERVICE

3 And the *king* **sovereign**
spake **said** unto Ashpenaz
the *master* **rabbi** of his eunuchs,
that he should bring
certain of the *children* **sons** of *Israel* **Yisra El,**
and of the *king's* **sovereign's** seed,
and of the *princes* **nobles;**
4 Children in whom was no blemish,
but *well favoured* **good visaged,**
and *skilful* **comprehending** in all wisdom,
and *cunning* **knowing** in knowledge,
and *understanding science* **discerning knowledge,**
and such as had *ability* **force** in them
to stand in the *king's palace* **sovereign's manse,**
and whom they might teach
the *learning* **scrolls** and the tongue
of the *Chaldeans* **Kesediym.**
5 And the *king appointed*
sovereign numbered them
a *daily provision* **day by day word**
of the *king's meat* **sovereign's delicacies,**
and of the wine which he drank:
so nourishing them three years,
that at the end *thereof*
they might stand *before* **at the face of** the *king* **sovereign.**
6 *Now* among these
were of the *children* **sons** of *Judah* **Yah Hudah,**
Daniel **Dani El,** *Hananiah* **Hanan Yah,**
Mishael **Misha El,** and *Azariah* **Azar Yah:**
7 Unto whom the *prince* **governor** of the eunuchs
gave **set** names:
for he *gave* **set** unto *Daniel* **Dani El**
the name of Belteshazzar **Belte Shats Tsar;**
and to *Hananiah* **Hanan Yah,** of Shadrach;
and to *Mishael* **Misha El,** of Meshach;
and to *Azariah* **Azar Yah,** of *Abednego* **Abed Nego.**
8 But *Daniel purposed* **Dani El set** in his heart
that he *would* **should** not *defile* **profane** *himself*
with the *portion* **delicacies** of the *king's meat* **sovereign,**
nor with the wine which he drank:
therefore he *requested* **besought**
of the *prince* **governor** of the eunuchs
that he might not *defile* **profane** *himself.*
9 *Now God* **Elohim** had
brought Daniel **given Dani El**
into *favour* **mercy** and *tender love* **mercies**
with **at the face of** the *prince* **governor** of the eunuchs.
10 And the *prince* **governor** of the eunuchs
said unto *Daniel* **Dani El,**
I fear my *lord* **adoni** the *king* **sovereign,**
who hath
appointed **numbered** your *meat* **food** and your drink:
for why should he see your faces *worse liking* **enraged**
than the children which are of your *sort* **circle?**
then shall ye *make* **cause** me *endanger* **to owe** my head
to the *king* **sovereign.**
11 Then said *Daniel* **Dani El**
to *Melzar* **the steward,**
whom the *prince* **governor** of the eunuchs
had *set over* **numbered**
Daniel **Dani El,** *Hananiah* **Hanan Yah,**
Mishael **Misha El,** and *Azariah* **Azar Yah,**
12 *Prove* **Test** thy servants, I beseech thee, ten days;
and let them give us *pulse* **herbs** to eat,
and water to drink.

NEBUKADNETS TSAR BESEIGES YERU SHALEM

1 In the third year of the sovereigndom
of Yah Yaqim sovereign of Yah Hudah,
Nebukadnets Tsar sovereign of Babel
comes to Yeru Shalem and besieges it:
2 and Adonay gives
Yah Yaqim sovereign of Yah Hudah
into his hand
with part of the instruments of the house of Elohim:
which he carried into the land of Shinar
to the house of his elohim;
and he brings the instruments
into the treasury of his elohim.

NEBUKADNETS TSAR CHOOSES SONS OF YISRA EL FOR SERVICE

3 And the sovereign
says to Ashpenaz the rabbi of his eunuchs,
to bring of the sons of Yisra El
and of seed of the sovereign and of the nobles;
4 children in whom *is* no blemish
—and of good visage
and comprehending in all wisdom
and knowing in knowledge
and discerning in knowledge;
and such as have inner force
to stand in the manse of the sovereign;
and to teach them
the scrolls and the tongue of the Kesediym.
5 And the sovereign numbers them
a day by day word
of the delicacies of the sovereign,
and of the wine he drinks:
thus nourishing them three years;
so that at the end
they stand at the face of the sovereign.
6 Among these, of the sons of Yah Hudah,
Dani El, Hanan Yah, Misha El, and Azar Yah:
7 to whom the governor of the eunuchs set names:
and he sets to Dani El, Belte Shats Tsar;
and to Hanan Yah, Shadrach;
and to Misha El, Meshach;
and to Azar Yah, Abed Nego.
8 And Dani El sets in his heart to not profane
with the delicacies of the sovereign
or with the wine he drinks:
and he beseeches the governor of the eunuchs
that he not profane:
9 and Elohim gives Dani El mercy and mercies
at the face of the governor of the eunuchs.
10 And the governor of the
eunuchs says to Dani El,
I fear my adoni the sovereign
who numbers your food and your drink:
for why sees he your faces enraged
more than the children of your circle?
You have me owe my head to the sovereign.
11 And Dani El says to the steward
whom the governor of the eunuchs numbers over
Dani El, Hanan Yah, Misha El, and Azar Yah,
12 Test your servants, I beseech you, ten days;
have them give us herbs to eat and water to drink:
13 Then let our *countenances* **visages**
be *looked upon* **seen** *before thee* **at thy face,**
and the *countenance* **visage** of the children that eat
of the *portion* **delicacies** of the *king's meat* **sovereign**:
and as thou seest, *deal* **work** with thy servants.
14 So he *consented* **hearkened** to them
in this *matter* **word,**
and *proved* **tested** them ten days.
15 And at the end of ten days
their *countenances* **visages**
appeared fairer **were seen better** and fatter in flesh
than all the children which did eat
the *portion* **delicacies** of the *king's meat* **sovereign.**
16 Thus *Melzar* **the steward**
took away the portion of **lifted** their *meat* **delicacies,**
and the wine that they should drink;
and gave them *pulse* **herbs.**
17 As for these four children,
God **Elohim** gave them
knowledge and *skill* **comprehension**
in all *learning* **scrolls** and wisdom:
and *Daniel had understanding in* **Dani El discerned**
all visions and dreams.
18 *Now* at the end of the days
that the *king* **sovereign** had said he should bring them in,
then the *prince* **governor** of the eunuchs brought them in
before Nebuchadnezzar **at the face of Nebukadnets Tsar.**
19 And the *king communed*
sovereign worded with them;
and among them all was found none
like *Daniel* **Dani El**, *Hananiah* **Hanan Yah,**
Mishael **Misha El**, and *Azariah* **Azar Yah**:
therefore stood they
before **at the face of** the *king* **sovereign.**
20 And in all *matters* **words** of wisdom
and *understanding* **of discernment,**
that the *king enquired* **sovereign besought** of them,
he found them ten *times* **hands** better than all
the *magicians* **horoscopists** and *astrologers* **enchanters**
that were in all his *realm* **sovereigndom.**
21 And *Daniel* **Dani El** continued
even unto the first year of *king Cyrus* **sovereign Koresh.**

DREAMS OF NEBUKADNETS TSAR

2 And in the second year of
the *reign* **sovereigndom**
of *Nebuchadnezzar* **Nebukadnets Tsar,**
Nebuchadnezzar **Nebukadnets Tsar** dreamed dreams,
wherewith his spirit *was troubled* **agitated,**
and his sleep brake from him.
2 Then the *king commanded* **sovereign said** to call
the *magicians* **horoscopists,**

and the *astrologers* **enchanters**,
and the sorcerers, and the *Chaldeans* **Kesediym**,
for to *shew* **tell** the *king* **sovereign** his dreams.
So they came
and stood *before* **at the face of** the *king* **sovereign**.
3 And the *king* **sovereign** said unto them,
I have dreamed a dream,
and my spirit *was troubled* **agitated** to know the dream.
4 Then *spake* **worded** the *Chaldeans* **Kesediym**
to the *king* **sovereign** in *Syriack* **Aramaic**,
O *king* **sovereign**, live *for ever* **eternally**:
tell **say to** thy servants the dream,
and we *will* **shall** shew the interpretation.
5 The *king* **sovereign** answered
and said to the *Chaldeans* **Kesediym**,
The *thing* **utterance** is gone from me:
if ye *will* **shall** not make known unto me the dream,
with the interpretation *thereof*,
ye shall be *cut* **served** in pieces,
and your houses shall be *made* **set** a *dunghill* **cesspool**.
6 But if ye shew the dream,
and the interpretation *thereof*,
ye shall *receive* **take from in front** of me
gifts and *rewards* **largess** and great *honour* **esteem**:
therefore shew me the dream,
and the interpretation *thereof*.
7 They answered *again* **secondly** and said,
Let the *king tell* **sovereign say to** his servants the dream,
and we *will* **shall** shew the interpretation of it.
8 The *king* **sovereign** answered and said,
I know of certainty that ye *would* **should** gain the time,
because ye see the *thing* **utterance** is gone from me.
13 then, at your face, see our visages
and the visage of the children
who eat of the delicacies of the sovereign: and
work with your servants as you see *fit*.
14 And he hearkens to them in this word
and tests them ten days:
15 and at the end of ten days
they see their visages better and fatter in flesh
than all the children
who eat the delicacies of the sovereign.
16 And the steward lifts their delicacies
and the wine they drink;
and gives them herbs.
17 As for these four children,
Elohim gives them knowledge and comprehension
in all scrolls and wisdom:
and Dani El discerns all visions and dreams.
18 And at the end of the days
the sovereign says to bring them in:
and the governor of the eunuchs
brings them in at the face of Nebukadnets Tsar:
19 and the sovereign words with them:
and among them all, no one was found
as Dani El, Hanan Yah, Misha El, and Azar Yah:
and they stand at the face of the sovereign.
20 And in all words of wisdom and of discernment
the sovereign beseeches of them
he finds them ten hands better
than all the horoscopists and enchanters
in all his sovereigndom:
21 and Dani El continues
to the first year of sovereign Koresh.

Dreams Of Nebukadnets Tsar

2 And in the second year
of the sovereigndom of Nebukadnets Tsar,
Nebukadnets Tsar dreams dreams
which agitate his spirit;
and his sleep breaks from him:
2 and the sovereign says to call
the horoscopists and the enchanters
and the sorcerers and the Kesediym
to tell the sovereign his dreams.
And they come
and stand at the face of the sovereign:
3 and the sovereign says to them,
I dreamed a dream
and my spirit agitates to know the dream.
4 And the Kesediym word to
the sovereign in Aramaic,
O sovereign, live eternally:
say the dream to your servants
and we show the interpretation.
5 The sovereign answers
and says to the Kesediym,
The utterance is gone from me:
if you make not known to me
the dream with the interpretation,
they serve you in pieces,
and set your houses a cesspool:
6 and if you show the dream
and the interpretation,
you take from in front of me
gifts and largess and great esteem:
so show me the dream and the interpretation.
7 They answer secondly and say,
May the sovereign say the dream to his servants
and we show the interpretation thereof.

8 The sovereign answers and says,
I know for certain that you *are* gaining time,
because you see the utterance is gone from me:
9 But if ye *will* **shall** not make
known unto me the dream,
there is but—one decree for you:
for ye have prepared *lying* **false**
and *corrupt words* **ruinous utterances**
to *speak before* **say in front of** me,
till the time be changed:
therefore *tell* **say to** me the dream,
and I shall know
that ye can shew me the interpretation *thereof.*
10 The *Chaldeans* **Kesediym** answered
before **in front of** the *king* **sovereign**, and said,
There is not a man upon the *earth* **dry**
that can shew the *king's matter* **sovereign's utterance**:
therefore **because** there is no *king* **sovereign**,
lord **great**, nor *ruler* **dominator**,
that asked *such things* **utterances as these**
at any *magician* **horoscopist**,
or *astrologer* **enchanter**, or *Chaldean* **Kesediym**.
11 And it is *a rare thing* **an esteemed utterance** that the
king requireth **sovereign asketh**, and there is none other
that can shew it *before* **in front of** the *king* **sovereign**,
except the *gods* **elahim**,
whose *dwelling* **whirling** is not with flesh.
12 *For this cause* **Therefore** the
king was angry **sovereign raged**
and **was** very *furious* **enraged**,
and *commanded* **said** to destroy
all the *wise men* **magi** of *Babylon* **Babel**.
13 And the decree *went forth* **emerged**
that the *wise men* **magi** should be *slain* **severed**;
and they *sought* **requested**
Daniel **Dani El** and his *fellows* **companions**
to be *slain* **severed**.
14 Then *Daniel answered* **Dani El responded**
with counsel and *wisdom* **taste**
to *Arioch* **Aryoch** the *captain* **great**
of the *king's guard* **slaughterers of the sovereign**,
which *was gone forth* **emerged**
to *slay* **sever** the *wise men* **magi** of *Babylon* **Babel**:
15 He answered and said to *Arioch* **Aryoch**
the *king's captain* **sovereign's dominator**,
Why is the decree *so hasty* **severe**
from the king **in front of the sovereign**?
Then *Arioch* **Aryoch**
made the *thing* **utterance** known to *Daniel* **Dani El**.
16 Then *Daniel went in* **Dani El entered**,
and *desired* **requested** of the *king* **sovereign**
that he *would* **should** give him *time* **an appointment**,
and that he *would* **should** shew the *king* **sovereign**
the interpretation.
17 Then *Daniel* **Dani El** went to his house,
and made the *thing* **utterance** known
to *Hananiah* **Hanan Yah**, *Mishael* **Misha El**,
and *Azariah* **Azar Yah**, his companions:
18 That they *would desire* **should request** mercies
of the God **in front of Elah** of *heaven* **the heavens**
concerning this *secret* **mystery**;
that *Daniel* **Dani El** and his *fellows* **companions**
should not *perish* **destruct** with the *rest* **remainder**
of the *wise men* **magi** of *Babylon* **Babel**.

DANI EL EXPOSES THE MYSTERY

19 Then was the *secret revealed* **mystery exposed**
unto *Daniel* **Dani El** in a night vision.
Then *Daniel* **Dani El**
blessed *the God* **Elah** of *heaven* **the heavens**.
20 *Daniel* **Dani El** answered and said,
Blessed be the name of *God* **Elah**
for ever and ever **from eternity until eternity**:
for wisdom and might are his:
21 And he changeth the times and the seasons:
he *removeth kings* **passeth by sovereigns**,
and *setteth up kings* **raiseth sovereigns**:
he giveth wisdom unto the *wise* **magi**,
and *knowledge* **perception**
to them that know *understanding* **discernment**:
22 He *revealeth* **exposeth**
the *deep* **profound** and *secret things* **hidden**:
he knoweth what is in the darkness,
and the light *dwelleth with him* **he releaseth**.
9 and if you not make known to me the dream
—one decree for you:
for you prepare false and ruinous utterances
to say in front of me,
until the change of time:
so say to me the dream,
so that I know you show me the interpretation.
10 The Kesediym answer in front of the sovereign,
and say,
There is not a man on the dry
who can show the utterance of the sovereign:
because no sovereign, great, or dominator,
asks utterances as these
of any horoscopist or enchanter or Kesediym:
11 and it is an esteemed
utterance the sovereign asks;

and there is no one other
who can show it in front of the sovereign
—except the elahim who whirl not with flesh.
12 So the sovereign rages—very enraged;
and says to destroy all the magi of Babel:
13 and the decree emerges to sever the magi;
and they request to sever
Dani El and his companions.
14 Then Dani El responds with counsel and taste
to Aryoch the great
of the slaughterers of the sovereign
—who emerges to sever the magi of Babel.
15 He answers Aryoch the
dominator of the sovereign,
and says,
Why is the decree in front of the sovereign so severe?
Then Aryoch makes the utterance known to Dani El:
16 and Dani El enters,
and requests of the sovereign
to give him an appointment,
to show the sovereign the interpretation.
17 Then Dani El goes to his house,
and makes the utterance known
to Hanan Yah, Misha El, and Azar Yah
his companions:
18 to request mercies in front
of Elah of the heavens
concerning this mystery;
so that Dani El and his companions not destruct
with the remainder of the magi of Babel.

Dani El Exposes The Mystery

19 Then in a night vision
the mystery is exposed to Dani El;
and Dani El blesses Elah of the heavens:
20 Dani El answers and says,
Blessed—the name of Elah from eternity to eternity:
for wisdom and might are his:
21 and he changes the times and the seasons:
he passes sovereigns by, and raises sovereigns:
he gives wisdom to the magi,
and perception to them who know discernment:
22 he exposes the profound and the hidden:
he knows what is in the darkness,
and releases the light.
23 I thank thee, and *praise* **laud** thee,
O thou *God* **Elah** of my fathers,
who hast given me wisdom and might,
and hast made known unto me now
what we *desired* **requested** of thee:
for thou hast *now* made known unto us
the *king's matter* **sovereign's utterance.**
24 Therefore
Daniel went in **Dani El entered** unto *Arioch* **Aryoch,**
whom the *king* **sovereign** had *ordained* **numbered**
to destroy the *wise men* **magi** of *Babylon* **Babel:**
he went and said thus unto him;
Destroy not the *wise men* **magi** of *Babylon* **Babel:**
bring **enter** me in *before* **front of** the *king* **sovereign,**
and I *will* **shall** shew unto the *king* **sovereign**
the interpretation.
25 Then *Arioch* **Aryoch** *brought*
in Daniel **entered Dani El**
before **in front of** the *king in haste* **sovereign hastily,**
and said thus unto him,
I have found a *man* **mighty**
of the *captives* **sons of the exiles** of *Judah* **Yah Hudah,**
that *will* **shall** make known unto the *king* **sovereign**
the interpretation.
26 The *king* **sovereign** answered
and said to *Daniel* **Dani El,**
whose name was *Belteshazzar* **Belte Shats Tsar,**
Art thou able to make known unto me
the dream which I have seen,
and the interpretation *thereof*?
27 *Daniel* **Dani El** answered
in *the presence* **front** of the *king* **sovereign,** and said,
The *secret* **mystery**
which the *king* **sovereign** hath *demanded* **asked**
cannot the *wise men* **magi,** the *astrologers* **enchanters,**
the *magicians* **horoscopists,** the *soothsayers* **discerners,**
shew unto the *king* **sovereign;**
28 *But* **However**
there is *a God* **an Elah** in *heaven* **the heavens**
that *revealeth secrets* **exposeth mysteries,**
and maketh known
to *the king Nebuchadnezzar* **sovereign**
Nebukadnets Tsar
what shall be the *latter* **final** days.
Thy dream, and the visions of thy head upon thy bed,
are these;
29 As for thee, O *king* **sovereign,**
thy thoughts **thine intentions**
came into thy mind **ascended** upon thy bed,
what should *come to pass hereafter* **become after this:**
and he that *revealeth secrets* **exposeth mysteries**
maketh known to thee what shall *come to pass* **become.**
30 But as for me,
this *secret* **mystery** is not *revealed* **exposed** to me
for *any* wisdom that I have **in me** *more* than any living,

but for *their sakes* **words** that shall make known
the interpretation to the *king* **sovereign**,
and that thou mightest know
the *thoughts* **intentions** of thy heart.

Dani El Recalls The Mystery

31 Thou, O *king* **sovereign**, sawest,
and behold *a* **one** great image.—This great image,
whose *brightness* **cheerfulness** was excellent,
stood before **rose up in front of** thee;
and the *form thereof* **appearance** was *terrible* **terrifying**.
32 This image's head was of fine gold,
his breast and his arms of silver,
his *belly* **inwards** and his *thighs* **flanks** of *brass* **copper**,
33 His legs of iron,
his feet *part of* **from** iron and *part of* **from** clay.
34 Thou sawest till that a stone was cut out
without **not by** hands,
which *smote* **struck** the image
upon his feet *that were* of iron and clay,
and *brake* **pulverized** them *to pieces*.
35 Then was the iron, the clay, the *brass* **copper**,
the silver, and the gold,
broken to pieces together **pulverized as one**,
and became like the chaff of the
summer threshingfloors;
and the wind *carried* **bore** them *away*,
that no place was found for them:
23 I thank you, and laud you,
O you, Elah of my fathers,
who gives me wisdom and might
and now makes known to me
what we request of you:
that you make known to us
the utterance of the sovereign.
24 So Dani El enters to Aryoch,
whom the sovereign numbered
to destroy the magi of Babel:
he goes and says thus to him:
Destroy not the magi of Babel:
enter me in front of the sovereign
and I show the interpretation to the sovereign.
25 Then Aryoch hastily enters Dani El
in front of the sovereign, and says thus to him,
I found a mighty *one*
of the sons of the exiles of Yah Hudah
to make known the interpretation to the sovereign.
26 The sovereign answers and says to Dani El
—whose name *is* Belte Shats Tsar,
Are you able to make known to me
the dream I saw?—and the interpretation?
27 Dani El answers in front
of the sovereign, and says,
The mystery the sovereign asks
the magi, the enchanters,
the horoscopists, the discerners,
cannot show to the sovereign;
28 but there is an Elah in the heavens
who exposes mysteries,
and makes known to sovereign Nebukadnets Tsar
what becomes in the final days.
Your dream
and the visions of your head on your bed are these:
29 As for you, O sovereign,
the intentions that ascended on your bed,
What becomes after this?
—and he who exposes mysteries
makes known to you what becomes.
30 As for me,
this mystery is not exposed to me
for wisdom that I have in me
any more than for any *one* living,
but for words to make
the interpretation known to the sovereign,
so that you know the intentions of your heart.

Dani El Recalls The Mystery

31 You, O sovereign, saw, and behold,
one great image—this great image
whose excellent cheerfulness rises in front of you:
and the appearance terrifies.
32 This head of the image, of fine gold;
his breast and his arms, of silver;
his inwards and his flanks, of copper;
33 his legs, of iron;
his feet, of iron and of clay:
34 you see until a stone is cut—not by hands
which strikes the image on his feet of iron and clay
and pulverizes them:
35 then the iron, the clay,
the copper, the silver and the gold
pulverize as one,
and become
as the chaff of the summer threshingfloors;
and the wind bears them,
and no place is found for them:
and the stone that *smote* **struck** the image
became a great *mountain* **rock**,
and filled the whole earth.

DANI EL INTERPRETS THE MYSTERY

36 This is the dream;
and we *will tell* **shall say** the interpretation *thereof*
before the king **in front of the sovereign**.
37 Thou, O *king* **sovereign**,
art a *king* **sovereign** of *kings* **sovereigns**:
for *the God* **Elah** of *heaven* **the heavens**
hath given thee a *kingdom* **sovereigndom**,
power, and *strength* **empowerment**, and *glory* **esteem**.
38 And *wheresoever* **everywhere**
the *children* **sons** of men *dwell* **whirl**,
the *beasts* **live beings** of the field
and the *fowls* **flyers** of the *heaven* **heavens**
hath he given into thine hand,
and hath made thee *ruler* **dominate** over them all.
Thou art this head of gold.
39 And *after thee* **in thy place**
shall arise another *kingdom* **sovereigndom**
inferior to thee **from thee of earth**,
and another third *kingdom* **sovereigndom**
of *brass* **copper**,
which shall *bear rule* **dominate** over all the earth.
40 And the fourth *kingdom* **sovereigndom**
shall be *strong* **mighty** as iron:
forasmuch **because that** as iron
breaketh in pieces **pulverizeth** and *subdueth* **crusheth**
all *things*:
and as iron that *breaketh* **shattereth** all these,
shall it *break in pieces* **pulverize** and *bruise* **shatter**.
41 And whereas thou sawest
the feet and *toes* **digits**,
part of **from** potters' clay, and *part of* **from** iron,
the *kingdom* **sovereigndom** shall be divided;
but **from** there shall be in it of the strength of the iron,
forasmuch **because that** as thou sawest the iron
mixed **comingled** with miry clay.
42 And *as* the *toes* **digits** of the feet
were *part of* **from** iron, and *part of* **from** clay,
so the *kingdom* **sovereigndom** shall be
partly strong **from might**, and *partly* **from** broken.
43 And whereas thou sawest iron
mixed **comingled** with miry clay,
they shall *mingle themselves* **become comingled**
with the seed of men:
but they shall not *cleave one to another* **be this with that**,
even **behold** as iron is not *mixed* **comingled** with clay.
44 And in the days of these *kings* **sovereigns**
shall *the God* **Elah** of *heaven* **the heavens**
set up **raise** a *kingdom* **sovereigndom**,
which shall *never* **not** be *destroyed* **despoiled eternally**:
and the *kingdom* **sovereigndom**
shall not be left to other people,
but it shall *break in pieces* **pulverize** and consume
all these *kingdoms* **sovereigndoms**,
and it shall *stand for ever* **be raised eternally**.
45 *Forasmuch* **Because that** as
thou sawest that the stone
was cut out of the *mountain without* **rock not by** hands,
and that it *brake in pieces* **pulverized** the iron,
the *brass* **copper**, the clay, the silver, and the gold;
the great *God* **Elah**
hath made known to the *king* **sovereign**
what shall *come to pass hereafter* **become after this**:
and the dream is certain,
and the interpretation *thereof sure* **trustworthy**.

NEBUKADNETS TSAR PROMOTES DANI EL

46 Then *the king Nebuchadnezzar*
sovereign Nebukadnets Tsar
fell upon his face,
and *worshipped Daniel* **prostrated to Dani El**,
and *commanded* **said**
that they should *offer* **libate** an *oblation* **offering**
and *sweet odours* **savour of rest** unto him.
47 The *king* **sovereign** answered
unto *Daniel* **Dani El**,
and said, *Of* **From** a truth *it is*,
that your *God* **Elah** is *a God* **an Elah** of *gods* **elahim**,
and a *Lord of kings* **master of sovereigns**,
and *a revealer* **an exposer** of *secrets* **mysteries**,
seeing **that** thou couldest *reveal*
expose this *secret* **mystery**.
and the stone that strikes the image
becomes a great rock and fills the whole earth.

DANI EL INTERPRETS THE MYSTERY

36 This is the dream
and we say the interpretation in front of the sovereign:
37 You, O sovereign, are a sovereign of sovereigns:
for Elah of the heavens gives you a sovereigndom—
power and empowerment and esteem:
38 and everywhere the sons of men whirl;
and he gives the live beings of the field
and the flyers of the heavens into your hand,
and has you dominate over them all:
you are this head of gold.
39 And in your stead
rises another sovereigndom of earth
and another, a third sovereigndom of copper
who dominates over all the earth.

40 And the fourth sovereigndom
becomes mighty as iron:
because as iron pulverizes and crushes all:
and as iron shatters all these,
it pulverizes and shatters.
41 And as to what you saw—the feet and digits,
of clay of the potters, and of iron,
the sovereigndom becomes divided;
for the strength of the iron becomes therein
just as you saw the iron comingled with miry clay.
42 And the digits of the feet, of iron and of clay,
thus the sovereigndom
—becomes mighty, and becomes partly broken.
43 And as you saw iron comingled with miry clay,
they become comingled with the seed of men:
but they become not this with that
—behold, as iron is not comingled with clay.
44 And in the days of these sovereigns
Elah of the heavens raises a sovereigndom,
which despoils not eternally:
and the sovereigndom *is* not left to other people,
it pulverizes and consumes all these sovereigndoms
and it *is* raised eternally.
45 Because, as you saw,
the stone cut from the rock, not by hands,
and it pulverizes the iron, the copper, the clay,
the silver, and the gold;
the great Elah makes known to the sovereign
what becomes after this:
and the dream is certain,
and the interpretation trustworthy.

NEBUKADNETS TSAR PROMOTES DANI EL

46 Then sovereign Nebukadnets Tsar
falls on his face,
and prostrates to Dani El,
and says for them to libate an offering
and savour of rest to him.
47 The sovereign answers Dani El, and says,
Of a truth, your Elah is an Elah of elahim,
and a master of sovereigns,
and an exposer of mysteries,
that you can expose this mystery.
48 Then the *king* **sovereign**
made Daniel a great man **greatened Dani El**,
and gave him many great gifts,
and *made* **had** him *ruler* **dominate**
over the whole *province* **jurisdiction** of *Babylon* **Babel**,
and *chief* **great** of the *governors* **prefects**
over all the *wise men* **magi** of *Babylon* **Babel**.
49 Then *Daniel* **Dani El** requested
of the *king* **sovereign**,
and he *set* **numbered**
Shadrach, Meshach, and *Abednego* **Abed Nego**,
over the *affairs* **service**
of the *province* **jurisdiction** of *Babylon* **Babel**:
but Daniel **and Dani El** *sat*
in the *gate* **portal** of the *king* **sovereign**.

THE IMAGE OF GOLD OF NEBUKADNETS TSAR

3 *NEBUCHADNEZZAR* **Nebukadnets Tsar**
the *king* **sovereign** made an image of gold,
whose height was *threescore* **sixty** cubits,
and the breadth *thereof* six cubits:
he *set it up* **raised it** in the *plain* **valley** of Dura,
in the *province* **jurisdiction** of *Babylon* **Babel**.
2 Then *Nebuchadnezzar* **Nebukadnets Tsar**
the *king* **sovereign**
sent to gather together the *princes* **satraps**,
the *governors* **prefects**, and the *captains* **governors**,
the *judges* **mighty diviners**, the treasurers,
the *counsellors* **decreers**, the sherriffs,
and all the *rulers* **dominators**
of the *provinces* **jurisdictions**,
to come to the *dedication* **hanukkah** of the image
which *Nebuchadnezzar* **Nebukadnets Tsar**
the *king* **sovereign** had *set up* **raised**.
3 Then the *princes* **satraps**, the *governors* **prefects**,
and *captains* **governors**, the *judges* **mighty diviners**,
the treasurers, the counsellors, the sheriffs,
and all the *rulers* **dominators**
of the *provinces* **jurisdictions**
were gathered together
unto the *dedication* **hanukkah** of the image
that *Nebuchadnezzar* **Nebukadnets Tsar**
the *king* **sovereign** had *set up* **raised**;
and they *stood before* **rose in front of** the image
that *Nebuchadnezzar* **Nebukadnets Tsar**
had *set up* **raised**.
4 Then an *herald* **announcer**
cried aloud **called out with valour**,
To you *it is commanded* **they say**,
O people, nations, and *languages* **tongues**,
5 That at what time
ye hear the *sound* **voice** of the *cornet* **horn**,
flute, harp, sackbut, psaltery, *dulcimer* **symphonia**,
and all *kinds* **species** of *musick* **psalming**,
ye fall down and *worship* **prostrate to** the golden image
that *Nebuchadnezzar* **Nebukadnets Tsar**
the *king* **sovereign** hath *set up* **raised**:

6 And whoso
falleth not down and *worshippeth* **prostrateth**
shall the same *hour* **blink**
be *cast* **hurled** into the midst of a burning fiery furnace.
7 Therefore at that *time* **appointment,**
when **that** all the people
heard the *sound* **voice** of the *cornet* **horn,**
flute, harp, sackbut, psaltery,
and all *kinds* **species** of *musick* **psalming,**
all the people, the nations, and the *languages* **tongues,**
fell down and *worshipped* **prostrated**
to the golden image
that *Nebuchadnezzar* **Nebukadnets Tsar**
the *king* **sovereign** had *set up* **raised.**
8 *Wherefore* **Therefore** at that *time* **appointment**
certain Chaldeans came near **mighty**
Kesediym approached, and *accused*
chewed out the *Jews* **Yah Hudiym.**
9 They *spake* **answered** and said to
the king Nebuchadnezzar **sovereign Nebukadnets Tsar,**
O *king* **sovereign,** live *for ever* **eternally.**
10 Thou, O *king* **sovereign,** has *made* **set** a decree,
that every man that shall hear
the *sound* **voice** of the *cornet* **horn,**
flute, harp, sackbut, psaltery, and *dulcimer* **symphonia,**
48 Then the sovereign greatens Dani El
and gives him many great gifts;
and has him dominate
over the whole jurisdiction of Babel
and the great of the prefects
—over all the magi of Babel.
49 And Dani El requests of the sovereign,
and he numbers Shadrach, Meshach, and Abed Nego
over the service of the jurisdiction of Babel:
and Dani El in the portal of the sovereign.

THE IMAGE OF GOLD OF NEBUKADNETS TSAR

3 Nebukadnets Tsar the sovereign
makes an image of gold
its height, sixty cubits; its breadth, six cubits:
he raises it in the valley of Dura,
in the jurisdiction of Babel.
2 And Nebukadnets Tsar the sovereign
sends to gather together
the satraps, the prefects and the governors,
the mighty diviners, the treasurers,
the decreers, the sheriffs
and all the dominators of the jurisdictions
to come to the hanukkah of the image
Nebukadnets Tsar the sovereign raised.
3 Then the satraps, the prefects and governors,
the mighty diviners, the treasurers,
the decreers, the sheriffs
and all the dominators of the jurisdictions
gather together to the hanukkah of the image
Nebukadnets Tsar the sovereign raised;
and they rise in front of the image
that Nebukadnets Tsar raised.
4 And an announcer calls out with valour,
To you they say,
O people, nations, and tongues,
5 at the time you hear the voice of the horn,
flute, harp, sackbut, psaltery, symphonia,
and all species of psalming,
fall down and prostrate to the golden image
Nebukadnets Tsar the sovereign raised:
6 and whoever falls not down and prostrates
that same blink
is hurled midst a burning fiery furnace.
7 Therefore at that appointment,
all the people hear the voice of the horn,
flute, harp, sackbut, psaltery,
and all species of psalming,
and all the people, the nations and the tongues
fall down and prostrate to the golden image
Nebukadnets Tsar the sovereign raised.
8 Therefore at that appointment
mighty Kesediym approach
and chew out the Yah Hudiym;
9 they answer,
yes, they say to sovereign Nebukadnets Tsar,
O sovereign, live eternally:
10 You, O sovereign, set a decree,
that every man who hears the voice of the horn,
flute, harp, sackbut, psaltery, and symphonia,
and all *kinds* **species** of *musick* **psalming,**
shall fall down and *worship* **prostrateth**
to the golden image:
11 And whoso
falleth not down and *worshippeth* **prostrateth,**
that he should be *cast* **hurled**
into the midst of a burning fiery furnace.
12 There are *certain Jews* **mighty Yah Hudiym**
whom thou has *set* **numbered** over the *affairs* **service**
of the *province* **jurisdiction** of *Babylon* **Babel,**
Shadrach, Meshach, and *Abednego* **Abed Nego;**
these *men* **mighty,** O *king* **sovereign,**
have not *regarded* **set their taste to** thee:
they serve not thy *gods* **elahim,**
nor *worship* **prostrate to** the golden image

which thou hast *set up* **raised.**
13 Then *Nebuchadnezzar* **Nebukadnets Tsar**
in *his rage* **quiver** and fury
commanded **said** to bring
Shadrach, Meshach, and *Abednego* **Abed Nego.**
Then they brought these *men* **mighty**
before **in front of** the *king* **sovereign.**
14 *Nebuchadnezzar* **Nebukadnets Tsar**
spake **answered** and said unto them,
Is it *true* **your intent,**
O Shadrach, Meshach, and *Abednego* **Abed Nego,**
do not ye serve my *gods* **elahim,**
nor *worship* **prostrate**
to the golden image which I have *set up* **raised?**
15 Now if ye be *ready* **prepared**
that at what time ye hear the sound of the *cornet* **horn,**
flute, harp, sackbut, psaltery, and *dulcimer* **symphonia,**
and all *kinds* **species** of *musick* **psalming,**
ye fall down and *worship* **prostrate**
to the image which I have made; *well*:
but if ye *worship* **prostrate** not,
ye shall be *cast* **hurled** the same *hour* **blink**
into the midst of a burning fiery furnace;
and who is that *God* **Elah**
that shall *deliver* **liberate** you out of my hands?
16 Shadrach, Meshach, and *Abednego* **Abed Nego,**
answered and said to the *king* **sovereign,**
O *Nebuchadnezzar* **Nebukadnets Tsar,**
we *are not careful to answer* **need not respond to** thee
in this *matter* **decision.**
17 If it be so, our *God* **Elah** whom we serve
is able to *deliver* **liberate** us
from the burning fiery furnace,
and he *will deliver* **shall liberate** us
out of **from** thine hand, O *king* **sovereign.**
18 But if not, be it known unto
thee, O *king* **sovereign,**
that we *will* **shall** not serve thy *gods* **elahim,**
nor *worship* **prostrate to** the golden image
which thou has *set up* **raised.**
19 Then was *Nebuchadnezzar* **Nebukadnets Tsar**
full **filled** of fury,
and the *form* **image** of his *visage* **face**
was changed against
Shadrach, Meshach, and *Abednego* **Abed Nego:**
therefore he *spake* **answered,** and *commanded* **said**
that they should *heat* **kindle** the furnace
one seven times more than it was wont to be heated
seven above the usual kindling.
20 And he *commanded* **said**
to the most mighty *men* **mighty of valour**
that were *in* **among** his *army* **valiant**
to *bind* **shackle**
Shadrach, Meshach, and *Abednego* **Abed Nego,**
and to *cast* **hurl** them into the burning fiery furnace.
21 Then these *men* **mighty** were *bound* **shackled**
in their *coats* **mantles,** their *hosen* **undergarments,**
and their hats, and their *other garments* **robes,**
and were *cast* **hurled**
into the midst of the burning fiery furnace.
22 Therefore
because the *king's commandment* **sovereign's utterance**
was *urgent* **severe,**
and the furnace exceeding *hot* **kindled,**
the flame of the fire *slew* **severed** those *men* **mighty**
and all species of psalming,
falls down and prostrates to the golden image:
11 and whoever falls not down and prostrates
is hurled midst a burning fiery furnace:
12 there are mighty Yah Hudiym
whom you numbered
over the service of the jurisdiction of Babel
—Shadrach, Meshach, and Abed Nego:
these mighty, O sovereign,
set not their taste to you:
they neither serve your elahim
nor prostrate to the golden image you raised.
13 Then Nebukadnets Tsar, in quiver and fury,
says to bring Shadrach, Meshach, and Abed Nego.
—then they bring these mighty
in front of the sovereign.
14 Nebukadnets Tsar answers and says to them,
Is it your intent,
O Shadrach, Meshach, and Abed Nego,
to neither serve my elahim
nor prostrate to the golden image I raised?
15 Now behold, if you *are* prepared,
at the time you hear the sound of the horn,
flute, harp, sackbut, psaltery and symphonia
and all species of psalming,
you fall down and prostrate to the image I made—
and behold, if you prostrate not,
at that same blink
you are hurled midst a burning fiery furnace!
Who is that Elah who liberates you from my hands?
16 Shadrach, Meshach, and Abed Nego answer
and say to the sovereign,
O Nebukadnets Tsar,
we need not respond to you in this decision:
17 and so be it,

our Elah whom we serve
is able to liberate us from the burning fiery furnace,
and liberate us from your hand, O sovereign.
18 And behold, *if* not, know this, O sovereign,
that we neither serve your elahim
nor prostrate to the golden image you raised.
19 Then Nebukadnets Tsar fills with fury,
and changes the image of his face
against Shadrach, Meshach and Abed Nego:
he answers and says
for them to kindle the furnace
seven above the usual kindling.
20 And to the most mighty mighty of valour
among his valiant,
he says to shackle
Shadrach, Meshach, and Abed Nego,
and to hurl them into the burning fiery furnace.
21 Then they shackle these
mighty in their mantles,
their undergarments and their hats and their robes
and hurl them midst the burning fiery furnace.
22 So because the utterance of
the sovereign *is so* severe
and the furnace exceedingly kindled
the flame of the fire severs the mighty
that took up Shadrach,
Meshach and *Abednego* **Abed Nego**.
23 And these three *men* **mighty**,
Shadrach, Meshach, and *Abednego* **Abed Nego**, fell down *bound* **shackled**
into the midst of the burning fiery furnace.
24 Then *Nebuchadnezzar* **Nebukadnets Tsar**
the *king* **sovereign** *was astonied* **marvelled**,
and rose up *in haste* **hastily**,
and *spake* **answered**, *and said* **saying** unto his cousellors,
Did not we *cast* **hurl** three *men* **mighty** bound
into the midst of the fire?
They answered and said unto the *king* **sovereign**,
True **Certainly**, O *king* **sovereign**.
25 He answered and said,
Lo **Behold**, I see four *men loose* **mighty released**,
walking in the midst of the fire,
and they have no *hurt* **damage**;
and the *form* **appearance** of the fourth
is like the *Son* **Bar** of *God* **Elah**.
26 Then *Nebuchadnezzar* **Nebukadnets Tsar**
came near **approached** the *mouth* **portal**
of the burning fiery furnace,
and spake **answered**, and said,
Shadrach, Meshach, and *Abednego* **Abed Nego**,
ye servants of *the most high God* **Elyon Elah**,
come forth **emerge**, and come *hither.*
Then Shadrach, Meshach, and *Abednego* **Abed Nego**,
came forth of **emerged from** the midst of the fire.
27 And the *princes* **satraps**, *governors* **prefects**,
and *captains* **governors**,
and the *king's* **sovereign's** counsellors,
being gathered together, saw these *men* **mighty**,
upon whose bodies
the fire *had no power* **domininated not**,
nor was an hair of their head singed,
neither were their *coats* **mantles** changed,
nor the *smell* **scent** of fire had passed on them.
28 *Then Nebuchadnezzar* **Nebukadnets Tsar**
spake **answered**, and said,
Blessed be *the God* **Elah** of
Shadrach, Meshach, and *Abednego* **Abed Nego**,
who hath sent his angel
and *delivered* **liberated** his servants
that *trusted in* **attended** him,
and have changed the *king's word* **sovereign's utterance**,
and *yielded* **gave** their bodies,
that they might not serve nor *worship* **prostrate**
to any *god* **elah**, except their own *God* **Elah**.

THE DECREE OF NEBUKADNETS TSAR

29 *Therefore I make* **I set** a decree,
That every people, nation, and *language* **tongue**,
which *speak any thing amiss* **say misleadingly**
against *the God* **Elah** of
Shadrach, Meshach, and *Abednego* **Abed Nego**,
shall be *cut* **served** in pieces,
and their houses
shall be *made a dunghill* **equated to a cesspool**:
because **that** there is no other *God* **Elah**
that can *deliver after this sort* **rescue thus**.
30 Then the *king* **sovereign**
promoted **prospered**
Shadrach, Meshach, and *Abednego* **Abed Nego**,
in the *province* **jurisdiction** of *Babylon* **Babel**.

THE PROCLAMATION OF NEBUKADNETS TSAR

4 *NUBUCHADNEZZAR* **Nebukadnets Tsar**
the *king* **sovereign**,
unto all people, nations, and *languages* **tongues**,
that *dwell* **whirl** in all the earth;
Peace **Shalom** be *multiplied* **increased** unto you.
2 *I thought it good* **It was**
glorifying in front of me
to shew the *signs* **omens** and *wonders* **marvels**

that the *high God* **Elyon Elah** hath
wrought **served** toward me.
3 How great *are* his *signs* **omens**!
and how mighty *are* his *wonders* **marvels**!
his *kingdom* **sovereigndom**
is an *everlasting kingdom* **eternal sovereigndom**, and
his dominion is from generation to generation.
who take Shadrach, Meshach and Abed Nego.
23 And these three mighty,
Shadrach, Meshach, and Abed Nego
fall down shackled midst the burning fiery furnace.
24 Then Nebukadnets Tsar the sovereign
marvels and rises hastily, and answers,
saying to his cousellors,
Hurled we not three mighty bound midst the fire?
They answer and say to the sovereign,
Certainly, O sovereign.
25 He answers and says,
Behold, I see four mighty released,
walking midst the fire with no damage;
and the appearance of the fourth is as the Bar of Elah.
26 Then Nebukadnets Tsar
approaches the portal of the burning fiery furnace;
and he answers and says,
Shadrach, Meshach, and Abed Nego,
you servants of Elyon Elah,
emerge, and come.
—then Shadrach, Meshach and Abed Nego
emerge from midst the fire.
27 And they gather together,
these satraps, prefects and governors
and the counsellors of the sovereign,
to see these mighty
on whose bodies neither the fire domininates
nor an hair of their head singes
nor their mantles change
nor the scent of fire passes on them.
28 Nebukadnets Tsar answers and says,
Blessed—Elah
of Shadrach, Meshach, and Abed Nego
who sent his angel
to liberate his servants who attend him;
and changes the utterance of the sovereign;
and gives their bodies
that they neither serve nor prostrate to any elah
except their own Elah.

THE DECREE OF NEBUKADNETS TSAR

29 I set a decree,
To every people, nation, and tongue,
who say misleadingly against the Elah
of Shadrach, Meshach and Abed Nego
that they be served in pieces;
and equate their houses to a cesspool:
because that there is no other Elah
who can rescue thus.
30 Then the sovereign prospers
Shadrach, Meshach, and Abed Nego,
in the jurisdiction of Babel.

THE PROCLAMATION OF NEBUKADNETS TSAR

4 Nebukadnets Tsar the sovereign:
to all people, nations, and tongues
whirling in all the earth:
Shalom be increased to you.
2 It *is* glorifying in front of me
to show the omens and marvels
Elyon Elah serves toward me.
3 How great his omens!
And how mighty his marvels!
His sovereigndom *is* an eternal sovereigndom,
and his dominion from generation to generation.

THE DREAM OF NEBUKADNETS TSAR OF THE TREE

4 I *Nebuchadnezzar* **Nebukadnets Tsar**
was at rest **serenized** in mine house,
and *flourishing* **verdant** in my *palace* **manse**:
5 I saw a dream which *made* **terrified** me *afraid*,
and the *thought* **conceptions** upon my bed and
the visions of my head *troubled* **terrified** me.
6 *Therefore made* I **set** a decree to *bring in* **enter**
all the *wise men* **magi** of *Babylon* **Babel**
before me **in front of me,**
that they might make known unto me
the interpretation of the dream.
7 Then *came in* **entered** the
magicians **horoscopists**,
the *astrologers* **enchanters**, the *Chaldeans* **Kesediym**,
and the *soothsayers* **discerners**:
and I *told* **said** the dream *before* **in front of** them;
but they did not make known unto me
the interpretation *thereof.*
8 *But at the last* **Until finally**
Daniel **Dani El** came in *before* **in front of** me,
whose name was *Belteshazzar* **Belte Shats Tsar**,
according to the name of my *god* **elah,**
and in whom is the spirit of the holy *gods* **elahim**:
and *before* **in front of** him I *told* **said** the dream, *saying,*
9 O *Belteshazzar* **Belte Shats Tsar**

master **great** of the *magicians* **horoscopists,**
because I know
that the spirit of the holy *gods* **elahim** is in thee,
and no *secret troubleth* **mystery distresseth** thee,
tell **say to** me the visions of my dream that I have seen,
and the interpretation *thereof.*
10 Thus were the visions of mine head in my bed;
I saw, and behold a tree in the midst of the earth,
and the height *thereof* was great.
11 The tree *grew* **greatened,**
and *was strong* **empowered,**
and the height *thereof*
reached **spread** unto *heaven* **the heavens,**
and the sight *thereof*
to the *end* **consummation** of all the earth:
12 The *leaves thereof were*
fair **foliage was beautiful,**
and the fruit *thereof* much,
and in it was *meat* **food** for all:
the *beasts* **live beings** of the field
had shadow **shaded** under it,
and the *fowls* **birds** of the *heaven* **heavens**
dwelt **whirled** in the *boughs* **branches** *thereof,*
and all flesh was *fed* **nourished** of it.
13 I saw in the visions of my head upon my bed,
and, behold, a *watcher* **waker** and an holy one *came*
down **descended** from *heaven* **the heavens;**
14 He *cried aloud* **called out**
with valour, and said thus,
Hew **Cut** down the tree, and *cut* **chop** off his branches,
shake off his *leaves* **foliage,** and scatter his fruit:
let the *beasts get away* **live beings flee** from under it,
and the *fowls* **birds** from his branches:
15 *Nevertheless* **But**
leave the stump of his roots in the earth,
even with a band of iron and *brass* **copper,**
in the *tender grass* **sprouts** of the field;
and let it be *wet* **dyed**
with the dew of *heaven* **the heavens,**
and *let* his portion *be* with the *beasts* **live beings**
in the *grass* **herbage** of the earth:
16 Let his heart be changed from man's,
and let a *beast's* **live being's** heart be given unto him;
and let seven times pass over him.
17 This *matter* **decision**
is by the decree of the *watchers* **wakers,**
and the *demand* **mandate**
by the *word* **edict** of the holy ones:
to the *intent* **word** that the living may know
that *the most High ruleth* **Elyon is dominator**
in the *kingdom* **sovereigndom** of men,
and giveth it to whomsoever he *will* **willeth,**
and *setteth up* **raiseth** over it the *basest* **lowliest** of men.
18 This dream
I *king Nebuchadnezzar* **sovereign Nebukadnets Tsar**
have seen.

THE DREAM OF NEBUKADNETS TSAR OF THE TREE

4 I Nebukadnets Tsar
being serene in my house and verdant in my manse:
5 I see a dream which terrifies me;
and the conceptions on my bed and the
visions of my head terrify me:
6 and I set a decree to have all the magi of Babel
enter in front of me,
to make known to me the interpretation of the dream:
7 then the horoscopists, the enchanters,
the Kesediym and the discerners enter:
and I say the dream in front of them;
and they make not known to me the interpretation:
8 until finally Dani El comes in front of me
—whose name *is* Belte Shats Tsar
according to the name of my elah
—and in whom *is* the spirit of the holy elahim:
and I say the dream in front of him,
9 O Belte Shats Tsar, great of the horoscopists,
because I know the spirit of the holy elahim *is* in you,
and no mystery distresses you,
say to me the visions of the dream I saw,
and the interpretation.
10 Thus *are* the visions of my head in my bed;
I see, and behold, a tree midst the earth,
and the height *is* great:
11 the tree greatens and empowers;
and the height spreads to the heavens,
and the sight to the consummation of all the earth:
12 the foliage *is* beautiful and the fruit much,
and food therein for all:
the live beings of the field shade under it
and the birds of the heavens whirl in its branches
and all flesh nourishes thereof.
13 I see, in the visions of my head on my bed,
and behold, a waker and a holy one
descend from the heavens;
14 he calls out with valour, and says thus:
Cut the tree and chop his branches; shake
its foliage and scatter its fruit:
so that the live beings flee from under it
and the birds from his branches:

15 but leave the stump of its roots in the earth,
even with a band of iron and copper
in the sprouts of the field
—dyed with the dew of the heavens;
and his portion with the live beings
in the herbage of the earth:
16 change his heart from that of a man
and give him a heart of a live being;
and seven times pass over him.
17 This decision *is* by the decree of the wakers;
and the mandate by the edict of the holy ones:
to the word so that the living know
Elyon *is* dominator in the sovereigndom of men,
and gives it to whomever he wills;
and raises the lowliest of men over it.
18 This dream, I sovereign Nebukadnets Tsar saw:
Now thou, O *Belteshazzar* **Belte Shats Tsar**,
declare **say** the interpretation *thereof*,
forasmuch as **because that**
all the *wise men* **magi** of my *kingdom* **sovereigndom**
are not able to *make known unto me* **have me know**
the interpretation:
but thou art able;
for the spirit of the holy *gods* **elahim** is in thee.

Dani El Interprets The Dream Of The Tree

19 Then *Daniel* **Dani El**,
whose name was *Belteshazzar* **Belte Shats Tsar**,
was *astonied* **astonished** for one *hour* **blink**,
and his *thoughts troubled* **intentions terrified** him.
The *king spake* **sovereign answered**, and said,
Belteshazzar **Belte Shats Tsar**,
let not the dream, or the interpretation *thereof*,
trouble **terrify** thee.
Belteshazzar **Belte Shats Tsar** answered and said,
My *lord* **master**, the dream be to them that hate thee,
and the interpretation *thereof* to thine enemies.
20 The tree that thou sawest,
which *grew* **greatened**, and *was strong* **empowered**,
whose height
reached **spread** unto the *heaven* **heavens**,
and the sight *thereof* to all the earth;
21 Whose *leaves were fair* **foliage was beautiful**,
and the fruit *thereof* much,
and in it was *meat* **food** for all;
under which
the *beasts* **live beings** of the field *dwelt* **whirled**,
and upon whose branches
the *fowls* **birds** of the *heaven* **heavens**
had their habitation **tabernacled**:
22 It is thou, O *king* **sovereign**,
that art *grown* **greatened**
and *become strong* **empowered**:
for thy greatness is *grown* **greatened**,
and *reacheth* **spreadeth** unto *heaven* **the heavens**,
and thy dominion to the *end*
consummation of the earth.
23 And whereas the *king* **sovereign**
saw a *watcher* **waker** and an holy one
coming down **descending** from *heaven* **the heavens**,
and saying,
Hew **Cut** the tree down, and *destroy* **despoil** it;
yet **but**
leave the stump of the roots *thereof* in the earth,
even with a band of iron and *brass* **copper**,
in the *tender grass* **sprouts** of the field;
and let it be *wet* **dyed**
with the dew of *heaven* **the heavens**,
and *let* his portion
be with the *beasts* **live beings** of the field,
till seven times pass over him;
24 This is the interpretation, O *king* **sovereign**,
and this is the decree of the *most High* **Elyon**,
which is *come* **happened**
upon my *lord* **master** the *king* **sovereign**:
25 That they shall *drive* **expel** thee from men,
and thy *dwelling* **whirling**
shall be with the *beasts* **live beings** of the field,
and they shall *make* **cause** thee
to *eat* **feed** on *grass* **herbage** as *oxen* **bulls**,
and they shall *wet* **dye** thee
with the dew of *heaven* **the heavens**,
and seven times shall pass over thee,
till thou know that *the most High* **Elyon**
ruleth **dominateth** in the *kingdom*
sovereigndom of men,
and giveth it to whomsoever he *will* **willeth**.
26 And whereas they *commanded* **said**
to leave the stump of the tree roots;
thy *kingdom* **sovereigndom**
shall be *sure* **permanent** unto thee,
after **from** that thou shalt *have known* **know**
that the heavens *do rule* **dominate**.
27 *Wherefore* **Therefore**, O *king* **sovereign**,
let my *counsel* **ruling** be *acceptable* **glorifying** unto thee,
and break off thy sins by *righteousness* **justness**,
and *thine iniquities* **thy perverseness**
by *shewing mercy* **granting charism** to the *poor* **humble**;
and you, O Belte Shats Tsar, say the interpretation;

because all the magi of my sovereigndom
are not able to have me know the interpretation:
and you can;
for the spirit of the holy elahim is in you.

Dani El Interprets The Dream Of The Tree

19 Then Dani El, whose name *is* Belte Shats Tsar,
is astonished for one blink
and his intentions terrify him.
The sovereign answers and says,
Belte Shats Tsar,
terrify not at the dream or the interpretation.
Belte Shats Tsar answers and says,
My master, the dream *is* to them who hate you;
and the interpretation to your enemies.
20 The tree you saw,
which greatens, and empowers,
whose height spreads to the heavens,
and the sight to all the earth;
21 whose foliage *is* beautiful, and the fruit much,
with food therein for all;
under which the live beings of the field whirl,
and on whose branches
the birds of the heavens tabernacle:
22 it is you, O sovereign,
who greatens and empowers:
for your greatness greatens
and spreads to the heavens,
and your dominion to the consummation of the earth.
23 And whereas the sovereign
saw a waker and an holy one
descend from the heavens,
and saying, Cut the tree, and despoil it;
but leave the stump of the roots in the earth
even with a band of iron and copper
in the sprouts of the field;
and dyed with the dew of the heavens,
and his portion with the live beings of the field,
until seven times pass over him.
24 This is the interpretation, O sovereign,
and this is the decree of the Elyon
which happens to my master the sovereign:
25 and they expel you from men
and you whirl with the live beings of the field;
and they have you feed on herbage as bulls and
they dye you with the dew of the heavens
and seven times pass over you,
until you know that Elyon
dominates in the sovereigndom of men,
and gives it to whomever he wills.
26 And whereas they say
to leave the stump of the tree roots;
your sovereigndom *is* permanent to you;
after you know that the heavens dominate.
27 Therefore, O sovereign,
my ruling *is* glorious to you;
and break off your sins by justness,
and your perverseness
by granting charism to the humble;
if **whether** it may be
a lengthening of thy *tranquillity* **serenity**.

Interpretation Of Dani El Fulfilled

28 All this *came* **happened** upon
the king Nebuchadnezzar **sovereign Nebukadnets Tsar**.
29 At the end of twelve months
he walked in the *palace* **manse**
of the *kingdom* **sovereigndom** of *Babylon* **Babel**.
30 The *king spake* **sovereign answered**, and said,
Is not this great *Babylon* **Babel**, that I have built
for the house of the *kingdom* **sovereigndom**
by the *might* **empowerment** of my power,
and for the *honour* **esteem** of my majesty?
31 While the *word* **utterance**
was in the *king's* **sovereign's** mouth,
there fell a voice from *heaven* **the heavens**, *saying*,
O *king Nebuchadnezzar* **sovereign Nebukadnets Tsar**,
to thee *it is spoken* **they are saying**;
The *kingdom* **sovereigndom** is *departed* **passed**
from thee.
32 And they shall *drive* **expel** thee from men,
and thy *dwelling* **whirling**
shall be with the *beasts* **live beings** of the field:
they shall *make* **cause** thee
to *eat grass* **feed on herbage** as *oxen* **bulls**,
and seven times shall pass over thee,
until thou know
that the *most High ruleth* **Elyon is dominator**
in the *kingdom* **sovereigndom** of men,
and giveth it to whomsoever he *will* **willeth**.
33 The same *hour* **blink**
was the *thing fulfilled* **utterance consummated**
upon *Nebuchadnezzar* **Nebukadnets Tsar**:
and he was *driven* **expelled** from men,
and *did eat grass* **fed on herbage** as *oxen* **bulls**,
and his body was *wet* **dyed**
with the dew of *heaven* **the heavens**,
till his hairs were *grown* **greatened** like eagles' *feathers*,
and his nails like birds' *claws*.

34 And at the end of the days
I *Nebuchadnezzar* **Nebukadnets Tsar**
lifted up mine eyes unto *heaven* **the heavens,**
and *mine understanding* **perception** returned unto me,
and I blessed the *most High* **Elyon,**
and I *praised* **lauded** and *honoured* **esteemed** him
that liveth *for ever* **eternally,**
whose dominion is an *everlasting* **eternal** dominion,
and his *kingdom* **sovereigndom**
is from generation to generation:
35 And *the inhabitants of* **they**
that whirl on the earth
are *reputed* **machinated** as *nothing* **nought:**
and he doeth *according to his will* **as he willeth**
in the army **among the valiant** of *heaven* **the heavens,**
and *among*
the inhabitants of **them that whirl on** the earth:
and none can tay his hand,
or say unto him, What *doest* **servest** thou?
36 At the same *time* **appointment**
my *reason* **perception** returned unto me;
and for the *glory* **esteem** of my *kingdom* **sovereigndom,**
mine *honour* **majesty** and *brightness* **cheerfulness**
returned unto me;
and my counsellors and my *lords sought* **nobles**
requested unto me;
and I was *established* **restored**
in my *kingdom* **sovereigndom,**
and excellent *majesty* **greatness** was added unto me.
37 Now I *Nebuchadnezzar* **Nebukadnets Tsar**
praise **laud** and *extol* **exalt** and *honour* **esteem**
the *King* **Sovereign** of *heaven* **the heavens,**
all whose *works* **acts** are truth,
and his ways *judgment* **plead:**
and those that walk in *pride* **arrogance**
he is able to abase.

The Feast Of Bel Shats Tsar

5 *Belshazzar* **Bel Shats Tsar,** the *king* **sovereign**
made a great feast to a thousand of his *lords* **nobles,**
and drank *wine* **fermentation**
before **in front of** the thousand.
whether there be a lengthening of your serenity.

Interpretation Of Dani El Fulfilled

28 And all this happens on
sovereign Nebukadnets Tsar.
29 At the end of twelve months
he walks in the manse of the sovereigndom of Babel:
30 the sovereign answers and says,
Is not this great Babel, which I built,
for the house of the sovereigndom
by the empowerment of my power,
and for the esteem of my majesty?
31 While the utterance
is still in the mouth of the sovereign,
a voice falls from the heavens,
O sovereign Nebukadnets Tsar,
to you they are saying;
the sovereigndom passes from you;
32 and they expel you from men;
and you whirl with the live beings of the field;
and feed on herbage as bulls:
and seven times pass over you;
until you know that the Elyon is dominator
in the sovereigndom of men,
and gives it to whomever he wills.
33 The same blink
the utterance consummates on Nebukadnets Tsar:
and he *is* expelled from men
and feeds on herbage as bulls;
and his body *is* dyed with the dew of the heavens,
until his hairs greaten as eagles and his nails as birds.
34 And at the end of the days,
I, Nebukadnets Tsar, lift my eyes to the heavens,
and perception returns to me,
and I bless Elyon,
and I laud and esteem him who lives eternally
—whose dominion is an eternal dominion
and his sovereigndom from generation to generation:
35 and all who whirl on the earth are machinated
as nought: and he does as he wills
among the valiant of the heavens and they
who whirl on the earth: and no one can strike
his hand, or say to him, What serve you?
36 At the same appointment
my perception returns to me;
and for the esteem of my sovereigndom,
my majesty and cheerfulness return to me;
and my counsellors and my nobles request to me;
and I *am* restored in my sovereigndom
and excellent greatness *is* added to me.
37 Now I, Nebukadnets Tsar,
laud and exalt and esteem
the Sovereign of the heavens
all whose acts are truth,
and his ways plead:
and they who walk in arrogance,
he is able to abase.

THE FEAST OF BEL SHATS TSAR

5 Bel Shats Tsar the sovereign
makes a great feast to a thousand of his nobles;
and drinks fermentation in front of the thousand.
2 *Belshazzar* **Bel Shats Tsar,**
whiles he tasted the *wine* **fermentation,**
commanded **said** to bring the golden and silver vessels
which his father *Nebuchadnezzar* **Nebukadnets Tsar**
had *taken* **removed** out of the *temple* **manse**
which was in *Jerusalem* **Yeru Shalem;**
that the *king* **sovereign,** and his *princes* **nobles,**
his *wives* **mistresses,** and his concubines,
might drink *therein.*
3 Then they brought the golden vessels
that were *taken* **removed**
out of the *temple* **manse** of the house of *God* **Elah**
which was at *Jerusalem* **Yeru Shalem;**
and the *king* **sovereign,** and his *princes* **nobles,**
his *wives* **mistresses,** and his concubines, drank in them.
4 They drank *wine* **fermentation,**
and *praised* **lauded** the *gods* **elahim** of gold, and of silver,
of *brass* **copper,** of iron, of *wood* **timber,** and of stone.

THE SCRIBING ON THE WALL

5 In the same *hour* **blink**
came forth fingers **emerged digits** of a man's hand,
and *wrote* **inscribed**
over against **in front of** the *candlestick* **menorah**
upon the plaister of the wall
of the *king's palace* **sovereign's manse:**
and the *king* **sovereign** saw the *part* **palm** of the hand
that *wrote* **inscribed.**
6 Then the *king's countenance*
sovereign's cheerfulness
was changed,
and his *thoughts troubled* **intentions terrified** him,
so that the *joints* **vertebrae** of his loins
were *loosed* **released,**
and his knees *smote* **knocked** one against another.
7 The *king cried aloud* **sovereign**
called out with valour
to *bring in* **enter** the *astrologers* **enchanters,**
the *Chaldeans* **Kesediym,** and the
soothsayers **discerners.**
And the *king spake* **sovereign answered,**
and said to the *wise men* **magi** of *Babylon* **Babel,**
Whosoever **Whatever man**
shall *read* **call out** this *writing* **inscribing,**
and shew me the interpretation *thereof,*
shall be *clothed* **enrobed** with *scarlet* **purple,**
and have a *chain* **necklace** of gold about his neck,
and shall be the third
ruler **to dominate** in the *kingdom* **sovereigndom.**
8 Then *came in* **entered**
all the *king's wise men* **sovereign's magi:**
but they could not *read* **call out** the *writing* **inscribing,**
nor make known to the *king* **sovereign**
the interpretation *thereof.*
9 Then was *king Belshazzar*
sovereign Bel Shats Tsar
greatly *troubled* **terrified,**
and his *countenance* **cheerfulness** was changed in him,
and his *lords* **nobles** were *astonied* **perplexed.**
10 *Now* the *queen* **sovereigness**
by reason **because** of the *words* **utterances**
of the *king* **sovereign** and his *lords* **nobles**
came **entered** into the banquet house:
and the *queen spake* **sovereigness answered** and said,
O *king* **sovereign,** live *for ever* **eternally:**
let not *thy thoughts trouble* **thine intentions terrify** thee,
nor let thy *countenance* **cheerfulness** be changed:
11 There is a *man* **mighty** in
thy *kingdom* **sovereigndom,**
in whom is the spirit of the holy *gods* **elahim;**
and in the days of thy father
light and *understanding* **comprehension** and wisdom,
like the wisdom of the *gods* **elahim,** was found in him;
whom
the king Nebuchadnezzar **sovereign Nebukadnets Tsar**
thy father, the *king* **sovereign,** *I say,* thy father,
made master **raised great** of the *magicians* **horoscopists,**
astrologers **enchanters,** *Chaldeans* **Kesediym,**
and *soothsayers* **discerners;**
12 *Forasmuch* **Because that** as an excellent spirit,
and *knowledge* **perception,**
and *understanding* **comprehension,**
2 Bel Shats Tsar, as he tastes the fermentation,
says to bring the golden and silver vessels
his father Nebukadnets Tsar
removed from the manse in Yeru Shalem;
for the sovereign and his nobles,
his mistresses and his concubines to drink.
3 Then they bring the golden
vessels they removed
from the manse of the house of Elah at Yeru Shalem;
and the sovereign and his nobles,
his mistresses and his concubines drink in them.
4 They drink fermentation;
and laud the elahim of gold and of silver,
of copper, of iron, of timber and of stone.

The Scribing On The Wall

5 In the same blink
digits of the hand of a man emerge,
and inscribe in front of the menorah
on the plaster of the wall
of the manse of the sovereign:
and the sovereign
sees the palm of the hand that inscribes:
6 then the cheerfulness of the sovereign changes
and his intentions terrify him
—so that the vertebrae of his loins release,
and his knees knock one against another.
7 The sovereign calls out with valour
to have the enchanters
the Kesediym and the discerners enter:
and the sovereign answers,
and says to the magi of Babel,
Whatever man calls out this inscribing
and shows me the interpretation
enrobes with purple
with a necklace of gold around his neck
and dominates—third in the sovereigndom.
8 Then all the magi of the sovereign enter:
but they can neither call out the inscribing
nor make known the interpretation to the sovereign.
9 Then sovereign Bel Shats Tsar terrifies greatly
and his cheerfulness changes in him;
and his nobles *are* perplexed.
10 The sovereigness,
because of the utterances
of the sovereign and his nobles,
enters into the banquet house:
and the sovereigness answers and says,
O sovereign, live eternally:
may neither your intentions terrify you,
nor your cheerfulness change:
11 there is a mighty in your sovereigndom
in whom is the spirit of the holy elahim;
and in the days of your father
light and comprehension and wisdom,
as the wisdom of the elahim, *was* found in him;
whom sovereign Nebukadnets Tsar your father
—the sovereign—your father raised
—the great of the horoscopists,
enchanters, Kesediym and discerners;
12 because of the excellent spirit
and perception and comprehension
interpreting of dreams,
and *shewing* **solving** of *hard sentences* **enigmas**,
and *dissolving* **unraveling** of *doubts* **riddles**,
were found in the same *Daniel* **Dani El**,
whom the *king named* **sovereign set the name**
Belteshazzar **Belte Shats Tsar**:
now let *Daniel* **Dani El** be called,
and he *will* **shall** shew the interpretation.
13 Then *was Daniel brought in* **Dani El entered**
before **in front of** the *king* **sovereign**.
And the *king* **sovereign**
spake **answered** and said unto *Daniel* **Dani El**,
Art thou that *Daniel* **Dani El**,
which art of the *children* **sons** of the *captivity* **exiles**
of *Judah* **Yah Hudah**,
whom the *king* **sovereign** my father
brought out of *Jewry* **Yah Hudah**?
14 I have even heard of thee,
that the spirit of *the gods* **elahim** is in thee,
and that light and *understanding* **comprehension**
and excellent wisdom is found in thee.
15 And now the *wise men* **magi**,
the *astrologers* **enchanters**,
have been *brought in before* **entered in front of** me,
that they should *read* **call out** this *writing* **inscribing**,
and make known unto me the interpretation *thereof*:
but they could not
shew the interpretation of the *thing* **utterance**:
16 And I have heard of thee,
that thou canst *make* **interpret** interpretations,
and *dissolve doubts* **unravel riddles**:
now if thou canst *read* **call out** the *writing* **inscribing**,
and make known to me the interpretation *thereof*,
thou shalt be *clothed* **enrobed** with *scarlet* **purple**,
and have a *chain* **necklace** of gold about thy neck,
and shalt be the third *ruler* **to dominate**
in the *kingdom* **sovereigndom**.

Dani El Interprets The Inscribing

17 Then *Daniel* **Dani El** answered
and said *before* **in front of** the *king* **sovereign**,
Let thy gifts be to thyself,
and give thy *rewards* **largess** to another;
yet **however**
I will read **shall call out** the *writing* **inscribing**
unto the *king* **sovereign**,
and make known to him the interpretation.
18 O thou *king* **sovereign**,
the most high God **Elyon Elah**
gave *Nebuchadnezzar* **Nebukadnets Tsar** thy father
a *kingdom* **sovereigndom**, and *majesty* **greatness**,
and *glory* **esteem**, and *honour* **majesty:**
19 And *for the majesty* **from the greatness**

that he gave him,
all people, nations, and *languages* **tongues**
trembled **became agitated**
and *feared before* **terrified in front of** him:
whom he *would* **willed,** he *slew* **severed**;
and whom he *would* **willed,** he *kept alive* **let live**;
and whom he *would* **willed,** he *set up* **lifted**;
and whom he *would* **willed,** he *put down* **abased**.
20 But when his heart was lifted up,
and his *mind* **spirit**
hardened **empowered** in *pride* **seething**,
he was deposed from his *kingly* **sovereigndom** throne,
and they *took* **passed** his *glory* **esteem** from him:
21 And he was *driven* **expelled**
from the sons of men;
and his heart
was *made like the beasts* **equated to live beings**,
and his *dwelling* **whirling**
was with the *wild asses* **onagers**:
they fed him with *grass like oxen* **herbage as bulls**,
and his body was *wet* **dyed**
with the dew of *heaven* **the heavens**;
till he knew that *the most high God* **Elyon Elah**
ruled **is dominator** in the *kingdom*
sovereigndom of men,
and that he *appointeth* **raiseth** over it
whomsoever he *will* **willeth**.
22 And thou his *son* **bar**, O
Belshazzar **Bel Shats Tsar**,
hast not *humbled* **abased** thine heart,
interpreting of dreams and solving of enigmas
and unraveling of riddles found in the same Dani El
—to whom the sovereign set the name
Belte Shats Tsar:
now call Dani El, and he shows the interpretation.
13 Then Dani El enters in front of the sovereign;
and the sovereign answers and says to Dani El,
Are you that Dani El
of the sons of the exiles of Yah Hudah
whom the sovereign my father
brought from Yah Hudah?
14 I hear of you, that the spirit of elahim is in you,
and that light and comprehension
and excellent wisdom *is* found in you:
15 and now the magi, the enchanters,
entered in front of me to call out this inscribing,
and make known the interpretation to me:
but they cannot show
the interpretation of the utterance:
16 and I—I hear of you,
that you can interpret interpretations
and unravel riddles:
now behold, *if* you can call out the inscribing
and make known the interpretation to me
I enrobe you with purple
with a necklace of gold around your neck;
and to dominate—third in the sovereigndom.

Dani El Interprets The Inscribing

17 Then Dani El answers
and says in front of the sovereign,
Your gifts are yours
and give your largess to another;
however I call out the inscribing to the sovereign
and have him know the interpretation.
18 You, O sovereign,
Elyon Elah gave Nebukadnets Tsar your father
a sovereigndom and greatness
and esteem and majesty:
19 and from the greatness he gave him,
all people, nations and tongues
became agitated and terrified in front of him:
whom he willed, he severed;
and whom he willed, enlivened;
and whom he willed, he lifted;
and whom he willed, he abased:
20 and when he lifted his heart
and empowered his spirit in seething
he *was* deposed from the throne of his sovereigndom,
and his esteem passed from him
21 —expelled from the sons of men;
and his heart *was* equated to live beings,
and his whirling *was* with the onagers:
they fed him with herbage as bulls,
and his body *was* dyed with the dew of the heavens;
until he knew that Elyon Elah
is dominator in the sovereigndom of men,
and that he raises over it whomever he wills.
22 And you his bar, O Bel Shats Tsar,
have not abased your heart
though **because that** thou knewest all this;
23 But hast lifted up thyself
against the *Lord* **Master** of *heaven* **the heavens**;
and they have brought the vessels of his house
before **in front of** thee,
and thou, and thy *lords* **nobles**,
thy *wives* **mistresses**, and thy concubines,
have drunk *wine* **fermentation** in them;
and thou hast *praised* **lauded** the *gods* **elahim** of silver,
and gold, of *brass* **copper**, iron, *wood* **timber**, and stone,

which see not, nor hear, nor know:
and *the God* **Elah** in whose hand thy breath is,
and whose are all thy ways,
hast thou not *glorified* **esteemed**:
24 Then was the *part* **palm** of the hand
sent *from* **in front of** him;
and this *writing* **inscribing** was *written* **signed**.
25 And this is the *writing* **inscribing**
that was *written* **signed**,
MENE/**NUMBERED**, MENE/**NUMBERED**,
TEKEL/**BALANCED**, UPHARSIN/**SPLIT**.
26 This is the interpretation of the *thing* **utterance**:
MENE/**NUMBERED**;
God **Elah** hath numbered thy *kingdom* **sovereigndom**,
and *finished it* **shalamed**.
27 TEKEL/**BALANCED**;
Thou art *weighed* **balanced** in the balances,
and art found *wanting* **deficient**.
28 PERES/**SPLIT**;
Thy *kingdom* **sovereigndom** is *divided* **split**,
and given to the *Medes* **Maday** and Persians.
29 Then *commanded Belshazzar*
said Belte Shats Tsar,
and they *clothed Daniel* **enrobed Dani El**
with *scarlet* **purple**,
and *put* a *chain* **necklace** of gold about his neck,
and *made a proclamation* **announced** concerning him,
that he should be the third *ruler* **dominator**
in the *kingdom* **sovereigndom**.
30 In that night was *Belshazzar* **Bel Shats Tsar**,
the *king* **sovereign** of the *Chaldeans* **Kesediym**
slain **severed**.
31 And *Darius* **Daryavesh** the *Median* **Maday**
took the *kingdom* **sovereigndom**,
being about threescore **a son of sixty** and two years *old*.

Daryavesh Raises One Hundred And Twenty Satraps

6 It *pleased Darius* **was glorifying**
in front of Daryavesh
to *set* **raise** over the *kingdom* **sovereigndom**
an hundred and twenty *princes* **satraps**,
which should be over the whole *kingdom* **sovereigndom**;
2 And over these three *presidents* **eunuchs**;
of whom *Daniel* **Dani El** was first:
that *the princes* **these satraps**
might give *accounts* **decrees** unto them,
and the *king* **sovereign** should have no damage.
3 Then this *Daniel* **Dani El**
was preferred **became preeminent**
above the *presidents* **eunuchs** and *princes* **satraps**,
because an excellent spirit was in him;
and the *king* **sovereign** thought to *set* **raise** him
over the whole *realm* **sovereigndom**.

Daryavesh Raises A Bond

4 Then the *presidents* **eunuchs** and *princes* **satraps**
sought to find *occasion* **pretext** against *Daniel* **Dani El**
concerning the *kingdom* **sovereigndom**;
but they could find
none occasion **no pretext** nor *fault* **ruining**;
forasmuch as **because that** he was *faithful* **trustworthy**,
neither was there any error or *fault*
ruining found in him.
5 Then said these *men* **mighty**,
We shall not find any *occasion* **pretext**
against this *Daniel* **Dani El**,
except **therefore** we find it against him
concerning the *law* **decree** of his *God* **Elah**.
6 Then these *presidents*
eunuchs and *princes* **satraps**
assembled together **conspired** to the *king*
sovereign, and said thus unto him,
King Darius **Sovereign Daryavesh**,
live *for ever* **eternally**.
7 All the *presidents* **eunuchs** of
the *kingdom* **sovereigndom**,
the *governors* **prefects**, and the *princes* **satraps**,
even though you know all this;
23 and you lift yourself
against the Master of the heavens;
and they bring the vessels of his house in front of you;
and you and your nobles,
your mistresses and your concubines
drink fermentation in them;
and you laud the elahim of silver and gold,
of copper, iron, timber and stone,
which neither see nor hear nor know:
and Elah in whose hand your breath *is*,
and whose all your ways *are*,
you esteem not.
24 Then the palm of the hand
is sent in front of him;
and this inscribing *is* signed:
25 and this is the inscribing that *is* signed,
MENE/NUMBERED, MENE/NUMBERED,
TEKEL/BALANCED, UPHARSIN/SPLIT.
26 This is the interpretation of the utterance:
MENE/NUMBERED;
Elah numbers your sovereigndom,

and shalams:
27 TEKEL/BALANCED;
You *are* balanced in the balances,
and found deficient:
28 PERES/SPLIT;
Your sovereigndom *is* split,
and given to the Maday and Persians.
29 Then Belte Shats Tsar says
to enrobe Dani El with purple,
with a necklace of gold around his neck;
and announces concerning him,
to become the third dominator in the sovereigndom.
30 In that night,
Bel Shats Tsar the sovereign of the Kesediym
is severed.
31 And Daryavesh the Maday
takes the sovereigndom
—a son of sixty—two years.

Daryavesh Raises One Hundred And Twenty Satraps

6 And so it is glorifying in front of Daryavesh
to raise a hundred and twenty satraps
over the sovereigndom
—three over the whole sovereigndom
2 and over these eunuchs,
—of whom Dani El *is* one
—that these satraps give decrees to them,
that the sovereign have no damage.
3 Then this Dani El
becomes preeminent over the eunuchs and satraps
because of the excellent spirit in him;
and the sovereign thinks to raise him
over the whole sovereigndom.

Daryavesh Raises A Bond

4 Then the eunuchs and satraps
seek to find a pretext against Dani El
concerning the sovereigndom;
but they can find no pretext or ruining
because he *is* trustworthy;
nor find any error or ruining in him.
5 Then these mighty say,
We find not any pretext against this Dani El;
except we find against him
concerning the decree of his Elah.
6 Then these eunuchs and satraps
conspire to the sovereign;
and say thus to him,
Sovereign Daryavesh, live eternally.
7 All the eunuchs of the sovereigndom
the prefects and the satraps
the counsellors, and the *captains* **governors**,
have consulted together
to *establish* **raise up** a royal statute,
and to *make a firm a decree* **empower an edict**,
that whosoever shall *ask* **request** a *petition* **request**
of any *God* **Elah** or man *for* **until** thirty days,
save **except** of thee, O *king* **sovereign**,
he shall be *cast* **hurled** into the *den* **dugout** of lions.
8 Now, O *king* **sovereign**,
establish **raise** the *decree* **bond**,
and sign the *writing* **inscribing**, that it be not changed,
according to the *law* **decree**
of the *Medes* **Maday** and Persians,
which *altereth* **passeth** not.
9 *Wherefore* **Therefore then**
king Darius **sovereign Daryavesh**
signed the *writing* **inscribing** and the *decree* **bond**.
10 Now when *Daniel* **Dani El** knew
that the *writing* **inscribing** was signed,
he *went* **entered** into his house;
and his windows being open in his *chamber* **upper room**
toward *Jerusalem* **Yeru Shalem**,
he kneeled upon his knees
three *times* **appointments** a day,
and prayed,
and *gave thanks* **spread hands**
before **in front of** his *God* **Elah**,
as he did *aforetime* **formerly**.
11 Then these *men assembled* **mighty conspired**,
and found *Daniel* **Dani El**
praying and making supplication **requesting charism**
before **in front of** his *God* **Elah**.
12 Then they *came near* **approached**,
and *spake before* **said in front of** the *king* **sovereign**
concerning the *king's decree* **sovereign's bond**;
Hast thou not signed a *decree* **bond**,
that every man that shall *ask a petition* **request**
of any *God* **Elah** or man *within* **until** thirty days,
save **except** of thee, O *king* **sovereign**,
shall be cast into the *den* **dugout** of lions?
The *king* **sovereign** answered and said,
The *thing* **utterance** is *true* **certain**,
according to the *law* **decree**
of the *Medes* **Maday** and Persians, which altereth not.
13 Then answered they
and said *before* **in front of** the *king* **sovereign**,
That *Daniel* **Dani El**, which is of the *children* **sons**
of the *captivity* **exile** of *Judah* **Yah Hudah**,

regardeth not **his taste to** thee, O *king* **sovereign**,
nor the decree that thou hast signed,
but *maketh* **requesteth** his *petition* **request**
three *times* **appointments** a day.
14 Then the *king* **sovereign**,
when he heard these *words* **utterances**,
was sore displeased **much stank** with himself,
and set his *heart* **anxiety** on *Daniel* **Dani El**
to *deliver* **liberate** him:
and he laboured till the *going down* **downing** of the sun
to *deliver* **rescue** him.
15 Then these *men* **mighty**
assembled **conspired** unto the *king* **sovereign**,
and said unto the *king* **sovereign**,
Know, O *king* **sovereign**,
that the *law* **decree** of the *Medes* **Maday** and Persians is,
That no *decree* **bond** nor *statute* **edict**
which the *king establisheth* **sovereign raiseth**
may be changed.

Dani El In The Dugout

16 Then the *king commanded* **sovereign said**,
and they brought *Daniel* **Dani El**,
and *cast* **hurled** him into the *den* **dugout** of lions.
Now the *king spake* **sovereign answered**
and said unto *Daniel* **Dani El**,
Thy *God* **Elah**
whom thou servest *continually* **perpetually**,
he *will deliver* **shall liberate** thee.
17 And *a* **one** stone was brought,
and *laid* **set** upon the mouth of the *den* **dugout**;
and the *king* **sovereign** sealed it with his own signet,
and with the signet of his *lords* **nobles**;
the counsellors and the governors
consulted together to raise a royal statute
and to empower an edict
—that whoever requests a request
of any Elah or man until thirty days,
except of you, O sovereign,
be hurled into the dugout of lions:
8 now, O sovereign, raise the bond,
and sign the inscribing, that it not change,
according to the decree of the Maday and Persians
which passes not.
9 —so sovereign Daryavesh
signs the inscribing and the bond.
10 And Dani El, knowing the inscribing *is* signed,
enters into his house,
opens his windows in his upper room
toward Yeru Shalem,
he kneels on his knees three appointments a day,
and prays and spreads hands in front of his Elah,
as he did formerly.
11 Then these mighty conspire;
and find Dani El
requesting charism in front of his Elah:
12 then they approach in front of the sovereign
and say concerning the bond of the sovereign;
Signed you not a bond,
that every man who requests
of any Elah or man until thirty days,
except of you, O sovereign,
be cast into the dugout of lions?
The sovereign answers and says,
The utterance is certain,
according to the decree of the Maday and Persians
which alters not.
13 Then they answer
and say in front of the sovereign,
That Dani El of the sons of the exile of Yah Hudah
neither regards this taste to you, O sovereign,
nor the decree you signed;
but requests his request three appointments a day.
14 Then when the sovereign hears these utterances,
he stinks much with himself,
and sets his anxiety on Dani El to liberate him:
and he labors until the downing of the sun
to rescue him.
15 Then these mighty conspire to the sovereign
and say to the sovereign,
Know, O sovereign,
the decree of the Maday and Persians
—that any bond or edict the sovereign raises
is not changed.

Dani El In The Dugout

16 Then the sovereign says to bring Dani El;
and they hurl him into the dugout of lions.
The sovereign answers and says to Dani El,
Your Elah, whom you serve perpetually,
he liberates you.
17 And they bring one stone
and set it on the mouth of the dugout;
and the sovereign seals it with his own signet
and with the signet of his nobles;
that *the purpose* **his will** might not be changed
concerning *Daniel* **Dani El**.
18 Then the *king* **sovereign**
went to his *palace* **manse**,
and *passed the night* **lodged overnight** fasting:

neither were instruments *of musick*
brought before **entered in front of** him:
and his sleep *went* **fled** from him.
19 Then the *king* **sovereign** arose
very early in the morning **in the splendour of dawn,**
and went *in haste* **hastily** unto the *den* **dugout** of lions.
20 And when he *came to*
approached the *den* **dugout,**
he cried with a *lamentable* **contorting** voice
unto *Daniel* **Dani El:**
and the *king spake* **sovereign answered**
and said to *Daniel* **Dani El,**
O *Daniel* **Dani El,** servant of the living *God* **Elah,**
is thy *God* **Elah,** whom thou servest continually,
able to *deliver* **liberate** thee from the lions?

Dani El Liberated From The Dugout

21 Then *said Daniel* **uttered Dani El**
unto the *king* **sovereign,**
O *king* **sovereign,** live *for ever* **eternally.**
22 My *God* **Elah** hath sent his angel,
and hath shut the lions' mouths,
that they have not *hurt* **despoiled** me:
forasmuch as before **because that in front of** him
innocency **purity** was found in me;
and also *before* **in front of** thee,
O *king* **sovereign,** have I done no *hurt* **wickedness.**
23 Then was the *king* **sovereign**
exceeding *glad* **rejoiced** for him,
and *commanded* **said**
that they should take *Daniel up* **Dani El**
out of the *den* **dugout.**
So *Daniel* **Dani El** was taken *up* out of the *den* **dugout,**
and no *manner of hurt* **damage** was found upon him,
because he *believed* **trusted** in his *God* **Elah.**
24 And the *king commanded* **sovereign said,**
and they brought those *men* **mighty**
which had *accused Daniel* **chewed out Dani El,**
and they *cast* **hurled** them into the *den* **dugout** of lions,
them, their *children* **sons,** and their *wives* **women;**
and *had the mastery of* **the lions dominated** them,
and *brake all* **pulverized** their bones *in pieces*
or ever **ere** they *came* **happened**
at the bottom of the *den* **dugout.**

The Decree Of Daryavesh

25 Then *king Darius* **sovereign Daryavesh**
wrote **inscribed**
unto all people, nations, and *languages* **tongues,**
that *dwell* **twirl** in all the earth;
Peace **Shalom** be *multiplied* **increased** unto you.
26 I *make* **set in front of me** a decree,
That in every dominion of my *kingdom* **sovereigndom**
men *tremble* **become agitated** and *fear* **terrify**
before the God **in front of the Elah** of *Daniel* **Dani El:**
for he is the living *God* **Elah,**
and *stedfast for ever* **permanent eternally,**
and his *kingdom* **sovereigndom**
that which shall not be *destroyed* **despoiled,**
and his dominion shall be
even unto the *end* **consummation.**
27 He *delivereth* **liberateth** and rescueth,
and he *worketh signs* **doeth omens** and *wonders* **marvels**
in *heaven* **the heavens** and in earth,
who hath *delivered Daniel* **liberated Dani El**
from the *power* **hand** of the lions.
28 So this *Daniel* **Dani El** prospered
in the *reign* **sovereigndom** of *Darius* **Daryavesh,**
and
in the *reign* **sovereigndom** of *Cyrus* **Koresh** the Persian.

The Dream Of Dani El, Of Four Live Beings

7 In the first year
of *Belshazzar* **Bel Shats Tsar**
king **sovereign** of *Babylon* **Babel**
Daniel had **Dani El saw** a dream and visions of his head
upon his bed:
then he *wrote* **inscribed** the dream,
and *told* **said** the sum of the *matters* **utterances.**
that his will concerning Dani El not change.
18 Then the sovereign goes to his manse
and lodges overnight fasting;
and his instruments enter not in front of him
and his sleep flees from him.
19 Then the sovereign rises in the splendor of dawn
and goes hastily to the dugout of lions:
20 and he approaches the dugout
and with a contorted voice, cries to Dani El:
and the sovereign answers and says to Dani El,
O Dani El, servant of the living Elah,
is your Elah, whom you serve continually,
able to liberate you from the lions?

Dani El Liberated From The Dugout

21 Then Dani El utters to the sovereign,
O sovereign, live eternally.
22 My Elah sent his angel,
and shut the mouths of the lions
that they not despoil me:

because, in front of him,
purity *is* found in me; and also in front of you,
O sovereign, I did no wickedness.
23 Then the sovereign rejoices exceedingly for him;
and says to take Dani El from the dugout:
and they take Dani El from the dugout;
and they find no damage on him,
because he trusted in his Elah.
24 And the sovereign says
to bring those mighty who chewed out Dani El;
and they hurl them into the dugout of lions
—them, their sons and their women;
and the lions dominate them
and pulverize their bones
ere they happen at the bottom of the dugout

THE DECREE OF DARYAVESH

25 Then sovereign Daryavesh
inscribes to all people, nations and tongues
who twirl in all the earth,
Shalom be increased to you.
26 I set a decree in front of me,
that in every dominion of my sovereigndom
that men agitate and terrify
in front of the Elah of Dani El:
for he is the living Elah and eternally permanent;
and his sovereigndom despoils not,
and his dominion *is* to the consummation.
27 He liberates and rescues;
and he does omens and marvels
in the heavens and in earth
—who liberated Dani El from the hand of the lions.
28 And this Dani El prospers
in the sovereigndom of Daryavesh;
and in the sovereigndom of Koresh the Persian.

THE DREAM OF DANI EL, OF FOUR LIVE BEINGS

7 In the first year of Bel Shats
Tsar sovereign of Babel
Dani El sees a dream and visions of his head
on his bed:
then he inscribes the dream
and says the sum of the utterances:
2 *Daniel spake* **Dani El answered** and said,
I saw in my vision by night, and, behold,
the four winds of the *heaven* **heavens**
strove **rushed** upon the great sea.
3 And four great *beasts* **live beings** *came up* **ascended**
from the sea, *diverse* **changed** one from another.
4 The first was like a lion, and had eagle's wings:
I *beheld* **saw** till the wings *thereof* were plucked,
and it was lifted up from the earth,
and *made stand* **raised** upon the feet as a man,
and a man's heart was given to it.
5 And behold another *beast* **live being**,
a second, like to a bear,
and it raised up itself on *one* **its** side,
and it had three ribs
in the mouth of it between the teeth of it:
and they said thus unto it, Arise, devour much flesh.
6 After this I *beheld* **saw**, and *lo* **behold** another,
like a leopard,
which had upon the back of it four wings of a *fowl* **flyer**;
the *beast* **live being** had also four heads;
and dominion was given to it.
7 After this I saw in the night visions, and
behold a fourth *beast* **live being**, *dreadful*
terrifying and *terrible* **burly**,
and *strong exceedingly* **exceedingly mighty**;
and it had great iron teeth:
it devoured and *brake in pieces* **pulverized**,
and *stamped* **trampled**
the *residue* **survivors** with the feet of it:
and it was *diverse* **changed**
from all the *beasts* **live beings**
that were *before* **in front of** it;
and it had ten horns.
8 I *considered* **was comprehending** the horns,
and, behold,
there *came up among* **ascended between** them
another little horn,
before **in front of** whom there were
three of the first horns *plucked up by the roots* **uprooted**:
and, behold, in this horn were eyes like the eyes of man,
and a mouth *speaking* **uttering** great *things*.

DANI EL SEES THE ANCIENT OF DAYS

9 I *beheld* **saw** till the thrones
were *cast down* **hurled**,
and the Ancient of days did sit,
whose *garment* **robe** was white as snow,
and the hair of his head like the *pure* **clean** wool:
his throne was like the fiery flame,
and his wheels as *burning* **flaming** fire.
10 A fiery *stream issued* **river flowed**
and *came forth* **emerged** from *before* **in front of** him:
thousand thousands ministered unto him,
and ten thousand times ten thousand **a myriad myriads**
stood before **rose up in front of** him:

the judgment was set,
and the *books* **scrolls** were opened.
11 I *beheld* **saw** then
because of the voice of the great *words* **utterances**
which the horn *spake* **uttered**:
I *beheld even* **saw**
till the *beast* **live being** was *slain* **severed**,
and his body destroyed, and given to the burning flame.
12 *As concerning* the *rest* **survivors**
of the *beasts* **live beings**,
they had their dominion *taken* **pass** away:
yet their lives were *prolonged* **given**
for a season **until an appointment** and time.

DANI EL SEES THE SON/BAR OF MAN

13 I saw in the night visions, and, behold,
one like the Son/**Bar** of man
came **coming** with the clouds of *heaven* **the heavens**,
and *came* **coming** to the Ancient of days,
and they *brought* **approached** him *near*
before **in front of** him.
14 And there was given him dominion,
and *glory* **esteem**, and a *kingdom* **sovereigndom**,
that all people, nations, and *languages* **tongues**,
should serve him:
2 Dani El answers and says,
I see in my vision by night, and behold,
the four winds of the heavens rush on the great sea:
3 and four great live beings ascend from the sea,
changed one from another.
4 The first like a lion with wings of an eagle:
I see until the wings *are* plucked;
and it lifts from the earth
and it raises on its feet as a man;
and it *is* given the heart of a man.
5 And behold, another live being,
a second, like a bear:
and it raises itself on its side;
with three ribs in its mouth between its teeth:
and they say thus to it,
Rise, devour much flesh.
6 After this I see, and behold,
another like a leopard:
and on its back, four wings of a flyer;
the live being also having four heads;
and it *is* given dominion.
7 After this I see in the night visions,
and behold, a fourth live being,
terrifying and burly, and exceedingly mighty,
with great iron teeth:
it devours and pulverizes and tramples
the survivors with its feet:
and it *is* changed
from all the live beings in front of it
—with ten horns.
8 I am comprehending the horns, and behold,
another little horn ascends between them;
in front of whom three of the first horns uproot:
and behold, in this horn, eyes like the eyes of man,
and a mouth uttering greatly.

DANI EL SEES THE ANCIENT OF DAYS

9 I see until the thrones are hurled:
and the Ancient of days sits
with robe as white snow,
and the hair of his head as clean wool;
his throne as a fiery flame
and his wheels as flaming fire.
10 A fiery river flows
and emerges from in front of him:
a thousand thousands minister to him,
and a myriad myriads rise in front of him:
the judgment is set,
and the scrolls are opened.
11 I see, then,
because of the voice of the great utterances
the horn utters:
I see until the live being is severed
and his body destroyed
and given to the burning flame:
12 the survivors of the live beings,
pass their dominion away:
yet their lives *are* given
until an appointment and time.

DANI EL SEES THE SON/BAR OF MAN

13 I see in the night visions,
and behold, like the Son/Bar of man, comes with
the clouds of the heavens, and comes to the Ancient
of days, and they approach in front of him:
14 and he is given dominion
and esteem and a sovereigndom
—so that all people, nations and tongues serve him:
his dominion is an *everlasting* **eternal** dominion,
which shall not pass away,
and his *kingdom* **sovereigndom**
that which shall not be *destroyed* **despoiled**.
15 I *Daniel* **Dani El** was grieved in my spirit
in the midst of my *body* **sheath**,
and the visions of my head *troubled* **terrified** me.

Dani El Interprets The Utterances

16 I *came near* **approached**
unto one of them that *stood by* **rose,**
and *asked* **requested of** him the
truth **certainty** of all this.
So he *told* **said to** me, and made me know
the interpretation of the *things* **utterances.**
17 These great *beasts* **live beings,**
which are four, are four *kings* **sovereigns,**
which shall arise out of the earth.
18 But the *saints* **holy** of *the most High* **Elyon**
shall take the *kingdom* **sovereigndom,**
and *possess* **hold** the *kingdom* **sovereigndom**
for ever **eternally,**
even *for ever* **eternally** and *ever* **eternally.**
19 Then I *would* **willed to** know the *truth* **certainty**
of the fourth *beast* **live being,**
which was *diverse* **changed** from all the others,
exceeding *dreadful* **terrifying,**
whose teeth were of iron, and his nails of *brass* **copper;**
which devoured, *brake in pieces* **pulverized,**
and *stamped* **trampled** the *residue*
survivors with his feet;
20 And of the ten horns that were in his head,
and of the other which *came up* **ascended,**
and *before* **in front of** whom three fell;
even of that horn that had eyes,
and a mouth that *spake* **uttered** very great *things,*
whose *look* **vision** was *more stout* **greater**
than his *fellows* **companions.**
21 I *beheld* **saw,**
and the same horn made war with the *saints* **holy,**
and prevailed against them;
22 *Until* the Ancient of days came,
and *judgment* **the pleading of the cause**
was given to the *saints* **holy** of *the most High* **Elyon;**
and the *time came* **appointment happened**
that the *saints* **holy**
possessed **held** the *kingdom* **sovereigndom.**
23 Thus he said, The fourth *beast* **live being**
shall be the fourth *kingdom* **sovereigndom** upon earth,
which shall be *diverse* **changed** from all kingdoms,
and shall devour the whole earth,
and shall tread it down, and *break* **pulverize** it *in pieces.*
24 And the ten horns out of
this *kingdom* **sovereigndom**
are ten *kings* **sovereigns** that shall arise:
and another shall rise after them;
and he shall be *diverse* **changed** from the first,
and he shall *subdue* **abase** three *kings* **sovereigns.**
25 And he shall *speak great words* **utter utterances**
against **concerning** the *most High* **Elyon,**
and shall wear out the *saints* **holy**
of *the most High* **Elyon,**
and *think* **willeth** to change
times **appointments** and *laws* **decrees:**
and they shall be given into his hand
until a time and times and the dividing of time.
26 But the *judgment* **pleaded** *shall sit* **is set,**
and they shall *take* **pass** away his dominion,
to *consume* **desolate** and to destroy it
unto the *end* **consummation.**
27 And the *kingdom* **sovereigndom** and dominion,
and the greatness of the *kingdom* **sovereigndom**
under the whole *heaven* **heavens,**
shall be given to the people
of the *saints* **holy** of *the most High* **Elyon,**
whose *kingdom* **sovereigndom**
is an *everlasting kingdom* **eternal sovereigndom,**
and all dominions shall serve and
obey **hearken unto** him.
28 *Hitherto* **Until thus**
is the *end* **conclusion** of the *matter* **utterance.**
As for me Daniel **I—Dani El,**
my *cogitations* **intentions** much *troubled* **terrified** me,
and my *countenance* **cheerfulness** changed in me:
but I *kept* **guarded** the *matter* **utterance** in my heart.
his dominion *is* an eternal dominion
which passes not away;
and his sovereigndom despoils not.
15 I Dani El grieve in my spirit midst my sheath,
and the visions of my head terrify me.

Dani El Interprets The Utterances

16 I approach one of them who rises,
and request of him the certainty of all this:
and he says to me
and has me know the interpretation of the utterances.
17 These great live beings, four,
are four sovereigns rising from the earth:
18 and the holy of Elyon take the sovereigndom,
and hold the sovereigndom eternally
—even eternally and eternally.
19 Then I will to know
the certainty of the fourth live being,
who *is* changed from all the others
—exceeding terrifying,
—teeth of iron and his nails of copper;
who devours, pulverizes
and tramples the survivors with his feet;

20 and of the ten horns in his head, and of the other
which ascends, and in front of whom three fall;
even of that horn with eyes
and a mouth uttering very great;
whose vision *is* greater than his companions.
21 I see,
and the same horn makes war with the holy;
and prevails against them;
22 the Ancient of days comes,
and gives the pleading of the cause
to the holy of Elyon;
and the appointment so happens
that the holy hold the sovereigndom.
23 Thus he says, The fourth live being
becomes the fourth sovereigndom on earth
which *is* changed from all kingdoms;
and it devours the whole earth,
and treads it down, and pulverizes it.
24 And the ten horns from this sovereigndom
are ten sovereigns who rise:
and another rises after them
—changed from the first;
and he abases three sovereigns:
25 and he utters utterances concerning the Elyon
and wears out the holy of Elyon;
and wills to change appointments and decrees:
and they are given into his hand
until a time and times and the dividing of time.
26 And the pleading is set,
and they pass away his dominion,
to desolate and to destroy it to the consummation:
27 and the sovereigndom and dominion,
and the greatness of the sovereigndom
under the whole heavens,
is given to the people of the holy of Elyon,
whose sovereigndom is an eternal sovereigndom;
and all dominions serve and hearken to him.
28 So, thus is the conclusion of the utterance.
I—Dani El,
my intentions terrify me much
and my cheerfulness changes in me:
but I guarded the utterance in my heart.

The Vision Of Dani El: Of The Ram And The Buck

8 In the third year of the *reign* **sovereigndom**
of *king Belshazzar* **sovereign Bel Shats Tsar**
a vision *appeared unto* **was seen by** me,
even unto me *Daniel* **Dani El,**
after that which *appeared unto* **was seen by** me
at the *first* **beginning.**
2 And I saw in a vision; and
it *came to pass* **became,**
when I saw, that I was at Shushan in the palace,
which is in the *province* **jurisdiction** of Elam;
and I saw in a vision, and I was by the river of Ulai.
3 Then I lifted up mine eyes,
and saw, and, behold,
there stood *before* **at the face of** the river
a **one** ram which had *two* horns:
and the *two* horns were high;
but one was higher than the *other* **second,**
and the higher *came up* **ascended** last.
4 I saw the ram *pushing*
westward **butting seaward,**
and northward, and southward;
so that no *beasts* **live beings**
might stand *before him* **at his face,**
neither *was there any* that could *deliver* **rescue**
out of his hand;
but he *did* **worked** according to his *will* **pleasure,**
and *became great* **greatened.**
5 And as I *was considering* **discerned,** behold,
an he goat **a buck of the doe goats**
came from the *west* **dusk**
on the face of the whole earth,
and touched not the *ground* **earth:**
and the *goat* **buck** had a *notable* horn **of vision**
between his eyes.
6 And he came to the ram *that*
had two **master of** horns,
which I had seen standing *before* **at the face of** the river,
and ran unto him in the fury of his *power* **force.**
7 And I saw him *come* **touch**
close *unto* **beside** the ram,
and he was *moved with choler* **embittered** against him,
and smote the ram, and brake his two horns:
and there was no *power* **force** in the ram
to stand *before him* **at his face,**
but he cast him down to the *ground* **earth,**
and *stamped upon* **trampled** him:
and there was none
that could *deliver* **rescue** the ram out of his hand.
8 Therefore the *he goat* **buck of the doe goats**
waxed very great **greatened mightily:**
and when he was *strong* **mighty,**
the great horn was broken;
and for it *came up* **ascended a vision of** four *notable ones*
toward the four winds of *heaven* **the heavens.**
9 And out of one of them came forth a little horn,

which *waxed exceeding great* **greatened exceedingly,**
toward the south, and toward the *east* **rising,**
and toward the *pleasant land* **splendour.**
10 And it *waxed great* **greatened,**
even to the host of *heaven* **the heavens;**
and it *cast down* **felled** *some* of the host and of the stars
to the *ground* **earth,**
and *stamped upon* **trampled** them.
11 Yea, he *magnified* **greatened** *himself*
even to the *prince* **governor** of the host,
and by him
the *daily sacrifice* **continual** was *taken away* **lifted,**
and the place of the *sanctuary* **holies** was cast down.
12 And an host was given him
against the *daily sacrifice* **continual**
by reason of *transgression* **rebellion,**
and it cast down the truth to the *ground* **earth;**
and it *practised* **worked,** and prospered.
13 Then I heard one *saint* **holy one** speaking,
and *another saint* **one holy one**
said unto *that certain saint* **such a one** which spake,
How long shall be the vision
concerning **of** the *daily sacrifice* **continual,**
and the *transgression* **rebellion** of *desolation* **desolating,**
to give both the *sanctuary* **holies** and the host
to be *trodden under foot* **trampled?**
14 And he said unto me,
Unto two thousand and three hundred

The Vision Of Dani El: Of The Ram And The Buck

8 In the third year
of the sovereigndom of sovereign Bel Shats Tsar
a vision was seen by me—Dani El,
after the *one* that was seen by me at the beginning.
2 And I see in a vision; and so be it,
I see, and I *am* at Shushan in the palace,
in the jurisdiction of Elam:
and I see in a vision, and I *am* by the river of Ulai:
3 and I lift my eyes and see, and behold,
there at the face of the river
stands one ram with horns:
and the horns *are* high;
but one *is* higher than the second
and the higher ascends last:
4 I see the ram butting seaward
and northward and southward;
so that live beings neither stand at his face,
nor *are* rescued from his hand;
and he works as he pleases; and greatens.
5 And I discern, and behold,
a buck of the doe goats comes from the dusk
on the face of the whole earth,
and touches not the earth:
and the buck has a horn of vision between his eyes:
6 and he comes to the ram master of horns
—whom I see standing at the face of the river;
and runs to him in the fury of his force:
7 and I see him touch close beside the ram
and he embitters against him;
and smites the ram and breaks his two horns: and
the ram has no force to stand at his face; and he
casts him to the earth and tramples him: there
is no one to rescue the ram from his hand.
8 And the buck of the doe goats greatens mightily:
and when he is mighty, the great horn breaks;
and a vision of four
ascends toward the four winds of the heavens:
9 and from one of them, comes a little horn
which greatens exceedingly,
toward the south and toward the rising
and toward the splendor:
10 and it greatens to the host of the heavens;
and it fells
some of the host and of the stars to the earth,
and tramples them.
11 Yes, he greatens, even to
the governor of the host;
and he lifts the continual
and casts down the place of the holies:
12 and he gives a host against the continual
by reason of rebellion,
and casts down the truth to the earth;
and it works and prospers.
13 And I heard a holy one speaking,
and a holy one says to such a one who speaks,
How long *ere* the vision of the continual,
and the rebellion of desolating,
gives both the holies and the host a trampling?
14 And he says to me,
Until two thousand and three hundred
days **evening mornings;**
then shall the *sanctuary* **holies** be *cleansed* **justified.**

A Mighty Interprets The Vision

15 And **so be** it *came to pass,*
when I, *even* I *Daniel* **Dani El,** had seen the vision,
and sought for *the meaning* **discernment,**
then, behold,
there stood before me

as the *appearance* **visage** of a *man* **mighty**.
16 And I heard a *man's* **human** voice
between *the banks of* Ulai,
which called, and said, *Gabriel* **Gabri El**,
make **cause** this *man* **one**
to *understand* **discern** the vision.
17 So he came *near* **beside** where I stood:
and when he came,
I *was afraid* **frightened**, and fell upon my face:
but he said unto me,
Understand **Discern**, O son of *man* **humanity**:
for at the time of the end shall be the vision.
18 *Now* as he was *speaking* **wording** with me,
I was *in a deep sleep* **sleeping soundly**
on my face toward the *ground* **earth**:
but he touched me, and *set* **stood** me *upright* **standing**.
19 And he said, Behold,
I *will make* **shall cause** thee **to** know
what shall be in the last end of the *indignation* **rage**:
for at the *time appointed* **season** the end shall be.
20 The ram which thou sawest
having two **master of** horns
are the *kings* **sovereigns** of *Media* **Maday** and Persia.
21 And the *rough goat* **buck buck**
is the *king* **sovereign** of *Grecia* **Yavan**:
and the great horn that is between his eyes
is the first *king* **sovereign**.
22 *Now* that being broken,
whereas four stood *up for it* **in its stead,**
four *kingdoms* **sovereigndoms** shall stand *up*
out of the *nation* **goyim**, but not in his *power* **force**.
23 And in the *latter time* **finality**
of their *kingdom* **sovereigndom**,
when the *transgressors* **rebels**
are *come to the full* **consummated**,
a *king* **sovereign** of *fierce countenance* **strong face**,
and *understanding dark sentences* **discerning riddles**,
shall stand *up*.
24 And his *power* **force** shall be mighty,
but not by his own *power* **force**:
and he shall *destroy wonderfully* **ruin marvelously**,
and shall prosper, and *practise* **work**,
and shall *destroy* **ruin** the mighty
and the *holy people* **people of the holy one**.
25 And through his *policy* **comprehension** also
he shall cause *craft* **deceit** to prosper in his hand;
and he shall *magnify* **greaten** *himself* in his heart,
and by *peace* **serenity** shall *destroy* **ruin** many:
he shall also stand *up*
against the *Prince* **Governor** of *princes* **governors**;
but he shall be broken *without* **by a final** hand.
26 And the vision of the evening and the morning
which was *told* **said** is *true* **in truth**:
wherefore shut thou up the vision;
for it shall be for many days.
27 And I *Daniel* **Dani El**
fainted, and was **became** sick *certain* **for** days;
afterward I rose up,
and *did* **worked** the *king's business* **sovereign's work**;
and I was *astonished* **stunned** at the vision,
but none *understood* **discerned** it.

DANI EL DISCERNS THE SCROLL OF THE SEVENTY WEEKS

9 In the first year
of *Darius* **Daryavesh** the son of
Ahasuerus **Achach Rosh**,
of the seed of the *Medes* **Maday**,
which *was made king* **reigned sovereign**
over the *realm* **sovereigndom** of
the *Chaldeans* **Kesediym**;
2 In the first year of his reign
I *Daniel understood* **Dani El discerned** by *books* **scrolls**
the number of the years,
whereof the word of *the LORD* **Yah Veh**
evening mornings;
then the holies *is* justified.

A MIGHTY INTERPRETS THE VISION

15 And so be it,
I—I Dani El see the vision and seek discernment,
and behold,
there stands in front of me as the visage of a mighty:
16 and I hear a human voice between Ulai,
and he calls and says,
Gabri El, this one discerns the vision.
17 So he comes beside where I stand:
and he comes, and I frighten and fall on my face:
and he says to me,
Discern, O son of humanity:
for the vision of the time of the end.
18 And as he words with me,
I sleep soundly on my face toward the earth:
and he touches me, and in standing, stands me:
19 and he says, Behold,
I have you know
what becomes in the last end of the rage
at the season of the end.
20 The ram you see—the master of horns
are the sovereigns of Maday and Persia:

21 and the buck buck, the sovereign of Yavan:
and the great horn between his eyes,
the first sovereign;
22 that, being broken, four stand in its stead
—four sovereigndoms from the goyim stand
—but not in his force.
23 And in the finality of their sovereigndom,
the rebels *are* consummated,
and a sovereign of strong face and discerning riddles
stands:
24 and his force *is* mighty
—and not by his own force:
and he ruins marvelously and prospers and works;
and ruins the mighty and the people of the holy one:
25 and through his comprehension
deceit also prospers in his hand;
and he greatens in his heart
and by serenity ruins many:
he also stands against the Governor of governors;
and *is* broken by a final hand.
26 And the vision of the evening and the morning
is said in truth:
and you, you shut up the vision;
for it *is* for many days.
27 And I Dani El, am sick for days,
I rise and work the work of the sovereign
—stunned at the vision; and no one discerns it.

Dani El Discerns The Scroll Of The Seventy Weeks

9 In the first year
of Daryavesh the son of Achach Rosh
of the seed of the Maday,
who reigns sovereign
over the sovereigndom of the Kesediym;
2 in the first year of his reign
I Dani El discern by scrolls
the number of the years the word of Yah Veh
came to *Jeremiah* **Yirme Yah** the prophet,
that he *would accomplish* **should fulfill** seventy years
in the *desolations* **parched areas**
of *Jerusalem* **Yeru Shalem**.
3 And I *set* **gave** my face
unto *the Lord God* **Adonay Elohim**,
to seek by prayer and supplications,
with fasting, and *sackcloth* **saq**, and ashes:
4 And I prayed unto *the LORD*
Yah Veh my *God* **Elohim**,
and *made* **spread** my *confession* **hands**, and said,
I beseech O *Lord* **Adonay**,
the great and *dreadful God* **awesome El**,
keeping **guarding** the covenant and mercy
to them that love him, and to them
that *keep* **guard** his *commandments* **misvoth**;
5 We have sinned,
and have *committed iniquity* **perverted**,
and have done wickedly, and have rebelled,
even by *departing* **turning aside**
from thy *precepts* **misvoth** and from thy judgments:
6 Neither have we hearkened
unto thy servants the prophets,
which *spake* **worded** in thy name
to our *kings* **sovereigns**,
our *princes* **governors**, and our fathers,
and to all the people of the land.
7 O *Lord* **Adonay**,
righteousness belongeth **justness** unto thee,
but unto us *confusion* **shame** of faces, as at this day;
to the men of *Judah* **Yah Hudah**,
and to the *inhabitants* **settlers** of
Jerusalem **Yeru Shalem**,
and unto all *Israel* **Yisra El**,
that are near, and *that are* far *off*,
through all the *countries* **lands**
whither thou hast driven them,
because of their *trespass* **treason**
that they have *trespassed* **treasoned** against thee.
8 O *Lord* **Adonay**,
to us *belongeth confusion* **be shame** of face,
to our *kings* **sovereigns**, to our *princes* **governors**,
and to our fathers,
because we have sinned against thee.
9 To *the Lord* **Adonay** our *God* **Elohim** *belong* **be** mercies
and forgivenesses, though we have rebelled against him;
10 Neither have we *obeyed*
hearkened unto the voice
of *the LORD* **Yah Veh** our *God* **Elohim**,
to walk in his *laws* **torah**,
which he *set before us* **gave at our face**
by **the hand of** his servants the prophets.
11 Yea, all *Israel* **Yisra El**
have *transgressed* **trespassed** thy *law* **torah**,
even by *departing* **turning aside**,
that they might not *obey* **hearken unto** thy voice;
therefore the *curse* **oath** is poured upon us,
and the oath that is *written* **inscribed**
in the *law* **torah** of *Moses* **Mosheh**
the servant of *God* **Elohim**,
because we have sinned against him.
12 And he hath *confirmed* **raised** his words,

which he *spake* **worded** against us,
and against our judges that judged us,
by bringing upon us a great evil:
for under the whole *heaven* **heavens**
hath not been *done* **worked**
as hath been *done* **worked** upon *Jerusalem* **Yeru Shalem.**
13 As it is *written* **inscribed**
in the *law* **torah** of *Moses* **Mosheh,**
all this evil is come upon us:
yet *made* **stroked** we not *our prayer* **the face**
before the LORD **of Yah Veh** our *God* **Elohim,**
that we might turn from our *iniquities* **perversities,**
and *understand* **comprehend** thy truth.
14 Therefore
hath *the LORD* **Yah Veh** watched upon the evil,
and brought it upon us:
for *the LORD* **Yah Veh** our *God* **Elohim**
is *righteous* **just** in all his works which he *doeth* **worketh:**
for we *obeyed* **hearkened** not **unto** his voice.
was to Yirme Yah the prophet,
concerning fulfilling the parched areas
of Yeru Shalem—seventy years.
3 And I give my face to Adonay Elohim,
to seek by prayer and supplications;
with fasting and saq and ashes.
4 And I pray to Yah Veh my Elohim,
and spread my hands, and say,
I beseech, O Adonay, great and awesome El,
who guards the covenant and mercy
to them who love him
and to them who guard his misvoth;
5 we sinned and perverted
and did wickedly and rebelled
—by turning aside
from your misvoth and from your judgments:
6 we hearkened not to your servants the prophets,
who worded in your name to our sovereigns,
our governors and our fathers
and to all the people of the land.
7 O Adonay, justness to you;
and shame of faces to us, as this day;
to the men of Yah Hudah
and to the settlers of Yeru Shalem
and to all Yisra El, near and far,
through all the lands you drove them,
because of the treason they treasoned against you.
8 Adonay, shame of face to us
—to our sovereigns, to our governors
and to our fathers,
because we sinned against you.
9 To Adonay our Elohim,
mercies and forgivenesses
though we rebelled against him;
10 we hearkened not
to the voice of Yah Veh our Elohim
—to walk in the torah he gave at our face
by the hand of his servants the prophets.
11 Yes, all Yisra El trespassed your torah,
even by turning aside
to not hearken to your voice;
so the oath pours on us
—the oath inscribed in the torah
of Mosheh the servant of Elohim,
because we sinned against him.
12 And he raises the words he worded against us
and against our judges who judge us,
by bringing a great evil on us
—as never worked under the whole heavens
as he works on Yeru Shalem:
13 as inscribed in the torah of Mosheh,
all this evil comes on us:
yet we stroke not the face of Yah Veh our Elohim
to turn from our perversities
and comprehend your truth:
14 and Yah Veh watches on the evil,
and brings it on us:
for Yah Veh our Elohim
is just in all the works he works:
for we hearken not to his voice.
15 And now, *O Lord* **Adonay** our *God* **Elohim,**
that hast brought thy people forth
out of the land of *Egypt* **Misrayim**
with a *mighty* **strong** hand,
and hast *gotten* **worked** thee *renown* **a name,**
as at this day;
we have sinned, we have done wickedly.
16 *O Lord* **Adonay,**
according to all thy *righteousness* **justness,**
I beseech thee,
let thine *anger* **wrath** and thy fury be turned away
from thy city *Jerusalem* **Yeru**
Shalem, thy holy mountain:
because for our sins,
and for the *iniquities* **perversities** of our fathers,
Jerusalem **Yeru Shalem** and thy people
are *become* a reproach to all that are **round** about us.
17 Now therefore, O our *God* **Elohim,**
hear the prayer of thy servant, and his supplications,
and cause thy face to *shine* **lighten**
upon thy *sanctuary* **holies** that is desolate,

for *the Lord's* **Adonay's** sake.
18 O my *God* **Elohim,**
incline **spread** thine ear, and hear;
open thine eyes,
and *behold* **see** our *desolations* **desolated,**
and the city which is called by thy name:
for we do not *present* **fell** our supplications
before thee **at thy face**
for our *righteousnesses* **justnesses,**
but for thy great mercies.
19 *O Lord* **Adonay**, hear; *O Lord* **Adonay**, forgive;
O Lord **Adonay**, hearken and *do* **work**;
defer **delay** not, for thine own sake, *O* my *God* **Elohim**:
for thy city and thy people are called by thy name.
20 And whiles I was speaking, and praying,
and *confessing* **spreading my hands for** my sin
and the sin of my people *Israel* **Yisra El,**
and *presenting* **felling** my supplication
before the LORD **at the face of Yah Veh** my *God* **Elohim**
for the holy mountain of my *God* **Elohim;**
21 Yea, whiles I was speaking in prayer,
even the man *Gabriel* **Gabri El,**
whom I had seen in the vision at the beginning,
being *caused to fly swiftly* **wearied in weariness,**
touched me
about the time of the evening *oblation* **offering.**
22 And *he informed me* **discerned,**
and *talked* **worded** with me, and said,
O *Daniel* **Dani El,**
I am now come forth to *give* **cause** thee
skill and understanding **to comprehend discernment.**
23 At the beginning of thy supplications
the *commandment* **word** came forth,
and I am come to *shew* **tell** *thee*;
for thou art *greatly beloved* **desired:**
therefore *understand* **discern** the *matter* **word,**
and *consider* **discern** the vision.

The Vision Of The Seventy Weeks

24 Seventy weeks are *determined*
cut upon thy people
and upon thy holy city,
to *finish* **restrain** the *transgression* **rebellion,**
and to *make an end of* **seal up** sins,
and to *make reconciliation* **kapar/atone**
for *iniquity* **perversity,**
and to bring in *everlasting*
righteousness **eternal justness,**
and to seal up the vision and *prophecy* **the prophet,**
and to anoint the *most Holy* **holy of holies.**
25 Know therefore and *understand* **comprehend,**
that from the
going forth **proceeding** of the *commandment* **word**
to restore and to build *Jerusalem* **Yeru Shalem**
unto the Messiah the *Prince* **Eminent** shall be
seven weeks, and *threescore* **sixty** and two weeks:
the *street* **broadway** shall be
built again **restored and rebuilt,**
and the *wall* **trench,**
even in *troublous* times **of distress.**
26 And after *threescore* **sixty** and two weeks
shall Messiah be cut off,
15 And now, Adonay our Elohim,
who brought your people from the land of Misrayim
with a strong hand,
and worked yourself a name, as this day;
we sin; we do wickedly.
16 Adonay, according to all your justness,
I beseech you,
turn away your wrath and your fury
from your city Yeru Shalem—your holy mountain:
because,
for our sins and for the perversities of our fathers
Yeru Shalem and your people
are a reproach to all, all around us:
17 and now, O our Elohim,
hear the prayer of your servant and his supplications;
and lighten your face on your holies
that *are* desolate for sake of Adonay.
18 O my Elohim, spread your ear and hear;
open your eyes and see our desolated;
and the city on whom your name is called:
for we fell not our supplications at your face
because of our our justnesses
—but because of your great mercies.
19 Adonay, hear; Adonay, forgive;
Adonay, hearken and work;
delay not, for your own sake, my Elohim:
for your city and your people
on whom your name is called.
20 And as I speak and pray
and spread my hands for my sin
and for the sin of my people Yisra El;
and fell my supplication
at the face of Yah Veh my Elohim
for the holy mountain of my Elohim;
21 yes, as I speak in prayer,
the man Gabri El,
whom I saw in the vision at the beginning,
wearied in weariness,

touches me about the time of the evening offering:
22 and discerns, and words with me, and says,
O Dani El,
I now come forth
to have you comprehend discernment:
23 at the beginning of your supplications
the word came forth,
and I come to tell; for you are desired:
so discern the word and discern the vision.

The Vision Of The Seventy Weeks

24 Seventy weeks are cut on your people
and on your holy city
to restrain the rebellion
and to seal up sins
and to kapar/atone for perversity
and to bring in eternal justness
and to seal up the vision and the prophet
and to anoint the holy of holies.
25 So know and comprehend,
that from the proceeding of the word
to restore and to build Yeru Shalem
to the Messiah, the Eminent
is seven weeks and sixty—two weeks
—to restore and rebuild the broadway and the trench
even in times of distress.
26 And after sixty—two weeks
Messiah *is* cut off;
but not for himself:
and the people of the *prince* **eminent** that shall come
shall *destroy* **ruin** the city and the *sanctuary* **holies**;
and the end *thereof* shall be with *a flood* **an overflowing**,
and unto the end of the war
desolations are *determined* **appointed**.
27 And he shall *confirm* **empower**
the **a** covenant with many *for* one week:
and in the *midst* **half** of the week
he shall cause the sacrifice and the *oblation* **offering**
to *cease* **shabbathize**,
and for the *overspreading* **wing** of abominations
he shall *make it* desolate **it**,
even until the *consummation* **final finish**,
and that *determined* **appointed**
shall be poured upon the *desolate* **desolated**.

The Vision Of Dani El Of One Human And Michah El

10 In the third year of *Cyrus* **Koresh**
king **sovereign** of Persia
a *thing* **word** was *revealed* **exposed** unto *Daniel* **Dani El**,
whose name was called *Belteshazzar* **Belte Shats Tsar**;
and the *thing* **word** was *true* **in truth**,
but the *time appointed* **hostility** was *long* **great**:
and he *understood* **discerned** the *thing* **word**,
and had *understanding* **discernment** of the vision.
2 In those days I *Daniel* **Dani El**
was mourning three *full* weeks **of days**.
3 I ate no *pleasant* bread **of desire**,
neither came flesh nor wine in my mouth,
in anointing, neither did I anoint myself *at all*,
till three *whole* weeks **of days** were fulfilled.
4 And in the four and twentieth
day of the first month,
as I was by the *side* **hand** of the great
river, which is *Hiddekel* **Hiddeqel**;
5 Then I lifted up mine eyes, and *looked* **saw**,
and behold *a certain* **one** man *clothed* **enrobed** in linen,
whose loins were girded with fine *gold* **ore** of Uphaz:
6 His body also was like the beryl,
and his face as the *appearance* **visage** of lightning,
and his eyes as *lamps* **flambeaus** of fire,
and his arms and his feet
like in *colour to polished brass* **eye as burnished copper**,
and the voice of his words like the voice of a multitude.
7 And I *Daniel* **Dani El** alone saw the vision:
for the men that were with me saw not the vision;
but **nevertheless**
a great *quaking* **trembling** fell upon them,
so that they fled to hide themselves.
8 Therefore I *was left* **remained** alone,
and saw this great vision,
and there remained no *strength* **force** in me:
for my *comeliness* **majesty** was turned in me
into *corruption* **ruin**,
and I retained no *strength* **force**.
9 Yet heard I the voice of his words:
and when I heard the voice of his words,
then was I *in a deep sleep* **sleeping soundly** on my face,
and my face toward the *ground* **earth**.
10 And, behold, an hand touched me,
which *set* **staggered** me upon my knees
and *upon* the palms of my hands.
11 And he said unto me,
O *Daniel* **Dani El,** a man *greatly beloved* **desired**,
understand **discern** the words that
I *speak* **word** unto thee,
and **in standing,** stand *upright*:
for unto thee am I now sent.
And when he had *spoken* **worded** this word unto me,
I stood trembling.

12 Then said he unto me, *Fear*
Awe not, *Daniel* **Dani El**:
for from the first day
that thou didst *set* **give** thine heart
to *understand* **discern**,
and to *chasten* **humble** thyself
before **at the face of** thy *God* **Elohim**,
thy words were heard, and I am come for thy words.
13 But the *prince* **governor**
of the *kingdom* **sovereigndom** of Persia
withstood **stood against** me one and twenty days:
but not for himself:
and the people of the eminent who comes
ruins the city and the holies;
and the end is with an overflowing;
and to the end of the war
desolations are appointed.
27 And he empowers a covenant with many
—one week:
and in the half of the week
he shabbathizes the sacrifice and the offering;
and for the wing of abominations
he desolates it even until the final finish;
and pours what *is* appointed on the desolate.

The Vision Of Dani El Of One Human And Michah El

10 In the third year of Koresh sovereign of Persia
a word is exposed to Dani El,
whose name *is* called Belte Shats Tsar;
and the word *is* truth and the hostility *is* great:
and he discerns the word
and discernment of the vision.
2 In those days I, Dani El
mourn three weeks of days:
3 I neither eat bread of desire
nor flesh and wine come into my mouth;
and in anointing, I anoint not myself
until the fulfilling of three weeks of days:
4 and in the twenty—fourth
day of the first month,
I am by the hand of the great river Hiddeqel;
5 and I lift my eyes and see;
and behold, one man enrobed in linen, with
loins girded with fine ore of Uphaz:
6 and his body as the beryl;
and his face as the visage of lightning;
and his eyes as flambeaus of fire;
and his arms and his feet
as the eye of burnished copper;
and the voice of his words as the voice of a multitude.
7 And I, Dani El alone see the vision;
and the men with me see not the vision:
and a great trembling falls on them;
so that they flee to hide themselves:
8 and I alone remain and see this great vision;
and no force remains in me:
for the majesty in me turns into ruin
and I retain no force:
9 yet I hear the voice of his words:
and I hear the voice of his words,
and I sleep soundly on my face
with my face toward the earth:
10 and behold, a hand touches me,
which staggers my knees and the palms of my hands.
11 And he says to me, O Dani El, a man desired,
discern the words I word to you,
in standing, stand:
for I am now sent to you.
—and when he words this word to me,
I stand trembling.
12 And he says to me, Awe not, Dani El:
for from the first day you gave your heart to discern
and to humble yourself at the face of your Elohim,
I heard your words;
and I come because of your words:
13 and the governor of the sovereigndom of Persia
stands against me twenty—one days:
but, *lo* **behold**, *Michael* **Michah El**,
one of the *chief princes* **head governors**,
came to help me;
and I remained there
with **beside** the *kings* **sovereigns** of Persia.
14 *Now* I am come
to *make* **cause** thee *understand* **to discern**
what shall befall thy people in the latter days:
for yet the vision is for *many* days.
15 And when he had *spoken* **worded** such words
unto me,
I *set* **gave** my face toward the *ground* **earth**,
and I became *dumb* **mute**.
16 And, behold, *one like the similitude* **a likeness**
of the sons of *men* **humanity** touched my lips:
then I opened my mouth, and *spake* **worded**,
and said unto him that stood *before* **in front of** me,
O my *lord* **adoni**,
by the vision my *sorrows* **pangs** are turned upon me,
and I have retained no *strength* **force**.
17 For how can the servant
of *this my lord* **my adoni**

talk with this my lord **word this with my adoni**?
for as for me, *straightway* **at this time**
there *remained* **stood** no *strength* **force** in me,
neither *is* **remained** there breath *left* in me.
18 Then there came again and touched me
one like the *appearance* **visage** of a *man* **human**,
and he strengthened me,
19 And said, O man *greatly beloved* **desired**,
fear **awe** not:
peace **shalom** be unto thee, be strong, yea, be strong.
And when he had *spoken* **worded** unto me,
I was strengthened, and said,
Let my *lord speak* **adoni word**;
for thou hast strengthened me.
20 Then said he,
Knowest thou wherefore I come unto thee?
and now *will* **shall** I return
to fight with the *prince* **governor** of Persia:
and when I am gone forth, *lo* **behold**,
the *prince* **governor** of *Grecia* **Yavan** shall come.
21 But I *will shew* **shall tell** thee
that which is *noted* **signified**
in the *scripture* **inscribing** of truth:
and there is none that holdeth with me in these *things*,
but *Michael* **Michah El** your *prince* **governor**.

The Sovereigns Of The North And The South

11 Also I
in the first year of *Darius* **Daryavesh** the *Mede* **Maday**,
even I, **I** stood to *confirm* **strengthen him**
and to *strengthen him* **be his stronghold**.
2 And now *will I shew* **shall I tell** thee the truth.
Behold,
there shall stand *up* yet three *kings* **sovereigns** in Persia;
and the fourth shall be
far richer **enriched in greater riches** than they all:
and by his strength through his riches
he shall *stir up* **waken** all
against the *realm* **sovereigndom** of *Grecia* **Yavan**.
3 And a mighty *king* **sovereign** shall stand *up*,
that shall *rule* **reign** with great *dominion* **reign**,
and *do* **work** according to his *will* **pleasure**.
4 And when he shall stand *up*,
his *kingdom* **sovereigndom** shall be broken,
and shall be *divided* **halved**
toward the four winds of *heaven* **the heavens**;
and not to his posterity,
nor according to his *dominion* **reign**
which he *ruled* **reigned**:
for his *kingdom* **sovereigndom**
shall be *plucked up* **uprooted**,
even for others beside those.
5 And the *king* **sovereign** of
the south shall be strong,
and *one* of his *princes* **governors**;
and he shall be strong above him,
and *have dominion* **reign**;
his *dominion* **reign** shall be a great *dominion* **reign**.
6 And in the end of years
they shall *join themselves together* **unite**;
and behold, Michah El, one of the head governors,
comes to help me;
and I remain there beside the sovereigns of Persia.
14 I come so that you discern
what befalls your people in the latter days:
for the vision is yet for days.
15 And he words such words to me,
and I give my face toward the earth, and I *am* mute:
16 and behold,
a likeness of the sons of humanity touches my lips:
and I open my mouth and word,
and say to him standing in front of me,
O my adoni, because of the vision,
my pangs turn on me and I retain no force.
17 For how can the servant of my adoni
word this with my adoni?
For as for me, at this time,
neither force stands in me,
yes, nor breath remains in me.
18 And as the visage of a human
comes again and touches me and strengthens me,
19 and says, O man desired,
awe not; shalom to you:
be strong; yes, be strong.
And when he words to me, I strengthen, and say,
My adoni, word;
for you strengthened me.
20 And he says, Know you why I come to you?
And now I return to fight with the governor of Persia:
and when I go, behold,
the governor of Yavan comes:
21 but I tell you
what is signified in the inscribing of truth:
and no one holds with me in these
except Michah El your governor.

The Sovereigns Of The North And The South

11 And I, in the first year of Daryavesh the Maday,

I stand to strengthen him and as his stronghold:
2 and now, I tell you the truth:
behold, three sovereigns still stand in Persia;
and the fourth enriches in greater riches than they all:
and by his strength and through his riches
he wakens all against the sovereigndom of Yavan:
3 and a mighty sovereign stands
who reigns with great reign;
and works according to his pleasure:
4 and he stands,
and his sovereigndom breaks in half
toward the four winds of the heavens:
and neither to his posterity
nor according to the reign he reigns:
for his sovereigndom uproots,
—and for others beside these.
5 And the sovereign of the south
—even his governors strengthen;
and he strengthens above him and reigns:
he reigns a great reign.
6 And in the end of years they unite;
for the *king's* **sovereign's** daughter of the south
shall come to the *king* **sovereign** of the north
to *make an agreement* **work a straightness**:
but she shall not retain the *power* **force** of the arm;
neither shall he stand, nor his arm:
but she shall be given up,
and they that brought her, and he that *begat* **birthed** her,
and he that strengthened her in these times.
7 But out of a branch of her roots
shall *one* stand *up* in his *estate* **station**,
which shall come with *an army* **the valiant**,
and shall enter into the *fortress* **stronghold**
of the *king* **sovereign** of the north,
and shall *deal* **work** against them, and shall prevail:
8 And shall also carry captives
into *Egypt* **Misrayim**
their *gods* **elohim**, with their *princes* **libations**,
and with their *precious vessels* **instruments of desire**
of silver and of gold;
and he shall *continue* **stand** more years
than the *king* **sovereign** of the north.
9 So the *king* **sovereign** of the south
shall come into his *kingdom* **sovereigndom**,
and shall return into his own *land* **soil**.
10 But his sons shall be *stirred up* **throttled**,
and shall *assemble* **gather**
a multitude of *great forces* **valiant**:
and **in coming,** *one* shall *certainly* come,
and overflow, and pass through:
then shall he return, and be *stirred up* **throttled**,
even to his *fortress* **stronghold**.
11 And the *king* **sovereign** of the south
shall be *moved with choler* **embittered**,
and shall come forth and fight with him,
even with the *king* **sovereign** of the north:
and he shall *set forth* **cause** a great multitude **to stand**;
but the multitude shall be given into his hand.
12 And when he hath *taken*
borne away the multitude,
his heart shall be lifted *up*;
and he shall *cast down many ten thousands* **fell myriads**:
but he shall not be strengthened *by it*.
13 For the *king* **sovereign** of the north shall return,
and shall *set forth* **stand** a multitude
greater than the former,
and **in coming,** shall *certainly* come
after certain **at the end of times, even** years
with a great *army* **valiant**
and with much *riches* **acquisitions**.
14 And in those times there shall many stand *up*
against the *king* **sovereign** of the south:
also the *robbers* **sons of tyrants** of thy people
shall *exalt* **lift** themselves to *establish* **stand** the vision;
but they shall *fall* **falter**.
15 So the *king* **sovereign** of the north shall come,
and *cast up* **pour** a *mount* **mound**,
and *take* **capture** the most *fenced* **fortified** cities:
and the arms of the south shall not withstand,
neither his chosen people,
neither shall there be any *strength* **force** to withstand.
16 But he that cometh against him
shall *do* **work** according to his own *will* **pleasure**,
and none shall stand *before him* **at his face**:
and he shall stand in the *glorious* land **of splendour**,
which by his hand shall be *consumed* **fully finished**.
17 He shall also set his face to enter
with the *strength* **power**
of his whole *kingdom* **sovereigndom**,
and *upright ones* **straight** with him;
thus shall he *do* **work**:
and he shall give him the daughter of women,
corrupting **to ruin** her:
but she shall not stand *on his side*, neither be for him.
18 After this
shall he *turn* **set** his face unto the *isles* **islands**,
and shall take many:
but a *prince* **commander** for his own behalf
shall cause *the* **his** reproach *offered by him*
to *cease* **shabbathize**;

without his own reproach
he shall cause it to turn upon him.
and a daughter of the sovereign of the south
comes to the sovereign of the north
to work a straightness:
and she retains not the force of the arm;
and neither stands he nor his arm:
and she *is* given
—she, and they who bring her
and he who birthed her,
and he who strengthened her in these times.
7 And from a branch of her roots
one who stands in his station
comes with the valiant
and enters into the stronghold
of the sovereign of the north;
and works against them and prevails:
8 and also carries captives into Misrayim
—their elohim with their libations
and with their instruments of desire
of silver and of gold:
and he stands more years
than the sovereign of the north:
9 and the sovereign of the south comes into his
sovereigndom, and returns to his own soil:
10 and his sons throttle themselves
and gather a multitude of valiant:
and in coming, they come
and overflow and pass through:
and he returns,
and they throttle themselves to his stronghold.
11 And the sovereign of the south embitters
and comes and fights him
with the sovereign of the north:
and he withstands a great multitude;
and the multitude *is* given into his hand.
12 And he bears away the multitude,
and his heart lifts;
and he fells myriads:
but he strengthens not.
13 For the sovereign of the north returns
and withstands a multitude greater than the former;
and in coming, comes at the end of times
—even years with a great valiant
and with much acquisitions.
14 And in those times
many withstand the sovereign of the south:
and the sons of tyrants of your people
lift themselves to withstand the vision;
and they falter.
15 And the sovereign of the north
comes and pours a mound
and captures the most fortified cities:
and neither the arms of the south withstand,
nor his chosen people,
neither is there any force to withstand:
16 and he who comes against him
works according to his own pleasure;
and no one stands at his face:
and he stands in the land of splendor,
fully finished by his hand.
17 And he sets his face to enter
with the power of his whole sovereigndom,
and with his straight *ones*;
thus he works:
and he gives him the daughter of women
to ruin her:
and neither she stands, nor he.
18 After this he sets his face to the islands,
and takes many:
and a commander
shabbathizes his reproach of himself
and turns his own reproach on him:
19 Then he shall turn his face
toward the *fort* **stronghold** of his own land:
but he shall *stumble* **falter** and fall, and not be found.
20 Then shall stand *up* in his *estate* **station**
a raiser of **an exactor who passeth** taxes
in the *glory* **majesty** of the *kingdom* **sovereigndom**:
but within *few days* **one day**
he shall be *destroyed* **broken**,
neither in *anger* **wrath**, nor in *battle* **war**.
21 And in his *estate* **station**
shall stand *up a vile person* **a despised**,
to whom they shall not give
the *honour* **majesty** of the *kingdom* **sovereigndom**:
but he shall come in *peaceably* **serenity**,
and *obtain* **hold** the *kingdom* **sovereigndom**
by *flatteries* **soothings**.
22 And with the arms of *a flood* **an overflowing**
shall they be *overflown* **overflowed**
from *before him* **his face**,
and shall be broken;
yea, also the *prince* **eminent** of the covenant.
23 And after *the league made with* **joining** him
he shall work deceitfully:
for he shall *come up* **ascend**,
and shall become *strong* **mighty**
with a small *people* **goyim**.
24 He shall enter *peaceably* **in serenity**

even upon the *fattest places* **fatness**
of the *province* **jurisdiction**;
and he shall *do* **work** that
which his fathers have not *done* **worked**,
nor his fathers' fathers;
he shall scatter among them
the *prey* **plunder**, and spoil, and *riches* **acquisitions**:
yea, and he shall
forecast **fabricate** his *devices* **fabrications**
against the *strong holds* **fortresses**, even for a time.
25 And he shall *stir up* **waken**
his *power* **force** and his *courage* **heart**
against the *king* **sovereign** of the south
with a great *army* **valiant**;
and the *king* **sovereign** of the south
shall be *stirred up* **throttled** to *battle* **war**
with a *very* **mighty** great and mighty *army* **valiant**;
but he shall not stand:
for they shall *forecast devices* **fabricate fabrications**
against him.
26 Yea,
they that feed of *the portion of his meat* **his delicacies**
shall *destroy* **break** him,
and his *army* **valiant** shall overflow:
and many shall fall down *slain* **pierced**.
27 And both of these *kings'* **sovereign's** hearts
shall be to *do mischief* **vilify**,
and they shall *speak* **word** lies at one table;
but it shall not prosper:
for yet the end shall be at the *time appointed* **season**.
28 Then shall he return into his land
with great *riches* **acquisitions**;
and his heart shall be against the holy covenant;
and he shall *do exploits* **work**,
and return to his own land.
29 At the *time appointed* **season** he shall return,
and come toward the south;
but it shall not be as the former, or as the latter.
30 For the ships of *Chittim*
Kittim shall come against him:
therefore he shall be *grieved* **dejected**, and return,
and *have indignation* **rage** against the holy covenant:
so shall he *do* **work**;
he shall even return,
and *have intelligence* **discern** with them
that forsake the holy covenant.
31 And arms shall stand on his part,
and they shall *pollute* **profane** the *sanctuary* **holies**
of *strength* **the stronghold**,
and shall *take away* **turn aside**
the *daily sacrifice* **continual**,
and they shall *place* **give** the abomination
that *maketh desolate* **desolateth**.

19 and he turns his face
toward the stronghold of his own land:
and he falters and falls, and they find him not.
20 And in his station
stands *one* who passes an exactor of taxes
in the majesty of the sovereigndom:
and within one day he *is* broken
—neither in wrath nor in war.
21 And in his station stands *one*—despised
to whom they give not
the majesty of the sovereigndom:
and he comes in serenity,
and holds the sovereigndom by soothings.
22 And with the arms of an overflowing
they overflow at his face, and break; yes,
and also the eminent of the covenant.
23 And after joining him, he works deceitfully:
for he ascends mightily with a small goyim.
24 He enters in serenity
even on the fatness of the jurisdiction;
and he works what neither his fathers worked,
nor the fathers of his fathers;
and he scatters
the plunder and spoil and acquisitions among them:
yes, and he fabricates his fabrications
against the fortresses—even for a time:
25 and he wakens his force and his heart
against the sovereign of the south
with a great valiant;
and the sovereign of the south throttles to war
with a mighty great and mighty valiant;
and he withstands not:
for they fabricate fabrications against him:
26 yes, they who feed of his delicacies, break him;
and his valiant overflow and many fall pierced.
27 And the hearts of both of these sovereign vilify;
and at one table they word lies;
and it prospers not:
for yet the end *is* in season.
28 And he returns to his land
with great acquisitions
and with his heart against the holy covenant;
and he works and returns to his own land:
29 he returns in season
and comes toward the south;
and not as in the former or as in the latter:
30 for the ships of Kittim come against him:

so he *is* dejected and returns;
and rages against the holy covenant:
thus he works; and returns;
and discerns with them
concerning them who forsake the holy covenant.
31 And arms stand up for him
and profane the holies of the stronghold
and turn aside the continual;
and they give the abomination that desolates.
32 And such as *do wickedly* **declare wicked**
against the covenant
shall he *corrupt* **profane** by *flatteries* **soothings**:
but the people that *do* know their *God* **Elohim**
shall *be strong* **strengthen**, and *do exploits* **work**.
33 And they that *understand* **comprehend**
among **of** the people
shall *instruct many* **have many discern**:
yet they shall *fall* **falter** by the sword, and by flame,
by captivity, and by *spoil* **plunder**, *many* days.
34 *Now* when they shall *fall* **falter**,
they shall be *holpen* **helped** with a little help:
but many shall *cleave* **join** to them
with *flatteries* **soothings**.
35 And *some* of them *of*
understanding **that comprehend**
shall *fall* **falter**,
to *try* **refine** them, and to purge,
and to *make* **whiten** them *white*,
even to the time of the end:
because it is yet for a *time appointed* **season**.
36 And the *king* **sovereign**
shall *do* **work** according to his *will* **pleasure**;
and he shall exalt himself,
and *magnify* **greaten** himself above every *god* **el**,
and shall *speak marvellous things* **word marvels**
against *the God* **El** of *Gods* **Elohim**,
and shall prosper
till the *indignation* **rage** be *accomplished* **concluded**:
for that that is *determined* **appointed**
shall be *done* **worked**.
37 Neither shall he *regard* **discern**
the *God* **Elohim** of his fathers, nor the desire of women,
nor *regard* **discern** any *god* **elohah**:
for he shall *magnify* **greaten** himself above all.
38 But in his *estate* **station**
shall he honour the *God* **Elohah** of *forces* **strongholds**
and *a god* **an elohah** whom his fathers knew not
shall he honour with gold, and silver,
and with *precious* **esteemed** stones,
and *pleasant things* **desires**.
39 Thus shall he *do* **work**
in the *most strong holds* **fortresses of strongholds**
with a strange *god* **elohah**,
whom he shall *acknowledge* **recognize**
and *increase* **abound** with *glory* **honour**:
and he shall cause them to *rule* **reign** over many,
and shall *divide* **allot** the *land* **soil** for *gain* **price**.
40 And at the time of the end
shall the *king* **sovereign** of the south *push at* **butt** him:
and the *king* **sovereign** of the north shall come
against him like a whirlwind **and whirl him away**,
with chariots, and with *horsemen* **cavalry**,
and with many ships;
and he shall come into the *countries* **lands**,
and shall overflow and pass over.
41 He shall enter also
into the *glorious* land **of splendour**,
and many *countries* shall *be overthrown* **falter**:
but these shall escape out of his hand,
even Edom, and Moab,
and the *chief* **first** of the *children* **sons** of Ammon.
42 He shall *stretch forth* **spread** his hand also
upon the *countries* **lands**:
and the land of *Egypt* **Misrayim** shall not escape.
43 But he shall *have power* **reign**
over the **hidden** treasures of gold and of silver,
and over all the *precious things*
desires of *Egypt* **Misrayim**:
and the *Libyans* **Lubiym** and the *Ethiopians* **Kushiym**
shall be at his *steps* **paces**.
44 But *tidings* **reports**
out of the *east* **rising** and out of the north
shall *trouble* **terrify** him:
therefore he shall go forth with great fury
to *destroy* **desolate**,
and *utterly to make away* **to devote** many.
45 And he shall plant
the *tabernacles* **tents** of his *palace*
pavilion between the seas
in the *glorious* holy mountain **of splendour**;
yet he shall come to his end, and none shall help him.
32 And they who declare wicked the covenant
he profanes by soothings:
and the people who know their Elohim
strengthen and work:
33 and of the people who comprehend,
many discern:
yet they falter by the sword and by the flame
by captivity and by plunder—days:
34 and in their faltering,

are helped with a little help:
and many join them with soothings.
35 And they who comprehend, falter
in order to refine them and to purge
and to whiten them to the time of the end:
because it *is* yet for a season.
36 And the sovereign works
according to his pleasure;
and exalts himself
and greatens himself above every el
and words marvels against the El of elohim,
and prospers until the rage concludes:
until that appointed is worked.
37 He neither discerns the Elohim of his fathers
nor the desire of women;
nor discerns any elohah:
for he greatens himself above all.
38 And in his station
he honors the elohah of strongholds
—an elohah whom his fathers knew not
he honors with gold and silver
and with esteemed stones and desires:
39 thus he works in the fortresses of strongholds
with a strange elohah
—whom he recognizes and abounds with honor:
and he has them reign over many
and allots the soil for a price.
40 And at the time of the end
the sovereign of the south butts him:
and the sovereign of the north
comes and whirls him away
with chariots and with cavalry and with many ships;
and he comes into the lands
and overflows and passes over:
41 and he enters into the land of splendor
and many falter:
and these escape from his hand:
Edom and Moab and the first of the sons of Ammon:
42 and he spreads his hand on the lands:
and the land of Misrayim escapes not:
43 and he reigns
over the hidden treasures of gold and of silver
and over all the desires of Misrayim:
with the Lubiym and the Kushiym at his paces.
44 And the reports from the
rising and from the north
terrify him:
and he goes with great fury
to desolate and to devote many:
45 and he plants the tents of his pavilion
between the seas
in the holy mountain of splendor;
and he comes to his end and no one helps him.

THE TIME OF TRIBULATION

12 And at that time shall
Michael **Michah El** stand up,
the great *prince* **governor**
which standeth for the *children* **sons** of thy people:
and there shall be a time of *trouble* **tribulation**,
such as never was since there was a *nation* **goyim**
even to that same time:
and at that time thy people shall *be delivered* **escape**,
every one that shall be found
written **inscribed** in the *book* **scroll**.

THE RESURRECTION

2 And **the** many *of them*
that sleep in the *dust of the earth*
soil of dust shall awake,
some to *everlasting* **eternal** life,
and some to *shame* **reproach**
and *everlasting* **eternal** contempt.
3 And they that *be wise* **comprehend**
shall *shine* **have brilliancy**
as the *brightness* **brilliance** of the *firmament* **expanse**;
and they that *turn* **justify** many *to righteousness*
as the stars *for ever and ever* **eternally and eternally**.

THE SCROLL OF DANI EL SEALED

cp Apocalypse 22:10

4 But thou, O *Daniel* **Dani El**,
shut up the words, and seal the *book* **scroll**,
even to the time of the end:
many shall *run to and fro* **flit**,
and knowledge shall *be increased* **abound**.
5 Then I *Daniel looked* **Dani El saw**, and, behold,
there stood other two,
the one on this side of the *bank* **lip** of the river,
and the *other* **one** on that side of the *bank* **lip** of the river.
6 And *one* said to the man
clothed **enrobed** in linen,
which was *upon* **above** the waters of the
river, *How long* **Until when** shall it be
to the end of these *wonders* **marvels**?
7 And I heard the man *clothed* **enrobed** in linen,
which was *upon* **above** the waters of the river,
when he *held* **lifted** *up* his right *hand* and his left *hand*
unto *heaven* **the heavens**,

and *sware* **oathed** by him that liveth *for ever* **eternally**
that it shall be
for a *time* **season**, *times* **seasons**, and an half;
and when he shall have *accomplished* **finished**
to scatter the *power* **hand** of the holy people,
all these *things* shall be finished.
8 And I heard, but I *understood* **discerned** not:
then said I, O my *Lord* **Adonay**,
what shall be the end of these *things*?
9 And he said, Go thy way, *Daniel* **Dani El**:
for the words are closed up and sealed
till the time of the end.
10 Many shall be purified,
and *made white* **whitened**, and *tried* **refined**;
but the wicked shall do wickedly:
and none of the wicked shall *understand* **discern**;
but the *wise* **enwisened**
shall *understand* **comprehendingly discern**.
11 And from the time that the
daily sacrifice **continual**
shall be *taken away* **turned aside**,
and the abomination that *maketh desolate* **desolateth**
set up **be given**,
there shall be a thousand two hundred and ninety days.
12 *Blessed* **Blithesome** is he that waiteth,
and *cometh to* **toucheth**
the thousand three hundred and five and thirty days.
13 But go thou thy way till the end be:
for thou shalt rest,
and stand in thy *lot* **pebble** at the end of the days.

THE TIME OF TRIBULATION

12 And at that time
Michah El the great governor stands
—who stands for the sons of your people:
and there becomes a time of tribulation,
such as never became since there *was* a goyim
until that time:
and at that time your people escape
—every one found inscribed in the scroll.

THE RESURRECTION

2 And the many sleeping in the soil of dust awake
—some to eternal life;
and some to reproach and eternal contempt:
3 and they who comprehend
with brilliance as the brilliance of the expanse;
and they who justify many
as the stars eternally and eternally.

THE SCROLL OF DANI EL SEALED

cp Apocalypse 22:10

4 And you, O Dani El,
shut the words and seal the scroll
to the time of the end
—many flit and knowledge abounds.
5 Then I, Dani El see, and behold,
two others stand there
—the one on this side of the lip of the river and
the one on that side of the lip of the river:
6 and he says to the man enrobed in linen
above the waters of the river,
Until when end these marvels?
7 And I hear the man enrobed in linen
above the waters of the river;
and he lifts his right and his left to the heavens
and oaths by him who lives eternally,
For a season, seasons, and an half
—at the finishing
of the scattering of the hand of the holy people
all these finish.
8 And I hear, but I discern not:
and I say, O my Adonay,
what *is* the end of these?
9 And he says, Go your way, Dani El:
for the words are closed and sealed
until the time of the end:
10 many purify themselves and whiten and refine;
and the wicked *do* wickedly:
and no one of the wicked discerns;
and the enwisened discern comprehendingly.
11 And from the time they turn aside the continual
and give the abomination that desolates
is a thousand two hundred and ninety days.
12 Blithesome—he who awaits
and touches
the thousand three hundred and thirty—five days.
13 And you, go your way until the end:
and then you rest
and stand in your pebble at the end of the days.

The Word Of Yah Veh To Hoshea

1 The word of *the LORD* **Yah Veh**
that came unto Hosea **being to Hoshea**, the son of Beeri,
in the days of *Uzziah* **Uzzi Yah**, *Jotham* **Yah Tham**,
Ahaz **Ach Az**, and *Hesekiah* **Yechizqi Yah**,
kings **sovereigns** of *Judah* **Yah Hudah**,
and in the days of *Jeroboam* **Yarob Am**
the son of *Joash* **Yah Ash**,
king **sovereign** of *Israel* **Yisra El**.

Hoshea Marries Gomer

2 The beginning
of the word of *the LORD* **Yah Veh** by *Hosea* **Hoshea**.
And *the LORD* **Yah Veh** said to *Hosea* **Hoshea**,
Go, take unto thee a *wife* **woman** of whoredoms
and children of whoredoms:
for the land hath *committed great whoredom* **whored**,
departing from *the LORD* **Yah Veh**.

Gomer Births Yizre El

3 So he went and took Gomer
the daughter of Diblaim;
which conceived, and *bare* **birthed** him a son.
4 And *the LORD* **Yah Veh** said unto him,
Call his name *Jezreel* **Yizre El**;
for yet a little *while*,
and I *will avenge* **shall visit** the blood of *Jezreel* **Yizre El**
upon the house of *Jehu* **Yah Hu**,
and *will* **shall** cause to *cease* **shabbathize**
the *kingdom* **sovereigndom** of the
house of *Israel* **Yisra El**.
5 And **so be** it *shall come to pass* at that day,
that I *will* **shall** break the bow of *Israel* **Yisra El**
in the valley of *Jezreel* **Yizre El**.

Gomer Births Lo Ruchamah

6 And she conceived again,
and *bare* **birthed** a daughter.
And *God* **he** said unto him,
Call her name *Lo—ruhamah* **Lo Ruchamah**:
for *I will no more have* **shall not add to** mercy *upon*
the house of *Israel* **Yisra El**;
but **in bearing,** I *will* **shall** *utterly take* bear them away.
7 But I *will have* **shall** mercy
upon the house of *Judah* **Yah Hudah**,
and *will* **shall** save them
by *the LORD* **Yah Veh** their *God* **Elohim**,
and *will* **shall** not save them by bow, nor by sword,
nor by *battle* **war**, by horses, nor by *horsemen* **cavalry**.

Gomer Births Lo Ammi

8 *Now* when she had weaned
Lo—ruhamah **Lo Ruchamah**,
she conceived, and *bare* **birthed** a son.
9 Then said *God* **He**,
Call his name *Loammi* **Lo Ammi**:
for ye are not my people,
and I *will* **shall** not be *your God* **yours**.

From Lo Ammi To Sons Of El

10 Yet the number of the *children*
sons of *Israel* **Yisra El**
shall be as the sand of the sea,
which cannot be measured nor *numbered* **scribed**;
and **so be** it *shall come to pass*,
that in the place where it was said unto them,
Ye are not my people **Lo Ammi**,
there it shall be said unto them,
Ye are the sons of the living *God* **El**.
11 Then shall the *children*
sons of *Judah* **Yah Hudah**
and the *children* **sons** of *Israel* **Yisra El**
be gathered together,
and *appoint* **set** themselves one head,
and they shall *come up* **ascend** out of the land:
for great shall be the day of *Jezreel* **Yizre El**.

The Judgment Of Yah Veh

2 Say ye unto your brethren, Ammi/**My people**;
and to your sisters, Ruhamah/**Mercied**.
2 Plead with your mother, plead:
for she is not my *wife* **woman**,
neither am I her *husband* **man**:
let her *therefore put away* **turn aside** her whoredoms
out of her sight **from her face**,
and her adulteries from between her breasts;
3 Lest I strip her naked,
and set her as in the day that she was *born* **birthed**,
and *make* **set** her as a wilderness,
and set her like a *dry* **parched** land,
and *slay* **deathify** her with thirst.

The Word Of Yah Veh To Hoshea

1 The word of Yah Veh
being to Hoshea the son of Beeri
in the days of
Uzzi Yah, Yah Tham, Ach Az and Yechizqi Yah,
sovereigns of Yah Hudah,
and in the days of Yarob Am
the son of Yah Ash sovereign of Yisra El.

HOSHEA MARRIES GOMER

2 The beginning of the word
of Yah Veh by Hoshea:
And Yah Veh says to Hoshea,
Go, take to yourself a woman of whoredoms
and children of whoredoms:
for the land whores from Yah Veh.

GOMER BIRTHS YIZRE EL

3 And he goes
and takes Gomer the daughter of Diblaim
who conceives and births him a son.
4 And Yah Veh says to him,
Call his name Yizre El/El Seeds;
for yet a little,
and I visit the blood of Yizre El
on the house of Yah Hu,
and shabbathize
the sovereigndom of the house of Yisra El.
5 And so be it, at that day,
I break the bow of Yisra El in the valley of Yizre El.

GOMER BIRTHS LO RUCHAMAH

6 And she conceives again, and births a daughter:
and he says to him,
Call her name Lo Ruchamah/Not Mercied:
for I add not to mercy the house of Yisra El;
for in bearing, I bear them away:
7 and I mercy the house of Yah Hudah,
and save them by Yah Veh their Elohim;
and save them not by bow, or by sword,
or by war, by horses, or by cavalry.

GOMER BIRTHS LO AMMI

8 And she weans Lo Ruchamah
and conceives and births a son.
9 Then he says,
Call his name Lo Ammi/Not My People:
for you are not my people,
and I am not yours.

FROM LO AMMI TO SONS OF EL

10 And the number of the sons of Yisra El
is as the sand of the sea
—neither measured nor scribed:
and so be it,
in the place where it says to them, Lo Ammi
there it says to them,
You are the sons of the living El:
11 and the sons of Yah Hudah
and the sons of Yisra El
gather together,
and set themselves one head,
and they ascend from the land:
for great *is* the day of Yizre El.

THE JUDGMENT OF YAH VEH

2 Say to your brothers, Ammi/My people;
and to your sisters, Ruchamah/Mercied.
2 Plead with your mother—plead:
for she *is* neither my woman nor I her man:
have her turn aside her whoredoms from her face
and her adulteries from between her breasts;
3 lest I strip her naked
and set her as in the day she was birthed;
and set her as a wilderness
and set her as a parched land
and deathify her with thirst:
4 And I *will* **shall** not *have*
mercy *upon* her *children* **sons**;
for they be the *children* **sons** of whoredoms.
5 For their mother hath *played the harlot* **whored**:
she that conceived them hath done shamefully:
for she said, I *will* **shall** go after my lovers,
that give me my bread and my water,
my wool and my flax, mine oil and my drink.
6 Therefore, behold,
I *will* **shall** hedge up thy way with thorns,
and *make* **wall** a wall, that she shall not find her paths.
7 And she shall *follow after* **pursue** her lovers,
but she shall not overtake them;
and she shall seek them,
but shall not find them:
then shall she say,
I *will* **shall** go and return to my first *husband* **man**;
for then was it better with me than *now* **at this time**.
8 For she did not know that I gave her *corn* **crop**,
and *wine* **juice**, and oil,
and *multiplied* **abounded** her silver and gold,
which they *prepared* **worked** for Baal.
9 Therefore *will* **shall** I return,
and take away my *corn* **crop** in the time *thereof*,
and my *wine* **juice** in the season *thereof*,
and *will recover* **shall rescue** my wool and my flax
given to cover her nakedness.
10 And now
will **shall** I *discover* **expose** her *lewdness* **vulva**
in the *sight* **eyes** of her lovers,
and *none* **no man**

shall *deliver* **rescue** her out of mine hand.
11 I *will* **shall** also
cause all her *mirth* **joy** to *cease* **shabbathize**,
her *feast days* **celebrations**, her new moons,
and her *sabbaths* **shabbaths**,
and all her *solemn feasts* **seasons**.
12 And I *will destroy* **shall desolate**
her vines and her fig trees,
whereof she hath said,
These are my *rewards* **payoffs**
that my lovers have given me:
and I *will make* **shall set** them a forest,
and the *beasts* **live beings** of the field shall eat them.
13 And I *will* **shall** visit upon
her the days of Baalim,
wherein she *burned incense* **incensed** to them,
and she *decked* **adorned** herself
with her *earrings* **noserings** and her *jewels* **ornaments**,
and she went after her lovers, and forgat me,
saith the LORD **an oracle of Yah Veh**.

THE RESTORATION OF YAH VEH

14 Therefore, behold, I *will allure* **shall entice** her,
and *bring* **carry** her into the wilderness,
and *speak* **word** comfortably unto her.
15 And I *will* **shall** give her
her vineyards from thence,
and *the valley of Achor* **Gaymek Achor**
for *a door* **an opening** of hope:
and she shall *sing* **answer** there,
as in the days of her youth,
and as in the day when she *came up* **ascended**
out of the land of *Egypt* **Misrayim**.
16 And it shall be at that day,
saith the LORD **an oracle of Yah Veh**,
that thou shalt call me Ishi/**My man**;
and shalt call me no more Baali/**My Baal**.
17 For I *will take away* **shall turn aside**
the names of Baalim out of her mouth,
and they shall no more be remembered by their name.
18 And in that day
will I make **shall I cut** a covenant for them
with the *beasts* **live beings** of the field
and with the *fowls* **flyers** of *heaven* **the heavens**,
and with the *creeping things* **creepers** of the *ground* **soil**:
and I *will* **shall** break the bow
and the sword and the *battle* **war** out of the earth,
and *will make* **shall cause** them
to lie down *safely* **confidently**.
19 And I *will* **shall** betroth thee unto me
for ever **eternally**;
yea, I *will* **shall** betroth thee unto me
4 and I not mercy her sons;
for they *are* the sons of whoredoms:
5 for their mother whores:
she who conceived them shames
—for she says, I go after my lovers
who give me my bread and my water;
my wool and my flax; my oil and my drink:
6 so behold,
I hedge your way with thorns,
and wall a wall that she not find her paths:
7 and she pursues her lovers
and overtakes them not;
and she seeks them
and finds them not.
And she says, I go and return to my first man;
for it *was* better with me than at this time.
8 —and she knows not
that I gave her crop and juice and oil;
and abounded her silver and gold
which they worked for Baal.
9 So I return and take away my crop in time
and my juice in season;
and rescue my wool and my flax
which covers her nakedness.
10 And now I expose her vulva
in the eyes of her lovers,
and no man rescues her from my hand.
11 I also shabbathize all her joy
—her celebrations, her new moons,
and her shabbaths, and all her seasons:
12 and I desolate her vines and her fig trees
whereof she says,
These are my payoffs my lovers give me:
and I set them a forest
and the live beings of the field eat them:
13 and I visit on her the days of Baalim,
wherein she incenses to them;
and adorns herself
with her noserings and her ornaments,
and goes after her lovers, and forgets me
—an oracle of Yah Veh.

THE RESTORATION OF YAH VEH

14 So behold, I entice her;
and carry her into the wilderness
and word comfortably to her:
15 and I give her her vineyards from there
and Gaymek Achor for an opening of hope:

and there she answers
as in the days of her youth
—as in the day she ascended
from the land of Misrayim.
16 And so be it, at that day,
—an oracle of Yah Veh
that you call me Ishi/My Man;
and call me no more Baali/My Baal.
17 For I turn aside
the names of Baalim from her mouth,
—no more remembered by name:
18 and in that day,
I cut a covenant for them
with the live beings of the field
and with the flyers of the heavens
and with the creepers of the soil:
and I break the bow and the sword
and the war from the earth
and lay them down confidently:
19 and I betroth you to me eternally;
yes, I betroth you to me
in *righteousness* **justness**, and in judgment,
and in *lovingkindness* **mercy**, and in mercies.
20 I *will* **shall** even betroth thee unto me
in *faithfulness* **trustworthiness**:
and thou shalt know *the LORD* **Yah Veh**.
21 And **so be** it *shall come to pass*, in that day,
I *will hear* **shall answer**,
saith the LORD **an oracle of Yah Veh**,
I *will hear* **shall answer** the heavens,
and they shall *hear* **answer** the earth;
22 And the earth shall *hear* **answer** the *corn* **crop**,
and the *wine* **juice**, and the oil;
and they shall *hear Jezreel* **answer Yizre El**.
23 And I *will sow* **shall seed**
her unto me in the earth;
and I *will have mercy* **shall Mercy/Ruchamah**
upon her that had not obtained mercy
Not Mercied/Lo Ruchamah;
and I *will* **shall** say to
them which were not my people
Not My People/Lo Ammi,
Thou art my people **My People/Ammi**;
and they shall say, *Thou art my God* **My Elohim**.

The Reconciliation Of Hoshea

3 Then said *the LORD* **Yah Veh** unto me, Go yet,
love a woman beloved of her friend, yet an adulteress,
according to the love of *the LORD* **Yah Veh**
toward the *children* **sons** of *Israel* **Yisra El**,
who *look to* **face** other *gods* **elohim**,
and love *flagons* **cakes** of *wine* **grapes**.
2 So I bought her to me for fifteen *pieces of* silver,
and *for an homer* **a chomer** of barley,
and *an half homer* **a lethech** of barley:
3 And I said unto her,
Thou shalt *abide* **settle** for me many days;
thou shalt not *play the harlot* **whore**,
and thou shalt not be for another man:
so *will* **shall** I also be for thee.
4 For the *children* **sons** of *Israel* **Yisra El**
shall *abide* **settle** many days
without a king **with no sovereign**,
and *without a prince* **no governor**,
and without a **no** sacrifice,
and without an image **no monolith**,
and without an **no** ephod,
and without **no** teraphim:
5 Afterward
shall the *children* **sons** of *Israel* **Yisra El** return,
and seek *the LORD* **Yah Veh** their *God* **Elohim**,
and David their *king* **sovereign**;
and shall fear *the LORD* **Yah Veh** and his goodness
in the latter days.

The Controversy Of Yah Veh

4 Hear the word of *the LORD* **Yah Veh**,
ye *children* **sons** of *Israel* **Yisra El**:
for *the LORD* **Yah Veh** hath a controversy
with the *inhabitants* **settlers** of the land,
because there is no truth, nor mercy,
nor knowledge of *God* **Elohim** in the land.
2 By *swearing* **oathing**, and lying, and *killing* **murder**,
and stealing, and *committing adultery* **adulterizing**,
they *break out* **separate**, and blood toucheth blood.
3 Therefore shall the land mourn,
and every one that *dwelleth* **settleth** therein
shall languish,
with the *beasts* **live beings** of the field,
and with the *fowls* **flyers** of *heaven* **the heavens**;
yea, the fishes of the sea also
shall be *taken away* **gathered**.
4 Yet let no man strive, nor reprove *another* **man**:
for thy people are as they that strive with the priest.
5 Therefore shalt thou *fall* **falter** in the day,
and the prophet also
shall *fall* **falter** with thee in the night,
and I *will destroy* **shall sever** thy mother.
6 My people are *destroyed*
severed for lack of knowledge:

because thou hast *despised* **spurned** knowledge,
I *will* **shall** also *reject* **spurn** thee,
that thou shalt be no priest to me:
seeing thou hast forgotten the *law*
torah of thy *God* **Elohim**,
in justness and in judgment;
and in mercy and in mercies:
20 and betroth you to me in trustworthiness:
and you know Yah Veh:
21 and so be it, in that day, I answer
—an oracle of Yah Veh—I answer the
heavens and they answer the earth;
22 and the earth answers the crop
and the juice and the oil; and they answer Yizre El:
23 and I seed her to me in the earth;
and I have Mercy/Ruchamah
on Not Mercied/Lo Ruchamah;
and to Not My People/Lo Ammi,
I say My People/Ammi;
and they say, My Elohim.

THE RECONCILIATION OF HOSHEA

3 Then Yah Veh says to me,
Go again; love a woman beloved of her friend,
and an adulteress,
according to the love of Yah Veh
toward the sons of Yisra El,
who face other elohim and love cakes of grapes.
2 So I buy her for myself for fifteen silver
and a chomer of barley and a lethech of barley:
3 and I say to her,
You, settle for me many days;
neither whore,
nor become for another man:
and thus I also for you.
4 The sons of Yisra El settle for many days
with no sovereign and no governor;
no sacrifice, no monolith,
no ephod, no teraphim:
5 afterward the sons of Yisra El return
and seek Yah Veh their Elohim
and David their sovereign;
and fear Yah Veh and his goodness in the latter days.

THE CONTROVERSY OF YAH VEH

4 Hear the word of Yah Veh,
you sons of Yisra El:
because of a controversy of Yah Veh
with the settlers of the land;
because there is neither truth nor mercy
nor knowledge of Elohim in the land:
2 oathing and lying and murder
and stealing and adulterizing separate;
and blood touches blood.
3 So the land mourns
and every one settling therein languishes
with the live beings of the field
and with the flyers of the heavens;
yes, the fishes of the sea *are* gathered:
4 yet neither strive with man nor reprove man:
for your people are as they who strive with the priest.
5 And you falter in the day
and the prophet also falters with you in the night;
and I sever your mother.
6 My people *are* severed for lack of knowledge:
because you spurn knowledge,
I also spurn you from priesting to me:
seeing you forget the torah of your Elohim,
I *will* **shall** also forget thy *children* **sons**.
7 *As they were increased*
According to their abundance,
so they sinned against me:
therefore *will* **shall** I change their *glory* **honour**
into *shame* **abasement**.
8 They eat *up* the sin of my people,
and they *set* **lift** their *heart* **soul**
on their *iniquity* **perversity**.
9 And there shall be, like people, like priest:
and I *will punish* **shall visit upon** them for their ways,
and *reward them* **return** their *doings* **exploits**.
10 For they shall eat,
and not *have enough* **be satisfied**:
they shall *commit whoredom* **whore**,
and shall not *increase* **break forth**:
because they have *left off* **forsaken**
to *take heed to the LORD* **guard unto Yah Veh**.
11 Whoredom and wine and *new wine* **juice**
take away the heart.
12 My people ask *counsel* at their *stocks* **trees**,
and their staff *declareth* **telleth** unto them:
for the spirit of whoredoms hath
caused them to *err* **stray**,
and they have *gone a whoring* **whored**
from under their *God* **Elohim**.
13 They sacrifice upon the tops of the mountains,
and *burn* incense upon the hills,
under oaks and poplars and *elms* **terebinth**,
because the shadow *thereof* is good:

therefore your daughters shall *commit whoredom* **whore,**
and your *spouses* **brides**
shall *commit adultery* **adulterize.**
14 I *will* **shall** not *punish* **visit upon** your daughters
when they *commit whoredom* **whore,**
nor your *spouses* **brides**
when they *commit adultery* **adulterize:**
for themselves are separated with whores,
and they sacrifice with *harlots* **hallowed whores:**
therefore the people that *doth* **discerneth** not *understand*
shall fall.
15 Though thou, *Israel* **Yisra**
El, *play the harlot* **whoreth,**
yet let not *Judah offend* **Yah Hudah become guilty;**
and come not ye unto Gilgal,
neither *go ye up to Bethaven* **ascend ye to Beth Aven,**
nor *swear* **oath,** *The LORD* **Yah Veh** liveth.
16 For *Israel slideth back* **Yisra El rebelleth**
as a *backsliding* **revolting** heifer:
now *the LORD will feed* **Yah Veh shall tend** them
as a lamb in *a large place* **an expanse.**
17 *Ephraim* **Ephrayim** is joined to idols:
let **leave** him alone.
18 Their *drink* **potion** is *sour* **turned:**
they have *committed whoredom* **whored** continually:
her *rulers* **bucklers** with *shame* **abasement** do love,
Give ye.
19 The wind hath bound her up in her wings,
and they shall be *ashamed* **shamed**
because of their sacrifices.

THE JUDGMENT OF YAH VEH AGAINST YISRA EL

5 Hear ye this, O priests;
and hearken, ye house of *Israel* **Yisra El;**
and *give ye ear* **hearken,** O house of the *king* **sovereign;**
for judgment is toward you,
because ye have been a snare on *Mizpah* **Mispeh,**
and a net spread upon Tabor.
2 And the *revolters* **deviates**
are profound to make **have deepened to** slaughter,
though I have been a *rebuker* **discipliner** of them all.
3 I know *Ephraim* **Ephrayim,**
and *Israel* **Yisra El** is not *hid* **concealed** from me:
for *now,* O *Ephraim* **Ephrayim,**
thou *committest whoredom* **whorest,**
and *Israel* **Yisra El** *is defiled* **fouleth.**
4 They *will* **shall** not *frame*
give their *doings* **exploits**
to turn unto their *God* **Elohim:**
for the spirit of whoredoms is in the midst of them,
and they have not known *the LORD* **Yah Veh.**
5 And the *pride* **pomp** of *Israel* **Yisra El**
doth testify **answereth** to his face:
I also forget your sons.
7 According to their abundance,
thus they sin against me:
so I change their honor into abasement.
8 They eat the sin of my people,
and they lift their soul on their perversity:
9 and so be it, as people, as priest:
and I visit on them for their ways,
and return their exploits.
10 For they eat, and satisfy not:
they whore, and not break forth:
because they forsake to guard to Yah Veh.
11 Whoredom and wine and juice
take away the heart:
12 my people ask at their trees,
and their staff tells them:
for the spirit of whoredoms strays them
and they whore from under their Elohim:
13 they sacrifice on the mountain tops
and incense on the hills;
under oaks and poplars and terebinth
because the shadow is good:
so your daughters whore
and your brides adulterize.
14 I neither visit on your daughters
when they whore;
nor your brides
when they adulterize:
for they separate with whores
and they sacrifice with hallowed whores:
a people who discerns not, falls.
15 Though you, Yisra El, whore,
and you, O Yah Hudah,
neither guilt nor come to Gilgal;
neither ascend to Beth Aven
nor oath, Yah Veh lives.
16 For Yisra El rebels as a revolting heifer;
now Yah Veh tends them as a lamb in an expanse:
17 Ephrayim joins with idols; leave him alone:
18 their potion turns; they whore continually:
her bucklers love abasement:
19 the wind binds her in her wings,
and they shame because of their sacrifices.

THE JUDGMENT OF YAH VEH AGAINST YISRA EL

5 Hear this, O priests;
and hearken, you house of Yisra El;
and hearken, O house of the sovereign:
for judgment is toward you
because you become a snare on Mispeh,
and a net spread over Tabor:
2 and the deviates deepen to slaughter,
and I discipline them all.
3 I know Ephrayim,
and Yisra El is not concealed from me:
for you, O Ephrayim, whore
and Yisra El fouls:
4 they give not their exploits
to return to their Elohim:
for the spirit of whoredoms is midst them
and they know not Yah Veh:
5 and the pomp of Yisra El answers to his face:
therefore shall *Israel* **Yisra El** and *Ephraim* **Ephrayim**
fall **falter** in their *iniquity* **perversity**;
Judah **Yah Hudah** also shall *fall* **falter** with them.
6 They shall go with their
flocks and with their herds
to seek *the LORD* **Yah Veh**;
but they shall not find *him*;
he hath withdrawn himself from them.
7 They have dealt *treacherously* **covertly**
against *the LORD* **Yah Veh**:
for they have *begotten* **birthed** strange *children* **sons**:
now shall a month *devour* **consume** them
with their *portions* **allotments**.
8 *Blow* **Blast** ye the *cornet*
shophar in *Gibeah* **Gibah**,
and the trumpet in Ramah:
cry aloud **shout** at *Bethaven* **the house of mischief**,
after thee, O *Benjamin* **Ben Yamin**.
9 *Ephraim* **Ephrayim** shall be desolate
in the day of rebuke:
among the *tribes* **scions** of *Israel* **Yisra El**
have I made known
that which shall *surely* be **trustworthy**.
10 The *princes* **governors** of *Judah* **Yah Hudah**
were like them that remove the *bound* **border**:
therefore I will **I shall** pour out my wrath
upon them like water.
11 *Ephraim* **Ephrayim**
is oppressed and *broken* **crushed** in judgment,
because he *willingly walked* **willed to walk**
after the *commandment* **misvah**.
12 Therefore *will* **shall** I be
unto *Ephraim* **Ephrayim**
as a moth,
and to the house of *Judah* **Yah Hudah** as rottenness.
13 When *Ephraim* **Ephrayim** saw his sickness,
and *Judah* **Yah Hudah** saw his *wound* **sore**,
then went *Ephraim* **Ephrayim** to the *Assyrian* **Ashshuri**,
and sent to *king Jareb* **sovereign Yareb to plead**:
yet could he not heal you,
nor cure you of your *wound* **sore**.
14 For I *will* **shall** be unto *Ephraim* **Ephrayim**
as a **roaring** lion,
and as a *young lion* **whelp**
to the house of *Judah* **Yah Hudah**:
I, *even* I, *will* **shall** tear and go away;
I *will take* **shall bear** away,
and none shall rescue *him*.
15 I *will* **shall** go and return to my place,
till they acknowledge their *offence* **having guilted**,
and seek my face:
in their *affliction* **tribulation** they
will **shall** seek me early.

THE CALL TO YISRA EL TO RETURN TO YAH VEH

6 Come, and let us return
unto *the LORD* **Yah Veh**:
for he hath torn, and he *will* **shall** heal us; he
hath smitten, and he *will* **shall** bind us *up*.
2 After two days *will* he *revive* **shall enliven** us:
in the third day he *will* **shall** raise us *up*, and
we shall live *in his sight* **at his face**.
3 Then shall we know,
if we *follow on* **pursue** to know *the LORD* **Yah Veh**:
his *going forth* **proceeding**
is prepared as the *morning* **dawn**;
and he shall come unto us as the *rain* **downpour**,
as the *latter and former* **after** rain
poureth unto the earth.

THE RESPONSE OF YAH VEH

4 O *Ephraim* **Ephrayim**, what
shall I *do* **work** unto thee?
O *Judah* **Yah Hudah**, what shall I *do* **work** unto thee?
for your *goodness* **mercy** is as a morning cloud,
and as the early dew it goeth away.
5 Therefore have I hewed them by the prophets;
I have *slain* **slaughtered** them

by the *words* **sayings** of my mouth:
and thy judgments are as the light that goeth forth.
6 For I desired mercy, and not sacrifice;
and the knowledge of *God* **Elohim** more
than *burnt offerings* **holocausts**.
7 But they like *men* **humanity**
have *transgressed* **trespassed** the covenant:
there have they dealt *treacherously* **covertly** against me.
8 *Gilead* **Gilad** is a city of them
that *work iniquity* **do mischief**,
and *is polluted* **trippeth** with blood.
and Yisra El and Ephrayim falter in their perversity;
Yah Hudah also falters with them.
6 With their flocks and with their herds
they go to seek Yah Veh;
and find not:
he withdraws himself from them.
7 They deal covertly against Yah Veh:
for they birth strange sons:
now a month consumes them with their allotments.
8 You, blast the shophar in Gibah
and the trumpet in Ramah:
shout at the house of mischief,
After you, O Ben Yamin!
9 Ephrayim becomes desolate
in the day of rebuke:
among the scions of Yisra El
I make known the trustworthy.
10 The governors of Yah Hudah become removers
of the border: I pour my wrath on them as water.
11 Ephrayim *is* oppressed; crushed in judgment;
because he wills to walk after the misvah.
12 So I *am* to Ephrayim as a moth
and to the house of Yah Hudah as rottenness.
13 And Ephrayim sees his sickness
and Yah Hudah sees his sore;
and Ephrayim goes to the Ashshuri
and sends to sovereign Yareb to plead:
yet he can neither heal you
nor cure you of your sore.
14 For I *am* to Ephrayim as a roaring lion
and as a whelp to the house of Yah Hudah:
I—I tear and go away; I bear away;
and no one rescues:
15 I go and return to my place,
until they acknowledge their guilting
and seek my face:
in their tribulation they seek me early.

THE CALL TO YISRA EL TO RETURN TO YAH VEH

6 Come, and return to Yah Veh:
for he tears, and he heals us;
he smites, and he binds us:
2 after two days he enlivens us;
in the third day he raises us;
and we live at his face.
3 And we know—we pursue to know Yah Veh:
as the dawn
he prepares his proceeding;
and he comes to us as the downpour
—as the after rain pouring to the earth.

THE RESPONSE OF YAH VEH

4 O Ephrayim, what work I to you?
O Yah Hudah, what work I to you?
For your mercy *is* as a morning cloud,
and as the early dew, goes away.
5 So I hew them by the prophets;
I slaughter them by the sayings of my mouth:
and your judgments *are* as the light that comes forth.
6 For I desire mercy and not sacrifice;
and the knowledge of Elohim more than holocausts.
7 And they, as humanity, trespass the covenant:
there they deal covertly against me.
8 Gilad is a city of doers of mischief
and trips with blood:
9 And as troops *of robbers wait for* **await** a man,
so the *company* **commune** of priests
murder in the way *by consent* **to** Shechem:
for they *commit lewdness* **work intrigue**
10 I have seen *an horrible thing* **horror**
in the house of *Israel* **Yisra El**:
there is the whoredom of *Ephraim* **Ephrayim**,
Israel **Yisra El** is defiled.
11 Also, O *Judah* **Yah Hudah**,
he hath set an harvest for thee,
when I returned the captivity of my people.
7 When I *would* **should** have
healed *Israel* **Yisra El**,
then the *iniquity* **perversity** of *Ephraim* **Ephrayim**
was discovered **exposed**,
and the *wickedness* **evil** of *Samaria* **Shomeron**:
for they *commit* **do** falsehood;
and the thief *cometh in* **enters**,
and the troop *of robbers*
spoileth without **strippeth in the outways**.
2 And they *consider* **say** not in their hearts

that I remember all their *wickedness* **evil**:
now their own *doings* **exploits**
have *beset* **surrounded** them *about*;
they are *before* **in front of** my face.
3 They *make* **cheer**
the *king glad* **sovereign** with their *wickedness* **evil**,
and the *princes* **governors** with their *lies* **deceptions**.
4 They are all adulterers,
as an oven *heated* **burning** by the baker,
who *ceaseth* **shabbathizeth** from *raising* **waking**
after he hath kneaded the dough, until it be leavened.
5 In the day of our *king* **sovereign**
the *princes* **governors** have *made* **stroked** him *sick*
with *bottles of* wine **of fury**;
he *stretched* **drew** out his hand with scorners.
6 For they have *made ready* **approached;**
their heart *like* **is** an oven, *whiles* they
lie in wait **lurk all night**:
their baker sleepeth *all the night*;
in the morning it burneth as a flaming fire.
7 They are all *hot* **heated** as an oven,
and have *devoured* **consumed** their judges;
all their *kings* **sovereigns** are fallen:
there is none among them that calleth unto me.
8 *Ephraim* **Ephrayim,**
he hath *mixed himself* **mingled** among the people;
Ephraim **Ephrayim** is *a cake* **an ashcake** not turned.
9 Strangers have *devoured*
consumed his *strength* **force**,
and he knoweth it not:
yea, *gray hairs are* **greyness be** here and there upon him,
yet he knoweth not.
10 And the *pride* **pomp** of *Israel* **Yisra El**
testifieth **answereth** to his face:
and they do not return
to *the LORD* **Yah Veh** their *God* **Elohim**,
nor seek him for all this.
11 *Ephraim* **Ephrayim** also
is like a *silly* **deluded** dove without heart:
they call to *Egypt* **Misrayim**, they go to *Assyria* **Ashshur**.
12 When they shall go,
I *will* **shall** spread my net upon them;
I *will* **shall** bring them down
as the *fowls* **flyers** of the *heaven* **heavens**;
I *will chastise* **shall discipline** them,
as *their congregation hath heard*
reported to their witness.
13 Woe unto them! for they have fled from me:
destruction **ravage** unto them!
because they have *transgressed* **rebelled** against me:
though I have redeemed them,
yet they have *spoken* **worded** lies against me.
14 And they have not cried
unto me with their heart,
when they howled upon their beds:
they *assemble* **sojourn** *themselves*
for *corn* **crop** and *wine* **juice**,
and they *rebel* **turn aside** against me.
15 Though I have
bound **disciplined** and strengthened their arms,
yet do they *imagine mischief* **fabricate evil** against me.
16 They return, but not to *the most High* **Elyon**:
9 and as troops await a man,
a commune of priests
murders in the way to Shechem:
for they work intrigue.
10 I see horror in the house of Yisra El:
—the whoredom of Ephrayim,
Yisra El defiles.
11 Also, O Yah Hudah,
I set a harvest for you
when I restore the captivity of my people.
7 When I heal Yisra El,
then I expose the perversity of Ephrayim
and the evil of Shomeron;
for they do falsehood:
and the thief enters
and the troop strips in the outways:
2 and they say not in their hearts
that I remember all their evil:
their own exploits surround them;
they are in front of my face:
3 they cheer the sovereign with their evil
and the governors with their deceptions:
4 they are all adulterers
—as an oven burning by the baker
who shabbathizes from waking
after he kneads the dough, until it leavens.
5 In the day of our sovereign
the governors stroke him with wine of fury;
he draws his hand with scorners:
6 for they approach; their heart is an oven:
they lurk all night; their baker sleeps: in the
morning it burns as a flaming fire.
7 They all heat as an oven
and consume their judges;
all their sovereigns fall:
not one among them calls to me.
8 Ephrayim, he mingles among the people;
Ephrayim is an ashcake not turned.

9 Strangers consume his
force and he knows it not:
yes, greyness here and there on him
yet he knows not.
10 And the pomp of Yisra El answers to his face:
and they neither return to Yah Veh their Elohim
nor seek him for all this:
11 and Ephrayim is as a
deluded dove without heart:
they call to Misrayim; they go to Ashshur:
12 they go, and I spread my net over them;
I bring them down as the flyers of the heavens;
I discipline them as reported to their witness.
13 Woe to them! For they flee from me:
ravage to them—because they rebel against me:
and I—I redeem them;
yet they word lies against me:
14 and they cry not to me with their heart
but howl on their beds:
they sojourn for crop and juice
and they turn aside against me.
15 Though I discipline and strengthen their arms,
yet they fabricate evil against me:
16 they return, but not to Elyon:
they are like a deceitful bow:
their *princes* **governors** shall fall by the sword
for the rage of their tongue:
this shall be their derision
in the land of *Egypt* **Misrayim.**

8 *Set* the *trumpet* **shophar** to thy *mouth* **palate.**
He shall come
as an eagle against the house of *the LORD* **Yah Veh,**
because they have *transgressed* **trespassed** my covenant,
and *trespassed* **rebelled** against my *law* **torah.**
2 *Israel* **Yisra El** shall cry unto me,
My *God* **Elohim,** we know thee.
3 *Israel* **Yisra El** hath cast off
the thing that **which** is good:
the enemy shall pursue him.
4 They have set up *kings*
sovereigns, but not by me:
they have *made princes* **dominated,** and I knew it not:
of their silver and their gold
have they *made* **worked** them idols,
that they may be cut off.
5 Thy calf, O *Samaria*
Shomeron, hath cast *thee* off;
mine anger **my wrath** is kindled against them:
how long *will* **shall** it be
ere they *attain to* **be capable of** innocency?
6 For from *Israel* **Yisra El** was it also:
the *workman made* **engraver worked** it;
therefore it is not *God* **Elohim:**
but the calf of *Samaria* **Shomeron**
shall be *broken in pieces* **shattered.**
7 For they have *sown* **seeded** the wind,
and they shall *reap* **harvest** the *whirlwind* **hurricane:**
it hath no stalk:
the *bud* **sprout** shall *yield* **work** no *meal* **flour:**
if so be it *yield* **work,** the strangers shall swallow it *up.*
8 *Israel* **Yisra El** is swallowed *up:*
now shall they be among the *Gentiles* **goyim**
as *a vessel* **an instrument** wherein is no *pleasure* **delight.**
9 For they are *gone up*
ascended to *Assyria* **Ashshur,**
a wild *ass* **runner** alone by himself:
Ephraim **Ephrayim** hath hired lovers.
10 Yea, though they have hired
among the *nations* **goyim,**
now *will* **shall** I gather them,
and they shall *sorrow* **be pierced** a little
for the burden of the *king* **sovereign**
of *princes* **governors.**
11 Because *Ephraim* **Ephrayim**
hath *made many* **abounded sacrifice** altars to sin,
sacrifice altars shall be unto him to sin.
12 I have *written* **inscribed** to him
the *great things* **myriads of greatnesses** of my *law* **torah,**
but they were *counted* **fabricated** as *a* strange *thing.*
13 They sacrifice flesh
for the sacrifices of *mine offerings* **my holocausts,**
and eat *it;*
but the LORD **Yah Veh**
accepteth them not **is not pleased with them;**
now *will* **shall** he remember their *iniquity* **perversity,**
and visit their sins:
they shall return to *Egypt* **Misrayim.**
14 For *Israel* **Yisra El** hath
forgotten his *Maker* **Worker,**
and buildeth *temples* **manses;**
and *Judah* **Yah Hudah**
hath *multiplied fenced* **abounded fortified** cities:
but I *will* **shall** send a fire upon his cities,
and it shall *devour* **consume** the *palaces* **citadels** *thereof.*

9 *Rejoice* **Cheer** not, O *Israel* **Yisra El,**
for *joy* **twirling,** as *other* people:
for thou hast *gone a whoring* **whored**
from thy *God* **Elohim,**
thou hast loved a *reward* **payoff**
upon every *cornfloor* **crop threshingfloor.**

2 The *floor* **threshingfloor**
and the *winepress* **trough**
shall not *feed* **tend** them,
and the *new wine* **juice** shall *fail* **deceive** in her.
3 They shall not *dwell* **settle**
in the *LORD'S* land **of Yah Veh**;
but *Ephraim* **Ephrayim** shall return to *Egypt* **Misrayim**,
and they shall eat *unclean things* **the foul**
in *Assyria* **Ashshur**.
4 They shall not *offer* **libate** wine *offerings*
to *the LORD* **Yah Veh**,
they are as a deceitful bow:
their governors fall by the sword
for the rage of their tongue:
this *is* their derision in the land of Misrayim.

8 A shophar to your palate
—as an eagle against the house of Yah Veh:
because they trespass my covenant
and rebel against my torah.
2 They cry to me,
My Elohim, we—Yisra El, know you!
3 Yisra El casts off the good:
an enemy pursues him.
4 they set sovereigns, but not by me:
they set dominators, and I know not:
they work idols of their silver and their gold
and cut themselves off.
5 Cast your calf, O Shomeron;
my wrath kindles against them:
how long ere they *are* capable of innocency?
6 For even of Yisra El:
the engraver works it; and it *is* not of Elohim:
for the calf of Shomeron shatters.
7 For they seed the wind
and harvest the hurricane:
there *is* no stalk; the sprout works no flour:
and if it works, strangers swallow it.
8 Yisra El is swallowed:
they are now among the goyim
as an instrument wherein *is* no delight:
9 for they ascend to Ashshur
—a wild runner alone by himself:
Ephrayim hires lovers.
10 Yes, though they hire among the goyim
I now gather them;
and they *are* pierced a little
by the burden of the sovereign of governors.
11 Because Ephrayim abounds
sacrifice altars to sin,
they are his sacrifice altars to sin.
12 I inscribe to him
the myriads of greatnesses of my torah,
they fabricate them as strange:
13 they sacrifice flesh
for the sacrifices of my holocausts,
and eat;
Yah Veh *is* not pleased with them;
now he remembers their perversity
and visits their sins:
they return to Misrayim.
14 And Yisra El forgets his
Worker and builds manses
and Yah Hudah abounds fortified cities:
and I send a fire on his cities
and it consumes the citadels.

9 Neither cheer, O Yisra El; nor twirl as people:
for you whore from your Elohim,
you love a payoff on every crop threshingfloor.
2 The threshingfloor and
the trough, they tend not
and the juice in her deceives:
3 they settle not in the land of Yah Veh;
and Ephrayim returns to Misrayim,
and they eat the foul in Ashshur.
4 They neither libate wine to Yah Veh,
neither shall they *be pleasing unto* **please** him:
their sacrifices shall be unto them
as the bread of *mourners* **mischief**;
all that eat *thereof* shall be *polluted* **fouled**:
for their bread for their soul
shall not come into the house of *the LORD* **Yah Veh**.
5 What *will* **shall** ye *do* **work**
in the *solemn* **season** day,
and in the day
of the *feast* **celebration** of *the LORD* **Yah Veh**?
6 For, *lo* **behold**,
they are gone because of *destruction* **ravage**:
Egypt **Misrayim** shall gather them *up*,
Memphis **Moph** shall *bury* **entomb** them:
the *pleasant places* **desirables** for their silver,
nettles **thistles** shall possess them:
thorns shall be in their *tabernacles* **tents**.
7 The days of visitation *are come* **approach**,
the days of *recompence are come* **satisfaction approach**;
Israel **Yisra El** shall know *it*:
the prophet is a fool,
the *spiritual* man **of the spirit** is *mad* **insane**,
for the *multitude* **abundance**
of *thine iniquity* **thy perversity**,
and the great *hatred* **enmity**.

8 The *watchman* **watcher** of *Ephraim* **Ephrayim**
was with my *God* **Elohim**:
but the prophet is a snare of a *fowler* **snarer**
in all his ways,
and *hatred* **enmity** in the house of his *God* **El**.
9 They have *deeply* **deepened,**
corrupted themselves **they have ruined,**
as in the days of *Gibeah* **Gibah**:
therefore he *will* **shall** remember
their *iniquity* **perversity,**
he *will* **shall** visit their sins.
10 I found *Israel* **Yisra El** like
grapes in the wilderness;
I saw your fathers
as the firstripe in the fig tree at her *first time* **beginning**:
but they went to *Baalpeor* **Baal Peor,**
and separated themselves unto *that* shame;
and their abominations were according as they loved.
11 *As for Ephraim* **Ephrayim,**
their *glory* **honour** shall fly *away* like a *bird* **flyer,**
from the birth,
and from the *womb* **belly**, and from the conception.
12 Though they *bring up*
nourish their *children* **sons,**
yet *will* **shall** I bereave them,
that there shall not be a *man left* **human**:
yea,
woe also to them when I *depart* **turn aside** from them!
13 *Ephraim* **Ephrayim,** as I saw *Tyrus* **Sor,**
is *planted* **transplanted**
in a *pleasant place* **habitation of rest**:
but *Ephraim* **Ephrayim** shall bring
forth his *children* **sons**
to the *murderer* **slaughterer.**
14 Give them, O *LORD* **Yah Veh**:
what *wilt* **shalt** thou *give*?
give them *a miscarrying* **an aborting**
womb and dry breasts.
15 All their *wickedness* **evil** is in Gilgal:
for there I hated them:
for the *wickedness* **evil** of their *doings* **exploits**
I *will* **shall** drive them out of mine house,
I *will* **shall add not to** love them *no more*:
all their *princes* **governors** are revolters.
16 *Ephraim* **Ephrayim** is smitten,
their root is *dried up* **withered,**
they shall *bear* **work** no fruit:
yea, though they *bring forth* **birth,**
yet *will* **shall** I slay
even the *beloved fruit* **desire** of their *womb* **belly.**
17 My *God will cast* **Elohim**
shall spurn them *away*,
because they did not hearken unto him:
and they shall be wanderers
among the *nations* **goyim.**

10 *Israel* **Yisra El** is an *empty* **evacuating** vine,
he *bringeth forth* **equateth** fruit unto himself:
according to the *multitude* **abundance** of his fruit
he hath *increased* **abounded** the **sacrifice** altars;
according to the goodness of his land
they have made goodly *images* **monoliths.**
nor please him:
their sacrifices *are* to them as the bread of mischief;
all who eat *are* fouled:
for their bread for their soul
comes not into the house of Yah Veh.
5 What work you in the day of the season
and in the day of the celebration of Yah Veh?
6 For behold, they are gone because of ravage:
Misrayim gathers them; Moph entombs them:
as for the desirables of their silver,
thistles possess them: thorns *are* in their tents.
7 The days of visitation approach,
the days of satisfaction approach;
Yisra El knows:
the prophet is a fool: the man of the spirit *is* insane,
because of the abundance of your perversity
and the great enmity.
8 Ephrayim is the watcher of my Elohim:
the prophet is a snare of the snarer in all his ways;
and enmity *is* in the house of his El.
9 They deepen; they ruin as in the days of Gibah:
he remembers their perversity; he visits their sins.
10 I find Yisra El as grapes in the wilderness;
I see your fathers
as the firstripe in the fig tree at her beginning:
they—they go to Baal Peor,
and separate themselves to shame
—their abominations are as their love.
11 Ephrayim is as a fowl
their honor flies from the birth
and from the belly and from the conception.
12 Though they nourish their sons,
yet I bereave them—without a human:
yes also, woe to them when I turn aside from them!
13 Ephrayim, as I saw Sor,
is transplanted in a habitation of rest:
and Ephrayim brings his sons to the slaughterer.
14 Give them, O Yah Veh!
What give you?

Give them an aborting womb and dry breasts.
15 All their evil *is* in Gilgal;
surely, there I hated them:
for the evil of their exploits
I drive them from my house;
I add not to love them:
all their governors are revolters.
16 Ephrayim *is* smitten:
their root withers; they work no fruit:
yes, though they birth,
yet I slay the desire of their belly.
17 My Elohim spurns them,
because they hearken not to him:
and they become wanderers among the goyim.

10 Yisra El is an evacuated vine,
he equates fruit to himself: as the abundance of
his fruit he abounds the sacrifice altars; as the
goodness of his land they make goodly monoliths:
2 Their heart is *divided* **allotted**;
now shall they
be found faulty **acknowledge having guilted**:
he shall break *down* **the neck of** their altars,
he shall *spoil* **ravage** their *images* **monoliths**.
3 For now they shall say, We
have no *king* **sovereign,**
because we *feared* **awed** not *the LORD* **Yah Veh**; what
then should a *king do* **sovereign work a** to us?
4 They have *spoken* **worded** words,
swearing falsely **oathing vainly**
in *making* **cutting** a covenant:
thus judgment springeth *up*
as *hemlock* **rosh** in the furrows of the field.
5 The *inhabitants* **fellow tabernaclers**
of *Samaria* **Shomeron** shall *fear* **sojourn**
because of the *calves* **heifers** of *Bethaven* **Beth Aven**:
for the people *thereof* shall mourn over it,
and the *priests* **ascetics** *thereof* that *rejoiced* **twirled** on it,
for the *glory* **honour** *thereof*,
because it is *departed* **exiled** from it.
6 It shall be also *carried* **borne**
unto *Assyria* **Ashshur**
for a oblation **an offering**
to *king Jareb* **sovereign Yareb to plead**:
Ephraim **Ephrayim**
shall *receive* **take** shame,
and *Israel* **Yisra El**
shall *be ashamed* **shame** of his own counsel.
7 As for *Samaria* **Shomeron,**
her *king* **sovereign** is *cut off* **severed**
as the *foam* **raging** upon the **face of the** water.
8 The *high places* **bamahs** also of Aven,
the sin of *Israel* **Yisra El**, shall be *destroyed* **desolated**:
the thorn and the thistle
shall *come up* **ascend** on their **sacrifice** altars;
and they shall say to the mountains, Cover us;
and to the hills, Fall on us.
9 O *Israel* **Yisra El,**
thou hast sinned from the days of *Gibeah* **Gibah**:
there they stood:
the *battle* **war** in *Gibeah* **Gibah**
against the *children* **sons** of *iniquity* **wickedness**
did not overtake them.
10 *It is in my desire* **I yearn**
that I should *chastise* **bind** them;
and the people shall *be gathered* **gather** against them,
when *they* **I** shall bind *themselves* **them**
in their two *furrows* **eyes.**
11 And *Ephraim* **Ephrayim** is
as an heifer that is taught,
and loveth to *tread out the corn* **thresh**;
but I passed over upon her *fair* **good** neck:
I *will make Ephraim* **shall cause Ephrayim**
to *ride* **be ridden;**
Judah **Yah Hudah** shall plow,
and *Jacob* **Yaaqov** shall *break his clods* **harrow.**
12 *Sow* **Seed** to yourselves in
righteousness **justness,**
reap in **harvest to your mouth** mercy;
break up **till** your *fallow ground* **tillage**:
for it is time to seek *the LORD* **Yah Veh,**
till he come
and *rain righteousness* **pour justness** upon you.
13 Ye have plowed wickedness,
ye have *reaped iniquity* **harvested wickedness**;
ye have eaten the fruit of *lies* **deceptions**:
because thou didst *trust* **confide** in thy way,
in the *multitude* **abundance** of thy mighty *men.*
14 Therefore shall *a tumult* **an uproar** arise
among thy people,
and all thy fortresses shall be *spoiled* **ravaged,**
as Shalman *spoiled Betharbel* **ravaged Beth Arb El**
in the day of *battle* **war**:
the mother was *dashed in pieces* **splattered**
upon her *children* **sons.**
15 *So* **Thus** shall *Bethel do* **Beth El work** unto you
because **at the face of the evil**
of your *great wickedness* **evil**:
in *a morning* **the dawn**
shall the king of Israel utterly be cut off
in severing,

the sovereign of Yisra El shall be severed.
2 their heart is allotted;
now they acknowledge having guilted:
he breaks the neck of their altars;
he ravages their monoliths.
3 For now they say, We have no sovereign,
because we awe not Yah Veh.
What then works a sovereign to us?
4 They word words;
oathing vainly in cutting a covenant:
thus judgment springs as rosh
in the furrows of the field:
5 the fellow tabernaclers of Shomeron sojourn
because of the heifers of Beth Aven:
for the people mourn over it;
and the ascetics twirl on it:
for the honor *is* exiled from it:
6 also it is borne to Ashshur
as an offering to sovereign Yareb to plead:
Ephrayim shames
and Yisra El shames of his own counsel.
7 As for Shomeron,
her sovereign *is* severed
as the raging on the face of the water.
8 And the bamahs of Aven,
the sin of Yisra El, desolates:
the thorn and the thistle
ascend on their sacrifice altars;
and they say to the mountains, Cover us!
and to the hills, Fall on us!
9 O Yisra El, you sinned from the days of Gibah:
there they stood:
the war in Gibah overtook them not
because of the sons of wickedness.
10 I yearn to bind them;
and when I bind their two eyes
the people gather against them.
11 And Ephrayim is as an heifer that is taught
—who loves to thresh;
and I—I pass over on her good neck:
Ephrayim, I ride;
Yah Hudah plows; and Yaaqov harrows.
12 Seed to yourselves in justness;
harvest to your mouth mercy;
till your tillage:
for it is time to seek Yah Veh,
until he comes and pours justness on you.
13 You plow wickedness; you harvest wickedness:
you eat the fruit of deceptions:
because you confide in your way
—in the abundance of your mighty.
14 And an uproar rises among your people;
and ravages all your fortresses
as Shalman ravaged Beth Arb El in the day of war:
—the mother splattered on her sons.
15 Thus Beth El works to you
at the face of the evil of your evil:
in the dawn
in severing, sever the sovereign of Yisra El.

11 When *Israel* **Yisra El** was a *child* **lad**,
then I loved him,
and called my son out of *Egypt* **Misrayim**.
2 As they called them, so they
went from *them* **their face**:
they sacrificed unto Baalim,
and *burned incense* **incensed** to *graven images* **sculptiles**.
3 I *taught Ephraim* **caused**
Ephrayim also to *go* **tread**,
taking them by their arms;
but they knew not that I healed them.
4 I drew them with cords of a *man* **human**,
with *bands* **ropes** of love:
and I was to them
as they that *take off* **lift** the yoke on their jaws,
and I *laid meat* **spread** unto them **to eat**.
5 He shall not return into the
land of *Egypt* **Misrayim**,
and the *Assyrian* **Ashshuri** shall be his *king*
sovereign, because they refused to return.
6 And the sword shall *abide* **whirl** on his cities,
and shall *consume* **finish off** his branches,
and *devour them* **consume**, because
of their own counsels.
7 And my people
are *bent* **prone** to *backsliding from me* **apostasy**:
though they called them to *the most High* **Elyon**,
none at all *would* **should** exalt him.
8 How shall I give thee up, *Ephraim* **Ephrayim**?
how shall I *deliver* **buckler** thee, *Israel* **Yisra El**?
how shall I *make* **give** thee as Admah?
how shall I *set* **set** thee as *Zeboim* **Seboim**?
mine heart is turned within me,
my *repentings are kindled* **solaces yearn** together.
9 I *will* **shall** not *execute* **work**
the *fierceness* **fuming** of *mine anger* **my wrath**,
I *will* **shall** not return to *destroy*
Ephraim **ruin Ephrayim**:
for *I am God* **I—El**, and not man;
the Holy One in the midst of thee:
and I *will* **shall** not enter into the city.

10 They shall walk after *the LORD* **Yah Veh**:
he shall roar like a lion:
when he shall roar,
then the *children* **sons** shall tremble
from the *west* **seaward**.
11 They shall tremble as a bird
out of *Egypt* **Misrayim**,
and as a dove out of the land of *Assyria* **Ashshur**:
and I *will place* **shall settle** them in their houses,
saith the LORD **an oracle of Yah Veh**.
12 *Ephraim compasseth* **Ephrayim**
surroundeth me *about*
with *lies* **deceptions**,
and the house of *Israel* **Yisra El** with deceit:
but *Judah yet ruleth* **Yah Hudah**
rambles on with *God* **El**,
and is *faithful* **trustworthy** with the *saints* **holy**.

12 *Ephraim feedeth* **Ephrayim grazeth** on wind,
and *followeth after* **pursueth** the *east wind* **easterly**:
he daily increaseth **every day he aboundeth** lies
and *desolation* **ravage**;
and they *do make* **cut** a covenant
with the *Assyrians* **Ashshuri**,
and oil is *carried* **borne** into *Egypt* **Misrayim**.
2 *The LORD* **Yah Veh**
hath also a controversy with *Judah* **Yah Hudah**,
and *will punish Jacob* **shall visit upon Yaaqov**
according to his ways;
according to his *doings* **exploits**
will **shall** he *recompense* **return** him.
3 He *took* **tripped** his brother by the heel
in the *womb* **belly**,
and by his strength
he *had power* **prevailed** with *God* **Elohim**:
4 Yea, he *had power* **dominated** over the angel,
and prevailed:
he wept,
and *made supplication unto him* **was granted charism**:
he found him in *Bethel* **Beth El**,
and there he *spake* **worded** with us;
5 Even *the LORD God of hosts*
Yah Veh Elohim Sabaoth;
the LORD **Yah Veh** is his memorial.
6 Therefore *turn* **return** thou to thy *God* **Elohim**:
keep **guard** mercy and judgment,
and *wait on* **await** thy *God* **Elohim** continually.

11 Because Yisra El *is* a lad, I love him;
and from Misrayim I call my son.
2 They call them; they go from their face:
they sacrifice to Baalim and incense to sculptiles.
3 And I tread Ephrayim
—taking them by their arms;
and they know not that I heal them
4 —draw them with human cords
—with ropes of love:
and I *am* to them
as they who lift the yoke on their jaws;
and I spread to them; and they eat.
5 He returns not to the land of Misrayim,
and the Ashshuri *is* his sovereign
—because they refuse to return:
6 and the sword whirls on his cities
and finishes off his branches and consumes
because of their own counsels.
7 And my people *are* prone to apostasy:
though they call Elyon to themselves,
no one at all exalts him.
8 How give I you up, Ephrayim?
How buckler I you, Yisra El? How give I you as
Admah? How set I you as Seboim? My heart
turns within me; my solaces yearn together.
9 I neither work the fuming of my wrath
nor return to ruin Ephrayim:
for I *am* El, and not man;
the Holy One among you:
and I enter not the city.
10 They walk after Yah Veh; he roars as a lion:
when he roars,
the sons from the seaward tremble:
11 they tremble as a bird from Misrayim
and as a dove from the land of Ashshur:
and I settle them in their houses
—an oracle of Yah Veh.
12 Ephrayim surrounds me with deceptions
and the house of Yisra El with deceit:
and Yah Hudah rambles on with El
and is trustworthy with the holy.

12 Ephrayim grazes on wind
and pursues the easterly;
every day he abounds lies and ravages:
and they cut a covenant with the Ashshuri
and bear oil to Misrayim.
2 And Yah Veh has a controversy with Yah Hudah
and visits on Yaaqov according to his ways
—according to his exploits he returns to him.
3 He tripped his brother by the heel in the belly;
and by his strength he prevailed with Elohim:
4 Yes, he dominated over the angel
and prevailed by weeping and *was* granted charism: he
found him in Beth El and there he worded with us;

5 even Yah Veh Elohim Sabaoth;
Yah Veh *is* his memorial.
6 And you, return to your Elohim;
guard mercy and judgment
and await your Elohim continually.
7 He is *a merchant* **Kenaan,**
the balances of deceit are in his hand:
he loveth to oppress.
8 And *Ephraim* **Ephrayim** said,
Yet I am *become rich* **enriched,**
I have found me out *substance* **strength:**
in all my labours
they shall find none *iniquity* **perversity** in me
that were sin.
9 And I that *am the LORD*
Yah Veh thy *God* **Elohim**
from the land of *Egypt* **Misrayim**
will **shall** yet *make* **cause** thee
to *dwell* **settle** in *tabernacles* **tents,**
as in the days of the *solemn feast* **seasons.**
10 I have also *spoken* **worded** by the prophets,
and I have *multiplied* **abounded** visions,
and used *similitudes* **comparisons,**
by the *ministry* **hand** of the prophets.
11 Is there *iniquity* **mischief** in *Gilead* **Gilad**?
surely they are vanity:
they sacrifice *bullocks* **oxen** in Gilgal;
yea, their **sacrifice** altars
are as heaps in the furrows of the fields.
12 And *Jacob* **Yaaqov**
fled into the *country* **field** of *Syria* **Aram,**
and *Israel* **Yisra El** served for a *wife* **woman,**
and for a *wife* **woman** he *kept sheep* **guarded.**
13 And by a prophet
the LORD brought Israel **Yah Veh ascended Yisra El**
out of *Egypt* **Misrayim,**
and by a prophet was he *preserved* **guarded.**
14 *Ephraim* **Ephrayim**
provoked **vexed** him *to anger*
most bitterly **with bitterness:**
therefore shall he *leave* **abandon** his blood upon him,
and his reproach
shall his *Lord return* **Adonay returneth** unto him.

13 When *Ephraim* **Ephrayim**
spake trembling **worded in terror,**
he *exalted* **lifted** himself in *Israel* **Yisra El;**
but when he *offended* **had guilted** in Baal, he died.
2 And now they **add to** sin *more and more,*
and have *made* **worked** them
molten images **moltens** of their silver,
and idols
according to their own *understanding* **discerning,**
all of it the work of the *craftsmen* **engravers:**
they say of them,
Let *the men* **humanity** that *sacrifice* **sacrificeth**
kiss the calves.
3 Therefore they shall be as the morning cloud
and as the early dew that passeth away,
as the chaff that is
driven with the whirlwind **stormed**
out of the *floor* **threshingfloor,**
and as the smoke out of the *chimney* **window.**
4 Yet *I am the LORD* **I—Yah Veh** thy *God* **Elohim**
from the land of *Egypt* **Misrayim,**
and thou shalt know no *god but* **elohim beside** me:
for there is no saviour *beside* **except** me.
5 I did know thee in the wilderness,
in the land of great *drought* **droughts.**
6 According to their pasture,
so were they *filled* **satiated;**
they were *filled* **satiated,** and their heart was
exalted; therefore have they forgotten me.
7 Therefore I *will* **shall** be
unto them as a **roaring** lion:
as a leopard by the way *will* **shall** I observe them:
8 I *will* **shall** meet them
as a bear that is bereaved *of her whelps,*
and *will rend* **shall rip** the *caul* **treasure** of their heart,
and there *will* **shall** I devour them like a **roaring** lion:
the wild *beast* **live being of the**
field shall *tear* **split** them.
9 O *Israel* **Yisra El,** thou hast
destroyed **ruined** thyself;
but in me is thine help.
10 *I will be thy king:* **Where is thy sovereign**
where is any other that may save **that saveth** thee
in all thy cities?
and thy judges of whom thou saidst,
Give me a *king* **sovereign** and *princes* **governors?**
7 Kenaan—the balances of deceit *are* in his hand;
he loves to oppress:
8 and Ephrayim says, Surely I enrich:
I find my strength in all my labors
they find no one perversity in me—sin.
9 And I—Yah Veh your Elohim
from the land of Misrayim;
and I return you to settle in tents
as in the days of the seasons.
10 And I word by the prophets,
and I abound visions,

and by the hand of the prophets
use comparisons.
11 Is there mischief in Gilad?
surely they are vanity:
they sacrifice oxen in Gilgal;
yes, their sacrifice altars *are* as heaps
in the furrows of the fields.
12 And Yaaqov flees into the field of Aram,
and Yisra El serves for a woman:
yes, for a woman he guards.
13 And by a prophet
Yah Veh ascends Yisra El from Misrayim,
—guarded by a prophet.
14 Ephrayim vexes himself with bitterness:
and he abandons his blood on him,
and Adonay returns his reproach to him.

13 When Ephrayim words in terror,
he lifts himself in Yisra El;
When he guilts in Baal, he dies.
2 And now they add to sin
and work themselves moltens of their silver
—idols according to their own discerning
all the work of the engravers:
of humanity who sacrifices,
they say, Kiss the calves.
3 So they are as the morning cloud
and as the early dew that passes away:
as the chaff stormed from the threshingfloor
and as the smoke from the window.
4 Yet I—Yah Veh your Elohim
from the land of Misrayim
and you know no elohim except me:
for there is no saviour except me.
5 I—I knew you in the wilderness,
in the land of great droughts.
6 According to their pasture, they satiate;
—satiate, and exalt their heart;
so they forget me.
7 And I *am* to them as a roaring lion:
as a leopard by the way I observe them:
8 I meet them as a bear bereaved
and rip the treasure of their heart;
and there I devour them as a roaring lion:
as the wild live being of the field, split them.
9 O Yisra El, you ruin yourself;
but your help is in me.
10 Where is your sovereign
who saves you in all your cities?
And your judges of whom you say,
Give me a sovereign and governors?
11 I gave thee a *king* **sovereign**
in *mine anger* **my wrath,**
and took him away in my wrath.
12 The *iniquity* **perversity** of *Ephraim* **Ephrayim**
is bound *up*; his sin is hid.
13 The *sorrows* **pangs** of a
travailing **birthing** woman
shall come upon him: he is an unwise son;
for he should not stay
long in the place of the breaking forth
the time of the matrix
of *children* **sons.**
14 I *will* **shall** ransom them
from the *power* **hand** of *the grave* **sheol;**
I *will* **shall** redeem them from death:
O death, *I will be thy plagues* **where are thy pestilences;**
O *grave* **sheol,** *I will be thy destruction* **where is thy ruin:**
repentance **sighing** shall be hid from mine eyes.
I Corinthians 15:55
15 Though he *be fruitful* **bear**
fruit among his brethren,
an east wind shall come,
the *wind* **wind/Spirit** of *the LORD* **Yah Veh**
shall *come up* **ascend** from the wilderness,
and his *spring* **fountain** shall *become dry* **shame,**
and his fountain shall *be dried up* **parch:**
he shall spoil the treasure
of all pleasant *vessels* **instruments.**
16 *Samaria* **Shomeron**
shall become desolate **hath guilted;**
for she hath rebelled against her *God* **Elohim:**
they shall fall by the sword:
their *infants* **sucklings**
shall be *dashed in pieces* **splattered,**
and their women *with child* **having conceived**
shall be *ripped up* **split.**

YAH VEH APPEALS TO YISRA EL

14 O *Israel* **Yisra El,**
return unto *the LORD* **Yah Veh** thy *God* **Elohim;**
for thou hast *fallen* **faltered**
by *thine iniquity* **thy perversity.**
2 Take with you words, and
turn to *the LORD* **Yah Veh:**
say unto him, *Take away* **Bear** all *iniquity* **perversity,**
and *receive us graciously* **take goodly:**
so *will* **shall** we *render* **shalam**
the *calves* **bullocks** of our lips.
3 *Asshur* **Ashshur** shall not save us;
we *will* **shall** not ride upon horses:

neither *will* **shall** we say any more
to the work of our hands,
Ye are our gods **Our elohim**:
for in thee
the *fatherless findeth mercy* **orphan is mercied**.
4 I *will* **shall** heal their *backsliding* **apostasy**,
I *will* **shall** love them *freely* **voluntarily**:
for *mine anger* **my wrath** is turned away from him.
5 I *will* **shall** be as the dew unto *Israel* **Yisra El**:
he shall *grow* **blossom** as the lily,
and *cast forth* **smite** his roots as Lebanon.
6 His *branches* **sprouts** shall spread,
and his *beauty* **majesty** shall be as the olive *tree*,
and his *smell* **scent** as Lebanon.
7 They that *dwell* **settle** under
his shadow shall return;
they shall *revive* **enliven** as the *corn* **crop**,
and *grow* **blossom** as the vine:
the *scent* **memorial** *thereof*
shall be as the wine of Lebanon.
8 *Ephraim shall say* **Ephrayim**,
What have I to do any more with idols?
I have *heard him* **answered**, and observed him:
I am like a green fir tree. From me is thy fruit found.
9 Who is wise,
and he shall *understand* **discern** these *things*?
prudent **discerning**, and he shall know them?
for the ways of *the LORD* **Yah Veh** are *right* **straight**,
and the just shall walk in them:
but the *transgressors* **rebels** shall *fall* **falter** therein.
11 I give you a sovereign in my wrath;
and take him in my wrath:
12 the perversity of Ephrayim
is bound; his sin is hid:
13 pangs of a birthing woman come on him:
he is an unwise son;
for he stays not to the time of the matrix of sons.
14 I ransom them from the hand of sheol;
I redeem them from death:
O death, where *are* your pestilences;
O sheol, where *is* your ruin:
sighing *is* hid from my eyes.
I Corinthians 15:55
15 Though he bears fruit among his brothers,
an east wind comes;
the wind/Spirit of Yah Veh
ascends from the wilderness;
and his fountain shames; and his fountain parches:
he spoils the treasure of all pleasant instruments.
16 Shomeron guilts;
for she rebelled against her Elohim:
they fall by the sword:
their sucklings splatter
and their conceiving women split.

YAH VEH APPEALS TO YISRA EL

14 O Yisra El, return to Yah Veh your Elohim;
for you falter by your perversity.
2 Take with you words, and turn to Yah Veh:
say to him, Bear all perversity and take the goodly:
thus we shalam the bullocks of our lips.
3 Neither Ashshur saves us;
nor ride we on horses:
nor say we any more to the work of our hands,
Our elohim:
for in you the orphan *is* mercied.
4 I heal their apostasy; I love them voluntarily:
for my wrath turns from him.
5 I become as the dew to Yisra El:
he blossoms as the lily
and smites his roots as Lebanon:
6 his sprouts spread
and his majesty becomes as the olive
and his scent as Lebanon.
7 They who settle under his shadow return;
they enliven as the crop and blossom as the vine:
their memorial *is* as the wine of Lebanon.
8 Ephrayim,
What have I to do any more with idols?
I—I answer and observe him:
I *am* as a green fir tree: from me your fruit *is* found.
9 Who is wise, and discerns these?
Discerns, and knows them?
For straight *are* the ways of Yah Veh
and the just walk therein:
and the rebels falter therein.

Introduction

1 The word of *the LORD* **Yah Veh**
that came to *Joel* **Yah El** the son of *Pethuel* **Pethu El.**
2 Hear this, ye *old men* **elders,**
and *give ear* **hearken,**
all ye *inhabitants* **settlers** of the land.
Hath this been in your days,
or even in the days of your fathers?

The Land Desolated

3 *Tell* **Scribe** ye your *children* **sons** of it,
and *let your children tell* **your sons** their *children* **sons,**
and their *children* **sons** another generation.
4 That which the palmerworm hath left
hath the locust eaten;
and that which the locust hath left
hath the cankerworm eaten;
and that which the cankerworm hath left
hath the caterpiller eaten.
5 Awake, ye *drunkards* **intoxicants,** and weep;
and howl, all ye drinkers of wine,
because of the *new wine* **squeezed juice;**
for it is cut off from your mouth.
6 For a *nation* **goyim**
is come up **hath ascended** upon my land,
strong **mighty,** and without number,
whose teeth are the teeth of a lion,
and he hath the *cheek teeth* **molars**
of a *great* **roaring** lion.
7 He hath *laid* **set** my vine *waste* **desolate,**
and *barked* **chipped away** my fig tree:
in stripping, he hath *made* **stripped** it *clean bare,*
and cast it away;
the *branches* **tendrils** *thereof* are *made white* **whitened.**
8 Lament like a virgin girded with *sackcloth* **saq**
for the *husband* **master** of her youth.
9 The *meat* offering and the
drink offering **libation**
is cut off from the house of *the LORD* **Yah Veh;** the
priests, the *LORD'S* ministers of **Yah Veh,** mourn.
10 The field is *wasted* **ravaged,**
the *land* **soil** mourneth;
for the *corn is wasted* **crop ravageth:**
the *new wine is dried up* **juice withereth,**
the oil languisheth.
11 Be ye ashamed, O ye *husbandmen* **cultivators;**
howl, O ye vinedressers, for the wheat and for the barley;
because the harvest of the field is *perished* **destroyed.**
12 The vine *is dried up* **withereth,**
and the fig tree languisheth;
the pomegranate tree, the palm tree also,
and the apple tree,
even all the trees of the field, *are* withered:
because *joy* **rejoicing** is withered *away*
from the sons of *men* **humanity.**

Call To Repentance

13 Gird *yourselves,* and *lament* **mourn,** ye priests:
howl, ye ministers of the **sacrifice** altar:
come, *lie all night* **stay overnight** in *sackcloth* **saq,**
ye ministers of my *God* **Elohim:**
for the *meat* offering and the *drink offering* **libation**
is withholden from the house of your *God* **Elohim.**

The Day Of Yah Veh

14 *Sanctify* **Hallow** ye a fast,
call a *solemn* **private** assembly,
gather the elders
and all the *inhabitants* **settlers** of the land
into the house of *the LORD* **Yah Veh** your *God* **El,**
and cry unto *the LORD* **Yah Veh,**
15 *Alas* **Aha** for the day!
for the day of *the LORD* **Yah Veh** is *at hand* **nearby,**
and as a *destruction* **ravage** from *the Almighty* **Shadday**
shall it come.
16 Is not the *meat* **food** cut off
before **in front of** our eyes,
yea, joy **cheerfulness** and *gladness* **twirling**
from the house of our *God* **Elohim?**
17 The *seed is rotten* **kernels rot** under their clods,
the *garners* **treasuries** *are laid* desolate,
the *barns* **granaries** are broken *down;* for
the *corn is withered* **crop withereth.**
18 How *do the beasts groan* **the animals sigh!**
the *herds* **droves** of cattle are perplexed,

Introduction

1 The word of Yah Veh
being to Yah El the son of Pethu El:
2 Hear this, you elders;
and hearken, all you settlers of the land:
becomes this in your days?
Or in the days of your fathers?

The Land Desolated

3 Scribe thereof to your sons;
and your sons to their sons;
and their sons to another generation.
4 What the palmerworm leaves, the locust eats;

and what the locust leaves, the cankerworm eats;
and what the cankerworm leaves, the caterpiller eats.
5 Waken, you intoxicants, and weep;
and howl, all you drinkers of wine:
because the squeezed juice
is cut off from your mouth.
6 For a goyim ascends on my land
—mighty and without number:
whose teeth, the teeth of a lion;
and the molars of a roaring lion.
7 He sets my vine desolate
and chips away my fig tree:
in stripping, he strips and casts away;
the tendrils whiten.
8 Lament as a virgin girt with saq
for the master of her youth:
9 the offering and the libation
is cut off from the house of Yah Veh;
the priests, the ministers of Yah Veh, mourn:
10 the field *is* ravaged; the soil mourns;
for the crop *is* ravaged:
the juice withers; the oil languishes.
11 Shame, O you cultivators!
Howl, O you vinedressers!
for the wheat and for the barley;
because the harvest of the field is destroyed.
12 The vine withers and the fig tree languishes;
—pomegranate tree,
also palm tree and apple tree
—all trees of the field wither:
because rejoicing withers from the sons of humanity.

Call To Repentance

13 Gird and mourn, you priests!
Howl, you ministers of the sacrifice altar!
Come, stay overnight in saq,
you ministers of my Elohim:
for the offering and the libation
is withheld from the house of your Elohim.

The Day Of Yah Veh

14 Hallow a fast! Call a private assembly!
Gather the elders and all the settlers of the land
into the house of Yah Veh your El,
and cry to Yah Veh,
15 Aha for the day!
for the day of Yah Veh *is* nearby,
and comes as a ravage from Shadday.
16 Is not the food cut off in front of our eyes?
Cheerfulness and twirling
from the house of our Elohim?
17 The kernels rot under their clods;
the treasuries desolate;
the granaries break;
for the crop withers.
18 How the animals sigh!
The droves of cattle perplex,
because they have no pasture;
yea, the *flocks* **droves** of *sheep* **flocks**
are *made desolate* **guilted**.
19 O *LORD* **Yah Veh**, to thee
will I cry **shall I call out**:
for the fire
hath *devoured* **consumed** the *pastures*
folds of the wilderness,
and the flame
hath *burned* **inflamed** all the trees of the field.
20 The *beasts* **animals** of the field
cry **yearn** also unto thee:
for the *rivers* **reservoirs** of waters
are dried up **withered**,
and the fire
hath *devoured* **consumed** the *pastures*
folds of the wilderness.

2 *Blow* **Blast** ye the *trumpet*
shophar in *Zion* **Siyon**,
and *sound an alarm* **shout** in my holy mountain:
let all the *inhabitants* **settlers** of the land *tremble* **quiver**:
for the day of *the LORD* **Yah Veh** cometh,
for it is *nigh at hand* **nearby**;
2 A day of **dripping** darkness
and of *gloominess* **darkness**,
a day of clouds and of thick darkness,
as the *morning* **dawn** spread upon the mountains:
a great people and a *strong* **mighty**;
there hath not been *ever* **eternally** the like,
neither shall **add to** be *any more* after it,
even to the years
of *many generations* **generation and generation**.
3 A fire *devoureth before them*
consumeth at their face;
and behind them a flame *burneth* **inflameth**:
the land is as the garden of Eden
before them **at their face**,
and behind them a desolate wilderness;
yea, and *nothing shall escape them*
there shall be no escapees.
4 The *appearance* **visage** of them
is as the *appearance* **visage** of horses;
and as *horsemen* **cavalry**, so shall they run.

5 Like the *noise* **voice** of chariots
on the tops of mountains
shall they *leap* **dance**,
like the *noise* **voice** of a flame of fire
that *devoureth* **consumeth** the stubble,
as a *strong* **mighty** people set in *battle* **war** array.
6 *Before* **In front of** their face
the people shall *be much pained* **writhe**: all
faces shall gather *blackness* **flushness.**
7 They shall run like mighty *men*;
they shall *climb* **ascend** the wall like men of war;
and they shall march every *one* **man** on his ways,
and they shall not *break* **entangle** their *ranks* **paths**:
8 Neither shall *one* **man** thrust *another* **brother**;
they shall walk
every one **all the mighty** in *his path* **their highway**:
and when they fall upon the sword,
they shall not be *wounded* **cropped.**
9 They shall run to and fro in the city;
they shall run upon the wall,
they shall *climb up* **ascend** upon the houses;
they shall enter in at the windows like a thief.
10 The earth shall quake *before them* **at their face**;
the heavens shall *tremble* **quake**:
the sun and the moon shall *be dark* **darken,**
and the stars
shall *withdraw* **gather** their *shining* **brilliance**:
11 And *the LORD* **Yah Veh**
shall *utter* **give** his voice
before **at the face of** his *army* **valiant**:
for his camp is *very* **mighty** great:
for he is *strong* **mighty** that *executeth* **worketh** his word:
for the day of *the LORD* **Yah Veh** is great
and *very terrible* **mighty awesome**;
and who can *abide* **contain** it?
12 Therefore also now,
saith the LORD **an oracle of Yah Veh,**
turn ye *even* to me with all your heart,
and with fasting,
and with weeping, and with *mourning* **chopping**:
13 And *rend* **rip** your heart,
and not your *garments* **clothes,**
and turn unto *the LORD* **Yah Veh** your *God* **Elohim**:
because they have no pasture;
yes, the droves of flocks have guilted.
19 O Yah Veh, to you I call out:
for the fire consumes the folds of the wilderness;
and the flame inflames all the trees of the field;
20 also the animals of the field yearn to you:
for the reservoirs of waters wither,
and the fire consumes the folds of the wilderness.

2 Blast the shophar in Siyon!
And shout in my holy mountain!
All the settlers of the land quiver:
for the day of Yah Veh approaches—nearby:
2 a day of dripping darkness and of darkness;
a day of clouds and of thick darkness
as the dawn spread on the mountains:
a great people and a mighty;
neither became the like eternally
nor adds to become afterward
to the years of generation and generation.
3 A fire consumes at their face;
and behind them a flame inflames:
the land *is* as the garden of Eden at their face,
and behind them a desolate wilderness;
yes, and there are no escapees.
4 Their visage *is* as the visage of horses;
and as cavalry, thus they run:
5 as the voice of chariots on the mountain tops,
they dance;
—as the voice of a flame of fire consumes the stubble
—as a mighty people set in war array.
6 In front of their face the people writhe:
all faces gather flushness:
7 they run as the mighty;
they ascend the wall as men of war;
and every man marches on his ways:
and they neither entangle their paths
8 nor man thrust brother:
they walk all their mighty in the highway:
and when they fall on the sword, they are not cut off.
9 They run to and fro in the city;
they run on the wall;
they ascend on the houses;
they enter at the windows as a thief:
10 the earth quakes at their face;
the heavens quake;
the sun and the moon darken;
and the stars gather their brilliance:
11 and Yah Veh gives his voice
at the face of his valiant;
for his camp is mighty great:
for he who works his word *is* mighty:
for the day of Yah Veh *is* great and mighty awesome;
and who can contain it?
12 And also now
—an oracle of Yah Veh
you, turn to me with all your heart,
and with fasting
and with weeping and with chopping:

13 and rip your heart and not your clothes;
and turn to Yah Veh your Elohim:
for he is *gracious* **charismatic** and merciful,
slow to *anger* **wrath**, and of great *kindness* **mercy**,
and *repenteth him of* **he sigheth concerning** the evil.
14 Who knoweth**?** *if he will return*—**He returneth**
and repent **yea, he sigheth**,
and *leave a blessing* **leaveth a blessing** behind him;
even a meat—**an** offering and a *drink offering* **libation**
unto *the LORD* **Yah Veh** your *God?* **Elohim.**
15 *Blow* **Blast** the *trumpet* **shophar** in *Zion* **Siyon**,
sanctify **hallow** a fast, call a *solemn* **private** assembly:
16 Gather the people, *sanctify*
hallow the congregation,
assemble **gather** the elders,
gather the *children* **sucklings**,
and those that suck the breasts:
let the bridegroom go forth of his chamber,
and the bride out of her *closet* **canopy**.
17 Let the priests, the ministers
of *the LORD* **Yah Veh**,
weep between the porch and the **sacrifice** altar,
and let them say, Spare thy people, O *LORD* **Yah Veh**,
and give not thine *heritage* **inheritance** to reproach,
that the *heathen* **goyim** should *rule* **reign** over them:
wherefore should they say among the people,
Where is their *God* **Elohim**?
18 Then *will the LORD* **shall Yah Veh**
be jealous for his land,
and *pity* **compassion** his people.
19 Yea, *the LORD will* **let Yah Veh** answer
and say unto his people,
Behold, I *will* **shall** send you *corn* **crop**,
and *wine* **juice**, and oil,
and ye shall be satisfied therewith:
and I *will* **add** no more *make* **to give** you a reproach
among the *heathen* **goyim**:
20 But I *will* **shall** remove far off from you
the northern *army*,
and *will* **shall** drive him
into a land *barren* **parched** and desolate,
with his face toward the east sea,
and his *hinder part* **end** toward the *utmost* **latter** sea,
and his stink shall *come up* **ascend**,
and his *ill savour* **stench** shall *come up* **ascend**,
because he hath *done great things* **greatened to work**.
21 *Fear* **Awe** not, O *land* **soil**;
be glad **twirl** and *rejoice* **cheer**:
for *the LORD* **Yah Veh**
will do great things **shall work greatly**.
22 *Be* **Awe** not *afraid*, ye *beasts* **animals** of the field:
for the *pastures* **folds** of the wilderness do
spring, for the tree beareth her fruit,
the fig tree and the vine
do yield **give** their *strength* **valuables**.
23 *Be glad* **Twirl** then, ye
children **sons** of *Zion* **Siyon**,
and *rejoice* **cheer**
in *the LORD* **Yah Veh** your *God* **Elohim**:
for he hath given you
the *former rain moderately* **early pour in justness**,
and he *will* **shall** cause to *come* **bring** down for you
the *rain* **downpour**,
the *former* **early** rain, and the *latter* **after** rain
in the first *month*.
24 And the *floors* **threshingfloors**
shall be *full of wheat* **filled with grain**,
and the *fats* **troughs** shall overflow
with *wine* **juice** and oil.
25 And I *will restore* **shall shalam** to you
the years that the locust hath eaten, the cankerworm,
and the caterpiller, and the palmerworm,
my great *army* **valiant** which I sent among you.
26 And ye shall eat *in plenty*,
eat and *be satisfied* **satiate**,
and *praise* **halal**
the name of *the LORD* **Yah Veh** your *God* **Elohim**,
that hath *dealt wondrously* **worked**
marvelously with you:
and my people shall never *be ashamed* **shame eternally**.
27 And ye shall know
that I am in the midst of *Israel* **Yisra El**,
and that *I am the LORD* **I—Yah Veh** your *God* **Elohim**,
and none else:
and my people shall *never be ashamed*
not shame eternally.
for he *is* charismatic and merciful
slow to wrath and of great mercy;
and he sighs concerning the evil.
14 Who knows?
He returns; yes, he sighs:
and leaves a blessing behind him
—an offering and a libation
to Yah Veh your Elohim.
15 Blast the shophar in Siyon!
Hallow a fast! Call a private assembly!
16 Gather the people! Hallow the congregation!
Gather the elders! Gather the sucklings!
And they who suck the breasts!
Have the bridegroom come from his chamber!

And the bride from her canopy!
17 Have the priests, the ministers of Yah Veh,
weep between the porch and the sacrifice altar;
and have them say, Spare your people, O Yah Veh!
And give not your inheritance to reproach
so that the goyim reign over them!
Why have them say among the people,
Where is their Elohim?
18 And Yah Veh is jealous for his land
and compassions his people:
19 yes, Yah Veh answers to his people,
Behold, I send you crop and juice and oil
and satisfy you therewith:
and I add not to give you
as a reproach among the goyim:
20 and I remove the northern far from you;
and drive him into a land parched and desolate;
with his face toward the east sea
and his end toward the latter sea;
and his stink ascends; and his stench ascends,
because he greatens to work.
21 Awe not, O soil; twirl and cheer:
for Yah Veh works greatly.
22 Awe not, you animals of the field:
for the folds of the wilderness spring up,
for the tree bears her fruit;
the fig tree and the vine give their valuables.
23 And twirl, you sons of Siyon;
and cheer in Yah Veh your Elohim:
for he gives you the early pour in justness,
and he brings down the downpour for you
—the early rain and the after rain in the first.
24 And the threshingfloors fill with grain
and the troughs overflow with juice and oil.
25 And I shalam to you
the years the locust eats
—the cankerworm
and the caterpiller and the palmerworm
—the great valiant I sent among you.
26 And you eat—eat and satiate;
and halal the name of Yah Veh your Elohim
who works marvelously with you:
and my people shame not eternally.
27 And you know I *am* midst Yisra El,
and I—Yah Veh your Elohim—and no one else:
and my people shame not eternally.

The Spirit Of Yah Veh Pours On All Flesh

28 And **so be** it *shall come to pass*, afterward,
that I *will* **shall** pour out my spirit upon all flesh;
and your sons and your daughters shall prophesy,
your *old men* **elders** shall dream dreams,
your *young men* **youths** shall see visions:
29 And also
upon the servants and upon the *handmaids* **maids**
in those days *will* **shall** I pour *out* my spirit.

Signs Of Omens

30 And I *will shew wonders* **shall give omens**
in the heavens and in the earth,
blood, and fire, and *pillars* **columns** of smoke.
31 The sun shall be turned into darkness,
and the moon into blood,
before **at the face of the coming**
of the great and *terrible* **awesome**
day of *the LORD* **Yah Veh** *come.*
32 And **so be** it *shall come to pass,*
that whosoever
shall call on the name of *the LORD* **Yah Veh**
shall be *delivered* **rescued**:
for in mount *Zion* **Siyon** and in *Jerusalem* **Yeru Shalem**
shall be *deliverance* **an escape**,
as *the LORD* **Yah Veh** hath said,
and in the *remnant* **survivors**
whom *the LORD* **Yah Veh** shall call.

The Goyim Judged

3 For, behold, in those days, and in that time,
when I shall *bring again* **return** the captivity
of *Judah* **Yah Hudah** and *Jerusalem* **Yeru Shalem**,
2 I *will* **shall** also gather all *nations* **goyim**,
and *will* **shall** bring them down
into *the valley of Jehoshaphat* **Gay Yah Shaphat**,
and *will* **shall** plead with them there
for my people and for my *heritage* **inheritance**
Israel **Yisra El**,
whom they have scattered among the *nations* **goyim**,
and *parted* **allotted** my land.
3 And they *have cast lots*
handle pebbles for my people;
and have given a *boy* **child** for *an harlot* **a whore**,
and sold a *girl* **child** for wine, that they might drink.
4 Yea, and what have ye to do with me,
O *Tyre* **Sor**, and *Zidon* **Sidon**,
and all the *coasts* **regions** of *Palestine* **Pelesheth**?
will **shall** ye *render* **deal** me *a recompence* **shalam**?
and if ye *recompense* **deal** me,
swiftly and *speedily* **quickly**
will **shall** I return your *recompence* **dealing**
upon your own head;

5 Because ye have taken my silver and my gold,
and have carried into your *temples* **manses**
my goodly *pleasant things* **desirables**:
6 The *children also* **sons** of *Judah* **Yah Hudah**
and the *children* **sons** of *Jerusalem* **Yeru Shalem**
have ye sold unto the *Grecians* **sons of Yavaniy**,
that ye might remove them far from their border.
7 Behold, I *will raise* **shall waken** them
out of the place whither ye have sold them,
and *will* **shall** return your *recompence* **dealing**
upon your own head:
8 And I *will* **shall** sell your
sons and your daughters
into the hand of the *children* **sons** of *Judah* **Yah Hudah**,
and they shall sell them to the *Sabeans* **Shebaiym**,
to a *people* **goyim** far off:
for *the LORD* **Yah Veh** hath *spoken* **worded** *it*.
9 *Proclaim ye* **Call ye out** this
among the *Gentiles* **goyim**;
Prepare **Hallow** war, wake up the mighty *men*,
let all the men of war draw near;
let them *come up* **ascend**:
10 *Beat* **Forge** your plowshares into swords,
and your *pruninghooks* **psalmpicks** into *spears* **javelins**:
let the *weak* **vanquished** say, I am *strong* **mighty**.
11 *Assemble yourselves* **Hurry**,
and come, all ye *heathen* **goyim**,
and gather yourselves together round about:
thither cause thy mighty ones to *come down* **descend**,
O *LORD* **Yah Veh**.
12 Let the *heathen* **goyim** be wakened,

The Spirit Of Yah Veh Pours On All Flesh

28 And so be it, afterward,
I pour my spirit on all flesh;
and your sons and your daughters prophesy;
your elders dream dreams;
your youths see visions:
29 and also on the servants and on the maids
in those days I pour my spirit.

Signs Of Omens

30 And I give omens
in the heavens and in the earth
—blood and fire and columns of smoke:
31 the sun turns into darkness
and the moon into blood
at the face of the coming
the great and awesome day of Yah Veh.
32 And so be it,
whoever calls on the name of Yah Veh
is rescued:
for in mount Siyon and in Yeru Shalem
is an escape,
as Yah Veh says,
and in the survivors whom Yah Veh calls.

The Goyim Judged

3 For behold, in those days, and in that time,
when I restore the captivity
of Yah Hudah and Yeru Shalem,
2 then I gather all the goyim
and bring them down
to Gay Yah Shaphat/Valley Yah Judges;
and there plead with them
for my people and for my inheritance Yisra El
—whom they scattered among the goyim
and allotted my land.
3 And they handle pebbles for my people;
and give a child for a whore,
and sell a child for wine to drink.
4 Yes, and what do you with me,
O Sor and Sidon and all the regions of Pelesheth?
Deal you me shalam?
And if you deal me,
I return your dealing
swiftly and quickly on your own head;
5 because you took my silver and my gold
and carried to your manses
—my goodly desirables:
6 and you sold the sons of Yah Hudah
and the sons of Yeru Shalem
to the sons of Yavaniy
—to remove them far from their border.
7 Behold, I waken them from
the place you sold them;
and return your dealing on your own head:
8 and I sell your sons and your daughters
into the hand of the sons of Yah Hudah;
and they sell them to the Shebaiym
—to a goyim far off:
for Yah Veh has worded.
9 Call this out among the goyim!
Hallow war! Waken the mighty!
Draw all the men of war near! Ascend them!
10 Forge your plowshares into swords
and your psalmpicks into javelins! Have
the vanquished say, I *am* mighty.
11 Hurry and come, all you goyim!

And gather yourselves together all around:
and there have your mighty ones descend,
O Yah Veh.
12 Waken, O goyim;
and *come up* **ascend**
to *the valley of Jehoshaphat* **Gay Yah Shaphat**:
for there *will* **shall** I sit
to judge all the *heathen* **goyim** round about.
13 *Put ye in* **Spread** the sickle,
for the harvest is *ripe* **ripened**:
come, *get you down* **descend ye**;
for the *press is full* **winepress filleth**,
the *fats* **troughs** overflow;
for their *wickedness* **evil** is great.
14 Multitudes, multitudes in the valley of decision:
for the day of *the LORD* **Yah Veh** is near
in the valley of decision.
15 The sun and the moon shall be darkened,
and the stars
shall *withdraw* **gather** their *shining* **brilliance**.
16 *The LORD* **Yah Veh** also
shall roar out of *Zion* **Siyon**,
and *utter* **give** his voice from *Jerusalem* **Yeru Shalem**;
and the heavens and the earth shall *shake* **quake**:
but *the LORD* **Yah Veh**
will **shall** be the *hope* **refuge** of his people,
and the *strength* **stronghold**
of the *children* **sons** of *Israel* **Yisra El**.
17 So shall ye know
that *I am the LORD* **I—Yah Veh** your *God* **Elohim**
dwelling **tabernacling** in *Zion* **Siyon**, my holy mountain:
then shall *Jerusalem* **Yeru Shalem** be holy,
and there shall no strangers pass through her any more.
18 And **so be** it *shall come to pass*, in that day,
that the mountains
shall *drop down new wine* **drip squeezed juice**,
and the hills shall *flow* **go** with milk,
and all the *rivers* **reservoirs** of *Judah* **Yah Hudah**
shall *flow* **go** with waters,
and a fountain shall *come forth* **go**
of **from** the house of *the LORD* **Yah Veh**,
and shall *water* **wet** the *valley* **wadi** of Shittim.
19 *Egypt* **Misrayim** shall be a desolation,
and Edom shall be a desolate wilderness,
for the violence
against the *children* **sons** of *Judah* **Yah Hudah**,
because they have *shed* **poured** innocent blood
in their land.
20 But *Judah* **Yah Hudah**
shall *dwell for ever* **settle eternally**,
and *Jerusalem* **Yeru Shalem**
from generation to generation.
21 For I *will cleanse* **shall exonerate** their blood
that I have not *cleansed* **exonerated**:
for *the LORD* **Yah Veh**
dwelleth **tabernacleth** in *Zion* **Siyon**.

and ascend to Gay Yah Shaphat/Valley Yah Judges:
for there I sit to judge all the goyim all around.
13 Spread the sickle; for the harvest ripens:
come, descend; for the winepress fills: the
troughs overflow; for their evil is great.
14 Multitudes,
multitudes in the valley of decision:
for the day of Yah Veh is near
in the valley of decision.
15 The sun and the moon darken
and the stars gather their brilliance:
16 and Yah Veh roars from Siyon
and gives his voice from Yeru Shalem:
and the heavens and the earth quake:
and Yah Veh *is* the refuge of his people,
and the stronghold of the sons of Yisra El.
17 Thus you know I—Yah Veh your Elohim
tabernacling in Siyon, my holy mountain:
then Yeru Shalem becomes holy,
and strangers pass through her no more.
18 And so be it, in that day,
the mountains drip squeezed juice;
and the hills go with milk;
and all the reservoirs of Yah Hudah go with waters;
and a fountain goes from the house of Yah Veh
and wets the wadi of Shittim.
19 Misrayim becomes a desolation
and Edom becomes a desolate wilderness
for their violence against the sons of Yah Hudah
—because they poured innocent blood in their land.
20 And Yah Hudah settles eternally,
and Yeru Shalem from generation to generation.
21 For I exonerate their blood
which I had not exonerated:
for Yah Veh tabernacles in Siyon.

INTRODUCTION

1 The words of Amos,
who was among the *herdmen* **branders** of *Tekoa* **Teqoa**,
which he saw concerning *Israel* **Yisra El**
in the days of *Uzziah* **Uzzi Yah**
king **sovereign** of *Judah* **Yah 1-ludah**,
and in the days of *Jeroboam* **Yarob Am**
the son of *Joash* **Yah Ash** *king*
sovereign of *Israel* **Yisra El**,
two years *before* **ere the face of** the *earthquake* **quake**.
2 And he said, *The LORD* **Yah Veh**
will **shall** roar from *Zion* **Siyon**,
and *utter* **give** his voice from *Jerusalem* **Yeru Shalem**;
and the *habitations* **folds** of the *shepherds* **tenders**
shall mourn,
and the top of *Carmel* **Karmel/orchard** shall wither.
3 Thus saith *the LORD* **Yah Veh**;
For three
transgressions **rebellions** of *Damascus* **Dammeseq**,
and for four,
I *will* **shall** not *turn away the punishment*
thereof **restore them**;
because they have threshed *Gilead* **Gilad**
with *threshing instruments* **sickles** of iron:
4 But I *will* **shall** send a fire
into the house of *Hazael* **1-laza El**,
which shall *devour* **consume**
the *palaces* **citadels** of *Benhadad* **Ben 1-ladad**.
5 I *will* **shall** break also the bar
of *Damascus* **Dammeseq**,
and cut off the *inhabitant* **settler**
from the *plain* **valley** of Aven,
and him that *holdeth* **upholdeth** the sceptre
from the house of Eden:
and the people of *Syria* **Aram**
shall *go into captivity* **be exiled** unto *Kir* **Qir**,
saith *the LORD* **Yah Veh**.
6 Thus saith *the LORD* **Yah Veh**;
For three *transgressions* **rebellions** of *Gaza* **Azzah**,
and for four,
I *will* **shall** not *turn away the punishment*
thereof **restore them**;
because they *carried away captive* **exiled**
the *whole captivity* **complete exiles**,
to *deliver* **shut** them up to Edom:
7 But I *will* **shall** send a fire
on the wall of *Gaza* **Azzah**,
which shall *devour* **consume** the *palaces* **citadels** *thereof*:
8 And I *will* **shall** cut off the *inhabitant* **settler**
from Ashdod,
and him that *holdeth* **upholdeth** the *sceptre* **scion**
from Ashkelon,
and I *will* **shall** turn mine hand against *Ekron* **Eqron**:
and the *remnant* **survivors** of the
Philistines **Peleshethiym**
shall *perish* **destruct**,
saith *the Lord GOD* **Adonay Yah Veh**.
9 Thus saith *the LORD* **Yah Veh**;
For three *transgressions* **rebellions** of *Tyrus* **Sor**,
and for four,
I *will* **shall** not *turn away the punishment*
thereof **restore them**;
because they delivered *up*
the *whole captivity* **complete exiles** to Edom,
and remembered not the *brotherly* covenant **of brethren**:
10 But I *will* **shall** send a fire
on the wall of *Tyrus* **Sor**,
which shall devour the *palaces* **citadels** *thereof*.
11 Thus saith *the LORD* **Yah Veh**;
For three *transgressions* **rebellions** of Edom,
and for four,
I *will* **shall** not *turn away the punishment*
thereof **restore them**;
because he did pursue his brother with the sword,
and *did cast off all pity* **ruined mercies**,
and his *anger* **wrath** did tear *perpetually* **eternally**,
and he *kept* **guarded** his wrath *for ever* **in perpetuity**:
12 But I *will* **shall** send a fire upon Teman,
which shall devour the *palaces* **citadels** of Bozrah.
13 Thus saith *the LORD* **Yah Veh**;
For three *transgressions* **rebellions**
of the *children* **sons** of Ammon,
and for four,
I *will* **shall** not *turn away the punishment*
thereof **restore them**;
because they have
ripped up **split** the women with child of *Gilead* **Gilad**,
that they might enlarge their border:
14 But I *will* **shall** kindle a
fire in the wall of Rabbah,

INTRODUCTION

1 The words of Amos,
being among the branders of Teqoa,
which he sees concerning Yisra El
in the days
of Uzzi Yah sovereign of Yah Hudah;
and in the days

of Yarob Am the son of Yah Ash sovereign of Yisra El,
two years ere the face of the quake.
2 And he says,
Yah Veh roars from Siyon
and gives his voice from Yeru Shalem;
and the folds of the tenders mourn
and the top of Karmel/orchard withers.
3 Thus says Yah Veh:
For three rebellions of Dammeseq,
and for four, I restore them not;
because of threshing Gilad with sickles of iron:
4 and I send a fire to the house of Haza El
to consume the citadels of Ben Hadad:
5 and I break the bar of Dammeseq
and cut off the settler
from the valley of Aven;
and he who upholds the sceptre
from the house of Eden:
and exile the people of Aram to Qir,
says Yah Veh.
6 Thus says Yah Veh:
For three rebellions of Azzah,
and for four, I restore them not;
because of exiling the complete exiles
to shut them up to Edom:
7 and I send a fire on the wall of Azzah
to consume the citadels:
8 and I cut off the settler from Ashdod
and he who upholds the scion from Ashkelon;
and I turn my hand against Eqron:
and destroy the survivors of the Peleshethiym,
says Adonay Yah Veh.
9 Thus says Yah Veh:
For three rebellions of Sor,
and for four, I restore not;
because of delivering the complete exiles to Edom
and remember not the covenant of brothers:
10 and I send a fire on the wall of Sor,
to consume the citadels.
11 Thus says Yah Veh:
For three rebellions of Edom,
and for four, I restore them not;
because of pursuing his brother with the sword
and ruining his mercies
and tearing his wrath eternally;
and guarding his wrath in perpetuity:
12 and I send a fire on Teman,
to consume the citadels of Bozrah.
13 Thus says Yah Veh:
For three rebellions of the sons of Ammon,
and for four, I restore them not;
because of splitting the women with child of Gilad,
to enlarge their border:
14 and I kindle a fire in the wall of Rabbah
and it shall devour the *palaces* **citadels** *thereof*,
with *shouting* **shouts** in the day of *battle* **war**,
with a *tempest* **storm**
in the day of the *whirlwind* **hurricane**:
15 And their *king* **sovereign**
shall go into *captivity* **exile**,
he and his *princes* **governors** together,
saith *the LORD* **Yah Veh**.

Judgment On Yah Hudah And Yisra El

2 Thus saith *the LORD* **Yah Veh**;
For three *transgressions* **rebellions** of Moab,
and for four,
I *will* **shall** not *turn away the punishment*
thereof **restore them**;
because he burned the bones
of the *king* **sovereign** of Edom into lime:
2 But I *will* **shall** send a fire upon Moab,
and it shall *devour* **consume**
the *palaces* **citadels** of *Kirioth* **Qerioth**:
and Moab shall die with *tumult* **an uproar**,
with *shouting* **shouts**,
and with the *sound* **voice** of the *trumpet* **shophar**:
3 And I *will* **shall** cut off the
judge from the midst *thereof*,
and *will slay* **shall slaughter**
all the *princes* **governors** *thereof* with him,
saith *the LORD* **Yah Veh**.
4 Thus saith *the LORD* **Yah Veh**;
For three *transgressions* **rebellions** of *Judah* **Yah Hudah**,
and for four,
I *will* **shall** not *turn away the punishment*
thereof **restore them**;
because they have *despised* **spurned**
the *law* **torah** of *the LORD* **Yah Veh**,
and have not *kept* **guarded** his *commandments* **statutes**,
and their lies caused them to *err* **stray**,
after the which their fathers have walked:
5 But I *will* **shall** send a fire
upon *Judah* **Yah Hudah**,
and it shall *devour* **consume**
the *palaces* **citadels** of *Jerusalem* **Yeru Shalem**.
6 Thus saith *the LORD* **Yah Veh**;
For three *transgressions* **rebellions** of *Israel* **Yisra El**,
and for four,

I *will* **shall** not *turn away the punishment*
thereof **restore them**;
because they sold the *righteous* **just** for silver,
and the *poor* **needy** for a pair of shoes;
7 That *pant* **gulp** after the dust of the earth
on the head of the poor,
and *turn aside* **pervert** the way of the *meek* **humble**:
and a man and his father
will **shall** go in unto the *same maid* **lass**,
to profane my holy name:
8 And they *lay themselves down* **spread**
upon clothes laid to pledge
by **beside** every **sacrifice** altar,
and they drink the wine of the condemned
in the house of their *god* **elohim**.
9 Yet *destroyed* **desolated** I the *Amorite* **Emoriy**
before them **at their face**,
whose height was like the height of the cedars,
and he was *strong* **powerful** as the oaks;
yet I *destroyed* **desolated** his fruit from above,
and his roots from beneath.
10 Also I *brought* **ascended** you *up*
from the land of *Egypt* **Misrayim**,
and *led* **carried** you forty years through the wilderness,
to possess the land of the *Amorite* **Emoriy**.
11 And I raised up of your sons for prophets,
and of your *young men* **youths** for *Nazarites* **Separatists**.
Is it not even thus, O ye *children* **sons** of *Israel* **Yisra El**?
saith the LORD **an oracle of Yah Veh**.
12 But ye gave the *Nazarites*
Separatists wine to drink;
and *commanded* **misvahed** the prophets, saying,
Prophesy not.
13 Behold, I am pressed under you,
as a *cart* **wagon** is pressed that is full of *sheaves* **omers**.
14 Therefore the flight shall
perish **destruct** from the swift,
and the strong shall not strengthen his force, neither
shall the mighty *deliver himself* **rescue his soul**:
15 Neither shall he stand
that *handleth* **manipulateth** the bow;
and he that is swift of foot shall
not *deliver* **rescue** *himself*:
to consume the citadels
with shouts in the day of war;
with a storm in the day of the hurricane: 15
and their sovereign goes into exile
—he and his governors together,
says Yah Veh.

JUDGMENT ON YAH HUDAH AND YISRA EL

2 Thus says Yah Veh:
For three rebellions of Moab,
and for four, I restore them not;
because of burning the bones
of the sovereign of Edom into lime:
2 and I send a fire on Moab,
to consume the citadels of Qerioth:
and Moab dies with an uproar
—with shouts and with the voice of the shophar:
3 and I cut off the judge from among them
and slaughter all the governors with him,
says Yah Veh.
4 Thus says Yah Veh;
For three rebellions of Yah Hudah,
and for four, I restore them not;
because of spurning the torah of Yah Veh,
and not guarding his statutes;
and their lies stray them
—after the which their fathers walked:
5 and I send a fire on Yah Hudah,
to consume the citadels of Yeru Shalem.
6 Thus says Yah Veh:
For three rebellions of Yisra El,
and for four, I restore them not;
because of selling the just for silver
and the needy for a pair of shoes;
7 who gulp after the dust of the earth
on the head of the poor,
and pervert the way of the humble:
and a man and his father going in to the lass
to profane my holy name:
8 and they spread on clothes laid to pledge
beside every sacrifice altar;
and drink the wine of the condemned
in the house of their elohim.
9 And I—I desolate the Emoriy at their face,
whose height *is* as the height of the cedars
as powerful as the oaks;
and I desolate his fruit from above
and his roots from beneath.
10 And I ascended you from the land of Misrayim;
and carried you forty years through the wilderness
to possess the land of the Emoriy:
11 and I raised of your sons for prophets
and of your youths for Separatists.
Is it not even thus, O you sons of Yisra El?
—an oracle of Yah Veh.
12 And you have the Separatists drink wine;

and misvah the prophets, saying,
Prophesy not.
13 Behold, I press you under
—press as a wagon full of omers.
14 and the flight destructs from the swift:
neither the strong strengthens his force
nor the mighty rescues his soul:
15 neither stands he who manipulates the bow;
nor rescues he who is swift of foot:
neither shall he that rideth the horse
deliver himself **rescue his soul.**
16 And he that is *courageous* **strong of heart**
among the mighty
shall flee away naked in that day, *saith*
the LORD **an oracle of Yah Veh.**

The Word Of Yah Veh Against The Sons Of Yisra El

3 Hear this word
that *the LORD* **Yah Veh** hath *spoken* **worded** against you,
O *children* **sons** of *Israel* **Yisra El,**
against the whole family which I *brought up* **ascended**
from the land of *Egypt* **Misrayim,** saying,
2 You only have I known of all
the families of the *earth* **soil:**
therefore I *will punish* **shall visit upon** you
for all your *iniquities* **perversities.**
3 Can two walk together,
except they *be agreed* **congregate?**
4 *Will* **Shall** a lion roar in the forest,
when he hath no prey?
will a young lion cry **shall a whelp give voice**
out of his *den* **habitation,**
if **except** he have *taken nothing* **captured?**
5 *Can* **Falleth** a bird *fall* in a snare upon the earth,
where no *gin* **snare** is for him?
shall one *take up* **ascend** a snare from the *earth* **soil,**
and *have taken nothing at all*
if in capturing, it hath not captured?
6 Shall a *trumpet be blown*
shophar blast in the city,
and the people not *be afraid* **tremble?**
shall there be evil in a city,
and *the LORD* **Yah Veh** hath not *done* **worked** it?
7 Surely *the Lord GOD* **Adonay Yah Veh**
will do nothing **shall work no word,**
but he *revealeth* **exposeth** his *secret* **private counsel**
unto his servants the prophets.
8 The lion hath roared, who
will **shall** not *fear* **awe?**
the Lord GOD **Adonay Yah Veh** hath *spoken* **worded,**
who *can but* **doth not** prophesy?
9 *Publish* **Let it be heard**
in the *palaces* **citadels** at Ashdod,
and in the *palaces* **citadels** in the
land of *Egypt* **Misrayim,**
and say, Assemble yourselves
upon the mountains of *Samaria* **Shomeron,**
and *behold* **see** the great *tumults* **confusions**
in the midst *thereof,*
and the oppressed in the midst *thereof.*
10 For they know not
to *do right* **work straightforwardness,**
saith the LORD **an oracle of Yah Veh,**
who *store up* **treasure** violence and *robbery* **ravage**
in their *palaces* **citadels.**
11 Therefore thus saith *the*
Lord GOD **Adonay Yah Veh;**
An adversary there shall *be* **A tribulator**
—even round about the land;
and he shall bring down thy strength from thee,
and thy *palaces* **citadels** shall be *spoiled* **plundered.**
12 Thus saith *the LORD* **Yah Veh;**
As the *shepherd* **tender**
taketh **rescueth** out of the mouth of the lion
two legs, or a piece of an ear;
so shall the *children* **sons** of *Israel* **Yisra El**
be *taken out* **rescued**
that *dwell* **settle** in *Samaria* **sShomeron**
in the *corner* **edge** of a bed,
and in *Damascus* **Dammeseq** in a *couch* **bedstead.**
13 Hear ye,
and *testify* **witness** in the house of *Jacob* **Yaaqov,**
saith the Lord GOD **an oracle of Adonay Yah Veh,**
the God of hosts **Elohim Sabaoth,**
14 That in the day that I shall visit
the *transgressions* **rebellions** of *Israel* **Yisra El** upon him
I *will* **shall** also visit the **sacrifice**
altars of *Bethel* **Beth El:**
and the horns of the **sacrifice** altar shall be cut off,
and fall to the *ground* **earth.**
15 And I *will* **shall** smite the winter house
with the summer house;
and the houses of ivory shall *perish* **destruct,**
and the great houses shall *have an end* **be consummated,**
saith the LORD **an oracle of Yah Veh.**
nor rescues he his soul who rides the horse:
16 and among the mighty, he who is strong of heart
flees away naked in that day
—an oracle of Yah Veh.

The Word Of Yah Veh Against The Sons Of Yisra El

3 Hear this word that Yah Veh words against you,
O sons of Yisra El
—against the whole family
I ascended from the land of Misrayim, saying,
2 You only, know I of all the families of the soil:
so I visit on you for all your perversities.
3 Walk two together, unless they congregate?
4 Roars a lion in the forest, when he has no prey?
Gives a whelp his voice from his habitation
unless he captures?
5 Falls a bird in a snare on the earth
where he has no snare?
Ascends a snare from the soil
and in capturing, captures not?
6 Blasts a shophar in the city and the people tremble not?
Becomes there evil in a city and Yah Veh worked it not?
7 Surely Adonay Yah Veh works no word;
unless he exposes his private counsel
to his servants the prophets.
8 The lion roars, who awes not?
Adonay Yah Veh words, who prophesies not?
9 O that it be heard in the citadels at Ashdod
and in the citadels in the land of Misrayim,
and say, Assemble yourselves
on the mountains of Shomeron,
and see the great confusions in the midst
and the oppressed in the midst.
10 For they know not to work straightforwardness
—an oracle of Yah Veh
who treasure violence and ravage in their citadels.
11 So thus says Adonay Yah Veh:
A tribulator surrounds the land
and he brings down your strength
and plunders your citadels.
12 Thus says Yah Veh:
As the tender rescues from the mouth of the lion
two legs or a piece of an ear,
thus *are* the sons of Yisra El rescued
who settle in Shomeron in the edge of a bed;
and in Dammeseq in a bedstead.
13 Hearken and witness in the house of Yaaqov
—an oracle of Adonay Yah Veh Elohim Sabaoth
14 in the day I visit the
rebellions of Yisra El on him
I also visit the sacrifice altars of Beth El:
and cut off the horns of the sacrifice altar
to fall to the earth:
15 and I smite the winter house
with the summer house;
and destroy the houses of ivory,
and consummate the great houses
—an oracle of Yah Veh.

Yisra El Unrepentant

4 Hear this word, ye *kine* **heifers** of Bashan,
that are in the mountain of *Samaria* **Shomeron,**
which oppress the poor, which crush the needy,
which say to their *masters* **adonim,**
Bring, and let us drink.
2 *The Lord GOD* **Adonay Yah Veh**
hath *sworn* **oathed** by his holiness,
that, *lo* **behold**, the days shall come upon you,
that he *will take* **shall lift** you *away* with hooks,
and your posterity with fishhooks.
3 And ye shall go out at the breaches,
every cow at that which is before her **women in front**;
and ye shall cast them into the palace,
saith the LORD **an oracle of Yah Veh.**
4 Come to *Bethel* **Beth El**, and *transgress* **rebel**;
at Gilgal *multiply transgression* **abound rebellion**;
and bring your sacrifices *every* **at** morning,
and your tithes after three years **of days**:
5 And *offer a sacrifice of thanksgiving*
incense with spread hands with *leaven* **fermentation,**
and *proclaim* **call out**
and *publish the free offerings* **let**
the voluntaries be heard:
for *this liketh you* **thus have ye loved,**
O ye *children* **sons** of *Israel* **Yisra El,**
saith the Lord GOD **an oracle of Adonay Yah Veh.**
6 And I also have given you
cleanness **innocency** of teeth in all your cities,
and *want* **lack** of bread in all your places:
yet have ye not returned unto me,
saith the LORD **an oracle of Yah Veh.**
7 And also I have withholden
the *rain* **downpour** from you,
when there were yet three months to the harvest:
and I caused it to rain upon one city,
and caused it not to rain upon *another* **one** city:
one *piece* **allotment** was rained upon,
and the *piece* **allotment** whereupon it rained not
withered.
8 So two or three cities wandered unto one city,
to drink water; but they were not satisfied:
yet have ye not returned unto me,
saith the LORD **an oracle of Yah Veh.**

9 I have smitten you with
blasting and *mildew* **pale green**:
when your gardens and your vineyards
and your fig trees and your *olive trees* **olives**
increased **abounded**,
the palmerworm devoured *them*:
yet have ye not returned unto me,
saith the LORD **an oracle of Yah Veh**.
10 I have sent among you the pestilence
after the manner **by the way** of *Egypt* **Misrayim**:
your *young men* **youths**
have I *slain* **slaughtered** with the sword,
and have taken away your horses;
and I have *made* **caused** the stink of your camps
to *come up* **ascend** unto your nostrils:
yet have ye not returned unto me,
saith the LORD **an oracle of Yah Veh**.
11 I have *overthrown some of* **turned against** you,
as *God* **Elohim**
overthrew *Sodom* **Sedom** and *Gomorrah* **Amorah**,
and ye were as a *firebrand* **brand**
plucked **rescued** out of the burning:
yet have ye not returned unto me,
saith the LORD **an oracle of Yah Veh**.
12 Therefore thus *will I do* **shall I work** unto thee,
O *Israel* **Yisra El**:
and because I *will do* **shall work** this unto thee,
prepare to meet thy *God* **Elohim**, O *Israel* **Yisra El**.
13 For, *lo* **behold**,
he that formeth the mountains, and createth the wind,
and *declareth* **telleth** unto *man* **humanity**
what is his *thought* **meditation**,
that *maketh* **worketh** the *morning* **dawn** darkness,
and treadeth upon the *high places* **bamahs** of the earth,
The LORD, The God of hosts **Yah Veh Elohim Sabaoth**,
is his name.

YISRA EL UNREPENTANT

4 Hear this word, you heifers of Bashan
in the mountain of Shomeron
—who oppress the poor; who crush the needy;
who say to their adonim,
Bring, and we drink.
2 Adonay Yah Veh oaths by his holiness,
that behold, days come on you,
that he lifts you with hooks
and your posterity with fishhooks:
3 and you go out at the breaches
—women in front;
and you cast them into the palace
—an oracle of Yah Veh.
4 Come to Beth El, and rebel;
abound rebellion at Gilgal:
and bring your sacrifices at morning,
and your tithes after three years of days:
5 and incense with fermentation
with spread hands
and call out that the voluntaries be heard:
for thus you loved, O you sons of Yisra El
—an oracle of Adonay Yah Veh.
6 And I also
—I gave you innocency of teeth in all your cities
and lack of bread in all your places:
yet you returned not to me
—an oracle of Yah Veh.
7 And I also
—I withheld the downpour from you,
when yet three months to the harvest:
and I, on one city, rained;
and on one city, rained not:
—one allotment, rained on;
and the allotment not rained on withers:
8 and two or three cities wander to one city
to drink water;
and they satiated not:
yet you returned not to me
—an oracle of Yah Veh.
9 I smote you with blasting and pale green
when your gardens and your vineyards
and your fig trees and your olives abounded;
and the palmerworm devoured:
yet you returned not to me
—an oracle of Yah Veh.
10 I sent the pestilence among you
by the way of Misrayim:
I slaughtered your youths with the sword
and took away your horses;
and I ascended the stink of your camps
to your nostrils:
yet you returned not to me
—an oracle of Yah Veh.
11 I turned against you,
as Elohim overthrew Sedom and Amorah,
—as a brand rescued from the burning:
yet you returned not to me
—an oracle of Yah Veh.
12 So thus I work to you, O Yisra El:
and because I work this to you,
prepare to meet your Elohim, O Yisra El.
13 For behold,

he who formed the mountains and created the wind,
who tells his meditation to humanity,
who works the dawn darkness,
who treads on the bamahs of the earth,
Yah Veh Elohim Sabaoth *is* his name.

THE LAMENTATION OF YAH VEH AGAINST YISRA EL

5 Hear ye this word which
I *take up* **lift** against you,
even a lamentation, O house of *Israel* **Yisra El**.
2 The virgin of *Israel* **Yisra El** is fallen;
she shall *no more* **add not to** rise:
she is forsaken upon her *land* **soil**;
there is none to raise her up.
3 For thus saith *the Lord GOD* **Adonay Yah Veh**;
The city that went out by a thousand
shall leave an hundred,
and that which went forth by an hundred
shall leave ten,
to the house of *Israel* **Yisra El**.
4 For thus saith *the LORD* **Yah Veh**
unto the house of *Israel* **Yisra El**,
Seek ye me, and ye shall live:
5 But seek not *Bethel* **Beth**
El, nor enter into Gilgal,
and pass not to *Beersheba* **Beer Sheba**:
for **in exiling,**
Gilgal shall *surely go into captivity* **be exiled**,
and *Bethel* **Beth El** shall come to *nought* **mischief**.
6 Seek *the LORD* **Yah Veh**, and *ye* shall live;
lest he *break out* **prosper** like fire
in the house of *Joseph* **Yoseph**,
and *devour it* **consume**,
and there be none to quench it in *Bethel* **Beth El**.
7 Ye who turn judgment to wormwood,
and leave off *righteousness* **justness** in the earth,
8 Seek him that *maketh the*
seven stars **worketh Kimah**
and *Orion* **Kesil**,
and turneth the shadow of death into the morning,
and maketh the day dark with night:
that calleth for the waters of the sea,
and poureth them out upon the face of the earth:
The LORD **Yah Veh** is his name:
9 That *strengtheneth* **releaseth** the *spoiled* **ravaged**
against the strong,
so that the *spoiled* shall **ravaged**
come against the fortress.
10 They hate him
that *rebuketh* **reproveth** in the *gate* **portal**,
and they abhor him
that *speaketh uprightly* **wordeth integriously**.
11 Forasmuch therefore
as your *treading* **trampling** is upon the poor,
and ye take from him burdens of *wheat* **grain**:
ye have built houses of hewn stone,
but ye shall not *dwell* **settle** in them;
ye have planted *pleasant* vineyards **of desire**,
but ye shall not drink wine of them.
12 For I know
your *manifold transgressions* **great rebellions**
and your mighty sins:
they *afflict* **tribulate** the just,
they take a *bribe* **koper/atonement**,
and they *turn aside* **pervert** the *poor* **needy**
in the *gate* **portal** *from their right*.
13 Therefore the *prudent* **comprehending**
shall keep *silence* **still** in that time; for it is an evil time.
14 Seek good, and not evil, that ye may live:
and so *the LORD, the God of hosts*
Yah Veh Elohim Sabaoth,
shall be with you, as ye have *spoken* **said**.
15 Hate the evil, and love the good,
and *establish* **set** judgment in the *gate* **portal**:
it may be that **perhaps**
the LORD God of hosts **Yah Veh Elohim Sabaoth**
will be gracious **shall grant charism**
unto the *remnant* **survivors** of *Joseph* **Yoseph**.

THE DAY OF YAH VEH

16 Therefore
the LORD, the God of hosts, the Lord,
Yah Veh Elohim Sabaoth Adonay saith thus;
Wailing **Chopping** shall be in all streets;
and they shall say in all the *highways* **outways**,
Alas! alas! **Hah! Hah!**
and they shall call the *husbandman* **cultivator**
to mourning,
and such as *are skilful of* **know** lamentation
to *wailing* **chopping**.

THE LAMENTATION OF YAH VEH AGAINST YISRA EL

5 Hear this word I lift against you!
A lamentation, O house of Yisra El.
2 The virgin of Yisra El—
fallen; she adds not to rise:
forsaken on her soil
she has no one to raise her up.

3 For thus says Adonay Yah Veh:
The city that comes by a thousand
leaves a hundred;
and that which comes by a hundred
leaves ten to the house of Yisra El.
4 For thus says Yah Veh to the house of Yisra El:
Seek me, and live:
5 neither seek Beth El nor enter Gilgal
nor pass through Beer Sheba:
for in exiling, Gilgal *is* exiled,
and Beth El becomes for mischief.
6 Seek Yah Veh, and live;
lest he prospers as fire in the house of Yoseph
and consumes;
and no one in Beth El to quench it.
7 You who turn judgment to wormwood,
and leave off justness in the earth,
8 seek him who works Kimah and Kesil
and turns the shadow of death into the morning
and makes the day dark with night:
who calls for the waters of the sea
and pours them on the face of the earth:
Yah Veh *is* his name:
9 —who releases the ravaged against the strong,
so that the ravaged come against the fortress.
10 They hate him who reproves in the portal
and they abhor him who words integriously:
11 so because you trample on the poor
and take his burdens of grain; you
build houses of hewn stone,
and you settle not therein; you plant vineyards
of desire, and you drink not their wine.
12 For I know your great rebellions
and your mighty sins:
they tribulate the just;
they take a koper/atonement;
and they pervert the needy in the portal.
13 So, in that time,
the comprehending keep still; for it is an evil time.
14 Seek good, and not evil, so that you live:
and so be it, as you say,
Yah Veh Elohim Sabaoth *is* with you.
15 Hate the evil and love the good
and set judgment in the portal:
perhaps Yah Veh Elohim Sabaoth
grants charism to the survivors of Yoseph.

THE DAY OF YAH VEH

16 So, thus says Yah Veh Elohim Sabaoth Adonay:
Chopping *is* in all streets;
and in all the outways, they say, Hah! Hah!
and they call the cultivator to mourning
and such as know lamentation to chopping:
17 And in all vineyards shall be *wailing* **chopping**:
for I *will* **shall** pass *through thee* **in your midst**,
saith *the LORD* **Yah Veh**.
18 *Woe* **Ho** unto you
that desire the day of *the LORD* **Yah Veh**!
to what end is it for you?
the day of *the LORD* **Yah Veh** is darkness, and not light.
19 As if a man did flee from **the face of** a lion,
and a bear met him;
or went into the house,
and *leaned* **propped** his hand on the wall,
and a serpent bit him.
20 Shall not the day of *the LORD* **Yah Veh**
be darkness, and not light?
even very dark, and no *brightness* **brilliance** in it?
21 I hate, I *despise* **spurn** your
feast days **celebrations**,
and I *will* **shall** not *smell* **scent**
in your *solemn* **private** assemblies.
22 Though ye *offer* **holocaust** me
burnt offerings **holocausts** and your *meat* offerings,
I *will* **shall** not *accept them* **be pleased**:
neither *will* **shall** I *regard* **scan**
the *peace offerings* **shelamim** of your *fat beasts* **fatlings**.
23 *Take* **Turn** thou *away* **aside** from me
the *noise* **roar** of thy songs;
for I *will* **shall** not hear
the *melody* **psalm** of thy *viols* **bagpipes**.
24 But let judgment *run down* **roll** as waters,
and *righteousness* **justness**
as a *mighty stream* **perennial wadi**.
25 Have ye *offered* **brought near** unto me
sacrifices and offerings in the wilderness forty years,
O house of *Israel* **Yisra El**?
26 But ye have borne the *tabernacle*
sukkoth/brush arbor
of your *Moloch* **sovereign** and *Chiun* **Kiun** your images,
the star of your *god* **elohim**,
which ye *made* **worked** to yourselves.
27 Therefore
will **shall** I cause you to go into *captivity* **exile**
beyond *Damascus* **Dammeseq**,
saith *the LORD* **Yah Veh**,
whose name is *The God of hosts* **Elohim Sabaoth**.

Ho To Them Who Relax In Siyon

6 *Woe* **Ho** to them that *are*
at ease **relax** in *Zion* **Siyon**,
and *trust* **confide** in the mountain
of *Samaria* **Shomeron**,
which are *named* **appointed**
chief **firstlings** of the *nations* **goyim**,
to whom the house of *Israel* **Yisra El** came!
2 Pass ye unto *Calneh* **Kalneh**, and see;
and from thence go ye to Hamath the *great* **rabbi**:
then go down **descend** to Gath
of the *Philistines* **Peleshethiym**:
be they better than these *kingdoms* **sovereigndoms**?
or their border greater than your border?
3 Ye that *put far* **cast** away the evil day,
and cause the *seat* **settlement** of violence to come near;
4 That lie upon beds of ivory,
and *stretch* **spread** themselves upon
their *couches* **bedsteads**,
and eat the *lambs* **rams** out of the flock,
and the calves out of the midst of the stall;
5 That *chant* **chatter**
to the *sound* **mouth** of the *viol* **bagpipe**,
and *invent* **fabricate** to themselves
instruments of *musick* **song**,
like David;
6 That drink wine in *bowls* **sprinklers**,
and anoint themselves with the
chief **firstlings** ointments:
but they are not *grieved* **worn**
for the *affliction* **breach** of *Joseph* **Yoseph**.
7 Therefore now shall they *go captive* **be exiled**
with the first that *go captive* **be exiled**,
and the *banquet* **feast of revelling**
of them that *stretched* **spread** themselves
shall be *removed* **turned aside**.
8 *The Lord GOD* **Adonay Yah Veh**
hath *sworn* **oathed** by *himself* **his soul***,

*Yah Veh is the soul of the triune deity
Read: Yirme Yah 51:14

17 and in all vineyards, chopping:
for I pass midst you, says Yah Veh.
18 Ho to you who desire the day of Yah Veh!
To what end is it for you?
The day of Yah Veh is darkness, and not light
19 —as a man flees the face of a lion
and a bear meets him;
or goes into the house and props his hand on the wall
and a serpent bites him:
20 *Is* not the day of Yah Veh
darkness and not light?
—even very dark with no brilliance therein?
21 I hate, I spurn your celebrations,
and I scent not your private assemblies.
22 Though you holocaust
your holocausts and offerings to me,
I *am* neither pleased
nor scan I the shelamim of your fatlings:
23 turn aside the roar of your songs from me
for I hear not the psalm of your bagpipes:
24 and judgment rolls as waters
and justness as a perennial wadi.
25 Brought you near to me
sacrifices and offerings in the wilderness forty years
O house of Yisra El?
26 Yes, you bore
the sukkoth/brush arbor of your sovereign
and Kiun, the star of your elohim,
the images you worked to yourselves.
27 So I exile you beyond Dammeseq,
says Yah Veh,
whose name *is* Elohim Sabaoth.

Ho To Them Who Relax In Siyon

6 Ho to them who relax in Siyon
and confide in the mountain of Shomeron
—the appointed firstlings of the goyim
to whom the house of Yisra El comes!
2 Pass to Kalneh, and see;
and from there go to Hamath the rabbi:
descend to Gath of the Peleshethiym:
Are they better than these sovereigndoms?
Or their border greater than your border?
3 You who cast away the evil day;
who bring near the settlement of violence;
4 who lie on beds of ivory
and spread themselves on their bedsteads;
and eat the rams from the flock
and the calves from midst the stall;
5 who chatter to the mouth of the bagpipe
who, as David,
fabricate to themselves instruments of song;
6 who drink wine in sprinklers
and anoint themselves with the firstlings ointments;
who are not worn out for the breach of Yoseph:
7 so now they *are* exiled
with the first of the exiles,
and the feast of revelling
of them who spread themselves *is* turned aside.

8 Adonay Yah Veh oaths by his soul*

*Yah Veh is the soul of the triune deity
Read: Yirme Yah 51:14

saith the LORD the God of hosts
an oracle of Yah Veh Elohim Sabaoth,
I *abhor* **loathe** the *excellency* **pomp** of *Jacob* **Yaaqov,**
and hate his *palaces* **citadels:**
therefore *will I deliver* **shall I shut** up the city
with *all that is therein* **the fulness thereof.**
9 And **so be** it *shall come to pass,*
if there remain ten men in one house, that they shall die.
10 And *a man's* **his** uncle shall *take* **bear** him *up,*
and he that *burneth* **cremateth** him,
to bring out the bones out of the house,
and shall say unto him
that is by the *sides* **flanks** of the house,
Is there yet any with thee?
and he shall say, *No* **Final.**
Then shall he say, *Hold thy tongue* **Hush:**
for we may not *make mention of* **memorialize**
the name of *the LORD* **Yah Veh.**
11 For, behold,
the LORD commandeth **Yah Veh misvaheth,**
and he *will* **shall** smite the great house
with *breaches* **dewdrops,**
and the little house with *clefts* **fissures.**
12 Shall horses run upon the rock?
will **shall** one plow *there* with oxen?
for ye have turned judgment into *gall* **rosh,**
and the fruit of *righteousness* **justness**
into *hemlock* **wormwood:**
13 Ye which *rejoice* **cheer** in
a *thing* **word** of nought,
which say,
Have we not taken to us horns by our own strength?
14 But, behold,
I *will* **shall** raise *up* against you a *nation* **goyim,**
O house of *Israel* **Yisra El,**
saith the LORD the God of hosts
an oracle of Yah Veh Elohim Sabaoth;
and they shall afflict you from the entering in of Hemath
unto the *river* **wadi** of the *wilderness* **plain.**

WARNING VISIONS

7 Thus *hath the Lord GOD* **Adonay Yah Veh**
shewed unto me **hath me see;**
and, behold, he formed *grasshoppers* **grubbers**
in the beginning of the *shooting up* **ascending**
of the *latter* **after** growth;
and, *lo* **behold,** it was the latter growth
after the *king's mowings* **sovereign's shearings.**
2 And **so be** it *came to pass,*
that when they had *made an end of* **finished** eating
the *grass* **herbage** of the land,
then I said, *O Lord GOD* **Adonay Yah Veh,**
forgive, I beseech thee:
by whom **how** shall *Jacob* **Yaaqov** arise? for he is small.
3 *The LORD repented* **Yah Veh sighed** for this:
It shall not be, saith *the LORD* **Yah Veh.**
4 Thus *hath the Lord GOD* **Adonay Yah Veh**
shewed unto me **hath me see:**
and, behold, *the Lord GOD* **Adonay Yah Veh**
called to contend by fire,
and it *devoured* **consumed** the great *deep* **abyss,**
and did eat up *a part* **an allotment.**
5 Then said I, O *Lord GOD* **Adonay Yah Veh,**
cease, I beseech thee:
by whom **How** shall *Jacob* **Yaaqov** arise? for he is small.
6 *The LORD repented* **Yah Veh sighed** for this:
This also shall not be,
saith *the Lord GOD* **Adonay Yah Veh.**
7 Thus he *shewed* **hath** me **see:** and, behold,
the Lord stood **Adonay stationed** upon a wall
made by a plumbline, with a plumbline in his hand.
8 And *the LORD* **Yah Veh** said unto me,
Amos, what seest thou?
And I said, A plumbline.
Then said *the LORD* **Yah Veh Adonay,**
Behold, I *will* **shall** set a plumbline
in the midst of my people *Israel* **Yisra El:**
I *will* **shall** not *again* **add to** pass by them any more:
9 And the *high places* **bamahs** of *Isaac* **Yischaq**
shall be *desolate* **desolated,**
—an oracle of Yah Veh Elohim Sabaoth.
I loathe the pomp of Yaaqov and hate his citadels:
so I shut up the city with the fulness thereof.
9 And so be it,
if ten men remain in one house, they die:
10 and his uncle and his cremater lift him
to bring the bones from the house,
and say to him who is by the flanks of the house,
Are there yet any with you?
And he says, Final.
Then he says, Hush:
for we memorialize not the name of Yah Veh.
11 For, behold, Yah Veh misvahs;
and he smites the great house with dewdrops
and the little house with fissures:
12 Run horses on the rock?

Plows one with oxen?
For you turn judgment into rosh
and the fruit of justness into wormwood.
13 You who have no word of cheer,
who say, Have we not, by our own strength,
taken horns to ourselves?
14 Surely behold, I raise a goyim against you,
O house of Yisra El
—an oracle of Yah Veh Elohim Sabaoth
and they afflict you from the entering in of Hemath
to the wadi of the plain.

WARNING VISIONS

7 Thus Adonay Yah Veh shows me;
and behold, he forms grubbers
in the beginning of the ascending of the after growth;
and behold, it *is* the latter growth
after the shearings of the sovereign.
2 And so be it,
they finish eating the herbage of the land,
and I say, Adonay Yah Veh,
forgive, I beseech you:
How rises Yaaqov? For he is small.
3 Yah Veh sighs for this:
So be it not, says Yah Veh.
4 Thus Adonay Yah Veh shows me:
and behold, Adonay Yah Veh calls to contend by fire;
and it consumes the great abyss
and eats an allotment.
5 And I say, O Adonay Yah Veh,
cease, I beseech you:
How rises Yaaqov? For he is small.
6 Yah Veh sighs for this also:
So be it not, says Adonay Yah Veh.
7 Thus he has me see: and behold,
Adonay stations a plumb line on a wall
and a plumb line in his hand.
8 And Yah Veh says to me, Amos, what see you?
And I say, A plumbline.
Then Yah Veh Adonay says,
Behold, I set a plumbline among my people Yisra El:
I add not to pass by them any more:
9 and *I* desolate the bamahs of Yischaq
and the *sanctuaries* **holies** of *Israel* **Yisra El**
shall be *laid waste* **parched**;
and I *will* **shall** rise
against the house of *Jeroboam*
Yarob Am with the sword.
10 Then *Amaziah* **Amas Yah**
the priest of *Bethel* **Beth El**
sent to *Jeroboam* **Yarob Am**
king **sovereign** of *Israel* **Yisra El**, saying,
Amos hath conspired against thee
in the midst of the house of *Israel* **Yisra El**:
the land is not able to *bear* **contain** all his words.
11 For thus Amos saith,
Jeroboam **Yarob Am** shall die by the sword,
and **in exiling,**
Israel **Yisra El** shall *surely be led away captive* **be exiled**
out of their own *land* **soil**.
12 Also *Amaziah* **Amas Yah** said unto Amos,
O thou seer, go,
flee thee *away* into the land of *Judah* **Yah Hudah**,
and there eat bread, and prophesy there:
13 But **add not to** prophesy *not again*
any more at *Bethel* **Beth El**:
for it is the *king's chapel* **holies of the sovereigndom**,
and it is the *king's court* **house of the sovereign**.
14 Then answered Amos, and
said to *Amaziah* **Amas Yah**,
I was no prophet, neither was I a prophet's son;
but I was an herdman,
and a *gatherer* **pincher** of *sycomore fruit* **sycomores**:
15 And *the LORD* **Yah Veh** took me
as I followed the flock,
and *the LORD* **Yah Veh** said unto me,
Go, prophesy unto my people *Israel* **Yisra El**.
16 Now therefore
hear thou the word of *the LORD* **Yah Veh**:
Thou sayest, Prophesy not against *Israel* **Yisra El**,
and *drop* **drip** not
thy word against the house of *Isaac* **Yischaq**.
17 Therefore thus saith *the LORD* **Yah Veh**;
Thy *wife* **woman** shall *be an harlot* **whore** in the city,
and thy sons and thy daughters shall fall by the sword,
and thy *land* **soil** shall be *divided* **allotted** by line;
and thou shalt die in a *polluted land* **foul soil**:
and **in exiling,**
Israel **Yisra El** shall *surely go into captivity* **be exiled**
forth of **from** his *land* **soil**.

THE BASKET OF SUMMER FRUIT

8 Thus *hath the Lord GOD* **Adonay Yah Veh**
shewed unto me **hath me see**:
and behold a basket of summer fruit.
2 And he said, Amos, what seest thou?
And I said, A basket of summer fruit.
Then said *the LORD* **Yah Veh** unto me,
The end is come upon my people of *Israel* **Yisra El**;
I *will* **shall** not *again* **add to** pass by them any more.

3 And the *songs* **songstresses** of the *temple* **manse**
shall be howlings in that day,
saith the Lord GOD **an oracle of Adonay Yah Veh**:
there shall be many *dead bodies* **carcases** in every place;
they shall cast them forth *with silence* **hushed**.
4 Hear this, O ye that *swallow up* **gulp** the needy,
even to make the *poor* **humble** of the land
to *fail* **shabbathize**,
5 Saying,
When *will* **shall be** the new moon *be gone* **passed**,
that we may *sell corn* **market for kernels**?
and the *sabbath* **shabbath**,
that we may *set forth wheat* **open grain**,
making **lessening** the ephah *small*,
and **greatening** the shekel *great*,
and *falsifying* **twisting** the balances by deceit?
6 That we may *buy* **chattel** the poor for silver,
and the needy for a pair of shoes;
yea, and *sell* **market for kernels**
the *refuse* **chaff** of the *wheat* **grain**?
7 *The LORD* **Yah Veh** hath *sworn* **oathed**
by the *excellency* **pomp** of *Jacob* **Yaaqov**,
Surely *I will never* **shall not in perpetuity**
forget any of their works.
8 shall not the land *tremble* **quake** for this,
and every one mourn that *dwelleth* **settleth** therein?
and parch the holies of Yisra El;
and I rise against the house of Yarob Am
with the sword.
10 And Amas Yah the priest of Beth El
sends to Yarob Am sovereign of Yisra El,
saying, Amos conspires against you
among the house of Yisra El:
the land is not able to contain all his words.
11 For Amos says thus:
Yarob Am dies by the sword,
and in exiling, Yisra El *is* exiled from their own soil.
12 Also Amas Yah says to Amos,
O you seer, go, flee into the land of Yah Hudah,
and there eat bread, and there prophesy:
13 and add not to prophesy any more at Beth El:
for it is the holies of the sovereigndom
and it is the house of the sovereign.
14 Then Amos answers and says to Amas Yah,
I *am* neither a prophet nor a son of a prophet;
but I *am* a herdman and a pincher of sycomores:
15 and as I follow the flock,
Yah Veh takes me and Yah Veh says to me,
Go, prophesy to my people Yisra El.
16 And now, hear the word of Yah Veh:
You say, Neither prophesy against Yisra El
nor drip against the house of Yischaq.
17 So Yah Veh says thus:
Your woman whores in the city
and your sons and your daughters fall by the sword
and your soil *is* allotted by line;
and you die in a foul soil:
and in exiling, Yisra El *is* exiled from his soil.

THE BASKET OF SUMMER FRUIT

8 Thus Adonay Yah Veh shows me,
and behold, a basket of summer fruit:
2 and he says, Amos, what see you?
And I say, A basket of summer fruit.
And Yah Veh says to me,
The end comes on my people of Yisra El;
I add not to pass by them any more.
3 And the songstresses of the
manse howl in that day
—an oracle of Adonay Yah Veh:
with many carcases in every place;
they cast them forth:
Hush!
4 Hear this, O you who gulp the needy,
who shabbathize the humble of the land,
5 saying,
When passes the new moon, to market kernels?
—the shabbath, to open grain?
—to lessen the ephah and greaten the shekel?
—to twist the balances by deceit?
6 —to chattel the poor for silver
and the needy for a pair of shoes?
—to market kernels, the chaff of the grain?
7 Yah Veh oaths by the pomp of Yaaqov,
Surely I forget none of their works in perpetuity.
8 Quakes not the land for this?
And every one who settles therein mourns?
and it shall *rise up* **ascend** wholly as a *flood* **light**;
and it shall be *cast out* **expelled** and drowned,
as by the *flood* **river** of *Egypt* **Misrayim**.
9 And **so be** it *shall come to pass*, in that day,
saith the Lord GOD **an oracle of Adonay Yah Veh**,
that I *will* **shall** cause the sun to *go
down* **descend** at noon,
and I *will* **shall** darken the earth in the *clear* **light of** day:
10 And I *will* **shall** turn your *feasts* **celebrations**
into mourning,
and all your songs into lamentation;
and I *will bring up sackcloth* **shall ascend saq**
upon all loins,

and baldness upon every head;
and I *will make* **shall set** it
as the mourning of an only *son*,
and the end *thereof* as a bitter day.
11 Behold, the days come,
saith the Lord GOD **an oracle of Adonay Yah Veh,**
that I *will* **shall** send a famine in the land,
not a famine of bread, nor a thirst for water,
but of hearing the words of *the LORD* **Yah Veh**:
12 And they shall wander from sea to sea,
and from the north even to the *east* **rising**,
they shall *run to and fro* **flit**
to seek the word of *the LORD* **Yah Veh**,
and shall not find *it*.
13 In that day
shall the *fair* **beautiful** virgins and *young men* **youths**
faint **languish** for thirst.
14 They that *swear* **oath**
by the *sin* **guilt** of *Samaria* **Shomeron**,
and say, Thy *god* **elohim**, O Dan, liveth;
and, The *manner* **way** of *Beersheba* **Beer Sheba** liveth;
even they shall fall, and never rise *up* again.

JUDGMENT OF YAH VEH

9 I saw *the Lord* **Adonay**
standing **stationed** upon the **sacrifice** altar:
and he said, Smite the lintel of the door,
that the *posts* **thresholds** may *shake* **quake**:
and *cut* **crop** them in the head, all of them;
and I *will slay* **shall slaughter** the last of them
with the sword:
he that fleeth of them shall not flee away,
and *he that escapeth* **any escapee** of them
shall not be *delivered* **rescued**.
2 Though they dig into *hell* **sheol,**
thence shall mine hand take them;
though they *climb up* **ascend** to *heaven* **the heavens,**
thence *will* **shall** I bring them down:
3 And though they hide themselves
in the top of *Carmel* **Karmel/orchard,**
I *will* **shall** search and take them out thence;
and though they be hid from my *sight* **eyes**
in the *bottom* **floor** of the sea,
thence *will I command* **shall I misvah** the serpent,
and he shall bite them:
4 And though they go into captivity
before **at the face of** their enemies,
thence *will I command* **shall I misvah** the sword,
and it shall *slay* **slaughter** them:
and I *will* **shall** set mine eyes upon them for evil,
and not for good.
5 And *the Lord GOD of hosts*
Adonay Yah Veh Sabaoth
is he that toucheth the land, and it shall melt,
and all that *dwell* **settle** therein shall mourn:
and it shall *rise up* **ascend** wholly like a *flood* **river**;
and shall be drowned,
as *by* the *flood* **river** of *Egypt* **Misrayim.**
6 It is he
that buildeth his *stories* **steps** in the *heaven* **heavens,**
and hath founded his *troop* **band** in the earth;
he that calleth for the waters of the sea,
and poureth them out upon the face of the earth:
The LORD **Yah Veh** is his name.
7 Are ye not
as *children* **sons** of the *Ethiopians* **Kushiym** unto me,
O *children* **sons** of *Israel* **Yisra El?**
saith the LORD **an oracle of Yah Veh.**
And it all ascends as a light
and expels and drowns as by the river of Misrayim.
9 And so be it, in that day,
—an oracle of Adonay Yah Veh
that I decend the sun at noon
and I darken the earth in the light of day:
10 and I turn your celebrations into mourning
and all your songs into lamentation;
and I ascend saq on all loins
and baldness on every head;
and I set it as the mourning of an only *one*
and the end as a bitter day.
11 Behold, days come,
—an oracle of Adonay Yah Veh
and I send a famine in the land
—neither a famine of bread nor a thirst for water;
but of hearing the words of Yah Veh:
12 and they wander from sea to sea
and from the north even to the rising;
and they flit to seek the word of Yah Veh
and find not.
13 In that day
the beautiful virgins and youths languish for thirst;
14 they who oath by the guilt of Shomeron,
and say, Your elohim, O Dan, lives! and,
The way of Beer Sheba lives!
—even they fall and never rise again.

JUDGMENT OF YAH VEH

9 I see Adonay stationed on the sacrifice altar;
and he says, Smite the lintel of the door,
so as to quake the thresholds:

and crop them in the head—all of them;
and I slaughter the last of them with the sword:
and he who flees, flees not to them,
and the escapee escapes not to them.
2 And if they dig into sheol
my hand takes them from there;
and if they ascend to the heavens
I bring them down from there:
3 and if they hide in the top of Karmel/orchard
I search and take them from there;
and if they hide from my eyes in the floor of the sea
I misvah the serpent to bite them there;
4 and if they go into captivity
at the face of their enemies,
I misvah the sword to slaughter them there:
and I set my eyes on them for evil
and not for good.
5 And Adonay Yah Veh Sabaoth
is he who touches the land, and it melts,
and all that settle therein mourn:
and it all ascends as a river
and drowns as the river of Misrayim.
6 He who builds his steps in the heavens
and founds his band in the earth;
he who calls for the waters of the sea
and pours them on the face of the earth;
Yah Veh *is* his name.
7 Are you not as sons of the Kushiym to me,
O sons of Yisra El?
—an oracle of Yah Veh.
Have not I *brought up Israel* **ascended Yisra El**
out of the land of *Egypt* **Misrayim**?
and the *Philistines* **Peleshethiym** from *Caphtor* **Kaphtor**,
and the *Syrians* **Aramiym** from *Kir* **Qir**?
8 Behold, the eyes of *the Lord*
GOD **Adonay Yah Veh**
are upon the sinful *kingdom* **sovereigndom**,
and I *will destroy* **shall desolate** it
from off the face of the *earth* **soil**;
saving **finally,** that **in desolating,**
I *will* **shall** not *utterly destroy* **desolate**
the house of *Jacob* **Yaaqov**,
saith the LORD **an oracle of Yah Veh.**
9 For, *lo* **behold**, I *will command* **shall misvah**,
and I *will sift* **shall shake** the house of *Israel* **Yisra El**
among all *nations* **goyim**,
like as *corn* is *sifted* **shaken** in a sieve,
yet shall not *the least grain* **a kernel** fall upon the earth.
10 All the sinners of my people
shall die by the sword,
which say,
The evil shall not *overtake* **approach**
nor *prevent* **confront** us.

The Restoration Of Yisra El

11 In that day *will* **shall** I raise *up*
the *tabernacle* **sukkoth/brush arbor** of David
that is fallen,
and *close up* **wall** the breaches *thereof*;
and I *will* **shall** raise *up* his ruins,
and I *will* **shall** build it as in the **original** days *of old*:
12 That they may possess the
remnant **survivors** of Edom,
and of all the *heathen* **goyim**,
which are called by my name,
saith the LORD **an oracle of Yah Veh**
that *doeth* **worketh** this.
13 Behold, the days come,
saith the LORD **an oracle of Yah Veh,**
that the *plowman* **plower**
shall *overtake* **approach** the *reaper* **harvester**,
and the treader of grapes him that *soweth* **draweth** seed;
and the mountains
shall *drop sweet wine* **drip squeezed juice**,
and all the hills shall melt.
14 And I *will bring again* **shall return**
the captivity of my people of *Israel* **Yisra El**,
and they shall build the *waste* **desolated** cities,
and *inhabit* **settle** them;
and they shall plant vineyards,
and drink the wine *thereof*;
they shall also *make* **work** gardens,
and eat the fruit of them.
15 And I *will* **shall** plant them upon their *land* **soil**,
and they shall no more
be *pulled up* **uprooted** out of their *land* **soil**
which I have given them,
saith *the LORD* **Yah Veh** thy *God* **Elohim**.
Ascended I not Yisra El from the land of Misrayim?
And the Peleshethiym from Kaphtor?
And the Aramiym from Qir?
8 Behold, the eyes of Adonay Yah Veh
on the sinful sovereigndom;
and I desolate it from off the face of the soil:
finally,
in desolating, I desolate not the house of Yaaqov
—an oracle of Yah Veh.

9 For behold, I misvah,
and I shake the house of Yisra El among all goyim
as shaken in a sieve;
yet not a kernel falls on the earth.
10 All the sinners of my people die by the sword,
who say,
The evil neither approaches nor confronts us.

The Restoration Of Yisra El

11 In that day
I raise the fallen sukkoth/brush arbor of David
and wall the breaches;
and I raise his ruins
and I build it as in the original days:
12 so that they possess the survivors of Edom
and of all the goyim on whom my name is called
—an oracle of Yah Veh who works this.
13 Behold, days come,
—an oracle of Yah Veh
that the plower approaches the harvester
and the treader of grapes the drawer of seed;
and the mountains drip squeezed juice
and all the hills melt:
14 and I restore the captivity
of my people of Yisra El:
and they build the desolated cities and settle them;
and they plant vineyards and drink the wine;
and work gardens and eat their fruit:
15 and I plant them on their soil
—no more uprooted from the soil I give them,
says Yah Veh your Elohim.

THE VISION OF OBAD YAH CONCERNING EDOM

1 The vision of *Obadiah* **Obad Yah**.
Thus saith *the Lord GOD* **Adonay Yah Veh**
concerning Edom;
We have heard a *rumour* **report**
from *the LORD* **Yah Veh**,
and an ambassador is sent among the *heathen* **goyim**,
Arise ye, and let us rise up against her in *battle* **war**.
2 Behold,
I have *made* **given** thee small among the *heathen* **goyim**:
thou art *greatly* **mightily** despised.
3 The *pride* **arrogance** of thine
heart hath deceived thee,
thou that *dwellest* **tabernaclest** in the clefts of the rock,
whose *habitation* **settlement** is high;
that saith in his heart,
Who shall bring me down to the *ground* **earth**?
4 Though thou *exalt* **heighten** *thyself* as the eagle,
and though thou set thy nest among the stars,
thence *will* **shall** I *bring* **descend** thee *down*,
saith the LORD **an oracle of Yah Veh**.
5 If thieves came to thee, if
robbers **ravagers** by night,
(how art thou cut off!)
would **should** they not have stolen
till they had *enough* **satiated**?
if the *grapegatherers* **clippers** came to thee,
would **should** they not
leave *some grapes* **gleanings**?
6 How *are the things of Esau*
Esav hath been searched *out*!
how are his *hidden things sought up* **treasures bulged**!
7 All the men of thy *confederacy* **covenant**
have *brought* **sent** thee *even* to the border:
the men that were at *peace* **shalom** with thee
have deceived thee, and prevailed against thee;
they *that eat* **set** thy bread
have laid a wound under **to estrange** thee:
there is *none understanding* **no discernment** in him.
8 shall I not in that day,
saith the LORD **an oracle of Yah Veh**,
even destroy the wise *men* out of Edom,
and *understanding* **discernment**
out of the mount of *Esau* **Esav**?
9 And thy mighty *men*, O
Teman, shall be dismayed,
to the end that every *one* **man** of the mount of *Esau* **Esav**
may be cut off by *slaughter* **severing**.
10 For thy violence against
thy brother *Jacob* **Yaaqov**
shame shall cover thee,
and thou shalt be *cut off for ever* **severed eternally**.
11 In the day that thou stoodest on the other side,
in the day that the strangers
carried away captive **captured** his *forces* **valiant**,
and *foreigners* **strangers** entered into his *gates* **portals**,
and *cast lots* **handled pebbles**
upon *Jerusalem* **Yeru Shalem**,
even thou wast as one of them.
12 But thou shouldest not have *looked* **seen**
on the day of thy brother
in the day that he became *a stranger* **estranged**;
neither shouldest thou have *rejoiced* **cheered**
over the *children* **sons** of *Judah* **Yah Hudah**
in the day of their destruction;
neither shouldest thou
have *spoken proudly* **greatened thy mouth**
in the day of *distress* **tribulation**.
13 Thou shouldest not have entered
into the *gate* **portal** of my people
in the day of their calamity;
yea, thou shouldest not have *looked* **seen**
on their *affliction* **evil** in the day of their calamity,
nor have *laid hands* **spread** on their *substance* **valiant**
in the day of their calamity;
14 Neither shouldest thou
have stood in the crossway,
to cut off those of his *that did escape* **escapees**;
neither shouldest thou have *delivered* **shut** up
those of his *that did remain* **survivors**
in the day of *distress* **tribulation**.
15 For the day of *the LORD* **Yah Veh**
is near upon all the *heathen* **goyim**:
as thou hast *done* **worked**,
it shall be *done* **worked** unto thee:
thy *reward* **dealing** shall return upon thine own head.

THE VISION OF OBAD YAH CONCERNING EDOM

1 The vision of Obad Yah:
Thus says Adonay Yah Veh concerning Edom:
We hear a report from Yah Veh,
and an ambassador is sent among the goyim,
Rise; yes, rise against her in war.
2 Behold, I give you little among the goyim;
you are mightily despised:
3 the arrogance of your heart deceives you
—you who tabernacle in the clefts of the rock;

whose settlement is high;
he says in his heart,
Who descends me to the earth?
4 Though you heighten as the eagle
and though you set your nest among the stars,
I descend you from there
—an oracle of Yah Veh.
5 If thieves come to you, if ravagers by night
—how you are cut off
steal they not until they satiate?
If the clippers come to you,
leave they not gleanings?
6 How Esav is searched!
How his treasures bulge!
7 All the men of your covenant
send you to the border:
the men at shalom with you
deceive you and prevail against you;
they set your bread under you to estrange you:
there is no discernment in him.
8 In that day,
—an oracle of Yah Veh
destroy I not the wise from Edom?
And discernment from the mount of Esav?
9 And your mighty, O Teman, dismay,
so that every man of the mount of Esav
is cut off by severing.
10 For your violence against your brother Yaaqov,
shame covers you;
and you *are* severed eternally.
11 In the day you stand on the other side,
in the day the strangers capture his valiant,
and strangers enter his portals,
and handle pebbles on Yeru Shalem,
even you *are* as one of them:
12 and you neither see the day of your brother
—the day he is estranged;
nor cheer over the sons of Yah Hudah
in the day of their destruction;
nor greaten your mouth in the day of tribulation.
13 nor enter the portal of my people
in the day of their calamity;
yes, nor see their evil
in the day of their calamity;
nor spread over their valiant
in the day of their calamity;
14 nor stand in the crossway to cut off his escapees;
nor shut up his survivors in the day of tribulation.
15 For the day of Yah Veh is near on all the goyim:
as you work, as worked to you:
your dealing returns on your own head:
16 For as ye have drunk upon my holy mountain,
so shall all the *heathen* **goyim** drink continually,
yea, they shall drink, and they shall *swallow down* **gulp**,
and they shall be as though they had not been.
17 But upon mount *Zion* **Siyon**
shall be *deliverance* **an escape**,
and there shall be *holiness* **a holies**;
and the house of *Jacob* **Yaaqov**
shall possess their possessions.
18 And the house of *Jacob* **Yaaqov** shall be a fire,
and the house of *Joseph* **Yoseph** a flame,
and the house of *Esau* **Esav** for stubble,
and they shall *kindle* **inflame** in them,
and *devour* **consume** them;
and there shall not be any *remaining* **survivors**
of the house of *Esau* **Esav**;
for *the LORD* **Yah Veh** hath *spoken it* **worded**.
19 And they of the south
shall possess the mount of *Esau* **Esav**;
and they of the *plain* **lowland**
the *Philistines* **Peleshethiym**:
and they shall possess the fields of *Ephraim* **Ephrayim**,
and the fields of *Samaria* **Shomeron**:
and *Benjamin* **Ben Yamin** shall possess *Gilead* **Gilad**.
20 And the *captivity* **exiles** of *this host* **the valiant**
of the *children* **sons** of *Israel* **Yisra El**
shall possess that of the *Canaanites* **Kenaaniym**,
even unto *Zarephath* **Sarephath**;
and the *captivity* **exiles** of *Jerusalem* **Yeru Shalem**,
which is in Sepharad,
shall possess the cities of the south.
21 And saviours
shall *come up* **ascend** on mount *Zion* **Siyon**
to judge the mount of *Esau* **Esav**;
and the *kingdom* **sovereigndom**
shall be *the LORD'S* **Yah Veh's**.
16 for as you drink on my holy mountain
thus all the goyim drink continually
—yes, they drink and they gulp,
and they become as though they had never become.
17 And on mount Siyon becomes an escape
and there becomes a holies;
and the house of Yaaqov possesses their possessions.
18 And so be it,
the house of Yaaqov becomes a fire
and the house of Yoseph a flame
and the house of Esav a stubble;
and they inflame among them, and consume them;
so that there are no survivors of the house of Esav;

for Yah Veh has worded.
19 And they of the south
possess the mount of Esav;
and they of the lowland the Peleshethiym:
and they possess the fields of Ephrayim
and the fields of Shomeron:
and Ben Yamin possesses Gilad:
20 and the exiles of the valiant
of the sons of Yisra El,
the Kenaaniym to Sarephath;
and the exiles of Yeru Shalem in Sepharad,
possess the cities of the south.
21 And saviours ascend on mount Siyon
to judge the mount of Esav;
and the sovereigndom becomes to Yah Veh.

THE WORD OF YAH VEH TO YONAH

1 *Now* the word of *the LORD* **Yah Veh**
came unto *Jonah* **Yonah** the son of *Amittai* **Amittay**,
saying,
2 Arise, go to Nineveh, that great city,
and *cry* **call out** against it;
for their *wickedness* **evil**
is come up before me **hath ascended at my face.**

YONAH FLEES FROM YAH VEH

3 But *Jonah* **Yonah** rose up to flee unto Tarshish
from the *presence* **face** of *the LORD* **Yah Veh**,
and *went down* **descended** to *Joppa* **Yapho**;
and he found a ship going to Tarshish:
so he *paid* **gave** the *fare* **hire** *thereof*,
and *went down* **descended** into it,
to go with them unto Tarshish
from the *presence* **face** of *the LORD* **Yah Veh.**
4 But *the LORD* **Yah Veh**
sent out **cast** a great wind into the sea,
and there was a *mighty tempest* **great storm** in the sea,
so that the ship was *like* **fabricated** to be broken.
5 Then the mariners were *afraid* **awed**,
and cried every man unto his *god* **elohim**,
and cast *forth* the *wares* **instruments**
that were in the ship
into the sea, to lighten it of them.
But *Jonah was gone down* **Yonah descended**
into the *sides* **flanks** of the ship;
and he lay, and was *fast asleep* **sleeping soundly**.
6 So the *shipmaster came to*
great sailer approached him,
and said unto him, What meanest
thou, O **sound** sleeper?
arise, call upon thy *God* **Elohim**,
if so be that *God will think* **Elohim shall shine** upon us,
that we *perish* **destruct** not.
7 And they said every *one*
man to his *fellow* **friend**,
Come, and let us *cast lots* **fell pebbles**,
that we may know
for whose cause **on whose account** this evil is upon us.
So they *cast lots* **felled pebbles**,
and the *lot* **pebble** fell upon *Jonah* **Yonah**.
8 Then said they unto him,
Tell us, we *pray* **beseech** thee,
for whose cause this evil is upon us;
What is *thine occupation* **thy work**?
and whence comest thou?

what is thy *country* **land**? and of what people art thou?
9 And he said unto them, I *am* an Hebrew;
and I fear *the LORD* **Yah Veh**,
the God **Elohim** of *heaven* **the heavens**,
which *hath made* **worked** the sea and the dry *land*.
10 Then were the men *exceedingly*
afraid **greatly awed**,
and said unto him, Why hast thou *done* **worked** this?
For the men knew that he fled
from the *presence* **face** of *the LORD* **Yah Veh**,
because he had told them.
11 Then said they unto him,
What shall we *do* **work** unto thee,
that the sea may *be calm* **subside** unto us?
for the sea wrought, and *was tempestuous* **stormed**.

YONAH SWALLOWED BY A GREAT FISH

12 And he said unto them,
Take me up, and cast me forth into the sea;
so shall the sea *be calm* **subside** unto you:
for I know that *for* **on** my *sake* **account**
this great *tempest* **storm** is upon you.
13 Nevertheless the men *rowed* **paddled** hard
to *bring it* **return** to the *land* **dry**;
but they could not:
for the sea wrought,
and *was tempestuous* **stormed** against them.
14 Wherefore
they *cried* **called out** unto *the LORD* **Yah Veh**, and said,
We beseech thee, O *LORD* **Yah Veh**,
we beseech thee,
let us not *perish* **destruct** for this man's *life* **soul**,
and *lay* **give** not upon us innocent blood:
for thou, O *LORD* **Yah Veh**,
hast *done* **worked** as it *pleased* **delighted** thee.
15 So they *took up Jonah* **lifted Yonah**,
and cast him forth into the sea:

THE WORD OF YAH VEH TO YONAH

1 And so be the word of Yah Veh
to Yonah the son of Amittay, saying,
2 Rise, go to Nineveh, that great city,
and call out against it;
for their evil ascends at my face.

YONAH FLEES FROM YAH VEH

3 And Yonah rises to flee
from the face of Yah Veh
to Tarshish;
and descends to Yapho;
and he finds a ship going to Tarshish:
so he gives the hire and descends into it
to go with them to Tarshish
from the face of Yah Veh.
4 And Yah Veh casts a great wind on the sea,
and there is a great storm in the sea,
so that the ship fabricates to be broken:
5 and the mariners awe
and every man cries to his elohim;
and cast the instruments in the ship into the sea
to lighten it by them:
and Yonah descends into the flanks of the ship;
and he lies down and sleeps soundly:
6 and the great sailer approaches him,
and says to him, What mean you, O sound sleeper?
Rise, call on your Elohim,
if so be that Elohim shine on us that we not destruct.
7 And every man says to his friend,
Come, and we fell pebbles,
so that we know on whose account this evil *is* on us.
—and they fell pebbles
and the pebble falls on Yonah.
8 And they say to him, Tell us, we beseech you,
for whose cause this evil *is* on us!
What is your work? And whence come you?
What is your land? And of what people are you?
9 And he says to them, I—a Hebrew;
and I fear Yah Veh Elohim of the heavens,
who worked the sea and the dry.
10 And the men awe an awe,
and say to him, Why work you this?
—for the men know
he flees from the face of Yah Veh
—because he told them.
11 And they say to him,
What work we to you, to subside the sea to us?
—for the sea works and storms.

YONAH SWALLOWED BY A GREAT FISH

12 And he says to them,
Take me and cast me into the sea;
and thus the sea subsides to you:
for I know that on my account
this great storm *is* on you.
13 And the men paddle hard to return to the dry;
and they cannot:
for the sea works and storms against them.
14 And they call out to Yah Veh, and say,
We beseech you, O Yah Veh, we beseech you,
that we not destruct for the soul of this man,

and give not innocent blood on us:
for you, O Yah Veh, work as it delights you.
15 So they lift Yonah, and cast him into the sea
and the sea *ceased* **stood** from her raging.
16 Then the men
feared the LORD exceedingly **awed Yah Veh greatly**,
and *offered* **sacrificed** a sacrifice
unto *the LORD* **Yah Veh**,
and *made* **vowed** vows.
17 *Now the LORD* **Yah Veh**
had *prepared* **numbered** a great fish
to swallow up *Jonah* **Yonah**.
And *Jonah* **Yonah** was in the *belly* **inwards** of the fish
three days and three nights.

THE PRAYER OF YONAH, THE ANSWER OF YAH VEH

2 Then *Jonah* **Yonah**
prayed unto *the LORD* **Yah Veh** his *God* **Elohim**
out of the fish's *belly* **inwards**,
2 And said, I *cried* **called out**
by reason **because** of *mine affliction* **my tribulation**
unto *the LORD* **Yah Veh**,
and he *heard* **answered** me;
out of the belly of *hell* **sheol** cried I,
and thou heardest my voice.
3 For thou hadst cast me into the deep,
in the midst of the seas;
and the *floods compassed* **rivers surrounded** me *about*:
all thy *billows* **breakers** and thy waves passed over me.
4 Then I said,
I am *cast out of* **expelled from** thy *sight* **eyes**;
yet I *will* **shall** look again toward thy holy *temple* **manse**.
5 The waters *compassed* **surrounded** me *about*,
even to the soul:
the *depth closed* **abyss surrounded** me *round about*,
the *weeds* **reeds** were *wrapped* **bound** about my head.
6 I *went down* **descended**
to the *bottoms* **bases** of the mountains;
the earth with her bars was about me *for ever* **eternally**:
yet hast thou *brought up* **ascended** my life
from *corruption* **the pit of ruin**,
O *LORD* **Yah Veh** my *God* **Elohim**.
7 When my soul *fainted* **languished** within me
I remembered *the LORD* **Yah Veh**:
and my prayer came in unto thee,
into thine holy *temple* **manse**.
8 They that observe *lying* **vain** vanities
forsake their own mercy.
9 But I *will* **shall** sacrifice unto thee
with the voice of *thanksgiving* **spread hands**;
I *will pay* **shall shalam** that that I have vowed.
Salvation is of *the LORD* **Yah Veh**.
10 And *the LORD spake* **Yah**
Veh said unto the fish,
and it vomited out *Jonah* **Yonah** upon the dry *land*.

THE SECOND WORD OF YAH VEH TO YONAH

3 And the word of *the LORD* **Yah Veh**
came unto *Jonah the second time* **Yonah secondly**,
saying,
2 Arise, go unto Nineveh, that great city,
and *preach* **call out** unto it
the *preaching* **calling out** that I *bid* **word** thee.
3 So *Jonah* **Yonah** arose, and went unto Nineveh,
according to the word of *the LORD* **Yah Veh**.
Now Nineveh was *an exceeding* **a** great city **of Elohim**
of three days' *journey* **walk**.
4 And *Jonah* **Yonah** began to enter into the city
a **one** day's *journey* **walk**,
and he *cried* **called out**, and said,
Yet forty days,
and Nineveh shall be *overthrown* **turned against**.
5 So the *people* **men** of Nineveh
believed God **trusted Elohim**,
and *proclaimed* **called out** a fast,
and *put on sackcloth* **enrobed saq**,
from the greatest of them even to
the *least* **lesser** of them.
6 For word *came* **touched**
unto the *king* **sovereign** of Nineveh,
and he arose from his throne,
and he *laid* **passed** his *robe* **mighty mantle** from him,
and covered him with *sackcloth* **saq**, and sat in ashes.
7 And he caused it to be *proclaimed* **cried out**
and *published* **said** through Nineveh
by the *decree* **taste** of the *king* **sovereign** and his nobles,
and the sea stands from her raging:
16 and the men awe an awe to Yah Veh
and sacrifice a sacrifice and vow vows to Yah Veh:
17 and Yah Veh numbers a great fish
to swallow Yonah:
and Yonah is in the inwards of the fish
three days and three nights.

THE PRAYER OF YONAH, THE ANSWER OF YAH VEH

2 And Yonah prays to Yah Veh his Elohim
from the inwards of the fish,

2 and says, Because of my tribulation
I call to Yah Veh; and he answers me:
from the belly of sheol I cry; and you hear my voice:
3 for you cast me into the deep, midst the seas;
and the rivers surround me:
all your breakers and your waves pass over me.
4 Then I—I say, I am expelled from your eyes;
yet I look again toward your holy manse:
5 the waters surround me to the soul;
the abyss surrounds me;
the reeds bind around my head:
6 I descend to the bases of the mountains;
the earth with her bars around me eternally:
yet you ascend my life from the pit of ruin,
O Yah Veh my Elohim.
7 When my soul languishes within me
I remember Yah Veh:
and my prayer comes in to you
—into your holy manse.
8 They who observe vain vanities
forsake their own mercy;
9 and I sacrifice to you
with the voice of spread hands;
I shalam what I vow:
salvation *is* of Yah Veh.
10 And Yah Veh says to the fish,
and it vomits Yonah on the dry.

THE SECOND WORD OF YAH VEH TO YONAH

3 And so be the word of Yah Veh
to Yonah secondly, saying,
2 Rise, go to Nineveh, that great city;
and call out to it the calling I word you.
3 And Yonah rises, and goes to Nineveh
according to the word of Yah Veh
—Nineveh is a great city of Elohim
of a walk of three days.
4 And Yonah begins to enter the city
a walk of one day;
and he calls out, and says,
Yet forty days, and Nineveh *is* turned against.
5 So the men of Nineveh trust Elohim
and call a fast and enrobe saq
—from their greatest even to their lesser.
6 And word touches to the sovereign of Nineveh;
and he rises from his throne
and passes his mighty mantle from him
and covers himself with saq and sits in ashes:
7 and he cries throughout Nineveh,
saying by the taste of the sovereign and his nobles,
saying,
Let neither *man* **humanity** nor *beast*
animal, herd nor flock,
taste *any thing* **aught**:
let them not *feed* **graze**, nor drink water:
8 But let *man* **humanity** and *beast* **animal**
be covered with *sackcloth* **saq**,
and *cry mightily* **call out severely** unto *God* **Elohim**:
yea, let them turn every *one* **man** from his evil way,
and from the violence that is in their *hands* **palms**.
9 Who *can tell* **knoweth**
if *God will* **Elohim shall** turn and *repent* **sigh**,
and turn away from his *fierce anger* **fuming wrath**,
that we *perish* **destruct** not?
10 And *God* **Elohim** saw their works,
that they turned from their evil way;
and *God repented* **Elohim sighed** of the evil,
that he had *said* **worded**
that he *would do* **should work** unto them;
and he *did* **worked** it not.

THE ANGER OF YONAH;
THE MERCY OF YAH VEH

4 But it *displeased Jonah exceedingly*
was greatly evil to Yonah,
and he was very angry.
2 And he prayed unto *the*
LORD **Yah Veh**, and said,
I *pray* **beseech** thee, O *LORD* **Yah Veh,**
was not this my *saying* **word,**
when I was yet in my *country* **soil?**
Therefore I *fled before* **anticipated to flee** unto Tarshish:
for I knew that thou art a *gracious God* **charismatic El,**
and merciful, slow to anger, and of great *kindness* **mercy,**
and *repentest* **sighest** thee of the evil.
3 Therefore now, O *LORD* **Yah Veh,**
take, I beseech thee, my *life* **soul** from me;
for it is better for me to die than to live.
4 Then said *the LORD* **Yah Veh,**
Doest thou well—**please** to be *angry* **inflamed?**
5 So *Jonah* **Yonah** went out of the city,
and sat on the east *side* of the city,
and there *made* **worked** him
a *booth* **sukkoth/brush arbor,**
and sat under it in the shadow,
till he might see what *would* **should** become of the city.
6 And *the LORD God* **Yah Veh Elohim**
prepared **numbered** a gourd,
and *made* **caused** it
to *come up* **ascend** over *Jonah* **Yonah,**

that it might be a shadow over his head,
to *deliver* **rescue** him from his *grief* **evil**.
So Jonah was exceeding glad
In cheering, Yonah greatly cheered of the gourd.
7 But *God prepared* **Elohim**
numbered a *worm* **maggot**
when the *morning rose* **dawn ascended**
the *next day* **morrow,**
and it smote the gourd that it withered.
8 And **so be** it *came to pass,*
when the sun did arise,
that *God* **Elohim**
prepared **numbered** a vehement east wind;
and the sun *beat* **smote** upon the head of *Jonah* **Yonah,**
that he *fainted* **languished,**
and *wished in himself* **asked of his soul** to die, and said,
It is better for me to die than to live.
9 And *God* **Elohim** said to *Jonah* **Yonah,**
Doest thou well—**please** to be *angry* **inflamed**
for the gourd?
And he said,
I *do* well—**please** to be *angry* **inflamed,** *even* unto death.
10 Then said *the LORD* **Yah Veh,**
Thou hast *had pity on* **spared** the gourd,
for the which thou hast not laboured,
neither *madest it grow* **nourished;**
which *came up in* **was a son of** a night,
and *perished in* **destructed a son of** a night:
11 And should not I spare Nineveh, that great city,
wherein *are more than* **abound**
sixscore thousand persons **twelve myriads of humanity**
that *cannot discern* **know not**
between their right *hand* and their left *hand;*
and *also much cattle* **many animals?**
saying,
Neither humanity nor animal, herd nor flock,
tastes aught:
neither grazes, nor drinks water:
8 and humanity and animal covers with saq
and calls out severely to Elohim:
yes, every man turns from his evil way
and from the violence in their palms.
9 Who knows?
Perhaps Elohim turns and sighs
—turns from his fuming wrath, and we destruct not!
10 And Elohim sees their works
—that they turn from their evil way;
and Elohim sighs of the evil
he worded to work to them;
and he works it not.

THE ANGER OF YONAH; THE MERCY OF YAH VEH

4 And it *is* greatly evil to Yonah
and he *is* very angry:
2 and he prays to Yah Veh, and says,
I beseech you, O Yah Veh,
was this not my word when I was yet in my soil?
So I anticipated to flee to Tarshish:
for I knew you *are* an El
—charismatic and merciful,
slow to anger and of great mercy;
and you sigh of the evil:
3 and now, O Yah Veh, I beseech you,
take my soul from me;
for it is better for me to die than to live.
4 And Yah Veh says,
Is your inflaming well—pleasing?
5 And Yonah goes from the city
and sits on the east of the city;
and works himself a sukkoth/brush arbor
and sits under its shadow
until he sees what becomes of the city.
6 And Yah Veh Elohim numbers a gourd
and ascends it over Yonah,
to become a shadow over his head
to rescue him from his evil:
and in cheering, Yonah cheers greatly for the gourd.
7 And Elohim numbers a maggot
at the ascending of the dawn on the morrow;
and it smites the gourd that it withers:
8 and so be it, when the sun rises,
Elohim numbers a vehement east wind;
and the sun smites on the head of Yonah
so that he languishes;
and asks of his soul to die, and says,
It is better for me to die than to live.
9 And Elohim says to Yonah,
Is your inflaming over the gourd well—pleasing?
And he says,
My inflaming is well—pleasing—even to death.
10 Then Yah Veh says,
You spared the gourd,
for which you neither labored nor nourished;
becoming a son of a night
and destructing a son of a night:
11 and I—spare I not Nineveh, that great city,
wherein twelve myriads of humanity abound
—who know not between their right and their left
—and many animals?

The Word Of Yah Veh Against Shomeron And Yeru Shalem

1 The word of *the LORD* **Yah Veh**
that came to *Micah* **Michah** the *Morasthite* **Moreshethiy**
in the days of *Jotham* **Yah Tham**,
Ahaz **Ach Az**, and *Hesekiah* **Yechizqi Yah**,
kings **sovereigns** of *Judah* **Yah Hudah**,
which he saw concerning
Samaria **Shomeron** and *Jerusalem* **Yeru Shalem**.
2 Hear, all ye people;
hearken, O earth, and all **the fulness** *that* therein *is*:
and let *the Lord GOD be* **Adonay Yah Veh**
witness against you,
the Lord **Adonay** from his holy *temple* **manse**.
3 For, behold,
the LORD **Yah Veh** cometh forth out of his place,
and *will come down* **shall descend**,
and tread upon the *high places* **bamahs** of the earth.
4 And the mountains shall
be molten **melt** under him,
and the valleys shall *be cleft* **split**,
as wax *before* **at the face of** the fire,
and as the waters
that are poured down a *steep place* **descent**.
5 For the *transgression* **rebellion** of *Jacob* **Yaaqov**
is all this,
and for the sins of the house of *Israel* **Yisra El**.
What is the *transgression* **rebellion** of *Jacob* **Yaaqov**?
is it not *Samaria* **Shomeron**?
and what
are the *high places* **bamahs** of *Judah* **Yah Hudah**?
are they not *Jerusalem* **Yeru Shalem**?
6 *Therefore* I *will make*
Samaria **shall set Shomeron**
as an heap of the field,
and as plantings of a vineyard:
and I *will* **shall** pour down the stones *thereof*
into the valley,
and I *will discover* **shall expose** the foundations *thereof*.
7 And all the *graven images* **sculptiles** *thereof*
shall be *beaten to pieces* **crushed**,
and all the *hires* **payoffs** *thereof*
shall be burned with the fire,
and all the idols *thereof will I lay* **shall I set** desolate:
for she gathered it of the *hire* **payoff**
of *an harlot* **a whore**,
and they shall return
to the *hire* **payoff** of *an harlot* **a whore**.
8 Therefore I *will wail* **shall chop** and howl,
I *will* **shall** go stripped and naked:
I *will make* **shall work** a *wailing* **chopping**
like the *dragons* **monsters**,
and mourning as the **daughters of the** owls.
9 For her wound is incurable;
for it is come unto *Judah* **Yah Hudah**;
he *is come* **toucheth** unto the *gate* **portal** of my people,
even to *Jerusalem* **Yeru Shalem**.
10 *Declare* **Tell** ye it not at Gath,
in weeping, weep ye not *at all*:
in the house of Aphrah
roll **in wallowing, wallow** thyself in the dust.
11 Pass ye away,
thou *inhabitant* **settler** of *Saphir* **Shaphir**,
having thy shame naked:
the *inhabitant* **settler** of *Zaanan* **Saanan** came not forth
in the *mourning* **chopping** of *Bethezel* **Beth Ha Esel**;
he shall *receive* **take** of you his standing.
12 For the *inhabitant* **settler** of Maroth
waited carefully for **awaited** good:
but evil *came down* **descended** from *the LORD* **Yah Veh**
unto the *gate* **portal** of *Jerusalem* **Yeru Shalem**.
13 O thou *inhabitant* **settler** of Lachish,
bind **yoke** the chariot to the *swift beast* **stallion**:
she is the beginning of the sin
to the daughter of *Zion* **Siyon**:
for the *transgressions* **rebellions** of *Israel* **Yisra El**
were found in thee.
14 Therefore shalt thou give presents
to *Moreshethgath* **Moresheth Gath**:
the houses of Achzib shall be a lie
to the *kings* **sovereigns** of *Israel* **Yisra El**.
15 Yet *will* **shall** I bring *an*
heir **a successor** unto thee,

The Word Of Yah Veh Against Shomeron And Yeru Shalem

1 The word of Yah Veh
being to Michah the Moreshethiy
in the days of Yah Tham, Ach Az and Yechizqi Yah
sovereigns of Yah Hudah,
which he sees
concerning Shomeron and Yeru Shalem.
2 Hear, all you people;
hearken, O earth, and all the fulness thereof:
Adonay Yah Veh witnesses against you
—Adonay from his holy manse.
3 For behold,
Yah Veh comes from his place and descends
and treads on the bamahs of the earth:

4 and the mountains melt under him
and the valleys split
—as wax at the face of the fire
and as the waters pour down a descent:
5 all this *is* for the rebellion of Yaaqov
and for the sins of the house of Yisra El.
What *is* the rebellion of Yaaqov?
Is it not Shomeron?
And what are the bamahs of Yah Hudah?
Are they not Yeru Shalem?
6 I set Shomeron as a heap of the field
—as plantings of a vineyard:
and I pour the stones into the valley
and I expose the foundations;
7 and crush all the sculptiles
and burn all the payoffs with the fire
and desolate all the idols;
for she gathers from the payoff of a whore
and to the payoff of a whore they return:
8 for this I chop and howl;
I go stripped and naked:
I work a chopping as the monsters
and a mourning as the daughters of the owls:
9 for her wound *is* incurable;
for it comes to Yah Hudah:
he touches to the portal of my people
—to Yeru Shalem.
10 Tell it not at Gath;
in weeping, weep not:
in the house of Aphrah;
in wallowing, wallow yourself in the dust.
11 Pass on, you settler of Shaphir,
naked *one* of shame:
the settler of Saanan goes not;
in the chopping of Beth Ha Esel;
he takes his standing from you.
12 For the settler of Maroth awaits good;
for evil descends from Yah Veh
to the portal of Yeru Shalem.
13 You, settler of Lachish,
yoke the chariot to the stallion;
she is the beginning of sin to the daughter of Siyon
—for *all* the rebellions of Yisra El found in you.
14 So give presents to Moresheth Gath:
the houses of Achzib *are* a lie
to the sovereigns of Yisra El.
15 Yet I bring a successor to you,
O *inhabitant* **settler** of Mareshah:
he shall come unto Adullam
the *glory* **honour** of *Israel* **Yisra El.**
16 *Make* **Balden** thee *bald*, and *poll* **shear** thee
for *thy delicate children* **the sons of thy delights**;
enlarge thy baldness as the eagle;
for they are *gone into captivity* **exiled** from thee.

2 *Woe* **Ho** to them
that *devise iniquity* **fabricate mischief**,
and *work* **do** evil upon their beds!
when the morning is light, they *practise* **work** it,
because it is in the *power* **el** of their hand.
2 And they *covet* **desire** fields,
and *take* **strip** them *by violence*;
and houses, and *take* **bear** them away:
so they oppress a *man* **mighty** and his house,
even a man and his *heritage* **inheritance**.
3 Therefore thus saith *the LORD* **Yah Veh**;
Behold, against this family *do I devise* **I fabricate** an evil,
from which ye shall not *remove* **depart** your necks;
neither shall *ye* go haughtily: for this time is evil.
4 In that day
shall one take *up* a *parable* **proverb** against you,
and lament with a *doleful* lamentation **of lamentations**,
and say, **In ravaging,** We be *utterly spoiled* **ravaged**:
he hath changed the *portion* **allotment** of my people:
how hath he *removed* **departed** it from me!
turning away **in restoring,**
he hath *divided* **allotted** our fields.
5 Therefore thou shalt have none
that shall cast a cord by *lot* **pebble**
in the congregation of *the LORD* **Yah Veh**.
6 *Prophesy* ye **drip** not,
say they to them that prophesy **they drip**:
they shall not *prophesy* **drip*** to them,
that they shall not *take* **remove** shame.
*drip: as in dripping words.
7 *O thou that art named*
the house of *Jacob* **Yaaqov sayeth,**
is the spirit of *the LORD* **Yah Veh** straitened?
are these his *doings* **exploits**?
do not my words *do good to* **well—please** him
that walketh *uprightly* **straight**?
8 *Even of late* **From yesterday**
my people is risen up as an enemy:
ye *pull off* **strip** the *robe* **mighty mantle**
with the *garment* **clothes**
from them that pass by *securely* **confidently**
as men *averse* **returning** from war.
9 The women of my people
have ye *cast out* **expelled**
from their *pleasant* houses **of delights**;
from their *children* **sucklings**

have ye taken away my *glory for ever* **majesty eternally.**
10 Arise ye, and depart; for this is not *your* rest:
because it is *polluted* **fouled**, it shall *destroy* **despoil** you,
even with a sore destruction—**a forceful despoiling.**
11 If a man walking in the
spirit and falsehood do lie,
saying, I will prophesy **I shall drip** unto thee
of wine and of *strong drink* **intoxicants**;
he shall *even be the prophet of* **drip unto** this people.

YAH VEH GATHERS THE SURVIVORS OF YISRA EL

12 *I will surely assemble* **In gathering, I shall gather,**
O *Jacob* **Yaaqov**, all of thee;
I will surely gather **In gathering, I shall gather**
the *remnant* **survivors** of *Israel* **Yisra El**;
I *will put* **shall set** them together
as the *sheep* **flock** of *Bozrah* **the fold,**
as the *flock* **drove** in the midst of their fold:
they shall *make great noise* **quake**
by reason **because** of *the multitude of men* **humanity.**
13 The *breaker* **separater** is *come up* **ascended**
before them **at their face:**
they have *broken up* **separated,**
and have passed through the *gate* **portal,**
and are gone out by it:
and their *king* **sovereign** shall pass
before them **at their face,**
and *the LORD* **Yah Veh** on the head of them.

THE WORD OF YAH VEH TO YAAQOV AND YISRA EL

3 And I said, Hear, I *pray* **beseech** you,
O settler of Mareshah:
he comes to Adullam, the honor of Yisra El.
16 Balden yourselves and shear yourselves
for the sons of your delights:
enlarge your baldness as the eagle
for they exile from you.

2 Ho to them who fabricate mischief
—who work evil on their beds!
In the light of the morning, they work
because it *is* in the el of their hand:
2 and they desire fields and strip them;
and houses, and bear them away:
and oppress a mighty and his house
—even a man and his inheritance.
3 So thus says Yah Veh:
Behold, I fabricate an evil against this family
from which you neither depart your necks
nor go haughtily:
for this *is* a time of evil.
4 In that day, one takes a proverb against you
and laments with a lamentation of lamentations
and says, In ravaging, we *are* ravaged:
he changes the allotment of my people.
How he removes it from me!
In restoring, he allots our fields.
5 So you have no one to cast a cord by pebble
in the congregation of Yah Veh:
6 you drip* not; they drip:
they drip not to you,
they remove not shame.
*drip: as in dripping words.
7 The house of Yaaqov says,
Becomes the spirit of Yah Veh strait?
Are these his exploits?
My words,
well—please they not him who walks straight?
8 From yesterday my people rise as an enemy:
you strip the mighty mantle with the clothes
from them who pass by confidently
as men returning from war:
9 you expel the women of my people
from their houses of delights;
from their sucklings
you take away my majesty eternally.
10 Rise and depart; for this not rest:
because of foulness, it despoils you
—a forceful despoiling.
11 If a man walking with spirit/wind
and with falsehood lies, *saying*,
I drip to you of wine and of intoxicants;
he drips to this people.

YAH VEH GATHERS THE SURVIVORS OF YISRA EL

12 In gathering, I gather Yaaqov—all of you;
in gathering, I gather the survivors of Yisra El;
I set them together as the flock of the fold;
as the drove among their fold:
they quake because of humanity.
13 The separater ascends at their face:
they separate and pass through the portal;
yes, they go through it:
and their sovereign passes at their face,
and Yah Veh at their head.

THE WORD OF YAH VEH TO YAAQOV AND YISRA EL

3 And I say, Hear, I beseech you,
O heads of *Jacob* **Yaaqov**,
and ye *princes* **commanders**
of the house of *Israel* **Yisra El**;
Is it not for you to know judgment?
2 Who hate the good, and love the evil;
who *pluck off* **strip** their skin from off them,
and their flesh from off their bones;
3 Who also eat the flesh of my people,
and *flay* **strip** their skin from off them;
and they break their bones,
and *chop* **spread** them *in pieces*,
as for the *pot* **caldron**, and as flesh within the caldron.
4 Then shall they cry unto *the LORD* **Yah Veh**,
but he *will* **shall** not *hear* **answer** them:
he *will* **shall** even hide his face from them at that time,
as they have *behaved* **vilified** *themselves ill*
in their *doings* **exploits**.
5 Thus saith *the LORD* **Yah**
Veh concerning the prophets
that *make* **cause** my people *err* **to stray**,
that bite with their teeth, and *cry* **call out**, *Peace* **Shalom**;
and he that *putteth* **giveth** not into their mouths,
they even *prepare* **hallow** war against him.
6 Therefore night shall be unto you,
that ye shall not have a vision;
and it shall be *dark* **darkness** unto you,
that ye shall not divine;
and the sun shall go down over the prophets,
and the day shall be *dark* **darkened** over them.
7 Then shall the seers *be ashamed* **shame**,
and the diviners *confounded* **blush**:
yea, they shall all cover their *lips* **upper lip**;
for there is no answer of *God* **Elohim**.
8 But *truly* I am *full* **filled** of *power* **force**
by the spirit of *the LORD* **Yah Veh**,
and of judgment, and of might,
to declare unto *Jacob* **Yaaqov** his *transgression* **rebellion**,
and to *Israel* **Yisra El** his sin.
9 Hear this, I *pray* **beseech** you,
ye heads of the house of *Jacob* **Yaaqov**,
and *princes* **commanders** of the house of *Israel* **Yisra El**,
that abhor judgment, and pervert all *equity* **straightness**.
10 They build up *Zion* **Siyon** with blood,
and *Jerusalem* **Yeru Shalem** with *iniquity* **wickedness**.
11 The heads *thereof* judge for *reward* **bribes**,
and the priests *thereof* teach for *hire* **price**,
and the prophets *thereof* divine for *money* **silver**:
yet *will* **shall** they lean upon *the LORD* **Yah Veh**,
and say **saying**, Is not *the LORD* **Yah Veh** among us?
none evil can come upon us.
12 Therefore shall *Zion* **Siyon** for your sake
be plowed *as* a field,
and *Jerusalem* **Yeru Shalem** shall become heaps,
and the mountain of the house
as the *high places* **bamahs** of the forest.

THE SOVEREIGNDOM OF THE FINAL DAYS

4 But in the *last* **final** days
so be it *shall come to pass*,
that the mountain of the house of *the LORD* **Yah Veh**
shall be established in the top of the mountains,
and it shall be *exalted* **lifted** above the hills;
and people shall flow unto it.
2 And many *nations* **goyim** shall come,
and say, Come, and let us *go up* **ascend** to
the mountain of *the LORD* **Yah Veh**,
and to the house of *the God* **Elohim** of *Jacob* **Yaaqov**;
and he *will* **shall** teach us of his ways,
and we *will* **shall** walk in his paths:
for the *law* **torah** shall go forth of *Zion* **Siyon**,
and the word of *the LORD* **Yah Veh**
from *Jerusalem* **Yeru Shalem**.
3 And he shall judge among many people,
and *rebuke strong nations* **reprove**
mighty goyim afar off;
and they shall *beat* **forge** their swords into plowshares,
and their spears into *pruninghooks* **psalmpicks**:
nation **goyim** shall not lift *up* a sword
against *nation* **goyim**,
neither shall they learn war any more.
4 But they shall sit every man
under his vine and under his fig tree;
O heads of Yaaqov
and you commanders of the house of Yisra El;
Is it not for you to know judgment?
2 —Who hate the good and love the evil?
Who strip their skin from off them and
their flesh from off their bones?
3 Who eat the flesh of my people?
They strip their skin
and they break their bones;
and spread them as for the caldron
and as flesh within the caldron.
4 Then they cry to Yah Veh,
and he answers them not:
he even hides his face from them at that time,

as they vilify in their exploits.
5 Thus says Yah Veh
concerning the prophets who stray my people
—who bite with their teeth
and call out, Shalom;
who give not into their mouths,
and hallow war against him.
6 So your night *is without* a vision
and darkness *without* a divination:
and the sun goes down over the prophets
and the day darkens over them:
7 and the seers shame and the diviners blush:
yes, they all cover their upper lip;
for there is no answer, O Elohim.
8 And I *am* filled of force by the spirit of Yah Veh;
and of judgment and of might
to declare to Yaaqov his rebellion
and to Yisra El his sin.
9 Hear this, I beseech you,
you heads of the house of Yaaqov
and commanders of the house of Yisra El
—who abhor judgment and pervert all straightness
10 —who build Siyon with blood
and Yeru Shalem with wickedness.
11 The heads judge for a bribe
and the priests teach for a price,
and the prophets divine for silver:
yet they lean on Yah Veh, saying,
Is not Yah Veh among us?
Evil approaches us not!
12 So because of you
Siyon *is* plowed as a field
and Yeru Shalem becomes heaps;
and the mountain of the house
as the bamahs of the forest.

THE SOVEREIGNDOM OF THE FINAL DAYS

4 And so be it, in the final days,
the mountain of the house of Yah Veh
is established in the top of the mountains
and lifted above the hills;
and people flow into it.
2 And many goyim come, and say, Come!
Ascend to the mountain of Yah Veh
and to the house of Elohim of Yaaqov;
and he teaches us of his ways
and we walk in his paths:
for from Siyon comes a torah
and the word of Yah Veh from Yeru Shalem:
3 and he judges among many people
and reproves mighty goyim afar off:
and they forge their swords into plowshares
and their spears into psalmpicks:
goyim neither lift a sword against goyim
nor learn war any more:
4 and every man sits under his
vine and under his fig tree;
and none shall make them *afraid* **tremble**:
for the mouth of *the LORD of hosts* **Yah Veh Sabaoth**
hath *spoken it* **worded**.
5 For all people *will* **shall** walk
every *one* **man** in the name of his *god* **elohim**,
and we *will* **shall** walk
in the name of *the LORD* **Yah Veh** our *God* **Elohim**
for ever **eternally** and *ever* **eternally**.
6 In that day,
saith the LORD **an oracle of Yah Veh**,
will I assemble her **shall I gather those** that *halteth* **limp**,
and I *will* **shall** gather *her that is driven out* **the expelled**,
and *her* **those** that I have *afflicted* **vilified**;
7 And I *will make her* **shall**
set those that *halted* **limp**
a *remnant* **survivor**,
and *her* **those** that *was* **were** cast far off
a *strong nation* **mighty goyim**:
and *the LORD* **Yah Veh** shall reign over them
in mount *Zion* **Siyon** from henceforth,
even *for ever* **eternally**.
8 And thou, O *tower of the flock* **Migdal Eder**,
the *strong hold* **mound** of the daughter of *Zion* **Siyon**,
unto thee shall it come, even the first *dominion* **reign**;
the *kingdom* **sovereigndom**
shall come to the daughter of *Jerusalem* **Yeru Shalem**.
9 Now why dost thou *cry out aloud* **shout a shout**?
is there no *king* **sovereign** in thee?
is thy counsellor *perished* **destroyed**?
for pangs *have taken* **hold** thee
as a woman *in travail* **birthing**.
10 *Be in pain* **Writhe**, and
labour to bring forth **birth**,
O daughter of *Zion* **Siyon**,
like a woman *in travail* **birthing**:
for now shalt thou go forth out of the city,
and thou shalt *dwell* **tabernacle** in the field,
and thou shalt go *even* to *Babylon* **Babel**;
there shalt thou be *delivered* **rescued**;
there *the LORD* **Yah Veh** shall redeem thee
from the *hand* **palm** of thine enemies.
11 Now also
many *nations* **goyim** are gathered against thee,

that say, Let her be *defiled* **profaned**,
and let our eye *look* **see** upon *Zion* **Siyon**.
12 But they know not
the *thoughts* **fabrications** of *the LORD* **Yah Veh**,
neither *understand* **discern** they his counsel:
for he shall gather them
as the *sheaves* **omers** into the *floor* **threshingfloor**.
13 Arise and thresh, O daughter of *Zion* **Siyon**:
for I *will make* **shall set** thine horn iron,
and I *will make* **shall set** thy hoofs *brass* **copper**:
and thou shalt *beat in pieces* **pulverize** many people:
and I *will consecrate* **shall devote** their **greedy** gain
unto *the LORD* **Yah Veh**,
and their *substance* **valuables**
unto the *Lord* **Adonay** of the whole earth.

THE BIRTH OF THE ETERNAL DOMINATOR

5 Now *gather thyself in troops* **troop together**,
O daughter of troops:
he hath *laid* **set** siege against us:
they shall smite the judge of *Israel* **Yisra El**
with a *rod* **scion** upon the cheek.
2 But thou, *Bethlehem Ephratah*
Beth Lechem Ephrath,
though thou be
little among the thousands of *Judah* **Yah Hudah**,
yet out of thee shall he come forth unto me
that is to be *ruler* **sovereign** in *Israel* **Yisra El**;
whose *goings forth* **proceedings**
have been from *of old* **antiquity**,
from *everlasting* **days eternal**.
3 Therefore *will* **shall** he give them up,
until the time that she which *travaileth* **birtheth**
hath *brought forth* **birthed**:
then the remnant of his brethren
shall return unto the *children* **sons** of *Israel* **Yisra El**.
4 And he shall stand and *feed* **tend**
in the strength of *the LORD* **Yah Veh**,
in the *majesty* **pomp**
of the name of *the LORD* **Yah Veh** his *God* **Elohim**;
and no one trembles them:
for the mouth of Yah Veh Sabaoth has worded.
5 For all people
—every man walks in the name of his elohim,
and we walk in the name of Yah Veh our Elohim
eternally and eternally.
6 In that day,
—an oracle of Yah Veh
I gather the limping and I gather the expelled
and those whom I vilified;
7 and I set the limping, a survivor;
and the cast off, a mighty goyim:
and Yah Veh reigns over them in mount Siyon
from now on—even eternally.
8 And you, O Migdal Eder,
the mound of the daughter of Siyon,
to you it comes—even the first reign;
the sovereigndom comes
to the daughter of Yeru Shalem.
9 Now, why shout you a shout?
Is there no sovereign in you?
Is your counsellor destroyed?
For pangs hold you as a woman birthing.
10 Writhe, and birth, O daughter of Siyon,
as a woman birthing:
for now you go from the city
and you tabernacle in the field
and you go to Babel—there to be rescued:
there Yah Veh redeems you
from the palm of your enemies.
11 And now, many goyim gather against you,
who say, She profanes!
—but our eye sees on Siyon.
12 They neither know the fabrications of Yah Veh
nor discern his counsel:
for he gathers them as the omers
into the threshingfloor.
13 Rise and thresh, O daughter of Siyon:
for I set your horn iron
and I set your hoofs copper;
and you pulverize many people:
and I devote their greedy gain to Yah Veh,
and their valuables to the Adonay of the whole earth.

THE BIRTH OF THE ETERNAL DOMINATOR

5 Now, troop together, O daughter of troops:
he sets a siege against us:
with a scion on the cheek
they smite the judge of Yisra El.
2 But you, Beth Lechem Ephrath,
being little among the thousands of Yah Hudah,
from you he comes to me
to become sovereign in Yisra El;
whose proceeds *are* from antiquity
—from days eternal.
3 So he gives them up,
until the time that she who is to birth, births:
and the remnant of his brothers
returns to the sons of Yisra El:

4 and he stands and tends
in the strength of Yah Veh
in the pomp of the name of Yah Veh his Elohim:
and they shall *abide* **settle**:
for now shall he *be great* **greaten**
unto the *ends* **finalities** of the earth.
5 And this *man* shall be the *peace* **shalom**,
when the *Assyrian* **Ashshuriy** shall come into our land:
and when he shall tread in our *palaces* **citadels**,
then shall we raise against him seven *shepherds* **tenders**,
and eight *principal men* **libated of humanity**.
6 And they shall *waste* **tend**
the land of *Assyria* **Ashshur** with the sword,
and the land of Nimrod
in the *entrances* **openings** *thereof*:
thus shall he *deliver* **rescue** us
from the *Assyrian* **Ashshuri**,
when he cometh into our land,
and when he treadeth within our borders.
7 And the *remnant* **survivors** of *Jacob* **Yaaqov**
shall be in the midst of many people
as a dew from *the LORD* **Yah Veh**,
as the showers upon the *grass* **herbage**,
that *tarrieth* **awaiteth** not for man,
nor waiteth for the sons of *men* **humanity**.
8 And the remnant of *Jacob* **Yaaqov**
shall be among the *Gentiles* **goyim**
in the midst of many people
as a lion among the *beasts* **animals** of the forest,
as a *young lion* **whelp**
among the *flocks* **droves** of *sheep* **flocks**:
who, if he *go* **pass** through,
both *treadeth down* **trampleth**, and teareth in pieces,
and none *can deliver* **rescueth**.
9 Thine hand shall be lifted *up*
upon *thine adversaries* **thy tribulators**, and
all thine enemies shall be cut off.
10 And **so be** it *shall come to pass* in that day,
saith the LORD **an oracle of Yah Veh**,
that I *will* **shall** cut off thy horses
out of the midst of thee,
and I *will* **shall** destroy thy chariots:
11 And I *will* **shall** cut off the cities of thy land,
and *throw down* **demolish** all thy *strong holds* **fortresses**:
12 And I *will* **shall** cut off *witchcrafts* **sorceries**
out of thine hand;
and thou shalt have no *more soothsayers* **cloudgazers**:
13 Thy *graven images* **sculptiles**
also *will* **shall** I cut off,
and thy *standing images* **monoliths**
out of the midst of thee;
and thou shalt no more
worship **prostrate to** the work of thine hands.
14 And I *will pluck up* **shall**
uproot thy *groves* **asherah**
out of the midst of thee:
so *will I destroy* **shall I desolate** thy cities.
15 And I *will execute vengeance*
shall work avengement
in *anger* **wrath** and fury upon the *heathen* **goyim**,
such as they have not heard.

THE CONTROVERSY OF YAH VEH WITH YISRA EL

6 Hear ye *now* **I beseech,** what
the LORD **Yah Veh** saith;
Arise, contend thou before the mountains,
and let the hills hear thy voice.
2 Hear ye, O mountains,
the *LORD'S* controversy **of Yah Veh,**
and ye *strong* **perennial** foundations of the earth:
for *the LORD* **Yah Veh**
hath a controversy with his people,
and he *will plead with Israel* **shall reprove Yisra El**.
3 O my people, what have I
done **worked** unto thee?
and wherein have I wearied thee?
testify **answer** against me.
4 For I *brought* **ascended** thee *up*
out of the land of *Egypt* **Misrayim,**
and redeemed thee out of the house of servants;
and I sent *before thee* **ere thy face**
Moses **Mosheh**, *Aaron* **Aharon**, and *Miriam* **Miryam**.
5 O my people, remember *now* **I beseech,**
what *Balak king* **Balaq sovereign** of Moab
consulted **counselled,**
and what Balaam the son of Beor answered him
from Shittim unto Gilgal;
that ye may know
the *righteousness* **justness** of *the LORD* **Yah Veh**.
and there they settle:
for now he greatens to the finalities of the earth:
5 and thus is this one of shalom.
And when the Ashshuriy come into our land
—when he treads in our citadels,
then we raise seven tenders against him,
and eight libated humans:
6 and they tend the land of
Ashshur with the sword,

and the land of Nimrod in the openings:
thus he rescues us from the Ashshuri
when he comes into our land
and when he treads within our borders.
7 And so be the survivors of Yaaqov
among many people
—as dew from Yah Veh
—as the showers on the herbage,
who neither awaits man
nor awaits the sons of humanity.
8 And so be the remnant of
Yaaqov among the goyim
among many people
—as a lion among the animals of the forest
—as a whelp among the droves of flocks:
who, if he passes through, both tramples and tears;
and no one rescues.
9 Lifted *is* your hand over your tribulators,
and all your enemies cut off.
10 And so be it, in that day,
—an oracle of Yah Veh
that I cut off your horses from your midst
and I destroy your chariots:
11 and I cut off the cities of your land
and demolish all your fortresses:
12 and I cut off sorceries from your hand
so that you have no cloudgazers:
13 and I cut off your sculptiles and your monoliths
from your midst;
and you prostrate no more to the work of your hands:
14 and I uproot your asherah from your midst
thus I desolate your cities:
15 and in wrath and fury
I work avengement on the goyim
such as they never heard.

THE CONTROVERSY OF YAH VEH WITH YISRA EL

6 Hear, I beseech, what Yah Veh says;
Rise! Contend in front of the mountains
so that the hills hear your voice.
2 Hear the controversy of Yah Veh,
O mountains,
and you perennial foundations of the earth:
for Yah Veh has a controversy with his people
and he reproves Yisra El.
3 O my people, what work I to you?
And wherein weary I you?
Answer against me.
4 For I ascended you from the land of Misrayim
and redeemed you from the house of servants;
and ere your face
I sent Mosheh, Aharon, and Miryam.
5 O my people, remember, I beseech,
what Balaq sovereign of Moab counselled
and what Balaam the son of Beor answered him
from Shittim to Gilgal;
so that you know the justness of Yah Veh.
6 Wherewith shall I *come before*
the LORD **confront Yah Veh**,
and bow myself *before* **in front of** the high *God* **Elohim**?
shall I *come before* **confront** him
with *burnt offerings* **holocausts**,
with *calves of a year old* **yearling sons**?
7 *Will the LORD* **Shall Yah Veh** be pleased
with thousands of rams,
or with *ten thousands* **myriads** of *rivers* **wadies** of oil?
shall I give my *firstborn* **birstbirthed**
for my *transgression* **rebellion**,
the fruit of my *body* **belly** for the sin of my soul?
8 He hath *shewed* **told** thee, O *man* **humanity**,
what is good;
and what doth *the LORD* **Yah Veh** require of thee,
but to *do justly* **work judgment**, and to love mercy,
and to walk humbly with thy *God* **Elohim**?
9 *The LORD'S* **Yah Veh's** voice
crieth **calleth out** unto the city,
and the *man of wisdom* **counsellor** shall see thy name:
hear ye the rod, and who hath *appointed* **congregated** it.
10 Are there yet the treasures of wickedness
in the house of the wicked,
and the *scant measure* **emaciated ephah**
that *is abominable* **enrageth**?
11 Shall I *count them pure* **purify them**
with the wicked balances,
and with the *bag* **pouch** of deceitful *weights* **stones**?
12 For the rich *men thereof*
are *full* **filled** of violence,
and the *inhabitants* **settlers** *thereof*
have spoken *lies* **falsehoods**,
and their tongue is deceitful in their mouth.
13 Therefore also
will I make thee sick **shall I stroke thee** in smiting thee,
in *making* **desolating** thee *desolate* because of thy sins.
14 Thou shalt eat, but not be *satisfied* **satiated**;
and thy *casting down* **hunger**
shall be in the midst of thee;
and thou shalt *take hold* **remove**,
but shalt not *deliver* **escape**;
and that which *thou deliverest* **escapeth**

will **shall** I give up to the sword.
15 Thou shalt *sow* **seed**, but
thou shalt not *reap* **harvest**;
thou shalt tread the olives,
but thou shalt not anoint thee with oil;
and *sweet wine* **juice**, but shalt not drink wine.
16 For the statutes of Omri are *kept* **guarded**,
and all the works of the house of *Ahab* **Ach Ab**,
and ye walk in their counsels;
that I should *make* **give** thee a desolation,
and the *inhabitants* **settlers** *thereof* an hissing:
therefore ye shall bear the reproach of my people.

WOE IS YISRA EL

7 Woe is me!
for I am as *when they have gathered* **the ingathering of** the summer fruits,
as the *grapegleanings* **gleanings** of the *vintage* **crop**:
there is no cluster to eat:
my soul desired the *firstripe* **firstling** fruit.
2 The *good man* **merciful**
is *perished* **destructed** out of the earth:
and there is none *upright* **straight**
among *men* **humanity**:
they all *lie in wait* **lurk** for blood;
they hunt every man his brother with a net.
3 That they may do evil
with both *hands earnestly* **palms well—pleasingly**,
the *prince* **governor** asketh,
and the judge *asketh for a reward* **for satisfaction**;
and the great *man*,
he uttereth his mischievous desire
wordeth the mischief of his soul:
so they *wrap* **pervert** it *up*.
4 The best of them is as a *brier* **thorn**:
the most upright is sharper
straighter than a thorn hedge:
the day of thy *watchmen* **watchers** and thy visitation cometh;
now shall be their perplexity.
5 Trust ye not in a friend,
put **confide** ye not *confidence* in a *guide* **chiliarch**:
6 With what confront I Yah Veh?
And bow myself in front of the high Elohim?
Confront I him with holocausts?
With yearling sons?
7 Please Yah Veh with thousands of rams?
With myriads of wadies of oil?
Give I my firstbirthed for my rebellion
—the fruit of my belly for the sin of my soul?
8 He tells you, O humanity, what is good.
And what requires Yah Veh of you
—except to work judgment and to love mercy
and to walk humbly with your Elohim?
9 The voice of Yah Veh calls to the city,
and the counsellor sees your name: Hear
the rod; and he who congregates it.
10 Are there yet treasures of wickedness
in the house of the wicked?
And the emaciated ephah that enrages?
11 Purify I them with balances of wickedness?
And with the pouch of stones of deceit?
12 —whose the rich are filled of violence
and the settlers speak falsehoods;
and their tongue is deceitful in their mouth?
13 And I also, in smiting you, I stroke you
—desolate you because of your sins.
14 You eat, and satiate not;
and hunger *is* among you;
and you remove, but escape not;
and whatever escapes, I give to the sword.
15 You—you seed, and you harvest not;
you—you tread the olive,
and you anoint not with oil;
and juice, and you drink not the wine.
16 And you guard the statutes of Omri
and all the works of the house of Ach Ab;
and you walk in their counsels:
and I give you for a desolation,
and the settlers for a hissing:
and you bear the reproach of my people.

WOE IS YISRA EL

7 Woe is me!
As the ingathering of the summer fruits;
as the gleanings of the crop;
there is no cluster to eat:
my soul desires the firstling fruit:
2 the merciful destruct from the earth;
and no one among humanity is straight:
they all lurk for blood;
every man hunts his brother with a net
3 to do evil with both palms well—pleasingly, the
governor and the judge ask for satisfaction; and
the great words of the mischief of his soul:
thus they pervert.
4 Their best is as a thorn;
straighter than a thorn hedge:
the day of your watchers and your visitation comes
—now their perplexity.

5 Neither trust in a friend
nor confide in a chiliarch:
keep **guard** the *doors* **opening** of thy mouth
from her that lieth in thy bosom.
6 For the son *dishonoureth* **disgraceth** the father,
the daughter riseth *up* against her mother,
the daughter in law against her mother in law;
a man's enemies are the men of his own house.

The Survivors In The Final Days

7 Therefore
I *will look* **shall watch** unto *the LORD* **Yah Veh**;
I *will wait for the God* **shall await Elohim**
of my salvation:
my *God will* **Elohim shall** hear me.
8 *Rejoice* **Cheer** not against me, O mine enemy:
when I fall, I shall arise;
when I sit in darkness,
the LORD **Yah Veh** shall be a light unto me.
9 I *will* **shall** bear the *indignation* **rage**
of *the LORD* **Yah Veh**,
because I have sinned against him,
until he plead my *cause* **plea**,
and *execute* **work** judgment for me:
he *will* **shall** bring me forth to the light,
and I shall *behold* **see** his *righteousness* **justness**.
10 Then *she that is* mine enemy shall see *it*,
and shame shall cover her which said unto me,
Where is *the LORD* **Yah Veh** thy *God* **Elohim**?
mine eyes shall *behold* **see** her:
now shall she be *trodden down* **trampled**
as the mire of the *streets* **outways**.
11 In the day that thy walls are to be built,
in that day shall the *decree* **statute** be far removed.
12 In that day *also*
he shall come even to thee from *Assyria* **Ashshur**,
and from the *fortified* cities **of siege**,
and *from* the *fortress* **siege** even to the river,
and from sea to sea, and *from* mountain to mountain.
13 Notwithstanding the land shall be desolate
because of them that *dwell* **settle** therein,
for the fruit of their *doings* **exploits**.
14 *Feed* **Tend** thy people with thy *rod* **scion**,
the flock of thine *heritage* **inheritance**,
which *dwell solitarily* **tabernacle alone**
in the *wood* **forest**,
in the midst of *Carmel* **Karmel/orchard**:
let them *feed* **graze** in Bashan and *Gilead* **Gilad**,
as in the **original** days *of old*.
15 According to the days
of thy coming out of the land of *Egypt* **Misrayim**
will I shew unto him marvellous things
shall I have him see marvels.
16 The *nations* **goyim** shall see
and be *confounded* **shamed** at all their might:
they shall *lay* **set** their hand upon their mouth,
their ears shall *be deaf* **deafen**.
17 They shall lick the dust like a serpent,
they shall *move* **quiver** out of their *holes* **strongholds**
like *worms* **creepers** of the earth:
they shall *be afraid* **fear**
of the LORD **Yah Veh** our *God* **Elohim**,
and shall *fear* **awe** because of thee.
18 Who is *a God* **an El** like unto thee,
that *pardoneth iniquity* **beareth perversity**,
and passeth by the *transgression* **rebellion**
of the *remnant* **survivors** of his *heritage* **inheritance**?
he *retaineth* **holdeth** not his *anger* **wrath**
for ever **eternally**,
because he delighteth *in* mercy.
19 He *will* **shall** turn again,
he *will have compassion upon* **shall mercy** us;
he *will* **shall** subdue our *iniquities* **perversities**;
and thou *wilt* **shalt** cast all their sins
into the *depths* **deep** of the sea.
20 Thou *wilt perform* **shalt give**
the truth to *Jacob* **Yaaqov**,
and the mercy to Abraham,
which thou hast *sworn* **oathed** unto our fathers
from the days of *old* **antiquity**.
guard the opening of your mouth
from her who lies in your bosom:
6 for son disgraces father;
daughter rises against her mother;
the daughter in law against her mother in law;
the enemies of a man are the men of his own house.

The Survivors In The Final Days

7 And I—I watch to Yah Veh;
I await Elohim of my salvation:
my Elohim hears me.
8 Cheer not against me, O my enemy:
when I fall, I rise;
when I sit in darkness Yah Veh *is* my light.
9 I bear the rage of Yah Veh
because I sinned against him;
until he pleads my plea
and works my judgment:
he brings me to the light and I see his justness.

10 And my enemy sees;
and shame covers her who says to me,
Where is Yah Veh your Elohim?
My eyes see her:
now she becomes for trampling
as the mire of the outways.
11 In the day to build your walls
—in that day the statute *is* far removed:
12 —in that day he even comes to you
from Ashshur and from the cities of siege
—the siege even to the river
and from sea to sea and mountain to mountain:
13 and the land becomes desolate
because of them who settle therein—
for the fruit of their exploits.
14 Tend your people with your scion
—the flock of your inheritance
who tabernacle alone in the forest
midst Karmel/orchard:
they graze in Bashan and Gilad
as in the original days.
15 According to the days
of your coming from the land of Misrayim
I have him see marvels.
16 The goyim see and shame at all their might:
they set their hand on their mouth;
—deafen their ears:
17 they lick the dust as a serpent;
they quiver from their strongholds
as creepers of the earth:
they fear Yah Veh our Elohim
and awe because of you.
18 Who is an El like to you,
who bears perversity,
and passes by the rebellion
of the survivors of his inheritance?
he holds not his wrath eternally
because he delights mercy.
19 He restores; he mercies us:
he subdues our perversities.
You cast all their sins into the deep of the sea;
20 You give truth to Yaaqov; mercy to Abraham
—which you oathed to our fathers
from the days of antiquity.

THE BURDEN OF NINEVEH

1 The burden of Nineveh.
The *book* **scroll** of the vision
of *Nahum* **Nachum** the *Elkoshite* **Elqoshiy**.
2 *God* **El** is jealous,
and *the LORD revengeth* **Yah Veh avengeth**;
the LORD revengeth **Yah Veh avengeth**,
and is *furious* **a master of fury**;
the LORD will take vengeance on **Yah Veh shall avenge**
his *adversaries* **tribulators**,
and he *reserveth wrath* **guardeth** for his enemies.
3 *The LORD* **Yah Veh** is slow to *anger* **wrath**,
and great in *power* **force**,
and **in exonerating,**
will **shall** not *at all acquit the wicked* **exonerate:**
the LORD **Yah Veh** hath his way
in the *whirlwind* **hurricane** and in the *storm* **whirling**,
and the clouds are the dust of his feet.
4 He rebuketh the sea, and
maketh it dry **withereth**,
and drieth *up* all the rivers:
Bashan languisheth, and *Carmel* **Karmel/orchard**,
and the *flower* **blossom** of Lebanon languisheth.
5 The mountains quake at him, and the hills melt,
and the earth is *burned* **lifted** at his *presence* **face**,
yea, the world, and all that *dwell* **settle** therein.
6 Who can stand
before **at the face of** his *indignation* **rage**?
and who *can abide* **rise**
in the *fierceness* **fuming** of his *anger* **wrath**?
his fury is poured out like fire,
and the rocks are *thrown* **pulled** down by him.
7 *The LORD* **Yah Veh** is good,
a *strong hold* **strength** in the day of *trouble* **tribulation**;
and he knoweth them that *trust* **seek refuge** in him.
8 But with an *overrunning flood*
overpassing overflowing
he *will make an utter end* **shall work a final finish**
of the place *thereof*,
and darkness shall pursue his enemies.
9 What do ye *imagine* **fabricate**
against *the LORD* **Yah Veh**?
he *will make an full end* **shall work a final finish:**
affliction **tribulation** shall not rise *up* the second *time*.
10 For while they be *folden*
together **entwined** as thorns,
and while they *are drunken* **carouse** as
drunkards **carousers**, they shall be *devoured*
consumed as stubble fully dry.
11 There is one come out of thee,
that *imagineth* **fabricateth** evil
against *the LORD* **Yah Veh,**
a *wicked counsellor* **counsellor of Beli Yaal**.
12 Thus saith *the LORD* **Yah Veh**;
Though they be *quiet* **at shalom**, and likewise many,
yet thus shall they be *cut down* **shorn,**
when he shall pass through.
Though I have *afflicted* **humbled** thee,
I *will afflict* **shall humble** thee no more.
13 For now *will* **shall** I break
his yoke **pole** from off thee,
and *will burst* **shall tear** thy bonds *in sunder.*
14 And *the LORD* **Yah Veh**
hath *given a commandment* **misvahed** concerning thee,
that no more of thy name be *sown* **seeded**:
out of the house of thy *gods* **elohim**
will **shall** I cut off
the *graven image* **sculptile** and the molten *image*:
I *will make* **shall set** thy *grave* **tomb**;
for thou art *vile* **abased**.
15 Behold upon the mountains
the feet of him that *bringeth good tidings* **evangelizeth**,
that *publisheth peace* **hearkeneth shalom**!
O *Judah* **Yah Hudah**,
keep **celebrate** thy *solemn feasts* **celebrations**,
perform **shalam** thy vows:
for *the wicked* **Beli Yaal**
shall *no more* **not add to** pass through thee;
he is utterly cut off.

THE FALL OF NINEVEH

2 He that *dasheth in pieces* **shattereth**
is *come up before* **ascended in front of** thy face:
keep **guard** the *munition* **rampart**, watch the way,
make **strengthen** thy loins *strong*,
fortify **strengthen** thy power mightily.

THE BURDEN OF NINEVEH

1 The burden of Nineveh:
The scroll of the vision of Nachum the Elqoshiy.
2 El *is* jealous and Yah Veh avenges;
Yah Veh avenges and is a master of fury:
Yah Veh avenges his tribulators
and he guards for his enemies:
3 Yah Veh *is* slow to wrath and great in force;
and in exonerating, Yah Veh exonerates not:
his way *is* in the hurricane and in the whirling
and clouds *are* the dust of his feet:

4 he rebukes the sea
and withers and dries all the rivers:
Bashan and Karmel/orchard languish;
and the blossom of Lebanon languishes:
5 the mountains quake at him and the hills melt
and the earth lifts at his face
—yes, the world and all who settle therein.
6 Who stands at the face of his rage?
And who rises in the fuming of his wrath?
He pours his fury as fire
and pulls down the rocks.
7 Yah Veh *is* good,
a strength in the day of tribulation;
and he knows them who seek refuge in him.
8 And with an overpassing overflowing
he works a final finish of the place;
and darkness pursues his enemies.
9 What fabricate you against Yah Veh?
He works a final finish:
tribulation rises not secondly.
10 For while they entwine as thorns,
and while they carouse as carousers, they
are consumed as stubble fully dry.
11 From you
comes one who fabricates evil against Yah Veh
—a counsellor of Beli Yaal.
12 Thus says Yah Veh:
Though at shalom, and thus so many,
yet thus they *are* shorn when he passes through.
Though I humbled you, I humble you no more.
13 And now I break his yoke pole upon you,
and tear away your bonds:
14 and Yah Veh misvahs concerning you,
that your name *is* seeded no more:
from the house of your elohim
I cut off the sculptile and the molten:
I set your tomb; for you are abased.
15 Behold, on the mountains
the feet of him who evangelizes,
who hearkens, Shalom!
O Yah Hudah, celebrate your celebrations!
Shalam your vows!
for Beli Yaal adds not to pass through you;
he is utterly cut off.

The Fall Of Nineveh

2 He who shatters ascends in front of your face:
guard the rampart; watch the way;
strengthen your loins;
strengthen your power mightily:
2 For *the LORD* **Yah Veh** hath turned away
the *excellency* **pomp** of *Jacob* **Yaaqov**,
as the *excellency* **pomp** of *Israel* **Yisra El**:
for the *emptiers* **evacuators**
have *emptied* **evacuated** them *out*,
and *marred* **ruined** their vine *branches* **twigs**.
3 The *shield* **buckler** of his mighty *men*
is *made red* **reddened**,
the valiant men are in **dyed** scarlet:
the chariots shall be **fiery**
with *flaming torches* **cleavers of fire**
in the day of his preparation,
and the fir trees shall be *terribly* shaken.
4 The chariots shall *rage*
halal in the *streets* **outways**,
they shall *justle one against another*
prowl in the broad ways:
they shall seem like torches **their visage as flambeaus**,
they shall run like the lightnings.
5 He shall *recount* **remember** his *worthies* **mighty**:
they shall *stumble* **falter** in their *walk* **way**;
they shall make haste to the wall *thereof*,
and the *defence* **covering** shall be prepared.
6 The gates of the rivers shall be opened,
and the *palace* **manse** shall be *dissolved* **melted**.
7 And *Huzzab* **it is set:**
she shall be *led away captive* **exiled/exposed**,
she shall be *brought up* **ascended**,
and her maids shall *lead* **drive** her
as with the voice of doves,
tabering **tambourining** upon their *breasts* **hearts**.
8 But Nineveh is of *old* **days** like a pool of water:
yet they shall flee away.
Stand, stand, *shall they cry*; but none shall look back.
9 *Take* **Plunder** ye the *spoil of* silver,
take **plunder** the *spoil of* gold:
for there is none end of the *store*
structure and *glory* **honour**
out of all the *pleasant furniture* **vessels of desire**.
10 She is empty, and void, and *waste* **wasted**:
and the heart melteth, and the
knees *smite together* **knock**,
and much pain is in all loins,
and the faces of them all gather *blackness* **flushness**.
11 Where is the *dwelling* **habitation** of the lions,
and the *feedingplace* **pasture** of the *young lions* **whelps**,
where the lion, *even* the *old* **roaring** lion, walked,
and the lion's whelp,
and none *made* **trembleth** them *afraid*?
12 The lion did tear in pieces
enough for his whelps,

and strangled for his lionesses,
and filled his holes with prey,
and his *dens* **habitations** with *ravin* **prey**.
13 Behold, I am against thee,
saith the LORD of hosts **an oracle of Yah Veh Sabaoth**,
and I *will* **shall** burn her chariots in the smoke,
and the sword shall *devour* **consume**
thy *young lions* **whelps**:
and I *will* **shall** cut off thy prey from the earth,
and the voice of thy *messengers* **angels**
shall no more be heard.

HO TO NINEVEH

3 *Woe* **Ho** to the bloody city!
it is all full of *lies* **deceptions** and *robbery* **tyranny**;
the prey departeth not;
2 The *noise* **voice** of a whip,
and the *noise* **voice**
of the *rattling* **quake** of *the wheels* **a wheel**,
and of the pransing horses,
and of the *jumping* **dancing** chariots.
3 The horseman *lifteth up* **ascendeth** both
the *bright* **flame of the** sword
and the *glittering* **lightning** spear:
and there is *a multitude* **an abundance** of *slain* **pierced**,
and *a great number* **the heaviness** of carcases;
and there is none end of their corpses;
they *stumble* **falter** upon their corpses:
4 Because of the multitude of the whoredoms
of the *wellfavoured harlot* **whore of good charism**,
the *mistress* **baalah** of *witchcrafts* **sorceries**,
that selleth *nations* **goyim** through her whoredoms,
and families through her *witchcrafts* **sorceries**.
2 for Yah Veh turns away the pomp of Yaaqov
as the pomp of Yisra El:
for the evacuators evacuate them
and ruin their vine twigs:
3 the buckler of his mighty reddens;
the valiant men *are* in dyed scarlet:
and fiery chariots with cleavers of fire
in the day of his preparation;
and the fir trees shake.
4 The chariots halal in the outways;
they prowl in the broadways:
their visage as flambeaus;
they run as the lightnings.
5 He remembers his mighty;
they falter in their walk;
they hasten to the wall
and prepare the covering:
6 the gates of the rivers open
and the manse melts.
7 And it is set:
she is exiled/exposed;
she ascends;
and her maids drive her as with the voice of doves
tambourining on their hearts.
8 And Nineveh is as a pool
of water from days *ago*:
yet they flee.
Stand! Stand! And no one looks back.
9 Plunder the silver; plunder the gold:
for there is no end of the structure and honor
of all the vessels of desire;
10 she is empty and void and wasted:
and the heart melts and the knees knock
and much pain in all loins;
and all their faces gather flushness.
11 Where is the habitation of the lions?
And the pasture of the whelps?
Where walks the lion? The roaring lion?
And the whelp of the lion?
And no one trembles?
12 The lion tears enough pieces for his whelps
and strangles for his lionesses;
and fills his holes with prey
and his habitations with prey.
13 Behold, I *am* against you
—an oracle of Yah Veh Sabaoth
and I burn her chariots in the smoke
and the sword consumes your whelps:
and I cut off your prey from the earth
and the voice of your angels *is* heard no more.

HO TO NINEVEH

3 Ho to the bloody city!
Full of deceptions and tyranny;
the prey departs not:
2 The voice of a whip
and the voice of the quake of a wheel
and of the pransing horses
and of the dancing chariots!
3 The horseman ascends both
—the flame of the sword and the lightning spear:
and there *is* an abundance of pierced
and the heaviness of carcases;
and there is no end of their corpses:
they falter on their corpses.
4 Because of the multitude of the whoredoms
of the whore of good charism,

the baalah of sorceries,
who sells goyim through her whoredoms,
and families through her sorceries.
5 Behold, I am against thee,
saith the LORD of hosts **an oracle of Yah Veh Sabaoth**;
and I *will discover* **shall expose** thy *skirts* **drapings**
upon thy face,
and I *will shew the nations* **shall have the goyim see**
thy nakedness,
and the *kingdoms* **sovereigndoms**
thy *shame* **abasement**.
6 And I *will* **shall** cast
abominable filth **abominations** upon thee,
and *make* **wither** thee *vile*,
and *will* **shall** set thee as a *gazingstock* **spectacle**.
7 And **so be** it *shall come to pass*,
that all they that *look upon* **see** thee shall flee from thee,
and say, Nineveh is *laid waste* **ravaged**:
who *will bemoan* **shall wag over** her?
whence shall I seek *comforters* **sighers** for thee?
8 *Art thou better* **Well—pleasest thou**
more than *populous No* **No Ammon**,
that *was situate* **settled** among the rivers,
that had the waters round about it,
whose *rampart* **trench** was the sea,
and her wall was from the sea?
9 *Ethiopia* **Kush** and *Egypt* **Misrayim**
were her *strength* **might**,
and *it was infinite* **there was no end**;
Put and *Lubim* **Lubiym** were thy helpers.
10 Yet was she *carried away* **exiled**,
she went into captivity:
her *young children* **sucklings** also
were *dashed in pieces* **splattered**
at the top of all the *streets* **outways**:
and they *cast lots* **handled pebbles**
for her honourable men,
and all her great *men* were *bound* **chained** in chains.
11 Thou also shalt be *drunken* **intoxicated**:
thou shalt be *hid* **concealed**,
thou also shalt seek *strength* **a stronghold**
because of the enemy.
12 All thy *strong holds* **fortresses**
shall be like fig trees with the *firstripe figs* **firstlings**:
if they be shaken,
they shall *even* fall into the mouth of the eater.
13 Behold, thy people in the
midst of thee are women:
the gates of thy land
in opening,
shall be *set wide open* **opened** unto thine enemies:
the fire shall *devour* **consume** thy bars.
14 *Draw* **Bail** thee waters for the siege,
fortify **strengthen** thy *strong holds* **fortresses**:
go into *clay* **mire** and tread the morter,
make strong **strengthen** the brickkiln.
15 There shall the fire *devour* **consume** thee;
the sword shall cut thee off,
it shall eat thee *up* like the cankerworm:
make **multiply** thyself *many* as the cankerworm,
make **multiply** thyself *many* as the locusts.
16 Thou hast *multiplied* **abounded** thy merchants
above the stars of *heaven* **the heavens**:
the cankerworm *spoileth* **spreadeth**,
and *fleeth away* **flieth**.
17 Thy *crowned* **princes** are as the locusts,
and thy *captains* **officers**
as the *great grasshoppers* **grubbing grubbers**,
which *camp* **encamp** in the *hedges* **walls** in the cold day,
but when the sun ariseth they flee away,
and their place is not known where they are.
18 Thy *shepherds* **tenders** slumber,
O *king* **sovereign** of *Assyria* **Ashshur**:
thy *nobles* **mighty** shall *dwell in the dust* **tabernacle**:
thy people is scattered upon the mountains,
and *no man* **no one** gathereth *them*.
19 There is no healing of thy *bruise* **break**;
thy wound *is grievous* **worn**:
all that hear the *bruit* **report** of thee
shall clap the *hands* **palms** over thee:
for upon whom
hath not thy *wickedness* **evil** passed continually?
5 Behold, I *am* against you
—an oracle of Yah Veh Sabaoth
and I expose your drapings on your face,
and I have the goyim see your nakedness
and the sovereigndoms your abasement:
6 and I cast abominations on you
and wither you and set you as a spectacle.
7 And so be it,
all who see you, flee from you;
and say, Nineveh *is* ravaged:
Who wags over her?
Where seek I sighers for you?
8 Well—please you more than No Ammon
who settles among the rivers surrounded by waters?
Whose trench *is* the sea? And the sea her wall?
9 Kush and Misrayim her might
and without end;
and Put and Lubiym your helpers.

10 Yet was she *is* exiled; she goes into captivity:
even her sucklings splatter
at the top of all the outways:
and they handle pebbles for her honorable men
and chain all her great in chains.
11 Even you intoxicate; you become concealed:
even you seek a stronghold because of the enemy.
12 All your fortresses *are* fig trees of the firstlings:
if you shake, they fall into the mouth of the devourer.
13 Behold, your people among you *are* women:
in opening,
the gates of your land open to your enemies:
the fire consumes your bars.
14 Bail waters for the siege;
strengthen your fortresses:
go into mire and tread the morter;
strengthen the brickkiln:
15 there the fire consumes you;
the sword cuts you off;
deviours you as the cankerworm:
multiply yourself as the cankerworm;
multiply yourself as the locusts.
16 You abound your merchants
above the stars of the heavens:
the cankerworm spreads and flies.
17 Your princes *are* as the locusts
and your officers as the grubbing grubbers
who encamp in the walls in the cold day;
and when the sun rises they flee,
and the place where they are is not known.
18 Your tenders slumber, O sovereign of Ashshur;
your mighty tabernacle:
your people scatter on the mountains
and no one gathers.
19 There is no healing of your breach;
your wound *is* worn:
all who hear your report
clap their palms over you:
for on whom passes not your evil continually?

The First Burden Of Habakkuk

1 The burden which Habakkuk
the prophet did see.
2 O *LORD* **Yah Veh,**
how long shall I cry, and thou *wilt* **shalt** not hear!
even cry out unto thee of violence,
and thou *wilt* **shalt** not save!
3 Why dost thou *shew me*
iniquity **have me see mischief,**
and cause me to *behold grievance* **scan at toil**?
for *spoiling* **ravage** and violence are *before* **in front of** me:
and there are that *raise up* **lift** strife and contention.
4 Therefore the *law* **torah** is *slacked* **exhausted,**
and judgment
doth never go forth **goeth not in perpetuity**:
for the wicked
doth compass about **surroundeth** the *righteous* **just**;
therefore *wrong* **twisted** judgment proceedeth.

The Response Of Yah Veh

5 *Behold* **See** ye among the *heathen* **goyim,**
and *regard* **look,** and *wonder* **marvel** marvellously:
for I *will* **shall** work a work in your days
which ye *will* **shall** not *believe* **trust,**
though it be *told you* **scribed.**
6 For, *lo* **behold,** I raise *up*
the *Chaldeans* **Kesediym,**
that bitter and hasty *nation* **goyim,**
which shall *march* **walk**
through the *breadth* **expanse** of the land,
to possess the *dwellingplaces* **tabernacles**
that are not theirs.
7 They are terrible and *dreadful* **awesome**:
their judgment and their *dignity* **exalting**
shall proceed of themselves.
8 Their horses also are swifter than the leopards,
and are *more fierce* **sharper** than the evening wolves:
and their *horsemen* **cavalry** shall spread themselves,
and their *horsemen* **cavalry** shall come from far;
they shall fly as the eagle that hasteth to eat.
9 They shall come all for violence:
their faces
shall *sup up as the east wind* **suck the easterly,**
and they shall gather the captivity as the sand.
10 And they shall *scoff at the*
kings **ridicule sovereigns,**
and the *princes* **potentates**
shall be a *scorn* **laughingstock** unto them:
they shall *deride* **ridicule** every *strong hold* **fortress**;
for they shall heap dust, and *take* **capture** it.
11 Then shall his *mind* **spirit** change,
and he shall pass over, and *offend* **shall guilt,**
imputing this his *power* **force** unto his *god* **elohah.**

The Second Burden Of Habakkuk

12 Art thou not from *everlasting* **antiquity,**
O *LORD* **Yah Veh** my *God* **Elohim,** mine Holy One?
we shall not die.
O *LORD* **Yah Veh,**
thou hast *ordained* **set** them for judgment;
and, O *mighty God* **Rock,**
thou hast *established* **founded** them
for *correction* **reproving.**
13 Thou art of purer eyes than to *behold* **see** evil,
and canst not look on *iniquity* **toil**:
wherefore lookest thou
upon them that deal *treacherously* **covertly,**
and *holdest thy tongue* **hushest** when the wicked
devoureth the man that is **swallow him**
that is more **just** *righteous than he*?
14 And *makest men* **workest humanity**
as the fishes of the sea,
as the *creeping things* **creepers,**
that have no *ruler* **sovereign** over them?
15 They *take up* **ascend** all of
them with the *angle* **hook,**
they catch them in their net,
and gather them in their drag **net**:
therefore they *rejoice* **cheer** and *are glad* **twirl.**
16 Therefore they sacrifice unto their net,
and *burn* incense unto their drag **net**;
because by them their *portion* **allotment** is fat,
and their *meat plenteous* **food fattened.**
17 shall they therefore *empty* **drag** their net,
and not spare continually
to *slay* **slaughter** the *nations* **goyim**?

The First Burden Of Habakkuk

1 The burden Habakkuk the prophet sees:
2 O Yah Veh, how long cry I, and you hear not!
—even cry out to you of violence, and you save not?
3 Why show me mischief,
and have me to scan at toil?
With ravage and violence in front of me?
And strife and contention lifting themselves?
4 So the torah *is* exhausted
and judgment goes not in perpetuity:
for the wicked surround the just;
so twisted judgment proceeds.

THE RESPONSE OF YAH VEH

5 See among the goyim and look;
and marvel marvellously:
for he works a work in your days which you trust not
though it *is* scribed.
6 For, behold, I raise the Kesediym,
that bitter and hasty goyim,
to walk through the expanse of the land;
to possess the tabernacles which *are* not theirs:
7 —terrible and awesome:
their judgment and their exalting
proceeds from themselves:
8 with horses swifter than leopards
and sharper than the evening wolves:
and their cavalry spread themselves
and their cavalry comes from afar;
they fly as the eagle hastening to devour:
9 they all come for violence;
their faces suck the easterly
and they gather the captivity as the sand.
10 And they ridicule sovereigns,
and potentates *are* their laughingstock:
they ridicule every fortress;
for they heap dust and capture it.
11 Then his spirit passes on and he passes over;
yes, he guilts
his force *is* unto his elohah.

THE SECOND BURDEN OF HABAKKUK

12 Are you not from antiquity,
O Yah Veh my Elohim, my Holy One?
We die not, O Yah Veh:
you set them for judgment;
and O Rock, you founded them for reproof:
13 —eyes, purer than to see evil,
that cannot look on toil:
Why look on them who deal covertly?
And hush
when the wicked swallow him who *is* more just?
14 Works humanity as the fishes of the sea?
As the creepers who have no sovereign over them?
15 He ascends them all with the hook;
he catches them in their net
and gathers them in their dragnet:
so he cheers and twirls:
16 so he sacrifices to his net
and incenses to his dragnet;
because by them his allotment *is* fat,
and his food fattens.
17 So drags he not his net?
And spares he not
from continually slaughtering the goyim?

2 I *will* **shall** stand upon my *watch* **guard**,
and set me upon the *tower* **rampart**,
and *will* **shall** watch to see
what he *will say* **shall word** unto me,
and what I shall *answer* **respond**
when I am reproved **upon my reproof**.

THE RESPONSE OF YAH VEH

2 And *the LORD* **Yah Veh** answered me, and said,
Write **Inscribe** the vision,
and *make it plain* **explain it** upon *tables* **slabs**,
that he may run that *readeth it* **calleth out**.
3 For the vision is yet for *an*
appointed time **a season**,
but at the end it shall *speak* **breathe**, and
not lie: though it tarry, wait for it;
because **in coming**, it *will surely* **shall** come,
it *will* **shall** not *tarry* **delay**.
4 Behold,
his soul which is *lifted up* **swollen**
is not *upright* **straight** in him:
but the just shall live by his *faith* **trustworthiness**.
5 Yea also,
because he *transgresseth* **dealeth covertly** by wine,
he is *a proud man* **an arrogant mighty**,
neither *keepeth at home* **resteth in his habitation**,
who enlargeth his *desire* **soul** as *hell* **sheol**,
and is as death, and cannot be satisfied,
but gathereth unto him all *nations* **goyim**,
and *heapeth* **gathereth** unto him all people:
6 Shall not all these
take up a parable **lift a proverb** against him,
and a *taunting proverb* **satire riddle**
against him, and say,
Woe **Ho** to him
that *increaseth* **aboundeth** that which is not his!
how long?
and to him that *ladeth* **heavieth** himself
with *thick clay* **heavy pledges**!
7 Shall they not rise *up suddenly* **in a blink**
that shall bite thee,
and awake that shall *vex* **agitate** thee,
and thou shalt be for *booties* **plunder** unto them?
8 Because thou hast spoiled many *nations* **goyim**,
all the remnant of the people shall spoil
thee; because of *men's* **human** blood,
and for the violence of the land,
of the city, and of all that *dwell* **settle** therein.
9 *Woe* **Ho** to him that *coveteth* **greedily gaineth**

an evil *covetousness* **greedy gain** to his
house, that he may set his nest on high,
that he may be *delivered* **rescued**
from the *power* **palm** of evil!
10 Thou hast *consulted*
counselled shame to thy house
by *cutting* **scraping** off many people,
and hast sinned against thy soul.
11 For the stone shall cry out of the wall,
and the *beam* **crossbeam** out of the timber
shall answer *it*.
12 *Woe to him that buildeth a town with*
Ho to the builder of a city by blood,
and stablisheth a city by *iniquity* **wickedness**!
13 Behold,
is it not of *the LORD of hosts* **Yah Veh Sabaoth**
that the *people* **nations** shall labour
in the very **for sufficient** fire,
and the people shall weary themselves
for *very* **sufficient** vanity?
14 For the earth shall be filled with the knowledge
of the *glory* **honour** of *the LORD* **Yah Veh**,
as the waters cover the sea.
15 *Woe* **Ho** unto him
that giveth his *neighbour* **friend** drink,
that *puttest* **scrapest** thy *bottle* **skin** *to him*,
and *makest* **intoxicatest** him *drunken* also,
that thou mayest look on their *nakedness* **pudenda**!
16 Thou art *filled* **satiated**
with shame—**abasement** for *glory* **honour**:
drink thou also,
and *let thy foreskin be uncovered* **be uncircumcised**:

2 I stand on my guard
and set myself on the rampart;
and watch to see what he words to me;
and what I respond to my reproof.

The Response Of Yah Veh

2 And Yah Veh answers me, and says,
Inscribe the vision; and explain on slabs;
so that he who runs calls out:
3 for the vision is yet for a season;
and at the end it breathes and lies not:
though it tarries, await;
because in coming, it comes;
it delays not.
4 Behold, one swells up!
his soul within is not straight:
and the just lives by his trustworthiness.
5 Yes also, because he deals covertly by wine;
arrogant *is* the mighty
—who rests not in his habitation—who enlarges his soul
as sheol; and as death, *is* never satisfied: and gathers all
goyim to himself, and gathers all people to himself.
6 They, all of them,
lift they not a proverb against him?
and a satire riddle against him?
and say,
Ho to him who abounds in what *is* not his!
How long?
And to him who heavies himself with heavy pledges!
7 Rise they not in a blink—they who bite you?
And waken—they who agitate you?
And you become their plunder?
8 Because you spoil many goyim
all the remnant of the people spoil you
—because of human blood
and for the violence of the land;
of the city and all who settle therein.
9 Ho to him who greedily gains
an evil greedy gain to his house
—to set his nest on high
—to rescue himself from the palm of evil!
10 You counsel shame to your house
by scraping off many people
and sin against your soul.
11 For the stone cries from the wall:
and the crossbeam of timber answers.
12 Ho to him who builds a city by blood
—who establishes a city by wickedness!
13 Behold, is it not from Yah Veh Sabaoth
that the nations labor for sufficient fire?
And the people weary themselves
for sufficient vanity?
14 For the earth fills with the knowledge
of the honor of Yah Veh
as the waters cover the sea.
15 Ho to him who gives his friend drink
—who scrapes the *wine* skin
—who also intoxicates
just to look at their pudenda!
16 You satiate—abasement for honor:
and you drink and be uncircumcised:
the cup of *the LORD'S* **Yah Veh's** right *hand*
shall be turned unto thee,
and *shameful spewing* **an abasement**
shall be on thy *glory* **honour**.
17 For the violence of Lebanon shall cover thee,
and the *spoil* **ravage** of *beasts* **animals**,
which *made* **terrified** them *afraid*
because of *men's* **human** blood,
and for the violence of the land,

of the city, and of all that dwell therein.
18 What profiteth the *graven image* **sculptile**
that the *maker* **former** *thereof* hath *graven* **sculpted** it;
the molten *image*, and a teacher of *lies* **falsehoods**,
that the *maker* **former** of his *work* **form**
trusteth **confideth** therein,
to *make dumb* **work mute** idols?
19 *Woe* **Ho** unto him
that saith to the *wood* **timber**, Awake;
to the *dumb* **silent** stone, *Arise* **Awake**, it shall teach!
Behold, it is *laid over* **manipulated** with gold and silver,
and there is no *breath* **spirit** at all in the midst of it.
20 But *the LORD* **Yah Veh** is
in his holy *temple* **manse**:
let all the earth keep silence *before him* **at his face**.

The Lyric Poem Of Habakkuk

3 A prayer of Habakkuk the prophet
upon Shigionoth **A Lyric Poem**.
2 O *LORD* **Yah Veh**, I have
heard thy *speech* **report**,
and was *afraid* **awed**:
O *LORD* **Yah Veh**,
revive **enliven** thy *work* **deeds** in the midst of the years,
in the midst of the years make known;
in *wrath* **quivering** remember mercy.
3 *God* **Elohah** came from Teman,
and the Holy One from mount Paran.
Selah.
His *glory* **majesty** covered the heavens,
and the earth was *full of* **filled with** his *praise* **halal**.
4 And *his brightness* **brilliance** was as the light;
he had horns *coming* out of his hand:
and there was the hiding of his *power* **strength**.
5 *Before him* **At his face** went the pestilence,
and burning coals went forth at his feet.
6 He stood,
and *measured* **shook** the earth:
he *beheld* **saw**,
and *drove asunder* **loosed** the *nations* **goyim**;
and the *everlasting* **eternal** mountains were scattered,
the perpetual hills *did bow* **prostrated**:
his ways are everlasting.
7 I saw the tents of *Cushan*
Kushan in *affliction* **mischief**:
and the curtains of the land of *Midian* **Midyan**
did tremble **quivered**.
8 Was *the LORD displeased* **Yah Veh inflamed**
against the rivers?
was *thine anger* **thy wrath** against the rivers?
was thy wrath against the sea,
that thou didst ride upon thine horses
and thy chariots of salvation?
9 **In exposing,** Thy bow was
made quite naked **exposed**,
according to the oaths of the tribes **the rods oathed**,
even thy word **saying**.
Selah.
Thou *didst cleave* **splittest** the earth with rivers.
10 The mountains saw thee,
and they *trembled* **writhed**:
the *overflowing* **flooding** of the water passed by:
the *deep uttered* **abyss gave** his voice,
and lifted *up* his hands on high.
11 The sun and moon
stood still in their *habitation* **residence**:
at the light of thine arrows they went,
and at the *shining* **brilliance** of thy glittering spear.
12 Thou *didst march* **paced** through the land
in *indignation* **rage**,
thou *didst thresh* **threshed** the *heathen* **goyim**
in *anger* **wrath**.
13 Thou wentest forth for the
salvation of thy people,
even for salvation with *thine anointed* **thy Messiah**;
thou *woundedst* **struck** the head
out of the house of the wicked,
the cup of the right of Yah Veh turns to you,
and an abasement *is* on your honor.
17 For the violence of Lebanon covers you,
and the ravage of animals terrifies them
because of human blood;
and for the violence of the land,
of the city, and of all who dwell therein.
18 What profit *is* the sculptile
to the former who sculpts
—or the molten, to a teacher of falsehoods,
Confides the former of its form to work mute idols?
19 Ho to him
who says to the timber, Waken!
—to the silent stone, Waken! It teaches!
Behold, it *is* manipulated with gold and silver,
and there *is* no spirit at all in its midst.
20 And Yah Veh *is* in his holy manse:
silence at his face, all the earth.

The Lyric Poem Of Habakkuk

3 A prayer of Habakkuk the prophet:
A Lyric Poem.
2 O Yah Veh, I hear your report, and awe:
O Yah Veh, enliven your deeds midst the years,
midst the years make known;

in quivering, remember mercy.
3 Elohah comes from Teman
and the Holy One from mount Paran.
Selah.
His majesty covers the heavens and
the earth fills with his halal:
4 with brilliance as the light;
his horns from his hand:
and there, the secret of his strength.
5 At his face goes the pestilence;
and burning coals go at his feet:
6 he stands, and measures the earth;
he sees, and loosens the goyim.
And the eternal mountains scatter;
the perpetual hills prostrate:
his ways *are* eternal.
7 I see the tents of Kushan in mischief:
the curtains of the land of Midyan quiver.
8 Yah Veh, inflame you against the rivers?
Your wrath against the rivers?
Your wrath against the sea
—so that you ride on your horses
and your chariots of salvation?
9 In exposing, you expose your bow;
the rods oath, saying,
Selah.
You split the earth with rivers;
10 the mountains see you, and writhe:
the flooding of the water passes by;
the abyss gives his voice:
and he lifts his hands on high.
11 The sun and moon stand still in their residence:
at the light, your arrows come
—at the brilliance of your glittering spear.
12 You pace through the land in rage;
you thresh the goyim in wrath:
13 you come for the salvation of your people
—for salvation with your Messiah;
you strike the head of the house of the wicked,

exeGeses ready research BIBLE

by *discovering* **stripping naked**
the foundation unto the neck.
Selah.
14 Thou *didst strike* **pierced**
through with his *staves* **rods**
the head of his *villages* **suburbs**:
they *came out as a whirlwind* **stormed** to scatter me:
their *rejoicing* **jumping for joy**
was as to *devour* **consume** the *poor*
secretly **humble covertly**.
15 Thou *didst walk* **treaded** through the sea
with thine horses,
through the heap of great waters.
16 When I heard, my belly *trembled* **quivered**;
my lips quivered at the voice:
rottenness entered into my bones,
and I *trembled* **quivered** in myself,
that I might rest in the day of *trouble* **tribulation**:
when he *cometh up* **ascendeth** unto the people,
he *will invade* **shall troop against** them with his troops.
17 Although the fig tree shall not blossom,
neither shall *fruit* **produce** be in the vines;
the labour of the olive shall *fail* **deceive**,
and the fields shall *yield* **work** no *meat* **food**;
the flock shall be cut off from the fold,
and there shall be no herd in the stalls:
18 Yet I *will rejoice* **shall jump for joy**
in *the LORD* **Yah Veh**,
I *will joy* **shall twirl** in *the God* **Elohim** of my salvation.
19 *The LORD God* **Yah Veh Adonay**
is my *strength* **valour**,
and he *will make* **shall set** my feet like hinds' *feet*,
and he *will make* **shall cause** me
to *walk* **tread** upon *mine high places* **my bamahs**.
To *the chief singer* **his eminence**
on my *stringed instruments* **strummers**.
by stripping the foundation, naked to the neck.
Selah.
14 With his *own* rods
you pierce through the head of his suburbs:
they storm to scatter me:
they jump for joy to consume the humble covertly.
15 You tread through the sea with your horses
—through the heap of great waters.
16 I hear; my belly quivers;
my lips quiver at the voice:
rottenness enters my bones;
and I quiver in myself
that I rest in the day of tribulation:
he ascends to the people;
he troops against them with his troops.
17 Although neither the fig tree blossoms
nor produce among the vines; the labor of the olive
deceives and the fields work no food; the flock *is* cut
off from the fold, and there *is* no herd in the stalls:
18 yet I jump for joy in Yah Veh;
I twirl in Elohim of my salvation.
19 Yah Veh Adonay *is* my valour
and he sets my feet as the hinds;
and he has me tread on my bamahs.
To his eminence,
with my strummers.

INTRODUCTION

1 The word of *the LORD* **Yah Veh**
which came unto *Zephaniah* **Sephan Yah**
the son of *Cushi* **Kushiy**,
the son of *Gedaliah* **Gedal Yah**,
the son of *Amariah* **Amar Yah**,
the son of *Hizkiah* **Yechizqi Yah**,
in the days of *Josiah* **Yoshi Yah** the son of Amon,
king **sovereign** of *Judah* **Yah Hudah**.

IMPENDING DOOM

2 *I will utterly consume* **In
gathering, I shall gather** all *things*
from off the *land* **face of the soil**,
saith the LORD **an oracle of Yah Veh**.
3 I *will consume* **shall gather**
man **humanity** and *beast* **animal**;
I *will consume* **shall gather**
the *fowls* **flyers** of the *heaven* **heavens**,
and the fishes of the sea,
and the stumblingblocks with the wicked:
and I *will* **shall** cut off *man* **humanity**
from *off* **the face of** the *land* **soil**,
saith the LORD **an oracle of Yah Veh**.
4 I *will* **shall** also *stretch out* **spread** mine hand
upon *Judah* **Yah Hudah**,
and upon all
the *inhabitants* **settlers** of *Jerusalem* **Yeru Shalem**;
and I *will* **shall** cut off the *remnant* **survivors** of Baal
from this place,
and the name of the *Chemarims*
ascetics with the priests;
5 And them that *worship* **prostrate
to** the host of *heaven* **the heavens**
upon the *housetops* **roofs**;
and them that *worship* **prostrate**
and that *swear* **oath** by *the LORD* **Yah Veh**,
and that *swear* **oath** by Malcham;
6 And them that are *turned back* **apostatized**
from *the LORD* **Yah Veh**;
and *those* that have not sought *the LORD* **Yah Veh**,
nor enquired for him.
7 *Hold thy peace* **Hush**
at the *presence* **face** of *the Lord GOD* **Adonay Yah Veh**:
for the day of *the LORD* **Yah Veh** is *at hand* **nearby**:
for *the LORD* **Yah Veh** hath prepared a sacrifice,
he hath *bid* **hallowed** his *guests* **called out ones**.
8 And **so be** it *shall come to pass*
in the day of the *LORD'S* sacrifice **of Yah Veh**,
that I *will punish* **shall visit upon** the *princes* **governors**,
and the *king's children* **sovereign's sons**,
and all such
as are *clothed* **enrobed** with strange *apparel* **robes**.
9 In the same day also *will I
punish* **shall I visit upon**
all those that leap on the threshold,
which fill their *masters'* **adoniym's** houses
with violence and deceit.
10 And **so be** it *shall come to pass* in that day,
saith the LORD **an oracle of Yah Veh**,
that there shall be the *noise* **voice** of a cry
from the fish *gate* **portal**,
and an howling from the second,
and a great *crashing* **breaking** from the hills.
11 Howl, ye *inhabitants* **settlers**
of *Maktesh* **Machtesh**,
for all the *merchant* people **of Kenaan** are cut
down; all they that bear silver are *cut off* **severed**.
12 And **so be** it *shall come to pass* at that time,
that I *will* **shall** search *Jerusalem* **Yeru Shalem**
with *candles* **lamps**,
and *punish* **visit upon** the men
that are *settled* **curdled** on their *lees* **dregs**:
that say in their heart,
The LORD will **Yah Veh shall** not *do good* **well—please**,
neither *will* **shall** he *do evil* **vilify**.
13 Therefore
their *goods* **valuables** shall become a *booty* **plunder**,
and their houses a desolation:
they shall also build houses, but not *inhabit them* **settle**;
and they shall plant vineyards, but
not drink the wine *thereof*.

THE GREAT DAY OF YAH VEH

14 The great day of *the LORD*
Yah Veh is near, *it is* near,

INTRODUCTION

1 The word of Yah Veh
being to Sephan Yah the son of Kushiy
the son of Gedal Yah the son of Amar Yah
the son of Yechizqi Yah
in the days of Yoshi Yah the son of Amon
sovereign of Yah Hudah.

IMPENDING DOOM

2 In gathering, I gather all
from off the face of the soil
—an oracle of Yah Veh.

3 I gather humanity and animal;
I gather the flyers of the heavens
and the fishes of the sea,
and the stumblingblocks with the wicked:
and I cut off humanity from the face of the soil
—an oracle of Yah Veh.
4 And I spread my hand on Yah Hudah
and on all the settlers of Yeru Shalem;
and I cut off the survivors of Baal from this place;
and the name of the ascetics with the priests;
5 and they who prostrate
to the host of the heavens on the roofs;
and they who prostrate and oath by Yah Veh,
and oath by Malcham;
6 and they who apostatize from Yah Veh
—who neither seek Yah Veh nor enquire of him.
7 Hush at the face of Adonay Yah Veh:
for the day of Yah Veh *is* nearby:
for Yah Veh prepares a sacrifice;
he hallows his called ones.
8 And so be it, in the day of
the sacrifice of Yah Veh,
I visit on the governors
and on the sons of the sovereign
and all such as enrobe with strange robes.
9 In the same day,
I also visit on all who leap on the threshold
—who fill the houses of their adoniym
with violence and deceit.
10 And so be it, in that day,
—an oracle of Yah Veh
the voice of a cry from the fish portal
and an howling from the second
and a great breaking from the hills.
11 Howl, you settlers of Machtesh,
for all the people of Kenaan are cut down;
all who bear silver are severed.
12 And so be it, at that time,
I search Yeru Shalem with lamps;
and visit on the men who curdle on their dregs
—who say in their heart,
Yah Veh neither well—pleases nor vilifies.
13 And their valuables become a plunder,
and their houses a desolation:
and they build houses, and settle not;
and they plant vineyards, and drink not the wine.

THE GREAT DAY OF YAH VEH

14 The great day of Yah Veh *is* near—near
and hasteth *greatly* **mightily**,
even the voice of the day of *the LORD* **Yah Veh**:
the mighty *man* shall *cry* **whoop** there bitterly.
15 That day is a day of wrath,
a day of *trouble* **tribulation** and distress,
a day of *wasteness* **devastation** and *desolation* **ruin,**
a day of darkness and *gloominess* **darkness,**
a day of clouds and *thick* **dripping** darkness,
16 A day of the *trumpet* **shophar** and *alarm* **blast**
against the *fenced* **fortified** cities,
and against the high *towers* **corners**.
17 And I *will bring distress upon men*
shall tribulate humanity,
that they shall walk like blind *men*,
because they have sinned against *the LORD* **Yah Veh**:
and their blood shall be poured out as dust,
and their *flesh* **eating** as the dung **ball**.
18 Neither their silver nor their gold
shall be able to *deliver* **rescue** them
in the day of t*he LORD'S* **Yah Veh's** wrath;
but the whole land shall be *devoured* **consumed**
by the fire of his jealousy:
for he shall *make* **work**
even a *speedy riddance* **hasty final finish** of
all them that *dwell* **settle** in the land.

THE CALL OF YAH VEH TO THE GOYIM

2 Gather yourselves *together*, yea, gather *together*,
O *nation* **goyim** not *desired* **yearned for;**
2 *Before* **Ere** the *decree bring forth* **statute births,**
before **ere** the day pass as the chaff,
before **ere** the *fierce anger* **fuming wrath**
of *the LORD* **Yah Veh** come upon you,
before **erc** the day
of the *LORD'S anger* **wrath of Yah Veh** come upon you.
3 Seek ye *the LORD* **Yah Veh,**
all ye *meek* **humble** of the earth,
which have *wrought* **done** his judgment;
seek *righteousness* **justness**, seek *meekness* **humility**:
it may *be* **perhaps** ye shall be hid
in the day of the *LORD'S anger* **wrath of Yah Veh.**
4 For *Gaza* **Azzah** shall be forsaken,
and Ashkelon a desolation:
they shall drive out Ashdod at the noon *day*,
and *Ekron* **Eqron** shall be *rooted up* **uprooted.**
5 *Woe* **Ho** unto the *inhabitants* **settlers**
of the sea *coast* **boundary,**
the *nation* **goyim** of the *Cherethites* **Kerethiym**!
the word of *the LORD* **Yah Veh** is against you;
O *Canaan* **Kenaan,**
the land of the *Philistines* **Peleshethiym,**

I *will* **shall** even destroy thee,
that there shall be no *inhabitant* **settler.**
6 And the sea *coast* **boundary**
shall be *dwellings* **habitations of rest**
and *cottages* **meadows** for *shepherds* **tenders,**
and *folds* **walls** for flocks.
7 And the *coast* **boundary** shall be
for the *remnant* **survivors**
of the house of *Judah* **Yah Hudah;**
they shall *feed* **graze** thereupon:
in the houses of Ashkelon
shall they *lie down* **crouch** in the evening:
for *the LORD* **Yah Veh** their *God*
Elohim shall visit them,
and turn away their captivity.
8 I have heard the reproach of Moab,
and the revilings of the *children* **sons** of Ammon,
whereby they have reproached my people,
and *magnified* **greatened** *themselves* against their border.
9 Therefore *as* I live,
saith the LORD of hosts **an oracle of Yah Veh Sabaoth,**
the God **Elohim** of *Israel* **Yisra El,**
Surely Moab shall be as *Sodom* **Sedom,**
and the *children* **sons** of Ammon as *Gomorrah* **Amorah,**
even the *breeding* **possession** of nettles, and saltpits,
and *a perpetual* **an eternal** desolation:
the *residue* **survivors** of my people
shall *spoil* **plunder** them,
and the remnant of my *people* **goyim**
shall *possess* **inherit** them.
and the voice of the day of Yah Veh hastens mightily:
the mighty whoop there bitterly:
15 a day of wrath—that day; a day of tribulation
and distress; a day of devastation and ruin;
a day of darkness and darkness;
a day of clouds and dripping darkness
16 a day of the shophar and blast
against the fortified cities and against the high corners.
17 And I tribulate humanity
and they walk as the blind:
because they sin against Yah Veh
and pour blood as dust
and eat the dung ball.
18 Even their silver, even their gold
cannot rescue them
in the day of the wrath of Yah Veh;
and in the fire of his jealousy
consumes the whole land:
for he even works a hasty final finish
of all who settle in the land.

THE CALL OF YAH VEH TO THE GOYIM

2 Gather yourselves;
yes, gather, O goyim not yearned for:
2 ere the birth of the statute;
ere the day pass as the chaff;
ere the fuming wrath of Yah Veh comes on you;
ere the day of the wrath of Yah Veh comes on you.
3 Seek Yah Veh, all you humble of the earth,
who do his judgment:
seek justness; seek humility:
perhaps you *are* hidden
in the day of the wrath of Yah Veh.
4 For Azzah *is* forsaken and
Ashkelon a desolation:
they drive out Ashdod at noon and uproot Eqron.
5 Ho to the settlers of the sea boundary
—the goyim of the Kerethiym!
the word of Yah Veh *is* against you;
O Kenaan, the land of the Peleshethiym:
I even destroy you, without settler.
6 And the sea boundary
becomes habitations of rest
and meadows for tenders
and walls for flocks:
7 and the boundary becomes for the survivors
of the house of Yah Hudah to graze thereon:
in the houses of Ashkelon
they crouch in the evening:
for Yah Veh their Elohim visits them
and restores their captivity.
8 I hear the reproach of Moab
and the revilings of the sons of Ammon
—whereby they reproach my people,
and greaten against their border:
9 so, I live
—an oracle of Yah Veh Sabaoth Elohim of Yisra El.
Surely Moab *is* as Sedom
and the sons of Ammon as Amorah
—the possession of nettles and saltpits
—an eternal desolation:
the survivors of my people plunder them
and the remnant of my goyim inherit them.
10 This shall they have for their *pride* **pomp,**
because they have reproached
and *magnified* **greatened** *themselves* against the people
of *the LORD of hosts* **Yah Veh Sabaoth.**
11 *The LORD* **Yah Veh**
will **shall** be *terrible* **awesome** unto them:
for he *will famish* **shall emaciate**

all the *gods* **elohim** of the earth;
and *men* shall *worship* **prostrate to** him,
every *one* **man** from his place,
even all the *isles* **islands** of the *heathen* **goyim**.
12 Ye *Ethiopians* **Kushiym** also,
ye shall be *slain* **pierced** by my sword.
13 And he *will stretch out* **shall spread** his hand
against the north,
and destroy *Assyria* **Ashshur**;
and *will make* **shall set** Nineveh a desolation,
and *dry* **parch** like a wilderness.
14 And *flocks* **droves** shall *lie down* **crouch**
in the midst of her,
all the *beasts* **live beings** of the *nations* **goyim**:
both the *cormorant* **pelican** and the bittern
shall *lodge* **stay overnight** in the upper lintels of it;
their voice shall sing in the windows;
desolation **parch** shall be in the thresholds:
for he shall *uncover* **strip naked** the cedar work.
15 This is the *rejoicing* city **of jumping for joy**
that *dwelt carelessly* **settled confidently**,
that said in her heart, I *am*, and there is none beside me:
how is she become a desolation,
a **resting** place for *beasts to lie down in* **live beings**!
every one that passeth by her shall hiss,
and wag his hand.

HO TO YERU SHALEM

3 *Woe* **Ho** to her
that *is filthy* **rebelleth** and *polluted* **profaneth**,
to—the oppressing city!
2 She *obeyed* **hearkened** not **unto** the voice;
she *received* **took** not *correction* **discipline**;
she *trusted* **confided** not in *the LORD* **Yah Veh**;
she *drew* **approached** not *near to* her *God* **Elohim**.
3 Her *princes* **governors**
within her are roaring lions;
her judges are evening wolves;
they *gnaw* **craunch** not *the bones*
till *the morrow* **morning**.
4 Her prophets are *light* **frothy**
and *treacherous persons* **covert men**:
her priests have *polluted* **profaned** the *sanctuary* **holies**,
they have *done violence to* **violated** the *law* **torah**.
5 The just *LORD* **Yah Veh** is in the midst *thereof*;
he *will* **shall** not *do iniquity* **work wickedness**:
every morning **by morning**
doth he bring **he giveth** his judgment to light,
he *faileth* **lacketh** not;
but the *unjust* **wicked** knoweth no shame.
6 I have cut off the *nations* **goyim**:
their *towers* **corners** are *desolate* **desolated**;
I *made* **parched** their *streets waste* **outways**,
that none passeth by:
their cities are destroyed,
so that there is no man,
that there is *none inhabitant* **no settler**.
7 I said, Surely thou *wilt fear* **shalt awe** me,
thou *wilt receive instruction* **shalt take discipline**;
so their *dwelling* **habitation** should not be cut off,
howsoever I punished **all that I visited upon** them:
but **surely** they rose early,
and *corrupted* **ruined** all their *doings* **exploits**.

THE JUDGMENT OF THE GOYIM

8 Therefore wait ye upon me,
saith the LORD **an oracle of Yah Veh**,
until the day that I rise *up* to the prey:
for my *determination* **judgment**
is to gather the *nations* **goyim**,
that I may *assemble* **gather** the
kingdoms **sovereigndoms**,
to pour upon them *mine indignation* **my rage**,
even all my *fierce anger* **fuming wrath**:
for all the earth
shall be *devoured* **consumed** with the fire of my jealousy.
10 This *is* for their pomp,
because they reproach and greaten
against the people of Yah Veh Sabaoth.
11 Yah Veh *is* awesome against them:
for he emaciates all the elohim of the earth;
and every man prostrates to him from his place
—all the islands of the goyim.
12 Also you, O Kushiym
you, pierced by my sword.
13 And he spreads his hand against the north
and destroys Ashshur;
and sets Nineveh as a desolation
and parches as a wilderness:
14 and droves crouch among her
—all the live beings of the goyim: both
the pelican and the bittern
stay overnight in the upper lintels thereof;
their voice sings in the windows;
parch *is* in the thresholds:
for he strips naked the cedar work
15 —this—the city of jumping for joy
who settles confidently
—who says in her heart,
I—and there is no one beside me!

How she becomes a desolation
—a resting place for live beings!
every one who passes by her
hisses and wags his hand.

HO TO YERU SHALEM

3 Ho to her who rebels and profanes,
—the oppressing city!
2 She hearkens not to the voice;
she takes not discipline;
she confides not in Yah Veh;
she approaches another Elohim.
3 Her governors within her *are* roaring lions;
her judges *are* evening wolves;
they craunch not until morning:
4 her prophets *are* frothy and covert men;
her priests profane the holies;
they violate the torah:
5 Yah Veh *is* just among her;
he works not wickedness:
morning by morning he gives his judgment to light;
he lacks not:
and the wicked shame not.
6 I cut off the goyim; desolate their corners:
I parch their outways so no one passes by:
destroy their cities
—without man; without settler.
7 I say, Only, awe me;
you, take discipline
that I not cut off your habitation
from all I visit on her:
but they rise early and ruin all their exploits.

THE JUDGMENT OF THE GOYIM

8 So await me
—an oracle of Yah Veh
until the day I rise to the prey:
for my judgment *is* to gather goyim;
to gather sovereigndoms;
to pour my rage on them—all my fuming wrath:
for I consume all the earth
with the fire of my jealousy.
9 For then *will* **shall** I turn to the people
a *pure language* **purified lip,**
that they may all
call upon the name of *the LORD* **Yah Veh,**
to serve him with one *consent* **shoulder.**
10 From beyond the rivers of *Ethiopia* **Kush**
my *suppliants* **entreaters,**
even the daughter of my *dispersed* **scattered,**
shall bring mine offering.
11 In that day shalt thou not be *ashamed* **shamed**
for all thy *doings* **exploits,**
wherein thou hast *transgressed* **rebelled** against me:
for then I *will take away* **shall turn aside**
out of the midst of thee
them that *rejoice* **jump for joy** in thy *pride* **pomp,**
and thou shalt *no more* **not add**
to be *haughty* **lifted**
because of my holy mountain.

THE SURVIVORS OF YISRA EL

12 I *will* **shall** also leave in the midst of thee
an *afflicted* **humbled** and poor people,
and they shall *trust* **seek refuge**
in the name of *the LORD* **Yah Veh.**
13 The *remnant* **survivors** of *Israel* **Yisra El**
shall not *do iniquity* **work wickedness,**
nor *speak* **word** lies;
neither shall a deceitful tongue be found in their mouth:
for they shall *feed* **graze** and *lie down* **crouch,**
and none shall *make* **tremble** them *afraid.*
14 Sing, O daughter of *Zion* **Siyon;**
shout, O *Israel* **Yisra El;**
be glad **cheer** and *rejoice* **jump for joy** with all the heart,
O daughter of *Jerusalem* **Yeru Shalem.**
15 *The LORD* **Yah Veh**
hath *taken away* **turned aside** thy judgments,
he hath *cast out* **faced** thine enemy:
the *king* **sovereign** of *Israel* **Yisra El,**
even the LORD **Yah Veh,** is in the midst of thee:
thou shalt not see evil any more.
16 In that day it shall be said
to *Jerusalem* **Yeru Shalem,**
Fear **Awe** thou not:
and to Zion **Siyon,**
Let not thine hands *be slack* **slacken.**
17 *The LORD* **Yah Veh** thy *God* **Elohim**
in the midst of thee is mighty;
he *will* **shall** save,
he *will* **shall** rejoice over thee with *joy* **cheerfulness;**
he *will rest* **shall hush** in his love,
he *will joy* **shall twirl** over thee with *singing* **shouting.**
18 I *will* **shall** gather *them that*
are sorrowful **the grieved**
for the *solemn assembly* **congregation,** who are of
thee, to whom the reproach of it was a burden.
19 Behold, at that time
I *will undo* **shall work** all that *afflict* **humble** thee:
and I *will* **shall** save her that *halteth* **limpeth,**

and gather her that was *driven out* **expelled**;
and I *will get* **shall set** them
praise **for a halal** and *fame* **a name**
in every land
where they have been put to **of their** shame.
20 At that time *will* **shall** I bring you *again*,
even in the time that I gather you:
for I *will make* **shall give** you a name and a *praise* **halal**
among all people of the earth,
when I *turn back* **return** your captivity
before **in front of** your eyes,
saith *the LORD* **Yah Veh**.
9 For then I restore a purified lip to the people
so that they all call on the name of Yah Veh
to serve him with one shoulder.
10 From beyond the rivers of Kush
my entreaters, the daughter of my scattered,
bring my offering.
11 In that day you shame not
for all the exploits you rebel against me:
for then I turn aside from among you
all who jump for joy in your pomp;
and you add not to lift yourself
because of my holy mountain.

THE SURVIVORS OF YISRA EL

12 And I leave midst you
a humbled and poor people;
and they seek refuge in the name of Yah Veh:
13 the survivors of Yisra El
neither work wickedness nor word lies;
nor *is* a deceitful tongue found in their mouth:
for they graze and crouch and no one trembles.
14 Sing, O daughter of Siyon! Shout, O Yisra El!
Cheer and jump for joy with all the heart,
O daughter of Yeru Shalem!
15 Yah Veh turns aside your judgments;
he faces your enemy:
the sovereign of Yisra El, Yah Veh, *is* midst you:
you see no evil any more.
16 In that day they say to Yeru Shalem, Awe not!
Siyon, slacken not your hands!
17 Yah Veh your Elohim midst you *is* mighty;
he saves; he rejoices over you with cheerfulness;
he hushes in his love;
he twirls over you with shouting.
18 I gather the grieved from the congregation
who became from you;
whose reproach *was* a burden.
19 Behold, at that time,
I work all who humble you:
and I save her who limps,
and gather her who *was* expelled;
and I set them for a halal and a name
in every land of their shame.
20 At that time, I bring you,
even in the time I gather you:
for I give you a name and a halal
among all people of the earth,
when I restore your captivity in front of your eyes,
says Yah Veh.

THE PEOPLE DISRUPT BUILDING THE HOUSE OF YAH VEH

1 In the second year of *Darius* **Daryavesh**
the *king* **sovereign**,
in the sixth month, in the first day of the month,
came the word of *the LORD* **Yah Veh**
by *Haggai* **the hand of Haggay** the prophet
unto *Zerubbabel* **Zerub Babel**
the son of *Shealtiel* **Shealti El**,
governor **captain** of *Judah* **Yah Hudah**,
and to *Joshua* **Yah Shua** the son of *Josedech* **Yah Sadaq**,
the *high* **great** priest, saying,
2 Thus *speaketh* **saith**
the LORD of hosts **Yah Veh Sabaoth**, saying,
This people say, The time *is* **approached** not *come*,
the time that the *LORD'S* house **of Yah Veh**
should be built.

THE DISCIPLINE OF YAH VEH FOR THE DISRUPTED WORK

3 Then came the word of *the LORD* **Yah Veh**
by **the hand of** *Haggai* **Haggay** the prophet, saying,
4 Is it time for you,
O ye, to *dwell* **settle** in your cieled houses,
and this house *lie waste* **parch**?
5 Now therefore
thus saith *the LORD of hosts* **Yah Veh Sabaoth**;
Consider **Set thy heart on** your ways.
6 Ye have sown *much* **aboundingly**,
and *bring* **brought** in little;
ye eat, but ye have *not enough* **no satisfaction**;
ye drink, but ye are not *filled with drink* **intoxicated**;
ye *clothe* **enrobe** you, but there is none *warm* **heated**;
and he that *earneth wages* **hireth**
earneth wages **hireth**
to put it into a *bag with holes* **pierced bundle**.
7 Thus saith *the LORD of hosts* **Yah Veh Sabaoth**;
Consider **Set thy heart on** your ways.
8 *Go up* **Ascend** to the mountain,
and bring *wood* **timber**,
and build the house;
and I *will take pleasure* **shall be pleased** in it,
and I *will* **shall** be *glorified* **honoured**,
saith *the LORD* **Yah Veh**.
9 Ye *looked for much* **faced aboundingly**,
and, *lo* **behold**, it came to little;
and when ye brought it home, I *did blow* **puffed** upon it.
Why **Wherefore**?
saith the LORD of hosts **an oracle of Yah Veh Sabaoth**.
Because of mine house that is *waste* **parched**,
and ye run every man unto his own house.
10 Therefore the *heaven* **heavens** over you
is stayed from dew,
and the earth is stayed from her *fruit* **produce**.
11 And I called for a *drought* **parch** upon the land,
and upon the mountains, and upon the *corn* **crop**,
and upon the *new wine* **juice**, and upon the oil,
and upon that which the *ground* **soil** bringeth forth,
and upon *men* **humanity**, and upon *cattle* **animals**,
and upon all the labour of the *hands* **palms**.

THE WORK BEGINS AGAIN

12 Then *Zerubbabel* **Zerub Babel**
the son of *Shealtiel* **Shealti El**,
and *Joshua* **Yah Shua** the son of *Josedech* **Yah Sadaq**,
the *high* **great** priest,
with all the *remnant* **survivors** of the people,
obeyed **hearkened unto** the voice
of *the LORD* **Yah Veh** their *God* **Elohim**,
and the words of *Haggai* **Haggay** the prophet,
as *the LORD* **Yah Veh** their *God* **Elohim** had sent him,
and the people *did fear* **awed**
before the LORD **at the face of Yah Veh**.
13 Then *spake Haggai* **said Haggay**
the *LORD'S messenger* **angel of Yah Veh**
in the *LORD'S message* **evangelism of Yah Veh**
unto the people, saying,
I am with you,
saith the LORD **an oracle of Yah Veh**.
14 And *the LORD* **Yah Veh**
stirred up **wakened** the spirit of *Zerubbabel* **Zerub Babel**
the son of *Shealtiel* **Shealti El**, governor
of *Judah* **Yah Hudah**,
and the spirit of *Joshua* **Yah Shua**

THE PEOPLE DISRUPT BUILDING THE HOUSE OF YAH VEH

1 In the second year of Daryavesh the sovereign,
in the sixth month, in the first day of the month,
so be the word of Yah Veh
by the hand of Haggay the prophet
to Zerub Babel
the son of Shealti El captain of Yah Hudah
and to Yah Shua the son of Yah Sadaq the great priest,
saying,
2 Thus say Yah Veh Sabaoth, saying,
This people say, The time approaches not
—the time to build the house of Yah Veh.

THE DISCIPLINE OF YAH VEH FOR THE DISRUPTED WORK

3 So be the word of Yah Veh
by the hand of Haggay the prophet, saying,
4 Is it time for you
—you, to settle in your cieled houses
and this house a parch?
5 And now, thus says Yah Veh Sabaoth:
Set your heart on your ways.
6 You seed aboundingly, and bring in little;
you eat, and you satiate not;
you drink, and you intoxicate not;
you enrobe, and no one heats up;
and he who hires *himself out*
hires to put it into a pierced bundle.
7 Thus says Yah Veh Sabaoth:
Set your heart on your ways:
8 ascend to the mountain
and bring timber and build the house;
and please me and honor me,
says Yah Veh.
9 You face aboundingly,
and behold, little;
and when you bring it home, I puff thereon:
Why?
—an oracle of Yah Veh Sabaoth
because my house *is* parched,
and you, every man runs to his own house:
10 so the heavens over you stay from her dew
and the earth stays from her produce:
11 and I call a parch on the land
and on the mountains and on the crop
and on the juice and on the oil
and on whatever the soil brings forth;
and on humanity and on animals
and on all the labor of the palms.

THE WORK BEGINS AGAIN

12 And Zerub Babel the son of Shealti El
and Yah Shua the son of Yah Sadaq the great priest
with all the survivors of the people
hearken to the voice of Yah Veh their Elohim
and the words of Haggay the prophet
as Yah Veh their Elohim sends him:
and the people awe at the face of Yah Veh.
13 And Haggay the angel of Yah Veh
in the evangelism of Yah Veh
says to the people, saying, I *am* with you
—an oracle of Yah Veh.
14 And Yah Veh wakens the spirit of Zerub Babel
the son of Shealti El governor of Yah Hudah,
and the spirit of Yah Shua
the son of *Josedech* **Yah Sadaq**, the *high* **great** priest,
and the spirit of all the *remnant* **survivors** of the people;
and they came and *did* **worked** work
in the house of *the LORD of hosts* **Yah Veh Sabaoth**,
their *God* **Elohim**,
15 In the four and twentieth
day of the sixth month,
in the second year
of *Darius* **Daryavesh** the *king* **sovereign**.

THE NEW HOUSE

2 In the seventh *month*,
in the one and twentieth *day* of the month,
came the word of *the LORD* **Yah Veh**
by **the hand of** the prophet *Haggai* **Haggay**, saying,
2 Speak now to *Zerubbabel* **Zerub Babel**
the son of *Shealtiel* **Shealti El**,
governor of *Judah* **Yah Hudah**,
and to *Joshua* **Yah Shua** the son of *Josedech* **Yah Sadaq**,
the *high* **great** priest,
and to the *residue* **survivors** of the people, saying,
3 Who *is left* **surviveth** among you
that saw this house in her first *glory* **honour**?
and how *do ye* see **ye** it now?
is it not in your eyes
in comparison of it **likened** as *nothing* **nought**?
4 Yet now *be strong* **prevail**,
O *Zerubbabel* **Zerub Babel**,
saith the LORD **an oracle of Yah Veh**;
and *be strong* **prevail**, O *Joshua* **Yah Shua**,
son of *Josedech* **Yah Sadaq**, the *high* **great** priest;
and *be strong* **prevail**, all ye people of the land,
saith the LORD **an oracle of Yah Veh**,
and work: for I am with you,
saith the LORD of hosts **an oracle of Yah Veh Sabaoth**:
5 According to the word that
I *covenanted* **cut** with you
when ye came out of *Egypt* **Misrayim**,
so my spirit *remaineth* **standeth** among you:
fear **awe** ye not.
6 For thus saith *the LORD*
of hosts **Yah Veh Sabaoth**;
Yet once, it is a little while,
and I *will shake* **shall quake** the heavens,
and the earth, and the sea,
and the *dry land* **parched areas**;
7 And I *will shake* **shall quake** all *nations* **goyim**,
and the desire of all *nations shall*
come **goyim approaches**:

and I *will* **shall** fill this house with *glory* **honour,**
saith *the LORD of hosts* **Yah Veh Sabaoth.**
8 The silver is mine, and the gold is mine,
saith the LORD of hosts **an oracle of Yah Veh Sabaoth.**
9 The *glory* **honour** of this latter house
shall be greater than of the former,
saith the LORD of hosts **an oracle of Yah Veh Sabaoth:**
and in this place *will* **shall** I give *peace* **shalom,**
saith *the LORD of hosts* **Yah Veh Sabaoth.**

THE TORAH CONCERNING THE HALLOWED

10 In the four and twentieth
day of the ninth *month,*
in the second year of *Darius* **Daryavesh,**
came the word of *the LORD* **Yah Veh**
by *Haggai* **the hand of Haggay** the prophet, saying,
11 Thus saith *the LORD of hosts* **Yah Veh Sabaoth;**
Ask *now* **I beseech,** the priests *concerning* the *law* **torah,**
saying,
12 If *one* **a man** bear holy flesh
in the *skirt* **wing** of his *garment* **clothes,**
and with his *skirt do* **wing** touch bread,
or pottage, or wine, or oil, or any *meat* **food,**
shall it be *holy* **hallowed?**
And the priests answered and said, No.
13 Then said *Haggai* **Haggay,**
If *one that is unclean by a dead body* **a fouled dead soul**
touch any of these,
shall it be *unclean* **fouled?**
And the priests answered and said,
It shall be *unclean* **fouled.**
14 Then answered *Haggai* **Haggay,** and said,
So is this people,
and so is this *nation before me* **goyim at my face,**
saith the LORD **an oracle of Yah Veh;**
and so is every work of their hands;
and that which they *offer* **oblate** there is *unclean* **fouled.**
15 And *now* **I beseech,** I pray you,
the son of Yah Sadaq the great priest,
and the spirit of all the survivors of the people;
and they come and work the work
in the house of Yah Veh Sabaoth their Elohim 15
in the twenty—fourth day of the sixth month,
in the second year of Daryavesh the sovereign.

THE NEW HOUSE

2 In the seventh, in the
twenty—first of the month,
so be the word of Yah Veh
by the hand of the prophet Haggay, saying,
2 Speak now to Zerub Babel
the son of Shealti El governor of Yah Hudah,
and to Yah Shua
the son of Yah Sadaq the great priest,
and to the survivors of the people, saying,
3 Who among you survives
—who saw this house in her first honor?
And how see you now?
Likens it not in your eyes as naught?
4 And now prevail, O Zerub Babel
—an oracle of Yah Veh
and prevail, O Yah Shua
son of Yah Sadaq the great priest;
and prevail all you people of the land
—an oracle of Yah Veh
and work: for I *am* with you
—an oracle of Yah Veh Sabaoth
5 according to the word I cut with you
when you came from Misrayim,
thus my spirit stands among you: awe not.
6 For thus says Yah Veh Sabaoth:
Yet once, in a little *while,*
and I quake the heavens and the earth and the sea
and the parched areas;
7 and I quake all goyim
and the desire of all goyim approaches:
and I fill this house with honor,
says Yah Veh Sabaoth.
8 The silver *is* mine, and the gold *is* mine
—an oracle of Yah Veh Sabaoth.
9 So be the honor of this latter house
—greater than the former
—an oracle of Yah Veh Sabaoth
and in this place I give shalom,
says Yah Veh Sabaoth.

THE TORAH CONCERNING THE HALLOWED

10 In the twenty—fourth of the ninth,
in the second year of Daryavesh,
so be the word of Yah Veh
by the hand of Haggay the prophet, saying,
11 Thus says Yah Veh Sabaoth:
Ask, I beseech, the priests *of* the torah, saying,
12 If a man bears holy flesh
in the wing of his clothes,
and with his wing touches bread
or pottage or wine or oil or any food,
is it hallowed?
And the priests answer and say, No.
13 Then Haggay says,
If a fouled dead soul touches any of these,

is it fouled?
And the priests answer and say, Fouled.
14 And Haggay answers and says,
Thus *is* this people and thus *is* this goyim at my face
—an oracle of Yah Veh
and thus *is* every work of their hands;
and what they oblate there *is* fouled.
15 And I beseech, I pray you,
consider **set thy heart** from this day and upward,
from before **ere** a stone was *laid* **set** upon a stone
in the *temple* **manse** of *the LORD* **Yah Veh**:
16 Since *those days were* **then**,
when one came to an heap of twenty *measures*,
there were *but* ten:
when one came to the *pressfat* **trough**
for to draw out fats **to strip** fifty *vessels* out of the press,
there were *but* twenty.
17 I smote you with blasting
and with *mildew* **pale green**
and with hail in all the *labours* **works** of your hands;
yet ye turned not to me,
saith the LORD **an oracle of Yah Veh**.
18 *Consider now* **Set thy heart I beseech,**
from this day and upward,
from the four and twentieth day of the ninth *month*,
even from the day that the foundation
of *the LORD'S temple* **Yah Veh's manse**
was *laid* **founded**,
consider it **set thy heart**.
19 Is the seed yet in the *barn* **granary**?
yea, as yet the vine, and the fig tree,
and the pomegranate, and the olive tree,
hath not *brought forth* **borne**:
from this day *will* **shall** I bless *you*.
20 And *again* **secondly** the
word of *the LORD* **Yah Veh**
came unto *Haggai* **Haggay**
in the four and twentieth *day* of the month, saying,
21 Speak to *Zerubbabel* **Zerub Babel**,
governor of *Judah* **Yah Hudah**, saying,
I *will shake* **shall quake** the heavens and the earth;
22 And I *will overthrow* **shall overturn** the throne
of *kingdoms* **sovereigndoms**,
and I *will destroy* **shall desolate** the strength
of the *kingdoms* **sovereigndoms** of the *heathen* **goyim**;
and I *will overthrow* **shall overturn** the chariots,
and *those that ride in them* **their riders**;
and the horses and their riders shall *come down* **topple**,
every *one* **man** by the sword of his brother.
23 In that day,
saith the LORD of hosts **an oracle of Yah Veh Sabaoth**,
will **shall** I take thee,
O *Zerubbabel* **Zerub Babel**, my servant,
the son of *Shealtiel* **Shealti El**,
saith the LORD **an oracle of Yah Veh**,
and *will make* **shall set** thee as a *signet* **seal**:
for I have chosen thee,
saith the LORD of hosts **an oracle of Yah Veh Sabaoth**.

set your heart from this day and upward,
ere you set stone on stone in the manse of Yah Veh:
16 From now on,
when one comes to an heap of twenty,
and it becomes ten:
when one comes to the trough
to strip fifty from the press,
and it becomes twenty.
17 I smite you with blasting and with pale green
and with hail in all the works of your hands;
yet you turn not to me
—an oracle of Yah Veh.
18 Set your heart, I beseech,
from this day and upward,
from the twenty—fourth day of the ninth,
from the day of founding the foundation
of the manse of Yah Veh,
set your heart.
19 *Is* the seed yet in the granary?
Yes, as yet the vine and the fig tree
and the pomegranate and the olive tree
have not borne:
from this day I bless.
20 And secondly
so be the word of Yah Veh to Haggay
in the twenty—fourth of the month, saying,
21 Speak to Zerub Babel governor of Yah Hudah,
saying, I quake the heavens and the earth;
22 and I overturn the throne of sovereigndoms;
and I desolate the strength
of the sovereigndoms of the goyim;
and I overturn the chariots and their riders:
and the horses and their riders topple
—every man by the sword of his brother.
23 In that day
—an oracle of Yah Veh Sabaoth
I take you, O Zerub Babel
my servant the son of Shealti El
—an oracle of Yah Veh
and set you as a seal:
for I choose you
—an oracle of Yah Veh Sabaoth.

YAH VEH IS ENRAGED WITH THE FATHERS

1 In the eighth month,
in the second year of *Darius* **Daryavesh**,
came the word of *the LORD* **Yah Veh**
unto *Zechariah* **Zechar Yah**,
the son of *Berechiah* **Berech Yah**,
the son of Iddo the prophet, saying,
2 **In being enraged,**
The LORD **Yah Veh** hath been *sore displeased* **enraged**
with your fathers.
3 *Therefore* say thou unto them,
Thus saith *the LORD of hosts* **Yah Veh Sabaoth**;
Turn ye unto me,
saith *the LORD of hosts* **Yah Veh Sabaoth**,
and I *will* **shall** turn unto you,
saith the LORD of hosts **an oracle of Yah Veh Sabaoth**.
4 Be ye not as your fathers,
unto whom the former prophets have *cried* **called out**,
saying, Thus **saying thus:**
saith the LORD of hosts **an oracle of Yah Veh Sabaoth**;
Turn ye *now* **I beseech,** from your evil *ways* **exploits**,
and from your evil *doings* **exploits**:
but they *did* **heard** not *hear*,
nor *hearken* **hearkened** unto me,
saith the LORD **an oracle of Yah Veh**.
5 Your fathers, where are they?
and the prophets, *do they live for*
ever **live they eternally**?
6 But my words and my statutes,
which I *commanded* **misvahed** my servants the prophets,
did they **overtook** not *take hold of* your fathers?
and they returned and said,
Like as *the LORD of hosts* **Yah Veh Sabaoth**
thought **intrigued** to *do* **work** unto us,
according to our ways,
and *according to* our *doings* **exploits**,
so hath he *dealt* **worked** with us.

THE RIDER ON THE RED HORSE

7 Upon the four and twentieth
day of the eleventh month,
which is the month *Sebat* **Shebat**,
in the second year of *Darius* **Daryavesh**,
came the word of *the LORD* **Yah Veh**
unto *Zechariah* **Zechar Yah**,
the son of *Berechiah* **Berech Yah**,
the son of Iddo the prophet, saying,
8 I saw by night,
and behold a man riding upon a red horse,
and he stood among the myrtle trees
that were in the *bottom* **shade**;
and behind him were there red horses,
speckled **bay**, and white.
9 Then said I, O my *lord* **adoni**, what are these?
And the angel that *talked* **worded** with me said unto me,
I *will shew thee* **shall have thee see** what these be.
10 And the man that stood among the myrtle trees
answered and said,
These are they whom *the LORD* **Yah Veh** hath sent
to walk to and fro through the earth.
11 And they answered the
angel of *the LORD* **Yah Veh**
that stood among the myrtle trees, and said,
We have walked to and fro through the earth,
and, behold,
all the earth *sitteth still* **settleth**, and *is at rest* **resteth**.
12 Then the angel of *the LORD* **Yah Veh**
answered and said,
O *LORD of hosts* **Yah Veh Sabaoth**,
how long *wilt* **shalt** thou not
have mercy *on Jerusalem* **Yeru Shalem**
and *on* the cities of *Judah* **Yah Hudah**,
against which thou hast *had indignation* **been enraged**
these *threescore and ten* **seventy** years?
13 And *the LORD* **Yah Veh**
answered the angel that *talked* **worded** with me
with good words
and *comfortable words* **words of solaces**.
14 So the angel that *communed* **worded** with me
said unto me, *Cry* **Call** thou **out**, saying, Thus
saith *the LORD of hosts* **Yah Veh Sabaoth**;
I am jealous/**zealous**
for *Jerusalem* **Yeru Shalem** and for *Zion* **Siyon**

YAH VEH IS ENRAGED WITH THE FATHERS

1 In the eighth month,
in the second year of Daryavesh,
so be the word of Yah Veh to Zechar Yah
the son of Berech Yah the son of Iddo the prophet,
saying,
2 In enraging, Yah Veh enraged over your fathers.
3 You, say to them, Thus says Yah Veh Sabaoth:
You, turn to me, says Yah Veh Sabaoth,
and I turn to you
—an oracle of Yah Veh Sabaoth.
4 Become not as your fathers
to whom the former prophets called out,
saying thus:
—an oracle of Yah Veh Sabaoth

Turn, I beseech, from your evil ways
and from your evil exploits!
—and they neither heard nor hearkened to me
—an oracle of Yah Veh.
5 Your fathers, where *are* they?
And the prophets, live they eternally?
6 Only, my words and my statutes
which I misvahed to my servants the prophets,
overtook they not your fathers?
And they return and say,
As Yah Veh Sabaoth intrigues to work to us,
according to our ways and our exploits,
works he thus with us.

The Rider On The Red Horse

7 On the twenty—fourth day
of the eleventh month, the month Shebat,
in the second year of Daryavesh,
so be the word of Yah Veh to Zechar Yah
the son of Berech Yah the son of Iddo the prophet,
saying,
8 I see by night, and behold,
a man riding on a red horse;
and he stands among the myrtle trees, in the shade;
and behind him, horses—red, bay, and white.
9 And I say, O my adoni, what are these?
And the angel wording with me says to me,
I—I have you see what these *are*.
10 And the man standing among the myrtle trees
answers and says,
These are they whom Yah Veh sends
to walk to and fro through the earth.
11 And they answer the angel of Yah Veh
standing among the myrtle trees, and say,
We walk to and fro through the earth,
and behold, all the earth settles and rests.
12 And the angel of Yah Veh answers and says,
O Yah Veh Sabaoth,
how long mercy you not
Yeru Shalem and the cities of Yah Hudah,
against whom you enraged these seventy years?
13 And Yah Veh answers the angel
who *is* wording with me
with words of good and words of solaces.
14 And the angel wording with me
says to me, Call out, saying,
Thus says Yah Veh Sabaoth:
I am jealous/zealous for Yeru Shalem and for Siyon
with a great jealousy/**zeal**.
15 And **in my enraging,**
I am *very sore displeased* **greatly enraged**
with the *heathen* **goyim** that *are at ease* **relax**:
for I was but a little *displeased* **enraged,**
and they helped *forward the affliction* **for the evil**.
16 Therefore thus saith *the LORD* **Yah Veh**;
I am returned to *Jerusalem* **Yeru Shalem** with mercies:
my house shall be built in it,
saith the LORD of hosts **an oracle of Yah Veh Sabaoth,**
and a line shall be *stretched forth* **spread**
upon *Jerusalem* **Yeru Shalem.**
17 *Cry yet* **Call out**, saying,
Thus saith *the LORD of hosts* **Yah Veh Sabaoth**;
My cities through *prosperity* **good**
shall yet be *spread abroad* **scattered**;
and *the LORD* **Yah Veh**
shall yet *comfort Zion* **sigh over Siyon,**
and shall yet choose *Jerusalem* **Yeru Shalem**.

The Four Horns

18 Then lifted I up mine eyes, and saw,
and behold four horns.
19 And I said unto the angel
that *talked* **worded** with me,
What be these?
And he *answered* **said to** me,
These are the horns
which have *scattered Judah* **winnowed Yah Hudah,**
Israel **Yisra El**, and *Jerusalem* **Yeru Shalem**.

The Four Engravers

20 And *the LORD* **Yah Veh**
shewed me **had me see** four *carpenters* **engravers**.
21 Then said I, What come these to *do* **work**?
And he spake, saying,
These are the horns
which have *scattered Judah* **winnowed Yah Hudah,**
so that no **mouth of** man *did lift up* **lifted** his head:
but these are come to *fray* **tremble** them,
to *cast out* **hand toss** the horns of the *Gentiles* **goyim,**
which lifted *up* their horn
over the land of *Judah* **Yah Hudah**
to *scatter* **winnow** it.

The Man With The Measuring Line

2 I lifted up mine eyes again, and *looked* **saw,**
and behold a man with a measuring line in his hand.
2 Then said I, Whither goest thou?
And he said unto me,
To measure *Jerusalem* **Yeru Shalem,**
to see what is the breadth *thereof*,

and what is the length *thereof.*
3 And, behold,
the angel that *talked* **worded** with me went forth,
and another angel went out to meet him,
4 And said unto him, Run,
speak **word** to *this young man* **yonder lad**, saying,
Jerusalem **Yeru Shalem** shall be *inhabited* **settled**
as *towns without walls* **suburbs**
for the *multitude* **abundance** of *men* **humanity**
and *cattle therein* **animals in her midst**:
5 For I,
saith the LORD **an oracle of Yah Veh,**
will **shall** be unto her a wall of fire round about,
and *will* **shall** be the *glory* **honour** in the midst of her.
6 Ho, ho, *come forth*, and flee
from the land of the north,
saith the LORD **an oracle of Yah Veh**:
for I have spread you *abroad*
as the four winds of the *heaven* **heavens**,
saith the LORD **an oracle of Yah Veh.**
7 *Deliver* **Rescue** thyself, *O Zion* **Ho Siyon**,
that *dwellest* **settlest** with the daughter of *Babylon* **Babel.**
8 For thus saith *the LORD*
of hosts **Yah Veh Sabaoth**;
After the *glory* **honour** hath he sent me
unto the *nations* **goyim** which spoiled you:
for he that toucheth you
toucheth the *apple* **pupil** of his eye.
9 For, behold, I *will* **shall**
shake mine hand upon them,
and they shall be a spoil to their servants:
and ye shall know
that *the LORD of hosts* **Yah Veh Sabaoth** hath sent me.
10 *Sing* **Shout** and *rejoice* **cheer,**
O daughter of *Zion* **Siyon:**
with a great jealousy/zeal:
15 and in my enraging,
I enrage greatly with the goyim who relax:
for I was but a little enraged,
and they helped for evil.
16 So thus says Yah Veh:
I return to Yeru Shalem with mercies:
build my house therein
—an oracle of Yah Veh Sabaoth
and spread a line on Yeru Shalem:
17 call out, saying,
Thus says Yah Veh Sabaoth: My cities scatter
through good; and Yah Veh still sighs over
Siyon, and still chooses Yeru Shalem.

THE FOUR HORNS

18 Then I lift my eyes, and see,
and behold, four horns:
19 and I say to the angel wording with me,
What *are* these?
And he says to me,
These *are* the horns that winnow Yah Hudah,
Yisra El, and Yeru Shalem.

THE FOUR ENGRAVERS

20 And Yah Veh shows me four engravers:
21 and I say, What approach these to work?
And he speaks, saying,
These *are* the horns that winnow Yah Hudah,
so that no mouth of man lifts his head:
and these approach to tremble them,
to hand toss the horns of the goyim,
whio lift their horn over the land of Yah Hudah
to winnow it.

THE MAN WITH THE MEASURING LINE

2 And I lift my eyes, and see:
and behold, a man with a measuring line in his hand:
2 and I say, Where go you?
And he says to me, To measure Yeru Shalem,
to see what the breadth and what the length *are.*
3 And behold, the angel wording with me comes;
and another angel comes to meet him,
4 and says to him, Run!
Word to yonder lad, saying,
Yeru Shalem settles the suburbs
because of the abundance of humanity
and animals midst her:
5 and I
—an oracle of Yah Veh
—I am to her a wall of fire all around,
and I am for honor midst her.
6 Ho, ho, and flee from the land of the north
—an oracle of Yah Veh
for I spread you as the four winds of the heavens
—an oracle of Yah Veh.
7 Rescue yourself, Ho, Siyon,
who settles with the daughter of Babel.
8 For thus says Yah Veh Sabaoth:
After the honor he sends me
to the goyim who spoiled you:
for he who touches you touches the pupil of his eye.
9 For, behold, I shake my hand on them,
and they become a spoil to their servants: and
you know that Yah Veh Sabaoth sent me.

10 Shout and cheer, O daughter of Siyon:
for, *lo* **behold**, I come,
and I *will dwell* **shall tabernacle** in the midst of thee,
saith the LORD **an oracle of Yah Veh**.
11 And many *nations* **goyim**
shall be joined to *the LORD* **Yah Veh** in that day,
and shall be my people:
and I *will* **shall** dwell in the midst of thee,
and thou shalt know
that *the LORD of hosts* **Yah Veh Sabaoth**
hath sent me unto thee.
12 And *the LORD* **Yah Veh** shall
inherit *Judah* **Yah Hudah**
his *portion* **allotment** in the holy *land* **soil**,
and shall choose *Jerusalem* **Yeru Shalem** again.
13 *Be silent* **Hush**, O all flesh,
before the LORD **at the face of Yah Veh**:
for he *is raised up* **awaketh** out of his holy habitation.

YAH SHUA THE GREAT PRIEST

3 And he *shewed me* **had me see**
Joshua **Yah Shua** the *high* **great** priest
standing *before* **at the face of**
the angel of *the LORD* **Yah Veh**,
and Satan standing at his right
hand to *resist* **oppose** him.
2 And *the LORD* **Yah Veh** said unto Satan,
The LORD **Yah Veh** rebuke thee, O Satan;
even *the LORD* **Yah Veh**
that hath chosen *Jerusalem* **Yeru Shalem**
rebuke thee:
is not this a brand *plucked* **rescued** out of the fire?
3 *Now Joshua* **Yah Shua**
was *clothed* **enrobed** with *filthy garments* **dungy clothes**,
and stood *before* **at the face of** the angel.
4 And he answered and *spake* **said**
unto those that stood *before him* **at his face**, saying,
Take away **Turn aside** the *filthy garments* **dungy clothes**
from him.
And unto him he said, *Behold* **See**,
I have caused *thine iniquity* **thy perversity**
to pass from thee,
and I *will clothe* **shall enrobe** thee
with change of *raiment* **mantles**.
5 And I said,
Let them set a *fair mitre* **pure turban** upon his head.
So they set a *fair mitre* **pure turban** upon his head,
and *clothed* **enrobed** him with *garments* **clothes**.
And the angel of *the LORD* **Yah Veh** stood by.
6 And the angel of *the LORD* **Yah Veh**
protested **witnessed** unto *Joshua* **Yah Shua**, saying,
7 Thus saith *the LORD of hosts* **Yah Veh Sabaoth**;
If thou *wilt* **shalt** walk in my ways,
and if thou *wilt keep* **shalt guard** my *charge* **guard**,
then thou shalt also *judge* **plead the cause in** my house,
and shalt also *keep* **guard** my courts,
and I *will* **shall** give thee places to walk
among these that stand by.

THE SPROUT

8 Hear *now* **I beseech**,
O *Joshua* **Yah Shua** the *high* **great** priest, thou,
and thy *fellows* **friends** that sit *before thee* **at thy face**:
for they are men *wondered at* **of omens**:
for, behold,
I *will* **shall** bring forth my servant
the *BRANCH* **SPROUT**.
9 For behold the stone
that I have *laid* **given**
before Joshua **at the face of Yah Shua**;
upon one stone shall be seven eyes:
behold,
I *will* **shall** engrave the *graving* **engraving** *thereof*,
saith the LORD of hosts **an oracle of Yah Veh Sabaoth**,
and I *will remove* **shall depart**
the *iniquity* **perversity** of that land
in one day.
10 In that day,
saith the LORD of hosts **an oracle of Yah Veh Sabaoth**,
shall ye call every man his *neighbour* **friend**
under the vine and under the fig tree.

THE GOLDEN MENORAH AND THE TWO OLIVES

4 And the angel that *talked* **worded** with me
came again **returned**, and waked me,
as a man that is wakened out of his sleep.
for behold, I come and I tabernacle among you
—an oracle of Yah Veh.
11 And many goyim join Yah Veh in that day,
and become my people:
and I dwell midst you;
and you know that Yah Veh Sabaoth sent me to you:
12 And Yah Veh inherits Yah Hudah,
his allotment on the holy soil,
and again chooses Yeru Shalem.
13 Hush, O all flesh, at the face of Yah Veh:
for he wakens from his holy habitation.

YAH SHUA THE GREAT PRIEST

3 And he shows me Yah Shua the great priest
standing at the face of the angel of Yah Veh; and
Satan standing at his right to oppose him.
2 And Yah Veh says to Satan,
Yah Veh rebuke you, O Satan;
Yah Veh who chooses Yeru Shalem
rebukes you:
Is not this a brand rescued from the fire?
3 Yah Shua enrobes with dungy clothes
and stands at the face of the angel:
4 and he answers and says to them
standing at his face, saying, Turn
aside his dungy clothes.
And to him he says, See,
I pass your perversity from you;
and I enrobe you with change of mantles.
5 He also says,
Set a pure turban on his head.
—and they set a pure turban on his head,
and enrobe him with clothes.
And the angel of Yah Veh stands by;
6 and the angel of Yah Veh witnesses to Yah Shua,
saying,
7 Thus says Yah Veh Sabaoth:
If you walk in my ways and if you guard my guard,
then you also plead the cause in my house
and also guard my courts;
and I give you places to walk
among these standing by.

THE SPROUT

8 Hear I beseech, O Yah Shua the great priest
—you and your friends sitting at your face:
for they are men of omens:
for behold, I bring forth my servant the SPROUT.
9 For behold, the stone I give
at the face of Yah Shua;
on one stone *are* seven eyes:
behold, I engrave the engraving
—an oracle of Yah Veh Sabaoth
and I depart the perversity from that land in one day.
10 In that day,
—an oracle of Yah Veh Sabaoth
you, have every man call his friend
under the vine and under the fig tree.

THE GOLDEN MENORAH AND THE TWO OLIVES

4 And the angel wording with me
returns and wakens me
—as a man wakens from his sleep:
2 And said unto me, What seest thou?
And I said, I *have looked* **saw**, and behold,
a *candlestick* **menorah** all of gold,
with a bowl upon the top of it,
and his seven lamps thereon,
and seven *pipes* **tubes** to the seven lamps,
which are upon the top *thereof*:
3 And two *olive trees* **olives** by it,
one upon the right *side* of the bowl,
and *the other* **one** upon the left *side thereof.*
4 So I answered
and *spake* **said** to the angel that *talked* **worded** with me,
saying, What are these, my *lord* **Adonay**?
5 Then the angel that *talked* **worded** with me
answered and said unto me,
Knowest thou not what these be?
And I said, No, my *lord* **Adonay**.
6 Then he answered and
spake **said** unto me, saying,
This is the word of *the LORD* **Yah Veh**
unto *Zerubbabel* **Zerub Babel**, saying,
Not by *might* **valour**, nor by *power* **force**,
but by my spirit,
saith *the LORD of hosts* **Yah Veh Sabaoth**.
7 Who art thou, O great mountain?
before Zerubbabel **at the face of Zerub
Babel** thou shalt become a plain:
and he shall bring forth the headstone *thereof*
with *shoutings* **clamors**,
crying, Grace, grace **Charism, charism** unto it.
8 Moreover
the word of *the LORD* **Yah Veh** came unto me, saying,
9 The hands of *Zerubbabel* **Zerub Babel**
have laid the foundation of this house;
his hands shall also *finish it* **clip**;
and thou shalt know
that *the LORD of hosts* **Yah Veh Sabaoth**
hath sent me unto you.
10 For who hath *despised* **disrespected**
the day of *small things* **the lesser**?
for they shall *rejoice* **cheer**,
and shall see the *plummet* **tin weight**
in the hand of *Zerubbabel* **Zerub Babel:**
with those seven;

they are the eyes of *the LORD* **Yah Veh**,
which *run to and fro* **flit** through the whole earth.
11 Then answered I, and said unto him,
What are these two *olive trees* **olives**
upon the right *side* of the *candlestick* **menorah**
and upon the left *side thereof*?
12 And I answered *again*
secondly, and said unto him,
What be these two olive branches
which *through* **by the hand of** the two golden *pipes* **tubes**
empty **pour out** the golden *oil* out of themselves?
13 And he *answered* **said to** me *and said* **saying**,
Knowest thou not what these be?
And I said, No, my *lord* **Adonay**.
14 Then said he,
These are the two *anointed ones* **sons of oil**,
that stand by the *Lord* **Adonay** of the whole earth.

THE FLYING ROLL

5 Then I turned, and lifted up mine eyes,
and *looked* **saw**, and behold**,** a flying roll.
2 And he said unto me, What seest thou? And I
answered **said**, I see a flying roll; the length *thereof*
is twenty cubits, and the breadth *thereof* ten cubits.
3 Then said he unto me,
This is the *curse* **oath**
that goeth forth over the face of the whole earth:
for every one that stealeth shall be *cut off* **exonerated**
as on this side *according to it* **thus**;
and every one that *sweareth* **oatheth**
shall be *cut off* **exonerated**
as on that side *according to it* **thus**.
4 I *will* **shall** bring it forth,
saith the LORD of hosts **an oracle of Yah Veh Sabaoth**,
and it shall enter into the house of the thief,
and into the house of him
that *sweareth* **oatheth** falsely by my name:

2 and says to me, What see you?
And I say, I see, and behold,
a menorah all of gold
with a bowl on the top of it
and his seven lamps on it
and seven tubes to the seven lamps on the top:
3 and two olives by it;
one on the right of the bowl and one on the left.
4 And I answer and say to
the angel wording with me,
saying, What are these, my Adonay?
5 And the angel wording with me
answers and says to me,
Know you not what these *are*?
And I say, No, my Adonay.
6 And he answers and says to me, saying,
This is the word of Yah Veh to Zerub Babel, saying,
Neither by valour nor by force;
but by my spirit, says Yah Veh Sabaoth.
7 Who are you, O great mountain?
at the face of Zerub Babel you *are but* a plain:
and he brings forth the headstone with clamors,
Charism! Charism to it!
8 And so be the word of Yah Veh to me, saying,
9 The hands of Zerub Babel founded this house;
and his hands clip;
and you know Yah Veh Sabaoth sent me to you.
10 For who disrespects the day of the lesser?
they cheer,
and see the tin weight in the hand of Zerub Babel:
these seven *are* the eyes of Yah Veh
flitting through the whole earth.
11 And I answer and say to him,
What *are* these two olives
on the right and on the left of the menorah?
12 And I answer secondly, and say to him,
What *are* these two olive branches
by the hand of the two golden tubes
pouring the golden *oil* from themselves?
13 And he says to me, saying,
Know you not what these *are*?
And I say, No, my Adonay.
14 And he says,
These are the two sons of oil
standing by the Adonay of the whole earth.

THE FLYING ROLL

5 And I turn and lift my eyes and see;
and behold, a flying roll:
2 and he says to me, What see you?
And I say, I see a flying roll;
the length twenty cubits and the breadth ten cubits.
3 And he says to me,
This *is* the oath
going over the face of the whole earth:
for every one who steals *is* exonerated
as on this side, thus;
and every one who oaths *is* exonerated
as on that side, thus.
4 I bring it forth
—an oracle of Yah Veh Sabaoth
and it enters into the house of the thief
and into his house who oaths falsely by my name:

and it shall *remain* **stay overnight**
in the midst of his house,
and shall *consume* **finish** it **off**
with the timber *thereof* and the stones *thereof.*

THE EPHAH

5 Then the angel that *talked*
worded with me went forth,
and said unto me, Lift *up now* thine eyes,
and see what is this that goeth *forth.*
6 And I said, What is it?
And he said, This is an ephah that goeth forth.
He said *moreover,*
This is their *resemblance* **eye** through all the earth.
7 And, behold, there was lifted
up a *talent* **round** of lead:
and this is *a* **one** woman
that sitteth in the midst of the ephah.
8 And he said, This is wickedness.
And he cast it into the midst of the ephah;
and he cast the *weight* **stone** of lead
upon the mouth *thereof.*
9 Then lifted I up mine eyes,
and *looked* **saw**, and, behold,
there came out two women,
and the wind was in their wings;
for *they* **these** had wings like the wings of a stork:
and they lifted up the ephah
between the earth and **between** the *heaven* **heavens**.
10 Then said I to the angel that
talked **worded** with me,
Whither do these *bear* **carry** the ephah?
11 And he said unto me,
To build it an house in the land of Shinar:
and it shall be established,
and set there upon her own *base.*

THE FOUR CHARIOTS

6 And I turned, and lifted up mine eyes,
and *looked* **saw**, and, behold,
there came four chariots
out from between two mountains;
and the mountains were mountains of *brass* **copper**.
2 in the first chariot were red horses;
and in the second chariot *black* **dark** horses;
3 And in the third chariot white horses;
and in the fourth chariot grisled and *bay* **strong** horses.
4 Then I answered
and said unto the angel that *talked* **worded** with me,
What are these, my *lord* **Adonay**?
5 And the angel answered and said unto me,
These are the four *spirits* **spirits/winds** of the heavens,
which go forth from standing
before the Lord **in front of Adonay** of all the earth.
6 The *black* **dark** horses which are therein
go forth into the north *country* **land**;
and the white go forth after them;
and the grisled go forth toward the south *country* **land**.
7 And the *bay* **strong** went forth,
and sought to go that **in walking,**
they might walk *to and fro* through the earth:
and he said, Get you hence,
in walking, walk *to and fro* through the earth.
So **in walking,** they walked *to and fro* through the earth.
8 Then cried he upon me,
and *spake* **worded** unto me,
saying, *Behold* **See**,
these that go toward the north *country* **land**
have *quieted* **rested** my spirit in the north *country* **land**.

YAH SHUA CROWNED

9 And the word of *the LORD*
Yah Veh came unto me,
saying,
10 Take of *them of the captivity* **the exile**,
even of *Heldai* **Helday**, of *Tobijah* **Tobi Yah**,
and of *Jedaiah* **Yeda Yah**,
which are come from *Babylon* **Babel**,
and come thou the same day,
and go into the house of *Josiah* **Yoshi Yah**
the son of *Zephaniah* **Sephan Yah**;
11 Then take silver and gold,
and *make* **work** crowns,
and set them upon the head of *Joshua* **Yah Shua**
the son of *Josedech* **Yah Sadaq**, the *high* **great** priest;
12 And *speak* **say** unto him, saying,
Thus *speaketh the LORD of hosts* **saith Yah Veh Sabaoth**,
saying,
and it stays overnight midst his house
and finishes it off with the timber and the stones.

THE EPHAH

5 And the angel wording with me
comes and says to me,
Lift your eyes, and see what this is that goes.
6 And I say, What is it?
And he says, This is the ephah coming.
And he says, This is their eye through all the earth.
7 And behold, a round of lead lifting:

and this is one woman sitting midst the ephah.
8 And he says, This is wickedness!
—and he casts it midst the ephah;
and he casts the stone of lead on the mouth.
9 And I lift my eyes and see, and behold,
two women come with the wind in their wings;
—wings as the wings of a stork:
and they lift the ephah
between the earth and between the heavens.
10 Then I say to the angel wording with me,
Where carry they the ephah?
11 And he says to me,
To build a house in the land of Shinar:
and to establish and set there on her own.

The Four Chariots

6 And I turn and lift my eyes and see,
and behold,
four chariots coming from between two mountains;
and the mountains *are* mountains of copper.
2 In the first chariot, red horses;
and in the second chariot, dark horses;
3 and in the third chariot, white horses;
and in the fourth chariot, grisled and strong horses.
4 And I answer
and say to the angel wording with me,
What are these, my Adonay?
5 And the angel answers and says to me,
These are the four spirits/winds of the heavens,
coming from standing
in front of Adonay of all the earth:
6 the dark horses therein go into the north land;
and the white go after them;
and the grisled go toward the south land:
7 and the strong go,
and seek to go walking—walking through the earth:
and he says, Go!
In walking, walk through the earth.
—and in walking, they walk through the earth.
8 And he cries on me, and words to me, saying,
See, these going toward the north land
rest my spirit in the north land.

Yah Shua Crowned

9 And so be the word of Yah Veh to me, saying,
10 Take of the exiles
—of Helday, of Tobi Yah and of Yeda Yah
who come from Babel,
and come the same day,
and go into the house of Yoshi Yah
the son of Sephan Yah:
11 and take silver and gold, and work crowns;
and set them on the head of Yah Shua
the son of Yah Sadaq the great priest;
12 snd say to him, saying,
Thus says Yah Veh Sabaoth:
saying,
Behold the man whose name is The *BRANCH* **SPROUT**;
and he shall *grow up* **sprout** out of his place,
and he shall build
the *temple* **manse** of *the LORD* **Yah Veh**:
13 Even he
shall build the *temple* **manse** of *the LORD* **Yah Veh**;
and he shall bear the *glory* **majesty**,
and shall sit and *rule* **reign** upon his throne;
and he shall be a priest upon his throne:
and the counsel of *peace* **shalom**
shall be between them both.
14 And the crowns shall be to Helem,
and to *Tobijah* **Tobi Yah**, and to *Jedaiah* **Yeda Yah**,
and to Hen the son of *Zephaniah* **Sephan Yah**,
for a memorial
in the *temple* **manse** of *the LORD* **Yah Veh**.
15 And they that are far off shall come
and build in the *temple* **manse** of *the LORD* **Yah Veh**,
and ye shall know
that *the LORD of hosts* **Yah Veh Sabaoth**
hath sent me unto you.
And this shall *come to pass* **become**,
if **in hearkening,** ye *will diligently obey* **shall hearken**
unto the voice of *the LORD* **Yah Veh** your *God* **Elohim**.

Concerning Fasting

7 And **so be** it *came to pass*,
in the fourth year of *king Darius* **sovereign Daryavesh**,
that the word of *the LORD* **Yah Veh**
came unto *Zechariah* **Zechar Yah**
in the fourth *day* of the ninth month,
even in *Chisleu* **Kislav**;
2 When they had sent unto the house of *God* **El**
Sherezer **Shareser** and *Regemmelech* **Regem Melech**,
and their men,
to *pray before the LORD* **stroke the face of Yah Veh**,
3 And to *speak* **say** unto the priests which were in
the house of *the LORD of hosts* **Yah Veh Sabaoth**,
and to the prophets, saying,
should I weep in the fifth month,
separating myself,
as I have *done* **worked** these so many years?
4 Then came the word

of *the LORD of hosts* **Yah Veh Sabaoth** unto me, saying,
5 Speak unto all the people of
the land, and to the priests,
saying,
When ye fasted and *mourned* **chopped**
in the fifth and seventh *month,*
even those seventy years,
did ye at all fast **in fasting, fasted ye** unto me,
even to me?
6 And when ye *did eat* **ate**, and
when ye *did drink* **drank**,
did not ye eat for yourselves **ate ye not**,
and *drink* **drank ye not** for *yourselves* **them**?
7 *Should ye not hear* **Are not these** the words
which *the LORD* **Yah Veh** hath *cried* **called out**
by **the hand of** the former prophets,
when *Jerusalem* **Yeru Shalem**
was *inhabited* **settled** and *in prosperity* **serene**,
and the cities *thereof* round about her,
when *men inhabited* **they settled** the south
and the *plain* **lowland**?
8 And the word of *the LORD* **Yah Veh**
came unto *Zechariah* **Zechar Yah**, saying,
9 Thus *speaketh* **saith**
the LORD of hosts **Yah Veh Sabaoth**, saying,
Execute true judgment **Judge judgment in truth**,
and *shew* **work** mercy and *compassions* **mercies**
every man to his brother:
10 And oppress not the widow,
nor the *fatherless* **orphan**,
the *stranger* **sojourner**, nor the *poor* **humble**;
and let *none* **no man** of you *imagine* **fabricate** evil
against his brother in your heart.
11 But they refused to hearken,
and *pulled away the* **gave a revolting** shoulder,
and *stopped* **made heavy** their ears,
that they should not hear.
12 Yea, they *made* **set** their hearts
as *an adamant stone* **a brier**,
lest they should hear the *law* **torah**,
Behold the man whose name *is* The SPROUT;
and he sprouts from his place
and he builds the manse of Yah Veh:
13 yes, he builds the manse of Yah Veh;
and he bears the majesty
and sits and reigns on his throne;
and he becomes a priest on his throne:
and the counsel of shalom
becomes between them both.
14 And the crown *is* to Helem
and to Tobi Yah and to Yeda Yah
and to Hen the son of Sephan Yah,
for a memorial in the manse of Yah Veh.
15 And they who are far off
come and build in the manse of Yah Veh;
and you know Yah Veh Sabaoth sends me to you.
And so be it,
if in hearkening,
you hearken to the voice of Yah Veh your Elohim.

CONCERNING FASTING

7 And so be it,
in the fourth year of sovereign Daryavesh,
so be the word of Yah Veh to Zechar Yah
in the fourth of the ninth month, in Kislav;
2 and Beth El
sends Shareser and Regem Melech and their men
to stroke the face of Yah Veh;
3 and to say
to the priests in the house of Yah Veh Sabaoth
and to the prophets, saying,
Weep I, in the fifth month, separating myself,
as I worked these so many years?
4 And so be the word of Yah Veh Sabaoth to me,
saying,
5 Speak to all the people of the land
and to the priests, saying,
When you fasted and chopped
in the fifth and seventh
—even these seventy years,
in fasting, fasted you to me—me?
6 And when you ate and when you drank
ate you not,
and drank you not for yourselves?
7 Are not these the words Yah Veh called out
by the hand of the former prophets
when Yeru Shalem settled serene?
And the cities all around her
when they settled the south and the lowland?
8 And so be the word of Yah Veh to Zechar Yah,
saying,
9 Thus says Yah Veh Sabaoth:
saying, Judge judgment in truth,
and every man,
work mercy and mercies to his brother:
10 and oppress not
widow and orphan, sojourner and humble;
and no man of you
fabricate evil against his brother in your heart.
11 And they refuse to hearken;

and give a revolting shoulder
and heavy their ears that they hear not.
12 Yes, they set their hearts as a brier
lest they hear the torah
and the words which *the LORD of hosts* **Yah Veh Sabaoth**
hath sent in his spirit by **the hand of** the former prophets:
therefore came a great *wrath* **rage**
from *the LORD of hosts* **Yah Veh Sabaoth.**
13 Therefore it is *come to pass* **become,**
that as he *cried* **called out,**
and they *would* **should** not hear;
so they *cried* **called out**, and I *would* **should** not hear,
saith *the LORD of hosts* **Yah Veh Sabaoth:**
14 But I *scattered* **stormed** them *with a whirlwind*
among all the *nations* **goyim** whom they knew not.
Thus the land *was desolate* **desolated** after them,
that no *man* **one** passed through nor returned:
for they *laid the pleasant* **set the** land **of desire** desolate.

The New Relationship Of Yah Veh With Yisra El

8 Again the word
of *the LORD of hosts* **Yah Veh Sabaoth**
came *to me*, saying,
2 Thus saith *the LORD of hosts* **Yah Veh Sabaoth;**
I was jealous/**zealous** for *Zion* **Siyon**
with great jealousy/**zeal,**
and I was jealous/**zealous** for her
with great fury.
3 Thus saith *the LORD* **Yah Veh;**
I am returned unto *Zion* **Siyon,**
and *will dwell* **shall tabernacle**
in the midst of *Jerusalem* **Yeru Shalem:**
and *Jerusalem* **Yeru Shalem** shall
be called a city of truth;
and the mountain of *the LORD of hosts* **Yah Veh Sabaoth**
the holy mountain.
4 Thus saith *the LORD of hosts* **Yah Veh Sabaoth;**
There shall yet
old men **eldermen** and *old women* **elderwomen**
dwell **settle** in the *streets* **broadways**
of *Jerusalem* **Yeru Shalem,**
and every man with his *staff* **crutch** in his hand
for *very age* **abundance of days.**
5 And the *streets* **broadways** of the city
shall be *full* **filled** of boys and girls
playing in the *streets* **broadways** *thereof.*
6 Thus saith *the LORD of hosts* **Yah Veh Sabaoth;**
If it be marvellous
in the eyes of the *remnant* **survivors** of this people
in these days,
should it **not** also be marvellous in mine eyes?
saith the LORD of hosts **an oracle of Yah Veh Sabaoth.**
7 Thus saith *the LORD of hosts* **Yah Veh Sabaoth;**
Behold, I *will save* **am the saviour of** my people
from the *east country* **land of the rising,**
and from the *west country*
land of the entrance of the sun;
8 And I *will* **shall** bring them,
and they shall *dwell* **tabernacle**
in the midst of *Jerusalem* **Yeru Shalem:**
and they *shall* be my people,
and *I will be* **I am** their *God* **Elohim,**
in truth and in *righteousness* **justness.**
9 Thus saith *the LORD of hosts* **Yah Veh Sabaoth;**
Let your hands be strong,
ye that hear in these days
these words by the mouth of the prophets,
which were in the day that the foundation
of the house of *the LORD of hosts* **Yah Veh Sabaoth**
was *laid* **founded,**
that the *temple* **manse** might be built.
10 For *before* **at the face of** these days
there was no hire for *man* **humanity,**
nor any hire for *beast* **animal;**
neither *was* there any *peace* **shalom** to him
that went out or came in
because of the *affliction* **tribulation:**
for I *set* **send** all *men* **humanity**
every *one* **man** against his *neighbour* **friend.**
11 But now
I *will* **shall** not be
unto the *residue* **survivors** of this people
as in the former days,
saith the LORD of hosts **an oracle of Yah Veh Sabaoth.**
12 For the seed shall be *prosperous* **at shalom;**
the vine shall give her fruit,
and the words Yah Veh Sabaoth sends his spirit
by the hand of the former prophets:
and so be it,
a great rage from Yah Veh Sabaoth.
13 and so be it,
as he calls, and they hearken not;
thus they call, and I hearken not,
says Yah Veh Sabaoth:
14 and I storm them among all the goyim
whom they know not:

and thus desolate the land after them,
so that one neither passes through nor returns:
for they desolate their land of desire.

The New Relationship Of Yah Veh With Yisra El

8 And so be the word of Yah Veh Sabaoth, saying,
2 Thus says Yah Veh Sabaoth:
I *am* jealous/zealous for Siyon with great jealousy/zeal
and I *am* jealous/zealous for her with great fury.
3 Thus says Yah Veh: I return to Siyon,
and tabernacle midst Yeru Shalem:
and call Yeru Shalem,
The City of Truth;
and the mountain of Yah Veh Sabaoth,
The Holy Mountain.
4 Thus says Yah Veh Sabaoth:
and eldermen and elderwomen
still settle there in the broadways of Yeru Shalem;
and every man with his crutch in his hand
because of abundance of days:
5 and the broadways of the city
fill with boys and girls playing in the broadways.
6 Thus says Yah Veh Sabaoth:
If it *is* marvellous
in the eyes of the survivors of this people
in these days,
is it not also marvellous in my eyes?
—an oracle of Yah Veh Sabaoth.
7 Thus says Yah Veh Sabaoth:
Behold, I *am* the saviour of my people
from the land of the rising
and from the land of the entrance of the sun:
8 and I bring them,
and they tabernacle midst Yeru Shalem:
and they become my people,
and I am their Elohim in truth and in justness.
9 Thus says Yah Veh Sabaoth:
Strengthen your hands
you, who in these days,
hear these words by the mouth of the prophets,
of the day of founding the house of Yah Veh Sabaoth,
to build the manse.
10 For ere the face of these days
there was neither hire for humanity,
nor any hire for animal;
nor any shalom to him who comes or goes
because of the tribulation:
for I sent all humanity
—every man against his friend.
11 And now
I *am* not to the survivors of this people
as in the former days
—an oracle of Yah Veh Sabaoth.
12 For the seed has shalom;
the vine gives her fruit
and the *ground* **earth** shall give her *increase* **produce**,
and the heavens shall give their dew;
and I *will* **shall** cause
the *remnant* **survivors** of this people
to possess all these *things*.
13 And **so be** it *shall come to pass*,
that as ye were *a curse* **an abasement**
among the *heathen* **goyim**,
O house of *Judah* **Yah Hudah**,
and house of *Israel* **Yisra El**;
so *will* **shall** I save you, and ye shall be a blessing:
fear **awe** not, *but let* **strengthen** your hands *be strong*.
14 For thus saith *the LORD*
of hosts **Yah Veh Sabaoth**;
As I *thought* **intrigued** to *punish* **vilify** you,
when your fathers *provoked* **enraged** me *to wrath*,
saith *the LORD of hosts* **Yah Veh Sabaoth**,
and I *repented* **sighed** not:
15 So *again* have I *thought*
turned back and intrigued
in these days to *do* well—**please**
unto Jerusalem **Yeru Shalem**
and *to* the house of *Judah* **Yah Hudah**:
fear **awe** ye not.
16 These are the *things* **words**
that ye shall *do* **work**;
Speak **Word** ye every man
the truth to his *neighbour* **friend**;
execute the judgment of truth **judge truth and judgment**
and peace **shalom** in your *gates* **portals**:
17 And let *none* **no man** of you
imagine **fabricate** evil in your hearts
against his *neighbour* **friend**;
and love no false oath:
for all these are *things* **those** that I hate,
saith the LORD **an oracle of Yah Veh**.
18 And the word of *the LORD*
of hosts **Yah Veh Sabaoth**
came unto me, saying,
19 Thus saith *the LORD of hosts* **Yah Veh Sabaoth**;
The fast of the fourth *month*, and the fast of the fifth,
and the fast of the seventh, and the fast of the tenth,
shall be to the house of *Judah* **Yah Hudah**
joy **rejoicing** and *gladness* **cheerfulness**,

and *cheerful feasts* **good seasons;**
therefore love the truth and *peace* **shalom.**
20 Thus saith *the LORD of hosts* **Yah Veh Sabaoth;**
It shall yet come to pass,
that there shall **yet** come people,
and the *inhabitants* **settlers** of many cities:
21 And the *inhabitants* **settlers** of one *city*
shall go to *another* **one**, saying,
Let us go speedily
to *pray before the LORD* **stroke the face of Yah Veh,**
and to seek *the LORD of hosts* **Yah Veh Sabaoth:**
I *will* **shall** go also.
22 Yea, many people and *strong*
nations **mighty goyim**
shall come to seek *the LORD of hosts* **Yah Veh Sabaoth**
in *Jerusalem* **Yeru Shalem,**
and to *pray before the LORD* **stroke the face of Yah Veh.**
23 Thus saith *the LORD of hosts* **Yah Veh Sabaoth;**
In those days **so be** it *shall come to pass,*
that ten men shall take hold
out of all *languages* **tongues** of the *nations* **goyim,**
even shall take hold of the *skirt* **wing**
of *him that is a Jew* **a man Yah Hudiy,**
saying, We *will* **shall** go with you:
for we have heard that *God* **Elohim** is with you.

THE BURDEN OF YAH VEH

9 The burden of the word of *the LORD* **Yah Veh**
in the land of Hadrach,
and *Damascus* **Dammeseq** shall be the rest *thereof:*
when the eyes of *man* **humanity,**
as of all the *tribes* **scions** of *Israel* **Yisra El,**
shall be toward *the LORD* **Yah Veh.**
2 And Hamath also shall border thereby;
Tyrus **Sor**, and *Zidon* **Sidon,**
though it be *very wise* **mightily enwisened.**
3 And *Tyrus* **Sor**
did build **built** herself a *strong hold* **rampart,**
and heaped *up* silver as the dust,
and *fine gold* **ore** as the mire of the *streets* **outways.**
4 Behold, *the Lord will* **Adonay shall** cast her out,
and the earth gives her produce
and the heavens give their dew:
and I have the survivors of this people
to possess all these.
13 And so be it,
as you *were* an abasement among the goyim,
O house of Yah Hudah and house of Yisra El,
thus I save you, and you become a blessing:
awe not; strengthen your hands.
14 For thus says Yah Veh Sabaoth:
As I intrigued to vilify you
when your fathers enraged me,
says Yah Veh Sabaoth,
and I sighed not:
15 thus in these days,
I return to intrigue and well—please Yeru Shalem
and the house of Yah Hudah.
Awe not.
16 These are the words you work;
Every man of you, word truth to his friend;
judge truth and judgment of shalom in your portals:
17 and no man of you
fabricate evil in your hearts against his friend;
and love no false oath:
for all these are those that I hate
—an oracle of Yah Veh.
18 And so be the word of Yah Veh Sabaoth to me,
saying,
19 Thus says Yah Veh Sabaoth:
The fast of the fourth and the fast of the fifth
and the fast of the seventh and the fast of the tenth
are for rejoicing and cheerfulness and good seasons;
to the house of Yah Hudah:
so love truth and shalom.
20 Thus says Yah Veh Sabaoth:
People and settlers of many cities still come:
21 and the settlers of one come to one, saying,
We go speedily to stroke the face of Yah
Veh and to seek Yah Veh Sabaoth:
I go—even I.
22 Yes, many people and mighty goyim
come to seek Yah Veh Sabaoth in Yeru Shalem
and to stroke the face of Yah Veh.
23 Thus says Yah Veh Sabaoth:
In those days, so be it,
ten men from all tongues of the goyim,
take hold—even take hold of the wing of a man
—a Yah Hudiy,
saying, We go with you:
for we hear that Elohim *is* with you.

THE BURDEN OF YAH VEH

9 The burden of the word of Yah Veh
against the land of Hadrach
and Dammeseq its place of rest:
when the eyes of humanity
and all the scions of Yisra El
are toward Yah Veh;
2 and Hamath borders thereby;

and Sor and Sidon enwisen mightily:
3 and Sor builds herself a rampart;
and heaps silver as the dust
and ore as the mire of the outways.
4 Behold, Adonay casts her out
and he *will* **shall** smite her *power* **valiant** in the sea;
and she shall be *devoured* **consumed** with fire.
5 Ashkelon shall see *it*, and *fear* **awe**;
Gaza **Azzah** also shall see *it*,
and *be very sorrowful* **writhe mightily**, and *Ekron* **Eqron**;
for her expectation shall be ashamed;
and the *king* **sovereign**
shall *perish* **destruct** from *Gaza* **Azzah**,
and Ashkelon shall not be *inhabited* **settled**.
6 And a *bastard* **mongrel**
shall *dwell* **settle** in Ashdod,
and I *will* **shall** cut off
the *pride* **pomp** of the *Philistines* **Peleshethiym**.
7 And I *will take away* **shall turn aside**
his blood out of his mouth,
and his abominations from between his teeth:
but he that *remaineth* **surviveth**,
even he, shall be for our *God* **Elohim**,
and he shall be
as a *governor* **chiliarch** in *Judah* **Yah Hudah**,
and *Ekron* **Eqron** as a *Jebusite* **Yebusiy**.
8 And I *will* **shall** encamp about mine house
because of the *army* **station**,
because of him that passeth by,
and because of him that returneth:
and no *oppressor* **exactor**
shall pass through them any more:
for now have I seen with mine eyes.

The Saving Sovereign

9 *Rejoice greatly* **Twirl mightily**,
O daughter of *Zion* **Siyon**;
shout, O daughter of *Jerusalem* **Yeru Shalem**:
behold, thy *King* **Sovereign** cometh unto thee:
he is just, and *having salvation* **saving**;
lowly **humble**, and riding upon *an ass* **a burro**,
and upon a colt the *foal of an ass* **son of a she burro**.
10 And I *will* **shall** cut off
the chariot from *Ephraim* **Ephrayim**,
and the horse from *Jerusalem* **Yeru Shalem**,
and the *battle* **war** bow shall be cut off:
and he shall *speak peace* **word shalom**
unto the *heathen* **goyim**:
and his dominion shall be from sea *even* to sea,
and from the river *even* to the *ends*
finalities of the earth.
11 As for thee also,
by the blood of thy covenant
I have sent forth thy prisoners
out of the *pit* **well** wherein is no water.
12 Turn you to the *strong hold* **fortress**,
ye prisoners of hope:
even to day *do I declare* **I tell**
that I *will render* **shall return** double unto thee;
13 When I have bent *Judah* **Yah Hudah** for me,
filled the bow with *Ephraim* **Ephrayim**,
and *raised up* **wakened** thy sons, O *Zion* **Siyon**,
against thy sons, O *Greece* **Yavan**,
and *made* **set** thee as the sword of a mighty *man*.
14 And *the LORD* **Yah Veh** shall be seen over them,
and his arrow shall go forth as the lightning:
and *the Lord GOD* **Adonay Yah Veh**
shall *blow* **blast** the *trumpet* **shophar**,
and shall go with *whirlwinds* **storms** of the south.
15 *The LORD of hosts* **Yah Veh**
Sabaoth shall defend them;
and they shall *devour* **consume**,
and subdue with sling stones;
and they shall drink, and make a noise as through wine;
and they shall be filled like *bowls* **sprinklers**,
and as the corners of the **sacrifice** altar.
16 And *the LORD* **Yah Veh** their *God* **Elohim**
shall save them in that day as the flock of his people:
for they shall be as the stones of *a crown* **separatism**,
lifted up **raised** as an ensign upon his *land* **soil**.
17 For how great is his goodness,
and how great is his beauty!
corn **crop**
shall make the *young men cheerful* **youths flourish**,
and *new wine* **juice** the *maids* **virgins**.

The Provision Of Yah Veh

10 Ask ye of *the LORD* **Yah Veh** rain
in the time of the *latter* **after** rain;
and smites her valiant in the sea;
and fire consumes her:
5 Ashkelon sees and awes;
Azzah also sees and writhes mightily;
and Eqron shames for her expectation;
and the sovereign destructs from Azzah,
and Ashkelon settles not:
6 and a mongrel settles in Ashdod,
and I cut off the pomp of the Peleshethiym:
7 and I turn aside his blood from his mouth,

and his abominations from between his teeth:
and he who survives, even he *is* for our Elohim;
and he becomes as a chiliarch in Yah Hudah,
and Eqron as a Yebusiy.
8 And I encamp around my house
because of those stationed
—because of him who passes by,
and because of him who returns:
and no exactor passes through them any more:
for now I see with my eyes.

THE SAVING SOVEREIGN

9 Twirl mightily, O daughter of Siyon!
Shout, O daughter of Yeru Shalem!
Behold, your Sovereign comes to you:
he is just and saving;
humble—and riding on a burro
and on a colt the son of a she burro.
10 And I cut off the chariot from Ephrayim
and the horse from Yeru Shalem
and cut off the bow of war:
and he words shalom to the goyim:
with his dominion from sea to sea
and from the river to the finalities of the earth.
11 And you,
by the blood of your covenant
I sent your prisoners from the well without water.
12 Turn to the fortress, you prisoners of hope:
even today I tell you that I return double to you;
13 when I bend Yah Hudah for me,
fill the bow with Ephrayim,
and waken your sons, O Siyon,
against your sons, O Yavan,
and set you as the sword of a mighty.
14 And Yah Veh is seen over them,
and his arrow comes as the lightning:
and Adonay Yah Veh blasts the shophar
and comes with storms of the south:
15 Yah Veh Sabaoth defends them;
and they consume, and subdue with sling stones;
and they drink, and make a noise as through wine;
and they fill up as sprinklers
and as the corners of the sacrifice altar.
16 And Yah Veh their Elohim
saves them in that day
as the flock of his people:
for they raise the stones of separatism
as an ensign on his soil.
17 How great his goodness
and how great his beauty!
crop flourishes the youths; and juice the virgins.

THE PROVISION OF YAH VEH

10 Ask rain of Yah Veh
in the time of the after rain!
so *the LORD* **Yah Veh**
shall *make bright clouds* **work lightnings**,
and give them *showers* **downpours** of *rain* **downpour**,
to every *one grass* **man herbage** in the field.
2 For the *idols* **teraphim**
have *spoken vanity* **worded mischief**,
and the diviners have seen a *lie* **falsehood**,
and have *told false* **worded vain** dreams;
they *comfort* **sigh** in vain:
therefore they went their way as a flock,
they *were troubled* **answered**,
because **that** there was no *shepherd* **tender**.
3 *Mine anger* **My wrath**
was kindled against the *shepherds* **tenders**,
and I *punished* **visited** the **he** goats:
for *the LORD of hosts* **Yah Veh Sabaoth**
hath visited his *flock* **drove**
the house of *Judah* **Yah Hudah**,
and hath *made* **set** them
as his *goodly* horse **of majesty** in the battle.
4 Out of him came forth the corner,
out of him the *nail* **stake**, out of him the battle bow,
out of him every *oppressor* **exactor** together.
5 And they shall be as mighty *men*,
which *tread down their enemies* **trample**
in the mire of the *streets* **outways** in the battle:
and they shall fight,
because *the LORD* **Yah Veh** is with them,
and the riders on horses shall be *confounded* **shamed**.
6 And *I will strengthen* **prevail mightily**
shall the house of *Judah* **Yah Hudah**,
and I *will* **shall** save the house of *Joseph* **Yoseph**,
and I *will bring them again to place* **shall resettle** them;
for I *have* mercy *upon* them:
and they shall be as though I had not cast them off:
for *I am the LORD* **I—Yah Veh** their *God* **Elohim**,
and *will hear* **shall answer** them.
7 And *they of Ephraim* **Ephrayim**
shall be like a mighty *man*,
and their heart shall *rejoice* **cheer** as through wine:
yea, their *children* **sons** shall see it, and *be glad* **cheer**;
their heart shall *rejoice* **twirl** in *the LORD* **Yah Veh**.
8 I *will* **shall** hiss for them, and gather them;
for I have redeemed them:
and they shall *increase* **abound**
as they have *increased* **abounded**.

9 And I *will sow* **shall seed**
them among the people:
and they shall remember me *in far countries* **afar off**;
and they shall live with their *children* **sons**,
and *turn again* **return**.
10 I *will bring* **shall return** them *again also*
out of the land of *Egypt* **Misrayim**,
and gather them out of *Assyria* **Ashshur**;
and I *will* **shall** bring them
into the land of *Gilead* **Gilad** and Lebanon;
and *place* shall not be found for them.
11 And he shall pass through the sea
with *affliction* **tribulation**,
and shall smite the waves in the sea,
and all the deeps of the river shall *dry up* **wither**:
and the *pride* **pomp** of *Assyria* **Ashshur**
shall be brought down,
and the *sceptre* **scion** of *Egypt* **Misrayim**
shall *depart away* **turn aside**.
12 And *I will strengthen them*
they shall prevail mightily
in *the LORD* **Yah Veh**;
and they shall walk up and down in his name,
saith the LORD **an oracle of Yah Veh**.

THE RAVAGE OF LEBANON

11 Open thy doors, O Lebanon,
that the fire may *devour* **consume** thy cedars.
2 Howl, fir tree; for the cedar is fallen;
because the mighty are *spoiled* **ravaged**:
howl, O ye oaks of Bashan;
for the forest of the *vintage* **crop** *is*
come down **be toppled**.
3 There is a voice of the howling
of the *shepherds* **tenders**;
for their *glory is spoiled* **mighty be ravaged**:
a voice of the roaring of *young lions* **whelps**;
for the *pride* **pomp** of *Jordan* **Yarden**
is spoiled **be ravaged**.

Yah Veh works lightnings
and gives them downpours of downpour
—herbage to every man in the field:
2 because the teraphim words mischief,
and the diviners see a falsehood
and word vain dreams;
they sigh in vain:
so they go their way as a flock,
they answer that there is no tender.
3 My wrath kindles against the tenders,
and I visit the he goats:
for Yah Veh Sabaoth visits his drove
—the house of Yah Hudah
and sets them as his horse of majesty in the battle.
4 From him comes the corner;
from him the stake;
from him the battle bow;
from him every exactor together:
5 and they become as the mighty
who trample in the mire of the outways in the battle:
and they fight, for Yah Veh *is* with them,
and the riders on horses shame.
6 And the house of Yah Hudah prevails mightily,
and I save the house of Yoseph and I resettle them;
for I mercy them:
and they become as though I cast them not off:
for I—Yah Veh their Elohim,
and I answer them.
7 And Ephrayim is as the mighty;
and their heart cheers as through wine:
yes, their sons see, and cheer;
their heart twirls in Yah Veh.
8 I hiss for them, and gather them;
for I redeemed them:
and in abounding, they abound:
9 and I seed them among the people:
and they remember me afar off;
and they live with their sons, and return.
10 I return them from the land of Misrayim,
and gather them from Ashshur;
and I bring them into the land of Gilad and Lebanon;
and naught *is* found for them.
11 And he passes through the sea with tribulation
and smites the waves in the sea;
and all the deeps of the river wither:
and they bring down the pomp of Ashshur,
and the scion of Misrayim turns aside:
12 and they prevail mightily in Yah Veh;
and they walk up and down in his name
—an oracle of Yah Veh.

THE RAVAGE OF LEBANON

11 Open your doors, O Lebanon,
and fire consumes among your cedars.
2 Howl, fir tree; for the cedar falls;
because the mighty *are* ravaged!
Howl, O you oaks of Bashan;
for the forest of the crop topples!
3 A voice of howling of the tenders;
for their mighty *are* ravaged!
A voice of the roaring of whelps;

for the pomp of Yarden *is* ravaged.
4 Thus saith *the LORD* **Yah Veh** my *God* **Elohim**;
Feed **Tend** the flock of the slaughter;
5 Whose *possessors slay*
chattelers slaughter them,
and *hold themselves not guilty* **have not guilted**:
and they that sell them say,
Blessed be *the LORD* **Yah Veh**; for I am *rich* **enriched**:
and their own *shepherds pity* **tenders spare** them not.
6 For I *will* **shall** no more
pity **spare** the *inhabitants* **settlers** of the land,
saith the LORD **an oracle of Yah Veh**:
but, *lo* **behold**,
I *will deliver the men* **shall present humanity**
every one **each man** into his *neighbour's* **friend's** hand,
and into the hand of his *king* **sovereign**:
and they shall *smite* **crush** the land,
and out of their hand I *will* **shall** not *deliver* **rescue** them.
7 And I *will feed* **shall tend** the flock of slaughter,
even you **thus**, O *poor* **humble** of the flock.
And I took unto me two staves;
the one I called *Beauty* **Pleasantness**,
and the *other* **one** I called Bands;
and I *fed* **tended** the flock.
8 Three *shepherds* **tenders** also
I *cut* **chopped** off in one month;
and my soul lothed them,
and their soul also *abhorred* **lothed** me.
9 Then said I, I *will* **shall** not *feed* **tend** you:
that that dieth, let it die;
and that that is to be cut off, let it be cut off;
and let *the rest* **them that survive**
eat every one **each woman eat** the flesh of *another* **sister**.
10 And I took my staff, *even Beauty* **Pleasantness**,
and cut it asunder,
that I might break my covenant
which I had *made* **cut** with all the people.
11 And it was broken in that day:
and so the *poor* **humble** of the flock
that *waited upon* **guarded** me
knew that it was the word of *the LORD* **Yah Veh**.
12 And I said unto them,
If *ye think* **it be** good **in thine eyes**,
give *me* my *price* **hire**;
and if not, *forbear* **cease**.
So they weighed for my *price* **hire** thirty *pieces of* silver.
13 And *the LORD* **Yah Veh** said unto me,
Cast it unto the *potter* **former**:
a *goodly price* **mighty estimation**
that I was *prised* **appraised** at of them.
And I took the thirty *pieces* of silver,
and cast them to the *potter* **former**
in the house of *the LORD* **Yah Veh**.
14 Then I cut asunder *mine other* **my second** staff,
even Bands,
that I might break the brotherhood
between *Judah* **Yah Hudah** and *Israel* **between Yisra El**.
15 And *the LORD* **Yah Veh** said unto me,
Take unto thee yet
the instruments of a foolish *shepherd* **tender**.
16 For, *lo* **behold**,
I *will* **shall** raise up a *shepherd* **tender** in the land,
which shall not visit those that be cut off,
neither shall seek the *young one* **lad**,
nor heal that that is broken,
nor *feed* **sustain** that that *standeth still* **be stationed**:
but he shall eat the flesh of the fat,
and *tear* **craunch** their *claws in pieces* **hoofs**.
17 *Woe* **Ho** to the idol *shepherd* **tender**
that *leaveth* **forsaketh** the flock!
the sword shall be upon his arm, and upon his right eye:
his arm shall *be clean dried up* **wither**,
and **in dimming,**
his right eye shall be *utterly darkened* **dimmed**.

THE SIEGE OF YERU SHALEM

12 The burden of the word of *the LORD* **Yah Veh**
for *Israel* **Yisra El**,
saith the LORD **an oracle of Yah Veh**,
which *stretcheth forth* **spreadeth** the heavens,
and layeth the foundation of the earth,
and formeth the spirit of *man* **humanity** within him.
4 Thus says Yah Veh my Elohim:
Tend the flock of the slaughter;
5 whose chattelers slaughter them,
and they guilt not:
and they who sell them say,
Blessed—Yah Veh; for I enrich:
and their own tenders spare them not.
6 For I spare the settlers of the land no more
—an oracle of Yah Veh.
And behold,
I present humanity
—each man to the hand of his friend
and to the hand of his sovereign;
and they crush the land:
and from their hand I rescue them not:
7 and I tend the flock of slaughter
—even you, O humble of the flock.
And I take two staves to myself;

the one I call Pleasantness
and the one I call Bands:
and I tend the flock.
8 And in one month, I chop off three tenders;
and my soul loathes them,
and their soul also loathes me.
9 Then I say, I tend you not:
what dies, dies;
and what *is* cut off, *is* cut off;
and of them who survive,
each woman eats the flesh of sister.
10 And I take my staff, Pleasantness, and cut it,
to break the covenant I cut with all the people:
11 and I break it in that day:
and thus the humble of the flock
who guard me know it *is* the word of Yah Veh.
12 And I say to them,
If good in your eyes, give me my hire;
and if not, cease.
—and they weigh for my hire thirty silver.
13 And Yah Veh says to me,
Cast it to the former:
—a mighty appraisal I *am* appraised by them.
—and I take the thirty silver
and cast them to the former in the house of Yah Veh.
14 Then I cut my second staff, Bands,
to break the brotherhood
between Yah Hudah and between Yisra El.
15 And Yah Veh says to me,
Take to yourself again
the instruments of a foolish tender:
16 for, behold, I raise a tender in the land,
who neither visits the cut off,
nor seeks the lad,
nor heals the broken,
nor sustains the stationed:
and he eats the flesh of the fat
and craunches their hoofs.
17 Ho to the idol tender
who forsakes the flock!
the sword *is* on his arm and on his right eye:
his arm withers,
and in dimming, his right eye dims.

THE SIEGE OF YERU SHALEM

12 The burden of the word of Yah Veh for Yisra El
—an oracle of Yah Veh
who spread the heavens and founded the earth
and formed the spirit of humanity within him:
2 Behold, I *will make Jerusalem*
shall set Yeru Shalem
a *cup* **bason** of *trembling* **staggering**
unto all the people round about,
when they shall be in the siege
both against *Judah* **Yah Hudah**
and against *Jerusalem* **Yeru Shalem.**
3 And in that day
will I make Jerusalem **shall I set Yeru Shalem**
a *burdensome* stone **of burden** for all *people* **goyim:**
all that burden themselves with it
in incising, shall be *cut in pieces* **incised,**
though all the people of the earth
be gathered *together* against it.

THE LIBERATION OF YERU SHALEM

4 In that day,
saith the LORD **an oracle of Yah Veh,**
I *will* **shall** smite
every horse with *astonishment* **consternation,**
and his rider with *madness* **insanity:**
and I *will* **shall** open mine eyes
upon the house of *Judah* **Yah Hudah,**
and *will* **shall** smite
every horse of the people with blindness.
5 And the *governors* **chiliarchs**
of *Judah* **Yah Hudah**
shall say in their heart,
The *inhabitants* **settlers** of *Jerusalem* **Yeru Shalem**
shall be my strength
in *the LORD of hosts* **Yah Veh**
Sabaoth their *God* **Elohim.**
6 In that day *will* I *make* **shall I set**
the *governors* **chiliarchs** of *Judah* **Yah Hudah**
like an *hearth* **laver** of fire among the *wood* **timber,**
and like a *torch* **flambeau** of fire in *a sheaf* **an omer;**
and they shall *devour* **consume** all
the people round about,
on the right *hand* and on the left:
and *Jerusalem* **Yeru Shalem**
shall be *inhabited* **settled** again in her own place,
even in *Jerusalem* **Yeru Shalem.**
7 *The LORD* **Yah Veh** also
shall save the tents of *Judah* **Yah Hudah** first,
that the *glory* **adornment** of the house of David
and the *glory* **adornment**
of the *inhabitants* **settlers** of *Jerusalem* **Yeru Shalem**
do not magnify themselves **greaten not**
against *Judah* **Yah Hudah.**
8 In that day shall *the LORD* **Yah Veh**

defend the *inhabitants* **settlers** of
Jerusalem **Yeru Shalem**;
and he that *is feeble* **faltereth** among them at that day
shall be as David;
and the house of David shall be as *God* **Elohim**,
as the angel of *the LORD* **Yah Veh**
before **at the face of** them.
9 And **so be** it *shall come to pass* in that day,
that I *will* **shall** seek
to *destroy* **desolate** all the *nations* **goyim** that
come against *Jerusalem* **Yeru Shalem**.

THE SPIRIT OF CHARISM

10 And I *will* **shall** pour upon the house of David,
and upon the *inhabitants* **settlers**
of *Jerusalem* **Yeru Shalem**,
the spirit of *grace* **charism** and of supplications:
and they shall look upon me whom they have pierced,
and they shall *mourn* **chop** for him,
as one *mourneth* **choppeth** for his only *son*,
and shall be *in bitterness* **embittered** for him,
as one that is *in bitterness* **embittered**
for his *firstborn* **birstbirthed**.

THE CHOPPING IN YERU SHALEM

11 In that day
shall there *be a great mourning* **greaten a chopping**
in *Jerusalem* **Yeru Shalem**,
as the *mourning* **chopping**
of *Hadadrimmon* **Hadad Rimmon**
in *the valley of Megiddon* **Gay**
Megiddo/Valley of Troops.
12 And the land shall *mourn* **chop**,
every family **families by families** apart; the
family of the house of David apart,
and their *wives* **women** apart;
the family of the house of Nathan apart,
and their *wives* **women** apart;
13 The family of the house of Levi apart,
2 Behold, I set Yeru Shalem a bason of staggering
to all the people all around,
in the siege
both against Yah Hudah and against Yeru Shalem:
3 and in that day,
I set Yeru Shalem a stone of burden for all goyim:
all who burden themselves with it
in incising, incise themselves,
and all the people of the earth gather against it.

THE LIBERATION OF YERU SHALEM

4 In that day,
—an oracle of Yah Veh
I smite every horse with consternation
and his rider with insanity:
and I open my eyes on the house of Yah Hudah
and smite every horse of the people with blindness.
5 And the chiliarchs of Yah
Hudah say in their heart,
The settlers of Yeru Shalem
are my strength in Yah Veh Sabaoth their Elohim.
6 In that day I set the chiliarchs of Yah Hudah
as a laver of fire among the timber;
and as a flambeau of fire in an omer;
and they consume all the people all around
on the right and on the left:
and Yeru Shalem settles again in her own place
—in Yeru Shalem:
7 and Yah Veh saves the tents of Yah Hudah first,
so that the adornment of the house of David
and the adornment of the settlers of Yeru Shalem
greaten not against Yah Hudah.
8 In that day,
Yah Veh defends the settlers of Yeru Shalem;
and so be it,
the faltering among them at that day *are* as David;
and the house of David as Elohim
—as the angel of Yah Veh at their face.
9 And so be it, in that day,
I seek to desolate all the goyim
who come against Yeru Shalem.

THE SPIRIT OF CHARISM

10 And I pour on the house of David,
and on the settlers of Yeru Shalem,
the spirit of charism and of supplications:
and they look on me whom they pierced,
and they chop for him as one chops for his only,
and embitter over him
as one embitters for his firstbirthed.

THE CHOPPING IN YERU SHALEM

11 In that day,
a chopping greatens in Yeru Shalem,
as the chopping of Hadad Rimmon
in Gay Megiddo/Valley of Troops:
12 and the land chops
—families by families apart:
the family of the house of David apart

and their women apart;
the family of the house of Nathan apart
and their women apart;
13 the family of the house of Levi apart
and their *wives* **women** apart;
the family of *Shimei* **Shimiy** apart,
and their *wives* **women** apart;
14 All the families that *remain* **survive**,
every family **families by families** apart,
and their *wives* **women** apart.

THE FOUNTAIN FOR SIN AND FOR EXCLUSION

13 In that day there shall be a fountain opened
to the house of David
and to the *inhabitants* **settlers** of *Jerusalem* **Yeru Shalem**
for sin and for *uncleanness* **exclusion**.
2 And **so be** it *shall come to pass* in that day,
saith the LORD of hosts **an oracle of Yah Veh Sabaoth**,
that I *will* **shall** cut off the names of the idols
out of the land,
and they shall no more be remembered:
and also I *will* **shall** cause the prophets
and the *unclean* spirit **of foulness** to pass out of the land.
3 And **so be** it *shall come to pass*,
that when any **man** shall yet prophesy,
then his father and his mother that *begat* **birthed** him
shall say unto him, Thou shalt not live;
for thou *speakest lies* **wordest falsehoods**
in the name of *the LORD* **Yah Veh**:
and his father and his mother that *begat* **birthed** him
shall thrust him through when he prophesieth.
4 And **so be** it *shall come to pass* in that day,
that the prophets shall *be ashamed* **shame**
every one **each man** of his vision,
when he hath prophesied;
neither shall they *wear* **enrobe**
a *rough garment* **mighty mantle of hair** to deceive:
5 But he shall say, I am no prophet,
I am *an husbandman* **a man that serveth the soil**;
for man taught me to keep cattle **a human chatteler**
from my youth.
6 And one shall say unto him,
What are these wounds in thine hands?
Then he shall *answer* **say**,
Those with which I was *wounded* **smitten**
in the house of my *friends* **beloved**.
7 Awake, O sword, against my *shepherd* **tender**,
and against the *man* **mighty** that is my *fellow* **friend**,
saith the LORD of hosts **an oracle of Yah Veh Sabaoth**:
smite the *shepherd* **tender**,
and the *sheep* **flock** shall be scattered:
and I *will* **shall** turn mine hand
upon the *little ones* **belittled**.
8 And **so be** it *shall come to*
pass, that in all the land,
saith the LORD **an oracle of Yah Veh**,
two *parts* **mouths** therein shall be cut off and *die* **expire**;
but the third shall *be left* **remain** therein.
9 And I *will* **shall** bring the
third *part* through the fire,
and *will* **shall** refine them as silver is refined,
and *will try* **shall proof** them as gold is *tried* **proofed**:
they shall call on my name,
and I *will hear* **shall answer** them:
I *will* **shall** say, *It is my people* **My people**:
and they shall say,
The LORD is my God **Yah Veh, My Elohim**.

THE GATHERING OF THE GOYIM

14 Behold, the day of *the LORD* **Yah Veh** cometh,
and thy spoil
shall be *divided* **allotted** in the midst of thee.
2 For I *will* **shall** gather all *nations* **goyim**
against *Jerusalem* **Yeru Shalem** to battle;
and the city shall be *taken* **captured**,
and the houses *rifled* **plundered**,
and the women *ravished* **lain with and raped**;
and half of the city shall go forth into *captivity* **exile**,
and the *residue* **remnant** of the people
shall not be cut off from the city.
3 Then shall *the LORD* **Yah Veh** go forth,
and fight against those *nations* **goyim**,
as *when* **the day** he fought in the day of *battle* **war**.

THE RETURN OF YAH VEH

4 And his feet shall stand in that day
upon the mount of Olives,
and their women apart;
the family of Shimiy apart
and their women apart:
14 —all the families who survive
families by families apart and their women apart.

THE FOUNTAIN FOR SIN AND FOR EXCLUSION

13 And so be it, in that day,
a fountain opens to the house of David
and to the settlers of Yeru Shalem
for sin and for exclusion.
2 And so be it, in that day,

—an oracle of Yah Veh Sabaoth
I cut off the names of the idols from the land,
—no more remembered:
and also I pass the prophets
and the spirit of foulness from the land.
3 And so be it,
any man who still prophesies,
his father and his mother who birthed him
say to him, You live not!
—for you word falsehoods in the name of Yah Veh:
and his father and his mother who birthed him
thrust him through when he prophesies.
4 And so be it, in that day,
each man of the prophets shames for his vision
when he prophesies;
they enrobe not a mighty mantle of hair to deceive.
5 And *one* says, I *am* no prophet,
I *am* a man who serves the soil;
a human chatteler from my youth.
6 And *one* says to him,
What are these wounds in your hands?
And he says,
Because I was smitten in the house of my beloved.
7 Waken, O sword, against my tender,
and against the mighty, my friend
—an oracle of Yah Veh Sabaoth:
smite the tender, and the flock scatters:
and I turn my hand on the belittled.
8 And so be it, in all the land
—an oracle of Yah Veh
two mouths therein *are* cut off—they expire;
and the third remains therein:
9 and I bring the third through the fire and refine them
as the refining of silver, and proof them as the proofing
of gold: they call on my name, and I answer them:
I say, My people:
and they say, Yah Veh, My Elohim.

THE GATHERING OF THE GOYIM

14 Behold, the day of Yah Veh approaches,
to allot your spoil among you:
2 and I gather all goyim to
battle against Yeru Shalem;
and capture the city and plunder the houses;
and rape the women:
and half of the city goes into exile,
and not cut off the remnant of the people
from the city.
3 And Yah Veh comes and
fights against those goyim,
as the day he fought in the day of war.

THE RETURN OF YAH VEH

4 And in that day,
his feet stand on the mount of Olives
which is before Jerusalem **at the face of Yeru Shalem**
on the *east* **rising,**
and the mount of Olives
shall *cleave* **split** in *the midst thereof* **half**
toward the east **eastward** and *toward the west* **seaward,**
and there shall be a *very* **mighty** great valley;
and half of the mountain
shall *remove toward the north* **depart northward,**
and half of it *toward the south* **southward.**
5 And ye shall flee to the valley of the mountains;
for the valley of the mountains
shall *reach* **touch** unto *Azal* **Asel**: yea,
ye shall flee, like as ye fled
from *before* **the face of** the *earthquake* **quake**
in the days of *Uzziah* **Uzzi Yah**
king **sovereign** of *Judah* **Yah Hudah**:
and *the LORD* **Yah Veh** my *God* **Elohim** shall come,
and all the *saints* **holy** with thee.
6 And **so be** it *shall come to pass* in that day,
that the light shall not be *clear* **esteemed,**
nor *dark* **curdled**:
7 But it shall be one day
which shall be known to *the LORD* **Yah Veh,**
not day, nor night:
but **and so be** it *shall come to pass,*
that at evening time it shall be light.
8 And it shall be in that day,
that living waters
shall go out from *Jerusalem* **Yeru Shalem;**
half of them toward the *former* **ancient** sea,
and half of them toward the *hinder* **latter** sea:
in summer and in winter shall it be.
9 And *the LORD* **Yah Veh** shall be *king* **sovereign**
over all the earth:
in that day shall there be one *LORD* **Yah Veh,**
and his name one.
10 All the land shall be *turned*
surrounded as a plain
from Geba to Rimmon south of *Jerusalem* **Yeru Shalem**:
and it shall be lifted *up,*
and *inhabited* **settled** in her place,
from *Benjamin's gate* **the portal of Ben Yamin**
unto the place of the first *gate* **portal,**
unto the corner *gate* **portal,**
and from the tower of *Hananeel* **Hanan El**
unto the *king's winepresses* **sovereign's troughs.**
11 And *men* shall *dwell* **settle** in it,

and there shall be no more *utter destruction* **devotement**;
but *Jerusalem* **Yeru Shalem**
shall be *safely inhabited* **confidently settled**.
12 And this shall be the plague wherewith *the*
LORD **Yah Veh** *will* **shall** smite all the people
that have *fought* **hosted** against *Jerusalem* **Yeru Shalem**;
Their flesh shall *consume away* **dissolve**
while they stand upon their feet,
and their eyes shall *consume away* **dissolve**
in their holes,
and their tongue shall *consume away* **dissolve**
in their mouth.
13 And **so be** it *shall come to pass* in that day,
that a great *tumult* **confusion** from *the LORD* **Yah Veh**
shall be among them;
and they shall lay hold *every one* **each man**
on the hand of his *neighbour* **friend**,
and his hand shall *rise up* **ascend**
against the hand of his *neighbour* **friend**.
14 And *Judah* **Yah Hudah** also
shall fight at *Jerusalem* **Yeru Shalem**;
and the *wealth* **valuables**
of all the *heathen* **goyim** round about
shall be gathered *together*,
gold, and silver, and *apparel* **clothes**,
in *great* **mighty** abundance.
15 And so shall be the plague of the horse,
of the mule, of the camel, and of the *ass* **burro**,
and of all the *beasts* **animals**
that shall be in these *tents* **camps**,
as this plague.
at the face of Yeru Shalem on the rising:
and the mount of Olives splits in half
—eastward and seaward
—a mighty great valley;
and half of the mountain departs northward
and half southward:
5 and you flee to the valley of the mountains;
for the valley of the mountains touches to Asel:
yes, you flee,
as you fled the face of the quake
in the days of Uzzi Yah sovereign of Yah Hudah:
and Yah Veh my Elohim approaches
—all the holy with you.
6 And so be it, in that day,
that the light neither esteems nor curdles:
7 and so be it, in one day,
known *only* to Yah Veh,
neither day nor night:
and so be it,
that at evening time it becomes light:
8 and so be it, in that day,
that living waters come from Yeru Shalem;
half of them toward the ancient sea
and half of them toward the latter sea:
and it becomes summer and winter.
9 And Yah Veh becomes sovereign
over all the earth:
in that day,
there is one Yah Veh; and his name one.
10 All the land surrounds as a plain
from Geba to Rimmon south of Yeru Shalem:
and it lifts and settles in her place
from the portal of Ben Yamin
to the place of the first portal to the corner portal;
and from the tower of Hanan El
to the troughs of the sovereign.
11 And they settle in her,
and is no more devotement;
and Yeru Shalem settles confidently.
12 And this is the plague
wherewith Yah Veh smites all the people
who host against Yeru Shalem:
their flesh dissolves as they stand on their feet;
and their eyes dissolve in their holes;
and their tongue dissolve in their mouth.
13 And so be it, in that day,
there is a great confusion from Yah Veh
among them:
and each man lays hold on the hand of his friend;
and ascends his hand against the hand of his friend:
14 and Yah Hudah also fights at Yeru Shalem;
and they gather the valuables
of all the goyim all around
—gold and silver and clothes in mighty abundance.
15 And so be the plague of the horse,
of the mule, of the camel and of the burro;
and so be all the animals in these camps
—as this plague.
16 And **so be** it *shall come to pass*,
that every one that *is left* **remaineth**
of all the *nations* **goyim**
which came against *Jerusalem* **Yeru Shalem**
shall *even go up from* **ascend sufficiently** year to year
to *worship* **prostrate to** the *King* **Sovereign**,
the LORD of hosts **Yah Veh Sabaoth**,
and to *keep* **celebrate** the *feast* **celebration**
of *tabernacles* **sukkoth/brush arbors**.
17 And it shall be,
that whoso *will* **shall** not *come up* **ascend**

of *all* the families of the earth
unto *Jerusalem* **Yeru Shalem**
to *worship* **prostrate to** the *King* **Sovereign**,
the LORD of hosts **Yah Veh Sabaoth**,
even upon them shall be no *rain* **downpour**.
18 And if the family of *Egypt*
go **Misrayim ascend** not *up*,
and come not,
that have no rain; **then not on them**
there shall be the plague,
wherewith *the LORD* **Yah Veh**
will **shall** smite the *heathen* **goyim**
that *come* **ascend** not *up*
to *keep* **celebrate** the *feast* **celebration**
of *tabernacles* **sukkoth/brush arbors**.
19 This shall be
the punishment **for the sin** of *Egypt* **Misrayim**,
and *the punishment* **for the sin** of all *nations* **goyim**
that *come* **ascend** not *up*
to keep **celebrate** the *feast* **celebration**
of *tabernacles* **sukkoth/brush arbors**.
20 In that day shall there be
upon the *bells* **jinglers** of the horses,
HOLINESS UNTO *THE LORD* **YAH VEH**;
and the *pots* **caldrons**
in the *LORD'S* house **of Yah Veh**
shall be like the *bowls* **sprinklers**
before **at the face of** the **sacrifice** altar.
21 Yea, every *pot* **caldron**
in *Jerusalem* **Yeru Shalem** and in *Judah* **Yah Hudah**
shall be *holiness* **holy**
unto *the LORD of hosts* **Yah Veh Sabaoth**:
and all they that sacrifice shall come and take of them,
and *seethe* **stew** therein:
and in that day
there shall be no more the *Canaanite* **Kenaaniy**
in the house of *the LORD of hosts* **Yah Veh Sabaoth**.
16 And so be it,
every one of all the goyim who remain
who come against Yeru Shalem
ascend sufficiently year by year
to prostrate to the Sovereign Yah Veh Sabaoth;
and to celebrate the celebration
of sukkoth/brush arbors.
17 And so be it,
whoever, of the families of the earth,
who ascend not to Yeru Shalem
to prostrate to the Sovereign Yah Veh Sabaoth,
even on them *is* downpour.
18 And if the family of Misrayim
neither ascend nor come,
then the plague is on them
wherewith Yah Veh smites the goyim
who ascend not to celebrate the celebration
of sukkoth/brush arbors:
19 so be it for the sin of Misrayim
and for the sin of all goyim
who ascend not celebrate the celebration
of sukkoth/brush arbors.
20 In that day there is on the jinglers of the horses,
HOLINESS TO YAH VEH.
And so be the caldrons in the house of Yah Veh
—as the sprinklers at the face of the sacrifice altar:
21 and so be every caldron
in Yeru Shalem and in Yah Hudah
—holy to Yah Veh Sabaoth:
and all who sacrifice come and take thereof,
and stew therein:
and in that day,
the Kenaaniy is no more
in the house of Yah Veh Sabaoth.

THE LOVE OF YAH VEH FOR YISRA EL

1 The burden of the word of *the LORD* **Yah Veh**
to *Israel* **Yisra El** by **the hand of** Malachi.
2 I have loved you,
saith the LORD **an oracle of Yah Veh**.
Yet ye say, Wherein hast thou loved us?
Was not *Esau Jacob's* **Esav Yaaqov's** brother?
saith *the LORD* **Yah Veh**:
yet I loved *Jacob* **Yaaqov**,
3 And I hated *Esau* **Esav**,
and *laid* **set** his mountains
and his *heritage* **inheritance** waste
for the *dragons* **monsters** of the wilderness.
4 Whereas Edom saith, We are impoverished,
but we *will* **shall** return
and build the *desolate places* **parched areas**;
thus saith *the LORD of hosts* **Yah Veh Sabaoth**, They
shall build, but I *will throw* **shall break** down; and
they shall call them, The border of wickedness, and,
The people against whom *the LORD* **Yah Veh**
hath indignation for ever **be enraged eternally**.
5 And your eyes shall see, and ye shall say,
The LORD will **Yah Veh shall** be *magnified* **greatened**
from the border of *Israel* **Yisra El**.

PRIESTS PROFANE THE SACRIFICE ALTAR

6 A son honoureth his father,
and a servant his *master* **adoni**:
if then I be a father, where is mine honour?
and if I be *a master* **an adoni**,
where is my *fear* **awesomeness**?
saith *the LORD of hosts* **Yah Veh Sabaoth** unto you,
O priests, that despise my name.
And ye say, Wherein have we despised thy name?
7 Ye *offer polluted* **bring profaned** bread
upon *mine* **my sacrifice** altar;
and ye say, Wherein have we *polluted* **profaned** thee?
In that ye say **Saying**,
The table of *the LORD* **Yah Veh** is *contemptible* **despised**.
8 And if ye *offer* **bring near** the blind for sacrifice,
is it not evil?
and if ye *offer* **bring near** the lame and sick, is it not evil?
offer **oblate** it *now* **I beseech,** unto thy governor;
will **shall** he be pleased with thee,
or *accept* **lift** thy *person* **face**?
saith *the LORD of hosts* **Yah Veh Sabaoth**.
9 And now, I *pray* **beseech** you,
beseech God **stroke the face of El**
that he *will be gracious* **shall grant charism** unto us:
this hath been by your *means* **hand**:
will **shall** he *regard* **lift** your *persons* **faces**?
saith *the LORD of hosts* **Yah Veh Sabaoth**.
10 Who is there even among you
that *would* **should** shut the doors *for nought*?
neither do ye *kindle fire on mine* **light my sacrifice** altar
for nought **gratuitously**.
I have no *pleasure* **delight** in you,
saith *the LORD of hosts* **Yah Veh Sabaoth**,
neither *will I accept* **shall** an offering
at your hand **please me**.
11 For from the rising of the sun
even unto the *going down* **entry** of the same
my name shall be great among the *Gentiles* **goyim**;
and in every place
incense shall be *offered* **brought near** unto my name,
and a pure offering:
for my name shall be great among the *heathen* **goyim**,
saith *the LORD of hosts* **Yah Veh Sabaoth**.
12 But ye have profaned it, *in that ye say* **saying**,
The table of *the LORD* **Yah Veh** is *polluted* **profaned**;
and the fruit *thereof*,
even his *meat* **food**, is contemptible.
13 Ye said also, Behold, what
a weariness is it **trouble**!
and ye have *snuffed* **puffed** at it,
saith *the LORD of hosts* **Yah Veh Sabaoth**;
and ye brought that which was *torn* **stripped**,
and the lame, and the sick;
thus ye brought an offering:
should *I accept* this of your hand **please**?
saith *the LORD* **Yah Veh**.

THE LOVE OF YAH VEH FOR YISRA EL

1 The burden of the word of Yah Veh
to Yisra El by the hand of Malachi.
2 I loved you
—an oracle of Yah Veh.
Yet you say, Wherein loved you us?
Was not Esav the brother of Yaaqov? says Yah Veh;
Yet I loved Yaaqov:
3 and I hated Esav;
and set his mountains and his inheritance waste
for the monsters of the wilderness.

4 Because Edom says, We are impoverished,
and we return and build the parched areas.
Thus says Yah Veh Sabaoth:
They build, and I break down;
and they call them,
The border of wickedness:
and,
The people against whom Yah Veh enrages eternally.
5 And your eyes see, and you say,
Yah Veh greatens from the border of Yisra El.

PRIESTS PROFANE THE SACRIFICE ALTAR

6 A son honors his father,
and a servant his adoni:
and if I *am* a father, where is my honor?
and if I *am* an adoni, where is my awesomeness?
Yah Veh Sabaoth says to you,
O priests, who despise my name,
you say, Wherein despise we your name?
7 You bring profane bread on my sacrifice altar;
and you say, Wherein profane we you?
saying, The table of Yah Veh *is* despised.
8 And if you bring the blind
for sacrifice, is it not evil?
And if you bring the lame and sick, is it not evil?
Oblate it, I beseech, to your governor;
Is he pleased with you? Or lifts he your face?
says Yah Veh Sabaoth.
9 And now, I beseech you, stroke the face of El
so that he grant us charism:
this being from your hand,
Lifts he your faces?
says Yah Veh Sabaoth.
10 Who, even among you, shuts the doors?
Yes, you light my sacrifice altar gratuitously;
I neither delight in you,
says Yah Veh Sabaoth,
nor an offering at your hand pleases me.
11 For from the rising of the sun
even to the entry of the same
my name *is* great among the goyim;
and in every place
incense *is* brought to my name,
and a pure offering:
for my name *is* great among the goyim,
says Yah Veh Sabaoth.
12 And you profane it, saying,
The table of Yah Veh *is* profane;
and the fruit, his food, contemptible.
13 You also say, Behold, what trouble!
and you puff at it,
says Yah Veh Sabaoth;
and you bring the stripped and the lame and the sick.
Thus bring you an offering: of your hand that pleases?
says Yah Veh.
14 But cursed be the deceiver,
which hath in his *flock* **drove** a male,
and voweth, and sacrificeth
unto *the Lord corrupt thing* **Adonay** a **ruin**:
for I am a great *King* **Sovereign**,
saith *the LORD of hosts* **Yah Veh Sabaoth**,
and my name is *dreadful* **awesome**
among the *heathen* **goyim**.

A MISVAH FOR THE PRIESTS

2 And now, O ye priests,
this *commandment* **misvah** is for you.
2 If ye *will* **shall** not hear,
and if ye *will* **shall** not *lay* **set** it to heart,
to give *glory* **honour** unto my name,
saith *the LORD of hosts* **Yah Veh Sabaoth**,
I *will* **shall** even send a curse upon you,
and I *will* **shall** curse your blessings:
yea, I have cursed them already,
because ye *do not lay* **set** it **not** to heart.
3 Behold, I *will corrupt* **shall rebuke** your seed,
and *spread* **winnow** dung upon your faces,
even the dung of your *solemn feasts* **celebrations**;
and one shall *take* **bear** you away with it.
4 And ye shall know
that I have sent this *commandment* **misvah** unto you,
that my covenant might be with Levi,
saith *the LORD of hosts* **Yah Veh Sabaoth**.
5 My covenant was with him
of life and *peace* **shalom**;
and I gave them to him for the *fear* **awesomeness**
wherewith he *feared* **awed** me,
and was *afraid before* **terrified at the face of** my name.
6 The *law* **torah** of truth was in his mouth,
and *iniquity* **perversity** was not found in his lips:
he walked with me
in *peace* **shalom** and *equity* **straightness**
and *did turn* **turned** many away from iniquity.
7 For the priest's lips should
keep **guard** knowledge,
and they should seek the *law* **torah** at his
mouth: for he is the *messenger* **angel**
of *the LORD of hosts* **Yah Veh Sabaoth**.

8 But ye are *departed* **turned aside** out of the way;
ye have caused many to *stumble* **falter** at the *law* **torah**;
ye have *corrupted* **ruined** the covenant of Levi,
saith *the LORD of hosts* **Yah Veh Sabaoth.**
9 Therefore have I also *made* **given** you
contemptible **despised** and *base* **lowly**
before all the people,
according as **your mouth**
ye have not *kept* **guarded** my ways,
but have *been partial* **lifted thy face**
in **against** the *law* **torah.**
10 Have we not all one father?
hath not one *God* **El** created us?
why *do we deal treacherously* **deal we covertly**
every man against his brother,
by profaning the covenant of our fathers?
11 *Judah* **Yah Hudah** hath
dealt *treacherously* **covertly,**
and an *abomination is committed* **abhorrence be worked**
in *Israel* **Yisra El** and in *Jerusalem* **Yeru Shalem**;
for *Judah* **Yah Hudah** hath profaned
the holiness of *the LORD* **Yah Veh** which he loved,
and hath married the daughter of a strange *god* **el.**
12 *The LORD will* **Yah Veh shall** cut off the man
that *doeth* **worketh** this,
the master **him that waketh**
and *the scholar* **him that answereth,**
out of the *tabernacles* **tents** of *Jacob* **Yaaqov,**
and him that *offereth* **bringeth near** an offering
unto *the LORD of hosts* **Yah Veh Sabaoth.**
13 And this have ye done *again* **secondly,**
covering the **sacrifice** altar of *the LORD* **Yah Veh**
with tears, with weeping, and with *crying out* **shrieking,**
insomuch
that he *regardeth* **faceth** not the offering any more,
or *receiveth* **taketh** it with *good will* **pleasure**
at your hand.
14 Yet ye say, *Wherefore* **Why**?
Because *the LORD* **Yah Veh** hath *been witness* **witnessed**
between thee and **between** the *wife* **woman** of thy youth,
14 And cursed *is* the deceiver
who has a male in his drove;
and vows and sacrifices a ruin to Adonay:
for I am a great Sovereign, says Yah Veh Sabaoth;
and my name *is* awesome among the goyim.

A Misvah For The Priests

2 And now, to you O priests, this misvah.
2 If you hear not and if you set not to heart
to give honor to my name,
says Yah Veh Sabaoth,
I send a curse on you and I curse your blessings:
yes, I also curse, because you set it not to heart.
3 Behold, I rebuke your seed
and winnow dung on your faces—
the dung of your celebrations;
to bear you away with it.
4 And you know I send this misvah to you,
so that my covenant becomes with Levi,
says Yah Veh Sabaoth.
5 My covenant with him becomes life and shalom;
and I give them to him
for the awesomeness with which he awes me,
and because he terrifies at the face of my name.
6 The torah of truth being in his mouth,
and no perversity found in his lips:
he walks with me in shalom and straightness
and turns many away from iniquity.
7 For the lips of the priest guard knowledge
and they seek the torah at his mouth: for
he is the angel of Yah Veh Sabaoth.
8 And you turn aside from the way;
you falter many at the torah;
you ruin the covenant of Levi;
says Yah Veh Sabaoth.
9 So I also give you
despised and lowly in front of all the people
because according to your mouth
you guard not my ways,
and lift faces against the torah.
10 Have we not all one father?
Has not one El created us?
Why deal we covertly, every man against his brother,
by profaning the covenant of our fathers?
11 Yah Hudah deals covertly,
and works an abhorrence
in Yisra El and in Yeru Shalem;
for Yah Hudah profanes the holiness of Yah Veh
which he loved,
and married the daughter of a strange el.
12 Yah Veh cuts off the man who works this
—he who wakens and he who answers
from the tents of Yaaqov;
and he who brings near an offering
to Yah Veh Sabaoth.
13 And secondly, you do this:
you cover the sacrifice altar of Yah Veh

with tears, with weeping and with shrieking;
because there is no more facing the offering
or taking it *with* pleasure at your hand.
14 And you say, Why?
Because Yah Veh witnesses
between you and between the woman of your youth
exeGeses ready research BIBLE
against whom thou hast dealt *treacherously* **covertly**:
yet is she thy companion,
and the *wife* **woman** of thy covenant.
15 And *did not he make* **worked he not** one?
Yet had he the *residue of the* spirit **of survival**.
And wherefore one?
That he might seek a *godly* seed **of Elohim**.
Therefore take heed to **Guard** your spirit,
and let none deal *treacherously* **covertly**
against the *wife* **woman** of his youth.
16 For *the LORD* **Yah Veh**,
the God **Elohim** of *Israel* **Yisra El**,
saith that he hateth *putting* **sending** away:
for one covereth violence with his *garment* **robe**,
saith *the LORD of hosts* **Yah Veh Sabaoth**:
therefore take heed to **guard** your spirit,
that ye deal not *treacherously* **covertly**.
17 Ye have *wearied the LORD* **belaboured Yah Veh**
with your words.
Yet ye say, Wherein have we *wearied* **belaboured** him?
When ye say **Saying**,
Every one that *doeth* **worketh** evil
is good in the *sight* **eyes** of *the LORD* **Yah Veh**,
and he delighteth in them;
or, Where is the *God* **Elohim** of judgment?

PROPHECY OF THE ANGEL OF YAH VEH AND HIS ADONAY

3 Behold, I *will* **shall** send my *messenger* **angel**,
and he shall *prepare* **face** the way *before me* **at my face**:
and the *Lord* **Adonay**, whom ye seek,
shall suddenly come to his *temple* **manse**,
even the *messenger* **angel** of the covenant,
whom ye delight in:
behold, he shall come,
saith *the LORD of hosts* **Yah Veh Sabaoth**.
Matthaios 11:10, Markos 1:2, Loukas 7:27
2 But who may *abide* **sustain** the day of his coming?
and who shall stand when he *appeareth* **be seen**?
for he is like a refiner's fire, and like fullers' soap:
3 And he shall sit as a refiner
and purifier of silver:
and he shall purify the sons of Levi,
and purge them as gold and silver,
that they may *offer* **bring near** unto *the LORD* **Yah Veh**
an offering in *righteousness* **justness**.
4 Then shall the offering
of *Judah* **Yah Hudah** and *Jerusalem* **Yeru Shalem**
be pleasant unto the LORD **please Yah Veh**,
as in the *days of old for ever* **original eternal days**,
and as in *former* **ancient** years.
5 And I *will come near to* **shall**
approach you to judgment;
and I *will* **shall** be a *swift* **hasty** witness
against the sorcerers,
and against the adulterers,
and against false *swearers* **oathers**,
and against those
that oppress the hireling in his *wages* **hire**,
the widow, and the *fatherless* **orphan**,
and that *turn aside* **pervert** the *stranger* **sojourner**
from his right,
and *fear* **awe** not me,
saith *the LORD of hosts* **Yah Veh Sabaoth**.
6 For *I am the LORD* **I—Yah Veh**, I change not;
therefore ye sons of *Jacob* **Yaaqov**
are not *consumed* **finished off**.

TITHING

7 Even from the days of your fathers
ye are *gone away* **turned aside**
from *mine ordinances* **my statutes**,
and have not *kept* **guarded** them.
Return unto me, and I *will* **shall** return unto you,
saith *the LORD of hosts* **Yah Veh Sabaoth**.
But ye said, Wherein shall we return?
8 *Will a man rob God* **Shall**
a human defraud Elohim?
Yet ye have *robbed* **defrauded** me.
But **And** ye say, Wherein have we
robbed **defrauded** thee?
In tithes and *offerings* **exaltments**.
against whom you dealt covertly:
yet is she your companion
and the woman of your covenant.
15 And worked he not one?
Yet he has the spirit of survival.
And why one?
To seek a seed of Elohim.
Guard your spirit
that no one deal covertly

against the woman of his youth.
16 For Yah Veh Elohim of Yisra El
says that he hates sending away:
for one covers violence with his robe,
says Yah Veh Sabaoth:
guard your spirit,
that you not deal covertly.
17 You belabor Yah Veh with your words:
yet you say, Wherein belabor we him?
By saying,
Every one who works evil
is good in the eyes of Yah Veh,
and he delights in them!
—or, Where is the Elohim of judgment?

PROPHECY OF THE ANGEL OF YAH VEH AND HIS ADONAY

3 Behold, I send my angel,
and he faces the way at my face:
and the Adonay, whom you seek,
suddenly comes to his manse
—even the angel of the covenant
in whom you delight!
Behold, he comes,
says Yah Veh Sabaoth.
Matthaios 11:10, Markos 1:2, Loukas 7:27
2 And who measures the day of his coming?
And who stands when he *is* seen?
—for he is as the fire of a refiner
and as the soap of a fullers:
3 and he sits as a refiner and purifier of silver:
and he purifies the sons of Levi
and purges them as gold and silver,
so that they bring near an offering in justness
to Yah Veh.
4 nd the offering of Yah Hudah and Yeru Shalem
pleases Yah Veh
—as in the original eternal days
and as in ancient years.
5 And I approach you for judgment;
and I become a hasty witness against the sorcerers
and against the adulterers and against false oathers
and against those who oppress the hireling in his hire
—the widow and the orphan;
and who pervert the sojourner and awe me not,
says Yah Veh Sabaoth.
6 For I—Yah Veh; I change not:
so you sons of Yaaqov are not finished off.

TITHING

7 Even from the days of your fathers
you turn aside from my statutes
and guard them not.
Return to me and I return to you,
says Yah Veh Sabaoth.
And you say, Return in what?
8 A human, defrauds he Elohim?
—yet you defraud me.
And you say, Wherein defraud we you?
In tithes and exaltments.
9 Ye are cursed with a curse:
for ye have *robbed* **defrauded** me,
even this whole *nation* **goyim**.
10 Bring ye all the tithes into the
storehouse **treasure house**,
that there *may* be *meat* **prey** in mine house,
and *prove* **proof** me *now* **I beseech,** herewith,
saith *the LORD of hosts* **Yah Veh Sabaoth**,
if I *will* **shall** not open you
the windows of *heaven* **the heavens**,
and pour you out a blessing,
that **until** there shall not be
room enough to receive it sufficient.
11 And I *will* **shall** rebuke the
devourer for your sakes,
and he shall not *destroy* **ruin** the
fruits of your *ground* **soil**;
neither shall your vine *cast* **abort** her fruit
before the time in the field,
saith *the LORD of hosts* **Yah Veh Sabaoth**.
12 And all *nations* shall **goyim**
call you *blessed* **blithesome**:
for ye shall be a delightsome land,
saith *the LORD of hosts* **Yah Veh Sabaoth**.
13 Your words have *been stout*
prevailed against me,
saith *the LORD* **Yah Veh**.
Yet ye say,
What have we *spoken so much* **worded** against thee?
14 Ye have said, It is vain to serve *God* **Elohim**:
and what *profit* **greedy gain** is it
that we have *kept* **guarded** his *ordinance* **guard**,
and that we have walked *mournfully* **darkly**
before the LORD of hosts **at the face of Yah Veh Sabaoth**?
15 And now we call the *proud*
arrogant *happy* **blithesome**;
yea, they that work wickedness *are set up* **built**;
yea, they that *tempt God* **proof Elohim**

are even *delivered* **rescued.**

THE SCROLL OF REMEMBRANCE

16 Then they that *feared the LORD* **awed Yah Veh**
spake often one **worded man** to *another* **friend**:
and *the LORD* **Yah Veh** hearkened, and heard *it*,
and a *book* **scroll** of remembrance
was *written before him* **inscribed at his face**
for them that *feared the LORD* **awed Yah Veh**,
and that *thought upon* **fabricated** his name.
17 And they shall be mine,
saith *the LORD of hosts* **Yah Veh Sabaoth**,
in that day when I *make up* **work** my
jewels **peculiar treasure**;
and I *will* **shall** spare them,
as a man spareth his own son that serveth him.
18 Then shall ye return, and *discern* **see**
between the *righteous* **just** and the wicked,
between him that serveth *God* **Elohim**
and **between** him that serveth him not.

THE DAY OF YAH VEH

4 For, behold, the day *cometh* **approacheth**,
that shall *burn* **inflame** as an oven;
and all the *proud* **arrogant**,
yea, and all that *do* **work** wickedly, shall be stubble:
and the day that *cometh* **approacheth**
shall burn them *up*,
saith *the LORD of hosts* **Yah Veh Sabaoth**,
that it shall leave them neither root nor branch.

THE SUN OF JUSTNESS

2 But unto you that fear my name
shall the Sun of *righteousness* **justness** arise
with healing in his wings;
and ye shall go forth, and grow up as calves of the stall.
3 And ye shall *tread down* **trample** the wicked;
for they shall be ashes under the soles of your feet
in the day that I shall *do* **work** *this*,
saith *the LORD of hosts* **Yah Veh Sabaoth**.
4 Remember ye the *law* **torah**
of *Moses* **Mosheh** my servant,
which I *commanded* **misvahed** unto him in Horeb
for all *Israel* **Yisra El**, *with* the statutes and judgments.

ELI YAH THE PROPHET

5 Behold, I *will* **shall** send you
Elijah **Eli Yah** the prophet
before **ere the face of** the *coming* **approaching**
of the great and *dreadful* **awesome**
day of *the LORD* **Yah Veh**:
6 And he shall turn the heart of the fathers
to the *children* **sons**,
and the heart of the *children* **sons** to their fathers,
lest **ere** I come and smite the earth
with a *curse* **devotement**.
9 You *are* cursed with a curse:
for you defraud me—this whole goyim.
10 Bring all your tithes into the treasure house,
that there be prey in my house;
and proof me, I beseech, herewith,
says Yah Veh Sabaoth,
if I not open the windows of the heavens to you
and pour a blessing
until you not have sufficient.
11 And for your sakes, I rebuke the devourer
that he neither ruin the fruits of your soil;
nor your vine abort her fruit ere its time in the field,
says Yah Veh Sabaoth.
12 And all goyim call you blithesome:
for you become a delightsome land,
says Yah Veh Sabaoth.
13 Your words prevail against me, says Yah Veh.
Yet you say, What word we against you?
14 You say, It *is* vain to serve Elohim!
and, What greedy gain is it to guard his guard,
and to walk darkly at the face of Yah Veh Sabaoth?
15 And now we call the arrogant, blithesome;
yes, those working wickedness are built up;
yes, they proof Elohim, and escape.

THE SCROLL OF REMEMBRANCE

16 Then they who awe Yah Veh
word man to friend:
and Yah Veh hearkens and hears
and inscribes a scroll of remembrance at his face
of them who awe Yah Veh
and of them who fabricate his name.
17 And they are mine, says Yah Veh Sabaoth,
in that day, when I work my peculiar treasure;
and I spare them
as a man spares his own son who serves him:
18 and you return and see
between the just and the wicked,
between him who serves Elohim
and between him who serves him not.

The Day Of Yah Veh

4 For behold,
the day approaches that inflames as an oven;
and all the arrogant,
yes, and all who work wickedly, become stubble:
and the day that approaches burns them,
says Yah Veh Sabaoth,
that it leaves them neither root nor branch.

The Sun Of Justness

2 And to you who fear my name,
the Sun of justness rises with healing in his wings;
and you go, and grow as calves of the stall:
3 and you trample the wicked;
for they become ashes under the soles of your feet,
in the day I work,
says Yah Veh Sabaoth.
4 Remember the torah of Mosheh my servant,
that I misvahed to him in Horeb
for all Yisra El,
the statutes and judgments.

Eli Yah The Prophet

5 Behold, I send you Eli Yah the prophet
ere the face of the approaching
of the great and awesome day of Yah Veh:
6 and he turns the heart of the fathers to the sons
and the heart of the sons to their fathers
ere I come and smite the earth with a devotement.

www.ingramcontent.com/pod-product-compliance
Lightning Source LLC
Chambersburg PA
CBHW051105100526
44583CB00045B/2519

* 9 7 8 1 6 3 9 5 0 1 3 9 7 *